WITHDRAWN

Hoover's Handbook of World Business 2024

Hoover's Handbook of World Business 2024 is intended to provide readers with accurate and authoritative information about the enterprises covered in it. Hoover's researched all companies and organizations profiled, and in many cases contacted them directly so that companies represented could provide information. The information contained herein is as accurate as we could reasonably make it. In many cases we have relied on third-party material that we believe to be trustworthy, but were unable to independently verify. We do not warrant that the book is absolutely accurate or without error. Readers should not rely on any information contained herein in instances where such reliance might cause financial loss. The publisher, the editors, and their data suppliers specifically disclaim all warranties, including the implied warranties of merchantability and fitness for a specific purpose. This book is sold with the understanding that neither the publisher, the editors, nor any content contributors are engaged in providing investment, financial, accounting, legal, or other professional advice.

The financial data (Historical Financials sections) in this book are from a variety of sources. Mergent Inc., provided selected data for the Historical Financials sections of publicly traded companies. For private companies and for historical information on public companies prior to their becoming public, we obtained information directly from the companies or from trade sources deemed to be reliable. Hoover's, Inc., is solely responsible for the presentation of all data.

Many of the names of products and services mentioned in this book are the trademarks or service marks of the companies manufacturing or selling them and are subject to protection under US law. Space has not permitted us to indicate which names are subject to such protection, and readers are advised to consult with the owners of such marks regarding their use. Hoover's is a trademark of Hoover's, Inc.

Copyright © 2024 by Dun & Bradstreet. All rights reserved. No part of this book may be reproduced or transmitted in any form or by any means, electronic or mechanical, including by photocopying, facsimile transmission, recording, rekeying, or using any information storage and retrieval system, without permission in writing from Hoover's, except that brief passages may be quoted by a reviewer in a magazine, in a newspaper, online, or in a broadcast review.

10 9 8 7 6 5 4 3 2 1

Publishers Cataloging-in-Publication Data

Hoover's Handbook of World Business 2024

    Includes indexes.

    ISBN: 979-8-89251-050-9

    ISSN 1055-7199

    1. Business enterprises — Directories. 2. Corporations — Directories.

HF3010 338.7

U.S. AND WORLD BOOK SALES
Mergent Inc.

580 Kingsley Park Drive
Fort Mill, SC
29715
Phone: 704-559-6961
e-mail: skardon@ftserussell.com
Web: www.mergentbusinesspress.com

Abbreviations

AB – Aktiebolag (Swedish)*
ADR – American Depositary Receipts
AG – Aktiengesellschaft (German)*
AFL-CIO – American Federation of Labor and Congress of Industrial Organizations
AMEX – American Stock Exchange
A/S – Aktieselskab (Danish)*
ASA – Allmenne Aksjeselskaper (Norwegian)*
ATM – asynchronous transfer mode; automated teller machine
CAD/CAM – computer-aided design/computer-aided manufacturing manufacturing
CASE – computer-aided software engineering
CD-ROM – compact disc – read-only memory
CEO – chief executive officer
CFO – chief financial officer
CMOS – complementary metal oxide semiconductor
COMECON – Council for Mutual Economic Assistance
COO – chief operating officer
DAT – digital audio tape
DOD – Department of Defense
DOE – Department of Energy
DOT – Department of Transportation
DRAM – dynamic random-access memory
DVD – digital versatile disc/digital video disc
EC – European Community
EPA – Environmental Protection Agency
EPS – earnings per share
EU – European Union
EVP – executive vice president
FCC – Federal Communications Commission
FDA – Food and Drug Administration

FDIC – Federal Deposit Insurance Corporation
FTC – Federal Trade Commission
GATT – General Agreement on Tariffs and Trade
GmbH – Gesellschaft mit beschränkter Haftung (German)*
GNP – gross national product
HDTV – high-definition television
HMO – health maintenance organization
HR – human resources
HTML – hypertext markup language
ICC – Interstate Commerce Commission
IMF – International Monetary Fund
IPO – initial public offering
IRS – Internal Revenue Service
KGaA – Kommanditgesellschaft auf Aktien (German)*
LAN – local-area network
LBO – leveraged buyout
LNG – liquefied natural gas
LP – limited partnership
Ltd. – Limited
MFN – Most Favored Nation
MITI – Ministry of International Trade and Industry (Japan)
NAFTA – North American Free Trade Agreement
Nasdaq – National Association of Securities Dealers Automated Quotations
NATO – North Atlantic Treaty Organization
NV – Naamlose Vennootschap (Dutch)*
NYSE – New York Stock Exchange
OAO – open joint stock company (Russian)
OAS – Organization of American States

OECD – Organization for Economic Cooperation and Development
OEM – original equipment manufacturer
OOO – limited liability company (Russian)
OPEC – Organization of Petroleum Exporting Countries
OS – operating system
OTC – over-the-counter
P/E – price to earnings ratio
PLC – public limited company (UK)*
RAM – random-access memory
R&D – research and development
RISC – reduced instruction set computer
ROA – return on assets
ROI – return on investment
ROM – read-only memory
SA – Société Anonyme (French)*; Sociedad(e) Anónima (Spanish and Portuguese)*
SA de CV – Sociedad Anónima de Capital Variable (Spanish)*
SEC – Securities and Exchange Commission
SEVP – senior executive vice president
SIC – Standard Industrial Classification
SpA – Società per Azioni (Italian)*
SPARC – scalable processor architecture
SVP – senior vice president
VAR – value-added reseller
VAT – value-added tax
VC – venture capitalist
VP – vice president
WAN – wide-area network
WWW – World Wide Web
ZAO – closed joint stock company (Russian)
z o.o. – z ograniczona odpowiedzialnoscia (Polish)*

---

* These abbreviations are used in companies' names to convey that the companies are limited liability enterprises; the meanings are usually the equivalent of corporation or incorporated.

Mergent Inc.

Executive Managing Director: John Pedernales

Publisher and Managing Director of Print Products: Thomas Wecera

Director of Print Products: Charlot Volny

Quality Assurance Editor: Wayne Arnold

Production Research Assistant: Davie Christna

Data Manager: Allison Shank

MERGENT CUSTOMER SERVICE-PRINT

Support and Fulfillment Manager: Stephanie Kardon Phone: 704-559-6961
email: skardon@ftserussell.com
Web: www.mergentbusinesspress.com

ABOUT MERGENT INC.

For over 100 years, Mergent, Inc. has been a leading provider of business and financial information on public and private companies globally. Mergent is known to be a trusted partner to corporate and financial institutions, as well as to academic and public libraries. Today we continue to build on a century of experience by transforming data into knowledge and combining our expertise with the latest technology to create new global data and analytical solutions for our clients. With advanced data collection services, cloud-based applications, desktop analytics and print products, Mergent and its subsidiaries provide solutions from top down economic and demographic information, to detailed equity and debt fundamental analysis. We incorporate value added tools such as quantitative Smart Beta equity research and tools for portfolio building and measurement. Based in the U.S., Mergent maintains a strong global presence, with offices in New York, Charlotte, San Diego, London, Tokyo, Kuching and Melbourne. Mergent, Inc. is a member of the London Stock Exchange plc group of companies. The Mergent business forms part of LSEG's Information Services Division, which includes FTSE Russell, a global leader in indexes.

Contents

List of Lists	vi
Companies Profiled	vii
About *Hoover's Handbook of World Business 2024*	xi
Using Hoover's Handbooks	xii
A List-Lover's Compendium	1a
The Companies	1
The Index of Company Executives	691

List of Lists

HOOVER'S RANKINGS

The 100 Largest Companies by Sales in Hoover's Handbook of World Business 2024..........................2a
The 100 Most Profitable Companies in Hoover's Handbook of World Business 2024..........................3a
The 100 Largest Employers in Hoover's Handbook of World Business 2024..........................4a

Companies Profiled

Company	Page
A.P. Moller - Maersk A/S	1
AB Electrolux (Sweden)	2
AB SKF	3
ABB Ltd	5
ABN AMRO Bank NV	7
Absa Group Ltd (New)	8
Abu Dhabi Islamic Bank	9
Accenture plc	9
Acer Inc	11
ACS Actividades de Construccion y Servicios, S.A.	13
Adecco Group AG	14
Adidas AG	15
Adient Plc	17
Adyen N.V.	18
Aegon Ltd	18
Aeon Co Ltd	20
AGC Inc	21
Ageas NV	21
AGL Energy Ltd	21
AIA Group Ltd.	22
AIB Group PLC	23
Air Canada Inc	24
Airbus SE	25
Aisin Corporation	27
Ajinomoto Co., Inc. (Japan)	28
AKBANK	29
Akita Bank Ltd (The) (Japan)	30
Akzo Nobel NV (Netherlands)	30
Alcon Inc	32
ALD SA	32
Alfresa Holdings Corp Tokyo	32
Alibaba Group Holding Ltd	33
Alimentation Couche-Tard Inc	34
Allianz SE	36
Alpek SAB de CV	38
Alpha Services & Holdings SA	38
AltaGas Ltd	39
Aluminum Corp of China Ltd.	40
Ambev SA	40
Amcor plc	40
America Movil SAB de CV	42
AMMB Holdings BHD	43
Ampol Ltd	44
ANA Holdings Inc	45
Anglo American Platinum Ltd	45
Anglo American Plc	46
Anheuser-Busch InBev SA/NV	48
Anhui Conch Cement Co Ltd	48
Aon plc (Ireland)	49
Aozora Bank Ltd	49
Aptiv Corp	50
Aptiv PLC	50
Arca Continental SAB de CV	51
ArcelorMittal SA	53
Arch Capital Group Ltd	55
Arkema S.A.	56
Asahi Group Holdings Ltd.	57
Asahi Kasei Corp	57
ASE Technology Holding Co Ltd	57
Ashtead Group Plc	58
ASML Holding NV	59
ASSA ABLOY AB	61
Assicurazioni Generali S.p.A.	62
Associated British Foods Plc	63
AstraZeneca Plc	65
Athene Holding Ltd (New)	67
Atlas Copco AB (Sweden)	68
Australia & New Zealand Banking Group Ltd	71
Autoliv Inc	71
Aviva Plc	71
Awa Bank, Ltd.	73
AXA SA	73
AXIS Capital Holdings Ltd	74
BAE Systems Plc	74
Baidu Inc	76
Balfour Beatty Plc	76
Baloise Holding AG	78
Banco Bilbao Vizcaya Argentaria SA (BBVA)	79
Banco Bradesco SA	80
Banco de Chile	80
Banco Itau Chile	81
Banco Santander Brasil SA	81
Banco Santander Chile	83
Banco Santander Mexico SA, Institucion de Banca Multiple, Grupo Financiero Santander Mexico	83
Banco Santander SA (Spain)	84
BanColombia SA	84
Bangkok Bank Public Co., Ltd. (Thailand)	85
Bank Millennium SA	86
Bank of Communications Co., Ltd.	86
Bank of East Asia Ltd.	87
Bank of Ireland Group plc	88
Bank of Iwate, Ltd. (The) (Japan)	89
Bank of Kyoto Ltd (Japan)	89
Bank of Montreal (Quebec)	90
Bank of Nagoya, Ltd.	90
Bank of Nova Scotia Halifax	90
Bank of Queensland Ltd	92
Bank of Saga, Ltd. (The) (Japan)	92
Bank of the Philippine Islands	93
Bank of the Ryukyus, Ltd.	93
Bank Polska Kasa Opieki SA	93
Barclays Bank Plc	94
Barclays PLC	95
Barrick Gold Corp.	97
BASF SE	98
Bausch Health Companies Inc	100
BAWAG Group AG	102
Bayer AG	102
Bayerische Motoren Werke AG	104
BCE Inc	105
BDO Unibank Inc.	107
Beiersdorf AG	107
BHP Group Ltd	109
Blom Bank SAL	110
BlueScope Steel Ltd.	110
BNP Paribas (France)	112
Boc Hong Kong Holdings Ltd	114
Bouygues S.A.	115
BP PLC	117
Braskem S A	118
Brenntag SE	119
BRF S.A.	119
Bridgestone Corp (Japan)	120
British American Tobacco Plc	121
Brookfield Business Partners LP	123
Brookfield Corp	123
Brookfield Infrastructure Partners LP	124
BT Group Plc	124
Bunzl Plc	126
BYD Co Ltd	128
C.P. All Public Co Ltd	128
Canadian Imperial Bank Of Commerce (Toronto, Ontario)	129
Canadian National Railway Co	130
Canadian Natural Resources Ltd	131
Canadian Pacific Kansas City Ltd	132
Canadian Tire Corp Ltd	133
Canadian Western Bank	135
Canon Inc	135
Capgemini SE	136
Carlsberg A/S (Denmark)	136
Carnival Plc	138
Casino Guichard Perrachon S.A.	139
Cathay Financial Holding Co	141
Ceconomy AG	142
Cemex S.A.B. de C.V.	143
Cenovus Energy Inc	145
Central Japan Railway Co.	146
Centrica Plc	146
CGI Inc	148
Chiba Bank, Ltd	150
Chiba Kogyo Bank, Ltd. (The)	150
China Communications Constructions Group Ltd	150
China Construction Bank Corp	151
China Gas Holdings Ltd.	152
China Life Insurance Co Ltd	153
China Mobile Limited	153
China Petroleum & Chemical Corp	154
China Resources Land Ltd	155
China Resources Power Holdings Co Ltd	156
China Shenhua Energy Co., Ltd.	157
China Southern Airlines Co Ltd	158
China Steel Corp	159
Chow Tai Fook Jewellery Group Ltd.	159
Chubb Ltd	160
Chubu Electric Power Co Inc	161
Chugai Pharmaceutical Co Ltd	162
Chugoku Bank, Ltd. (The)	163
Chugoku Electric Power Co., Inc. (The)	163
CIMB Group Holdings Bhd	164
CITIC Ltd	164
CK Hutchison Holdings Ltd	165
CLP Holdings Ltd	166
Clydesdale Bank PLC	167
CNH Industrial NV	168
Co-operative Bank plc	168
Coca-Cola Europacific Partners plc	169
Coca-Cola FEMSA SAB de CV	170
Coca-Cola HBC AG	171
Coles Group Ltd (New)	172
Commercial Bank of Qatar	172
Commercial International Bank (Egypt) SAE	172
Commerzbank AG	173
Commonwealth Bank of Australia	173
Compagnie de Saint-Gobain	175
Compagnie Financiere Richemont SA	175
Compagnie Generale des Etablissements Michelin SCA	177
Compal Electronics Inc	177
Companhia Siderurgica Nacional	178
Compania de Distribucion Integral Logista Holdings SA	179
Compass Group PLC	179
Computacenter Plc	180
Constellium SE (France)	182
Continental AG (Germany, Fed. Rep.)	183
Corporacion Nacional del Cobre de Chile	184
Cosmo Energy Holdings Co Ltd	184
Covestro AG	185
CrediCorp Ltd.	185
Credit Agricole SA	185
CRH Plc	186
CSL Ltd	187

vii

Companies Profiled (continued)

Company	Page
Currys plc	188
Cushman & Wakefield PLC	189
Dai Nippon Printing Co Ltd	189
Dai-ichi Life Holdings Inc	190
Daiichi Sankyo Co Ltd	190
Daikin Industries Ltd	191
Dairy Farm International Holdings Ltd	192
Daito Trust Construction Co., Ltd.	193
Daiwa House Industry Co Ltd	194
Danone	195
Danske Bank A/S	197
Datang International Power Generation Co Ltd	199
DBS Group Holdings Ltd.	199
DCC Plc	200
Denso Corp	201
Dentsu Group Inc	203
Deutsche Bank AG	204
Deutsche Lufthansa AG (Germany, Fed. Rep.)	206
Deutsche Post AG	207
Deutsche Telekom AG	208
Diageo Plc	210
DiDi Global Inc	212
DKSH Holding Ltd	212
DNB BANK ASA	213
Dole plc	213
Downer EDI Ltd	214
DS Smith Plc	215
DSV AS	216
E Sun Financial Holdings Co Ltd	216
E.ON SE	217
East Japan Railway Co.	219
Easyjet Plc	220
Eaton Corp plc	220
Ecopetrol SA	221
EDP Energias de Portugal S.A.	222
Electric Power Development Co., Ltd. (Japan)	223
Empire Co Ltd	224
Empresa Nacional del Petroleo (Chile)	225
Enbridge Inc	225
Endesa S.A.	226
Enel Americas SA	228
Enel Societa Per Azioni	228
Eneos Holdings Inc	230
Engie SA	231
ENI S.p.A.	233
ENN Energy Holdings Ltd	235
EQB Inc	236
Equinor ASA	236
Ericsson	236
Erste Group Bank AG	237
EssilorLuxottica	239
Etablissements FR Colruyt SA Halle	240
Eurobank Ergasias Services & Holdings SA	240
Everest Group Ltd	241
Evergreen Marine Corp Taiwan Ltd	242
Evraz PLC	243
Exor NV	243
Fairfax Financial Holdings Ltd	243
Far Eastern International Bank	244
Far Eastern New Century Corp	245
Fast Retailing Co., Ltd.	245
Faurecia SE (France)	246
Federal Bank Ltd (The) (India)	248
Ferguson PLC (New)	248
FIDEA Holdings Co. Ltd.	249
FIH Mobile Ltd	249
First Abu Dhabi Bank PJSC	250
FirstRand Ltd.	250
Flex Ltd	251
Flutter Entertainment plc	253
Fomento Economico Mexicano, S.A.B. de C.V.	253
Fortescue Ltd	255
Fortis Inc	256
Fortum OYJ	256
Fresenius Medical Care AG (New)	258
Fresenius SE & Co KGaA	260
FUJIFILM Holdings Corp	262
Fujitsu Ltd	263
Fukui Bank Ltd.	263
Gail India Ltd	263
Galp Energia, SGPS, SA	264
Gazprom Neft PJSC	265
Geely Automobile Holdings Ltd	267
Gerdau S.A.	267
Glencore PLC	268
Great-West Lifeco Inc	269
Grupo Aval Acciones Y Valores SA	271
Grupo Bimbo SAB de CV (Mexico)	271
Grupo Financiero Banorte S.A. BDE C V	273
GSK plc	273
Gunma Bank Ltd (The)	275
Hachijuni Bank, Ltd. (Japan)	275
Hang Seng Bank Ltd.	276
Hannover Rueckversicherung SE	276
Hanwa Co Ltd (Japan)	277
HDFC Bank Ltd	277
Heidelberg Materials A G	278
Heineken Holding NV (Netherlands)	280
Heineken NV (Netherlands)	280
Helleniq Energy Holdings S A	280
Helvetia Holding AG	282
Henkel AG & Co KGAA	282
Hermes International SCA	284
Hino Motors, Ltd.	286
Hirogin Holdings Inc	286
Hitachi Construction Machinery Co Ltd	287
Hitachi, Ltd.	287
Hokkoku Financial Holdings Inc	287
Hokuhoku Financial Group Inc	288
Holcim Ltd (New)	288
Hon Hai Precision Industry Co Ltd	290
Honda Motor Co Ltd	291
HSBC Bank Plc	293
HSBC Holdings Plc	293
Huaneng Power International Inc	295
Hyakugo Bank Ltd. (Japan)	296
Hyakujushi Bank, Ltd.	296
Hydro-Quebec	296
Hyundai Motor Co., Ltd.	297
IA Financial Corp Inc	299
Iberdrola SA	300
ICICI Bank Ltd (India)	300
ICL Group Ltd	301
Idemitsu Kosan Co Ltd	302
IHI Corp	303
Iida Group Holdings Co., Ltd.	303
Impala Platinum Holdings Ltd.	304
Imperial Brands PLC	304
Imperial Oil Ltd	304
Inchcape PLC	306
Industria De Diseno Textil (Inditex) SA	307
Industrial and Commercial Bank of China Ltd	309
Infineon Technologies AG	310
Infosys Ltd.	311
ING Groep NV	312
Inpex Corp.	314
Intact Financial Corp	315
International Consolidated Airlines Group SA	316
International Distributions Services Plc	316
Intesa Sanpaolo S.P.A.	318
Investec plc	319
Isuzu Motors, Ltd. (Japan)	320
Itau Unibanco Holding S.A.	322
ITOCHU Corp (Japan)	323
J Sainsbury PLC	324
Japan Airlines Co Ltd JAL	326
Japan Post Bank Co Ltd	326
Japan Post Holdings Co Ltd	327
Japan Post Insurance Co Ltd	327
Japan Tobacco Inc.	327
Jardine Matheson Holdings Ltd.	329
JBS SA	330
JD Sports Fashion PLC	332
JD.com, Inc.	333
Jeronimo Martins S.G.P.S. SA	333
JFE Holdings Inc	334
Jiangxi Copper Co., Ltd.	335
JinkoSolar Holding Co., Ltd.	336
Johnson Controls International plc	336
Johnson Matthey Plc	337
JSC VTB Bank	339
JTEKT Corp	340
Juroku Financial Group Inc	341
Kajima Corp. (Japan)	341
Kansai Electric Power Co., Inc. (Kansai Denryoku K. K.) (Japan)	342
Kao Corp	343
Kawasaki Heavy Industries Ltd	344
KBC Group NV	345
KDDI Corp	345
KE Holdings Inc	345
Keiyo Bank, Ltd. (The) (Japan)	346
Kering SA	346
Kingfisher PLC	348
Kirin Holdings Co Ltd	350
Kobe Steel Ltd	351
Koc Holdings AS	352
Komatsu Ltd	354
Kone OYJ	354
Koninklijke Ahold Delhaize NV	355
Koninklijke Philips NV	357
Korea Electric Power Corp	358
Kubota Corp. (Japan)	358
Kuehne & Nagel International AG	359
Kyocera Corp	360
Kyushu Electric Power Co Inc	361
L'Air Liquide S.A. (France)	362
L'Oreal S.A. (France)	362
Larsen & Toubro Ltd	363
Laurentian Bank of Canada	363
Legal & General Group PLC	363
Lenovo Group Ltd	365
Lewis (John) Partnership Plc	367
LG Chem Ltd (New)	368
LG Display Co Ltd	368
LG Electronics Inc	370
LG Energy Solution Ltd	371
LIXIL Corp	371
Lloyds Banking Group Plc	372
Loblaw Companies Ltd	374
London Stock Exchange Group Plc	374
lululemon athletica inc	376
LVMH Moet Hennessy Louis Vuitton	378
LY Corp	380
LyondellBasell Industries NV	380
Macquarie Bank Ltd	380
Macquarie Group Ltd	381
Magna International Inc	383
Magnit PJSC	385
Mahindra & Mahindra Ltd	385
Manulife Financial Corp	385
Mapfre SA	386
Marks & Spencer Group PLC	386
Marubeni Corp.	388
Mazda Motor Corp. (Japan)	390
McKesson Europe AG	391
Mediobanca Banca Di Credito Finanziario SpA	392
Medipal Holdings Corp	394
Medtronic PLC	395
Meituan	395
Melrose Industries Plc	395
MercadoLibre Inc	395
Mercedes-Benz AG	397
Merck KGaA (Germany)	398
Metro Inc	400
Minebea Mitsumi Inc	401
Mitsubishi Chemical Group Corp	402
Mitsubishi Corp	403

Companies Profiled (continued)

Company	Page
Mitsubishi Electric Corp	403
Mitsubishi Estate Co Ltd	403
Mitsubishi HC Capital Inc	404
Mitsubishi Heavy Industries Ltd	405
Mitsubishi Materials Corp.	406
Mitsubishi Motors Corp. (Japan)	406
Mitsubishi Shokuhin Co., Ltd.	407
Mitsubishi UFJ Financial Group Inc	407
Mitsui & Co., Ltd.	409
Mitsui Chemicals Inc (Japan)	410
Mitsui Fudosan Co Ltd	410
Mitsui OSK Lines Ltd	411
Miyazaki Bank, Ltd. (The)	412
MMC Norilsk Nickel PJSC	412
MOL Magyar Olaj es Gazipari Reszvenytar	413
Molson Coors Beverage Co	415
MS&AD Insurance Group Holdings	415
MTN Group Ltd (South Africa)	416
Muenchener Rueckversicherungs-Gesellschaft AG (Germany)	417
Murata Manufacturing Co Ltd	418
Musashino Bank, Ltd.	420
Nanto Bank, Ltd.	420
National Australia Bank Ltd.	421
National Bank of Canada	422
National Grid plc	423
National Westminster Bank Plc	425
NatWest Group PLC	426
NEC Corp	427
Nedbank Group Ltd	427
Neste Oyj	428
Nestle SA	430
NetEase, Inc	433
New World Development Co. Ltd.	433
NH Foods Ltd	434
Nidec Corp	435
Nine Dragons Paper (Holdings) Limited	436
Nintendo Co., Ltd.	437
Nippon Express Holdings Inc	438
Nippon Paint Holdings Co Ltd	438
Nippon Paper Industries Co Ltd	439
Nippon Steel Corp (New)	439
Nippon Steel Trading Corp	441
Nippon Telegraph & Telephone Corp (Japan)	442
Nippon Yusen Kabushiki Kaisha	443
Nissan Motor Co., Ltd.	443
NN Group NV (Netherlands)	445
Nokia Corp	446
Nomura Holdings Inc	447
Nordea Bank ABp	449
Norsk Hydro ASA	450
North Pacific Bank Ltd	452
Novartis AG Basel	452
Novatek Joint Stock Co	453
Novo-Nordisk AS	454
Novolipetsk Steel	455
NTT Data Group Corp	457
Nutrien Ltd	457
NXP Semiconductors NV	457
Obayashi Corp	458
Ogaki Kyoritsu Bank, Ltd.	460
Oita Bank Ltd (Japan)	460
Oji Holdings Corp	460
OMV AG (Austria)	462
Orange	463
Orbia Advance Corp SAB De CV	465
Origin Energy Ltd	466
Orix Corp	467
Orsted A/S	468
Osaka Gas Co Ltd (Japan)	469
OSB Group plc	470
Otsuka Holdings Co., Ltd.	471
Paltac Corp	471
Pan Pacific International Holdings Corp	471
Panasonic Holdings Corp	472
Parkland Corp	473
PDD Holdings Inc	474
Permanent TSB Group Holdings Plc	474
Pernod Ricard S.A. (France)	475
Persol Holdings Co Ltd	477
PetroChina Co Ltd	477
Petroleo Brasileiro SA	478
Petroleos Mexicanos (Pemex) (Mexico)	480
Phoenix Group Holdings PLC	482
Ping An Insurance (Group) Co of China Ltd.	482
Piraeus Financial Holdings SA	483
PJSC Magnitogorsk Iron & Steel Works	484
POSCO Holdings Inc	484
Power Corp. of Canada	486
Prudential Plc	487
PT Bank Mandiri Persero Tbk	489
PT Telekomunikasi Indonesia (Persero) TBK	490
PTT Exploration & Production Public Co Ltd	491
PTT Global Chemical Public Co Ltd	491
PTT Public Co Ltd	492
Publicis Groupe S.A.	493
Puma SE	495
Qatar Islamic Bank	496
QBE Insurance Group Ltd.	496
Raiffeisen Bank International Ag Wien	497
Rakuten Group Inc	497
Ramsay Health Care Ltd. (Australia)	498
Reckitt Benckiser Group Plc	499
Recruit Holdings Co Ltd	499
Reliance Industries Ltd	499
RELX PLC	500
RenaissanceRe Holdings Ltd.	501
Renault S.A. (France)	501
Renesas Electronics Corp	502
Repsol S.A.	503
Resona Holdings Inc Osaka	504
Resonac Holdings Corp	505
Rexel S.A.	506
Ricoh Co Ltd	507
Rio Tinto Ltd	508
Rio Tinto Plc	510
Roche Holding Ltd	512
Rogers Communications Inc	513
Rolls-Royce Holdings Plc	515
Rosneft Oil Co OJSC (Moscow)	517
Royal Bank Canada (Montreal, Quebec)	518
Royal Bank of Canada (Montreal, Quebec)	518
Royal DSM NV	520
RWE AG	522
Ryanair Holdings Plc	523
Safran SA	524
Saipem SpA	525
Samsung Electronics Co Ltd	526
San-In Godo Bank, Ltd. (The) (Japan)	527
Sandoz Group AG	527
Sandvik AB (Sweden)	527
Sanofi	528
SAP SE	530
Saputo Inc	532
Saras Raffinerie Sarde SpA	533
Sasol Ltd.	533
Sberbank Of Russia	534
SBI Shinsei Bank Ltd	535
Schindler Holding AG	536
Schlumberger Ltd	537
Schroders PLC	538
SCOR S.E. (France)	539
Sea Ltd	541
SEB SA	541
Seiko Epson Corp Suwa	542
Sekisui Chemical Co Ltd	544
Sekisui House, Ltd. (Japan)	544
Seven & i Holdings Co. Ltd.	545
SG Holdings Co Ltd	546
Shanghai Electric Group Co Ltd	546
Sharp Corp (Japan)	547
Shell plc	548
Shiga Bank, Ltd.	550
Shikoku Bank, Ltd. (Japan)	550
Shimizu Corp.	550
Shin-Etsu Chemical Co., Ltd.	551
Shizuoka Bank Ltd (Japan)	552
Shoprite Holdings, Ltd.	553
Siam Cement Public Co. Ltd.	553
Siam Commercial Bank Public Co Ltd (The)	554
Sibanye Stillwater Ltd	555
Siemens AG (Germany)	555
Siemens Energy AG	557
Siemens Gamesa Renewable Energy SA	557
Sika AG	558
Singapore Telecommunications Ltd	558
Sinopec Shanghai Petrochemical Co., Ltd.	559
Sinopharm Group Co., Ltd.	560
Sinovac Biotech Ltd	560
Sistema PJSFC	560
Skandinaviska Enskilda Banken	562
Smurfit Kappa Group PLC	563
Societe Generale	565
Sodexo	565
SoftBank Corp (New)	567
Sojitz Corp	567
Sompo Holdings Inc	569
Sony Group Corp	570
South African Reserve Bank	573
Spotify Technology SA	573
SSE PLC	574
Standard Bank Group Ltd	574
Standard Chartered Plc	576
State Bank of India	577
Steel Authority of India Ltd	578
Stellantis NV	579
STMicroelectronics NV	579
Stora Enso Oyj	580
Subaru Corporation	582
Sumitomo Chemical Co., Ltd.	583
Sumitomo Corp. (Japan)	584
Sumitomo Electric Industries, Ltd. (Japan)	584
Sumitomo Forestry Co., Ltd. (Japan)	586
Sumitomo Metal Mining Co Ltd	586
Sumitomo Mitsui Financial Group Inc Tokyo	587
Sumitomo Mitsui Trust Holdings Inc	588
Sun Hung Kai Properties Ltd	589
Sun Life Assurance Company of Canada	589
Sun Life Financial Inc	590
Suncor Energy Inc	591
Suncorp Group Ltd.	592
Suntory Beverage & Food Ltd.	593
Suruga Bank, Ltd.	593
Suzuken Co Ltd	593
Suzuki Motor Corp. (Japan)	594
Svenska Handelsbanken	595
Swatch Group AG (The)	597
Swedbank AB	597
Swire (John) & Sons Ltd.	597
Swire Pacific Ltd.	598
Swiss Life Holding AG	600
Swiss Re Ltd	600
SwissCom AG	601
T&D Holdings Inc	601
Taisei Corp	602
Taiwan Semiconductor Manufacturing Co., Ltd.	602
Takeda Pharmaceutical Co Ltd	604
Tata Motors Ltd	605
Tata Steel Ltd	606
TC Energy Corp	607
TDK Corp	609
TE Connectivity Ltd	610
Techtronic Industries Co. Ltd.	611
Teck Resources Ltd	612
Telecom Italia SpA	613
Telefonica SA	615
Telenor ASA	615

Companies Profiled (continued)

Teleperformance SA ... 617	Toyota Industries Corporation (Japan) ... 641	Wesfarmers Ltd. ... 665
Telstra Group Ltd ... 617	Toyota Motor Corp ... 642	West Japan Railway Co ... 666
TELUS Corp ... 619	Toyota Tsusho Corp ... 643	Weston (George) Ltd ... 666
Tenaris SA ... 620	Trane Technologies plc ... 644	Westpac Banking Corp ... 668
Tencent Holdings Ltd. ... 620	TSB Banking Group Plc ... 644	WH Group Ltd ... 670
Ternium S A ... 621	TUI AG ... 645	Willis Towers Watson Public Ltd Co ... 670
Tesco PLC ... 622	Turkiye Garanti Bankasi AS ... 646	Wipro Ltd ... 670
Teva Pharmaceutical Industries Ltd ... 622	UBS Group AG ... 647	Wistron Corp ... 672
TFI International Inc ... 623	Ultrapar Participacoes SA ... 648	Woodside Energy Group Ltd ... 673
Thales ... 625	Umicore SA ... 649	Woolworths Group Ltd ... 674
ThyssenKrupp AG ... 627	Unicredito SpA ... 651	WPP Plc (New) ... 676
Tochigi Bank Ltd. ... 629	Unilever Plc ... 652	WSP Global Inc ... 678
Toho Bank, Ltd. (The) ... 629	United Overseas Bank Ltd. (Singapore) ... 653	Yamada Holdings Co Ltd ... 679
Toho Holdings Co Ltd ... 629	Vale SA ... 654	Yamagata Bank Ltd. (The) ... 679
Tohoku Electric Power Co., Inc. (Japan) ... 630	Valeo SE ... 656	Yamaha Motor Co Ltd ... 679
Tokio Marine Holdings Inc ... 631	Vedanta Ltd ... 656	Yamanashi Chuo Bank, Ltd. (Japan) ... 681
Tokyo Century Corp ... 632	Vestas Wind Systems A/S ... 656	Yamato Holdings Co., Ltd. ... 681
Tokyo Electric Power Company Holdings Inc ... 633	Vinci SA ... 657	YangMing Marine Transport Corp ... 682
Tokyo Electron, Ltd. ... 634	Vipshop Holdings Ltd ... 660	Yankuang Energy Group Co Ltd ... 682
Tokyo Gas Co Ltd ... 634	Vivendi SE ... 660	Yapi Ve Kredi Bankasi AS ... 683
Toppan Inc ... 635	Vodafone Group Plc ... 661	Yorkshire Building Society ... 684
Toray Industries, Inc. ... 636	voestalpine AG ... 662	YPF SA ... 685
Toronto Dominion Bank ... 636	Volkswagen AG ... 663	Yue Yuen Industrial (Holdings) Ltd. ... 686
Toshiba Corp ... 638	Volvo AB ... 663	Zte Corp. ... 687
TotalEnergies SE ... 639	Vontobel Holding AG ... 665	Zurich Insurance Group AG ... 688
Toyota Boshoku Corp ... 640	Welcia Holdings Co Ltd ... 665	

About Hoover's Handbook of World Business 2024

This edition of Hoover's Handbook of World Business is focused on its mission of providing you with premier coverage of the global business scene. Featuring 300 of the world's most influential companies based outside of the United States, this book is one of the most complete sources of in-depth information on large, non-US-based business enterprises available anywhere.

Hoover's Handbook of World Business is one of our four-title series of handbooks that covers, literally, the world of business. The series is available as an indexed set, and also includes Hoover's Handbook of American Business, Hoover's Handbook of Private Companies, and Hoover's Handbook of Emerging Companies. This series brings you information on the biggest, fastest-growing, and most influential enterprises in the world.

HOOVER'S ONLINE FOR BUSINESS NEEDS

In addition to Hoover's widely used MasterList and Handbooks series, comprehensive coverage of more than 40,000 business enterprises is available in electronic format on our Web site at www.hoovers.com. Our goal is to provide our customers the fastest path to business with insight and actionable information about companies, industries, and key decision makers, along with the powerful tools to find and connect to the right people to get business done. Hoover's has partnered with other prestigious business information and service providers to bring you all the right business information, services, and links in one place.

We welcome the recognition we have received as the premier provider of high-quality company information — online, electronically, and in print — and continue to look for ways to make our products more available and more useful to you.

We believe that anyone who buys from, sells to, invests in, lends to, competes with, interviews with, or works for a company should know all there is to know about that enterprise. Taken together, this book and the other Hoover's products and resources represent the most complete source of basic corporate information readily available to the general public.

HOW TO USE THIS BOOK

This book has four sections:

1. "Using Hoover's Handbooks" describes the contents of our profiles and explains the ways in which we gather and compile our data.

2. "A List-Lover's Compendium" contains lists of the largest, fastest-growing, and most valuable companies of global importance.

3. The company profiles section makes up the largest and most important part of the book — 300 profiles of major business enterprises, arranged alphabetically.

4. Three indexes complete the book. The first sorts companies by industry groups, the second by headquarters location. The third index is a list of all the executives found in the Executives section of each company profile.

Using Hoover's Handbooks

SELECTION OF THE COMPANIES PROFILED

The 300 profiles in this book include a variety of international enterprises, ranging from some of the largest publicly traded companies in the world — Daimler AG, for example — to Malaysia's largest and oldest conglomerate, Sime Darby Berhad. It also includes many private businesses, such as Bertelsmann AG and LEGO, as well as a selection of government-owned entities, such as Mexico's Petróleos Mexicanos. The companies selected represent a cross-section of the largest, most influential, and most interesting companies based outside the United States.

In selecting these companies, we followed several basic criteria. We started with the global giants, including Toyota and Royal Dutch Shell, and then looked at companies with substantial activity in the US, such as Vivendi and Diageo. We also included companies that dominate their industries (e.g., AB Electrolux, the world's #1 producer of household appliances), as well as representative companies from around the world (an Indian conglomerate, Tata; two firms from Finland, Nokia and Stora Enso Oyj; and two companies from Russia, OAO Gazprom and OAO LUKOIL). Companies that weren't necessarily global powerhouses but that had a high profile with consumers (e.g., IKEA) or had interesting stories (Virgin Group) were included. Finally, because of their truly global reach, we added the Big Four accounting firms (even though they are headquartered or co-head quartered in the US).

ORGANIZATION

The profiles are presented in alphabetical order. You will find the commonly used name of the enterprise at the beginning of the profile; the full, legal name is found in the Locations section. For some companies, primarily Japanese, the commonly translated English name differs from the actual legal name of the company, so both are provided. (The legal name of Nippon Steel Corporation is Shin Nippon Seitetsu Kabushiki Kaisha.) If a company name starts with a person's first name (e.g., George Weston Limited), it is alphabetized under the first name. We've also tried to alphabetize companies where you would expect to find them — for example, Deutsche Lufthansa is in the L's and Grupo Televisa can be found under T.

The annual financial information contained in the profiles is current through fiscal year-ends occurring as late as June 2023. We have included certain nonfinancial developments, such as officer changes, through September 2023.

OVERVIEW

In the first section of the profile, we have tried to give a thumbnail description of the company and what it does. The description will usually include information on the company's strategy, reputation, and ownership. We recommend that you read this section first.

HISTORY

This extended section, which is present for most companies, reflects our belief that every enterprise is the sum of its history and that you have to know where you came from in order to know where you are going. While some companies have limited historical awareness, we think the vast majority of the enterprises in this book have colorful backgrounds. We have tried to focus on the people who made the enterprises what they are today. We have found these histories to be full of twists and ironies; they make fascinating reading.

EXECUTIVES

Here we list the names of the people who run the company, insofar as space allows. We have shown age and pay information where available, although most non-US companies are not required to report the level of detail revealed in the US.

Although companies are free to structure their management titles any way they please, most modern corporations follow standard practices. The ultimate power in any corporation lies with the shareholders, who elect a board of directors, usually including officers or "insiders," as well as individuals from outside the company. The chief officer, the person on whose desk the buck stops, is usually called the chief executive officer

(CEO) in the US. In other countries, practices vary widely. In the UK, traditionally, the Managing Director performs the functions of the CEO without the title, although the use of the term CEO is on the rise there. In Germany it is customary to have two boards of directors: a managing board populated by the top executives of the company and a higher-level supervisory board consisting of outsiders.

As corporate management has become more complex, it is common for the CEO to have a "right-hand person" who oversees the day-to-day operations of the company, allowing the CEO plenty of time to focus on strategy and long-term issues. This right-hand person is usually designated the chief operating officer (COO) and is often the president of the company. In other cases one person is both chairman and president.

We have tried to list each company's most important officers, including the chief financial officer (CFO) and the chief legal officer. For companies with US operations, we have included the names of the US CEO, CFO, and top human resources executive, where available.

The people named in the Executives section are indexed at the back of the book.

The Executives section also includes the name of the company's auditing (accounting) firm, where available.

LOCATIONS

Here we include the company's full legal name and its headquarters, street address, telephone and fax numbers, and Web site, as available. We also list the same information for the US office for each company, if one exists. Telephone numbers of foreign offices are shown using the standardized conventions of international dialing. The back of the book includes an index of companies by headquarters location.

In some cases we have also included information on the geographic distribution of the company's business, including sales and profit data. Note that these profit numbers, like those in the Products/Operations section below, are usually operating or pretax profits rather than net profits. Operating profits are generally those before financing costs (interest income and payments) and before taxes, which are considered costs attributable to the whole company rather than to one division or part of the world. For this reason the net income figures (in the Historical Financials section) are usually much lower, since they are after interest and taxes. Pretax profits are after interest but before taxes.

PRODUCTS/OPERATIONS

This section lists as many of the company's products, services, brand names, divisions, subsidiaries, and joint ventures as we could fit. We have tried to include all its major lines and all familiar brand names. The nature of this section varies by company and the amount of information available. If the company publishes sales and profit information by type of business, we have included it (in US dollars).

COMPETITORS

In this section we have listed enterprises that compete with the profiled company. This feature is included as a quick way to locate similar companies and compare them. Because of the difficulty in identifying companies that only compete in foreign markets, the list of competitors is still weighted to large international companies with a strong US presence.

HISTORICAL FINANCIALS

Here we have tried to present as much data about each enterprise's financial performance as we could compile in the allocated space. Financial data for all companies is presented in US dollars, using the appropriate exchange rate at fiscal year-end.

While the information presented varies somewhat from industry to industry, it is less complete in the case of private companies that do not release data (although we have always tried to provide annual sales and employment). The following information is generally present.

A five-year table, with relevant annualized compound growth rates, covers:
- Sales — fiscal year sales (year-end assets for most financial companies)
- Net income — fiscal year net income (before accounting changes)
- Net profit margin — fiscal year net income as a percent of sales (as a percent of assets for most financial firms)
- Employees — fiscal year-end or average number of employees
- Stock price — the fiscal year close
- P/E — high and low price/earnings ratio
- Dividends per share — fiscal year dividends per share

The information on the number of employees is intended to aid the reader interested in knowing whether a company has a long-term trend of increasing or decreasing employment. As far as we know, we are the only company that publishes this information in print format.

The numbers on the left in each row of the Historical Financials section give the month and the year in which the company's fiscal year actually ends. Thus, a company with a September 30, 2018, year-end is shown as 9/18.

In addition, we have provided in graph form a stock price history for companies that trade on the major US exchanges. The graphs, covering up to five years, show the range of trading between the high and the low price, as well as the closing price for each fiscal year. For public companies that trade on the OTC or Pink Sheets or that do not trade on US exchanges, we graph net income. Generally, for private companies, we have graphed net income, or, if that is unavailable, sales.

Key year-end statistics in this section generally show

the financial strength of the enterprise, including:
- Debt ratio (long-term debt as a percent of shareholders' equity)
- Return on equity (net income divided by the average of beginning and ending common shareholders' equity)
- Cash and cash equivalents
- Current ratio (ratio of current assets to current liabilities)
- Total long-term debt (including capital lease obligations)
- Number of shares of common stock outstanding
- Dividend yield (fiscal year dividends per share divided by the fiscal year-end closing stock price)
- Dividend payout (fiscal year dividends divided by fiscal year EPS)
- Market value at fiscal year-end (fiscal year-end closing stock price multiplied by fiscal year-end number of shares outstanding)
- Fiscal year sales for financial institutions.

Per share data has been adjusted for stock splits. The data for public companies with sponsored American Depositary Receipts has been provided to us by Morningstar, Inc. Other public company information was compiled by Hoover's, which takes full responsibility for the content of this section.

In the case of private companies that do not publicly disclose financial information, we usually did not have access to such standardized data. We have gathered estimates of sales and other statistics from numerous sources.

Hoover's Handbook of World Business

A List-Lover's Compendium

The 100 Largest Global Public Companies by Sales in Hoover's Handbook of World Business 2024

Rank	Company	Sales ($mil)
1	China Petroleum & Chemical Corp	$480,989
2	PetroChina Co Ltd	$469,537
3	Shell plc	$323,183
4	Volkswagen AG	$298,232
5	Toyota Motor Corp	$278,966
6	TotalEnergies SE	$263,310
7	Glencore PLC	$255,984
8	Samsung Electronics Co Ltd	$235,341
9	Industrial and Commercial Bank of China Ltd	$217,576
10	Hon Hai Precision Industry Co Ltd	$216,489
11	BP PLC	$211,397
12	Stellantis NV	$209,940
13	China Construction Bank Corp	$197,828
14	Mercedes-Benz AG	$169,705
15	Mitsubishi Corp	$161,969
16	JD.com, Inc.	$151,658
17	Equinor ASA	$150,806
18	Enel Societa Per Azioni	$150,078
19	ENI S.p.A.	$142,784
20	HSBC Holdings Plc	$134,708
21	China Mobile Limited	$133,612
22	Honda Motor Co Ltd	$126,949
23	Alibaba Group Holding Ltd	$126,358
24	CITIC Ltd	$126,029
25	Bayerische Motoren Werke AG	$125,907
26	E.ON SE	$124,729
27	Deutsche Telekom AG	$124,019
28	Petroleos Mexicanos (Pemex) (Mexico)	$121,809
29	Rosneft Oil Co OJSC (Moscow)	$116,674
30	Eneos Holdings Inc	$112,749
31	Allianz SE	$111,600
32	Nestle SA	$111,591
33	Mitsui & Co., Ltd.	$107,417
34	Petroleo Brasileiro SA	$105,513
35	ITOCHU Corp (Japan)	$104,708
36	China Communications Constructions Group Ltd	$104,408
37	Deutsche Post AG	$100,862
38	Engie SA	$100,252
39	Hyundai Motor Co., Ltd.	$98,991
40	AXA SA	$98,852
41	Banco Santander SA (Spain)	$98,779
42	Nippon Telegraph & Telephone Corp (Japan)	$98,630
43	PTT Public Co Ltd	$97,464
44	Reliance Industries Ltd	$97,241
45	Brookfield Corp	$95,924
46	LVMH Moet Hennessy Louis Vuitton	$95,423
47	BASF SE	$93,269
48	Koninklijke Ahold Delhaize NV	$92,902
49	Japan Post Holdings Co Ltd	$92,609
50	BNP Paribas (France)	$91,426
51	Credit Agricole SA	$88,725
52	Sony Group Corp	$86,644
53	Seven & i Holdings Co. Ltd.	$86,357
54	Royal Bank of Canada (Montreal, Quebec)	$85,320
55	Royal Bank Canada (Montreal, Quebec)	$85,320
56	Siemens AG (Germany)	$82,395
57	Hitachi, Ltd.	$81,699
58	A.P. Moller - Maersk A/S	$81,529
59	Repsol S.A.	$80,902
60	Tencent Holdings Ltd.	$80,385
61	Sinopharm Group Co., Ltd.	$80,037
62	Nissan Motor Co., Ltd.	$79,563
63	Tesco PLC	$78,825
64	Muenchener Rueckversicherungs-Gesellschaft AG (Germany)	$76,741
65	Bank of Communications Co., Ltd.	$76,306
66	Toyota Tsusho Corp	$73,946
67	Toronto Dominion Bank	$73,819
68	Alimentation Couche-Tard Inc	$71,856
69	Idemitsu Kosan Co Ltd	$71,000
70	Taiwan Semiconductor Manufacturing Co., Ltd.	$70,608
71	Roche Holding Ltd	$70,188
72	Jiangxi Copper Co., Ltd.	$69,569
73	Marubeni Corp.	$69,005
74	ArcelorMittal SA	$68,275
75	Korea Electric Power Corp	$67,945
76	Vinci SA	$66,791
77	Aeon Co Ltd	$66,657
78	Unilever Plc	$66,017
79	Barclays PLC	$65,415
80	Accenture plc	$64,111
81	Lloyds Banking Group Plc	$63,907
82	JBS SA	$62,930
83	Panasonic Holdings Corp	$62,911
84	LG Electronics Inc	$62,892
85	Dai-ichi Life Holdings Inc	$62,868
86	Airbus SE	$62,761
87	Lenovo Group Ltd	$61,946
88	BYD Co Ltd	$61,470
89	Assicurazioni Generali S.p.A.	$60,968
90	Societe Generale	$60,900
91	Nippon Steel Corp (New)	$59,883
92	Rio Tinto Ltd	$59,617
93	POSCO Holdings Inc	$59,402
94	Anheuser-Busch InBev SA/NV	$59,380
95	Tokyo Electric Power Company Holdings Inc	$58,555
96	Iberdrola SA	$57,619
97	Brookfield Business Partners LP	$55,068
98	Compagnie de Saint-Gobain	$54,745
99	Bayer AG	$54,191
100	Rio Tinto Plc	$54,041

SOURCE: MERGENT INC., DATABASE, APRIL 2024

The 100 Largest Global Public Companies by Income in Hoover's Handbook of World Business 2024

Rank	Company	Net Income ($mil)
1	Industrial and Commercial Bank of China Ltd	$52,254
2	China Construction Bank Corp	$46,844
3	Samsung Electronics Co Ltd	$33,031
4	A.P. Moller - Maersk A/S	$29,198
5	Equinor ASA	$28,746
6	Taiwan Semiconductor Manufacturing Co., Ltd.	$27,387
7	Tencent Holdings Ltd.	$27,286
8	Petroleo Brasileiro SA	$25,679
9	HSBC Holdings Plc	$23,533
10	PetroChina Co Ltd	$21,652
11	Rio Tinto Ltd	$21,094
12	Stellantis NV	$20,597
13	TotalEnergies SE	$20,526
14	Deutsche Telekom AG	$19,702
15	Shell plc	$19,359
16	Toyota Motor Corp	$18,405
17	China Mobile Limited	$18,294
18	Glencore PLC	$17,320
19	LVMH Moet Hennessy Louis Vuitton	$16,806
20	Sberbank Of Russia	$16,656
21	Volkswagen AG	$15,878
22	Mercedes-Benz AG	$15,795
23	BP PLC	$15,239
24	Novartis AG Basel	$14,850
25	ENI S.p.A.	$14,831
26	Bayerische Motoren Werke AG	$14,014
27	Roche Holding Ltd	$13,744
28	Nestle SA	$13,399
29	Bank of Communications Co., Ltd.	$13,357
30	BHP Group Ltd	$12,921
31	Vodafone Group Plc	$12,863
32	Novo-Nordisk AS	$12,436
33	Ping An Insurance (Group) Co of China Ltd.	$12,143
34	Rosneft Oil Co OJSC (Moscow)	$11,759
35	BNP Paribas (France)	$10,889
36	Royal Bank Canada (Montreal, Quebec)	$10,744
37	Alibaba Group Holding Ltd	$10,586
38	Royal Bank of Canada (Montreal, Quebec)	$10,574
39	Banco Santander SA (Spain)	$10,258
40	China Shenhua Energy Co., Ltd.	$10,092
41	Rio Tinto Plc	$10,058
42	CITIC Ltd	$9,684
43	China Petroleum & Chemical Corp	$9,610
44	Nippon Telegraph & Telephone Corp (Japan)	$9,108
45	Chubb Ltd	$9,028
46	Mitsubishi Corp	$8,865
47	ASML Holding NV	$8,682
48	Evergreen Marine Corp Taiwan Ltd	$8,632
49	Mitsui & Co., Ltd.	$8,489
50	Sinovac Biotech Ltd	$8,467
51	Siemens AG (Germany)	$8,421
52	Vale SA	$8,230
53	Reliance Industries Ltd	$8,014
54	Nippon Yusen Kabushiki Kaisha	$7,602
55	UBS Group AG	$7,457
56	Toronto Dominion Bank	$7,389
57	Allianz SE	$7,196
58	Unilever Plc	$7,185
59	AXA SA	$7,129
60	Bank of Nova Scotia Halifax	$7,066
61	Sony Group Corp	$7,036
62	Lloyds Banking Group Plc	$6,958
63	Unicredito SpA	$6,897
64	Accenture plc	$6,871
65	Banco Bilbao Vizcaya Argentaria SA (BBVA)	$6,856
66	SAP SE	$6,799
67	ING Groep NV	$6,735
68	Gazprom Neft PJSC	$6,704
69	Barclays PLC	$6,702
70	Commonwealth Bank of Australia	$6,679
71	Ecopetrol SA	$6,514
72	MMC Norilsk Nickel PJSC	$6,512
73	GSK plc	$6,280
74	Suncor Energy Inc	$6,258
75	Canadian Natural Resources Ltd	$6,211
76	DBS Group Holdings Ltd.	$6,113
77	L'Oreal S.A. (France)	$6,094
78	ITOCHU Corp (Japan)	$6,010
79	Sanofi	$5,981
80	Mitsui OSK Lines Ltd	$5,977
81	YangMing Marine Transport Corp	$5,968
82	AstraZeneca Plc	$5,955
83	NatWest Group PLC	$5,908
84	Deutsche Bank AG	$5,900
85	Credit Agricole SA	$5,806
86	Novatek Joint Stock Co	$5,765
87	Deutsche Post AG	$5,723
88	Itau Unibanco Holding S.A.	$5,616
89	Anheuser-Busch InBev SA/NV	$5,341
90	Shin-Etsu Chemical Co., Ltd.	$5,317
91	Tata Steel Ltd	$5,300
92	Nippon Steel Corp (New)	$5,210
93	Petroleos Mexicanos (Pemex) (Mexico)	$5,131
94	HDFC Bank Ltd	$5,095
95	KDDI Corp	$5,086
96	Cathay Financial Holding Co	$5,038
97	Novolipetsk Steel	$5,036
98	Hon Hai Precision Industry Co Ltd	$5,031
99	Honda Motor Co Ltd	$4,891
100	Hitachi, Ltd.	$4,873

SOURCE: MERGENT INC., DATABASE, APRIL 2024

The 100 Largest Global Public Employers in Hoover's Handbook of World Business 2024

Rank	Company	Employees
1	Hon Hai Precision Industry Co Ltd	826,608
2	Accenture plc	733,000
3	Volkswagen AG	675,805
4	Deutsche Post AG	600,278
5	JD.com, Inc.	450,679
6	China Mobile Limited	449,934
7	Sodexo	429,941
8	Industrial and Commercial Bank of China Ltd	427,587
9	Aeon Co Ltd	425,421
10	Jardine Matheson Holdings Ltd.	425,000
11	Koninklijke Ahold Delhaize NV	414,000
12	Nippon Telegraph & Telephone Corp (Japan)	381,653
13	Japan Post Holdings Co Ltd	377,047
14	Toyota Motor Corp	375,235
15	Teleperformance SA	360,980
16	Capgemini SE	359,567
17	China Construction Bank Corp	352,588
18	Infosys Ltd.	343,234
19	Reliance Industries Ltd	342,982
20	Tesco PLC	336,926
21	Sumitomo Electric Industries, Ltd. (Japan)	334,716
22	Hitachi, Ltd.	322,525
23	Fomento Economico Mexicano, S.A.B. de C.V.	320,752
24	Siemens AG (Germany)	320,000
25	Fresenius SE & Co KGaA	316,078
26	Yue Yuen Industrial (Holdings) Ltd.	310,000
27	CK Hutchison Holdings Ltd	300,000
28	Sberbank Of Russia	287,866
29	Vinci SA	271,648
30	Nestle SA	270,000
31	Stellantis NV	258,275
32	Wipro Ltd	250,000
33	JBS SA	250,000
34	State Bank of India	244,250
35	Brookfield Corp	240,000
36	Alibaba Group Holding Ltd	235,216
37	Panasonic Holdings Corp	233,391
38	HSBC Holdings Plc	220,861
39	Loblaw Companies Ltd	220,000
40	Weston (George) Ltd	220,000
41	Dairy Farm International Holdings Ltd	216,000
42	Yamato Holdings Co., Ltd.	210,197
43	Banco Santander SA (Spain)	206,462
44	Woolworths Group Ltd	200,364
45	EssilorLuxottica	200,121
46	Deutsche Telekom AG	199,652
47	Continental AG (Germany, Fed. Rep.)	199,038
48	Honda Motor Co Ltd	197,039
49	Denso Corp	195,471
50	BNP Paribas (France)	193,122
51	Casino Guichard Perrachon S.A.	188,811
52	CGI Inc	183,000
53	Ramsay Health Care Ltd. (Australia)	179,000
54	Magna International Inc	179,000
55	America Movil SAB de CV	176,014
56	Flex Ltd	172,108
57	Compagnie de Saint-Gobain	170,714
58	Seven & i Holdings Co. Ltd.	167,248
59	Mercedes-Benz AG	166,056
60	Industria De Diseno Textil (Inditex) SA	164,997
61	International Distributions Services Plc	162,360
62	CITIC Ltd	161,408
63	Allianz SE	159,253
64	Mitsubishi UFJ Financial Group Inc	158,100
65	Faurecia SE (France)	157,460
66	NTT Data Group Corp	155,531
67	ITOCHU Corp (Japan)	155,403
68	Aptiv Corp	155,000
69	Anheuser-Busch InBev SA/NV	154,540
70	Aptiv PLC	154,000
71	Mitsubishi Electric Corp	149,655
72	Nissan Motor Co., Ltd.	147,119
73	Shoprite Holdings, Ltd.	142,602
74	Aisin Corporation	142,245
75	Glencore PLC	141,625
76	HDFC Bank Ltd	141,579
77	Orange	139,698
78	Fujitsu Ltd	135,793
79	Airbus SE	134,267
80	Associated British Foods Plc	133,487
81	Compagnie Generale des Etablissements Michelin SCA	132,213
82	Jeronimo Martins S.G.P.S. SA	131,094
83	Empire Co Ltd	131,000
84	ICICI Bank Ltd (India)	130,542
85	Bridgestone Corp (Japan)	129,262
86	Nidec Corp	128,002
87	Unilever Plc	128,000
88	ArcelorMittal SA	126,756
89	Bouygues S.A.	124,651
90	Nippon Steel Corp (New)	121,990
91	ACS Actividades de Construccion y Servicios, S.A.	120,827
92	Wesfarmers Ltd.	120,000
93	Bayerische Motoren Werke AG	118,909
94	NEC Corp	118,527
95	Societe Generale	117,576
96	Petroleos Mexicanos (Pemex) (Mexico)	116,063
97	Banco Bilbao Vizcaya Argentaria SA (BBVA)	115,675
98	Suzuki Motor Corp. (Japan)	114,903
99	Sinopharm Group Co., Ltd.	114,766
100	WPP Plc (New)	114,173

SOURCE: MERGENT INC., DATABASE, APRIL 2024

Hoover's Handbook of World Business

The Companies

A.P. Moller - Maersk A/S

A.P. Moller - Maersk is an integrated container logistics company, connecting, protecting, and simplifying trade to help customers grow and succeed. Operating in about 130 countries, the conglomerate specializes in global container shipping and related services. It operates through Maersk Line Business (Maersk Line, Safmarine and Sealand ? A Maersk company) together with the Hamburg Süd brands (Hamburg Süd and Aliança), Maersk Oil Trading as well as strategic transhipment hubs under the APM Terminals brand. Other activities include marine towing and salvage through Svitzer and refrigerated containers manufactured by Maersk Container Industry. The US is the company's largest single market with over 20% of sales.

Operations

A.P. Moller ? Maersk has four segments: Ocean, Logistics & Services, Terminals & Towage, and Manufacturing & Others.

Ocean segment, which consist of approximately 75% of company's revenue, Ocean includes the ocean activities of Maersk Liner Business (Maersk Line, Safmarine and Sealand ? A Maersk Company) together with the Hamburg Süd brands (Hamburg Süd and Aliança), as well as strategic transhipment hubs under the APM Terminals brand.

Logistics & Services segment with the logistics and supply chain management services, container inland services, inland haulage activities (intermodal), trade finance services and freight forwarding. It consist of some 15% of total revenue.

Terminals & Towage includes gateway terminals involving landside activities (being port activities where the customers are mainly the carriers), and towage services under the Svitzer brand. It consists of approximately 10% of revenue.

Manufacturing & others represent the remaining in the company's revenue. It includes the activities of Maersk Container Industry, Maersk Supply Service and others.

Geographic Reach

Denmark-based company, A.P. Moller ? Maersk operates in some 130 countries, worldwide. It operates in USA, Australia, France, Nigeria, China and Hong Kong, UK, Germany, Netherlands, Brazil, Singapore, etc. USA is the leading country which consist of over 20% of total revenue.

Sales and Marketing

Maersk offers global and local logistics solutions to industries such as retail, chemical, fashion and lifestyle, automotive, technology and electronics, as well as pharma and healthcare logistics.

Financial Performance

The company's revenue for fiscal 2021 increased to $61.8 billion compared from the prior year with $39.7 billion.

Profit for fiscal 2021 increased to $18.0 billion compared from the prior year with $2.9 billion.

Cash held by the company at the end of fiscal 2021 increased to $5.8 billion. Cash provided by operations was $22.0 billion while cash used for investing and financing activities were $8.3 billion and $7.9 billion, respectively.

Strategy

The company's transformation strategy towards becoming the global integrator of container logistics, building long-term customer relationships for reliable and differentiated transportation services, was validated in 2021 by supporting contract customers' supply chains alleviating bottlenecks through investing in additional equipment and increasing the capacity allocated to contracted volumes.

The record-high financial performance of 2021 has enabled the company to accelerate the investment in its long-term transformation, digitization and decarburization, while at the same time providing our shareholders with solid cash returns.

Company Background

Founded by Peter Mærsk Møller and his son Arnold Peter Møller, A.P. Møller - Mærsk styles the company and family name as "Mærsk" but uses "Maersk" for the names of most of its subsidiaries. A.P. Møller - Mærsk's main shareholder is The A.P. Møller and Chastine Mc-Kinney Møller Foundation, which was established by company founder A.P. Møller in 1953.

EXECUTIVES

Chief Executive Officer, Soren Skou
Chief Financial Officer, Patrick Jany
Chief People Officer, Susana Elvira
Chief Technology & Information Officer, Navneet Kapoor
Ocean & Logistics Chief Executive Officer, Vincent Clerc
APM Terminals Chief Executive Officer, Morten Henrick Engelstoft
Fleet & Strategic Brands Chief Executive Officer, Henriette Hallberg Thygesen
Corporate Affairs General Counsel, Corporate Affairs Head, Caroline Pontoppidan
Independent Non-Executive Chairman, Jim Hagemann Snabe
Vice-Chairman, Ane Maersk Mc-Kinney Uggla
Independent Director, Bernard Ladislas Bot
Independent Director, Marc Engel
Independent Director, Arne Karlsson
Independent Director, Blythe S.J. Masters
Independent Director, Amparo Moraleda
Director, Thomas Lindegaard Madsen
Director, Jacob Andersen Sterling
Director, Robert Mærsk Uggla
Auditors : PricewaterhouseCoopers Statsautoriseret Revisionspartnerselskab

LOCATIONS

HQ: A.P. Moller - Maersk A/S
Esplanaden 50, Copenhagen K DK-1263
Phone: (45) 33 63 33 63
Web: www.maersk.com

2017 Sales

	% of total
USA	16
China and Hong Kong	6
United Kingdom	4
Germany	3
India	3
Netherlands	3
Brazil	2
Turkey	2
Denmark	1
Singapore	1
Other countries	59
Total	100

PRODUCTS/OPERATIONS

2017 Sales

	$ mil.	% of total
Maersk Line	24,299	74
APM Terminals	4,138	13
Damco	2.668	8
Maersk Container Industry	1,016	3
Svitzer	659	2
Other businesses, unallocated and eliminations	(1,835)	-
Total	30,945	100

Selected Business Areas

Container shipping & related
    Damco (freight forwarding and supply chain management services)
    Maersk Container Industry (manufacturing of dry and refrigerated containers)
    Maersk Line (global container shipping)
    MCC Transport (intra-Asia container shipping)
    Safmarine (Africa, Middle East, and Indian subcontinent container shipping)
    Seago Line
    SeaLand
    Svitzer (specialized marine services, including towing, salvage, and emergency response)
Terminal activities
    APM Terminals (port operations, inland transportation, and container repair)

COMPETITORS

ANDEAVOR LLC
AltaGas Ltd
ENLINK MIDSTREAM, INC.
EXPEDITORS INTERNATIONAL OF WASHINGTON, INC.
EXTERRAN CORPORATION
MAERSK INC.
PAR PACIFIC HOLDINGS, INC.
PHILLIPS 66
SURGUTNEFTEGAZ, PAO
XPO LOGISTICS, INC.

HISTORICAL FINANCIALS
Company Type: Public

Income Statement   FYE: December 31

	REVENUE ($mil)	NET INCOME ($mil)	NET PROFIT MARGIN	EMPLOYEES
12/22	81,529	29,198	35.8%	104,260
12/21	61,787	17,942	29.0%	85,375
12/20	39,740	2,850	7.2%	83,624
12/19	38,890	(84)	—	86,279
12/18	39,019	3,169	8.1%	80,220
Annual Growth	20.2%	74.2%	—	6.8%

2022 Year-End Financials
Debt ratio: 4.3%   No. of shares ($ mil.): 17
Return on equity: 53.8%   Dividends
Cash ($ mil.): 10,057   Yield: —
Current Ratio: 3.01   Payout: 0.0%
Long-term debt ($ mil.): 3,774   Market value ($ mil.): 198

	STOCK PRICE ($) FY Close	P/E High/Low	PER SHARE ($) Earnings	Dividends	Book Value
12/22	11.22	0	01,595.00	1.30	3,632
12/21	17.92	0 0	938.00	0.17	2,379
12/20	11.11	0 0	145.00	0.81	1,538
12/19	7.18	— —	(4.00)	0.82	1,398
12/18	6.24	0 0	152.00	0.08	1,571
Annual Growth	15.8%	— —	80.0%	101.0%	23.3%

AB Electrolux (Sweden)

AB Electrolux is a top maker of household appliances worldwide that sells approximately 60 million household products annually. Electrolux cranks out washing machines, stoves, refrigerators, and freezers under the Electrolux (accounts for about 35% of the company's revenue), Frigidaire (nearly 30%), and AEG (approximately 15%) names. The company operates in approximately 120 markets around the world. Electrolux's largest market is the US accounting for some 30% of its revenue. AB Electrolux was founded in 1919, by Axel Wenner-Gren.

Operations
AB Electrolux's operations are divided into four reportable segments: Europe (about 40% of sales); North America (more than 30%); Latin America (roughly 15%), and Asia-Pacific, Middle East and Africa (nearly 15%).

All these segments produce appliances for the consumer market, and products comprise mainly of refrigerators, freezers, cookers, dryers, washing machines, dishwashers, microwave ovens, vacuum cleaner and other small appliances.

Overall, sales from product areas include taste with around 60%, care with some 30%, and wellbeing with about 10%.

Geographic Reach
Stockholm-based, AB Electrolux boasts a global reach, as its products are sold in more than 120 markets. The US is the company's biggest single market, representing about 30% of sales, followed by Brazil with around 10% of sales, and after that, no other country accounts for more than 10% of sales.

Sales and Marketing
Electrolux sells to a substantial number of customers in the form of large retailers, buying groups, and independent stores.

Financial Performance
Company's revenue for fiscal 2021 increased by 8% to SEK 125.6 billion compared from the prior year with SEK 116.0 billion.

Cash held by the company at the end of fiscal 2021 decreased to SEK 10.9 billion. Cash provided by operations was SEK 7.1 billion while cash used for investing and financing activities were SEK 6.8 billion and SEK 4.9 billion, respectively. Main uses of cash were for capital expenditure in property, plant and equipment; and redemption of shares.

Strategy
Electrolux's strategy for profitable growth is firmly based in the market trends that drive the development of a changing household appliance market. Sustainability is integrated in its strategy and therefore in everything the company do. Developing sustainable consumer experience innovation and increasing efficiency through digitalization, modularized products and automated and flexible manufacturing are its key drivers for profitable growth. Company's strong balance sheet allows Electrolux to invest in those drivers to create value through innovative products that are efficiently produced, while delivering strong direct shareholder returns. The primary financial priority is achieving its financial targets of an operating margin of at least 6% and a return on net assets of over 20%, over a business cycle. Once established, Electrolux's objective is sales growth of at least 4% annually, over a business cycle.

Mergers and Acquisitions
In mid-2021, Electrolux agreed to acquire La Compagnie du SAV (CSAV), the main French independent service provider (ISP) specialized in repairing domestic appliances. The acquisition is fully in line with the Electrolux Group strategy to offer outstanding experiences to consumers, ensuring they get the most out of their appliances during the complete lifecycle of the product. With this acquisition, the company further strengthens its service network in France allowing them to meet the growing market demand in the after-sales service area in the best possible way. Financial terms were not disclosed.

HISTORY
Swedish salesman Axel Wenner-Gren saw an American-made vacuum cleaner in a Vienna, Austria, store window in 1910 and envisioned selling the cleaners door-to-door, a technique he had learned in the US. Two years later he worked with fledgling Swedish vacuum cleaner makers AB Lux and Elektromekaniska to improve their existing designs. The two companies merged to form AB Electrolux in 1919. When the board of the new company balked at Wenner-Gren's suggestion to mass-produce vacuum cleaners, he guaranteed Electrolux's sales through his own sales company.

In the 1920s the company used the "Every home -- an Electrolux home" slogan as Wenner-Gren drove his sales force on and launched new sales companies in Europe and North and South America. He scored a publicity coup by securing the blessing of Pope Pius XI to vacuum the Vatican, gratis, for a year. By the end of the 1920s, Electrolux had purchased most of Wenner-Gren's sales companies (excluding Electrolux US) and had gambled on refrigerator technology and won. By buying vacuum cleaner maker Volta (Sweden, 1934), it gained retail distribution.

Despite the loss of Eastern European subsidiaries during WWII, the company did well until the 1960s, when it backed an unpopular refrigeration technology. Swedish electrical equipment giant ASEA, controlled by Marcus Wallenberg, bought a large stake in Electrolux in 1964, and in 1967 he installed Hans Werthén as chairman. Werthén slashed overhead and sold the company's minority stake in Electrolux US to Consolidated Foods. (The US Electrolux business was taken private in 1987.)

Since 1970 Electrolux has bought more than 300 companies (many of them troubled appliance makers), updated their plants, and gained global component manufacturing efficiencies. Acquisitions included National Union Electric (Eureka vacuum cleaners, US, 1974), Tappan (appliances, US, 1979), Zanussi (appliances, industrial products; Italy; 1984), White Consolidated Industries (appliances, industrial products; US; 1986), and Lehel (refrigerators, Hungary, 1991). By 1996 the company had acquired a 41% interest in Refrigeração Paraná, Brazil's #2 manufacturer of appliances. (Electrolux owned it all by 1998.)

To better focus on its "white goods" (washers, refrigerators, etc.), in 1996 Electrolux began selling noncore businesses. In 1997, under new CEO Michael "Mike the Knife" Treschow, the company launched a restructuring plan involving the closing of about 25 plants and the elimination of more than 12,000 jobs, mostly in Europe. The plan worked: Electrolux's profits more than quadrupled in 1998. Also that year the company launched a joint venture in India with Voltas Limited, forming that country's largest refrigerator manufacturer.

Electrolux acquired the European operations of chainsaw maker McCulloch in 1999. To strengthen its Asian presence, Electrolux teamed up with Toshiba for future collaboration on household appliances. Also that year the company said it would sell its vending machine unit and professional refrigeration business. That year AB Electrolux agreed to buy the major appliance business of Email Ltd., Australia's top household appliance maker.

In January 2002 it finalized the sale of its leisure appliance operations -- mostly refrigerators for recreational vehicles -- to private equity firm EQT Northern Europe. In April 2002 Electrolux CEO Michael Treschow resigned (but remained as a director) and was replaced by board member Hans Stråberg. The firm acquired Diamant Boart International, a world-leading manufacturer and distributor of diamond tools and related equipment, in June 2002.

As part of a restructuring effort to combat the effects of diminishing consumer demand and higher material costs, Electrolux cut nearly 5,000 jobs (about 6% of its workforce) during 2003.

Electrolux relaunched its flagship brand of vacuum cleaners in North America during 2004, having bought the rights from long-unaffiliated vacuum maker Electrolux LLC (now Aerus). Also that year former CEO Michael Treschow reappeared in a leadership position, assuming the role of chairman. Treschow left the company again in 2007. Hans Straberg, who had joined Electrolux in 1983, was appointed CEO of the business in 2002.

The firm exited its outdoor segment, which consisted of chainsaws and lawn and garden equipment (Husqvarna, Jonsered brands) and diamond tools (Dimas, Diamant Boart names) through a spinoff in 2006.

EXECUTIVES

President, Chief Executive Officer, Director, Jonas Samuelson
Executive Vice President Chief Executive Officer, Therese Friberg
Executive Vice President Chief Commercial Officer, Anna Ohlsson-Leijon
General Counsel, Secretary, Ulrika Elfving
Chairman, Staffan Bohman
Director, Petra Hedengran
Director, Henrik Henriksson
Director, Ulla Litzen
Director, Karin Overbeck
Director, Fredrik Persson
Director, David Porter
Director, Viveca Brinkenfeldt Lever
Director, Peter Ferm
Director, Wilson Quispe
Auditors : PricewaterhouseCoopers AB

LOCATIONS

HQ: AB Electrolux (Sweden)
S:t Goransgatan 143, Stockholm SE-105 45
Phone: (46) 8 738 60 00   **Fax:** (46) 8 738 74 61
Web: www.electroluxgroup.com

2018 Sales

	% of total
USA	31
Brazil	10
Germany	5
Australia	4
Sweden	5
Switzerland	2
Canada	2
United Kingdom	3
France	4
Italy	4
Other	30
Total	100

PRODUCTS/OPERATIONS

2018 Sales

	% of total
Major Appliances, North America	31
Major Appliances Europe, Middle East and Africa	35
Latin America	14
Asia/Pacific	7
Homecare and Small Domestic Appliances	6
Professional Products	7
Total	100

Selected Products and Brands
Consumer durables
    Core A
        Floorcare products
Professional products
        Foodservice equipment
        Laundry equipment

COMPETITORS

ABB Ltd
Atlas Copco AB
Axel Johnson AB
BUNZL PUBLIC LIMITED COMPANY
GKN LIMITED
Neles Oyj
RUSSELL HOBBS, INC.
SEB SA
Svenska Cellulosa AB SCA
WHIRLPOOL CORPORATION

HISTORICAL FINANCIALS
Company Type: Public

Income Statement   FYE: December 31

	REVENUE ($mil)	NET INCOME ($mil)	NET PROFIT MARGIN	EMPLOYEES
12/22	13,002	(127)	—	50,769
12/21	13,867	516	3.7%	51,590
12/20	14,192	805	5.7%	47,543
12/19	12,790	269	2.1%	48,652
12/18	13,867	425	3.1%	54,419
Annual Growth	(1.6%)	—	—	(1.7%)

2022 Year-End Financials
Debt ratio: 2.8%   No. of shares ($ mil.): 270
Return on equity: (-7.5%)   Dividends
Cash ($ mil.): 1,692   Yield: —
Current Ratio: 0.98   Payout: 387.6%
Long-term debt ($ mil.): 2,770   Market value ($ mil.): 7,377

	STOCK PRICE ($) FY Close	P/E High/Low		PER SHARE ($) Earnings	Dividends	Book Value
12/22	27.32	9	5	0.46	1.78	5.87
12/21	48.61	4	2	1.79	7.44	7.25
12/20	46.10	3	1	2.80	5.12	7.97
12/19	48.96	7	5	0.93	1.78	8.44
12/18	42.37	5	3	1.47	1.91	8.45
Annual Growth	(10.4%)	—	—	(25.3%)	(1.8%)	(8.7%)

AB SKF

One of the world's leading makers of roller and ball bearings, SKF produces a variety of bearings and units, as well as seals, mechatronics (electromechanical tools and systems), and lubrication systems, and related products and services. SKF's products are used all over the world and in a large variety of rotating applications, ranging from renewable energy, such as wind and ocean power, to heavy industries like mining, metal, and pulp and paper. Its products are also used in cars and commercial vehicles, as well as in bicycles, skateboards and household appliances. It operates in about 130 countries worldwide and has around 17,000 distributor locations.

Operations
SKF's divided into two divisions: Industrial & Automotive.

The Industrial segment accounts for more than 70% of total revenue and offers a broad product range of bearings, seals and lubrication systems. It also offers rotating shaft services and solutions for machine health assessment, reliability engineering and remanufacturing.

The Automotive segment (about 30%) offers customized bearings, seals and related products for wheel-end, driveline, e-powertrain, engine, suspension and steering applications to manufacturers of cars, light and heavy trucks, trailers, buses and two-wheelers.

Geographic Reach
Based in Sweden, SKF is present in about 130 countries. It has some 15 technology centers and more than 75 manufacturing sites in over 20 countries, and direct sales channels in about 70 countries.

About 40% of SKF's revenue comes from Europe, Middle East and Africa, while around 30% comes from Asia and Pacific and nearly 30% of combined revenue comes from the Americas region.

Sales and Marketing
The Industrial segment supplies more than 40 industries globally with products and services, both directly and indirectly through a network of more than 7,000 distributors.

Its Automotive segment supplies the vehicle aftermarket with spare parts, both directly and indirectly through a network of more than 10,000 distributors. The OEM manufacturers account for about 80% of the total bearings market, while the independent vehicle aftermarket accounts for the remainder.

Financial Performance
Net sales for fiscal 2022 increased to SEK96.9 billion compared from the prior year with SEK 81.7 billion.

Profit for fiscal 2022 increased to SEK 4.6 billion compared from the prior year with SEK 7.6 billion.

HOOVER'S HANDBOOK OF WORLD BUSINESS 2024

Cash held by the company at the end of fiscal 2022 decreased to SEK 10.3 billion. Cash provided by operations was SEK 5.6 billion while cash used for investing and financing activities were SEK 5.3 billion and SEK 3.4 billion, respectively. Main uses of cash were additions to property, plant and equipment; and cash dividends to shareholders of AB SKF and non-controlling interests.

Strategy

In the beginning of 2022, SKF presented a new strategic framework based on two concepts: intelligent and clean. These concepts will guide the company on its journey to become an even more focused, innovative and profitable industrial player.

To deliver on its ambitions, the company identified four growth enablers: scaling the pace and impact of technology development; digitalizing the full value chain; continuing to invest in automation and regionalization; and organization and leadership.

SKF's broad business reach gives the company a platform to drive profitable growth, as it allows the company to continuously target the most attractive opportunities. Within these growth areas, strong market demand matches its ability to differentiate and provide customer value. This means that the company are well positioned to accelerate profitable growth.

Mergers and Acquisitions

In early 2022, SKF has completed the acquisition of Laser Cladding Venture n.v. (LCV), an additive manufacturing company based in Belgium. LCV is a niche engineering start-up specialized in various additive manufacturing technologies and processes, which can be applied to support SKF's service and remanufacturing offering. Additive manufacturing will play an important role in developing tomorrow's value proposition to support customers' future application needs. In addition, additive manufacturing will facilitate a circular economy approach which supports SKF's ambition to provide solutions that minimizes the overall CO2 footprint.

In 2021, SKF has completed the acquisition of EFOLEX AB, a Gothenburg-based manufacturer of the Europafilter-branded industrial lubrication and oil filtration systems. Thomas Fröst, President, Industrial Technologies, says: "In addition to being an interesting stand-alone product, the Europafilter technology is a good strategic fit with SKF RecondOil's Double Separation Technology offer and will widen our overall lubrication management capabilities."

Also in 2021, SKF has completed the acquisition of Rubico Consulting AB, an industrial consultancy firm based in Luleå, Sweden. Rubico Consulting AB specialises in visualisation and analysis of signal data. This expertise will be integrated into SKF's offer around the rotating shaft, as well as powering new technology areas such as bearings with fiber-optic sensors.

HISTORY

SKF began as the brainchild of Sven Wingquist, a maintenance engineer at the Swedish textile company Gamlestadens Fabriker. Displeased with imported bearings used in Gamlestadens Fabriker's factories, Wingquist (with resources allotted by Fabriker) founded Svenska Kullagerfabriken (SKF) in 1907 and produced bearings from his own workshop. In 1910 SKF had one factory in Sweden; the following year, the company established another in the UK.

SKF reaped the financial benefits of being based in a neutral country during WWI, selling its products to both the Allied and Central powers. In 1914 subsidiaries were established in Belgium, the Netherlands, and Russia. Two years later SKF bought a steel works company in Sweden to supply the company with steel. Also in 1916 SKF opened a plant in the US. By 1918 the company had 12 factories and its sales force spanned 100 countries. An economic slump sagged the company's sales in the early 1920s. SKF's Volvo subsidiary entered the automobile manufacturing industry in 1926 and acted as SKF's testing unit until it was spun off in 1935.

The onset of the Great Depression allowed SKF to purchase some of its German competitors. In 1929 SKF's stock began trading internationally, and the company purchased Swedish machine toolmaker Lidkopings Mekaniska Verkstad. In the thick of the Depression, SKF concentrated its efforts on R&D, and in 1932 it patented two spherical rolling-bearing products.

The company enjoyed a few prosperous years after the Depression, but WWII and harder times were lurking. During the war the Allies bombed SKF's Schweinfurt and Canstatt factories. The company's reconstruction efforts included building manufacturing plants in Spain, Canada, and the Netherlands, followed by expansion into Brazil and India. By 1950 the company boasted 18 factories with 65% of its workforce operating outside Sweden. In 1957 the company added a new ball and roller factory (one of its biggest buildings) to its ranks. SKF built a research center in the US in 1963. In 1969 astronaut Neil Armstrong took photos of the historic moon landing with a camera fitted with SKF bearings.

EXECUTIVES

President, Chief Executive Officer, Executive Director, Rickard Gustafson
Digital Transformation Senior Vice President, Operations Senior Vice President, Joakim Kandholm
Technology Development Chief Technology Officer, Technology Development Senior Vice President, Victoria Van Camp
Finance Chief Financial Officer, Finance Senior Vice President, Niclas Rosenlew
General Counsel, Senior Vice President, Legal and Compliance, Mathias Lyon
People Experience and Communication Senior Vice President, Ann-Sofie Zaks
Independent Chairman, Hans Straberg
Independent Director, Hock Goh
Independent Director, Barb J. Samardzich
Independent Director, Colleen C. Repplier
Independent Director, Geert Follens
Independent Director, Hakan Buskhe
Independent Director, Susanna Schneeberger
Director, Jonny Hilbert
Director, Zarko Djurovic
Director, Thomas Eliasson
Director, Steve Norrman
Auditors : Deloitte AB

LOCATIONS

HQ: AB SKF
Hornsgatan 1, Gothenburg SE-415 50
Phone: (46) 31 337 10 00   **Fax:** (46) 31 337 28 32
Web: www.skf.com

PRODUCTS/OPERATIONS

2016 Sales by Division

	% of total
Industrial Market	70
Automotive Market	30
Total	100

2016 Sales

	% of total
Europe excl. Sweden	38
North America (incl. Mexico)	25
Asia-Pacific	26
Latin America	6
Middle East/Africa	3
Sweden	2
Total	100

Selected Products

Bearing housings
Bearing units
Composite dry sliding bearings & FW bushings
Coupling systems
High-precision bearings
Hydraulic seals
Industrial shaft seals
Rolling bearings
Spherical plain bearings & rod ends

Selected Markets

Aerospace
Agriculture
Bicycle
Cars
Compressors
Construction
Drive-by-wire
Electric motors & generators
Electric motors for consumer goods
Electric power tools
Food & beverage
Home appliance
HPI, oil & gas
Industrial fans
Industrial pumps
Industrial transmission
Machine tool
Marine
Material handling
Medical & healthcare
Metals industry
Mining, mineral processing, & cement
Plastic & rubber

Printing machines
Pulp & paper
Racing
Railways
Skates
Traditional electric power generation
Trucks, trailers, & buses
Two wheelers
Wind energy

Selected Services
Asset management services
Condition monitoring
Energy & sustainability management
Mechanical maintenance
Operator driven reliability (ODR)
Remanufacturing services
SKF certified electric motor rebuilder
SKF certified maintenance partners
SKF distributor network
SKF engineering consultancy services
SKF logistics services
Training

COMPETITORS

ABB Ltd
Atlas Copco AB
Axel Johnson AB
BUNZL PUBLIC LIMITED COMPANY
GKN LIMITED
KAYDON CORPORATION
Neles Oyj
Svenska Cellulosa AB SCA
THE TIMKEN COMPANY
thyssenkrupp AG

HISTORICAL FINANCIALS

Company Type: Public

Income Statement — FYE: December 31

	REVENUE ($mil)	NET INCOME ($mil)	NET PROFIT MARGIN	EMPLOYEES
12/22	9,344	430	4.6%	42,641
12/21	9,021	809	9.0%	42,602
12/20	9,161	526	5.7%	40,963
12/19	9,246	597	6.5%	43,360
12/18	9,575	813	8.5%	44,428
Annual Growth	(0.6%)	(14.7%)	—	(1.0%)

2022 Year-End Financials

Debt ratio: 1.6%
Return on equity: 9.3%
Cash ($ mil.): 988
Current Ratio: 2.45
Long-term debt ($ mil.): 1,752
No. of shares ($ mil.): 455
Dividends
Yield: —
Payout: 71.1%
Market value ($ mil.): 6,946

	STOCK PRICE ($) FY Close	P/E High/Low		PER SHARE ($) Earnings	Dividends	Book Value
12/22	15.26	2	1	0.95	0.67	10.99
12/21	23.79	2	1	1.78	0.74	10.58
12/20	25.66	3	2	1.15	0.30	9.22
12/19	20.17	2	1	1.31	0.65	8.38
12/18	15.13	1	1	1.78	0.65	8.23
Annual Growth	0.2%	—	—	(14.7%)	0.8%	7.5%

ABB Ltd

ABB is a leading global technology company with a comprehensive and increasingly digitalized offering of electrification, motion and automation solutions. About half of its customers are industrial customers, serving production facilities and factories worldwide from process industries such as oil and gas, pulp and paper as well as mining, automotive, food and beverage, and consumer electronics. Operating for more than 130 years, Zurich, Switzerland-based ABB has operations in about 100 countries worldwide. The company completed its divestment of its Power Grids business to Hitachi in 2020.

Operations

ABB operates through four segments: Electrification Products, Motion, Process Automation, and Robotics & Discrete Automation.

Electrification Products generates over 45% of ABB's sales and manufactures products and services such as electric vehicle charging infrastructure, renewable power solutions, modular substation packages, distribution automation products, switchboard and panelboards, switchgear, UPS solutions, circuit breakers, measuring and sensing devices, control products, wiring accessories, enclosures and cabling systems and intelligent home and building solutions, designed to integrate and automate lighting, heating, ventilation, security and data communication networks.

Motion segment produces more than 20% of sales and manufactures and sells motors, generators, drives, wind converters, mechanical power transmissions, complete electrical powertrain systems and related services and digital solutions for a wide range of applications in industry, transportation, infrastructure, and utilities.

Process Automation accounts for more than 20% of sales and develops integrated automation and electrification systems and solutions, digital solutions, artificial intelligence applications for the process and hybrid industries, as well as services such as remote monitoring, preventive maintenance, and cybersecurity services.

The Robotics & Discrete Automation division sells robotics, controllers, software, function packages, cells, programmable logic controllers (PLC), industrial PCs (IPC), servo motion, engineered manufacturing solutions, turn-key solutions and collaborative robot solutions for a wide range of applications. It pulls in over 10% of sales.

Geographic Reach

Zurich, Switzerland-based ABB's operations extend to more than 100 countries across Europe (more than 35% of sales), the Asia, Middle East and Africa (AMEA) region and the Americas (each accounting for over 30% of sales).

ABB has properties in the US, Austria, Italy, Finland, Sweden, and Switzerland.

Sales and Marketing

ABB's business areas deliver products to customers through a global network of channel partners, end-customers, direct sales force, third-party channels, as well as through system integrators and machine builders. Most of the business's revenue is derived from sales through channel partners like distributors and wholesalers, as well as installers, OEMs and system integrators. The company's customer base is comprised of production facilities and factories from product industries (oil and gas, pulp and paper, mining), discrete industries (automotive, food and beverage, consumer electronics), including customers that operate in the transport and infrastructure market.

Financial Performance

Note: Growth rates may differ after conversion to US Dollars.

ABB's performance for the past five years has fluctuated from year to year but had an overall upward trend with 2021 as its highest performing year over the period.

ABB's revenue in 2021 was $28.9 billion, an increase of 11% compared to $26.1 million in 2020. Revenues increased across all Business Areas, recovering from the pandemic-related impacts of the previous year. The Electrification and Robotics & Discrete Automation Business Areas reported strong growth, largely driven by the short-cycle businesses.

Net income in 2021 decreased by $600 million to $4.5 billion compared to the prior year's $5.1 billion.

ABB's cash position for the end of 2021 amounted to $4.5 billion. The company's operating activities generated $3.3 billion. Investing activities provided $2.3 billion, while financing activities used $4.9 billion. ABB's primary cash uses were for purchases of treasury stock and dividends paid.

Mergers and Acquisitions

In 2021, ABB acquired ASTI Mobile Robotics for $190 million. ASTI is a global leader in the growth of Autonomous Mobile Robot (AMR) market with a broad portfolio of vehicles and software. The acquisition of ASTI enables ABB to deliver unique automation portfolio, further expanding into new industry segments.

HISTORY

Asea Brown Boveri (ABB) was formed in 1988 when two giants, ASEA AB of Sweden and BBC Brown Boveri of Switzerland, combined their electrical engineering and equipment businesses. Percy Barnevik, head of ASEA, became CEO.

ASEA was born in Stockholm in 1883 when Ludwig Fredholm founded Electriska Aktiebolaget to manufacture an electric dynamo created by engineer Jonas Wenstrom. In 1890 the company merged with Wenstrom's brother's firm to form Allmanna Svenska Electriska Aktiebolaget (ASEA), a pioneer in industrial electrification. Early in the 1900s ASEA began its first railway electrification project. By the 1920s it was providing locomotives and other equipment to Sweden's national railway, and by the next decade ASEA was one of Sweden's largest electric equipment manufacturers. In 1962 it bought 20% of appliance maker Electrolux. ASEA created the nuclear power venture ASEA-ATOM with the Swedish government in 1968 and bought full control in 1982.

BBC Brown Boveri was formed in 1891 as the Brown, Boveri, and Company partnership between Charles Brown and Walter Boveri in Baden, Switzerland. It made power generation equipment and produced the first steam turbines in Europe in 1900. BBC entered Germany (1893), France (1894), and Italy (1903) and diversified into nuclear power equipment after WWII.

By 1988 BBC, the bigger company, had a West German network that ASEA, the more profitable company, coveted. Both had US joint ventures. In an unusual merger, ASEA (which became ABB AB) and BBC (later ABB AG) continued as separate entities sharing equal ownership of ABB. Barnevik crafted a unique decentralized management structure under which national subsidiaries were closely linked to their local customers and labor forces. In six years ABB took over more than 150 companies worldwide.

An ABB-led consortium built one of the world's largest hydroelectric plants in Iran in 1992, and in 1995 ABB merged its transportation segment into Adtranz (a joint venture with Daimler-Benz) to form the world's #1 maker of trains.

Tragedy struck in 1996. Robert Donovan, CEO of ABB's US subsidiary, died in a plane crash along with Commerce Secretary Ron Brown and other executives on a trade mission. Donovan's death hastened the US unit's restructuring.

In 1997 Barnevik gave up the title of CEO, remaining as chairman, and was succeeded by Göran Lindahl, an engineer who worked his way up the ranks at ASEA. (Barnevik remained chairman until 2001.) After 1997 profits dipped drastically, Lindahl scrapped Barnevik's vaunted regional matrix structure in favor of one organized by product areas under a strong central management. Though the Asian financial crisis slowed orders, ABB still pulled in large contracts, including one to build the world's largest cracker plant in Texas in 1998.

In 1999 ABB acquired Elsag Bailey, a Dutch maker of industrial control systems, for about $1.5 billion, and sold its 50% stake in Adtranz to DaimlerChrysler for about $472 million. ABB and France's ALSTOM combined their power generation businesses to form the world's largest power plant equipment maker. That year ABB AB and ABB AG were at last united under a single stock through holding company ABB Ltd.

ABB scaled back its power plant-related activities in 2000. The company sold its nuclear power business to BNFL for $485 million and its 50% stake in ABB Alstom Power to ALSTOM for $1.2 billion. (Areva acquired ALSTOM's transmission and distribution business in 2004.) In 2001 Lindahl resigned and Jürgen Centerman, head of the company's automation business, replaced him. Centerman promptly reorganized ABB's industrial operations into four segments based on customer type and two based on product type.

Also in 2001 ABB acquired French company Entrelec, a supplier of industrial automation and control products. With economic slowdowns occurring in the company's key markets, ABB announced plans in 2001 to cut 12,000 jobs over 18 months. Later that year, amid rising numbers of asbestos claims against US subsidiary Combustion Engineering, ABB took a $470 million fourth-quarter charge to cover asbestos liabilities. The claims charged asbestos exposures stemming from products supplied before the mid-1970s by Combustion Engineering, which ABB acquired in 1990.

In 2002 ABB found itself embroiled in controversy after revealing not only a record loss but also payments of large pensions to former chairman Barnevik and former chief executive Lindahl. The former executives agreed that year to return a part (about $82 million) of their pension payouts to ABB. That year the company, which faced $4.4 billion in debts after industry slumps affected its sales of power systems and equipment, industrial automation, and controls, sold part of its financial services unit to GE Commercial Finance for $2.3 billion.

The day after the company sold its structured finances unit, ABB's chief executive, Jürgen Centerman, resigned and was replaced by the chairman, Jürgen Dormann. That year ABB sold its metering business to Germany-based Ruhrgas for $244 million.

In 2003, as part of its settlement with asbestos plaintiffs, ABB placed Combustion Engineering into bankruptcy. Later that same year the company announced that it would sell its Sirius International reinsurance business to the Bermuda-based White Mountains; the deal was completed in 2004 for about $425 million. ABB also sold its upstream oil, gas, and petrochemicals unit to Candover Partners, 3i, and J.P. Morgan Partners for $925 million in 2004. (To clear the way for the sale, ABB also agreed to pay US regulators $16 million in fines to settle bribery cases at US-based ABB Vetco Gray and Scotland-based ABB Vetco UK. The subsidiaries -- part of the petroleum business that was sold -- allegedly paid off government officials in Angola, Kazakhstan, and Nigeria in order to win oil contracts between 1998 and 2003.)

Sulzer CEO Fred Kindle succeeded Dormann as ABB's CEO in 2005. (Dormann remained chairman until his retirement in 2007.) The company made a number of small dispositions in 2005, including its Japanese control valves business, its foundry business, and several cable and power line businesses.

ABB ended years of litigation -- and a major corporate headache -- when it reached a settlement on an asbestos liability case related to US subsidiary Combustion Engineering in 2006. As part of the settlement, ABB committed more than $1.4 billion to pay settled claims.

After consolidating its remaining businesses into the two areas, power technologies and automation technologies, ABB restructured its operations into five divisions in 2006: Power Products, Power Systems, Automation Products, Process Automation, and Robotics. It took further steps to streamline operations and position itself for growth, for example by moving its main robotics operation from Detroit to Shanghai.

In 2006 ABB voluntarily disclosed to the US Department of Justice and the SEC that the company made payments in the Middle East that might have violated anti-bribery laws. The following year ABB disclosed similar suspect payments at subsidiaries in Asia, Europe, and South America.

Kindle left ABB in 2008 due to what the company called "irreconcilable differences" concerning the leadership of the company; former GE Healthcare CEO Joe Hogan became CEO of ABB later that year.

In 2008 the company dug deeper into its investment purse, spending $653 million to complete 12 deals. Most notably, ABB purchased Kuhlman Electric, a US-based transformer manufacturer, from The Carlyle Group for $513 million, including assumed debt. Kuhlman Electric was integrated into ABB's Power Products division in North America, and deepens ABB's geographic footprint and product offerings in the industrial and electric utility sectors.

ABB's bunch of businesses has been peeled back, too. Several divestitures were completed in 2008 and 2007; ABB exited its 50% interest in South Africa's ABB Powertech Transformers to Powertech, owned by the Altron Group, for $11 million. In 2007 ABB sold subsidiary ABB Lummus Global to Chicago Bridge & Iron Co. for some $870 million in cash, as well as its Building Systems business in Germany, and power plant interests in India and Morocco to Abu Dhabi National Oil. Power Lines businesses in Brazil and Mexico were also put on the sale block for $20 million.

ABB plowed in $209 million in 2009, adding eight new operations. Among them, the company acquired the assets of Sinai Engineering, a designer and provider of services for electrical generation and transmission systems planning, as well as construction management. The transaction, completed through its US ABB, Inc., expanded ABB's presence in western Canada. On the other side of the world, ABB picked up South Africa's Westingcorp (Pty) Ltd. The move ramped up ABB's line of power capacitors (machines that add to a system's power quality and energy efficiency) and opened the door to local and global electric utilities and mining markets.

ABB in mid-2010 acquired K-TEK, a maker of level detection technology used in the oil and gas industry, as well as water and other industries. Its instrumentation and sensing technologies, which number more than 350,000 installations, enhanced ABB's slate of measurement products, part of its Process Automation division. The deal garnered K-TEK's facilities in the US, the Netherlands, China, India, and South Africa.

ABB picked up US software provider Insert Key Solutions in late 2010. Its combination with the earlier acquisition of Ventyx (valued at approximately $1 billion) from Vista Equity Partners created a comprehensive portfolio of software for managing asset-intensive businesses engaged in the utility, energy, and communications industries. Ventyx and Insert Key Solutions joined ABB's network management business.

EXECUTIVES

Chief Executive Officer, Bjorn Rosengren
Chief Financial Officer, Executive Vice President, Timo Ihamuotila
Chief Human Resources Officer, Carolina Granat
Chief Human Resources Officer, Sylvia Hill
Chief Communications Officer, Theodor Swedjemark
General Counsel, Maria Varsellona
Motion Business President, Morten Wierod
Business President, Tarak Mehta
Business President, Sami Atiya
Business President, Peter Terwiesch
Chairman, Peter R. Voser
Vice-Chairman, Jacob Wallenberg
Director, Jennifer Xin-Zhe Li
Director, Lars Forberg
Director, Matti Alahuhta
Director, Geraldine Matchett
Director, David Constable
Director, Gunnar Brock
Director, Frederico Fleury Curado
Director, David W. Meline
Director, Satish Pai

Auditors: KPMG AG

LOCATIONS

HQ: ABB Ltd
Affolternstrasse 44, P.O. Box 8131, Zurich CH-8050
Phone: (41) 43 317 7111 **Fax:** (41) 43 317 7992
Web: www.abb.com

2018 Sales

	$ mil.	% of total
Asia, Middle East and Africa	9,491	34
Europe	10,129	37
The Americas	8,042	29
Total	27,662	100

PRODUCTS/OPERATIONS

2018 Sales

	$ mil.	% of total
Electrification Products	11,686	41
Robotics and Motion	9,147	32
Industrial Automation	7,394	26
Corporate and Other	273	1
Inter-segment elimination	(838)	-
Total	27,662	100

Selected Products

Electrification Products
   Modular substation packages
   Distribution automation
   Measuring and sensing devices
   Circuit breakers
   Control products
   Wiring accessories
   Cabling systems
   KNX systems
Robotics and Motion
   Robots
   Robot automation solutions
   Controllers
   Electrical motors and generators
   Mechanical power transmission products
   Low- and medium-voltage drive
Industrial Automation
   Performance optimization
   Automation solutions
   System 800xA
   PLC Automation
   Decathlon Software
   Turbochargers

COMPETITORS

ASSA ABLOY AB
Atlas Copco AB
ENERPAC TOOL GROUP CORP.
EXPRO INTERNATIONAL GROUP LIMITED
Fortum Oyj
GKN LIMITED
Neles Oyj
SCHNEIDER ELECTRIC SE
Siemens AG
TEAM, INC.

HISTORICAL FINANCIALS

Company Type: Public

Income Statement   FYE: December 31

	REVENUE ($mil)	NET INCOME ($mil)	NET PROFIT MARGIN	EMPLOYEES
12/23	32,235	3,745	11.6%	107,900
12/22	29,446	2,475	8.4%	105,100
12/21	28,945	4,546	15.7%	104,400
12/20	26,134	5,146	19.7%	105,600
12/19	27,978	1,439	5.1%	144,400
Annual Growth	3.6%	27.0%	—	(7.0%)

2023 Year-End Financials

Debt ratio: 19.1%   No. of shares ($ mil.): 1,841
Return on equity: 28.6%   Dividends
Cash ($ mil.): 5,819   Yield: —
Current Ratio: 1.18   Payout: 45.6%
Long-term debt ($ mil.): 5,221   Market value ($ mil.): 81,579

	STOCK PRICE ($) FY Close	P/E High/Low		PER SHARE ($) Earnings	Dividends	Book Value
12/23	44.30	22	15	2.01	0.92	7.28
12/22	30.46	30	19	1.30	0.88	6.85
12/21	38.17	17	12	2.25	0.85	7.96
12/20	27.96	11	6	2.43	1.61	7.72
12/19	24.09	36	27	0.67	0.79	6.34
Annual Growth	16.5%	—		31.6%	3.9%	3.5%

ABN AMRO Bank NV

EXECUTIVES

Chief Executive Officer, Chairman, Robert A.J. Swaak
Chief Financial Officer, Vice-Chairman, Lars Kramer
Chief Risk Officer, Director, Tanja Cuppen
Chief Innovation & Technology Officer, Director, Carsten Bittner
Corporate Banking Chief Commercial Officer, Director, Dan Dorner
Wealth Management Chief Commercial Officer, Director, Choy van der Hooft-Cheong
Personal & Business Banking Chief Commercial Officer, Director, Annerie Vreugdenhil
Auditors: Ernst & Young Accountants LLP

LOCATIONS

HQ: ABN AMRO Bank NV
Gustav Mahlerlaan 10, Amsterdam 1082 PP
Phone: —
Web: www.abnamro.com

HISTORICAL FINANCIALS

Company Type: Public

Income Statement   FYE: December 31

	REVENUE ($mil)	NET INCOME ($mil)	NET PROFIT MARGIN	EMPLOYEES
12/22	11,716	1,995	17.0%	20,038
12/21	11,427	1,393	12.2%	19,957
12/20	12,962	(55)	—	19,234
12/19	14,237	2,297	16.1%	17,977
12/18	19,026	2,527	13.3%	18,830
Annual Growth	(11.4%)	(5.7%)	—	1.6%

2022 Year-End Financials

Debt ratio: —   No. of shares ($ mil.): 897
Return on equity: 8.3%   Dividends
Cash ($ mil.): 65,006   Yield: —
Current Ratio: —   Payout: 34.8%
Long-term debt ($ mil.): —   Market value ($ mil.): 12,404

Absa Group Ltd (New)

Absa Group is one of the largest financial services groups in South Africa with operations in a dozen African countries. The group offers a range of banking and financial services including deposits, loans, credit cards, insurance, financial planning, and investment banking services. Its Absa Securities UK subsidiary in London launched its international operations and the group is currently working to procure licenses in the US. With an extensive branch network, a team of 41,000 banking professionals and a customer base of over 12 million, it is one of Africa's most respected banks.

Operations
The group's reportable segments are: RBB, CIB, Head Office, Treasury and other operations; and Barclays separation.

RBB (some 70% of sales) offers retail, business banking and insurance products within South Africa and Absa Regional Operations.

CIB (over 25%) offers corporate and investment banking solutions in South Africa and Absa Regional Operations.

Head Office, Treasury and other operations (less than 5%) consists of various non-banking activities and includes investment income earned by the group, as well as income earned by Absa Manx Holdings and Corporate Real Estate Services. Barclays separation Barclays PLC contributed R12.1 billion to the group in June 2017, primarily in recognition of the investments required for the group to separate from Barclays PLC.

Overall, more than 60% of sales were generated from its interest income, while about 40% were generated from non-interest income.

Geographic Reach
Headquartered in Johannesburg, the group operates in more than 10 African countries, UK, and the US. The group has majority stakes in banks in Botswana, Ghana, Kenya, Mauritius, Mozambique, Seychelles, South Africa, Tanzania, Uganda and Zambia. There are also representative offices in New York, London, Namibia and Nigeria as well as bank assurance operations in Botswana, Kenya, Mozambique, South Africa and Zambia.

Sales and Marketing
The group interacts with its customers and clients through a combination of physical and electronic channels, offering a comprehensive range of banking services.

Financial Performance
The group had a net interest income of R36.9 billion in 2021, a 2% increase from the previous year's net interest income of R36 billion.

In 2021, the group had a net profit of R26.7 billion, a 158% increase from the previous year's net profit of R10.4 billion.

The company's cash at the end of 2021 was R20.3 billion. Operating activities generated R6.5 billion, while investing activities used R3.5 billion, mainly for purchase of intangible assets. Financing activities used another R515 million, primarily for payment of dividends.

Strategy
The company's capital management strategy, which is in line with and in support of the group's strategy, is to create sustainable value for shareholders within the boundaries imposed by the group's risk appetite. The group's capital management priorities are to:

Create sustainable value for shareholders while maintaining sufficient capital supply for growth, with capital ratios within the Board-approved risk appetite and above minimum levels of regulatory capital.

Maintain adequate capital buffers to allow for the removal of the COVID-19 pandemic capital relief and subsequent uplift in the pillar 2A requirement from 1 January 2022.

Monitor and assess upcoming regulatory developments that may affect the capital position. These include the Basel III enhancements, including FRTB; the proposed amendments to the regulations relating to banks; the resolution framework and the financial conglomerate supervisory framework in South Africa.

EXECUTIVES
Financial director, Executive Director, Jason P Quinn
Chief Executive Officer, Executive Director, Arrie Rautenbach
Interim Chief Financial Director, Executive Director, Punkie E. Modise
Secretary, Nadine R. Drutman
Chairman, Independent Non-Executive Director, Sello Moloko
Independent Non-Executive Director, Tasneem Abdool-Samad
Independent Non-Executive Director, Nonhlanhla S. Mjoli-Mncube
Independent Non-Executive Director, John J. Cummins
Independent Non-Executive Director, Alex B. Darko
Independent Non-Executive Director, Rose A. Keanly
Independent Non-Executive Director, Swithin J. Munyantwali
Independent Non-Executive Director, Dhanasagree Naidoo
Independent Non-Executive Director, Francis Okomo-Okello
Independent Non-Executive Director, Ihronn Rensburg
Independent Non-Executive Director, Rene van Wyk
Non-Executive Director, Fulvio Tonelli
Auditors : PricewaterhouseCoopers Inc.

LOCATIONS
HQ: Absa Group Ltd (New)
7th Floor, Absa Towers West, 15 Troye Street, Johannesburg 2001
Phone: (27) 11 350 4000
Web: www.absa.africa

PRODUCTS/OPERATIONS

2016 Sales
	% of total
RBB	71
CIB	22
WIMI	7
Total	100

2016 Sales
	% of total
Interest income	58
Non-interest income	42
Total	100

COMPETITORS
AMUNDI PIONEER ASSET MANAGEMENT USA, INC.
BANK HAPOALIM LTD.
BEKB / BCBE Finanz AG
Bâloise Holding AG
NEDBANK GROUP LTD
PUTNAM INVESTMENTS, LLC
SANLAM LTD
SEI INVESTMENTS COMPANY
WOODBURY FINANCIAL SERVICES, INC.
Zurich Insurance Group AG

HISTORICAL FINANCIALS
Company Type: Public

Income Statement — FYE: December 31

	ASSETS ($mil)	NET INCOME ($mil)	INCOME AS % OF ASSETS	EMPLOYEES
12/22	105,956	1,214	1.1%	35,451
12/21	102,911	1,114	1.1%	35,267
12/20	104,343	400	0.4%	36,737
12/19	99,627	1,015	1.0%	38,472
12/18	89,627	967	1.1%	40,856
Annual Growth	4.3%	5.8%		(3.5%)

2022 Year-End Financials
Return on assets: 1.1%
Return on equity: 15.1%
Long-term debt ($ mil.): —
No. of shares ($ mil.): 827
Sales ($ mil.): 9,341
Dividends
Yield: —
Payout: 68.5%
Market value ($ mil.): 18,989

	STOCK PRICE ($) FY Close	P/E High/Low		PER SHARE ($) Earnings	Dividends	Book Value
12/22	22.95	1	1	1.46	1.00	10.14
12/21	19.48	1	1	1.34	0.31	9.81
12/20	16.25	3	1	0.48	0.64	9.51
12/19	20.62	2	1	1.22	1.21	9.73
12/18	21.99	2	1	1.16	1.27	9.20
Annual Growth	1.1%			5.9%	(5.8%)	2.5%

	STOCK PRICE ($) FY Close	P/E High/Low		PER SHARE ($) Earnings	Dividends	Book Value
12/22	13.82	8	5	2.09	0.73	27.15
12/21	14.74	12	7	1.37	0.62	26.48
12/20	9.78	—	—	0.00	0.00	27.40
12/19	18.15	10	8	2.31	1.44	25.65
Annual Growth	(8.7%)	—		(2.5%)	(15.6%)	1.4%

Abu Dhabi Islamic Bank

EXECUTIVES

Chief Executive Officer, Tirad Mahmoud
Retail Banking Global Head, S. Sarup
Wholesale Banking Global Head, A. Usmani
Strategic Clients & Community Banking Head, A. Abdullah
Region Officer, W. Al Khazraji
Shari'a Global Head, O. Kilani
Risk Global Head, M. Husain
Technology Global Head, Operations Global Head, M. Khan
Internation Expansion Head, A. Z. Alshehhi
Chief Financial Officer, A. Moir
Chief Operating Officer, N. Saliba
Risk Review Head, Audit Head, A. Kanan
Subsidiary Officer, A. Qadir Khanani
Corporate Governance Global Head, Compliance Global Head, B. Ahmed
Region Officer, A. Abrahim
Region Officer, N. Loutfy
Human Resources Global Head, N. Powar
Chairman, Jawaan Awaidha Suhail Al Khaili
Vice-Chairman, Khaled Abdulla Neamat Khouri
Auditors : Deloitte & Touche (M.E.)

LOCATIONS

HQ: Abu Dhabi Islamic Bank
P.O. Box 313, Abu Dhabi
Phone: —
Web: www.adib.co.ae

HISTORICAL FINANCIALS

Company Type: Public

Income Statement — FYE: December 31

	ASSETS ($mil)	NET INCOME ($mil)	INCOME AS % OF ASSETS	EMPLOYEES
12/23	52,505	1,361	2.6%	0
12/22	45,886	976	2.1%	0
12/20	34,803	436	1.3%	0
12/19	34,305	707	2.1%	0
12/18	34,089	680	2.0%	0
Annual Growth	9.0%	14.9%	—	—

2023 Year-End Financials

Return on assets: 2.7%
Return on equity: 21.0%
Long-term debt ($ mil.): —
No. of shares ($ mil.): 3,632
Sales ($ mil.): 3,374
Dividends
Yield: —
Payout: 55.6%
Market value ($ mil.): —

Accenture plc

Accenture is a leading global professional services company that helps the world's leading businesses, governments, and other organizations build their digital core, optimize their operations, accelerate revenue growth, and enhance citizen services. The company has over 721,000 employees in more than 120 countries. The company provides a range of services, solutions, and assets across Strategy & Consulting, Technology, Operations, Industry X, and Song (formerly Interactive). Accenture generates more than 45% of its revenue in North America.

Operations

Accenture's business is divided into five operating groups based on client industries: Products (consumer goods, retail, travel, life sciences); Financial Services; Communications, Media & Technology; Health & Public Service (private and public health organizations, educational institutions); and Resources (chemicals, energy, forestry, mining, and metals).

Products account for the largest share in the company's total revenue (about 30%), followed by communications, media & technology (some 20%), financial services (about 20%), health & public service (nearly 20%), and resources (almost 15%).

In addition to reporting revenues by geographic markets, the company also reports revenues by two types of work: consulting (some 55% of sales) and outsourcing (around 45%).

Geographic Reach

Dublin-based Accenture serves clients in more than 120 countries. The company's geographic markets, North America (more than 45% of the company's revenue), Europe (around 35%) and Growth Markets (some 20%), bring together integrated service teams, which typically consist of industry and functional experts, technology and capability specialists and professionals with local market knowledge and experience, to meet client needs.

To get close to the action, Accenture has major offices in the world's leading business centers, including in the US (Boston, Chicago, New York, and San Francisco), Europe (Dublin, Frankfurt, London, Madrid, Milan, Paris, and Rome), and the Asia/Pacific region (Bangalore, Beijing, Manila, Mumbai, SÃ£o Paolo, Shanghai, Singapore, Sydney, and Tokyo), among others. In total, we have facilities and operations in more than 200 cities in around 50 countries around the world.

Sales and Marketing

Accenture's clients span from Forbes Global 2000 companies, governments, and government agencies. The company's advertising costs were $119.2 million, $171.8 million, and $57.7 million for fiscal 2022, 2021, and 2020, respectively.

Financial Performance

The company's revenues increased by $11.1 billion to $61.6 billion in fiscal 2022 compared to $50.5 billion in the prior fiscal year. Revenues for fiscal 2022 increased 22% in US dollars and 26% in local currency compared to fiscal 2021. During fiscal 2022, revenue growth in local currency was very strong across all geographic markets, industry groups, and types of work.

The company's net income increased to $6.9 billion in fiscal 2022 compared to $5.9 billion in fiscal 2021.

Cash held by the company at the end of 2022 amounted to $7.9 billion. Operating activities provided $9.5 billion. Investing and financing activities used $4.3 billion and $5.3 billion, respectively. Main uses for cash were purchases of businesses and investments; and purchases of shares.

Strategy

The core of Accenture's growth strategy is delivering 360Â° value to its clients, people, shareholders, partners and communities. The company's strategy defines the areas in which it will drive growth, build differentiation via 360Â° value and enable its business to create that value every day. It defines 360Â° value as delivering the financial business case and unique value a client may be seeking, and striving to partner with its clients to achieve greater progress on inclusion and diversity, reskill and upskill its clients' employees, help clients achieve their sustainability goals, and create meaningful experiences, both with Accenture and for the customers and employees of our clients.

Accenture brings industry-specific solutions and services as well as cross-industry expertise and leverages its scale and global footprint, innovation capabilities, and strong ecosystem partnerships together with its assets and platforms, including MyWizard, MyNav, and SynOps, to deliver tangible value for its clients.

Mergers and Acquisitions

In early 2023, Accenture completed its acquisition of SKS Group, a consulting firm for banks in Germany, Austria, and Switzerland to modernize their infrastructure and adhere to regulatory requirements. The acquisition expands the company's technology, consulting, and regulatory services capabilities, while improving its services to banks, such as national promotional banks that provide financial and development assistance to local businesses and communities. The deal includes all of SKS Group's businesses. Financial terms of the transaction were not disclosed.

Also in early 2023, Accenture acquired Morphus, a privately held Brazil-based cyber defense, risk management and cyber threat intelligence services provider, expanding its practice capabilities in Brazil and Latin America. The acquisition expands Accenture's portfolio and marks the launch of a Cyber Industry practice in Latin America led by seasoned former CISOs from Morphus. The new offerings also expand Accenture's position in Growth Markets in Morphus's primary industry groups: communications media and technology, financial services, energy, retail and aviation. Financial terms were not disclosed.

In 2023, Accenture completed its

acquisition of Inspirage, an integrated Oracle Cloud specialist firm with an emphasis in supply chain management, headquartered in Bellevue, Washington. The acquisition further enhances Accenture's Oracle Cloud capabilities, helping it accelerate innovation for clients through emerging technologies, such as touchless supply chain and digital twins. Financial terms of the transaction were not disclosed.

In late 2022 Accenture acquired Fiftyfive5, a customer insights and advisory business. The move will strengthen Accenture Song's (formerly Accenture Interactive) ability to help clients tap data insights and performance marketing to accelerate growth and innovation across Australia and New Zealand. Terms of the transaction were not disclosed.

Also in late 2022, Accenture completed its acquisition of the people and business assets of Allgemeines Rechenzentrum GmbH (ARZ), a technology service provider focused on the banking sector in Austria. The acquisition of ARZ's business capabilities expands Accenture's cloud-based banking offerings, ranging from core banking services to online banking, as well as regulatory services for clients across Europe. Accenture has also signed a series of agreements to deliver technology services to ARZ's existing customers. Financial terms of the transaction were not disclosed.

In 2022, Accenture acquired Illinois-based Blackcomb Consultants, a leading independent Guidewire partner in North America. The acquisition enhances Accenture's ability to deliver Guidewire solutions to insurers globally to help them become "cloud-first" businesses. Guidewire's end-to-end technology platform combines digital, core analytics and artificial intelligence capabilities across the underwriting, billing, claims and customer relationship management functions, helping property and casualty (P&C) insurers reimagine their operations in the cloud. Terms of the transaction were not disclosed.

HISTORY

Accenture traces its history back to the storied accounting firm of Arthur Andersen & Co. Founded by Northwestern University professor and accounting legend Arthur Andersen in 1913, the firm's expanding scope of operations led it into forensic accounting and advising clients on financial reporting processes, forming the basis for a management consulting arm. Arthur Andersen led the firm until his death in 1947. His successor, Leonard Spacek, split off the consulting operations as a separate unit in 1954.

The consulting business grew quickly during the 1970s and 1980s, thanks in part to an orgy of US corporate re-engineering. By 1988 consulting accounted for 40% of Andersen's sales. Chafing at sharing profits with the auditors (who faced growing price pressures and a rising tide of legal action due to the accounting irregularities of their clients), the consultants sought more power within the firm. The result was a 1989 restructuring that established Andersen Worldwide (later Andersen) as the parent of two independent units, Arthur Andersen and Andersen Consulting (AC). The growing revenue imbalance between the operations remained unresolved, however, and a year later Arthur Andersen poured gas on the flames by establishing its own business consultancy.

Meanwhile, AC continued to expand during the 1990s by forming practices focused on manufacturing, finance, and government. It addressed the shift from mainframes to PCs by forming alliances with technology heavyweights Hewlett-Packard, Sun Microsystems, and Microsoft. In 1996 AC teamed up with Internet service provider BBN (acquired by GTE in 1997) to form ServiceNet, a joint venture to develop Internet commerce and other systems.

The Andersen family feud took a turn for the worse in 1997 with the retirement of CEO Lawrence Weinbach. A deadlocked vote for a new leader led the board to appoint accounting partner Robert Grafton as CEO, angering the consulting partners. Later that year AC asked the International Chamber of Commerce to negotiate a breakup of Andersen Worldwide. George Shaheen, to whom many attributed the heightened tensions between the units, resigned as CEO of AC in 1999 and was replaced by Joe Forehand.

While the separation dispute dragged on, the consulting business grew and diversified amid increasing consolidation in the industry. In 1999 the company moved into e-commerce venture funding with the formation of Andersen Consulting Ventures, and in 2000 it inked partnership deals with Microsoft (Microsoft system implementation services), Sun Microsystems (for B2B Internet office supply sales), and BT (Internet-based human resources services).

That year an international arbitrator finally approved AC's separation from its parent, ruling that the consultancy must change its name and pay Andersen Worldwide $1 billion (far less than the $15 billion demanded by the accounting partners). Renamed Accenture, the company went public in 2001. While the new name (a made-up word) might have struck some as a marketing challenge, having an identity distinct from that of its former parent proved to be a stroke of luck for Accenture. Andersen broke apart in 2002 after becoming embroiled in the accounting scandals of energy giant Enron.

In 2004 Accenture successfully bid on a $10 billion, 10-year contract to create a system to identify visitors and immigrants coming into the country. Dubbed US-VISIT (United States Visitor and Immigrant Status Indicator Technology), the system was to be employed by the Department of Homeland Security to prevent terrorists from entering the US. However, Accenture's bid nearly ran afoul of congressional critics who tried to pass spending amendments barring firms headquartered outside the US from winning security-related business.

Forehand stepped down as CEO of Accenture in 2004 and was replaced by company veteran William Green. Forehand remained chairman until he retired in 2006, when Green was named to that post, as well.

Accenture acquired Capgemini's North American health practice in 2005 for $175 million in order to strengthen its offerings to hospitals and health care systems. In 2006 the firm expanded its outsourcing operations by buying NaviSys, a leading provider of software for the life insurance industry, along with key assets of Kansas-based accountant Savista.

In mid-2008, Accenture swallowed up ATAN, an industrial and automation services provider based in Brazil that caters to the mining, energy, and utilities sectors. It also obtained SOPIA, a Tokyo-based consulting firm specializing in Oracle systems integration. During that year Accenture added to its transportation and travel services operations (located within its Products Division) when it bought AddVal Technology. AddVal provided software and technology used for freight order management, and the deal enhanced Accenture's ability to integrate and simplify its clients' freight management services capabilities.

In late 2009 Accenture looked to solidify its position in a vital market when it obtained the Symbian professional services unit of Nokia. The unit offers engineering and support services for the Symbian operating system, one of the world's most widely used operating systems for smart phones. The acquired operations provided a broad range of embedded software services for mobile devices and were rebranded Accenture Embedded Mobility Services.

Accenture obtained RiskControl, a consulting firm based in Brazil, in early 2010. Also that year Accenture bought Beijing Genesis Interactive Technology Company, an embedded software firm providing mobile software outsourcing services to companies in China. The acquisitions furthered Accenture's penetration into the cutting-edge smart phone support services market.

Focusing on beefing up its Financial Services segment, in 2011 Accenture acquired Duck Creek Technologies, a provider of software and tools catering to the insurance and health care sectors. At the time of the transaction, Duck Creek served about 60 clients throughout North America and the UK.

At the beginning of 2011, Pierre Nanterme, the former head of the company's financial services operations, was promoted to become the company's newest CEO. Green remains with Accenture as chairman.

EXECUTIVES

Chair, Chief Executive Officer, Director, Julie Spellman Sweet, $1,250,000 total compensation
Chief Financial Officer, Kathleen R. McClure, $975,000 total compensation
Chief Operating Officer, John Walsh
Chief Compliance Officer, General Counsel, Corporate Secretary, Joel Unruch
Region Officer, Melissa A. Burgum
Division Officer, Leo Framil
Division Officer, Yusuf Tayob
Division Officer, Gianfranco Casati, $1,108,990 total compensation
Region Officer, Jean-Marc Ollagnier
Lead Independent Director, Director, Gilles C. Pelisson, $90,000 total compensation
Director, Jaime Ardila, $40,978 total compensation
Director, Nancy McKinstry
Director, Beth E. Mooney
Director, Paula A. Price
Director, Venkata S.M. Renduchintala
Director, Arun Sarin
Director, Tracey T. Travis
Director, Alan Jope
Auditors : KPMG LLP

LOCATIONS

HQ: Accenture plc
 1 Grand Canal Square, Grand Canal Harbour, Dublin 2
Phone: (353) 1 646 2000
Web: www.accenture.com

2018 Sales

	% of total
North America	45
Europe	33
Growth Markets	19
Total	100

PRODUCTS/OPERATIONS

2018 sales

	% of total
Communications, Media & Technology	19
Financial Services	20
Health & Public Service	16
Products	26
Resources	14
Reimbursement	5
Total	100

2018 sales

	% of total
Consulting	52
Outsourcing	43
Reimbursement	5
Total	100

Selected Practice Areas
Communications and high technology
 Communications
 Electronics and high technology
 Media and entertainment
Products
 Automotive
 Consumer goods and services
 Health and life sciences
 Industrial equipment
 Retail
 Transportation and travel services
Financial services
 Banking
 Capital markets
 Insurance
Resources
 Chemicals
 Energy
 Natural resources
 Utilities
Government

Selected Services
Business consulting
 Customer relationship management
 Finance and performance management
 Human performance
 Strategy
 Supply chain management
Outsourcing
 Application outsourcing
 Business process outsourcing (BPO)
 Customer contact
 Finance and accounting
 Human resources
 Learning
 Procurement
 Infrastructure outsourcing
Systems integration and technology
 Enterprise architecture
 Information management
 Infrastructure consulting
 Intellectual property
Research and developmen

COMPETITORS

AMDOCS LIMITED
ATOS SE
BT GROUP PLC
CAPGEMINI
CAPGEMINI NORTH AMERICA, INC.
CEGID GROUP
DATATEC LTD
DIMENSION DATA HOLDINGS LTD
STEFANINI, INC.
WIPRO LIMITED

HISTORICAL FINANCIALS
Company Type: Public

Income Statement   FYE: August 31

	REVENUE ($mil)	NET INCOME ($mil)	NET PROFIT MARGIN	EMPLOYEES
08/23	64,111	6,871	10.7%	733,000
08/22	61,594	6,877	11.2%	721,000
08/21	50,533	5,906	11.7%	624,000
08/20	44,327	5,107	11.5%	506,000
08/19	43,215	4,779	11.1%	492,000
Annual Growth	10.4%	9.5%	—	10.5%

2023 Year-End Financials
Debt ratio: 0.3%   No. of shares ($ mil.): 628
Return on equity: 28.7%   Dividends
Cash ($ mil.): 9,045   Yield: —
Current Ratio: 1.30   Payout: 41.5%
Long-term debt ($ mil.): 43 Market value ($ mil.): —

Acer Inc

Founded in 1976, Acer is now one of the world's top ICT companies and has a presence in over 160 countries. As Acer evolves with the industry and changing lifestyles, it is focused on enabling a world where hardware, software and services will fuse with one another, creating ecosystems and opening up new possibilities for consumers and businesses alike. Acer products include servers, storage systems, monitors, projectors, gaming products and esports platform, gadgets and apparel and cloud services. The company sells through resellers and distributors worldwide. Taiwan generates about 20% of Acer's total revenue.

Operations
The company's reportable segments comprise the device business group (IT Hardware Products; accounts for about 85% of total revenue) and other business groups (more than 15%). The IT Hardware Products engages mainly in the research, design, and marketing of personal computers, IT products, and tablet products. Other business groups mainly engage in the activities of e-commerce, cloud services, sales and distribution of smart devices, distributors and agency, new energy devices, and handheld devices, as well as real estate services.

Overall, Acer generates about 70% of its total revenue from personal computers and some 30% from peripherals and other products.

Geographic Reach
Acer has a presence in more than 160 countries. Its home country, Taiwan accounts for about 20% of Acer's total revenue, while the USA brings in some 20%, and Mainland China for around 5%. Other countries earn almost 55% of total revenue.

Sales and Marketing
Acer primarily sells and markets its multi-branded IT products through distributors in different geographic areas.

Financial Performance
Acer's revenue for the past five fiscal years experienced increases and decreases starting from NTD242.3 billion, NTD234.3 billion, NTD277.1 billion, NTD319.0 billion and NTD275.4, for 2018 to 2022, respectively.

Company revenue for fiscal 2022 decreased to NTD275.4 billion compared form the prior year with NTD319.0 billion. The decrease was primarily due to lower IT Hardware products sales.

Net income for fiscal 2022 decreased to NTD5.0 billion compared from the prior year with NTD10.9 billion. The decrease was primarily due to higher revenues.

Cash held by the company at the end of fiscal 2022 increased to NTD46.8 billion. Cash provided by operations was NTD5.9 billion while cash used for investing and financing activities were NTD903.0 million and NTD5.8 billion, respectively. Main uses of cash were purchase of financial assets measured at fair value through other comprehensive income; and decrease in short-term borrowings.

Strategy
Acer is constantly evolving with the industry and changing lifestyles by continuing to push for innovation in existing businesses, while expanding to new territories. In the PC and displays business, Acer is committed to

strengthening the foundations with technological innovations such as its state-of-the-art thermal cooling solutions, and designing unique product lines for the specific needs of gamers, education, and more. At the same time, Acer's strategy is to explore new opportunities, expand into adjacent territories, and cultivate multiple business engines. Acer is encouraging employees to think outside the box by promoting intrapreneurship.

Acer continues to research and develop customer-centric products, and explore beyond boundaries to identify and incubate micro trends that have potential for growth. Its strategy is to grow its multiple business engines for the group's long-term sustainability, and this strategy has been making progress. Currently, Acer has nine public subsidiaries: Acer Gadget, Acer Gaming, Highpoint Service Network, Acer Medical, Acer Cyber Security, Acer Synergy Tech, Weblink International Inc., Acer e-Enabling Service Business, and AOPEN.

HISTORY

Acer founder and chairman Stan Shih, respected enough for his business acumen to once be considered for the premiership of Taiwan, designed that country's first desktop calculator in the early 1970s. The company's precursor, Multitech International, was launched in 1976 with $25,000 by Shih and four others who called themselves the "Gardeners of Microprocessing." In 1980 Multitech introduced the Dragon Chinese-language terminal, which won Taiwan's top design award; in 1983 it introduced an Apple clone and its first IBM-compatible PC. Multitech set up AcerLand, Taiwan's first and largest franchised computer retail chain, in 1985.

The company changed its name to Acer (the Latin word for "sharp, acute, able, and facile") in 1987 and went public on the Taiwan exchange the next year. Acer got into the semiconductor market in 1989 when it entered into a joint venture with Texas Instruments (named TI-Acer) to design and develop memory chips in Taiwan. In 1990 Acer's US subsidiary, Acer America, paid $90 million for Altos Computer Systems, a US manufacturer of UNIX systems.

During the prosperous 1980s Acer increased its management layers and slowed the decision-making process. In late 1990 the company restructured, trimming its workforce by 8% (about 400 employees), including two-thirds of headquarters. The layoff was unprecedented -- being asked to resign from a job in Taiwan carries a social stigma. Shih wrote a letter to all those affected, explaining the plight of the company. The following year Acer began its decentralization plan to create a worldwide confederation of publicly owned companies.

Acer suffered its first loss in 1991 on revenues of almost $1 billion, partly because of increased marketing budgets in the US and Europe and continuing investment in TI-Acer. The company bounced back in 1993, with 80% of its profit coming from that joint venture.

The Aspire PC, available in shades of gray and green, was unveiled in 1995. In 1996 the company expanded into consumer electronics, introducing a host of new, inexpensive videodisc players, video telephones, and other devices in order to boost global market share. In 1997 Acer purchased TI's notebook computer business. A slowdown in memory chip sales, plus a financial slide at Acer America, cost the firm $141 million, but Acer finished the year in the black.

Shih stepped down as president in 1998 to focus on restructuring. The company ended its venture with TI, buying TI's 33% stake and renaming the unit Acer Semiconductor Manufacturing. The company also began making information appliances, introducing a device able to play CD-ROMs via TV sets and perform other task-specific functions. Continued losses due to a highly competitive US market caused a drop in profits for 1998.

In 1999 Acer sold a 30% stake in its struggling Acer Semiconductor Manufacturing affiliate to Taiwan Semiconductor Manufacturing Company (TSMC completed its purchase of the remaining 70% of the business, which was renamed TSMC-Acer Semiconductor Manufacturing, the following year.) The competitive heat and the rise of under-$1,000 PCs took a toll that year when Acer cut US jobs, streamlined operations, and withdrew from the US retail market. The company intensified its focus on providing online software, hardware, and support for users, launching a digital services business and a venture capital operation to invest in promising Internet startups.

The company suffered a financial blow in 2000 when large customer IBM cancelled an order for desktop computers. Late that year, after continued losses in a slowing PC market, the company announced it would cut more jobs in the US and Germany and close an unspecified number of plants worldwide.

Acer saw major streamlining in 2001, when it spun off its contract manufacturing operations (renamed Wistron), as well as its consumer electronics and peripherals business (renamed BenQ). Slumping sales in a weakening computer hardware market prompted Acer's restructuring efforts. In addition to clarifying the structure of Acer's sizable operations, the separation of Acer's branded operations and Wistron served to eliminate possible customer concerns about a conflict of interest between the two businesses.

In 2005 president J. T. Wang succeeded Shih as CEO. In 2007 Acer sold its electronic components distribution subsidiary, Sertek, to Yosun Industrial. It also acquired Gateway for $710 million that year. President Gianfranco Lanci took over for Wang as CEO in 2008.

Acer acquired E-TEN, a Taiwan-based developer of smartphones, also in 2008. E-TEN markets products under its own brand and designs devices for OEMs.

EXECUTIVES

Chairman, Chief Executive Officer, Executive Chairman, Jason Chen
Co-Chief Operating Officer, Tiffany Huang
Co-Chief Operating Officer, Jerry Kao
Corporate Vice-President, President, Emmanuel Fromont
President, Ben Wan
President, Gregg Prendergast
President, Andrew Hou
President, Victor Chien
Chief Technology Officer, RC Chang
Corporate Governance Officer, Lydia Wu
Chief Financial Officer, Meggy Chen
Accounting Officer, Sophia Chen
President, Non-Independent Executive Director, Maverick Shih
Non-Independent Director, Stan Shih
Non-Independent Director, George Huang
Non-Independent Director, Phillip Peng
Independent Director, F.C. Tseng
Independent Director, Ji-Ren Lee
Independent Director, Ching-Hsiang Hsu
Auditors : KPMG

LOCATIONS

HQ: Acer Inc
7F-5, No. 369, Fuxing N. Rd., Songshan Dist., Taipei 105
Phone: (886) 2 2719 5000   **Fax:** (886) 2 8712 5519
Web: www.acer-group.com

2015 Sales

	% of total
Americas	21
Mainland China	11
Taiwan	8
Others	60
Total	100

2015 Sales

	% of total
Personal Computers	79
Peripherals and others	21
Total	100

PRODUCTS/OPERATIONS

Selected Products
Computers (desktop, handheld, netbook, notebook, server, tablet)
Digital cameras
Digital projectors
LCD televisions
Monitors (cathode-ray tube and liquid-crystal display)
Smartphones

COMPETITORS

AGILYSYS, INC.
ARROW ELECTRONICS, INC.
CDW CORPORATION
COMPUCOM SYSTEMS, INC.

DELL INC.
GATEWAY, INC.
LENOVO GROUP LIMITED
SCANSOURCE, INC.
TECH DATA CORPORATION
WESTERN DIGITAL CORPORATION

HISTORICAL FINANCIALS

Company Type: Public

Income Statement — FYE: December 31

	REVENUE ($mil)	NET INCOME ($mil)	NET PROFIT MARGIN	EMPLOYEES
12/21	11,521	393	3.4%	0
12/20	9,860	214	2.2%	1,627
12/19	5,800	87	1.5%	1,600
12/18	7,921	100	1.3%	7,338
12/17	8,002	94	1.2%	7,046
Annual Growth	9.5%	42.7%	—	—

2021 Year-End Financials

Debt ratio: 0.2%
Return on equity: 17.5%
Cash ($ mil.): 1,611
Current Ratio: 1.35
Long-term debt ($ mil.): 364
No. of shares ($ mil.): 3,001
Dividends
Yield: —
Payout: 149.8%
Market value ($ mil.): 28,150

	STOCK PRICE ($) FY Close	P/E High/Low		PER SHARE ($) Earnings	Dividends	Book Value
12/21	9.38	3	1	0.13	0.19	0.77
12/20	4.26	2	2	0.07	0.12	0.71
12/19	2.80	4	3	0.03	0.08	0.64
12/18	3.75	5	3	0.03	0.09	0.63
12/17	2.02	—	—	0.03	0.07	0.64
Annual Growth	46.8%	—	—	42.7%	30.1%	4.7%

ACS Actividades de Construccion y Servicios, S.A.

Founded in 1983, ACS, Actividades de Construcció³n y Servicios, AS is one of Spain's largest construction and infrastructure groups. The company's activities include civil engineering, installation and maintenance of energy facilities, transport services, and highway management. ACS has grown by investing in such firms as former construction rival Dragados and Germany-based infrastructure giant HOCHTIEF. Its largest market is North America accounting for about 60% of its revenue.

Operations

ACS divides its business into three segments: Construction, Services and Concessions.

ACS's Construction segment, which generates nearly 95% of the company's revenue, consists of Dragados and HOCHTIEF. The companies operate in a diverse range of sectors, including public works (highways, railways, ports, and airports), social value (residential buildings, social facilities, and installations), infrastructure services (transport, communications, energy, resources, and defense), and mining.

The Services segment, which generates more than 5% of revenue, includes the business of Clece, which offers comprehensive maintenance of buildings, public places or organizations, as well as assistance for people.

The Concessions segment consist of IRIDIUM and Abertis. IRIDIUM is the ACS company that continues leading international activity in the infrastructure sector, primarily transportation. Abertis is one of the leading international operators in toll road management, in which the group has a 50% holding (30% direct and 20% indirect, through HOCHTIEF).

Geographic Reach

ACS is based in Madrid, Spain and has operations in Argentina, Australian, Austria, Canada, Chile, Czech Republic, Germany, India, Indonesia, Mexico, New Zealand, Peru, Poland, Portugal, Singapore, Slovak Republic, Spain, The Netherlands, UK and US.

Its largest market is North America, generating around 60% of revenue and followed by Asia Pacific for more than 20%. The remaining revenues are produced in Spain (about 10%), South America (about 5%), Rest of Europe (over 5%).

Financial Performance

Company's revenue for fiscal 2021 decreased to EUR 27.8 billion compared from the prior year with EUR 27.9 billion.

Profit for fiscal 2021 increased to EUR 3.0 billion compared from the prior year with EUR 542.3 million.

Strategy

The ACS Group operates in an increasingly complex and competitive environment that entails numerous risks and uncertainties, forcing the company to adapt its strategy to the challenges and opportunities that arise in a highly dynamic global sector.

The ACS Group has consolidated a leading business model worldwide in its sector, featuring extensive diversification in terms of geography and business activity, thanks to its strategy of pursuing global leadership, optimizing the profitability of the resources employed and promoting sustainable development. These three pillars ensure the generation of shared value for all its stakeholders and sustainable and profitable growth for its shareholders.

Mergers and Acquisitions

In 2022, ACS has reached an agreement through its subsidiary IRIDIUM, for the acquisition of a 44.65% stake in the SH-288 toll lane concession in Houston, United States for nearly EUR 900 million. With this increase, acquired from the infrastructure funds InfraRed Capital Partners, Northleaf Capital Partners and Star America, the Spanish company now holds 66.27% of the capital invested in the project and takes control of the concession. With this transaction, the ACS strengthens its position as controlling shareholder of the SH-288 toll lane, from which it consolidates its leadership in the infrastructure market in the US, and from which it advances in its expansion strategy in the North American concessions market.

HISTORY

In war-torn Europe in 1942, the Spanish construction company Obras y Construcciones Industriales (Ocisa) was born. The company soon began a 50-year association with Spain's hydroelectric industry, marked by the completion of the dam and reservoir project Presa de Bachimana in 1950. The company built nine more dam and reservoir projects in Spain (including Presa de la Llosa, completed in 1997).

As the demand for public works projects decreased and competition increased, Spanish constructors began working abroad, especially in Latin America, where Ocisa was contracted in 1975 to create an irrigation tunnel in Venezuela's Andes.

A six-year economic expansion measured by the success of Spain's "Big Seven" construction companies, including #5 Ocisa, reached its end in 1992 when the Spanish government, the country's biggest builder, was forced to cut spending on infrastructure. This triggered consolidation in Spain's construction industry, including Ocisa's 1993 acquisition of Construcciones Padros, in which Ocisa held a 25% stake. Adopting the new name OCP Construcciones, it also absorbed the assets of its installation and assembly subsidiary, Compania de la Distribucion de Electricidad (Grupo Cobra).

The slowdown in public works projects continued and companies sought additional pooling of resources and diversification of activities at home and abroad. In 1996 OCP bought a 40% stake in the state-owned construction firm Auxini, increased to 100% a year later. Also in 1997 the OCP group, led by its president, Florentino Perez, acquired Gines Navarro Construcciones, controlled (79%) by the powerful investment group led by brothers Carlos and Juan March. The two companies combined to create Spain's third-largest construction group, Actividades de Construcciones y Servicios, or Grupo ACS.

EXECUTIVES

Vice-Chairman, Antonio Garcia Ferrer
Executive Chairman, Chief Executive Officer, Director, Florentino Perez Rodriguez
Secretary, Director, Jose Luis del Valle Perez
Director, Agustin Batuecas Torrego
Director, Antonio Botella Garcia
Director, Javier Echenique Landiribar
Director, Carmen Fernandez Rozado
Director, Emilio Garcia Gallego

Director, Joan-David Grima Terre
Director, Mariano Hernandez Herreros
Director, Pedro Lopez Jimenez
Director, Catalina Minarro Brugarolas
Director, Maria Soledad Perez Rodriguez
Director, Miquel Roca Junyent
Director, Jose Eladio Seco dominguez
Auditors : KPMG Auditores, S.L.

LOCATIONS

HQ: ACS Actividades de Construccion y Servicios, S.A.
Avenida de PÃo XII, 102, Madrid 28036
Phone: (34) 91 343 9200   **Fax:** (34) 91 343 9456
Web: www.grupoacs.com

2017 Sales

	% of total
North America	45
Asia/Pacific	29
Spain	13
Rest of Europe	7
South Africa	5
Africa	1
Total	100

PRODUCTS/OPERATIONS

2017 Sales

	% of total
Construction	78
Industrial Services	18
Environment	4
Total	100

Selected Subsidiaries

Concessions
    Concesiones Viarias Chile, S.A. (infrastructures)
    Iridium Concesiones de Infraestructuras S.A.
Construction
    Acainsa, S.A. (real estate development)
    Ave Lalin
    Consorcio Tecdra, S.A.
    Constructora Norte Sur, S.A. (48%, Chile)
    Desaladora Barcelona (28%)
    Guadarrama Iv (33%)
    Inmobiliaria Alabega, S.A. (real estate development)
    Isla Verde Ute (35%)
    Soterram. Basurto Ute Tecsa-Necso (50%)
    Terminal Aeropuerto (70%)
Environment
    Consenur, S.A. (management and treatment of hospital waste)
    Empordanesa de Neteja, S.A. (urban solid waste management and street cleaning)
    Mapide, S.A. (interior cleaning)
    Publimedia Sistemas Publicitarios, S.L. (advertising services)
    RetraOil, S.L. (treatment of oils and marpoles)
    Servicios Generales de Jaén, S.A. (75%, water)
    Somasur, S.A. (intermediary company, Morocco)
    Urbaser de Méjico, S.A. (collection of urban solid waste and street cleaning)
    Urbaser Valencia, C.A. (collection of urban solid waste and street cleaning)
    Ute Ecoparc V (20%, USW treatment)
    Vertederos de Residuos, S.A. (84%, VERTRESA, collection of urban solid waste and street cleaning)
Industrial Services
    ACS Industrial Services LLC (energy production, US)
    Actividades de Servicios e Instalaciones Cobra, S.A. (auxiliary energy and communications distribution, Guatemala)
    Andasol 1, S.A. (energy production)
    API Movilidad S.A. (road maintenance)
    BTOB Construccion Ventures, S.L. (administrative management)
    Central Térmica de Mejillones S.A. (engineering, supply, and construction, Chile)
    Cobra Ingeniería de Montajes, S.A. (installations and assembly)
    Cobra Perú, S.A. (auxiliary energy and communications distribution)
    Coinsal Instalaciones y Servicios, S.A. de C.V. (installations and assembly, El Salvador)
    Cymi Holding S.A. (securities holding company, Brazil)
    Dragados Gulf Construction Ltd. (Saudi Arabia)
    Emurtel, S.A. (50%, electrical installations)
    Enq, S.L. (electrical installations)
    Etra Catalu?a, S.A. (electrical installations)
    Extresol-1 S.L. (energy production)
    Gerovitae La Guancha, S.A. (senior social and health center operations)
    Humiclima Est, S.A. (air conditioning)
    Incro, S.A. (50%, engineering)
    Infraest. Energéticas Medioambi. Extreme?as S.L. (services)
    Instalaciones y Servicios Codeven, C.A. (air conditioning)
    Mantenimiento y Montajes Industriales, S.A. (industrial maintenance and assemblies)
    Mexsemi, S.A. de C.V. (99.7%, assemblies, Mexico)
    Opade Organizac. y Promoc de Actividades Deportivas, S.A. (athletic activities organization and promotion)
    Parque Eólico Marmellar, S.L. (70%, energy production)
    Portumasa, S.A. (manufacture and sale of electical equipment, Portugal)
    Semi Maroc, S.A. (99.7%, assemblies)
    Serveis Catalans, Serveica, S.A. (electrical installations)
    SICE LLC. (design, construction, installation, and maintenance of traffic and trade)
    Sistemas Radiantes F. Moyano, S.A. (telecommunications)
    Tecnotel de Canarias, S.A. (air conditioning)
    Ute C.T. Andasol 1 (80%, fossil fuel plant)
    Venezolana de Limpiezas Indust. C.A. (83%, VENELIN, Venezuela)
Services
    Valdemingomez 2000, S.A. (34%, Valdemingómez degasification)

COMPETITORS

ACCIONA, SA
CARILLION PLC
CIMIC GROUP LIMITED
HENRY BOOT PLC
MATRIX SERVICE COMPANY
OBRASCON HUARTE LAIN SA
TETRA TECH UK CONSULTING GROUP LIMITED
THE SUNDT COMPANIES INC
TUTOR PERINI CORPORATION
WINSUPPLY INC.

HISTORICAL FINANCIALS

Company Type: Public

Income Statement   FYE: December 31

	REVENUE ($mil)	NET INCOME ($mil)	NET PROFIT MARGIN	EMPLOYEES
12/21	31,627	3,446	10.9%	120,827
12/20	43,349	704	1.6%	181,699
12/19	44,210	1,080	2.4%	194,036
12/18	42,243	1,047	2.5%	191,823
12/17	42,201	961	2.3%	181,527
Annual Growth	(7.0%)	37.6%	—	(9.7%)

2021 Year-End Financials

Debt ratio: 33.0%   No. of shares ($ mil.): 320
Return on equity: 61.7%   Dividends
Cash ($ mil.): 12,737   Yield: —
Current Ratio: 1.43   Payout: 4.3%
Long-term debt ($ mil.): 9,758   Market value ($ mil.): 1,708

	STOCK PRICE ($) FY Close	P/E High/Low		PER SHARE ($) Earnings	Dividends	Book Value
12/21	5.33	1	1	10.46	0.46	22.37
12/20	6.64	5	2	1.96	0.02	12.42
12/19	7.91	4	3	2.87	1.74	13.37
12/18	7.70	4	3	2.71	1.30	12.86
12/17	7.79	4	3	2.42	0.00	11.22
Annual Growth	(9.1%)	—		44.1%	—	18.8%

Adecco Group AG

Adecco is the world's largest employment agency, serving about 100,000 clients. The bulk of Adecco's business is providing temporary staffing, permanent placement and outsourcing under the brands Adecco and Adia. Adecco does most of its business in Europe, particularly France, but it has operations globally. Pontoon, General Assembly and LHH is Adecco's HR outsourcing business, fulfilling an organization's staffing needs. The company offers its services through its 39,000 employees and 3.5 million associates. Adecco traces its roots to 1957 and has a history of growing through mergers and acquisitions.

Operations

Company service lines are: Flexible Placement (accounts for more than 75% of revenue); Permanent Placement (less than 5%); Career Transition (less than 5%); Outsourcing, Consulting, & Other Services (more than 15%); and Training, Up-skilling & Re-skilling (less than 5%).

Flexible Placement place associates with organizations on a temporary basis, providing flexibility to employers and new opportunities to candidates. The company manage the entire recruitment process from candidate search and screening, through onboarding and training, to payroll and administration.

Permanent Placement help employers to recruit talent for permanent roles, securing the skills needed for an organization's ongoing success. The company source candidates, screen CVs, conduct interviews and assessments, and advise hiring managers.

Career Transition support organizations and their employees through changes that require individuals to transition out of their existing roles.

Outsourcing, Consulting & Other Services also offer a full spectrum of complementary HR solutions, including: Outsourcing ? staffing and managing the entirety of a labor-intensive activity, such as warehouse logistics or IT support; Consulting ? providing technical experts for project-related work; Managed Service Programmes (MSPs) ?managing all parts of the flexible workforce at organizations using a large number of contingent workers; and Recruitment Process Outsourcing (RPO) ? handling the entire hiring process for employers recruiting large numbers of permanent employees.

Training, Up-skilling & Re-skilling offer training, up-skilling and re-skilling both as standalone services and in combination with other solutions, such as placements or as part of a broader workforce transformation offering.

Geographic Reach

The company operates in four regions on around 60 countries. Company's revenue mainly from its operations in EMEA with more than 65% followed by Americas and Asia Pacific were around 20% and more than 10%, respectively.

Sales and Marketing

Adecco provides temporary staffing, permanent placement, career transitioning, outsourcing, talent development and other services to more than 100,000 clients.

Financial Performance

Company's revenue for fiscal 2022 increased by 13% to EUR 23.6 billion compared from the prior year with EUR 20.9 billion. The increase was primarily due to higher revenues on every service lines aside from career transitions.

Net income for fiscal 2022 decreased to EUR 342 million compared from the prior year with EUR 586 million. The decrease was primarily due to lower EBITA excluding one-off, offsetting the increase in revenues.

Cash provided by operations was EUR 543 million while cash used for investing and financing activities were EUR 1.4 billion and EUR 1.38 billion, respectively.

Strategy

The Adecco Group's Future@Work strategy aims to positively impact the work lives of even more individuals, and further enable the growth of its clients and the wider economies in which the company operate.

The company's strategy was designed to address the megatrends transforming the world of work. Since then, increased political and economic volatility and the impacts of the Covid-19 pandemic have accelerated many of the shifts already underway. In the developed labour markets, 2022 was characterized by a global scarcity of talent, the need to up skill workers to navigate the green and digital transitions, and the rise of the human-centric organization.

EXECUTIVES

Chief Executive Officer, Alain Dehaze
Chief Financial Officer, Coram Williams
Chief Sales and Marketing Officer, Valerie Beaulieu
Communications Chief of Staff and Communications Officer, Corporate
Communications Chief of Staff and Communications Officer, Corporate
Communications Senior Vice President,
Communications Senior Vice President,
Corporate Communications Head,
Communications Head, Stephan Howeg
Chief Human Resources Officer, Gordana Landen
Chief Digital Officer, Teppo Paavola
Chief Information Officer, Ralf Weissbeck
President, Christophe Catoir
Modis President, Jan Gupta
LHH (Talent Solutions) President, Gaelle de la Fosse
Chairman, Independent Non-Executive Director, Jean-Christophe Deslarzes
Non-Executive Chairman, Independent Non-Executive Director, Kathleen Taylor
Independent Non-Executive Director, Rachel Duan
Independent Non-Executive Director, Ariane Gorin
Independent Non-Executive Director, Alexander Gut
Independent Non-Executive director, Didier R. Lamouche
Independent Non-Executive Director, David Prince
Independent Non-Executive Director, Regula Wallimann
Auditors : Ernst & Young Ltd.

LOCATIONS

HQ: Adecco Group AG
Bellerivestrasse 30, Zurich 8008
Phone: (41) 44 878 88 88   **Fax:** (41) 44 829 88 88
Web: www.adeccogroup.com

2018 sales

	%
France	24
North America & UK&I General Staffing	13
North America & UK&I Professional Staffing	14
Germany, Austria, Switzerland	9
Benelux & Nordics	9
Italy	8
Japan	5
Iberia	5
Rest of the World	11
Career Transition & Talent Development	2
Total	**100**

PRODUCTS/OPERATIONS

2018 sales

	%
General Staffing	
Office	23
Industrial	53
Professional Staffing	
IT	11
Engineering & Technical	4
Finance & Legal	4
Medical & Science	2
Solutions	
Career Transition & Talent Development	2
BPO	1
Total	**100**

Selected Brands
Adecco
Badenoch & Clark
Modis
Spring Professional

Selected Services
Career Transition
Outsourcing, Talent Development, and other services
Permanent Placement
Temporary Staffing

COMPETITORS

BLACKROCK, INC.
Bâloise Holding AG
GROUPE CRIT
ICAHN ENTERPRISES L.P.
IMPELLAM GROUP PLC
LafargeHolcim Ltd
MANPOWERGROUP INC.
SEI INVESTMENTS COMPANY
Swiss Re AG
TRUEBLUE, INC.

HISTORICAL FINANCIALS

Company Type: Public

Income Statement   FYE: December 31

	REVENUE ($mil)	NET INCOME ($mil)	NET PROFIT MARGIN	EMPLOYEES
12/21	23,711	663	2.8%	32,625
12/20	24,007	(120)	—	30,264
12/19	26,303	816	3.1%	34,662
12/18	27,332	524	1.9%	34,774
12/17	28,362	944	3.3%	33,787
Annual Growth	(4.4%)	(8.5%)	—	(0.9%)

2021 Year-End Financials

Debt ratio: 29.6%   No. of shares ($ mil.): 165
Return on equity: 16.7%   Dividends
Cash ($ mil.): 3,453   Yield: 3.2%
Current Ratio: 1.63   Payout: 19.2%
Long-term debt ($ mil.): 3,113   Market value ($ mil.): 4,221

	STOCK PRICE ($) FY Close	P/E High/Low		PER SHARE ($) Earnings	Dividends	Book Value
12/21	25.57	9	6	4.07	0.83	25.99
12/20	33.27	—	—	(0.75)	0.78	24.44
12/19	31.64	7	5	5.02	0.74	27.29
12/18	23.50	14	8	3.17	1.23	25.07
12/17	38.33	9	8	5.59	0.96	25.83
Annual Growth	(9.6%)	—	—	(7.6%)	(3.5%)	0.1%

Adidas AG

adidas' broad and diverse portfolio in both the Sport Performance and Sport Inspired categories ranges from major global sports to regional grassroot events and local sneaker culture. The German sportswear company sells sports shoes, apparel, and equipment sporting its iconic three-stripe logo in some 160 countries. One of the top sporting goods manufacturers worldwide (along with NIKE and Under Armour), adidas focuses on football, soccer, basketball, running, and training gear and apparel as well as lifestyle goods. Founder Adi Dassler, brother of PUMA creator Rudi, began making shoes in Germany in the early 1920s. Majority of its sales were generated in EMEA.

Operations

adidas operates predominantly in one industry segment ? the design, distribution and marketing of athletic and sports lifestyle products.

Its five operating segments are EMEA, North America, Greater China, Asia Pacific, and Latin America. The EMEA segment brings in more than 35% of sales, followed by North America with about 25%, Greater China with more than 20%, Asia Pacific with approximately 10%, and Latin America with over 5%.

Overall, adidas brand generates about 55% of sales from footwear, around 40% from apparel, and nearly 5% from accessories and gear.

Geographic Reach

Based in Germany, it sells its products through nearly 2,200 stores worldwide. Its e-commerce operation reaches customers in about 60 countries worldwide.

adidas outsources nearly all its manufacturing. Its nearly 115 independent manufacturing partners were producing in about 235 manufacturing facilities. The majority (roughly 70%) of its independent manufacturing partners are located in Asia. Indonesia represented the company's largest sourcing country with about 35% of the total volume, followed by Vietnam with approximately 30%, and China with some 15%

Sales and Marketing

The company expands its portfolio of partners, which already includes BeyoncÃ©, Jerry Lorenzo, Kanye West, Pharrell Williams, Stella McCartney, and Yohji Yamamoto, all of whom continue to play a significant role in wowing its consumers on the lifestyle side. Likewise, the company continues to leverage its partnerships with the biggest symbols in sport, be it with teams like Bayern Munich or Real Madrid, athletes like Lionel Messi or Mikaela Shiffrin, or events like the Boston and Berlin Marathons.

Financial Performance

In 2021, adidas AG net sales increased 12% to EUR 4.5 billion compared to EUR 4 billion in the prior year.

Net income for fiscal 2021 increased by 220% to EUR 1.9 billion compared to the prior year's net income of EUR 578 million.

Cash held by the company at the end of fiscal 2021 increased to EUR 3.8 billion. Cash provided by operations activities totaled EUR 3.2 billion. Investing activities used EUR 424 million, mainly for purchase of property, plant and equipment. Financing activities used another EUR 3 million, primarily for the repurchase of adidas AG shares

Strategy

At the beginning of 2021, the company launched its new strategy 'Own the Game' for the period until 2025. As part of this strategy, adidas is focusing its growth efforts on the three strategic markets Greater China, EMEA, and North America. To be able to execute this strategy successfully, adidas has changed its organizational structure. Since January 1, 2021, adidas manages Greater China as a separate market. The remaining Asia-Pacific (APAC) market now comprises Japan, South Korea, Southeast Asia, and the Pacific region. The change reflects the increasing importance of Greater China as a growth market for the company. In addition, adidas created the EMEA (Europe, Middle East, and Africa) market. To better leverage economies of scale, the company has integrated the former markets Europe, Russia/CIS, and Emerging Markets into the newly formed EMEA market. The markets North America and Latin America remain unchanged.

Company Background

adidas was founded in 1924 by Adi Dassler (hence "adi-das") in the small German town of Herzogenaurach. It found fame early on when US sprinter Jesse Owens won four gold medals at the 1936 Olympics in Berlin while wearing adidas running spikes. Adi's brother Rudolf left the company in acrimonious circumstances in 1947 and formed Puma, also in Herzogenaurach; the two companies entered into an intense rivalry (later eclipsed by the adidas-NIKE rivalry). adidas became a public company in 1995 and in 2006 acquired Reebok, which as of 2019 is the only non-adidas apparel brand used by the company.

HISTORY

adidas grew out of an infamous rift between German brothers Adi and Rudi Dassler, who created athletic shoe giants adidas and Puma. As WWI was winding down, Adi scavenged for tires, rucksacks, and other refuse to create slippers, gymnastics shoes, and soccer cleats at home. His sister cut patterns out of canvas. By 1926 the shoes' success allowed the Dasslers to build a factory. At the 1928 Amsterdam Olympics, German athletes first showcased Dassler shoes to the world. In 1936 American Jesse Owens sprinted to Olympic gold in Dassler's double-striped shoes.

Business boomed until the Nazis commandeered the Dassler factory to make boots for soldiers. Although both Rudi and Adi were reportedly members of the Nazi party, only Rudi was called to service. Adi remained at home to run the factory. When Allied troops occupied the area, Adi made friends with American soldiers -- even creating shoes for a soldier who wore them at the 1946 Olympics. Rudi came home from an American prison camp and joined his brother; together they scavenged the war-torn landscape for tank materials and tents to make shoes.

Soon a dispute between the brothers split the business. Rumors circulated that Rudi resented that Adi had failed to use his American connections to help spring him from prison camp. Rudi set up his own factory, facing Adi across the River Aurach. The brothers never spoke to each other again, except in court. Rudi's company was named Puma, and Adi's became adidas. Adi added a third stripe to the Dassler's trademark shoe, while Rudi chose a cat's paw in motion. Thus began one of the most intense rivalries in Europe. The children of Puma and adidas employees attended separate elementary schools, and the employees even distinguished themselves by drinking different beers.

With Adi's innovations throughout the late 1940s and 1950s (such as the replaceable-cleat soccer shoe), adidas came to dominate the world's athletic shoe market. In the late 1950s it capitalized on the booming US market, overtaking the canvas sneakers made by P.F. Flyers and Stride Rite (Keds). The company also initiated the practice of putting logos on sports bags and clothing.

adidas continued to expand globally in the 1960s and 1970s to maintain its dominant position. However, a flood of new competitors following the 1972 Munich Olympics and the death of Adi in 1978 signaled the end of an era. As NIKE and Reebok captured the North American market during the 1980s, adidas made one of its biggest missteps -- it turned down a sneaker endorsement offer from a young Michael Jordan in 1984.

French politician and entrepreneur Bernard Tapie bought the struggling company in 1989, but he stepped down in 1992 amid personal, political, and business scandals. The next year Robert Louis-Dreyfus became CEO. He shifted production to Asia, pumped up the advertising budget, and brought in former NIKE marketing geniuses to re-establish the company's identity.

adidas became adidas-Salomon in 1997 with its $1.4 billion purchase of Salomon, a French maker of skis and other sporting goods. The company also opened its first high-profile store in Portland, Oregon, that year. In a 1998 reorganization, Louis-Dreyfus sacked Jean-Francois Gautier as Salomon's president in the wake of disappointing sales, particularly from TaylorMade Golf, Salomon's golf subsidiary.

Amid a 10% slide in revenue, several key executives decided to leave the company in 2000, including adidas America CEO Steve Wynne. Citing poor health, Louis-Dreyfus soon followed (but remained as chairman); he was replaced by the new CEO of adidas America, Ross McMullin, who soon after was diagnosed with cancer. Later that year the company announced it would consolidate its apparel under the Heritage label to reinforce its position in the burgeoning casual wear market.

In 2001 Louis-Dreyfus retired as chairman and in March COO Herbert Hainer became chief executive. That year adidas-Salomon opened adidas Originals retail stores in Tokyo and Berlin; that was followed with a New York City store in 2002. Despite slumping sales in the US amid deep discounting by competitors, adidas announced in 2003 that it would not offer discounts and still intended to capture 20% of the country's shoe market.

Britain's Barclays Bank PLC became adidas' largest shareholder in 2004, raising its stake to 5.4%. The company changed its name in 2006 to adidas AG.

In May 2008 adidas AG won a $305 million award from a federal jury in Oregon for trademark violation of its three-stripe design by Collective Brands, the operator of the Payless and Stride Rite shoe-store chains.

In November 2011 adidas acquired outdoor specialist Five Ten, a leading brand in the technical outdoor markets and outdoor action sports community, for $25 million.

EXECUTIVES

Chief Executive Officer, Kasper Bo Rorsted
Chief Financial Officer, Executive Board Member, Harm Ohlmeyer
Global Human Resources Executive Board Member, Amanda Rajkumar
Global Brands Executive Board Member, Brian Grevy
Global Operations Executive Board Member, Martin Shankland
Global Sales Executive Board Member, Roland Auschel
Chairman, Thomas Rabe
Deputy Chairman, Udo Muller
Deputy Chairman, Ian Gallienne
Director, Kathrin Menges
Director, Herbert Kauffmann
Director, Gunter Weigl
Director, Jing Ulrich
Director, Nassef Sawiris
Director, Bodo Uebber
Director, Roswitha Hermann
Director, Frank Scheiderer
Director, Michael Storl
Director, Christian Klein
Director, Beate Rohrig
Director, Petra Auerbacher
Director, Roland Nosko
Auditors : KPMG AG Wirtschaftsprüfungsgesellschaft

LOCATIONS

HQ: Adidas AG
Adi-Dassler-Strasse 1, Herzogenaurach 91074
Phone: (49) 91 32 84 0 **Fax:** (49) 91 32 84 2241
Web: www.adidas-group.com

2018 Sales

	% of total
Asia/Pacific	33
Europe	27
North America	21
Latin America	7
Emerging Markets	5
Russia/CIS	3
Other Businesses	4
Total	100

PRODUCTS/OPERATIONS

2018 Sales by Product

	% of total
Footwear	58
Apparel	38
Hardware	4
Total	100

2018 Sales by Brand

	% of total
adidas	92
Reebok	8

	% of total
Total	100

COMPETITORS

CONVERSE INC.
DR MARTENS AIRWAIR GROUP LIMITED
FILA U.S.A., INC.
LOTTO SPORT ITALIA SPA
NIKE, INC.
REEBOK INTERNATIONAL LTD.
SAUCONY, INC.
SKECHERS U.S.A., INC.
SOLE TECHNOLOGY, INC.
TOD'S SPA

HISTORICAL FINANCIALS

Company Type: Public

Income Statement   FYE: December 31

	REVENUE ($mil)	NET INCOME ($mil)	NET PROFIT MARGIN	EMPLOYEES
12/22	24,042	653	2.7%	59,258
12/21	24,033	2,395	10.0%	61,401
12/20	24,354	530	2.2%	62,285
12/19	26,542	2,218	8.4%	59,533
12/18	25,096	1,949	7.8%	57,016
Annual Growth	(1.1%)	(23.9%)	—	1.0%

2022 Year-End Financials

Debt ratio: 18.3%   No. of shares ($ mil.): 178
Return on equity: 9.7%   Dividends
Cash ($ mil.): 852   Yield: —
Current Ratio: 1.27   Payout: 35.6%
Long-term debt ($ mil.): 3,146   Market value ($ mil.): 12,094

	STOCK PRICE ($) FY Close	P/E High/Low		PER SHARE ($) Earnings	Dividends	Book Value
12/22	67.74	41	15	3.57	1.27	29.86
12/21	144.00	17	13	12.34	1.30	44.43
12/20	182.99	88	46	2.71	3.68	40.61
12/19	162.80	17	10	11.23	1.34	38.94
12/18	104.34	15	11	9.64	1.12	36.67
Annual Growth	(10.2%)	—		(22.0%)	3.2%	(5.0%)

Adient Plc

Adient is the world's largest global automotive seating supplier. It manufactures complete seating systems, frames, mechanisms, seat components, trims, and fabrics that are installed in a myriad of passenger cars, trucks, and SUVs. To secure its global penetration, the company has major market positions in the Americas, Europe, and China, and has longstanding relationships with the largest global auto manufacturers, including Ford, GM, Toyota, and Volkswagen. Adient was spun off from Johnson Controls, a maker of car batteries and automotive interior parts, in late 2016. The company's largest market is the US, which generates about 45% of the company's revenue.

Operations

Adient manages its business on a geographic basis and operates in the following three reportable segments: Americas (about 45% of revenue), which is inclusive of North America and South America; Europe, Middle East, and Africa (about 35%), and Asia Pacific/China (nearly 20%).

Adient designs and manufactures a full range of seating systems and components for passenger cars, commercial vehicles and light trucks, including vans, pick-up trucks and sport/crossover utility vehicles. Adient's technologies extend into virtually every area of automotive seating solutions including complete seating systems, frames, mechanisms, foam, head restraints, armrests, and trim covers.

Geographic Reach

Based in Plymouth, Michigan, Adient operates approximately 205 wholly- and majority-owned manufacturing or assembly facilities in about 30 countries. Additionally, it has partially-owned affiliates in China, Asia, Europe, and North America. The company also has approximately 40 administrative locations.

The US accounts for around 45% of revenue. EMEA generates about 35% (almost 5% comes from Germany).

Sales and Marketing

Adient is a supplier to all of the global OEMs and has longstanding relationships with premier automotive manufacturers including Ford Motor, General Motors, Toyota, Nissan, Volkswagen, BMW, and Volvo, among others.

Adient also supplies growing Chinese OEMs BAIC Motor, Chery Automobile, Changan Automobile, FAW Group, Proton Holdings Berhad, Ashok Leyland, Tata Motors, and Zhejiang Geely. It sells to Tata Motors in India and to newer auto manufacturers such as Tesla Motors in the US.

Financial Performance

Adient recorded net sales of $14.1 billion for fiscal 2022, representing an increase of $441 million when compared to fiscal 2021. The increase in net sales is attributable to higher overall production volumes in the Americas, operational footprint changes primarily related to the consolidation of CQADNT in China and favorable material economics recoveries.

Net loss attributable to Adient was $120 million for fiscal 2022, compared to an income of $1.1 billion for fiscal 2021. The net loss in fiscal 2022 is primarily attributable to operational inefficiencies resulting from supply chain disruptions including higher freight cost, overall higher input costs, lower overall production volumes in EMEA, and lower equity income resulting from prior year divestitures of certain affiliates in China.

The company's cash at the end of 2022 was $947 million. Operating activities generated $274 million, while investing activities generated $484 million. Financing activities used $1.3 billion, primarily for repayment of long-term debt.

Strategy

Adient's strategy is focused on seven key areas: Global Manufacturing Footprint; Operational Efficiencies; Longstanding

Customer Relationships with Leading Global OEMs; Product Innovation and Process Leadership; Global Development Network; Leadership Position in China; and Platform for Global Growth.

Company Background

Adient was established in October 2016 when it separated from Johnson Controls (then knows as Johnson Controls Automotive Experience) and began trading on the New York Stock Exchange as a stand-alone company.

Operating independently, the company set out making acquisitions to drive growth. In 2017, it acquired Futuris, an automotive seating company focused on West Coast automakers.

EXECUTIVES

Chairman, Director, Frederick A. Henderson, $293,333 total compensation
President, Chief Executive Officer, Director, Douglas G. Del Grosso
Executive Vice President, Chief Financial Officer, Jerome J. Dorlack
Senior Vice President, General Counsel, Secretary, Heather M. Tiltmann
Vice President, Chief Accounting Officer, Principal Accounting Officer, Gregory S. Smith
Region Officer, James D. Conklin
Region Officer, Jiang Huang
Region Officer, Michel Berthelin
Director, Julie L. Bushman
Director, Peter H. Carlin
Director, Rick T. Dillon
Director, Richard A. Goodman
Director, Jose M. Gutierrez
Director, Jodi Euerle Eddy
Director, Barb J. Samardzich
Auditors : PricewaterhouseCoopers LLP

LOCATIONS

HQ: Adient Plc
3 Dublin Landings, North Wall Quay, Dublin 1 D01 H104
Phone: (354) 734 254 5000
Web: www.adient.com

2018 Sales

	$ mil	% of total
United States	6,118	35
Germany	1,464	8
Mexico	1,177	7
Other European countries	5,519	32
Other foreign countries	3,161	18
Total	17,439	100

PRODUCTS/OPERATIONS

Selected Products
Complete vehicle seats
Commercial vehicle seats
Structures and mechanisms
Seat foam
Seat fabrics
Seat trims

2018 Sales

	$ mil.	% of total
Seating	15,704	84
Seat Structures and Mechanisms (SS&M)	3,003	16
Reconciling Items	(1,268)	-
Total	17,439	100

HISTORICAL FINANCIALS

Company Type: Public

Income Statement FYE: September 30

	REVENUE ($mil)	NET INCOME ($mil)	NET PROFIT MARGIN	EMPLOYEES
09/23	15,395	205	1.3%	70,000
09/22	14,121	(120)	—	75,000
09/21	13,680	1,108	8.1%	75,000
09/20	12,670	(547)	—	77,000
09/19	16,526	(491)	—	83,000
Annual Growth	(1.8%)	—	—	(4.2%)

2023 Year-End Financials

Debt ratio: 26.9% No. of shares ($ mil.): 93
Return on equity: 9.5% Dividends
Cash ($ mil.): 1,110 Yield: —
Current Ratio: 1.15 Payout: 0.0%
Long-term debt ($ mil.): 2,401 Market value ($ mil.): —

Adyen N.V.

EXECUTIVES

Chief Executive Officer, Pieter Willem van der Does
Chief Commerce Officer, Roelant Prins
Chief Financial Officer, Ingo Jeroen Uytdehaage
Chief Operating Officer, Kamran Zaki
Chief Legal and Compliance Officer, Mariette Bianca Swart
Chief Technology Officer, Alexander Matthey
Independent Chairman, Pieter Sipko Overmars
Independent Director, Delfin Rueda Arroyo
Independent Director, Pamela A. Joseph
Independent Director, Caoimhe Keogan
Director, Joep van Beurden
Auditors : PricewaterhouseCoopers Accountants N.V.

LOCATIONS

HQ: Adyen N.V.
Simon Carmiggeltstraat 6-50, Amsterdam 1011 DJ
Phone: (31) 85 888 8138
Web: www.adyen.com

HISTORICAL FINANCIALS

Company Type: Public

Income Statement FYE: December 31

	REVENUE ($mil)	NET INCOME ($mil)	NET PROFIT MARGIN	EMPLOYEES
12/22	9,543	602	6.3%	3,332
12/21	6,785	531	7.8%	2,180
12/20	4,469	320	7.2%	1,747
12/19	2,982	229	7.7%	1,182
12/18	1,892	150	7.9%	873
Annual Growth	49.8%	41.5%	—	39.8%

2022 Year-End Financials

Debt ratio: — No. of shares ($ mil.): 30
Return on equity: 26.7% Dividends
Cash ($ mil.): 6,966 Yield: —
Current Ratio: 1.42 Payout: 0.0%
Long-term debt ($ mil.): — Market value ($ mil.): 428

	STOCK PRICE ($) FY Close	P/E High/Low		PER SHARE ($) Earnings	Dividends	Book Value
12/22	13.80	1	1	19.41	0.00	83.14
12/21	26.32	4	2	17.33	0.00	66.19
12/20	46.40	6	2	10.44	0.00	49.25
12/19	16.46	2	2	7.50	0.00	32.43
Annual Growth	(5.7%)			26.8%		26.5%

Aegon Ltd

Dutch life insurance giant Aegon serves more than 31.7 million customers worldwide. Its subsidiaries, which include Transamerica and Scottish Equitable plc, operates primarily in the US, the Netherlands, and the UK, offering insurance or reinsurance business, pensions, asset management or services. Aegon has insurance operations in the Americas, Europe, and Asia and are also active in savings and asset management operations, accident and health insurance, general insurance and to a limited extent banking operations. Aegon stretches back all the way to 1844 where it offered loans from a converted saloon in San Francisco to help Dutch people pay for funerals.

Operations

Aegon operates through five segments: Americas, Aegon the Netherlands, Aegon UK, Aegon International, and Aegon Asset Management (AAM).

The Americas is its biggest market, representing roughly 50% of revenue. It operates primarily under the Transamerica brand in the US and has operations in Brazil and Canada. Transamerica provides a wide range of life insurance, long-term care (LTC) insurance and voluntary benefits (including supplemental health insurance), retirement plans, recordkeeping and advisory services, annuities, mutual funds and other long-term savings and investment products.

Accounting for about 25% of revenue, Aegon UK provides a broad range of investment, retirement solutions and protection products to individuals, advisers and employers. Aegon UK accesses customers through wealth advisers and the Workplace and has a market-leading position in each with 3.9 million customers and GBP 215 billion assets under administration (AUA).

Aegon the Netherlands (some 15%) provide of life, non-life, banking and services business. It also operates several other brands, including Knab, TKP Pensioen, and Robidus. Aegon the Netherlands' primary subsidiaries are: Aegon Bank N.V.Aegon Cappital B.V.; Aegon Hypotheken B.V.; Aegon

Levensverzekering N.V.; Aegon Schadeverzekering N.V.; and Aegon Spaarkas N.V.; among others.

Aegon International consists of the two growth markets, China and Spain & Portugal, Aegon's business in Central and Eastern Europe, the high-net-worth life insurance business and some smaller ventures in Asia. International also operates in Brazil and be responsible for all three growth markets of Aegon. Aegon International accounts for less than 10% of revenue.

Aegon Asset Management is a global active investment manager, serving institutional and private investors. It offers fixed income, equities, real estate, absolute return, liability-driven, and multi-asset solutions. The segment accounts for less than 5% of total revenue.

Overall, premium income accounts for about 60% of revenue, while investment income generates some 30% and fee and commission income accounts for around 10%.

Geographic Reach

Based in The Hague, the Netherlands, Aegon operates in The Netherlands, UK, Spain, China, Hong Kong, Indonesia, Japan, Thailand, Hungary, Poland, Romania, and Turkey. It has operations in US through Transamerica, while Transamerica Life Bermuda in Bermuda, Hong Kong, and Singapore. Its Aegon Asset Management operates from US, the Netherlands, the UK, China, Japan, Germany, Hungary, and Spain.

Sales and Marketing

Aegon primarily sells its products and services through brokers, agents, independent financial advisors, employee, benefit consultants, and banks. It also does some direct selling. Aegon's partnership with Banco Santander allows Aegon to sell products through the Spanish banking giant's branch network.

Aegon Asset Management uses several sales and distribution channels, including affiliated companies, direct to institutional clients, independent investment advisors, investment consultants, joint ventures, and third-party investment platforms.

Financial Performance

Company's revenue for fiscal 2021 decreased to EUR 25.2 billion compared from the prior year with EUR 25.7 billion.

Net income for fiscal 2021 increased to EUR 1.7 billion compared from the prior year with EUR 55 million.

Cash held by the company at the end of fiscal 2021 decreased to EUR 6.9 billion. Cash provided by financing activities was EUR 300 million while cash used for operations and investing activities were EUR 1.8 billion and EUR 54 million, respectively.

Strategy

The company are creating a more focused business portfolio to deliver success for Aegon and its stakeholders as it move toward its vision. A central element of this approach is the reallocation of capital from its Financial Assets to its Strategic Assets in its three core markets, as well as its three growth markets, and Aegon Asset Management. The company want to be seen as leading with contemporary propositions and outstanding, digitally enabled, customer service.

HISTORY

AEGON traces its roots to 1844, when former civil servant and funeral society agent J. Oosterhoff founded Algemeene Friesche, a burial society for low-income workers. The next year a similar organization, Groot-Noordhollandsche, was founded. These companies later became insurers and expanded nationwide. Meanwhile Olveh, a civil servants' aid group, was founded in 1877. The three companies merged in 1968 to form mutual insurer AGO.

AEGON's other operations came from different traditions. Vennootschap Nederland was founded in 1858 as a tontine (essentially a death pool, with the survivors taking the pot) by Count A. Langrand-Dumonceau, an ex-French Foreign Legionnaire from Belgium. In 1913 the company merged with Eerste Nederlandsche, whose accident and health division had been previously spun off as Nieuwe Eerste Nederlandsche.

A year after Vennootschap was founded, C. F. W. Wiggers van Kerchem founded a similar scheme, Nillmij, in the Dutch East Indies. The government promoted Nillmij to colonial civil servants and military people, and for a while the company enjoyed a monopoly in the colony. Nillmij's Indonesian operations were nationalized after independence in 1957, but its Dutch subsidiaries continued to operate. All insurers were hit by fast-growing postwar government social programs. As a result, industry consolidation came early to the Netherlands. In 1969 Eerste Nederlandsche, Nieuwe Eerste Nederlandsche, and Nillmij merged to form Ennia.

AGO demutualized in 1978 and became AGO Holding N.V., which was owned by Vereniging AGO. Meanwhile, the shrinking Dutch insurance market forced companies to look overseas. AGO moved into the US in 1979 by buying Life Investors; by 1982 half of its sales came from outside the Netherlands. Ennia, meanwhile, expanded in Europe (it entered Spain in 1980) and the US (buying Arkansas-based National Old Line Insurance in 1981).

AGO and Ennia merged in 1983 to form AEGON. Vereniging AGO became Vereniging AEGON and received a 49% stake in the combined entity. (This stake was later reduced.) The company made more purchases at home and abroad and spent much of the rest of the decade assimilating operations.

AEGON's US units accounted for about 40% of sales in the mid-1980s, and the firm increased that figure with acquisitions. In 1986 it bought Baltimore-based Monumental Corp. (life and health insurance) and expanded the company's US penetration.

This left AEGON underrepresented in Europe, as deregulation paved the way for economic union, and social service cutbacks spurred opportunities in private financial planning in the region. So in the 1990s AEGON began buying European companies, including Regency Life (UK, 1991) and Allami Biztosito (Hungary, 1992). It formed an alliance with Mexico's Grupo Financiero Banamex in 1994. This reduced its reliance on US sales. It continued buying specialty operations in the US, particularly asset management lines.

In 1997 AEGON began to concentrate on life insurance and financial services and shed its other operations. It bought the insurance business of Providian (now part of Washington Mutual) and sold noncore lines, such as auto coverage. The next year it sold FGH Bank (mortgages) to Germany's Bayerische Vereinsbank (now Bayerische Hypotheken und Vereinsbank) and in 1999 sold auto insurer Worldwide Insurance.

That year AEGON expanded further in the US with the $9.7 billion purchase of Transamerica and bought the life and pensions businesses of the UK's Guardian Royal Exchange. In 2000 the company sold Labouchere N.V., a Dutch banking subsidiary, to Dexia. Also in 2000 AEGON acquired UK-based third-party administrator HS Administrative Services.

Following the Transamerica acquisition, the company divested several assets to focus on life insurance and pensions. In 2003 and 2004 diverse parts of Transamerica Finance (including its real estate tax unit and trailer leasing business) were sold to various companies, including First American, GE Commercial Finance, and a joint venture held by Goldman Sachs and Cerberus Capital Management.

EXECUTIVES

Chairman, Chief Executive Officer, Lard Friese
Chief Financial Officer, Matthew J. Rider
Chief Technology Officer, Mark Bloom
Chief Risk Officer, Allegra van Hovell-Patrizi
Chief Transformation Officer, Duncan Russell
General Counsel, Onno van Klinken
Chairman, Director, William L. Connelly
Vice Chair, Director, Coerien M. Wortmann-Kool
Director, Mark A. Ellman
Director, Ben J. Noteboom
Director, Caroline Ramsay
Director, Thomas Wellauer
Director, Dona D. Young
Auditors : PricewaterhouseCoopers Accountants N.V.

LOCATIONS

HQ: Aegon Ltd
Aegonplein 50, The Hague 2591 TV

Phone: (31) 70 344 54 58
Web: www.aegon.com

2018 sales

	%
Europe	49
Americas	45
Asia	4
Asset Management	2
Total	100

PRODUCTS/OPERATIONS

2018 Sales

	% of total
Premiums	67
Investment income	24
Fees & commissions	9
Other	—
Total	100

COMPETITORS

AVIVA PLC
Achmea B.V.
Bâloise Holding AG
ING Groep N.V.
MMC VENTURES LIMITED
NN Group N.V.
Randstad N.V.
The Bank of Nova Scotia
Wolters Kluwer N.V.
Zurich Insurance Group AG

HISTORICAL FINANCIALS

Company Type: Public

Income Statement   FYE: December 31

	ASSETS ($mil)	NET INCOME ($mil)	INCOME AS % OF ASSETS	EMPLOYEES
12/21	529,997	2,241	0.4%	22,271
12/20	544,688	(179)	—	22,322
12/19	494,408	1,391	0.3%	23,757
12/18	449,641	813	0.2%	26,543
12/17	474,614	2,959	0.6%	28,318
Annual Growth	2.8%	(6.7%)	—	(5.8%)

2021 Year-End Financials

Return on assets: 0.4%   Dividends
Return on equity: 7.8%   Yield: —
Long-term debt ($ mil.): —   Payout: 14.8%
No. of shares ($ mil.): 2,572   Market value ($ mil.): 12,710
Sales ($ mil.): 52,535

	STOCK PRICE ($) FY Close	P/E High/Low		PER SHARE ($) Earnings	Dividends	Book Value
12/21	4.94	5	4	1.06	0.16	11.52
12/20	3.95	—	—	(0.11)	0.07	11.59
12/19	4.53	10	7	0.63	0.34	13.45
12/18	4.65	24	16	0.33	0.32	12.70
12/17	6.30	6	5	1.37	0.31	11.04
Annual Growth	(5.9%)	—	—	(6.1%)	(15.7%)	1.1%

Aeon Co Ltd

Japanese giant AEON CO conduct various business operations centering on retail store operations, including financial services operations, shopping center development operations, and services and specialty store operations. The company operates more than 20,000 stores/locations in about 15 countries across some 15 countries. Its home, country, Japan, accounts for the majority of AEON's revenue. AEON traces its roots back to 1970 as JUSCO Co., Ltd.

Operations

AEON operates through eight business segments: GMS; Supermarket; Discount Store; Financial Services; Health and Wellness; Shopping Center Development; Services and Specialty Store; International Business and Others.

The GMS Business accounts for about 35% of revenue and includes general merchandise stores (GMS), specialty stores that sell packaged lunches and ready-to-eat meals.

The Supermarket Business (over 25% of revenue) operates community-rooted supermarkets, small-sized stores, and convenience stores while enhancing its lineups of everyday necessities focused on foodstuffs and services.

The Health & Wellness Business (more than 10%) operates drugstores and dispensing pharmacies to help support the health of local residents. In addition to broadening the product lineups from medical products and daily necessities to health food products, it is expanding its services to include dispensing for home care patients.

The Services and Specialty Store Business operates facilities management services, amusement services, food services, specialty stores that sell family casual apparel and footwear, flat-rate discount store business, and other related businesses.

The Financial Services Business (around 5% of revenue) offers integrated financial services that combine credit, banking, insurance services, and e-money WAON cards. Operations extend to Asian countries.

The Shopping Center Development Business (some 5%) develops and operates community-friendly shopping malls in Japan, China, and ASEAN countries. In cooperation with other segments, it is working to enhance its services and facilities.

The Discount Store Business (some 5%) includes discount stores and implements low-cost measures such as consolidating product purchasing and integrating logistics and is working to realize management that thoroughly pursues lower prices.

International Business (about 5%) includes retail stores in the ASEAN region and China, offering products and services tailored to the needs and lifestyles of the respective countries and regions.

Other Businesses include mobile marketing business, digital and other related businesses. It is in charge of product development and quality control for Aeon's Topvalu brand, as well as establishing infrastructure such as logistics, computer systems, and IT.

Geographic Reach

Based in Chiba, Japan, AEON operates in about 20,000 stores/locations in about 15 countries in Asia.

Its home country, Japan, accounts for more than 90% of revenue, while ASEAN, China and other market account for the remaining 10%.

Financial Performance

Company's revenue for fiscal 2022 increased by 2% to ¥51.9 billion compared from the prior year with ¥50.7 billion.

Net income for fiscal 2022 increased to ¥122.8 billion compared from the prior year with ¥53.2 billion.

Cash held by the company at the end of fiscal 2022 decreased to ¥1.1 trillion. Cash provided by operations was ¥204.5 billion while cash used for investing and financing activities were ¥343.9 billion and ¥2.2 billion, respectively. Main uses of cash were purchase of non-current assets and repayments of long-term loans payable.

Company Background

AEON's predecessor company Jusco was established in 1969 through a joint venture of three of other entities. It launched its retail development business that year and five years later introduced AEON's first private-brand product, J-Cup.

In 1976 Jusco was listed on the Tokyo, Osaka, and Nagoya Stock Exchanges. The company expanded into financial services and specialty retail in the 1980s and opened its first store outside Japan (in Malaysia). By the end of the decade Jusco Group was renamed AEON Group (Jusco Co. took the AEON Co. name in 2001).

AEON became a holding company in 2008.

EXECUTIVES

Representative Executive Officer, Chairman, Director, Motoya Okada
President, Representative Executive Officer, Director, Akio Yoshida
Vice-Chairman, Motohiro Fujita
Executive Vice President, Executive Officer, Director, Yuki Habu
Executive Vice President, Hiroyuki Watanabe
Executive Vice President, Mitsuko Tsuchiya
Outside Director, Takashi Tsukamoto
Outside Director, Peter Child
Outside Director, Carrie Yu
Outside Director, Makoto Hayashi
Auditors : Deloitte Touche Tohmatsu LLC

LOCATIONS

HQ: Aeon Co Ltd
1-5-1 Nakase, Mihama-ku, Chiba 261-8515
Phone: (81) 43 212 6042
Web: www.aeon.info

2018 Sales

	% of total
Japan	92
ASEAN	4
China	3
Other	1
Total	100

PRODUCTS/OPERATIONS

2018 Sales

	% of total
General Merchandise Stores	34
Supermarkets	36
Services and Specialty Stores	9
Health and Wellness Stores	8
Shopping Center Development	4
Financial Services	4
International Business	5
Total	**100**

Selected Store Names
Abilities Jusco (CDs, DVDs, and books)
Asbee (shoe stores)
Blue Grass (apparel for teenage girls)
Claire's Nippon (women's clothing)
Cox (family casual clothing)
HapYcom (drugstores)
Home Wide Corp. (home centers)
JUSCO (apparel, food, and household item superstores)
JUS-Photo (film developing)
Laura Ashley Japan (clothing and home furnishings)
Maxvalu (supermarkets)
Mega Sports (Sports Authority stores)
MINISTOP (convenience stores)
MYCAL Corporation (supermarkets)
My Basket (small-scale supermarkets)
Nustep (family footwear stores)
Petcity (pets & pet supplies)
Sports Authority (sporting goods)

COMPETITORS

BESTWAY (HOLDINGS) LIMITED
CECONOMY AG
DAI-ICHI LIFE HOLDINGS, INC.
ICELAND FOODS GROUP LIMITED
Itausa S/A
Lululemon Athletica Canada Inc
MAPFRE, SA
SEVEN & I HOLDINGS CO., LTD.
WAYFAIR INC.
WESFARMERS LIMITED

HISTORICAL FINANCIALS

Company Type: Public

Income Statement — FYE: February 28

	REVENUE ($mil)	NET INCOME ($mil)	NET PROFIT MARGIN	EMPLOYEES
02/23	66,657	156	0.2%	425,421
02/22	75,440	56	0.1%	420,663
02/21	80,921	(667)	—	408,567
02/20	79,146	246	0.3%	420,165
02/19	76,884	213	0.3%	419,912
Annual Growth	(3.5%)	(7.5%)	—	0.3%

2023 Year-End Financials
Debt ratio: 0.2%   No. of shares ($ mil.): 857
Return on equity: 2.1%   Dividends
Cash ($ mil.): 9,575   Yield: 1.3%
Current Ratio: 1.03   Payout: 139.6%
Long-term debt ($ mil.): 15,086   Market value ($ mil.): 15,924

	STOCK PRICE ($) FY Close	P/E High/Low		PER SHARE ($) Earnings	Dividends	Book Value
02/23	18.58	1	1	0.18	0.26	8.48
02/22	22.12	4	3	0.07	0.32	9.76
02/21	33.60	—	—	(0.79)	0.34	10.75
02/20	18.17	1	1	0.29	0.32	11.57
02/19	21.33	1	1	0.25	0.29	11.75
Annual Growth	(3.4%)	—	—	(7.4%)	(2.5%)	(7.8%)

AGC Inc

EXECUTIVES

Chairman, Director, Takuya Shimamura
President, Chief Executive Officer, Representative Director, Yoshinori Hirai
Executive Vice President, Chief Financial Officer, Chief Compliance Officer, Representative Director, Shinji Miyaji
Senior Managing Executive Officer, Chief Technology Officer, Representative Director, Hideyuki Kurata
Outside Director, Hiroyuki Yanagi
Outside Director, Keiko Honda
Outside Director, Isao Teshirogi
Auditors: KPMG AZSA LLC

LOCATIONS

HQ: AGC Inc
1-5-1 Marunouchi, Chiyoda-ku, Tokyo 100-8405
Phone: (81) 3 3218 5603   Fax: 404 446-4295
Web: www.agc.com

HISTORICAL FINANCIALS

Company Type: Public

Income Statement — FYE: December 31

	REVENUE ($mil)	NET INCOME ($mil)	NET PROFIT MARGIN	EMPLOYEES
12/22	15,450	(23)	—	62,279
12/21	14,745	1,075	7.3%	60,420
12/20	13,702	317	2.3%	60,368
12/19	13,982	409	2.9%	60,286
12/18	13,848	814	5.9%	58,853
Annual Growth	2.8%	—	—	1.4%

2022 Year-End Financials
Debt ratio: 0.2%   No. of shares ($ mil.): 222
Return on equity: (-0.2%)   Dividends
Cash ($ mil.): 1,591   Yield: —
Current Ratio: 1.59   Payout: 0.0%
Long-term debt ($ mil.): 2,967   Market value ($ mil.): 1,446

	STOCK PRICE ($) FY Close	P/E High/Low		PER SHARE ($) Earnings	Dividends	Book Value
12/22	6.51	—	—	(0.11)	0.36	47.51
12/21	9.62	0	0	4.84	0.25	51.44
12/20	6.95	0	0	1.43	0.22	48.82
12/19	7.11	0	0	1.84	0.22	48.10
12/18	6.56	0	0	3.62	0.20	46.69
Annual Growth	(0.2%)	—	—	15.4%	0.4%	

Ageas NV

EXECUTIVES

Chief Executive Officer, Director, Bart De Smet
Chief Financial Officer, Christophe Boizard
Chief Risk Officer, Kurt De Schepper
Chairman, Jozef De Mey
Vice-Chairman, Guy de Selliers de Moranville
Director, Frank Arts
Director, Ronny Brueckner
Director, Shaoliang Jin
Director, Bridget F. McIntyre
Director, Roel Nieuwdorp
Director, Lionel Perl
Director, Jan Zegering Hadders
Auditors : PwC Reviseurs d'Entreprises SRL / PwC Bedrijfsrevisoren BV

LOCATIONS

HQ: Ageas NV
Bolwerklaan 21, Brussels 1210
Phone: (32) 2 557 57 11   Fax: (32) 2 557 57 50
Web: www.ageas.com

HISTORICAL FINANCIALS

Company Type: Public

Income Statement — FYE: December 31

	ASSETS ($mil)	NET INCOME ($mil)	INCOME AS % OF ASSETS	EMPLOYEES
12/22	107,129	1,079	1.0%	13,388
12/21	125,794	956	0.8%	10,101
12/20	136,742	1,400	1.0%	10,045
12/19	122,885	1,099	0.9%	10,741
12/18	116,451	926	0.8%	11,009
Annual Growth	(2.1%)	3.9%	—	5.0%

2022 Year-End Financials
Return on assets: 0.9%   Dividends
Return on equity: 10.3%   Yield: —
Long-term debt ($ mil.): —   Payout: 54.1%
No. of shares ($ mil.): 183 Market value ($ mil.): 8,180
Sales ($ mil.): 11,089

	STOCK PRICE ($) FY Close	P/E High/Low		PER SHARE ($) Earnings	Dividends	Book Value
12/22	44.54	10	7	5.85	3.17	44.09
12/21	51.85	14	10	5.12	4.19	72.60
12/20	53.39	11	5	7.44	2.16	75.85
12/19	59.28	12	8	5.70	1.71	66.12
12/18	44.71	13	11	4.71	1.70	55.45
Annual Growth	(0.1%)	—	—	5.6%	16.8%	(5.6%)

AGL Energy Ltd

EXECUTIVES

Managing Director, Chief Executive Officer, Executive Director, Graeme Hunt
Chief Operating Officer, Markus Brokhof
Chief Customer Officer, Jo Egan
Chief People Officer, Amanda Lee
Chief Financial Officer, Damien Nicks
Secretary, General Counsel, Melinda Hunter
Chairman, Independent Non-Executive Director, Peter R. Botten
Independent Non-Executive Director, Mark Bloom
Independent Non-Executive Director, Graham Cockroft
Independent Non-Executive Director, Patricia McKenzie
Independent Non-Executive Director, Diane L. Smith-Gander

Independent Non-Executive Director, Vanessa (Fernandes) Sullivan

Auditors : Deloitte Touche Tohmatsu

LOCATIONS

HQ: AGL Energy Ltd
   Level 24, 200 George Street, Sydney, New South Wales 2000

Phone: (61) 2 9921 2999   **Fax:** (61) 2 9921 2552
Web: www.agl.com.au

HISTORICAL FINANCIALS

Company Type: Public

Income Statement   FYE: June 30

	REVENUE ($mil)	NET INCOME ($mil)	NET PROFIT MARGIN	EMPLOYEES
06/23	9,371	(836)	—	3,881
06/22	9,095	591	6.5%	3,897
06/21	8,213	(1,544)	—	4,398
06/20	8,333	695	8.3%	4,167
06/19	9,280	634	6.8%	3,750
Annual Growth	0.2%	—	—	0.9%

2023 Year-End Financials

Debt ratio: 12.5%   No. of shares ($ mil.): 672
Return on equity: (-21.7%)   Dividends
Cash ($ mil.): 97   Yield: 0.5%
Current Ratio: 1.09   Payout: 0.0%
Long-term debt ($ mil.): 1,877   Market value ($ mil.): 4,891

	STOCK PRICE ($) FY Close	P/E High/Low		PER SHARE ($) Earnings	Dividends	Book Value
06/23	7.27	—	—	(1.24)	0.04	5.04
06/22	5.75	5	3	0.90	0.22	6.66
06/21	6.30	—	—	(2.50)	0.54	6.63
06/20	11.67	9	7	1.08	0.65	8.88
06/19	13.96	12	9	0.97	0.78	9.01
Annual Growth	(15.1%)	—	—	—	(51.7%)	(13.5%)

AIA Group Ltd.

The AIA Group Limited and its subsidiaries comprise the largest independent publicly listed pan-Asian life insurance group. The life insurance and wealth management company operates in about 20 markets across Asia and the Pacific. It offers life insurance, credit insurance, employee benefits, and pension services to its corporate clients. For individuals, the company provides basic life insurance along with savings, investment, and retirement products. Founded in 1919, it was the original business that would later grow to become American International Group (AIG), and was a cornerstone of that company's Asia-based operations. However, in 2010 AIG spun off the business through a public offering. Majority of its sales were generated in Hong Kong.

Operations

AIA's reportable segments are Hong Kong (including Macau; about 40% of sales)), Mainland China (nearly 20%), Thailand (over 10%), Singapore (including Brunei; around 10%)), Malaysia (some 5%), Other Markets (roughly 15%), and Group Corporate Centre. Except for the latter segment, they all writes life insurance business, providing life insurance, accident and health insurance and savings plans to customers in its local market, and distributes related investment and other financial services products. Through its extensive network of agents, partners, and employees across the region, AIA serves more than 39 million individual policyholders and more than 16 million participating members of group insurance schemes.

Overall, about 75% of sales were generated from premiums and free income, while the rest were generated from investment return and others.

Geographic Reach

The company has operations in about 20 countries in the Asia/Pacific region with the notable exception of Japan. (It owns branches and subsidiaries in Hong Kong, Thailand, Singapore, Malaysia, China, Korea, the Philippines, Australia, Indonesia, Taiwan, Vietnam, New Zealand, Macau, Brunei, Sri Lanka; it also owns a minority stake in an Indian joint venture and has a representative office in Myanmar.)

The company is headquartered in Hong Kong.

Sales and Marketing

AIA markets its products through agents, partners, and employees throughout the region and serves the holders of more than 39 million individual policies and over 16 million participating members of group insurance schemes.

Financial Performance

Company's revenue for fiscal 2021 decreased to $47.5 billion compared from the prior year with $50.4 billion.

Profit for fiscal 2021 increased to $7.5 billion compared from the prior year with $5.8 billion.

Cash held by the company at the end of fiscal 2021 decreased to $4.7 billion. Cash provided by operations was $3.9 billion while cash used for investing and financing activities were $2.8 billion and $1.7 billion, respectively. Main uses of cash were for prepayment for investment in an associate; and dividends paid.

Strategy

In February 2022, the company announced the establishment of new business, Amplify Health, in partnership with Discovery Limited (Discovery), its long-standing partner in AIA Vitality. AIA's vision is for Amplify Health to be a leading digital health technology and integrated solutions business, transforming how individuals, corporates, payors and providers experience and manage health insurance and healthcare delivery, improving the health and wellness outcomes of patients and communities across Asia. Amplify Health will accelerate AIA's health and wellness strategy, leveraging an array of health technology assets, proprietary data analytics and extensive health expertise transferred from Discovery, a global leader in value-based healthcare.

Mergers and Acquisitions

In late 2022, IA Group Limited has agreed to acquire 100 per cent of the shares in MediCard Philippines, Inc., a leading Health Maintenance Organisation (HMO) in the Philippines providing health insurance and healthcare services to more than 920,000 members across corporate and individual plans. The acquisition brings assets and capabilities across healthcare provision, administration and management, accelerating AIA's Integrated Health Strategy in the Philippines. MediCard has an extensive medical service network of over 1,000 partner hospitals and clinics, and 26 high-quality MediCard-owned clinics located in key cities across the Philippines that offer a broad suite of services across primary care, diagnostics, laboratory tests and minor surgeries. Terms were not disclosed.

In early 2022, AIA Group Limited as agreed to acquire 100 per cent of the shares in Blue Cross (Asia-Pacific) Insurance Limited and 80 per cent of the shares in Blue Care JV (BVI) Holdings Limited ("Blue Care") from The Bank of East Asia, Limited. Blue Cross is a well-established insurer in Hong Kong focused on providing leading health insurance products. Blue Care operates medical centers with a large medical network in Hong Kong. AIA and BEA have also agreed to extend the scope of their existing exclusive bancassurance partnership. Through the acquisition of Blue Cross, their partnership will include a 15-year agreement covering personal lines general insurance products. This will provide a comprehensive suite of AIA's insurance solutions, including health insurance, to BEA's personal banking customers in Hong Kong. Terms were not disclosed.

Company Background

Founded in Shanghai in 1919 by Cornelius Vander Starr, AIA was the original business that would later grow to become American International Group (AIG), and was a cornerstone of that company's Asia-based operations. However, in 2010 AIG spun off the business through a public offering.

EXECUTIVES

Chief Executive Officer, President, Executive Director, Yuan Siong Lee
Independent Non-Executive Chairman,
Independent Non-Executive Director, Edmund Sze-Wing Tse
Independent Non-Executive Director, Jack Chak-Kwong So
Independent Non-Executive Director, Chung-Kong Chow
Independent Non-Executive Director, John Barrie Harrison

Independent Non-Executive Director, George Yong-Boon Yeo
Independent Non-Executive Director, Lawrence Juen-Yee Lau
Independent Non-Executive Director, Swee-Lian Teo
Independent Non-Executive Director, Narongchai Akrasanee
Independent Non-Executive Director, Cesar Velasquez Purisima
Independent Non-Executive Director, Jane Jie Sun
Auditors : PricewaterhouseCoopers

LOCATIONS
HQ: AIA Group Ltd.
35/F, AIA Central, No. 1 Connaught Road Central,
Phone: —
Web: www.aia.com

2018 Sales by Segment

	% of total
Hong Kong	41
Thailand	14
China	13
Singapore	11
Malaysia	6
Other Markets	14
Group Corporate Centre	1
Total	100

PRODUCTS/OPERATIONS

2018 Sales

	$ mil.	% of total
Net premiums & fee income	31,913	88
Investment return	4,077	11
Other	30	1
Total	36,297	100

COMPETITORS
Achmea B.V.
CNA FINANCIAL CORPORATION
INSURANCE AUSTRALIA GROUP LIMITED
LIVERPOOL VICTORIA FRIENDLY SOCIETY LTD
MAPFRE, SA
Manulife Financial Corporation
PartnerRe Ltd.
QBE INSURANCE GROUP LIMITED
Samsung Life Insurance Co., Ltd.
Sun Life Financial Inc

HISTORICAL FINANCIALS
Company Type: Public

Income Statement — FYE: December 31

	ASSETS ($mil)	NET INCOME ($mil)	INCOME AS % OF ASSETS	EMPLOYEES
12/22	303,048	282	0.1%	25,405
12/21	339,874	7,427	2.2%	23,981
12/20	326,121	5,779	1.8%	23,000
12/19	284,132	6,648	2.3%	23,000
12/18	229,806	3,163	1.4%	22,000
Annual Growth	7.2%	(45.4%)	—	3.7%

2022 Year-End Financials
Return on assets: —
Return on equity: 0.5%
Long-term debt ($ mil.): —
No. of shares ($ mil.): 11,734
Sales ($ mil.): 19,078
Dividends
Yield: —
Payout: 3504.6%
Market value ($ mil.): 521,342

	STOCK PRICE ($) FY Close	P/E High/Low	PER SHARE ($) Earnings	Dividends	Book Value
12/22	44.43	228 91	479 0.02	0.70	3.25
12/21	40.32	90 65	0.61	0.66	5.00
12/20	49.13	103 66	0.48	0.61	5.23
12/19	42.09	82 57	0.55	0.63	4.76
12/18	32.88	146 114	0.26	0.48	3.23
Annual Growth	7.8%	—	(47.3%)	9.9%	0.1%

AIB Group PLC

Allied Irish Banks (AIB), one of Ireland's largest banks and private employers, is looking beyond the Emerald Isle for its proverbial pot o' gold. The company offers retail and commercial accounts and loans, life insurance, financing, leasing, pension, and trust services through a network of 200 branches, 74 EBS Limited offices, 10 business centers, and 755 ATMs. The company's capital markets division offers commercial treasury services, corporate finance, and investment banking services. In the US, AIB specializes in financial services for the not-for-profit sector.

Operations
Over the years AIB has reorganized into a more simplified structure in which its divisions were integrated and its AIB and First Trust operations were more closely aligned. To attract additional customers, the bank also introduced mobile banking services to its offerings.

HISTORY
Allied Irish Banks was formed in 1966 by the "trinity" of Provincial Bank (founded 1825), The Royal Bank (founded 1836), and Munster and Leinster (founded 1885 but with origins back to the late 1600s). Both AIB and its then-larger rival, Bank of Ireland, had to consolidate in order to compete with North American banks entering Ireland. From its start, AIB sought to expand overseas, and by 1968 it had an alliance with Canada's Toronto-Dominion Bank.

In the 1970s AIB expanded its branch network to England and Scotland. The 1980s saw AIB boost its presence in the US market (it had already debuted AIB branches) with the acquisition of First Maryland Bancorp.

The Irish Parliament's Finance Act of 1986 instituted a withholding tax known as the Deposit Interest Retention Tax (DIRT) for Irish residents. Consequently (with a wink and a nod), AIB and other banks let customers create bogus non-resident accounts to avoid paying DIRT. An investigation indicated that, at one point, AIB's branch in Tralee had 14,700 non-resident accounts on its rolls -- more than half the local population. After tax authorities began probing, many of the accounts in question were reclassified as "resident," and customers had to pay the taxes on them. In 1991 AIB was reprimanded, but neither the bank nor its customers have paid the remaining $100 million tax bill.

Tom Mulcahy, who integrated AIB's treasury, investment, and international banking activities, became chief executive in 1994. Mulcahy, a respected leader, envisioned AIB as an international, Ireland-based bank.

In 1995 AIB bought UK-based investment fund manager John Govett from London Pacific Group (now Berkeley Technology Limited). Mulcahy moved AIB the same year into Eastern Europe with a stake in Poland-based Wielkopolski Bank Kredytowy (or WBK).

AIB was busy in 1999. It gained a toehold in Asia by entering a cross-marketing agreement with Singapore's Keppet TatLee bank, a survivor of the region's financial crisis. Liberalized Singapore banking laws allowed AIB the right to buy one-quarter of the bank by 2001. AIB also bought an 80% stake of Bank Zachodni in Poland in 1999.

That year AIB merged First Maryland Bancorp and its other US holdings into the renamed Allfirst Financial, a sizable mid-Atlantic states bank.

To consolidate its power in Eastern Europe, in 2001 AIB merged its Polish banks (Wielkopolski Bank Kredytowy and Bank Zachodni) into Bank Zachodni WBK. That year Mulcahy retired but was appointed by the Irish government to take over as chairman of troubled airline Aer Lingus.

AIB lost nearly $700 million from 1996 to 2002, apparently from bogus foreign exchange transactions made by rogue trader John Rusnak, who pleaded guilty to bank fraud.

In 2003 AIB sold troubled Maryland-based bank Allfirst Financial to M&T Bank Corporation. As part of the deal, AIB assumed ownership of more than 20% of M&T, becoming the company's largest shareholder. Under AIB's direction Allfirst had grown into a major regional player, with about 250 branches in Maryland, Pennsylvania, Virginia, and Washington, DC.

In the midst of the global financial crisis, the Irish government injected ?2 billion ($2.8 billion) into AIB in exchange for a 25% share in voting rights in 2008. Ireland also provided capital for Bank of Ireland and Irish Bank Resolution Corporation to help stabilize the plunging Irish financial system. AIB also sought capital from the private sector.

EXECUTIVES

Chief Operating Officer, Andrew Mcfarlane
Chief Executive Officer, Executive Director, Colin Hunt
Chief Enterprise Development Officer, C. J. Berry
Chief Financial Officer, Executive Director, Donal Galvin
Chief People Officer, Geraldine Casey
Chief Technology Officer, Fergal Coburn
General Counsel, Helen Dooley

Chief Risk Officer, Michael Frawley
Corporate Affairs and Strategy Director, Mary Whitelaw
Secretary, Conor Gouldson
Independent Non-Executive Chairman, Jim Pettigrew
Deputy Chairman, Independent Non-Executive Director, Brendan McDonagh
Independent Non-Executive Director, Anik Chaumartin
Independent Non-Executive Director, Basil Geoghegan
Independent Non-Executive Director, Tanya Horgan
Independent Non-Executive Director, Sandy Kinney Pritchard
Independent Non-Executive Director, Elaine Maclean
Independent Non-Executive Director, Andy Maguire
Independent Non-Executive Director, Helen Normoyle
Independent Non-Executive Director, Ann O'Brien
Independent Non-Executive Director, Fergal O'Dwyer
Independent Non-Executive Director, Jan Sijbrand
Independent Non-Executive Director, Ranjit Singh
Auditors : Deloitte Ireland LLP

LOCATIONS
HQ: AIB Group PLC
10 Molesworth Street, Dublin 2
Phone: (353) 1 660 0311   **Fax:** 212 515-6710
Web: www.aibgroup.com

PRODUCTS/OPERATIONS
2013 Sales

	% of total
Interest and similar income	86
Fee and commission income	11
Others	3
Total	100

COMPETITORS
AIB GROUP (UK) P.L.C.
BANKINTER SOCIEDAD ANONIMA
BARCLAYS PLC
Bank of Canada
Bank of Ireland
FEDERAL RESERVE BANK OF CHICAGO
FEDERAL RESERVE BANK OF KANSAS CITY
FEDERAL RESERVE BANK OF NEW YORK
PERMANENT TSB PUBLIC LIMITED COMPANY
RESERVE BANK OF INDIA

HISTORICAL FINANCIALS
Company Type: Public

Income Statement   FYE: December 31

	ASSETS ($mil)	NET INCOME ($mil)	INCOME AS % OF ASSETS	EMPLOYEES
12/22	138,581	819	0.6%	9,590
12/21	144,737	732	0.5%	8,916
12/20	135,474	(943)	—	9,193
12/19	110,662	367	0.3%	9,520
12/18	104,827	1,250	1.2%	9,831
Annual Growth	7.2%	(10.0%)	—	(0.6%)

2022 Year-End Financials
Return on assets: 0.5%
Return on equity: 5.9%
Long-term debt ($ mil.): —
No. of shares ($ mil): 2,673
Sales ($ mil.): 3,716
Dividends
Yield: —
Payout: 0.0%
Market value ($ mil.): —

Air Canada Inc

Air Canada is Canada's largest airline and the largest provider of scheduled passenger services in the Canadian market, the Canada-US trans-border market and in the international market to and from Canada. It serves some 185 destinations on six continents, primarily in Canada and the US. It extends its network as part of the Star Alliance global marketing group, which is led by United Airlines and Lufthansa. Jetz is Air Canada's premier charter aviation service provider delivering superior Business Class service to satisfy the travel needs of professional sports teams, entertainment groups and corporate clients. About 35% of its passenger revenue comes from its domestic operations.

Operations
Passenger revenue (more than 85% of the company's total revenue) and Cargo revenue (nearly 10%) are recognized when transportation is provided, it also includes revenue, fees, and surcharges from passenger-related services such as excess baggage and seat selection.

Other revenue (more than 5%) is comprised of revenues from the sale of the ground portion of vacation packages, ground handling services, onboard sales, and loyalty programs.

Geographic Reach
Headquartered in Quebec, Air Canada has an average of about 945 daily scheduled flights to some 185 direct destinations on six continents. It bolstered its international reach by relaunching 34 routes across the Atlantic and Pacific oceans including to Paris, Amsterdam, Tel Aviv, and Tokyo from Toronto. Service to Casablanca, Algiers, Nice, Rome, Tel Aviv, and Tokyo, from Montréal, resumed as well. From Vancouver, it operated flights to Dublin, Frankfurt, and Zurich, and service between Halifax and London Heathrow was introduced in midspring. The company generated over 30% of passenger revenues in Canada, the Atlantic has around 30%, while US trans-border and the Pacific accounts for the rest.

Sales and Marketing
The company offers the Aeroplan program, which is s Canada's premier travel loyalty program. Aeroplan helps members travel more and offers the ability to earn or redeem points on all Air Canada fights as well as the world's largest airline partner network, encompassing over 40 airlines serving hundreds of destinations across the globe. Members earn points with Aeroplan's more than 150 financial, retail, and travel partners, including online shopping via the Aeroplan eStore. In addition to flights, members also have access to an extensive range of merchandise, hotel, and car rental rewards.

Financial Performance
The company's revenue for fiscal 2022 increased by 158% to C$16.6 billion compared from the prior year with C$6.4 billion.

Net loss for fiscal 2022 decreased to C$1.7 billion compared from the prior year with C$3.6 billion.

Cash held by the company at the end of fiscal 2022 increased to C$2.7 billion. Cash provided by operating activities was C$2.4 billion while cash used for financing and investing activities were C$1.6 billion and C$2.5 billion, respectively.

Strategy
Over the past decade, Air Canada has aimed to be a sustainable global champion by pursuing profitable international growth opportunities and leveraging its competitive attributes, identifying and implementing cost reduction and revenue enhancing initiatives, engaging customers by continually enhancing their travel experience and by consistently achieving customer service excellence, and fostering positive culture change.

Now, Air Canada is evolving its business to better prepare for the future. As part of these efforts, it is introducing "Rise Higher", its newly articulated business imperatives, intended to elevate everything about its business. As it embarks on this next chapter, Air Canada will: fund its future by staying vigilant on costs, seizing on opportunities, and making the right strategic investments; reach new frontiers, by embracing its competitive strengths to grow the business by expanding its international reach, and continually exploring new opportunities; elevate its customers, and support the creation of meaningful customer experiences and human connections by leveraging innovations in technology, loyalty and products; and foster a collaborative workplace that respects diverse cultures and languages, while making impactful contributions to society.

Mergers and Acquisitions
In 2022, Air Canada acquired 30 extra-long range (XLR) versions of the Airbus A321neo aircraft. The aircraft has sufficient range to serve all North American and select transatlantic markets, while offering customers added comfort and improving the carrier's fuel efficiency to advance its environmental programs. The acquisition of the state-of-the-art Airbus A321XLR is an important element of this strategy and will drive Air Canada core priorities of elevating the customer experience, advancing its environmental goals, network expansion and increasing its overall cost efficiency.

EXECUTIVES

Chairman, Vagn Ove Sorensen
President, Chief Executive Officer, Calin Rovinescu
Deputy Chief Executive, Chief Financial Officer, Michael S. Rousseau
Director, Christie J. B. Clark
Auditors : PricewaterhouseCoopers LLP

LOCATIONS

HQ: Air Canada Inc
7373 Cote-Vertu Boulevard West, Saint-Laurent, Quebec H4S 1Z3
Phone: —
Web: www.aircanada.com

2018 Sales

	% of total
Canada	30
U.S. transborder	22
Atlantic	26
Pacific	15
Other	7
Total	100

PRODUCTS/OPERATIONS

2018 Sales

	% of total
Passenger	90
Cargo	4
Other	6
Total	100

COMPETITORS

AMERICAN AIRLINES GROUP INC.
DELTA AIR LINES, INC.
EASYJET PLC
INTELSAT INFLIGHT LLC
INTERNATIONAL CONSOLIDATED AIRLINES GROUP SA
SOUTHWEST AIRLINES CO.
SPIRIT AIRLINES, INC.
UNITED AIRLINES HOLDINGS, INC.
UNITED AIRLINES, INC.
WestJet Airlines Ltd

HISTORICAL FINANCIALS

Company Type: Public

Income Statement   FYE: December 31

	REVENUE ($mil)	NET INCOME ($mil)	NET PROFIT MARGIN	EMPLOYEES
12/23	16,472	1,717	10.4%	0
12/22	12,241	(1,256)	—	30,478
12/21	5,024	(2,828)	—	25,775
12/20	4,581	(3,649)	—	21,113
12/19	14,691	1,133	7.7%	32,903
Annual Growth	2.9%	10.9%		

2023 Year-End Financials

Debt ratio: 34.6%
Return on equity: —
Cash ($ mil.): 6,451
Current Ratio: 1.03
Long-term debt ($ mil.): 9,805
No. of shares ($ mil.): 358
Dividends
Yield: —
Payout: 0.0%
Market value ($ mil.): 5,062

	STOCK PRICE ($) FY Close	P/E High/Low		PER SHARE ($) Earnings	Dividends	Book Value
12/23	14.12	3	2	4.50	0.00	1.68
12/22	14.42	—	—	(3.51)	0.00	(3.21)
12/21	16.71	—	—	(8.05)	0.00	0.02
12/20	17.90	—	—	(12.94)	0.00	4.05
12/19	37.35	7	4	4.18	0.00	12.81
Annual Growth	(21.6%)	—	—	1.9%	—	(39.9%)

Airbus SE

Airbus has built on its strong European heritage to become truly international ? with roughly 180 locations and 18,000 direct suppliers globally. The company constantly innovates to provide efficient and technologically-advanced solutions in aerospace, defense, and connected services. In commercial aircraft, the company offers modern and fuel-efficient airliners and associated services. The company is also a European leader in defense and security and one of the world's leading space businesses. In helicopters, the company provides the most efficient civil and military rotorcraft solutions and services worldwide. Europe generates more than 30% of Airbus' total revenue.

Operations

Airbus has three operating divisions: Airbus, Airbus Defence and Space, and Airbus Helicopters.

The Airbus segment accounts for about 70% of the company's revenue, is one of the world's leading aircraft manufacturers of passenger and freighter aircraft and related services.

The Airbus Defence and Space segment (some 20% of revenue) is Europe's number one defense and space enterprise and among the world's top ten space businesses. Its three core business groups are Military Aircraft; Space Systems; and Connected Intelligence. Airbus Defence and Space develops, produces and maintains cutting-edge products, systems and services, enabling governments, institutions and commercial customers to protect people and resources.

Airbus Helicopters (more than 10%) is a global leader in the civil and military rotorcraft market. Its product range includes light single-engine, light twin-engine, medium, and medium-heavy rotorcraft, which are adaptable to all kinds of mission types based on customer needs. Airbus Helicopters delivered more than 360 helicopters in 2022.

Geographic Reach

Airbus is headquartered in the Netherlands but has its main operational base in Toulouse, France. The company's global presence includes France, Germany, Spain, and the UK, fully-owned subsidiaries in the US, China, Japan, India, and in the Middle East, and spare parts centres in Hamburg, Frankfurt, Washington, Beijing, Dubai and Singapore. It also has engineering and training centres in Toulouse, Miami, Mexico, Wichita, Hamburg, Bangalore, Beijing and Singapore, as well as an engineering centre in Russia.

The Commercial Aircraft division has operations in France, Germany, Spain and the UK, as well as subsidiaries in the US, China, Japan, India, and the Middle East. The Defence and Space division is headquartered in Munich, Germany with main production facilities in France, Germany, Spain and the UK, and also has engineering centers and offices in more than 40 countries.

Airbus' customer base is geographically diversified with, customers in the Asia/Pacific region accounting for around 30% of total revenue, the same with Europe at roughly 30%, followed by North America for about 20%, Middle East (about 10%), and Latin America (5%).

Sales and Marketing

More than 3,100 operators currently fly Airbus Helicopters' rotorcraft in over 150 countries. Airbus Helicopters' principal military clients are Ministries of Defence (MoDs) in Europe, Asia, the US and Latin America. In the civil and parapublic sector, Airbus Helicopters has a leading market share in Europe, the Americas and Asia-Pacific.

Financial Performance

Airbus Group's performance for the past three years has increased year-over-year, ending with 2022 as its highest performing year over the period.

Revenues for 2022 increased by EUR6.6 billion to EUR58.8 billion, as compared to 2021's revenue of EUR52.1 billion.

Net profit for fiscal year end 2022 increased to EUR4.1 billion, as compared to the prior year's net profit of EUR4.2 billion.

The company held EUR9.4 billion at end of 2022. Operating activities provided EUR5.5 billion to the coffers. Investing activities used EUR2.6 billion, while financing activities provided EUR4.5 billion. Main cash uses were for industrial capital expenditure and M&A activities.

Strategy

As part of its business strategy, the company may acquire or divest businesses and/or form joint ventures or strategic alliances. Executing acquisitions and divestments can be difficult and costly due to the complexities inherent in integrating or carving out people, operations, technologies and products. There can be no assurance that any of the businesses that the company intends to acquire or divest can be integrated or carved out successfully, as timely as originally planned or that they will perform well and deliver the expected synergies or cost savings once integrated or separated. In addition, regulatory, administrative or other contractual conditions can prevent transactions from being finalized. The company's business, results of operations and financial condition may be materially affected if these transactions will not be successfully completed or do not produce the expected benefits.

Company Background

Airbus dates back to the formation of Airbus Industry GIE (later Airbus SAS) in 1970, a European effort to establish a civil aviation company capable of competing with the US hegemony of Boeing, Lockheed, and McDonnell Douglas. It launched the A300 in 1974, and, after a big win when Eastern Air Lines bought its aircraft, by 1980 Airbus trailed only Boeing among the world's commercial jet makers. The European Aeronautic Defence and Space Company NV was established in the Netherlands in 2000 to consolidate various European aviation businesses, including Eurocopter Group, a leader helicopter manufacturer. It changed its name to Airbus in 2014 in respect of its main subsidiary.

HISTORY

The growth of the European Aeronautic Defence and Space Company -- EADS -- is overshadowed by the long history of its components and by the obstacles overcome to cement the deal: The French and the Germans historically aren't overly fond of each other, so how did it come to pass that Germany's DaimlerChrysler Aerospace AG (DASA) and France's Aerospatiale Matra put aside their differences to band together with Spain's Construcciones AeronÃuticas SA (CASA)?

The US aerospace sector in the 1990s saw many companies consolidate, scrambling to make their way in the post-Cold War era. Boeing, the largest aerospace company in the world, got that way by acquiring a number of operations, including Rockwell International's aerospace and defense operations (1995), and most importantly, McDonnell Douglas in a $16 billion deal (1997). In the same era, defense giant Lockheed merged with Martin Marietta (1995) and acquired Loral (1997). These US companies had it relatively easy -- they all paid taxes to Uncle Sam, but acquisition deals in Europe were stymied by concerns over national security and privatization because much of Europe's defense industry was government-owned.

Spurred into action by their US rivals, DASA and British Aerospace (now BAE SYSTEMS) -- partners in Airbus -- began merger talks in 1997. Fearful of being left out in the cold, France's government-owned Aerospatiale -- another Airbus partner -- began talks to merge with Matra, a French defense company controlled by LagardÃre. Weeks after the Aerospatiale-Matra deal was announced in 1998, the chairman of DASA's parent company, JÃœrgen Schrempp, met with LagardÃre's CEO, Jean-Luc LagardÃre, and proposed a three-way deal. It never occurred and in 1999 the BAE SYSTEMS and DASA deal fell through, as well.

Later that year Schrempp and LagardÃre met again and laid the groundwork for a merger between DASA and Aerospatiale Matra. Less than three weeks after the Aerospatiale-Matra merger was completed, LagardÃre found itself pitching the DASA/Aerospatiale Matra merger idea to a stunned French government (which still held a 48% stake in Aerospatiale Matra). Marathon negotiations ensued. Late in the year Spain's Construcciones AeronÃuticas SA (CASA) agreed to become part of EADS.

In 2000 EADS went public and Airbus announced that it would abandon its consortium structure in favor of incorporation. The next year EADS began pushing for a consolidation of army and naval equipment manufacturing among EU countries similar to the aerospace consolidation that created EADS. For Airbus, the long-sought switch from consortium to corporation finally occurred in July 2001 when Airbus S.A.S. was incorporated.

EADS bought out BAE SYSTEMS' 25% share in their Astrium joint venture in 2003. In October 2004 EADS agreed to acquire US defense electronics maker Racal Instruments as part of its plan to increase defense sales in the US. Rumors surfaced the next month that EADS was discussing a merger deal with French defense company Thales.

In December 2004 EADS and BAE SYSTEMS gave Airbus the green-light to build the superjumbo, twin-deck A380, a plane that competes directly with Boeing's upcoming 787 Dreamliner. A few months later in early 2005, EADS was given preferred bidder status for the UK's Royal Air Force aerial refueling tanker contract. The program was valued at approximately $25 billion.

Claiming victory at last in 2006, Airbus beat Boeing on deliveries (434 vs. 398), but Boeing racked up a record 1,004 plane orders, while Airbus notched only 790. Moreover EADS' shares took a pounding in 2006 on Airbus' announcement that deliveries of the A380 would be delayed by six or seven months due to manufacturing glitches. A group of EADS shareholders cried foul and filed suit when it was revealed that co-CEO NoÃ«l Forgeard and five other EADS directors exercised stock options weeks before an internal investigation into the delays was launched. Two weeks later Forgeard fell on his sword and resigned. Louis Gallois, former chairman of SociÃ©tÃ© Nationale des Chemins de Fer FranÃ§ais (SNCF), France's state railway company, was named to replace him. The same fate befell Airbus boss Gustav Humbert, who was replaced by Christian Streiff, a former executive at French building materials concern, Compagnie de Saint-Gobain.

The production logjams at Airbus also prompted some of the company's airline customers to seek compensation in lieu of taking their business elsewhere (Boeing). EADS forecast that the production delays at Airbus would be a $2.5 billion drain on profits over four years. In the wake of the additional delivery delays, Airbus CEO Christian Streiff was sent packing after only three months on the job. EADS Co-CEO Louis Gallois was named as his replacement.

In 2006 Daimler announced plans to gradually reduce its stake in EADS from about 30% to half that amount. Later that year EADS acquired Sofrelog of France (a maker of maritime monitoring systems). Russian bank Vneshtorgbank (100% controlled by the Russian government) also purchased a 5% stake in EADS for about $1.17 billion. The stake did not entitle Vneshtorgbank to a board seat, but the move was expected to strengthen cooperation between EADS and the re-emerging Russian aerospace industry.

After long negotiations, EADS shifted in 2007 to a new management structure aimed at cutting down on the damaging political bickering between its German and French management and shareholder factions. Politicians like German Chancellor Angela Merkel and French President Nicolas Sarkozy touted the compromise as a success. Others, namely labor forces, were more skeptical -- calling the latest management shake-up just another round of musical chairs that leaves the power struggles between Paris and Munich largely unresolved.

EADS continued to expand into emerging markets, especially regions including Asia, the Middle East, and North and South America. Deliveries included the company's (long-delayed) A380 model, launched with Singapore Airlines in late 2008. Adding to Airbus's standing, the all-new A350-XWB (made for the most part of lighter-weight composite materials) sliced into about two-thirds of jet demand in the Middle East. It also forged alliances and won contracts in Brazil, China, Japan, and North America.

Airbus launched a cost-cutting initiative in 2008 that slashed some 10,000 jobs. Dubbed Power8, the plan marched out cost-saving measures that aimed to reduce development cycles by two years and boost overall productivity by 20%. Central to Power8 was the spinoff of some of Airbus's manufacturing facilities to new partners. Partner funding of planes like the A350-XWB (spurred by assurances of subcontract work) plus plant sales risked an ongoing row between Airbus and unions, as well as factory owners -- stakeholders who feared plant divestitures and more job cuts. That year EADS captured its first big US military contract when Airbus North America was given the opportunity to make US Army light utility helicopters.

The company was awarded a contract to replace outdated KC-135 refueling tankers, in conjunction with Northrop Grumman, for the US Air Force -- an upset protested by rival bidder Boeing. Soon after, the Government Accountability Office (GAO) announced its findings of flaws in the bidding process. EADS and Northrop Grumman dropped out of the bidding in early 2010, with EADS vowing not to submit a proposal unless it was assured that it had a fair chance to win. By late summer -- after US president Obama assured French president Nicolas Sarkozy that the Pentagon tanker bidding process would be fair -- EADS announced that it would consider once again to enter into the bidding war. The contract to build the US tanker, valued at approximately $35 billion, went to Boeing in early 2011.

In September 2012 EADS (now the Airbus Group) announced it was considering a merger with UK-based BAE Systems, a global provider of sensors, flight controls, and aircraft. However, the proposed $45 billion merger -- which would have created the largest global aerospace and defense player on the planet, both in total sales and market value -- was called off weeks later after it failed to pass European governmental and regulatory hurdles.

Preparing to capitalize on demand, Airbus Group hammered out its Vision 2020 goals, under which it pursues the world's #1 position in air and space platforms, systems, and services. Services are targeted to achieve a 25% share of the business in less than 10 years. To this end, Airbus Group has been scouting deals in the services sector. In August 2011 it agreed to purchase Vizada, a global satellite-based mobile communication services provider, from French private-equity Apax France. The whopping ?673 million ($969 million) deal bolsters Airbus Group's subsidiary Astrium, a top contractor of space-technology wares in Europe, and furthers opportunities beyond Europe with maritime, aerospace, as well as land, media, and other commercial customers. Hard on its heels, Airbus Group took over more than 98% of Canada-based Vector Aerospace for C$625 million (about $341 million). Vector joins Eurocopter as a standalone business, adding a multi-platform aviation repair and overhaul business.

EXECUTIVES

Chief Executive Officer, Executive Director, Guillaume Faury
Chief Financial Officer, Dominik Asam
Chief Human Resources Officer, Thierry Baril
Chief Operating Officer, Alberto Gutierrez
Communications and Corporate Affairs Executive Vice President, Julie Kitcher
Chief Technical Officer, Sabine Klauke
Chief Commercial Officer, Christian Scherer
General Counsel, Secretary, John Harrison
Chairman, Independent Non-Executive Director, Rene Obermann
Independent Non-Executive Director, Victor Chu
Independent Non-Executive Director, Jean-Pierre Clamadieu
Independent Non-Executive Director, Ralph D. Crosby

Independent Non-Executive Director, Mark B. Dunkerley
Independent Non-Executive Director, Stephen Gemkow
Independent Non-Executive Director, Catherine Guillouard
Independent Non-Executive Director, Maria Amparo Moraleda Martinez
Independent Non-Executive Director, Claudia Nemat
Independent Non-Executive Director, Irene Rummelhoff
Independent Non-Executive Director, Anthony Wood
Auditors : Ernst & Young Accountants LLP

LOCATIONS

HQ: Airbus SE
Mendelweg 30, Leiden 2333 CS
Phone: (31) 71 5245 600   **Fax:** (31) 71 5232 807
Web: www.airbusgroup.com

2018 Sales

	% of total
Asia Pacific	37
Europe	28
North America	17
Middle East	10
Latin America	2
Other countries	6
Total	100

PRODUCTS/OPERATIONS

2018 Sales

	% of total
Airbus	74
Airbus Defence and Space	17
Airbus Helicopters	9
Other HQ / Consolidation	-
Total	100

Selected Products

Commercial Aircraft
    A series passenger aircraft
    ACJ series corporate jets
    Beluga cargo planes
Helicopters
    H series helicopters
    ACH corporate helicopters
    Tiger attack helicopter
    NH90 military helicopter
    Hforce weapons system
Defence and Space
    A400M airlifter aircraft
    A330 MRTT tanker/transport aircraft
    Eurofighter Typhoon fighter jet
    Zephyr High Altitude Pseudo-Satellite (HAPS)
    Unmanned aircraft systems
    Earth observation
    Ariane rocket launchers
    Orion human spacecraft
    Bartolomeo space platform

COMPETITORS

AEGON N.V.
BAE SYSTEMS PLC
BRITISH AIRWAYS PLC
Chicago Bridge & Iron Company N.V.
Frank's International N.V.
ING Groep N.V.
MMC VENTURES LIMITED
ROYAL DUTCH SHELL plc
Randstad N.V.
THE BOEING COMPANY

HISTORICAL FINANCIALS

Company Type: Public

Income Statement   FYE: December 31

	REVENUE ($mil)	NET INCOME ($mil)	NET PROFIT MARGIN	EMPLOYEES
12/22	62,761	4,535	7.2%	134,267
12/21	59,025	4,768	8.1%	126,495
12/20	61,256	(1,390)	—	131,349
12/19	79,130	(1,529)	—	134,931
12/18	72,956	3,497	4.8%	133,671
Annual Growth	(3.7%)	6.7%	—	0.1%

2022 Year-End Financials

Debt ratio: 11.8%   No. of shares ($ mil.): 787
Return on equity: 37.8%   Dividends
Cash ($ mil.): 16,899   Yield: —
Current Ratio: 1.20   Payout: 5.1%
Long-term debt ($ mil.): 11,354   Market value ($ mil.): 23,359

	STOCK PRICE ($) FY Close	P/E High/Low		PER SHARE ($) Earnings	Dividends	Book Value
12/22	29.66	6	4	5.76	0.30	17.56
12/21	31.91	6	4	6.07	1.70	13.64
12/20	27.32	—	—	(1.78)	0.00	10.09
12/19	36.75	—	—	(1.96)	0.35	8.58
12/18	23.78	8	6	4.49	0.35	14.36
Annual Growth	5.7%		—	6.4%	(3.6%)	5.2%

Aisin Corporation

The AISIN Group (Aisin Seiki Co., Ltd.) offers a wide range of products covering nearly all components that comprise an automobile through its high level technical capabilities. The company's main business offers automotive-related products such as transmissions, brakes, and engine and car navigation systems. Its energy and home business offers items for more comfortable living, with products that include heating and cooling systems and shower toilets with jet sprays. The company has approximately 200 consolidated subsidiaries and companies worldwide. The company generates about 60% of its revenue from its Japan.

Operations

The company consists of segments by location of the company based on the manufacture and sale of automobile parts and set four reportable segments: Japan (about 60%), North America (nearly 15%), Europe (more than 5%) and China (about 10%).

Geographic Reach

Based in Japan, AISIN has operations all over the globe. It has about 75 subsidiaries in Japan and roughly 130 internationally.

Sales and Marketing

AISIN's major customers are Stellantis, Volkswagen, Audi, Suzuki, Volvo, Mitsubishi, Honda, Nissan and BMW, among others.

Financial Performance

In 2022, the company reported a revenue of Â¥3.9 trillion, an 11% increase from the previous year's revenue of Â¥3.5 trillion.

The company had a net income of Â¥167.5 billion in 2022, a 31% increase from the previous year's net income of Â¥220 billion.

The company's cash at the end of 2022 was Â¥386.9 billion. Operating activities generated Â¥193.3 billion, while investing activities used Â¥205 billion, mainly for purchase of property, plant and equipment. Financing activities used another Â¥135.9 billion, primarily for repayment of long-term loans payable as well as cash dividends paid.

Company Background

Aisin Seiki traces its roots to 1943 when Tokai Hikoki was founded to produce airplane engines for the Japanese war effort. After the war, the company switched to manufacturing sewing machines and auto parts. Aisin Seiki took its present name in 1965 after Tokai Hikoki merged with Shinkawa Kogyo.

EXECUTIVES

President, Representative Director, Moritaka Yoshida
Representative Director, Kenji Suzuki
Representative Director, Shintaro Ito
Director, Yoshihisa Yamamoto
Outside Director, Michiyo Hamada
Outside Director, Seiichi Shin
Outside Director, Koji Kobayashi
Outside Director, Tsuguhiko Hoshino
Auditors : PricewaterhouseCoopers Aarata LLC

LOCATIONS

HQ: Aisin Corporation
 2-1 Asahi-machi, Kariya, Aichi 448-8650
Phone: (81) 566 24 8265
Web: www.aisin.com

PRODUCTS/OPERATIONS

2019 Sales

	% of total
Aisin Seiki Group	39
Aisin AW Group	36
Advics Group	13
Aisin Takaoka Group	7
Other	5
Total	100

Selected Products
Automotive
 Chassis and vehicle safety systems
 Body products
 ICT and electronics
Energy System
 GHP
 Cogeneration system
Life and Amenity
 Bed, furniture, and fabric (ASLEEP)
 House remodeling service (Livelan)
 Home-use sewing machine
 Cogeneration system
 Shower-toilet seat
 Audio equipment

COMPETITORS

ALLISON TRANSMISSION HOLDINGS, INC.
BORGWARNER INC.
DANA INCORPORATED
DENSO CORPORATION
Dongfeng Motor Group Co., Ltd
Hyundai Mobis Co., Ltd
REGAL BELOIT CORPORATION
Robert Bosch Gesellschaft mit beschrÃ¤nkter Haftung
TENNECO INC.
WABCO HOLDINGS INC.

HISTORICAL FINANCIALS
Company Type: Public

Income Statement   FYE: March 31

	REVENUE ($mil)	NET INCOME ($mil)	NET PROFIT MARGIN	EMPLOYEES
03/23	33,057	282	0.9%	142,245
03/22	32,205	1,166	3.6%	143,006
03/21	31,842	954	3.0%	139,832
03/20	34,864	221	0.6%	144,334
03/19	36,508	994	2.7%	148,359
Annual Growth	(2.5%)	(27.0%)	—	(1.0%)

2023 Year-End Financials
Debt ratio: 0.2% No. of shares ($ mil.): 269
Return on equity: 2.1% Dividends
Cash ($ mil.): 2,385 Yield: —
Current Ratio: 1.55 Payout: 121.6%
Long-term debt ($ mil.): 5,171 Market value ($ mil.): —

Ajinomoto Co., Inc. (Japan)

Ajinomoto is the world's leading manufacturer of amino acids and operates a wide array of global businesses centered on its Food Products and AminoScience businesses. The company makes and sells other seasonings, as well as soups and ready-to-eat meals, frozen foods, coffee, and sweeteners available in Japan and across the globe. It also plans to concentrate on specialty products, such as AjiPro-L, a lysine formulation for dairy cows. Ajinomoto generates about 55% of its revenue outside of Japan. The company started in 1908 when Dr. Kikunae Ikeda discovered that the umami component of kombu (kelp) broth is glutamic acid.

Operations

The company operates in three reportable segments: Seasonings and Foods (about 55% of sales), Healthcare and Others (over 20%), and Frozen Foods (about 20%).

The Seasonings and Foods segment includes sauce and seasonings such as Umami seasonings AJI-NO-MOTO, HON-DASHI, Cook Do, Ajinomoto KK ConsommÃ©, Pure Select Mayonnaise, Ros Dee, and more, as well as quick nourishment and solution and ingredients.

Its Healthcare and Others includes Amino acids for pharmaceuticals and foods, culture media, medical foods, as well as Bio-Pharma Services, Specialty Chemicals, and others.

Its Frozen Foods segment includes Chinese dumplings, Cooked rice, Noodles, Desserts, Shumai, Processed chicken, and others.

Geographic Reach

Tokyo-based Ajinomoto generates about 45% of revenue from its home country; major international markets include the US, Thailand, and Europe.

Sales and Marketing

Ajinomoto serves food manufacturers, and pharmaceutical and chemical companies, among other customers.

Financial Performance

During the fiscal year ended March 31, 2021, the company's consolidated sales fell 3% year-on-year, or Â¥28.5 billion, to Â¥1.1 trillion. This was because there was a continued decline in sales of restaurant and industrial use products mainly in Seasonings and Foods and Frozen Foods due to the impact of lockdowns and other measures in conjunction with the COVID-19 global pandemic, even though a trend of recovery can be seen in demand for products for use in foodservice, while sales of home-use products increased due to the expansion in at-home dining demand.

In 2021, the company had a net income of Â¥59.4 billion, a 215% increase from the previous year's net income of Â¥18.8 billion. This was primarily due to a lower volume of cost of sales for the year.

The company's cash at the end of 2021 was Â¥181.6 billion. Operating activities generated Â¥165.7 billion, while investing activities used Â¥66.2 billion, mainly for purchase of property, plant and equipment. Financing activities used another Â¥60.4 billion, primarily for purchase of shares in subsidiaries not resulting in change of scope of consolidation.

Strategy

In early 2020, the Ajinomoto Group entered into a contract to transfer the entire equity stake held by the group corresponding to 51% of the outstanding shares in Fuji Ace Co., Ltd., a packaging materials manufacturing and sales company in Thailand, to Fuji Seal International, Inc. and other entities, and transferred the equity stake on March 6, 2020. Accordingly, together with the logistics business, which had previously been classified under discontinued operations, profit related to the packaging business in the fiscal year ended March 31, 2020, has been restated as profit from discontinued operations, and the discontinued operations have been presented separately from continuing operations.

Company Background

Ajinomoto Group traces its history to the 1909 introduction of umami seasoning AJI-NO-MOTO by Saburosuke Suzuki II. The company spent decades expanding sales of the seasoning before diversifying into other products during the second half of the 20th century.

HISTORY

In 2002 the company acquired Shimizu Pharmaceutical Co., which included a line of kidney dialysis products. In 2003 Ajinomoto started selling its products in China. That year it, opened a dried Western-style soup and dried scallop-flavor seasoning operation called Shanghai Ajinomoto Seasoning Co. Also in 2003 Ajinomoto sold its interest in the seven processed-food joint ventures it had with Unilever. The deal was completed in 2004.

Always expanding its product offerings, in 2005 the company introduced Glyna brand dietary supplement made with the amino acid, glycine.

In 2006 the company expanded its sauces and frozen foods array with the purchase of the AMOY brand and operations from Danone. In addition to seasonings, AMOY makes chilled convenience foods (such as dim sum) under the AMOY and Royal Dragon brands.

Ajinomoto was founded in 1888 to harvest iodine from seaweed.

EXECUTIVES

Representative Executive Officer, President, Chief Executive Officer, Director, Taro Fujie
Representative Executive Officer, Executive Vice President, Chief Innovation Officer, Director, Hiroshi Shiragami
Senior Managing Executive Officer, Director, Tatsuya Sasaki
Senior Managing Executive Officer, Yoshiteru Masai
Senior Managing Executive Officer, Chief Digital Officer; Chief Transformation Officer, Takayuki Koda
Outside Director, Kimie Iwata
Outside Director, Joji Nakayama
Outside Director, Atsushi Toki
Outside Director, Mami Indo
Outside Director, Yoko Hatta
Outside Director, Scott Trevor Davis
Director, Takeshi Saito
Director, Takumi Matsuzawa
Auditors : KPMG AZSA LLC

LOCATIONS

HQ: Ajinomoto Co., Inc. (Japan)
  1-15-1 Kyobashi, Chuo-ku, Tokyo 104-8315
Phone: (81) 3 5250 8111
Web: www.ajinomoto.co.jp

2017 Sales

	% of total
Japan	45
Other	55
Total	100

PRODUCTS/OPERATIONS

2017 Sales

	% of total
International Food Products	43
Japan Food Products	35
Life Support	12
Healthcare	10
Total	100

COMPETITORS

ANNIE'S, INC.
CALAVO GROWERS, INC.
GENERAL MILLS, INC.
GLANBIA PUBLIC LIMITED COMPANY
INGREDION INCORPORATED
MCCORMICK & COMPANY, INCORPORATED
Marfrig Global Foods S/A
PT. INDOFOOD SUKSES MAKMUR TBK
SENSIENT TECHNOLOGIES CORPORATION
UNITED NATURAL FOODS, INC.

HISTORICAL FINANCIALS
Company Type: Public

Income Statement   FYE: March 31

	REVENUE ($mil)	NET INCOME ($mil)	NET PROFIT MARGIN	EMPLOYEES
03/23	10,204	706	6.9%	43,318
03/22	9,449	622	6.6%	42,947
03/21	9,676	536	5.5%	42,535
03/20	10,133	173	1.7%	41,528
03/19	10,180	268	2.6%	44,186
Annual Growth	0.1%	27.4%	—	(0.5%)

2023 Year-End Financials
Debt ratio: 0.1%
Return on equity: 12.9%
Cash ($ mil.): 996
Current Ratio: 1.81
Long-term debt ($ mil.): 1,796
No. of shares ($ mil.): 529
Dividends
Yield: 1.2%
Payout: 34.0%
Market value ($ mil.): 18,650

	STOCK PRICE ($) FY Close	P/E High/Low		PER SHARE ($) Earnings	Dividends	Book Value
03/23	35.21	0	0	1.32	0.44	10.90
03/22	28.47	0	0	1.15	0.45	10.52
03/21	20.68	0	0	0.98	0.30	10.20
03/20	19.20	1	0	0.32	0.30	9.04
03/19	16.02	0	0	0.48	0.30	10.04
Annual Growth	21.8%	—	—	28.5%	9.9%	2.1%

AKBANK

Akbank provides corporate investment banking, commercial banking, SME banking, consumer banking, payment systems, treasury transactions, private banking, and international banking services. The bank provides these services in Turkey through nearly 720 branches, about 5,000 ATMs, and more than 600 point-of-sale terminals. Internationally, Akbank operates branches in Germany and in Malta; Akbank, shares is listed are listed in Borsa Istanbul (BIST). Overseas, the bank's 'Level 1' ADR depository receipts are traded on the USTC market. Subsidiaries provide non-banking financial, capital-market, and wealth management are carried out by the Bank affiliates such as AK investment, AK asset management, and Aklease. The bank was founded in 1948.

EXECUTIVES

Vice-Chairman, Executive Director, Eyup Engin
Chief Executive Officer, Director, Sabri Hakan Binbasgil
Executive Director, Ahmet Fuat Ayla
SME Banking Executive Vice President, Bulent Oguz
Consumer Banking and Digital Solutions Executive Vice President, Human Resources
Executive Vice President, Strategy Executive Vice President, Burcu Civelek Yuce
Credit Monitoring and Collections Executive Vice President, Ege Gultekin
Corporate & Investment Banking Executive Vice President, Levent Celebioglu
Technology Executive Vice President, Gokhan Gokcay
Commercial Banking Executive Vice President, Cetin Duz
Chief Financial Officer, Turker Tunali
Private Banking and Wealth Management Executive Vice President, Sahin Alp Keler
Credit Allocation Executive Vice President, Yunus Emre Ozben
Special Credits Executive Vice President, Zeynep Ozturk
Treasury Executive Vice President, Gamze Sebnem Muratoglu
People and Culture Executive Vice President, Pinar Anapa
General Counsel, Berna Avdan
Chairman, Suzan Sabanci Dincer
Director, Yaman Toruner
Director, Emre Derman
Director, Ozgur Demirtas
Director, Orhun Kostem
Director, Tugrul Belli
Director, Levent Demirag
Auditors : PwC Bagimsiz Denetim ve Serbest Muhasebeci Mali Musavirlik A.S.

LOCATIONS

HQ: AKBANK
  Sabanci Center 4, Istanbul, Levent 34330
Phone: (90) 212 385 55 55   Fax: (90) 212 319 52 52
Web: www.akbank.com.tr

PRODUCTS/OPERATIONS

2014 Sales

	% of total
Interest income	81
Fee and commission received	16
Dividend income	-
Other operating income	3
Total	100

Selected Businesses
AKAssetmanagement
AKLease
AKInvestment
AKbank AG
Akbank Dubai Limited

COMPETITORS

AL RAJHI BANKING AND INVESTMENT CORPORATION
Bank of Communications Co.,Ltd.
CAIXABANK SA
ICICI BANK LIMITED
Industrial and Commercial Bank of China Limited
QATAR NATIONAL BANK (Q.P.S.C.)
Shinhan Financial Group Co., Ltd.
TURKIYE GARANTI BANKASI ANONIM SIRKETI
TURKIYE IS BANKASI ANONIM SIRKETI
Woori Finance Holdings Co., Ltd.

HISTORICAL FINANCIALS
Company Type: Public

Income Statement — FYE: December 31

	ASSETS ($mil)	NET INCOME ($mil)	INCOME AS % OF ASSETS	EMPLOYEES
12/22	61,287	3,206	5.2%	13,247
12/21	57,028	906	1.6%	12,606
12/20	64,340	822	1.3%	12,862
12/19	65,088	903	1.4%	13,136
12/18	67,035	1,079	1.6%	13,367
Annual Growth	(2.2%)	31.3%	—	(0.2%)

2022 Year-End Financials
Return on assets: 6.2%
Return on equity: 52.2%
Long-term debt ($ mil.): —
No. of shares ($ mil.): 520,000
Sales ($ mil.): 8,233
Dividends
Yield: —
Payout: 267.4%
Market value ($ mil.): 1,061,840

	STOCK PRICE ($) FY Close	P/E High/Low	PER SHARE ($) Earnings	Dividends	Book Value
12/22	2.04	18 6	0.01	0.02	0.02
12/21	1.05	62 32	0.00	0.02	0.01
12/20	1.90	199 105	0.00	0.00	0.02
12/19	2.71	261 165	0.00	0.47	0.02
12/18	2.48	297 145	0.00	0.15	0.02
Annual Growth	(4.7%)	—	23.0%	(42.5%)	(6.5%)

Akita Bank Ltd (The) (Japan)

EXECUTIVES

President, Representative Director, Akihiro Araya
Director, Masato Tsuchiya
Director, Tsuyoshi Minakawa
Director, Hiroyoshi Miura
Director, Kosuke Ashida
Outside Director, Yoshiyuki Tsuji
Outside Director, Junichi Sakaki
Outside Director, Naofumi Nakata
Outside Director, Tamaki Kakizaki
Director, Masahiko Sato
Outside Director, Masahiro Morohashi
Outside Director, Kenichi Kobayashi
Outside Director, Kyoko Omoteyama
Auditors : Deloitte Touche Tohmatsu LLC

LOCATIONS

HQ: Akita Bank Ltd (The) (Japan)
 3-2-1 Sanno, Akita 010-8655
Phone: (81) 18 863 1212
Web: www.akita-bank.co.jp

HISTORICAL FINANCIALS
Company Type: Public

Income Statement — FYE: March 31

	ASSETS ($mil)	NET INCOME ($mil)	INCOME AS % OF ASSETS	EMPLOYEES
03/21	31,508	24	0.1%	2,011
03/20	27,920	28	0.1%	2,081
03/19	27,311	37	0.1%	2,148
03/18	29,634	44	0.2%	2,176
03/17	26,655	42	0.2%	2,191
Annual Growth	4.3%	(12.8%)	—	(2.1%)

2021 Year-End Financials
Return on assets: —
Return on equity: 1.5%
Long-term debt ($ mil.): —
No. of shares ($ mil.): 17
Sales ($ mil.): 393
Dividends
Yield: —
Payout: 0.0%
Market value ($ mil.): —

Akzo Nobel NV (Netherlands)

Akzo Nobel is a Dutch multinational and is one of the leading global paints and coatings companies of the world, and a top producer of specialty chemicals. The company which is headquartered in Netherlands has operations in over 150 countries. AzkoNobel serves a variety of industries including aerospace, automotive, chemical, electronics, mining, and oil & gas. Nearly 30% of the company's total sales comes from Asia. The company was founded in 1646.

Operations
AkzoNobel's Performance Coatings segment is a supplier of performance coatings with strong brands and technologies. Its high quality products are used to protect and enhance everything from ships, cars, aircraft, yachts and architectural components (structural steel, building products, flooring) to consumer goods (mobile devices, appliances, beverage cans, furniture) and oil and gas facilities. The segment accounts for approximately 60% of the company's revenue.

The company's Decorative Paints, supply a variety of quality products for every situation and surface, including paints, lacquers and varnishes. It also offers a range of mixing machines and color concepts for the building and renovation industry. Its specialty coatings for metal, wood and other building materials are the reference to the market. The segment accounts for approximately 40% of the total revenue.

Geographic Reach
The Netherlands-based AkzoNobel operates in more than 150 countries.

The company has sales across the world. Majority of its sales comes from EMA (some 50%), followed by the Asia Pacific region (about 30%). North America brings in just over 10% of sales, while South America accounts for nearly 10%.

Sales and Marketing
AzkoNobel serves a variety of industries including aerospace, automotive, chemical, electronics, mining, and oil & gas ,vehicle refinishes, water, wood coatings, and yacht.

Financial Performance
Akzo Nobel's performance for the past five years have continued to decrease year-over-year from 2017 but has recovered for 2021.

Revenue in 2021 increased by EUR1 billion to EUR9.6 billion as compared to 2020's revenue of EUR8.5 billion.

Net income increased by EUR 199 million to ?829 million for fiscal year end 2021 as compared to the prior year's net income of EUR 630 million.

Cash holdings decreased by more than half to EUR 1.1 billion. Operations provided a cash inflow of EUR 805 million. Investing activities used EUR 134 million and EUR 974 million, respectively. Main cash uses were for capital expenditures and share buyback.

Company Background
The company was founded in 1646.

HISTORY

The Akzo side of Akzo Nobel traces its roots to two companies -- German rayon and coatings maker Vereinigte Glanzstoff-Fabriken (founded 1899) and Dutch rayon maker Nederlandsche Kunstzijdebariek (founded 1911 and known as NK or Enka). In 1928 NK built a plant near Asheville, North Carolina, in what later became the town of Enka. The two companies merged in 1929 to create Algemene Kunstzijde-Unie (AKU).

In 1967 two Dutch companies merged to form Koninklijke Zout-Organon (KZO). Two years later KZO bought US-based International Salt and merged with AKU to form Akzo. In the 1980s Akzo focused on building its chemicals, coatings, and pharmaceuticals businesses. Akzo sold its paper and pulp business to Nobel in 1993. A few months later the company reclaimed that business when it bought Nobel.

Best remembered for the prizes that bear his name (which were first awarded in 1901 through a bequest in his will), Alfred Nobel invented the blasting cap in 1863, making it possible to control the detonation of nitroglycerin. He then persuaded Stockholm merchant J. W. Smitt to help him finance Nitroglycerin Ltd. to make and sell the volatile fluid (1864). Nobel's quest to improve nitroglycerin led to his invention of dynamite in 1867.

After Nobel's death in 1896, Nitroglycerin Ltd. remained an explosives maker, and in 1965 it changed its name to Nitro Nobel. In 1978 Swedish industrialist Marcus Wallenberg bought Nitro Nobel for his KemaNord chemical group, known afterward as KemaNobel. Within six years industrialist Erik Penser controlled both KemaNobel and armaments maker Bofors, and he merged them in 1984 as Nobel Industries.

Risky investments led Penser to ruin in 1991. His holdings, including Nobel, were taken over by a government-owned bank and conveyed into Securum, a state-owned holding company (which still owns 18% of Akzo Nobel). In 1992 Nobel spun off its consumer-goods segment.

Akzo bought Nobel in 1994. Although the company had good financial results in 1995, it faced pressure from rising costs for raw materials and a difficult foreign-exchange environment. Akzo announced major closings and layoffs -- it sold its polyethylene packaging resin business and moved some clothing-grade rayon operations to Poland.

The merger between Akzo and Nobel was legally completed in 1996. That year the company introduced Puregon, a fertility drug, and Remeron, touted as a replacement for Prozac, in the US and other countries. In 1997 Akzo Nobel put most of its worst-performing segment, fibers, into a joint venture with Turkish conglomerate Sabanci. It also sold its North American salt unit to Cargill.

Akzo Nobel acquired Courtaulds (coatings, sealants, and fibers) in 1998 and changed the firm's name to Akzo Nobel UK. AkzoNobel also bought BASF deco, the European decorative-coatings business of BASF Coatings. Akzo Nobel combined its fiber business with AkzoNobel UK to form a new division, Acordis. AkzoNobel then sold Acordis to investment firm CVC Capital Partners in 1999 for $859 million (AkzoNobel retains a minority share). That year AkzoNobel bought Hoechst's animal-health unit, Hoechst Roussel Vet, for $712 million. In 2000 the company bought Dexter Corporation's aircraft coatings business.

In 2001 Akzo Nobel sold its medical diagnostics division to French drugmaker bioMérieux-Pierre Fabre. Later that year the company picked up the vehicle refinishes business of MAC Specialty Coatings of the US. It also agreed to sell its printing inks business to a private equity firm.

CEO Cees van Lede retired in mid-2003, succeeded by Hans Wijers, who immediately set about restructuring, cutting costs, and erasing debt. By year's end more than 3,300 jobs were cut and AkzoNobel had sold off three big chemical units: catalysts (to Albemarle for about $750 million), coating resins, and phosphorous chemicals (to Ripplewood Holdings for another $270 million).

The fruits of those sell-offs came with 2005 acquisitions in Germany, France, and Switzerland. The last purchase, of Swiss Lack, made Akzo Nobel the largest paint company in Switzerland as well. The following year the company made a bigger buy, that of Canadian coatings maker Sico for $285 million.

Also in 2006 Akzo Nobel decided to pare down its operations further with the sale of its inks and adhesive resins business to Hexion Specialty Chemicals. The business was concentrated in Europe but had strong international operations as well. The deal brought the company about $100 million.

Early in 2006 Akzo announced plans to split off its pharmaceuticals segment, Organon. It originally planned to float a minority share early in 2007 and then fully separate the new company by 2009. In a surprise move, however, Schering-Plough came in and bought the unit for $14.4 billion.

In what turned out to be a major turning point for the company, Akzo Nobel approached UK coatings and chemicals maker ICI with a $14 billion takeover offer in late 2007. ICI's board rejected the price tag as insufficient. Akzo Nobel countered, twice, and ended up agreeing to a deal worth $16 billion. As part of the deal, Henkel bought the adhesives and electronic materials businesses of ICI subsidiary National Starch and Chemical. The buy of ICI built up Akzo's coatings business even further. The acquired businesses have great strength in retail decorative paints and in North America, both areas in which Akzo Nobel's coatings business had been lacking.

Another business acquired in the deal was Akzo Nobel's new Chemicals Pakistan division, which was composed of the company's majority holdings in two publicly traded companies. Those subsidiaries made soda ash, polyester fibers, and pure terephthalic acid (PTA). In 2009, though, the company sold its 75% stake in the subsidiary that makes PTA to Korean manufacturer KP Chemical.

Akzo Nobel subsidiary National Starch acquired Penford Australia's specialty grain wet milling and manufacturing facility in 2009, expanding National Starch's reach into the Asia/Pacific region. However, in 2010 Corn Products International (renamed Ingredion) acquired National Starch for $2.7 billion.

In 2010 Akzo Nobel acquired the powder coatings business of Dow Chemical Company. The deal brought technological know-how and significant synergy potential to Akzo Nobel's Powder Coatings line and enhanced the company's position in the US.

As part of its three-year performance improvement program launched in late 2011, Azko Nobel restructured business lines, such as its European and North American decorative paints and its performance coatings' wood finishes and adhesives. The company has managed to raise prices enough in 2012 to offset most of the raw material price increases. Although the costs of titanium dioxide continue to rise, Akzo Nobel has been successful in passing on most of its raw material cost increases.

In early 2012 the company completed its acquisition of Boxing Oleochemicals, a leading Chinese surfactants producer. Boxing makes nitrile amines and derivatives, used for industrial and consumer applications ranging from asphalt additives to fabric softeners. The buy enhances Azko Nobel's position in specialty surfactants and broadens its reach in Asia. Boxing's operations will be integrated into the company's Surface Chemistry unit.

In early 2012 the company also moved to strengthen its packaging coatings operations by trying to acquire the part of Italy's Packaging Coatings Metlac Group it doesn't own (it holds a 49% stake). However, the UK's office of Fair Trading put the brakes on the deal because of competition concerns and referred the case to the UK's Competition Commission. Both Metlac and Akzo Nobel supply metal packaging coatings used in food and beverage cans.

In 2012 Akzon Nobel split its ICI Pakistan subsidiary into two new companies: AkzoNobel Pakistan Limited (comprising the paints and specialty chemicals business) and ICI Pakistan Limited (comprising all other businesses of ICI Pakistan). In the process, AkzoNobel maintains 76% control of the paints business while seeking a buyer for ICI Pakistan.

To expand its industrial coatings business, Akzo Nobel acquired Germany-based Schramm Holding in 2011. Akzo Nobel believes the acquisition makes it the global leader for specialty plastic coatings for the lucrative market serving mobile devices, laptops, TVs, and auto interiors. Also in 2011, Akzo Nobel opened a new coatings plant in India.

That year the company's Decorative Paints unit expanded with the company's entry into a partnership in China with Quangxi CAVA Titanium Industry Co. to ensure a supply of titanium dioxide. It also invested ?110 million ($135 million) in 2011 in a replacement manufacturing plant in the North East of England.

To raise cash to pay down debt, in 2012 AkzoNobel divested its North American Decorative Paints business to PPG Industries for $1.05 billion.

EXECUTIVES

Chief Executive Officer, Chairman, Thierry F.J. Vanlancker
Chief Financial Officer, Maarten de Vries
Chief Human Resources Officer, Joelle Boxus
Chief Manufacturing Officer, David Prinselaar
Chief Supply Chain Officer, Karen-Marie Katholm
Independent Chairman, Nils Smedegaard Andersen
Independent Deputy Chairman, Member, Byron E. Grote
Independent Member, Pamela J. Kirby
Independent Member, Jolanda Poots-Bijl
Independent Member, Dick Sluimers
Independent Member, Patrick W. Thomas
Auditors : PricewaterhouseCoopers Accountants N.V.

LOCATIONS

HQ: Akzo Nobel NV (Netherlands)
 Christian Neefestraat 2, P.O. Box 75730, Amsterdam 1070 AS
Phone: (31) 88 969 7555   **Fax:** (31) 20 502 7666

Web: www.akzonobel.com

2016 Sales

	% of total
Asia	26
US and Canada	17
Latin America	9
The Netherlands	5
Other European countries	38
Other regions	5
Total	**100**

PRODUCTS/OPERATIONS

2016 sales

	% of total
Performance Coatings	40
Specialty Chemicals	33
Decorative Paints	27
Total	**100**

Selected Brands
AkzoNobel
Awlgrip
Biostyle
Coral
Dissolvine
Dulux
Ecosel
Expancel
Flexa
Hammerite
Levasil
Sadolin
Sikkens

Selected Products
Specialty chemicals
    Base chemicals
        Functional chemicals
        Polymer chemicals
        Pulp and paper chemicals
        Surfactants
Decorative paints
Performance coatings
    Car refinishes
    Industrial finishes
    Marine and protective coatings
    Powder coatings

COMPETITORS

BASF SE
Evonik Industries AG
Evonik Operations GmbH
HERAEUS HOLDING Gesellschaft mit beschränkter Haftung
PPG INDUSTRIES, INC.
RECKITT BENCKISER GROUP PLC
SOLVAY FRANCE
SYNTHOMER PLC
THE DOW CHEMICAL COMPANY
thyssenkrupp AG

HISTORICAL FINANCIALS

Company Type: Public

Income Statement   FYE: December 31

	REVENUE ($mil)	NET INCOME ($mil)	NET PROFIT MARGIN	EMPLOYEES
12/22	11,584	375	3.2%	35,200
12/21	10,851	938	8.6%	32,800
12/20	10,468	773	7.4%	32,200
12/19	10,414	605	5.8%	33,800
12/18	10,599	7,643	72.1%	34,500
Annual Growth	2.2%	(52.9%)	—	0.5%

2022 Year-End Financials
Debt ratio: 41.1%   No. of shares ($ mil.): 174
Return on equity: 7.2%   Dividends
Cash ($ mil.): 1,548   Yield: —
Current Ratio: 1.09   Payout: 25.6%
Long-term debt ($ mil.): 3,347   Market value ($ mil.): 3,890

	STOCK PRICE ($) FY Close	P/E High/Low		PER SHARE ($) Earnings	Dividends	Book Value
12/22	22.31	18	10	2.15	0.55	26.54
12/21	36.74	9	7	5.05	0.62	33.81
12/20	36.06	11	6	4.03	0.56	37.00
12/19	34.05	14	10	2.83	1.99	35.72
12/18	26.64	1	1	29.86	7.21	52.89
Annual Growth	(4.3%)	—	—	(48.2%)	(47.4%)	(15.8%)

Alcon Inc

EXECUTIVES

Chief Executive Officer, Executive Director, David J. Endicott
Chief Financial Officer, Timothy C. Stonesifer
Senior Vice President, Chief Information & Transformation Officer, Sue-Jean Lin
Chairman, F. Michael Ball
Independent Director, Lynn Dorsey Bleil
Independent Director, Thomas H. Glanzmann
Independent Director, D. Keith Grossman
Independent Director, Scott Harlan Maw
Independent Director, Karen J. May
Independent Director, Ines Poschel
Independent Director, Arthur Cummings
Independent Director, Dieter Spalti
Auditors : PricewaterhouseCoopers LLP

LOCATIONS

HQ: Alcon Inc
   Rue Louis-d'Affry 6, Fribourg 1701
Phone: (41) 817 293 0450   **Fax:** (41) 817 916 2652
Web: www.alcon.com

HISTORICAL FINANCIALS

Company Type: Public

Income Statement   FYE: December 31

	REVENUE ($mil)	NET INCOME ($mil)	NET PROFIT MARGIN	EMPLOYEES
12/23	9,455	974	10.3%	25,315
12/22	8,717	335	3.8%	25,178
12/21	8,291	376	4.5%	24,389
12/20	6,833	(531)	—	23,655
12/19	7,508	(656)	—	22,142
Annual Growth	5.9%	—	—	3.4%

2023 Year-End Financials
Debt ratio: 16.0%   No. of shares ($ mil.): 493
Return on equity: 4.8%   Dividends
Cash ($ mil.): 1,094   Yield: —
Current Ratio: 2.28   Payout: 12.2%
Long-term debt ($ mil.): 4,594   Market value ($ mil.): —

ALD SA

EXECUTIVES

Chief Executive Officer, Tim Albertson
Deputy Chief Executive, Gilles Bellemere
Deputy Chief Executive, John Saffrett
Chief Financial Officer, Gilles Momper
Administrative Director, Hans van Beeck
Director, Chairman, Philippe Heim
Independent Director, Xavier Durand
Independent Director, Patricia Lacoste
Independent Director, Nathalie Leboucher
Independent Director, Christophe Périllat
Director, Delphine Garcin-Meunier
Director, Bernardo Sanchez-Incera
Director, Didier Haugel
Director, Karine Destrebohn
Auditors : ERNST & YOUNG et Autres

LOCATIONS

HQ: ALD SA
   Corosa Building, 1-3 Rue Eugène et Armand Peugeot Corosa, Rueil-Malmaison 92800
Phone: (33) 1 58 98 79 31
Web: www.aldautomotive.com

HISTORICAL FINANCIALS

Company Type: Public

Income Statement   FYE: December 31

	REVENUE ($mil)	NET INCOME ($mil)	NET PROFIT MARGIN	EMPLOYEES
12/21	11,861	988	8.3%	6,893
12/20	12,192	625	5.1%	6,606
12/19	10,977	633	5.8%	6,715
12/18	10,274	636	6.2%	6,520
12/17	9,909	680	6.9%	6,303
Annual Growth	4.6%	9.8%		2.3%

2021 Year-End Financials
Debt ratio: 77.7%   No. of shares ($ mil.): 403
Return on equity: 19.4%   Dividends
Cash ($ mil.): 172   Yield: —
Current Ratio: 0.43   Payout: 50.0%
Long-term debt ($ mil.): 14,302   Market value ($ mil.): —

Alfresa Holdings Corp Tokyo

Alfresa Holdings distributes prescription drugs, medical tests and devices, and over-the-counter (OTC) supplements on a wholesale basis in the Japanese market. The firm is Japan's largest pharmaceuticals wholesaler, holding as the third largest in the world. It also has an overseas business development arm, which targets other Asian markets for growth. Its offerings also include OTC drugs, diagnostic reagents, and health foods. Its manufacturing division researches, develops, manufactures, and markets these items as well as active pharmaceutical ingredients (APIs) used by other firms to make drugs.

Operations

Alfresa operates in four primary segments: Ethical Pharmaceuticals Wholesaling, Self-Medication Products Wholesaling, Manufacturing, and Medical-Related (dispensing pharmacies).

The group's Ethical Pharmaceuticals Wholesaling segment contributes more than 85% of the group's total revenue. In addition to selling prescription drugs, tests, medical devices, and other products, it provides services to hospitals, clinics, pharmacies, and other customers.

The Self-Medication Products Wholesaling segment provides OTC drugs, health foods, supplements, and other items to drugstores and pharmacies. It brings in some 10% of the group's revenue.

The smallest segments are Manufacturing and Medical-Related. Manufacturing develops and manufactures drugs, APIs, tests, medical devices, and other products, while Medical-Related provides dispensing pharmacy services. Each segment provides the remainder of Alfresa's total revenue.

Geographic Reach

Alfresa is headquartered in Tokyo and is ranked three as the largest pharmaceutical market in the world. The company seeks to expand in other parts of Asia, particularly in China and Vietnam. In China, the Group established joint venture REMEJE PHARMACEUTICALS (CHINA) CO., LTD. in 2005 as a representative office for pharmaceuticals and healthcare-related products. In Vietnam, the Group established joint venture Alfresa Codupha Healthcare Vietnam Co., Ltd. (Alcopha) in 2013 to conduct import and sales mainly of medical devices and materials and diagnostic reagents, and is gradually setting up a stable management foundation. There are more than 200 warehouse in Japan and in overseas.

Sales and Marketing

Alfresa's customers include hospitals, medical care facilities, drugstores, and pharmacies. Company's products and services offer to over 100,000 customers throughout Japan.

Financial Performance

The Group's net sales increased 1% due to growth in sales volumes for hepatitis C therapeutic agents and anticancer drugs.

The company's net income increased by Â¥9.7 billion to Â¥61.2 billion, compared to Â¥51.6 billion from the prior year. The increase was primarily due to the 68% increase on their other income.

Cash held by the company in 2019 increased by Â¥9.5 billion to Â¥205.1 billion, compared to Â¥195.6 billion in the prior year. Cash from operations was Â¥46.9 billion, while cash used for investing and financing activities were Â¥12.9 billion and Â¥24.9 billion, respectively.

Strategy

Alfresa's basic approach to financial and capital strategy under the 19?21 Mid-term Management Plan is to raise corporate value by pursuing the optimal balance of financial soundness, capital efficiency, and shareholder returns. In particular, the company will press forward even further with investments and measures to promote growth, based on issues identified in the previous plan.

The Alfresa Group uses capital cost as a management indicator, measuring and updating provisional figures each year while referring to information from multiple external professional organizations. In addition to monitoring the profitability of existing businesses, they also refer to the latest cost of capital when making investment decisions and evaluating businesses or investment securities.

Mergers and Acquisitions

Company Background

Alfresa was created in 2003 from the combination of wholesalers Azwell and Fukujin.

EXECUTIVES

President, Representative Director, Ryuji Arakawa
Executive Vice President, Director, Seiichi Kishida
Executive Vice President, Director, Yusuke Fukujin
Director, Shigeki Ohashi
Director, Toshiki Tanaka
Director, Hisashi Katsuki
Director, Koichi Shimada
Outside Director, Takeshi Hara
Outside Director, Manabu Kinoshita
Outside Director, Toshie Takeuchi
Outside Director, Kimiko Kunimasa
Auditors : KPMG AZSA LLC

LOCATIONS

HQ: Alfresa Holdings Corp Tokyo
1-1-3 Otemachi, Chiyoda-ku, Tokyo 100-0004
Phone: (81) 3 5219 5100
Web: www.alfresa.com

PRODUCTS/OPERATIONS

2018 Sales by Segment

	% of total
Ethical Pharmaceuticals Wholesaling	88
Self-Medication Products Wholesaling	10
Pharmaceutical Manufacturing	1
Medical-Related	1
Total	100

COMPETITORS

ALLERGAN LIMITED
APTARGROUP, INC.
CATALENT, INC.
CONSORT MEDICAL LIMITED
ENDO INTERNATIONAL PUBLIC LIMITED COMPANY
MEDIPAL HOLDINGS CORPORATION
PERRIGO COMPANY PUBLIC LIMITED COMPANY
STERIS LIMITED
SUZUKEN CO., LTD.
TOHO HOLDINGS CO.,LTD.

HISTORICAL FINANCIALS

Company Type: Public

Income Statement   FYE: March 31

	REVENUE ($mil)	NET INCOME ($mil)	NET PROFIT MARGIN	EMPLOYEES
03/22	21,257	264	1.2%	14,282
03/21	23,511	221	0.9%	14,468
03/20	24,859	371	1.5%	14,562
03/19	23,843	376	1.6%	14,718
03/18	24,512	335	1.4%	14,629
Annual Growth	(3.5%)	(5.7%)	—	(0.6%)

2022 Year-End Financials

Debt ratio: —   No. of shares ($ mil.): 202
Return on equity: 6.6%   Dividends
Cash ($ mil.): 1,483   Yield: —
Current Ratio: 1.27   Payout: 0.0%
Long-term debt ($ mil.): —   Market value ($ mil.): —

Alibaba Group Holding Ltd

The group operates four operating segments: Core Commerce (over 85% of sales), Cloud Computing (about 10%), Digital Media and Entertainment (some 5%), and Innovation Initiatives and others. The Core Commerce segment is comprised of platforms operating in retail and wholesale commerce in China, retail and wholesale commerce ? cross-border and global, logistics services, local consumer services and others. The Cloud Computing segment is comprised of Alibaba Cloud, which offers a complete suite of cloud services to customers worldwide, including elastic computing, database, storage, network virtualization services, large scale computing, security, management and application services, big data analytics, a machine learning platform and IoT services.

Operations

The group operates four operating segments: Core Commerce (over 85% of sales), Cloud Computing (about 10%), Digital Media and Entertainment (some 5%), and Innovation Initiatives and others.

The Core Commerce segment is comprised of platforms operating in retail and wholesale commerce in China, retail and wholesale commerce ? cross-border and global, logistics services, local consumer services and others.

The Cloud Computing segment is comprised of Alibaba Cloud, which offers a complete suite of cloud services to customers worldwide, including elastic computing, database, storage, network virtualization services, large scale computing, security, management and application services, big data analytics, a machine learning platform and IoT services.

The Digital Media and Entertainment businesses leverage its deep data insights to serve the broader interests of consumer through its key distribution platform, Youku, and through Alibaba Pictures and its other diverse content platforms that provide online videos, films, live events, news feeds, literature and music, among other areas.

The Innovation Initiatives and others segment includes businesses such as Amap, DingTalk, Tmall Genie and others.

Geographic Reach

Headquartered in Zheijiang Province, China, Alibaba has other offices in mainland China, Hong Kong S.A.R., Singapore and the US. It maintains data centers in a number of countries including China, Indonesia, Malaysia, India, Australia, Singapore, Dubai, Germany, the UK, Japan, and the US.

Sales and Marketing

As Taobao Marketplace is China's largest mobile commerce destination, with a large and growing social community and an exceptionally wide range of product offerings, and Tmall is the world's largest third-party online and mobile commerce platform for brands and retailers, Alibaba wide consumer recognition of its brands and enjoy significant organic traffic through word-of-mouth.

Financial Performance

Total revenue increased by 41% from RMB509.7 billion in the fiscal year 2020 to RMB717.3 billion in the fiscal year 2021. The increase was mainly driven by revenue growth across all its business segments.

As a result of the foregoing, the Alibaba Group's net income increased by 2% from RMB140.4 billion in the fiscal year 2020 to RMB143.3 billion in the fiscal year 2021.

Cash held by the Alibaba Group at the end of fiscal year 2021 increased to RMB356.5 billion. Cash provided by operations and financing activities were RMB231.8 billion and RMB30.1 billion, respectively. Cash used for investing activities was RMB244.2 billion, mainly due to an increase in short-term investments, net.

Strategy

Alibaba continues to innovate in the areas of business models, products and services, and technology to create value for both consumers and businesses. It is focused on the following key areas: Drive User Growth and Engagement; Empower Businesses to Facilitate Digital Transformation and Improve Operational Efficiency; and Continue to Innovate.

Alibaba Group Holding intends to further address the consumption needs of users in less developed areas, and to provide individuals at different income levels with access to quality merchandise and services suitable to their consumption capabilities.

The group also intends to make its offerings available to more users outside of China as the group implements its globalization initiatives. Starting with Southeast Asia, Alibaba Group Holdings aims to serve users around the world with localized operations as well as cross-border commerce with access to Chinese manufacturers and consumers.

The group's diverse commerce platforms and extensive consumer insights, combined with its cloud computing technologies, New Retail supply chain management and sales and marketing systems, form a critical foundation that facilitates digital transformation for businesses. Alibaba Group Holdings refer to this foundation as the Alibaba Business Operating System, or ABOS.

Mergers and Acquisitions

In 2020, Alibaba Group acquired additional effective equity interest in Sun Art for a cash consideration of $3.6 billion (RMB24.1 billion). Upon the completion of the transaction, the group's effective equity interest in Sun Art increased to approximately 67% and Sun Art became a consolidated subsidiary of the group. In late 2020, the Alibaba Group acquired additional ordinary shares of Sun Art from public shareholders for a cash consideration of HK$4.9 billion (RMB4.1 billion) through a mandatory general offer as required under the Hong Kong Code on Takeovers and Mergers, which resulted in a reduction in noncontrolling interests amounting to RMB4.6 billion. Upon the completion of the mandatory general offer, the group's effective equity interest in Sun Art further increased to approximately 74%.

EXECUTIVES

Chief Executive Officer, Chairman, Director, Daniel Yong Zhang
Executive Vice-Chairman, Joseph Chung Tsai
President, Director, J. Michael Evans
Chief Financial Officer, Toby Hong Xu
Chief People Officer, Jane Fang Jiang
Chief Technology Officer, Zeming Wu
General Counsel, Sara Siying Yu
Industrial E-commerce Chief Executive Officer, Community E-commerce Chief Executive Officer, Taobao and Tmall Group Chief Executive Officer, Trudy Shan Dai
Independent Director, Wan Ling Martello
Independent Director, Weijian Shan
Independent Director, Irene Yun-Lien Lee
Independent Director, Albert Kong Ping Ng
Independent Director, Kabir Misra
Director, Maggie Wei Wu
Independent Director, Jerry Yang
Auditors : PricewaterhouseCoopers

LOCATIONS

HQ: Alibaba Group Holding Ltd
26/F Tower One, Times Square, 1 Matheson Street, Causeway Bay,
Phone: (852) 2215 5100 **Fax:** (852) 2215 5200
Web: www.alibabagroup.com

PRODUCTS/OPERATIONS

2016 Sales

	% of total
China commerce	
Retail	79
Wholesale	4
International commerce	
Retail	2
Wholesale	6
Cloud computing	3
Others	6
Total	**100**

HISTORICAL FINANCIALS

Company Type: Public

Income Statement   FYE: March 31

	REVENUE ($mil)	NET INCOME ($mil)	NET PROFIT MARGIN	EMPLOYEES
03/23	126,358	10,586	8.4%	235,216
03/22	134,497	9,814	7.3%	254,941
03/21	109,499	22,986	21.0%	251,462
03/20	71,805	21,051	29.3%	117,600
03/19	56,135	13,091	23.3%	101,958
Annual Growth	22.5%	(5.2%)		23.2%

2023 Year-End Financials

Debt ratio: 1.3%   No. of shares ($ mil.): 20,526
Return on equity: 7.4%   Dividends
Cash ($ mil.): 28,085   Yield: —
Current Ratio: 1.81   Payout: 0.0%
Long-term debt ($ mil.): 21,686   Market value ($ mil.): 2,097,348

	STOCK PRICE ($) FY Close	P/E High/Low	PER SHARE ($) Earnings	Dividends	Book Value
03/23	102.18	34 19	0.50	0.00	7.08
03/22	108.80	88 27	0.45	0.00	7.07
03/21	226.73	47 29	1.04	0.00	6.66
03/20	194.48	32 20	0.98	0.00	5.01
03/19	182.45	47 32	0.62	0.00	3.59
Annual Growth	(13.5%)		(5.3%)		18.5%

Alimentation Couche-Tard Inc

Alimentation Couche-Tard is a global leader in the convenience sector across the globe, operating the brands Couche-Tard, Circle K and Ingo. The company offers fast and friendly service, providing convenience products; including food and hot and cold beverages, and mobility services, including road transportation fuel and charging solutions for electric vehicles. While most of its sales are rung up in the US, it operates in Europe, as well as about 15 countries in other parts of the world through license agreements. Most of the company's revenue comes from sales of road transportation fuel. Alimentation Couche-Tard, which is French for "food for those who go to bed late," has expanded through acquisitions around the world.

Operations

In Couche-Tard's global operations, Circle K, Couche-Tard, and Ingo have been its key brands.

In-store merchandise sales primarily comprise the sale of tobacco products and alternative tobacco products, beverages, beer, wine, fresh food offerings including quick service restaurants, candy and snacks and grocery items. These revenues are recognized at the time of the transaction since control of goods and services is considered transferred when customer makes payment and takes possession of the sold item. Merchandise sales also include the wholesale of merchandise and goods to certain independent operators and franchisees made from its distribution centers and commissaries, which are generally recognized upon delivery to its customers. Service revenues primarily include car wash revenues, commissions on the sale of lottery tickets, fees from automatic teller machines, sales of calling cards, sales of gift cards and revenues from electric vehicles charging stations.

Overall, road transportation fuel brings in more than 70% of the company's revenue, while merchandise and services accounts for over 25%.

Geographic Reach

Headquartered in Quebec, Canada, Couche-Tard's network is comprised of about 9,095 convenience stores throughout North America, including more than 7,980 stores with road transportation fuel dispensing. Its North American network consists of over 15 business units, including nearly 15 in the US covering more than 45 states and three in Canada covering all 10 provinces. The company has operations throughout the Scandinavian countries (Norway, Sweden, and Denmark), in the Baltic countries (Estonia, Latvia, and Lithuania), as well as in Ireland, and have an important presence in Poland. Under licensing agreements, more than 1,800 stores are operated under the Circle K banner in about 15 other countries and territories (Cambodia, Egypt, Guam, Guatemala, Honduras, Indonesia, Jamaica, Macau, Mexico, New Zealand, Saudi Arabia, the United Arab Emirates, and Vietnam), which brings the worldwide total network to more than 14,000 stores.

The US generates about 65% of company's revenue. Europe and other region provides about 20% and the remainder comprised of Canada's revenue.

Sales and Marketing

The company launched its EasyPay loyalty program in all US markets, providing everyday fuel discounts to its most loyal customer. Couche-Tard recognizes sales of merchandise and goods to certain independent operators and franchisees made from the company's distribution centers and sales of road transportation fuel upon delivery to its customers.

Financial Performance

The company had a total revenue of $62.8 billion in 2022, a 37% increase from the previous year's total revenue of $45.8 billion.

In 2022, the company had net earnings of $2.68 billion, a 1% decrease from the previous year's net earnings of $2.7 billion.

The company's cash at the end of 2022 was $2.1 billion. Operating activities generated $3.9 billion, while investing activities used $1.8 billion, mainly for purchase of property and equipment, intangible assets and other assets. Financing activities used another $3 billion, primarily for share repurchases.

Strategy

For fiscal 2023, as the company reaches the last milestone of its 5-year strategy, the company will continue to enhance its offer to meet its customer's needs, making their lives a little easier every day. Despite supply chain and labor challenges, the company remains focused on its convenience and mobility business by refining its fresh food program, pursuing opportunities to expand the flexibility in the company's supply chain and growing its electric vehicles offer to keep the company's position as a global leader in the future of electric charging solutions. The company stands ready to seek out additional acquisition opportunities and nurture the culture of discipline and entrepreneurship that has been its trademark as it is close to reaching its five-year ambition of doubling the business. In this rapidly evolving environment, the roll out of the Values We Live By and actions taken toward them are proofs of the company's commitment into increasing employee engagement, diversity and inclusion as well as sustainability which remains at the forefront of its priorities and a lens to the business.

Mergers and Acquisitions

In late 2021, Couche-Tard acquired approximately 19 convenience stores and two non-operating properties across the state of New Mexico. The assets are owned and operated by Pic Quik, a successful company originally founded in 1958. With this acquisition, the company will be able to build on its strong network in the state and grow its mission of making its customers' lives a little easier every day.

In-mid 2021, Couche-Tard announced it is moving forward with a binding agreement for the acquisition of convenience and fuel retail sites from ARS Fresno LLC and certain affiliated companies. The transaction includes approximately 35 high quality locations currently operated under the Porter's brand and located predominately in Oregon and Western Washington. "We are excited to bring the Porter's stores and team members into the Couche-Tard family. These locations have strong fuel and convenience assets with a track record of growth and a network of experienced employees. With this transaction, we look forward to growing in the pacific northwest and making our customers' lives a little easier everyday in that region." said Brian Hannasch, President and Chief Executive Officer of Alimentation Couche-Tard.

EXECUTIVES

Executive Chairman, Director, Alain Bouchard
President, Chief Executive Officer, Director, Brian P. Hannasch
Chief Technology Officer, Deborah Hall Lefevre
Chief Marketing Officer, Kevin A. Lewis
Chief People Officer, Ina Strand
Chief Financial Officer, Claude Tessier
Development and Construction, North America Executive Vice President, Darrell L. Davis
Operations, Europe Executive Vice President, Hans-Olav Hoidahl
Operations, North America, and Global Commercial Optimization Executive Vice President, Timothy Alexander Miller
Operations Senior Vice President, Niall Anderton
Operations Senior Vice President, Brian Bednarz
Global Shared Services Senior Vice President, Kathleen K. Cunnington
Operations Senior Vice President, Rick Johnson
Operations Senior Vice President, Jorn Madsen
Merchandising Senior Vice President,
Operations Senior Vice President, Dennis Tewell
Operations Senior Vice President, Stephane Trudel
Global Fuels Senior Vice President, Andrew Brewer
Senior Vice President, General Counsel, Corporate Secretary, Valery Zamuner
Lead Director, Melanie Kau
Director, Jean Bernier
Director, Eric Boyko
Director, Jacques D'Amours
Director, Richard Fortin
Director, Marie-Josee Lamothe
Director, Janice L. Fields
Director, Monique F. Leroux
Director, Real Plourde
Director, Daniel Rabinowicz
Director, Louis Tetu
Auditors : PricewaterhouseCoopers LLP

LOCATIONS

HQ: Alimentation Couche-Tard Inc
4204 boul. Industriel, Laval, Quebec H7L 0E3
Phone: 450 662-6632   **Fax:** 450 662-6630
Web: www.corpo.couche-tard.com

2018 Sales

	$ mil.	% of total
US	34,178	67
Europe	10,315	20
Canada	6,901	13
Total	51,394	100

PRODUCTS/OPERATIONS

2018 Sales

	$ mil.	% of total
Road Transportation Fuel	37,116	72
Merchandise and Services	12,976	25
Other	1,302	3
Total	51,394	100

HOOVER'S HANDBOOK OF WORLD BUSINESS 2024

COMPETITORS

7-ELEVEN, INC
AHOLD U.S.A., INC.
ARO LIQUIDATION, INC.
CASEY'S GENERAL STORES, INC.
CST BRANDS, LLC
DELHAIZE AMERICA, LLC
EG GROUP LIMITED
SUPERVALU INC.
VILLAGE SUPER MARKET, INC.
WOOLWORTHS GROUP LIMITED

HISTORICAL FINANCIALS

Company Type: Public

Income Statement — FYE: April 30

	REVENUE ($mil)	NET INCOME ($mil)	NET PROFIT MARGIN	EMPLOYEES
04/23	71,856	3,090	4.3%	100,000
04/22	62,809	2,683	4.3%	26,000
04/21	45,760	2,705	5.9%	124,000
04/20	54,132	2,353	4.3%	131,000
04/19	59,117	1,833	3.1%	109,000
Annual Growth	5.0%	13.9%	—	(2.1%)

2023 Year-End Financials

Debt ratio: 20.3%
Return on equity: 24.3%
Cash ($ mil.): 834
Current Ratio: 1.10
Long-term debt ($ mil.): 5,888
No. of shares ($ mil.): 981
Dividends
Yield: —
Payout: 6.7%
Market value ($ mil.): 49,006

	STOCK PRICE ($) FY Close	P/E High/Low	PER SHARE ($) Earnings	Dividends	Book Value
04/23	49.94	17 13	3.06	0.21	12.80
Annual Growth					

Allianz SE

One of the world's biggest insurers, Allianz SE offers a range of insurance products and services ? including property-casualty, life/health, asset management, and corporate ? through subsidiaries, ventures, and affiliates operating all over the globe (Allianz SE and its subsidiaries are collectively known as the Allianz Group). Based in Munich, Germany, the company serves some 126 million customers in such key markets as France, Morocco, Italy, Luxembourg, Switzerland, and the US. In addition to selling insurance, Allianz provides retail and institutional asset management services through Allianz Asset Management, private equity investment through Allianz Capital Partners.

Operations

Allianz primarily operates through three business segments ? life/health, property/casualty, and asset management ? which are further divided, primarily by geography, into eleven reportable segments.

The company offers a wide range of property-casualty and life/health insurance, motor, accident, property, general liability, travel insurances, and assistance services. The life/health business segment offers savings and investment products in addition to life and health policies. Allianz generates 50% to 55% of its revenue from its life/health segment. The property/casualty segment accounts for more than 40% of revenue. These two segments do most of their business in France, Germany, Italy, and the US.

The asset management segment, which generates roughly 5% of revenue, is a global provider of institutional and retail asset management products and services to third-party investors. It also provides investment management services to the Allianz Group's insurance operations. The products for retail and institutional customers include equity and fixed-income funds as well as multi-assets and alternative products. The United States, Canada, Europe, and the Asia-Pacific region represent the primary asset management markets. In all, around 30% were generated from German Speaking Countries and Central & Eastern Europe, about 30% from Western & Southern Europe and Asia Pacific, nearly 20% from Global Insurance Lines & Anglo Markets, Middle East and Africa, about 10% each from Iberia & Latin America and Allianz Partners, and USA, and the rest are from asset management.

Geographic Reach

Headquartered in Munich, Germany, Allianz operates in more than 70 countries, with most of its operations in Europe. It also operates in the Asia Pacific region, Africa, and the Americas, and operates its business from Munich and from branch offices in Rome (Italy), Casablanca (Morocco), Singapore, Labuan (Malaysia), Wallisellen (Switzerland), Vienna (Austria), and Dublin (Ireland).

Sales and Marketing

The company offers its products and services to about 126 million customers in more than 70 countries.

Financial Performance

Allianz' revenues grew by almost 6% to EUR149 billion and its operating profit increased by 25% to EUR13.4 billion. These results were driven by a strong performance across all its businesses. In the company's Property-Casualty business, Allianz generated solid revenues of EUR62.3 billion and an operating profit of EUR5.7 billion.

Allianz' cash at the end of 2021 was EUR24.2 billion. Operating activities generated EUR25.1 billion, while investing activities used EUR19.8 billion. Financing activities used another EUR3.8 billion.

Strategy

Allianz continues to drive initiatives addressing the five dimensions of its Renewal Agenda: Customer Centricity, Digital by Default, Technical Excellence, Growth Engines and Inclusive Meritocracy. To realize its growth ambition and accelerate the company's value creation, it has defined five additional strategic areas of focus:

Transforming the Life/Health and Asset Management franchise: Fully address protection and savings needs and accelerate transformation to a capital efficient model, both leveraging its strengths in Asset Management.

Expanding Property & Casualty leadership position: Beat the best players in each market, building on productivity gains and scale, in retail motor and beyond.

Boosting growth through scalable platforms: Scale the company's customer-facing platforms and build new operating platforms to grow its business volume and margin.

Deepening the global vertical integration and execution of agility: Verticalize operating models across lines of business to unleash value from skills and scale.

Reinforcing capital productivity and resilience: Retain industry-leading financial strength and unlock further value creation potential through an improved risk/return profile and an active management and reduction of tail risk exposure.

Mergers and Acquisitions

In early 2022, Allianz Real Estate has acquired a brand new LEED Platinum & WELL Gold office complex in Barcelona in an off-market transaction from seller Meridia Capital, a leading Spanish fund manager and real estate investment specialist. The 29,000 sqm asset, composed of two buildings of 13 and seven floors, is located in the 22@ business district, an established sub-market attracting prime tenants looking for modern, adaptable Class A offices not available in Barcelona's traditional CBD. Terms were not disclosed.

Also in early 2022, Allianz Ayudhya Capital PCL (AYUD) has entered into an agreement to acquire 100% of shares of Aetna Thailand, a prominent player in the Thai health insurance market. The acquisition reaffirms the company's commitment to further invest and expand its health insurance business to benefit customers in Thailand. Terms were not disclosed.

Also in 2022, Allianz Real Estate, acting on behalf of several Allianz group companies, has acquired a new, Grade A, 70,000 sqm logistics facility in Norrköping, Sweden, for approx. EUR 85 million from Infrahubs Holding, a leading Swedish logistics developer. The newly completed asset is located in the logistics 'golden triangle' connecting the four Nordic capitals of Copenhagen, Oslo, Helsinki and Stockholm. It is situated in a strategic micro location in Norrköping, with a major motorway, harbor, rail connection and airport all within a 15-minute drive. It is fully let to prime tenant PostNord on a long-term lease. Terms were not disclosed.

In late 2021, Allianz acquired a majority stake in Jubilee Insurance Company of Uganda Limited, East Africa's largest insurance group. The stake acquired by Allianz represents 29,700,000 ordinary shares of Jubilee Insurance Company of Uganda. JHL will retain a 34% stake, or 15,300,000 ordinary shares, in the company. The General Business of Jubilee Insurance Company of Uganda Limited will change its name in due course to Jubilee Allianz General Insurance Company Limited, subject to approvals.

Also in late 2021, Allianz acquired Aviva Italia S.p.A., the Italian property & casualty (P&C) insurance entity of the Aviva Group, from Aviva Italia Holding S.p.A. The transaction, which is worth about 330 million euros, involved a portfolio equally distributed between motor and non-motor business segments with gross written premiums of about 400 million euros. The completion of the transaction further strengthens Allianz S.p.A.'s No.3 position in the Italian P&C insurance industry, increasing the company's market share by approximately one percentage point.

In mid-2021, Allianz Australia announced the completion of the transaction to acquire Westpac's general insurance business, and commenced a 20-year exclusive agreement to distribute general insurance products to Westpac customers. As part of the agreement, more than 350 Westpac general insurance employees have now officially joined Allianz, bringing with them a suite of talents and industry knowledge that will help Allianz to continue to grow and innovate. The agreement, worth A$725 million, sees the expansion of Allianz's product offering available through Westpac.

Company Background

In 1890, Allianz is founded in Munich, Germany by insurance specialist Carl Thieme and banker Wilhelm Finck. In 1893, Allianz opened its office in London for international operations headed by Carl Schreiner. By the year 1938, the employee strength reached to a number of 24,000. The Munich headquarters of Allianz was destroyed by bombs during the World War II. The expansions went through with the establishment of more branches in many countries of the world like Spain, Brazil, the Netherlands.

HISTORY

Carl Thieme founded Allianz in Germany in 1890. That year the company took part in the creation of the Calamity Association of Accident Insurance Companies, a consortium of German, Austrian, Swiss, and Russian firms, to insure international commerce.

By 1898 Thieme had established offices in the UK, Switzerland, and the Netherlands. His successor, Paul von der Nahmer, expanded Allianz into the Balkans, France, Italy, Scandinavia, and the US. After a hiatus during WWI, Allianz returned to foreign markets.

In WWII, Allianz insured Auschwitz, Dachau, and other death camps. Company documents show Allianz wasn't worried about risk at the SS troop-guarded camps. After the German defeat, the victors seized Allianz's foreign holdings, except for a stake in Spain's Plus Ultra. In the 1950s Allianz repurchased confiscated holdings in Italian and Austrian companies.

Allianz saturated the German market and began a full-scale international drive in the late 1950s and 1960s. It became Europe's largest insurer through a series of acquisitions beginning in 1973. Allianz formed Los Angeles-based Allianz Insurance in 1977.

In 1981 Allianz launched a takeover (which turned hostile) of the UK's Eagle Star insurance company. After a 1983 bidding joust with Britain's B.A.T Industries (now part of Zurich Financial Services), Allianz withdrew.

The firm consoled itself by shopping. In 1984 it won control of Riunione Adriatica di Sicurtà (Ras), Italy's second-largest insurance company. Two years later the firm bought Cornhill (now Allianz Insurance plc) on its third try. As the Iron Curtain crumbled, Allianz in 1989 acquired 49% of Hungaria Biztosito. Its drang nach Osten continued the next year after national reunification, when it gained control of Deutsche Versicherungs AG, East Germany's insurance monopoly. Allianz that year became the first German insurer licensed in Japan; it also bought the US's Fireman's Fund Insurance.

Natural disasters led to large claims and set the company back in 1992, the first time in 20 years it lost money from its German operations. Allianz restructured operations that year; profits surged in 1993, mostly from international business.

Allianz expanded in Mexico in 1995, forming a life and health insurance joint venture with Grupo Financiero BanCrecer (now owned by Grupo Financiero Banorte). The company set up an asset management arm in Hong Kong in 1996 with an eye to further Asian expansion, getting a license in China the next year. In 1997 after Holocaust survivors sued Allianz and other insurers for failing to pay on life policies after WWII, Allianz agreed to participate in a repayment fund.

In 1998 Allianz bought control of Assurances Générales de France; it was the white knight that prevented Assicurazioni Generali from taking the company. In 1999 Allianz said it would restructure some of its insurance operations, including spinning off its marine and aviation lines, to better compete in the multinational market. That year US subsidiary Allianz Life bought Life USA Holding. In 2000 Allianz bought 70% of PIMCO Advisors Holdings to strengthen its asset management operations. That year the company continued its push into Asia, buying a 12% stake in Hana Bank of South Korea and planning to boost its ownership of Malaysia British Assurance Life. Also in 2000 Allianz acquired Dutch insurer Zwolsche Algemeene.

Allianz remained acquisitive in 2001, buying US investment manager Nicholas-Applegate and taking a majority stake in ROSNO, one of Russia's largest insurers. Also that year it bought a nearly 96% stake in German banking giant Dresdner and acquired the remainder the following year.

Allianz paid out claims of some $1.3 billion relating to the terrorist attacks on the World Trade Center. The company set up a terrorism insurance unit, offering coverage primarily for companies within the European Union.

EXECUTIVES

Chief Executive Officer, Oliver Bate
Management Board Member, Sergio Balbinot
Management Board Member, Sirma Baoshnakova
Management Board Member, Barbara Karuth-Zelle
Management Board Member, Klaus-Peter Rohler
Management Board Member, Ivan De La Sota
Management Board Member, Giulio Terzariol
Management Board Member, Gunther Thallinger
Management Board Member, Christopher G. Townsend
Management Board Member, Renate Wagner
Management Board Member, Andreas Wimmer
Chairman, Michael Diekmann
Vice-Chairwoman, Gabriele Burkhardt-Berg
Vice-Chairman, Director, Herbert Hainer
Director, Primiano Di Paolo
Director, Sophie Boissard
Director, Christine Bosse
Director, Rashmy Chatterjee
Director, Friedrich Eichiner
Director, Jean-Clade Le Goaer
Director, Martina Grundler
Director, Frank Kirsch
Director, Jurgen Lawrenz
Auditors : PricewaterhouseCoopers GmbH Wirtschaftsprüfungsgesellschaft

LOCATIONS

HQ: Allianz SE
Königinstrasse 28, Munich 80802
Phone: (49) 89 38 00 0 **Fax:** (49) 89 38 00 3425
Web: www.allianz.com

2018 sales

	% of total
Western & Southern Europe	32
US	11
Germany	27
Specialty insurance	16
Growth markets	9
Broker markets	4
Total	100

PRODUCTS/OPERATIONS

2018 sales

	% of total
Life/Health	54
Property/Casualty	41
Asset Management	5
Total	100,

Selected Operations and Brands
Allianz
Allianz Global Corporate and Specialty
Allianz Global Investors
Allianz Worldwide Care
Euler Hermes

PIMCO

COMPETITORS

AEGON N.V.
AMERICAN INTERNATIONAL GROUP, INC.
AVIVA PLC
AXA
Generali Deutschland AG
PRUDENTIAL PUBLIC LIMITED COMPANY
RSA INSURANCE GROUP PLC
STANDARD LIFE ABERDEEN PLC
Talanx AG
Zurich Insurance Group AG

HISTORICAL FINANCIALS

Company Type: Public

Income Statement   FYE: December 31

	ASSETS ($mil)	NET INCOME ($mil)	INCOME AS % OF ASSETS	EMPLOYEES
12/22	1,091,010	7,196	0.7%	159,253
12/21	1,289,680	7,481	0.6%	155,411
12/20	1,300,940	8,354	0.6%	150,269
12/19	1,135,320	8,885	0.8%	147,268
12/18	1,027,890	8,545	0.8%	142,460
Annual Growth	1.5%	(4.2%)	—	2.8%

2022 Year-End Financials

Return on assets: 0.6%
Return on equity: 10.2%
Long-term debt ($ mil.): —
No. of shares ($ mil.): 401
Sales ($ mil.): 111,600
Dividends
 Yield: —
 Payout: 4.5%
Market value ($ mil.): 8,614

	STOCK PRICE ($) FY Close	P/E High/Low	PER SHARE ($) Earnings	Dividends	Book Value
12/22	21.45	2 1	17.37	0.80	136.90
12/21	23.61	2 1	17.92	0.81	221.68
12/20	24.65	2 1	20.03	0.72	240.73
Annual Growth	(6.7%)	—	(3.5%)	2.7%	(13.2%)

Alpek SAB de CV

EXECUTIVES

Chief Executive Officer, Jose de Jesus Valdez Simancas
Chief Financial Officer, Jose Carlos Pons de la Garza
Human Capital Senior Vice President, Armando Ramos Cantu
Chairman, Armando Garza Sada
Director, Ana Laura Magaloni
Director, Francisco Jose Calderon Rojas
Director, Alvaro Fernandez Garza
Director, Rodrigo Fernandez Martinez
Director, Francisco Rogelio Garza Egloff
Director, Andres E. Garza Herrera
Director, Merici Garza Sada
Director, Pierre Francis Haas Garcia
Director, Jose Antonio Rivero Larrea
Director, Enrique Zambrano Benitez
Director, Jaime Zabludovsky Kuper
Auditors : Galaz, Yamazaki, Ruiz Urquiza, S.C.

LOCATIONS

HQ: Alpek SAB de CV
 Avenida Gomez Morin Sur No. 1111, Col. Carrizalejo, San Pedro Garza García, Nuevo Leon 66254
Phone: —
Web: www.alpek.com

HISTORICAL FINANCIALS

Company Type: Public

Income Statement   FYE: December 31

	REVENUE ($mil)	NET INCOME ($mil)	NET PROFIT MARGIN	EMPLOYEES
12/22	10,856	702	6.5%	0
12/21	7,640	379	5.0%	0
12/20	5,736	157	2.7%	6,200
12/19	6,325	349	5.5%	6,004
12/18	6,841	693	10.1%	5,797
Annual Growth	12.2%	0.3%	—	—

2022 Year-End Financials

Debt ratio: 1.5%
Return on equity: 30.3%
Cash ($ mil.): 322
Current Ratio: 1.47
Long-term debt ($ mil.): 1,603
No. of shares ($ mil.): 2,107
Dividends
 Yield: —
 Payout: 2.6%
Market value ($ mil.): —

Alpha Services & Holdings SA

Alpha Bank is the second-largest bank in Greece (after National Bank of Greece). It provides business and personal banking services through more than 650 branches in Greece and hundreds more in Cyprus, Albania, Bulgaria, Romania, Serbia, and Ukraine, as well as in New York, London, and Jersey in the UK Channel Islands. In addition to loans, deposit accounts, and credit cards, the Alpha Bank group also offers retail banking, asset management, investment banking, private banking, insurance, brokerage, leasing, and factoring. Founded in 1879, Alpha Bank has been buffeted by economic turmoil in Greece. Still, it acquired Emporiki Bank S.A. from Crédit Agricole in mid-2013.

EXECUTIVES

Growth and Innovation General Manager, Executive Director, Spyros N. Filaretos
Chief Executive Officer, Executive Director, Vassilios E. Psaltis
Chief Risk Officer General Manager, Spyridon A. Andronikakis
Chief Financial Officer General Manager, Lazaros A. Papagaryfallou
Chief Legal and Governance Officer General Manager, Nikolaos V. Salakas
Chief Transformation Officer General Manager, Anastasia Ch. Sakellariou
Chief Operating Officer General Manager, Stefanos N. Mytilinaios
Secretary, Eirini E. Tzanakaki
Non-Executive Chairman, Vasileios T. Rapanos
Independent Non-Executive Director, Dimitris C. Tsitsiragos
Independent Non-Executive Director, Jean L. Cheval
Independent Non-Executive Director, Carolyn G. Dittmeier
Independent Non-Executive Director, Richard R. Gildea
Independent Non-Executive Director, Elanor R. Hardwick
Independent Non-Executive Director, Shahzad A. Shahbaz
Independent Non-Executive Director, Jan A. Vanhevel
Non-Executive Director, Efthimios O. Vidalis
Non-Executive Director, Johannes Herman Frederik G. Umbgrove
Auditors : Deloitte Certified Public Accountants S.A.

LOCATIONS

HQ: Alpha Services & Holdings SA
 40 Stadiou Street, Athens GR-102 52
Phone: (30) 210 326 0000   **Fax:** (30) 210 326 5438
Web: www.alpha.gr

2015 Sales

	% of total
Greece	84
Other countries	16
Total	100

PRODUCTS/OPERATIONS

2015 Gross Sales

	% of total
Retail banking	47
Corporate banking	36
South Eastern Europe	14
Asset management and insurance	3
Total	100

2015 Sales

	% of total
Interest and similar income	87
Fee and commission income	11
Other income	2
Total	100

Selected Services

Bancassurance
Business Banking
Cards
Consumer Loans
Deposit Accounts
Housing Loans
Investment Products
Private Banking

COMPETITORS

ABC INTERNATIONAL BANK PLC
BANK OF CYPRUS PUBLIC COMPANY LIMITED
EMPORIKI BANK OF GREECE S.A.
EUROBANK ERGASIAS SERVICES AND HOLDINGS S.A.
Ing Belgique
OTP Bank Nyrt.
PIRAEUS FINANCIAL HOLDINGS S.A.
THE ROYAL BANK OF SCOTLAND INTERNATIONAL LTD
Volkswagen Bank Gesellschaft mit beschränkter Haftung
Wüstenrot & Württembergische AG

HISTORICAL FINANCIALS

Company Type: Public

Income Statement — FYE: December 31

	ASSETS ($mil)	NET INCOME ($mil)	INCOME AS % OF ASSETS	EMPLOYEES
12/22	83,327	424	0.5%	8,460
12/21	83,028	(3,289)	—	8,939
12/20	85,979	127	0.1%	10,528
12/19	71,248	108	0.2%	10,530
12/18	69,864	60	0.1%	11,314
Annual Growth	4.5%	62.7%	—	(7.0%)

2022 Year-End Financials

Return on assets: 0.5%
Return on equity: 6.4%
Long-term debt ($ mil.): —
No. of shares ($ mil.): 2,348
Sales ($ mil.): 3,131
Dividends Yield: —
Payout: 0.5%
Market value ($ mil.): 552

	STOCK PRICE ($) FY Close	P/E High/Low		PER SHARE ($) Earnings	Dividends	Book Value
12/22	0.23	2	1	0.18	0.00	2.85
12/21	0.31	—	—	(1.70)	0.00	2.92
12/20	0.29	9	2	0.08	0.00	6.60
12/19	0.56	9	4	0.07	0.00	6.14
12/18	0.29	21	9	0.03	0.00	6.02
Annual Growth	(4.9%)	—	—	51.4%	—	(17.1%)

AltaGas Ltd

AltaGas is a Canada-based energy infrastructure company that gathers, generates, processes, stores and sells natural gas and NGLs to customers across North America. Altgas serves approximately 1.7 million customers across Virginia, Maryland, Michigan, the District of Columbia, and Alaska. The company transacts more than 1.2 billion cubic feet (bcf) of natural gas and NGLs, including gas gathering and processing, NGL extraction and fractionation, logistics, liquids handling, and global export. About 75% of the company's total sales comes from the US. AltaGas was founded in 1994.

Operations

AltaGas operates in mainly two segments, Utilities and Midstream.

The Utilities segment, which accounts for 35% of the company's revenue, owns and operates franchised, cost-of-service, rate-regulated natural gas distribution and storage utilities that are focused on providing safe, reliable, and affordable energy to its customers.

The Midstream segment (about 65%) is the North American platform connects customers and market. This includes wellhead to tidewater, focused on providing customers with safe and reliable service and connectivity that facilitates the best outcome for the customers' businesses.

The Corporate/Other segment consists of the company's corporate activities and a small portfolio of gas-fired power generation and distribution assets capable of generating 508 MW of power primarily in the state of California.

Geographic Reach

AltaGas generates about 65% of the company's revenue from Canada, with the US accounting for the remainder.

Sales and Marketing

AltaGas sells natural gas and power directly to some 1.7 million residential, commercial, and industrial customers.

Financial Performance

AltaGas' performance for the past five years has increased year-over-year with 2022 as its highest performing year over the period.

The company's revenue increased by $3.5 billion to $14.1 billion in 2022, an increase from 2021's revenue of $10.6 billion.

AltaGas net income for fiscal year end 2022 also increased to $523 million, as compared to the prior year's net income of $283 million.

Cash held by the company at the end of the year was at $64 million. Operating activities generated $539 million. Investing activities used $997 million, while financing activities provided $435 million. Main cash uses were for capital expenditures for property, plant, and equipment, as well as repayment of long-term debt.

Strategy

The majority of 2022 capital expenditures are expected to focus on projects within the Utilities platform that are anticipated to deliver stable and transparent rate base growth, positive risk-adjusted returns, and safe, reliable service for customers.

In 2022, AltaGas' capital expenditures for the Utilities segment will focus primarily on accelerated pipe replacement programs, customer growth, and system betterment. In the Midstream segment, capital expenditures are anticipated to primarily relate to facility turnarounds, maintenance and administrative capital, optimization of existing assets, investment in Environment, Social & Governance (ESG) initiatives, and new business development.

Mergers and Acquisitions

In mid-2022, AltaGas announced the purchase of 25.97% equity ownership of Petrogas Energy Corp. from Idemitsu Canada Corporation, a wholly owned subsidiary of Idemitsu Kosan Co., Ltd., for total cash considerations of C$285 million. The Petrogas acquisition, along with the planned sale of AltaGas' Alaska Utilities that was announced in late May, is representative of the Company's opportunistic capital recycling strategy to achieve corporate objectives and create long-term value for all stakeholders, as has been demonstrated over the past three years.

Company Background

AltaGas was founded in 1994.

EXECUTIVES

Chief Financial Officer, Executive Vice President, D. James Harbilas
Chief Administrative Officer, Executive Vice President, Corine R. K. Bushfield
Chief Legal Officer, Executive Vice President, Bradley B. Grant
Executive Vice President, Randy W. Toone
Utilities Executive Vice President, Utilities President, Donald M. Jenkins
Commercial Strategy and Business Development Executive Vice President, Fredrick K. Dalena
Chief Executive Officer, Director, Randall L. Crawford
Independent Non-Executive Chairman, Pentti O. Karkkainen
Independent Director, Victoria A. Calvert
Independent Director, David W. Cornhill
Independent Director, Allan L. Edgeworth
Independent Director, Daryl H. Gilbert
Independent Director, Robert B. Hodgins
Independent Director, Cynthia Johnston
Independent Director, Phillip R. Knoll
Independent Director, Linda G. Sullivan
Independent Director, Nancy G. Tower
Director, Terry D. McCallister
Auditors: Ernst & Young LLP

LOCATIONS

HQ: AltaGas Ltd
1700, 355 - 4th Avenue S.W., Calgary, Alberta T2P 0J1
Phone: —
Web: www.altagas.ca

2014 Sales

	% of total
Canada	66
U.S.	34
Total	100

PRODUCTS/OPERATIONS

2014 Net Sales

	% of total
Utilities	41
Power	15
Gas	44
Total	100

COMPETITORS

ATMOS ENERGY CORPORATION
CHESAPEAKE ENERGY CORPORATION
CIMAREX ENERGY CO.
DOMINION ENERGY QUESTAR CORPORATION
ENLINK MIDSTREAM, INC.
Enbridge Inc
NRG ENERGY, INC.
OVINTIV EXPLORATION INC.
SOUTHWESTERN ENERGY COMPANY
WPX ENERGY, INC.

HISTORICAL FINANCIALS
Company Type: Public

Income Statement FYE: December 31

	REVENUE ($mil)	NET INCOME ($mil)	NET PROFIT MARGIN	EMPLOYEES
12/22	10,416	386	3.7%	3,045
12/21	8,301	222	2.7%	2,926
12/20	4,387	15	0.4%	2,984
12/19	4,219	5	0.1%	2,801
12/18	3,125	(13)	—	2,881
Annual Growth	35.1%	—	—	1.4%

2022 Year-End Financials
Debt ratio: 28.8% No. of shares ($ mil.): 281
Return on equity: 7.2% Dividends
Cash ($ mil.): 39 Yield: —
Current Ratio: 1.36 Payout: 75.1%
Long-term debt ($ mil.): 6,428 Market value ($ mil.): 4,842

	STOCK PRICE ($) FY Close	P/E High/Low	PER SHARE ($) Earnings	Dividends	Book Value
12/22	17.20	16 12	1.04	0.78	19.58
12/21	21.64	26 18	0.64	0.78	19.47
12/20	14.72	10 4	1.37	0.76	19.79
12/19	15.22	6 4	2.13	0.74	19.85
12/18	10.14	— —	(1.65)	1.53	18.73
Annual Growth	14.1%	— —	—	(15.4%)	1.1%

Aluminum Corp of China Ltd.

EXECUTIVES

Executive Director, President, Runzhou Zhu
Chief Financial Officer, Secretary, Non-Executive Director, Jun Wang
Supervisor, Shulan Shan
Staff Supervisor, Xiaoguang Guan
Staff Supervisor, Xuguang Yue
Supervisory Committee Chairman, Guohua Ye
Independent Non-Executive Director, Lijie Chen
Independent Non-executive Director, Shihai Hu
Chairman (Acting), Non-executive Director, Hong Ao
Independent Non-executive Director, Dazhuang Li
Auditors : Ernst & Young Hua Ming LLP

LOCATIONS

HQ: Aluminum Corp of China Ltd.
  No. 62, North Xizhimen Street, Haidian District, Beijing 100082
Phone: (86) 10 8229 8560 **Fax:** (86) 10 8229 8158
Web: www.chalco.com.cn

HISTORICAL FINANCIALS
Company Type: Public

Income Statement FYE: December 31

	REVENUE ($mil)	NET INCOME ($mil)	NET PROFIT MARGIN	EMPLOYEES
12/22	42,180	607	1.4%	0
12/21	42,489	800	1.9%	0
12/20	28,438	113	0.4%	0
12/19	27,316	122	0.4%	0
12/18	26,204	126	0.5%	65,211
Annual Growth	12.6%	48.0%	—	—

2022 Year-End Financials
Debt ratio: 5.1% No. of shares ($ mil.): —
Return on equity: 7.5% Dividends
Cash ($ mil.): 2,791 Yield: —
Current Ratio: 0.87 Payout: 263.2%
Long-term debt ($ mil.): 7,158 Market value ($ mil.): —

	STOCK PRICE ($) FY Close	P/E High/Low	PER SHARE ($) Earnings	Dividends	Book Value
12/22	10.28	72 30	0.03	0.09	0.00
12/21	13.73	83 27	0.05	0.00	0.00
12/20	8.68	353 180	0.00	0.00	0.00
12/19	8.69	290 193	0.01	0.00	0.00
12/18	7.82	415 171	0.01	0.00	0.00
Annual Growth	7.1%	— —	—	52.6%	—

Ambev SA

EXECUTIVES

Co-Chairman, Carlos Alves de Brito
Co-Chairman, Victorio Carlos de Marchi
Chief Sales and Marketing Officer, Chief Executive Officer, Jean Jereissati Neto
Investor Relations and Shared Services Officer Chief Financial Officer, Investor Relations and Shared Services Officer Officer, Lucas Machado Lira
Legal and Compliance Executive Officer, Leticia Rudge Barbosa Kina
Sales Executive Officer, Sales Chief People Officer, Ricardo Morais Pereira de Melo
Commercial Executive Officer, Eduardo Braga Cavalcanti de Lacerda
Supply Executive Officer, Logistics Executive Officer, Supply Chief Industrial Officer, Logistics Chief Industrial Officer, Mauricio Nogueira Soufen
Logistics Executive Officer, Paulo Andre Zagman
Corporate Affairs Executive Officer, Ricardo Goncalves Melo
Procurement Executive Officer, Rodrigo Figueiredo de Souza
Information Technology Chief Technology Officer, Information Technology Executive Officer, Eduardo Eiji Horai
Marketing Executive Officer, Daniel Wakswaser Cordeiro
Non-Alcoholic Beverages Executive Officer, Pablo Firpo
Sales Chief Sales Officer, Sales Executive Officer, Daniel Cocenzo

Director, Milton Seligman
Director, Roberto Moses Thompson Motta
Director, Lia Machado de Matos
Director, Fernando Mommensohn Tennenbaum
Director, Fabio Colletti Barbosa
Director, Vicente Falconi Campos
Director, Nelson Jose Jamel
Independent Director, Claudia Quintella Woods
Independent Director, Antonio Carlos Augusto Ribeiro Bonchristiano
Independent Director, Marcos de Barros Lisboa
Alternate Director, Michel Dimitrios Doukeris
Alternate Director, Carlos Eduardo Klutzenschell Lisboa
Auditors : PricewaterhouseCoopers Auditores Independentes Ltda

LOCATIONS

HQ: Ambev SA
  Rua Dr. Renato Paes de Barros, 1017 - 3rd Floor, Sao Paulo 04530-001
Phone: (55) 11 2122 1200
Web: www.ambev.com.br

HISTORICAL FINANCIALS
Company Type: Public

Income Statement FYE: December 31

	REVENUE ($mil)	NET INCOME ($mil)	NET PROFIT MARGIN	EMPLOYEES
12/21	13,073	2,273	17.4%	52,806
12/20	11,240	2,191	19.5%	50,479
12/19	13,085	2,930	22.4%	51,352
12/18	12,942	2,840	21.9%	49,617
12/17	14,459	2,213	15.3%	51,432
Annual Growth	(2.5%)	0.7%	—	0.7%

2021 Year-End Financials
Debt ratio: 0.1% No. of shares ($ mil.): 15,738
Return on equity: 16.1% Dividends
Cash ($ mil.): 2,983 Yield: 3.8%
Current Ratio: 0.99 Payout: 77.0%
Long-term debt ($ mil.): 47 Market value ($ mil.): 44,068

	STOCK PRICE ($) FY Close	P/E High/Low	PER SHARE ($) Earnings	Dividends	Book Value
12/21	2.80	4 3	0.14	0.11	0.94
12/20	3.06	5 3	0.14	0.07	0.90
12/19	4.66	7 5	0.18	0.10	0.97
12/18	3.92	9 5	0.18	0.13	0.92
12/17	6.46	14 10	0.14	0.15	0.88
Annual Growth	(18.9%)	— —	0.8%	(7.8%)	1.6%

Amcor plc

Amcor is a global leader in developing and producing responsible packaging for food, beverage, pharmaceutical, medical, home and personal-care, and other products. It divides business into two segments, Flexibles and Rigid Packaging. The reportable segments produce flexible packaging, rigid packaging, specialty cartons, and closure products, which are sold to customers participating in a range of attractive end use areas throughout Europe,

North America, Latin America, Africa, and the Asia Pacific regions. About 50% of Amcor's revenue comes from North America. Its history dates to the 1860s when Samuel Ramsden, a young stone mason from Yorkshire, arrived in Australia with his bride to seek his fortune.

Operations

The company's business is organized and presented in the two reportable segments: Flexibles and Rigid Packaging.

Flexibles segment accounts for more than 75% of revenue and manufactures flexible and film packaging in the food and beverage, medical and pharmaceutical, fresh produce, snack food, personal care, and other industries.

Rigid Packaging (nearly 25%) makes rigid containers for a broad range of predominantly beverage and food products, including carbonated soft drinks, water, juices, sports drinks, milk-based beverages, spirits and beer, sauces, dressings, spreads and personal care items, and plastic caps for a wide variety of applications.

Geographic Reach

Based in Zurich, Switzerland, Amcor operates through a sprawling network of around 220 sites spanning some 45 countries.

It caters to a diverse group of regions: North America (accounts for nearly 50% of revenue), Europe (around 30%), Latin America (more than 10%) and Asia Pacific (some 10%).

Sales and Marketing

The company's sales are made through a variety of distribution channels, but primarily through its direct sales force. Its technically trained sales force is supported by product development engineers, design technicians, field service technicians, and customer service teams.

Financial Performance

Net sales increased by $1.7 billion, or by 13% to $14.5 billion in fiscal year 2022, compared to fiscal year 2021.

In 2021, the company had a net income of $815 million, a 14% decrease from the previous year's net income of $951 million.

The company's cash at the end of 2021 was $775 million. Operating activities generated $1.5 billion, while investing activities used $527 million, mainly for purchase of property, plant, and equipment, and other intangible assets. Financing activities used another $891 million, primarily for repayment of long-term debt.

Strategy

The company's business strategy consists of three components: a focused portfolio, differentiated capabilities, and its aspiration to be the leading global packaging company. To fulfill this aspiration, it is determined to win for customers, employees, shareholders, and the environment.

Focused portfolio. The company's portfolio of businesses share certain important characteristics:

A focus on primary packaging for fast-moving consumer goods,

Good industry structure,

Attractive relative growth, and

Multiple paths for the company to win through its leadership position, scale, and ability to differentiate its product offering through innovation.

Company Background

Amcor's beginnings can be traced to the 1860s when Samuel Ramsden established a paper mill in Melbourne. The company's predecessor, Australian Paper Manufacturers (APM) Ltd., was established by the 1926 merger of some of Australia's more significant paper companies, including the Australian Paper Mills Company and Sydney Paper Mills. APM, the name by which the company was known until it was changed to Amcor in 1986, began producing pulp in 1938.

During WWII, 70% of APM's production was dedicated to the manufacture of ammunition and war equipment, but the company continued to expand its paper mills. At the close of the war, it was the country's largest paper and pulp company and had a monopoly on Australia's wrapping paper and board markets.

APM expanded its paper offerings during the 1960s to include tissue products when it formed Kimberly-Clark Australia, a joint venture with US-based Kimberly-Clark. The late 1970s, however, brought about significant diversification for the company when APM purchased Brown & Dureau, a company with holdings in international trading, automotive, retailing, and aviation industries. APM continued to expand its operations during the 1980s with acquisitions that included Containers Packaging (1982) and James Hardie Containers (1986). Also in 1986 the APM changed its name to Amcor Limited and made a slew of plant acquisitions from companies such as Reed Corrugated Containers, J Fielding & Co., United Packages, and Tasmanian Fibre Containers.

HISTORY

Amcor's beginnings can be traced to the 1860s when Samuel Ramsden established a paper mill in Melbourne. The company's predecessor, Australian Paper Manufacturers (APM) Ltd., was established by the 1926 merger of some of Australia's more significant paper companies, including the Australian Paper Mills Company and Sydney Paper Mills. APM, the name by which the company was known until it was changed to Amcor in 1986, began producing pulp in 1938.

During WWII, 70% of APM's production was dedicated to the manufacture of ammunition and war equipment, but the company continued to expand its paper mills. At the close of the war, it was the country's largest paper and pulp company and had a monopoly on Australia's wrapping paper and board markets.

APM expanded its paper offerings during the 1960s to include tissue products when it formed Kimberly-Clark Australia, a joint venture with US-based Kimberly-Clark. The late 1970s, however, brought about significant diversification for the company when APM purchased Brown & Dureau, a company with holdings in international trading, automotive, retailing, and aviation industries. APM continued to expand its operations during the 1980s with acquisitions that included Containers Packaging (1982) and James Hardie Containers (1986). Also in 1986 the APM changed its name to Amcor Limited and made a slew of plant acquisitions from companies such as Reed Corrugated Containers, J Fielding & Co., United Packages, and Tasmanian Fibre Containers.

EXECUTIVES

Chairman, Independent Non-Executive Director, Graeme R. Liebelt

Finance Executive Vice President, Finance Chief Financial Officer, Michael Casamento

Amcor Flexibles Europe, Middle East and Africa President, Peter Konieczny

Amcor Rigid Plastics President, Michael Schmitt

Amcor Rigid Packaging President, Eric V. Roegner

Strategic Development Executive Vice President, Ian G. Wilson

Secretary, Julie F. McPherson

Corporate Secretary, Corporate General Counsel, Corporate Vice President, Rebecca Farrell

Finance Chief Executive Officer, Finance Managing Director, Director, Ronald S. Delia

Independent Non-Executive Director, Deputy Chairman, Armin Meyer

Independent Non-Executive Director, Karen J. Guerra

Independent Non-Executive Director, Jeremy L. Sutcliffe

Director, Andrea Bertone

Director, Nicholas Tom Long

Director, David T. Szczupak

Director, Phillip Weaver

Director, Arun Nayar

Auditors : PricewaterhouseCoopers AG

LOCATIONS

HQ: Amcor plc
83 Tower Road North, Warmley, Bristol BS30 8XP
Phone: (44) 117 975 3200
Web: www.amcor.com

2015 Sales

	% of total
Western Europe	32
North America	31
Australia & New Zealand	5
Emerging markets	32
Total	100

PRODUCTS/OPERATIONS

2018 Sales	% of total
Flexibles	70
Rigid Plastics	30
Total	100

Selected Products Boxes Cartons Fiber packaging Glass packaging Wine bottles Metal packaging Cans Closures Packaging papers Plastic packaging Closures Flexibles Plastic bottles, jars, and containers

COMPETITORS

AGI-SHOREWOOD GROUP US, LLC
AMCOR FLEXIBLES NORTH AMERICA, INC.
GRAPHIC PACKAGING HOLDING COMPANY
GREIF, INC.
H. S. CROCKER COMPANY, INC.
Hong Kong Sainuo International Co., Ltd. Shanghai Representative Office
LDI LTD., LLC
PACKAGING DYNAMICS CORPORATION
SONOCO PRODUCTS COMPANY
TSL ENGINEERED PRODUCTS, LLC

HISTORICAL FINANCIALS
Company Type: Public

Income Statement — FYE: June 30

	REVENUE ($mil)	NET INCOME ($mil)	NET PROFIT MARGIN	EMPLOYEES
06/23	14,694	1,048	7.1%	35,000
06/22	14,544	805	5.5%	37,000
06/21	12,861	939	7.3%	39,000
06/20	12,467	612	4.9%	47,000
06/19	9,458	430	4.5%	50,000
Annual Growth	11.6%	24.9%	—	(8.5%)

2023 Year-End Financials

Debt ratio: 39.7%
Return on equity: 25.8%
Cash ($ mil.): 689
Current Ratio: 1.19
Long-term debt ($ mil.): 6,653
No. of shares ($ mil.): 1,447
Dividends
  Yield: —
  Payout: 0.0%
Market value ($ mil.): —

America Movil SAB de CV

AmÃ©rica MÃ³vil is Latin America's leading telecommunications services provider with about 286.5 million subscribers in some 25 countries. In Mexico, the company has about 80.5 million wireless subscribers to its Telcel and Telmex brands. Its second largest market is Brazil, where it has some 70.5 million subscribers through Claro. AmÃ©rica MÃ³vil also provides fixed-line service in Central America and the Caribbean. While the company's operations are centered in Latin America, in Eastern Europe through A1. The company also offers broadband, Pay TV, and IT services. Billionaire Carlos Slim HelÃº owns most of AmÃ©rica MÃ³vil. About 40% of its revenue is generated in Mexico.

Operations

The company provides telecommunications services which include mobile and fixed-line voice services, wireless and fixed data services, internet access and Pay TV, over the top and other related services. The company also sells equipment, accessories and computers.

Its voice services provided by the company, both wireless and fixed, mainly include the following: airtime, local, domestic and international long-distance services, and network interconnection services. Data services include value added, corporate networks, data and internet services. Pay TV represents basic services, as well as pay per view and additional programming and advertising services. AMX provides other related services to advertising in telephone directories, publishing and call center services. The company also provides video, audio and other media content that is delivered through the internet directly from the content provider to the end user.

Overall, about 85% of sales were generated from its services, while equipment accounts for the rest.

Geographic Reach

The company generates about 40% of revenue from Mexico, with Brazil accounting for more than 15%, and Colombia generates roughly 10% of revenue.

The company's other markets are the Southern Cone (Argentina, Chile, Paraguay and Uruguay) and Europe (Austria, Belarus, Bulgaria, Croatia, Macedonia, Serbia and Slovenia). Those regions combine for approximately 20% combined of revenue. The remaining revenue (about 25% combined revenues) comes from the Andean Region (Ecuador and Peru), Central America (Costa Rica, El Salvador, Guatemala, Honduras, Nicaragua, and Panama), and the Caribbean (the Dominican Republic and Puerto Rico).

The company is headquartered in Mexico.

Sales and Marketing

AmÃ©rica MÃ³vil reaches customers through a network of retailers and service centers for retail customers and a dedicated sales force for corporate customers. The company counts some 402,000 points of sale and more than 3,300 customer service centers. America Movil's subsidiaries also sell their services and products online.

For the years ended 2019, 2020, and 2021, advertising expenses were M$13.1 million, M$11.2 million and M$12.0 million, respectively

Financial Performance

The company reported an operating revenue of M$855.5 billion in 2021, a 2% increase from the previous year's operating revenue of M$839.7 billion.

In 2021, the company had a net income of M$4.6 billion, a 16% increase from the previous year's net income of M$4 billion.

The company's cash at the end of 2021 was M$38.7 billion. Operating activities generated M$258.2 billion, while investing activities used M$76.5 billion, primarily for purchase of property, plant and equipment. Financing activities used another M$177.4 billion, primarily for repayment of loans.

Strategy

America Movil continues to seek ways to optimize its portfolio, including by finding investment opportunities in telecommunications and related companies worldwide, including in markets where the company are already present, and it often have several possible acquisitions under consideration. The company may pursue opportunities in Latin America or in other areas in the world.

In late 2021, the company announced that it entered into an agreement with Cable & Wireless Panama, S.A., an affiliate of Liberty Latin America LTD., to sell 100% of its interest in the company's subsidiary Claro Panama, S.A. The transaction excludes (i) all telecommunication towers owned indirectly by AmÃ©rica MÃ³vil in Panama and (ii) the Claro trademarks. The agreed purchase price is US$200 million on a cash/ debt free basis. The closing of the transaction is subject to customary conditions for this type of transactions, including obtaining required governmental approvals.

Mergers and Acquisitions

In early 2022, AmÃ©rica MÃ³vil and its Brazilian subsidiary Claro S.A. closed the acquisition of its portion of Grupo Oi's Brazilian assets pursuant to the purchase agreement entered between Grupo Oi, as seller, and Claro, TelefÃ³nica Brasil S.A. and TIM S.A., as purchasers. Claro will pay R$3,572 milllion brazilian reais as total consideration for such acquisition. In addition, Claro has paid R$188 milllion brazilian reais for transition services to be provided by Grupo Oi to Claro during the following twelve months. The transaction creates additional value for Claro, its clientes and its shareholders, through increased growth, generation of operating efficiencies and improvements in service quality.

Company Background

AmÃ©rica MÃ³vil was formed in 2000 from a spinoff from Telmex, which was at the time Mexico's largest local and long-distance phone service provider. In late 2006, AmÃ©rica MÃ³vil acquired majority owner AmÃ©rica Telecom in a move to streamline the structure of the company and to free up assets for share buybacks or dividends.

HISTORY

The company was formed in 2000 as a result of a spinoff from Telmex, which was at the time Mexico's largest local and long-distance phone service provider. In late 2006, AmÃ©rica MÃ³vil acquired majority owner AmÃ©rica Telecom in a move to streamline the structure of the company and to free up assets for share buybacks or dividends.

The company expanded its presence in the Caribbean region in 2007 with the acquisition of Puerto Rico Telephone from Verizon Communications and a handful of other shareholders for nearly $2 billion. The next year it bought Jamaican wireless service provider Oceanic Digital Jamaica and became licenced to provide wireless services in Panama.

Also in 2008, the company rebranded its operations in Argentina, Paraguay, and Uruguay to its Claro brand, which América Móvil now uses for all of its operations in Central America and the Caribbean. That year it bought Estesa Holding, a cable TV and data services provider in Nicaragua, for $48 million. The acquisition of Estesa boosted América Móvil's cable television and broadband offerings and gave the company greater access to the Nicaraguan market.

EXECUTIVES

Chief Executive Officer, Director, Daniel Hajj Aboumrad
Chief Financial Officer, Carlos Jose Garcia Moreno Elizondo
General Counsel, Corporate Secretary, Alejandro Cantu Jimenez
Chief Fixed-line Operations Officer, Director, Oscar Von Hauske Solis
Chief Wireless Operations Officer, Angel Alija Guerrero
Corporate Pro-Secretary, Rafael Robles Miaja
Chairman, Carlos Slim Domit
Vice-Chairman, Patrick Slim Domit
Independent Director, Director, Ernesto Vega Velasco
Independent Director, Director, Pablo Roberto Gonzalez Guajardo
Independent Director, Director, David Ibarra Munoz
Independent Director, Director, Antonio Cosio Pando
Independent Director, Director, Rafael Moises Kalach Mizrahi
Independent Director, Director, Luis Alejandro Soberon Kuri
Independent Director, Director, Francisco Medina Chavez
Director, Arturo Elias Ayub
Director, Vanessa Hajj Slim
Auditors : Mancera, S.C.

LOCATIONS

HQ: America Movil SAB de CV
Lago Zurich 245, Plaza Carso/Edificio Telcel, Colonia Ampliacion Granada, Mexico City, Miguel Hidalgo 11529
Phone: (52) 55 2581 3700 **Fax:** (52) 55 2581 4422
Web: www.americamovil.com

2015 Sales

	% of total
Mexico wireless	22
Brazil	19
US	12
Mexico fixed	11
Southern cone	8
Europe	8
Colombia	7
Andean region	6
Central America	4
Caribbean	3
Total	100

PRODUCTS/OPERATIONS

2018 Sales

	% of total
Mexico Wireless	21
Brazil	18
US	14
Southern Cone	10
Europe	9
Telmex	9
Colombia	7
Andean Region	5
Central America	4
Caribbean	3
Total	100

2018 Sales

	% of total
Services	83%
Equipment	17%
Total	

Selected Operations

América Móvil Peru (8.3 million subscribers)
AM Wireless Uruguay (800,000 subscribers)
AMX Argentina (17 million subscribers)
AMX Paraguay (500,000 subscribers)
Claro Chile (3.6 million subscribers)
Claro Panama (100,000 subscribers)
Codetel (Dominican Republic, 4.8 million subscribers)
Comcel (Colombia, 27.7 million subscribers)
Conecel (Ecuador, 9.4 million subscribers)
CTE (El Salvador, 800,000 subscribers)
ENITEL (Nicaragua, 2.2 million subscribers)
Oceanic (Jamaica, 400,000 subscribers)
Sercom Honduras (1.4 million subscribers)
TELPRI (Puerto Rico 1.6 million subscribers)
TracFone (US, 14.4 million subscribers)
Telgua (Guatemala, 1.2 million subscribers)

COMPETITORS

AT&T INC.
Altice Europe N.V.
CELLNEX TELECOM SA.
GLOBANT S.A.
ILIAD
LIBERTY GLOBAL PLC
MILLICOM INTERNATIONAL CELLULAR S.A.
SBA COMMUNICATIONS CORPORATION
TELEFONICA, SA
VODAFONE GROUP PUBLIC LIMITED COMPANY

HISTORICAL FINANCIALS

Company Type: Public

Income Statement   FYE: December 31

	REVENUE ($mil)	NET INCOME ($mil)	NET PROFIT MARGIN	EMPLOYEES
12/22	43,160	3,892	9.0%	176,014
12/21	41,842	9,410	22.5%	181,205
12/20	51,179	2,358	4.6%	186,851
12/19	53,243	3,579	6.7%	191,523
12/18	52,797	2,673	5.1%	194,431
Annual Growth	(4.9%)	9.8%	—	(2.5%)

2022 Year-End Financials

Debt ratio: 1.6%   No. of shares ($ mil.): 63,325
Return on equity: 19.9%   Dividends
Cash ($ mil.): 1,722   Yield: —
Current Ratio: 0.74   Payout: 36.9%
Long-term debt ($ mil.): 20,880 Market value ($ mil.): —

AMMB Holdings BHD

From the a.m. to the p.m., AmBank Group is on the job, providing financial services to customers throughout Malaysia. AMMB Holdings (which trades as AmBank Group) controls dozens of subsidiaries and affiliates, providing individuals and businesses with a range of financial services and products through some 175 offices. The company operates in several segments: retail, business, and investment banking; insurance; and Islamic financial services. Services include asset management, commercial banking, futures trading, leasing, mortgage lending, offshore banking, property trust management, retail financing, and securities services.

EXECUTIVES

Chief Internal Auditor, Kim Mon Thein
Chief Operating Officer, Ross Neil Foden
Chief Risk Officer, Nigel Christopher William Denby
Chief Financial Officer, Mandy Simpson
Chief Information Officer, Charles Keng Lock Tan
Secretary, Phaik Gunn Koid
Non-Independent Non-Executive Director, Shayne Cary Elliott
Non-Independent Non-Executive Director, Gilles Plante
Independent Non-Executive Director, Clifford Francis Herbert
Independent Non-Executive Director, Larry Nyap Liou Gan
Non-Independent Non-Executive Director, Mark David Whelan
Non-Independent Non-Executive Director, Kim Wai Soo
Auditors : Messrs Ernst & Young PLT

LOCATIONS

HQ: AMMB Holdings BHD
22nd Floor, Bangunan AmBank Group, No. 55, Jalan Raja Chulan, Kuala Lumpur 50200
Phone: (60) 3 2036 2633   **Fax:** (60) 3 2032 1914
Web: www.ambankgroup.com

COMPETITORS

AXA ADVISORS, LLC
CORCENTRIC, LLC
NEWABLE INVESTMENTS LIMITED
Siemens Financial Services GmbH
W.H. IRELAND GROUP PLC

HISTORICAL FINANCIALS

Company Type: Public

Income Statement   FYE: March 31

	ASSETS ($mil)	NET INCOME ($mil)	INCOME AS % OF ASSETS	EMPLOYEES
03/21	41,041	(922)	—	0
03/20	39,184	310	0.8%	0
03/19	38,908	368	0.9%	0
03/18	35,679	292	0.8%	10,000
03/17	30,438	299	1.0%	10,672
Annual Growth	7.8%	—	—	—

2021 Year-End Financials

Return on assets: (-2.2%)   Dividends
Return on equity: (-23.0%)   Yield: —
Long-term debt ($ mil.): —   Payout: 0.0%
No. of shares ($ mil.): 3,008   Market value ($ mil.): —
Sales ($ mil.): 389

Ampol Ltd

Ampol Limited supplies the country's largest branded petrol and convenience network as well as refining, importing and marketing fuels and lubricants. Ampol supplies fuel to around 80,000 customers in diverse markets across the Australian economy, including defence, mining, transport, marine, agriculture, aviation and other commercial sectors. Across its retail network, Ampol serves more than three million customers every week with fuel and convenience products. Its ability to service its broad customer base is supported by its robust supply chain and strategic infrastructure positions across the country, which includes more than 25 terminals, five major pipelines, over 55 depots, around 1,925 branded sites, and one refinery located in Lytton, Queensland.

Operations
The company operates through two reportable segments: Fuels and Infrastructure and Convenience Retail.

The Fuels and Infrastructure segment (over 75%) includes revenues and costs associated with the integrated wholesale fuels and lubricants supply for the company, including the nternational businesses. This includes Lytton refining, Bulk Fuels sales, Trading and Shipping, Infrastructure, and the Gull and Seaoil businesses.

The Convenience Retail segment (about 25% of revenue) includes revenues and costs associated with fuels and shop offerings at Ampol's network of stores, including royalties and franchise fees on remaining franchise stores.

Overall, Diesel accounted for nearly 50% the company's total revenues; petrol for about 30%; and jet fuel, over 5%.

Geographic Reach
The company operates in Australia, New Zealand, and Singapore.

Its sourcing capabilities and geographic reach have significantly expanded in recent years, with strong growth observed in third-party fuel volumes in 2020 and storage in the South East Asian region providing scope for our Trading and Shipping business to deliver strong returns on working capital in volatile market conditions.

Sales and Marketing
The recently established Houston office has been supporting Ampol's Singapore team with investigating new international markets and identifying sourcing improvement opportunities, and they will continue to work together to identify further growth potential. Its Trading and Shipping operations play a key role in our success, sourcing petroleum products from global markets that connect to customer needs in both Australia and other international markets.

The company has interests in associates primarily for the marketing, sale and distribution of fuel products. It has interests in joint arrangements primarily for the marketing, sale and distribution of fuel products and the operation of convenience stores.

Financial Performance
Revenue from the sale of goods was $15 billion in 2020 compared to $22.1 billion in the prior year. Total revenue decreased due to a 17% decline in Australian sales volumes resulting from reduced demand as a result of the COVID-19 pandemic. Australian Dollar product prices are also on average 34% lower than 2019. Lower product prices in 2020 were driven by lower weighted average Dated Brent crude oil price (2020: US$42/bbl vs 2019: US$64/bbl).

Net loss after tax attributable to equity holders of the parent entity was $484.9 million in 2020 compared to a net profit of $382.8 million in 2019. There was an inventory loss of $360 million after tax or $514 million before tax in 2020. Over time revenues will increase/decrease as the price of products changes, this includes impacts from the AUD/USD exchange rate movements.

Cash at the end of fiscal year 2020 was $367.6 million. Operations and investing activities provided $267.6 million and $462.6 million, respectively, while financing activities used $391.8 million mainly for repayment of borrowings.

Strategy
The revitalization of the iconic Ampol brand is a key part of the company's business strategy. It provides a unique opportunity to re-engage its people, reinforce its customer connections and redefine the identity of the company. As it looks towards its future and executing its strategy, the reinvigoration of Ampol allows the company to enhance its market-leading position in transport fuels, execute on the convenience market opportunity and reaffirm its commitment to communities.

As the company delivers the rebrand works across its retail network, it is refreshing the shopfronts of its company-controlled sites to align with its format strategy. This includes transitioning its shops to its Foodary brand and the continued rollout of its Ampol Woolworths Metro format.

The company had made strong progress since it announced the return of Ampol in December 2019. It opened its first two Ampol retail sites in Sydney in August, with a total of 26 sites rebranded across the country in 2020. It is on track to rebrand its entire network of more than 1,900 sites by the end of 2022.

In 2020, Ampol reached several milestones in its International growth strategy, with the opening of a new Trading and Shipping office in Houston and the expansion of its international storage program supported by favourable market conditions.

Company Background
Growing its business to keep up with demand, in 2011 Caltex Australia dissolved the Vitalgas Pty Ltd joint venture agreement by acquiring the stake held by Origin Energy Holdings for $4.1 million. The unit then became Calgas Pty Ltd.

It also bought Graham Bailey Pty Ltd for $19.1 million. Bailey is Australia's leading provider of marine fuel, remote infrastructure, and related services, with operations in all major Australian ports and a network of 16 sites from the south of Western Australia through to Darwin, in the Northern Territories.

EXECUTIVES

Managing Director, Chief Executive Officer, Executive Director, Matthew Halliday
Chief Financial Officer, Greg Barnes
Z Energy Executive General Manager, Michael Bennetts
Fuels and Infrastructure Executive General Manager, Andrew Brewer
International and New Business Executive General Manager, Brent Merrick
Retail Australia Executive General Manager, Kate Thomson
Chairman, Independent Non-Executive Director, Steven Gregg
Independent Non-Executive Director, Simon Allen
Independent Non-Executive Director, Mark P. Chellew
Independent Non-Executive Director, Melinda Conrad
Independent Non-Executive Director, Elizabeth Donaghey
Independent Non-Executive Director, Michael Ihlein
Independent Non-Executive Director, Gary Smith
Independent Non-Executive Director, Penny Winn
Auditors: KPMG

LOCATIONS

HQ: Ampol Ltd
29-33 Bourke Road, Alexandria, New South Wales 2015
Phone: 800 240 398
Web: www.ampol.com.au

PRODUCTS/OPERATIONS

2011 Sales

	% of total
Refining & supply	53
Marketing	47
Total	100

Major Subsidiaries
Caltex Australia Petroleum Pty Ltd
Caltex Lubricating Oil Refinery Pty Ltd
Caltex Petroleum Distributors Pty Ltd
Caltex Refineries (NSW) Pty Ltd
Caltex Refineries (Qld) Pty Ltd

COMPETITORS

ADAMS RESOURCES & ENERGY, INC.
COMPANHIA BRASILEIRA DE PETROLEO IPIRANGA
CROSSAMERICA PARTNERS LP
GLOBAL PARTNERS LP
MACQUARIE INFRASTRUCTURE CORPORATION
PAKISTAN STATE OIL COMPANY LIMITED

RS ENERGY K.K.
SASOL LTD
SPRAGUE RESOURCES LP
WORLD FUEL SERVICES CORPORATION

HISTORICAL FINANCIALS
Company Type: Public

Income Statement   FYE: December 31

	REVENUE ($mil)	NET INCOME ($mil)	NET PROFIT MARGIN	EMPLOYEES
12/22	26,173	541	2.1%	8,790
12/21	15,682	406	2.6%	0
12/20	11,924	(375)	—	8,200
12/19	15,645	268	1.7%	7,644
12/18	15,338	395	2.6%	6,629
Annual Growth	14.3%	8.2%	—	7.3%

2022 Year-End Financials
Debt ratio: 12.7%   No. of shares ($ mil.): 238
Return on equity: 23.7%   Dividends
Cash ($ mil.): 85   Yield: —
Current Ratio: 1.16   Payout: 89.1%
Long-term debt ($ mil.): 1,458   Market value ($ mil.): 9,382

	STOCK PRICE ($) FY Close	P/E High/Low	Earnings	Dividends	Book Value
12/22	39.37	15 11	2.26	2.02	10.36
12/21	43.43	20 16	1.69	1.01	9.35
12/20	44.00	— —	(1.50)	1.00	9.15
12/19	44.00	— —	1.06	1.22	9.15
12/18	44.00	— —	1.52	1.56	9.13
Annual Growth	(2.7%)	—	10.5%	6.5%	3.2%

ANA Holdings Inc

ANA Holdings is the parent of All Nippon Airways, one of Japan's leading carriers along with Japan Airlines. With a fleet of more than 305 aircraft, ANA flies to around 100 airports worldwide. It extends its network through code-sharing with members of the Star Alliance, an airline marketing partnership that includes such carriers as United Continental's United Airlines and Continental, and Lufthansa. (Code-sharing enables airlines to sell tickets on one another's flights.) Besides passenger service, ANA's air transportation operations include cargo and mail hauling and aircraft maintenance and ground support. The company also sells travel packages and operates hotels. Majority of its sales were generated from Japan.

Operations
ANA's reportable segments are Air Transportation (some 70% of net sales), Airline Related (around 15%), Trade and Retail (over 5%), and Travel Services (about 5%).

Air Transportation conducts domestic and International passenger operations, cargo and mail operations, and other transportation services. Airline Related conducts air transportation-related operations, such as airport passenger and ground handling services and maintenance services.

Trade and Retail conducts mainly imports and exports goods related to air transportation and is involved in in-store and non-store retailing. Travel Services conducts operations centering on the development and sales of travel plans. It also conducts planning and sales of branded travel packages using air transportation.

Geographic Reach
Headquartered in Tokyo, Japan, the company also has operations in the Americas, Europe, China, and Asia. Over 70% of sales were generated from Japan, while it generated about 30% from overseas.

Financial Performance
The company reported a revenue of Â¥1 trillion, a 1197% increase from the previous year's total revenue of Â¥728.7 billion.

In 2021, the company had a net loss of Â¥143.6 billion, a 65% improvement from the previous year's net loss of Â¥404.3 billion.

The company's cash at the end of 2021 was Â¥621 billion. Investing activities generated Â¥230 billion, while investing activities used Â¥76.4 billion. Financing activities provided another Â¥93.6 billion.

Company Background
Two domestic Japanese air carriers that started in 1952 -- Nippon Helicopter and Aeroplane Transport and Far East Airlines -- consolidated operations in 1957 as All Nippon Airways (ANA).

EXECUTIVES
Chairman, Representative Director, Shinya Katanozaka
Vice-Chairman, Director, Yuji Hirako
President, Representative Director, Koji Shibata
Executive Vice President, Representative Director, Ichiro Fukuzawa
Director, Juichi Hirasawa
Director, Emiko Kajita
Director, Shinichi Inoue
Outside Director, Ado Yamamoto
Outside Director, Izumi Kobayashi
Outside Director, Eijiro Katsu
Outside Director, Masumi Minegishi
Auditors : Deloitte Touche Tohmatsu LLC

LOCATIONS
HQ: ANA Holdings Inc
1-5-2 Higashi-Shimbashi, Minato-ku, Tokyo 105-7140
Phone: (81) 3 6748 1001
Web: www.anahd.co.jp

2014 Sales
	% of total
Japan	86
Overseas	14
Total	100

PRODUCTS/OPERATIONS

2014 Sales
	% of total
Air transportation	73
Airline related	11
Travel services	8
Trade and Retail	6
Other businesses	2
Total	100

COMPETITORS
AIR FRANCE - KLM
ATLAS AIR WORLDWIDE HOLDINGS, INC.
Azul S/A
CATHAY PACIFIC AIRWAYS LIMITED
EASYJET PLC
Grupo Aeroportuario del Sureste, S.A.B. de C.V.
INTERNATIONAL CONSOLIDATED AIRLINES GROUP SA
SWISSPORT GB LIMITED
THOMAS COOK GROUP PLC
UNITED AIRLINES, INC.

HISTORICAL FINANCIALS
Company Type: Public

Income Statement   FYE: March 31

	REVENUE ($mil)	NET INCOME ($mil)	NET PROFIT MARGIN	EMPLOYEES
03/23	12,820	671	5.2%	42,794
03/22	8,388	(1,180)	—	44,221
03/21	6,581	(3,654)	—	49,607
03/20	18,187	254	1.4%	49,448
03/19	18,586	1,000	5.4%	47,074
Annual Growth	(8.9%)	(9.5%)	—	(2.4%)

2023 Year-End Financials
Debt ratio: 0.4%   No. of shares ($ mil.): 470
Return on equity: 10.7%   Dividends
Cash ($ mil.): 4,532   Yield: —
Current Ratio: 1.76   Payout: 0.0%
Long-term debt ($ mil.): 10,455   Market value ($ mil.): 2,054

	STOCK PRICE ($) FY Close	P/E High/Low	Earnings	Dividends	Book Value
03/23	4.37	0 0	1.28	0.00	13.76
03/22	4.13	— —	(2.51)	0.00	13.93
03/21	4.83	— —	(9.77)	0.00	19.33
03/20	5.06	0 0	0.76	0.14	29.19
03/19	7.42	0 0	2.99	0.11	29.65
Annual Growth	(12.4%)	—	(19.1%)	—	(17.5%)

Anglo American Platinum Ltd

Gold may glitter, but some see pizzazz in platinum. Anglo American Platinum (Amplats) which is 80%-owned by natural resources giant Anglo American, is the world's largest miner of platinum group metals, or PGMs, such as platinum, palladium, and rhodium. The company produces around 2.4 million ounces of platinum and about 1.4 million ounces of palladium annually. Its reserves include about 879 million ounces comprising platinum, palladium, rhodium, and gold. PGMs are used in catalytic converters, electronics, fuel cells, industrial processes (as catalysts), and jewelry. Amplats operates the Unki Mine in Zimbabwe, explores in Brazil through joint-ventures, and also has exploration activities in Russia.

EXECUTIVES

Chief Executive Officer, Executive Director, Natascha Viljoen

Finance Director, Executive Director, Craig W. Miller

Secretary, Elizna Viljoen

Chairman, Independent Non-Executive Director, Norman Bloe Mbazima

Lead Independent Non-Executive Director, Peter Mageza

Independent Non-Executive Director, Roger J. Dixon

Independent Non-Executive Director, Thabi Leoka

Independent Non-Executive Director, Nombulelo T. Moholi

Independent Non-Executive Director, Dhanasagree Naidoo

Independent Non-Executive Director, John M. Vice

Non-Executive Director, Nolitha Fakude

Non-Executive Director, Anik Michaud-Ahmed

Non-Executive Director, Duncan Graham Wanblad

Auditors: PricewaterhouseCoopers Inc.

LOCATIONS

HQ: Anglo American Platinum Ltd
 144 Oxford Road, Melrose, Rosebank 2196
Phone: (27) 11 373 6111 **Fax:** (27) 11 373 5111
Web: www.angloamericanplatinum.com

PRODUCTS/OPERATIONS

Business
Bathopele Mine
Khomanani Mine
Thembelani Mine
Khuseleka Mine
Siphumelele Mine
Tumela Mine
Dishaba Mine
Union Mine
Mogalakwena Mine
Unki Platinum Mine
Twickenham Platinum Mine
Der Brochen
Modikwa Platinum Mine
Aquarius Platinum Mine
Aquarius Platinum Mine
Mototolo Platinum Mine
Bafokeng-Rasimone Platinum Mine (BRPM)
Bokoni Platinum Mine
Pandora Mine
Process Operations
Concentrators
Smelters
Rustenburg Base Metals
Precious Metals Refiners
Group Performance Data
Products and Services
Platinum
Palladium
Rhodium
Ruthenium
Iridium
Cobalt sulphate
Copper
Nickel
Chrome ore

COMPETITORS

AMALGAMATED METAL CORPORATION PLC
Boliden AB
IMPALA PLATINUM HOLDINGS LTD
Industrias Peñoles, S.A.B. de C.V.
PETROPAVLOVSK PLC

HISTORICAL FINANCIALS

Company Type: Public

Income Statement   FYE: December 31

	REVENUE ($mil)	NET INCOME ($mil)	NET PROFIT MARGIN	EMPLOYEES
12/22	9,695	2,904	30.0%	0
12/21	13,457	4,953	36.8%	0
12/20	9,390	2,067	22.0%	0
12/19	7,088	1,317	18.6%	25,268
12/18	5,186	474	9.1%	24,789
Annual Growth	16.9%	57.3%	—	—

2022 Year-End Financials

Debt ratio: —
Return on equity: 49.4%
Cash ($ mil.): 1,748
Current Ratio: 1.55
Long-term debt ($ mil.): 1
No. of shares ($ mil.): 264
Dividends
 Yield: 0.1%
 Payout: 14.6%
Market value ($ mil.): 3,693

	STOCK PRICE ($) FY Close	P/E High/Low	PER SHARE ($) Earnings	Dividends	Book Value
12/22	13.95	0 0	11.02	1.62	21.60
12/21	19.32	0 0	18.80	1.87	24.23
12/20	16.20	0 0	7.85	0.42	20.22
12/19	15.75	0 0	5.00	0.14	16.06
12/18	6.08	0 0	1.80	0.07	12.19
Annual Growth	23.1%	—	57.3%	123.3%	15.4%

Anglo American Plc

Anglo American is a leading global mining company, with a world class portfolio of mining and processing operations and undeveloped resources in 15 countries. Annually, it produces 14.9 Mt of metallurgical coal, around 63.8 Mt of iron ore, about 647 kt of copper from two mines, and some 32.3 Mct of diamond. Though present in five continents, Anglo American has a major presence in Asia where it generates most of the sales. De Beers produces a third of the world's rough diamonds. Entrepreneur Ernest Oppenheimer establishes Anglo America in 1917.

Operations

The company operates through eight reportable segments: Platinum Group Metals (about 35% of sales), Iron Ore (around 25%), Copper (some 15%), De Beers (nearly 15%), Metallurgical Coal (over 5%), Nickel, Manganese and Crop Nutrients, as well as a Corporate function (generated the rest). Segments predominantly derive revenue as follows ? Platinum Group Metals: platinum group metals and nickel; Iron Ore: iron ore; Copper: copper; De Beers: rough and polished diamonds; Coal: metallurgical coal and thermal coal; Nickel and Manganese: nickel, manganese ore and alloys.

Geographic Reach

The company's most significant presence is in Asia, accounting to over 60% of sales, in which China generates around 25%. Its other productive assets can be found in South Africa, Australia, Botswana, Brazil, Canada, Chile, Colombia, Namibia, Peru, and Zimbabwe, among others. Anglo America is headquartered in London, UK.

Sales and Marketing

The company's customers operate in some of the world's most critical and diverse industries ? from automotive to steelmaking, from technology and jewelry to energy production. It engages with customers through business and industry forums.

Financial Performance

The company's revenue in 2021 increased to $41.6 billion compared to $25.4 billion in the prior year.

Net income in 2021 increased to $17.6 billion compared to $5.5 billion in the prior year.

Cash held by the company at the end of 2021 increased to $9.1 billion. Operating activities provided $16.7 billion while investing and financing activities used $5.6 billion and $9.4 billion, respectively. Main cash uses were expenditures on property, plant and equipment, interest paid and dividends paid.

Strategy

Anglo American offers an increasingly differentiated investment proposition centered around sustainable performance and high quality, responsible growth of 35% over the next decade. First and foremost is its Quellaveco copper project in Peru, expected to come on stream in mid-2022, where the company has also increased early production plans to create additional value.

The greater proportion of its output and investment capital is focused on what Anglo American call future-enabling products ? with thermal coal moving out of the portfolio, replaced by growth in Copper, PGMs and Crop Nutrients. The company are well positioned to run the business sustainably and ? being disciplined with its capital ? to grow production as a foundation for future returns.

HISTORY

In 1905 the Oppenheimers, a German family with a major interest in the Premier Diamond Mining Company of South Africa, began buying some of the region's richest gold-bearing land. The family formed Anglo American Corporation of South Africa in 1917 to raise money from J. P. Morgan and other US investors. The name was chosen to disguise the company's German background during WWI.

Under Ernest Oppenheimer the company bought diamond fields in German Southwest Africa (now Namibia) in 1920, breaking the De Beers hegemony in diamond production. Oppenheimer's 1928 negotiations with Hans

Merensky, the person credited with the discovery of South Africa's "platinum arc," led to Anglo American's interest in platinum.

The diamond monopoly resurfaced in 1929 when Anglo American won control of De Beers, formed by Cecil Rhodes in 1888 with the help of England's powerful Rothschild family.

Anglo American and De Beers had become the largest gold producers in South Africa by the 1950s. They were also major world producers of coal, uranium, and copper. In the 1960s and 1970s, Anglo American expanded through mergers and cross holdings in industrial and financial companies. It set up Luxembourg-based Minorco to own holdings outside South Africa and help the company avoid sanctions placed on firms doing business in the apartheid country.

Minorco sold its interest in Consolidated Gold Fields in 1989, and in 1990 it bought Freeport-McMoRan Gold Company (US). In 1993 Minorco bought Anglo American's and De Beers' South American, European, and Australian operations as part of a swap that put all of Anglo American's non-African assets, except diamonds, in Minorco's hands. Some analysts claimed the company had moved the assets to protect them from possible nationalization by the new, black-controlled South African government. The company spun off insurer African Life to a group of black investors in 1994.

Anglo American bought a stake in UK-based conglomerate Lonrho (now Lonmin) in 1996. In 1997 Anglo American made mining acquisitions in Zambia, Colombia, and Tanzania and began reorganizing its gold and diamond operations. In 1998 the company's First National and Southern Life financial units merged with Rand Merchant Bank's Momentum Life Assurers to form FirstRand. (Anglo American has divested most of its interest in FirstRand.)

The company moved to the UK in 1999 and began trading on the London Stock Exchange in an effort to reach international investors. When it was based in South Africa, Anglo American was unable to send its money overseas (the result of boycotts connected to that country's apartheid policies), so it bulked up on South African interests. Anglo American has evolved such that it can depend on product and geographic diversity to weather global economic turmoil. South African operations now make up less than half of the company's total sales, and its base metals and platinum units each account for about a quarter of sales.

In 2000 the company bought UK building materials company Tarmac plc and later sold Tarmac America to Greece-based Titan Cement for $636 million. That year De Beers paid $590 million for Anglovaal Mining's stake in De Beers' flagship Venetia diamond mine and $900 million for Royal Dutch Shell's Australian coal mining business. On the disposal side, Anglo American sold its 68% stake in LTA and its 14% stake in Li & Fung, a Hong Kong trading company. Harry Oppenheimer died that year at the age of 92.

In a surprising move, in early 2001 Anglo American announced that it had formed a consortium with Central Holding (the Oppenheimer family) and Debswana Diamond to acquire De Beers. In February De Beers agreed to be acquired in a deal worth about $17.6 billion. The deal -- giving Anglo American and Central Holding 45% each and Debswana a 10% stake -- was completed in June 2001.

In 2002 Anglo American and Japan-based conglomerate Mitsui pooled their Australian coal resources; Anglo American owns 51% of the joint venture. The company also completed a $1.3 billion deal that year for Chilean copper assets (two mines and a smelter) formerly owned by Exxon Mobil. In 2003 the company eyed the red hot iron ore market when it acquired a controlling stake in South Africa-based iron producer Kumba Resources.

Anglo American sold its 20% stake in Gold Fields to Norilsk Nickel in 2004 and reduced its stake in AngloGold Ashanti to 42% from its former 51% in 2006, then to below 20% the following year, and finally entirely in 2009. In divesting its gold interests, Anglo American seemed to capitulate to demands from the investor community and the idea that the gold industry is sufficiently different from the rest of the mining industry as to necessitate separate management.

The company set up new units in 2009 along product and geographical lines. The new divisions consisted of platinum (South Africa), copper (Chile), nickel (Brazil), metallurgical coal (Australia), thermal coal (South Africa), Kumba Iron Ore (of which Anglo American owned 65%, South Africa), and Iron Ore Brazil. The change capped off several years of reorganization and divestment.

In 2009 the board of Anglo American rejected an offer to merge with rival Xstrata (renamed Glencore in 2014). Although Xstrata called the bid a "merger of equals" based on similar capitalization sizes, Anglo American's board was not convinced of the benefits of the $68 billion all stock deal. Although Anglo American used to have a majority stake in AngloGold Ashanti, it divested its remaining shares in 2009.

In 2010 Anglo American, through its subsidiary Anglo Zinc, completed the divestment of its zinc assets to Vedanta Resources subsidiary Sterlite Industries in a $1.3 billion deal. That year the company also sold Tarmac's aggregates businesses in France, Germany, Poland, and the Czech Republic, as well as its French and Belgian concrete products operations, for $483 million.

Nicky Oppenheimer, grandson of the founder, retired from the board in 2011.

EXECUTIVES

Strategy Chief Executive Officer, Business Development Chief Executive Officer, Executive Director, Duncan Graham Wanblad
Financial Director, Executive Director, Stephen W. Pearce
People and Organization Director, Didier Charreton
Technical Director, Matthew Daley
South Africa Director, Nolitha Fakude
Base Metals Chief Executive Officer, Ruben Fernandes
Crop Nutrients Chief Executive Officer, Tom McCulley
Corporate Relations and Sustainable Impact Director, Anik Michaud-Ahmed
Kumba Iron Ore Chief Executive Officer, Bulk Commodities Chief Executive Officer, Themba M. Mkhwanazi
Strategy and Business Development Director, Helena Nonka
Marketing Chief Executive Officer, Peter Whitcutt
General Counsel, Secretary, Richard Price
Chairman, Non-Executive Director, Stuart J. Chambers
Senior Independent Director, Non-Executive Director, Ian Tyler
Independent Non-Executive Director, Ian R. Ashby
Independent Non-Executive Director, Marcelo Bastos
Independent Non-Executive Director, Hilary Maxson
Independent Non-Executive Director, Hixonia Nyasulu
Independent Non-Executive Director, Nonkululeko Merina Cheryl Nyembezi-Heita
Auditors : PricewaterhouseCoopers LLP

LOCATIONS

HQ: Anglo American Plc
17 Charterhouse Street, London EC1N 6RA
Phone: (44) 20 7968 8888   **Fax:** (44) 20 7968 8500
Web: www.angloamerican.com

PRODUCTS/OPERATIONS

2018 sales

	% of total
Coal	26
De Beers	20
Platinum Group Metals	19
Copper	17
Iron Ore	12
Nickel and Manganese	6
Corporate and other	-
Total	100

Selected Subsidiaries
Platinum
    Anglo Platinum Corporation Limited (75%, South Africa)
Base Metals
Anglo American Sur (75%, copper mines, Chile)
    Empresa Minera de Mantos Blancos SA (copper, Chile)
    Minera Loma de Níquel, CA (91%, nickel, Venezuela)
    Minera Quellaveco SA (80%, copper, Peru)
    Minera Sur Andes Limitada (copper, Chile)

Coal
 Anglo Coal (South Africa)
  Anglo Coal (Callide) Pty Limited (Australia)
 Ferrous Metals and Industries
  Kumba Resources Limited (65%; coal, iron ore, heavy minerals; South Africa)
 Industrial Minerals
  Copebras Limitada (phosphate products, Brazil)
 Diamonds
  De Beers S.A. (45%)

COMPETITORS

2020410 LIMITED
BHP GROUP PLC
Barrick Gold Corporation
CLOSE BROTHERS GROUP PLC
Eurofima Europäische Gesellschaft für die Finanzierung von Eisenbahnmaterial
KBC Groupe
LONMIN LIMITED
NATIONAL BANK OF GREECE S.A.
STANDARD CHARTERED PLC
WESTERN SELECTION P.L.C.

HISTORICAL FINANCIALS

Company Type: Public

Income Statement FYE: December 31

	NET REVENUE ($mil)	NET INCOME ($mil)	NET PROFIT MARGIN	EMPLOYEES
12/23	30,652	283	0.9%	0
12/22	35,118	4,514	12.9%	62,000
12/21	41,554	8,562	20.6%	62,000
12/20	30,902	2,089	6.8%	64,000
12/19	29,870	3,547	11.9%	63,000
Annual Growth	0.6%	(46.9%)		

2023 Year-End Financials

Debt ratio: 25.4%
Return on equity: 1.0%
Cash ($ mil.): 6,088
Current Ratio: 1.85
Long-term debt ($ mil.): 15,172
No. of shares ($ mil.): 1,212
Dividends
 Yield: —
 Payout: 265.2%
Market value ($ mil.): 15,130

	STOCK PRICE ($) FY Close	P/E High/Low		PER SHARE ($) Earnings	Dividends	Book Value
12/23	12.48	98	46	0.23	0.61	20.67
12/22	19.61	7	4	3.68	1.44	22.56
12/21	20.58	4	2	6.84	1.67	22.84
12/20	16.80	10	4	1.67	0.35	20.85
12/19	14.45	5	4	2.76	0.53	18.08
Annual Growth	(3.6%)	—	—	(46.3%)	3.6%	3.4%

Anheuser-Busch InBev SA/NV

EXECUTIVES

Co-Chairman, Chief Executive Officer, Carlos Alves de Brito
Legal, Commercial and M&A Chief Legal and Corporate Affairs Officer, Legal, Commercial and M&A Secretary, Legal, Commercial and M&A Vice President, John Blood
Chief Financial Officer, Chief Technology Officer, Felipe Dutra
Chief People and Transformation Officer, David Almeida
Chief Disruptive Growth Officer, Pedro Earp
Chief Non-Alcohol Beverages Officer, Lucas Herscovici
Chief Supply Officer, Peter Kraemer
Chief Procurement Officer, Maurice Anthony Milikin
Chief Owned-Retail Officer, Pablo Panizza
Chief Legal Officer, Chief Corporate Affairs Officer, Director, Sabine Chalmers
Chief Supply Officer, Claudio Braz Ferro
General Counsel, Katherine Barrett
Region Officer, Ricardo Tadeu
Director, Maria Asuncion Aramburuzabala
Independent Director, Martin J. (Marty) Barrington
Independent Director, M. Michele Burns
Independent Director, Xiaozhi Liu
Director, Paul Cornet de Ways-Ruart
Director, Claudio Garcia
Director, William F. Gifford
Director, Paulo Alberto Lemann
Director, Alejandro Santo Domingo Davila
Director, Elio Leoni Sceti
Director, Cecilia Sicupira
Director, Gregoire de Spoelberch
Director, Marcel Herrmann Telles
Director, Alexandre Van Damme
Auditors : PwC Bedrijfsrevisoren BV / Reviseurs d'Entreprises SRL

LOCATIONS

HQ: Anheuser-Busch InBev SA/NV
Brouwerijplein 1, Leuven 3000
Phone: (32) 16 27 61 11   **Fax:** (32) 16 50 61 11
Web: www.ab-inbev.com

HISTORICAL FINANCIALS

Company Type: Public

Income Statement FYE: December 31

	NET REVENUE ($mil)	NET INCOME ($mil)	NET PROFIT MARGIN	EMPLOYEES
12/23	59,380	5,341	9.0%	154,540
12/22	57,786	5,969	10.3%	166,632
12/21	54,304	4,670	8.6%	169,339
12/20	46,881	1,405	3.0%	163,695
12/19	52,329	9,171	17.5%	170,000
Annual Growth	3.2%	(12.6%)		(2.4%)

2023 Year-End Financials

Debt ratio: 35.6%
Return on equity: 6.8%
Cash ($ mil.): 10,332
Current Ratio: 0.63
Long-term debt ($ mil.): 74,163
No. of shares ($ mil.): 1,983
Dividends
 Yield: —
 Payout: 31.6%
Market value ($ mil.): 128,195

	STOCK PRICE ($) FY Close	P/E High/Low		PER SHARE ($) Earnings	Dividends	Book Value
12/23	64.62	25	20	2.60	0.82	41.26
12/22	60.04	23	15	2.91	0.53	37.00
12/21	60.55	34	23	2.28	1.17	34.66
12/20	69.91	119	50	0.69	1.45	34.49
12/19	82.04	22	14	4.53	2.01	38.65
Annual Growth	(5.8%)	—	—	(13.0%)	(20.0%)	1.6%

Anhui Conch Cement Co Ltd

Put this company to your ear and you can hear the money. Anhui Conch Cement is China's largest cement producer as measured by sales and production volume. The company has more than 15 clinker plants and 20 cement grinding mills in China. Its products include various grades of portland cement, portland blast furnace slag cement, compound cement, and high-grade commodity clinker sold under the Conch brand. Anhui Conch Cement's products have been used in the construction of a number of large-scale infrastructure projects in Shanghai, including the Oriental Pearl Television Tower and Shanghai Pudong Airport. Outside of China, the company distributes its products to Europe, the Americas, and Southeast Asia.

EXECUTIVES

Deputy General Manager, Supervisor, Pengfei Wang
Assistant General Manager, General Manager, Executive Director, Bin Wu
Secretary, Board Secretary (Hong Kong), Buyu Zhao
Deputy General Manager, Executive Director, Qunfeng Li
Deputy General Manager, Xiaobo Li
Deputy General Manager, Qiubi Ke
Supervisory Committee Chairman, Xiaoming Wu
Board Secretary, Board Secretary (Acting), Shui Yu
Staff Supervisor, Tiantian Liu
Chairman (Acting), Vice Chairman, Jianchao Wang
Non-executive Director, Executive Director, Feng Ding
Independent Non-executive Director, Daguang Liang
Independent Non-executive Director, Yunyan Zhang
Independent Non-executive Director, Xiaorong Zhang
Chairman, Cheng Wang
Auditors : KPMG Huazhen LLP

LOCATIONS

HQ: Anhui Conch Cement Co Ltd
39 Wenhua Road, Wuhu City, Anhui Province 241000
Phone: (86) 553 8398976   **Fax:** (86) 553 8398931
Web: www.conch.cn

2015 Sales by Region

	% of total
Central China	31
East China	27
South China	20
West China	21
Overseas	1
Total	100

PRODUCTS/OPERATIONS

2015 Sales by Principal Activities

	% of total
Cliker and cement products	98
Materials and other products	1
Service income	1
Total	100

COMPETITORS

BUZZI UNICEM USA INC
GIANT CEMENT HOLDING, INC.
LEHIGH CEMENT COMPANY LLC
PT. INDOCEMENT TUNGGAL PRAKARSA TBK
Taiwan Cement Corporation

HISTORICAL FINANCIALS

Company Type: Public

Income Statement — FYE: December 31

	REVENUE ($mil)	NET INCOME ($mil)	NET PROFIT MARGIN	EMPLOYEES
12/22	19,137	2,270	11.9%	0
12/21	26,454	5,240	19.8%	0
12/20	26,947	5,371	19.9%	0
12/19	22,567	4,827	21.4%	0
12/18	18,667	4,334	23.2%	0
Annual Growth	0.6%	(14.9%)	—	—

2022 Year-End Financials

Debt ratio: 1.3%
Return on equity: 8.5%
Cash ($ mil.): 8,387
Current Ratio: 2.98
Long-term debt ($ mil.): 1,449
No. of shares ($ mil.): —
Dividends
  Yield: —
  Payout: 349.9%
Market value ($ mil.): —

	STOCK PRICE ($) FY Close	P/E High/Low		PER SHARE ($) Earnings	Dividends	Book Value
12/22	17.29	9	5	0.43	1.50	0.00
12/21	25.05	5	4	0.99	1.43	0.00
12/20	30.98	6	5	1.01	1.22	0.00
12/19	36.51	6	4	0.91	1.06	0.00
12/18	23.99	6	4	0.82	0.80	0.00
Annual Growth	(7.9%)	—	—	(14.9%)	17.2%	—

Aon plc (Ireland)

EXECUTIVES

Chairman, Director, Lester B. Knight
President, Eric C. Andersen, $900,000 total compensation
Chief Executive Officer, Director, Gregory C. Case, $1,500,000 total compensation
Global Finance Executive Vice President, Global Finance Chief Financial Officer, Christa Davies, $900,000 total compensation
Executive Vice President, Secretary, General Counsel, Darren Zeidel
Chief People Officer, Division Officer, Lisa Stevens
Chief Operating Officer, Mindy F. Simon
Chief Digital Officer, James Platt
Director, Jin-Yong Cai
Director, Jeffrey C. Campbell
Director, Fulvio Conti
Director, Cheryl A. Francis
Director, Adriana Karaboutis
Director, Richard C. Notebaert
Director, Gloria Santona
Director, Sarah E. Smith
Director, Byron Spruell
Director, Carolyn Y. Woo
Auditors: Ernst & Young LLP

LOCATIONS

HQ: Aon plc (Ireland)
Metropolitan Building, James Joyce Street, Dublin 1 60601
Phone: (353) 1 266 6000
Web: www.aon.com

COMPETITORS

AVIVA PLC
AXA
CINCINNATI FINANCIAL CORPORATION
CNO FINANCIAL GROUP, INC.
MAPFRE, SA
MS&AD INSURANCE GROUP HOLDINGS, INC.
STANDARD LIFE ABERDEEN PLC
Sampo Oyj
THE HARTFORD FINANCIAL SERVICES GROUP, INC.
TOWERGATE PARTNERSHIPCO LIMITED

HISTORICAL FINANCIALS

Company Type: Public

Income Statement — FYE: December 31

	REVENUE ($mil)	NET INCOME ($mil)	NET PROFIT MARGIN	EMPLOYEES
12/23	13,376	2,564	19.2%	50,000
12/22	12,479	2,589	20.7%	50,000
12/21	12,193	1,255	10.3%	50,000
12/20	11,066	1,969	17.8%	50,000
12/19	11,013	1,532	13.9%	50,000
Annual Growth	5.0%	13.7%	—	0.0%

2023 Year-End Financials

Debt ratio: 33.0%
Return on equity: —
Cash ($ mil.): 778
Current Ratio: 1.00
Long-term debt ($ mil.): 9,995
No. of shares ($ mil.): 198
Dividends
  Yield: —
  Payout: 19.2%
Market value ($ mil.): —

Aozora Bank Ltd

Aozora Bank is building its banking business to reach the blue skies above. Aozora (which means blue sky in Japanese) recently extricated itself from a multi-year government bailout and is focused on continuing its journey towards better times. Aozora has about 20 regional offices in Japan several overseas, with a strong presence in its home town of Tokyo. The bank provides a host of retail and business banking services, as well as corporate banking services (loans and derivative products, consulting and advisory) and specialty finance and financial markets offerings.

Operations

Aozora Bank operates several segments: Retail Banking, Institutional Banking, Specialized Banking, and Financial Markets.

Retail Banking offers typical products and services to both consumer and commercial clients, including deposit accounts, checking accounts, and mortgages. Through a network of branch offices, internet banking, phone banking, and ATMs co-locating in Japan Post Bank locations, it provides many avenues for its customers to transact business. This segment leverages two of the Bank's subsidiaries, Aozora Securities and Aozora Investment Management.

Institutional Banking addresses the needs to corporations by offering advice on capital policy and business recovery, support for overseas expansion, and consultancy around management and general business activities. This segment also serves the needs of fellow Japanese financial institutions.

Specialized Banking focuses on financing for real estate deals and business recovery. It also houses the international business which works on syndicated loans, corporate loans, project financing, and other customer needs in primarily North America and Asia.

The Financial Markets segment invests the Aozora Bank's money in such opportunities as derivatives, equities, and fixed income, ensuring that the risk of its investments stay within the guideline risk objectives and constraints of the Aozora Bank group.

Geographic Reach

Tokyo-headquartered Aozora Bank operates 21 offices in Japan (7 in Tokyo), and one each in China (Shanghai), Hong Kong, Singapore, London, and New York City. It extends its geographic reach through business alliance partners operating in Taiwan, the Philippines, Indonesia, and Thailand.

Financial Performance

Note: Financial results are denoted in Japanese currency, the Yen (Â¥).

Revenue declined 7% in FY2016 to Â¥85.3 billion. The fall was due to decreases in net interest income, lower fees and commissions, and an almost 50% slip in other ordinary income.

Despite lower revenue, favorable comparison against the prior year's deferred taxes helped net income to stay in line with the prior year, about Â¥44 billion.

Strategy

Aozora has a six-pronged strategy whose primary objective is to diversify its income sources. Its retail banking segment is looking to provide more products and services to seniors and mass affluent customers. It wants to expand its business with SMEs (small-medium enterprises) and other corporate customers. It has designs on deepening its existing relationships with regional Japanese financial institutions. Aozora wants to grow business in its Specialty Finance and its International Business segment, and finally it wants to pursue diversified global investments for its own cache of cash to address its own internal risk compliance needs.

It is only a few years beyond exiting a government-funded public bail out that occurred in the late 1990's. With all the public funds now paid back, Aozora has a bit more freedom of movement to pursue growth and expansion objectives.

EXECUTIVES

President, Chief Executive Officer, Representative Director, Kei Tanikawa
Executive Vice President, Representative Director, Koji Yamakoshi
Executive Vice President, Representative Director, Hideto Oomi
Senior Managing Executive Officer, Chief Risk Officer, Director, Masayoshi Ohara
Outside Director, Ippei Murakami
Outside Director, Sakie Fukushima Tachibana
Outside Director, Hideyuki Takahashi
Outside Director, Hideaki Saito
Auditors : Deloitte Touche Tohmatsu LLC

LOCATIONS

HQ: Aozora Bank Ltd
 6-1-1 Kojimachi, Chiyoda-ku, Tokyo 102-8660
Phone: (81) 3 6752 1111
Web: www.aozorabank.co.jp

PRODUCTS/OPERATIONS

Selected affiliates
ABN Advisors
Aozora Asia Pacific Finance Limited
Aozora Europe Limited
Aozora Investments Management
Aozora Loan Services
Aozora Real Estate Investment Advisors
Aozora Regional Consulting Co., Ltd.
Aozora Securities
Aozora Trust Bank
AZB Funding
AZB Funding 2
AZB Funding 3
AZB Funding 4 Limited

COMPETITORS

AKBANK TURK ANONIM SIRKETI
AUSTRALIA AND NEW ZEALAND BANKING GROUP LIMITED
BANK OF YOKOHAMA,LTD.,
Bank of Communications Co.,Ltd.
China Minsheng Banking Corp., Ltd.
DEUTSCHE BANK AG
Hana Financial Group Inc.
MIZUHO FINANCIAL GROUP, INC.
QATAR NATIONAL BANK (Q.P.S.C.)
YORKSHIRE BANK PUBLIC LIMITED COMPANY

HISTORICAL FINANCIALS
Company Type: Public

Income Statement — FYE: March 31

	ASSETS ($mil)	NET INCOME ($mil)	INCOME AS % OF ASSETS	EMPLOYEES
03/23	53,940	65	0.1%	2,619
03/22	55,317	287	0.5%	2,525
03/21	53,437	261	0.5%	2,477
03/20	48,823	259	0.5%	2,433
03/19	47,452	326	0.7%	2,390
Annual Growth	3.3%	(33.1%)	—	2.3%

2023 Year-End Financials
Return on assets: 0.1%
Return on equity: 1.8%
Long-term debt ($ mil.): —
No. of shares ($ mil.): 116
Sales ($ mil.): 1,376
Dividends
 Yield: —
 Payout: 52.7%
Market value ($ mil.): 528

	STOCK PRICE ($) FY Close	P/E High/Low		Earnings	Dividends	Book Value
03/23	4.53	0	0	0.56	0.30	28.20
03/22	5.36	0	0	2.46	0.29	34.74
03/21	5.94	0	0	2.24	0.29	38.27
03/20	4.69	0	0	2.22	0.35	33.75
03/19	6.13	0	0	2.79	0.39	34.74
Annual Growth	(7.3%)	—		(33.1%)	(6.9%)	(5.1%)

Aptiv Corp

EXECUTIVES

Chairman, Director, Rajiv L. Gupta
President, Chief Executive Officer, head, Holding/Parent Company Officer, Director, Kevin P. Clark
Director, Nancy E. Cooper
Director, Richard L. Clemmer
Director, Sean O. Mahoney
Director, Merit E. Janow
Director, Robert K. Ortberg
Director, Nicholas M. Donofrio
Director, Paul M. Meister
Director, Joseph L. Hooley
Director, Colin J. Parris
Director, Ana G. Pinczuk
Auditors : Ernst & Young LLP

LOCATIONS

HQ: Aptiv Corp
 5 Hanover Quay, Grand Canal Dock, Dublin D02 VY79
Phone: (353) 1 259 7013

HISTORICAL FINANCIALS
Company Type: Public

Income Statement — FYE: December 31

	REVENUE ($mil)	NET INCOME ($mil)	NET PROFIT MARGIN	EMPLOYEES
12/21	15,618	590	3.8%	155,000
12/20	13,066	1,804	13.8%	0
12/19	14,357	990	6.9%	0
Annual Growth	4.3%	(22.8%)	—	—

2021 Year-End Financials
Debt ratio: 22.6%
Return on equity: 7.2%
Cash ($ mil.): 3,139
Current Ratio: 2.01
Long-term debt ($ mil.): 4,059
No. of shares ($ mil.): 270
Dividends
 Yield: —
 Payout: 0.0%
Market value ($ mil.): —

Aptiv PLC

Aptiv, formerly known as Delphi Automotive, is a leading global technology and mobility architecture company primarily serving the automotive sector. The company's main business is designing and assembling a car's electrical architecture, including its wiring assemblies, cabling, and safety distribution. Aptiv also makes advanced electrical systems and software, such as those involved in autonomous driving and vehicle connectivity. Aptiv is one of the largest vehicle technology suppliers and its customers include the 25 largest automotive original equipment manufacturers (OEMs) in the world. The company has approximately 22,000 scientists, engineers and technicians focused on developing market relevant product solutions for its customers, as well as more than 130 major manufacturing facilities and about 10 major technical centers. The US generates about 40% of Aptiv's total sales.

Operations

Aptiv's business is organized into two segments: Signal and Power Solutions, and Advanced Safety and User Experience.

The Signal and Power Solutions segment generates nearly 75% of sales and designs, manufactures, and assembles electrical architecture for automobiles including engineered component products, connectors, wiring assemblies and harnesses, cable management, electrical centers and hybrid high voltage, and safety distribution systems.

The Advanced Safety and User Experience accounts for about 25% of sales and provides critical technologies and services to enhance vehicle safety, security, comfort, and convenience, including sensing and perception systems, electronic control units, multi-domain controllers, vehicle connectivity systems, cloud-native software platforms, application software, autonomous driving technologies, and end-to-end DevOps tools.

Geographic Reach

Domiciled in Jersey, UK, Aptiv has operations in around 50 countries. It has more than 123 manufacturing facilities and over 10 major technical centers (four in North America, five in the Asia/Pacific region, and two in EMEA). The company's revenue is well diversified: the US generates nearly 40% of revenue; the EMEA region brings in about 30%, and the Asia-Pacific region around 30%. Latin America accounts for the remainder.

Sales and Marketing

Aptiv's customer base includes all 25 of the largest automotive OEMs in the world; Stellantis and General Motors are Aptiv's two biggest customers and account for around 10% of the company's sales each year. Other customers include Mercedez-Benz, Ford, Geely, Daimler, SAIC, Tesla, BMW, Toyota, and Tata Motors.

Financial Performance

Aptiv's performance for the past five years has fluctuated with a decrease from its first two years, then increasing year-over-year since then.

Total net sales for 2022 increased 12% compared to 2021. Its volumes increased 14%

for the period, which reflects increased global automotive production of 5% (5% on an AWM basis), which was partially offset by unfavorable foreign currency impacts, primarily related to the Euro and Chinese Yuan Renminbi. The increase in volumes is primarily attributable to increases in all regions.

Net income for 2022 decreased to $590 million compared to the prior year's $609 million.

Cash held by the company at the end of 2022 increased to $1.6 billion. Operating activities provided $1.3 billion. Investing activities used $5.2 billion, while financing activities provided $2.4 billion. Main cash uses were for business acquisition costs and accounts receivables.

Strategy

Aptiv believes it is well-positioned for growth from increasing global vehicle production volumes. Aptiv is focused on accelerating the commercialization of active safety, autonomous driving, enhanced user experiences, and connected services, providing the software, advanced computing platforms, and networking architecture required to do so. The company has successfully created a competitive cost structure while investing in research and development to grow its product offerings, which are aligned with the high-growth industry mega-trends, and re-aligned its manufacturing footprint into an efficient, low-cost regional service model, focused on increasing Aptiv's profit margins.

Mergers and Acquisitions

In 2022, Aptiv acquired Wind River for $3.5 billion in cash. Wind River is a global leader in delivering software for the intelligent edge. The acquisition allows Aptiv to accelerate the journey to a software-defined future of the automotive industry.

Company Background

The company's return to the public markets and eventual profitability hasn't been easy. Delphi has struggled financially for years; it was only sporadically profitable for after being spun off in 1999. Delphi filed for bankruptcy in 2005 and emerged four years later as a heavily indebted private company owned by its investors, Elliot Management, GM, and Silver Point Capital. By that time it had laid off more than 75,000 workers, closed more than 70 sites, reduced its products lines from 119 to 33, exited 11 businesses, and had its pension (primarily for UAW workers) frozen and taken over by federal Pension Benefit Guaranty Corporation (PBGC). (In the end, the union workers' pension was kept afloat by taxpayers as part of the 2009 auto industry bailout).

In 2011, Delphi was finally able to pay off GM for its $3.8 billion stake and PBGC for the $594 million it owed. The two transactions were funded with cash and $2.5 billion of new bank debt as part of a $3 billion credit facility from by investment bank J.P. Morgan Securities. The company makes about half of what it made five years ago, and plans the use the proceeds from its IPO to fund operations, buy equipment, and repay more debt.

Paying off GM helped pave the way for the company's return to health, and a new business strategy to show investors doesn't hurt, either. Admittedly, Delphi has much leaner operations after its restructuring and moved the bulk of its operations outside the US to emerging markets where overall costs, especially labor costs, are lower. Delphi no longer has any UAW employees on its payroll; outside the US, it relies on non-salary and temporary workers to manage a flexible workforce.

EXECUTIVES

Chairman, Director, Rajiv L. Gupta
President, Chief Executive Officer, Director, Kevin P. Clark, $1,375,000 total compensation
Senior Vice President, Chief Financial Officer, Joseph R. Massaro, $790,500 total compensation
Senior Vice President, Chief Technology Officer, Division Officer, Glen De Vos
Senior Vice President, Division Officer, David Paja, $603,275 total compensation
Senior Vice President, Chief Compliance Officer, General Counsel, Secretary, David M. Sherbin, $595,000 total compensation
Senior Vice President, Chief Human Resources Officer, Mariya K. Trickett
Vice President, Chief Accounting Officer, Allan J. Brazier
Director, Nancy E. Cooper
Director, Nicholas M. Donofrio
Director, Joseph L. Hooley
Director, Sean O. Mahoney
Director, Paul M. Meister
Director, Robert K. Ortberg
Director, Colin J. Parris
Director, Ana G. Pinczuk
Director, Lawrence A. Zimmerman
Director, Frank J. Dellaquila
Director, Richard L. Clemmer
Auditors : Ernst & Young LLP

LOCATIONS

HQ: Aptiv PLC
5 Hanover Quay, Grand Canal Dock, Dublin D02 VY79
Phone: (353) 1 259 7013
Web: www.delphi.com

2018 Sales

	$ mil.	% of total
United States	5,390	37
Europe, Middle East & Africa	4,689	33
Asia/Pacific	3,916	27
South America	2700	2
Total	14,335	100

PRODUCTS/OPERATIONS

2018 Sales by Segment

	$ mil.	% of total
Signal and Power Solutions	10,402	72
Advanced Safety and User Experience	4,078	28
Total	14,435	100

Selected Products
Automotive Industry
Connection Systems
Driver Interface
Electrical/Electronic Architecture
Hybrid & Electric Vehicle Products
Infotainment
Safety Electronics
Sensors

COMPETITORS

ALLISON TRANSMISSION HOLDINGS, INC.
COBRA ELECTRONICS CORPORATION
DELTEX MEDICAL GROUP PLC
IRVING PLACE CAPITAL, LLC
JOHNSON CONTROLS INTERNATIONAL PUBLIC LIMITED COMPANY
KIRKLAND'S, INC.
LeasePlan Corporation N.V.
TRACTOR SUPPLY COMPANY
ULTA SALON, COSMETICS & FRAGRANCE, INC.
VERIZON COMMUNICATIONS INC.

HISTORICAL FINANCIALS

Company Type: Public

Income Statement — FYE: December 31

	REVENUE ($mil)	NET INCOME ($mil)	NET PROFIT MARGIN	EMPLOYEES
12/23	20,051	2,938	14.7%	154,000
12/22	17,489	594	3.4%	160,000
12/21	15,618	590	3.8%	155,000
12/20	13,066	1,804	13.8%	151,000
12/19	14,357	990	6.9%	141,000
Annual Growth	8.7%	31.3%	—	2.2%

2023 Year-End Financials

Debt ratio: 25.4%
Return on equity: 28.8%
Cash ($ mil.): 1,640
Current Ratio: 1.72
Long-term debt ($ mil.): 6,204
No. of shares ($ mil.): 279
Dividends
Yield: —
Payout: 0.0%
Market value ($ mil.): —

Arca Continental SAB de CV

Arca Continental is Latin America's second-largest Cola-Cola bottler and among the largest in the world. Besides the production, distribution, and sale of the world's most popular soft drink, Arca distributes other Coca-Cola brands such as Ciel and Dasani waters, in addition to the snack brands Bokados in Mexico, Inalecsa in Ecuador, and Wise and Deep River in the US. Arca's footprint spans approximately 45 production centers and nearly 360 distribution centers. It serves over 125 million customers across northern and western Mexico, Ecuador, Peru, Northern Argentina, and southwestern US. Arca Continental was formed by the 2011 merger of Mexico's Embotelladoras Arca and Grupo Continental. Mexico generates the majority of the company's sales.

Operations

The company's Beverages (including carbonated, non-carbonated, dairy beverages and carboy, and individual format purified water) which produces, distributes, and sells TCCC brand beverages in different territories in Mexico, US, Argentina, Ecuador, and Peru as well as Santa Clara dairy beverages in Mexico and Toni in Ecuador. The company's portfolio of beverages and dairy products includes cola and flavored soft drinks, individual purified and flavored water, dairy beverages and other carbonated and non-carbonated beverages in sundry presentations.

Geographic Reach

Headquartered in Mexico, the company has operations in the northern and western regions of Mexico, as well as in Ecuador, Peru, in the northern region of Argentina, and the southwestern region of the US. The Mexico generates more than 40% of sales, followed by the US with nearly 40%, Peru with nearly 10%, Ecuador with over 5%, and Argentina with approximately 5%.

Sales and Marketing

The company serves over 125 million people in the northern and western regions of Mexico, Ecuador, Peru, in the northern region of Argentina, and the southwestern region of the US.

The company advertising and promotional expenses, including public relations were M$3.1 million and M$3.0 million both in 2021 and 2020, respectively.

Financial Performance

The company had net sales amounting to M$183.4 billion in 2021, an 8% increase from the previous year's net sales of M$169.3 billion.

In 2021, the company had a net income of M$12.3 billion, a 20% increase from the previous year's net income of M$10.3 billion.

The company's cash at the end of 2021 was M$32.1 billion. Operating activities generated M$30.7 billion, while investing activities used M$7.1 billion, mainly for acquisition of property, plant and equipment. Financing activities used another M$19.3 billion, primarily for payments of current and non-current debt.

Strategy

Arca Continental's business strategy allows it to align its activities with the mission of generating maximum value for stakeholders, with a clear focus on customers and the consumer as the source and destination of shared value.

The company accelerates its digital innovation agenda and employing advanced analytics tools, to ensure the continuous evolution of its business.

It is also constantly looking for savings and efficiencies that allow it to continue generating value for the business. The company is disciplined in its spending to ensure the most profitable investments that drive long-term business growth and sustainability. As part of its principles and through each of its activities, Arca Continental promotes the creation of value for the communities in which it operates and with which it interacts.

EXECUTIVES

Chief Executive Officer, Arturo Guitierrez Hernandez
Chief Commercial and Digital Officer, Jose Borda Noriega
Chief Corporate Affairs and Sustainability Officer, Guillermo Garza Martinez
Chief Financial Officer, Emilio Marcos Charur
Chief Human Resources Officer, Denise Martinez Aldana
Technical Operations Chief Technical and Supply Chain Officer, Alejandro Molina Sanchez
Chief Strategic Planning Officer, Alejandro Rodriguez Saenz
Legal Secretary, Legal General Counsel, Jaime Sanchez Fernandez
Non-Executive Chairman, Jorge Humberto Santos Reyna
Honorary Life Chairman, Non-Executive Director, Manuel L. Barragan Morales
Vice-Chairman, Non-Executive Director, Luis Arizpe Jimenez
Vice-Chairman, Non-Executive Director, Miguel Angel Rabago Vite
Independent Non-Executive Director, Juan Carlos Correa Ballesteros
Independent Non-Executive Director, Felipe Cortes Font
Independent Non-Executive Director, Ernesto Lopez de Nigris
Independent Non-Executive Director, Daniel H. Sayre
Independent Non-Executive Director, Adrian Jorge Lozano Lozano
Independent Non-Executive Director, Armando Solbes Simon
Non-Executive Director, Alejandro Jose Arizpe Narro
Non-Executive Director, Alfonso J. Barragan Rodriguez
Non-Executive Director, Alejandro M. Elizondo Barragan
Non-Executive Director, Francisco Rogelio Garza Egloff
Non-Executive Director, Roberto Garza Velazquez
Non-Executive Director, Johnny Robinson Lindley Suarez
Non-Executive Director, Rodrigo Alberto Gonzalez Barragan
Non-Executive Director, Cynthia H. Grossman
Non-Executive Director, Alberto Sanchez Palazuelos
Non-Executive Director, Bernardo Gonzalez Barragan
Non-Executive Director, Jesus Viejo Gonzalez
Non-Executive Director, Marcela Villareal Fernandez
Auditors : Mancera, S.C. (a member practice of Ernst & Young Global Limited)

LOCATIONS

HQ: Arca Continental SAB de CV
Avenida San Jeronimo 813 Pte., Monterrey, Nuevo Leon 64640
Phone: (52) 81 8151 1400
Web: www.arcacontal.com

2018 sales

	%
Mexico	40
United States	36
Peru	11
Ecuador	8
Argentina	5
Total	100

PRODUCTS/OPERATIONS

Selected Products and Brands
Bottled water
   Ciel
   Ciel Aquarius
   Ciel Dasani
   Ciel Naturae
   Purasol
   Sierrazul Mineral Water
   Topo Chico Mineral Water
Carbonated soft drinks
   Coca-Cola
   Coca-Cola Caffeine Free
   Coca-Cola Light
   Coca-Cola Zero
   Delaware Punch
   Don Diego Sangria
   Fanta
   Fresca
   Joya
   Joya Light
   Manzana Lift
   Sangría Se?orial
   Senzao
   Sprite
   Sprite 0
   Squirt
   Topo Chico Grapefruit
   Topo Chico Sangría
   Topo Chico Sangría Light
Other products
   Frutier
   Minute Maid Forte
   Minute Maid Revita
   Nestea
   POWERade

HISTORICAL FINANCIALS

Company Type: Public

Income Statement   FYE: December 31

	REVENUE ($mil)	NET INCOME ($mil)	NET PROFIT MARGIN	EMPLOYEES
12/22	10,730	792	7.4%	0
12/21	9,084	600	6.6%	0
12/20	8,635	517	6.0%	57,976
12/19	8,723	506	5.8%	63,359
12/18	8,083	442	5.5%	0
Annual Growth	7.3%	15.7%		

2022 Year-End Financials

Debt ratio: 0.9%   No. of shares ($ mil.): 1,744
Return on equity: 13.0%   Dividends
Cash ($ mil.): 1,418   Yield: —
Current Ratio: 1.37   Payout: 69.4%
Long-term debt ($ mil.): 2,081   Market value ($ mil.): —

ArcelorMittal SA

ArcelorMittal is one of the world's leading integrated steel and mining companies. It produces a broad range of high-quality finished and semi-finished steel products. Specifically, ArcelorMittal produces flat products, including sheet and plate, and long products, including bars, rods and structural shapes. It also produces pipes and tubes for various applications. ArcelorMittal sells its products primarily in local markets and to a diverse range of customers in approximately 155 countries, including the automotive, appliance, engineering, construction, and machinery industries. In mid-2022, ArcelorMittal signed an agreement with the shareholders of Companhia SiderÃºrgica do PecÃ©m (CSP) to acquire CSP for an enterprise value of approximately $2.2 billion. The company generates the majority if its revenue in Europe.

Operations

ArcelorMittal reports its business in the following five reportable segments corresponding to continuing activities: Europe, Brazil, NAFTA, ACIS, and Mining.

Europe accounts for more than 50% of total revenue, produces flat, long, and tubular products. Flat products include hot-rolled coil, cold-rolled coil, coated products, tinplate, plate, and slab. These products are sold primarily to customers in the automotive, general, and packaging sectors. In 2021, shipments from Europe totaled approximately 33.2 million tonnes.

Brazil (about 15%) produces flat, long, and tubular products. Flat products include slabs, hot-rolled coil, cold-rolled coil, and coated steel. Long products comprise sections, wire rod, bar and rebars, billets, and wire drawing. In 2021, shipments from Brazil totaled approximately 11.7 million tonnes.

NAFTA (approximately 15%) produces flat, long, and tubular products. Flat products include slabs, hot-rolled coil, cold-rolled coil, coated steel products, and plate and are sold primarily to customers in the following sectors: automotive, energy, construction packaging and appliances and via distributors and processors. Flat product facilities are located at two integrated and mini-mill sites located in two countries. Long products include wire rod, sections, rebar, billets, blooms, and wire drawing. Long production facilities are located at two integrated and mini-mill sites located in two countries. In 2021, shipments from NAFTA totaled approximately 9.6 million tonnes.

ACIS (over 10%) produces a combination of flat, long, and tubular products. It has five flat and long production facilities in three countries. In 2021, shipments from ACIS totaled approximately 10.4 million tonnes, with shipments made on a worldwide basis.

Mining generates some 5% of total revenue, provides the company's steel operations with high quality and low-cost iron ore reserves and also sells mineral products to third parties. The company's mines are located in North America and Africa. In 2021, iron ore production in the Mining segment totaled approximately 26.2 million tonnes.

Overall, flat products bring in approximately 55% of the company's revenue, followed by long products with nearly 25%. Tubular products, mining products, and other account for the rest.

Geographic Reach

Headquartered in Luxembourg City, ArcelorMittal has steel-making operations in about 15 countries on four continents, including more than 35 integrated and mini-mill steel-making facilities.

The company has iron ore mines in Brazil, Bosnia, Canada, Kazakhstan, Liberia, Mexico, Ukraine and the US, with coal mining in Kazakhstan and the US.

ArcelorMittal's logistics network includes some 15 owned or partially owned deep-water ports and linked railway sidings.

The company generates approximately 55% of its revenue in Europe. The Americas bring in about 35% of revenue, while Asia and Africa account for the remainder.

Sales and Marketing

ArcelorMittal's markets are all those that consume steel as an input, including the automotive, appliance, engineering, construction, energy, and machinery markets. It sells its steel products primarily in local markets and through its centralized marketing organization to a diverse range of customers in approximately 155 countries. The company prefers to sell exports through its international network of sales agencies to ensure that all ArcelorMittal products are presented to the market in a cost-efficient and coordinated manner.

Financial Performance

The company had revenues of $76.6 billion, a 44% increase from the previous year's revenue of $53.3 billion.

In 2021, the company had a net income of $15.6 billion, a 2793% improvement from the previous year's net loss of $578 million.

The company's cash at the end of 2021 was $4.2 billion. Operating activities generated $9.9 billion, while investing activities used $340 million, mainly for purchase of property, plant and equipment and intangibles. Financing activities used another $10.9 billion, primarily for share buyback.

Strategy

ArcelorMittal's success is built on its core values of sustainability, quality and leadership and the entrepreneurial boldness that has empowered its emergence as the first truly global steel and mining company. Acknowledging that a combination of structural issues and macroeconomic conditions will continue to challenge returns in its sector, the company has adapted its footprint to the new demand realities, intensified its efforts to control costs and repositioned its operations to outperform its competitors.

Against this backdrop, ArcelorMittal's strategy is to leverage four distinctive attributes that will enable it to capture leading positions in the most attractive areas of the steel industry value chain, from mining at one end to distribution and first-stage processing at the other: Global scale and scope; Unmatched technical capabilities; Diverse portfolio of steel and related businesses, particularly mining; and Financial capability.

Mergers and Acquisitions

In mid-2022, ArcelorMittal announced that it signed an agreement with the shareholders of Companhia SiderÃºrgica do PecÃ©m (CSP) to acquire CSP for an enterprise value of approximately $2.2 billion. CSP is a world-class operation, producing high-quality slab at a globally competitive cost. The acquisition expands the company's position in the high-growth Brazilian steel industry and it adds approximately 3 million tonnes of high-quality and cost-competitive slab capacity, with the potential to supply slab intra-group or to sell into North and South America.

Also in mid-2022, ArcelorMittal acquired a majority stake in voestalpine's state-of-the-art HBI facility in Texas. The acquisition valued the Corpus Christi operations at approximately $1 billion. The state-of-the-art plant is one of the largest of its kind in the world. It has an annual capacity of two million tonnes of HBI, which is a premium, compacted form of Direct Reduced Iron (DRI) developed to overcome issues associated with shipping and handling DRI. The transaction enhances the company's ability to produce the high-quality input materials required for low-carbon emissions steelmaking, and reinforces the company's position as a world leader in DRI production.

HISTORY

ArcelorMittal is the product of decades of steelmaking by India's Mittal family. In 1967 patriarch Mohan Mittal unsuccessfully tried to open a steel mill in Egypt. He and his four younger brothers then set up a steel company in India, but squabbles pushed Mohan to chart his own course, eventually giving rise to an empire that flourished under the Ispat name. Mohan's son Lakshmi began working part-time at the family steel mill while in school; he started full-time at 21, after graduating in 1971.

Mohan set up an operation in Indonesia in 1975 (Ispat Indo) and put Lakshmi in charge. The next year, fueled by ambitions and held back by government regulations in India, Lakshmi formed Ispat International in Jakarta, Indonesia, to focus on expansion through acquisitions. He spent the next decade strengthening the Indonesian operations and perfecting the minimill process using direct-reduced iron (DRI).

Ispat took advantage of the recessionary late 1980s and early 1990s by making a string of acquisitions. In 1988 it took over the management of Trinidad and Tobago's state steel companies (bought in 1994; renamed Caribbean Ispat).

In 1992 Ispat bought Mexico's third-largest (albeit bankrupt) steel and DRI producer. Two years later it acquired Canada's Sidbec-Dosco steelmaker. Also that year Lakshmi took exclusive control of international operations, leaving his brothers Pramod and Vinod to control the Indian divisions.

The mid-1990s brought more acquisitions: In 1995 Ispat bought Germany's Hamburger Stahlwerks and a mill in Kazakhstan. The next year it purchased Ireland's only steelmaker, Irish Steel. Lakshmi moved to London in 1996 and purchased a home on Bishops Avenue, known as "millionaire's row." (Saudi Arabia's King Fahd was a neighbor.)

In 1997 the company bought the long-product (wire rod) division of Germany's Thyssen AG (renamed Ispat Stahlwerk Ruhrort and Ispat Walzdraht Hochfeld). It also completed a $776 million IPO.

Ispat acquired Chicago-based Inland Steel in 1998 (and renamed it Ispat Inland), including the steel-finishing operations of I/N Tek (60% Inland-owned joint venture with Nippon Steel) and I/N Kote (50% Inland-owned joint venture with NSC).

In 1999 Ispat formed a joint venture with Mexican steelmaker Grupo Imsa to make flat-rolled steel to sell throughout most of the Americas. It also paid $96 million for France-based Usinor's Unimétal, Tréfileurope, and Sociétè Métallurgique de Révigny subsidiaries, which specialize in carbon long products. That year Ispat Inland became the target of a US federal criminal grand jury investigation and a related civil lawsuit for allegedly defrauding the Louisiana Highway Department. (The case was settled for $30 million, with the cost split between Ispat Inland and Contech Construction Products Inc. of Ohio.)

In 2000 the company responded to a downturn in the steel industry by starting a Web-based joint venture with Commerce One to connect buyers and sellers in the worldwide metals market. It also offered to buy VSZ, Slovakia's #1 steelworks, but was outbid by U.S. Steel.

After struggling with heavy debt, high labor and energy costs, new environmental regulations, and EU steel quotas in 2001, Ispat closed down its subsidiary, Irish Ispat, which accounted for about 2% of the parent company's steel production.

In 2002 the company's 51%-owned pipe making subsidiary, Productura Mexicana de Tuberia, sold almost all of its production assets.

The present ArcelorMittal was forged in 2004 when Ispat International (of which the Mittal family owned 70%) purchased LNM Holdings (wholly owned by the Mittals) for $13 billion. In 2006, the former Mittal Steel agreed to buy rival Arcelor for about $34 billion to create ArcelorMittal.

Mittal Steel had established its hold on the world steel market through its 2005 purchase of the US-based International Steel Group (ISG) for $4.5 billion. The purchase made the company the largest steel producer (ahead of U.S. Steel and Nucor) in the US, a market that had long been a targeted area for expansion for CEO Mittal. Once the deal closed, the company combined ISG's operations with those of subsidiary Ispat Inland to form a single North American entity, Mittal Steel USA (now ArcelorMittal USA).

Also in 2005, Mittal Steel acquired a 93% stake in Ukrainian state-run steel company KryvorizhStal with the winning $4.84 billion bid in an auction held by the Ukrainian government. The price was high, but Mittal was anxious to gain a stronger foothold in the region -- and to keep its rivals away from KryvorizhStal. (This fact, incidentally, went a long way to convincing Mittal it needed to combine with Arcelor; the competition for acquisitions was driving prices dramatically upward.)

The company also began to broaden its portfolio outside the steel industry, dipping its toe into the energy business. In mid-2005 Mittal formed two joint ventures with India's government-controlled Oil & Natural Gas Corporation: one to buy stakes in foreign oil and gas projects, the other involved in oil and gas trading and shipping. The ventures began to look for business in places like Indonesia, Kazakhstan, Angola, and Trinidad and Tobago.

After consolidating his family's various steel interests in the early part of this decade, Mittal began work on the steel industry as a whole and was soon the world's largest steel producer.

By 2006, Mittal Steel no longer was content to be merely the world's largest steel producer; it wanted to dominate the market. The company announced an offer to the shareholders of Arcelor, then the industry's #2 player, to buy that company and, in the process, create the world's first 100-million-ton steel producer. Arcelor, and seemingly half the governments of Western Europe, initially fought the attempt.

Mittal improved its proposed price, however, and Arcelor's board finally approved the offer when Mittal also made ownership/corporate governance concessions. The combined company is 43% owned by the Mittal family. After a few months of a transitional management team arrangement, Lakshmi Mittal took over as CEO of the combined company toward the end of 2006.

In 2009 ArcelorMittal completed its acquisition of the laser-welding steel activities of Noble International, a leader in the niche industry. It also acquired Mexican steel producer Sicarsta for nearly $1.5 billion, an acquisition that, combined with its Lazaro Cardenas, created Mexico's largest steel company.

In 2011, the company spun off its stainless and specialty steels steel operations into Aperam, which immediately became the world's sixth-largest stainless steel producer. ArcelorMittal made the decision in 2010 to spin off its stainless steel units in Europe and Brazil after determining that they were underperforming and would better thrive as a separate business.

After spinning its wheels in an escalating bidding war, in 2011 ArcelorMittal joined rival Nunavut Iron Ore in making a joint acquisition of Canada-based Baffinland Iron Mines for $594 million. Both companies sought access to Baffinland's Mary River Project, an undeveloped deposit of iron ore on sparsely populated North Baffin Island located inside the Arctic Circle, as a source of raw materials. The venture faces stiff challenges, including building an infrastructure around the mine's formidable location, and shipping the ore out to Europe and other production sites.

Also that year, the company bought a 40% stake in G Steel Public Company, greatly expanding its presence in Asia. G Steel produces about 2.5 million ton of steel annually at its two slab-rolling plants in Thailand. The deal was part of ArcelorMittal's strategy of establishing a presence in emerging markets with with the potential for future growth.

In 2012 ArcelorMittal expanded its presence in China by increasing its stake in a joint venture with Valin Group, known as Valin ArcelorMittal Automotive (VAMA), from 33% to 49%. VAMA is trying to enhance its position in China as a supplier of high-strength steels and products for the automotive market. The joint venture, scheduled to become operational in 2014, will increase its planned capacity from 1.2 million tons to 1.5 million tons.

That year it sold New Jersey-based Skyline Steel, a North American steel foundation and piling products distributor, and specialty steel plate and bar producer Astralloy to US-based Nucor for $605 million.

EXECUTIVES

Chairman, Executive Chairman, Director,
Lakshmi N. Mittal

Strategy Chief Executive Officer, Mergers & Acquisitions Chief Executive Officer, Director,
Aditya Mittal

Finance Chief Financial Officer, Finance Executive Vice President, Genuino M. Christino

Executive Vice President, Stefan Buys

Executive Vice President, Jefferson de Paula

Executive Vice President, Geert Van Poelvoorde
Executive Vice President, John Brett
Corporate Business Optimization Executive Vice President, Corporate Business Optimization Head, Bradley Davey
Executive Vice President, Vijay Goyal
Executive Vice President, Dilip Oommen
Executive Vice President, Stephanie Werner-Dietz
Secretary, Henk Scheffer
Lead Independent Non-Executive Director, Bruno Lafont
Independent Non-Executive Director, Tye Burt
Independent Non-Executive Director, Karyn F. Ovelmen
Independent Non-Executive Director, Karel de Gucht
Independent Non-Executive Director, Etienne Schneider
Independent Non-Executive Director, Clarissa Lins
Non-Independent Director, Vanisha Mittal Bhatia
Non-Independent Director, Michel Wurth
Auditors : Ernst & Young S.A.

LOCATIONS

HQ: ArcelorMittal SA
24-26, Boulevard d'Avranches, Luxembourg L-1160
Phone: (352) 4792 1   **Fax:** (352) 4792 2235
Web: www.arcelormittal.com

2018 Sales

	$ mil.	% of total
Europe	38,263	50
Americas	29.068	38
Asia & Africa	8,702	12
Total	76,033	100

PRODUCTS/OPERATIONS

2018 Sales

	$ millions	% of total
NAFTA	20,332	25
Europe	40,488	49
Brazil	8,711	11
ACIS	7.961	10
Mining	4,211	5
Others and eliminations	(5,670)	-
Total	76,033	100

2018 sales

	% of total
Flat products	61
Long products	21
Tubular products	3
Mining products	1
Others	14
Total	100

Segments and Selected Products

Flat Carbon Europe
    Coated products
    Coil
    Cold-rolled
    Hot-rolled
    Plate
    Slab
    Tin plate
Flat Carbon Americas
    Coated products
    Steel
    Plate
    Coil
    Cold-rolled
    Hot-rolled
    Slabs
Long Carbon Americas & Europe
    Billets
    Blooms
    Rebar
    Sections
    Wire rod
Asia, Africa & Comonwealth of Independent States
    Flat products
    Long products
    Pipes
    Tubes
ArcelorMittal Steel Solutions & Services (in-house trading and distribution arm)

COMPETITORS

AK STEEL HOLDING CORPORATION
DC ALABAMA, INC.
ELKEM HOLDING, INC.
NIPPON DENKO CO., LTD.
NLMK, PAO
Posco Co.,Ltd.
READING ALLOYS, INC.
SEVERSTAL, PAO
TATA STEEL EUROPE LIMITED
thyssenkrupp AG

HISTORICAL FINANCIALS

Company Type: Public

Income Statement   FYE: December 31

	REVENUE ($mil)	NET INCOME ($mil)	NET PROFIT MARGIN	EMPLOYEES
12/23	68,275	919	1.3%	126,756
12/22	79,844	9,302	11.7%	154,352
12/21	76,571	14,956	19.5%	157,909
12/20	53,270	(733)	—	167,743
12/19	70,615	(2,391)	—	191,248
Annual Growth	(0.8%)	—	—	(9.8%)

2023 Year-End Financials

Debt ratio: 11.4%   No. of shares ($ mil.): 819
Return on equity: 1.7%   Dividends
Cash ($ mil.): 7,686   Yield: —
Current Ratio: 1.53   Payout: 34.3%
Long-term debt ($ mil.): 8,369   Market value ($ mil.): 23,259

	STOCK PRICE ($) FY Close	P/E High/Low		PER SHARE ($) Earnings	Dividends	Book Value
12/23	28.39	30	20	1.09	0.37	65.86
12/22	26.22	4	2	10.18	0.32	66.00
12/21	31.83	3	2	13.49	0.26	53.91
12/20	22.90	—	—	(0.64)	0.00	35.42
12/19	17.54	—	—	(2.42)	0.17	38.06
Annual Growth	12.8%	—	—	—	21.8%	14.7%

Arch Capital Group Ltd

Arch Capital Group offers property/casualty insurance and reinsurance through subsidiaries in Bermuda, Canada, Europe, Asia, and the US. Its insurance subsidiaries offer marine and aviation, professional liability, health care liability, and other specialty lines. The company's US subsidiary, Arch Insurance Group specializes in excess and surplus lines coverage. The company's Arch Re reinsurance subsidiaries focus on property/casualty coverage, including catastrophe and some specialty lines. The company distributes its products through both wholesale and retail brokers.

HISTORY

Fortuitous timing helped the company as it transformed itself starting in 2000 when what was Arch-US sold off the assets of its Risk Capital Reinsurance to Folksamerica Reinsurance. It retained the core of the company and used it to form Arch Capital Group. As a freshly formed company, it did not face the load of claims that hit more established insurers following the events of September 11, 2001. Arch Capital Group commenced underwriting in October 2001 and capitalized on soaring rates and the need for fresh reinsurers. Earlier in that year, the company had formed Arch Reinsurance Ltd (Bermuda) and had acquired other insurance operations to

As part of its transformation the company has sold off operations that no longer fit, including its non-standard automobile business, merchant banker Hales & Company, which specialized in insurance mergers and acquisitions, and property/casualty insurer American Independent Insurance.

EXECUTIVES

Chief Executive Officer, Chairman, Director, Constantine P. Iordanou, $587,121 total compensation

Vice-Chairman, John M. Pasquesi

President, Chief Operating Officer, Subsidiary Officer, Marc Grandisson, $982,576 total compensation

Executive Vice President, Chief Financial Officer, Treasurer, Francois Morin, $563,406 total compensation

Executive Vice President, Chief Risk Officer, Mark Donald Lyons, $291,667 total compensation

Senior Vice President, Chief Investment Officer, Subsidiary Officer, W. Preston Hutchings, $483,333 total compensation

Chief Executive Officer, David E. Gansberg

Subsidiary Officer, David H. McElroy, $650,000 total compensation

Subsidiary Officer, Michael R. Murphy

Subsidiary Officer, Timothy J. Olson

Subsidiary Officer, Nicolas Papadopoulo, $750,000 total compensation

Subsidiary Officer, Louis T. Petrillo

Subsidiary Officer, Maamoun Rajeh, $650,000 total compensation

Subsidiary Officer, John F. Rathgeber

Subsidiary Officer, Andrew T. Rippert, $700,000 total compensation

Senior Advisor, Director, John D. Vollaro, $312,500 total compensation

Director, John L. Bunce

Director, Eric W. Doppstadt

Director, Laurie S. Goodman

Director, Yiorgos Lillikas
Director, Louis J. Paglia
Director, Brian S. Posner
Director, Eugene S. Sunshine
Auditors : PricewaterhouseCoopers LLP

LOCATIONS

HQ: Arch Capital Group Ltd
  Waterloo House, Ground Floor, 100 Pitts Bay Road, Pembroke HM 08
Phone: (1) 441 278 9250   Fax: (1) 441 278 9255
Web: www.archcapgroup.com

COMPETITORS

AMWINS GROUP, INC.
ARROWPOINT CAPITAL CORP.
Argo Group International Holdings, Ltd.
BEAZLEY GROUP LIMITED
BESSO LIMITED
CNA FINANCIAL CORPORATION
Endurance Specialty Holdings Ltd
GUY CARPENTER & COMPANY, LLC
ODYSSEY RE HOLDINGS CORP.
WELLS FARGO INSURANCE SERVICES, INC.

HISTORICAL FINANCIALS

Company Type: Public

Income Statement — FYE: December 31

	ASSETS ($mil)	NET INCOME ($mil)	INCOME AS % OF ASSETS	EMPLOYEES
12/23	58,906	4,443	7.5%	0
12/22	47,990	1,476	3.1%	5,800
12/21	45,100	2,156	4.8%	5,200
12/20	43,282	1,405	3.2%	4,500
12/19	37,885	1,636	4.3%	4,300
Annual Growth	11.7%	28.4%	—	—

2023 Year-End Financials
Return on assets: 8.3%
Return on equity: 28.4%
Long-term debt ($ mil.): —
No. of shares ($ mil.): 373
Sales ($ mil.): 13,234
Dividends
Yield: —
Payout: 0.0%
Market value ($ mil.): —

Arkema S.A.

A major player in specialty chemicals, Arkema manufactures high performance materials like polymers and additives, industrial specialty products like fluorochemicals and hydrogen peroxide, as well as coating resins and plastic additives. With presence in some 55 countries, Arkema's around 140 production sites are spread across Europe, North America, and Asia. The company is especially focused on bio-based products, lightweight materials, water management, electronics solutions, and home efficiency and insulation. Its branded polymer products include PEKK, Orgasol, and Pebax. Majority of sales were generated from Europe including France.

Operations

Arkema is structured into three coherent and complementary segments dedicated to Specialty Materials (Advanced Materials with over 30% of sales, Coating Solutions with about 30%, and Adhesive Solutions with about 25%) as well as a competitive and well-positioned Intermediates segment (some 15%).

Products have included high performance polymers and performance additives for Advanced Materials; construction and consumer and industrial assembly for Adhesive Solutions; and coating resins and additives for Coating Solutions.

Geographic Reach

Geographically, the rest of Europe, NAFTA (USA, Canada, and Mexico) and Asia generated roughly 30% of sales each. Arkema has some 140 production sites in some 55 countries. It also has some 15 R&D sites and approximately 1,600 researchers.

The company is based in France.

Sales and Marketing

The company's end markets have included general industry generated about 30% of total sales, paints and coatings with some 20%; building and construction and consumer goods with each having some 15%, and electrics, electronics and energy, as well as automotive and transportation, each accounts for over 5%.

Financial Performance

Note: Growth rates may differ after conversion to US Dollars.

The company's revenue for fiscal 2021 increased to EUR 9.5 billion compared to EUR 7.9 billion in the prior year.

Net income for fiscal 2021 increased to EUR 282 million compared to EUR 103 million in the prior year.

Cash held by the company at the end of fiscal 2021 increased to EUR 2.3 billion. Cash provided by operations and investing activities were EUR 915 million and EUR 473 million, respectively. Cash used for financing activities was EUR 652 million, mainly for purchase of treasury shares.

Strategy

As part of this new phase of transformation, and in order to achieve its organic growth target of between 3% and 3.5% on average per year over the period 2020-2024, Arkema will leverage its recent production unit start-ups and continue its ambitious investment policy in high-growth countries. These projects, the most significant of which concerns the expansion of its specialty polyamides in Asia, will support growth in demand in several key end-markets, such as consumer goods, new energies and clean mobility.

Technological innovation is at the heart of Arkema's strategy and a key growth driver. It enables the group to address major economic and societal challenges through solutions that contribute to the United Nations' Sustainable Development Goals.

The company aims to more than double the organic growth of its Specialty Materials between 2020 and 2024 through bolt-on acquisitions. Priority will be given to Adhesive Solutions with, on average, two to three small transactions per year supplemented by one to three medium-sized acquisitions over the period.

Mergers and Acquisitions

In mid- 2022, Arkema announced to acquire Polimeros Especiales, a leading emulsion resins producer in Mexico. This planned acquisition is fully in line with Arkema's strategy to expand its Coating Solutions segment in growing markets and in low-volatile organic compound solutions. Waterborne is one of Arkema's key solventfree technologies, together with powder, ultraviolet/light emitting diode/electron beam and high-solid systems. Terms were not disclosed.

Also in mid-2022, Arkema finalizes the acquisition of Permoseal in South Africa, a leader in adhesive solutions for DIY, packaging and construction. Permoseal's well-known brands will complement Bostik's offering in the region and strengthen its positions in South Africa's and Sub-Saharan Africa's dynamic industrial, construction and DIY markets. Terms were not disclosed.

In early 2022, Arkema finalizes the acquisition Ashland performance adhesives. This acquisition also allows to upgrade the 2024 profitability target for Arkema's Adhesive Solutions segment, which now aims for an EBITDA margin above 17%, among the very best in the industry, with sales of over EUR 3 billion.

Also in early 2022, Arkema strengthens its engineering adhesives with the acquisition Shanghai Zhiguan Polymer Materials (PMP) which specialized in hot-melt adhesives for the consumer electronics market. This project is in line with Bostik's strategy to build a strong position in the attractive engineering adhesives market and to accelerate its development in the fast-growing electronics market, especially in Asia. Terms were not disclosed.

EXECUTIVES

Chairman, Chief Executive Officer, Executive Chairman, Thierry Le Henaff
Chief Operating Officer, Marc Schuller
Industry and Corporate Social Responsibility Executive Vice President, Luc Benoit-Cattin
Strategy Executive Vice President, Bernard Boyer
Chief Financial Officer, Marie-Jose Donsion
Human Resources Executive Vice President, Communications Executive Vice President, Thierry Parmentier
Senior Independent Director, Independent Director, Helene Moreau-Leroy
Independent Director, Sebastien Moynot
Independent Director, Marie-Ange Debon
Independent Director, Ilse Henne
Independent Director, Ian Hudson
Independent Director, Victoire de Margerie
Independent Director, Thierry Pilenko

Independent Director, Philippe Sauquet
Director, Jean-Marc Bertrand
Director, Isabelle Boccon-Gibod
Director, Laurent Mignon
Director, Nathalie Muracciole
Director, Nicholas Patalano
Director, Susan Rimmer
Auditors : KPMG Audit

LOCATIONS

HQ: Arkema S.A.
420, rue d'Estienne d'Orves, Colombes, Cedex 92705
Phone: (33) 1 49 00 80 80 **Fax:** (33) 1 49 00 83 96
Web: www.arkema.com

2015 sales

	% of total
Europe	38
North America	33
Asia	24
Other	5
Total	100

PRODUCTS/OPERATIONS

2015 sales

	% of total
Coating Solutions	24
High Performance Materials	44
Industrial Specialties	32
Total	100

Selected Products
Industrial Chemicals
  Acrylics
  Fluorochemicals
  Hydrogen peroxide
  PMMA
  Thiochemicals
Performance Products
  Functional additives (additives and organic peroxides)
  Specialty Chemicals
  Technical polymers
Vinyl Products
  Chlorine/Soda
  Pipes and profiles
  PVC
  Vinyl compounds

COMPETITORS

DCC PUBLIC LIMITED COMPANY
Evonik Industries AG
FLUIDRA, SA
GOODWIN PLC
KRATON CORPORATION
MINERALS TECHNOLOGIES INC.
MITSUBISHI CHEMICAL HOLDINGS CORPORATION
MPM HOLDINGS INC.
REXEL
VALLOUREC

HISTORICAL FINANCIALS
Company Type: Public

Income Statement
FYE: December 31

	REVENUE ($mil)	NET INCOME ($mil)	NET PROFIT MARGIN	EMPLOYEES
12/22	12,335	1,030	8.4%	21,100
12/21	10,774	1,481	13.8%	20,209
12/20	9,675	407	4.2%	20,576
12/19	9,810	609	6.2%	20,507
12/18	10,096	809	8.0%	20,010
Annual Growth	5.1%	6.2%	—	1.3%

2022 Year-End Financials
Debt ratio: 25.8% No. of shares ($ mil.): 74
Return on equity: 14.1% Dividends
Cash ($ mil.): 1,700 Yield: —
Current Ratio: 1.98 Payout: 23.8%
Long-term debt ($ mil.): 2,734 Market value ($ mil.): 6,717

	STOCK PRICE ($) FY Close	P/E High/Low		PER SHARE ($) Earnings	Dividends	Book Value
12/22	89.78	11	6	13.62	3.25	104.22
12/21	141.75	8	6	19.29	3.04	96.46
12/20	115.93	30	14	4.86	2.42	83.02
12/19	106.42	17	13	7.20	2.81	77.40
12/18	84.98	14	9	10.10	2.67	74.77
Annual Growth	1.4%	—	—	7.8%	5.0%	8.7%

Asahi Group Holdings Ltd.

EXECUTIVES

Chairman, Director, Akiyoshi Koji
President, Chief Executive Officer, Representative Director, Atsushi Katsuki
Chief Human Resources Officer, Executive Officer, Director, Keizo Tanimura
Chief Financial Officer, Executive Officer, Director, Kaoru Sakita
Senior Managing Executive Officer, Ryoichi Kitagawa
Senior Managing Executive Officer, Taemin Park
Outside Director, Christina L. Ahmadjian
Outside Director, Kenichiro Sasae
Outside Director, Tetsuji Ohashi
Outside Director, Mari Matsunaga
Auditors : KPMG AZSA LLC

LOCATIONS

HQ: Asahi Group Holdings Ltd.
1-23-1 Azumabashi, Sumida-ku, Tokyo 130-8602
Phone: (81) 3 5608 5116
Web: www.asahigroup-holdings.com

HISTORICAL FINANCIALS
Company Type: Public

Income Statement
FYE: December 31

	REVENUE ($mil)	NET INCOME ($mil)	NET PROFIT MARGIN	EMPLOYEES
12/22	19,056	1,150	6.0%	36,565
12/21	19,425	1,333	6.9%	36,685
12/20	19,673	900	4.6%	36,699
12/19	19,241	1,309	6.8%	35,996
12/18	19,280	1,373	7.1%	34,663
Annual Growth	(0.3%)	(4.3%)	—	1.3%

2022 Year-End Financials
Debt ratio: 0.2% No. of shares ($ mil.): 506
Return on equity: 7.9% Dividends
Cash ($ mil.): 284 Yield: —
Current Ratio: 0.58 Payout: 37.7%
Long-term debt ($ mil.): 8,575 Market value ($ mil.): —

Asahi Kasei Corp

EXECUTIVES

Chairman, Director, Hideki Kobori
President, Representative Director, Director, Koshiro Kudo
Senior Managing Executive Officer, Director, Kazushi Kuse
Representative Director, Toshiyasu Horie
Director, Hiroki Ideguchi
Director, Masatsugu Kawase
Outside Director, Tsuneyoshi Tatsuoka
Outside Director, Tsuyoshi Okamoto
Outside Director, Yuko Maeda
Outside Director, Chieko Matsuda
Auditors : PricewaterhouseCoopers Aarata LLC

LOCATIONS

HQ: Asahi Kasei Corp
1-1-2 Yuraku-cho, Chiyoda-ku, Tokyo 100-0006
Phone: (81) 3 6699 3030
Web: www.asahi-kasei.co.jp

HISTORICAL FINANCIALS
Company Type: Public

Income Statement
FYE: March 31

	REVENUE ($mil)	NET INCOME ($mil)	NET PROFIT MARGIN	EMPLOYEES
03/23	20,471	(685)	—	48,897
03/22	20,234	1,330	6.6%	46,751
03/21	19,020	720	3.8%	44,497
03/20	19,821	957	4.8%	40,689
03/19	19,598	1,332	6.8%	39,283
Annual Growth	1.1%	—	—	5.6%

2023 Year-End Financials
Debt ratio: 0.2% No. of shares ($ mil.): 1,387
Return on equity: (-5.4%) Dividends
Cash ($ mil.): 1,885 Yield: 3.7%
Current Ratio: 1.63 Payout: 0.0%
Long-term debt ($ mil.): 4,350 Market value ($ mil.): 19,402

	STOCK PRICE ($) FY Close	P/E High/Low		PER SHARE ($) Earnings	Dividends	Book Value
03/23	13.98	—	—	(0.49)	0.53	8.99
03/22	17.26	0	0	0.96	0.61	10.00
03/21	23.30	0	0	0.52	0.62	9.55
03/20	14.03	0	0	0.69	0.64	9.02
03/19	20.72	0	0	0.95	0.67	8.93
Annual Growth	(9.4%)	—	—	—	(5.7%)	0.1%

ASE Technology Holding Co Ltd

Advanced Semiconductor Engineering (ASE) helps chip makers wrap up production. The company is one of the world's leading providers of semiconductor packaging services; it also designs and manufactures interconnect materials and provides front-end and final chip testing services through its subsidiary ASE Test. The company provides electronic manufacturing services through Universal Scientific Industrial (USI), and it owns ISE Labs, an engineering test services provider in Silicon Valley. Customers in the US account for about 65% of ASE's sales. The company has more than 240 customers around the world; some of the largest include Broadcom, Microsoft, NVIDIA, and STMicroelectronics.

EXECUTIVES

Chairman, Chief Executive Officer, Director, Jason C. S. Chang
Vice-Chairman, President, Director, Richard H. P. Chang
Worldwide Marketing & Strategy Chief Operating Officer, Director, Tien Wu
Chief Corporate Governance Officer, Chief Administrative Officer, Du-Tsuen Uang
Chief Financial Officer, Director, Joseph Tung
Independent Director, Shen-Fu Yu
Independent Director, Tai-Lin Hsu
Independent Director, Mei-Yueh Ho
Director, Bough Lin
Director, Chi-Wen Tsai
Director, Raymond Lo
Director, Tien-Szu Chen
Director, Jeffrey Chen
Director, Rutherford Chang
Auditors : PricewaterhouseCoopers

LOCATIONS

HQ: ASE Technology Holding Co Ltd
  26, Chin 3rd Road, Kaohsiung 811
Phone: (886) 2 6636 5678   **Fax:** (886) 2 2757 6121
Web: www.aseglobal.com

2016 Sales

	% of total
US	68
Taiwan	14
Asia	9
Europe	8
Others	1
Total	100

PRODUCTS/OPERATIONS

2017 Sales

	% of total
EMS	46
Packaging	43
Testing	9
Other	2
Total	100

2017 Sales

	% of total
IC Wire Bonding	49
Bumping, Flip Chip, WLP, and SiP	30
Discrete and Other	11
Total	100

Selected Services
Material offerings
  Substrates
Packaging
  Ball grid array (BGA)
  Chip scale package (CSP)
  Dual-in-line
  Flip chip (flipping chip to connect with substrate)
  Pb free solution (lead-free)
  Pin grid array (PGA)
  Plastic-leaded chip carrier packages (PLCCs)
  Quad flat packages (QFP)
  SiP (system in package)
  Small-outline plastic J-bend packages (SOJ)
  Small-outline plastic packages (SOP)
  Thin quad flat packages (TQFP)
  Thin small-outline plastic packages (TSOP)
Testing
  Electrical design validation
  Failure analysis
  Front-end engineering testing
  Logic/mixed-signal final testing
  Memory final testing
  Reliability analysis
  Software program development
  Wafer probing
Other
  Burn-in testing
  Dry pack
  Tape and reel

Selected Subsidiaries and Affiliates
ASE Japan
ASE Korea
ASE Holding Electronics (Philippines), Incorporated
ASE Malaysia
ASE Test
Hung Ching (real estate development)
ISE Labs, Inc. (engineering and testing, US)
Universal Scientific Industrial Co., Ltd. (contract electronics manufacturing)

COMPETITORS

ADVANTEST AMERICA CORPORATION (DEL)
ALTERA CORPORATION
AMKOR TECHNOLOGY, INC.
ELECTRO SCIENTIFIC INDUSTRIES, INC.
GSI TECHNOLOGY, INC.
INFINITI SOLUTIONS PRIVATE LIMITED
MOSYS, INC.
Orient Semiconductor Electronics,Ltd.
PSEMI CORPORATION
VENTURE CORPORATION LIMITED

HISTORICAL FINANCIALS

Company Type: Public

Income Statement FYE: December 31

	REVENUE ($mil)	NET INCOME ($mil)	NET PROFIT MARGIN	EMPLOYEES
12/21	20,586	2,172	10.6%	95,727
12/20	16,973	959	5.7%	101,981
12/19	13,801	569	4.1%	96,528
12/18	12,133	825	6.8%	93,891
12/17	9,795	775	7.9%	68,753
Annual Growth	20.4%	29.4%	—	8.6%

2021 Year-End Financials

Debt ratio: 1.1%
Return on equity: 25.6%
Cash ($ mil.): 2,747
Current Ratio: 1.35
Long-term debt ($ mil.): 5,761
No. of shares ($ mil.): 4,282
Dividends
  Yield: 2.7%
  Payout: 76.3%
Market value ($ mil.): 33,447

	STOCK PRICE ($) FY Close	P/E High/Low		PER SHARE ($) Earnings	Dividends	Book Value
12/21	7.81	1	0	0.49	0.22	2.14
12/20	5.84	1	1	0.22	0.09	1.80
12/19	5.56	1	1	0.13	0.11	1.56
12/18	3.75	1	1	0.19	0.14	1.56
Annual Growth	27.7%	—		26.5%	11.2%	8.2%

Ashtead Group Plc

Ashtead is an international equipment rental company with national networks in the US, UK and Canada, trading under the name Sunbelt Rentals. It offers a full range of construction and industrial equipment across a wide variety of applications to a diverse customer base. It operates about 900 branches in the US. In UK, it is the largest rental company with over 190 stores and about 80 stores in Canada. Ashtead hires out everything from air compressors, pumps, scaffolding, and welders to aerial work platforms, road compactors, generators, and temporary traffic management equipment. Its US Market accounts for more than 80% of sales.

Operations

The company operates in one class of business, which is the rental of equipment divided to three business units, Sunbelt US, Sunbelt UK, and Sunbelt Canada. Ashtead's rental solutions cover situations such as non-residential construction, facilities management, disaster relief (pumps and power generation), major event management (power and lighting), climate control (cooling, heating, and dehumidification), scaffolding, and traffic management.

Geographic Reach

Headquartered in Cheapside, the US generates more than 80% of Ashtead's total revenue; the UK accounting for more than 10% and Canada account for roughly 5%. It has over 900 full-service Sunbelt stores in North America (including some 75 in Canada).

Financial Performance

Note: Growth rates may differ after conversion to US Dollars.

Ashtead group's performance for the past five years have continued to increase year over year with the last two years almost stagnant.

The group's revenue for the year decreased by £22 million to £5 billion in 2021 as compared to 2020's revenue of £5.1 billion.

Profit for the fiscal year 2021 also decreased to £697.4 million as compared to the prior year's net profit of £739.7 million.

Cash held by the company at the end of 2021 decreased to £19.2 million. Cash provided by operations was £1.4 billion. Investing activities and financing activities used £233 million and £1.4 billion, respectively. Main cash uses were for acquisitions of businesses and redemption of loans.

Strategy

For 2021, the company introduced its strategic plan Sunbelt 3.0, which despite the impact of COVID-19, is ambitious and reflects what the company believes is possible for them. Even under normal circumstances, the company's business is still cyclical and the company has made a business model that capitalizes on that. The company seeks to make the most of the structural growth opportunities available, particularly in the US and Canada. From 2011 to 2021, the company achieved a compounded annual growth rate of 16% and plans to achieve more through Sunbelt 3.0.

HISTORY

The Ashtead Group was founded in 1947 as Ashtead Plant Hire Company, a conventional industrial and plant equipment rental firm focused on the UK market. In 1984, when a buyout group led by Peter Lewis and George Burnett acquired it, the company had only 60 employees. The Ashtead Group went public in 1986. In 1990 the company made its first major excursion outside the UK with the acquisition of Sunbelt Rentals, based in the southeastern US.

The company underwent a growth spurt in the early 1990s. The UK construction industry was enduring a major recession, and hard times prompted firms to outsource their plant hire equipment. The company also went after clients from less-affected areas, such as water utilities and local government. In response, Ashtead doubled its sales force and invested heavily in new equipment.

The firm set up its Ashtead Technology unit in Aberdeen in 1993 to provide the oil exploration industry in the North Sea with specialized equipment (such as survey, inspection, video, and instruments) and technical advice. It later set up an Ashtead Technology branch in Singapore.

Still growing through acquisitions in 1996, Ashtead first bought Leada Acrow, a plant hire firm active in Ireland and the UK, then acquired McLean Rentals in the US, doubling the size of its Sunbelt Rentals operations. In 1997 Ashtead Technology set up a Houston office to serve oil exploration companies in the Gulf of Mexico.

Also in 1997, Ashtead acquired UK-based Sheriff Holdings, its first purchase of a publicly listed company, and subsequently disposed of that firm's waste disposal and heavy-equipment hire units. That year Ashtead launched an ambitious plan to up its number of UK rental offices from 146 to 300 by the year 2000.

The company acquired equipment renter UK Plant in 1999. It also began looking for a US merger partner in 1999, but instead bought 19 more US branches and opted to go it alone. In 2000 Ashtead acquired BET USA, Rentokil Initial's chain of rental equipment outlets in the US. That year it added to its US presence by acquiring environmental equipment group Response Rentals.

It took Ashtead just three months to integrate BET USA into its Sunbelt operations. In 2001 the company continued its US expansion by opening about 25 additional equipment outlets. In 2002, Ashtead restructured its UK-based A-Plant operations by selling off the subsidiary's low-performing assets. It also disposed of its A-Plant operations in Ireland in 2003.

EXECUTIVES

Sunbelt Chief Executive Officer, Executive Director, Brendan Horgan
Chief Financial Officer, Executive Director, Michael Pratt
Secretary, Eric Watkins
Non-Executive Chairman, Non-Executive Director, Paul Walker
Senior Independent Non-Executive Director, Non-Executive Director, Angus G. Cockburn
Independent Non-Executive Director, Jill Easterbrook
Independent Non-Executive Director, Tanya D. Fratto
Independent Non-Executive Director, Lucinda J. Riches
Independent Non-Executive Director, Lindsley Ruth
Auditors : Deloitte LLP

LOCATIONS

HQ: Ashtead Group Plc
100 Cheapside, London EC2V 6DT
Phone: (44) 20 7726 9700
Web: www.ashtead-group.com

2016 Sales

	% of total
North America	86
UK	14
Total	100

PRODUCTS/OPERATIONS

2016 Sales

	% of total
Sunbelt	86
A-Plant	14
Total	100

Selected Subsidiaries
Sunbelt Rentals, Inc. (US)
Ashtead Plant Hire Company Limited (A-Plant)

Selected Operations
A-Plant and Sunbelt Rental Equipment
    Aerial work platforms
    Air compressors
    Air nailers
    Ground-care products
    Lifting and handling equipment (forklifts, manlifts, scissorlifts)
    Paint sprayers
    Power generation equipment
    Pumps
    Tractors and trailers
    Traffic systems
    Trenchers
    Welders
    Woodworking tools
Sunbelt Specialty Services
    Convention services
    Generator rentals
    Pile driving services
    Pump rentals

COMPETITORS

AAON, INC.
AARON'S, LLC
AGGREKO PLC
H&E EQUIPMENT SERVICES, INC.
HARSCO CORPORATION
HERC HOLDINGS INC.
MIND TECHNOLOGY, INC.
RENTOKIL INITIAL PLC
TRUE VALUE COMPANY, L.L.C.
WINMARK CORPORATION

HISTORICAL FINANCIALS
Company Type: Public

Income Statement   FYE: April 30

	REVENUE ($mil)	NET INCOME ($mil)	NET PROFIT MARGIN	EMPLOYEES
04/23	9,667	1,617	16.7%	25,347
04/22	7,962	1,251	15.7%	21,752
04/21	6,997	969	13.9%	18,826
04/20	6,325	925	14.6%	19,284
04/19	5,853	1,036	17.7%	17,803
Annual Growth	13.4%	11.8%	—	9.2%

2023 Year-End Financials
Debt ratio: 36.5%   No. of shares ($ mil.): 438
Return on equity: 29.3%   Dividends
Cash ($ mil.): 29   Yield: —
Current Ratio: 1.01   Payout: 85.6%
Long-term debt ($ mil.): 6,595   Market value ($ mil.): 100,910

	STOCK PRICE ($) FY Close	P/E High/Low		PER SHARE ($) Earnings	Dividends	Book Value
04/23	230.15	76	45	3.66	3.14	13.70
04/22	206.46	124	73	2.80	2.32	11.38
04/21	260.42	175	75	2.16	2.01	10.07
04/20	108.65	87	39	2.02	1.94	8.19
04/19	111.65	77	50	2.15	1.69	7.30
Annual Growth	19.8%	—	—	14.2%	16.8%	17.1%

ASML Holding NV

ASML Holding is a global innovation leader in the chip industry that provides chipmakers with hardware, software, and services to mass produce patterns on silicon through lithography. ASML's products include EUV (extreme ultraviolet) lithography systems, DUV (deep ultraviolet) lithography systems, refurbished systems, and metrology and inspection systems. ASML staffs some 60 offices in three continents. More than 90% of its revenue comes from chip manufacturers in Asia and its customers include the world's biggest chipmakers. The company was founded in 1984.

Operations
ASML has one reportable segment, for the development, production, marketing, sales, upgrading and servicing of advanced semiconductor equipment systems, consisting of lithography, metrology and inspection systems.

System sales account for over 70% of the total sales, while service and field option sales account for the rest.

Geographic Reach
Netherlands-based ASML generates about 90% of its total revenue from Asia, of which Taiwan accounts nearly 40%, followed by

South Korea, China, and Japan. The US accounts for about 10%, while EMEA accounts for less than 5%.

Sales and Marketing

In 2021, two customers exceed more than 10% of total net sales, totaling EUR 12.5 billion, or more than 65%, of total net sales. ASML's comprehensive portfolio supports customers across the semiconductor industry from mass- producing advanced Logic and Memory chips to creating novel 'More than Moore' applications or cost-effective manufacturing of mature chip technologies.

Financial Performance

ASML achieved another record year in 2021, with total net sales increasing by EUR 4.6 billion, 33.1%, reflecting an increase in Net system sales of 32.3%, and an increase in Net service and field options sales of 35.4% compared to 2020. The increase in net sales was driven by a strong increase in demand from the company's customers across all technologies.

Net income in 2021 amounted to EUR 5.9 billion, or 31.6% of total net sales, representing EUR 14.36 basic net income per ordinary share, compared to net income in 2020 of EUR 3.4 billion.

The company had EUR 6.9 billion in cash in 2021 compared to EUR 6 billion the year before. Operating activities provided EUR 10.8 billion, while investing activities used EUR 72 million and financing activities used EUR 9.9 billion. Main cash uses were dividends paid, purchase of treasury shares, purchase of short-term investments, intangible assets, and property, plant and equipment.

Strategy

To realize ASML's long-term strategy vision within the semiconductor industry, the company continues to drive its core strategy, which it defines around five major pillars: strengthen customer trust, holistic lithography and applications, DUV competitiveness, EUV 0.33 NA for manufacturing and EUV 0.55 NA insertion.

HISTORY

ASML Holding's pedigree is as good as its timing was bad. The company was formed in 1984 under the name ASM Lithography Holding as a joint venture between Advanced Semiconductor Materials (ASM; now ASM International) and the Scientific and Industrial Equipment Division of Philips. ASML had already begun selling a wafer stepper (a device that transfers reticle patterns onto silicon wafers) when the joint venture was announced.

Unfortunately, the chip industry was headed into one of its infamous slumps. Startup costs dogged both ASM and Philips. Though the industry downturn abated by 1987, the financial stresses created by the slump led ASM to sell its 50% stake in ASML to Philips in 1988.

Philips offered a minority stake in ASML to the public in 1995. By 1998 ASML was battling Canon for the stepper industry's #2 spot. Also that year the company formed a unit to develop lithography equipment for makers of thin-film heads (used in recording and data storage), MEMS (microelectromechanical systems), and compound semiconductors.

In 1999 ASML joined with Applied Materials and Lucent Technologies (now Alcatel-Lucent) to form SCALPEL, an alliance formed to speed development of electron beam lithography. Also that year the company bought MicroUnity Systems' MaskTools unit (optical proximity correction technology). In 2000 Doug Dunn, a former CEO of the Philips Consumer Electronics Division, became ASML's president and CEO.

ASML later agreed to acquire Silicon Valley Group (SVG) in a deal valued at about $1.6 billion. In 2001, after many delays -- and opposition from some US business groups -- the US government cleared the way for the merger. As part of the deal, ASML and SVG were given six months to sell SVG's Tinsley unit, which made highly specialized optical gear for sensitive aerospace and military applications. Late in the year, ASML sold Tinsley to privately held SSG Precision Optronics (now L-3 SSG-Tinsley).

Also in 2001 Philips sold off nearly three-fourths of its remaining 24% stake in ASML. Later that year ASML cut 1,400 jobs -- about one-sixth of its workforce -- in the face of the worst downturn yet in the worldwide chip industry. That year the company also changed its name from ASM Lithography Holding to ASML Holding.

In 2004 Dunn retired as CEO. He was succeeded by Eric Meurice, a veteran executive of THOMSON, Dell, and Intel. ASML and Nikon reached a legal settlement on global patent litigation that year, including a cross-licensing agreement. The settlement called for ASML to make an initial payment of $60 million to Nikon, followed by payments of $9 million a year for three years.

Intel and Toshiba, two of the biggest chip makers in the world, licensed ASML's Scattering Bar Technology in 2005, technology that helped improve wafer yield results using ASML equipment. In 2007 ASML acquired Brion Technologies, a developer of software for photolithography optimization, for $270 million in cash. Founded in 2002, Brion became a wholly owned subsidiary of ASML.

EXECUTIVES

Chair, President, Chief Executive Officer, Peter T. F. M. Wennink
Technology Vice Chair, Product Vice Chair, Technology President, Product President, Technology Chief Technology Officer, Product Chief Technology Officer, Martin A. Van den Brink
Executive Vice President, Chief Financial Officer, Roger J. M. Dassen
Executive Vice President, Chief Operations Officer, Frederic J. M. Schneider-Maunoury
Chair, Director, Gerard J. Kleisterlee
Independent Director, Antoinette P. Aris
Independent Director, Mark D. M. Durcan
Independent Director, Johannes M. C. Stork
Independent Director, Terri L. Kelly
Independent Director, Birgit Conix
Independent Director, Rolf-Dieter Schwalb
Independent Director, Warren D. A. East
Auditors: KPMG Accountants N.V.

LOCATIONS

HQ: ASML Holding NV
De Run 6501, Veldhoven 5504 DR
Phone: (31) 40 268 3000
Web: www.asml.com

2018 Sales

	% of total
Korea	34
Taiwan	18
United States	18
China	17
EMEA	6
Japan	5
Singapore	2
Total	100

PRODUCTS/OPERATIONS

2018 Sales

	% of total
Net system sales	75
Net service and field option sales	25
Total	100

COMPETITORS

ASM International N.V.
CYMER, INC.
Chicago Bridge & Iron Company N.V.
Frank's International N.V.
Gemalto B.V.
LATTICE SEMICONDUCTOR CORPORATION
LyondellBasell Industries N.V.
MMC VENTURES LIMITED
NXP Semiconductors N.V.
Signify N.V.

HISTORICAL FINANCIALS

Company Type: Public

Income Statement — FYE: December 31

	REVENUE ($mil)	NET INCOME ($mil)	NET PROFIT MARGIN	EMPLOYEES
12/23	30,523	8,682	28.4%	42,416
12/22	22,614	6,006	26.6%	39,086
12/21	21,065	6,658	31.6%	32,016
12/20	17,155	4,361	25.4%	28,073
12/19	13,271	2,910	21.9%	24,900
Annual Growth	23.1%	31.4%	—	14.2%

2023 Year-End Financials

Debt ratio: 12.8%
Return on equity: 70.4%
Cash ($ mil.): 7,758
Current Ratio: 1.50
Long-term debt ($ mil.): 5,129
No. of shares ($ mil.): 393
Dividends
Yield: —
Payout: 0.0%
Market value ($ mil.): —

ASSA ABLOY AB

ASSA ABLOY is a global producer access solutions such as mechanical and electronic security products and security doors. ASSA ABLOY offering covers products and services related to openings such as locks, doors, gates and entrance automation solutions. It is also experts in trusted identities like keys, cards, tags, mobile and biometric identity verification systems. The company's products secure institutional and commercial buildings (hotels, offices, hospitals, schools). It also serves the residential market. The company offers its services through the ASSA ABLOY master brand and HID or Yale. Its operations span some 70 countries and generates its revenue in North America at around 50% of total sales.

Operations

Through ASSA ABLOY's divisions, the company is able to offer a complete range of innovative access solutions, including mechanical and electromechanical locks, cylinders, keys, tags, security doors, identification products and automated entrances.

The company has four product groups, with mechanical locks, lock systems and fittings (more than 20% of the company's revenue), entrance automation (more than 30%), electromechanical and electronic locks (about 30%), and security doors and hardware (about 20%).

Geographic Reach

ASSA ABLOY has both global and local presence with about 1,000 sites which includes more than 150 R&D sites and about 180 production facilities in more than 70 countries.

The North America market sales account for about 50% of the company's revenue, followed by Europe at about 35%. Other markets include Asia (about 10%), and Oceania, South America, and Africa (all accounting for less than 10%).

Sales and Marketing

The majority of the company's sales go through distributors. Most markets are fragmented where they sell their products to several distributors. The company works proactively with these distributors in product marketing and product development.

Financial Performance

ASSA ABLOY's performance for the past five years has fluctuated but had an overall increase, ending with 2022 as its highest performing year over the period.

The company's revenue increased by SEK25.8 billion to SEK120.8 billion for 2022, as compared to 2021's revenue of SEK95 billion.

ASSA ABLOY's net income for fiscal year end 2022 also increased to SEK13.3 billion, as compared to the prior year's net income of SEK10.9 billion.

The company held about SEK3.4 billion at the end of the year. Operating activities provided SEK14.4 billion to the coffers. Investing activities and financing activities used SEK10.6 billion and SEK4.7 billion, respectively. Main cash uses were for investments in subsidiaries and dividends.

Strategy

ASSA ABLOY's strategy has the company's common strategic framework and objectives, including continuing with successful acquisitions, growing in emerging markets, increasing service penetration, actively upgrading installed base, and generating more recurring revenue.

Mergers and Acquisitions

In 2022, ASSA ABLOY has signed an agreement to acquire Control iD, a leading developer of hardware and software solutions for access control and time & attendance in Brazil. The acquisition provides a great opportunity for the company to further develop its commercial and residential access control solutions and services to many different markets and applications in Brazil.

In mid-2022, ASSA ABLOY has signed an agreement to acquire VHS Plastik Metal (VHS), a leading manufacturer of hardware systems for windows and doors based in Turkey. "We are very excited about the acquisition of VHS. This transaction is a step change to our existing trading business in Turkey and reinforces our long-term commitment to the local market. VHS offers a strong range of window and door hardware products that will complement our offer in Turkey," says Neil Vann, Executive Vice President of ASSA ABLOY and Head of EMEIA Division.

Also in 2022, ASSA ABLOY has acquired J Newton Enterprises Inc, a leading pedestrian door distributor and service company in Florida. "I am very pleased to welcome J Newton Enterprises into the ASSA ABLOY Group. This acquisition delivers on our strategy to reinforce our current offering within entrance automation," says Nico Delvaux, President and CEO of ASSA ABLOY.

ASSA ABLOY completed eight acquisition in 2021, mainly to strengthen and expand its core operations. Of particular significance was its purchase of the US-based Hardware and Home Improvement (HHI), a division of Spectrum Brands. It is a leading provider of security, plumbing, and builders' hardware products to the North American residential segment with a diversified product offering of locksets, faucets, and buildersÂ´ hardware. The acquisition advances ASSA ABLOY strategy to strengthen its position by adding complementary products to the core business and it will further accelerate the transformation from mechanical to digital solutions.

Company Background

The current incarnation of the company was formed following the spinoff of Assa AB from security group Securitas. Assa subsequently acquired lockmaster Abloy from Finnish company WÃ¤rtsilÃ¤; the two merged to form ASSA ABLOY in 1994.

Abloy traces its roots to 1907, when Emil Henriksson, a young precision mechanic from Helsinki, noticed that the principle of rotating detainer discs inside cash register cylinders could also be applied to locks. He patented his invention in 1919 under the name Henriksson's Patent Lock.

Assa's history goes back even farther, to 1881, when 29-year old August Stenman put himself in debt to buy the Thunell hinge factory in the town of Eskilstuna, Sweden.

EXECUTIVES

President, Chief Executive Officer, Nico Delvaux
Executive Vice President, Chief Financial Officer, Erik Pieder
Executive Vice President, Lucas Boselli
Executive Vice President, Simon Ellis
Executive Vice President, Chief Human Resources Officer, Maria Romberg Ewerth
Executive Vice President, Massimo Grassi
Executive Vice President, Bjorn Lidefelt
Executive Vice President, Stephanie Ordan
Executive Vice President, Martin Poxton
Executive Vice President, Neil Vann
Chairman, Independent Director, Lars Renstrom
Vice-Chairman, Independent Director, Carl Douglas
Independent Director, Johan Hjertonsson
Independent Director, Sofia Schorling Hogberg
Independent Director, Eva Karlsson
Independent Director, Lena Olving
Independent Director, Joakim Weidemanis
Independent Director, Susanne Pahlen Aklundh
Director, Rune Hjalm
Director, Mats Persson
Deputy Director, Bjarne Johansson
Deputy Director, Nadja Wikstrom
Auditors : Ernst & Young AB

LOCATIONS

HQ: ASSA ABLOY AB
Klarabergsviadukten 90, Stockholm SE-107 23
Phone: (46) 8 506 485 00   **Fax:** (46) 8 506 485 85
Web: www.assaabloy.com

2014 Sales

	% of total
Europe	41
North America	36
Asia	16
Oceania	4
South America	2
Africa	1
Total	100

PRODUCTS/OPERATIONS

Assicurazioni Generali S.p.A.

Assicurazioni Generali is one of the largest global players in the insurance industry. Present in some 50 countries, Generali's core businesses are involved in both life and property/casualty insurance (including accident, health, motor, fire, marine/aviation, and reinsurance). Generali is one of the major global players in the insurance and asset management sector. In more earthbound realms, the company targets individuals and small to midsized businesses, and has been in business since 1831. It generated majority of its sales from Italy.

Operations

The company operates in four segments: Life (over 40% of operating sales), Property & Casualty (some 40% of sales), Asset Management (approximately 10%), and Holding and other business (nearly 10%).

Activities of Life segment include saving and protection business, both individual and for family, as well as unit linked products with investment purposes and complex plans for multinationals. Investment vehicles and entities supporting the activities of Life companies are also reported in this segment.

Activities of Non-life segment or the Property & Casualty segment include both motor and non-motor businesses, among which motor third party liabilities, casualty, accident, and health. It also includes more sophisticated covers for commercial and industrial risks and complex plans for multinationals. Investment vehicles and entities supporting the activities of Non-life companies are also reported in this segment.

The Asset management segment operates as a supplier of products and services both for the insurance companies of the Generali Group and for third-party customers identifying investment opportunities and sources of income for all of its customers, simultaneously managing risks.

The Holding and other business is a heterogeneous pool of activities different form insurance and asset management and in particular it includes banking activities, expenses related to the management and coordination activities, the group's business financing as well as other activities that the group considers ancillary to the core insurance business.

Generali also promotes its financial services operations, including Banca Generali, which offer such services as wealth management and bank insurance products.

Geographic Reach

Headquartered in Italy, the company primarily operates in Western Europe, especially in Italy (some 30% of operating sales), Austria, CEE and Russia (about 15%), Germany (some 15%), France (roughly 15%), and International (over 10%, which include Spain, and Switzerland). Generali also operates in Asia (including China, Hong Kong, India, Indonesia, Japan, the Philippines, Singapore, Thailand, Malaysia, and Vietnam), Central and South America, and the Middle East; it also has offices in India and China.

Sales and Marketing

Generali serves some 68 million customers around the world. It sells through channels including its own global network of agents as well as financial advisors, and brokers. It also sells by telephone and online.

Financial Performance

Generali's revenue for fiscal 2021 increased by 14% to EUR 1.1 billion compared from the prior year with EUR 993 million. The increase in Assets Under Management (AUM) - driven by positive net inflows - the good performance of financial markets and the growth in revenues of the companies which are part of the multi-boutique platform.

Net income for fiscal 2021 increased by 30% to EUR 504 million compared from the prior year with EUR 386 million.

Cash held by the company at the end of fiscal 2021 increased to EUR 8.4 billion. Cash provided by operations was EUR 17.5 billion while cash used for investing and financing activities were EUR 16.3 billion and EUR 677 million, respectively. Main uses of cash were for net cash flows from available for sale financial assets, and dividends payment.

Strategy

Generali's IT security strategy, named Cyber Security Transformation Program 2, 2020-2022, aims to further increase its security posture through the adoption of innovative and advanced solutions and the progressive standardization and centralization of the company security services. The company engage more than 40 countries and business units through 27 projects. Generali is strengthening the company resilience thanks to the enhancement of its ability to prevent, identify and respond to potential cyber-attacks, and increasing assessments to ensure adequate security levels to its business initiatives based on new technologies, like cloud and Internet of Things technologies.

HISTORY

Assicurazioni Generali was founded as Assicurazioni Generali Austro-Italiche in 1831 by a group of merchants led by Giuseppe Morpurgo in the Austro-Hungarian port of Trieste. Formed to provide insurance to the city's bustling trade industry, the company offered life, marine, fire, flood, and shipping coverage. That year Morpurgo established what he intended to be Generali's headquarters in Venice. (While the company maintained offices in both cities, Trieste ultimately won out.)

By 1835 Generali had opened 25 offices in Central and Western Europe; it had also expelled Morpurgo. The firm moved into

---

2014 Sales

	% of total
EMEA	25
Americas	21
Asia/Pacific	14
Global Technologies	13
Entrance Systems	27
Total	100

2014

	% of total
Mechanical locks, lock systems & accessories	30
Entrance automation	27
Electromechanical & electronic locks	23
Security doors & hardware	20
Total	100

Selected Products
Access control and identification
ASSA ABLOY Mobile Keys
Door automatics
Door closers
Electromechanical and electronic locks
Hotel locks and security
Mechanical locks and hardware
Security doors

COMPETITORS

AMERICAN SCIENCE AND ENGINEERING, INC.
APTIV PLC
AVAYA INC.
CARILLION PLC
DIEBOLD NIXDORF, INCORPORATED
G4S PLC
HALMA PUBLIC LIMITED COMPANY
INGENICO GROUP
INNERWORKINGS, INC.
TEAM, INC.

HISTORICAL FINANCIALS

Company Type: Public

Income Statement — FYE: December 31

	REVENUE ($mil)	NET INCOME ($mil)	NET PROFIT MARGIN	EMPLOYEES
12/22	11,644	1,281	11.0%	52,463
12/21	10,486	1,203	11.5%	50,934
12/20	10,727	1,122	10.5%	48,471
12/19	10,107	1,074	10.6%	48,992
12/18	9,389	307	3.3%	48,353
Annual Growth	5.5%	42.9%	—	2.1%

2022 Year-End Financials

Debt ratio: 1.9%
Return on equity: 17.0%
Cash ($ mil.): 329
Current Ratio: 1.20
Long-term debt ($ mil.): 1,978
No. of shares ($ mil.): 1,110
Dividends
Yield: —
Payout: 17.7%
Market value ($ mil.): 11,885

	STOCK PRICE ($) FY Close	P/E High/Low		PER SHARE ($) Earnings	Dividends	Book Value
12/22	10.70	1	1	1.15	0.20	7.46
12/21	15.27	2	1	1.08	0.22	6.91
12/20	12.30	2	1	1.01	0.21	6.49
12/19	11.65	1	1	0.97	0.18	5.72
12/18	8.87	4	3	0.28	0.19	5.22
Annual Growth	4.8%	—	—	42.9%	2.2%	9.4%

Africa and Asia in the 1880s. In 1900 Generali began selling injury and theft insurance. In 1907 Generali's Prague office provided the young, experimental writer Franz Kafka his first job. (He found it disagreeable and quit after a few months.)

During WWI the firm's Venice office pledged allegiance to Italy, while the office in Trieste (still part of Austria-Hungary) stayed loyal to the Hapsburgs. After the war Trieste was absorbed by the new Italian republic. Under Edgardo Morpurgo, Generali expanded further in the 1920s, managing 30 subsidiaries and operating in 17 countries. As fascist Italy aligned itself with Germany in the 1930s, adoption of anti-Semitic laws caused Morpurgo and a number of other high-ranking Jewish employees to flee the country. In 1938 Generali moved its headquarters to Rome (but moved them back to Trieste after war's end).

The firm maintained steady business both before and during Nazi occupation in WWII; in 1945, however, the Soviets seized all Italian properties in Eastern Europe, including 14 Generali subsidiaries. In 1950 Generali invaded the US market, offering shipping and fire insurance and reinsurance. Generali established a cooperative agreement with Aetna Life and Casualty (now Aetna Inc.) in 1966, further cementing its US connections.

In 1988 Generali tried to acquire French insurer Compagnie du Midi. Foreshadowing Generali's later dealings with Istituto Nazionale delle Assicurazioni (INA), Midi escaped Generali's grasp through a merger with AXA. As the Iron Curtain frayed in 1989, Generali formed AB Generali Budapest through a joint venture with a Hungarian insurer. In 1990 the firm opened an office in Tokyo through an agreement with Taisho Marine and Fire Insurance (which became Mitsui Marine & Fire Insurance and is now Mitsui Sumitomo Insurance). By 1993 Generali had become Italy's largest insurer.

In 1997 the firm was accused, along with other major European insurers, of not paying on policies of Holocaust victims. (It moved to settle claims in 1999.)

EXECUTIVES

Chief Executive Officer, Executive Director, Philippe Donnet
Secretary, Giuseppe Catalano
Chairman, Gabriele Galateri di Genola
Deputy Vice-Chairman, Non-Independent Director, Francesco Gaetano Caltagirone
Vice-Chairman, Director, Clemente Rebecchini
Independent Director, Romolo Bardin
Independent Director, Paolo Di Benedetto
Independent Director, Alberta Figari
Independent Director, Ines Mazzilli
Independent Director, Antonella Mei-Pochtler
Independent Director, Diva Moriani
Independent Director, Roberto Perrotti
Independent Director, Sabrina Pucci
Director, Lorenzo Pellicioli
Auditors : KPMG S.p.A.

LOCATIONS

HQ: Assicurazioni Generali S.p.A.
Piazza Duca degli Abruzzi 2, Trieste 34132
Phone: (39) 40 671402 **Fax:** (39) 40 671600
Web: www.generali.com

2018 Sales

	% of total
Italy	3
Germany	15
France	13
Austria, CEE & Russia	14
International	
Spain	5
Switzerland	5
Americas and Southern Europe	2
Asia	1
Europ Assistance	2
Investments, Asset & Wealth Management	10
Total	100

PRODUCTS/OPERATIONS

2018 Sales by Segment

	% of total
Life	57
Property/casualty	37
Holding & other	6
Total	100

COMPETITORS

AEGON N.V.
AIA GROUP LIMITED
Korean Reinsurance Company
METLIFE, INC.
NIPPON LIFE INSURANCE COMPANY
OLD COMPANY 20 LIMITED
REINSURANCE GROUP OF AMERICA, INCORPORATED
RFIB GROUP LIMITED
THE GUARDIAN LIFE INSURANCE COMPANY OF AMERICA
Zurich Insurance Group AG

HISTORICAL FINANCIALS

Company Type: Public

Income Statement — FYE: December 31

	NET ASSETS ($mil)	INCOME ($mil)	INCOME AS % OF ASSETS	EMPLOYEES
12/23	563,341	4,150	0.7%	81,879
12/22	554,369	3,110	0.6%	82,061
12/21	663,526	3,222	0.5%	74,621
12/20	668,517	2,140	0.3%	72,644
12/19	577,746	2,997	0.5%	71,936
Annual Growth	(0.6%)	8.5%	—	3.3%

2023 Year-End Financials

Return on assets: 0.7%
Return on equity: 16.5%
Long-term debt ($ mil.): —
No. of shares ($ mil.): 1,542
Sales ($ mil.): 60,968
Dividends
Yield: —
Payout: 15.6%
Market value ($ mil.): 16,306

	STOCK PRICE ($) FY Close	P/E High/Low		PER SHARE ($) Earnings	Dividends	Book Value
12/23	10.57	5	4	2.68	0.42	20.80
12/22	8.88	6	4	1.97	0.37	11.18
12/21	10.59	6	4	2.01	0.58	21.07
12/20	8.75	10	5	1.34	0.21	23.48
12/19	10.47	6	5	1.89	0.33	20.29
Annual Growth	0.2%	—	—	9.2%	6.4%	0.6%

Associated British Foods Plc

Associated British Foods (ABF) is a highly diversified group, with a wide range of food and ingredient businesses, including its own low-cost high-street fashion chain Primark. ABF also makes and markets grocery products, sugar, ingredients, and agricultural products. Some of its well-known brands include Twinings, Ovomaltine, Patak's, Blue Dragon, Kingsmill, and Silver Spoon, among others. Other divisions churn out sugar, specialty oils, and animal feed. ABF's activities span nearly 55 countries worldwide and provide its services through about 130,000 employees. Roughly 40% of the company's revenue is generated within the UK.

Operations

ABF's business is divided into Retail, Groceries, Sugar, Ingredients, and Agriculture.

The Groceries segment, responsible for approximately 30% of sales, manufactures products such as hot beverages, sugar and sweeteners, vegetable oils, and bread and baked goods. Its brands include hot beverages Twinings (tea) and Ovaltine (hot chocolate), Silver Spoon and Billington's (sugar), Jordans and Dorset Cereals (breakfast cereals), Mazola (corn oil), and others.

The Agriculture and Ingredients segments generate around 10% each of sales and manufacture animal feed and bakery ingredients, respectively.

However, despite its focus on food, ABF's largest segment by revenue is Retail. The segment owns low-cost high-street chain Primark.

Geographic Reach

Based in the UK, ABF has direct operations in around 55 countries across Europe, Africa, the Americas, the Asia/Pacific region, and Australia. ABF generates close to 35% of its annual sales in the UK and another nearly 35% in countries in Europe and Africa. The Asia/Pacific region the Americas the remaining more than 15%, each.

The Sugar business operates about 30 factory plants in ten countries, enabling the segment to produce about 4.5 million tons of sugar, annually. Its operations dominate regions including Africa, the UK, Spain, and north east China. Primark operates in about 15 countries.

Sales and Marketing

ABF's branded products are sold through supermarkets and other retail outlets and via wholesale and foodservice channels.

Financial Performance

Note: Growth rates may differ after conversion to US Dollars.

The company's performance for five years has fluctuated but overall had a downslope trend with 2021 as its lowest performing year over the five-year period.

ABF's revenue for 2021 decreased by about £53 million to about £13.8 billion compared with £13.9 billion in the prior year. All its food businesses delivered growth and in aggregate sales were 5% ahead of last year at constant currency. Primark sales in both years were impacted by trading restrictions and store closures as a result of government measures taken to contain the spread of COVID-19. The periods of closure were longer this year compared to the last financial year and sales declined by 5% at constant currency as a result.

Net income for the year ended 2021 increased by about £23 million to £478 million from £455 million in the prior year.

The company's cash for the year ended 2021 was £2.2 billion. Operating activities generated £1.4 billion. Investing activities and financing activities used £561 million and £512 million, respectively. Main cash uses were for purchases of property, plant, and equipment; and repayment of lease liabilities.

Strategy

Associated British Foods' strategy includes a long-term view, organic and acquisition growth; a devolved operating model; entrepreneurial flair; capital discipline; prudent balance sheet management; commitment to ethical conduct; and a sustainable business practice. All these are then applied to the company's five business segments through framework for collaboration, disciplined capital allocation, material risk assessment, and strategic engagement. As a result, the efforts of Associated British Foods enabled long-term value for its customers, employees, investors, shareholders, suppliers, communities, and governments.

HISTORY

When Garfield Weston took over his father's company upon the elder Weston's death in 1924, George Weston Limited was one of Canada's largest bakeries. Ten years later, taking advantage of the cheap prices afforded by a worldwide depression, Garfield purchased a biscuit-making division from Scottish baker Mitchell & Muir and opened a factory in Edinburgh. He promptly purchased other UK bakeries and grouped them in 1935 as Allied Bakeries.

Allied went public that year, with the Weston family controlling most of its shares. The company's early accomplishments included the introduction of sliced bread to the UK. By 1940 Allied had acquired more than 30 bakeries and had become Britain's largest baker by introducing inexpensive biscuits to the masses.

Garfield's son Garry joined Allied's board of directors in 1948. The following year the company acquired two Australian firms: Gold Crust Bakeries and Gartelle White. It also bought the Ryvita Company, a maker of crispbread. Placed under Garry's control, Ryvita eventually became a household name in the UK. Garry also helped the Burton's biscuit division launch the popular Wagon Wheels chocolate biscuits in 1951. Three years later he was sent to Australia to oversee the company's operations there.

To control the entire food-selling process, Allied moved into retailing during the 1950s, acquiring famous London department store Fortnum & Mason (later acquired by the Weston family). The company was renamed Associated British Foods (ABF) in 1960. During the 1960s ABF opened Primark clothing stores and bought the Fine Fare chain of supermarkets. By the time Garry returned to the UK to become CEO in 1966, his father had thrown together a number of businesses that made everything from flour to parrot food. To achieve a stronger focus, Garry sold many of these.

Growth continued internally. In 1970 ABF opened the largest bakery in Western Europe in Glasgow, Scotland. Frozen foods were added in 1978, the year Garfield died. The company's Twinings Tea subsidiary opened its first North American factory in 1980. Two years later ABF formed AB Ingredients to make new ingredients and additives for baked goods. The company sold the Fine Fare chain to Dee Corp. (now Somerfield) in 1986, and the following year it formed AB Technology to develop high-tech improvements for food processing.

After nearly 25 years without a major acquisition, in 1991 the company purchased British Sugar, one of the UK's two sugar processors, from Berisford, a diversified holdings firm. In 1995 the company acquired AC Humko, a manufacturer of specialty oils in the US, from Kraft. The next year ABF sold its supermarkets in the Irish Republic and Northern Ireland to the UK's biggest supermarket chain, Tesco. Peter Jackson was appointed CEO in 1999. That year the company acquired German baking ingredients producer Rohr Enzymes and bought several mills from Dalgety Feed.

In 2000 ABF sold its UK ice-cream business to Richmond Foods (now R&R Ice Cream). Deputy chairman Harry Bailey took over as chairman when Garry became ill. ABF sold Burtons Biscuits (Wagon Wheels) that year to investment firm HM Capital Partners (then called Hicks, Muse, Tate & Furst) for about $187 million, and it bought several Procter & Gamble commercial shortening and oil brands. In 2001 ABF sold AB Coatings, its food coatings business, and Nelsons, its jam and preserves business. Also that year the company agreed to buy the UK bakery ingredients business of the Kerry Group.

In 2002 ABF's subsidiary, ACH Food Companies, purchased 19 of Unilever's North American brands, including Mazola corn oil, Argo and Kingsford's corn starches, Karo corn syrup, and Henri's salad dressings. Also in 2002 ABF acquired the food and beverages business of Novartis, with the exception of Puerto Rican and US assets. (Brands included Caotina, Ovomaltine, and Ovaltine.) Later in the year the company sold off its Allied Glass Containers business to management.

In 2003 ABF sold six UK flour mills to Archer Daniels Midland. In 2004 the company acquired Unilever's Mexican oils and fats brands, including Inca, Mazola, and Capullo, in a $110 million cash transaction. Later that year it acquired Irish feed ingredients companies Vistavet and Nutrition Services Ltd. ABF's subsidiary ACH Food Companies also acquired the global yeast, herbs, and spice businesses of Australian company Burns, Philp. The acquisition included Burns, Philp's Fleischmann's Yeast brand and herb and spice company Tone Brothers.

In 2004 chief executive Peter Jackson unexpectedly announced he was stepping down. A member of ABF's founding and controlling family, George Weston, was chosen to succeed Jackson. (The Weston family also controls Canadian food processor and supermarket operator George Weston Limited).

ABF's Allied Grain unit formed a joint venture with Banks Cargill Agriculture, Frontier, in 2005. Frontier's products include grains and oilseeds. The 2005 purchase of retailer Littlewoods' stores added to ABF's Primark retail department-store operations.

In 2006 AFB bought the ethnic foods business of Heinz subsidiary, HP Foods; it also acquired a 51% stake in South Africa's largest sugar producer, Illovo, for $599 million in cash. The next year, it acquired Indian food maker, Patak's. Its meal-accompaniment products, Blue Dragon and Westmill Foods add to ABF's other ethnic cuisine offerings. The acquisition included Patak's assets and brands in all countries with the exception of India.

Already a player in the breakfast-food sector both in the US and internationally, in 2007 the company added to its branded food product offerings with the acquisition of Jordans, a UK maker of breakfast cereals, cereal bars, muesli, and oat porridge.

EXECUTIVES

Chief Executive Officer, Executive Director, George Garfield Weston

Financial Director, Executive Director, John G. Bason

Secretary, Paul Lister
Chairman, Director, Michael McLintock
Senior Independent Director, Independent Non-Executive Director, Ruth Cairnie
Independent Non-Executive Director, Graham Allan
Independent Non-Executive Director, Wolfhart Hauser
Independent Non-Executive Director, Heather Rabbatts
Independent Non-Executive Director, Richard Reid
Non-Executive Director, Emma Adamo
Auditors : Ernst & Young LLP

LOCATIONS

HQ: Associated British Foods Plc
Weston Centre, 10 Grosvenor Street, London W1K 4QY
Phone: (44) 20 7399 6500 **Fax:** (44) 20 7399 6580
Web: www.abf.co.uk

2018 Sales

	% of total
UK	38
Europe & Africa	38
Asia/Pacific	14
The Americas	10
Total	100

PRODUCTS/OPERATIONS

2018 Sales

	%
Retail	48
Grocery	22
Sugar	12
Ingredients	9
Agriculture	9
Total	100

Selected Products and Brands

Agriculture
    Animal feeds (AB Agri)
Grocery
    Bread, baked goods, and cereal
        Allinson breads
        Burgen breads
        Jordans cereals
        Kingsmill breads
        Ryvita rye crispbread
        Speedibake bakery products
        Sunblest bread, snacks, and rolls
        Tip Top bread and baked goods (Australia)
    Herbs and spices
        Durkee (US)
        Gravies
        Sauces
        Seasonings
        Soup bases
        Spices
        Spice Islands (US)
        Seasonings
        Spices
        Tone's spices (US)
    Hot beverages, sugar, and sweeteners
        Billington's cane sugars
        Jacksons of Picadilly teas
        Karo corn syrup
        Ovaltine
        Silver Spoon sugar (UK)
        La Tisaniere teas and infusions (France)
        Twinings teas
    Meat
        Don Deligoods (Australia)
        KRC (Australia)
    Vegetable oils
        Capullo canola oil (Mexico)
        Mazola corn oil (US)
    World foods
        Blue Dragon (Asian)
        Patak's (Indian)
    Other
        Askeys ice cream and dessert accompaniments
        Baking Mad
        Baking advice
        Recipes
        Tips
        Crusha milkshake mix
Ingredients
    Specialty ingredients
    Enzymes
    Specialty proteins and lipids
    Yeast extracts
    Yeast and bakery ingredients
    Argo corn starch
Retail clothing
    Primark
    Accessories
    Childrenswear
    Footwear
    Homeware
    Hosiery
    Lingerie
    Menswear
    Womenswear
Sugar
    Beet sugar

COMPETITORS

BAKKAVOR GROUP PLC
BOPARAN HOLDCO LIMITED
Bunge Limited
DANONE
GENERAL MILLS, INC.
George Weston Limited
KRAFT HEINZ FOODS COMPANY
PARMALAT FINANZIARIA SPA
RECKITT BENCKISER GROUP PLC
UNITED BISCUITS TOPCO LIMITED

HISTORICAL FINANCIALS

Company Type: Public

Income Statement   FYE: September 16

	REVENUE ($mil)	NET INCOME ($mil)	NET PROFIT MARGIN	EMPLOYEES
09/23	24,501	1,295	5.3%	133,487
09/22	19,380	798	4.1%	132,273
09/21	19,156	659	3.4%	127,912
09/20	17,875	583	3.3%	133,425
09/19	19,704	1,093	5.5%	138,097
Annual Growth	5.6%	4.3%	—	(0.8%)

2023 Year-End Financials

Debt ratio: 3.7%   No. of shares ($ mil.): 767
Return on equity: 9.2%   Dividends
Cash ($ mil.): 1,807   Yield: —
Current Ratio: 1.83   Payout: 27.5%
Long-term debt ($ mil.): 488   Market value ($ mil.): 19,782

	STOCK PRICE ($) FY Close	P/E High/Low		PER SHARE ($) Earnings	Dividends	Book Value
09/23	25.76	20	12	1.66	0.46	17.92
09/22	15.16	28	17	1.01	0.48	16.49
09/21	26.26	57	37	0.83	0.07	17.29
09/20	24.83	60	35	0.74	0.39	15.16
09/19	29.35	30	23	1.38	0.50	14.87
Annual Growth	(3.2%)	—	—	4.7%	(2.3%)	4.8%

AstraZeneca Plc

A global, science-led, patient-focused pharmaceutical company, AstraZeneca specializes in drugs for cardiovascular, renal and metabolism, respiratory and immunology, oncology, rare disease and other therapy areas. The company's biggest sellers include cholesterol reducer Crestor, cardiovascular drug Brilinta, acid reflux remedy Nexium, and Symbicort for asthma. AstraZeneca also markets drugs that aim to treat high cholesterol, diabetes, pain, and various cancers. The company has operations in the UK, US, Sweden, and China, among others, and its products are sold in more than 100 countries. Majority of its sales were generated outside the UK.

Operations

AstraZeneca operates as a single operating segment that researches, develops, manufactures, and commercializes biopharmaceuticals. Its research focuses on five therapy areas: Oncology; Cardiovascular, Renal & Metabolism; Respiratory & Immunology, Rare Disease; and Other Medicines and COVID-19.

Oncology brings in some 35% of total sales. Its major products include Faslodex for breast cancer and Zoladex for breast and prostate cancers.

The Cardiovascular, Renal, & Metabolism group is brings in around 21% of total sales. Its major products include Crestor for high cholesterol and Brilinta for the treatment of coronary syndromes and prevention of further coronary events. Other drugs include Farxiga, Onglyza, Bydureon, and Byetta (for type-2 diabetes); Symlin (diabetes); Seloken/Toptol-XL and Atacand (hypertension, heart failure, and angina).The Respiratory & Immunology unit brings in around 15% of total sales, largely from the sales of asthma drug Symbicort (the company's single biggest earner).

The Rare Disease, with about 10%.

The Other Medicines (around 5%) and COVID-19 segment (brings in about 10% of total sales) produces drugs in the areas of autoimmunity, infection, neuroscience, and gastroenterology. Its leading drugs include acid reflux medication Nexium and schizophrenia treatment Seroquel.

Geographic Reach

Cambridge, UK-based AstraZeneca has operations in Europe, Americas, Asia, Africa and Australasia region.

The Americas is AstraZeneca's most lucrative region, accounting for over 35% of sales. The Asia/Pacific region, Africa, and Australasia together represent nearly 35% of sales, Europe around 20%, and the company's native UK generate about 10% of sales.

Sales and Marketing

AstraZeneca markets its products to physicians through sales and marketing teams who are active in more than 100 countries.

Financial Performance

AstraZeneca's revenue increased 41% from $25.9 million in 2020 to $36.5 million in 2021. Growth was well balanced across AstraZeneca's strategic areas of focus with double-digit growth in all major regions, including Emerging Markets, despite some headwinds in China.

In 2021, the company's net income was $265 million, a $3.0 billion decrease from the previous year's net income of $3.1 billion. The decrease was due to large expenses in selling, general and administrative and in research and development.

The company's cash at the end of 2021 was $6 billion. Operating activities generated $6 billion, while investing activities used $11.1 billion, mainly for acquisition of subsidiaries. Financing activities generated another $3.6 billion.

Strategy

AstraZeneca, in early 2022, announced plans to open a new site at the heart of the Cambridge, MA, life sciences and innovation hub.

The new site will be a strategic R&D centre for AstraZeneca, as well as Alexion's new corporate headquarters. The site will bring together approximately 1,500 R&D, commercial and corporate colleagues into a single purpose-built space in Kendall Square, Cambridge, MA.

The site, scheduled for completion in 2026, will be in close proximity to several major academic, pharma and biotech institutions, inspiring greater collaboration and innovation potential, and providing access to future talent. The move reinforces AstraZeneca's commitment to the greater Boston area, with over 570,000 square feet of R&D and commercial space, and room for expansion for the future.

Mergers and Acquisitions

In late 2021, AstraZeneca's Alexion has exercised its option to acquire all remaining equity in Caelum Biosciences for CAEL-101, a potentially first-in-class fibril-reactive monoclonal antibody (mAb) for the treatment of light chain (AL) amyloidosis. AL amyloidosis is a rare disease in which misfolded amyloid proteins build up in organs throughout the body, including the heart and kidneys, causing significant organ damage and failure that may ultimately be fatal. Alexion will pay Caelum the agreed option exercise price of approximately $150 million, with the potential for additional payments of up to $350 million upon achievement of regulatory and commercial milestones.

In mid-2020, AstraZeneca completed the acquisition of Alexion Pharmaceuticals, Inc. (Alexion). The closing of the acquisition marks the company's entry into medicines for rare diseases and the beginning of a new chapter for AstraZeneca. AstraZeneca now has an enhanced scientific presence in immunology and, through Alexion's innovative complement-biology platform and robust pipeline, will continue to pioneer the discovery and development of medicines for patients with rare diseases. Rare diseases represent a significant unmet medical need and becomes a high-growth opportunity for the company. The total consideration paid to the Alexion shareholders was approximately $13.3 billion in cash and 236,321,411 new AstraZeneca shares.

HISTORY

AstraZeneca forerunner Imperial Chemical Industries (ICI) was created from the 1926 merger of four British chemical companies -- Nobel Industries; Brunner, Mond and Company; United Alkali; and British Dyestuffs -- in reaction to the German amalgamation that created I. G. Farben. ICI plunged into research, recruiting chemists, engineers, and managers and forming alliances with universities. Between 1933 and 1935, at least 87 new products were created, including polyethylene.

Fortunes declined as competition increased after WWII. In 1980 ICI posted losses and cut its dividend for the first time. In 1982 turnaround artist John Harvey-Jones shifted ICI from bulk chemicals to high-margin specialty chemicals such as pharmaceuticals and pesticides. That business became Zeneca, which ICI spun off in 1993.

The takeover specter loomed large over the company during its first year. Zeneca had several drugs in its pipeline, but it also had expiring patents on others, making them fair game for competitors. Bankrolled by its agrochemical business, Zeneca forged alliances with other pharmaceutical firms. In 1994 it entered a marketing alliance with Amersham International (now Amersham) to sell Metastron, a nuclear-medicine cancer agent. The next year Zeneca formed a joint venture with Chinese companies Advanced Chemicals and Tianli to make textile-coating chemicals.

In 1995 Glaxo was forced to sell a migraine drug candidate to complete its merger with Wellcome. Zeneca's gamble in buying the then-unproven drug (Zomig) paid off when the product gained US FDA approval two years later.

By 1997 Zeneca completed its gradual acquisition of Salick Health Care, formed to create more humane cancer treatment programs. The purchase followed a trend of large drug firms moving into managed care, which raised concerns that centers might be pressured to use their parent companies' drugs, but Zeneca maintained that Salick would remain independent except to the extent that it offered an opportunity to evaluate treatments.

In 1998 Zeneca got the FDA's OK to sell its brand of tamoxifen (Nolvadex) to women at high risk of contracting breast cancer. In 1999 it sued Eli Lilly to protect Nolvadex against Lilly's marketing claim that its osteoporosis treatment Evista reduced breast cancer risk, a use for which it was not approved.

In 1999 Zeneca completed its purchase of Sweden's Astra to form AstraZeneca. That year the firm sold its specialty chemicals unit, Zeneca Specialties, to Cinven Group and Investcorp. With its agricultural business stagnated due to crippled markets in Asia and Europe, AstraZeneca announced plans to merge the unit with the agrochemicals business of Novartis and spun it off as Syngenta.

In 2013 AstraZeneca sold its only non-pharma business, Aptium Oncology, an operator of cancer treatment centers in the US. This came on the heels of selling its other non-core units Astra Tech (medical devices) and Dentsply Sirona (dental implant systems).

EXECUTIVES

Chief Executive Officer, Executive Director, Pascal Soriot

Chief Financial Officer, Executive Director, Aradhana Sarin

Chief Strategy Officer, Marc Dunoyer

Chief Human Resources Officer, General Counsel, Chief Compliance Officer, Jeff Pott

Vaccines & Immune Therapies Executive Vice President, Iskra Reic

BioPharmaceuticals R&D Executive Vice President, Menelas Pangalos

Oncology R&D Executive Vice President, Susan Galbraith

Oncology Business Unit Executive Vice President, David Fredrickson

BioPharmaceuticals Business Unit Executive Vice President, Ruud Dobber

International and China President Executive Vice President, Leon Wang

Sustainability Executive Vice President, Sustainability Chief Compliance Officer, Katarina Ageborg

Information Technology Executive Vice President, Operations Executive Vice President, Sustainability Executive Vice President, Pam P. Cheng

Independent Non-Executive Chairman, Director, Leif Johansson

Senior Independent Non-Executive Director, Philip Broadley

Independent Non-Executive Director, Andreas Rummelt

Independent Non-Executive Director, Euan Ashley

Independent Non-Executive Director, Michel Demare

Independent Non-Executive Director, Deborah DiSanzo

Independent Non-Executive Director, Diana Layfield

Independent Non-Executive Director, Sherilyn S. McCoy

Independent Non-Executive Director, Tony Mok

Independent Non-Executive Director, Nazneen Rahman
Non-Executive Director, Marcus Wallenberg, $99,000 total compensation
Auditors : PricewaterhouseCoopers LLP

LOCATIONS

HQ: AstraZeneca Plc
1 Francis Crick Avenue , Cambridge Biomedical Campus, Cambridge, England CB2 0AA
Phone: (44) 20 3749 5000   **Fax:** (44) 1223 352 858
Web: www.astrazeneca.com

2018 sales

	%
The Americas	39
Asia, Africa, and Australasia	33
Continental Europe	17
UK	11
Total	100

PRODUCTS/OPERATIONS

2018 Sales

	$ mil.	% of total
Products		
Cardiovascular, Renal & Metabolism	6,710	30
Respiratory	4,911	22
Oncology	46,028	27
Other	3,400	16
Externalization	1,041	10
Total	22,090	100

Selected Products

Cardiovascular
  Atacand (angiotensin II antagonist for hypertension and heart failure)
  Brilinta (acute coronary syndromes and events in high-risk post myocardial infarction)
  Crestor (statin for cholesterol-lowering drug)
  Onglyza (type 2 diabetes)
  Plendil (calcium antagonist for hypertension and angina)
  Seloken/Toprol-XL (beta-blocker for blood pressure, heart failure, angina)
  Zestril (ACE inhibitor for hypertension, other)
Gastrointestinal
  Losec/Prilosec (acid reflux disease)
  Nexium (acid reflux disease)
Infection and Other Products
  FluMist (intranasal flu vaccine)
  Merrem/Meronem (intravenous antibiotic for serious hospital infections)
  Synagis (for respiratory syncytial virus, or RSV, in infants)
Neuroscience
  Diprivan (general anesthetic)
  Local anesthetics (Carbocaine, Citanest, Naropin, Xylocaine)
  Seroquel (anti-psychotic for schizophrenia and bipolar)
  Zomig (migraines)
Oncology
  Arimidex (aromatase inhibitor for breast cancer)
  Casodex (anti-androgen for prostate cancer)
  Faslodex (oestrogen receptor antagonist for breast cancer)
  Iressa (kinase inhibitor for non-small cell lung cancer)
  Nolvadex (breast cancer)
  Zoladex (LHRH agonist for prostate and breast cancer)
Respiratory & Inflammation
  Oxis (beta-agonist for asthma and chronic obstructive pulmonary disease)
  Pulmicort (anti-inflammatory for asthma)
  Rhinocort (topical nasal anti-inflammatory)
  Symbicort (anti-inflammatory and bronchodilator in one inhaler for asthma and chronic obstructive pulmonary disease)

Selected Subsidiaries

AstraZeneca AB (Sweden)
AstraZeneca BV (The Netherlands)
AstraZeneca Canada Inc.
AstraZeneca do Brasil Limitada
AstraZeneca Farmaceutica Spain SA
AstraZeneca GmbH (Germany)
AstraZeneca KK (Japan)
AstraZeneca LP (US)
AstraZeneca Pharmaceuticals Co., Limited (China)
AstraZeneca Pharmaceuticals LP (US)
AstraZeneca Pty Limited (Australia)
AstraZeneca SAS (France)
AstraZeneca SpA (Italy)
AstraZeneca UK Limited
IPR Pharmaceuticals Inc. (Puerto Rico)
MedImmune, L.L.C. (US)
Novexel SA (France)
NV AstraZeneca SA (Belgium)
Zeneca Holdings Inc. (US)

COMPETITORS

ASTELLAS PHARMA LTD.
Boehringer Ingelheim International GmbH
Evotec SE
NICOX SA
Roche Holding AG
SANOFI
SINCLAIR PHARMA LIMITED
Theratechnologies Inc
VECTURA GROUP PLC
VECTURA GROUP SERVICES LIMITED

HISTORICAL FINANCIALS

Company Type: Public

Income Statement
FYE: December 31

	REVENUE ($mil)	NET INCOME ($mil)	NET PROFIT MARGIN	EMPLOYEES
12/23	45,811	5,955	13.0%	89,900
12/22	44,351	3,288	7.4%	83,500
12/21	37,417	112	0.3%	83,100
12/20	26,617	3,196	12.0%	76,100
12/19	24,384	1,335	5.5%	70,600
Annual Growth	17.1%	45.3%	—	6.2%

2023 Year-End Financials

Debt ratio: 27.2%
Return on equity: 15.6%
Cash ($ mil.): 5,840
Current Ratio: 0.82
Long-term debt ($ mil.): 22,365
No. of shares ($ mil.): 1,550
Dividends
Yield: —
Payout: 37.2%
Market value ($ mil.): 104,403

	STOCK PRICE ($) FY Close	P/E High/Low		PER SHARE ($) Earnings	Dividends	Book Value
12/23	67.35	20	16	3.81	1.42	25.25
12/22	67.80	34	25	2.11	1.42	23.90
12/21	58.25	798	590	0.08	1.37	25.34
12/20	49.99	25	15	2.44	1.37	11.90
12/19	49.86	49	34	1.03	1.37	10.00
Annual Growth	7.8%	—	—	38.7%	0.9%	26.0%

Athene Holding Ltd (New)

Athene is a leading financial services company specializing in retirement services that issues, reinsures, and acquires retirement savings products designed for the increasing number of individuals and institutions seeking to fund retirement needs. It generates attractive financial results for its policyholders and shareholders by combining its two core competencies of sourcing long-term, generally illiquid liabilities and investing in a high-quality investment portfolio, which takes advantage of the illiquid nature of the company's liabilities. Through its operating subsidiaries, the company serves customers in all 50 states by providing products in the retirement savings market. Athene went public in December 2016. In early 2022, Athene and Apollo completed their merger in an all-stock transaction that implies a total equity value of approximately $11 billion for Athene.

Operations

Athene operates its core business strategies out of one reportable segment, Retirement Services. In addition to Retirement Services (brings in more than 55% of the company's revenue), it reports certain other operations in Corporate and Other (about 5%). The segment is comprised of the company's US and Bermuda operations that issue and reinsure retirement savings products and institutional products. It has retail operations, which provide annuity retirement solutions to its policyholders. Retirement Services also has reinsurance operations, which reinsure fixed indexed annuities (FIA), multi-year guaranteed annuities (MYGA), traditional one-year guarantee fixed deferred annuities, immediate annuities and institutional products from its reinsurance partners. In addition, the company's institutional operations, including funding agreement activities and pension group annuity operations, are included in its Retirement Services segment. Corporate and Other includes certain other operations related to the company's corporate activities, including corporate allocated expenses, merger and acquisition costs, debt costs, certain integration and restructuring costs, certain stock-based compensation, and intersegment eliminations. Non-operating adjustments account for the rest.

Its four distribution channels include retail, flow reinsurance, institutional, and acquisitions and block reinsurance. It conducts business primarily through its non-US reinsurance subsidiaries, to which AHL's other insurance subsidiaries and third-party ceding companies directly and indirectly reinsure a portion of their liabilities, including Athene Life Re Ltd. (ALRe), a Bermuda exempted company, and Athene Life Re International Ltd. (ALReI), and Athene USA Corporation, an Iowa corporation (together with its subsidiaries, AUSA).

Geographic Reach

Athene is headquartered in Bermuda.

Sales and Marketing

Athene distributes annuity products through a variety of channels including banks, broker dealers, and independent marketing organizations.

Financial Performance

The company had a revenue of $26.3 billion, a 78% increase from the previous year's revenue of $14.8 billion. This was primarily due to a higher volume of non-controlling interests, VIE expenses and other adjustments to revenues.

In 2021, the company had a net income of $3.7 billion, a 157% increase from the previous year's net income of $1.4 billion. This was primarily due to a higher sales volume for the year.

The company's cash at the end of 2021 was $10.4 billion. Operating activities generated $10.3 billion, while investing activities used $27.9 billion, mainly for purchases of available-for-sale securities. Financing activities provided another $19.6 billion.

Strategy

The key components of the company's long-term growth strategy are as follows:

Expand its Organic Distribution Channels. The company plans to grow organically by expanding its retail, flow reinsurance and institutional distribution channels with a focus on international expansion, particularly in Asia. These organic channels generally allow the company to adjust its product mix to originate liabilities that meet the company's return targets in diverse market environments.

Pursue Attractive Inorganic Growth Opportunities. The company plans to continue leveraging its expertise in sourcing and evaluating inorganic transactions to grow its business profitably.

Expand The Company's Product Offering. It seeks to build products that meet its policyholders' retirement savings objectives, such as accumulation, income and legacy planning.

Leverage Its Merger with Apollo in 2022. The company intends to leverage its merger with Apollo in 2022 and beyond to source high-quality assets with attractive risk-adjusted returns.

EXECUTIVES

Chairman, Chief Executive Officer, Chief Investment Officer, James R. Belardi, $863,750 total compensation
President, Subsidiary Officer, Grant Kvalheim, $750,000 total compensation
Executive Vice President, Chief Financial Officer, Martin P. Klein, $625,000 total compensation
Executive Vice President, General Counsel, John L. Golden
Executive Vice President, Chief Risk Officer, Douglas Niemann
Executive Vice President, Chief Operating Officer, Chief Actuary, Michael S. Downing
Senior Vice President, Corporate Controller, Principal Accounting Officer, Sarah VanBeck
Corporate Secretary, Natasha Scotland Courcy

Director, Lead Independent Director, Marc A. Beilinson
Director, Robert L. Borden
Director, Mitra Hormozi
Director, Scott M. Kleinman
Director, Brian Leach
Director, Gernot Lohr
Director, H. Carl McCall
Director, Matthew R. Michelini
Director, Manfred Puffer
Director, Marc J. Rowan
Director, Lawrence J. Ruisi
Director, Lynn C. Swann
Director, Hope Schefler Taitz
Director, Arthur Wrubel
Director, Fehmi Alexander Zeko
Auditors : DELOITTE & TOUCHE LLP

LOCATIONS

HQ: Athene Holding Ltd (New)
Second Floor, Washington House, 16 Church Street, Hamilton HM 11
Phone: (1) 441 279 8400
Web: www.athene.com

PRODUCTS/OPERATIONS

2015 Sales

	$ mil.	% of total
Net investment income	2,608	85
Product charges	248	8
Premiums & other	230	7
Adjustments		(470)
Total	2,616	100

HISTORICAL FINANCIALS

Company Type: Public

Income Statement — FYE: December 31

	NET ASSETS ($mil)	INCOME ($mil)	INCOME AS % OF ASSETS	EMPLOYEES
12/22	246,047	(4,162)	—	1,718
12/21	235,149	3,859	1.6%	1,403
12/20	202,771	1,541	0.8%	1,350
12/19	146,875	2,172	1.5%	1,325
12/18	125,505	1,053	0.8%	1,275
Annual Growth	18.3%	—	—	7.7%

2022 Year-End Financials

Return on assets: (-1.7%)
Return on equity: (-39.5%)
Long-term debt ($ mil.): —
No. of shares ($ mil.): 203
Sales ($ mil.): 7,623
Dividends
Yield: —
Payout: 0.0%
Market value ($ mil.): —

Atlas Copco AB (Sweden)

Atlas Copco is a pioneer and a technology driver, and industries all over the world rely on its expertise. The company's market-leading compressors, vacuum solutions, generators, pumps, power tools and assembly systems can be found everywhere. As a global, industrial company based in Stockholm, Sweden, the company has customers in more than 180 countries and over 49,000 employees. The company's industrial ideas empower its customers to grow and drive society forward. Atlas Copco is characterized by focused businesses in selected market segments, high customer focus through a decentralized organization, global presence, a stable service business, professional people, and an asset-light and flexible manufacturing setup.

Operations

The company has four business areas: compressor technique (generates about 45% of revenue), vacuum technique (nearly 30%), industrial technique (more than 15%), and power technique (nearly 15%).

The Compressor Technique business area provides compressed air solutions; industrial compressors, gas and process compressors and expanders, air and gas treatment equipment, air management systems, and service through a global network.

The Vacuum Technique business area provides vacuum products, exhaust management systems, valves and related products, and service through a global network.

The Industrial Technique business area provides industrial power tools, assembly and machine vision solutions, quality assurance products, software, and service through a global network.

The Power Technique business area provides portable air and power, industrial and portable flow solutions through products such as mobile compressors, generators, light towers, industrial and portable pumps, along with a number of complementary products. It also offers specialty rental and provides service through a global network.

Geographic Reach

The company generates nearly 40% from Asia/Oceania, more than 25% from Europe, about 25% from North America, about 5% from Africa/Middle East, and less than 5% from South America.

Sales and Marketing

The company's business area continued to invest in innovation and market presence in targeted markets and segments. One example of increased geographical presence was the opening of three new rental depots for the Specialty Rental business.

The global market for industrial power tools and assembly systems with related services has a large number of participants with a wide range of products in different applications such as assembly of parts, drilling and material removal. Customers are found in industries such as the automotive industry, off-highway vehicles, the electronics industry, aerospace, appliances, the energy sector, and general industrial manufacturing. In particular, the business area has been successful in developing advanced electric industrial tools and systems that assist customers in achieving fastening according to their specifications and minimizing errors and interruptions in production.

Financial Performance

The Group's revenues increased 27% to a record MSEK 141 325 (110 912), corresponding to a 12% organic increase. Currency had a positive effect of 12%, and acquisitions contributed with 3% during the year.

Profit before tax increased 28% to MSEK 30 044 (23 410). Excluding items affecting comparability, profit before tax was MSEK 29 893 (24 097), corresponding to margin of 21.2% (21.7).

Cash at the end of the year was MSEK 11 254. Operating activities generated MSEK 21 377 while investing and financing activities used MSEK 15 503 and MSEK 14 651.

Strategy

To succeed in its mission, Atlas Copco strives for a leading position in selected markets and segments. This is achieved through innovations and by delivering leading differentiated technology. With products and services critical to the customers' operations, Atlas Copco strives to support customers in their success. To support profitable growth over a business cycle, the company aims to have an agile balance sheet and focuses on markets with high service potential.

Acquisitions are an important part of the company's strategy for growth. The combination of organic growth and successful acquisitions has shaped it into the Group we are today, and it continues to look for new technologies and segments that complement its current offering.

Mergers and Acquisitions

In mid-2022, Atlas Copco acquired Les pompes Ã vide TECHNI-V-AC inc. TECHNI-V-AC is a distributor of Atlas Copco vacuum equipment and a service provider, in Canada. The acquisition will further strengthen Atlas Copco Vacuum Technique's presence in Canada. The company will operationally become part of the Vacuum Technique Service Division within the Vacuum Technique Business Area. The purchase price is not disclosed.

In 2022, Atlas Copco acquired CAS Products Ltd (CAS). The company specializes in sales, installation and service of compressed air systems and the main customers are industrial and service companies. CAS has a strong market presence in the North West region of England and this acquisition will enable to further develop Atlas Copco's brand portfolio. The company will become part of the service division within the Compressor Technique Business Area. The purchase price is not disclosed.

Also in 2022, Atlas Copco completed the acquisition of Pumpenfabrik Wangen GmbH, a German manufacturer of progressive cavity pumps used for transferring fluids mainly in the biogas and wastewater sectors. The company also manufactures twin-screw pumps used in sectors like food and beverage and cosmetics. This acquisition creates a solid foundation for further growth in new industrial pump segments. The acquired business will become part of the Power and Flow division within Atlas Copco's Power Technique Business Area. The purchase price is not disclosed.

In 2021, Atlas Copco has acquired AEP, a French distributor of compressors and provider of service. The company has a strong market presence in Paris and the ÃŽle-de-France region. Said Vagner Rego, Business Area President Compressor Technique. "By this acquisition we will reinforce our commitment to better serve our customers and strengthen our capabilities for the growing market of small- and medium-size companies." The purchase price is not material relative to Atlas Copco's market capitalization and is not disclosed.

In mid-2021, Atlas Copco has acquired CPC Pumps International Inc., a Canada-based company that specializes in the design, manufacturing, and servicing of custom-engineered, mission critical centrifugal pumps. The acquisition adds complementary assets to the company's portfolio and strengthens its market position. The purchase price is not material relative to Atlas Copco's market capitalization and is not disclosed.

Also in 2021, Atlas Copco has acquired IBVC Vacuum, S.L.U, known as Iberica Vacuum. The company's customers are mainly industrial and scientific companies as well as universities and research institutes in Spain and Portugal. Said Geert Follens, Business Area President Vacuum Technique. "Through this acquisition we will get the opportunity to better serve current customers and further strengthen our market presence for the Edwards brand in this key region of Southern Europe." The purchase price is not material relative to Atlas Copco's market capitalization and is not disclosed.

HISTORY

Eduard FrÃ¤nckel, chief engineer of Swedish Rail, founded the company in 1873 to make railroad equipment. It had a successful start by making wagons and railroad carriages. By 1876, however, competition had forced the company to diversify into producing steel bridge structures and frames for buildings and church towers. While this strategy worked for awhile, by 1887 losses forced FrÃ¤nckel to leave the company, and in 1891 the business went into liquidation.

Financier A. O. Wallenberg, whose financial backing had helped found the company, was its largest shareholder. He restructured Atlas and provided the loans needed to keep it alive. When Wallenberg died in 1886, his son, K. A. Wallenberg, took his seat as a director and recruited Oscar Lamm as managing director. Lamm reversed the company's fortunes, shifting it into the production of steam engines and machine tools. In 1892 Marcus Wallenberg became a board member and ran Atlas alongside Lamm.

Under Lamm and Wallenberg, the company bought the Swedish rights to produce Rudolf Diesel's engine and formed a new company (with Wallenberg's brother, Knut) -- AB Diesels Motorer. Lamm's nephew, Gunnar Jacobsson, became managing director of New Atlas in 1909. Demand increased for the company's diesel engines and machine tools before and during WWI. So in 1917 the company produced its last steam locomotive and merged AB Diesels and Atlas into one company -- AB Atlas Diesel -- with Jacobsson as its managing director.

The diesel engine business slumped after the war. Marcus Wallenberg, who had claimed chairmanship in 1933, was forced to provide loans to Atlas to keep it afloat. When Jacobsson retired in 1940, Wallenberg hired Walter Wehtje as managing director and shifted the company away from its money-losing diesel engine operations and into producing air compressors.

WWII forced Sweden to increase its farm acreage in order to sustain its population. The effort utilized the company's compressors and air tools to remove large boulders from rock-strewn fields. After the war Atlas focused on increasing exports. To compete, it provided technical services with its products, and by the late 1940s business had increased tenfold. The company dropped its unprofitable diesel engine line in 1948, and in 1956 it changed its name to Atlas Copco.

Developing ergonomic designs for its power tools provided rich dividends in the 1960s. In 1968 the company restructured into mining and construction, airpower, and tools segments. Tom Wachtmeister became CEO in 1975, and in 1980 the company made several purchases in the US to strengthen its revenues. Atlas Copco acquired Chicago Pneumatic Tool Co. (1987) and became the world's largest maker of air compressors in the process.

Michael Treschow, the managing director of Atlas Copco Tools AB, replaced Wachtmeister as CEO in 1991. He carried on the company's acquisition policy until he left in 1997 and was succeeded by Giulio Mazzalupi. In 1997 Atlas Copco bought Prime Service, one of the US's largest equipment rental companies, and in 1999 it bought US-based Rental Service Corporation (RSC) and its more than 290 equipment rental centers. The next year RSC bought 11 companies, as well. In early 2001 Atlas Copco acquired Masons Holdings Ltd., a UK-based generator manufacturer and renamed the company Atlas Copco Masons.

Atlas Copco expanded its construction and mining technique business in 2002 with the acquisitions of Krupp Berco Bautechnik GmbH (a Germany-based manufacturer of hydraulic demolition equipment for the mining and construction industries) and its sister company in France from ThyssenKruppTechnologies AG. Giulio Mazzalupi was succeeded as president and CEO that year by Gunnar Brock.

In mid-2004, citing limited synergies within the manufacturing and selling of electric tools versus Atlas Copco's other businesses, Atlas Copco announced the selling of Atlas Copco Electric Tools (Germany) and Milwaukee Electric Tool to Techtronic Industries for $713 million. The deal became official in January 2005.

In late 2006 Atlas Copco exited its Rental Service division when it sold most of its stake in RSC Equipment Rental to Ripplewood Holdings and Oak Hill Capital Management for about $3.4 billion. Atlas Copco retains about a 14% stake in RSC.

The decision to explore options for its Rental Service unit came in early 2006 as the company determined its rental operations were not a good strategic fit with its manufacturing activities. With operations limited to North America, Rental Service needed international expansion to grow. Atlas Copco decided investing further in Rental Services was not the best strategy for the company.

While 2005 was a decent year for Atlas Copco -- with high raw materials and purchased goods costs offset by price increases and improvements in operating efficiency -- 2006 was the best year in the company's history. All of the company's major geographic markets turned in double-digit growth. Orders from continuing operations increased by 23%. Revenue grew by 20% and operating profit grew by 33%.

Atlas Copco grew its compressor business through targeted acquisitions in China and North America, but greater still was organic growth fueled by new products, improvements in its sales and distribution network, and focus on the aftermarket.

The construction and mining division also grew through the acquisition of Swedish compaction and paving equipment maker Dynapac AB in early 2007. The division also experienced strong global demand for equipment, as well as consumables, such as drill bits and drill steel.

In 2008 the company's multiple acquisitions included mining industry service company PT Fluidcom Jaya, in Indonesia, and the European air compressor rental business of Aggreko. Atlas Copco also invested in the southeastern US market, purchasing Industrial Power Sales, a distributor of tools, assembly systems, and material handling equipment, and Grimmer Industries' booster and portable compressor business.

CEO and president Gunnar Brock stepped down in mid-2009. Ronnie Leten assumed the position to lead the company through recovery from the economic recession. Leten previously served as president of Compressor Technique.

During 2010 Atlas Copco acquired Austria's Hartl, a maker of mobile crushing and screening equipment, and Netherlands-based Cirmac International, which specializes in renewable energy technologies, used to upgrade biogas to natural gas. More significant, Atlas Copco purchased Quincy Compressor from EnPro Industries for $190 million. Quincy complements Atlas Copco's core products with a portfolio of branded compressors (reciprocating and rotary screw) and vacuum pumps, as well as its presence in the US and China. Smaller acquisitions included H&F Drilling Supplies in the UK; Servis. A.C., a compressor service provider in the Czech Republic; a remaining 75% stake in Indian companies Focus Rocbit and Prisma Roctools; and Compressor Engineering, a UK distributor and service provider for compressed air equipment.

Among the bolt-on businesses that broaden Atlas Copco's network, in fall 2010 the company took over the sales and marketing operations of its distributor in Michigan, Kramer Air Tool. The deal followed acquisitions of distributors in the southern US, Tooling Technologies, the northwestern US, American Air Products, and Louisiana-based Premier Equipment.

In mid-2011 Atlas Copco acquired Spain-based GESAN S.A., a manufacturer of diesel and petrol generators. The deal gives it a better foothold with a distributor network that reaches 85 countries, with Russia and other parts of Europe and Africa as principal markets

EXECUTIVES

President, Chief Executive Officer, Executive Director, Mats Rahmstrom
Chief Legal Officer Senior Vice President, Eva Klasen
Business Area President Compressor Technique Senior Executive Vice President, Vagner Rego
Business Area President Vacuum Technique Senior Executive Vice President, Geert Follen
Business Area President Industrial Technique Senior Executive Vice President, Henrik Elmin
Business Area President Power Technique Senior Executive Vice President, Andrew Walker
Chief Financial Officer Senior Vice President, Peter Kinnart
Chief Human Resources Officer Senior Vice President, Cecilia Sandberg
Chief Communications Officer Senior Vice President, Sara Hagg Liljedal
Chairman, Independent Director, Hans Straberg
Independent Director, Staffan Bohman
Independent Director, Johan Forssell
Independent Director, Helene Mellquist
Independent Director, Anna Ohlsson-Leijon
Independent Director, Gordon Riske
Independent Director, Peter Wallenberg
Director, Benny Larsson
Director, Mikael Bergstedt
Deputy Director, Thomas Nilsson
Deputy Director, Helena Hemstrom
Auditors: Ernst & Young AB

LOCATIONS

HQ: Atlas Copco AB (Sweden)
SE-105 23, Stockholm
Phone: (46) 8 743 80 00   **Fax:** (46) 8 643 37 18
Web: www.atlascopcogroup.com

2018 Sales

	% of total
Europe	31
Asia & Australia	35
North America	24
Africa & Middle East	6
South America	4
Total	100

PRODUCTS/OPERATIONS

2018 Sales

	% of total
Compressor Technique	46
Vacuum Technique	23
Industrial Technique	19
Power Technique	12
Total	100

Selected Products

Compressor Technique
    Air dryers, coolers, filters
    Air treatment and gas purification equipment
    Air management systems
    Compressors (gas and process)
    Compressors (oil-free and oil-injected stationary)
    Compressors (portable)
    Electric power generators
    Specialty rental services
    Turbo expanders
Construction and Mining Technique
    Construction and demolition tools
    Drilling equipment (surface)
    Drilling tools (rock)
    Exploration drilling
    Loading equipment
    Mobile crushers and screeners
    Raiseboring equipment
    Rigs (underground rock drilling)
    Rigs (surface drilling)
    Road construction equipment
    Rock reinforcement and bolting
    Tunneling and mining equipment
    Water well, gas, coal bed methane
Industrial Technique
    Aftermarket products, software, and service
    Air motors
    Air assembly tools
    Drills
    Electrical assembly tools
    Fixtured applications
    Grinding
    Hoist and trolleys
    Pneumatic power tools and systems
    Power tools (industrial)

COMPETITORS

AB Electrolux
AB SKF
ABB Ltd
BUNZL PUBLIC LIMITED COMPANY
ENERPAC TOOL GROUP CORP.
GKN LIMITED
INGERSOLL RAND INC.
JOHN CRANE INC.
Neles Oyj
TEAM, INC.

HISTORICAL FINANCIALS
Company Type: Public

Income Statement					FYE: December 31

	REVENUE ($mil)	NET INCOME ($mil)	NET PROFIT MARGIN	EMPLOYEES
12/22	13,623	2,263	16.6%	48,951
12/21	12,242	2,001	16.3%	42,862
12/20	12,213	1,808	14.8%	40,160
12/19	11,153	1,776	15.9%	38,774
12/18	10,653	11,860	111.3%	36,862
Annual Growth	6.3%	(33.9%)	—	7.3%

2022 Year-End Financials
Debt ratio: 1.8%
Return on equity: 31.8%
Cash ($ mil.): 1,084
Current Ratio: 1.31
Long-term debt ($ mil.): 1,953
No. of shares ($ mil.): 4,868
Dividends
  Yield: —
  Payout: 204.0%
Market value ($ mil.): 57,447

	STOCK PRICE ($) FY Close	P/E High/Low		PER SHARE ($) Earnings	Dividends	Book Value
12/22	11.80	13	2	0.46	0.95	1.58
12/21	69.31	19	13	0.41	1.27	1.53
12/20	51.08	18	11	0.37	0.77	1.34
12/19	40.15	12	7	0.37	0.66	1.18
12/18	23.93	2	1	2.44	11.90	0.98
Annual Growth	(16.2%)	—	—	(34.0%)	(46.9%)	12.8%

Australia & New Zealand Banking Group Ltd

EXECUTIVES

Chief Executive Officer, Managing Director, Executive Director, Shayne C. Elliott
Digital and Australia Transformation Group Executive, Australia Retail Group Executive, Maile Carnegie
Group Chief Risk Officer, Kevin Corbally
International Chief Financial Officer, Farhan Faruqui
Technology and Group Services Group Executive, Technology Group Executive, Gerard Florian
Talent and Culture and Service Centers Group Executive, Kathryn van der Merwe
Institutional Group Executive, Mark Whelan
General Counsel, Ken Adams
Secretary, Simon M. Pordage
Chairman, Independent Non-Executive Director, Paul D. O'Sullivan
Independent Non-Executive Director, Ilana R. Atlas
Independent Non-Executive Director, Jane Halton
Independent Non-Executive Director, John P. Key
Independent Non-Executive Director, Graeme R. Liebelt
Independent Non-Executive Director, John T. Macfarlane
Independent Non-Executive Director, Christine O'Reilly
Auditors : KPMG

LOCATIONS
HQ: Australia & New Zealand Banking Group Ltd
ANZ Centre Melbourne, Level 9, 833 Collins Street, Docklands, Victoria 3008
Phone: (61) 3 9273 5555   **Fax:** (61) 3 8542 5252
Web: www.anz.com

HISTORICAL FINANCIALS
Company Type: Public

Income Statement					FYE: September 30

	ASSETS ($mil)	NET INCOME ($mil)	INCOME AS % OF ASSETS	EMPLOYEES
09/23	716,750	4,601	0.6%	40,342
09/22	701,781	4,601	0.7%	39,196
09/21	704,263	4,433	0.6%	40,221
09/20	741,812	2,545	0.3%	38,579
09/19	662,905	4,022	0.6%	39,060
Annual Growth	2.0%	3.4%	—	0.8%

2023 Year-End Financials
Return on assets: 0.6%
Return on equity: 10.4%
Long-term debt ($ mil.): —
No. of shares ($ mil.): 3,001
Sales ($ mil.): 34,864
Dividends
  Yield: —
  Payout: 33.8%
Market value ($ mil.): —

Autoliv Inc

EXECUTIVES

Chairman, Director, Jan Carlson, $986,646 total compensation
President, Chief Executive Officer, Director, Mikael Bratt, $875,957 total compensation
Quality Executive Vice President, Svante Mogefors
Legal Affairs Executive Vice President, Legal Affairs General Counsel, Legal Affairs Secretary, Anthony J. Nellis
Sustainability Executive Vice President, Human Resources Executive Vice President, Sherry Vasa
Operations Executive Vice President, Magnus Jarlegren
Finance Executive Vice President, Finance Chief Financial Officer, Fredrik Westin
Supply Chain Management Executive Vice President, Christian Swahn
Chief Technology Officer, Jordi Lombarte
Region Officer, Bradley Murray, $414,099 total compensation
Region Officer, Jennifer Cheng
Region Officer, Frithjof R. Oldorff
Director, Laurie Brlas
Director, Hasse Johansson
Director, Leif Johansson
Director, David E. Kepler
Director, Franz-Josef Kortum
Director, Min Liu
Director, Xiaozhi Liu
Director, James M. Ringler
Director, Thaddeus J. (Ted) Senko
Auditors : Ernst & Young AB

LOCATIONS
HQ: Autoliv Inc
Klarabergsviadukten 70, Section B7, Box 70381, Stockholm SE-107 24
Phone: (46) 8 587 20 600
Web: www.autoliv.com

COMPETITORS
ADIENT PUBLIC LIMITED COMPANY
ALLISON TRANSMISSION HOLDINGS, INC.
APTIV PLC
DANA INCORPORATED
DENSO INTERNATIONAL AMERICA, INC.
Hyundai Mobis Co., Ltd
JOHNSON CONTROLS, INC.
LEAR CORPORATION
TENNECO INC.
WABCO HOLDINGS INC.

HISTORICAL FINANCIALS
Company Type: Public

Income Statement					FYE: December 31

	REVENUE ($mil)	NET INCOME ($mil)	NET PROFIT MARGIN	EMPLOYEES
12/23	10,475	488	4.7%	70,300
12/22	8,842	423	4.8%	69,100
12/21	8,230	435	5.3%	60,600
12/20	7,447	186	2.5%	68,000
12/19	8,547	461	5.4%	65,000
Annual Growth	5.2%	1.4%	—	2.0%

2023 Year-End Financials
Debt ratio: 22.3%
Return on equity: 18.8%
Cash ($ mil.): 498
Current Ratio: 0.98
Long-term debt ($ mil.): 1,324
No. of shares ($ mil.): 82
Dividends
  Yield: —
  Payout: 46.5%
Market value ($ mil.): 9,102

	STOCK PRICE ($) FY Close	P/E High/Low		PER SHARE ($) Earnings	Dividends	Book Value
12/23	110.19	19	14	5.72	2.66	30.94
12/22	76.58	22	14	4.85	2.58	30.30
12/21	103.41	22	17	4.96	1.88	30.10
12/20	92.10	44	19	2.14	1.86	27.56
12/19	84.41	16	12	5.29	2.48	24.18
Annual Growth	6.9%	—	—	2.0%	1.8%	6.4%

Aviva Plc

Aviva is the UK's leading Savings, Retirement, Investments and Insurance business, helping 18.5 million customers across its core markets of the UK, Ireland and Canada. It also has international investments in Singapore, China and India. Aviva has a total of £401 billion assets under management. Aviva Investors is a global asset manager that combines its insurance heritage, investment capabilities and sustainability expertise to deliver wealth and retirement outcomes that matter most to investors. The company traces its history back to 1696.

Operations
Aviva divides its business into the

following segments: UK & Ireland Life (about 50%), General Insurance (some 50%), Aviva Investors, and International investments.

The UK & Ireland Life operations are life insurance, long-term health and accident insurance, savings, pensions and annuity business.

General Insurance include UK and Ireland and Canada. The principal activities of its UK & Ireland General Insurance operations are the provision of insurance cover to individuals and businesses, for risks associated mainly with motor vehicles, property and liability (such as employers' liability and professional indemnity liability) and medical expenses. The principal activity of its Canada General Insurance operation is the provision of personal and commercial lines insurance products principally distributed through insurance brokers.

Aviva Investors operates in a number of international markets, in particular the UK, North America and Asia Pacific. Aviva Investors manages policyholders' and shareholders' invested funds, provides investment management services for institutional pension fund mandates and manages a range of retail investment products. These include investment funds, unit trusts, open-ended investment companies and individual savings accounts.

International investments comprise its long-term business operations in China, India and Singapore.

Net earned premiums are by far Aviva's biggest revenue source at 90% and the rest arising from fees and commission income.

Geographic Reach
Based in UK, Aviva has operations in Ireland, Canada, China, India, and Singapore.

Sales and Marketing
In Canada, it has a strong, long-standing relationship with its network of over 800 independent brokers and a partnership with Royal Bank of Canada (RBC), the largest bank and most valuable brand in Canada, with a significant portion of high net worth customers.

Financial Performance
Note: Growth rates may differ after conversion to US Dollars.

The company's revenue for fiscal 2021 decreased to Â£15.9 billion compared from the prior year with Â£16.3 billion.

Cash held by the company at the end of fiscal 2021 decreased to Â£11.9 billion. Cash provided by investing activities was Â£74 million while cash used for operations and financing activities were Â£2.9 billion and Â£4.4 billion, respectively.

Strategy
Aviva's strategy is to invest for profitable growth and to deliver on its ambition to be the clear market leader in the UK and Ireland.

Despite 2021 being another COVID-19 impacted year, its service has remained market-leading, supported by its ongoing investment in digital journeys and effective transition to a hybrid-working model. The company are well placed in the evolution of mobility, as customers increasingly switch to Electric Vehicles (EVs). Aviva currently insure around 1 in 8 Battery Electric Vehicles (BEV) & Hybrid vehicles in the UK and have an ambition to be the leading EV insurer.

Mergers and Acquisitions
In 2022, Aviva announced the acquisition of Succession Wealth for a consideration of Â£385 million. Succession Wealth is a leading national independent financial advice firm with approximately 200 planners advising on Â£9.5 billion of assets, delivering high-quality advice to around 19,000 clients throughout the UK. The transaction significantly enhances Aviva's presence in the fast-growing UK wealth market as more people seek advice for their retirement and savings options.

HISTORY
When insurers hiked premiums after the 1861 Great Tooley Street Fire of London, merchants formed Commercial Union Fire Insurance (CU). It opened offices throughout the UK and in foreign ports and soon added life (1862) and marine (1863) coverage.Over the next 20 years, CU's foreign business thrived. The firm had offices across the US by the 1880s. In the 1890s CU entered Australia, India, and Southeast Asia. Foreign business eventually accounted for some 75% of CU's sales.

CU went shopping in the 20th century, adding accident insurer Palatine Insurance Co. of Manchester in 1900 and rescuing two companies ruined by San Francisco's 1906 earthquake and fire. CU recovered from the Depression with the help of a booming auto insurance market, and spent most of the 1930s and WWII consolidating operations to cut costs.

Profits suffered in the 1950s as CU faced increased competition in the US. To boost sales, it merged with both multi-line rival North British and Mercantile and life insurer Northern and Employers Assurance in the early 1960s. While US business continued to lag in the 1970s, the company's European business grew.

From 1982 to 1996, CU cut its operations in the US, entered new markets (Poland, 1992; South Africa and Vietnam, 1996), and sold its New Zealand subsidiaries (1995). As competition in the UK increased, the company in 1997 reorganized and merged with General Accident in 1998.

General Accident & Employers Liability Assurance Association (GA) was formed in 1885 in Perth, Scotland, to sell workers' compensation insurance. Within a few years, GA had branches in London and Scotland. It diversified into insurance for train accidents (1887), autos (1896), and fire (1899); in 1906 its name changed to General Accident Fire and Life Assurance.

GA expanded into Australia, Europe, and Africa at the turn of the century. After WWI, the company's auto insurance grew along with car ownership. During the 1930s the company entered the US auto insurance market. WWII put a stop to GA's growth.

The company expanded after the war, forming Pennsylvania General Fire Insurance Association (1963) and acquiring the UK's Yorkshire Insurance Co. (1967). By the 1980s about one-third of its sales came from the US.

After 1986 GA acquired some 500 real estate brokerage agencies to cross-sell its home and life insurance. To increase presence in Asia and the Pacific, the company in 1988 acquired NZI Corp., a New Zealand banking and insurance company whose failing operations cost GA millions. At the same time, new US government regulations and a series of damaging storms hammered the company.

In response GA cut costs, posting a profit by 1993. As the industry consolidated, the company bought nonstandard auto insurer Sabre (1995), life insurer Provident Mutual (1996), and General Insurance Group Ltd. in Canada (1997). Unable to compete on its own, GA merged with CU to form CGU in 1998.

After the merger, CGU added personal pension plans and entered alliances to sell insurance in Italy and India. Merger costs and exceptional losses for 1998 hit operating profits hard. In 1999 CGU upped its stake in French bank SociÃ©tÃ© GÃ©nÃ©rale to about 7% to help it fend off a hostile takeover attempt by Banque Nationale de Paris (now BNP Paribas).

In 2000 CGU merged with rival Norwich Union to form CGNU and made plans to exit the Canadian life and the US general insurance businesses. In 2001 CGNU sold its US property/casualty operations to White Mountains Insurance.

In an attempt to strengthen its brand name, the company changed its name to Aviva in 2002. Following the name change, the company merged and rebranded many of its subsidiaries. Aviva also made changes to its Asian operations in 2004, selling its general insurance business in Asia to Mitsui Sumitomo Insurance.

Back home, Aviva acquired UK-based automotive service company RAC in 2005 (sold to The Carlyle Group in 2011) to gain access to its auto insurance and loan businesses. To get to the meaty middle, Aviva stripped off RAC's non-core businesses, including its fleet services, which it sold to VT Group in 2006. At around the same time, the company also divested its 50% ownership in Lex Vehicle Leasing to HBOS (which later merged with Lloyds TSB to become Lloyds Banking Group).

As part of an effort to focus on the Aviva brand, the company changed the long-time UK brand name of Norwich Union to Aviva UK in 2009.

airframes are the Eurofighter Typhoon, the Hawk Advanced Jet Trainer, and the Tornado.

Electronic Systems generates over 20% of sales and comprises the US- and UK-based electronics activities, including electronic warfare systems, navigation systems, electro-optical sensors, military and commercial digital engine and flight controls, precision guidance and seeker solutions, next-generation military communications systems and data links, persistent surveillance capabilities, space electronics and electric drive propulsion systems.

Platforms and Services (US) accounts for more than 15% of sales and designs and manufactures naval ships and submarines and compatible combat systems and equipment. The segment also provides an array of associated services including training, maintenance, and modernization programs to support ships and equipment.

Maritime generates over 15% of sales and comprises the Group's UK-based maritime and land activities. Maritime programmes include the construction of seven Astute Class submarines for the Royal Navy, as well as the design and production of the Royal Navy's Dreadnought Class submarine and Type 26 frigate. Land UK's munitions business designs, develops and manufactures a comprehensive range of munitions products serving a number of customers including its main customer, the UK Ministry of Defense.

Cyber & Intelligence accounts nearly 10% of sales and comprises the US-based Intelligence & Security business and UK-headquartered Applied Intelligence business, and covers the Group's cyber security, secure government and commercial financial security activities.

Overall, BAE generates nearly 55% of sales from Air, around 25% from Maritime, around 15% from Land and about 5% from Cyber.

Geographic Reach

London, UK-based BAE Systems has major operations in the UK, US, Australia, and Saudi Arabia.

The US generates over 45% of sales, the UK almost 20%, Saudi Arabia close to 15%, and Australia less than 5%, among others.

Sales and Marketing

BAE's largest customers are governments but also sells to large prime contractors and commercial businesses. The company engages third parties to assist sales and marketing activities of BAE.

Financial Performance

The company had a total revenue of Â£19.5 billion, a 1% increase from the previous year's revenue of Â£19.3 billion. The increase was primarily due to a higher sales volume in the company's air segment.

In 2021, the company had a net income of Â£1.9 billion, a 39% increase from the previous year's net income of Â£1.4 billion.

The company's cash at the end of 2021 was Â£2.9 billion. Operating activities generated Â£2.4 billion, while financing activities used $2.3 billion, primarily for equity dividends paid. Investing activities generated another Â£66 million.

Strategy

BAE's strategy consists of:

Sustaining and growing its defense business; Continuing to grow business in adjacent markets; Developing and expanding international business; Inspiring and developing a diverse workforce to drive success; Enhancing financial performance and delivering sustainable growth in shareholder value; and Advancing and integrating its sustainability agenda.

Mergers and Acquisitions

In early 2022, BAE Systems has completed the acquisition of Bohemia Interactive Simulations (BISim) for $200 million. Bohemia Interactive Simulations (BISim) is a global software developer of simulation training solutions for military organizations based in Orlando Florida. With the successful completion of this acquisition, BAE Systems customers would have access to the company's extensive and proven system integration experience complemented by BISim's innovative training products and solutions to enhance military readiness for the US and its allies.

In late 2021, BAE Systems has acquired In-Space Missions, a UK company that designs, builds and operates satellites and satellite systems. The acquisition will combine BAE Systems' experience in highly secure satellite communications with In-Space Missions' full lifecycle satellite capability, to make a compelling sovereign UK space offer. This acquisition is part of BAE Systems' strategy to develop breakthrough technologies, pursuing bolt-on acquisitions where they complement existing capabilities and provide an opportunity to accelerate technology development in key areas Terms were not disclosed.

In early 2021, BAE Systems acquires Pulse Power and Measurement Limited; an independent developer of high-end electronics, based in Shrivenham. PPM has a strong track record of working within the defence and communications sector, cyber security and commercial test and research markets in both the UK and USA and it strongly complements BAE Systems' digital and data capabilities. Terms were not disclosed.

Company Background

Post-Wright brothers and pre-WWII, a host of aviation companies sprang up to serve the British Empire -- too many to survive after the war, when the empire contracted. Parliament took steps in 1960 to save the industry by merging companies to form larger, stronger entities -- Hawker-Siddeley Aviation and British Aircraft Corporation (BAC).

Hawker-Siddeley, made up of aircraft and missiles divisions, was created by combining A.V. Roe, Gloster Aircraft, Hawker Aircraft, Armstrong Whitworth, and Folland Aircraft. It attained fame in the 1960s for developing the Harrier "jump jet."

BAC was formed from the merger of Bristol Aeroplane, English Electric, and Vicker-Armstrong. In 1962 it joined France's Aerospatiale to build the supersonic Concorde and became a partner in ventures to develop the Tornado and Jaguar fighters. The cost of these ventures, plus the commercial failure of the Concorde, was more than the company could bear. Realizing British aviation was again in trouble, the British government nationalized BAC and Hawker-Siddeley in 1976 and merged them in 1977 with Scottish Aviation to form British Aerospace (BAe).

HISTORY

Post-Wright brothers and pre-WWII, a host of aviation companies sprang up to serve the British Empire -- too many to survive after the war, when the empire contracted. Parliament took steps in 1960 to save the industry by merging companies to form larger, stronger entities -- Hawker-Siddeley Aviation and British Aircraft Corporation (BAC).

Hawker-Siddeley, made up of aircraft and missiles divisions, was created by combining A.V. Roe, Gloster Aircraft, Hawker Aircraft, Armstrong Whitworth, and Folland Aircraft. It attained fame in the 1960s for developing the Harrier "jump jet."

BAC was formed from the merger of Bristol Aeroplane, English Electric, and Vicker-Armstrong. In 1962 it joined France's Aerospatiale to build the supersonic Concorde and became a partner in ventures to develop the Tornado and Jaguar fighters. The cost of these ventures, plus the commercial failure of the Concorde, was more than the company could bear. Realizing British aviation was again in trouble, the British government nationalized BAC and Hawker-Siddeley in 1976 and merged them in 1977 with Scottish Aviation to form British Aerospace (BAe).

EXECUTIVES

Chief Executive Officer, Executive Director, Charles Woodburn

Financial Director, Executive Director, Brad Greve

President, Executive Director, Tom Arseneault

General Counsel, Ed Gelsthorpe

Secretary, David Parkes

Chairman, Director, Roger Carr

Chair Designate, Non-Executive Director, Cressida Hogg

Non-Executive Director, Nick Anderson

Non-Executive Director, Crystal E. Ashby

Non-Executive Director, Elizabeth Corley

Non-Executive Director, Jane Griffiths

Senior Independent Director, Non-Executive Director, Christopher M. Grigg

Non-Executive Director, Ewan Kirk

Non-Executive Director, Stephen W. Pearce
Non-Executive Director, Nicole W. Piasecki
Non-Executive Director, Mark Sedwill
Auditors : Deloitte LLP

LOCATIONS
HQ: BAE Systems Plc
 6 Carlton Gardens, London SW1Y 5AD
Phone: (44) 1252 373232
Web: www.baesystems.com

2018 Sales
	% of total
US	46
UK	22
Saudi Arabia	15
Rest of Europe	7
Rest of Middle East	4
Australia	3
Canada	3
Rest of Asia and Pacific	—
Total	100

PRODUCTS/OPERATIONS
2018 Sales
	% of total
Air	33
Electronic Systems	23
Maritime	17
Platforms & Services (US)	17
Cyber & Intelligence	10
Total	100

COMPETITORS
AEROVIRONMENT, INC.
Airbus SE
GENERAL DYNAMICS CORPORATION
GULFSTREAM AEROSPACE CORPORATION
KAMAN CORPORATION
LOCKHEED MARTIN CORPORATION
NAVAL GROUP
ROLLS-ROYCE HOLDINGS PLC
TEXTRON INC.
THE BOEING COMPANY

HISTORICAL FINANCIALS
Company Type: Public

Income Statement — FYE: December 31

	REVENUE ($mil)	NET INCOME ($mil)	NET PROFIT MARGIN	EMPLOYEES
12/22	25,590	1,915	7.5%	84,000
12/21	26,308	2,369	9.0%	86,200
12/20	26,307	1,772	6.7%	89,600
12/19	24,172	1,949	8.1%	87,800
12/18	21,476	1,276	5.9%	78,000
Annual Growth	4.5%	10.7%	—	1.9%

2022 Year-End Financials
Debt ratio: 20.1% No. of shares ($ mil.): 3,070
Return on equity: 17.0% Dividends
Cash ($ mil.): 3,740 Yield: —
Current Ratio: 1.08 Payout: 193.8%
Long-term debt ($ mil.): 6,246 Market value ($ mil.): 129,405

	STOCK PRICE ($) FY Close	P/E High/Low	PER SHARE ($) Earnings	Dividends	Book Value
12/22	42.15	83 51	0.61	1.18	4.40
12/21	29.79	60 45	0.74	1.29	3.17
12/20	27.15	90 54	0.55	1.17	1.97
12/19	30.28	67 50	0.61	1.11	2.23
12/18	23.42	112 73	0.40	1.11	2.22
Annual Growth	15.8%	—	11.1%	1.5%	18.7%

Baidu Inc

Baidu wants to increase Web search results success one hundred times over. Baidu, which means a "hundred times," is a leading Chinese-language Internet search engine (Baidu.com), with about 80% of the search market in China. (Google is Baidu's main competitor, with about 20% of the Chinese market.) Baidu offers news, MP3, video, and image search. It earns nearly all of its revenues through online advertising services. In order to reap the rewards of a market that consists of a whopping 470 million Internet users, the company has had to accept a massive government bureaucracy and its censorship rules. Baidu also operates in the Japanese market through Japanese-language search service Baidu Japan.

EXECUTIVES
Chief Executive Officer, Chairman, Executive Director, Robin Yanhong Li
Chief Financial Officer, Rong Luo
Chief Technology Officer, Haifeng Wang
Executive Vice President, Dou Shen
Senior Vice President, General Counsel, Victor Zhixiang Liang
Human Resources and Administrative Senior Vice President, Shanshan Cui
Independent Director, James Ding
Independent Director, Brent Callinicos
Independent Director, Yuanqing Yang
Independent Director, Jixun Foo
Auditors : Ernst & Young Hua Ming LLP

LOCATIONS
HQ: Baidu Inc
 Baidu Campus, No. 10 Shangdi 10th Street, Haidian District, Beijing 100085
Phone: (86) 10 5992 8888 **Fax:** (86) 10 5992 0000
Web: www.baidu.com

PRODUCTS/OPERATIONS
2015 Sales
	% of total
Online marketing services	96
Other	4
Total	100

Selected Products and Services
Baidu-Hexun Finance (financial information)
Baidu Hi (instant messaging)
Baidu Image Search (searches within an index of nearly 80 million images)
Baidu Local Search (online search for local business information)
Baidu MP3 Search (links to nearly four million songs and other multimedia)
Baidu News (links to news from about 1,000 sources)
Baidu Post Bar (message boards)
Baidu Safety Center (virus scanning, system repair, online security evaluations)
Baidu Search Ranking (lists top search terms based on daily search queries)
Baidu Union (network of third-party Web sites)
Baidu Web Directory (browses and searches through websites)
Baidu Web Search (web search using Chinese language search terms)

HISTORICAL FINANCIALS
Company Type: Public

Income Statement — FYE: December 31

	REVENUE ($mil)	NET INCOME ($mil)	NET PROFIT MARGIN	EMPLOYEES
12/23	18,984	2,764	14.6%	39,800
12/22	17,927	1,095	6.1%	41,300
12/21	19,609	1,610	8.2%	45,500
12/20	16,371	3,435	21.0%	41,000
12/19	15,436	295	1.9%	37,779
Annual Growth	5.3%	74.9%	—	1.3%

2023 Year-End Financials
Debt ratio: 2.7% No. of shares ($ mil.): 2,805
Return on equity: 8.3% Dividends
Cash ($ mil.): 3,558 Yield: —
Current Ratio: 3.01 Payout: 0.0%
Long-term debt ($ mil.): 8,090 Market value ($ mil.): 334,070

	STOCK PRICE ($) FY Close	P/E High/Low	PER SHARE ($) Earnings	Dividends	Book Value
12/23	119.09	23 15	0.97	0.00	12.25
12/22	114.38	62 32	0.36	0.00	11.58
12/21	148.79	97 38	0.55	0.00	12.05
12/20	216.24	27 11	1.24	0.00	10.43
12/19	126.40	3 2	8.04	0.00	679.86
Annual Growth	(1.5%)	—	(41.0%)	—	(63.4%)

Balfour Beatty Plc

Balfour Beatty is a leading international infrastructure group that finances, develops, builds, maintains and operates the increasingly complex and critical infrastructure that supports national economies and deliver projects at the heart of local communities. The company provides infrastructure and commercial services including engineering, design, construction, and maintenance. Balfour Beatty works on a range of project types including roads and railways, schools, military housing, hospitals, and airports. It also provides financing and is an active participant in public-private partnerships. The US units include Balfour Beatty Infrastructure and Balfour Beatty Construction. The UK accounts for approximately 45% of sales.

Operations
Balfour Beatty divides its business into three operating units: Construction Services, Support Services, and Infrastructure Investments.

Construction Services is Balfour Beatty's largest business contributing more than 80% of its revenue. The company's construction activities include building, refurbishment and fit-out, mechanical and electrical services, civil and ground engineering, and rail engineering.

Support Services, which brings in about 15% of revenue, maintains and refurbishes existing assets, such as power transmission lines, gas and water conduits, rail, highways, robust core business by expanding the portfolio of services for its customers.

Baloise also made huge progress with strengthening, optimizing and diversifying its core business. In the life business, it is continuing to improve the business mix by focusing on risk and unit-linked products. The company also capitalized on the opportunities for growth in Switzerland presented by the withdrawal of a competitor. The strategic reallocation of the non-life portfolio in Germany is having a positive impact. The German business's turnaround is reflected in a considerable increase in new customers.

The 2019 results for the Luxembourg business unit were also robust. Baloise unlocked opportunities and possibilities in Belgium's attractive non-life insurance market when it acquired insurance company Fidea NV in the first half of the year. The announced acquisition of Athora's non-life insurance portfolio will also markedly strengthen the market position of the Belgian business. These two acquisitions will underpin Belgium's role as a second key pillar within the Baloise Group alongside the Swiss business. They will also help to diversify the business. The Athora portfolio will significantly strengthen Baloise's position in the Wallonia region of Belgium.

Mergers and Acquisitions

In 2020, As part of a strategic partnership, Baloise Asset Management is acquiring a stake in Zurich-based asset manager Tolomeo Capital AG. With this transaction, Baloise Asset Management will further strengthen its position as one of Switzerland's leading rule-based asset managers. In addition, it will exploit synergies and complementary capabilities in areas such as automated investment solutions and alternative investments. Terms were not disclosed.

In 2020, Baloise has acquired two plots of land as part of the Giessen development in Dübendorf. Plans for the approximately 35,000 square metre site include the construction of 500 new homes, as well as commercial units and green spaces, by 2026. The acquisition of the land and the planned development expands Baloise's investment portfolio of rented property in highly attractive locations. Terms were not disclosed.

In 2019, As part of its Simply Safe strategy, Baloise Asset Management, part of the Baloise Group, has acquired a stake in business start-up Brainalyzed, a specialist in machine learning and artificial intelligence (AI). Following a two-year partnership and its first experiences with swarm-based artificial intelligence, Baloise has decided to invest in the company. Brainalyzed's innovative approach to AI will help Baloise Asset Management to successfully expand its third-party asset management business.

Company Background

The Basler Versicherungs-Gesellschaft gegen Feuerschaden (Baloise Insurance Company for Fire Damage) is founded in 1863. Today, it is known as the Baloise Group and operates in four countries under the umbrella of Bâloise Holding Ltd. At the time of its greatest geographical expansion, around 1938, it had offices in about 50 countries worldwide.

HISTORY

In 1863 15 business leaders in Basel, Switzerland, formed the Bâloise Fire Insurance Company. This was followed in 1864 by the formation of the Baloise transportation and life insurance companies.

Bâloise-Holding was created in 1962 as a holding company for the previously independent insurance entities. In 1971, it merged all of its non-life companies into the Baloise Insurance Group.

Under its then-new chairman and president Rolf Schäuble, Bâloise-Holding began in 1993 to reorganize its operations as it implemented a new corporate strategy. Key components of the strategy included a focus on the company's core European markets and a pattern of discarding less-profitable businesses. In 1998 Bâloise-Holding sold off its US operations.

Strengthening its position as a full-fledged financial services company, in 2000 Bâloise acquired Swiss bank Solothurner (now Bâloise Bank SoBa).

The same year it purchased Belgian bank HBK-Spaarbank, Belgian insurer Amazon Insurance N.V., and Swiss regional bank Solothurner Bank SoBa.

EXECUTIVES

Chairman, Andreas Burckhardt
Director, Andreas Beerli
Director, Thomas Pleines
Auditors : Ernst & Young Ltd.

LOCATIONS

HQ: Baloise Holding AG
Aeschengraben 21, Basel CH-4002
Phone: (41) 58 285 89 42   **Fax:** (41) 58 285 70 70
Web: www.baloise.com

2014 Sales

	% of total
Switzerland	48
Germany	18
Belgium	17
Luxembourg	16
Other	1
Total	100

PRODUCTS/OPERATIONS

2014 Sales

	% of total
Non-life insurance	47
Life	53
Total	100

Selected Subsidiaries
Austria
    Basler Versicherungen (insurance and pension products for private and business clients)
Belgium
    Mercator Verzekeringen (personal and property insurance for individuals and small to mid-sized businesses)
Germany
    Basler Versicherungen (personal and property insurance for individuals, small and mid-sized enterprises, and selected industrial clients)
    Deutscher Ring (insurance and pension products for individuals)
Luxembourg
    Bâloise Assurances (life, personal, and property insurance for private and business clients)
Switzerland
    Bâloise Bank SoBa (banking products and services)
    Basler Versicherungen (insurance and pension products for individuals and small to mid-sized enterprises)

COMPETITORS

AEGON N.V.
AMUNDI
AMUNDI PIONEER ASSET MANAGEMENT USA, INC.
Achmea B.V.
Credit Suisse Group AG
LafargeHolcim Ltd
Sampo Oyj
Swiss Life Holding AG
Swiss Re AG
Zurich Insurance Group AG

HISTORICAL FINANCIALS

Company Type: Public

Income Statement   FYE: December 31

	ASSETS ($mil)	NET INCOME ($mil)	INCOME AS % OF ASSETS	EMPLOYEES
12/21	98,572	644	0.7%	0
12/20	100,330	493	0.5%	7,693
12/19	90,015	718	0.8%	7,646
12/18	82,193	531	0.6%	7,203
12/17	86,605	561	0.6%	7,286
Annual Growth	3.3%	3.5%	—	—

2021 Year-End Financials

Return on assets: 0.6%	Dividends
Return on equity: 8.2%	Yield: —
Long-term debt ($ mil.): —	Payout: 2.8%
No. of shares (mil.): 45	Market value ($ mil.): 717
Sales ($ mil.): 11,369	

	STOCK PRICE ($) FY Close	P/E High/Low		PER SHARE ($) Earnings	Dividends	Book Value
12/21	15.87	1	1	14.30	0.41	176.76
12/20	14.38	2	2	10.93	0.42	176.01
12/19	18.13	1	1	15.51	0.36	152.44
12/18	14.92	1	1	11.30	0.32	130.30
12/17	15.24	1	1	11.76	0.31	136.98
Annual Growth	1.0%	—	—	5.0%	7.4%	6.6%

Banco Bilbao Vizcaya Argentaria SA (BBVA)

EXECUTIVES

Digital Banking Group Executive Chairman, Corporate Development Group Executive Chairman, Strategy Group Executive Chairman, Group Executive Chairman, Carlos Torres Vila
Chief Executive Officer, Executive Director, Onur Genc
Accounting Chief Financial Officer, Finance Chief Financial Officer, Accounting Head, Finance Head, Jaime Saenz de Tejada Pulido
General Secretary, Domingo Armengol Calvo
General Secretary, Non-Executive Director, Jose Maldonado Ramos
Deputy Chairman, Independent Director, Jose Miguel Andres Torrecillas
Lead Independent Director, Juan Pi Llorens
Independent Non-Executive Director, Jaime Felix Caruana Lacorte
Independent Non-Executive Director, Raul Catarino Galamba de Oliveira
Independent Non-Executive Director, Belen Garijo Lopez
Independent Non-Executive Director, Sunir Kumar Kapoor
Independent Non-Executive Director, Lourdes Maiz Carro
Independent Non-Executive Director, Ana Cristina Peralta Moreno
Independent Non-Executive Director, Ana Leonor Revenga Shanklin
Independent Non-Executive Director, Jan Paul Marie Francis Verplancke
Non-Executive Director, Susana Rodriguez Vidarte
Non-Executive Director, Carlos Vicente Salazar Lomelin
Auditors : Ernst & Young, S.L

LOCATIONS
HQ: Banco Bilbao Vizcaya Argentaria SA (BBVA)
Calle Azul 4, Madrid 28050
Phone: (34) 91 537 7000   **Fax:** (34) 91 537 6766
Web: www.bbva.com

HISTORICAL FINANCIALS
Company Type: Public

Income Statement   FYE: December 31

	ASSETS ($mil)	NET INCOME ($mil)	INCOME AS % OF ASSETS	EMPLOYEES
12/22	761,665	6,856	0.9%	115,675
12/21	750,295	5,266	0.7%	110,432
12/20	903,501	1,601	0.2%	123,174
12/19	784,465	3,943	0.5%	126,973
12/18	774,941	6,097	0.8%	125,627
Annual Growth	(0.4%)	3.0%	—	(2.0%)

2022 Year-End Financials
Return on assets: 0.9%   Dividends
Return on equity: 14.1%   Yield: —
Long-term debt ($ mil.): —   Payout: 35.0%
No. of shares ($ mil.): 6,024   Market value ($ mil.): 36,208
Sales ($ mil.): 48,369

	STOCK PRICE ($) FY Close	P/E High/Low	Earnings	Dividends	Book Value
12/22	6.01	7	4	1.06	0.37	8.33
12/21	5.87	11	6	0.76	0.16	7.60
12/20	4.94	47	19	0.17	0.28	8.22
12/19	5.58	14	10	0.53	0.29	8.22
12/18	5.29	12	7	0.87	0.30	8.15
Annual Growth	3.2%			5.0%	5.5%	0.6%

Banco Bradesco SA

EXECUTIVES
Chief Executive Officer, Octavio de Lazari
Executive Vice President, Marcelo de Araujo Noronha
Executive Vice President, Andre Rodrigues Cano
Executive Vice President, Cassiano Ricardo Scarpelli
Executive Vice President, Eurico Ramos Fabri
Executive Vice President, Rogerio Pedro Camara
Managing Executive Officer, Chief Risk Officer, Moacir Nachbar
Managing Executive Officer, Walkiria Schirrmeister Marchetti
Managing Executive Officer, Bruno D'Avila Melo Boetger
Managing Executive Officer, Guilherme Muller Leal
Managing Executive Officer, Joao Carlos Gomes da Silva
Managing Executive Officer, Glaucimar Peticov
Managing Executive Officer, Jose Ramos Rocha Neto
Executive Deputy Officer, Antonio Jose da Barbara
Executive Deputy Officer, Edson Marcelo Moreto
Executive Deputy Officer, Jose Sergio Bordin
Investor Relations Executive Deputy Officer, Investor Relations Officer, Leandro de Miranda Araujo
Executive Deputy Officer, Roberto de Jesus Paris
Executive Deputy Officer, Edilson Wiggers
Executive Deputy Officer, Oswaldo Tadeu Fernandes
Chairman, Director, Luiz Carlos Trabuco Cappi
Vice-Chairman, Director, Carlos Alberto Rodrigues Guilherme
Independent Director, Samuel Monteiro dos Santos Junior
Independent Director, Walter Luis Bernardes Albertoni
Independent Director, Paulo Roberto Simoes da Cunha
Director, Denise Aguiar Alvarez Valente
Director, Milton Matsumoto
Director, Alexandre da Silva Gluher
Director, Mauricio Machado de Minas
Auditors : KPMG Auditores Independentes Ltda.

LOCATIONS
HQ: Banco Bradesco SA
Cidade de Deus S/N – Vila Yara, Sao Paulo, Osasco 06029-900
Phone: (55) 11 2194 0922   **Fax:** (55) 11 3684 3213
Web: www.bradesco.com.br

HISTORICAL FINANCIALS
Company Type: Public

Income Statement   FYE: December 31

	ASSETS ($mil)	NET INCOME ($mil)	INCOME AS % OF ASSETS	EMPLOYEES
12/22	340,318	3,968	1.2%	88,381
12/21	300,673	4,158	1.4%	87,274
12/20	308,971	3,049	1.0%	89,575
12/19	342,942	5,229	1.5%	97,329
12/18	336,384	4,272	1.3%	98,605
Annual Growth	0.3%	(1.8%)	—	(2.7%)

2022 Year-End Financials
Return on assets: 1.2%   Dividends
Return on equity: 13.6%   Yield: —
Long-term debt ($ mil.): —   Payout: 16.7%
No. of shares ($ mil.): 5,330   Market value ($ mil.): 15,351
Sales ($ mil.): 45,022

	STOCK PRICE ($) FY Close	P/E High/Low	Earnings	Dividends	Book Value
12/22	2.88	2	1	0.35	0.06	5.61
12/21	3.42	2	1	0.41	0.13	5.54
12/20	5.26	5	2	0.30	0.08	5.76
12/19	8.95	6	4	0.51	0.33	6.90
12/18	9.89	7	4	0.42	0.14	6.57
Annual Growth	(26.5%)			(4.1%)	(19.6%)	(3.9%)

Banco de Chile

Banco de Chile proffers a place for pesos. Chile's second-largest bank after Banco Santander Chile, it has some 300 branches and 1,400 ATMs in its home country, as well as operations in Argentina, Brazil, China, Mexico, and the US. In addition to corporate and retail banking, the company offers (through subsidiaries) mutual funds, brokerage, insurance, financial planning, factoring, and other services. The Luksic family, through such entities as Quiñenco and Sociedad Matriz Banco de Chile, controls a majority of the bank. In 2008 Citigroup bought a 10% stake in the bank (with an option to acquire more) from Quiñenco and merged its Chilean operations into Banco de Chile.

EXECUTIVES
Chief Executive Officer, Eduardo Ebensperger Orrego
Chief Financial Officer, Rolando Sanchez Arias
General Counsel, Secretary, Alfredo Villegas Montes
Chairman, Pablo Granito Lavin
Vice-Chairman, Director, Andronico Luksic Craig
Director, Vice-Chairman, Julio Santiago Figueroa
Independent Director, Jaime Estevez Valencia
Independent Director, Alfredo Cutiel Ergas Segal
Director, Hernan Buchi Buc
Director, Jean Paul Luksic Fontbona

Director, Andres Ergas Heymann
Director, Francisco Perez Mackenna
Director, Samuel Libnic
Director, Raul A. Anaya Elizalde
Auditors : EY Audit SpA

LOCATIONS

HQ: Banco de Chile
Paseo Ahumada 251, Santiago
Phone: (56) 2 637 1111   **Fax:** (56) 2 653 5156
Web: www.bancochile.cl

COMPETITORS

BANCO BILBAO VIZCAYA ARGENTARIA SOCIEDAD ANONIMA
BANCO DE GALICIA Y BUENOS AIRES S.A.U.
BANCO SANTANDER RIO S.A.
BANK OF AYUDHYA PUBLIC COMPANY LIMITED
BDO UNIBANK, INC.
Bolivar Banco C.A.
CHANG HWA COMMERCIAL BANK, LTD.
METROPOLITAN BANK & TRUST COMPANY
QNB FINANSBANK ANONIM SIRKETI
UNITED OVERSEAS BANK LIMITED

HISTORICAL FINANCIALS
Company Type: Public

Income Statement   FYE: December 31

	ASSETS ($mil)	NET INCOME ($mil)	INCOME AS % OF ASSETS	EMPLOYEES
12/23	63,190	1,408	2.2%	12,550
12/22	64,429	1,643	2.6%	12,550
12/21	60,358	1,239	2.1%	12,284
12/20	64,084	565	0.9%	13,134
12/19	55,648	819	1.5%	13,562
Annual Growth	3.2%	14.5%	—	(1.9%)

2023 Year-End Financials
Return on assets: 2.2%
Return on equity: 24.6%
Long-term debt ($ mil.): —
No. of shares ($ mil.): 101,017
Sales ($ mil.): 5,579
Dividends
Yield: —
Payout: 10847.0%
Market value ($ mil.): 2,331,472

	STOCK PRICE ($) FY Close	P/E High	P/E Low	Earnings	Dividends	Book Value
12/23	23.08	2	1	0.01	1.51	0.06
12/22	20.82	2	1	0.02	1.26	0.06
12/21	15.71	2	1	0.01	0.37	0.06
12/20	20.38	6	4	0.01	0.63	0.06
12/19	20.99	5	4	0.01	0.79	0.05
Annual Growth	2.4%	—	—	14.5%	17.5%	2.9%

Banco Itau Chile

As Chile's oldest operating bank, CORPBANCA has been processing, procuring, and protecting pesos since 1871. Through its network of more than 120 branches (which operate under the CorpBanca and Banco Condell banners) across Chile, the bank offers the conventional range of commercial and retail banking services. It also owns and operates 500-plus ATMs in Chile. CorpBanca also has a New York branch. It additionally offers mutual fund management, financial advisory, and insurance brokerage services.

Key subsidiaries include Corredores de Seguros, an insurance provider, and Corredores de Bolsa, a securities brokerage. Itau Unibanco acquired CORPBANCA in April 2016.

EXECUTIVES

Chief Executive Officer, Gabriel Amado de Moura
Chief Financial Officer, Rodrigo Luis Rosa Couto
Chief Compliance Officer, Cristobal Ortega Soto
Chief Risk Officer, Mauricio Baeza Letelier
Chief Audit Officer, Emerson Bastian Vergara
Itau Corpbanca Colombia Chief Executive Officer, Baruc Saez
Wholesale Banking Corporate Director, Christian Tauber Dominguez
Retail Banking Corporate Director, Julian Acuna Moreno
Treasury Corporate Director, Pedro Silva Yrarrazaval
Operations Corporate Director, Digital Business Development Corporate Director, Jorge Novis Neto
Information Technology Corporate Director, Eduardo Neves
Human Resources Corporate Director, People and Management Performance Corporate Director, Marcela Leonor Jimenez Pardo
General Counsel, Cristian Toro Canas
Chairman, Director, Jorge Andres Saieh Guzman
Vice-Chairman, Director, Ricardo Villela Marino
Director, Jorge Selume Zaror
Director, Fernando Aguad Dagach
Director, Gustavo Arriagada Morales
Director, Matias Granata
Director, Milton Maluhy Filho
Director, Rogerio Carvalho Braga
Director, Pedro Samhan Escandar
Director, Fernando Concha Ureta
Director, Bernard Pasquier
Auditors : PricewaterhouseCoopers Consultores Auditores SpA

LOCATIONS

HQ: Banco Itau Chile
Presidente Riesco 5537, Santiago, Las Condes
Phone: (56) 2 660 1701   **Fax:** (56) 2 660 2476
Web: www.itau.cl

PRODUCTS/OPERATIONS

Selected Subsidiaries
Corp Legal S.A.
CorpBanca Administradores General de Fondos S.A.
CorpBanca Agencia de Valores S.A.
CorpBanca Asesorías Financieras S.A.
CorpBanca Corredores de Seguros S.A.
CorpBanka Corredores de Bolsa S.A.
SMU Corp S.A.

COMPETITORS

CTBC Financial Holding Co., Ltd.
DnB ASA
Itau Unibanco Holding S/A
SINOPAC FINANCIAL HOLDINGS COMPANY LIMITED
THANACHART CAPITAL PUBLIC COMPANY LIMITED

HISTORICAL FINANCIALS
Company Type: Public

Income Statement   FYE: December 31

	ASSETS ($mil)	NET INCOME ($mil)	INCOME AS % OF ASSETS	EMPLOYEES
12/22	47,015	516	1.1%	5,163
12/21	44,131	320	0.7%	7,770
12/20	49,924	(1,137)	—	8,364
12/19	45,602	154	0.3%	8,987
12/18	42,251	246	0.6%	9,179
Annual Growth	2.7%	20.3%	—	(13.4%)

2022 Year-End Financials
Return on assets: 1.1%
Return on equity: 13.5%
Long-term debt ($ mil.): —
No. of shares ($ mil.): 973,518
Sales ($ mil.): 3,839
Dividends
Yield: —
Payout: 0.0%
Market value ($ mil.): 3,144,463

	STOCK PRICE ($) FY Close	P/E High	P/E Low	Earnings	Dividends	Book Value
12/22	3.23	8	6	0.00	0.00	0.00
12/21	2.90	11	6	0.00	0.00	0.00
12/20	4.95	—	—	0.00	0.00	0.01
12/19	8.61	63	34	0.00	0.00	0.01
12/18	13.60	45	36	0.00	0.00	0.01
Annual Growth	(30.2%)	—	—	2.5%	—	(18.6%)

Banco Santander Brasil SA

Banco Santander (Brazil) is the third largest private bank in Brazil and the only international bank with scale in the country. The bank, part of Spain's Banco Santander, provides financial services through over 1,985 branches, primarily in Brazil's south and southeast. Santander Brasil also offers wholesale banking to large corporations. Additional services include asset management, private banking, and insurance. It operates in the retail and wholesale segments with high value-added offerings, which enables it to provide a wide range of products and services for individuals, small and medium-sized enterprises and wholesale. The Santander Group was founded in Spain in 1857, and established a representative office in Brazil, followed by the opening of its first branch in 1982.

Operations

The company operates through two segments: Commercial Banking (approximately 90% of sales), and Global Wholesale Banking (some 10%).

Commercial Banking provides services and products to individuals and companies (except for global corporate customers who are managed by its Global Wholesale Banking). The revenue from this segment is derived from the banking and financial products and services available to its account and non-account holders.

Global Wholesale Banking offers a wide range of national and international tailored financial services and structured solutions for its global corporate customers, comprised mostly of local and multinational corporations.

Overall, around 70% of sales through net interest income, while fee and commission income generated about 30%. In addition, its loan portfolio includes commercial and Industrial (some 50%), installment loans to individuals (roughly 40%), real estate (around 10%), and lease financing.

Geographic Reach

The company is headquartered in Sao Paulo, Brazil, and has four major administrative operational centers. It also has some 385 properties for the activities of its banking network and rent 1,719 properties for the same purpose.

Sales and Marketing

The company offers its financial services and products to its customers through our multichannel distribution network composed of: physical channels, such as branches, mini-branches and ATMs; call centers; and digital channels, such as Internet banking and mobile banking. The company provides its complete portfolio of products and services to its 30 million active customers.

Financial Performance

Total Income amounted to R$63.9 billion in 2021, an increase of 33% in comparison with the year ended December 31, 2020, primarily due to the effects of the hedge for investment abroad, which had a significant impact in 2020 due to the exchange rate variation and the growth of the net interest income due to the increase in the volume of the credit portfolio.

In 2021, the company had a net income of R$15.5 billion, a 16% increase from the previous year's net income of R$13.4 billion.

The company's cash at the end of 2021 was R$32.7 billion. Operating activities generated R$6.8 billion, while investing activities used R$1.9 billion, mainly for investments in tangible and intangible assets. Financing activities used another R$658.5 million, primarily for payments of other long-term financial liabilities.

Strategy

The company's strategy is centered on endeavoring to generate profitable, recurring, and sustainable growth. It believes the expansion of its customer base over the years is due to the company's ability to capture new customers and increase their loyalty. It has achieved this by offering a comprehensive portfolio of products and services, with a particular emphasis on quality and a constant drive to improve customer satisfaction. The company serves customers through multi-channel solutions which it believes enables it to provide a tailored and human service which is responsive to the needs of customers. The company relies on four integrated service channels to do offer its services to our customers: digital, remote, physical and external channels.

Company Background

The parent company listed approximately 15% of its shares of its Brazilian unit on the New York Stock Exchange in a 2009 IPO. It turned out to be the world's largest IPO that year raising some R$13 billion ($8 billion). The proceeds from the offering have been used to drive growth by funding new branches and lending. It is also growing its insurance and credit card businesses; the company recently began offering its Santander-Ferrari credit card.

In late 2010 Santander rebranded its Brazilian brands -- Banco Real and Santander Brasil -- under the same name and platform. (It completed similar restructuring efforts in the UK and Mexico.) The parent company has high hopes for its Latin American operations, especially in the high-growth markets of Brazil and Mexico. As such, Santander is committed to investing in those units as it solidifies its position as a leading global bank.

Santander Brasil is the result of the 2006 merger of Banco Santander banks Banco Santander Brasil, Banco Santander Meridional, and Banco do Estado de SÃ£o Paulo. The company added to its Brazilian bank empire when it acquired Banco Real in 2008. At the time, Banco Real was the fourth largest non government-owned Brazilian bank. The acquisition boosted Santander Brasil into the top three of banks in Brazil (along with Banco Bradesco and ItaÃº Unibanco)

Brazil is a promising region of the world for banking. The country was a resilient market during the economic downturn. Employment levels rose and a new middle class emerged. As the Brazilian economy expands Santander Brasil expects lending and overall demand for banking services to grow.

EXECUTIVES

Vice-Chairman, Chief Executive Officer, Sergio Agapito Lires Rial
Vice President Executive Officer, Alberto Monteiro de Queiroz Netto
Investor Relations Vice President Executive Officer, Investor Relations Officer, Angel Santodomingo Martell
Vice President Executive Officer, Alessandro Tomao
Vice President Executive Officer, Antonio Pardo de Santayana Montes
Vice President Executive Officer, Carlos Rey de Vicente
Vice President Executive Officer, Ede Ilson Viani
Vice President Executive Officer, Jean Pierre Dupui
Vice President Executive Office, Juan Sebastian Moreno Blanco
Vice President Executive Officer, Mario Roberto Opice Leao
Vice President Executive Officer, Patricia Souto Audi
Vice President Executive Officer, Vanessa de Souza Lobato Barbosa
Chairman, Alvaro Antonio Cardoso de Souza
Independent Director, Pedro Augusto de Melo
Independent Director, Deborah Patricia Wright
Independent Director, Deborah Stern Vieitas
Independent Director, Marília Artimonte Rocca
Director, Jose Antonio Alvarez Alvarez
Director, Jose de Paiva Ferreira
Director, Jose Maria Nus Badia
Auditors : PricewaterhouseCoopers Auditores Independentes Ltda.

LOCATIONS

HQ: Banco Santander Brasil SA
Avenida Presidente Juscelino Kubitschek, 2041, Suite 281, Block A, Condominio WTORRE JK - Vila Nova Conceicao, Sao Paulo 04543-011
Phone: (55) 11 3174 8589   **Fax:** (55) 11 3174 6751
Web: www.santander.com.br

PRODUCTS/OPERATIONS

2013 Sales

	% of total
Interest and similar income	82
Fee and commission income	17
Gains on financial transactons	1
Total	100

COMPETITORS

BANCO BILBAO VIZCAYA ARGENTARIA SOCIEDAD ANONIMA
BANCO POPULAR ESPAÃ‘OL SA (EXTINGUIDA)
BANCO SANTANDER SA
BNP PARIBAS
Banco do Brasil S/A
COMMONWEALTH BANK OF AUSTRALIA
INTESA SANPAOLO SPA
NATWEST GROUP PLC
Nordea Bank AB
UNICREDIT SPA

HISTORICAL FINANCIALS

Company Type: Public

Income Statement   FYE: December 31

	REVENUE ($mil)	NET INCOME ($mil)	NET PROFIT MARGIN	EMPLOYEES
12/22	26,580	2,701	10.2%	52,603
12/21	17,174	2,786	16.2%	48,834
12/20	13,661	2,583	18.9%	44,599
12/19	22,879	4,081	17.8%	47,819
12/18	21,040	3,241	15.4%	48,012
Annual Growth	6.0%	(4.5%)		2.3%

2022 Year-End Financials

Debt ratio: —   No. of shares ($ mil.): 3,787
Return on equity: 13.2%   Dividends
Cash ($ mil.): 4,160   Yield: —
Current Ratio: —   Payout: 94.6%
Long-term debt ($ mil.): —   Market value ($ mil.): 20,415

	STOCK PRICE ($) FY Close	P/E High/Low	PER SHARE ($) Earnings	Dividends	Book Value
12/22	5.39	4	3	0.35	0.33	5.50
12/21	5.37	4	3	0.36	0.46	4.98
12/20	8.64	6	3	0.33	0.56	5.36
12/19	12.13	6	5	0.52	0.47	6.32
12/18	11.13	7	4	0.41	0.46	6.16
Annual Growth	(16.6%)	—	—	(4.3%)	(8.4%)	(2.8%)

Banco Santander Chile

Banco Santander-Chile (Santander-Chile) is a leading commercial bank in Chile. Established in 1978, it is a standalone subsidiary of the Santander Group. From more than 285 branches and 1,645 ATMs throughout Chile, the bank provides a broad range of commercial and retail banking services to its customers, including Chilean peso and foreign currency denominated loans to finance a variety of commercial transactions, trade, foreign currency forward contracts and credit lines and a variety of retail banking services, including mortgage financing. In addition to its traditional banking operations, Santander-Chile offers a variety of financial services, including financial leasing, financial advisory services, mutual fund management, securities brokerage, insurance brokerage, and investment management. The bank had total assets of Ch$68.4 trillion (US$80.5 billion) and total deposits of Ch$27.1 trillion (US$31.9 billion) in 2022.

EXECUTIVES

Chairman, President, Executive Chairman, Claudio Melandri Hinojosa
First Vice President, Director, Rodrigo Montes Vergara
Second Vice President, Director, Orlando Poblete Iturrate
Chief Executive Officer, Roman Blanco
Retail Banking Director, Pedro Orellana
Corporate and Investment Banking Director, Andres Trautmann
Middle Market Director, Luis Araya
Chief Financial Officer, Emiliano Muratore
Financial Controller, Guillermo Sabater
Risk Director, Franco Rizza
Technology Director, Operations Director, Ricardo Bartel
Human Resources Director, Communications Director, Maria Eugenia de la Fuente Nunez
Administration and Global Payments Director, Sergio Avila
Clients and Service Quality Director, Claudia Heimpell
Internal Audit Director, Oscar Gomez
Wealth Management and Insurance Director, Jorge Valencia
Chief Accounting Officer, Jonathan Covarrubias
General Counsel, Cristian Florence
Director, Felix de Vicente Mingo
Director, Alfonso Gomez Morales
Director, Ana Dorrego
Director, Rodrigo Echenique Gordillo
Director, Lucia Santa Cruz Sutil
Director, Juan Pedro Santa Maria Perez
Auditors : PricewaterhouseCoopers Consultores Auditores SpA

LOCATIONS

HQ: Banco Santander Chile
Bandera 140, 20th Floor, Santiago
Phone: (11) 562 320 2000 **Fax:** (11) 562 696 1679
Web: www.santander.cl

COMPETITORS

BANCA ANTONVENETA SPA
BANCO BBVA ARGENTINA S.A.
BANCO ESPAÃ'OL DE CREDITO SA (EXTINGUIDA)
BANCO SANTANDER RIO S.A.
BANK OF THE JAMES FINANCIAL GROUP, INC.
Banque Nationale du Canada
CREDIT INDUSTRIEL ET COMMERCIAL
HMN FINANCIAL, INC.
QNB CORP.
SlovenskÃ¡ sporitelna, a.s.

HISTORICAL FINANCIALS
Company Type: Public

Income Statement — FYE: December 31

	ASSETS ($mil)	NET INCOME ($mil)	INCOME AS % OF ASSETS	EMPLOYEES
12/23	80,515	656	0.8%	0
12/22	79,782	923	1.2%	9,389
12/21	74,930	988	1.3%	9,988
12/20	78,367	770	1.0%	10,470
12/19	68,620	839	1.2%	11,200
Annual Growth	4.1%	(6.0%)	—	—

2023 Year-End Financials
Return on assets: 0.8%
Return on equity: 11.5%
Long-term debt ($ mil.): —
No. of shares ($ mil.): 188,446
Sales ($ mil.): 5,955
Dividends Yield: —
Payout: 32941.0%
Market value ($ mil.): 3,672,813

	STOCK PRICE ($) FY Close	P/E High/Low	PER SHARE ($) Earnings	Dividends	Book Value
12/23	19.49	7	5	0.00	1.15	0.03
12/22	15.84	5	4	0.00	1.09	0.03
12/21	16.29	5	3	0.01	1.03	0.03
12/20	18.99	9	5	0.00	0.65	0.03
12/19	23.07	9	7	0.00	0.83	0.02
Annual Growth	(4.1%)	—	—	(6.0%)	8.4%	6.4%

Banco Santander Mexico SA, Institucion de Banca Multiple, Grupo Financiero Santander Mexico

Grupo Financiero Santander, which operates primarily through Banco Santander (Mexico) bank, is among the top five largest financial services firms in Mexico based on net income, assets, and deposits. It offers retail and commercial banking, as well as asset management, brokerage and custody services (through subsidiary Casa de Bolsa Santander), and securities underwriting. Banco Santander Mexico serves more than 12 million customers with approximately 1,300 branches across the country. Grupo Financiero Santander is 75%-owned by Spanish banking giant Grupo Santander.

Operations
The company's retail banking segment is its largest, bringing in about 85% of total revenue. Wholesale banking, which includes the broker-dealer operations, brings in most of the rest.

EXECUTIVES

Chief Financial Officer, Didier Mena Campos
Intervention and Control Management Deputy General Director, Emilio de Eusebio Saiz
Risk Deputy General Manager, Ricardo Alonso Fernandez
Staff Deputy General Director, Marketing Deputy General Director, Research Deputy General Director, Strategy Deputy General Director, Public Affairs Deputy General Director, Staff Chief, Marketing Chief, Research Chief, Strategy Chief, Public Affairs Chief, Rodrigo Brand de Lara
Business and Institutional Banking Deputy General Director, Pablo Fernando Quesada Gomez
Business Strategy Deputy General Director, Client Services Deputy General Director, Alejandro Diego Cecchi Gonzalez
Corporate Resources and Recoveries Deputy General Director, Executive Director, Carlos Hajj Aboumrad
Digital and Innovation Deputy General Director, Digital Banking Deputy General Director, Maria Fuencisla Gomez Martin
Chief Executive Officer, Executive President, Director, Hector Blas Grisi Checa
Human Resources Executive Director, Juan Ignacio Echeverria Fernandez

Process Executive Director, Operations
Executive Director, Jesus Santiago Martin Juarez
Consumer Strategy Executive Director, Francisco Jesus Moza Zapatero
Internal Audit Chief Audit Executive, Juan Ramon Jimenez Lorenzo
Deputy General Legal Director, Secretary, Fernando Borja Mujica
Independent Chairman, Laura Renee Diez Barroso de Azcarraga
Independent Director, Cesar Augusto Montemayor Zambrano
Independent Director, Barbara Garza Laguera Gonda
Independent Director, Antonio Puron Mier y Teran
Independent Director, Fernando Benjamin Ruiz Sahagun
Independent Director, Alberto Torrado Martinez
Independent Director, Maria de Lourdes Melgar Palacios
Director, Magdalena Sofia Salarich Fernandez de Valderrama
Director, Francisco Javier Garcia-Carranza Benjumea
Auditors : PricewaterhouseCoopers, S.C.

LOCATIONS

HQ: Banco Santander Mexico SA, Institucion de Banca Multiple, Grupo Financiero Santander Mexico
Avenida Prolongacion Paseo de la Reforma 500, Colonia Lomas de Santa Fe, Alcaldía Álvaro Obregón, Ciudad de México 01219
Phone: (52) 55 5269 1925   **Fax:** (52) 55 5269 2701
Web: www.santander.com.mx

PRODUCTS/OPERATIONS

2014 Sales

	%
Retail Banking	85
Global Wholesale Banking	13
Corporate Activities	2
Total	100

2014 Sales

	%
Interest income and similar income	75
Fee and commission income	21
Gains/(losses) on financial assets and liabilities (net)	3
Other operating income	1
Total	100

COMPETITORS

GRUPO FINANCIERO GALICIA S.A.
Grupo Financiero BBVA Bancomer, S.A. de C.V.
Grupo Financiero Banorte, S.A.B. de C.V.
Grupo Financiero HSBC, S.A. de C.V.
Grupo Financiero Inbursa, S.A.B. de C.V.

HISTORICAL FINANCIALS

Company Type: Public

Income Statement FYE: December 31

	ASSETS ($mil)	NET INCOME ($mil)	INCOME AS % OF ASSETS	EMPLOYEES
12/21	82,077	1,017	1.2%	25,276
12/20	92,501	954	1.0%	21,183
12/19	77,567	1,077	1.4%	15,857
12/18	71,639	984	1.4%	16,016
12/17	67,471	948	1.4%	15,116
Annual Growth	5.0%	1.8%	—	13.7%

2021 Year-End Financials

Return on assets: 1.1%
Return on equity: 13.1%
Long-term debt ($ mil.): —
No. of shares ($ mil.): 6,786
Sales ($ mil.): 6,626
Dividends
 Yield: 2.8%
 Payout: 128.9%
Market value ($ mil.): 38,279

	STOCK PRICE ($) FY Close	P/E High/Low		PER SHARE ($) Earnings	Dividends	Book Value
12/21	5.64	2	2	0.15	0.16	1.18
12/20	5.15	3	1	0.14	0.00	1.14
12/19	6.78	3	2	0.16	0.33	1.05
12/18	6.16	3	2	0.14	0.29	0.92
12/17	7.31	4	3	0.14	0.00	0.86
Annual Growth	(6.3%)	—	—	1.8%	—	8.1%

Banco Santander SA (Spain)

EXECUTIVES

Executive Chairman, Executive Director, Ana Patricia Botin-Sanz de Sautuola y O'Shea
Chief Executive Officer, Vice-Chairman, Executive Director, Jose Antonio Alvarez Alvarez
Executive Director, Sergio A. L. Rial
Chief Risk Officer, Keiran Foad
Global Wholesale Banking Chief Financial Officer, Jose Antonio Garcia Cantera
Risk Chief Audit Executive, Juan Guitard Marin
Chief Compliance Officer, Senior Executive Vice President, Marjolien van Hellemondt-Gerdingh
Secretary, Jaime Perez Renovales
Vice-Chairman, Lead Independent Director, Independent Non-Executive Director, Bruce Carnegie-Brown
Independent Non-Executive Director, Homaira Akbari
Independent Non-Executive Director, Alvaro Cardoso de Souza
Independent Non-Executive Director, Sol Daurella Comadran
Independent Non-Executive Director, Henrique de Castro
Independent Non-Executive Director, Gina Diez Barroso
Independent Non-Executive Director, Ramiro Mato Garcia-Ansorena
Independent Non-Executive Director, Ramon Martin Chavez Marquez
Independent Non-Executive Director, Belen Romana Garcia
Independent Non-Executive Director, Pamela Walkden
Non-Executive Director, Javier Botin-Sanz de Sautuola y O'Shea
Non-Executive Director, Luis Isasi Fernandez de Bobadilla
Auditors : PricewaterhouseCoopers Auditores, S.L.

LOCATIONS

HQ: Banco Santander SA (Spain)
Ciudad Grupo Santander, Madrid, Boadilla del Monte 28660
Phone: (34) 91 289 32 80   **Fax:** (34) 91 257 12 82
Web: www.santander.com

COMPETITORS

BANCO BILBAO VIZCAYA ARGENTARIA SOCIEDAD ANONIMA
BANCO DE SABADELL SA
BANCO POPULAR ESPAÑOL SA (EXTINGUIDA)
BANKIA SA
BANKINTER SOCIEDAD ANONIMA
CAIXA GERAL DE DEPÓSITOS, S.A.
CAIXABANK SA
HSBC HOLDINGS PLC
NATWEST GROUP PLC
UNICREDIT SPA

HISTORICAL FINANCIALS

Company Type: Public

Income Statement FYE: December 31

	ASSETS ($mil)	NET INCOME ($mil)	INCOME AS % OF ASSETS	EMPLOYEES
12/22	1,852,690	10,258	0.6%	206,462
12/21	1,806,270	9,195	0.5%	197,070
12/20	1,851,060	(10,764)	—	191,189
12/19	1,709,630	7,314	0.4%	196,419
12/18	1,671,150	8,943	0.5%	202,713
Annual Growth	2.6%	3.5%	—	0.5%

2022 Year-End Financials

Return on assets: 0.5%
Return on equity: 10.9%
Long-term debt ($ mil.): —
No. of shares ($ mil.): 16,794
Sales ($ mil.): 98,779
Dividends
 Yield: —
 Payout: 34.2%
Market value ($ mil.): 49,543

	STOCK PRICE ($) FY Close	P/E High/Low		PER SHARE ($) Earnings	Dividends	Book Value
12/22	2.95	7	5	0.57	0.20	5.67
12/21	3.29	9	6	0.49	0.07	5.67
12/20	3.05	—	—	(0.66)	0.10	5.78
12/19	4.14	14	10	0.41	0.19	6.76
12/18	4.48	15	10	0.51	0.20	6.80
Annual Growth	(9.9%)	—	—	2.8%	(0.7%)	(4.5%)

BanColombia SA

Bancolombia has a wealth of services for wealthy and average Colombians alike. Serving more than 6.4 million customers, Bancolombia is the #1 bank in Colombia, with more than 700 branches and some 2300 ATMs throughout the country. Its Banagrícola division has another 100 branches located in El Salvador. The bank provides traditional commercial and retail banking services, including deposit accounts, loans and mortgages, credit and debit cards, and cash management. It also offers asset management, insurance, investment banking, and brokerage services. In addition to its core Colombia and El Salvador operations, the bank is also present in the US, Panama, and Peru. Bancolombia traces its roots back to 1945.

EXECUTIVES

Corporate Innovation & Digital Transformation Chief Executive Officer, Juan Carlos Mora Uribe

Legal Vice President, Mauricio Rosillo Rojas
Business Vice President, Retail & SME Banking Vice President, Maria Cristina Arrastia Uribe
Corporate Services Vice President, Jaime Alberto Villegas Gutierrez
Risk Management Vice President, Rodrigo Prieto Uribe
Internal Audit Vice President, Jose Mauricio Rodriguez
Innovation Vice President, Cipriano Lopez Gonzalez
Financial Vice President, Financial Chief Financial Officer, Jose Humberto Acosta
Chief Legal Officer, General Counsel, Claudia Echavarria Uribe
Independent Director, Luis Fernando Restrepo Echavarria
Independent Director, Andres Felipe Mejia Cardona
Independent Director, Sylvia Escovar Gomez
Independent Director, Arturo Condo Tamayo
Non-Independent Director, Juan David Escobar Franco
Director, Gonzalo Alberto Perez Rojas
Director, Silvina Vatnick
Auditors : PwC Contadores y Auditores S.A.S.

LOCATIONS

HQ: BanColombia SA
Carrera 48 # 26-85, Avenida Los Industriales, Medellin
Phone: (57) 4 404 1837
Web: www.grupobancolombia.com

PRODUCTS/OPERATIONS

2013 Sales

	% of total
Interest income	
Loans	65
Financial leases	9
Investment sercurities	5
Fees and other service income	
Credit and debit card fees	7
Commissions from banking services	4
Collections and payment fees	3
Trust activities	2
Checking fees	1
Others	4
Total	100

Selected Subsidiaries

Banca de Inversion Bancolombia S.A. (investment banking)
Bancolombia (Panamá), S.A.
Bancolombia Puerto Rico
Factoring Bancolombia S.A. (99.97%)
Fiduciaria Bancolombia S.A. (trust services, 98.8%)
Inversiones Financieras Banco Agricola S.A. (investments, 98.4%)
Leasing Bancolombia S.A.
Patrimonio Autonomo CV Sufinanciamiento (loan management)
Valores Bancolombia S.A. (securities brokerage)

COMPETITORS

ARAB BANK PLC
BANCO SANTANDER RIO S.A.
Banque de Montréal
CREDITO BERGAMASCO SPA
ISRAEL DISCOUNT BANK OF NEW YORK
METROPOLITAN BANK & TRUST COMPANY
MUFG AMERICAS HOLDINGS CORPORATION
ORIENTAL BANK OF COMMERCE
The Toronto-Dominion Bank

UNION BANK OF INDIA

HISTORICAL FINANCIALS
Company Type: Public

Income Statement — FYE: December 31

	ASSETS ($mil)	NET INCOME ($mil)	INCOME AS % OF ASSETS	EMPLOYEES
12/22	72,722	1,398	1.9%	33,140
12/21	71,217	1,004	1.4%	31,245
12/20	74,672	80	0.1%	30,633
12/19	71,879	949	1.3%	31,075
12/18	67,799	818	1.2%	31,040
Annual Growth	1.8%	14.3%	—	1.7%

2022 Year-End Financials
Return on assets: 2.1%
Return on equity: 19.0%
Long-term debt ($ mil.): —
No. of shares ($ mil.): 509
Sales ($ mil.): 7,308
Dividends
Yield: —
Payout: 151.3%
Market value ($ mil.): 14,547

	STOCK PRICE ($) FY Close	P/E High/Low		PER SHARE ($) Earnings	Dividends	Book Value
12/22	28.54	0	0	1.47	2.22	15.81
12/21	31.59	0	0	1.06	0.25	15.54
12/20	40.18	0	0	0.10	1.54	15.22
12/19	54.79	0	0	1.01	1.24	16.06
12/18	38.10	0	0	0.87	1.35	15.02
Annual Growth	(7.0%)	—	—	13.9%	13.3%	1.3%

Bangkok Bank Public Co., Ltd. (Thailand)

Bangkok Bank wants to protect the baht you've got. One of the largest commercial banks in Thailand, Bangkok Bank provides a variety of banking services to individual and commercial clients, including checking and savings accounts, loans, Internet banking, and treasury and investment banking services. It operates about 1,200 branches serving 16 million customers throughout Thailand, about a dozen other Southeast Asian countries, the UK, and the US. The bank was founded in 1944 in response to the difficulty Thai businessmen encountered in receiving credit facilities from foreign banks; it has since had a hand in developing its homeland's industry and agriculture.

EXECUTIVES

Chairman, Executive Chairman, Executive Director, Deja Tulananda
Executive Director, Amorn Chandarasomboon
Executive Director, Singh Tangtatswas
Executive Director, Charamporn Jotikasthira
Executive Director, Pichet Durongkaveroj
Senior Executive Vice President, Executive Director, Suvarn Thansathit
President, Executive Director, Chartsiri Sophonpanich
Senior Executive Vice President, Executive Director, Chansak Fuangfu
Senior Executive Vice President, Executive Director, Boonsong Bunyasaranand
Senior Executive Vice President, Executive Director, Chong Toh
Senior Executive Vice President, Corporate Secretary, Executive Director, Kobsak Pootrakool
Senior Executive Vice President, Executive Director, Niraman Laisathit
Chairman, Non-Executive Director, Phornthep Phornprapha
Independent Director, Siri Jirapongphan
Independent Director, Chatchawin Charoen-Rajapark
Independent Director, Arun Chirachavala
Independent Director, Chokechai Niljianskul
Independent Director, Bundhit Eua-arporn
Independent Director, Parnsiree Amatayakul
Independent Director, Predee Daochai
Auditors : Deloitte Touche Tohmatsu Jaiyos Audit Co., Ltd.

LOCATIONS

HQ: Bangkok Bank Public Co., Ltd. (Thailand)
333 Silom Road, Bangrak, Bangkok 10500
Phone: (66) 0 2645 5555 **Fax:** (66) 0 2230 2453
Web: www.bangkokbank.com

COMPETITORS

ARAB BANK PLC
AUSTRALIA AND NEW ZEALAND BANKING GROUP LIMITED
BANK OF AYUDHYA PUBLIC COMPANY LIMITED
Bank Of Shanghai Co., Ltd.
FIRST NATIONAL BANK ALASKA
HANG SENG BANK, LIMITED
NATIONAL BANK OF KUWAIT S.A.K.P.
STANDARD CHARTERED PLC
UNITED OVERSEAS BANK LIMITED
VIETNAM TECHNOLOGICAL AND COMMERCIAL JOINT STOCK BANK

HISTORICAL FINANCIALS
Company Type: Public

Income Statement — FYE: December 31

	ASSETS ($mil)	NET INCOME ($mil)	INCOME AS % OF ASSETS	EMPLOYEES
12/22	127,989	848	0.7%	0
12/21	130,662	799	0.6%	0
12/20	127,696	573	0.4%	0
12/19	107,989	1,202	1.1%	0
12/18	96,345	1,092	1.1%	25,287
Annual Growth	7.4%	(6.1%)	—	—

2022 Year-End Financials
Return on assets: 0.6%
Return on equity: 5.8%
Long-term debt ($ mil.): —
No. of shares ($ mil.): 1,908
Sales ($ mil.): 5,481
Dividends
Yield: —
Payout: 0.0%
Market value ($ mil.): 41,269

	STOCK PRICE ($) FY Close	P/E High/Low		PER SHARE ($) Earnings	Dividends	Book Value
12/22	21.62	1	1	0.44	0.44	7.66
12/21	18.69	1	1	0.42	0.44	7.78
12/20	20.59	3	2	0.30	0.70	7.86
12/19	27.50	2	1	0.63	0.85	7.52
12/18	32.00	2	2	0.57	0.81	6.69
Annual Growth	(9.3%)	—	—	(6.1%)	(14.1%)	3.5%

Bank Millennium SA

Bank Millennium provides a variety of banking and financial services in Poland. Along with such bread-and-butter banking offerings as deposit accounts andÂ lending, Bank Millennium offers brokerage, investment funds, leasing services, and pension and savings plans. The company has nearly 500 locations and more thanÂ 500 ATMs around Poland. Bank Millennium is the primary member of the Bank Millennium Group, which also includes Millennium Leasing, Millennium Brokerage House, and Millennium TFI (investment funds). Banco Comercial PortuguÃªs owns 66% of the company.

EXECUTIVES

Management Chairman, Joao Nuno Lima Bras Jorge
Management Deputy Chairman, Fernando Cardoso Rodrigues Bicho
Secretary, Deputy Chairman, Dariusz Rosati
Chairman, Boguslaw Kott
Deputy Chairman, Nuno Manuel da Silva Amado
Director, Miguel Maya Dias Pinheiro
Director, Jose Miguel Bensliman Schorcht da Silva Pessanha
Director, Alojzy Nowak
Director, Grzegorz Jedrys
Director, Anna Jakubowski
Director, Lingjiang Xu
Director, Miguel de Campos Pereira de Bragança
Director, Agnieszka Hryniewicz-Bieniek
Director, Andrzej Kozminski
Auditors : PricewaterhouseCoopers Polska spolka z ograniczona odpowiedzialnoscia Audyt sp.k.

LOCATIONS

HQ: Bank Millennium SA
ul.Stanislawa Zaryna 2A, Warsaw 02-593
Phone: (48) 22 598 40 31   **Fax:** (48) 22 598 2563
Web: www.bankmillennium.pl

COMPETITORS

BANK BPH S A
BANK POLSKA KASA OPIEKI S A
DEUTSCHE BANK POLSKA S A
FIDUCIARY TRUST COMPANY INTERNATIONAL
SITIBANK, AO

HISTORICAL FINANCIALS

Company Type: Public

Income Statement   FYE: December 31

	ASSETS ($mil)	NET INCOME ($mil)	INCOME AS % OF ASSETS	EMPLOYEES
12/23	32,028	146	0.5%	6,872
12/22	25,216	(234)	—	0
12/21	25,606	(328)	—	0
12/20	26,336	6	0.0%	0
12/19	25,846	147	0.6%	0
Annual Growth	5.5%	(0.2%)		

2023 Year-End Financials
Return on assets: —
Return on equity: —
Long-term debt ($ mil.): —
No. of shares ($ mil.): 1,213
Sales ($ mil.): 2,604
Dividends
Yield: —
Payout: 0.0%
Market value ($ mil.): —

Bank of Communications Co., Ltd.

Founded in 1908, Bank of Communications (BoCom) is one of the note-issuing banks with the longest history in modern China. It offers services in corporate and personal banking and treasury. Its products and services include deposits and loans, supply chain finance, cash management, international settlement and trade financing, investment banking, asset custody, wealth management, bank cards, private banking, treasury businesses. BoCom operates nearly 250 branches in Mainland China and about 25 branches, subsidiary banks, with nearly 70 overseas operating outlets in around 20 countries in the Americas, Asia, Australia, and Europe. Most of its revenue comes from its domestic operations. HSBC Holdings has close to a 20% interest in BoCom.

Operations

BoCom organizes its operations into four main business segments.

Its corporate banking segment generates approximately 45% of overall revenue. The business mainly comprises corporate loans, bills, trade financing, corporate deposits, and remittance.

BoCom's personal banking unit brings in about 45% of revenue and mainly comprises personal loans, personal deposits, credit cards and remittance.

The bank's Treasury business generates nearly 10% of revenue and includes money market placements and takings, financial investment, and securities sold under repurchase agreements.

The bank's major subsidiaries include: BoCom Schroder Fund Management, BoCom International Trust, BoCom Financial Leasing, BoCom MSIG Life Insurance, China BoCom Insurance, BoCom International holdings, BoCom Financial Asset Investment, and Bocom Wealth Management. Its rural banks include Dayi BoCom Xingmin Rural Bank, Zhejiang Anji BoCom Rural Bank, Xinjiang Shihezi BoCom Rural bank, and QingDao Laoshan BoCom Rural Bank.

Its interest income accounts for a total of approximately 60% while its non-interest income including commissions and fees accounts for a total of approximately 40%.

Geographic Reach

In addition to its nearly 250 branches in Mainland China, Shanghai-based BoCom has roughly 70 overseas operating outlets in nearly 20 countries in the Americas, Asia, Australia, and Europe. It has overseas subsidiaries, branches, and representative offices in major cities including Hong Kong, New York, London, Singapore, Tokyo, Frankfurt, Luxembourg, and Sydney.

Yangtze River Delta generates the largest geographical revenue of BoCom (over 35%), followed by Central China that accounts for nearly 15%, head office (some 15%) and the remaining revenues came from Bohai Rim Economic Zone, Pearl River Delta, Western China, North Eastern China, and from overseas countries.

Sales and Marketing

The bank provides comprehensive one-stop wealth management solutions for corporate, government institutions and interbank financial customers through intelligent financial service, and digital transformation.

Financial Performance

Note: Growth rates may differ after conversion to US Dollars.

BoCom's revenue has been rising consistently for the last five years. BoCom's revenue grew 37% between 2017 and 2021. Its net income followed the same trend within the last five years.

BoCom's interest income for 2021 increased by RMB 8.5 billion or 2.3% to RMB 377.6 billion, due to subsequent increases in the company's income from loans and advances to customers. This segment increased RMB 15 billion, or 6%, to RMB 266.4 billion.

BoCom reported a net profit of RMB 87.6 billion in 2021, a 12% from RMB 78.3 billion in 2020. The increase in profits comes from the increase in the company's income, as well as equity investments in the year.

The company's cash and equivalents at the end of the year totaled RMB 194.3 billion, a RMB 112,812 billion decrease from the year prior. Operating activities used RMB 34.8 billion that year, compared to RMB 149.4 billion generated from 2020. Investing activities used another RMB 75.5 billion, mainly for financial investments and purchases in property and equipment. Financing activities provided RMB 1.3 billion from equity instruments and debt securities.

Strategy

BoCom continues its commitment to the strategic objective of "building the first-tier bank with wealth management characteristics and global competitive capabilities in the world," by focusing on the new development stage, carrying out a new vision for development comprehensively, and devoting to accelerating the high-quality development in the progress of serving to create a new development pattern.

Furthermore, the company has leveraged

the advantage of its "Shanghai Base," to improve its management mechanism and strengthen business development. It has also constructed a "New Digital BoCom" focused on keeping in line with the overall development context of digital economy, deepening the financial supply-side reform, increasing resource investment, and creating new growth points of business value. BoCom has also created four business features that increase its appeal to consumers: inclusive finance, trade finance, sci-tech finance, and wealth finance. Lastly, the company has been improving its five professional capabilities: customer operations, technology empowerment, risk management, cooperative operation, and resource allocation.

Company Background

In 2007, with its purchase of an 85% stake in Hubei International Trust and Investment, BoCom entered the trust industry. Soon after, it began also to cater to the insurance industry with the launch of BoCommLife Insurance, a joint venture with the Commonwealth Bank of Australia. BoCom is among the nation's first commercial banks allowed to tap into the insurance industry.

EXECUTIVES

Outside Supervisor, Xinyu Tang
Outside Supervisor, Zhihua Xia
Supervisor, Xueqing Wang
Outside Supervisor, Yao Li
Board Secretary, Sheng Gu
Staff Supervisor, Xingshe Guan
Outside Supervisor, Hanwen Chen
Supervisor, Minsheng Zhang
President, Vice Chairman, Jun Liu
Outside Supervisor, Jiandong Ju
Staff Supervisor, Bing Feng
Staff Supervisor, Zhihong Lin
Chief Risk Officer, Hua Lin
Non-executive Director, Haoyang Liu
Independent Non-executive Director, Zhiwei Yang
Independent Non-executive Director, Zhanyun Hu
Independent Non-executive Director, Haoyi Cai
Chairman (Acting), Executive Director, Vice Chairman, Chairman, Deqi Ren
Non-executive Director, Junkui Chen
Non-executive Director, Shaozong Chen
Independent Non-executive Director, Lei Shi
Non-executive Director, Hongjun Song
Non-executive Director, Longcheng Li
Independent Non-executive Director, Xiaohui Li
Non-executive Director, Yijian Liao
Independent Non-executive Director, Xiangdong Zhang
Non-executive Director, Baosheng Chang
Non-executive Director, Linping Wang
Auditors : KPMG Huazhen LLP

LOCATIONS

HQ: Bank of Communications Co., Ltd.
No. 188, Yin Cheng Zhong Road, Pudong New District, Shanghai 200120
Phone: (86) 21 58766688   **Fax:** (86) 21 58798398
Web: www.bankcomm.com

2018 Sales

	% of total
Northern China	11
Northeastern China	3
Eastern China	36
Central and Southern China	18
Western China	8
Overseas	6
Head Office	18
Total	100

PRODUCTS/OPERATIONS

2018 Sales

	% of total
Corporate Banking	46
Personal Banking	36
Treasury Business	11
Other business	7
Total	100

2018 Sales

	% of total
Net interest income	85
Fee and commission income	10
Net gains arising from trading activities	2
Insurance business income	1
Others	2
Total	100

Selected Services

Personal Banking
    Personal Savings in Local and Foreign Currencies
    Bank Card
    Personal Lending
    Wealth Management
    Precious Metals and Commodities
Corporate & International
    Wealth Management
    Corporate Transaction Banking
    Finance Services
    Investment Banking Services
    Offshore Banking
    Precious Metals and Commodities
    Corporate Forex Wealth Management
    Document Settlement
    Remittance and Bill Services
    Trade Finance
Interbank Financing
    Interbank Cooperation
    Banksecurities Cooperation
    Bankfutures Cooperation
    Institutional Financial Management and Insurance Service
    Factor Markets
    Precious Metals and Commodities

HISTORICAL FINANCIALS

Company Type: Public

Income Statement   FYE: December 31

	ASSETS ($mil)	NET INCOME ($mil)	INCOME AS % OF ASSETS	EMPLOYEES
12/22	1,883,330	13,357	0.7%	91,823
12/21	1,837,520	13,795	0.8%	90,238
12/20	1,635,660	11,968	0.7%	90,716
12/19	1,423,580	11,106	0.8%	87,828
12/18	1,385,690	10,704	0.8%	89,542
Annual Growth	8.0%	5.7%	—	0.6%

2022 Year-End Financials

Return on assets: 0.7%
Return on equity: 9.2%
Long-term debt ($ mil.): —
No. of shares ($ mil.): 74,262
Sales ($ mil.): 76,306
Dividends
Yield: —
Payout: 0.0%
Market value ($ mil.): —

Bank of East Asia Ltd.

Bank of East Asia (BEA) is dedicated to providing comprehensive wholesale banking, personal banking, wealth management, and investment services to its customers in Hong Kong, Mainland China, and other major markets around the world. BEA also operates one of the largest branch networks in Hong Kong, with about 55 branches, around 45 SupremeGold Centres, and three i-Financial Centres throughout the city. Products and services include syndicated loans, trade finance, deposit-taking, foreign currency savings, remittances, mortgage loans, consumer loans, credit cards, Cyberbanking, retail investment and wealth management services, private banking, Renminbi services, foreign exchange margin trading, broking services, Mandatory Provident Fund services, and general and life insurance.

Operations

The group has nine reportable segments.

Mainland China operations mainly include the back office unit for Mainland China operations in Hong Kong, all subsidiaries and associates operating in Mainland China, except those subsidiaries carrying out data processing and other back office operations for Hong Kong operations in Mainland China. It accounts for about 30% of total revenue.

Corporate Banking includes corporate lending and loan syndication, asset based lending, commercial lending, securities lending and trade financing activities with correspondent banks and corporates in Hong Kong. Corporate Banking brings in around 20% of total revenue.

Personal Banking includes branch operations, personal internet banking, consumer finance, property loans and credit card business to individual customers in Hong Kong. It accounts for about 20% of total revenue.

Others (more than 5% of total revenue) mainly include insurance business, trust business, securities & futures broking and corporate financial advisory carried out by subsidiaries operating in Hong Kong and other supporting units of Hong Kong operations located outside Hong Kong.

Overseas operations mainly include the back office unit for overseas banking operations in Hong Kong, Macau Branch, Taiwan Branch and all branches, subsidiaries and associates operating in overseas. Overseas operations generate more than 10% of total revenue.

Treasury Markets (less than 5%) include treasury operations and securities dealing in Hong Kong. C

entralized operations include supporting units of banking operations in Hong Kong. It accounts for some 5% of total revenue.

Corporate management (less than 5%) absorbs the regulatory capital cost of loan capital issued by the bank and receives, from Hong Kong operations, the interest income on business activities funded by capital instruments issued by the bank.

Overall, net interest income accounts for more than 65% of total revenue.

Geographic Reach

With about 150 outlets worldwide, BEA operates an extensive international network covering Hong Kong and the rest of Greater China, Southeast Asia, the UK, and the US.

BEA China maintains a strong presence in Mainland China, with about 30 branches and some 40 sub-branches covering some 40 cities.

Financial Performance

The company reported a net interest income of HK$11.2 billion in 2021, a 3% decrease from the previous year's net interest income of HK$11.6 billion.

In 2021, the company had a net income of HK$5.3 billion, a 46% increase from the previous year's net income of HK$3.6 billion. This was primarily due to a lower volume of impairment losses for the year.

The company's cash at the end of 2021 was HK$120.6 billion. Operating activities HK$9.7 billion, while investing activities provided HK$2.7 billion. Financing activities used another HK$6.6 billion, primarily for redemption of loan capital.

Strategy

While the company focuses on the resilience of its business, the company is also investing for the future. Online banking and digital innovation have changed the playing field for financial services. Digital transformation is part of the company's long-term strategy, ensuring that it is prepared for the digital challenges of tomorrow.

The company also has made important changes to its international network, sharpening its focus on corporate banking in Singapore, Macau and the UK. This initiative produced the desired results, with steady growth in business. Linking Hong Kong and the Mainland with the company's international network remains a key aspect of its strategy going forward.

As well as strengthening internal collaboration, the company has continued to foster mutually beneficial partnerships with like-minded organizations. In 2021, the company entered into a ground-breaking bancassurance agreement with AIA Group Limited. Its shared vision and excellent working relationship ensured that the company's partnership enjoyed a highly promising start.

EXECUTIVES

Chairman, Director, David Kwok-po Li
Co-Chief Executive Officer, Executive Director, Adrian David Man-kiu Li
Co-Chief Executive Officer, Executive Director, Brian David Li Man-bun
Deputy Chief Executive, Chief Investment Officer, Samson Kai-cheong Li
Deputy Chief Executive, Chief Operating Officer, Hon-shing Tong
Secretary, Alson Chun-tak Law
Deputy Chairman, Non-Executive Director, Arthur Kwok Cheung Li
Deputy Chairman, Independent Non-Executive Director, Allan Chi-yun Wong
Independent Non-Executive Director, Meocre Kwon-wing Li
Independent Non-Executive Director, William Junior Guiherme Doo
Independent Non-Executive Director, David Tak-yeung Mong
Independent Non-Executive Director, Rita Lai Tai Fan Hsu
Independent Non-Executive Director, Delman Lee
Independent Non-Executive Director, Henry Tang
Non-Executive Director, Francisco Javier Serrado
Non-Executive Director, Daryl Win Kong Ng
Non-Executive Director, Aubrey Kwok-sing Li
Non-Executive Director, Winston Yau-lai Lo
Non-Executive Director, Stephen Charles Kwok-sze Li
Non-Executive Director, Masayuki Oku
Auditors : KPMG

LOCATIONS

HQ: Bank of East Asia Ltd.
  10 Des Voeux Road Central,
Phone: (852) 3608 3608   **Fax:** (852) 3608 6000
Web: www.hkbea.com

PRODUCTS/OPERATIONS

2014 Sales

	% of total
Interest income	83
Non-interest income	17
Total	100

COMPETITORS

CHIBA BANK,LTD., THE
CIMB GROUP HOLDINGS BERHAD
DBS GROUP HOLDINGS LTD
HONG LEONG BANK BERHAD
KB Financial Group Inc.
OVERSEA-CHINESE BANKING CORPORATION LIMITED
PUBLIC BANK BHD
PUBLIC FINANCIAL HOLDINGS LIMITED
SHIZUOKA BANK, LTD., THE
UNITED OVERSEAS BANK LIMITED

HISTORICAL FINANCIALS

Company Type: Public

Income Statement   FYE: December 31

	ASSETS ($mil)	NET INCOME ($mil)	INCOME AS % OF ASSETS	EMPLOYEES
12/22	113,274	559	0.5%	8,453
12/21	116,370	675	0.6%	8,824
12/20	114,077	466	0.4%	9,539
12/19	111,111	418	0.4%	9,846
12/18	107,181	831	0.8%	9,796
Annual Growth	1.4%	(9.4%)	—	(3.6%)

2022 Year-End Financials

Return on assets: 0.4%   Dividends
Return on equity: 3.9%   Yield: —
Long-term debt ($ mil.): —   Payout: 65.9%
No. of shares ($ mil.): 2,680   Market value ($ mil.): 3,082
Sales ($ mil.): 4,112

	STOCK PRICE ($) FY Close	P/E High/Low		PER SHARE ($) Earnings	Dividends	Book Value
12/22	1.15	1	1	0.17	0.11	5.08
12/21	1.43	2	1	0.20	0.07	5.08
12/20	2.13	2	2	0.13	0.06	4.99
12/19	2.18	4	2	0.11	0.10	4.83
12/18	3.18	2	1	0.26	0.12	4.52
Annual Growth	(22.4%)			(10.5%)	(2.7%)	3.0%

Bank of Ireland Group plc

EXECUTIVES

Chief Executive Officer, Executive Director, Myles O'Grady
Chief Financial Officer, Mark Spain
Chief People Officer, Matt Elliott
Chief Risk Officer, Stephen Roughton-Smith
Staff Head of Corporate Affairs, Staff Chief, Oliver Wall
Transformation Director, Enda Johnson
Corporate Governance Secretary, Corporate Governance Head, Sarah McLaughlin
Chairman, Non-Executive Director, Patrick Kennedy
Deputy Chairman, Senior Independent Director, Independent Non-Executive Director, Richard Goulding
Independent Non-Executive Director, Giles Andrews
Independent Non-Executive Director, Ian Buchanan
Independent Non-Executive Director, Evelyn Bourke
Independent Non-Executive Director, Eileen Fitzpatrick
Independent Non-Executive Director, Fiona Muldoon
Independent Non-Executive Director, Steve Pateman
Non-Executive Director, Michele Greene
Auditors : KPMG

LOCATIONS

HQ: Bank of Ireland Group plc
40 Mespil Road, Dublin 4 D04 C2N4
Phone: —
Web: www.bankofireland.com

HISTORICAL FINANCIALS

Company Type: Public

Income Statement — FYE: December 31

	ASSETS ($mil)	NET INCOME ($mil)	INCOME AS % OF ASSETS	EMPLOYEES
12/22	161,621	949	0.6%	10,153
12/21	175,742	1,186	0.7%	8,696
12/20	164,155	(910)	—	9,782
12/19	148,074	433	0.3%	10,440
12/18	141,625	710	0.5%	10,367
Annual Growth	3.4%	7.5%	—	(0.5%)

2022 Year-End Financials

Return on assets: 0.5%
Return on equity: 7.6%
Long-term debt ($ mil.): —
No. of shares ($ mil.): 1,069
Sales ($ mil.): 4,940
Dividends
Yield: —
Payout: 4.3%
Market value ($ mil.): 9,985

	STOCK PRICE ($) FY Close	P/E High/Low	PER SHARE ($) Earnings	Dividends	Book Value
12/22	9.34	13 7	0.82	0.04	11.85
12/21	5.80	7 4	1.03	0.06	11.86
12/20	3.95	— —	(0.89)	0.00	10.92
12/19	5.40	19 10	0.40	0.13	10.06
12/18	5.62	17 9	0.66	0.09	9.84
Annual Growth	13.5%	— —	5.5%	(21.9%)	4.8%

Bank of Iwate, Ltd. (The) (Japan)

Operating on the island of Honshu, The Bank of Iwate is certainly nothing to sneeze at. The bank boasts about 110 branches, more than 90 of them in its home Iwate prefecture on the island of Honshu. Besides the usual banking services such as deposits and credit cards, Bank of Iwate also provides leasing and clerical outsourcing. It has been focusing on lending to small and midsized firms and enhancing customer convenience. Ever on guard against the encroachment of major banks, Bank of Iwate has teamed with two other regional banks, Aomori Bank and Akita Bank, to create an investment trust. The Bank of Iwate was founded in 1932 as Iwate Shokusan Bank. It took on its present name in 1960.

EXECUTIVES

Chairman, Director, Masahiro Takahashi
President, Representative Director, Sachio Taguchi
Senior Managing Executive Officer, Director, Motomu Sato
Director, Yasushi Sasaki
Director, Kensei Ishikawa
Director, Shinji Niisato
Director, Toru Iwayama
Outside Director, Atsushi Takahashi
Outside Director, Fumio Ube
Outside Director, Atsushi Miyanoya
Director, Yuji Chiba
Director, Shuichi Fujiwara
Outside Director, Shinobu Obara
Outside Director, Etsuko Sugawara
Outside Director, Masakazu Watanabe
Auditors : KPMG AZSA LLC

LOCATIONS

HQ: Bank of Iwate, Ltd. (The) (Japan)
1-2-3 Chuodori, Morioka, Iwate 020-8688
Phone: (81) 19 623 1111   **Fax:** (81) 19 652 6751
Web: www.iwatebank.co.jp

COMPETITORS

BANK OF NAGOYA, LTD., THE
BANK OF THE RYUKYUS, LIMITED
EIGHTEENTH BANK, LIMITED., THE
Erste Group Bank AG
Portigon AG

HISTORICAL FINANCIALS

Company Type: Public

Income Statement — FYE: March 31

	ASSETS ($mil)	NET INCOME ($mil)	INCOME AS % OF ASSETS	EMPLOYEES
03/21	34,689	26	0.1%	1,939
03/20	32,109	34	0.1%	1,994
03/19	31,689	37	0.1%	2,057
03/18	33,495	52	0.2%	2,116
03/17	31,773	90	0.3%	2,128
Annual Growth	2.2%	(26.7%)	—	(2.3%)

2021 Year-End Financials

Return on assets: —
Return on equity: 1.4%
Long-term debt ($ mil.): —
No. of shares ($ mil.): 17
Sales ($ mil.): 409
Dividends
Yield: —
Payout: 36.5%
Market value ($ mil.): —

Bank of Kyoto Ltd (Japan)

For financial services in Kyoto, proper protocol might involve a visit to The Bank of Kyoto. The regional bank serves Kyoto and neighboring prefectures through some 165 branch offices. The bank serves businesses, particularly small and medium-sized local companies, as well as individual consumers. In addition to traditional deposit banking and lending, The Bank of Kyoto and its subsidiaries offer credit cards, leasing, stock brokerage, and business consulting services. The bank has worked to expand its operations beyond its home base and has opened branches to the north in the Kinki Region. Founded in 1941, the bank has about $81 billion in assets and ranks as Kyoto Prefecture's largest retail bank.

Geographic Reach

The Bank of Kyoto operates 110 branches in Kyoto Prefecture, 28 in Osaka Prefecture, a dozen in Shiga, eight in Hyogo, and seven branches in Nara.

Strategy

The Bank of Kyoto is aggressively opening branches to expand its reach beyond Kyoto Prefecture. Since opening its first branch at Kusatsu in Shiga Prefecture in 2000, the bank has opened branches in five neighboring prefectures (Kyoto, Osaka, Shiga, Nara, and Hyogo).

EXECUTIVES

President, Representative Director, Nobuhiro Doi
Senior Managing Director, Representative Director, Toshiro Iwahashi
Director, Mikiya Yasui
Director, Hiroyuki Hata
Director, Minako Okuno
Outside Director, Junko Otagiri
Outside Director, Chiho Oyabu
Outside Director, Eiji Ueki
Auditors : Deloitte Touche Tohmatsu LLC

LOCATIONS

HQ: Bank of Kyoto Ltd (Japan)
700 Yakushimae-cho, Karasuma-dori, Matsubara-Agaru, Shimogyo-ku, Kyoto 600-8652
Phone: (81) 75 361 2211   **Fax:** (81) 75 343 1276
Web: www.kyotobank.co.jp

COMPETITORS

AICHI BANK, LTD.,
EIGHTEENTH BANK, LIMITED., THE
HOKKOKU BANK, LTD., THE
NANTO BANK,LTD., THE
NISHI-NIPPON CITYBANK,LTD.

HISTORICAL FINANCIALS

Company Type: Public

Income Statement — FYE: March 31

	ASSETS ($mil)	NET INCOME ($mil)	INCOME AS % OF ASSETS	EMPLOYEES
03/22	100,389	169	0.2%	3,901
03/21	110,851	152	0.1%	3,951
03/20	92,846	187	0.2%	3,969
03/19	87,274	286	0.3%	4,092
03/18	89,263	181	0.2%	4,154
Annual Growth	3.0%	(1.8%)	—	(1.6%)

2022 Year-End Financials

Return on assets: 0.1%
Return on equity: 1.8%
Long-term debt ($ mil.): —
No. of shares ($ mil.): 75
Sales ($ mil.): 1,047
Dividends
Yield: —
Payout: 36.6%
Market value ($ mil.): —

Bank of Montreal (Quebec)

EXECUTIVES

Chairman, Director, George A. Cope
Vice-Chairman, Thomas E. Flynn
Chief Executive Officer, Director, Darryl White
Chief Risk Officer, Patrick Cronin
Chief Strategy and Operations Officer, Cameron Fowler
People and Culture Chief Human Resources Officer, People and Culture Head, Mona Malone
Chief Technology Officer and Operations Officer, Steve Tennyson
Chief Financial Officer, Tayfun Tuzun
BMO Capital Markets Group Head, Dan Barclay
North American Commercial Banking Group Head, David B. Casper
North American Personal and Business Banking Group Head, Ernie Johannson
BMO Wealth Management Group Head, Deland Kamanga
General Counsel, Sharon Haward-Laird
President, Sophie Brochu
Advisor, Simon A. Fish
Director, Janice M. Babiak
Director, Craig Broderick
Director, Christine A. Edwards
Director, Martin S. Eichenbaum
Director, David Harquail
Director, Linda S. Huber
Director, Eric Richer La Fleche
Director, Lorraine Mitchelmore
Auditors : KPMG LLP

LOCATIONS

HQ: Bank of Montreal (Quebec)
129 rue Saint-Jacques, Montreal, Quebec H2Y 1L6
Phone: 416 436-9388
Web: www.bmo.com

HISTORICAL FINANCIALS

Company Type: Public

Income Statement — FYE: October 31

	ASSETS ($mil)	NET INCOME ($mil)	INCOME AS % OF ASSETS	EMPLOYEES
10/23	935,185	3,156	0.3%	55,767
10/22	833,662	9,906	1.2%	46,722
10/21	799,970	6,079	0.8%	43,863
10/20	713,601	3,645	0.5%	43,360
10/19	646,974	4,211	0.7%	45,513
Annual Growth	9.6%	(7.0%)	—	5.2%

2023 Year-End Financials

Return on assets: 0.3%
Return on equity: 5.8%
Long-term debt ($ mil.): —
No. of shares ($ mil.): 720
Sales ($ mil.): 49,238
Dividends
Yield: 0.1%
Payout: 102.1%
Market value ($ mil.): 7,296

	STOCK PRICE ($) FY Close	P/E High/Low		PER SHARE ($) Earnings	Dividends	Book Value
10/23	10.12	15	1	4.11	4.19	77.24
10/22	73.42	4	0	14.63	3.98	76.78
10/21	1.88	1	0	9.37	3.43	71.85
10/20	8.72	2	0	5.68	3.19	65.87
10/19	17.35	6	2	6.57	3.08	60.66
Annual Growth	(12.6%)			(11.1%)	8.0%	6.2%

Bank of Nagoya, Ltd.

Camrys and Corollas aren't the only "big wheels" you'll find in Nagoya. The prefecture is home to The Bank of Nagoya, as well as automaker Toyota and other vehicle manufacturers. The regional bank has more than 105Â branches in and around its home area, as well as locations in other major Japanese cities and two representative offices in China. The Bank of Nagoya focuses on serving the businesses of the region, as well as individual consumers. In addition to deposit banking and lending, the bank and its subsidiaries offer such products and services as leasing, credit cards, and securities trading. The Bank of Nagoya was established in 1949.

EXECUTIVES

Chairman, Director, Kazumaro Kato
President, Representative Director, Director, Ichiro Fujiwara
Representative Director, Masao Minamide
Director, Satoru Hattori
Director, Katsutoshi Yamamoto
Director, Kazu Kondo
Director, Hideki Mizuno
Director, Mitsuru Yoshihashi
Outside Director, Takehisa Matsubara
Outside Director, Hisako Munekata
Director, Tomoaki Oka
Outside Director, Nobuyoshi Hasegawa
Outside Director, Takao Kondo
Outside Director, Masatoshi Sakaguchi
Auditors : KPMG AZSA LLC

LOCATIONS

HQ: Bank of Nagoya, Ltd.
3-19-17 Nishiki, Naka-ku, Nagoya, Aichi 460-0003
Phone: (81) 52 951 5911   **Fax:** (81) 52 961 6605
Web: www.meigin.com

COMPETITORS

BANK OF IWATE, LTD., THE
BANK OF SAGA, LTD., THE
BANK OF THE RYUKYUS, LIMITED
EIGHTEENTH BANK, LIMITED., THE
JUROKU BANK,LTD., THE

Bank of Nova Scotia Halifax

HISTORICAL FINANCIALS

Company Type: Public

Income Statement — FYE: March 31

	ASSETS ($mil)	NET INCOME ($mil)	INCOME AS % OF ASSETS	EMPLOYEES
03/22	42,444	95	0.2%	2,586
03/21	44,369	96	0.2%	2,394
03/20	36,250	42	0.1%	2,396
03/19	35,191	55	0.2%	2,445
03/18	36,103	54	0.2%	2,486
Annual Growth	4.1%	15.0%	—	1.0%

2022 Year-End Financials

Return on assets: 0.2%
Return on equity: 4.5%
Long-term debt ($ mil.): —
No. of shares ($ mil.): 17
Sales ($ mil.): 642
Dividends
Yield: —
Payout: 18.5%
Market value ($ mil.): —

Scotiabank is a leading bank in the Americas that provides personal and commercial banking, wealth management and private banking, corporate and investment banking, and capital markets. Through its Canadian Banking, it serves customers through its network of about 955 branches, more than 3,765 automated banking machines (ABMs), and the internet, mobile, telephone banking, and specialized sales teams. Canadian Banking also provides an alternative self-directed banking solution to over 2 million Tangerine Bank customers. The bank services include deposit accounts, loans, insurance, brokerage, asset management, wealth management, foreign exchange services, equity underwriting, and trust services. The majority of its total revenue (about 60%) comes from customers in Canada.

Operations

Scotiabank has its business lines: Canadian Banking, International Banking, Global Banking and Markets and Global Wealth Management.

The International Banking business (about 20% of the revenue) provides products and services similar to the Canadian Banking segment, but with nearly 10 million Retail, Corporate and Commercial customers.

Canadian Banking serves more than 10 million retail, small business, and commercial banking clients. It interacts with its customers through a network of over 950 physical branches and more than 3,765 ATMs, along with mobile and digital banking platforms. The segment provides financial advice and solutions such as debit & credit cards, checking accounts, home mortgages, and insurance products. The segment generates above 40% of all revenue and earnings.

Global Banking and Markets (GBM) (above 20%) provides corporate clients with lending and transaction services, investment banking advice and access to capital markets. GBM is a full-service wholesale bank in the Americas, with operations in about 20 countries, serving clients across Canada, the US, Latin America, Europe and Asia-Pacific.

Global Wealth Management (more than 15%) is focused on delivering comprehensive wealth management advice and solutions to clients across Scotiabank's footprint. Global Wealth Management serves over 2 million investment fund and advisory clients across 13 countries ? managing over $500 billion in assets.

Geographic Reach

Toronto, Canada-based Scotiabank generates over 50% of its revenue from Canada. Its southern neighbor, the US, accounts for less than 5% of revenue, while its major South American markets such as Mexico, Peru, Chile, Brazil, and Colombia combine to bring in some 45%.

It also has operations in Europe and the Caribbean, with a relatively large presence in Panama, Costa Rica, and Dominican Republic. Within Asia, it runs its business in China, India, Hong Kong, Japan, Thailand, Singapore, and others.

Sales and Marketing

Scotiabank serves nearly 50% of its loans to residential mortgages, and more than 35% from business and government. Canadian Banking serves customers through its network of branches, automated banking machines, online, mobile and telephone banking, and specialized sales teams. Its business clients operate in several industries, including real estate & construction, financial services, wholesale & retail, energy, automotive, healthcare, technology, media, agriculture and others.

Financial Performance

In the past five years, Scotiabank's revenue rose 13% to C$21.3 billion in fiscal 2021 (ended October) from C$27.2 billion in fiscal 2017. Its net income increased by 17% to C$9.9 billion in fiscal 2021 from C$8.2 billion in fiscal 2017.

In fiscal 2021, the company posted a total revenue of C$31.3 billion, a decrease of C$84 million from the prior year. Net interest income was C$16.9 billion, a decrease of C$359 million or 2%. The negative impact of foreign currency translation of 3%, together with lower margins and the impact of divested operations, more than offset positive increases from strong asset growth in Canadian Banking and higher contribution from asset/liability management activities. Non-interest income was up C$275 billion or 2% to C$14.3 billion.

Net income was C$9.9 billion in fiscal 2021, up 45% from C$6.8 billion in fiscal 2020 due primarily to lower provision for credit losses, as a result of a more favorable credit and macroeconomic outlook.

Cash at the end of fiscal 2021 was C$9.7 billion, down by C$1.4 million from the prior year. Operating activities used C$12.8 billion, while financing activities used another C$2.8 billion. Investing activities generated C$14.7 billion. Main cash uses were cash dividends paid and distribution paid, redemption of preferred shares, and payment of lease liabilities.

Strategy

As economies in the region rebounded throughout the year, International Banking launched a series of initiatives to strengthen the business, recover profitability, and invest across its footprint to develop its full potential.

Underpinning the long-term strategy is the focus on being the preferred choice for customers, leveraging digital engagement to deliver superior customer experiences, while driving operational efficiency and outpacing the competition in priority businesses, enabled by a diverse and talented winning team.

EXECUTIVES

Chief Executive Officer, President, Director, Brian J. Porter
Chief Human Resources Officer, Group Head, Barbara F. Mason
Chief Financial Officer, Group Head, Rajagopal Viswanathan
Chief Compliance Officer, Executive Vice President, Nicole Frew
Chief Risk Officer, Philip Thomas
Global Banking and Markets Chief Operating Officer, Global Banking and Markets Executive Vice President, Loretta Marcoccia
Chief Digital Officer, Executive Vice President, Shawn Rose
Global Capital Markets Co-Group Head, Global Banking and Markets Co-Group Head, Global Capital Markets Head, Global Banking and Markets Head, Jake Lawrence
Global Corporate and Investment Banking Co-Group Head, Global Banking and Markets Co-Group Head, Global Corporate and Investment Banking Head, Global Banking and Markets Head, James Neate
International Banking and Digital Transformation Group Head, Ignacio Deschamps
Global Wealth Management Group Head, Glen Gowland
Canadian Banking Group Head, Dan Rees
Technology & Operations Group Head, Michael Zerbs
Executive Vice President, General Counsel, Ian Arellano
Executive Vice President, Chief Auditor, Paul Baroni
Finance and Strategy Executive Vice President, Anique Asher
Canadian Business Banking Executive Vice President, Stephen Bagnarol
Canadian Wealth Management Executive Vice President, Alex Besharat
Global Operations Executive Vice President, Tracy Bryan
Financial Crimes Risk Management & Group Chief Anti-Money Laundering Officer Executive Vice President, Stuart Davis
Retail Distribution Executive Vice President, John Doig
Chile Executive Vice President, Chile Country Head, Diego Masola
Executive Vice President, Group Treasurer, Tom McGuire
Executive Vice President, President, Gillian Riley
Executive Vice President, Country Head, Mexico, Adrian Otero Rosiles
Peru Executive Vice President, Peru Country Head, Francisco Sardon
Caribbean, Central America and Uruguay Executive Vice President, Anya M. Schnoor
Canadian Business Banking Executive Vice President, Kevin Teslyk
Finance Executive Vice President, Maria Theofilaktidis
Business Technology Executive Vice President, Business Technology Global Chief Information Officer, Ashley Veasey
Retail Customer Executive Vice President, Terri-Lee Weeks
Director, Chairman, Aaron W. Regent
Director, Nora A. Aufreiter
Director, Guillermo E. Babatz
Director, Una M. Power
Director, L. Barry Thomson
Director, Scott B. Bonham
Director, Daniel H. Callahan
Director, Lynn K. Patterson
Director, Michael D. Penner
Director, Calin Rovinescu
Director, Susan L. Segal
Director, Benita M. Warmbold
Auditors : KPMG LLP

LOCATIONS

HQ: Bank of Nova Scotia Halifax
1709 Hollis Street, Halifax, Nova Scotia B3J 1W1
Phone: 416 866-3672
Web: www.scotiabank.com

PRODUCTS/OPERATIONS

FY2017 Revenue

	% of total
Interest	
Loans	62
Securities & Deposits with financial institutions	5
Non-interest	
Banking	11
Wealth management	9
Trading	4
Underwriting and other advisory	2
Non-trading foreign exchange	2
Net gain on sale of investment securities	2
Insurance underwriting income, net of claims	2
Net income from investments in associated corporations	1
Others	3
Total	100

FY2017 Revenue	% of total
Canadian Banking	46
International Banking	37
Global Banking and Markets	17
Total	100

Selected Canadian Subsidiaries
BNS Capital Trust
BNS Investment Inc.
    Montreal Trust Company of Canada
    Scotia Merchant Capital Corporation
Dundee Bank of Canada
Maple Trust Company
National Trustco Inc.
    The Bank of Nova Scotia Trust Company
    National Trust Company
RoyNat Inc.
Scotia Capital Inc.
    1548489 Ontario Limited
    Scotia iTrade Corp.
Scotia Asset Management L.P.
Scotia Capital, Inc.
Scotia Dealer Advantage Inc.
Scotia Insurance Agency Inc.
Scotia Life Insurance Company
Scotia Mortgage Corporation
Scotia Securities Inc.
Scotiabank Capital Trust
Scotiabank Subordinated Notes Trust.
Scotiabank Tier 1 Trust

Selected International Subsidiaries
The Bank of Nova Scotia Berhad (Malaysia)
The Bank of Nova Scotia International Limited (Bahamas)
    The Bank of Nova Scotia Asia Limited (Singapore)
    The Bank of Nova Scotia Trust Company (Bahamas) Ltd.
    Scotiabank & Trust (Cayman) Ltd. (Cayman Islands)
        BNS (Colombia) Holdings Limited
        Grupo BNS de Costa Rica, S.A.
        Scotia Insurance (Barbados) Limited
        Scotiabank (Bahamas) Limited
        Scotiabank (British Virgin Islands) Limited
        Scotiabank Caribbean Treasury Limited (Bahamas)
        Scotiabank (Hong Kong) Limited
        Scotiabank (Ireland) Limited
Scotia Group Jamaica Limited (72%)
    The Bank of Nova Scotia Jamaica Limited
    Scotia DBG Investments Limited (77%, Jamaica)
Grupo Financiero Scotiabank Inverlat, S.A. de C.V. (97%, Mexico)
Nova Scotia Inversiones Limitada (Chile)
    Scotiabank Chile, S.A.
Scotia Capital (USA) Inc.
Scotia Holdings (US) Inc.
    The Bank of Nova Scotia Trust Company of New York
        Scotiabanc Inc. (US)
Scotia International Limited (Bahamas)
    Scotiabank Anguilla Limited
Scotiabank de Puerto Rico
Scotiabank El Salvador, S.A.
Scotiabank Europe plc (UK)
Scotiabank Peru S.A.A.
Scotiabank Trinidad and Tobago Limited

COMPETITORS
AEGON N.V.
Achmea B.V.
Banco do Brasil S/A
ING Groep N.V.
Kardan N.V.
MMC VENTURES LIMITED
NN Group N.V.
QATAR NATIONAL BANK (Q.P.S.C.)
The Toronto-Dominion Bank
Unilever N.V.

HISTORICAL FINANCIALS
Company Type: Public

Income Statement   FYE: October 31

	ASSETS ($mil)	NET INCOME ($mil)	INCOME AS % OF ASSETS	EMPLOYEES
10/22	987,499	7,066	0.7%	90,979
10/21	959,182	7,602	0.8%	89,488
10/20	854,331	4,947	0.6%	92,001
10/19	824,597	6,231	0.8%	101,813
10/18	760,436	6,367	0.8%	97,629
Annual Growth	6.8%	2.6%		(1.7%)

2022 Year-End Financials
Return on assets: 0.7%   Dividends
Return on equity: 13.4%   Yield: 6.4%
Long-term debt ($ mil.): —   Payout: 62.3%
No. of shares ($ mil.): 1,191   Market value ($ mil.): 57,567
Sales ($ mil.): 34,291

	STOCK PRICE ($) FY Close	P/E High/Low		PER SHARE ($) Earnings	Dividends	Book Value
10/22	48.32	9	6	5.87	3.14	44.98
10/21	65.56	9	6	6.23	2.91	47.16
10/20	41.56	11	6	3.98	2.71	42.27
10/19	57.33	9	7	5.07	2.62	42.15
10/18	53.71	9	8	5.19	2.55	40.49
Annual Growth	(2.6%)	—	—	3.1%	5.3%	2.7%

Bank of Queensland Ltd

EXECUTIVES
Chief Executive Officer, Managing Director, Executive Director, George Frazis
Retail Banking Group Executive, Martine Jager
Business Banking Group Executive, Chris Screen
People and Culture Group Executive, Debra Eckersley
Chief Financial Officer, Executive Director, Racheal Kellaway
Chief Operating Officer, Paul Newham
Chief Risk Officer, David Watts
Chief Information Officer, Craig Ryman
General Counsel, Secretary, Nicholas Alllton
Secretary, Fiona Daly
Chairman, Independent Non-Executive Director, Patrick Allaway
Independent Non-Executive Director, Deborah Kiers
Independent Non-Executive Director, Bruce Carter
Independent Non-Executive Director, Warwick Martin Negus
Independent Non-Executive Director, Karen Penrose
Independent Non-Executive Director, Mickie Rosen
Independent Non-Executive Director, Jenny Fagg
Auditors : PricewaterhouseCoopers

LOCATIONS
HQ: Bank of Queensland Ltd
Level 6, 100 Skyring Terrace, Newstead, Queensland 4006
Phone: (61) 7 3212 3844
Web: www.boq.com.au

HISTORICAL FINANCIALS
Company Type: Public

Income Statement   FYE: August 31

	ASSETS ($mil)	NET INCOME ($mil)	INCOME AS % OF ASSETS	EMPLOYEES
08/22	68,520	292	0.4%	3,040
08/21	66,989	270	0.4%	2,218
08/20	41,710	84	0.2%	2,021
08/19	37,412	200	0.5%	2,098
08/18	38,260	242	0.6%	2,039
Annual Growth	15.7%	4.7%		10.5%

2022 Year-End Financials
Return on assets: 0.4%   Dividends
Return on equity: 6.6%   Yield: 6.0%
Long-term debt ($ mil.): —   Payout: 126.2%
No. of shares ($ mil.): 645   Market value ($ mil.): 5,954
Sales ($ mil.): 1,689

	STOCK PRICE ($) FY Close	P/E High/Low		PER SHARE ($) Earnings	Dividends	Book Value
08/22	9.23	20	14	0.41	0.55	7.11
08/21	12.77	20	12	0.46	0.38	7.10
08/20	8.47	56	24	0.18	0.39	6.85
08/19	12.31	20	16	0.47	0.87	6.41
08/18	16.01	23	16	0.59	1.16	7.02
Annual Growth	(12.9%)			(8.4%)	(16.8%)	0.3%

Bank of Saga, Ltd. (The) (Japan)

The Bank of Saga could probably tell plenty of stories about the people and businesses it serves, butÂ it's most likely too circumspect to be so loose-of-lip. The regional bank serves consumers and businesses through its approximately 110 branches; someÂ 65 offices are inÂ Japan's Saga prefecture, about 40 are in Fukuoka prefecture, and others are located in Nagasaki and Tokyo. Founded in 1955, the bank capitalizes on its location convenient to the Asian mainland, serving companies that do business internationally. In addition to traditional deposit and lending services, the bank and its subsidiaries offer such products and services as business matching and venture capital.

EXECUTIVES
Chairman, Director, Yoshihiro Jinnouchi
President, Representative Director, Hideaki Sakai
Senior Managing Director, Representative Director, Kingo Tominaga
Director, Kazuyuki Tsutsumi
Director, Shinzaburo Nakamura

Director, Toru Unoike
Director, Shigeyuki Yamasaki
Director, Hidemitsu Muta
Director, Hiroshi Koso
Outside Director, Naoto Furutachi
Outside Director, Kentaro Tomiyoshi
Auditors : Ernst & Young ShinNihon LLC

LOCATIONS

HQ: Bank of Saga, Ltd. (The) (Japan)
2-7-20 Tojin, Saga 840-0813
Phone: (81) 952 24 5111
Web: www.sagabank.co.jp

COMPETITORS

BANK OF NAGOYA, LTD., THE
BANK OF THE RYUKYUS, LIMITED
EIGHTEENTH BANK, LIMITED., THE
JUROKU BANK,LTD., THE
TAIWAN COOPERATIVE BANK

HISTORICAL FINANCIALS
Company Type: Public

Income Statement — FYE: March 31

	ASSETS ($mil)	NET INCOME ($mil)	INCOME AS % OF ASSETS	EMPLOYEES
03/21	27,555	22	0.1%	1,705
03/20	23,582	22	0.1%	1,790
03/19	22,306	23	0.1%	1,862
03/18	22,801	62	0.3%	1,917
03/17	20,886	25	0.1%	1,921
Annual Growth	7.2%	(3.7%)	—	(2.9%)

2021 Year-End Financials
Return on assets: —
Return on equity: 2.0%
Long-term debt ($ mil.): —
No. of shares ($ mil.): 16
Sales ($ mil.): 376
Dividends
Yield: —
Payout: 47.9%
Market value ($ mil.): —

Bank of the Philippine Islands

Bank of the Philippine Islands is one of that country's largest lenders. The universal bank has more than 800 branches in its homeland, as well as locations in Hong Kong, Italy, and the US. It provides asset management and trust services, mutual funds, electronic banking, and brokerage services in addition to standard commercial and consumer deposits, loans, and credit cards. The bank also performs investment banking services such as corporate finance and advisory. Giant Philippine conglomerate Ayala controls the Bank of the Philippine Islands, which sells insurance provided by other Ayala divisions.

EXECUTIVES

President, Chief Executive Officer, Executive Director, Jose Teodoro K. Limcaoco
Chief Financial Officer, Senior Vice President, Chief Sustainability Officer, Eric Roberto M. Luchangco
Executive Vice President, Chief Operating Officer, Ramon L. Jocson
Executive Vice President, Maria Theresa D. Marcial
Executive Vice President, Marie Josephine M. Ocampo
Executive Vice President, Juan Carlos L. Syquia
Senior Vice President, Chief Credit Officer, Joseph Anthony M. Alonso
Senior Vice President, Treasurer, Dino R. Gasmen
Senior Vice President, Chief Risk Officer, Marita Socorro D. Gayares
Senior Vice President, Chief Customer Officer, Chief Marketing Officer, Mary Catherine Elizabeth P. Santamaria
Senior Vice President, Chief Audit Executive, Rosemarie B. Cruz
Senior Vice President, Chief Compliance Officer, Noravir A. Gealogo
Secretary, Angela Pilar B. Maramag
Chairman, Non-Executive Director, Jaime Augusto Zobel de Ayala
Vice-Chairman, Non-Executive Director, Cezar Peralta Consing
Lead Independent Director, Independent Director, Ignacio R. Bunye
Independent Director, Janet Har Ang Guat
Independent Director, Cesar Velasquez Purisima
Independent Director, Maria Dolores B. Yuvienco
Non-Executive Director, Rene G. Banez
Non-Executive Director, Romeo L. Bernardo
Non-Executive Director, Ramon R. del Rosario
Non-Executive Director, Octavio Victor R. Espiritu
Non-Executive Director, Aurelio R. Montinola
Auditors : Isla Lipana & Co.

LOCATIONS

HQ: Bank of the Philippine Islands
Ayala North Exchange, Tower One, 6796 Ayala Avenue corner Salcedo St., Legaspi Village, Makati City 1229
Phone: 8 246 5902
Web: www.bpi.com.ph

COMPETITORS

ARAB BANK PLC
BANK OF AYUDHYA PUBLIC COMPANY LIMITED
HANG SENG BANK, LIMITED
METROPOLITAN BANK & TRUST COMPANY
RIYAD BANK

HISTORICAL FINANCIALS
Company Type: Public

Income Statement — FYE: December 31

	ASSETS ($mil)	NET INCOME ($mil)	INCOME AS % OF ASSETS	EMPLOYEES
12/22	46,812	711	1.5%	17,573
12/21	47,502	468	1.0%	19,181
12/20	46,485	445	1.0%	19,952
12/19	43,546	568	1.3%	21,429
12/18	39,703	439	1.1%	18,911
Annual Growth	4.2%	12.8%	—	(1.8%)

2022 Year-End Financials
Return on assets: 1.5%
Return on equity: 12.9%
Long-term debt ($ mil.): —
No. of shares ($ mil.): 4,919
Sales ($ mil.): 2,457
Dividends
Yield: —
Payout: 24.1%
Market value ($ mil.): —

Bank of the Ryukyus, Ltd.

EXECUTIVES

Chairman, Representative Director, Tokei Kinjo
President, Representative Director, Yasushi Kawakami
Senior Managing Director, Representative Director, Keishi Fukuhara
Director, Yasushi Tokashiki
Director, Ryoji Toyoda
Director, Ken Shimabukuro
Outside Director, Masanori Fukuyama
Outside Director, Kanako Tomihara
Outside Director, Masaharu Harazaki
Auditors : Ernst & Young ShinNihon LLC

LOCATIONS

HQ: Bank of the Ryukyus, Ltd.
2-1 Higashimachi, Naha, Okinawa 900-0034
Phone: (81) 98 866 1212
Web: www.ryugin.co.jp

HISTORICAL FINANCIALS
Company Type: Public

Income Statement — FYE: March 31

	ASSETS ($mil)	NET INCOME ($mil)	INCOME AS % OF ASSETS	EMPLOYEES
03/22	25,196	45	0.2%	1,877
03/21	25,090	23	0.1%	1,889
03/20	22,438	45	0.2%	1,916
03/19	21,577	55	0.3%	2,016
03/18	22,213	82	0.4%	1,945
Annual Growth	3.2%	(13.7%)	—	(0.9%)

2022 Year-End Financials
Return on assets: 0.1%
Return on equity: 4.1%
Long-term debt ($ mil.): —
No. of shares ($ mil.): 42
Sales ($ mil.): 473
Dividends
Yield: —
Payout: 26.7%
Market value ($ mil.): —

Bank Polska Kasa Opieki SA

Bank Polska Kasa Opieki, better known as Bank Pekao (from its initials P.K.O.), offers retail, corporate, and investment banking services, primarily in Poland. It also provides leasing and asset management services. Branches can also be found in France and the Ukraine. In addition to traditional deposit products, Bank Pekao offers loans, leasing and factoring services, custodial services, currency exchange, and foreign trade facilitation. Originally founded as a state-owned bank to provide banking services to Polish emigrants, Bank Pekao is now controlled by Italian bank UniCredit, which holds approximately 53% of its shares.

EXECUTIVES

President, Leszek Skiba
Vice President, Jaroslaw Fuchs
Vice President, Marcin Gadomski
Vice President, Jerzy Kwiecinski
Vice President, Pawel Straczynski
Vice President, Blazej Szczecki
Vice President, Wojciech Werochowski
Vice President, Piotr Zborowski
Vice President, Magdalena Zmitrowicz
Chairwoman, Beata Kozlowska-Chyla
Deputy Chairman, Joanna Dynysiuk
Deputy Chairman, Malgorzata Sadurska
Director, Sabina Bigos-Jaworowska
Director, Justyna Glebikowska-Michalak
Director, Michal Kaszynski
Director, Marian Majcher
Director, Marcin Izdebski
Secretary, Stainslaw Ryszard Kaczoruk
Auditors : KPMG Audyt SpÃ³lka z ograniczona odpowiedzialnoscia sp.k.

LOCATIONS

HQ: Bank Polska Kasa Opieki SA
Grzybowska Street 53/57, Warsaw 00-844
Phone: (48) 22 656 00 00 **Fax:** (48) 22 656 00 04
Web: www.pekao.com.pl

COMPETITORS

BANK BPH S A
BANK MILLENNIUM S A
DEUTSCHE BANK POLSKA S A
DOICHE BANK, OOO
SITIBANK, AO

HISTORICAL FINANCIALS

Company Type: Public

Income Statement — FYE: December 31

	ASSETS ($mil)	NET INCOME ($mil)	INCOME AS % OF ASSETS	EMPLOYEES
12/22	64,072	391	0.6%	14,642
12/21	59,454	551	0.9%	14,702
12/20	59,903	303	0.5%	14,994
12/19	53,593	570	1.1%	15,678
12/18	50,910	609	1.2%	16,714
Annual Growth	5.9%	(10.5%)	—	(3.3%)

2022 Year-End Financials

Return on assets: —
Return on equity: —
Long-term debt ($ mil.): —
No. of shares ($ mil.): 262
Sales ($ mil.): 3,398
Dividends
Yield: —
Payout: 0.0%
Market value ($ mil.): —

Barclays Bank Plc

Barclays Bank is the flagship subsidiary of global financial group Barclays PLC. Barclays Bank UK PLC is the ring-fenced bank within the Barclays PLC. The Barclays Bank UK contains the majority of the Barclays PLC's Barclays UK division, including the Personal Banking, Business Banking and Barclaycard Consumer UK businesses other than the Barclays Partner Finance business. The bank serve customers across a wide range of retail banking needs, from credit card users, to start-up businesses, to homebuyers getting on the property ladder for the first time. The Barclays Bank UK PLC is supported by the Barclays PLC service company, Barclays Execution Services Limited (BX), which provides technology, operations and functional services to businesses across the Barclays PLC.

Operations

Barclays Bank UK operates through three reportable segments: Personal Banking, Barclaycard Consumer UK and Business Banking.

Personal Banking which comprises Personal and Premier banking, Mortgages, Savings, Investments and Wealth management. The segment accounts for about 60% of revenue.

Business Banking which offers products, services and specialist advice to clients ranging from start-ups to medium-sized businesses and is where the ESHLA loan portfolio is held. The segment makes up some 20% of revenue.

Barclaycard Consumer UK (more than 20%) which comprises the Barclaycard UK consumer credit cards business.

Overall, net interest income earns more than 75% of total revenue, while net fee and commission income accounts for nearly 20% and investment income and net trading income account for about 5% of combined revenue.

Geographic Reach

The Barclays Bank UK operates through branches, offices and subsidiaries in the UK.

Financial Performance

The company's revenue for fiscal 2021 increased to Â£6.9 billion compared from the prior year with Â£5.0 billion.

Profit for fiscal 2021 increased to Â£2.2 billion compared from the prior year with Â£381 million.

Cash held by the company at the end of fiscal 2021 increased to Â£73.4 billion. Cash provided by operations and investing activities were Â£29.0 billion and Â£6.4 billion, respectively. Cash used for financing activities was Â£785 million, mainly for redemption of subordinated debt.

Strategy

Barclay are focused on the following areas:

Providing exceptional service and insights to customers: Barclays aim to provide simple, relevant and prompt services and propositions for its customers so they have greater choice and access to money management capabilities.

Driving technology and digital innovation: The company continue to invest in its digital capabilities, upgrading its systems, moving to cloud technology and implementing automation of manual processes.

Continuing to grow its business: The company are pursuing partnership opportunities to build and deliver better propositions and services for its customers. The company aim to use the Barclays platform to provide better service to Barclays customers and open up new income streams.

Evolving its societal purpose: Barclays are working to support the communities it serve. Barclays are focused on financial inclusion and recognize its role in supporting people and businesses make the transition to a low-carbon economy.

EXECUTIVES

Chief Executive Officer, Executive Director, C. S. Venkatakrishnan
Secretary, Stephen Shapiro
Chairman, Nigel Higgins
Executive Director, Anna Cross
Independent Non-Executive Director, Mohamed A. El-Erian
Independent Non-Executive Director, Robert Berry
Independent Non-Executive Director, Dawn Fitzpatrick
Independent Non-Executive Director, Mike Ashley
Independent Non-Executive Director, Mary Francis
Independent Non-Executive Director, Diane Lynn Schueneman
Auditors : KPMG LLP

LOCATIONS

HQ: Barclays Bank Plc
1 Churchill Place, London E14 5HP
Phone: (44) 20 7116 3170
Web: www.barclays.com

2018 sales

	%
United Kingdom	33
Americas	51
Europe	11
Asia	4
Africa and Middle East	1
Total	100

PRODUCTS/OPERATIONS

2018 sales

	%
Corporate and Investment Bank	70
Consumer, Cards and Payments	30
Head Office	-
Total	100

2018 sales

	%
Net Interest Income	23
Net Fee and Commission Income	41
Net Trading Income	32
Net Investment Income	3
Other Income	1
Total	100

COMPETITORS

ABC INTERNATIONAL BANK PLC
BANCA COMERCIALA ROMANA SA
CREDIT SUISSE (UK) LIMITED
EUROBANK ERGASIAS SERVICES AND HOLDINGS S.A.

INFINITY FOREIGN EXCHANGE LTD
KLEINWORT BENSON (CHANNEL ISLANDS) LIMITED
NEDBANK GROUP LTD
National Bank Financial & Co Inc
SARASIN & PARTNERS LLP
THE ROYAL BANK OF SCOTLAND PUBLIC LIMITED COMPANY

HISTORICAL FINANCIALS

Company Type: Public

Income Statement — FYE: December 31

	ASSETS ($mil)	NET INCOME ($mil)	INCOME AS % OF ASSETS	EMPLOYEES
12/22	1,448,850	4,393	0.3%	21,900
12/21	1,430,940	5,561	0.4%	20,200
12/20	1,446,220	2,420	0.2%	20,900
12/19	1,157,700	2,799	0.2%	20,500
12/18	1,120,610	1,066	0.1%	22,400
Annual Growth	6.6%	42.5%	—	(0.6%)

2022 Year-End Financials

Return on assets: 0.3%
Return on equity: 6.3%
Long-term debt ($ mil.): —
No. of shares ($ mil.): 2,342
Sales ($ mil.): 32,893
Dividends
Yield: —
Payout: 0.0%
Market value ($ mil.): 33,077

	STOCK PRICE ($) FY Close	P/E High/Low	PER SHARE ($) Earnings	Dividends	Book Value
12/22	14.12	— —	0.00	0.00	30.30
12/21	18.53	— —	0.00	0.00	32.50
12/20	16.79	— —	0.00	0.00	31.29
12/19	15.12	— —	0.00	0.00	28.53
12/18	46.99	— —	0.00	0.00	26.00
Annual Growth	(26.0%)	— —	—	—	3.9%

Barclays PLC

Raising the bar for global finance, Barclays owns one of Europe's largest banks, a top market-making investment bank, the top UK credit card, and an international wealth management firm. The bank offers their services to individuals and small businesses. Its flagship Barclays Bank has some 700 branches in the UK as well as operations throughout Europe, Africa, the Middle East, and the Americas. In addition to holding one of the world's largest investment banks, the company's Barclaycard arm is one of the UK's leading credit card providers and provides consumer lending and payment processing services, primarily in Europe.

Operations

Barclays PLC and Barclays Bank PLC operate two segments, Barclays UK, which is made up of its retail banking, consumer credit cards, wealth, and corporate banking businesses serving retail customers and business banking customers in the UK; and Barclays International, which consists of its corporate banking franchise, its investment bank, its credit cards business in the US (Barclaycard US) and abroad, its international wealth management services, and its merchant payment services offered through its corporate banking and Barclaycard business.

Geographic Reach

Barclays have 50% of its revenue was generated in the UK, while another 30% came from the Americas. The rest of its revenue came from the rest of Europe (10%) and Asia (5%).

Sales and Marketing

The company spent EUR 399 million, EUR 330 million, and EUR 425 million for the years 2021, 2020, and 2019, respectively, for marketing and advertising.

Financial Performance

Note: Growth rates may differ after conversion to US dollars. This analysis uses financials from the company's annual report.

Barclays' performance for the past five years has steadily increased year-over-year, ending with 2021 as its highest performing year over the period.

The company's total income increased by EUR 174 million to EUR 21.9 billion for 2021 as compared to 2020's total income of EUR 21.8 billion.

Barclays held cash of about EUR 259.2 billion by the end of 2021. Operating activities provided EUR 48.9 billion. Investing activities and financing activities provided EUR 4.3 billion and EUR 107 million, respectively.

Strategy

Barclays' strategy included the diversification of its business to deliver double-digit returns in hand with its strategic priorities: Delivering next-generation, digitized consumer financial services; delivering sustainable growth in the CIB; and capturing opportunities as the company transitions to the low-carbon economy. These are done through the investment in digital capabilities to improve the bank's services and expanding unsecured lending in the bank's market regions. Barclays prioritizes digital investment and expanding CIB internationally, including the Middle East and China. Lastly, the company uses its financial and capital market expertise to support the scale-up of low-carbon technologies.

Company Background

Legal troubles have caused headwinds for Barclays's bottom line in recent years. In mid-2012, the company admitted to manipulating the London Interbank Offered Rate (LIBOR), a benchmark for daily global short-term interest rates. The bank repeatedly manipulated the LIBOR in order to make its funding position look stronger than it actually was; the rigging also helped the bank make money on credit derivatives. Chairman Martin Agius and CEO Bob Diamond both resigned as a result of the developments, and the company paid US and UK regulators some £290 million ($453 million) in settlement fines. Shortly after the LIBOR scandal, the UK's Serious Fraud Office launched an inquiry into payments Barclays made to sovereign investor Qatar Holding in 2008. At the behest of regulators, Barclays ringfenced its UK consumer bank from its riskier investment banking assets in 2018.

HISTORY

Barclays first spread its wings in 1736 when James Barclay united his family's goldsmithing and banking businesses. As other family members joined the London enterprise, it became known as Barclays, Bevan & Tritton (1782).

Banking first became regulated in the 19th century. To ward off takeovers, 20 banks combined with Barclays in 1896. The new firm, Barclay & Co., began preying on other banks. Within 20 years it bought 17, including the Colonial Bank, chartered in 1836 to serve the West Indies and British Guiana (now Guyana). The company, renamed Barclays Bank Ltd. in 1917, weathered the Depression as the UK's #2 bank.

Barclays began expanding again after WWII, and by the late 1950s it had become the UK's top bank. It had a computer network by 1959, and in 1966 it introduced the Barclaycard in conjunction with Bank of America's BankAmericard (now Visa).

In 1968 the UK's Monopolies Commission barred Barclays' merger with two other big London banks, but had no objections to a two-way merger, so Barclays bought competitor Martins.

Barclays moved into the US consumer finance market in 1980 when it bought American Credit, 138 former Beneficial Finance offices, and Bankers Trust's branch network.

During the 1980s, London banks faced competition from invading overseas banks, local building societies, and other financial firms. Banking reform in 1984 led to formation of a holding company for Barclays Bank PLC.

To prepare for British financial deregulation in 1986, Barclays formed Barclays de Zoete Wedd (BZW) by merging its merchant bank with two other London financial firms. Faced with sagging profits, Barclays sold its California bank in 1988 and its US consumer finance business in 1989.

In 1990 Barclays bought private German bank Merck, Finck & Co. and Paris bank L'Européenne de Banque. The company countered 1992's bad-loan-induced losses by accelerating a cost-cutting program begun in 1989. To appease stockholders, chairman and CEO Andrew Buxton (a descendant of one of the bank's founding families) gave up his CEO title, hiring Martin Taylor (previously CEO of textile firm Courtaulds) for the post.

The company sold its Australian retail banking business in 1994, then began trimming other operations, including French corporate banking and US mortgage operations. However, it bought the Wells Fargo Nikko Investment Company to boost Asian operations.

Barclays' piecemeal sale of BZW signaled

its failure to become a global investment banking powerhouse. In 1997 it sold BZW's European investment banking business to Credit Suisse First Boston, retaining the fixed-income and foreign exchange business. (Credit Suisse bought Barclays' Asian investment banking operations in 1998.)

Losses in Russia and a $250 million bailout of US hedge fund Long-Term Capital Management hit Barclays Capital in 1998. Taylor resigned that year in part because of his radical plans for the bank. Sir Peter Middleton stepped in as acting CEO; Barclays later tapped Canadian banker Matthew Barrett for the post. (Middleton also became chairman upon Buxton's retirement.)

Barclays in 1999 started a move toward online banking at the expense of traditional branches. The company announced free lifetime Internet access for new bank customers.

In 2000 the bank ruffled feathers when it announced the closure of about 170 mostly rural UK branches. Also in 2000 the company sold its Dial auto leasing unit to ABN AMRO and bought Woolwich plc. The following year Barclay's closed its own life insurance division, opting instead to sell the life insurance and pension products of London-based Legal & General Group.

In 2004 chief executive Barrett was named Barclays' chairman, succeeding Peter Middleton who became chairman of Centre for Effective Dispute Resolution (CEDR) and later, chancellor of the University of Sheffield.

After exiting the South African market in 1987 over apartheid concerns, Barclays returned in a big way in 2005, buying a majority stake (about 57%) in the Absa Group, one of the country's largest retail banks. The deal also represented the largest-ever direct foreign investment there. The next year Barclays sold its South African businesses, including corporate, international retail, and commercial operations, to Absa.

The company entered the US credit card market when it bought Juniper Financial (now Barclays Bank Delaware) from Canadian Imperial Bank of Commerce (CIBC) in 2004. In a previous hook-up with CIBC, Barclays merged its Caribbean banking business with CIBC's to create an 85-branch regional bank, FirstCaribbean International Bank, with each company owning 44%; Barclays sold its stake to CIBC in 2006.

In 2005 the bank sold its vendor finance businesses in the UK and Germany to CIT Group. Barclays said that the sale will allow it to focus on its commercial leasing business.

The bank moved to assimilate its Woolwich acquisition in 2006 when it closed 200 branches and consolidated Woolwich branches into existing Barclays locations. It retained the Woolwich mortgage brand but switched account holders to Barclays accounts.

The company and HSBC formed a joint venture that manages their cash handling operations in the UK. Named Vaultex, the joint venture acquired Loomis Cash Management in 2007.

Marcus Agius succeeded the retiring Matthew Barrett as chairman in 2007.

Although the company withdrew its bid for Dutch banking giant ABN AMRO (narrowly escaping that troubled deal), in 2008 it bought Russian bank Expobank from Petropavlovsk Finance. Expobank was one of the largest ATM networks in Russia and part of the booming consumer banking industry there. Also that year, Barclays sold noncore business Barclays Life and its portfolio of some 760,000 life and pension policies to Swiss Re for £753 million ($1.5 billion).

The group chose not to participate in the UK's bank bailouts as the global financial crisis intensified in late 2008 but pursued its own capital-raising plan. Through the deal, sovereign investment fund Qatar Investment Authority became the bank's largest shareholder with a 5% stake.

In 2009 it shut down US-based subprime mortgage lender EquiFirst, which it had purchased from Regions Financial before it fell victim to the mortgage bust.

Later that year, it sold a majority of Barclays Global Investors to American money manager BlackRock for £9.5 billion ($15 billion). In exchange, it gained a 20% stake in the new BlackRock, with some $3 trillion under management for institutional clients around the world. The deal provided the bank with much-needed cash and cleared the way for a commercial partnership with BlackRock.

Another major transaction was the £1 billion ($1.8 billion) acquisition of Lehman Brothers' North American operations, a deal which made Barclays Capital one of the world's largest investment banks.

EXECUTIVES

Chief Executive Officer, Executive Director, C. S. Venkatakrishnan
Finance Director, Executive Director, Anna Cross
Chief Operating Officer, Alistair Currie
Interim Group Chief Compliance Officer, Matthew Fitzwater
Group Human Resources Director, Tristram Roberts
Group Chief Risk Officer, Taalib Shah
Chief Information Officer, Craig Bright
Chief Internal Auditor, Lindsay O'Reilly
Group General Counsel, Secretary, Stephen Shapiro
Independent Chairman, Non-Executive Director, Nigel Higgins
Senior Independent Non-Executive Director, Brian Gilvary
Independent Non-Executive Director, Mike Ashley
Independent Non-Executive Director, Robert Berry
Independent Non-Executive Director, Tim J. Breedon
Independent Non-Executive Director, Dawn Fitzpatrick
Independent Non-Executive Director, Mary Francis
Independent Non-Executive Director, Crawford Gillies
Independent Non-Executive Director, Marc Moses
Independent Non-Executive Director, Diane Lynn Schueneman
Independent Non-Executive Director, Julia Wilson
Auditors: KPMG LLP

LOCATIONS

HQ: Barclays PLC
  1 Churchill Place, London E14 5HP
Phone: (44) 20 7116 1000
Web: www.barclays.com

2018 Sales

	% of total
UK	52
Americas	36
Europe	8
Africa and Middle East	3
Asia	1
Total	100

PRODUCTS/OPERATIONS

2018 Sales

	% of total
Barclays International	66
Barclays UK	34
Head Office	—
Total	100

COMPETITORS

CREDIT SUISSE (USA), INC.
HSBC HOLDINGS PLC
JPMORGAN CAZENOVE HOLDINGS
LLOYDS BANKING GROUP PLC
MERRILL LYNCH & CO., INC.
MORGAN STANLEY
NATWEST GROUP PLC
RAYMOND JAMES FINANCIAL, INC.
THE GOLDMAN SACHS GROUP INC
UBS FINANCIAL SERVICES INC.

HISTORICAL FINANCIALS

Company Type: Public

Income Statement — FYE: December 31

	ASSETS ($mil)	NET INCOME ($mil)	INCOME AS % OF ASSETS	EMPLOYEES
12/23	1,883,040	6,702	0.4%	92,400
12/22	1,822,230	7,136	0.4%	87,400
12/21	1,865,570	9,674	0.5%	81,600
12/20	1,841,690	3,252	0.2%	83,000
12/19	1,505,740	4,323	0.3%	80,800
Annual Growth	5.7%	11.6%	—	3.4%

2023 Year-End Financials

Return on assets: 0.3%
Return on equity: 7.5%
Long-term debt ($ mil.): —
No. of shares ($ mil.): 15,154
Sales ($ mil.): 65,415
Dividends
  Yield: —
  Payout: 112.3%
Market value ($ mil.): 119,418

	STOCK PRICE ($)	P/E	PER SHARE ($)		
	FY Close	High/Low	Earnings	Dividends	Book Value
12/23	7.88	35 24	0.34	0.39	5.99
12/22	7.80	34 21	0.36	0.28	5.18
12/21	10.35	29 19	0.49	0.16	5.57
12/20	7.99	115 49	0.12	0.14	5.17
12/19	9.52	70 50	0.19	0.35	4.91
Annual Growth	(4.6%)	— —	16.5%	2.6%	5.1%

Barrick Gold Corp.

Barrick Gold is a sector-leading gold and copper producers, with proved reserves among the largest in the industry. It has interests in about 15 producing gold mines in about 20 countries, the most significant assets being in Nevada, US (Carlin, Cortez and Turquoise Ridge), Mali (Loulo-Gounkoto), and Democratic Republic of Congo (Kibali). Barrick also have all the shares in Acacia, which owns gold mines and exploration properties in Africa. The company have ownership interests in producing copper mines in Chile, Saudi Arabia and Zambia. Barrick Gold was formed via the 2019 merger of Barrick and Randgold. Majority of its sales were generated in the US.

Operations
Barrcik Gold's presentation of its reportable operating segments consists of about 10 gold mines (Carlin, Cortez, Turquoise Ridge, Pueblo Viejo, Loulo-Gounkoto, Kibali, Veladero, Porgera, North Mara and Bulyanhulu). The remaining operating segments, including its copper mines, remaining gold mines and project, have been grouped into an "other" category.

Gold sales accounts for approximately 90% of revenue followed by Copper sales and others which accounts for the remainder of revenue.

Geographic Reach
Barrick Gold has major operations in about 20 countries in in North and South America, Africa, Papua New Guinea and Saudi Arabia.

Headquartered in Toronto, Ontario in Canada, more than 50% of the company's sales were generated in the US, Dominican Republic with nearly 10%, Mali with around 10%, while Tanzania, and Zambia generated nearly 10% each.

Sales and Marketing
The company has three customers that individually account for more than 10% of the total revenue. These customers represent approximately 25%, 15%, and 10% of total revenue.

Financial Performance
The company had a revenue of $12 billion in 2021, a 5% dip from the previous year's revenue of $12.6 billion.

In 2021, the company had a net income of $3.3 billion, a 9% decrease from the previous year's net income of $3.6 billion.

The company's cash at the end of 2021 was $5.3 billion. Operating activities generated $4.4 billion, while investing activities used $1.9 billion, primarily for capital expenditures. Financing activities used another $2.4 billion, mainly for disbursements to non-controlling interests.

Strategy
The company plans for the long term and continuously invest in sustainable growth, with resource-based plans for all its mines and worldwide exploration programs designed to deliver a steady stream of new business opportunities. It partners with stakeholders to achieve the best outcomes.

Barrick's strategy is to operate as business owners by attracting and developing world-class people who understand and are involved in the value chain of the business, act with integrity and are tireless in their pursuit of excellence. The company are focused on returns to its stakeholders by optimizing free cash flow, managing risk to create long-term value for its shareholders and partnering with host governments and its local communities to transform their country's natural resources into sustainable benefits and mutual prosperity. Barrick aim to achieve this through the following: Asset Quality; Operational Excellence; and Sustainable Profitability.

Mergers and Acquisitions
In late 2021, Twiga Minerals Corporation (Twiga), a joint venture between Barrick and the Government of Tanzania, has announced the acquisition of new prospecting licences in Tanzania by Bulyanhulu Gold Mine Limited (Bulyanhulu), a subsidiary of Barrick. Under the terms of the Purchase Agreement, the consideration payable by Bulyanhulu is $6 million.

HISTORY

Barrick Gold started in 1983 when Peter Munk merged three small mining and oil and gas companies as Barrick Resources Corp. and took the company public. (Saudi Arabia's Khashoggi family also owned a stake.) The company's early mining activities included stakes in Camflo Mines Ltd., the Renabie Mine in Ontario, and the Valdez Creek Mine in Alaska. Its oil and gas properties and interest in two coal mines were sold in the mid-1980s.

Barrick Resources grew rapidly by buying up North American gold mines. It was renamed American Barrick Resources in 1985 after it acquired the Goldstrike Property (with total reserves of 16 million ounces of gold). In 1988 American Barrick had seven producing mines in Alaska, Nevada, and Utah, as well as in Ontario and Quebec. That year the company opened the Holt-McDermott Mine, the first property it would develop from exploration through to production. Also in 1988 American Barrick completed a $23 million ore-processing complex at Goldstrike. The next year it began mining Goldstrike's Betze deposit.

American Barrick discussed merging with Newmont Mining in 1991, but the talks were called off. In 1994 it purchased Lac Minerals Ltd., which included Chilean mines in South America's richest gold belt. By 1995, when the company was renamed Barrick Gold, it had become the largest gold producer outside South Africa. Also in 1995 the company acquired a 40% stake in the High Desert Property, now the Newmont/Barrick HD joint venture, in Nevada.

Barrick paid $800 million in 1996 for Arequipa Resources, which had struck gold at the Pierina Mine in the Peruvian Andes. It also bought Chile's Pascua Mine and continued developing projects in Argentina.

Barrick had a stroke of luck in early 1997 when talks to develop the Busang project in Indonesia with fellow Canadian firm Bre-X Minerals failed. Bre-X's project was discovered to be what many consider the mining industry's greatest fraud. (A 1998 lawsuit, however, claimed that Barrick knew Bre-X's "find" was phony but kept that knowledge to itself.)

When gold prices plunged in 1997, Barrick announced plans to close mines in Chile and the US -- cutting about 42% of its workforce. Mercur was closed in late 1997. With gold still in the cellar in 1998, milling operations were suspended at the Pinson Mine in Nevada. Former oil executive Paul Melnuk, a longtime Munk associate, succeeded Munk in 1998 as president and CEO but resigned the next year. Munk continued as chairman. Barrick also reached a joint venture agreement with Anglo American's gold subsidiary, AngloGold, to develop Barrick's potential gold properties in Congo, Mali, Niger, and Senegal -- thus reducing Barrick's exposure in the unstable region.

In 1999 Barrick expanded into Africa with its $281 million acquisition of Sutton Resources, owner of the Bulyanhulu property. It also exchanged some land in the Carlin Trend with Newmont.

Barrick's hedging practices, which have become its distinguishing feature, came under attack from investors in 2000, despite company estimates that it earned an additional $391 million through hedging in 1999 and another $300 million in 2000.

In 2000 Barrick acquired Canadian gold exploration company Pangea Goldfields, including operations in Peru and near Bulyanhulu in Tanzania. Production began at Barrick's Bulyanhulu mine in 2001. The company joined the flurry of industry consolidation in late 2001 when it acquired 125-year-old Homestake Mining (US) in a $2.3 billion share exchange. The deal places Barrick in a three-way race for market dominance with rivals Newmont and AngloGold.

The company announced a rich strike at

its Alto Chicama gold property in Peru in 2002. Barrick closed its El Indio, Bousquet, McLaughlin, Ruby Hill, and Agua de la Falda mines in 2002. In 2004 Barrick made inroads into Russia when it acquired a stake in Highland Gold Mining. The company's Holt-McDermott Mine in Canada was divested in that year.

Barrick's $10 billion purchase of Placer Dome enlarged its current mining operations in Australia, Chile, Tanzania, and the US. Following the acquisition, the company sold off certain Placer Dome subsidiaries (primarily in Canada) to Goldcorp for $1.6 billion. It also sold Placer Dome's 50% interest in the South African South Deep site to Gold Fields for another $1.5 billion.

EXECUTIVES

Chief Financial Officer, Senior Executive Vice President, Graham P. Shuttleworth
Strategic Matters Senior Executive Vice President, Kevin Thomson
Chief Executive Officer, President, Director, Mark Bristow
Executive Chairman, Non-Independent Director, John Lawson Thornton
Independent Director, Christopher L. Coleman
Independent Director, Brian L. Greenspun
Independent Director, Andrew J. Quinn
Independent Director, Anne Kabagambe
Independent Director, Loreto Silva
Director, J. Brett Harvey
Director, Hongyu Cai
Director, Gustavo A. Cisneros
Director, J. Michael Evans
Director, Isela Costantini
Auditors : PricewaterhouseCoopers LLP

LOCATIONS

HQ: Barrick Gold Corp.
 Brookfield Place, TD Canada Trust Tower, 161 Bay Street, Suite 3700, Toronto, Ontario M5J 2S1
Phone: 416 307 7405   **Fax:** 416 861 9717
Web: www.barrick.com

2018 Sales

	% of total
United States	42
Dominican Republic	18
Tanzania	9
Argentina	5
Peru	6
Australia	6
Zambia	7
Papua New Guinea	4
Canada	3
Total	100

PRODUCTS/OPERATIONS

2018 Sales

	% of total
Gold	91
Copper	7
Other	2
Total	100

2018 sales by mine

	%
Barrick Nevada	37
Pueblo Viejo	18
Acacia	9
Veladero	5
Lagunas Norte	5
Turquoise Ridge	5
Other mines	21
Total	100

Selected Mining Properties

North America
  Cortez (Nevada)
  Eskay Creek (British Columbia)
  Goldstrike Property (Nevada)
  Hemlo (50%, Ontario)
  Marigold (33%, Nevada)
  Round Mountain (50%, Nevada)
Africa
  Bulyanhulu (Tanzania)
  Tulawaka (70%, Tanzania)
Australia/Pacific
  Cowal (New South Wales)
  Kalgoorlie (50%, Western Australia)
  Porgera Mine (95%, Papua New Guinea)
  Plutonic (Western Australia)
  Yilgarn South (Western Australia)
South America
  Lagunas Norte (Peru)
  Pierina Mine (Peru)
  Veladero Project (Argentina)

COMPETITORS

ANGLO AMERICAN PLC
ANGLOGOLD ASHANTI LTD
COEUR MINING, INC.
FREEPORT-MCMORAN INC.
Franco-Nevada Corporation
Golden Star Resources Ltd
HECLA MINING COMPANY
LONMIN LIMITED
NEWMONT CORPORATION
Newmont Goldcorp Corporation

HISTORICAL FINANCIALS

Company Type: Public

Income Statement   FYE: December 31

	REVENUE ($mil)	NET INCOME ($mil)	NET PROFIT MARGIN	EMPLOYEES
12/23	11,397	1,272	11.2%	0
12/22	11,013	432	3.9%	0
12/21	11,985	2,022	16.9%	0
12/20	12,595	2,324	18.5%	20,000
12/19	9,717	3,969	40.8%	0
Annual Growth	4.1%	(24.8%)	—	—

2023 Year-End Financials

Debt ratio: 10.3%
Return on equity: 5.5%
Cash ($ mil.): 4,148
Current Ratio: 3.16
Long-term debt ($ mil.): 4,715
No. of shares ($ mil.): 1,755
Dividends
Yield: —
Payout: 55.5%
Market value ($ mil.): 31,758

	STOCK PRICE ($) FY Close	P/E High/Low	PER SHARE ($) Earnings	Dividends	Book Value
12/23	18.09	28 20	0.72	0.40	13.30
12/22	17.18	107 55	0.24	0.65	12.97
12/21	19.00	22 15	1.14	0.78	13.41
12/20	22.78	23 12	1.31	0.31	13.13
12/19	18.59	9 5	2.26	0.20	12.05
Annual Growth	(0.7%)	—	(24.9%)	18.9%	2.5%

BASF SE

Through its more than 111,000 employees globally, BASF offers chemistry products to different sectors. The company's portfolio is divided into the Chemicals, Materials, Industrial Solutions, Surface Technologies, Nutrition & Care and Agricultural Solutions segments and serves nearly all sectors. Based in Germany, BASF's manufacturing footprint spans more than 90 countries and around 250 production sites worldwide. From basic chemicals to high value-added products and system solutions -- serves around 80,000 customers globally.

Operations

The company operates through six segments: Surface Technologies (Catalysts and Coatings), Materials (Performance Materials and Monomers), Chemicals (Petrochemicals and Intermediates), Industrial Solutions (Dispersions & Pigments and Performance Chemicals), Agricultural Solutions, Nutrition & Care (Care Chemicals and Nutrition & Health), and Others.

The Surface Technologies segment products includes catalysts and battery materials for the automotive and chemical industries, surface treatments, colors and coatings. This segment accounts for about 25% of the total revenue.

The Materials segment (generates some 20%) offers advanced materials and its precursors for new applications and systems. Its product portfolio includes isocyanates and polyamides as well as inorganic basic products and specialties for plastics and plastics processing.

The Chemicals segment brings in around 15% of sales and makes basic chemicals and intermediates, contributing to the organic growth of key value chains. Alongside internal transfers, customers include the chemical and plastics industries.

The Industrial Solutions segment develops and markets ingredients and additives for industrial applications, such as polymer dispersions, pigments, resins, electronic materials, antioxidants and additives. The segment represents more than 10% of total sales.

The Agricultural Solutions (10% of revenue) provides fungicides, herbicides, insecticides and biological crop protection, and seed treatment. It offers farmers innovative solutions, including those based on digital technologies, combined with practical advice.

Geographic Reach

BASF is based in the industrial city of Ludwigshafen, Germany, and has operations in around 90 countries.

BASF's manufacturing sites are highly efficient "Verbund" sites, including its Ludwigshafen site, which is the world's largest chemicals plant. BASF's total production footprint totals around 240 sites worldwide.

Germany is BASF's largest single market at roughly 10% of total sales, the rest of the Europe were about 40%. North America accounts for about 30% and Asia about 30% of sales.

Sales and Marketing

BASF boasts a global base of around 80,000 customers, ranging from major global customers and medium-sized businesses to end consumers.

BASF established its five global service units. The five global units are Global Procurement, Global Engineering Services and Global Digital Services, Global Business Services, and the European Site & Verbund Management.

Financial Performance

Note: Growth rates may differ after conversion to US Dollars.

Although BASF SE's performance for the span of five years had some fluctuations, the performance had an overall growth with 2022 as its highest performing year over the period.

Revenue for 2022 increased by EUR 8.7 billion to EUR 87.3 billion compared to EUR 78.6 billion in the prior uear.

The company recorded a net loss of EUR4.9 billion for the fiscal year end 2022, as compared to the prior year's net income of EUR 207 million.

BASF's cash at the end of the year was EUR 2.5 billion. The company's operations produced a cash inflow of EUR 7.7 billion. Investing activities and financing activities used EUR 3.8 billion and EUR 4 billion, respectively. Main cash uses were for payments made for property, plant and equipment, as well as payments for dividends.

Strategy

BASF is passionate about chemistry and its customers. The company's customers are at the center of everything the company does, with its products and technology, growing profitably and at the same time, creating value for society and the environment.

Company Background

Originally named Badische Anilin & Soda-Fabrik, BASF AG was founded in Mannheim, Germany, by jeweler Frederick Englehorn in 1861. Unable to find enough land for expansion in Mannheim, BASF moved to nearby Ludwigshafen in 1865. The company was a pioneer in coal tar dyes, and it developed a synthetic indigo in 1897. Its synthetic dyes rapidly replaced more expensive organic dyes. BASF scientist Fritz Haber synthesized ammonia in, giving BASF access to the market for nitrogenous fertilizer. The company moved into petrochemicals and became a leading manufacturer of plastic and synthetic fiber.

HISTORY

Originally named Badische Anilin & Soda-Fabrik, BASF AG was founded in Mannheim, Germany, by jeweler Frederick Englehorn in 1861. Unable to find enough land for expansion in Mannheim, BASF moved to nearby Ludwigshafen in 1865. The company was a pioneer in coal tar dyes, and it developed a synthetic indigo in 1897. Its synthetic dyes rapidly replaced more expensive organic dyes.

BASF scientist Fritz Haber synthesized ammonia in 1909, giving BASF access to the market for nitrogenous fertilizer (1913). Haber received a Nobel Prize in 1918 but was later charged with war crimes for his work with poison gases. Managed by Carl Bosch, another Nobel Prize winner, BASF joined the I.G. Farben cartel with Bayer, Hoechst, and others in 1925 to create a German chemical colossus. Within the cartel BASF developed polystyrene, PVC, and magnetic tape. Part of the Nazi war machine, I.G. Farben made synthetic rubber and used labor from the Auschwitz concentration camp during WWII.

After the war I.G. Farben was dismantled. BASF regained its independence in 1952 and rebuilt its war-ravaged factories. Strong postwar domestic demand for basic chemicals aided its recovery, and in 1958 BASF launched a US joint venture with Dow Chemical. (BASF bought out Dow's half in 1978.) The company moved into petrochemicals and became a leading manufacturer of plastic and synthetic fiber.

In the US the company purchased Wyandotte Chemicals (1969), Chemetron (1979), and Inmont (1985), among others. To expand its natural gas business in Europe, in 1991 the company signed deals with Russia's Gazprom and France's Elf Aquitaine. BASF bought Mobil's polystyrene-resin business and gained almost 10% of the US market.

BASF bought Imperial Chemical's polypropylene business in 1994 and became Europe's second-largest producer of the plastic. The next year the company paid $1.4 billion for the pharmaceutical arm of UK retailer Boots.

In 1997 BASF formed a joint venture with PetroFina (now TOTAL); in 2001 the venture opened the world's largest liquid steam cracker, in Port Arthur, Texas.

BASF made seven major acquisitions in 1998, including the complexing business of Ciba Specialty Chemicals. It also made six divestitures, which included its European buildings-paints operations, sold to Nobel N.V.

In 1999 the US fined the company $225 million for its part in a worldwide vitamin price-fixing cartel (in 2001 the European Commission fined it another $260 million, bringing the total expected cost of fines, out-of-court settlements, and legal expenses to about $800 million). BASF also faced a class-action suit as a result of the scheme. That year the company moved into oil and gas exploration in Russia through a partnership agreement with Russia's Gazprom. BASF also merged its textile operations into Bayer and Hoechst's DyStar joint venture, forming a $1 billion company that is a world-leading dye maker.

BASF completed its acquisition of Rohm and Haas' industrial coatings business in 2000 and bought the Cyanamid division (herbicides, fungicides, and pesticides) of American Home Products (now Wyeth). That year BASF expanded its superabsorbents business by paying $656 million for US-based Amcol International's Chemdal International unit.

Rather than attempt to compete in the rapidly consolidating pharmaceutical industry, in 2001 BASF sold its midsized Knoll Pharmaceutical unit to Abbott Laboratories for about $6.9 billion. It also announced that it was closing 10 plants and cutting about 4,000 jobs (4% of its workforce).

BASF sold its fibers unit in 2003 to focus on core chemical operations, which it added to throughout the next few years. For example, it bought a portion of Bayer's agchem businesses for $1.3 billion when European antitrust regulators mandated the Bayer divestment following its acquisition of Aventis CropScience. BASF also acquired Honeywell Specialty Materials' engineering plastics business in exchange for its fibers division. BASF's acquisition later that year of MSA's Callery Chemical Division strengthened BASF's line of inorganics, which it planned to focus on providing to the pharmaceutical industry. Other acquisitions included Ticona's nylon 66 business and Sunoco's plasticizers unit.

That year also brought chairman JĀœrgen Hambrecht's announcement that the company would push forward with a restructuring of its North American business. The focus of the plan was to save more than $250 million over the next three years. Included among the steps were job cuts of approximately 1,000 and the relocation of its North American headquarters (though remaining in New Jersey) in late 2004. (The move to smaller facilities was enabled by the sale of Knoll Pharmaceuticals in 2001, which reduced operations at the home base.)

BASF sold Basell, its petrochemical JV with Shell, in 2005. The two companies had announced in 2004 that they planned to exit the polyolefins business with the sale of Basell. The deal was finalized late the next year. Investment group Access Industries came in with the winning bid of about $5.7 billion. That company's name was changed to LyondellBasell after its 2007 acquisition of Lyondell Chemical Company.

The company opened two Verbund sites in Asia -- one in Nanjing, China, and the other in Kuantan, Malaysia. The Chinese site delivered its first product in early 2005 and began operating fully in the middle of that year. It's the centerpiece and primary operation of BASF-YPC, a joint venture with Sinopec that was formed in 2000. BASF's goal is to achieve 70% of its sales in the region from local production by 2015; that figure hovered at about 60% in 2008.

The company also legally changed its name from BASF Aktiengesellschaft to BASF SE in 2008. The move made formal BASF's transition to a European company, as opposed to one organized in Germany.

In 2009 BASF spent about $4 billion to acquire Swiss chemicals giant Ciba. Following a review phase of Ciba's operations and their fit within the structure of BASF, the company began integrating Ciba into its performance products segment; this entailed the sale or closure of almost half of Ciba's 55 manufacturing facilities and the loss of about 3,700 of its employees. As part of that strategy, BASF SE sold the Regulatory and Safety Testing businesses of Ciba's Expert Services unit to London-based Intertek Group in 2010.

Also in 2010, BASF acquired specialty chemicals company Cognis GmbH in a $3.8 billion deal. Cognis gave BASF a boost in entering several high-margin business lines, such as personal care and cosmetics.

EXECUTIVES

Executive Chairman, Martin Brudermuller
Vice-Chairman, Chief Financial Officer, Hans-Ulrich Engel
Executive Director, Saori Dubourg
Executive Director, Michael Heinz
Executive Director, Markus Kamieth
Executive Director, Melanie Maas-Brunner
Independent Director, Kurt Wilhelm Bock
Independent Director, Sinischa Horvat
Independent Director, Thomas Carell
Independent Director, Dame Alison J. Carnwath
Independent Director, Liming Chen
Independent Director, Tatjana Diether
Independent Director, Waldemar Helber
Independent Director, Anke Schaferkordt
Independent Director, Roland Strasser
Director, Franz Fehrenbach
Director, Denise Schellemans
Director, Michael Vassiliadis
Auditors : KPMG AG Wirtschaftsprufungsgesellschaft

LOCATIONS

HQ: BASF SE
   Carl-Bosch-Strasse 38, Ludwigshafen 67056
Phone: (49) 621 60 0   **Fax:** (49) 621 602525
Web: www.basf.com

2018 Sales

	% of total
Europe	
Germany	29
Other Countries	16
North America	27
Asia Pacific	22
South America, Africa, Middle East	6
Total	100

PRODUCTS/OPERATIONS

2018 Sales

	% of total
Functional Materials & Solutions	34
Performance Products	25
Chemicals	26
Agricultural Solutions	10
Other	5
Total	100

Selected Products

Chemicals
   Inorganics
   Ammonia
   Formaldehyde
   Melamine
   Sulfuric acid
   Urea
   Intermediates
   Performance chemicals
   Water-based resins
   Petrochemicals
   Feedstocks
   Industrial gases
   Plasticizers
   Specialty chemicals
Plastics
   Engineering plastics
   Foams
   Polyamides and intermediates
   Polyurethanes
   Styrenics
Functional Solutions
   Catalysts
   Battery materials
   Chemical catalysts
   Coatings
   Automotive coatings
   Decorative paints
   Industrial coatings
   Pigments
   Construction chemicals
Performance Products
   Automotive fluids
   Care chemicals
   Paper chemicals
   Pharma ingredients
   Textile chemicals
Agricultural Solutions
   Crop protection
   Fungicides
   Herbicides
   Insecticides

COMPETITORS

AMERICAN PACIFIC CORPORATION
ASPEN AEROGELS, INC.
CMC MATERIALS, INC.
ELEMENT SOLUTIONS INC
ELEMENTIS PLC
SIGMA-ALDRICH CORPORATION
SOLUTIA INC.
Solvay
THE DOW CHEMICAL COMPANY
THE LUBRIZOL CORPORATION

HISTORICAL FINANCIALS

Company Type: Public

Income Statement   FYE. December 31

	REVENUE ($mil)	NET INCOME ($mil)	NET PROFIT MARGIN	EMPLOYEES
12/22	93,269	(669)	—	111,481
12/21	88,962	6,251	7.0%	111,047
12/20	72,592	(1,300)	—	110,302
12/19	66,597	9,454	14.2%	117,628
12/18	71,775	5,390	7.5%	118,371
Annual Growth	6.8%	—	—	(1.5%)

2022 Year-End Financials

Debt ratio: 24.6%   No. of shares ($ mil.): 893
Return on equity: (-1.5%)   Dividends
Cash ($ mil.): 2,687   Yield: —
Current Ratio: 1.83   Payout: 0.0%
Long-term debt ($ mil.): 16,225   Market value ($ mil.): 11,005

	STOCK PRICE ($) FY Close	P/E High/Low		PER SHARE ($) Earnings	Dividends	Book Value
12/22	12.31	—	—	(0.75)	0.65	47.28
12/21	17.53	3	3	6.79	1.38	50.27
12/20	19.68	—	—	(1.41)	0.67	45.07
12/19	18.72	2	2	10.27	0.64	50.73
12/18	17.59	5	3	5.85	0.66	43.71
Annual Growth	(8.5%)	—	—	—	(0.3%)	2.0%

Bausch Health Companies Inc

Bausch Health is a multinational, specialty pharmaceutical and medical device company that develops, manufactures and markets primarily in the therapeutic areas of gastroenterology (GI) and dermatology, a broad range of branded, generic and branded generic pharmaceuticals, over-the-counter (OTC) products and medical aesthetic devices and, through its majority ownership of Bausch + Lomb Corporation (Bausch + Lomb), branded, and branded generic pharmaceuticals, OTC products and medical devices (contact lenses, intraocular lenses, ophthalmic surgical equipment) in the therapeutic area of eye health. The company's products are marketed directly or indirectly in approximately 100 countries. The US and Puerto Rico generate some 60% of total revenue.

Operations

Bausch Health operates through five segments: Bausch + Lomb, Salix, International, Diversified Products, and Solta Medical.

The Bausch + Lomb segment includes its global Bausch + Lomb eye-health business. Its global Bausch + Lomb eye-health business includes its Global Vision Care, Global Surgical, Global Consumer and Global Ophthalmic Pharmaceuticals product. It accounts for about 45% of revenue.

The Salix segment (roughly 25%) offers gastrointestinal products in the US, including irritable bowel treatment Xifaxan.

The International segment, with the exception of its Bausch + Lomb products and Solta products, includes sales in Canada, Europe, Asia, Australia, Latin America, Africa and the Middle East of branded pharmaceutical products, branded generic pharmaceutical products and OTC products, which accounts for over 10% of total revenue.

Bausch Health's Diversified Products segment includes neurology and therapeutic drugs, dental products, and generics. Its portfolio includes antidepressant Wellbutrin, Mysoline for seizures, Syprine for Wilson's disease treatment, and NeutraSal for dry mouth. The segment accounts for more than 10% of total revenue.

The Solta Medical segment consists of global sales of Solta Medical (Solta) aesthetic medical devices. The segment accounts for less than 5% of total revenue.

Geographic Reach

The US and Puerto Rico market account for some 60% of its total revenue. Its next five-largest markets ? China, Canada, Poland, Mexico, and Japan ? contribute fairly equally to a total of more than 15%.

Bausch Health's global corporate headquarters are located in Laval, Quebec, Canada, and its US headquarters are in Bridgewater, New Jersey. The company also owns or has an interest in manufacturing plants or properties outside the US, including Canada, Mexico, and certain countries in Europe, Asia and South America.

Sales and Marketing

Bausch Health's top customers are AmerisourceBergen (nearly 20% of revenue), McKesson (about 15% of revenue), and Cardinal Health (almost 15%). Other customers include hospitals, physicians, and pharmacies.

The company promotes its products through its own sales force and sells through wholesalers. As part of its marketing program for pharmaceuticals, it uses direct to customer advertising, direct mailings, advertise in trade, social media and medical periodicals, exhibit products at medical conventions and sponsor medical education symposia.

The company's advertising costs were $518 million, $ 515 million, and $451 million, for 2022, 2021, and 2020, respectively.

Financial Performance

The company reported a total revenue of $8.1 billion, a 4% decrease from the previous year's total revenue. The decrease was primarily driven by the unfavorable impact of foreign currencies.

In 2022, the company had a net loss of $225 million, a 76% improvement from the previous year's net loss of $948 million.

Cash held by the company at the end of fiscal 2022 was $564 million. Operating activities used $728 million, while investing activities used $303 million, mainly for purchases of property, plant and equipment. Financing activities used another $474 million, primarily for repayments of long-term debt.

Strategy

Bausch Health's strategy is to focus its business on core therapeutic classes that offer attractive growth opportunities. Within its chosen therapeutic classes, the company prioritizes durable products which it believes have the potential for strong operating margins and evidence of growth opportunities. The company believes this strategy has reduced complexity in its operations and maximizes the value of its: eye-health, GI and dermatology businesses, which collectively now represent a substantial portion of its revenues. Bausch Health has found and continues to believe there is significant opportunity in these businesses and the company believes its existing portfolio, commercial footprint and pipeline of product development projects positions the company to successfully compete in these markets and provide it with the greatest opportunity to build value for its shareholders.

Company Background

The company began as Biovail Corporation, which was formed in 2000 from the combination of TXM Corporation and Biovail Corporation International. In 2010 it acquired Valeant Pharmaceuticals International and took the Valeant name.

It changed its name to Bausch Health Companies in 2018.

HISTORY

In 2010 the company, then named Biovail Corporation, acquired the former Valeant Pharmaceuticals for $3.3 billion and took on the Valeant name. The purchase widened its neurological offerings, as well as its dermatology and over-the-counter (OTC) lines and its international distribution network. Both companies were already undergoing restructuring efforts to focus on core offerings, and the new Valeant further cut operational expenses through post-merger integration efforts, including a 25% reduction of the combined workforce.

Valeant and Biovail combined operations in a reverse-merger transaction that aimed to enhance shareholder value and widen product offerings. Valeant had historically been focused on developing improved versions of existing drugs using its oral drug-delivery technologies; however, due to increased competition in the drug-delivery technologies marketplace, the company began shifting its focus to proprietary CNS therapies. Both Ultram ER and Cardizem LA (a long-acting version of Sanofi's blood pressure therapy Cardizem) started facing competition from generic versions in 2009 and 2010.

The combined company retained the Biovail headquarters in Canada, as well as the Biovail corporate structure, but Michael Pearson, CEO of the old Valeant, took the reins of the new Valeant (replacing former Biovail CEO Bill Wells).

In addition to meeting growth targets, the company's name change to Valeant following the merger could also signify a desire to disassociate itself with some past troubles associated with the Biovail name. While operating as Biovail, the company and some of its former executives were charged with accounting fraud in 2008 by the SEC, which claimed that the company misled investors over earnings and losses. The company paid a fine to settle the SEC charges; it also paid fines to settle similar allegations from the Ontario Securities Commission (OSC), a Canadian regulatory body, in 2009.

Biovail founder Eugene Melnyk was one of the charged executives who left the company during the investigations. After the company began restructuring efforts to focus on CNS operations, Melnyk (who was then the company's largest shareholder with about 18% of stock) fought against the new plan and waged an unsuccessful proxy fight aimed at returning the company to its original focus on difficult-to-manufacture generics and brand extensions. In 2010 Melnyk gave up his fight and sold off his holdings in the company he had founded.

Valeant (then named Biovail) bought the US marketing rights for top selling neurology drug Wellbutrin XL back from GSK in 2009, reversing its previous strategy of solely relying on partnerships to sell its drugs in the US. (GSK continued to handle international marketing of the drug.) The $510 million asset purchase fed the company's strategy of focusing on CNS therapies, and the firm hoped that off-patent sales of Wellbutrin XL would generate significant cash to support its R&D programs. The deal also gave Valeant the right to produce an authorized generic version of Wellbutrin XL. The company also launched its new depression therapy, Aplenzin, through a marketing arrangement with French drugmaker Sanofi in 2009.

In mid-2009 Valeant acquired the worldwide rights to the entire portfolio of tetrabenazine products (including international Xenazine rights) from Cambridge Laboratories for $230 million. It also gained several early stage CNS drug development programs through the deal, including a tetrabenazine program for the treatment of Tourette syndrome. The company netted more CNS drugs in 2010 with the purchase of certain compounds from Cortex Pharmaceuticals.

In 2010 Valeant sold its noncore contract research division to Lambda Therapeutic Research for $6 million.

EXECUTIVES

Chairperson, Director, John A. Paulson

Chief Executive Officer, Director, Thomas J. Appio, $730,385 total compensation

Executive Vice President, General Counsel, Seana Carson

Executive Vice President, General Counsel, Christina M. Ackermann, $647,539 total compensation

Subsidiary Officer, Sam A. Eldessouky

Senior Vice President, Chief Accounting Officer, Interim Chief Financial Officer, Controller, John S. Barresi

Division Officer, Joseph F. Gordon, $501,731 total compensation

Director, Thomas W. Ross

Director, Brett M. Icahn
Director, Sarah B. Kavanagh
Director, Steven D. Miller
Director, Richard C. Mulligan
Director, Robert N. Power
Director, Russel C. Robertson
Director, Amy B. Wechsler
Auditors : PricewaterhouseCoopers LLP

LOCATIONS

HQ: Bausch Health Companies Inc
 2150 St. Elzéar Blvd. West, Laval, Quebec H7L 4A8
Phone: 514 744-6792
Web: www.bauschhealth.com

2018 Sales

	$ mil.	% of total
US & Puerto Rico	5,011	60
China	361	4
Canada	319	4
Japan	226	3
Poland	218	3
Mexico	211	3
France	205	2
Egypt	178	2
Germany	170	2
Russia	154	2
UK	117	1
Italy	85	1
Spain	83	1
Other	1,042	12
Total	8,380	100

PRODUCTS/OPERATIONS

2018 Sales

	$ mil.	% of total
Bausch + Lomb/International	4,664	56
Salix	1,749	21
Diversified Products	1,342	16
Ortho Dermatologics	625	7
Total	8,380	100

2018 Sales

	$ mil.	% of total
Pharmaceuticals	4,032	48
Devices	1,640	20
OTC	1,412	17
Branded and other generics	1,187	14
Other	109	1
Total	8,380	100

COMPETITORS

ABBVIE INC.
AKORN, INC.
ALLERGAN LIMITED
BRISTOL-MYERS SQUIBB COMPANY
CELGENE CORPORATION
ENDO HEALTH SOLUTIONS INC.
ENDO INTERNATIONAL PUBLIC LIMITED COMPANY
Old API Wind-down Ltd
TAKEDA PHARMACEUTICAL COMPANY LIMITED
TEVA PHARMACEUTICAL INDUSTRIES LIMITED

HISTORICAL FINANCIALS
Company Type: Public

Income Statement FYE: December 31

	REVENUE ($mil)	NET INCOME ($mil)	NET PROFIT MARGIN	EMPLOYEES
12/23	8,757	(592)	—	20,270
12/22	8,124	(225)	—	19,900
12/21	8,434	(948)	—	19,600
12/20	8,027	(560)	—	21,600
12/19	8,601	(1,788)	—	21,700
Annual Growth	0.5%	—	—	(1.7%)

2023 Year-End Financials

Debt ratio: 81.9%   No. of shares ($ mil.): 365
Return on equity: —   Dividends
Cash ($ mil.): 947   Yield: —
Current Ratio: 1.30   Payout: 0.0%
Long-term debt ($ mil.): 21,938   Market value ($ mil.): 2,929

	STOCK PRICE ($) FY Close	P/E High/Low	PER SHARE ($) Earnings	Dividends	Book Value
12/23	8.02	— —	(1.62)	0.00	(2.79)
12/22	6.28	— —	(0.62)	0.00	(1.91)
12/21	27.61	— —	(2.64)	0.00	(0.29)
12/20	20.80	— —	(1.58)	0.00	1.51
12/19	29.92	— —	(5.08)	0.00	3.02
Annual Growth	(28.0%)		—	—	—

BAWAG Group AG

EXECUTIVES

Chief Executive Officer, Anas Abuzaakouk
Chief Financial Officer, Enver Sirucic
Chief Risk Officer, Stefan Barth
Chief Investment Officer, Andrew Wise
Chairperson, Egbert Fleischer
Deputy Chairperson, Kim Fennebresque
Director, Frederick S. Haddad
Director, Adam Rosmarin
Director, Ingrid Streibel-Zarfl
Director, Verena Spitz
Auditors : KPMG Austria Wirtschaftspruefungs- und Steuerberatungsgesellschaft

LOCATIONS

HQ: BAWAG Group AG
 Wiedner Gürtel 11, Vienna A-1100
Phone: (43) 5 99 05 0
Web: www.bawaggroup.com

COMPETITORS

MEDIOLANUM SPA
Sampo Oyj
THOMAS COOK GROUP PLC
Talanx AG
VIRGIN MONEY UK PLC

HISTORICAL FINANCIALS
Company Type: Public

Income Statement FYE: December 31

	ASSETS ($mil)	NET INCOME ($mil)	INCOME AS % OF ASSETS	EMPLOYEES
12/21	63,752	543	0.9%	3,716
12/20	65,203	348	0.5%	4,071
12/19	51,267	515	1.0%	3,696
12/18	51,187	499	1.0%	3,474
12/17	55,227	559	1.0%	3,437
Annual Growth	3.7%	(0.7%)	—	2.0%

2021 Year-End Financials

Return on assets: 0.8%   Dividends
Return on equity: 10.9%   Yield: —
Long-term debt ($ mil.): —   Payout: 58.7%
No. of shares ($ mil.): 88   Market value ($ mil.): —
Sales ($ mil.): 1,937

Bayer AG

Bayer, one of the leading life science companies around the world, makes prescription products and works in oncology, hematology, ophthalmology through its Pharmaceuticals division; OTC products like Claritin and Canesten via its Consumer Health division; and crop protection and pest control via its Crop Science division. Its top selling pharmaceuticals include oral anticoagulant Xarelto and eye disease medicine Eylea. About 30% of the company's revenue is generated from the US.

Operations

Bayer operates in three reportable segments: Crop Science, Pharmaceuticals and Consumer Health.

The Crop Science segment does business in seeds and plant traits, crop protection, digital solutions and customer services. Main products and brands include Adengo, Asgrow, BioAct, Dekalb, Fox, Maxforce, Seminis, Climate FieldView and Deltapine.

Pharmaceuticals division includes development, production and marketing of prescription products, especially for cardiology and women's health; specialty therapeutics in the areas of oncology, hematology, ophthalmology and ? in the medium term ? cell and gene therapy; diagnostic imaging equipment and the necessary contrast agents. Among its products and brands are Adalat, Betaferon, Cipr, Eylea, Medrad Stellant, Nexavar and Visanne.

The Consumer Health business includes development, production and marketing of mainly nonprescription (over-the-counter) products in the dermatology, nutritional supplements, digestive health, allergy, cough and cold, and pain and cardiovascular risk prevention categories. In addition to Alka-Seltzer, Bepanthen and Canesten, its main products and brands also include Elevit, Iberogast, Redoxon, Supradyn and One A Day.

Geographic Reach

Bayer, headquartered in Leverkusen,

Germany, generates approximately 35% of sales from North America, its largest geographical segment. It also generates significant revenue in Europe, the Middle East and Africa (around 30%) and the Asia/Pacific region (roughly 20%). Latin America brings in nearly 15% of sales. The US is Bayer's single largest geography at around 30% of sales.

Bayer has operations in the Americas, Africa, Asia Pacific and the Middle East. Overall, Bayer comprises approximately 375 consolidated companies operating in about 85 countries around the world.

Sales and Marketing

Bayer's pharmaceuticals products are distributed primarily through wholesalers, pharmacies and hospitals, while Crop Science products are sold through wholesalers and retailers or directly to farmers, and it markets pest and weed control products and services to professional users outside the agriculture industry. The Consumer Health division's well-known and established brands are sold through pharmacies and pharmacy chains, supermarkets, online retailers and other large and small retailers.

Financial Performance

Note: Growth rates may differ after conversion to US Dollars.

Total reported net sales in 2021 increased by EUR2.7 billion, or 7%, year on year to EUR44.1 billion.

In 2021, the company had a net income of EUR1 billion, a 110% improvement from the previous year's net loss of EUR10.5 billion. This was primarily due to a higher volume of sales for the year, as well as a lower volume of cost of goods.

The company's cash at the end of 2021 was EUR4.6 billion. Operating activities generated EUR5.1 billion, while financing activities used EUR5.6 billion, mainly for retirements of debt. Investing activities provided another EUR855 million.

Strategy

Bayer focuses on four strategic levers to deliver attractive returns for shareholders while also making a positive contribution to society and the environment:

Bayer develops innovative products and solutions and leverage cutting-edge research to address unmet societal challenges. It is also continuing to drive the digitalization of its entire value chain.

Bayer drives the operational performance of its business by optimizing its resource allocation and cost base.

Sustainability is an integral part of the company's business strategy, operations and compensation system. Through its businesses, Bayer contributes significantly to the United Nations' Sustainable Development Goals (SDGs). It also pursues resolute, science-based climate action along its entire value chain.

As a global leader in health and nutrition, Bayer continues to develop its business. The company creates value with strategy-based resource allocation focused on profitable growth. It is active in regulated and highly profitable sectors that are driven by innovation and in which we have the objective to grow ahead of the competition.

HISTORY

Friedrich Bayer founded Bayer in Germany in 1863 to make synthetic dyes. Research led to such discoveries as Antinonin (synthetic pesticide, 1892), aspirin (1897), and synthetic rubber (1915).

Under Carl Duisberg, Bayer allegedly made the first poison gas used by Germany in WWI. During the war the US seized Bayer's US operations and trademark rights and sold them to Sterling Drug.

In 1925 Bayer, BASF, Hoechst, and other German chemical concerns merged to form I.G. Farben Trust. Their photography businesses, combined as Agfa, also joined the trust. Between wars Bayer developed polyurethanes and the first sulfa drug, Prontosil (1935).

During WWII the trust took over chemical plants of Nazi-occupied countries, used slave labor, and helped make Zyklon B gas used to kill people at Auschwitz. At war's end Bayer lost its 50% of Winthrop Laboratories (US) and Bayer of Canada (to Sterling Drug). The 1945 Potsdam Agreement called for the breakup of I.G. Farben, and Bayer AG emerged in 1951 as an independent company with many of its original operations, including Agfa.

After rebuilding in West Germany, Bayer AG and Monsanto formed a joint venture (Mobay, 1954); Bayer AG later bought Monsanto's share (1967). In the 1960s the company offered more dyes, plastics, and polyurethanes, and added factories worldwide. Agfa merged with Gevaert (photography, Belgium) in 1964; Bayer AG retained 60%. Over the next 25 years it acquired Miles Labs (Alka-Seltzer, US, 1978), the rest of Agfa-Gevaert (1981), Compugraphic (electronic imaging, US, 1989), and Nova's Polysar (rubber, Canada, 1990).

Bayer AG integrated its US holdings under the name Miles in 1992 (renamed Bayer Corporation in 1995). The next year it introduced its first genetically engineered product, Kogenate hemophilia treatment. It regained US rights to the Bayer brand and logo in 1994 by paying SmithKline Beecham $1 billion for the North American business of Sterling Winthrop.

EXECUTIVES

Chairman, Chief Executive Officer, Chief Sustainability Officer, Director, Werner Baumann
Transformation and Talent Management Board Member, Sarena S. Lin
Finance Management Board Member, Wolfgang Nickl
Pharmaceuticals Management Board Member, Stefan Oelrich
Crop Science Management Board Member, Rodrigo Santos
Consumer Health Management Board Member, Heiko Schipper
Director, Johanna W Faber
Chairman, Norbert Winkeljohann
Vice-Chairman, Director, Oliver Zuehlke
Director, Paul Achleitner
Director, Simone Bagel-Trah
Director, Horst Baier
Director, Norbert W. Bischofberger
Director, Andre Van Broich
Director, Ertharin Cousin
Director, Thomas Elsner
Director, Colleen A. Goggins
Director, Robert Gundlach
Director, Heike Hausfeld
Director, Reiner Hoffmann
Director, Fei-Fei Li
Director, Frank Lollgen
Director, Petra Reinbold-Knape
Director, Andrea Sacher
Director, Michael Schmidt-KieBling
Director, Alberto Weisser
Director, Otmar D. Wiestler
Auditors : Deloitte GmbH Wirtschaftsprufungsgesellschaft

LOCATIONS

HQ: Bayer AG
    Kaiser-Wilhelm-Allee 1, Leverkusen 51368
Phone: (49) 214 30 33022
Web: www.bayer.com

2017 Sales

	% of total
Europe/Middle East/Africa	38
North America	29
Asia/Pacific	22
Latin America	11
Total	100

2017 Sales

	% of total
United States	24
Germany	10
China	7
Brazil	5
Other	54
Total	100

PRODUCTS/OPERATIONS

2017 Sales

	% of total
Pharmaceuticals	50
Crop Science	28
Consumer Health	17
Animal Health	5
Total	100

Selected Operations and Products

HealthCare
    Animal health products
    Diabetes care products
    Consumer care products (over-the-counter drugs)
    Pharmaceuticals
CropScience
    BioScience (biotechnology and seeds)

Crop protection (insecticides and herbicides)
Environmental science (lawn care and non-agricultural pesticides)

Selected Brands
HealthCare
    Adalat (cardiovascular medication)
    Advantage (animal health)
    Aleve/Flanax (analgesic)
    Alka-Seltzer (analgesic and antacid)
    Aspirin (analgesic)
    Aspirin Cardio (cardiovascular)
    Avalox/Avelox (antibiotic)
    Bepanthen/Bepanthol (skin care treatment)
    Betaferon/Betaseron (multiple sclerosis medication)
    Baytril (animal health infections)
    Breeze/Contour (diabetes care glucose meters)
    Canesten (antifungal)
    Cipro/Ciprobay (antibiotic)
    Glucobay (diabetes treatment)
    Iopamiron (diagnostic imaging)
    Kogenate (hematology/cardiology)
    Levitra (impotence drug)
    Magnevist (diagnostic imaging)
    Mirena (contraceptive)
    Nexavar (oncology)
    One-A-Day (vitamins)
    Supradyn (multivitamin)
    Ultravist (diagnostic imaging)
    Yasmin/Yasminelle/YAZ (contraceptive)
CropScience
    Confidor/Gaucho/Admire/Merit (insecticides/seed treatment)
    Flint/Stratego/Sphere/Nativo (fungicides)
    Poncho (seed treatment)
    Ficam/Maxforce/Esplanade/K-Othrine
(Environmental Science)

COMPETITORS

BAYER CORPORATION
BRISTOL-MYERS SQUIBB COMPANY
Bausch Health Companies Inc
CIPLA LIMITED
ENDO HEALTH SOLUTIONS INC.
HIKMA PHARMACEUTICALS PUBLIC LIMITED COMPANY
JOHNSON & JOHNSON
MERCK & CO., INC.
MERCK KG auf Aktien
Novartis AG

HISTORICAL FINANCIALS

Company Type: Public

Income Statement   FYE: December 31

	REVENUE ($mil)	NET INCOME ($mil)	NET PROFIT MARGIN	EMPLOYEES
12/22	54,191	4,432	8.2%	101,369
12/21	49,893	1,131	2.3%	99,637
12/20	50,809	(12,880)	—	101,459
12/19	48,890	4,593	9.4%	107,435
12/18	45,333	1,941	4.3%	110,838
Annual Growth	4.6%	22.9%	—	(2.2%)

2022 Year-End Financials

Debt ratio: 34.3%
Return on equity: 11.5%
Cash ($ mil.): 5,522
Current Ratio: 1.08
Long-term debt ($ mil.): 34,417
No. of shares ($ mil.): 982
Dividends
  Yield: —
  Payout: 7.9%
Market value ($ mil.): 12,634

STOCK PRICE ($) FY Close	P/E High/Low		PER SHARE ($) Earnings	Dividends	Book Value
12/22 12.86	4	3	4.51	0.36	42.15
12/21 13.26	16	12	1.15	0.41	38.04
12/20 14.84	—	—	(13.11)	0.53	38.13
12/19 20.28	5	4	4.68	1.51	54.10
12/18 17.57	18	10	2.06	0.96	56.46
Annual Growth (7.5%)	—		21.6%	(22.0%)	(7.0%)

Bayerische Motoren Werke AG

Bayerische Motoren Werke, better known as BMW, is the leading automaker in the premium segment worldwide. It manufactures and sells around 2.5 million premium-brand cars and off-road vehicles each year under the BMW, MINI, and Rolls-Royce names. Spare parts and accessories are also offered. Its vehicles and products are sold worldwide through company branches, independent dealers, subsidiaries, and importers. In addition, the company also offers car leasing and credit financing for both retail and corporate fleet customers, as well as dealer financing and insurance. BMW also makes motorcycles. BMW generates the majority of its sales internationally.

Operations

The BMW Group comprises three main segments: Automotive, Motorcycles, and Financial Services. An "Other Entities" segment consists of holding companies and group financing companies.

The Automotive segment contributes about 75% of total group revenue and sells BMW-branded cars, MINI-branded cars, and the 100-year-old, luxury Rolls-Royce line. Financial Services, which account for some 25% of sales, offers credit financing and leasing to retail customers through companies, as well as through co-operation agreements with local financial services providers and importers. Motorcycles (less than 5%% of sales) are geared toward premium markets with models in the sport, tour, roadster, heritage, adventure and urban mobility categories.

Overall, nearly 70% of sales were generated from sales of products and related goods, nearly 15% from products previously leased to customers, and some 10% from lease installments.

Geographic Reach

Based in Munich, Germany, BMW operates 30-plus production and assembly plants in about 15 countries and racks up sales in more than 110 countries. The company also operates almost 45 dedicated sales subsidiaries and financial services locations and nearly 15 R&D centers worldwide.

BMW's cars are popular worldwide, pulling in billions in sales from Europe, North America, Asia, and other major markets. It generates nearly 45% of its revenue in Europe and nearly% in Asia (primarily in China). The US contributes almost 20% of revenues.

Sales and Marketing

BMW sells around 2.5 million cars. Its sales network comprises around 3,500 BMW, 1,600 MINI, and some 150 Rolls-Royce dealerships. In Germany, cars are sold through BMW branches and independent dealerships. Outside Germany, vehicles are distributed through subsidiaries and independent importers. Motorcycles are sold by more than 1,200 dealerships and importers in over 90 countries.

Financial Performance

The company had revenues of EUR 111.2 billion in 2021, a 12% increase from the previous year's revenue of EUR 99 billion.

In 2021, the company had a net profit of EUR 16.1 billion, a 36% increase from the previous year's net profit of EUR 5.2 billion.

The company's cash at the end of 2021 was EUR 16 billion. Operating activities generated EUR 15.9 billion, while investing activities used EUR 6.4 billion, mainly for total investment in intangible assets and property, plant and equipment. Financing activities used another EUR 6.7 billion, primarily for repayment of non-current financial liabilities.

Strategy

In the BMW Group's view, a key prerequisite for a company's profitability is that its activities are compatible with external economic, ecological and social interests. Conversely, profitability is the prerequisite for a company's ability to develop sustainable and innovative technologies, ensure job security, and cooperate with all its business partners along a value chain that is striving to become increasingly sustainable.

For this reason, since the financial year 2020, the BMW Group has kept stakeholders informed of its business performance by reporting on an integrated basis. With the Integrated Group Report 2021, we aim to provide a clear and comprehensive insight into the BMW Group and explain its activities in a transparent, comprehensible and measurable manner. It is well aware that integrated reporting is among the subjects of an ongoing discussion currently taking place between stakeholders, regulators and reporting entities. The status achieved to date is therefore still subject to constant review and continuous improvement.

Mergers and Acquisitions

In early 2022, he BMW Group has acquired a stake in its partner Kinexon. The two companies have been working together for several years in order to advance the comprehensive digitalisation of the BMW Group production network. The premium carmaker announced that it has now acquired a minority stake in the innovative, Munich-based software company through its own venture capital company, BMW i Ventures. Kinexon's high-precision real-time locating systems are also designed for use in competitive sports and applied by numerous sport clubs of FiFA and NBA which record the movement data of athletes and their equipment through wearables. The BMW Group and Kinexon GmbH have agreed not to disclose any acquisition details.

In early 2022, he BMW Group welcomes a new addition to its portfolio, as the ALPINA brand becomes part of the company. The BMW Group will secure the rights to the ALPINA brand ? bringing even greater diversity to its own luxury-car range. BMW AG and ALPINA Burkard Bovensiepen GmbH + Co. KG have reached an agreement to this effect that will secure the long-term future of the ALPINA brand as well as the Burkard Bovensiepen GmbH und Co. KG. ALPINA Burkard Bovensiepen GmbH + Co. KG is a German vehicle manufacturer based in Buchloe. Terms were not disclosed.

HISTORY

BMW's logo speaks to its origin: a propeller in blue and white, the colors of Bavaria. In 1913 Karl Rapp opened an aircraft-engine design shop near Munich. He named it Bayerische Motoren Werke (BMW) in 1917. The end of WWI brought German aircraft production to a halt, and BMW shifted to making railway brakes until the 1930s. BMW debuted its first motorcycle, the R32, in 1923, and the company began making automobiles in 1928 after buying small-car company Fahrzeugwerke Eisenach.

In 1933 BMW launched a line of larger cars. The company built aircraft engines for Hitler's Luftwaffe in the 1930s and stopped all auto and motorcycle production in 1941. BMW chief Josef Popp resisted and was ousted. Under the Nazis, the company operated in occupied countries, built rockets, and developed the world's first production jet engine.

With its factories dismantled after WWII, BMW survived by making kitchen and garden equipment. In 1948 it introduced a one-cylinder motorcycle, which sold well as cheap transportation in postwar Germany. BMW autos in the 1950s were large and expensive and sold poorly. When motorcycle sales dropped, the company escaped demise in the mid-1950s by launching the Isetta, a seven-foot, three-wheeled "bubble car."

In the 1970s BMW's European exports soared, and the company set up a distribution subsidiary in the US. The company also produced larger cars that put BMW on par with Mercedes-Benz.

EXECUTIVES

Chairman, Director, Oliver Zipse

Purchasing and Supplier Network Executive Board Member, Joachim Post
Human Resources, Labour Relations Director Executive Board Member, Ilka Horstmeier
Production Executive Board Member, Milan Nedeljkovic
Customer, Brands, Sales Executive Board Member, Pieter Nota
Finance Executive Board Member, Nicolas Peter
Development Executive Board Member, Frank Weber
General Counsel, Andreas Liepe
Chairman, Norbert Reithofer
Deputy Chairman, Manfred Schoch
Deputy Chairman, Stefan Quandt
Deputy Chairman, Stefan Schmidt
Director, Deputy Chairman, Kurt Wilhelm Bock
Director, Bernhard Ebner
Director, Jens Kohler
Director, Anke Schaferkordt
Director, Marc R. Bitzer
Director, Heinrich Hiesinger
Director, Christiane Benner
Director, Thomas Wittig
Director, Vishal Sikka
Director, Susanne Klatten
Director, Dominique Mohabeer
Director, Sibylle Wankel
Director, Johann Horn
Director, Christoph Schmidt
Director, Rachel Claire Empey
Director, Werner Zierer
Auditors : PricewaterhouseCoopers GmbH

LOCATIONS

HQ: Bayerische Motoren Werke AG Aktiengesellschaft, Munich 80788
Phone: (49) 89 382 0   **Fax:** (49) 89 3895 5858
Web: www.bmwgroup.com

2018 Sales

	% of total
Europe	
Germany	14
Rest of Europe	32
Americas	
US	17
Rest of Americas	4
Asia	
China	19
Rest of Asia	11
Other Regions	3
Total	100

PRODUCTS/OPERATIONS

2018 Sales

	% of total
Automotive	74
Financial services	24
Motorcycles	2
Elimination	-
Total	100

Selected Products

Automobiles
  BMW
    1 Series
    3 Series
    5 Series
    6 Series
    7 Series
    X3, X5, X6 sports utility vehicles
    M Models
    Z4
  MINI Electric
  MINI Cooper
  MIMI Hatch
  MIMI Clubman
  Rolls-Royce Phantom
  Rolls-Royce Wraith
  Rolls-Royce Dawn
Motorcycles
  BMW

COMPETITORS

ALLISON TRANSMISSION HOLDINGS, INC.
BMW OF NORTH AMERICA, LLC
CUMMINS INC.
Daimler AG
Hyundai Mobis Co., Ltd
LEAR CORPORATION
MOTORCAR PARTS OF AMERICA, INC.
NISSAN MOTOR CO.,LTD.
VOLKSWAGEN AG
WABCO HOLDINGS INC.

HISTORICAL FINANCIALS

Company Type: Public

Income Statement — FYE: December 31

	REVENUE ($mil)	NET INCOME ($mil)	NET PROFIT MARGIN	EMPLOYEES
12/21	125,907	14,014	11.1%	118,909
12/20	121,489	4,633	3.8%	120,726
12/19	117,003	5,518	4.7%	133,778
12/18	111,634	8,150	7.3%	134,682
12/17	118,291	10,333	8.7%	129,932
Annual Growth	1.6%	7.9%	—	(2.2%)

2021 Year-End Financials

Debt ratio: 30.5%   No. of shares ($ mil.): 601
Return on equity: 18.3%   Dividends
Cash ($ mil.): 18,119   Yield: 1.6%
Current Ratio: 1.13   Payout: 2.3%
Long-term debt ($ mil.): 48,956   Market value ($ mil.): 20,107

	STOCK PRICE ($) FY Close	P/E High/Low		PER SHARE ($) Earnings	Dividends	Book Value
12/21	33.40	2	1	21.25	0.54	139.82
12/20	29.35	5	3	7.03	0.64	124.14
12/19	27.12	4	3	8.39	0.93	110.64
12/18	26.97	3	2	12.39	1.13	109.50
12/17	34.67	3	2	15.73	1.01	107.75
Annual Growth	(0.9%)	—		7.8%	(14.7%)	6.7%

BCE Inc

BCE is Canada's largest provider of telecommunications services. The operates an extensive local access network in Ontario, QuÃ©bec, the Atlantic provinces and Manitoba, as well as in Canada's Northern Territories. It provides a complete suite of wireless communications, wireline voice and data, including Internet access and TV, product and service offerings to residential, business and wholesale customers. BCE has 9.9 million mobile subscribers with nationwide mobile voice and data services. It also had approximately 2.5 million mobile connected device subscribers. The company's brands include Bell, Fibe (internet protocol TV), TSN (sports network), and CraveTV.

Operations

BCE operates in three segments: Bell Wireless, Bell Wireline and Bell Media.

Bell Wireline, which generates about 50% of BCE's revenue, provides data, internet access, TV, and local and long distance telephone, as well as well as other communications services and products. It serves Bell's residential, small and medium-sized business and enterprise customers in Ontario's and Quebec's metro areas.

Bell Wireless accounts for almost 40% of BCE's revenue with wireless voice and data communication products and services to Bell's residential, small and medium-sized business and large enterprise customers across Canada.

Bell Media brings in some 15% of BCE's revenue. The segment encompasses about 35 conventional TV stations; more than 25 specialty TV channels, including TSN, Space, Discovery, and RDS; four national pay-TV services, including The Movie Network (TMN); and some 110 licensed radio stations in almost 60 markets across Canada. The segment also offers out-of-home advertising with billboards and digital formats.

Geographic Reach

BCE provides local access network in Ontario, QuÃ©bec, the Atlantic provinces and Manitoba, as well as in Canada's Northern Territories.

The company's broadband fiber network, consists of fiber-to-the-node (FTTN) and fiber-to-the-premise (FTTP) locations, covers about 10 million homes and businesses in Ontario, QuÃ©bec, the Atlantic provinces, and Manitoba.

Sales and Marketing

BCE delivers its products and services to residential wireless and wireline customers through more than 1,000 Bell, Virgin Plus, Lucky Mobile and The Source retail locations; national retailers such as Best Buy, Walmart, Loblaws and Glentel's WIRELESSWAVE, Tbooth wireless and WIRELESS etc., as well as a network of regional and independent retailers in all regions; call centre representatives; its websites, including bell.ca, virginplus.ca, luckymobile.ca and thesource.ca; and door-to-door sales representatives. It also offers customers the convenience of One Bill for Internet, TV, home phone, wireless and smart home services.

In 2023, Bell and Staples announced a multi-year exclusive agreement to sell Bell, Virgin Plus and Lucky Mobile wireless and wireline services through Staples stores across Canada for consumers and small businesses, starting in the first half of 2023.

Financial Performance

(Figures are in Canadian dollars and might differ from other sources due to exchange rates).

Total operating revenues for 2022 was C$24.2 billion, a 3% increase from the previous year's total operating revenues of C$23.4 billion.

In 2022, the company had a net income of C$2.9 billion, a 1% increase from the previous year's net income of C$2.9 billion.

The company's cash at the end of 2022 was C$99 million. Operating activities generated C$8.4 billion, while investing activities used C$5.5 billion, mainly for capital expenditures. Financing activities used another C$3 billion, primarily for cash dividends paid on common shares.

Strategy

BCE's strategy builds on its longstanding strengths in networks, service innovation and content creation, and positions the company for continued growth and innovation leadership. Its primary business objectives are to grow its subscriber base profitably and to maximize revenues, operating profit, free cash flow and return on invested capital by further enhancing its position as the foremost provider in Canada of comprehensive communications services to residential, business and wholesale customers, and as Canada's leading content creation company.

It seeks to take advantage of opportunities to leverage its networks, infrastructure, sales channels, and brand and marketing resources across its various lines of business to create value for its customers and other stakeholders. Its strategy is centred on its disciplined focus and execution of six strategic imperatives that position the company to deliver continued success in a fast-changing communications marketplace. The six strategic imperatives that underlie BCE's business plan are: build the best networks; drive growth with innovative services; deliver the most compelling content; champion customer experience; operate with agility and cost efficiency; engage and invest in its people and create a sustainable future.

Mergers and Acquisitions

In 2022, Bell completed its acquisition of Distributel, a national independent communications provider offering a wide range of consumer, business and wholesale communications services for cash consideration of $303 million ($282 million net of cash acquired) and $39 million of estimated additional cash consideration contingent on the achievement of certain performance objectives. The acquisition of Distributel is expected to support growth in Bell's residential and business customers. Distributel's results are included in those of its Bell Wireline segment.

Also in 2022, BCE acquired EBOX, an Internet, telephone and television service provider based in Longueuil, QuÃ©bec. Bell will maintain the EBOX brand and operations, and EBOX will continue providing compelling telecommunications services for consumers and businesses in QuÃ©bec and parts of Ontario. The acquisition of EBOX will further strengthen Bell's presence in QuÃ©bec, a key market for its business.

Company Background

Alexander Graham Bell experimented with the telephone in his native Canada before moving to the US in the mid-1870s. His father sold his Canadian patent rights to National Bell Telephone which combined with Canada's Hamilton District Telegraph to form Bell Telephone Company of Canada. Known as Bell Canada, it received a charter in 1880 and settled in Montreal. By 1882 it had 40 exchanges. AT&T owned 48% of the company in 1890, but by 1925 Canadians owned 95% of Bell Canada. (AT&T severed all ties in 1975.)

HISTORY

Alexander Graham Bell experimented with the telephone in his native Canada before moving to the US in the mid-1870s. His father sold his Canadian patent rights to National Bell Telephone which combined with Canada's Hamilton District Telegraph to form Bell Telephone Company of Canada. Known as Bell Canada, it received a charter in 1880 and settled in Montreal. By 1882 it had 40 exchanges. AT&T owned 48% of the company in 1890, but by 1925 Canadians owned 95% of Bell Canada. (AT&T severed all ties in 1975.)

EXECUTIVES

Regulatory Officer Chief Executive Officer, Legal Chief Executive Officer, Regulatory Officer President, Legal President, Director, Mirko Bibic

Vice-Chairman, Wade Oosterman

Corporate Services Chief Human Resources Officer, Corporate Services Executive Vice President, Nikki Moffat

Executive Vice President, Chief Financial Officer, Glen LeBlanc

Executive Vice President, Chief Legal & Regulatory Officer, Robert Malcolmson

Independent Director, Cornell Wright
Independent Director, Katherine Lee
Independent Director, Monique F. Leroux
Independent Director, Jennifer Tory
Independent Director, Louis P. Pagnutti
Director, David F. Denison
Director, Robert P. Dexter
Director, Sheila A. Murray
Director, Gordon M. Nixon
Director, Calin Rovinescu
Director, Karen Sheriff
Director, Robert C. Simmonds
Auditors : Deloitte LLP

LOCATIONS

HQ: BCE Inc
 1 Carrefour Alexander Graham-Bell, Building A, 8th Floor, Verdun, Quebec H3E 3B3
Phone: 800-339-6353   **Fax:** 514-786-3970
Web: www.bce.ca

PRODUCTS/OPERATIONS

2018 Sales

	% of total
Bell Wireline	52
Bell Wireless	35
Bell Media	13
Total	100

2018 Sales

	% of total
Services:	
Data	32
Wireless	27
Voice	14
Media	11
Other services	1
Products:	
Wireless	9
Data	2
Wireless	2
Total	100

COMPETITORS

AT&T INC.
FRONTIER COMMUNICATIONS CORPORATION
KT Corporation
Koninklijke KPN N.V.
Manitoba Telecom Services Inc
Rogers Communications Inc
SK Telecom Co.,Ltd.
SPRINT CORPORATION
TELECOM ITALIA O TIM SPA
TELUS Corporation

HISTORICAL FINANCIALS

Company Type: Public

Income Statement — FYE: December 31

	REVENUE ($mil)	NET INCOME ($mil)	NET PROFIT MARGIN	EMPLOYEES
12/23	18,614	1,566	8.4%	45,132
12/22	17,874	2,008	11.2%	44,610
12/21	18,410	2,126	11.6%	49,781
12/20	17,972	1,961	10.9%	50,704
12/19	18,402	2,334	12.7%	52,100
Annual Growth	0.3%	(9.5%)	—	(3.5%)

2023 Year-End Financials

Debt ratio: 37.9% No. of shares ($ mil.): 912
Return on equity: 9.7% Dividends
Cash ($ mil.): 582 Yield: —
Current Ratio: 0.65 Payout: 169.7%
Long-term debt ($ mil.): 23,490 Market value ($ mil.): 35,925

	STOCK PRICE ($) FY Close	P/E High/Low		PER SHARE ($) Earnings	Dividends	Book Value
12/23	39.38	22	16	1.72	2.92	16.73
12/22	43.95	18	14	2.20	2.72	17.98
12/21	52.04	18	14	2.35	2.79	19.55
12/20	42.80	19	13	2.17	2.50	18.23
12/19	46.35	15	12	2.59	2.39	17.90
Annual Growth	(4.0%)	—	—	(9.7%)	5.1%	(1.7%)

BDO Unibank Inc.

"BDO" could stand for "Big Darn Operation," but instead, it's short for Banco de Oro Unibank, the latest iteration of a merger that took place in 2007 between two Filipino entities, Banco de Oro Universal Bank and Equitable PCI Bank. Since 1968, Banco de Oro has provided corporate, commercial, retail, and investment banking services throughout the country. Established in 1938, Equitable PCI brings to the coupling its commercial banking, small and middle market lending, trust, leasing, and remittances expertise. Combined, BDO operates a network of more than 680 branches and some 1,200 ATMs in Metro Manila, as well as the Luzon, Mindanao, and Visayas provinces.

EXECUTIVES

Vice-Chairman, Executive Vice-Chairman, Executive Director, Jesus A. Jacinto
President, Chief Executive Officer, Executive Director, Nestor V. Tan
Comptroller, Executive Vice President, Lucy C. Dy
Treasurer, Executive Vice President, Dalmacio D. Martin
Office Chief, Staff Chief, Office President, Staff President, Office Senior Vice President, Staff Senior Vice President, Lazaro Jerome C. Guevarra
Chief Interal Auditor, Senior Vice President, Estrellita V. Ong
Chief Compliance Officer, Senior Vice President, Federico P. Tancongco
Secretary, Edmundo L. Tan
Assistant Secretary, Sabino E. Acut
Assistant Secretary, Alvin C. Go
Chairman, Non-Executive Director, Teresita T. Sy
Lead Independent Director, Director, Dioscoro I. Ramos
Independent Director, Vipul Bhagat
Independent Director, Estela P. Bernabe
Independent Director, George T. Barcelon
Independent Director, Vicente S. Perez
Non-Executive Director, Walter C. Wassmer
Non-Executive Director, Jones M. Castro
Non-Executive Director, Josefina N. Tan
Auditors : Punongbayan & Araullo

LOCATIONS

HQ: BDO Unibank Inc.
BDO Corporate Center, 7899 Makati Avenue, Makati City 0726
Phone: (63) 2 840 7000
Web: www.bdo.com.ph

COMPETITORS

ARAB BANK PLC
BANCO POPULAR ESPAÑOL SA (EXTINGUIDA)
BANK OF AYUDHYA PUBLIC COMPANY LIMITED
Banco de Chile
CHANG HWA COMMERCIAL BANK, LTD.
FUNDACION CAJA MEDITERRANEO
HANG SENG BANK, LIMITED
Itau Unibanco Holding S/A
METROPOLITAN BANK & TRUST COMPANY
QNB FINANSBANK ANONIM SIRKETI

HISTORICAL FINANCIALS

Company Type: Public

Income Statement — FYE: December 31

	ASSETS ($mil)	NET INCOME ($mil)	INCOME AS % OF ASSETS	EMPLOYEES
12/22	73,251	1,025	1.4%	39,323
12/21	71,074	839	1.2%	38,873
12/20	70,243	587	0.8%	38,756
12/19	62,975	872	1.4%	38,510
12/18	57,545	622	1.1%	36,387
Annual Growth	6.2%	13.3%	—	2.0%

2022 Year-End Financials

Return on assets: 1.4% Dividends
Return on equity: 12.9% Yield: —
Long-term debt ($ mil.): — Payout: 128.9%
No. of shares ($ mil.): 5,264 Market value ($ mil.): 109,797
Sales ($ mil.): 4,325

	STOCK PRICE ($) FY Close	P/E High/Low		PER SHARE ($) Earnings	Dividends	Book Value
12/22	20.86	2	2	0.19	0.25	1.57
12/21	24.95	3	2	0.19	0.15	1.89
12/20	22.24	5	3	0.13	0.14	1.86
12/19	32.08	3	2	0.20	0.13	1.66
12/18	25.32	4	3	0.14	0.13	1.43
Annual Growth	(4.7%)	—	—	8.1%	17.5%	2.4%

Beiersdorf AG

Beiersdorf is one of the world's leading companies in the consumer goods industry. Its success is based on its strong portfolio of internationally leading brands. The company makes anti-aging products under the Caviar Collection, Eucerin, and La Prairie brands. Its body care brands include such items as Labello, 8x4, and Florena. Beiersdorf offers plasters and wound care products under Hansaplast, Aquaphor, and Coppertone. Under the tesa name, the company offers highly innovative self-adhesive system and product solutions for industry, craft businesses, and consumers. Coffee and cigarettes firm maxingvest (formerly Tchibo Holding) owns a majority stake in Beiersdorf. Europe accounts for about 50% of the company's revenue.

Operations

Beiersdorf operates two business units: Consumer and tesa. Consumer is by far the larger of the two, at approximately 80% of total sales. The division's brands include Nivea, the most significant for the company, Eucerin and La Prairi. It also sells Libello and Hansaplast, which are trusted by consumers around the globe.

The tesa business, which accounts for some 20%, concentrates on developing high-quality self-adhesive system and product solutions for industry, craft businesses, and end consumers.

Geographic Reach

The German-headquartered company has customers in more than 100 countries. In addition to the large skin research center in

Hamburg, its global research and development network also includes two large innovation centers in China (Shanghai) and the US (New Jersey) as well as four development centers in Mexico, Brazil, India, and Japan. Europe accounts for about 50% of total sales, followed by Africa, Asia and Australia with over 30%, and Americas with approximately 20%.

Sales and Marketing
Beiersdorf's marketing and selling expenses were approximately EUR 2.7 billion and EUR 2.5 billion in 2021 and 2020, respectively.

Financial Performance
Company's revenue for fiscal 2021 increased to EUR 7.6 billion compared from the prior year with EUR 7.0 billion.

Profit for fiscal 2021 increased to EUR 655 million compared from the prior year with EUR 577 million.

Cash held by the company at the end of fiscal 2021 increased to EUR 1.04 billion. Cash provided by operations was EUR 993 million while cash used for investing and financing activities were EUR 845 million and EUR 141 million, respectively.

Strategy
In 2019, the company formulated its C.A.R.E+ business strategy. This is designed to ensure competitive, sustainable growth and respond to a fast-changing environment defined by megatrends such as digitalization and sustainability. Already identified by Beiersdorf as key issues before the pandemic, these are topics whose importance has only increased as a result of COVID-19. Since the launch of C.A.R.E+, the company have systematically implemented and refined this business strategy further, focusing on innovation, digitalization, sustainability, and growth. These focus areas are reflected in its strategic priorities: strengthen its brands by enriching their purpose; fast forward digital transformation; win with skin care; unlock white spot potential; fuel the growth through increased productivity; and build on strong foundations: Culture ? Core Values ? Capabilities ? Care Beyond Skin.

Mergers and Acquisitions
In early 2022, Beiersdorf successfully completed the acquisition of Chantecaille Beaute Inc., USA, a leading prestige beauty company, for an enterprise value between $590 million and $690 million. "Through the acquisition of Chantecaille, we are bolstering our portfolio in prestige beauty and strengthening our position, especially in the United States, China and Korea, which is a priority of our C.A.R.E.+ strategy," said Vincent Warnery, Chief Executive Officer of Beiersdorf.

HISTORY

Hamburg pharmacist Paul Carl Beiersdorf began Beiersdorf in 1882 when he received a patent for his method of making guttapercha plaster gauze, a medicated dressing. After his son committed suicide in 1890, Beiersdorf sold his laboratory to pharmacist Oskar Troplowitz. (The founder himself committed suicide in 1896.)

Under Troplowitz, the innovative company came up with Leukoplast, the first sticking plaster, in 1901. In 1909 Beiersdorf launched Labello, the first lip balm in a push tube. The company also got into adhesive tapes and toothpaste. In 1911 Beiersdorf introduced NIVEA, a pure white skin cream that was the first water-in-oil emulsion product. Troplowitz died in 1918.

Beiersdorf had factories in Argentina, Australia, Denmark, France, Mexico, Russia, and the US by the beginning of WWI, and exports accounted for more than 40% of its sales. That all came to a halt during the war, but Beiersdorf soon rebuilt its international operations.

The company put NIVEA into its well-known blue packaging in the 1920s, and it launched Hansaplast, the first ready-to-use plaster, in 1922. The company's innovations continued when it introduced tesa, the first transparent adhesive film, in 1936. Insurer Allianz took a stake in Beiersdorf in the mid-1930s.

Beiersdorf suffered at home and abroad during WWII. In Hitler's Germany it was targeted as a Jewish company, while Allied countries seized its assets elsewhere. In the 1950s, while introducing new products (8 x 4 deodorizing soap in 1951, atrix hand cream in 1955), the company began reacquiring the international rights to its brands. The process would take almost half a century, starting in the Netherlands in 1952 and ending with the acquisition of a Polish company in 1998.

Beiersdorf set up a joint venture with Japanese personal care products maker Kao in 1971. The Herz family, owners of German coffee company Tchibo Holding, bought about one-fourth of Beiersdorf in 1974. Beiersdorf restructured that year to focus its operations on three main product groups: cosmetics and skin care, pharmaceuticals, and adhesives.

Over the years the company allowed its number of brands and products to mushroom without thought for the economies of scale that come from focusing on a limited number of major names and lines. In 1989 Beiersdorf began reducing its number of products, cutting loose several noncore businesses, and refocusing on skin care, especially the NIVEA brand.

Those moves continued when Rolf Kunisch became CEO in 1994. By early 2000 Beiersdorf's market value had tripled under Kunisch. In 2002 Beiersdorf purchased Florena Cosmetic GmbH, which had made Beiersdorf cosmetic products under contract prior to the sale. In May 2005 Thomas-Bernd Quaas succeeded Kunisch, who retired as chairman.

In June 2006 the company established Beiersdorf Middle East, based in the United Arab Emirates. The new affiliate will serve 16 countries across the Middle East, and North and West Africa.

In February 2007 the company sold its Hirtler soap factory in South Baden to the Dutch personal and household care group Budelpack International.

In December 2008 the firm sold its Futuro health supports (wraps, braces, and elastic bandages) and compression hosiery product line to 3M. Beiersdorf acquired Futuro in 1996.

EXECUTIVES

Chairman, Chief Executive Officer, Vincent Warnery
Executive Board Member, Oswald Barckhahn
Executive Board Member, Astrid Hermann
Executive Board Member, Thomas Ingelfinger
Executive Board Member, Zhengrong Liu
Executive Board Member, Grita Loebsack
Executive Board Member, Ramon A. Mirt
Executive Board Member, Patrick Rasquinet
Director, Chairman, Reinhard Pollath
Deputy Chairman, Martin Hansson
Director, Deputy Chairwoman, Manuela Rousseau
Director, Hong Chow
Director, Reiner Hansert
Director, Wolfgang Herz
Director, Andreas Kohn
Director, Jan Koltze
Director, Christine Martel
Director, Olaf Papier
Director, Frederic Pflanz
Director, Kirstin Weiland
Auditors : Ernst & Young GmbH Wirtschaftspruefungsgesellschaft

LOCATIONS

HQ: Beiersdorf AG
Unnastrasse 48, Hamburg 20245
Phone: (49) 40 4909 0   **Fax:** (49) 40 4909 3434
Web: www.beiersdorf.com

2015 Sales

	% of total
Europe	51
Africa/Asia/Australia	30
Americas	19
Total	100

PRODUCTS/OPERATIONS

2015 Sales

	% of total
Consumer	83
tesa	17
Total	100

Selected Brands
8x4
Eucerin
Florena
Hansaplast
La Prairie
Labello
NIVEA
NIVEA FOR MEN

SBT
SLEK
tesa

Selected Products
Deodorants
Hand care
Lip care
Skin care
tesa
Fastening systems
Masking systems
Packaging systems

COMPETITORS

AVON PRODUCTS, INC.
BEIERSDORF, INC.
BUNZL PUBLIC LIMITED COMPANY
COLGATE-PALMOLIVE COMPANY
KAO CORPORATION
RECKITT BENCKISER GROUP PLC
REVLON, INC.
SHISEIDO COMPANY, LIMITED
THE PROCTER & GAMBLE COMPANY
TUPPERWARE BRANDS CORPORATION

HISTORICAL FINANCIALS

Company Type: Public

Income Statement — FYE: December 31

	REVENUE ($mil)	NET INCOME ($mil)	NET PROFIT MARGIN	EMPLOYEES
12/21	8,632	722	8.4%	20,567
12/20	8,621	687	8.0%	20,306
12/19	8,592	806	9.4%	20,654
12/18	8,283	833	10.1%	20,059
12/17	8,458	805	9.5%	18,595
Annual Growth	0.5%	(2.7%)	—	2.6%

2021 Year-End Financials

Debt ratio: 1.1% No. of shares ($ mil.): 226
Return on equity: 9.7% Dividends
Cash ($ mil.): 1,172 Yield: 1.0%
Current Ratio: 1.39 Payout: 3.2%
Long-term debt ($ mil.): 119 Market value ($ mil.): 4,670

	STOCK PRICE ($) FY Close	P/E High/Low		PER SHARE ($) Earnings	Dividends	Book Value
12/21	20.59	9	7	3.18	0.21	34.29
12/20	23.45	11	8	3.03	0.10	33.76
12/19	23.89	8	6	3.56	0.10	30.03
12/18	21.35	7	6	3.68	0.10	28.39
12/17	23.65	8	7	3.55	0.11	26.97
Annual Growth	(3.4%)	—	—	(2.7%)	16.7%	6.2%

BHP Group Ltd

BHP Billiton Plc, (changed name to BHP Group Plc, now BHP Group (UK) Ltd) is one half of a dual-listed mining giant. It is headquartered in London; the other part of the company, BHP Group Limited, is based in Australia. Although they maintain separate listings, the companies are managed as a single entity and have the same management team and board of directors. One of the largest diversified natural resources companies, it ranks among the world's top producers of iron ore and coal (thermal and metallurgical). Other products include aluminum, copper, nickel, silver, uranium, and potash. BHP also has crude oil and natural gas holdings. China generated majority of its sales.

Operations

The company operates in three segments: Iron Ore (over 45% of sales), Copper (around 25%), and Coal (about 25%).

The Iron Ore segment includes the mining of iron ore. The Copper segment includes the mining of copper, silver, zinc, molybdenum, uranium and gold. The Coal segment includes the mining of metallurgical coal and energy coal.

Geographic Reach

The dual listed company is headquartered in Australia and London. It also has a commercial offices in Singapore, as well as share registrars and transfer offices in Australia, UK, South Africa, New Zealand, and the US.

China generated around 55% of sales, Japan with about 15%, India with nearly 10%, South Korea and Rest of Asia with over 5% each, while the rest were generated from Australia, Europe, North America, and South America.

Financial Performance

The company reported a total revenue of $65.1 billion in 2022, a 14% increase from the previous year's total revenue of $56.9 billion. This increase was mainly due to higher average realised prices for metallurgical coal, thermal coal, copper and nickel, partially offset by lower average realised prices for iron ore.

In 2022, the company had a net income of $30.9 billion, a 173% increase from the previous year's net income of $11.3 billion.

The company's cash at the end of 2022 was $17.2 billion. Operating activities generated $32.2 billion, while investing activities used $7 billion, mainly for purchases of property, plant and equipment. Financing activities used another $22.8 billion, primarily for dividends paid.

Strategy

The company will manage the most resilient long-term portfolio of assets, in highly attractive commodities, and will grow value through being excellent at operations, discovering and developing resources, acquiring the right assets and options, and capital allocation. Through its differentiated approach to social value, the company will be a trusted partner who creates value for all stakeholders.

Company Background

From two small mining companies founded in the mid-1800s to the eventual merger of Broken Hill Proprietary and Billiton in 2001, today BHP is a leader in the resources industry. BHP began as a silver, lead and zinc mining company in Broken Hill, Australia in 1885. Billiton goes back further, to 1851, as a tin mining company in the island of Belitung in Indonesia. Over the next century, it expanded into businesses like oil & gas, nickel, diamond mining and marketing, and potash businesses, with varying success stories. In 2015, BHP decided to simplify its vast portfolio by spinning off some of its metals and mining businesses into a global company South32.

HISTORY

After starting out on its own in 1860, Billiton was subsequently bought, first by Royal Dutch Shell, and then by Gencor, only to end up on its own once again. In 1860 a group of Dutch shareholders formed Billiton NV. The company bought the rich tin deposits of Billiton island (now part of Indonesia), for which it was named. The business grew to include tin and lead smelting in the Netherlands. Billiton NV began mining bauxite in the 1940s, but WWII caused a production slowdown.

While demand for petroleum products exploded in the 1950s and 1960s, in 1970 the industry nose-dived. Royal Dutch Shell (formed from the merger of Royal Dutch and Shell Transport and Trading) responded by diversifying, buying Billiton NV, which it renamed Billiton International. Shell had gotten its start in commodities in the 1880s, selling Russian oil of the Rothschilds to the Far East. Royal Dutch formed in 1890, after buying the rights to drill for oil in the Dutch East Indies. The two companies merged in 1907.

The 1970 Billiton purchase helped Royal Dutch Shell make up for the 1970s oil shortage and rationing that had resulted from OPEC's crude oil price hikes. Slow worldwide economic growth, a major recession, and oil and chemicals overcapacity impacted the company in the late 1970s and early 1980s.

Royal Dutch Shell sold Billiton in 1994 to Gencor, which had been formed in 1980 by the merger of General Mining and Finance Corporation and Union Corporation. General Mining began mining gold in South Africa in the 1890s, and Gencor continued its predecessors' metals and manufacturing operations. Gencor, however, spent the early 1980s focused on manufacturing because it anticipated a downturn in base metals. But the recession, inflation, and high interest rates stifled Gencor's success, and the company became known as an unfocused conglomerate. In 1986 a newly appointed chairman separated Gencor's manufacturing and mining interests.

By 1989 Gencor had cut its staff and reorganized. That year it bought 31% of South Africa's Richards Bay aluminum smelter. Within two years Gencor had become a holding company with a primary interest in mining. In 1993 the firm unbundled its non-mining activities. With the end of apartheid in 1994, Gencor was able to expand abroad. Its purchase of Billiton catapulted its presence into 13 countries, but in 1996 the metals market spiraled downward.

Billiton was spun off by Gencor in 1997. It took over all of Gencor's nonprecious metal interests, including its aluminum, titanium, ferroalloy, and coal assets. That year Billiton combined its nickel interests with QNI of Australia. Making good on its plan to buy new base metals assets, Billiton entered a joint venture in 1998 to explore for lead and zinc with Ireland's Ennex. Billiton also sold its metals brokerage subsidiary to Metallgesellschaft AG (Germany).

In 1999 Billiton announced that it would invest in smaller companies with promising properties and limit its own in-house exploration operations. It entered joint ventures with PT Taraco Mining to explore for coal in Indonesia and with Comet Resources to develop the Ravensthorpe Nickel Project in Western Australia.

Billiton's offer for a 21% stake in the Gove bauxite-alumina project in Australia was bested by Alcan in 2000. The company agreed to pay Alcoa about $1.5 billion for its majority stake in the Worsley alumina refinery in Australia. With Anglo American and Glencore International (now Glencore Xstrata), it acquired a 50% stake in Colombia's Cerrejon Zona Norte coal mine for $384 million; it then bought Canadian mining company Rio Algom (copper, molybdenum, uranium, and coal) for $1.2 billion.

In 2001 Billiton closed the purchase of Alcoa's share of the Worsley smelter. The same year Billiton agreed to be acquired by Aussie natural resources company BHP Ltd. to form a dual-listed entity -- known collectively as BHP Billiton -- consisting of BHP Billiton Limited (run from Melbourne) and BHP Billiton plc (run from London). The deal closed in June 2001.

EXECUTIVES

Chief Executive Officer, Non-Independent Director, Mike Henry
Chief Financial Officer, David M. Lamont
Chief Operating Officer, Edgar Basto
Chief Legal, Governance and External Affairs Officer, Caroline Cox
Chief People Officer, Jad Vodopija
Chief Development Officer, Johan van Jaarsveld
Staff Chief Technical Officer, Laura Tyler
Chief Commercial Officer, Vandita Pant
Americas President, Ragnar Udd
Australia President, Australia Senior Executive Officer, Geraldine Slattery
Secretary, Stefanie Wilkinson
Chairman, Independent Non-Executive Director, Ken N. MacKenzie
Senior Independent Director, Independent Non-Executive Director, Gary J. Goldberg
Independent Non-Executive Director, Terry J. Bowen
Independent Non-Executive Director, Malcolm Broomhead
Independent Non-Executive Director, Xiaoqun Clever
Independent Non-Executive Director, Ian Cockerill

Independent Non-Executive Director, John Mogford
Independent Non-Executive Director, Christine O'Reilly
Independent Non-Executive Director, Dion J. Weisler
Independent Non-Executive Director, Catherine Tanna
Independent Non-Executive Director, Michelle A. Hinchliffe
Auditors: Ernst & Young

LOCATIONS

HQ: BHP Group Ltd
Level 18, 171 Collins Street, Melbourne, Victoria 3000
Phone: (61) 03 9609 3333   **Fax:** (61) 03 9609 3015
Web: www.bhp.com

2015 Sales

	$ in mil	% of total
Australia	2,205	5
United Kingdom	230	1
Rest of Europe	2,235	5
China	16,337	36
Japan	4,863	11
Rest of Asia	4,734	11
North America	7,990	17
South America	1,342	3
Southern Africa	10	-
Rest of world	322	1
India	1,680	4
South Korea	2,688	6
Total	44,636	100

PRODUCTS/OPERATIONS

2015 Sales

	$ in mil	% of total
Iron Ore	14,753	33
Petroleum and Potash	11,447	26
Copper	11,453	26
Coal	5,885	13
Group and unallocated items	1,098	2
Total	44,636	100

COMPETITORS

ANGLESEY MINING PLC
ANGLO PACIFIC GROUP PLC
BARRICK TZ LIMITED
BHP GROUP LIMITED
FREEPORT-MCMORAN INC.
POLYMETAL INTERNATIONAL PLC
RIO TINTO PLC
VEDANTA RESOURCES LIMITED
Vale S/A
WEATHERLY INTERNATIONAL PUBLIC LIMITED COMPANY

HISTORICAL FINANCIALS

Company Type: Public

Income Statement   FYE: June 30

	REVENUE ($mil)	NET INCOME ($mil)	NET PROFIT MARGIN	EMPLOYEES
06/23	53,817	12,921	24.0%	42,319
06/22	65,098	30,900	47.5%	39,210
06/21	60,817	11,304	18.6%	34,478
06/20	42,931	7,956	18.5%	31,589
06/19	44,288	8,306	18.8%	28,926
Annual Growth	5.0%	11.7%	—	10.0%

2023 Year-End Financials

Debt ratio: 19.6%   No. of shares ($ mil.): 5,064
Return on equity: 28.8%   Dividends
Cash ($ mil.): 12,428   Yield: 8.8%
Current Ratio: 1.23   Payout: 310.9%
Long-term debt ($ mil.): 12,674   Market value ($ mil.): 302,193

	STOCK PRICE ($) FY Close	P/E High/Low		PER SHARE ($) Earnings	Dividends	Book Value
06/23	59.67	28	19	2.55	5.27	8.79
06/22	56.18	13	9	6.09	7.00	8.88
06/21	72.83	36	21	2.23	3.12	10.14
06/20	49.73	37	20	1.57	2.86	9.48
06/19	58.11	36	27	1.60	6.60	9.34
Annual Growth	0.7%			12.3%	(5.5%)	(1.5%)

Blom Bank SAL

Auditors: Ernst & Young p.c.c.

LOCATIONS

HQ: Blom Bank SAL
Verdun, Rachid Karami Street, BLOM Bank Bldg., P.O. Box 11-1912, Beirut, Riad El Solh 1107 2807
Phone: (961) 1 743 300   **Fax:** (961) 1 738 946
Web: www.blombank.com

HISTORICAL FINANCIALS

Company Type: Public

Income Statement   FYE: December 31

	ASSETS ($mil)	NET INCOME ($mil)	INCOME AS % OF ASSETS	EMPLOYEES
12/21	26,468	4	0.0%	3,326
12/20	29,716	1	—	4,620
12/19	33,295	109	0.3%	4,853
12/18	36,740	507	1.4%	0
12/17	32,544	482	1.5%	0
Annual Growth	(5.0%)	(69.1%)		

2021 Year-End Financials

Return on assets: —   Dividends
Return on equity: 0.1%   Yield: —
Long-term debt ($ mil.): —   Payout: 0.0%
No. of shares ($ mil.): 206   Market value ($ mil.): —
Sales ($ mil.): 1,374

BlueScope Steel Ltd.

BlueScope Steel is a global leader in metal coating and painting for building and construction. Principally focused on the Asia-Pacific region, the group manufactures and markets a wide range of branded products that include pre-painted COLORBOND steel, zinc/aluminum alloy-coated ZINCALUME steel and the LYSAGHT range of building products. BlueScope's vertically integrated operations for flat steel products in Australia and New Zealand produce value-added metallic coated and painted products, together with hot rolled coil, cold rolled coil, steel plate and pipe and tube. The company has approximately 100 facilities in more than 20 countries, and generates approximately 40% of revenue in North America.

Operations

BlueScope has five operating segments: Australian Steel Products (ASP); North Star BlueScope Steel; Building Products Asia and North America; Buildings & Coated Products North America; and New Zealand & Pacific Islands (Previously called New Zealand & Pacific Steel).

ASP generates more than 40% of the company's total sales and it produces and markets a range of high value coated and painted flat steel products for Australian building and construction customers as well as providing a broader offering of commodity flat steel products.

North Star BlueScope Steel is a single site electric arc furnace producer of hot rolled coil in Ohio US. It accounts for about 25% of revenue.

Building Products Asia and North America is technology leader in metal coated and painted steel building products, principally focused on the Asia-Pacific region, with a wide range of branded products that include pre-painted COLORBOND steel, zinc/aluminum alloy-coated ZINCALUME steel and the LYSAGHT range of products. This segment produces more than 20% of the sales.

Buildings & Coated Products North America (about 10% of revenue) is a leader in engineered building solutions, servicing the low-rise non-residential construction needs of customers from an engineering and manufacturing base in North America.

New Zealand & Pacific Islands accounts for the remaining revenue and it consists of three primary business areas: New Zealand Steel, Pacific Steel, and BlueScope Pacific Islands. This segment also includes the Waikato North Head iron sands mine which supplies iron sands to the Glenbrook Steelworks and for export.

Overall, building products bring in about 50% of the company's revenue, followed by steelmaking products, which contribute nearly 35%, and engineered building solutions, which generate more than 10%. Properties and others account for the rest.

Geographic Reach

Melbourne, Australia-based, BlueScope has operations in North America (approximately 40% of revenue), Australia (some 35%), Asia (almost 15%), and New Zealand (approximately 5%). Others account for the rest.

ASP segment's main manufacturing facilities are at Port Kembla (NSW) and Western Port (Victoria). North Star BlueScope is strategically located near its customers and in one of the largest scrap markets in North America.

Building Products Asia and North America segment has an extensive footprint of metallic coating, painting and steel building product operations in Thailand, Indonesia, Vietnam, Malaysia, India and North America, primarily servicing the residential and non-residential building and construction industries across Asia, and the non-residential building and construction industry in North America.

Sales and Marketing

BlueScope's ASP products are primarily sold to the Australian domestic market, with some volume exported. This segment also operates pipe and tube manufacturing, and a network of roll-forming and distribution sites throughout Australia, acting as a major steel product supplier to the building and construction, manufacturing, transport, agriculture and mining industries.

Financial Performance

Note: Growth rates may differ after conversion to US Dollars.

The company reported a revenue of A$19 billion, a 48% increase from the previous year's revenue of A$12.9 billion. The increase in sales revenue from continuing operations was primarily due to higher selling prices driven by higher global steel prices, combined with ongoing strong demand and favourable impacts from a weaker Australian dollar exchange rate.

In 2022, the company had a net income of A$2.8 billion, a 135% increase from the previous year's net income of A$1.2 billion.

The company's cash at the end of 2022 was A$1.7 billion. Operating activities generated $2.5 billion, while investing activities used A$1.8 billion, mainly for payments for purchase of businesses. Financing activities used another A$1.1 billion, primarily for share buybacks.

Strategy

BlueScope's strategy sets out how the company will deliver on its Purpose and deliver strong returns and sustainable outcomes over the next five years and beyond. Its strategy drives transformation and growth, while continuing to deliver on core expectations for its stakeholders. Core elements of its strategy include investment in carbon reduction technologies, product and service innovation, and delivering a safe, inclusive and diverse workplace.

Mergers and Acquisitions

In mid-2022, BlueScope acquired Coil Coatings business from Cornerstone Building Brands for $500 million. Coil Coatings is the second largest metal painter in the US, with a total capacity of around 900,000 tons per annum across seven facilities, predominantly serving commercial, and industrial construction applications. BlueScope Managing Director and CEO Mark Vassella said, "The acquisition of Coil Coatings is a significant step forward in our growth plans for North America. It almost triples our US metallic coating and painting capacity to over 1.3 million metric tonnes per annum, from around 475,000 tonnes per annum at present, and gives us immediate and direct access to the large and growing Eastern US region."

In late 2021, BlueScope acquired the ferrous scrap steel recycling business of MetalX for approximately $240 million. Announcing the acquisition, Managing Director and CEO Mark Vassella said, "The US is a key focus for BlueScope's future growth. The MetalX ferrous acquisition adds to our extensive US asset footprint of over $3.0 billion, which spans steelmaking, steel coating and painting, engineered building systems and industrial property development. And we have current and intended expansion projects totalling up to $1.5 billion, including the North Star expansion project."

Company Background

BlueScope was formed as an independent company in 2002; called BHP Steel at the time, it was spun off when BHP and Billiton merged to form BHP Billiton.

The company traces its roots back to the 1915 establishment of the Australian steel industry.

EXECUTIVES

Chief Executive Officer, Managing Director, Executive Director, Mark Royce Vassella
Chief Financial Officer, Tania J. Archibald
Hot Rolled Products Chief Executive Officer, Pat Finan
BlueScope Buildings Chief Executive, Alec Highnam
Australian Steel Products Chief Executive Officer, John Nowlan
Climate Change Chief Executive Officer, New Zealand and Pacific Islands Chief Executive Officer, Gretta Stephens
NS BlueScope Chief Executive Officer, Connell Zhang
Chief Legal Officer, Company Secretary, Debra J. Counsell
Group Counsel – Secretariat, Secretary, Penny S. Grau
Chairman, Independent Non-Executive Director, John Andrew Bevan
Independent Non-Executive Director, Penelope Binham-Hall
Independent Non-Executive Director, Ewen Graham Wolseley Crouch
Independent Non-Executive Director, Rebecca P. Dee-Bradbury
Independent Non-Executive Director, Kathleen Marie Conlon
Independent Non-Executive Director, Richard Mark Hutchinson
Independent Non-Executive Director, Jennifer Margaret Lambert
Auditors : Ernst & Young

LOCATIONS

HQ: BlueScope Steel Ltd.
Level 24, 181 William Street, Melbourne, Victoria 3000
Phone: (61) 3 9666 4000   **Fax:** (61) 3 9666 4111
Web: www.bluescope.com

PRODUCTS/OPERATIONS

2016 sales	% of total
Australian Steel Products	46
BlueScope Buildings	18
Building Products ASEAN, Nth Am & India	18
New Zealand & Pacific Steel	9
Hot Rolled Products North America	9
Total	100

SELECTED BRANDS
LYSAGHT STEEL BUILDING PRODUCTS,
COLORBOND STEEL.
COLORSTEEL,
ZINCALUME STEEL
GALVABOND STEEL
GALVASPAN STEEL
BLUESCOPE ZACS
SUPERDYMA
BUTLER
VARCO PRUDEN
ECOBUILDTM
PROBUILD

COMPETITORS
ALERIS CORPORATION
AMPCO-PITTSBURGH CORPORATION
CARPENTER TECHNOLOGY CORPORATION
COMMERCIAL METALS COMPANY
HARSCO CORPORATION
HBIS Company Limited
NIPPON STEEL NISSHIN CO., LTD.
RELIANCE STEEL & ALUMINUM CO.
TIMKENSTEEL CORPORATION
UNITED STATES STEEL CORPORATION

HISTORICAL FINANCIALS
Company Type: Public

Income Statement — FYE: June 30

	REVENUE ($mil)	NET INCOME ($mil)	NET PROFIT MARGIN	EMPLOYEES
06/23	12,075	668	5.5%	33,000
06/22	13,092	1,933	14.8%	0
06/21	9,684	895	9.2%	0
06/20	7,760	66	0.9%	0
06/19	8,809	711	8.1%	0
Annual Growth	8.2%	(1.6%)	—	—

2023 Year-End Financials
Debt ratio: 1.0%
Return on equity: 9.9%
Cash ($ mil.): 986
Current Ratio: 1.95
Long-term debt ($ mil.): 120
No. of shares ($ mil.): 453
Dividends
Yield: 2.2%
Payout: 103.5%
Market value ($ mil.): 31,058

	STOCK PRICE ($) FY Close	P/E High/Low		PER SHARE ($) Earnings	Dividends	Book Value
06/23	68.50	32	23	1.43	1.51	15.28
06/22	55.22	15	9	3.90	2.50	14.35
06/21	83.50	36	18	1.76	0.45	11.37
06/20	40.32	262	172	0.13	0.40	8.92
06/19	39.88	33	20	1.31	0.43	9.31
Annual Growth	14.5%			2.1%	37.0%	13.2%

BNP Paribas (France)

One of Europe's leading provider of banking and financial services, BNP Paribas and its many subsidiaries offer a wide range of retail and corporate and investment banking services across Europe, North America, Africa, and the Asia/Pacific region. Additional services include corporate vehicle leasing, digital banking and investment services, and private banking and wealth management. BNP Paribas operates in Italy through BNL banca commerciale and in Belgium via BNP Paribas Fortis. In the US, the company owns BancWest. BNP Paribas earns roughly 75% of its revenue from customers in Europe (mainly in France, Belgium, Italy, and Luxembourg). BNP has EUR 422 billion in assets. The company was founded in 1822.

Operations
BNP Paribas operates two core businesses: Retail Banking & Services and Corporate & Institutional Banking.

Retail Banking & Services operates in more than 60 countries and accounts for about 70% of the bank's total revenue. The segment consists of its domestic retail banking networks in France, Italy (BNL bc), Belgium (CPBB), and Luxembourg (CPBL), as well as certain specialized retail banking divisions (Personal Investors, Leasing Solutions, Personal Finance, Arval, and New Digital Businesses). BNP Paribas is the leading private bank in France, and #1 for cash management and professional equipment financing in Europe. BNL bc holds a residential mortgage market share of around 7% in Italy and a 4% household current account market share.

International Financial Services consists of all BNP Paribas Group's retail banking businesses outside the euro zone, split between Europe-Mediterranean and BancWest in the United States. It also includes personal finance, insurance, and wealth and asset management activities.

Corporate and Institutional Banking generates the over 30% of revenue. It consists of three divisions. Global Banking provides services in Europe, the Middle East, Africa, the Asia/Pacific region, and Americas, as well as corporate finance activities. Global Markets offers fixed income, currency and commodities, and equity and prime services. Securities Services caters to management companies, financial institutions, and other corporations.

Broadly speaking, the company makes about 45% of its net revenue from interest (after interest expense). Net commission income brings in about 25% and the rest arises from gains on financial instruments and available-for-sale financial assets, insurance and other activities that generate more than 30% of revenues combined.

Geographic Reach
While it caters to some 65 countries, Paris-based BNP focuses mainly on four domestic markets where it holds leading positions: Belgium, France, Italy and Luxembourg. Europe is the bank's largest market, accounting for some 75% of revenue. North America contributed more than 10%, while the Asia/Pacific and Africa region and other countries contributed about 15% combined.

In France, BNP Paribas' retail network consists of some 1,700 branches and some 4,255 ATMs. Its private banking network consists of numerous centers throughout France, eleven wealth management offices, about 40 business centers for SME, mid-cap and key account customers, including five specialized divisions (Innovation, Real Estate, Images & Media, Institution, Non-profit Organizations & Foundations, Banking & Financial Services.

In Italy, through BNL banca commerciale, BNP Paribas operates about 705 branches, 1,700 ATMs, about 35 private banking centers, roughly 45 small business centers, over 40 branches dealing with SMEs, large corporates, local authorities, and public sector organizations, and a few trade centers for cross-border activities and investment desks that assist local and international companies with direct investments in Italy.

BNP Paribas' Belgium unit operates around 385 branches, some 1,215 ATMs, around 15 centers of dedicated structure, around 225 Fintro franchises, over 655 retail outlets in partnership with Bpost Bank.

In Luxembourg, it supports its 180,000 customers via about branches, over 95 ATMs, and five private banking centers.BancWest is active in some 25 Western and Mid-Western US states. It operates around 515 branches.

The Europe-Mediterranean segment operates a network in about 1,600 branches across 14 countries, including Turkey, Poland, Ukraine, Morocco, Tunisia, Algeria, and seven countries in Sub-Saharan Africa.

Sales and Marketing
BNP Paribas supports all its customers - individuals, associations, entrepreneurs, SMEs, and institutions.

Financial Performance
The company's revenue for fiscal 2021 increased by 4% to EUR 46.2 billion compared from the prior year with EUR 44.3 billion.

Net income for fiscal 2021 increased to EUR 9.5 billion compared from the prior year with EUR 7.1 billion.

Cash held by the company at the end of fiscal 2021 increased to EUR 362.4 billion. Cash provided by operations and financing activities were EUR 42.4 billion and EUR 14.5 billion, respectively. Cash used for investing activities was EUR 1.2 billion.

Strategy
BNP Paribas Personal Finance has developed an active partnership strategy an active strategy of partnerships with retail chains, automotive manufacturers and dealers, e-commerce merchants and other financial institutions (banking and insurance), drawing on its experience and its ability to integrate services tailored to the activity and commercial policy of its third parties.

Mergers and Acquisitions
In early 2022, BNP Paribas has completed the acquisition of Floa, a subsidiary of Casino

group. It is a French leader for web and mobile payment solutions that makes customers' life easier through payment facilities. By capitalising on its European footprint, coupled with BNP Paribas' expertise and the broad spectrum of different business lines, it will be able to envisage a wider deployment across Europe. Terms were not disclosed.

HISTORY

BNP Paribas Group's predecessor Banque Nationale de Paris (BNP) is the progeny of two state banks with parallel histories; each was set up to jump-start the economy after a revolution in 1848.

For a century, Paris-based Comptoir National d'Escompte de Paris (CNEP) bounced between private and public status, depending on government whim. It was the #3 bank in France from the late 19th century through the 1950s.

Banque National pour le Commerce et l'Industrie (BNCI) started in Alsace, a region that was part of Germany from the Franco-Prussian War until WWI. BNCI served as an economic bridge between Germany and France, which had to give the bank governmental resuscitation during the Depression. By the 1960s BNCI had passed CNEP in size.

French leader Charles de Gaulle expected banking to drive post-WWII reconstruction, and in 1945 CNEP and BNCI were nationalized. In 1966 France's finance minister merged them and they became BNP. That year the company started an association with Dresdner Bank of Germany, under which the two still operate joint ventures, primarily in Eastern Europe.

By 1993 privatization was again in vogue, and BNP was cut loose by the government. It expanded outside France to ameliorate the influences of the French economy and government. Even before it was privatized, BNP was involved in such politically charged actions as the bailout of OPEC money repository Banque Arabe and the extension of credit to Algeria's state oil company Sonatrach.

The privatized BNP looked overseas in the late 1990s. In 1997 alone, it won the right to operate in New Zealand, bought Laurentian Bank and Trust of the Bahamas, took control of its joint venture with Egypt's Banque du Caire, and opened a subsidiary in Brazil.

BNP bought failed Peregrine Investment's Chinese operations in 1998. That year the bank also expanded in Peru, opened an office in Algeria, opened a representative office in Uzbekistan, set up an investment banking subsidiary in India, and bought Australian stock brokerage operations from Prudential.

After a decade of globe-trotting, BNP brought it on home in 1999 and set off a year of tumult in French banking. As France's other two large banks (Société Générale and Paribas) made plans to merge, BNP decided it would absorb both banks as a means to get a bigger chunk of the to-be-privatized Crédit Lyonnais and to protect France from Euro-megabank penetration by creating the globe's largest bank.

Executives at Société Générale (SG) had other ideas, forming a cartel called "Action Against the BNP Raid." Meanwhile, BNP tried to boost to controlling stakes its holdings in the two banks. (In Europe's cross-ownership tradition, the target banks also owned part of BNP.) France's central bank tried unsuccessfully to negotiate a deal (the government supported the triumvirate merger). A war of words was played out in the media, and finally shareholders had to vote on the proposals. In the end, BNP won control of Paribas, but not SG. As BNP prepared to integrate a reluctant Paribas into its operations, regulators ordered BNP to relinquish its stake in SG. The newly merged company was dubbed BNP Paribas Group.

In 2000 BNP Paribas and Avis Group launched a fleet-management joint venture. BNP also bought 150 shopping centers from French retailer Carrefour and the 40% of merchant bank Cobepa that it didn't already own. In 2001 BNP Paribas took full control of US-based BancWest. The company bought United California Bank from UFJ Holdings (now part of Mitsubishi UFJ Financial Group) the following year.

The bank opened up a second "home market" when it bought Italy's Banca Nazionale del Lavoro (BNL) for $11 billion in 2006.

Two of the French bank's most transformative acquisitions included the deal to buy Italian bank Banca Nazionale del Lavoro in 2006 and the 75% purchase of Fortis Bank (which also included a 25% stake in Fortis Insurance). Both deals boosted BNP Paribas' retail banking business across Europe. Retail banking is now responsible for more than 60% of BNP Paribas' revenues.

In addition to the Fortis and BNL acquisitions, BNP Paribas looked to grow in new markets. BNP Paribas acquired Sahara Bank in Libya and a 51% stake in UkrSibbank, one of Ukraine's leading banks.

In 2008, as the world's economies struggled to stay afloat, the French government agreed to inject ?10.5 billion ($14 billion) into the nation's top six banks, including BNP Paribas. The government didn't receive shares in the banks it assisted; rather, the capital injections were meant to help reenergize lending activities in France. A year after receiving the cash, BNP Paribas announced plans to repay the government's aid.

In 2009, after a couple of false starts and a seven-month saga, BNP Paribas acquired control of Fortis Banque (also known as Fortis Bank). Fortis' Dutch operations were excluded from the transaction. The deal further cemented BNP Paribas as a top European bank. Fortis Bank was nationalized in October 2008 to prevent its collapse, and the takeover by BNP Paribas was delayed and revised to satisfy Fortis shareholders and other interested parties. Upon the closing of the deal, BNP Paribas became the market leader in Belgium and Luxembourg. The Belgian government gained more than 10% of BNP Paribas in the transaction.

BNP Paribas complimented its 2009 acquisition of Fortis with the purchase of private bank Insinger de Beaufort.

In 2011 BNP Paribas continued its strategy of expanding in high growth markets and acquired a majority of South Africa's Cadiz Securities. BNP Paribas also owns Banque Internationale pour le Commerce et l'Industrie, which is active in six African nations, and a majority of Türk Ekonomi Bankasi in Turkey. BNP Paribas has been expanding in China, Egypt, Israel, and Russia as well.

In 2012 the company sold the bulk of its controlling stake in real estate firm Klépierre to US mall owner Simon for some ?1.5 billion (around $2 billion) to further raise its capital levels.

EXECUTIVES

Chief Executive Officer, Executive Director, Jean-Laurent Bonnafe
Chief Financial Officer, Lars Machenil
Chief Risk Officer, Frank Roncey
Chief Information Officer, Bernard Gavgani
Chief Operating Officer, Executive Director, Juliette Brisac
Chairman, Jean Lemierre
Independent Director, Jacques Aschenbroich
Independent Director, Pierre-Andre de Chalendar
Independent Director, Monique Cohen
Independent Director, Wouter De Ploey
Independent Director, Hugues Epaillard
Independent Director, Rajna Gibson-Brandon
Independent Director, Marion Guillou
Independent Director, Daniela Schwarzer
Independent Director, Sandrine Verrier
Independent Director, Michel J. Tilmant
Independent Director, Field Wicker-Miurin
Director, Lieve Logghe
Director, Christian Noyer
Auditors : Mazars

LOCATIONS

HQ: BNP Paribas (France)
  16, Boulevard des Italiens, Paris 75009
Phone: (33) 1 40 14 45 46   **Fax:** (33) 1 42 98 21 22
Web: www.bnpparibas.com

2018 Sales

	% of total
Europe	75
North America	11
Asia & Pacific	7
Others	7
Total	100

PRODUCTS/OPERATIONS

2018 Sales

	% of total
Retail Banking & Services:	
Domestic Markets	
French Retail Banking	14
Belgian Retail Banking	8
BNL banca commerciale	7
Other Domestic Markets activities	7
International Financial Services	
Personal Finance	13
International Retail Banking	
BancWest	6
Wealth and Asset Management	6
EuropeMediterranean	8
Insurance	6
Corporate & Institutional Banking:	
Global Markets	11
Corporate Banking	9
Securities Services	5
Other Activities:	—
Total	100

2018 Sales

	% of total
Net interest income	49
Net commission income	22
Net gain on financial instruments at fair value through profit or loss	14
Net gain on available-for-sale financial assets and other financial assets not measured at fair value	1
Net income from insurance activities	10
Net income from other activities	4
Total	100

COMPETITORS

AUSTRALIA AND NEW ZEALAND BANKING GROUP LIMITED
COMMONWEALTH BANK OF AUSTRALIA
CoÃ¶peratieve Rabobank U.A.
HSBC HOLDINGS PLC
NATWEST GROUP PLC
Nordea Bank AB
Royal Bank Of Canada
STANDARD CHARTERED PLC
Skandinaviska Enskilda Banken AB
UNICREDIT SPA

HISTORICAL FINANCIALS

Company Type: Public

Income Statement · FYE: December 31

	ASSETS ($mil)	NET INCOME ($mil)	INCOME AS % OF ASSETS	EMPLOYEES
12/22	2,847,810	10,889	0.4%	193,122
12/21	2,981,830	10,739	0.4%	189,765
12/20	3,054,100	8,673	0.3%	193,319
12/19	2,430,470	9,176	0.4%	198,816
12/18	2,337,160	8,618	0.4%	202,625
Annual Growth	5.1%	6.0%	—	(1.2%)

2022 Year-End Financials

Return on assets: 0.3%
Return on equity: 8.5%
Long-term debt ($ mil.): —
No. of shares ($ mil.): 1,233
Sales ($ mil.): 91,426
Dividends
Yield: —
Payout: 23.8%
Market value ($ mil.): 35,116

	STOCK PRICE ($) FY Close	P/E High/Low		PER SHARE ($) Earnings	Dividends	Book Value
12/22	28.47	5	3	8.33	1.99	105.46
12/21	34.79	5	3	8.22	1.57	108.16
12/20	26.61	6	3	6.52	1.36	110.83
12/19	29.69	5	4	6.97	1.68	96.59
12/18	22.54	7	4	6.56	1.76	93.03
Annual Growth	6.0%	—		6.1%	3.1%	3.2%

Boc Hong Kong Holdings Ltd

BOC Hong Kong (Holdings) is the parent of Bank of China (Hong Kong), which has more than 190 branches, 280 automated banking centers, and over 1,000 self-service machines in Hong Kong. The bank serves retail customers, small entrepreneurs, and corporate customers, providing loans, trade related products and other credit facilities, investment and insurance products. It also operates banknote printing business. Bank of China, which is controlled by the Chinese government, owns about two-thirds of BOC Hong Kong.

Operations

BOC Hong Kong (Holdings) operates under four operating segments: Personal Banking, Corporate Banking, Treasury, and Insurance.

Both Corporate Banking (about 40% of revenue), and Personal Banking (about 30% of revenue) provide general banking services including various deposit products, overdrafts, loans, and other credit facilities, investment and insurance products, and foreign currency and derivative products. Corporate Banking serves corporate clients, while Personal Banking serves retail customers.

Treasury (about 30% of revenue) manages the funding and liquidity, interest rate, and foreign exchange positions of the bank in addition to proprietary trades. The Insurance segment represents the business mainly relating to life insurance products, including individual life insurance and group life insurance products.

Overall, BOC Hong Kong (Holdings) generates more than 50% of its revenue from interest income, followed by insurance premiums for about 25% of revenue, and commissions about for 15%.

Geographic Reach

Hong Kong-based, BOC Hong Kong (Holdings) has operations in the US, Singapore, and China. It also has branches in Thailand, Malaysia, Vietnam, the Philippines, Indonesia, Cambodia, Laos, and Brunei.

Sales and Marketing

BOC Hong Kong (Holdings)'s five largest customers accounted less than 30% of total interest income and other operating income of the bank in 2019.

Financial Performance

In 2019, BOCHK's annual profit hit a new high of HK$34.1 billion, representing a growth of 4% year-on-year.

Cash held by the company at the end of 2019 decreased to HK$331.7 billion compared to HK$626.1 billion in the prior year. Cash used for operations, investing activities and financing activities were HK$268.7 billion, HK$3.3 billion and HK$18.5 billion, respectively.

Strategy

BOCHK's strategic goal is to "Build a Top-class, Full-service and Internationalised Regional Bank". Capitalising on its advantages as a major commercial banking group in Hong Kong, BOCHK aims to increase local market penetration and actively expand its business in the Southeast Asian region. The company strive to provide customers with comprehensive, professional and high-quality services. As one of the three note-issuing banks and the sole clearing bank for Renminbi ("RMB") business in Hong Kong, BOCHK has strong market positions in all major businesses. Its strong RMB franchise has made the company the first choice for customers in RMB business.

EXECUTIVES

Vice-Chairman, Chief Executive Officer, Executive Director, Yu Sun
Deputy Chief Executive, Haifeng Xu
Deputy Chief Executive, Man Chan
Chief Risk Officer, Xin Jiang
Chief Financial Officer, Chenggang Liu
Secretary, Nan Luo
Vice-Chairman, Non-Executive Director, Jin Liu
Independent Non-Executive Director, Eva Cheng
Independent Non-Executive Director, Koon Shum Choi
Independent Non-Executive Director, Anita Yuen Mei Fung
Independent Non-Executive Director, Beng Seng Koh
Independent Non-Executive Director, Quinn Yee Kwan Law
Independent Non-Executive Director, Sunny Wai Kwong Lee
Independent Non-Executive Director, Savio Wai-Hok Tung
Non-Executive Director, Jingzhen Lin
Auditors : PricewaterhouseCoopers

LOCATIONS

HQ: Boc Hong Kong Holdings Ltd
53rd Floor, Bank of China Tower, 1 Garden Road,
Phone: (852) 2846 2700   **Fax:** (852) 2810 5830
Web: www.bochk.com

PRODUCTS/OPERATIONS

2014 Sales

	% of total
Interest income	58
Fee and commission income	17
Gross earned premiums	20
Net trading gain	3
Others	2
Total	100

COMPETITORS

AUSTRALIA AND NEW ZEALAND BANKING GROUP LIMITED
BANK OF AYUDHYA PUBLIC COMPANY LIMITED
CHANG HWA COMMERCIAL BANK, LTD.
CIMB GROUP HOLDINGS BERHAD
HANG SENG BANK, LIMITED
HSBC HOLDINGS PLC
OVERSEA-CHINESE BANKING CORPORATION LIMITED
PUBLIC FINANCIAL HOLDINGS LIMITED
SINOPAC FINANCIAL HOLDINGS COMPANY LIMITED
UNITED OVERSEAS BANK LIMITED

HISTORICAL FINANCIALS

Company Type: Public

Income Statement — FYE: December 31

	ASSETS ($mil)	NET INCOME ($mil)	INCOME AS % OF ASSETS	EMPLOYEES
12/22	472,826	3,471	0.7%	14,832
12/21	466,704	2,945	0.6%	14,553
12/20	428,359	3,416	0.8%	14,915
12/19	388,613	4,133	1.1%	14,668
12/18	377,026	4,085	1.1%	14,046
Annual Growth	5.8%	(4.0%)	—	1.4%

2022 Year-End Financials

Return on assets: 0.7%
Return on equity: 8.3%
Long-term debt ($ mil.): —
No. of shares ($ mil.): 10,572
Sales ($ mil.): 12,574
Dividends
Yield: —
Payout: 870.5%
Market value ($ mil.): 717,046

	STOCK PRICE ($) FY Close	P/E High/Low		PER SHARE ($) Earnings	Dividends	Book Value
12/22	67.82	33	24	0.33	2.86	3.96
12/21	66.29	35	27	0.28	3.16	3.90
12/20	60.13	30	21	0.32	3.67	3.83
12/19	69.18	30	21	0.39	3.70	3.67
12/18	73.94	35	24	0.39	3.28	3.39
Annual Growth	(2.1%)	—	—	(4.0%)	(3.4%)	4.0%

Bouygues S.A.

Bouygues is the fifth largest construction group in the world. It is a diversified services group operating in markets with strong growth potential. Present in more than 80 countries, it provides a range of general and expert services to the group's business segments in areas such as finance, communication, sustainable development, patronage, new technologies, insurance, legal affairs, and human resources. Its road, buildings, and property development contracting services operate through Bouygues Construction, road builder Colas, and property developer Bouygues Immobilier. The group also owns around 90% stake in Bouygues Telecom. Bouygues' principal owners are brothers Martin and Oliver Bouygues and the company's employees. Bouygues generates the majority of its sales from France.

Operations

Bouygues is a diversified industrial group with five main business segments: Bouygues Construction, Colas, Bouygues Telecom, Bouygues Immobilier, and TF1.

Bouygues Construction, which accounts for almost 35% of sales, is a benchmark player in sustainable construction through the construction of many eco-neighborhoods, low-carbon buildings and structures certified against the best world eco-standards, as well as through rehabilitation of sites to reach positive-energy status.

Colas generates approximately 35%. Its three main activities are: roads, construction materials, and railways. It also includes transport of water and energy in France. Colas has significant additional construction materials production and recycling activities, which it operates via a network of quarries as well as emulsion, asphalt, and ready-mix concrete plants.

Bouygues Telecom accounts for nearly 20% of sales and has been providing the best technology to make its customer's digital lives richer and more intense. Its vocation is to provide high-quality networks, products and services adapted to the needs and expectations of its 25 million customers.

Bouygues Immobilier produces around 5% of sales and is one of France's leading property developers, developing residential, commercial, and office buildings.

TF1, which generates about 5% of sales, offers unique range if unencrypted and pay-TV content and services that responds to the people's new ways of consuming media.

Geographic Reach

Paris-based Bouygues' largest market is France, which accounts for approximately 60% of its total sales. Europe excluding France contributes almost 20% of total sales and Americas more than 10%. The firm is also active in Africa, the Asia Pacific region, Central America, and the Middle East. While the company does business in around 80 countries worldwide, it is mainly active in developed nations.

Sales and Marketing

The company serves a wide range of customers, from private and public TV channels to the streaming platforms. Bouygues Telecom provides high-quality networks, products and services tailored to the needs of approximately 26 million customers.

Financial Performance

Company's revenue for fiscal 2022 increased by 8% to EUR 37.6 billion compared from the prior year with EUR 34.7 billion.

Profit for fiscal 2021 increased to EUR 1.3 billion compared from the prior year with EUR 770 million.

Cash held by the company at the end of fiscal 2021 increased to EUR 6.2 billion. Cash provided by operations was EUR 3.6 billion while cash used for investing and financing activities were EUR 1.2 billion and EUR 284 million, respectively.

Strategy

The Bouygues group's business segments drive growth over the long term because they all meet essential needs, such as housing, transportation, generating and saving energy, bringing people closer together, communication, information and entertainment. Furthermore, their diversity helps cushion the impact of less positive business cycles, as the group proved throughout the Covid pandemic.

Bouygues also strives to maintain a robust financial structure in order to ensure its independence and preserve its model over time. For example, the company's construction businesses tie up a small amount of capital and generate a high level of cash. Bouygues' gearing, corresponding to net debt over shareholders' equity, stood at 7% at end-2021.

Mergers and Acquisitions

In 2021, Bouygues announced that a new milestone has been completed in the creation of a new global leader in multi-technical services, with the signing of the Equans share purchase agreement with Engie. The acquisition will accelerate Bouygues' development in the strong growth potential multi-technical services sector, at the convergence between the energy, digital and industrial transitions.

Company Background

HISTORY

With the equivalent of $1,700 in borrowed money, Francis Bouygues, son of a Paris engineer, started Entreprise Francis Bouygues in 1952 as an industrial works and construction firm in the Paris region of France. Within four years his firm had expanded into property development.

By the mid-1960s Bouygues had entered the civil engineering and public works sectors and developed regional construction units across France. In 1970 it was listed on the Paris stock exchange. Four years later the company established Bouygues Offshore to build oil platforms.

In 1978 the firm built Terminal 2 of Paris' Charles de Gaulle airport. Three years later it won the contract to construct the University of Riyadh in Saudi Arabia (then the world's largest building project at 3.2 million sq. ft.), which was completed in 1984. That year Bouygues acquired France's #3 water supply company, Saur, and power transmission and supply firm ETDE.

Expansion continued in 1986 with the purchase of the Screg Group, which included Colas, France's top highway contractor. The next year the company led a consortium to buy 50% of newly privatized network Société Télévision Française 1 (TF1). Bouygues became the largest shareholder with a 25% stake (increased to 40% by 1999). In 1988 the company began building the Channel Tunnel (completed 1994) and moved into its new ultramodern headquarters, dubbed Challenger, in Saint-Quentin-en-Yvelines, outside Paris.

After rumors of failing health, Francis Bouygues resigned as chairman in 1989. His son Martin took over as chairman and CEO, although the patriarch, called France's "Emperor of Concrete," remained on the board until his death in 1993.

Despite fears that the group would suffer without its founder's leadership, Bouygues continued to grow with the 1989 acquisition of a majority interest in Grands Moulins de Paris, France's largest flour milling firm (sold 1998). In 1990 it purchased Swiss construction group Losinger.

The company entered the telecom industry in 1993 with a national paging network and added a mobile phone license a year later. In 1996 the group listed 40% of Bouygues Offshore's shares on the New York and Paris stock exchanges. Also that year it launched mobile phone operator Bouygues Telecom and entered a partnership with Telecom Italia.

By 1999 Bouygues Telecom had reached 2 million customers, and Bouygues bought back a 20% share held by the UK's Cable and Wireless to increase its stake to nearly 54%. That year Bouygues Offshore bought Norwegian engineering firm Kvaerner, and the group spun off its construction sector, creating Bouygues Construction.

After word circulated that Deutsche Telekom wanted to acquire the group's telecom unit, Bouygues became the target of takeover rumors. Francois Pinault, France's richest businessman, became Bouygues' largest non-family shareholder when he increased his stake to 14% (later reduced to about 2%). Pinault's biggest rival, Bernard Arnault, upped his stake to more than 9% of the group, fueling speculation of a battle over control of the board.

In 2001 the company pulled out of France's auction for a third-generation wireless license and remained the only European incumbent mobile carrier without a major domestic investment in 3G technology (until 2009). The next year the company agreed to buy Telecom Italia's stake in Bouygues Telecom, increasing Bouygues' ownership in the mobile operator from 54% to more than 65%. In 2002 the company sold its 51% stake in oil field platform construction unit Bouygues Offshore to Italian oil services group Saipem, which announced plans to bid for the remaining shares.

However, talks with German utility giant E.ON over the sale of Bouygues' Saur subsidiary failed that year, after E.ON decided to focus instead on its electricity and gas operations.

In 2005 Bouygues was more successful when it sought to sell Saur piecemeal. It sold several divisions of the subsidiary (Coved, Saur France, Saur International, and Stereau) to French private equity firm PAI Partners but retained the African and Italian (Sigesa-Crea) divisions of the firm.

Bouygues bought the French government's 21% stake in ALSTOM for $2.5 billion in 2006. The deal was approved on the condition that it not try to control the company for at least three years. Bouygues did build up its holding after the acquisition, though, eventually holding 29% of the shares.

In 2008 property developer Bouygues Immobilier expanded with the acquisition of Urbis, a French rival. That year Colas bought the Gouyer Group of companies (distribution of construction materials) in Martinique and Guadeloupe, while Bouygues Telecom acquired a fixed-line network that allowed it to launch the Bbox broadband router and Internet services that include VoIP, e-mail, Internet access, and television; the telecom unit also gained the previously denied right to offer the iPhone 3G.

EXECUTIVES

Chief Executive Officer, Olivier Roussat
Deputy Chief Executive, Director, Edward Bouygues
Deputy Chief Executive, Chief Financial Officer, Pascal Grange
Human Resources Senior Vice President,
Human Resources Director, Jean-Manuel Soussan
Chairman, Director, Martin Bouygues
Non-Independent External Director, Alexandre De Rothschild
Independent Director, Pascaline de Dreuzy
Independent Director, Clara Gaymard
Independent Director, Colette Lewiner
Independent Director, Benoit Maes
Independent Director, Rose-Marie Van Lerberghe
Director, Olivier Bouygues
Director, Cyril Bouygues
Director, Bernard Allain
Director, Beatrice Besombes
Director, Raphaelle Deflesselle
Director, Michele Vilain
Auditors : Mazars

LOCATIONS

HQ: Bouygues S.A.
   32 avenue Hoche, Paris 75008
Phone: (33) 1 44 20 10 00
Web: www.bouygues.com

2018 Sales

	% of total
Europe	
France	61
European Union	11
Other countries	5
North America	11
Asia-Pacific	5
Africa	3
Central and South America	1
Middle East	1
Oceania	3
Total	100

PRODUCTS/OPERATIONS

2018 Sales

	% of total
Colas	37
Bouygues Construction	34
Bouygues Telecom	15
Bouygues Immobilier	8
TF1	6
Total	100

Selected Subsidiaries and Affiliates

Construction
   Autoroute de liaison Seine-Sarthe SA (33%)
   Bouygues Bâtiment Ile-de-France SA (99.9%)
   Bati-Rénov SA (99.3%)
   Bouygues Bâtiment International SA (99.9%)
   Bouygues Thai Ltd (49%)
   DTP Singapour Pte Ltd (99.9%)
   Kohler Investment SA (Luxembourg, 99.9%)
   Bouygues Construction SA (99.9%)
   ETDE SA (99.9%)
   Exprimm IT (99.9%)
   Icel Maidstone Ltd (UK, 99.9%)
   Quille SA (99.9%)
   Westminster Local Education Partnership Ltd (UK, 80%)
Media
   Métro France Publications (15%)
   Télévision Française 1 SA (TF1, 43%)
   TF1 Vidéo (43%)
   TV Breizh (43%)
Property
   Bouygues Immobilier
   Parque Empresearial Cristalia SL
   SNC Bouygues Immobilier Entreprises Île-de-France
Roads
   Cofiroute (16%)
   Colas Guadeloupe (97%)
   Colas Hungaria (97%)
   Colas Polska (97%)
   Colas SA (96%)
   Spac (97%)
Telecommunications
   Bouygues Telecom SA (90%)

COMPETITORS

ACCIONA, SA
ACS, ACTIVIDADES DE CONSTRUCCION Y SERVICIOS, SA
CAPGEMINI
EIFFAGE
FERROVIAL SA
ORANGE
STRABAG SE
TELECOM ITALIA O TIM SPA
TELEFONICA, SA
VINCI

HISTORICAL FINANCIALS

Company Type: Public

Income Statement FYE: December 31

	REVENUE ($mil)	NET INCOME ($mil)	NET PROFIT MARGIN	EMPLOYEES
12/21	42,607	1,273	3.0%	124,651
12/20	42,660	854	2.0%	129,018
12/19	42,676	1,329	3.1%	130,450
12/18	40,929	1,501	3.7%	129,275
12/17	39,623	1,300	3.3%	119,836
Annual Growth	1.8%	(0.5%)	—	1.0%

2021 Year-End Financials

Debt ratio: 19.0%
Return on equity: 10.4%
Cash ($ mil.): 7,358
Current Ratio: 1.04
Long-term debt ($ mil.): 6,570
No. of shares ($ mil.): 382
Dividends
Yield: 7.1%
Payout: 7.4%
Market value ($ mil.): 2,772

	STOCK PRICE ($) FY Close	P/E High/Low		PER SHARE ($) Earnings	Dividends	Book Value
12/21	7.25	3	2	3.34	0.52	32.99
12/20	8.50	5	4	2.25	0.26	33.33
12/19	8.40	3	2	3.56	0.23	30.76
12/18	7.94	3	2	4.07	0.24	29.94
12/17	6.56	—	—	3.61	0.24	28.98
Annual Growth	2.5%	—	—	(1.9%)	21.7%	3.3%

BP PLC

BP is one of the largest oil and gas companies in the world. The company explores, produces, and sells oil and gas, fuels, lubricants, wind power, and biofuels. BP's main brands include the eponymous BP brand, which appears on rigs, offices, and gas stations, gas station-specific brands Amoco (US) and Aral (Germany), lubricant brand Castrol, and gas station convenience store brands ampm and Wild Bean CafÃ©. The company's reportable segments are now gas & low carbon energy, oil production & operations, customers & products, and Rosneft. It has operations throughout the world, but generates most of its revenue from outside of the US.

Operations

BP has four major operating segments: Customers & Products (over 80% of sales), Gas & Low Carbon Energy (more than 15%), Oil Production & Operations, and Rosneft.

The Customers & Products segment comprises its customer-focused businesses, spanning convenience and mobility, which includes fuels retail and next-gen offers such as electrification, as well as aviation, midstream, and Castrol lubricant. It also includes its oil products businesses, refining & trading.

The Gas & Low Carbon Energy segment comprises regions with upstream business that predominantly produce natural gas, gas marketing and trading activities and the company's solar, wind, and hydrogen businesses.

The Oil Production & Operations segment comprises regions with upstream activities that predominantly produce crude oil.

The Rosneft segment was unchanged and continues to include equity-accounted earnings from the company's investment in Rosneft.

Overall, oil products generate about 65% of sales, followed by natural gas, LNG and NGLs with some 15%, crude oil, non-oil products and other revenues from contracts with customers, and other operating revenues account for the rest.

Geographic Reach

Headquartered in London, BP has LNG activities located in Abu Dhabi, Angola, Australia, Indonesia, and Trinidad. In Europe, BP is active in the North Sea and the Norwegian Sea. In addition, BP also has activities in Abu Dhabi, Azerbaijan, China, India, Indonesia, Iraq, Kuwait, Oman, and Russia.

Its upstream activities in Americas are located in deepwater Gulf of Mexico, the Lower 48 states, Canada, and Mexico. It also has oil and gas activities in Argentina, Brazil and Trinidad & Tobago and through PAEG, a joint venture that is owned by BP (50%) and Bridas Corporation (50%), in Argentina, Bolivia, and Uruguay. Furthermore, the company also has activities in Africa strategically located in Algeria, Angola, CÃ´te d'Ivoire, Egypt, The Gambia, Libya, Mauritania, SÃ£o TomÃ© & PrÃncipe, and Senegal.

In terms of revenue, the US is the company's largest market, generating about 35% of total revenue.

Sales and Marketing

BP primarily sells oil and gas through pipelines and by ship, truck and rail, serving more than 12 million retail customers, including end-use consumers, B2B customers, and distributors.

Major company brands include eponymous BP, as well as AMOCO, ampm, Aral, and Castrol. With more than 2.5 million customers visit an Aral service station, Aral is one of the most recognized brands in Germany, while BP and Castrol are leading brands of motor oil and lubricants. The US retail brand ampm has more than 1,000 locations throughout the US west coast.

Financial Performance

The company's revenue in 2021 increased to $157.7 billion compared from the prior year with $105.9 billion. Revenue in 2021 were higher due to higher gas marketing and trading revenues, higher realizations, and higher production.

Net income in 2021 was $15.2 billion compared to a net loss of $24.9 billion in the prior year.

Cash held by the company at the end of 2021 decreased to $30.7 billion. Operating activities provided $23.6 billion while investing and financing activities used $5.7 billion and $18.1 billion, respectively. Main cash uses were expenditure on property, plant and equipment, intangible and other assets; and repayments of long-term financing.

Strategy

The company is focused on performing while transforming to: grow value and returns; deliver compelling distributions; and invest in the energy transition and drive down emissions.

It is driving returns, high-grading its portfolio and lowering the company's emissions, through three focus areas: oil and gas, refining and bioenergy. As the world seeks lower carbon fuels, the company sees opportunities to leverage its portfolio of assets and customer base ? with bioenergy as one of its transition growth engines.

Mergers and Acquisitions

In late 2022, BP acquired Archaea Energy, a leading provider of renewable natural gas (RNG), marking a milestone in the growth of the company's strategic bioenergy business. "We see enormous opportunity to grow our bioenergy business by bringing Archaea fully into bp," said Dave Lawler, chairman and president bp America. "The talent, expertise and passion of their team has let them achieve incredible growth so far, and we're excited to support the next chapter in line with our strategy." Together with around $800 million net debt, the total enterprise value is approximately $4.1 billion.

Company Background

BP's history dates back to efforts of British companies to capitalize on discoveries of rich oil deposits in Middle East in the late 19th and early 20th Centuries. These included the Anglo-Persian Oil Company (later the Anglo-Iranian Oil Company), in which the British Government took a majority share in 1914. It became British Petroleum in 1954, and, following a number of other acquisitions, became BP in 2000. BP's modern history is marked by the 2010 Deepwater Horizon disaster, a massive spill in the Gulf of Mexico that resulted in the highest fines and penalties in the history of the US.

EXECUTIVES

Chairman, Helge Lund

Chief Executive Officer, Executive Director, Bernard Looney

Finance Chief Financial Officer, Executive Director, Murray Auchincloss

Customers and Products Executive Vice President, Emma Delaney

Gas and low carbon energy Executive Vice President, Anja Dotzenrath

Regions, corporates and solutions Executive Vice President, William Lin

Innovation and Engineering Executive Vice President, Leigh-Ann Russell

Production & Operations Executive Vice President, Production, Transformation and Carbon Executive Vice President, Gordon Birrell

Trading and shipping Executive Vice President, Carol Howle

Strategy, sustainability and ventures Executive Vice President, Giulia Chierchia

People and Culture Executive Vice President, Kerry Dryburgh

Legal Executive Vice President, Eric Nitcher

Secretary, Ben J.S. Mathews

Senior Independent Non-Executive Director, Paula Rosput Reynolds

Independent Non-Executive Director, Hina Nagarajan

Independent Non-Executive Director, Pamela Daley

Independent Non-Executive Director, Melody Meyer

Independent Non-Executive Director, Tushar Morzaria

Independent Non-Executive Director, Karen A. Richardson

Independent Non-Executive Director, John Sawers

Independent Non-Executive Director, Johannes Teyssen

Independent Non-Executive Director, Amanda Blanc

Independent Non-Executive Director, Satish Pai

Auditors : Deloitte LLP

LOCATIONS

HQ: BP PLC
  1 St. James's Square, London SW1Y 4PD
Phone: (44) 20 7496 4000   Fax: (44) 20 7496 4630
Web: www.bp.com

2018 Sales

	% of total
US	33
Other countries	67
Total	100

PRODUCTS/OPERATIONS

2018 Sales

	% of total
Downstream	91
Upstream	9
Other businesses and corporate	—
Total	100

Major Operations
Refining and marketing
   Marketing
   Refining
   Supply and trading
   Transportation and shipping
Exploration and production
   Field development
   Gas processing and marketing
   Oil and gas exploration
   Pipelines and transportation
Gas and power
   Natural gas marketing and trading
   Natural gas liquids
Chemicals
   Chemical intermediates
   Feedstock
   Performance products
   Polymers
Other
   Coal mining
   Solar power

Selected Subsidiaries
Atlantic Richfield Co
BP America Inc. (US)
BP Amoco Chemcal Company (US)
BP Oil Australia
BP Exploration Operating Company
BP Espa?a (Spain)
BP International
BP Norge (Norway)
BP Oil New Zealand
BP Shipping
BP Southern Africa (South Africa)
Burmah Castrol
The Standard Oil Company (US)

COMPETITORS

Alfa, S.A.B. de C.V.
CHEVRON CORPORATION
CONOCOPHILLIPS
EG GROUP LIMITED
Equinor ASA
IBERDROLA, SOCIEDAD ANONIMA
OPHIR ENERGY LIMITED
REPSOL SA.
SASOL LTD
TOTAL SE

HISTORICAL FINANCIALS
Company Type: Public

Income Statement   FYE: December 31

	REVENUE ($mil)	NET INCOME ($mil)	NET PROFIT MARGIN	EMPLOYEES
12/23	211,397	15,239	7.2%	87,800
12/22	245,025	(2,487)	—	66,300
12/21	162,319	7,565	4.7%	65,900
12/20	180,626	(20,305)	—	63,600
12/19	282,423	4,026	1.4%	70,100
Annual Growth	(7.0%)	39.5%		5.8%

2023 Year-End Financials

Debt ratio: 18.5%   No. of shares ($ mil.): 16,823
Return on equity: 22.1%   Dividends
Cash ($ mil.): 33,030   Yield: —
Current Ratio: 1.21   Payout: 191.6%
Long-term debt ($ mil.): 48,670   Market value ($ mil.): 595,560

	STOCK PRICE ($) FY Close	P/E High	P/E Low	Earnings	Dividends	Book Value
12/23	35.40	47	38	0.86	1.65	4.18
12/22	34.93	—	—	(0.13)	1.36	3.76
12/21	26.63	80	55	0.37	1.27	3.84
12/20	20.52	—	—	(1.00)	1.87	3.52
12/19	37.74	228	182	0.20	2.44	4.86
Annual Growth	(1.6%)	—	—	44.4%	(9.4%)	(3.7%)

Braskem S A

Braskem is a South American giant, the continent's largest petrochemical company. The company is part of the chemical and petrochemical industry, which has a significant share in several supply chains and is essential for economic development. It is the only integrated petrochemical company for the first and second generation of thermoplastic resins in Brazil. Braskem produces thermoplastic resins (polyethylene, polypropylene, and polyvinyl Chloride). The company also makes aromatics like benzene, ethylene, propylene, and butadiene. It has five polypropylene plants in the US and two polypropylene plants in Germany. Brazil accounts for the majority of its sales.

Operations

Braskem has a broad and diversified portfolio of chemical and petrochemical products. The company has a global installed capacity of approximately 21.4 million tons per year.

The company's business operations were organized into three segments, which corresponded to its principal production processes, products, and services.

Brazil segment includes production and sale of chemicals at the chemical complex; supply of electricity and other inputs produced in these complexes to second-generation producers located in the petrochemical complexes; production and sale of PE, including the production of "green PE" from renewable resources, and PP produced by the company in Brazil; and production and sale of PVC and caustic soda. The USA and Europe segment includes its production, operations, and sale of polypropylene. Mexico segment includes the company's production, operations, and sale of ethylene, HDPE (high-density polyethylene), and LDPE (low-density polyethylene) in Mexico.

By products, PE/PP accounts for about 70% of the company's revenue. Ethylene, propylene; naphtha, condensate and crude oil; benzene, toluene and xylene; PVC/caustic soda/ EDC; ETBE/gasoline; butadiene; cumene; solvents; and other products represent the remaining.

Geographic Reach

Headquartered I Brazil, the company operates industrial units installed in Brazil, US, Mexico, and Germany. Brazil accounts for about 65% of sales, while other major markets and other countries (including US, Europe, and Mexico) account for nearly 35%. The company operates in and sells its products into several countries, such as Brazil, Argentina, Colombia, Chile, the US, Germany, Netherlands, Mexico, and Singapore.

Sales and Marketing

The company serves customers in markets and sectors including food packaging, adhesives, agribusiness, rubber, fuel, construction, industrial, retail, automotive, personal care and cleaning, agribusiness, and health, among others.

Financial Performance

The company's revenue for fiscal 2021 increased to R$105.6 billion compared from the prior year with R$58.5 billion.

Profit for fiscal 2021 increased to R$18.0 billion compared from the prior year with a loss of R$9.7 billion.

Cash held by the company at the end of fiscal 2021 decreased to R$8.7 billion. Cash provided by operations was R$20.4 billion while cash used for investing and financing activities were R$3.4 billion and R$17.0 billion, respectively.

Strategy

The key pillars of Braskem's strategy include: grow renewables and recycling; grow the existing business with productivity and competitiveness; continue to innovate; strengthen its governance; and responsible capital allocation and shareholder remuneration.

The company intend to continue to invest in its current business to maintain productivity and competitiveness, focusing on operational efficiency and excellence, commercial and logistics effectiveness, cost leadership, and differentiation through its relationships with clients.

Mergers and Acquisitions

In mid-2022, Braskem entered into an agreement for the acquisition of shares and the subscription of new shares in Wise Plãsticos S.A., a company engaged in mechanical recycling. Braskem will acquire an equity interest of 61.1% in the share capital of Wise for an estimated amount of R$121 million. The transaction represents yet another step by Braskem in its strategy to invest in the circular economy by developing sustainable and innovative solutions based on opportunities to improve the plastics recycling chain, which includes the challenge of recycling in Brazil.

EXECUTIVES

Chief Executive Officer, Director, Roberto Lopes Pontes Simoes
Chief Financial Officer, Pedro van Langendonck Teixeira de Freitas
Executive Officer, Edison Terra Filho
Executive Officer, Marcelo Arantes de Carvalho
Executive Officer, Marcelo de Oliveira Cerqueira
Executive Officer, Daniel Sales Correa
Chairman, Jose Mauro Mettrau Carneiro da Cunha
Vice-Chairman, Joao Cox Neto
Independent Director, Gesner Jose de Oliveira Filho
Independent Director, Paulo Roberto Vales de Souza
Independent Director, Julio Soares de Moura Neto
Independent Director, Andrea da Motta Chamma
Director, Roberto Faldini
Director, Joao Pinheiro Nogueira Batista
Director, Rogerio Bautista da Nova Moreira
Director, Marcelo Klujsza
Auditors : KPMG Auditores Independentes Ltda.

LOCATIONS

HQ: Braskem S A
Rua Lemos Monteiro, 120 – 24º andar, Butanta, Sao Paulo 05501-050
Phone: (55) 11 3576 9000   **Fax:** (55) 11 3576 9532
Web: www.braskem.com.br

2014 Sales

	% of total
Brazil	57
United States	20
Other countries	23
Total	100

PRODUCTS/OPERATIONS

2014 Sales

	% of total
Basic Petrochemicals	45
Polyolefins	33
USA and Europe	14
Vinyls	5
Chemical Distribution and others	3
Total	100

Selected Products

Basic Petrochemicals
    Benzene
    Butadiene
    Butene-1
    Ethylene
    Isoprene
    Mixed xylene
    Ortho-xylene
    Para-xylene
    Propylene
    Toluene
    Methyl tertiary-butyl ether (MTBE)
Polyolefins
    Polyethylene
    Polyethylene terephthalate (PET)
    Polyvinyl chloride (PVC)

COMPETITORS

AJINOMOTO CO., INC.
ARKEMA
CALAVO GROWERS, INC.
LyondellBasell Industries N.V.
MEDIFAST, INC.
SAMWORTH BROTHERS (HOLDINGS) LIMITED
SENSIENT TECHNOLOGIES CORPORATION
TERRAVIA HOLDINGS, INC.
TRINSEO S.A.
VISCOFAN SA

HISTORICAL FINANCIALS

Company Type: Public

Income Statement   FYE: December 31

	REVENUE ($mil)	NET INCOME ($mil)	NET PROFIT MARGIN	EMPLOYEES
12/22	18,252	(63)	—	8,668
12/21	18,953	2,509	13.2%	8,312
12/20	11,272	(1,288)	—	7,993
12/19	13,016	(632)	—	7,940
12/18	14,944	728	4.9%	8,008
Annual Growth	5.1%	—	—	2.0%

2022 Year-End Financials

Debt ratio: 10.1%   No. of shares ($ mil.): 451
Return on equity: (-4.4%)   Dividends
Cash ($ mil.): 2,357   Yield: —
Current Ratio: 1.42   Payout: 0.0%
Long-term debt ($ mil.): 8,478   Market value ($ mil.): 4,155

	STOCK PRICE ($) FY Close	P/E High/Low		PER SHARE ($) Earnings	Dividends	Book Value
12/22	9.20	—	—	(0.08)	0.56	3.07
12/21	21.09	1	0	3.15	2.59	3.13
12/20	9.01	—	—	(1.62)	0.00	(0.94)
12/19	14.80	—	—	(0.79)	0.37	2.69
12/18	24.46	9	6	0.92	1.77	3.73
Annual Growth	(21.7%)	—	—	—	(25.0%)	(4.8%)

Brenntag SE

EXECUTIVES

Chief Transformation Officer, Ewout van Jarwaarde
Chief Financial Officer, Kristin Neumann
Chief Executive Officer, Christian Kohlpaintner
Chief Operating Officer, Henri Nejade
Chief Operating Officer, Steven Terwindt
Independent Director, Chairwoman, Doreen Nowotne
Independent Director, Deputy Chairman, Andreas Rittstieg
Director, Stefanie Berlinger
Director, Wijnand P. Donkers
Director, Ulrich M. Harnacke
Director, Richard Ridinger
Auditors : PricewaterhouseCoopers GmbH Wirtschaftsprufungsgesellschaft

LOCATIONS

HQ: Brenntag SE
Messeallee 11, Essen 45131
Phone: (49) 201 6496 2100   **Fax:** (49) 201 6496 2003
Web: www.brenntag.de

HISTORICAL FINANCIALS

Company Type: Public

Income Statement   FYE: December 31

	REVENUE ($mil)	NET INCOME ($mil)	NET PROFIT MARGIN	EMPLOYEES
12/21	16,279	507	3.1%	17,236
12/20	14,452	572	4.0%	17,237
12/19	14,395	523	3.6%	17,492
12/18	14,372	527	3.7%	16,616
12/17	14,077	432	3.1%	15,416
Annual Growth	3.7%	4.1%	—	2.8%

2021 Year-End Financials

Debt ratio: 25.6%   No. of shares ($ mil.): 154
Return on equity: 12.0%   Dividends
Cash ($ mil.): 797   Yield: 1.1%
Current Ratio: 1.41   Payout: 6.0%
Long-term debt ($ mil.): 1,845   Market value ($ mil.): 2,792

	STOCK PRICE ($) FY Close	P/E High/Low		PER SHARE ($) Earnings	Dividends	Book Value
12/21	18.07	7	5	3.27	0.21	28.68
12/20	15.76	5	2	3.71	0.18	28.20
12/19	10.80	4	3	3.39	0.17	25.55
12/18	8.71	4	3	3.41	0.17	24.29
12/17	12.60	6	4	2.81	0.16	23.07
Annual Growth	9.4%	—	—	3.9%	6.8%	5.6%

BRF S.A.

EXECUTIVES

Chief Executive Officer, Lorival Nogueira Luz
Chief Financial Officer, Chief Investor Relations Officer, Carlos Alberto Bezerra de Moura
Operations and Procurement Officer, Vinicius Guimaraes Barbosa

Comercial Brazil Market Vice President, Sidney Rogerio Manzaro
Human Resources and Shared Services Vice President, Alessandro Rosa Bonorino
Quality and Sustainability Vice President, Neil Hamilton dos Guimaraes Peixoto
Sales & Operations Planning and Supply Chain Vice President, Leonardo Campo Dall'Orto
Chairman, Pedro Pullen Parente
Vice-Chairman, Director, Augusto Marques da Cruz Filho
Director, Dan Ioschpe
Director, Flavia Buarque de Almeida
Director, Flavia Maria Bittencourt
Director, Jose Luiz Osorio
Director, Luiz Fernando Furlan
Director, Ivandre Montiel da Silva
Director, Marcelo Feriozzi Bacci
Director, Roberto Rodrigues
Auditors : KPMG Auditores Independentes Ltda.

LOCATIONS

HQ: BRF S.A.
Av. das Nacoes Unidas, 14.401 - 22nd to 25th Floors, Torre A2, Condominio Parque da Cidade, Vila Gertrudes, Sao Paulo 04794-000
Phone: (55) 11 2322 5005   Fax: (55) 11 2322 5740
Web: www.brf-global.com

HISTORICAL FINANCIALS

Company Type: Public

Income Statement
FYE: December 31

	REVENUE ($mil)	NET INCOME ($mil)	NET PROFIT MARGIN	EMPLOYEES
12/22	10,174	(598)	—	96,259
12/21	8,674	75	0.9%	100,176
12/20	7,599	292	3.8%	101,002
12/19	8,320	40	0.5%	92,842
12/18	7,778	(1,146)	—	105,621
Annual Growth	6.9%	—	—	(2.3%)

2022 Year-End Financials

Debt ratio: 7.7%
Return on equity: (-32.0%)
Cash ($ mil.): 1,537
Current Ratio: 1.19
Long-term debt ($ mil.): 3,713
No. of shares ($ mil.): 1,078
Dividends
Yield: —
Payout: 0.0%
Market value ($ mil.): 1,703

	STOCK PRICE ($) FY Close	P/E High/Low	PER SHARE ($) Earnings	Dividends	Book Value
12/22	1.58	— —	(0.57)	0.00	1.98
12/21	4.09	10 7	0.09	0.00	1.88
12/20	4.20	4 1	0.36	0.00	2.05
12/19	8.70	48 23	0.05	0.00	2.38
12/18	5.68	— —	(1.41)	0.00	2.21
Annual Growth	(27.4%)		—	—	(2.8%)

Bridgestone Corp (Japan)

Founded in 1931, Bridgestone is one rolling stone that gathers no moss. Vying with Michelin to be the world's largest tire maker, Bridgestone makes tires for a variety of vehicle types. In addition to passenger and commercial vehicle tires, the company makes tires for construction and mining vehicles, agricultural machinery, and aircraft. It also manufactures a range of non-tire products, including consumer products like golf balls and bicycles, polyurethane foam for industrial applications, and adhesive film for the solar industry. Bridgestone operates approximately 160 production and development bases in more than 150 countries throughout the world. It generates nearly 50% of revenue from the Americas.

Operations

Its tire business offers tires and tubes for passenger cars, trucks, buses, aircraft, construction and off-road mining vehicles, industrial and agricultural machinery, motorcycles, scooters and other vehicles. Its solution business offers tire-centric solutions and retail & service: Business to provide added value to products through product and tire-related data. Moreover, its Diversified Products Business offers Chemical and industrial products: Industrial rubber products, building materials, hoses and other products.

Geographic Reach

Based in Japan, Bridgestone operates through about 160 manufacturing plants and development facilities. It sells its products in more than 150 countries worldwide. The Americas is Bridgestone's largest market, generating nearly 45% of total sales. Other major markets include Japan (over 25%), Europe (20%), China/Asia Pacific (over 10%).

Financial Performance

Note: Growth rates may differ after conversion to US Dollars.

The company's revenue has fluctuated over the last five years. Its revenue declined about 11% between 2017 and 2021.

Meanwhile, the company's revenue increased by about 8% to Â¥3.3 trillion in 2021 from Â¥3.0 trillion in 2020 after recording sales increase in all its geographic location except in China and Asia Pacific.

Free cash flow at the end of fiscal year 2021 was Â¥413.2 billion. Operations provided Â¥281.5 million while investing activities provided another Â¥131.7 billion.

Strategy

Bridgestone plans to invest Â¥700 billion in strategic resources by 2023 to evolve into a "strong" Bridgestone with an "aggressive approach" and "challenging" spirit. This includes investments of Â¥350 billion each in strategic investments and expenses and in M&A, corporate venture capital (CVC), strategic partnership, and other co-creation activities.

It further strengthens its core businesses while balancing strategic growth investments for expansion of growth businesses and in exploratory business, and skillfully scrutinizes and invests in business opportunities. In 2021, the company strengthened the premium business strategy in its core business, while executing strategic growth investments to support the expansion of its solutions business.

To accelerate further growth looking ahead to 2030 and beyond in line with the "Bridgestone E8 Commitment," it is "laying foundations for future growth," executing strategic growth investments focused around the tire business (core business) and the solutions business (growth business). In the tire business, Bridgestone is building and implementing the ENLITEN business strategy as the core of its new tire business strategy. Until now, it has been expanding ENLITEN as an innovative tire technology optimized for EVs.

Company Background

In 1906 Shojiro Ishibashi and his brother Tokujiro assumed control of the family's clothing business. They focused on making tabi, traditional Japanese footwear, and in 1923 began working with rubber for soles. In 1931 Shojiro formed Bridgestone to make tires and during that decade the company began producing auto tires, airplane tires, and golf balls.

HISTORY

In 1906 Shojiro Ishibashi and his brother Tokujiro assumed control of the family's clothing business. They focused on making tabi, traditional Japanese footwear, and in 1923 began working with rubber for soles. In 1931 Shojiro formed Bridgestone (Ishibashi means "stone bridge" in Japanese) to make tires, and during that decade the company began producing auto tires, airplane tires, and golf balls. Bridgestone followed the Japanese military to occupied territories, where it built plants. The company's headquarters moved to Tokyo in 1937.

Although Bridgestone lost all of its overseas factories during WWII, its Japanese plants escaped damage. The company began making bicycles in 1946 and signed a technical assistance pact with Goodyear five years later, enabling Bridgestone to import badly needed technology. In the 1950s and 1960s, Bridgestone started making nylon tires and radials and again set up facilities overseas, mostly elsewhere in Asia. The company benefited from the rapid growth in Japanese auto sales in the 1970s. Shojiro died at age 87 in 1976.

EXECUTIVES

Representative Executive Officer, Global Chief Executive Officer, Director, Shuichi Ishibashi
Representative Executive Officer, Joint Global Chief Operating Officer, Director, Masahiro Higashi
Joint Global Chief Operating Officer, Executive Officer, Paolo Ferrari

Senior Managing Director, Global Chief Technology Officer, Executive Officer, Masato Banno
Outside Director, Scott Trevor Davis
Outside Director, Yuri Okina
Outside Director, Kenichi Masuda
Outside Director, Kenzo Yamamoto
Outside Director, Yojiro Shiba
Outside Director, Yoko Suzuki
Outside Director, Yukari Kobayashi
Outside Director, Yasuhiro Nakajima
Director, Akira Matsuda
Director, Tsuyoshi Yoshimi
Auditors : Deloitte Touche Tohmatsu LLC

LOCATIONS

HQ: Bridgestone Corp (Japan)
 3-1-1 Kyobashi, Chuo-ku, Tokyo 104-8340
Phone: (81) 3 6836 3162   Fax: 615 937-3621
Web: www.bridgestone.co.jp

2018 Sales

	% of total
The Americas	47
Japan	19
Europe, Russia, the Middle East and Africa	18
Other	16
Total	100

PRODUCTS/OPERATIONS

2018 Sales

	% of total
Tires	83
Diversified products	17
Total	100

Selected Products

Tires and tubes
  Bridgestone tires
  Firestone tires
  Primewell tires
  Fuzion tires
  Agricultural
  Aircraft
  Buses
  Cars
  Trucks
  Commercial vehicles
  Construction and mining vehicles
  Motorcycles
Diversified products
  Bicycles, bicycle tires and accessories
  Chemical and industrial
  Adhesive and anti-reflective film for glass and flat-panel displays
  Conveyor belts
  Electronic paper for still image display
  High-performance films
  Hydraulic hoses
  Marine fenders
  Panel type water tank
  Polyurethane foam
  Rubber tracks
  Seismic isolators
  Single crystal wafers for semiconductor devices
  Roofing and wall systems
  Rubber lining, flashing and membrane
  Golf clubs
  Sporting goods
  Golf balls
  Golf clubs
  Services
  Fleet management
  Maintenance and repair
  Consumer credit

HISTORICAL FINANCIALS

Company Type: Public

Income Statement   FYE: December 31

	REVENUE ($mil)	NET INCOME ($mil)	NET PROFIT MARGIN	EMPLOYEES
12/22	31,191	2,279	7.3%	129,262
12/21	28,199	3,423	12.1%	135,636
12/20	29,053	(226)	—	138,036
12/19	32,473	2,695	8.3%	143,589
12/18	33,192	2,652	8.0%	143,509
Annual Growth	(1.5%)	(3.7%)	—	(2.6%)

2022 Year-End Financials

Debt ratio: 0.1%
Return on equity: 10.7%
Cash ($ mil.): 3,937
Current Ratio: 2.31
Long-term debt ($ mil.): 2,622
No. of shares ($ mil.): 684
Dividends
 Yield: —
 Payout: 40.5%
Market value ($ mil.): —

British American Tobacco Plc

British American Tobacco (BAT) is a leading consumer-centric, multi-category consumer goods company that provides tobacco and nicotine products to millions of consumers worldwide. The company sold approximately 637 billion cigarette sticks and some 18 billion OPT a year, sold in more than 175 markets across more than 50 countries. BAT sells five global cigarette brands (including Dunhill, Kent, Rothmans, Lucky Strike, and Pall Mall). The company is a leading FTSE company with truly international credentials. The company operates across the US; Americas and Sub-Saharan Africa; Europe and North Africa; and Asia-Pacific and Middle East. Additionally, BAT owns Reynolds American. Most of BAT's revenue comes from the US.

Operations

British American Tobacco (BAT) offers combustible portfolio (including but not limited to Kent, Dunhill, Lucky Strike, Pall Mall, Rothmans, Camel (US), Newport (US), Natural American Spirit (US)) which accounts for about 85% of sales; new category portfolio (being Vapour, THP, and Modern Oral) which accounts for about 10%, and the company's traditional oral portfolio accounts for around 5%.

Geographic Reach

Based in London, UK, BAT operates more than 40 cigarette factories in approximately 40 countries. The US is its largest market, accounting for about 45% of sales, followed by Europe and North Africa at about 25% of sales, Asia/Pacific and Middle East at about 15% of sales, and Americas and Sub-Saharan Africa at approximately 15% of sales.

Sales and Marketing

BAT sells its products through more than 175 markets with over 11 million points of sale, reaching more than 150 million consumers daily.

Financial Performance

Revenue declined 0.4% to £25.7 billion compared to 2020 (while 2020 was marginally lower than 2019, down 0.4% to £25.8 billion).

In 2021, the company had a net loss of £7 billion, a 206% drop from the previous year's net income of £6.6 billion.

The company's cash at the end of 2021 was £2.5 billion. Operating activities generated £9.7 billion, while investing activities used £1.1 billion, mainly for purchases of property, plant and equipment. Financing activities used another £8.7 billion, primarily for dividends paid to owners of the parent.

Strategy

In 2021, 12% of company revenue was from non-combustible products. This was achieved through a multi-category approach which is the very essence of its purpose to build A Better Tomorrow ? providing adult consumers with a range of enjoyable and less risky choices for every mood and moment.

High Growth Segments. Driven by the company's unique and data-driven consumer insight platform (PRISM), it will focus on product categories and consumer segments across its global business that have the best potential for long-term sustainable growth;Priority Markets. By relying on a rigorous market prioritization system (MAPS), the company will focus the strengths of its unparalleled retail and marketing reach, as well as its regulatory and scientific expertise, on those markets and marketplaces with the greatest opportunities for growth;

For over a century, the company has built trusted and powerful brands that satisfy consumers and serve as a promise for quality and enjoyment. It will build the brands of the future by focusing on fewer, stronger and global brands across all its product categories, delivered through the company's deep understanding and segmenting of consumers.

Company Background

In fall 2011 it purchased Colombia's second-largest cigarette maker, Productora Tabacalera de Colombia (Protabaco) for $452 million. Protabaco's brands include Mustang (the country's #2 selling cigarette), Premier, and President. The deal elevates BAT from third place to second in Colombia's cigarette market.

HISTORY

After a year of vicious price-cutting between Imperial Tobacco (UK) and James Buchanan Duke's American Tobacco in the UK, Imperial counterattacked in the US. To end the cigarette price war in the UK, the firms created British American Tobacco (BAT) in 1902. The truce granted Imperial the British market, American the US market, and they jointly owned BAT in the rest of the world.

With Duke in control, BAT expanded into new markets. In China it was selling 25 billion cigarettes a year by 1920. When the Communist revolution ended BAT's operations in China, the company lost more than 25% of its sales (although China later reemerged as a major export market for the company's cigarettes).

A 1911 US antitrust action forced American to sell its interest in BAT and opened the US market to the company. BAT purchased US cigarette manufacturer Brown & Williamson in 1927 and continued to grow through geographic expansion until the 1960s. In 1973 BAT and Imperial each regained control of its own brands in the UK and Continental Europe. Imperial sold the last of its stake in BAT in 1980.

Fearing that mounting public concern over smoking would limit the cigarette market, BAT acquired nontobacco businesses; it changed its name to B.A.T Industries in 1976. The acquisitions of retailers Saks (1973), Argos (UK, 1979), Marshall Field (1982), and later, insurance firms, diversified the company's sales base. After a 1989 hostile takeover bid from Sir James Goldsmith, it sold its retail operations, and retained its tobacco and financial services.

In 1994 B.A.T acquired the former American Tobacco for $1 billion. In 1997 the company acquired Cigarrera de Moderna (with 50% of Mexico's cigarette sales) and formed a joint venture with the Turkish tobacco state enterprise, Tekel.

B.A.T's tobacco operations were spun off in 1998 as British American Tobacco (BAT). The financial services operations were merged with Zurich Insurance in a transaction that created two holding companies: Allied Zurich (UK) and Zurich Allied (Switzerland). With the changes, Martin Broughton became chairman of BAT.

The company in 1999 paid $8.2 billion to buy Dutch cigarette company Rothmans International (Rothmans, Dunhill) from Switzerland's Compagnie Financiere Richemont and South Africa's Rembrandt Group -- both controlled by Anton Rupert. With the purchase, BAT received a controlling stake in Canada's Rothmans, Benson & Hedges (RBH).

In early 2000 BAT bought the 58% of Canada's Imasco it didn't already own. Imasco sold off its financial services and BAT received Imasco's Imperial Tobacco unit (not related to the UK's Imperial Brands) in the deal. (Formerly called Imperial Tobacco Company of Canada, Imasco was created in 1908 with help from BAT.) BAT also unloaded its share of RBH via a public offering.

In 2001 BAT bought the 40.5% of its BAT Australasia subsidiary (formed in 1999 through the Rothmans merger) it didn't already own. Broughton announced that year that the Chinese government had approved development plans that would allow the company to build a factory in China. The company also announced it would build the first foreign-owned cigarette factory in South Korea, at that time the world's #8 tobacco market.

Increasing its Latin American regional presence, BAT purchased a controlling stake in Peru's top tobacco company, Tabacalera Nacional, and several of its suppliers in 2003. However, two months later BAT said it would not make the million-dollar investment in the company. The announcement came soon after Peru raised taxes on cigarettes. By the end of the year, BAT had purchased tobacco manufacturer Ente Tabacchi Italiani S.p.A. from the Italian government. BAT sold the distribution end of its Italian business to CompaÃ±Ãa de DistribuciÃ³n Integral Logista in 2004, the same year that Broughton retired; the company named Jan du Plessis as chairman and Paul Adams as CEO.

In June 2009 the company acquired an 85% stake in Indonesia's fourth largest cigarette maker PT Bentoel Internasional Investama Tbk for £303 million ($494 million) from Rajawali Group. Later that year Richard Burrows became chairman; he replaced du Plessis, who had become chairman of Rio Tinto. Replacing Adams, Nicandro Durante became CEO in early 2011. BAT in fall 2011 acquired Colombia's second-largest cigarette maker, Productora Tabacalera de Colombia (Protabaco) for $452 million.

EXECUTIVES

Asia-Pasific and Middle East President, Guy Meldrum
Chief Executive Officer, Executive Director, Jack Marie Henry David Bowles
Chief Growth Officer, Kingsley Wheaton
Research and Science Designate Director, James Murphy
Digital and Information Director, Javed Iqbal
Transformation Director, Finance Director, Group Transformation Director, Executive Director, Tadeu Luiz Marroco
Legal & External Affairs Director, Legal & External Affairs General Counsel, Jerome B. Abelman
Operations Director, Zafar Khan
Talent and Culture Designate Director, Talent, Culture and Inclusion Director, Hae In Kim
Research and Science Director, David O'Reilly
New Categories Director, Paul Lageweg
Americas and Sub-Saharan Africa Regional Director, Luciano Comin
Asia-Pacific and Middle East Regional Director, Michael Dijanosic
Asia-Pacific and Middle East Regional Director, Europe Regional Director, Eastern Europe, Middle East and Africa Regional Director, Johan Vandermeulen
Secretary, Paul McCrory
Chairman, Non-Independent Director, Luc Jobin
Senior Independent Director, Sue Farr
Independent Non-Executive Directo, Dimitri Panayotopoulos
Independent Non-Executive Director, Karen Guerra
Independent Non-Executive Director, Holly Keller Koeppel
Independent Non-Executive Director, Savio Ming Sang Kwan
Independent Non-Executive Director, J. Darrell Thomas
Independent Non-Executive Director, Krishnan Anand
Independent Non-Executive Director, Veronique Laury
Auditors : KPMG LLP

LOCATIONS

HQ: British American Tobacco Plc
Globe House, 4 Temple Place, London WC2R 2PG
Phone: (44) 20 7845 1000   **Fax:** (44) 20 7240 0555
Web: www.bat.com

2018 sales

	%
US	39
Europe and North Africa	24
Asia/Pacific and Middle East	20
Americas	17
Total	100

PRODUCTS/OPERATIONS

2018 sales

	%
Combustible Portfolio	63
Potentially Risk-Reduced Products	
Vapor	1
THP	2
Modern Oral	-
Traditional Oral	4
Other	30
Total	100

Selected Brands
Benson & Hedges
Camel Snus
Craven 'A'
Dunhill
glo
Granit
Grizzly
John Player Gold Leaf
Kent
Kool
Lucky Strike
Lyft
Kodiak
Mocca
Pall Mall
Peter Stuyvesant
Player's Gold Lead
Rothmans
State Express 555
Viceroy
VIP
Vogue
Vuse
Vype

COMPETITORS

800-JR CIGAR, INC.
AMCON DISTRIBUTING COMPANY
BRITISH AMERICAN TOBACCO JAPAN, LTD.
BRITISH AMERICAN TOBACCO SOUTH AFRICA (PTY) LTD

COMPAÄIA DE DISTRIBUCION INTEGRAL LOGISTA SAU
IMPERIAL BRANDS PLC
JAPAN TOBACCO INC.
JT International SA
PYXUS INTERNATIONAL, INC.
SWISHER INTERNATIONAL GROUP INC.

HISTORICAL FINANCIALS
Company Type: Public

Income Statement — FYE: December 31

	REVENUE ($mil)	NET INCOME ($mil)	NET PROFIT MARGIN	EMPLOYEES
12/23	34,771	(18,310)	—	46,725
12/22	33,291	8,024	24.1%	77,951
12/21	34,613	9,165	26.5%	82,868
12/20	35,176	8,734	24.8%	89,182
12/19	34,172	7,532	22.0%	94,846
Annual Growth	0.4%	—	—	(16.2%)

2023 Year-End Financials
Debt ratio: 42.7% No. of shares ($ mil.): 2,230
Return on equity: (-22.4%) Dividends
Cash ($ mil.): 5,937 Yield: —
Current Ratio: 0.91 Payout: 0.0%
Long-term debt ($ mil.): 45,124 Market value ($ mil.): 65,330

	STOCK PRICE ($) FY Close	P/E High/Low	PER SHARE ($) Earnings	Dividends	Book Value
12/23	29.29	— —	(8.24)	2.93	30.04
12/22	39.98	15 12	3.51	2.63	40.69
12/21	37.41	13 11	3.98	2.94	39.52
12/20	37.49	17 12	3.81	2.68	37.38
12/19	42.46	17 13	3.29	2.58	36.92
Annual Growth	(8.9%)	— —	—	3.2%	(5.0%)

Brookfield Business Partners LP

EXECUTIVES
Chief Executive Officer, Cyrus Madon
Chief Financial Officer, Jaspreet Dehl
Secretary, Jane Sheere
Non-Independent Chairman, Non-Independent Director, Jeffrey Miles Blidner
Lead Independent Director, John S. Lacey
Independent Director, David C. Court
Independent Director, Anthony Gardner
Independent Director, David Hamill
Independent Director, Don Mackenzie
Independent Director, Patricia L. Zuccotti
Non-Independent Director, Stephen J. Girsky
Auditors : Deloitte LLP

LOCATIONS
HQ: Brookfield Business Partners LP
73 Front Street, 5th Floor, Hamilton HM 12
Phone: (441) 294 3309
Web: www.brookfield.com

HISTORICAL FINANCIALS
Company Type: Public

Income Statement — FYE: December 31

	REVENUE ($mil)	NET INCOME ($mil)	NET PROFIT MARGIN	EMPLOYEES
12/23	55,068	482	0.9%	72,000
12/22	57,545	55	0.1%	47,000
12/21	46,587	258	0.6%	90,000
12/20	37,635	(91)	—	67,315
12/19	43,032	43	0.1%	67,030
Annual Growth	6.4%	83.0%	—	1.8%

2023 Year-End Financials
Debt ratio: 51.3% No. of shares ($ mil.): 143
Return on equity: 29.0% Dividends
Cash ($ mil.): 3,252 Yield: —
Current Ratio: 1.04 Payout: 3.8%
Long-term debt ($ mil.): 39,492 Market value ($ mil.): —

Brookfield Corp

Brookfield Corporation (formerly Brookfield Asset Management) has about $825 billion in assets under management, including real estate, renewable power, infrastructure, credit and private equity. Brookfield is also one of the world's largest investors in renewable power, owning more than 8,000 power-generating facilities including wind and solar plants with a total of approximately 24,000 megawatts of installed capacity. With operations in more than 30 countries on five continents, most of the company's revenue is generated from outside of Canada.

Operations
Brookfield has six core business segments: Private Equity, Infrastructure, Real Estate, Infrastructure, Renewable Power and Transition, Asset Management, and Corporate Activities.

The Private Equity segment invests in a broad range of industries, with a focus on business services, infrastructure services, and industrial operations. It accounts for about 65% of total revenue.

The Infrastructure segment develops, owns, and operates the company's infrastructure assets including utility, transport, energy, data infrastructure, and sustainable resource holdings. It accounts for some 15% of revenue.

The Real Estate segment develops, owns, and operates the company's retail, office, core retail, LP investments and other properties. The segment brings in around 15% of total revenue.

Renewable Power and Transition segment includes the ownership, operation and development of hydroelectric, wind, utility-scale solar power generating assets and distributed energy & sustainable solutions. It brings in more than 5% of revenue.

The Asset Management segment include long-term private funds, perpetual strategies and liquid strategies on behalf of the company's investors, as well as its share of the asset management activities of Oaktree Capital Management.

The Corporate Activities segment manages investment of cash and financial assets, as well as the management of corporate leverage, including corporate borrowings and preferred equity.

Geographic Reach
Toronto-based Brookfield has a wide variety of holdings around the world, with operations in the Asia/Pacific region, Europe, the Middle East, North America, and South America. More than 25% of its revenue comes from its business in the UK. Its next largest markets are the US (some 25% of revenue), Canada, (more than 10%), Australia, Brazil , India, and Colombia.

Financial Performance
In 2022, the company had a total revenue of $92.8 billion, a 22% increase from the previous year's total revenue of $75.7 billion. This was primarily attributable to the higher volume of revenue from contracts with customers for the year.

Net income was $2.1 billion in 2022, a 48% decrease from the previous year's net income of $4 billion. This was primarily due to the higher volume of direct costs for the year.

Cash held by the company at the end of fiscal 2022 was $14.4 billion. Financing activities generated $32.5 billion, while investing activities used $39.7 billion, mainly for financial assets and other. Operating activities provided another $8.8 billion.

Strategy
The company predominantly invests in real assets across renewable power and transition, infrastructure, private equity, real estate, and credit.

Brookfield's invests where it can bring its competitive advantages to bear, such as its significant and perpetual capital base, its global presence and reputation, and synergies across the company's strategies.

Company Background
Brookfield Asset Management was established in 1899 as the SÃ£o Paulo Railway, Light and Power Company. In the 1950s the company began investing in real assets, and in the 1990s it scooped up major commercial properties in New York and Boston. It also invested in renewable energy holdings. The group established its first third-party fund in 2001, launching its asset management operations.

In 2017 Brookfield Renewable Partners partnered with other investors to acquire 51% of TerraForm Power, a portfolio of solar and wind power assets, for a total commitment of $656 million. Later that year, the investors acquired all of TerraForm Global, another renewable power portfolio with assets in Brazil, China, and India, for a total of $750 million. Also in 2017, the company acquired a portfolio of manufactured housing communities in the US for $768 million.

EXECUTIVES

Chief Executive Officer, Executive Director, J. Bruce Flatt
Chief Financial Officer, President, Nicholas Goodman
Independent Non-Executive Chairman, Frank J. McKenna
Vice-Chairman, Brian D. Lawson
Vice-Chairman, Director, Jeffrey Miles Blidner
Independent Director, M. Elyse Allan
Independent Director, Angela F. Braly
Independent Director, Janice R. Fukakusa
Independent Director, Maureen Kempston-Darkes
Independent Director, Rafael Miranda Robredo
Independent Director, Hutham S. Olayan
Independent Director, Seek Ngee Huat
Independent Director, Diana L. Taylor
Director, Jack L. Cockwell
Director, Howard S. Marks
Director, Lord O'Donnell
Auditors : Deloitte LLP

LOCATIONS

HQ: Brookfield Corp
Brookfield Place, Suite 100, 181 Bay Street, P.O. Box 762, Toronto, Ontario M5J 2T3
Phone: 416 363-9491 **Fax:** 416 363-2856
Web: www.brookfield.com

2017 Sales

	$ mil.	% of total
UK	15,106	37
US	8,284	20
Canada	5,883	14
Australia	4,405	11
Brazil	3,206	8
Other	3,902	10
Total	40,786	100

PRODUCTS/OPERATIONS

2017 Sales by Segment

	$ mil.	% of total
Private Equity	24,220	60
Real Estate	6,824	17
Infrastructure	3,859	10
Renewable Power	2,788	7
Residential Development	2,447	6
Corporate Activities	362	—
Asset Management	286	—
Total	40,786	100

Selected Subsidiaries

Brookfield Infrastructure Partners L.P. (70%)
Brookfield Office Properties Inc. (32%)
Brookfield Renewable Partners L.P. (40%)
Brookfield Residential Properties (31%)
Norbord Inc. (40%)

COMPETITORS

ALEXANDER & BALDWIN, INC.
BRIXMOR PROPERTY GROUP INC.
FOREST CITY ENTERPRISES, L.P.
HEIWA REAL ESTATE CO.,LTD.
HIGHWOODS PROPERTIES, INC.
INDUS REALTY TRUST, INC.
JEFFERIES FINANCIAL GROUP INC.
PROLOGIS, INC.
THE BLACKSTONE GROUP INC
TRAMMELL CROW COMPANY

HISTORICAL FINANCIALS

Company Type: Public

Income Statement FYE: December 31

	REVENUE ($mil)	NET INCOME ($mil)	NET PROFIT MARGIN	EMPLOYEES
12/23	95,924	1,130	1.2%	240,000
12/22	92,769	2,056	2.2%	200,000
12/21	75,731	3,966	5.2%	180,000
12/20	62,752	(134)	—	150,000
12/19	67,826	2,807	4.1%	151,000
Annual Growth	9.1%	(20.3%)	—	12.3%

2023 Year-End Financials

Debt ratio: 2.5%   No. of shares ($ mil.): 1,523
Return on equity: 2.5%   Dividends
Cash ($ mil.): 11,222   Yield: —
Current Ratio: 0.91   Payout: 45.9%
Long-term debt ($ mil.): 12,160   Market value ($ mil.): 61,121

	STOCK PRICE ($) FY Close	P/E High/Low	PER SHARE ($) Earnings	Dividends	Book Value
12/23	40.12	66 46	0.61	0.28	30.05
12/22	31.46	50 25	1.19	0.56	27.81
12/21	60.38	25 15	2.39	0.52	29.55
12/20	41.27	— —	(0.12)	0.48	23.72
12/19	57.80	33 21	1.73	0.43	23.20
Annual Growth	(8.7%)	—	(23.0%)	(10.0%)	6.7%

Brookfield Infrastructure Partners LP

Unlike consumers, Brookfield Infrastructure is looking to get more than electricity and gas out of utility companies. An investor in infrastructure-related assets, Brookfield owns and operates utility, energy, timber, and transportation companies in the Americas, Europe, and the Asia-Pacific region. It routinely acquires minority or majority interests in such companies, invests in capital and operational improvements to boost its assets' returns, and then sells off its ownership interests. Its assets include gas and electricity transmission companies in Chile, Canada, and the US; a rail system in Australia; and timberlands in the Pacific Northwest. Brookfield was formed in 2007.

Geographic Reach

Australia generates 45% of the company's total revenue, while the UK accounts for 31%. Other major markets include Columbia (10%), Canada (7%), Chile (6%), and the US (1%).

EXECUTIVES

Chief Executive Officer, Sam Pollock
Chief Financial Officer, David Krantz
Chief Operating Officer, Ben Vaughan
Chair, Director, Anne C. Schaumburg
Director, Jeffrey Miles Blidner
Director, William Cox
Director, Roslyn Kelly
Director, Daniel Muniz Quintanilla
Director, Suzanne P. Nimocks
Auditors : Deloitte LLP

LOCATIONS

HQ: Brookfield Infrastructure Partners LP
73 Front Street, Fifth Floor, Hamilton HM 12
Phone: (1) 441 294 3309
Web: www.brookfieldinfrastructure.com

PRODUCTS/OPERATIONS

Selected Assets

BBI Port Acquisitions (UK) Limited (Sea port in the UK)
Dalrymple Bay Coal Terminal, Australia
Euroports, Europe and China (Sea ports)
Great Lakes Power Transmission L.P., Canada
International Energy Group, Europe
International Energy Group, Europe (Liquid petroleum gas distributor)
Island Timberlands Limited Partnership, Canada
Longview Timber Holdings, Corp., U.S.
Natural Gas Pipeline Company of America, U.S.
Powerco Limited, New Zealand
Transelec Chile S.A., Chile
WestNet Rail, Australia (Rail lines operator)

COMPETITORS

Archer Limited
BayWa AG
DCC PUBLIC LIMITED COMPANY
Itausa S/A
SONEPAR

HISTORICAL FINANCIALS

Company Type: Public

Income Statement FYE: December 31

	REVENUE ($mil)	NET INCOME ($mil)	NET PROFIT MARGIN	EMPLOYEES
12/23	17,931	367	2.0%	0
12/22	14,427	341	2.4%	52,000
12/21	11,537	766	6.6%	44,000
12/20	8,885	324	3.6%	41,000
12/19	6,597	211	3.2%	0
Annual Growth	28.4%	14.8%		

2023 Year-End Financials

Debt ratio: 45.5%   No. of shares ($ mil.): 654
Return on equity: 5.8%   Dividends
Cash ($ mil.): 1,857   Yield: —
Current Ratio: 0.68   Payout: 1092.8%
Long-term debt ($ mil.): 39,876   Market value ($ mil.): —

BT Group Plc

BT Group is one of the world's leading communications services companies. The company provides solutions for its customers in over 180 countries, such as broadband, mobile, TV, networking, IT services and related services and applications. BT operates through four customer-facing units: Consumer, Global, Enterprise, and Openreach. BT also builds, owns, and operates the UK's largest fixed and mobile networks, which support the country's digital ambition. BT designs, markets, sells and supports committed spend year to date higher than our spend in 2020, making it another successful year and one of the most acquisitive years in our history. The acquisitions demonstrate the opportunities for growth in digital channels, with Workwear Express a strong online driven business and Hydropac a specialist in packaging products that support online focused customers."

HISTORY

Bunzl's earliest predecessor was a Czechoslovakian haberdashery that opened its doors in 1854. The company moved its operations to Austria in 1883 and expanded into rag trading and textile and paper manufacturing. The firm went by Bunzl & Biach, but it was run by the Bunzl family. In the late 1920s the company began making cigarette filters from crepe paper.

Hitler annexed Austria in 1938, but the Jewish Bunzl family had planned ahead by moving the headquarters from Vienna to Switzerland in 1936. The firm also had a subsidiary in London that served as an alternate base; when the company's Austrian assets were seized during Nazi occupation, family members sought refuge in the UK, Switzerland, and the US. Hugo Bunzl, who had championed the idea of making cigarette filters, wound up in the UK. In 1940 he founded Tissue Papers Ltd. to make tissue, crepe paper, and cigarette filters. The family regained its Austrian operations in 1946, and Tissue Papers began distributing the Austrian paper products. Its name was changed to Bunzl Pulp & Paper Ltd. in 1952.

Filter-tipped cigarettes became more popular after the war, and Eastman Kodak soon developed cellulose acetate tow filters. Bunzl began using the material in 1954, the same year it set up American Filtrona Corporation, its US subsidiary. Medical research began to identify cigarette smoking as a health risk, and filters soared in popularity. Bunzl stepped up production and soon became the world leader in cigarette filters. Its paper and packaging business also grew, and the company went public in 1957.

Bunzl continued to grow steadily, thanks to cigarette filter sales. Growth slowed, however, and governments began restricting cigarette advertising. The company began to diversify in the late 1960s; through product development and acquisitions it was able to offer self-adhesive labels, tapes, plastic tubes, and polythene film and bags.

In 1970 Bunzl Pulp & Paper took over its Austrian progenitor, Bunzl & Biach. The purchase brought Bunzl more fully into papermaking and reduced its dependence on cigarette filters. By the latter half of the decade, many cigarette companies were making their own filters, and competition from Eastern Europe was hurting the company's paper margins. To compensate, Bunzl expanded its plastics operations into pipes; it also had a disastrous foray into data processing.

In 1980 Bunzl sold its Austrian paper business, and the waning filter business once again made up the lion's share of profits. The company bought into the specialized paper and plastic distribution business through acquisitions during the early 1980s. By the end of 1984, sales had more than quintupled, with filters responsible for less than 20% of profits. Bunzl made about 70 more purchases between 1985 and 1987, but it had integration problems and began to sell companies even as it was picking them up.

The company focused on its core operations in the 1990s, although goodwill charges related to divestitures and a reassessment of past charges led to a loss in 1994. In 1997 Bunzl created Bunzl Extrusion with the reacquisition of American Filtrona (it had operated separately since 1984). Bunzl also bought Grocery Supply Systems (supermarket disposables) that year. In the first half of 1998, Bunzl spent about $60 million on acquisitions that included UK paper distributor The Paper Company and Netherlands-based extruded-plastics maker Enitor BV. In 1999 Bunzl bought Provend Group PLC, a leading provider of vending supplies (beverage-vending machines) and catering disposables in the UK. The following year the company enhanced its outsourcing holdings by acquiring Shermond Products Limited, a UK-based health care and hygiene product supplier.

In an effort to diversify its product offerings, in 2001 Bunzl expanded its food supplies business (utensils, catering supplies) in the US and Europe. In 2002 Bunzl further expanded its European food outservices business with its acquisition of Lockhart (catering supplies) from Sodexo, whose client base complements Bunzl's in the UK.

Bunzl split off its Filtrona operations in 2005 (since renamed Essentra), creating two publicly traded companies where there previously had been only one.

In 2010, Bunzl purchased Clean Care A/S, a supplier of cleaning and hygiene consumable products based in Denmark. A few months later it snatched up Weita Holding, a similar firm catering to Switzerland. The previous year Bunzl bought W.K. Thomas, an airlines and catering foodservices distributor, and Industrial Supplies, cleaning and hygiene products distributor. Part of the King UK group, W.K. Thomas and Industrial Supplies were in administration (the UK's bankruptcy program).

In August 2011 the company sold its vending business in the UK (acquired in 1999) at a loss (Â£56 million).

EXECUTIVES

Chief Executive Officer, Executive Director, Frank van Zanten
Human Resources Director, Diana Breeze
Chief Financial Officer, Executive Director, Richard Allan Howes
Corporate Development Director, Andrew Mooney
North America Chief Executive Officer, Jim McCool
U.K. and Ireland Managing Director, Andrew Tedbury
Continental Europe Managing Director, Alberto Grau
Latin America Managing Director, Jonathan Taylor
Asia Pacific Managing Director, Kim Hetherington
Chief Information Officer, Mark Jordan
Secretary, Suzanne Jefferies
Chairman, Non-Executive Director, Peter Ventress
Senior Independent Director, Non-Executive Director, Vanda Murray
Independent Non-Executive Director, Lloyd Pitchford
Independent Non-Executive Director, Stephan Nanninga
Independent Non-Executive Director, Vinodka Murria
Non-Executive Director, Pamela J. Kirby
Auditors : PricewaterhouseCoopers LLP

LOCATIONS

HQ: Bunzl Plc
York House, 45 Seymour Street, London W1H 7JT
Phone: (44) 20 7725 5000   **Fax:** (44) 20 7725 5001
Web: www.bunzl.com

2018 Sales

	% of total
North America	58
Europe	
Continental	20
UK & Ireland	14
Rest of world	8
Total	100

PRODUCTS/OPERATIONS

2018 Sales by Market

	% of total
Food service	29
Grocery	26
Cleaning & hygiene	12
Retail	11
Safety	12
Health care	7
Other	3
Total	100

COMPETITORS

Clariant AG
GKN LIMITED
Huhtamäki Oyj
Kesko Oyj
Neles Oyj
SPICERS LIMITED
Svenska Cellulosa AB SCA
UNIFIRST CORPORATION
UNILEVER PLC
WESFARMERS LIMITED

HISTORICAL FINANCIALS
Company Type: Public

Income Statement — FYE: December 31

	REVENUE ($mil)	NET INCOME ($mil)	NET PROFIT MARGIN	EMPLOYEES
12/22	14,493	571	3.9%	21,883
12/21	13,861	596	4.3%	20,406
12/20	13,798	586	4.3%	19,239
12/19	12,316	461	3.7%	18,984
12/18	11,592	416	3.6%	18,846
Annual Growth	5.7%	8.2%	—	3.8%

2022 Year-End Financials
Debt ratio: 35.6%
Return on equity: 19.2%
Cash ($ mil.): 1,810
Current Ratio: 1.40
Long-term debt ($ mil.): 1,894
No. of shares ($ mil.): 337
Dividends
Yield: —
Payout: 37.4%
Market value ($ mil.): 11,163

	STOCK PRICE ($) FY Close	P/E High/Low	PER SHARE ($) Earnings	Dividends	Book Value
12/22	33.06	27 22	1.69	0.63	9.70
12/21	39.79	31 22	1.78	0.70	8.80
12/20	34.00	28 13	1.75	0.66	7.77
12/19	27.80	33 24	1.38	0.58	6.84
12/18	30.72	32 25	1.25	0.58	6.43
Annual Growth	1.9%	—	7.9%	2.2%	10.8%

BYD Co Ltd

EXECUTIVES
President, Chairman, Chuanfu Wang
Supervisory Committee Chairman, Junqing Dong
Staff Supervisor, Zhen Wang
Supervisor, Jiangfeng Huang
Board Secretary, Qian Li
Chief Financial Officer, Accountant General, Yalin Zhou
Supervisor, Yongzhao Li
Staff Supervisor, Mei Tang
Vice Chairman, Xiangyang Lv
Non-executive Director, Zuoquan Xia
Independent Director, Hongping Cai
Independent Director, Yanbo Jiang
Independent Director, Min Zhang
Auditors: Ernst & Young Hua Ming (LLP)

LOCATIONS
HQ: BYD Co Ltd
Unit 1712, 17th Floor, Tower 2, Grand Central Plaza, No. 138 Shatin Rural Commmittee Road, New Territories,
Phone: —
Web: www.byd.com.cn

COMPETITORS
AUDI AG
EXIDE TECHNOLOGIES, LLC
GEELY AUTOMOBILE HOLDINGS LIMITED
INCI GS YUASA AKU SANAYI VE TICARET ANONIM SIRKETI
NISSAN MOTOR CO.,LTD.
TATA MOTORS LIMITED
TESLA, INC.

TOYOTA AUTO BODY CO.,LTD.
TOYOTA MOTOR CORPORATION
TOYOTA MOTOR CORPORATION AUSTRALIA LIMITED

HISTORICAL FINANCIALS
Company Type: Public

Income Statement — FYE: December 31

	REVENUE ($mil)	NET INCOME ($mil)	NET PROFIT MARGIN	EMPLOYEES
12/22	61,470	2,409	3.9%	0
12/21	34,045	479	1.4%	0
12/20	23,943	647	2.7%	0
12/19	18,357	232	1.3%	0
12/18	18,907	404	2.1%	0
Annual Growth	34.3%	56.3%	—	—

2022 Year-End Financials
Debt ratio: 0.6%
Return on equity: 16.1%
Cash ($ mil.): 7,461
Current Ratio: 0.72
Long-term debt ($ mil.): 1,100
No. of shares ($ mil.): —
Dividends
Yield: —
Payout: 2.9%
Market value ($ mil.): —

	STOCK PRICE ($) FY Close	P/E High/Low	PER SHARE ($) Earnings	Dividends	Book Value
12/22	49.14	14 7	0.83	0.02	0.00
12/21	67.50	77 34	0.17	0.04	0.00
12/20	52.77	36 6	0.22	0.01	0.00
12/19	9.92	28 19	0.07	0.05	0.00
12/18	12.60	20 11	0.14	0.03	0.00
Annual Growth	40.5%	—	57.3%	(8.7%)	—

C.P. All Public Co Ltd

EXECUTIVES
Vice-Chairman, Executive Director, Pittaya Jearavisitkul
Chairman, Vice-Chairman, Executive Director, Korsak Chairasmisak
Vice-Chairman, Executive Director, Piyawat Titasattavorakul
Vice-Chairman, Chief Executive Officer, Executive Director, Tanin Buranamanit
Managing Director (Co), Yuthasakk Poomsurakul
Executive Director, Umroong Sanphasitvong
Managing Director (Co), Vichai Janjariyakun
Accounting Senior Vice President, Finance Senior Vice President, Taweesak Kaewrathtanapattama
Corporate Asset and Facilities Management Senior Vice President, Vichien Chuengviroj
Human Resources Senior Vice President, Lawan Tienghongsakiul
Accounting Chief Financial Officer, Finance Chief Financial Officer, Accounting Senior Vice President, Finance Senior Vice President, Kriengchai Boonpoapichart
Distribution Center Function Senior Vice President, Ampa Yongpisanpop
Marketing Senior Vice President, Nipaporn Ackarapolpanich
Operations Senior Vice President, Thupthep Jiraadisawong
Information Technology Vice President, Wiwat Pongritsakda
Purchasing Vice President, Phaphatsorn Thanasorn
Finance Vice President, Accounting Vice President, Finance Deputy Chief Financial Officer, Accounting Deputy Chief Financial Officer, Ronnakitt Pojamarnpornchai
Finance Secretary, Accounting Secretary, Finance Vice President, Accounting Vice President, Supot Shitgasornpongse
Chairman, Non-Executive Director, Soopakij Chearavanont
Vice-Chairman, Non-Executive Director, Suphachai Chearavanont
Independent Non-Executive Director, Phatcharavat Wongsuwan
Independent Non-Executive Director, Prasobsook Boondech
Independent Non-Executive Director, Padoong Techasarintr
Independent Non-Executive Director, Pridi Boonyoung
Independent Non-Executive Director, Nampung Wongsmith
Independent Non-Executive Director, Kittipong Kittayarak
Non-Executive Director, Adirek Sripratak
Non-Executive Director, Narong Chearavanont
Non-Executive Director, Prasert Jarupanich
Auditors: KPMG Phoomchai Audit Ltd.

LOCATIONS
HQ: C.P. All Public Co Ltd
313 C.P. Tower, 24th Floor, Silom Road, Kwang Silom, Khet Bangrak, Bangkok 10500
Phone: (66) 2 677 9000   **Fax:** (66) 2 679 0050
Web: www.cpall.co.th

HISTORICAL FINANCIALS
Company Type: Public

Income Statement — FYE: December 31

	REVENUE ($mil)	NET INCOME ($mil)	NET PROFIT MARGIN	EMPLOYEES
12/21	17,717	391	2.2%	0
12/20	18,257	537	2.9%	0
12/19	19,172	750	3.9%	0
12/18	16,317	646	4.0%	0
12/17	15,022	611	4.1%	0
Annual Growth	4.2%	(10.5%)	—	—

2021 Year-End Financials
Debt ratio: 1.2%
Return on equity: 12.9%
Cash ($ mil.): 2,784
Current Ratio: 0.77
Long-term debt ($ mil.): 9,398
No. of shares ($ mil.): 8,983
Dividends
Yield: —
Payout: 0.0%
Market value ($ mil.): 162,594

	STOCK PRICE ($) FY Close	P/E High/Low	PER SHARE ($) Earnings	Dividends	Book Value
12/21	18.10	19 13	0.04	0.21	0.35
12/20	21.00	23 9	0.06	0.34	0.36
12/19	23.75	14 7	0.08	0.32	0.35
12/18	12.62	— —	0.07	0.04	0.29
12/17	12.62	— —	0.07	0.03	0.26
Annual Growth	9.4%	—	(11.6%)	58.6%	7.9%

Canadian Imperial Bank Of Commerce (Toronto, Ontario)

Canadian Imperial Bank of Commerce (CIBC) is one of North America's leading financial institution. It serves about 11 million clients in Canada, the US, and around the world. Through four strategic business units ? the Canadian Personal and Business Banking; the Canadian Commercial Banking and Wealth Management; the US Commercial Banking and Wealth Management; and Capital Market. CIBC provides a range of financial products and services to individuals, small businesses, and commercial, corporate, and institutional customers. CIBC generates around 80% of revenue in Canada.

Operations
CIBC organizes its operations into four main business segments. The largest, Canadian Personal and Small Business Banking, generates more than 40% of the company's total revenues and provides financial advice, products, and services through a team of advisors to personal and small business clients.

The Canadian Commercial Banking and Wealth Management division (about 30% of revenues) and U.S. Commercial Banking and Wealth Management (10%) both offer relationship-oriented commercial and private banking and wealth management services to middle-market companies, entrepreneurs, and high-net-worth individuals and families.

Capital Markets (more than 20%) sells integrated global markets products and services, investment banking advice, corporate banking, and research to corporate, government, and institutional clients globally.

Geographic Reach
Based in Toronto, Canada, CIBC does about 80% of its business in Canada.

Although working to increase its footprint in the US, US operations currently represent about 15% of sales. The company also does business in the Caribbean (close to 10% of total revenues). It generates less just less than 5% of sales in other countries.

Sales and Marketing
CIBC provides financial products and services to 11 million individual, small business, commercial, corporate and institutional clients from Canada and around the world.

Financial Performance
Note: Growth rates may differ after conversion to US dollars.

CIBC's performance for the span of five years beginning in 2017 have seen an upward trend with 2021 as its highest performing year.

The company's revenue increased by C$1.3 billion million to C$20 billion compared to C$18.7 billion in the prior year. Net interest income was up $415 million or 4% from 2020, primarily due to volume growth across its businesses and higher trading revenue, partially offset by lower product spreads as a result of changes in the interest rate environment and the impact of foreign exchange translation.

Net income also increased significantly by C$2.7 billion to $C6.4 billion compared to the prior year's C$3.8 billion. Net income was affected by a $125 million increase in legal provisions (Corporate and Other) and $12 million ($9 million after-tax) in transaction and integration-related costs associated with the acquisition of the Canadian Costco credit card portfolio (Canadian Personal and Business Banking).

Cash held by the bank at the end of the year was C$34.6 billion. Operation activities used C$3.3 billion. Financing activities and investing activities used C$1.9 billion and C$3.5 billion, respectively. Main cash uses were for repayment of loans, payment of dividends and distributions, and purchases of securities measured/designated at FVOCI and amortized cost.

Strategy
The company aims on building a modern and relationship-oriented bank. Through the company's efforts, superior client experience and top-tier shareholder returns will be delivered while maintaining its financial strength. The company prioritizes; further strengthening its Canadian customer franchise; maintaining and growing its resilient North American Commercial Banking, Wealth Management, and Capital Markets Businesses; and accelerating ongoing investments in growth initiatives.

HISTORY

In 1858 Bank of Canada was chartered; Toronto financier William McMaster bought the charter in 1866 when investors failed to raise enough money to open it and changed the name to Canadian Bank of Commerce.

The firm opened in 1867, bought the Gore Bank of Hamilton (1870), and expanded within seven years to 24 branches in Ontario, as well as Montreal and New York. Led by Edmund Walker, the bank spread west of the Great Lakes with the opening of a Winnipeg, Manitoba, branch in 1893 and joined the Gold Rush with branches in Dawson City, Yukon Territory, and Skagway, Alaska, in 1898.

As the new century began, the bank's purchases spanned the breadth of Canada, from the Bank of British Columbia (1901) to Halifax Banking (1903) and the Merchants Bank of Prince Edward Island (1906). More buys followed in the 1920s; the bank's assets peaked in 1929 and then plunged during the Depression. It recovered during WWII.

In 1961 Canadian Bank of Commerce merged with Imperial Bank of Canada to become Canadian Imperial Bank of Commerce (CIBC). Imperial Bank was founded in 1875 by Henry Howland; it went west to Calgary and Edmonton and became known as "The Mining Bank." It bought Barclays Bank (Canada) in 1956.

As the energy and agriculture sectors declined in the early 1980s, two of CIBC's largest borrowers, Dome Petroleum and tractor maker Massey-Ferguson, defaulted on their loans. Deregulation opened investment banking to CIBC, which in 1988 bought a majority share of Wood Gundy, one of Canada's largest investment dealers; CIBC also purchased Merrill Lynch Canada's retail brokerage business.

In 1992 CIBC added substantially to its loss reserves (resulting in an earnings drop of 98%) to cover real estate losses from developer Olympia & York and others. This launched more cost-cutting as the company reorganized by operating segments.

Deregulation allowed CIBC to begin selling insurance in 1993; the company built a collection of life, credit, personal property/casualty, and nonmedical health companies.

In 1996 the bank formed Intria, a processing and technical support subsidiary. The next year CIBC Wood Gundy became CIBC World Markets, and CIBC bought securities firm Oppenheimer & Co. and added its stock underwriting and brokerage abilities to CIBC World Markets.

In 1998 increasing foreign competition prompted CIBC and Toronto-Dominion to plan a merger (as did Royal Bank of Canada and Bank of Montreal); the government halted both plans, citing Canada's already highly concentrated banking industry.

Spurned, the bank overhauled its operations to spark growth in the late 1990s. To cut costs it eliminated some 4,000 jobs and sold its more than $1-billion real estate portfolio. It teamed with the Winn-Dixie (1999) and Safeway (2000) supermarket chains to operate electronic branches in the US. The firm scaled back its disappointing international operations and began selling its insurance units.

In 2000 CIBC created Amicus as a holding company for CIBC World Markets' retail electronic banking business. The following year the bank sold its merchant card services business to US-based Global Payments.

In 2002 the company snagged US-based Merrill Lynch's Canadian retail brokerage, asset management, and securities operations, renaming it CIBC Asset Management Inc. That same year CIBC merged its Caribbean banking business with that of UK-based Barclays to create FirstCaribbean Bank.

The next year CIBC sold the Oppenheimer private client and asset-management divisions to Fahnestock Viner (now Oppenheimer Holdings). It sold Juniper Financial, a Delaware-based credit card issuer, to Barclays for some $293 million in 2004.

In 2004 and again in 2006, CIBC was sued by creditors of Internet telecommunications company Global Crossing, stating that the bank had engaged in insider trading to the tune of $2 billion. Creditors demanded a return of the proceeds. CIBC denied the claims, but in 2006 two units of the bank agreed to pay $17.4 million to investors in the ill-fated telecom.

More trouble came in 2005 when CIBC agreed to pay some $2.4 billion in an investor class-action suit to resolve claims that the company helped notorious energy trader Enron to conceal losses.

EXECUTIVES

Chief Executive Officer, President, Director, Victor G. Dodig
Chief Risk Officer, Senior Executive Vice President, Shawn Beber
Chief Legal Officer, Executive Vice President, Kikelomo Lawal
Chief Financial Officer and Enterprise Strategy, Senior Executive Vice President, Hratch Panossian
Senior Executive Vice President, Group Head, Michael G. Capatides
Capital Markets and Direct Financial Services Senior Executive Vice President, Capital Markets and Direct Financial Services Group Head, Harry Culham
Personal and Business Banking Senior Executive Vice President, Personal and Business Banking Group Head, Laura Dottori-Attanasio
Commercial Banking and Wealth Management Senior Executive Vice President, Commercial Banking and Wealth Management Group Head, Jon Hountalas
Technology, Infrastructure and Innovation Senior Executive Vice President, Technology, Infrastructure and Innovation Group Head, Christina Kramer
People, Culture and Brand Senior Executive Vice President, People, Culture and Brand Group Head, Sandy Sharman
Corporate Director, Katharine Berghuis Stevenson
Corporate Director, Patrick D. Daniel
Corporate Director, Christine E. Larsen
Corporate Director, Jane L. Peverett
Corporate Director, Nicholas D. Le Pan
Corporate Director, Martine Turcotte
Corporate Director, Nanci E. Caldwell
Corporate Director, Mary Lou Maher
Corporate Director, Kevin J. Kelly
Director, Charles J. G. Brindamour
Director, Luc Desjardins
Director, Barry L. Zubrow
Director, Michelle L. Collins
Auditors: Ernst & Young LLP

LOCATIONS

HQ: Canadian Imperial Bank Of Commerce (Toronto, Ontario)
81 Bay Street, CIBC Square, Toronto, Ontario M5J 0E7

Phone: 416 980-3096 **Fax:** 416 980-7012
Web: www.cibc.com

2017 Sales

	% of total
Canada	83
Caribbean	8
US	7
Other Countries	2
Total	100

PRODUCTS/OPERATIONS

2017 Sales

	% of total
Canadian Personal and Small Business Banking	52
Canadian Commercial Banking and Wealth Management	22
Capital Markets	17
US Commercial Banking and Wealth Management	5
Corporate and other	4
Total	100

PRODUCT CATEGORIES

Financial advice
Mobile banking
Online banking
Mobile investment consulting
Mobile wallets
Business Plus credit cards
Digital cart
Simplii Financial
Wealth management services
CIBC Integrated Payments service
CIBC Active Global Currency Pool
Commercial banking services
CIBC Global Money Transfer service
International Student Pay

COMPETITORS

AUSTRALIA AND NEW ZEALAND BANKING GROUP LIMITED
Banque de Montréal
COMMONWEALTH BANK OF AUSTRALIA
HUNTINGTON BANCSHARES INCORPORATED
ING Groep N.V.
KEYCORP
Royal Bank Of Canada
STANDARD CHARTERED PLC
The Toronto-Dominion Bank
U.S. BANCORP

HISTORICAL FINANCIALS

Company Type: Public

Income Statement   FYE: October 31

	ASSETS ($mil)	NET INCOME ($mil)	INCOME AS % OF ASSETS	EMPLOYEES
10/23	705,555	3,611	0.5%	48,074
10/22	690,521	4,551	0.7%	50,427
10/21	678,140	5,204	0.8%	0
10/20	578,505	2,849	0.5%	43,853
10/19	494,688	3,868	0.8%	45,157
Annual Growth	9.3%	(1.7%)	—	1.6%

2023 Year-End Financials

Return on assets: 0.5%
Return on equity: 9.6%
Long-term debt ($ mil.): —
No. of shares ($ mil.): 931
Sales ($ mil.): 40,145
Dividends
Yield: 7.2%
Payout: 93.1%
Market value ($ mil.): 32,839

	STOCK PRICE ($) FY Close	P/E High/Low	PER SHARE ($) Earnings	Dividends	Book Value
10/23	35.27	9 7	3.73	2.55	41.15
10/22	45.41	18 6	4.89	2.52	40.53
10/21	121.26	18 12	5.64	2.36	40.98
10/20	74.62	21 12	3.09	2.19	34.61
10/19	85.26	16 13	4.25	2.10	32.73
Annual Growth	(19.8%)	—	(3.2%)	4.9%	5.9%

Canadian National Railway Co

Canadian National Railway (CN) is Canada's #1 railroad and one of the largest in North America. It operates a network of about 19,500 route miles of track spanning Canada's Eastern and Western coasts with the U.S. South. Crossing the continent north-south and east-west, CN hauls such freight as coal, forest products, petroleum and chemicals, and grain and fertilizers. It operates about 25 intermodal terminals, which transfer freight between truck and train, and over 40 warehousing and distribution facilities. Other transportation services include international freight forwarding. CN's revenues are fairly balanced among Canadian traffic, US traffic, transborder traffic, and overseas traffic.

Operations

The company's services are: Rail, Intermodal, Trucking, and Marine.

Rail includes services related to equipment, customs brokerage service, transloading and distribution, business development & real estate; and private car storage.

Intermodal includes services related to temperature controlled cargo, port partnerships, transloading and distribution, logistic sparks, customs brokerage, trucking, and moving grain in container.

Trucking has more than 1,050 owner operators, plus a fleet of 8,000 chassis and 8,000 containers. Trucking offers door-to-door service, import and export dray, interline services, and specialized services.

The company's marine services extend beyond where trucks and track stop, offering its customers marine shipping in regions like the Great Lakes and Newfoundland and Labrador.

Geographic Reach

The company is headquartered at Quebec, Canada. CN's rail network of approximately 20,000 route-miles of track, shipping globally through the many ports it services on three coasts, or leveraging about 25 strategically located Intermodal terminals across its network.

Sales and Marketing

CN serves companies under the industries of: automotive, coal, fertilizers, food &

beverages, forest products, dimensional, grain, metals & minerals, petroleum & chemicals, and consumer goods.

Financial Performance

The company's revenue in 2021 increased to C$14.5 billion compared to C$13.8 billion in the prior year.

Net income in 2021 increased to C$4.9 billion compared to C$3.6 billion in the prior year.

Cash held by the company at the end of 2021 increased to C$1.3 billion. Operating activities C$7.0 billion while investing and financing activities used C$2.9 billion and C$3.9 billion, respectively. Main cash uses were property additions and purchase of common shares by share trusts. Main cash uses were additions of property, repayment of debt and repurchases of common stock.

EXECUTIVES

Chair, Director, Robert Pace
Vice Chair, Director, Shauneen Bruder
President, Chief Executive Officer, Director, Jean-Jacques Ruest
Rail Centric Supply Chain Senior Vice President, James Cairns
Corporate Services Chief Legal Officer, Corporate Services Executive Vice President, Sean Finn
Executive Vice President, Chief Financial Officer, Ghislain Houle
Senior Vice President, Chief Human Resources Officer, Dorothea Klein
Senior Vice President, Doug MacDonald
Executive Vice President, Chief Information and Technology Officer, Dominique Malenfant
Senior Vice President, Chief Strategy Officer, Helen Quirke
Network Operations and Transportation Senior Vice President, Rance Randle
Consumer Product Supply Chain Senior Vice President, Keith Reardon
Executive Vice President, Chief Operating Officer, Robert E. Reilly
Network Operations Senior Vice President, Mechanical and Engineering Senior Vice President, Doug Ryhorchuk
Director, Jean Charest
Director, Denise Gray
Director, Justin M. Howell
Director, Kevin G. Lynch
Director, Margaret A. McKenzie
Director, James E. O'Connor
Director, Jo-ann dePass Olsovsky
Director, Robert L. Phillips
Director, Laura Stein
Auditors : KPMG LLP

LOCATIONS

HQ: Canadian National Railway Co
935 de La Gauchetiere Street West, Montreal, Quebec H3B 2M9
Phone: 888 888-5909
Web: www.cn.ca

2016 sales

	% of total
Canada	66
U.S.	34
Total	100

PRODUCTS/OPERATIONS

2016 sales

	% of total
Rail freight revenues	94
Other revenues	6
Total	100

COMPETITORS

BNSF RAILWAY COMPANY
CELADON GROUP, INC.
CSX CORPORATION
EAST JAPAN RAILWAY COMPANY
GATX CORPORATION
GENESEE & WYOMING INC.
KANSAS CITY SOUTHERN
N.V. Nederlandse Spoorwegen
UNION PACIFIC CORPORATION
UNION PACIFIC RAILROAD COMPANY

HISTORICAL FINANCIALS

Company Type: Public

Income Statement — FYE: December 31

	REVENUE ($mil)	NET INCOME ($mil)	NET PROFIT MARGIN	EMPLOYEES
12/23	12,696	4,243	33.4%	24,987
12/22	12,649	3,784	29.9%	23,971
12/21	11,366	3,840	33.8%	22,604
12/20	10,853	2,797	25.8%	24,381
12/19	11,455	3,237	28.3%	25,975
Annual Growth	2.6%	7.0%	—	(1.0%)

2023 Year-End Financials

Debt ratio: 26.5%
Return on equity: 27.1%
Cash ($ mil.): 697
Current Ratio: 0.61
Long-term debt ($ mil.): 12,171
No. of shares ($ mil.): 642
Dividends
Yield: —
Payout: 37.0%
Market value ($ mil.): 80,742

	STOCK PRICE ($) FY Close	P/E High/Low		PER SHARE ($) Earnings	Dividends	Book Value
12/23	125.63	15	13	6.44	2.38	23.62
12/22	118.88	17	14	5.50	2.17	23.56
12/21	122.86	19	14	5.41	1.97	25.48
12/20	109.85	23	15	3.93	1.73	21.73
12/19	90.45	17	13	4.48	1.62	19.45
Annual Growth	8.6%	—	—	9.5%	10.2%	5.0%

Canadian Natural Resources Ltd

Canadian Natural is a Canadian based senior independent energy company engaged in the acquisition, exploration, development, production, marketing and sale of crude oil, natural gas and NGLs. The company's principal core regions of operations are western Canada, the UK sector of the North Sea and Offshore Africa. In addition, the company has major interests in oil sands production in Canada. Canadian Natural Resources has reported proved reserves of more than 12.8 billion barrels of oil, bitumen, and natural gas liquids, including about 7.0 billion barrels of synthetic crude oil, and approximately 12.2 trillion cu. ft. of natural gas, and produced an average of nearly 1 million barrels of oil equivalent per day. The company was founded in 1989.

Operations

Canadian Natural Resources generates some 55% of its revenue through three geographic segment activities (North America, North Sea and Offshore Africa). These include the exploration, development, production and marketing of crude oil, natural gas liquids and natural gas. The company's Oil Sands Mining and Upgrading activities, account for about 45% of revenue, are reported in a separate segment from exploration and production activities. Midstream and Refining activities include the company's pipeline operations, an electricity co-generation system and NWRP.

Geographic Reach

Canadian Natural Resources' exploration and production activities are conducted in three geographic segments: North America (accounts for over 50% of total revenue); and North Sea and Offshore Africa (less than 5%).

The company is headquartered in Calgary, Alberta with about 15 domestic operating locations. It also has about 5 international offices in Central Africa, the UK, and West Africa.

Sales and Marketing

Canadian Natural Resources customers are mainly in the crude oil and natural gas industry.

Financial Performance

Note: Growth rates may differ after conversion to US Dollars.

The company reported a revenue C$32.9 billion, an 88% increase from the previous year's revenue of C$17.5 billion.

For 2021, the company reported net earnings of C$7.7 billion compared with a net loss of C$435 million for 2020.

The company's cash at the end of 2021 was C$744 million. Operating activities generated C$14.5 billion, while financing activities used C$10.2 billion, mainly for repayment issuance of bank credit facilities and commercial paper. Investing activities used another C$3.7 billion, primarily for net expenditures on property, plant and equipment.

Strategy

Canadian Natural Resources' objectives are to increase crude oil and natural gas production, reserves, cash flow and net asset value on a per common share basis through the economic and sustainable development of its existing crude oil and natural gas properties and through the discovery and/or acquisition of new reserves. The company strives to meet these objectives in a sustainable and responsible way, maintaining a commitment to environmental stewardship and safety excellence.

The company strives to meet these objectives by having a defined growth and value enhancement plan for each of its products and segments. The company takes a balanced approach to growth and investments and focuses on creating long-term shareholder value.

The company's three-phase crude oil marketing strategy includes: blending various crude oil streams with diluents to create more attractive feedstock; supporting and participating in pipeline expansions and/or new additions; and supporting and participating in projects that will increase the downstream conversion capacity for heavy crude oil and bitumen (thermal oil).

Strategic accretive acquisitions are a key component of the company's strategy. The company has used a combination of internally generated cash flows and debt and equity financing to selectively acquire properties generating future cash flows in its core areas. The company's financial discipline, commitment to a strong balance sheet, and capacity to internally generate cash flows provides the means to responsibly and sustainability grow in the long term.

Mergers and Acquisitions

In late 2021, Canadian Natural Resources Limited has completed its acquisition of Storm Resources Ltd. for a cash consideration of $6.28 per share. The acquired production, infrastructure and land complements Canadian Natural's natural gas assets in the Northeast British Columbia area, providing the Company further opportunities to leverage synergies within our diversified portfolio.

Company Background

The company was founded in 1989.

EXECUTIVES

Chairman, Executive Chairman, Director, N. Murray Edwards
President, Director, Tim S. McKay
Marketing Senior Vice President, Bryan C. Bradley
Corporate Development Senior Vice President, Ronald K. Laing
Safety, Risk Management and Innovation Senior Vice President, Pamela A. McIntyre
Finance Chief Financial Officer, Finance Senior Vice President, Mark A. Stainthorpe
Legal Vice President, Legal General Counsel, Legal Corporate Secretary, Paul M. Mendes
Director, Catherine M. Best
Director, M. Elizabeth Cannon
Director, Dawn L. Farrell
Director, Christopher L. Fong
Director, Gordon D. Giffin
Director, Wilfred A. Gobert
Director, Steve W. Laut
Director, Frank J. McKenna
Director, David A. Tuer
Director, Annette M. Verschuren

Auditors: PricewaterhouseCoopers LLP

LOCATIONS

HQ: Canadian Natural Resources Ltd
2100, 855 - 2nd Street S.W., Calgary, Alberta T2P 4J8
Phone: 403 517-6700   **Fax:** 403 517-7350
Web: www.cnrl.com

2015 Sales

	% of total
Exploration and Production	
North America	68
North Sea	5
offshore Africa	4
Oil sands mining and upgrading	22
Midstream	1
Total	100

COMPETITORS

BERRY PETROLEUM COMPANY, LLC
Cenovus Energy Inc
Crescent Point Energy Corp
HKN, INC.
Husky Energy Inc
Korea National Oil Corporation
MURPHY OIL CORPORATION
NOBLE ENERGY, INC.
OCCIDENTAL PETROLEUM CORPORATION OF CALIFORNIA
Twin Butte Energy Ltd

HISTORICAL FINANCIALS

Company Type: Public

Income Statement   FYE: December 31

	REVENUE ($mil)	NET INCOME ($mil)	NET PROFIT MARGIN	EMPLOYEES
12/23	27,136	6,211	22.9%	10,272
12/22	31,275	8,086	25.9%	0
12/21	23,599	6,017	25.5%	9,735
12/20	13,267	(341)	—	9,993
12/19	17,563	4,159	23.7%	10,180
Annual Growth	11.5%	10.5%		0.2%

2023 Year-End Financials

Debt ratio: 10.7%
Return on equity: 21.1%
Cash ($ mil.): 661
Current Ratio: 0.96
Long-term debt ($ mil.): 7,408
No. of shares ($ mil.): 1,072
Dividends
Yield: —
Payout: 49.5%
Market value ($ mil.): 70,264

	STOCK PRICE ($) FY Close	P/E High/Low		PER SHARE ($) Earnings	Dividends	Book Value
12/23	65.52	9	7	5.64	2.79	28.02
12/22	55.53	7	4	7.04	3.40	25.60
12/21	42.25	7	3	5.07	1.59	24.83
12/20	24.05	—	—	(0.29)	1.26	21.48
12/19	32.35	7	5	3.49	1.13	22.64
Annual Growth	19.3%		—	12.8%	25.4%	5.5%

Canadian Pacific Kansas City Ltd

With operations stretching from Vancouver to New York, Canadian Pacific Railway (CP) hauls freight roughly about a 15,000-mile network in Canada and the US. The company also serves more than 10 ports on west and east coasts. US units include Soo Line Railroad and Dakota, Minnesota & Eastern Railroad, which operate in the Midwest; and Delaware and Hudson Railway, which operates in the Northeast. Freight hauled by CP includes intermodal containers, coal, grain, and industrial and consumer products. The company also provides logistics services and land transportation via partners.

Operations

The company only operates one segment, which is rail transportation. This segment is then broken down to its line of businesses: Bulk (40%), Merchandise (about 40%), and intermodal (more than 20%).

Bulk commodities typically move in large volumes across long distance. It includes the transportation of grain, coal, potash, and fertilizers. Merchandise freight transports industrial and consumer products such as energy, chemicals and plastics, metals, minerals and consumer products, automotive, and forest products. Lastly, intermodal traffic consists of retail goods in overseas containers that can be transported by train, ship, and truck, and in domestic containers that can be moved by train and truck.

Geographic Reach

Calgary-based Canadian Pacific Railway Limited also has a main dispatch center and primary dispatching facility in Canada. The company operates in both Canada and the US, with its domestic operations accounting for 75% of the company's operations, and the US accounting for 25%.

Financial Performance

Canadian Pacific Railway's performance for the past five years have seen an upward trend, with a slight fluctuation over the last three years but still ending with 2021 as its highest performing year over the period.

The company's revenues for 2020 increased by CAD 285 million to CAD 7.9 billion as compared to 2020's revenue of CAD 7.7 billion.

Net income for the fiscal year end 2021 also increased by CAD 408 million to CAD 2.8 billion as compared to the prior year's net income of CAD 2.4 billion.

The company held CAD 82 million at the end of 2021. The company's operating activities provided CAD 3.7 billion. Investing activities used CAD 13.7 billion while financing activities provided CAD 9.9 billion. Main cash uses were for an investment in Kansas City Southern and additions to properties.

Strategy

Since 2012, the company has been transforming its operations by investing in the network and precise execution of a scheduled railroading model that lower costs, optimizes assets, and provides a better, more competitive service. Canadian Pacific Railway continues this transformation through focusing on five key foundations: Providing services; controlling costs; optimizing assets; operating safely; and developing people.

EXECUTIVES

Chairman, Director, Isabelle Courville
President, Chief Executive Officer, Director, Keith Edward Creel, $1,158,750 total compensation
Executive Vice President, Chief Financial Officer, Nadeem S. Velani, $460,000 total compensation
Executive Vice President, Chief Marketing Officer, John Kenneth Brooks
Operations Executive Vice President, Mark Redd
Strategic Planning and Technology Transformation Senior Vice President, James Dominic Luther Clements
Senior Vice President, Chief Risk Officer, Laird Joseph Pitz, $437,720 total compensation
Market Strategy and Asset Management Vice President, Mike Foran
Vice President, Chief Information Officer, Pam Arpin
Chief Legal Officer, Corporate Secretary, Jeffrey Jerom Ellis
Human Resources Chief Culture Officer, Human Resources Vice President, Chad Rolstad
Director, John Russell Baird
Director, Gillian H. Denham
Director, Edward R. Hamberger
Director, Matthew H. Paull
Director, Jane L. Peverett
Director, Andrea Robertson
Director, Gordon T. Trafton
Auditors : Ernst & Young LLP

LOCATIONS

HQ: Canadian Pacific Kansas City Ltd
7550 Ogden Dale Road S.E., Calgary, Alberta T2C 4X9
Phone: 403 319-7000   **Fax:** 403 319-6770
Web: www.cpr.ca

2015 Sales

	% of total
Canada	69
US	31
Total	100

PRODUCTS/OPERATIONS

2015 Sales

	% of total
Freight	98
Non-freight	2
Total	100

Selected Freight Products

Bulk
   Grain
   Barley
   Canola
   Durum
   Flax
   Oats
   Rye
   Spring wheat
   Coal
   Metallurgical coal
   Petroleum coke
   Thermal coal
   Sulphur and fertilizers
Intermodal
Merchandise
   Industrial and consumer products
   Aggregates
   Chemicals
   Ethanol
   Plastics
   Mine
   Non-coal energy-related products
   Steel
   Automotive
   Automotive parts
   Domestic vehicles
   Import vehicles
   Pre-owned vehicles
   Forest products
   Lumber
   Paper products
   Panel
   Wood pulp

COMPETITORS

ALASKA RAILROAD CORPORATION
CSX CORPORATION
Compagnie des Chemins de Fer Nationaux du Canada
FLORIDA EAST COAST RAILWAY, L.L.C.
INTERSTATE DISTRIBUTOR CO.
IOWA INTERSTATE RAILROAD, LLC
PASCHALL TRUCK LINES, INC.
RAILWORKS CORPORATION
Rumo Malha Sul S/A
UNION PACIFIC RAILROAD COMPANY

HISTORICAL FINANCIALS

Company Type: Public

Income Statement
FYE: December 31

	REVENUE ($mil)	NET INCOME ($mil)	NET PROFIT MARGIN	EMPLOYEES
12/23	9,472	2,962	31.3%	19,927
12/22	6,517	2,600	39.9%	12,754
12/21	6,277	2,239	35.7%	11,834
12/20	6,055	1,919	31.7%	11,890
12/19	5,983	1,873	31.3%	12,694
Annual Growth	12.2%	12.1%	—	11.9%

2023 Year-End Financials

Debt ratio: 21.2%
Return on equity: 9.7%
Cash ($ mil.): 350
Current Ratio: 0.53
Long-term debt ($ mil.): 14,599
No. of shares ($ mil.): 932
Dividends
Yield: —
Payout: 13.5%
Market value ($ mil.): 73,692

	STOCK PRICE ($) FY Close	P/E High/Low		PER SHARE ($) Earnings	Dividends	Book Value
12/23	79.06	20	17	3.18	0.43	33.58
12/22	74.59	22	17	2.79	0.56	30.90
12/21	71.94	91	15	3.28	0.60	28.57
12/20	346.69	97	57	2.82	0.56	8.62
12/19	254.95	74	52	2.69	0.48	7.92
Annual Growth	(25.4%)	—	—	4.2%	(2.8%)	43.5%

Canadian Tire Corp Ltd

Don't be fooled by its name: Canadian Tire sells much more than tires. About 490 Canadian Tire general merchandise stores run by a network of associate dealers across Canada sell automotive, home, and sports and leisure products, including bicycles. The company's 90-plus PartSource auto parts stores cater to automotive do-it-yourselfers and professionals, while its roughly 385-location Mark's Work Wearhouse chain offers work and casual apparel and footwear for men and women. Its Canadian Tire Petroleum subsidiary runs 300 gas bar locations, making it one of the country's largest independent gasoline retailers. Established in 1922, Canadian Tire also owns Canada's largest sporting goods retailer, FGL Sports.

Operations

Canadian Tire operates three business segments: Retail, CT REIT, and Financial Services.

The Retail segment (which made up 89% of Canadian Tire's total revenue in fiscal 2015, ended January) includes the business from its Canadian Tire, PartSource, Canadian Tire Petroleum (CTP), Mark's, and various FGL Sports stores. Its Canadian Tire stores make up about half of its total revenue, and are operated by independent business owner dealers. Its CTP stores sell fuel and related products from about 300 agent operated gas bars that boast 296 convenience stores and over 80 car wash stations. The company's 415 FGL Sports stores sell sports-related footwear, apparel, and equipment under the Sport Chek, Hockey Experts, Sports Experts, National Sports, Intersport, Pro Hockey Life, and Atmosphere banners.

The Financial Services segment (8% of revenue) markets a range of Canadian Tire-branded credit cards through its subsidiary Canadian Tire Financial Services (CTFS). (One in five Canadian households had a Canadian Tire credit card in 2014.) CTFS's subsidiary, Canadian Tire Bank, offers personal loans and lines of credit; high-interest and tax-free savings accounts; insurance plans; and warranty products. Scotiabank acquired a 20% stake in the company's financial services business in October 2014, which raised nearly $477 million in net proceeds for Canadian Tire.

The CT REIT segment (3% of revenue) owned 273 properties spanning 20 million square feet of gross leasable area across all provinces and two territories in Canada as of early 2015. Its property portfolio included Canadian Tire stores, retail centers anchored by Canadian Tire stores, company distribution centers, a mixed-use commercial property, and devleopment lands where future Canadian Tire stores could be built.

Geographic Reach

Canadian Tire's retail outlets blanket the country with a store network that served about 90% of Canada's population in 2014. The company has representative offices in the Pacific Rim related to product sourcing, logistics, and vendor management. Its four distribution facilities are in Brampton, Ontario; Calgary, Alberta; and Montreal, Quebec.

Sales and Marketing

Canadian Tire's supply chain partners

include common carrier trucking companies, third-party logistics companies, ocean carriers, and railways.

Financial Performance

Note: Growth rates may differ after conversion to US dollars. This analysis uses financials from the company's annual report.

Canadian Tire's annual revenues and profits have been trending higher since 2009 with a growing total store base and rising same-store sales.

The company's revenue climbed 6% to C$12.5 billion ($10.7 billion) in fiscal 2015 (ended January 3, 2015), mostly thanks to a combination of 6% Retail sales growth from strong performance from its Canadian Tire and FGL Sports stores; and 5% Financial Services business growth as credit card sales and balances grew. Its Retail business grew for a variety of factors: its Canadian Tire's retail sales improved with enhanced assortments and new products; its automotive business posted strong results through the year; its FGL Sports sales grew thanks to strong same-store sales at its Sport Chek locations and new store openings; and Mark's sales grew thanks to new marketing campaigns that promoted new assortments and national brands in men's casual wear and footwear.

Revenue growth in FY2015 drove Canadian Tire's net income up 13% to C$639.3 million ($548 million) for the year. The company's operating cash levels fell 36% to C$574.8 million ($492.5 million) despite higher earnings, due to unfavorable working capital changes mostly related to merchandise inventories.

Strategy

Canadian Tires' President and CEO laid out a handful of priorities in late 2015 as the company's strategy for growth. These included: continuing to strengthen the company's brands; growing its relationships with its independently-owned Canadian Tire Dealers; embracing the new world of retail by utilizing in-store digital and digital marketing practices and building its e-commerce channel; becoming more productive and efficient; and continuing to look for inorganic growth opportunities, building upon its successful acquisitions of the Forzani Group (now FGL Sports) and Mark's Work Wearhouse it made in the past.

Some of the company's other priorities, outlined in 2015, included: renovating its Canadian Tire stores with expanded Living categories and better store design; building Mark's market share in the overall casual apparel and casual footwear market with a specific focus on menswear in the jeans, outwear, and casual footwear categories; and expanding its FGL Sports' Sport Check store network -- especially adding new, large urban flagship concept stores -- while closing over 100 other retail locations by 2017.

To boost traffic and customer retention within its existing stores, Canadian Tires has been pushing its "My Canadian Tire Money" card and mobile app loyalty program. The program, launched in October 2014, not only gives customers reward points for shopping at the Canadian Tire-affiliated stores, but also provides allows the company to leverage customer shopping data to build new retail strategies and personalized relationships over the long term.

HISTORY

In 1922 brothers John and Alfred Billes bought Hamilton Tire and Garage in Toronto, a city with 40,000 cars at the time. In addition to the usual repair parts, tires, and batteries, the brothers also provided a homemade brand of antifreeze. They fired up earnings even more by renting spaces in their heated garage so drivers in that cold land wouldn't have trouble starting their cars in the morning.

Five years after buying the garage, the Billes brothers incorporated as Canadian Tire. Aptly named, the company began fielding requests for auto parts from across the country. In 1928 Canadian Tire published a French-English bilingual catalog that is still distributed to 9 million homes.

The Great Depression had little effect on the company as more Canadians sought to hold on to their cars (numbering a million in 1930) rather than buy new ones. For these many do-it-yourself auto mechanics, Canadian Tire introduced the super-lastic tire guarantee, the first time in the country a tire was guaranteed for other than the manufacturers' defects. Also in the 1930s the company opened its first associate store, in Hamilton, Ontario, forming the pattern for many such stores to come.

The 1950s saw Canadian Tire roll out a chain of gas stations and introduce a cash bonus coupon called Canadian Tire Money that gas-buying customers could redeem on store merchandise. In the early 1960s customers could earn Tire Money at retail stores, as well as gas stations.

Tiring of its core product, the company began diversifying its line, selling small appliances and other housewares. In the early 1970s tires and other auto supplies accounted for half of Canadian Tire's sales; by 1978 those products accounted for about 35%.

In the next decade the company found itself going south. In 1982 it bought the Texas-based White Stores chain. After disappointing results, however, Canadian Tire had sold all its US stores by 1986.

In 1994 Canadian Tire introduced its Next Generation stores with expanded offerings and a more customer-friendly format. In another innovation five years later, the company announced plans to launch a chain of 200 PartSource stores aimed at garage professionals and advanced do-it-yourselfers. In 2000 Canadian Tire launched an e-commerce site that now markets 15,000 products.

In order to focus on its own credit card, the company sold its credit card management operations to Citigroup-owned Associates Financial Services of Canada in 2001. Also that year Canadian Tire acquired the Mark's Work Wearhouse apparel chain.

In 2002 the company built and opened 20 stores; in 2003 19 stores were opened.

Tom Gauld, formerly president of Canadian Tire Financial Services, succeeded Wayne Sales and president and CEO of Canadian Tire in April 2006. Sales remained on the board of directors as vice chairman.

In September 2008 Canadian Tire sold 11 of its retail properties to two commercial real estate firms for a combined $164 million and change. The sale is part of the company's plan to sell and lease back a dozen of its properties for $174 million.

In January 2009 Gauld retired and was succeeded as CEO by director Stephen Wetmore.

In August 2011 Canadian Tire acquired Canada's largest sporting goods retailer, The Forzani Group, for C$771 million (nearly US$800 million). Forzani, which owns the Sport Chek and Athletes World chains, among others, will operate as a separate business unit as part of the acquisition.

The 2011 acquisition of the Forzani Group -- the first major purchase by CEO Stephen Wetmore -- was designed to shore up the retailer's position in sporting goods and apparel and give it more competitive heft as it prepared for the 2013 arrival of the US's #2 discounter, Target Corp, in Canada.

EXECUTIVES

President, Chief Executive Officer, Director, Greg Hicks

Executive Vice President, Chief Financial Officer, Gregory G. Craig

Executive Vice President, Strategic Advisor, General Counsel, James R. Christie

International Executive Vice President, Mahes S. Wickramasinghe

Executive Vice President, Chief Human Resources Officer, John E. Pershing

Non-Executive Chairman, Director, Maureen J. Sabia

Director, Eric T. Anderson

Corporate Director, R. Jamie Anderson

Director, Martha G. Billes

Director, Owen G. Billes

Corporate Director, Diana L. Chant

Corporate Director, David C. Court

Corporate Director, Mark E. Derbyshire

Corporate Director, Steve Frazier

Director, Norman Jaskolka

Director, Patrick J. Connolly

Director, Sylvain Leroux

Director, Donald A. Murray

Director, J. Michael Owens

Corporate Director, Nadir Patel

Corporate Director, Cynthia M. Trudell
Auditors : Deloitte LLP

LOCATIONS

HQ: Canadian Tire Corp Ltd
2180 Yonge Street, Toronto, Ontario M4P 2V8
Phone: 416 480-3000   **Fax:** 416 544-7715
Web: www.corp.canadiantire.ca

PRODUCTS/OPERATIONS

2015 Stores

	No.
Canadian Tire Stores	493
FGL Sports	436
Mark's Work Wearhouse	383
Gas bars	297
PartSource	91
Total	1,700

2015 Revenue

	% of total
Canadian Tire Retail	89
Financial services	8
CT Reit	3
Eliminations	—
Total	100

Selected Products

Automotive
    Batteries and accessories
    Car radio and video systems and parts
    Car security systems
    Emergency road kits
    Lighting and electrical products
    Test and tune supplies and equipment
    Tires
    Truck and trailer accessories
    Wiper blades
Garden and patio
    Barbecues and accessories
    Fertilizers
    Garden tools
    Garden wear
    Patio furniture
    Pest control supplies
    Sheds
    Wheelbarrows and carts
Home products
    Bathroom cabinets and other supplies
    Batteries
    Cleaning supplies
    Electrical
    Electronics
    Home décor
    Kitchen products
    Laundry products
    Lighting products
    Mailboxes
    Pet supplies
    Plumbing supplies
    Safety and security products
    Storage and organization products
Sports and recreation
    Baseball
    Bicycles
    Camping equipment and supplies
    Curling
    Fishing equipment and supplies
    Golf equipment and supplies
    Skateboard and scooters
    Snowshoeing
    Sport and duffel bags
Workshop
    Carpentry tools
    Electrical products
    Generators
    Power tool accessories
    Shop vacuums
    Welding and soldering equipment and supplies

COMPETITORS

ADVANCE AUTO PARTS, INC.
AUTOZONE, INC.
BRIDGESTONE RETAIL OPERATIONS, LLC
CARPARTS.COM, INC.
COSTCO WHOLESALE CORPORATION
HALFORDS GROUP PLC
MURPHY USA INC.
SPARTANNASH COMPANY
THE GOODYEAR TIRE & RUBBER COMPANY
TRUE VALUE COMPANY, L.L.C.

HISTORICAL FINANCIALS

Company Type: Public

Income Statement   FYE: December 30

	REVENUE ($mil)	NET INCOME ($mil)	NET PROFIT MARGIN	EMPLOYEES
12/23	12,566	160	1.3%	33,806
12/22*	13,169	772	5.9%	34,606
01/22	12,791	885	6.9%	33,892
01/21*	11,673	590	5.1%	31,786
12/19	11,100	594	5.4%	31,574
Annual Growth	3.2%	(27.9%)	—	1.7%

*Fiscal year change

2023 Year-End Financials

Debt ratio: 23.4%   No. of shares ($ mil.): 55
Return on equity: 3.8%   Dividends
Cash ($ mil.): 234   Yield: —
Current Ratio: 1.77   Payout: 182.5%
Long-term debt ($ mil.): 3,322   Market value ($ mil.): 5,907

	STOCK PRICE ($) FY Close	P/E High	P/E Low	PER SHARE ($) Earnings	Dividends	Book Value
12/23	106.20	38	26	2.85	5.21	75.26
12/22*	104.46	8	6	13.01	4.33	72.00
01/22	143.52	9	7	14.43	3.69	66.89
01/21*	131.85	11	4	9.66	3.57	58.08
12/19	105.57	9	8	9.61	3.17	52.02
Annual Growth	0.1%	—	—	(26.2%)	13.2%	9.7%

*Fiscal year change

Canadian Western Bank

EXECUTIVES

Chairman, Independent Director, Robert L. Phillips
Chief Executive Officer, President, Independent Director, Christopher H. Fowler
Finance Executive Vice President, Finance Chief Financial Officer, R. Matthew Rudd
Human Resources Executive Vice President, Human Resources and Corporate Communications Executive Vice President, Kelly S. Blackett
Banking Executive Vice President, Stephen Murphy
Business Transformation Executive Vice President, M. Glen Eastwood
Chief Financial Officer, Executive Vice President, Carolyn J. Graham

Chief Information Officer, Executive Vice President, Darrell R. Jones
Executive Vice President, Chief Risk Officer, Carolina Parra
Senior Vice President, General Counsel, Corporate Secretary, Bindu Cudjoe
Independent Director, Andrew J. Bibby
Independent Director, Marie Y. Delorme
Independent Director, Maria Filippelli
Independent Director, Linda M. O. Hohol
Independent Director, Robert A. Manning
Independent Director, E. Gay Mitchell
Independent Director, Sarah A. Morgan-Silvester
Independent Director, Margaret J. Mulligan
Independent Director, Irfhan A. Rawji
Independent Director, Ian M. Reid
Independent Director, H. Sanford Riley
Auditors : KPMG LLP

LOCATIONS

HQ: Canadian Western Bank
Suite 3000, 10303 Jasper Avenue N.W., Canadian Western Bank Place, Edmonton, Alberta T5J 3X6
Phone: 780 423-8888   **Fax:** 780 423-8897
Web: www.cwb.com

HISTORICAL FINANCIALS

Company Type: Public

Income Statement   FYE: October 31

	ASSETS ($mil)	NET INCOME ($mil)	INCOME AS % OF ASSETS	EMPLOYEES
10/23	30,602	253	0.8%	2,505
10/22	30,325	246	0.8%	2,712
10/21	30,214	288	1.0%	2,789
10/20	25,512	203	0.8%	2,505
10/19	23,856	217	0.9%	2,278
Annual Growth	6.4%	3.9%	—	2.4%

2023 Year-End Financials

Return on assets: 0.8%   Dividends
Return on equity: 9.0%   Yield: 4.7%
Long-term debt ($ mil.): —   Payout: 53.4%
No. of shares ($ mil.): 96   Market value ($ mil.): 1,990
Sales ($ mil.): 1,805

	STOCK PRICE ($) FY Close	P/E High	P/E Low	PER SHARE ($) Earnings	Dividends	Book Value
10/23	20.64	6	5	2.44	0.96	30.19
10/22	17.32	9	5	2.48	0.95	28.96
10/21	31.98	9	6	3.02	0.94	32.00
10/20	18.36	9	4	2.15	0.86	28.75
10/19	25.67	8	6	2.31	0.81	25.63
Annual Growth	(5.3%)	—	—	1.4%	4.2%	4.2%

Canon Inc

EXECUTIVES

Chairman, Chief Executive Officer, Director, Fujio Mitarai
Executive Vice President, Chief Financial Officer, Director, Toshizo Tanaka

Printing Business Executive Vice President, Printing Business Chief Technology Officer, Director, Toshio Homma
Outside Director, Kunitaro Saida
Outside Director, Yusuke Kawamura
Auditors : Deloitte Touche Tohmatsu LLC

LOCATIONS
HQ: Canon Inc
30-2, Shimomaruko 3-chome, Ohta-ku, Tokyo 146-8501
Phone: (81) 3 3758 2111   **Fax:** (81) 3 5482 9680
Web: www.global.canon/en

HISTORICAL FINANCIALS
Company Type: Public

Income Statement — FYE: December 31

	REVENUE ($mil)	NET INCOME ($mil)	NET PROFIT MARGIN	EMPLOYEES
12/22	30,594	1,851	6.1%	0
12/21	30,521	1,865	6.1%	184,034
12/20	30,661	808	2.6%	181,897
12/19	33,096	1,152	3.5%	187,041
12/18	35,936	2,298	6.4%	195,056
Annual Growth	(3.9%)	(5.3%)	—	—

2022 Year-End Financials
Debt ratio: —
Return on equity: 8.1%
Cash ($ mil.): 2,747
Current Ratio: 1.58
Long-term debt ($ mil.): 18
No. of shares ($ mil.): 1,015
Dividends
Yield: —
Payout: 49.4%
Market value ($ mil.): 22,016

	STOCK PRICE ($) FY Close	P/E High/Low	PER SHARE ($) Earnings	Dividends	Book Value
12/22	21.68	0 0	1.80	0.89	23.26
12/21	24.43	0 0	1.78	0.77	23.87
12/20	19.41	0 0	0.77	1.12	23.89
12/19	27.35	0 0	1.08	1.47	23.31
12/18	27.60	0 0	2.13	1.52	23.81
Annual Growth	(5.9%)	—	(4.2%)	(12.5%)	(0.6%)

Capgemini SE

EXECUTIVES
Chairman, Paul Hermelin
Chief Executive Officer, Director, Aiman Ezzat
Chief Financial Officer, Carole Ferrand
Chief Human Resources Officer, Anne Lebel
Chief Operating Officer, Executive Board Member, Olivier Sevillia
Independent Director, Xiaoqun Clever
Independent Director, Maria Ferraro
Independent Director, Sian Herbert-Jones
Independent Director, Belen Moscoso del Prado Lopez-Doriga
Independent Director, Xavier Musca
Independent Director, Frederic Oudea
Independent Director, Patrick Pouyanne
Independent Director, Olivier Roussat
Independent Director, Tanja Rueckert
Independent Director, Kurt Sievers
Director, Pierre Goulaieff
Director, Herve Jeannin
Director, Lucia Sinapi-Thomas
Auditors : Mazars

LOCATIONS
HQ: Capgemini SE
11, rue de Tilsitt, Paris 75017
Phone: (33) 1 47 54 50 00   **Fax:** (33) 1 47 54 50 25
Web: www.capgemini.com

HISTORICAL FINANCIALS
Company Type: Public

Income Statement — FYE: December 31

	REVENUE ($mil)	NET INCOME ($mil)	NET PROFIT MARGIN	EMPLOYEES
12/22	23,491	1,652	7.0%	359,567
12/21	20,554	1,309	6.4%	324,684
12/20	19,450	1,174	6.0%	269,769
12/19	15,859	961	6.1%	219,314
12/18	15,113	835	5.5%	211,313
Annual Growth	11.7%	18.6%	—	14.2%

2022 Year-End Financials
Debt ratio: 28.3%
Return on equity: 17.0%
Cash ($ mil.): 4,060
Current Ratio: 1.28
Long-term debt ($ mil.): 6,039
No. of shares ($ mil.): 171
Dividends
Yield: —
Payout: 5.4%
Market value ($ mil.): 5,732

	STOCK PRICE ($) FY Close	P/E High/Low	PER SHARE ($) Earnings	Dividends	Book Value
12/22	33.34	5 4	9.39	0.51	60.43
12/21	48.94	7 4	7.54	0.47	55.72
12/20	30.83	6 2	6.81	0.31	44.47
12/19	24.36	5 3	5.61	0.38	55.93
12/18	19.53	6 4	4.87	0.40	51.33
Annual Growth	14.3%	—	17.8%	6.6%	4.2%

Carlsberg A/S (Denmark)

Carlsberg A/S, the owner of Carlsberg Breweries, is one of the world's leading brewers. The company's beer portfolio spans its core beer brands, including local power brands and international premium brands, craft and speciality brands, and alcohol-free brews. In addition to the worldwide brewing operations of its flagship subsidiary, Carlsberg also operates the Carlsberg Research Center, a world-leading laboratory for brewing-oriented research. Although most of the company's revenue comes from the sale of Carlsberg beers, it also sells the Tuborg brand (one of the best-selling beers in Norway). The company is majority-owned by the Carlsberg Foundation, established in 1876 by founder J.C. Jacobsen, which promotes the arts, sciences, and social work in Denmark. It generates the majority of its revenue in western Europe. Carlsberg was established in 1847 by brewer J.C. Jacobsen.

Operations
Carlsberg's revenue arises primarily from the sale of beverages to its customers. Other revenue by category is sales of products other than beverages that do not drive any volume, such as merchandise, services, by products etc. The company has more than 140 brands in its beer portfolio, which spans core beer brands, craft and speciality, and alcohol-free brews.

Overall, beer revenue generates nearly 80% of the company's sales, while other beverages (encompassing both alcoholic and nonalcoholic beverages) account for the rest.

Geographic Reach
Based in Denmark, Carlsberg is present in more than 100 countries around the world. Western Europe accounts for around 45% of the company's revenue, Asia provides nearly 30%, while Central & Eastern Europe bring in approximately 25%.

Sales and Marketing
The company's regions provide an attractive exposure to mature and emerging markets. It has a number 1 or 2 position in more than 20 markets, and around 70% of its volumes are sold in these markets. Its customers range from on-trade to off-trade, from online to offline. The company's online business-to-business platform, available in ten markets across its three regions, serving more than 40,000 customers.

Financial Performance
Revenue increased by 13.8% to DKK 66.6 billion (2020: DKK 58.5 billion). Revenue was positively impacted by the recovery of the on-trade in some markets due to fewer restrictions in 2021 than in 2020 and solid growth of premium products.

In 2021, the company had a net income of DKK 6.8 billion, a 14% increase from the previous year's net income of DKK 6 billion.

The company's cash at the end of 2021 was DKK 8.3 billion. Operating activities generated DKK 13.3 billion, while investing activities used DKK 4.4 billion, mainly for acquisition of property, plant and equipment and intangible assets. Financing activities used another DKK 8.9 billion, primarily for share buy-back.

Strategy
The company's SAIL'22 strategy has served it well since its launch in 2016, resulting in a strong and resilient company. SAIL'22 has focused on improving its business organically. Since 2016, it has guided the company's actions, setting clear priorities for how it brews for a better today and tomorrow. While providing a clear overall direction for the company's business, SAIL'22 has been a "living" strategy. Since its launch in March 2016, it has continuously adjusted the application of the strategy to reflect learnings and also the market environment, which has significantly changed, especially with COVID-19. Coupled with a significantly strengthened performance management culture and a good organizational balance

between markets, regions and central functions, the company has been able to leverage scale while remaining close to local consumers and customers.

HISTORY

Carlsberg stems from the amalgamation of two proud Danish brewing concerns. Captain J. C. Jacobsen founded the first of these in Copenhagen; his father had worked as a brewery hand before acquiring his own small brewery in 1826. Studious and technically minded, J. C. inherited the brewery in 1835. He opened the Carlsberg Brewery (named for his son Carl) in 1847 and exported his first beer (to the UK) in 1868. J. C. established the Carlsberg Foundation in 1876 to conduct scientific research and oversee brewery operations.

Carl, who conflicted with his father over brewery operations, opened a new facility (New Carlsberg) adjacent to his dad's in 1881. Both men bestowed gifts upon their city, such as a church, an art museum, a royal castle renovation, and Copenhagen Harbor's famous Little Mermaid statue. Father and son willed their breweries to the foundation, which united them in 1906.

Tuborgs Fabrikker was founded in 1873 by a group of Danish businessmen who wanted to establish a major industrial project (including a brewery) at Tuborg Harbor. Philip Heyman headed the group and in 1880 spun off all operations but the brewery.

Carlsberg and Tuborg became Denmark's two leading brewers. After WWII, both began marketing their beers outside the country. Between 1958 and 1972 they tripled exports and established breweries in Europe and Asia. Both brewers' desire to grow internationally influenced their decision to merge, which they did in 1969 as United Breweries.

During the 1980s the firm diversified, forming Carlsberg Biotechnology in 1983 to extend its research to other areas. It strengthened its position in North America through licenses with Anheuser-Busch (1985) and John Labatt (1988). United Breweries reverted to the old Carlsberg name in 1987.

Carlsberg and Allied-Lyons (which became Allied Domecq before being acquired by Pernod Ricard in 2005) combined their UK brewing, distribution, and wholesaling operations under the name Carlsberg-Tetley (now Carlsberg UK) in 1992, creating the UK's third-largest brewer (behind Bass and Courage).

The firm teamed up with India's United Breweries in 1995 to distribute Carlsberg beer on the subcontinent. Bass acquired Allied's 50% of Carlsberg-Tetley in 1996 but sold its stake to Carlsberg in 1997 upon orders from regulators. Also in 1997 Carlsberg and Coca-Cola set up Coca-Cola Nordic Beverages to bottle and distribute soft drinks in Nordic countries. That year Poul Svanholm retired after 25 years as CEO; he was replaced by JÃ¯rn Jensen.

Carlsberg acquired a 60% stake in Finnish brewer Sinebrychoff in 1998. Carlsberg then sold a 60% stake in Vingaarden to Finland's Oy Rettig (1999), sold its remaining 43% share of the Tivoli amusement park to Danish tobacco group Skandinavisk Tobakskompagni (2000), and reduced its 64% holding in Royal Scandinavia to 28% (2000). Carlsberg bought the beverage operations of Swedish firm FeldschlÃ¶sschen HÃ¶rlimann in 2000 and agreed to combine brewing businesses with Norway-based Orkla in a deal worth $1.5 billion; Carlsberg Breweries was formed in February 2001 after both agreed to divest several brands and distribution rights to gain regulatory approval.

Carlsberg stopped production at Coca-Cola Nordic Beverages (the company still exists but has no operations) in 2001 because of conflicts with Orkla's Pepsi bottling contracts in Sweden and Norway; Carlsberg and Coca-Cola continued to produce and sell Coke in Denmark and Finland. Nils S. Andersen became the company's president and CEO that year.

In 2002 Carlsberg sold 32% of its Lithuanian brewery to Russia's Baltic Beverage Holding, a joint venture between Carlsberg and Scottish & Newcastle. That year Carlsberg also signed an agreement giving Carib Brewery Ltd., part of the ANSA McAl Group, the rights to brew and distribute Carlsberg Beer in selected areas of the Caribbean.

In 2003 Carlsberg Breweries acquired an additional 27.5% stake in Pirinsko Pivo, a Bulgarian brewery, bringing its overall ownership to 94.5%. That same year, it purchased the Chinese brewers Dali and Kunming. The following year the group acquired the Germany-based beer brewer and distributor Holsten-Brauerei.

In 2007 Nils Andersen left to become CEO at A.P. MÃ¸ller - MÃ¦rsk; he was replaced by JÃ¸rgen Rasmussen.

In November 2012 Carlsberg acquired all the outstanding shares of Russian brewer Pivovarennaya kompaniya Baltika.

EXECUTIVES

Chief Executive Officer, Cees't Hart
Chief Financial Officer, Ulrica Fearn
Asia Executive Vice President, Joao Abecasis
Strategy and Digital Executive Vice President, Soren Brinck
Commercial, Asia Executive Vice President, Group Sales, Marketing & Innovation Executive Vice President, Asia Executive Vice President, Western Europe Executive Vice President, Graham James Fewkes
Chief Human Resources Officer, Joris Huijsmans
Central & Eastern Europe Executive Vice President, Commercial Development Executive Vice President, Lars Lehmann
Supply Chain Executive Vice President, Victor Shevtsov

Chair, Independent Non-Executive Director, Henrik Poulsen
Deputy Chair, Non-Independent Non-Executive Director, Majken Schultz
Independent Non-Executive Director, Mikael Aro
Independent Non-Executive Director, Magdi Batato
Independent Non-Executive Director, Lilian Fossum Biner
Independent Non-Executive Director, Richard Burrows
Independent Non-Executive Director, Punita Lal
Non-Independent Non-Executive Director, Carl Bache
Non-Independent Non-Executive Director, Soren-Peter Fuchs Olesen
Independent Director, Lars Fruergaard Jorgensen
Supervisory Board Member, Hans S. Andersen
Supervisory Board Member, Eva Vilstrup Decker
Supervisory Board Member, Erik Lund
Supervisory Board Member, Olayide Oladokun
Supervisory Board Member, Tenna Skov Thorsted
Supervisory Board Member, Finn Lok
Supervisory Board Member, Peter Petersen
Supervisory Board Member, Lars Stemmerik
Auditors : PricewaterhouseCoopers Statsautoriseret Revisionsaktieselskab

LOCATIONS

HQ: Carlsberg A/S (Denmark)
1 J. C. Jacobsens Gade, Copenhagen V 1799
Phone: (45) 3327 3300 **Fax:** (45) 3327 4701
Web: www.carlsberggroup.com

2017 Sales

	% of total
Western Europe	59
Eastern Europe	18
Asia	23
Total	100

PRODUCTS/OPERATIONS

Selected BrandsCarlsbergTuborgGrimbergenKronenbourg 1664Somersby

COMPETITORS

ABI SAB GROUP HOLDING LIMITED
ASTELLAS PHARMA LTD.
ASTRAZENECA PLC
Anheuser-Busch InBev
Anheuser-Busch InBev
FPInnovations
SEMATECH, INC.
SENOMYX, INC.
SINCLAIR PHARMA LIMITED
Theratechnologies Inc

HISTORICAL FINANCIALS

Company Type: Public

Income Statement   FYE: December 31

	REVENUE ($mil)	NET INCOME ($mil)	NET PROFIT MARGIN	EMPLOYEES
12/22	10,091	(152)	—	38,906
12/21	10,141	1,041	10.3%	39,375
12/20	9,656	994	10.3%	40,010
12/19	9,903	987	10.0%	41,248
12/18	9,585	814	8.5%	40,837
Annual Growth	1.3%	—	—	(1.2%)

2022 Year-End Financials

Debt ratio: 3.4%   No. of shares ($ mil.): 137
Return on equity: (-2.8%)   Dividends
Cash ($ mil.): 1,172   Yield: —
Current Ratio: 0.70   Payout: 0.0%
Long-term debt ($ mil.): 3,111   Market value ($ mil.): 3,644

	STOCK PRICE ($) FY Close	P/E High	P/E Low	PER SHARE ($) Earnings	Dividends	Book Value
12/22	26.53	—	—	(1.09)	0.47	33.36
12/21	34.72	1	1	7.21	0.48	47.13
12/20	32.13	1	1	6.78	0.41	44.68
12/19	29.79	1	0	6.52	0.37	44.12
12/18	21.25	1	1	5.32	0.37	45.57
Annual Growth	5.7%	—	—	—	6.3%	(7.5%)

Carnival Plc

Operating as a dual-listed company with US-based Carnival Corporation, it is the one of the world's largest leisure travel companies with operations in North America, Australia, Europe and Asia, with about 10 cruise lines, a fleet of over 90 ships and a total passenger capacity of some 243,180. Carnival serves UK passengers (and Australia) primarily through P&O Cruises, while brands such as AIDA and Costa Cruises serve travelers across the rest of Europe. In North America, Carnival operates Princess Cruise Lines, Holland America, Seabourn, P&O Cruises Australia and its flagship Carnival Cruise Lines. Carnival also owns ocean liner operator Cunard, which is the epitome of British refinement for travelers who relish the line's impeccable White Star Services, fine dining, sophisticated adventure, and the legacy of historic voyages and transatlantic travel. The company generates around 55% of its sales from North America.

Operations

The company is a leisure travel company with a portfolio of nine of the world's leading cruise lines. With operations in North America, Australia, Europe and Asia, our portfolio features ? Carnival Cruise Line, Princess Cruises, Holland America Line, P&O Cruises (Australia), Seabourn, Costa Cruises, AIDA Cruises, P&O Cruises (UK) and Cunard.

Carnival Cruise Line is the most popular cruise brand in North America and operates about 25 ships designed to foster exceptionally fun and memorable vacation experiences a an outstanding value. Princess Cruises is the world's thord largest cruise line based on guest capacity and the company's ships are renowned for its innovative design and wide array of choices in dining, entertainment and amenities. The Holland America Line's premium fleet of some 10 spacious, elegant mid-sized ships feature sophisticated five-star dining, extensive entertainment and activities, innovative culinary enrichment programs and compelling worldwide itineraries. The P&O Cruises (Australia) provides a quintessential holiday experience for Australians and New Zealanders, taking them to some of the world's most idyllic and hard-to-reach places across Asia and the South Pacific.

The Seabourn provides ultraluxury cruising vacations in a unique, small-ship style that focuses on genuine, intuitive service, all-suite accommodations, superb cuisine and unique experiences in destinations worldwide. AIDA Cruises is one of the fastest growing and commercially most successful tourism businesses in Germany. The P&O Cruises (UK) has a fleet of five ships. It combines genuine service, a sense of occasion and attention to detail; and ensures passengers have the holiday of a lifetime. The Cunard is the epitome of British refinement for travelers who relish the line's impeccable White Star Services, fine dining, sophisticated adventure, and the legacy of historic voyages and transatlantic travel.

The company operates in four segments: NAA cruise operations, which accounts for about 60% of total sales; EA cruise operations, which brings in more than 35%; Cruise support, which includes portfolio of leading port destinations; and Tour and other, which represents the hotel and transportation operations of Holland America Princess Alaska Tours operations.

Overall, Carnival generates over 50% of total sales from passenger tickets, and about 50% from onboard & other.

Geographic Reach

Headquartered in Florida, US and Southampton, UK, Carnival's largest market is North America, which represents around 55% of sales. Other major markets include Europe (over 40%) and Australia and Asia (less than 5%).

Sales and Marketing

Carnival sells its cruises through travel agents, tour operators, company vacation planners and its websites.

Financial Performance

The company's revenue for fiscal 2021 decreased to $1.9 billion compared from the prior year with $5.6 billion.

Net income for fiscal 2021 increased to $9.5 billion compared form the prior year with $10.2 billion.

Cash held by the company at the end of fiscal 2021 decreased to $9.0 billion. Cash provided by financing activities was $6.9 billion while cash used for operations and investing activities were $4.1 billion and $3.5 billion, respectively.

EXECUTIVES

Chairman, Director, Micky M. Arison, $906,400 total compensation
President, Chief Executive Officer, Chief Climate Officer, Independent Non-Executive Director, Joshua Ian Weinstein
Chief Financial Officer, Chief Accounting Officer, David Bernstein, $750,000 total compensation
Chief Risk Officer, Chief Compliance Officer, Richard Brilliant
General Counsel, Enrique Miguez
Senior Vice President, Secretary, Arnaldo Perez, $450,000 total compensation
Independent Non-Executive Director, Jonathon Band
Independent Non-Executive Director, Jason Glen Cahilly
Independent Non-Executive Director, Helen Deeble
Independent Non-Executive Director, Jeffrey J. Gearhart
Independent Non-Executive Director, Katie Lahey
Independent Non-Executive Director, Stuart Subotnick
Independent Non-Executive Director, Laura A. Weil
Independent Non-Executive Director, Randall J. Weisenburger
Independent Non-Executive Director, Sara Mathew
Auditors: PricewaterhouseCoopers LLP

LOCATIONS

HQ: Carnival Plc
Carnival House, 100 Harbour Parade, Southampton SO15 1ST
Phone: (44) 23 8065 5000
Web: www.carnivalplc.com

2015 Sales

	$ mil.	% of total
North America Cruise Brands	9,866	62
EAA Cruise Brands	5,636	36
Cruise support	119	1
Tour & other	226	1
Adjustments	(133)	-
Total	15,714	100

2015 Sales

	$ mil.	% of total
North America	8,015	51
Europe	5,133	33
Australia & Asia	2,256	14
Others	310	2
Total	15,714	100

PRODUCTS/OPERATIONS

2015 Sales

	$ mil.	% of total
Cruise		
Passenger tickets	11,601	74
Onboard & other	3,887	25
Tour & other	226	1
Total	15,714	100

Selected Cruise Ships

AIDA
    AIDAaura (launched in 2003; 1,266 passengers)

AIDAbella (2008; 2,050)
AIDAcara (1996; 1,180)
AIDAdiva (2007; 2,050)
AIDAvita (2002; 1,266)
Carnival Cruise Lines
  Carnival Conquest (2002; 2,966)
  Carnival Destiny (1996; 2,634)
  Carnival Freedom (2007; 2,966)
  Carnival Glory (2003; 2,966)
  Carnival Legend (2002; 2,118)
  Carnival Liberty (2005; 2,966)
  Carnival Miracle (2004; 2,118)
  Carnival Pride (2001; 2,118)
  Carnival Spirit (2001; 2,118)
  Carnival Splendor (2008; 2,998)
  Carnival Triumph (1999; 2,750)
  Carnival Valor (2004; 2,966)
  Carnival Victory (2000; 2,750)
  Ecstasy (1991; 2,050)
  Elation (1998; 2,050)
  Fantasy (1990; 2,054)
  Fascination (1994; 2,050)
  Holiday (1985; 1,450)
  Imagination (1995; 2,050)
  Inspiration (1996; 2,050)
  Paradise (1998; 2,048)
  Sensation (1993; 2,050)
Costa Cruises
  Costa Allegra (1992; 784)
  Costa Atlantica (2000; 2,114)
  Costa Classica (1991; 1,302)
  Costa Europa (1986; 1,488)
  Costa Fortuna (2003; 2,702)
  Costa Magica (2004; 2,702)
  Costa Marina (1990; 762)
  Costa Mediterranea (2003; 2,114)
  Costa Romantica (1993; 1,344)
  Costa Serena (2007; 2,978)
  Costa Victoria (1996; 1,928)
Cunard Line
  Queen Mary 2 (2003; 2,592)
  Queen Victoria (2007; 1,980)
  Queen Elizabeth (2010; 2,092)
Holland America Line
  Amsterdam (2000; 1,380)
  Eurodam (2008; 2,104)
  Maasdam (1993; 1,258)
  Noordam (2006; 1,918)
  Oosterdam (2003; 1,848)
  Prinsendam (1988; 792)
  Rotterdam (1997; 1,316)
  Ryndam (1994; 1,260)
  Statendam (1993; 1,258)
  Veendam (1996; 1,258)
  Volendam (1999; 1,432)
  Westerdam (2004; 1,916)
  Zaandam (2000; 1,432)
  Zuiderdam (2002; 1,848)
Ibero Cruises
  Grand Celebration (1987; 1,494)
  Grand Mistral (1999; 1,244)
  Grand Voyager (2000; 834)
Ocean Village
  Ocean Village (1989; 1,578)
  Ocean Village Two (1990; 1,708)
P&O Cruises
  Arcadia (2005; 2,016)
  Artemis (1984; 1,200)
  Aurora (2000; 1,870)
  Oceana (2000; 2,016)
  Oriana (1995; 1,818)
  Ventura (2008; 3,078)
P&O Cruises Australia
  Pacific Dawn (1991; 1,596)
  Pacific Sun (1986; 1,480)
Princess Cruise Lines
  Caribbean Princess (2004; 3,100)
  Coral Princess (2002; 1,974)
  Crown Princess (2006; 3,080)
  Dawn Princess (1997; 1,998)
  Diamond Princess (2004; 2,678)
  Emerald Princess (2007; 3,080)
  Golden Princess (2001; 2,598)
  Grand Princess (1998; 2,592)
  Island Princess (2003; 1,974)
  Pacific Princess (1999; 676)
  Royal Princess (2001; 710)
  Ruby Princess (2008; 3,080)
  Sapphire Princess (2004; 2,678)
  Sea Princess (1998; 2,016)
  Star Princess (2002; 2,598)
  Sun Princess (1995; 2,022)
  Tahitian Princess (2000; 676)
Seabourn
  Seabourn Legend (1992; 208)
  Seabourn Pride (1988; 208)
  Seabourn Spirit (1989; 208)

COMPETITORS

Azul S/A
BENETEAU
CARNIVAL CORPORATION
EASYJET PLC
EUROPCAR MOBILITY GROUP
INTERNATIONAL CONSOLIDATED AIRLINES GROUP SA
JUST EAT LIMITED
NORWEGIAN CRUISE LINE HOLDINGS LTD.
ROYAL CARIBBEAN CRUISES LTD.
THOMAS COOK GROUP PLC

HISTORICAL FINANCIALS

Company Type: Public

Income Statement — FYE: November 30

	REVENUE ($mil)	NET INCOME ($mil)	NET PROFIT MARGIN	EMPLOYEES
11/23	21,593	(74)	—	2,000
11/22	12,168	(6,093)	—	87,000
11/21	1,908	(9,501)	—	40,000
11/20	5,595	(10,236)	—	70,000
11/19	20,825	2,990	14.4%	106,000
Annual Growth	0.9%	—	—	(62.9%)

2023 Year-End Financials

Debt ratio: 62.2% No. of shares ($ mil.): 1,264
Return on equity: (-1.0%) Dividends
Cash ($ mil.): 2,426 Yield: —
Current Ratio: 0.46 Payout: 0.0%
Long-term debt ($ mil.): 28,483 Market value ($ mil.): 17,039

	STOCK PRICE ($) FY Close	P/E High/Low		PER SHARE ($) Earnings	Dividends	Book Value
11/23	13.48	—	—	(0.06)	0.00	5.44
11/22	8.94	—	—	(5.16)	0.00	5.61
11/21	16.19	—	—	(8.46)	0.00	10.69
11/20	17.67	—	—	(13.20)	0.50	18.91
11/19	42.58	14	9	4.32	2.00	37.08
Annual Growth	(25.0%)	—	—	—	—	(38.1%)

Casino Guichard Perrachon S.A.

One of the world's leading food retailers, Casino Group owns and operates more than 11,500 stores , including hypermarkets (mostly GÃ©ant), supermarkets (Casino and Monoprix, to name a few), restaurants (Casino Shop), and discount stores (Leader Price). Its model is built on five pillars: a portfolio of buoyant formats in France; a leading food and non-food E-commerce offering; the development of new growth drivers; significant shareholding in major retailers in Latin America; and strengthening of the company's structure through major financial and strategic plans. Most of its stores are in France, but it has outlets in Cameroon, Uruguay, Brazil, Colombia, and Argentina.

Operations

Its retail operations bring revenue from France of around 45%, from Latam retail over 45%, and mpre than 5% revenue from e-commerce.

France Retail segment comprises retail operating segments (mainly the sub-group banners Casino, Monoprix, Franprix and VindÃ©mia). The Latam Reatil comprises food retailing operating segments in Latin America (mainly the GPA and AssaÃ food banners and the Ã‰xito, Disco-Devoto and Libertad sub-group banners). The E-commerce segment comprises the Cdiscount and the Cnova N.V. holding company.

Of its over 11,500 stores, about 5,730 are convenience stores, over 940 are Franprix, about 840 Monoprix point of sale, about 430 Casino supermarkets, and Casino hypermarkets.

Geographic Reach

Casino is headquartered in France. It has more than 230 affiliated stores and around 230 stores operating in North Africa and Middle East, as well as in Sub-Saharan Africa and in more than 30 countries, including France, Colombia, Brazil, Argentina, Uruguay, Senegal, Cote d'Ivoire, Cameroon, Madagascar, and Mauritius.

Financial Performance

In 2021, the company reported a net sales of EUR 30.5 billion, a 4% decrease from the previous year's net sales of EUR 31.9 billion.

Net loss for fiscal 2021 decreased to EUR 530 million compared from the prior year with EUR 664 million.

The company's cash at the end of 2021 was EUR 2.2 billion. Operating activities generated EUR 1.5 billion, while investing activities used EUR 1.1 billion, mainly for acquisition of property, plant and equipment, intangible assets and investment property. Financing activities used another EUR 848 million, primarily for repayments of loans and borrowings.

Strategy

In France, Casino Group stands out for its portfolio of buoyant formats encompassing a mix of premium, convenience, supermarket and hypermarket banners. At 31 December 2021, Casino Group comprised about 8,320 stores in France, including some 6,070 franchises.

The food retail sector in France has for several years been undergoing profound changes due to a shift in consumer habits and regional trends. Consumers nowadays have new expectations with regard to the environment, such as product traceability and animal welfare, but also to practicality, leading to major changes in their consumption habits. They tend now to prefer urban convenience formats. Economic and demographic territorial trends are highly uneven from one region to another, with major urban hubs mainly situated in the ÃŽle-de-France, RhÃ´ne-Alpes and Provence Alpes CÃ´te d'Azur areas of France, where the company has a particularly strong presence.

Casino is concentrating on the buoyant premium and convenience formats and reducing its exposure to discount stores. In November 2020, the company completed the sale to Aldi France of 545 Leader Price stores, 2 Casino supermarkets and 3 warehouses.

Company Background

Casino is controlled by Euris, which is controlled by Jean-Charles Naouri, Casino's chairman and CEO.

HISTORY

Frenchman Geoffroy Guichard married Antonia Perrachon, a grocer's daughter, in 1889 in Saint-Ã‰tienne, France. Three years later Geoffroy took over his father-in-law's general store (a converted "casino" or musical hall). In 1898 the company became SociÃ©tÃ© des Magasins du Casino. By 1900, when it became a joint stock company, Casino had 50 stores; it opened its 100th store in 1904. That year the company introduced its first private-label product: canned sardines. In 1917 Guichard named his two sons, Mario and Jean, as managers.

By WWI there were about 215 branches, more than 50 in Saint-Ã‰tienne. From 1919 to the early 1920s, the company opened several factories to manufacture goods such as food, soap, and perfumes. In 1925 the elder Guichard retired, leaving the day-to-day operations of Casino to his two sons. (Geoffroy died in 1940.) WWII took a heavy toll on the company: About 70 Casino stores were leveled and another 450 were damaged.

The company began opening cafeterias in 1967, and in 1976 it formed Casino USA to run them. Casino USA bought an interest in the California-based Thriftimart volume retailer in 1983, renaming the company after Thriftimart's Smart & Final warehouse stores.

Casino grew by acquiring companies across France, including CEDIS (16 hypermarkets, 116 supermarkets, and 722 smaller stores in eastern France; 1985) and La Ruche Meridionale (18 hypermarkets and 112 supermarkets in southern France, 1990). Casino bought nearly 300 hypermarkets and supermarkets from Rallye SA in 1992, giving Rallye about 30% of the company. The company opened its first hypermarket in Warsaw, Poland, in 1996.

Rival PromodÃ¨s made a roughly $4.5 billion hostile takeover bid for Casino in 1997. Guichard family members voted against the PromodÃ¨s offer, instead backing a $3.9 billion friendly offer from Rallye (increasing their stake to nearly 50%). Casino also launched a massive counterattack -- buying more than 600 Franprix and Leader Price supermarket stores from food manufacturer TLC Beatrice and acquiring a 21% stake in hypermarket chain Monoprix. PromodÃ¨s withdrew its bid four months later.

Casino expanded internationally in the late 1990s, acquiring stakes in food retailers in Argentina (Libertad), Uruguay (Disco), Colombia (Almacenes Exito SA), Brazil (Companhia Brasileira de DistribuiÃ§Ã£o), and Thailand (Big C, the country's largest retailer). It also opened its first hypermarket in Taichung, Taiwan.

Expansion in France included a joint venture (called Opera), formed in 1999 with retailer Cora SA to buy food and nonfood goods for the Casino and Cora stores, and the acquisition of 100 convenience stores (converted to the Petit Casino banner) in southwest France from retailer Guyenne et Gascogne.

Casino acquired 100 Proxi convenience stores in southeast France in 2000 from Montagne (most became Vival franchises) and more than 400 convenience stores (Eco Service and others) from Auchan. Casino also bought 51% of French online retailer Cdiscount.com (CDs, videos, CD-ROMs, and DVDs), and upped its ownership in several of its international supermarket operations, including gaining 100% ownership of Libertad. It also increased its ownership of Monoprix to 49%.

In July 2002 Casino bought a 38% stake in Laurus NV, its financially troubled Dutch rival. Laurus operates nearly 2,000 supermarkets in the Netherlands, Spain, and Belgium. (Soon after, Casino sold Laurus's unprofitable stores in Spain and Belgium.) Also in 2002 the company sold its wine division, Les Chais Beaucairois, to wine and spirits company Marie Brizard for $22 million.

Chief executive Pierre Bouchut unexpectedly left Casino in March 2005. Jean-Charles Naouri, the company's chairman and controlling shareholder, replaced him. In May Casino took joint control of Brazil's leading food retailer, Companhia Brasileira de DistribuiÃ§Ã£o, along with the family of AbÃlio Diniz. Previously, Casino held a minority stake in the supermarket chain. Casino spun off some of its shopping center assets in an October IPO for part of its real estate assets in France, including shopping mall properties adjacent to its hypermarket and supermarkets, as well as the land under its cafeterias.

In 2006 the French supermarket operator spun off its property company Mercialys. (Following the IPO, Casino holds about a 60% stake in Mercialys.) In January 2006 Casino increased its stake in Colombia's biggest retailer Exito to nearly 39%. The company in July sold its 19 hypermarkets in Poland to METRO AG, its German rival, for about $1.1 billion as part of its asset disposal program. In September Casino sold its 50% stake in its Taiwanese subsidiary, Far Eastern GÃ©ant, to its joint venture partner Far Eastern Department Stores.

Real estate sales continued in late 2007 with the announcement that Casino plans to sell nearly $930 million in assets, including 255 grocery stores in France. The retailer says it plans to use the proceeds from the sale of these "mature" assets for high-potential projects in France and abroad. In May 2007 Casino sold its 55% stake of the California-based Smart & Final warehouse grocery chain to Apollo Management for $813 million, thereby exiting the US market.

Casino acquired in July 2008 about 90% of the French textile maker International Textiles Associes (or INTEXA) from members of the Broyer family. Also, Casino exercised its option in 2008 to increase its share in Dutch supermarket operator Super de Boer (formerly Laurus, acquired in 2002) to a majority stake. However, in December 2009 Casino sold its 57% stake in Super de Boer to Dutch rival Jumbo Groep Holding for ?552.5 (nearly $800 million).

In November 2009 Casino acquired the remaining shares of Leader Price and Franprix chains from the Baud family, bringing its ownership stake up to 100% in both chains.

EXECUTIVES

Chairman, Chief Executive Officer, Director,
Jean-Charles Naouri
Chief Financial Officer, Executive Director,
David Lubek
Strategic Planning Chief Operating Officer, Strategic Planning Director, Strategic Planning Committee Secretary, Julien Lagubeau
E-commerce Executive Director, Emmanuel Grenier
Supply Chain Executive Director, Merchandising Executive Director, Supply Chain Director, Merchandising Director, Supply Chain Subsidiary Officer, Merchandising Subsidiary Officer, Herve Daudin
CSR and Engagement Director, Matthieu RichÃ©
Human Resources Director, RaphaÃ«le Hauzy
Subsidiary Officer, Carlos Mario Giraldo Moreno
Subsidiary Officer, Tina Schuler
General Secretary, Guillaume AppÃ©re
Independent Director, Frederic Saint-Geours
Independent Director, Maud Bailly
Independent Director, Thierry Billot
Independent Director, Beatrice Dumurgier
Independent Director, Christiane Feral-Schuhl
Independent Director, Nathalie Andrieux
Director, Matignon Diderot
Director, Franck Hattab
Director, Alexis Ravalais
Director, Societe Carpinienne de Participations
Director, Josseline de Clausade
Director, FonciÃ¨re Euris

Director, Thomas Piquemal
Director, Fimalac Marc de Lacharrière
Director, Odile Muracciole
Director, Didier Carlier
Director, David de Rothschild
Director, Didier Lévêque
Auditors : KPMG S.A

LOCATIONS

HQ: Casino Guichard Perrachon S.A.
1, Cours Antoine Guichard, Saint-Etienne, Cedex 1 42008
Phone: (33) 4 77 45 31 31   **Fax:** (33) 4 77 45 38 38
Web: www.groupe-casino.fr

PRODUCTS/OPERATIONS

2015 Stores

	No.
France	10,627
International	
Argentina	27
Uruguay	65
Brazil	2,181
Colombia	1,668
Thailand	734
Vietnam	42
Total	15,344

2015 type of Stores (France)

	No.
Casino hypermarket	128
Supermarkets	441
Monoprix	698
Franprix	867
Leader price	810
Convenience stores	6,916
Indian ocean	146
Other Activities	621
Total	10,627

2015 Sales

	% of Total
France Retail	41
Latam Retail	32
Latam Electronics	11
Asia	9
E-Commerce	7
Total	100

Selected Operations

Banque du Groupe Casino (60%, financial services)
Big C (36%, Thailand)
Casino Enterprise (non-food operations)
Cativen (66%, Venezuela)
Cdiscount.com (67%, e-commerce)
Companhia Brasileira de Distribuição (34%, Brazil)
Devoto (97%, supermarkets, Uruguay)
Exito Colombia SA (55%, supermarkets, hypermarkets)
Franprix (supermarkets)
Géant (hypermarkets)
Imagica (photo and digital imaging processing)
Leader Price (supermarkets)
Libertad (hypermarkets, Argentina)
Vindémia (supermarkets; Madagascar, Mauritius, Réunion)

COMPETITORS

7-ELEVEN, INC
AUCHAN HOLDING
CARREFOUR
Grupo Comercial Chedraui, S.A.B. de C.V.
KERING
KINGFISHER PLC
Koninklijke Ahold Delhaize N.V.
RALLYE
STAGE STORES, INC.
Victoria Retail Group B.V.

HISTORICAL FINANCIALS

Company Type: Public

Income Statement   FYE: December 31

	REVENUE ($mil)	NET INCOME ($mil)	NET PROFIT MARGIN	EMPLOYEES
12/22	36,317	(337)	—	188,811
12/21	35,147	(599)	—	196,307
12/20	39,899	(1,087)	—	202,955
12/19	39,644	(1,607)	—	209,696
12/18	42,527	(61)	—	214,458
Annual Growth	(3.9%)	—		(3.1%)

2022 Year-End Financials

Debt ratio: 30.5%   No. of shares ($ mil.): 108
Return on equity: (-11.3%)   Dividends
Cash ($ mil.): 2,674   Yield: —
Current Ratio: 0.71   Payout: 0.0%
Long-term debt ($ mil.): 7,701 Market value ($ mil.): —

Cathay Financial Holding Co

One of the largest financial services company in Taiwan, Cathay Financial Holding Co. owns companies involved in banking, insurance, brokerage, and more. Cathay consists of three principal operating subsidiaries: Cathay Life Insurance Co., Ltd., offering life insurance products; Cathay United Bank Ltd., providing wealth management, consumer banking, corporate banking and investment services; Cathay Century Insurance Co., Ltd., providing motor, fire, marine, engineering, and property & casualty insurance. All told, the company has more than 700 locations and claims a customer base of more than 13 million customers. Cathay was founded in 2001.

Operations

Cathay Financial operates through four main segments: banking; life insurance; property insurance; and securities.

The life insurance operating segment (more than 85% of total revenue) is engaged in interest-sensitive sales of traditional insurance, investment-linked insurance and annuity insurance and providing financial planning services and policy loan services.

The banking operating segment (some 10%) is engaged in permitted businesses of commercial banks provided by the Banking Act of the Republic of China, foreign exchange business, guarantee business, advisory service of foreign currency investments, trust business, offshore banking units and other financial business of investments from returning expatriates.

The property insurance operating segment is engaged in fire insurance, marine insurance, land and air insurance, liability insurance, Guarantee insurance, reinsurance and other insurance.

The securities operating segment is engaged in brokerage, dealership, and underwriting business and is dedicated to capabilities of research, development and design to provide security financial services with a variety of new financial products.

Geographic Reach

Taiwan-based, Cathay continues to deepen its overseas presence, establishing a vast network of business locations across Greater China and Southeast Asia, and continues to strengthen local business management and promote digital services. The company has regional offices in Taiwan, Mainland China, Hong Kong, Vietnam, Singapore, Cambodia, Malaysia, Philippines, Myanmar, Europe, Japan and the US.

Sales and Marketing

With a comprehensive network of 700 branches and nearly 30 thousand sales forces, Cathay services more than 13 million customers.

Financial Performance

The company reported a total revenue of NT$ 194.9 billion in 2021, a 2% increase from the previous year's total revenue of NT$ 190.9 billion.

In 2021, the company had a net income of NT$ 139.5 billion, an 89% increase from the previous year's net income of NT$ 74.6 billion.

The company's cash at the end of 2021 was NT$ 692 billion. Operating activities generated NT$ 72.5 billion, while investing activities used NT$ 12.9 billion, mainly for acquisition of financial assets. Financing activities used another NT$ 25 billion, primarily for dividends paid.

Strategy

The company's business strategy will continue to respond to rapidly changing market conditions. Going forward, Cathay FHC will continue to improve its regional expansion, accelerate digital transformation and business innovation, and leverage its financial competencies to achieve sustainable finance while accounting for robust business development and risk management.

EXECUTIVES

Chairman, Hong-Tu Tsai
President, Director, Chang-Ken Lee
Chief Auditor, Senior Executive Vice President, Chih-Jung Kung
Chief Financial Officer, Senior Executive Vice President, Grace Chen
Senior Executive Vice President, David P. Sun
Chief Investment Officer, Senior Executive Vice President, Sophia Cheng
Senior Executive Vice President, Chung-Yi Teng
Chief Risk Officer, Executive Vice President, Ching Lu Huang
Chief Information Officer, Senior Executive Vice President, Chia-Sheng Chang
Senior Executive Vice President, Jian-Hsing Wu
Senior Executive Vice President, Hsiang-Hsin Tsai
Senior Executive Vice President, Tsung-Hsien Tsai
Senior Executive Vice President, Xu-Jie Yao

Chief Corporated Governance Officer, Executive Vice President, Deh-Yen Weng
Chief Compliance Officer, Executive Vice President, Judie Hsu
Vice-Chairman, Tsu-Pei Chen
Director, Cheng-Ta Tsai
Director, Chen-Chiu Tsai
Director, Chi-Wei Joong
Director, Andrew Ming-Jian Kuo
Director, Tiao-Kuei Huang
Director, Ming-ho Hsiung
Independent Director, Feng-Chiang Miau
Independent Director, Edward Yung Do Way
Independent Director, Li-Ling Wang
Independent Director, Tang-Chieh Wu
Auditors : Deloitte & Touche

LOCATIONS

HQ: Cathay Financial Holding Co
No. 296, Jen Ai Road, Section 4, Taipei
Phone: (886) 2 2708 7689   **Fax:** (886) 2 2325 2488
Web: www.cathayholdings.com

COMPETITORS

Banque Nationale du Canada
CIMB GROUP HOLDINGS BERHAD
CMB WING LUNG BANK LIMITED
CTBC Financial Holding Co., Ltd.
Grupo Financiero BBVA Bancomer, S.A. de C.V.
HollisWealth Inc
MEGA FINANCIAL HOLDING COMPANY LIMITED
NOMURA INTERNATIONAL PLC
VOYA SERVICES COMPANY
Wüstenrot & Württembergische AG

HISTORICAL FINANCIALS

Company Type: Public

Income Statement — FYE: December 31

	ASSETS ($mil)	NET INCOME ($mil)	INCOME AS % OF ASSETS	EMPLOYEES
12/21	418,748	5,038	1.2%	57,100
12/20	389,666	2,653	0.7%	0
12/19	336,205	2,096	0.6%	0
12/18	301,605	1,682	0.6%	0
12/17	298,176	1,898	0.6%	0
Annual Growth	8.9%	27.6%		

2021 Year-End Financials
Return on assets: 1.2%
Return on equity: 15.5%
Long-term debt ($ mil.): —
No. of shares ($ mil.): 13,169
Sales ($ mil.): 9,268
Dividends
Yield: —
Payout: 0.0%
Market value ($ mil.): —

Ceconomy AG

Ceconomy (formerly Metro) is Europe's leading consumer electronics retailer. Through the retail brands Media Markt and Saturn, Ceconomy sells thousands of electronic items such as gaming, household appliances, smart home, telecommunications, computer, photo, as well as an option to rent rather than buy appliances for about 1,020 stores in more than 10 European countries, including its home market. Its other businesses include digital advertising company, Deutsche Technikberatung, which offers installation assistance, connection and troubleshooting of electronic devices at home. Ceconomy holds about 25% stake in Fnac Darty, France's largest electronics retailer. The company generates the majority of its sales in Germany, Austria, Switzerland, and Hungary.

Operations

As the central management holding company, Ceconomy covers basic functions such as finance, accounting, controlling, legal and compliance. The focus of the operating business is the MediaMarktSaturn Retail Group, to which the MediaMarkt and Saturn brands belong.

MediaMarkt operates as an independent retail brand within the MediaMarktSaturn Retail Group. It combines the advantages of in-store and online retail under the umbrella of a trusted brand, complemented by opportunities for mobile, app-based shopping.

Saturn operates as an independent retail brand under the umbrella of the MediaMarktSaturn Retail Group. It links its in-store business in Germany closely with its online shop and mobile shopping via app.

Deutsche Technikberatung (DTB) stands for professional assistance for the installation, connection and troubleshooting of electronic devices at home.

Overall, product sales bring in approximately 95% of the company revenue, while services and solutions accounts for some 5%.

Geographic Reach

Germany is home to approximately 405 of Dusseldorf-based Ceconomy's total base of about 1,020 stores. Its second biggest presence is in Italy, with nearly 120 stores, while its remaining stores are relatively well diversified across more than 10 other countries in Western/Southern Europe, Eastern Europe, and Central Europe, as well as Turkey.

Ceconomy reports sales under three regions: DACH (Germany, Austria, Switzerland, and Hungary), which accounts for nearly 55% of the sales; Western Europe (about 35%); and Eastern Europe and other countries (more than 10%, combined).

Sales and Marketing

Ceconomy has approximately 2.5 billion customer touchpoints per year. In addition, the company has strong and loyal customer base with some 29 million loyalty club members.

Financial Performance

The company had a total revenue of EUR21.4 billion, a 3% increase from the previous year's total revenue of EUR20.8 billion.

Reported company EBIT increased significantly by EUR407 million to EUR326 million in the past financial year 2021.

The company's cash at the end of 2021 was EUR1.6 billion. Operating activities generated EUR450 million, while investing activities used another EUR263 million, financial investments and securities. Financing activities used another EUR77 million, primarily for redemption of lease liabilities.

Strategy

In a technology-driven world, CECONOMY's vision is to be the first choice ? for consumers as well as business partners ? as a trusted retailer with tailored solutions. This is founded on an omni-channel model focused on the customer experience. At the same time, sustainability is an essential part of the corporate strategy, which is why a holistic sustainability strategy is being developed and consistently implemented. Sustainability is to be integrated into all of CECONOMY's processes in accordance with the United Nations Sustainable Development Goals, namely by amending internal processes, reducing the company's emissions and shaping working conditions.

There are three key pillars to CECONOMY's strategy:

Create and efficient organization and structure. The stores will be relieved of administrative tasks so that they can direct their efforts more intensively towards customers. The relocation of these activities to the headquarters of the country organizations also supports the central management of important processes, including product range management, purchasing and logistics;

Build a unique value proposition. CECONOMY employs an omni-channel model in order to offer customers a unique value proposition and thus increase their satisfaction and loyalty. This is based primarily on three factors: Firstly, a seamless omni-channel experience, including in the form of personalized customer experiences, both online and in store. Secondly, an optimized supply chain, including centralized procurement and continuous improvements in logistics, which in turn means higher availability of goods and faster delivery times. Thirdly, the performance promise is based on optimized category management, which aligns product range more closely to customer needs; and

Accelerate growth path. In addition to the expansion of product range categories to innovative new areas of technology, relationships with business customers and manufacturers will thus come further to the fore in the future.

HISTORY

Otto Beisheim founded METRO SB-Grossmarkte in the German town of Mulheim in 1964. A wholesale business serving commercial customers, it operated under the name METRO Cash & Carry. Three years later Beisheim received backing from the owners of Franz Haniel & Cie (an industrial company founded in 1756) and members of the Schmidt-Ruthenbeck family (also in wholesaling). This allowed METRO to expand rapidly in Germany and, in 1968, into the Netherlands under the name Makro Cash & Carry via a partnership with Steenkolen Handelsvereeniging (SHV). During the 1970s the company expanded its wholesaling operations within Europe and moved into retailing.

METRO's foray into retailing was aided during the next decade by the acquisition of department store chain Kaufhof AG. By the 1980s the rise of specialty stores had many department stores on the defensive, and Kaufhof's owners sold it to METRO and its investment partner, Union Bank of Switzerland.

As METRO's ownership interest in Kaufhof rose above 50%, the chain began converting some of its stores from department stores into fashion and sporting goods sellers. Kaufhof began acquiring a stake in computer manufacturer and retailer Vobis in 1989. In 1993 METRO, now operating as METRO Holding AG, acquired a majority interest in supermarket company Asko Deutsche Kaufhaus, which owned the Praktiker building materials chain. The reclusive Beisheim retired from active management the following year.

To cut costs and prepare for expansion into Asia, in 1996 METRO Holding merged its German retail holdings -- Kaufhof; Asko; another grocery operation, Deutsche SB Kauf; and its German cash-and-carry operations -- into one holding company, METRO AG.

EXECUTIVES

Labor Chief Executive Officer, Labor Director, Karsten Wildberger
Chief Financial Officer, Florian Wieser
Chairman, Thomas Dannenfeldt
Vice-Chairwoman, Sylvia Woelke
Director, Katrin Adt
Director, Wolfgang Baur
Director, Kirsten Joachim Breuer
Director, Karin Dohm
Director, Daniela Eckardt
Director, Sabine Eckhardt
Director, Thomas Fernkorn
Director, Florian Funck
Director, Ludwig Glosser
Director, Doreen Huber
Director, Jurgen Kellerhals
Director, Stefanie Nutzenberger
Director, Claudia Plath
Director, Jens Ploog
Director, Lasse Putz
Director, Erich Schuhmacher
Director, Jurgen Schulz
Director, Christoph Vilanek
Auditors : KPMG AG Wirtschaftsprüfungsgesellschaft

LOCATIONS

HQ: Ceconomy AG
Kaistrasse 3, Duesseldorf 40221
Phone: (49) 211 5408 7125
Web: www.ceconomy.de

2018 Sales

	% of total
DACH (Germany, Austria, Switzerland, Hungary)	58
Western/Southern Europe	32
Eastern Europe	8
Others	2
Total	100

2018 stores

Germany	432
Austria	52
Switzerland	27
Hungary	29
Belgium	28
Greece	12
Italy	115
Luxembourg	2
Netherlands	49
Portugal	10
Spain	86
Poland	86
Turkey	71
Sweden	28
Others	28
Total	1,022

PRODUCTS/OPERATIONS

Selected Operations
Consumer Electronics
 Media Markt
 Saturn
Other OperationsiBoodJukeRetail Media GroupDeutsche Teknikberatung

COMPETITORS

A123 SYSTEMS LLC
ANIXTER INTERNATIONAL INC.
CRESCENT ELECTRIC SUPPLY COMPANY
FACILITY SOLUTIONS GROUP, INC.
GENERAL SUPPLY & SERVICES, INC.
GRAYBAR ELECTRIC COMPANY, INC.
Otto (GmbH & Co KG)
SEQUANS COMMUNICATIONS
STAPLES, INC.
SUPERDRY PLC

HISTORICAL FINANCIALS

Company Type: Public

Income Statement — FYE: September 30

	REVENUE ($mil)	NET INCOME ($mil)	NET PROFIT MARGIN	EMPLOYEES
09/22	21,219	(122)	—	44,584
09/21	24,725	(268)	—	45,841
09/20	24,390	(271)	—	47,727
09/19	23,404	133	0.6%	55,259
09/18	24,807	(245)	—	61,827
Annual Growth	(3.8%)	—	—	(7.8%)

2022 Year-End Financials

Debt ratio: 27.0%
Return on equity: (-19.3%)
Cash ($ mil.): 749
Current Ratio: 0.91
Long-term debt ($ mil.): 2,128
No. of shares ($ mil.): 485
Dividends
 Yield: 11.2%
 Payout: 0.0%
Market value ($ mil.): 108

	STOCK PRICE ($) FY Close	P/E High/Low		PER SHARE ($) Earnings	Dividends	Book Value
09/22	0.22	—	—	(0.30)	0.02	1.18
09/21	0.80	2	1	0.75	0.00	2.31
09/20	0.96	—	—	(0.76)	0.00	1.60
09/19	1.09	4	2	0.37	0.00	2.33
09/18	1.35	—	—	(0.74)	0.04	2.23
Annual Growth	(36.3%)			—	(10.3%)	(14.7%)

Cemex S.A.B. de C.V.

CEMEX is a leading vertically integrated heavy building materials company focused on four core businesses?Cement, Ready-Mix Concrete, Aggregates, and Urbanization Solutions. It is a global building materials company that provides high-quality products and reliable services to customers and communities in more than 50 countries. The majority of its sales come from cement; the company has about 15 cement plants and more than 100 cement distribution centers throughout Mexico. CEMEX operates in North America as well as in Africa, Asia, Europe, the Middle East, and South America. The US is the company's largest market with around 30% of sales.

Operations

Cemex' operations include the Cement segment (accounts for more than 40% of the industry revenue), Ready-mix concrete segment (about 35%), Aggregates (about 15%), and Urbanization Solutions (more than 10%).

The company manufactures cement through a closely controlled chemical process, which uses their professional knowledge and experience to develop customized products designed to satisfy its client's specific requirements and that also foster sustainable construction. The ready-mix concrete segment develops solutions based on their thorough knowledge and application of ready-mix concrete technology.

The aggregates segment, enables the company to be one of the world's largest suppliers of aggregates, which is used for a wide array of applications such as construction and maintenance of highways, walkways, parking lots, airport runways, and railways. Lastly, the Urbanization Solutions segment is a portfolio of related businesses that complements the company's value offering of products and solutions, looking to connect with the broader metropolis ecosystem, address urbanization challenges, and provide means to all stakeholders in the construction value chain to enable sustainable urbanization.

Geographic Reach

Cemex maintains business relationships in more than 50 countries globally, with Mexico and the EMEAA accounting for about 30%, each. The company also has operations in Mexico, accounting for more than 20%. The company has cement production facilities in Mexico, the US, the UK, Germany, Spain, Poland, the Czech Republic, Croatia, Egypt, the Philippines, the UAE, Colombia, Panama, Nicaragua, Guatemala, the Dominican Republic, Puerto Rico, Trinidad and Tobago, Jamaica and Barbados.

Financial Performance

Cemex' performance for the past five years has fluctuated but had an overall increase with 2022 as its highest performing year over the period.

The company's revenue increased by $1.2 billion to $15.6 billion for 2022, as compared to 2021's revenue of $14.4 billion.

Cemex' net income for fiscal year end 2022 increased to $858 million, as compared to the company's net income of $753 million.

The company held $495 million at the end of the year. Operating activities provided $1.5 billion to the coffers. Investing activities and financing activities used $732 million and $961 million, respectively. Main cash uses were for purchase of property, machinery and equipment, as well as debt repayments.

Strategy

To achieving its mission, its strategy is to create value by building and managing a global portfolio of integrated cement, ready-mix concrete, aggregates and Urbanization Solutions businesses. The company's five strategic priorities, in no particular order, are: Health and Safety; Customer Centricity; Innovation; Sustainability; and Operating EBITDA Growth.

HISTORY

The foundation of CEMEX began with -- what else? -- cement. Lorenzo Zambrano founded Cementos Hidalgo in northern Mexico in 1906. In 1931 the company merged with Cementos Portland Monterrey and was renamed Cementos Mexicanos, from which its current name, CEMEX, is derived.

During the 1960s the company expanded into the cities of Ciudad Valles and TorreÃ³n by building plants; it moved into MÃ©rida in 1966 by acquiring Cementos Maya. The founder's grandson, also named Lorenzo Zambrano, joined the company in 1968. CEMEX became a true national force during the 1970s by acquiring more plants, including one in central Mexico.

CEMEX went public in 1976. With its acquisition of Cementos Guadalajara and its three plants, it became Mexico's top cement maker. After serving in several engineering positions and as VP of operations, Zambrano was named CEO in 1985. He had worked at CEMEX as a teenager in the early 1960s and claims he knew he wanted to work for CEMEX since he was 14.

Zambrano set about making CEMEX an international player. Already an exporter, the company boosted its exporting business by purchasing Cementos AnÃ¡huac in 1987. Two years later CEMEX sealed its position as the top Mexican cement maker by acquiring that country's #2 cement company, Cementos Tolteca. CEMEX then bought its first non-Mexican operations in 1992, adding Valenciana de Cementos and Sanson, Spain's largest cement makers. Two years later CEMEX added Vencemos (Venezuela's top cement business), Cemento Bayano (Panama), and a plant in Texas.

The globalization of CEMEX helped the company weather several peso devaluations during the 1990s, including one in late 1994. The company continued to expand abroad, adding Cementos Nacionales (Dominican Republic) in 1995 and Cementos Diamante and Samper (both in Colombia) in 1996. Those deals made the company the world's third-largest cement producer.

After claiming more of the European and Latin American cement markets, CEMEX turned its attention to the Pacific Rim, where it made investments in Rizal Cement Company in the Philippines in 1997 and PT Semen Gresik in Indonesia in 1998 (it sold its 25% stake in 2006).

A booming US economy fueled residential and commercial construction in fiscal 1999, lifting CEMEX to record sales. In 2000 CEMEX gained significant size when it acquired US cement maker Southdown for $2.8 billion. The company sold its Kentucky and Missouri operations to Rinker Materials, a unit of Australia's CSR Ltd, in 2001.

In mid-2002 CEMEX bought Puerto Rican Cement Company (PRCC) for around $180 million. The next year CEMEX acquired Mineral Resource Technologies and Dixon-Marquette Cement in the US. In 2005 CEMEX added extensive European operations with the acquisition of UK-based ready-mix cement giant RMC Group. The deal, worth about $5.8 billion, instantly made CEMEX a leader in Europe.

The company also acquired Rinker, Australia's biggest building material manufacturer, for more than $14 billion in 2007. In 2008 CEMEX sold most of its stake in telecom company Axtel and later its Canary Islands operations, garnering a combined $474 million for debt payments. In 2009 CEMEX (still struggling under the weight of debt and facing declining sales) sold its Australian operations to Holcim for nearly $2 billion. In 2011 CEMEX bought Ready Mix USA's interest in the companies' two joint ventures, which have operations in the Southeast US.

EXECUTIVES

Finance Chief Executive Officer, Planning Chief Executive Officer, Development Chief Executive Officer, Non-Independent Director, Fernando Angel Gonzalez Olivieri

Finance and Administration Chief Financial Officer, Finance and Administration Executive Vice President, Maher Al-Haffar

Corporate Communications Executive Vice President, Public Affairs Executive Vice President, Investor Relations Executive Vice President, Louisa P. Rodriguez

Administration Executive Vice President, Strategic Planning and Business Development Executive Vice President, Strategic Planning and Business Development Chief Financial Officer, Administration Chief Financial Officer, Jose Antonio Gonzalez Flores

Organization Executive Vice President, Administration Executive Vice President, Digital and Organization Development Executive Vice President, Luis Hernandez Echavez

Corporate Affairs Executive Vice President, Risk Management Executive Vice President, Mauricio Doehner Cobian

Legal Senior Vice President, Roger Saldana Madero

Comptrollership Vice President, Rafael Garza Lozano

CEMEX USA President, Jaime Muguiro Dominguez

CEMEX Mexico President, Ricardo Naya Barba

CEMEX Europe, Middle East, Africa & Asia President, Sergio Mauricio Menendez Medina

CEMEX South, Central America and the President, Jesus Vicente Gonzalez Herrera

Chairman, Non-Independent Director, Rogelio Zambrano Lozano

Independent Director, Armando J. Garcia Segovia

Independent Director, Rodolfo Garcia Muriel

Independent Director, Francisco Javier Fernandez Carbajal

Independent Director, Armando Garza Sada

Independent Director, David Martinez Guzman

Independent Director, Everardo Elizondo Almaguer

Independent Director, Ramiro Gerardo Villarreal Morales

Independent Director, Gabriel Jaramillo Sanint

Independent Director, Isabel María Aguilera Navarro

Non-Independent Director, Marcelo Zambrano Lozano

Auditors : KPMG Cardenas Dosal, S.C.

LOCATIONS

HQ: Cemex S.A.B. de C.V.
Avenida Ricardo Margain Zozaya 325, Colonia Valle del Campestre, San Pedro Garza Garcia, Nuevo Leon 66265
Phone: (52) 81 8888 8888   **Fax:** (52) 81 8888 4417
Web: www.cemex.com

2018 Sales

	% of total
United States	26
Europe	26
Mexico	24
South, Central America & Caribbean	14
Asia, Middle East and Africa	10
Total	100

PRODUCTS/OPERATIONS

2018 Sales

	% of total
Cement	45
Ready mix	39
Aggregates	16
Total	100

Selected Subsidiaries
CEMEX México, S. A. de C.V.
    CEMEX Espa?a, S.A. (Spain)
    Assiut Cement Company (Egypt)
    Cement Bayano, S.A. (Panama)
    CEMEX Asia Holdings Ltd. (Singapore)
    APO Cement Corporation (Philippines)
    CEMEX (Thailand) Co., Ltd.
    Solid Cement Corporation (Philippines)
    CEMEX Colombia, S.A.
    CEMEX (Costa Rica), S.A.
    CEMEX de Puerto Rico, Inc
    CEMEX Dominicana, S.A. (Dominican Republic)
    CEMEX France Gestion (S.A.S.)
    CEMEX Corp. (US)
    CEMEX Venezuela, S.A.C.A.
CEMEX U.K.
    CEMEX Austria AG
    CEMEX Czech Republic, s.r.o.
    CEMEX Deutschland AG. (Germany)
    CEMEX Holdings (Israel) Limited
    CEMEX Investments Limited (UK)
    CEMEX Polska sp. Z.o.o. (Poland)
    CEMEX SIA (Latvia)
    Readymix plc (Ireland)

COMPETITORS

BUZZI UNICEM SPA
Dyckerhoff GmbH
HeidelbergCement AG
LOMA NEGRA COMPAÃIA INDUSTRIAL ARGENTINA S.A.
LafargeHolcim Ltd
SOJITZ CORPORATION
TEXAS INDUSTRIES, INC.
TITAN AMERICA LLC
VISCOFAN SA
Votorantim Cimentos S/A

HISTORICAL FINANCIALS

Company Type: Public

Income Statement   FYE: December 31

	REVENUE ($mil)	NET INCOME ($mil)	NET PROFIT MARGIN	EMPLOYEES
12/23	17,388	182	1.0%	46,124
12/22	15,577	858	5.5%	41,663
12/21	14,548	753	5.2%	46,210
12/20	12,970	(1,467)	—	41,663
12/19	13,130	143	1.1%	40,640
Annual Growth	7.3%	6.2%	—	3.2%

2023 Year-End Financials

Debt ratio: 21.9%   No. of shares ($ mil.): 43,524
Return on equity: 1.6%   Dividends
Cash ($ mil.): 624   Yield: —
Current Ratio: 0.74   Payout: 0.0%
Long-term debt ($ mil.): 6,203   Market value ($ mil.): 337,319

	STOCK PRICE ($) FY Close	P/E High/Low	PER SHARE ($) Earnings	Dividends	Book Value
12/23	7.75	1993 981	0.00	0.00	0.27
12/22	4.05	346 162	0.02	0.00	0.24
12/21	6.78	520 302	0.02	0.00	0.22
12/20	5.17	— —	(0.03)	0.00	0.18
12/19	3.78	1797 932	0.00	0.10	0.21
Annual Growth	19.7%	— —	7.9%	—	7.1%

Cenovus Energy Inc

Cenovus Energy is the second-largest Canadian oil and natural gas producer. The company is also known as the second-largest Canadian- based refiner and upgrader. The company's major operations include oil sands plays of Alberta; thermal and crude oil and natural gas projects across Western Canada; crude oil production in Newfoundland and Labrador; and natural gas and liquids production in China and Indonesia. Cenovus' upstream assets produce an average of more than 586,600 barrels of oil per day. The Canadian market generated around 50% of sales. The company was incorporated in 1938 as The Husky Refining Company.

Operations

Cenovous Energy operates in two segments, namely Upstream (about 50%) and Downstream (more than 50%).

The Upstream segment includes the operation of Oil Sands, Conventional, and Offshore. These operations include the development and production of bitumen and heavy oil in northern Alberta and Saskatchewan; assets rich in NGLs and natural gas within the Elmworth-Wapiti, Kaybob-Edson, Clearwater and Rainbow Lake operating in Alberta and British Columbia; and the operations, exploration and development activities in China and the East Cost of Canada, respectively. The Downstream segment includes the company's Canadian manufacturing and US manufacturing.

Geographic Reach

Cenovus is a Canadian-based integrated energy company headquartered in Calgary, Alberta. The company has operations in Canada, the US, and China. Canada and the US are the largest markets of the company.

Financial Performance

Cenovus Energy's performance for the past five years has fluctuated with a decreased from 2019 to 2020, then increasing significantly since then, ending with 2022 as their highest performing year over the period.

The company recorded an increase of $22.9 billion to $71.8 billion for 2022, as compared to 2021's revenue of $48.8 billion.

Cenovus also recorded an increase in its net income in fiscal year end 2022 to $6.5 billion, as compared to the prior year's net income of $587 million.

The company held $4.5 billion at the end of the year. Operating activities generated $11.4 billion to the coffers. Investing activities provided $9.1 billion, while financing activities used $7.7 billion. Main cash uses were for capital investment and repayment of long-term debt.

Strategy

The company's strategy is focused on maximizing shareholder value through competitive cost structures and optimizing margins, while delivering top-tier safety performance and sustainability leadership. The company prioritizes Free Funds Flow generation through all price cycles to manage our balance sheet, increase shareholder returns through dividend growth and share repurchases, reinvest in our business and diversify our portfolio.

Mergers and Acquisitions

In mid-2022, Cenovus Energy, through its US operating business, has reached an agreement to purchase bp's 50% interest in the bp-Husky Toledo Refinery in Ohio. Cenovus has owned the other 50% of the refinery since its combination with Husky Energy in 2021. Cenovus's US operating business will assume operatorship from bp upon closing of the transaction, which is expected before the end of 2022, dependent on the satisfaction of closing conditions. Total consideration includes US$300 million in cash.

Also in 2022, Cenovus Energy has reached an agreement to purchase the remaining 50% of the Sunrise oil sands project in northern Alberta from bp. Total consideration for the transaction includes $600 million in cash. Full ownership of Sunrise further enhances Cenovus's core strength in the oil sands. Sunrise has been operated by the company since the beginning of 2021, following the Husky Energy transaction, and Cenovus is now in the early stages of applying its oil sands operating model at this asset.

Company Background

Cenovus Energy was formed in late 2009 as a spinoff from major Canada-based oil and gas player EnCana.

The split allowed EnCana to focus almost exclusively on natural gas exploration and development in North America, while Cenovus took on responsibilities as an integrated oil company, with the intent of boosting its production and refining capacities. An expansion at the Wood River refinery in Illinois is placed Cenovus among the leading heavy oil refiners in the US. The coker and refinery upgrade (completed in late 2011) increased its crude oil refining capacity and more than doubled its heavy crude oil refining capacity.

In 2010 Cenovus reported an improvement in revenues and income, as the result of global economy bouncing back from a recession, which produced higher commodity prices and demand, driving up sales of the company's products.

EXECUTIVES

Chief Financial Officer, Executive Vice President, Jeffrey R. Hart

Chief Executive Officer, President, Executive Director, Non-Independent Director, Alexander J. Pourbaix

Chief Operating Officer, Executive Vice President, Jonathan M. McKenzie

Stakeholder Engagement Chief Sustainability Officer, Stakeholder Engagement Senior Vice President, Rhona M. DelFrari

Downstream Executive Vice President, Keith A. Chiasson

Safety & Operations Technical Services Executive Vice President, P. Andrew Dahlin

Upstream – Thermal, Major Projects & Offshore Executive Vice President, Norrie C. Ramsay
Strategy & Corporate Development Executive Vice President, Karamjit S. Sandhar
Corporate Services Executive Vice President, Sarah Walters
Upstream – Conventional & Integration Executive Vice President, J. Drew Zieglgansberger
Legal Senior Vice President, Legal General Counsel, Legal Corporate Secretary, Gary F. Molnar
Independent Director, Chair, Keith A. MacPhail
Independent Director, Keith M. Casey
Independent Director, Jane E. Kinney
Independent Director, Harold N. Kvisle
Independent Director, Eva L. Kwok
Independent Director, Richard J. Marcogliese
Independent Director, Claude Mongeau
Independent Director, Wayne E. Shaw
Independent Director, Rhonda I. Zygocki
Non-Independent Director, Frank J. Sixt
Director, Canning K. N. Fok
Auditors : PricewaterhouseCoopers LLP

LOCATIONS

HQ: Cenovus Energy Inc
4100, 225 – 6 Avenue S.W., Calgary, Alberta T2P 1N2
Phone: —
Web: www.cenovus.com

PRODUCTS/OPERATIONS

2014 Sales

	% of total
Refining & marketing	62
Upstream	
Oil sands	23
Conventional	15
Total	100

2014 Sales

	% of total
Canada	52
United States	48
Total	100

COMPETITORS

AMPLIFY ENERGY CORP.
Advantage Oil & Gas Ltd
BERRY PETROLEUM COMPANY, LLC
CONTANGO OIL & GAS COMPANY
Husky Energy Inc
MURPHY OIL CORPORATION
PETROQUEST ENERGY, INC.
TALOS PETROLEUM LLC
WARREN RESOURCES, INC.
WHITING PETROLEUM CORPORATION

HISTORICAL FINANCIALS

Company Type: Public

Income Statement — FYE: December 31

	REVENUE ($mil)	NET INCOME ($mil)	NET PROFIT MARGIN	EMPLOYEES
12/23	39,386	3,100	7.9%	0
12/22	49,464	4,769	9.6%	5,998
12/21	36,397	460	1.3%	5,938
12/20	10,388	(1,868)	—	2,413
12/19	15,497	1,684	10.9%	2,361
Annual Growth	26.3%	16.5%	—	—

2023 Year-End Financials

Debt ratio: 10.2%
Return on equity: 14.6%
Cash ($ mil.): 1,680
Current Ratio: 1.56
Long-term debt ($ mil.): 5,362
No. of shares ($ mil.): 1,871
Dividends
Yield: —
Payout: 24.7%
Market value ($ mil.): 31,167

	STOCK PRICE ($) FY Close	P/E High/Low	PER SHARE ($) Earnings	Dividends	Book Value
12/23	16.65	10 7	1.60	0.40	11.57
12/22	19.41	7 4	2.37	0.34	10.68
12/21	12.28	48 21	0.21	0.07	9.26
12/20	6.04	— —	(1.52)	0.13	10.68
12/19	10.15	6 4	1.37	0.16	12.00
Annual Growth	13.2%	—	4.0%	25.3%	(0.9%)

Central Japan Railway Co.

Central Japan Railway, known as JR Central, provides passenger transportation throughout a network of some 1,970 km (1,221 miles) of track and about 405 stations. The company's shinkansen (high-speed) lines connect the metropolitan areas of Tokyo, Nagoya, and Osaka. In addition, JR Central operates a dozen conventional rail lines, mainly in the Nagoya and Shizuoka areas, and provides bus services. The company also earns revenue from department store and hotel operations; food and beverage sales; leasing real estate near its train stations; and travel agency services. JR Central was one of seven companies formed in the 1987 privatization of Japanese National Railways.

EXECUTIVES

Chairman, Representative Director, Shin Kaneko
President, Representative Director, Shunsuke Niwa
Executive Vice President, Representative Director, Kentaro Takeda
Executive Vice President, Representative Director, Akihiko Nakamura
Executive Vice President, Representative Director, Mamoru Uno
Executive Vice President, Representative Director, Hiroshi Suzuki
Executive Vice President, Representative Director, Atsuhito Mori
Advisor, Director, Koei Tsuge
Outside Director, Haruo Kasama
Outside Director, Taku Oshima
Outside Director, Tsuyoshi Nagano
Outside Director, Hiroko Kiba
Outside Director, Joseph P. Schmelzeis
Auditors : Deloitte Touche Tohmatsu LLC

LOCATIONS

HQ: Central Japan Railway Co.
1-1-4 Meieki, Nakamura-ku, Nagoya, Aichi 450-6101
Phone: (81) 52 564 2620   **Fax:** 202 429-1917
Web: www.jr-central.co.jp

PRODUCTS/OPERATIONS

2014 Sales

	% of total
Transportation	70
Merchandise & other	12
Real Estate	4
Other	14
Total	100

COMPETITORS

CSX CORPORATION
Compagnie des Chemins de Fer Nationaux du Canada
EAST JAPAN RAILWAY COMPANY
GENESEE & WYOMING INC.
HANKYU HANSHIN HOLDINGS,INC.
KANSAS CITY SOUTHERN
N.V. Nederlandse Spoorwegen
RZHD, PAO
TAISEI CORPORATION
UNION PACIFIC CORPORATION

HISTORICAL FINANCIALS

Company Type: Public

Income Statement — FYE: March 31

	REVENUE ($mil)	NET INCOME ($mil)	NET PROFIT MARGIN	EMPLOYEES
03/23	10,513	1,647	15.7%	37,076
03/22	7,687	(426)	—	37,800
03/21	7,437	(1,820)	—	38,231
03/20	16,993	3,665	21.6%	38,715
03/19	16,959	3,961	23.4%	37,927
Annual Growth	(11.3%)	(19.7%)	—	(0.6%)

2023 Year-End Financials

Debt ratio: 0.4%
Return on equity: 5.9%
Cash ($ mil.): 5,065
Current Ratio: 3.72
Long-term debt ($ mil.): 31,859
No. of shares ($ mil.): 985
Dividends
Yield: 0.8%
Payout: 0.0%
Market value ($ mil.): 11,751

	STOCK PRICE ($) FY Close	P/E High/Low	PER SHARE ($) Earnings	Dividends	Book Value
03/23	11.93	0 0	1.67	0.10	28.66
03/22	13.00	— —	(0.43)	0.12	29.75
03/21	15.08	— —	(1.85)	0.13	33.40
03/20	16.30	0 0	3.74	0.14	35.84
03/19	23.25	0 0	4.04	0.13	31.82
Annual Growth	(15.4%)	—	(19.8%)	(6.8%)	(2.6%)

Centrica Plc

Centrica is a leading energy services and solutions company centered on supplying the energy needs of its more than 10 million customer accounts mainly in the UK, Ireland and North America via three major brands? British Gas, Bord Gáis Energy, and Centrica Business Solutions. It is one of the largest electricity and gas supplier in the UK. It also offers related installation, repair and maintenance services, digital smart technologies (the Hive). The company holds a 69% interest in Spirit Energy, an exploration and production company that is a joint venture.

Operations

The company operates through six operating segments which are:

British Gas Services & Solutions (around 5% of revenue) offers installation, repair and maintenance of domestic central heating and related appliances, and the provision of fixed-fee maintenance/breakdown service and insurance contracts in the UK; and the supply of new technologies and energy efficiency solutions in the UK.

British Gas Energy (around 35% of revenues) supplies gas and electricity to residential and small business customers in the UK.

Bord Gáis Energy (accounts for around 5% of revenue) supplies gas and electricity to residential, commercial and industrial customers in the Republic of Ireland; installation, repair and maintenance of domestic central heating and related appliances in the Republic of Ireland; and power generation in the Republic of Ireland.

Centrica Business Solutions (approximately 10% of revenue) supplies gas and electricity to business customers in the UK; and the supply of energy services and solutions to large organizations in all geographies in which the company operates, and the development and operation of large-scale power assets in the UK.

Energy Marketing & Trading (approximately 40%) offers procurement, trading and optimization of energy in the UK and Europe; the global procurement and sale of LNG; and the generation of power from the Spalding combined cycle gas turbine tolling contract (the contract ended in 2021).

Upstream (about 10%) facilitates the production and processing of oil and gas principally within Spirit Energy; and the sale of power generated from nuclear assets in the UK.

Geographic Reach
The company is headquartered at Windsor, Berkshire.

Sales and Marketing
The company caters to approximately 10 million residential customers.

Financial Performance
Company's revenue for fiscal 2022 increased to GBP23.7 billion compared from the prior year with GBP14.7 billion. The increase was primarily due to higher revenues on its every segment especially on British Gas Energy segment and Energy Marketing & Trading.

Net loss for fiscal 2022 was GBP636 million compared from the prior year with a net income of GBP1.2 billion. The losses was primarily due to higher expenses offsetting the increase in revenues.

Cash held by the company at the end of fiscal 2022 decreased to GBP4.2 billion. Cash provided by operations was GBP1.3 billion while cash used for investing and financing activities were GBP566 million and GBP917 million, respectively. Main uses of cash were purchase of securities and repayment of borrowings and capital element of leases

Strategy
Centrica's strategy is driven by our Purpose to help customers live sustainably, simply and affordably.

As the pace of change continues to accelerate, the company are responding by focusing colleagues and technology on helping businesses and households to use energy more efficiently and sustainably. Centrica recognize the need to help enable a more flexible energy system and are deploying a range of technologies to help build the grid of the future with both electric and hydrogen technologies.

Company Background
Centrica traces its roots back to British Gas, which is one of the oldest companies in the world, with a history stretching back over 200 years. However, the company as it stands today only dates back to 1986, when the gas industry was privatized and British Gas Plc was formed, with a "tell Sid" campaign encouraging customers to buy shares in the company.

In 1997, Centrica was founded when British Gas was split into two separate companies.

HISTORY

William Murdock invented gas lighting in 1792. In 1812 the Gas Light and Coke Company of London was formed as the world's first gas supplier to the public, and by 1829 the UK had 200 gas companies.

In the second half of the 19th century, the gas industry began looking for new uses for the fuel. Gas stoves were introduced in 1851, the geyser water heater was invented in 1868, and in 1880 the first gas units to heat individual rooms were developed.

Gas companies countered the emerging electricity industry by renting gas stoves at low prices and installing gas fittings (stove, pipe, and lights) in poor homes with no installation charges or deposits. By 1914 the UK had 1,500 gas suppliers.

The electricity industry soon made major strikes against the gas industry's dominance. In 1926 the government began reorganizing the fragmented electricity supply industry, building a national power grid and establishing the Central Electricity Generating Board to oversee it.

The gas industry was nationalized in 1949, and 1,050 gas suppliers were brought under the control of the British Gas Council. Still, the gas industry was losing. Supplying gas was more expensive than generating electricity: Gas was seen as a power supply of the past. The Gas Council sought to change that image through an aggressive marketing campaign in the 1960s, touting gas as a modern, clean fuel. Other factors played a part in its re-emergence: The Clean Air Act of 1956 steadily reduced the use of coal for home heating, liquefied natural gas was discovered in the North Sea, and OPEC raised oil prices in the 1970s. When natural gas was introduced, most of the old gasworks were demolished, and the British Gas Council (which became the British Gas Corp. in 1973) set about converting, free of charge, every gas appliance in the UK to natural gas.

As Margaret Thatcher's government began privatizing state industries, the British Gas Corp. was taken public in 1986. Freed from government control, British Gas expanded its international exploration and production activities. When the US gas industry began deregulating, British Gas formed joint venture Accord Energy in 1994 with US gas trader Natural Gas Clearinghouse (now NGC) to sell gas on the wholesale market.

With the opening of the UK gas-supply market (which began regionally in 1996 and went nationwide in 1998), British Gas split into two public companies to avoid a conflict of interest between its supply business and its monopoly transportation business. In 1997 it spun off Centrica, the retail operations, and BG (now BG Group), which received the transportation business and the international exploration and production operations.

The UK electricity supply market began opening up to competition in 1998, and Centrica won 750,000 UK electricity customers, most of them also gas customers. In 1999 it bought The Automobile Association, which it sold to venture capitalists in 2004. In 2000 Centrica began offering telecom services in the UK.

Centrica moved into North America in 2000 by purchasing two Canadian companies: natural gas retailer Direct Energy Marketing and gas production company Avalanche Energy. It gained a 28% stake in US marketing firm Energy America through the Direct Energy transaction and purchased the remaining 72% from US firm Sempra Energy the next year. Continuing its non-domestic strategy, Centrica bought a 50% interest in Belgium energy supplier Luminus.

The firm purchased 60% of the 1,260-MW Humber Power station in 2001, its first domestic power plant interest. It also acquired the UK operations of Australia's One.Tel, and it bought Enron's European retail supply business, Enron Direct, for $137 million.

In 2002 Centrica purchased the retail energy services business of Canadian pipeline company Enbridge for $637 million; it also agreed to acquire another Enron-controlled company, US retail energy supplier NewPower Holdings, for $130 million. But Centrica withdrew its offer to buy NewPower a month after the deal was announced because of concerns about NewPower's potential Enron-related liabilities. Later that year Centrica acquired 200,000 retail customer accounts in Ohio and Pennsylvania from NewPower.

In 2004 the company brought all its UK

HOOVER'S HANDBOOK OF WORLD BUSINESS 2024

upstream activities together under Centrica Energy.

In 2005, Centrica acquired Oxxio, the Netherlands #4 energy supplier.

To pursue green energy options, in 2007 British Gas launched British Gas New Energy.

In 2007 Centrica acquired Newfield Exploration's North Sea assets for $486 million and in 2008 it acquired its first gas and oil assets in the Norwegian North Sea for $375 million (from Marathon Oil).

Growing it retail business, in 2008 Centrica acquired Electricity Direct, a UK commercial retail supplier serving nearly 1 million customers.

In 2008 Centrica's British Gas unit acquired 40,000 small and mid-sized business customers from UK retail energy provider BizzEnergy in the wake of the latter's sudden financial collapse.

Centrica began in 2012 a program to save £500 million ($788 million) in costs over the next two years by identifying efficiencies. Although the company plans to continue investing for further growth, it has already started cutting 2,300 positions company-wide, as well as implementing a pay freeze across much of the group. It set out to develop a better relationship with its customers by simplifying the purchase of gas and electricity. It also decided to make the cost of delivery more transparent by giving its customers a breakdown on their bill of the actual costs of providing the energy.

Through its aggressive acquisition strategy in North America, the company has gained more than 6 million retail power and gas supply customers in less than a decade as part of its Direct Energy operations. Building on its portfolio of offerings, in 2011 it acquired Illinois-based Home Warranty of America (HWA) for £30 million ($48 million). HWA provides whole home warranty plans to more than 70,000 customers through a network of 4,000 contractors.

Direct Energy also made three acquisitions in 2011 for its residential energy supply business in North America: Gateway Energy Services, First Choice Power, and Vectren Retail. The deals, part of the company's strategy of acquiring smaller suppliers and buying in deregulated markets, added more than 750,000 customers.

In a major move to grow its upstream business and its Norwegian operations, Centrica completed a £936 million ($1.5 billion) deal in 2012 to acquire Norwegian assets from Statoil and ConocoPhillips. Combined, the new assets will increase the company's reserves by almost 40% and its production by more than 30%. The acquisition includes proved and probable reserves of 117 million barrels of oil equivalent and production of 34,000 barrels of oil evalent per day. The buy also makes Centrica one of Norway's fastest growing companies, with a third of its gas and oil production originating from that region. The company's upstream operations also have a presence in Trinidad and the Netherlands.

In spite of the growth of Centrica's gas assets, the company decided to raise its gas and electricity prices by 17% in late 2011 to cover the rising wholesale commodity prices in the first half of the year. Mild weather that year led to a decline per household averaging 21% less in gas and 4% less in electricity consumption. With lower residential demand, customer bills were 4% lower on average in 2011. Consumer complaints over higher prices for heating homes in the UK led to protests at the offices of utility companies and at town halls early in 2012.

EXECUTIVES

Group Chief Executive, Executive Director, Chris O'Shea
Group Chief Financial Officer, Executive Director, Kate Ringrose
Chairman, Scott Wheway
Senior Independent Non-Executive Director, Stephen Alan Michael Hester
Independent Non-Executive Director, Amber Rudd
Independent Non-Executive Director, Kevin O'Byrne
Independent Non-Executive Director, Carol Arrowsmith
Independent Non-Executive Director, Pam Kaur
Independent Non-Executive Director, Heidi Mottram
Auditors: Deloitte LLP

LOCATIONS

HQ: Centrica Plc
Millstream, Maidenhead Road, Windsor, Berkshire SL4 5GD
Phone: — —
Web: www.centrica.com

PRODUCTS/OPERATIONS

2017 Sales by Geography

	£ mil	% of total
UK	13,506	48
US	9,579	34
Rest of Europe	3,301	12
Others	1,637	6
Total	28,023	100

2017 Sales by Segment

	£ mil	% of total
Centrica Business	15,111	54
Centrica Consumer	12,108	43
Exploration & Production	671	2
Centrica Storage	133	1
Total		28,023

COMPETITORS

DYNEGY INC.
FortisBC Energy Inc
IBERDROLA, SOCIEDAD ANONIMA
Pacific Northern Gas Ltd.
SEMPRA ENERGY
SOUTHWEST GAS CORPORATION
SOUTHWEST GAS HOLDINGS, INC.
TALLGRASS ENERGY PARTNERS, LP
UNS ENERGY CORPORATION
Union Gas Limited

HISTORICAL FINANCIALS

Company Type: Public

Income Statement   FYE: December 31

	REVENUE ($mil)	NET INCOME ($mil)	NET PROFIT MARGIN	EMPLOYEES
12/22	28,580	(941)	—	19,954
12/21	19,870	1,630	8.2%	19,704
12/20	16,716	55	0.3%	25,753
12/19	29,942	(1,350)	—	29,147
12/18	37,901	233	0.6%	31,780
Annual Growth	(6.8%)	—	—	(11.0%)

2022 Year-End Financials

Debt ratio: 16.7%   No. of shares ($ mil.): 5,877
Return on equity: (-46.2%)   Dividends
Cash ($ mil.): 5,828   Yield: —
Current Ratio: 0.95   Payout: 0.0%
Long-term debt ($ mil.): 3,621   Market value ($ mil.): 26,801

	STOCK PRICE ($) FY Close	P/E High/Low	PER SHARE ($) Earnings	Dividends	Book Value
12/22	4.56	— —	(0.16)	0.04	0.21
12/21	3.85	18 12	0.28	0.00	0.55
12/20	2.47	732 243	0.01	0.00	0.23
12/19	4.86	— —	(0.24)	0.49	0.28
12/18	6.87	257 197	0.04	0.57	0.71
Annual Growth	(9.7%)	—	—	(47.0%)	(26.3%)

CGI Inc

Founded in 1976, CGI is among the largest information technology (IT) and business consulting services firms in the world. The company delivers a full range of services, including business consulting, strategic IT and systems integration, managed IT and business process services, and intellectual property to help clients accelerate digitization, achieve immediate cost savings, and drive revenue growth. CGI delivers end-to-end services that cover the full spectrum of technology delivery; from digital strategy and architecture to solution design, development, integration, implementation, and operations. The company generates sine 15% of total revenue.

Operations

The company's secure and flexible end-to-end services include strategic IT and business consulting, systems integration, IT managed services and intellectual property solutions. Its uses its systems integration capabilities to advance clients' IT modernization efforts, and its managed IT and business process services help clients mitigate cost pressures while driving more value from their technology supply chains.

Overall, Managed IT and Business Process Services account for about 55% of revenue and Business consulting, strategic IT consulting and systems integration for some 45%.

Geographic Reach

Based in Canada, CGI has a network of 400 local offices across North America, South America, Europe, Middle East, and Africa (EMEA), and Asia/Pacific.

The US accounts for about 30% of revenue, followed by the Nordic region (Sweden and Finland), about 15%, Canada, around 15%, France, nearly 15%, and the UK for more than 10%.

Financial Performance

For the year ended September 30, 2021, revenue was C$12.1 billion, a decrease of C$37.3 million, or 0.3% over the same period last year. On a constant currency basis, revenue increased by C$132.1 million or 1.1%. The increase was mainly due to growth within the government, financial services and communications & utilities vertical markets, mainly driven by the Central and Eastern Europe, Canada and Western and Southern Europe segments, as well as recent business acquisitions.

In 2021, the company had net earnings of C$1.4 billion, a 22% increase from the previous year's net earnings of C$ 1.1 billion.

The company's cash at the end of 2021 was C$1.7 billion. Operating activities generated C$2.1 billion, while investing activities used C$397.5 billion, mainly for purchase of property, plant and equipment. Financing activities used another C$1.7 billion, primarily for repayment of long-term debt.

Strategy

CGI's strategy is executed through a unique business model that combines client proximity with an extensive global delivery network to deliver the following benefits:

Local relationships and accountability: The company lives and works near clients to provide a high level of responsiveness, partnership, and innovation. Its local CGI members speak the company's clients' language, understand their business environment, and collaborate to meet their goals and advance their business.

Global reach: The company's local presence is complemented by an expansive global delivery network that ensures its clients have 24/7 access to best-fit digital capabilities and resources to meet their end-to-end needs.

Committed experts: One of the company's key strategic goals is to be its clients' partner and expert of choice. To achieve this, CGI invests in developing and recruiting professionals with extensive industry, business and in-demand technology expertise.

Comprehensive quality processes: CGI's investment in quality frameworks and rigorous client satisfaction assessments has resulted in a consistent track record of on-time and within-budget project delivery. With regular reviews of engagements and transparency at all levels, the company ensures that client objectives and its own quality objectives are consistently followed at all times. This thorough process enables CGI to generate continuous improvements for all stakeholders by applying corrective measures as soon as they are required.

Corporate social responsibility: In 2021, CGI accelerated its Corporate Social Responsibility engagement through various key initiatives, including the release of its global CSR report, and by committing to achieve net-zero carbon emissions by 2030.

Mergers and Acquisitions

In 2022, CGI, through its subsidiary CGI France SAS ("CGI France") announced the completion of the acquisition of all the shares of Umanis held by MURA (controlled by M. Laurent Piepszownik) and the Pouligny Family. CGI France acquired 2,428,749 shares in Umanis and now holds a total of 16,983,876 shares, representing 91.54% of the company's capital and at least 91.42% of voting rights. "The combination of CGI's operations and those of Umanis will further deepen our presence and positioning across Western and Southern Europe. This transaction is consistent with the metro market merger element of our Build and Buy strategy for delivering profitable inorganic growth, while acting as a catalyst for future organic growth," said George Schindler, CGI President and CEO.

Also in 2022, CGI has completed, through its subsidiary CGI France SAS ("CGI France"), the previously announced acquisition of Harwell Management, a leading management consulting firm specializing in financial services for the French market. The acquisition increases CGI's capabilities within its CGI Business Consulting business across several key financial services sectors, including retail banking, corporate and investment banking, capital markets, insurance, and other specialized banking services, such as energy trading and asset management.

In late 2021, CGI announced that its subsidiary, CGI Technology and Solutions Australia Pty Limited, has signed an agreement to acquire Unico, a technology consultancy and systems integrator based in Melbourne, Australia. The acquisition will grow CGI's footprint in Australia, with a focus on the Melbourne metro market, and in key industry sectors, including communications, government, utilities and financial services.

Also in 2021, CGI announced that it is acquiring Cognicase Management Consulting (CMC), a leading provider of technology and management consulting services and solutions for over 25 years, primarily in the Spanish market. The acquisition will deepen CGI's footprint in Spain and will strengthen the company's client-proximity model. CMC will bring CGI increased capacity to better serve its clients and help them accelerate their digitization. CMC's proven industry expertise and solutions complement CGI's end-to-end services, ranging from comprehensive consulting capabilities to systems integration and managed IT services.

In 2021. CGI announced that CGI Federal Inc. acquired Array Holding Company, Inc. (ARRAY), a leading digital services provider that optimizes mission performance for the U.S. Department of Defense and other government organizations. The merger expands CGI Federal's footprint into strategic markets, such as the U.S. Air Force and Space Command and add to its digital modernization and DevOps capabilities.

HISTORY

Serge Godin founded CGI Group in 1976 after stints at several computer consulting firms. Godin convinced his best friend, André Imbeau, to join him after CGI won its second contract. Two years later Jean Brassard, who awarded the duo their first government contract, came aboard. CGI (Conseillers en Gestion et Informatique) was born in Godin's basement, but the company grew quickly; within 10 years CGI was among the top five information technology (IT) services firms in Canada.

CGI grew rapidly during the 1980s as it won contracts that ranged from providing facilities management for oil powerhouse Ultramar to installing a software system for tracking inmates in federal prisons. CGI boosted its revenues and headcount in 1986 when it acquired fellow consulting firm BST Group. That year the company went public. In 1988 CGI moved into military consulting with its acquisition of Intellitech, a secure data communications specialist.

CGI turned its acquisitive eye south in 1991, buying US-based Software Professionals. The company bolstered its roster of private-sector customers (it already counted Molson and Johnson & Johnson among its clients) when it won a major contract with Alcan Aluminium in 1993.

EXECUTIVES

Chairman, Executive Chairman, Serge Godin
Strategic Planning and Corporate Development Co-Chair, Strategic Planning and Corporate Development Executive Vice President, Co-Chair, Director, Julie Godin
President, Chief Executive Officer, George D. Schindler
President, Chief Operating Officer, Jean-Michel Baticle
Executive Vice President, Chief Financial Officer, Francois Boulanger
Executive Vice President, Chief Business Engineering Officer, Mark Boyajian
Executive Vice President, Chief Human Resources Officer, Bernard Labelle
Legal and Economic Affairs Executive Vice President, Legal and Economic Affairs Corporate Secretary, Benoit Dube
Auditors : PricewaterhouseCoopers LLP

LOCATIONS

HQ: CGI Inc
1350 Rene-Levesque Blvd. West, 25th Floor, Montreal, Quebec H3G 1T4
Phone: —
Web: www.cgi.com

SERVICES OFFERED BY CGI
Consulting
Systems integration
Management of IT and business functions

2015 Sales

	% of total
U.S.	28
Canada	16
France	15
UK	12
Sweden	7
Finland	7
Rest of World	15
Total	**100**

PRODUCTS/OPERATIONS

2018 sales

	% of total
System Integration and Consulting	52
Management of IT and Business Functions	48
Total	**100**

COMPETITORS

ATOS SYNTEL INC.
CAPGEMINI
CMTSU LIQUIDATION, INC
COMPUTACENTER PLC
COMPUTER TASK GROUP, INCORPORATED
EBIX, INC.
IGATE CORP.
INFOSYS LIMITED
SOPRA STERIA GROUP
VIRTUSA CORPORATION

HISTORICAL FINANCIALS
Company Type: Public

Income Statement — FYE: September 30

	REVENUE ($mil)	NET INCOME ($mil)	NET PROFIT MARGIN	EMPLOYEES
09/23	10,644	1,214	11.4%	183,000
09/22	9,364	1,067	11.4%	0
09/21	9,517	1,074	11.3%	0
09/20	9,086	835	9.2%	76,000
09/19	9,144	953	10.4%	77,500
Annual Growth	3.9%	6.2%	—	24.0%

2023 Year-End Financials
Debt ratio: 14.6%
Return on equity: 20.9%
Cash ($ mil.): 1,167
Current Ratio: 1.06
Long-term debt ($ mil.): 1,445
No. of shares ($ mil.): 233
Dividends
Yield: —
Payout: 0.0%
Market value ($ mil.): 22,964

	STOCK PRICE ($) FY Close	P/E High/Low	PER SHARE ($) Earnings	Dividends	Book Value
09/23	98.49	15 11	5.11	0.00	26.54
09/22	75.24	14 11	4.40	0.00	22.26
09/21	84.76	17 12	4.25	0.00	22.32
09/20	67.77	20 12	3.14	0.00	20.90
09/19	79.14	17 12	3.44	0.00	19.34
Annual Growth	5.6%	—	10.4%	—	8.2%

Chiba Bank, Ltd

EXECUTIVES

Chairman, Representative Director, Hidetoshi Sakuma
Chief Executive Officer, President, Representative Director, Tsutomu Yonemoto
Senior Managing Executive Officer, Chief Business Officer, Director, Kiyomi Yamazaki
Senior Managing Executive Officer, Chief Strategy Officer, Chief Digital Transformation Officer, Director, Mutsumi Awaji
Chief Human Resources Officer, Director, Takashi Makinose
Chief Risk Officer, Director, Masayasu Ono
Chief Information Officer, Kazunari Tanaka
Outside Director, Yuko Tashima
Outside Director, Yasuko Takayama
Outside Director, Takahide Kiuchi
Auditors : Ernst & Young ShinNihon LLC

LOCATIONS

HQ: Chiba Bank, Ltd
1-2 Chiba-Minato, Chuo-ku, Chiba 260-8720
Phone: (81) 43 245 1111
Web: www.chibabank.co.jp

HISTORICAL FINANCIALS
Company Type: Public

Income Statement — FYE: March 31

	ASSETS ($mil)	NET INCOME ($mil)	INCOME AS % OF ASSETS	EMPLOYEES
03/23	148,574	452	0.3%	6,709
03/22	157,064	448	0.3%	6,841
03/21	161,646	448	0.3%	6,917
03/20	143,804	442	0.3%	6,884
03/19	135,124	455	0.3%	6,942
Annual Growth	2.4%	(0.2%)	—	(0.8%)

2023 Year-End Financials
Return on assets: 0.3%
Return on equity: 5.6%
Long-term debt ($ mil.): —
No. of shares ($ mil.): 724
Sales ($ mil.): 2,090
Dividends
Yield: —
Payout: 0.0%
Market value ($ mil.): —

Chiba Kogyo Bank, Ltd. (The)

If industriousness is a virtue, Chiba Kogyo Bank hopes to capitalize on the goodness of its home prefecture. The bank, with more than 70 locations, serves the industry-heavy prefecture of Chiba, which is adjacent to Tokyo. Chiba Kogyo bank provides a range of traditional banking services to businesses and individuals. Subsidiaries are active in such areas as home lending, credit cards, leasing, and computer equipment sales and maintenance. Approximately 40 % of the bank's voting stock is controlled by Mizuho Financial Group and affiliated entities.

EXECUTIVES

Chairman, Representative Director, Shunichi Aoyagi
President, Representative Director, Hitoshi Umeda
Deputy President, Representative Director, Ryuichi Matsumaru
Director, Yasumitsu Kanda
Director, Katsumi Shirai
Outside Director, Hisako Toya
Outside Director, Testuro Sugiura
Outside Director, Eiji Yamada
Auditors : Ernst & Young ShinNihon LLC

LOCATIONS

HQ: Chiba Kogyo Bank, Ltd. (The)
2-1-2 Saiwai-cho, Mihama-ku, Chiba 261-0001
Phone: (81) 43 243 2111
Web: www.chibakogyo-bank.co.jp

COMPETITORS

AICHI BANK, LTD..
DAISHI HOKUETSU BANK, LTD.
EHIME BANK, LTD., THE
JUROKU BANK,LTD., THE
OITA BANK,LTD., THE

HISTORICAL FINANCIALS
Company Type: Public

Income Statement — FYE: March 31

	ASSETS ($mil)	NET INCOME ($mil)	INCOME AS % OF ASSETS	EMPLOYEES
03/22	29,353	52	0.2%	2,241
03/21	29,336	43	0.1%	2,319
03/20	26,267	41	0.2%	2,402
03/19	25,413	46	0.2%	2,479
03/18	25,798	63	0.2%	2,518
Annual Growth	3.3%	(4.7%)	—	(2.9%)

2022 Year-End Financials
Return on assets: 0.1%
Return on equity: 3.6%
Long-term debt ($ mil.): —
No. of shares ($ mil.): 59
Sales ($ mil.): 421
Dividends
Yield: —
Payout: 18.7%
Market value ($ mil.): —

China Communications Constructions Group Ltd

EXECUTIVES

Supervisor, Yongbin Wang
Staff Supervisor, Yanmin Yao
Supervisor, Sen Li
Board Secretary, Changjiang Zhou
Chief Financial Officer, Hongbiao Zhu
President, Executive Director, Haihuai Wang

Supervisory Committee Chairman, Xi'an Zhao
Independent Non-executive Director, Long Huang
Non-executive Director, Maoxun Liu
Independent Non-executive Director, Weifeng Wei
Independent Non-executive Director, Changhong Zheng
Chairman, Tongzhou Wang
Executive Director, Xiang Liu
Auditors : PricewaterhouseCoopers Zhong Tian LLP

LOCATIONS

HQ: China Communications Constructions Group Ltd
85 De Sheng Men Wai Street, Xicheng District, Beijing 100088
Phone: (86) 10 8201 6562 **Fax:** (86) 10 8201 6524
Web: www.ccccltd.cn

HISTORICAL FINANCIALS
Company Type: Public

Income Statement — FYE: December 31

	REVENUE ($mil)	NET INCOME ($mil)	NET PROFIT MARGIN	EMPLOYEES
12/22	104,408	2,769	2.7%	0
12/21	107,998	2,834	2.6%	0
12/20	95,957	2,477	2.6%	0
12/19	79,731	2,889	3.6%	0
12/18	71,365	2,861	4.0%	0
Annual Growth	10.0%	(0.8%)	—	—

2022 Year-End Financials

Debt ratio: 4.5% No. of shares ($ mil.): —
Return on equity: 7.0% Dividends
Cash ($ mil.): 16,353 Yield: —
Current Ratio: 0.93 Payout: 0.0%
Long-term debt ($ mil.): 53,745 Market value ($ mil.): —

China Construction Bank Corp

China Construction Bank (CCB) is a leading large-scale commercial bank in China. The bank provides customers with comprehensive financial services. With about 14,740 banking outlets and 349,600 staff members, the bank serves hundreds of millions of personal and corporate customers. The bank has subsidiaries in various sectors, including fund management, financial leasing, trust, insurance, futures, pension and investment banking, and has more than 200 overseas entities covering around 30 countries and regions.

Operations

CCB operates three core business segments: Corporate Banking (about 40% of total sales), Personal Banking (more than 45%), and Treasury operations (almost 10% of total sales.

Corporate banking segment represents the provision of a range of financial products and services to corporations, government agencies and financial institutions. The products and services include corporate loans, trade financing, deposit taking and wealth management services, agency services, financial consulting and advisory services, cash management services, remittance and settlement services, custody services and guarantee services, etc.

Personal banking segment represents the provision of a range of financial products and services to individual customers. The products and services comprise personal loans, deposit taking and wealth management services, card business, remittance services and agency services, etc.

The Treasury business covers the group's treasury operations. The treasury enters into inter-bank money market transactions, repurchase and resale transactions, and invests in debt securities. It also trades in derivatives and foreign currencies for its own account. The treasury carries out customer-driven derivatives, foreign currency and precious metal trading. Its function also includes the management of the group's overall liquidity position, including the issuance of debt securities.

Others These represent equity investments and the revenues, results, assets and liabilities of overseas branches and subsidiaries.

Broadly speaking, the company generates over 80% of its net operating income from net interest income (mostly on loans and advances), while the rest comes from net fee and commission income from bank card fees.

Geographic Reach

Headquartered in Beijing, CCB has branches across 30 countries and regions and has some 200 overseas entities. It divides its operations in six Chinese regions, plus head office and Overseas segments: Yangtze River Delta (more than15% of sales), Pearl River Delta (more than 15%), Bohai Rim (15%), Central (more than 10%), Western (more than 15%), Northeastern (under 5%), and Head Office (more than 20%).

Sales and Marketing

The bank set up some 65 new outlets, including around 30 county-level outlets, and expanded into eight new counties. It continued to optimize the self-service channel network, and had more than 79,140 ATMs, around 25,530 self-service banks, including some 11,350 off-premise self-service banks, and 48,735 smart teller machines. By the end of 2020, the bank had established more than 250 inclusive finance (small business) service centers and small business centers, and over 1,500 personal loan centers.

It launched innovated convenient service models such as "Smart Handling" and "CCB Doorstep Service", and significantly enhanced the online and offline collaboration capacity, which was manifested by the facts that around 30 counter businesses could be completed by retrieving account QR code through mobile banking APP instead of providing physical media, and 75 products were offered through "online order, centralized processing, physical distribution and doorstep service". It leveraged the WeChat official account "CCB Banking Centre" to effectively expand the service radius and efficiency of outlets.

Financial Performance

CCB's operating income grew by more than 25% over the past five years since 2016.

In fiscal 2020, the company's revenue, consisting of net interest income, net fee and commission income, and other net non-interest income, increased 5% to RMB714.2 billion. Net interest income increased by RMB38.8 billion over 2019. In this amount, an increase of RMB63.9 billion was due to the movements of average balances of assets and liabilities, and a decrease of RMB25.1 million was due to the movements of average yields and costs.

Net income grew nearly 2% to RMB271 billion.

Cash and cash equivalents at the end of 2020 was RMB878.9 billion. Cash from operations decreased to RMB580.7 billion, while investing and financing activities used RMB642.2 billion and RMB89.9 billion, respectively. Main cash uses were purchase of investment securities, dividends paid, and repayment of borrowings.

Strategy

The company seeks to become a world-class bank by providing the best service to its customers, maximizing shareholder value and providing excellent career opportunities to its employees. CCB intends to focus its efforts on its target customers, products and geographical regions.

Customers. CCB intends to strengthen its historically strong relationships with its large corporate customers by focusing on industry leaders in strategic industries such as power, telecommunications, oil and gas, and infrastructure, as well as major financial institutions and government agencies, and by selectively developing relationships with small- and medium-enterprise customers. In the personal banking segment, it intends to increase its revenue from high-income retail customers, while capitalizing on its cost efficiency and economies of scale to serve its mass market customers more efficiently.

Products. CCB intends to develop its wholesale and retail products with a focus on fee-based businesses, including payment and settlement services, personal wealth management and corporate treasury management. The company intends to grow proactively its personal banking business with a focus on residential mortgages and diverse savings products, and to build an industry-leading credit card business.

Geographic regions. CCB intends to prioritize its efforts in the major cities of the more developed geographical markets of the Yangtze River Delta, Pearl River Delta and Bohai Rim regions. It also intends to accelerate its development in the capital cities of inland provinces in China.

Company Background

In 2009, CCB acquired two-thirds of Hefei Xingtai Trust for 3.4 billion Yuan ($497 million). The deal gave CCB entry to the trust management business; Hefei Xingtai was renamed CCB Trust.

The bank entered the insurance business with its acquisition of Dutch financial company ING's 50% stake of Pacific Antai Life Insurance. In late 2010, CCB increased its ownership to 51%, making it Pacific Antai's controlling shareholder.

EXECUTIVES

President, Vice Chairman, Executive Director, Jinliang Zhang
Chief Financial Officer, Liurong Sheng
Chief Risk Officer, Yuanguo Cheng
Chief Supervisor, Yongqing Wang
Executive Vice President, Executive Director, Yong Cui
Outside Supervisor, Xijun Zhao
Outside Supervisor, Shenglin Ben
Outside Supervisor, Huan Liu
Supervisor, Hong Lin
Staff Supervisor, Yi Wang
Staff Supervisor, Jun Liu
Secretary, Changmiao Hu
Chairman, Executive Director, Guoli Tian
Executive Director, Zhihong Ji
Independent Non-Executive Director, Kenneth Patrick Chung
Independent Non-Executive Director, Cohen Bill William
Independent Non-executive Director, McCarthy M.C.
Independent Non-executive Director, Independent Director, Wheeler Graham
Independent Non-Executive Director, Antony Kam Chung Leung
Independent Non-executive Director, Independent Director, Madeleine Michel
Non-Executive Director, Jiandong Xu
Non-Executive Director, Bo Tian
Non-Executive Director, Yang Xia
Non-Executive Director, Min Shao
Non-Executive Director, Fang Liu
Non-executive Director, Lu Li
Auditors : Ernst & Young

LOCATIONS

HQ: China Construction Bank Corp
28/F., CCB Tower, 3 Connaught Road Central, Central,
Phone: (852) 39186939 **Fax:** (852) 39186001
Web: www.ccb.com

2016 sales

	%
Yangtze River Delta	16
Pearl River Delta	14
Bohai Rim	16
Central	17
Western	16
Northeastern	5
Head Office	12
Overseas	3
Total	100

PRODUCTS/OPERATIONS

2016 Revenue

	% of total
Interest	75
Fees & commissions	20
Other	5
Total	100

Selected Subsidiaries
CCB Principal Asset Management Co., Ltd.
CCB International (Holdings) Limited
China Construction Bank (Asia) Corporation Limited
China Construction Bank (London) Limited
China Construction Bank Financial Leasing Corporation Limited
Sino-German (75%)
Sino-German Bausparkasse Co. Ltd.

COMPETITORS

AKBANK TURK ANONIM SIRKETI
BANK OF INDIA
CANARA BANK
China Merchants Bank Co., Ltd.
HSBC USA, INC.
ICICI BANK LIMITED
Industrial and Commercial Bank of China Limited
SHINSEI BANK, LIMITED
Shinhan Financial Group Co., Ltd.
TURKIYE IS BANKASI ANONIM SIRKETI

HISTORICAL FINANCIALS

Company Type: Public

Income Statement   FYE: December 31

	ASSETS ($mil)	NET INCOME ($mil)	INCOME AS % OF ASSETS	EMPLOYEES
12/22	5,015,760	46,844	0.9%	352,588
12/21	4,765,420	47,872	1.0%	351,252
12/20	4,301,410	40,583	0.9%	349,671
12/19	3,655,560	37,764	1.0%	347,156
12/18	3,376,230	36,450	1.1%	345,971
Annual Growth	10.4%	6.5%	—	0.5%

2022 Year-End Financials
Return on assets: 0.9%   Dividends
Return on equity: 11.8%   Yield: —
Long-term debt ($ mil.): —   Payout: 484.6%
No. of shares ($ mil.): 250,011   Market value ($ mil.): 3,105,137
Sales ($ mil.): 197,828

	STOCK PRICE ($) FY Close	P/E High/Low	Earnings	Dividends	Book Value
12/22	12.42	11 9	0.19	0.90	1.66
12/21	13.74	15 11	0.19	0.85	1.63
12/20	15.02	18 13	0.16	0.76	1.45
12/19	17.30	17 14	0.15	0.75	1.27
12/18	16.30	21 15	0.15	0.74	1.15
Annual Growth	(6.6%)	—	6.3%	4.9%	9.6%

China Gas Holdings Ltd.

EXECUTIVES

Chairman, Xiao Yun Li
Vice-Chairman, Ying Xu
Managing Director, Director, Ming Hui Liu
Executive Director, Director, Wei Wei Zhu
Executive Director, Director, Jin Long Ma
Secretary, Doris Yan Tung Yang
Director, Zhuo Zhi Feng
Director, Joe Yamagata
Director, R. K. Goel
Director, Joong Ho Kim
Director, William Rackets
Director, Yu Hua Zhao
Director, Er Wan Mao
Director, Cynthia Sin Yue Wong
Auditors : Deloitte Touche Tohmatsu

LOCATIONS

HQ: China Gas Holdings Ltd.
Room 1601, 16th Floor, Capital Centre, 151 Gloucester Road, Wanchai.
Phone: —
Web: www.chinagasholdings.com.hk

HISTORICAL FINANCIALS

Company Type: Public

Income Statement   FYE: March 31

	REVENUE ($mil)	NET INCOME ($mil)	NET PROFIT MARGIN	EMPLOYEES
03/21	9,000	1,347	15.0%	0
03/20	7,679	1,185	15.4%	59,462
03/19	7,565	1,047	13.8%	51,000
03/18	6,731	776	11.5%	48,000
03/17	4,117	533	13.0%	41,000
Annual Growth	21.6%	26.1%		

2021 Year-End Financials
Debt ratio: 4.5%   No. of shares ($ mil.): 5,212
Return on equity: 22.8%   Dividends
Cash ($ mil.): 1,066   Yield: 1.4%
Current Ratio: 1.09   Payout: 587.6%
Long-term debt ($ mil.): 4,079   Market value ($ mil.): 540,471

	STOCK PRICE ($) FY Close	P/E High/Low	Earnings	Dividends	Book Value
03/21	103.69	52 33	0.26	1.52	1.28
03/20	86.98	64 42	0.23	1.38	0.98
03/19	89.70	72 41	0.21	1.04	0.86
03/18	90.45	76 29	0.15	0.81	0.73
03/17	39.69	50 36	0.11	0.56	0.53
Annual Growth	27.1%	—	24.2%	28.6%	24.6%

China Life Insurance Co Ltd

China Life Insurance Company (China Life) is a leading life insurance company in China. The company is a leading provider of individual and group life insurance, annuity, and accident and health insurance in China. With a controlling stake in China Life Pension Company and significant stake in China Life Property and Casualty Insurance Company, the company has expanded into other insurance-related areas. Through China Life Asset Management, the company has investment assets of RMB 4.98 trillion. China Life has approximately 317 million long-term individual and group life insurance policies, annuity contracts and long-term health insurance policies in force. It also provides both individual and group accident and short-term health insurance policies and services.

Operations

China Life operates through three principal business segments: Life insurance (accounts for about 80% of revenue); Health (some 15%) insurance and Accident insurance (less than 5%).

Life insurance, which offers participating and non-participating life insurance and annuities to individuals and groups; Health insurance, which offers short-term and long-term health insurance to individuals and groups; and Accident insurance, which offers short-term and long-term accident insurance to individuals and groups.

Overall, net premiums earned generates some 75% of revenue, while investment income brings in more than 20% and other miscellaneous accounts for the remaining revenue.

Geographic Reach

China Life is based in Beijing, China.

Sales and Marketing

The company's distribution network reaches almost every county in China. Throughout China, it has approximately 820,000 exclusive agents operating in approximately 15,000 field offices for its individual products and approximately 45,000 direct sales representatives for group products. China Life has a multi-channel distribution network selling individual and group insurance products through intermediaries, primarily non-dedicated agencies located in over 49,000 outlets of commercial banks.

Financial Performance

The company reported a revenue of RMB 824.9 billion, a 2% increase from the previous year's revenue of RMB 805 billion.

As of December 31, 2021, equity attributable to equity holders was RMB 478.6 billion, an increase of 6%, from RMB 450.1 billion as of December 31, 2020. This was primarily due to the combined impact of total comprehensive income and profit distributions during 2021.

The company's cash at the end of 2021 was RMB 60.4 billion. Operating activities generated RMB 286.4 billion, while investing activities used RMB 393.7 billion, mainly for debt investments. Financing activities provided another RMB 111.1 billion.

Strategy

In 2021, in line with its general development strategy, the company developed and introduced 160 new products, including: 53 long-term insurance products consisting of 12 life insurance products, eight annuity products and 33 health insurance products; and 107 short-term insurance products consisting of two accident insurance products and 105 health insurance products.

Company Background

China Life's history goes back to 1949, when its predecessor People's Insurance Company of China (PICC) was established. The unified national insurer was created just 20 days after the founding of new China. In 2003, PICC was dissolved and replaced by four state-owned firms, including China Life. The company went public that year, listing on the Hong Kong Stock Exchange and the New York Stock Exchange. It listed on the Shanghai Stock Exchange in 2007.

HISTORY

China Life listed on the NYSE in what would become one of the largest IPOs of 2003, valued at more than $3 billion. The company's IPO, however, was tarnished by subsequent revelations of improper accounting prior to the company's going public; several US lawsuits were filed, but in 2006 the SEC's investigation came to an end with no action taken.

EXECUTIVES

Vice President, President, Executive Director, Non-executive Director, Hengxuan Su
Chief Risk Officer, Supervisor, Yuzeng Jia
Board Secretary, Vice President, Executive Director, Mingguang Li
Staff Supervisor, Qingyang Cao
Supervisor, Bing Han
Staff Supervisor, Xiaoqing Wang
Person-in-charge of Finance, Xiumei Huang
Chairman, Bin Wang
Non-executive Director, Changqing Yuan
Independent Director, Xin Tang
Executive Director, Dairen Lin
Independent Director, Jieke Bai
Independent Director, Aishi Liang
Non-executive Director, Junhui Wang
Independent Director, Zhiquan Lin
Auditors : Ernst & Young Hua Ming LLP

LOCATIONS

HQ: China Life Insurance Co Ltd
16 Financial Street, Xicheng District, Beijing 100033

Phone: (86) 10 63631191 **Fax:** (86) 10 66575112
Web: www.e-chinalife.com

PRODUCTS/OPERATIONS

2017 Sales by Segment

	% of total
Life Insurance	86
Health Insurance	11
Accident Insurance	2
Other	1
Total	100

COMPETITORS

AFLAC INCORPORATED
CITIZENS, INC.
Kyobo Life Insurance Co., Ltd.
MAPFRE, SA
MASSACHUSETTS MUTUAL LIFE INSURANCE COMPANY
MUTUAL OF OMAHA INSURANCE COMPANY
PRINCIPAL FINANCIAL GROUP, INC.
PRUDENTIAL FINANCIAL, INC.
Tower Group International Ltd
UNUM GROUP

HISTORICAL FINANCIALS

Company Type: Public

Income Statement — FYE: December 31

	ASSETS ($mil)	NET INCOME ($mil)	INCOME AS % OF ASSETS	EMPLOYEES
12/22	761,307	4,650	0.6%	0
12/21	770,414	8,020	1.0%	0
12/20	650,191	7,685	1.2%	0
12/19	535,586	8,376	1.6%	0
12/18	473,141	1,656	0.4%	102,817
Annual Growth	12.6%	29.4%	—	—

2022 Year-End Financials

Return on assets: 0.6%
Return on equity: 7.0%
Long-term debt ($ mil.): —
No. of shares ($ mil.): —
Sales ($ mil.): 31,608
Dividends
Yield: —
Payout: 0.0%
Market value ($ mil.): —

China Mobile Limited

China Mobile Limited is a top-tier provider of telecommunications and related services in mainland China. It is renowned for its world-class telecommunications and information operations, which boast the largest network and customer base globally. The company is also a market leader in profitability, brand value, and market value ranking. Its services include voice, data, broadband, dedicated lines, IDC, cloud computing, IoT, and others in the Customer, Home, Business, and New (CHBN) markets. China Mobile Limited has about 975 million mobile customers and around 272 million wireline broadband subscribers. The majority stake of the state-controlled China Mobile Communications Corporation (CMCC) is held through an intermediary subsidiary, China Mobile (Hong Kong) Group Limited. The company was established in 1997.

Operations

China Mobile provides telecommunications services (such as voice and data services), telecommunication-related products (such as handsets), customer point rewards, and/or other promotional goods/services.

China Mobile's telecommunications services, include wireless data traffic services (account for more than 45%), applications and information services (about 20%), wireline broadband services (around 10%), voice services (nearly 10%), and SMS & MMS services (less than 5%). Sales of products and others account for almost 15%.

The company has three popular brands: "GoTone", "M-zone", and "Easy Own". In addition, it launched new initiatives including "Home Data Information Communications Technology," or HDICT, an integrated family management and service solution provided with the comprehensive application of home data, information, and communications technology.

The company also accelerated the implementation of "5G+" by formulating well-coordinated development of 5G and 4G. It constructed and began operating more than 1.285 million 5G base stations and launched 5G commercial services in all prefecture-level cities, selected counties, and key areas in China.

Geographic Reach
Hong Kong based, China Mobile has its presence in about 30 cities, autonomous regions, and directly-administered municipalities in China.

Sales and Marketing
The majority of China Mobile's operating revenue is from contracts with the customers. In general, the company serves individual and corporate customers.

Financial Performance
The company's revenue has been rising in the last few years. It has an overall increase of 27% between 2018 and 2022.

In 2022, the company had a total revenue of RMB 937.3 billion, a 10% increase from the previous year's total revenue of RMB 848.3 billion. Overall, its efforts in fostering digital transformation revenue as the "second curve" have yielded remarkable results. These services have become a key growth driver contributing to a more balanced, stable and healthy overall revenue structure.

Net income was RMB 125.6 billion in 2022, an 8% increase from the previous year's net income of RMB 116.3 billion.

Cash held by the company at the end of 2022 was RMB 167.1 billion. Operating activities generated RMB 280.8 billion, while investing activities used RMB 238.1 billion, mainly for payment for property, plant and equipment. Financing activities used another RMB 120.5 billion, primarily for dividends paid to the company's equity shareholders.

Strategy
With a focus on innovation, entrepreneurship and creation, the company synergistically developed the four segments: international business, equity investment, digital content and FinTech, accelerating breakthroughs in emerging areas. As a result, the revenue contribution of key business segments increased significantly. In 2022, its "New" market revenue achieved very rapid growth, reaching RMB 38.5 billion, up 26.9% year-on-year. In terms of international business, the company deepened the synergies between international and domestic markets, speeding up the export of high-quality and mature capabilities to overseas markets and achieving breakthroughs in 5G industry solutions. It further optimized the deployment of international resources, creating a thriving international cooperation ecosystem. Alongside improved globalized operations, the company's international business revenue reached RMB16.7 billion, up 25.4% year-on-year. In terms of equity investment, adhering to a focus on value contribution, ecosystem formation and synergy creation, the company delved into critical sectors through the two-pronged approach of direct investment and investing through funds.

Company Background
China Mobile Limited was incorporated in Hong Kong on 3 September 1997. The Company was listed on the New York Stock Exchange ("NYSE") and The Stock Exchange of Hong Kong Limited ("HKEX" or the "Stock Exchange") on 22 October 1997 and 23 October 1997, respectively.

EXECUTIVES

Executive Director, Chairman, Jie Yang
Chief Executive Officer, Executive Director, Xin Dong
Executive Director, Yuhang Wang
Chief Financial Officer, Executive Director, Ronghua Li
Vice President, Huidi Li
Vice President, Tongqing Gao
Vice President, Qin Jian
Vice President, Dachun Zhao
Secretary, Grace Wong
Independent Non-Executive Director, Moses Mo Chi Cheng
Independent Non-Executive Director, Paul Man Yiu Chow
Independent Non-Executive Director, Stephen K.W. Yiu
Independent Non-Executive Director, Qiang Yang
Auditors : KPMG Huazhen LLP

LOCATIONS

HQ: China Mobile Limited
60th Floor, The Center, 99 Queen's Road Central.
Phone: (852) 3121 8888   **Fax:** (852) 2511 9092
Web: www.chinamobileltd.com

PRODUCTS/OPERATIONS

2015 Sales

	% of total
Telecommunication Services	
Voice Services	56
Data Services	33
Other	5
Other products & services	6
Total	100

2015 Sales

	% of total
Revenue from telecommunications services	87
Revenue from sales of products and others	13
Total	100

COMPETITORS

IBASIS, INC.
IDT CORPORATION
NTT DOCOMO, INC.
SINGAPORE TELECOMMUNICATIONS LIMITED
SMARTONE TELECOMMUNICATIONS HOLDINGS LIMITED
SPARK NEW ZEALAND LIMITED
SPOT MOBILE INTERNATIONAL LTD.
SYNIVERSE HOLDINGS, INC.
TATA TELESERVICES LIMITED
TELSTRA CORPORATION LIMITED

HISTORICAL FINANCIALS
Company Type: Public

Income Statement   FYE: December 31

	REVENUE ($mil)	NET INCOME ($mil)	NET PROFIT MARGIN	EMPLOYEES
12/21	133,612	18,294	13.7%	449,934
12/20	117,437	16,489	14.0%	454,332
12/19	107,199	15,325	14.3%	464,656
12/18	107,122	17,123	16.0%	459,152
12/17	113,795	17,561	15.4%	464,656
Annual Growth	4.1%	1.0%	—	(0.8%)

2021 Year-End Financials
Debt ratio: —
Return on equity: 9.8%
Cash ($ mil.): 38,424
Current Ratio: 1.02
Long-term debt ($ mil.): —
No. of shares ($ mil.): 20,475
Dividends
 Yield: —
 Payout: 116.3%
Market value ($ mil.): —

China Petroleum & Chemical Corp

China Petroleum and Chemical Corporation (Sinopec Corp.) is one of the largest integrated energy and chemical companies in China. Its principal operations include the exploration and production, pipeline transportation and sale of petroleum and natural gas; the production, sale, storage and transportation of refinery products, petrochemical products, coal chemical products, synthetic fibre, and other chemical products; the import and export, including an import and export agency business, of petroleum, natural gas, petroleum products, petrochemical and chemical products, and other commodities and technologies; and research, development and application of technologies and information. Equipped with a well-developed refined oil products sales network, the group is the largest supplier of refined oil products in China; and in terms of ethylene production capacity, the group takes the first position in China, and has a well-established marketing network for chemical products. Sinopec Corp. generates some 80% of revenue from Mainland China.

Operations

The group operates through four main segments: Refining; Marketing and distribution; Chemicals; and Exploration and production. Corporate and others (more than 25% of revenue), which largely comprises the trading activities of the import and export companies of the group and research and development undertaken by other subsidiaries.

Refining, which processes and purifies crude oil, that is sourced from the exploration and production segment of the group and external suppliers, and manufactures and sells petroleum products to the chemicals and marketing and distribution segments of the group and external customers. The segment generates some 30% of revenue.

Marketing and distribution, which owns and operates oil depots and service stations in the PRC, and distributes and sells refined petroleum products (mainly gasoline and diesel) in the PRC through wholesale and retail sales networks. The segment accounts for nearly 30% of revenue.

Chemicals, which manufactures and sells petrochemical products, derivative petrochemical products and other chemical products mainly to external customers. The segment makes up for around 10% of revenue.

Exploration and production, which explores and develops oil fields, produces crude oil and natural gas and sells such products to the refining segment of the group and external customers. The segment brings in almost 5% of revenue.

Geographic Reach

Based in Beijing, Sinopec generates vast majority of its revenue from Mainland China. The group operates some 30 refineries in China.

Sales and Marketing

All of its retail sales are made through a network of service stations and petroleum shops operated under the Sinopec brand.

Financial Performance

The company reported a total revenue of RMB 2.7 trillion in 2021, a 30% increase from the previous year's total revenue of RMB 2.1 trillion.

In 2021, the company had a net income of RMB 72 billion, a 115% increase from the previous year's net income of RMB 33.4 billion.

The company's cash at the end of 2021 was RMB 60.4 billion. Operating activities generated RMB 225.2 billion, while investing activities used RMB 121.3 billion, mainly for capital expenditures. Financing activities used another RMB 84.7 billion, primarily for repayments of bank and other loans.

EXECUTIVES

President, Chairman, Non-Executive Director, Acting Chairman, Yongsheng Ma
President, Executive Director, Baocai Yu
Chief Financial Officer, Donghua Shou
Vice President, Secretary, Wensheng Huang
Supervisor, Zhenying Jiang
Staff Supervisor, Defang Li
Staff Supervisor, Yaohuan Chen
Supervisor, Hongjin Guo
Staff Supervisor, Dapeng Lv
Supervisor, Zhaolin Yin
Supervisory Committee Chairman, Shaofeng Zhang
Supervisor, Zhiguo Zhang
Supervisor, Lianggong Lv
Supervisor, Fasen Qiu
Supervisor, Po Wu
Supervisor, Yalin Zhai
Chairman, Yuzhuo Zhang
Executive Director, Hongbin Liu
Executive Director, Yonglin Li
Executive Director, Yiqun Ling
Independent Non-executive Director, Hongbin Cai
Independent Non-executive Director, Jianing Wu
Independent Non-executive Director, Mingjian Bi
Independent Non-executive Director, Dan Shi
Non-executive Director, Dong Zhao
Auditors : PricewaterhouseCoopers Zhong Tian LLP

LOCATIONS

HQ: China Petroleum & Chemical Corp
No. 22 Chaoyangmen North Street, Chaoyang District, Beijing 100728
Phone: (86) 10 5996 0028   **Fax:** (86) 10 5996 0386
Web: www.sinopec.com

2015 Sales

	% of total
Mainland China	78
Others	22
Total	100

PRODUCTS/OPERATIONS

2015 Sales

	% of total
Marketing and distribution	34
Refining	28
Chemicals	10
Exploration and production	4
Corporate and others	24
Total	100

COMPETITORS

Bankers Petroleum Ltd
Cenovus Energy Inc
FIELDPOINT PETROLEUM CORPORATION
Husky Energy Inc
JAPAN PETROLEUM EXPLORATION CO.,LTD.
KUWAIT PETROLEUM CORPORATION S.A.K
NIGERIAN NATIONAL PETROLEUM CORPORATION (NNPC)
OIL REFINERIES LTD
QATAR PETROLEUM
TransAtlantic Petroleum Corp

HISTORICAL FINANCIALS

Company Type: Public

Income Statement — FYE: December 31

	REVENUE ($mil)	NET INCOME ($mil)	NET PROFIT MARGIN	EMPLOYEES
12/22	480,989	9,610	2.0%	0
12/21	431,727	11,216	2.6%	0
12/20	322,004	5,034	1.6%	0
12/19	426,286	8,276	1.9%	402,206
12/18	420,334	9,172	2.2%	423,543
Annual Growth	3.4%	1.2%		—

2022 Year-End Financials

Debt ratio: 1.0%
Return on equity: 8.4%
Cash ($ mil.): 21,026
Current Ratio: 0.78
Long-term debt ($ mil.): 15,649
No. of shares ($ mil.): —
Dividends
Yield: —
Payout: 0.0%
Market value ($ mil.): —

China Resources Land Ltd

China Resources Land (CR Land) is a strategic business unit responsible for city construction and operation under China Resources Group, a Fortune Global 500 company, and is also a front-runner of comprehensive urban investors, developers and operators in mainland China. It primarily develops properties in urban areas of China such as Beijing, Shanghai, Shenzhen, and Chengdu. It covers a wide range of business: residential development, investment property, urban redevelopment, property management, senior housing, leasing apartment, industrial funds, industrial property, cultural sports and educational property, cinema, construction, decoration, electromechanical and furniture etc. CR Land was established in 1994 via reconstructing.

Operations

The company operates in four segments: Development Properties for Sale (over 85% of sales), Property Investments and Management (more than 5%), Construction, and Decoration Services and Others (some 5%), and Hotel Operations.

The Development Properties for Sale segment represents the income generated from development and sales of residential properties, office and commercial premises.

The Property Investments and Management segment represents the lease of investment properties, which are self-developed or under subleases by the group to generate rental income and to gain from the appreciation in the properties' values in the long term, together with income generated from property management and related services for investment properties.

The Construction, Decoration Services and Others segment represents the income generated from construction and decoration services, property management and related services for residential properties, urban development and operation, leasing apartment, senior housing, cinema and others.

The Hotel Operations segment represents the income generated from hotel accommodation and catering services.

Geographic Reach

Headquartered in Hong Kong, the company has operations in Beijing, Shanghai, Shenzhen, Guangzhou, Hangzhou, Nanjing and Chengdu.

Sales and Marketing

The company's five largest suppliers and five largest customers together accounted for less than 30% of its purchases and sales respectively.

Financial Performance

CR Land's revenues for the past five years have consistently increased annually, rising over 100% between 2017 and 2021. Profits also followed a similar trajectory, overall increasing 65% in the same period.

The company achieved 18% growth in revenue with RMB 212.1 billion in 2021, from RMB 179.6 billion the year prior. The increase was due to an influx in revenue from customer contracts, rental income, and segment revenue.

Profit for the year amounted to RMB 32.4 billion, a 9% increase from RMB 29.8 billion the year prior. The rise in profit can be attributable to the increase in revenue for the year, as well as a decline in the company's income tax expense.

Cash at the end of the year was RMB 106.8 billion, a RMB 19.4 billion increase from RMB 87.5 billion the year prior. Operations provided RMB 7.0 billion, while financing activities contributed another RMB 40.2 billion from notes issuances and capital contributions from non-controlling interests. Investing activities used RMB 27.8 billion, mainly for properties investments, financial assets acquisitions, and time deposits acquisitions.

Strategy

CR Land has continued to develop its strategic roadmap during the 14th Five-Year Plan period (2021-2025), keeping pace with national strategies and opening new grounds for development.

Guided by the company's goal of "reshaping CR Land to achieve high-quality development," the company ensured high product quality through innovation and standardization. It set up a special technology promotion team as the quality gatekeeper and implemented 25 regional benchmark projects. Meanwhile, the company has stepped up its digital transformation pace and launched a comprehensive exploration of smart cities, taking full advantage of scientific innovation and digital capabilities to enable advanced corporate operations. In 2021, CR Land compiled the CR Land Smart Community Design Standard to realize data connectivity through a cohesive standard, shortening the duration of projects.

EXECUTIVES

Chairman, Executive Director, Xin Li
Vice-Chairman, Executive Director, Chief Operating Officer, Dawei Zhang
Chief Financial Officer, Executive Director, Shiqing Guo
Executive Director, Senior Vice President, Chief Strategy Officer, Ji Xie
Executive Director, Senior Vice President, Chief Human Resources Officer, President, Bingqi Wu
Secretary, Frank Yiu Fung So
Independent Non-Executive Director, Bosco Hin Ngai Ho
Independent Non-Executive Director, Andrew Y. Yan
Independent Non-Executive Director, Peter Kam To Wan
Independent Non-Executive Director, Wei Zhong
Independent Non-Executive Director, Sun Zhe
Non-Executive Director, Xiaoyong Liu
Non-Executive Director, Jian Dou
Non-Executive Director, Hong Cheng
Auditors : Ernst & Young

LOCATIONS

HQ: China Resources Land Ltd
46th Floor, China Resources Building, 26 Harbour Road, Wanchai,
Phone: (852) 2877 2330   **Fax:** (852) 2877 9068
Web: www.crland.com.hk

PRODUCTS/OPERATIONS

2015 sales

	% of total
Sales of developed properties	90
Property investment & management	6
Hotel operations	1
Construction, decoration services & others	3
Total	100

COMPETITORS

AGILE GROUP HOLDINGS LIMITED
HANG LUNG GROUP LIMITED
MITSUBISHI ESTATE COMPANY, LIMITED
MITSUI FUDOSAN CO., LTD.
NEW WORLD DEVELOPMENT COMPANY LIMITED
SINO LAND COMPANY LIMITED
SUN HUNG KAI PROPERTIES LIMITED
THE GALE COMPANY L L C
UOL GROUP LIMITED
YANLORD LAND GROUP LIMITED

HISTORICAL FINANCIALS

Company Type: Public

Income Statement   FYE: December 31

	REVENUE ($mil)	NET INCOME ($mil)	NET PROFIT MARGIN	EMPLOYEES
12/22	30,014	4,072	13.6%	55,311
12/21	33,410	5,103	15.3%	49,478
12/20	27,458	4,557	16.6%	48,414
12/19	21,231	4,120	19.4%	51,976
12/18	17,619	3,523	20.0%	46,518
Annual Growth	14.2%	3.7%	—	4.4%

2022 Year-End Financials

Debt ratio: 2.9%
Return on equity: 11.9%
Cash ($ mil.): 13,849
Current Ratio: 1.35
Long-term debt ($ mil.): 22,592
No. of shares ($ mil.): 7,130
Dividends
Yield: —
Payout: 0.0%
Market value ($ mil.): —

China Resources Power Holdings Co Ltd

China Resources Power helps to keep the lights on. Known as CR Power, it develops, operates, and manages large coal-fired power plants in China, holding shares in more than 35 power plants. It also has wind farms, hydroelectric projects, and other renewable energy projects. Facilities boast a combined generation capacity of more than 26,000 MW. About 42% of its power is generated in eastern China, 24% in central China, 18% in southern China, and 10% in northern China. Its service areas include some of China's wealthiest provinces, including Guangdong, Hebei, Henan, Hunan, Jiangsu, and Zhejiang provinces. CR Power is a subsidiary of China Resources Holdings, which is also parent to China Resources Beer.

EXECUTIVES

President, Executive Director, Baofeng Shi
Vice-Chairman, Executive Director, Junzheng Zhang
Senior Vice President, Executive Director, Secretary, Xiao Bing Wang
Chairman, Non-Executive Director, Chuandong Wang
Independent Non-Executive Director, Elsie Oi sie Leung
Independent Non-Executive Director, Raymond Kuo Fung Ch'ien
Independent Non-Executive Director, Jack Chak Kwong So
Independent Non-Executive Director, Yuchuan Yang
Non-Executive Director, Guixin Liu
Non-Executive Director, Guoyong Chen
Auditors : Deloitte Touche Tohmatsu

LOCATIONS

HQ: China Resources Power Holdings Co Ltd
Rooms 2001-2002, 20th Floor, China Resources Building, 26 Harbour Road, Wanchai,
Phone: (852) 2593 7530   **Fax:** (852) 2593 7531
Web: www.cr-power.com

COMPETITORS

CALPINE CORPORATION
Huadian Power International Corporation Limited
Huaneng Power International, Inc.
KANSAI ELECTRIC POWER COMPANY, INCORPORATED, THE
TALEN ENERGY CORPORATION

HISTORICAL FINANCIALS

Company Type: Public

Income Statement   FYE: December 31

	REVENUE ($mil)	NET INCOME ($mil)	NET PROFIT MARGIN	EMPLOYEES
12/22	13,254	903	6.8%	22,340
12/21	11,515	204	1.8%	21,252
12/20	8,971	978	10.9%	21,611
12/19	8,701	846	9.7%	21,746
12/18	9,823	504	5.1%	21,629
Annual Growth	7.8%	15.7%	—	0.8%

2022 Year-End Financials

Debt ratio: 6.0%
Return on equity: 8.2%
Cash ($ mil.): 990
Current Ratio: 0.61
Long-term debt ($ mil.): 11,974
No. of shares ($ mil.): 4,810
Dividends
Yield: —
Payout: 0.0%
Market value ($ mil.): 132,047

	STOCK PRICE ($) FY Close	P/E High/Low	Earnings	Dividends	Book Value
12/22	27.45	32 15	0.19	0.43	2.19
12/21	48.15	146 46	0.04	1.16	2.36
12/20	15.18	14 10	0.20	1.01	2.30
12/19	18.70	23 13	0.18	0.68	1.95
12/18	28.22	37 28	0.11	1.60	1.86
Annual Growth	(0.7%)	—	15.3%	(28.1%)	4.2%

China Shenhua Energy Co., Ltd.

China Shenhua Energy Company (CSEC) is principally engaged in the production and sale of coal and electricity, railway, port and shipping transportation, and coal-to-olefins businesses in China. CSEC operates five major mines. The Shendong Mines account for close to two-thirds of its total coal production, which is about 185 million tons a year. It is the largest listed coal company in China and globally with the sales volume of coal reaching more than 447 million tonnes and commercial coal production volume reaching approximately 282.7 million tonnes. CSEC owns and operates four railway lines and port facilities for the transportation of its coal. The company also operates some 15 power plants total installed capacity of close to 30,245 MW. Almost all of its sales account to China.

Operations

The company operates six segments: Coal (over 70% of sales), Power (over 20%), Railway, Port, Shipping, and Coal Chemical (accounts for the remaining).

Coal operations produce coal from surface and underground mines, and the sale of coal to external customers, the power operations segment and the coal chemical operations segment.

Power operations use coal from the coal operations segment and external suppliers, thermal power, wind power, water power and gas power to generate electric power for the sale to coal operations segment and external customers.

Railway operations provide railway transportation services to the coal operations segment, the power operations segment, the coal chemical operations segment and external customers.

Port operations provide loading, transportation and storage services to the coal operations segment and external customers. The company charges service fees and other expenses, which are reviewed and approved by the relevant government authorities.

Shipping operations provide shipment transportation services to the power operations segment, the coal operations segment and external customers.

Coal chemical operations use coal from the coal operations segment to first produce methanol and further process into polyethylene and polypropylene, together with other by-products, for sale to external customers.

Geographic Reach

The company is headquartered in China where it generates almost all of it sales.

Sales and Marketing

The company sells its coal under long-term supply contracts, which allow periodical price adjustments, and at spot market. It also sells its polyethylene at spot market.

The total revenue from the top five customers of the group accounts for some 35% of the revenue of the group, including the revenue of the group from its largest customer accounting for around 25% of the revenue of the group. The largest customer of the group was China Energy (including its subsidiaries), the controlling shareholder of the company. The group mainly sells coal products and provides coal transportation service to the company.

Financial Performance

Except in 2019, the company's revenue has been rising in the last few years. It has an overall growth of 37% between 2015 and 2019.

The company had a revenue of RMB 241.9 billion, an 8% decrease from the previous year. The decrease was primarily due to lower sales volume in the company's Power, Port, and Coal Chemical Segments.

Profit for the year ended 2019 totaled RMB 49.8 billion.

The company's cash for the year ended 2019 was RMB 41.8 billion. Operating activities generated RMB 63.1 billion, while investing activities used RMB 46.3 billion, primarily for purchases of wealth management products included in prepaid expenses and other current assets. Financing activities used another RMB 37.2 billion, primarily for dividends paid to equity holders of the company.

Strategy

Over the past year, guided by the overall development strategy requirement of "One Target, Three Models and Five Strategies, and Seven First-class" of China Energy, the company took active measures to identify its strategic positioning, defined its development goals, and organized the promotion of strategy research for development, the development of world-class demonstration enterprises and the preparation of the "14th five-year" plan, which charted the course and laid a solid foundation for the long-term development of the company.

EXECUTIVES

Secretary, Qing Huang
Supervisor, Dayu Zhou
Chief Financial Officer, Shancheng Xu
General Manager, Executive Director, Jiping Yang
Staff Supervisor, Changyan Zhang
Deputy General Manager, Staff Director, Xingzhong Wang
Supervisory Committee Chairman, Meijian Luo
Deputy General Manager, Zhiming Li
Chairman, Xiangxi Wang
Independent Non-executive Director, Zhongen Bai
Independent Non-executive Director, Hanwen Chen
Non-executive Director, Jinzhong Jia
Executive Director, Mingjun Xu
Independent Non-executive Director, Guoqiang Yuan

Auditors : Deloitte Touche Tohmatsu Certified Public Accountants LLP

LOCATIONS

HQ: China Shenhua Energy Co., Ltd.
22 Andingmen Xibinhe Road, Dongcheng District, Beijing 100011
Phone: (86) 10 5813 3399   **Fax:** (86) 10 5813 1804
Web: www.csec.com

2008 Sales

	% of total
China	91
Other countries	9
Total	100

COMPETITORS

DOMINION ENERGY, INC.
FLORIDA POWER & LIGHT COMPANY
GREAT PLAINS ENERGY INCORPORATED
THE SOUTHERN COMPANY
WEC ENERGY GROUP INC.

HISTORICAL FINANCIALS

Company Type: Public

Income Statement   FYE: December 31

	REVENUE ($mil)	NET INCOME ($mil)	NET PROFIT MARGIN	EMPLOYEES
12/22	49,942	10,092	20.2%	0
12/21	52,801	7,918	15.0%	0
12/20	35,665	5,989	16.8%	0
12/19	34,760	6,215	17.9%	0
12/18	38,396	6,377	16.6%	0
Annual Growth	6.8%	12.2%	—	—

2022 Year-End Financials

Debt ratio: 1.1%
Return on equity: 18.0%
Cash ($ mil.): 24,715
Current Ratio: 2.14
Long-term debt ($ mil.): 6,072
No. of shares ($ mil.): —
Dividends
Yield: 0.1%
Payout: 264.3%
Market value ($ mil.): —

	STOCK PRICE ($) FY Close	P/E High/Low	PER SHARE ($) Earnings	Dividends	Book Value
12/22	11.46	4 2	0.51	1.34	0.00
12/21	9.33	4 3	0.40	0.95	0.00
12/20	7.47	5 3	0.30	1.01	0.00
12/19	8.33	5 3	0.31	0.42	0.00
12/18	8.64	5 4	0.32	0.47	0.00
Annual Growth	7.3%	— —	12.2%	30.2%	

China Southern Airlines Co Ltd

One of China's top three airline companies, along with China Eastern Airlines and Air China, China Southern Airlines operates a fleet of about 880 passenger and cargo transport aircraft, including Boeing models 787, 777, & 737 series and Airbus models A380, 330, 320, 350 series and ARJ21, from its hub in Guangzhou and about 20 branches regional bases. China Southern Airlines has over 843 thousand flights during the year. The company generates most of its sales domestically.

Operations

China Southern Airlines' scope of business includes: provision of services of domestic, regional and international scheduled and unscheduled air transportation of passenger, cargo, mail and luggage; provision of services of general aviation; provision of services of aircraft repair and maintenance; acting as an agency of domestic and foreign airlines; offering airlines catering services (operated by branch office only); and conducting other aviation and relevant businesses, among others.

The company generates about 95% of sales from traffic activities. The remaining is from other operating activities including commission, general aviation, and hotel and tour operations.

The company has two reportable operating segments; Airline Transportation Operations (around 95% of sales) and other segments (about 5%), according to internal organization structure, managerial needs and internal reporting system. Airline transportation operations comprises the Group's passenger and cargo and mail operations. Other segments includes hotel and tour operation, air catering services, ground services, cargo handling and other miscellaneous services.

Geographic Reach

China Southern Airlines headquarters is located in Guangzhou. It has about 20 branches in Beijing, Shenzhen, and other cities and almost 10 holding aviation subsidiaries including Xiamen Airlines. The company has set up CSAGA in Zhuhai, and has set up around 20 domestic offices in Hangzhou, Qingdao and other places, and approximately 55 overseas offices in Sydney, New York and other places. It generates some 75% of total sales from domestic operations, about 25% from international, and the rest were generated from Hong Kong, Macau & Taiwan.

Sales and Marketing

The company's top 5 customers account for less than 30%% of the company's total revenue. Its advertising and promotion expenses were RMB 140 million and RMB 121 million in 2021 and 2020, respectively.

Financial Performance

The company's revenue in 2021 increased by 10% to RMB101.6 billion compared to RMB 92.6 billion in the prior year.

Net loss in 2021 increased to RMB12.1 billion compared to the prior year's RMB10.8 billion.

Cash held by the company at the end of fiscal 2021 decreased to RMB21.5 billion. Operating and financing activities provided RMB7.7 billion and RMB4.2 billion, respectively. Investing activities used RMB15.8 billion, mainly for acquisition of property, plant and equipment and other asset.

Strategy

During the reporting period, the company made progress in deepening reform and implemented its development strategies one by one. China Southern Airlines formulated the overarching approach for high quality development, coordinated and prepared the development plan for the "14th Five-Year Plan"; promoted downward penetration of governance reform, developed authorization management system from the Board to the management; deeply drove the adjustment and optimization of five major structures for fleet, market, manpower, industry, assets and liabilities; thoroughly promoted the contractual management of the tenure system, promoted the downward penetration of the market-oriented operation mechanism; propelled the development of "marketization, integration, industrialization and internationalization" of aircraft maintenance; proceeded with the non-public issuance of shares.

EXECUTIVES

President, General Manager, Chairman, Vice Chairman, Xulun Ma
Executive Vice President, General Manager, Executive Director, Vice Chairman, Wensheng Han
Executive Vice President, Deputy General Manager, Zhengrong Zhang
Executive Vice President, Deputy General Manager, Laijun Luo
Deputy General Manager, Executive Vice President, Jidong Ren
Executive Vice President, Deputy General Manager, Yong Cheng
Executive Vice President, Deputy General Manager, Zhixue Wang
Executive Vice President, Chief Engineer, Deputy General Manager, Tongbin Li
Secretary, Bing Xie
Staff Supervisor, Juan Mao
Supervisory Committee Chairman, Jiashi Li
Supervisor, Xiaochun Lin
Deputy General Manager, Yingxiang Wu
Chief Financial Officer, Deputy General Manager, Accountant General, Yong Yao
Independent Non-executive Director, Huizhong Gu
Independent Non-executive Director, Changyue Liu
Independent Non-executive Director, Wei Guo
Independent Non-executive Director, Yan Yan
Auditors : PricewaterhouseCoopers Zhong Tian LLP

LOCATIONS

HQ: China Southern Airlines Co Ltd
278 Ji Chang Road, Guangzhou, Guangdong Province 510405
Phone: (86) 20 8612 4462 **Fax:** (86) 20 8665 9040
Web: www.csair.com

2014 Sales

	% of total
Domestic	77
International	21
Hong Kong, Macau & Taiwan	2
Total	100

PRODUCTS/OPERATIONS

2014 Sales

	% of total
Traffic revenue	96
Other	4
Total	100

Selected Services

Excess baggage
Carry-on baggage
Delayed/damaged/lost baggage
Checked Baggage
Restrictions on baggage transportation
Special baggage

COMPETITORS

Air China Limited
China Airlines Ltd.
China Eastern Airlines Corporation Limited
EVA AIRWAYS CORPORATION
Hainan Airlines Holding Co., Ltd.
JET AIRWAYS (INDIA) LIMITED
KENYA AIRWAYS PLC
Korean Airlines Co., Ltd.
POLSKIE LINIE LOTNICZE LOT S A
PT. GARUDA INDONESIA TBK

HISTORICAL FINANCIALS
Company Type: Public

Income Statement   FYE: December 31

	REVENUE ($mil)	NET INCOME ($mil)	NET PROFIT MARGIN	EMPLOYEES
12/22	12,619	(4,737)	—	0
12/21	16,010	(1,906)	—	0
12/20	14,152	(1,657)	—	0
12/19	22,178	380	1.7%	0
12/18	20,880	433	2.1%	0
Annual Growth	(11.8%)	—	—	—

2022 Year-End Financials
Debt ratio: 6.0%
Return on equity: (-60.1%)
Cash ($ mil.): 2,933
Current Ratio: 0.23
Long-term debt ($ mil.): 4,992
No. of shares ($ mil.): —
Dividends
Yield: —
Payout: 0.0%
Market value ($ mil.): —

China Steel Corp

China Steel Corporation (CSC) manufactures and sells steel products and engages in mechanical, communications, and electrical engineering. The company's main products are steel plates, bars, wire rods, hot-rolled and cold-rolled coils. CSC also makes electro galvanized coils, electrical steel coils, hot and cold rolled coils, and hot-dip galvanized coils. CSC was founded in late 1971. About 90% of the company's total revenue comes from Taiwan.

Operations
The company operates in two segments: Steel department (around 80% of sales), and Shipping Department. Others generated the rest of sales.

The Steel department manufactures and sells steel products, including the Corporation, Dragon Steel Corporation (DSC), Chung Hung Steel Corporation (CHS), CSC Steel Sdn. Bhd (CSCM), China Steel and Nippon Steel Vietnam Joint Stock Company (CSVC) and China Steel Corporation India Pvt. Ltd. (CSCI), while the Shipping department include cargo handling, vessel shipping and trade in vessels, including China Steel Express Corporation (CSE), CSE Transport Corporation (CSEP), CSEI Transport (Panama) Corporation (CSEIP) and Kaoport Stevedoring Corporation (KPC).

By products, steel generated around 80% of sales, followed by construction contract, service and other revenue (some 10%), and non-ferrous materials with nearly 10%.

In all, sales of goods generated about 95% of sales.

Geographic Reach
CSC is headquartered in Kaohsiung, Taiwan and has offices in Taipei, Taiwan and Osaka, Japan.

About 90% of the revenue comes from Taiwan, followed by Vietnam, Malaysia, China, and India, among others.

Sales and Marketing
Presently CSC and its nearly 25 subsidiaries constitute in five business areas: steel, engineering and construction, industrial materials, logistics, and services & investments.

Financial Performance
Revenues of the company at the end of 2021 increased by 49% to NT$468 billion compared to $314.8 billion. The increase was primarily due to higher sales volume across the company's segments.

The company had a net profit of about NT$62.1 billion for 2021 compared to $885.9 million in the prior year.

Cash held by the company at the end of 2021 was at NT$19 billion. Cash provided by operations amounted to NT$71.3 billion. Investing activities and financing activities used NT$16.2 billion and NT$48.6 billion, respectively. Main cash uses were acquisition of property, plant and equipment, repayments of long-term bank borrowings.

Company Background
China Steel Corporation was founded in late 1971.

EXECUTIVES
Chairman, Chao-Tung Wong
President, Jih-Gang Liu
Executive Vice President, Director, K.L. Du
Administration Vice President, H Li
Technology Vice President, Y.S. Chen
Production Vice President, Director, J.Y. Song
Engineering Vice President, T.R. Jeng
Finance Vice President, K.H. Chang
Planning Vice President, K.T. Lee
Director, Jhaoyi Chen
Director, Liangdong Fan
Director, Jhengyi Wong
Director, Jhaojin Wei
Director, Zuen Jhang
Director, Dingpeng Liang
Director, Kunyi Li
Auditors : Deloitte & Touche

LOCATIONS
HQ: China Steel Corp
1 Chung-Kang Road, Siaogang District, Kaohsiung 81233
Phone: (886) 7 802 1111   **Fax:** (886) 7 537 3570
Web: www.csc.com.tw

PRODUCTS/OPERATIONS
2015 Sales
	% of total
Sales revenues	97
Service & other revenues	3
Total	100

Selected Products
Cold-rolled products
Color sheets
Electrical steel coils
Hot-rolled products
Steel bar
Steel plates
Wire rods

Selected Subsidiaries
China Prosperity Development Corporation
China Steel Express Corporation
China Steel Global Trading Corporation
China Steel Security Corporation
C. S. Aluminum Corporation
Gains Investment Corporation
HIMAG Magnetic Corporation

COMPETITORS
Anshan Iron And Steel Group Co., Ltd.
ArcelorMittal Dofasco G.P.
CALIFORNIA STEEL INDUSTRIES, INC.
Jiangsu Shagang Group Co., Ltd.
REPUBLIC STEEL
STEEL TECHNOLOGIES LLC
TERNIUM ARGENTINA S.A.
USS-POSCO INDUSTRIES, A CALIFORNIA JOINT VENTURE
Villaceros
Wugang Group Co., Ltd.

HISTORICAL FINANCIALS
Company Type: Public

Income Statement   FYE: December 31

	REVENUE ($mil)	NET INCOME ($mil)	NET PROFIT MARGIN	EMPLOYEES
12/21	16,914	2,241	13.2%	0
12/20	11,201	31	0.3%	0
12/19	12,233	294	2.4%	0
12/18	13,100	799	6.1%	28,648
12/17	11,702	570	4.9%	28,332
Annual Growth	9.6%	40.8%	—	—

2021 Year-End Financials
Debt ratio: 0.9%
Return on equity: 19.3%
Cash ($ mil.): 865
Current Ratio: 1.30
Long-term debt ($ mil.): 3,726
No. of shares ($ mil.): 15,414
Dividends
Yield: —
Payout: 7.5%
Market value ($ mil.): —

Chow Tai Fook Jewellery Group Ltd.

EXECUTIVES
Managing Director, Director, Kent Siu-Kee Wong
Chairman, Henry Kar-Shun Cheng
Executive Director, Director, Adrian Chi-Kong Cheng
Executive Director, Director, Conroy Chi-Heng Cheng
Executive Director, Director, Sai-Cheong Chan
Executive Director, Director, Albert Hiu-Sang Chan
Financial Director, Secretary, Director, Hamilton Ping-Hei Cheng
Executive Director, Director, Peter Chi-Keung Suen
General Counsel, Lauren Guet-Lan Tan
Other Director, Alan Yee-Pong Chan
Other, Barry Kim-Pun Wong
Controller, Kit-Sang Li
Honorary Chairman, Yu-Tung Cheng
Director, Wilson Kam-Biu Cheng
Director, Tong-Fat Koo
Director, Victor Kwok-King Fung

Director, Gordon Che-Keung Kwong
Director, Jeffrey Kin-Fung Lam
Director, Raymond Ching-Fai Or
Auditors : PricewaterhouseCoopers

LOCATIONS

HQ: Chow Tai Fook Jewellery Group Ltd.
33/F, New World Tower, 16-18 Queen's Road Central,
Phone: (852) 2524 3166   **Fax:** (852) 2526 9178
Web: www.chowtaifook.com

HISTORICAL FINANCIALS

Company Type: Public

Income Statement — FYE: March 31

	REVENUE ($mil)	NET INCOME ($mil)	NET PROFIT MARGIN	EMPLOYEES
03/21	9,025	775	8.6%	27,900
03/20	7,319	374	5.1%	29,700
03/19	8,492	583	6.9%	30,400
03/18	7,537	521	6.9%	29,200
03/17	6,594	393	6.0%	29,450
Annual Growth	8.2%	18.5%	—	(1.3%)

2021 Year-End Financials

Debt ratio: 2.4%
Return on equity: 21.1%
Cash ($ mil.): 775
Current Ratio: 1.90
Long-term debt ($ mil.): 231
No. of shares ($ mil.): 10,000
Dividends
  Yield: —
  Payout: 412.0%
Market value ($ mil.): 152,500

	STOCK PRICE ($) FY Close	P/E High/Low		PER SHARE ($) Earnings	Dividends	Book Value
03/21	15.25	25	11	0.08	0.32	0.40
03/20	7.37	39	22	0.04	0.78	0.34
03/19	10.01	31	17	0.06	0.74	0.39
03/18	11.40	29	23	0.05	0.51	0.43
03/17	9.82	31	20	0.04	0.66	0.41
Annual Growth	11.6%	—	—	18.5%	(16.5%)	(0.8%)

Chubb Ltd

Chubb Limited sells commercial and personal property and casualty insurance, personal accident and supplemental health insurance (A&H), reinsurance, and life insurance to a diverse group of clients. The world's largest publicly traded property/casualty insurer, Chubb primarily provides those lines of insurance to commercial and personal customers in some 55 countries and territories. The company's Chubb Tempest Re businesses provide reinsurance to property/casualty insurers in North America and Europe. Chubb holds total assets of approximately $200 billion.

Operations

Chubb operates through six primary business segments: North America Commercial P&C Insurance, Overseas General Insurance, North America Personal P&C (property and casualty) Insurance, Life Insurance, North America Agricultural Insurance, and Global Reinsurance.

The largest segments are North America Commercial P&C Insurance (about 40% of net premiums earned) and Overseas General Insurance (about 30% of net premiums earned).

North America Commercial P&C Insurance serves large institutional customers, corporations, and small- and mid-sized companies in the US, Canada, and Bermuda. It also includes the company's Westchester and Chubb Bermuda wholesale and specialty units.

Overseas General Insurance is composed of Chubb International and Chubb Global Markets, the company's international specialty and excess and surplus business. Chubb International operates in Europe, the Asia Pacific region, Far East, Eurasia and Africa, and Latin America. It offers property and casualty, accident and health, specialty, and personal lines products. Chubb Global Markets offers specialty insurance and includes Chubb's Lloyd's of London Syndicate 2488.

North America Personal P&C Insurance (about 15% of net premiums) provides affluent and high-net-worth consumers in the US and Canada with property, liability, travel, and recreational marine coverage insurance and services.

The Life Insurance segment (more than 5% of net premiums) operates through Chubb Life, Chubb Tempest Life Re, and the North American supplemental A&H and life business of Combined Insurance. It offers individual life and group benefit insurance, primarily in developing markets.

North America Agricultural Insurance, also active in the US and Canada, provides a variety of coverage including crop insurance, primarily Multiple Peril Crop Insurance (MPCI) and crop-hail insurance through Rain and Hail Insurance Service (Rain and Hail) as well as farm and ranch and specialty P&C commercial insurance products and services through its Chubb Agribusiness unit. It accounts for approximately 5% of net premiums.

Global Reinsurance is the company's smallest segment, bringing in less than 5% of net earned premiums. It includes Chubb Tempest Re Bermuda, Chubb Tempest Re USA, Chubb Tempest Re International, and Chubb Tempest Re Canada. Global Reinsurance markets its reinsurance products worldwide primarily through reinsurance brokers under the Chubb Tempest Re brand name and provides a broad range of traditional and non-traditional reinsurance coverage to a diverse array of primary P&C companies.

Geographic Reach

Chubb has offices around the world, including North America (Philadelphia, Pennsylvania; Wilmington, Delaware; Whitehouse Station, New Jersey; and Simsbury, Connecticut), Europe (including its headquarters in Switzerland), Bermuda, Latin America, Asia Pacific, and Japan. It generates around 70% of net premiums from North America. Chubb Global Markets operates out of Lloyd's of London, the world-renowned specialty insurance market.

Sales and Marketing

Chubb's customers range from individuals (including wealthy individuals) and small businesses to multi-national corporations and other insurance companies. Most of the company's business is conducted through company agents or third-party insurance brokers or agents.

Chubb's products are generally offered through a North American network of independent agents and brokers, as well as eTraditional, which are digital platforms where the company electronically quote, bind, and issue for agents and brokers. An example of this is the Chubb Marketplace.

Chubb has counted most of the Fortune 1000 as clients for many years.

Financial Performance

The company's revenue for fiscal 2021 increased by 14% to $41.0 billion compared from the prior year with $36.0 billion.

Net income was a record $8.5 billion compared with $3.5 billion in 2020. Net income in 2021 was driven by record P&C underwriting results, including growth in net premiums earned and improvements in its loss and loss expense ratios.

Cash held by the company at the end of fiscal 2021 decreased to $1.81 billion. Cash provided by operations was $11.1 billion while cash used for investing and financing activities were $6.7 billion and $4.4 billion, respectively.

Company Background

In early 2016 the former ACE Limited acquired the US's Chubb Corporation for $28 billion and took the Chubb name.

EXECUTIVES

Executive Vice Chairman, President, Chief Operating Officer, Executive Vice-Chairman, John W. Keogh, $963,462 total compensation
Chairman, President, Chief Executive Officer, Director, Evan G. Greenberg, $1,400,000 total compensation
Vice-Chairman, Division Officer, John J. Lupica, $854,615 total compensation
Finance Executive Vice President, Finance Chief Financial Officer, Peter Enns
Executive Vice President, General Counsel, Secretary, Joseph F. Wayland
Chief Accounting Officer, Principal Accounting Officer, Subsidiary Officer, Annmarie T. Hagan
Region Officer, Subsidiary Officer, Paul J. Krump, $859,231 total compensation
Director, Michael G. Atieh
Director, Sheila P. Burke
Director, Mary A. Cirillo
Lead Director, Director, Michael P. Connors
Director, ?Robert J. Hugin
Director, Robert W. Scully

Director, Eugene B. Shanks
Director, Theodore E. Shasta
Director, David H. Sidwell
Director, Olivier Steimer
Director, ?Frances F. Townsend
Auditors : PricewaterhouseCoopers LLP

LOCATIONS

HQ: Chubb Ltd
  Baerengasse 32, Zurich CH-8001
Phone: (41) 43 456 7600
Web: www.chubb.com

PRODUCTS/OPERATIONS

2018 Sales by Segment

	$ mil.	% of total
Net premiums earned		
North America Commercial P&C Insurance	12,402	37
Overseas General Insurance	8,612	26
North America Personal P&C Insurance	4,593	14
Life Insurance	2,218	6
North America Agricultural Insurance	1,569	5
Global Reinsurance	670	2
Net investment income	3,305	10
Net realized gains	(652)	-
Total	32,717	100

COMPETITORS

ACTIS CAPITAL LIMITED
AMERIPRISE FINANCIAL, INC.
CARILLION PLC
CASS INFORMATION SYSTEMS, INC.
MILESTONE CAPITAL PARTNERS LLP
MS&AD INSURANCE GROUP HOLDINGS, INC.
REGIONAL MANAGEMENT CORP.
REINSURANCE GROUP OF AMERICA, INCORPORATED
WALKER & DUNLOP, INC.
XL GROUP PUBLIC LIMITED COMPANY

HISTORICAL FINANCIALS

Company Type: Public

Income Statement — FYE: December 31

	ASSETS ($mil)	NET INCOME ($mil)	INCOME AS % OF ASSETS	EMPLOYEES
12/23	230,682	9,028	3.9%	40,000
12/22	199,144	5,313	2.7%	34,000
12/21	200,054	8,539	4.3%	31,000
12/20	190,774	3,533	1.9%	31,000
12/19	176,943	4,454	2.5%	33,000
Annual Growth	6.9%	19.3%	—	4.9%

2023 Year-End Financials

Return on assets: 4.2%
Return on equity: 16.4%
Long-term debt ($ mil.): —
No. of shares ($ mil.): 405
Sales ($ mil.): 49,735
Dividends
  Yield: —
  Payout: 15.5%
Market value ($ mil.): —

Chubu Electric Power Co Inc

Chubu Electric Power is Japan's an electric utility. The company supplies power to about 16 million people in central Japan's Chubu region, a manufacturing region in Japan that includes Nagoya. The company has biomass, hydroelectric, nuclear, wind, and solar power generating facilities, and it has a capacity of more than 33,400 MW. In addition, the company offers services utilizing renewable energy that align with customer needs towards the realization of a low-carbon society, including the CO2-free menu service. In response to deregulation, Chubu Electric Power has moved into newer industries, including IT, natural gas supply, real estate management, and overseas consulting.

Operations

The company operate its business into three reportable segment: Customer Service & Sales, Power Network and JERA.

Customer Service & Sales focuses on expansion of total energy services centered on gas & electric power. Power Network is focus on provision of power network services and JERA focuses on fuel upstream and procurement to power generation and wholesale of electricity and gas.

Electricity (90% of total revenue) has about 210 power generation facilities in Japan, a transmission line that runs more than 12,200 kilometers, a distribution line that runs more than 133,300 kilometers, and nearly 930 transformer substations.

Other (15%) provides energy services such as the sale of gas and liquefied natural gas (LNG) and the provision of co-generation systems.

Geographic Reach

The company's headquarter is located in Higashi-shincho, Higashi-ku, Nagoya.

In addition to Japan, the company has offices in Australia, Mexico, UAE, The Netherlands, India, Canada, Indonesia, Philippines, Mexico, Oman, Thailand, Taiwan, Qatar, Vietnam, and the US.

Sales and Marketing

The company supplies electricity to residential, commercial, and industrial customers via transmission and distribution lines.

Moreover, the company created new forms of community which are connected home service, Korekara Denki (energy services based on customer participation), smart pole service and regional information bank.

Financial Performance

Note: Growth rates may differ after conversion to US Dollars.

In 2019, consolidated operating revenue increased by 1% from the previous consolidated fiscal year to 3.1 trillion yen, mainly due to an increase in fuel cost adjustment charge and increase in surcharge and grant based on Act on Special Measures Concerning Procurement of Electricity from Renewable Energy Sources by Electric Utilities.

The company's net income in 2019 fell by 3.9 billion yen to 62.2 billion yen from 66 billion yen in the prior year.

Cash held by the company at the end of 2019 decreased by 402.5 billion yen to 147.6 billion yen compared to 550.1 billion yen in the prior year. Cash provided by operations was 255.9 billion while cash used for investing and financing activities were 647.6 billion yen and 5.9 billion yen, respectively.

Strategy

In April 2020, the Chubu Electric Power Group split off their power transmission and distribution business. At the same time, the company split off their sales business and put into practice business model that separates power generation from sales. With each of their businesses dealing with customers and society and developing independently, they are more certain to deliver good-quality, environmentally friendly energy that is essential for their daily lives and business in a safer, more affordable and more stable manner.

Building on this foundation, along with energy the company will provide new services that exceed the expectations of their customers and society, while utilizing digital technology, through the creation of community support infrastructure. Through these activities, they will contribute to the resolution of social issues, including the achievement of a low-carbon society, which is an urgent issue worldwide.

Mergers and Acquisitions

In 2019, Mitsubishi Corporation and Chubu Electric Power Co., Inc. were selected as the preferred buyers in a bid for the Dutch Energy Company "Eneco".

Both MC and Chubu have since been completing the acquisition procedures. The total value of this acquisition is 4.1 billion euros (500 billion yen).

Eneco is an integrated energy company that is actively engaged in renewable power generation projects.

EXECUTIVES

Chairman, Representative Director, Satoru Katsuno
President, Chief Executive Officer, Representative Director, Kingo Hayashi
Executive Vice President, Chief Financial Officer, Chief Compliance Officer, Representative Director, Hitoshi Mizutani
Executive Vice President, Chief Information Officer, Director, Hisanori Ito
Senior Managing Executive Officer, Chief Nuclear Officer, Representative Director, Ichiro Ihara
Outside Director, Takayuki Hashimoto
Outside Director, Tadashi Shimao
Outside Director, Mitsue Kurihara
Outside Director, Yoko Kudo
Auditors : KPMG AZSA LLC

LOCATIONS

HQ: Chubu Electric Power Co Inc
  1 Higashi-shincho, Higashi-ku, Nagoya, Aichi 461-8680
Phone: (81) 52 951 8211
Web: www.chuden.co.jp

PRODUCTS/OPERATIONS

2016 Sales

	% of total
Electric power	90
Energy	3
Other	7
Total	100

COMPETITORS

CHUGOKU ELECTRIC POWER COMPANY,INCORPORATED,THE
GEORGIA POWER COMPANY
KANSAI ELECTRIC POWER COMPANY, INCORPORATED, THE
KYUSHU ELECTRIC POWER COMPANY, INCORPORATED
MUNICIPAL ELECTRIC AUTHORITY OF GEORGIA
PG&E CORPORATION
TOHOKU ELECTRIC POWER COMPANY,INCORPORATED
TOKYO ELECTRIC POWER COMPANY HOLDINGS, INCORPORATED
Uniper SE
Vattenfall AB

HISTORICAL FINANCIALS

Company Type: Public

Income Statement — FYE: March 31

	REVENUE ($mil)	NET INCOME ($mil)	NET PROFIT MARGIN	EMPLOYEES
03/23	29,933	287	1.0%	28,367
03/22	22,239	(353)	—	28,365
03/21	26,510	1,329	5.0%	28,238
03/20	28,244	1,505	5.3%	28,448
03/19	27,406	717	2.6%	30,321
Annual Growth	2.2%	(20.5%)	—	(1.7%)

2023 Year-End Financials

Debt ratio: 0.3%
Return on equity: 1.8%
Cash ($ mil.): 2,712
Current Ratio: 0.93
Long-term debt ($ mil.): 18,103
No. of shares ($ mil.): 756
Dividends
Yield: —
Payout: 98.9%
Market value ($ mil.): —

Chugai Pharmaceutical Co Ltd

Chugai Pharmaceutical develops therapies for bone metabolism and blood disorders, cancer, infectious diseases, immune system disorders, kidney, and brain diseases. Products include Alcensa, an oral, small molecule targeted molecular therapy; EEdirol, a vitamin D3 preparation born out of Chugai's many years of research in vitamin D, is an agent that improves bone metabolism in addition to calcium metabolism; and Hemlibra is a bispecific antibody that employs Chugai's innovative antibody engineering technologies. Chugai Pharmaceuticals has foreign operations in Asia, Europe, and North America through subsidiaries and branch locations. Chugai Pharmaceutical generates more than 50% of its revenue from Japan.

Swiss drugs group Roche owns about 60% of Chugai Pharmaceutical.

Operations

The group has a single business of pharmaceuticals, which consists of research and development of new prescription medicines and subsequent manufacturing, marketing and distribution activities.

Geographic Reach

Based in Japan, Chugai has research laboratories in Gotemba, Yokohama, Kamakura and Ukima. It also has three plants located in Ukima, Fujieda and Utsunomiya. Overseas, Chugai Pharma USA, Inc. (US); Chugai Pharma Europe Ltd. (UK); Chugai Pharma Science (Beijing) Co., Ltd. (China); and Chugai Pharma Taiwan Ltd. (Taiwan) are engaged in clinical development and submission of applications in their respective countries. Chugai Pharmabody Research Pte. Ltd. (Singapore) is engaged in pharmaceutical research and development.

Its home country, Japan, generates more than 50% of revenue.

Financial Performance

The company reported a total revenue of Â¥999.8 billion, a 27% increase from the previous year's total revenue of Â¥786.9 billion.

In 2021, the company had a net income of Â¥303 billion, a 41% increase from the previous year's net income of Â¥214.7 billion.

The company's cash at the end of 2021 was Â¥267.8 billion. Operating activities generated Â¥279.6 billion, while investing activities used Â¥118.9 billion, mainly for purchases of marketable securities. Financing activities used another Â¥107.4 billion, primarily for dividends paid to Chugai shareholders.

Strategy

With a view toward realizing the Envisioned Future set out in its Mission Statement, the company has formulated and implemented "TOP I 2030," a growth strategy to achieve this goal since 2021, while materializing the vision of what it means to be a top innovator by 2030. Its envisioned Top Innovator in 2030: 1. "Expectation from patients all over the world" A company with drug discovery capabilities that meet the world's highest standards, and which offers hope to patients around the world, that "Chugai will surely create new treatments" 2. "Attracting talent and players from around the world" A company that attracts passionate talent from all over the world, and inspire players involved in healthcare around the world to think they can create something new by partnering with Chugai 3. "Role model for the world" A company that serves as a global role model, due to recognition for its ESG initiatives through its business activities, and by playing a leading role in solving social issues.

EXECUTIVES

President, Chief Executive Officer, Representative Director, Osamu Okuda
Director, Hisafumi Yamada
Director, Toshiaki Itagaki
Outside Director, Mariko Y Momoi
Outside Director, Fumio Tateishi
Outside Director, Hideo Teramoto
Director, Christoph Franz
Director, James H. Sabry
Director, Teresa A. Graham
Auditors : KPMG AZSA LLC

LOCATIONS

HQ: Chugai Pharmaceutical Co Ltd
2-1-1 Nihonbashi-Muromachi, Chuo-ku, Tokyo 103-8324
Phone: (81) 3 3281 6611   Fax: (81) 3 3281 2828
Web: www.chugai-pharm.co.jp

PRODUCTS/OPERATIONS

Selected Subsidiaries
C&C Research Laboratories (Korea)
Chugai Pharma Europe Ltd. (UK)
Chugai Pharma Marketing Ltd. (UK)
Chugai Pharma (Shanghai) Consulting Co., Ltd.
Chugai Pharma Taiwan Ltd.
Chugai Pharma U.K. Ltd.
Chugai Sanofi-Aventis S.N.C. (France)
Chugai U.S.A., Inc.
 Chugai Pharma U.S.A., LLC
Fuji-Gotemba Research Laboratories
Kamakura Research Laboratories
Ukima Research Laboratories

Selected Products
Actemra (rheumatoid arthritis)
Alfarol (osteoporosis)
Epogin (anemia related to chronic renal failure)
Granocyte/Neutrogin (neutropenia associated with chemotherapy)
Sigmart (anti-anginal agent)

COMPETITORS

CYCLACEL PHARMACEUTICALS, INC.
GLAXOSMITHKLINE ARGENTINA S.A.
Helix BioPharma Corp
NEUROCRINE BIOSCIENCES, INC.
PROVECTUS BIOPHARMACEUTICALS, INC.
SAMARITAN PHARMACEUTICALS, INC.
Swedish Orphan Biovitrum AB (Publ)
TOLERX, INC.
UCB Pharma GmbH
XENCOR, INC.

HISTORICAL FINANCIALS

Company Type: Public

Income Statement — FYE: December 31

	REVENUE ($mil)	NET INCOME ($mil)	NET PROFIT MARGIN	EMPLOYEES
12/22	9,561	2,841	29.7%	7,771
12/21	8,685	2,632	30.3%	7,664
12/20	7,635	2,083	27.3%	7,555
12/19	6,320	1,451	23.0%	7,394
12/18	5,272	841	16.0%	7,432
Annual Growth	16.0%	35.6%	—	1.1%

2022 Year-End Financials

Debt ratio: —
Return on equity: 28.6%
Cash ($ mil.): 1,686
Current Ratio: 3.15
Long-term debt ($ mil.): —
No. of shares ($ mil.): 1,645
Dividends
Yield: —
Payout: 19.0%
Market value ($ mil.): 20,842

	STOCK PRICE ($) FY Close	P/E High/Low		PER SHARE ($) Earnings	Dividends	Book Value
12/22	12.67	0	0	1.73	0.33	6.57
12/21	16.36	0	0	1.60	0.27	6.28
12/20	26.60	3	0	1.27	1.57	5.78
12/19	185.57	2	1	0.88	1.90	4.79
12/18	116.08	2	2	0.51	1.19	4.19
Annual Growth	(42.5%)	—	—	35.5%	(27.5%)	11.9%

Chugoku Bank, Ltd. (The)

Chugoku Bank hopes to attract individuals and businesses who are looking to bank on the sunny side. The Japanese regional bank serves the Okayama prefecture (known as 'the sunny land') and the neighboring areas of Ehime, Hiroshima, Hyogo, Kagawa, and Tottori through some 150 offices and a network of ATMs. The bank also boasts overseas operations, with offices in China, Hong Kong, Singapore, and the US. Chugoku Bank subsidiaries and affiliates are involved in such businesses as asset management, credit cards, credit guarantees, financing, leasing, and pre-paid cards. Japan Trustee Services Bank, Ltd., owns a majority stake in the bank.

EXECUTIVES

Chairman, Director, Masato Miyanaga
President, Representative Director, Sadanori Kato
Senior Managing Director, Representative Director, Koji Terasaka
Senior Managing Director, Representative Director, Ikuhide Harada
Director, Shinichi Taniguchi
Director, Tatsuo Hiramoto
Director, Hiroyuki Ohara
Director, Hiromichi Kato
Outside Director, Yoshio Sato
Outside Director, Akira Kodera
Director, Hiromichi Ando
Director, Kotaro Kogame
Outside Director, Hiromichi Furuya
Outside Director, Toshihide Saito
Outside Director, Kazuhiro Tanaka
Outside Director, Yukiyo Kiyono
Auditors : KPMG AZSA LLC

LOCATIONS

HQ: Chugoku Bank, Ltd. (The)
1-15-20 Marunouchi, Kita-ku, Okayama 700-8628
Phone: (81) 86 223 3111   **Fax:** 212 371-7173
Web: www.chugin.co.jp

PRODUCTS/OPERATIONS

Selected Subsidiaries
CBS Company, Limited
Chugin Asset Management Company, Limited
Chugin Securities Co., Ltd.
The Chugin Card Company, Limited
The Chugin Credit Guarantee Co., Limited
The Chugin Lease Company, Limited
The Chugin Operation Center, Co., Limited

COMPETITORS

BANK OF AYUDHYA PUBLIC COMPANY LIMITED
DAISHI HOKUETSU BANK, LTD.
EHIME BANK, LTD., THE
HACHIJUNI BANK, LTD., THE
METROPOLITAN BANK & TRUST COMPANY

HISTORICAL FINANCIALS
Company Type: Public

Income Statement   FYE: March 31

	ASSETS ($mil)	NET INCOME ($mil)	INCOME AS % OF ASSETS	EMPLOYEES
03/22	83,923	151	0.2%	4,769
03/21	82,666	130	0.2%	4,818
03/20	75,056	109	0.1%	4,885
03/19	74,530	146	0.2%	4,933
03/18	79,739	200	0.3%	5,012
Annual Growth	1.3%	(6.8%)	—	(1.2%)

2022 Year-End Financials
Return on assets: 0.1%
Return on equity: 3.2%
Long-term debt ($ mil.): —
No. of shares ($ mil.): 185
Sales ($ mil.): 1,059
Dividends
  Yield: —
  Payout: 28.4%
Market value ($ mil.): —

Chugoku Electric Power Co., Inc. (The)

The Chugoku Electric Power Co. has provided a stable supply of electricity to support the foundations of people's lives and of industry. The company's main business is the generation, transmission, and distribution of electric power. The company has ten regional utility companies in Japan. The company's 114 power plants generate about 11,540 MW; traditional thermal plants generate about 70% of its power. The Chugoku company's power plant portfolio includes a life-extending method for high-temperature steam-pipes at a thermal power plant. The company was established in 1951.

Operations
The company's operating segments are Comprehensive Energy (about 65% of sales); Power Transmission and Distribution (over 25%); and Information and Telecommunications (less than 5%).

With movement toward decarbonization gaining pace across the world and rising tension over international energy security, the environment surrounding its power generation business continues to see great change. As a Group, it is working to develop a power source mix in line with the S + 3E policy (Safety + Energy Security, Economic Efficiency and Environment), while engaging in efforts aimed at decarbonization and enhanced competitiveness.

A wide range of changes are impacting operations in its power transmission and distribution business, including the increasing frequency and severity of natural disasters, the tight situation surrounding nationwide power supply and demand, and the increasing usage volumes of renewable energy.

In addition, here are growing opportunities to use information and communications technology in all areas of business and life due to progress in fields such as AI, IoT, and 5G, and the COVID-19 crisis has once again underlined its importance.

Geographic Reach
The company has 114 electric power stations (11,540 MW) The company is headquartered in Hiroshima, Japan, and regional offices in Tattori, Shimane, Okayama, Yamaguchi, and Tokyo, in Japan.

Financial Performance
The company and its consolidated subsidiaries recognized operating revenues of ¥1.1 trillion in the consolidated statement of operations for the current fiscal year.

In 2021, the company had a net loss of ¥39.7 billion, a 373% improvement from the previous year's net income of $14.6 billion.

The company's cash at the end of 2021 was ¥66.5 billion. Operating activities generated ¥310 million, while investing activities used ¥206.4 billion, mainly for purchase of property. Financing activities provided another ¥212.6 billion.

EXECUTIVES

Chairman, Representative Director, Mareshige Shimizu
President, Chief Executive Officer, Representative Director, Natsuhiko Takimoto
Executive Vice President, Representative Director, Shigeru Ashitani
Executive Vice President, Representative Director, Toshio Takaba
Director, Tatsuo Kitano
Director, Toru Funaki
Outside Director, Makoto Furuse
Director, Norimasa Tamura
Outside Director, Etsuko Nosohara
Outside Director, Noriko Otani
Outside Director, Eiichi Kuga
Auditors : KPMG AZSA LLC

LOCATIONS

HQ: Chugoku Electric Power Co., Inc. (The)
4-33 Komachi, Naka-ku, Hiroshima 730-8701
Phone: (81) 82 241 0211
Web: www.energia.co.jp

PRODUCTS/OPERATIONS

2016 Sales

	% of total
Electric power	84
Comprehensive energy supply	3
Information and telecommunications	3
Other	10
Total	100

2016 Sales	% of total
Electric	90
Other	10
Total	100

COMPETITORS

ALLIANT ENERGY CORPORATION
ASSOCIATED ELECTRIC COOPERATIVE, INC.
CHUBU ELECTRIC POWER CO.,INC.
GEORGIA POWER COMPANY
HOKKAIDO ELECTRIC POWER COMPANY, INCORPORATED
KANSAI ELECTRIC POWER COMPANY, INCORPORATED, THE
KYUSHU ELECTRIC POWER COMPANY, INCORPORATED
MUNICIPAL ELECTRIC AUTHORITY OF GEORGIA
TOHOKU ELECTRIC POWER COMPANY,INCORPORATED
TOKYO ELECTRIC POWER COMPANY HOLDINGS, INCORPORATED

HISTORICAL FINANCIALS

Company Type: Public

Income Statement — FYE: March 31

	REVENUE ($mil)	NET INCOME ($mil)	NET PROFIT MARGIN	EMPLOYEES
03/22	9,344	(326)	—	12,949
03/21	11,808	131	1.1%	13,050
03/20	12,412	829	6.7%	13,163
03/19	12,433	103	0.8%	13,418
03/18	12,383	195	1.6%	13,485
Annual Growth	(6.8%)	—		(1.0%)

2022 Year-End Financials

Debt ratio: 0.6%
Return on equity: (-6.2%)
Cash ($ mil.): 547
Current Ratio: 0.49
Long-term debt ($ mil.): 17,137
No. of shares ($ mil.): 360
Dividends
Yield: —
Payout: 0.0%
Market value ($ mil.): —

CIMB Group Holdings Bhd

CIMB Group is the second-largest financial services firm in Malaysia, behind Maybank. It is the holding company for CIMB Bank, CIMB Investment Bank, and CIMB Islamic, which provide retail and commercial banking and financial services to 13 million customers throughout Southeast Asia. While it has a presence in 17 countries (including a CIMB Securities office in New York City), the bank's main markets are Malaysia, Indonesia, Singapore, Thailand, and Cambodia. Altogether the group has more than 1,050 branches. CIMB Group's offerings include corporate and consumer banking, investment banking, Islamic banking, stock brokerage, asset management, and insurance. It was established in 1924 as Bian Chiang Bank.

Mergers and Acquisitions

CIMB Investment Bank became one of the largest investment banking franchises in Asia in 2012 with the acquisition of most of the Asian investment banking business of the Royal Bank of Scotland. The acquisition gave CIMB a presence in Taiwan and Australia and expanded its operations in Hong Kong, India, and China. RBS kept its business in South Korea.

EXECUTIVES

Chief Legal Officer, Chief Compliance Officer, Chief Integrity and Governance Officer, Kwan Keen Yew
Chief Risk Officer, Vera Handajani
Chief People Officer, Chief Sustainability Officer, Gurdip Singh Sidhu
Corporate Treasurer, Kok Wei Chu
Senior Independent Non-Executive Director, Su Yin Teoh
Independent Non-Executive Director, Robert Neil Coombe
Independent Non-Executive Director, Shulamite N. K. Khoo
Independent Non-Executive Director, Yuet Mee Ho
Non-Independent Non-Executive Director, Kok Kwan Lee
Auditors: PricewaterhouseCoopers PLT

LOCATIONS

HQ: CIMB Group Holdings Bhd
Level 13, Menara CIMB, Jalan Stesen Sentral 2, Kuala Lumpur Sentral, Kuala Lumpur 50470
Phone: (60) 3 2261 8888   **Fax:** (60) 3 2261 0099
Web: www.cimb.com

COMPETITORS

BGEO GROUP LIMITED
DBS GROUP HOLDINGS LTD
Grupo Financiero Banorte, S.A.B. de C.V.
HSBC HOLDINGS PLC
NOMURA INTERNATIONAL PLC
OVERSEA-CHINESE BANKING CORPORATION LIMITED
PUBLIC BANK BHD
SAVILLS PLC
UNITED OVERSEAS BANK LIMITED
Wüstenrot & Württembergische AG

HISTORICAL FINANCIALS

Company Type: Public

Income Statement — FYE: December 31

	ASSETS ($mil)	NET INCOME ($mil)	INCOME AS % OF ASSETS	EMPLOYEES
12/22	151,397	1,235	0.8%	33,252
12/21	149,362	1,031	0.7%	33,265
12/20	149,600	296	0.2%	34,183
12/19	140,119	1,114	0.8%	35,265
12/18	129,223	1,350	1.0%	36,104
Annual Growth	4.0%	(2.2%)		(2.0%)

2022 Year-End Financials

Return on assets: 0.8%
Return on equity: 8.9%
Long-term debt ($ mil.): —
No. of shares ($ mil.): 10,665
Sales ($ mil.): 6,273
Dividends
Yield: —
Payout: 49.9%
Market value ($ mil.): —

CITIC Ltd

CITIC Limited is one of China's largest conglomerates and a constituent of the Hang Seng Index. CITIC has grown in step with the country's rise and modernization. It has built a remarkable portfolio of businesses in comprehensive financial services, advanced intelligent manufacturing, advanced materials, new consumption and new-type urbanization. CITIC Limited is now 58% owned by CITIC Group and the rest is held by independent shareholders. More than 85% of its revenue comes from mainland China.

Operations

CITIC operates through five reportable segments: Advanced Materials; Comprehensive financial services; New Consumption; New-type urbanizations; and Advanced intelligent manufacturing.

Advanced materials segment (around 40%) includes exploration, processing and trading of resources and energy products, including crude oil, coal and iron ore, as well as manufacturing of special steels.

Comprehensive financial services segment accounts for about 35% of total revenue, includes banking, trust, asset management, securities and insurance services.

New consumption segment (nearly 10%) includes motor and food and consumer products business, telecommunication services, publication services, modern agriculture, and others.

New-type urbanization segment includes development, sale and holding of properties, contracting and design services, infrastructure services, environmental services and others. The segment generates less than 10% of total revenue.

Advanced intelligent manufacturing segment (more than 5%) includes manufacturing of heavy machineries, specialized robotics, aluminum wheels, aluminum casting parts and other products.

Overall, net interest income accounts for about 25% of total revenue, while sales of goods and services account for around 65% and net fee and commission income and other revenue account for the remaining 10%.

Geographic Reach

Headquartered in Hong Kong, CITIC earned more than 85% of revenue from mainland China while Hong Kong, Taiwan and Macau and other countries generate about 15% of combined revenue.

Financial Performance

Company's revenue for fiscal 2021 increased by 28% to HK$708.9 billion compared from the prior year with HK$552.9 billion.

Profit for fiscal 2021 increased to HK$70.2 billion compared from the prior year with HK$80.9 billion.

Cash held by the company at the end of fiscal 2021 decreased to HK$357.6 billion.

Cash provided by financing activities was HK$208.2 billion while cash used for operations and investing activities were HK$40.7 billion and HK$267.5 billion, respectively.

Strategy

In 2021, over 2.50 million tons of new products were developed and sold, representing 17% of the total sales volume and a 12% increase in sales of these products as compared to 2020. The company obtained 313 patents including 72 invention patents during the year. During the period, the company established the Technology Department to set up 29 "bottleneck" projects around strategic emerging industries, with two projects being completed within the year. For example, it participated in the "localization of bogie bearings for high-speed EMUs" project, and successfully resolved the "bottleneck" concerning the sourcing of key materials for high speed railways, achieving "zero" imports for these materials.

EXECUTIVES

Executive Director, Chairman, Hexin Zhu
Vice-Chairman, President, Executive Director, Guohua Xi
Executive Director, Zhengjun Liu
Executive Director, Guoquan Wang
Independent Non-Executive Director, Francis Wai Keung Siu
Independent Non-Executive Director, Jinwu Xu
Independent Non-Executive Director, Anthony Francis Neoh
Independent Non-Executive Director, Gregory Lynn Curl
Independent Non-Executive Director, Toshikazu Tagawa
Non-Executive Director, Yi Li
Non-Executive Director, Yang Yu
Non-Executive Director, Lin Zhang
Non-Executive Director, Xiaoping Yang
Non-Executive Director, Jiang Tang
Auditors : PricewaterhouseCoopers

LOCATIONS

HQ: CITIC Ltd
32nd Floor, CITIC Tower, 1 Tim Mei Avenue, Central,
Phone: (852) 2820 2111   **Fax:** (852) 2877 2771
Web: www.citic.com

2015 Sales

	% of total
Mainland China	87
Hong Kong and Macau	6
Overseas	7
Total	100

PRODUCTS/OPERATIONS

2015 Sales

	% of total
Financial Services	49
Manufacturing	14
Resources and energy	11
Real estate	7
Engineering contracting	4
Others	15
Total	100

COMPETITORS

AUSTRALIA AND NEW ZEALAND BANKING GROUP LIMITED
Agricultural Bank of China Limited
BLUESCOPE STEEL LIMITED
Bank Of China Limited
China Construction Bank Corporation
HSBC USA, INC.
INVESTCORP HOLDINGS B.S.C
Industrial and Commercial Bank of China Limited
KOBE STEEL, LTD.
UNITED STATES STEEL CORPORATION

HISTORICAL FINANCIALS

Company Type: Public

Income Statement   FYE: December 31

	REVENUE ($mil)	NET INCOME ($mil)	NET PROFIT MARGIN	EMPLOYEES
12/22	126,029	9,684	7.7%	161,408
12/21	116,053	9,004	7.8%	136,637
12/20	93,327	7,304	7.8%	135,304
12/19	94,188	6,922	7.3%	287,910
12/18	88,459	6,414	7.3%	273,344
Annual Growth	9.3%	10.8%	—	(12.3%)

2022 Year-End Financials

Debt ratio: —   No. of shares ($ mil.): 29,090
Return on equity: 10.1%   Dividends
Cash ($ mil.): 132,537   Yield: —
Current Ratio: —   Payout: 25.1%
Long-term debt ($ mil.): —   Market value ($ mil.): —

CK Hutchison Holdings Ltd

CK Hutchison Holdings is a renowned multinational conglomerate committed to development, innovation and technology in many different sectors and one of the largest companies listed on the Hong Kong Exchanges and Clearing (HKEX) main board. It operates a variety of businesses in about 50 countries across the world. Its holdings include companies in ports, retail, infrastructure, energy, telecommunications, finance and investments and others. The company has majority stakes in companies including Hutchison Telecommunications Hong Kong Holdings, Hutchison Telecommunications (Australia), CK Infrastructure Holdings, and Hutchison China MediTech. CK Hutchison traces its roots to a dispensary company that opened in the 1800s in Guangzhou, China. More than 50% of the company's total sales is generated from Europe.

Operations

CK Hutchison Holdings' operations are diversified across five core businesses: retail (approximately 40%), telecommunications (about 25% of sales), infrastructure (about 15%), and ports and related services and energy (about 10% each). The company also reports a finance & investments and others segment (accounts for the remaining sales).

Doing business as A.S. Watson Group, the retail division is the largest health and beauty retailer in Asia and Europe by store number with about 140 million loyalty member base. With more than 16,300 locations in about 30 markets, the unit's brands include health and beauty company Watsons (operating in Asian and European markets), ICI PARIS XL (a European perfume and cosmetics company), and PARKnSHOP (a supermarket chain in Greater China). In addition, it includes electronics and electrical appliances. It also manufactures and distributes bottled water and beverage products in Hong Kong and Mainland China.

Telecommunications has three divisions: 3 Group Europe, Hutchison Telecommunications Hong Kong Holdings and Hutchison Asia Telecommunications. It is also a pioneer of mobile data communication technologies and an operator and innovator of converged telecommunication and digital services with businesses in six countries across Europe. While, HTHKH holds the Group's interests in mobile operations in Hong Kong and Macau. HAT holds the Group's interests in the mobile operations in Indonesia, Vietnam and Sri Lanka.

The company's infrastructure division comprises the company's interest in CK Infrastructure Holdings Limited (CKI) and the economic benefits deriving from its direct holdings in six co-owned infrastructure investments with CKI. CKI is the largest publicly listed infrastructure company on the SHEK. Its industries include energy, transportation, waste management, waste-to-energy, household infrastructure, and water in Hong Kong, China, the UK, continental Europe, Australia, New Zealand, the US and Canada.

Its ports and related services is the world's leading port investor, developer and operator, the division holds interests in more than 50 ports comprising about 290 operational berths in about 25 countries, including container terminals operating in six of the 10 busiest container ports in the world. The division handled a total throughput of approximately 88.0 million twenty-foot equivalent units. It also engages in river trade, cruise terminal operations and ports related logistic services.

Geographic Reach

More than half of the Hong Kong-based CK Hutchison Holdings' revenue comes from Europe. Hong Kong, Mainland China, and Canada provide nearly 20% of combined revenue. It garners about 15% of revenue from Asia, Australia, and other countries.

Global finance operations and investments represent the remainder of its revenue stream.

Sales and Marketing

The company's five largest suppliers combined and the revenue from sales of goods or rendering of services attributable to the company's five largest customers combined was less than 30% of the total value of company purchases and total company revenue.

Financial Performance

Note: Growth rates may differ after conversion to US dollars.

In 2021, the company had a revenue of HK$445.4 billion, a 10% increase from the previous year's total revenue of HK$403.8 billion.

The company's profit for the year was HK$33.5 billion, a 15% increase from the previous year.

The company's cash at the end of 2021 was HK$153.1 billion. Operating activities provided HK$52.2 billion, while investing activities used HK$550 million, mainly for cash flows used in investing activities. Financing activities used another HK$54.5 billion, mainly for repayment of borrowings.

Strategy

The principal objective of the company is to enhance long-term total return for its shareholders. To achieve this objective, the group focuses on achieving recurring and sustainable earnings, cash flow and dividend growth without compromising the group's financial strength and stability.

The group executes disciplined management of revenue growth, margin and costs, capital and investments to return ratio targets, earnings and cash flow accretive merger and acquisition activities, as well as organic growth in sectors or geographies where the group has strong management experience and resources. Technology transformation also remains a key initiative of the group to capture new cost and revenue opportunities in all businesses.

At the same time, the group is committed to maintaining long-term investment grade ratings, preserving strong liquidity and flexibility, sustaining a long and balanced debt maturity profile and actively managing cash flow and working capital. The group explores opportunities to enhance shareholders' returns, which include potential telecom infrastructure divestures and solidifying strategic alliances with global technology partners.

Mergers and Acquisitions

In mid-2021, CK Hutchison announced that the CK Hutchison Group entered into a binding agreement with Swire Pacific Limited (Swire Pacific) to acquire 50% interest in Hongkong United Dockyards Limited (HUD) from Swire Pacific. HUD integrates the extensive dockyard expertise and traditions of its two founding shareholders, and provides multi-disciplinary marine services and engineering solutions in Asia. Following the acquisition of 50% interest from Swire Pacific, HUD will become wholly-owned by members of the CK Hutchison Group.

Company Background

CK Hutchison Holdings' original precursor company was a small dispensary opened in Guangzhou in 1828. The company moved to Hong Kong in 1841 and took the name HK Dispensary. The company was renamed A.S. Watson in 1863. British expatriate John Duflon Hutchison took over the company in the last quarter of the 19th century.

Auditors: PricewaterhouseCoopers

LOCATIONS

HQ: CK Hutchison Holdings Ltd
  48th Floor, Cheung Kong Center, 2 Queen's Road Central,
Phone: (852) 2128 1188   **Fax:** (852) 2128 1705
Web: www.ckh.com.hk

2018 Sales

	% of total
Hong Kong	10
Mainland China	9
Europe	47
Canada	12
Asia, Australia, and Others	14
Finance & Investments and Others	8
Total	100

PRODUCTS/OPERATIONS

2018 Sales

	% of total
Ports and Related Services	8
Retail	37
Infrastructure	14
Husky Energy	12
3 Group Europe	17
Hutchison Telecommunications Hong Kong Holdings	2
Hutchison Asia Telecommunications	2
Finance & Investments and Others	8
Total	100

HISTORICAL FINANCIALS

Company Type: Public

Income Statement FYE: December 31

	REVENUE ($mil)	NET INCOME ($mil)	NET PROFIT MARGIN	EMPLOYEES
12/22	33,680	4,706	14.0%	300,000
12/21	36,014	4,293	11.9%	300,000
12/20	34,361	3,759	10.9%	300,000
12/19	38,400	5,115	13.3%	300,000
12/18	35,383	4,979	14.1%	300,000
Annual Growth	(1.2%)	(1.4%)	—	0.0%

2022 Year-End Financials

Debt ratio: 3.2% No. of shares ($ mil.): 3,830
Return on equity: 6.9% Dividends
Cash ($ mil.): 17,717 Yield: —
Current Ratio: 1.27 Payout: 0.0%
Long-term debt ($ mil.): 27,812 Market value ($ mil.): —

CLP Holdings Ltd

The CLP Group is one of the largest investor-owned power businesses in Asia-Pacific with investments in Hong Kong, Mainland China, Australia, India, Southeast Asia and Taiwan. Its business spans every major segment of the electricity value chain including retail, transmission and distribution, along with a diversified portfolio of generation assets. As of 2022, its generation capacity in operation and under construction across the Asia-Pacific region stood at some 19,980 MW on an equity basis, supplemented with an additional about 5,100 MW of long-term purchases and energy storage capacity. CLP was founded in 1901, generates the majority of its revenue from Hong Kong.

Operations

The company operates in Hong Kong, Mainland China, India, Southeast Asia, Taiwan, and Australia.

In Hong Kong, CLP Holdings generates, and distributes electricity to more than 2.5 million customers. Nearly 40% of local sales is derived from the Commercial sector, nearly 30% from Infrastructure and Public Services, over 25% from Residential, and some 5% from Manufacturing.

In Mainland China it is one of the largest external independent power producers with a focus on clean and low-carbon energy, including nuclear and renewables.

In India, the company has a diversified generation portfolio comprising coal, gas, and renewable energy (including wind).

In Southeast Asia and Taiwan, CLP Holdings has interests in Taiwan's Ho-Ping Power Station and the Lopburi solar project in Thailand.

In Australia, CLP Holdings has one of the largest integrated energy companies. EnergyAustralia provides gas and electricity to about 2.5 million customers.

About 50% of sales were generated from Hong Kong electricity business, while energy businesses outside Hong Kong accounts for the rest. Overall, about 90% of sales were generated from electricity, gas and others account for some 5% each.

Geographic Reach

The company is headquartered in Hong Kong where it operates a vertically-integrated electricity supply business providing a highly-reliable supply of electricity to 80% of the city's population. Outside Hong Kong, the company invest in the energy sector in Mainland China, India, Southeast Asia, Taiwan and Australia.

It generates nearly 50% of sales in Hong Kong, about 45% in Australia, and the remaining were generated from India, Mainland China, and others.

Sales and Marketing

Sales to the company's five largest customers together represented less than 30%

of the company's total turnover during the year. The company serves over 5 million customer accounts.

Financial Performance

Note: Growth rates may differ after conversion to US Dollars.

The company's net revenue increased by 17% to HK$48 billion in 2022, as sales from the Hong Kong electricity business, energy businesses outside Hong Kong, and others all increased that year.

The company recorded loss in total earnings of HK$4.9 billion in 2022 compared to an earning of HK$4.6 billion from the prior year after recording loss in Australia.

Cash and cash equivalents at the end of the year were HK$3.7 billion, HK$3.5 billion lower from the year prior. Operating activities used HK$2.8 billion in 2022, and investing activities used another HK$9.3 billion, mainly for capital expenditures. Financing activities provided HK$5.9 billion, mostly from proceeds from long-term borrowings.

Strategy

CLP powers the sustainable development of communities in which it operates by providing safe, reliable and affordable electricity to its customers with minimal impact to the environment. It aims to be the leading responsible energy provider in the Asia-Pacific region, from one generation to the next.

CLP looks to leverage new and emerging technologies to aid the progressive decarbonization of its portfolio, empower its customers in making better energy choices, enhance the performance of its operations, and to evolve and grow its business along with the transition. The company launched a revised version of its Climate Vision 2050 in 2019, further updating its strategy for existing and future investments.

As it transitions to a Utility of the Future, it is further digitalizing its operations, which is another strategic priority of CLP. It is focused on opportunities that will deliver robust performance from today's asset base well into the medium term in addition to sustainable results from low-carbon solutions in the longer term. In the past year, these strategies continued to steer the company forward amid the fluctuations in both its business and operating environment.

In 2019, CLP launched Smart Energy Connect, the first online energy app store in Asia. The app offers a range of innovative and practical applications to help businesses and organizations in the region manage energy use in a greener and the smarter way.

Company Background

Digitalisation is at the heart of the new strategy with new software systems planned to strengthen risk management and incident reporting. CLP meanwhile continued efforts to reduce the risks of working at height and other hazardous activities, improving processes to increase worker safety.

CLP continued to engage with capital providers to communicate its strategy on sustainability and climate change, participating in a range of initiatives such as the Asia Investor Group on Climate Change's Asian Utilities Engagement Program. CLP presented its views on governance for climate action at events including the Climate Change Conference hosted by the Hong Kong Chartered Governance Institute in January, and a symposium organised by global environmental disclosure organisation CDP in March.

CLP strengthened efforts to improve safety in the first half of 2022, launching a new multi-year health, safety and environment (HSE) strategy with a focus on designing safer work processes through improved organisational learning.

The new HSE strategy will enhance capabilities across the business ? from senior managers to frontline workers ? to increase safety and operational resilience through increased understanding of work activities and improvements to systems and processes. A key objective of the strategy is to prevent fatalities and life-changing incidents.

EXECUTIVES

Chief Executive Officer, Executive Director, Richard Kendall Lancaster
Chief Financial Officer, Nicolas Alain Marie Tissot
Chief Human Resources Officer, Eileen Burnett-Kant
Chief Corporate Development Officer, Quince Wai Yan Chong
Secretary, General Counsel, Chief Administrative Officer, David John Simmonds
Chairman, Non-Executive Director, Michael David Kadoorie
Non-Executive Vice-Chairman, William Elkin Mocatta
Independent Non-Executive Director, Zia Mody
Independent Non-Executive Director, Christina Gaw
Independent Non-Executive Director, Chunyuan Gu
Independent Non-Executive Director, Roderick I. Eddington
Independent Non-Executive Director, May Siew Boi Tan
Independent Non-Executive Director, Fanny Fan Chiu Fun Law
Independent Non-Executive Director, Nicholas Charles Allen
Non-Executive Director, Philip Lawrence Kadoorie
Non-Executive Director, John Andrew Harry Leigh
Non-Executive Director, Andrew Clifford Winawer Brandler
Auditors : PricewaterhouseCoopers

LOCATIONS

HQ: CLP Holdings Ltd
 8 Laguna Verde Avenue, Hung Hom, Kowloon,
Phone: (852) 2678 8228 **Fax:** (852) 2670 4448
Web: www.clpgroup.com

PRODUCTS/OPERATIONS

Selected Subsidiaries and Affiliates

Castle Peak Power Company Limited (CAPCO, 70%, electricity generation)
CLP Australia Holdings Pty Ltd (electric transmission and distribution utility)
CLP Engineering Limited (energy construction services)
CLP India (integrated energy, India)
CLP Power Asia Limited (independent power projects)
 CLP Power China Limited (independent power projects)
 CLP Power International Limited (independent power projects)
CLP Power Hong Kong Limited (electric transmission and distribution utility)
CLP Properties Limited (real estate)
Hong Kong Nuclear Investment Company Limited (HKNIC, electricity generation)
TRUenergy (integrated energy, Australia)

COMPETITORS

DUKE ENERGY OHIO, INC.
ELECTRICITE DE FRANCE
ENERGY TRANSFER LP
ENGIE
KINDER MORGAN INC
Korea Gas Corporation
PNM RESOURCES, INC.
TC Energy Corporation
Uniper SE
Ãrsted A/S

HISTORICAL FINANCIALS

Company Type: Public

Income Statement — FYE: December 31

	REVENUE ($mil)	NET INCOME ($mil)	NET PROFIT MARGIN	EMPLOYEES
12/22	12,915	118	0.9%	8,318
12/21	10,766	1,088	10.1%	8,116
12/20	10,265	1,477	14.4%	8,060
12/19	11,004	598	5.4%	7,960
12/18	11,673	1,730	14.8%	7,634
Annual Growth	2.6%	(48.8%)	—	2.2%

2022 Year-End Financials

Debt ratio: 3.2% No. of shares ($ mil.): 2,526
Return on equity: 0.8% Dividends
Cash ($ mil.): 549 Yield: —
Current Ratio: 0.78 Payout: 765.9%
Long-term debt ($ mil.): 6,146 Market value ($ mil.): 18,342

	STOCK PRICE ($) FY Close	P/E High/Low		PER SHARE ($) Earnings	Dividends	Book Value
12/22	7.26	28	18	0.05	0.36	5.36
12/21	10.07	3	3	0.43	0.36	5.74
12/20	9.19	2	2	0.58	0.36	5.73
12/19	10.43	7	5	0.24	0.36	5.36
12/18	11.29	2	2	0.68	0.31	5.51
Annual Growth	(10.5%)	—		(48.7%)	3.9%	(0.7%)

Clydesdale Bank PLC

Founded in 1838, the full-service, Scotland-based Clydesdale Bank is owned by Virgin Money UK. Along with standard personal and business services such as deposit accounts, lending, credit cards, and financial advice, the bank also dabbles in agribusiness and private banking. Clydesdale has a proud history of innovation and support for Scottish industry and communities. Sister firm, Yorkshire Bank, also operates as a National Australia Bank brand in the UK.

Operations

Clydesdale Bank offers personal, private and business banking services.

The personal banking products and services include current accounts, credit cards, savings, loans, mortgages, and insurance. Private banking included mortgages for private customers. Its business banking products include day-to-day banking, savings, and loans and finances.

EXECUTIVES

Chief Financial Officer, Executive Director, Ian Smith
Secretary, James Peirson
Secretary, Lorna McMillan
Chief Executive Officer, Executive Director, David Duffy
Non-Executive Director, Clive Adamson
Non-Executive Director, David Bennett
Non-Executive Director, Paul Coby
Non-Executive Director, Geeta Gopalan
Non-Executive Director, Adrian Grace
Non-Executive Director, Fiona MacLeod
Non-Executive Director, Jim Pettigrew
Non-Executive Director, Darren Pope
Non-Executive Director, Teresa Robson-Capps
Non-Executive Director, Amy Stirling
Non-Executive Director, Tim Wade
Auditors : Ernst & Young LLP

LOCATIONS

HQ: Clydesdale Bank PLC
30 St Vincent Place, Glasgow, Scotland G1 2HL
Phone: (44) 141 248 7070   **Fax:** (44) 141 204 0828
Web: www.cbonline.co.uk

COMPETITORS

DBRS Limited
HIFX EUROPE LIMITED
METRO BANK PLC
MUFG AMERICAS HOLDINGS CORPORATION
PRIMARY CAPITAL LIMITED
PROVIDENT FINANCIAL PLC
SCHRODERS PLC
The Toronto-Dominion Bank
YORKSHIRE BANK PUBLIC LIMITED COMPANY
ZIONS BANCORPORATION

HISTORICAL FINANCIALS

Company Type: Public

Income Statement — FYE: September 30

	ASSETS ($mil)	NET INCOME ($mil)	INCOME AS % OF ASSETS	EMPLOYEES
09/21	119,970	636	0.5%	7,415
09/20	115,853	(320)	—	8,256
09/19	112,156	(262)	—	8,703
09/18	56,841	(311)	—	5,769
09/17	58,002	(393)	—	6,040
Annual Growth	19.9%	—		5.3%

2021 Year-End Financials

Return on assets: 0.5%
Return on equity: 8.9%
Long-term debt ($ mil.): —
No. of shares ($ mil.): 12,431
Sales ($ mil.): 2,739
Dividends
 Yield: —
 Payout: 0.0%
Market value ($ mil.): —

CNH Industrial NV

EXECUTIVES

Chairman, Executive Director, Suzanne Heywood
Chief Executive Officer, Executive Director, Scott W. Wine
Financial Services Chief Financial Officer, Financial Services President, Financial Services
Chief Sustainability Officer, Oddone Incisa della Rocchetta
Chief Digital Officer, Parag Garg
Chief Information Officer, Interim Chief Technology & Quality Officer, Marc Kermisch
Chief Human Resources Officer, Kevin Barr
Chief Legal Officer, Chief Compliance Officer, Roberto Russo
Chief Diversity & Inclusion, Sustainability and Transformation Officer, Kelly Manley
Chief Supply Chain Officer, Tom Verbaeten
Corporate Development Senior Vice President, Michele Lombardi
Internal Audit Senior Vice President, Carlo De Bernardi
Communications Senior Vice President, Laura Overall
Agriculture President, Derek Neilson
Asia Pacific President, Chun Woytera
Europe, Middle East & Africa President, Carlo Alberto Sisto
Senior Independent Non-Executive Director, Leo W. Houle
Independent Non-Executive Director, Howard W. Buffett
Independent Non-Executive Director, Asa Tamsons
Independent Non-Executive Director, Catia Bastioli
Independent Non-Executive Director, John B. Lanaway
Independent Non-Executive Director, Vagn Ove Sorensen
Non-Executive Director, Alessandro Nasi
Auditors : Ernst & Young LLP

LOCATIONS

HQ: CNH Industrial NV
25 St. James's Street, London SW1A 1HA
Phone: (44) 207 925 1964   **Fax:** 630 887-2344
Web: www.cnhindustrial.com

HISTORICAL FINANCIALS

Company Type: Public

Income Statement — FYE: December 31

	REVENUE ($mil)	NET INCOME ($mil)	NET PROFIT MARGIN	EMPLOYEES
12/23	24,687	2,371	9.6%	40,220
12/22	23,551	2,029	8.6%	40,070
12/21	33,428	1,723	5.2%	71,895
12/20	26,032	(493)	—	64,016
12/19	28,079	1,422	5.1%	63,499
Annual Growth	(3.2%)	13.6%		(10.8%)

2023 Year-End Financials

Debt ratio: 59.0%
Return on equity: 31.5%
Cash ($ mil.): 5,045
Current Ratio: 9.41
Long-term debt ($ mil.): 27,326
No. of shares ($ mil.): 1,290
Dividends
 Yield: —
 Payout: 0.0%
Market value ($ mil.): —

Co-operative Bank plc

The Co-operative Bank is the first UK high street bank to introduce a customer-led Ethical Policy which sets out the way it does business. It provides a full range of banking products and services to retail and SME (Small and Medium Sizes Enterprises) customers. The bank also offers insurance and investments such as ISAs, mortgages, credit cards, and loans. The company was founded in 1872 as the Loans and Deposits department of Co-operative Wholesale Society.

Operations

The company offers products to both retail and business banking customers, which together are referred to as its core customer segments. The Retail segment accounts for about 85%, while SME generated over 15%.

The Retail segment offers high street, telephony and online services, including current accounts, savings, mortgages, personal loans and credit cards. The SME segment offers banking services for small and medium-sized businesses, charities and social enterprises including current accounts, savings, loans, overdrafts and credit cards. Overall, approximately 90% of sales were generated from net interest income.

Geographic Reach

The company is headquartered in Manchester, UK.

Sales and Marketing

The company caters to retail and SME (Small and Medium Sizes Enterprises) customers.

Financial Performance

The company's revenue for fiscal 2021 increased to Â£361.5 million compared to Â£307.3 million in the prior year.

Net income for fiscal 2021 was Â£31.1 million compared to a net loss of Â£103.7 million in the prior year.

Cash held by the company at the end of

fiscal 2021 increased to Â£5.7 billion. Operating activities provided Â£1.7 billion while investing and financing activities used Â£123.5 million and Â£48 million, respectively. Main cash uses were purchase of investment securities; and interest paid on Tier 2 notes and senior unsecured debt.

Strategy

The company aims to establish sustainable advantage by trusting in its customer-led Ethical Policy, its co-operative values and its committed colleagues, whilst removing cost and income inhibitors.

EXECUTIVES

Chief Executive Officer, Executive Director, Andrew Bester
Chief Operating Officer, Executive Director, Chris Davis
Chief Financial Officer, Executive Director, Nick Slape
Chairman, Robert G. Dench
Independent Non-Executive Director, Glyn Michael Smith
Senior Independent Director, Derek Weir
Independent Non-Executive Director, Bill Thomas
Independent Non-Executive Director, Sue Harris
Non-Independent Non-Executive Director, Morteza Mahjour
Independent Non-Executive Director, Sally-Ann Hibberd
Auditors : Ernst & Young LLP

LOCATIONS

HQ: Co-operative Bank plc
P.O. Box 101, 1 Balloon Street, Manchester M60 4EP
Phone: (44) 161 832 3456 **Fax:** (44) 161 829 4475
Web: www.co-operativebank.co.uk

PRODUCTS/OPERATIONS

2016 Sales

	% of total
Interest receivable and similar income	86
Fee and commission income	14
Total	100

COMPETITORS

CREDITO EMILIANO SPA
CTBC Financial Holding Co., Ltd.
EASTERN VIRGINIA BANKSHARES, INC.
FIRST NATIONAL CORPORATION
OLD POINT FINANCIAL CORPORATION
PRINCETON NATIONAL BANCORP, INC.
QNB CORP.
THE CITIZENS NATIONAL BANK OF MERIDIAN (INC)
THE ROYAL BANK OF SCOTLAND PUBLIC LIMITED COMPANY
UNION BANK OF INDIA

HISTORICAL FINANCIALS
Company Type: Public

Income Statement				FYE: December 31
	ASSETS ($mil)	NET INCOME ($mil)	INCOME AS % OF ASSETS	EMPLOYEES
12/21	39,518	265	0.7%	2,630
12/20	34,935	(130)	—	2,890
12/19	30,948	(202)	—	3,357
12/18	29,496	(87)	—	3,547
12/17	33,078	314	1.0%	3,965
Annual Growth	4.5%	(4.1%)	—	(9.8%)

2021 Year-End Financials
Return on assets: 0.7%
Return on equity: 12.2%
Long-term debt ($ mil.): —
No. of shares ($ mil.): 9,029
Sales ($ mil.): 702
Dividends
Yield: —
Payout: 0.0%
Market value ($ mil.): —

Coca-Cola Europacific Partners plc

Producing one of the world's most recognizable consumer brands for European consumers, Coca-Cola Europacific Partners (formerly known as Coca-Cola European Partners) (CCEP), bottles and distributes a variety of Coca-Cola-brand beverages, including Coca-Cola trademarked soft drinks like Coca-Cola, Diet Coke, and Sprite, as well as energy drinks (Monster), waters (Smartwater), juices (Minute Maid), sports drinks (Powerade), and ready-to-drink teas (Nestea). CCEP operates in nearly 15 Western European countries and nearly 30 other countries serving approximately 1.75 million customers. On average, the group sells approximately 16.4 billion liters of products annually. CCEP was formed in 2016 from the merger of Coca-Cola Enterprises, Coca-Cola Iberian Partners, and Coca-Cola ErfrischungsgetrÃ¤nke AG. Coca-Cola Europacific Partners is its new name as Coca-Cola Amatil (Amatil) and Coca-Cola European Partners (CCEP) joined together in 2021. CCEP generates about 25% of sales in Great Britain.

Operations

The group derives its revenues through a single business activity, which is making, selling and distributing non-alcoholic ready to drink beverages. It operates solely in developed markets in Western Europe and has a homogenous product portfolio across its geographic territories.

CCEP's products include Coca-Cola, Sprite, Fanta, (sparkling); Monster, Powerade, Burn, (energy drinks); Smartwater, Aquarius (Hydration); Costa, Nestea, (Tea and Coffee); and Minute Maid and Tropico (Juices).

CCEP works with franchise partners to offer consumers a wide range of drinks for every taste and occasion, with or without sugar. By brand category volume of sales, Coca-Cola brands bring in about 60%, followed by flavors, mixers and energy, with some 25%, hydration category, with more than 5%, and RTD tea, RTD coffee, juices, and other, with around 10%.

The group operates about 15 thousand vehicles of various types, the majority of which are leased. It also owns approximately 1.6 million pieces of cold drink equipment, principally coolers, and vending machines.

Geographic Reach

Headquartered in the UK, CCEP operates across about 15 European countries, including France, Germany, the UK, Belgium, the Netherlands, Norway, Spain, Portugal, and Sweden. Great Britain is the group's biggest market, accounting for about 25% of total sales. Iberia (Spain, Portugal, and Andorra) and Germany represent around 20% each and France (France and Monaco) pulls in more than 15%.

The group has approximately 45 production sites.

Sales and Marketing

CCEP has a powerful distribution network, reaching customers from convenience stores, supermarkets, bars, restaurants, sports venues and wholesaler, in Europe.

CCEP relies extensively on advertising and sales promotions to market its products. It advertises in all major media to promote sales in the local areas it serves. The group also benefits from regional, local and global advertising programs. It takes part in various programs and arrangements with customers to increase the sale of products. These include arrangements under which allowances can be earned by customers for attaining agreed sales levels or for participating in specific marketing programs.

Financial Performance

Note: Growth rates may differ after conversion to US Dollars.

The company's revenue for fiscal 2021 increased by 30% to EUR 13.8 billion compared from the prior year with EUR 10.6 billion.

Profit for fiscal 2021 increased to EUR 1.4 billion compared from the prior year with EUR 695 million.

Cash held by the company at the end of fiscal 2021 decreased to EUR 1.4 billion. Cash provided by operations and financing activities were EUR 2.1 billion and EUR 3.3 billion, respectively. Cash used for investing activities was EUR 5.6 billion, mainly for acquisition of bottling operations.

Strategy

CCEP's strategy is based on seven growth platforms: growing the sparkling category and its share where it leads; Building share where it's don't lead; doubling its energy business; building a platform for growth in coffee; smart revenue growth management; utilize digital, data and analytics as a competitive differentiator; and winning channel strategy and outlet coverage to drive unrivalled execution.

Capturing the growth in digital commerce has been an important area of focus and investment for CCEP. It has leveraged the growth in e-commerce by supporting its customers with unique online price/pack offers, upweighted marketing and dedicated digital teams in each of its markets.

Mergers and Acquisitions

Coca-Cola Europacific Partners is the new name of the group as Coca-Cola Amatil (Amatil) and Coca-Cola European Partners (CCEP) join together following completion of the acquisition in mid-2021. The group will continue to be listed on Euronext Amsterdam, the New York Stock Exchange, London Stock Exchange and on the Spanish Stock Exchanges, and will continue to trade under the symbol CCEP.

Company Background

CCEP was formed in 2016 from the merger of Coca-Cola Enterprises, Inc. (which operated in Belgium, France, Great Britain, Luxembourg, Monaco, the Netherlands, Norway, and Sweden), Coca-Cola Iberian Partners S.A.U. (Andorra, Spain, and Portugal) and Coca-Cola ErfrischungsgetrÃ„nke GmbH (Germany). The merger of the three companies makes CCEP one of the largest consumer packaging companies in Europe.

EXECUTIVES

Chief Executive Officer, Executive Director, Damian P. Gammell

Chief Financial Officer, Nik Jhangiani

Chief Customer Service and Supply Chain Officer, Jose Antonio Echeverria

Chief Information Officer, Peter Brickley

Chief Commercial Officer, Stephen Lusk

Chief Public Affairs, Communications and Sustainability Officer, Ana Callol

Chief Integration Officer, Victor Rufart

Chief People and Culture Officer, Veronique Vuillod

General Counsel, Secretary, Clare Wardle

Chairman, Sol Daurella

Senior Independent Director, Independent Non-Executive Director, Thomas H. Johnson

Independent Non-Executive Director, Jan Bennink

Independent Non-Executive Director, John Bryant

Independent Non-Executive Director, Christine Cross

Independent Non-Executive Director, Nathalie Gaveau

Independent Non-Executive Director, Dagmar P. Kollmann

Independent Non-Executive Director, Mark Philip Price

Independent Non-Executive Director, Dessi Temperley

Independent Non-Executive Director, Garry Watts

Non-Executive Director, Manolo Arroyo

Non-Executive Director, Jose Ignacio Comenge Sanchez-Real

Non-Executive Director, Alvaro Gomez-Trenor Aguilar

Non-Executive Director, Alfonso Libano Daurella

Non-Executive Director, Mario Rotllant Sola

Non-Executive Director, Brian Smith

Auditors : Ernst & Young LLP

LOCATIONS

HQ: Coca-Cola Europacific Partners plc
Pemberton House, Bakers Road, Uxbridge UB8 1EZ
Phone: (44) 1895 231 313
Web: www.ccep.com

2018 Sales

	% of total
Spain/Portugal/Andorra	23
Great Britain	20
Germany	20
France/Monaco	15
Luxembourg	9
Netherlands	5
Norway	4
Sweden	3
Iceland	1
Total	100

HISTORICAL FINANCIALS

Company Type: Public

Income Statement   FYE: December 31

	REVENUE ($mil)	NET INCOME ($mil)	NET PROFIT MARGIN	EMPLOYEES
12/23	20,271	1,848	9.1%	32,000
12/22	18,498	1,610	8.7%	33,100
12/21	15,577	1,118	7.2%	33,000
12/20	13,016	611	4.7%	22,000
12/19	13,492	1,223	9.1%	17,498
Annual Growth	10.7%	10.9%	—	16.3%

2023 Year-End Financials

Debt ratio: 43.1%
Return on equity: 21.6%
Cash ($ mil.): 1,571
Current Ratio: 0.91
Long-term debt ($ mil.): 11,182
No. of shares ($ mil.): 459
Dividends
Yield: —
Payout: 54.2%
Market value ($ mil.): —

Coca-Cola FEMSA SAB de CV

Coca-Cola FEMSA is the largest franchise bottler of Coca-Cola trademark beverages in the world in terms of sales volume with a wide portfolio of around 130 leading multi-category brands and some 2 million points of sale through about 50 bottling plants and about 270 distribution centers in approximately 10 Latin America. The company produces, markets, and distributes soft drinks, such as Coca-Cola, Ciel, and Powerade, as well as Santa Clara, Del Valle, Shangri-la, Topo Chico, and Ades. Coca-Cola FEMSA also distributes its products across Central America, Columbia, Venezuela, and parts of Argentina and Brazil. Mexico and Central America bring in nearly 60% of the company's revenue.

Operations

The company produces, markets, sells, and distributes mainly Coca-Cola trademark beverages. The Coca-Cola trademark beverages include: sparkling beverages (colas and flavored sparkling beverages), waters and other beverages (including juice drinks, coffee, teas, milk, value-added dairy, sports drinks, energy drinks, alcoholic beverages and plant-based drinks). In addition, it distributes and sells Heineken-owned brand beer products, Estrella Galicia and TherezÃ³polis beer products in its Brazilian territories and Monster products in all of the countries where the company operates.

Overall, product sales bring in almost all of the company's revenue. Services rendered and other operating revenue account for the remainder.

Geographic Reach

Headquartered in Mexico City, Coca-Cola FEMSA operates in 10 countries, including nine countries of Latin America (Argentina, Brazil, Colombia, Costa Rica, Guatemala, Mexico, Nicaragua, Panama, Venezuela, and Uruguay). It has more than 185 distribution centers in Mexico and Central America (Mexico, Guatemala, Nicaragua, Costa Rica, and Panama) and nearly 75 distribution centers in South America (Colombia, Brazil, Argentina, and Uruguay).

Sales and Marketing

Coca-Cola FEMSA uses several sales and distribution models depending on market and geographic conditions and the customer's profile: the pre-sale system; the conventional truck route system; sales through digital platforms to access technologically enabled customer; the telemarketing system; and sales through third-party wholesalers and other distributors of its products.

The company advertises in all major communications media. Its principal channels are small retailers, on-premise accounts, such as restaurants and bars, supermarkets and third party distributors.

In addition to its fleet of trucks, the company distributes its products in certain locations through electric carts and hand-trucks in order to comply with local environmental and traffic regulations. In some of its territories, the company relies on third parties to transport its finished products from the company's bottling plants to its distribution centers and, in some cases, directly to its customers.

Financial Performance

Its consolidated total revenues increased by 6.1% to Ps.194.8 billion in 2021 as compared to 2020, mainly as a result of its pricing initiatives, coupled with favorable price-mix effects and volume growth.

In 2021, the company had a net income of Ps.15.7 billion in 2021, as compared to Ps.10.3 billion in 2020. This 52.4% increase was mainly driven by solid operating results coupled with a decrease in its comprehensive financial result.

The company's cash at the end of 2021 was Ps. 47.2 billion. Operating activities generated Ps. 32.7 billion, while investing activities used Ps. 9.5 billion, mainly for acquisitions of long-lived assets. Financing activities used another Ps. 20.3 billion, primarily for repayment of borrowings.

Strategy

The company is transforming itself to thrive in the current evolving global business environment. It has strengthened its longstanding relationship with The Coca-Cola Company by together updating and enhancing the following main objectives: growth principles, relationship economics, potential new businesses and ventures, and digital strategy.

To consolidate the company's position as a global leader in its industry and strengthen the company's value proposition for retail clients and end consumers, the company is working across six strategic corridors: build out an open omnichannel platform, develop a customer-centric winning portfolio, foster an agile, digital-savvy, people-centric culture, place sustainability at the center of its organization, digitize its core, and actively pursue value-enhancing acquisitions.

The company seeks to accelerate its revenue growth through the introduction of new categories, products and presentations that better meet its consumers' needs and preferences, while maintaining its core products and improving its profitability. To address its consumers' diverse lifestyles, it has developed new products through innovation and have expanded the availability of low- and non-caloric beverages by reformulating and broadening itsproduct portfolio to reduce added sugar and offering smaller presentations of its products.

EXECUTIVES

Chief Executive Officer, Director, John Anthony Santa Maria Otazua
Chief Financial Officer, Constantino Spas Montesinos
Mexico Chief Operating Officer, Washington Fabricio Ponce Garcia
Latin America Chief Operating Officer, Latin America Strategic Planning Officer, Eduardo Guillermo Hernández Pena
Brazil Chief Operating Officer, Ian Marcel Craig Garcia
Human Resources Officer, Karina Paola Awad Perez
Corporate Affairs Officer, Jose Ramon de Jesus Martinez Alonso
Supply Chain and Engineering Officer, Rafael Ramos Cass
Commercial Development Officer, Rafael Alberto Suarez Olaguibel
Digital and Technology Officer, Ignacio Echevarria Mendiguren

General Counsel, Carlos Luis Diaz Saenz
Secretary, Carlos Eduardo Aldrete Ancira
Chairman, Jose Antonio Fernandez Carbajal
Independent Director, Ricardo Guajardo Touche
Independent Director, Enrique F. Senior Hernandez
Independent Director, Luis Rubio Freidberg
Independent Director, Daniel Javier Servitje Montull
Independent Director, Luis Alfonso Nicolau Gutierrez
Independent Director, Charles H. McTier
Independent Director, Victor Alberto Tiburcio Celorio
Independent Director, Francisco Zambrano Rodriguez
Independent Director, Alfonso Gonzales Migoya
Director, Federico Jose Reyes Garcia
Director, Miguel Eduardo Padilla Silva
Director, Jose Luis Cutrale
Director, Jose Octavio Reyes Lagunes
Director, John Murphy
Director, James Leonard Dinkins
Auditors : Mancera, S.C. (a member practice of Ernst & Young Global Limited)

LOCATIONS

HQ: Coca-Cola FEMSA SAB de CV
Mario Pani No. 100, Colonia Santa Fe Cuajimalpa, Alcadia Cuajimalpa de Morelos, Mexico 05348
Phone: (52) 55 1519 6179
Web: www.coca-colafemsa.com

2016 Sales

	% of total
Mexico and central America	49
South America (excluding Venezuela)	40
Venezuela	11
Total	100

PRODUCTS/OPERATIONS

Selected Products and Brands

Colas
  Coca-Cola
  Coca-Cola Light
  Coca-Cola Zero
Flavored sparking beverages
  Aquarius Fresh
  Chinotto
  Crush
  Fanta
  Fresca
  Frescolita
  Hit
  Kuat
  Lift
  Mundet
  Quatro
  Simba
  Sprite
Juices and nectars
  Del Prado
  Estrella Azul
  Jugos del Valle
Milk and dairy products
  D'Oro
  Estrella Azul
  Vaquita
  Vita Slim
Water
  Alpina
  Brisa
  Ciel
  Crystal
  Kin
  Manantial
  Nevada
Other
  Aquarius (flavored water)
  Cepita
  Hi-C
  Jugos del Valle (juice-gased beverage)
  Kaiser (beer in Brazil)
  Matte Leão (ready to drink tea)
  Nestea
  Powerade (isotonic)

COMPETITORS

ASAHI GROUP HOLDINGS,LTD.
COCA - COLA HELLENIC BOTTLING COMPANY S.A.
DANONE
Embotelladora Andina S.A.
Fomento EconÃ³mico Mexicano, S.A.B. de C.V.
Grupo Lala, S.A.B. de C.V.
Quilmes Industrial (QUINSA) SA
SUNTORY HOLDINGS LIMITED
THE COCA-COLA COMPANY
THE PHILADELPHIA COCA-COLA BOTTLING COMPANY

HISTORICAL FINANCIALS

Company Type: Public

Income Statement
FYE: December 31

	REVENUE ($mil)	NET INCOME ($mil)	NET PROFIT MARGIN	EMPLOYEES
12/22	11,588	972	8.4%	97,211
12/21	9,527	768	8.1%	83,754
12/20	9,241	518	5.6%	82,334
12/19	10,278	639	6.2%	82,186
12/18	9,272	707	7.6%	83,364
Annual Growth	5.7%	8.3%	—	3.9%

2022 Year-End Financials

Debt ratio: 1.4%
Return on equity: 15.4%
Cash ($ mil.): 2,058
Current Ratio: 1.37
Long-term debt ($ mil.): 3,584
No. of shares ($ mil.): 16,806
Dividends
  Yield: —
  Payout: 4607.3%
Market value ($ mil.): 1,140,836

	STOCK PRICE ($) FY Close	P/E High/Low		PER SHARE ($) Earnings	Dividends	Book Value
12/22	67.88	62	48	0.06	2.66	0.38
12/21	54.79	62	46	0.05	2.44	0.35
12/20	46.10	101	64	0.03	2.14	0.35
12/19	60.62	96	77	0.04	1.84	0.39
12/18	60.84	90	68	0.04	1.70	0.38
Annual Growth	2.8%	—	—	8.2%	11.8%	0.2%

Coca-Cola HBC AG

EXECUTIVES

Chief Executive Officer, Executive Director, Zoran Bogdanovic
Group Chief Operating Officer, Naya Kalogeraki
Chief Financial Officer, Ben Almanzar
Chief Supply Officer, Ivo Bjelis
Chief People and Culture Officer, Sanda Parezanovic
Supply Chain Chief Corporate Affairs and Sustainability Officer, Marcel Martin
Chief Customer and Commercial Officer, Barbara Tonz

Digital Commerce Business Development Director, Vitaliy Novikov
Chief Digital and Technology Officer, Mourad Ajarti
Strategy and Transformation Director Director, Spyros Mello
Chief Corporate Development Officer, General Counsel, Secretary, Jan Gustavsson
Non-Executive Chairman, Anastassis G. David
Senior Independent Non-Executive Director, Reto Francioni
Independent Non-Executive Director, Charlotte J. Boyle
Independent Non-Executive Director, Olusola David-Borha
Independent Non-Executive Director, Anna Diamantopoulou
Independent Non-Executive Director, William W. Douglas
Independent Non-Executive Director, Alexandra Papalexopoulou
Non-Executive Director, Henrique Braun
Non-Executive Director, Anastasios I. Leventis
Non-Executive Director, Christodoulos Leventis
Non-Executive Director, Bruno Pietracci
Non-Executive Director, Ryan Rudolph
Auditors : PricewaterhouseCoopers S.A.

LOCATIONS

HQ: Coca-Cola HBC AG
Turmstrasse 26, Steinhausen CH-6312
Phone: (41) 41 726 0110
Web: www.coca-colahellenic.com

HISTORICAL FINANCIALS
Company Type: Public

Income Statement — FYE: December 31

	REVENUE ($mil)	NET INCOME ($mil)	NET PROFIT MARGIN	EMPLOYEES
12/22	9,824	443	4.5%	33,043
12/21	8,113	619	7.6%	26,787
12/20	7,525	509	6.8%	27,722
12/19	7,888	547	6.9%	28,389
12/18	7,623	512	6.7%	28,884
Annual Growth	6.5%	(3.5%)	—	3.4%

2022 Year-End Financials
Debt ratio: 35.4%
Return on equity: 12.9%
Cash ($ mil.): 768
Current Ratio: 1.24
Long-term debt ($ mil.): 3,130
No. of shares ($ mil.): 366
Dividends
 Yield: —
 Payout: 69.0%
Market value ($ mil.): —

Coles Group Ltd (New)

EXECUTIVES

Chief Executive Officer, Managing Director, Executive Director, Steven Cain
Chief Financial Officer, Leah Weckert
Chief Operating Officer, Greg Davis
Chief Operating Officer, Matthew Swindells
Property & Export Chief Officer, Thinus Keeve
Chief Marketing Officer, Lisa Ronson
Chief People Officer, Kris Webb
Chief Information & Digital Officer, Roger Sniezek
Chief Legal Officer, David Brewster
Chief Executive Online & Corporate Affairs, Alister Jordan
Secretary, Daniella Pereira
Chairman, Independent Non-Executive Director, James Graham
Non-Executive Director, David Cheesewright
Independent Non-Executive Director, Jacqueline Chow
Independent Non-Executive Director, Abigail Pip Cleland
Independent Non-Executive Director, Richard J. Freudenstein
Independent Non-Executive Director, Wendy Stops
Independent Non-Executive Director, Zlatko Todorcevski
Auditors : Ernst & Young

LOCATIONS

HQ: Coles Group Ltd (New)
800-838 Toorak Road, Hawthorn East, Victoria 3123
Phone: (61) 3 9829 5111
Web: www.colesgroup.com.au

HISTORICAL FINANCIALS
Company Type: Public

Income Statement — FYE: June 27

	REVENUE ($mil)	NET INCOME ($mil)	NET PROFIT MARGIN	EMPLOYEES
06/21	29,558	763	2.6%	0
06/20	25,971	672	2.6%	0
06/19	26,949	1,005	3.7%	0
06/18	28,904	1,165	4.0%	0
Annual Growth	0.7%	(13.2%)	—	—

2021 Year-End Financials
Debt ratio: 4.8%
Return on equity: 37.1%
Cash ($ mil.): 597
Current Ratio: 0.59
Long-term debt ($ mil.): 867
No. of shares ($ mil.): 1,334
Dividends
 Yield: —
 Payout: 81.0%
Market value ($ mil.): —

Commercial Bank of Qatar

EXECUTIVES

Chief Executive Officer, Joseph Abraham
Auditors : Ernst & Young

LOCATIONS

HQ: Commercial Bank of Qatar
P.O. Box 3232, Doha
Phone: (974) 4449 0000   **Fax:** (974) 4449 0070
Web: www.cbq.com.qa

HISTORICAL FINANCIALS
Company Type: Public

Income Statement — FYE: December 31

	ASSETS ($mil)	NET INCOME ($mil)	INCOME AS % OF ASSETS	EMPLOYEES
12/22	46,461	772	1.7%	0
12/21	45,457	633	1.4%	0
12/20	42,199	357	0.8%	0
12/19	40,532	555	1.4%	0
12/18	37,107	456	1.2%	0
Annual Growth	5.8%	14.0%	—	—

2022 Year-End Financials
Return on assets: 1.6%
Return on equity: 11.3%
Long-term debt ($ mil.): —
No. of shares ($ mil.): 4,047
Sales ($ mil.): 2,591
Dividends
 Yield: —
 Payout: 0.0%
Market value ($ mil.): —

Commercial International Bank (Egypt) SAE

EXECUTIVES

Chief Executive Officer, Executive Director, Hussein Abaza
Deputy Chief Risk Officer, Hanan El Borollossy
Chairman, Hisham Ezz Al arab
Lead Director, Jawaid Mirza
Independent Non-Executive Director, Paresh Sukthankar
Independent Non-Executive Director, Magda Habib
Independent Non-Executive Director, Mark Richards
Independent Non-Executive Director, Rajeev K. L. Kakar
Independent Non-Executive Director, Amani Abou-Zeid
Non-Executive Director, Bijan Khosrowshahi
Auditors : Saleh, Barsoum & Abdel Aziz - Grant Thornton

LOCATIONS

HQ: Commercial International Bank (Egypt) SAE
Nile Tower, 21/23 Charles de Gaulle Street, Cairo, Giza
Phone: (20) 2 3747 2000   **Fax:** (20) 2 3570 3632
Web: www.cibeg.com

HISTORICAL FINANCIALS
Company Type: Public

Income Statement — FYE: December 31

	ASSETS ($mil)	NET INCOME ($mil)	INCOME AS % OF ASSETS	EMPLOYEES
12/22	25,678	650	2.5%	7,700
12/21	31,709	844	2.7%	7,308
12/20	27,212	651	2.4%	7,071
12/19	24,131	736	3.1%	6,900
12/18	19,120	533	2.8%	6,759
Annual Growth	7.7%	5.1%	—	3.3%

2022 Year-End Financials

Return on assets: 2.8%
Return on equity: 23.5%
Long-term debt ($ mil.): —
No. of shares ($ mil.): 2,982
Sales ($ mil.): 2,428
Dividends
  Yield: —
  Payout: 17.7%
Market value ($ mil.): 3,490

	STOCK PRICE ($) FY Close	P/E High	P/E Low	PER SHARE ($) Earnings	PER SHARE ($) Dividends	Book Value
12/22	1.17	0	0	0.19	0.03	0.92
12/21	3.21	1	1	0.26	0.00	1.48
12/20	3.71	2	1	0.20	0.05	1.28
12/19	5.06	2	1	0.23	0.04	1.10
12/18	4.15	1	1	0.20	0.03	0.81
Annual Growth	(27.1%)	—	—	(1.0%)	2.9%	3.0%

Commerzbank AG

EXECUTIVES

Chairman, Manfred Knof
Deputy Chairman, Chief Financial Officer, Bettina Orlopp
Chief Risk Officer, Marcus Chromik
Corporate Clients, Michael Kotzbauer
Human Resources Managing Director, Sabine Mlnarsky
Chief Operating Officer, Jorg Oliveri del Castillo-Schulz
Private and Small-Business Customers Managing Director, Thomas Schaufler
Honorary Chairman, Klaus-Peter Muller
Chairman, Helmut Gottschalk
Deputy Chairman, Uwe Tschage
Director, Heike Anscheit
Director, Alexander Boursanoff
Director, Gunnar de Buhr
Director, Stefan Burghardt
Director, Frank Czichowski
Director, Sabine U. Dietrich
Director, Jutta A. Donges
Director, Monika Fink
Director, Stefan Jennes
Director, Kerstin Jerchel
Director, Burkhard Keese
Director, Alexandra Krieger
Director, Daniela Mattheus
Director, Caroline Seifert
Director, Robin J. Stalker
Director, Gertrude Tumpel-Gugerell
Director, Frank Westhoff
Director, Stefan Wittmann
Auditors : KPMG AG Wirtschaftsprufungsgesellschaft

LOCATIONS

HQ: Commerzbank AG
  Kaiserplatz, Frankfurt am Main 60261
Phone: (49) 69 136 20   **Fax:** (49) 69 28 53 89
Web: www.commerzbank.com

HISTORICAL FINANCIALS

Company Type: Public

Income Statement   FYE: December 31

	ASSETS ($mil)	NET INCOME ($mil)	INCOME AS % OF ASSETS	EMPLOYEES
12/22	509,925	1,532	0.3%	42,378
12/21	535,421	486	0.1%	45,387
12/20	622,133	(3,522)	—	46,724
12/19	520,555	723	0.1%	48,512
12/18	529,503	990	0.2%	49,410
Annual Growth	(0.9%)	11.5%	—	(3.8%)

2022 Year-End Financials

Return on assets: 0.3%
Return on equity: 4.8%
Long-term debt ($ mil.): —
No. of shares ($ mil.): 1,252
Sales ($ mil.): 13,343
Dividends
  Yield: —
  Payout: 0.0%
Market value ($ mil.): 11,710

	STOCK PRICE ($) FY Close	P/E High	P/E Low	PER SHARE ($) Earnings	PER SHARE ($) Dividends	Book Value
12/22	9.35	10	6	1.06	0.00	25.60
12/21	7.59	35	24	0.26	0.00	26.08
12/20	6.45	—	—	(2.86)	0.00	26.93
12/19	6.07	18	10	0.57	0.14	26.33
12/18	6.66	23	9	0.79	0.23	25.80
Annual Growth	8.9%	—	—	7.6%	—	(0.2%)

Commonwealth Bank of Australia

Commonwealth Bank of Australia (CBA) offers retail, private, business, and institutional banking services, funds management, insurance, and investment services. CBA's brands include Bankwest, Colonial First State, online brokerage CommSec, and ASB Bank, which provides banking, investment, and financial services. CBA serves over 15 million customers via about 1,000 branch offices and nearly 2,500 ATMs in Australia. In addition, CBA operates in Australia, New Zealand, United Kingdom, the United States, China, Japan, Europe, Singapore, Hong Kong and Indonesia. CBA offers life insurance and a provider of home loans in Australia. It has total assets of A$1.1 trillion.

Operations

Broadly speaking, Commonwealth Bank of Australia (CBA) generates around 80% of its revenue from interest income from its various banking divisions and New Zealand operations. Other banking income provides about 20% of total revenue. Income from fund management and insurance income account for the remainder.

Its Retail Banking unit provides deposit, home loan, and consumer loan products to retail customers and small businesses. The Business Banking division provides personalized banking services to Agribusiness customers and high-net-worth individuals, as well as margin lending through CommSec and retail banking products and servicing to non-relationship managed small business customers.

Institutional Banking and Markets provides debt and equity capital raising, financial and commodities price risk management, and transactional banking services to corporate, institutional, and government clients.. Its New Zealand division includes the banking and funds management business operating in New Zealand under the company's brand.

Geographic Reach

Commonwealth Bank of Australia generates around 85% of its revenue from customers in Australia and more than 10% in New Zealand. It has minority investments in China and Vietnam.

Sales and Marketing

Commonwealth Bank of Australia provides financial education to school children in Australia through its Start Smart program, which has reached more than four million pupils since its inception. It also funds the Commonwealth Bank Teaching Awards and Evidence For Learning.

CBA has 7.6 million active digital customers. CBA uses CommBank app, and the Customer Engagement Engine which uses artificial intelligence to analyze data and serve customers with the information and services that are most relevant to them.

Advertising, marketing and loyalty costs were A$412 million, A$424 million, and A$443 million for the years 2021, 2020, and 2019, respectively.

Financial Performance

Commonwealth Bank of Australia's (CBA) performance for the past five years have fluctuated with slight dips and growth from year-to-year.

CBA's operating income for 2021 increased by about A$385 million to A$24.2 billion as compared to 2020's net profit of A$23.8 billion.

The group's statutory net profit after tax for the financial year 2021 (ended June) was A$10.2 billion as compared to the prior year's net income of A$7.4 billion.

CBA had A$87.4 billion by the end of the year. Operating activities provided A$41.3 billion. Investing activities and financing activities provided A$871 million and A$18.3 billion, respectively.

Strategy

CBA's strategy is to become a simpler, better bank that delivers balanced and sustainable outcomes for the customers, community, people and shareholders. CBA is becoming a simpler bank by focusing on the core banking businesses and simplifying the organization to reduce costs and create the capacity to invest, while also reducing risk and making it easier for the customers and people to get things done.

The four execution priorities are:

Leadership in Australia's recovery and transition; Reimagined products and services; Global best digital experiences and technology; and Simpler, better foundations.

As part of the Bank's strategic priorities, it has committed to playing a leadership role in supporting Australia's economic recovery and transition to a sustainable economy. In addition to considering the risks of climate change, its strategy also seeks to harness the significant existing and emerging opportunities to help its customers reduce their emissions and adapt to climate change.

Mergers and Acquisitions

HISTORY

The Commonwealth Bank Act of 1911 allowed banks to conduct both savings bank and central bank functions and paved the way for the founding of the Commonwealth Bank of Australia the next year. The bank initially operated through a single main office and in nearly 500 post offices in Victoria; it spread out through the entire country over the next few years.

The young bank was drafted during WWI to help the federal government organize war loans and a merchant shipping fleet. In 1919 the bank took over responsibility for issuing notes from the Federal Treasury. In 1928 it created the Commonwealth Savings Bank from its savings department.

Australia -- heavily indebted to British lenders -- was devastated by the Great Depression. As banks failed, the Commonwealth Bank picked up several other institutions, including the state banks in Western Australia and New South Wales. During those years Commonwealth took on more and more of the functions of a central bank.

During WWII the bank again came to the aid of its country, acting as an agent for the federal government. After the war, when the Australian economy stabilized, the bank began offering home loans.

After years of controversy, in 1959 two bank acts formally separated the Commonwealth Bank's central bank and savings functions. The Reserve Bank of Australia took over the central bank functions in 1960, and the trading and savings operations were taken over by the new Commonwealth Development Bank, later renamed the Commonwealth Banking Corporation (a subsidiary of Commonwealth Bank of Australia).

The bank concentrated on expansion and diversification in the 1970s, establishing travel, home insurance, and financing (CBFC, 1978); it set its sights on technology in the 1980s, expanding its credit card offerings and introducing electronic banking.

The US's 1987 stock market crash again affected Australia's banks, which spent almost a decade recovering. Luckily for Commonwealth Bank, it wasn't the hardest hit.

In 1988 Commonwealth Bank moved into life insurance and investment services, forming subsidiaries Commonwealth Life and Commonwealth Management Services (now together known as CBA Financial Services). In 1989 the bank bought 75% of New Zealand-based ASB Bank.

Commonwealth faced a bevy of challenges, including banking deregulation that began in 1982, foreign competition, and 1990's banking-law amendments allowing banks to be publicly traded. All of these factors influenced Commonwealth's decision to reorganize. The government sold approximately 30% of its stake in 1991, in part to help Commonwealth fund its acquisition of the State Bank of Victoria. The government sold the rest of its stake in 1996.

That year the company's push into electronic banking bore fruit -- some 60% of all its banking transactions were online; that figure later rose to 80%. The company moved into e-commerce in 1999, putting out a call for an overseas partner; Commonwealth's stated goal was to generate one-quarter of its income outside Australia. Also that year Commonwealth and a division of The Bank of Nova Scotia joined forces to form a commodities trading group specializing in metals. In 2000 the company bought Australian financial services firm Colonial Limited.

In late 2008 the company acquired Australia-based BankWest from British bank HBOS (now part of Lloyds Banking Group). The US$1.5 billion deal included insurer and asset manager St. Andrew's (which was later sold) and bolstered CBA's presence in western Australia. Its 2008 acquisitions of BankWest from HBOS bolstered its position in western Australia.

In 2010 CBA entered the Chinese insurance market with the launch of a joint venture with Bank of Communications.

In 2011, the bank opened branches in China, India, and Indonesia and bought a 20% sake in Vietnam International Bank. Also that year, the bank continued to strengthen its ties to China, signing a referral agreement with Agricultural Bank of China to capture potential customers.

EXECUTIVES

Retail Banking Services Chief Executive Officer, Retail Banking Services Managing Director, Executive Director, Matthew Comyn
Corporate Affairs Deputy Chief Executive, David Cohen
Chief Risk Officer, Nigel Williams
Enterprise Services Group Executive, Enterprise Services Chief Information Officer, Pascal Boillat
Financial Services Group Executive, Financial Services Chief Financial Officer, Alan Docherty
Legal & Group Governance Group Executive, Legal & Group Governance General Counsel, Carmel Mulhern
Program Delivery Group Executive, Scott Wharton
Business and Private Banking Group Executive, Mike Vacy Lyle
Retail Banking Services Group Executive, Angus Sullivan
Human Resources Group Executive, Sian Lewis
Institutional Banking and Markets Group Executive, Andrew Hinchli
Marketing and Corporate affairs Group Executive, Priscilla Sims Brown
Chairman, Non-Executive Director, Catherine Livingstone
Independent Non-Executive Director, Anne Templeman-Jones
Independent Non-Executive Director, Paul O'Malley
Independent Non-Executive Director, Genevieve Bell
Independent Non-Executive Director, Shirish Apte
Independent Non-Executive Director, Mary Padbury
Independent Non-Executive Director, Wendy Stops
Independent Non-Executive Director, Rob Whitfield
Auditors : PricewaterhouseCoopers

LOCATIONS

HQ: Commonwealth Bank of Australia
Commonwealth Bank Place South, Level 1, 11 Harbour Street, Sydney, New South Wales 2000
Phone: (61) 2 9378 2000   **Fax:** (61) 2 9118 7192
Web: www.commbank.com.au

2017

	%
Australia	83
New Zealand	11
Other locations	5
Total	100

PRODUCTS/OPERATIONS

2017

	%
Interest income	60
Other banking income	19
Premiums from insurance contracts	10
Funds management income	8
Investment revenue (funds management	2
Investment revenue (insurance	1
Total	100

2017 Sales by Segment

	A$ million	% of total
Retail banking services	10,511	43
Business & private banking	3,840	16
Institutional banking & markets	2,893	12
Wealth Management	2,393	10
New Zealand	2,191	9
Bankwest	1,874	8
IFS and Other Divisions	904	4
Total		100

Selected Brands
ASB (New Zealand)
Bankwest
Colonial First State
CommInsure
CommSec
FirstChoice
Sovereign

COMPETITORS

AUSTRALIA AND NEW ZEALAND BANKING GROUP LIMITED
KEYCORP
NATIONAL AUSTRALIA BANK LIMITED
NATWEST GROUP PLC
Nordea Bank AB
Royal Bank Of Canada
Skandinaviska Enskilda Banken AB
The Toronto-Dominion Bank
U.S. BANCORP
WESTPAC BANKING CORPORATION

HISTORICAL FINANCIALS

Company Type: Public

Income Statement — FYE: June 30

	ASSETS ($mil)	NET INCOME ($mil)	INCOME AS % OF ASSETS	EMPLOYEES
06/23	829,312	6,679	0.8%	53,754
06/22	836,076	7,410	0.9%	53,395
06/21	819,639	7,641	0.9%	50,278
06/20	694,917	6,602	1.0%	48,167
06/19	684,171	6,005	0.9%	48,238
Annual Growth	4.9%	2.7%	—	2.7%

2023 Year-End Financials

Return on assets: 0.8%
Return on equity: 13.9%
Long-term debt ($ mil.): —
No. of shares ($ mil.): 1,674
Sales ($ mil.): 32,401
Dividends
 Yield: 4.0%
 Payout: 68.3%
Market value ($ mil.): 112,126

	STOCK PRICE ($) FY Close	P/E High/Low		PER SHARE ($) Earnings	Dividends	Book Value
06/23	66.96	12	10	3.86	2.72	28.46
06/22	62.00	12	10	4.14	2.72	29.48
06/21	75.03	14	8	4.05	1.80	33.33
06/20	48.13	11	7	3.59	2.74	27.91
06/19	58.19	12	9	3.28	2.97	27.58
Annual Growth	3.6%			4.2%	(2.2%)	0.8%

Compagnie de Saint-Gobain

EXECUTIVES

Chief Executive Officer, Director, Benoit Bazin
Corporate Strategy Vice President, Noemie Chocat
CEO of the Northern Europe Region Senior Vice President, Patrick Dupin
CEO of the Southern Europe, Middle East, Africa Region Senior Vice President, Thierry Fournier
CEO of the Latin America Region Senior Vice President, Javier Gimeno
Marketing & Development Vice President, Cordula Gudduschat
Chief Innovation Officer, Anne Hardy
Technology & Industrial Performance Senior Vice President, Benoit d'iribarne
Human Resources & Corporate Social Responsibility Senior Vice President, Claire Pedini
Communication Vice President, Laurance Pernot
Chief Digital and Information Officer, Ursula Soritsch-Renier
Chief Financial Officer, Sreedhar N.
Corporate Secretary, Director, Antoine Vignial
Chairman, Director, Pierre-Andre de Chalendar
Lead Independent Director, Jean-Dominique Senard
Independent Director, Jean-Francois Cirelli
Independent Director, Thierry Delaporte
Independent Director, Lina Ghotmeh
Independent Director, Ieda Gomes Yell
Independent Director, Pamela Knapp
Independent Director, Agnes Lemarchand
Independent Director, Dominique Leroy
Independent Director, Anne-Marie Idrac
Employee Director, Lydie Cortes
Employee Director, Philippe Thibaudet
Director, Sibylle Daunis-Opfermann
Director, Gilles Schnepp
Auditors : KPMG S.A

LOCATIONS

HQ: Compagnie de Saint-Gobain
Tour Saint-Gobain, 12, place de l'Iris, Courbevoie 92400
Phone: (33) 1 47 62 30 00
Web: www.saint-gobain.com

HISTORICAL FINANCIALS

Company Type: Public

Income Statement — FYE: December 31

	REVENUE ($mil)	NET INCOME ($mil)	NET PROFIT MARGIN	EMPLOYEES
12/22	54,745	3,207	5.9%	170,714
12/21	50,041	2,853	5.7%	167,816
12/20	46,810	559	1.2%	167,552
12/19	47,826	1,578	3.3%	170,643
12/18	47,873	480	1.0%	181,001
Annual Growth	3.4%	60.7%	—	(1.5%)

2022 Year-End Financials

Debt ratio: 22.1%
Return on equity: 13.8%
Cash ($ mil.): 6,551
Current Ratio: 1.24
Long-term debt ($ mil.): 9,573
No. of shares ($ mil.): 511
Dividends
 Yield: —
 Payout: 5.6%
Market value ($ mil.): 4,991

	STOCK PRICE ($) FY Close	P/E High/Low		PER SHARE ($) Earnings	Dividends	Book Value
12/22	9.76	2	1	6.19	0.35	47.43
12/21	14.05	3	2	5.39	0.32	44.98
12/20	9.14	12	5	1.04	0.00	41.43
12/19	8.17	3	2	2.90	0.30	40.21
12/18	6.59	14	8	0.87	0.31	37.76
Annual Growth	10.3%	—	—	63.3%	3.4%	5.9%

Compagnie Financiere Richemont SA

Compagnie Financiere Richemont is one of the world's leading luxury goods groups. It is the owner of prestigious Maisons, recognized for its excellence in jewelry, watches, fashion and accessories, and distinguished by their craftsmanship and creativity. It markets Cartier jewelry, Piaget and Baume & Mercier watches, Montblanc pens, and Chloe haute coture. Richemont also owns jeweler Van Cleef & Arpels. Customers can get their hands on Richemont's finery at its more than 2,295 boutiques scattered across five continents, as well as online. Richemont was founded in Switzerland in 1940s by South African Johann Rupert. Majority of its sales were generated in the Asia-Pacific.

Operations

The company operates in three segments: Jewellery Maisons (around 60% of sales), Specialist Watchmakers (about 20%), and Online Distributors (nearly 15%). Others account for the rest of the sales.

The Jewellery Maisons designs, manufactures and distributes jewellery products; these comprise Buccellati, Cartier, and Van Cleef & Arpels.

The Specialist Watchmakers' primary activity includes the design, manufacture and distribution of precision timepieces. The group's Specialist Watchmakers comprise A. Lange & Söhne, Baume & Mercier, IWC Schaffhausen, Jaeger-LeCoultre, Panerai, Piaget, Roger Dubuis, and Vacheron Constantin.

The Online Distributors' primary activity is the online sale of luxury goods. This segment comprises Watchfinder and YNAP.

Other operating segments include Alaïa, Chloé, dunhill, Montblanc, Peter Millar, Purdey, Serapian, AZ Factory, investment property companies, and other manufacturing entities.

By product, Richemont generates about 45% of its sales from jewelry and more than 30% from watches. Clothing and leather goods and accessories account for around 10% each. Other items, such as writing instruments bring in the remainder.

Richemont is supported by regional and central functions structured around the world to provide specialized support in terms of distribution, finance, legal, IT, and administration.

Geographic Reach

Headquartered in Geneva, Switzerland, Richemont generates about 40% of its sales from the Asia Pacific region, its biggest geography. Europe accounts for nearly 25%, the Americas with more than 20%, the Middle

East and Africa with around 10%, and Japan with roughly 5%. It has over 2,295 monobrand boutiques in around 35 locations.

Sales and Marketing
Richemont generates more than 55% of sales through its retail channel and the rest from its wholesale and royalty income, and online retail channels.

Financial Performance
The company had revenues amounting to £19.2 billion in 2021, a 46% increase from the previous year's revenue of £13.1 billion. The company had higher sales volumes across all of its segments (retail, wholesale and royalty income, and online retail).

In 2021, the company had an operating profit of £3.4 billion, a 129% increase from the previous year's operating profit of £1.5 billion.

The company's cash at the end of 2021 was £4.6 billion. Operating activities generated £4.6 billion, while investing activities used £2.3 billion, mainly for investment in money market and externally managed funds. Financing activities used another £1.8 billion, primarily for dividends paid.

Strategy
To meet stakeholders' evolving expectations, the company's Transformational CSR Strategy ('Strategy') was elaborated by the CSR Committee in collaboration with its Maisons and support functions. The strategy includes the company's commitments over the short, medium and long term. It has grouped these commitments into Foundational, Aspirational and Transformational. Foundational commitments were largely delivered by December 2021, while Aspirational and Transformational commitments are targeted for delivery by December 2022 and 2025, respectively. Together, the Strategy and its commitments represent Richemont's Movement for Better Luxury.

The strategy's four focus areas, people, sourcing, environment and communities, work together towards Better Luxury. The strategy's three transversal issues, governance, engagement and innovation, bind those focus areas together. The company's strategy's four focus areas, people, sourcing, environment and communities, work together towards Better Luxury. The strategy's three transversal issues, governance, engagement and innovation, bind those focus areas together.

Mergers and Acquisitions
In mid-2021, Richemont has acquired 100% of Delvaux, the renowned Belgian luxury leather goods Maison, in a private transaction. Delvaux is the oldest luxury leather goods Maison in the world. It has a unique heritage, expressed through the richness of its archives, and distinguishes itself through its exceptional savoir faire and creativity. Delvaux's leather pieces are crafted by skilled artisans in its workshops across Belgium and France, and mostly sold across a highly qualitative network of 50 boutiques worldwide. Richemont's acquisition will position Delvaux for its next stage of development, by enabling Delvaux to leverage the Group's global presence and digital capabilities, to develop its omnichannel opportunities and customer engagement. Terms were not disclosed.

HISTORY
Anton Rupert started a tobacco company in the late 1940s that eventually became the Rembrandt Group, a tobacco and liquor giant in South Africa with other diverse holdings. To avoid possible antiapartheid sanctions, in 1988 Rupert and his son, Johann, spun off Rembrandt's non-South African holdings.

Those holdings included 33% of UK-based tobacco firm Rothmans International (Benson & Hedges). Rothmans had a controlling stake in Dunhill Holdings (tobacco and accessories), and it had acquired piecemeal a major stake in jeweler Cartier in the 1970s and 1980s. The Rembrandt spin off, based in Zug, Switzerland, and named Compagnie Financière Richemont, went public in 1988.

Richemont increased its stake in Rothmans in 1990 to about 63% by purchasing Philip Morris' shares. The next year Richemont expanded into new areas, buying South African pay-TV station M-Net and, through a joint venture, acquiring 49% of Horn & Hardart (which became Hanover Direct in 1993). Dunhill acquired the Karl Lagerfeld fashion house in 1992.

In part to shelter the company from UK taxes, in 1993 Richemont's assets were split into two publicly traded companies: Rothmans International (tobacco) and Vendôme Luxury Group, which combined Dunhill's fashion holdings and Cartier. (Vendôme is a square in Paris where many expensive Cartier items are sold.) Richemont retained majority interests in both firms.

In 1995 Richemont acquired the shares of Rothmans it didn't already own and merged it with Rembrandt's South African tobacco holdings. Richemont also merged M-Net with two other television companies to form Network Holdings (NetHold) in exchange for a 50% stake in that firm.

The next year Richemont bought Swiss luxury watchmaker Vacheron Constantin, and it sold most of NetHold to French pay-TV operator Canal+ in exchange for 15% of Canal+ (now owned by Vivendi Universal). (It sold that stake in 1999.) The company in 1997 bought French leather goods company Lancel and sold Karl Lagerfeld SA to the designer. Richemont increased its stake in Hanover Direct that year by purchasing the shares of its joint venture it didn't own. It also bought out Vendôme's minority shareholders in 1997, making the company a wholly owned subsidiary.

Richemont exited tobacco in 1999 by merging its tobacco holdings with British American Tobacco (BAT), the world's #2 cigarette company, in exchange for a 35% stake in BAT (including the shares owned by Remgro, formerly Rembrandt). That year Richemont also purchased 60% of Van Cleef & Arpels, a manufacturer and retailer of watches and jewelry with over 40 stores. It wrapped up the year by taking a 20% stake in online jewelry retailer Adornis.com (which shut down in late 2000).

In 2000 Richemont bought Swiss luxury watch dial manufacturer Stern Group and later, Mannesmann AG's Les Manufactures Horlogeres SA luxury watch unit. Beating a host of rivals (including LVMH), Richemont acquired the Jaeger-LeCoultre, IWC, and A. Lange & Söhne luxury watch brands; the purchase positioned the company to control the market for watches costing more than $1,500.

Chloé designer Stella McCartney left the company in 2001 to launch her own label with Gucci. Also in 2001 the company purchased an additional 20% of Van Cleef & Arpels, raising its stake in the company to 80%. Additionally that year Richemont wrote down to zero its investment in catalog marketer Hanover Direct's (Domestications, Silhouettes) common stock.

The company spun off its jointly held 30% stake in BAT in October 2008. The spinoff was timed to coincide with a potentially penalizing change in Luxembourg tax law that would have left Richemont vulnerable to the ebbs and flows in upscale purchasing.

After five years at the helm, CEO Norbert Platt retired at the end of 2009. He cited health concerns as the reason for his retirement.

In June 2010 Richemont completed its acquisition of more than 93% of the shares in Net-A-Porter Limited. NET-A-PORTER operates as an independent entity alongside Richemont's other luxury goods businesses.

EXECUTIVES
Chief Executive Officer, Director, Jerome Lambert
Chief Financial Officer, Director, Burkhart Grund
Secretary, Swen H. Grundmann
Chairman, Director, Johann Rupert
Non-Executive Deputy Chairman, Non-Executive Director, Josua Malherbe
Non-Executive Director, Nikesh Arora
Lead Independent Director, Non-Executive Director, Clay Brendish
Non-Executive Director, Jean-Blaise Eckert
Non-Executive Director, Keyu Jin
Non-Executive Director, Wendy N. Luhabe
Non-Executive Director, Jeff Moss
Non-Executive Director, Vesna Nevistic
Non-Executive Director, Guillaume Pictet
Non-Executive Director, Maria Ramos
Non-Executive Director, Anton Rupert

Non-Executive Director, Patrick Thomas
Non-Executive Director, Jasmine M. Whitbread
Auditors : PricewaterhouseCoopers SA

LOCATIONS

HQ: Compagnie Financiere Richemont SA
50 Chemin de la Chenaie, Geneva, Bellevue 1293
Phone: (41) 22 721 3500   **Fax:** (41) 22 721 3550
Web: www.richemont.com

2018 Sales

	% of total
Asia-Pacific	40
Europe	27
Americas	16
Middle East and Africa	8
Japan	9
Total	100

PRODUCTS/OPERATIONS

2018 Sales

	□ mil	% of total
Jewelry Maisons	6,447	59
Specialist Watchmakers	2,714	25
Other businesses (apparel & leather & accessories)	1,818	17
Total	10,979	100

2018 Sales

	% of total
Retail	63
Wholesale	37
Total	100

2018 Sales

	% of total
Jewelry	41
Watches	40
Leather goods	7
Clothing	4
Writing instruments	4
Other	4
Total	100

Major Brands
A. Lange & Söhne (watches)
Alaia
Alfred Dunhill (menswear and accessories)
Baume & Mercier (watches)
Cartier (jewelry and watches)
Chloé (womenswear, jewelry, fragrances, and accessories)
Dunhill
Giampiero Bodino (jewelry)
IWC (watches)
Jaeger-LeCoultre (watches)
Lancel (leather goods)
Montblanc (writing instruments)
Officine Panerai (watches)
Peter Millar
Piaget (watches)
Purdey (firearms)
Roger Dubuis (watches)
Vacheron Constantin (watches)
Van Cleef & Arpels (jewelry and watches)

COMPETITORS

FRENCH CONNECTION GROUP PLC
KERING
KINGFISHER PLC
Koninklijke Ahold Delhaize N.V.
LAURA ASHLEY HOLDINGS PLC
LEVI STRAUSS & CO.
MUSGRAVE GROUP PUBLIC LIMITED COMPANY
RECKITT BENCKISER GROUP PLC
TIFFANY & CO.
The Swatch Group AG

HISTORICAL FINANCIALS
Company Type: Public

Income Statement   FYE: March 31

	REVENUE ($mil)	NET INCOME ($mil)	NET PROFIT MARGIN	EMPLOYEES
03/23	21,682	340	1.6%	33,959
03/22	21,291	2,302	10.8%	35,853
03/21	15,418	1,526	9.9%	34,760
03/20	15,598	1,022	6.6%	34,728
03/19	15,710	3,129	19.9%	35,640
Annual Growth	8.4%	(42.6%)	—	(1.2%)

2023 Year-End Financials
Debt ratio: 31.3%   No. of shares ($ mil.): 518
Return on equity: 1.6%   Dividends
Cash ($ mil.): 11,883   Yield: 1.3%
Current Ratio: 2.47   Payout: 40.0%
Long-term debt ($ mil.): 6,469   Market value ($ mil.): 8,269

	STOCK PRICE ($) FY Close	P/E High	P/E Low	PER SHARE ($) Earnings	Dividends	Book Value
03/23	15.96	29	18	0.59	0.22	39.76
03/22	12.61	4	3	4.01	0.16	42.68
03/21	9.57	4	2	2.69	0.10	40.60
03/20	5.37	5	3	1.80	0.12	36.60
03/19	7.26	2	1	5.53	0.11	37.14
Annual Growth	21.8%	—	—	(42.9%)	18.6%	1.7%

Compagnie Generale des Etablissements Michelin SCA

EXECUTIVES

Managing Chairman, Florent Menegaux
Chief Financial Officer, Yves Chapot
Manufacturing Executive Vice President, Pierre-Louis Dubourdeau
Research & Development Executive Vice President, Eric Philippe Vinese
Distribution, Services and Solutions, Strategy, Innovation and Partnerships Executive Vice President, Lorraine Frega
Engagement and Brands Executive Vice President, Adeline Challon-Kemoun
Personnel Executive Vice President, People Executive Vice President, Jean-Claude Pats
Urban and Long-Distance Transportation and European Regions Executive Vice President, Benedicte De Bonnechose
Automotive, Motorsports, Experiences and Americas Regions Executive VIce President, Scott Clark
High-Tech Materials Executive Vice President, Maude Portigliatti
Specialties and Africa/India/Middle East, China, East Asia and Australia Regions Executive Vice President, Serge Lafon
Chairman, Non-Independent Director, Barbara Dalibard
Non-Independent Non-Executive Director, Jean-Christophe Laourde
Non-Independent Non-Executive Director, Delphine Roussy
Senior Independent Director, Independent Director, Thierry Le Henaff
Independent Director, Jean-Pierre Duprieu
Independent Director, Aruna Jayanthi
Independent Director, Anne-Sophie De La Bigne
Independent Director, Patrick De La Chevardiere
Independent Director, Monique F. Leroux
Independent Director, Wolf-Henning Scheider
Independent Director, Jean-Michel Severino
Auditors : PricewaterhouseCoopers Audit

LOCATIONS

HQ: Compagnie Generale des Etablissements Michelin SCA
23, place des Carmes-Dechaux, Clermont-Ferrand 63000
Phone: (33) 4 73 32 20 00
Web: www.michelin.com

HISTORICAL FINANCIALS
Company Type: Public

Income Statement   FYE: December 31

	REVENUE ($mil)	NET INCOME ($mil)	NET PROFIT MARGIN	EMPLOYEES
12/22	30,535	2,137	7.0%	132,213
12/21	26,932	2,087	7.7%	124,767
12/20	25,121	775	3.1%	123,642
12/19	27,097	1,965	7.3%	127,187
12/18	25,226	1,920	7.6%	117,393
Annual Growth	4.9%	2.7%	—	3.0%

2022 Year-End Financials
Debt ratio: 19.7%   No. of shares ($ mil.): 714
Return on equity: 12.4%   Dividends
Cash ($ mil.): 2,759   Yield: —
Current Ratio: 1.67   Payout: 20.4%
Long-term debt ($ mil.): 5,025   Market value ($ mil.): 9,919

	STOCK PRICE ($) FY Close	P/E High	P/E Low	PER SHARE ($) Earnings	Dividends	Book Value
12/22	13.89	12	4	2.98	0.61	25.59
12/21	32.79	13	9	2.90	1.01	23.73
12/20	25.72	31	19	1.08	0.45	21.73
12/19	24.45	11	8	2.71	0.83	20.78
12/18	19.60	13	8	2.65	0.83	19.33
Annual Growth	(8.2%)	—	—	3.0%	(7.5%)	7.3%

Compal Electronics Inc

Compal Electronics is one of the world's largest notebook computer manufacturers, counting Dell, Lenovo, and Acer as customers. Compal also makes mobile phone handsets, LCD and 3D TVs, and computer displays as well as a growing list of server computers, tablets, and media players. The Taiwan-based company operates in China, as well as in other countries including Vietnam and India. The US is its biggest single market, accounting for about 40% of sales.

Operations

Compal operates two segments: the Information Technology product segment (over 95% of sales), which is primarily engaged in the development, manufacture and sale of information technology products and mobile communication products; and the Strategy Integrate Product segment (nearly 5%) is primarily engaged in the research, development, manufacture and sale of networking products.

The company gets virtually all of its revenue from its 5C segment.

Geographic Reach

Based in Taiwan, Compal has sites in China, the US, Vietnam, and Brazil, as well as in Poland and India. In terms of sales, US accounts for about 40%, followed by China with nearly 15%.

Financial Performance

Compal's revenue for fiscal 2022 decreased by 13% to NT$1.1 billion compared from the prior year with NT1.2 billion. The decrease was primarily due to lower revenues on IT Products segment offsetting the increase on Strategically Integrated Product segment.

Net income for fiscal 2022 decreased to NT$10.7 billion, a 39% decrease compared to the prior year with NT$17.5 billion.

The company's cash at the end of 2022 was NT$79.7 billion. Operating activities generated NT$58.6 billion, while investing activities used NT$9.9 billion, mainly for acquisition of property, plant and equipment. Financing activities used another NT$49.4 billion, primarily for repayments of long-term borrowings.

Strategy

The company's strategic focuses are: adapt to market changes, respond epidemic situation, strengthen innovative design concepts, maintain the focus on product difference to meet market needs; enhance operational efficiency, to further increase its product competitiveness and push the sales growth rate higher than the market average; improve logistics management and flexibility to shorten delivery times; consolidate material supply to fulfill OEMs' demands; elaborate different market strategies for different product markets; diversified production sites to mitigate geopolitical risk and strengthen cost competitiveness; pay close attention to market trends and evolution in smart devices and develop product concepts suitable for OEM customers and the market; and many more.

Company Background

Established in 1984, Compal has grown to its present scale with outstanding management and solid R&D capacity. To meet client needs from design to manufacturing, Compal manufacture 5C products such as notebook computers, tablets, wearable devices, smart phones. In 2007, Compal established its second offshore manufacturing base in Vietnam, in light of prospective emerging market demand, the company proceeded to set up an NB service center in Poland and another NB manufacturing plant in Brazil. In order to achieve the objective of optimized production capacity and high product quality.

EXECUTIVES

Chairman, Rock Sheng-Hsiun Hsu
Vice-Chairman, Medica John Kevin
President, Chief Executive Officer, Director, Ray Jui-Tsung Chen
Managing Director, Director, Wen-Bin Hsu
Executive Vice President, Director, Wunjhong Shen
Executive Vice President, Director, Yongcing Jhang
Executive Vice President, Director, Zongbin Wong
Senior Vice President, Director, Shaozu Gong
Senior Vice President, Tingjyun Jhou
Senior Vice President, Jyunde Shen
Senior Vice President, Guochuan Chen
Senior Vice President, Peiyuan Chen
Senior Vice President, Ciouruei Wei
Senior Vice President, Ying Jhang
Vice President, Mingjhih Jhang
Vice President, Jhihcyuan Jheng
Vice President, Chief Financial Officer, Gary Lu
Vice President, Mingsing Syu
Vice President, Shihtong Wang
Vice President, Renciou Shao
Vice President, Bosyong Jhang
Vice President, Jinwun Liao
Vice President, Tianming Chen
Vice President, Tianyuan Cai
Vice President, Zihping Liao
Vice President, Jhaosian Jhang
Vice President, Botang Wang
Vice President, Dajyun Wang
Vice President, Mingsong Lin
Vice President, Siguan Chen
Vice President, Dunyi Cai
Vice President, Zongming Wang
Vice President, Fucyuan Jhang
Vice President, Jiouhong Wang
Vice President, Huajhao Chen
Vice President, Jisiang Ma
Vice President, Yongnan Jhang
Vice President, Shengsyong Chen
Director, Pinghe Ciou
Director, Guangnan Lin
Director, Jyongci Syu
Director, Cilin Wei
Auditors : KPMG

LOCATIONS

HQ: Compal Electronics Inc
No. 581 & 581-1, Ruiguang Road, Neihu District, Taipei 11492

Phone: (886) 2 8797 8588 **Fax:** (886) 2 2659 1566
Web: www.compal.com

2017 Sales

	% of total
United States	38
Mainland China	13
Netherlands	11
Germany	4
UK	4
Others	30
Total	100

PRODUCTS/OPERATIONS

2017 Sales

	% of total
IT Product Segment	98
Strategically Integrated Product Segment	2
Total	100

2017 Sales

	% of total
5C Electronic Products	100
Others	-
Total	100

COMPETITORS

CONCURRENT TECHNOLOGIES PLC
DELL TECHNOLOGIES INC.
Diebold Nixdorf AG
INVENTEC CORPORATION
PEGATRON CORPORATION
Quanta Computer Inc.
SIGMA DESIGNS, INC.
SUPER MICRO COMPUTER, INC.
Samsung Electronics Co., Ltd.
ZYTRONIC PLC

HISTORICAL FINANCIALS

Company Type: Public

Income Statement
FYE: December 31

	REVENUE ($mil)	NET INCOME ($mil)	NET PROFIT MARGIN	EMPLOYEES
12/21	44,628	456	1.0%	0
12/20	37,325	333	0.9%	0
12/19	32,748	232	0.7%	0
12/18	31,640	291	0.9%	0
12/17	29,935	193	0.6%	0
Annual Growth	10.5%	23.9%		

2021 Year-End Financials

Debt ratio: 1.0%   No. of shares ($ mil.): 4,407
Return on equity: 11.5%   Dividends
Cash ($ mil.): 2,714   Yield: —
Current Ratio: 1.21   Payout: 237.2%
Long-term debt ($ mil.): 332   Market value ($ mil.): —

Companhia Siderurgica Nacional

EXECUTIVES

Chairman, President, Chief Executive Officer, Benjamin Steinbruch
Chief Investor Relations Officer, Chief Financial Officer, Marcelo Cunha Ribeiro

Executive Officer, David Moise Salama
Executive Officer, Luis Fernando Barbosa Martinez
Executive Officer, Pedro Gutemberg Quariguasi Netto
Director, Fabiam Franklin
Director, Yoshiaki Nakano
Director, Antonio Bernardo Vieira Maia
Director, Miguel Ethel Sobrinho
Auditors : Grant Thornton Auditores Independentes

LOCATIONS

HQ: Companhia Siderurgica Nacional
Av. Brigadeiro Faria Lima 3400, 20Âº andar, SÃ£o Paulo, SP 04538-132
Phone: (55) 11 3049 7454   **Fax:** (55) 11 3049 7212
Web: www.csn.com.br

HISTORICAL FINANCIALS
Company Type: Public

Income Statement — FYE: December 31

	REVENUE ($mil)	NET INCOME ($mil)	NET PROFIT MARGIN	EMPLOYEES
12/21	8,597	2,199	25.6%	24,660
12/20	5,788	730	12.6%	23,196
12/19	6,327	445	7.0%	24,869
12/18	5,918	1,307	22.1%	24,857
12/17	5,591	3	0.1%	25,189
Annual Growth	11.4%	416.1%	—	(0.5%)

2021 Year-End Financials
Debt ratio: 7.3%
Return on equity: 81.1%
Cash ($ mil.): 2,987
Current Ratio: 1.43
Long-term debt ($ mil.): 4,848
No. of shares ($ mil.): 1,341
Dividends
  Yield: 7.8%
  Payout: 20.3%
Market value ($ mil.): 5,957

	STOCK PRICE ($) FY Close	P/E High/Low	PER SHARE ($) Earnings	Dividends	Book Value
12/21	4.44	1 0	1.60	0.35	2.72
12/20	5.95	2 0	0.53	0.07	1.38
12/19	3.45	3 2	0.32	0.23	1.83
12/18	2.19	1 1	0.95	0.17	1.62
12/17	2.45	506 232	0.00	0.00	1.56
Annual Growth	16.0%	—	— 414.3%	—	14.8%

Compania de Distribucion Integral Logista Holdings SA

EXECUTIVES

Chief Executive Officer, Inigo Meiras
Secretary, Director, Rafael de Juan Lopez
Chairman, Gregorio Maranon y Bertran de Lis
Independent Director, Alain Minc
Independent Director, Jaime Carvajal Hoyos
Director, Amal Pramanik
Director, John Michael Jones
Independent Director, Cristina Garmendia Mendizabal
Director, John Matthew Downing
Director, Richard Guy Hathaway
Auditors : Ernst & Young, S.L.

LOCATIONS

HQ: Compania de Distribucion Integral Logista Holdings SA
Calle Trigo 39, Poligono Industrial Polvoranca, Madrid, Leganes 28914
Phone: (34) 91 481 98 00
Web: www.grupologista.com

HISTORICAL FINANCIALS
Company Type: Public

Income Statement — FYE: September 30

	REVENUE ($mil)	NET INCOME ($mil)	NET PROFIT MARGIN	EMPLOYEES
09/22	11,174	193	1.7%	5,533
09/21	12,520	201	1.6%	5,851
09/20	12,363	184	1.5%	5,956
09/19	11,070	179	1.6%	5,980
09/18	10,976	181	1.7%	5,803
Annual Growth	0.4%	1.7%	—	(1.2%)

2022 Year-End Financials
Debt ratio: —
Return on equity: 36.6%
Cash ($ mil.): 213
Current Ratio: 0.90
Long-term debt ($ mil.): —
No. of shares ($ mil.): 131
Dividends
  Yield: —
  Payout: 0.0%
Market value ($ mil.): —

Compass Group PLC

Compass Group is the world's largest contract foodservices provider, with operations in in around 40 countries and manage the business across three geographic regions and five main sectors. It provides hospitality and foodservice for a variety of businesses and such public-sector clients as cultural institutions, hospitals, and schools. The company also provides operations in sporting and leisure venues, exhibit centers, visitor attractions and major events as well as support services to major companies in the oil, gas, mining and construction industries. Its foodservice brands include Chartwells, Medirest, and Levy Restaurants.

Operations

Compass Group trades under some 15 brands. These include Eurest, Restaurant Associates, Flik, Canteen and Bon Appetit (business and industry); medirest, morrison and crothall (healthcare and seniors); Chartwells, Flik and Bon Appetit (education); Levy (sports and leisure); and ESS (defense, offshore, and remote).

Business & Industry accounts for nearly 35% of sales, provides nutritious foods while healthcare and seniors, generates about over 25% of sales provides public and private sectors with quality assurance of food and some support services.

Education (about 20% of sales) provides dining solutions and support in academic fields from kindergarten to college.

Other segment includes Sports & Leisure (about 15% of sales) operates at some sporting and leisure venues, exhibition centres, visitor attractions and major events. Defense, Offshore, and Remote (about 10% of sales) provides food and some support services to major companies in the oil, gas, mining and construction industries.

Geographic Reach

UK-Based Compass Group operates primarily in North America, Europe and other regions worldwide. North America is the company's biggest territory, accounting for over 65% of sales. Europe (generates over 20% of sales. Other countries bring in the remaining some 10% of sales.

Sales and Marketing

Compass Group operates in five sectors: business & industry (nearly 35% of sales), healthcare & seniors (over 25%), education (about 20%), sports & leisure (about 15%), and defense, offshore & remote (less than 10%).

Financial Performance

Compass Group's revenue increased by 42.5% to Â£25.5 billion from Â£17.9 billion the year prior. The company experienced growth across all segments through the year, led by its Healthcare & Senior Living segment which generated Â£6.8 billion that year.

Profit for the year was Â£1.1 billion, representing an over 200% increase from last year's profit of Â£357 million. The growth was primarily due to increases related to revenue for the year.

Cash and equivalents at the end of the year were Â£1.7 billion, a Â£78 million increase from the year prior. Operations provided Â£1.6 billion to the coffers, while investing and financing activities used Â£874 million and Â£693 million, respectively. The company's main cash uses in 2022 were purchases of property, plant, and equipment; purchases of shares; and dividends paid.

Strategy

Compass Group's strategy is to focus on food services and targeted support services, particularly from first-time outsourcing. Its model for creating value remains unchanged based on its three key strategic pillars of People, Performance, and Purpose.

The company has a meaningful purpose, and part of this is providing great food to millions of people across the world. This makes people healthier and happier and helps them perform better. Compass believes that the best people will deliver the best service, enabling it to deliver the best results.

Its approach to sectorisation and sub-sectorisation remains high for its business. Winning in different sectors requires different skills and processes, and increased customization at scale will continue to be a key driver of its success.

EXECUTIVES

Chief Executive Officer, Executive Director, Dominic Blakemore
Chief Financial Officer, Executive Director, Palmer Brown
Group Chief Commercial Officer, Shelley Roberts
Group Chief People Officer, Deborah Lee
North America Chief Operating Officer, Executive Director, Gary Green
Asia Pacific Regional Managing Director, Mark Van Dyck
Latin America Regional Managing Director, James Meaney
UK & Ireland Regional Managing Director, Robin Mills
General Counsel, Secretary, Alison Yapp
Non-Executive Chairman, Paul Steven Walsh
Independent Non-Executive Director, Senior Independent Director, John Bryant
Independent Non-Executive Director, Carol Arrowsmith
Independent Non-Executive Director, Stefan Bomhard
Independent Non-Executive Director, Ian Meakins
Independent Non-Executive Director, Anne-Francoise Nesmes
Independent Non-Executive Director, Nelson Silva
Independent Non-Executive Director, Ireena Vittal
Non-Executive Director, John Bason
Non-Executive Director, Arlene Isaacs-Lowe
Non-Executive Director, Sundar Raman
Auditors : KPMG LLP

LOCATIONS

HQ: Compass Group PLC
  Compass House, Guildford Street, Chertsey, Surrey KT16 9BQ
Phone: (44) 1932 573 000
Web: www.compass-group.com

2018 Sales

	%
North America	59
Europe	25
Rest of the World	16
Total	100

PRODUCTS/OPERATIONS

2018 sales

	%
Business & Industry	39
Healthcare & Seniors	24
Education	18
Sports & Leisure	12
Defence, Offshore, and Remote	7
Total	100

Selected Operating Units

All Leisure (sports and leisure venues)
Bon Appétit Management Company (on-site dining services)
Canteen (vending services)
Chartwells (education foodservices)
Crothall (health care facilities management)
ESS (offshore and remote foodservices)
Eurest (corporate foodservice)
FLIK (upscale foodservices)
Levy Restaurants (fine dining, sports and leisure events)
Medirest (health care services)
Morrison Management Specialists (health care foodservice)
Restaurant Associates Managed Services (corporate dining and sporting and leisure events)
Scolarest (education foodservices)

COMPETITORS

ARAMARK
BELRON INTERNATIONAL LIMITED
CANNAE HOLDINGS, INC.
DARDEN RESTAURANTS, INC.
EMPRESARIA GROUP PLC
MITCHELLS & BUTLERS PLC
ROARK CAPITAL GROUP INC.
SENTINEL CAPITAL PARTNERS, L.L.C.
SODEXO
TTEC HOLDINGS, INC.

HISTORICAL FINANCIALS

Company Type: Public

Income Statement   FYE: September 30

	REVENUE ($mil)	NET INCOME ($mil)	NET PROFIT MARGIN	EMPLOYEES
09/23	38,028	1,610	4.2%	0
09/22	28,158	1,228	4.4%	513,707
09/21	24,081	480	2.0%	478,070
09/20	25,580	170	0.7%	548,143
09/19	30,627	1,366	4.5%	596,452
Annual Growth	5.6%	4.2%		

2023 Year-End Financials

Debt ratio: 23.5%   No. of shares ($ mil.): 1,715
Return on equity: 23.8%   Dividends
Cash ($ mil.): 1,033   Yield: —
Current Ratio: 0.75   Payout: 45.1%
Long-term debt ($ mil.): 2,798   Market value ($ mil.): 41,766

	STOCK PRICE ($) FY Close	P/E High	P/E Low	Earnings	Dividends	Book Value
09/23	24.35	37	29	0.92	0.42	3.67
09/22	19.77	35	26	0.69	0.27	3.68
09/21	20.90	112	71	0.27	0.19	3.68
09/20	15.09	334	152	0.10	0.47	3.44
09/19	25.75	38	27	0.86	0.46	2.58
Annual Growth	(1.4%)	—	—	1.8%	(2.3%)	9.2%

Computacenter Plc

Computacenter is one of the UK's largest technology product distributors. The company provides hardware and software from such leading vendors as Cisco, HPE, Microsoft, NetApp, Samsung, VMware, and Dell Technologies. It sells products to large enterprises and government agencies in the UK, France, Germany, Malaysia, Spain, and South Africa. Computacenter helps its customers to source, transform, and manage their technology infrastructure, to deliver digital transformation, enabling people and their business. Founders and directors Peter Ogden and Sir Philip Hulme remain major shareholders. Computacenter generates most of its revenue from Germany.

Operations

Computacenter has an integrated offering which provides three complementary entry points for its customers.

Technology Sourcing, brings in about 80% of revenue, is the company's traditional core business. It helps customers to determine their technology needs and, supported by the company's technology partners, it provides the commercial structures, integration and supply chain services to meet those needs reliably.

Managed Services generates about 15% of the company's revenue. It maintains, supports, and manages IT infrastructure and operations for its customers, to improve quality and flexibility while reducing costs.

Under the Professional Services, the company provides structured solutions and expert resources to help its customers to select, deploy and integrate digital technology, to achieve their business goals. Professional Services accounts for the remaining revenue.

Geographic Reach

The company is based in the UK and operates nine locations up and down the country. It is also present in eight countries, including Hungary, Poland, Malaysia and South Africa. Germany generates approximately 30% of revenue, followed by the UK and the North America with nearly 30% each, France gives in some 10%, and the rest comes from other countries.

Sales and Marketing

Computacenter serves more than 3.7 million customers. Its target market is the largest 1,000 corporate and government organizations.

Financial Performance

Note: Growth rates may differ after conversion to US Dollars.

The company's revenues increased by 24% to £6.8 billion in 2021.

In 2021, the company had a net income of £248 million, a 20% increase from the previous year's net income of £206.6 million.

The company's cash at the end of 2021 was £273.2 million. Operating activities generated £224.3 million, while investing activities used £25 million, mainly for purchases of property, plant and equipment. Financing activities used another £228.4 million, primarily for repayment of loans and credit facility.

Strategy

Computacenter's strategic priorities are to lead with and grow its services business; improve its services productivity and enhance its competitiveness; retain and maximize the relationship with its customers over the long term; and innovative its services offerings to build future growth opportunities.

Mergers and Acquisitions

In mid-2022, Computacenter acquired one of the fastest-growing value-added resellers in the US, Business IT Source (BITS). BITS employs around 100 people and has headquarters and integration center in Buffalo Grove, Illinois. "Our US business continues to grow organically but we will take additional opportunities to improve our positioning. BITS gives us a much stronger presence in the Midwest of the United States and brings some great people, customers and leadership to our business. The Buffalo Grove Integration Center will allow us to serve more of our Midwest regional customers locally over time, helping us to meet our sustainability goals. I am confident that the BITS leadership will seize the opportunity to continue their current growth momentum." said Mike Norris, Computacenter Group CEO.

HISTORY

Computacenter's story is nothing if not about timing. It began at the dawn of the PC revolution, and blossomed because the company's two founders were already awake. Management consultant Philip Hulme and ex-Morgan Stanley executive Peter Ogden formed Computacenter in 1981. The UK entrepreneurs, who met while seeking MBAs at Harvard University in the early 1970s, started their computer distribution business after perceiving a need among large corporations for computer systems more adaptable than the wall-sized, expensive mainframes then in vogue.

By 1983, thanks mainly to the birth of IBM's PC, Computacenter was generating sales of £1.5 million. The next year Computacenter created a sibling company called Computasoft to specialize in financial-sector applications. By 1984 Computacenter had six branch stores. In 1989 it joined the International Computer Group, a joint venture formed that year to cater to international organizations with global service concerns.

Investcorp, a development capital firm for a consortium of rich Arab investors, bought 30% of Computacenter in 1990. (Investcorp sold its stake in 1995 at a strong profit.) The company continued to ride the corporate networked PC trend and in 1993 logged $526 million in sales and cemented its reputation as the UK's #1 desktop services firm.

Michael Norris, who began at Computacenter as a junior salesman in 1984, was named CEO in 1994. Using his background as one of the company's star sellers, Norris intensified Computacenter's organic growth. The company also reengineered its maintenance business that year. Computacenter suffered a bit of infamy in 1994 after four people were murdered during a robbery on a yacht in the Caribbean. The yacht, named for the company, was owned by Odgen.

In 1995 Computacenter won the largest desktop contract in Europe, signing an agreement with British Telecommunications. That year the company bought French firm Networx SA and made it a majority-owned Computacenter subsidiary. The company in 1996 beefed up its technical acumen to include consulting and major networking support. Sales that year exceeded $1.3 billion.

Sales reached the $1.8 billion mark in 1997, and the company bought German firm BITService and revamped it into a German subsidiary. Computacenter went public in 1998 in the midst of a high-tech stock frenzy that made 30 of its employees millionaires overnight. The already wealthy Hulme and Ogden donated most of their money to individual charitable trusts.

Also in 1998, in a continuing effort to expand its services, Computacenter forged an alliance with Microsoft to supply planning and support services to Windows NT customers. That year the company founded its e-commerce division, iGroup, which develops Internet commerce strategies and provides Web site monitoring and hosting services.

In 1999 Computacenter signed a three-year contract renewal with British Telecommunications (now BT Group) to provide the telecom giant with systems maintenance and e-commerce implementation services. Later that year Computacenter launched Biomni, a 50-50 joint venture with Computasoft (now Dealogic), to develop business-to-business software for electronic trading networks.

Citing reasons of unprofitability, Computacenter discontinued operations in Germany in 2001, selling its German arm to GE Capital IT Solutions. (It acquired GE's IT business units in the UK and France as part of the deal.) The company also closed its UK-based iGroup business that year. Computacenter reentered Germany in 2003 with its acquisition of GE CompuNet; it also acquired GE Capital IT Solutions Austria that year, although it , although in 2005 Computacenter sold its Austrian business to S&T System Integration & Technology Distribution. Also in 2005 it reduced its ownership stake in Biomni to more than 38%. The remainder is owned by Lowkin Limited.

Computacenter acquired Thesaurus Computer Services, a provider of mainframe and data center managed services based in the UK, in 2009. The purchase added new customers and expanded Computacenter's service capabilities for IBM servers, software, storage systems, and mainframes. That year the company also acquired Germany-based becom Informationssysteme, a distributor of large IBM systems.

EXECUTIVES

Chief Executive Officer, Executive Director,
Mike J. Norris
Financial Director, Executive Director, F. Anthony Conophy
Secretary, Simon Pereira
Independent Non-Executive Chairman,
Independent Non-Executive Director, Peter Ryan
Senior Independent Non-Executive Director, Ros Rivaz
Independent Non-Executive Director, Ljiljana Mitic
Independent Non-Executive Director, Rene Haas
Independent Non-Executive Director, Pauline Campbell
Non-Executive Director, Philip Hulme
Non-Executive Director, Peter Ogden
Auditors : KPMG LLP

LOCATIONS

HQ: Computacenter Plc
 Hatfield Avenue, Hatfield, Hertfordshire AL10 9TW
Phone: (44) 1707 631000
Web: www.computacenter.com

2015 Sales

	% of total
UK	46
Germany	39
France	13
Belgium	2
Total	100

PRODUCTS/OPERATIONS

2015 Sales by Business Type

	% of total
Data center & networking	26
Contractual services	24
Workplace	22
Software	11
Third-party services	9
Professional services	8
Total	100

2015 Sales

	% of total
Supply chain revenue	67
Services	
Managed services	24
Professional services	9
Total	100

Selected Services

Consulting and integration
 Integration
 Project management
Managed and support services
 Data centers
 Desktop
 Disaster recovery
 Help desk
 Networks
Supply chain services
 Configuration and deployment
 Consulting
 Procurement
 Software license management
 Technology disposal

COMPETITORS

CAPITA PLC
CERIDIAN LLC
CGI Inc
COMPUCOM SYSTEMS, INC.
COMPUTER TASK GROUP, INCORPORATED
HAYS PLC
IGATE CORP.
INFOSYS LIMITED
SUMTOTAL SYSTEMS LLC
WIPRO LIMITED

HISTORICAL FINANCIALS
Company Type: Public

Income Statement FYE: December 31

	REVENUE ($mil)	NET INCOME ($mil)	NET PROFIT MARGIN	EMPLOYEES
12/21	9,064	249	2.8%	17,992
12/20	7,425	209	2.8%	16,764
12/19	6,672	134	2.0%	15,816
12/18	5,557	103	1.9%	15,117
12/17	5,123	109	2.1%	14,026
Annual Growth	15.3%	22.8%	—	6.4%

2021 Year-End Financials
Debt ratio: 2.2%   No. of shares ($ mil.): 114
Return on equity: 27.0% Dividends
Cash ($ mil.): 384   Yield: —
Current Ratio: 1.21   Payout: 41.2%
Long-term debt ($ mil.): 22 Market value ($ mil.): —

Constellium SE (France)

Constellium (borne out of Rio Tinto Alcan's Engineered Products division) makes specialty rolled and extruded aluminum products, from tin cans for food to the metal frames for automobiles and airplanes. Constellium's proprietary materials include Surfalex, an alloy developed for auto bodies, and AIRWARE, a lightweight, specialty aluminum-lithium alloy for aerospace applications. While headquartered in the Netherlands for tax purposes, Constellium has more than 25 manufacturing plants in China, Czech Republic, France, Germany, Slovakia, Switzerland, and the US. Most of its business is in Europe. The company went public in the US in 2013.

IPO
Constellium plans to use the proceeds from its $333 million IPO for general corporate purposes, such as working capital, paying down debt, and possibly making an acquisition.

Operations
Constellium operates through three segments: Packaging and Automotive Rolled Products (43% of sales in 2012), Aerospace and Transportation (33% of sales), and Automotive Structures and Industry (24% of sales). For its Packaging and Automotive Rolled Products, the company is the top supplier of aluminum cans (for beer, carbonated beverages, and canned food) in Europe. Automotive rolled products include the structural framework for cars and heat exchangers. Customers for its packaging products include Amcor, Ball, and Crown Holdings, while automotive customers include Audi, BMW, Daimler, Peugeot, and ThyssenKrupp.

The Aerospace and Transportation segment makes highly customized aluminum plates, sheets, and extruded products (such as landing gear) for the aerospace and defense industry. Customers in this segment include Airbus, Boeing, Bombardier, Dassault, Embraer, and Lockheed Martin.

The Automotive Structures and Industry segment makes aluminum bumpers, dashboard frames, and other parts for the auto industry, as well as extruded parts for building, energy, rail, and other industrial applications. Customers in this segment include major automakers as well as industrial manufacturers such as Alstom, Ansaldo, Bosch, and Siemens.

Geographic Reach
Constellium has more than 25 manufacturing plants in China, Czech Republic, France, Germany, Slovakia, Switzerland, and the US. Europe is its largest market in terms of revenue, accounting for more than three-quarters of sales in 2012, but its products are sold in more than 60 countries.

Sales and Marketing
Constellium sells its products either directly or through distributors; it has sales offices in 10 countries in Asia, Europe, and the US. Its 10 largest customers account for more than 40% of revenues.

Financial Performance
Overall sales grew 2% in 2012, despite lower prices per pound for aluminum. That year the company shipped more than 1,033 kilo tons by volume of aluminum products, down from 1,058 kilo tons in 2011. 2012 was also the first year without the Alcan International Network business segment. Constellium sold the specialty chemicals and raw materials supply chain services division to Sweden-based CellMark.

Strategy
The company's strategy involves including making investments in higher-margin product categories, such as its building a state-of-the-art plant to make AIRWARE for aerospace customers. These higher-margin products are designed specifically for certain customers; they're not off-the-shelf materials that can be purchased from a competitor.

Constellium is also looking expand in China. Currently the company's two plants in China are joint ventures with Engley Auto Parts.

EXECUTIVES

Chief Executive Officer, Executive Director, Jean-Marc Germain
Manufacturing Excellence Chief Technical Officer, Manufacturing Excellence Senior Vice President, Jack Clark
Chief Human Resources Officer, Senior Vice President, Philip Ryan Jurkovic
Chief Financial Officer, Executive Vice President, Peter R. Matt
Aerospace and Transportation business unit President, Ingrid Joerg
Packaging and Automotive Rolled Products business unit President, Strategy, Business Development, Research & Development President, Peter Basten
Automotive Structures and Industry business unit President, Philippe Hoffmann
Sustainability Senior Vice President, Public Affairs Senior Vice President, Communications Senior Vice President, Nicolas Brun
Senior Vice President, General Counsel, Secretary, Jeremy Leach
Chairman, Independent Non-Executive Director, Richard B. Evans
Independent Non-Executive Director, Guy Maugis
Independent Non-Executive Director, Werner P. Paschke
Independent Non-Executive DIrector, Michiel Brandjes
Independent Non-Executive Director, Peter F. Hartman
Independent Non-Executive Director, John Ormerod
Independent Non-Executive Director, Lori A. Walker
Independent Non-Executive Director, Martha Finn Brooks
Independent Non-Executive Director, Stephanie Frachet
Auditors : PricewaterhouseCoopers Audit

LOCATIONS
HQ: Constellium SE (France)
   Washington Plaza, 40-44 rue Washington, Paris 75008
Phone: (33) 1 73 01 46 00
Web: www.constellium.com

COMPETITORS
ARD Holdings S.A.
BARNES GROUP INC.
Chicago Bridge & Iron Company N.V.
Frank's International N.V.
HES Beheer B.V.
KAISER ALUMINUM CORPORATION
Koninklijke Nedschroef Holding B.V.
LyondellBasell Industries N.V.
STANDEX INTERNATIONAL CORPORATION
Unilever N.V.

HISTORICAL FINANCIALS
Company Type: Public

Income Statement FYE: December 31

	REVENUE ($mil)	NET INCOME ($mil)	NET PROFIT MARGIN	EMPLOYEES
12/22	8,672	321	3.7%	12,500
12/21	6,963	290	4.2%	12,000
12/20	5,992	(25)	—	12,000
12/19	6,632	66	1.0%	13,200
12/18	6,511	215	3.3%	13,000
Annual Growth	7.4%	10.5%	—	(1.0%)

2022 Year-End Financials
Debt ratio: 40.8%   No. of shares ($ mil.): 144
Return on equity: 59.9% Dividends
Cash ($ mil.): 177   Yield: —
Current Ratio: 1.21   Payout: 0.0%
Long-term debt ($ mil.): 1,858 Market value ($ mil.): —

Continental AG (Germany, Fed. Rep.)

Continental offers safe, efficient, intelligent and affordable solutions for vehicles, machines, traffic and transportation. It is divided into four group sectors: Automotive, Tires, ContiTech, and Contract Manufacturing. These comprise a total of 17 business areas. Customers outside Germany generate some 80% of company's total revenue. The Continental-Caoutchouc-und Gutta-Percha Compagnie is founded in Hanover in 1871 as a joint stock company. The company offers its products to automotive original-equipment businesses and industrial businesses.

Operations

Continental operates through four segments: Automotive; Tires; ContiTech, and Contract Manufacturing.

Automotive segment is the largest segment accounting for more than 40%, offers technologies for passive-safety, brake, chassis, motion and motion-control systems.

Tires segment is the largest segment accounting for about 25% and offers digital tire monitoring and tire management systems. With its premium portfolio in the car, truck, bus, two-wheel and specialty tire segment, tires stand for innovative solutions in tire technology.

ContiTech (more than 10%) develops and manufactures cross-materials, environmentally friendly and intelligent products and systems for the automotive industry, railway engineering, mining, agriculture and other key industries.

Contract Manufacturing (less than 5%) is the contract manufacturing of products by Continental companies for Vitesco Technologies.

Geographic ReachWith roughly 520 locations in about 60 countries, Continental does half of its business in Europe (about 20% in Germany), while the other half is divided between North America and Asia. Continental is headquartered in Hanover, Germany.

Sales and Marketing

With about 60% total revenue, automotive manufacturers are Continental's most important customer group. In the tires segment, sales to dealers and end users represent the largest share of the tire-replacement business. In the ContiTech business area, important customers come from both the automotive industry and other key industries such as railway engineering, machine and plant construction, mining and the replacement business. Vistesco Technologies constitutes the sole customers.

Financial Performance

Consolidated net sales increased by 16% to EUR 39.4 billion in 2022 compared to EUR 33.8 billion. However, 2022's net income decreased to EUR 66.6 million, as compared to the prior year's net income of $1.4 billion.

The company's cash at the end of 2022 was EUR 3 billion. Operating activities generated EUR 2.3 billion. Investing activities used EUR 2.2 billion, while financing activities provided EUR 90.6 million. Main cash uses were for capital expenditures on property, plant and equipment, and software, as well as cash flow from continuing operations.

Strategy

In 2022, the company systematically realigned its entire organizational structure and its management processes. The company's strategy is based on three cornerstones: Strengthening operational performance; Differentiating the portfolio; and Turning change into opportunity.

Mergers and Acquisitions

In late 2022, Continental acquired Backes Transportbandservice AB. The company from Växjö is a leading service provider for the material handling industry in the southeast of Sweden. The acquisition is another step to further strengthen Continental's industrial business in the region.

Also in late 2022, Continental acquired the conveyor and maintenance company Vulk & Montage, based in Karlstad, Sweden. This acquisition complements the portfolio of Continental and establishes the technology company in the heart of Sweden's industrial area.

In 2022, Continental acquired family-owned belting manufacturer WCCO Belting headquartered in Wahpeton, North Dakota, USA. With this acquisition, the technology company complements its conveyor belting customer portfolio and strengthens its Conveying Solutions business in the agricultural industry. Additionally, equipment manufacturers, distributors, dealers, and farmers will benefit from a combined product and service portfolio generating a full multi-tier offering that will enable better support and service.

HISTORY

A group of financiers and industrialists with interests in the rubber industry founded Continental-Caoutchouc und Gutta-Percha Compagnie in Hanover, Germany, in 1871. The company's products included solid tires for carriages and bicycles, rubberized fabrics, and various consumer items.

In 1892 Continental was the first German maker of pneumatic bicycle tires. During this period the budding automobile and motorcycle industries created fresh demand for solid tires. Continental began producing pneumatic tires for automobiles in 1898. By 1904 Continental was first to develop a treaded tire. Between 1905 and 1913 Continental expanded into Australia, Denmark, Italy, Norway, Romania, Sweden, and the UK by forming marketing subsidiaries. However, the onset of WWI caused a shift to military production and the overseas sales network dissolved.

Poor overall economic conditions atrophied postwar tire industry growth, and by the late 1920s the company merged several German rubber firms to create a much larger and stronger Continental. In 1929 the company changed its name to Continental Gummi-Werke AG.

EXECUTIVES

Chairman, Nikolai Setzer
Information Technology Executive Director, Finance and Controlling Executive Director, Katja Durrfeld
Tires Group Sector Executive Director, Christian Kotz
ContiTech Executive Director, Philip Nelles
Human Resources Executive Director, Ariane Reinhart
Chairman, Wolfgang Reitzle
Vice-Chairman, Christiane Benner
Director, Hasan Allak
Director, Stefan E. Buchner
Director, Gunter Dunkel
Director, Francesco Grioli
Director, Michael Iglhaut
Director, Satish Khatu
Director, Isabel Corinna Knauf
Director, Carmen Loffler
Director, Sabine Neuss
Director, Rolf Nonnenmacher
Director, Dirk Nordmann
Director, Lorenz Pfau
Director, Klaus Rosenfeld
Director, George F.W. Schaeffler
Director, Maria-Elisabeth Schaeffler
Director, Joerg Schoenfelder
Director, Stefan Scholz
Director, Elke Volkmann
Director, Siegfried Wolf
Auditors : PricewaterhouseCoopers GmbH Wirtschaftsprüfungsgesellschaft

LOCATIONS

HQ: Continental AG (Germany, Fed. Rep.)
Vahrenwalder Strasse 9, Hanover D-30165
Phone: (49) 511 938 01 **Fax:** (49) 511 938 81 770
Web: www.continental.com

2017 Sales

	% of total
Europe	
Germany	20
Europe excluding Germany	29
North America	25
Asia	22
Other cegions	4
Total	100

PRODUCTS/OPERATIONS

2017 Sales

	% of total
Automotive Group	
Chassis & safety	22
Interior	21
Powertrain	17
Rubber Group	
Tires (passenger & light truck)	26
ContiTech	14
Total	**100**

Selected Automotive Group Products
Chassis and Safety
    Chassis components
    Electronic brake systems
    Hydraulic brake systems
    Passive safety and ADAS
    Sensors
Interior
    Body and security
    Commercial vehicles and aftermarket
    Connectivity
    Instrumentation and displays
    Interior modules
    Multimedia
Powertrain
    Engine systems
    Fuel supply
    Hybrid electric vehicle
    Sensors and actuators
    Transmissions

Selected Rubber Group Products
ContiTech
    Air spring systems
    Benecke-Kaliko group
    Conveyor belt group
    Elastomer coatings
    Fluid technology
    Power transmission group
    Vibration control
Tires
    Commercial vehicles
    Off-road vehicles
    Passenger and light truck
    Motorcycles
    Bicycles

COMPETITORS

BRIDGESTONE CORPORATION
DANA INCORPORATED
DENSO CORPORATION
GKN LIMITED
HUSCO INTERNATIONAL, INC.
NHK SPRING CO., LTD.
Robert Bosch Gesellschaft mit beschränkter Haftung
STRATTEC SECURITY CORPORATION
TENNECO INC.
TOYOTA BOSHOKU CORPORATION

HISTORICAL FINANCIALS
Company Type: Public

Income Statement   FYE: December 31

	REVENUE ($mil)	NET INCOME ($mil)	NET PROFIT MARGIN	EMPLOYEES
12/22	42,090	71	0.2%	199,038
12/21	38,217	1,646	4.3%	190,875
12/20	46,296	(1,180)	—	236,386
12/19	49,938	(1,375)	—	241,458
12/18	50,851	3,317	6.5%	243,226
Annual Growth	(4.6%)	(61.7%)	—	(4.9%)

2022 Year-End Financials
Debt ratio: 19.0%
Return on equity: 0.5%
Cash ($ mil.): 3,191
Current Ratio: 1.14
Long-term debt ($ mil.): 3,252
No. of shares ($ mil.): 200
Dividends
  Yield: —
  Payout: 46.5%
Market value ($ mil.): 1,194

	STOCK PRICE ($) FY Close	P/E High/Low		PER SHARE ($) Earnings	Dividends	Book Value
12/22	5.97	32	15	0.35	0.16	70.80
12/21	10.54	2	1	8.24	2.49	68.99
12/20	14.96	—	—	(5.90)	0.24	75.25
12/19	12.83	—	—	(6.88)	0.37	86.42
12/18	13.78	4	1	16.59	0.39	102.21
Annual Growth	(18.9%)	—		(61.8%)	(19.3%)	(8.8%)

Corporacion Nacional del Cobre de Chile

Codelco is a different kind of high-energy copper top. State-owned Corporación Nacional del Cobre de Chile (Codelco) is one of the world's top producers of copper, its reserves represents around 5% of global copper reserves. Its core business is exploring, developing and exploiting mineral resources, processing them to produce refined copper and by-products, and then marketing them to customers around the world. The company operates through seven mining divisions: Chuquicamata, Ministro Hales, Radomiro Tomic, Gabriela Mistral, Salvador, Andina, El Teniente, as well as the Ventanas Smelter and Refinery. It produces and markets refined products such as copper cathodes with 99.9% purity, which are obtained in its electrorefining and electrowinning processes, unrefined products including copper concentrates, roasted copper concentrates, anodes and blister (metallic material with a purity of around 99.5%, which is used as raw material for the production of copper cathodes), and by-products which includes molybdenum, its main by-product, a key input in the manufacture of special steels; sulfuric acid, which has the property of dissolving various types of metals and substances; gold, silver and rhenium.

EXECUTIVES

Chairman, Gerardo Jofre Miranda
Director, Fernando Porcile Valenzuela
Director, Marcos Lima Aravena
Director, Marcos Buchi Buc
Director, Jorge Bande Bruck
Director, Juan Luis Ossa Bulnes
Director, Andres Tagle Dominguez
Director, Raimundo Espinoza Concha
Director, Jaime Gutierrez Castillo
Auditors: PricewaterhouseCoopers

LOCATIONS

HQ: Corporacion Nacional del Cobre de Chile
Huerfanos 1270, Santiago
Phone: (56) 2 690 3000   **Fax:** (56) 2 690 3288

Web: www.codelco.com

PRODUCTS/OPERATIONS

2015 Sales

	% of total
El Teniente	21
Chuquicamata	18
R. Tomic	14
M. Hales	14
Andina	9
G. Mistral	6
Ventanas	5
Salvador	4
Other	9
Total	**100**

2015 Sales

	% of total
Asia	
China	25
Other	18
America	16
Europe	12
Other	29
Total	**100**

COMPETITORS

ASARCO LLC
FREEPORT-MCMORAN INC.
First Quantum Minerals Ltd
Inmet Mining Corporation
Lundin Mining Corporation
MONTERRICO METALS LIMITED
Nexa Resources
Southern Perú Copper Corporation Sucursal del Perú
THOMPSON CREEK METALS COMPANY USA
Vale S/A

HISTORICAL FINANCIALS
Company Type: Public

Income Statement   FYE: December 31

	REVENUE ($mil)	NET INCOME ($mil)	NET PROFIT MARGIN	EMPLOYEES
12/22	17,018	345	2.0%	0
12/21	21,024	1,942	9.2%	0
12/20	14,173	242	1.7%	15,267
12/19	12,524	6	0.1%	16,726
12/18	14,308	155	1.1%	18,036
Annual Growth	4.4%	22.1%		

2022 Year-End Financials
Debt ratio: 37.3%
Return on equity: 3.2%
Cash ($ mil.): 1,026
Current Ratio: 1.73
Long-term debt ($ mil.): 16,689
No. of shares ($ mil.): —
Dividends
  Yield: —
  Payout: 0.0%
Market value ($ mil.): —

Cosmo Energy Holdings Co Ltd

EXECUTIVES

President, Representative Director, Hiroshi Kiriyama
Senior Managing Executive Officer, Representative Director, Takayuki Uematsu
Chief Development Officer, Noriko Rzonca
Director, Shigeru Yamada
Director, Junko Takeda

Outside Director, Ryuko Inoue
Outside Director, Takuya Kurita
Outside Director, Yasuko Takayama
Outside Director, Keiichi Asai
Director, Toshiyuki Mizui
Auditors : KPMG AZSA LLC

LOCATIONS

HQ: Cosmo Energy Holdings Co Ltd
  1-1-1 Shibaura, Minato-ku, Tokyo 105-8302
Phone: (81) 3 3798 9338   **Fax:** (81) 3 3798 3841
Web: ceh.cosmo-oil.co.jp

HISTORICAL FINANCIALS
Company Type: Public

Income Statement — FYE: March 31

	REVENUE ($mil)	NET INCOME ($mil)	NET PROFIT MARGIN	EMPLOYEES
03/22	20,063	1,141	5.7%	10,322
03/21	20,169	775	3.8%	10,390
03/20	25,223	(259)	—	10,155
03/19	25,015	479	1.9%	9,700
03/18	23,760	685	2.9%	9,842
Annual Growth	(4.1%)	13.6%	—	1.2%

2022 Year-End Financials
Debt ratio: 0.2%
Return on equity: 35.5%
Cash ($ mil.): 660
Current Ratio: 0.91
Long-term debt ($ mil.): 2,021
No. of shares ($ mil.): 84
Dividends
  Yield: —
  Payout: 7.1%
Market value ($ mil.): 1,907

	STOCK PRICE ($) FY Close	P/E High/Low		PER SHARE ($) Earnings	Dividends	Book Value
03/22	22.50	—	—	11.42	0.82	44.24
03/21	22.50	0	0	7.78	0.72	34.62
Annual Growth	0.0%	—	—	10.1%	3.3%	6.3%

Covestro AG

EXECUTIVES

Chief Executive Officer, Markus Steilemann
Chief Commercial Officer, Sucheta Govil
Chief Technology Officer, Klaus O. Schafer
Labor Chief Financial Officer, Labor Director, Thomas Toepfer
Independent Chairman, Richard Pott
Vice-Chairman, Petra Kronen
Independent Director, Christine Bortenlanger
Independent Director, Lise Kingo
Independent Director, Rolf Nonnenmacher
Independent Director, Regine Stachelhaus
Independent Director, Patrick W. Thomas
Director, Irena Kustner
Director, Ulrich Liman
Director, Petra Reinbold-Knape
Director, Marc Stothfang
Director, Frank Werth
Auditors : KPMG AG

LOCATIONS

HQ: Covestro AG
  Kaiser-Wilhelm-Allee 60, Leverkusen 51373
Phone: (49) 214 6009 2000   **Fax:** (49) 214 6009 3000
Web: www.covestro.com

HISTORICAL FINANCIALS
Company Type: Public

Income Statement — FYE: December 31

	REVENUE ($mil)	NET INCOME ($mil)	NET PROFIT MARGIN	EMPLOYEES
12/22	19,190	(290)	—	17,985
12/21	18,000	1,829	10.2%	17,909
12/20	13,139	563	4.3%	16,501
12/19	13,935	619	4.4%	17,201
12/18	16,738	2,087	12.5%	16,770
Annual Growth	3.5%	—	—	1.8%

2022 Year-End Financials
Debt ratio: 21.3%
Return on equity: (-3.6%)
Cash ($ mil.): 1,279
Current Ratio: 2.18
Long-term debt ($ mil.): 3,108
No. of shares ($ mil.): 189
Dividends
  Yield: —
  Payout: 0.0%
Market value ($ mil.): 3,694

	STOCK PRICE ($) FY Close	P/E High/Low		PER SHARE ($) Earnings	Dividends	Book Value
12/22	19.45	—	—	(1.52)	1.30	39.84
12/21	30.90	4	3	9.47	1.05	45.09
12/20	30.65	13	6	3.04	0.50	35.63
12/19	22.77	10	7	3.39	0.98	31.97
12/18	25.00	6	3	10.83	0.98	33.48
Annual Growth	(6.1%)	—	—	—	7.3%	4.4%

CrediCorp Ltd.

EXECUTIVES

Chairman, Executive Chairman, Director, Luis Enrique Romero Belismelis
Chief Executive Officer, Walter Bayly
Deputy Chief Executive, Gianfranco Ferrari
Deputy Chief Executive, Alvaro Correa
Chief Risk Officer, Reynaldo Llosa
Chief Financial Officer, Cesar Rios
Chief Corporate Audit Officer, Jose Esposito
Chief Compliance and Ethics Officer, Barbara Falero
Chief Human Resources Officer, Bernardo Sambra
Deputy Secretary, Miriam Bottger
Vice-Chairman, Raimundo Morales Dasso
Independent Director, Patricia Lizarraga Guthertz
Independent Director, Irzio Pinasco Menchelli
Independent Director, Antonio Abruna Puyol
Independent Director, Alexandre Gouvea
Independent Director, Maite Aranzabal Harreguy
Director, Fernando Fort Marie
Director, Leslie Pierce Diez Canseco
Auditors : Gaveglio, Aparicio y Asociados S.C.R.L.

LOCATIONS

HQ: CrediCorp Ltd.
  Calle Centenario 156, La Molina, Lima 12
Phone: (51) 1 313 2014   **Fax:** (51) 1 313 2121
Web: www.grupocredicorp.com

HISTORICAL FINANCIALS
Company Type: Public

Income Statement — FYE: December 31

	ASSETS ($mil)	NET INCOME ($mil)	INCOME AS % OF ASSETS	EMPLOYEES
12/22	62,340	1,219	2.0%	36,968
12/21	61,348	898	1.5%	36,358
12/20	65,582	95	0.1%	36,806
12/19	56,649	1,286	2.3%	35,828
12/18	52,450	1,178	2.2%	34,024
Annual Growth	4.4%	0.9%	—	2.1%

2022 Year-End Financials
Return on assets: 1.9%
Return on equity: 16.7%
Long-term debt ($ mil.): —
No. of shares ($ mil.): 79
Sales ($ mil.): 6,054
Dividends
  Yield: —
  Payout: 25.8%
Market value ($ mil.): —

Credit Agricole SA

EXECUTIVES

Chief Executive Officer, Executive Director, Philippe Brassac
Deputy Chief Executive Officer, Executive Director, Xavier Musca
Chief Financial Officer, Jerome Grivet
Chief Risk Officer, Alexandra Boleslawski
Innovation, Digital Transformation and IT Group Head, Jean-Paul Mazoyer
Insurance Head, Philippe Dumont
Development, Client and Human Head, Michel Ganzin
Retail Banking Subsidiaries Head, Michel Mathieu
Savings Management and Property Head, Yves Perrier
Specialised Financial Services Head, Stephane Priami
Major Clients Head, Jacques Ripoll
Compliance Head, Martine Boutinet
Human Resources Head, Benedicte Chretien
Internal Audit Head, Michel Le Masson
Group for Italy Head, Giampiero Maioli
Corporate Secretary, Veronique Faujour
Chairman, Dominique Lefebvre
Deputy Chairman, Raphael Appert
Independent Director, Caroline Catoire
Independent Director, Marie-Claire Daveu
Independent Director, Laurence Dors
Independent Director, Francoise Gri
Independent Director, Monica Mondardini
Independent Director, Catherine Pourre
Director, Pascale Berger
Director, Pierre Cambefort
Director, Daniel Epron
Director, Jean-Pierre Gaillard
Director, Nicole Gourmelon

Director, Jean-Paul Kerrien
Director, Christiane Lambert
Director, Pascal Lheureux
Director, Gerard Ouvrier-Buffet
Director, Louis Tercinier
Director, Philippe de Waal
Director, Francois Heyman
Director, Simone Vedie
Director, Agnes Audier
Auditors : ERNST & YOUNG et Autres

LOCATIONS
HQ: Credit Agricole SA
12 place des Etats-Unis, Montrouge, Cedex 92127
Phone: (33) 1 43 23 52 02
Web: www.credit-agricole.com

HISTORICAL FINANCIALS
Company Type: Public

Income Statement — FYE: December 31

	ASSETS ($mil)	NET INCOME ($mil)	INCOME AS % OF ASSETS	EMPLOYEES
12/22	2,315,120	5,806	0.3%	71,652
12/21	2,347,430	6,614	0.3%	75,975
12/20	2,721,530	5,754	0.2%	142,159
12/19	1,984,650	5,438	0.3%	75,423
12/18	1,860,250	5,038	0.3%	73,346
Annual Growth	5.6%	3.6%		(0.6%)

2022 Year-End Financials
Return on assets: 0.2%
Return on equity: 8.1%
Long-term debt ($ mil.): —
No. of shares ($ mil.): 3,006
Sales ($ mil.): 88,725
Dividends
Yield: 0.1%
Payout: 31.2%
Market value ($ mil.): 15,696

	STOCK PRICE ($) FY Close	P/E High/Low	PER SHARE ($) Earnings	Dividends	Book Value
12/22	5.22	4 3	1.80	0.56	22.96
12/21	7.08	4 3	2.08	0.48	25.52
12/20	6.24	— —	0.00	0.98	50.31
12/19	7.23	5 3	1.66	0.39	24.49
12/18	5.33	6 4	1.59	0.37	23.53
Annual Growth	(0.5%)	— —	3.1%	11.1%	(0.6%)

CRH Plc

CRH manufactures and supplies a diverse range of integrated building materials, products and innovative end-to-end solutions, which can be found throughout the built environment, from major public infrastructure projects to commercial buildings and residential homes. CRH has over 3,160 operating locations and a presence in around 30 countries, CRH has become the top supplier of building materials in North America and the largest heavyside materials business in Europe. The largest Irish company, CRH was formed in 1970 and has grown quickly in recent years thanks to a relentless acquisition program. The majority of its revenue comes from outside of Ireland.

Operations

CRH operates in three operating segments: Americas materials (around 45% of revenue), Europe materials (amore than 30%), and Building products (around 25%).

Americas Materials segment provide solutions for the construction and RMI of public infrastructure, homes and commercial buildings across North America. Its businesses in the US and Canada utilize an extensive network of reserve backed quarry locations, to provide asphalt paving services and to produce and supply a range of materials including cement, aggregates, ready mixed concrete and asphalt.

Europe Materials segment provides solutions for the construction of public infrastructure, homes and commercial buildings to customers in construction markets across some 20 countries in Europe and two countries in Asia. An extensive network of quarry and production locations adjacent to attractive local construction markets produce cement, lime, aggregates, asphalt, ready mixed concrete and concrete products, as well as providing paving and construction services.

Building products segment includes businesses operating across a portfolio of building product related platforms including architectural products, infrastructure products, and construction accessories. Its businesses offer a diverse range of products including brickwork supports that keep walls standing, glazing systems that hold glass in place, products that collect, connect and protect vital utility infrastructure and pavers, blocks and patio products used to pave our city centres and create unique outdoor living spaces.

Geographic Reach

Ireland-based CRH operates in about 30 countries, on four continents. The US accounts for about 60% of its revenue, while the UK for some 15%, and less than 5% of its revenue from its home country, Ireland.

Sales and Marketing

CRH markets its products to infrastructure (about 40% of total revenue), residential (some 35%), and non-residential (about 25%) demand for repair, maintenance and new build construction projects.

Financial Performance

The company reported a total revenue of $32.7 billion in 2022, a 12% increase from the previous year's total revenue of $29.2 billion. This was primarily due to the higher volume of sales in the company's Americas Materials and Building Products segments.

In 2022, the company had a net income of $3.9 billion, a 48% increase from the previous year's net income of $2.6 billion.

The company's cash at the end of 2022 was $5.9 billion. Operating activities generated $4 billion, while investing activities used $884 million, mainly for acquisition of subsidiaries. Financing activities used another $2.7 billion, primarily for treasury shares/own shares purchased.

Mergers and Acquisitions

In 2022, CRH has reached an agreement with TorQuest Partners and Caisse de dépôt et placement du Québec (CDPQ) to acquire Barrette Outdoor Living, Inc. (Barrette), North America's leading provider of residential fencing and railing solutions for an enterprise value of $1.9 billion. The transaction follows the recent divestment of CRH's Building Envelope business and demonstrates the continued execution of the group's strategy to create shareholder value through active portfolio management and the efficient allocation and reallocation of capital.

Company Background

The Group resulted from the merger in 1970 of two leading Irish public companies, Cement Limited (established in 1936) and Roadstone Limited (incorporated in 1949). Cement Limited manufactured and supplied cement while Roadstone Limited was primarily involved in the manufacture and supply of aggregates, readymixed concrete, mortar, coated macadam, asphalt and contract surfacing to the Irish construction industry.

EXECUTIVES

Chief Executive Officer, Executive Director, Albert Manifold
Group Finance Director, Executive Director, Senan Murphy
Secretary, N. Colgan
Chairman, Non-Executive Director, Richard Boucher
Senior Independent Director, Gillian L. Platt
Non-Executive Director, Richard H. Fearon
Non-Executive Director, Johan Karlstrom
Non-Executive Director, Shaun Kelly
Non-Executive Director, Lamar McKay
Non-Executive Director, Heather Ann McSharry
Non-Executive Director, Mary K. Rhinehart
Non-Executive Director, Lucinda J. Riches
Non-Executive Director, Siobhan Talbot
Auditors : Deloitte Ireland LLP

LOCATIONS
HQ: CRH Plc
Stonemason's Way, Rathfarnham, Dublin D16 KH51
Phone: (353) 1 404 1000   **Fax:** (353) 1 404 1007
Web: www.crh.com

2018 sales

	%
United States	45
Rest of Europe	25
UK	12
Benelux	9
Ireland	2
Rest of the World	7
Total	100

CSL Ltd

CSL is a leading global biotechnology company with a dynamic portfolio of life-saving medicines, including those that treat hemophilia and immune deficiencies, as well as vaccines to prevent influenza. The biopharmaceutical holding company operates through two main subsidiaries: CSL Behring develops plasma-derived and recombinant products used to treat infections, bleeding disorders, and autoimmune diseases, while Seqirus is a leading influenza vaccine provider in the world. CSL operates in more than 100 countries and generates around 50% of revenue from the US operations.

Operations

CSL's operating segments are CSL Behring and Seqirus.

CSL Behring accounts for nearly 85% of total revenue, manufactures, markets, and develops plasma therapies (plasma products and recombinants), conducts early stage research on plasma and non-plasma therapies, excluding influenza, receives license and royalty income from the commercialization of intellectual property and undertakes the administrative and corporate function required to support the company.

Seqirus (more than 15%) manufactures and distributes non-plasma biotherapeutic products and develops influenza related products.

Geographic Reach

Although the group's research and development, manufacturing, sales, and distribution operations are spread throughout the world, it operates predominantly in six geographic areas, namely Australia, China, Germany, the UK, Switzerland, and its largest market, the US.

CSL's head office is located in Melbourne, Australia.

Financial Performance

The company's revenue for fiscal 2021 increased to $10.3 billion compared from the prior year with $9.2 billion.

Profit for fiscal 2021 increased to $2.4 billion compared from the prior year with $2.1 billion.

Cash held by the company at the end of fiscal 2021 decreased to $1.7 billion. Cash provided by operations was $3.6 billion while cash used for investing and financing activities were $1.7 billion and $1.4 billion, respectively.

Strategy

CSL's 2030 strategy was developed to maximize its capabilities and advantages in a competitive and changing world. Historically and to this day, CSL have the most efficient supply chain from collections through to finished product for plasma-derived protein therapeutics, a business that has grown sustainably in recent years and does not face patent cliffs. The company's differentiated cell-based influenza products offer communities improved protection against seasonal influenza and its extensive experience in rare disease allows the company to focus on patients in its core therapeutic areas, delivering next generation innovative products across multiple platforms.

The company believe the 2030 strategy is resilient in the face of the challenges today and will make it stronger. CSL's efforts over the last year have focused on maintaining its leadership position and preparing for strong growth when market forces become favorable.

EXECUTIVES

Chief Executive Officer, Managing Director, Non-Independent Executive Director, Paul Perreault
Legal Executive Vice President, Legal General Counsel, Greg Boss
Executive Vice President, Chief Commercial Officer, Bill Campbell
Executive Vice President, Chief Digital Information Officer, Mark Hill
Chief Financial Officer, Joy Linton
Chief Operating Officer, Paul McKenzie
Research & Development Executive Vice President, Research & Development Chief Medical Officer, Research & Development Head, Bill Mezzanotte
Executive Vice President, Chief Human Resources Officer, Elizabeth Walker
Corporate Governance Secretary, Corporate Governance Head, Fiona Mead
Chairman, Independent Non-Executive Director, Brian A. McNamee
Independent Non-Executive Director, Bruce Brook
Independent Non-Executive Director, Megan Clark
Independent Non-Executive Director, Carolyn Hewson
Independent Non-Executive Director, Duncan Maskell
Independent Non-Executive Director, Marie E. McDonald
Independent Non-Executive Director, Alison Mary Watkins
Non-Independent Non-Executive Director, Andrew Cuthbertson
Auditors : Ernst & Young

LOCATIONS

HQ: CSL Ltd
655 Elizabeth Street, Melbourne, Victoria 3000
Phone: (61) 3 9389 1911   **Fax:** (61) 3 9389 1434
Web: www.csl.com.au

2013 Sales

	% of total
US	38
Germany	19
Australia	15
Switzerland	3
Rest of the world	31
Total	100

2018 Sales

	% of total
Europe	
Heavyside	28
Distribution	14
Lightside	6
Americas	
Materials	33
Distribution	9
Asia	2
Total	100

PRODUCTS/OPERATIONS

2018 sales

	%
Cement, lime and cement products	12
Aggregates, asphalt, and readymixed products	27
Construction contract activities	21
Construction accessories	2
Perimeter protection, shutters & awnings, and network access products	2
Architectural and precast products	17
Architectural glass and glazing systems and wholesale hardware distribution	6
General Builders Merchants, DIY, and Sanitary, Heating & Plumbing	14
Total	100

Selected Activities and Products

Materials
    Aggregates
    Agricultural and chemical lime
    Asphalt
    Cement
    Concrete products
    Ready-mixed concrete
Products
    Architectural concrete
    Building products
    Building envelope products
    Construction accessories
    Clay facing bricks, pavers, and blocks
    Structural concrete
Distribution
    Builders merchants
    DIY stores

COMPETITORS

CARR'S GROUP PLC
DCC PUBLIC LIMITED COMPANY
DIPLOMA PLC
Evonik Industries AG
HARSCO CORPORATION
Itausa S/A
LIXIL CORPORATION
LafargeHolcim Ltd
SUMMIT MATERIALS, INC.
WESFARMERS LIMITED

HISTORICAL FINANCIALS

Company Type: Public

Income Statement				FYE: December 31
	REVENUE ($mil)	NET INCOME ($mil)	NET PROFIT MARGIN	EMPLOYEES
12/22	32,723	3,847	11.8%	77,520
12/21	30,981	2,565	8.3%	77,446
12/20	27,587	1,122	4.1%	77,099
12/19	28,213	2,165	7.7%	86,951
12/18	30,679	2,882	9.4%	89,831
Annual Growth	1.6%	7.5%	—	(3.6%)

2022 Year-End Financials

Debt ratio: 21.3%
Return on equity: 18.3%
Cash ($ mil.): 5,936
Current Ratio: 1.67
Long-term debt ($ mil.): 8,145
No. of shares ($ mil.): 744
Dividends
Yield: —
Payout: 25.2%
Market value ($ mil.): —

PRODUCTS/OPERATIONS

2013 Sales

	% of total
CSL Behring	88
biotherapiesCSL	9
Intellectual property licensing	3
Total	100

COMPETITORS

ASTRAZENECA PLC
CSL BEHRING L.L.C.
ENZO BIOCHEM, INC.
KYOWA KIRIN CO., LTD.
MERIDIAN BIOSCIENCE, INC.
NICOX SA
SA GENFIT
SANGAMO THERAPEUTICS, INC.
TRANSGENE
VECTURA GROUP PLC

HISTORICAL FINANCIALS

Company Type: Public

Income Statement — FYE: June 30

	REVENUE ($mil)	NET INCOME ($mil)	NET PROFIT MARGIN	EMPLOYEES
06/23	13,310	2,194	16.5%	64,130
06/22	10,561	2,254	21.3%	30,398
06/21	10,310	2,375	23.0%	25,415
06/20	9,150	2,102	23.0%	27,009
06/19	8,538	1,918	22.5%	25,000
Annual Growth	11.7%	3.4%	—	26.6%

2023 Year-End Financials

Debt ratio: 33.7%
Return on equity: 14.4%
Cash ($ mil.): 1,548
Current Ratio: 2.01
Long-term debt ($ mil.): 11,172
No. of shares ($ mil.): 482
Dividends
  Yield: 1.1%
  Payout: 22.6%
Market value ($ mil.): 44,503

	STOCK PRICE ($) FY Close	P/E High/Low	PER SHARE ($) Earnings	Dividends	Book Value
06/23	92.26	24 19	4.53	1.03	32.73
06/22	92.00	24 18	4.80	1.01	30.26
06/21	106.35	23 18	5.21	0.96	18.42
06/20	99.84	25 16	4.62	0.85	14.38
06/19	75.78	20 14	4.23	0.79	11.59
Annual Growth	5.0%	— —	1.8%	6.9%	29.6%

Currys plc

Currys (formerly Dixons Carphone) is a leading omni-channel retailer of technology products and services with approximately 830 stores and some 715 million website visits in eight countries. It operates under a variety of brand names, including Currys, PC World, Dixons, Carphone Warehouse, and Elkjop. Currys sells mobile phones and other white goods, and also offers related support and repair services. The UK generates more than 50% of Currys' revenue. In mid-2021, Dixons Carphone changed its name to Currys. The company was founded by Henry Curry in 1884 as a bicycle-building business.

Operations

Currys' UK & Ireland operations bring in roughly 55% of revenue. The segment comprises the operations of Currys, Carphone Warehouse, iD Mobile and B2B operations.

Its Nordics brands, worth approximately 40% of revenue, include operations in Norway, Sweden, Finland, and Denmark with franchise operations in Iceland, Greenland, and the Faroe Islands. Consists of ongoing operations in Greece and Cyprus, the company's Greece segment brings in about 5% of revenue.

Overall, sale of goods brings in about 90% of the company's revenue, followed by commission with more than 5%, support services with less than 5%, while other services account for the rest.

Geographic Reach

Currys' home market is the UK. The company is active in eight countries, including the Nordics and Greece. The UK generates more than 50% of revenue, followed by Sweden with about 15%, and Norway with more than 10% of revenue, and the rest comes from other countries.

Sales and Marketing

Currys sells its products through its store network and e-commerce channel.

Financial Performance

Note: Growth rates may differ after conversion to US Dollars.

The company had revenues amounting to £10.1 billion, a 2% dip from the previous year's revenue of £10.3 billion.

In fiscal 2022, the company had a net income of £135 million, a 10% increase from the previous year's net income of £123 million.

The company's cash for the year ended 2022 was £124 million. Operating activities generated £428 million, while investing activities used £134 million, mainly for acquisition of property, plant & equipment and other intangibles. Financing activities used another £340 million, primarily for capital repayment of lease liabilities.

Strategy

Omni-channel is the company's strategy to create a seamless shopping journey across all channels. Whether it is online, in its 830 stores or using a combination of both channels, the company will provide customers with an easy and connected shopping experience across its full range of products and services. The last 12 months have shown the company just how important it is to have stores and online working seamlessly together to provide customers a full experience.

HISTORY

Recognizing the lucrative future of wireless communications, 25-year-old Charles Dunstone, a former NEC mobile phone sales manager, started The Carphone Warehouse in 1989, opening his first store in 1990. By 1993 the company had 17 stores and a mail-order operation.

In 1996 the company entered the Paris and Dublin markets, marking its first non-UK operations. The next year it entered Madrid.

In 1998 Carphone Warehouse acquired GEAB Teleshop, a phone retailer in Sweden with 36 stores. The business was renamed GEAB The Phone House and was the first purchase of what would become a three-year buying spree of wireless retailers throughout Europe. Later that year it bought Dutch mobile phone retailer and wholesaler Comprotel Groep BV (32 stores). That year the company also opened stores in Belgium and Germany.

In 1999 the company opened two stores in Poland and others in the Czech Republic, Switzerland, Italy, and Hungary. Later that year it acquired the UK business of Tandy (268 consumer electronics and mobile phone stores), Società Commerciale Telecom/Telephonie (45 phone stores in France), and about 30 stores from four retailers in Portugal (Polirent, Computer World, Eurotransmitte, and PVP). Also in 1999 the company launched MViva, an Internet portal aimed at serving wireless customers.

Continuing with acquisitions throughout 2000, Carphone Warehouse bought 46 stores in Spain from ACJM SL (trading as Viva Voce); acquired 76 stores in Germany from Otto Boenicke; took over Dutch mobile phone retailer Road Phone N.V., including its 18 stores; and purchased eight Time & Light stores in Belgium. Also in 2000 the company opened stores in Turkey and Israel.

Beyond acquisitions and new store openings, the company was also busy in 2000 with its service operations; it purchased the UK operations of Cellcom Limited, a cellular service provider, and started a content deal with AOL Europe for MViva. Carphone Warehouse acquired AOL Europe's minority stake in MViva in August 2002.

In late 2000 Carphone Warehouse began selling about 60 of its Tandy stores. It boosted its London presence in 2001 to some 130 stores with the purchase of 13 stores from rival Odyssey Corporation Administration. In 2002 it acquired Opal Telecom (a fixed-line telecommunications network provider to businesses) and added this offering to its retail stores.

The company's TalkTalk brand expanded its product line in 2004 with the launch of its broadband service. Carphone Warehouse introduced TalkTalk in 2003 as an alternative to services offered by the UK's telecommunications giant BT Group. In 2004 Spain-based Xtra Telecom was acquired by the company.

In 2005 Carphone Warehouse bought One.Tel from Centrica for about $254 million. The company acquired the UK customer base of AOL's Internet access business from Time Warner in 2006 for about $688 million. Best Buy acquired a 50% interest in Carphone Warehouse's European and US retail interests for approximately $2.2 billion (£1.1 billion) in 2008. In October the firm's business-to-business division Opal acquired its long-term partner V Networks.

Carphone Warehouse in May 2008 had offered more than $1 billion to acquire Tiscali's British broadband assets. However, Carphone Warehouse pulled out of the bidding for Tiscali six months later. (Previously, the company made a major move to beef up its broadband offerings when it acquired Time Warner's British AOL unit for some $688 million in 2006.) Under the terms of a joint venture with Best Buy formed in mid-2008, Carphone Warehouse sold half of its retail business to the US consumer electronics giant for about $2.2 billion. The deal was meant to transform Carphone Warehouse from primarily a seller of mobile phones in the UK to a big-box retailer of consumer electronics through its interest in Best Buy Europe Group. Co-founder David Ross resigned from the company in late 2008. In July 2009 the company's TalkTalk Group acquired the UK operations of Italy's Tiscali.

EXECUTIVES

Chief Executive Officer, Executive Director, Alex Baldock
Chief Financial Officer, Executive Director, Jonny Mason
Secretary, General Counsel, Nigel Paterson
Chairman, Non-Executive Director, Ian Livingston
Deputy Chairman, Senior Independent Director, Tony DeNunzio
Independent Non-Executive Director, Andrea Gisle Joosen
Independent Non-Executive Director, Eileen Burbidge
Independent Non-Executive Director, Fiona C. McBain
Independent Non-Executive Director, Gerry Murphy
Auditors : Deloitte LLP

LOCATIONS

HQ: Currys plc
1 Portal Way, London W3 6RS
Phone: (44) 203 110 3251
Web: www.dixonscarphone.com

2016 Sales

	% of total
UK & Ireland	66
Nordics	27
Southern Europe	6
Connected World Services	1
Total	100

PRODUCTS/OPERATIONS

2016 Sales

	£ mil	% total
UK & Ireland	6,404	66
Nordics	2,632	27
Southern Europe	550	6
Connected World Services	152	1
Total	9,738	100

HISTORICAL FINANCIALS
Company Type: Public

Income Statement FYE: April 30

	REVENUE ($mil)	NET INCOME ($mil)	NET PROFIT MARGIN	EMPLOYEES
04/22*	12,732	89	0.7%	33,532
05/21	14,386	16	0.1%	36,087
05/20*	12,746	(204)	—	42,209
04/19	13,458	(412)	—	42,990
04/18	14,493	228	1.6%	43,760
Annual Growth	(3.2%)	(21.0%)	—	(6.4%)

*Fiscal year change

2022 Year-End Financials
Debt ratio: 1.5% No. of shares ($ mil.): 1,100
Return on equity: 2.9% Dividends
Cash ($ mil.): 158 Yield: —
Current Ratio: 0.79 Payout: 52.5%
Long-term debt ($ mil.): 100 Market value ($ mil.): —

Cushman & Wakefield PLC

EXECUTIVES

Executive Chairman, Director, Brett White, $950,000 total compensation
President, Andrew R. McDonald
President, Chief Executive Officer, Chief Operating Officer, Director, Michelle M. MacKay
Executive Vice President, Chief Financial Officer, Principal Accounting Officer, Neil O. Johnston
Strategic Planning Executive Vice President, Strategic Planning Chief Investment Officer, Nathaniel Robinson
Lead Director, Director, Timothy D. Dattels
Director, Jonathan J. Coslet
Director, Anthony Miller
Director, Lincoln Pan
Director, Angela A. Sun
Director, Jodie W. McLean
Director, Billie L. Williamson
Auditors : KPMG LLP

LOCATIONS

HQ: Cushman & Wakefield PLC
125 Old Broad Street, London EC2N 1AR
Phone: (44) 20 3296 3000
Web: www.cushmanwakefield.com

HISTORICAL FINANCIALS
Company Type: Public

Income Statement FYE: December 31

	REVENUE ($mil)	NET INCOME ($mil)	NET PROFIT MARGIN	EMPLOYEES
12/23	9,493	(35)	—	52,000
12/22	10,105	196	1.9%	52,000
12/21	9,388	250	2.7%	50,000
12/20	7,843	(220)	—	50,000
12/19	8,751	0	0.0%	53,000
Annual Growth	2.1%	—	—	(0.5%)

2023 Year-End Financials
Debt ratio: 41.8% No. of shares ($ mil.): 227
Return on equity: (-2.1%) Dividends
Cash ($ mil.): 767 Yield: —
Current Ratio: 1.17 Payout: 0.0%
Long-term debt ($ mil.): 3,096 Market value ($ mil.): —

Dai Nippon Printing Co Ltd

EXECUTIVES

Chairman, Representative Director, Yoshitoshi Kitajima
President, Representative Director, Yoshinari Kitajima
Senior Managing Director, Representative Director, Kenji Miya
Senior Managing Director, Representative Director, Masato Yamaguchi
Senior Managing Executive Officer, Sakae Hikita
Senior Managing Executive Officer, Motoharu Kitajima
Senior Managing Executive Officer, Satoru Inoue
Senior Managing Executive Officer, Mitsuru Tsuchiya
Senior Managing Executive Officer, Toshiki Sugimoto
Director, Hirofumi Hashimoto
Director, Masafumi Kuroyanagi
Director, Toru Miyake
Director, Minako Miyama
Outside Director, Tsukasa Miyajima
Outside Director, Kazuyuki Sasajima
Outside Director, Yoshiaki Tamura
Outside Director, Hiroshi Shirakawa
Auditors : ARK LLC

LOCATIONS

HQ: Dai Nippon Printing Co Ltd
1-1-1 Ichigaya-Kagacho, Shinjuku-ku, Tokyo 162-8001
Phone: (81) 3 6735 0129
Web: www.dnp.co.jp

COMPETITORS

CLIPPER MAGAZINE, LLC
MACDERMID, INCORPORATED
MPAC Industries Corporation
NELSONS LABELS (MANCHESTER) LIMITED
NOCOPI TECHNOLOGIES, INC.
PANTONE LLC
SHARP CORPORATION
TOPPAN PRINTING CO., LTD.
VERICO TECHNOLOGY LLC
WESTROCK PACKAGING, INC.

Dai-ichi Life Holdings Inc

HISTORICAL FINANCIALS
Company Type: Public

Income Statement — FYE: March 31

	REVENUE ($mil)	NET INCOME ($mil)	NET PROFIT MARGIN	EMPLOYEES
03/23	10,310	643	6.2%	55,693
03/22	11,050	798	7.2%	54,363
03/21	12,060	226	1.9%	54,817
03/20	12,914	640	5.0%	48,192
03/19	12,655	(322)	—	47,449
Annual Growth	(5.0%)	—	—	4.1%

2023 Year-End Financials
Debt ratio: 0.1%
Return on equity: 7.8%
Cash ($ mil.): 1,850
Current Ratio: 2.01
Long-term debt ($ mil.): 854
No. of shares ($ mil.): 261
Dividends
Yield: 1.6%
Payout: 9.9%
Market value ($ mil.): 3,672

	STOCK PRICE ($) FY Close	P/E High/Low	PER SHARE ($) Earnings	Dividends	Book Value
03/23	14.04	0 0	2.41	0.23	31.22
03/22	11.77	0 0	2.92	0.29	33.36
03/21	10.55	0 0	0.81	0.30	33.57
03/20	10.48	0 0	2.17	0.30	30.03
03/19	11.97	— —	(1.07)	0.29	29.80
Annual Growth	4.1%	—	—	(5.0%)	1.2%

EXECUTIVES
Chairman, Director, Seiji Inagaki
President, Chief Executive Officer, Representative Director, Tetsuya Kikuta
Senior Managing Executive Officer, Yuji Tokuoka
Senior Managing Executive Officer, Chief Information Officer, Chief Digital Officer, Stephen Barnham
Managing Executive Officer, Chief Sustainability Officer, Director, Hidehiko Sogano
Chief Risk Officer, Hideyuki Ohashi
Chief Financial Officer, Taisuke Nishimura
Chief Compliance Officer, Webster Coates
Chief Communications Officer, Kyoko Wada
Representative Director, Hitoshi Yamaguchi
Director, Hiroshi Shoji
Director, Toshiaki Sumino
Outside Director, Koichi Maeda
Outside Director, Yuriko Inoue
Outside Director, Yasushi Shingai
Outside Director, Bruce Miller
Director, Takahiro Shibagaki
Director, Fusakazu Kondo
Outside Director, Rieko Sato
Outside Director, Ungyong Shu
Outside Director, Koichi Masuda
Auditors : KPMG AZSA LLC

LOCATIONS
HQ: Dai-ichi Life Holdings Inc
1-13-1 Yurakucho, Chiyoda-ku, Tokyo 100-8411
Phone: (81) 3 3216 1222
Web: www.dai-ichi-life-hd.com

HISTORICAL FINANCIALS
Company Type: Public

Income Statement — FYE: March 31

	REVENUE ($mil)	NET INCOME ($mil)	NET PROFIT MARGIN	EMPLOYEES
03/23	62,868	1,443	2.3%	60,997
03/22	64,360	3,365	5.2%	62,260
03/21	67,746	3,285	4.8%	64,823
03/20	57,965	298	0.5%	63,719
03/19	59,981	2,032	3.4%	62,938
Annual Growth	1.2%	(8.2%)	—	(0.8%)

2023 Year-End Financials
Debt ratio: —
Return on equity: 5.2%
Cash ($ mil.): 18,998
Current Ratio: —
Long-term debt ($ mil.): —
No. of shares ($ mil.): 987
Dividends
Yield: 3.3%
Payout: 43.5%
Market value ($ mil.): 18,019

	STOCK PRICE ($) FY Close	P/E High/Low	PER SHARE ($) Earnings	Dividends	Book Value
03/23	18.26	0 0	1.42	0.61	21.86
03/22	21.44	0 0	3.15	0.51	35.24
03/21	13.02	0 0	2.94	0.57	38.97
03/20	12.10	1 0	0.26	0.54	30.71
03/19	16.62	0 0	1.75	0.52	29.17
Annual Growth	2.4%	—	(5.1%)	3.9%	(7.0%)

Daiichi Sankyo Co Ltd

Daiichi Sankyo is a leader in the Japanese pharmaceuticals business. The company manufactures prescription drugs, including treatments for cardiovascular, bone and joint, autoimmune, metabolic, and infectious diseases. Products include Olmetec for hypertension, Loxonin for inflammation, Efient for patients with acute coronary syndrome, and edoxaban to help prevent venous thromboembolism. Providing innovative products and services in more than 20 countries, Daiichi Sankyo generates nearly 55% of its revenue from Japan.

Operations
Daiichi Sankyo operates in a single segment, Pharmaceutical Operation. It earns around 95% of revenue from prescription drugs and healthcare (OTC) products account for more than 5%.

Geographic Reach
Based in Japan, the company operates in more than 20 countries in Europe, the Americas, and Asia. Japan accounts for around 55% of total revenue, while North America generates nearly 25%, Europe and other regions bring in also some 25%.

Sales and Marketing
Its largest customer, Alfresa Holdings Corporation, accounts for more than 10% if revenue.

Financial Performance
Company's revenue for fiscal 2022 increased to Â¥1.0 trillion compared from the prior year with Â¥962.5 million.

Profit for fiscal 2022 decreased to Â¥73.5 billion compared from the prior year with Â¥74.1 billion.

Cash held by the company at the end of fiscal 2022 increased to Â¥662.5 billion. Cash provided by operations and investing activities were Â¥139.2 billion and Â¥212.3 billion, respectively. Cash sued for financing activities were Â¥86.2 billion, mainly for dividends paid.

Strategy
Align with Vision 2025 and looking beyond 2025, Daiichi Sankyo set "3 and Alpha" Strategy, in which R&D resources are concentrated to its leading ADCs in oncology; DS-8201, DS-1062, U3-1402, as a major pillar of its R&D activities. Oncology is a major disease known to have high morbidity and mortality rate around the world. The company are taking steps forward to bring patients who still suffer in the realm of oncology the medication they need as early as possible.

Daiichi Sankyo also aim to bring innovative medicines in "Alpha", which in its terms states disease areas where patients suffer from lack of effective treatments or sufficient treatments yet to be developed in oncology and rare diseases.

Company Background
Daiichi Sankyo was formed when Sankyo purchased rival Daiichi Pharmaceutical for more than $7 billion in 2005. The two companies merged their operations into the newly formed Daiichi Sankyo, creating a top pharmaceutical manufacturer in Japan. Since the merger, the company has focused primarily on prescription and consumer drugs and has been exiting its chemical and animal health operations.

EXECUTIVES
Chairman, Chief Executive Officer, Representative Director, Sunao Manabe
President, Chief Operating Officer, Representative Director, Hiroyuki Okuzawa
Senior Managing Executive Officer, Representative Director, Shoji Hirashima
Senior Managing Executive Officer, Chief Information Officer, Director, Masahiko Ohtsuki
Senior Managing Executive Officer, Director, Takashi Fukuoka
Outside Director, Kazuaki Kama
Outside Director, Sawako Nohara
Outside Director, Yasuhiro Komatsu
Outside Director, Takaaki Nishii
Auditors : KPMG AZSA LLC

LOCATIONS
HQ: Daiichi Sankyo Co Ltd
3-5-1 Nihonbashi-Honcho, Chuo-ku, Tokyo 103-8426

Phone: (81) 3 6225 1111
Web: www.daiichisankyo.co.jp

2015 Sales

	% of total
Japan	60
US	25
Europe	8
Other countries	7
Total	**100**

COMPETITORS

ADARE PHARMACEUTICALS, INC.
ASTRAZENECA PLC
Boehringer Ingelheim International GmbH
CIPLA LIMITED
EISAI CO., LTD.
IONIS PHARMACEUTICALS, INC.
Roche Holding AG
SHIONOGI & CO., LTD.
SUMITOMO DAINIPPON PHARMA CO., LTD.
UNITED THERAPEUTICS CORPORATION

HISTORICAL FINANCIALS

Company Type: Public

Income Statement — FYE: March 31

	REVENUE ($mil)	NET INCOME ($mil)	NET PROFIT MARGIN	EMPLOYEES
03/23	9,599	819	8.5%	17,435
03/22	8,590	550	6.4%	16,458
03/21	8,692	686	7.9%	16,033
03/20	9,044	1,189	13.1%	15,348
03/19	8,395	843	10.0%	14,887
Annual Growth	3.4%	(0.7%)	—	4.0%

2023 Year-End Financials

Debt ratio: —
Return on equity: 7.8%
Cash ($ mil.): 3,318
Current Ratio: 2.82
Long-term debt ($ mil.): 763
No. of shares ($ mil.): 1,917
Dividends
Yield: 0.5%
Payout: 50.1%
Market value ($ mil.): 70,041

	STOCK PRICE ($) FY Close	P/E High/Low	PER SHARE ($) Earnings	Dividends	Book Value
03/23	36.53	1 0	0.43	0.21	5.66
03/22	21.78	1 0	0.29	0.24	5.79
03/21	29.41	2 1	0.35	0.24	6.00
03/20	68.31	1 1	0.61	0.21	6.19
03/19	50.64	1 1	0.43	0.21	5.81
Annual Growth	(7.8%)	— —	(0.3%)	0.0%	(0.6%)

Daikin Industries Ltd

Founded in 1924, Daikin Industries is the #1 air conditioning company in the world. Daikin makes air conditioning and refrigeration products for residential and industrial use. Residential products include heat pumps, gas furnaces, and air conditioners; industrial products range from infrared ceramic space heaters to marine vessel air conditioners. Daikin also manufactures and sells chemicals (fluorocarbons, fluopolymers, fluoropaints, and semiconductor-etching products, among others), oil hydraulics for machinery, and products such as aircraft parts for defense organizations. The US is the company's largest market, generating more than 30% of its revenue.

Operations

Daikin conducts its operation through four businesses: Air Conditioning, which accounts for about 90% of the company's revenue, Chemicals accounts for more than 5%, and Oil Hydraulics and Defense Systems accounts for the rest.

Daikin's Air Conditioning business provides air-conditioning systems to factories, ships, vehicles, buildings, and residential housing. It offers a variety of air conditioning products such as room air conditioning systems, air purifiers, heat pump hot water and room heating systems, freezers, marine-type container refrigerators, and air conditioning systems for facilities and plants, among others.

The Chemicals business offers a lineup of about 1,800 fluorine compounds including fluocarbon gas, fluoropolymers, and fluoroelastomers, which are developed to support various industries such as semiconductors, EVs, information and communication technology, and new energy.

The Oil Hydraulics business develops and manufactures environmentally-conscious oil hydraulic pumps and oil hydraulic units under the themes of higher machine precision, quieter operation, and further miniaturization. Its unique hydraulic technologies will contribute to the development of the industry by offering outstanding energy-conservation performance and unleashing the potential power control.

The Defense Systems business designs and manufactures various products for Japan's Ministry of Defense (MOD), including aircraft parts and missile components and fuses, particularly for ammunition used in training. It also engages in the manufacturing and sales of home-use oxygen therapy equipment as well as in the supply of oxygen concentrators, which require the highest levels of reliability, performance, functionality, and quality.

Geographic Reach

Osaka, Japan-based, Daikin has expanded its global business to over 170 countries, comprising more than 110 production bases focused on market-localized production.

Daikin's largest market is the US, representing more than 30% of its revenue, followed by Europe with nearly 20%, Japan with more than 15%, Asia and Oceania with about 15%, and the rest comes from other markets.

Sales and Marketing

Daikin sells its products through its network of dealers who engage directly with the users of its products.

Financial Performance

Company's revenue for fiscal 2023 increased to JPY4.0 trillion compared from the prior year with JPY3.1 trillion. The increase was primarily due to higher revenues on its segment aside from its defense systems.

Strategy

In 2021, Daikin formulated Strategic Management Plan FUSION 25, which covers the period from 2021 to fiscal 2025. Recognizing the opportunities presented by medium- and long-term trends and the changes in its business environment since the formulation of its initial FUSION 25 strategic management plan.

Mergers and Acquisitions

In early 2022, Daikin acquired Duplomatic MS S.p.A, an Italian hydraulic equipment manufacturer, for 220 EURmillion. With this acquisition, Daikin intends to realize energy savings in the field of industrial equipment in Europe by integrating the business foundation of Duplomatic with its own specialty of environmental technologies to reduce environmental load and contribute to a sustainable society.

Company Background

Daikin Industries traces its roots back to 1924. Founded in Osaka, Japan as Osaka Kinzolu Kogyosho Limited Partnership, the company began as a town factory with no more than 15 employees making radiator tubes for aircraft. In 1933, the company began doing research on flourine refrigerants and later began manufacturing a methyl chloride type refrigerator dubbed the Mifujirator. With the successful development of fluorocarbon gas, the company began mass-producing the Mifujirator starting in 1942. It introduced Japan's first packaged air conditioner for commercial use and began marketing the first residential window air conditioner in 1958. The company was renamed Daikin Kogyo Co. Ltd. in 1963 and later to the current Daikin Industries Ltd. in 1982.

EXECUTIVES

Chairman, Director, Noriyuki Inoue
President, Chief Executive Officer, Representative Director, Masanori Togawa
Executive Vice President, Representative Director, Ken Tayano
Executive Vice President, Director, Takashi Matsuzaki
Senior Managing Director, Director, Kanwal Jeet Jawa
Executive Vice President, Director, Masatsugu Minaka
Outside Director, Tatsuo Kawada
Outside Director, Akiji Makino
Outside Director, Shingo Torii
Outside Director, Yuko Arai
Auditors : Deloitte Touche Tohmatsu LLC

LOCATIONS

HQ: Daikin Industries Ltd
Osaka Umeda Twin Towers South, 1-13-1 Umeda, Kita-ku, Osaka 530-0001
Phone: (81) 6 6147 6864
Web: www.daikin.co.jp

2018 sales

	% of total
Japan	24
USA	24
China	17
Asia and Oceania	15
Europe	14
Other regions	6
Total	100

PRODUCTS/OPERATIONS

2018 Sales

	% of total
Air conditioning	89
Chemicals	9
Other	2
Total	100

Selected Products and Operations
Air Conditioning and Refrigerator Division
    Split/multi-split type air conditioners
    Unitary (ducted split)
    Air to water heat pump systems
    Heating systems
    Air purifiers
    Medium/low temperature refrigeration
    Sky/air (packaged air conditioners for shops and small offices)
        Ventilation products
        Control systems
        Commercial air cleaners
        Commercial air conditioners
        Container refrigeration
        Large-scale refrigerators
        Marine vessel air conditioners and refrigerators
        Marine-type container refrigeration units
        Room air cleaners
        Room air conditioners
Chemical Division
    Equipment and systems
    Fluorocarbon gas
    Synthesized products
Oil Hydraulics Division
    Centralized lubrication units and systems
    Oil hydraulic products for industrial machinery
    Oil hydraulic products for mobile equipment
Defense Systems Division
    Aircraft components
    Ammunition
    Warheads for aerial torpedoes

COMPETITORS

AAON, INC.
AIR SYSTEM COMPONENTS, INC.
DOVER CORPORATION
Danfoss A/S
EVOQUA WATER TECHNOLOGIES CORP.
GOODMAN MANUFACTURING COMPANY, L.P.
MESTEK, INC.
REGAL BELOIT CORPORATION
TRANE INC.
WELBILT, INC.

HISTORICAL FINANCIALS

Company Type: Public

Income Statement   FYE: March 31

	REVENUE ($mil)	NET INCOME ($mil)	NET PROFIT MARGIN	EMPLOYEES
03/23	29,894	1,935	6.5%	107,127
03/22	25,560	1,789	7.0%	97,476
03/21	22,518	1,411	6.3%	93,102
03/20	23,494	1,572	6.7%	89,957
03/19	22,404	1,707	7.6%	86,472
Annual Growth	7.5%	3.2%	—	5.5%

2023 Year-End Financials

Debt ratio: 0.1%   No. of shares ($ mil.): 292
Return on equity: 12.2%   Dividends
Cash ($ mil.): 4,637   Yield: 0.8%
Current Ratio: 1.67   Payout: 2.4%
Long-term debt ($ mil.): 2,358   Market value ($ mil.): 5,240

	STOCK PRICE ($) FY Close	P/E High/Low	Earnings	Dividends	Book Value
03/23	17.90	0 0	6.61	0.16	57.41
03/22	18.18	0 0	6.11	0.15	55.40
03/21	20.21	0 0	4.82	0.15	51.47
03/20	11.98	0 0	5.37	0.16	45.24
03/19	11.69	0 0	5.83	0.13	43.77
Annual Growth	11.2%	—	3.2%	4.3%	7.0%

Dairy Farm International Holdings Ltd

The cows may be out to pasture, but Dairy Farm International Holdings has a barn full of retail operations; some 6,400 stores in about 10 countries in Asia. The company owns supermarkets, hypermarkets, health and beauty stores, convenience shops, and home furnishing stores in China, Hong Kong, India, Indonesia, Malaysia, Macau, Singapore, South Korea, Taiwan, and Vietnam. It also has a 50% interest in Hong Kong's leading chain restaurant Maxim's. Jardine Matheson Holdings, controlled by the Keswick family, owns more than 75% of Dairy Farm International Holdings, which began in 1886 as a dairy with 80 imported cows providing fresh milk for Hong Kong.

Geographic Reach

Dairy Farm is incorporated in Bermuda and operates in North Asia (Hong Kong, mainland China, Macau and Taiwan), East Asia (Malaysia, Indonesia, Vietnam and Brunei), and South Asia (Singapore, Cambodia, the Philippines and India).

Financial Performance

Dairy Farm's net sales increased by 6% from 2013 to 2014 primarily due to increased sales from its food, health, and beauty business. Food revenue increased due to additional sales from its supermarkets/hypermarkets and convenience stores. Its net income, however, decreased from 2013 to 2014 due to a rise in administration and other operating expenses.

Strategy

In order to grow, Dairy Farm continues to expand its store network across all formats and renovate existing stores to enhance the shopping experience for its customers. During 2014, Dairy Farm opened 124 net new stores and acquired 238 retail outlets. The company continues to expand its operations in Hong Kong and Vietnam, and it is also growing its casual dining and Japanese restaurant chains in Hong Kong and mainland China.

Company Background

Determined to have fresh, pure milk, a group of Hong Kong businessmen in 1886 established a farm and stocked it with a herd of imported British dairy cows. Climate change and disease were early hurdles, but by 1892 Dairy Farm's production had grown large enough to warrant building an ice house distribution center. As the European population of Hong Kong grew, Dairy Farm added fresh butter imported from Australia (1899), frozen meats, and a retail store (1904). Additional businesses grew around Dairy Farm through the 1920s, including food processing, a delicatessen, and more retail stores.

EXECUTIVES

Chief Executive Officer, Executive Director, Ian McLeod
Chief Financial Officer, Non-Executive Director, Clem Constantine
Secretary, Jonathan Lloyd
Human Resources Director, Judith Nelson
Managing Director, Executive Director, John Witt
Non-Executive Chairman, Ben Keswick
Non-Executive Director, Mark Greenberg
Non-Executive Director, George Joseph Ho
Non-Executive Director, Adam Keswick
Non-Executive Director, Delman Lee
Non-Executive Director, Anthony J. L. Nightingale
Non-Executive Director, Y. K. Pang
Non-Executive Director, Jeremy Parr
Non-Executive Director, Percy Weatherall
Non-Executive Director, Clive Schlee
Auditors : PricewaterhouseCoopers LLP

LOCATIONS

HQ: Dairy Farm International Holdings Ltd
11/F Devon House, Taikoo Place, 979 King's Road,
Quarry Bay, P.O. Box 286, G.P.O.,
Phone: (852) 2299 1888   **Fax:** (852) 2299 4888
Web: www.dairyfarmgroup.com

2013 Sales

	$ mil.	% of total
North Asia	5,496.0	53
East Asia	2,869.3	28
South Asia	1,992.1	19
Total	10,357.4	100

PRODUCTS/OPERATIONS

2013 Sales

	$ mil.	% of total
Supermarkets/hypermarkets	5,974.9	58
Convenience stores	1,780.9	17
Health & beauty stores	2,179.9	21
Home furnishings stores	421.7	4
Total	10,357.4	100

Selected Operations
Supermarkets and hypermarkets
    Cold Storage (Malaysia and Singapore)
    Foodworld (India)
    Giant (Brunei, Indonesia, Malaysia and Singapore)
    Hero (Indonesia)
    Jasons Marketplace (Hong Kong, Singapore and Taiwan)

Market Place (Hong Kong)
Oliver's The Delicatessen (Hong Kong)
Shop N Save (Singapore)
ThreeSixty (Hong Kong)
Wellcome (Hong Kong, Taiwan and Vietnam)
Convenience Stores
7-Eleven (Southern China, Hong Kong, Macau, and Singapore)
Starmart (Indonesia)
Health and Beauty
Guardian (Indonesia, Malaysia, Singapore, and Brunei)
Health and Glow (India)
Mannings (Hong Kong, Macau and China)
Restaurants
Maxim's (China, Hong Kong)
Starbucks
Other
IKEA (Hong Kong and Taiwan)

COMPETITORS

ASSOCIATED BRITISH FOODS PLC
CARDENAS MARKETS LLC
GROCERY OUTLET INC.
LAWSON, INC.
MOY PARK LIMITED
SEVEN-ELEVEN JAPAN CO., LTD.
TAWA SUPERMARKET, INC.
THE FRESH MARKET INC
WAWA, INC.
WAYNE FARMS LLC

HISTORICAL FINANCIALS

Company Type: Public

Income Statement — FYE: December 31

	REVENUE ($mil)	NET INCOME ($mil)	NET PROFIT MARGIN	EMPLOYEES
12/22	9,174	(114)	—	216,000
12/21	9,015	102	1.1%	230,000
12/20	10,268	271	2.6%	220,000
12/19	11,192	323	2.9%	230,000
12/18	11,749	92	0.8%	230,000
Annual Growth	(6.0%)	—	—	(1.6%)

2022 Year-End Financials

Debt ratio: 54.2%
Return on equity: (-10.3%)
Cash ($ mil.): 230
Current Ratio: 0.39
Long-term debt ($ mil.): 2,548
No. of shares ($ mil.): 1,353
Dividends
  Yield: —
  Payout: 0.0%
Market value ($ mil.): 19,536

	STOCK PRICE ($) FY Close	P/E High/Low		PER SHARE ($) Earnings	Dividends	Book Value
12/22	14.44	—	—	(0.09)	0.33	0.70
12/21	14.23	311	169	0.08	0.66	0.94
12/20	20.97	146	86	0.20	0.90	0.98
12/19	28.45	196	117	0.24	0.96	0.89
12/18	44.23	688	574	0.07	0.96	1.07
Annual Growth	(24.4%)	—	—	—	(23.4%)	(10.1%)

Daito Trust Construction Co., Ltd.

You can trust Daito to land on the right side of a property deal. Daito Trust Construction provides a unique service to Japanese landowners ? the ability to develop a tailored business plan to unlock long-term value in their land. In Japan, it is customary to pass land to succeeding generations. Passing it to heirs triggers tax consequences and sometimes places it in the hands of people who don't know what to do with it. Daito, and its subsidiaries, designs a plan to develop the land ? such as building a high-rise apartment complex ? and then constructs the building, recruits tenants, manages the property, remits payment to the landowner and keeps a little for its own profit. Since the inception of this business model in 1980 it has built more than 170,000 buildings, worked with 80,000 landowners, and exceeded 1 million units under management.

Operations

Daito Trust Construction's core business model is comprised of two segments, construction and real estate. The construction segment diagnoses potential land uses, designs a building & funding plan, proposes the plan to the landowner and once agreed to, constructs the building. The real estate segment recruits tenants and manages leases and the property for a 35-year term.

Much of the group's operations occur within three companies: Daito Trust Construction, Daito Kentaku Leasing, and Daito Kentaku Partners. Other subsidiaries provide tangential services, Daito Energy installs solar power panels on the roofs its buildings (> 13,000); Gaspal Group designs, builds, and delivers natural gas to nearly households (> 300,000); and Care Partner operates elderly & nursery care facilities. It also owns finance and insurance businesses.

Geographic Reach

Tokyo-headquartered Daito performs much of its business in Japan's major cities. It has branched out in recent years into Malaysia, where it owns the Le Meridien Kuala Lumpur Hotel, and into the US, where it owns an apartment building co-developed with a US-based partner.

Financial Performance

Note: Financial results are denoted in Japanese currency, the Yen (Â¥).

Daito Construction has produced consistently upward revenue for over a decade, rising each year from 2007 to 2017, from Â¥564 billion to Â¥1.5 trillion. Net income over that same period nearly doubled, increasing from Â¥42 million to more than Â¥80 million.

In FY2017 (ended March 31, 2017), Daito generated Â¥1.5 trillion (about US$13.8 billion). Revenue for the year improved in all categories ? completed construction contracts, real estate sales, and other business revenue ? resulting in a 6% rise year-over-year.

Net income jumped 22% to Â¥82.5 billion (about US$760 million). The company managed expenses well, improving its gross margin two percentage points. With the increased revenue and lower expenses, the firm registered a nice earnings boost compared to FY2016.

Cash at the end of the year was Â¥200 million, an increase of Â¥18 million. Operating activities contributed Â¥124 million to cash, most of it from net income. Investing activities used Â¥33 million to purchase tangible assets (property, plant, equipment), investment securities, and intangible assets. Financing activities depleted cash by Â¥72 million, mostly to issue stock dividends to shareholders and to repurchase company stock.

Strategy

Daito Construction's strategy is slow and steady. It operates somewhat like a real estate investment trust, generating stable revenue and income year after year, spinning off a large portion of earnings to shareholders and investing the rest into growing its portfolio of properties. The company's business model varies, however, in that it works with existing landowners to determine what kind of property to build, and that it limits its time frame by instituting a 35-year leases with its landowners.

The group is enjoying nice economic tailwinds brought about by a growing economy, low interest rates brought about in early 2015 by the Bank of Japan, and increasing demand for single-person households. Demand for rental housing is expected to be brisk in coming years.

From business perspective, Daito's core competencies in construction and real estate will continue to aid the expansion of its portfolio. Its trajectory of units under management has been impressive, growing from 600,000 in 2010 to 800,0000 in 2013, and exceeding 1,000,000 in 2017.

The group also expects to expand its other operations in energy, nursing care, childcare, and overseas investments.

EXECUTIVES

President, Representative Director, Kei Takeuchi
Director, Yoshihiro Mori
Director, Masafumi Tate
Director, Tsukasa Okamoto
Director, Yutaka Amano
Director, Yoshimasa Tanaka
Outside Director, Mami Sasaki
Outside Director, Atsushi Iritani
Director, Shuji Kawai
Outside Director, Masa Matsushita
Outside Director, Takashi Shoda
Outside Director, Kenji Kobayashi
Auditors : Ernst & Young ShinNihon LLC

LOCATIONS

HQ: Daito Trust Construction Co., Ltd.
2-16-1 Konan, Minato-ku, Tokyo 108-8211
Phone: (81) 3 6718 9111
Web: www.kentaku.co.jp

COMPETITORS

FLETCHER KING PLC

FORESTAR GROUP INC.
MAPELEY ESTATES LIMITED
PIRES INVESTMENTS PLC
REALOGY HOLDINGS CORP.

HISTORICAL FINANCIALS
Company Type: Public

Income Statement — FYE: March 31

	REVENUE ($mil)	NET INCOME ($mil)	NET PROFIT MARGIN	EMPLOYEES
03/23	12,445	528	4.2%	22,010
03/22	13,014	572	4.4%	21,785
03/21	13,447	562	4.2%	21,549
03/20	14,613	832	5.7%	21,916
03/19	14,368	812	5.7%	21,754
Annual Growth	(3.5%)	(10.2%)	—	0.3%

2023 Year-End Financials
Debt ratio: 0.1%
Return on equity: 18.4%
Cash ($ mil.): 2,092
Current Ratio: 2.00
Long-term debt ($ mil.): 588
No. of shares ($ mil.): 68
Dividends
Yield: 3.9%
Payout: 12.7%
Market value ($ mil.): 1,653

	STOCK PRICE ($) FY Close	P/E High/Low		PER SHARE ($) Earnings	Dividends	Book Value
03/23	24.00	0	0	7.74	0.96	43.77
03/22	26.55	0	0	8.39	1.09	43.19
03/21	29.15	0	0	8.21	1.29	39.89
03/20	23.02	0	0	12.03	1.43	37.99
03/19	34.93	0	0	10.94	1.36	37.16
Annual Growth	(9.0%)	—	—	(8.3%)	(8.4%)	4.2%

Daiwa House Industry Co Ltd

Daiwa House Industry is one of the leading companies in housing, construction and real estate industries. Its businesses build, lease, sell, and manage rental properties, single-family houses, condominiums, and commercial buildings. Daiwa's other businesses include energy efficiency and construction support services as well as operation of hotels and sports clubs. Daiwa has offices located in Osaka, Nagoya and Tokyo, and more than 55 branches. It also owns and operates nine factories and manages autonomous group companies in about 30 countries. The company was founded by Nobuo Ishibashi in 1955 with "industrialization of construction" as a corporate philosophy.

Operations
Daiwa House Industry's revenue is diversified across seven business segments.

Through its Logistics, Business and Corporate Facilities Business segment (some 25% of sales), Daiwa develops and builds logistics, manufacturing, and medical and nursing-care facilities, and builds, manages, and operates temporary facilities.

Rental Housing segment (over 20%) conducts rental housing development, construction, management, operation, and real estate agency services.

Daiwa's Commercial Facilities business (over 15%) develops, builds, manages, and operates commercial facilities.

In its Single-Family Houses division (about 15%), Daiwa engages in construction by order of single-family houses and the sale of a package of new house and land.

Via its Condominiums segment (about 10%) Daiwa develops, sells, and manages condominiums.

The company engages in renovation and real estate agency services through its Existing Homes business (less than 5%).

Daiwa's Other Businesses division generated around 10%.

Geographic Reach
Headquartered in Osaka, Japan, Daiwa House Industry has offices in Japan, over 55 branches, nine factories, and research and training centers in Nara, Osaka, and Tokyo. The company also has international offices in China, Taiwan, Indonesia, Philippines, Vietnam, Myanmar, and Mexico.

Sales and Marketing
Daiwa House Industry is emphasizing constructions that ameliorate societal needs in Japan, including nursing homes, environmentally friendly housing, food-industry facilities, offices, hotels, fitness, health and leisure, and medical buildings, among others.

Financial Performance
The company's revenue in fiscal 2022 increased by 8% to JPY4.4 trillion compared to JPY 4.1 trillion in the prior year.

Net income in fiscal 2022 increased by 16% to JPY225.3 billion compared to JPY 195.1 billion in the prior year.

Cash held by the company at the end of fiscal 2022 decreased to JPY 326.3 billion. Operating and financing activities provided JPY 336.4 billion and JPY 24.4 billion, respectively. Investing activities used JPY 467.4 billion.

Strategy
In the Logistics, Business and Corporate Facilities Business segment, the company worked to enhance the company's business scope by constructing a variety of facilities to suit the differing business needs of its corporate customers, and by providing total support services that enable customers to utilize their assets most effectively. To nurture business pillars besides logistics facilities development, which has driven earnings growth, Daiwa launched the "DPDC" (D Project Data Center) brand and also worked on, as part of an initiative for organizing an infrastructure for people's daily life, Toyama Public Wholesale Market Redevelopment Project, as a first project to support the redevelopment of aging municipal wholesale markets, and one of Japan's largest onshore salmon farms.

Company Background
Founded in 1955 by Nobuo Ishibashi, Daiwa House Industry first developed homes that could be quickly built using steel pipe frameworks to withstand natural disasters. The technique was first used for warehouses, depots, and offices primarily for the Japanese National Railways and the Japanese government. The company went on to develop study rooms that that could be built in three hours, larger prefabricated houses targeting newlyweds, and eventually large-scale residential complexes.

EXECUTIVES
President, Chief Executive Officer, Chief Operating Officer, Representative Director, Keiichi Yoshii
Executive Vice President, Chief Financial Officer, Representative Director, Takeshi Kosokabe
Executive Vice President, Representative Director, Yoshiyuki Murata
Senior Managing Executive Officer, Director, Keisuke Shimonishi
Director, Hirotsugu Otomo
Director, Kazuhito Dekura
Director, Yoshinori Ariyoshi
Director, Toshiya Nagase
Outside Director, Yukiko Yabu
Outside Director, Yukinori Kuwano
Outside Director, Miwa Seki
Outside Director, Kazuhiro Yoshizawa
Outside Director, Yujiro Ito
Auditors : Ernst & Young ShinNihon LLC

LOCATIONS
HQ: Daiwa House Industry Co Ltd
3-3-5 Umeda, Kita-ku, Osaka 530-8241
Phone: (81) 6 6225 7804   **Fax:** (81) 6 6342 1399
Web: www.daiwahouse.co.jp

PRODUCTS/OPERATIONS
2017 Sales

	% of total
Rental housing	26
Logistics, Business, and Corporate Facilities	22
Commercial Facilities	16
Single-Family Housing	10
Condominiums	7
Existing Homes	3
Other Businesses	16
Total	100

COMPETITORS
BOWMER AND KIRKLAND LIMITED
INSTALLED BUILDING PRODUCTS, INC.
LENDLEASE CORPORATION LIMITED
LINDUM GROUP LIMITED
LIXIL CORPORATION
MITSUBISHI ESTATE COMPANY, LIMITED
MITSUI FUDOSAN CO., LTD.
RENEW HOLDINGS PLC.
RUSSELL ARMER LIMITED
SHIMIZU CORPORATION

HISTORICAL FINANCIALS
Company Type: Public

Income Statement   FYE: March 31

	REVENUE ($mil)	NET INCOME ($mil)	NET PROFIT MARGIN	EMPLOYEES
03/23	36,852	2,315	6.3%	72,505
03/22	36,498	1,852	5.1%	70,716
03/21	37,270	1,761	4.7%	71,299
03/20	40,351	2,152	5.3%	70,344
03/19	37,415	2,144	5.7%	67,174
Annual Growth	(0.4%)	1.9%	—	1.9%

2023 Year-End Financials
Debt ratio: 0.2%   No. of shares ($ mil.): 658
Return on equity: 14.3%   Dividends
Cash ($ mil.): 2,688   Yield: 4.0%
Current Ratio: 2.13   Payout: 0.0%
Long-term debt ($ mil.): 11,296   Market value ($ mil.): 15,530

	STOCK PRICE ($) FY Close	P/E High/Low		PER SHARE ($) Earnings	Dividends	Book Value
03/23	23.57	0	0	3.52	0.96	26.03
03/22	26.00	0	0	2.83	1.08	25.33
03/21	29.54	0	0	2.68	1.04	25.33
03/20	24.62	0	0	3.24	1.10	23.96
03/19	31.82	0	0	3.22	1.02	21.71
Annual Growth	(7.2%)	—	—	2.2%	(1.4%)	4.6%

Danone

Danone is one of the largest dairy food and water producers in the world. The company is organized around three core activities: Essential Dairy and Plant-Based Products, Specialized Nutrition, and Waters. The #1 maker of fresh dairy products worldwide, Danone sells dozens of global and regional yogurt brands, including top-sellers Danone and Activia, functional brands like Actimel and Danonino, and Greek yogurt brand Oikos. The company's evian, Volvic, and Aqua water brands (among others) make it #2 worldwide in bottled water, and Danone is also the world's #2 baby nutrition company. Danone products are available in more than 120 countries around the globe. The company generates the majority of its revenue in Europe and NORAM region.

Operations
Danone has three principal product categories: Essential Dairy and Plant-Based (EDP), Specialized Nutrition, and Waters.

EDP carries out the production and distribution of fresh fermented dairy products and other dairy specialties; plant-based products and drinks (from soy, almond, hazelnut, rice, oat, and coconut); and coffee creamers. Its main brands in the segment are Activia, Actimel, Alpro, Danonino, Oikos, and Prostokvashino. Danone generates about 55% of total sales from EDP.

Specialized Nutrition comprises two units, Early Life Nutrition and Medical Nutrition. Early Life produces and distributes specialized nutrition for babies and young children, particularly infant milk formula products. Global brands include Aptamil and Nutrilion while market-specific products include Cow&Gate, BlÃ©dina, Bebelac, Malyutka, and Dumex. Advanced Medical Nutrition produces specialized nutrition for those with certain illnesses or weakened by age under the umbrella brand of Nutricia. The business accounts for approximately 30% of sales.

The Waters business bottles and sells natural, flavored, and vitamin-enhanced waters under the global brands Evian and Volvic and local brands such as Aqua, Mizone, Bonafont, and Villavicencio. It generates around 15% of sales.

Geographic Reach
Paris-based Danone is a force in dairy, water, and nutrition products in more than 120 countries worldwide. Overall, Danone rings up more than 55% of sales from Europe and NORAM and nearly 45% from Asia-Pacific, Greater China, and Latin America.

Danone operates approximately 190 production plants and some 400 distribution centers worldwide.

Sales and Marketing
Danone works hand-in-hand with suppliers, product distributors, retail companies, startups, NGOs and policymakers to find innovative solutions.

Financial Performance
Note: Growth rates may differ after conversion to US Dollars.

The company had net sales of EUR 24.3 billion in 2021, a 3% increase from the previous year's net sales of EUR 23.6 billion

Strategy
In 2022, the company's CEO Antoine de Saint-Affrique, alongside a strengthened leadership team, presented a new strategic plan: "Renew Danone" to enable the company to reconnect with sustainable profitable growth model. This plan is the result of a strategic review carried out during several months of meetings and discussions between 2021 and 2022 with the company's partners and other stakeholders around the world and from all parts of the business, but also its farmers, customers, and investors.

To reconnect with a sustainable profitable growth model, the company's actions will focus on an end-to-end step-up in the quality of execution, a strengthened innovation model geared for scale and impact, and increased investments in consumer value, as well as brands and commercial development.

Mergers and Acquisitions
In early 2021, Danone acquired plant-based pioneer Follow Your Heart. The transaction was a share purchase agreement, in which the French dairy giant bought 100% of the shares of Earth Island, Follow Your Heart's parent company. The acquisition of Follow Your Heart helps bolster the company's plant-based portfolio, which also includes brands Silk and So Delicious. Financial details were not disclosed.

HISTORY

In 1965 Antoine Riboud replaced his uncle as chairman of family-run Souchon-Neuvesel, a Lyons, France-based maker of glass bottles. Antoine quickly made a mark in this field -- he merged the firm with Boussois, a major French flat-glass manufacturer, creating BSN in 1966.

Antoine enlarged BSN's glass business and filled the company's bottles by acquiring well-established beverage and food concerns. In 1970 BSN purchased Brasseries Kronenbourg (France's largest brewer), SociÃ©tÃ© EuropÃ©enne de Brasseries (another French brewer), and Evian (mineral water, France). The 1972 acquisition of Glaverbel (Belgium) gave BSN 50% of Europe's flat-glass market. The next year BSN merged with France's Gervais Danone (yogurt, cheese, Panzani pasta; founded in 1919 and named after founder Isaac Carasso's son Daniel). This moved the company into pan-European brand-name foods.

Increasing energy costs depressed flat-glass earnings, so BSN began divesting its flat-glass businesses. In the late 1970s it acquired interests in brewers in Belgium, Spain, and Italy.

BSN bought Dannon, the leading US yogurt maker (co-founded by Daniel Carasso, who had continued making Danone yogurt in France until WWII), in 1982. It established a strong presence in the Italian pasta market by buying stakes in Ponte (1985) and Agnesi (1986). BSN also purchased Generale Biscuit, the world's #3 biscuit maker (1986), and RJR Nabisco's European cookie and snack-food business (1989).

In a series of acquisitions starting in 1986, BSN took over Italy and Spain's largest mineral water companies and several European pasta makers and other food companies. Adopting the name of its leading international brand, BSN became Groupe Danone in 1994.

Antoine's son, Franck, succeeded him as chairman in 1996 and restructured the company to focus on three core businesses: dairy, beverages (specifically water and beer), and biscuits. By 1997 Danone had begun shedding non-core grocery products. The company simultaneously stepped up acquisitions of dairy, beer, biscuit, and water companies in developing markets.

The 1998 purchase of AquaPenn Spring Water for $112 million doubled its US water-bottling production capacity. Danone in 1999 completed a merger and subsequent sale of part of its BSN Emballage glass-packaging unit to UK buyout firm CVC Capital Partners for $1.2 billion; Danone retained 44% ownership. Thirsty for the #2 spot in US bottled water sales, Danone gulped down McKesson Water (the #3 bottled water firm in the US, after Nestlé and Suntory) for $1.1 billion in 2000.

Also in 2000 Danone's joint venture Finalrealm (which includes several European equity firms), along with Burlington Biscuits, Nabisco, and HM Capital Partners (then called Hicks, Muse, Tate & Furst), acquired 87% of leading UK biscuit maker United Biscuits. Danone then bought Naya (bottled water, Canada) and sold its brewing operations (#2 in Europe) to Scottish & Newcastle (later acquired by Heineken and Carlsberg) for more than $2.6 billion.

During 2001 Danone announced restructuring would shutter two LU biscuit plants and eliminate about 1,800 jobs; the move met with strikes and legal battles. That same year, having been bumped to the #2 spot in the US yogurt market (after General Mills' Yoplait brand), Danone acquired 40% of Stonyfield Farm, the #4 yogurt brand in the US, and ultimately came to own 84% of the company.

The company launched 2002 with a series of beverage acquisitions, including Frucor (New Zealand) and Zywiec Zdroj (the top brand of water in Poland). Danone then struck a deal handing Coca-Cola the distribution and marketing of Evian in North America and formed a joint venture with Coke to distribute its lower-end water brands. Antoine Riboud died that same year at the age of 83.

Danone divested noncore companies during 2002, including the sale of its Italian meat and cheese business, Galbani, and its Kro Beer Brands (Kronenbourg, 1664 brands) to Scottish & Newcastle. Then, typical of its consolidation strategy, later in 2002 Danone acquired the home and office water delivery companies Chateaud'eau (France), Patrimoine des Eaux du Quebec (Canada), and Canada's Sparkling Spring (now Aquaterra).

In 2004 Danone sold its 10% interest in the Australian dairy firm National Foods. Later that year it announced an alliance with Japanese dairy group Yakult Honsha to focus both companies' efforts with probiotics. Danone is a 20% shareholder of Yakult and has agreed not to increase its share holdings of Yakult for five years and not to pursue majority control for another five. Also in 2004 Danone acquired the Mexican bottled water company, Arco Iris.

While its dairy and water businesses bubbled along nicely, Danone found its cookies crumbling. Opting for a new recipe, in 2004 it joined with Argentine food giant ARCOR Group to merge both companies' biscuits operations in South America. Later that same year, Danone sold off its W&R Jacob Ltd. biscuits operations in Ireland to local company Fruitfield Foods. It also sold Italaquae, its Italian bottled water business, to LGR Holding.

Long after its departure from brewing, in 2004 Danone was fined ?1.5 million for forming a beer distribution cartel along with Heineken in 1996. In 2005 Danone and Coca-Cola ended their 2002 water-distribution joint venture, with Coke buying out Danone's 49% share for about $100 million.

In 2005 Danone got out of the brewing business altogether, with the sale of its 33% stake in Spanish brewer Mahou. It sold its HP Foods Group, including Amoy, Lea & Perrins, and HP sauce brands, to Heinz and its biscuits businesses in the UK and Ireland. That year it sold its US home and office water-delivery company, DS Waters of America, to investment firm Kelso & Company. Danone has increased its ownership of Russian dairy and beverage company Wimm-Bill-Dann Foods to almost 20%.

Due to slow sales for its chilled products and competition from lower-priced brands, in 2006 Danone introduced Senjà (a soy-based yogurt) in France. It acquired Egyptian fresh dairy products company Olait (which it renamed Danone Dairy Egypt) and Algerian bottled water company Tessala. On the Asian front, Danone acquired 23% of fruit-drink company China Huiyuan Juice Group and 51% of Wahaha. (It sold its interest in Huiyuan Juice in 2010.) In the Ukraine, it bought fresh dairy company JSC Molochnyi Zavod. In the US, it launched the Activia brand yogurt.

Because it wants to introduce more organic products in Europe, in 2006 Danone announced the spending of $66 million on the expansion of its subsidiary Stonyfield Farm's New Hampshire production plant. (That year, Stonyfield bought a 34% interest in Irish organic dairy, Glenisk.)

In 2006 Danone sold its Amoy Asian sauce and chilled foods business to Ajinomoto, exiting the sauce business altogether. It then sold virtually all of its grocery activities, glass-container business, its cheese and cured meat activities (Galbani), and its beer activities in Europe. It also sold New Zealand biscuits maker Griffins Food to investment firm Pacific Equity Partners.

Danone paid ?12 billion (about $16 billion) for Numico, maker of infant food and medical nutrition (nutritional bars and shakes) in 2007. The Numico products (Cow & Gate, Dumex, Mellin, milupa, NUTRICIA) joined Danone's blédina baby-food brand to create a wide array of well-known nutritional products for babies and adults. The purchase made Danone the largest baby-food maker in Europe.

Prior to announcing the Numico purchase, Danone announced the sale of its cookie business to Kraft Foods; that deal closed in late 2007. At the time, some analysts saw Danone as ripe for a takeover; hence, the Numico deal was construed as a way for Danone to remain independent. (The acquisition was viewed as helping ward off predators who might have been attracted to the cash that Danone accrued as a result of the Kraft deal.) As part of its strategy to divest itself of all biscuit/cookie activities, in 2009 the company ended its Indian joint venture with the Wadia Group. Danone sold its 50% interest in the operation, ABI Holdings, to Wadia.

Strengthening its business in Asia, in 2007 Danone acquired all of the Japanese joint venture with Ajinomoto and Calpis that it did not already own. Renamed Danone Japan, the operation manufactures fresh products for the expanding Japanese dairy market.

Saying it wanted to "regain room for maneuver[ing]," in 2007 it sold off its 20% stake in and terminated its distribution agreement with Shanghai-based Bright Dairy. Danone cited no specifics surrounding the move, but the company has had legal disputes with various joint-venture partners in China and India recently, relating to how its brands are marketed and produced.

In late 2007 the company exited its joint venture with Chinese company Mengniu Dairy Group, citing time frame and other condition difficulties. (Both companies agreed to the termination of the venture, which was initiated in 2006.) Turning to South America that same year, Danone acquired a 70% holding in Chile's fresh dairy company, Vialat.

Among its divestments in 2008, in order to fulfill European Union requirements for its acquisition of Numico, the company sold off its French baby milk and baby drinks businesses to Groupe Lactalis. That year it also sold its subsidiary, Frucor, a maker of non-alcoholic beverages in New Zealand and Australia, as well as its international brands V and Mizone (with the exception of in China and Indonesia) to Suntory for some ?600 million ($780 million).

Danone took full control of its South African joint venture, Danone Clover, in 2009. It purchased Clover's 45% stake for R1,085 ($145 million). (Clover is one of South Africa's largest dairy companies.) Other partnerships include a joint venture with Weight Watchers formed in 2008. The 51% Weight Watchers-49% Danone operation provides weight-management services to the People's Republic of China.

Following its acquisition of a controlling interest in a venture with Russia's Unimilk in 2010, Danone sold its 18.4% stake in Wimm-Bill-Dann Foods back to the Russian dairy and juice producer for $470 million.

EXECUTIVES

Chief Executive Officer, Antoine de Saint-Affrique
Chief Financial, Technology and Data Officer, Juergen Esser
Chief Operating Officer, Vikram Agarwal
Chief Human Resources Officer, Roberto di Bernardini
Chief Sustainability and Strategic Business Development Officer, Henri Bruxelles
Chief Growth Officer, Nigyar Makhmudova
Chief Sustainability and Strategic Business Development Officer, Isabelle Esser
North America Chief Executive Officer, Shane Grant
International Chief Executive Officer, Veronique Penchienati-Bosetta
General Secretary, Laurent Sacchi
Chairman, Independent Director, Gilles Schnepp
Honorary Chairman, Franck Riboud
Independent Director, Lead Independent Director, Jean-Michel Severino
Independent Director, Guido Barilla
Independent Director, Clara Gaymard
Independent Director, Michel Landel
Independent Director, Gaelle Olivier
Independent Director, Serpil Timuray
Independent Director, Lionel Zinsou-Derlin
Non-Independent Director, Cecile Cabanis
Director, Frederic Boutebba
Director, Bettina Theissig
Auditors : PricewaterhouseCoopers Audit

LOCATIONS

HQ: Danone
17, Boulevard Haussmann, Paris 75009
Phone: (33) 1 44 35 20 20   **Fax:** (33) 1 44 35 26 95
Web: www.danone.com

2018 Sales

	% of total
Asia-Pacific, Latin America, Middle East, Africa & CIS	45
Europe and NORAM	55
Total	**100**

PRODUCTS/OPERATIONS

2018 sales

	%
Essential Dairy & Plant-Based (North America)	20
Essential Dairy & Plant-Based (International)	33
Specialized Nutrition	29
Waters	18
Total	**100**

COMPETITORS

ASSOCIATED BRITISH FOODS PLC
Fresh Del Monte Produce Inc.
GENERAL MILLS, INC.
Grupo Lala, S.A.B. de C.V.
Nestlé S.A.
PARMALAT FINANZIARIA SPA
PEPSICO, INC.
RECKITT BENCKISER GROUP PLC
SUNTORY HOLDINGS LIMITED
UNITED BISCUITS TOPCO LIMITED

HISTORICAL FINANCIALS

Company Type: Public

Income Statement FYE: December 31

	REVENUE ($mil)	NET INCOME ($mil)	NET PROFIT MARGIN	EMPLOYEES
12/21	27,482	2,177	7.9%	98,105
12/20	28,988	2,400	8.3%	101,911
12/19	28,391	2,165	7.6%	102,449
12/18	28,230	2,690	9.5%	105,783
12/17	29,581	2,940	9.9%	104,843
Annual Growth	(1.8%)	(7.2%)	—	(1.6%)

2021 Year-End Financials

Debt ratio: 40.4%
Return on equity: 11.4%
Cash ($ mil.): 745
Current Ratio: 1.09
Long-term debt ($ mil.): 14,082
No. of shares ($ mil.): 638
Dividends
  Yield: 7.6%
  Payout: 13.2%
Market value ($ mil.): 7,906

	STOCK PRICE ($) FY Close	P/E High/Low		PER SHARE ($) Earnings	Dividends	Book Value
12/21	12.39	5	4	3.33	0.95	30.64
12/20	13.10	6	4	3.67	0.48	30.61
12/19	16.49	6	5	3.31	0.43	29.83
12/18	13.98	5	4	4.16	0.44	28.92
12/17	16.77	4	4	4.69	0.42	27.49
Annual Growth	(7.3%)	—	—	(8.2%)	22.7%	2.7%

Danske Bank A/S

Danske Bank is the largest financial services provider in Denmark, and one of the largest financial institutions in the Nordic countries. It serves approximately 3.3 million personal and business customers, as well as about 2,060 corporate and institutional customers in eight countries. The bank's core markets include Denmark, Finland, Norway, and Sweden. It offers a wide range of services in the fields of banking, mortgage finance, insurance, pension, real-estate brokerage, asset management and trading in fixed income products, foreign exchange, and equities. Danske Bank's roots go back to 1871, when Den Danske Landmandsbank was founded. The bank generates the majority of its revenue in Denmark.

Operations

Danske Bank operates four business units, a Non-core unit and a Group Functions unit.

Personal & Business Customers, brings in about 60% of the bank's revenue, serves personal customers and small and medium-sized corporates across all Nordic markets.

Large Corporates & Institutions serves large corporate and institutional customers across all Nordic markets. It provides about 20% of the bank's revenue.

Danica Pension specializes in pension schemes, life insurance policies, and health insurance policies in Denmark and Norway.

Northern Ireland (generates approximately 5%) serves retail and commercial customers through a network of branches and business centers in Northern Ireland alongside digital channels.

Non-core includes certain customer segments that are no longer considered part of the core business. The Non-core unit is responsible for the controlled winding-up of this part of the loan portfolio. The portfolio consists primarily of loans to customers in the Baltics and liquidity facilities for Special Purpose Vehicles (SPVs) and conduit structures.

Geographic Reach

Denmark accounts for about 45% of Copenhagen-based Danske Bank's total revenue. Sweden brings in nearly 25%, followed by Norway with almost 20%. Finland, Ireland, the UK, Germany, Baltics, and Poland account for the rest.

Sales and Marketing

Danske Bank serves retail and commercial customers, as well as companies and institutional investors through a network of branches, business centers, and digital channels.

Financial Performance

Note: Growth rates may differ after conversion to US dollars.

Danske Bank's revenues have been fluctuating over the past five years. The bank has had a decline of about 40% from 2017 to 2020. The significant decline can be attributed to recent economical hindrances such as the COVID-19 pandemic: despite economic recovery, government support packages in Denmark contributed to the subdued credit demand in the country's banking sector.

The company's total income in 2021 was up 4% to DKK 42.6 billion from DKK 40.9 billion in 2020. The increase was driven mainly by a strong performance in its capital markets activities on the back of good customer activity, and it continues to support customers with advisory services and capital.

Net interest income amounted to DKK 22 billion in 2021 from DKK 22.2 billion in 2020. It saw a positive impact from the deposit repricing initiatives at Personal & Business Customers Denmark that were implemented during 2021. At Large Corporates & Institutions, the company saw higher activity-driven net interest income and higher net interest income from undrawn committed credit facilities, which compensated for the decline in net interest income from lower average lending volumes.

Danske Bank ended 2021 with total cash and cash equivalents of DKK 363 billion. Operating activities used DKK 37.6 billion, used mainly for deposits, amounts due to credit institutions and banks, and issued bonds. Investing activities used another DKK 1.6 billion for acquisition of tangible and intangible assets. Financing activities also used DKK 1.4 billion, mainly for redemptions of non-preferred senior bonds, subordinated debt, and equity accounted capital.

Strategy

Danske Bank has reached the mid-point

period for its strategic transformation plan. The company will continue to enhance its services and products to customers as well as support innovation in the society. The company updated its 2023 ambitions by strengthening its position to deliver long-term sustainable value creation. Danske Bank is also extending the timeline for reaching amore normalized compliance cost level to 2025 to allow it to sustain the resilience of Danske Bank.

As the next step in Danske Bank's ongoing transformation, it announced in January 2022 a further fine-turning of the organization. Going forward, the commercial activities will be organized in three business units: Personal Customers, Business Customers, and Large Corporates & Institutions. The aim is to become even more customer-centric and to enhance the commercial focus as well as to accelerate execution of the 2023 plan.

Mergers and Acquisitions

In 2021, Danske Bank has entered into an agreement with OP Financial Group in Finland and the consortium of banks behind Vipps in Norway to merge the three mobile payment providers MobilePay, Vipps, and Pivo. The ambition is to create Europe's best and most comprehensive digital wallet. Serving 11 million users and over 330,000 shops and web shops, the company will be one of the largest bank-owned mobile payment providers in Europe. In addition, the parties plan to invest heavily in e-commerce, which has been growing rapidly in recent years, and to ensure users access to mobile cross-border payments. The banks behind Vipps will own 65% of the new parent company, Vipps AS, Danske Bank will own 25%, and the OP Financial Group will own 10%.

HISTORY

Leathersmith-turned-stock trader Gottlieb Gedalia founded Den Danske Landmandsbank, Hypothek- og Vexelbank i KjÃ¸benhavn (The Danish Farmer's Bank, Mortgage, and Exchange Bank of Copenhagen. It would change its name four times before finally settling on the less-verbose Danske Bank.

Even in its early years, Danske Bank never restricted itself to purely agricultural concerns, preferring to offer a wide range of banking services that appealed to farmers, merchants, and businessmen alike. Isak GlÃ¼ckstadt, who managed the bank from 1872 until his death in 1910, guided the bank to prominence in Copenhagen's corporate landscape, where it became a leading commercial bank. GlÃ¼ckstadt's son, Emil, succeeded his father as managing director in 1910. Despite his best efforts, Danske Bank could not cope with the strains of WWI and the Depression; the Danish government had to rescue the firm from bankruptcy. But the bank survived German occupation during WWII mostly unscathed.

During the 1960s and 1970s Denmark's government encouraged Danish banks to expand internationally. Danske Bank pounced on the opportunity by forming consortium banks with such Nordic neighbors as Skandinaviska Enskilda Banken (aka S-E-Banken). Danske Bank stayed ahead of its competitors through acquisitions, including the purchase of two large Danish banks in 1990, making it Denmark's largest bank.

By 1990 the bank also had made its presence felt worldwide, but Asian economic crises in the early 1990s caused the bank's international subsidiaries to fall short of expectations. After restructuring its international business, the bank focused more energy on its Nordic customers. It bought Sweden's Ã–stgÃ¶ta Enskilda in 1998 and Norway's Fokus Bank in 1999. In 2000 Danske bought fellow Danish Bank BG Bank. Danske also added a Finnish asset management company and a majority interest in Pol-Can Bank of Poland in the same year. In 2001 Danske and BG trimmed down redundant branches.

Danske Bank bought the banking operations of Finnish insurer Sampo for more than $5 billion in 2007. The acquisition brought in more than 150 branches in Finland, Estonia, Latvia, and Lithuania. It followed Danske Bank's 2005 acquisitions of National Irish Bank and Northern Bank from National Australia Bank for some $1.8 billion.

EXECUTIVES

Chief Executive Officer, Carsten Rasch Egeriis
Chief Risk Officer, Magnus Agustsson
Chief People Officer, Karsten Breum
Chief Financial Officer, Stephen Engels
Chief Operating Officer, France Woelders
Chairman, Independent Director, Martin Blessing
Vice-Chairman, Non-Independent Director, Jan Thorsgaard Nielsen
Independent Director, Jacob Dahl
Independent Director, Raija-Leena Hankonen-Nybom
Independent Director, Bente Avnung Landsnes
Independent Director, Allan Polack
Independent Director, Carol Sergeant
Independent Director, Helle Valentin
Non-Independent Director, Lars-Erik Brenoe
Director, Bente Bang
Director, Kirsten Ebbe Brich
Director, Aleksandras Cicacovas
Director, Louise Aggerstrom Hansen
Auditors: Deloitte Statsautoriseret Revisionspartnerselskab

LOCATIONS

HQ: Danske Bank A/S
Holmens Kanal 2-12, Copenhagen K DK-1092
Phone: (45) 33 44 00 00 **Fax:** 212 370-9564
Web: www.danskebank.com

PRODUCTS/OPERATIONS

2017 Sales

	% of total
Net interest income	49
Net fee income	32
Net trading income	16
Other income	3
Total	100

2017 Sales by Segment

	% of total
Personal Banking	25
Business Banking	23
Corporate & Institutions	23
Wealth Management	17
Northern Ireland	4
Other Activities	5
Eliminations	(2)
Reclassification	3
Total	100

COMPETITORS

Banque de MontrÃ©al
CoÃ¶peratieve Rabobank U.A.
DEUTSCHE BANK AG
ING Groep N.V.
Nordea Bank AB
Skandinaviska Enskilda Banken AB
Svenska Handelsbanken AB
The Toronto-Dominion Bank
U.S. BANCORP
UniCredit Bank AG

HISTORICAL FINANCIALS

Company Type: Public

Income Statement   FYE: December 31

	ASSETS ($mil)	NET INCOME ($mil)	INCOME AS % OF ASSETS	EMPLOYEES
12/22	540,456	(740)	—	21,022
12/21	599,002	1,897	0.3%	21,754
12/20	677,815	666	0.1%	22,376
12/19	565,217	2,146	0.4%	22,006
12/18	548,803	2,132	0.4%	20,683
Annual Growth	(0.4%)		—	0.4%

2022 Year-End Financials

Return on assets: (-0.1%)   Dividends
Return on equity: (-3.0%)   Yield: —
Long-term debt ($ mil.): —   Payout: 0.0%
No. of shares ($ mil.): 850   Market value ($ mil.): 8,382
Sales ($ mil.): 15,206

	STOCK PRICE ($) FY Close	P/E High/Low	PER SHARE ($) Earnings	Dividends	Book Value
12/22	9.85	— —	(0.86)	0.09	27.06
12/21	8.66	1 1	2.22	0.11	31.51
12/20	8.21	2 1	0.78	0.33	32.59
12/19	8.05	1 0	2.51	0.43	30.02
12/18	9.99	1 1	2.53	0.56	29.29
Annual Growth	(0.4%)		—	(35.9%)	(2.0%)

Datang International Power Generation Co Ltd

Datang Power is a powerful player in the Chinese power market. Datang International Power Generation (Datang Power), formerly Beijing Datang Power Generation, operates and develops power plants (primarily coal-fired), sells electricity, and provides power equipment maintenance services. One of China's top independent power producers, with a generating capacity of 39,190 MW (coal-fired, wind powered, and hydroelectric facilities), Datang Power owns and operates four power plants and manages more than 50 power and power-related companies in 18 provinces. In 2013 it added 1,240 MW of renewable energy capacity. Government-owned China Datang Corp. owns about 35% of Datang Power (which also has chemical and coal assets).

EXECUTIVES

Staff Supervisor, Deputy General Manager, Hong Guo
Accountant General, Quancheng Liu
Staff Supervisor, Genle Liu
Staff Supervisor, Bo Song
Deputy General Manager, Fugui Bai
Deputy General Manager, Qiying Wang
Deputy General Manager, Zheng Chang
Deputy General Manager, Wenwei Duan
Deputy General Manager, Yong Wan
Independent Non-executive Director, Dongxiao Niu
Non-executive Director, Bo Qu
Non-executive Director, Yongxing Sun
Auditors : ShineWing (HK) CPA Limited

LOCATIONS

HQ: Datang International Power Generation Co Ltd
No. 9 Guangningbo Street, Xicheng District, Beijing 100033
Phone: (86) 10 88008800   Fax: (86) 10 88008111
Web: www.dtpower.com

PRODUCTS/OPERATIONS

2015 Sales

	% of total
Sales of electricity	90
Sales of chemical products	3
Heat supply	2
Sales of coal	—
Others	5
Total	100

2015 Sales

	% of total
Power generation Segment	93
Chemical segment	3
Coal segment	—
Other segments	4
Total	100

COMPETITORS

CHINA POWER INTERNATIONAL DEVELOPMENT LIMITED
COGENTRIX ENERGY POWER MANAGEMENT LLC
ELECTRICITY GENERATING AUTHORITY OF THAILAND
Maxim Power Corp.
TAIWAN POWER COMPANY

HISTORICAL FINANCIALS

Company Type: Public

Income Statement   FYE: December 31

	REVENUE ($mil)	NET INCOME ($mil)	NET PROFIT MARGIN	EMPLOYEES
12/22	16,934	(59)	—	0
12/21	16,288	(1,459)	—	0
12/20	14,619	464	3.2%	0
12/19	13,718	153	1.1%	0
12/18	13,577	179	1.3%	33,483
Annual Growth	5.7%	—	—	—

2022 Year-End Financials

Debt ratio: 8.4%
Return on equity: (-0.6%)
Cash ($ mil.): 1,470
Current Ratio: 0.42
Long-term debt ($ mil.): 16,699
No. of shares ($ mil.): —
Dividends
Yield: —
Payout: 0.0%
Market value ($ mil.): —

DBS Group Holdings Ltd.

Founded in 1968, DBS is a leading financial services group in Asia with a presence in about 20 markets. The bank is focused on leveraging digital technology to reimagine banking to provide its customers a full range of services in consumer banking, wealth management, and institutional banking. Headquartered and listed in Singapore, DBS has a growing presence in the three key Asian axes of growth: Greater China (less than 10% of total income), Southeast Asia and South Asia (roughly 10%). The bank serves more than 11.8 million consumer-banking/wealth management customers and more than 340,000 million institutional banking customers. DBS has approximately S$686 billion of total assets.

Operations

DBS Group reports in four major business segments are: Institutional Banking, Consumer Banking/Wealth Management, Treasury Markets, and others.

Institutional Banking (more than 40% of total income) provides financial services and products to institutional clients including bank and non-bank financial institutions, government-linked companies, large corporates and small and medium-sized businesses. The business focuses on broadening and deepening customer relationships. Products and services comprise the full range of credit facilities from short-term working capital financing to specialized lending. It also provides global transactional services such as cash management, trade finance and securities and fiduciary services, treasury and markets products, corporate finance and advisory banking as well as capital markets solutions.

Consumer Banking/Wealth Management (over 35%) provides individual customers with a diverse range of banking and related financial services. The products and services available to customers include current and savings accounts, fixed deposits, loans and home finance, cards, payments, investment, and insurance products.

Treasury Markets' activities (about 10%) primarily include structuring, market-making and trading across a broad range of treasury products. The Others segment (accounts for the rest) encompasses the results of corporate decisions that are not attributed to business segments as well as the contribution of LVB as its activities have not been aligned with the group's segment definitions.

Geographic Reach

Headquartered in Singapore, DBS generates majority of its income from Singapore (about 65%) where its head office is located while more than 15% comes from Hong Kong. The rest of greater China and South and Southeast Asia bring in less than 10% each, and the rest of the world account for the rest.

Hong Kong comprises mainly DBS Bank (HK) Limited and DBS HK branch. Rest of Greater China comprises mainly DBS Bank (China) Ltd, DBS Bank (Taiwan) Ltd and DBS Taipei branch. South and Southeast Asia comprises mainly PT Bank DBS Indonesia, DBS Bank India Limited (including LVB balances post-amalgamation) and DBS Labuan branch.

Sales and Marketing

Throughout the year, DBS maintains active engagement of its stakeholders with enhanced content and contextualized marketing. It interacts with customers through multiple channels including digital banking, call centers and branches. It communicates with its employees using multiple channels to ensure they are aligned with its strategic priorities. This also allows the company to be up to date with their concerns.

Financial Performance

The company had a net interest income of S$8.4 billion in 2021, a 7% decrease from the previous year's net interest income of S$8.4 billion.

In 2021, the company had a net income of S$7.8 billion, a 45% increase from the previous year's net income of S$5.4 billion.

The company's cash at the end of 2021 was S$46.7 billion. Operating activities generated S$7.7 billion, while investing activities used S$1.6 billion, primarily for acquisition of interests in associates and joint ventures. Financing activities used another S$2.6 billion, mainly for dividends paid to shareholders of the company.

Strategy

In the last decade, DBS focused on technology transformation to build a robust and scalable foundation. The Covid-19 pandemic validated its strategy. At the onset of the pandemic, the company's staff swiftly switched to remote working without any loss of productivity, continued delivering on its book of work and experimented with emerging technologies such as 5G, Internet of Things (IoT) and blockchain. DBS doubled down on its technology investments to create further distance between the company and its competitors, which allowed DBS to move into a new chapter of transformation to deliver superior customer experiences.

Mergers and Acquisitions

In mid-2021, DBS Group Holdings announced that its wholly-owned subsidiary, DBS Bank Ltd (DBS), entered into an agreement and obtained approvals from Monetary Authority of Singapore (MAS) and China Banking and Insurance Regulatory Commission, Shenzhen Office (Shenzhen CBIRC) to subscribe for a 13% stake in Shenzhen Rural Commercial Bank Corporation Limited ("SZRCB") for RMB 5,286 million (S$1,079 million). The investment is in line with the group's strategy of investing in its core markets and accelerates its expansion in the rapidly growing Greater Bay Area (GBA).

EXECUTIVES

Chief Executive Officer, Executive Director, Piyush Gupta
Chief Financial Officer, Sok Hui Chng
Technology & Operations Chief Information Officer, Technology & Operations Head, Jimmy Keng Joo Ng
Chief Risk Officer, Kian Tiong Soh
Secretary, Chia-Yin Teoh
Secretary, Marc Tan
Non-Independent Non-Executive Director, Chairman, Peter Lim Huat Seah
Independent Non-Executive Director, Bonghan Cho
Independent Non-Executive Director, Punita Lal
Independent Non-Executive Director, Judy Lee
Independent Non-Executive Director, Anthony Weng Kin Lim
Independent Non-Executive Director, Sai Choy Tham
Non-Executive Director, Lead Independent Director, Olivier Tse Ghow Lim
Non-Independent Non-Executive Director, Kai Fong Chng
Non-Independent Non-Executive Director, Tian Yee Ho
Auditors : PricewaterhouseCoopers LLP

LOCATIONS

HQ: DBS Group Holdings Ltd.
   12 Marina Boulevard, Marina Bay Financial Centre Tower 3, 018982

Phone: (65) 6878 8888   **Fax:** 213 627-0228
Web: www.dbs.com

2016 Sales

	% of total
Singapore	66
Hong Kong	18
Rest of the greater China	7
South and Southeast Asia	6
Rest of the world	3
Total	100

PRODUCTS/OPERATIONS

2016 Sales

	% of total
Institutional Banking	45
Consumer Banking/wealth management	37
Treasury	10
Others	8
Total	100

2016 Sales

	% of total
Interest income	64
Net fee and commission income	20
Net Trading income	12
Net income from investment securities	3
Other income	1
Total	100

Selected Subsidiaries

DBS Bank
   Bank of the Philippines Islands (20.3%)
   Cholamandalam DBS Finance Limited (37.4%)
   DBS Asia Capital Limited
   DBS Asset Management Ltd
   DBS Diamond Holdings Ltd
   DBS Bank (Hong Kong) Limited
   Hutchison DBS Card Ltd (50%)
   DBSN Services Pte. Ltd.
   DBS Vickers Securities (Singapore) Pte Ltd
   The Islamic Bank of Asia Limited (50%)
   PT Bank DBS Indonesia (99%)

COMPETITORS

BANK OF AYUDHYA PUBLIC COMPANY LIMITED
CIMB GROUP HOLDINGS BERHAD
GREAT EASTERN HOLDINGS LIMITED
Grupo Financiero Banorte, S.A.B. de C.V.
HSBC HOLDINGS PLC
NOMURA INTERNATIONAL PLC
OVERSEA-CHINESE BANKING CORPORATION LIMITED
SAVILLS PLC
UNITED OVERSEAS BANK LIMITED
Wüstenrot & Württembergische AG

HISTORICAL FINANCIALS

Company Type: Public

Income Statement   FYE: December 31

	ASSETS ($mil)	NET INCOME ($mil)	INCOME AS % OF ASSETS	EMPLOYEES
12/22	554,675	6,113	1.1%	36,000
12/21	508,263	5,041	1.0%	33,000
12/20	491,732	3,571	0.7%	29,000
12/19	430,308	4,750	1.1%	28,000
12/18	404,458	4,095	1.0%	0
Annual Growth	8.2%	10.5%	—	—

2022 Year-End Financials

Return on assets: 1.1%   Dividends
Return on equity: 14.3%   Yield: —
Long-term debt ($ mil.): —   Payout: 174.4%
No. of shares ($ mil.): 2,572   Market value ($ mil.): 260,740
Sales ($ mil.): 16,188

STOCK PRICE ($) FY Close	P/E High/Low	PER SHARE ($) Earnings	Dividends	Book Value
12/22	101.37	35 28	2.35	4.10	16.50
12/21	97.36	37 29	1.93	2.81	16.60
12/20	76.05	44 28	1.37	2.73	16.21
12/19	77.16	34 28	1.83	4.16	14.84
12/18	69.73	42 31	1.58	4.98	14.12
Annual Growth	9.8%	—	10.5%	(4.7%)	4.0%

DCC Plc

DCC is a leading international sales, marketing, and support services company. It is organized into four divisions: Retail & Oil, Technology, Liquid Petroleum Gas (LPG), and Healthcare. It distributes to end users or resellers in nearly 20 countries, sourcing product wholesale from refineries and manufacturers. DCC operates through dozens of subsidiaries including Butagaz, Exertis, Certas Energy, and Flogas. It also trades under the Esso brand under license in Norway. DCC generates the majority of its revenue from customer in the UK. DCC was founded in 1976 as a venture capital company before expanding into commodity distribution.

Operations

DCC operates under four reportable segments: DCC Retail & Oil, DCC Technology, DCC LPG, and DCC Healthcare.

DCC Retail & Oil generates approximately 55% of revenue. The segment is the leading provider of transport and heating energy, lower emission fuels and biofuels, and related services to consumers and businesses across Europe and has a key focus on being a market leader in providing sustainable energy solutions to consumers.

DCC Technology brings up about 25% of revenue. It is a leading route-to-market and supply chain partner for global technology brands and customers. The segment provides a broad range of consumer, business and enterprise technology products and services to retailers, resellers and integrators and domestic appliances and lifestyle products to retailers and consumers.

DCC LPG gives in approximately 15% of revenue. It supplies LPG in cylinder and bulk format to residential, commercial and industrial customers. In addition, the segment continues to develop a broader customer offering through the supply of natural gas, power and renewables products, plus a range of specialty gases such as refrigerants and medical gases.

DCC Healthcare segment generates about 5% of revenue. It provides products and services to healthcare providers and health and beauty brand owners.

Geographic Reach

Dublin-based, DCC generates more than 35% of its revenue from the UK, followed by France which gives in about 20%, Ireland and

North America contribute nearly 10% each, and the rest comes from other countries.

Sales and Marketing

DCC has a diverse customer base. Its hydrocarbon businesses serve domestic, agriculture, commercial, aviation, and marine customers, and gas stations. The Technology division's customers are physical and online retailers, resellers, and value added retailers. The Heathcare segment serves health and beauty brand owners, specialist retailers, and direct sales/mail order companies.

Financial Performance

Note: Growth rates may differ after conversion to US Dollars.

Revenue for the year amounted to £17.7 billion, a 32% increase from 2021's revenue of £13.4 billion.

The profit for the year attributable to owners of the Parent Company amounted to £312.3 million (2021: £292.6 million).

The company's cash for the year ended 2022 was £1.3 billion. Operating activities generated £451.8 million, while investing activities used £867.4 million, mainly for acquisition of subsidiaries. Financing activities provided another £21.5 million, primarily for dividends paid to owners of the Parent Company.

Strategy

The company's strategy informs how it enables people and businesses to grow and progress and achieve its long-term strategic objective, which is to build a growing, sustainable and cash-generative business which consistently provides returns on capital well in excess of the company's cost of capital. The company does this by developing high quality sales, marketing and support services businesses within industries that provide essential products and services to society. Its businesses create sustainable competitive advantage within these industries by building leading positions in selected sectors, focusing on value creation for their stakeholders, and benefiting from group expertise in areas such as capital deployment and risk management.

Mergers and Acquisitions

In late 2021, DCC announced that DCC Technology completed the acquisition of Almo Corporation ("Almo" or the "Business"). The acquisition was based on an initial enterprise value of approximately $610 million (£462 million) on a cash-free, debt-free basis. The transaction represents DCC's largest acquisition to date and materially expands DCC Technology's successful and growing North American business.

Company Background

In early 2020, DCC Healthcare acquired Minnesota based, Amerilab Technologies Inc. a specialist provider of contract manufacturing and related services in effervescent nutritional products for $85 million. The acquisition is part of the company's step to build a business of scale in the world's largest health supplements and nutritional products market.

In late 2019, DCC Healthcare acquired Florida-based, Ion Labs, Inc. a contract manufacturer of nutritional products for $60 million. This acquisition represented a significant step in DCC Health & Beauty Solutions' strategy to build a material presence in the attractive US health supplements and nutritional products market.

EXECUTIVES

Chief Executive Officer, Executive Director, Donal Murphy
Chief Financial Officer, Executive Director, Kevin Lucey
Information Technology Chief Information Officer, Peter Quinn
Control Director, Financial Planning Director, Finance Director, Conor Murphy
Human Resources Head, Nicola McCracken
Secretary, General Counsel, Darragh Byrne
Non-Executive Chairman, Director, John Moloney
Non-Executive Director, Senior Independent Director, Mark Breuer
Non-Executive Director, Caroline Dowling
Non-Executive Director, Tufan Erginbilgic
Non-Executive Director, David C. Jukes
Non-Executive Director, Pamela J. Kirby
Non-Executive Director, Jane Ann Lodge
Non-Executive Director, Cormac Michael Mccarthy
Non-Executive Director, Mark Ryan
Auditors : KPMG

LOCATIONS

HQ: DCC Plc
DCC House, Leopardstown Road, Foxrock, Dublin D18 PK00
Phone: (353) 1 279 9400   **Fax:** (353) 1 283 1017
Web: www.dcc.ie

2018 sales

	%
United Kingdom	54
France	19
Ireland	6
Other	21
Total	100

PRODUCTS/OPERATIONS

2018 Sales

	% of total
Retail & Oil	65
Technology	22
LPG	10
Healthcare	4
Total	100

COMPETITORS

CARR'S GROUP PLC
DIPLOMA PLC
EG GROUP LIMITED
FLUIDRA, SA
MRC GLOBAL INC.
NOW INC.
REXEL
THERMON GROUP HOLDINGS, INC.
VALLOUREC
WESFARMERS LIMITED

HISTORICAL FINANCIALS

Company Type: Public

Income Statement   FYE: March 31

	REVENUE ($mil)	NET INCOME ($mil)	NET PROFIT MARGIN	EMPLOYEES
03/22	23,270	409	1.8%	15,341
03/21	18,464	402	2.2%	13,199
03/20	18,228	303	1.7%	12,773
03/19	19,946	343	1.7%	12,418
03/18	20,044	367	1.8%	10,430
Annual Growth	3.8%	2.7%	—	10.1%

2022 Year-End Financials

Debt ratio: 27.5%   No. of shares ($ mil.): 98
Return on equity: 11.2%   Dividends
Cash ($ mil.): 1,829   Yield: —
Current Ratio: 1.37   Payout: 17.2%
Long-term debt ($ mil.): 2,537   Market value ($ mil.): 4,094

	STOCK PRICE ($) FY Close	P/E High/Low	PER SHARE ($) Earnings	Dividends	Book Value
03/22	41.50	— —	4.15	0.72	38.65
03/21	41.50	16 9	4.08	0.68	36.98
03/20	32.15	— —	3.08	0.64	31.22
03/19	41.92	— —	3.66	0.57	31.87
03/18	41.92	— —	4.11	0.57	25.87
Annual Growth	(0.3%)	— —	0.2%	5.8%	10.6%

Denso Corp

Since its founding in 1956, Denso Corporation has made quality products and services. The company continues to lead changes in the mobility domain and repeatedly pursuing innovations and new creations. Industries include chemistry, physics, electronic engineering, and software. The company also manufactures semiconductors. Globally, the company has 170,000 employees and cater to customer through its segments: electrification; powertrain; thermal; mobility; and sensor systems & semiconductors.

Operations

Denso's operations are divided into seven segments: Electrification Systems (about 20%); Powertrain Systems (more than 20%); Thermal Systems (about 25%); Mobility Systems (more than 20%); Sensor Systems & Semiconductors (about 5%); and Industrial Solutions and Food Value Chain (around 5%)

The electrification systems segment produces HEV and BEV drive systems, power supply and related products for vehicles that are eco-friendly. In addition, the segment also manufactures electric power steering motors, control bake motors, and electric control units (ECU).

The powertrain systems segment develops and manufactures gasoline and diesel engine management systems as well as engine-related products such as variable cam timing (VCT) systems. The thermal systems segment produces air-conditioning systems for cars and buses.

The mobility segment develops electronic systems, human-machine interface (HMI), telematics control units (TCUs), advanced driver assistance systems (ADAS).

The sensor systems segment & semiconductors manufacture microelectronic devices such as in-vehicle power semiconductors, semiconductor sensors, and integrated circuits (ICs).

The industrial solutions segment makes automated equipment, modules, and industrial-use robots while the food value chain segment manufactures and sells turnkey solutions for horticultural facilities (consulting and cloud services related to greenhouse materials).

Geographic Reach
Based in Japan, DENSO operates globally in regions North America (about 20%), Europe (10%), and Asia (about 25%).

Financial Performance
Note: Growth rates may differ after conversion to US Dollars.

For the past five years, Denso's performance have fluctuated with fiscal year ended 2022 as its highest performing year over the period.

The company's revenue increased by Â¥579 billion to Â¥ 5.5 trillion in 2022 as compared to Â¥4.9 trillion in 2021.

Denso's net income for 2022 increased to Â¥7.4 trillion as compared to the prior year's net income of Â¥6.8 trillion.

The company held Â¥ 867.8 billion at the end of the year. Operating activities provided Â¥395.6 billion. Investing activities and financing activities used Â¥301.6 billion and Â¥59.5 billion, respectively.

Company Background
Originally the in-house parts supplier for Toyota, Nippondenso Co. (the predecessor to DENSO) was spun off by Toyota in 1949. Nippondenso remained dependent upon Toyota for sales, as it still does today.

In 1966 Nippondenso established sales offices in the US, then turned to Europe, establishing a branch office Germany in 1970. It later went on to establish subsidiaries in the US, Canada, Europe, and Asia. In 1984, Nippondenso joined with Allen Bradley Co. (US) to develop factory automation equipment. The company changed its name to DENSO CORPORATION in 1996. In 2001 the company merged its industrial equipment subsidiaries (bar code scanners and factory automation robots), and spun them off as majority-owned subsidiary DENSO Wave (now part of the company's non-automotive business segment). In 2006 DENSO added four new Chinese production facilities that make navigation systems, air conditioner compressors, instrument panels, and oil filters. It has also established technical centers in China and Thailand.

Over the years, DENSO has partnered with rival parts suppliers Bosch and Aisin Seiki and carmaker Toyota Motor, forming joint ventures and alliances to collaborate on the development of emerging technologies such as advanced safety features and automated driving.

HISTORY
Originally the in-house parts supplier for Toyota, Nippondenso Co. (the predecessor to DENSO) was spun off by Toyota in 1949 because Toyota no longer wanted the burden of Nippondenso's troubled financial performance. Nippondenso remained dependent upon Toyota for sales, and members of Toyota's controlling family, the Toyodas, remained involved in management. Nippondenso established a technological partnership with Germany's Robert Bosch in 1953.

As part of its plan to become a major supplier to North American carmakers, in 1966 Nippondenso established a sales office in Chicago and branch offices in Los Angeles and Detroit. It then turned to Europe, establishing a branch office in Stuttgart, Germany, in 1970. The following year the company established its first overseas subsidiary, Nippondenso of Los Angeles (now DENSO Sales California). In 1972 the company established three more foreign subsidiaries, in Australia, Canada, and Thailand. A European subsidiary (now DENSO Europe) was established in the Netherlands in 1973.

Nippondenso began consignment production for what is now known as Asmo Co., a maker of electric motors, in 1978. In 1984 the company joined with Allen Bradley Co. (US) to develop factory automation equipment. That year the predecessor to DENSO Manufacturing Michigan, one of the company's largest international subsidiaries, was established. Nippondenso expanded into Spain in 1989 by opening a plant in Barcelona.

In 1990 the company formed NDM Manufacturing (now DENSO Manufacturing UK), a joint venture (25%-owned) with Magneti Marelli of Italy, for the manufacture of automotive air conditioning and heating systems. The following year Nippondenso and AT&T formed a joint venture for the development of integrated circuit (IC) cards.

Nippondenso established several Chinese manufacturing joint ventures during the mid-1990s. In 1994 the company was recognized by the Guinness Book of Records as the maker of the world's smallest car, the DENSO Micro Car.

The company changed its name to DENSO CORPORATION in 1996. In 1999 it acquired the rotating machines business of Magneti Marelli. The next year DENSO agreed to buy out Magneti Marelli's share in the companies' automotive air conditioning and heating joint venture (the deal was completed in 2001).

In 2001 DENSO ceased production of wireless phones in order to focus on making onboard car information systems. Also in 2001 the company merged its industrial equipment subsidiaries (bar code scanners and factory automation robots), and spun them off as majority-owned subsidiary DENSO Wave.

DENSO joined forces with Robert Bosch GmbH in 2003 to form a joint venture for the development of car navigation and multimedia systems.

In 2006 DENSO added four new Chinese production facilities that make navigation systems, air conditioner compressors, instrument panels, and oil filters. It has also established technical centers in China and Thailand.

EXECUTIVES
Chairman, Representative Director, Director, Koji Arima
President, Representative Director, Director, Shinnosuke Hayashi
Executive Vice President, Representative Director, Director, Yasushi Matsui
Director, Kenichiro Ito
Director, Akio Toyoda
Outside Director, Shigeki Kushida
Outside Director, Yuko Mitsuya
Outside Director, Joseph P. Schmelzeis
Auditors : Deloitte Touche Tohmatsu LLC

LOCATIONS
HQ: Denso Corp
1-1 Showa-cho, Kariya, Aichi 448-8661
Phone: (81) 566 61 7910
Web: www.denso.co.jp

2019 Sales

	% of total
Japan	43
Asia	23
North America	22
Europe	11
Others	1
Total	100

PRODUCTS/OPERATIONS
2019 Sales

	% of total
Thermal Systems	26
Powertrain Systems	24
Mobility Systems	17
Electrification Systems	15
Electronic Systems	12
Other Automotive	2
FA-New Business	4
Total	100

Products & Services
Electronics
Powertrain ECU (electronic control unit) designSemiconductor sensorPower cardsAcoustic vehicle alerting systemsBody control computers
Powertrain
VCTCommon rail systemsSpark plugExhaust gas sensorHigh pressure pumps
Thermal
CondensersRadiatorsBus air-conditionersRefrigeration unitsWater cooled intercoolers
Mobility
Milimeter-wave radarIntegrated cockpit systems

COMPETITORS

AUTOCAM CORPORATION
DANA INCORPORATED
DENSO INTERNATIONAL AMERICA, INC.
EATON CORPORATION PUBLIC LIMITED COMPANY
FUEL SYSTEMS SOLUTIONS, INC.
HILITE INTERNATIONAL, INC.
Hyundai Mobis Co., Ltd
JOHNSON CONTROLS, INC.
Robert Bosch Gesellschaft mit beschrÃ¤nkter Haftung
TENNECO INC.

HISTORICAL FINANCIALS

Company Type: Public

Income Statement — FYE: March 31

	REVENUE ($mil)	NET INCOME ($mil)	NET PROFIT MARGIN	EMPLOYEES
03/23	48,063	2,362	4.9%	195,471
03/22	45,344	2,169	4.8%	197,951
03/21	44,585	1,129	2.5%	196,126
03/20	47,475	627	1.3%	202,363
03/19	48,424	2,298	4.7%	206,521
Annual Growth	(0.2%)	0.7%	—	(1.4%)

2023 Year-End Financials

Debt ratio: 0.1%
Return on equity: 7.2%
Cash ($ mil.): 5,509
Current Ratio: 1.82
Long-term debt ($ mil.): 4,398
No. of shares ($ mil.): 1,497
Dividends
Yield: 4.6%
Payout: 0.0%
Market value ($ mil.): 42,235

	STOCK PRICE ($) FY Close	P/E High/Low	PER SHARE ($) Earnings	Dividends	Book Value
03/23	28.20	0 0	1.56	0.66	21.94
03/22	31.84	0 0	1.41	0.67	23.15
03/21	33.35	0 0	0.73	0.66	22.67
03/20	15.86	1 0	0.40	0.64	20.19
03/19	19.52	0 0	1.47	0.31	20.95
Annual Growth	9.6%	— —	1.5%	21.1%	1.2%

Dentsu Group Inc

Dentsu ensures not only group governance, but also empowers all group companies and their individuals who create value and innovation. Its numerous agencies provide creative services for thousands of clients in more than 145 countries and regions across five continents. Dentsu offers a host of marketing and communications services, including public relations, content services, creative services, and other services. Approximately 45% of the company's revenue comes from Japan. The company conducts business outside of Japan through its London-based Dentsu International Limited. Dentsu was founded in 1901 as Japan Advertising and Telegraphic Service.

Operations

Dentsu reports within two business segments: Japan business (around 45%) and International business (about 55% of sales).

Within Japan, Dentsu operates a number of business domains in which DJN will transform its current Advertising, Creative, Marketing and Promotions, Digital, Media, Content and other domains into four new business domains. These domains are AX (Advertising Transformation), BX (Business Transformation), CX (Customer Experience Transformation) and DX (Digital Transformation). In the International business segment, the group is in the process of consolidating more than 160 agency brands into six global leadership brands within Dentsu International (hereinafter "DI"). By transforming iots organizational structure into a more integrated and efficient one, it offers solutions that are ideas-led, data-driven and technology-enabled.

The company's stable of marketing agencies includes Carat, iProspect, Isobar, 360i, and Merkle, among numerous others.

With regards to the company's products and services, its advertising business virtually generates almost all of Dentsu's revenue (more than 90%). The business provides various advertising through media including newspapers, magazines, radio, television, internet, sales promotion, movies, out-of-home, and public transportation information service, which gives in about 10% of revenue, offers sales of information-related products. The company also provides clients with event marketing, creative services, marketing, public relations, and contents services.

Geographic Reach

Tokyo-based Dentsu conducts approximately 55% of its business outside of Japan, doing so through its Dentsu International, based in London. The Americas account for roughly 25% of the company's total revenue, followed by the EMEA region (Europe, Middle East & Africa) at over 20% and APAC (Asia Pacific) at approximately 10%.

Financial Performance

Net revenue increased by 17% year on year (14% year on year after factoring out the effects of foreign exchange rates) to Â¥976.6 billion. The main causes of the increase in net revenue were increased organic growth (by Â¥112,756 million; or by 13.1% on a consolidated basis, 17.9% in DJN, 9.7% in DI), increased effect of foreign exchange rates (by Â¥25,721 million), and increased effect of acquisitions (by Â¥3,059 million).

In 2021, the company had a net income of Â¥208.8 billion, a 248% improvement from the previous year's net income of Â¥141.1 billion.

The company's cash at the end of 2021 was Â¥723.5 billion. Operating activities generated Â¥139.7 billion, while financing activities used Â¥232.2 billion, primarily for payments for acquisition of interest in subsidiaries from. Investing activities provided another Â¥262.2 billion.

Strategy

To address more sophisticated and complex clients' challenges, the company has designed its strategy centering on the Integrated Growth Solutions, which are comprehensive solutions by optimally combining the company's unique and diverse capabilities. Going forward, by leveraging growth and expansion of the Customer Transformation & Technology area including growth through M&A, the company will integrate a diverse range of capabilities in the Marketing Communication field and further enhance them as solutions that help clients achieve topline growth.

Dentsu has expanded its capabilities and diversified its revenue sources during its history of development. The Marketing Communication field includes the Creative, Media and Content business domains, whereas the Customer Transformation & Technology area includes the Marketing Technology, Customer Experience Management, Commerce, System Integration, and Transformation & Growth Strategy domains. Such diverse service coverage has driven the Group's competitive advantages. Further, consumer intelligence based on its unique data base (which is the data analytics and insight that leads to an understanding of consumer behavior) underpins these diverse capabilities. On top of that, the company has forged alliances with technology companies and platformers, and has increased and expanded resources for helping clients introduce or utilize marketing technology or analysis tools of these partners. its resources are demonstrating market competitiveness in size and quality.

Mergers and Acquisitions

In mid-2022, Dentsu Group has entered an agreement to acquire a majority stake in Extentia, a global technology and services firm with a focus on enterprise mobility, cloud engineering, and user experiences. Extentia will join Merkle, a leading technology-enabled, data-driven customer experience management (CXM) company within Dentsu Group's international business, Dentsu International. Extentia has nearly 800 staff in Pune and Bangalore, India. With this acquisition, Extentia further bolsters Merkle's existing Salesforce capabilities, adding scale and additional geography in India. Terms were not disclosed.

Also in mid-2022, Dentsu Group has entered an agreement to acquire Pexlify, a leading Salesforce consultancy based in the UK and Ireland. Pexlify will join Merkle, a leading technology-enabled, data-driven customer experience management (CXM) company within Dentsu Group's international business, Dentsu International. With this acquisition, Pexlify further bolsters Merkle's existing Salesforce capabilities, adding scale and additional geography in the UK and Ireland for B2B and B2C clients. It adds expertise in Salesforce Sales, Service, and Experience Cloud solutions and further expands Merkle's existing offering in Salesforce Commerce and Marketing Clouds. Terms were not disclosed.

In early 2022, Dentsu Group has acquired

additional shares of the digital marketing operations company Dig into Inc. This announcement makes Dig into a wholly owned subsidiary of Dentsu Group. Dig into becomes part of Dentsu Japan Network (DJN), which is responsible for the Dentsu Group's business in Japan. The consolidation will allow for deeper cooperation with Dentsu Digital Inc., the company at the core of DJN's digital marketing activities, and contribute to the sustainable business growth of client companies. Terms were not disclosed.

In mid-2021, Dentsu Group has entered an agreement to acquire LiveArea, a global customer experience and commerce agency, subject to customary closing conditions, based in the US. LiveArea is a division of PFSweb Inc. LiveArea will join Merkle, a leading technology-enabled, data-driven customer experience management (CXM) company within Dentsu Group's international business, Dentsu International. With this acquisition, LiveArea bolsters Merkle's global experience and commerce capabilities and furthers Merkle's position as a go to experience partner for businesses around the world. Terms were not disclosed.

Company Background

Seeing a need for a Japanese wire service, Sino-Japanese war correspondent Hoshiro Mitsunaga founded Telegraphic Service Co. in 1901. Mitsunaga let newspapers pay their wire service bills with advertising space, which his advertising agency, Japan Advertising (also founded in 1901) resold. He merged the two companies as Nihon Denpo-Tsushin Sha (Japan Telegraphic Communication Company) in 1907. Known as Dentsu for short (the name was officially changed in 1955), the company gained Japanese rights to the United Press wire in 1908 and began extracting even more favorable advertising rates from its clients. With its mix of content and advertising, Dentsu became a leading Japanese communications business.

HISTORY

Seeing a need for a Japanese wire service, Sino-Japanese war correspondent Hoshiro Mitsunaga founded Telegraphic Service Co. in 1901. Mitsunaga let newspapers pay their wire service bills with advertising space, which his advertising agency, Japan Advertising (also founded in 1901) resold. He merged the two companies as Nihon Denpo-Tsushin Sha (Japan Telegraphic Communication Company) in 1907. Known as Dentsu for short (the name was officially changed in 1955), the company gained Japanese rights to the United Press wire in 1908 and began extracting even more favorable advertising rates from its clients. With its mix of content and advertising, Dentsu became a leading Japanese communications business. But in 1936 Japan's government consolidated all news services into its propaganda machine, Domei, taking half of Dentsu's stock. During WWII all of Japan's advertising agencies were combined into 12 entities. Following the war, US occupation forces dismantled Domei, and its 50% holding in Dentsu stock was transferred to two new press agencies, Kyodo and Jiji.

Hideo Yoshida, who became president of Dentsu in 1947, began the task of rebuilding the company, currying favor by employing the sons of politicians and business leaders. He also helped build the television industry in Japan by investing in start-up broadcasters. Their gratitude translated into preferential treatment for Dentsu, leading to its decades-long domination of Japanese TV advertising.

By 1973 Dentsu had become the world's largest advertising agency, but the company's growth stalled with the slowing Japanese economy. Slow to expand overseas, foreign billings accounted for just 7% of revenues in 1986 (and despite growth initiatives the company has yet to make lasting progress in this area). The next year Saatchi & Saatchi passed Dentsu as the world's #1 advertising group. Young & Rubicam/Dentsu later joined with Havas' Eurocom to form HDM Worldwide (named after Havas, Dentsu, and Y&R's Marsteller).

Dentsu rebounded with Japan's economic boom in the late 1980s, but the company continued to struggle abroad. Eurocom pulled out of HDM Worldwide in 1990, and the newly named Dentsu, Young & Rubicam Partnerships reorganized to focus on North America, Asia, and Australia. Dentsu joined with Collett Dickenson Pearce to maintain its presence in Europe after HDM's demise. Restructuring in 1996 created several new units, including one to focus on the Olympics, and in 1997 the company set up the Interactive Solution Center to focus on digital media.

The company agreed to buy UK ad agency Harari Page in 1998 and announced plans for its own public offering. Dentsu took a 20% stake in Bcom3 (formerly BDM) in 2000, the new advertising holding company formed by the merger of The Leo Group and MacManus Group. It also formed a Japanese Internet services joint venture with US consulting company marchFIRST. After marchFIRST's demise Dentsu gained full ownership of the company and renamed it DentsuFUSE.

The following year Dentsu reorganized its US and European units and purchased US ad firm Oasis International Group and became a publicly listed company in late 2001.

In April 2009 chairman and CEO Tateo Mataki retired, making way for Tatsuyoshi Takashima, who was the company's president and COO. Years later, Tadashi Ishii became the company's most recent president and CEO.

EXECUTIVES

Chairman of Board, Director, Timothy Andree
President, Chief Executive Officer, Executive Officer, Director, Hiroshi Igarashi
Executive Vice President, Chief Financial Officer, Executive Officer, Director, Arinobu Soga
Deputy Chief Financial Officer, Director, Nick Priday
Outside Director, Gan Matsui
Outside Director, Paul Candland
Outside Director, Andrew House
Outside Director, Keiichi Sagawa
Outside Director, Mihoko Sogabe
Outside Director, Yuka Matsuda
Auditors : KPMG AZSA LLC

LOCATIONS

HQ: Dentsu Group Inc
1-8-1 Higashi-Shimbashi, Minato-ku, Tokyo 105-7050
Phone: (81) 3 6217 6600
Web: www.group.dentsu.com

2015 Sales

	% of Sales
Japan	42
International	58
Total	100

PRODUCTS/OPERATIONS

2015 Sales

	%of Sales
Advertising	93
Information Service	7
Other Business	-
Total	100

HISTORICAL FINANCIALS

Company Type: Public

Income Statement   FYE: December 31

	REVENUE ($mil)	NET INCOME ($mil)	NET PROFIT MARGIN	EMPLOYEES
12/22	9,439	454	4.8%	69,066
12/21	9,430	941	10.0%	64,832
12/20	9,112	(1,548)	—	64,533
12/19	9,651	(745)	—	66,400
12/18	9,261	821	8.9%	62,608
Annual Growth	0.5%	(13.8%)		2.5%

2022 Year-End Financials

Debt ratio: 0.1%   No. of shares ($ mil.): 265
Return on equity: 6.9%   Dividends
Cash ($ mil.): 4,581   Yield: —
Current Ratio: 1.15   Payout: 125.0%
Long-term debt ($ mil.): 3,313   Market value ($ mil.): 8,294

	STOCK PRICE ($) FY Close	P/E High/Low		PER SHARE ($) Earnings	Dividends	Book Value
12/22	31.25	0	0	1.68	2.11	25.17
12/21	35.80	0	0	3.36	1.29	26.79
12/20	30.05			(5.54)	0.89	26.07
12/19	34.24			(2.65)	1.70	32.43
12/18	44.77	0	0	2.91	1.64	33.79
Annual Growth	(8.6%)			(12.8%)	6.5%	(7.1%)

Deutsche Bank AG

Deutsche Bank AG is one of the leading financial groups in the world and in Germany. It operates around 1,700 retail branch locations in some 60 countries across five continents. Deutsche Bank serves private individuals, corporate customers and institutional clients with a wide variety of investment, financial and related products and services. The bank's asset management business holds over EUR 1.3 billion in assets under management. Deutsche Bank generates most of its revenue from outside of Germany. The company was founded in 1870.

Operations

The company operates in six operating segments: Investment Bank (IB), Private Bank (PB), Corporate Bank (CB), Asset Management (AM), Capital Release Unit (CRU) and Corporate & Other (C&O).

IB includes Deutsche Bank's Origination & Advisory businesses. It also includes Fixed Income, Currency (FIC) Sales & Trading, which includes their Global Credit Trading, Foreign Exchange, Rates and Emerging Markets Debt businesses.

PB serves personal and private clients, wealthy individuals, entrepreneurs and families. In its international businesses it also focus on commercial clients. It is organized along two business divisions: Private Bank Germany and International Private Bank. Its product range includes payment and account services, credit and deposit products as well as investment advice including a range of Environmental, Social and Governance (ESG) products.

CB is focused on serving corporate clients, including the German "Mittelstand", larger and smaller sized commercial and business banking clients in Germany as well as multinational companies.

The Asset Management operates under the DWS brand. It is unchanged from Deutsche Bank's previous segmentation and provides investment solutions to individual investors and institutions with a diversified range of Active, Passive and Alternative Asset Management products and services.

New Capital Release Unit's (CRU) principal objectives are to liberate capital consumed by low return assets and businesses that earn insufficient returns or activities that are no longer core to its strategy by liberating capital in an economically rational manner. In addition, the CRU is focused on reducing costs.

Geographic Reach

Headquartered in Frankfurt, the financial capital of Germany (and continental Europe), Deutsche is active in around 60 countries worldwide.

Sales and Marketing

The global coverage function in the Corporate Bank focuses on international Large Corporate Clients and is organized into two units: Coverage and Risk Management Solutions.

Coverage includes multi-product generalists covering headquarter level and subsidiaries via global, regional and local coverage teams. Coverage of the IB's clients is provided by the Institutional Client Group, which houses their debt sales team and works in conjunction with Finance Solutions Group in the Corporate Bank, covering capital markets and Treasury solutions.

Private Bank Germany business and Private & Commercial Business International have similar distribution channels. Those include branch network, supported by customer call centers and self-service terminals; advisory centers of the Deutsche Bank brand in Germany, Italy and Spain, which connects branch network with digital offerings; online and mobile banking including Digital Platform, through which they provide a transaction platform for banking, brokerage and self-services, combined with a multi-mobile offering for smartphones and tablets; and lastly, financial advisors, as an additional service channel in collaboration with self-employed financial advisors as well as sales and cooperation partners.

Financial Performance

The bank's performance for the past five years has fluctuated with a downward trend for the first half then continuing to recover in the latter part of the period.

Net revenues for the company were EUR 25.4 billion in 2021, an increase of EUR 1.4 billion, or 6 % compared to 2020. Net revenues in the Core Bank increased by 5 % to EUR 25.4 billion. Net revenues in the Corporate Bank (CB) of EUR 5.2 billion remained flat year-on-year as business volume growth and deposit repricing offset interest rate headwinds.

The company reported a net profit of EUR 2.5 billion for fiscal year end 2021 as compared to the prior year's net profit of EUR 600 million.

Cash held by the company at the end of fiscal 2021 increased to EUR 179.9 billion. Operating activities used EUR 3 billion. Investing activities and financing activities provided EUR 23.6 billion and EUR 1.6 billion, respectively. Main cash uses were for loans at amortized cost and non-trading financial assets mandatory at fair value through profit and loss.

Strategy

The bank's ongoing strategic transformation was designed to refocus their Core Bank around market leading businesses, which operate in growing markets with attractive return potential. The bank continues to deliver on cost reduction targets; continuing its portfolio and cost reduction and completion of Prime Finance transfer in the Capital Release Unit segment.

Company Background

Deutsche Bank was founded in 1870 in Berlin by Adelbert Delbrück, a private banker, and Ludwig Bamberger, a politician and currency expert. Shortly after, it opened its first international branches in China (Shanghai and Yokohama) and the UK (London). In its first century of activity significant events included financing steel company Krupp (which became ThyssenKrupp), the Northern Pacific Railroad, and film company UFA (which made films including Fritz Lang's Metropolis). Deutsche dipped its toe into investment banking in the late 1980s and by the late 1990s the bank was dead-set on taking on global leaders in investment banking such as JPMorgan and Goldman Sachs. Deutsche responded slowly to the 2008 financial crisis, stumbling from net loss to net loss, before CEO Christian Sewing in 2019 cut a fifth of its workforce and retrenched the bank with downwardly revised investment banking ambitions.

HISTORY

Georg von Siemens opened Deutsche Bank in Berlin in 1870. Three years later the firm opened an office in London and was soon buying other German banks. In the late 1800s Deutsche Bank helped finance Germany's electrification (carried out by Siemens AG) and railroad construction in the US and the Ottoman Empire. Von Siemens ran the bank until his death in 1901.

The bank survived post-WWI financial chaos by merging with Disconto-Gesellschaft and later helped finance the Nazi war machine. After the war, the Allies split the company into 10 banks; it became extinct in Soviet-controlled East Germany.

The bank was reassembled in 1957 and primarily engaged in commercial banking, often taking direct interests in its customers. It added retail services in the 1960s. In 1975, to prevent the Shah of Iran from gaining a stake in Daimler-Benz (now Daimler), the bank bought 29% of that company.

The firm opened an investment banking office in the US in 1971 and a branch office in 1978. In the 1980s it expanded geographically, buying Bank of America's Italian subsidiary (1986) and UK merchant bank Morgan Grenfell (1989); it also moved into insurance, creating life insurer DB Leben (1989).

Terrorists killed chairman Alfred Herrhausen, a symbol of German big business, in 1989. After German reunification in 1990, successor Hilmar Kopper oversaw the bank's reestablishment in eastern Germany.

In 1994 Deutsche Bank bought most of ITT's commercial finance unit. That year the company suffered scandal when real estate developer Jurgen Schneider borrowed more than DM1 billion and disappeared; he was later found and returned to Germany.

The company grew its global investment banking operations in 1995 under its Morgan Grenfell subsidiary. Corporate culture clashes prompted Deutsche Bank to take greater control of the unit and restructure it in 1998.

Deutsche Bank's global aspirations

suffered a setback in 1998 when losses on investments in Russia trimmed its bottom line. Still trying to put WWII behind it, the bank accepted responsibility for its wartime dealing in gold seized from Jews but has rejected liability to compensate victims of Nazi forced labor who toiled in industrial companies in which it holds stakes.

In 1999 the bank acquired Bankers Trust. Despite a decision to divest its industrial portfolio, that year the company bought Tele Columbus, the #2 cable network in Germany, and Piaggio, the Italian maker of the famed Vespa motor scooter. On the banking front, Deutsche Bank bought Chase Manhattan's Dutch auction business and sought a foothold in Japan through alliances with Nippon Life Insurance and Sakura Bank (now part of Sumitomo Mitsui Banking).

In 2000 the company agreed to merge with Dresdner Bank (after which they would spin off their retail banking businesses), but the merger collapsed, in part over the fate of investment banking subsidiary Dresdner Kleinwort Benson. German mega-insurer Allianz bought Dresdner in 2001. Deutsche Bank's reorganization plans the same year saw the bank eliminate 2,600 jobs worldwide and realign its businesses into two divisions. Deutsche Bank also bought Banque Worms from French insurer AXA.

Looking for a steady supply of cash, in 2001 Deutsche Bank's Morgan Grenfall Private Equity bought 3,000 English pubs owned by UK-based conglomerate Whitbread plc. In 2002 more shuffling of the executive board members allowed Deutsche Bank to grow in the international Anglo-American style, rather than as a domestic player.

In 2004 Deutsche Bank acquired Berkshire Mortgage (now Deutsche Bank Berkshire Mortgage), one of the top multifamily residential lenders in the US. The next year it bought Russian financial services company United Financial Group and combined its depositary business with its own.

The year 2006 was a bad year for the company from a public relations standpoint. Fallout from former chairman Rolf Breuer's remarks regarding the financial stability of banking client Kirch Holding led to a shake-up in the executive suite and the board that year. Later, UK financial regulators charged the bank an $11.1 million fine for market misconduct related to trading activity in 2004. In the US the IRS investigated the bank for alleged abusive tax shelters.

The bank also took a public relations hit when its CEO, Josef Ackermann, went on trial for illegal bonuses during his tenure at Mannesmann.

To boost its lending operations in the US, the company bought MortgageIT, a real estate investment trust, for some ?285 million ($430 million) in 2007. The timing wasn't great: the subsidiary suffered a major loss, a victim of the US subprime mortgage crisis. Also that year Deutsche Bank acquired Abbey Life from Lloyds Banking Group for some ?1 billion ($2 billion.) This acquisition fared better than MortgageIT, finishing out the year in the black.

Deutsche Bank's expansion was slowed in 2008 when its proposed acquisition of some of ABN AMRO's assets -- including corporate and commercial units, parts of Hollandische Bank Unie, and a factoring company -- from Fortis was canceled.

On the heels of a global expansion which began in earnest in 2002, Deutsche Bank was hit hard by the worldwide financial crisis. The company reported a fourth-quarter loss of ?4.8 billion in 2008, largely due to declines in its trading and asset management businesses. Its Americas business, primarily the US operations, was hit the hardest by far.

But in 2009 Deutsche Bank's growth seemed to pick back up again as it acquired Dresdner Bank's global agency securities lending business from Commerzbank. The business was merged with Deutsche's trust and securities services unit. The deal expanded Deutsche Bank's custody platform.

EXECUTIVES

Chief Executive Officer, Chairman, Director, Christian Sewing
Chief Transformation Officer, Director, Fabrizio Campelli
Chief Operating Officer, Director, Frank Kuhnke
Chief Technology, Data and Innovation Officer, Director, Bernd Leukert
Chief Financial Officer, Director, James von Moltke
Chief Risk Officer, Director, Stuart Wilson Lewis
Chief Administrative Officer, Director, Stefan Simon
Germany Regional Chief Executive Officer, Germany President, Director, Karl von Rohr
Regional CEO Americas, Director, Christiana Riley
Director, Alexander von zur Muhlen
Auditors : Ernst & Young GmbH Wirtschaftsprüfungsgesellschaft

LOCATIONS

HQ: Deutsche Bank AG
  Taunusanlage 12, Frankfurt am Main 60325
Phone: (49) 69 910 00   **Fax:** (49) 69 910 34 225
Web: www.db.com

2018 Sales

	% of total
Germany	38
Americas	22
UK	14
Rest of Europe, Middle East and Africa	13
Asia/Pacific	13
Other	.
Total	100

PRODUCTS/OPERATIONS

2018 Sales

	% of total
Corporate & Investment Bank	51
Private & Commercial Bank	40
Asset Management	9
Other	
Total	100

COMPETITORS

AUSTRALIA AND NEW ZEALAND BANKING GROUP LIMITED
Bank Of China Limited
COMMERZBANK AG
DZ BANK AG Deutsche Zentral-Genossenschaftsbank, Frankfurt am Main
ING Groep N.V.
NATIONAL AUSTRALIA BANK LIMITED
Raiffeisen Zentralbank Ö-sterreich Aktiengesellschaft
UBS AG
UniCredit Bank AG
WESTPAC BANKING CORPORATION

HISTORICAL FINANCIALS

Company Type: Public

Income Statement FYE: December 31

	ASSETS ($mil)	NET INCOME ($mil)	INCOME AS % OF ASSETS	EMPLOYEES
12/22	1,427,750	5,900	0.4%	0
12/21	1,499,380	2,774	0.2%	82,969
12/20	1,626,110	592	0.0%	84,659
12/19	1,456,980	(6,051)	—	87,597
12/18	1,543,880	305	0.0%	91,737
Annual Growth	(1.9%)	109.6%		

2022 Year-End Financials

Return on assets: 0.4%   Dividends
Return on equity: 8.0%   Yield: —
Long-term debt ($ mil.): —   Payout: 0.0%
No. of shares ($ mil.): —   Market value ($ mil.): —
Sales ($ mil.): 40,435

Deutsche Lufthansa AG (Germany, Fed. Rep.)

EXECUTIVES

Executive Board Chairman, Executive Board Chief Executive Officer, Executive Board Executive Board Member, Carsten Spohr
Chief Financial Officer, Executive Board Member, Ulrik Svensson
Executive Board Member, Thorsten Dirks
Logistics Executive Board Member, Information Technology Executive Board Member, Group Airlines Executive Board Member, Logistics Chief Officer, Group Airlines Chief Officer, Information Technology Chief Officer, Harry Hohmeister
Legal Affairs Executive Board Member, Legal Affairs Chief Human Resources Officer, Bettina Volkens
Supervisory Board Honorary Chairman, Juergen Weber

Supervisory Board Supervisory Board Member, Wolfgang Mayrhuber

Supervisory Board Member, Chairman, Karl-Ludwig Kley

Supervisory Board Deputy Chairman, Supervisory Board Supervisory Board Member, Supervisory Board Employee Representative, Christine Behle

Supervisory Board Member, Nicoley Baublies

Supervisory Board Member, Jorg Cebulla

Supervisory Board Member, Herbert Hainer

Supervisory Board Member, Carsten Knobel

Supervisory Board Member, Martin Koehler

Supervisory Board Member, Employee Representative, Doris Krueger

Supervisory Board Member, Employee Representative, Eckhard Lieb

Supervisory Board Member, Employee Representative, Jan-Willem Marquardt

Supervisory Board Member, Employee Representative, Ralf Mueller

Supervisory Board Member, Martina Merz

Supervisory Board Member, Monika Ribar

Supervisory Board Member, Miriam E. Sapiro

Supervisory Board Member, Employee Representative, Andreas Strache

Supervisory Board Member, Employee Representative, Christina Weber

Supervisory Board Member, Employee Representative, Birgit Weinreich

Supervisory Board Member, Matthias Wissmann

Supervisory Board Member, Stephan Sturm

Auditors : Ernst & Young GmbH Wirtschaftpruefungsgesellschaft

LOCATIONS

HQ: Deutsche Lufthansa AG (Germany, Fed. Rep.)
Lufthansa Aviation Center (LAC), Airportring, Frankfurt 60546
Phone: (49) 69 696 0   **Fax:** (49) 69 696 33422
Web: www.lufthansagroup.com

COMPETITORS

AIR FRANCE - KLM
ALASKA AIR GROUP, INC.
ATLAS AIR WORLDWIDE HOLDINGS, INC.
Air Canada
CATHAY PACIFIC AIRWAYS LIMITED
DELTA AIR LINES, INC.
INTERNATIONAL CONSOLIDATED AIRLINES GROUP SA
JAPAN AIRLINES CO.,LTD.
UNITED AIRLINES HOLDINGS, INC.
UNITED AIRLINES, INC.

HISTORICAL FINANCIALS

Company Type: Public

Income Statement   FYE: December 31

	REVENUE ($mil)	NET INCOME ($mil)	NET PROFIT MARGIN	EMPLOYEES
12/22	35,377	844	2.4%	109,509
12/21	19,151	(2,479)	—	105,290
12/20	16,892	(8,253)	—	110,065
12/19	41,664	1,361	3.3%	138,353
12/18	41,656	2,477	5.9%	135,534
Annual Growth	(4.0%)	(23.6%)	—	(5.2%)

2022 Year-End Financials

Debt ratio: 32.3%
Return on equity: 12.3%
Cash ($ mil.): 1,911
Current Ratio: 0.86
Long-term debt ($ mil.): 11,993
No. of shares ($ mil.): 1,195
Dividends
Yield: —
Payout: 0.0%
Market value ($ mil.): 9,845

	STOCK PRICE ($) FY Close	P/E High/Low		Earnings	Dividends	Book Value
12/22	8.24	13	9	0.70	0.00	7.51
12/21	7.13	—	—	(3.38)	2.90	4.21
12/20	13.13	—	—	(15.35)	0.00	2.77
12/19	18.15	10	6	2.86	0.64	23.82
12/18	22.95	8	4	5.24	0.67	22.80
Annual Growth	(22.6%)	—	—	(39.5%)	—	(24.2%)

Deutsche Post AG

Deutsche Post AG (operating as Deutsche Post DHL Group) is Europe's largest postal service, the company is also one of the world's leading providers of express delivery, freight transport, supply chain management, and e-commerce solutions. Deutsche Post trades under two brand names, Deutsche Post and DHL. The company does business in Europe (its largest market), the Americas, Middle East, Africa and Asia Pacific. Its Post & Parcel Germany division deliver around 6.2 million parcels about 48 million letter per working day.

Operations

Deutsche Post operates through five divisions: Express; Post and Parcel Germany; Global Forwarding, Freight; Supply Chain and e-Commerce solutions.

The Express division (about 30% of sales) delivers urgent documents through its core product, Time Definite International (TDI), which offers pre-defined delivery times.

Deutsche Post's Global Forwarding and Freight division (about 30%) brokers transport services between customers and freight carriers by air, ocean and ground transportation. The division's business units are Global Forwarding and Freight Post and Parcel Germany contributes about 20% of total sales and transports, sorts and delivers documents and goods in and outside of Germany. Its business units are called Post Germany, Parcel Germany and International.

The Supply Chain segment (more than 15%) delivers customized supply chain solutions to its customers based on globally standardised modular components including warehousing, transport and value-added services.

Lastly, the eCommerce solutions generating more than 5% of the total revenue, are geared towards providing high-quality solutions, particularly to customers in the rapidly growing e-commerce sector. Its core activities include national last-mile parcel delivery in selected countries. It also supplies cross-border non-TDI services.

Geographic Reach

Based in Bonn, Germany, Deutsche Post delivers to almost everywhere in the world. Germany accounts for about 25% of total sales; wider Europe contributes roughly 30%. The rest arises mainly from the Americas, the Asia Pacific region and Middle East/ Africa.

Sales and Marketing

The company's products and services are targeted towards both private and business customers and range from physical and hybrid letters to special products for the merchandise delivery, and include additional services such as registered mail, cash on delivery and insured items. The company markets through retail outlets, post boxes, mail centers, paketshops, salespoints, letter and parcel delivery, parcel centers, packstations, and real estate for network expansion.

Financial Performance

Note: Growth rates may differ after conversion to US Dollars.

Deutsche Post's performance for the past five years has increased year-over-year with 2022 as its highest performing year over the period.

In fiscal year end 2022, the revenue increased by EUR 12.7 billion to EUR 94.4 billion, as compared to 2021's revenue of EUR 81.7 billion.

Consolidated net profit increased by EUR 306 million to EUR 5.4 billion for fiscal year end 2022, as compared to the prior year's net income of EUR 5.1 billion.

The company's cash at the end of 2022 was EUR 3.8 billion. Operating activities generated EUR 8.4 billion. Investing activities and financing activities used EUR 3.2 billion and EUR 7.4 billion, respectively. Main cash uses were for property, plant, and equipment intangible assets and repayment of non-current financial liabilities.

Strategy

The company announced Strategy 2025 in October 2019. It draws on the successful elements of Strategy 2015 and 2020, which established the company as the world's leading logistics company. Building on this strong foundation, Strategy 2025 helps the company to cement and grow that leading position as the pace of change in the world around it accelerates.

It defined its strategic goals in a comprehensive process in which the company worked with relevant stakeholders including employees, customers, suppliers and investors. Its Strategy House illustrates the most important elements of its strategy and how they are connected.

Strategy 2025 navigated the company safely through the volatile, fast-changing environment brought about by the global pandemic. As part of a yearly assessment, the company undertook a detailed review of its corporate strategy and found it not only to be fundamentally sound, but that it had also made Deutsche Post DHL Group more resilient in the face of the pandemic. That resilience is the result of disciplined and consistent execution of the company's Group strategy, with each and every element playing a key role.

HISTORY

The German postal system was established in the 1490s when German emperor Maximilian I ordered a reliable and regular messenger service to be set up between Austria (Innsbruck, where the emperor had his court) and the farther reaches of his Holy Roman Empire: the Netherlands, France, and Rome. The von Tassis (later renamed Taxis) family of Italy was responsible for running the network. Family members settled in major cities across Europe to expand the postal business.

Although the family operated what was officially an exclusively royal mail service, by the early 1500s the company was also delivering messages for private patrons. In 1600 a family member who served as general postmaster was authorized to collect fees for private mail deliveries. By the early 19th century, Thurn und Taxis, as the company was then called, was the leading postal service in the Holy Roman Empire, serving more than 11 million people.

The dissolution of the Holy Roman Empire, prompted by Napoleon's military adventures, led to the creation of a federation of 39 independent German states. Thurn und Taxis had to make agreements with members of the separate states, including Austria and Prussia. After Austria's defeat in 1866 by Prussia, the confederation was dissolved and all Thurn und Taxis postal systems were absorbed by Prussia. When Bismarck's Prussian-led German Reich was established in 1870, the new postal administration (Reichspostverwaltung) began issuing postage stamps valid across Germany.

After Germany was defeated in WWII and split into two nations in 1949, two postal systems were established: Deutsche Post (East Germany) and Deutsche Bundespost (West Germany). The fall of the Berlin Wall in 1989 preceded a reunion of the two German states in 1990. That year Deutsche Post, led by chairman Klaus Zumwinkel, was integrated into Deutsche Bundespost.

EXECUTIVES

Chief Executive Officer, Member, Tobias Meyer
Member, Oscar de Bok
Member, Pablo Ciano
Member, Nikola Hagleitner
Member, Melanie Kreis
Member, Thomas Ogilvie
Member, John Pearson
Member, Tim Scharwath
Chairman, Nikolaus von Bomhard
Deputy Chairman, Andrea Kocsis

Director, Ingrid Deltenre
Director, Heinrich Hiesinger
Director, Luise Holscher
Director, Simone Menne
Director, Lawrence Rosen
Director, Stefan Schulte
Director, Katja Windt
Director, Stefan B. Wintels
Director, Jorg von Dosky
Director, Gabriele Gulzau
Director, Thomas Held
Director, Mario Jacubasch
Director, Thorsten Kuhn
Director, Ulrike Lennartz-Pipenbacher
Director, Yusuf Ozdemir
Director, Stephan Teuscher
Director, Stefanie Weckesser
Auditors : PricewaterhouseCoopers GmbH Wirtschaftprufungsgesellschaft

LOCATIONS

HQ: Deutsche Post AG
 Zentrale - Investor Relations, Bonn 53250
Phone: (49) 228 182 6 3636   **Fax:** (49) 228 182 6 3919
Web: www.dpdhl.de

2018 Sales

	% of total
Europe	
Germany	30
Europe (excluding Germany)	30
Americas	18
Asia/Pacific	18
Other regions	4
Total	100

PRODUCTS/OPERATIONS

2018 Sales

	% of total
PeP	29
Express	25
Global Forwarding, Freight	23
Supply Chain	21
Corporate Center/Other	2
Total	100

Selected Services
Mail and package delivery
Dialogue marketing services
Time Definite International (TDI) express delivery
Air freight
Freight forwarding services
Contract logistics
Ocean freight
Outsourcing and system solutions for the mail business

COMPETITORS

AEGIS COMMUNICATIONS GROUP, LLC
APAC CUSTOMER SERVICES, INC.
Deutsche Telekom AG
Otto (GmbH & Co KG)
PLANET PAYMENT, INC.
PostNL N.V.
SERCO GROUP PLC
SPICERS LIMITED
Telia Company AB
VIAD CORP

HISTORICAL FINANCIALS

Company Type: Public

Income Statement FYE: December 31

	REVENUE ($mil)	NET INCOME ($mil)	NET PROFIT MARGIN	EMPLOYEES
12/22	100,862	5,723	5.7%	600,278
12/21	92,526	5,719	6.2%	592,263
12/20	81,990	3,656	4.5%	571,974
12/19	71,117	2,945	4.1%	546,924
12/18	70,486	2,376	3.4%	547,459
Annual Growth	9.4%	24.6%	—	2.3%

2022 Year-End Financials
Debt ratio: 9.9%
Return on equity: 25.3%
Cash ($ mil.): 4,047
Current Ratio: 0.99
Long-term debt ($ mil.): 6,769
No. of shares ($ mil.): 1,239
Dividends
 Yield: —
 Payout: 29.7%
Market value ($ mil.): 46,465

	STOCK PRICE ($) FY Close	P/E High/Low		PER SHARE ($) Earnings	Dividends	Book Value
12/22	37.50	14	7	4.62	1.37	20.03
12/21	64.08	17	11	4.54	2.22	17.39
12/20	49.84	21	10	2.90	1.05	13.65
12/19	37.82	18	12	2.35	1.24	12.83
12/18	27.33	28	16	1.90	1.37	12.62
Annual Growth	8.2%			24.9%	0.1%	12.2%

Deutsche Telekom AG

Deutsche Telekom (DT) is one of the world's leading integrated telecommunications companies, with some 245 million mobile customers, 25 million fixed-network lines, and more than 20 million broadband lines. Operating as T-Mobile in the US and in certain other European countries, the company offers fixed-network and mobile communications services and products, as well as information and communication technology (ICT). It offers its consumers fixed-network/ broadband, mobile, internet, and internet-based TV products and services, as well as ICT solutions for its business and corporate customers. DT generates majority of sales in the US.

Operations

Deutsche Telekom's operations have five operating segments with the US, followed by Germany accounting for majority of the company's revenues.

The company's three segments involve Germany, the US, and Europe, which comprises all fixed-network and mobile business activities in these regions.

Deutsche Telekom's Systems Solutions operating segment offers a focuses a B2B product and solution portfolio under the T-Systems brand. The segment complements it with its horizontal offerings for advisory, cloud services, and digitalization solutions.

The Group Development segment actively

manages entities, subsidiaries, and equity investments to grow their value while giving them the entrepreneurial freedom they need to promote their continued strategic development. Lastly, the Group Headquarters and Group Services segment comprises of all group units that cannot be allocated directly to one of the operating segments.

Geographic Reach

Deutsche Telekom operates in Germany, the US, and Europe with US accounting for about 65% of the company's revenue.

Sales and Marketing

The company has some 248 million mobile customers, 26 million fixed-network lines, and 22 million broadband customers.

Financial Performance

Deutsche Telekom's annual report increased by EUR 6.6 billion to EUR 114.4 billion in 2022, an increase of 6.1% in 2022, as compared to 2021's revenue of EUR 107.8 billion.

The company's net profit for fiscal year end 2022 also increased to EUR8 billion, as compared to the prior year's net profit of EUR 4.2 billion.

Deutsche Telekom held about EUR 5.8 billion at the end of the year. Operating activities provided EUR 35.8 billion to the coffers. Investing activities and financing activities used EUR 22.3 billion and EUR 15.4 billion, respectively. Main cash uses were for property, plant, and equipment and repayment of current financial liabilities.

Strategy

The company remain very successful on the market making Deutsche Telekom by far the leading telecommunications company in Europe in terms of market capitalization, revenue, and earnings. In the Western tech-sphere, the company is well positioned to implements its Leading Digital Telco strategy. No other telecommunications company has a comparable footprint with its own networks on both side of the Atlantic, in Europe and the United States.

HISTORY

Deutsche Telekom was formed by the 1989 separation of West Germany's telecommunications services from the nation's postal system, Deutsche Post. Dating back to the 15th century (when the Thurn und Taxis private postal system was created for German principalities), the service expanded to cover Austria, France, the Netherlands, and most of Germany by the 1850s. After the 1866 Austro-Prussian War, it became part of the North German Postal Confederation. When the German Empire was formed in 1871, the postal operation became the Deutsche Reichspost (later the Bundespost). Shortly thereafter, the newly invented telephone was introduced in Germany.

Post-WWI inflation shook the Bundespost, and the government allowed it to try new organizational structures. A 1924 law allowed the state-run service to operate as a quasi-commercial company. After WWII the American-British zone returned postal authority to Germans, and in 1949 the USSR established the state of East Germany.

Only by the 1960s did West Germany's postal and phone services meet modern standards. Privatization of the Bundespost became a political cause when many complained about the monopoly's cost and inefficiency. Efforts to privatize the agency (named Deutsche Telekom in 1989) intensified with the 1990 German reunification. Faced with updating the antiquated phone system of the former East Germany, however, political opposition to taking Deutsche Telekom public faded.

The company began operating T-D1, its mobile phone network, in 1992, and the next year it launched T-Online, now Germany's largest online service provider. In 1996 Deutsche Telekom finally went public and raised more than $13 billion in Europe's largest IPO. It also launched Global One with France Telecom (renamed Orange) and Sprint (now Sprint Nextel); as part of the partnership, Deutsche Telekom took a 10% stake in Sprint.

In 1998 European Union (EU) member countries opened their phone markets to competition, and Deutsche Telekom's long-distance market share quickly eroded. Under EU pressure, in 1999 the company said it would sell its cable network, which it divided into nine regional units.

EXECUTIVES

Management Board Chairman, Control Chairman, Finance Chairman, Management Board Chief Executive Officer, Control Chief Executive Officer, Finance Chief Executive Officer, Timotheus Hottges
Legal Affairs Management Board Member, Human Resources Management Board Member, Birgit Bohle
Finance Management Board Member, Finance Chief Financial Officer, Christian P. Illek
Technology and Innovation Management Board Member, Claudia Nemat
Chairman, Supervisory Board Member, Frank Appel
Deputy Chairman, Supervisory Board Member, Frank Sauerland
Supervisory Board Member, Guenther Braunig
Supervisory Board Member, Odysseus D. Chatzidis
Supervisory Board Member, Constantin Greve
Supervisory Board Member, Katja Hessel
Supervisory Board Member, Lars Hinrichs
Supervisory Board Member, Helga Jung
Supervisory Board Member, Nicole Koch
Supervisory Board Member, Dagmar P. Kollmann
Supervisory Board Member, Petra Steffi Kreusel
Supervisory Board Member, Harald Kruger
Supervisory Board Member, Kerstin Marx
Supervisory Board Member, Susanne Schottke
Supervisory Board Member, Lothar M. Schroder
Supervisory Board Member, Nicole Seelemann-Wandtke
Supervisory Board Member, Karl-Heinz Streibich
Supervisory Board Member, Margret Suckale
Supervisory Board Member, Karin Topel
Supervisory Board Member, Stefan B. Wintels
Auditors : Deloitte GmbH Wirtschaftsprüfungsgesellschaft

LOCATIONS

HQ: Deutsche Telekom AG
 Friedrich-Ebert-Allee 140, Bonn 53113
Phone: (49) 228 181 49494   **Fax:** (49) 228 181 94004
Web: www.telekom.com

2017 Sales

	% of total
US	48
Europe	
Germany	28
Other European countries	15
System Solutions	7
Group Development	2
Total	100

PRODUCTS/OPERATIONS

2017 Sales

	% of total
Telecommunications	90
ICT solutions	9
Other	1
Total	100

COMPETITORS

Deutsche Post AG
IDT CORPORATION
Magyar Telekom Plc.
OOREDOO Q.P.S.C
ORANGE
SPRINT CORPORATION
TDC A/S
TELEFONICA, SA
Telenor ASA
VODAFONE GROUP PUBLIC LIMITED COMPANY

HISTORICAL FINANCIALS

Company Type: Public

Income Statement   FYE: December 31

	REVENUE ($mil)	NET INCOME ($mil)	NET PROFIT MARGIN	EMPLOYEES
12/23	124,019	19,702	15.9%	199,652
12/22	121,967	8,545	7.0%	206,759
12/21	123,140	4,726	3.8%	216,528
12/20	123,955	5,103	4.1%	226,291
12/19	90,417	4,341	4.8%	210,533
Annual Growth	8.2%	46.0%	—	(1.3%)

2023 Year-End Financials

Debt ratio: 39.9%   No. of shares ($ mil.): 4,978
Return on equity: 33.7%   Dividends
Cash ($ mil.): 8,056   Yield: —
Current Ratio: 1.01   Payout: 18.9%
Long-term debt ($ mil.): 105,115   Market value ($ mil.): 120,134

	STOCK PRICE ($) FY Close	P/E High/Low		PER SHARE ($) Earnings	Dividends	Book Value
12/23	24.13	7	6	3.95	0.75	12.66
12/22	19.98	13	10	1.72	0.65	10.43
12/21	18.51	25	19	0.98	1.33	9.72
12/20	18.27	23	15	1.08	0.65	9.29
12/19	16.29	22	19	0.92	1.49	7.48
Annual Growth	10.3%	—		44.0%	(15.8%)	14.1%

Diageo Plc

Diageo is a global leader in beverage alcohol with an outstanding collection of brands across spirits and beer, boasting a portfolio of world-renowned brands such as Smirnoff vodka, Captain Morgan rum, Johnnie Walker whisky, Baileys Irish cream, and Tanqueray gin. It also makes beer, including Guinness, and wine. With more than 200 global, local, and luxury brands, the company sells its products in more than 180 countries around the world. Diageo rings up sales in virtually every country in the world and has about 140 production sites globally. North America is its largest market, accounting for about 40% of total sales.

Operations

Diageo groups its products into three main alcohol types: spirits, beer, and ready-to-drink.

Spirits comprise most of the company's revenue, generating more than 80%. Beer accounts for about 15% of sales and ready-to-drink products (such as premixed gin and tonic) generate about 5%. Other products, including wine, bring in the remaining sales.

Breaking it down further, scotch accounts for about 25% of sales, followed by beer (approximately 15%) and vodka (some 10%).

Its brands are also split into categories such as Global (brands available in most of the world, such as Smirnoff and Johnnie Walker), Local Stars (individual to one market and providing a platform for growth), and Reserve (luxury, exclusive brands at the above-premium price point, such as Ciroc and Casamigos).

Geographic Reach

Based in the UK, Diageo owns and operates sites in Scotland (more than 45) and North America (over 10) footprint including malting, distilling, maturation, packaging, office and engineering and co-product plants (high level). It also has approximately 15 ports in the UK and six in the North America.

The company generates about 40% of sales in North America, with Europe and Turkey and the Asia-Pacific region adding another 20% each. Diageo generates about 10% of sales in Africa and nearly 10% in Latin America and the Caribbean.

Diageo has offices and production facilities in North America, Latin America and Caribbean, Europe, Africa, and the Asia/Pacific region. It sells products in more than 180 markets in these regions. The company's broad geographic footprint protects it from instability in one or multiple of its operating environments.

Sales and Marketing

The company works with a wide range of customers, including big and small customers, on- and off-trade, retailers, wholesalers and distributors, and digital and e-commerce.

Financial Performance

Note: Growth rates may differ after conversion to US Dollars.

The company's net sales for fiscal 2021 increased to EUR12.7 billion compared with EUR11.8 billion in the prior year.

Profit for fiscal 2021 increased to EUR2.8 billion compared with EUR1.5 billion in the prior year.

Cash held by the company at the end of fiscal 2021 decreased to EUR2.7 billion. Cash provided by operations was EUR3.7 billion investing and financing activities used EUR1.1 billion and EUR1.6 billion, respectively. Main cash uses were purchase of property, plant and equipment and computer software; and equity dividends paid.

Strategy

The company's six strategic priorities are: sustain quality growth, embed everyday efficiency, invest smartly, promote positive drinking, pioneer grain-to-glass sustainability, and champion inclusion and diversity.

In 2021, the company: Launched innovations across its global giant brands to recruit new consumers and unlock new occasions, including Guinness Nitro Cold Brew Coffee, Captain Morgan Sliced Apple, Smirnoff Seltzers and Baileys Apple Pie; Enhanced Guinness 0.0 product quality through the introduction of a new filtration process and additional quality assurance measures, leading to product re-launch in Summer 2021 ; Expanded no- and lower choices with launch of Tanqueray 0.0%, Gordon's 0.0% and Baileys Deliciously Light; and ? Accelerated development of e-commerce capabilities, including further development of its direct to consumer e-commerce platforms, such as HaigClub.com, TheBar.com and Seedlip.com.

Mergers and Acquisitions

In early 2022, Diageo acquired 21Seeds, a rapidly growing flavored tequila infused with the juice of real fruits. The brand is available in three varieties: Valencia Orange, Grapefruit Hibiscus and Cucumber JalapeÃ±o. This acquisition is in line with the company's strategy to acquire high growth brands in fast growing categories.

In early 2022, Diageo completed the acquisition of Casa UM, owner of premium artisanal mezcal brand, Mezcal UniÃ³n. Mezcal UniÃ³n is a 100% handcrafted mezcal brand from Oaxaca, Mexico.

In early 2021, Diageo acquired Far West Spirits, owner of the Lone River Ranch Water (Lone River) brand. Lone River is a hard seltzer that takes inspiration from the popular classic Texan "Ranch Water" cocktail. This acquisition is very much in keeping with the company's strategy to acquire high growth brands in fast growing categories.

In a separate transaction in early 2021, Diageo completed the acquisition of Chase Distillery. This acquisition brings the award-winning Chase Original Potato Vodka and seven premium plus gins, including Chase GB Gin, Pink Grapefruit & Pomelo Gin and Rhubarb & Bramley Apple Gin into the Diageo portfolio.

Also in early 2021, Diageo acquired Loyal 9 Cocktails, a rapidly growing spirits-based ready to drink brand, from Sons of Liberty Spirits Company. Loyal 9's vodka-based ready to drink cocktails have quickly captured the hearts of New England consumers. It combines the appeal of indulgent full flavor lemonade and "Americana", with high-quality ingredients and 9% ABV.

Company Background

Diageo was created by Guinness and GrandMet's 1997 merger.

Guinness began business in 1759 when Arthur Guinness leased a small brewery in Dublin, Ireland. Guinness began specializing in porters in 1799. Managed by the third generation of Guinnesses, the company went public as a London-based firm in 1886.

GrandMet was established by Maxwell Joseph. In 1931 he began acquiring properties for resale, but WWII slowed his progress. He started buying hotels in 1946, and by 1961 GrandMet had gone public.

HISTORY

Diageo -- from the Latin word for "day" and the Greek word for "world" -- was born from Guinness and GrandMet's 1997 merger to fight flat liquor sales and spirited competitors.

Guinness began business in 1759 when Arthur Guinness leased a small brewery in Dublin, Ireland. Guinness began specializing in porters in 1799. Managed by the third generation of Guinnesses, the company went public as a London-based firm in 1886.

In the 1950s managing director Hugh Beaver was credited with conceiving the Guinness Book of Records . During the 1970s Guinness bought more than 200 companies, with disappointing results. Guinness refocused on brewing and distilling operations in the late 1980s by selling noncore businesses and acquiring firms such as Schenley (Dewar's). In 1988 and 1989 it bought 24% of LVMH MoÃ«t Hennessy Louis Vuitton (later exchanged for 34% of LVMH's wine and spirits business). More acquisitions followed in the 1990s, capped by Guinness' 1997 announcement of its $19 billion merger with Grand Metropolitan.

GrandMet was established by Maxwell

Joseph. In 1931 he began acquiring properties for resale, but WWII slowed his progress. He started buying hotels in 1946, and by 1961 GrandMet had gone public.

Diversification began in 1970 with the purchases of catering firms, restaurants, and betting shops. In the early 1970s, in what was the largest British takeover to that time, GrandMet bought brewer Truman Hanburg, followed by Watney Mann, which owned International Distillers & Vintners, makers of Bailey's, Bombay Gin, and J&B.

GrandMet looked overseas through the 1970s, taking over the Liggett Group, a US cigarette maker (sold 1986) whose Paddington unit was the US distributor of J&B Scotch. In 1987 it bought Heublein (Smirnoff, Lancers, JosÃ© Cuervo). Two years later it bought The Pillsbury Company (Burger King and Green Giant) in a hostile takeover.

In 1997 Guinness and GrandMet combined, creating Diageo and dividing the companies and brands among four divisions: The Pillsbury Company, Burger King, Guinness, and United Distillers & Vintners.

In 2000 COO Paul Walsh, a former Pillsbury CEO, took over as CEO of both Diageo and its newly combined alcoholic beverage division, Guinness/UDV. Also that year Diageo, along with fellow wine and spirits producer Pernod Ricard, agreed to pay $8.2 billion to Vivendi for the Seagram's drinks business that holds several brands, including Crown Royal, VO Canadian whiskies, and Sterling Vineyards.

In 2001 Diageo sold its Guinness World Records business to media company Gullane Entertainment for $63 million. That year the company also completed its sale of Pillsbury to General Mills. After months of wrangling with the FTC, Diageo finally won regulatory approval for the Seagram's drinks purchase from Vivendi in 2001. The company gained the Crown Royal, and VO Canadian brands through this purchase.

In 2002 Diageo completed the sale of its Malibu rum brand to Allied Domecq for about $796 million; the deal also sealed Diageo's ownership of the Captain Morgan rum brand, as Allied Domecq agreed to drop its lawsuit involving Captain Morgan. Diageo discontinued marketing its Captain Morgan Gold rum drink in the US later that year because of disappointing sales.

Also in 2002 Diageo sold Burger King for $1.5 billion to a group composed of Texas Pacific Group, Bain Capital, and Goldman Sachs Capital Partners. Diageo's decision to sell its Pillsbury unit and its Burger King business (the #2 burger chain, after McDonald's) was part of the company's new focus on its spirits, wine, and beer businesses. The Pillsbury divestiture gave the company a 33% stake in General Mills (Diageo sold nearly half of its shares in October 2004). Also in 2002 Diageo and Pernod Ricard, which together own rights to the Seagram's brand, sold Seagram's line of nonalcoholic mixers to The Coca-Cola Company.

In 2003 Diageo and Jose Cuervo said they would jointly sell Don Julio and Tres Magueyes tequilas. Diageo also joined with Heineken to purchase 30% of InBev's (now Anheuser-Busch InBev's) Namibia Breweries in southern Africa. The brewery will make Heineken and Beck's beer.

Diageo said in 2003 that it would launch a low-alcohol version of its highly popular Baileys Irish Cream. Known as Baileys Glide, the drink is made with Irish whiskey, but Diageo said it would be manufactured in Germany. Also that year Diageo reopened the George Dickel distillery in Tullahoma, Tennessee. In addition, Diageo cut 150 jobs in 2003 from its Guinness operation amid declining sales of the well-known stout.

In 2005 Diageo and Heineken formed a partnership for the production and distribution of Guinness in Russia. The company also acquired The Chalone Wine Group in 2005 for about $260 million. It added the winery into Diageo's current US wine operations, which are organized under Diageo Chateau & Estate Wines. Diageo also acquired Netherlands distiller Ursus Vodka for an undisclosed amount and added Bushmills Irish whiskey to its stable, with the purchase of the brand from Pernod Ricard for $363 million. It also agreed to stay out of any negotiations regarding the takeover of Allied Domecq. (In 2005 Pernod Ricard acquired Allied Domecq.) That year it also disposed of its 4% holdings in General Mills, saying the investment was not congruent with its business strategy.

In 2007 the company acquired about a 45% stake in Quanxing, which distills the traditional premium Chinese liquor baijiu.

In 2008 Diageo formed a 50-50 joint venture with Dutch vodka maker Ketel One, paying ?610 million ($900 million) for its interest. The partnership followed Diageo's abandoned plans to bid on Absolut vodka maker V&S Group. (Ultimately the V&S Group was auctioned off to Pernod Ricard by its owner, the Swedish government.) Also that year Diageo took full ownership of D Distribution, the Russian distributor of the Smirnoff and Smirnov brands. It paid about $30 million for the remaining 25% stake held by Alfa Group.

Diageo saw its leadership change in 2008 when Lord James Blyth of Rowington, stepped down as chairman. He was replaced by Franz Humer, who previously served as CEO of F. Hoffmann-La Roche.

Meanwhile, Diageo has signaled an interested in acquiring Moet Hennessy, the spirits and wine subsidiary of French luxury conglomerate LVMH; however, LVMH is not inclined to sell. Diageo owns about 35% of MoÃ«t Hennessy. Undeterred from building its liqueurs portfolio, Diageo in mid-2010 increased its interest in the London Group, which supplies the premium NUVO brand of liqueurs, to a little more than 70%. London Group was created through a joint venture between Diageo and New York entrepreneur Raphael Yakoby.

EXECUTIVES

North America & Global Supply Chief Executive Officer, Executive Director, Debra Crew
Chief Financial Officer, Executive Director, Lavanya Chandrashekar
Chief Marketing Officer, Cristina Diezhandino
Chief Human Resources Officer, Louise Prashad
Global Supply Chain & Procurement President, Global Supply Chain & Procurement Chief Sustainability Officer, Ewan Andrew
Europe President, Soraya Benchikh
Latin America and Caribbean President, Alvaro Cardenas
Africa President, Dayalan Nayager
Asia Pacific & Global Travel President, John O'Keeffe
North America President, Claudia Schubert
Global Corporate Relations Director Director, Daniel Mobley
General Counsel, Secretary, Tom Shropshire
Chairman, Non-Executive Director, Javier Ferran
Non-Executive Director, Senior Independent Director, Susan Kilsby
Independent Non-Executive Director, Karen Blackett
Independent Non-Executive Director, Melissa Bethell
Independent Non-Executive Director, Valerie Chapoulaud-Floque
Independent Non-Executive Director, John Manzoni
Independent Non-Executive Director, Nicola S. Mendelsohn
Independent Non-Executive Director, Alan J. H. Stewart
Independent Non-Executive Director, Ireena Vittal
Auditors : PricewaterhouseCoopers LLP

LOCATIONS

HQ: Diageo Plc
16 Great Marlborough Street, London W1F 7HS
Phone: (44) 20 7947 9100
Web: www.diageo.com

2019 Sales

	% of total
North America	35
Europe & Turkey	23
Asia-Pacific	21
Africa	12
Latin America & Caribbean	9
Total	100

PRODUCTS/OPERATIONS

2019 Sales

	% of sales
Spirits	69
Beer	16
Ready-to-drink	6
Other	9
Total	100

Selected Brands

Strategic brands
- Baileys Original Irish Cream liqueur
- Buchanan's De Luxe Scotch whiskey
- Captain Morgan rum
- Cîroc vodka
- Crown Royal Canadian whisky
- Don Julio
- Guinness stout
- J&B Scotch whiskey
- Johnnie Walker Scotch whisky
- Ketel One vodka
- Smirnoff vodka
- Tanqueray London Dry and Tanqueray No. TEN gin
- Windsor Premier Scotch whisky

COMPETITORS

ANHEUSER-BUSCH COMPANIES, LLC
BEAM SUNTORY INC.
CASTLE BRANDS INC.
CONSTELLATION BRANDS, INC.
CRAFT BREW ALLIANCE, INC.
Companhia de Bebidas das Americas Ambev
FOSTER'S GROUP PTY LTD
MOLSON COORS BEVERAGE COMPANY
NEW BELGIUM BREWING COMPANY, INC.
THE BOSTON BEER COMPANY INC

HISTORICAL FINANCIALS

Company Type: Public

Income Statement — FYE: June 30

	REVENUE ($mil)	NET INCOME ($mil)	NET PROFIT MARGIN	EMPLOYEES
06/23	21,644	4,722	21.8%	30,237
06/22	18,713	3,934	21.0%	27,987
06/21	17,656	3,688	20.9%	27,650
06/20	14,418	1,728	12.0%	27,775
06/19	16,324	4,009	24.6%	28,420
Annual Growth	7.3%	4.2%	—	1.6%

2023 Year-End Financials

Debt ratio: 58.6%
Return on equity: 47.8%
Cash ($ mil.): 1,820
Current Ratio: 1.63
Long-term debt ($ mil.): 18,720
No. of shares ($ mil.): 2,459
Dividends
  Yield: 2.0%
  Payout: 185.0%
Market value ($ mil.): 426,734

	STOCK PRICE ($) FY Close	P/E High/Low	PER SHARE ($) Earnings	Dividends	Book Value
06/23	173.48	122 102	2.08	3.62	4.02
06/22	174.12	143 115	1.69	3.94	3.78
06/21	191.69	171 118	1.57	3.71	3.74
06/20	134.39	297 178	0.73	3.43	3.24
06/19	172.31	133 97	1.65	3.35	4.48
Annual Growth	0.2%	— —	5.9%	2.0%	(2.6%)

DiDi Global Inc

EXECUTIVES

Chairman, Chief Executive Officer, Will Wei Cheng
President, Director, Jean Qing Liu
Senior Vice President, Division Officer, Director, Stephen Jingshi Zhu
Capital Markets Vice President, Capital Markets Head, David Peng Xu
Public Communications Vice President, Min Li
Compliance Vice President, Risk Control Vice President, Rui Wu
Chief Financial Officer, Alan Yue Zhuo
Chief Technology Officer, Bob Bo Zhang
Chief Mobility Safety Officer, Jinglei Hou
Division Officer, Shu Sun
Director, Martin Chi Ping Lau
Director, Daniel Yong Zhang
Director, Adrian Perica
Independent Director, Gaofei Wang
Independent Director, Yusuo Wang
Auditors : PricewaterhouseCoopers Zhong Tian LLP

LOCATIONS

HQ: DiDi Global Inc
 No. 1 Block B, Shangdong Digital Valley, No. 8 Dongbeiwang West Road, Beijing, Haidian District
Phone: (86) 10 8304 3181

HISTORICAL FINANCIALS

Company Type: Public

Income Statement — FYE: December 31

	REVENUE ($mil)	NET INCOME ($mil)	NET PROFIT MARGIN	EMPLOYEES
12/22	20,408	(3,447)	—	20,870
12/21	27,380	(7,772)	—	24,396
12/20	21,671	(1,607)	—	15,914
12/19	22,245	(1,398)	—	14,214
12/18	19,668	(2,177)	—	13,563
Annual Growth	0.9%	—	—	11.4%

2022 Year-End Financials

Debt ratio: 0.6%
Return on equity: (-22.9%)
Cash ($ mil.): 3,023
Current Ratio: 2.52
Long-term debt ($ mil.): 21
No. of shares ($ mil.): 1,196
Dividends
  Yield: —
  Payout: 0.0%
Market value ($ mil.): 3,806

	STOCK PRICE ($) FY Close	P/E High/Low	PER SHARE ($) Earnings	Dividends	Book Value
12/22	3.18	— —	(2.95)	0.00	11.54
12/21	4.98	— —	(11.98)	0.00	14.92
Annual Growth	(36.1%)	— —	—	—	(6.2%)

DKSH Holding Ltd

DKSH Holding is a leading Market Expansion Services provider that delivers growth for companies in Asia and beyond. Its consumer goods unit markets luxury, fashion, food, and lifestyle products. Its health care unit distributes pharmaceuticals, consumer health, and over-the-counter health products, as well as medical devices and offers services including product registration, marketing and sales, and capillary physical distribution. Its technology unit covers a broad range of capital investment goods and analytical instruments for which it offers marketing, sales, distribution, and after-sales services. Formed in 2002, DKSH operates in countries across Asia, Europe, and the Americas. Majority of its sales were generated in Thailand.

Operations

The company operates through several primary segments: Healthcare (some 50% of sales), Consumer Goods (about 35%), Performance Materials (over 10%), and Technology (about 5%).

DKSH Business Unit Healthcare is the leading Market Expansion Services provider for healthcare companies seeking to grow their business in Asia. Custom-made offerings comprise registration, regulatory services, market entry studies, importation, customs clearance, marketing and sales, physical distribution, invoicing and cash collection. Products available through DKSH Healthcare include ethical pharmaceuticals, consumer health and over-the-counter (OTC) products, as well as medical devices.

DKSH Business Unit Consumer Goods is Asia's leading Market Expansion Services provider with a focus on fast moving consumer goods, food services, luxury goods, fashion and lifestyle products, as well as hair and skin cosmetics. The Business Unit's comprehensive Market Expansion Services extend from product feasibility studies and registration to importation, customs clearance, marketing and merchandising, sales, warehousing, physical distribution, invoicing, cash collection and after-sales services.

DKSH Business Unit Performance Materials is a leading specialty chemicals distributor and provider of Market Expansion Services for performance materials, covering Europe, North America and the whole of Asia. The Business Unit sources, markets and distributes a wide range of specialty chemicals and ingredients for pharmaceutical, personal care, food & beverage, as well as various industrial applications.

DKSH Business Unit Technology is the leading provider of Market Expansion Services covering a broad range of capital investment goods and analytical instruments. The Business Unit offers total solutions in the areas of infrastructure, industrial materials and supplies, precision and textile machinery, semiconductors, photovoltaic and electronics, agriculture, hospitality as well as specialized industrial applications.

Geographic Reach

DKSH is based in Zurich and generated some 30% of sales from Thailand, about 20% from Malaysia and Singapore, around 20% in Greater China.

Sales and Marketing

The company serves specialty chemicals, food and beverage, pharmaceutical and personal care industries.

Financial Performance

Net sales grew by 2% to CHF 11.3 billion in 2022 from CHF 11.1 billion in 2021. All four Business Units improved their performance. Accordingly, the Group's EBIT margin reached 3% compared to 3% in 2021 and 2% in 2020.

Net income for fiscal 2022 decreased to CHF284.7 million compared from the prior year with CHF304.9 million.

Cash held by the company at the end of fiscal 2022 decreased to CHF636.4 million. Cash provided by operations and financing activities were CHF321.9 million and CHF182.0 million, respectively. Cash used for investing activities was CHF513.1 million, mainly for acquisitions.

Strategy

Acquisitions will continue to be a crucial part of DKSH's strategy as they provide us with access to attractive business segments and expand its market position across its Business Units.

Another key aspect of the company's strategy is digitalization. DKSH keep driving digital business models and leveraging data and analytics to increase efficiencies and offer higher service levels to its clients and customers. In addition, based on its proven omni-channel approach, its eCommerce sales have increased three-fold compared to pre-pandemic levels of 2019.

EXECUTIVES

Global Business Development Vice President, Bijay Singh
Chief Executive Officer, Stefan P. Butz
Chief Financial Officer, Bernhard Schmitt
Corporate Affairs Head, Strategic Investments Head, Stephen Ferraby
Secretary, Laurent Sigismondi
Non-Executive Chairman, Independent Non-Executive Director, Marco Gadola
Independent Non-Executive Director, Wolfgang Baier
Independent Non-Executive Director, Jack Clemons
Independent Non-Executive Director, Frank Ch. Gulich
Independent Non-Executive Director, Annette G. Kohler
Independent Non-Executive Director, Hans Christoph Tanner
Independent Non-Executive Director, Eunice Zehnder-Lai
Non-Independent Non-Executive Director, Adrian T. Keller
Non-Independent Non-Executive Director, Andreas W. Keller
Auditors : Ernst & Young Ltd

LOCATIONS

HQ: DKSH Holding Ltd
  Wiesenstrasse 8, P.O. Box 888, Zurich 8034
Phone: (41) 44 386 7272   **Fax:** (41) 44 386 7282
Web: www.dksh.com

PRODUCTS/OPERATIONS

2014 Sales

	% of total
Consumer goods	42
Healthcare	46
Performance Materials	8
Technology	4
Total	100

2014 Sales

	% of total
Thailand	34
Greater China	30
Malaysia/Singapore	20
Other	16
Total	100

COMPETITORS

ARKEMA
AirBoss of America Corp
CFAO
DCC PUBLIC LIMITED COMPANY
Evonik Industries AG
FLUIDRA, SA
LIXIL CORPORATION
N L INDUSTRIES, INC.
REXEL
VALHI, INC.

HISTORICAL FINANCIALS
Company Type: Public

Income Statement   FYE: December 31

	REVENUE ($mil)	NET INCOME ($mil)	NET PROFIT MARGIN	EMPLOYEES
12/23	13,228	217	1.6%	27,062
12/22	12,270	217	1.8%	0
12/21	12,166	245	2.0%	31,453
12/20	12,196	178	1.5%	32,447
12/19	11,978	178	1.5%	33,353
Annual Growth	2.5%	5.1%	—	(5.1%)

2023 Year-End Financials
Debt ratio: 14.9%
Return on equity: 10.5%
Cash ($ mil.): 821
Current Ratio: 1.40
Long-term debt ($ mil.): 560
No. of shares ($ mil.): 64
Dividends
Yield: —
Payout: 80.3%
Market value ($ mil.): —

DNB BANK ASA

EXECUTIVES

Corporate Banking Norway Chief Executive Officer, Corporate Banking Norway Executive Vice President, Kjerstin R. Braathen
Chief Financial Officer, Ida Lerner
Chief Compliance Officer, Mirella E. Grant
Personal Banking Executive Vice President, Ingjerd Blekeli Spiten
Corporate Banking Executive Vice President, Harald Serck-Hanssen
Wealth Management Executive Vice President, Hakon Hansen
Marketing Executive Vice President, Alexander Opstad
Payments & Innovation Executive Vice President, Benjamin Kristoffer Golding
People Executive Vice President, Anne Sigrun Moen
Group Risk Management Executive Vice President, Sverre Krog
Technology & Services Executive Vice President, Maria Ervik Lovold
Corporate Communications Executive Vice President, Communications & Sustainability Executive Vice President, Thomas Midteide
Chairman, Olaug Svarva
Vice-Chairman, Svein Richard Brandtzæg
Non-Independent Director, Lillian Hattrem
Non-Independent Director, Stian Tegler Samuelsen
Non-Independent Director, Eli Solhaug
Director, Gro Bakstad
Director, Julie Galbo
Director, Jens Peter Due Olsen
Director, Jaan Ivar Semlitsch
Director, Kim Wahl
Auditors : Ernst & Young AS

LOCATIONS
HQ: DNB BANK ASA
  Dronning Eufemias gate 30, BjÃ‚rvika, Oslo 0191
Phone: (47) 915 03000
Web: www.dnb.no/en

COMPETITORS
CENKOS SECURITIES PLC
CREDITO EMILIANO SPA
CTBC Financial Holding Co., Ltd.
FIRST INTERNATIONAL BANK OF ISRAEL LTD
Hana Financial Group Inc.
ISRAEL DISCOUNT BANK OF NEW YORK
Itau Unibanco Holding S/A
LEGAL & GENERAL GROUP PLC
THANACHART CAPITAL PUBLIC COMPANY LIMITED
Woori Finance Holdings Co., Ltd.

HISTORICAL FINANCIALS
Company Type: Public

Income Statement   FYE: December 31

	ASSETS ($mil)	NET INCOME ($mil)	INCOME AS % OF ASSETS	EMPLOYEES
12/21	330,770	2,765	0.8%	9,659
12/20	342,601	2,196	0.6%	9,311
12/19	317,848	2,799	0.9%	9,336
12/18	303,559	2,686	0.9%	9,638
12/17	329,086	2,544	0.8%	9,561
Annual Growth	0.1%	2.1%	—	0.3%

2021 Year-End Financials
Return on assets: 0.8%
Return on equity: 9.9%
Long-term debt ($ mil.): —
No. of shares ($ mil.): 1,550
Sales ($ mil.): 7,706
Dividends
Yield: 8.8%
Payout: 109.3%
Market value ($ mil.): 35,581

	STOCK PRICE ($) FY Close	P/E High/Low		PER SHARE ($) Earnings	Dividends	Book Value
12/21	22.95	2	1	1.78	2.03	17.81
Annual Growth	—			—	—	—

Dole plc

EXECUTIVES

Executive Chairman, Director, Carl McCann
Chief Executive Officer, Director, Rory Byrne

Chief Operating Officer, Director, Johan Lindén
Chief Financial Officer, Director, Frank Davis
Director, Timothy M. George
Director, Rose B. Hynes
Director, Imelda Hurley
Director, Michael Meghen
Director, Helen Nolan
Director, Jimmy P. Tolan
Director, Kevin Toland
Auditors : KPMG

LOCATIONS

HQ: Dole plc
29 North Anne Street, Dublin 7 D07 PH36
Phone: (353) 1 887 2600
Web: www.doleplc.com

HISTORICAL FINANCIALS

Company Type: Public

Income Statement — FYE: December 31

	REVENUE ($mil)	NET INCOME ($mil)	NET PROFIT MARGIN	EMPLOYEES
12/22	9,228	86	0.9%	37,422
12/21	6,454	(7)	—	38,500
12/20	4,345	52	1.2%	40,000
12/19	4,166	55	1.3%	0
12/18	4,392	36	0.8%	0
Annual Growth	20.4%	24.0%		

2022 Year-End Financials

Debt ratio: 26.7%
Return on equity: 7.7%
Cash ($ mil.): 228
Current Ratio: 1.10
Long-term debt ($ mil.): 1,127
No. of shares ($ mil.): 94
Dividends
  Yield: —
  Payout: 35.1%
Market value ($ mil.): —

Downer EDI Ltd

Downer EDI works to keep things working. The company provides engineering and infrastructure management for public and private entities throughout Australia, New Zealand, Asia, and the Pacific. It offers a range of engineering services that includes design, project and facilities management, operations, consulting, and maintenance. The company is organized along six divisions: Transport Services; Technology and Communications Services; Utilities Services; Engineering, Construction, and Maintenance; Mining; and Rail. Although Downer EDI's footprint covers the Asia/Pacific region, Australian operations account for more than 80% of its revenue.

Operations

The group's Transport Services segment is the largest, contributing 27% of net sales in fiscal 2015 (ended June). That segment provides construction, development, management, and maintenance services for highways, railroads, light rails, ports, and airports in Australia and New Zealand. Closely following is the Engineering, Construction, and Maintenance segment (25% of net sales), which specializes in plant services and providing consulting services to minerals and metals customers. Mining (21%) provides contract mining services including planning, drilling, and blasting.

Meanwhile, the Rail division is engaged in the supply, maintenance, and provision of components to the freight and passenger rail sector in Australia, and Utilities Services provides asset life-cycle services to energy clients in Australia and New Zealand. Finally, Technology and Communications Services offers end-to-end infrastructure management services to telecom customers (also in Australia and New Zealand).

Geographic Reach

Downer EDI primarily operates in Australia and New Zealand, but its operations also reach the Asia/Pacific region, South America, and southern Africa.

Sales and Marketing

The company serves a range of sectors that includes transportation, telecom, utilities, mining, and rail customers. Its customer roster, past and present, includes Chevron, Bechtel, Fluor, FOXTEL, and Vodafone.

Financial Performance

Note: Growth rates may differ after conversion to US dollars.

Revenues, which had been climbing through 2012, have slipped since then. In fiscal 2015 (ended June), revenue fell 5% to A$7 billion, versus A$7.4 billion in 2014. The Mining and Rail divisions experienced slowdowns that year due to factors including a fall in commodity prices, the completion of major projects, and reduced volumes on existing contracts.

Lower sales led to a drop in net income that year. Profits had been on the rise for three years but fell 3% to A$210.2 million in 2015. To improve its bottom line, Downer EDI has been focusing on reducing its plant and equipment costs (by increasingly using leased equipment and better utilizing its owned assets).

Cash flow from operations fell 17% to A$486.5 million in 2015.

Strategy

Downer EDI has been facing a challenging time in the market, as fewer jobs are available to the industry overall. One of the company's key strategies is to focus on providing additional services to its existing customers, including pursuing overseas contracts for those same customers. Acquisitions and capital expenditures help support this strategy, as does a focus on driving efficiency across the organization. In early 2014, the company sold its New Zealand consulting arm Spiire NZ to Calibre Group for NZ$2.2 million.

In 2015 the company secured a 10-year maintenance deal with Pacific National through which it will provide management services for more than 300 locomotives.

Downer EDI has also formed strategic joint ventures with partners such as Bombadier and Caterpillar to boost its presence in the passenger and freight market.

Mergers and Acquisitions

In 2014 Downer EDI acquired design and construction firm Tenix Holding, which serves the power and water sectors in Australia and New Zealand, for $A300 million. It also bought VEC Civil Engineering and VEC Plant & Equipment, which primarily build bridges and other concrete structures in Tasmania. That purchase added new expertise to the firm.

Previously, in 2013, the company bought the operations of Scarriff Pipelines and Scarriff Construction for A$4 million. Scarriff's primary activity is maintaining water pipelines.

EXECUTIVES

Chief Executive Officer, Managing Director, Executive Director, Grant Anthony Fenn
Australian Operations Chief Operating Officer, Sergio Cinerari
Chief Financial Officer, Michael J. Ferguson
New Zealand Chief Executive Officer, S. L. Killeen
Spotless Chief Executive Officer, Peter J. Tompkins
General Counsel, Secretary, Robert Regan
Secretary, Peter J. Lyons
Chairman, Independent Non-Executive Director, Richard Michael Harding
Independent Non-Executive Director, Philip Stuart Garling
Independent Non-Executive Director, Teresa G. Handicott
Independent Non-Executive Director, Nicole M. Hollows
Independent Non-Executive Director, Peter Lawrence Watson
Auditors : KPMG

LOCATIONS

HQ: Downer EDI Ltd
Level 2, Triniti III, Triniti Business Campus, 39 Delhi Road, North Ryde, Sydney, New South Wales 2113
Phone: (61) 2 9468 9700   **Fax:** (61) 2 9813 8915
Web: www.downergroup.com

2015 Sales

	% of total
Australia	81
New Zealand and Pacific	18
Africa	1
Asia	0
South America	0
Other	0
Total	100

PRODUCTS/OPERATIONS

2015 Sales

	% of total
Rendering of services	64
Mining services	21
Construction contracts	11
Sale of goods	3
Other revenue	1
Other income	0
Total	100

2015

	mil $	%
DI-AU	3,669.4	52
Mining	1,532.4	22
DI-NZ	1,202.0	17
Rail	611.6	9
Unallocated	4.5	0
Total	7,019.9	100

COMPETITORS

CARILLION PLC
CH2M HILL COMPANIES, LTD.
COSTAIN GROUP PLC
JACOBS ONE LIMITED
Petrofac Limited
SNC-Lavalin Group Inc
Stantec Inc
TEAM, INC.
WILLBROS GROUP, INC.
WORLEY LIMITED

HISTORICAL FINANCIALS

Company Type: Public

Income Statement   FYE: June 30

	REVENUE ($mil)	NET INCOME ($mil)	NET PROFIT MARGIN	EMPLOYEES
06/21	8,654	136	1.6%	44,000
06/20	8,682	(102)	—	0
06/19	8,960	183	2.0%	0
06/18	8,872	52	0.6%	0
06/17	5,583	139	2.5%	0
Annual Growth	11.6%	(0.6%)	—	—

2021 Year-End Financials

Debt ratio: 13.8%
Return on equity: 6.6%
Cash ($ mil.): 609
Current Ratio: 1.03
Long-term debt ($ mil.): 889
No. of shares ($ mil.): 695
Dividends
Yield: —
Payout: 84.6%
Market value ($ mil.): —

DS Smith Plc

DS Smith provides sustainable fibre-based packaging across Europe and North America which is supported by recycling and paper-making operations. It plays a central role in the value chain across sectors including FMCG, industrials and e-commerce. It is a leading international sustainable packaging company, with innovative packaging solutions made from recycled and/or recyclable material. It also manufactures corrugated case material (CCM), which is the paper used for conversion into corrugated board. It provides a full recycling and waste management service. We are Europe's largest cardboard and paper recycler and are also one of the leading full-service recycling and waste management companies in Europe.

Operations

The company's business operates in four geographic segments: Northern Europe, Southern Europe, Eastern Europe, and North America.

Northern Europe (generates nearly 40% of revenue) includes Belgium, Denmark, Finland, Germany, Netherlands, Norway, Sweden, Switzerland and United Kingdom. Southern Europe (nearly 40% of revenue) includes France, Italy, Portugal and Spain. Eastern Europe (more than 15%) includes Austria, Bosnia and Herzegovina, Bulgaria, Croatia, Czechia, Estonia, Greece, Hungary, Latvia, Lithuania, North Macedonia, Poland, Romania, Serbia, Slovakia, Slovenia and TuÂ¨rkiye. North America generates nearly 10%.

Geographic Reach

The company generates its revenue from various locations including the UK (more than 15% of revenue), France (about 15%), Iberia (more than 10%), Italy (more than 10%), Germany (nearly 10%), USA (nearly 10%), and others (nearly 30%).

Sales and Marketing

The company's customers are largely fast-moving consumer goods (FMCG) companies that produce goods typically sold in supermarkets and via e-commerce channels. It makes corrugated packaging for some of the largest global food brands, online retailers and industrial customers and sells paper and recycling materials to third parties.

Financial Performance

For the 12-month period, revenue grew to Â£8.2 billion (2021/22: Â£7.2 billion), up 11% on a constant currency basis and 14% on a reported basis; with the decline in box volumes (Â£295 million) more than offset by higher selling prices (Â£1.2 billion) across the company which reflect the lag in recovery of the increases in input costs during the period 2021 to 2023.

Profit for the year 2023 was Â£502 million compared to Â£280 million in 2022.

Cash at the end of the year was Â£368 million. Operations generated Â£866 million while investing and financing activities used Â£526 million and Â£728 million, respectively.

Strategy

The company's strategy is based on balancing the requirements of its core stakeholders. The company's strategic pillars include delighting its customers, realizing the potential of its people, and leading the way in sustainability.

The company is working with large customers in resilient sectors such as FMCG and aiming to grow share with these customers. It is also focusing on embeddingdiversityand inclusion by expanding resource groups and local networks. It is designing out waste and pollution and keeping materials in use while decarbonizing its operations and value chain.

HISTORY

Capitalizing on the wartime demand for cigarettes, David Solomon Smith and his cousin began manufacturing cigarette cartons in London in 1940. (Smith was chairman of his company until 1991.) The enterprise went public in 1960, but little changed until 1983, when Richard Brewster and others bought a 29% stake. Brewster became CEO and began acquiring other paper and packaging makers. After some small deals, including Western Board Mills (1984) and Abbitrin (1985), David S. Smith picked up St. Regis in 1986 and Kemsley Mill in 1988. By the time Brewster left the company in 1991, it was the UK's leading papermaker.

Peter Williams became the new CEO and continued down the acquisition trail. Notable purchases include French packaging company Kaysersberg in 1992 and Spicers, an office-products wholesaler, in 1993. In 1996 David S. Smith added Biber Paper Converting and its subsidiary, John Dickinson Stationery (sold in 2005).

Despite rosy mid-decade predictions for the future of the paper industry, by 1997 profits had begun a downward slide, thanks to the pound's strength and industry overcapacity. After three straight years of declining profits, David S. Smith said in 1999 that it was willing to consider being acquired. However, an increase in sales and successful restructuring efforts significantly improved the company's position in 2000.

With increased profits, David S. Smith resumed its expansion activities. In 2000 the company acquired Packaging Systems LLC, also known as Rapak, a leading supplier of bag-in-box liquid packaging, based in Chicago. The next year it added a Spicers division in Germany to increase its European office product sales. David S. Smith also formed alliances with Georgia-Pacific on packaging and S.P. Richards on wholesale office products in the US, and wants to spend $142 million on acquisitions to strengthen its position in the paper and packaging markets. In September 2001 the company changed its name to DS Smith plc.

In 2008 the company acquired the New Thames Mill and the adjacent Grovehurst Energy from M-real Corp. and subsequently converted the mill to manufacture lightweight CCM. In 2010 DS Smith sold its corrugated packaging operations in Turkey for around Â£4.8 million (about $7.6 million).

EXECUTIVES

Chief Executive Officer, Executive Director, Miles Roberts
Financial Director, Executive Director, Adrian Marsh
General Counsel, Secretary, Iain Simm
Chairman, Gareth Davis
Non-Executive Director, Celia Baxter
Non-Executive Director, Chris Britton
Non-Executive Director, Alina Kessel
Non-Executive Director, David Robbie
Non-Executive Director, Louise Smalley
Non-Executive Director, Rupert Soames
Auditors : Deloitte LLP

LOCATIONS

HQ: DS Smith Plc
350 Euston Road, London NW1 3AX

Phone: (44) 20 7756 1800
Web: www.dssmith.com

2019 sales

	%
UK	18
Western Europe	28
DCH and Northern Europe	18
Central Europe and Italy	26
North America	10
Total	**100**

PRODUCTS/OPERATIONS

Selected Subsidiaries
UK Packaging
    DS Smith Paper Limited
    DS Smith Logistics Limited
    DS Smith Packaging Limited
Office Products Wholesaling
    Spicers France SAS
    Spicers (Ireland) Limited
    Spicers Limited
    Spicers Belgium NV
Continental European Corrugated Packaging
    DS Smith Kaysersberg S.A.S. (France)
    DS Smith Polska S.A. (Poland)
    Otor S.A. (France)
    Toscana Ondulati SpA (Italy)
Plastic Packaging
    Cartón Plástico s.a. (Spain)
    David S. Smith America Inc. (US)
    DS Smith Plastics Limited
    DSS Rapak Inc. (US)
    DS Smith Ducaplast S.A.S. (France)
    DW Plastics NV (Belgium)
    Rapak GmbH (Germany)
    StePac L.A. Limited (Israel)

COMPETITORS

AMCOR FLEXIBLES NORTH AMERICA, INC.
DEVRO PLC
EPWIN GROUP PLC
Franz Haniel & Cie. GmbH
ILLINOIS TOOL WORKS INC.
RECKITT BENCKISER GROUP PLC
RENISHAW P L C
SMURFIT KAPPA GROUP PUBLIC LIMITED COMPANY
SONOCO PRODUCTS COMPANY
thyssenkrupp AG

HISTORICAL FINANCIALS

Company Type: Public

Income Statement   FYE: April 30

	REVENUE ($mil)	NET INCOME ($mil)	NET PROFIT MARGIN	EMPLOYEES
04/22	9,088	351	3.9%	29,856
04/21	8,311	269	3.2%	29,309
04/20	7,563	659	8.7%	29,397
04/19	8,028	356	4.4%	27,574
04/18	7,914	355	4.5%	27,097
Annual Growth	3.5%	(0.3%)	—	2.5%

2022 Year-End Financials
Debt ratio: 27.2%   No. of shares ($ mil.): 1,373
Return on equity: 7.2%   Dividends
Cash ($ mil.): 1,027   Yield: —
Current Ratio: 0.87   Payout: 73.8%
Long-term debt ($ mil.): 1,745   Market value ($ mil.): —

DSV AS

EXECUTIVES

Chief Executive Officer, Jens Bjorn Andersen
Vice Chief Executive Officer, Chief Operating Officer, Jens H. Lund
Chief Financial Officer, Michael Ebbe
Chairman, Director, Thomas Plenborg
Deputy Chairman, Director, Jorgen Moller
Director, Annette Sadolin
Director, Beat Walti
Director, Marie-Louise Aamund
Director, Birgit Woidemann Norgaard
Director, Niels Smedegaard
Director, Tarek Sultan Al-Essa
Auditors : PricewaterhouseCoopers Statsautoriseret Revisionspartnerselskab

LOCATIONS

HQ: DSV AS
  Hovedgaden 630, Hedehusene 2640
Phone: (45) 43 20 30 40
Web: www.dsv.com

HISTORICAL FINANCIALS

Company Type: Public

Income Statement   FYE: December 31

	REVENUE ($mil)	NET INCOME ($mil)	NET PROFIT MARGIN	EMPLOYEES
12/23	22,408	1,830	8.2%	73,577
12/22	33,847	2,523	7.5%	76,283
12/21	27,745	1,705	6.1%	77,958
12/20	19,122	701	3.7%	56,621
12/19	14,231	556	3.9%	61,216
Annual Growth	12.0%	34.7%		4.7%

2023 Year-End Financials
Debt ratio: 2.2%   No. of shares ($ mil.): 209
Return on equity: 17.5%   Dividends
Cash ($ mil.): 958   Yield: —
Current Ratio: 1.11   Payout: 37.8%
Long-term debt ($ mil.): 2,972   Market value ($ mil.): 18,371

	STOCK PRICE ($) FY Close	P/E High/Low	PER SHARE ($) Earnings	Dividends	Book Value
12/23	87.81	2 1	8.49	3.21	48.81
12/22	79.39	1 1	10.94	2.62	47.41
12/21	117.38	3 1	7.34	2.02	48.81
12/20	84.02	5 2	3.04	1.37	34.58
12/19	57.83	3 2	2.77	1.12	32.46
Annual Growth	11.0%	—	32.4%	30.0%	10.7%

E Sun Financial Holdings Co Ltd

Here comes the E.Sun, and I say it's providing banking and financial services in Taiwan. Established in 2002 to consolidate the operations of E.Sun Bank and other subsidiaries, E.Sun provides commercial banking, venture capital, securities trading, and other financial services to businesses and individuals throughout the country. The group depends on commercial banking services for its bread and butter (90% of annual revenues) and carries out additional financial operations through six subsidiaries. An attempt to acquire Taiwan Business Bank in 2005 broke down amid union protests. A year later the group allied with Singapore's Temasek which would eventually control 6% through Fullerton Financial Holdings.

EXECUTIVES

Chairman, Director, Yung-Jen Huang
President, Director, Yung-Hsung Hou
Deputy President, Jiaw-Hwang Shy
Deputy President, Chief Brand Officer, Director, Wu-Lin Duh
Chief Information Officer, Chief Risk Officer, Heng-Hwa Yang
Senior Executive Vice President, Tung-Long Kuo
Senior Executive Vice President, Joe Huang
General Auditor, Wei-Chin Chien
Chief Strategy Officer, Joseph N.C. Huang
Chief Human Resources Officer, J.C. Wang
Senior Executive Vice President, Suka Chen
Chief Accounting Officer, Kuan-Her Wu
Executive Vice President, Scott Chou
Executive Vice President, Mao-Cin Chen
Chief Marketing Officer, Shuei-Ping Wan
Executive Vice President, Jih-Hsiung Tseng
Director, Jackson Mai
Director, Tai-Chi Lee
Director, Chen-En Ko
Director, Chi-Jen Lee
Director, Jen-Jen Chang Lin
Director, Ron-Chu Chen
Director, Jian-Li Wu
Director, Fei-Long Tsai
Auditors : Deloitte & Touche

LOCATIONS

HQ: E Sun Financial Holdings Co Ltd
  14F., No.117 & 1F, No. 115, Sec.3, Minsheng E. Rd.,
  Songshan District, Taipei
Phone: (886) 2 2175 1313
Web: www.esunfhc.com.tw

COMPETITORS

Hana Financial Group Inc.
MITSUBISHI UFJ FINANCIAL GROUP, INC.
MIZUHO FINANCIAL GROUP, INC.
SUMITOMO MITSUI TRUST HOLDINGS, INC.
Shinhan Financial Group Co., Ltd.

HISTORICAL FINANCIALS

Company Type: Public

Income Statement   FYE: December 31

	ASSETS ($mil)	NET INCOME ($mil)	INCOME AS % OF ASSETS	EMPLOYEES
12/21	116,689	743	0.6%	0
12/20	105,748	641	0.6%	0
12/19	83,449	0	0.0%	0
12/18	74,801	558	0.7%	0
12/17	69,957	497	0.7%	0
Annual Growth	13.6%	10.6%		

2021 Year-End Financials

Return on assets: 0.6%
Return on equity: 10.9%
Long-term debt ($ mil.): —
No. of shares ($ mil.): 14,794
Sales ($ mil.): 2,434
Dividends
Yield: —
Payout: 0.0%
Market value ($ mil.): —

E.ON SE

E.ON is one of Europe's largest operators of energy networks and energy infrastructure and a provider of innovative customer solutions for some 51 million customers. The company's operations are energy networks and customer solutions. Its non-strategic operations are reported under non-core Business. With customers in Germany, Denmark, Sweden, Italy, the UK, Czech Republic, Hungary, Romania, Slovakia, and Turkey, E.ON boasts 700,000 kilometers of energy networks in Germany, and about 14.9 million connection points for power in its service territory. About 55% of E.ON's total revenue comes from Germany.

Operations

E.ON operates through two segments: Customer Solutions (over 60% of sales) and Energy Networks (about 20%). Non-strategic operations are reported under Non-Core Business; corporate functions and equity interests managed directly by E.ON SE are reported under Corporate Functions/Other (about 20% combined).

Customer solutions segment serves as the platform for working with E.ON's customers to actively shape Europe's energy transition. This includes supplying customers in Europe (excluding Turkey) with power, gas, and heat and offering products and services that enhance their energy efficiency and autonomy and provide other benefits.

Energy Networks consists of E.ON's power and gas distribution networks and related activities. It is subdivided into three regional markets: Germany, Sweden, and East-Central Europe/Turkey (which consists of the Czech Republic, Hungary, Romania, Poland, Croatia, Slovakia, and the stake in Enerjisa Enerji in Turkey, which is accounted for using the equity method).

The Non-Core Business segment t consists of the E.ON Group's non-strategic activities. This applies to the operation and dismantling of nuclear power stations in Germany (which is managed by the PreussenElektra unit) and the generation business in Turkey. The Corporate Functions' main task is to lead the E.ON Group. This involves charting E.ON's strategic course and managing and funding its existing business portfolio. Corporate Functions' tasks include optimizing E.ON's overall business across countries and markets from a financial, strategic, and risk.

Overall, electricity generates about 70% of total revenue, while gas for some 25% and other for over 5% of total revenue.

Geographic Reach

E.ON's corporate headquarters is in Essen, Germany. E.ON has a presence in Germany, Norway, Denmark, the Netherlands, the United Kingdom, Belgium, France, Poland, Czech Republic, Italy, Austria, Slovakia, Croatia, Slovenia, Romania, Hungary and Italy.

About 55% of E.ON's total revenue comes from Germany.

Sales and Marketing

The company's customers are across all categories: residential, small and medium-sized enterprises, large commercial and industrial, and public entities.

Financial Performance

The company reported a revenue of EUR 77.4 billion, a 27% increase from the previous year's revenue of EUR 60.9 billion.

In 2021, the company had a net income of EUR 5.3 billion, a 318% increase from the previous year's net income of $1.3 billion

The company's cash at the end of 2021 was EUR 3.6 billion. Operating activities generated EUR 4.1 billion, while investing activities used EUR 5.4 billion, primarily for purchases of investments in Intangible assets and property, plant and equipment. Financing activities provided another EUR 2.3 billion.

Strategy

The year 2021 was a year of fundamental redirection for E.ON. Following the successful integration of innogy, in April 2021 Leonhard Birnbaum succeeded Johannes Teyssen as CEO. Two other new Management Board members were appointed as well: Victoria Ossadnik (for Digitalization) and Patrick Lammers (for Customer Solutions). The new management team designed an updated strategy to prepare the entire E.ON Group for the decade ahead. In 2021 E.ON moved forward on the sustainable course that it had set early on and, as part of the updated strategy, defined new growth ambitions. Its main focus was to propel socially responsible sustainability and Europe's energy transition in the digital age. Both?the energy transition and sustainability?are among the key drivers of future growth in E.ON's core businesses: energy networks and customer solutions. Networks form the backbone of the energy transition and make a significant contribution to its success. Sustainable products and services for cities, municipalities, industry, and households enable E.ON to support its customers on their journey to climate neutrality.

The transition toward a new, climate-neutral, and distributed energy world is accelerating and will also spur a decade of growth for the entire energy sector. Being an energy company with about 51 million customers in Europe (including customers in Turkey and at ZSE in Slovakia) will enable E.ON to benefit from this transition and simultaneously to play a key role in shaping Europe's decarburization. A few months ago, E.ON aligned its strategy with three priorities? sustainability, digitalization and growth?and set a new course with a clear vision for the Company's future. In the years ahead, E.ON will become the sustainable platform for Europe's green energy transition. It will also use digitalization to master the increasing complexity of the entire energy system.

HISTORY

VEBA (originally Vereinigte Elektrizitats- und Bergwerks AG) was formed in 1929 in Berlin to consolidate Germany's state-owned electricity and mining interests. These operations included PreussenElektra, an electric utility formed by the German government in 1927; Hibernia, a coal mining firm founded in 1873; and Preussag, a mining and smelting company founded in 1923.

In the 1930s VEBA produced synthetic gasoline (essential to the German war machine) from coal at its Hibernia plant. In 1938 the company and chemical cartel I. G. Farben set up Chemische Werke Hüls to make synthetic rubber. After WWII, VEBA's assets in western Germany were transferred to the government, and several executives were arrested. Preussag was spun off in 1959.

In 1965 the government spun off VEBA to the public. That year the company entered trading and transportation by buying Stinnes, one of West Germany's largest industrial companies. In 1969 VEBA transferred its coal mining interests to Ruhrkohle and a few years later moved into oil exploration and development. The company shortened its name to VEBA in 1970.

The West German government sold its remaining stake in VEBA in 1987. In a changed regulatory environment, large investors were able to accumulate big portions of stock, and their dissatisfaction with the company's lackluster results made it a takeover target. In response, new chairman Ulrich Hartmann began cutting noncore businesses and reducing staff.

In 1990 VEBA began accumulating mobile communications, networking, and cable TV companies. It allied with the UK's Cable and Wireless (C&W) in 1995 to develop a European mobile phone business, but in 1997 C&W sold its interest to VEBA (as part of the deal, VEBA gained a 10% stake in C&W, which it sold in 1999). In anticipation of the 1998 deregulation of the German telecom market, VEBA and RWE merged their German telecom businesses in 1997.

VEBA acquired a 36% stake in Degussa, a specialty chemicals company, in 1997; two years later Degussa merged with Hüls to form a separately traded chemical company called Degussa-Hüls, in which VEBA took a 62% stake. VEBA sold a 30% stake in Stinnes to the public in 1999. The company's telecom venture sold its fixed-line telephone business, its cable TV unit, and its stake in mobile phone operator E-Plus.

These moves, however, were just the prelude to a bigger deal: a $14 billion merger agreement between VEBA and fellow German conglomerate VIAG. The partners announced plans to dump noncore businesses and beef up their energy and chemicals holdings. VEBA and VIAG completed their merger in 2000, and the combined company adopted the name E.ON. The companies' utilities businesses were combined into E.ON Energie, and their chemicals units were brought together as Degussa.

To gain regulatory approval to form E.ON, VEBA and VIAG agreed to sell their stakes in German electric utilities Bewag and VEAG and coal producer LAUBAG. E.ON sold its VEAG and LAUBAG interests, along with semiconductor and electronics distribution units, in 2000 and sold Bewag in 2001.

In 2001 E.ON agreed to acquire UK electricity generator Powergen (now E.ON UK), and it sold off nonutility operations, including Degussa and Veba Oel. E.ON swapped a 51% stake in Veba Oel for BP's 26% stake in German natural gas supplier Ruhrgas (now E.ON Ruhrgas). E.ON also sold Klöckner to UK steel trader Balli and sold its stake in silicon wafer maker MEMC to buyout firm Texas Pacific Group.

In 2002 E.ON sold its VAW Aluminum unit to Norwegian conglomerate Norsk Hydro in a $2.8 billion deal. Regulators moved to prevent E.ON from acquiring BP's stake in Ruhrgas in 2002, but BP agreed to pay for the Veba Oel stake in cash if necessary, and the swap was completed later that year. E.ON also acquired Vodafone and ThyssenKrupp's stakes in Ruhrgas in 2002, and it sold its remaining stake in Veba Oel to BP.

Also in 2002 E.ON completed its purchase of Powergen (which included its US subsidiary LG&E Energy) for about $8 billion, and it sold its 65% stake in logistics company Stinnes to German railroad operator Deutsche Bahn. In late 2002 E.ON acquired the UK energy supply and generation businesses of TXU Europe in a $2.5 billion deal.

The following year E.ON swapped its majority stake in chemical maker Degussa with coal group RAG for RAG's 18% interest in Ruhrgas. It completed its acquisition of Ruhrgas by purchasing the combined 40% stake held by Royal Dutch Shell, Exxon Mobil, and TUI (formerly Preussag). It also sold subsidiary Viterra's energy services unit (gas and water meters) to CVC Capital Partners.

In 2005 the company acquired the Enfield power station in the UK for $250.2 million.

In 2007 E.ON acquired Ireland-based wind farm company Airtricity for $1.4 billion.

Pursuing growth in new geographic markets, in 2007 E.ON acquired Russia-based power utility OGK-4 for almost $6 billion. Outmaneuvered by its rivals, in 2008 it dropped its $56 billion bid to buy Endesa S.A., Spain's largest electric utility, settling for the purchase of a number of Endesa's generation assets in Spain and Italy.

In 2009, to counter EDF's acquisition of British Energy, E.ON and RWE formed a joint venture to develop 6,000 MW of nuclear power capacity in the UK.

That year, prompted by the regulatory requirements of the European Commission, E.ON and GDF SUEZ agreed to swap generating assets to allow for more competition in their major markets. It sold 860 MW of Germany-based conventional power plants, 132 MW of hydroelectric plants, and access to 770 MW of nuclear power. In return GDF SUEZ sold to E.ON a similar amount of power generation capacity in France and the Benelux countries. In 2010, also to meet EU anti-monopoly regulations, it sold grid operator Transpower to Dutch giant TenneT for $1.1 billion and it swapped 5,000 MW of generation capacity with EDF and EnBW.

In 2010 the company sold E.ON U.S., which operates Kentucky's two major utilities, for $7.6 billion. Its US assets were no longer considered a core part of its growth strategy, and the sale helped to pay down debt. To raise cash, that year it also sold its 3.5% stake in Gazprom to Russian investment bank Vnesheconombank for $4.4 billion.

EXECUTIVES

Integration Chairman, Integration Chief Executive Officer, Leonhard Birnbaum
Chief Financial Officer, Marc Spieker
Digital Chief Operating Officer, Victoria Ossadnik
Networks Chief Operating Officer, Thomas Konig
Commercial Chief Operating Officer, Patrick Lammers
Director, Anke Groth
Chairman, Karl Ludwig Kley
Director, Katja Bauer
Deputy Chairman, Enrich Clementi
Deputy Chairman, Christoph Schmitz
Director, Klaus Frohlich
Director, Ulrich Grillo
Director, Eugen-Gheorghe Luha
Director, Miroslav Pelouch
Director, Szilvia Pinczesne Marton
Director, Stefan May
Director, Rene Pohls
Director, Andreas Schmitz
Director, Rolf Martin Schmitz
Director, Fred Schulz
Director, Karen de Segundo
Director, Elisabeth Wallbaum
Director, Deborah Wilkens
Director, Ewald Woste
Director, Albert Zettl
Auditors : KPMG AG Wirtschaftsprufungsgesellschaft

LOCATIONS

HQ: E.ON SE
Brusseler Platz 1, Essen D-45131
Phone: (49) 211 184 00 **Fax:** (49) 211 45 79 5 01
Web: www.eon.com

2016 Sales

	% of total
Germany	57
United Kingdom	20
Europe (other)	16
Sweden	6
Other	1
Total	100

PRODUCTS/OPERATIONS

2016 Sales

	% of total
Customer Solutions	53
Energy Networks	38
Renewables	3
Non-Core Business	3
Corporate Functions/Other	3
Total	100

2016 Sales

	% of total
Electricity	78
Gas	17
Other	5
Total	100

COMPETITORS

BERKSHIRE HATHAWAY ENERGY COMPANY
DYNEGY INC.
ELECTRICITE DE FRANCE
ENEL SPA
ENERGIA GROUP NI HOLDINGS LIMITED
Fortum Oyj
IBERDROLA, SOCIEDAD ANONIMA
INTERNATIONAL POWER LTD.
SEMPRA TEXAS HOLDINGS CORP.
Vattenfall AB

HISTORICAL FINANCIALS

Company Type: Public

Income Statement — FYE: December 31

	REVENUE ($mil)	NET INCOME ($mil)	NET PROFIT MARGIN	EMPLOYEES
12/22	124,729	1,955	1.6%	71,613
12/21	88,444	5,309	6.0%	72,169
12/20	75,682	1,248	1.6%	78,126
12/19	46,443	1,758	3.8%	78,948
12/18	34,327	3,690	10.8%	43,302
Annual Growth	38.1%	(14.7%)		13.4%

2022 Year-End Financials

Debt ratio: 27.2% No. of shares ($ mil.): 2,610
Return on equity: 13.0% Dividends
Cash ($ mil.): 10,013 Yield: —
Current Ratio: 1.39 Payout: 52.2%
Long-term debt ($ mil.): 30,935 Market value ($ mil.): 25,817

	STOCK PRICE ($) FY Close	P/E High/Low		PER SHARE ($) Earnings	Dividends	Book Value
12/22	9.89	19	11	0.75	0.39	6.51
12/21	13.94	8	5	2.04	0.42	5.23
12/20	11.06	36	25	0.48	0.38	2.32
12/19	10.67	17	13	0.76	0.35	3.91
12/18	9.87	8	6	1.71	0.26	3.04
Annual Growth	0.1%			(18.6%)	10.2%	21.0%

East Japan Railway Co.

If you want to ride the rails into Tokyo, you could find yourself cruising at 168 mph aboard a bullet train operated by East Japan Railway, better known as JR East. The company serves more than 15 million people daily and carries passengers on more than 7,400 km of track in the eastern half of the Japanese mainland, including the Tokyo area. JR East's Shinkansen (bullet-train) lines connect metropolitan Tokyo with other major cities. Besides its transportation-related operations, JR East generates revenue from leasing restaurant and retail space in its stations and from managing shopping centers and office buildings on property that has been developed near its stations.

Operations
East Japan Railway has four operating segments: Transportation, Retail & Services, Real Estate & Hotels, and Other.

The Transportation segment includes passenger transportation operations, which are centered on railway operations, as well as travel agency services, cleaning services, station operations, facilities maintenance operations, and railcar manufacturing and maintenance. The segment accounts for almost 70% of the company's total revenue.

The Retail & Services segment consists of JR East's life-style service business that includes retail sales and restaurant operations, wholesale businesses, a truck transportation business, and advertising and publicity. The segment accounts for more than 15% of revenue.

The Real Estate & Hotels segment encompasses JR East's life-style service business that includes shopping center operations, leasing of office buildings and other properties, and hotel operations. This segment accounts for more than 10% of total revenue.

JR East's Other segment consists of IT & Suica, which includes credit cards and information processing among other businesses. The segment accounts for nearly 5% of total revenue.

Geographic Reach
The railway business of JR East spans the eastern half of the Hons Shinkansen network, which connects Tokyo with regional cities in five directions.

The company is headquartered in Tokyo, Japan. It also has offices internationally located in New York, Paris, London and Singapore.

Sales and Marketing
JR East major customers was omitted as no single outside customer contributes about 10% or more to company's total sales.

The average number of passengers per day is about 17 million.

Financial Performance
Note: Growth rates may differ after conversion to US Dollars.

As a result of the company's initiatives, during the fiscal year under review, operating revenues increased 2% year on year, to Â¥3.0 trillion ($27.0 billion).

JR East profit attributable to owners of parent increased 2%, to Â¥295.2 billion ($2,660 million), mainly due to higher income before income taxes.

In fiscal 2019, net cash provided by operating activities totaled Â¥663.8 billion ($6.0 billion), Â¥40.4 billion less than in the previous fiscal year. This result was mainly due to an increase in major receivables. Net cash used in investing activities amounted to Â¥594.4 billion ($5.3 billion), Â¥52.6 billion more than in the previous fiscal year. This result was mainly due to an increase in payments for purchases of fixed assets. Net cash used in financing activities came to Â¥120.7 billion ($1.1 billion), Â¥14.4 billion less than in the previous fiscal year. This result was mainly due to an increase in proceeds from procurement of interest-bearing debt.

Strategy
In July 2018, the company announced the Group Management Vision "Move Up 2027" and entered the second year.

The goal of "Move Up 2027" is to create a service that integrates transportation services, lifestyle services, and IT/Suica, starting from "people". This is a service that only JR East has because it has a multi-layered, "real" network that supports the living infrastructure. The group will build an ecosystem centered on "people" who continue to create new value by fusing technological innovation and big data.

"Move Up2027" will finally enter the full-scale execution phase. Following the lifestyle service business growth vision "NEXT10" formulated in 2017, in 2018, the company started "Medium-term Vision for Service Quality Reforms 2020" and "Group Safety Plan 2023", and newly established "Technology Innovation Promotion Division". JR East have steadily laid the foundation for the strong promotion of "Reform 2027". In the future, based on these, JR East will put the transition from the "railway infrastructure starting point" to the "human starting point" on track. To realize the future depicted in "Move Up 2027," it will concretely accelerate measures in line with the three focus points of "safety," "life," and "happiness of employees and their families."

EXECUTIVES

Chairman, Director, Tetsuro Tomita
President, Representative Director, Yuji Fukasawa
Executive Vice President, Representative Director, Yoichi Kise
Executive Vice President, Representative Director, Katsumi Ise
Executive Vice President, Representative Director, Chiharu Watari
Director, Atsuko Itoh
Director, Hitoshi Suzuki
Outside Director, Motoshige Itoh
Outside Director, Reiko Amano
Outside Director, Hiroko Kawamoto
Outside Director, Toshio Iwamoto
Outside Director, Takashi Kinoshita
Director, Masaki Ogata
Outside Director, Kimitaka Mori
Outside Director, Hiroshi Koike
Auditors: KPMG AZSA LLC

LOCATIONS
HQ: East Japan Railway Co.
2-2-2 Yoyogi, Shibuya-ku, Tokyo 151-8578
Phone: (81) 3 5334 1111
Web: www.jreast.co.jp

PRODUCTS/OPERATIONS

2017 Sales

	% of total
Transportation	64
Retail & Services	18
Real Estate & Hotels	11
Other	7
Total	100

COMPETITORS

CENTRAL JAPAN RAILWAY COMPANY
CSX CORPORATION
Compagnie des Chemins de Fer Nationaux du Canada
FIRSTGROUP PLC
GENESEE & WYOMING INC.
HUB GROUP, INC.
KANSAS CITY SOUTHERN
N.V. Nederlandse Spoorwegen
TRAVELCENTERS OF AMERICA INC.
UNION PACIFIC CORPORATION

HISTORICAL FINANCIALS
Company Type: Public

Income Statement — FYE: March 31

	REVENUE ($mil)	NET INCOME ($mil)	NET PROFIT MARGIN	EMPLOYEES
03/23	18,061	745	4.1%	93,425
03/22	16,269	(780)	—	96,316
03/21	15,936	(5,219)	—	98,158
03/20	27,145	1,827	6.7%	98,415
03/19	27,107	2,665	9.8%	99,034
Annual Growth	(9.7%)	(27.3%)	—	(1.4%)

2023 Year-End Financials
Debt ratio: 0.4%
Return on equity: 4.0%
Cash ($ mil.): 1,615
Current Ratio: 0.69
Long-term debt ($ mil.): 30,745
No. of shares ($ mil.): 377
Dividends
Yield: 1.3%
Payout: 0.0%
Market value ($ mil.): 3,481

	STOCK PRICE ($) FY Close	P/E High/Low	PER SHARE ($) Earnings	Dividends	Book Value
03/23	9.22	0 0	1.98	0.12	49.18
03/22	9.61	— —	(2.07)	0.15	52.14
03/21	11.89	— —	(13.84)	0.21	60.63
03/20	12.61	0 0	4.84	0.24	76.76
03/19	16.05	0 0	6.98	0.22	72.60
Annual Growth	(12.9%)	— —	(27.0%)	(13.5%)	(9.3%)

Easyjet Plc

easyJet is a low-cost European point-to-point airline that uses its cost advantage, operational efficiency and leading positions in primary airports to deliver low fares, seamlessly connecting Europe with the warmest welcome in the sky. The low-fare airline operates over 925 routes from nearly 155 airports. easyJet operates from about 30 crew bases on the European continent and in the UK, including London's Gatwick, and Luton airports. The company is the No. 1 airline brand in the UK, France, and Switzerland. Its fleet consists of about 310 primarily Airbus jets. The carrier was established in 1995 by Sir Stelios Haji-Ioannou and its largest market is the UK. The company generated almost all of its sales in the Europe.

Operations
easyJet partners with key suppliers to deliver many of its operational and commercial activities. Airbus is its sole aircraft supplier. The company operates in two segments: Airline, which generated over 95% of the company's sales and Holidays with less than 5%. Airline business operates easyJet's route network and the holiday's business, which sells holiday packages. Overall, Passenger accounts for about 70% of the company's total sales. The remaining is produced by Ancillary.

Geographic Reach
easyJet is based in Bedfordshire, UK and operates in about 35 countries. The company flies about 310 aircraft, about 175 of which are registered in the UK, about 120 in Austria, and over 25 in Switzerland. In addition to the UK, its core markets are France, Italy, and Switzerland.

Customers based in the UK account for about 30% of revenue. Southern Europe account for nearly 45% of revenue. Northern Europe and other regions account for the remaining nearly 30%.

Sales and Marketing
The company serves some 20 million customers around the world.

Financial Performance
Revenue for the full year 2021 decreased 52% to Â£1.5 billion from 2020's Â£3 billion.

In 2021, the company had a net loss of Â£858 million, a 20% improvement from the previous year's net loss of Â£1.1 billion.

The company's cash at the end of 2021 totaled Â£3.5 billion, a 55% increase from the previous year's cash of Â£2.3 billion. Operating activities used Â£1 billion, while investing activities generated Â£719 million. Financing activities generated another Â£1.6 billion.

Strategy
easyJet has prioritized six strategic initiatives that will continue to build on its structural advantages in the European aviation market and enable the company to lead the recovery as travel returns. The initiatives include: Network strategy; Customer excellence; Product portfolio evolution; easyJet holidays; Cost focus; and Sustainability.

Company Background
Greek-Cypriot entrepreneur Sir Stelios Haji-Ioannou, the son of a shipping magnet, founded easyJet in 1995 after leaving his father's company. He launched the no-frills airline from London Luton Airport using two rented 737s, a small crew wearing orange sweatshirts, and Â£29 one-way fares to Glasgow advertised as 'fly to Scotland for the price of a pair of jeans.'

EXECUTIVES

Chief Executive Officer, Executive Director, Johan Lundgren
Chief Financial Officer, Executive Director, Kenton Jarvis
Chief Operating Officer, Peter Bellew
People Group Director, Ella Bennett
Chief Data and Information Officer, Stuart Birrell
Chief Commercial Officer, Sophie Dekkers
Markets and Marketing Group Director, Thomas Haagensen
General Counsel, Secretary, Maaike de Bie
Non-Executive Chairman, Robert John Orr Barton
Chair Designate, Non-Executive Director, Stephen Alan Michael Hester
Senior Independent Non-Executive Director, Julie Southern
Independent Non-Executive Director, Andreas Bierwirth
Independent Non-Executive Director, Catherine Biner Bradley
Independent Non-Executive Director, Nicholas Leeder
Independent Non-Executive Director, Moni Mannings
Independent Non-Executive Director, David Robbie
Auditors: PricewaterhouseCoopers LLP

LOCATIONS

HQ: Easyjet Plc
Hangar 89, London Luton Airport, Luton, Bedfordshire LU2 9PF
Phone: (44) 1582 525019
Web: www.easyjet.com

2015 Sales

Europe	% of total
UK	47
Southern Europe	31
Northern Europe	20
Other regions	2
Total	100

HISTORICAL FINANCIALS
Company Type: Public

Income Statement — FYE: September 30

	REVENUE ($mil)	NET INCOME ($mil)	NET PROFIT MARGIN	EMPLOYEES
09/23	10,014	397	4.0%	0
09/22	6,367	(186)	—	13,951
09/21	1,960	(1,153)	—	12,389
09/20	3,860	(1,384)	—	14,566
09/19	7,860	429	5.5%	14,751
Annual Growth	6.2%	(2.0%)		

2023 Year-End Financials
Debt ratio: 23.6%
Return on equity: 12.1%
Cash ($ mil.): 3,584
Current Ratio: 1.00
Long-term debt ($ mil.): 1,791
No. of shares ($ mil.): 753
Dividends
Yield: —
Payout: 10.5%
Market value ($ mil.): 3,871

	STOCK PRICE ($) FY Close	P/E High/Low		PER SHARE ($) Earnings	Dividends	Book Value
09/23	5.14	15	8	0.52	0.06	4.54
09/22	3.30	—	—	(0.25)	0.00	3.70
09/21	9.29	—	—	(2.14)	1.51	4.68
09/20	6.44	—	—	(3.40)	0.49	5.33
09/19	14.48	19	12	1.08	0.75	9.26
Annual Growth	(22.8%)			(16.6%)	(48.0%)	(16.3%)

Eaton Corp plc

EXECUTIVES

Chairman, Chief Executive Officer, Director, Craig Arnold, $1,200,004 total compensation
Executive Vice President, Chief Financial Officer, Thomas B. Okray
Division Officer, Heath B. Monesmith
Executive Vice President, Chief Legal Officer, Taras G. Szmagala
Executive Vice President, Chief Human Resources Officer, Ernest W. Marshall
Senior Vice President, Controller, Daniel Roy Hopgood
Division Officer, Paulo Ruiz
Division Officer, Joao V. Faria
Division Officer, Nandakumar Cheruvatath
Director, Olivier C. Leonetti
Director, Silvio Napoli
Director, Gregory R. Page
Director, Sandra Pianalto
Director, Robert V. Pragada
Director, Lori J. Ryerkerk
Director, Gerald B. Smith
Director, Dorothy C. Thompson
Director, Darryl L. Wilson
Auditors: Ernst & Young LLP

LOCATIONS

HQ: Eaton Corp plc
Eaton House, 30 Pembroke Road, Dublin 4 44114-2584
Phone: (353) 1 637 2900
Web: www.eaton.com

HISTORICAL FINANCIALS

Company Type: Public

Income Statement — FYE: December 31

	REVENUE ($mil)	NET INCOME ($mil)	NET PROFIT MARGIN	EMPLOYEES
12/23	23,196	3,218	13.9%	94,000
12/22	20,752	2,462	11.9%	92,000
12/21	19,628	2,144	10.9%	86,000
12/20	17,858	1,410	7.9%	92,000
12/19	21,390	2,211	10.3%	101,000
Annual Growth	2.0%	9.8%	—	(1.8%)

2023 Year-End Financials

Debt ratio: 24.1%
Return on equity: 17.8%
Cash ($ mil.): 488
Current Ratio: 1.51
Long-term debt ($ mil.): 8,244
No. of shares ($ mil.): 399
Dividends
Yield: —
Payout: 42.8%
Market value ($ mil.): —

Ecopetrol SA

Ecopetrol performs crude oil and natural gas exploration, production, refining, and transportation. The largest company in Colombia (where it accounts for 60% of national production and is one of the world's largest oil companies), Ecopetrol has two large refineries (Barrancabermeja and Cartagena) strategically located to supply the domestic market and to export oil and oil products to the southern US. Ecopetrol explores for oil and gas across Colombia, and is expanding internationally through exploration partnerships in Brazil, Peru, and the US Gulf of Mexico. In 2022, the company reported proved reserves of more than 2 billion barrels of oil equivalent. Majority of its sales were generated from Colombia.

Operations

Ecopetrol's operating segments include: Exploration and Production (about 45%); Transport and Logistics (about 45%); Refining, Petrochemical and Biofuels (about 10%); and Electric Power Transmission and Toll Roads Concessions (5%).

The Exploration and production segment includes activities related to the exploration and production of oil and gas. The Transport and logistics segment includes activities associated with the transport and distribution of hydrocarbons and derivative products in operation. The Refining, petrochemicals, and biofuels segment mainly includes activities performed at the Barrancabermeja and Catagena refineries, where crude oil from production fields is refined or processed. In addition, the segment includes distribution of natural gas and LPG activities performed by Invercolsa Group. Lastly, the Electric power transmission and toll roads concessions include activities of supplying electric power transmission services, design, development, construction, operation, and maintenance of road and energy infrastructure projects.

Geographic Reach

Ecopetrol is headquartered in Bogota, Colombia. Colombia accounts for more than 50% of the company's revenue. This is followed by the US (about 20%) and Asia (about 15%). The company also has operations in Central America and the Caribbean, South America, and Europe.

Financial Performance

Ecopetrol's performance for the past five years has fluctuated, but had an overall increase with 2022 as its highest performing year over the period.

Revenues increased by COP67.7 trillion to COP159.6 trillion for 2022, as compared to 2021's revenue of COP91.9 trillion.

Ecopetrol's net income for fiscal year end 2022 increased to COP35.2 trillion, as compared to 2021's revenue of COP17.6 trillion.

The company held COP15.4 trillion at the end of the year. Operating activities generated COP36.2 trillion to the coffers. Investing activities and financing activities used COP18.1 trillion and COP18.9 trillion, respectively. Main cash uses were for investment in natural and environmental resources, and repayment of borrowings.

Strategy

Ecopetrol Group published its long-term strategy (the "2040 Strategy"), also referred to as "Energy that Transforms", being the first company in the oil and gas industry in Latin America to disclose a roadmap for the next 20 years. The strategy aims to address comprehensively current environmental, social, and governance priorities, while maintaining its focus on generating sustainable value for all its stakeholders. The objective of this long-term strategy is to consolidate an agile and dynamic organization that promptly adapts to the changes faced by the energy industry.

EXECUTIVES

Chief Executive Officer, Felipe Bayon Pardo
Supply & Services Chief Operating Officer,
Supply & Services Vice President, Alberto Consuegra Granger
Downstream Segment Chief Financial Officer, Jaime Caballero Uribe
Development Vice President, Production Vice President, Regional Development Vice President, Jorge Elman Osorio Franco
Exploration Vice President, Jorge Arturo Calvache Archila
Projects & Engineering Vice President, Jurgen Gerardo Loeber Rojas
Commercial & Marketing Vice President, Pedro Fernando Manrique Gutierrez
Strategy & New Business Vice President, New Business Vice President, Juan Manuel Rojas Payan
Gas Vice President, Yeimy Baez
Health, Safety and Environment Vice President, Mauricio Galvis Jaramillo
Refining and Industrial Processes Vice President, Walter Fabian Canova
Legal Affairs Vice President, Legal Affairs General Counsel, Fernan Ignacio Bejarano Arias
Compliance Vice President, Compliance Officer, Maria Juliana Alban Duran
Human Resources Vice President, Alejandro Arango Lopez
Sustainable Development Vice President, Diana Hoyos Escobar
Supply & Services Vice President, Carlos Andres Santos Nieto
Digital Vice President, Ernesto Gutierrez de Pineres
Secretary General, Monica Jimenez Gonzalez
Non-Independent Director, German Eduardo Quintero Rojas
Independent Director, Cecilia Maria White Velez
Independent Director, Luis Guillermo Echeverri Velez
Independent Director, Juan Emilio Posada Echeverri
Independent Director, Sergio Restrepo Isaza
Independent Director, Luis Santiago Perdomo Maldonado
Independent Director, Esteban Piedrahita Uribe
Independent Director, Hernando Ramirez Plazas
Independent Director, Carlos Gustavo Cano Sanz
Auditors: Ernst & Young Audit S.A.S.

LOCATIONS

HQ: Ecopetrol SA
Carrera 13 No. 36-24, Bogota
Phone: (57) 310 315 8600
Web: www.ecopetrol.com.co

2013 Sales

	% of total
Colombia	38
US	29
Asia	16
Europe	7
Central America and Caribbean	5
South America	3
Others	2
Total	100

PRODUCTS/OPERATIONS

2013 Sales

	% of total
Exploration & production	59
Refining activities	34
Transportation & logistics	7
Total	100

COMPETITORS

Equinor ASA
ISRAMCO, INC.
LUKOIL, PAO
MURPHY OIL CORPORATION
NOBLE ENERGY, INC.
OMV Aktiengesellschaft
PETROBRAS AMERICA INC.
PHILLIPS 66
SASOL LTD
SURGUTNEFTEGAZ, PAO

HISTORICAL FINANCIALS

Company Type: Public

Income Statement — FYE: December 31

	REVENUE ($mil)	NET INCOME ($mil)	NET PROFIT MARGIN	EMPLOYEES
12/22	32,899	6,514	19.8%	18,903
12/21	22,575	3,844	17.0%	18,378
12/20	14,674	463	3.2%	13,977
12/19	21,765	4,184	19.2%	15,157
12/18	21,131	3,505	16.6%	12,228
Annual Growth	11.7%	16.8%	—	11.5%

2022 Year-End Financials

Debt ratio: —
Return on equity: 40.8%
Cash ($ mil.): 3,174
Current Ratio: 1.36
Long-term debt ($ mil.): 19,156
No. of shares ($ mil.): 41,116
Dividends
 Yield: 0.1%
 Payout: 1138.0%
Market value ($ mil.): 430,492

	STOCK PRICE ($) FY Close	P/E High/Low	PER SHARE ($) Earnings	Dividends	Book Value
12/22	10.47	0 0	0.16	1.80	0.43
12/21	12.89	0 0	0.09	0.09	0.41
12/20	12.91	1 0	0.01	1.30	0.35
12/19	19.96	0 0	0.10	1.78	0.40
12/18	15.88	0 0	0.09	0.61	0.41
Annual Growth	(9.9%)	— —	16.8%	31.0%	1.1%

EDP Energias de Portugal S.A.

EDP - Energias de Portugal is a multinational and vertically-integrated utility company that generates, transmits, distributes, and supplies electricity and gas to some 9.1 million customers. EDP is one of the largest wind energy production company in the world with a part of its energy is produced from renewable resources. EDP (a major wind energy player), which has a combined generating capacity of about 20 GW from its domestic hydroelectric, coal, solar, and wind-powered plants. Around 45% of the company's sales were generated in Portugal.

Operations

EDP's business segments include Renewables (about 10%), Networks (more than 5%), and Client Solutions and Energy Management (about 85%).

The renewables segment corresponds to the activity of producing electricity through renewable energy sources, with emphasis on hydro, wind, and solar.

The networks segment corresponds to the electricity distribution and transmission activity, including regulated energy retailers.

Lastly, the client solutions and energy management include the: production of electricity using non-renewable energy sources, with emphasis on coal and gas; commercialization of electricity and gas and energy solutions services to customers; and the intermediation business responsible for managing the purchase and sale of energy in the Iberian and Brazilian markets, as well as for the respective hedging operations.

Geographic Reach

Majority of EDP's operations come from Portugal, accounting for about 45% of the company's revenue. Spain is the second largest market for the company accounting for about 35%. Other markets include Brazil and the US.

Sales and Marketing

The company distributes around 60 TWh of electricity through overhead and underground lines to some 9.4 million electricity and gas customers.

Financial Performance

EDP's performance for the past five years has fluctuated with a decreasing trend in the first half of the period, then increasing since 2020, ending with 2022 as its highest performing year over the period.

EDP's revenue increased by EUR 5.7 billion to EUR 20.6 billion for 2022, as compared to 2021's revenue of EUR 15.0 billion.

The company's net income increased by EUR 22.3 million to EUR 679.0 million, as compared to the prior year's net income of EUR 656.7 million.

About EUR 4.9 billion was held by the group at the end of the year. Operating activities provided EUR 3.8 billion to the coffers. Investing activities used EUR 3.2 billion, while financing activities provided EUR 1.1 billion. Main cash uses were for acquisition of assets or subsidiaries and payments relating to financial debt, including collateral deposits.

Strategy

Digital transformation is part of EDP's strategy that revolves around three key points, namely, digital strategy, digital products, and digital culture. The company aims to: set priorities for digital transformation and ambitious targets in close collaboration with the business, and monitoring developments with an integrated overview; accelerate the digitalization of business with the introduction of new technologies and digital tools, which create value for all EDP stakeholders; and driving the adoption of new, agile, and collaborative ways of working, and the attraction, development, and retention of talent.

HISTORY

EDP - Energias de Portugal has its roots in the several power enterprises that sprouted throughout the country during the infancy of electricity. The first recorded event in Portugal's electrification was the import of six voltaic arc lamps in 1878. The nation's first large-scale project saw the light in 1893 when the city of Braga was illuminated by the Sociedade de Electricidade do Norte de Portugal.

Electricity grew throughout the 1900s in the form of municipal concession contracts for distribution and government-licensed power plants. Large-scale power stations were not in effect in Portugal until after 1947, when Companhia Nacional de Electricidade was formed to interconnect the small generating systems dotting the nation. From the 1950s to mid-1970s, new companies were formed to bring electricity to various parts of Portugal.

The original Electricidade de Portugal was founded in the wake of a leftist revolution during the 1970s in Portugal. In what became known as the Captain's Revolution, military officers overthrew the Portuguese government, which had been a dictatorship since 1933. The new government, dominated by Marxists, nationalized Portugal's industries, including its generation, transmission, and distribution companies, in 1975. The next year the Portuguese government created Electricidade de Portugal to unify the recently nationalized companies.

A new Social Democrat government came to power in 1987 and decided to denationalize Portuguese industry, including EDP. The company reorganized into four major sectors in 1994: production (headed by its CPPE subsidiary), transmission, distribution, and services (led by its REN subsidiary, which operated the national grid, four regional utilities, and 10 services units). EDP was the holding company.

Seeking opportunities opened up by the privatization of Brazil's state-owned electricity distributor, EDP joined a consortium with Spain's Endesa and Chile's Chilectra to buy 70% of Rio de Janeiro distributor CERJ in 1996. The next year EDP gained a license to help build a hydro plant in Brazil. By 1998 the Endesa-led consortium had gained control of another Brazilian distributor, Coelce.

The Portuguese government floated 30% of EDP in 1997, raising $1.76 billion. In a joint venture with the UK's PowerGen and Germany's Siemens, EDP formed TurbogÁjs to operate a power plant that would produce 20% of Portugal's electricity.

In 1998 EDP forged an alliance with Spain's Iberdrola and bought 80% of Guatemalan utility EEGSA. That year EDP and SÃ£o Paulo utility CPFL gained control of SÃ£o Paulo distributor Bandeirante. In 1999 EDP acquired stakes in two other Brazilian distributors. It also joined the UK's Thames Water to develop projects in Portugal, Chile, and Brazil and bought 45% of Chilean water and sewage company Essel. (EDP exchanged its stake in Essel for Thames Water's interest in the Portuguese joint venture in 2002.) The Portuguese state reduced its stake in EDP to about 50% in 1999.

Stepping up its telecommunications activities in 2000, EDP made its telecom unit, Onitelecom (ONI), fully operational and agreed to share a fiber-optic network on the Iberian Peninsula with Spain's Iberdrola. (In 2006, however, the company sold its stake in

ONI.) Also in 2000 the Portuguese government acquired a majority stake in EDP's REN unit, and EDP combined its four power distribution utilities into one unit (EDP DistribuiÃ§Ã£o).

In 2001 EDP and Spanish savings bank Cajastur jointly bid to buy HidrocantÃ¡brico, one of Spain's leading utilities. EDP won control of 20% of HidrocantÃ¡brico, while German utility Energie Baden-WÃ¼rttemberg (EnBW) won control of 60%. The following year, after a fierce bidding war, the two companies agreed that EDP would control the majority share (40%), while EnBW would own only 35%.

The company changed its name from EDP - Electricidade de Portugal to EDP - Energias de Portugal in 2004.

Since 2007 the company has sold much of its holdings in other firms to pay down debt. Divestment deals include a 30% stake in Portugal's national transmission grid operator, Rede ElÃ©ctrica Nacional (REN); a 40% stake in TURBOGÁS - Produtora EnergÃ©tica, the company behind the construction of gas power station Tapada do Outeiro; and a 27% stake in PORTUGEN - Energia, which is in charge of operating Tapada do Outeiro. In 2011 it sold a 7.7% stake in Brazil's Ampla Energia to a subsidiary of Spain's Endesa for ? 85 million ($121 million).

EXECUTIVES

Executive Chairman, Miguel Stilwell De Andrade
Executive Director, Miguel Nuno Simoes Nunes Ferreira Setas
Executive Director, Chief Financial Officer, Rui Manuel Rodrigues Lopes Teixeira
Executive Director, Ana Paula Garrido de Pina Marques
Executive Director, Vera de Morais Pinto Pereira Carneiro
Secretary, Ana Rita Pontífice Ferreira de Almeida Corte-Real
Independent Non-Executive Chairman, Joao Luis Ramalho de Carvalho Talone
Independent Director, Joao Carvalho das Neves
Independent Director, Maria del Carmen Fernandez Rozado
Independent Director, Laurie Fitch
Independent Director, Esmeralda da Silva Santos Dourado
Independent Director, Helena Sofia Silva Borges Salgado Fonseca Cerveira Pinto
Independent Director, Sandrine Dixson-Decleve
Independent Director, Zili Shao
Independent Director, Luis Maria Viana Palha da Silva
Non-Independent Director, Dingming Zhang
Non-Independent Director, Shengliang Wu
Non-Independent Director, Ignacio Herrero Ruiz
Non-Independent Director, Zhang Hui
Non-Independent Director, Miguel Espregueira Mendes Pereira Leite
Non-Independent Director, Felipe Fernandez Fernandez
Non-Independent Director, Fernando Maria Masaveu Herrero
Auditors : PricewaterhouseCoopers & Associados - Sociedade de Revisores Oficiais de Contas, Lda.

LOCATIONS

HQ: EDP Energias de Portugal S.A.
Avenida 24 de Julho, 12, Lisbon, Poente 1249-300
Phone: (351) 21 001 25 00 **Fax:** (351) 21 001 28 99
Web: www.edp.pt

2014 Sales

	% of total
Portugal	51
Spain	27
Brazil	18
US	2
Other	2
Total	100

PRODUCTS/OPERATIONS

2014 Sales

	% of total
Electricity and Network access	87
Gas and Network access	10
Revenue from assets assigned to concessions	3
Sales of CO2 licences	0
Other	0
Total	100

COMPETITORS

Alpiq Holding SA
ENDESA SA
ENEL SPA
GROUPE CRIT
IBERDROLA, SOCIEDAD ANONIMA
LafargeHolcim Ltd
PHAROL - SGPS, S.A.
SONAE - SGPS, S.A.
Schindler Holding AG
Weatherford International Ltd.

HISTORICAL FINANCIALS

Company Type: Public

Income Statement FYE: December 31

	REVENUE ($mil)	NET INCOME ($mil)	NET PROFIT MARGIN	EMPLOYEES
12/22	22,055	725	3.3%	13,211
12/21	16,958	743	4.4%	12,236
12/20	15,277	982	6.4%	11,610
12/19	16,092	574	3.6%	11,660
12/18	17,496	594	3.4%	11,631
Annual Growth	6.0%	5.1%	—	3.2%

2022 Year-End Financials

Debt ratio: 36.4% No. of shares ($ mil.): 3,947
Return on equity: 7.4% Dividends
Cash ($ mil.): 5,233 Yield: —
Current Ratio: 0.88 Payout: 1100.1%
Long-term debt ($ mil.): 16,856 Market value ($ mil.): 196,524

	STOCK PRICE ($) FY Close	P/E High/Low	PER SHARE ($) Earnings	Dividends	Book Value
12/22	49.79	326 237	0.18	2.00	2.40
12/21	54.77	376 288	0.19	3.42	2.67
12/20	65.64	309 181	0.26	3.18	2.98
12/19	43.08	314 239	0.16	2.13	2.74
12/18	34.85	291 217	0.16	2.27	2.83
Annual Growth	9.3%	— —	3.2%	(3.1%)	(4.0%)

Electric Power Development Co.. Ltd. (Japan)

The dryly named electric utility Electric Power Development Co. has a much more fun nickname -- J-POWER. With a generating capacity of 16,380 MW, the company supplies power used all over Japan. It has 67 hydroelectric plants, as well as some thermal and geothermal plants, and owns a transmission network that covers 2,400 km. J-POWER acts as a wholesale electric utility, selling to other electric power companies. Established by the Japanese government in 1952, J-POWER went through the privatization process, finally achieving full privatization and trading on the Tokyo Stock Exchange in 2004. The company is also sometimes referred to as EPDC.

EXECUTIVES

Chairman, Representative Director, Toshifumi Watanabe
President, Representative Director, Hitoshi Kanno
Executive Vice President, Representative Director, Hiroyasu Sugiyama
Executive Vice President, Director, Osamu Hagiwara
Executive Vice President, Director, Yoshikazu Shimada
Executive Vice President, Director, Hiroshi Sasatsu
Executive Vice President, Director, Isshu Kurata
Director, Takaya Nomura
Director, Ryoji Sekine
Outside Director, Tomonori Ito
Outside Director, John Buchanan
Outside Director, Takashi Yokomizo
Director, Naori Fukuda
Outside Director, Hiroshi Fujioka
Outside Director, Kiyoshi Nakanishi
Outside Director, Kimiko Oga
Auditors : Ernst & Young ShinNihon LLC

LOCATIONS

HQ: Electric Power Development Co.. Ltd. (Japan)
6-15-1 Ginza, Chuo-ku, Tokyo 104-8165
Phone: (81) 3 3546 2211 **Fax:** (81) 3 3546 9532
Web: www.jpower.co.jp

PRODUCTS/OPERATIONS

2015 Sales

	% of total
Electric power business	78
Electric power - Related business	4
Overseas business	15
Other business	3
Total	100

COMPETITORS

CALIFORNIA INDEPENDENT SYSTEM OPERATOR CORPORATION
CHUBU ELECTRIC POWER CO.,INC.
Electrabel
PUERTO RICO ELECTRIC POWER AUTHORITY
TransAlta Corporation

HISTORICAL FINANCIALS
Company Type: Public

Income Statement — FYE: March 31

	REVENUE ($mil)	NET INCOME ($mil)	NET PROFIT MARGIN	EMPLOYEES
03/23	13,829	853	6.2%	7,078
03/22	8,916	572	6.4%	7,146
03/21	8,210	201	2.5%	7,156
03/20	8,417	389	4.6%	7,262
03/19	8,103	417	5.2%	7,190
Annual Growth	14.3%	19.6%	—	(0.4%)

2023 Year-End Financials
Debt ratio: 0.4%
Return on equity: 11.3%
Cash ($ mil.): 2,567
Current Ratio: 1.78
Long-term debt ($ mil.): 12,519
No. of shares ($ mil.): 183
Dividends
 Yield: —
 Payout: 0.0%
Market value ($ mil.): —

Empire Co Ltd

Empire Company Limited (Empire) comprises an empire of supermarkets, food distribution, and real estate investments. The company operates through wholly-owned subsidiary Sobeys, a chain of more than 1,600 food and drug stores across Canada under names such as Sobeys, Safeway, FreshCo, and IGA, as well as more than 350 retail fuel locations. Additionally, the company distributes food to its own stores and other retailers. Empire invests in commercial real estate through stakes in real estate investment trust Crombie REIT and residential property developer Genstar. Empire and its subsidiaries, franchisees, and affiliates employ approximately 130,000 people.

Operations
Empire's business is organized in two reportable segments ? Food Retailing and Investments and Other Operations.

Empire's Food Retailing business consists of wholly-owned subsidiary Sobeys Inc. Banners include Foodland, Thrifty Foods, Longo's, and Lawtons Drugs. The segment consists of company-owned, franchised, and affiliated stores and locations. Virtually, all of Empire's revenue is generated by this segment.

The Investments and Other Operations segment principally consists of real estate investments and various other corporate operations. It includes a more than 40% stake in both Crombie REIT and Genstar.

Geographic Reach
Headquartered in Stellarton, Nova Scotia, Empire operates retail stores and fuel locations in every province in Canada. Its stake in real estate investment trust Crombie REIT allows the company to profit from income-producing properties such as shopping centers, freestanding stores, and mixed-use developments in urban and suburban markets in Canada. Its Genstar, California-based, has operations in Ontario, Western Canada, and the US.

Sales and Marketing
The company has AIR MILES loyalty program for its customers. AIR MILES are earned by Sobeys customers based on purchases in stores. The company pays a per point fee under the terms of the agreement with AIR MILES. Longo's Thank You Rewards program allows members to earn points on their purchases at Longo's stores.

Financial Performance
The company's revenue in 2021 increased to C$410.3 million compared to C$390.0 million in the prior year.

Net income in 2021 increased to C$811.3 million compared to the prior year's C$764.2 million.

Cash held by the company at the end of 2021 decreased to C$812.3 million. Cash provided by operations was C$2.1 billion while cash used for investing and financing activities were C$891.4 million and C$1.3 billion, respectively. Main cash uses were purchases of property, equipment and investment property, repayments of long-term debt and dividends paid.

Strategy
In the first quarter of fiscal 2021, the company launched Project Horizon, a three-year strategy focused on core business expansion and the acceleration of e-commerce. The company remains on track to achieve an incremental $500 million in annualized EBITDA and an improvement in EBITDA margin of 100 basis points by fiscal 2023 by growing market share and building on cost and margin discipline. The company expects to generate a compound average growth rate in earnings per share of at least 15% over Project Horizon's three-year timeframe.

In fiscal 2021, Project Horizon benefits were achieved from the expansion and renovation of the company's store network, the addition of new stores, improvement in store operations and merchandising from data analytics along with continued efficiencies gained through strategic sourcing initiatives.

Mergers and Acquisitions
In mid-2021, Empire, through a wholly-owned subsidiary, completed the purchase of 51% of Longo's, a long-standing, family-built network of specialty grocery stores in the Greater Toronto Area (GTA) of Ontario, and the Grocery Gateway e-commerce business. The Longo's culture is so closely aligned with the company. Empire acquired Longo's issued and outstanding shares based on a total enterprise value of $700 million.

Company Background
J. W. Sobey started a butcher shop and meat delivery business in Nova Scotia in 1907 later expanding to a full-service grocery operation in 1924. By 1939, Sobeys had six grocery stores in Nova Scotia and continue to grow by promising low prices and introducing new products and concepts into the Sobey grocery business. On a trip through the US in the 1940s, Sobey executives witnessed first-hand the operation of a new type of grocery store?the supermarket. Sobeys introduced the first supermarket in Nova Scotia in 1947.

While continuing to build its grocery operation, Sobeys began investing in real estate, carried out as the Empire Company. Empire went public on the Toronto Stock Exchange in 1983. At the same time, the Sobeys chain was folded into Empire. In 1987, Sobeys opened its first store in Ontario; by the early 1990s, Sobeys had expanded in Ontario and into Quebec.

The 1998 acquisition of The Oshawa Group (owner of the IGA and Price Chopper grocery chains) tripled the size of Sobeys and made its food service distributorship the largest in Canada. Later that year, Empire took Sobeys public again, retaining a majority stake in the grocery business. In 2000, Empire sold its 25% stake in US-based grocery retailer Hannaford Bros. Co. to Delhaize America for more than $800 million in cash and stock.

In 2013, Sobeys bought more than 200 Safeway stores in Western Canada for a whopping $5.8 billion. An anti-competition ruling against the company in 2014 prompted Sobeys to sell off its one remaining Price Chopper store to the North West Company.

EXECUTIVES

President, Chief Executive Officer, Executive Director, Michael Medline
Chief Financial Officer, Michael Vels
Director, Chairman, James M. Dickson
Director, Cynthia J. Devine
Director, Sharon Driscoll
Director, Gregory Josefowicz
Director, Sue Lee
Director, William Linton
Director, Martine Reardon
Director, Frank C. Sobey
Director, John R. Sobey
Director, Karl R. Sobey
Director, Paul D. Sobey
Director, Robert G. C. Sobey
Director, Martine Turcotte
Auditors : PricewaterhouseCoopers LLP

LOCATIONS

HQ: Empire Co Ltd
115 King Street, Stellarton, Nova Scotia B0K 1S0
Phone: 902 752-8371 **Fax:** 902 755-6477
Web: www.empireco.ca

PRODUCTS/OPERATIONS

Related Businesses
Pharmacy
Wholesale
Fuel/Convenience

Liquor
Private Label Brands
Loyalty Reward Programs
Real Estate

COMPETITORS

AMIRA C FOODS INTERNATIONAL DMCC
ITOCHU CORPORATION
MITSUBISHI CORPORATION
Migros-Genossenschafts-Bund
SPARTANNASH COMPANY
SUPERVALU INC.
SYSCO CORPORATION
Sobeys Inc
UNITED NATURAL FOODS, INC.
US FOODS, INC.

HISTORICAL FINANCIALS
Company Type: Public

Income Statement   FYE: May 6

	REVENUE ($mil)	NET INCOME ($mil)	NET PROFIT MARGIN	EMPLOYEES
05/23	22,694	508	2.2%	131,000
05/22	23,635	580	2.5%	130,000
05/21	23,107	571	2.5%	134,000
05/20	19,074	416	2.2%	63,000
05/19	18,780	287	1.5%	60,000
Annual Growth	4.8%	15.3%	—	21.6%

2023 Year-End Financials
Debt ratio: 4.6%
Return on equity: 13.4%
Cash ($ mil.): 163
Current Ratio: 0.77
Long-term debt ($ mil.): 675
No. of shares ($ mil.): 253
Dividends
Yield: —
Payout: 25.0%
Market value ($ mil.): 6,747

	STOCK PRICE ($) FY Close	P/E High/Low	PER SHARE ($) Earnings	Dividends	Book Value
05/23	26.64	12 9	1.96	0.49	15.21
05/22	33.09	13 10	2.18	0.47	14.80
05/21	31.54	13 9	2.12	0.42	13.42
05/20	21.60	12 8	1.53	0.34	10.41
05/19	22.21	16 12	1.05	0.33	10.95
Annual Growth	4.7%	—	16.7%	10.6%	8.6%

Empresa Nacional del Petroleo (Chile)

EXECUTIVES

Chairman, Laurence Golborne Riveros
Vice-Chairman, Hernan Cheyre Valenzuela
Director, Ramon Jara Araya
Director, Jorge Matute Matute
Director, Miguel Moreno Garcia
Director, Ivan Antonio Perez Pavez
Director, Rodolfo Krause Lubascher
Director, Manuel Francisco Gana Eguiguren
Director, Axel Juan Christensen de la Cerda
Auditors : Deloitte Auditores Consultores Limitada

LOCATIONS

HQ: Empresa Nacional del Petroleo (Chile)
 Av. Apoquindo 2929 Floor 5, Piso 5, Santiago, Las Condes
Phone: (56) 2 280 3318   Fax: (56) 2 234 9201

Web: www.enap.cl

HISTORICAL FINANCIALS
Company Type: Public

Income Statement   FYE: December 31

	REVENUE ($mil)	NET INCOME ($mil)	NET PROFIT MARGIN	EMPLOYEES
12/22	12,324	575	4.7%	0
12/21	7,654	141	1.9%	3,312
12/20	4,891	(89)	—	0
12/19	7,628	5	0.1%	0
12/18	8,304	(230)	—	0
Annual Growth	10.4%	—	—	—

2022 Year-End Financials
Debt ratio: 51.8%
Return on equity: 43.6%
Cash ($ mil.): 449
Current Ratio: 1.69
Long-term debt ($ mil.): 3,895
No. of shares ($ mil.): —
Dividends
Yield: —
Payout: 0.0%
Market value ($ mil.): —

Enbridge Inc

Enbridge is one of the biggest pipeline operators in North America. The company move about 30% of the crude oil produced in North America, Enbridge transport nearly 20% of the natural gas consumed in the U.S., and it also operate North America's third-largest natural gas utility by consumer count. The company also invests in renewable energy, with investments in North American and European renewable energy totaling approximately 2,175 MW of installed capacity. In all, the Canada accounts for over 50% of Enbridge's revenue.

Operations
Enbridge activities are carried out through five business segments: Liquids Pipelines (more than 20%); Gas Transmission and Midstream (around 10%); Gas Distribution and Storage (about 15%); Renewable Power Generation (less than 5%); and Energy Services (approximately 55%).

Liquids Pipelines consists of pipelines and terminals in Canada and the US that transport and export various grades of crude oil and other liquid hydrocarbons.

Gas Transmission and Midstream consists of its investments in natural gas pipelines and gathering and processing facilities in Canada and the US, including US Gas Transmission, Canadian Gas Transmission, US Midstream and other assets.

Gas Distribution and Storage consists of its natural gas utility operations, the core of which is Enbridge Gas Inc. (Enbridge Gas), which serves residential, commercial and industrial customers throughout Ontario. This business segment also includes natural gas distribution activities in QuÃ©bec.

Renewable Power Generation consists primarily of investments in wind and solar assets, as well as geothermal, waste heat recovery, and transmission assets.

The Energy Services businesses in Canada and the US provide physical commodity marketing and logistical services to North American refiners, producers, and other customers.

Geographic Reach
Enbridge Inc. is headquartered in Calgary, Canada. We have a workforce of more than 12,000 people, primarily in the United States and Canada.

Sales and Marketing
The company serves residential, commercial and industrial customers.

Financial Performance
Company's revenue for fiscal 2022 increased to CAD 53.3 billion compared from the prior year with CAD47.1 billion. The increase was primarily due to higher revenues on every segments.

Net income for fiscal 2022 decreased to CAD2.6 billion compared from the prior year with CAD5.8 billion. The decrease was primarily due to higher expenses offsetting the increase on revenues.

Cash held by the company at the end of fiscal 2022 increased to CAD907 million. Cash provided by operations was CAD11.2 billion while cash used for investing and financing activities were CAD5.3 billion and CAD5.4 billion, respectively. Main uses of cash were debenture and term note repayments and capital expenditures.

Strategy
Enbridge's strategy is underpinned by a deep understanding of energy supply and demand fundamentals. Through disciplined capital allocation that is aligned with its outlook on energy markets, Enbridge have become an industry leader with a diversified portfolio across both conventional and lower-carbon energies. The company's assets have reliably generated low-risk, resilient cash flows through many commodity and economic cycles.

In order to continue to be an industry leader and value creator going forward, Enbridge maintain a robust strategic planning approach. The company regularly conduct scenario and resiliency analysis on both its assets and business strategy. The copany test various value enhancement and maximization options, and it regularly engage with its Board of Directors (the Board) to ensure alignment and maintain active oversight, including updates and discussions throughout the year and a dedicated annual Strategic Planning session. Going forward, Enbridge plan to use this comprehensive approach to guide its investment and portfolio decisions.

Mergers and Acquisitions
In 2023, Enbridge Inc. announced that it has entered into three separate definitive agreements with Dominion Energy, Inc. to acquire EOG, Questar and PSNC for an aggregate purchase price of US$14.0 billion (CDN$19 billion), comprised of $US9.4 billion of cash consideration and US$4.6 billion of assumed debt, subject to customary closing adjustments. Upon the closings of the three

transactions, Enbridge will add gas utility operations in Ohio, North Carolina, Utah, Idaho and Wyoming, representing a significant presence in the U.S. utility sector.

In 2023, Enbridge Inc. announced that a wholly-owned subsidiary, it has entered into a definitive agreement with FortisBC Holdings Inc. to acquire its interest in FortisBC Midstream Inc., which holds a 93.8% interest in Aitken Creek Gas Storage facility and a 100% interest in Aitken Creek North Gas Storage facility (collectively, Aitken Creek Storage) for $400 million, subject to customary closing adjustments.

Company Background

Enbridge is an early pioneer in the development of oil production in Western Canada. The company was born in 1949 when crude oil was discovered in Leduc No. 1. Starting life as the Interprovincial Pipe Line Company, it was conceived as a pipeline that will carry Alberta crude to refineries in Regina.

In 1950, it sold some 3 million barrels of oil. By 2018, the company will sell close to that volume every day.

Enbridge merged with Spectra in early 2017 to create one of the largest energy infrastructure company in North America with an enterprise value of approximately US $126 billion.

EXECUTIVES

Chairman, Director, Pamela L. Carter
President, Chief Executive Officer, Director, Gregory L. Ebel
Executive Vice President, Chief Accounting Officer, Patrick R. Murray
Executive Vice President, Division Officer, Colin K. Gruending
Canadian Operations Executive Vice President, Finance Executive Vice President, System Performance & Solutions Executive Vice President, Finance Division Officer, System Performance & Solutions Division Officer, Canadian Operations Division Officer, Cynthia L. Hansen
Engineering, Procurement & Construction & Project Services Executive Vice President, Major Projects Executive Vice President, Project Services Executive Vice President, Corporate Services Executive Vice President, Byron C. Neiles
Strategy and Power Senior Vice President, Matthew Akman
Senior Vice President, Chief Accounting Officer, Subsidiary Officer, Melissa M. LaForge
Vice President, Corporate Secretary, Karen K.L. Uehara
Director, Mayank (Mike) M. Ashar
Director, Gaurdie E. Banister
Director, Susan M. Cunningham
Director, Teresa S. Madden
Director, Stephen S. Poloz
Director, Jane Rowe
Director, Dan C. Tutcher

Auditors : PricewaterhouseCoopers LLP

LOCATIONS

HQ: Enbridge Inc
200, 425 - 1st Street S.W., Calgary, Alberta T2P 3L8
Phone: 403 231-3900 **Fax:** 403 231-5929
Web: www.enbridge.com

2018 Sales

	% of total
US	59
Canada	41
Total	100

PRODUCTS/OPERATIONS

2018 Sales

	% of total
Commodity sales	60
Transportation and other services	31
Gas distribution	9
Total	100

Selected Subsidiaries and Affiliates

Gas Pipelines, Processing and Energy Services
    Aux Sable Liquids Products Inc. (43%)
    Alliance Pipeline Limited Partnership (50%)
    Tlbury Solar Project
    Vector Pipeline Limited Partnership (60%)
Gas Distribution
    Enbridge Gas Distribution
    Enbridge Gas New Brunswick (63%)
    Gazifère Inc.
    Niagara Gas Transmission Limited
Liquids Pipelines
    Chicap Pipe Line Company (44%)
    Enbridge Energy Partners, L.P. (13%)
    Enbridge Pipelines (Athabasca) Inc.
    Enbridge Pipelines (North Dakota) Inc.
    Enbridge Pipelines (NW) Inc.
    Enbridge Pipelines (Toledo) Inc.
    Enbridge Pipelines Inc.
    Frontier Pipeline Company (78%)
    Mustang Pipe Line Partners (30%)
    Olympic Pipe Line (85%)
Sponsored Investments
    Enbridge Income Fund (72%)
    Enbridge Energy Partners L.P. (25.5%)
Corporate
    Noverco Inc. (39%)
    Gaz Métropolitain and Company, Limited Partnership (71%)
    Vermont Gas Systems, Inc.

COMPETITORS

ATMOS ENERGY CORPORATION
AltaGas Ltd
BUCKEYE PARTNERS, L.P.
ENABLE MIDSTREAM PARTNERS, LP
ENBRIDGE ENERGY PARTNERS, L.P.
ETP LEGACY LP
GENESIS ENERGY, L.P.
NUSTAR ENERGY L.P.
PLAINS ALL AMERICAN PIPELINE, L.P.
PLAINS GP HOLDINGS, L.P.

HISTORICAL FINANCIALS

Company Type: Public

Income Statement   FYE: December 31

	REVENUE ($mil)	NET INCOME ($mil)	NET PROFIT MARGIN	EMPLOYEES
12/23	32,931	4,670	14.2%	0
12/22	39,417	2,220	5.6%	11,100
12/21	36,957	4,859	13.1%	10,900
12/20	30,698	2,641	8.6%	11,200
12/19	38,449	4,381	11.4%	11,300
Annual Growth	(3.8%)	1.6%	—	—

2023 Year-End Financials

Debt ratio: 34.0%   No. of shares ($ mil.): 2,125
Return on equity: 10.2%   Dividends
Cash ($ mil.): 4,515   Yield: —
Current Ratio: 0.83   Payout: 125.0%
Long-term debt ($ mil.): 56,369   Market value ($ mil.): 76,543

	STOCK PRICE ($) FY Close	P/E High/Low	PER SHARE ($) Earnings	Dividends	Book Value
12/23	36.02	15 11	2.14	2.68	21.82
12/22	39.10	35 28	0.95	2.54	21.87
12/21	39.08	15 11	2.25	2.68	23.57
12/20	31.99	30 18	1.16	2.42	23.79
12/19	39.77	15 13	2.02	2.22	25.05
Annual Growth	(2.4%)	—	1.5%	4.9%	(3.4%)

Endesa S.A.

Endesa provides power to some 10.6 million electricity customers and approximately 1.6 million gas customers. A subsidiary of Italian power giant Enel, Endesa is a leading electric utility in Spain and has a gross installed capacity of some 24,230 MW from nuclear, hydroelectric, and renewable energy plants. Endesa is the primary electricity company in Chile, Argentina, Colombia and Peru and also operates in Brazil. The company is also investing heavily in renewable energy to meet Spain's commitment to greenhouse gas reduction. Spain accounts for the Majority of the company's sales.

Operations

The company's segments include Generation and Supply (about 85% of sales), Distribution (about 15%) and Structure (nearly 5%), which mainly includes balances and transactions of holding companies and financing and service provision companies.

Geographic Reach

Its registered offices and headquarters are at Madrid. About 90% of sales were generated in Spain, Portugal with some 5%, and France, Germany, Italy, UK, Netherlands, and Other accounts for the rest.

Sales and Marketing

ENDESA maintains relationships with a large number of customers, 10.6 million electricity customers and 1.6 million gas customers.

Financial Performance

Income in 2019 totaled ?20.2 billion, ?37 million (-0.2%) less than that of 2018.

The company's net income for 2019 decreased to ?180 million compared to ?1.4 billion in the prior year.

Cash held by the company at the end of 2019 increased by ?18 million to ?31 million compared to ?13 million in the prior year. Cash provided by operations was ?2.2 billion, while cash used for investing and financing activities were ?30 million and ?2.1 billion, respectively.

Strategy

Development of the electricity grid has long been a fundamental pillar of ENDESA's strategy. Projected investment, driven by the electrification of demand and the inclusion of renewable energies, aims to improve grid quality and efficiency, reducing operating costs, and increasing the value of assets through investments in smart grids and the pursuit of excellence.

To this end, ENDESA continues with its investment effort aimed at becoming the reference digital operator, and for this it will allocate Euros 1,100 million in the 2019-2022 period to the development, automation and modernization of the network. This amount represents approximately 55% of the Euros 2,000 million total investment envisaged for this business in the plan.

HISTORY

When dictator Francisco Franco set about rebuilding Spain after the Civil War, Empresa Nacional de Electricidad (Endesa) was formed in 1944 under the state-run Instituto Nacional de Industria (INI). The nation's lack of power facilities sparked the company into building hydroelectric plants. In the 1950s the US, fighting the Cold War, financed Spain's industrial boom, which Endesa aided by building coal-fired plants, including Compostilla (on line in 1961).

When inflation plagued Spain in the late 1950s, the government cut off INI's funding. INI and its companies then borrowed heavily from banks. Spain then passed the Stabilization Act in 1959 to make INI companies self-financing, though they were still government-owned. In the 1960s many of Spain's rural areas were undeveloped, so the government instituted and funded a plan to build power infrastructure.

In 1972 Endesa acquired the As Pontel and Teruel facilities, where it began constructing fossil fuel plants. However, the energy crisis of the early 1970s kept the plants from operating until 1976 and 1979, respectively.

After Franco's death in 1975, King Juan Carlos moved Spain into Europe's free market union. In preparation for the liberalization of the energy markets, INI and Endesa reorganized in 1983 and shifted INI's holdings in regional electric utilities (Eneco, Enher, Gesa, and Unelco) to Endesa.

After the government halted its nuclear power program in 1984, many private electric companies were left with bad investments. Endesa was brought in to bail them out by taking over power plants; to repay Endesa, they were forced to buy Endesa's electricity. The 1985 asset swaps also brought regional power companies Erz and Fecsa into Endesa's grasp.

In 1986 Spain joined the European Community; two years later the government sold 20% of Endesa to the public. In the early 1990s Endesa went into coal production when it purchased ENCASUR (1990), and it continued buying interests in private power companies, including Viesgo and Sevillana.

The government floated more of the company in 1997, and the utility became Endesa, S.A. Its eye on Latin American opportunity, Endesa bought a 29% stake in Chile's largest power company, Enersis. It also branched into telecommunications by grabbing a small stake in RetevisiÃ³n.

Endesa was fully privatized in 1998, the year Spain's deregulation process began. The next year Endesa paid some $2.6 billion to buy the outstanding shares of its regional units and merge them into the company, as part of its larger effort to reorganize and cut its costs and workforce. Endesa also increased its stake in Enersis to more than 60%.

In 2000 Endesa began restructuring its regional electric utilities into separate generation and distribution units. Also that year, Endesa, Telecom Italia, and UniÃ³n Fenosa combined their Spanish telecom holdings to form the Auna joint venture. (Telecom Italia later sold its stake to Santander Central Hispano.) Endesa also agreed to acquire rival Spanish utility Iberdrola, but the companies cancelled the transaction in 2001.

In 2001 Endesa completed the purchase of a 30% interest in French generation company SNET. The company also acquired one of Italian utility Enel's power production units (Elettrogen). Endesa sold its New Viesgo unit (a spinoff composed of regional electric utility Electra de Viesgo, which served 500,000 customers and had 2,400 MW of generation assets) to Enel in 2002.

Endesa branched out into new territories to prepare for the deregulation of Spain's electric utility market, which took full effect in 2003.

In 2005 Endesa sold its major stake in Auna to France Telecom (since renamed Orange).

The company found itself the target of takeover bids by other European power companies seeking to bulk up in the wake of the deregulation of the European power and gas markets. In 2007 E.ON and Gas Natural made bids of $47-plus billion and $26-plus billion, respectively, for Endesa. That year Enel and Acciona jumped into the fray, buying about 70% and 25% of the company, respectively, when Gas Natural dropped out of the bidding. E.ON dropped out in 2008 in return for buying some power plants and shareholdings in Italy, Spain, and France from Endesa. In 2009 Enel bought Acciona's stake.

In 2009 Endesa had a generating capacity of more than 3,700 MW of wind power, or about 10% of the Spanish wind power market. In another major move to promote renewable energy, in 2010 the company agreed to develop about 550 recharging locations in Barcelona, Madrid, and Seville to power electric cars.

EXECUTIVES

Chief Executive Officer, Executive Director, Jose Damian Bogas Galvez
Secretary, Francisco Borja Acha Besga
Independent Chairman, Juan Sanchez-Calero Guilarte
Vice-Chairman, Francesco Starace
Independent Director, Maria Eugenia Bieto Caubet
Independent Director, Ignacio Garralda Ruiz de Velasco
Independent Director, Pilar Gonzalez de Frutos
Independent Director, Alicia Koplowitz Romero de Joseu
Independent Director, Francisco de Lacerda
Director, Antonio Cammisecra
Director, Maria Patrizia Grieco
Director, Alberto de Paoli
Auditors : KPMG Auditores, S.L.

LOCATIONS

HQ: Endesa S.A.
Calle Ribera Del Loira 60, Madrid 28042
Phone: (34) 91 213 10 00   **Fax:** (34) 91 563 81 81
Web: www.endesa.com

2009 Sales

	% of total
Europe	
Spain & Portugal	68
Latin America	32
Total	100

COMPETITORS

ACCIONA, SA
E.ON UK PLC
EDP ESPAÃ'A SAU
ENEL SPA
Electrabel
IBERDROLA, SOCIEDAD ANONIMA
KOC HOLDING ANONIM SIRKETI
RWE AG
SHV Holdings N.V.
TECHNIP

HISTORICAL FINANCIALS

Company Type: Public

Income Statement   FYE: December 31

	REVENUE ($mil)	NET INCOME ($mil)	NET PROFIT MARGIN	EMPLOYEES
12/22	35,134	2,713	7.7%	18,516
12/21	23,654	1,624	6.9%	9,258
12/20	21,574	1,710	7.9%	9,591
12/19	22,632	191	0.8%	9,952
12/18	23,127	1,622	7.0%	9,763
Annual Growth	11.0%	13.7%	—	17.4%

2022 Year-End Financials

Debt ratio: 39.5%   No. of shares ($ mil.): 1,058
Return on equity: 46.4%   Dividends
Cash ($ mil.): 930   Yield: —
Current Ratio: 0.96   Payout: 13.7%
Long-term debt ($ mil.): 12,500   Market value ($ mil.): 9,902

	STOCK PRICE ($) FY Close	P/E High/Low		PER SHARE ($) Earnings Dividends		Book Value
12/22	9.36	5	3	2.56	0.35	5.61
12/21	11.52	11	7	1.54	0.78	5.75
12/20	14.43	12	9	1.62	0.61	8.48
12/19	13.86	89	75	0.18	0.57	8.15
12/18	11.62	9	8	1.53	0.56	9.77
Annual Growth	(5.3%)	—		13.7%	(11.1%)	(13.0%)

Enel Americas SA

One of the largest publicly listed companies in the electricity sector in South America, Enel AmÃ©ricas (formerly Enersis AmÃ©ricas) is engaged in the generation, transmission, and distribution of electricity in Argentina, Brazil, Colombia, Costa Rica, Guatemala, Panama, and Peru through its subsidiaries and affiliates. Its distribution companies provide power to some 26.2 million customers. Its 60%-owned Enel GeneraciÃ³n Chile is Chile's largest power generator. The company had around 15,925 MW of net installed generation capacity and approximately 26.2 million distribution customers. The company was founded in 1981 when the CompaÃ±Ãa Chilena de Electricidad S.A. created a new corporate structure, which gave birth to a parent company and three subsidiaries.

Operations

The company operates through two segments: Distribution Business (over 70% of sales), of which Brazil had more than 50%, Columbia with some 10% and Argentina and Peru with some 5% each; and Generation and Transmission Business (about 30%), of which Brazil had some 15%, Columbia with about 10%, Peru with less than 5%, and Argentina and Central America with the rest.

The Distribution Business is conducted in Argentina through Edesur; in Brazil through Enel DistribuciÃ³n RÃo S.A., Enel DistribuciÃ³n CearÃ¡ S.A., Enel DistribuciÃ³n Goias and Enel DistribuciÃ³n Sao Paulo (formerly Eletropaulo); in Colombia through Codensa; and in Peru through Enel DistribuciÃ³n PerÃº.

The Generation and Transmission Business is conducted in Argentina through Enel Trading Argentina (formerly Cemsa), Central Dock Sud, Enel GeneraciÃ³n Costanera, Enel GeneraciÃ³n El ChocÃ³n and Enel Green Power Argentina S.A.; in Brazil through through its subsidiaries, EGP Cachoeira Dourada, Enel CIEN, Enel Green Power Proyectos I (Volta Grande), Fortaleza, Enel Trading Brasil S.A. and the EGP Group companies; in Colombia through subsidiary Emgesa and Enel Green Power Colombia S.A.S ESP; in Peru through subsidiaries Enel GeneraciÃ³n PerÃº, Enel GeneraciÃ³n Piura, Chinango and Enel Green Power Peru S.A.C and in Central America by our subsidiaries Enel Green Power Costa Rica S.A., Enel Green Power Guatemala S.A. and Enel Power PanamÃ¡ S.R.L.

Geographic Reach

Headquartered in Santiago, Chile, the company is engaged in the generation, transmission, and distribution of electricity in Argentina, Brazil, Colombia, Costa Rica, Guatemala, Panama, and Peru.

Sales and Marketing

The company has approximately 26.2 million distribution customers.

Financial Performance

The company reported a total revenue of $16.2 billion in 2021.

In 2021, the company had a net income of $741 million, a 10% decrease from the previous year's net income of $825 million.

The company's cash at the end of 2021 was $1.4 billion. Operating activities generated $2.6 billion, while investing activities used $1.9 billion, mainly for other payments to acquire equity or debt instruments of other entities. Financing activities provided another $2.7 billion.

EXECUTIVES

Chief Executive Officer, Maurizio Bezzeccheri
Administration, Finance and Control Officer, Aurelio Ricardo Bustilho de Oliveira
Planning and Control Officer, Bruno Stella
Internal Audit Manager, Raffaele Cutrignelli
Communications Officer, Jose Miranda Montecinos
General Counsel, Secretary, Domingo Valdes Prieto
Chairman, Francisco Borja Acha Besga
Director, Livio Gallo
Director, Enrico Viale
Director, Patricio Gomez Sabaini
Director, Domingo Cruzat Amunátegui
Vice-Chairman, Jose Antonio Vargas Lleras
Director, Hernan Somerville Senn
Auditors : KPMG Auditores Consultores SPA

LOCATIONS

HQ: Enel Americas SA
Santa Rosa 76, Santiago 833099
Phone: (56) 2 2353 4400   **Fax:** (56) 2 378 4790
Web: www.enelamericas.com

PRODUCTS/OPERATIONS

2016 Sales
	% of total
Distribution	67
Generation and Transmission	33
Total	100

2016 Sales
	% of total
Brazil	36
Colombia	30
Peru	17
Argentina	17
Total	100

Selected Subsidiaries

Ampla Energía e Serviços (distribution, generation, and transmission, Brazil)
Centrais Elétricas Cachoeira Dourada (distribution, generation, and transmission, Brazil)
Chilectra (distribution)
Compañía Americana de Multiservicios (CAM, electricity support services and engineering)
Edelnor (distribution, Peru)
Edesur (distribution, Argentina)
Endesa Brasil Consolidated (distribution, generation, and transmission, Brazil)
Endesa Chile (generation)
Endesa Fortaleza (distribution, generation, and transmission, Brazil)
Inmobiliaria Manso de Velasco (IMV, real estate)
Synapsis (information and telecommunications)

COMPETITORS

CMS ENERGY CORPORATION
CONSOLIDATED EDISON, INC.
CPS ENERGY
Corporacion Nacional del Cobre de Chile
Enel Generacion Chile S.A.
GESTORE DEI MERCATI ENERGETICI SPA
Innergex Inc
PG&E CORPORATION
SCANA CORPORATION
TRANSPORTADORA DE GAS DEL SUR S.A.

HISTORICAL FINANCIALS

Company Type: Public

Income Statement   FYE: December 31

	REVENUE ($mil)	NET INCOME ($mil)	NET PROFIT MARGIN	EMPLOYEES
12/21	16,192	740	4.6%	16,461
12/20	12,192	825	6.8%	16,731
12/19	14,314	1,614	11.3%	17,295
12/18	13,184	1,201	9.1%	18,364
12/17	10,540	709	6.7%	11,393
Annual Growth	11.3%	1.1%		9.6%

2021 Year-End Financials
Debt ratio: 17.6%   No. of shares ($ mil.): 107,280
Return on equity: 7.0%   Dividends
Cash ($ mil.): 1,396   Yield: —
Current Ratio: 0.91   Payout: 94.0%
Long-term debt ($ mil.): 4,905   Market value ($ mil.): —

Enel Societa Per Azioni

Enel is the largest private renewable energy operator in the world, with some 53.4 GW of managed capacity, and the largest private electricity distribution company globally, with 74 million end users connected to the world's most advanced digitalized grids. It manages the largest customer base in the world among private companies, with more than 69 million customers. Enel's portfolio of power stations includes hydroelectric, wind, thermal, electricity, and other renewables. More than half of Enel's revenue comes from its home country, Italy. Enel was founded in 1962 with the fusion of more than a thousand energy producers.

Operations

Enel reports six business segments, three of which are its leading revenue earners ? End-user markets (around 35%), Thermal generation and trading (some 30% of total revenue), and Infrastructure and Networks (about 20%). The three other segments, Enel Green Power (about 10%), as well as Enel X and Services, bring in a combined less than 5% of revenue.

Geographic Reach

Based in Italy, Enel is primarily present in more than 30 countries from Europe to Latin America, North America, Africa, Asia, and Oceania.

Enel's largest market, Italy, bringing in over 50% of total sales, while Iberia with about 25%, and Americas (North and Latin) with around 25%.

Sales and Marketing

The company serves some 69 million retail customers, some 45 million end users with active smart meters, and some 75 million end users.

Financial Performance

The company's revenue in 2021 increased by 33% to EUR 88.0 billion compared from the prior year with EUR 66.0 billion.

Profit in 2021 remained the same with EUR 6.7 billion.

Cash held by the company at the end of 2021 increased to EUR 9.0 billion. Cash provided by operations and financing activities were EUR10.1 billion and EUR3.8 billion, respectively. Cash used for investing activities was EUR10.9 billion, mainly for investments in property, plant and equipment.

Strategy

The Plan underpinning the early achievement of this ambitious goal is based on the implementation of certain key strategic steps: the plan to abandon coal and gas generation by 2027 and 2040 respectively, replacing the thermal generation portfolio with new renewables capacity and exploiting the hybridization of renewables with storage solutions; by 2040, 100% of the electricity sold by the company will be generated from renewables and by the same year the company will exit the retail gas sales business.

n support of our long-term targets, in 2022-2024 the company expects to directly invest around EUR 45 billion, of which EUR 43 billion through the Ownership model, mainly in expanding and upgrading grids and in developing renewables and about EUR 2 billion through the Stewardship model, while mobilizing ?8 billion in investment from third parties.

Mergers and Acquisitions

In mid-2022, Enel through its wholly-owned subsidiary Enel X, and Intesa Sanpaolo S.p.A., acting through its subsidiary Banca 5 S.p.A. finalized the acquisition from Schumann Investments S.A., a company controlled by the international private equity fund CVC Capital Partners Fund VI, of 70% of the share capital of Mooney Group S.p.A., a fintech company operating in proximity banking and payments. Specifically, after having obtained the required administrative authorizations, Enel X acquired 50% of Mooney's share capital, whereas Banca 5, which previously owned a 30% stake of Mooney, increased its participation to 50%, placing Mooney under the joint control of both parties. Terms were not disclosed.

HISTORY

Italy's energy consumption doubled in the 1950s as the country experienced a period of rapid industrialization and urbanization. A tight-knit oligopoly controlled the electric power industry and included Edison, SADE, La Centale, SME, and Finelettrica. The economic boom pushed into the 1960s, and the Italian government created Enel (Ente Nazionale per l'Energia Elettrica) in 1962 to nationalize the power industry. In 1963 Enel began gradually buying some 1,250 electric utilities. About 160 municipal utilities and the larger independents, such as Edison, were left out of the takeover.

The company spent the late 1960s and early 1970s connecting Italy's unwieldy transmission network and building new power plants, including the La Spezia thermoelectric plant (600 MW). Construction costs, coupled with the high prices Enel was required to pay for its takeover targets, caused the utility to become steeped in debt. The Arab oil embargoes of the early 1970s made matters worse, and the Italian government helped Enel with an endowment in 1973.

The energy crisis also prompted Enel to build its first nuclear power plant, Caorso, which came on line in 1980. However, nuclear power was short-lived in Italy: After the 1986 Chernobyl accident, a national referendum forced Enel to deactivate its nukes in 1987. The firm also stepped up its development of renewable energy sources in the 1980s.

Meanwhile, Enel opened its Centro Nazionale de Controllo (CNC) in Rome in 1985 to supervise Italy's power grid. The next year the company turned its first profit.

To begin disassembling Enel's monopoly, the Italian government in 1992 opened the power generation market to outside producers and converted Enel into a joint stock company (with the state holding all of the shares). Following the European Union's 1997 directive to deregulate Europe's power industry, Enel unbundled its utility activities and began trimming its staff.

Italy's Bersani Decree (passed in 1999) outlined the restructuring process: Enel was ordered to divest 25% of its capacity (15,000 MW) and turn over a portion of its municipal distribution networks to local governments to enhance competition in the country's power market. Accordingly, it transferred management of the national transmission grid to an independent government-owned operator, Gestore della Rete di Trasmissione Nazionale (GRTN), and reduced its customer count by approximately 1 million through municipal distribution asset sales.

Enel had already begun to diversify. It started Wind Telecomunicazioni, a joint venture with France Telecom -- later renamed Orange-- and Deutsche Telekom in 1998. (Deutsche Telekom sold its stake to the other partners in 2000.) Wind first offered fixed-line and mobile telecom services to corporations; it extended the services to residential users in 1999. In addition, Enel began building water infrastructure to serve local distributors and purchased three water operations in southern Italy.

Also in 1999 the government floated 32% of Enel in one of the world's largest IPOs at the time. The next year the company bought Colombo Gas (a northern Italian gas distributor with about 75,000 customers) and it transferred control of its transmission network to Gestore della Rete di Trasmissione Nazionale (an independent government-owned operator), while retaining ownership of the assets.

Enel bought fixed-line telephone company Infostrada from Vodafone in 2001, acquired two more Italian gas distributors, and sold its 5,400-MW Elettrogen generation unit to Spain's Endesa for $2.3 billion. That year Enel put its 7,000-MW Eurogen generation unit on the auction block. The high bidder, with a $2.6 billion offer, was a consortium backed by Fiat and Électricité de France; the sale was completed in 2002.

Also in 2002, Enel merged Infostrada into Wind Telecomunicazioni to create one of Italy's top telecom companies, it purchased Camuzzi Gazometri's gas distribution business (Italy's second-largest) for $870 million from Mill Hill Investments, and it bought Endesa's Viesgo unit (2,400 MW of generating capacity and 500,000 power customers) for about $1.8 billion.

Enel sold its final generation divestment company, Interpower (2,600 MW), to a consortium of utilities (including Belgian utility Electrabel and Italian utility ACEA) for about $880 million in 2003.

That year Enel purchased France Telecom's 27% stake in Wind for $1.4 billion, making the unit a wholly owned subsidiary. (Enel had flirted with the idea of taking Wind public but instead sold the unit in 2006 to the Egypt-based Weather Investments consortium, which had the backing of Orascom Telecom's chairman and CEO, Naguib Sawiris.)

The Italian government began the second round of Enel's privatization process in 2003 by selling a 7% stake to Morgan Stanley for more than $2.3 billion. In 2004 the government further reduced its stake by nearly 20% through a public offering of shares.

In 2005 it acquired power distribution and sales businesses in Romania and in 2006 in Slovakia.

With Italian regulators requiring that Enel divest 80% of its Terna subsidiary (which holds the company's power transmission assets) by 2007, Enel spun off 50% of the unit in an IPO in 2004. The following year it divested another 44%, and the company reduced its holding to about 5% by January 2006. Grid management and operational functions were also transferred from GRTN back to Terna.

In 2008 the company set Enel Green Power to develop wind, solar, geothermal and biomass projects. By 2009 it was operating alternative energy plants worldwide with a generating capacity of 4,700 MW. In 2010 Enel Green Power acquired Pagoda Wind Power, which is developing 4,000 MW of wind projects in California.

In what could have been a large cross-border deal, Enel considered making a bid for France's SUEZ (now GDF SUEZ) utility company. Perhaps in reaction to the news of Enel's interest, France's Gaz de France made a bid for SUEZ (consummated in 2008), a move that Italy called protectionist.

Unperturbed by its failure to secure SUEZ, the company took control of Spain's power giant Endesa in 2007, increasing its market share as a European power player. Hoping to pay down what had become a heavy debt load, the company in 2009 sold an 80% stake in gas distributor Enel Rete Gas for $666 million.

In 2012, Enel Green Power consolidated its position in the Greek renewable industry through the launching of two new plants - a wind farm and a photovoltaic plant - both located in the Peloponnese region.

EXECUTIVES

Chief Executive Officer, Director, Francesco Starace
Secretary, Silvia Alessandra Fappani
Chairman, Michele Crisostomo
Director, Cesare Calari
Director, Costanza Esclapon de Villeneuve
Director, Samuel Leupold
Director, Alberto Marchi
Director, Mariana Mazzucato
Director, Mirella Pellegrini
Director, Anna Chiara Svelto
Auditors : KPMG SpA

LOCATIONS

HQ: Enel Societa Per Azioni
Viale Regina Margherita, 137, Rome 00198
Phone: (39) 6 8509 3184   Fax: (39) 6 8509 5810
Web: www.enel.com

2018 sales

	%
Italy	50
Iberia	26
South America	19
Europe and Euro-Mediterranean Affairs	3
North and Central America	2
Africa, Asia, and Oceania	—
Total	100

PRODUCTS/OPERATIONS

2018 Sales

	% of total
Thermal Generation and Trading	41
End-user markets	35
Infrastructure and Networks	16
Enel Green Power	4
Enel X	1
Services	3
Total	100

2018 sales

	%
Sale of electricity	57
Transport of Electricity	14
Fees from network operators	1
Transfers from institutional market operators	2
Sales of gas	6
Transport of gas	1
Sale of fuel	11
Other	8
Total	100

COMPETITORS

ATLANTIA SPA
COHORT PLC
DENTSU INTERNATIONAL LIMITED
E.ON SE
ERG SPA
HILL INTERNATIONAL, INC.
IBERDROLA, SOCIEDAD ANONIMA
MACE LIMITED
Vattenfall AB
WS ATKINS LIMITED

HISTORICAL FINANCIALS

Company Type: Public

Income Statement   FYE: December 31

	REVENUE ($mil)	NET INCOME ($mil)	NET PROFIT MARGIN	EMPLOYEES
12/22	150,078	3,884	2.6%	65,124
12/21	99,610	3,609	3.6%	66,279
12/20	79,755	3,203	4.0%	66,717
12/19	90,188	2,440	2.7%	68,253
12/18	86,659	5,484	6.3%	69,272
Annual Growth	14.7%	(8.3%)	—	(1.5%)

2022 Year-End Financials

Debt ratio: 43.5%   No. of shares ($ mil.): 10,159
Return on equity: 12.4%   Dividends
Cash ($ mil.): 11,792   Yield: —
Current Ratio: 0.91   Payout: 138.5%
Long-term debt ($ mil.): 72,831   Market value ($ mil.): 54,252

	STOCK PRICE ($) FY Close	P/E High/Low	PER SHARE ($) Earnings	Dividends	Book Value
12/22	5.34	51 28	0.16	0.22	3.01
12/21	7.96	33 24	0.35	0.24	3.30
12/20	10.15	40 25	0.32	0.22	3.42
12/19	7.85	38 27	0.24	0.18	3.36
12/18	5.81	13 10	0.54	0.16	3.57
Annual Growth	(2.1%)	—	(26.1%)	8.5%	(4.2%)

Eneos Holdings Inc

Japan's ENEOS Holdings (formerly JXTG Holdings) is an integrated energy holding company that combines the businesses of two of the country's top oil refiners Nippon Oil and Nippon Mining Holdings, which merged to become a powerhouse with diverse operations in petroleum refining and marketing, oil and natural gas exploration and production, and metals (mainly copper). It manages group companies and subsidiaries engaged in the energy business; oil and natural gas exploration, development, and production business; and metals business; and operations incidental to said businesses. Established in 2010, majority of its sales were generated in Japan.

Operations

ENEOS Holdings operates through four segments: Energy (around 80% of sales), Metals (over 10%), Oil and Natural gas E&P (less than 5%), and Other (some 5%).

The Energy segment is engaged in petroleum refining & marketing, basic chemical products, electricity, lubricants, high-performance materials, gas, hydrogen, and renewable energy.

The Metals segment includes copper foils, precision rolled products, precision-fabricated products, thin-film materials, development and exploration of non-ferrous metal resources, non-ferrous metal products (e.g. copper, precious metals, tantalum, and niobium), non-ferrous metal recycling and industrial waste treatment, titanium, and electric wires.

The Oil and Natural gas E&P segment includes oil and natural gas exploration, development and production.

Other segment includes asphalt paving, civil engineering work, construction work, land transportation, real estate leasing business, and affairs common to the ENEOS Group companies including fund procurement.

Geographic Reach

Headquartered in Tokyo, Japan, it generated over 75% of sales from Japan, while China generated around 5%. The rest of the sales were generated from other countries.

Sales and Marketing

The ENEOS does not have any external customer whose revenue exceeds 10% of the ENEOS' total revenue.

Financial Performance

The company's revenue for fiscal 2022 increased to JPY 10.9 trillion compared from the prior year with JPY 7.7 trillion.

Profit for fiscal 2022 increased to JPY 579.1 billion compared from the prior year with JPY 112.9 billion.

Cash held by the company at the end of fiscal 2022 increased to JPY 524.0 billion. Cash provided by operations and financing activities were JPY 209.5 billion and JPY 226.0 billion, respectively. Cash used for investing activities was JPY 349.9 billion, mainly for purchase of property, plant and equipment.

Mergers and Acquisitions

In late 2021, ENEOS Holdings announced that its consolidated subsidiary ENEOS Corporation has decided to acquire the entire issued shares of Japan Renewable Energy Corporation, indirectly owned by the

Infrastructure business within Goldman Sachs Asset Management and an affiliate of GIC Private Limited. JRE has been one of the leading renewable energy companies in Japan that engages in renewable power generation business across the full value chain from project development to operation and maintenance of renewable power plants. ENEOS will establish a system that stably and efficiently supplies CO2-free electricity to customers by combining fluctuating renewable energy power supplies with energy management system (EMS), which optimally controls electricity by utilizing storage battery and electric vehicle (EV). Terms were not disclosed.

Company Background

The merger of Nippon Oil and Nippon Mining in 2010 was spurred on by changes in the Japanese oil industry, including excess refining capacity due to the continued decline in domestic demand for refined petroleum products, a growing consumer awareness of environmental issues and alternative energy options, and a sluggish Japanese economy. Such trends prompted the two to consider restructuring and integrating their businesses to strengthen competitiveness. Following the merger JX Nippon set up upstream oil business JX Nippon Oil & Gas Exploration and metals unit JX Nippon Mining and Metals as operating subsidiaries.

Petroleum refining and marketing will continue to be a core segment that JX Holdings plans to expand further throughout Asia and arpund the world. However, it may also look for future opportunities to engage in new energy markets, such as fuel cells and photovoltaic power generation, to keep up with the growing green trend.

In 2012, the company's wholly owned subsidiary, JX Nippon Exploration and Production (U.K.) Limited signed sale and purchase agreements to acquire an extensive portfolio of non-operated oil and gas assets in the UK Continental Shelf from ENI. The assets give JX a substantial long-term oil and gas production base in the UK.

EXECUTIVES

Chairman, Director, Katsuyuki Ota
President, Representative Director, Takeshi Saito
Executive Vice President, Representative Director, Yasushi Yatabe
Executive Vice President, Representative Director, Tomohide Miyata
Executive Vice President, Chief Digital Officer, Director, Hideki Shiina
Executive Vice President, Director, Keitaro Inoue
Director, Toshiya Nakahara
Director, Seiichi Murayama
Outside Director, Yasumi Kudo
Outside Director, Tetsuro Tomita
Outside Director, Toshiko Oka
Director, Shingo Nishimura

Director, Tomoo Shiota
Outside Director, Seiichiro Nishioka
Outside Director, Yuko Mitsuya
Outside Director, Hiroko Kawasaki
Auditors : Ernst & Young ShinNihon LLC

LOCATIONS

HQ: Eneos Holdings Inc
1-1-2 Otemachi, Chiyoda-ku, Tokyo 100-8162
Phone: (81) 3 6257 7075
Web: www.hd.eneos.co.jp

2014 Sales

	% of total
Japan	74
China	19
Other countries	7
Total	100

PRODUCTS/OPERATIONS

2014 Sales

	% of total
Energy	87
Metals	8
Oil & natural gas exploration & production	2
Other	3
Total	100

COMPETITORS

CLEAN TECH ASSETS LIMITED
Evonik Industries AG
HUNTING PLC
IDEMITSU KOSAN CO.,LTD.
NEWMARKET CORPORATION
REPSOL SA.
SASOL LTD
SURGUTNEFTEGAZ, PAO
TOTAL SE
VALLOUREC

HISTORICAL FINANCIALS

Company Type: Public

Income Statement   FYE: March 31

	REVENUE ($mil)	NET INCOME ($mil)	NET PROFIT MARGIN	EMPLOYEES
03/23	112,749	1,079	1.0%	57,625
03/22	89,789	4,415	4.9%	55,282
03/21	69,162	1,029	1.5%	55,114
03/20	92,231	(1,731)	—	55,359
03/19	100,499	2,910	2.9%	54,978
Annual Growth	2.9%	(22.0%)	—	1.2%

2023 Year-End Financials

Debt ratio: 0.2%
Return on equity: 5.0%
Cash ($ mil.): 2,338
Current Ratio: 1.41
Long-term debt ($ mil.): 15,387
No. of shares ($ mil.): 3,025
Dividends
Yield: —
Payout: 95.6%
Market value ($ mil.): 20,997

	STOCK PRICE ($) FY Close	P/E High/Low	PER SHARE ($) Earnings	Dividends	Book Value
03/23	6.94	0 0	0.35	0.33	7.10
03/22	7.45	0 0	1.37	0.39	7.30
03/21	9.21	0 0	0.32	0.40	6.52
03/20	7.21	— —	(0.53)	0.41	6.61
03/19	9.00	0 0	0.86	0.36	7.36
Annual Growth	(6.3%)	—	(20.2%)	(2.1%)	(0.9%)

Engie SA

Engie is a European and world leader in low-carbon electricity production, centralized and decentralized energy networks, and associated services. The company relies on its key business lines (Renewables, Decentralized infrastructure, Client Solutions, Thermal Generation and Energy Supply) to offer its customers competitive, high value-added solutions that enable them to achieve their carbon-neutrality targets. Engie operates electricity power plants, natural gas terminals, and storage facilities in less than 30 countries.

Operations

Engie has four Global Business Units (GBU) associated with the its four main business lines (Thermal and Supply with some 30% of sales, Energy Solutions with over 15%, Networks with over 10%, and Renewables with around 5%) and two operating entities (Nuclear and Global Energy Management and Sales (GEMS)).

Thermal encompasses all the company's centralized power generation activities using thermal assets, whether contracted or not. It includes the operation of power plants fueled mainly by gas or coal, as well as pump-operated storage plants. The energy produced is fed into the grid and sold either on the open or regulated market or to third parties through electricity sale agreements. It also includes the financing, construction and operation of desalination plants, whether or not connected to power plants as well as the development of hydrogen production capacities. Supply encompasses all the company's activities relating to the sale of gas and electricity to end customers, whether professional or individual. It also includes all the activities in services for residential clients.

Energy Solutions encompasses the construction and management of decentralized energy networks to produce low-carbon energy (heating and cooling networks, distributed power generation plants, distributed solar power parks, low-carbon mobility, low-carbon cities and public lighting, etc.) and related services (energy efficiency, technical maintenance, sustainable development consulting).

Networks comprises the company's electricity and gas infrastructure activities and projects. These activities include the management and development of gas and electricity transportation networks and natural gas distribution networks in and outside of Europe, natural gas underground storage in Europe, and regasification infrastructure in France and Chile.

Renewables comprises all centralized renewable energy generation activities, including financing, construction, operation and maintenance of renewable energy facilities, using various energy sources such as hydroelectric, onshore wind, photovoltaic solar, biomass, offshore wind, and geothermal.

The energy produced is fed into the grid and sold either on the open or regulated market or to third parties through electricity sale agreements.

Geographic Reach

Engie has activities in some 30 countries. Europe accounts for about 45% of sales, with France alone accounts for some 25%. The US and Canada, Latin America, Asia, Middle East and Africa accounts for the remaining of sales. Its headquarters are located in France.

Sales and Marketing

Engie provides gas and electricity to end-customers worldwide, with around 22 million contracts. Nearly half of its customers are located outside France.

Financial Performance

The company reported a revenue of EUR 57.9 billion, a 31% increase from the previous year's revenue of EUR 44.3 billion. This was primarily due to a higher volume of sales in the company's.

In 2021, the company had a net income of EUR 3.8 billion, a 521% improvement from the previous year's net loss of EUR 893 million. The EUR 5.2 billion increase compared to 2020 was mainly linked to the higher net recurring income company share and lower impairment loses.

The company's cash at the end of 2021 was EUR 13.9 billion. Operating activities generated EUR 7.3 billion, while investing activities used EUR 11 billion, mainly for acquisitions of property, plant and equipment and intangible assets. Financing activities provided another EUR 4.8 billion.

Strategy

Engie's strategy is focused on accelerating the energy transition. In 2021 the company reaffirmed its operating strategy and undertook a deep re-organization. It laid the foundations for long-term, sustainable growth in line with its stated purpose. Everything is in place to make 2022 a year of aggressive growth.

Mergers and Acquisitions

In late 2021, Engie and Crédit Agricole Assurances announced an agreement to acquire a 97.33% stake of Eolia Renovables from Canada-based Alberta Investment Management Corporation. The transaction includes the ownership and operation of 899 MW of operating assets and a 1.2 GW pipeline of renewable projects. The acquisition is set to boost the company's presence in the Spanish renewables market and accelerate the company's growth and reach its target of 50 GW of renewable capacity by 2025. The transaction will have a ?0.4 billion net financial debt impact for ENGIE.

HISTORY

The first canal in Egypt was dug in the 13th century BC, but it was Napoleon who revived the idea of a shorter trade route to India: a canal through Egypt linking the Gulf of Suez with the Mediterranean. Former French diplomat and engineer Ferdinand de Lesseps formed Compagnie Universelle du Canal Maritime de Suez in 1858 to build and eventually operate the canal, which opened 11 years later. Egypt's modernization had pushed it into debt and increased its ties to the British government, which, by 1875, had acquired a 44% stake in the company.

For more than 80 years the Suez Canal was a foreign enclave, protected by the British Army since 1936. After Egypt's puppet government fell, and as Gamal Abd Al-Nasser assumed power in 1956, British troops exited the Canal Zone, which Egypt quickly nationalized. Israel, Britain, and France attacked, but the UN arranged a truce and foreign forces withdrew, leaving the Suez in Egypt's control.

With no canal to operate, Universelle du Canal Maritime de Suez became Compagnie Financière de Suez in 1958. A year later it created a bank (which became Banque Indosuez in 1974).

In 1967 Financière de Suez became the largest shareholder in Société Lyonnaise des Eaux et de L'Eclairage, a leading French water company. Formed in 1880, Lyonnaise des Eaux had stakes in water (Northumbrian Water) and energy (Elyo). After France's energy firms were nationalized in 1946, Lyonnaise des Eaux dipped deeper into the water industry by acquiring Degrémont (now Ondeo-Degrémont) in 1972. It also purchased stakes in waste management (SITA, 1970) and heating systems (Cofreth, 1975).

In the 1980s Lyonnaise des Eaux expanded in Spain, the UK, and the US, and diversified into cable TV (1986) and broadcast TV (1987). It merged with construction firm Dumez in 1990.

Meanwhile, Financière de Suez became a financial power when it won a controlling stake in Société Générale de Belgique (SGB) in 1988 and bought Groupe Victoire in 1989. But the two buys left the firm (renamed Compagnie de Suez in 1990) deeply in debt.

Losing money, Compagnie de Suez disposed of Victoire (1994) and then the valuable Banque Indosuez (1996). In 1996 the company bought a controlling stake in Belgium's top utility, Tractebel (now SUEZ-TRACTEBEL). Compagnie de Suez and Lyonnaise des Eaux merged in 1997 to create Suez Lyonnaise des Eaux. The following year Suez Lyonnaise acquired the rest of SGB and bought the European and Asian operations of waste management giant Browning-Ferris Industries; it also began divesting noncore operations.

Suez Lyonnaise in 1999 expanded its core businesses, primarily in the US. The company bought Calgon (water treatment, US) and Nalco Chemical (water treatment chemicals, US), then merged Calgon into Nalco to form Ondeo Nalco. (The company's name was changed back to Nalco when it was divested in 2003.)

In 2000 Suez Lyonnaise bought United Water Resources (now United Water) and acquired the rest of SITA. Through its Elyo subsidiary, Suez Lyonnaise bought out minority shareholders in US-based Trigen Energy. The company also merged its construction unit, Groupe GTM, with French construction rival VINCI; Suez Lyonnaise then sold the VINCI shares that it received from the transaction.

The next year the company shortened its name to Suez (later modified to SUEZ) as part of a global rebranding effort. It also united its water services operations under the ONDEO brand. In 2002 SUEZ made Tractebel a wholly owned subsidiary by purchasing the remaining publicly held shares. Also in 2002, SUEZ sold minority stakes in communications equipment manufacturer Sagem (now SAFRAN), steelmaker Arcelor, and motorway operator Autopistas Concesionaria Española (ACESA).

SUEZ divested most of its 11% stake in Belgian insurance firm Fortis for nearly $2 billion in 2003. It also sold its 79% stake in cable company Coditel that year. In 2003 the company merged Tractebel and SGB (Tractebel's former holding company) to form SUEZ-TRACTEBEL.

Gaz de France was founded in 1946 by the French government to consolidate the more than 500 (mostly coal-fired) gas works that had existed before WWII. From 1949 on, Gaz de France focused on upgrading gas plants and local transmission networks. Its first long-distance pipeline was built in 1953, linking Paris to the Lorraine coal gas fields. With the development of the Lacq gas field in southwestern France, annual gas sales increased by 300% between 1957 and 1962.

By 1965 nearly half of the French population was supplied with natural gas. Spurred on by the loss of its Algerian colony, which held major oil and gas assets, the French government pushed for new gas supplies to supplement its Lacq resources. Gaz de France was able to secure a contract with Algerian natural gas supplier Sonatrach in 1965, and in 1967 it signed an import contract with Dutch supplier Gasunie. The company also diversified in the 1960s, helping to build a natural gas liquefaction plant in Algeria and a receiving terminal in Le Havre. It also helped pioneer gas storage engineering.

Following the price shock of the Arab oil embargo of the early 1970s, Gaz de France stepped up its search for alternative suppliers, including contracts with Russia's largest gas producer Soyouzgazexport (in 1976, 1980, and 1984) and four separate Norwegian producers, Efofisk (1977), Stafjord (1985), Heimdal (1986), and Gullfaks (1987). The company also renewed contracts with its Dutch and Algerian suppliers.

During the 1990s Gaz de France expanded

its international operations as deregulation in the industry accelerated. In 1994 the company gained a foothold in eastern Germany's gas sector by buying gas production and storage company Erdgas Erdol GmbH (EEG). Three years later Gaz de France acquired Italian heating and related services firm Agip Servizi and was awarded a joint venture contract to distribute gas in Berlin in 1997 and in the suburbs of Mexico City in 1998.

Through contracts for North Sea oil and gas with Elf Aquitaine (now owned by TOTAL FINA ELF), British-Borneo, and Ruhrgas in 1999, the company increased its natural gas supplies. It also established new gas supply contracts with Nigeria and Qatar.

For the first time in its history, Gaz de France became an offshore field operator in 2000 by acquiring exploration and production company TransCanada International Netherlands and a 39% stake in Noordgastransport BV, an offshore gas pipeline operator.

In 2001, through the purchase of a 10% interest in Petronet LNG, Gaz de France embarked on a project to import liquefied natural gas from Qatar to India.

France's energy and environmental services giants came together when SUEZ merged with Gaz de France in 2008 to form GDF SUEZ. As part of the merger agreement, and in order to clear hurdles set up by the EU competition policy, SUEZ then spun off its waste and water unit, SUEZ Environnement.

Following the 2008 merger of Gaz de France with SUEZ, in a move to expand geographically, GDF SUEZ acquired a 90% stake in Izmit Gaz Dagitim San Ve Tic AS (Turkey's third-largest natural gas distributor) for $232 million.

In 2009 the company made further geographic realignments, prompted by the regulatory requirements of the European Commission, for GDF SUEZ and Germany's E.ON to allow for more competition in their major markets by swapping some generation capacity. It acquired from E.ON 860 MW of Germany-based conventional power plants, 132 MW of hydroelectric plants, and through subsidiary Electrabel, access to 770 MW of nuclear power. In return GDF SUEZ sold to E.ON a similar amount of power generation capacity in France and the Benelux countries.

Ramping up its nuclear assets, in 2011 GDF SUEZ formed a joint venture with IBERDROLA and Scottish and Southern Energy. NuGeneration planned to develop up to 3,600 MW of nuclear power in the UK. Late in 2011 SSE announced plans to sell its 25 percent in NuGen to GDF SUEZ and IBERDROLA and return to its renewable energy strategy.

EXECUTIVES

Chief Executive Officer, Executive Director, Catherine MacGregor

Human Resources Executive Vice President, Jean-Sebastien Blanc
Transformation and Geographies Executive Vice President, Frank Demaille
Digital and Information Systems Executive Vice President, Yves Le Gelard
Finance, Corporate Social Responsibility and Procurement Executive Vice President, Pierre-Francois Riolacci
Executive Vice President, Jerome Stubler
Corporate Secretariat, Strategy, Research and Innovation, and Communication Executive Vice President, Claire Waysand
Chairman, Independent Director, Jean-Pierre Clamadieu
Independent Director, Fabrice Bregier
Independent Director, Francoise Malrieu
Independent Director, Ross McInnes
Independent Director, Marie-Jose Nadeau
Independent Director, Peter Ricketts
Director, Stephanie Besnier
Director, Patrice Durand
Director, Mari-Noelle Jego-Laveissiere
Director, Christophe Agogue
Director, Alain Beullier
Director, Philippe Lepage
Director, Jacinthe Delage
Auditors : ERNST & YOUNG et Autres

LOCATIONS

HQ: Engie SA
 1, Place Samuel de Champlain, Courbevoie 92400
Phone: (33) 1 44 22 00 00
Web: www.engie.com

2018 Sales

	% of total
Europe	
France	41
Belgium	10
Other EU countries	26
Other European countries	1
Asia, Middle East, and Oceania	8
North America	6
South America	7
Africa	1
Total	100

COMPETITORS

CLP HOLDINGS LIMITED
ENEL SPA
ENERGY TRANSFER LP
Fortum Oyj
IBERDROLA, SOCIEDAD ANONIMA
Infraestructura Energética Nova, S.A.B. de C.V.
KINDER MORGAN INC
TC Energy Corporation
THE WILLIAMS COMPANIES INC
Ørsted A/S

HISTORICAL FINANCIALS
Company Type: Public

Income Statement FYE: December 31

	REVENUE ($mil)	NET INCOME ($mil)	NET PROFIT MARGIN	EMPLOYEES
12/22	100,252	231	0.2%	96,454
12/21	65,496	4,143	6.3%	170,000
12/20	68,422	(1,885)	—	172,703
12/19	67,431	1,104	1.6%	171,103
12/18	69,394	1,182	1.7%	249,795
Annual Growth	9.6%	(33.5%)	—	(21.2%)

2022 Year-End Financials
Debt ratio: 17.3% No. of shares ($ mil.): 2,420
Return on equity: 0.6% Dividends
Cash ($ mil.): 16,629 Yield: —
Current Ratio: 1.11 Payout: 1041.0%
Long-term debt ($ mil.): 27,343 Market value ($ mil.): 34,568

	STOCK PRICE ($) FY Close	P/E High/Low		PER SHARE ($) Earnings	Dividends	Book Value
12/22	14.28	196	133	0.09	0.89	15.11
12/21	14.78	11	9	1.65	0.65	17.30
12/20	15.30	—	—	(0.87)	0.65	14.70
12/19	16.17	50	41	0.38	1.26	15.39
12/18	14.32	46	35	0.42	0.84	16.88
Annual Growth	(0.1%)	—	—	(33.0%)	1.6%	(2.7%)

ENI S.p.A.

Eni is a global energy company with a high technological content, engaged in the entire value chain: from exploration, development, and extraction of oil and natural gas, to the generation of electricity from cogeneration and renewable sources, traditional and bio refining and chemical, and the development of circular economy processes. Downstream, its portfolio of refineries, transmission networks and power generation plants sell fuels/biofuels, chemical products, lubricants, and gas & power. Outside its home country of Italy, Eni is active Africa, Europe, and North America as well as other productive gas regions such as Kazakhstan and Venezuela. Europe, which accounts for most of Eni's sales, is home to about 5,315 service stations.

Operations

Eni has five reporting segments: Refining & Marketing and Chemicals (over 50% of sales); Global Gas & LNG Portfolio (more than 20%); Exploration & Production (beyond 10%); Plenitude & Power (about 15%) and Corporate and Other activities.

The Refining & Marketing and Chemicals segment includes the supply, processing, distribution and marketing of fuels and chemicals. The results of the Chemicals segment were aggregated with the Refining & Marketing performance in a single reportable segment, because these two operating segments have similar economic returns. It comprises the activities of trading oil and products with the aim to execute the transactions on the market in order to balance the supply and stabilize and cover the commercial margins.

The Global Gas &LNG Portfolio (GGP) segment includes the supply and sale of wholesale natural gas via pipeline, international transport and purchase and marketing of LNG. It includes gas trading activities finalized to hedging and stabilizing the trade margins, as well as optimizing the gas asset portfolio.

The Exploration & Production segment includes the research, development and production of oil, condensates and natural gas, forestry conservation (REDD+) and CO2 capture and storage projects.

The Plenitude & Power segment includes the retail sales of gas, electricity and related services, production and wholesale sales of electricity from thermoelectric and renewable plants, services for E-mobility. It also includes trading activities of CO2 emission certificates and forward sale of electricity with a view to hedging/optimizing the margins of the electricity.

The Corporate and Other activities includes the main business support functions, in particular holding, central treasury, IT, human resources, real estate services, captive insurance activities, research and development, new technologies, business digitalization and the environmental activity developed by the subsidiary Eni Rewind.

Geographic Reach

Based in Rome, Italy, Eni is active in about 70 countries worldwide across Europe (Italy, Norway, and the UK), Africa (Algeria, Angola, Congo, Egypt, Ghana, Libya, Mozambique, Nigeria), the US, Venezuela, and Kazakhstan. Eni's about 5,315 service stations are located in Europe.

Europe accounts for nearly 75% of annual sales, Africa and Asia with around 10% of sales each and the Americas gives in roughly 5% of sales.

Sales and Marketing

The company's customers include households, large residential accounts (hospitals, schools, public administration buildings, offices) and small and medium-sized businesses.

Financial Performance

The company's revenue in 2021 increased by 73% to EUR 77.8 billion compared to EUR 44.9 billion in the prior year.

Profit in 2021 was EUR 5.8 billion compared to a net loss of EUR 8.6 billion in the prior year.

Cash held by the company at the end of 2021 decreased to EUR 8.3 billion. Operating activities provided EUR 12.9 billion while investing and financing activities used EUR 12.0 billion and EUR 2.0 billion, respectively. Main uses cash of were dividends paid, repayments of long-term debt and capital expenditures.

Strategy

Eni's strategy is defined in a scenario for the next four years characterized by a Brent price supported by current market dynamics, with a demand growth expected to recover pre-pandemic levels by 2022 and a limited supply from the production issues and financial discipline of the international oil companies.

Overall, the 2022-2025 plan projects a company with robust fundamentals and growing profitability, thanks to the transformation strategy implemented in response to downturn that, on the one hand, increased the resilience of traditional businesses and their ability to generate cash, and, on the other hand, created the conditions for a phase of strong development of the transition business, based on the integration of technologies, on new business models and on the closer collaboration with stakeholders. The expected results in the next four years will make Eni's carbon neutrality strategy by 2050 more solid, thanks to the growing visibility of the intermediate targets and the steps closer.

Mergers and Acquisitions

In 2022, Eni has agreed to acquire BP business in Algeria, including the two gas-producing concessions "In Amenas" and "In Salah" (45.89% and 33.15% working interest respectively). This acquisition has a great strategic value to further contribute to Europe's gas needs and further strengthens Eni's presence in Algeria, a major gas producer and a key country in for Eni. Terms were not disclosed.

In mid-2022, Eni has acquired the company Export LNG Ltd, which owns the Tango FLNG floating liquefaction facility, from Exmar group. The facility will be used by Eni in the Republic of Congo, as part of the activities of the natural gas development project in the Marine XII block, in line with Eni's strategy to leverage gas equity resources. Terms were not disclosed.

In early 2022, Eni, through Eni gas e luce, which will become Plenitude this year, has acquired the Greek company Solar Konzept Greece ("SKGR") from Solar Konzept International which is majority owned by Aquila Capital, a sustainable investment and asset development company, based in Hamburg, Germany. SKGR owns a photovoltaic plants' development platform in Greece. SKGR's portfolio includes a pipeline of projects at various stages of development, totalling around 800 MW. These projects form the basis for further development in the country. Terms were not disclosed.

In mid-2021, ni, through Eni gas e luce, today signed an agreement to acquire 100% of Be Power S.p.A., which through its subsidiary Be Charge is the second largest Italian operator with over 5 thousand electric vehicle charging points on public land. Be Power owns the Be Charge branded charging infrastructures installed on public and private land and holds the relevant concessions. With the acquisition of Be Power, Eni takes a leadership position in a market at the heart of the European Union's energy transition strategy. Terms were not disclosed.

HISTORY

Although the Italian parliament formed Ente Nazionale Idrocarburi (National Hydrocarbon Agency) in 1953, Enrico Mattei is the true father of Eni. In 1945 Mattei, a partisan leader during WWII, was appointed northern commissioner of Agip, a state-owned petroleum company founded in 1926 by Mussolini, and ordered to liquidate the company. Mattei instead ordered the exploration of the Po Valley, where workers found methane gas deposits in 1946.

When Eni was created in 1953, Mattei was named president. His job was to find energy resources for an oil-poor country. He initiated a series of joint ventures with several Middle Eastern and African nations, offering better deals than his large oil company rivals, which he dubbed the Seven Sisters.

Mattei didn't stick to energy: By the time he died in a mysterious plane crash in 1962, Eni had acquired machinery manufacturer Pignone, finance company Sofid, Milan newspaper Il Giorno, and textile company Lane Rossi. Eni grew during the 1960s, partly because of a deal made for Soviet crude in 1958 and a joint venture with Esso in 1963. It also expanded its chemical activities.

By the early 1970s losses in Eni's chemical and textile operations, the oil crisis, and the Italian government's dumping of unprofitable companies on Eni hurt its bottom line. Former finance minister Franco Reviglio took over in 1983 and began cutting inefficient operations.

EniChem merged with Montedison, Italy's largest private chemical company, in 1988, but clashes between the public agency and the private company made Montedison sell back its stake in 1990. Eni became a joint stock company in 1992, but the government retained a majority stake.

Franco Bernabe took over Eni following a 1993 bribery scandal and began cutting noncore businesses. The Italian government began selling Eni stock in 1995. In 1996 Eni signed on to develop Libyan gas resources and build a pipeline to Italy. A year later the company merged its Agipa exploration and production subsidiary into its main operations. Eni also took a 35% stake in Italian telecom company Albacom (which has since been sold to British Telecom Group).

The government cut its stake in Eni from 51% to 38% in 1998. That year Vittorio Mincato, a company veteran, succeeded Bernabe as CEO. In 1999 Eni and Russia's RAO Gazprom, the world's largest natural gas production firm, agreed to build a controversial $3 billion natural gas pipeline stretching from Russia to Turkey. Eni agreed to invest $5.5 billion to develop oil and gas reserves in Libya; it also sold interests in

Saipem and Nuovo Pignone, as well as some of its Italian service stations.

In 2000 Eni paid about $910 million for a 33% stake in Galp, a Portuguese oil and gas company that also has natural gas utility operations. Also that year Eni bought British-Borneo Oil & Gas in a $1.2 billion deal, and in 2001 it paid $4 billion for UK independent exploration and production company LASMO, topping a bid by US-based Amerada Hess.

The Italian government sold off another 5% of Eni in 2001, reducing its stake to about 30%, and announced that it was considering selling its entire investment. In an effort to reduce noncore holdings, the company sold property management subsidiary Immobiliare Metanopoli to Goldman Sachs. Also that year Eni sold a minority stake in its gas pipeline unit, Snam Rete Gas, to the public.

In 2002 Eni entered discussions to acquire Enterprise Oil, but lost out to a rival bid from Royal Dutch Shell. Later that year Eni's oil field services unit Saipem gained control of Bouygues Offshore. In 2006 Eni and Gazprom formed an international alliance to launch joint mid and downstream gas projects, and collaborate in upstream and in technological activities.

EXECUTIVES

Energy Evolution Chief Operating Officer, Giuseppe Ricci
Natural Resources Chief Operating Officer, Alessandro Pultri
Chief Financial Officer, Francesco Gattei
Human Capital and Procurement Coordination Chief Services & Stakeholder Relations Officer, Claudio Granata
Technology Director, Research & Development Director, Digital Director, Francesca Zarri
Commercial Negotiations Director, Legal Affairs Director, Stefano Speroni
Internal Audit Director, Gianfranco Cariola
Governance Director, Corporate Affairs Director, Corporate Governance Director, Corporate Governance Senior Executive Vice President, Governance Senior Executive Vice President, Corporate Affairs Senior Executive Vice President, Roberto Ulissi
Chief Executive Officer, Director, Claudio Descalzi
External Communication Director, Erika Mandraffino
International Affairs Director, Public Affairs Director, Lapo Pistelli
Integrated Risk Management Director, Grazia Fimiani
Integrated Compliance Counsel, Legal & Regulatory Compliance Counsel, Integrated Compliance Secretary, Legal & Regulatory Compliance Secretary, Integrated Compliance Director, Legal & Regulatory Compliance Director, Luca Franceschini
Non-Executive Chairman, Lucia Calvosa
Independent Non-Executive Director, Ada Lucia De Cesaris
Independent Non-Executive Director, Pietro A. Guindani
Independent Non-Executive Director, Karina A. Litvack
Independent Non-Executive Director, Emanuele Piccinno
Independent Non-Executive Director, Nathalie Tocci
Independent Non-Executive Director, Raphael Loius L. Vermeir
Non-Executive Director, Filippo Giansante
Auditors : PricewaterhouseCoopers SpA

LOCATIONS

HQ: ENI S.p.A.
 Piazzale Enrico Mattei 1, Rome 00144
Phone: (39) 6 59821 **Fax:** (39) 6 59822575
Web: www.eni.com

2018 Sales

	% of total
Europe	
Italy	33
Other EU countries	27
Other countries	9
Asia	13
Africa	11
Americas	7
Total	100

PRODUCTS/OPERATIONS

2018 Sales

	% of total
Gas & power	57
Refining & marketing and chemicals	30
Exploration & production	13
Corporate & other activities	-
Total	100

Selected Subsidiaries and Affiliates

Distrigas NV (gas, Belgium)
EniPower SpA (power generation)
Italgas SpA (natural gas supply)
Saipem SpA (42.9%, oil field services)
Snam Rete Gas SpA (52.5%, gas pipeline)
Snamprogetti SpA (contracting and engineering)

COMPETITORS

COMPAÑIA ESPAÑOLA DE PETROLEOS SAU
COSMO OIL CO., LTD.
GAZPROM NEFT, PAO
HELLENIC PETROLEUM S.A.
LUKOIL, PAO
MOL Magyar Olaj- és Gázipari Nyilvánosan Működő Részvénytársaság
NK ROSNEFT, PAO
OMV Aktiengesellschaft
Petroleo Brasileiro S A Petrobras
Suncor Energy Inc

HISTORICAL FINANCIALS

Company Type: Public

Income Statement FYE: December 31

	REVENUE ($mil)	NET INCOME ($mil)	NET PROFIT MARGIN	EMPLOYEES
12/22	142,784	14,831	10.4%	32,188
12/21	88,026	6,588	7.5%	32,689
12/20	55,162	(10,597)	—	31,495
12/19	79,762	166	0.2%	32,053
12/18	88,109	4,725	5.4%	31,701
Annual Growth	12.8%	33.1%	—	0.4%

2022 Year-End Financials

Debt ratio: 18.9%
Return on equity: 27.9%
Cash ($ mil.): 10,845
Current Ratio: 1.26
Long-term debt ($ mil.): 20,692
No. of shares ($ mil.): 3,345
Dividends
Yield: —
Payout: 30.7%
Market value ($ mil.): 95,879

	STOCK PRICE ($) FY Close	P/E High/Low		PER SHARE ($) Earnings	Dividends	Book Value
12/22	28.66	8	6	4.22	1.30	17.48
12/21	27.65	18	12	1.81	1.11	14.21
12/20	20.60	—	—	(2.97)	0.85	12.85
12/19	30.96	895	726	0.04	1.33	15.03
12/18	31.50	33	26	1.32	1.37	16.22
Annual Growth	(2.3%)	—	—	33.8%	(1.4%)	1.9%

ENN Energy Holdings Ltd

EXECUTIVES

Chairman, Executive Director, Yusuo Wang
Vice-Chairman, Executive Director, Hongtao Zheng
President, Executive Director, Xiaojing Wu
Chief Human Resources Officer, Jin Zhang
Chief Financial Officer, Jianfeng Liu
Executive Vice President, Liang Xiong
Chief Digital Officer, Zhenping Huang
Senior Vice President, Li Su
Financial Controller, Nini Mu
Secretary, Mui Yin Leung
Executive Director, Dongzhi Wang
Independent Non-Executive Director, Zhixiang Ma
Independent Non-Executive Director, Po Kwong Yuen
Independent Non-Executive Director, Quinn Yee Kwan Law
Independent Non-Executive Director, Catherine Yu Yu Yien
Non-Executive Director, Zizheng Wang
Non-Executive Director, Yongsheng Jin
Non-Executive Director, Yuying Zhang
Auditors : Deloitte Touche Tohmatsu

LOCATIONS

HQ: ENN Energy Holdings Ltd
 Room 3101–04, 31st Floor, Tower 1, Lippo Centre, No. 89 Queensway,
Phone: (852) 2528 5666 **Fax:** (852) 2865 7204
Web: www.ennenergy.com

HISTORICAL FINANCIALS
Company Type: Public

Income Statement   FYE: December 31

	REVENUE ($mil)	NET INCOME ($mil)	NET PROFIT MARGIN	EMPLOYEES
12/21	14,666	1,221	8.3%	0
12/20	10,950	959	8.8%	0
12/19	10,086	814	8.1%	0
12/18	8,824	409	4.6%	0
12/17	7,417	430	5.8%	0
Annual Growth	18.6%	29.8%		

2021 Year-End Financials
Debt ratio: 3.1%
Return on equity: 23.3%
Cash ($ mil.): 1,367
Current Ratio: 0.66
Long-term debt ($ mil.): 1,266
No. of shares ($ mil.): 1,127
Dividends
  Yield: 1.9%
  Payout: 140.9%
Market value ($ mil.): 86,199

	STOCK PRICE ($) FY Close	P/E High	P/E Low	Earnings	Dividends	Book Value
12/21	76.46	13	9	1.08	1.50	5.00
12/20	58.88	11	6	0.85	0.81	4.15
12/19	43.72	9	7	0.72	0.56	3.31
12/18	35.31	17	10	0.37	0.50	2.77
12/17	28.90	12	7	0.40	0.39	2.41
Annual Growth	27.5%	—	—	28.4%	39.9%	20.1%

EQB Inc

EXECUTIVES
Chairman, Director, David M. B. LeGresley
President, Chief Executive Officer, Executive Director, Andrew Moor
Senior Vice President, Chief Risk Officer, Ron Tratch
Senior Vice President, Chief Financial Officer, Chadwick Westlake
Senior Vice President, Chief Information Officer, Dan Dickinson
Senior Vice President, Chief Human Resources Officer, Jody Sperling
Senior Vice President, Darren Lorimer
Senior Vice President, Mahima Poddar
Director, Eric Beutel
Director, Michael R. Emory
Director, Susan Ericksen
Director, Diane Giard
Director, Kishore Kapoor
Director, Yongah Kim
Director, Lynn McDonald
Director, Rowan Saunders
Director, Vincenza Sera
Director, Michael P. Stramaglia
Auditors : KPMG LLP

LOCATIONS
HQ: EQB Inc
  Equitable Bank Tower, 30 St. Clair Avenue West, Suite 700, Toronto, Ontario M4V 3A1
Phone: —
Web: www.equitablebank.ca

HISTORICAL FINANCIALS
Company Type: Public

Income Statement   FYE: December 31

	ASSETS ($mil)	NET INCOME ($mil)	INCOME AS % OF ASSETS	EMPLOYEES
12/22	37,817	195	0.5%	1,685
12/21	28,390	226	0.8%	1,161
12/20	24,147	172	0.7%	925
12/19	21,803	154	0.7%	900
12/18	18,385	118	0.6%	669
Annual Growth	19.8%	13.4%	—	26.0%

2022 Year-End Financials
Return on assets: 0.6%
Return on equity: 11.7%
Long-term debt ($ mil.): —
No. of shares ($ mil.): 37
Sales ($ mil.): 1,231
Dividends
  Yield: —
  Payout: 16.0%
Market value ($ mil.): 1,560

	STOCK PRICE ($) FY Close	P/E High	P/E Low	Earnings	Dividends	Book Value
12/22	41.53	8	4	5.58	0.89	49.90
12/21	54.56	14	7	6.56	0.58	45.00
12/20	76.06	13	6	5.09	0.58	38.35
12/19	84.98	15	8	4.60	0.50	33.55
12/18	43.67	10	8	3.55	0.40	28.39
Annual Growth	(1.2%)	—	—	12.0%	22.6%	15.1%

Equinor ASA

EXECUTIVES
Technology, Projects & Drilling President, Technology, Projects & Drilling Chief Executive Officer, Anders Opedal
Development & Production International Chief Financial Officer, Development & Production International Executive Vice President, Torgrim Reitan
Safety, Security and Sustainability Executive Vice President, Jannicke Nilsson
Exploration and Production Norway Executive Vice President, Kjetil Hove
Global Strategy & Business Development Executive Vice President, Exploration and Production International Executive Vice President, Alasdair Cook
Technology, Projects and Drilling Executive Vice President, Projects, Drilling and Procurement Executive Vice President, Geir Tungesvik
Marketing, Midstream & Processing Executive Vice President, Irene Rummelhoff
Renewables Executive Vice President, Pal Eitrheim
Executive Vice President, Chief Technical Officer, Hege Skryseth
Legal and Compliance Executive Vice President, Legal and Compliance General Counsel, Siv Helen Rygh Torstensen
Communications Executive Vice President, Jannik Lindbaek
People and Organization Executive Vice President, Aksel Stenerud

---

Independent Non-Executive Chairman, Jon Erik Reinhardsen
Deputy Chair, Independent Non-Executive Director, Anne Drinkwater
Independent Non-Executive Director, Rebekka Glasser Herlofsen
Independent Non-Executive Director, Jonathan Lewis
Independent Non-Executive Director, Finn Bjorn Ruyter
Independent Non-Executive Director, Tove Andersen
Non-Executive Director, Stig Laegreid
Non-Executive Director, Per Martin Labraten
Non-Executive Director, Hilde Mollerstad
Independent Director, Haakon Bruun-Hanssen
Auditors : Ernst & Young AS

LOCATIONS
HQ: Equinor ASA
  Forusbeen 50, Stavanger N-4035
Phone: (47) 51 99 00 00   **Fax:** (47) 51 99 00 50
Web: www.equinor.com

HISTORICAL FINANCIALS
Company Type: Public

Income Statement   FYE: December 31

	REVENUE ($mil)	NET INCOME ($mil)	NET PROFIT MARGIN	EMPLOYEES
12/22	150,806	28,746	19.1%	21,500
12/21	90,924	8,563	9.4%	21,126
12/20	45,818	(5,510)	—	21,245
12/19	64,357	1,843	2.9%	21,412
12/18	79,593	7,535	9.5%	20,525
Annual Growth	17.3%	39.8%	—	1.2%

2022 Year-End Financials
Debt ratio: 18.0%
Return on equity: 61.8%
Cash ($ mil.): 15,579
Current Ratio: 1.77
Long-term debt ($ mil.): 24,141
No. of shares ($ mil.): 3,121
Dividends
  Yield: —
  Payout: 18.6%
Market value ($ mil.): 111,797

	STOCK PRICE ($) FY Close	P/E High	P/E Low	Earnings	Dividends	Book Value
12/22	35.81	5	3	9.03	1.68	17.29
12/21	26.33	11	6	2.63	0.56	12.07
12/20	16.42	—	—	(1.69)	0.71	10.43
12/19	19.91	43	29	0.56	1.01	12.36
12/18	21.17	13	9	2.27	0.91	12.91
Annual Growth	14.0%	—	—	41.2%	16.6%	7.6%

Ericsson

EXECUTIVES
President, Chief Executive Officer, Director, Borje E. Ekholm
Business Area Networks Executive Vice President, Fredrik Jejdling
Chief People Officer, Senior Vice President, MajBritt Arfert
Senior Vice President, Chief Legal Officer, Secretary, Scott Dresser

Senior Vice President, Chief Technology Officer, Erik Ekudden
Global Operations Senior Vice President, Moti Gyamlani
Market Area North America Senior Vice President, Niklas Heuveldop
Market Area North East Asia Senior Vice President, Chris Houghton
Market Area Europe and Latin America Senior Vice President, Jenny Lindqvist
Senior Vice President, Chief Marketing and Communications Officer, Stella Medlicott
Senior Vice President, Chief Financial Officer, Carl Mellander
Market Area South East Asia Senior Vice President, Nunzio Mirtillo
Business Area Enterprise Wireless Solutions Senior Vice President, George Mulhern
Business Area Cloud Software and Services Senior Vice President, Per Narvinger
Market Area Middle East and Africa Senior Vice President, Fadi Pharaon
Business Area Global Communications Platform Senior Vice President, Rory P. Read
Business Area Technologies and New Businesses Senior Vice President, Asa Tamsons
Chairman, Ronnie Leten
Deputy Chairman, Helena Stjernholm
Deputy Chairman, Jacob Wallenberg
Director, Jon Fredrik Baksaas
Director, Jan Carlson
Director, Nora M. Denzel
Director, Carolina Dybeck Happe
Director, Eric A. Elzvik
Director, Kurt Jofs
Director, Kristin S. Rinne
Auditors : Deloitte AB

LOCATIONS

HQ: Ericsson
Torshamnsgatan 21, Kista, Stockholm SE-164 83
Phone: (46) 10 719 0000
Web: www.ericsson.com

HISTORICAL FINANCIALS

Company Type: Public

Income Statement — FYE: December 31

	REVENUE ($mil)	NET INCOME ($mil)	NET PROFIT MARGIN	EMPLOYEES
12/23	26,302	(2,641)	—	99,952
12/22	26,177	1,805	6.9%	105,529
12/21	25,642	2,504	9.8%	101,322
12/20	28,443	2,139	7.5%	100,824
12/19	24,425	238	1.0%	99,417
Annual Growth	1.9%	—	—	0.1%

2023 Year-End Financials

Debt ratio: 1.6%
Return on equity: (-22.6%)
Cash ($ mil.): 3,514
Current Ratio: 1.20
Long-term debt ($ mil.): 2,918
No. of shares ($ mil.): 3,330
Dividends
Yield: —
Payout: 0.0%
Market value ($ mil.): 20,980

	STOCK PRICE ($) FY Close	P/E High/Low		PER SHARE ($) Earnings	Dividends	Book Value
12/23	6.30	—	—	(0.79)	0.27	2.96
12/22	5.84	2	1	0.54	0.24	3.90
12/21	10.87	2	1	0.75	0.23	3.61
12/20	11.95	3	1	0.64	0.16	3.19
12/19	8.78	16	12	0.07	0.11	2.68
Annual Growth	(8.0%)	—	—	—	25.8%	2.5%

Erste Group Bank AG

Erste Group Bank is the holding company of Erste Bank, Austria's first savings bank founded in 1819. However, the company has grown beyond its home country to number around 2,090 branches throughout Central and Eastern European that serve more than 16 million customers. The company has operating subsidiaries in Austria, Croatia, the Czech Republic, Hungary, Slovakia, Serbia, and Romania, as well as an indirect presence in four other countries in the region. Erste Group banks provide financial services, such as savings and lending to individuals and small to medium-size businesses. About half of its sales were generated from Austria.

Operations

The company operates in two geographic segments: Austria and Central and Eastern Europe, both generated half of the company's sales.

Its Austria segment comprises of the Erste Bank Oesterreich & Subsidiaries (EBOe & Subsidiaries) which includes the Erste Bank der oesterreichischen Sparkassen AG (Erste Bank Oesterreich) and its main subsidiaries (e.g. sBausparkasse, Salzburger Sparkasse, Tiroler Sparkasse, Sparkasse Hainburg); the Savings Banks segment which includes those savings banks that are members of the Haftungsverbund (cross-guarantee system) of the Austrian savings banks sector; and other Austria segment comprises Erste Group Bank AG (Holding) with its Corporates and Group Markets business, Erste Group Immorent GmbH, Erste Asset Management GmbH and Intermarket Bank AG.

Its Central and Eastern Europe (CEE) consists of the following six operating segments covering Erste Group's banking subsidiaries located in the respective CEE countries: Czech Republic (comprising Ceská sporitelna Group), Slovakia (comprising Slovenská sporitelna Group), Romania (comprising Banca Comerciala Română Group), Hungary (comprising Erste Bank Hungary Group), Croatia (comprising Erste Bank Croatia Group) and Serbia (comprising Erste Bank Serbia Group).

Overall, net interest income generated around 65% of sales, net fee & commission income with nearly 30%, and net trading result and gains/losses from financial instruments at FVPL with roughly 5%.

In addition, some 45% were generated from retail, about 25% from savings bank, over 20% from corporates, and group markets with nearly 10%.

Geographic Reach

Vienna, Austria-based, Erste Bank is home to some 820 branches in Austria, the most of any country. The Czech Republic has nearly 420 Erste branches, Romania with around 325, Slovakia with some 200, Croatia around 135, Hungary some 105, and Serbia over 85.

Sales and Marketing

The company serves some 3.9 million customers in Austria, 4.5 million in Czech Republic, 2.1 million in Slovakia, 0.9 million in Hungary, 2.9 million in Romania, 0.5 million in Serbia, and 1.3 million in Croatia.

Advertising and marketing expenses for the years 2021 and 2020 EUR 167.5 million and EUR 154.6 million, respectively.

Financial Performance

The company's revenue in 2021 increased to EUR 7.3 billion compared to EUR 6.8 billion in the prior year.

Net income in 2021 increased to EUR 2.4 billion compared to EUR 1.0 billion in the prior year.

Cash held by the company at the end of 2021 increased to EUR 45.5 billion. Operating activities provided EUR 11.4 billion while investing and financing activities used EUR 483.4 million and EUR 1.3 billion, respectively. Main cash uses were property and equipment and intangible assets; and dividends paid to equity holders of the parent.

Strategy

Erste Group strives to be the leading retail and corporate bank in the eastern part of the European Union, including Austria. To achieve this goal, Erste Group aims to support its retail, corporate and public sector customers in realizing their ambitions and ensuring financial health by offering excellent financial advice and solutions, lending responsibly and providing a safe harbor for deposits. Erste Group's business activities will continue to contribute to economic growth and financial stability and thus to prosperity in its region.

In all of its core markets in the eastern part of the European Union, Erste Group pursues a balanced business model focused on providing the best banking services to each of its customers. In this respect, digital innovations are playing an increasingly important role. The sustainability of the business model is reflected in the bank's ability to fund customer loans by customer deposits, with most customer deposits being stable retail deposits. The sustainability of the bank's strategy is reflected in long-term client trust, which underpins strong market shares in almost all of Erste Group's core markets. However, market leadership is not an end in itself. Market leadership creates value only when it goes hand in hand with positive economies of scale and contributes to the long-term success of the company.

HISTORY

In 1819 a bank was born, and its name was Erste oesterreichische Spar-Cassa. Called Die Erste for short, the bank was Austria's first commercial and savings bank. Unlike Austria's community savings banks, Die Erste was independent -- not backed by government guarantees.

For more than 150 years, Die Erste operated as a local savings bank serving Vienna. Then in 1979 the Austrian government passed a law that would alter the face of the banking industry in that country. The Banking Act of 1979 placed banks and savings institutions in direct competition with each other by allowing them both to take part in all aspects of the banking business. As a result of the enhanced competition, Die Erste began expanding its domestic branch network.

Meanwhile, the Austrian savings banks had established their own central institution in 1937 and called it Girovereinigung der Ã–sterreichischen Sparkassen, or Girozentrale for short. Girozentrale focused on managing the liquidity reserves of the savings banks and helping them with their syndication and securities businesses. The bank also endeavored to improve the non-cash payment system and to promote mortgage savings. Concentrating on international and investment banking rather than retail banking, Girozentrale eventually became the country's third-largest bank.

Throughout the late 1980s and into the 1990s, rumors began to spread about a possible merger between Girozentrale and Die Erste (both were associated with the nation's conservative People's Party). In 1992 Girozentrale merged with Ã–sterreichisches Credit-Institut (Ã–CI) to create GiroCredit, giving the central savings bank a branch network for the first time. But it also made GiroCredit a direct competitor with its two largest shareholders -- Bank Austria (now part of HypoVereinsbank) and Die Erste, who were also fierce competitors with each other.

Between 1992 and 1994 Die Erste and Bank Austria struggled to find a solution to the problem of GiroCredit's ownership. In 1994 Bank Austria emerged the victor by winning the majority stake in GiroCredit in a move that was characterized by Die Erste as "unfriendly."

Throughout the next two years Die Erste attempted to secure a stake in Creditanstalt, Austria's second-biggest bank, as the Austrian government began moves to privatize it. Die Erste acted as a part of a consortium of Austrian, German, and Italian entities interested in obtaining stakes in the bank. But in 1997 Bank Austria won that battle too, managing to take over Creditanstalt. In turn, Die Erste bought Bank Austria's majority stake in GiroCredit. The resulting company was given the name Erste Bank, which went public that year in the largest stock issue in Austrian history. In 1998 it became the first major Austrian company to allow for the election of small shareholder representatives to its supervisory board.

In 2000 Erste Bank bought a majority stake in CeskÃ Sporitelna, the largest retail bank in the Czech Republic, from the Czech government. Later in the year the Slovak government allowed Erste Bank to become a major shareholder in the previously state-owned SlovenskÃ sporitel'na. Erste Bank was also one of several Austrian banks to be accused by the European Commission of fixing foreign exchange fees.

In 2001 Erste Bank took control of SlovenskÃ Sporitel'na and acquired majority ownership of Tiroler Sparkasse Bank AG. The following year Erste Bank took full control of Czech Republic-based Czeska Sporitelna. Ever acquisitive, in 2005 the company completed its acquisition of Serbia's Novosadska banka.

Erste in 2006 acquired Romanian bank Banca Comerciala Romana, the largest bank in that country, and previously state-owned.

Erste switched to a holding company structure in 2008. That year the company also sold most of its insurance business to Vienna Insurance Group.

EXECUTIVES

Chairman, Willibald Cernko
Chief Corporates and Markets Officer, Info Bleier
Chief Financial Officer, Stefan Dorfler
Chief Risk Officer, Alexandra Habeler-Drabek
Chief Operating Officer, David O'Mahony
Chief Platform Officer, Maurizio Poletto
Chairman, Friedrich Rodler
1st Vice Chairman, Maximilian Hardegg
2nd Vice Chairwoman, Elisabeth Krainer Senger-Weiss
Supervisory Board Member, Christine Catasta
Supervisory Board Member, Henrietta Egerth-Stadlhuber
Supervisory Board Member, Alois Flatz
Supervisory Board Member, Hikmet Ersek
Supervisory Board Member, Marion Khuny
Supervisory Board Member, Friedrich Santner
Supervisory Board Member, Michael Schuster
Supervisory Board Member, Andras Simor
Supervisory Board Member, Michele F. Sutter-Rudisser
Supervisory Board Member, Martin Grieber
Supervisory Board Member, Markus Haag
Supervisory Board Member, Regina Haberhauer
Supervisory Board Member, Andreas Lachs
Supervisory Board Member, Barbara Pichler
Supervisory Board Member, Jozef Pinter
Supervisory Board Member, Karin Zeisel
Auditors : Sparkassen-Prufungsverband (Prufungsstelle)

LOCATIONS

HQ: Erste Group Bank AG
Am Belvedere 1, Vienna A-1100
Phone: (43) 5 0100 10100
Web: www.erstegroup.com

PRODUCTS/OPERATIONS

2017 Sales

	% of total
Net interest income	67
Net fee & commission income	36
Net trading result	1
Total	100

Selected Subsidiaries
Banca Comerciala Romana S.A. (BCR)
Ceská Sporitelna (Czech Republic)
Erste Bank a.d. Novi Sad (Serbia)
Erste Bank Croatia (Erste & Steiermärkische Bank d.d.)
Erste Bank der oesterreichen Sparkassen AG
    Autoleasing EBV
    Sparkasse Salzburg
    Wohnbaubank
Erst Bank Hungary Nyrt.
Erste Bank Ukraine (formerly Bank Prestige)
Slovenská sporitelna, a.s. (Slovakia)

COMPETITORS

Bayerische Landesbank
COMMERZBANK AG
DEUTSCHE BANK AG
DZ BANK AG Deutsche Zentral-Genossenschaftsbank, Frankfurt am Main
KfW
Nordea Bank AB
Portigon AG
Raiffeisen Zentralbank Ã–sterreich Aktiengesellschaft
UniCredit Bank AG
WESTPAC BANKING CORPORATION

HISTORICAL FINANCIALS

Company Type: Public

Income Statement   FYE: December 31

	ASSETS ($mil)	NET INCOME ($mil)	INCOME AS % OF ASSETS	EMPLOYEES
12/22	345,902	2,311	0.7%	44,957
12/21	347,967	2,177	0.6%	44,596
12/20	340,442	961	0.3%	45,690
12/19	275,856	1,650	0.6%	47,284
12/18	271,173	2,053	0.8%	47,397
Annual Growth	6.3%	3.0%	—	(1.3%)

2022 Year-End Financials
Return on assets: 0.6%   Dividends
Return on equity: 11.5%   Yield: —
Long-term debt ($ mil.): —   Payout: 11.0%
No. of shares ($ mil.): 407   Market value ($ mil.): 6,492
Sales ($ mil.): 14,869

	STOCK PRICE ($) FY Close	P/E High/Low		PER SHARE ($) Earnings	Dividends	Book Value
12/22	15.95	5	2	5.16	0.57	50.75
12/21	23.90	6	3	4.72	0.58	50.24
12/20	15.16	14	6	1.93	0.00	52.48
12/19	18.76	7	5	3.63	0.76	42.97
12/18	16.53	6	4	4.60	0.68	40.29
Annual Growth	(0.9%)		—	2.9%	(4.3%)	5.9%

EssilorLuxottica

EssilorLuxottica is one of the world's leading makers of ophthalmic lenses, frames, and sunglasses for both wholesale and retail customers. The vertically-integrated company offers lens technology (including the Varilux and Transitions brands), eyewear (Ray-Ban and Oakley, among other brands), and retail brands such as LensCrafters and Sunglass Hut. In all, it has more than 150 brands and some 18,000 retail locations. The company operates worldwide but generates more 45% of its sales from North America. Essilor International merged with Luxottica, the world's largest eyewear maker, in 2018 to form EssilorLuxottica.

Operations

EssilorLuxottica operates through two new segments: Professional Solutions (PS) and Direct to Consumer (DTC).

The DTC segment (more than 50%) represents the retail business of the company. The supply of the company's products and services directly to the end consumer either through the network of physical stores operated by the company (brick and mortar) or the online channel (e-commerce).

The PS segment (almost 50%) represents the wholesale business of the company. The supply of the company's products and services to all the professionals of the eyecare industry (distributors, opticians, independents, third-party e-commerce platforms, etc.).

Overall, products generate nearly 95% of total revenue, while managed vision care, eye-exam and related professional fees, and franchisee royalties account for the remaining 5%.

Geographic Reach

EssilorLuxottica is based in Paris, France, and has manufacturing and logistics facilities, distribution networks and human capital well balanced and diversified across more than 150 countries.

More than 45% of the company's revenue comes from North America, about 45% generated from EMEA, while roughly 10% of revenue comes from Asia Pacific, and around 5% from Latin America.

Sales and Marketing

EssilorLuxottica serves eye care professionals across the globe, including independent opticians as well as optometrists, cooperatives, central purchasing agencies and retail optical banners.

Financial Performance

The company reported a total revenue of EUR 24.5 billion in 2022, a 24% increase from the previous year's total revenue of EUR 19.8 billion. The company had higher volumes of sales in both of its segments.

Net income for 2022 was EUR 2.2 billion, a 49% increase from the previous year's net income of EUR 1.4 billion. This was primarily due to the higher volume of sales for the year.

The company's cash at the end of 2022 was EUR 2 billion. Operating activities generated EUR 4.8 billion, while investing activities used EUR 2.6 billion, mainly for purchase of property, plant and equipment and intangible assets. Financing activities used another EUR 3.6 billion, primarily for cash payments for principal portion of lease liabilities.

Strategy

EssilorLuxottica leverages over 170 years of pioneering innovation, operational excellence, entrepreneurial spirit and international mindset. It develops eye care and eyewear solutions that meet the world's growing vision care demands and changing consumer lifestyles, while inventing new ways to reach people who suffer from uncorrected vision. The company's business model covers the industry's value chain and draws on the complementary expertise of two industry pioneers, one in advanced lens technologies and the other in the craftsmanship of iconic eyewear. It offers a set of solutions for consumers and eye care professionals, focusing on the quality of its products and services as a strategic differentiating factor.

The creation of the perfect complete pair has become a reality, with both glasses and frames designed and manufactured in an integrated way from the very start. Each frame has a unique and perfectly fitted lens to accompany it, leading to a seamless brand experience with Ray-Ban Authentic being the company's most prominent example.

Mergers and Acquisitions

In 2022, EssilorLuxottica acquired US-based lab network Walman Optical, a leading lab partner to vision care practices around the country. The acquisition draws on EssilorLuxottica's focus on product and service innovation to create growth opportunities for Walman Optical.

HISTORY

EssilorLuxxotica's roots go back to the 1849 formation of the Association Confraternelle des Ouvriers Lunetiers, a workers cooperative of eyeglass makers that became the Societe des Lunetiers, then S & L, and finally in the 20th century, Essel. An Essel engineer invented the Varilux lens in 1959.

Increased international competition in the 1960s spurred the 1972 merger of Essel and rival Silor, a maker of lenses and frames. Silor, founded by optician Georges Lissac, brought with it the Orma shock-resistant organic glass lens it had developed in 1956.

After the merger, Essilor focused on international expansion, setting its sights first on the US. Building on its parents' established presence in that country, the company partnered with biomedical firm Milton Roy to open a plant in 1974; Essilor bought out its partner the next year. The company went public in 1975.

Throughout the 1970s and 1980s the firm continued to expand its geographic reach and improve and expand its products. By the end of the 1980s Essilor had become a prominent player in the optics market.

Essilor experienced a sales slump in the early 1990s and responded by cutting jobs and restructuring operations worldwide. Sales of Varilux lenses, plus the introduction of a new product line (Crizal antireflective lenses) in 1992, helped the firm rebound by the mid-1990s. Essilor then continued its global expansion, entering or expanding its presence in such countries as Australia, China, India, and the US through acquisitions and joint ventures with Oakley (1996), Gerber Scientific (1997), Bausch & Lomb (1997), and SRF (1998), and Nikon (1999), among others.

EXECUTIVES

Chief Executive Officer, Non-Independent Director, Francesco Milleri
Deputy Chief Executive, Non-Independent Director, Paul du Saillant
Executive Chairman, Non-Independent Director, Leonardo del Vecchio
Independent Director, Marie-Christine Coisne-Roquette
Independent Director, José Gonzalo
Independent Director, Nathalie von Siemens
Independent Director, Andrea Zappia
Independent Director, Cristina Scocchia
Independent Director, Swati A. Piramal
Independent Director, Jean-luc Biamonti
Non-Independent Director, Margot Bard
Non-Independent Director, Juliette Favre
Non-Independent Director, Romolo Bardin
Director, Léonel Pereira Ascenção
Employees Director, Sébastien Brown
Auditors : Mazars

LOCATIONS

HQ: EssilorLuxottica
147, rue de Paris, Charenton-le-Pont 94220
Phone: (33) 1 49 77 42 24
Web: www.essilorluxottica.com

2018 Pro Forma Sales

	% of total
North America	52
Europe	25
Asia, Oceania, and Africa	17
Latin America	6
Total	100

PRODUCTS/OPERATIONS

2018 Pro Forma Sales

	% of total
Lenses & optical instruments	39
Retail	36
Wholesale	19
Sunglasses & readers	5
Equipment	1
Total	100

COMPETITORS

BAUSCH & LOMB INCORPORATED
COOPERVISION, INC.

ESSILOR OF AMERICA, INC.
LUXOTTICA GROUP SPA
Lululemon Athletica Canada Inc
NATIONAL VISION HOLDINGS, INC.
SIGNET ARMORLITE, INC.
STAAR SURGICAL COMPANY
THE COOPER COMPANIES INC
U.S. VISION, INC.

HISTORICAL FINANCIALS
Company Type: Public

Income Statement — FYE: December 31

	REVENUE ($mil)	NET INCOME ($mil)	NET PROFIT MARGIN	EMPLOYEES
12/22	26,160	2,298	8.8%	200,121
12/21	22,433	1,655	7.4%	193,371
12/20	17,708	104	0.6%	151,017
12/19	19,524	1,209	6.2%	152,954
12/18	12,366	1,244	10.1%	152,740
Annual Growth	20.6%	16.6%	—	7.0%

2022 Year-End Financials
Debt ratio: 15.9%
Return on equity: 5.9%
Cash ($ mil.): 2,093
Current Ratio: 0.97
Long-term debt ($ mil.): 8,292
No. of shares ($ mil.): 445
Dividends
  Yield: —
  Payout: 25.5%
Market value ($ mil.): 40,338

	STOCK PRICE ($) FY Close	P/E High/Low	PER SHARE ($) Earnings	Dividends	Book Value
12/22	90.58	21 15	5.16	1.32	89.83
12/21	106.91	33 20	3.71	1.34	90.29
12/20	77.76	467 298	0.23	0.70	90.62
12/19	76.59	32 22	2.74	1.14	89.45
12/18	63.16	18 14	4.67	0.92	88.30
Annual Growth	9.4%	— —	2.5%	9.3%	0.4%

Etablissements FR Colruyt SA Halle

Colruyt and its subsidiaries carry names that are well-known in Belgium France, and Luxembourg. Retail still accounts for more than four fifths of its revenue, but Colruyt is also active in wholesale, foodservice and production of renewable energy. Colruyt also possesses experience and expertise in areas such as technology, IT and communication, as well as production and packaging of meat, coffee, cheese and wine. Colruyt Group consists of over forty brands for individuals and businesses including Bio-planet, Cru, Dreambaby, Spar Colruyt Group, ZEB, Fiets, Eoly Cooperative, SmartWithFood, Collibri Foundation, Solucious, Symeta, Parkwind, Boni Selection, and Colex. The company traces its roots back in 1928 Franz Colruyt starts a colonial wholesale goods business (selling things such as coffee, salt and sugar) in Lembeek, to serve grocers in Brussels and the surrounding area.

EXECUTIVES

Executive Chairman, Chief Executive Officer, Jef Colruyt
Chief Financial Officer, Stefaan Vandamme
Secretary, Kris Castelein
Non-Executive Director, Francois Gillet
Non-Executive Director, Dries Colpaert
Non-Executive Director, Hilde Cerstelotte
Non-Executive Director, Frans Colruyt
Non-Executive Director, Wim Colruyt
Independent Director, Astrid de Lathauwer
Independent Director, Chantal De Vrieze
Independent Director, Rika Coppens
Auditors: EY Bedrijfsrevisoren BV

LOCATIONS

HQ: Etablissements FR Colruyt SA Halle
Edingensesteenweg 196, Halle B-1500
Phone: (32) 2 363 55 45   Fax: (32) 2 360 02 07
Web: www.colruytgroup.com

2016 Sales

	% of total
Belgium	87
France	13
Total	100

PRODUCTS/OPERATIONS

2016 Sales

	% of total
Retail	77
Wholesale and Foodservice	17
Other Activities	6
Total	100

Selected Brands
Retail:
  Bio-Planet
  ColliShop
  Colruyt
  DreamBaby
  DreamLand
  OKay

Wholesale:
Belgium:
  Alvo
  Eurospar
  Spar
France:
  CocciMarket
  Coccinelle
  Panier Sympa

Foodservice:
  Collivery
  Foodinvest
  Pro à Pro

Other:
  DATS 24 (gas stations)
  Intrion (engineering)
  Symeta (print & document management)
  WE-Power (renewable energy)

COMPETITORS

DIERBERGS MARKETS, INC.
FOOD 4 LESS OF SOUTHERN CALIFORNIA, INC.
GROCERY OUTLET INC.
HOUCHENS INDUSTRIES, INC.
JETRO CASH AND CARRY ENTERPRISES, LLC
PALMER & HARVEY MCLANE LIMITED
SAVE MART SUPERMARKETS DISC
SHOPPERS FOOD WAREHOUSE CORP.
SUPER CENTER CONCEPTS, INC.
THE C D HARTNETT COMPANY

HISTORICAL FINANCIALS
Company Type: Public

Income Statement — FYE: March 31

	REVENUE ($mil)	NET INCOME ($mil)	NET PROFIT MARGIN	EMPLOYEES
03/22	11,155	318	2.9%	32,996
03/21	11,649	487	4.2%	32,945
03/20	10,496	472	4.5%	30,631
03/19	10,594	429	4.1%	29,903
03/18	11,132	459	4.1%	29,388
Annual Growth	0.1%	(8.7%)	—	2.9%

2022 Year-End Financials
Debt ratio: 18.8%
Return on equity: 11.5%
Cash ($ mil.): 195
Current Ratio: 0.80
Long-term debt ($ mil.): 722
No. of shares ($ mil.): 128
Dividends
  Yield: 2.4%
  Payout: 50.9%
Market value ($ mil.): —

Eurobank Ergasias Services & Holdings SA

Eurobank Ergasias has a lot of branches for shaking the money tree. The bank operates some 500 branches, business centers, and ATMs in its home country Greece and about 1,250 more in about half-a-dozen other central and southeastern European countries. In addition to traditional retail banking and consumer lending, Eurobank offers business banking, factoring, insurance, leasing, investment banking, and wealth management services. The bank was founded in 1990 as Euromerchant Bank. Swiss-based EFG Bank European Financial Group owns about 44% of Eurobank.

EXECUTIVES

Chief Executive Officer, Director, Fokion C. Karavias
Deputy Chief Executive, Stavros E. Ioannou
Deputy Chief Executive, Konstantinos V. Vassiliou
Deputy Chief Executive, Andreas D. Athanassopoulos
Deputy Group Company Secretary, Veronique Karalis
Chairperson, Non-Executive Director, Georgios P. Zanias
Non-Executive Director, Bradley Paul L. Martin
Vice-Chairperson, Non-Executive Director, Georgios K. Chryssikos
Non-Independent Non-Executive Director, Cinzia V. Basile
Non-Independent Non-Executive Director, Irene C. Rouvitha-Panou
Non-Independent Non-Executive Director, Alice K. Gregoriadi
Non-Independent Non-Executive Director, Efthymia P. Deli

Non-Independent Non-Executive Director,
Rajeev K. L. Kakar

Non-Independent Non-Executive Director,
Jawaid A. Mirza

Auditors : KPMG Certified Auditors S.A.

LOCATIONS

HQ: Eurobank Ergasias Services & Holdings SA
8 Othonos Street, Athens 105 57
Phone: (30) 214 40 61000 **Fax:** (30) 210 323 3866
Web: www.eurobank.gr

COMPETITORS

BANK OF CYPRUS PUBLIC COMPANY LIMITED
BARCLAYS BANK PLC
NORTHERN BANK LIMITED
PIRAEUS FINANCIAL HOLDINGS S.A.
STANDARD CHARTERED PLC

HISTORICAL FINANCIALS

Company Type: Public

Income Statement — FYE: December 31

	ASSETS ($mil)	NET INCOME ($mil)	INCOME AS % OF ASSETS	EMPLOYEES
12/22	87,002	1,420	1.6%	0
12/21	88,117	371	0.4%	11,935
12/20	83,121	(1,488)	—	11,501
12/19	72,711	142	0.2%	13,456
12/18	66,402	104	0.2%	13,162
Annual Growth	7.0%	92.1%	—	—

2022 Year-End Financials

Return on assets: 1.6%
Return on equity: 21.8%
Long-term debt ($ mil.): —
No. of shares ($ mil.): 3,710
Sales ($ mil.): 4,328
Dividends
  Yield: —
  Payout: 0.0%
Market value ($ mil.): 1,929

	STOCK PRICE ($) FY Close	P/E High/Low	PER SHARE ($) Earnings	Dividends	Book Value
12/22	0.52	2 1	0.38	0.00	1.91
12/21	0.48	6 3	0.10	0.00	1.69
12/20	0.35	— —	(0.41)	0.00	1.74
12/19	0.48	14 6	0.04	0.00	2.02
12/18	0.25	15 6	0.05	0.00	2.64
Annual Growth	19.9%	— —	70.0%	—	(7.8%)

Everest Group Ltd

Everest Re Group is the holding company for Everest Reinsurance Company (Everest Re), an underwriter of property/casualty reinsurance and insurance. Everest Re markets its reinsurance products to US and international insurance companies, both directly and through independent brokers. Under the reinsurance arrangements, Everest Re assumes the risks on policies written by its clients. The company offers specialized underwriting in several areas, including property/casualty, marine, aviation, and surety and accident and health.

Operations

Everest Re's reporting segments are Insurance Operations and Reinsurance Operations.

The Reinsurance operation (some 75% of gross written premium) writes worldwide property and casualty reinsurance and specialty lines of business, on both a treaty and facultative basis, through reinsurance brokers, as well as directly with ceding companies. Business is written in the US, Bermuda, and Ireland offices, as well as, through branches in Canada, Singapore, UK and Switzerland. The Insurance operation generates some 25% of gross written premiums and writes property and casualty insurance directly and through brokers, surplus lines brokers and general agents within the US, Canada and Europe through its offices in the US, Bermuda, Canada, Europe and South America.

The company generates roughly 90% from premiums, while net investment income with some 10% and net realized capital gains account for the rest.

Geographic Reach

Everest Re is co-headquartered in Bermuda and New Jersey. It has offices in Bermuda, Brussels, Atlanta, Boston, Houston, Indianapolis, Los Angeles, California, Florida, Chicago, Dublin, London, Miami, New York, Sao Paulo, Singapore, Toronto, and Zurich.

The company's international business is conducted through its Everest Re units in Canada, Brazil, and Singapore, as well as through its Bermuda Re and Everest International units. Everest Re Group's traditional insurance offerings are provided in the US through Everest Security, Everest Denali, Everest Premier, Everest National Insurance and Everest Indemnity Insurance.

Sales and Marketing

The company writes business on a worldwide basis for many different customers and lines of business, thereby obtaining a broad spread of risk. The company is not substantially dependent on any single customer, small group of customers, line of business or geographic area. For the 2021 calendar year, no single customer (ceding company or insured) generated about 5% of the company's gross written premiums. Roughly 65%, around 30% and over 5% of the company's 2021 gross written premiums were written in the broker reinsurance, direct reinsurance, and insurance markets, respectively.

Financial Performance

The company had a total revenue of $1.4 billion, a 161% increase from the previous year's total revenue of $542.8 million.

In 2021, the company had a net income of $1.4 billion, a 168% increase from the previous year's net income of $514 million.

The company's cash at the end of 2021 was $3.3 million. Operating activities generated $296 million, while investing activities used a $48.4 million, primarily for cost of other invested assets acquired. Financing activities used another $245.2 million.

Strategy

Everest Re's business strategy is to sustain its leadership position within targeted reinsurance and insurance markets, provide effective management throughout the property and casualty underwriting cycle and thereby achieve an attractive return for its shareholders. The company's underwriting strategies seek to capitalize on its financial strength and capacity, global franchise, stable and experienced management team, diversified product and distribution offerings, underwriting expertise and disciplined approach, efficient and low-cost operating structure, and effective enterprise risk management practices.

The company offers treaty and facultative reinsurance and admitted and non-admitted insurance. Its products include the full range of property and casualty reinsurance and insurance coverages, including marine, aviation, surety, errors and omissions liability, directors' and officers' liability, medical malpractice, other specialty lines, accident and health, and workers' compensation.

The company's underwriting strategies emphasize underwriting profitability over premium volume. Key elements of this strategy include careful risk selection, appropriate pricing through strict underwriting discipline and adjustment of its business mix in response to changing market conditions. The company focuses on reinsuring companies that effectively manage the underwriting cycle through proper analysis and pricing of underlying risks and whose underwriting guidelines and performance are compatible with its objectives.

Commencing in 2015, the Everest Re initiated a strategic build out of its insurance platform through the investment in key leadership hires which in turn has brought significant underwriting talent and stronger direction in achieving its insurance program strategic goals of increased premium volume and improved underwriting results. Recent growth is coming from highly diversified areas including newly launched lines of business, as well as product and geographic expansion in existing lines of business. The company is building a world-class insurance platform capable of offering products across lines and geographies, complementing its leading global reinsurance franchise. As part of this initiative, the company launched a new syndicate through Lloyd's of London and formed Ireland Insurance, providing access to additional international business and new product opportunities to further diversify and broaden its insurance portfolio going forward.

EXECUTIVES

Chairman, Director, Joseph V. Taranto, $1,007,692 total compensation

President, Chief Executive Officer, Subsidiary Officer, Director, Juan Carlos Andrade Ortiz, $1,250,000 total compensation

Executive Vice President, Division Officer, Mike Karmilowicz
Executive Vice President, Chief Financial Officer, Mark Kociancic
Executive Vice President, Chief Operating Officer, Division Officer, James Williamson
Interim General Counsel, Brent Hoffman
Lead Director, Director, William F. Galtney
Director, John J. Amore
Director, John A. Graf
Director, Meryl D. Hartzband
Director, Geraldine (Gerri) Losquadro
Director, Roger M. Singer
Director, John A. Weber
Director, Hazel M. McNeilage
Auditors : PricewaterhouseCoopers LLP

LOCATIONS

HQ: Everest Group Ltd
Seon Place - 4th Floor, 141 Front Street, P.O. Box HM 845, Hamilton HM 19
Phone: (1) 441 2950006   **Fax:** (1) 441 2954828
Web: www.everestre.com

PRODUCTS/OPERATIONS

2017 Gross Written Premiums by Segment

	% of total
US Reinsurance	36
Insurance	29
International	18
Bermuda	17
Total	100

COMPETITORS

AVIVA PLC
BRIT LIMITED
Chubb Limited
Fairfax Financial Holdings Limited
MAPFRE, SA
MS&AD INSURANCE GROUP HOLDINGS, INC.
REINSURANCE GROUP OF AMERICA, INCORPORATED
RSA INSURANCE GROUP PLC
TOWERGATE PARTNERSHIPCO LIMITED
XL GROUP PUBLIC LIMITED COMPANY

HISTORICAL FINANCIALS

Company Type: Public

Income Statement — FYE: December 31

	ASSETS ($mil)	NET INCOME ($mil)	INCOME AS % OF ASSETS	EMPLOYEES
12/23	49,399	2,517	5.1%	0
12/22	39,966	597	1.5%	2,428
12/21	38,185	1,379	3.6%	1,947
12/20	32,788	514	1.6%	1,746
12/19	27,324	1,009	3.7%	1,603
Annual Growth	16.0%	25.7%	—	—

2023 Year-End Financials

Return on assets: 5.6%
Return on equity: 23.2%
Long-term debt ($ mil.): —
No. of shares ($ mil.): 43
Sales ($ mil.): 14,587

Dividends
Yield: —
Payout: 11.2%
Market value ($ mil.): —

Evergreen Marine Corp Taiwan Ltd

A hardy perennial of the transportation industry, Evergreen Marine has sprouted into one of the world's largest container shipping companies. With a fleet of about 160 container vessels that specialize in transporting perishable goods, Evergreen Marine has more than 240 service locations that cover some 80 countries. Its busiest routes are between the Asia/Pacific region and North America. The company is part of founder Dr. Yung-fa Chang's diverse business empire known as Evergreen Group; affiliates include passenger and freight carrier EVA Airways and companies engaged in container manufacturing, shipbuilding, port operations, real estate development, and engineering.

HISTORY

Former Taiwanese sailor Chang Yung-fa founded Evergreen Marine in 1968 with a secondhand cargo vessel. Japanese trading group Marubeni lent Chang $450,000 for the startup.

Chang's Chinese given name translates as "evergreen" or "prospering." (The company's ship names all begin with "Ever.") In 1975 the company established a Panamanian subsidiary, Evergreen Group (later Evergreen International), to oversee a fleet sailing under the Panamanian flag.

As Evergreen Marine was expanding its fleet, it was also expanding its routes. It opened a Japanese office in 1969, began routes between Southeast Asia and the US West Coast in 1975, and added routes to the Red Sea, the Mediterranean, and the Persian Gulf in the late 1970s.

Evergreen Marine announced in 1982 that it would increase its fleet and support services, and two years later it launched around-the-world routes. The company also formed its Uniglory Marine shipping affiliate in 1984.

By 1986 investments in both vessels and technology had made Evergreen Marine the most cost-effective shipper in the world. That year it formed Evergreen International USA (later Evergreen America) to oversee operations in the US, Canada, and the Caribbean; it opened a German office to coordinate operations in northern Europe and the Mediterranean. Under pressure from Taiwan's government, Chang took Evergreen Marine public in 1987.

Chang formed EVA Airways in 1991, with routes from Taipei, Taiwan, to Bangkok, Seoul, and Vienna. Before EVA was formed, Taiwan, lacking formal relations with many governments, had ceded several of state-owned China Airlines' routes to foreign carriers. As a private company EVA was given those routes. By 1993 EVA was flying to Los Angeles and Paris.

Uniglory increased many of its inter-Asian shipping routes to a twice-weekly schedule in 1996 after it gave Evergreen Marine its Far East-South Africa-South America routes. In 1997 Uniglory's feeder boxship Uni-Order sailed directly from Taiwan to China, the first Taiwanese ship to do so in nearly 50 years. That year Evergreen Marine won approval to invest $5.5 million in a venture to build an inland container depot in South China.

Evergreen Marine expanded its fleet by ordering more than a dozen cargo vessels in 1995 and 1996; EVA took delivery of two Boeing 747s and a McDonnell Douglas MD-90 in 1996 and ordered six long-range aircraft in 1997. Evergreen Marine opened a transshipment hub in 1997 near Colon, Panama -- the first of five planned worldwide and the base for its north-south expansion. However, the currency crisis of 1997 and 1998 that hammered Asian economies prompted Evergreen Marine to temporarily halt new vessel orders in 1998. Instead, the company boosted its fleet and its European presence that year by acquiring 163-year-old Italian shipping company Lloyd Triestino.

In 1999 Evergreen Marine teamed up with rival COSCO to launch a joint service linking Asian ports with South Africa and South America. The next year it allied with Crowley, APL, and Lykes to trade between the east coasts of the Americas.

Evergreen Marine formed a consortium with two other Taiwanese shipping companies in 2001 to build and operate a container shipment/warehousing center at Taipei Harbor. The next year, in a move that caused ripples in the shipping industry, Evergreen shifted its business away from Singapore's main port, operated by PSA Corporation, to the neighboring port of Tanjung Pelepas in Malaysia, which offered cheaper rates.

In another controversial move, Chang re-registered transport companies under holding company Evergreen Group (including Evergreen Marine, EVA Airways, and Uniglory Marine) as British and Italian companies in 2002. The move was seen as a step toward establishing trade with mainland China. Chang, who had come under fire for advocating the establishment of trade links to China, then resigned his post as a senior adviser to Taiwan president Chen Shui-bian.

The east coast operations of Evergreen Marine's US affiliate were shut down for a month in 2003 because of a work stoppage by the International Longshoremen's Association.

EXECUTIVES

Chairman, President, Cheng-Yung Chang
Director, Chang kuo-cheng
Director, Chang yang-fa
Director, Kuo shiuan-yu
Director, Lin sun-san
Director, Wang long-shung

Auditors : PricewaterhouseCoopers

LOCATIONS

HQ: Evergreen Marine Corp Taiwan Ltd
No. 166, Sec. 2, Minsheng East Road, Taipei 104
Phone: (886) 2 2505 7766   **Fax:** (886) 2 2505 5256
Web: www.evergreen-marine.com

COMPETITORS

BRAMBLES LIMITED
CROWLEY MARITIME CORPORATION
DFDS A/S
EURONAV MI II INC.
INTERNATIONAL SHIPHOLDING CORPORATION
KAWASAKI KISEN KAISHA, LTD.
Panalpina Welttransport (Holding) AG
SEACOR HOLDINGS INC.
SEASPAN CORPORATION
YANG MING MARINE TRANSPORT CORPORATION

HISTORICAL FINANCIALS

Company Type: Public

Income Statement — FYE: December 31

	REVENUE ($mil)	NET INCOME ($mil)	NET PROFIT MARGIN	EMPLOYEES
12/21	17,675	8,632	48.8%	8,103
12/20	7,368	867	11.8%	0
12/19	6,366	3	0.1%	0
12/18	5,533	9	0.2%	0
12/17	5,078	236	4.7%	0
Annual Growth	36.6%	145.9%	—	—

2021 Year-End Financials
Debt ratio: 0.4%
Return on equity: —
Cash ($ mil.): 3,893
Current Ratio: 2.60
Long-term debt ($ mil.): 1,676
No. of shares ($ mil.): 5,265
Dividends
  Yield: —
  Payout: 0.0%
Market value ($ mil.): —

Evraz PLC

EXECUTIVES

Business Development Chief Executive Officer, Commerce Chief Executive Officer, Executive Director, Aleksey Ivanov
Chief Financial Officer, Executive Director, Nikolay Ivanov
Head of the Coal Division Vice President, Andrey Davydov
Head of the Vanadium Division Vice President, Alexander Erenburg
EVRAZ North America President, EVRAZ North America Chief Executive Officer, James Skip Herald
Corporate Strategy and Performance Management Vice President, Alexander Kuznetsov
Information Technology Vice President, Artem Natrusov
Head of the Urals Division Vice President, Denis Novozhenov
Health, Safety and Environment Vice President, Konstantin Rubin
Human Resources Vice President, Elena Samsonova
Corporate Communications Vice President, Vsevolod Sementsov
Technologies Development Vice President, Sergey Sergienko
Sales Vice President, Logistics Vice President, Ilya Shirokobrod
Head of the Siberia Division Vice President, Alexey Soldatenkov
Legal Vice President, Corporate Governance Vice President, Property Vice President, Yanina Staniulenaite
Compliance with Business Procedures and Asset Protection Vice President, Sergey Vasiliev
Secretary, Prism Cosec
Non-Executive Chairman, Director, Alexander Abramov
Senior Independent Non-Executive Director, Michael Peat
Independent Non-Executive Director, Maria Gordon
Independent Non-Executive Director, Karl Gruber
Independent Non-Executive Director, Deborah Gudgeon
Independent Non-Executive Director, Alexander Izosimov
Independent Non-Executive Director, Stephen T. Odell
Independent Non-Executive Director, James Rutherford
Independent Non-Executive Director, Sandra M. Stash
Non-Executive Director, Alexander Frolov
Non-Executive Director, Eugene Shvidler
Non-Executive Director, Eugene Tenenbaum
Auditors : Ernst & Young LLP

LOCATIONS

HQ: Evraz PLC
2 Portman Street, London W1H 6DU
Phone: (44) 20 7832 8990
Web: www.evraz.com

HISTORICAL FINANCIALS

Company Type: Public

Income Statement — FYE: December 31

	REVENUE ($mil)	NET INCOME ($mil)	NET PROFIT MARGIN	EMPLOYEES
12/21	13,486	3,034	22.5%	71,591
12/20	9,754	848	8.7%	67,339
12/19	11,905	326	2.7%	66,734
12/18	12,836	2,406	18.7%	65,890
12/17	10,827	699	6.5%	76,020
Annual Growth	5.6%	44.3%	—	(1.5%)

2021 Year-End Financials
Debt ratio: 35.9%
Return on equity: —
Cash ($ mil.): 1,027
Current Ratio: 1.62
Long-term debt ($ mil.): 3,440
No. of shares ($ mil.): 1,458
Dividends
  Yield: —
  Payout: 60.3%
Market value ($ mil.): —

Exor NV

EXECUTIVES

Chairman, Chief Executive Officer, John Elkann
Vice-Chairman, Non-Executive Director, Alessandro Nasi
Chief Financial Officer, Enrico Vellano
Senior Non-Executive Director, Marc J. Bolland
Non-Executive Director, Melissa Bethell
Non-Executive Director, Laurence Debroux
Non-Executive Director, Ginevra Elkann
Non-Executive Director, António Horta-Osorio
Non-Executive Director, Andrea Agnelli
Non-Executive Director, Joseph Y. Bae
Auditors : Ernst & Young Accountants LLP

LOCATIONS

HQ: Exor NV
Gustav Mahlerplein 25, Amsterdam, North Holland 1082 MS
Phone: (31) 20 240 2 220   **Fax:** (31) 20 240 2 738
Web: www.exor.com

HISTORICAL FINANCIALS

Company Type: Public

Income Statement — FYE: December 31

	REVENUE ($mil)	NET INCOME ($mil)	NET PROFIT MARGIN	EMPLOYEES
12/21	38,049	1,943	5.1%	19
12/20	146,684	(36)	0.0%	23
12/19	161,403	3,427	2.1%	23
12/18	164,100	1,542	0.9%	22
12/17	171,937	1,668	1.0%	21
Annual Growth	(31.4%)	3.9%	—	(2.5%)

2021 Year-End Financials
Debt ratio: —
Return on equity: 11.5%
Cash ($ mil.): 8,947
Current Ratio: —
Long-term debt ($ mil.): —
No. of shares ($ mil.): 231
Dividends
  Yield: —
  Payout: 5.5%
Market value ($ mil.): —

Fairfax Financial Holdings Ltd

Fairfax Financial Holdings is a holding company whose corporate objective is to build long term shareholder value by achieving a high rate of compound growth in book value per share over the long term. The company is one of the largest property and casualty companies in the world with $27.6 billion in gross premiums written, all operating in a decentralized structure with outstanding management focused on disciplined underwriting. Chairman and CEO Prem Watsa control 43.9% of the voting rights of Fairfax Financial. Majority of its net premiums earned were generated in the US.

Operations

Fairfax operations are divided into two segments: Property and Casualty Insurance and Reinsurance and Life insurance and Run-off.

Property and Casualty Insurance segment divided into three business units: North American Insurers, Global Insurers and Reinsurers, and International Insurers and

Reinsurers. North America Insurers provides a full range of commercial insurance in property, casualty, and specialty risks, principally within the US and Canada through Northbridge, Crum & Forster, and Zenith National. Global Insurers and Reinsurers provides diverse insurance and reinsurance coverage to its global customers including specialty insurance, treaty and facultative reinsurance and other risk management solutions through Allied World, Brit, and Odyssey Group. International Insurers and Reinsurers provides coverage for diverse insurance and reinsurance risk in local markets, primarily across Asia, Europe (excl. UK), and Latin America. The International Insurers and Reinsurers reporting segment's business is underwritten by individual companies within Fairfax Asia, Fairfax Latin America and Fairfax Central and Eastern Europe, as well as Group Re, Bryte Insurance, and Eurolife's property and casualty insurance operations.

Life insurance and Run-off segment is comprised of Eurolife's life insurance operations and US Run-off, which includes TIG Insurance Company.

Geographic Reach
Fairfax's corporate office is located in Toronto, Canada. It also has operations in the US, in which accounts for around 65% of net premiums earned, while international accounts for more than 15%, and the remaining accounts for Canada, and Asia.

Sales and Marketing
The company uses brokers to distribute its business and, in some instances, will distribute through agents or directly to customers. The company may also conduct business through third parties such as managing general agents where it is cost effective to do so and where the company can control the underwriting process to ensure its risk management criteria are met. Each of these channels has its own distinct distribution characteristics and customers.

Financial Performance
The company's operating activities used $4.4 million, while investing activities provided $384.8 million. Financing activities used another $1.3 million, primarily for purchases of subsidiary shares from non-controlling interests.

Strategy
The company may periodically and opportunistically acquire other insurance and reinsurance companies or execute other strategic initiatives developed by management. The company may periodically explore opportunities to make strategic investments in all or part of certain businesses or companies.

Company Background
Fairfax was founded in 1985 by Chairman and CEO V. Prem Watsa.

EXECUTIVES

Chairman, Chief Executive Officer, Director, V. Prem Watsa
Vice President, Chief Financial Officer, Jennifer Allen
Vice President, Chief Operating Officer, Peter Clarke
International Operations Vice President, Jean Cloutier
Administrative Services Vice President, Vinodh Loganadhan
Strategic Investments Vice President, Bradley Martin
Vice President, Chief Actuary, Olivier Quesnel
Corporate Affairs Vice President, Corporate Affairs Secretary, Eric Salsberg
Corporate Development Vice President, John Varnell
Vice President, Mike Wallace
Lead Director, R. William McFarland
Director, Anthony F. Griffiths
Director, Robert J. Gunn
Director, David L. Johnston
Director, Karen L. Jurjevich
Director, Christine N. McLean
Director, Timothy R. Price
Director, Brandon W. Sweitzer
Director, Lauren C. Templeton
Director, Benjamin P. Watsa
Director, William C. Weldon
Auditors: PricewaterhouseCoopers LLP

LOCATIONS
HQ: Fairfax Financial Holdings Ltd
95 Wellington Street West, Suite 800, Toronto, Ontario M5J 2N7
Phone: 416 367-4941
Web: www.fairfax.ca

Sales 2016
	% of total
United States	62
Canada	13
Asia	11
International	14
Total	100

PRODUCTS/OPERATIONS

2016 Sales
	% of total
Casualty	56
Property	32
Specialty	12
Total	100

2016 Sales
	% of total
OdysseyRe	24
Crum & Forster	21
Brit	20
Northbridge	11
Zenith National	8
Fairfax Asia	7
Runoff	2
Other	7
Total	100

Selected Subsidiaries
Insurance
    Asian Insurance
        Falcon Insurance Company (Hong Kong) Ltd.
        First Capital Insurance Limited (Singapore)
    Canadian Insurance
        Northbridge Financial Corporation
        Commonwealth Insurance Company
        Federated Holdings of Canada Limited
        Lombard General Insurance Company of Canada
        Markel Insurance Company of Canada
    U.S. Insurance
        Crum & Forster Holdings Corporation
Reinsurance
    CRC (Bermuda) Reinsurance Limited
    Odyssey Re Holdings Corp.
    Polish Re (Poland)
    Wentworth Insurance Company Ltd. (Barbados)
Runoff
    nSpire Re Limited
    RiverStone Group LLC
    RiverStone Holdings Limited
    TRG Holding Corporation

COMPETITORS
ADVENT INTERNATIONAL CORPORATION
AMTRUST FINANCIAL SERVICES, INC.
Chubb Limited
EATON VANCE CORP.
FRANKLIN RESOURCES, INC.
HOULIHAN LOKEY, INC.
INVESCO LTD.
MS&AD INSURANCE GROUP HOLDINGS, INC.
Onex Corporation
STANDARD & POOR'S FINANCIAL SERVICES LLC

HISTORICAL FINANCIALS
Company Type: Public

Income Statement   FYE: December 31

	ASSETS ($mil)	NET INCOME ($mil)	INCOME AS % OF ASSETS	EMPLOYEES
12/23	91,985	4,332	4.7%	51,044
12/22	92,125	1,147	1.2%	47,040
12/21	86,645	3,401	3.9%	39,040
12/20	74,054	218	0.3%	41,044
12/19	70,508	2,004	2.8%	44,043
Annual Growth	6.9%	21.3%		3.8%

2023 Year-End Financials
Return on assets: 4.7%
Return on equity: 21.8%
Long-term debt ($ mil.): —
No. of shares ($ mil.): 23
Sales ($ mil.): 15,439
Dividends
    Yield: —
    Payout: 5.7%
Market value ($ mil.): 21,916

	STOCK PRICE ($) FY Close	P/E High/Low	Earnings	PER SHARE ($) Dividends	Book Value
12/23	920.76	5 3	173.24	10.00	964.21
12/22	594.12	13 10	43.49	10.00	691.25
12/21	492.13	4 3	122.25	10.00	664.31
12/20	340.94	72 35	6.29	10.00	513.67
12/19	469.11	7 6	69.79	10.00	520.37
Annual Growth	18.4%		25.5%	0.0%	16.7%

Far Eastern International Bank

EXECUTIVES
Managing Director, Independent Director, Hsiao Hui Wang
Executive Director, Shaw Y. Wang

Executive Director, Tsung-Ming Chung
Director, Chairperson, Ching-Ing Hou
Vice-Chairman, Douglas Tong Hau
Independent Director, Bing Shen
Independent Director, Susan Chang
Director, Humphrey Cheng
Director, James Wu
Director, Shih-Chun Hsu
Director, Min-Teh Yu
Auditors : Deloitte & Touche

LOCATIONS

HQ: Far Eastern International Bank
26F & 27F, No. 207, Sec. 2, Dunhua S. Road, Taipei, Taipei 106
Phone: (886) 2 2378 6868   **Fax:** (886) 2 2377 9000
Web: www.feib.com.tw

HISTORICAL FINANCIALS

Company Type: Public

Income Statement — FYE: December 31

	ASSETS ($mil)	NET INCOME ($mil)	INCOME AS % OF ASSETS	EMPLOYEES
12/21	26,114	106	0.4%	0
12/20	24,199	89	0.4%	0
12/19	21,874	121	0.6%	0
12/18	20,511	115	0.6%	0
12/17	19,405	96	0.5%	2,754
Annual Growth	7.7%	2.5%	—	—

2021 Year-End Financials

Return on assets: 0.4%
Return on equity: 5.9%
Long-term debt ($ mil.): —
No. of shares ($ mil.): 3,569
Sales ($ mil.): 496
Dividends
 Yield: —
 Payout: 51.8%
Market value ($ mil.): —

Far Eastern New Century Corp

Far Eastern New Century (FENC) touts global prominence in polyester and textile production, brand name, and technology. It makes and markets semi-finished and finished goods, including yarns, fabrics, bed sheets, towels, and knitted apparel. The company is Asia's #1 producer of polyester polymer and polyethylene terephthalate (PET) resin, used in a variety of items from beer bottles to mechanical rubber. It prints and dyes cloth as well as makes films. Its products are used by known brands such as Adidas, Nike, H&M, Levi's. The company roots its history back in 1942 when Yu-Ziang Hsu founded Far Eastern Knitting Factory Co., Ltd. in Shanghai, it is part of the Far Eastern Group, a Taiwan-based conglomerate with around 250 affiliated companies.

EXECUTIVES

Director, Champion Lee
Auditors : Deloitte & Touche

LOCATIONS

HQ: Far Eastern New Century Corp
36F, Taipei Metro Tower 207, Section 2, Tun Hwa South Road, Taipei
Phone: (886) 2 27338000   **Fax:** (886) 2 27367184
Web: www.fenc.com

2013 Sales

	% of total
Asia	60
America	25
Europe	11
Others	4
Total	100

PRODUCTS/OPERATIONS

2013 Sales

	% of total
Telecommunications	33
Polyester	29
Petrochemical	19
Textile	13
Property	3
Investment & other	3
Total	100

COMPETITORS

Barmag Liegenschaften GmbH & Co. KG
CAROLINA MILLS, INCORPORATED
COATS HOLDINGS LTD
Gamma Holding B.V.
NATIONAL SPINNING CO., INC.
PHARR YARNS, LLC
TORAY INDUSTRIES,INC.
UNIFI, INC.
UNITIKA LTD.
Weiqiao Textile Company Limited

HISTORICAL FINANCIALS

Company Type: Public

Income Statement — FYE: December 31

	REVENUE ($mil)	NET INCOME ($mil)	NET PROFIT MARGIN	EMPLOYEES
12/21	8,624	349	4.1%	0
12/20	7,357	286	3.9%	0
12/19	8,355	358	4.3%	4,833
12/18	7,476	393	5.3%	0
12/17	7,346	272	3.7%	0
Annual Growth	4.1%	6.5%	—	—

2021 Year-End Financials

Debt ratio: 1.5%
Return on equity: 4.7%
Cash ($ mil.): 1,247
Current Ratio: 1.16
Long-term debt ($ mil.): 7,219
No. of shares ($ mil.): 5,352
Dividends
 Yield: —
 Payout: 0.0%
Market value ($ mil.): —

Fast Retailing Co., Ltd.

Fast Retailing is the world's third-largest manufacturer and retailer of private-label apparel in terms of sales. It operates multiple fashion brands including UNIQLO, GU, and Theory. UNIQLO, the company's pillar brand, generates approximately Â¥1.92 trillion in annual sales from nearly 2,395 stores in approximately 25 countries and regions. Driven by the company's LifeWear concept for ultimate everyday clothing, UNIQLO offers unique products made from high-quality, highly functional materials at reasonable prices by managing everything from procurement and design to production and retail sales. Meanwhile, the company's fun, low-priced GU fashion brand generates annual global sales of approximately Â¥246 billion, primarily in Japan. The company was established in 1963.

Operations

The company operates in four business segments: UNIQLO International, UNIQLO Japan, GU, and Global Brands.

UNIQLO is Fast Retailing's mainstay brand offering basic casualwear at reasonable prices. UNIQLO International operates approximately 1,585 stores and contributes about 50% of the company's total revenue. UNIQLO Japan (approximately 35%) operates about 810 stores.

GU generates more than 10% of sales through nearly 450 stores. Its Global Brands business (some 5%) operates through around 720 stores and features clothing under the GU, Theory, Comptoir des Cotonniers, Princesse tam.tam, and J brand operations.

Geographic Reach

Based in Japan, the company operates more than 3,560 stores across Japan, Greater China, Southeast Asia and Oceania, the US and Canada, Europe, and Russia.

Sales and Marketing

The company conducts its global clothing operations through both physical stores and e-commerce channels. Online sales in Japan accounted for about 40% of Fast Retailing's total sales. It also has online sales in Greater China, Taiwan, South Korea, the UK, the US, Australia, and Singapore, among other places.

Financial Performance

The company's revenue for fiscal 2022 increased to Â¥2.3 trillion compared to Â¥2.1 trillion in the prior year.

Profit for fiscal 2022 increased to Â¥284.8 billion compared to Â¥175.7 billion in the prior year.

Cash held by the company at the end of fiscal 2022 increased to Â¥1.4 trillion. Cash provided by operations was Â¥430.8 billion while cash used for investing and financing activities were Â¥212.2 billion and Â¥213.1 billion, respectively. Main cash uses were amounts deposited into bank deposits with original maturities of three months or longer; and repayments of lease liabilities.

EXECUTIVES

Chairman, President, Chief Executive Officer, Representative Director, Tadashi Yanai
Chief Financial Officer, Director, Takeshi Okazaki
Outside Director, Nobumichi Hattori
Outside Director, Masaaki Shintaku
Outside Director, Naotake Ono
Outside Director, Kathy Mitsuko Koll

Outside Director, Joji Kurumado
Outside Director, Yutaka Kyoya
Director, Kazumi Yanai
Director, Koji Yanai
Auditors : Deloitte Touche Tohmatsu LLC

LOCATIONS

HQ: Fast Retailing Co., Ltd.
Midtown Tower, 9-7-1 Akasaka, Minato-ku, Tokyo 107-6231
Phone: (81) 3 6865 0050
Web: www.fastretailing.com

PRODUCTS/OPERATIONS

2018 sales

	% of total
UNIQLO International	42
UNIQLO Japan	41
GU	10
Global Brands	7
Total	100

COMPETITORS

B&M European Value Retail S.A.
BURBERRY GROUP PLC
CECONOMY AG
EG GROUP LIMITED
HANESBRANDS INC.
LIXIL CORPORATION
LightInTheBox Holding Co., Ltd.
PORTMEIRION GROUP PUBLIC LIMITED COMPANY
SUPERDRY PLC
UNY GROUP HOLDINGS CO.,LTD.

HISTORICAL FINANCIALS

Company Type: Public

Income Statement   FYE: August 31

	REVENUE ($mil)	NET INCOME ($mil)	NET PROFIT MARGIN	EMPLOYEES
08/23	18,970	2,031	10.7%	59,871
08/22	16,582	1,969	11.9%	113,689
08/21	19,416	1,546	8.0%	118,725
08/20	19,070	857	4.5%	128,492
08/19	21,542	1,529	7.1%	137,281
Annual Growth	(3.1%)	7.4%	—	(18.7%)

2023 Year-End Financials

Debt ratio: —
Return on equity: 17.5%
Cash ($ mil.): 6,193
Current Ratio: 2.98
Long-term debt ($ mil.): —

No. of shares ($ mil.): 306
Dividends
Yield: 1.5%
Payout: 5.1%
Market value ($ mil.): 6,998

	STOCK PRICE ($) FY Close	P/E High/Low	PER SHARE ($) Earnings	Dividends	Book Value
08/23	22.82	0 0	6.61	0.35	40.73
08/22	58.68	0 0	6.42	0.43	36.71
08/21	65.71	0 0	5.04	0.45	33.17
08/20	59.87	0 0	2.80	0.44	29.65
08/19	58.49	0 0	4.99	0.15	28.83
Annual Growth	(21.0%)	—	7.3%	24.0%	9.0%

Faurecia SE (France)

Faurecia is one of the world's largest automotive seat makers. In addition to car seats, it also manufactures emission control systems, vehicle interiors and doors, and front-end systems. Although Europe accounts for about 45% of overall revenue, it supplies most major carmakers, including GM, Ford, and Volkswagen. Faurecia is a global leader in its four areas of business: seating, interiors, Clarion Electronics and clean mobility. The company's strong technological offering provides carmakers with solutions for the cockpit of the future and sustainable mobility. Faurecia was formed in 1997 with the takeover of Bertrand Faure by PSA-owned ECIA to create a global automotive player. In 2021, with the merger of PSA and FCA and the creation of Stellantis, a new chapter began in Faurecia's history.

Operations

Faurecia operates four business units: Seating; Interiors; Clean Mobility; and Clarion Electronics.

Seating (roughly 40% of revenue) design and manufacture of complete vehicle seats, seating frames and adjustment mechanisms; Interiors (about 30%) design, manufacture and assembly of instrument panels and complete cockpits, door panels and modules, and acoustic systems; Clean Mobility (more than 25%) design and manufacture of exhaust systems, solutions for fuel cell electric vehicles, and after treatment solutions for commercial vehicles; and Clarion Electronics (about 5%) design and manufacture of display technologies, driver assistance systems and cockpit electronics.

Geographic Reach

Based in Paris, France, Faurecia has around 300 industrial sites and more than 75 R&D centers located in more than 40 different countries. Europe is the company's largest market at some 45% of overall revenue, followed by North America and Asia at some 25% of revenue, each. South America and the rest of the world accounts for the remaining 5% of revenue.

Sales and Marketing

Faurecia works with some of the biggest names in the automotive industry. Its five main customers represent about 55% of revenue. Stellantis and VW lead the way with more than 15% of revenue each, followed by Ford (about 10%), Renault-Nissan (about 10%) and GM (around 5%).

Financial Performance

Note: Growth rates may differ after conversion to US Dollars.

Sales reached EUR15.6 billion in 2021 compared to EUR14.4 billion in 2020. This represents an increase of 8% on a reported basis and 9% at constant scope & currencies.

In 2021, the company had a net income of EUR861.7 million, a 106% increase from the previous year's net income of EUR418.4 million.

The company's cash at the end of 2021 was EUR4.9 billion. Operating activities generated EUR1.4 billion, while investing activities used EUR1.3 billion, mainly for capitalized development costs. Financing activities provided another EUR1.6 billion.

Strategy

On February 7, 2022, Faurecia launched FORVIA, the new company name combining Faurecia and HELLA, representing the 7th largest automotive technology supplier. As detailed in a press release issued on that day, FORVIA will be structured around six Business Groups with leading positions, all with full accountability, consolidating Product Lines and Regional Divisions. Five of them, "Seating", "Interiors", "Clean Mobility", "Electronics" and "Lighting", have sales already exceeding 3 billion euros while the newly-created "Lifecycle Solutions" will grow this segment to a leading position. "Seating", "Interiors", "Clean Mobility" will be based in Nanterre (France) and "Electronics", "Lighting" and "Lifecycle Solutions" will be based in Lippstadt (Germany). Global support functions will be deployed at Group, Business Group, Product & Business Division and Plant levels. FORVIA will provide customers with an offer of high technology products and solutions that is organized around 24 differentiating Product Lines and address all the automotive industry megatrends.

Mergers and Acquisitions

In 2022, Faurecia announced its completed the acquisition of Hella, a major automotive player in lighting and electronics based in Lippstadt, Germany. Patrick Koller, Chief Executive Officer of Faurecia, declared: "Today, Hella and Faurecia are opening the first chapter of the newly combined group. This transforming acquisition brings together two complementary and profitable companies to create the 7th largest global automotive supplier with a highly advanced technology portfolio. Our 2025 combined group sales ambitions of EUR33 billion represents a significant leverage and we will now work together effectively to immediately start implementing the significant and confirmed synergies that have been identified and create sustainable value for all our stakeholders."

In 2021, Faurecia has acquired designLED. The Scotland-based company, specialized in advanced backlighting technologies, will strengthen Faurecia's offer for display technologies and enrich its immersive experiences for the Cockpit of the Future.

In early 2021, Faurecia successfully completed the final closing of its acquisition of CLD, one of the leading Chinese manufacturers of hydrogen tanks. Headquartered in ShenYang, CLD has around 200 employees and 2 plants in Liaoning with a capacity of 30,000 tanks per year. Through the acquisition of CLD and thanks to the certification of Type IV tanks, Faurecia will further energize its momentum for hydrogen mobility in China.

HISTORY

Bertrand Faure opened his workshop in Levallois-Perret, France, in 1914 to manufacture cushions and spring backs for automotive seats; spring pads were developed in 1929. The company diversified into bedding in 1954. The following year it opened a factory near Etampes.

Throughout the 1960s and 1970s, Bertrand Faure continued to grow through geographic and product-line expansion. The company boosted its metal and foam seat-making operations in France, and in 1971 it expanded into Germany with the purchase of automotive seating component manufacturer Schmitz. Faure bought French bedding maker MÃ©rinos in 1973 and then changed its company name to EpÃ©da-Bertrand Faure. Between 1977 and 1978 EpÃ©da-Bertrand Faure expanded its automotive seating business through acquisitions in Spain and Portugal.

EpÃ©da-Bertrand Faure diversified into the luggage business with the 1982 purchase of Delsey. That year the company was floated on the French stock exchange. In 1983 EpÃ©da-Bertrand Faure further strengthened its car-seat business in France with the purchase of Autocoussin (structures and foam) and Cousin FrÃ¨res (mechanisms). Another plant in Germany was opened in 1986 to supply BMW. That year EpÃ©da-Bertrand Faure invested in Canadian CASE, a leading North American maker of car-seat mechanisms. The company also reorganized its automotive activities under the name Bertrand Faure Automobile.

EpÃ©da-Bertrand Faure acquired Luchaire, a defense materials and aerospace and automotive equipment manufacturer, in 1987. The following year the company bought automotive seating structures maker Sicam (Italy) and seating foam and structures firm Molaflex (Portugal). In 1989 the company forged joint ventures in the UK, Japan, and Canada for the manufacture of car seating.

By 1990 the company had reorganized into four product segments: automotive seats, bedding, luggage, and aerospace equipment. The automotive seating business was conducted under the name Bertrand Faure, while the rest of the group changed its name to EBF. Bertrand Faure purchased RHW, a leading German maker of car seats, in 1991.

The following year EBF's board of directors decided to focus the company on automotive seating and initiated a vast restructuring plan. EBF sold its bedding concerns in 1994. As part of its restructuring, EBF changed its name back to Bertrand Faure. Two years later Bertrand Faure opened offices in Beijing and SÃ£o Paulo.

Peugeot S.A. subsidiary ECIA and Bertrand Faure merged in 1999 to form Faurecia. In 2000 Faurecia bolstered its North American presence by purchasing US-based automotive exhaust system maker AP Automotive Systems; it renamed the subsidiary Faurecia Exhaust Systems. The company acquired Sommer Allibert's car interiors business early in 2001.

Expanding in Asia, Faurecia purchased Chang Heung Precision Co. Ltd., a Korean maker of exhaust systems, in 2003.

Since 2004 the headcount at high-cost Western European locations has been reduced, while headcount in low-cost regions has increased.

In 2006 the company opened a new plant in China for the manufacture of automotive seats and interior modules for Ford.

In 2006 CEO Pierre Levi stepped down amid a corruption scandal involving Faurecia employees who allegedly offered kickbacks to managers at customers, including Volkswagen and BMW. CFO Frank Imbert was named interim CEO, then director Gregoire Olivier followed as CEO. Yann DelabriÃ¨re succeeded him in early 2007.

In 2007 sales in North America grew by 42%. The company opened seven new plants in the US in 2006 and 2007 -- in Michigan (seats, interior modules, front end modules), Ohio (interior modules and exhaust systems), and South Carolina (seats).

In Asia, Faurecia's sales grew by 21% in 2007 over the previous year. To keep up momentum Faurecia continues to invest in the region.

EXECUTIVES

Chief Executive Officer, Director, Patrick Koller
Communications Executive Vice President, Victoria Chanial
Chief Financial Officer Executive Vice President, Olivier Durand
Americas Region Executive Vice President, Nik Endrud
Faurecia Automotive Seating Executive Vice President, Frank Huber
Faurecia Clean Mobility Executive Vice President, Olivier Lefebvre
Faurecia Interiors Executive Vice-Chairman, Jean-Paul Michel
Digital Transformation and Strategy Executive Vice President, Christopher Mokwa
Sales and Program Management Executive Vice-Chairman, Thorsetn Muschal
Operations Executive Vice President, Christophe Schmitt
Human Resources Executive Vice President, Jean-Pierre Sounillac
Asia Executive Vice President, Francois Tardif
Executive Vice President, General Counsel, Secretary, Nolwenn Delaunay
Chairman, Independent Director, Michel de Rosen
Independent Director, Judy Curran
Independent Director, Odile Desforges
Independent Director, Penelope A. Herscher
Independent Director, Valerie Landon
Independent Director, Jean-Bernard Levy
Independent Director, Yan Mei
Independent Director, Denis Mercier
Independent Director, Peter Mertens
Director, Jurgen Berhend
Director, Robert Peugeot
Director, Daniel Bernardino
Director, Emmanuel Pioche
Auditors : Mazars

LOCATIONS

HQ: Faurecia SE (France)
23-27, avenue des Champs-Pierreux, Â Nanterre (Hauts-de-Seine) 92000
Phone: (33) 1 72 36 70 00 **Fax:** (33) 1 72 36 70 07
Web: www.faurecia.com

2016 Sales

	% of total
Europe	52
North America	28
Asia	16
South America	3
Rest of the World	1
Total	100

PRODUCTS/OPERATIONS

2016 Sales

	% total
Clean Mobility	39
Automotive Seating	35
Interior Systems	26
Total	100

2016 Sales by Customer

	% of total
VW Group	15
Ford group	14
Renault-Nissan	12
Peugeot S.A.	11
GM	8
Daimler	6
BMW	4
Others	30
Total	100

COMPETITORS

ADIENT PUBLIC LIMITED COMPANY
Franz Haniel & Cie. GmbH
GKN LIMITED
LEAR CORPORATION
Magna International Inc
PEUGEOT SA
RENISHAW P L C
Rheinmetall Automotive AG
VALEO
thyssenkrupp AG

HISTORICAL FINANCIALS

Company Type: Public

Income Statement   FYE: December 31

	REVENUE ($mil)	NET INCOME ($mil)	NET PROFIT MARGIN	EMPLOYEES
12/22	27,190	(407)	—	157,460
12/21	17,677	(89)	—	111,140
12/20	17,984	(464)	—	113,931
12/19	19,949	662	3.3%	115,496
12/18	20,069	802	4.0%	114,693
Annual Growth	7.9%	—	—	8.2%

2022 Year-End Financials

Debt ratio: 36.1%   No. of shares ($ mil.): 197
Return on equity: (-9.5%)   Dividends
Cash ($ mil.): 4,486   Yield: —
Current Ratio: 0.99   Payout: 0.0%
Long-term debt ($ mil.): 9,725   Market value ($ mil.): —

Federal Bank Ltd (The) (India)

Auditors: Borkar & Muzumdar

LOCATIONS

HQ: Federal Bank Ltd (The) (India)
Federal Towers, P.O. Box No. 103, Aluva, Kerala 683 101
Phone: (91) 484 2623620 29 **Fax:** (91) 484 2623119
Web: www.federalbank.co.in

HISTORICAL FINANCIALS

Company Type: Public

Income Statement — FYE: March 31

	ASSETS ($mil)	NET INCOME ($mil)	INCOME AS % OF ASSETS	EMPLOYEES
03/22	27,832	260	0.9%	12,790
03/21	26,320	227	0.9%	12,592
03/20	23,012	209	0.9%	12,496
03/19	22,219	190	0.9%	12,227
03/18	20,482	143	0.7%	12,112
Annual Growth	8.0%	16.0%		1.4%

2022 Year-End Financials

Return on assets: 0.9%
Return on equity: 10.8%
Long-term debt ($ mil.): —
No. of shares ($ mil.): 2,102
Sales ($ mil.): 2,178
Dividends
Yield: —
Payout: 0.0%
Market value ($ mil.): —

Ferguson PLC (New)

Ferguson PLC is one of the world's largest distributors of heating and plumbing supplies to professional contractors. The company distributes heating and cooling equipment, plumbing supplies, pipes, valves, safety equipment, and fire protection products, as well as building materials in North America and Europe. Key customers include building contractors, plumbing and heating engineers, and industrial and mechanical contractors. In 2019, the company announced it was spinning off its Wolseley subsidiary as a separate public company. Wolseley will focus on the UK market, while Ferguson will concentrate solely on customers in the UK.

HISTORY

In the late 1800s Irishman Frederick Wolseley immigrated to Australia, where he developed the world's first mechanical sheep shearer. In 1889 he formed Wolseley Sheep Shearing Machine Company. Herbert Austin, a young engineer who perfected Wolseley's machine, moved back to England and became manager of the company's Birmingham factory when the company relocated there in 1893.

In 1895 Austin, amazed by an automobile exhibition he attended in Paris, obtained an advance from the company to develop an automobile; it went into production in 1901. The car manufacturing operations were separated from the company's other machinery operations and soon were bought by Vickers. (Austin went out on his own in 1905 and began producing cars under his own name -- the venerable Austin line.)

By the middle of the century, Wolseley Sheep Shearing had grown to include central heating and plumbing products distribution. In 1958 it joined with Geo. H. Hughes to form Wolseley-Hughes. At the time the company was a small manufacturer with 11 distribution depots.

The company's watershed transition began in 1976, when Jeremy Lancaster took over the chairmanship from his father. (In the 20 years that Lancaster was chairman, profits rose from about $6 million in 1976 to more than $350 million in 1996.) In the late 1970s the company began expanding rapidly through acquisitions. In 1982 it went public and acquired Ferguson Enterprises, a leading distributor of plumbing supplies on the US's East Coast. The acquisition marked the company's first substantial US purchase. Three years later the company formed Wolseley Centers, which distributed building products under the names Plumb Center, Controls Center, and Pipeline Center. In 1986 the company changed its name to Wolseley plc. Acquisitions that year included Carolina Builders Corporation and M.P. Harris & Co. Late 1980s acquisitions included Familian (1987), the largest plumbing supplier on the US's West Coast, and Familian Northwest (1988).

Wolseley then looked across the English Channel. In 1992 it bought Brossette, France's largest specialist distributor of plumbing supplies. The company moved further eastward in 1994, acquiring Ã–AG Group (now Wolseley Austria), Austria's largest wholesale plumbing supply business. In addition to 40 Austrian branches, Ã–AG also had five branches in both Hungary and Germany and four in the Czech Republic. The Ã–AG deal solidified Wolseley's position as the world's #1 plumbing and heating merchant.

Wolseley turned its attention back to the US in the mid-1990s, buying a half-dozen companies, including Building Material Supply. John Young became CEO that year when Jeremy Lancaster retired from the company.

In 1998 the company began integrating California-based Familian and Virginia-based Ferguson Enterprises -- together responsible for more than half of Wolseley's US distribution revenues -- under Ferguson's management. The company continued making acquisitions that year and the next, including its first Italian company (Manzardo, plumbing and heating supplies); it also grew by opening new outlets. Wolseley sold some of its burner and boiler manufacturing operations in 1999.

Chairman Richard Ireland became acting chief executive in June 2000 with the retirement of Young for health reasons. That year the company sold most of its manufacturing businesses. It sold its remaining boiler and burner manufacturing businesses in early 2001. In May 2001 Ferguson Enterprises CEO Charles Banks was named group chief executive.

Also in 2001 Wolseley bought the heating and plumbing operations of Westburne Group (from France-based Rexel, a distributor of electrical equipment) for $356 million to further expand in the US. In 2002 Wolseley bought Clayton Acquisition, a Florida-based wholesale distributor of waterworks, for $110 million. Additionally in 2002 the company bought Wasco, a Dutch heating-equipment supplier, for $58 million to expand in Europe. In December of that year Ireland was replaced as chairman by deputy chairman John Whybrow.

In July 2003 Wolseley bought Pinault Bois & Materiaux (now PB & M), which distributes lumber and building supplies in France, from Pinault-Printemps-Redoute. Wolseley acquired three North American businesses, JM Lumber, Liberty Equipment & Supply, and Nuroc Plumbing and Heating Supplies, in September 2003.

The company acquired Tobler Management [now Wolseley (Schweiz)], a Swiss HVAC wholesaler, from CapVis in December 2003. PB & M acquired Groupe Simoni, a French building materials distributor, in January 2004. Wolseley expanded its Irish business through the August 2004 acquisition of Brooks Group, an Irish building supply company, from UPM-Kymmene. Capping an acquisitive year, Wolseley also acquired Parnell-Martin Management and Record Supply Company in the US and TAPS Wholesale Bath Centre in Canada in December 2004.

Overall, in the fiscal year ended July 2005, the company spent £431 million on 26 acquisitions.

In April 2006 Wolseley acquired Brandon Hire for £72 million. The acquisition of DT Group in September brought Wolseley into new markets in Denmark, Finland, Norway, and Sweden. In October the company purchased Woodcote - stavebni materialy a.s., a general builders merchant with operations in the Czech Republic, Croatia, Hungary, Poland, Romania, and Slovakia. Overall, in fiscal 2006 the company added 279 new locations.

In August 2007 Wolseley purchased Davidson Pipe Company in the US, thereby gaining access to the New York metropolitan market.

In 2008 the company acquired Gama Myjava in Slovakia.

In May 2009 Wolseley sold a 51% stake in BMC Stock to The Gores Group, LLC, a US private equity firm. In June, Ian Meakins joined Wolseley as CEO. He succeeded Claude "Chip" Hornsby, who resigned from the position after three years.

In July 2011 the company sold its Electric Center business to Edmundson Electrical. In November Wolseley sold its remaining 49% stake in Stock Building Supply to Gores Group.

In 2017 the company changed its name from Wolseley PLC to Ferguson PLC.

EXECUTIVES

Director, Kevin Murphy
Chief Financial Officer, Director, Mike Powell
Corporate Communications Executive Director, Investor Relations Executive Director, Mark Fearon
Auditors: Deloitte LLP

LOCATIONS

HQ: Ferguson PLC (New)
1020 Eskdale Road, Winnersh Triangle, Wokingham, Berkshire RG41 5TS
Phone: (44) 0118 927 3800   **Fax:** (44) 118 929 8701
Web: www.fergusonplc.com

2011 Sales

	% of total
North America	
US	40
Canada	6
UK	18
Nordic region	16
France	14
Central Europe	6
Total	100

PRODUCTS/OPERATIONS

2011 Sales by Market

	% of total
Residential repair, maintenance & improvement	36
Non-residential repair, maintenance & improvement	21
Residential new construction	20
Non-residential new construction	16
Civil infrastructure	7
Total	100

2011 Sales by Product

	% of total
Plumbing, heating & air conditioning	40
Building materials	30
Civil/waterworks, commercial & industrial	28
Other	2
Total	100

Selected Products
Building materials
  Beams and trusses
  Bricks, blocks, and aggregates
  Cement
  Doors and frames
  Glass
  Insulation
  Plaster and plasterboard
  Roofing materials
  Tiles and flooring
  Timber products
Civil/waterworks, industrial, and commercial
  Carbon and stainless steel pipes, valves, and fittings
  Drainage pipes
  Underground pressure pipes
Plumbing, heating, and air conditioning
  Air conditioning equipment
  Baths and showers
  Boilers and burners
  Brassware
  Control equipment
  Copper tubing
  Heat pumps
  Hot water cylinders
  Plastic pipes and fittings
  Radiators and valves
  Sanitaryware
  Solar equipment
  Ventilation equipment
Other
  Electrical cables
  Lighting
  Wiring
  Services
  Customer inventory management
  Installation
  Maintenance

Selected Subsidiaries
CFM
  Heating appliances, Luxembourg
DT Group
  Building materials, Denmark
Ferguson Enterprises Inc.
  Wholesale distribution of plumbing, heating, and piping products, US
Manzardo SpA
  Heating and plumbing equipment, Italy
OAG AG
  Heating and plumbing products, Austria
PB&M
  Building materials and wood distribution, France
Tobler
  Heating and plumbing products, Switzerland
Wasco Holding BV
  Heating equipment, The Netherlands
Wolseley Canada
  Wholesale distribution of plumbing, heating, and ventilation products, Canada
Wolseley France
  Building materials, plumbing, and heating products, France
Wolseley UK Limited
  Construction products, UK
Woodcote Group
  Construction materials, Czech Republic

COMPETITORS

FERGUSON UK HOLDINGS LIMITED
GEORGE T. SANDERS CO.
HAJOCA CORPORATION
INTERLINE BRANDS, INC.
SID HARVEY INDUSTRIES, INC.

HISTORICAL FINANCIALS

Company Type: Public

Income Statement — FYE: July 31

	REVENUE ($mil)	NET INCOME ($mil)	NET PROFIT MARGIN	EMPLOYEES
07/23	29,734	1,889	6.4%	35,000
07/22	28,566	2,122	7.4%	36,000
07/21	22,792	1,508	6.6%	29,538
07/20	21,819	961	4.4%	34,637
07/19	22,010	1,108	5.0%	35,939
Annual Growth	7.8%	14.3%	—	(0.7%)

2023 Year-End Financials
Debt ratio: 23.5%
Return on equity: 38.9%
Cash ($ mil.): 601
Current Ratio: 1.67
Long-term debt ($ mil.): 3,711
No. of shares ($ mil.): 204
Dividends
  Yield: —
  Payout: 32.8%
Market value ($ mil.): —

FIDEA Holdings Co. Ltd.

EXECUTIVES

Representative Executive Officer, President, Chief Executive Officer, Director, Yuichi Tao
Executive Vice President, Chief Financial Officer, Chief Technology Officer, Norio Miyashita
Senior Managing Executive Officer, Chief Marketing Officer, Masahiro Niino
Managing Executive Officer, Chief Risk Officer, Tadahiko Onoyama
Managing Executive Officer, Chief Investment Officer, Hidenori Asami
Executive Officer, Chief Compliance Officer, Hitoshi Kudo
Director, Arata Ito
Director, Masahiko Matsuta
Director, Hideo Togashi
Director, Satoru Nishibori
Outside Director, Shoichi Ogawa
Outside Director, Kyoichi Fukuda
Outside Director, Yutaka Hori
Outside Director, Hiroshi Konno
Outside Director, Tomoko Nunoi
Outside Director, Wataru Hirose
Outside Director, Fumio Kai
Auditors: Ernst & Young ShinNihon LLC

LOCATIONS

HQ: FIDEA Holdings Co. Ltd.
3-1-24 Chuo, Aoba-ku, Sendai, Miyagi 980-0021
Phone: (81) 22 290 8800
Web: www.fidea.co.jp

HISTORICAL FINANCIALS

Company Type: Public

Income Statement — FYE: March 31

	ASSETS ($mil)	NET INCOME ($mil)	INCOME AS % OF ASSETS	EMPLOYEES
03/22	26,843	28	0.1%	2,335
03/21	29,094	29	0.1%	2,538
03/20	25,011	12	0.0%	2,724
03/19	24,663	34	0.1%	2,928
03/18	26,010	40	0.2%	3,105
Annual Growth	0.8%	(8.0%)	—	(6.9%)

2022 Year-End Financials
Return on assets: 0.1%
Return on equity: 3.0%
Long-term debt ($ mil.): —
No. of shares ($ mil.): 18
Sales ($ mil.): 420
Dividends
  Yield: —
  Payout: 50.4%
Market value ($ mil.): —

FIH Mobile Ltd

EXECUTIVES

Chairman, Chief Executive Officer, Samuel Wai Leung Chin
Executive Director, Director, Yu Yang Chih

Business Development Vice President, Tom Hsu
Tang Chen
Vice President, Yi Hsin Pao
Treasurer, Jonathan Chung Chang Hsu
Chief Accounting Officer, Danny Kam Wah Tam
Secretary, Wan Mui Tang
Director, Jimmy Ban Ja Chang
Director, Hsiao Ling Gou
Director, Jin Ming Lee
Director, Fang Ming Lu
Director, Siu Ki Lau
Director, Daniel Joseph Mehan
Director, Fung Ming Chen
Auditors : Deloitte Touche Tohmatsu

LOCATIONS

HQ: FIH Mobile Ltd
No. 4 Minsheng Street, Tucheng District, New Taipei 236
Phone: —
Web: www.fihmobile.com

HISTORICAL FINANCIALS
Company Type: Public

Income Statement — FYE: December 31

	REVENUE ($mil)	NET INCOME ($mil)	NET PROFIT MARGIN	EMPLOYEES
12/22	9,394	(72)	—	44,055
12/21	8,582	56	0.7%	73,993
12/20	8,934	(173)	—	70,381
12/19	14,378	(12)	—	85,729
12/18	14,929	(857)	—	97,484
Annual Growth	(10.9%)	—	—	(18.0%)

2022 Year-End Financials
Debt ratio: 12.3%
Return on equity: (-3.6%)
Cash ($ mil.): 1,825
Current Ratio: 1.21
Long-term debt ($ mil.): —
No. of shares ($ mil.): 7,938
Dividends
  Yield: —
  Payout: 0.0%
Market value ($ mil.): —

First Abu Dhabi Bank PJSC

Auditors : KPMG Lower Gulf Limited

LOCATIONS

HQ: First Abu Dhabi Bank PJSC
FAB Building, Khalifa Business Park 1 Al Qurum, P. O. Box 6316, Abu Dhabi
Phone: —
Web: www.bankfab.com

HISTORICAL FINANCIALS
Company Type: Public

Income Statement — FYE: December 31

	ASSETS ($mil)	NET INCOME ($mil)	INCOME AS % OF ASSETS	EMPLOYEES
12/23	318,212	4,467	1.4%	0
12/19	223,817	3,409	1.5%	5,451
12/18	202,621	3,270	1.6%	0
12/17	182,156	2,486	1.4%	0
12/16	114,538	1,441	1.3%	0
Annual Growth	15.7%	17.5%	—	—

2023 Year-End Financials
Return on assets: —
Return on equity: —
Long-term debt ($ mil.): —
No. of shares ($ mil.): 11,041
Sales ($ mil.): 19,669
Dividends
  Yield: —
  Payout: 49.6%
Market value ($ mil.): —

FirstRand Ltd.

FirstRand, through its portfolio of integrated financial services businesses, operates in South Africa, certain markets in sub-Saharan Africa, the UK, and India. Boasting some R2,004 billion in assets, the company is the largest financial institution by market capitalization in Africa. The company's FirstRand Bank Holdings operates FirstRand Bank and First National Bank (FNB) in southern Africa, as well as asset financing firm WesBank and investment bank Rand Merchant Bank. FirstRand owns and operates some 735 FNB branches and around 5,700 ATMs mostly in South Africa, and the rest of Africa. Majority of its sales were generated from South Africa.

Operations

FirstRand operates three main segments or franchises. Its Retail and Commercial consists of First National Bank (FNB) business, about 65% of FirstRand's normalized earnings and WesBank with over 5%. FNB represents the group's activities in the retail and commercial segments in South Africa and several countries in the rest of Africa. Its rest of Africa portfolio represents a mix of mature businesses with significant scale and market share, including Namibia, Botswana and Eswatini, and growing businesses in Mozambique, Zambia, Lesotho and Ghana. WesBank represents the group's activities in instalment credit, fleet management and related services in the retail, commercial and corporate segments of South Africa.

Its Rand Merchant Bank (RMB) business (about 20% of earnings) comprised the corporate and investment banking segments in South Africa, the UK, the African continent and India. RMB offers corporate finance, leveraged finance, resource sector solutions, infrastructure sector solutions, real estate finance, debt capital markets, debt trade solutions, sponsor services, corporate broking, loan syndications, coverage, advisory, corporate transactional banking and principal investments.

Aldemore, some 10%, is a UK specialist lender focusing on lending in six areas: asset finance, invoice finance, SME commercial mortgages (including property development), residential mortgages, buy-to-let mortgages and vehicle finance (MotoNovo).

Broadly speaking, some 70% of FirstRand's total revenue came from interest income, while another around 20% came from fee and commission income. The rest of its revenue came from fair value gains (approximately 5%), insurance income, (less than 5%), and other non-interest revenue (two percent).

Geographic Reach

Headquartered in South Africa, FNB had some 735 branches. Its rest of Africa portfolio represents a mix of mature businesses with significant scale and market share, including Namibia, Botswana and Eswatini, and growing businesses in Mozambique, Zambia, Lesotho and Ghana.

South Africa accounts for over 75%, while other Africa and UK accounts for the rest.

Financial Performance

The company reported a total revenue of R24.3 billion in 2022, a 203% increase from the previous year's total revenue of R8 billion.

In 2022, the company had a net income of R33.6 billion, a 22% increase from the previous year's net income of R27.5 billion.

The company's cash at the end of 2022 was R9.8 billion. Operating activities generated R39.7 billion, while investing activities used R3.3 billion, mainly for acquisition of property and equipment. Financing activities used another R2.5 billion, primarily for capital repaid on Tier 2 liabilities.

Company Background

FirstRand was formed in 1998 when Rand Merchant Bank Holdings (RMBH) and mining company Anglo American Corporation merged their financial services operations. RMB Holdings still held a 33.9% stake in the company as of early 2016.

EXECUTIVES

Chief Executive Officer, Executive Director, Alan Patrick Pullinger
Finance Director, Executive Director, H. S. Kellan
Chief Operating Officer, Executive Director, M. Vilakazi
Secretary, C. Low
Chairman, Independent Non-Executive Director, W. R. Jardine
Independent Non-Executive Director, G. G. Gelink
Independent Non-Executive Director, R. M. Loubser
Independent Non-Executive Director, T. S. Mashego
Independent Non-Executive Director, P. D. Naidoo
Independent Non-Executive Director, Z. Roscherr
Independent Non-Executive Director, S. P. Sibisi
Independent Non-Executive Director, L. L. von Zeuner
Independent Non-Executive Director, T. Winterboer
Non-Executive Director, J. P. Burger
Auditors : PricewaterhouseCoopers Inc.

LOCATIONS

HQ: FirstRand Ltd.
4 Merchant Place, Corner Fredman Drive & Rivonia Road, Sandton 2196
Phone: (27) 11 282 1808   **Fax:** (27) 11 282 8088
Web: www.firstrand.co.za

PRODUCTS/OPERATIONS

2015 Sales

	% of total
Interest	
Advances	54
Other	5
Non interest	
Fees & commissions	29
Fair value income	7
Gains less losses from investing activities	2
Other	3
Total	100

Selected Subsidiaries
First National Bank Holdings (Botswana) Limited
First National Bank of Lesotho Limited
First National Bank of Namibia Limited (61%)
First National Bank of Swaziland Limited
First National Bank of Zambia Limited
FirstCorp Merchant Bank Holdings Limited
FirstRand Bank Limited
Firstrand Finance Company Limited
FNB Insurance Brokers (Pty) Limited
RMB Asset Finance Limited
RMB Investment and Advisory (Pty) Limited
WesBank

COMPETITORS
BRITISH ARAB COMMERCIAL BANK PUBLIC LIMITED COMPANY
BYLINE BANCORP, INC.
CANARA BANK
LIONTRUST ASSET MANAGEMENT PLC
MITSUBISHI UFJ FINANCIAL GROUP, INC.
PCF GROUP PLC
RESONA HOLDINGS, INC.
Shinhan Financial Group Co., Ltd.
Woori Finance Holdings Co., Ltd.
YAPI VE KREDI BANKASI ANONIM SIRKETI

HISTORICAL FINANCIALS
Company Type: Public

Income Statement — FYE: June 30

	REVENUE ($mil)	NET INCOME ($mil)	NET PROFIT MARGIN	EMPLOYEES
06/23	11,714	1,973	16.8%	0
06/22	10,337	2,052	19.9%	48,059
06/21	11,258	1,924	17.1%	47,413
06/20	10,022	1,046	10.4%	49,233
06/19	12,202	2,177	17.8%	48,780
Annual Growth	(1.0%)	(2.4%)	—	—

2023 Year-End Financials
Debt ratio: —
Return on equity: 20.2%
Cash ($ mil.): 9,230
Current Ratio: —
Long-term debt ($ mil.): —
No. of shares ($ mil.): 5,606
Dividends
  Yield: —
  Payout: 59.1%
Market value ($ mil.): —

Flex Ltd

Flex is the diversified manufacturing partner of choice that helps market-leading brands design, build and deliver innovative products that improve the world. Flex's services range from design engineering, to manufacturing and assembly, to logistics, to innovation services and power modules. It makes and assembles printed circuit board assembly, and assembly of systems and subsystems that incorporate printed circuit boards and complex electromechanical components. Flex covers a lot of ground around the world, operating in more than 100 locations in approximately 30 countries. The majority of the company's revenue comes from international markets.

Operations
Flex's three operating and reportable segments are Flex Agility Solutions (FAS), Flex Reliability Solutions (FRS) and Nextracker.

The FAS segment comprises more than 50% of the company's sales. It is optimized for longer product lifecycles requiring complex ramps with specialized production models and critical environments.

The FRS segment is optimized for longer product lifecycles requiring complex ramps with specialized production models and critical environments. It contributes more than 40% of the sales.

Nextracker (more than 5%), the leading provider of intelligent, integrated solar tracker and software solutions used in utility-scale and ground-mounted distributed generation solar projects around the world. Nextracker's products enable solar panels to follow the sun's movement across the sky and optimize plant performance.

Geographic Reach
Flex operates a network of more than 100 facilities in approximately 30 countries across four continents. Its extensive network of innovation labs, design centers, manufacturing and services sites in the world's major consumer and enterprise products markets are located in Asia, the Americas, and Europe.

The company's headquarters is in Changi South Lane, Singapore and its headquarters in US is in San Jose, California.

Customers in China and Mexico account for more than 20% of sales each and US customers supplying more than 15%. Brazil, Malaysia, Hungary, and other countries account for the rest.

Sales and Marketing
Flex delivers technology innovation, supply chain and manufacturing solutions to various industries including cloud, communications, enterprise, automotive, industrial, consumer devices, lifestyle, healthcare, and energy.

Its ten largest customers account for about 35% of sales.

Financial Performance
Net sales for fiscal year 2023 increased approximately 17%, or $4.3 billion, to $30.3 billion from the prior year. The increase in sales was notable in all three segments.

In fiscal year 2023, the company had a net income of $1.0 billion, a 10% increase from the previous year's net income $936 million, due to lower income taxes in fiscal year 2023, offset by the absence of an approximate $150 million noncash gain recorded in fiscal year 2022 related to certain tax credits in Brazil and higher interest expense in fiscal year 2023.

The company's cash at the end of fiscal year 2023 was $3.3 billion. Operating activities generated $950 million, while investing activities used $604 million, mainly for purchases of property and equipment. Financing activities provided another $2 million.

Strategy
Flex helps customers responsibly build products that create value and improve people's lives. It does this by providing its customers with product development lifecycle services, from innovation, design, and engineering, to manufacturing, supply chain solutions, logistics, and circularity offerings. Its strategy is to enable and scale innovation for customers, maintain its leadership in its capabilities, and build extended offerings in high-growth industries and markets.

Flex focuses on hiring and retaining the world's best talent to maintain the company's competitiveness and world-class capabilities. It has taken steps to attract the best engineering, functional and operational leaders and have accelerated efforts to develop the future leaders of the company.

Flex believes that building strong partnerships with customers and delivering on its commitments strengthens trust and customer retention. Its customers come first, and it has a relentless focus on delivering distinctive products and services in a cost-effective manner with fast time to market. Flex is highly collaborative and leverages its global system and processes to operate with speed and responsiveness to provide customers with a reliant supply chain partner.

Flex focuses on companies that are leaders in their industry and value the company's superior capabilities in design, manufacturing, and supply chain services. It focuses on high growth industries and markets where it has distinctive competence and compelling value propositions. Flex's market-focused approach to managing business increases customers' competitiveness by leveraging its deep vertical industry and cross-industry expertise, as well as global scale, regional presence and agility to respond to changes in market dynamics.

The company continues to invest in maintaining the leadership of its world-class manufacturing and services capabilities including automation, new product introduction and large-scale manufacturing.

HISTORY
Flextronics International, formed in 1990, followed two earlier contract manufacturers named Flextronics formed in 1969 and 1980. The latter iteration used acquisitions to expand throughout Asia and the US. In 1988 it opened the first US-managed contract electronics plant in China, and that year sales topped $200 million.

But acquisitions burdened Flextronics

with debt and left it with disparate operations. It divested its US-based manufacturing operations and laid off 75% of its workforce. The company brought in a management team to sell its healthy Asian operations to pay off debt. These operations formed the current incarnation of Flextronics International.

A revitalized Flextronics, based in Singapore, went public in 1994. It quickly joined the industry rush toward consolidation and globalization. Acquisitions included nCHIP (California, 1996), FICO Plastics (Hong Kong, 1997), Neutronics Electronic Industries (Austria, 1997), and Kyrel EMS Oyj (Finland and France, 1999).

In 2000 Flextronics acquired rival The DII Group, which propelled the company to the #4 spot in contract manufacturing (behind Solectron, SCI Systems, and Celestica). The company was also selected by Microsoft to build the software juggernaut's Xbox video game console. Later that year Motorola and Flextronics signed one of the largest outsourcing deals ever, worth an estimated $30 billion over five years. The company expanded further in Asia when it acquired JIT Holdings, a Singapore-based electronics manufacturer.

In 2001 Flextronics announced a deal with telecommunications giant Ericsson; under the pact Flextronics assumed management of Ericsson's mobile phone manufacturing operations worldwide. Later that year the company announced that it would cut its workforce by about 10%, and that the multibillion-dollar deal with Motorola unraveled due to a continuing market slowdown. Flextronics also repurchased Motorola's 5% stake in the company.

Also that year Flextronics bought Telcom Global Solutions, a supplier of planning and design services for telecommunications providers. Flextronics later announced a deal with Xerox to acquire Xerox facilities in Brazil, Canada, Malaysia, and Mexico for about $220 million, and to provide manufacturing services to Xerox for five years. Later that year the company laid off 10,000 workers -- about 15% of its staff -- in a cost-cutting move. Flextronics also acquired a 91% stake in Orbiant, a telephone network services spinoff of Swedish telecom giant Telia, for $100 million in cash (along with future payments pegged to the unit's performance).

In 2002 the company made a deal with CASIO COMPUTER, under which Flextronics bought two CASIO plants in Asia, then supplied the Japanese electronics maker with finished products in a three-year pact. Also that year the company significantly expanded its presence in southern China with the purchase of Hong Kong-based NatSteel Broadway (printed circuit boards, plastic and metal components) for about $367 million.

In 2004 Flextronics took over optical, wireless, and enterprise manufacturing, as well as optical design operations from Nortel Networks in a four-year supply deal generating about $2.5 billion in annual revenues. Flextronics later closed several former Nortel facilities in Canada, France, and Northern Ireland.

Flextronics also acquired a majority ownership stake in India-based software services provider Hughes Software Systems (HSS) in 2004. The following year Flextronics purchased Agilent's mobile communications camera module business. The company sold its semiconductor division to AMIS Holdings (now part of ON Semiconductor), and its Flextronics Network Services division was merged with a company called Telavie and renamed Relacom; Flextronics retained a 30% stake.

Flextronics set plans in 2005 to build an industrial park in Chennai, India, to supplement its existing operations on the subcontinent, where it previously employed more than 5,000 people. The development added to the two manufacturing facilities and three design centers Flextronics had in India.

To focus on its core electronics manufacturing services business in 2006, Flextronics sold its Flextronics Software Systems business (renamed Aricent) to an affiliate of KKR for about $900 million in cash and notes. Flextronics retained a 15% equity interest in the software development business, which was primarily based in India (it sold the remaining stake in 2009). Divestitures of its software and semiconductor businesses took a small chunk out of the company's revenues -- $278 million in fiscal 2006.

Flextronics then acquired International DisplayWorks, a contract manufacturer of small LCDs and LCD modules for cell phones and other consumer electronics, for stock valued at approximately $243 million. International DisplayWorks became a wholly owned subsidiary of Flextronics, operating within the company's Components Group. Also in 2006, nLight Corp. acquired the assets of Flextronics Photonics, including a line of fiber-coupled and hybrid microelectronic devices.

In 2007 Flextronics purchased rival contract manufacturer Solectron in a deal valued at $3.6 billion. The combination vaulted the company into the position of the second-largest contract electronics manufacturer in the world, trailing only Hon Hai Precision Industry, the maker of products for Apple, Dell, and many other companies.

The next year it bought contract disposable device maker Avail Medical Products, a private company with around $250 million in sales, to further the expansion of its Flextronics Medical segment. Also in 2008 Flextronics inked a deal to acquire Elcoteq's ZAO Elcoteq subsidiary and plant in St. Petersburg, Russia. Flextronics, however, later terminated the transaction and was forced to pay a fee for noncompletion.

In 2009 it sold its stake in Aricent, a privately held communications software company, to investment firms KKR and CPP Investment Board for about $250 million. The sale was part of a plan to sell noncore assets as Flextronics tried to bolster its balance sheet during the economic downturn. At the end of the year it bought SloMedical S.R.O., a leading maker of disposable medical devices for the European market. In addition to adding disposable devices for the medical and surgical market in Eastern Europe, SloMedical (based in Slovenia) gave Flextronics an FDA-compliant, clean room-enabled production site with low production costs.

In 2012 Flextronics acquired Stellar Microelectronics, an EMS provider based in California that specializes in custom packaging services for the aerospace, defense, and medical manufacturing markets, as part of a plan to expand services for the highly regulated markets. Also that year, Flextronics sold its Vista Point camera module business to Tessera Technologies' subsidiary DigitalOptics; the sale included the brand, intellectual property, and China-based manufacturing assets.

EXECUTIVES

Chairman, Director, Michael D. Capellas
Chief Executive Officer, Director, Revathi Advaithi, $165,865 total compensation
Executive Vice President, General Counsel, Scott Offer, $559,116 total compensation
Chief Financial Officer, Paul R. Lundstrom
Chief Accounting Officer, Daniel Wendler
Division Officer, Kwang Hooi Tan
Division Officer, Rebecca Sidelinger
Division Officer, Michael Hartung
Director, Maryrose T. Sylvester
Director, Erin L. McSweeney
Director, Charles K. Stevens
Director, Lay Koon Tan
Director, William D. Watkins
Director, Michael E. Hurlston
Director, John D. Harris
Director, Patrick J. Ward
Auditors : Deloitte & Touche LLP

LOCATIONS

HQ: Flex Ltd
  2 Changi South Lane, 486123
Phone: (65) 6876 9899
Web: www.flex.com

2018 Sales

	$ mil.	% of total
China	6,649	25
Mexico	4,539	17
US	3,106	12
Brazil	2,181	8
Malaysia	1,996	8
India	1,805	7
Other countries	5,935	23
Total	26,211	100

PRODUCTS/OPERATIONS

2018 Sales

	$ mil.	% of total
Communications & Enterprise Compute	8,336	32
Consumer Technologies Group	6,836	26
Industrial & emerging industries	6,813	24
High reliability solutions	4,829	18
Total	26,211	100

Selected Services

Assembly and manufacturing
    Box build (complete systems)
    Complex electromechanical components
    Printed circuit boards (PCBs)
    Subsystems (including those that incorporate PCBs)
Engineering
    Design
    Prototyping
    Test development
Materials procurement and management
    Planning
    Purchasing
    Warehousing
Network support
    Installation and maintenance of telecommunications systems and corporate networks
Packaging
Plastic and metal components
Product distribution
Recycling and refurbishment
Testing of PCBs, subsystems, and systems
Warranty repair

COMPETITORS

ATOS SE
AVAGO TECHNOLOGIES LIMITED
CAPGEMINI
Celestica Inc
JABIL INC.
JOHNSON CONTROLS INTERNATIONAL PUBLIC LIMITED COMPANY
REXEL
SANMINA CORPORATION
SPIRENT COMMUNICATIONS PLC
TT ELECTRONICS PLC

HISTORICAL FINANCIALS

Company Type: Public

Income Statement   FYE: March 31

	REVENUE ($mil)	NET INCOME ($mil)	NET PROFIT MARGIN	EMPLOYEES
03/23	30,346	793	2.6%	172,108
03/22	26,041	936	3.6%	172,648
03/21	24,124	613	2.5%	167,201
03/20	24,209	87	0.4%	160,000
03/19	26,210	93	0.4%	200,000
Annual Growth	3.7%	70.7%	—	(3.7%)

2023 Year-End Financials

Debt ratio: 18.0%   No. of shares ($ mil.): 450
Return on equity: 16.7%   Dividends
Cash ($ mil.): 3,294   Yield: —
Current Ratio: 1.48   Payout: 0.0%
Long-term debt ($ mil.): 3,691   Market value ($ mil.): —

Flutter Entertainment plc

Flutter Entertainment (formerly Paddy Power Betfair) is a leading bookmaker serving bettors in Ireland and the UK through about 250 retail betting outlets. The company offers betting on a wide range of sporting events, including cricket, football, horse racing, and rugby, as well as American and other international sports. It also takes bets online and over the phone. Flutter Entertainment also offers other online games, including bingo, casino games, and poker. In addition to its domestic and UK activities, the company operates betting in Australia through subsidiary Sportsbet. Having merged with Betfair in 2016, Flutter continued its quest to consolidate the online gaming industry when it agreed to merge with Stars Group, a Canadian online gambling company in 2019.

EXECUTIVES

Chief Financial Officer, Executive Director, Jonathan S. Hill
Chief Executive Officer, Executive Director, Peter Jackson
Secretary, Edward Traynor
Independent Chairman, Non-Executive Director, Gary McGann
Senior Independent Director, Holly Keller Koeppel
Independent Non-Executive Director, Nancy Cruickshank
Independent Non-Executive Director, Nancy Dubuc
Independent Non-Executive Director, Alfred F. Hurley
Independent Non-Executive Director, David A. Lazzarato
Non-Executive Director, Richard Flint
Non-Executive Director, Carolan Lennon
Independent Non-Executive Director, Atif Rafiq
Independent Non-Executive Director, Mary Turner
Independent Non-Executive Director, Holly Keller Koeppel
Auditors: KPMG

LOCATIONS

HQ: Flutter Entertainment plc
Belfield Office Park, Beech Hill Road, Clonskeagh, Dublin 4
Phone: (353) 1 905 1000   **Fax:** (353) 1 905 1001
Web: www.flutter.com

COMPETITORS

2016 GCG LIMITED
ACN 066 441 067 PTY LTD
BET365 GROUP LIMITED
CATALYST MEDIA GROUP PLC
OPENBET LIMITED
SPORTECH PLC
SPORTING INDEX LIMITED
SPORTINGBET LIMITED
TABCORP HOLDINGS LIMITED
VICTOR CHANDLER LIMITED

HISTORICAL FINANCIALS

Company Type: Public

Income Statement   FYE: December 31

	REVENUE ($mil)	NET INCOME ($mil)	NET PROFIT MARGIN	EMPLOYEES
12/22	9,261	(363)	—	18,736
12/21	8,134	(560)	—	15,798
12/20	6,023	51	0.9%	12,550
12/19	2,826	190	6.7%	8,890
12/18	2,391	257	10.8%	7,702
Annual Growth	40.3%	—	—	24.9%

2022 Year-End Financials

Debt ratio: 32.8%   No. of shares ($ mil.): 176
Return on equity: (-2.9%)   Dividends
Cash ($ mil.): 2,517   Yield: —
Current Ratio: 0.87   Payout: 0.0%
Long-term debt ($ mil.): 6,671   Market value ($ mil.): 12,013

	STOCK PRICE ($) FY Close	P/E High/Low		PER SHARE ($) Earnings	Dividends	Book Value
12/22	68.22	—	—	(2.06)	0.00	69.79
12/21	79.66	—	—	(3.19)	0.00	78.67
12/20	104.30	363	122	0.39	0.00	85.48
12/19	61.79	34	20	2.37	0.30	66.07
12/18	40.71	25	16	3.02	2.51	63.20
Annual Growth	13.8%	—	—	—	—	2.5%

Fomento Economico Mexicano, S.A.B. de C.V.

Fomento Económico Mexicano or FEMSA is a top soft drink bottler and convenience store operator in Latin America. Its Coca-Cola FEMSA subsidiary is the world's largest Coca-Cola bottler. FEMSA bottles Coca-Cola, Sprite, other soft drinks, juices, and water in around 10 Latin American countries. The company operates more than 565 service stations located in more than 15 states throughout Mexico and it also owns about 20,430 OXXO convenience stores in Colombia, Chile, Mexico, and Peru, primarily in the northern part of the country, through its FEMSA Comercio subsidiary. The company generates the majority of its revenue in Mexico and Central America.

Operations

The company's business units include Coca-Cola FEMSA (about 35% of sales), and FEMSA Comerico which is divided to Proximity Division (nearly 35%), Health Division (around 15%), Logistics and Distribution (about 10%), Fuel Division (more than 5%), and other businesses (account for the rest).

Coca-Cola FEMSA includes the delivery of beverages, the rendering of manufacturing services, logistic and administrative services. Proximity Division includes mainly the commercialization of spaces into within stores, and revenues related to promotions and financial services. It operates the largest chain of small-format stores in Mexico and Latin America including as some of its principal products as beers, cigarettes, sodas, other beverages and snacks. Health Division's core products include patent and generic formulas of medicines, beauty products, medical supplements, housing, and personnel care products. Logistics and distribution includes rendering a wide range of logistic services and maintenance of vehicles to subsidiaries and customers. The revenues in this business are integrated from the sale of consumables in the janitorial, sanitary supply, and packaging industry in the US. Fuel Division's core products are sold in the retail service stations as fuels, diesel, motor oils and other car care products. Other businesses involves the production, commercialization of refrigerators including its delivery and installation and offering of integral maintenance services at the point of sale. It also includes the design, manufacturing, and recycling of plastic products. In addition, it includes the sale of equipment for food processing, storage and weighing.

Geographic Reach

Headquartered in Nuevo León, Mexico, FEMSA operates in Argentina, Brazil, Colombia, Costa Rica, Guatemala, Mexico, Nicaragua, Panama, and Ecuador. Subsidiary Coca-Cola FEMSA operates in Argentina, Brazil, Central America, Colombia, Mexico, and Venezuela. Mexico and Central America bring in nearly 60% of the company's revenue, while South America accounts for the rest.

Sales and Marketing

FEMSA relies extensively on advertising, sales promotions and retailer support programs to target the particular preferences of its consumers. It advertises in all major communications media. Its principal channels are small retailers, on-premise accounts, such as restaurants and bars, supermarkets and third-party distributors.

The company's advertising and promotional expenses amounted to approximately Ps. 7,586, Ps. 7,471, and Ps. 8,840 for the years ended 2021, 2020, and 2019, respectively.

Financial Performance

FEMSA's consolidated total revenues increased about 13% to Ps. 556.3 billion in 2021 compared to Ps. 493.0 billion in 2020. Coca-Cola FEMSA's total revenues increased 6% to Ps. 194.8 billion, mainly as a result of pricing initiatives, coupled with favorable price-mix effects and volume growth.

Consolidated net income was Ps. 37.7 billion in 2021 compared to Ps. 3.8 billion in 2020, reflecting higher income from operations across its business units; higher other income; and an increase in its share of profit of equity accounted investees.

Cash held by the company at the end of fiscal 2021 increased to Ps.97.4 billion. Operating activities provided Ps.53.2 billion while investing and financing activities used Ps.46.2 billion and Ps.37.0 billion, respectively. Main cash uses were interest paid, dividends paid, purchase of investments and acquisitions of property, plant and equipment.

Strategy

FESMA currently operate in Mexico, Central America, South America and in the US, including some of the most populous metropolitan areas in Latin America?which provides the company with opportunities to create value through both an improved ability to execute its strategies in both complex and developed markets. It has also increased its capabilities to operate and succeed in other geographic regions by improving management skills to obtain a precise understanding of local consumer needs. Going forward, FESMA intend to use those capabilities to continue our expansion, both geographically and within its current business verticals, such as non-alcoholic beverages, small box retail, logistics and distribution, and other ancillary businesses, as well as taking advantage of potential opportunities across its current markets to leverage its capability set.

Additionally, FESMA is leveraging the competitive advantages and strong market position of its businesses to build innovative digital businesses in the financial services industry to address the financial needs of its customers and business partners, with an efficient and comprehensive value proposition. Moreover, through OXXO Premia, the company is developing OXXO's first customer loyalty program that will allow the company to further connect with its customers, while rewarding them for their loyalty and day-to-day purchases at OXXO, other FEMSA formats, and beyond.

Mergers and Acquisitions

In early 2022, FEMSA successfully closed the acquisition of OK Market, a small-format proximity store chain in Chile, after receiving the necessary regulatory approvals. The transaction will add 134 locations to FEMSA's proximity business existing footprint in this important market, to reach a total of 258 locations. With this transaction, FEMSA increases its commitment as a proximity store operator in Chile, improving its scale and ability to better serve its Chilean consumers.

HISTORY

FEMSA's 2005 purchase of Panamerican Beverages (Panamco) through its Coca-Cola subsidiary gave the company access to markets in Brazil, Colombia, Costa Rica, Guatemala, Nicaragua, Panama, and Venezuela.

EXECUTIVES

Executive Chairman, Jose Antonio Fernandez Carbajal
Chief Executive Officer, Director, Miguel Eduardo Padilla Silva
Chief Corporate Officer, Francisco Camacho Beltran
Strategic Business Chief Executive Officer,
Strategic Businesses Chief Executive Officer,
Strategic Business Vice President, Strategic Businesses Vice President, Alfonso Garza Garza
Corporate Affairs Vice President, Roberto Campa Cifrian
Administration and Corporate Control Vice President, Gerardo Estrada Attolini
Finance and Corporate Development Director, Eugenio Garza y Garza
General Counsel, Secretary, Carlos Eduardo Aldrete Ancira
Independent Director, Ricardo Guajardo Touche
Independent Director, Luis Alberto Moreno Mejia
Independent Director, Ricardo Ernesto Saldivar Escajadillo
Independent Director, Alfonso Gonzalez Migoya
Independent Director, Michael Larson
Independent Director, Robert Edwin Denham
Independent Director, Victor Alberto Tiburcio Celorio
Director, Javier Gerardo Astaburuaga Sanjines
Director, Eva Maria Garza Laguera Gonda
Director, Mariana Garza Laguera Gonda
Director, Jose Fernando Calderon Rojas
Director, Alfonso Garza Garza
Director, Bertha Paula Michel Gonzalez
Director, Alberto Bailleres Gonzalez
Director, Francisco Javier Fernandez Carbajal
Director, Barbara Garza Laguera Gonda
Auditors: Mancera, S.C., a member practice of Ernst & Young Global Limited

LOCATIONS

HQ: Fomento Economico Mexicano, S.A.B. de C.V.
General Anaya No. 601 Pte., Colonia Bella Vista, Monterrey, Nuevo Leon 64410
Phone: (52) 818 328 6167   **Fax:** (52) 818 328 6080
Web: www.femsa.com

2014

Geography	mil (pesos)	%
Mexico and Central America	186,736	71
South America	69,172	26
Venezuela	8,835	3
Consolidation adjustments	(1,294)	-
Total	263,449	100

PRODUCTS/OPERATIONS

2014

Business Unit	mil (pesos)	%
Coca-Cola FEMSA	147,298	53
FEMSA Comercio	109,624	40
Other	20,069	7
Consolidation Adjustments	(13,542)	-
Total	263,449	100

COMPETITORS

América Móvil, S.A.B. de C.V.
Anheuser-Busch InBev
Anheuser-Busch InBev
Controladora Mabe, S.A. de C.V.
Grupo Bimbo, S.A.B. de C.V.

Grupo Comercial Chedraui, S.A.B. de C.V.
Grupo Lala, S.A.B. de C.V.
NATURGY ENERGY GROUP SA.
SUNTORY HOLDINGS LIMITED
THE EDRINGTON GROUP LIMITED

HISTORICAL FINANCIALS

Company Type: Public

Income Statement — FYE: December 31

	REVENUE ($mil)	NET INCOME ($mil)	NET PROFIT MARGIN	EMPLOYEES
12/21	27,205	1,393	5.1%	320,752
12/20	24,810	(97)	—	320,618
12/19	26,782	1,094	4.1%	314,656
12/18	23,888	1,219	5.1%	297,073
12/17	23,373	2,152	9.2%	295,097
Annual Growth	3.9%	(10.3%)	—	2.1%

2021 Year-End Financials

Debt ratio: 1.3%
Return on equity: 11.3%
Cash ($ mil.): 4,763
Current Ratio: 1.69
Long-term debt ($ mil.): 9,094
No. of shares ($ mil.): 17,891
Dividends
Yield: 1.4%
Payout: 1607.1%
Market value ($ mil.): 1,390,320

	STOCK PRICE ($) FY Close	P/E High/Low		PER SHARE ($) Earnings	Dividends	Book Value
12/21	77.71	62	47	0.07	1.11	0.72
12/20	75.77	90	56	0.05	1.43	0.67
12/19	94.51	98	85	0.05	1.48	0.74
12/18	86.05	80	68	0.06	1.39	0.73
12/17	93.90	44	37	0.11	1.29	0.71
Annual Growth	(4.6%)	—	—	(10.3%)	(3.8%)	0.3%

Fortescue Ltd

Fortescue Metals Group is one of the world's lowest cost iron ore producers. The company, Australia's third-largest miner (behind Rio Tinto and BHP Billiton), has more than 1.7 billion tons of iron ore reserves; it began production in 2008 and produced about 180 million tons in fiscal 2022. It shipments has already been sold to steel producers around the world, including Chinese steel producers. As one of the world's largest producers of iron ore, Fortescue's wholly owned and integrated operations in the Pilbara include the Chichester, Solomon and Western mining hubs. Majority of its sales were generated in China.

Operations

Fortescue Metals operates through two segments: Iron Ore, which generated all of its sales, and FFI. Iron ore includes exploration, development, production, processing, sale and transportation of iron ore, and the exploration for other minerals. The FFI includes undertaking activities in the development of green electricity, green hydrogen and green ammonia projects in both Australia and globally.

The company's wholly owned and integrated operations in the Pilbara include the Chichester, Solomon and Western mining hubs.

The Chichester Hub in the Chichester Ranges includes the Cloudbreak and Christmas Creek mines and has an annual production capacity of approximately 100 million tonnes per annum (mtpa) from three ore processing facilities (OPFs).

The Solomon Hub in the Hamersley Ranges is located 60km north of Tom Price and 120km to the west of its Chichester Hub. It comprises the Firetail, Kings Valley and Queens Valley mines which together have a production range of 65 to 70mtpa. The expansion to Queens Valley has enabled continued production of the Kings Fines product.

Its Western hub includes its newest mine at Eliwana commenced operations in December 2020 and includes a 30mtpa dry OPF and 143km of rail linking the mine to its Hamersley rail line.

Overall, Iron Ore generated about 90% of sales, while shipping revenues generated the rest.

Geographic Reach

Based in Australia, Fortescue Metals' primary market is China, accounted for about 90% of the company's total sales.

Sales and Marketing

The company generated $1.3 billion and $1.8 billion from its top two customers which generated over 5% and some 10% of the company's total sales.

Financial Performance

Company's revenue for fiscal 2022 decreased to $17.4 billion compared from the prior year with $22.3 billion. The decrease was mainly due to less sales of iron ore.

Cash held by the company at the end of fiscal 2022 decreased to $5.2 billion. Cash provided by operations was $6.6 billion while cash used for investing and financing activities were $3.1 billion and $5.1 billion, respectively. Main uses of cash were payments for property, plant and equipment; and dividends paid.

Strategy

The company continue to look for other opportunities for automation and artificial intelligence to drive greater efficiency across the business, including the use of data to predict outcomes and optimise performance, the expansion of autonomy to fixed plant and non-mining equipment and the application of relocatable conveyor technology.

Mergers and Acquisitions

In late 2021, Fortescue Future Industries (FFI) has acquired the commercial assets of Xergy Inc and Xergy One Ltd. (Xergy) to form FFI Ionix Inc. A wholly owned subsidiary of FFI and based in the United States, FFI Ionix will operate as a technology development company focused on global technology leadership and commercialisation of hydrogen technologies, including ion exchange membranes for water electrolysis, electrochemical compression, water transmission and fuel cells. Terms were not disclosed.

Company Background

Fortescue Metals was formed in 2003 after its majority shareholder, The Metal Group, purchased Allied Mining & Processing.

EXECUTIVES

Chief Executive Officer, Managing Director, Executive Director, Elizabeth Anne Gaines
Deputy Chief Executive, Julie Shuttleworth
Chief Operating Officer, Greg Lilleyman
Chief Financial Officer, Ian Wells
Chief General Counsel, Peter Ernest Huston
Joint Secretary, Alison Terry
Secretary, Cameron Wilson
Non-Executive Director, Non-Executive Chairman, Andrew Forrest
Lead Independent Director, Non-Executive Director, Deputy Chairman, Mark Barnaba
Non-Executive Director, Sebastian Coe
Non-Executive Director, Jennifer Morris
Non-Executive Director, Jean Baderschneider
Non-Executive Director, Zhang Ya-Qin
Non-Executive Director, Penny Bingham-Hall
Non-Executive Director, Zhiqiang Cao
Auditors : PricewaterhouseCoopers

LOCATIONS

HQ: Fortescue Ltd
Level 2, 87 Adelaide Terrace, East Perth, Western Australia 6004
Phone: (61) 8 6218 8888   **Fax:** (61) 8 6218 8880
Web: www.fortescue.com

2015 Sales

	% of total
China	94
Others	6
Total	100

PRODUCTS/OPERATIONS

2015 Sales

	% of total
Sales of iron ore	97
Sales of joint venture ore	1
Other revenue	2
Total	100

COMPETITORS

BHP GROUP LIMITED
CLEVELAND-CLIFFS INC.
Galiano Gold Inc
LONMIN LIMITED
PEABODY ENERGY CORPORATION
Teck Resources Limited
VEDANTA LIMITED
Vale S/A
Western Magnesium Corporation
Zijin Mining Group Company Limited

HISTORICAL FINANCIALS

Company Type: Public

Income Statement   FYE: June 30

	REVENUE ($mil)	NET INCOME ($mil)	NET PROFIT MARGIN	EMPLOYEES
06/23	16,871	4,798	28.4%	0
06/22	17,390	6,197	35.6%	0
06/21	22,284	10,295	46.2%	10,164
06/20	12,820	4,735	36.9%	0
06/19	9,965	3,187	32.0%	0
Annual Growth	14.1%	10.8%		

2023 Year-End Financials

Debt ratio: 16.3%
Return on equity: 27.1%
Cash ($ mil.): 4,287
Current Ratio: 2.47
Long-term debt ($ mil.): 4,528
No. of shares ($ mil.): 3,075
Dividends
  Yield: —
  Payout: 112.3%
Market value ($ mil.): —

Fortis Inc

Fortis is a leading regulated electric and gas utility holding company in North America. Its approximately 10 utilities, most of which are the sole supplier of electricity or gas in its respective territories, serve about 3.4 million customers across five Canadian provinces, nine US states, and three Caribbean countries. Primary subsidiaries include ITC, UNS Energy, and Central Hudson in the US and FortisBC Energy, FortisAlberta, and Newfoundland Power in Canada. Fortis has grown significantly in recent years as a result of acquisitions. Over 50% of sales were generated from the US.

Operations

Electric and gas revenue includes revenue from the sale and/or delivery of electricity and gas, transmission revenue, and wholesale electric revenue, all based on regulator-approved tariff rates including the flow through of commodity costs.

Other services revenue includes: management fee revenue at UNS Energy for the operation of Springerville Units 3 and 4; revenue from storage optimization activities at Aitken Creek; and revenue from other services that reflect the ordinary business activities of Fortis' utilities.

Geographic Reach

The company is headquartered at St. John, Canada. Fortis' largest geographical market was the United States with more than 50% of the total revenue; followed by Canada and Caribbean with around 40% and 5%, respectively.

Sales and Marketing

Fortis serves up to 3.4 million electric and gas utility customers.

Financial Performance

Fortis' revenue for fiscal 2022 increased to CAD11.0 billion compared to the prior year with CAD9.4 billion. The increase in revenue, net of foreign exchange, was due primarily to: higher flow-through costs in customer rates, driven by higher commodity prices; Rate Base growth; and higher retail and wholesale electricity sales, as well as transmission revenue, at UNS Energy, partially offset by the normal operation of regulatory deferrals at FortisBC Energy.

Net income for fiscal 2022 increased to CAD1.5 billion compared to the prior year with CAD1.4 billion. The increase was primarily due to higher revenues offsetting the increase in expenses.

Cash held by the company at the end of fiscal 2022 increased CAD209 million. Cash provided by operations and financing activities were CAD3.1 billion and CAD1.0 billion, respectively. Cash used for investing activities was CAD4.1 billion, mainly for additions to property, plant and equipment.

EXECUTIVES

President, Chief Executive Officer, Director, David G. Hutchens
Executive Vice President, Chief Financial Officer, Jocelyn H. Perry
Sustainability Executive Vice President, Sustainability Chief Human Resources Officer, Nora M. Duke
Eastern Canadian and Caribbean Operations Executive Vice President, Operations & Innovation Executive Vice President, Gary J. Smith
Capital Markets and Business Development Senior Vice President, Stuart I. Lochray
Vice President, Controller, Karen J. Gosse
Investor Relations Vice President, Stephanie A. Amaimo
Vice President, Chief Information Officer, Ronald J. Hinsley
Corporate Affairs Vice President, Communications Vice President, Karen M. McCarthy
Vice President, General Counsel, Regan P. O'Dea
Executive Vice President, Chief Legal Officer, Secretary, James R. Reid
Independent Chair, Independent Director, Douglas J. Haughey
Independent Director, Maura J. Clark
Independent Director, Tracey C. Ball
Independent Director, Lawrence T. Borgard
Independent Director, Margarita K. Dilley
Independent Director, Gianna M. Manes
Independent Director, Jo Mark Zurel
Director, Pierre J. Blouin
Director, Paul J. Bonavia
Director, Julie A. Dobson
Auditors: Deloitte LLP

LOCATIONS

HQ: Fortis Inc
Fortis Place, Suite 1100, 5 Springdale Street, St. John's, Newfoundland & Labrador A1E 0E4
Phone: 709 737-2800   **Fax:** 709 737-5307
Web: www.fortisinc.com

PRODUCTS/OPERATIONS

2018 Sales

ITC	19
UNS Energy	24
Central Hudson Canada	11
FortisBC Energy	13
Newfoundland Power	8
Fortis Alberta	7
FortisBC Electric	4
Maritime Electric	2
FortisOntario	2
Caribbean Caribbean Utilities	3
FortisTCI	1
Other Services	5
Other & Alternative	1
Total	**100**

COMPETITORS

ATMOS ENERGY CORPORATION
BERKSHIRE HATHAWAY ENERGY COMPANY
DOMINION ENERGY, INC.
DYNEGY INC.
HAWAIIAN ELECTRIC INDUSTRIES, INC.
ONCOR ELECTRIC DELIVERY COMPANY LLC
SEMPRA ENERGY
SOUTHWESTERN ENERGY COMPANY
TUCSON ELECTRIC POWER COMPANY
Uniper SE

HISTORICAL FINANCIALS

Company Type: Public

Income Statement   FYE: December 31

	REVENUE ($mil)	NET INCOME ($mil)	NET PROFIT MARGIN	EMPLOYEES
12/23	8,689	1,186	13.7%	9,598
12/22	8,165	1,030	12.6%	9,242
12/21	7,418	1,015	13.7%	9,095
12/20	7,017	1,000	14.3%	8,961
12/19	6,744	1,322	19.6%	8,970
Annual Growth	6.5%	(2.7%)		1.7%

2023 Year-End Financials

Debt ratio: 34.3%
Return on equity: 7.3%
Cash ($ mil.): 471
Current Ratio: 0.67
Long-term debt ($ mil.): 20,803
No. of shares ($ mil.): 490
Dividends
  Yield: —
  Payout: 73.7%
Market value ($ mil.): 20,178

	STOCK PRICE ($) FY Close	P/E High/Low		PER SHARE ($) Earnings	Dividends	Book Value
12/23	41.13	15	12	2.34	1.72	33.07
12/22	40.04	17	13	2.06	1.60	32.25
12/21	48.27	18	15	2.05	1.64	31.90
12/20	40.82	18	13	2.04	1.45	31.46
12/19	41.52	11	9	2.90	1.38	30.72
Annual Growth	(0.2%)			(5.3%)	5.8%	1.9%

Fortum OYJ

Fortum is a European energy company with activities in more than 40 countries. It is also one of the world's largest producers of carbon dioxide-free electricity in Europe. The company has a total of more than 50,295 MW generation capacity in areas such as Finland, Sweden, Russia, Germany, the UK, and Netherlands. Further, the company produces power such as hydropower, nuclear power, combined heat and power, condensing power, wind power, and solar power. The company also has significant operations in a growth area, Russia, including 11.3 MW of power generation capacity in 2021. (Russia accounted for about less than 5% of Fortum's total revenues that year). The Finnish government owns over 50% of Fortum. The company generated majority of its sales outside UK.

Operations

Fortum operates through five reporting segments: Uniper (about 95% of sales); Generation (roughly 5%); Consumer Solutions; Russia; and City Solutions (about 5% combined).

The Uniper segment is a leading international energy company. Its business is the secure provision of energy related services, and its main activities include power generation in Europe and Russia, as well as global energy trading and optimization, which comprises Uniper's three businesses: The European Generation; Global Commodities; and Russian Power Generation.

The Generation segment is responsible for Nordic power generation. It comprises CO2 free nuclear, hydro, and wind power generation, as well as power portfolio optimization, trading, market intelligence, thermal power for the capacity reserve, and global nuclear services.

The consumer Solutions segment is responsible for the electricity and gad retail businesses in the Nordics, Poland and Spain, including the customer service and invoicing businesses.

The Russia segment comprises power and heat generation and sales in Russia.

The City Solutions is responsible for sustainable solutions for urban areas. It comprises heating, cooling, waste-to-energy, and other circular economy solutions, as well as solar power generation, services, and development of new biomass-based businesses.

Overall, gas sales generated about 55% of sales, and power sales with some 30%.

Geographic Reach

Finland-based company, it has operations in more than 40 countries through its about 20,000 professionals. Some of these countries include Finland, Sweden, Russia, Poland, Norway, Great Britain, Estonia, and India.

Its largest geographic sales is the UK, over 25% of the company's revenue. Followed by Germany (around 20%), Nordics (some 10%), and other Europe (over 30%).

Sales and Marketing

Fortum has 2.2 million customers across different brands.

Financial Performance

The company's revenue in 2021 increased by 129% to EUR 12.4 billion compared to EUR 49.0 billion in the prior year.

Net Loss in 2021 was EUR 114 million compared to a net profit of EUR 1.9 billion in the prior year.

Cash held by the company at the end of 2021 increased to EUR 7.6 billion. Operating and financing activities provided EUR 5.0 billion and EUR 6.0 billion, respectively. Investing activities used EUR 5.7 billion, mainly for change in margin receivables.

Strategy

In November 2021, the Swedish Energy Agency presented a proposal on a national hydrogen strategy.

The strategy focuses on "colour-blind" fossil-free hydrogen with a target to have 5 GW of installed electrolyser capacity by 2030 and an additional 10 GW of capacity by 2045. The strategy is currently being processed in the Ministry of Infrastructure, but it is still unclear when it will be adopted as the official Swedish hydrogen strategy.

Company Background

The Loviisa power plant was the first nuclear power plant in Finland. The power plant has two units: unit 1 started operating in February 1977, and unit 2 in November 1980. The units are VVER-440 type pressurized water reactors.

HISTORY

The 1998 betrothal of two Finnish state-controlled businesses created the country's largest enterprise, and even the European Union extended its blessing. Called Fortum, the new company combined the oil, gas, and chemical businesses of Neste with electric utility Imatran Voima Oy (IVO).

IVO was founded in 1932, when it built its first hydroelectric power plant (100 MW). The utility began expanding rapidly in the 1960s, when it built a giant coal-fired plant (then the largest in the Nordic region) and extended its transmission lines to the Soviet Union and Sweden. It built Finland's first nuclear reactor in 1977 at Lovissa.

The utility introduced district heating services in 1982 and began developing combined heat and power plants in the 1980s. The company began acquiring stakes in power projects around the world in the late 1980s, and by the early 1990s it was involved in power projects in the Czech Republic, Germany, Poland, and Russia, as well as in Asia.

The Nordic energy industry was deregulated in the mid-1990s. IVO, which had already acquired several small Finnish utilities, bought Sweden's Gullspangs Kraft in 1997, picking up 5,000 MW of generating capacity.

Neste was created in 1948 as Finland's state-controlled oil and gas enterprise. Since Finland imported all of its oil products, WWII left the country with shortages and forced a rationing policy. Neste's job was to develop storage facilities for fuel oil; however, a major fire in 1949 prompted the company to look beyond storage.

Department of Industry director Uolevi Raade pushed for a national refinery, and the Finnish parliament approved the plan in 1954. Raade became president of Neste in 1955, and the refinery opened two years later. A second refinery opened in 1967. Lacking a stable natural gas source, Neste began taking gas deliveries from the Soviet Union in 1971.

Neste entered the petrochemicals arena in 1972, when it began producing ethylene, polyethylene, and polyvinylchloride. In the early 1980s the company added service stations to its operations, buying three Finnish petroleum marketers. Continuing to buy oil abroad, Neste had nearly 20 tankers in its fleet by the mid-1980s.

In 1994 Neste and Russia's Gazprom set up Gasum, a joint venture responsible for natural gas production and transportation. Partially privatized in 1995, Neste reorganized and cut its workforce by a third. By the end of 1996 the Finnish government held an 83% stake in Neste.

After the 1998 merger, Fortum sold 50% of its stake in Gasum (reducing its stake to 25%) in 1999 to comply with merger conditions. It also sold Neste Chemicals to private equity fund Industri Kapital.

In 2000 Fortum acquired Stora Enso's power plants in Sweden and Finland. It also grabbed a 49% stake in Ishavskraft, a Norwegian electricity sales company, and acquired German utility group Wesertal. The next year, Fortum acquired Estonian power company Saue Thermo and sold its shares in Hungarian power generator Budapesti ErĂ¶mĂ¼ and Latvian gas company Latvijas Gaze.

In 2001 the company also acquired full ownership of Birka Energi, the Swedish utility that serves Stockholm. In 2002 the company divested its oil and gas assets in Oman.

In 2003 Fortum sold its Norwegian oil and gas business (Fortum Petroleum) to Eni.

In 2005 Fortum acquired a 60% interest in Suomijos Energija, a Lithuania-based company providing heat generation through natural gas and biofuel firing, from Finnish firm Kotkan Energia. The transaction increased Fortum's holding in Suomijos to 70%, and expanded its municipal and industrial heating operations. Fortum renamed the company Fortum Heat Lietuva.

Also in 2005 the company spun off its oil and gas operations as Neste Oil Oy.

In 2007 the company launched a project to build up to eight 2-3 MW wind power plants in the Rosa Finnmark area of Sweden.

In 2008 the company acquired Siberia based Russian Territorial Generating Company 10 (TGC 10), which has significant power generation assets. By 2009 some 92% of Fortum's power generation in EU countries came from non-carbon emission power sources (renewable and nuclear power plants).

As part of its wind energy push, in 2008

Fortum and Finland's National Forest Enterprise (Metsähallitus) signed a deal to reserve state-owned Pitkämatala and Maakrunni sea areas offshore of the municipalities of Kemi, Simo, and Ii for the development of large scale wind power farms. In 2009 the two partners also agreed to develop wind farms onshore in Northern Finland, in the Kuolavaara-Keulakkopää area, located in the Kittilä and Sodankylä municipalities.

Also on the renewables front, in 2010 the company acquired a 40% stake in the Blaiken wind power project, with the remaining 60% held by the Swedish energy company Skelleftea Kraft. The Blaiken Vind joint venture will be a wind farm to be constructed in the Blaiken region in northern Sweden, with a maximum of 100 wind turbines and a capacity of 250 MW.

EXECUTIVES

Chief Executive Officer, President, Tapio Kuula
Executive Vice President, Division Officer, Aleksander Chuvaev
Executive Vice President, Division Officer, Timo Karttinen
Executive Vice President, Division Officer, Per Langer
Executive Vice President, Division Officer, Matti Ruotsala
Executive Vice President, Chief Financial Officer, Juha Laaksonen
Corporate Relations and Sustainability Executive Vice President, Anne Brunila
Human Resources Senior Vice President, Mikael Frisk
Research & Development Senior Vice President, Corporate Strategy Senior Vice President, Maria Paatero-Kaarnakari
Chairman, Matti Lehti
Deputy Chairman, Sari Baldauf
Director, Esko Aho
Director, Ilona Ervasti-Vaintola
Director, Birgitta Johansson-Hedberg
Director, Joshua Larson
Director, Christian Ramm-Schmidt
Auditors: Deloitte Oy

LOCATIONS

HQ: Fortum OYJ
Keilaniementie 1, Espoo FI-00048
Phone: (358) 10 452 9151   **Fax:** (358) 10 45 24447
Web: www.fortum.com

2014 Sales

	% of total
Nordic	68
Russia	22
Poland	5
Estonia	1
Others	4
Total	100

PRODUCTS/OPERATIONS

2014 Sales

	% of total
Power and Technology	40
Heat, Electricity Sales and Solutions	25
Russia	20
Distribution	14
Other	1
Netting of Nord Pool transactions	-
Eliminations	-
Total	100

2014 Sales

	% of total
Power Sales (excluding indirect tax)	64
Heat Sales	16
Network transmissions	15
Others	5
Total	100

COMPETITORS

ABB Ltd
ESSAR ENERGY LIMITED
EXPRO INTERNATIONAL GROUP LIMITED
GKN LIMITED
IBERDROLA, SOCIEDAD ANONIMA
INTERNATIONAL POWER LTD.
KCA DEUTAG ALPHA LIMITED
LUKOIL, PAO
Neles Oyj
Vattenfall AB

HISTORICAL FINANCIALS

Company Type: Public

Income Statement — FYE: December 31

	REVENUE ($mil)	NET INCOME ($mil)	NET PROFIT MARGIN	EMPLOYEES
12/22	9,403	(2,580)	—	7,712
12/21	127,221	836	0.7%	19,140
12/20	60,155	2,237	3.7%	19,933
12/19	6,115	1,663	27.2%	8,191
12/18	6,003	965	16.1%	8,286
Annual Growth	11.9%	—	—	(1.8%)

2022 Year-End Financials

Debt ratio: 34.7%
Return on equity: (-24.4%)
Cash ($ mil.): 4,185
Current Ratio: 1.08
Long-term debt ($ mil.): 3,800
No. of shares ($ mil.): 888
Dividends
Yield: —
Payout: 0.0%
Market value ($ mil.): 2,905

	STOCK PRICE ($) FY Close	P/E High/Low	PER SHARE ($) Earnings	Dividends	Book Value
12/22	3.27	— —	(2.91)	0.24	9.22
12/21	6.30	8 5	0.94	0.27	15.46
12/20	4.71	3 1	2.52	0.24	17.90
12/19	5.09	3 2	1.88	0.25	16.41
12/18	4.17	5 4	1.09	0.25	15.27
Annual Growth	(5.9%)		(1.2%)	(11.8%)	

Fresenius Medical Care AG (New)

Fresenius Medical Care is one of the largest dialysis providers in the world. Its staff treats about 345,425 patients at more than 4,170 dialysis clinics worldwide. The company provides dialysis care and related services to persons who suffer from ESKD as well as other health care services. The company supplies dialysis clinics it owns, operates or manages with a broad range of products and also sell dialysis products to other dialysis service providers. Fresenius Medical Care sells its health care products to customers in around 150 countries and it also use them in its own health care service operations. Fresenius SE owns 32.2% of Fresenius Medical Care. North America generates approximately 70% of the company's revenue.

Operations

Health care services account for a majority of total revenue. The company provides hemodialysis treatments through its global network of more than 4,170 dialysis clinics, as well as on an as-needed basis for contracted hospitals. Its clinics also offer services for home dialysis patients, the majority of whom receive PD treatment. For these patients, the company provide materials, training and patient support services, including clinical monitoring, follow-up assistance and arranging for delivery of the supplies to the patient's residence.

Health care products, accounting for about 20% of revenue, include hemodialysis machines, dialyzers, peritoneal dialysis cyclers, hemodialysis concentrates, bloodlines, and water treatment systems. It also makes renal pharmaceuticals, apherisis (blood cleansing) products, liver support therapies, and acute cardiopulmonary products.

Geographic Reach

With a majority of its operations in the US (North America accounts for approximately 70% of revenue), Fresenius Medical Care is increasing its presence in other regions, including EMEA, Asia-Pacific and Latin America. The company has dialysis clinic operations in about 50 countries, while its dialysis products segment serves customers in around 150 countries.

Fresenius Medical Care's corporate headquarters is in Bad Homburg, Germany. The North America operations are based in Waltham, Massachusetts, while the Asia-Pacific headquarters is located in Hong Kong and the Latin America headquarters is in Rio de Janeiro.

Sales and Marketing

In the US, Fresenius Medical Care's core health care segment relies generally with third party payors, such as Medicare, Medicaid or commercial insurers. Outside the US, the reimbursement arrangement is usually made through national or local government programs with reimbursement rates established by statute or regulation.

The company markets its products and services for individuals with renal diseases of which around 3.8 million patients worldwide regularly undergo dialysis treatment.

Financial Performance

Note: Growth rates may differ after conversion to US Dollars.

In 2021, the company had a revenue of

EUR 17.6 billion, a 1% decrease from the previous year's revenue of EUR 17.9 billion.

The company had a net income of EUR 1.2 billion, a 15% increase from the previous year's net income of EUR 1.4 billion.

The company's cash at the end of 2021 was EUR 1.5 billion. Operating activities generated EUR 2.5 billion, while investing activities used EUR 1.2 billion, mainly for purchases of property, plant and equipment and capitalized development costs. Financing activities used another EUR 1 billion, primarily for repayments of long-term debt.

Strategy

In 2020, the company updated its strategy to leverage its core strategic competencies in order to achieve the company's goal of providing health care for chronically and critically ill patients across the renal care continuum (Strategy 2025), which encompasses new renal care models, value-based care models, chronic kidney disease and transplantation as well as future innovations. Accordingly, it has adjusted the presentation of consolidated and operating segment data to reflect the integration of Dialysis and Care Coordination, now referred to as "other health care services," in its business model. Therefore, the company does not present Dialysis and other health care services metrics separately. As such, other health care services information previously presented separately for the North America Segment and the Asia-Pacific Segment is now included within the corresponding Health Care metric. This presentation also more closely aligns its external financial reporting with the manner in which management reviews financial information to make operating decisions and evaluate performance of its business.

Company Background

Fresenius Medical Care was formed in 1996 by the merger of Fresenius AG's dialysis systems division with chemical maker W. R. Grace's National Medical Care (NMC) dialysis services division. Fresenius traces its roots back to the 1462 founding of Hirsch Pharmacy in Frankfurt (acquired by the Fresenius family in the 18th century) and its 1966 entry into the dialysis equipment market. NMC was founded in 1968 by Constantine Hampers, who opened his first dialysis clinic in Boston in 1971.

In 1998 Fresenius Medical Care expanded its clinics through the purchase of NEOMEDICA and expanded its laboratory services by buying Spectra Laboratories. Subsequent acquisitions expanded international operations.

In 2005 the company transformed its structure from a corporation to a share-limited partnership; the restructuring included a name change from Fresenius Medical Care AG to Fresenius Medical Care AG & Co. KGaA.

The company acquired US rival Renal Care Group, which had 460 locations, in 2006. Later acquisitions added dialysis medications and dialysis filter cartridges.

In 2017 Fresenius Medical Care acquired day-hospital operator Cura Group to further expand in Australia's dialysis market.

HISTORY

Fresenius Medical Care was formed in 1996 by the merger of Fresenius AG's dialysis systems division with National Medical Care (NMC). While Fresenius traces its roots back to the 1462 founding of Hirsch Pharmacy in Frankfurt (the Fresenius family gained control of the company in the 18th century) and its 1966 entry into the dialysis equipment market, NMC was founded in 1968 by Constantine Hampers, who recognized that for-profit companies could provide dialysis services more cheaply than not-for-profit hospitals. He opened his first clinic in Boston (it grew to some 600 clinics) and took the company public in 1971. In 1984, he sold the company to chemical maker W. R. Grace, which was on a diversification binge, but attempted to buy it back after 10 contentious years.

The birth of Fresenius Medical was also mired in legal muck. NMC was under investigation for fraudulent Medicare billing and illegal kickbacks, and its manufacturing operations were restricted by court order. Fresenius Medical put an end to the fraud, but the ongoing investigation took its toll on its bottom line.

In 1997 a US federal court lifted the manufacturing injunction against NMC. That year Fresenius Medical grew its US clinic practices with the purchase of NEOMEDICA and expanded its laboratory services by buying Spectra Laboratories. The next year it sold its diagnostic services and home care divisions to concentrate on its core dialysis operations. In 1998 it also partnered with Kaiser Permanente, a leading not-for-profit HMO, to run dialysis clinics and provide other services to patients. Growth continued the next year with key acquisitions in such regions as western Europe, South Korea, and the US.

Fresenius Medical was finally able to put its NMC woes behind it in 2000 when it settled the Medicare fraud suit for some $425 million. Undaunted, the firm also acquired the non-US operations of rival DaVita (formerly Total Renal Care). The next year it bought the perfusion services business of Edwards Lifesciences.

In 2005 the company transformed its structure from a corporation to a share-limited partnership; the restructuring included the formation of the company's general partner, Fresenius Medical Care Management AG, and a name change from Fresenius Medical Care AG to Fresenius Medical Care AG & Co. KGaA.

In a larger than usual transaction, the company also acquired US rival Renal Care Group, which had 460 locations, in 2006. The deal was valued at $3.5 billion and made Fresenius Medical Care the top US dialysis center operator (despite the required divestiture of some 100 centers to clear the deal). Fresenius Medical Care also later sold the former RCG laboratory operations.

Also in 2006 the company purchased the 50% stake in venture Renaissance Health Care that it didn't already own and the 20% stake in Optimal Renal Care (a former venture with health care provider Kaiser Permanente) and merged Optimal Renal Care into Renaissance Health Care; the combined entity was renamed KidneyTel.

Fresenius Medical Care acquired its first dialysis medication, the PhosLo brand calcium acetate, and related assets from Nabi Biopharmaceuticals in 2006. The following year it acquired privately held Renal Solutions, which makes filter cartridges that can be used in home dialysis, a growing field in the hemodialysis market.

In 2007, the company sealed its position in the Asian dialysis market with the acquisition of a majority stake in Taiwan-based Jiate Excelsior.

In 2008 it entered drug distribution agreement with pharma companies Luitpold and Galenica to expand its therapeutic offerings.

To further cement its position in Asia, in 2010 the company agreed to purchase Asia Renal Care from Bumrungrad International to expand its operations in Taiwan, Singapore, and other Asia/Pacific countries. It also established operations in countries including Japan, Korea, and Russia that year.

Also in 2010 it expanded its home care offerings by purchasing the peritoneal (abdominal) dialysis operation of Gambro and the assets of home therapy device development firm Xcorporeal.

Fresenius Medical Care continued its growth efforts in 2011 when it acquired Dutch firm Euromedic International's dialysis business, International Dialysis Centers (IDC), for some ?485 million ($647 million). The purchase gave Fresenius about 70 clinics in Central and Eastern Europe.

In 2017 Fresenius Medical Care acquired day-hospital operator Cura Group to further expand in Australia's dialysis market.

EXECUTIVES

Chairman, Chief Executive Officer, Rice Powell
Chief Financial Officer, Helen Giza
Global Chief Medical Officer, Franklin W. Maddux
Chairman, Stephan Sturm
Vice-Chairman, Dieter Schenk
Director, Gerd Krick
Director, Rolf A. Classon
Director, William P. Johnson
Director, Rachel Claire Empey
Auditors : PricewaterhouseCoopers GmbH

LOCATIONS

HQ: Fresenius Medical Care AG (New)
Else-Kroener-Strasse 1, Bad Homburg 61346
Phone: (49) 6172 608 2522   **Fax:** (49) 6172 609 2301
Web: www.fmc-ag.com

2011 Sales

	% of total
North America	
Dialysis care	57
Dialysis products	6
International	
Dialysis products	19
Dialysis care	17
Total	**100**

PRODUCTS/OPERATIONS

2011 Payer Breakdown

	% of total
Medicare ESRD program	46
Private/alternative payers	43
Medicaid & other government sources	6
Hospitals	5
Total	**100**

Selected Acquisitions

2012
Liberty Dialysis Holdings ($1.7 billion, US dialysis clinics under Liberty and Renal Advantage brands)
2011
American Access Care Holdings ($385 million, US vascular access centers)
International Dialysis Centers (IDC, €485 million or $647 million, Central and Eastern European dialysis Centers and former division of Euromedic)
2010
Asia Renal Care (dialysis centers in Taiwan, Singapore, and other Asia/Pacific countries, former unit of Bumrungrad International)
Peritoneal dialysis operations (former unit of Gambro)
Xcorporeal (home therapy devices)

COMPETITORS

AMERISOURCEBERGEN CORPORATION
CHINDEX INTERNATIONAL, INC.
COOPERSURGICAL, INC.
DAVITA INC.
FRESENIUS MEDICAL CARE HOLDINGS, INC.
Fresenius SE & Co. KGaA
HENRY SCHEIN, INC.
OWENS & MINOR, INC.
PATTERSON COMPANIES, INC.
TRIVIDIA HEALTH, INC.

HISTORICAL FINANCIALS

Company Type: Public

Income Statement   FYE: December 31

	REVENUE ($mil)	NET INCOME ($mil)	NET PROFIT MARGIN	EMPLOYEES
12/23	21,546	552	2.6%	112,382
12/22	20,717	719	3.5%	128,044
12/21	19,941	1,097	5.5%	122,909
12/20	21,918	1,429	6.5%	125,364
12/19	19,622	1,346	6.9%	120,659
Annual Growth	2.4%	(20.0%)	—	(1.8%)

2023 Year-End Financials

Debt ratio: 25.8%
Return on equity: 3.6%
Cash ($ mil.): 1,554
Current Ratio: 1.42
Long-term debt ($ mil.): 7,708
No. of shares ($ mil.): 293
Dividends
Yield: —
Payout: 70.0%
Market value ($ mil.): 6,112

	STOCK PRICE ($) FY Close	P/E High/Low	PER SHARE ($) Earnings	Dividends	Book Value
12/23	20.83	16 10	1.88	1.32	51.42
12/22	16.34	15 6	2.46	1.20	50.92
12/21	32.46	12 9	3.75	1.07	49.05
12/20	41.56	12 8	4.86	0.50	47.00
12/19	36.83	11 8	4.45	0.45	45.00
Annual Growth	(13.3%)	—	(19.3%)	30.8%	3.4%

Fresenius SE & Co KGaA

Fresenius is one of the world's leading healthcare companies. The company offers a wide range of dialysis and infusion products and services through its four core business segments, which operate as legally independent entities: Fresenius Medical Care, Fresenius Kabi, Fresenius Helios, and Fresenius Vamed. The company's Medical Care division specializes in treating chronic kidney failure in more than 4,100 dialysis clinics Fresenius Kabi provides nutrition, infusion, and IV therapies and related equipment. Fresenius Helios is Europe's leading private healthcare provider, while Fresenius Vamed offers facility management, project development, and other services to hospitals and health facilities. Fresenius has operations in more than 100 countries and the Europe is its biggest market.

Operations

Of its four segments, Medical Care is Fresenius' largest segment accounting for more than 45% of total revenue. Helios brings in over 25%, Kabi for some 20% of revenue, and Vamed for about 5%.

Fresenius Medical Care is the world's largest provider of products and services for individuals with renal diseases of which more than 3.9 million patients worldwide regularly undergo dialysis treatment. Through its network of more than 4,100 dialysis clinics, Fresenius Medical Care provides dialysis treatments for about 344,685 patients around the globe. Fresenius Medical Care is also the leading provider of dialysis products such as hemodialysis machines, dialyzers and related disposable products.

Fresenius Helios s is Europe's leading private hospital operator, with more than 85 acute care hospitals, about 240 outpatient care centers with 600 accredited doctor's licenses, six prevention centers and about 20 occupational medicine centers. Fresenius Helios includes Helios Kliniken in Germany, QuirÃ³nsalud in Spain and Latin America and the Eugin Group with a global network of reproductive clinics.

Fresenius Kabi's product portfolio comprises a comprehensive range of IV generic drugs, infusion therapies and clinical nutrition products as well as the devices for administering these products.. The company's products and services are used to help care for critically and chronically ill patients.

Fresenius Vamed is a leading global provider of services for hospitals and other health care facilities. It provides project development, planning, technical and operation management, and turnkey construction services to hospitals and other health care facilities around the world.

Geographic Reach

Headquartered in Bad Homburg, Germany. Europe is Fresenius' largest market at about 45% of revenue, followed by North America (some 40%), Asia/Pacific region (about 10%), Latin America (about 5%) and Africa (less than 5% of revenue).

Fresenius has an international distribution network and operates more than 90 production facilities. The largest of these are located in the US, China, Germany, Japan, and Sweden.

Sales and Marketing

Fresenius provides products and services for dialysis, hospitals, and outpatient medical care. In addition, Fresenius focuses on hospital operations. It also manages projects and provides services for hospitals and other health care facilities worldwide. More than 300,000 employees have dedicated themselves to the service of health.

Financial Performance

Note: Growth rates may differ after conversion to US Dollars.

Revenue has been rising for Fresenius in the last five years. It has a 22% overall increase between 2018 and 2022.

The company reported a total revenue of EUR40.8 billion, a 9% increase from the previous year's total revenue of EUR37.5 billion. At constant currency, this was mainly driven by organic growth in EMEA, including the effects of hyperinflation in Turkiye, Asia-Pacific and Latin America, which was partially offset by the impact of COVID-19 on organic growth in North America.

In 2022, the company had a net income of EUR1.4 billion, a 25% decrease from the previous year's net income of EUR1.8 billion.

The company's cash at the end of 2022 was EUR2.7 billion. Operating activities generated EUR4.2 billion, while investing activities used EUR2.6 billion, mainly for purchases of property, plant and equipment and capitalized development costs. Financing activities used another EUR1.6 billion, primarily for repayments of short-term debt.

Strategy

The company offers healthcare products and services for critically and chronically ill individuals, in line with the megatrends of health and demographics. The company improves people's lives by providing high-quality and affordable healthcare. In doing so, the company considers significant paradigm shifts in the healthcare environment with regards to biologic products and therapies, technological change and new forms of data generation, processing and usage. Its goal is to expand Fresenius' position as a leading global provider of products, services, and therapies for critically and chronically ill people. At the same time, the company wants to grow profitably and use its capital efficiently, in order to create value for its stakeholders and enable the company to continue investing in better medicine.

Mergers and Acquisitions

In 2022, Fresenius Kabi closed the acquisition of Ivenix, Inc. (Ivenix), a specialized infusion therapy company. Ivenix adds a next-generation infusion therapy platform for the significant US market to Fresenius Kabi's portfolio and provides the company with key capabilities in hospital connectivity. The combination of Ivenix's leading hardware and software products with Fresenius Kabi's offering in intravenous fluids and infusion devices will create a comprehensive and leading portfolio of premium products, forming a strong basis to enable sustainable growth in the high-value MedTech space. The purchase price is a combination of US$240 million upfront payment and milestone payments, strictly linked to the achievement of commercial and operating targets.

In early 2022, The Eugin Group, part of Fresenius Helios, acquires a majority stake in the Delaware Institute for Reproductive Medicine (DIRM), a renowned fertility center in the US state of Delaware that has been established for 35 years. With this acquisition, Eugin further expands its existing network in the US and expects to generate additional synergies and operational efficiencies. A number of key physicians will remain minority shareholders in DIRM. Terms of the transaction were not disclose.

Company Background

Fresenius can trace its lineage all the way back to an apothecary founded in 1462 in Frankfurt. A few centuries later in the 1870s the business was bought by the Fresenius family, and in 1912 Eduard Fresenius began making medicines based on purified water, his speciality. WWII -- and Eduard's death in 1946 -- almost destroyed the company, which was saved by his 26-year-old daughter Else. She and her new husband Hans Kroner rebuilt the company and turned it into a global infusions solutions company, including developing its own dialysis machines in the 1970s. Over the coming decades the company expanded by acquisitions, notable National Medical Care in 1996, which became Fresenius Medical Care, today the company's biggest business. Else's charitable foundation, Else Kroner-Fresenius-Stiftung, is Germany's largest charitable foundation.

HISTORY

Fresenius was founded as the Hirsch Pharmacy in 1462. The Fresenius family took over its ownership in the 18th century and converted it into a pharmaceutical manufacturing entity in 1912.

Fresenius entered the dialysis equipment market in 1966. The company formed its Fresenius Medical Care unit in 1996 when it merged its dialysis systems division with National Medical Care (NMC).

In 1999 Fresenius formed its Fresenius Kabi division by combining its infusion pharmaceutical operations with the former infusion solution business of drugmaker Pharmacia & Upjohn, which it acquired the previous year.

The company conducted a number of expansion efforts within the Kabi division in the following decade, including the 2007 purchase of IV drug manufacturing firms Labesfal (Portugal) and Filaxis (Argentina), as well as German medical device maker Clinico. Also that year the company bought the artificial colloid product business of Kyorin to build up a presence in the Tokyo market.

It then purchased Indian oncology drug manufacturer Dabur Pharma in 2008. Also that year the unit expanded its reach in the US market for injectable drugs by acquiring US generics maker APP Pharmaceuticals for $3.7 billion plus debt.

Following the acquisition of German private clinic operator Helios Kliniken, Fresenius refreshed its acute care operations by separating its hospital division (Fresenius ProServe) into two business segments, Fresenius Helios and Fresenius Vamed, in 2008.

EXECUTIVES

Management Board Chief Executive Officer, Management Board Member, Stephan Sturm
Chief Financial Officer, Rachel Claire Empey
Fresenius Medical Care Member, Fresenius Medical Care North America Member, Management Board Member, Fresenius Medical Care North America Chief Executive Officer, Management Board Chief Executive Officer, Fresenius Medical Care Chief Executive Officer, Rice Powell
Management Board Member, Fresenius Helios Member, Management Board Chief Executive Officer, Fresenius Helios Chief Executive Officer, Francesco De Meo
Fresenius Vamed Member, Management Board Member, Fresenius Vamed Chief Executive Officer, Management Board Chief Executive Officer, Ernst Wastler
Management Board Member, Sebastian Biedenkopf
Management Board Member, Michael Sen
Chair, Wolfgang Kirsch
Deputy Chairman, Michael Diekmann
Deputy Chairman, Grit Genster
Supervisory Board Member, Michael Albrecht
Supervisory Board Member, Stephanie Balling
Supervisory Board Member, Bernd Behlert
Supervisory Board Member, Konrad Kolbl
Supervisory Board Member, Frauke Lehmann
Supervisory Board Member, Iris Low-Friedrich
Supervisory Board Member, Klaus-Peter Mueller
Supervisory Board Member, Susanne Zeidler
Supervisory Board Member, Oscar Romero De Paco
Supervisory Board Member, Heinrich Hiesinger
Auditors : PricewaterhouseCoopers GmbH Wirtschaftsprüfungsgesellschaf

LOCATIONS

HQ: Fresenius SE & Co KGaA
Else-Kroener-Strasse 1, Bad Homburg D-61352
Phone: (49) 6172 608 0   **Fax:** (49) 6172 608 2488
Web: www.fresenius.com

2017 Sales

	% of total
North America	45
Europe	41
Asia Pacific	9
Latin America & other regions	4
Africa	1
Total	100

PRODUCTS/OPERATIONS

2017 Sales

	% of total
Fresenius Medical Care	52
Fresenius Kabi	19
Fresenius Helios	26
Fresenius Vamed	3
Corporate/Other	(-)
Total	100

Selected Services

Fresenius Medical Care
   Dialysis facility operation
   Disease management
   Disposable dialysis supplies
   Hemodialysis equipment
   Peritoneal dialysis equipment
Fresenius Kabi
   Blood volume replacement
   Enteral nutrition
   Infusion and IV devices
   Infusion therapies
   IV generic drugs
   Parenteral nutrition
   Tranfusion products
Fresenius Helios
   HELIOS Kliniken Group (61 private hospitals, Germany)
Fresenius Vamed
   Construction management
   Facility planning
   Maintenance services
   Operational management
   Project development
   Staff recruitment and training

COMPETITORS

AMERISOURCEBERGEN CORPORATION
CAREFUSION CORPORATION
CONMED CORPORATION
DAVITA INC.
Fresenius Medical Care AG & Co. KGaA
HOLOGIC, INC.
NXSTAGE MEDICAL, INC.
OLYMPUS CORPORATION
ROCKWELL MEDICAL, INC.
VOLCANO CORPORATION

HISTORICAL FINANCIALS

Company Type: Public

Income Statement — FYE: December 31

	REVENUE ($mil)	NET INCOME ($mil)	NET PROFIT MARGIN	EMPLOYEES
12/21	42,467	2,057	4.8%	316,078
12/20	44,522	2,094	4.7%	311,269
12/19	39,756	2,114	5.3%	294,134
12/18	38,398	2,321	6.0%	276,750
12/17	40,620	2,174	5.4%	273,249
Annual Growth	1.1%	(1.4%)	—	3.7%

2021 Year-End Financials

Debt ratio: 32.3%
Return on equity: 10.1%
Cash ($ mil.): 3,128
Current Ratio: 1.16
Long-term debt ($ mil.): 18,817
No. of shares ($ mil.): 558
Dividends
Yield: 3.5%
Payout: 4.5%
Market value ($ mil.): 5,574

	STOCK PRICE ($) FY Close	P/E High/Low		PER SHARE ($) Earnings	Dividends	Book Value
12/21	9.98	4	3	3.69	0.35	38.50
12/20	11.65	5	3	3.76	0.17	37.31
12/19	13.96	4	3	3.79	0.15	33.80
12/18	12.15	6	3	4.16	0.15	31.73
12/17	19.43	7	6	3.90	0.12	29.93
Annual Growth	(15.3%)	—	—	(1.3%)	30.1%	6.5%

FUJIFILM Holdings Corp

Fujifilm is a global leader, offering a wide variety of products and services, and has committed to solving society's greatest challenges. With about 280 companies, Fujifilm provides products and services of Healthcare (Medical Systems, Consumer Healthcare, Pharmaceuticals, Bio CDMO, and Regenerative Medicine), Materials (Advanced Materials, Graphic Systems & Inkjets, and Recording Media), Business Solution (Office & Business Solutions), and Imaging (Photo Imaging and Optical Device and Electronic Imaging). Customers overseas account for about 60% revenue.

Operations

Fujifilm operates through four segments: Healthcare; Business Innovation; Materials; and Imaging.

Healthcare segment provide diverse products and services such as medical devices, bio CDMO (biomedical Contract Development and Manufacturing Organization), pharmaceutical, regenerative medicine, and life sciences (cosmetics and supplements) in the three areas of Prevention, Diagnosis and Treatment.

Business Innovation segment provides office equipment such as multi-function devices and printers, as well as a variety of solutions and services for the businesses of various size, from large to small-and-medium. It also provides problem-solving document services tailored to diverse business formats and roles, including system integration, cloud service, business process outsourcing, and more.

Materials segment include electronic materials, display materials, industrial equipment, fine chemicals, recording media, equipment and materials for graphic communication, inks and industrial inkjet printheads.

Imaging segment provides products and services from input through output, from color films to instant cameras, developing and printing systems, color paper, photo printing services, and more. In addition to mirrorless digital cameras with uniquely high image quality thanks to its proprietary color reproduction technologies, it also provide TV and cinema lenses, surveillance camera, industrial lenses for production line inspection, and projectors.

Geographic Reach

Based in Tokyo, Japan, Fujifilm has office locations across Americas, Europe, Middle East, Africa, Asia and Oceania.

Fujifilm's domestic operations generate some 40% of revenue while overseas generate about 60%.

Financial Performance

In the fiscal year ended March 31, 2022, the Fujifilm Group recorded ¥2.5 trillion in consolidated revenue (up 15% year-over-year), reflecting sales increases mainly in the medical systems business, the bio CDMO business, the life sciences business and the electronic materials business.

In 2021, the company had a net income of ¥211.2 billion, a 17% increase from the previous year's net income of ¥181.2 billion.

The company's cash at the end of 2021 was ¥486.3 billion. Operating activities generated ¥323.9 billion, while investing activities used ¥153.5 billion, mainly for purchases of property, plant and equipment. Financing activities used another ¥105.2 billion, primarily for repayments of long-term debt.

Strategy

In the Healthcare segment, the medical systems business will drive sales growth to ensure increases in revenue and profit. In the life sciences field, it will position the bio CDMO business, which is expected to grow significantly in the medium to long term, as a priority business and aim to expand business by offering end-to-end values as a company supporting state-of-the-art therapeutic drug discovery. Also, with the aim of contributing to COVID-19 pandemic control, it will supply portable digital x-rays, diagnostic ultrasounds and other medical equipment, and undertake contract process development and manufacturing of vaccines, etc. for pharmaceutical companies.

In the Materials segment, it established the Advanced Materials Strategy Headquarters in October 2021 to expand the advanced materials business through cross-divisional strategy management and business portfolio establishment on a customer application basis, in addition to new business development over the medium to long term.

Mergers and Acquisitions

1

HISTORY

In 1934, Fuji Photo Film Co. was established through a government plan to build a domestic photographic film manufacturing industry in Japan. The new company inherited the split-off photographic film operations of Dainippon Celluloid Company Limited.

In 2006, Fuji Photo Film Co., Ltd. has been transformed into a holding company and renamed as Fujifilm Holdings Corp.

EXECUTIVES

Chairman, Director, Kenji Sukeno
President, Chief Executive Officer, Representative Director, Teiichi Goto
Chief Financial Officer, Director, Masayuki Higuchi
Chief Digital Officer, Seigo Sugimoto
Director, Naoki Hama
Director, Chisato Yoshizawa
Director, Yoji Ito
Outside Director, Kunitaro Kitamura
Outside Director, Makiko Eda
Outside Director, Tsuyoshi Nagano
Outside Director, Ikuro Sugawara
Auditors : KPMG AZSA LLC

LOCATIONS

HQ: FUJIFILM Holdings Corp
9-7-3 Akasaka, Minato ku, Tokyo 107-0052
Phone: (81) 3 6271 1111
Web: www.fujifilmholdings.com

2018 Sales

	% of total
Japan	41
Asia	27
Americas	19
Europe	13
Total	100

PRODUCTS/OPERATIONS

2018 Sales

	% of total
Document Solutions	43
Healthcare & Material Solutions	41
Imaging Solutions	16
Total	100

2018 Sales

	% of total
Sales	86
Rentals	14
Total	100

Selected Products

Document
  Color/Monochrome digital multifunction devices
  DocuWorks document handlingn software
  On-demand publishing systems

Computer publishing systems
Imaging
    Color photo printing paper and chemicals
    Digital cameras and accessories
    Instant films
    Digital minilabs/dry minilabs
    Motion picture films
    Photo lab equipment
    Photographic films
Healthcare and Material Solutions
    Digital mammography systems
    Synapse medical-use picture archiving and communications systems
    X-ray films
    Digital endoscopes
    Low-molecular pharmaceuticals
    functional cosmetics

COMPETITORS

DIPLOMA PLC
EASTMAN KODAK COMPANY
Evonik Industries AG
FLEX LTD.
KONICA MINOLTA, INC.
Koninklijke Philips N.V.
REXEL
RICOH COMPANY,LTD.
THE VITEC GROUP PLC.
TT ELECTRONICS PLC

HISTORICAL FINANCIALS
Company Type: Public

Income Statement — FYE: March 31

	REVENUE ($mil)	NET INCOME ($mil)	NET PROFIT MARGIN	EMPLOYEES
03/23	21,466	1,647	7.7%	83,513
03/22	20,764	1,736	8.4%	85,038
03/21	19,801	1,636	8.3%	83,006
03/20	21,327	1,151	5.4%	83,987
03/19	21,955	1,247	5.7%	82,841
Annual Growth	(0.6%)	7.2%	—	0.2%

2023 Year-End Financials
Debt ratio: 0.1%
Return on equity: 8.3%
Cash ($ mil.): 2,016
Current Ratio: 1.83
Long-term debt ($ mil.): 2,027
No. of shares ($ mil.): 401
Dividends
  Yield: 0.8%
  Payout: 11.1%
Market value ($ mil.): 20,352

	STOCK PRICE ($) FY Close	P/E High/Low	PER SHARE ($) Earnings	Dividends	Book Value
03/23	50.74	0 0	4.10	0.45	51.72
03/22	61.15	0 0	4.33	0.01	51.34
03/21	59.70	0 0	4.08	0.45	49.80
03/20	50.02	0 0	2.81	0.80	45.02
03/19	45.55	0 0	2.94	0.70	44.94
Annual Growth	2.7%	— —	8.7%	(10.7%)	3.6%

Fujitsu Ltd

EXECUTIVES

President, Chief Executive Officer, Representative Director, Takahito Tokita
Executive Vice President, Chief Operating Officer, Representative Director, Hidenori Furuta
SEVP, Chief Financial Officer, Director, Takeshi Isobe
Senior Advisor, Director, Masami Yamamoto
Outside Director, Chiaki Mukai
Outside Director, Atsushi Abe
Outside Director, Yoshiko Kojo
Outside Director, Kenichiro Sasae
Outside Director, Byron Gill
Auditors: Ernst & Young ShinNihon LLC

LOCATIONS
HQ: Fujitsu Ltd
  Shiodome City Center, 1-5-2 Higashi-Shimbashi, Minato-ku, Tokyo 105-7123
Phone: (81) 3 6252 2220
Web: www.fujitsu.com

HISTORICAL FINANCIALS
Company Type: Public

Income Statement — FYE: March 31

	REVENUE ($mil)	NET INCOME ($mil)	NET PROFIT MARGIN	EMPLOYEES
03/23	27,884	1,615	5.8%	135,793
03/22	29,488	1,501	5.1%	136,890
03/21	32,420	1,830	5.6%	138,698
03/20	35,539	1,474	4.1%	141,947
03/19	35,689	944	2.6%	145,845
Annual Growth	(6.0%)	14.4%	—	(1.8%)

2023 Year-End Financials
Debt ratio: —
Return on equity: 13.5%
Cash ($ mil.): 2,672
Current Ratio: 1.50
Long-term debt ($ mil.): 15
No. of shares ($ mil.): 188
Dividends
  Yield: 1.2%
  Payout: 4.1%
Market value ($ mil.): 5,083

	STOCK PRICE ($) FY Close	P/E High/Low	PER SHARE ($) Earnings	Dividends	Book Value
03/23	26.99	0 0	8.30	0.34	63.26
03/22	30.02	0 0	7.59	0.38	66.55
03/21	29.20	0 0	9.15	0.38	65.81
03/20	17.81	0 0	7.28	0.29	57.09
03/19	14.43	0 0	4.63	0.23	50.43
Annual Growth	17.0%	— —	15.7%	9.7%	5.8%

Fukui Bank Ltd.

Fukui Bank provides banking and other financial services in the Fukui prefecture of Japan. The regional bank serves both retail and commercial customers through nearly 100 branches and nine subsidiaries. Individuals, regional businesses, and public agencies use Fukui Bank for general banking, financial leasing, and real estate services among others. The bank was established in 1899.

EXECUTIVES

President, Representative Executive Officer, Director, Masahiro Hayashi
Representative Executive Officer, Senior Managing Director, Director, Toru Yuasa
Senior Managing Director, Representative Executive Officer, Director, Eiichi Hasegawa
Director, Osamu Watanabe
Director, Noriyuki Satake
Director, Masatake Yoshida
Outside Director, Kazuhiro Uchikami
Outside Director, Masaru Nambo
Outside Director, Yuko Mitsuya
Auditors: KPMG AZSA LLC

LOCATIONS
HQ: Fukui Bank Ltd.
  1-1-1 Junka, Fukui 910-8660
Phone: (81) 776 24 2030
Web: www.fukuibank.co.jp

COMPETITORS

AOMORI BANK,LTD., THE
CHUKYO BANK, LIMITED.
HIROSHIMA BANK, LTD., THE
SHIKOKU BANK LTD., THE
YAMAGATA BANK,LTD., THE

HISTORICAL FINANCIALS
Company Type: Public

Income Statement — FYE: March 31

	ASSETS ($mil)	NET INCOME ($mil)	INCOME AS % OF ASSETS	EMPLOYEES
03/21	31,730	23	0.1%	1,981
03/20	27,185	19	0.1%	2,012
03/19	25,307	28	0.1%	2,043
03/18	25,174	36	0.1%	2,062
03/17	23,251	37	0.2%	2,051
Annual Growth	8.1%	(11.4%)	—	(0.9%)

2021 Year-End Financials
Return on assets: —
Return on equity: 1.9%
Long-term debt ($ mil.): —
No. of shares ($ mil.): 24
Sales ($ mil.): 384
Dividends
  Yield: —
  Payout: 0.0%
Market value ($ mil.): —

Gail India Ltd

Incorporated in 1984, GAIL (India) Limited is a natural gas company with diversified interests across the natural gas value chain of trading, transmission, LPG production & transmission, LNG re-gasification, petrochemicals, city gas, E&P, etc. It owns and operates a network of around 14,615 km of natural gas pipelines spread across the country. It is working concurrently on execution of multiple pipeline projects to further enhance the spread. GAIL commands ~70% market share in gas transmission and has a Gas trading share of over 50% in India. GAIL and its Subsidiaries / JVs also have a formidable market share in City Gas Distribution.

Operations

GAIL currently aims to maximize the value potential of each portfolio by capitalizing on its market position and strengthening underdeveloped areas of value creation.

Natural Gas Transmission & Marketing portfolio has about 70% of natural gas transported in India and approximately 53% of natural gas sold in India.

City Gas Distribution operates in 61 geographical areas in India through subsidiaries and JV companies and maintains presence in metro cities. The portfolio serves CNG vehicles through 1689 CNG stations and supplies piped cooking gas to 5.08 million households.

Petrochemicals portfolio has a domestic market share of over 17% in polyethylene. It has a current marketing potfolio of 1.09 MTPA with a Petrochemicals Plant of BCPL at Lepetkata, Assam.

GAIL's Liquid Hydrocarbons Production and LPG Transmission has five gas processing plants with a capacity of 1,425 KTPA producing LPG, propane, pentane, naphtla, etc. It has LPG transmission capacity of 3.8 MTPA through some 2,040 km lPG pipelines.

Geographic Reach

GAIL is based India, and has two wholly owned subsidiaries in Singapore and the US. it has a representative office in Cairo to pursue business opportunities in Africa and the Middle East.

GAIL is a part of a consortium in two offshore exploration and production blocks in Myanmar and also holds a participating interest in the joint venture company - South East Asia Gas Pipeline Company Limited -- a transporter of gas produced from two blocks in Myanmar to China.

Sales and Marketing

GAIL markets its Gas Processing Unit's products --Liquefied Petroleum Gases (LPG), Propane, Pentane, Naphtha and by-products of polymer plant (Mixed Function Oxidases, Propylene and Hydrogenated C4 Mix). LPG is being sold exclusively to government-owned oil marketing companies while other products are sold directly to retail customers.

The company sells to a range of industries, including automotive, petrochemicals, industrial, fertilizer, and electric power utilities.

Financial Performance

GAIL's net sales have fluctuated over the last five years which declined towards 2021. Its net income followed the same trend between 2017 and 2021.

In fiscal year 2021, net sales decreased by 21% compared to the prior year after recording revenue decline in all its operations.

Net income fell by 35% in 2021 compared to the prior year.

Cash and cash equivalents at the end of 2021 was INR 1,506.59. Operations provide INR 8,993.4 while investing and financing activities used INR 4,993.04 crore and INR 3,470.62, respectively. Main cash used was mainly for investment in mutual fund and repayment of borrowings.

Strategy

GAIL undertook a detailed exercise in 2019 to develop 'Strategy 2030' to embark upon the next phase of value creation. Given the external headwinds, business environment, and market trends in the sector, in FY 2019-20, GAIL conducted a strategy revision exercise with sustainability imperatives and environmental risks as key considerations.

'Strategy 2030' focuses on building a robust and sustainable business portfolio for a dynamic business environment and an organization structure agile enough to unlock long-term growth opportunities. While COVID-19 pandemic did have a short-term impact on the strategic imperatives, the long-term focus areas on the company remain intact. Additionally, GAIS has identified five drivers that will define the future course of business: Expand presence across value chain; Organizational expertise & digital transformation; Diversify into sustainable and green energy; Offer enhanced value to consumers across verticals; and Expand global presence.

Digital strategy is one of the critical pillars of 'Strategy 2030'. GAIL has made significant investments in digital assets and new technologies, intending to address the company's future needs and to improve the overall efficiency. GAIL has taken various digital initiatives like the introduction of the digital worker for its robotic process automation, digitization of contactor payment processing, digitization of employee's payments etc., to give a boost the Digital Yatra, which GAIL has embarked upon to manage its operations digitally.

Company Background

The company started as a natural gas transmission company during the late 1980s.

GAIL is the pioneer of city gas distribution in India. It took many initiatives to introduce PNG for households and CNG for the transport sector to address the rising pollution levels. Pilot projects were launched in early 1990s in two metros Delhi and Mumbai through joint venture companies Indraprastha Gas Limited (IGL) and Mahanagar Gas Limited (MGL) leading to the start of commercial operation of city gas projects.

Auditors : A.R. & Co.

LOCATIONS

HQ: Gail India Ltd
16, Bhikaiji Cama Place, R. K. Puram, New Delhi 110066
Phone: (91) 11 26182955 **Fax:** (91) 11 26185941
Web: www.gailonline.com

PRODUCTS/OPERATIONS

Selected Joint Ventures
Aavantika Gas Limited (AGL)
Bhagyanagar Gas Limited (BGL)
Central U.P. Gas Limited (CUGL)
GAIL China Gas Global Energy Holdings Limited
Green Gas Limited (GGL)
Indraprastha Gas Limited (IGL)
Mahanagar Gas Limited (MGL)
Maharashtra Natural Gas Limited (MNGL)
ONGC Petro-additions Limited (OPaL)
Petronet LNG Limited (PLL)
Ratnagiri Gas and Power Private Limited (RGPPL)
Tripura Natural Gas Company Limited (TNGCL)

Selected Subsidiaries
Brahmaputra Cracker and Polymer Limited (BCPL)
GAIL Gas Limited
GAIL Global (Singapore) Pte Limited
GAIL GLOBAL (USA) INC., (GGUI)

2014

	%
NATURAL GAS TRADING	72
LPG & LIQUID HYDROCAR BONS	8
PETROCHE MICALS	6
NATURAL GAS	6
CITY GAS	4
UN- ALLOCABLE	3
TRANSMISSION SERVICES*	1
Total	

Products
Propane
Pentane
Naphtha
MFO
Hydrogenated C4 Mix
Propylene
Slop Oil

COMPETITORS

BG GROUP LIMITED
China National Petroleum Corporation
EQT CORPORATION
INDIAN OIL CORPORATION LIMITED
ISRAMCO, INC.
Korea Gas Corporation
Petrochina Company Limited
REX ENERGY CORPORATION
SASOL LTD
SURGUTNEFTEGAZ, PAO

HISTORICAL FINANCIALS

Company Type: Public

Income Statement FYE: March 31

	REVENUE ($mil)	NET INCOME ($mil)	NET PROFIT MARGIN	EMPLOYEES
03/22	12,415	1,618	13.0%	4,754
03/21	8,002	838	10.5%	4,705
03/20	9,811	1,247	12.7%	4,682
03/19	11,192	945	8.5%	4,529
03/18	8,531	737	8.6%	4,486
Annual Growth	9.8%	21.7%		1.5%

2022 Year-End Financials

Debt ratio: 0.1%   No. of shares ($ mil.): 4,440
Return on equity: 20.8% Dividends
Cash ($ mil.): 200   Yield: —
Current Ratio: 1.08   Payout: 164.7%
Long-term debt ($ mil.): 721 Market value ($ mil.): 53,551

	STOCK PRICE ($) FY Close	P/E High/Low		PER SHARE ($) Earnings	Dividends	Book Value
03/22	12.06	0	0	0.36	0.60	1.91
03/21	11.21	1	0	0.19	0.32	1.64
03/20	5.43	1	0	0.28	0.54	1.45
03/19	30.25	2	2	0.21	0.31	1.47
03/18	44.30	4	3	0.16	0.34	1.42
Annual Growth	(27.8%)			22.2%	15.1%	7.6%

Galp Energia, SGPS, SA

Portugal's primary oil and gas group, Galp Energia (formerly Petróleos de Portugal), produces, transports, refines, distributes, and sells crude oil, natural gas, and oil products. It operates mainly in Portugal and Spain, but also has operations in a half-dozen former Portuguese colonies. Although Galp Energia is primarily a refining and marketing company with more than 1,450 gas stations, it is seeking to expand its exploration and production efforts. The company has significant exploration and production activities in Angola, Brazil, and Portugal and holds gas and power infrastructure assets in Portugal. Italian energy giant Eni and Portuguese investment firm Amorim Energia each own 33% of the company.

EXECUTIVES

Chief Executive Officer, Chief Financial Officer, Vice-Chairman, Director, Filipe Silva
Non-Executive Chairwoman, Paula Amorim
Vice-Chairman, Lead Independent Director, Miguel Athayde Marques
Executive Director, Thore E. Kristiansen
Executive Director, Teresa Abecasis
Executive Director, Georgios Papadimitriou
Independent Non-Executive Director, Luis Todo Bom
Independent Non-Executive Director, Edmar de Almeida
Independent Non-Executive Director, Cristina Fonseca
Independent Non-Executive Director, Adolfo Mesquita Nunes
Independent Non-Executive Director, Javier Cavada Camino
Independent Non-Executive Director, Claudia Almeida e Silva
Non-Executive Director, Marta Amorim
Non-Executive Director, Francisco Teixeira Rego
Non-Executive Director, Carlos Pinto
Non-Executive Director, Jorge Seabra de Freitas
Non-Executive Director, Diogo Mendonca Rodrigues Tavares
Non-Executive Director, Rui Paulo Goncalves
Auditors : Ernst & Young Audit & Associados - SROC, S.A.

LOCATIONS

HQ: Galp Energia, SGPS SA
   Rua Tomas da Fonseca, Torre A, Lisbon 1600-209
Phone: (351) 217 242 500   **Fax:** (351) 217 242 965
Web: www.galp.com

PRODUCTS/OPERATIONS

2013 Sales

	% of total
Refining & marketing	83
Gas & power	17
Total	**100**

Selected Subsidiaries
Galp Power (electricity generation and sales)
Galpgeste (management and operation of service stations)
GDP Gás de Portugal
Petróleos de Portugal (Petrogal; exploration and production, refining, transport, distribution, and sales of oil products)
Sacor Maritima (marine transport)

Sopor (51%, distribution and sale of oil products)
Transgás Armazenagem (natural gas underground storage)

COMPETITORS

ATLAS COPCO USA HOLDINGS INC.
Alpiq Holding SA
CAMAC INTERNATIONAL CORPORATION
EDP - ENERGIAS DE PORTUGAL, S.A.
KUNLUN ENERGY COMPANY LIMITED
LafargeHolcim Ltd
SONAE - SGPS, S.A.
Weatherford International Ltd.
Westmount Energy Ltd
Winstar Resources Ltd

HISTORICAL FINANCIALS

Company Type: Public

Income Statement				FYE: December 31
	REVENUE ($mil)	NET INCOME ($mil)	NET PROFIT MARGIN	EMPLOYEES
12/22	29,009	1,575	5.4%	6,715
12/21	18,608	4	0.0%	6,152
12/20	14,197	(676)	—	6,114
12/19	19,017	436	2.3%	6,386
12/18	19,837	848	4.3%	6,360
Annual Growth	10.0%	16.7%	—	1.4%

2022 Year-End Financials
Debt ratio: 26.5%   No. of shares ($ mil.): 815
Return on equity: 40.8%   Dividends
Cash ($ mil.): 2,597   Yield: —
Current Ratio: 1.63   Payout: 14.1%
Long-term debt ($ mil.): 3,403   Market value ($ mil.): 5,478

	STOCK PRICE ($) FY Close	P/E High/Low		PER SHARE ($) Earnings	Dividends	Book Value
12/22	6.72	4	3	1.93	0.27	5.45
12/21	4.83	—	—	0.00	0.36	4.17
12/20	5.25	—	—	(0.81)	0.38	4.68
12/19	8.36	18	15	0.53	0.37	5.98
12/18	7.76	12	8	1.02	0.34	6.33
Annual Growth	(3.5%)	—	—	17.4%	(5.0%)	(3.7%)

Gazprom Neft PJSC

One of Russia's largest integrated oil companies, and its third-largest refiner, Gazprom Neft explores for, produces, refines, and markets petroleum products. Its retail operations include more than 1,800 gas stations. The company, with proved reserves of 2.8 billion barrels of oil equivalent, controls refineries in Moscow, Yaroslav, Serbia, and Omsk that produce more than 45.7 million tonnes of petroleum products per year. It refines about 80% of the oil it produces, a high ratio for Russia. Gazprom Neft also shares ownership of major natural gas project SeverEnergia with NOVATEK, the country's largest independent gas producer. State-owned gas giant Gazprom controls Gazprom Neft.

Operations

Gazprom Neft operates through two segments: Downstream and Upstream.

The Downstream segment processes crude oil into refined products. It also trades and transports crude oil and refined products. The segment brings in about two-thirds of the group's total revenue.

The Upstream segment explores, develops, produces, and sells crude oil and natural gas. It also provides oil fields services. The segment brings in about one-third of total sales.

Geographic Reach

Gazprom Neft operates in Russia and in other nations in Europe, the Middle East, South America, and Africa. The company exports to more than 50 countries around the world. Russia accounts for more than half of total revenue.

Its key refining facilities are located near Omsk, Moscow and Yaroslavl, and Serbia.

Financial Performance

Note: Growth rates may differ after conversion to US dollars.

With the steep decline in oil prices that hit the markets worldwide, Gazprom Neft's revenue fell in 2015 and 2016; revenue has been recovering in the years since. Net income has been growing as well, hitting record levels in 2017 and 2018.

In 2018, revenue increased 29% to 2.5 trillion RUB, thanks largely to recovering oil prices and to production growth at certain fields. Hydrocarbon production grew 7% that year, and oil product sales grew 4%. Aviation fuel sales alone rose 10%, due both to an increase in air traffic and to the company's expanded geographic coverage in that sector.

Net income rose 49% to 376.7 billion RUB in 2018. While revenue has been rising, the company is also implementing measures (such as utilizing new technologies) to operate more efficiently, which has boosted its bottom line.

The company ended 2018 with 247.6 billion RUB in net cash, some 150 billion RUB more than it had at the end of 2017. Operating activities provided 537.5 billion RUB in cash, while investing activities used 335 billion RUB and financing activities used another 56.5 billion RUB.

Strategy

Gazprom Neft has worked to become a global company over the past decade by expanding production and selling products around the world. It became Russia's third-largest oil producer in 2017.

Strategies to build business include expanding corporate sales, partnering with the largest consumers of petroleum products, growing its portfolio of gas stations, and digitizing business processes. The company is actively developing the first major domestic offshore project -- the Prirazlomnoye field in Russia's Arctic shelf -- and has production projects in other nations including Venezuela and Iraq.

Volume of conventional reserves has declined, which means that oil companies will need to increasingly concentrate on unconventional and complex segments (offshore, shale) where reserves are more difficult to recover. As a result, Gazprom Neft is heavily invested in technological projects that involve 3D modeling, artificial intelligence, big data, and cloud technologies.

Because the company has a number of foreign projects and is exploring additional geographies, it runs the risk of encountering political challenges. There is also the risk of having a competitive disadvantage in new markets. Gazprom Neft carefully assesses these risks when expanding.

HISTORY

In the aftermath of the fall of the Soviet Union in the early 1990s, Sibneft was formed in 1995 as part of Russia's privatization of state industries. Sibneft included western Siberian oil producer Noyabrskneftegas and the Omsk oil refinery. The Russian government was to retain a 51% stake for three years, while limiting foreign ownership to 15%. Finance Oil Company (FNK), controlled by business oligarch Boris Berezovsky, the man reportedly behind Sibneft's formation, gained a controlling stake in Sibneft. The new integrated oil company's prize asset was the Omsk refinery. Built in the mid-1980s, it was Russia's largest and most modern refinery.

In 1997 Sibneft became the first Russian company to issue a Eurobond. Despite an economic crisis in 1998, Sibneft continued to service all of its financial obligations. That year Sibneft made plans to merge with rival oil company Yukos (controlled by oligarch Mikhail Khodorkovsky), but falling oil prices led the two firms to scuttle the proposed union.

Also in 1998 Sibneft published a corporate governance charter, compiled by leading European experts to bring the company in line with international practices. This move was followed up with the appointment of three non-executives to the company's board of nine directors. A year later Sibneft became the first major Russian oil company to publish its financial accounts (audited by Arthur Andersen) according to US generally accepted accounting principles. In 1999 Sibneft also formed alliances with two Western oil services firms, US-based Schlumberger and Canadian-based BJ Services, to enhance its extraction of oil and gas.

During the 1999 Russian Duma elections, reclusive oligarch Roman Abramovich (who had acquired a 12% stake in Sibneft in 1996) claimed to control Sibneft, whereas Berezovsky (also elected to the Duma) was said to have only a background role in Sibneft.

The company announced plans in 2000 to invest $52 million to modernize the Omsk refinery, upgrading its capacity to produce lead-free gasoline. That year Sibneft also agreed to acquire majority stakes in two refined products retailers in the Urals region, which together controlled 132 service stations and 20 storage sites.

Sibneft lost out in its bid to gain control of Onako, another former state-owned oil company that was privatized in 2000. Sibneft had teamed up with two other oil companies, Yukos and Stroitransgaz (a unit of Russian gas giant Gazprom), to bid for Onako but lost out to rival Tyumen Oil Co. (TNK). However, Sibneft, which had gained control of a 40% stake in Onako's main oil producing subsidiary, Orenburgneft, reportedly made an arrangement with TNK to swap its Orenburgneft shares for a minority stake in Onako. Also in 2000, Sibneft and other Russian oil companies were investigated by Russian authorities after allegations of tax evasion.

In 2001 the company announced plans to search for oil in the Chukotka autonomous district. (Abramovich is the governor of Chukotka). This unexplored area has a similar geological structure to Alaska's oil-rich North Slope. Later that year Sibneft acquired a 36% stake in a Moscow refinery from oil giant LUKOIL, allowing the company to supply markets in European Russia.

In 2002 Sibneft opened its first gas station in Moscow.

Gazprom Neft (as Sibneft) was once controlled by UK-residing, Chelsea soccer club-owning Russian oligarch Roman Abramovich through investment company Millhouse Capital. In 2005 Gazprom bought its majority stake in Sibneft from Millhouse Capital for $11 billion. The company changed its name to Gazprom Neft the next year, and ENI acquired 20% of Gazprom Neft in 2007 following the bankruptcy of Yukos. Gazprom had the option to buy ENI's stake within two years and exercised that right in 2009, paying just more than $4 billion to ENI. Gazprom now directly owns or indirectly controls through subsidiaries about 95% of Gazprom Neft.

EXECUTIVES

Chairman, Chief Executive Officer, Executive Director, Alexander Valerievich Dyukov
Process Deputy Chairman, Sales Deputy Chairman, Logistics Deputy Chairman, Process Deputy Chief Executive, Sales Deputy Chief Executive, Logistics Deputy Chief Executive, Anatoly Cherner
Corporate Communications Deputy Chief Executive, Alexander Dybal
Security Deputy Chief Executive, Igor Antonov
Government Relations Deputy Chief Executive, Pavel Kolobkov
Corporate Affairs Deputy Chief Executive, Legal Deputy Chief Executive, Elena A. Ilyukhina
Foreign Asset Management Deputy Chief Executive, Administration Deputy Chief Executive, Kirill Kravchenko
Deputy Chairman, Vadim Yakovlev
Economics & Science Deputy Chief Executive, Economics & Science Member of the Management Board, Alexey Yankevich
Secretary, Viktoriya Nenadyshina
Non-Executive Chairman, Alexey Borisovich Miller
Non-Executive Director, Vitaly A. Markelov
Non-Executive Director, Sergey N. Menshikov
Non-Executive Director, Sergey I. Kuznets
Non-Executive Director, Famil K. Sadygov
Non-Executive Director, Alexander Ivanovich Medvedev
Non-Executive Director, Kirill Gennadievich Seleznev
Non-Executive Director, Vladimir Ivanovich Alisov
Non-Executive Director, Mikhail Leonidovich Sereda
Non-Executive Director, Elena Vladimirovna Mikhailova
Non-Executive Director, Valery Pavlovich Serdyukov
Non-Executive Director, Andrey Dmitriev
Non-Executive Director, Gennady Sukhov
Auditors : FBK, LLC

LOCATIONS

HQ: Gazprom Neft PJSC
3-5 Pochtamtskaya St., St. Petersburg 190000
Phone: (7) 812 363 31 52 **Fax:** (7) 812 363 31 51
Web: www.gazprom-neft.ru

2018 Sales

	% of total
Russian Federation	51
Commonwealth of Independent States	1
Export & international operations	44
Total	100

PRODUCTS/OPERATIONS

2018 Sales

	% of total
Petroleum products	67
Crude oil	29
Gas	1
Other	3
Total	100

2018 Sales by Segment

	% of total
Downstream	33
Upstream	67
Total	100

COMPETITORS

ADAMS RESOURCES & ENERGY, INC.
AEGEAN MARINE PETROLEUM S.A.
CRESTWOOD EQUITY PARTNERS LP
GAZPROM, PAO
KOCH INDUSTRIES, INC.
LUKOIL, PAO
MITSUI & CO., LTD.
MOTIVA ENTERPRISES LLC
NK ROSNEFT, PAO
THE PARKMEAD GROUP PLC

HISTORICAL FINANCIALS
Company Type: Public

Income Statement   FYE: December 31

	REVENUE ($mil)	NET INCOME ($mil)	NET PROFIT MARGIN	EMPLOYEES
12/21	40,863	6,704	16.4%	0
12/20	26,731	1,573	5.9%	82,960
12/19	39,933	6,430	16.1%	78,800
12/18	35,716	5,404	15.1%	66,500
12/17	32,136	4,380	13.6%	67,882
Annual Growth	6.2%	11.2%	—	—

2021 Year-End Financials
Debt ratio: 0.2%
Return on equity: 22.7%
Cash ($ mil.): 7,636
Current Ratio: 0.89
Long-term debt ($ mil.): 7,369
No. of shares ($ mil.): 4,718
Dividends
Yield: —
Payout: 0.0%
Market value ($ mil.): —

Geely Automobile Holdings Ltd

Geely Automobile is one of the top 10 automobile makers in China. It manufactures cars that are exported to more than 40 countries and makes automotive parts for use throughout China. Geely's nine manufacturing plants produce about two dozen sedan models sold under the brands GLEagle, Emgrand, and Englon. Its economy-model cars are sold from about 1,000 dealerships located across China; the export market accounts for about 25% of sales. It also owns two European car brands, Swedish car and truck company Volvo and the London Electric Vehicle Company (the maker of the black cabs that can be seen roving the city's streets). It sells over 1.2 million cars a year, its most popular models being the Geely Boyue, New Emgrand, New Vision, Emgrand GS, and Vision SUV.

EXECUTIVES

Chairman, Executive Director, Shu Fu Li
Vice-Chairman, Executive Director, Jian Yang
Vice-Chairman, Executive Director, Daniel Dong Hui Li
Chief Executive Officer, Executive Director, Sheng Yue Gui
Executive Director, Cong Hui An
Executive Director, Lawrence Siu Lung Ang
Executive Director, Mei Wei
Vice President, Adolph Yeung Chiu
Finance Secretary, Finance Controller, David Chung Yan Cheung
Independent Non-Executive Director, Dannis Cheuk Yin Lee
Independent Non-Executive Director, Alex Sau Hung Yeung
Independent Non-Executive Director, Qing Heng An
Independent Non-Executive Director, Yang Wang
Independent Non-Executive Director, Jocelyn Yin Shan Lam
Independent Non-Executive Director, Jie Gao
Auditors : Grant Thornton Hong Kong Limited

LOCATIONS
HQ: Geely Automobile Holdings Ltd
Room 2301, 23rd Floor, Great Eagle Centre, 23 Harbour Road, Wan Chai,
Phone: (852) 2598 3333   **Fax:** (852) 2598 3399
Web: www.geelyauto.com.hk

PRODUCTS/OPERATIONS
Selected Subsidiaries
Centurion Industries Limited
DSI Holdings Pty Limited
Jinan Geely Automobile Parts and Components Company Limited
Linkstate Overseas Limited
Luckview Group Limited
Value Century Group Limited
Zhejiang Geely Gearbox Limited

COMPETITORS
AMERICAN HONDA MOTOR CO., INC.
BRILLIANCE CHINA AUTOMOTIVE HOLDINGS LIMITED
Bayerische Motoren Werke AG
CONCEPT AUTOMOTIVE SERVICES LIMITED
MERCEDES-BENZ USA, LLC
SUBARU OF AMERICA, INC.
Spyker N.V.
TOYOTA MOTOR CORPORATION AUSTRALIA LIMITED
VOLVO CAR UK LIMITED
Volvo Group Canada Inc

HISTORICAL FINANCIALS
Company Type: Public

Income Statement   FYE: December 31

	REVENUE ($mil)	NET INCOME ($mil)	NET PROFIT MARGIN	EMPLOYEES
12/22	21,448	762	3.6%	49,000
12/21	16,005	763	4.8%	44,000
12/20	14,084	846	6.0%	38,000
12/19	13,997	1,176	8.4%	43,000
12/18	15,497	1,825	11.8%	52,400
Annual Growth	8.5%	(19.6%)	—	(1.7%)

2022 Year-End Financials
Debt ratio: 1.0%
Return on equity: 7.3%
Cash ($ mil.): 4,833
Current Ratio: 1.15
Long-term debt ($ mil.): 1,269
No. of shares ($ mil.): 10,056
Dividends
Yield: —
Payout: 42.0%
Market value ($ mil.): —

Gerdau S.A.

Gerdau is the leading manufacturer of long steel in North and South America. Gerdau believes it is one of the major global suppliers of special steel for the automotive industry. In Brazil, Gerdau also produces flat steel and iron ore, activities that are expanding Gerdau's product mix and the competitiveness of its operations. In addition, Gerdau believes it is one of Latin America's biggest recyclers and, worldwide, transforms millions of tonnes of scrap metal into steel every year, reinforcing its commitment to sustainable development in the regions where it operates. Gerdau's total consolidated installed annual capacity was approximately 17.7 million tonnes of crude steel and 15.9 million tonnes of rolled steel products. About half of its sales were generated from Brazil.

Operations
Gerdau's segments are:

Brazil business segment accounts for about 45% of total revenue and includes operations in Brazil, except Special Steels, and iron ore operation in Brazil.

North America business segment (some 35%) includes all operations in North America (Canada, US and Mexico), except special steel, in addition to associate and joint venture, both of which are located in Mexico.

Special Steel business segment includes the special steel operations in Brazil and the US. The segment generates about 15% of total revenue.

South America business segment (less than 10%) includes all operations in South America (Argentina, Peru, Uruguay and Venezuela), except the operations in Brazil, in addition to the joint ventures in the Dominican Republic and Colombia.

Its product mix includes crude steel (slabs, blooms and billets), which is sold to rolling plants; finished products for the construction industry, such as rebar, wire-rods, structural shapes, hot-rolled coils and heavy plates; finished industrial products, such as commercial rolled-steel bars, light profiles and wires; and agricultural products, such as stakes, smooth wire and barbed-wire. Gerdau also produces special steel items using cutting-edge technology.

Geographic Reach
The company operates in Argentina, Brazil, Canada, Colombia, the US, Mexico, Peru, the Dominican Republic, Uruguay, and Venezuela.

Brazil is the company's largest single market accounting for nearly 50% of total revenue, followed by North America market with around 40% and Latin America for some 10% of total revenue.

The company is headquartered in São Paulo, Brazil.

Sales and Marketing
Gerdau sells its products sells through independent distributors, direct sales, from the mills and its retail network.

Financial Performance
In 2021, net sales came to R$78.3 billion, up 79% from 2020, which were R$43.8 billion, reflecting the global upcycle in commodity prices, as well as the higher volumes sold. The volumes in 2021 increased 11% compared to 2020, where 12.7 million tons were sold and in 2020 11.5 million tons were sold.

In 2021, the company had a net income of R$15.6 billion, a 552% increase from the previous year's net income of R$2.4 billion.

The company's cash at the end of 2021 was R$4.2 billion. Operating activities generated R$16.6 billion, while investing activities used R$3 billion, mainly for purchases of property, plant and equipment. Financing activities used another R$10 billion, primarily for dividends and interest on capital paid as well as repayment of loans and financing.

Strategy

Gerdau remains focused on serving strategic markets that contribute results to its operation, analyzing the impacts and opportunities arising from the volatile international political-economic scenario and consolidating the presence of its entire product portfolio in these markets in 2022.

Company Background

In 2013 MetalÃºrgica Gerdau invested R$ 2.6 billion in fixed assets, mainly for projects already underway.

EXECUTIVES

Chief Executive Officer, Executive Director, Gustavo Werneck da Cunha

Executive Vice President, Chief Financial Officer, Investor Relations Officer, Harley Lorentz Scardoelli

Corporate Affairs Officer, General Counsel, Fabio Eduardo de Pieri Spina

Procurement Vice President, Fladimir Batista Lopes Gauto

Global Industrial Corporate Director, Hermenio Pinto Goncalves

Chairman, Director, Guilherme Chagas Gerdau Johannpeter

Director, Vice-Chairman, Andre Bier Gerdau Johannpeter

Vice-Chairman, Claudio Gerdau Johannpeter

Director, Aod Cunha de Moraes Junior

Director, Claudia Sender Ramirez

Director, Fernando Fontes Iunes

Director, Marcio Froes Torres

Director, Carlos Jose Da Costa Andre

Auditors: PricewaterhouseCoopers Auditores Independentes

LOCATIONS

HQ: Gerdau S.A.
Av. Dra. Ruth Cardoso, 8, 501 - 8 floor, Sao Paulo 05425-070
Phone: (55) 11 3094 6300 **Fax:** (55) 51 3323 2481
Web: www.gerdau.com

PRODUCTS/OPERATIONS

Selected Products
Billets
Blooms
Drawn products
Iron ore
Light and heavy structural shapes
Rebar
Round, square and flat bars
Shapes
Stainless steel
Wire rod

2015 Sales

	% of total
Brazil operation	29
North America operation	39
South America Operation	12
Special Steel operation	20
Total	100

2015 Sales

	% of total
Brazil	32
North America	45
Latin America	15
Europe/Asia	8
Total	100

COMPETITORS

Alfa, S.A.B. de C.V.
BayWa AG
CARR'S GROUP PLC
GOODWIN PLC
Gerdau S/A
HANWA CO.,LTD.
Itausa S/A
Nexa Resources
Vale S/A
thyssenkrupp AG

HISTORICAL FINANCIALS

Company Type: Public

Income Statement — FYE: December 31

	REVENUE ($mil)	NET INCOME ($mil)	NET PROFIT MARGIN	EMPLOYEES
12/22	15,584	2,160	13.9%	28,197
12/21	14,058	2,780	19.8%	27,739
12/20	8,436	455	5.4%	24,613
12/19	9,862	299	3.0%	24,787
12/18	11,893	593	5.0%	24,542
Annual Growth	7.0%	38.1%		3.5%

2022 Year-End Financials

Debt ratio: 3.2%
Return on equity: 25.7%
Cash ($ mil.): 468
Current Ratio: 2.32
Long-term debt ($ mil.): 1,793
No. of shares ($ mil.): 571
Dividends
Yield: 0.1%
Payout: 51.3%
Market value ($ mil.): 3,168

	STOCK PRICE ($) FY Close	P/E High/Low		PER SHARE ($) Earnings	Dividends	Book Value
12/22	5.54	1	1	1.23	0.63	15.25
12/21	4.92	1	0	1.62	0.57	13.37
12/20	4.67	3	1	0.27	0.05	10.39
12/19	4.90	7	4	0.17	0.07	11.73
12/18	3.76	3	2	0.35	0.07	3.91
Annual Growth	10.2%	—		37.4%	71.5%	40.5%

Glencore PLC

One of the world's largest natural resource companies, Glencore is active at every stage of commodity supply chain. It is a leading integrated producer and marketer of natural resources, with worldwide activities in the production, refinement, processing, storage, transport and marketing of metals and minerals and energy products. With presence in approximately 35 countries, and a diversified portfolio of more than 60 commodities, its operations span some 60 sites and facilities from crude oil production and coal mining, to custom metallurgical products, biofuels, and storage and handling of grains. Glencore was founded in 1974. The company's largest geographic market was Asia with around 40% of the total revenue.

IPO

Operations

The company offers products and services related to metals and minerals, energy, marketing, and recycling.

Metals and minerals, includes copper, cobalt, nickel, zinc and leak, ferroalloys, aluminum/alumina, and iron ore from third parties.

Energy is a major producer and marketer of coal, with mines in Australia, Africa and South America ? while its oil business is one of the leading marketers of crude oil, refined products and natural gas.

Marketing physically source commodities and products from our global supplier base ? and sells them to customers all over the world.

Glencore is a major recycler of end-of-life electronics, lithium-ion batteries, and other critical metal-containing products. The company has long been closing the loop for critical metals like copper, nickel, cobalt, zinc and precious metals.

Geographic Reach

Headquartered in Baar, Switzerland; Glencore have over 60 mining, metallurgical and oil production assets in more than 35 countries.

Sales and Marketing

Glencore's customers are industrial consumers, such as those in the automotive, steel, power generation, battery manufacturing and oil sectors. The company also provide financing, logistics and other services to producers and consumers of commodities.

Financial Performance

Glencore's revenue for fiscal 2022 increased to $256.0 billion compared to the prior year with $203.8 billion. The increase was primarily due to higher revenues on both segments offsetting the increase in intersegment eliminations.

Net income for fiscal 2022 increased to $22.9 billion compared to the prior year with $7.4 billion. The increase primarily due to higher revenues offsetting the increase in cost of goods sold.

Cash held by the company at the end of fiscal 2022 decreased to $2.0 billion. Cash provided by operations was $13.7 billion while cash used for investing and financing activities were $1.7 billion and $13.2 billion, respectively. Main uses of cash were purchase of property, plant and equipment; and distributions paid to equity holders of the Parent.

Mergers and Acquisitions

In 2023, Glencore International AG (Glencore) and Pan American Silver Corp.

(NYSE: PAAS, TSX: PAAS) (Pan American) announced they have reached an agreement for Glencore to acquire the 56.25% stake in the MARA Project (MARA or the Project) from Pan American. Under the terms of the agreement, Glencore will pay $475 million in cash upon closing and grant Pan American a copper Net Smelter Return (NSR) royalty of 0.75%.

In 2023, Glencore International AG (Glencore) and Pan American Silver Corp. (NYSE: PAAS, TSX: PAAS) (Pan American) announced they have reached an agreement for Glencore to acquire the 56.25% stake in the MARA Project (MARA or the Project) from Pan American. Under the terms of the agreement, Glencore will pay $475 million in cash upon closing and grant Pan American a copper Net Smelter Return (NSR) royalty of 0.75%.

Company Background

EXECUTIVES

Chief Executive Officer, Executive Director, Gary Nagle

Chief Financial Officer, Executive Director, Steven Kalmin

Secretary, John Burton

Independent Non-Executive Chairman, Non-Executive Director, Kalidas V. Madhavpeddi

Senior Independent Director, Non-Executive Director, Gill Marcus

Independent Non-Executive Director, Martin J. Gilbert

Independent Non-Executive Director, Patrice Merrin

Independent Non-Executive Director, Cynthia Blum Carroll

Independent Non-Executive Director, David Wormsley

Independent Non-Executive Director, Liz Hewitt

Non-Executive Director, Peter Coates

Auditors : Deloitte LLP

LOCATIONS

HQ: Glencore PLC
Baarermattstrasse 3, Baar CH-6340
Phone: (41) 41 709 2000   **Fax:** (41) 41 709 3000
Web: www.glencore.com

2018 Sales

	% of total
Asia	43
Europe	35
The Americas	17
Oceania	3
Africa	2
Total	100

PRODUCTS/OPERATIONS

2018 Sales

	% of total
Energy products	63
Metals and minerals	37
Corporate and other	—
Total	100

Selected Operations
Agricultural Products
 Barley
 Corn
 Meals
 Rice
 Sugar
 Wheat
Energy Products
 Coal
 Oil
Metals and Minerals
 Copper
 Ferroalloys
 Lead
 Nickel
 Zinc
Viterra, ($6.2 billion; Canada; grain merchant)

COMPETITORS

AKKA TECHNOLOGIES
CBOE GLOBAL MARKETS, INC.
COMPASS DIVERSIFIED HOLDINGS
Canaccord Genuity Group Inc
E D & F MAN HOLDINGS LIMITED
PEABODY ENERGY CORPORATION
ROYAL GOLD, INC.
TOTAL SE
VIRTU ITG HOLDINGS LLC
Zijin Mining Group Company Limited

HISTORICAL FINANCIALS

Company Type: Public

Income Statement   FYE: December 31

	REVENUE ($mil)	NET INCOME ($mil)	NET PROFIT MARGIN	EMPLOYEES
12/22	255,984	17,320	6.8%	141,625
12/21	203,751	4,974	2.4%	135,000
12/20	142,338	(1,903)	—	145,000
12/19	215,111	(404)	—	160,000
12/18	219,754	3,408	1.6%	158,000
Annual Growth	3.9%	50.1%	—	(2.7%)

2022 Year-End Financials

Debt ratio: 21.0%   No. of shares ($ mil.): 12,764
Return on equity: 38.7%   Dividends
Cash ($ mil.): 1,923   Yield: —
Current Ratio: 1.30   Payout: 81.7%
Long-term debt ($ mil.): 17,917   Market value ($ mil.): 170,028

	STOCK PRICE ($) FY Close	P/E High/Low		PER SHARE ($) Earnings	Dividends	Book Value
12/22	13.32	11	7	1.32	1.08	3.87
12/21	10.08	28	17	0.37	0.29	3.05
12/20	6.27	—	—	(0.14)	0.17	2.85
12/19	6.18	—	—	(0.03)	0.34	3.05
12/18	7.24	49	29	0.24	0.34	3.31
Annual Growth	16.5%	—	—	53.1%	33.5%	4.0%

Great-West Lifeco Inc

Great-West Lifeco is an international financial services holding company with interests in life insurance, health insurance, retirement and investment services, asset management and reinsurance businesses. The company operates in Canada, the US and Europe under the brands Canada Life, Empower, Putnam Investments, and Irish Life. Its companies have 215,000 advisor relationships, and thousands of distribution partners ? all serving its more than 33 million customer relationships across these regions. Power Corporation of Canada indirectly controlled 70.57% of the outstanding common shares of Great-West Lifeco.

Operations
The company operates through Canada, US, Europe and Capital Risk Solutions.

The Capital and Risk Solutions segment includes the Reinsurance business unit, which operates primarily in the US, Barbados, Bermuda and Ireland. Reinsurance products are provided through Canada Life and its subsidiaries. This includes both reinsurance and retrocession business transacted directly with clients or through reinsurance brokers. As a retrocessionaire, the company provides reinsurance to other reinsurers to enable those companies to manage their insurance risk. The segment accounts for about 45% of total revenue.

In Canada, Canada Life offers a broad portfolio of financial and benefit plan solutions for individuals, families, businesses and organizations through two primary business units: Individual Customer and Group Customer. Through the Individual Customer business unit, the company provides life, disability and critical illness insurance products as well as wealth savings and income products to individual customers. Through the Group Customer business unit, the company provides life, accidental death and dismemberment, disability, critical illness, health and dental protection, creditor insurance as well as retirement savings and income and annuity products and other specialty products to group clients in Canada. The segment accounts for some 30% off total revenue.

In the US, Empower is a leading provider of employer-sponsored retirement savings plans in the public/non-profit and corporate sectors that offers employer-sponsored defined contribution plans, administrative and recordkeeping services, individual retirement accounts, fund management as well as investment and advisory services. This includes the retirement services business of Massachusetts Mutual Life Insurance Company (MassMutual). Putnam provides investment management services and related administrative functions and distribution services, through a broad range of investment products, including the Putnam Funds, its own family of mutual funds, which are offered to individual and institutional investors. The segment accounts for some 15% of total revenue.

The Europe segment (about 10%) is comprised of three distinct business units serving customers in the UK, Ireland and Germany, offering protection and wealth management products, including payout annuity products. The UK and Germany business units operate under the Canada Life brand and the Ireland business unit operates under the Irish Life brand.

Overall, premiums account for about 80% of total revenue, while fee and net investment income account for about some 20% of combined revenue.

Geographic Reach
Based in Manitoba, Canada, Lifeco has operations in the US, Canada, and Europe.

Sales and Marketing
In Canada, Lifeco products are distributed through multiple channels: Advisor Solutions, managing general agencies (MGAs) and national accounts, and Financial Horizons Group. It is also distributed through an extensive network of group sales offices located across the country through brokers, consultants and financial security advisors.

Empower's products and services are marketed nationwide through its sales force, brokers, consultants, advisors, third-party administrators and financial institutions.

Financial Performance
The company's revenue for fiscal 2021 increased to C$64.4 billion compared from the prior year with C$60.6 billion.

Net income for fiscal 2021 increased to C$3.1 billion compared from the prior year with C$2.9 billion.

Cash held by the company at the end of fiscal 2021 decreased to C$6.1 billion. Cash provided by operations was C$10.4 billion while cash used for investing and financing activities were C$992 million and C$11.2 million, respectively.

Strategy
In 2022, Individual Customer will continue to advance on strategies to position for growth. The company will further establish the value propositions for advisors in all channels, providing them with strategies and tools for helping customers focus on achieving long-term financial security regardless of life stage and market fluctuations.

The company will continue to competitively develop, price and market its comprehensive range of individual insurance and individual wealth management products while maintaining its focus on sales and service support to customers and advisors in all channels. The company will also continue to monitor and respond to the impacts of long-term interest rates and fee income compression.

Mergers and Acquisitions
In late 2021, The Canada Life Assurance Company (Canada Life), a subsidiary of Great-West Lifeco Inc., has completed the previously announced acquisition of ClaimSecure Inc. (ClaimSecure). The completion of this acquisition increases the number of plan members served by Canada Life by 1.25 million individuals, including plan members and their dependents, with annual claims payments of more than C$1.2 billion. It also substantially enhances Canada Life's presence in the third-party administrator (TPA) and third-party payor (TPP) business segments. In addition, Canada Life becomes the first major Canadian insurer to own and operate a pharmacy benefits manager with national claims-paying technology capabilities.

In 2021, Great-West Lifeco Inc.'s (Lifeco) US subsidiary Empower Retirement (Empower) announced it has reached a definitive agreement to acquire Prudential Financial, Inc.'s (Prudential) full-service retirement business. Subject to regulatory approvals, Empower will acquire this business for a total transaction value of approximately C$4.45 billion (US$3.55 billion). The addition of this retirement business increases Empower's base to over 16.6 million participants, 71,000 workplace savings plans and approximately US$1.4 trillion in assets under administration. The deal also strengthens Empower's overall offering for participants and sponsors through additional expertise, an expanded product offering and new capabilities from Prudential.

Also in 2021, Great-West Lifeco announced its Colorado-based subsidiary, Empower Retirement (Empower), has completed the previously announced acquisition of the retirement services business of Massachusetts Mutual Life Insurance Company (MassMutual). With completion of the acquisition, Empower's reach in the US is expanded to more than 12 million retirement plan participants and assets to approximately US$884 billion on behalf of approximately 67,000 workplace savings plans.

EXECUTIVES

Executive Vice President, Chief Risk Officer, Graham R. Bird
Executive Vice President, General Counsel, Sharon C. Geraghty
Executive Vice President, Chief Financial Officer, Garry MacNicholas
Executive Vice President, Chief Human Resources Officer, Grace M. Palombo
Executive Vice President, Chief Information Officer, Steven M. Rullo
Executive Vice President, Global Chief Investment Officer, Raman Srivastava
Executive Vice President, Chief Actuary, Dervla Tomlin
Senior Vice President, Chief Internal Auditor, Nancy D. Russell
Senior Vice President, Chief Communications Officer, Chief Sustainability Officer, David B. Simmonds
Senior Vice President, Chief Compliance Officer, Anne C. Sonnen
Senior Vice President, Secretary, Chief Governance Officer, Jeremy W. Trickett
Strategy, Investments, Reinsurance and Corporate Development President, Strategy, Investments, Reinsurance and Corporate Development Head, Arshil Jamal
President, Chief Executive Officer, Director, Paul A. Mahon
Chair, Director, Robert Jeffrey Orr

Corporate Director, Deborah J. Barrett
Corporate Director, Marcel R. Coutu
Corporate Director, David G. Fuller
Corporate Director, Elizabeth C. Lempres
Corporate Director, Paula B. Madoff
Corporate Director, Siim A. Vanaselja
Corporate Director, T. Timothy Ryan
Director, Michael R. Amend
Director, Robin A. Bienfait
Director, Heather E. Conway
Director, Andre Desmarais
Director, Paul Desmarais
Director, Gary A. Doer
Director, Claude Genereux
Director, Susan J. McArthur
Director, Gregory D. Tretiak
Director, Brian E. Walsh
Auditors: Deloitte LLP

LOCATIONS

HQ: Great-West Lifeco Inc
100 Osborne Street North, Winnipeg, Manitoba R3C 1V3
Phone: 204 946-1190
Web: www.greatwestlifeco.com

2012 Sales

	$ mil.	% of total
US		
Asset management	23.8	40
Financial services	6.2	10
Canada		
Wealth management	9.4	16
Group insurance	7.5	12
Individual insurance	3.9	7
Europe		
Insurance & annuities	5.0	8
Reinsurance	4.0	7
Total	59.8	100

PRODUCTS/OPERATIONS

Selected Subsidiaries & Affiliates
The Great-West Life Assurance Company
    Canada Life Financial Corporation
    The Canada Life Assurance Company
    Canada Life Capital Corporation Inc.
    The Canada Life Group (U.K.) Limited
    Canada Life International Re Limited
    Canada Life Irish Holding Company Limited
    Crown Life Insurance Company
    Laketon Investment Management, Ltd.
    London Insurance Group
    London Life Insurance Company
    London Reinsurance Group Inc.
GWL&A Financial Inc. (US)
    Great-West Life & Annuity Insurance Company
    Advised Assets Group, LLC
    FASCore, LLC

COMPETITORS

AIG RETIREMENT SERVICES
AMERICAN NATIONAL INSURANCE COMPANY
Corporation Financiàre Power
GIBRALTAR LIFE INSURANCE CO., LTD., THE
GREAT-WEST LIFE & ANNUITY INSURANCE COMPANY
LINCOLN NATIONAL CORPORATION
NEW YORK LIFE INSURANCE COMPANY
PACIFIC LIFE INSURANCE COMPANY
SYMETRA FINANCIAL CORPORATION
Sun Life Financial Inc

HISTORICAL FINANCIALS
Company Type: Public

Income Statement   FYE: December 31

	ASSETS ($mil)	NET INCOME ($mil)	INCOME AS % OF ASSETS	EMPLOYEES
12/23	538,107	2,065	0.4%	33,500
12/22	518,664	2,476	0.5%	31,000
12/21	495,027	2,561	0.5%	28,000
12/20	471,620	2,415	0.5%	24,500
12/19	346,468	1,913	0.6%	24,000
Annual Growth	11.6%	1.9%	—	8.7%

2023 Year-End Financials
Return on assets: 0.3%
Return on equity: 9.8%
Long-term debt ($ mil.): —
No. of shares ($ mil.): 932
Sales ($ mil.): 24,606
Dividends
Yield: —
Payout: 70.9%
Market value ($ mil.): 30,882

	STOCK PRICE ($) FY Close	P/E High/Low	Earnings	Dividends	Book Value
12/23	33.12	11 8	2.21	1.57	21.71
12/22	23.14	9 6	2.55	1.45	23.02
12/21	30.02	9 7	2.64	1.42	22.96
12/20	23.00	9 5	2.49	1.38	20.34
12/19	25.66	11 8	1.91	1.27	18.78
Annual Growth	6.6%	—	3.7%	5.5%	3.7%

Grupo Aval Acciones Y Valores SA

EXECUTIVES

President, Luis Carlos Sarmiento Gutierrez
Chief Financial Officer, Diego Fernando Solano Saravia
Information Technology Chief, Rodolfo Velez Borda
Internal Control Chief, Rafael Eduardo Neira Torres
Legal Counsel Chief, Jorge Adrian Rincon Plata
Risk Management Officer Chief, Luz Karime Vargas Hurtado
Financial and Administrative Vice President, Accounting Vice President, Maria Edith Gonzalez Florez
Secretary, Luis Fernando Pabon Pabon
Chairman, Luis Carlos Sarmiento Angulo
Independent Director, Alvaro Velasquez Cock
Independent Director, Fabio Castellanos Ordonez
Independent Director, Esther America Paz Montoya
Director, Alejandro Figueroa Jaramillo
Director, Maria Lorena Gutierrez Botero
Director, Miguel Largacha Martinez
Auditors : KPMG S.A.S.

LOCATIONS

HQ: Grupo Aval Acciones Y Valores SA
Carrera 13 No. 26A-47, Bogota 110311
Phone: (57) 1 743 3222
Web: www.grupoaval.com

HISTORICAL FINANCIALS
Company Type: Public

Income Statement   FYE: December 31

	REVENUE ($mil)	NET INCOME ($mil)	NET PROFIT MARGIN	EMPLOYEES
12/21	9,470	810	8.6%	107,076
12/20	11,008	686	6.2%	104,862
12/19	10,891	923	8.5%	111,192
12/18	10,079	897	8.9%	91,191
12/17	8,281	657	7.9%	80,565
Annual Growth	3.4%	5.4%	—	7.4%

2021 Year-End Financials
Debt ratio: —
Return on equity: 15.1%
Cash ($ mil.): 9,003
Current Ratio: —
Long-term debt ($ mil.): —
No. of shares ($ mil.): 22,281
Dividends
Yield: 5.1%
Payout: 667.2%
Market value ($ mil.): 113,856

	STOCK PRICE ($) FY Close	P/E High/Low	Earnings	Dividends	Book Value
12/21	5.11	0 0	0.04	0.26	0.25
12/20	6.88	0 0	0.03	0.32	0.27
12/19	8.72	0 0	0.04	0.35	0.27
12/18	5.90	0 0	0.04	0.34	0.25
12/17	8.50	0 0	0.03	0.39	0.24
Annual Growth	(11.9%)	—	—	5.4%	(9.6%)	0.9%

Grupo Bimbo SAB de CV (Mexico)

Grupo Bimbo is the world's largest and leading baking company and an important player snack in Mexico. Offering more than 10,000 products under some 100 umbrella brands, Grupo Bimbo produces bread, cookies, and tortillas under the Tĩa Rosa, Bimbo, Wonder, and Marinela brands. With more than 3 million points of sale and approximately 1,600 sales centers in about 35 countries, the company operates about 205 bakeries and other plants. Not content with dominating the Latin American bread markets, the company also owns major operations in the US including Bimbo Bakeries USA. Half of its sales were generated in North America.

Operations
Grupo Bimbo makes snacks which include sliced bread, buns and rolls, pastries, cakes, cookies, English muffins, and tortillas though its sales centers. These products are sold under over 100 brand names, including Bimbo, Marinela, Sara Lee, Ricolina, Vital, and more.

Geographic Reach
Mexico-based, Grupo Bimbo operates facilities in about 35 countries worldwide. North America generates approximately 50% of company's revenue, followed by Mexico with about 30%, and Latin America and EAA countries account for the rest.

Sales and Marketing
Grupo Bimbo spent approximately $13.6 million, $12.6 million, and $11 million in advertising and promotional expense for years 2021, 2020, and 2019, respectively. Its largest customer accounts for about 15% of its net sales.

Financial Performance
Company's revenue for fiscal 2021 increased by 5% to Ps. 348.9 billion compared from the prior year with Ps. 331.1 billion.

Profit for fiscal 2021 increased to Ps. 26.7 billion compared from the prior year with Ps. 16.7 billion.

Cash held by the company at the end of fiscal 2021 decreased to Ps. 8.7 billion. Cash provided by operations was Ps. 45.8 billion while cash used for investing and financing activities were Ps. 32.5 billion and Ps. 14.1 billion, respectively. Main uses of cash were purchase of property, plant and equipment; and repayments of loans.

Strategy
The innovation and development of modern technologies, processes, and ingredients is an important factor in meeting its ambitions of improving its product offerings. The company continuously strive to drive technological solutions through joint efforts, thus allowing it to establish a close and synergistic relationship with various experts and universities to access know-how and scientific discoveries that may be applied to new state-of the-art technologies. It is then able to anticipate the needs of its consumers and prepare its response with short, medium, and long-term solutions in the field of nutrition.

Mergers and Acquisitions
In mid-2021, Grupo Bimbo reached an agreement to acquire the Brazil businesses of Switzerland-headquartered Aryzta AG. Financial terms of the transaction were not disclosed.

HISTORY

Starting with 10 trucks and bread in cellophane wrappers, in 1945 Lorenzo Servitje and associates, including Jaime Jorba, began deliveries of their Bimbo-brand breads around Mexico City.

Two years later distribution spread to three other cities. Steady growth for Grupo Industrial Bimbo followed during the 1950s and 1960s, with new plants opening in Guadalajara and Monterrey. In 1962 Jorba left the company, returned to Spain, and created Bimbo Espaĩa. In 1964, when Continental Bakeries introduced Wonder Bread to Mexico, Bimbo countered with a similarly positioned bread line using the licensed US Sunbeam brand.

By 1972 the company was firmly established as the bread-market leader in Mexico when it began making corn tortillas. The next year the company founded Frexport, its jam and jelly unit.

The company went public in 1980 but

remained firmly under the control of the Servitje family. A major leap in the company's vision for itself came when it created a bun for McDonald's. Bimbo won the exclusive contract to supply buns to Mexico's McDonald's in 1985. In 1986 Bimbo acquired rival Continental Bakeries' Wonder Bread brand in Mexico, thus securing a virtual monopoly on the Mexican packaged-bread market. Future growth would come from international expansion.

During the 1990s Bimbo began a steady stream of acquisitions and construction of plants in Guatemala (1990), Chile (1992), Venezuela (1993), and Peru (1998). Daniel Servitje Montull was named CEO of Bimbo in 1997.

The company began doing contract work in the mid-1990s for German confectioner Park Lane, leading up to its 1998 purchase of Park Lane; it also established a factory in the Czech Republic. However, the company's boldest move was its 1998 purchase of Mrs. Baird's, the largest family-owned US bakery, based in Fort Worth, Texas. The company formed Bimbo Bakeries USA to control the Mrs. Baird's business and move closer to its US competition. In 1999 it acquired the Four-S bakery business in California. Four-S came with the popular local Weber brand of bread.

In 1999 the company shortened its name to Grupo Bimbo. That year it was awarded the exclusive contract to supply buns to McDonald's in Colombia, Peru, and Venezuela.

During 2000 Grupo Bimbo completed the spinoff of its flour mills and processed jellies units, with the agreement that they would continue supplying Grupo Bimbo. Roberto Servitje AchÃ"tegui, grandson of founder Lorenzo Servitje, left the company that year to run a new company, Grupo Altex. In 2001 Bimbo bought Plus Vita, a fresh bread and baked goods business, from Bunge Alimentos (a subsidiary of agribusiness giant Bunge Limited). In 2001 Grupo Bimbo purchased a bread baking operation in Costa Rica from tortilla-giant and rival Gruma.

Grupo Bimbo purchased five western US Orowheat production facilities in 2002 from George Weston. The acquisition gave the company access to some well-known consumer brands including Thomas' English Muffins, Entenmann's, and Boboli. That year it also closed its Mrs. Baird's bakery facility in Dallas.

As part of its strategy to concentrate on its consumer businesses, in 2003 Bimbo sold its 42% stake in packaging business Novacel to French aluminum company Pechiney (now a part of Rio Tinto Alcan) for $38 million. It also closed its Dallas Orowheat bakery that year. Bimbo, along with a consortium of other companies, took over Argentinean bakery business CompaÃ±Ãa de Alimentos de Fargo in 2003. Bimbo's stake in Fargo is 30%.

In 2004 the company bought three Mexican confectionery companies: Joyco de MÃ©xico, Alimentos Duval, and Lolimen. Bimbo expanded into frozen bakery-product manufacturing that year, as well, when it formed a joint venture with Rich Products to produce frozen and partially baked goods under the Fripan brand name.

The number of Bimbo's acquisitions continued to increase during 2005 as the company bought Colombian bread maker Lalo, Chilean pastry manufacturer Lagos el Sur, Mexican pastry manufacturer PastelerÃas El Globo, and Mexican confectioner La Corona. It purchased two Uruguayan bakery companies in 2006 for about $7 million: Walter M. Doldan y Cia and Los Sorchantes.

Marking its entry into China, in 2006 the company purchased the Chinese unit of Spanish baker Panrico SA.

EXECUTIVES

Chairman, Chief Executive Officer, Daniel Javier Servitje Montull
Chief Financial Officer, Diego Gaxiola Cuevas
People Chief People Officer, Juan Muldoon Barrena
Chief Information and Transformation Officer,, Raul Ignacio Obregon Servitje
General Counsel, Secretary, Luis Miguel Briola Clement
Secretary, Norma Isaura Castaneda Mendez
Independent Director, Arturo Manuel Fernandez Perez
Independent Director, Edmundo Miguel Vallejo Venegas
Independent Director, Jaime A. El Koury
Independent Director, Jose Ignacio Perez Lizaur
Independent Director, Juana Francisca de Chantal Llano Cadav
Independent Director, Maria Luisa Jorda Castro
Independent Director, Rogelio M. Rebolledo Rojas
Director, Andres Obregon Servitje
Director, Guillermo Lerdo de Tejada Servitje
Director, Jaime Chico Pardo
Director, Javier de Pedro Espinola
Director, Lorenzo Sendra Creixell
Director, Luis Jorba Servitje
Director, María del Pilar Mariscal Servitje
Director, Maria Isabel Mata Torrallardona
Director, Marina De Tavira Servitje
Director, Mauricio Jorba Servitje
Auditors : Mancera, S.C. (Ernst & Young Global)

LOCATIONS

HQ: Grupo Bimbo SAB de CV (Mexico)
Prolongacion Paseo de la Reforma N1000, Colonia Pena Blanca Santa Fe, Delegacion Alvaro Obregon, Mexico City 01210
Phone: (52) 55 5268 6600 **Fax:** (525) 55 5268 6697
Web: www.grupobimbo.com

2014 Plants

	No.
US & Canada	85
Latin America	32
Mexico	39
Europe	10
Asia	1
Total	167

2014 Sales

	% of total
US & Canada	47
Mexico	38
Other countries	15
Total	100

PRODUCTS/OPERATIONS

Selected Brands
Asia
  Bimbo
Latin America
  Mexico
    Barcel
    Bimbo
    Clever
    Coronado
    Del Hogar
    El Globo
    La Corona
    Lonchibon
    Marinela
    Milpa Real
    Ricolino
    Suandy
    Tía Rosa
    Vero
  Other countries
    Bimbo Centroamerica
    Breddy
    Coronado Centroamerica
    Ideal
    La Mejor
    Lido
    Marinela
    Monarca
    Pix
    Schmidt
    Tulipan
Europe
  Bimbo
  Eagle
US
  Arnold
  Bimbo USA
  Boboli
  Brownberry
  Earthgrains
  Entenmann's
  Francisco
  Frenchbakery
  Heiner's
  Holsum
  Home Maid Bread
  Marinela USA
  Master
  Mickey
  Mrs. Baird's
  Old Country
  Old Home
  Orowea
  Rainbo
  Sara Lee
  Stroehmann
  Taystee
  Thomas'
  Tia Rosa USA

COMPETITORS

ASSOCIATED BRITISH FOODS PLC

BIG HEART PET BRANDS, INC.
EBRO FOODS, SA
GREENCORE GROUP PUBLIC LIMITED COMPANY
Grupo Lala, S.A.B. de C.V.
Koninklijke Ahold Delhaize N.V.
McCain Foods Limited
PARMALAT FINANZIARIA SPA
Tengelmann Warenhandelsgesellschaft KG
UNITED BISCUITS TOPCO LIMITED

HISTORICAL FINANCIALS
Company Type: Public

Income Statement — FYE: December 31

	REVENUE ($mil)	NET INCOME ($mil)	NET PROFIT MARGIN	EMPLOYEES
12/22	20,376	2,397	11.8%	0
12/21	17,063	778	4.6%	137,543
12/20	16,661	458	2.8%	148,746
12/19	15,429	333	2.2%	148,638
12/18	14,659	295	2.0%	138,432
Annual Growth	8.6%	68.8%	—	—

2022 Year-End Financials
Debt ratio: 1.2%
Return on equity: 42.4%
Cash ($ mil.): 629
Current Ratio: 0.71
Long-term debt ($ mil.): 3,966
No. of shares ($ mil.): 4,433
Dividends
Yield: —
Payout: 0.0%
Market value ($ mil.): 75,539

	STOCK PRICE ($) FY Close	P/E High/Low	PER SHARE ($) Earnings	Dividends	Book Value
12/22	17.04	2 1	0.54	0.23	1.43
12/21	13.25	4 3	0.17	0.18	1.06
12/20	9.00	5 3	0.10	0.08	0.93
12/19	7.01	7 5	0.07	0.08	0.84
12/18	8.30	8 6	0.06	0.06	0.87
Annual Growth	19.7%	—	71.0%	40.6%	13.3%

Grupo Financiero Banorte S.A. BDE C V

EXECUTIVES

Chief Executive Officer, Director, Jose Marcos Ramirez Miguel
Chief Financial Officer, Chief Operating Officer, Rafael Arana de la Garza
Chief Administrative Officer, Javier Beltran Cantu
Chief Legal Officer, Hector Avila Flores
Chief Audit Executive, Isaias Velazquez Gonzalez
Chairman, Carlos Hank Gonzalez
Independent Director, Alicia Alejandra Lebrija Hirshfeld
Independent Director, Everardo Elizondo Almaguer
Independent Director, Clemente Ismael Reyes Retana Valdes
Independent Director, Alfredo Elias Ayub
Independent Director, Adrian G. Sada Cueva
Independent Director, David Penaloza Alanis
Independent Director, Jose Antonio Chedraui Eguia
Independent Director, Alfonso de Angoitia Noriega
Independent Director, Thomas Stanley Heather Rodriguez
Director, Juan Antonio Gonzalez Moreno

Director, David Juan Villarreal Montemayor
Director, Carlos de la Isla Corry
Auditors: Galaz, Yamazaki, Ruiz Urquiza, S.C. (member of Deloitte Touche Tohmatsu Limited)

LOCATIONS
HQ: Grupo Financiero Banorte S.A. BDE C V
3000 Avenida Revolución, Monterrey, Nuevo Leon 64930
Phone: (52) 81 8319 6500
Web: www.banorte.com

HISTORICAL FINANCIALS
Company Type: Public

Income Statement — FYE: December 31

	ASSETS ($mil)	NET INCOME ($mil)	INCOME AS % OF ASSETS	EMPLOYEES
12/22	105,796	2,320	2.2%	26,455
12/21	90,522	1,714	1.9%	0
12/20	89,984	1,535	1.7%	29,920
12/19	83,511	1,930	2.3%	0
12/18	82,407	1,625	2.0%	30,548
Annual Growth	6.4%	9.3%	—	(3.5%)

2022 Year-End Financials
Return on assets: 2.3%
Return on equity: 19.3%
Long-term debt ($ mil.): —
No. of shares ($ mil.): 2,857
Sales ($ mil.): 17,576
Dividends
Yield: —
Payout: 0.0%
Market value ($ mil.): 102,370

	STOCK PRICE ($) FY Close	P/E High/Low	PER SHARE ($) Earnings	Dividends	Book Value
12/22	35.83	3 2	0.82	2.78	4.22
12/21	32.47	3 2	0.59	1.36	4.01
12/20	27.78	3 1	0.53	0.00	3.93
12/19	27.88	3 2	0.67	1.42	3.57
12/18	24.50	3 2	0.56	0.82	3.06
Annual Growth	10.0%	—	—	9.9%	35.9%	8.3%

GSK plc

GSK is a science-led global healthcare company. The company develop and deliver medicines, vaccines and consumer healthcare products that impact human health at scale. Its operations span the value chain from identifying, researching, developing and testing ground-breaking discoveries, to regulatory approval, manufacturing and commercialization. It delivers around 1.7 billion medicines, over 767 million vaccines and 3.7 consumer healthcare products. The US accounts for nearly 45% of the company's revenue.

Operations
GSK operates through three primary segments: Pharmaceuticals, Consumer Healthcare, and Vaccines. Pharmaceuticals is the largest by far, pulling approximately half of revenue.

The Pharmaceuticals division has a broad portfolio of innovative and established medicines in respiratory, HIV, immuno-inflammation and oncology. Asthma medication Advair has been GSK's primary money spinner for many years although it faces intensifying competition from biosimilars and generics. HIV drugs Trimueq and Tivicay are GSK's next biggest, while other respiratory drugs include Relvar/Breo Ellipta, Ventolin, and Flixotide. The division's R&D activity focuses on immunology, human genetics and advanced technologies.

GSK's Consumer Healthcare segment generates about 30% of revenue and produces products in the oral health, wellness, nutrition, and skin health categories. Its major brands include Advil, Voltaren, Centrum, Caltrate and Otrivin.

The Vaccines segment develops, produces and distributes around 2 million vaccines daily on the market in more than 160 countries. Meningitis vaccines Bexsero and Menveo are its biggest earner, followed by flu vaccine Fluarix and Shingles vaccine Shingrix. Vaccines account for around 20% of GSK's revenue.

Geographic Reach
Headquartered in London, GSK has a significant presence in the US and regional headquarters in Singapore.

GSK's Vaccines business has over 10 manufacturing sites, across nine countries. It has presence in more than 160 countries.

The US is GSK's largest market at nearly 45% of revenue. Europe generates about a quarter.

Sales and Marketing
GSK sells its products through a small number of wholesalers in addition to hospitals, pharmacies, physicians and other groups. Sales to the three largest wholesalers amounted to about 75% of the sales of the US Pharmaceuticals and Vaccines business.

Financial Performance
Note: Growth rates may differ after conversion to US dollars.

The company's revenue for fiscal 2021 increased to £34.11 billion compared from the prior year with £34.10 billion.

Net income for fiscal 2021 increased £5.1 billion compared from the prior year with £6.4 billion.

Cash held by the company at the end of fiscal 2021 decreased to £3.8 billion. Cash provided by operations was £8.0 billion while cash used for investing and financing activities were £1.8 billion and £7.6 billion, respectively.

Strategy
In recent years, the company have transformed GSK to improve performance, strengthen capabilities and prepare for a new future. GSK have done this by prioritizing Innovation, Performance and Trust.

Innovation is critical to how the company improve health and create financial value. In 2021, its total R&D expenditure was £5.3 billion, up by 3.5% AER on 2020. GSK have a robust late-stage R&D pipeline with many assets having the potential to be first or best in class. GSK continue to believe the rapid convergence of science and technology in biopharmaceuticals provides significant opportunity and is why its R&D will continue to focus on the science of the immune system, human genetics and use of advanced technologies.

Performance is delivered by investing effectively in its business and its people and executing competitively. GSK's ability to launch new products successfully and grow sales from its existing portfolio is key to its commercial success.

Trust underpins everything it do. GSK have maintained its acknowledged leadership in environmental, social and governance (ESG) issues, demonstrated by its sector-leading position in the Dow Jones Sustainability Index and its longstanding leadership in the Access to Medicine Index.

HISTORY

Englishman Joseph Nathan started an import-export business in New Zealand in 1873. He obtained the rights to a process for drying milk and began making powdered milk in New Zealand, selling it as baby food Glaxo.

Nathan's son Alec, dispatched to London to oversee baby food sales in Britain, increased Glaxo's name recognition by publishing the Glaxo Baby Book, a guide to child care. After WWI the company began distribution in India and South America.

In the 1920s Glaxo launched vitamin D-fortified formulations. It entered the pharmaceutical business with its 1927 introduction of Ostelin, a liquid vitamin D concentrate, and continued to grow globally in the 1930s, introducing Ostermilk (vitamin-fortified milk).

Glaxo began making penicillin and anesthetics during WWII; it went public in 1947. A steep drop in antibiotic prices in the mid-1950s led Glaxo to diversify; it bought veterinary, medical instrument, and drug distribution firms.

In the 1970s the British Monopolies Commission quashed both a hostile takeover attempt by Beecham and a proposed merger with retailer and drugmaker Boots. Glaxo launched US operations in 1978.

Glaxo shed nondrug operations in the 1980s to concentrate on pharmaceuticals. A 1981 marketing blitz launched antiulcer drug Zantac (to vie with SmithKline's Tagamet) in the US, where Glaxo's sales had been small. The company boosted outreach by contracting to use Hoffmann-La Roche's sales staff. The Zantac sales assault gave Glaxo leadership in US antiulcer drug sales.

Under CEO Sir Richard Sykes, Glaxo in 1995 made a surprise bid for UK rival Wellcome. Founded in 1880 by Americans Silas Burroughs and Henry Wellcome to sell McKesson-Robbins' products outside the US, Burroughs Wellcome and Co. began making its own products two years later. By the 1990s the company, which fostered Nobel Prize-winning researchers, led the world in antiviral medicines. Its primary drug products were Zovirax (launched 1981) and Retrovir (1987).

Though an earlier bid by Glaxo had been rejected, Sykes won the takeover with backing from Wellcome Trust, Wellcome's largest shareholder.

In 1997 the company formed a new genetics division, buying Spectra Biomedical and its gene variation technology. That year the company pulled diabetes drug Romozin (Rezulin in the US) from the UK market over concerns that it caused liver damage.

Glaxo in 1998 ended its joint venture with Warner-Lambert (begun 1993), selling its former partner the Canadian and US marketing rights to acid blocker Zantac 75.

In 1999 Glaxo trimmed its product line, pulling hepatitis treatment Wellferon because of slow sales and selling the US rights to several anesthesia products. It also cut some 3,400 jobs (half from the UK). Also that year Glaxo threatened to leave the UK after the National Health Service opted not to cover antiflu inhalant Relenza, claiming the drug is not cost-effective.

The FDA in 2000 approved Glaxo's Lotronex for irritable bowel syndrome, but several hospitalizations linked to the drug prompted the FDA to ask the company to withdraw it from the US market. Later that year Glaxo completed its merger with former UK rival SmithKline Beecham to create GlaxoSmithKline (GSK).

In 2015 GSK bought Novartis' Vaccines and Consumer Health business, and sold its cancer drugs business to the same company.

EXECUTIVES

Chief Executive Officer, Executive Director, Emma N. Walmsley
Chief Financial Officer, Executive Director, Iain Mackay
Chief Scientific Officer, Tony Wood
Human Resources Chief People Officer, Diana Conrad
Global Pharmaceuticals Chief Commercial Officer, Global Pharmaceuticals President, Luke Miels
Senior Vice President, General Counsel, Legal and Compliance, James Ford
Global Communications and CEO Office Senior Vice President, Sally Jackson
Corporate Development President, Corporate Development Chief Strategy Officer, David Redfern
Pharmaceuticals Supply Chain President, Regis Simard
Government Affairs President, Communications President, Global Affairs President, Phil Thomson
Global Health President, Deborah Waterhouse
Non-Executive Chairman, Jonathan Symonds
Senior Independent Non-Executive Director, Charles Bancroft
Independent Non-Executive Director, Anne Beal
Independent Non-Executive Director, Harry C. Dietz
Independent Non-Executive Director, Jesse Goodman
Independent Non-Executive Director, Urs Rohner
Independent Non-Executive Director, Vishal Sikka
Independent Non-Executive Director, Elizabeth McKee Anderson
Non-Executive Director, Hal V. Barron
Auditors: Deloitte LLP

LOCATIONS

HQ: GSK plc
980 Great West Road, Brentford, Middlesex TW8 9GS
Phone: (44) 20 8047 5000   **Fax:** (44) 20 8047 7807
Web: www.gsk.com

2017 Sales

	% of total
US	37
International	36
Europe	27
Total	100

PRODUCTS/OPERATIONS

2017 Sales

	% of total
Pharmaceuticals	57
Consumer healthcare	26
Vaccines	17
Total	100

Selected Products

Pharmaceuticals
  Respiratory
    Beconase (allergies)
    Becotide/Beclovent (asthma and chronic obstructive pulmonary disease)
    Flixonase/Flonase (allergies)
    Flixotide/Flovent (asthma and chronic obstructive pulmonary disease)
    Seretide/Advair (asthma and chronic obstructive pulmonary disease)
    Serevent (asthma and chronic obstructive pulmonary disease)
    Ventolin (asthma and chronic obstructive pulmonary disease)
    Veramyst/Avamys (rhinitis)
  Cardiovascular and urogenital
    Arixtra (deep vein thrombosis and pulmonary embolism)
    Avodart (prostatic hyperplasia)
    Benlysta (systemic lupus erychematosus, with HGS)
    Coreg CR (heart failure and hypertension)
    Fraxiparine (deep vein thrombosis and pulmonary embolism)
    Levitra (erectile dysfunction, with Bayer)
    Lovaza (coronary heart disease)
    Vesicare (overactive bladder)
    Volibris (pulmonary hypertension)
  Central nervous system disorders
    Horizant (post-herpetic neuralgia or restless leg syndrome)
    Imigran/Imitrex (migraines)
    Lamictal (epilepsy and bipolar disorder)
    Potiga/Trobalt (epilepsy and partial seizures)
    Requip (Parkinson's disease)
    Seroxat/Paxil (depression)
    Treximet (migraine)
    Wellbutrin SR (depression)
  ViiV Healthcare (HIV, with Pfizer)
    Combivir/Biovir (reverse transcriptase inhibitor for HIV/AIDS)
    Epivir/3TC (reverse transcriptase inhibitor for HIV/AIDS)
    Epizicom/Kivexa (combination of Epivir and Ziagen for HIV/AIDS)
    Lexiva/Telzir (protease inhibitor for HIV/AIDS)
    Selzentry (HIV)

Trizivir (three reverse transcriptase inhibitors for HIV/AIDS)
  Antibacterials
    Amoxil and Augmentin (antibiotics, non-US only)
  Dermatology
    Bactroban (skin infections)
    Duac (acne vulgaris)
    Zovirax (herpes infections, shingles, chicken pox, and cold sores)
  Antivirals
    Relenza (influenza)
    Hepsera (hepatitis B)
    Valtrex/Zelitrex (shingles and genital herpes)
    Zeffix/Septavir/Heptodin/Epivir HBV (hepatitis B)
  Vaccines
    Cervarix (human papilloma virus)
    Fluarix (influenza)
    FluLaval (influenza)
    Infanrix/Pediarix (diphtheria, tetanus, pertussis, polio, and hepatitis B)
    Rotarix (rotavirus)
    Synflorix (pneumonia)
    Twinrix (hepatitis A and hepatitis B)
  Metabolic
    Avandia, Avandamet (type 2 diabetes)
    Boniva/Bonviva (osteoporosis, with Roche)
Consumer products
  Over-the-counter medicines
    Abreva (cold sores)
    alli (weight loss)
    Breathe Right (nasal strips)
    Citrucel (laxative)
    Commit (smoking-cessation)
    Contac (respiratory product)
    Nicabate/NicoDerm/NiQuitin CQ (smoking-cessation)
    Nicorette (smoking-cessation)
    Panadol (analgesic)
    Tums (antacid)
  Oral care
    Aquafresh (toothpaste and toothbrushes)
    Corega (denture care)
    Dr Best (toothbrushes)
    Macleans (toothpaste)
    Odol (toothpaste)
    Polident (denture cleaner)
    Poli-Grip (denture adhesive)
    Sensodyne (toothpaste)
  Nutritional health care
    Horlicks (milk-based malted food and chocolate drinks)
    Lucozade (glucose energy drink)
    Ribena (line of juice drinks rich in vitamin C)

COMPETITORS

ASTRAZENECA PLC
BRISTOL-MYERS SQUIBB COMPANY
Bausch Health Companies Inc
Boehringer Ingelheim International GmbH
CIPLA LIMITED
ELI LILLY AND COMPANY
GILEAD SCIENCES, INC.
MERCK KG auf Aktien
MYLAN INC.
PFIZER INC.

HISTORICAL FINANCIALS
Company Type: Public

Income Statement — FYE: December 31

	REVENUE ($mil)	NET INCOME ($mil)	NET PROFIT MARGIN	EMPLOYEES
12/23	38,652	6,280	16.2%	70,212
12/22	35,301	18,004	51.0%	69,400
12/21	45,974	5,909	12.9%	90,096
12/20	46,535	7,845	16.9%	94,066
12/19	44,574	6,134	13.8%	99,437
Annual Growth	(3.5%)	0.6%	—	(8.3%)

2023 Year-End Financials
Debt ratio: 38.9%
Return on equity: 41.1%
Cash ($ mil.): 3,741
Current Ratio: 0.88
Long-term debt ($ mil.): 19,378
No. of shares ($ mil.): 4,056
Dividends
  Yield: —
  Payout: 92.2%
Market value ($ mil.): 150,325

	STOCK PRICE ($) FY Close	P/E High/Low	PER SHARE ($) Earnings	Dividends	Book Value
12/23	37.06	32 28	1.53	1.41	4.19
12/22	35.14	12 9	4.41	0.69	3.12
12/21	44.10	41 30	1.46	1.35	5.04
12/20	36.80	35 24	1.95	1.36	4.95
12/19	46.99	41 33	1.53	1.32	3.77
Annual Growth	(5.8%)	— —	0.0%	1.7%	2.7%

Gunma Bank Ltd (The)

Gunma Bank hopes that you have more than just a yen for its services. Through more than 140 branches, The Gunma Bank provides banking services in the Gunma prefecture and surrounding areasÂ of Japan through some 150 branches. The Gunma Bank also operates a subsidiary in Hong Kong and a branch in New York City. As the company's name might imply, the Gunma prefecture (known for its industry and agriculture-based economy)Â accounts for more than 80% of deposits. Besides deposits Gunma Bank's services include loans to companies, individuals, and the government, securities, insurance, and exchange. The Gunma Bank was founded in 1932.

EXECUTIVES

Chairman, Representative Director, Nobuyuki Horie
President, Representative Director, Akihiko Fukai
Senior Managing Director, Director, Hiroyuki Irisawa
Director, Akihiro Goto
Director, Tsutomu Takei
Director, Takeo Uchibori
Outside Director, Jun Kondo
Outside Director, Kuniko Nishikawa
Outside Director, Kazuhito Osugi
Auditors : Ernst & Young ShinNihon LLC

LOCATIONS

HQ: Gunma Bank Ltd (The)
194 Motosoja-machi, Maebashi, Gunma 371-8611
Phone: (81) 27 252 1111
Web: www.gunmabank.co.jp

COMPETITORS

BANK OF AYUDHYA PUBLIC COMPANY LIMITED
HACHIJUNI BANK, LTD., THE
NANTO BANK,LTD., THE
NISHI-NIPPON CITYBANK,LTD.
SHIGA BANK LTD., THE

HISTORICAL FINANCIALS
Company Type: Public

Income Statement — FYE: March 31

	ASSETS ($mil)	NET INCOME ($mil)	INCOME AS % OF ASSETS	EMPLOYEES
03/22	91,654	217	0.2%	4,588
03/21	95,875	121	0.1%	4,694
03/20	77,538	205	0.3%	4,730
03/19	73,504	210	0.3%	4,743
03/18	75,383	267	0.4%	4,737
Annual Growth	5.0%	(5.0%)	—	(0.8%)

2022 Year-End Financials
Return on assets: 0.2%
Return on equity: 4.9%
Long-term debt ($ mil.): —
No. of shares ($ mil.): 410
Sales ($ mil.): 1,255
Dividends
  Yield: —
  Payout: 0.0%
Market value ($ mil.): —

Hachijuni Bank, Ltd. (Japan)

EXECUTIVES

Chairman, Director, Takahiko Asai
President, Representative Director, Masaki Matsushita
Deputy President, Representative Director, Shohei Hidai
Director, Makoto Nakamura
Director, Hitoshi Nishizawa
Outside Director, Kayo Tashita
Outside Director, Miyako Hamano
Outside Director, Eiji Kanzawa
Outside Director, Takayuki Kanai
Auditors : Deloitte Touche Tohmatsu LLC

LOCATIONS

HQ: Hachijuni Bank, Ltd. (Japan)
178-8 Aza Okada, Oaza Nakagosho, Nagano 380-8682
Phone: (81) 26 227 1182
Web: www.82bank.co.jp

HISTORICAL FINANCIALS
Company Type: Public

Income Statement — FYE: March 31

	ASSETS ($mil)	NET INCOME ($mil)	INCOME AS % OF ASSETS	EMPLOYEES
03/23	97,336	181	0.2%	4,757
03/22	109,702	219	0.2%	4,855
03/21	109,828	202	0.2%	5,029
03/20	96,458	203	0.2%	5,101
03/19	94,375	203	0.2%	5,301
Annual Growth	0.8%	(2.8%)	—	(2.7%)

2023 Year-End Financials
Return on assets: 0.1%
Return on equity: 2.6%
Long-term debt ($ mil.): —
No. of shares ($ mil.): 471
Sales ($ mil.): 1,531
Dividends
  Yield: —
  Payout: 40.1%
Market value ($ mil.): —

Hang Seng Bank Ltd.

EXECUTIVES

Chief Operating Officer, Vivien Wai Man Chiu
Chief Financial Officer, Andrew Wing Lok Leung
Chief Compliance Officer, Christopher Hing Keung Tsang
Chief Executive Officer, Executive Director, Diana Ferreira Cesar
Commercial Banking Head, Donald Yin Shing Lam
Communications and Corporate Sustainability Head, May Kay Wong
Global Banking Head, Rose Mui Cho
Global Markets Head, Liz Tan Ling Chow
Human Resources Head, Elaine Yee Ning Wang
Strategy & Planning Head, Gilbert Man Lung Lee
Wealth and Personal Banking Head, Rannie Wah Lun Lee
Secretary, General Counsel, Godwin Chi Chung Li
Independent Non-Executive Chairman, Irene Yun Lien Lee
Independent Non-Executive Director, John Cho Chak Chan
Independent Non-Executive Director, Lai Yuen Chiang
Independent Non-Executive Director, Clement King Man Kwok
Independent Non-Executive Director, Kenneth Sing Yip Ng
Independent Non-Executive Director, Michael Wei Kuo Wu
Non-Executive Director, Kathleen Chieh Huey Gan
Non-Executive Director, David Yi Chien Liao
Non-Executive Director, Vincent Hong Sui Lo
Auditors : PricewaterhouseCoopers

LOCATIONS

HQ: Hang Seng Bank Ltd.
83 Des Voeux Road Central.
Phone: (852) 2198 1111 **Fax:** (852) 2868 4047
Web: www.hangseng.com

HISTORICAL FINANCIALS

Company Type: Public

Income Statement — FYE: December 31

	ASSETS ($mil)	NET INCOME ($mil)	INCOME AS % OF ASSETS	EMPLOYEES
12/22	242,992	1,304	0.5%	7,020
12/21	233,412	1,790	0.8%	9,331
12/20	226,987	2,152	0.9%	9,563
12/19	215,363	3,190	1.5%	10,331
12/18	200,623	3,091	1.5%	10,298
Annual Growth	4.9%	(19.4%)	—	(9.1%)

2022 Year-End Financials
Return on assets: 0.5%
Return on equity: 5.5%
Long-term debt ($ mil.): —
No. of shares ($ mil.): 1,911
Sales ($ mil.): 8,579
Dividends
  Yield: —
  Payout: 70.4%
Market value ($ mil.): 31,775

	STOCK PRICE ($) FY Close	P/E High/Low		PER SHARE ($) Earnings	Dividends	Book Value
12/22	16.62	4	3	0.64	0.45	12.34
12/21	18.26	3	2	0.89	0.71	12.36
12/20	17.30	3	2	1.08	0.80	12.35
12/19	20.62	2	2	1.64	0.92	12.01
12/18	22.38	2	2	1.59	0.81	10.82
Annual Growth	(7.2%)	—	—	(20.5%)	(13.9%)	3.3%

Hannover Rueckversicherung SE

Established in 1966, the Hannover Re Group today has a network of more than 170 subsidiaries, branches and representative offices worldwide. The group's German business is written by the subsidiary E+S RÃ¼ck. Hannover Re, with gross premium of more than EUR 27 billion, is the third-largest reinsurer in the world. It transacts all lines of property & casualty and life & health reinsurance and is present on all continents with more than 3,000 staff. Fifty percent of Hannover's is owned by Talanx AG.

Operations
The company operates through two operating segments: Property & casualty reinsurance (about 70% of premiums written) and Life & health reinsurance (around 30%).

Property & casualty reinsurance offers reinsurance services and risk solutions. Within the Hannover Re Group, these companies are Property & Casualty subsidiaries: Hannover ReTakaful, Bahrain, Hannover Re (Bermuda), Hannover Re (Ireland), Ireland, Hannover Re Africa, South Africa.

Life & health reinsurance segment offers risk solutions, financial solutions, and reinsurance services.

Geographic Reach
Headquartered at Hannover, Germany, the company has operations spread out in the Americas, Europe, and Asia.

Financial Performance
The company had total revenues of EUR 26.1 billion, a 13% increase from the previous year's total revenue of EUR 23 billion.

In 2021, the company had a net income of EUR 1.3 billion, a 42% increase from the previous year's net income of EUR 918.8 million.

The company's cash at the end of 2021 was EUR 1.4 billion. Financing activities generated EUR 277.5 million. Operating activities generated EUR 4.9 million, while investing activities used EUR 5.3 billion.

Strategy
The company's strategic initiatives are: customer excellence; innovation and digital strategy; Asia-Pacific growth; and talent management.

In the company's "Striving for sustainable outperformance" strong governance, risk management, integrated compliance and corporate social responsibility constitute the foundations for its growth as a reliable global reinsurance partner. Three performance drivers ? preferred business partner, innovation catalyst, and earnings growth ? are based on proven strengths and address the global trends affecting the insurance and reinsurance industry. Three performance enablers ? empowered people, a lean operating model and effective capital management ? have proven essential over the last decade for outperforming the industry average in terms of the return on equity. It has launched four strategic initiatives ? Customer Excellence, the Innovation and Digital Strategy, the Asia-Pacific Growth Initiative and Talent Management ? that it considers especially crucial and it intends to work on them intensively throughout the entire strategy cycle.

HISTORY

Hannover Re was founded in 1966 as the Aktiengesellschaft fÃ¼r Transport und RÃ¼ckversicherung (ATR) by the Feuerschadenverband Rheinisch-Westfaelischer Zechen (FSV), a mutual insurer specializing in fire damage, in the town of Bochum. Within five years, ATR had expanded into international reinsurance markets. In 1970 FSV merged with another mutual, HDI Haftpflichtverband der Deutschen Industrie, which owned reinsurer Eisen und Stahl RÃ¼ckversicherungs-AG. ATR's headquarters relocated to Hannover, and six years later it was renamed Hannover RÃ¼ckversicherungs-Gesellschaft.

Jointly managed by HDI, Hannover Re and Eisen und Stahl operated separately until 1996: Hannover Re targeted international markets, while Eisen und Stahl operated mostly within Germany.

Hannover Re maintained its foreign focus throughout the 1970s and 80s, expanding in Europe and South Africa, and making its first forays into the US. In 1990 the firm acquired US life insurer Reassurance Company of Hannover.

Hannover Re went public in 1994, selling 25% of its stock. Also that year the firm formed an Australian subsidiary. The next year Hannover Re acquired Eisen und Stahl (renamed E+S Ruck 1996), which then assumed total control of the company's domestic business.

In 1998 Hannover Re became the first reinsurer to securitize life insurance business (reinsurers often securitize non-life policies to protect against natural catastrophe risks) through an agreement with Interpolis, an Irish reinsurance subsidiary of the

Netherlands' Rabobank. Also that year the firm expanded its financial reinsurance business, reorganizing the Irish consortium it formed with another subsidiary of HDI into Hannover Re Advanced Solutions.

As various natural disasters offset earnings in Hannover Re's property & casualty division in 1998 and 1999, its life and health segment boomed. To facilitate further growth, the firm restructured these operations into a new subsidiary, Hannover Life Re. Also in 1999 the firm acquired the Clarendon Insurance Group of New York. In 2001 Hannover Re joined Inreon, an online reinsurance trading exchange set up by rivals Munich Re and Swiss Re. Also in 2001 the company established a Bermuda-based subsidiary, focused on catastrophe business. The following year Hannover Re split its stock in order to stimulate demand and become a more widely held company.

Like many other insurers, the company was hit hard by the attacks of September 11, 2001, falling stock markets, and, in 2005, damages in the Gulf of Mexico caused by hurricanes Katrina and Rita.

Late in 2006 China loosened its regulation of a number of industries, and insurance was one of them -- Hannover Re was one of the first to gain permission to enter the Chinese market for life and health reinsurance.

At about the same time, the company announced plans to cut down on its noncore business operations. The first move in this direction was the sale of its US-based Praetorian Group subsidiary to QBE's US-based subsidiary for a sum in excess of $800 million. Hannover Re used the proceeds to shore up its property/casualty and life/health reinsurance businesses.

EXECUTIVES

Chief Executive Officer, Jean-Jacques Henchoz
Chief Financial Officer, Roland Vogel
Member, Klaus Miller
Member, Michael Pickel
Member, Claude Chevre
Member, Silke Sehm
Member, Sven Althoff
Chairman, Torsten Leue
Deputy Chairman, Herbert K. Haas
Director, Natalie Bani Ardalan
Director, Frauke Heitmuller
Director, Ilka Hundeshagen
Director, Ursula Lipowsky
Director, Michael Ollmann
Director, Andrea Pollak
Director, Erhard Schipporeit
Auditors : PricewaterhouseCoopers GmbH WirtschaftsprÃ¼fungsgesellschaft

LOCATIONS

HQ: Hannover Rueckversicherung SE
 Karl-Wiechert-Allee 50, Hannover 30625

Phone: (49) 511 5604 0 **Fax:** (49) 511 5604 1188
Web: www.hannover-re.com

2013 Premiums Written

	% of total
Europe	
Germany	9
UK	19
France	4
Other countries	12
North America	
US	24
Other countries	5
Asia	12
Australia	6
Africa	3
Other regions	6
Total	100

COMPETITORS

ANTHEM, INC.
DELPHI FINANCIAL GROUP, INC.
ERGO Group AG
Generali Deutschland AG
MUTUAL OF OMAHA INSURANCE COMPANY
MÃ¼nchener RÃ¼ckversicherungs-Gesellschaft AG in MÃ¼nchen
PRUDENTIAL FINANCIAL, INC.
SCOR SE
Tower Group International Ltd
UNUM GROUP

HISTORICAL FINANCIALS
Company Type: Public

Income Statement				FYE: December 31
	ASSETS ($mil)	NET INCOME ($mil)	INCOME AS % OF ASSETS	EMPLOYEES
12/22	92,868	1,502	1.6%	3,519
12/21	93,834	1,393	1.5%	3,346
12/20	87,677	1,083	1.2%	3,218
12/19	80,116	1,441	1.8%	3,083
12/18	73,874	1,213	1.6%	3,317
Annual Growth	5.9%	5.5%	—	1.5%

2022 Year-End Financials
Return on assets: 1.6% Dividends
Return on equity: 14.0% Yield: —
Long-term debt ($ mil.): — Payout: 166.0%
No. of shares ($ mil.): 361 Market value ($ mil.): 35,848
Sales ($ mil.): 33,892

	STOCK PRICE ($) FY Close	P/E High/Low		PER SHARE ($) Earnings Dividends Book Value		
12/22	99.09	26	18	4.15	6.89	23.89
12/21	92.90	28	21	3.85	1.99	37.18
12/20	79.50	48	26	2.99	2.19	37.30
12/19	97.75	28	18	3.99	2.15	32.67
12/18	67.66	25	20	3.36	2.19	27.78
Annual Growth	10.0%	—	—	5.5%	33.2%	(3.7%)

Hanwa Co Ltd (Japan)

EXECUTIVES

President, Representative Director, Hironari Furukawa
Executive Vice President, Director, Yasumichi Kato
Senior Managing Executive Officer, Director, Hidemi Nagashima
Senior Managing Executive Officer, Director, Yoichi Nakagawa
Senior Managing Executive Officer, Director, Yasuharu Kurata
Senior Managing Executive Officer, Director, Yasushi Hatanaka
Senior Managing Director, Director, Yoichi Shinoyama
Outside Director, Ryuji Hori
Outside Director, Tatsuya Tejima
Outside Director, Kamezou Nakai
Outside Director, Junko Sasaki
Director, Takatoshi Kuchiishi
Director, Keiji Matsubara
Auditors : KPMG AZSA LLC

LOCATIONS

HQ: Hanwa Co Ltd (Japan)
 1-13-1 Tsukiji, Chuo-ku, Tokyo 104-8429
Phone: (81) 3 3544 2202 **Fax:** (81) 3 3544 2351
Web: www.hanwa.co.jp

HISTORICAL FINANCIALS
Company Type: Public

Income Statement				FYE: March 31
	REVENUE ($mil)	NET INCOME ($mil)	NET PROFIT MARGIN	EMPLOYEES
03/21	15,764	177	1.1%	5,696
03/20	17,572	(125)	—	5,455
03/19	18,733	125	0.7%	4,733
03/18	16,867	163	1.0%	4,211
03/17	13,541	146	1.1%	3,774
Annual Growth	3.9%	4.9%	—	10.8%

2021 Year-End Financials
Debt ratio: 0.3% No. of shares ($ mil.): 40
Return on equity: 11.1% Dividends
Cash ($ mil.): 459 Yield: —
Current Ratio: 1.62 Payout: 0.0%
Long-term debt ($ mil.): 2,023 Market value ($ mil.): —

HDFC Bank Ltd

EXECUTIVES

Chief Executive Officer, Managing Director, Sashidhar Jagdishan
Executive Director, Kaizad Bharucha
Chief Risk Officer, Jimmy Tata
Chief Information Officer, Ramesh Lakshminarayanan
Chief Human Resources Officer, Vinay Radzan
Business Finance & Strategy, Administration, Infrastructure, ESH & CSR Head, Ashima Bhat
Retail Assets and SLI Head, Retail Assets and SLI Head- Retail Assets, Arvind Kapil
Operations, ATM and Cash Management Product Head, Bhavesh Zaveri
Investment Banking, Private Banking, Capital Market and Financial Institutions Head, Rakesh Singh

Government, Institutional Business, BC Partnerships, Inclusive Banking and Start-ups Head, Smita Bhagat
Treasury-Sales, Analytics and Overseas Head, Arup Rakshit
Emerging Corporates Group Head, Raveesh K. Bhatia
Non-Executive Chairman, Independent Director, Atanu Chakraborty
Executive Director, Sashidhar Jagdishan
Independent Non-Executive Director, Malay Patel
Independent Non-Executive Director, Sunita Maheshwari
Independent Non-Executive Director, Umesh Chandra Sarangi
Non-Executive Director, Renu Karnad
Non-Executive Director, Sanjiv Sachar
Non-Executive Director, Sandeep Parekh
Auditors : KPMG Assurance and Consulting Services LLP

LOCATIONS

HQ: HDFC Bank Ltd
HDFC Bank House, Senapati Bapat Marg, Lower Parel, Mumbai 400013
Phone: (91) 22 3976 0711   Fax: (91) 22 2496 0737
Web: www.hdfcbank.com

HISTORICAL FINANCIALS

Company Type: Public

Income Statement — FYE: March 31

	ASSETS ($mil)	NET INCOME ($mil)	INCOME AS % OF ASSETS	EMPLOYEES
03/22	278,737	5,095	1.8%	141,579
03/21	245,736	4,455	1.8%	120,093
03/20	211,319	3,445	1.6%	116,971
03/19	191,923	3,180	1.7%	98,061
03/18	174,718	2,743	1.6%	88,253
Annual Growth	12.4%	16.7%		12.5%

2022 Year-End Financials

Return on assets: 1.9%
Return on equity: 16.5%
Long-term debt ($ mil.): —
No. of shares ($ mil.): 5,545
Sales ($ mil.): 21,171
Dividends
Yield: 0.3%
Payout: 24.8%
Market value ($ mil.): 340,108

	STOCK PRICE ($) FY Close	P/E High/Low	Earnings	Dividends	Book Value
03/22	61.33	1 1	0.92	0.21	5.96
03/21	77.69	1 1	0.81	0.09	5.35
03/20	38.46	3 1	0.63	0.41	4.57
03/19	115.91	3 2	0.59	0.27	4.33
03/18	98.77	3 2	0.52	0.24	3.48
Annual Growth	(11.2%)	— —	14.9%	(3.7%)	14.4%

Heidelberg Materials AG

HeidelbergCement is one of the world's largest building materials companies. Its products are used for the construction of houses, traffic routes, infrastructure, as well as commercial and industrial facilities, thus meeting the demands of a growing world population for housing, mobility, and economic development. Its core products cement, aggregates (sand, gravel, and crushed rock), ready-mixed concrete, and asphalt are homogeneous bulk goods. HeidelbergCement also offers services such as worldwide trading in cement and coal by sea. The company has around 600 mining sites and over 3,000 plants worldwide. All total it has some 2,570 locations across five continents.

Operations

HeidelbergCement extracts raw materials, produces building materials, conducts marketing, and distributes materials to customers. Specific activities include geological exploration of raw material deposits, purchasing or leasing the land where the deposits are located, obtaining mining concessions and environmental certifications, constructing manufacturing facilities in cooperation with external service providers, extracting raw materials, and facilities maintenance.

The company sold about 126.5 million metric tons of cement, some 306.4 million metric tons of aggregates, roughly 47.4 million cubic meters of ready-mixed concrete, and about 10.4 million metric tons of asphalt. It operates about 130 cement plants (plus some 20 as part of joint ventures), more than 600 quarries and aggregate pits, and around 1,410 ready-mixed concrete production sites worldwide.

Cement contributes more than 40% to total sales, ready-mixed concrete-asphalt some 25%, and aggregates about 20%. Other service-based joint ventures account for the remainder.

Geographic Reach

Headquartered in Germany, HeidelbergCement has operations in more than 50 countries. The company is divided into five geographic regions: Western and Southern Europe (more than 25% of total sales), North America (slightly less than 25%), Asia/Pacific (about 20%), Northern and Eastern Europe-Central Asia (about 15%), and Africa-Eastern Mediterranean Basin (about 10%). Trading subsidiary, HTC accounts for the remaining revenue. HCT supplies customers in about 70 countries from about 40 supplier countries. The majority of deliveries go to Africa, Asia, and North America. Key supplier countries include Turkey, Spain, Vietnam, Saudi Arabia and the USA.

The US is the company's largest market by country at around 20% of sales. Other major markets include the UK, Germany, Australia and France.

Sales and Marketing

HeidelbergCement's products are used for the construction of houses, traffic routes, infrastructure, and commercial and industrial facilities.

Financial Performance

Note: Growth rates may differ after conversion to US Dollars.

The company's revenue in 2021 increased by 6% to EUR 18.7 billion compared to EUR 17.6 billion in the prior year.

Net income in 2021 was EUR 1.9 billion compared to a net loss of EUR 1.9 billion in the prior year.

Cash held by the company at the end of 2021 increased to EUR 3.1 billion. Operting and financing activities were EUR 1.6 billion and EUR 2.8 billion, respectively. Investing activities used EUR 2.2 billion.

Strategy

Implementation of its "Beyond 2020" strategy, which HeidelbergCement first presented in September 2020, continues to move forward with great progress. Portfolio management is one important pillar of this strategy. The company are streamlining its country portfolio and prioritizing the strongest market positions. "Where we do not meet our return targets, we divest." Over the course of 2021, the company consistently pursued this strategy with the sale of business activities in Kuwait, Greece, Spain, and Sierra Leone, as well as at the West Coast of the USA. At the same time, it completed acquisitions in Australia, Italy, Tanzania, and the northwestern United States to improve its presence in existing profitable markets with high returns.

Company Background

HeidelbergCement traces its roots back to 1872, when Johann Philipp Schifferdecker, a wealthy brewer, went to Heidelberg, Germany, where his son was studying chemistry. Once there, he bought a bankrupt cement plant located on the Neckar River near Heidelberg.

HISTORY

HeidelbergCement AG's history began in 1872, when Johann Philipp Schifferdecker, a wealthy brewer, went to Heidelberg, Germany, where his son was studying chemistry. Once there he bought a bankrupt cement plant located on the Neckar River near Heidelberg in 1873. Schifferdecker named the firm Portland-Cement-Werk, Heidelberg, Schifferdecker & Sohne OHG.

The company's first year of operation, 1875, ended in a loss. The raw materials used to make its cement contained too much magnesium. To correct the problem, Schifferdecker leased a new limestone mine to obtain higher-quality raw materials. Transport presented a problem, and in 1883 Schifferdecker built a railroad to transport limestone to the plant. With these problems solved, the company built a second plant in 1888, the year that Schifferdecker died. The company went public the next year, and Schifferdecker's heirs renamed the firm Portland-Cementwerk Heidelberg, vormals Schifferdecker & Sohne.

A fire destroyed the company's plant in

1895, but the Schifferdeckers used the disaster as an opportunity to modernize the plant. The construction boom sparked at the turn of the century increased cement sales, and the enterprise continued to expand. In 1901 the company merged with its rival Mannheimer Portland-Cement-Fabrik AG to create Portland-Cementwerke Heidelberg und Mannheim AG.

Heidelberg-Mannheimer's plans for expansion died in WWI. From 1916 to 1923 the German government took control of the entire German cement industry. During that time the company merged with Stuttgarter Immobilien- und Bau- Geschaft AG, to create Portland-Cementwerke Heidelberg-Mannheim-Stuttgart AG.

After the war, peace did not bring prosperity to Germany. Hyperinflation made German cement 765 times more expensive than it had been in 1914. By 1926 the German economy had recovered, and one year later, the company converted its plants to electrical operations. The good times did not last long, however. As the Great Depression strangled the German economy, the company's cement shipments dropped by two-thirds from 1927 levels.

Just before WWII the company renamed itself Portland-Zementwerke Heidelberg AG. During the war the German cement industry was highly regulated by the German government. The destructive WWII years all but assured the renewed growth of the German cement industry, and Portland-Zementwerke Heidelberg grew steadily during the 1940s and 1950s. Annual shipments of 6 million tons were reached by 1965.

Peter Schumacher took over the company in 1971 and transformed it into an international enterprise with the 1977 acquisition of Pennsylvania-based Lehigh Portland Cement Company. That year the company adopted the name Heidelberger Zement AG. (Schumacher, who led the company for 25 years, died in 2002.)

During the 1980s Heidelberger Zement bought Atlas Cement Company and founded Addiment, Inc., in Georgia to market its building chemicals. The company also boosted its operations in Italy and France. It expanded into Eastern Europe in the early 1990s, and by 1997 had broadened its geographic reach to include acquisitions in countries such as China and Turkey.

Heidelberger Zement purchased Scancem, a Scandinavian cement operation, in 1999 to open up new markets in Africa, the Baltic States, and the UK. It also bolstered its building materials segment by increasing its stake in maxit Group, a Germany-based leader in the dry mortar business. In 2001 the company acquired majority stakes in regional cement makers Indocement Tunggal Prakarsa (Indonesia), Cesla (Russia), and Kryvyi Rih (Ukraine).

In 2003 the company moved its entire Heidelberg Building Materials Europe division under the maxit Group unit.

Spohn Group, run by long-time HeidelbergCement board members the Merckle family, acquired a majority stake in 2005.

In 2007 HeidelbergCement acquired UK's Hanson, one of the largest producers of aggregates in the world. The ?9 billion ($12 billion) acquisition helped position HeidelbergCement as a global integrated supplier of building materials and strengthened its materials base for aggregates.

Adolf Merckle committed suicide in 2009. His family later sold a large stake in HeidelbergCement.

EXECUTIVES

Executive Chairman, Member, Dominik von Achten
Chief Financial Officer, Member, Rene Aldach
Chief Sustainability Officer, Member, Nicola Kimm
Chief Digital Officer, Member, Dennis Lentz
Member, Kevin Gerard Gluskie
Member, Hakan Gurdal
Member, Ernest Jelito
Member, Jon Morrish
Member, Chris Ward
Chairman, Independent Director, Fritz-Juergen Heckmann
Deputy Chairman, Director, Heinz Schmitt
Independent Director, Ludwig Merckle
Independent Director, Tobias Merckle
Independent Director, Luka Mucic
Director, Barbara Breuninger
Director, Birgit Jochens
Director, Ines Ploss
Director, Peter Riedel
Director, Werner Schraeder
Director, Margret Suckale
Director, Marion Weissenberger-Eibl
Auditors : PricewaterhouseCoopers GmbH Wirtschaftpruefungsgesellschaft

LOCATIONS

HQ: Heidelberg Materials A G
Berliner Strasse 6, Heidelberg 69120
Phone: (49) 6221 481 13227   Fax: (49) 6221 481 13217
Web: www.heidelbergmaterials.com

2015 sales

	% of total
Western and Northern Europe	30
North America	27
Asia-Pacific	20
Eastern Europe-Central Asia	8
Africa-Mediterranean Basin	7
Group Services	8
Total	100

PRODUCTS/OPERATIONS

2015 sales

	% of total
Cement	40
Aggregates	20
Ready-mixed concrete-asphalt	27
Service-joint ventures other	13
Total	100

Selected Products

Cement
  Binders for geotechnology, environmental technology, and road construction
    Decorative concrete
    Fast-hardening cement
    Masonry cement
    Specialty cements for hydraulic engineering, sewage works construction, soil injection and masonry repair, and waste dump sealing
Concrete
  Light, heavy, and aerated concrete building blocks
  Pavers
  Prefab ceilings, walls, cellar units, and sewage works units
Building Materials
  Building chemicals
  Dry mortar
  Environmental technology
  Expanded clay
  Limestone and lime products
  Sand-lime bricks
  Special gypsums
Aggregates
Other
  Plaster
  Self-compacting concrete
  Steel-fiber concrete

COMPETITORS

Cemex, S.A.B. de C.V.
Dyckerhoff GmbH
HOLCIM (US) INC.
LafargeHolcim Ltd
Posco Co.,Ltd.
SOJITZ CORPORATION
TAIHEIYO CEMENT CORPORATION
TEXAS INDUSTRIES, INC.
TITAN AMERICA LLC
Votorantim Cimentos S/A

HISTORICAL FINANCIALS

Company Type: Public

Income Statement

FYE: December 31

	REVENUE ($mil)	NET INCOME ($mil)	NET PROFIT MARGIN	EMPLOYEES
12/22	22,846	1,705	7.5%	50,780
12/21	21,286	1,990	9.4%	51,209
12/20	21,556	(2,625)	—	53,122
12/19	21,264	1,224	5.8%	55,047
12/18	20,787	1,308	6.3%	57,939
Annual Growth	2.4%	6.8%	—	(3.2%)

2022 Year-End Financials

Debt ratio: 18.1%   No. of shares ($ mil.): 186
Return on equity: 9.9%   Dividends
Cash ($ mil.): 1,553   Yield: 0.2%
Current Ratio: 1.15   Payout: 0.0%
Long-term debt ($ mil.): 5,694   Market value ($ mil.): 2,107

	STOCK PRICE ($) FY Close	P/E High/Low		PER SHARE ($) Earnings	Dividends	Book Value
12/22	11.32	2	1	9.02	2.78	94.87
12/21	13.47	2	1	10.08	0.43	90.49
12/20	14.93	—	—	(13.23)	0.09	82.09
12/19	14.47	4	2	6.18	0.30	96.12
12/18	12.22	4	2	6.60	0.29	89.06
Annual Growth	(1.9%)	—	—	8.2%	75.9%	1.6%

Heineken Holding NV (Netherlands)

EXECUTIVES

Chairman, Chief Executive Officer, Director, Jean-Francois M. L. van Boxmeer
Executive Director, Charlene Lucille de Carvalho-Heineken
Executive Director, M. R. de Carvalho
Non-Executive Director, C. M. Kwist
Non-Executive Director, Jose Antonio Fernandez Carbajal
Non-Executive Director, A.A.C. de Carvalho
Auditors : Deloitte Accountants B.V.

LOCATIONS

HQ: Heineken Holding NV (Netherlands)
Tweede Weteringplantsoen 5, Amsterdam 1017 ZD
Phone: (31) 20 622 11 52 **Fax:** (31) 20 625 22 13
Web: www.heinekenholding.com

HISTORICAL FINANCIALS

Company Type: Public

Income Statement — FYE: December 31

	REVENUE ($mil)	NET INCOME ($mil)	NET PROFIT MARGIN	EMPLOYEES
12/21	24,834	1,882	7.6%	82,257
12/20	24,196	(125)	—	84,394
12/19	26,911	1,220	4.5%	85,853
12/18	25,733	1,100	4.3%	85,610
12/17	26,238	1,171	4.5%	80,425
Annual Growth	(1.4%)	12.6%	—	0.6%

2021 Year-End Financials

Debt ratio: 37.1%
Return on equity: 21.8%
Cash ($ mil.): 3,676
Current Ratio: 0.79
Long-term debt ($ mil.): 14,476
No. of shares ($ mil.): 288
Dividends
Yield: 0.9%
Payout: 6.6%
Market value ($ mil.): 13,566

	STOCK PRICE ($) FY Close	P/E High/Low	PER SHARE ($) Earnings	Dividends	Book Value
12/21	47.10	9 7	6.53	0.46	33.77
12/20	48.91	— —	(0.44)	0.74	28.14
12/19	48.75	14 11	4.23	0.75	31.16
12/18	43.15	15 12	3.82	0.72	28.46
12/17	49.45	15 11	4.06	0.66	27.61
Annual Growth	(1.2%)	—	12.6%	(8.5%)	5.2%

Heineken NV (Netherlands)

EXECUTIVES

Chairman, Chief Executive Officer, Dolf van den Brink
Chief Financial Officer, Executive Board Member, Harold van den Broek
Chief Commercial Officer, James Thompson
Chief Corporate Affairs and Transformation Officer, Stacey Tank
Chief People Officer, Yolanda Talamo
Chief Supply Chain Officer, Magne Setnes
Chief Digital and Technology Officer, Ronald den Elzen
Chairman, Supervisory Board Member, Jean-Marc Huet
Vice-Chairman, Supervisory Board Member, Jose Antonio Fernandez Carbajal
Supervisory Board Member, Maarten Das
Supervisory Board Member, Michel R. de Carvalho
Supervisory Board Member, Pamela Mars Wright
Supervisory Board Member, Marion Helmes
Supervisory Board Member, Rosemary L. Ripley
Supervisory Board Member, Helen Arnold
Supervisory Board Member, Nitin Paranjpe
Supervisory Board Member, Francisco Josue Camacho Beltran
Auditors : Deloitte Accountants B.V.

LOCATIONS

HQ: Heineken NV (Netherlands)
Tweede Weteringplantsoen 21, Amsterdam 1017 ZD
Phone: (31) 20 523 92 39 **Fax:** (31) 20 626 35 03
Web: www.theheinekencompany.com

HISTORICAL FINANCIALS

Company Type: Public

Income Statement — FYE: December 31

	REVENUE ($mil)	NET INCOME ($mil)	NET PROFIT MARGIN	EMPLOYEES
12/22	30,673	2,864	9.3%	86,390
12/21	24,834	3,762	15.1%	82,257
12/20	24,196	(250)	—	84,394
12/19	26,911	2,431	9.0%	85,853
12/18	25,733	2,179	8.5%	85,610
Annual Growth	4.5%	7.1%	—	0.2%

2022 Year-End Financials

Debt ratio: 31.5%
Return on equity: 14.5%
Cash ($ mil.): 2,953
Current Ratio: 0.78
Long-term debt ($ mil.): 12,803
No. of shares ($ mil.): 575
Dividends
Yield: —
Payout: 12.3%
Market value ($ mil.): 27,051

	STOCK PRICE ($) FY Close	P/E High/Low	PER SHARE ($) Earnings	Dividends	Book Value
12/22	47.02	12 9	4.97	0.61	36.30
12/21	56.55	10 8	6.53	0.46	34.13
12/20	55.84	— —	(0.44)	0.74	28.55
12/19	53.43	15 11	4.23	0.75	31.51
12/18	43.97	16 13	3.82	0.72	28.84
Annual Growth	1.7%	—	6.7%	(4.0%)	5.9%

Helleniq Energy Holdings S A

Hellenic Petroleum, which changed name to HELLENiQ Energy Holdings in 2022, is one of the leading energy groups in South East Europe, with activities spanning across the energy value chain and presence in six countries. Greece's largest company, HELLENiQ Energy operates three refineries: at Aspropyrgos, Elefsina, and Thessaloniki in Greece. In Greece, EKO's network of gas stations amounts to around 1,995; it has over 300 stations in Albania, Bulgaria, Cyprus, Georgia, Greece, Montenegro, and Serbia. The company is owned by Paneuropean Oil and Industrial Holdings S.A. (over 45%) and the Hellenic Republic Asset Development Fund (some 35%).

Operations

The company's main activities include Refining, Supply, and Trading of petroleum and petrochemical products, Fuels Marketing both in Greece and internationally, Renewable Energy Sources, Power Generation & Trading, as well as Supply, Distribution, and Trading of Natural Gas.

HELLENiQ ENERGY is active in the refining, supply and sales of oil products and petrochemicals through HELLENIC Petroleum Single Member Societe Anonyme Refining Supply and Sales Of Oil Products and Petrochemicals (HELLENIC PETROLEUM R.S.S.O.P.P. S.A.).

HELLENiQ ENERGY is active in the marketing and distribution of petroleum products, in Greece through its subsidiary Â EKO ABEE as well as internationally through its subsidiaries in Cyprus, Bulgaria, Serbia, Montenegro and Republic of North Macedonia.

Its Renewable Energy Sources operates through Hellenic Petroleum - Renewable Energy Sources SA (ELPE RES), of which its object of business is the production and trading of energy products produced by renewable energy sources.

The Electromobility Sources operates through ELPE Electromobility Services Provider S.A., a wholly owned subsidiary of the Group. ElpeFuture is active as a Provider of Electromobility Services, as a Charging Infrastructure Operator, and as a Transaction Processing Entity.

The Hellenic Petroleum Exploration and Production of Hydrocarbons develops activities and execute projects that involve every phase of the industry of hydrocarbon exploration and exploitation (upstream), as well as, to provide consulting services in related matters.

ASPROFOS, is the largest Greek engineering firm and energy consulting services provider in South-Eastern Europe. ASPROFOS supports HELLENiQ ENERGY investments particularly in the fields of refining and natural gas, through the provision of a broad range of technical, project management, and other related advisory services, while seeking to continuously expand the range of its services and broaden its client portfolio to include mainly international clients.

In petrochemicals business, DIAXON

PLASTIC PACKAGING MATERIALS SA, a company of HELLENiQ ENERGY, is the only producer in Greece of BOPP film, which is mainly used in the packaging industry.

In addition, its Power Generation & Natural Gas business includes ELPEDISON S.A. which is currently the second largest independent power producer in Greece with a total installed capacity of 840 MW.

Overall, exports generated about 45% of sales, domestic generated some 35%, while aviation & bunkering as well as international activities generated around 10% each.

Geographic Reach

Headquartered in Greece, the company is active in Southeast Europe, being one of the key marketing players, through with a total network of 300 petrol stations in Cyprus, Bulgaria, Serbia, Montenegro and Republic of North Macedonia.

Financial Performance

The company reported a total revenue of EUR 9.2 billion, a 59% increase from the previous year's total revenue EUR 5.8 billion.

In 2021, the company had a net income of EUR 337.4 million, a 185% improvement from the previous year's net loss of EUR 395.8 million.

The company's cash at the end of EUR 1.1 billion. Operating activities generated EUR 270.4 million, while investing activities used EUR 376 million, mainly for the purchase of property, plant and equipment & intangible assets. Financing activities used another EUR 61.3 million, primarily for repayments of borrowings.

Strategy

"Vision 2025" is based on 5 key pillars and is fully aligned with the European targets for reducing greenhouse gas emissions and developing new activities with low environmental footprint.

The first pillar revolves around redefining the company's strategy in terms of the environment, society and corporate governance (ESG), aiming mainly at reducing greenhouse gas emissions. Specifically, it seeks to improve the company's activities' scope 1 and scope 2 environmental footprint, (direct and indirect emissions respectively), by 50% by 2030, while developing options for reducing indirect environmental impacts (scope 3).

The second pillar focuses on increasing the company's economic value through substantial capital reallocation to new activities, as well as by increasing its core business competitiveness.

The next three pillars are based on upgrading corporate governance, establishing an appropriate corporate structure and adopting a new corporate identity, with the first two already completed and the third expected to be implemented soon.

HISTORY

Following discovery of the South Kavala gas field and Prinos oil field in the North Aegean Sea, the Greek government formed its own exploration company, Public Petroleum Corp. (DEP), in 1975. The company subsequently acquired control of the Hellenic Aspropyrgos Refinery (ELDA), a major refinery near Athens.

During the 1980s the state bought the Greek assets of Esso (now ExxonMobil), including a refinery and chemicals and marketing units. This Esso business (renamed EKO) set up two new oil-related enterprises: DEP-EKY (exploration and production) and DEPA (natural gas import and distribution). DEP retained control over crude imports, refining, and product trading. The company also set up engineering unit Asprofos, originally as a joint venture with Foster Wheeler Italiana, to upgrade and expand the Aspropyrgos Refinery. (Foster Wheeler sold its stake in 1988.) The refinery branched into petroleum marketing with the formation of another unit, ELDA-E.

Between 1991 and 1997 EKO expanded, establishing marketing activities in Georgia and acquiring Greek liquefied petroleum gas firm Petrolina. DEP and ELDA formed a petrochemical venture, and DEP-EKY joined a consortium to explore for oil and gas in western Greece.

In 1998 the Greek government restructured the oil and gas industry. DEP became Hellenic Petroleum Company, and other oil- and gas-related enterprises were merged into it. As part of the restructuring, EKO and ELDA merged their marketing segments to form EKO-ELDA, which acquired marketing unit G.MAMIDAKIS later that year. Although 85% of the natural gas company, DEPA, was transferred back to the government, Hellenic Petroleum retained the option to buy back shares.

Hellenic Petroleum was partially privatized in 1999, and the government kept a 75% stake (later reduced to 35%). Expanding in the Balkans, the company acquired control of the oil refinery in Skopje, Macedonia, that year, and bought 75% (later boosted to 86%) of Global, a petroleum marketing company in Albania. It also upped its stake in DEPA to 35% and began construction of polypropylene and propylene units.

In 2002 Hellenic Petroleum completed a crude oil pipeline linking its Macedonian refinery to its refinery at the Greek port of Thessaloniki. In 2003 it absorbed the operations of refining rival Petrola Hellas.

In 2008 the company acquired Opet Aygaz Bulgaria, which operates a network of 17 gas stations in Bulgaria. Building its assets at home, in 2009 Hellenic Petroleum acquired BP's network of 1,200 gas stations in Greece for about ?360 million ($515 million US). Formerly called BP Hellas, the company has been rebranded Hellenic Fuels, though the service stations will retain the BP brand for at least five years.

EXECUTIVES

Chief Executive Officer, Executive Director, Andreas Shiamishis
Chief Financial Officer, Christian Thomas
Executive Director, Gergios Alexopoulos
Non-Executive Chairman, Ioannis Papathanasiou
Independent Non-Executive Director, Theodoros Pantalakis
Independent Non-Executive Director, Spyridon Pantelias
Non-Executive Director, Theodoros-Achilleas Vardas
Non-Executive Director, Michael Kefalogiannis
Non-Executive Director, Alexandros Metaxas
Non-Executive Director, Ioannis Aivazis
Non-Executive Director, Loukas Papazoglou
Non-Executive Director, Alkiviades Psarras
Non-Executive Director, Constantinos Papagiannopoulos
Non-Executive Director, Georgios Papakonstantinou
Auditors : Ernst & Young Hellas

LOCATIONS

HQ: Helleniq Energy Holdings S A
8A Chimarras Str., Maroussi 15125
Phone: —
Web: www.helpe.gr

PRODUCTS/OPERATIONS

2014 Sales

	% of total
Refining	71
Marketing	26
Petrochemicals	3
Total	100

Selected Subsidiaries and Affiliates

ASPROFOS S.A. (infrastructure engineering company)
DEPA S.A. (35%, natural gas importation and distribution)
DIAXON A.B.E.E. (polypropylene film production)
GLOBAL PETROLEUM ALBANIA ShA. (99.9%, petroleum marketing)
OKTA CRUDE OIL REFINERY A. D. (51%, crude oil refinery, Macedonia)
VOLOS PET INDUSTRY S.A. (VPI, 35%, polyethylene terephthalate production)

COMPETITORS

COMPAÑIA ESPAÑOLA DE PETROLEOS SAU
COSMO OIL CO., LTD.
ENI SPA
IDEMITSU KOSAN CO.,LTD.
INDIAN OIL CORPORATION LIMITED
Imperial Oil Limited
LUKOIL, PAO
MOL Magyar Olaj- és Gázipari Nyilvánosan Működő Részvénytársaság
OMV Aktiengesellschaft
SURGUTNEFTEGAZ, PAO

HISTORICAL FINANCIALS
Company Type: Public

Income Statement   FYE: December 31

	REVENUE ($mil)	NET INCOME ($mil)	NET PROFIT MARGIN	EMPLOYEES
12/22	15,495	950	6.1%	3,519
12/21	10,438	381	3.7%	3,500
12/20	7,095	(485)	—	3,544
12/19	9,944	180	1.8%	2,975
12/18	11,187	242	2.2%	2,846
Annual Growth	8.5%	40.7%	—	5.4%

2022 Year-End Financials
Debt ratio: 35.5%
Return on equity: 37.6%
Cash ($ mil.): 961
Current Ratio: 0.95
Long-term debt ($ mil.): 1,530
No. of shares ($ mil.): 305
Dividends
  Yield: —
  Payout: 12.4%
Market value ($ mil.): —

Helvetia Holding AG

EXECUTIVES

Chief Executive Officer, Philipp Gmur
Chief Financial Officer, Annelis Luscher Hammerli
Chief Investment Officer, Andre Keller
Chief Technology Officer, Achim Baumstark
Chief Actuarial Officer, Beat Muller
Chief Corporate Center Officer, Roland Bentele
General Counsel, Secretary, Barbara Bolliger
Independent Non-Executive Chairwoman, Doris Russi Schurter
Independent Non-Executive Vice-Chairman, Hans C. Kunzle
Non-Executive Vice-Chairman, Thomas Schmuckli
Independent Non-Executive Director, Beat Fellmann
Independent Non-Executive Director, Ivo Furrer
Independent Non-Executive Director, Christoph Lechner
Independent Non-Executive Director, Gabriela Maria Payer
Independent Non-Executive Director, Andreas von Planta
Independent Non-Executive Director, Regula Wallimann
Non-Executive Director, Jean-Rene Fournier
Auditors : KPMG AG

LOCATIONS

HQ: Helvetia Holding AG
  Dufourstrasse 40, St. Gall CH-9001
Phone: (41) 58 280 50 00   Fax: (41) 58 280 50 01
Web: www.helvetia.com

HISTORICAL FINANCIALS
Company Type: Public

Income Statement   FYE: December 31

	REVENUE ($mil)	NET INCOME ($mil)	NET PROFIT MARGIN	EMPLOYEES
12/21	13,794	544	3.9%	12,128
12/20	11,707	300	2.6%	11,687
12/19	11,063	557	5.0%	6,829
12/18	9,301	439	4.7%	6,624
12/17	9,933	415	4.2%	6,592
Annual Growth	8.6%	7.0%	—	16.5%

2021 Year-End Financials
Debt ratio: —
Return on equity: 7.4%
Cash ($ mil.): 2,036
Current Ratio: —
Long-term debt ($ mil.): —
No. of shares ($ mil.): 52
Dividends
  Yield: —
  Payout: 0.7%
Market value ($ mil.): 156

	STOCK PRICE ($) FY Close	P/E High/Low		PER SHARE ($) Earnings	Dividends	Book Value
12/21	2.95	0	0	10.05	0.08	138.89
12/20	2.35	1	1	5.40	0.08	143.85
12/19	3.50	0	0	10.88	5.17	136.54
Annual Growth	(8.2%)	—	—	(2.0%)	(65.2%)	0.4%

Henkel AG & Co KGAA

Henkel operates globally with a well-balanced and diversified portfolio. The company makes branded products for laundry and homecare (Persil, All, Bref, and Somat), cosmetics and toiletries (Schwarzkopf, Dial, and Syoss) and many adhesives (Loctite, Pritt, and UniBond). Henkel's business is centered in Europe, with a growing presence in developing economies, such as Asia, Africa, the Middle East, and Latin America. Henkel owns subsidiaries in about 60 countries, with offices located nearly everywhere. Started in 1876, the company is owned by descendants of the founding Henkel family. The company generates most of its sales from Eastern Europe, Africa/Middle East, Latin America, and Asia.

Operations
Henkel divides its business into three units. Adhesive technologies accounts for about 50% of sales, which includes industrial adhesives as well as those for consumers, craftsmen, and building. Laundry & Home Care accounts for nearly 35% of sales; and Beauty Care accounts for about 20%. In early 2022, the company decided to merge the Laundry & Home Care and Beauty Care business into a new business unit: Henkel Consumer Brands.

Geographic Reach
The company's adhesive products have a worldwide presence. Emerging markets (Eastern Europe, Africa/Middle East, Latin America, and Asia, excluding Japan) generate about 40% of Henkel's sales. Henkel's business in Western Europe and North America is highly mature so it relies on its emerging markets for organic growth.

Henkel has around 175 manufacturing facilities that dot around 55 countries. Its largest plants are located in Düsseldorf, Germany (its headquarters), and in Bowling Green, Kentucky, US, and make detergents and household cleaning products, as well as adhesives.

Henkel's regional centers are located in Mexico, Brazil, Austria, Germany UAE, China, and US (Connecticut).

Sales and Marketing
Henkel is a strong partner for both brick-and-mortar and online retailers, with the capability to deliver considerable added value in both areas. Its products are sold mainly in brick-and-mortar stores, hair salons, third-party online platforms and direct-to-consumer channels. By business area, packaging and consumer goods bring in more than 30% of the company's total sales. Craftsmen, construction, and professional account for about 30%, automotive and metals generate more than 20%, and electronics and industrials account for the rest.

Henkel's customer base of customer base direct industry and retail clients is managed primarily by its own sales teams. Henkel's retail customers service the needs of private users, craftsmen and smaller industrial customers.

Financial Performance
Note: Growth rates may differ after conversion to US Dollars.

The company had sales of EUR 20.1 billion in 2021, a 4% increase from the previous year's sales of EUR 19.3 billion.

In 2021, the company had a net income of EUR 1.6 billion, a 15% increase from the previous year's net income of EUR 1.4 billion.

The company's cash at the end of 2021 was EUR 2.1 billion. Operating activities generated EUR 2.1 billion, while investing activities used EUR 479 million, mainly for purchase of intangible assets and property, plant and equipment. Financing activities used another EUR 1.3 billion, primarily for dividends and interest paid and received, as well as dividends paid to shareholders.

Strategy
The company continued to execute its Purposeful Growth agenda to lead the company successfully into the future. Henkel made great progresses in all areas of its strategy in 2021, despite the difficult economic and market environment.

In addition to active portfolio management, the company focused primarily on two aspects of its Purposeful Growth agenda: First, it became more competitive in the areas of innovation, sustainability and digitalization. And second, the company effectively strengthened its culture.

In pursuing an active portfolio management, at the beginning of 2020, the company identified brands and businesses with a total sales volume of more than one billion, euros, with the aim of divesting or discontinuing around half by the end of 2021. Since the beginning of 2020, the company has sold or discontinued brands and businesses representing an annual sales volume of around 0.5 billion euros ? thus achieving its goal. In addition, the acquisition of Swania in the first half of the year has strengthened its position in sustainable laundry and home care products in France.

To further improve the company's competitiveness, it focused on accelerating impactful innovations, on strengthening sustainability as a clear differentiator, and on increasing value creation for customers and consumers through digitalization.

Mergers and Acquisitions

In early 2022, Henkel signed an agreement to acquire the Asia-Pacific Hair Professional business of Shiseido. The acquisition comprises leading Professional brands such as Sublimic or Primience, endorsed by the licensed Shiseido Professional brand. Shiseido Professional is a salon-exclusive brand offering premium products for professional hairdressers in hair care, hair color and styling items as well as perm solutions. To support business growth through a strong partnership with Henkel, Shiseido will retain a 20% share in the legal entity in Japan.

In mid-2021, Henkel acquired Swania SAS, based in Nanterre, France, from Milestone Investisseurs and individual shareholders. Swania is the fastest-growing French independent player in the ecological home care market. Through this transaction, Henkel expands its position in the market for sustainable laundry and home care products and adds a highly complementary portfolio in very attractive and profitable market segments with a successful innovation track record. Both parties agreed to not disclose any financial details of the transaction.

Company Background

In 1876, Fritz Henkel and his two partners founded Henkel & Cie in Aachen, Germany. The company launched a laundry detergent based on sodium silicate, which they named "Universal-Washmittel". Henkel's first branded product was launched in 1878. In 1913, Henkel founded a subsidiary in Switzerland. Fritz passed in 1930 and was succeeded by his capable sons, Fritz Jr. and Hugo. Henkel became a limited company in 1975 and in 1985 it went public. Major product launches have included Persil (1907) and the Pritt stick (1969); it acquired Loctite in 1997. The company was renamed Henkel AG & Co in 2008.

HISTORY

In 1876 Fritz Henkel, a chemical plant worker, started Henkel & Cie in Aachen, Germany, to make a universal detergent. He moved the business to Düsseldorf in 1878 and launched Henkel's Bleaching Soda, one of Germany's first brand-name products. In the 1880s the company began making water glass, an ingredient of its detergent, which differs from soap in the way it emulsifies dirt. Henkel debuted Persil, a detergent that eliminated the need for rubbing or bleaching clothes, in 1907. Persil became a leading detergent in Germany.

Henkel set up an Austrian subsidiary in 1913. In response to a postwar adhesives shortage, the company started making glue for its own packaging and soon became Europe's leading glue maker. Henkel began making cleansers with newly developed phosphates in the late 1920s.

When Fritz died in 1930, Henkel stock was divided among his three children. In the 1930s the company sponsored a whaling fleet that provided fats for its products, and by 1939 the firm had 16 plants in Europe.

During WWII Henkel lost most of its foreign plants and made unbranded soap in Germany. After the war the company retooled its plants, branched out into personal care products, and competed with Unilever, Procter & Gamble, and Colgate-Palmolive for control of the German detergent market. (By 1968 Henkel dominated, with close to a 50% share.)

In 1960 Henkel bought its first US company, Standard Chemicals (renamed Henkel Corp. in 1971). Konrad Henkel, who took over in 1961, modernized the company's image by making changes in management structure and marketing techniques. Henkel patented a substitute for environmentally harmful phosphates, acquired 15% of Clorox in 1974, and bought General Mills' chemical business in 1977.

Henkel, owned at the time by 66 family members, went public with nonvoting shares in 1985. It bought US companies Nopco (specialty chemicals) and Parker Chemical (metal surface pretreatment) in 1987 and Emery, the #1 US oleochemicals maker, in 1989.

Henkel reorganized its product lines in 1991 by selling several noncore businesses. That year Henkel formed a partnership with Ecolab (of which it owned 24% -- later expanded to 50%); acquired interests in Hungary, Poland, Russia, and Slovenia; and introduced Persil in Spain and Portugal. In 1994 Henkel expanded into China and bought 25% of a Brazilian detergent maker.

The company's 1995 acquisition of Hans Schwarzkopf GmbH made Henkel the #1 hair-coloring manufacturer in Germany. The company bought Novamax Technologies, a US-based maker of metal-surface treatments, in 1996. The next year Henkel paid $1.3 billion for US adhesive giant Loctite, its biggest purchase to date. In 1998 it bought Ohio-based adhesive maker Manco to combine its US and Canadian consumer adhesive businesses (parts of Loctite and LePage, respectively) under Manco. Henkel pushed into the US toiletries market in 1998 by paying $93 million for DEP and creating a new subsidiary, Schwarzkopf & DEP Inc.

In 1999 Henkel created chemicals unit Cognis to focus primarily on palm kernel- and coconut oil-based products. To strengthen Cognis, Henkel bought Laboratoires Serobiologiques, a French producer of ingredients for the cosmetic and food industries, and divested specialty-paper chemicals operations. Henkel also formed a joint venture with soap maker Dial (Dial/Henkel LLC); the joint venture later bought the Custom Cleaner home dry cleaning business from Creative Products Resource.

Henkel picked up Yamahatsu Sangyo, a Japanese maker of hair colorants, in 2000. The company sold its Substral unit (fertilizer and plant care) to Scotts Company (now Scotts Miracle-Gro). In 2001 Henkel bought TOTAL's metal-treatment chemicals business. In addition, the company sold its Cognis specialty chemicals unit to private equity funds Schroeder Ventures and Goldman Sachs Capital Partners for about $2.2 billion. Also in 2001 Henkel said it would cut 2,500-3,000 jobs (about 5% of its workforce) over the next two years.

In 2003 Henkel purchased a majority stake in La Luz S.A., a Central American manufacturer and marketer of detergents and household cleaners. (Henkel entered the Latin American detergents market via Mexico in 2000.)

Henkel strengthened its adhesives business in Russia and North, Central, and Eastern Europe when it acquired Makroflex from YIT Construction Ltd. in July 2003. Makroflex, located in Finland and Estonia, developed and made old sealants and insulation materials for the construction industry.

In 2004 Henkel acquired Alberto-Culver's Indola European professional hair care business, which had logged about $55 million in recent annual sales. That year Henkel and US bleach giant Clorox agreed to a deal (in the form of an asset swap) that dissolved Henkel's nearly 30% stake in Clorox. The $2.8 billion transaction involved Henkel's purchase of Clorox's 20% stake in Henkel Iberica, a joint venture between the two in Portugal and Spain. Henkel also bought Clorox's stake in a pesticide company as part of the transaction and added Combat insecticides and Soft Scrub bathroom cleaner to its brand portfolio.

Henkel acquired Advanced Research Laboratories in 2004 and folded the company into its existing Schwarzkopf & Dep subsidiary, based in California. The deal boosted the company's share of the US hairstyling market. Henkel bought US-based Dial Corporation (Dial soap, Purex laundry products, Renuzit air fresheners) in 2004 for $2.9 billion in cash.

Also in 2004 Henkel bought 70% of Coventry's Chemtek, an independent firm that specializes in formulating and manufacturing liquid cleaners. The balance of the share is owned by Charteredbrands of Edinburgh.

To strengthen its foothold in the electronics market in China, Henkel in late 2005 bought a majority stake in Huawei Electronics Co. Ltd., a maker of epoxy molding compounds for semiconductors.

EXECUTIVES

Purchasing Chair, Carsten Knobel
Finance/Purchasing/Global Business Solutions Executive Vice President, Marco Swoboda
Human Resources and Infrastructure Services Executive Vice President, Sylvie Nicol
Adhesive Technologies Executive Vice President, Mark Dorn
Consumer Brands Executive Vice President, Wolfgang König
Honorary Chairman, Albrecht Woeste
Chairman, Simone Bagel-Trah
Vice-Chairwoman, Director, Birgit Helten-Kindlein
Director, Michael Baumscheiper
Director, Jutta Bernicke
Director, Lutz Bunnenberg
Director, Benedikt-Richard Freiherr von Herman
Director, Michael Kaschke
Director, Barbara Kux
Director, Simone Menne
Director, Andrea Pichottka
Director, Philipp Scholz
Director, Martina Seiler
Director, Dirk Thiede
Director, Edgar Topsch
Director, Michael Vassiliadis
Director, Poul Weihrauch
Auditors : PricewaterhouseCoopers GmbH Wirtschaftsprufungsgesellschaft

LOCATIONS

HQ: Henkel AG & Co KGAA
Henkelstrasse 67, Duesseldorf 40589
Phone: (49) 211 797 0   **Fax:** (49) 211 798 4040
Web: www.henkel.com

2018 Sales

	% of total
Western Europe	31
North America	25
Asia Pacific	17
Eastern Europe	14
Africa/Middle East	6
Latin America	6
Corporate	1
Total	100

PRODUCTS/OPERATIONS

2018 Sales

	% of total
Adhesive Technologies	50
Industrial Business	38
Consumers, Craftsmen, and Building	9
Laundry & Home Care	32
Beauty Care	20
Corporate	1
Total	100

Selected Brands

Adhesives, technologies
Ariasana
Ceresit
LePage
Loctite
Metylan
Pattex
Ponal
Pritt
Rubson
Sellotape
Sista
Solvite
Tangit
Technomelt
Teroson
UniBond

Cosmetics and toiletries
Aok
Barnängen
Clynol viton
Denivit
Diadermine
Dial
Dry Idea
Fa
La Toja
Licor del Polo
Neutromed
Right Guard
Schwarzkopf
Smooth 'N Shine
Syoss
Theramed
Tone
Vademecum

Laundry and homecare
Bref
Dixan
Mir
Persil
Perwoll
Pril
Pur
Purex
Soft Scrub
Somat
Spee
Vernel

COMPETITORS

AIR PRODUCTS AND CHEMICALS, INC.
Akzo Nobel N.V.
Beiersdorf AG
DIVERSEY, INC.
MACDERMID, INCORPORATED
NCH CORPORATION
OIL-DRI CORPORATION OF AMERICA
RECKITT BENCKISER GROUP PLC
S. C. JOHNSON & SON, INC.
THE CLOROX COMPANY

HISTORICAL FINANCIALS

Company Type: Public

Income Statement FYE: December 31

	REVENUE ($mil)	NET INCOME ($mil)	NET PROFIT MARGIN	EMPLOYEES
12/22	23,920	1,344	5.6%	0
12/21	22,711	1,849	8.1%	52,450
12/20	23,625	1,728	7.3%	52,950
12/19	22,583	2,340	10.4%	52,450
12/18	22,788	2,646	11.6%	53,000
Annual Growth	1.2%	(15.6%)	—	—

2022 Year-End Financials

Debt ratio: 9.4%
Return on equity: 6.3%
Cash ($ mil.): 1,162
Current Ratio: 1.14
Long-term debt ($ mil.): 1,971
No. of shares ($ mil.): —
Dividends
  Yield: —
  Payout: 10.3%
Market value ($ mil.): —

	STOCK PRICE ($) FY Close	P/E High/Low	PER SHARE ($) Earnings	Dividends	Book Value
12/22	16.13	7 5	3.15	0.33	0.00
12/21	19.72	6 5	4.26	0.69	85.89
12/20	24.18	8 5	3.96	0.33	83.98
12/19	23.57	21 4	5.38	0.36	80.05
12/18	98.36	23 18	6.08	0.40	75.01
Annual Growth	(36.4%)	—	(15.2%)	(4.6%)	—

Hermes International SCA

Hermès International is family-run, independent, and socially responsible. The company is committed to maintaining the majority of its production in France, through its more than 50 production sites, while developing its international distribution network of approximately 305 stores in some 45 countries. Hermès's watches, perfumes, and tableware are also sold through networks of specialized stores. The Hermès's adventure began in 1837 when the harness-maker Thierry Hermès opened a workshop in rue Basse-du-Rempart in Paris. The company generates the majority of its revenue in the Asia Pacific.

Operations

Hermès' Leather Goods & Saddlery encompasses bags for men and women, clutches, briefcases, luggage, small leather goods, diaries and writing objects, saddles, bridles and a full range of equestrian products and clothing. It provides about 45% of the company's revenue. The Ready-to-wear and Accessories métier is the company's second largest sector, representing approximately 25% of revenue. The other Hermès sectors include Jewellery and the Hermès Art of Living and Tableware, accounting for nearly 10% of the company's revenue. Silk and Textiles represent the fourth largest sector in the company, accounting for more than 5%. Perfume and Beauty, Watches, and other products account for the rest.

Logistics ships more than five million products to about 305 stores annually.

Geographic Reach

Headquartered in Paris, France, Hermès is present in approximately 45 countries. Asia Pacific (excluding Japan) provides more than 45% of the company's revenue, the Americas generate about 15%, Europe (excluding France) brings in approximately 15%, Japan and France contribute around 10% each, other countries account for less than 5%. With nearly 305 stores worldwide, the company has about 75 branches in Europe (including nearly 15 in France), more than 45 in the Americas (including around 30 in the US), approximately 95 in Asia (including some 30 in Japan), and six in Oceania. The company operates about 65 production sites, including more than 50 in France. It also operates production sites in Switzerland, the US, Australia, Italy, Portugal, and the UK.

Sales and Marketing

Hermès licenses exclusively to the company's subsidiaries. Its exclusive distribution network consists primarily of branches run by the company around the Hermès brand and e-commerce sites.

Financial Performance

The company reported a total revenue of EUR 9 billion, a 41% increase from the previous year's total revenue of EUR 6.4 billion.

In 2021, the company had a net income of EUR 2.4 billion, a 77% increase from the previous year's net income of EUR 1.4 billion.

The company's cash at the end of 2021 was EUR 6.7 billion. Financing activities generated EUR 3.4 billion, while investing activities used EUR 669 million, mainly for operating investments. Financing activities used another EUR 869 million, primarily for payment of dividends.

Strategy

The company, which had maintained its strategic investments in 2020, accelerated its projects in 2021. Operating investments amounted to EUR 532 million:

EUR 220 million was devoted to the renovation and expansion of its exclusive distribution network. This amount includes the construction of the future Madison 706 flagship in New York, the expansion of the Milan store in Italy, the opening of the Omotesando store in Japan and the relocation of the Beijing China World store or the expansion of Plaza 66 in Shanghai, China;

EUR 169 million was dedicated to production and métiers, mainly in Leather Goods but also in Tanneries, Textiles as well as Perfume and Beauty;

EUR 143 million was invested in information systems and digital but also in real estate projects to support the Group's growth.

Company Background

The company was founded in 1837 by Thierry Hermès

HISTORY

Hermès was founded in 1837 by harness-maker Thierry Hermès. The company won acclaim for its unique carriage design, and gained favor among European noblemen. The company's saddle stitch, notable for both its aesthetic and utilitarian qualities, became a trademark of sorts; Hermès craftsmen, working always by hand, spent 20 to 40 hours on custom-made saddles.

Thierry's son, Emile-Charles, followed in the family business. In 1879 he moved the company headquarters to 24, rue du Faubourg Saint Honoré, an address that was to become one of the most valuable pieces of real estate in all of Paris. His decision to move, however, was more practical than prescient. Emile-Charles simply moved his business to be nearer his wealthy customers in the carriage trade. In 1922 he sold his stake in the business to his brother Emile-Maurice.

Emile-Maurice, more than any other, was responsible for making the company what it is today. Something of a visionary, he saw the introduction of the automobile not only as a threat to the family's saddlery business, but also as an opportunity to diversify the business, and create accessories for a suddenly more mobile society. Under his direction, Hermès introduced travel-related leather goods, including saddlebags, luggage, wallets, handbags, and even jewelry. Emile also chose the well-known logo, that of a horse-drawn carriage, based on a drawing by Alfred De Dreux.

In the early 1900s, Emile brought the zipper to France when he purchased a two-year patent on the Canadian invention. Soon the zipper became associated with Hermès, and it appeared on handbags, jockey silks, and leather gloves. The company's line of leather apparel is said to have resulted from a design request for a zippered leather golf jacket by the Prince of Wales.

Ready-to-wear clothing was introduced in the 1920s as Emile handed the reins of the company to his son-in-law Robert Dumas. It was Robert who introduced the first Hermès scarf in 1937. Silk ties were introduced in 1949, and perfume in 1950. Robert continued to pursue diversification while maintaining the company's reputation for quality -- a difficult task, especially in the 1970s, when man-made materials like plastic and polyester dominated the fashion scene.

Robert Dumas died in 1978 and his son Jean-Louis took control. Previously a buyer for Bloomingdale's, Jean-Louis brought an outsider's eye to the company. He introduced young designers to strengthen the brand's youth appeal. He bought manufacturers of glassware, silverware, and tableware, as well as shoemaker John Lobb, in the 1980s. The company's sales skyrocketed, and Jean-Louis added stores in Asia, the Pacific Rim, and the US.

The company went public in 1993, with the family retaining more than 80%. In July 1999 Hermès took a 35% stake in the design business of its womenswear couturier Jean-Paul Gautier. In 2000 the company unveiled a New York store on Madison Avenue. Hermès also entered Portugal for the first time and construction began on a franchised store in Moscow. In December the company acquired about 31% of German camera and lens manufacturer Leica.

Hermès saw continued expansion in Asia, Europe, and the US in 2001. The company expanded its leather working business in 2002 and focused on promoting the craftsmen and women behind its products through public campaigns.

EXECUTIVES

Executive Chairman, Axel Dumas
Sales & Distribution Executive Vice President, Florian Craen
Communications Executive Vice President, Charlotte David
Artistic Executive Vice President, Pierre-Alexis Dumas
Corporate Development and Social Affairs Executive Vice President, Olivier Fournier
Leather Goods-Saddlery Executive Vice President, Catherine Fulconis
Métiers, Information Systems and Data Executive Vice President, Wilfried Guerrand
Finance Executive Vice President, Finance Chief Financial Officer, Eric du Halgouet
Human Resources Director, Sharon Macbeath
Manufacturing Division & Equity Investments Executive Vice President, Guillaume de Seynes
Perfume and Beauty Executive Vice President, Perfume and Beauty Chairwoman, Agnes de Villers
Chairman, Eric de Seynes
Vice-Chairman, Independent Director, Monique Cohen
Independent Director, Dominique Senequier
Independent Director, Estelle Brachlianoff
Independent Director, Alexandre Viros
Director, Dorothee Altmayer
Director, Charles-Eric Bauer
Director, Pureza Cardoso
Director, Matthieu Dumas
Director, Blaise Guerrand
Director, Julie Guerrand
Director, Olympia Guerrand
Director, Remy Kroll
Director, Renaud Mommeja
Auditors : Grant Thornton Audit

LOCATIONS

HQ: Hermes International SCA
24, rue du Faubourg-Saint-Honore, Paris 75008
Phone: (33) 1 40 17 49 20   **Fax:** (33) 1 40 17 49 94
Web: www.hermes.com

PRODUCTS/OPERATIONS

Selected Products
Gloves
Handbags
Home goods
Leather goods
Scarves
Stationery
Tableware

COMPETITORS

ARCADIA GROUP LIMITED
C. & J. CLARK INTERNATIONAL LIMITED
CHRISTIAN DIOR
FREDERICK'S OF HOLLYWOOD, INC.
LAURA ASHLEY HOLDINGS PLC
MANIFATTURE LANE GAETANO MARZOTTO & FIGLI SPA
N BROWN GROUP PLC
NATUZZI SPA
Procter & Gamble Deutschland GmbH

Tengelmann Warenhandelsgesellschaft KG

HISTORICAL FINANCIALS
Company Type: Public

Income Statement — FYE: December 31

	REVENUE ($mil)	NET INCOME ($mil)	NET PROFIT MARGIN	EMPLOYEES
12/22	12,391	3,596	29.0%	19,686
12/21	10,166	2,767	27.2%	17,595
12/20	7,841	1,700	21.7%	16,600
12/19	7,728	1,715	22.2%	15,417
12/18	6,832	1,608	23.5%	14,284
Annual Growth	16.0%	22.3%	—	8.3%

2022 Year-End Financials
Debt ratio: 0.2%
Return on equity: 30.8%
Cash ($ mil.): 9,852
Current Ratio: 3.94
Long-term debt ($ mil.): 37
No. of shares ($ mil.): 105
Dividends
 Yield: —
 Payout: 2.4%
Market value ($ mil.): 16,325

	STOCK PRICE ($) FY Close	P/E High/Low	PER SHARE ($) Earnings	Dividends	Book Value
12/22	154.80	5 3	34.27	0.85	125.99
12/21	175.53	8 4	26.37	0.55	101.67
12/20	108.12	8 5	16.21	0.85	86.61
12/19	75.40	5 4	16.34	0.51	70.77
12/18	55.25	5 4	15.33	1.08	60.45
Annual Growth	29.4%	—	22.3%	(5.9%)	20.2%

Hino Motors, Ltd.

Hino Motors introduced Japan's first truck in 1917. These days the company not only manufactures medium- and heavy-duty diesel trucks, but it also makes buses, special-purpose vehicles, and industrial diesel engines. Hino Motors dominates Japan's domestic truck market, beating out such competitors as Mitsubishi Motors and Isuzu Motors, and manufactures some 155,825 Hino-brand trucks and buses each year. Toyota Motor owns around 65% of the company.

Operations
The company's main business is the production and sales of trucks and buses, as well as production on commission for Toyota Motor Corporation and other services such as development and planning of related products. Domestic areas are covered by its company and domestic subsidiaries and overseas areas are covered by local overseas subsidiaries, with strategies created for each market for the services and products handled.

Overall, trucks and buses generated nearly 60% of sales, spare parts with about 10%, vehicles for Toyota with over 5%, and others which generated the rest.

Geographic Reach
Headquartered in Hino-shi, Tokyo, the company has operations in about 90 countries located in the Americas, Europe, Middles East, Asia and Oceania. Japan generated around 65% of sales, Asia with about 25%, and others with some 10%.

Financial Performance
The company's revenue for fiscal 2021 decreased to JPY 1.46 trillion compared to JPY 1.5 trillion in the prior year.

Net loss for fiscal 2021 decreased to JPY 1.9 billion compared to JPY 31.5 billion in the prior year.

Cash held by the company at the end of fiscal 2021 was JPY 54.7 billion. Operating activities provided JPY 108.4 billion while cash used for investing and financing activities were JPY 56.2 billion and JPY 38.4 billion, respectively. Main cash uses were purchase of property, plant and equipment; and decrease in short-term borrowings.

Strategy
The company's strategic focuses are providing Hino value and the world the company want to create; enhancing its business foundation in pursuit of sustainable growth. Enhancing its business foundation in pursuit of sustainable growth: growth and business structure changes leading up to 2025; growth scenario; new vehicle business; UIO business; and partnerships.

EXECUTIVES
President, Chief Executive Officer, Chief Human Resources Officer, Representative Director, Satoshi Ogiso
Senior Managing Executive Officer, Director, Naoki Sato
Outside Director, Motokazu Yoshida
Outside Director, Koichi Muto
Outside Director, Masahiro Nakajima
Outside Director, Shoko Kimijima
Director, Kenta Kon
Auditors : PricewaterhouseCoopers Aarata LLC

LOCATIONS
HQ: Hino Motors, Ltd.
 3-1-1 Hinodai, Hino, Tokyo 191-8660
Phone: (81) 42 586 5111 **Fax:** 248 699-9310
Web: www.hino.co.jp

2016 Sales
	% of total
Japan	66
Asia	21
Other	13
Total	100

PRODUCTS/OPERATIONS
2016 Sales
	% of total
Trucks and buses	53
Total Toyota brand	20
Service parts	6
Other	21
Total	100

Selected Overseas Subsidiaries and Affiliates
Hino Motor Sales Australia Pty. Ltd.
Hino Motor Sales U.S.A., Inc.
Hino Motors (Malaysia) Sdn. Bhd.
Hino Motors Sales (Thailand) Ltd.
Hinopak Motors Ltd. (Pakistan)
Shenyang Shenfei Hino Automobile Manufacturing Co., Ltd. (China)

COMPETITORS
Hyundai Motor Company
MAZDA MOTOR CORPORATION
MITSUBISHI MOTORS CORPORATION
NISSAN MOTOR CO.,LTD.
PEUGEOT SA
SUBARU CORPORATION
SUZUKI MOTOR CORPORATION
Scania AB
TOYOTA MOTOR CORPORATION
VOLKSWAGEN AG

HISTORICAL FINANCIALS
Company Type: Public

Income Statement — FYE: March 31

	REVENUE ($mil)	NET INCOME ($mil)	NET PROFIT MARGIN	EMPLOYEES
03/23	11,317	(883)	—	43,255
03/22	12,000	(696)	—	42,853
03/21	13,533	(67)	—	41,890
03/20	16,725	289	1.7%	44,188
03/19	17,891	495	2.8%	45,442
Annual Growth	(10.8%)	—	—	(1.2%)

2023 Year-End Financials
Debt ratio: 0.2%
Return on equity: (-28.4%)
Cash ($ mil.): 616
Current Ratio: 0.94
Long-term debt ($ mil.): 268
No. of shares ($ mil.): 574
Dividends
 Yield: —
 Payout: 0.0%
Market value ($ mil.): 2,279

	STOCK PRICE ($) FY Close	P/E High/Low	PER SHARE ($) Earnings	Dividends	Book Value
03/23	3.97	—	(1.54)	0.00	4.81
03/22	5.65	—	(1.21)	0.08	6.56
03/21	9.25	—	(0.12)	0.11	8.72
03/20	5.30	0 0	0.51	0.18	8.70
03/19	8.35	0 0	0.86	0.26	8.54
Annual Growth	(17.0%)	—	—	—	(13.4%)

Hirogin Holdings Inc

Few banks have deeper roots in the Hiroshima Prefecture than the Hiroshima Bank. Established in 1878, the bank serves Japan's Chugoku and Shikoku regions through more than 175 offices and 830 ATMs. Hiroshima organizes its business approach into three distinct areas: financial intermediation, risk management assistance, and information provision. It offers the traditional array of financial services, including investment and private banking products, real estate appraisal, banking software, venture capital support, and assistance with corporate restructuring.

EXECUTIVES
Chairman, Representative Director, Koji Ikeda
President, Representative Director, Toshio Heya
Senior Managing Executive Officer, Director, Akira Ogi
Director, Kazuo Kiyomune
Director, Fumitsugu Kariyada
Director, Yuji Eki

Outside Director, Kaori Maeda
Outside Director, Yoshinori Takahashi
Outside Director, Satoshi Miura
Auditors : KPMG AZSA LLC

LOCATIONS

HQ: Hirogin Holdings Inc
1-3-8 Kamiyacho, Naka-ku, Hiroshima -8691
Phone: (81) 82 247 5151
Web: www.hirogin.co.jp

COMPETITORS

AOZORA BANK,LTD.
EHIME BANK, LTD., THE
JUROKU BANK,LTD., THE
NANTO BANK,LTD., THE
TOCHIGI BANK.,LTD., THE

HISTORICAL FINANCIALS
Company Type: Public

Income Statement   FYE: March 31

	ASSETS ($mil)	NET INCOME ($mil)	INCOME AS % OF ASSETS	EMPLOYEES
03/21	99,432	194	0.2%	5,189
03/20	86,951	223	0.3%	4,729
03/19	80,841	230	0.3%	4,767
03/18	85,247	243	0.3%	4,792
03/17	79,362	279	0.4%	4,520
Annual Growth	5.8%	(8.6%)	—	3.5%

2021 Year-End Financials
Return on assets: 0.4%   Dividends
Return on equity: 8.6%   Yield: —
Long-term debt ($ mil.): —   Payout: 17.3%
No. of shares ($ mil.): 312   Market value ($ mil.): —
Sales ($ mil.): 1,047

Hitachi Construction Machinery Co Ltd

EXECUTIVES

Chairman, Representative Executive Officer, Director, Kotaro Hirano
Representative Executive Officer, Executive Vice President, Michifumi Tabuchi
Executive Vice President, Chief Strategy Officer, Naoyoshi Yamada
Senior Managing Executive Officer, Sonosuke Ishii
Senior Managing Executive Officer, Yusuke Kajita
Chief Financial Officer, Managing Executive Officer, Director, Keiichiro Shiojima
Chief Human Resources Officer, Managing Executive Officer, Seishi Toyoshima
Representative Executive Officer, President, Chief Operating Officer, Director, Masafumi Senzaki
Chief Technical Officer, Kazunori Nakamura
Chief Marketing & Sales Officer, Hidehiko Matsui
Chief Digital & Information Officer, Seimei Toonishi
Chief Procurement Officer, Yoshihiro Narukawa
Outside Director, Toshiko Oka

Outside Director, Kazushige Okuhara
Outside Director, Maoko Kikuchi
Outside Director, Takatoshi Hayama
Outside Director, Hidemi Moue
Outside Director, Toshinori Yamamoto
Outside Director, Joseph P. Schmelzeis
Auditors : Ernst & Young ShinNihon LLC

LOCATIONS

HQ: Hitachi Construction Machinery Co Ltd
2-16-1 Higashiueno, Taito-ku, Tokyo 110-0015
Phone: (81) 3 5826 8151
Web: www.hitachi-kenki.co.jp

HISTORICAL FINANCIALS
Company Type: Public

Income Statement   FYE: March 31

	REVENUE ($mil)	NET INCOME ($mil)	NET PROFIT MARGIN	EMPLOYEES
03/23	9,606	526	5.5%	27,697
03/22	8,426	623	7.4%	27,129
03/21	7,345	93	1.3%	26,836
03/20	8,579	379	4.4%	27,570
03/19	9,334	618	6.6%	27,118
Annual Growth	0.7%	(3.9%)	—	0.5%

2023 Year-End Financials
Debt ratio: 0.2%   No. of shares ($ mil.): 212
Return on equity: 11.0%   Dividends
Cash ($ mil.): 840   Yield: —
Current Ratio: 1.48   Payout: 33.3%
Long-term debt ($ mil.): 1,475   Market value ($ mil.): —

Hitachi, Ltd.

EXECUTIVES

Chairman, Outside Director, Katsumi Ihara
Executive Chairman, Representative Executive Officer, Director, Toshiaki Higashihara
President, Chief Executive Officer, Representative Executive Officer, Director, Keiji Kojima
Executive Vice President, Representative Executive Officer, Masakazu Aoki
Executive Vice President, Representative Executive Officer, Yoshihiko Kawamura
Executive Vice President, Representative Executive Officer, Alistair Dormer
Executive Vice President, Representative Executive Officer, Toshiaki Tokunaga
Senior Managing Executive Officer, Jun Abe
Senior Managing Executive Officer, Katsuya Nagano
Senior Managing Executive Officer, Representative Executive Officer, Hidenobu Nakahata
Senior Managing Executive Officer, Representative Executive Officer, Masahiko Hasegawa
Senior Managing Executive Officer, Claudio Facchin
Senior Managing Executive Officer, Mamoru Morita
Outside Director, Ravi Venkatesan

Outside Director, Cynthia Carroll
Outside Director, Ikuro Sugawara
Outside Director, Joe Harlan
Outside Director, Louise Pentland
Outside Director, Takatoshi Yamamoto
Outside Director, Hiroaki Yoshihara
Outside Director, Helmuth Ludwig
Director, Mitsuaki Nishiyama
Auditors : Ernst & Young ShinNihon LLC

LOCATIONS

HQ: Hitachi, Ltd.
1-6-6 Marunouchi, Chiyoda-ku, Tokyo 100-8280
Phone: (81) 3 3258 1111   **Fax:** 650 244-7037
Web: www.hitachi.co.jp

HISTORICAL FINANCIALS
Company Type: Public

Income Statement   FYE: March 31

	REVENUE ($mil)	NET INCOME ($mil)	NET PROFIT MARGIN	EMPLOYEES
03/23	81,699	4,873	6.0%	322,525
03/22	84,387	4,796	5.7%	368,247
03/21	78,837	4,530	5.7%	350,864
03/20	80,766	806	1.0%	301,056
03/19	85,608	2,009	2.3%	295,941
Annual Growth	(1.2%)	24.8%	—	2.2%

2023 Year-End Financials
Debt ratio: 0.1%   No. of shares ($ mil.): 937
Return on equity: 13.9%   Dividends
Cash ($ mil.): 6,256   Yield: —
Current Ratio: 1.15   Payout: 39.6%
Long-term debt ($ mil.): 7,817   Market value ($ mil.): 103,086

	STOCK PRICE ($) FY Close	P/E High/Low		PER SHARE ($) Earnings	Dividends	Book Value
03/23	109.95	0	0	5.13	2.04	39.58
03/22	100.13	0	0	4.96	1.88	36.90
03/21	92.45	0	0	4.68	1.79	32.93
03/20	57.45	1	1	0.83	1.74	30.13
03/19	64.87	0	0	2.08	1.45	30.51
Annual Growth	14.1%	—	—	25.4%	8.9%	6.7%

Hokkoku Financial Holdings Inc

Hokkoku Bank knows that not all of the gold in its hometown is in the bank vault. The regional bank is headquartered in Kanazawa (which translates to 'marsh of gold'), a city noted for its production of gold leaf. It serves the Ishikawa, Fukui, and Toyama prefectures (in the Hokuriku region) through 100-plus branches. It also has offices in Osaka, Nagoya, and Tokyo, as well as overseas in Shanghai and Singapore. Besides traditional deposit banking, Hokkoku Bank subsidiaries are engaged in leasing, credit cards, debt collection, business restructuring funding, revitalization, and credit guarantee. With total assets of $37 billion in fiscal 2013, the bank was founded in 1943 when three banks merged.

EXECUTIVES

President, Representative Director, Shuji Tsuemura
Representative Director, Kazuya Nakamura
Director, Koichi Nakada
Director, Yuji Kakuchi
Director, Nobuhiro Torigoe
Outside Director, Shigeru Nishii
Outside Director, Tadashi Onishi
Outside Director, Shuji Yamashita
Outside Director, Taku Oizumi
Outside Director, Naoko Nemoto
Auditors : Ernst & Young ShinNihon LLC

LOCATIONS

HQ: Hokkoku Financial Holdings Inc
2-12-6 Hirooka, Kanazawa, Ishikawa 920-8670
Phone: (81) 76 263 1111
Web: www.hfhd.co.jp

PRODUCTS/OPERATIONS

Selected Subsidiaries
The Hokkoku General Leasing Co., Ltd.
The Hokkoku Credit Service Co., Ltd.
The Hokkoku Credit Guarantee Co., Ltd.
The Hokkoku Management, Ltd.
The Hokkoku Servicer, Ltd.

COMPETITORS

BANK OF AYUDHYA PUBLIC COMPANY LIMITED
BANK OF THE RYUKYUS, LIMITED
HOKUETSU BANK, LTD., THE
NANTO BANK,LTD., THE
NISHI-NIPPON CITYBANK,LTD.

HISTORICAL FINANCIALS

Company Type: Public

Income Statement — FYE: March 31

	ASSETS ($mil)	NET INCOME ($mil)	INCOME AS % OF ASSETS	EMPLOYEES
03/22	46,961	77	0.2%	2,309
03/21	49,894	60	0.1%	2,265
03/20	46,957	67	0.1%	2,278
03/19	45,413	77	0.2%	2,309
03/18	44,948	95	0.2%	2,338
Annual Growth	1.1%	(5.2%)	—	(0.3%)

2022 Year-End Financials
Return on assets: 0.1%
Return on equity: 3.5%
Long-term debt ($ mil.): —
No. of shares ($ mil.): 26
Sales ($ mil.): 702
Dividends
Yield: —
Payout: 0.0%
Market value ($ mil.): —

Hokuhoku Financial Group Inc

Short on cash and passing through the Hokuriku or Hokkaido districts of Japan? You might want to check in with this group. The Hokuhoku Financial Group's core business is banking, primarily through its chief subsidiaries: The Hokuriku Bank and The Hokkaido Bank. Through both banks' approximately 325 branches, the financial services group targets the Toyama, Ishikawa, and Fukui Prefectures. In addition to banking, Hokuhoku Financial Group provides credit cards, leasing services, venture capital, and financing products. Hokuriku Bank (founded in 1877) merged with Hokkaido Bank in 2004 to form Hokuhoku Financial Group, which today operates in the Hokuriku and Hokkaido district and Tokyo, Osaka, and Nagoya.

EXECUTIVES

President, Representative Director, Hiroshi Nakazawa
Deputy President, Representative Director, Yuji Kanema
Director, Masahiko Kobayashi
Director, Yoshimasa Takada
Director, Yoshikazu Sakamoto
Director, Akira Sakai
Director, Yutaka Yokoi
Director, Hirokuni Kitagawa
Outside Director, Masaaki Manabe
Outside Director, Nobuya Suzuki
Outside Director, Kaoru Funamoto
Outside Director, Marie Ogawa
Auditors : Deloitte Touche Tohmatsu LLC

LOCATIONS

HQ: Hokuhoku Financial Group Inc
1-2-26 Tsutsumicho-dori, Toyama 930-8637
Phone: (81) 76 423 7331
Web: www.hokuhoku-fg.co.jp

PRODUCTS/OPERATIONS

Selected Subsidiaries and Affiliated Companies
Hokugin Lease Co., Ltd.
Hokugin Software Co., Ltd.
Hokuriku Capital Co., Ltd.
Hokuriku Card Co., Ltd.
Hokuriku Hosho Services Co., Ltd.
Nihonkai Services Co., Ltd.
The Hokkaido Bank, Ltd.
  Dogin Business Service, Ltd.
  Dogin Card Co., Ltd.
The Hokuriku Bank, Ltd.
  Hokugin Business Services Co., Ltd.
  Hokugin Corporate Co., Ltd.
  Hokugin Office Services Co., Ltd.
  Hokugin Real Estate Services Co., Ltd.
  Hokugin Shisankanri Co., Ltd.
  Hokuriku International Cayman Limited

COMPETITORS

E. SUN FINANCIAL HOLDING COMPANY, LTD.
Hana Financial Group Inc.
MITSUBISHI UFJ FINANCIAL GROUP, INC.
MIZUHO FINANCIAL GROUP, INC.
SINOPAC FINANCIAL HOLDINGS COMPANY LIMITED

HISTORICAL FINANCIALS

Company Type: Public

Income Statement — FYE: March 31

	ASSETS ($mil)	NET INCOME ($mil)	INCOME AS % OF ASSETS	EMPLOYEES
03/22	142,063	168	0.1%	7,414
03/21	150,242	192	0.1%	7,716
03/20	125,701	186	0.1%	7,983
03/19	119,067	219	0.2%	8,412
03/18	122,391	199	0.2%	8,751
Annual Growth	3.8%	(4.1%)	—	(4.1%)

2022 Year-End Financials
Return on assets: 0.1%
Return on equity: 3.2%
Long-term debt ($ mil.): —
No. of shares ($ mil.): 127
Sales ($ mil.): 1,494
Dividends
Yield: —
Payout: 23.8%
Market value ($ mil.): —

Holcim Ltd (New)

Holcim, formerly known as LafargeHolcim, is a global leader in innovative and sustainable building solutions. Holcim is the company behind some of the world's most trusted brands in the building sector including ACC, Aggregate Industries, Ambuja Cement, Disensa, Firestone Building Products, Geocycle, Holcim, Malarkey Roofing and Lafarge. Each year, Holcim produces around 470 million tons of building materials, in the form of cement, aggregates and asphalt products. It has a global presence managed through its offices scattered around approximately 70 countries. Holcim generates the majority of its revenue from Europe.

Operations

Holcim operates four business segments: Cement, Ready-Mix Concrete, Aggregates and Solutions & Products.

The Cement segment accounts for about 55% of total sales, produces typical masonry products to high-performance offerings tailored for specialized uses. It sells roughly 200.8 million tons of it to individuals buying bags of cement for businesses embarking on major construction projects.

The Ready-Mix segment (nearly 20%) delivers concrete in various forms, all of them ready for individuals and businesses to deploy for its specific projects. Holcim delivers around 46.5 million cubic meters annually.

The Aggregates segment (almost 15% of sales) provides the raw materials for concrete, masonry, and asphalt. It also produces base materials for roads, buildings, and landfills, including recycled aggregates (such as crushed concrete and asphalt left over from deconstruction activities). Holcim delivers about 269.9 million tons of aggregates each year.

Accounting for more than 10% of sales, Solutions & Products segment works closely with customers to define and deliver solutions tailored to customers' requirements.

All told, the company has around 2,300

plants, including about 1,375 ready-mix concrete, some 660 aggregates, and nabout 265 cement and grinding plants.

Geographic Reach

Switzerland-headquartered Holcim has a large asset presence in around 60 countries and boasts a market presence in just about every developed region on the globe.

Holcim's sales are well-balanced across the world's major regions. The company generates around 30% of its total sales from Europe; the Asia/Pacific regions accounts for more than 20%, North America brings in nearly 30% of total sales; and Latin America, Middle East and Africa together pull in the remaining some 20% of Holcim's total sales.

Financial Performance

Note: Growth rates may differ after conversion to US Dollars.

The company had net sales amounting to CHF 26.8 billion in 2021, a 16% increase from the previous year's net sales of CHF 23.1 billion. The record increase was driven by volume growth and strong pricing. Net sales growth was further supported by 7% of positive scope impact, mostly driven by the acquisition of Firestone Building Products (Firestone).

In 2021, the company had a net income of CHF 2.3 billion, a 35% increase from the previous year's net income of CHF 1.7 billion.

The company's cash at the end of 2021 was CHF 6.6 billion. Operating activities generated CHF 5 billion, while investing activities used CHF 4.7 billion, mainly for acquisition of participation in group companies. Financing activities provided another CHF 1.1 billion.

Strategy

With today's megatrends, from the rise in population and urbanization to improving living standards, Holcim will accelerate growth across all of its markets with leading profitability and cash flow. Holcim's profitable growth will be driven by innovative building solutions, from ECOPact green concrete to energy-efficient roofing systems. The company will lead cement's green transformation, with solutions like ECOPlanet, including the world's first cement with 20% construction & demolition waste inside. The company will further fuel its growth with bolt-on acquisitions in mature markets in the aggregates and ready-mix concrete businesses. Strengthening its performance, the company will scale up digitalization across its value chain, from operations and distribution to customer experience.

Mergers and Acquisitions

In 2022, Holcim has acquired Teko Mining Serbia, one of the country's largest independent aggregates companies with estimated 2022 net sales of over EUR 20 million. The acquisition includes Teko's four quarries and will strengthen Holcim's footprint in the dynamic Serbian market, complementing its recent acquisition of another aggregates operation in the region. Teko complements Holcim's existing cement and concrete operations perfectly, allowing to add aggregates and asphalt as part of its integrated offer in this highly dynamic market.

Also in 2022, Holcim acquired General Beton Romania S.R.L, a key national player in ready-mix concrete, with 2022 net sales (est.) of EUR 45 million. Miljan Gutovic, Region Head Europe Middle East Africa: "With this acquisition we will further expand the footprint of ECOPact green concrete, the first and most comprehensive sustainable concrete range in Romania. General Beton provides an excellent addition to our strong and diversified ready-mix concrete operations."

In mid-2022, Holcim completed the acquisition of PRB Group, France's biggest independent manufacturer of specialty building solutions. The acquisition is another exciting step in the expansion of Solutions & Products in the highly attractive repair and refurbishment market.

In 2021, Holcim has signed an agreement to acquire Malarkey Roofing Products, a leading company in the US residential roofing market. Jan Jenisch, CEO: "We are off to a strong start to our 'Strategy 2025 ? Accelerating Green Growth' with the acquisition of Malarkey Roofing Products, expanding our Solutions & Products business to become a global leader in roofing systems."

Also in 2021, Holcim completed the acquisition of Marshall Concrete Products, a longstanding and trusted supplier of concrete products and services in Minneapolis/St. Paul and the surrounding metropolitan area. This acquisition expands Holcim's footprint in the US. The acquisition enhances Holcim's current residential and light commercial offerings, benefiting all sectors served including infrastructure and industrial customers. Marshall Concrete Products and all its people will become a member of Holcim in the US.

In early 2021, LafargeHolcim (now known as Holcim) signed an agreement to acquire Firestone Building Products (FSBP), a leader in commercial roofing and building envelope solutions based in the US, for USD 3.4 billion. The acquisition of FSBP will strengthen LafargeHolcim's biggest market, the US, establishing a new growth profile, reaching USD 6 billion in annual net sales. Building on FSBP's strong organic growth, LafargeHolcim expects to accelerate its leadership through cross-selling opportunities and further bolt-on acquisitions. LafargeHolcim also aims to swiftly globalize the business, leveraging its European and Latin American footprint.

Also, in early 2021, Holcim announces the acquisition of Edile Commerciale and the signing of Cemex Rhone Alpes, both suppliers of ready-mix concrete and aggregates, ideally located in two of Europe's largest metropolitan areas, Milan, Italy, and Lyon, France. With 35 ready-mix concrete plants, these operations strengthen LafargeHolcim's position in two of the most dynamic and attractive areas in Europe, with strong demographic trends and key infrastructure projects. These two bolt-on acquisitions add to eight similar transactions carried out by LafargeHolcim in 2020, as a key driver of its growth strategy.

HISTORY

Cement company Aargauische Portlandcementfabrik Holderbank-Wildegg was founded near Zurich in 1912. Two years later Ernst Schmidheiny bought a stake in the company. His son and namesake later expanded the company beyond Switzerland, then grouped its interests under holding company "Holderbank" FinanciÃ¨re Glaris Ltd. in 1930. By WWII Holderbank had operations in Belgium, Egypt, Greece, Lebanon, and South Africa.

After the war Holderbank expanded into the Americas. It purchased Canada-based St. Lawrence Cement in 1953 and was listed on the Zurich stock exchange in 1958.

In 1970 the company swapped some assets with rival Swiss Cement-Industrie-Gesellschaft in a deal that increased Holderbank's presence in Costa Rica, Lebanon, Mexico, and West Germany. The company also converted several of its minority stakes into majority shareholdings. Thomas Schmidheiny became chairman of Holderbank's executive committee in 1978 and chairman of the board in 1984 upon his father's (Ernst's brother Max) retirement.

During a late-1980s market slump, Holderbank bought stakes in several US cement companies. It became the #1 US cement maker by purchasing Ideal Basic Industries in 1986. As the decade closed, Holderbank consolidated in Europe and in 1990 placed many of its US operations under holding company Holnam.

Holderbank then pushed into Central and Eastern Europe, where it gained production capacity in Hungary, among other countries. The company bought a 51% stake in Morocco-based Les Ciments de l'Oriental (CIOR) in 1993. Geographic diversity helped Holderbank weather depressed periods in regional markets, such as in Mexico, where profits dropped 83% from 1994 to 1995 during an economic crisis there.

The company picked up major acquisitions in Malaysia, the Philippines, Sri Lanka, and Thailand during a crippled economic period in Asia in the late 1990s. It also added capacity in the booming US market. Holderbank sought to invest in India in 1999, but the fragmented market there prevented it from finding a sizable company. Meanwhile, Holderbank continued searching for investments in China to expand its presence there. The following year the company became the majority shareholder of

Indonesian cement company, PT Semen Cibinong (now PT Holcim Indonesia). Its joint bid (with Portugal's Secil) for CIMPOR, the largest Portuguese cement manufacturer, got stuck in regulatory issues, however.

Holderbank changed its name to Holcim Ltd. in 2001. The name is derived from "Holderbank" (where it was founded) and "ciment" (French for cement). In 2002 Holcim's Thai subsidiary, Siam City Cement, acquired a controlling stake in TPI Polene, beating out rival CEMEX for the deal. Holcim acquired Spain-based Cementos de Hispania and disposed of Eternit AG business in 2003.

That year, when operations in Europe and North America showed little growth, the company looked toward emerging markets in Africa, Asia, and Latin America. Holcim tightened its hold on Holcim Apasco in Mexico by increasing its stake in the company from 69% to 93% in 2004; it later took full ownership.

In 2005 Holcim acquired UK-based construction products provider Aggregate Industries. The deal gave the group more than 140 quarries in the UK and US. It followed that up the following year with the purchases of aggregates producer Foster Yeoman in the UK and ready-mix concrete maker Meyer Material in the US.

In 2007, Holcim acquired control of Ambuja Cements in India; took a majority stake in the Croatian Plovanija Kamen cement plant and stone quarry; and bought building materials supplier Jurong Cement in Singapore.

The company acquired Tarmac Iberia from Anglo American for some ?148 million ($228 million) in 2008. The deal added about 50 ready-mixed concrete plants in Spain.

EXECUTIVES

Chief Executive Officer, Executive Director, Jan Jenisch
Chief Financial Officer, Geraldine Picaud
Chief Sustainability and Innovation Officer, Magali Anderson
Legal and Compliance Head, Mathias Gartner
Solutions & Products Business Unit Head, Jamie M. Gentoso
Human Resources Head, Feliciano Gonzalez Munoz
Europe Head, Miljan Gutovic
Asia, Middle East & Africa Head, Martin Kriegner
Latin America Head, Oliver Osswald
North America Head, Toufic Tabbara
Chairperson, Beat W. Hess
Vice-Chairman, Hanne Birgitte Breinbjerg Sorensen
Director, Philippe Block
Director, Kim Fausing
Director, Leanne Geale
Director, Ilias Laber
Director, Naina Lal Kidwai
Director, Patrick Kron
DIrector, Jurg Oleas
Director, Claudia Sender Ramirez
Auditors : Ernst & Young Ltd

LOCATIONS

HQ: Holcim Ltd (New)
  Grafenauweg 10, Zug, 6300
Phone: (41) 58 858 58 58   **Fax:** (41) 58 858 87 19
Web: www.holcim.com

2018 sales

	%
Asia Pacific	27
Europe	28
Latin America	10
Middle East & Africa	11
North America	21
Corporate/Eliminations	2
Total	100

PRODUCTS/OPERATIONS

2018 sales

	%
Cement	60
Aggregates	14
Ready-mix concrete	18
Products and Solutions	8
Total	100

COMPETITORS

Bâloise Holding AG
CRH PUBLIC LIMITED COMPANY
Cemex, S.A.B. de C.V.
GROUPE CRIT
HeidelbergCement AG
ICAHN ENTERPRISES L.P.
SONAE - SGPS, S.A.
Swiss Re AG
Weatherford International Ltd.
Zurich Insurance Group AG

HISTORICAL FINANCIALS

Company Type: Public

Income Statement   FYE: December 31

	REVENUE ($mil)	NET INCOME ($mil)	NET PROFIT MARGIN	EMPLOYEES
12/22	31,640	3,585	11.3%	60,422
12/21	29,396	2,517	8.6%	69,672
12/20	26,275	1,926	7.3%	67,409
12/19	27,642	2,323	8.4%	72,452
12/18	27,920	1,526	5.5%	77,055
Annual Growth	3.2%	23.8%	—	(5.9%)

2022 Year-End Financials

Debt ratio: 25.5%   No. of shares ($ mil.): 588
Return on equity: 11.7%   Dividends
Cash ($ mil.): 10,649   Yield: —
Current Ratio: 1.89   Payout: 7.1%
Long-term debt ($ mil.): 14,696   Market value ($ mil.): 6,056

	STOCK PRICE ($) FY Close	P/E High/Low		PER SHARE ($) Earnings	Dividends	Book Value
12/22	10.29	2	2	5.92	0.42	52.81
12/21	10.09	3	3	4.08	2.41	49.88
12/20	10.84	4	2	3.11	2.27	48.39
12/19	11.06	3	2	3.81	2.07	48.15
12/18	8.16	5	3	2.56	0.00	45.91
Annual Growth	6.0%	—	—	23.3%	—	3.6%

Hon Hai Precision Industry Co Ltd

Hon Hai Precision Industry Co., also known by its trade name, Foxconn, is the world's largest contract electronics manufacturer. It makes mobile phones, computers, servers, and TVs. It covers the four major product areas of consumer electronics, cloud network products, computer terminal products, components and others. The global company's customers include Apple, Cisco, Dell, and Amazon. Chairman Terry Gou founded Hon Hai in 1974 to make plastic switches for TVs.

Operations

The company generates about 98% of its revenue from 3C electronics (Computer, Communication, Consumer Electronics). Product segments include Smart Consumer Electronic Products; Cloud and networking Products; Computing Products; and Components and Others Product.

The Smart Consumer Electronic Products segment includes personal consumer electronic products such as smart phones, feature phones, and wearable devices. The Cloud and Networking segment includes enterprise and consumer network communication equipment including routers, servers, edge computing, data centers, satellite communications and other related equipment. The Computing Products segment includes lifestyle and work computing equipment, office and workplace computing products, including desktops, notebooks, tablets, office machines, and printers. Lastly, the Components and Other Products segment is composed of mainly connectors, mechanical parts and services.

Geographic Reach

Hon Hai has a wide range of product lines that is carried out in a regional production in more than 20 countries and more than 100 bases globally.

Financial Performance

Hon Hai's performance for the past five years has increased year-over-year with 2022 as its highest performing year over the period.

The company's revenue increased by NT$632 billion to NT$6.6 trillion for 2022, as compared to 2021's revenue of about NT$6 trillion.

Hon Hai's net income for fiscal year end 2022 also increased to NT$141.5 billion, as compared to the prior year's net income of NT$139.3 billion.

The company held NT$224.9 billion at the end of the year, with operating activities generating NT$4.1 trillion.

Company Background

Hon Hai Precision Industry Co., Ltd., or also knew to their business as Foxconn Technology Group or better known as

Foxconn, is a Taiwanese multinational electronics contract manufacturer headquartered in Tucheng, New Taipei City, Taiwan. It was founded in 1974 as Hon Hai Plastics Corporation, by Terry Gou, and later renamed as Hon Hai Precision Industry Co., Ltd., in 1982.

EXECUTIVES

Chairman, Terry Gou
Chief Financial Officer, Tetsai Huang
Chief Accounting Officer, Zongkai Jhou
Director, Jeng-wu Tai
Director, Sidney Lu
Director, Fangming Lyu
Director, Mark Chien
Director, Yuci Wu
Director, Chengyu Liu
Auditors : PricewaterhouseCoopers, Taiwan

LOCATIONS

HQ: Hon Hai Precision Industry Co Ltd
No. 66, Zhongshan Road, Tucheng Industrial Zone, Tucheng District, New Taipei
Phone: (886) 2 2268 3466
Web: www.foxconn.com

PRODUCTS/OPERATIONS

2017 Sales

	% of total
Ireland	30
US	29
China	9
Singapore	8
Japan	3
Taiwan	2
Others	19
Total	100

Selected Products
Cable assemblies
CD-ROMs
Connectors
E-book readers
Enclosures
Flat-panel displays
Game consoles
Handsets
Keyboards
LCD (liquid-crystal display) TVs
Mobile phones
Motherboards
Personal computers
Servers
Smartphones
Switches
Tablets
Thermal products

COMPETITORS

AMPHENOL CORPORATION
CTS CORPORATION
HIROSE ELECTRIC CO., LTD.
METHODE ELECTRONICS, INC.
OCLARO, INC.
QCEPT TECHNOLOGIES INC.
SIGMA DESIGNS, INC.
STMicroelectronics SA
Samsung Electronics Co., Ltd.
WOODHEAD INDUSTRIES, LLC

HISTORICAL FINANCIALS

Company Type: Public

Income Statement   FYE: December 31

	REVENUE ($mil)	NET INCOME ($mil)	NET PROFIT MARGIN	EMPLOYEES
12/21	216,489	5,031	2.3%	826,608
12/20	190,662	3,622	1.9%	0
12/19	178,459	3,851	2.2%	0
12/18	173,087	4,219	2.4%	0
12/17	158,733	4,678	2.9%	0
Annual Growth	8.1%	1.8%	—	—

2021 Year-End Financials
Debt ratio: 0.8%
Return on equity: 10.4%
Cash ($ mil.): 38,262
Current Ratio: 1.52
Long-term debt ($ mil.): 9,953
No. of shares ($ mil.): 13,862
Dividends
Yield: 2.7%
Payout: 58.0%
Market value ($ mil.): 102,448

	STOCK PRICE ($) FY Close	P/E High/Low		PER SHARE ($) Earnings	Dividends	Book Value
12/21	7.39	1	1	0.36	0.21	3.60
12/20	6.63	1	1	0.26	0.21	3.33
12/19	6.12	1	1	0.28	0.18	2.99
12/18	4.75	1	1	0.26	0.00	2.86
12/17	6.20	1	1	0.27	0.00	2.11
Annual Growth	4.5%	—	—	7.6%	—	14.3%

Honda Motor Co Ltd

Since its establishment, Honda has remained on the leading edge by creating new value and providing products of the highest quality at a reasonable price for worldwide customer satisfaction. Honda develops, manufactures and markets motorcycles, automobiles and power products globally. Honda's line of motorcycles includes everything from scooters to superbikes. The company's power products division makes commercial and residential machinery (lawn mowers, snow blowers, and tillers); portable generators; and outboard motors. More than half of Honda's sales comes from North America.

Operations

Four reporting segments comprise Honda Motor's operations: the Automobile business, Financial Services business, Motorcycle business, and Life Creation and other businesses.

Automobile business generates almost 65% of total sales. It offers vehicles that use gasoline engines of three, four or six-cylinder configurations, diesel engines, gasoline-electric hybrid systems and gasoline-electric plug-in hybrid systems. Honda also offers other alternative fuel-powered vehicles such as battery electric vehicles, fuel cell vehicles, and flexible fuel vehicles.

Financial Services generates nearly 20% of total sales. It offers retail lending, leasing to customers and other financial services, such as wholesale financing to dealers through finance subsidiaries.

Motorcycle Business generates about 15% of total sales. Honda produces a wide range of motorcycles, with engine displacement ranging from the 50cc class to the 1800cc class. Honda's motorcycle lineup uses internal combustion engine of air- or water-cooled, and in single, two, four or six-cylinder configurations. Honda also has electric vehicles in its lineup. Honda's motorcycle lineup consists of sports, business and commuter models.

Life Creation and Other Businesses generates less than 5% of total sales. Honda manufactured a variety of power products including general purpose engines, generators, water pumps, lawn mowers, riding mowers, robotic mowers, brush cutters, tillers, snow blowers, outboard marine engines, walking assist devices and portable battery inverter power sources.

Geographic Reach

Headquartered in Tokyo, Japan, Honda's major geographic areas are concentrated in North America (the US, Canada, and Mexico); Asia (Thailand, Indonesia, China, India, and Vietnam); Japan; and Europe (the UK, Germany, Italy, Belgium, France), as well as Brazil and Australia.

The Financial Services business provides financing and leasing through its subsidiaries in Japan, the US, Canada, the UK, Germany, Brazil and Thailand.

North America generates roughly 50% of net sales while Asia brings in over 25% of sales. Japan accounts about 15% and Europe and other regions generates less than 10% of sales combined.

Sales and Marketing

Most of Honda's products are distributed under the Honda trademarks in Japan and/or in overseas markets. In Japan, Honda produces and sells motorcycles, automobiles, and power products through its domestic sales subsidiaries and independent retail dealers. In overseas markets, Honda also provides motorcycles, automobiles, and power products through its principal foreign sales subsidiaries, which distribute Honda's products to local wholesalers and retail dealers.

It also sells spare parts and provides after-sales services through retail dealers directly or via its overseas operations, independent distributors and licensees.

Financial Performance

The company's revenue has declined in the last couple of years, following a trend of increase. It has a 6% overall decrease between 2017 and 2021. Its net income has been fluctuating in the same period with an overall increase of 7%.

Honda's consolidated sales revenue for the fiscal year 2022 (ended March), increased by Â¥1.4 trillion, or 11%, to Â¥14.6 trillion from the fiscal year 2021, due mainly to increase sales revenue in Motorcycle business and Financial services business operations as well as positive foreign currency translation effects.

Profit before income taxes increased by Â¥156.1 billion, or 17.1%, to Â¥1,070.1 billion from the previous fiscal year. Share of profit of investments accounted for using the equity method had a negative impact of Â¥70.2 billion, due mainly to recognition of reversal of impairment losses in previous fiscal year, which had been previously recognized on the investments in certain companies accounted for using the equity method.

The company's cash at the end of 2022 was Â¥3.7 trillion, a 33% increase from the previous year. Operating activities generated Â¥1.7 trillion, while investing activities used Â¥376.1 billion, mainly for payments for acquisitions of other financial assets. Financing activities used another Â¥615.7 billion, primarily for repayments of short-term financing liabilities.

Strategy

Honda will enhance the business strategy formulation function by steadily proceeding with the next initiatives, and build a highly competitive Mono-zukuri foundation to realize strong businesses.

In order to build strong businesses that can immediately respond to changes in the environment and can provide products that satisfy customer needs in a timely manner, Honda has established a unified operational structure which integrates S-E-D-B (Sales, Engineering, Development and Buying) areas. This enables the formulation of business strategies based on a big-picture view of product planning, development, buying/purchasing, engineering/production and sales, and the swift implementation of such strategies. At the same time, Honda will realize Mono-zukuri reform and stable production with high-precision development of new models through frontloading and operation which integrates the entire process from development through mass-production.

HISTORY

Soichiro Honda spent six years as an apprentice at Tokyo service station Art Shokai before opening his own branch of the repair shop in Hamamatsu in 1928. He also raced cars and in 1931 received a patent for metal spokes that replaced wood in wheels.

Honda started a piston ring company in 1937. During WWII the company produced metal propellers for Japanese bombers. When bombs and an earthquake destroyed most of his factory, Honda sold it to Toyota in 1945.

In 1946 Honda began motorizing bicycles with war-surplus engines. When this proved popular, Honda began making engines. The company was renamed Honda Motor Co. in 1948 and began producing motorcycles. Soichiro Honda hired Takeo Fujisawa in 1949 to manage the company so Honda could focus on engineering. Honda's innovative overhead valve design made its early 1950s Dream model a runaway success. In 1952 the smaller Cub, sold through bicycle dealers, accounted for 70% of Japan's motorcycle production.

Funded by a 1954 public offering and Mitsubishi Bank, Honda expanded capacity and began exporting. American Honda Motor Company was formed in Los Angeles in 1959, accompanied by the slogan "You meet the nicest people on a Honda" in a campaign crafted to counter the stereotypical biker image. Honda added overseas factories in the 1960s and began producing lightweight trucks, sports cars, and minicars.

The company began selling its tiny 600 model in the US in 1970, but it was the Civic, introduced in 1973, that first scored with the US car market. Three years later Honda introduced the Accord, which featured an innovative frame adaptable for many models. In 1982 Accord production started at the company's Ohio plant.

EXECUTIVES

President, Chief Executive Officer, Director, Toshihiro Mibe
Executive Vice President, Chief Operating Officer, Chief Brand Officer, Director, Seiji Kuraishi
Compliance Senior Managing Executive Officer, Compliance Chief Financial Officer, Compliance Officer, Director, Kohei Takeuchi
Risk Management Managing Executive Officer, Customer First Operations Managing Executive Officer, Risk Management Officer, Customer First Operations Officer, Noriya Kaihara
Managing Executive Officer, Noriaki Abe
Managing Executive Officer, Yasuhide Mizuno
Managing Executive Officer, Keiji Ohtsu
Chairman, Director, Toshiaki Mikoshiba
Independent Outside Director, Kunihiko Sakai
Independent Outside Director, Fumiya Kokubu
Independent Outside Director, Yoichiro Ogawa
Independent Outside Director, Kazuhiro Higashi
Independent Outside Director, Ryoko Nagata
Director, Asako Suzuki
Director, Masafumi Suzuki
Auditors : KPMG AZSA LLC

LOCATIONS

HQ: Honda Motor Co Ltd
1-1, Minami-Aoyama 2-chome, Minato-ku, Tokyo 107-8556
Phone: (81) 3 5412 1134
Web: www.honda.co.jp

2017 Sales

	% of total
North America	56
Asia	19
Japan	14
Europe	5
Other regions	6
Total	100

PRODUCTS/OPERATIONS

2017 Sales

	% of total
Automobiles	72
Financial Services	13
Motorcycles	12
Power products & other businesses	3
Total	100

Selected Acura Models
ILX sedan
TLX sedan
RLX sedan
RDX SUV
MDX SUV
NSX Supercar

Selected Honda Car and Truck Models
Passenger cars
Gold Wing
CB1100
CBR1000RR
CB1000R
VFR800F
Rebel
CB250R/CB300R
CB125R
CRF1000L Africa Twin
X-ADV
CRF250 Rally
PCX
SuperCub
Monkey

Selected ATVs
Utility ATVs
    TRX250X ATV sport
    TRX90X sport
    FourTrax Rincon
    FourTrax Foreman Rubicon 4x4
    FourTrax Rancher
    FourTrax Recon
    Pioner SxS
    Forza scooter
    PCX150 scooter
    Ruckus scooter
    Metropolitan scooter

Selected Power Products
Lawn mowers
Miimo robotic lawnmower
Marine motors
Portable generators
LiB-AID E500 portable power source
Pumps
Snowblowers
Tillers

COMPETITORS

Bayerische Motoren Werke AG
GKN LIMITED
MAHINDRA AND MAHINDRA LIMITED
MAZDA MOTOR CORPORATION
MITSUBISHI MOTORS CORPORATION
NISSAN MOTOR CO.,LTD.
SUBARU CORPORATION
TOYOTA MOTOR CORPORATION
VOLKSWAGEN AG
YAMAHA MOTOR CO., LTD.

HISTORICAL FINANCIALS
Company Type: Public

Income Statement   FYE: March 31

	REVENUE ($mil)	NET INCOME ($mil)	NET PROFIT MARGIN	EMPLOYEES
03/23	126,949	4,891	3.9%	197,039
03/22	119,640	5,812	4.9%	204,035
03/21	118,948	5,937	5.0%	211,374
03/20	137,549	4,198	3.1%	218,674
03/19	143,472	5,511	3.8%	219,722
Annual Growth	(3.0%)	(2.9%)	—	(2.7%)

2023 Year-End Financials
Debt ratio: 0.2%   No. of shares ($ mil.): 4,993
Return on equity: 6.0%   Dividends
Cash ($ mil.): 28,554   Yield: 3.5%
Current Ratio: 1.44   Payout: 35.3%
Long-term debt ($ mil.): 32,841 Market value ($ mil.): 132,265

	STOCK PRICE ($) FY Close	P/E High/Low		PER SHARE ($) Earnings	Dividends	Book Value
03/23	26.49	0	0	0.96	0.94	16.82
03/22	28.26	0	0	1.13	1.22	16.78
03/21	30.20	0	0	1.15	0.78	15.84
03/20	22.46	0	0	0.80	1.04	14.25
03/19	27.17	0	0	1.04	0.99	14.14
Annual Growth	(0.6%)	—	—	(2.0%)	(1.4%)	4.4%

HSBC Bank Plc

EXECUTIVES

Chief Executive Officer, Executive Director, James Emmet
Chief Financial Officer, Executive Director, James Fleurant
Secretary, Loren Wulfsohn
Chairman, Stephen O'Connor
Deputy Chairman, Independent Non-Executive Director, John F. Trueman
Independent Non-Executive Director, Andrew Wright
Independent Non-Executive Director, Yukiko Omura
Independent Non-Executive Director, Eric Strutz
Independent Non-Executive Director, Mary Marsh
Auditors : PricewaterhouseCoopers LLP

LOCATIONS

HQ: HSBC Bank Plc
 8 Canada Square, London E14 5HQ
Phone: (44) 20 7991 8888
Web: www.hsbc.co.uk

HISTORICAL FINANCIALS
Company Type: Public

Income Statement   FYE: December 31

	ASSETS ($mil)	NET INCOME ($mil)	INCOME AS % OF ASSETS	EMPLOYEES
12/21	804,041	1,402	0.2%	16,823
12/20	929,572	(2,030)	—	17,866
12/19	840,526	(1,337)	—	17,754
12/18	772,387	1,922	0.2%	30,437
12/17	1,106,040	2,443	0.2%	45,342
Annual Growth	(7.7%)	(13.0%)	—	(22.0%)

2021 Year-End Financials
Return on assets: 0.1%   Dividends
Return on equity: 4.4%   Yield: —
Long-term debt ($ mil.): —   Payout: 0.0%
No. of shares ($ mil.): 796   Market value ($ mil.): —
Sales ($ mil.): 16,223

HSBC Holdings Plc

HSBC is one of the largest banking and financial services organizations in the world. Alongside its home markets of Hong Kong and the UK, HSBC has subsidiaries throughout Europe, the wider Asia/Pacific region, the Middle East, Africa, and the Americas. All told, the company serves more than 40 million customers in about 65 countries. Its activities include wealth and personal banking, commercial banking, and global banking and markets. Its services are made possible through its 220,000 full-time staff catering to about 130 countries. HSBC was founded by the Scot Sir Thomas Sutherland in Hong Kong, then a British colony, in 1865 as was incorporated in the UK in 1991. Asian markets account for the majority of its sales.

Operations
HSBC operates three core business segments: Wealth and Personal Banking (about 45% of sales), Global Banking and Markets (some 30%), and Commercial Banking (around 25%).

The Wealth and Personal Banking (WPB) provides a full range of retail banking and wealth products to its customers from personal banking to ultra-high net worth individuals. Typically, customer offerings include retail banking products, such as current and savings accounts, mortgages and personal loans, credit cards, debit cards and local and international payment services. It also provides wealth management services, including insurance and investment products, global asset management services, investment management and Private Wealth Solutions for customers with more sophisticated and international requirements.

The Global Banking and Markets (GBM) provides tailored financial solutions to major government, corporate and institutional clients and private investors worldwide. The client-focused business lines deliver a full range of banking capabilities including financing, advisory and transaction services, a markets business that provides services in credit, rates, foreign exchange, equities, money markets and securities services, and principal investment activities.

The Commercial Banking (CMB) offers a broad range of products and services to serve the needs of its commercial customers, including small and medium-sized enterprises, mid-market enterprises and corporates. These include credit and lending, international trade and receivables finance, treasury management and liquidity solutions (payments and cash management and commercial cards), commercial insurance and investments. CMB also offers customers access to products and services offered by other global businesses, such as Global Banking and Markets, which include foreign exchange products, raising capital on debt and equity markets and advisory services.

Geographic Reach
London-based HSBC operates in around 65 countries. It generates over 45% its revenue from the Asia/Pacific region (including Hong Kong) and about 25% from Europe (including the UK). North America brings in around 10% of sales, Latin America about 10%, and the Middle East and North Africa around 5% as well.

Sales and Marketing
HSBC serves more than 40 million customers, ranging from individuals to large corporations and everything in between.

Financial Performance
HSBC Holdings' performance for the past five years have fluctuated from year to year but has overall decreased with 2021 as its lowest performing year over the period.

The company's operating income slightly decreased by $877 million to $49.6 billion in 2021 as compared to 2020's operating income of $50.4 billion.

Net income for fiscal year end 2021 decreased by $1.1 billion to $26.5 billion as compared to the prior year's net income of $27.6 billion.

Cash held by the company at the end of fiscal 2021 increased to $574 billion. Cash provided by operations was $104 billion. Investing activities provided $27.5 billion while financing activities used $10.8 billion. Main cash uses were from dividends paid to shareholders of the parent company and redemption of preference shares and other equity instruments.

Strategy
HSBC's strategy involves paving the way for them to accelerate execution of the growth opportunities across their businesses and international network, which in turn, help in the company's targets and ambitions. In line with the company's strategy, they set out aspirations in February 2021 to accelerate the shift of capital and resources to areas that have demonstrated the highest returns and where the company is strongest principally in

Asia.

Mergers and Acquisitions

In 2021, HSBC Insurance (Asia-Pacific) Holdings Ltd, an indirect wholly-owned subsidiary of HSBC Holdings plc (HSBC), has entered into an agreement to acquire 100% of the issued share capital of AXA Insurance Pte Limited (AXA Singapore) for US$529m. The proposed acquisition, which is subject to regulatory approval, is a key step in achieving HSBC's stated ambition of becoming a leading wealth manager in Asia, by expanding its insurance and wealth franchise in Singapore, a strategically important scale market for HSBC, and a major hub for its ASEAN wealth business. AXA Singapore is currently the 8th largest life insurer in Singapore by annualized new premiums, 5th largest property and casualty (P&C) insurer and a leading group health player.

Company Background

In Asia, HSBC sold its private banking operations in Japan to Credit Suisse in 2012. It also shut down its retail banking operations in Japan, though it continues to offer corporate banking there. HSBC sold its US credit card portfolio, worth some $30 billion, to Capital One in 2012, and sold 195 US bank branches, mainly in upstate New York, to First Niagara Financial Group for Â£613 million ($1 billion).

HISTORY

Scotsman Thomas Sutherland and other businessmen in 1865 opened the doors to Hongkong & Shanghai Bank, financing and promoting British imperial trade in opium, silk, and tea in East Asia. It soon established a London office and created an international branch network emphasizing China and East Asia. It claims to have been the first bank in Thailand (1888).

War repeatedly disrupted, but never demolished, the bank's operations. During WWII the headquarters were temporarily moved to London. (They moved back on a permanent basis in 1991.) The bank's chief prewar manager, Sir Vandeleur Grayburn, died in a Japanese POW camp. After the Communists took power in China in 1949, the bank gradually withdrew; by 1955 only its Shanghai office remained, and it was later closed. The bank played a key role in Hong Kong's postwar growth by financing industrialists who fled there from China.

In the late 1950s Hongkong & Shanghai Bank's acquisitions included the British Bank of the Middle East (founded 1889; now The Saudi British Bank) and Mercantile Bank (with offices in India and Southeast Asia). In 1965 the company bought 62% of Hang Seng, Hong Kong's #2 bank. It also added new subsidiaries, including Wayfoong (mortgage and small-business finance, 1960) and Wardley (investment banking, Hong Kong, 1972).

In the late 1970s and into the 1980s, China began opening to foreign business. The bank added operations in North America to capitalize on business between China and the US and Canada. Acquisitions included Marine Midland Bank (US, 1980), Hongkong Bank of Canada (1981), 51% of treasury securities dealer Carroll McEntee & McGinley (US, 1983), most of the assets and liabilities of the Bank of British Columbia (1986), and Lloyds Bank Canada (1990).

Following the 1984 agreement to return Hong Kong to China, Hongkong & Shanghai Bank began beefing up in the UK, buying London securities dealer James Capel & Co. (1986) and the UK's #3 bank, Midland plc (1992). In 1993 the company formed London-based HSBC Holdings and divested assets, most notably its interest in Hong Kong-based Cathay Pacific Airways.

HSBC then began expanding in Asia again, particularly in Malaysia, where its Hongkong Bank Malaysia became the country's first locally incorporated foreign bank. The company returned to China with offices in Beijing and Guangzhou. It also added new European branches.

Latin American banks acquired in 1997 were among the non-Asian operations that cushioned HSBC from the worst of 1998's economic crises. Nonetheless, The Hong Kong Monetary Authority took a stake in the bank to shore up the stock exchange and foil short-sellers.

In 1999 China's government made HSBC a loan for mainland expansion. That year the company was foiled in its attempt to buy South Korea's government-owned Seoulbank, but did buy the late Edmond Safra's Republic New York Corporation and his international bank holding company, Safra Republic Holdings (it negotiated a $450 million discount on the $10 billion deal after a Japanese probe of Republic's securities division caused delays).

The company unveiled several online initiatives in 2000, including Internet ventures with CK Hutchison Holdings and Merrill Lynch, and bought CCF (then called CrÃ‰dit Commercial de France, now HSBC France). However, HSBC's plans to buy a controlling stake in Bangkok Metropolitan Bank fell through before the year's end.

In 2001 HSBC agreed to pick up Barclays Bank's fund management operations in Greece. Later, in response to the slowing economy, it froze the salaries of 14,000 employees. Argentina's 2001 peso devaluation cost the company half a billion dollars in currency conversion losses alone. Total charges pertaining to Argentina equaled more than $1 billion that year.

HSBC expanded its consumer finance operations with the purchase of US-based Household International (now HSBC Finance) in 2003.

The next year HSBC acquired The Bank of Bermuda, as well as Marks and Spencer Financial Services (aka M&S Money), one of the UK's leading credit card issuers. It bought US credit card company Metris the following year.

HSBC's Latin American operations at this point were primarily in Argentina, Brazil, and Mexico. The company expanded its presence in Central America and the Caribbean with the 2006 purchase of Panama-based Banistmo, a banking group with offices in the Bahamas, Colombia, Costa Rica, El Salvador, Honduras, and Nicaragua.

HSBC sold its regional banking operations in France to Banque Populaire in 2008. The deal included eight banks with around 400 branches. Also that year the company canceled its proposed $6 billion acquisition of Lone Star's 51% stake in Korea Exchange Bank, a deal that had been held up for months by an investigation by the South Korean government. HSBC cited weakened asset values in the global financial markets for the cancellation.

Beset by mortgage defaults, the group closed its Decision One US-based wholesale subprime lending unit in 2007. In 2009 it shuttered its North American consumer lending business, placing related portfolios (excluding credit cards) in run-off. To further reduce its exposure to consumer credit, it sold a $4 billion car loan portfolio and servicing platform to an affiliate of Santander USA.

The company acquired a majority stake in Indonesian lender Bank Ekonomi in 2009, doubling its presence in the nation.

In 2010 HSBC sold HSBC Insurance Brokers to Marsh & McLennan in a Â£135 million ($218 million) cash-and-stock deal. As part of the transaction, the companies entered into a strategic partnership under which Marsh markets insurance and risk management services to HSBC's corporate and private clients ahead of other providers.

In late 2011 the Financial Services Authority (the UK regulator of financial services providers) fined HSBC Â£10.3 million after it was found that salespeople at its NHFA Limited subsidiary had sold inappropriate and unsuitable five-year bonds to nearly 3,000 elderly customers. HSBC, which had alerted the FSA once it was made aware of the issue, closed NHFA to new business that year.

EXECUTIVES

Chief Executive Officer, Executive Director, Noel Quinn

Wealth and Personal Banking Chief Executive Officer, Nuno Matos

Commercial Banking Chief Executive Officer, Global Commercial Banking Chief Executive Officer, Barry O'Byrne

Chief Financial Officer, Executive Director, Georges Elhedery

Chief Operating Officer, John M. Hinshaw

Chief Legal Officer, Bob Hoyt

Chief Human Resources Officer, Elaine Arden

Chief Communications Officer & Brand Officer, Steve John
Chief Sustainability Officer, Celine Herweijer
Chief Risk and Compliance Officer, Pam Kaur
Chief Governance Officer, Secretary, Aileen Taylor
Non-Executive Chairman, Non-Executive Director, Mark E. Tucker
Senior Independent Non-Executive Director, David Thomas Nish
Independent Non-Executive Director, Dame Carolyn Fairbairn
Independent Non-Executive Director, Rachel Duan
Independent Non-Executive Director, Geraldine Buckingham
Independent Non-Executive Director, James A. Forese
Independent Non-Executive Director, Steven Guggenheimer
Independent Non-Executive Director, Jose Antonio Meade Kuribrena
Independent Non-Executive Director, Eileen K. Murray
Independent Non-Executive Director, Jackson Pei Tai
Auditors : PricewaterhouseCoopers LLP

LOCATIONS

HQ: HSBC Holdings Plc
8 Canada Square, London E14 5HQ
Phone: (44) 20 7991 8888 **Fax:** (44) 20 7992 4880
Web: www.hsbc.com

2018 income

	% of total
Asia	49
Europe	30
North America	11
Latin America	5
MENA	5
Total	100

PRODUCTS/OPERATIONS

2018 Sales by Segment

	% of total
Retail banking & wealth management	40
Global banking & markets	29
Commercial banking	28
Global private banking	3
Total	100

Selected Subsidiaries

Hang Seng Bank Limited (62%, Hong Kong)
The Hong Kong and Shanghai Banking Corporation Limited
HSBC Asset Finance (UK) Ltd.
HSBC Bank Argentina S.A. (99.9%)
HSBC Bank A.S. (Turkey)
HSBC Bank Australia Limited
HSBC Bank Bermuda Limited
HSBC Bank Brasil S.A. - Banco Múltiplo
HSBC Bank Canada
HSBC Bank (China) Company Limited
HSBC Bank Egypt S.A.E. (95%)
HSBC Bank International Limited (Jersey)
HSBC Bank Malaysia Berhad
HSBC Bank Malta p.l.c. (70%)
HSBC Bank Middle East Limited
HSBC Bank (Panama) S.A.
HSBC Bank plc
HSBC Bank USA, N.A.
HSBC Finance Corporation (US)
HSBC France
HSBC Mexico S.A., Institución de Banca Múltiplo, Grupo Financiero HSBC (99.9%)
HSBC Private Banking Holdings (Suisse) S.A. (Switzerland)
HSBC Securities (USA) Inc.
HSBC Trinkaus & Burkhardt AG (80%, Germany)
Marks and Spencer Retail Financial Services Holdings Limited

COMPETITORS

AVIVA PLC
COMMONWEALTH BANK OF AUSTRALIA
CONCORDIA FINANCIAL GROUP, LTD.
Dexia
NATIONAL AUSTRALIA BANK LIMITED
NOMURA HOLDINGS, INC.
PRUDENTIAL PUBLIC LIMITED COMPANY
RSA INSURANCE GROUP PLC
STANDARD CHARTERED PLC
Street Capital Group Inc

HISTORICAL FINANCIALS

Company Type: Public

Income Statement   FYE: December 31

	ASSETS ($mil)	NET INCOME ($mil)	INCOME AS % OF ASSETS	EMPLOYEES
12/23	3,038,680	23,533	0.8%	220,861
12/22	2,966,530	16,035	0.5%	219,000
12/21	2,957,940	13,910	0.5%	219,697
12/20	2,984,160	5,139	0.2%	226,059
12/19	2,715,150	7,293	0.3%	235,351
Annual Growth	2.9%	34.0%	—	(1.6%)

2023 Year-End Financials

Return on assets: 0.7%
Return on equity: 12.6%
Long-term debt ($ mil.): —
No. of shares ($ mil.): 19,262
Sales ($ mil.): 134,708
Dividends
Yield: —
Payout: 230.7%
Market value ($ mil.): 780,911

	STOCK PRICE ($) FY Close	P/E High/Low		PER SHARE ($) Earnings	Dividends	Book Value
12/23	40.54	37	28	1.14	2.63	9.62
12/22	31.16	51	33	0.74	1.34	9.39
12/21	30.15	52	40	0.62	1.09	9.76
12/20	25.91	207	95	0.19	1.50	9.64
12/19	39.09	149	118	0.30	2.55	9.06
Annual Growth	0.9%	—	—	39.6%	0.8%	1.5%

Huaneng Power International Inc

Huaneng Power International is one of China's largest independent power producers. Its nearly 50 power plants in about 20 provinces have a capacity of more than 66,700 MW; nearly all of the company's power is produced from coal. Huaneng Power International, which is always expanding, also owns Singapore's electricity retailer Tuas Power. Huaneng Power International sells power to local utilities, primarily in China's coastal provinces. Huaneng International Power Development Corporation, a subsidiary of the China Huaneng Group, owns 36% of Huaneng Power International; China Huaneng Group, 16%. Huaneng Power International was formed in 1994.

EXECUTIVES

Deputy General Manager, General Manager, Vice President, Deputy Party Secretary, Director, Ping Zhao
Deputy General Manager, Vice President, Zhiyi Song
Deputy General Manager, Vice President, Jianmin Li
Deputy General Manager, Vice President, Ranxing Liu
Chief Accounting Officer, Accountant General, Lixin Huang
Secretary, Deputy General Manager, Chaoquan Huang
Vice President, Secretary, Deputy General Manager, Biquan Gu
Chief Accounting Officer, Deputy General Manager, Hui Zhou
Supervisor, Jianguo Gu
Supervisory Committee Vice Chairman, Xuan Mu
Staff Supervisor, Xiaojun Zhang
Staff Supervisor, Daqing Zhu
Deputy General Manager, Shuping Chen
General Engineer, Wei Liu
Supervisory Committee Chairman, Shuqing Li
Supervisor, Cai Ye
Staff Supervisor, Tong Zhu
Supervisor, Aidong Xia
Honorary Chairman, Chairman, Yinbiao Shu
Independent Director, Independent Non-executive Director, Mengzhou Xu
Independent Director, Independent Non-executive Director, Jizhen Liu
Independent Director, Independent Non-executive Director, Haifeng Xu
Independent Director, Independent Non-executive Director, Xianzhi Zhang
Director, Non-executive Director, Jian Huang
Director, Non-executive Director, Dabin Mi
Independent Director, Independent Non-executive Director, Qing Xia
Director, Non-executive Director, Chong Lin
Director, Non-executive Director, Heng Cheng
Chairman, Keyu Zhao
Director, Fei Lu
Director, Yu Teng
Director, Kui Wang
Director, Haifeng Li
Auditors : KPMG Huazhen LLP

LOCATIONS

HQ: Huaneng Power International Inc
Huaneng Building, 6 Fuxingmennei Street, Xicheng District, Beijing 100031
Phone: (86) 10 6322 6999 **Fax:** (86) 10 6322 6888
Web: www.hpi.com.cn

2013 Sales

	% of total
PRC power	89
Singapore	11
Total	100

COMPETITORS

CHINA POWER INTERNATIONAL DEVELOPMENT LIMITED
Huadian Power International Corporation Limited
INTERNATIONAL POWER LTD.
Korea Electric Power Gongsa (Naju)
TAIWAN POWER COMPANY

HISTORICAL FINANCIALS
Company Type: Public

Income Statement — FYE: December 31

	REVENUE ($mil)	NET INCOME ($mil)	NET PROFIT MARGIN	EMPLOYEES
12/22	35,764	(1,070)	—	0
12/21	32,228	(1,616)	—	0
12/20	25,907	697	2.7%	0
12/19	24,932	242	1.0%	0
12/18	24,695	209	0.8%	57,960
Annual Growth	9.7%	—	—	—

2022 Year-End Financials
Debt ratio: 8.5%
Return on equity: (-6.9%)
Cash ($ mil.): 2,489
Current Ratio: 0.51
Long-term debt ($ mil.): 27,648
No. of shares ($ mil.): —
Dividends
  Yield: —
  Payout: 0.0%
Market value ($ mil.): —

Hyakugo Bank Ltd. (Japan)

Serving its primary business base in the Mie Prefecture, Hyakugo Bank is a Japanese regional bank offering traditional banking services such as electronic, corporate, and consumer banking, as well as international and securities offerings. Hyakugo Bank serves its products through more than 100 branches and 26 sub-branches and also owns foreign offices in Singapore and Shanghai. Listed subsidiaries include Hyakugo Business Service Company, Hyakugo Staff Service Company, and Hyakugo Property Research Company. The bank goes all the way back to 1878, when it was established as The 105th National Chartered Bank.

EXECUTIVES

Chairman, Director, Toshiyasu Ito
President, Representative Director, Masakazu Sugiura
Senior Managing Executive Officer, Representative Director, Kei Yamazaki
Director, Satoru Fujiwara
Director, Masami Nanbu
Director, Tetsuya Kato
Outside Director, Nagahisa Kobayashi
Outside Director, Hisashi Kawakita
Outside Director, Keiko Nishioka
Outside Director, Atsushi Nakamura
Auditors : KPMG AZSA LLC

LOCATIONS

HQ: Hyakugo Bank Ltd. (Japan)
21-27 Iwata, Tsu, Mie 514-8666
Phone: (81) 59 227 2151
Web: www.hyakugo.co.jp

COMPETITORS

FIRST INTERNATIONAL BANK OF ISRAEL LTD
IYO BANK, LTD., THE
MICHINOKU BANK, LTD., THE
NANTO BANK,LTD., THE
TAIWAN BUSINESS BANK, LTD.

HISTORICAL FINANCIALS
Company Type: Public

Income Statement — FYE: March 31

	ASSETS ($mil)	NET INCOME ($mil)	INCOME AS % OF ASSETS	EMPLOYEES
03/22	63,700	110	0.2%	4,104
03/21	67,309	117	0.2%	4,185
03/20	59,303	105	0.2%	4,194
03/19	56,574	97	0.2%	4,238
03/18	54,072	110	0.2%	4,231
Annual Growth	4.2%	0.0%	—	(0.8%)

2022 Year-End Financials
Return on assets: 0.1%
Return on equity: 3.3%
Long-term debt ($ mil.): —
No. of shares ($ mil.): 253
Sales ($ mil.): 811
Dividends
  Yield: —
  Payout: 20.8%
Market value ($ mil.): —

Hyakujushi Bank, Ltd.

Businesses and individuals who say "Hi" to Hyakujushi Bank might find themselves saying " Hai " (yes) to the institution's banking and financial services offerings. One of Japan's regional banks, Hyakujushi Bank serves the Kagawa prefecture and about 10 other nearby prefectures through some 120 banking offices and a network of about 300 ATMs. (Most of the bank's loans originate outside its home base.) Hyakujushi Bank also has operations in Tokyo and Osaka. Hyakujushi Bank offers a variety of traditional banking services, including deposit banking and lending.

EXECUTIVES

President, Representative Director, Yujiro Ayada
Deputy President, Chief Compliance Officer, Representative Director, Ryohei Kagawa
Senior Managing Executive Officer, Representative Director, Kiichiro Oyama
Senior Managing Executive Officer, Kazuo Shiratori
Director, Masakazu Toyoshima
Director, Hiroyuki Kurokawa
Director, Hideaki Kanamoto
Director, Kazuhiro Tada
Director, Masashi Mori
Director, Toshiya Yoritomi
Director, Kazuhiro Kumihashi
Outside Director, Junichi Itoh
Outside Director, Yasuko Yamada

Outside Director, Nobuyuki Souda
Outside Director, Tomoko Fujimoto
Outside Director, Noriyuki Konishi
Auditors : Ernst & Young ShinNihon LLC

LOCATIONS

HQ: Hyakujushi Bank, Ltd.
5-1 Kamei-cho, Takamatsu, Kagawa 760-8574
Phone: (81) 87 831 0114
Web: www.114bank.co.jp

COMPETITORS

BANGKOK BANK PUBLIC COMPANY LIMITED
Bank Of Shanghai Co., Ltd.
HANG SENG BANK, LIMITED
KUMAMOTO BANK, LTD., THE
NISHI-NIPPON CITYBANK,LTD.

HISTORICAL FINANCIALS
Company Type: Public

Income Statement — FYE: March 31

	ASSETS ($mil)	NET INCOME ($mil)	INCOME AS % OF ASSETS	EMPLOYEES
03/22	47,249	96	0.2%	2,798
03/21	48,549	23	—	2,891
03/20	45,637	71	0.2%	2,978
03/19	44,206	50	0.1%	3,050
03/18	44,987	96	0.2%	3,164
Annual Growth	1.2%	0.0%	—	(3.0%)

2022 Year-End Financials
Return on assets: 0.2%
Return on equity: 4.0%
Long-term debt ($ mil.): —
No. of shares ($ mil.): 29
Sales ($ mil.): 601
Dividends
  Yield: —
  Payout: 17.6%
Market value ($ mil.): —

Hydro-Quebec

Hydro-Quebec has about 226,950 km of distribution lines and distributes electricity to approximately 4 million residential and commercial customers in Quebec. It generates about 37,250 MW of capacity from over 85 plants (including around 60 hydroelectric and nearly 25 thermal). Almost all of the company's power generation in 2021 came from renewable sources. The operator of one of North America's largest transmission networks (some 34,775 km), Hydro-Quebec also sells wholesale energy in the US and Canada.

Operations

The company has four divisions: Distribution (about 50% of sales), Generation (nearly 30%), Transmission (about 15%), and Construction (around 10%).

The Distribution segment includes activities related to the operation and development of Hydro-QuÃ©bec's distribution grid. It also includes retail electricity sales on the QuÃ©bec market, as well as customer services and the promotion of energy efficiency.

The Generation segment includes activities related to the operation and development of Hydro-QuÃ©bec's generating facilities, except in off-grid systems. It also includes electricity sales and arbitrage transactions on wholesale markets in northeastern North America.

The Transmission segment includes activities related to the operation and development of the main power transmission system, the marketing of system capacity and the management of power flows across Québec.

The Construction segment includes activities related to the design and execution of construction and refurbishment projects involving mainly power generation and transmission facilities.

Geographic Reach
Headquartered in Quebec, Canada, Hydro-Quebec Production operates in each of Quebec's over 15 administrative regions. It also serves wholesale customers in Canada and the US.

Sales and Marketing
Hydro-Québec grid delivers reliable electricity to over four million Québec customers and exports huge amounts of power to wholesale markets in the northeastern US and neighboring Canadian provinces.

Financial Performance
Revenue totaled C$14.5 billion, compared to C$13.6 billion a year earlier. This increase is due to a rise in net electricity sales in Québec, a surge in net electricity exports, a positive variance in the amounts recognized as other components of employee future benefit cost related to the Pension Plan and a reduction in financial expenses.

In 2021, the company had a net income of C$3.6 billion, a 55% increase from the previous year's net income of C$2.3 billion. The C$1.3 billion increase is due to unprecedented overall sales, a positive variance in the amounts recognized as other components of employee future benefit cost for the Pension Plan and a reduction in financial expenses.

The company's cash at the end of 2021 was C$1.3 billion. Operating activities generated C$5.1 billion, while investing activities used C$4.6 billion, mainly for additions to property, plant and equipment. Financing activities used another C$647 million, primarily for cash payments arising from credit risk management.

Strategy
In 2021, the company continued to strengthen its supply chain while increasing its strategic material stocks. The company attained these goals through different means, including weekly monitoring of at-risk items, placing orders months in advance, securing and boosting stock coverage, and optimizing its planning for equipment needs.

Mergers and Acquisitions
In late 2021, Innergex Renewable Energy Inc., and HQI US Holding LLC, a subsidiary of Hydro-Québec are pleased to announce the completion of the previously disclosed 50-50 joint acquisition of the 60 MW Curtis Palmer hydroelectric portfolio in the state of New York, for a total consideration of US$318.4 million ($393.4 million). The Facilities consists of two run-of-river hydroelectric facilities, Curtis Mills (12 MW) and Palmer Falls (48 MW). Curtis Palmer has a power purchase agreement for energy, RECs and capacity with Niagara Mohawk Power Corporation.

Company Background
In 2012 Hydro-Québec teamed up with Plug'nDrive Ontario to develop an electric vehicle public charging infrastructure offering cross-border charging stations in Québec and Ontario.

Under a 2010 energy agreement between the provinces of New Brunswick and Québec, Hydro-Québec acquired NB Power's generation assets (including seven hydroelectric power plants and two diesel peaking units) for $1.8 billion. In return, Hydro-Québec agreed to provide NB Power with an annual supply of 14 TWh of power under a long-term contract.

Hydro-Québec was formed in 1944 and is owned by the government of Québec.

EXECUTIVES

President, Chief Executive Officer, Director, Thierry Vandal
Corporate Affairs Executive Vice President, Corporate Affairs Secretary, Marie-Jose Nadeau
Technology Executive Vice President, Elie Saheb
Treasury & Pension Fund Vice President, Finance Vice President, Jean-Hugues Lafleur
Control Vice President, Accounting Vice President, Lise Croteau
Human Resources Vice President, Bruno Gingras
Chairman, Michael L. Turcotte
Director, Robert Sauve
Director, Gaston Blackburn
Director, Anik Brochu
Director, Carl Cassista
Director, Michelle Cormier
Director, Suzanne Gouin
Director, Isabelle Hudon
Director, Louis Lagasse
Director, Jacques Leblanc
Director, Michel Plessis-Belair
Director, Marie-France Poulin
Director, Martine Rioux
Director, Marie-Anne Tawil
Director, Emmanuel Triassi
Auditors : KPMG LLP

LOCATIONS
HQ: Hydro-Quebec
75, boulevard Rene-Levesque Quest, 20e Etage, Montreal, Quebec H2Z 1A4
Phone: 514 289-2211
Web: www.hydroquebec.com

PRODUCTS/OPERATIONS
2015 sales
	% of total
Distribution	86
Generation	13
Transmission	1
Corporate and Other Activities	-
Total	100

Selected Subsidiaries, Divisions, and Affiliates
Hydro-Québec Distribution (electricity distribution)
Hydro-Québec Equipment (engineering and construction)
   Société d'énergie de la Baie James (SEBJ, engineering and construction)
Hydro-Québec Production (electricity generation)
   Churchill Falls (Labrador) Corporation Limited (34%)
   Gestion Production HQ Inc.
   HQ Energy Marketing Inc. (energy trading and marketing)
   Bucksport Energy LLC (69%)
   HQ Energy Services (U.S.) Inc. (HQUS)
Hydro-Québec TransÉnergie (electricity transmission)
   Cedars Rapids Transmission Company, Limited
Hydro-Québec Technologie et Dévelopment Industriel (research and technology)
   Hydro-Québec CapiTech (venture capital investments)
   Institut de recherche d'Hydro-Québec (IREQ)

COMPETITORS
CITY OF AUSTIN
Centrais Eletricas Brasileiras S/A
ENERGY RESOURCES, CONSERVATION AND DEVELOPMENT COMMISSION
Hydro One Inc
NATIONAL POWER CORPORATION
NSTAR LLC
SOUTHWESTERN POWER ADMINISTRATION
TRI-STATE GENERATION AND TRANSMISSION ASSOCIATION, INC.
UNITED STATES DEPT OF ENERGY
WESTERN AREA POWER ADMINISTRATION

HISTORICAL FINANCIALS
Company Type: Public

Income Statement				FYE: December 31
	REVENUE ($mil)	NET INCOME ($mil)	NET PROFIT MARGIN	EMPLOYEES
12/21	11,405	2,798	24.5%	21,168
12/20	10,676	1,808	16.9%	20,011
12/19	10,767	2,244	20.8%	19,477
12/18	10,552	2,343	22.2%	19,904
12/17	10,743	2,270	21.1%	19,786
Annual Growth	1.5%	5.4%	—	1.7%

2021 Year-End Financials
Debt ratio: 47.2%
Return on equity: 15.9%
Cash ($ mil.): 1,018
Current Ratio: 0.57
Long-term debt ($ mil.): 36,470
No. of shares ($ mil.): 43
Dividends
  Yield: —
  Payout: 0.0%
Market value ($ mil.): —

Hyundai Motor Co., Ltd.

South Korea's leading carmaker, Hyundai Motor produces compact and luxury cars, SUVs, minivans, trucks, buses, and other commercial vehicles. Its cars are sold in 200 countries and produces more than 4.4 million units. Hyundai generates more than one-third of its sales each in South Korea and North America. The company manufactures and distributes motor vehicles and parts, operate vehicle financing and credit card processing, and manufacture trains. The company was founded in 1967.

Operations

The company has vehicle segment, finance segment and others segment. The vehicle segment is engaged in the manufacturing and sale of motor vehicles. The finance segment operates vehicle financing, credit card processing and other financing activities. Others segment includes the R&D, train manufacturing and other activities.

The Vehicle segment generated some 80% of sales, Finance segment with about 15%, and Others with the rest of sales. In addition, sale of goods generated some 85% of sales.

Geographic Reach

Headquartered in Seoul, South Korea. Hyundai's geographic areas are in Asia (excluding South Korea), North America, and Europe. South Korea generates some 35% of total sales while North America brings in soem 35 of total sales also, Europe gives about 20% of total sales, and Asia and other countries generates over 10% of total sales combined.

Financial Performance

The company reported a total revenue of KRW 117.6 trillion in 2021, a 13% increase from the previous year's total revenue of KRW 104 trillion.

In 2021, the company had a net income of KRW 5.7 billion, a 196% increase from the previous year's KRW 1.9 billion.

The company's cash at the end of 2021 was KRW 12.8 trillion. Financing activities generated KRW 8.8 trillion, while operating activities used KRW 1.2 trillion. Investing activities used another KRW 5.2 trillion, primarily for acquisitions of property, plant and equipment.

HISTORY

Hyundai Motor Company was established in 1967, and it initially began manufacturing cars and light trucks through a technology collaboration with Ford's UK operations. By the early 1970s Hyundai was ready to build cars under its own nameplate. The company debuted the subcompact Hyundai Pony in 1974 at Italy's annual Turin Motor Show.

The Pony was an instant domestic success and soon propelled Hyundai to the top spot among South Korea's carmakers. During the mid-1970s the company began exporting the Pony to El Salvador and Guatemala.

By the 1980s Hyundai was ready to shift into high gear and begin high-volume production in anticipation of penetrating more overseas markets. The company began exporting to Canada in 1983.

Hyundai introduced the Hyundai Excel in 1985. That year the company established its US subsidiary, Hyundai Motor America. By 1986 Hyundai was exporting Excels for sale in the US. Sales of the Excel soared the next year, so Hyundai decided to build a factory in Bromont, Quebec.

But by the time the factory was finished in 1989, consumers were tiring of the aging compact car and the quality problems that came with it. Hyundai closed the plant after just four years of operation.

The company introduced its first sports car, the Scoupe, in 1990. The following year it developed the first Hyundai-designed engine, called the Alpha. Two years later the carmaker unveiled its second-generation proprietary engine, the Beta.

By 1998 Hyundai was beginning to feel the pinch of the Asian economic crisis as domestic demand dropped drastically. However, the decrease in Korean demand was largely offset by exports. That year Hyundai took a controlling stake in Korean competitor Kia Motors.

In hopes of increasing its share of the Asian automotive market, Daimler AG took a 10% stake in Hyundai in 2000 (sold 2004). The deal included the establishment of a joint venture to manufacture commercial vehicles, as well as an agreement among Hyundai, Daimler, and Mitsubishi Motors to develop small cars for the global market.

In 2001 Hyundai decreased its stake in Kia Motors to about 46%.

The following year Daimler announced it would exercise its option to take a 50% stake in Hyundai's heavy truck business.

In 2004 Hyundai CEO Kim Dong-Jin was indicted in South Korea on charges that he violated campaign finance laws and engaged in managerial negligence. The charges stemmed from a general crackdown on campaign finance violations, during which more than a dozen members of South Korea's parliament were either indicted or detained. Later in 2004 Kim was convicted of the charges against him and sentenced to a suspended two-year prison term.

To increase its presence in the US, Hyundai completed construction of a new manufacturing plant, Hyundai Motor Manufacturing Alabama, in 2005. The plant's annual production was about 300,000 cars.

In 2006 Hyundai's legal woes persisted when two executives were arrested as part of a Korean bribery investigation. The pair were accused of creating a slush fund that was allegedly used to fund a lobbyist who sought favors for Hyundai from the South Korean government. Officials were also investigating whether the slush fund was created at the behest of Hyundai chairman Chung Mong-Koo.

Chung then was indicted and arrested on charges that he embezzled Hyundai company cash to finance bribes for Korean government officials in exchange for corporate favors. After two months of incarceration, Chung was released from jail on $1 million bail.

He was convicted early in 2007. Under Korean law, Chung faced a potential life sentence, but received only a three-year prison term as the judge in the case said Chung contributed hugely to the development of the Korean economy. During his trial Chung admitted some wrongdoing when he said "I admit to my guilt, to some extent." However, Chung appealed the conviction. Three other Hyundai officials were also convicted, but they received suspended sentences. Chung's son, Kia Motors boss Chung Eui-Sun, also was under investigation, but prosecutors did not indict him.

Later in 2007 Chung's three-year prison sentence was suspended by an appeals court, with a three-judge panel citing his importance to Korea's economy. The appellate judges, however, required the Hyundai executive to maintain a clean record for five years to avoid prison and to fulfill a promise he made to donate $1.1 billion of his personal assets to society.

EXECUTIVES

Chairman, Eui Sun Chung
President, Chief Executive Officer, Director, Won Hee Lee
President, Director, Albert Biermann
President, Director, Eon Tae Ha
Senior Vice President, Director, Sang-Hyun Kim
Independent Director, Eun Soo Choi
Independent Director, Dong Kyu Lee
Independent Director, Byung Kook Lee
Independent Director, Chi-Won Yoon
Independent Director, Eugene M. Ohr
Independent Director, Sang-Seung Yi
Auditors : KPMG Samjong Accounting Corp.

LOCATIONS

HQ: Hyundai Motor Co., Ltd.
12, Heolleung-ro, Seocho-gu, Seoul 06797
Phone: (82) 2 3464 1114 **Fax:** (82) 2 3463 3484
Web: www.hyundai-motor.com

2018 Sales

	% of total
South Korea	16
Overseas	84
Total	100

PRODUCTS/OPERATIONS

Selected Models
Commercial vehicles
    Aero (large city bus)
    Aero Town (medium bus)
    County (small bus)
    e-Mighty (light commercial truck)
    Super Aero City (bus)
    Universe (large coach bus)
Passenger cars
    Accent (compact coupe)
    Atos Prime (subcompact)
    Avante XD
    Azera (sedan)
    Elantra (sedan)
    Entourage (minivan)

Equus/Centennial (premium sedan)
Genesis (premium coupe)
Getz (compact sedan)
Santa Fe (SUV)
Sonata (sedan)
Tiburon (coupe)
Tucson (SUV)
Trajet (SUV)
Veracruz (SUV)

COMPETITORS

ALLISON TRANSMISSION HOLDINGS, INC.
AUTOLIV, INC.
Bayerische Motoren Werke AG
FCA US LLC
G N U INC
Kia Motors Corporation
LEAR CORPORATION
MOTORCAR PARTS OF AMERICA, INC.
Magna International Inc
SUBARU CORPORATION

HISTORICAL FINANCIALS

Company Type: Public

Income Statement — FYE: December 31

	REVENUE ($mil)	NET INCOME ($mil)	NET PROFIT MARGIN	EMPLOYEES
12/21	98,991	4,159	4.2%	0
12/20	95,557	1,308	1.4%	0
12/19	91,585	2,580	2.8%	0
12/18	86,836	1,352	1.6%	0
12/17	90,399	3,782	4.2%	68,590
Annual Growth	2.3%	2.4%	—	—

2021 Year-End Financials

Debt ratio: —
Return on equity: 6.8%
Cash ($ mil.): 10,769
Current Ratio: 1.38
Long-term debt ($ mil.): 62,391
No. of shares ($ mil.): 199
Dividends
Yield: —
Payout: 5.2%
Market value ($ mil.): —

IA Financial Corp Inc

Industrial Alliance Insurance and Financial Services (iA Financial Group) is one of the largest insurance and wealth management groups in Canada, with operations in the US. The group sells life, health, and disability insurance, as well as retirement savings plans and annuities, to individuals and employers across the country. To a much lesser extent, it offers life insurance products in parts of the US. The group manages mutual funds through its IA Clarington unit, and it brokers securities and funds through Investia, FundEX Investments, and iA Securities. iA Financial Group also sells auto and homeowners insurance. Its products are distributed by more than 50,000 representatives.

Operations

The group offer its products and services through Individual Wealth Management, Group Savings and Retirement, Individual Insurance, Group Insurance, US Operations and Other.

Individual Wealth Management offer individual products and services for savings plans, retirement funds and segregated funds, in addition to securities brokerage, trust operations and mutual funds. It accounts for more than 45% of total revenue.

Group Savings and Retirement offers group products and services for savings plans, retirement funds and segregated funds. It generates nearly 20% of total revenue.

Individual Insurance (roughly 15%) offer life, health, disability and mortgage insurance products.

Group Insurance (more than 10%) offers Life, health, accidental death and dismemberment, dental care and short and long-term disability insurance products for employee plans; creditor insurance, replacement insurance, replacement warranties, extended warranties and other ancillary products for dealer services; and specialized products for special markets.

The US Operations accounts for about 10% of total revenue and includes miscellaneous insurance products sold in the US such as life insurance products and extended warranties relating to dealer services.

Other include auto and home insurance products, services supporting the activities that have no link with key segments such as asset management and financing, company capital and some adjustments related to consolidation.

Overall, net premiums accounts for about 15% of total revenue, while investment income and other revenue account for the rest.

Geographic Reach

The group primarily operates in Canada and the US.

Sales and Marketing

Its products and services are offered to retail customers, businesses and groups.

Financial Performance

The group's revenue for fiscal 2021 increased to $15.5 billion compared from the prior year with $17.6 billion.

Net income for fiscal 2021 increased to $852 million compared from the prior year with $633 million.

Cash held by the group at the end of fiscal 2021 decreased to $1.5 billion. Cash provided by operations was $185 million while cash used for investing and financing activities were $294 million and $294 million, respectively. Main cash uses were for purchases of fixed and intangible assets and dividends paid on common shares.

Strategy

The group develops and sponsors mutual funds to implement investment strategies on behalf of investors, and earns management fees for providing these services.

EXECUTIVES

Executive Vice President, Chief Financial Officer, Chief Actuary, Jacques Potvin
President, Chief Executive Officer, Director, Yvon Charest
Executive Vice President, Normand Pepin
Investments Executive Vice President, Michel Tremblay
Senior Vice President, Chief Actuary, Rene Chabot
Sales Senior Vice President, Administration Senior Vice President, Bruno Michaud
Investor Relations Senior Vice President, Jacques Carriere
Business Development President, Business Development Chief Executive Officer, Business Development Senior Vice President, Denis Ricard
Human Resources Vice President, Jean-Francois Boulet
Legal Vice President, Legal Corporate Secretary, Douglas A. Carrothers
Information Systems Vice President, Guy Daneau
Internal Audit Vice President, Maurice Germain
Development Financial Services Vice President, Yvon Sauvageau
Assistant Secretary, Jennifer Dibblee
Assistant Secretary, France Beaudry
Chairman, John LeBoutillier
Director, Anne Belec
Director, Pierre Brodeur
Director, Robert Coallier
Director, L. G. Serge Gadbois
Director, Michel Gervais
Director, Lise Lachapelle
Director, Claude Lamoureux
Director, Francis P. McGuire
Director, Jim Pantelidis
Director, David R. Peterson
Director, Mary C. Ritchie
Auditors : Deloitte LLP

LOCATIONS

HQ: IA Financial Corp Inc
1080, Grande Allee West, P.O. 1907 Station Terminus, Quebec City, Quebec G1K 7M3
Phone: 418 684-5000 **Fax:** 418 684-5185
Web: www.ia.ca

PRODUCTS/OPERATIONS

2017 Sales by Segment

	% of total
Individual Insurance	36
Individual Wealth Management	30
Group Savings and Retirement	16
Group Insurance	15
Other	3
Total	100

Selected Subsidiaries

FundEX Investments Inc. (mutual fund broker)
IA American Life Insurance Company (US)
IA Clarington Investments Inc. (mutual fund management and promotion)
Investia Financial Services Inc. (mutual fund broker)
Solicour Inc. (financial services brokerage)
The Excellence Life Insurance Company (life and health insurance)

COMPETITORS

AMERICAN NATIONAL INSURANCE COMPANY
CINCINNATI FINANCIAL CORPORATION
China Pacific Insurance (Group) Co., Ltd.
MASSACHUSETTS MUTUAL LIFE INSURANCE COMPANY

NATIONAL GENERAL HOLDINGS CORP.
OHIO NATIONAL MUTUAL HOLDINGS, INC.
PRINCIPAL FINANCIAL GROUP, INC.
SECURIAN FINANCIAL GROUP, INC.
STANCORP FINANCIAL GROUP, INC.
SYMETRA FINANCIAL CORPORATION

HISTORICAL FINANCIALS
Company Type: Public

Income Statement — FYE: December 31

	ASSETS ($mil)	NET INCOME ($mil)	INCOME AS % OF ASSETS	EMPLOYEES
12/23	70,803	595	0.8%	0
12/22	64,643	622	1.0%	0
12/21	74,321	668	0.9%	0
12/20	67,909	497	0.7%	0
12/19	56,173	544	1.0%	6,800
Annual Growth	6.0%	2.3%	—	—

2023 Year-End Financials
Return on assets: 0.8%
Return on equity: 11.1%
Long-term debt ($ mil.): —
No. of shares ($ mil.): 99
Sales ($ mil.): 10,883
Dividends
 Yield: —
 Payout: 39.7%
Market value ($ mil.): 6,875

	STOCK PRICE ($) FY Close	P/E High/Low		PER SHARE ($) Earnings	Dividends	Book Value
12/23	69.00	9	8	5.64	2.24	53.29
12/22	56.91	8	6	5.66	1.92	50.39
12/21	56.86	8	5	6.05	1.63	52.89
12/20	46.16	10	5	4.48	1.52	47.78
12/19	32.01	5	5	4.91	1.36	44.01
Annual Growth	21.2%	—	—	3.5%	13.4%	4.9%

Iberdrola SA

EXECUTIVES

Chief Executive Officer, Executive Chairman, Jose Ignacio Sanchez Galan
Chief Financial Officer, Jose Sainz Armada
Internal Audit Managing Director, Sonsoles Rubio Reinoso
Legal Managing Director, Santiago Martinez Garrido
Business Managing Director, Armando Martinez Martinez
Purchasing & Insurance Managing Director, Asis Canales Abaitua
Renewable Energy Business Managing Director, Xabier Viteri Solaun
Liberalised Business Managing Director, Aitor Moso Raigoso
Control Managing Director, Risk Management Managing Director, Juan Carlos Rebollo Liceaga
Corporate Development Managing Director, Pedro Azagra Blazquez
Compliance Director, Maria Dolores Herrera Pereda
Networks Business Director, Elena Leon Munoz
Vice-Chairman, Lead Independent Director, Juan Manuel Gonzalez Serna
Independent Director, Maria Elena Antolin Raybaud
Independent Director, Jose Walfredo Fernandez
Independent Director, Manuel Moreu Munaiz
Independent Director, Xabier Sagredo Ormaza
Independent Director, Anthony L. Gardner
Independent Director, Sara de la Rica Goiricelaya
Independent Director, Nicola Mary Brewer
Independent Director, Regina Helena Jorge Nunes
Independent Director, Angel Jesus Acebes Paniagua
Independent Director, Maria Angeles Alcala Diaz
Independent Director, Isabel Garcia Tejerina
Other External Director, Inigo Victor de Oriol Ibarra
Other External Director, Francisco Martinez Corcoles
Other External Director, Samantha Barber
Auditors: KPMG Auditores, S.L.

LOCATIONS
HQ: Iberdrola SA
 Plaza Euskadi 5, Bilbao, Biscay 48009
Phone: (34) 944 151 411   **Fax:** (34) 944 663 194
Web: www.iberdrola.com

HISTORICAL FINANCIALS
Company Type: Public

Income Statement — FYE: December 31

	REVENUE ($mil)	NET INCOME ($mil)	NET PROFIT MARGIN	EMPLOYEES
12/22	57,619	4,634	8.0%	40,090
12/21	44,271	4,397	9.9%	38,702
12/20	40,678	4,431	10.9%	35,637
12/19	40,911	3,824	9.3%	34,306
12/18	40,168	3,451	8.6%	34,078
Annual Growth	9.4%	7.6%	—	4.1%

2022 Year-End Financials
Debt ratio: 37.1%
Return on equity: 10.6%
Cash ($ mil.): 4,921
Current Ratio: 0.81
Long-term debt ($ mil.): 42,528
No. of shares ($ mil.): 6,297
Dividends
 Yield: —
 Payout: 218.8%
Market value ($ mil.): 294,478

	STOCK PRICE ($) FY Close	P/E High/Low		PER SHARE ($) Earnings	Dividends	Book Value
12/22	46.76	76	59	0.69	1.50	6.97
12/21	47.21	98	68	0.65	1.55	7.29
12/20	57.50	105	70	0.67	1.45	6.94
12/19	41.31	82	59	0.59	1.23	6.65
12/18	32.09	69	56	0.53	1.22	6.86
Annual Growth	9.9%	—	—	6.5%	5.3%	0.4%

ICICI Bank Ltd (India)

ICICI Bank is a diversified financial services group offering a wide range of banking and financial services to corporate and retail customers through a variety of delivery channels, including bank branches, ATMs, call centers, internet and mobile phones. The bank has a network of about 5,420 branches and some 13,625 ATMs in India. Apart from banking products and services, the bank offers life and general insurance, asset management, securities broking, and private equity products and services through its specialized subsidiaries and affiliates. ICICI also offers agricultural and rural banking products. It earns interest and fee income from its commercial banking operations. ICICI generates the majority of its revenue from domestic operations.

Operations
ICICI operates three core business segments: retail banking, wholesale banking and treasury.

Retail Banking (30% of revenue) includes income from credit cards, debit cards, third party product distribution and the associated costs.

Wholesale Banking (30% of revenue) includes all advances to trusts, partnership firms, companies and statutory bodies, by the bank which are not included under Retail banking.

Treasury (40% of revenue) includes the entire investment and derivative portfolio of the Bank and ICICI Strategic Investments Fund.

Key subsidiaries include ICICI Prudential Life Insurance (the largest private sector life insurer in the country), ICICI Lombard General Insurance (property/casualty coverage), ICICI Prudential Asset Management (mutual funds), ICICI Securities (investment banking and brokerage), and ICICI Venture Funds Management (venture capital).

Geographic Reach
ICICI generates the majority of its total revenue in its home country. The bank has an international presence through its ICICI Bank UK and ICICI Bank Canada subsidiaries in the UK and Canada, respectively. It also has branches in China, Singapore, Dubai International Finance Centre, Hong Kong, the US (New York), South Africa and Bahrain. It has representative offices in the United Arab Emirates (Dubai, Abu Dhabi and Sharjah), Bangladesh, Nepal, Malaysia (Kuala Lumpur), US (Texas and California), Sri Lanka and Indonesia. Its subsidiary in the UK has a branch in Germany.

Sales and Marketing
The bank delivers products and services through various channels including branches, ATMs, mobile phones and the internet.

Financial Performance
Note: Growth rates may differ after conversion to US dollars.

The company reported a total revenue of INR 1 trillion, a 7% increase from the previous year's total revenue of INR 980.7 billion.

In 2021, the company had a net income of INR 233.4 billion, a 44% increase from the previous year's net income of INR 161.9 billion.

The company's cash at the end of 2021 was INR 1.7 trillion. Operating activities generated INR 550.5 billion, while investing activities used another INR 350.4 billion, mainly for purchase of held-to-maturity securities. Financing activities provided another INR 148.7 billion.

Strategy

The bank's strategic focus in fiscal 2022 continued to be on growth in core operating profit within the guardrails of risk and compliance. The bank's core operating profit grew by 22% during fiscal 2022 to INR 383.47 billion, through the focused pursuit of target market segments. The domestic loan portfolio grew by 18% year-on-year to INR 8.2 trillion. The bank grew its business with a focus on granularity and saw healthy growth across retail, small and medium enterprise and business banking portfolios, and in current and savings account deposits on a daily average basis. The bank's strategy of growing the loan portfolio in a granular manner is underpinned by a focus on risk and reward, with return of capital and containment of provisions below a defined percentage of core operating profit being key imperatives. While there are no targets for loan mix or segment-wise loan growth, the aim is to continue to grow the deposit franchise, maintain a stable and healthy funding profile and competitive advantage in cost of funds.

EXECUTIVES

Chief Executive Officer, Managing Director, Executive Director, Sandeep Bakhshi
Executive Director, Vishakha V. Mulye
Chief Financial Officer, Rakesh Jha
Executive Director, Anup Bagchi
Executive Director, Sandeep Batra
Secretary, Ranganath Athreya
Chairman, Independent Non-Executive Director, Girish Chandra Chaturvedi
Independent Non-Executive Director, Rama Bijapurkar
Independent Non-Executive Director, Uday M. Chitale
Independent Non-Executive Director, Neelam Dhawan
Independent Non-Executive Director, S. Madhavan
Independent Non-Executive Director, Hari L. Mundra
Independent Non-Executive Director, Radhakrishnan Nair
Independent Non-Executive Director, B. Sriram
Director, Lalit Kumar Chandel
Auditors : KPMG Assurance and Consulting Services LLP

LOCATIONS

HQ: ICICI Bank Ltd (India)
ICICI Bank Towers, Bandra-Kurla Complex, Mumbai 400 051
Phone: (91) 22 2653 1414   **Fax:** (91) 22 2653 1122
Web: www.icicibank.com

PRODUCTS/OPERATIONS

2015 Sales by Segment

	% of total
Treasury	39
Wholesale Banking	30
Retail Banking	30
Other Banking	1
Total	100

COMPETITORS

AKBANK TURK ANONIM SIRKETI
Bank of Communications Co.,Ltd.
CANARA BANK
China Construction Bank Corporation
HDFC BANK LIMITED
HSBC Bank Canada
Industrial and Commercial Bank of China Limited
MALAYAN BANKING BERHAD
STATE BANK OF INDIA
Woori Finance Holdings Co., Ltd.

HISTORICAL FINANCIALS

Company Type: Public

Income Statement   FYE: March 31

	ASSETS ($mil)	NET INCOME ($mil)	INCOME AS % OF ASSETS	EMPLOYEES
03/22	231,378	3,314	1.4%	130,542
03/21	215,099	2,512	1.2%	130,170
03/20	182,339	1,266	0.7%	131,232
03/19	179,030	614	0.3%	117,340
03/18	172,805	1,185	0.7%	112,360
Annual Growth	7.6%	29.3%	—	3.8%

2022 Year-End Financials

Return on assets: 1.5%
Return on equity: 14.7%
Long-term debt ($ mil.): —
No. of shares ($ mil.): 6,948
Sales ($ mil.): 20,897
Dividends
Yield: 0.2%
Payout: 12.0%
Market value ($ mil.): 131,610

	STOCK PRICE ($) FY Close	P/E High/Low		PER SHARE ($) Earnings	Dividends	Book Value
03/22	18.94	1	0	0.47	0.05	3.46
03/21	16.03	1	0	0.37	0.00	3.11
03/20	8.50	1	0	0.19	0.07	2.51
03/19	11.46	2	1	0.09	0.04	2.56
03/18	8.85	1	1	0.18	0.07	2.65
Annual Growth	21.0%	—	—	26.5%	(8.4%)	6.9%

ICL Group Ltd

Formerly Israel Chemicals Limited, ICL Group Ltd. (ICL) is a leading global specialty minerals and chemicals company that creates impactful solutions for humanity's sustainability challenges in global food, agriculture, and industrial markets. ICL leverages its unique bromine, potash and phosphate resources, its professional employees, and its strong focus on R&D and technological innovation to drive growth across its end markets. Bromine commonly is used in flame retardants, and potash is a common fertilizer. It is also a major producer of magnesium. Although most of the company's chemicals are produced in Israel (from the Dead Sea), it also mines for fertilizers in Spain and the UK. Around 30% of sales were generated in Europe.

Operations

ICL Group has four segments: Industrial Products (Bromine) (about 15% of the company revenue), Potash (about 30%), Phosphate Solutions (about 30%), and Growing Solutions (more than 20%).

The Industrial Products segments operates the bromine value chain, which includes elemental bromine and bromine compound for various industrial applications. The segment also operates several complementary businesses, mainly phosphorous-based flame retardants, and additional Dead Sea minerals for pharmaceutical, food, oil, and gas, and de-icing industries.

The Potash segment operates their potash value chain and includes primarily potash fertilizers and the magnesium business, a byproduct of potash production, which produces and sells pure magnesium and magnesium alloys, as well as chlorine and sylvinite.

The Phosphate Solutions segment is based on their potash value chain and includes specialty phosphate salts and acids for various food and industrial applications, as well as commodity phosphates, which are used mainly as fertilizers.

Lastly, the Growing Solutions segment includes the company's specialty fertilizers business. The segment is focused on expanding and strengthening their Growing Solutions offerings, by maximizing its existing capabilities and agronomic expertise.

Geographic Reach

The ICL Group is headquartered in Israel. Europe and Asia account for about 30% each. South America accounts for about 25%, followed by North America (15%). Brazil, China, and the US are ICL Group's largest markets.

Financial Performance

Although the ICL Group's performance for the past five years has seen fluctuations, performance increased year-over-year starting in 2020, with 2022 as its highest performing year over the period.

The company's revenue increased by $3.1 billion to $10 billion for 2022, as compared to 2021's revenue of $7 billion.

ICL's net income also increased significantly to $2.1 billion for fiscal year end 2022, as compared to the prior year's net income of $783 million.

The company held $417 million at the end of 2022. Operating activities used $723 million. Investing activities and financing activities used $754 million and $1.3 billion, respectively. Main cash uses were for purchases of property, plant and equipment and intangible assets and repayments of long-term debt.

Strategy

ICL Group's strategy is to strengthen or achieve a leadership position in each of its segments, either in terms of market share, value added, or cost competitiveness ? and to grow its businesses.

The company intends to build global leadership by developing and expanding its portfolio of essential and advanced crop nutrition products, digital solutions and integrated services, enabling farmers to increase yields, and provide for the ever-growing nutritional needs of the world. The company also intends to strengthen their positions in the food and industrial sectors.

Mergers and Acquisitions

In mid-2021, ICL, has completed the acquisition of Compass Minerals AmÃ©rica do Sul S.A., which includes the South American Plant Nutrition business of Compass Minerals, for approximately US$420 million. The South American Plant Nutrition business is the leading specialty plant nutrition business in Brazil and offers a broad range of solutions for plant nutrition and stimulation, covering all key Brazilian crops. The addition of the South American Plant Nutrition business will allow ICL to offer its customers the broadest and most advanced portfolio of plant nutrition products, covering the entire agricultural value chain.

In early 2021, ICL has entered into a definitive agreement to acquire Compass Minerals AmÃ©rica do Sul S.A., which includes the South American Plant Nutrition business of Compass Minerals ? after a planned carve-out of the existing water treatment and chemicals businesses ? for approximately R$2,207 million. The South American Plant Nutrition business is the leading specialty plant nutrition business in Brazil and offers a broad range of solutions for plant nutrition and stimulation, soil treatment, seed treatment and plant health, covering all key Brazilian crops. Upon completion of the acquisition, ICL expects it will be able to offer the broadest and most advanced portfolio of plant nutrition products covering the entire agricultural value chain.

EXECUTIVES

Chairman, Director, Executive Chairman, Yoav Doppelt
President, Chief Executive Officer, Raviv Zoller
Global Internal Audit Senior Vice President, Amir Meshulam
Executive Vice President, Anantha N. Desikan
Global Human Resources Chief People Officer,
Global Human Resources Executive Vice President, Ilana Fahima
Chief Financial Officer, Kobi Altman
Information Technology Senior Vice President, Miri Mishor
Senior Vice President, General Counsel, Lilach Geva-Harel
Independent External Director, Nadav Kaplan
Independent External Director, Ruth Ralbag
Independent Director, Lior Reitblatt
Independent Director, Reem Aminoach

Independent Director, Tzipi Ozer-Armon
Director, Aviad Kaufman
Director, Avisar Paz
Director, Ovadia Eli
Director, Sagi Kabla
Auditors : Somekh Chaikin (member firm of KPMG International)

LOCATIONS

HQ: ICL Group Ltd
 Millenium Tower, 23 Aranha Street, Tel Aviv 61202
Phone: (972) 3 684 4400 **Fax:** (972) 3 684 4427
Web: www.icl-group.com

Israel Chemicals has production facilities in China, Europe, Israel, South America, and the US.2015 Sales

	% of total
Europe	38
Asia	21
North America	23
South America	11
Rest of the World	7
Total	100

PRODUCTS/OPERATIONS

2015 Sales

	% of total
ICL Fertilizers	54
ICL Performance Products	26
ICL Industrial Products	20
Other products	-
Total	100

COMPETITORS

AMERICAN SOIL TECHNOLOGIES, INC.
ARAB POTASH COMPANY
Bayer CropScience AG
ETI MADEN ISLETMELERI GENEL MUDURLUGU
MARRONE BIO INNOVATIONS, INC.
MONSANTO COMPANY
NUFARM LIMITED
Sociedad Quimica y Minera de Chile S.A.
THAI CENTRAL CHEMICAL PUBLIC COMPANY LIMITED
THE CHEMOURS COMPANY

HISTORICAL FINANCIALS

Company Type: Public

Income Statement   FYE: December 31

	REVENUE ($mil)	NET INCOME ($mil)	NET PROFIT MARGIN	EMPLOYEES
12/22	10,015	2,159	21.6%	13,619
12/21	6,955	783	11.3%	13,233
12/20	5,043	11	0.2%	11,744
12/19	5,271	475	9.0%	12,117
12/18	5,556	1,240	22.3%	12,125
Annual Growth	15.9%	14.9%	—	2.9%

2022 Year-End Financials

Debt ratio: 21.7%   No. of shares ($ mil.): 1,289
Return on equity: 43.2%   Dividends
Cash ($ mil.): 417   Yield: —
Current Ratio: 1.75   Payout: 53.8%
Long-term debt ($ mil.): 2,042   Market value ($ mil.): —

Idemitsu Kosan Co Ltd

Idemitsu Kosan is one of top oil refiner in Japan (behind Nippon Oil). At its four refineries in Japan (processing 945,000 barrels per day) Idemitsu Kosan produces petroleum products, such as gasoline and other fuels, kerosene, and lubricants. It markets its fuel products through a network of some 6,200 service stations. The company is expanding its business globally in such areas as petroleum products, lubricants, asphalt, oil and gas development, renewable energy, coal, petrochemicals, and electronic materials. It was founded in Moji in 1911. Majority of its sales were generated from Japan.

Operations

Idemitsu Kosan has five reportable segments: Petroleum (about 80% of sales), Basic Chemicals (roughly 10%), Functional materials (around 5%), Resources (some 5%), and Power and Renewable Energy (less than 5%).

Petroleum segment includes production, sales, import/export, trading, etc. of refined petroleum products. Basic chemicals segment includes production, sales, etc. of olefin/aroma products. Functional Materials segment includes lubricants, performance chemicals, electronic materials, Functional paving material business, agricultural biotechnology products business, etc. Resources segment includes the exploration, development, production and sales of crude oil, natural gas and other energy resources such as coals. Power and Renewable Energy includes power generation (thermal power, solar power, wind power, etc.), sales of electricity, and solar cell business.

Geographic Reach

Headquartered in Tokyo, Japan, Idemitsu Kosan has offices in Africa, Asia (East, South East, and South West), Australia, Europe (including Russia), the Middle East, and North and South America. Japan generated about 75% of sales, Asia and Oceania with nearly 20%, and North America and Other regions with about 5% each.

Financial Performance

Net sales for the fiscal year ended March 31, 2022 decreased by Â¥58.4 billion, cost of sales decreased by Â¥52.1 billion, selling, general and administrative expenses decreased by Â¥7.1 billion, operating income increased by Â¥745 million and ordinary income and net income before income taxes increased by Â¥632 million, respectively.

In 2022, the company had a net income of Â¥388.1 billion, a 501% increase from the previous year's net income of Â¥64.6 billion.

The company's cash at the end of 2021 was Â¥139 billion. Operating activities generated Â¥146.1 billion, while investing activities used Â¥111.6 billion, mainly for purchases of tangible fixed assets. Financing activities used another Â¥30 billion, primarily for repayments of long-term loans payable.

Company Background

Pooling their LPG resources and expertise, in 2006 Idemitsu Kosan merged its LPG operations with those of Mitsubishi to form Astomos Energy.

EXECUTIVES

President, Chief Executive Officer, Representative Director, Shunichi Kito
Executive Vice President, Chief Operating Officer, Representative Director, Susumu Nibuya
Executive Vice President, Representative Director, Atsuhiko Hirano
Executive Vice President, Chief Financial Officer, Representative Director, Noriaki Sakai
Managing Executive Officer, Chief Digital Officer, Soichi Kobayashi
Director, Masahiko Sawa
Director, Masakazu Idemitsu
Director, Kazunari Kubohara
Outside Director, Takeo Kikkawa
Outside Director, Yumiko Noda
Outside Director, Maki Kado
Outside Director, Jun Suzuki
Auditors : Deloitte Touche Tohmatsu LLC

LOCATIONS

HQ: Idemitsu Kosan Co Ltd
1-2-1 Otemachi, Chiyoda-ku, Tokyo 100-8321
Phone: (81) 3 3213 3192
Web: www.idss.co.jp

2016 Sales

	% of total
Japan	75
Asia and Oceania	16
North America	6
Europe	2
Other	1
Total	100

PRODUCTS/OPERATIONS

2016 Sales

	% of total
Petroleum products	77
Petrochemical products	15
Resources	6
Others	2
Total	100

Products & Services
Agri-Bio
Electronic Materials
Lubricants
Packing Materials, Logistics, Plastics
Petrochemicals
Petroleum Transportation
Refinery & Plant
Renewable Energy
Research & Development
Resource Development
SUBSIDIARIES
AltaGas Idemitsu Joint Venture Limited Partnership
Apolloretailing Co.,Ltd.
Astomos Energy Corp.
Formosa Idemitsu Petrochemicals Corporation
Idemitsu Apollo Corporation
Idemitsu Australia Resources Pty Ltd
Idemitsu Canada Corporation
Idemitsu Canada Resouces Ltd.
Idemitsu Credit Co., Ltd.
Idemitsu Engineering Co., Ltd.
Idemitsu Insurance Service, Co.,Ltd.
Idemitsu International (Asia) Pte.Ltd.
Idemitsu Oita Geothermal Co.,Ltd.
Idemitsu Petroleum Norge AS
Idemitsu Petroleum UK Ltd.
Idemitsu Retail Marketing Co., Ltd.
Idemitsu SM (Malaysia) Sdn.Bhd.
Idemitsu Tanker Co., Ltd.
Idemitsu Unitech Co., Ltd.
Nghi Son Refinery and Petrochemical LLC
Prime Polymer Co., Ltd.
PS Japan Corp.
SDS Biotech K.K.

COMPETITORS

COSMO OIL CO., LTD.
ENEOS CORPORATION
GS Caltex Corporation
INDIAN OIL CORPORATION LIMITED
INNOSPEC INC.
NEWMARKET CORPORATION
Neste Oyj
RS ENERGY K.K.
SASOL LTD
THAI OIL PUBLIC COMPANY LIMITED

HISTORICAL FINANCIALS

Company Type: Public

Income Statement   FYE: March 31

	REVENUE ($mil)	NET INCOME ($mil)	NET PROFIT MARGIN	EMPLOYEES
03/23	71,000	1,904	2.7%	19,227
03/22	54,973	2,297	4.2%	19,003
03/21	41,152	315	0.8%	19,075
03/20	55,696	(211)	—	18,273
03/19	39,958	735	1.8%	13,398
Annual Growth	15.5%	26.9%	—	9.5%

2023 Year-End Financials

Debt ratio: 0.2%   No. of shares ($ mil.): 1,467
Return on equity: 16.7%   Dividends
Cash ($ mil.): 789   Yield: —
Current Ratio: 1.26   Payout: 0.0%
Long-term debt ($ mil.): 5,024   Market value ($ mil.): —

IHI Corp

EXECUTIVES

Chairman, Representative Director, Tsugio Mitsuoka
President, Chief Executive Officer, Representative Director, Hiroshi Ide
Executive Vice President, Representative Director, Masataka Ikeyama
Executive Vice President, Representative Director, Tsuyoshi Tsuchida
Director, Hideo Morita
Director, Akihiro Seo
Director, Jun Kobayashi
Director, Yasuaki Fukumoto
Outside Director, Yoshiyuki Nakanishi
Outside Director, Chieko Matsuda
Outside Director, Minoru Usui
Outside Director, Toshihiro Uchiyama
Auditors : Ernst & Young ShinNihon LLC

LOCATIONS

HQ: IHI Corp
3-1-1 Toyosu, Koto-ku, Tokyo 135-8710
Phone: (81) 3 6204 7065   **Fax:** (81) 3 6204 8800
Web: www.ihi.co.jp

HISTORICAL FINANCIALS

Company Type: Public

Income Statement   FYE: March 31

	REVENUE ($mil)	NET INCOME ($mil)	NET PROFIT MARGIN	EMPLOYEES
03/23	10,158	334	3.3%	28,486
03/22	9,642	543	5.6%	28,801
03/21	10,051	118	1.2%	29,149
03/20	12,772	118	0.9%	28,964
03/19	13,395	360	2.7%	29,286
Annual Growth	(6.7%)	(1.8%)	—	(0.7%)

2023 Year-End Financials

Debt ratio: 0.2%   No. of shares ($ mil.): 151
Return on equity: 10.9%   Dividends
Cash ($ mil.): 936   Yield: —
Current Ratio: 1.31   Payout: 30.5%
Long-term debt ($ mil.): 1,901   Market value ($ mil.): —

Iida Group Holdings Co., Ltd.

EXECUTIVES

Honorary Chairman, Director, Kazuhiko Mori
President, Representative Director, Masashi Kanei
Senior Managing Director, Representative Director, Hiroshi Nishino
Senior Managing Director, Director, Tadayoshi Horiguchi
Director, Shigeo Yamamoto
Director, Yoshinari Hisabayashi
Director, Shigeyuki Matsubayashi
Director, Kazuhiro Kodera
Outside Director, Toshihiko Sasaki
Outside Director, Eiichi Hasegawa
Outside Director, Nanako Murata
Auditors : Ernst & Young ShinNihon LLC

LOCATIONS

HQ: Iida Group Holdings Co., Ltd.
1-2-11 Nishikubo, Musashino, Tokyo 180-0013
Phone: (81) 422 60 8888   **Fax:** (81) 422 60 8890
Web: www.ighd.co.jp

HISTORICAL FINANCIALS

Company Type: Public

Income Statement   FYE: March 31

	REVENUE ($mil)	NET INCOME ($mil)	NET PROFIT MARGIN	EMPLOYEES
03/22	11,402	849	7.5%	12,815
03/21	13,151	752	5.7%	10,134
03/20	12,915	495	3.8%	9,693
03/19	12,145	591	4.9%	8,561
03/18	12,575	654	5.2%	7,736
Annual Growth	(2.4%)	6.7%	—	13.4%

Impala Platinum Holdings Ltd.

EXECUTIVES

Chief Executive Officer, Executive Director, Nicolaas Johannes Muller
Executive Director, Lee-Ann Samuel
Chief Financial Officer, Executive Director, Meroonisha Kerber
Secretary, Tabego T. Llale
Chairman, Independent Non-Executive Director, Mandla Sizwe Vulindlela Gantsho
Independent Non-Executive Director, Peter W. Davey
Independent Non-Executive Director, Dawn Earp
Independent Non-Executive Director, Alastair S. Macfarlane
Independent Non-Executive Director, Sydney Mufamadi
Independent Non-Executive Director, Babalwa Ngonyama
Independent Non-Executive Director, Mpho Elizabeth Kolekile Nkeli
Independent Non-Executive Director, Preston E. Speckmann
Independent Non-Executive Director, Z. Bernard Swanepoel
Non-Executive Director, Udo Lucht
Non-Executive Director, Boitumelo Koshane
Auditors : Deloitte & Touche

LOCATIONS

HQ: Impala Platinum Holdings Ltd.
  2 Fricker Road, Illovo 2196
Phone: (27) 11 731 9000   **Fax:** (27) 11 731 9254
Web: www.implats.co.za

HISTORICAL FINANCIALS

Company Type: Public

Income Statement FYE: June 30

	REVENUE ($mil)	NET INCOME ($mil)	NET PROFIT MARGIN	EMPLOYEES
06/21	9,063	3,289	36.3%	56,180
06/20	4,023	924	23.0%	0
06/19	3,429	103	3.0%	50,712
06/18	2,606	(776)	—	50,500
06/17	2,821	(629)	—	52,012
Annual Growth	33.9%	—		1.9%

2021 Year-End Financials

Debt ratio: —
Return on equity: 62.8%
Cash ($ mil.): 1,641
Current Ratio: 3.19
Long-term debt ($ mil.): (-16)
No. of shares ($ mil.): 813
Dividends
 Yield: 4.4%
 Payout: 18.7%
Market value ($ mil.): 13,488

2022 Year-End Financials

Debt ratio: 0.2%
Return on equity: 11.5%
Cash ($ mil.): 4,614
Current Ratio: 2.70
Long-term debt ($ mil.): 2,069
No. of shares ($ mil.): 288
Dividends
 Yield: —
 Payout: 0.0%
Market value ($ mil.): —

Imperial Brands PLC

EXECUTIVES

Chief Financial Officer, Executive Director, Lukas Paravicini
Chief Executive Officer, Executive Director, Stefan Bomhard
Global Supply Chain Officer, Javier Huerta
Chief Consumer Officer, Anindya Dascupta
Chief Strategy and Development Officer, Murray Mcgowan
Chief People and Culture Officer, Alison Clarke
Secretary, John Matthew Downing
Chairman, Therese Esperdy
Senior Independent Director, Sue Clark
Independent Non-Executive Director, Alan Johnson
Independent Non-Executive Director, Robert Kunze Concewitz
Independent Non-Executive Director, Simon Langelier
Independent Non-Executive Director, Steven P. Stanbrook
Independent Non-Executive Director, Jonathan Stanton
Independent Non-Executive Director, Diane de Saint Victor
Independent Non-Executive Director, Ngozi Edozien
Auditors : Ernst & Young LLP

LOCATIONS

HQ: Imperial Brands PLC
  121 Winterstoke Road, Bristol BS3 2LL
Phone: (44) 117 963 6636
Web: www.imperialbrandsplc.com

HISTORICAL FINANCIALS

Company Type: Public

Income Statement FYE: September 30

	REVENUE ($mil)	NET INCOME ($mil)	NET PROFIT MARGIN	EMPLOYEES
09/23	39,801	2,853	7.2%	25,200
09/22	35,927	1,732	4.8%	25,700
09/21	44,094	3,810	8.6%	30,300
09/20	41,773	1,917	4.6%	32,500
09/19	38,895	1,243	3.2%	32,700
Annual Growth	0.6%	23.1%	—	(6.3%)

2023 Year-End Financials

Debt ratio: 39.3%
Return on equity: 36.1%
Cash ($ mil.): 1,648
Current Ratio: 0.72
Long-term debt ($ mil.): 9,660
No. of shares ($ mil.): 898
Dividends
 Yield: —
 Payout: 55.9%
Market value ($ mil.): 18,379

	STOCK PRICE ($) FY Close	P/E High/Low		PER SHARE ($) Earnings	Dividends	Book Value
06/21	16.57	0	0	4.17	0.73	7.55
06/20	6.56	0	0	1.10	0.06	4.58
06/19	4.88	2	1	0.14	0.00	3.84
06/18	1.52	—	—	(1.08)	0.00	3.76
06/17	2.78	—	—	(0.88)	0.00	4.99
Annual Growth	56.2%			—		10.9%

Imperial Oil Ltd

Imperial Oil, one of Canada's largest oil integrated company behind Canadian Natural Resources, holds sway over a vast empire of oil and gas resources. Imperial is also a major producer of crude oil, largest petroleum refiner, marketer of petroleum products, and a major producer of petrochemicals. It sells petroleum products, including gasoline, heating oil, and diesel fuel, under the Esso name and other brand names. The company reported proved reserves in 2022 of about 2.2 billion barrels of oil-equivalent, including less than 5 million barrels of liquids, about 70 billion cu. ft. of natural gas, approximately 350 million barrels of synthetic oil, and roughly 1.8 billion barrels of bitumen.

Operations

Imperial Oil Limited has three segments: Upstream, Downstream, and Chemical.

Upstream operations include the exploration for, and production of, crude oil, natural gas, synthetic crude oil and bitumen. Downstream includes the transportation and refining of crude oil, blending of refined products and the distribution and marketing of those products. Lastly, the Chemical segment manufactures and markets various chemicals.

Geographic Reach

Imperial Oil Limited, headquartered in Alberta, Canada, with most of its operations in the provinces of Canada.

Sales and Marketing

The company sells gasoline to motorists at about 2,400 primarily Esso-branded gas stations across Canada.

It markets almost petroleum products throughout Canada to all types of customers. It also serves the Canadian agriculture, residential heating and small commercial markets and sells petroleum products to large industrial and commercial accounts as well as to other refiners and marketers.

Financial Performance

Imperial Oil Limited's performance for the past three years has seen an increase year-over-year with 2022 as its highest performing year over the period.

The company's revenue increased by CAN $1.9 billion to CAN $37.5 billion for 2022, as compared to 2021's revenue of CAN $37.5 billion.

Imperial Oil Limited recorded a net

	STOCK PRICE ($) FY Close	P/E High/Low		PER SHARE ($) Earnings	Dividends	Book Value
09/23	20.46	11	8	3.07	1.72	8.21
09/22	20.82	13	10	1.82	1.78	7.97
09/21	21.28	8	5	4.02	1.87	7.60
09/20	17.70	17	10	2.03	2.35	6.60
09/19	22.60	32	21	1.30	2.45	6.39
Annual Growth	(2.5%)			23.9%	(8.5%)	6.5%

income of CAN $7.3 billion for fiscal year end 2022, an increase compared to the prior year's net income of CAN $2.5 billion.

The company held about CAN $3.7 billion at the end of the year. Operating activities provided CAN $10.5 billion to the coffers. Investing activities and financing activities used CAN $618 million and CAN $8.3 billion, respectively. Main cash uses were for additions to property, plant, and equipment as well as common shares purchased.

Strategy

Imperial Oil Limited's strategy includes improving asset reliability, accelerating development and application of high impact technologies, maximizing value by capturing new business opportunities, managing existing portfolio, as well as pursuing sustainable improvements in organization efficiency and effectiveness. In addition, the company targets industry-leading performance in reliability, safety and operations integrity, as well as maximizing value from advanced technologies, capitalizing on integration across the company's businesses.

HISTORY

London, Ontario, boomed from the discovery of oil in the 1860s and 1870s, but when the market for Canadian kerosene became saturated in 1880, 16 refiners banded together to form the Imperial Oil Company.

The company refined sulfurous Canadian oil, nicknamed "skunk oil" for its powerful smell. Imperial faced tough competition from America's Standard Oil, which marketed kerosene made from lighter, less-odorous Pennsylvania crude. Guided by American expatriate Jacob Englehart, Imperial built a better refinery and hired a chemist to develop a process to clean sulfur from the crude.

By the mid-1890s Imperial had expanded from coast to Canadian coast. Cash-starved from its expansion, the company turned to old nemesis Standard Oil, which bought a controlling interest in Imperial in 1898. That interest is today held by Exxon Mobil.

After the turn of the century, Imperial began producing gasoline to serve the new automobiles. The horseless carriages were spooking the workhorses at the warehouse where fuel was sold, so an Imperial manager in Vancouver opened the first Canadian service station in 1907. The company marketed its gas under the Esso banner borrowed from Standard Oil.

An Imperial crew discovered oil in 1920 at Norman Wells in the remote Northwest Territories. In 1924 a subsidiary sparked a new boom with a gas well discovery in the Turner Valley area northeast of Edmonton. But soon Imperial's luck ran as dry as the holes it was drilling; it came away empty from the next 133 consecutive wells. That string ended in 1947 when it struck oil in Alberta at the Leduc No. 1. To get the oil to market, Imperial invested in the Interprovincial Pipe Line from Alberta to Superior, Wisconsin.

The company began research in 1964 to extract bitumen from the oil sands in Cold Lake, Alberta. During the 1970s oil crisis, Imperial continued to search for oil in northern Canada. It found crude on land near the Beaufort Sea (1970) and in its icy waters (1972). The company formed its Esso Resources Canadian Ltd. subsidiary in 1978 to oversee natural resources production.

In 1989 Texaco (acquired by Chevron in 2001), still reeling from a court battle with Pennzoil, sold Texaco Canada to Imperial. To diminish debt and comply with regulators, Imperial agreed to sell some of Texaco Canada's refining and marketing assets in Atlantic Canada, its interests in Interhome Energy, and oil and gas properties in western Canada.

Imperial reorganized in 1992, centralizing several units, and in 1993 closed its refinery at Port Moody, British Columbia. It sold most of its fertilizer business in 1994, disposed of 339 unprofitable gas stations in 1995, and the next year closed down Canada's northernmost oil refinery at Norman Wells.

In 1997 Imperial announced an ambitious program to expand Syncrude's oil sands bitumen upgrading plant. In 1998 Exxon agreed to buy Mobil, which had substantial Canadian oil assets. In 1999 Canada preapproved the potential merger of Imperial Oil and Mobil Canada. Later that year Exxon completed its purchase of Mobil to form Exxon Mobil.

Expanding its exploration and production assets, in 2007 Imperial and ExxonMobil Canada acquired exploration rights for a development parcel in the Beaufort Sea, and in 2008, in the Horn River area of northeastern British Columbia.

EXECUTIVES

Chairman, President, Chief Executive Officer, Director, Bradley W. Corson
Finance Senior Vice President, Administration Senior Vice President, Finance Controller, Administration Controller, Daniel E. Lyons
Downstream and Corporate Departments Vice President, Downstream and Corporate Departments Corporate Secretary, Downstream and Corporate Departments General Counsel, Ian R. Laing
Human Resources Vice President, Kristi L. Desjardins
Chemicals and Sarnia Chemical Plant Manager Vice President, Kimberly J. Haas
Western Canada Fuels Vice President, Imperial Oil Downstream Vice President, Imperial Oil Downstream Manager, Western Canada Fuels Manager, Jonathan R. Wetmore
Commercial and Corporate Development Vice President, Sherri L. Evers
Corporate Tax Director, Constance D. Gemmell
Treasurer, Kitty Lee
Assistant Controller, Bruce A. Jolly
Division Officer, Simon P. Younger
Director, David W. Cornhill
Director, Matthew R. Crocker
Director, Krystyna T. Hoeg
Director, Miranda C. Hubbs
Director, Jack M. Mintz
Director, David S. Sutherland
Auditors : PricewaterhouseCoopers LLP

LOCATIONS

HQ: Imperial Oil Ltd
505 Quarry Park Boulevard S.E., Calgary, Alberta T2C 5N1
Phone: 800 567-3776
Web: www.imperialoil.ca

PRODUCTS/OPERATIONS

2016 Sales

	% of total
Downstream	74
Upstream	22
Chemical	4
Total	100

COMPETITORS

CHEVRON CORPORATION
COSMO OIL CO., LTD.
DELEK US ENERGY, INC.
DELEK US HOLDINGS, INC.
GENESIS ENERGY, L.P.
HELLENIC PETROLEUM S.A.
HOLLYFRONTIER CORPORATION
MOL Magyar Olaj- és Gázipari Nyilvánosan Működő Részvénytársaság
SURGUTNEFTEGAZ, PAO
Suncor Energy Inc

HISTORICAL FINANCIALS

Company Type: Public

Income Statement — FYE: December 31

	REVENUE ($mil)	NET INCOME ($mil)	NET PROFIT MARGIN	EMPLOYEES
12/23	38,454	3,688	9.6%	5,300
12/22	44,120	5,427	12.3%	5,300
12/21	29,513	1,946	6.6%	5,400
12/20	17,583	(1,458)	—	5,800
12/19	26,187	1,689	6.5%	6,000
Annual Growth	10.1%	21.6%	—	(3.1%)

2023 Year-End Financials

Debt ratio: 7.6%
Return on equity: 21.9%
Cash ($ mil.): 651
Current Ratio: 1.26
Long-term debt ($ mil.): 3,026
No. of shares ($ mil.): 535
Dividends
Yield: —
Payout: 22.8%
Market value ($ mil.): 30,645

	STOCK PRICE ($) FY Close	P/E High/Low		PER SHARE ($) Earnings	Dividends	Book Value
12/23	57.19	7	5	6.41	1.46	31.29
12/22	48.74	5	3	8.49	1.08	28.37
12/21	36.10	10	5	2.73	0.82	25.17
12/20	19.03	—	—	(1.99)	0.66	22.92
12/19	26.47	11	8	2.21	0.64	25.06
Annual Growth	21.2%	—	—	30.5%	23.1%	5.7%

Inchcape PLC

Inchcape is the world's leading independent automotive distributor. Operating in the UK and over 40 markets in Europe, Asia, Australasia and the Pacific, Inchcape offers a wide variety of brands, including Audi, BMW, Jaguar, Land Rover, Mercedes, Subaru, Toyota, Volkswagen, and Volvo. Stretching back to the 1960s when it first began working in partnership with Toyota, it has fostered and maintained close relationships with some of the world's leading automotive manufacturers, as well as added new partnerships with many others over the decades. The company generates the majority of its sales outside the UK.

Operations

The company's business units are distribution, which brings in around 60% of revenue and retail (about 40%).

Its Distribution segment operations include exclusive distribution, sales and marketing activities of New Vehicles and Parts, as well as sale of the new and used vehicles together with logistics services where it may also be the exclusive distributor, alongside associated Aftersales activities of service, bodyshop repairs and parts sales.

The Retail segment includes the sale of New and Used Vehicles, together with associated Aftersales activities of service, bodyshop repairs and parts sales.

In all, about 95% of the company's sales came from goods, while the provision of services generated the rest.

Geographic Reach

Based in London, UK, Inchcape has operations across Europe (including UK; about 60% of sales), Asia Pacific (nearly 30%), and Americas and Africa (roughly 15%). The UK is its largest single market with some 25%, followed by Australia with nearly 13%, Russia with around 10%, and the rest comes from the rest of the world.

Sales and Marketing

The company has over 40 brand partners, which include Toyota, Jaguar, Land Rover, Suzuki, Mercedes-Benz, Volkswagen Group, BMW Group, and Subaru Corporation.

Financial Performance

The company's total revenue increased 12% from £6.8 billion in 2020 to £7.6 billion in 2021. This was primarily due to a higher volume of sales of goods for the year.

In 2021, the company had a net profit of £121.9 million.

The company's cash at the end of 2021 was £588.8 million. Operating activities generated £377 million, while financing activities used £212.7 million, mainly for the share buyback program. Investing activities generated another £13.2 million.

Strategy

Inchcape's strategy consists of:

Generating more value from existing markets and customers through route to market transformation. Success in providing OEMs with an omni-channel route to market will mean we sell more goods and services to consumers while reducing the cost of taking a vehicle to market for its partners.

Expanding into new and adjacent areas, capturing more value from the company's vehicles as well as others. This provides opportunities for Inchcape to create new solutions or take proven solutions from other markets to capture a greater part of the vehicle value chain; as well as

Using the company's core capabilities and market presence to expand and grow in new markets and with new partners. Manufacturers are now looking for partners in the markets they choose not to serve themselves, who have the scale to be able to exploit technology and data to deliver the omni-channel solution consumers are demanding.

HISTORY

Inchcape's roots are in an amalgam of shipping and trading companies. The most significant of these was Mackinnon Mackenzie & Company, which was formed in 1847 by William Mackinnon and Robert Mackenzie, two Scottish merchants, to trade and ship goods, such as cotton, primarily from India. The company founded Calcutta & Burmah Steam Navigation Company, which began carrying mail for the East India Company in 1856 and was renamed British India Steam Navigation Company (BI) in 1862. In 1874 Scotsman James Lyle Mackay joined Mackinnon Mackenzie in its Calcutta office. Mackay became a partner by saving one of the company's offices from bankruptcy, and in 1906 he spearheaded Mackinnon Mackenzie's acquisition of Binny's, a textile maker in south India. He gained knighthood for helping to solve India's currency problems, and then he took the name Baron Inchcape of Strathnaver when offered peerage in 1911 (in honor of Inchcape Rock near his hometown). Two years later Lord Inchcape became chairman and steered the merger of BI and another shipping giant, Peninsular & Oriental Steam Navigation Company.

Mackinnon Mackenzie acquired a number of trading businesses, including the Assam Company, India's oldest tea company, in 1915 (sold in 1991). The last MacKinnon heir died during WWI, and Lord Inchcape became the last surviving partner (he died in 1932). After WWII, Kenneth Mackay, the third Lord Inchcape, was confronted by the growing nationalism of newly independent countries in the Indian subcontinent, as well as outdated operations. He began reorganizing the family's shipping investments into a single UK-based public company. Disposals included 48% of Macneill & Barry (an agent for tea, coal, and jute) in 1949 and shipping partnerships in the 1950s. The remaining companies, flush with capital for growth, went public in 1958 as Inchcape.

Seeking less dependence on India, in 1967 the company expanded its geographical reach and began distributing automobiles when it acquired Borneo Company. It added luxury automobile distributor Mann Egerton in 1973. Inchcape entered insurance three years later with its acquisition of A. W. Bain Holdings, and it gained exclusive distribution of Toyota autos in the UK when it bought Pride & Clarke in 1978. The company began bottling Coca-Cola beverages in Chile in 1983.

By the late 1980s autos accounted for two-thirds of company sales. Inchcape purchased Middle East supermarket operator Spinneys in 1992. It then added to its insurance holdings with the purchase of Hogg Group in 1994 (sold 1996) and began bottling Coca-Cola in Russia that year. In 1995 Inchcape entered into a joint venture with Ricoh to distribute office equipment in the Asia/Pacific and also acquired a stake in The Coca-Cola Company's bottling operations in Peru.

Difficult economic conditions in some of the company's key markets led to a management shake-up in 1995, including the arrival of Lord Colin Marshall as chairman and Philip Cushing replacing Charles Mackay as CEO the next year. Inchcape then began selling its non-automobile businesses. In 1998 it sold its Russian bottling operations to Coca-Cola. In 1999 the company sold its shipping services division to investment firm Electra Fleming, its Asian marketing businesses to Li & Fung Distribution, and its bottling operations in Latin America to Chile's Embotelladora Arica for $750 million. Inchcape also sold its stake in its office equipment joint venture to Ricoh in mid-1999. Additionally in 1999 Peter Johnson was appointed CEO. John Egan became chairman in 2000.

Also in 2000 the company got involved with online car sales when wholly-owned subsidiary Autobytel UK was established. The next year Inchcape acquired the Bates Group, one of the UK's largest BMW/Audi dealers.

Inchcape discontinued the distribution of Ferrari and Maserati into the UK in 2004. The company will continue retailing these auto brands in the UK, however. Also that year Inchcape acquired two Mazda retailers in Estonia and two BMW/Mini dealerships in Poland as part of its strategy to expand in Eastern Europe.

In April 2005 Inchcape acquired six Mercedes-Benz dealerships in northwest England, making it the largest independent Mercedes-Benz dealer in the UK. Johnson replaced Egan as chairman at the end of the 2005, and André Lacroix, a former CEO of Euro Disney, took over as CEO.

In February 2006 the auto dealer purchased Keystar Motors in Brisbane, Australia. Also in 2006/early 2007 the acquisitive company purchased Lind

Automotive Group and European Motor Holdings plc in the UK. In February Inchcape sold Inchroy Credit Corp. -- its joint venture finance company in Hong Kong -- to Wing Hang Bank for about $181 million.

In July 2008 Inchcape acquired a 75.1% stake in Moscow-based Musa Motors Group for about $200 million. Musa operates 16 dealer centers for 10 brands in Moscow and the Moscow region (Musa Motors and Borishof), and a Rolls-Royce showroom in St. Petersburg. Also in 2008 the company purchased European Motor Holdings for nearly $520 million to enhance its UK business.

In May 2009, Ken Hanna succeeded Johnson as nonexecutive chairman of the company. Johnson left the firm after 15 years.

EXECUTIVES

Chief Executive Officer, Executive Director, Duncan Tait
Chief Financial Officer, Executive Director, Gijsbert de Zoeten
Secretary, Tamsin Waterhouse
Independent Chairman, Nigel M. Stein
Senior Independent Non-Executive Director, Jerry Buhlmann
Independent Non-Executive Director, Alex Jensen
Independent Non-Executive Director, Nayantara Bali
Independent Non-Executive Director, Jane Kingston
Independent Non-Executive Director, John Langston
Independent Non-Executive Director, Till Vestring
Auditors : Deloitte LLP

LOCATIONS

HQ: Inchcape PLC
22A St James's Square, London SW1Y 5LP
Phone: (44) 20 7546 0022   Fax: (44) 20 7546 0010
Web: www.inchcape.com

2015 Sales

	% of total
Australasia	25
North Asia	23
United Kingdom	18
South Asia	15
Emerging Markets	14
Europe	5
Total	100

PRODUCTS/OPERATIONS

2015 Sales

	% of total
Sale of goods	92
Provision of services	8
Total	100

COMPETITORS

AUTONATION, INC.
FIAT CHRYSLER AUTOMOBILES N.V.
FINISHMASTER, INC.
Ferguson plc
GROUP 1 AUTOMOTIVE, INC.
INVESTCORP HOLDINGS B.S.C
JAGUAR LAND ROVER LIMITED
JM FAMILY ENTERPRISES, INC.
Jim Pattison Group Inc
RAC GROUP LIMITED

HISTORICAL FINANCIALS
Company Type: Public

Income Statement   FYE: December 31

	REVENUE ($mil)	NET INCOME ($mil)	NET PROFIT MARGIN	EMPLOYEES
12/21	10,296	157	1.5%	14,427
12/20	9,331	(191)	—	15,915
12/19	12,386	426	3.4%	18,205
12/18	11,844	61	0.5%	18,150
12/17	12,087	363	3.0%	17,093
Annual Growth	(3.9%)	(18.8%)	—	(4.2%)

2021 Year-End Financials

Debt ratio: 8.2%   No. of shares ($ mil.): 383
Return on equity: 10.7%   Dividends
Cash ($ mil.): 803   Yield: —
Current Ratio: 1.20   Payout: 76.0%
Long-term debt ($ mil.): 283 Market value ($ mil.): —

Industria De Diseno Textil (Inditex) SA

Industria de Diseño Textil (Inditex) is one of the world's largest fashion retailers. Inditex sells on a global scale, with more than 6,475 shops under seven different banners: Zara, Bershka, Stradivarius, Pull & Bear, Massimo Dutti, Oysho, and Zara Home. The company's constant contact between the stores and online teams answer the popular trends by feeding back to designers on what are the customers' preferences. Amancio Ortega Gaona, one of the world's wealthiest men, founded Zara in 1975 and later created Inditex as a holding company. The company's largest market is Europe excluding Spain.

Operations

Inditex's seven brands ? Zara, Bershka, Stradivarius, Pull & Bear, Massimo Dutti, Oysho, and Zara Home ? have brick-and-mortar and online stores.

Zara is Inditex's primary brand and include Zara Home. It brings in nearly 70% of the company's revenue. Zara stores also include Radio Frequency Identification Technology (RFID), using cutting-edge systems to track the location of garments instantly and making those most in demand rapidly available to customers. Zara Home sells fashionable household products.

Bershka is Inditex's second-biggest earner, bringing in almost 10% of revenue. It targets a younger demographic at a lower price point. It has three main lines: Bershka, BSK and Man.

Its other brands, Massimo Dutti (upscale fashion), Oysho (lingerie and undergarments), Pull & Bear (teenagers and adults who have grown up with the brand), and Stradivarius, account for more than 20% of revenue combined.

Geographic Reach

Inditex is based in Spain. It owns or manages stores and franchises around the world divided to its seven major brands; Zara (more than 2,005 stores), Bershka (some 970), Stradivarius (approximately 915), Pull & Bear (about 865), Massimo Dutti (over 680), Oysho (nearly 555), and Zara Home (more than 480).

In Spain and the Rest of Europe its stores are almost all owned stores, while in the Americas and the Rest of the World it has a larger concentration of franchises. Europe (excluding Spain) is host to about 50% of Inditex's total store count, while Spain accounts for around 20%. Asia and other has about 20%, and the Americas hosts the remainder.

By revenue, Europe (excl. Spain) generates around 50% of sales, Spain brings in approximately 15%, the Americas for roughly 20%, and the Asia and rest of the world account for nearly 15%.

Sales and Marketing

The company sells its products in approximately 215 markets through its online platform or its stores in approximately 95 markets.

Financial Performance

Net sales reached EUR 27.7 billion, +36% versus 2020. Sales in constant currencies increased 37%. To provide a better comparison with pre-Covid levels, sales in constant currency grew 3% versus 2019.

In 2021, the company had a net income of EUR 4.2 billion, a 200% increase from the previous year's net income of EUR 1.4 billion.

The company's cash at the end of 2021 was EUR 7 billion. Operating activities generated EUR 6.8 billion, while investing activities used EUR 3.3 billion, mainly for changes in current financial investments. Financing activities used another EUR 3.9 billion, primarily for dividends.

Strategy

Inditex continues to see strong growth opportunities. The strategic initiatives to strengthen its global fully integrated store and online model are accelerating. Sustainability and digitalization are key parts of its strategy. Inditex plans to continue developing these key long-term priorities in order to maximize organic growth.

HISTORY

Holding company Industria de Diseño Textil (Inditex) got its start as Confecciones Goa in 1963, making women's lingerie and housecoats in La Coruña, Spain.

Founder Amancio Ortega learned the rag trade as a boy, when at age 13 he made deliveries for a shirtmaker. Managing a tailor shop when he was a young man, Ortega spied an expensive negligee for sale, and he thought he could make copies and sell them for half the price. From there he made nightshirts and pajamas before he opened the first Zara store in La Coruña in 1975, where Ortega began expanding his offerings for women.

Ortega formed Inditex as a holding company for his growing operations in 1985. Inditex ran nearly 100 Zara stores before venturing out of the country, to Portugal, in 1988. New York City and Paris stores opened in 1989.

The company created the Pull & Bear clothing chain in 1991. About that time Inditex purchased a 65% stake in the Massimo Dutti group. (Inditex owns it all now.) The group continued to open stores around the globe: Mexico in 1992, Greece in 1993, Belgium and Sweden in 1994, Malta and Cyprus in 1996, and Israel and Norway in 1997.

In 1998 Inditex opened the Berksha chain to lure young females. The company further expanded that year into Argentina, Japan, Lebanon, the UK, and Venezuela.

Inditex then acquired 90% of Stradivarius, a young women's chain with about 80 stores mostly in Spain. Meanwhile, that year Inditex moved into nine more countries: Bahrain, Brazil, Canada, Chile, Germany, the Netherlands, Poland, Saudi Arabia, and Uruguay.

In 2000 the company announced it would open 150 new stores in the next two years, including perhaps 40 in the US. Later in the year, however, the company said it would hold off on US expansion to concentrate on European growth. To fuel the growth of its Zara chain, Inditex floated 26% of the company in a public offering in May 2001.

Over the course of 2001, Inditex entered six new markets: the Czech Republic, Iceland, Ireland, Jordan, Luxembourg, and Puerto Rico.

In 2003 the first Zara Home stores opened and Inditex entered new markets in Malaysia, Russia, Slovakia, and Slovenia. The following year the group surpassed the 2,000 store count and entered Estonia, Hungary, Latvia, Lithuania, Morocco, Panama, and Romania.

Early in 2005 Inditex stopped selling fur items in all of its stores worldwide. In June Pablo Isla Álvarez de Tejera succeeded José María Castellano Ríos as chief executive of the Spanish fashion giant. Castellano remained a non-executive vice chairman of the company until September, when he resigned unexpectedly following a disagreement with Inditex's chairman Amancio Ortega over his failed bid for Fenosa, a Spanish utility company. Castellano's departure ended a 31-year partnership between the two men.

Overall, Inditex opened about 450 stores in 2005 and in the process became Europe's largest apparel retailer, ahead of Sweden's H&M Hennes & Mauritz.

In February 2006 the first Zara store opened its doors in Shanghai, the first Inditex shop in China.

In 2007 80% of new stores opened were located outside of Spain. Overall, the group added 560 stores in some 50 countries. Also in 2007 the group's Kiddy's Class business segment combined operations with Zara Childrenswear. In October, Zara Home launched an online shopping site. The online portal is a first for Inditex, which has focused on the international expansion of its fashion chains.

In 2009 Inditex signed a joint venture with the Tata Group to open stores in India beginning in 2010. Also in 2009 the firm opened its first stores in Syria. </p

EXECUTIVES

Chief Logistics Officer, Lorena Alba Castro
Chief Communications Officer, Raul Estradera Vazquez
Chief Executive Officer, Executive Director, Oscar Garcia Maceiras
Chief Infrastructure and Services Officer, Juan Jose Lopez Romero
Chief Information Technology Officer, Gabriel Moneo Marina
Chief Audit Officer, Paula Mouzo Leston
General Counsel, Secretary, Javier Monteoliva Diaz
Non-Executive Chairwoman, Marta Ortega Perez
Deputy Chairman, Non-Executive Director, Jose Arnau Sierra
Independent Non-Executive Director, Jose Luis Duran schulz
Independent Non-Executive Director, Rodrigo Echenique Gordillo
Independent Non-Executive Director, Denise Patricia Kingsmill
Independent Non-Executive Director, Anne Lange
Independent Non-Executive Director, Pilar Lopez Alvarez
Non-Executive Director, Amancio Ortega Gaona
Director, Flora Perez Marcote
Director, Emilio Saracho Rodriguez de Torres
Auditors : Ernst & Young, S.L.

LOCATIONS

HQ: Industria De Diseno Textil (Inditex) SA
Avda. de la Diputacion s/n, Edificio INDITEX, A Coruna, Arteixo 15143
Phone: (34) 98 118 5400
Web: www.inditex.com

2010 Sales

	% of total
Europe	
Spain	32
Other countries	46
America	10
Asia & other regions	12
Total	100

2010 Stores

	No.
Europe	
Spain	1,916
Other countries	2,006
Americas	390
Asia & other regions	595
Total	4,907

PRODUCTS/OPERATIONS

2015 Stores

	No.
Zara	2,162
Bershka	1,044
Pull & Bear	936
Stradivarius	950
Massimo Dutti	740
Oysho	607
Zara Home	502
Uterqüe	72
Total	7,013

2015 Sales

	% of total
Zara	65
Bershka	9
Massimo Dutti	7
Pull & Bear	7
Stradivarius	6
Zara Home	3
Oysho	2
Uterqüe	1
Total	100

COMPETITORS

ABERCROMBIE & FITCH CO.
BRODER BROS., CO.
CHANEL
GIORGIO ARMANI CORPORATION
H & M Hennes & Mauritz AB
PRADA USA CORP.
R. G. BARRY CORPORATION
TOMMY BAHAMA GROUP, INC.
Tengelmann Warenhandelsgesellschaft KG
YGM TRADING LIMITED

HISTORICAL FINANCIALS

Company Type: Public

Income Statement — FYE: January 31

	REVENUE ($mil)	NET INCOME ($mil)	NET PROFIT MARGIN	EMPLOYEES
01/23	35,285	4,474	12.7%	164,997
01/22	30,931	3,619	11.7%	165,042
01/21	24,746	1,341	5.4%	144,116
01/20	31,222	4,016	12.9%	176,611
01/19	30,036	3,956	13.2%	174,386
Annual Growth	4.1%	3.1%	—	(1.4%)

2023 Year-End Financials

Debt ratio: —
Return on equity: 25.2%
Cash ($ mil.): 6,024
Current Ratio: 1.80
Long-term debt ($ mil.): —
No. of shares ($ mil.): 3,111
Dividends
Yield: 2.1%
Payout: 24.9%
Market value ($ mil.): 48,605

	STOCK PRICE ($) FY Close	P/E High/Low	PER SHARE ($) Earnings	Dividends	Book Value
01/23	15.62	12 8	1.44	0.34	5.92
01/22	15.17	18 13	1.16	0.29	5.64
01/21	14.85	55 33	0.43	0.15	5.65
01/20	16.82	15 11	1.29	0.35	5.29
01/19	14.00	16 11	1.27	0.31	5.41
Annual Growth	2.8%		3.1%	2.0%	2.3%

Industrial and Commercial Bank of China Ltd

Boasting assets of roughly RMB$35 trillion, Industrial and Commercial Bank of China (ICBC) provides corporate, retail, and investment banking as well as asset management, pensions, financial leasing, insurance, and other financial services to 9.6 million corporate customers and 700 million personal customers, made possibly by about 7,500 domestic subsidiary employees and about 15,900 overseas employees. ICBC provides its products and services to corporations, government agencies, financial institutions, individual customers and other transactions. Industrial and Commercial Bank of China was founded on 1984.

Operations
Industrial and Commercial Bank of China (ICBC) operates three business segments. Corporate banking?which brings in roughly 50% of the bank's total operating income? provides traditional banking products, loans, trade financing, deposit-taking activities, corporate wealth management services, custody activities, and various other financial services to corporations, government agencies and financial institutions. Its personal banking division makes up about 40% of the bank's operating income and provides deposit, loan products as well as private banking services, card business, personal wealth management services and various types of personal intermediary services to individuals. Its treasury operations?which provide about 10% of total revenues?manage the bank's money market, foreign exchange, and investment securities.

In addition to these divisions, the bank also provides wealth management, asset custody, and pension services, and has a precious metals, franchise treasury, and asset securitization businesses.

Geographic Reach
Industrial and Commercial Bank of China (ICBC) is based in Beijing and generates more than 90% of its operating income from China, while the remainder comes from other countries and regions.

ICBC has subsidiaries and approximately 430 branches overseas. It has operations in Asia Pacific, Americas, and Europe.

Sales and Marketing
Industrial and Commercial Bank of China (ICBC) offers its services through its e-banking network, the internet, telephone, and self-service banking centers. It has about 15,800 outlets, more than 24,000 self-service banks, about 80,000 intelligent devices, and about 67,000 ATMs.

ICBC also caters to institutional customers in the fields of medical care, education, labor union, religion, public resources, land and resources, housing and construction.

Financial Performance
ICBC's performance for the past five years have continued to grow year-over-year with 2021 as its highest performing year over the period.

Operating income increased by RMB 60.8 billion to RMB 860.9 billion in 2021 as compared to 2020's revenue of RMB 800 billion.

The company's net profit for fiscal year end 2021 also saw an increase of RMB 32.5 billion to RMB 350.2 billion as compared to the prior year's net profit of RMB 317.7 billion.

ICBC's cash by the end of the year ended with RMB 1.4 trillion. Operations provided RMB 360.9 billion. Investing activities and financing activities used RMB 674.6 billion and RMB 11.6 billion, respectively. Main cash uses were purchases of financial investments and repayment on debt securities.

Strategy
For fiscal year end 2021, the company focused on four main parts of its strategy, namely, facilitating to build its name of being the 'No. 1 Personal Bank' promoting interactions with institutions such as the government, businesses, and consumption. The company also took a global response approach to extend global cash management services to more than 80 countries and regions. In addition, the company focused on building of two zones in Beijing as part of the company's strategy to sharpen its competitive edge. Lastly, the company implemented its Urban-Rural Collaborative Development Strategy wherein the company provided door-to-door services with portable intelligent terminals.

Mergers and Acquisitions
Company Background
Industrial and Commercial Bank of China (ICBC) was established in 1984 and went public in 2006. The bank ventured into the US broker-dealer business in 2010 when it acquired the Prime Dealer Services unit of Fortis Securities from BNP Paribas.

EXECUTIVES

Chief Risk Officer, Senior Executive Vice President, Executive Director, Jingwu Wang
Vice-Chairman, President, Senior Executive Vice President, Chief Risk Officer, Vice Chairman, Executive Director, Lin Liao
External Supervisor, Jie Zhang
Employee Supervisor, Xiangjiang Wu
Chief Supervisor, Liangbo Huang
Outside Supervisor, Lanbiao Liu
Chairman, Executive Director, Siqing Chen
Executive Director, Guoyu Zheng
Independent Non-Executive Director, Independent Director, Si Shen
Independent Non-Executive Director, Independent Director, Wellink Nout
Non-executive Director, Yongzhen Lu
Non-executive Director, Weidong Feng
Non-executive Director, Liqun Cao
Non-executive Director, Yifang Chen
Non-executive Director, Yang Dong
Independent Director, Zuliu Hu
Independent Director, Delin Chen
Auditors : Deloitte Touche Tohmatsu Certified Public Accountants LLP

LOCATIONS
HQ: Industrial and Commercial Bank of China Ltd
55 Fuxingmennei Avenue, Xicheng District, Beijing 100140
Phone: (86) 10 66106114   **Fax:** (86) 10 66107571
Web: www.icbc.com.cn

2018 Sales

	% of total
Mainland China	92
Overseas and other	8
Total	100

PRODUCTS/OPERATIONS
2018 Sales

	% of total
Interest	85
Non-interest	
Fees and commissions	15
Other	-
Total	100

2018 Sales by Segment

	% of total
Corporate banking	48
Personal banking	38
Treasury operations	13
Other	1
Total	100

Selected Services
Corporate banking services
Corporate Deposits and Loans
Institutional Banking
Investment Banking
Small and medium-sized enterprise business
Settlement and cash management
International settlement and trade finance
E-finance
ICBC Mobile
ICBC Mall
ICBC Link
Financing product line
Payment product line
Investment and wealth management product line
Personal banking services
Personal Finance
E-banking
Bank Card
Precious Metals
Private Banking
Global Market
Financial Asset Services
Wealth Management business
Asset Custody services
Pension services
Precious metal
Agency Treasury business
Asset securitization business
Agency sales
Treasury operations

Money Market activities
Investment
Financing
Channel and Development and Service Enhancement
Service enhancement
Consumer protection

COMPETITORS

AKBANK TURK ANONIM SIRKETI
BANK OF INDIA
Bank of Communications Co.,Ltd.
China Construction Bank Corporation
China Merchants Bank Co., Ltd.
HDFC BANK LIMITED
ICICI BANK LIMITED
Shinhan Financial Group Co., Ltd.
TURKIYE IS BANKASI ANONIM SIRKETI
Woori Finance Holdings Co., Ltd.

HISTORICAL FINANCIALS

Company Type: Public

Income Statement — FYE: December 31

	ASSETS ($mil)	NET INCOME ($mil)	INCOME AS % OF ASSETS	EMPLOYEES
12/22	5,741,660	52,254	0.9%	427,587
12/21	5,539,980	54,868	1.0%	434,089
12/20	5,098,440	48,301	0.9%	439,787
12/19	4,327,170	44,871	1.0%	445,106
12/18	4,027,100	43,277	1.1%	449,296
Annual Growth	9.3%	4.8%	—	(1.2%)

2022 Year-End Financials

Return on assets: 0.9%
Return on equity: 10.6%
Long-term debt ($ mil.): —
No. of shares ($ mil.): 356,406
Sales ($ mil.): 217,576
Dividends
Yield: —
Payout: 509.1%
Market value ($ mil.): 3,628,213

	STOCK PRICE ($) FY Close	P/E High/Low	PER SHARE ($) Earnings	Dividends	Book Value
12/22	10.18	12 9	0.14	0.72	1.42
12/21	11.23	16 11	0.15	0.69	1.44
12/20	12.81	19 12	0.13	0.62	1.24
12/19	15.37	18 14	0.12	0.61	1.08
12/18	14.16	21 16	0.12	0.61	0.95
Annual Growth	(7.9%)	—	4.2%	3.9%	10.6%

Infineon Technologies AG

Infineon Technologies is a world leader in semiconductor solutions. It develops, manufactures, and markets a large number of semiconductors and semiconductor-based solutions, focusing on key markets in the automotive, industrial, and consumer sectors. Its products range from standard components to special components for digital, analog, and mixed-signal applications, all the way to customer-specific solutions, together with the appropriate software. Its core business includes power semiconductors based on silicon (Si) in the form of IGBTs and MOSFETs. The company offer these as part of its extensive product portfolio to all relevant markets. Geographically, Greater China accounts for over 35% of the company's revenue.

Operations

The company operates in four segments: Automotive (around 45% of sales), Power & Sensor Systems (some 30%), Industrial Power Control (nearly 15%), and Connected Secure Systems (roughly 15%).

The Automotive segment is responsible for the semiconductor business for automotive electronics and for activities with memory products. The Power & Sensor Systems segment addresses more consumer-oriented applications and power supplies in general. In addition, activities in the area of radio frequency and sensor-based applications (including the recording of sensor data and interaction with machines and devices) fall within the sphere of responsibility of the Power & Sensor Systems segment. The Industrial Power Control segment concentrates on power semiconductors primarily used in industrial applications and renewable energy. Activities relating to traditional and new security applications, microcontrollers for non-automotive electronic applications and connectivity solutions are bundled in the Connected Secure Systems segment.

Geographic Reach

Headquartered in Germany, Infineon has regional headquarters in US (El Segundo, Milpitas and San Jose, California), Singapore, Shanghai and Tokyo.

Greater China is Infineon's largest single country market, accounting for over 35% of revenue. Customers in other parts of the Asia-Pacific region were around 15% of Infineon's revenue. The Europe, Middle East, and Africa and Americas market made up some 15% of revenue each. It also generates about 10% in Japan.

Financial Performance

The company reported a total revenue of EUR 14.2 billion in 2022, a 29% increase from the previous year's total revenue of EUR 11.1 billion.

In 2022, the company had a net income of EUR 2.2 billion, an 86% increase from the previous year's net income of EUR 1.2 billion.

The company's cash at the end of 2022 was EUR 1.4 billion. Operating activities generated EUR 4 billion, while investing activities used EUR 2.4 billion, mainly for purchases of financial investments. Financing activities used another EUR 2.4 billion, primarily for repayments of long-term financial debt.

Mergers and Acquisitions

In 2022, Infineon Technologies has acquired the Berlin-based startup Industrial Analytics. Infineon is thus strengthening its software and services business in artificial intelligence for predictive analysis relating to machinery and industrial equipment. Infineon is acquiring 100% of the company's shares. Both parties have agreed not to disclose the amount of the transaction.

Also in 2022, Infineon Technologies acquired NoBug Consulting SRL (Romania) and NoBug d.o.o. (Serbia). Founded in 1998, NoBug is a privately owned engineering company providing verification and design services for all the digital functionalities of semiconductor products. With approximately 120 engineers, NoBug Consulting SRL and NoBug d.o.o. are represented in Bucharest, Bra?ov, Ia?i (all Romania) and Belgrade (Serbia). By adding these R&D competence centers, Infineon is further accelerating the ability of its Connected Secure Systems (CSS) Division to work on complex IoT product developments. Thus, Infineon is building the basis for the IoT infrastructure of the future, enabling cybersecurity, AI and machine learning as well as robust connectivity. The parties have agreed not to disclose the purchase price.

HISTORY

Infineon Technologies was formed in 1999 from German industrial and electronics giant Siemens' semiconductor operations. Siemens, which was founded in 1847, began its semiconductor R&D program in 1952 -- just five years after scientists at Bell Laboratories invented the transistor. During the 1960s, Siemens' semiconductor operations developed chips for consumer electronics. By the early 1970s the company's facilities included chip factories in Malaysia and the Philippines. In 1985 Siemens released one of the first chipsets to comply with the ISDN communications standard. Five years later it released the first chipset for the Global System for Mobile Communications (GSM) cell phone standard.

Siemens in 1998 became one of the top 10 semiconductor companies by sales, despite falling DRAM prices that contributed to a loss for the year. In 1999 Siemens formed OSRAM Opto Semiconductor, an optoelectronics joint venture with its own subsidiary OSRAM. (Infineon subsequently sold its stake in the joint venture back to Siemens and exited the optoelectronics business.) Also in 1999, Siemens organized its semiconductor operations into a subsidiary, Infineon Technologies. Ulrich Schumacher, who had headed the semiconductor business, became Infineon's chairman and CEO. That year Infineon's alliance with IBM was converted into a joint venture, ALTIS Semiconductor.

In 2011 Infineon sold its wireless unit to Intel for about $1.4 billion in cash. Intel is looking to expand its offerings in the wireless market by purchasing what amounts to a complete portfolio of wireless chips, while Infineon wants to improve its results by concentrating on its core automotive, industrial, and security chip segments. The company had hoped to get around $2 billion for the wireless unit, which makes up around 30% of Infineon's total sales, but continues to lag behind wireless sector leaders QUALCOMM, Texas Instruments, and Broadcom.

EXECUTIVES

Chief Marketing Officer, Helmut Gasssel
Chief Financial Officer, Sven Schneider
Chief Executive Officer, Reinhard Ploss
Chief Digital Transformation Officer, Constanze Hufenbecher
Chief Operating Officer, Jochen Hanebeck
Chairman, Wolfgang Eder
Deputy Chairman, Johann Dechant
Director, Xiaoqun Clever
Director, Friedrich Eichiner
Director, Annette Engelfried
Director, Peter Gruber
Director, Hans-Ulrich Holdenried
Director, Susanne Lachenmann
Director, Geraldine Picaud
Director, Manfred Puffer
Director, Melanie Riedl
Director, Juergen Scholtz
Director, Kerstin Schulzendorf
Director, Ulrich Spiesshofer
Director, Margret Suckale
Director, Diana Vitale
Auditors : KPMG AG

LOCATIONS

HQ: Infineon Technologies AG
Am Campeon 1-15, Neubiberg D-85579
Phone: (49) 89 234 0   **Fax:** (49) 89 234 9552987
Web: www.infineon.com

2018 sales

	% of total
Germany	15
Greater China	34
Europe, Middle East, Africa	17
Americas	12
Asia-Pacific	15
Japan	7
Total	100

PRODUCTS/OPERATIONS

2018 sales

	% of total
Automotive	43
Power Management & Multi-market	31
Industrial Power Control	17
Digital Security Solutions	9
Other Operating Segments	—
Total	100

COMPETITORS

ADVANCED ENERGY INDUSTRIES, INC.
AMKOR TECHNOLOGY, INC.
BEL FUSE INC.
CYPRESS SEMICONDUCTOR CORPORATION
IXYS, LLC
PULSE ELECTRONICS CORPORATION
RENESAS ELECTRONICS AMERICA INC.
SOITEC
TDK CORPORATION
VICOR CORPORATION

HISTORICAL FINANCIALS
Company Type: Public

Income Statement   FYE: September 30

	REVENUE ($mil)	NET INCOME ($mil)	NET PROFIT MARGIN	EMPLOYEES
09/23	17,279	3,323	19.2%	58,590
09/22	13,859	2,124	15.3%	56,194
09/21	12,802	1,353	10.6%	50,288
09/20	10,030	430	4.3%	46,665
09/19	8,758	949	10.8%	41,418
Annual Growth	18.5%	36.8%	—	9.1%

2023 Year-End Financials
Debt ratio: 17.6%   No. of shares ($ mil.): 1,303
Return on equity: 19.6%   Dividends
Cash ($ mil.): 1,928   Yield: —
Current Ratio: 1.89   Payout: 8.9%
Long-term debt ($ mil.): 4,664 Market value ($ mil.): 43,245

	STOCK PRICE ($) FY Close	P/E High/Low		PER SHARE ($) Earnings	Dividends	Book Value
09/23	33.17	18	10	2.52	0.23	13.85
09/22	21.96	26	13	1.61	0.21	11.19
09/21	41.14	51	31	1.01	0.18	10.14
09/20	28.24	111	46	0.30	0.20	9.20
09/19	18.01	31	20	0.82	0.21	7.57
Annual Growth	16.5%	—	—	32.5%	1.7%	16.3%

Infosys Ltd.

Infosys is a leading provider of consulting, technology, outsourcing and next-generation digital services, enabling clients around the world to create and execute strategies for their digital transformation. The company also provides digital marketing, artificial intelligence, automation, analytics, engineering services, and Internet of Things services among others. Its subsidiary Infosys BPM provides business process outsourcing services. Infosys makes almost all of its sales overseas, with North America accounting for more than 60% of the total. Key industries served by the company are financial services, insurance, manufacturing, telecom, retail, and consumer goods.

Operations

The company's business segment are enterprises primarily in Financial Services and Insurance (over 30% of sales), enterprises in Retail (some 15%), enterprises in Communication (over 10%), enterprises in the Energy, Utilities, Resources and Services (over 10%), enterprises in Manufacturing (roughly 10%), enterprises in Hi-Tech (nearly 10%), enterprises in Life Sciences (over 5%), and all other segments account for the rest. The Financial Services reportable segments has been aggregated to include the Financial Services operating segment and Finacle operating segment because of the similarity of the economic characteristics. All other segments represent the operating segments of businesses in India, Japan, China, Infosys Public Services & other enterprises in Public Services.

About 95% of sales were generated from software services. Software products and platforms account for the rest.

Geographic Reach

The company, headquartered in Bengaluru, India, currently has presence in more than 245 locations across about 55 countries. Sales from North American markets account for more than 60%, followed by Europe with approximately 25%, India with less than 5%, and the rest of the world accounts for the remaining sales.

Sales and Marketing

The company organized its sales and marketing functions into teams, across nearly 55 countries around the world, focusing on delivering digital solutions for specific industries and geographies. It serves industries such as aerospace and defense, agriculture, automotive, communication services, consumer packaged goods, education, and engineering procurement and construction, among others.

Financial Performance

The company's revenue increased 20% from $13.6 billion in 2021 to $16.3 billion in 2022. This was primarily attributable to an increase in digital revenues, deal wins including large deals and volume increases across most of the segments.

In 2022, the company had a net income of $3 billion, a 19% increase from the previous year's net income of $2.5 billion.

The company's cash for the year ended 2022 was $2.3 billion. Operating activities generated $3.3 billion, while investing activities used $1 billion, mainly for liquid mutual fund units and fixed maturity plan securities. Financing activities used another $3.3 billion, mainly for payments of dividends.

Strategy

Infosys seeks to acquire or make strategic investments in complementary businesses, new and emerging technologies, services or products, or enter into strategic partnerships or alliances with third parties in order to enhance its business.

The company has made, and may in the future make, strategic investments in early-stage technology start-up companies in order to gain experience in or exploit niche technologies.

Mergers and Acquisitions

In mid-2022, Infosys announced a definitive agreement to acquire Denmark-based BASE life science, a leading technology and consulting firm in the life sciences industry, in Europe. The acquisition reaffirms the company's commitment to help global life sciences companies realize business value from cloud-first digital platforms and data, to speed-up clinical trials and scale drug development, positively impacting lives, and achieving better health outcomes.

In early 2022, Infosys completed the acquisition of oddity, a Germany-based digital marketing, experience, and commerce agency. The acquisition further strengthens Infosys' creative, branding and experience design capabilities, and demonstrates its continued commitment to co-create with clients, and help them navigate their digital transformation journey. oddity brings to Infosys a comprehensive service portfolio comprising digital-first brand management and communication, in-house production, including virtual and augmented reality, experience design and e-commerce services as well as its metaverse-ready set-up across Europe.

HISTORY

After receiving a master's degree in electrical engineering from one of India's highly regarded Institutes of Technology (Kanpur) in the 1960s, Narayana Murthy left for France and a job developing software for the air traffic control system at Paris' Charles de Gaulle airport.

During college Murthy had developed the belief that communism was the answer to his country's problems with poverty and corruption, a stance that was fortified during his time spent with Paris leftists in the 1970s. But while hitchhiking back to India in 1974, Murthy's Marxist sympathies eroded quickly after he was jailed in Hungary for allegedly disclosing state secrets while talking with Austrian tourists on a train. Murthy became a socialist at heart but capitalist in practice, setting out on a mission to create wealth rather than redistribute it.

That mission officially began in 1981, when Murthy convinced six fellow software engineers to start their own company. Infosys was founded that year with $250 in capital (mostly borrowed from their wives) and no idea of what it would sell.

From the beginning Murthy looked for business outside India, where he was able to sell customizable, inexpensive software to multinational corporations, such as Reebok and Nordstrom. But a lack of reputation and government regulations made business difficult for Infosys during the 1980s -- it took nine months just to get the company's first telephone line, and three years to import new computers. Infosys opened its first US office in 1987.

Many of the government regulations that had kept India's economy stagnant were lifted when reform swept the country in 1991. But this also opened the door for companies such as IBM (which had been asked to leave in 1977) and Digital Equipment (later acquired by Compaq) to enter India and lure away its best engineers. While no Indian company had ever done this before, Murthy initiated a stock option plan and other perks to retain his employees. Infosys went public in 1993. Morgan Stanley swooped in to salvage the undersubscribed IPO in a move that would later reap millions when Infosys' stock began to soar.

EXECUTIVES

Chief Executive Officer, Managing Director, Executive Director, Salil Parekh
Chief Financial Officer, Nilanjan Roy
Human Resources Group Head, Shaji Mathew
General Counsel, Chief Compliance Officer, Inderpreet Sawhney
Non-Independent Non-Executive Chairman, Nandan M. Nilekani
Lead Independent Non-Executive Director, D. Sundaram
Independent Non-Executive Director, Michael Gibbs
Independent Non-Executive Director, Bobby Parikh
Independent Non-Executive Director, Chitra Nayak
Independent Non-Executive Director, Govind Iyer
Auditors : Deloitte Haskins & Sells LLP

LOCATIONS

HQ: Infosys Ltd.
Electronics City, Hosur Road, Bengaluru, Karnataka 560 100
Phone: (91) 80 2852 0261   Fax: (91) 80 2852 0362
Web: www.infosys.com

2019 Sales

	% of total
North America	61
Europe	24
India	2
Rest of the World	13
Total	100

PRODUCTS/OPERATIONS

2019 Sales

	% of total
Software services	95
Software products	5
Total	100

2019 Sales by Market

	% of total
Financial services & insurance	32
Retail	16
Communication	13
Manufacturing	10
Life Sciences	6
All Other Segments	3
Total	100

Selected Services
Business process management
Custom application development
Engineering
Information technology consulting
Infrastructure management
Maintenance and production support
Management consulting
Operations and business process consulting
Package evaluation and implementation
Software re-engineering
Systems integration
Testing

COMPETITORS

ATOS SYNTEL INC.
CAPGEMINI
CGI Inc
COMPUTACENTER PLC
COMPUTER TASK GROUP, INCORPORATED
DHI GROUP, INC.
FORESCOUT TECHNOLOGIES, INC.
IGATE CORP.
VIRTUSA CORPORATION
WIPRO LIMITED

HISTORICAL FINANCIALS

Company Type: Public

Income Statement   FYE: March 31

	REVENUE ($mil)	NET INCOME ($mil)	NET PROFIT MARGIN	EMPLOYEES
03/23	18,212	2,981	16.4%	343,234
03/22	16,311	2,963	18.2%	314,015
03/21	13,561	2,613	19.3%	259,619
03/20	12,780	2,331	18.2%	242,371
03/19	11,799	2,199	18.6%	228,123
Annual Growth	11.5%	7.9%		10.8%

2023 Year-End Financials
Debt ratio: —   No. of shares ($ mil.): 4,136
Return on equity: 31.1%   Dividends
Cash ($ mil.): 1,481   Yield: 1.9%
Current Ratio: 1.81   Payout: 47.8%
Long-term debt ($ mil.): —   Market value ($ mil.): 72,139

	STOCK PRICE ($) FY Close	P/E High/Low		PER SHARE ($) Earnings	Dividends	Book Value
03/23	17.44	35	23	0.71	0.34	2.22
03/22	24.89	37	25	0.70	0.34	2.37
03/21	18.72	31	12	0.61	0.24	2.46
03/20	8.21	22	13	0.55	0.30	2.04
03/19	10.93	41	18	0.51	0.96	2.17
Annual Growth	12.4%			8.6%	(22.9%)	0.6%

ING Groep NV

ING Groep, with its tagline, "do your thing", offers banking services and activities for small and medium enterprises (SMEs) and mid-corporate clients. The group serves an estimate of about 40 million individual customers. Some of the group's services include payments, savings, insurance, investments, and lending products. ING made improvements and developments in its end-to-end digitalization in its operation as a result of the growing demand for digital and platform services. The group generates majority of its revenues from the Netherlands, Belgium, and Luxembourg. ING has its presence in more than 40 countries.

Operations

ING operates through six primary banking segments: Wholesale Banking (around 30%), Retail Netherlands (roughly 25%), Retail Other (about 20%), Retail Belgium (nearly 15%), Retail Germany (some 10%), and Corporate Line Banking.

ING's retail banking services countries are in the Market Leaders category (Netherlands, Belgium, and Germany). Most of its income is generated from the retail and private banking activities in these countries. Some of the products include savings accounts, business lending, mortgages, and other consumer lending in the Netherlands.

The group's wholesale banking offer products such as lending, debt capital markets, working capital solutions, export, finance, daily banking solutions, treasury, and risk solutions as well as corporate finance.

Geographic Reach

ING operates in more than 40 countries in Europe, North America, Latin America, Australia and the Asia region. Its revenue base is diversified, with the Netherlands, its largest single market, accounting for more than 30% of its total underlying banking income, followed by Belgium (more than 15%) and Germany (nearly 15%). Other important countries are Australia, Austria, Czech Republic, France, Germany, Italy, and Spain.

ING is headquartered in the Netherlands.

Sales and Marketing

ING serves approximately 40 million clients ranging from large companies to multinational corporations and financial institutions.

Financial Performance

ING's performance for the span of five years has continued to fluctuate.

The group's revenue decreased by ?669 million to ?17.6 billion compared to 2019's revenue of ?18.3 billion. The decrease was mainly due to the decrease in all its segments.

Net income decreased by ?495 million to ?13.6 billion compared to the prior year's net income of ?14.1 billion.

ING's cash held in 2020 at the end of the year amounted to ?111.5 billion. The bank's operations generated ?101.2 billion. Investing activities and financing activities used ?8.5 billion and ?34.7 billion, respectively. Main cash uses were for payment of securities at amortized cost and repayment of debt securities.

Strategy

ING's strategy revolves around its data-driven digital and mobile-first approach. With the effects of the global pandemic, the urgency to implement end-to-end digitalization was increased. This was to meet the growing demand for mobile banking as well as enhancing operational excellence.

The company's "Think Forward" strategy aims to empower its customers through earning primary relationship, mastering data, and being innovative through providing service to the changing customer needs. The group also incorporated banking to their platform for customers to be able to connect to the products and services of others in the banking sector. ING is building digital channels such as its OneApp, which is used by customers in the Netherlands, Belgium, and Germany.

Company Background

Prior to the economic meltdown, ING took aim at becoming a financial services player in all four corners of the world and made acquisitions accordingly. Along with much of the insurance industry, it shifted its base from traditional life insurance products to investment-backed products, which favor companies that can sell through banks. ING utilized its owns banks to distribute such products. The company also targeted expansion in growing economies such as South Korea, Turkey, and Thailand to meet anticipated consumer demand for new banking and retirement options. In more mature markets like North America and Europe, the company had the aging population in its sights and placed retirement planning and pensions as sources of future growth.

HISTORY

ING Groep's roots go back to 1845 when its earliest predecessor, the Netherlands Insurance Co., was founded. The firm began expanding geographically; in 1903 it added life insurance. In 1963 it merged with the century-old Nationale Life Insurance Bank to form Nationale-Nederland (NN). Over the next three decades, the company grew primarily through acquisitions in Europe, North America, and Australia. In 1986 NN became the first European life insurance company to be licensed in Japan.

Another predecessor, the Rijkspostspaarbank, was founded in 1881 to provide Dutch citizens with simple post office savings accounts. In 1918 the Postcheque-en Girondienst (giro) system was established to allow people to use vouchers drawn on their savings accounts to pay bills. This system became the main method of settling accounts (instead of bank checking accounts).

Rijkspostspaarbank and Postcheque merged in 1986 to become Postbank. Postbank merged in 1989 with the Nederlandse Middenstandsbank (founded 1927) to become NMB Postbank. The vast amounts of cash tied up in the post office savings and giro systems fueled NMB's business.

In 1991, as the European economic union became a reality and barriers between banking and insurance began to fall, NN merged with NMB Postbank to form Internationale Nederland Groep (ING). ING began cutting costs, shedding redundant offices and unprofitable operations in both its segments. In the US, where insurance and banking were legally divided, the company "debanked" itself in order to keep its more lucrative insurance operations (but retained the right to provide banking services to those operations).

ING sought to increase its investment banking and finance operations in the 1990s. In 1995 it took over UK-based Barings Bank (personal banker to the Queen of England) after Nicholas Leeson, a trader in Barings' Singapore office, lost huge sums of money in derivatives trading. The acquisition gave the firm a higher profile but cost more than anticipated and left it embroiled in lingering legal actions.

In 1996 ING bought Poland's Bank Slaski (the company had first entered Poland in 1994). The next year it expanded its securities business by acquiring investment bank Furman Selz, doubled its US life insurance operations by purchasing Equitable of Iowa, and listed on the NYSE. In 1998 ING's acquisition strategy again involved Europe and North America: It bought Belgium's Banque Bruxelles Lambert and Canadian life insurer Guardian Insurance Co. (from Guardian Royal Exchange, now part of AXA UK).

ING turned eastward in 1999, kicking off asset management operations in India and buying a minority stake in South Korea's HC&B (formerly Housing & Commercial Bank). In 2000 the company bulked up its North American operations with the purchase of 40% of Savia SA, a Mexican insurance concern. It also bought US firm ReliaStar Financial in a $6 billion deal and Charterhouse Securities from CCF (then called Crédit Commercial de France).

In 2004 ING realigned its management structure, dividing the company's operations into six business lines: Insurance Americas, Insurance Europe, Insurance Asia-Pacific, Wholesale Banking, Retail Banking, and ING Direct. ING boosted its North American insurance operations with the acquisition of Allianz's Canadian property and casualty operations.

The company struggled with investment banking arm ING Barings. The unit was reorganized and streamlined for cost-savings purposes, but ultimately was put on the block. Its Asian equities operations were sold to Macquarie Bank in 2004. Barings Private Equity Partners unit was sold to its management. The Barings investment management operations were sold, as well.

The company struggled with investment banking arm ING Barings. The unit was reorganized and streamlined for cost-savings purposes, but ultimately was put on the block. Its Asian equities operations were sold to Macquarie Bank in 2004. Barings Private Equity Partners unit was sold to its management. The Barings investment management operations were sold to MassMutual in 2005, while Northern Trust bought up its fund administration, trust, and custody operations.

ING sold most of ING BHF-Bank to Sal. Oppenheim during 2004. The next year ING turned over its US life reinsurance operations to Scottish Re and sold subsidiary Life Insurance Company of Georgia to Jackson National Life.

During 2005 ING acquired a 20% stake in the Bank of Beijing as part of a strategic alliance. In 2006 the company sold off its UK brokerage business, Williams de Broë, to The Evolution Group.

In 2008 the company acquired CitiStreet, a leading US administrator of defined-contribution retirement savings, pension, health, and other plans; it paid about $900 million for the firm.

After the global financial crisis hit in 2008, ING accepted a ?10 billion (more than $13 billion) bailout loan from the Dutch government. The bailout was intended to shore up the company's capital position and reassure wary investors. Strategic measures to further offset losses and repay debt were enacted in 2009 including layoffs and asset sales. CEO Michael Tilmant stepped down and was replaced by former chairman Jan Hommen. By the end of 2009, job cuts totaled about 10% of its workforce. The company also outlined plans to split the company in half by separating its insurance and banking operations.

Prior to the bailout, ING has already been working to simplify and streamline its operations through a "Back to Basics" strategy. Restructuring measures under the strategy include the refocusing of ING's banking operations on (mostly Central) Europe and the reduction of the company's US financial product offerings.

In early 2009 the company sold its ING Canada property/casualty business, which was then renamed Intact Financial. ING sold its life insurance joint venture stake in Australia and New Zealand to partner ANZ and offloaded its noncore annuity and mortgage businesses in Chile to life insurer Corp Group Vida Chile in late 2009. The company also sold its Taiwanese life insurance business to Fubon Financial Holding in a deal worth ?447 million ($600 million) in mid-2009. ING gained a 5% stake in Fubon through the deal, which it sold the following year for another ?395 million ($522 million).

In early 2010 ING completed sales of the company's Swiss Private Banking unit to Julius Baer for $506 million and its Asian Private Banking unit (operating in Hong Kong, the Philippines, and Singapore) to OCBC Bank for nearly $1.5 billion. In addition, the company sold its North American reinsurance operations to RGA and most of its US insurance brokerage operations to Lightyear Capital in early 2010. ING has also agreed to sell its stake in one of its Chinese life insurance ventures (Pacific Antai with China Pacific Insurance) to China Construction Bank.

In 2011 ING sold its Asian and European real estate investment management (REIM) operations, as well as select US REIM assets, for about $940 million to broker CBRE Group (formerly CB Richard Ellis Group). The firm sold its remaining US REIM assets to Lightyear Capital for some $100 million. Also that year the firm agreed to sell its Australian investment management business to UBS for an undisclosed sum.

Farther south, in 2011 the company sold its Latin American insurance operations to Columbian insurer GrupoSura for $3.7 billion.

The sale included insurance, savings, and investment management operations in Chile, Colombia, Mexico, Uruguay, and Peru. It also sold ING Car Least to BMW.

In 2016 the group exited the insurance business to focus on the European banking market.

EXECUTIVES

Chief Executive Officer, Steven van Rijswijk
Chief Financial Officer, Executive Director, Tanate Phutrakul
Chief Risk Officer, Ljiljana Cortan
Secretary, Cindy van Eldert-Klep
Director, Chairman, Hans G. J. Wijers
Director, Vice-Chairman, Mike Rees
Director, Jan Peter (J.P.) Balkenende
Director, Juan Colombas
Director, Harold Naus
Director, Herman Hulst
Director, Mariana Gheorghe
Director, Herna Verhagen
Director, Margarete Haase
Auditors : KPMG Accountants N.V.

LOCATIONS

HQ: ING Groep NV
  Bijlmerdreef 106, Amsterdam 1102 CT
Phone: (31) 20 564 7705
Web: www.ing.com

2018 sales

	%
Netherlands	32
Belgium	17
Germany	14
Other Challengers	10
Growth Markets	13
Wholesale Banking Rest of the World	13
Other	1
Total	100

PRODUCTS/OPERATIONS

2018 Sales

	% of total
Net interest income	76
Net fee and commission income	15
Valuation results & net trading income	6
Investment income	1
Share of results from associates and joint ventures	1
Other	1
Total	100

2018 sales

	%
Retail Banking	67
Wholesale Banking	32
Corporate Line Banking	1
Total	100

COMPETITORS

AEGON N.V.
AUSTRALIA AND NEW ZEALAND BANKING GROUP LIMITED
Achmea B.V.
MMC VENTURES LIMITED
NN Group N.V.
Randstad N.V.
Royal Bank Of Canada
The Bank of Nova Scotia
The Toronto-Dominion Bank
Wolters Kluwer N.V.

HISTORICAL FINANCIALS

Company Type: Public

Income Statement   FYE: December 31

	ASSETS ($mil)	NET INCOME ($mil)	INCOME AS % OF ASSETS	EMPLOYEES
12/21	1,074,420	6,735	0.6%	57,660
12/20	1,146,150	2,761	0.2%	55,901
12/19	997,600	4,382	0.4%	53,431
12/18	1,013,040	5,452	0.5%	52,233
12/17	1,011,600	6,549	0.6%	51,504
Annual Growth	1.5%	0.7%	—	2.9%

2021 Year-End Financials

Return on assets: 0.6%
Return on equity: 11.4%
Long-term debt ($ mil.): —
No. of shares ($ mil.): 3,775
Sales ($ mil.): 26,590
Dividends
  Yield: 4.2%
  Payout: 33.0%
Market value ($ mil.): 52,559

	STOCK PRICE ($) FY Close	P/E High/Low		PER SHARE ($) Earnings	Dividends	Book Value
12/21	13.92	10	5	1.73	0.59	15.61
12/20	9.44	24	9	0.71	0.15	16.24
12/19	12.05	14	9	1.12	0.62	14.70
12/18	10.66	16	9	1.40	0.64	14.44
12/17	18.46	14	11	1.69	0.65	14.94
Annual Growth	(6.8%)			0.6%	(2.2%)	1.1%

Inpex Corp.

INPEX explores for natural gas and oil in Indonesia and Australia, along with other oil-rich areas such as the Caspian Sea, Middle East, and South America. The company, which is focusing its efforts on cleaner-burning liquefied natural gas, exports its products from Indonesia to Japan, Singapore, and Malaysia. INPEX's projects reside in the Minami-Nagaoka gas field, one of the largest gas fields in Japan, and it operates additional liquefied natural gas terminals and units throughout the globe. The company operates through 70 subsidiaries and 20 associated companies.

Strategy

INPEX is researching new technologies designed to improve the efficiency of natural gas. The company is also exploring alternative fuels production including GTL (a replacement for gas oil) and DME (replacement for propane gas).

EXECUTIVES

Chairman, Representative Director, Toshiaki Kitamura
President, Representative Director, Takayuki Ueda
Executive Vice President, Director, Kenji Kawano
Senior Managing Executive Officer, Director, Kimihisa Kittaka
Senior Managing Executive Officer, Director, Nobuharu Sase

Director, Daisuke Yamada
Director, Toshiaki Takimoto
Outside Director, Jun Yanai
Outside Director, Norinao Iio
Outside Director, Atsuko Nishimura
Outside Director, Tomoo Nishikawa
Outside Director, Hideka Morimoto
Auditors : Ernst & Young ShinNihon LLC

LOCATIONS

HQ: Inpex Corp.
5-3-1 Akasaka, Minato-ku, Tokyo 107-6332
Phone: (81) 3 5572 0233
Web: www.inpex.co.jp

2016 Sales

	% of total
Japan	49
Asia & Oceania	37
UAE	10
Other	4
Total	100

2016 Sales

	% of total
Middle East & Africa	51
Asia & Oceania	30
Japan	11
Eurasia (Europe & NIS)	7
Americas	1
Total	100

PRODUCTS/OPERATIONS

2016 Sales

	% of total
Crude oil	67
Natural gas (excluding LPG)	30
LPG	1
Other	2
Total	100

COMPETITORS

Blackpearl Resources Inc
ERHC ENERGY INC.
Husky Energy Inc
IDEMITSU KOSAN CO.,LTD.
Ivanhoe Energy Inc
Keyera Corp
LIQUEFIED NATURAL GAS LIMITED
QATARGAS OPERATING COMPANY LIMITED
SENECA RESOURCES COMPANY, LLC
Trafina Energy Ltd

HISTORICAL FINANCIALS

Company Type: Public

Income Statement — FYE: December 31

	REVENUE ($mil)	NET INCOME ($mil)	NET PROFIT MARGIN	EMPLOYEES
12/22	17,641	3,326	18.9%	3,759
12/21	10,810	1,937	17.9%	3,658
12/20	7,480	(1,083)	—	3,715
12/19*	9,210	1,137	12.4%	3,721
03/19	8,771	867	9.9%	4,029
Annual Growth	19.1%	39.9%	—	(1.7%)

*Fiscal year change

2022 Year-End Financials

Debt ratio: 0.2%
Return on equity: 12.7%
Cash ($ mil.): 1,728
Current Ratio: 1.38
Long-term debt ($ mil.): 9,063
No. of shares ($ mil.): 1,265
Dividends
 Yield: —
 Payout: 0.0%
Market value ($ mil.): 13,958

Stock History

	STOCK PRICE ($) FY Close	P/E High/Low		PER SHARE ($) Earnings	Dividends	Book Value
12/22	10.68	0	0	2.43	0.89	21.93
12/21	8.77	0	0	1.34	0.29	19.57
12/20	5.41	—	—	(0.74)	0.39	18.18
12/19*	10.35	0	0	0.78	0.25	19.18
03/19	9.50	0	0	0.59	0.24	18.59
Annual Growth	3.0%	—	—	42.3%	38.1%	4.2%

*Fiscal year change

Intact Financial Corp

Intact Financial is the largest provider of property and casualty (P&C) insurance in Canada, a leading provider of global specialty insurance, and, with RSA, a leader in the UK and Ireland. In Canada, Intact provides repair and restoration services through its subsidiary On Side Restoration, a leading restoration company, restoring damaged homes and businesses. Intact also provides affinity insurance solutions through the Johnson Affinity Groups. Intact Financial generates its revenue in Canada. Intact Financial began in 1809 as The Halifax Fire Insurance Association.

IPO

Operations

Its Personal auto business accounts for about 30% of direct written premiums, personal property business accounts for about 25% of direct premiums written, while commercial insurance and specialty lines account for around 25% each.

The company has three reportable segments: Canada (more than 65% of direct written premiums), UK & International (more than 20%), and the US (about 10%).

In Canada, Intact distributes insurance under the Intact Insurance brand through a wide network of brokers, including its wholly-owned subsidiary BrokerLink, and directly to consumers through belairdirect. It also provide affinity insurance solutions through the Johnson Affinity Groups. Intact Public Entities is the MGA platform for distributing public entity insurance products in Canada. Coast Underwriters is its MGA specialized in Marine Insurance.

In the US, Intact Insurance Specialty Solutions provides a range of specialty insurance products and services through independent agencies, regional and national brokers, wholesalers and managing general agencies.

Across the UK, Ireland, and Europe, Intact Financial provides personal, commercial and specialty insurance solutions through the RSA brands.

Geographic Reach

Based in Toronto, Canada, Intact Financial operates across Canada, UK, Ireland, Europe, and the US.

Sales and Marketing

In the US, Intact Insurance Specialty Solutions provides a range of specialty insurance products and services through independent agencies, regional and national brokers, and wholesalers and managing general agencies.

Company Background

As ING Canada, the company went public in 2004 and used a portion of the proceeds from the IPO to acquire the Canadian operations of Allianz Group. After the IPO, Dutch insurance giant ING Groep held 70% of the company. It sold its holdings in 2008 to help offset losses elsewhere. Half of its holdings were sold to the public, while the other half went to institutional investors. Following the separation, the company changed its name to Intact Financial in 2009.

EXECUTIVES

Chief Executive Officer, Director, Charles J. G. Brindamour
Personal Lines Executive Vice President, Personal Lines Chief Operating Officer, Patrick Barbeau
Executive Vice President, Chief Legal Officer, Secretary, Frederic Cotnoir
Intact Insurance Executive Vice President, Debbie Coull-Cicchini
Sales and Marketing, Direct to Consumer Distribution Executive Vice President, Direct Distribution Executive Vice President, Sales and Marketing, Direct to Consumer Distribution Chief Marketing and Communications Officer, Direct Distribution Chief Marketing and Communications Officer, Anne Fortin
Global Specialty Lines Executive Vice President, Darren Godfrey
Executive Vice President, Chief Financial Officer, Louis Marcotte
Executive Vice President, Chief Risk & Actuarial Officer, Benoit Morissette
Intact Investment Management Inc. Executive Vice President, Intact Investment Management Inc. Managing Director, Werner Muehlemann
Executive Vice President, Chief People, Strategy and Climate Office, Carla J. Smith
Senior Vice President, Chief Internal Auditor, Sonya Cote
Chairman, Claude Dussault
Corporate Director, Emmanuel Clarke
Corporate Director, Jane E. Kinney
Corporate Director, Robert G. Leary
Corporate Director, Sylvie Paquette
Corporate Director, Timothy H. Penner
Corporate Director, Indira V. Samarasekera
Corporate Director, Frederick Singer
Corporate Director, William L. Young
Director, Janet De Silva
Director, Stuart J. Russell
Director, Carolyn A. Wilkin
Auditors : Ernst & Young LLP

LOCATIONS

HQ: Intact Financial Corp
700 University Avenue, Suite 1500, Toronto, Ontario
M5G 0A1
Phone: 866 464-2424
Web: www.intactfc.com

2015 Premiums

	% of total
Ontario	41
Quebec	27
Alberta	18
British Columbia	6
Rest of Canada	8
Total	100

PRODUCTS/OPERATIONS

2015 Premiums

	% of total
Personal auto	45
Commercial property & casualty	23
Personal property	23
Commercial auto	9
Total	100

COMPETITORS

AMERICAN FAMILY MUTUAL INSURANCE COMPANY, S.I.
AVIVA PLC
CINCINNATI FINANCIAL CORPORATION
FIRST ACCEPTANCE CORPORATION
GAINSCO, INC.
LIBERTY MUTUAL AGENCY CORPORATION
THE HANOVER INSURANCE GROUP INC
THE HARTFORD FINANCIAL SERVICES GROUP, INC.
THE PROGRESSIVE CORPORATION
THE TRAVELERS COMPANIES INC

HISTORICAL FINANCIALS

Company Type: Public

Income Statement — FYE: December 31

	ASSETS ($mil)	NET INCOME ($mil)	INCOME AS % OF ASSETS	EMPLOYEES
12/22	48,031	1,792	3.7%	28,500
12/21	52,093	1,622	3.1%	26,000
12/20	27,582	849	3.1%	0
12/19	24,798	579	2.3%	0
12/18	20,899	519	2.5%	14,000
Annual Growth	23.1%	36.3%	—	19.4%

2022 Year-End Financials

Return on assets: 3.6%
Return on equity: 15.6%
Long-term debt ($ mil.): —
No. of shares ($ mil.): 175
Sales ($ mil.): 15,001
Dividends
Yield: —
Payout: 29.7%
Market value ($ mil.): 25,616

	STOCK PRICE ($) FY Close	P/E High/Low		PER SHARE ($) Earnings	Dividends	Book Value
12/22	146.16	11	9	9.95	2.96	64.97
12/21	130.07	11	9	9.74	2.67	69.89
12/20	118.84	17	12	5.65	2.61	52.63
12/19	107.42	21	15	3.90	2.33	46.97
12/18	71.89	17	14	3.52	2.06	41.20
Annual Growth	19.4%	—	—	29.7%	9.5%	12.1%

International Consolidated Airlines Group SA

EXECUTIVES

Chief Executive Officer, Executive Director, Luis Gallego
Chief Information Officer, John Gibbs
Chief Financial Officer, Nicholas Cadbury
Chief People, Corporate Affairs and Sustainability Officer, Carolina Martinoli
Interim Chief Strategy Officer, Julio Rodriguez
General Counsel, Sarah Clements
Secretary, Alvaro Lopez-Jorrin
Deputy Secretary, Lucila Rodriguez
Chairman, Non-Executive Director, Javier Ferran
Senior Independent Director, Non-Executive Director, Heather Ann McSharry
Independent Non-Executive Director, Eva Castillo Sanz
Independent Non-Executive Director, Maurice Lam
Independent Non-Executive Director, Margaret Ewing
Independent Non-Executive Director, Lucy Nicola Shaw
Independent Non-Executive Director, Emilio Saracho
Independent Non-Executive Director, Peggy B. Bruzelius
Non-Executive Director, Giles Agutter
Non-Executive Director, Robin Phillips
Auditors : KPMG Auditores S.L.

LOCATIONS

HQ: International Consolidated Airlines Group SA
El Caserio, Iberia Zona Industrial 2, Camino de La Munoza s/n, Madrid 28042
Phone: (44) 20 8564 2800
Web: www.iairgroup.com

HISTORICAL FINANCIALS

Company Type: Public

Income Statement — FYE: December 31

	REVENUE ($mil)	NET INCOME ($mil)	NET PROFIT MARGIN	EMPLOYEES
12/22	24,635	460	1.9%	66,044
12/21	9,569	(3,319)	—	56,658
12/20	9,580	(8,496)	—	57,928
12/19	28,637	1,925	6.7%	64,642
12/18	27,949	3,303	11.8%	63,531
Annual Growth	(3.1%)	(38.9%)	—	1.0%

2022 Year-End Financials

Debt ratio: 28.2%
Return on equity: 30.1%
Cash ($ mil.): 10,252
Current Ratio: 0.79
Long-term debt ($ mil.): 9,919
No. of shares ($ mil.): 4,954
Dividends
Yield: —
Payout: 0.0%
Market value ($ mil.): 14,467

	STOCK PRICE ($) FY Close	P/E High/Low		PER SHARE ($) Earnings	Dividends	Book Value
12/22	2.92	51	26	0.07	0.00	0.43
12/21	3.81	—	—	(0.67)	0.00	0.19
12/20	4.36	—	—	(2.41)	0.85	0.32
12/19	16.55	21	12	0.95	1.33	3.86
12/18	15.58	13	10	1.57	0.51	3.86
Annual Growth	(34.2%)	—	—	(54.9%)	—	(42.1%)

International Distributions Services Plc

Royal Mail is an international business that provides postal and delivery services across our extensive networks. The company carries letters and other items daily to some 31 million addresses in the UK and around 40 countries internationally. Its combined parcels and letters UK network delivers the Universal Service. Royal Mail estimates that it visits around 60% of UK delivery points each day. Through its Local Collect network which consists of 11,100 Delivery Offices and Post Offices, Royal Mail the most accessible delivery operator in the UK. The enterprise, long government-owned, went public in late 2013.

Operations

The company consists of two principal operations. Its?UK-based operation which includes Royal?Mail?and Parcelforce Worldwide (Royal Mail; accounts for about 65% of sales) and its international operation, General Logistics?Systems (GLS; about 35%).

As the UK's sole designated Universal Service Provider, Royal Mail delivers a?'one-price-goes-anywhere' service on a range of letters and parcels six days a week. Parcelforce Worldwide is a leading provider of?express parcel?delivery services. The GLS is one of the largest ground-based providers of?deferred parcel?delivery services in?Europe with a growing presence in North America.

Geographic Reach

Based in London, Royal Mail operates throughout the UK and offers letter and parcel delivery services internationally. GLS has a growing international footprint which currently includes around 40 countries and nation states.

Sales and Marketing

The company provides a range of commercial services to consumers, sole traders, SMEs, large businesses and retailers, and other postal operators via our downstream network.

Financial Performance

The company had a revenue of Â£12.7 billion in 2021, a 1% increase from the previous year's revenue of Â£12.6 billion.

In 2021, the company had a net income of £612 million, a 1% decrease from the previous year's net income of £620 million.

The company's cash at the end of 2022 was £1.1 billion. Operating activities generated £1.2 billion, while investing activities used £759 million, mainly for purchase of property, plant and equipment. Financing activities generated another £401 million.

Strategy

To generate value for stakeholders, it is focused on building a more balanced and diverse parcels-led, international business. Recognizing that Royal Mail and GLS have different market positions, strengths and opportunities, the company has developed separate strategies to drive sustainable growth in each business and at all times meet changing customer needs.

HISTORY

Though the British Post Office was officially born in 1635, a royal postal service had been in operation long before that time. Organized by Henry VIII in 1512, it originally served only noblemen and merchants. But the public appetite for mail led to the 1635 Act of Parliament (under Charles I) that officially opened the service to the entire British public, to operate under the name Post Office.

During his reign Charles II passed the Post Office Charter of 1660 and dubbed Henry Bishop as Postmaster General. Bishop introduced the postmark to expedite delivery. Intracity delivery was launched in London in 1680, along with a citywide penny post.

Two problems over the years were the complex distance-based pricing schedule and the burden unexpected mail placed on the poor at a time when postage was paid cash on delivery. Rowland Hill burst onto the scene in 1837 with a treatise on postal reform: He pushed a cheap, uniform rate unrelated to distance, with postage to be prepaid.

Hill joined The Post Office to oversee his reforms, and the nationwide, flat-rate penny post was passed in 1840. He also introduced postage stamps to effect prepayment. Hill was finally named Post Office Secretary in 1854, and in the 1860s he introduced The Post Office savings banks to address underserved small savers. He retired in 1864, a giant of postal history.

A Hill contemporary was Anthony Trollope: Better known today for his novels, Trollope enjoyed a successful postal career from 1834 to 1867, introducing roadside postboxes to Britain in the mid-1850s.

The state bought out Britain's telegraph firms in 1870, assigning the operations to The Post Office. When the government acquired the UK's remaining private telephone operator, National Telephone Company, in 1912, the service became a model European PTT (postal, telephone, and telegraph monopoly).

After WWII, The Post Office enjoyed a decade of profits. But losses in 1955 made The Post Office realize its operations were too labor-intensive. It began using sorting machines in the mid-1950s and the postcode in 1959. The telephone arm rolled out subscriber trunk dialing in 1958, which enabled phone callers to dial without operator help.

The postal service initiated a modern banking service in 1968 called the Girobank. The next year The Post Office was established as an independent corporation (though still state-owned).

Margaret Thatcher's government spun off the telecommunications arm as British Telecom (now BT Group) in 1981; parts of the postal market were opened to competition. In 1986 The Post Office reorganized into four departments: Royal Mail Letters, Parcelforce, Girobank (sold in 1990), and Post Office Counters (which ran post offices as retail outlets).

During the 1990s the Royal Mail maintained a monopoly on mail costing less than a pound (until 2001, when EU regulations opened up this area to competition), but with other competition mounting The Post Office began to develop opportunities abroad. In 1994 it launched a US subsidiary to handle international bulk mail, and in 1999 it bought German Parcel and Der Kurier. Other acquisitions included the Williames group (Ireland, 1999), Citipost (US, 1999), and express mail carrier Crie (France, 2000). That year the company also agreed to create a joint venture with TNT Post Group and Singapore Post for international mail delivery.

Profits were hit in 2000, when The Post Office swallowed a write-down of some £570 million after the state decided to send benefits payments by direct deposit instead of by mail. The next year The Post Office changed its name to Consignia (derived from "consign") in tandem with its reorganization as a public limited company. The new name proved to be unpopular, however, and the company changed its name to Royal Mail Holdings in 2002.

The UK mail delivery market was officially opened to competition in 2006.

EXECUTIVES

Chief Executive Officer, Executive Director, Simon Thompson
Chief Financial Officer, Executive Director, Mick Jeavons
Secretary, General Counsel, Chief Risk and Governance Officer, Mark Amsden
Chief Operating Officer, Achim Dunnwald
Independent Non-Executive Chairman, Keith Williams
Executive Director, Martin Seidenberg
Senior Independent Non-Executive Director, Sarah Hogg

Independent Non-Executive Director, Rita Griffin
Independent Non-Executive Director, Maria da Cunha
Independent Non-Executive Director, Michael Findlay
Independent Non-Executive Director, Lynne Peacock
Auditors : KPMG LLP

LOCATIONS

HQ: International Distributions Services Plc
185 Farringdon Road, London EC1A 1AA
Phone: —
Web: www.internationaldistributionsservices.com

PRODUCTS/OPERATIONS

2019 Sales

	% of total
UK Parcels, International & Letters	73
General Logistics Systems	27
Total	100

COMPETITORS

Canada Post Corporation
Deutsche Post AG
Die Schweizerische Post AG
FEDEX OFFICE AND PRINT SERVICES, INC.
Koninklijke PostNL B.V.
LA POSTE
POSTE ITALIANE SPA
PostNL N.V.
SINGAPORE POST LIMITED
UNITED STATES POSTAL SERVICE

HISTORICAL FINANCIALS

Company Type: Public

Income Statement — FYE: March 27

	REVENUE ($mil)	NET INCOME ($mil)	NET PROFIT MARGIN	EMPLOYEES
03/22	16,774	807	4.8%	162,360
03/21	17,407	854	4.9%	158,592
03/20	13,242	196	1.5%	160,772
03/19	13,860	229	1.7%	161,978
03/18	14,358	365	2.5%	159,117
Annual Growth	4.0%	21.9%	—	0.5%

2022 Year-End Financials
Debt ratio: 10.8%
Return on equity: 12.1%
Cash ($ mil.): 1,500
Current Ratio: 1.10
Long-term debt ($ mil.): 1,150
No. of shares ($ mil.): 953
Dividends
Yield: —
Payout: 65.1%
Market value ($ mil.): 9,267

	STOCK PRICE ($) FY Close	P/E High/Low		PER SHARE ($) Earnings	Dividends	Book Value
03/22	9.72	26	14	0.81	0.53	7.38
03/21	14.30	24	5	0.85	0.00	6.62
03/20	3.27	41	20	0.20	0.30	6.87
03/19	6.21	95	35	0.23	0.32	6.05
03/18	14.86	63	40	0.36	0.00	6.26
Annual Growth	(10.1%)	—	—	22.2%	—	4.2%

Intesa Sanpaolo S.P.A.

The Intensa Sanpaolo group is one of the leading banking groups in Europe, offering services to business sectors such as retail, corporate, and wealth management. The group caters about 13.5 million customers through 4,3000 branches, domestically. The company has about 1,000 branches internationally, including subsidiary banks under its commercial banking in regions such as Central and Eastern Europe, the middle East, and North Africa. The group has six main business units; Bianca deo Territori, IMI Corporate & Investment Banking; International Subsidiary Banks; Private Banking; Asset Management; Insurance; and the UBI Group. The group was founded in January 2007, from the merger of Banca Intesa and Sanpaolo IMI.

Operations
The group has six main business units; Bianca deo Territori, IMI Corporate & Investment Banking; International Subsidiary Banks; Private Banking; Asset Management; Insurance; and the UBI Group.

The Banca del Territori account for more than 40% of the company's revenue. The IMI Corporate & Investment Banking, which accounts for more than 30% of the company's revenue, is responsible for corporate and transaction banking, investment banking and public finance and capital markets in Italy and internationally.

The International Subsidiary Banks Division (10%) manages the group's activities in foreign markets through commercial banking subsidiaries and associates, which are focuses in retail banking. The Private Banking segment (more than 10%) serves the top customer segment, which is comprised of private and high net worth individuals.

The Asset management division (less than 10%) develops the best asset management solutions for the group's customers. The Insurance division includes the following businesses: Intesa Sanpaolo Vita, Intesa Sanpaolo Life, Fideuran Vita, Intesa Sanpaolo Assicura, and Intesa Sanpaolo RBM Salute.

Geographic Reach
The group caters about 13.5 million customers through 4,3000 branches, domestically. It has about 1,000 branches internationally, including subsidiary banks under its commercial banking in regions such as Central and Eastern Europe, the middle East, and North Africa.

Italy accounts for about 80% of the company's operations with Europe accounting for more than 15%.

Sales and Marketing
Intensa Sanpaolo offers services to business sectors such as retail, corporate, and wealth management.

Financial Performance
Intesa's performance for the span of five years have slowly grown with the recent years seeing an upward trend.

For 2020, Intesa Sanpaolo's operating income grew 4.2% to ?19 billion as compared to 2019's operating income of about ?18.1 billion.

Net income increased by about 1% to ?7.7 billion in 2020 as compared to the prior year's net income of about ?7 billion.

Intesa Sanpaolo's cash position for 2020 amounted to ?9.8 billion. The bank's operations used ?2.1 billion. The group's investing activities used ?375 billion, while its financing activities provided ?152 million.

Strategy
Intesa Sanpaolo's strategy is geared towards solid and sustainable value creation for all stakeholders with whom the Bank has relations. It is aiming at a sharp increase in profitability and efficiency while preserving a low risk profile, deriving from solid revenue creation, continuous cost management and dynamic credit and risk management, with efficient use of capital and liquidity. Significant excess capital and high growth / high value businesses with a European scale allow Intesa Sanpaolo ample strategic flexibility.

Company Background
Intesa Sanpaolo is the result of the 2007 mega-merger between Banca Intesa and Sanpaolo IMI. After the merger, the company reshuffled its assets and sold off some branches in order to comply with antitrust orders and raise capital.

HISTORY

In Italy charity begins at home, and often heads to the financial institutions. In 1563 Turin citizens founded Compagnia di San Paolo, a foundation that provided education and dowries to orphaned girls and aid to impoverished nobility. In 1579 the organization began a pawn shop, the Monte di Pieta, or Mountain of Mercy (founded in 1519 and reopened by the Compagnia). The foundation grew over the next 200 years, fattened by bequests and inheritances from wealthy Piedmontese families.

The French Republican government in Piedmonte gradually took control of the foundation's operations and closed it in 1802. The Monte di Pieta was reopened in 1804 and under the French influence became more bank-like. In 1848 the charitable and financial operations were formally divided.

Industrialization came slowly to Italy after its unification in the 1860s (the country remained largely agricultural until after WWII), and the organization survived a banking crisis from 1887 to 1894 by operating conservatively. It contributed to the WWI effort by purchasing government bonds. In 1928 the foundation separated Monte di Pieta's credit and pawn operations and adopted the name Istituto di San Paolo di Torino - Beneficenza e Credito (San Paolo).

Specialized institutions were founded in the 1920s to finance utilities and transportation; one of them, La Centrale Societa per il Finanziamento di Imprese Elettriche e Telefoniche, was formed in 1925 to help finance Italy's energy and telecommunications industries. In 1965 this entity enlarged its focus and changed its name to La Centrale Finanziaria Generale, a forerunner of Banca Intesa.

La Centrale's interests in energy were transferred to ENEL, the state holding company, in 1985, leaving it with banking, finance, and insurance holdings. That year the bank merged with Nuovo Banco Ambrosiano, formerly Banco Ambrosiano.

Banco Ambrosiano was founded in 1896 by Guiseppi Tovino, whose good works and sturdy faith made him a saint (he was beatified in 1998). Betraying his legacy, in 1981 chairman Roberto Calvi was found hanging under the Blackfriars Bridge in London. Calvi, called "God's Banker" for his connections to the Vatican, left behind a tangle of debt, phony holding companies, and fraud that implicated the Catholic Church, brought down an archbishop, and involved a secretive Masonic lodge. Banco Ambrosiano was taken over by a group of creditor banks and its name was changed to Nuovo Banco Ambrosiano.

In 1989, Nuovo Banco Ambrosiano merged with its subsidiary, Banco Cattolica del Veneto, and became known as Banco Ambroveneto. It bought La Cassa di Risparmio delle Provincie Lombarde (Cariplo), Italy's biggest savings bank, in 1997; they merged to form Banca Intesa the following year. Cariplo was founded by the Austro-Hungarian government in 1823, when the region was still recovering from Napoleon's depredations. Count Giovanni Pietro Porro wanted to allow artisans and day laborers to set aside money, and the company remained true to that mission throughout Italy's unification and two world wars.

Italy began its race toward privatization in 1990 to counter the growing interest of foreign banks in the Italian market and help the nation meet the criteria for joining the European Union. In 1992 San Paolo was one of the first banks to sell a 20% stake in itself (it sold another 20% in 1997). The bank bought several regional and national banks over the next few years and in 1998 merged with investment bank Istituto Mobiliare Italiano, or IMI (founded 1931), to form Sanpaolo IMI.

Banca Intesa was the product of a combination of the staid Cassa di Risparmio delle Provincie Lombarde (Cariplo) and the somewhat more colorful Banco Ambroveneto, whose history helped inspire the plot of The Godfather, Part III . It took over Banca Commerciale Italiana (BCI, or Comit) in 2000, creating one of Italy's largest banks. Banca

Intesa integrated BCI to form IntesaBci the following year, and then in late 2002 rebranded as Banca Intesa.

Banca Intesa and Sanpaolo IMI merged in 2007. After the deal, antitrust authorities ordred the company to sell some 200 branches to France-based CrÃ©dit Agricole. In late 2008 the Italian banking group sold 36 branches to Veneto Banca for ?274 million ($401 million).

A good portion of its branches were acquired in 2007 when Intesa Sanpaolo increased its stake in Banca CR Firenze to some 60% in preparation for taking over the bank outright. Banca CR Firenze added about 550 locations in Tuscany and surrounding regions to Intesa Sanpaolo's network.

The next year the bank upped its stake in Cassa dei Risparmi di Forlì e della Romagna to about 70%, increasing its influence in northern Italy. During more reshuffling of assets, Intesa Sanpaolo sold a 30% stake in Cassa di Risparmio di Fano to Credito Valtellinese in 2009.

EXECUTIVES

Managing Director, Chief Executive Officer, Executive Director, Carlo Messina
Chairman, Gian Maria Gros-Pietro
Deputy Chairman, Paolo Andrea Colombo
Director, Franco Ceruti
Director, Roberto Franchini
Director, Anna Gatti
Director, Liana Logiurato
Director, Maria Mazzarella
Director, Fabrizio Mosca
Director, Milena Teresa Motta
Director, Luciano Nebbia
Director, Bruno Maria Parigi
Director, Bruno Picca
Director, Alberto Maria Pisani
Director, Livia Pomodoro
Director, Maria Alessandra Stefanelli
Director, Paola Tagliavini
Director, Daniele Zamboni
Director, Maria Cristina Zoppo
Auditors : EY S.p.A.

LOCATIONS

HQ: Intesa Sanpaolo S.P.A.
  Piazza San Carlo, 156, Torino 10121
Phone: (39) 011 555 1
Web: www.group.intesasanpaolo.com

2018 Sales
	% of total
Italy	80
Europe	16
Rest of the world	4
Total	100

PRODUCTS/OPERATIONS

2018 Sales
	% of total
Net interest income	41
Net fee and commission income	44
Profits on tradings	6
Income from insurance business	9
Total	100

2018 sales
	%
Banca del Territori	50
Corporate and Investment Banking	20
International Subsidiary Banking	10
Private Banking	10
Asset Management	4
Insurance	6
Total	100

Selected Subsidiaries
Banca CR Firenze
Banca dell'Adriatico
Banca di Credito Sardo
Banca di Trento e Bolzano
Banca Fideuram
Banca IMI
Banca Intesa
Banca Intesa Beograd
Banca Monte Parma
Banca Prossima
Banco di Napoli
Bank of Alexandria
Banka Koper
Cassa dei Risparmi di Forlì e della Romagna
Cassa di Risparmio del Friuli Venezia Giulia
Cassa di Risparmio del Veneto
Cassa di Risparmio della Provincia di Viterbo (CARIVIT)
Cassa di Risparmio di Civitavecchia
Cassa di Risparmio di Pistoia e della Lucchesia
Cassa di Risparmio di Rieti (CARIRI)
Cassa di Risparmio di Venezia
Cassa di Risparmio in Bologna
Casse di Risparmio dell'Umbria
CIB Bank
Epsilon Associati SGR
Equiter
Eurizon A.I. SGR
Eurizon Capital
IMI Fondi Chiusi SGR
IMI Investimenti
Infogroup

COMPETITORS

BANCA MONTE DEI PASCHI DI SIENA SPA
BANCO POPULAR ESPAÃ'OL SA (EXTINGUIDA)
BPER BANCA SPA
CoÃ¶peratieve Rabobank U.A.
DZ BANK AG Deutsche Zentral-Genossenschaftsbank, Frankfurt am Main
MEDIOBANCA S.P.A.
Nordea Bank AB
Skandinaviska Enskilda Banken AB
UNICREDIT SPA
UniCredit Bank AG

HISTORICAL FINANCIALS

Company Type: Public

Income Statement — FYE: December 31

	ASSETS ($mil)	NET INCOME ($mil)	INCOME AS % OF ASSETS	EMPLOYEES
12/22	1,042,070	4,650	0.4%	95,574
12/21	1,209,970	4,736	0.4%	97,698
12/20	1,230,500	4,021	0.3%	105,615
12/19	916,292	4,695	0.5%	59,998
12/18	902,094	4,638	0.5%	92,117
Annual Growth	3.7%	0.1%	—	0.9%

2022 Year-End Financials
Return on assets: 0.4%
Return on equity: 6.9%
Long-term debt ($ mil.): —
No. of shares ($ mil.): 18,964
Sales ($ mil.): 39,702
Dividends
Yield: —
Payout: 281.4%
Market value ($ mil.): 253,371

	STOCK PRICE ($) FY Close	P/E High/Low		PER SHARE ($) Earnings	Dividends	Book Value
12/22	13.36	81	45	0.25	0.69	3.47
12/21	15.63	80	56	0.25	1.01	3.72
12/20	14.15	106	54	0.22	0.04	4.17
12/19	15.73	67	51	0.27	0.96	3.59
12/18	13.42	91	52	0.27	1.03	3.54
Annual Growth	(0.1%)	—	—	(2.8%)	(9.5%)	(0.5%)

Investec plc

Investec plc is a financial services company providing private banking, asset management, brokerage, and investment banking, primarily to wealthy clients and financial institutions. The company operates three main business divisions: Wealth and Investment, Private Banking, and Corporate and Investment Banking. With about 15 offices across the UK, together with offices in the Channel Islands and Switzerland, Investec has funds under management (FUM) of Â£44.4 billion.

Operations

The company's four principal business divisions namely, Wealth & Investment, Private Banking, Corporate, Investment Banking, and Other and Group Investments.

Corporate and Investment Banking (accounts for about 60% of revenue) provides a wide range of products and services including specialized lending, treasury activities and institutional research and sales and trading. Wealth & Investment (nearly 35% of revenue) provides bespoke personal service to private clients, trusts, charities, intermediaries and pension schemes. Private Banking (more than 5%) provides lending, private capital, transactional banking, savings and foreign exchange. Other and Group Investments (around 5% of revenue) include investment and savings, financial planning and pensions and retirement.

Broadly speaking, Investec plc generate around 45% each of its total revenue from fee and commission income and net interest income, while some 5% from trading income and another 5% from investment and other income.

Geographic Reach

London-based Investec plc has 15 offices across the UK in Belfast, Birmingham, Bournemouth, Bristol, Cheltenham, Edinburgh, Exeter, Glasgow, Guernsey, Guildford, Leeds, Liverpool, London, Manchester and Sheffield.

Sales and Marketing

Investec plc's clients include domestic

and international private clients, clients of professional advisors, charities and trusts.

Financial Performance

The company reported a net interest income of Â£482.7 billion in 2021, a 21% increase from the previous year's net interest income of Â£399.7 million.

In 2021, the company had a net income of Â£235.9 million, a 238% increase from the previous year's net income of Â£69.8 million.

The company's cash at the end of 2021 was Â£6.8 billion. Operating activities generated Â£2.6 billion, while financing activities used Â£131.9 million, mainly for redemption of subordinated debt. Investing activities provided another Â£1.1 million.

Company Background

With its beginnings as a South African leasing company, Investec expanded into the UK in 2002. In 2010 it acquired UK asset manager Rensburg Sheppards (now Investec Wealth & Investment) boosting its funds under management by about half.

EXECUTIVES

Chief Executive Officer, Executive Director, Fani Titi
Financial Director, Executive Director, Nishlan Samujh
Secretary, David Miller
Chairman, Perry K.O. Crosthwaite
Senior Independent Non-Executive Director, Zarina BM Bassa
Independent Non-Executive Director, Henrietta Baldock
Independent Non-Executive Director, Philip A Hourquebie
Independent Non-Executive Director, David Friedland
Independent Non-Executive Director, Charles R Jacobs
Independent Non-Executive Director, Lord Malloch-Brown
Independent Non-Executive Director, Khumo L Shuenyane
Non-Executive Director, Ian R. Kantor
Non-Executive Director, Philisiwe G. Sibiya
Executive Director, James KC Whelan
Auditors : Ernst & Young LLP

LOCATIONS

HQ: Investec plc
 30 Gresham Street, London EC2V 7QP
Phone: (44) 20 7597 4000   **Fax:** (44) 20 7597 4491
Web: www.investec.com

PRODUCTS/OPERATIONS

FY2017 Operating Income

	% of total
Net Interest income	20
Fee and commission income	65
Trading income	10
Investment income	4
Others	1
Total	100

FY2017 Operating Income

	% of total
Speciality Banking	52
Wealth & Investment	22
Asset Management	26
Total	100

Selected Segments
Asset Management
Wealth & Investment
Specialist Banking

COMPETITORS

BANCO DE SABADELL SA
Bank of Communications Co.,Ltd.
Canaccord Genuity Group Inc
E TRADE FINANCIAL CORPORATION
EVERCORE INC.
LIONTRUST ASSET MANAGEMENT PLC
NUMIS CORPORATION PLC
OPPENHEIMER HOLDINGS INC.
RAYMOND JAMES FINANCIAL, INC.
STIFEL FINANCIAL CORP.

HISTORICAL FINANCIALS
Company Type: Public

Income Statement   FYE: March 31

	ASSETS ($mil)	NET INCOME ($mil)	INCOME AS % OF ASSETS	EMPLOYEES
03/23	70,891	995	1.4%	8,705
03/22	36,674	309	0.8%	0
03/21	34,143	96	0.3%	0
03/20	30,791	797	2.6%	0
03/19	29,653	247	0.8%	0
Annual Growth	24.3%	41.6%		

2023 Year-End Financials

Return on assets: 1.8%   Dividends
Return on equity: 21.2%   Yield: —
Long-term debt ($ mil.): —   Payout: 27.3%
No. of shares ($ mil.): 852   Market value ($ mil.): —
Sales ($ mil.): 5,487

Isuzu Motors, Ltd. (Japan)

Isuzu Motors is a leader in commercial vehicles and diesel engine. It consistently provided the innovative products and services with a focus on developing and manufacturing commercial vehicles (CVs), light commercial vehicles (LCVs), and diesel engines. It offers an array of products from light-duty pickup trucks to heavy-duty tractors. Its industrial engine can be found in Its vehicles sales accounts for about 70% of its revenue, majority of which came of its Japan market. The company traces its roots back in 1916.

Operations

The company compose a single business segment, primarily engaged in the manufacture and sale of vehicle (about 70% of the revenue), its engines and components (more than 5%), and industrial engine (less than 5%).

A manufacturer of commercial vehicles, Isuzu manufactures and sells trucks and buses. It contributes to the sustainable development of local communities and society by supporting the operation of vehicles throughout their life cycles, from introduction to after-sales service. The N-Series (ELF in Japan) launched in 1959, is its outstanding light-duty truck series.

It also manufactures and sells the D-MAX, a 1-ton pickup truck with proven performance and popularity around the world, and the MU-X PPV (Passenger Pickup Vehicle). Notably in Thailand, Isuzu's pickup manufacturing and export base, D-MAX enjoys overwhelming popularity for its beautiful styling and power. The development of the MU-X PPV (Passenger Pickup Vehicle) was derived from the D-MAX, further refining stability, comfort, safety and control, to meet the expectations and needs of customers around the world.

Geographic Reach

Headquartered in Kanagawa, Japan, Japan is the company's largest market, representing more some 35% of total sales. Other major market includes Asia generating nearly 30%. Other countries produces the remaining around 35%.

Financial Performance

Net sales rose by 606.1 billion yen 32% compared with the previous fiscal year to 2.5 trillion yen, which comprised 878.1 billion yen posted for Japan, up 17% year-on-year, and 1.6 trillion yen for the rest of the world, up 42% year-over-year.

In 2021, the company had a net income of Â¥42.7 million, a 66% decrease from the previous year's net income of Â¥126.2 million.

The company's cash at the end of 2021 was Â¥386.7 billion. Operating activities generated Â¥222.9 billion, while investing activities used Â¥93.4 billion, mainly for purchase of non-current assets. Financing activities used another Â¥55.3 billion, primarily for repayments of long-term borrowings.

HISTORY

After collaborating on car and truck production for 21 years, Tokyo Ishikawajima Shipbuilding and Engineering and Tokyo Gas and Electric Industrial formed Tokyo Motors, Inc. in 1937. The partners began producing the A truck (1918) and the A9 car (1922) under licenses from Wolseley (UK).

Tokyo Motors made its first truck under the Isuzu nameplate in 1938. It spun off Hino Heavy Industries in 1942. By 1943 the company was selling trucks powered by its own diesel engines, mostly to the Japanese military.

By 1948 the company was Japan's premier maker of diesel engines. It was renamed Isuzu (Japanese for "50 bells") in 1949. With generous public- and private-sector financing and truck orders from the US Army during the Korean War, Isuzu survived and refined its engine- and truck-making prowess. A pact with the Rootes Group (UK) enabled Isuzu to enter automaking. Beginning in 1953, Isuzu built Rootes' Hillman Minx in Japan.

Despite its strong reputation as a truck builder, Isuzu suffered financially, and by the late 1960s its bankers were shopping the company around to more stable competitors. GM, after witnessing rapid Japanese progress in US and Asian auto markets, bought about 34% of Isuzu in 1971. During the 1970s Isuzu launched the popular Gemini car and gained rapid entry to the US through GM, exporting such vehicles as the Chevy Luv truck and the Buick Opel.

As exports to GM waned, Isuzu set up its own dealer network in the US in 1981. That year GM CEO Roger Smith told a stunned Isuzu chairman Toshio Okamoto that Isuzu lacked the global scale GM was seeking. Smith asked Okamoto for help in buying a piece of Honda. After Honda declined and GM settled for 5% of Suzuki, Isuzu extended its GM ties, building the Geo Storm and establishing joint production facilities in the UK and Australia.

Despite a high-profile advertising campaign featuring Joe Isuzu, the company suffered in the 1980s in its efforts to gain any kind of significant share of the US passenger car market. Post-1985 yen appreciation hurt exports. Subaru-Isuzu Automotive, a joint venture with Fuji Heavy Industries, initiated production of Rodeos in Lafayette, Indiana, in 1989.

After Isuzu lost nearly $500 million in 1991 and 1992, it called on GM for help. GM responded by sending Donald Sullivan, a strategic business planning expert, to become Isuzu's #2 operations executive.

Isuzu signed a joint venture with Jiangxi Automobile Factory and ITOCHU in 1993 to build light-duty trucks in China. In 1994 Nissan and Isuzu agreed to cross-supply vehicles.

Isuzu weathered a public relations storm in 1996 when Consumer Reports magazine claimed that the top-selling Trooper sport utility vehicle was prone to tip over at relatively low speeds. Isuzu dismissed the report as unscientific, and the National Highway Traffic Safety Administration sided with the automaker. In 1997 the company sued the magazine for defamation. (Isuzu lost the case in 2000.) Also in 1997 Isuzu agreed to develop GM's diesel engines and began constructing a plant in Poland to supply engines to GM's Germany-based subsidiary Opel AG.

The next year GM and Isuzu announced a joint venture to make diesel engines in the US. Also in 1998 Isuzu announced restructuring plans that included cutting 4,000 jobs and reducing the number of its domestic marketing subsidiaries. In 1999 the plant in Poland opened and GM boosted its stake in Isuzu to 49%. Isuzu also agreed to form a joint venture with Toyota to manufacture buses.

Amid mounting losses and pressure from GM, Isuzu announced a management shakeup in 2001 that included naming GM chairman John Smith Jr. as special advisor and installing Randall Schwarz (GM truck group) as VP. Days later Isuzu announced its "Isuzu V plan," its sweeping cost-savings scheme that included job cuts and the closure of one factory.

The Isuzu V plan was revised in 2002 when the company announced GM would write off its entire stake while infusing Isuzu with about $84 million. Near the close of 2002 Isuzu agreed to sell its 49% stake in carmaking joint venture Subaru-Isuzu Automotive Inc. to Fuji Heavy Industries (FHI). When the deal was completed in January 2003, FHI renamed the company Subaru of Indiana Automotive Inc.

Isuzu had some rocky going in the early part of the 21st century. The company asked its creditor banks to forgive 100 billion yen (about $750 million) in debt in exchange for stakes in the company. As part of the plan, GM wrote off its entire stake in Isuzu, and reinfused the ailing carmaker with $84 million. The deal resulted in a recapitalized Isuzu and reduced GM's stake to 8%. Early in 2006 GM sold its 8% stake in Isuzu to entities including Mitsubishi Corporation, ITOCHU Corporation, and Mizuho Corporate Bank.

As 2006 wound near its close, Toyota Motor picked up a 6% stake in Isuzu Motors from Mitsubishi and ITOCHU. The two companies agreed to cooperate on engine technologies, with Isuzu focusing on small diesel engines and diesel emission controls and Toyota concentrating on environmental improvements to gasoline engines and alternative fuels.

EXECUTIVES

Chairman, Chief Executive Officer, Representative Director, Masanori Katayama
President, Chief Operating Officer, Representative Director, Shinsuke Minami
Executive Vice President, Director, Shinichi Takahashi
Senior Managing Executive Officer, Takashi Oodaira
Senior Managing Executive Officer, Satoshi Yamaguchi
Chief Financial Officer, Director, Naohiro Yamaguchi
Chief Risk Management Officer, Kenichi Asahara
Director, Shun Fujimori
Director, Tetsuya Ikemoto
Outside Director, Mitsuyoshi Shibata
Outside Director, Kozue Nakayama
Outside Director, Makoto Anayama
Director, Kenji Miyazaki
Director, Masao Watanabe
Outside Director, Kanji Kawamura
Outside Director, Kimie Sakuragi
Auditors: Ernst & Young ShinNihon LLC

LOCATIONS

HQ: Isuzu Motors, Ltd. (Japan)
1-2-5 Takashima, Nishi-ku, Yokohama, Kanagawa 220-8720
Phone: (81) 45 299 9305   **Fax:** 714 935-5200
Web: www.isuzu.co.jp

2016 Sales

	% of total
Japan	36
Thailand	18
Other	46
Total	**100**

PRODUCTS/OPERATIONS

2016 Sales

	% of total
Vehicles	72
Engines & components	5
Parts of overseas production	4
Other	19
Total	

Selected Vehicles and Brands

Buses
    Erga heavy-duty bus
    Erga Mio medium-duty bus
Commercial vehicles
    C&E Series heavy-duty trucks & tractors
    F Series medium-duty trucks
    N Series light-duty trucks
Diesel engines
    Automotive
    Industrial
    Marine
Pickup trucks & SUVs
    D-MAX
    MU-7 (Thailand)
    Panther (Indonesia)

Selected Subsidiaries and Affiliates

Anadolu Isuzu Otomotiv Sanayi Ve Ticaret AS (Turkey)
DMAX Ltd. (US)
Isuzu Australia Limited
Isuzu Motors Europe N.V. (Belgium)
Isuzu (China) Holding Co., Ltd.
Isuzu Commercial Truck of America, Inc.
Isuzu Commercial Truck of Canada, Inc.
Isuzu Motors America, LLC
Isuzu Motors Asia Ltd. (Singapore)
Isuzu Motors Co., (Thailand) Ltd.
Isuzu Motors Germany GmbH
Isuzu Motors Polska Sp. zo. o. (Poland)
Isuzu Philippines Corporation
Isuzu Truck (UK) Ltd.
P.T. Isuzu Astra Motor Indonesia
Qingling Motors Co., Ltd. (China)

COMPETITORS

FCA US LLC
FORD MOTOR COMPANY
HINO MOTORS, LTD.
Hyundai Motor Company
MAZDA MOTOR CORPORATION
NISSAN MOTOR CO.,LTD.
RENAULT
SUBARU CORPORATION
SUZUKI MOTOR CORPORATION
TOYOTA MOTOR CORPORATION

HISTORICAL FINANCIALS

Company Type: Public

Income Statement — FYE: March 31

	REVENUE ($mil)	NET INCOME ($mil)	NET PROFIT MARGIN	EMPLOYEES
03/23	23,993	1,139	4.7%	59,641
03/22	20,670	1,037	5.0%	58,619
03/21	17,233	385	2.2%	46,407
03/20	19,161	748	3.9%	46,925
03/19	19,406	1,024	5.3%	47,255
Annual Growth	5.4%	2.7%	—	6.0%

2023 Year-End Financials

Debt ratio: 0.1%
Return on equity: 12.1%
Cash ($ mil.): 2,880
Current Ratio: 1.76
Long-term debt ($ mil.): 2,740
No. of shares ($ mil.): 777
Dividends
 Yield: 4.4%
 Payout: 0.0%
Market value ($ mil.): 9,228

	STOCK PRICE ($) FY Close	P/E High/Low	PER SHARE ($) Earnings	Dividends	Book Value
03/23	11.87	0 0	1.47	0.53	12.64
03/22	12.93	0 0	1.34	0.44	12.63
03/21	10.81	0 0	0.52	0.27	12.50
03/20	6.46	0 0	1.01	0.35	11.89
03/19	13.14	0 0	1.36	0.32	11.37
Annual Growth	(2.5%)	— —	2.0%	13.5%	2.7%

Itau Unibanco Holding S.A.

Itaú Unibanco is the largest private bank in Brazil, the largest financial institution in Latin America, and one of the largest in the world by market cap. It offers financial products and services for different sectors of the economy and leaders in several segments in which it operates, whether in solutions for individuals, micro, small and medium-sized companies and very small companies. It provides investment banking, securities brokerage, and insurance services. Besides its network of about 3,645 branches and over 690 client site branches, the firm boasts operations in Brazil, Latin America and in about 20 countries. Banco Itaú merged with Unibanco in 2008 to become Itaú Unibanco.

Operations

The company has three business segments. These are Retail Banking (some 60% of the total sales), Wholesale Banking (approximately 30%), and Activities with the Market and Corporation (roughly 10%).

Retail Banking consists of business with retail customers, account holders and non-account holders, individuals and legal entities, high income clients (Itaú Uniclass and Personnalité), and the companies segment (microenterprises and small companies). It includes financing and credit offers made outside the branch network, in addition to credit cards and payroll loans.

Wholesale banking consists of products and services offered to middle-market companies, high net worth clients (Private Banking), and the operation of Latin American units and Itaú BBA, which is the unit responsible for business with large companies and investment banking operations.

Basically, corresponds to the result arising from capital surplus, subordinated debt surplus and the net balance of tax credits and debits. It also includes the financial margin on market trading, Treasury operating costs, and equity in earnings of companies not included in either of the other segments.

In addition, net interest income and non-interest income generated approximately 60% and 40% of the company's sales, respectively. It also generated some 60% of sales from interest margin, about 35% from banking services and charges, while income from insurance and private pension operations before claim and selling expenses and other generated the rest.

Geographic Reach

Headquartered in São Paulo, Brazil, it has its presence in Latin America, with operations in nearly 20 countries.

Sales and Marketing

Wholesale Banking looks after customers with high financial net worth (private banking) through units in Latin America, banking for middle-market and large companies and corporations through the activities of Itaú BBA, the unit responsible for corporate clients and in its role as an investment bank.

Retail Banking offers its services to account holders and non-account holders.

Financial Performance

Operating revenues increased by R$2.8 billion for 2021 compared to the same period of 2020. Net interest income increased by R$25,156 million, or 50.3%, for 2021 compared to the same period of 2020, mainly due to an increase of R$14.9 billion in interest and similar income, due to the increase of R$13.3 billion in loan operations income; an increase of R$10.1 billion in income of financial assets and liabilities at fair value through profit or loss, due to the lower negative effect during 2021, compared to the same period of 2020, of hedging instruments for its investments abroad. Non-interest income increased by 2.0% to R$51.2 billion for 2021 compared to the same period of 2020. This increase was mainly due to a 16.2%, or R$2.2 billion, increase in revenue from credit and debit cards, driven by higher revenues from the issuance of cards, as a consequence of higher income from debit and credit cards.

Net income attributable to the company increased by 41.6% to R$26.8 billion in 2021 from R$18.9 billion for the same period of 2020. This result is mainly due to a 26.1% increase in operating revenues and a 44.7% decrease in expected loss from financial assets and claims.

The company's cash at the end of 2021 was R$109.7 billion. Operating activities generated R$60.1 billion, while investing activities used R$4.8 billion, primarily for purchase of financial assets at amortized cost. Financing activities used another R$31.5 billion, primarily for redemptions in institutional markets.

Strategy

In 2021, the company began to implement a new retail strategy, called iVarejo 2030, with the objective of offering a better experience to customers, with complete, sustainable and increasingly digital solutions. It is changing into a "Phygital" bank, which stands for a digital bank with the convenience of the physical network. To support this transformation, the company restructured and expanded its digital branches, developed new services and tools used by its sales and relationship teams, aiming for greater efficiency in business generation and customer service. In order to grow its client base the company created a new strategy for client acquisition based on the 'acquiring manager', a professional that is fully dedicated to client hunting and business development.

EXECUTIVES

Chief Executive Officer, Milton Maluhy Filho
Chief Financial Officer, Officer, Alexsandro Broedel Lopes
Officer, Alexandre Grossmann Zancani
Officer, Andre Luis Teixeira Rodrigues
Officer, Carlos Fernando Rossi Constantini
Officer, Carlos Orestes Vanzo
Officer, Flavio Augusto Aguiar de Souza
Officer, Jose Virgilio Vita Neto
Officer, Marina Fagundes Bellini
Officer, Matias Granata
Officer, Pedro Paulo Giubbina Lorenzini
Officer, Ricardo Ribeiro Mandacaru Guerra
Officer, Sergio Guillinet Fajerman
Officer, Adriano Cabral Volpini
Officer, Alvaro Felipe Rizzi Rodrigues
Officer, Andre Balestrin Cestare
Officer, Daniel Sposito Pastore
Officer, Emerson Macedo Bortoloto
Officer, Eric Andre Altafim
Officer, Jose Geraldo Franco Ortiz Junior
Officer, Lineu Carlos Ferraz de Andrade
Officer, Luciana Nicola Schneider
Officer, Maria Blini de Carvalho
Officer, Mario Newton Nazareth Miguel
Officer, Paulo Sergio Miron
Officer, Renato Barbosa do Nascimento
Officer, Renato da Silva Carvalho
Officer, Renato Lulia Jacob
Officer, Rubens Fogli Netto
Officer, Tatiana Grecco
Officer, Teresa Cristina Athayde Marcondes Fontes
Non-Executive Co-Chairman, Pedro Moreira Salles

Non-Executive Co-Chairman, Roberto Egydio Setubal
Non-Executive Vice Chairman, Ricardo Villela Marino
Non-Executive Director, Alfredo Egydio Setubal
Non-Executive Director, Ana Lucia de Mattos Barretto Villela Villela
Non-Executive Director, Candido Botelho Bracher
Non-Executive Director, Joao Moreira Salles
Independent Director, Cesar Nivaldo Gon
Independent Director, Fabio Colletti Barbosa
Independent Director, Frederico Trajano Inacio Rodrigues
Independent Director, Maria Helena dos Santos Fernandes de Santana
Independent Director, Pedro Luiz Bodin de Moraes
Auditors : PricewaterhouseCoopers Auditores Independentes Ltda.

LOCATIONS
HQ: Itau Unibanco Holding S.A.
Praca Alfredo Egydio de Souza Aranha, 100, Sao Paulo 04344-902
Phone: (55) 11 2794 3547
Web: www.itau.com.br

PRODUCTS/OPERATIONS
2015 Sales

	% of total
Interest and similar income	73
Banking service fees	15
Income related to insurance and private pension	11
Other income	1
Total	100

COMPETITORS
ARAB BANK PLC
CTBC Financial Holding Co., Ltd.
DnB ASA
HANG SENG BANK, LIMITED
Hana Financial Group Inc.
ISRAEL DISCOUNT BANK OF NEW YORK
SINOPAC FINANCIAL HOLDINGS COMPANY LIMITED
STANDARD BANK GROUP LTD
THANACHART CAPITAL PUBLIC COMPANY LIMITED
TP ICAP LIMITED

HISTORICAL FINANCIALS
Company Type: Public

Income Statement   FYE: December 31

	ASSETS ($mil)	NET INCOME ($mil)	INCOME AS % OF ASSETS	EMPLOYEES
12/22	439,376	5,616	1.3%	0
12/21	371,309	4,801	1.3%	99,598
12/20	388,800	3,638	0.9%	56,444
12/19	407,363	6,745	1.7%	94,881
12/18	400,090	6,417	1.6%	100,300
Annual Growth	2.4%	(3.3%)	—	—

2022 Year-End Financials
Return on assets: 1.3%
Return on equity: 18.5%
Long-term debt ($ mil.): —
No. of shares ($ mil.): 4,298
Sales ($ mil.): 47,248
Dividends
Yield: —
Payout: 26.7%
Market value ($ mil.): 23,354

	STOCK PRICE ($) FY Close	P/E High/Low		PER SHARE ($) Earnings	Dividends	Book Value
12/22	4.71	2	1	0.57	0.15	6.41
12/21	3.75	2	1	0.49	0.14	5.53
12/20	6.09	4	2	0.37	0.22	5.55
12/19	9.15	4	3	0.69	0.64	6.87
12/18	9.14	5	3	0.66	0.55	7.11
Annual Growth	(15.3%)	—	—	(3.5%)	(27.6%)	(2.6%)

ITOCHU Corp (Japan)

Itochu Enex is totally immersed in Japan's oil and gas markets. The company operates some 45 subsidiaries. The home life segment supplies liquefied petroleum gas (LPG) to some 1.5 million homes and businesses throughout Japan. The company's car life and industrial materials divisions operate full service gas stations and sells gasoline, kerosene, and oil to service stations. The group is engaged in the sale of LPG, gasoline, Kerosene, diesel oil, fuel oil, asphalt, electricity, automobiles, and other goods.

Operations
The group operates four reportable segments: Car-Life (some 60% of sales), Industrial Business (approximately 20%), Home-Life, and Power & Utility (each accounts for some 10%).

The Car-Life division is engaged in sales and services involving LPG, kerosene, diesel oil, electricity, automobiles, car rental, and lifestyle, and automotive products, as well as in import/export of petroleum products and terminal tank rental.

The Industrial Business division is engaged in sales and service involving gasoline, kerosene, diesel oil, fuel oil, LPG, high grade urea solution AdBlue, GTL fuel, corporate fleet refuelling cards, asphalt, and marine fuels, as well as in the fly ash recycling business and slop recovery and recycling business.

The Home-Life division is engaged in sales and services involving LPG, kerosene, town gas, industrial gas, household equipment, smart energy equipment, remodelling, residential lithium-ion electricity storage systems, pressure resistance inspection for gas containers and welding materials.

The Power Utility division is engaged in the sale of electricity (coal-fired, natural gas-fired, wind, hydro, and photovoltaic power), and steam, as well as in providing district heating services, comprehensive energy services, electricity/heat supply services, electric power supply/demand management services, and asset management business.

Geographic Reach
The company is headquartered in Japan.

Sales and Marketing
The home-life division serves some 1.5 million customers throughout Japan, corporate users and some 2,700 distributors. The car-life division serves approximately 1,700 affiliated car-life stations. The industrial business division serves some 3,500 corporate users, domestic road construction companies, sea shippers and public agencies. The power and utility division serves corporations, individuals, electricity retailers, office buildings, and commercial facilities.

Financial Performance
The company's revenue in 2020 decreased to Â¥897.4 billion, due to a decrease of Â¥81.6 billion in the company's Car-Life segment.

Net income for 2020 increased to Â¥19.3 billion compared to Â¥17.9 billion in the prior year.

Cash held by the company at the end of 2020 increased to Â¥19.2 billion from Â¥18.7 billion in 2018. Cash provided by operations was Â¥28.1 billion while cash used for investing and financing activities were Â¥1.4 billion and Â¥26.2 billion, respectively. Main uses of cash were payments for purchases of property, plant and equipment and investment property.

Strategy
The company is implementing the two-year medium-term business plan "Moving 2020, Horizons", part of the growth strategy the company initiated based on the theme of "Moving". The strategies focus on: deepening connections, utilizing new tools, and expanding abroad.

Using all of its resources, the company is working to create new businesses, including the development of environment-related businesses. In 2019, Itochu Enex focuses on expanding sales of GTL fuel, and the use of this fuel has begun at New Yokohama City Hall and a major construction company.

EXECUTIVES
Chairman, Chief Executive Officer, Representative Director, Masahiro Okafuji
President, Chief Operating Officer, Representative Director, Keita Ishii
Executive Vice President, Chief Administrative Officer, Representative Director, Fumihiko Kobayashi
Executive Vice President, Chief Financial Officer, Representative Director, Tsuyoshi Hachimura
Executive Vice President, Representative Director, Hiroyuki Tsubume
Chief Digital & Information Officer, Managing Executive Officer, Tomoyuki Takada
Chief Strategy Officer, Representative Director, Hiroyuki Naka
Outside Director, Masatoshi Kawana
Outside Director, Makiko Nakamori
Outside Director, Kunio Ishizuka
Outside Director, Akiko Ito
Auditors : Deloitte Touche Tohmatsu LLC

LOCATIONS

HQ: ITOCHU Corp (Japan)
3-1-3 Umeda, Kita-ku, Osaka 530-8448
Phone: (81) 6 7638 2121   Fax: 212 818-8293
Web: www.itochu.co.jp

PRODUCTS/OPERATIONS

2014 Sales

	% of total
Energy Trade	25
Car-Life	59
Total Home-Life	13
Power and Utility	3
Other	-
Total	**100**

COMPETITORS

PETROLEUM TRADERS CORPORATION
RS ENERGY K.K
SAN-AI OIL CO.,LTD.
SUN COAST RESOURCES, INC.
TAUBER OIL COMPANY

HISTORICAL FINANCIALS

Company Type: Public

Income Statement   FYE: March 31

	REVENUE ($mil)	NET INCOME ($mil)	NET PROFIT MARGIN	EMPLOYEES
03/23	104,708	6,010	5.7%	155,403
03/22	101,066	6,743	6.7%	158,319
03/21	93,589	3,625	3.9%	171,829
03/20	101,179	4,618	4.6%	174,713
03/19	104,751	4,519	4.3%	158,517
Annual Growth	0.0%	7.4%	—	(0.5%)

2023 Year-End Financials

Debt ratio: 0.2%
Return on equity: 17.7%
Cash ($ mil.): 4,550
Current Ratio: 1.30
Long-term debt ($ mil.): 17,621
No. of shares ($ mil.): 1,456
Dividends
Yield: 2.9%
Payout: 25.6%
Market value ($ mil.): —

J Sainsbury PLC

J Sainsbury is one of the UK's largest food retailer operating about 600 supermarkets, more than 800 convenience stores throughout the UK, and an e-commerce offering. In addition to groceries, Sainsbury also sells apparel, homeware and cookware, and consumer electronics under Argos, Habitat, Tu, Nectar, and Sainsbury's Bank brands. Its Argos brand sells consumer goods through standalone stores, in Sainsbury's supermarkets and online. The company also offers consumer banking through Sainsbury's Bank, which provides banking and insurance products to its some 1.8 million customers.

Operations

J Sainsbury operates around 2,140 supermarkets, convenience stores, and Argos stores in the UK and Ireland, as well as its online business. The company is organized into two operating segments: Retail and Financial Services. The company's retailing business generates almost all of the company's total revenue. Financial Services include Sainsbury's Bank plc and Argos Financial Services entities, and provides its customers with affordable ways to manage its finances and reward them for their loyalty through Nectar. Argus operates in about 730 stores, nearly 600 Sainsbury's in supermarkets and more than 800 Sainsbury's in convenient stores. The company generates most of its sales from retail.

Geographic Reach

Based in London, Sainsbury trades predominantly in the UK and the Republic of Ireland.

Sales and Marketing

Two-thirds of the UK population have shopped with Sainsbury and over one million digital Nectar users regularly benefit from personalized offers with the company and with its Nectar partners. Within Argos, Sainsbury has 18.8 million active customers. In the company's Financial Services business, it has some 1.8 million active Sainsbury's Bank customers, and approximately 2.1 million Argos Financial Services customers.

Financial Performance

The company's revenue for fiscal 2022 increased by 10% to £375 million compared to £341 million in the fiscal 2021.

Net income for fiscal 2022 was £854 million compared to a net loss of £164 million in the prior year.

Cash held by the company at the end of fiscal 2022 decreased to £818 million. Operating activities was £1.0 billion while cash used for investing and financing activities were £649 million and £1.0 billion, respectively. Main cash uses were purchase of property, plant and equipment; and dividends paid on ordinary shares.

Strategy

The company is simplifying operations at pace and accelerating its cost saving programs in order to invest in improving food quality, increasing choice and innovation and consistently delivering value to customers. The company's portfolio brands Argos, Habitat, Tu, Nectar and Sainsbury's Bank support its core food business, delivering for customers and shareholders in their own right. The company will continue to pursue partnerships and to outsource where appropriate, benefitting from third parties that can make a positive impact for its customers.

Mergers and Acquisitions

In the same year it paid around £60 million to bring its long-running loyalty program Nectar into direct ownership. The scheme had been operated by the UK arm of Aimia Inc.

In February 2016 Sainsbury's acquired Home Retail Group for £1.3 billion (around $1.9 billion). Home Retail Group's Argos business is a leading consumer products retailer in the UK. The combined company makes Sainsbury's one of the UK largest food and non-food retailers, with over 90,000 products, 2,000 stores.

HISTORY

Newlyweds John James and Mary Ann Sainsbury established a small dairy shop in their London home in 1869. Customers flocked to the clean and efficient store, a far cry from most cluttered and dirty London shops. They opened a second store in 1876. By 1914, 115 stores had been opened, and the couple's sons had entered the business.

During WWI the company's stores established grocery departments to meet demand for preserved products, such as meat and jams, which were sold under the Sainsbury's label.

Mary Ann died in 1927 and John James the next year. Son John Benjamin, wholly devoted to the family business, took charge. (He is reported to have said on his deathbed, "Keep the stores well lit.") In the 1930s he engineered the company's first acquisition, the Thoroughgood stores.

Sales dropped by 50% during WWII, and some shops were destroyed by German bombing. Under third-generation leader Alan John Sainsbury, the company opened its first self-service store in 1950 in Croydon. The 75,000-sq.-ft. store opened in 1955 in Lewisham was considered to be the largest supermarket in Europe.

J Sainsbury went public in 1973. It established a joint venture with British Home Stores in 1975, forming the Savacentre hypermarkets (the company bought out its partner in 1989).

Sainsbury partnered with Grand Bazaar Innovation Bon Marche, of Belgium, in 1979 to establish Homebase, a do-it-yourself chain. (It bought the remaining 25% in 1996 and then sold the company in 2001, retaining only 18%.)

By 1983 most of Sainsbury's 229 stores were clustered in the south of England. A mature market and stiff competition forced the company to look elsewhere -- both overseas and close to home. It began buying out US-based Shaw's Supermarkets in New England and in 1984 opened its first Scottish hypermarket. By 1987 the grocer owned 100% of Shaw's, which had 60 stores in Massachusetts, Maine, and New Hampshire.

In 1991 Sainsbury came under competitive pressure from Tesco and the Argyll Group (later renamed Safeway plc), which also began building superstores. It responded with an expansion drive of its own, including opening its first Scottish supermarket (in Glasgow) the next year.

In 1994 the company purchased a $325 million stake in Maryland-based Giant Food. Sainsbury bought home improvement retailer Texas Homecare from UK leisure concern Ladbroke in 1995 and integrated it into its Homebase unit. The following year it bought 12 supermarkets in Connecticut from Dutch retailer Ahold Delhaize (the purchase lowered its profits for the year) and entered Northern Ireland.

A year later the company opened Sainsbury's Bank. Royal Ahold bought Giant Food, including Sainsbury's 20% stake, in 1998. David Sainsbury -- a great-grandson of the founders -- retired as chairman in 1998 to pursue politics, marking the first time a Sainsbury had not headed up the company in its more-than-a-century history.

As a cost-cutting effort in 1999, Sainsbury cut 2,200 jobs, more than half in management. It also launched its convenience store concept, called Sainsbury's Local. Also that year Sainsbury bought the 53-store Star Markets chain of Massachusetts, merging it into its Shaw's operations. In March 2000 Sir Peter Davis took over as CEO of Sainsbury's Supermarkets, replacing David Bremner.

In 2001 Sainsbury acquired 19 Grand Union stores in the US (17 of which were converted to the Shaw's banner), and opened 25 new stores in the UK. The company also exited the Egyptian market, and sold its home-and-garden chain Homebase to private equity firm Permira.

In 2002 Shaw's Supermarkets bought control of 18 stores in New England from bankrupt discounter Ames.

In November 2003 Sainsbury reached a Â£2 million out-of-court settlement with designer Jeff Banks over termination of his contract to revamp its clothing line in a bid to emulate rival ASDA's success with its George line of apparel.

In January 2004 the grocery chain acquired Swan Infrastructure (an Accenture affiliate), the company that ran its information technology systems, for about $1 billion. The move brought the grocers information technology operations, which were outsourced in 2000, back in-house.

In February 2004 Sainsbury acquired 54 Bells convenience stores. (Bells Stores was founded in 1968 by Les Bell and was owned by the Bell family until its acquisition.) Justin King (formerly of Marks & Spencer) joined Sainsbury as its CEO in March 2004, succeeding Sir Peter Davis, who became chairman of the board. In April Sainsbury sold JS USA Holdings, which operated 203 Shaw's and Star Markets stores in New England, to US grocery chain Albertson's in a deal worth about $2.4 billion. The retailer also disposed of JS Developments, its property development operation, in fiscal 2004. Davis stepped down as chairman of Sainsbury on July 1, 2004, one year ahead of schedule and following a prolonged dispute with investors that culminated in a fight over his compensation.

Philip Hampton (former finance director of Lloyds TSB (now Lloyds Banking Group), BT Group, and BG Group) joined Sainsbury as its new chairman on July 19, 2004. Hampton's appointment and experience with mergers and acquisitions fueled speculation that the struggling grocery chain may become a takeover target. In August Sainsbury acquired Jacksons Stores Ltd. and its wholly owned subsidiary Jacksons Stores 2002 Ltd. for about Â£100 million. In September Sainsbury agreed to pay ex-chairman Davis Â£2.6 million despite shareholder protests in July that forced the grocery retailer to withdraw a similar offer. At that time Lord Levene of Portsoken and Keith Butler-Wheelhouse, both nonexecutive directors of the company and members of the remuneration committee, resigned from the board.

In October 2004, Sainsbury said it was writing off Â£140 million against information technology systems and an another Â£120 million linked to ineffective supply-chain equipment as a result of a huge infrastructure investment program, instituted by ex-chairman Davis, that failed. In November the company acquired JB Beaumont, a convenience store chain with six stores in the East Midlands. In 2005 the grocery chain acquired the five-store SL Shaw chain in southeastern England. Sainsbury renamed the shops Sainsbury's Local. The acquisitions pushed Sainsbury's convenience store count to nearly 300 outlets throughout the UK, giving the company a 2% share of the convenience market.

The company sold 5% of its majority stake in Sainsbury's Bank in February 2007 to its joint venture partner HBOS for about Â£21 million ($40 million). As a result, the bank became a 50-50 joint venture between the two firms. Also in 2007 the company shutdown its online entertainment division, Sainsbury's Entertain You, which offered books, CDs, DVDs, videos, computer games, and a DVD rental service, citing stiff competition in the online arena. The company removed hydrogenated fats from its branded products in 2007.

In mid-2008 Qatar Holding-backed real estate investment group Delta Two increased its stake in Sainsbury to about 25%, fueling speculation that it may attempt to take over the British grocer. (In 2007 Delta Two made a bid to buy the remainder of the company, but withdrew the offering in November amid turmoil in the credit markets.) Delta Two was the second suitor to leave the grocery chain at the altar. The company and key shareholders from the founding Sainsbury family rebuffed a group of private equity investors led by CVC Capital earlier in the year.

In mid-2009 the grocery chain launched online sales of some 8,000 nonfood items, such as kitchenware and furniture. It also extended its online home grocery delivery service to an additional 200 stores. The company welcomed David Tyler, formerly chairman of Logica, as its new chairman in November 2009. Tyler succeeded Sir Philip Hampton.

In November 2010 the company launched Sainsbury's Entertainment, a digital download service that provides customers with access to more than 150,000 books, DVDs, Blu-rays, CDs, and games to purchase online.

EXECUTIVES

Chief Executive Officer, Executive Director, Simon Roberts
Chief Financial Officer, Executive Director, Kevin O'Byrne
Chief Digital Officer, Clodagh Moriarty
Chief Marketing Officer, Mark Given
Chief Information Officer, Phil Jordan
Food Commercial Director, Rhian Bartlett
Human Resources Director, Angie Risley
General Merchandise & Clothing Commercial Director, Paula Nickolds
Corporate Services Director, Corporate Services Secretary, Tim Fallowfield
Chairman, Non-Executive Director, Martin Scicluna
Senior Independent Director, Dame Susan Rice
Non-Executive Director, Brian J. Cassin
Non-Executive Director, Jo Harlow
Non-Executive Director, Adrian Hennah
Non-Executive Director, Tanuj Kapilashrami
Non-Executive Director, David Keens
Non-Executive Director, Keith Weed
Auditors : Ernst & Young LLP

LOCATIONS

HQ: J Sainsbury PLC
33 Holborn, London EC1N 2HT
Phone: —
Web: www.about.sainsburys.co.uk

PRODUCTS/OPERATIONS

2019 sales

	%
Retailing	9
Financial services	2
Total	100

2019 Stores

	No.
Sainsbury's Supermarkets	608
Convenience stores	820
Argos	
Standalone	594
In Sainsbury's	281
In Homebase	8
Habitat	16
Total	2,327

PRODUCTS
Summer
Fruit & veg
Meat & fish
Dairy, eggs & chilled
Bakery
Frozen
Food cupboard
Drinks
Health & beauty
Baby
Household
Pet
Home
Cook event
Electronics

COMPETITORS

ALBERTSONS COMPANIES, INC.
ASDA GROUP LIMITED
C&S WHOLESALE GROCERS, INC.
DAIEI, INC., THE

KINGFISHER PLC
Loblaw Companies Limited
SUPERVALU INC.
THE GREAT ATLANTIC & PACIFIC TEA COMPANY, INC.
WM MORRISON SUPERMARKETS P L C
WOOLWORTHS GROUP LIMITED

HISTORICAL FINANCIALS
Company Type: Public

Income Statement — FYE: March 4

	REVENUE ($mil)	NET INCOME ($mil)	NET PROFIT MARGIN	EMPLOYEES
03/23	37,777	248	0.7%	0
03/22	39,719	899	2.3%	181,000
03/21	40,138	(386)	—	180,000
03/20	37,734	197	0.5%	171,400
03/19	37,921	286	0.8%	179,900
Annual Growth	(0.1%)	(3.5%)	—	—

2023 Year-End Financials
Debt ratio: 3.0%
Return on equity: 2.6%
Cash ($ mil.): 1,582
Current Ratio: 0.68
Long-term debt ($ mil.): 723
No. of shares ($ mil.): —
Dividends
  Yield: —
  Payout: 567.3%
Market value ($ mil.): —

	STOCK PRICE ($) FY Close	P/E High/Low		PER SHARE ($) Earnings	Dividends	Book Value
03/23	12.69	145	89	0.11	0.60	0.00
03/22	13.16	61	40	0.38	0.51	4.85
03/21	12.80	—	—	(0.18)	0.57	4.12
03/20	11.11	215	161	0.08	0.54	4.58
03/19	11.69	196	128	0.12	0.48	5.01
Annual Growth	2.1%	—	—	(2.4%)	5.4%	—

Japan Airlines Co Ltd JAL

Japan Airlines (JAL) conducts domestic and international air transport businesses (passengers, cargo) by 15 consolidated subsidiaries and one affiliated company such as Japan Airlines, Japan Transocean Air, Japan Air Commuter, J-Air, Hokkaido Air System, and Ryuku Air Commuter. It has more than 130 domestic and about 80 international routes on a fleet comprising nearly 240 large, medium, small, and regional aircraft, mainly Boeings. Besides its scheduled passenger services, JAL carries air cargo, provides maintenance and ground-support services for airlines, sells packed tours, and provides credit cards.

Operations
Japan Airlines (JAL) divides its operations into two reportable segments: Air Transport (approximately 70% of sales) and Other (some 30%).

Air Transport comprises JAL's domestic and international passenger business. This segment also covers ground handling, aircraft maintenance, cargo, and airport peripheral businesses.

Domestic passenger accounts for the majority of the company's sales (about 35%), followed by cargo/mail (more than 30%), others which cover package tours, credit cards, agriculture, and business jet, among others (around 25%), and international passenger (some 10%).

Geographic Reach
Japan Airlines is based in Shinagawa-Ku, Tokyo. It directly serves more than 130 domestic and some 80 international routes.

Financial Performance
The revenue for the consolidated fiscal year increased 41.9% year over year to JPY 682.7 billion.

The loss attributable to owners of the parent was JPY 177.5 billion compared to the loss attributable to owners of the parent JPY 286.6 billion in the previous year).

Cash held by the company at the end of fiscal 2021 was JPY 494.2 million. Operating activities used JP Y103.5 million, while investing used another JPY 173.8 million. Financing activities generated JPY 359.3 million.

Strategy
Through business structure reform addressing market changes, JAL will reduce dependence on the full service carrier (FSC) business, and expand it LCC and non-airline businesses such as mileage.

As a result, JAL aims to achieve steady profit growth by 2023, when a return to 2019 demand levels is expected, and by 2025, the final year of Medium Term Management Plan, and to retrieve JPY43 billion of losses in the recovery phase, starting from JPY89 billion in EBIT in 2019.

Company Background
After WWII Japan was not allowed to form its own airline until the end of US occupation in 1951. That year a group of bankers led by Seijiro Yanagito founded Japanese Air Lines (JAL). JAL was essentially a revival of the prewar Nihon Koku Kabushiki Kaisha (Japan Air Transport Company), the national airline created by the Japanese government in 1928 and dissolved by the Allies in 1945. Since the Allied Peace Treaty forbade the airline to use Japanese flight crews, it leased both pilots and equipment from Northwest Airlines. In 1953 the airline was reorganized as Japan Airlines, with the government and the public owning equal shares.

EXECUTIVES

Chairman, Director, Yoshiharu Ueki
President, Representative Director, Yuji Akasaka
Executive Vice President, Representative Director, Shinichiro Shimizu
Senior Managing Executive Officer, Representative Director, Hideki Kikuyama
Senior Managing Executive Officer, Director, Ryuzo Toyoshima
Director, Tadayuki Tsutsumi
Outside Director, Eizo Kobayashi
Outside Director, Sonoko Hacchoji
Outside Director, Hiroyuki Yanagi
Auditors : KPMG AZSA LLC

LOCATIONS
HQ: Japan Airlines Co Ltd JAL
2-4-11 Higashi-Shinagawa, Shinagawa-ku, Tokyo 140-8637
Phone: (81) 3 5460 3121
Web: www.jal.com

2019 Sales
	% of total
Passenger	
Domestic	36
International	34
Incidental & other revenues	30
Total	100

PRODUCTS/OPERATIONS

2019 Sales
	% of total
Air Transportation	83
Other	17
Total	100

HISTORICAL FINANCIALS
Company Type: Public

Income Statement — FYE: March 31

	REVENUE ($mil)	NET INCOME ($mil)	NET PROFIT MARGIN	EMPLOYEES
03/23	10,328	258	2.5%	36,039
03/22	5,612	(1,459)	—	36,086
03/21	4,346	(2,589)	—	36,875
03/20	13,000	492	3.8%	36,797
03/19	13,429	1,361	10.1%	35,002
Annual Growth	(6.4%)	(34.0%)	—	0.7%

2023 Year-End Financials
Debt ratio: 0.3%
Return on equity: 4.2%
Cash ($ mil.): 4,799
Current Ratio: 1.38
Long-term debt ($ mil.): 6,108
No. of shares ($ mil.): 437
Dividends
  Yield: —
  Payout: 31.7%
Market value ($ mil.): 4,261

	STOCK PRICE ($) FY Close	P/E High/Low		PER SHARE ($) Earnings	Dividends	Book Value
03/23	9.75	0	0	0.59	0.19	14.02
03/22	9.30	—	—	(3.34)	0.00	15.05
03/21	11.21	—	—	(6.91)	0.00	19.58
03/20	9.14	0	0	1.43	0.51	29.93
03/19	17.58	0	0	3.90	0.51	30.16
Annual Growth	(13.7%)	—	—	(37.6%)	(22.0%)	(17.4%)

Japan Post Bank Co Ltd

EXECUTIVES

President, Representative Executive Officer, Director, Norito Ikeda
Executive Vice President, Representative Executive Officer, Director, Susumu Tanaka
Executive Vice President, Executive Officer, Yoshinori Hagino

Executive Vice President, Kunio Tanigaki
Senior Managing Executive Officer, Harumi Yano
Senior Managing Executive Officer, Takayuki Kasama
Senior Managing Director, Minoru Kotohda
Director, Hiroya Masuda
Director, Toshiyuki Yazaki
Outside Director, Ryoji Chubachi
Outside Director, Keisuke Takeuchi
Outside Director, Makoto Kaiwa
Outside Director, Risa Aihara
Outside Director, Hiroshi Kawamura
Outside Director, Kenzo Yamamoto
Outside Director, Shihoko Urushi
Outside Director, Keiji Nakazawa
Outside Director, Atsuko Sato
Auditors : KPMG AZSA LLC

LOCATIONS

HQ: Japan Post Bank Co Ltd
2-3-1 Otemachi, Chiyoda-ku, Tokyo 100-8793
Phone: (81) 3 3477 0111
Web: www.jp-bank.japanpost.jp

HISTORICAL FINANCIALS
Company Type: Public

Income Statement — FYE: March 31

	REVENUE ($mil)	NET INCOME ($mil)	NET PROFIT MARGIN	EMPLOYEES
03/23	15,499	2,440	15.7%	11,807
03/22	16,258	2,919	18.0%	15,465
03/21	17,581	2,529	14.4%	16,054
03/20	16,577	2,518	15.2%	16,383
03/19	16,663	2,403	14.4%	17,006
Annual Growth	(1.8%)	0.4%	—	(8.7%)

2023 Year-End Financials
Debt ratio: —
Return on equity: 3.2%
Cash ($ mil.): 561,533
Current Ratio: —
Long-term debt ($ mil.): —
No. of shares ($ mil.): 3,668
Dividends
Yield: —
Payout: 57.5%
Market value ($ mil.): —

Japan Post Holdings Co Ltd

EXECUTIVES

President, Representative Executive Officer, Chief Executive Officer, Director, Hiroya Masuda
Representative Executive Officer, Executive Vice President, Atsushi Iizuka
Senior Managing Executive Officer, Hiroaki Kawamoto
Senior Managing Executive Officer, Taneki Ono
Senior Managing Executive Officer, Yukihiko Yamashiro
Director, Norito Ikeda
Director, Kazuhide Kinugawa
Director, Tetsuya Senda
Outside Director, Kunio Ishihara
Outside Director, Charles Ditmars Lake

Outside Director, Michiko Hirono
Outside Director, Tsuyoshi Okamoto
Outside Director, Miharu Koezuka
Outside Director, Sakie Akiyama
Outside Director, Makoto Kaiami
Outside Director, Akira Satake
Outside Director, Takako Suwa
Auditors : KPMG AZSA LLC

LOCATIONS

HQ: Japan Post Holdings Co Ltd
2-3-1 Otemachi, Chiyoda-Ku, Tokyo 100-8791
Phone: (81) 03 3477 0111
Web: www.japanpost.jp

HISTORICAL FINANCIALS
Company Type: Public

Income Statement — FYE: March 31

	REVENUE ($mil)	NET INCOME ($mil)	NET PROFIT MARGIN	EMPLOYEES
03/22	92,609	4,124	4.5%	377,047
03/21	105,852	3,777	3.6%	390,775
03/20	110,089	4,456	4.0%	400,001
03/19	115,356	4,329	3.8%	407,488
03/18	121,676	4,337	3.6%	411,078
Annual Growth	(6.6%)	(1.3%)	—	(2.1%)

2022 Year-End Financials
Debt ratio: —
Return on equity: 3.8%
Cash ($ mil.): 651,652
Current Ratio: —
Long-term debt ($ mil.): —
No. of shares ($ mil.): 3,662
Dividends
Yield: 6.2%
Payout: 0.0%
Market value ($ mil.): —

Japan Post Insurance Co Ltd

EXECUTIVES

Representative Executive Officer, President, Director, Tetsuya Senda
Representative Executive Officer, Executive Vice President, Director, Noboru Ichikura
Senior Managing EXecutive Officer, Yasuaki Hironaka
Senior Managing Executive Officer, Atsushi Tachibana
Director, Tomoaki Nara
Director, Hiroya Masuda
Outside Director, Masako Suzuki
Outside Director, Tamotsu Saito
Outside Director, Kazuyuki Harada
Outside Director, Hisashi Yamazaki
Outside Director, Kaori Tonosu
Outside Director, Satoshi Tomii
Auditors : KPMG AZSA LLC

LOCATIONS

HQ: Japan Post Insurance Co Ltd
2-3-1 Otemachi, Chiyoda-ku, Tokyo 100-8794
Phone: (81) 3 3477 2383
Web: www.jp-life.japanpost.jp

HISTORICAL FINANCIALS
Company Type: Public

Income Statement — FYE: March 31

	REVENUE ($mil)	NET INCOME ($mil)	NET PROFIT MARGIN	EMPLOYEES
03/22	52,487	1,299	2.5%	10,291
03/21	60,649	1,500	2.5%	10,694
03/20	65,291	1,388	2.1%	10,802
03/19	70,167	1,087	1.6%	10,983
03/18	73,896	983	1.3%	11,009
Annual Growth	(8.2%)	7.2%	—	(1.7%)

2022 Year-End Financials
Debt ratio: —
Return on equity: 6.0%
Cash ($ mil.): 47,622
Current Ratio: —
Long-term debt ($ mil.): 2,466
No. of shares ($ mil.): 399
Dividends
Yield: —
Payout: 0.0%
Market value ($ mil.): —

Japan Tobacco Inc.

Japan Tobacco is a leading global tobacco company operating in about 75 markets, and its products are sold in more than 130 markets around the world. The company makes and sells globally recognized tobacco and cigarette brands like Winston, Camel, Mevius, and LD, as well as local cigarette brands. It has more than 100 worldwide brands, eight flagship brands, and four leading reduced-risk product brands. In addition to the tobacco business, the company operates pharmaceutical and processed food businesses. It has nearly 40 tobacco factories and nearly 25 processed food factories. Japan Tobacco was founded in 1985.

Operations

Japan Tobacco operates three businesses: tobacco (accounts for about 90% of the company's revenue), pharmaceutical (about 5%), and processed food business (less than 5%).

The tobacco business manufactures and offers tobacco products all around the world. Its leading brands include Winston, Camel, MEVIUS, and LD, as well as in RRP (Reduced-Risk Products), such as Ploom and Logic.

The pharmaceutical business focuses on the R&D, manufacturing, and sale of prescription drugs, concentrating on three specific therapeutic areas: Cardiovascular, Renal and Metabolism (CVRM); immunology; and neuroscience. Its products include CORECTIM Ointment 0.25% and CORECTIM Ointment 0.5%, Riona Tablets 250mg, and ENAROY Tablets 2 mg ? 4 mg, among others.

The processed food business manages the frozen and ambient food business, mainly for frozen noodles, frozen okonomiyaki (Japanese savory pancakes), packaged cooked rice, and the seasonings business, focusing on seasonings including yeast extracts. Major products include Reito-Sanuki-Udon (frozen noodles), Gottsu-umai okonomiyaki (Japanese savory pancakes), and HIMAX (yeast extract seasoning) in particular.

Geographic Reach

Tokyo, Japan-based, Japan Tobacco has nearly 40 factories for its tobacco business and nearly 25 factories for its processed foods business located in Japan and in more than 25 countries worldwide. Its subsidiary JT International SA is headquartered in Geneva, Switzerland. Additionally, the company also has offices in Africa, the Americas, Asia, Europe, and the Middle East.

Its key markets include Italy, Japan, Romania, Russia, Spain, Taiwan, the Philippines, the UK, and Turkey.

Sales and Marketing

Japan Tobacco sells its products through various channels, such as supermarkets, convenience stores, e-commerce sites, retailers, and authorized distributors. It also has a motivated salesforce with strong ties with trade.

Financial Performance

Japan Tobacco's for the past five fiscal years experienced decreases and increases starting from JPY2.2 trillion in 2018, to JPY2.2 trillion, JPY2.1 trillion, JPY2.3 trillion, and JPY2.7 trillion for fiscal years 2019 to 2022, respectively.

Company's revenue for fiscal 2022 increased by 14% to JPY2.7 trillion compared from the prior year with JPY2.3 trillion. The increase was primarily due to growing momentum in the tobacco business, the positive exchange effects of the weaker yen, and revenue growth for both the pharmaceutical and processed food businesses.

Cash held by the company at the end of fiscal 2022 increased to JPY866.9 billion. Cash provided by operations was JPY483.8 billion while cash used for investing and financing activities were JPY101.8 billion and JPY306.2 billion, respectively.

Strategy

In the second half of 2023, the company will accelerate the Ploom X expansion plan bringing the number of markets where it is on sale to 14 by year-end.

This builds on the successful rollout of Ploom X this April in Italy, the biggest HTS market in Europe, and in Lithuania, followed by Portugal in May.

Japan Tobacco expansion plan focus will be on established HTS markets, where the company can benefit from existing high levels of category awareness among adult consumers. This focused investment strategy will allow it to optimize its investments compared to markets where larger resources would be required to inform and convert adult consumers to HTS.

Company Background

Japan Tobacco is the result of the liberalization of the Japanese tobacco market in the mid-1980s. The government department that held a monopoly on the sale of tobacco products in Japan from 1898 was converted into a joint stock company and foreign companies were allowed to compete in the Japanese marketplace. The company changed significantly in the late 90s with the acquisition of R. J. Reynolds' non-US tobacco business, which included the brands Camel, Winston, and others. Around that time it also entered the pharmaceutical and processed foods business.

HISTORY

In 1898, roughly 325 years after tobacco was introduced in Japan, the nation's Ministry of Finance formed a bureau to monopolize its production to fund military and industrial expansion.

During WWII Japan's tobacco leaf imports from North and South America grew scarce and led to cigarette rationing. In 1949 the government began operating the tobacco production bureau as a business: the Japan Tobacco and Salt Public Corporation (in 1905 the bureau also became responsible for a salt monopoly).

The company launched Hope, the first Japanese-made filter cigarette, in 1957, and it became the world's best seller a decade later. In 1972 it began printing mild packaging "warnings": "Be careful not to smoke excessively for your health."

Japan Tobacco and Salt began selling Marlboro cigarettes licensed from Philip Morris in 1973. The Mild Seven brand (its current best-seller) went on sale in 1977; it became the world's #1 cigarette in 1981 but dropped to #2 (behind Marlboro) in 1993.

When its tobacco monopoly ended in 1985, the government established the firm as Japan Tobacco (a government-owned joint stock company). As competition from foreign imports increased, the firm came up with new means of making yen. It formed Japan Tobacco International (cigarette exports mainly to the US and Southeast Asia), moved into agribusiness and real estate operations, and, in 1986, created JT Pharmaceutical. In 1987 cigarette import tariffs ended, and importers lowered prices to match the company's; its sales and market share subsequently declined. During the late 1980s it introduced HALF TIME beverages and its first low-tar cigarettes (Mild Seven Lights is now the world's #1 light cigarette).

In 1992 Japan Tobacco bought its first overseas production facility, Manchester Tobacco (closed in 2001). Former Ministry of Finance official Masaru Mizuno became CEO that year -- and soon took up smoking. Also in 1992 the company and Agouron Pharmaceuticals agreed to jointly develop immune system drugs; in 1994 they added antiviral drugs. The government sold about 20% of the firm's stock to the public in 1994 and 13% in 1996. The firm began operating Burger King restaurants in Japan in 1996. Japan Tobacco bought Pillsbury Japan in 1998.

Japan Tobacco in 1999 paid nearly $8 billion for R.J. Reynolds International, the international tobacco unit of what was then RJR Nabisco. The company then renamed the unit, which has operations in 70 countries worldwide, JT International. It also bought the food products division of Asahi Chemical, Torii Pharmaceutical from Asahi Breweries, and the Unimat vending machine company.

Slowing sales prompted Japan Tobacco to announce in 2000 that it would reduce its workforce by 6,100 by 2005. Company exec Katsuhiko Honda became CEO that year (Mizuno remained as chairman) and said he'd push the government to sell its stake. Honda retired in 2006. In February 2001 the company announced plans to sell parts of its OTC drugs and health care businesses to Nichiiko Pharmaceutical to concentrate on prescription drugs. It also intends to sell all 25 of its Burger King outlets. In May Mizuno stepped down as chairman and was replaced by Takashi Ogawa.

In December 2001 Japan's Ministry of Finance recommended that it cut its holdings in the company from 66% to 50%; it would also allow the company to sell additional shares, which could further dilute the government's stake to as little as 33%. In 2002 Japan Tobacco completed the sale of its 25 Burger King outlets and its OTC drug business.

In January 2004 the company unveiled six new brands: Mild Seven One Menthol Box, Bitter Valley, Fuji Renaissance, Fuji Renaissance 100's, Hi-Lite Menthol, and BB Slugger. An added brand, Hope Menthol, currently being tested in the marketplace, also will see expanded availability. Japan Tobacco's Canadian subsidiary filed for bankruptcy protection in August 2004 following a billion-dollar smuggling claim by the Canadian government. Canada said that the company owed $1.4 billion in Canadian back taxes for allegedly smuggling cigarettes in 1998 and 1999.

Japan Tobacco in 2005 ended its agreement with Philip Morris to make and sell Marlboro cigarettes. The company closed 13 of its 25 manufacturing plants and six of its 30 sales branches by early 2006 as part of an effort to increase profits. These reductions slashed as many as 4,000 jobs from company payrolls as demand for cigarettes, partly depressed by higher taxes, continues to decline. Japan Tobacco is also using its own line of premium smokes to fill the gap left in the product line by the absence of Marlboro cigarettes. The company's deal with Philip Morris to sell Marlboro lapsed in 2005.

In April 2007 JT acquired Britain's Gallaher Group for about $15 billion. The purchase, which added Silk Cut and Benson & Hedges cigarette brands to its products portfolio, was the largest foreign acquisition by a Japanese company.

In January 2008 the company acquired a majority stake in Katokichi Co. for about $900 million. It then sold a 49% stake in the business to Nissin Foods, forming a joint venture. In April JT entered the seasonings business, acquiring a controlling stake in Fuji Foods.

At the end of 2008 Japan Tobacco placed Hans Group, its Australia-based chilled foods venture, and its subsidiaries into administration under the care of KordaMetha.

In 2009 Japan Tobacco acquired the UK's Tribac Leaf and Brazil-based leaf suppliers Kannenberg & Cia and Kannenberg, Barker, Hail & Cotton Tabacos.

EXECUTIVES

Chairman, Director, Mutsuo Iwai
Vice-Chairman, Director, Shigeaki Okamoto
President, Chief Executive Officer,
Representative Director, Masamichi Terabatake
Executive Vice President, Representative Director, Kiyohide Hirowatari
Executive Vice President, Representative Director, Kei Nakano
Senior Managing Executive Officer, Junichi Fukuchi
Chief Sustainability Officer, Hisato Imokawa
Chief Financial Officer, Nobuya Kato
Outside Director, Main Kohda
Outside Director, Yukiko Nagashima
Outside Director, Masato Kitera
Outside Director, Tetsuya Shoji
Auditors : Deloitte Touche Tohmatsu LLC

LOCATIONS

HQ: Japan Tobacco Inc.
4-1-1 Toranomon, Minato-ku, Tokyo 105-6927
Phone: (81) 3 6636 2914   **Fax:** 201 871-1417
Web: www.jti.co.jp

PRODUCTS/OPERATIONS

2018 Sales

	% of total
International tobacco	59
Japanese domestic tobacco	28
Processed food	7
Pharmaceutical	6
Total	100

COMPETITORS

ALTRIA GROUP, INC.
BRITISH AMERICAN TOBACCO P.L.C.
LORILLARD TOBACCO COMPANY, LLC
PHILIP MORRIS INTERNATIONAL INC.
PHILIP MORRIS USA INC.
PYXUS INTERNATIONAL, INC.
REYNOLDS AMERICAN INC.
Reemtsma Cigarettenfabriken Gesellschaft mit beschrÃ¤nkter Haftung
UNIVERSAL CORPORATION
VECTOR GROUP LTD.

HISTORICAL FINANCIALS

Company Type: Public

Income Statement   FYE: December 31

	REVENUE ($mil)	NET INCOME ($mil)	NET PROFIT MARGIN	EMPLOYEES
12/22	20,170	3,359	16.7%	59,366
12/21	20,196	2,940	14.6%	62,323
12/20	20,302	3,010	14.8%	64,981
12/19	20,039	3,207	16.0%	69,091
12/18	20,150	3,507	17.4%	70,586
Annual Growth	0.0%	(1.1%)	—	(4.2%)

2022 Year-End Financials

Debt ratio: 0.1%
Return on equity: 13.9%
Cash ($ mil.): 6,578
Current Ratio: 1.74
Long-term debt ($ mil.): 6,230
No. of shares ($ mil.): 1,774
Dividends
Yield: —
Payout: 30.7%
Market value ($ mil.): 17,802

	STOCK PRICE ($) FY Close	P/E High/Low		PER SHARE ($) Earnings	Dividends	Book Value
12/22	10.03	0	0	1.89	0.58	15.14
12/21	10.10	0	0	1.66	0.65	13.75
12/20	10.19	0	0	1.70	0.71	13.80
12/19	11.12	0	0	1.80	0.70	13.83
12/18	11.75	0	0	1.96	0.67	13.35
Annual Growth	(3.9%)	—	—	(0.8%)	(3.3%)	3.2%

Jardine Matheson Holdings Ltd.

Jardine Matheson Holdings (JMH) is a diversified Asian-based group founded in China in 1832. Comprised with a broad portfolio of market-leading businesses, which represent a combination of cash generating activities and long-term property assets that are closely aligned to the increasingly prosperous consumers of the region. JMH's subsidiaries include Jardine Pacific, Jardine Motors Group, and Jardine Cycle & Carriage. Other businesses include financial services, hotels (Mandarin Oriental), construction, mining, and transport services. Members of the Keswick family, descendants of the co-founder William Jardine, control JMH and Jardine Strategic through a complex ownership structure. The company generates the majority of its sales from customers in Southeast Asia.

Operations

Jardine Matheson operates it business into seven reportable segments: Astra, DFI Retail, Jardine Motors, Hongkong Land, Jardine Pacific, Jardine Cycle & Carriage, and Mandarin Oriental.

Astra generates the higher revenue with approximately 45% of sales, it offers automotive, financial services, heavy equipment, mining, construction and energy, agribusiness, infrastructure and logistics, IT and Property. With more than 240 subsidiaries, associated companies and other entities.

DFI Retail segment, accounts for some 25% of sales, operates under well-known brands across five divisions, being food (including Grocery Retail and Convenience Stores), health and beauty, home furnishings, restaurants, and other retailing.

Jardine Motors, with about 15% of sales, is currently comprised of Asian automotive businesses including Zung Fu Motors Group in Hong Kong and Macau, Cycle & Carriage in Singapore, Malaysia and Myanmar, Tunas Ridean in Indonesia, and Jardine Motors Group in the UK.

Hongkong Land (property investment, management and development with offices in Hong Kong, Singapore, Beijing, Jakarta and other major Asian cities) accounts for more than 5% of sales. Jardine Pacific (engineering and construction, aviation and transport services, and restaurants) and Jardine Cycle & Carriage (Singapore-listed investment holding company) and Mandarin Oriental (hotel investment with about 35 hotels and seven residences in about 25 countries and territories) both account for the rest.

Overall, motor vehicles accounts for more than 35% of sale, followed by retail and restaurants with over 25%, engineering, heavy equipment, mining and construction with more than 15%, property with over 5%, financial services with some 5%, and hotels and other account for the rest.

Geographic Reach

With its headquarters in Bermuda, Jardine Matheson also operates in more than 10 Asian countries and territories. The company operates mainly in Southeast Asia and Greater China. Southeast Asia and Greater China generate approximately 60% and about 30% of sales, respectively. The UK and other regions accounts for the rest.

Sales and Marketing

Jardine Matheson provides a wide range of businesses including motor vehicles and related operations, property investment and development, food retailing, health and beauty, home furnishings, engineering and construction, transport services, restaurants, luxury hotels, financial services, heavy equipment, mining, energy, and agribusiness. The company distributes its businesses by their subsidiaries and affiliate companies.

Financial Performance

Company's revenue for fiscal 2021 increased by 10% to $35.9 billion compared from the prior year with $32.6 billion.

Profit for fiscal 2021 increased to $1.9 billion compared from the prior year with a loss of $394 million.

Strategy

Company's works with its businesses to deliver on its strategic priorities of: actively evolving its company portfolio; enhancing leadership and entrepreneurialism; driving innovation and operational excellence; and embedding sustainability.

Mergers and Acquisitions

Jardine Matheson Holdings said that shareholders of Jardine Strategic Holdings Ltd approved its $5.5 billion purchase of the 15% stake it does not already own in the company at a special meeting. The acquisition allows the company to move ahead with its plans to simplify the parent company structure of the group.

Company Background

Jardine, Matheson & Co (JM & Co) was founded in Canton in July 1832 by Scots William Jardine and James Matheson. Jardine Matheson sent its first private shipments of tea to England in 1834. Following years after that, JM & Co completed the move of its main office to Hong Kong and opened its office in Shanghai. More offices were subsequently opened in Canton, Amoy and Foochow.

In the 1860s, JM & Co's trading activities were enhanced by the expansion of its shipping, banking and insurance interests. They moved its main office from East Point to Central Hong Kong in 1864.

JM & Co constructed the first railway line in China from Shanghai to Woosung in 1876.

By the 1910s, the heart of the business was in Shanghai, and from 1912 onwards the city was regarded as the Firm's headquarters. The Firm began to expand into new products and services to meet the needs of the growing industrialization of China.

EXECUTIVES

Chairman, Executive Chairman, Ben Keswick
Finance Executive Director, Executive Director, John Witt
Executive Director, Y. K. Pang
Executive Director, Adam Keswick
Finance Director, Executive Director, Graham Baker
Secretary, Jonathan Lloyd
Independent Non-Executive Director, Stuart Gulliver
Independent Non-Executive Director, Julian Hui
Independent Non-Executive Director, Michael Wei Kuo Wu
Non-Executive Director, David Hsu
Non-Executive Director, Anthony J. L. Nightingale
Non-Executive Director, Percy Weatherall
Auditors : PricewaterhouseCoopers LLP

LOCATIONS

HQ: Jardine Matheson Holdings Ltd.
48th Floor, Jardine House, G.P.O. Box 70,
Phone: (852) 2843 8288   **Fax:** (441) 292 4072
Web: www.jardines.com

2016 sales

	$ mil.	% of total
Southeast Asia	21,612	58
Greater China	12,495	34
UK	2,665	7
Other regions	279	1
Total	37,051	100

PRODUCTS/OPERATIONS

2016 Revenues

	$ mil.	% of total
Astra (automotive, financial services, agribusiness, heavy equipment & other)	13,610	37
Dairy Farm	11,201	30
Jardine Motors Group	5,197	14
Jardine Pacific	2,356	6
Jardine Cycle & Carriage	2,154	6
Hongkong Land	1,994	5
Mandarin Oriental	597	2
Adjustment	(58)	-
Total	37,051	100

2016 Revenues

	$ mil.	% of total
Motor vehicles	13,610	37
Retail and restaurants	11,201	30
Engineering, construction and mining contracting	5,197	14
Property	1989	5
Insurance broking and financial services	1357	4
Hotels	596	2
Others	3013	8
Total	37,051	100

Selected Major Subsidiaries and Affiliates

Astra International (automobile distribution and manufacturing, financial and IT services, heavy machinery)
Cycle & Carriage Ltd (69%, motor trading, Singapore)
Dairy Farm International Holdings Ltd (78%; supermarkets, hypermarkets, health and beauty and home furnishings stores, convenience stores and restaurants)
Honkong Land Holdings Ltd (50%, real estate)
Jardine Lloyd Thompson plc (32%, insurance and brokerage, UK)
Jardine Motors Group Holdings Ltd. (auto distribution, sales, and service; China, Hong Kong, Macao, and the UK)
Jardine Pacific Holdings Ltd. (transport services, engineering and construction, restaurants, and IT services)
Jardine Strategic Holdings Ltd. (81%, holding company)
Mandarin Oriental International Ltd. (74%, hotels)

HISTORICAL FINANCIALS

Company Type: Public

Income Statement
FYE: December 31

	REVENUE ($mil)	NET INCOME ($mil)	NET PROFIT MARGIN	EMPLOYEES
12/22	37,724	354	0.9%	425,000
12/21	35,862	1,881	5.2%	400,000
12/20	32,647	(394)	—	403,000
12/19	40,922	2,838	6.9%	464,000
12/18	42,527	1,732	4.1%	469,000
Annual Growth	(3.0%)	(32.8%)	—	(2.4%)

2022 Year-End Financials

Debt ratio: 18.2%   No. of shares ($ mil): 289
Return on equity: 1.2%   Dividends
Cash ($ mil.): 5,898   Yield: .
Current Ratio: 1.22   Payout: 164.7%
Long-term debt ($ mil.): 12,073   Market value ($ mil.): 14,661

	STOCK PRICE ($) FY Close	P/E High/Low	PER SHARE ($) Earnings	Dividends	Book Value
12/22	50.73	50 37	1.22	2.01	99.74
12/21	55.29	11 8	6.01	1.62	41.59
12/20	56.22	— —	(1.07)	1.62	40.59
12/19	55.25	9 7	7.56	1.62	41.41
12/18	69.05	15 12	4.59	1.52	35.74
Annual Growth	(7.4%)	—	(28.2%)	7.2%	29.2%

JBS SA

JBS is one of Brazil's largest multinationals, operating through a diversified global platform offering a variety of protein products and established prepared-food brands. The world's largest processor of animal protein has major operations in Brazil, as well as the US, Canada, Puerto Rico, Mexico, Europe, the UK, New Zealand, and Australia. It is also a significant producer of pork, poultry, and lamb. In addition to fresh and processed meat, JBS offers cooked and canned meats, ready-to-eat meals, as well as hides and dairy products. Its brands include Seara, Pilgrim's Pride, Primo, Moy Park, Swift, Doriana, DelÃcia, and Friboi. The company has more than 500 production units and commercial offices on five continents and in more than 20 countries.

Operations

JBS operates through five primary divisions: JBS Brazil, JBS USA Beef, JBS USA Pork, PPC (Pilgrim's Pride), and Seara.

JBS Brazil operations consist of producing beef, chicken, pork, fish and plant-based proteins, as well as prepared and frozen food products. It also operates in the leather segment and businesses associated with byproducts and waste from its operations. The business encompasses the companies Friboi, Swift, JBS Couro, and New Business.

JBS USA Beef, the company's largest segment includes (unsurprisingly) beef, lamb, and related operations in the US, as well as Canada and Australia.

JBS USA Pork is the world's second largest pork producer. It provides high-quality fresh, prepackaged, and ready to cook products including bacon, ham, sliced meats and pork cuts.

The Pilgrim's Pride division produces and sells fresh chicken and pork, branded value-added prepared and pre-packaged foods. Its focus is on the North American, Mexican, Puerto Rican and European markets. It has the capacity to process approximately 45 million chickens per week, as well as producing and selling fresh meats, prepared foods and prepackaged foods for high-added-value consumption.

With a broad product portfolio to serve all types of consumers, Seara is the market leader in frozen and plant-based foods, including high value-added businesses with a brand and a model that combines investment and innovation.

Geographic Reach

Brazil-based, JBS is present in more than 20 countries in five continents, with more than 500 production units and commercial offices dotted around Australia, Brazil, Canada, the US, Mexico, New Zealand, Argentina, Uruguay, the UK, and Europe. In addition, the company exports its products to approximately 190 countries around the world.

Sales and Marketing
JBS operates globally in both the B2B (business to business) and B2C (business to consumers) segments and now has approximately 275,000 customers worldwide. It uses different channels like social media and e-mail to market its product to the end consumers.

Financial Performance
The company's revenue for fiscal 2021 increased to R$350.7 billion compared from the prior year with R$270.2 billion.

Net income for fiscal 2021 increased to R$20.5 billion compared from the prior year with R$4.6 billion.

Strategy
JBS are one of Brazil's largest multinationals, operating through a diversified global platform offering a variety of protein products and established prepared-food brands. This strategy affords us greater operational flexibility, also mitigating risks posed by any trade barriers or health restrictions.

In the USA, the company invested in two major ventures in its plants in Missouri: JBS opened its cooked bacon unit in Moberly and began building a charcuterie plant making Italian delicacies and salami in Colombia, set to start operating in 2023.

There was a solid investment in expanding and modernizing Seara's plants and building new plants of JBS Biodiesel, Campo Forte (organo-mineral fertilizers), Colagen and Peptides and Zempack (metallic packaging).

Mergers and Acquisitions
In late 2021, JBS acquired Spanish company BioTech Foods, one of the global leaders in the development of biotechnology. The deal signals the company's entry into the cultivated protein market, which consists of producing food from animal cells and includes investment in building a new plant in Spain to scale up production. Along with the acquisition, JBS is also announcing the setting up of Brazil's first cultivated protein research & development (R&D) center. In all, JBS will channel $100 million to the two projects. The deal enables both companies to pool their strengths and accelerate the development of the cultivated protein market. The deal enables both companies to pool their strengths and accelerate the development of the cultivated protein market.

In mid-2021, JBS announced its plan to acquire 100% of Huon Aquaculture, Australia's second-largest salmon producer. Under terms of the transaction, JBS would pay A$3.85 per share of Huon Aquaculture, or approximately A$546 million ($400.5 million). "This is a strategic acquisition, which marks the entry of JBS into the aquaculture business," said Gilberto Tomazoni, global chief executive officer of JBS.

In early 2021, JBS entered into an agreement to purchase Vivera, Europe's third-largest plant-based food company, for an enterprise value of approximately ?341 million ($408.11 million). Vivera develops and produces a broad range of innovative plant-based meat replacement products for major retailers in over 25 countries across Europe, with relevant market share in the Netherlands, the UK and Germany. The deal includes three manufacturing facilities and a research and development center located in the Netherlands. The acquisition of Vivera strengthens and boosts JBS' global plant-based food platform.

HISTORY
After nearly two decades in operation, JBS began to expand its business significantly and steadily during the 1970s by purchasing independent slaughterhouses and cattle processing facilities throughout Brazil. These acquisitions continued through the end of the century at which point JBS also began to turn an acquisitive eye toward Argentina.

In 2005 the Brazilian meat giant took its first step abroad, buying 85% of Swift Armour, Argentina's largest beef processor, for $200 million.

In 2007 the company acquired US-based Swift Foods for $225 million and assumed its heavy debt load, estimated at more than $1 billion, a few months after going public on the Sao Paulo Stock Exchange.

In 2008 JBS acquired Australian-based beef producer Tasman Group for $107 million in cash. Also that year, it bought US processor Smithfield Beef from Smithfield Foods for $565 million. In Europe it formed a 50:50 joint venture with Italy's Cremonini and subsidiary Inalca, with plants in Italy, Russia and Africa, for $328 million.

In 2009 JBS filed with US regulators to hold a $2 billion initial public offering for JBS USA Holdings (It withdrew the proposed IPO in 2011.) Also in 2009 JBS acquired a 64% stake in restructured US poultry producer Pilgrim's Pride for $800 million. Prior to declaring bankruptcy in 2008, Pilgrim was the #1 US chicken producer and, despite selling off some of its operations, was still a huge poultry operation. Other than saying it hoped to increase Pilgrim's competitiveness both domestically and internationally, JBS made no other statement as to Pilgrim's future. In late 2009, JBS acquired Australia's Tatiara Meat Company from the Dutch company, VION Food Group, for $28 million. Tatiara is Australia's largest exporter of fresh lamb meat; it also offers value-added lamb products. It was integrated into JBS's Swift Australia operations. At home, JBS bought #2 Brazilian beef producer Bertin, with 38 plants at home and abroad, in an all-stock deal in 2009.

Eyeing acquisitions on the other side of the globe, JBS in September 2010 bought Australia's Rockdale Beef from joint owners Itoham Foods and Mitsubishi Corporation. The deal, valued at about $38 million, boosted the firm's processing capacity by some 550 cattle per day and secured its foothold in the country.

In February 2011 Wesley Batista succeeded his brother Joesley Batista as CEO of the company. Wesley, formerly head of the company's US subsidiary, is a 22-year veteran of JBS. Joesley Batista continued as chairman. In March JBS terminated its joint venture with Italy's Cremonini after a protracted dispute by selling its 50% stake in Inalca back to Cremonini for $304 million.

In March 2012 JBS, through its subsidiary JBS USA Holdings, increased its stake in Pilgrim's Pride to more than 75% through the purchase of nearly 19 million shares owned by Lonnie Bo Pilgrim for about $107 million.

EXECUTIVES
Chairman, Director, Joesley Mendonca Batista
Global Operations President, Global Operations Chief Executive Officer, Vice-Chairman, Director, Wesley Mendonca Batista
Global Chief Executive Officer, Gilberto Tomazoni
Institutional Relations Executive Director, Francisco de Assis e Silva
Control Executive Director, Administration Executive Director, Eliseo Santiago Perez Fernandez
Government Relations Director, Communications Director, Wilson Mello
Investor Relations Director, Jeremiah Alphonsus O'Callaghan
Region Officer, Wesley Batista
Subsidiary Officer, Andre Nogueira
Subsidiary Officer, Maxim Medvedovsky
Division Officer, Region Officer, Miguel Gularte
Division Officer, Russ Colaco
Director, Jose Batista Sobrinho
Director, Humberto Junqueira de Farias
Director, Joao Carlos Ferraz
Director, Carlos Alberto Caser
Director, Tarek Mohamed Noshy Nasr Mohamed Farahat
Director, Marcio Percival Alves Pinto
Auditors : Grant Thornton Auditores Independentes

LOCATIONS
HQ: JBS SA
Avenida Marginal Direita do Tiete, 500, Vila Jaguara, Sao Paulo 05118-100
Phone: (55) 11 3144 4000   **Fax:** (55) 11 3144 4279
Web: www.jbs.com.br

2017 Sales

	% of total
US	53
Asia	15
Brazil	12
Europe	5
Mexico	5
Other	10
Total	100

HISTORICAL FINANCIALS

Company Type: Public

Income Statement   FYE: December 31

	REVENUE ($mil)	NET INCOME ($mil)	NET PROFIT MARGIN	EMPLOYEES
12/21	62,930	3,676	5.8%	250,000
12/20	52,026	885	1.7%	250,000
12/19	50,880	1,509	3.0%	242,000
12/18	46,811	6	0.0%	230,000
12/17	49,255	161	0.3%	235,000
Annual Growth	6.3%	118.5%	—	1.6%

2021 Year-End Financials

Debt ratio: 8.0%
Return on equity: 48.6%
Cash ($ mil.): 4,393
Current Ratio: 1.40
Long-term debt ($ mil.): 14,463
No. of shares ($ mil.): 2,293
Dividends
Yield: 7.6%
Payout: 68.1%
Market value ($ mil.): 31,425

	STOCK PRICE ($) FY Close	P/E High/Low	Earnings	Dividends	Book Value
12/21	13.70	2 1	1.48	1.05	3.45
12/20	9.16	7 4	0.33	0.16	2.96
12/19	12.93	7 3	0.57	0.00	2.77
12/18	5.93	636 423	0.00	0.02	2.48
12/17	5.91	40 19	0.06	0.02	2.57
Annual Growth	23.4%	—	125.5%	182.0%	7.7%

JD Sports Fashion PLC

JD Sports Fashion is one of the leading global omnichannel retailer of sports, fashion and outdoor brands. The retailer operates more than 3,400 stores across about 25 brands that sell sport and athletic-inspired fashion apparel and footwear and outdoor clothing. Typical namesake JD Sports shops sell Adidas, Puma, and Nike brand footwear and clothing, among other brands, for men, women, and kids. Other banners The Finish Line in the US and Sprinter in Spain. It operates nearly 65 gyms locations under the JD Gyms name. Stephen Rubin's Pentland Group owns more than 50% of JD Sports Fashion. Most of JD Sports sales comes from the UK and Republic of Ireland.

Operations

JD Sports' operations are divided into two segments: Sports Fashion and Outdoor. Sports Fashion encompasses the retail of footwear and apparel in the sports fashion category across JD Sports' numerous brands and fascias. It operates nearly 3,155 stores and generates about 95% of total sales.

Outdoor, which brings in more than 5% of sales, covers apparel and footwear for hiking, camping, and mountaineering enthusiasts. It operates about 250 stores, mostly Millets, Go Outdoors, and Blacks.

Geographic Reach

Headquartered in Lancashire, England, JD Sports generates more than 40% of its sales in the UK and ROI, around 30% in North America, about 25% in Europe, and nearly 5% in elsewhere. It is active in more than 30 countries in total, including France, Germany, Spain, Malaysia, India, Australia, Canada, and Hong Kong. All in, the company trades from over 3,400 stores.

The company sources its products from nearly 20 countries. Its main sourcing regions continue to be Asia, India, Turkey, and Pakistan.

Sales and Marketing

JD Sports generates about 65% of its sales through its retail stores. Nearly 30% comes via multichannel and nearly 5% from other activities.

Its social engagement via high profile ambassadors has resulted in increased audience engagement. For example, the company's Christmas TV ad campaign was its most successful ever as the number one Christmas advert on YouTube with over 20 million views and was viewed more than 44 million times on TikTok. This helped make the JD Sports App the number one UK shopping app on both IOS & Android during the peak Christmas shopping period.

Financial Performance

Note: Growth rates may differ after conversion to US Dollars.

Total revenue for the company for the year increased by 39% to £8.6 billion with this increase significantly influenced by the impact of the recent acquisitions.

In 2021, the company had a net income of £459.6 million, a 101% increase from the previous year's net income of £229.2 million.

The company's cash at the end of 2021 was £1.3 billion. Operating activities generated £1.3 billion, while investing activities used £848.1 million, primarily for acquisition of subsidiaries. Financing activities used another £83.6 million, mainly for Repayment of interest-bearing loans and borrowings.

Strategy

The company's strategy is underpinned by the following pillars: Strong consumer connection; Excellence in physical retail & the international expansion of the JD brand; Omnichannel capability & technology; Environment, social & governance; and Brand & category width.

Mergers and Acquisitions

In late 2021, JD Sports acquired 80% of Greece-based Cosmos Sport S.A. Cosmos operates 57 stores in Greece and 3 in Cyprus. "This is another exciting acquisition for JD that further expands our presence in Europe. We welcome the highly experienced and knowledgeable Tsiknakis Family to the Group and we look forward to working with them on the development opportunities in the region", commented Peter Cowgill, Executive Chairman of JD Sports Fashion Plc.

In early 2021, JD Sports entered into a conditional agreement for the acquisition of 60% of Poland-based Marketing Investment Group S.A. (MIG). Commenting on the development, Peter Cowgill, Executive Chairman of JD Sports Fashion Plc, said: "This is an exciting acquisition for JD that will further build on the success of our international development strategy, expanding our operations into Central and Eastern Europe. We look forward to closing the transaction and welcoming the MIG team to the group."

Also in early 2021, JD Sports entered into a conditional agreement to acquire Baltimore-based athletic footwear and streetwear retailer DTLR Villa for approximately $495 million in cash (of which about $100 million will be used to repay existing company debt). The acquisition of DTLR will enhance the company's presence in the north and east of the US, and will be another important step in the group's evolution.

EXECUTIVES

Chief Executive Officer, Executive Director, Regis Schultz
Chief Financial Officer, Executive Director, Neil Greenhalgh
Secretary, General Counsel, Theresa Casey
Non-Executive Chairman, Andrew T. Higginson
Senior Independent Director, Non-Executive Director, Kath Smith
Non-Executive Director, Bert Hoyt
Non-Executive Director, Andy Long
Non-Executive Director, Suzi Williams
Non-Executive Director, Helen Ashton
Non-Executive Director, Mahbobeh Sabetnia
Non-Executive Director, Ian Dyson
Auditors: KPMG LLP

LOCATIONS

HQ: JD Sports Fashion PLC
Hollinsbrook Way, Pilsworth, Bury, Lancashire BL9 8RR
Phone: —
Web: www.jdplc.com

2018 Sales

	% of total
UK	65
Europe	30
Rest of world	5
Total	100

PRODUCTS/OPERATIONS

2018 Sales

	% of total
Sports Fashion	87
Outdoor	13
Total	100

Selected Brands

JD
size?
Footpatrol
Chausport
Sprinter
Perry
Aktiesport
Next Athleisure
Sport Zone

Scotts
Tessuti
Mainline
Get the Label
JD Gyms
Kukri
Focus
Source Lab
Kids Cavern
Nicholas Deakins
Blacks
Millets
Ultimate Outdoors
Go Outdoors

COMPETITORS

B&M European Value Retail S.A.
BURBERRY GROUP PLC
COMPAGNIE FINANCIERE RICHEMONT SA
FAST RETAILING CO., LTD.
FRASERS GROUP PLC
FRENCH CONNECTION GROUP PLC
GRAND VISION
PORTMEIRION GROUP PUBLIC LIMITED COMPANY
SKECHERS U.S.A., INC.
ZUMIEZ INC.

HISTORICAL FINANCIALS

Company Type: Public

Income Statement — FYE: January 28

	REVENUE ($mil)	NET INCOME ($mil)	NET PROFIT MARGIN	EMPLOYEES
01/23	12,521	176	1.4%	75,149
01/22	11,465	495	4.3%	67,831
01/21*	8,456	307	3.6%	54,385
02/20	8,020	322	4.0%	53,477
02/19	6,164	342	5.5%	48,852
Annual Growth	19.4%	(15.3%)	—	11.4%

*Fiscal year change

2023 Year-End Financials

Debt ratio: 1.7%   No. of shares ($ mil.): 5,183
Return on equity: 7.0%   Dividends
Cash ($ mil.): 1,957   Yield: —
Current Ratio: 1.59   Payout: 13.9%
Long-term debt ($ mil.): 46   Market value ($ mil.): 10,807

	STOCK PRICE ($) FY Close	P/E High/Low	PER SHARE ($) Earnings	Dividends	Book Value
01/23	2.09	88 36	0.03	0.00	0.51
01/22	2.41	228 34	0.10	0.00	0.50
01/21*	10.73	261 191	0.06	0.00	0.35
02/20	6.00	— —	0.07	0.00	0.33
02/19	6.00	116 110	0.07	0.00	0.27
Annual Growth	(23.2%)	— —	(16.5%)	1.8%	16.9%

*Fiscal year change

JD.com, Inc.

Online retailer JD.com wants to be China's answer to Amazon.com. The company sells books, electronics and computers, office and school supplies, home appliances, jewelry, automotive and industrial products, sporting goods, home and garden supplies, tools, and much more on its website. JD.com, which began selling electronics online, claims to be the largest direct sales company in China (measured by transaction volume), with a market share of nearly 47%. JD.com offers about 40 million SKUs and multiple delivery options, including next-day, three-hour, and night delivery. It operates about 85 warehouses in 36 Chinese cities. Founded in 2004 by its CEO Richard Liu, JD.com went public in 2014.

IPO

JD.com in May 2014 sold 93.7 million American depository shares priced at $19 each in an offering that raised $1.78 billion. The company plans to expand its fulfillment infrastructure by acquiring land use rights, building new warehouses, and purchasing shipping and delivery vehicles. It's also looking to invest in complementary businesses, assets, and technologies.

Operations

The Chinese e-tailer operates 86 warehouses in 36 cities across China. It counts 1,620 delivery stations in 495 cities. JD.com acquires products from suppliers and sells them directly to customers through its website and mobile applications. The company launched an online marketplace, which sells merchandise from third parties, in fall 2010 to broaden its selection of products. JD.com also offers services, such as advertising, transaction processing, and Internet financing.

Financial Performance

JD.com's sales have grown along with its product offering, although the company still operates at a loss. The e-tailer's gross merchandise volume (GMV) increased from RMB32.7 billion in 2011 to RMB73.3 billion in 2012 and RMB125.5 billion ($20.7 billion) in 2013. JD.com lost RMB1.3 billion, RMB1.7 billion and RMB 0.05 billion ($8 million) in 2011, 2012, and 2013, respectively. The company boasts 47.4 million active customer accounts and a market share of 46.5% in China.

Strategy

Unlike its larger rival Alibaba, JD.com maintains a significant amount of product inventory and owns much of its shipping and logistics network, a business model that has similarities to Internet colossus Amazon.com's core business. The company is building its mobile business. Currently, about 18% of its orders are made on mobile devices.

EXECUTIVES

Chief Executive Officer, Chairman, Executive Director, Richard Qiangdong Liu
JD Retail Chief Executive Officer, Lei Xu
Chief Financial Officer, Sandy Ran Xu
Chief Human Resources Officer, Pang Zhang
Independent Director, Ming Huang
Independent Director, Louis T. Hsieh
Independent Director, Dingbo Xu
Director, Martin Chi Ping Lau
Auditors: Deloitte Touche Tohmatsu Certified Public Accountants LLP

LOCATIONS

HQ: JD.com, Inc.
20th Floor, Building A, No. 18 Kechuang 11 Street,
Daxing District, Beijing 101111
Phone: (86) 10 8911 8888
Web: www.jd.com

HISTORICAL FINANCIALS

Company Type: Public

Income Statement — FYE: December 31

	REVENUE ($mil)	NET INCOME ($mil)	NET PROFIT MARGIN	EMPLOYEES
12/22	151,658	1,504	1.0%	450,679
12/21	149,889	(560)	—	385,357
12/20	114,033	7,554	6.6%	314,906
12/19	82,907	1,751	2.1%	227,730
12/18	67,170	(362)	—	178,927
Annual Growth	22.6%	—		26.0%

2022 Year-End Financials

Debt ratio: 1.0%   No. of shares ($ mil.): 3,135
Return on equity: 4.9%   Dividends
Cash ($ mil.): 12,337   Yield: —
Current Ratio: 1.32   Payout: 260.7%
Long-term debt ($ mil.): 4,382 Market value ($ mil.): 176,006

	STOCK PRICE ($) FY Close	P/E High/Low	PER SHARE ($) Earnings	Dividends	Book Value
12/22	56.13	22 12	0.47	1.21	9.86
12/21	70.07	— —	(0.18)	0.00	10.58
12/20	87.90	6 2	2.42	0.00	9.24
12/19	35.23	9 5	0.59	0.00	4.02
12/18	20.93	— —	(0.13)	0.00	3.00
Annual Growth	28.0%	— —	—	—	34.6%

Jeronimo Martins S.G.P.S. SA

Jerónimo Martins (JM) is a major Portuguese retailer with a network of about 4,910 stores dispersed across Portugal, Poland, and Colombia. In Portugal, the company has a leadership position in food distribution through the Pingo Doce chain and in the cash & carry segment with Recheio. In Poland, Biedronka is the biggest food distribution chain in the country with more than 3,200 stores, while in Colombia JM operates a network of more than 820 Ara-branded neighborhood stores. JM's specialized retail division consists of Hebe drugstores in Poland, as well as Jeronymo coffee shops and Hussel confectioners in Portugal. JM generates about 70% of its sales from Poland.

Operations

The company's Poland Retail segment generates approximately 70% of the company's revenue. The business unit operates under Biedronka banner. Portugal Retail segment, brings in some 20% of revenue, comprises the business unit of JMR (Pingo Doce supermarkets). Colombia Retail segment operates under Ara banner. It provides approximately 5% of the company's revenue. Portugal Cash & Carry segment (contributes nearly 5%) includes the wholesale business unit Recheio. Accounts for the rest, others, eliminations, and adjustments include business units with reduced materiality (coffee shops, chocolate stores, and agribusiness in Portugal, and health and beauty retail in Poland); the holding companies; and company's consolidation adjustments.

Geographic Reach

Jerónimo Martins is headquartered in Portugal and its main operations are in Portugal, Poland, and Colombia. JM generates about 70% of its revenue from Poland, followed by Portugal which brings up nearly 25%, and the rest comes from Colombia.

Sales and Marketing

Jerónimo Martins' advertising costs for the years 2021 and 2020 were approximately EUR 112 million and EUR 97 million, respectively.

Financial Performance

Note: Growth rates may differ after conversion to US Dollars.

Company's revenue for fiscal 2021 increased to EUR 20.9 billion compared from the prior year with EUR 19.3 billion.

Net income for fiscal 2021 increased to EUR 463 million compared from the prior year with EUR 312 million.

Cash held by the company at the end of fiscal 2021 increased to EUR 453.3 million. Cash provided by investing activities was EUR 526.8 million while cash used for operations and financing activities were EUR 62.1 million and EUR 182.0 million, respectively.

Strategy

The company's strategic vision is based on promoting profitable and sustainable growth, through three key guiding principles: Leadership: strong banners and brands that enable to achieve and reinforce leadership positions in the markets where it operates; Responsibility: continuous assessment of the impact of the business on the environment and society, an active and significant contribution towards improving the quality of life in the communities and towards sustainability as a whole; and Independence: careful management of the balance sheet and supply-chain to ensure the continuity of operations and autonomy in strategic decision-making.

Mergers and Acquisitions

In early 2021, Jerónimo Martins announced that its indirect wholly owned subsidiary, Jerónimo Martins – AgroAlimentar, S.A. (JMA), acquired shares representing approximately 66.68% of the share capital of Mediterranean Aquafarm, S.A., a company incorporated under Moroccan law. This acquisition embodies a partnership in Morocco that will allow JMA to continue developing its aquaculture network to produce sea bass, sea bream and meagre in offshore cages.

EXECUTIVES

Chairman, Chief Executive Officer, Director, Pedro Soares dos Santos
Independent Non-Executive Director, Antonio Pedro de Carvalho Viana-baptista
Independent Non-Executive Director, Clara Christina F. T. Streit
Independent Non-Executive Director, Elizabeth Ann Bastoni
Independent Non-Executive Director, Francisco Manuel Seixas da Costa
Independent Non-Executive Director, Maria Angela Holguin
Independent Non-Executive Director, Sergio Tavares Rebelo
Non-Executive Director, Andrzej Szlezak
Non-Executive Director, Artur Stefan Kirsten
Non-Executive Director, Jose Soares dos Santos
Auditors : Ernst & Young Audit & Associados – SROC, S.A.

LOCATIONS

HQ: Jeronimo Martins S.G.P.S. SA
  Rua Actor Antonio Silva, n.7, Lisboa 1649-033
Phone: (351) 21 753 20 00 **Fax:** (351) 21 752 61 74
Web: www.jeronimomartins.com

PRODUCTS/OPERATIONS

2017 Sales

	% of total
Poland Retail	68
Portugal Retail	25
Portugal Cash & Carry	6
Adjustments	(2)
Total	100

COMPETITORS

BESTWAY (HOLDINGS) LIMITED
DEXUS PROPERTY SERVICES PTY LIMITED
Dream Global Real Estate Investment Trust
EXPRESS, INC.
GROUPE CRIT
ICAHN ENTERPRISES L.P.
LafargeHolcim Ltd
SEVEN & I HOLDINGS CO., LTD.
SONAE - SGPS, S.A.
TOUPARGEL GROUPE

HISTORICAL FINANCIALS

Company Type: Public

Income Statement   FYE: December 31

	REVENUE ($mil)	NET INCOME ($mil)	NET PROFIT MARGIN	EMPLOYEES
12/22	27,112	630	2.3%	131,094
12/21	23,643	524	2.2%	123,458
12/20	23,678	383	1.6%	118,210
12/19	20,926	437	2.1%	115,428
12/18	19,853	459	2.3%	108,560
Annual Growth	8.1%	8.2%	—	4.8%

2022 Year-End Financials
Debt ratio: 4.2%   No. of shares ($ mil.): 628
Return on equity: 25.6%   Dividends
Cash ($ mil.): 1,902   Yield: —
Current Ratio: 0.60   Payout: 168.7%
Long-term debt ($ mil.): 254   Market value ($ mil.): 27,073

	STOCK PRICE ($) FY Close	P/E High/Low		PER SHARE ($) Earnings	Dividends	Book Value
12/22	43.08	53	41	1.00	1.69	3.96
12/21	46.71	65	39	0.83	1.50	4.10
12/20	34.03	82	66	0.61	0.81	3.92
12/19	33.16	57	38	0.70	0.73	3.53
12/18	23.02	63	37	0.73	1.45	3.24
Annual Growth	17.0%	—		8.2%	3.9%	5.2%

JFE Holdings Inc

JFE Holdings operates as a streamlined group headquarters responsible for strategic planning, risk management, accountability and corporate communications for all the subsidiaries and affiliates.. The "J" in JFE stands for Japan; "F" is for Fe, the chemical symbol for iron; and "E" stands for engineering. JFE Holdings' steel business unit, JFE Steel, accounts for some 65% of total sales and manufactures steel products such as bars, pipes, steel frames, tubes and stainless steel for the automotive, construction, and petroleum industries. JFE is among the world's largest steel companies, ranking behind ArcelorMittal, Japan's Nippon Steel & Sumitomo Metal, and China's Hebei Iron and Steel and Baosteel. The company was established in 2002. Majority of its sales were generated in Japan.

Operations

The company operates through three segments: Steel (JFE Steel Corporation; some 65% of sales), Trading (JFE Shoji Trade Corporation; some 25%), and Engineering (JFE Engineering Corporation, around 10%).

The JFE Steel provides high-value-added products that meet the diverse needs of its customers with its world-class technologies and product development capabilities, backed by a highly internationally competitive system based on two major integrated steelworks in Japan.

The JFE Shoji operates globally through supply chain networks across Japan and the world, handling a wide range of products with a focus on steel products, including steel raw materials, nonferrous metals, chemicals, fuel, equipment, ships, foods, and electronics.

The JFE Engineering provides technologies to effectively utilize diverse resources as green energy in the environmental and energy fields, and proactively engages in plant operation as well. It globally operates social infrastructure business, such as constructing bridges

Geographic Reach

Headquartered in Tokyo, Japan, the company has a global network of about 110 bases in over 20 countries. Japan generated about 65% of sales, while other countries generated the rest.

Sales and Marketing

The company had one customer that

generated some 10% of its sales which is the Marubeni-Itochu Steel Inc. and its group companies. Its steel products in Japan span many areas of demand which include building construction, civil engineering, automobiles, industrial machinery, and electrical machinery?and sales are made through a variety of channels.

Financial Performance

The company reported a net revenue of Â¥4.4 trillion in 2021, a 35% increase from the previous year's net revenue of Â¥3.2 trillion.

In 2021, the company had a net income of Â¥388.5 billion, a 7981% improvement from the previous year's net loss of Â¥4.9 billion.

The company's cash at the end of 2021 was Â¥101.8 billion. Operating activities generated Â¥298.7 billion, while investing activities used Â¥288 billion, mainly for purchase of property, plant and equipment, intangible assets, and investment property. Financing activities used another Â¥57.4 billion, primarily for repayments of long-term borrowings.

Mergers and Acquisitions

In mid-2022, JFE Shoji Corporation and its subsidiary JFE Shoji America Holdings agreed with the shareholders of California Expanded Metal Products Co. to acquire 100% of the share of CEMCO. CEMCO is one of the largest manufacturers in the United States of Steel Framing and Metal Lath for exterior and interior usage in construction market. JFE Shoji anticipates from the acquisition that CEMCO and subsidiaries relating to construction market under JFESAHD, JFE Shoji America LLC, Vest Inc. and Kelly Pipe Co., LLC will enhance synergies and capture demand of the construction market in North America. Terms were not disclosed.

In mid-2022, JFE Steel Corporation has acquired EcoLeaf, the Japan EPD Program by SuMPO, from the Sustainable Management Promotion Organization (SuMPO) in Japan for three products: tinplate, JFE Universal Brite (laminated steel sheet) and tin-free steel. Data visualization enabled by EcoLeaf will increase the transparency of environmental impact of JFE products. JFE Steel's tinplate, laminated steel sheets, tin-free steel sheets, including those for beverage and food cans, are essential materials that support everyday life in diverse settings. Terms were not disclosed.

EXECUTIVES

President, Chief Executive Officer, Representative Director, Koji Kakigi
Executive Vice President, Chief Financial Officer, Representative Director, Masashi Terahata
Senior Managing Executive Officer, Toshihiro Tanaka
Senior Managing Executive Officer, Shinji Iwayama
Representative Director, Yoshihisa Kitano
Director, Hajime Oshita
Director, Toshinori Kobayashi
Outside Director, Masami Yamamoto
Outside Director, Nobumasa Kemori
Outside Director, Yoshiko Ando
Auditors: Ernst & Young ShinNihon LLC

LOCATIONS

HQ: JFE Holdings Inc
2-2-3 Uchisaiwai-cho, Chiyoda-ku, Tokyo 100-0011
Phone: (81) 3 3597 4321
Web: www.jfe-holdings.co.jp

PRODUCTS/OPERATIONS

2015 Sales

	% of total
Steel	53
Engineering	38
Trading	9
Adjustment	-
Total	100

Selected Products
Electrical Steel
Energy
Environment
Iron Powders
Pipes and Tubes
Plates
Shapes
Sheets
Slag
Stainless
Steel Bars and Wire Rods
Steel Structure
Titanium

COMPETITORS

China Baowu Steel Group Corporation Limited
ELTHERINGTON GROUP LIMITED
Gerdau S/A
NIPPON STEEL CORPORATION
NIPPON STEEL NISSHIN CO., LTD.
Outokumpu Oyj
STEMCOR GLOBAL HOLDINGS LIMITED
VALLOUREC
thyssenkrupp AG
voestalpine High Performance Metals GmbH

HISTORICAL FINANCIALS
Company Type: Public

Income Statement   FYE: March 31

	REVENUE ($mil)	NET INCOME ($mil)	NET PROFIT MARGIN	EMPLOYEES
03/23	39,559	1,221	3.1%	64,241
03/22	35,886	2,368	6.6%	64,296
03/21	29,146	(197)	—	64,371
03/20	34,359	(1,821)	—	64,009
03/19	34,978	1,476	4.2%	62,083
Annual Growth	3.1%	(4.6%)	—	0.9%

2023 Year-End Financials
Debt ratio: 0.2%   No. of shares ($ mil.): 581
Return on equity: 7.9%   Dividends
Cash ($ mil.): 896   Yield: —
Current Ratio: 1.54   Payout: 28.5%
Long-term debt ($ mil.): 11,006   Market value ($ mil.): —

Jiangxi Copper Co., Ltd.

EXECUTIVES

Deputy General Manager, Chiwei Wang
Staff Supervisor, Kui Zhang
Deputy General Manager, Yunian Chen
Staff Supervisor, Min Zeng
Supervisor, Jianhua Zhang
Deputy General Manager, Xingeng Liao
Chief Financial Officer, Director, Tong Yu
General Manager, Board Secretary (Acting), Chairman, Director, Gaoqing Zheng
Deputy General Manager, Director, Fangyun Liu
Supervisor, Yongmin Guan
Supervisor, Donghua Wu
Deputy General Manager, Wenbo Jiang
Board Secretary, Deputy General Manager, Dongyang Tu
Director, Jianmin Gao
Director, Qing Liang
Director, Independent Director, Shutian Tu
Independent Director, Erfei Liu
Director, Bo Wang
Independent Director, Xike Liu
Independent Director, Xingwen Zhu
Independent Director, Feng Wang
Auditors: Deloitte Touche Tohmatsu Certified Public Accountants LLP

LOCATIONS

HQ: Jiangxi Copper Co., Ltd.
7666 Changdong Avenue, High and New Technology Development Zone, Nanchang, Jiangxi Province 330096
Phone: (86) 791 82710117 **Fax:** (86) 791 82710114
Web: www.jxcc.com

HISTORICAL FINANCIALS
Company Type: Public

Income Statement   FYE: December 31

	REVENUE ($mil)	NET INCOME ($mil)	NET PROFIT MARGIN	EMPLOYEES
12/22	69,569	868	1.2%	0
12/21	69,742	887	1.3%	0
12/20	48,708	354	0.7%	0
12/19	34,543	354	1.0%	0
12/18	31,299	355	1.1%	0
Annual Growth	22.1%	25.0%	—	—

2022 Year-End Financials
Debt ratio: 4.6%   No. of shares ($ mil.): —
Return on equity: 8.3%   Dividends
Cash ($ mil.): 4,653   Yield: —
Current Ratio: 1.32   Payout: 0.0%
Long-term debt ($ mil.): 1,414   Market value ($ mil.): —

JinkoSolar Holding Co., Ltd.

EXECUTIVES

Chief Executive Officer, Chairman, Xiande Li
Chief Financial Officer, Director, Haiyun Cao
Independent Director, Wing Keong Siew
Independent Director, Stephen Markscheid
Independent Director, Yingqiu Liu
Director, Kangping Chen
Director, Xianhua Li
Auditors : PricewaterhouseCoopers Zhong Tian LLP

LOCATIONS

HQ: JinkoSolar Holding Co., Ltd.
 1 Jingke Road, Shangrao Economic Development Zone, Jiangxi Province 334100
Phone: (86) 793 846 9699 **Fax:** (86) 793 846 1152
Web: www.jinkosolar.com

HISTORICAL FINANCIALS
Company Type: Public

Income Statement   FYE: December 31

	REVENUE ($mil)	NET INCOME ($mil)	NET PROFIT MARGIN	EMPLOYEES
12/22	12,049	89	0.7%	46,511
12/21	6,430	113	1.8%	31,030
12/20	5,371	35	0.7%	24,361
12/19	4,274	129	3.0%	15,195
12/18	3,640	59	1.6%	12,565
Annual Growth	34.9%	11.1%	—	38.7%

2022 Year-End Financials
Debt ratio: 6.3%
Return on equity: 4.5%
Cash ($ mil.): 1,484
Current Ratio: 1.05
Long-term debt ($ mil.): 2,042
No. of shares ($ mil.): 201
Dividends
 Yield: —
 Payout: 0.0%
Market value ($ mil.): 8,225

	STOCK PRICE ($) FY Close	P/E High/Low	Earnings	Dividends	Book Value
12/22	40.88	23 11	0.45	0.00	11.77
12/21	45.96	19 8	0.32	0.00	9.12
12/20	61.87	69 10	(0.21)	0.00	8.15
12/19	22.49	5 2	0.70	0.00	7.47
12/18	9.89	9 3	0.38	0.00	7.27
Annual Growth	42.6%	—	4.1%	—	12.8%

Johnson Controls International plc

Johnson Controls International Plc (Johnson Controls) is a global leader in smart, healthy and sustainable buildings, serving a wide range of customers in more than 150 countries. The company offers HVAC equipment, fire suppression, distributed energy storage, fire detection, industrial refrigeration, building automation and controls, digital solutions, residential and smart home security, and retail solutions, among others. Johnson Controls also provides technical services, energy-management consulting, and data-driven solutions. It serves customers in residential and non-residential building markets. Johnson Controls traces its roots back to 1885 as Johnson Electric Service Company. The US accounts for about 50% of the company's revenue.

Operations

Johnson Controls conducts its business through four business segments: Global Products, Building Solutions North America, Building Solutions EMEA/LA, and Building Solutions Asia Pacific.

The Global Products segment (more than 35% of total revenue) designs, manufactures and sells HVAC equipment, controls software and software services for residential and commercial applications to commercial, industrial, retail, residential, small business, institutional, and governmental customers worldwide. In addition, Global Products designs, manufactures and sells refrigeration equipment and controls globally. The Global Products business also designs, manufactures and sells fire protection, fire suppression and security products, including intrusion security, anti-theft devices, access control, and video surveillance and management systems, for commercial, industrial, retail, residential, small business, institutional and governmental customers worldwide. Global Products includes the Johnson Controls-Hitachi joint venture.

Accounting for about 35% of total revenue, Building Solutions North America segment designs, sells, installs and services HVAC, controls, building management, refrigeration, integrated electronic security and integrated fire-detection and suppression systems for commercial, industrial, retail, small business, institutional and governmental customers in the US and Canada. It also provides energy efficiency solutions and technical services, including inspection, scheduled maintenance, and repair and replacement of mechanical and controls systems, as well as data-driven "smart building" solutions, to non-residential building and industrial applications in the US and Canadian marketplace.

Building Solutions EMEA/LA segment designs, sells, installs, and services HVAC, controls, building management, refrigeration, integrated electronic security, integrated fire-detection and suppression systems, and provides technical services, including data-driven "smart building" solutions, to markets in Europe, the Middle East, Africa and Latin America. The segment accounts for about 15% of total revenue.

Building Solutions Asia Pacific segment (some 10% of revenue) designs, sells, installs, and services HVAC, controls, building management, refrigeration, integrated electronic security, integrated fire-detection and suppression systems, and provides technical services, including data-driven "smart building" solutions, to the Asia Pacific marketplace.

Geographic Reach

Johnson Controls has properties in over 60 countries throughout the world, with its world headquarters located in Cork, Ireland and its North American operational headquarters located in Milwaukee, Wisconsin.

The US generates about 50% of the company's total revenue, while Asia Pacific generates about 25%, followed by Europe at more than 15% and other non-US generates the remaining 10% of revenue.

Sales and Marketing

Johnson Controls serves a wide range of industries, including federal government, global marine and navy, residential, healthcare, education, industrial and manufacturing, local government, state government, sports and entertainment and transportation.

Financial Performance

The company reported a total revenue of $25.3 billion in 2022, a 7% increase from the previous year's total revenue of $23.7 billion. This was primarily due to the higher volume of products and systems sales for the year.

In 2022, the company had a net income of $1.5 billion, a 6% decrease from the previous year's net income of $1.6 billion.

Cash held by the company at the end of fiscal 2022 was $2 billion. Operating activities generated $2 billion, while investing activities used $693 million, mainly for capital expenditures. Financing activities used another $516 million, mainly for stock repurchases and retirements.

Strategy

The company's business strategy is to sustain and expand its position as a leader in smart and sustainable building solutions by offering a full spectrum of products and solutions for customer buildings across the globe. The company's core strategy remains focused on creating growth platforms, driving operational improvements and creating a high-performance culture. The company has strong positions in attractive and growing end-markets across HVAC, controls, fire, security and services, enhanced by its comprehensive product portfolio and substantial installed base. The company believes that it is well positioned to capitalize on the emerging and prevalent trends in the buildings industry, including decarbonization, healthy buildings/indoor environmental quality and smart buildings.

To capitalize on these trends, the company remains focused on maintaining leading positions in commercial HVAC and building management systems, as well as enabling growth through digital, to develop and leverage new digital technologies and capabilities into outcomes powered by its OpenBlue software platform. In furtherance of these goals, the Company has three strategic priorities:

Mergers and Acquisitions

In mid-2023, Johnson Controls acquired FM:Systems, a leading digital workplace management and Internet of Things (IoT) solutions provider for facilities and real estate professionals, for purchase price of $455 million. The acquisition adds complementary cloud-based software as a service (SaaS) digital workplace management capabilities to Johnson Controls' leading OpenBlue digital buildings software portfolio.

In 2023, Johnson Controls acquired Hybrid Energy AS, a growing provider of high-temperature energy management solutions with a focus on heat pumps for district heating and industrial processes. The acquisition will enable Johnson Controls to provide high-temperature heat pumps in rapidly growing district heating and industrial markets, especially in Europe. Financial terms of the transaction were not disclosed.

In 2022, Johnson Controls acquired zero trust cybersecurity provider ? Tempered Networks, based in Seattle, Washington. The acquisition gives Johnson Controls the capability to provide zero trust security within the fabric of its OpenBlue secure communications stack, advancing its vision of enabling fully autonomous buildings that are inherently resilient to cyberattack.

In early 2022, Johnson Controls completed the acquisition of California-based FogHorn, the leading developer of Edge AI software for the industrial and commercial Internet of Things (IoT) solutions. The acquisition accelerates Johnson Controls' innovation and vision for Smart Autonomous Buildings by pervasively integrating Foghorn's industry leading Edge AI platform throughout OpenBlue. Financial terms of the transaction were not disclosed.

HISTORY

Professor Warren Johnson developed the electric telethermoscope in 1880 so that janitors at Whitewater, Wisconsin's State Normal School could regulate room temperatures without disturbing classrooms. His device, the thermostat, used mercury to move a heat element that opened and shut a circuit. Milwaukee hotelier William Plankinton believed in the invention and invested $150,000 to start production.

The two men formed Johnson Electric Service Company in 1885. They sold the marketing, installation, and service rights to concentrate on manufacturing. Johnson also invented other devices such as tower clocks, and he experimented with the telegraph before becoming intrigued with the automobile and beginning production of steam-powered cars. He won the US Postal Service's first automotive contract, but never gained support within his own company. Johnson continued to look elsewhere for financing until his death in 1911.

The renamed Johnson Services regained full rights to its thermostats in 1912 and sold its other businesses. During the Depression it produced economy systems that regulated building temperatures. Johnson Services became a public company in 1940. During WWII it aided the war effort, building weather-data gatherers and radar test sets.

In the 1960s Johnson Services began developing centralized control systems for temperature, fire alarm, lighting, and security regulation. The company was renamed Johnson Controls in 1974.

EXECUTIVES

Chairman, Chief Executive Officer, Director, George R. Oliver, $1,500,000 total compensation
Executive Vice President, Chief Financial Officer, Olivier C. Leonetti
Executive Vice President, General Counsel, John Donofrio
Lead Independent Director, Director, Jurgen Tinggren
Director, Jean S. Blackwell
Director, Pierre E. Cohade
Director, Michael E. Daniels
Director, Webster Roy Dunbar
Director, Gretchen R. Haggerty
Director, Simone Menne
Director, Mark P. Vergnano
Director, John D. Young
Auditors : PricewaterhouseCoopers LLP

LOCATIONS

HQ: Johnson Controls International plc
One Albert Quay, Cork T12 X8N6
Phone: (353) 21 423 5000
Web: www.johnsoncontrols.com

2018 Sales

	$ mil.	% of total
US	14,625	46
Europe		
Germany	1,961	6
UK	1,139	4
Other European countries	3,005	10
China	2,166	7
Japan	1,903	6
Mexico	909	3
Rest of the world	5,692	18
Total	31,400	100

PRODUCTS/OPERATIONS

2018 Sales

	$ mil.	% of total
Building Solutions North America	8,679	28
Building Solutions EMEA/LA	3,696	12
Building Solutions Asia Pacific	2,553	8
Global Products	8,472	27
Power Solutions	8,000	25
Total	31,400	100

Selected Products

Automotive experience
    Electronics
        Body electronics
        Driver information
        HomeLink (wireless car-to-home connectivity)
        Infotainment and connectivity
    Interiors
        Cockpits and instrument panels
        Door panels
        Floor consoles
        Overhead products
    Seating
        Climate seat systems
        Foam
        Metal structures and mechanisms
        Seat safety
        Trim
Building efficiency
    Building management systems
    Fire safety products
    HVAC systems
    Refrigeration
    Security products
    Snowmaking equipment
    York equipment
Power solutions
    Absorbent glass mat technology
    Lead-acid batteries
    Lithium-ion batteries

HISTORICAL FINANCIALS

Company Type: Public

Income Statement   FYE: September 30

	REVENUE ($mil)	NET INCOME ($mil)	NET PROFIT MARGIN	EMPLOYEES
09/23	26,793	1,849	6.9%	100,000
09/22	25,299	1,532	6.1%	102,000
09/21	23,668	1,637	6.9%	101,000
09/20	22,317	631	2.8%	97,000
09/19	23,968	5,674	23.7%	104,000
Annual Growth	2.8%	(24.4%)	—	(1.0%)

2023 Year-End Financials

Debt ratio: 20.9%   No. of shares ($ mil.): 680
Return on equity: 11.2%   Dividends
Cash ($ mil.): 835   Yield: —
Current Ratio: 0.97   Payout: 53.9%
Long-term debt ($ mil.): 7,818   Market value ($ mil.): —

Johnson Matthey Plc

Johnson Matthey is a global leader in science that enables a cleaner and healthier world. It makes catalysts and licenses process designs and technologies that help customers in the chemicals and energy industries turn a wide range of feedstock into many of products that are essentials for modern life. Johnson Matthey supplies customers with pgms and are also a key supplier to other parts of John Matthey. Its key customers are chemical manufacturing companies, oil and gas companies, and other industrial customers and pgm-using industries. Its largest geographic sales is in Europe. The company was founded in 1817.

Operations

Johnson Matthey's operates through three operating segments:

Clean Air provides catalysts for emission control after-treatment systems to remove harmful emissions from vehicles and non-road equipment powered by diesel and gasoline. The segment accounts for around 45% of total revenue.

Efficient Natural Resources provides products and processing services for the efficient use and transformation of critical natural resources including oil, gas, biomass and platinum group metals to enable the decarbonisation of chemical value chains and provide circular economy solutions. The segment accounts for approximately 55% of revenue.

Other Markets is a portfolio of businesses with particular focus on potential growth and value realization opportunities. This includes Battery Systems, Fuel Cells, Diagnostic Services, Battery Materials and Green Hydrogen The segment accounts for less than 5% of total revenue

Geographic Reach

Headquartered in London, England; the company operates in more than 30 countries. Johnson Matthey have approximately 45 major manufacturing sites in South Africa to North Macedonia, the USA or China.

Company's largest geographic market was the United Kingdom with about 20% followed by the United States and Germany with more than 15% and around 10% of the total revenue, respectively.

Sales and Marketing

The company mainly serves automotive, chemicals, pharmaceuticals, oil and gas, and many more.

Financial Performance

Johnson Matthey's revenue for fiscal 2022 increased by 4% to GBP16.0 billion compared to the prior year with GBP15.4 billion. The increase was driven by a partial recovery in Clean Air and good performance in Efficient Natural Resources.

Net loss for fiscal 2022 was GBP101 million compared from the prior year with GBP205 million. The losses were primarily due to higher major impairment and restructuring charges offsetting the increase in revenues.

Cash held by the company at the end of fiscal 2022 decreased to GBP346 million. Cash provided by operations with GBP605 million while cash used for investing and financing activities was GBP260 million and GBP550 million, respectively. The main uses of cash were purchases of property, plant and equipment; and purchase of treasury shares.

Strategy

Johnson Matthey's are focusing its portfolio on its core competencies in metal chemistry, catalysis and process technology and divesting Value Businesses. Company's goal is to achieve a top three position in all its markets. Johnson Matthey's business structure supports this by allowing the company to maximize synergies across our four business units: Clean Air, Catalyst Technologies, Hydrogen Technologies, and PGM Services. Company's strategic priorities are to be: leading in the autocatalyst markets; the #1 in syngas-based chemicals and fuels technology; the market leader in performance components for hydrogen fuel cells and electrolysers; and the #1 global platinum group metals refiner.

Mergers and Acquisitions

In mid-2021, Johnson Matthey announced its acquisition of the assets and intellectual property of Oxis Energy Limited, based near Oxford, UK. Eugene McKenna, Managing Director Green Hydrogen, commented: "Acquiring Oxis Energy's assets enables us to support our customers as they meet the strong demand for proton exchange membrane electrolysers used to produce green hydrogen. Improving electrolyser efficiency and reducing the cost of hydrogen are key to the further development of the green hydrogen market and scaling up CCM manufacturing will help bring JM and our customers closer to achieving this goal."

HISTORY

Percival Johnson set up an assayer's shop in London in 1817. Using chemical and physical tests, he determined the amount of gold in a given bar and guaranteed his results by offering to buy the bars he assayed. Johnson then set up a gold refinery in the early 1830s and developed a method for extracting platinum group metals. As part of that process, he produced vitreous colors for pottery and glass, refined nickel, and silver nitrate for medical use and, later, for photographic uses.

George Matthey joined the company in 1838 and championed the platinum business, securing a steady supply of platinum from Russia. The company thrived on business generated by gold rushes in California (1849) and Australia (1851). It built a silver refinery to melt down European coinage and extract component metals, and in 1870 it bought a company that produced magnesium, antimony, vanadium, and aluminum. In 1891 the company became Johnson, Matthey & Co. Limited. Around the turn of the century, it bought rolling mills and began forming metals into sheet, tube, and wire to better serve jewelers.

During WWI Johnson, Matthey & Co. provided platinum catalysts and magnesium powder for explosives, and in WWII the company was appointed the government's agent for controlling platinum stocks. Johnson, Matthey & Co. expanded its international operations rapidly during the post-war boom, adding holdings in Australia, India, North America, and South Africa. It established subsidiaries in France and the Netherlands (1956), Italy (1959), Sweden (1960), Belgium (1961), and Austria (1962). The company also began conducting research on automotive catalytic converters to reduce pollution. It formed Johnson Matthey Bankers (JMB) to carry out its banking and trading activities.

A foray into the US jewelry business led to big losses in 1980, and the company pressed JMB to make higher-risk loans. JMB's contribution to profits went from less than 25% in 1981 (the year the company took its present name) to more than 60% in 1983. The bank ended up with so many bad loans that the Bank of England had to arrange a bailout in 1984. Gene Anderson, who became CEO in 1985, cut 3,000 jobs and reduced the number of divisions from 78 to 4. Profits rebounded, but Anderson resigned in 1989 after failing to persuade the board to diversify away from platinum.

During the 1990s the company invested heavily in its electronics division, which had been doing well since the 1989 acquisition of Cominco Electronic Materials (ultra-pure metals for microchips). By 1995 the division was responsible for about a third of Johnson Matthey's profits. In 1998 it bought Cookson Group's 50% share of its ceramics joint venture.

In 1998 Johnson Matthey shifted its focus to three core businesses: catalysts, colors and coatings, and precious metals. The next year it sold its electronic materials business, Johnson Matthey Electronics, to US-based AlliedSignal (now Honeywell International) and began looking for takeover opportunities in its core markets. In 2001 the company acquired pharmaceuticals manufacturers Meconic (now Macfarlan Smith; it's the UK's only maker of medical opiates -- cocaine and heroin) and Pharm-Eco, then used these acquisitions as the basis for a fourth division: Pharmaceutical Materials (now a part of its Fine Chemicals and Catalysts Division).

In 2002 the company acquired Cascade Biochem Limited to strengthen its Pharmaceutical Materials division, and metal catalyst company Synetix. CEO Chris Clark retired in 2003. He was succeeded by Neil Carson, former executive director of the precious metals and catalysts operations.

Following the sale of its Pigments & Dispersions unit to Rockwood Pigments in 2004, Johnson Matthey restructured its Colours and Coatings division by closing several of its manufacturing sites and transferring some operations to its Precious Metal Products division. The moves created what became the Ceramics division, the 2007 sale of which was the last in the dismantling of the Colours and Coatings division.

At the beginning of 2008, the company acquired the Argillon Group, which manufactured catalysts and advanced ceramic materials, from Ceramics Luxembourg (owned by KKR). Later that year, Johnson Matthey sold the acquired ceramic insulators alumina business for about $40 million.

In 2010 a Johnson Matthey subsidiary formed a joint venture with Aoxing Pharmaceutical to manufacture ingredients for narcotics and neurological drugs for the Chinese market. That same year, Johnson Matthey acquired Intercat, a supplier of fluid catalytic cracking services for the petroleum refining industry, for $56 million. It became part of Johnson Matthey's Process Technologies division's Ammonia, Methanol, Oil and Gas unit.

EXECUTIVES

Chief Executive Officer, Director, Robert J. MacLeod
Chief Financial Officer, Director, Stephen Oxley
Chief EHS and Operations Officer, Ron Gerrard
Chief Human Resources Officer, Annette M. Kelleher
Chief Technology Officer, Maurits van Tol
Clean Air Sector Chief Executive, Joan A. Braca
Battery Material Sector Chief Executive, Christian Gunther schwarz
Efficient Natural Resources Sector Chief Executive, Jane E. Toogood
General Counsel, Company Secretary, Nick Cooper
Chairman, Director, Patrick Thomas
Senior Independent Non-Executive Director, Director, John O'Higgins
Independent Non-Executive Director, Xiaozhi Liu
Independent Non-Executive Director, Jane Griffiths
Independent Non-Executive Director, Chris Mottershead
Independent Non-Executive Director, Doug Webb
Auditors : PricewaterhouseCoopers LLP

LOCATIONS

HQ: Johnson Matthey Plc
5th Floor, 25 Farringdon Street, London EC4A 4AB
Phone: (44) 20 7269 8400 **Fax:** (44) 20 7269 8433
Web: www.matthey.com

2015 Sales

	%
Europe	
UK	24
Germany	12
Rest of Europe	11
USA	25
Rest of North America	2
China (including Hong Kong)	11
Rest of Asia	10
Rest of World	5
Total	100

PRODUCTS/OPERATIONS

2015 Sales

	% of total
Precious Metals	56
Emission Control Technologies	33
Process Technologies	6
Fine Chemicals	4
New Businesses	1
Total	100

Businesses
Emission Control Technologies Division
Emission Control Technologies website
Stationary Emissions Control website
Process Technologies Division
Process Technologies website
Chemical Catalysts website
Johnson Matthey Formox website
Johnson Matthey Davy Technologies website
Tracerco website
Precious Metal Products Division
Services Businesses
Precious Metals Management
Global Precious Metal Refining website
Scavenging Technologies
PGM Database
Johnson Matthey & Brandenberger website
Manufacturing Businesses
Noble Metals website
Medical Device Components website
Metal Joining website
USA Jewellery Products
Advanced Glass Technologies website
Silver and Coating Technologies website
Chemical Products website
Piezoproducts website
Fine Chemicals Division
API Manufacturing
Johnnson Matthey Macfarlan Smith website
Johnson Matthey Pharmaceutical Materials - USA website
Johnson Matthey Pharma Services website

COMPETITORS

CHEVRON CORPORATION
CHEVRON PHILLIPS CHEMICAL COMPANY LLC
ETC SUNOCO HOLDINGS LLC
EXXON MOBIL CORPORATION
Evonik Industries AG
HERAEUS HOLDING Gesellschaft mit beschrÃ¤nkter Haftung
SHELL OIL COMPANY
SUN CAPITAL PARTNERS, INC.
W. R. GRACE & CO.
WORLD FUEL SERVICES CORPORATION

HISTORICAL FINANCIALS

Company Type: Public

Income Statement   FYE: March 31

	REVENUE ($mil)	NET INCOME ($mil)	NET PROFIT MARGIN	EMPLOYEES
03/23	18,476	341	1.8%	12,638
03/22	21,030	(132)	—	13,430
03/21	21,576	282	1.3%	14,582
03/20	18,008	315	1.7%	15,352
03/19	14,075	541	3.8%	14,795
Annual Growth	7.0%	(10.9%)	—	(3.9%)

2023 Year-End Financials

Debt ratio: 28.7%   No. of shares ($ mil.): 183
Return on equity: 11.0%   Dividends
Cash ($ mil.): 804   Yield: 3.7%
Current Ratio: 1.51   Payout: 99.3%
Long-term debt ($ mil.): 1,806   Market value ($ mil.): 9,061

	STOCK PRICE ($) FY Close	P/E High/Low		PER SHARE ($) Earnings	Dividends	Book Value
03/23	49.39	40	29	1.86	1.84	17.12
03/22	50.32	—	—	(0.69)	1.94	17.28
03/21	84.89	87	43	1.46	1.32	19.10
03/20	43.71	66	33	1.63	2.11	18.03
03/19	84.00	47	32	2.81	2.07	17.67
Annual Growth	(12.4%)	—	—	(9.8%)	(2.8%)	(0.8%)

JSC VTB Bank

VTB Bank offers a smorgasbord of financial services for corporate, financial, and retail clients in Russia, Western Europe, Africa, and Asia. It is a global provider of financial services, comprised of over 20 credit institutions and financial companies operating across all key areas of the financial market. The company also provides investment banking and services for financialn Russia, it performs banking operations through a parent company (VTB Bank) and a number of subsidiary banks ? Vozrozhdenie Bank, West Siberian Commercial Bank, Sarovbusinessbank ? as well as through the Post Bank joint venture. The Russian government owns 0over 90% of VTB.

Operations

VTB Bank operates three main business segments: Retail Business (RB), Corporate-Investment Banking (CIB), and Medium and Small Business.

The Retail Business global business line (about 45% of net income) specializes in banking services for individuals, providing a wide range of financial products and services that fully cover the needs of clients.

The CIB segment, which generates around 35% of the bank's net interest income, specializes in servicing major corporate clients through sales of lending, transaction and investment products as well as leasing and factoring services in Russia, the CIS countries, Europe, Asia and Africa.

The Medium and Small Business (MSB) global business line specializes in serving legal entities and individual entrepreneurs with annual revenues of up to RUB 25 billion per group of companies. This generated some 15% of the company's net interest income.

Overall, nearly 75% of sales were generated from its net income.

Geographic Reach

Moscow-based, VTB's main market is in Russia, though it also has a presence in nearly 20 other countries in the CIS (including Belarus, Ukraine, and Kazakhstan), Europe (Austria, Germany, France, the UK, Italy), Asia (China, Hong Kong, India, Singapore), the US, the Middle East (Dubai), and Africa.

Financial Performance

Note: Growth rates may differ after conversion to US Dollars.

VTB Bank achieved strong growth in key banking revenues, despite the challenging economic conditions. Net interest income increased by 21%, while net fee and commission income increased by 13% on the back of higher volumes of customer transactions on VTB's online platform as well as a significant increase in the volume of brokerage commissions.

The bank's net profit for 2020 declined 63% to R$75.3 billion from R$201.2 billion the year prior. Despite considerable increases in net interest income and net fee and commission income, increases in provision changes, staff costs and administrative expenses, and income tax contributed to the steep decline.

Cash at the end of the year was R$1.2 trillion, R$96.8 billion less from the year prior. Operating activities used R$158.8 billion, compared to an inflow of R$369.5 billion in 2019. Investing activities used another

R$687.3 billion, mainly for purchase of investment financial assets; intangible assets; and land, premises, and equipment. Financing activities contributed R$552.6 billion from proceeds from borrowings and funds from local central banks.

Strategy

VTB is focused on long-term and sustainable development, it has to adapt in response to new challenges, which means the evolution of the bank's business model, an increased focus on customers and their needs, acceleration of internal processes, and optimization of the bank's operating model. With this, VTB's 2022 strategy is centered around three pillars: the interests of its clients are the focus; intensive growth of the banking business, complemented by digital economy initiatives; and digitalization, advanced technologies, increased efficiency.

Customer usage of digital channels for their banking needs is expected to increase considerably: more than 50% of sales will be completely digital, and 100% of products will be available to customers through electronic channels by the end of 2022; more than 80% of service operations will move to remote channels. An important priority is the digitalization of internal processes, which will involve, in particular, the transition to a completely paperless internal workflow while maximizing the electronic workflow in relations with external counterparties.

VTB also plans to build an advanced operation and processing platform based on a next-generation microservice IT architecture that will create competitive advantages for the company in terms of the speed at which technological solutions are introduced and new services are brought to the market. Investments in technological products will be aimed at creating leading solutions in such areas as the use of biometric identification platforms, robotics and advanced analytics, and the virtualization of processes based on artificial intelligence technology, among others.

Key factors will be accelerating VTB's response to market changes and customer demand and promoting values within the corporate culture such as innovation, engagement, commitment to results and teamwork. The introduction and scaling of a new model of cross-functional teams will be an important drive for speeding up these processes.

Company Background

VTB Bank was formed in 1990 by the Bank of Russia. It went public in 2007, divesting about 20% of its shares to the public.

EXECUTIVES

Chairman, President, Director, Andrey L. Kostin
Chief Executive Officer, Director, Archil Kontselidze
Director, Anton V. Drozdov
Director, Aleksey V. Ulyukaev
Director, Kirill Gennadievich Androsov
Director, Arkady V. Dvorkovich
Director, Matias Warnig
Director, Alexei Savatyugin
Director, Sergey A. Storchak
Director, Yuri M. Medvedev
Director, Yves-Thibault de Silguy
Auditors : Ernst & Young LLC

LOCATIONS

HQ: JSC VTB Bank
11a Degtyarnyy Pereulok, Saint-Petersburg 191144
Phone: —
Web: www.vtb.com

PRODUCTS/OPERATIONS

2014 Sales

	% of total
Interest income	77
Non-interest gains	10
Net fee and commission income	6
Net insurance premium earned	4
Revenue from other non-banking activites	3
Total	100

HISTORICAL FINANCIALS

Company Type: Public

Income Statement				FYE: December 31
	REVENUE ($mil)	NET INCOME ($mil)	NET PROFIT MARGIN	EMPLOYEES
12/21	18,617	4,332	23.3%	0
12/20	16,584	1,077	6.5%	79,217
12/19	22,305	3,245	14.6%	82,300
12/18	17,321	2,571	14.8%	0
12/17	21,724	2,080	9.6%	0
Annual Growth	(3.8%)	20.1%		

2021 Year-End Financials

Debt ratio: —
Return on equity: 16.6%
Cash ($ mil.): 17,831
Current Ratio: —
Long-term debt ($ mil.): —
No. of shares ($ mil.): 12,960,000
Dividends
 Yield: —
 Payout: 11966.8%
Market value ($ mil.): —

JTEKT Corp

JTEKT is a giant manufacturer of ball bearings used in electrified powertrain units and automotive steering devices has indeed got talent. Other automotive parts made by JTEKT include ABS sensors, constant velocity (CV) joints, oil seals, steering gear systems, and driveshaft. It also builds machine tools, factory automation systems, and heat technology products, such as industrial furnaces and semiconductor manufacturing equipment. Its largest market, Japan, accounts for about 40% of revenue.

Operations

The JTEKT Corporation operates in three segments: automotive components, bearing, machine tools and mechatronics.

The automotive field accounts for about 70% of total revenue and provide major vehicle manufacturers around the world with steering systems responsible for maneuvering the car and drive parts to propel the car forward.

Bearings support the rotating parts of all the mechanical equipment. JTEKT's are active in wide range of domains with a particular focus on automotive. This segment generates more than 20% of the total company's revenue.

Machine tools and mechatronics support society across a diversity of sectors from automotive to steel, railway, aviation, aerospace, construction machinery, wind power, and more generation. It is responsible for the remaining 10% of the revenue.

Geographic Reach

Headquartered in Aichi, Japan is the company's largest market, representing almost 40% of the total revenue. Other major markets include Asia and Oceania, generating about 30%; and North America, over 20%. Europe accounts for around 10% of revenue.

Sales and Marketing

The company's products are primarily applied in the automobile, bearing and machine tool industries.

Financial Performance

The company reported a revenue of Â¥1.4 trillion in 2022, a 15% increase from the previous year's revenue of Â¥1.3 trillion.

In 2021, the company had a net income Â¥20.7 billion, a Â¥19.9 billion increase from the previous year's net income of Â¥800 million.

The company's cash at the end of 2021 was Â¥124.3 billion. Operating activities generated Â¥67 billion, while investing activities used Â¥25.3 billion, mainly for payment of Purchases of property, plant and equipment. Financing activities used another Â¥43.5 billion, primarily for repayment of long-term borrowings.

Company Background

JTEKT was formed on January 1, 2006, by a merger of Koyo Seiko Co. and Toyoda Machine Works.

EXECUTIVES

President, Representative Director, Kazuhiro Sato
Representative Director, Takumi Matsumoto
Representative Director, Koichi Yamanaka
Outside Director, Iwao Okamoto
Outside Director, Yuichiro Kato
Outside Director, Kazunari Kumakura
Auditors : PricewaterhouseCoopers Kyoto

LOCATIONS

HQ: JTEKT Corp
1-1 Asahi-machi, Kariya, Aichi 448-8652
Phone: (81) 566 25 7326   **Fax:** (81) 566 25 7311
Web: www.jtekt.co.jp

2014 Sales	% of total
Japan	44
North America	20
Asia, Oceania and other	20
Europe	16
Total	100

PRODUCTS/OPERATIONS

2014 Sales	% of total
Automotive components	59
Bearing	29
Machine tootls and mechatronics	12
Total	100

Selected Products
Bearings
    Automotive bearings & unit products
    Bearings for electric, electronic products
    Bearings for extreme special environments
    Bearings for general industrial equipment
    General purpose bearings
    Machine tool bearings
    Steel mill bearings
Driveline components
    4WD couplings
    CVT oil pumps
    Damper pulleys
    Driveshafts
    Propeller shafts
    Proportionately controlled AT & CVT valves
    TORSENs
Machine tools
    Grinders line up
    Horizontal spindle machining centers line up
Mechatronics
    General operation board
    Motion controllers
    Toyopuc
Sensor systems
Steering systems
    Components
    Electric power steering
    Hydraulic power steering

COMPETITORS
MOTION INDUSTRIES, INC.
NSK CORPORATION
NSK LTD.
NTN CORPORATION
PRIDGEON & CLAY, INC.
Robert Bosch Gesellschaft mit beschrÃ¤nkter Haftung
SCHAEFFLER TRANSMISSION, LLC.
STRATTEC SECURITY CORPORATION
TENNECO INC.
UNISON INDUSTRIES, LLC

HISTORICAL FINANCIALS
Company Type: Public

Income Statement   FYE: March 31

	REVENUE ($mil)	NET INCOME ($mil)	NET PROFIT MARGIN	EMPLOYEES
03/23	12,600	257	2.0%	51,087
03/22	11,743	170	1.4%	52,552
03/21	11,255	7	0.1%	53,775
03/20	13,071	(34)	—	56,639
03/19	13,733	222	1.6%	57,184
Annual Growth	(2.1%)	3.7%	—	(2.8%)

2023 Year-End Financials
Debt ratio: 0.1%
Return on equity: 5.3%
Cash ($ mil.): 929
Current Ratio: 1.72
Long-term debt ($ mil.): 1,559
No. of shares ($ mil.): 343
Dividends
   Yield: —
   Payout: 63.7%
Market value ($ mil.): 7,797

	STOCK PRICE ($) FY Close	P/E High/Low		PER SHARE ($) Earnings	Dividends	Book Value
03/23	22.73	0	0	0.75	0.48	14.61
03/22	22.44	0	0	0.50	0.40	14.96
03/21	31.82	13	7	0.02	0.65	14.51
03/20	21.14	—	—	(0.10)	1.22	13.41
03/19	36.54	1	0	0.65	1.20	14.12
Annual Growth	(11.2%)	—	—	3.7%	(20.6%)	0.8%

Juroku Financial Group Inc

The Juroku Bank is industriously working to serve its customers in the prefectures of Gifu and Aichi, both part of the industrial region of Chubu. The regional bank has about 150 offices in its primary service areas, as well as offices in Osaka and Tokyo, and overseas offices in Hong Kong and Shanghai. In addition to traditional deposit banking products and services, The Juroku Bank and its subsidiaries do business in such areas as credit cards, credit guarantees, investments, and leasing. The bank joined with five other regional banks to form the Tokai-Kinki PFI Financial Network, which is intended to help its member strengthen their abilities related to private finance initiatives.

EXECUTIVES

Chairman, President, Representative Director, Yukio Murase
Executive Vice President, Representative Director, Naoki Ikeda
Director, Yukiyasu Shiraki
Director, Akihide Ishiguro
Director, Shin Mishima
Director, Tsutomu Niimi
Outside Director, Yuji Kume
Outside Director, Kikuo Asano
Outside Director, Satoko Ito
Auditors : Deloitte Touche Tohmatsu LLC

LOCATIONS

HQ: Juroku Financial Group Inc
8-26 Kanda-machi, Gifu 500-8516
Phone: (81) 58 265 2111
Web: www.juroku.co.jp

COMPETITORS

AOZORA BANK,LTD.
BANK OF NAGOYA, LTD., THE
KAGOSHIMA BANK, LTD., THE
METROPOLITAN BANK & TRUST COMPANY
NANTO BANK,LTD., THE

HISTORICAL FINANCIALS
Company Type: Public

Income Statement   FYE: March 31

	ASSETS ($mil)	NET INCOME ($mil)	INCOME AS % OF ASSETS	EMPLOYEES
03/21	65,372	132	0.2%	3,624
03/20	59,626	118	0.2%	3,741
03/19	57,512	96	0.2%	3,911
03/18	57,413	93	0.2%	4,184
03/17	54,006	89	0.2%	4,319
Annual Growth	4.9%	10.3%	—	(4.3%)

2021 Year-End Financials
Return on assets: 0.2%
Return on equity: 3.9%
Long-term debt ($ mil.): —
No. of shares ($ mil.): 37
Sales ($ mil.): 1,005
Dividends
   Yield: —
   Payout: 22.8%
Market value ($ mil.): —

Kajima Corp. (Japan)

Kajima Corporation conducts construction, engineering, real estate development and other business globally. The company provides planning, development, design, engineering, capabilities and provide communities and customers around the world with urban and architectural spaces and infrastructure and built in highest standard. Kajima is growing its construction and real estate development businesses around the world through its global network of regional headquarters Kajima U.S.A. (KUSA); Kajima Asia Pacific Holdings (KAP); Kajima Europe (KE); Kajima Australia (KA); Chung-Lu Construction and Kajima China. Kajima was established in 1840 as Iwakichi Kajima.

Operations

Kajima consists of five reportable segments: Building Construction; Overseas Subsidiaries and Affiliates; Civil Engineering; Domestic Subsidiaries and Affiliates; and Real Estate Development and Other.

Building construction and Civil engineering segment are responsible for the construction business of the company. These segments account for about 55% of combined revenue.

Overseas Subsidiaries and Affiliates segment (around 30%) operates construction business, real estate development business and others overseas such as in North America, Europe, Asia, Oceania and other areas operated by overseas subsidiaries and affiliates.

Domestic Subsidiaries and Affiliates segment (about 15%) is responsible for the sales of construction materials, special construction and engineering services, comprehensive leasing business, building rental business and others mainly in Japan operated by domestic subsidiaries and affiliates.

Real Estate Development and Other segment include Real estate development business, architectural, structural and other design business and engineering business operated by the company.

Geographic Reach
Kajima is based in Japan. Its offices in Japan are located in the cities of Hokkaido, Tohoku, Kanto, Yokohama, Hokuriku, Chubu, Kansai, Shikoku, Chugoku, and Kyushu. Its international offices are in Taiwan, Singapore, Indonesia, Vietnam, Bangladesh, China, and Myanmar.

Financial Performance
The company reported a total revenue of ¥2.1 trillion in 2021, a 9% increase from the previous year's total revenue of ¥1.9 trillion. Both construction projects and Real estate and other generated higher revenues for the year.

In 2021, the company had a net income of ¥103.9 billion, a 5% increase from the previous year's net income of ¥98.5 billion.

The company's cash at the end of 2021 was ¥267.7 billion. Operating activities generated ¥30.2 billion, while investing activities used ¥51.2 billion, mainly for payment for purchases of property and equipment. Financing activities used another ¥20.9 billion, primarily for repayment of long-term loans.

Strategy
The company's strategy includes goals for 2030, as medium- to long-term objectives. To ensure progress toward these goals, the Kajima Group will (1) further strengthen core businesses; (2) strive to create new value; and (3) establish a strong management foundation and promote ESG measures for growth and transformation. Meanwhile, the company will develop and promote new measures and strategic investments as well as continue to move forward with existing measures.

Company Background
Founded in 1840, Kajima has had an illustrious and venerable history. It began earthquake remediation work in the early 1920s and built railroads and the first Western-style buildings in Japan.

EXECUTIVES

Chairman, Representative Director, Yoshikazu Oshimi
President, Representative Director, Hiromasa Amano
Executive Vice President, Representative Director, Keisuke Koshijima
Executive Vice President, Representative Director, Masaru Kazama
Executive Vice President, Director, Hiroshi Ishikawa
Executive Vice President, Takao Nomura
Executive Vice President, Koichi Matsuzaki
Senior Managing Executive Officer, Jun Matsushima
Senior Managing Executive Officer, Director, Takeshi Katsumi
Senior Managing Executive Officer, Director, Ken Uchida
Senior Managing Executive Officer, Takaharu Fukuda
Senior Managing Executive Officer, Norio Kita
Senior Managing Executive Officer, Takeshi Tadokoro
Senior Managing Executive Officer, Yoshihiko Riho
Senior Managing Executive Officer, Hiroshi Shoji
Outside Director, Kiyomi Saito
Outside Director, Yoichi Suzuki
Outside Director, Tamotsu Saito
Outside Director, Masami Iijima
Outside Director, Kazumine Terawaki
Auditors : Deloitte Touche Tohmatsu LLC

LOCATIONS

HQ: Kajima Corp. (Japan)
 1-3-1 Motoakasaka, Minato-ku, Tokyo 107-8388
Phone: (81) 3 5544 1111
Web: www.kajima.co.jp

2013 Sales

	% of total
Asia	
Japan	85
Other countries	7
North America	6
Europe	1
Other regions	
Total	

PRODUCTS/OPERATIONS

2013 Sales

	% of total
Construction	88
Real Estate & others	12
Total	100

2013 Sales

	% of total
Building construction	50
Civil Engineering	18
Real estate development and others	4
Others	28
Total	100

Selected Subsidiaries
Act Technical Support Inc. (sales and services)
Azuma Kanko Kaihatsu Co., Ltd. (hotels and leisure)
Chung-Lu Construction Co., Ltd. (Taiwan)
East Real Estate Co., Ltd.
Green Materials Recycle Corporation (sales and services)
Hawaiian Dredging Construction Company, Inc. (US)
Ilya Corporation (design and consulting)
Kajima Kress Co., Ltd. (procurement and construction)
Kajima Real Estate Investment Advisors Inc.
Kajima Tatemono Sogo Kanri Co., Ltd. (real estate development and management)
Public Relations Officer Corporation (sales and services)
Shinrinkohen Golf Club Co., Ltd.
Taiko Trading Co., Ltd. (procurement and construction)
Yaesu Book Center Co., Ltd. (culture)

COMPETITORS

BECHTEL GROUP, INC.
China Railway Engineering Group Co., Ltd.
China Railway Group Limited
GEE CONSTRUCTION LTD
HOCHTIEF AG
OBAYASHI CORPORATION
ORION GROUP HOLDINGS, INC.
SHIMIZU CORPORATION
STRABAG SE
VolkerWessels Nederland B.V.

HISTORICAL FINANCIALS
Company Type: Public

Income Statement FYE: March 31

	REVENUE ($mil)	NET INCOME ($mil)	NET PROFIT MARGIN	EMPLOYEES
03/23	17,956	839	4.7%	23,106
03/22	17,097	853	5.0%	22,806
03/21	17,224	889	5.2%	22,364
03/20	18,523	951	5.1%	22,114
03/19	17,827	991	5.6%	21,616
Annual Growth	0.2%	(4.1%)		1.7%

2023 Year-End Financials
Debt ratio: 0.1% No. of shares ($ mil.): 487
Return on equity: 11.1% Dividends
Cash ($ mil.): 2,145 Yield: 3.6%
Current Ratio: 1.33 Payout: 0.0%
Long-term debt ($ mil.): 1,902 Market value ($ mil.): 5,844

	STOCK PRICE ($) FY Close	P/E High/Low		PER SHARE ($) Earnings	Dividends	Book Value
03/23	12.00	0	0	1.71	0.44	16.22
03/22	12.01	0	0	1.71	0.50	15.76
03/21	14.28	0	0	1.74	0.47	15.61
03/20	10.76	0	0	1.85	0.47	14.20
03/19	14.89	0	0	1.91	0.47	13.08
Annual Growth	(5.3%)			(2.7%)	(1.5%)	5.5%

Kansai Electric Power Co., Inc. (Kansai Denryoku K. K.) (Japan)

As Japan's #2 electric utility (behind Tokyo Electric), Kansai Electric Power Company (KEPCO) provides electricity to customers in Japan's Kansai region. The utility has a generating capacity of 29.4 GW, which is produced at hydroelectric, coal, and nuclear power plants. As deregulation takes effect, KEPCO is moving into new business arenas, including retail natural gas sales in Japan. KEPCO is mainly engaged in electricity business, heat supply business, telecommunications business, gas supply business and more. It has over 100 companies, primarily in Japan. The company was founded in 1951.

Operations
KEPCO operates in four reportable: Energy (over 60% of sales), Transmission and Distribution (around 25%), IT/Communications (over 5%), and Life Business Solution (some 5%).

The Energy business provides new value through a variety of solutions including electricity, gas and utility services. The Transmission and Distribution business provides electricity in a secure and stable manner from a neutral and fair standpoint.

The IT/Communication business provides general telecommunication service. The Life/Business Solution business provides real estate related service and life and business related service.

Overall, electric products generated about 75% of sales.

Geographic Reach
KEPCO's supply area includes all of Osaka (headquarters), Hyogo, Kyoto, Nara, Shiga, Tokai, Hokuriku, Tokyo, and Wakayama.

Financial Performance
The company's revenue for fiscal 2022 decreased to JPY 2.9 trillion compared from the prior year with JPY 3.1 trillion.

Net income for fiscal 2022 decreased to JPY 85.8 billion compared from the prior year with JPY 109.0 billion.

Cash held by the company at the end of fiscal 2022 increased to JPY 490.5 billion. Cash provided by operations and financing activities were JPY 410.3 billion and JPY 318.8 billion, respectively. Cash used for investing activities was JPY 532.6 billion, mainly for purchases of property, plant, and equipment.

Company Background
The company was established in 1951. KEPCO has a longstanding relationship with Australia's North West Shelf liquefied natural gas (LNG) joint venture. One of the venture's first customers in 1989, the company in 2009 signed a new deal guaranteeing the Japanese utility some 3.3 million metric tons a year in LNG supply.

EXECUTIVES

Chairman, Outside Director, Sadayuki Sakakibara
Representative Executive Officer, President, Director, Nozomu Mori
Representative Executive Officer, Executive Vice President, Director, Koji Inada
Representative Executive Officer, Executive Vice President, Mikio Matsumura
Representative Executive Officer, Executive Vice President, Hitoshi Mizuta
Representative Executive Officer, Executive Vice President, Director, Makoto Araki
Outside Director, Takamune Okihara
Outside Director, Atsuko Kaga
Outside Director, Hiroshi Tomono
Outside Director, Kazuko Takamatsu
Outside Director, Fumio Naito
Outside Director, Seiji Manabe
Outside Director, Motoko Tanaka
Director, Yasuji Shimamoto
Director, Nobuhiro Nishizawa
Auditors : Deloitte Touche Tohmatsu LLC

LOCATIONS

HQ: Kansai Electric Power Co., Inc. (Kansai Denryoku K. K.) (Japan)
 3-6-16 Nakanoshima, Kita-ku, Osaka 530-8270
Phone: (81) 50 7105 9084
Web: www.kepco.co.jp

PRODUCTS/OPERATIONS

2016 Sales

	% of total
Electric power	86
IT/Communications	5
Other	9
Total	100

Selected Subsidiaries
Kanden Energy Solution Co., Inc
SAKAI LNG Corp
ECHIZEN ENELINE CO., INC
Osaka Bioenergy Co., Ltd
K-Opticom Corp
Kanden System Solutions Co., Inc
Kanden Realty & Development Co., Ltd.
Clearpass Co., Ltd
KANDEN AMENIX Corp
Kanden Community Co., Ltd
Kanden CS Forum Inc.
Kanden Oce Work Co., Inc
Kanden Power-Tech Corp
Kanden Business Support Corp.
San Roque Power Corporation
LNG EBISU Shipping Corporation
KPIC Netherlands, B.V.

COMPETITORS

CHUBU ELECTRIC POWER CO.,INC.
CHUGOKU ELECTRIC POWER COMPANY,INCORPORATED,THE
IBERDROLA, SOCIEDAD ANONIMA
KYUSHU ELECTRIC POWER COMPANY, INCORPORATED
PG&E CORPORATION
TALEN ENERGY CORPORATION
TOHOKU ELECTRIC POWER COMPANY,INCORPORATED
TOKYO ELECTRIC POWER COMPANY HOLDINGS, INCORPORATED
Uniper SE
Vattenfall AB

HISTORICAL FINANCIALS
Company Type: Public

Income Statement FYE: March 31

	REVENUE ($mil)	NET INCOME ($mil)	NET PROFIT MARGIN	EMPLOYEES
03/23	29,672	132	0.4%	42,255
03/22	23,445	705	3.0%	43,692
03/21	27,928	984	3.5%	44,179
03/20	29,334	1,197	4.1%	44,251
03/19	29,867	1,039	3.5%	45,699
Annual Growth	(0.2%)	(40.2%)	—	(1.9%)

2023 Year-End Financials
Debt ratio: 0.4%　　No. of shares ($ mil.): 893
Return on equity: 1.0%　　Dividends
Cash ($ mil.): 2,004　　Yield: —
Current Ratio: 0.79　　Payout: 0.0%
Long-term debt ($ mil.): 31,368　　Market value ($ mil.): —

Kao Corp

Kao (pronounced "cow") is one of Japan's leading makers of personal care, laundry, and cleaning products. Its brand names include Attack (a top laundry detergent in Japan), BiorÃ© (skin care), Laurier (sanitary napkins), Merries (disposable diapers), and PureOra (toothpaste). The company also manufactures Healthya brand beverages (green tea and water), cooking oils and fatty chemicals, printer and copier toner products, and plastics used in products such as athletic shoe soles. It operates through five reportable segments: the Hygiene and Living Care Business, the Health and Beauty Care Business, the Life Care Business, the Cosmetics Business, and the Chemical Business. Kao generates nearly 60% of sales from Japan.

Operations
Kao has five reportable segments: Hygiene and Living Care Business (approximately 35%), Health and Beauty Care Business (some 25%), Chemical Business (nearly 20%), Cosmetics Business (more than 15%), and Life Care Business (nearly 5%).

The company manufactures consumer products including fabric care products, home care products, sanitary products, skin care products, hair care products, personal health products, life care products, cosmetics, and chemical products including fatty alcohols, and surfactants.

Geographic Reach
Headquartered in Tokyo, the company generates nearly 60% of revenue from Japan. Asia brings in more than 20%, the Americas and Europe contribute about 10% each.

Sales and Marketing
The company delivers its products to customers through its sales companies and distributors in Japan and other countries.

Financial Performance
Note: Growth rates may differ after conversion of USD.

Company's revenue for fiscal 2021 increased to YEN 1.41 trillion compared from the prior year with YEN 1.38 trillion.

Net income for fiscal 2021 decreased to YEN 111.4 billion compared from the prior year with YEN 128.1 billion.

Cash held by the company at the end of fiscal 2021 decreased to YEN 336.1 billion. Cash provided by YEN 336.1 billion while cash used for investing and financing activities were YEN 67.2 billion and YEN 141.6 billion, respectively.

HISTORY

Tomiro Nagase founded the Kao Soap Company in 1887; shortly afterward, he began selling bars under the motto, "A Clean Nation Prospers." Kao's longtime rivalry with Procter & Gamble (P&G) was foreshadowed when it adopted a moon trademark in 1890 strikingly similar to the one chosen by P&G eight years earlier.

Kao moved into detergents in the 1940s. In the 1960s the company struck upon an idea that would vertically integrate it and set it apart from other consumer products manufacturers: It set up a network of wholesale distributors ("hansha") who sell only Kao products. The hansha system improved distribution time and cut costs by eliminating middlemen.

Yoshio Maruta, one of several chemical

engineers to run Kao, took over as president in 1971. Maruta presented himself as more Buddhist scholar than corporate honcho; during his 19 years at the top, he gave the company a wider vision through his emphasis on creativity and his insistence on an active learning environment. To encourage sharing of ideas, the company used open conference rooms for meetings and anyone interested could attend and participate in any meeting.

Under Maruta, Kao launched a string of successful products in new areas in the 1980s. In 1982 the company introduced its Sofina cosmetics line, emphasizing the line's scientific basis in a break from traditional beauty products marketing. The next year its Super Merries diapers (with a new design that reduced diaper rash) trounced P&G's Pampers in Japan. Its popular Attack laundry detergent (the first concentrated laundry soap) led the market within six months of its 1987 debut.

Seeking a way to enter the US market, Kao bought the Andrew Jergens skin care company -- based in Cincinnati, as is P&G -- in 1988. (It also purchased a chemical company to supply the materials to make Jergens' products.) P&G and Unilever braced themselves for the new competition, but Kao didn't deliver, releasing products like fizzy bath tablets that didn't sell well in a nation of shower-takers. In 1989 it bought a 75% interest in Goldwell, a German maker of hair care and beauty products sold through hair stylists. (By 1994 Kao owned all of Goldwell, which is now called Kao Professional Salon Services.)

In the mid-1980s Kao built a name for itself in the floppy disk market and became the top producer of 3.5-in. floppy disks in North America by 1990. However, competition crowded the field and drove the price of disks down. In 1997 the company stopped production of floppy disks in the US.

Chemical engineer Takuya Goto took over as president that year. Kao looked to other Asian markets and the US for potential consumers and found a willing audience in the US for its Bioré face strips. In 1998 Kao purchased Bausch & Lomb's skin care business, gaining the Curel and Soft Sense lotion brands.

In 2000 Kao established a joint venture with Novartis to make baby foods and over-the-counter drugs such as stomach medicines and other pain relief drugs. In 2001 Kao lost out on its offer for Clairol to P&G. Also in 2001 it formed a joint venture with Archer Daniels Midland to produce an anti-obesity diacylglycerol oil (used in margarine, cooking oil, salad dressing, and mayonnaise) and in 2002 began marketing it in the US under the brand name Enova. That year Kao dissolved its OTC-medicine-manufacturing joint venture with Novartis and renamed its Sofina cosmetics brand Prestige Cosmetics. Additionally in 2002 Kao acquired John Frieda Professional Hair Care through Andrew Jergens. (Andrew Jergens became Kao Brands in 2004.)

In 2004 Goto became chairman and Motoki Ozaki was promoted from president of the Global Fabric and Home Care division to president and CEO. The same year Kao broke off talks to purchase Kanebo.

In 2008 the company sold its fatty amine business to Akzo Nobel Surface Chemistry, a unit of Akzo Nobel.

EXECUTIVES

Chairman, Director, Michitaka Sawada
President, Representative Director, Yoshihiro Hasebe
Senior Managing Executive Officer, Representative Director, Masakazu Negoro
Senior Managing Executive Officer, Director, Toru Nishiguchi
Director, David J. Muenz
Outside Director, Osamu Shinobe
Outside Director, Chiaki Mukai
Outside Director, Nobuhide Hayashi
Outside Director, Eriko Sakurai
Outside Director, Takaaki Nishii
Auditors : Deloitte Touche Tohmatsu LLC

LOCATIONS

HQ: Kao Corp
1-14-10 Nihonbashi-Kayabacho, Chuo-ku, Tokyo 103-8210
Phone: (81) 3 3660 7111
Web: www.kao.com

PRODUCTS/OPERATIONS

2018 Sales

	% of total
Fabric & home care	23
Skin care & hair care	23
Chemical	18
Cosmetics	18
Human health care	18
Total	100

Selected Brand Names
Attack (laundry detergent)
Bioré (skin care)
Bub (shower gel)
Curel (skin care)
Essential (hair care)
Jergens (skin care)
Laurier (sanitary napkins)
Magiclean (household cleaner)
Merries (disposable diapers)
Primavista (makeup)
PureOra (toothpaste)
Quickle Wiper (household wipers)

COMPETITORS

BEIERSDORF, INC.
Beiersdorf AG
COLGATE-PALMOLIVE COMPANY
EDGEWELL PERSONAL CARE COMPANY
INTERNATIONAL FLAVORS & FRAGRANCES INC.
RECKITT BENCKISER GROUP PLC
REVLON, INC.
SHISEIDO COMPANY, LIMITED
THE CLOROX COMPANY
THE PROCTER & GAMBLE COMPANY

HISTORICAL FINANCIALS

Company Type: Public

Income Statement — FYE: December 31

	REVENUE ($mil)	NET INCOME ($mil)	NET PROFIT MARGIN	EMPLOYEES
12/22	11,770	652	5.5%	43,594
12/21	12,325	952	7.7%	44,722
12/20	13,408	1,223	9.1%	45,378
12/19	13,836	1,365	9.9%	45,796
12/18	13,713	1,397	10.2%	46,306
Annual Growth	(3.7%)	(17.3%)	—	(1.5%)

2022 Year-End Financials
Debt ratio: 0.1%
Return on equity: 8.8%
Cash ($ mil.): 2,035
Current Ratio: 1.66
Long-term debt ($ mil.): 471
No. of shares ($ mil.): 465
Dividends
Yield: —
Payout: 16.2%
Market value ($ mil.): 3,671

	STOCK PRICE ($) FY Close	P/E High/Low	PER SHARE ($) Earnings	Dividends	Book Value
12/22	7.88	0 0	1.39	0.23	15.84
12/21	10.45	0 0	2.00	0.26	17.66
12/20	15.44	0 0	2.54	0.25	18.60
12/19	16.58	0 0	2.82	0.23	16.40
12/18	14.90	0 0	2.86	0.11	15.34
Annual Growth	(14.7%)	—	(16.5%)	20.4%	0.8%

Kawasaki Heavy Industries Ltd

EXECUTIVES

Chairman, Director, Yoshinori Kanehana
President, Chief Executive Officer, Representative Director, Yasuhiko Hashimoto
Executive Vice President, Representative Director, Katsuya Yamamoto
Executive Vice President, Representative Director, Hiroshi Nakatani
Senior Managing Executive Officer, Hiroyoshi Shimokawa
Senior Managing Executive Officer, Motohiko Nishimura
Senior Managing Executive Officer, Hideko Shimamura
Outside Director, Jenifer Simms Rogers
Outside Director, Hideo Tsujimura
Outside Director, Katsuhiko Yoshida
Outside Director, Melanie Brock
Director, Akio Nekoshima
Director, Nobuhisa Kato
Outside Director, Atsuko Ishii
Outside Director, Ryoichi Saito
Outside Director, Susumu Tsukui
Auditors : KPMG AZSA LLC

LOCATIONS

HQ: Kawasaki Heavy Industries Ltd
Kobe Crystal Tower, 1-1-3 Higashi-Kawasakicho, Chuo-ku, Kobe, Hyogo 650-8680

Phone: (81) 78 371 9551   Fax: (81) 78 371 9568
Web: www.khi.co.jp

HISTORICAL FINANCIALS
Company Type: Public

Income Statement — FYE: March 31

	REVENUE ($mil)	NET INCOME ($mil)	NET PROFIT MARGIN	EMPLOYEES
03/23	12,956	398	3.1%	38,254
03/22	12,338	179	1.5%	36,587
03/21	13,443	(174)	—	36,691
03/20	15,120	171	1.1%	36,332
03/19	14,400	247	1.7%	35,691
Annual Growth	(2.6%)	12.6%	—	1.7%

2023 Year-End Financials
Debt ratio: 0.3%   No. of shares ($ mil.): 167
Return on equity: 10.0%   Dividends
Cash ($ mil.): 1,039   Yield: 1.6%
Current Ratio: 1.20   Payout: 0.0%
Long-term debt ($ mil.): 3,341   Market value ($ mil.): 1,496

	STOCK PRICE ($) FY Close	P/E High/Low	Earnings	Dividends	Book Value
03/23	8.91	0 0	2.38	0.15	25.77
03/22	7.43	0 0	1.07	0.07	23.47
03/21	9.98	— —	(1.05)	0.00	25.16
03/20	6.00	0 0	1.03	0.26	25.13
03/19	9.79	0 0	1.48	0.23	25.75
Annual Growth	(2.3%)	— —	12.5%	(11.0%)	0.0%

KBC Group NV

EXECUTIVES
Chief Executive Officer, Executive Director, Johan Thijs
Chief Innovation Officer, Erik Luts
Chief Financial Officer, Executive Director, Luc Popelier
Chief Risk Officer, Executive Director, Christine Van Rijsseghem
Chairman, Independent Director, Koenraad Debackere
Deputy Chairman, Non-Executive Director, Philippe Vlerick
Independent Non-Executive Director, Vladimira Papirnik
Non-Executive Director, Alain Bostoen
Non-Executive Director, Katelijn Callewaert
Non-Executive Director, Erik Clinck
Non-Executive Director, Sonja De Becker
Non-Executive Director, Franky Depickere
Non-Executive Director, Frank Donck
Non-Executive Director, Liesbet Okkerse
Non-Executive Director, Alicia Reyes Revuelta
Non-Executive Director, Theodoros Roussis
Non-Executive Director, Marc Wittemans
Auditors : PwC Bedrijfsrevisoren BV

LOCATIONS
HQ: KBC Group NV
  Havenlaan 2, Brussels 1080
Phone: (32) 2 429 49 16   **Fax:** (32) 2 429 44 16

Web: www.kbc.com

HISTORICAL FINANCIALS
Company Type: Public

Income Statement — FYE: December 31

	ASSETS ($mil)	NET INCOME ($mil)	INCOME AS % OF ASSETS	EMPLOYEES
12/22	380,087	2,929	0.8%	41,947
12/21	385,225	2,958	0.8%	40,428
12/20	393,645	1,767	0.4%	40,863
12/19	326,427	2,794	0.9%	37,854
12/18	325,016	2,943	0.9%	38,368
Annual Growth	4.0%	(0.1%)	—	2.3%

2022 Year-End Financials
Return on assets: 0.7%   Dividends
Return on equity: 12.5%   Yield: —
Long-term debt ($ mil.): —   Payout: 44.6%
No. of shares ($ mil.): 417   Market value ($ mil.): 13,420
Sales ($ mil.): 16,529

	STOCK PRICE ($) FY Close	P/E High/Low	Earnings	Dividends	Book Value
12/22	32.17	7 4	6.90	3.08	53.27
12/21	43.10	8 5	6.96	1.29	62.66
12/20	34.89	13 7	4.10	0.34	63.41
12/19	37.55	7 5	6.57	1.27	54.91
12/18	31.96	8 5	6.85	1.13	54.03
Annual Growth	0.2%	—	0.2%	28.4%	(0.4%)

KDDI Corp

EXECUTIVES
Chairman, Representative Director, Takashi Tanaka
President, Chief Executive Officer, Representative Director, Makoto Takahashi
Executive Vice President, Representative Director, Toshitake Amamiya
Senior Managing Executive Officer, Chief Technology Officer, Director, Kazuyuki Yoshimura
Senior Managing Executive Officer, Director, Yasuaki Kuwahara
Director, Hiromichi Matsuda
Outside Director, Goro Yamaguchi
Outside Director, Keiji Yamamoto
Outside Director, Shigeki Goto
Outside Director, Tsutomu Tannowa
Outside Director, Junko Okawa
Outside Director, Kyoko Okumiya
Auditors : PricewaterhouseCoopers Kyoto

LOCATIONS
HQ: KDDI Corp
  3-10-10 Iidabashi, Chiyoda-ku, Tokyo 102-8460
Phone: (81) 3 3347 0077   **Fax:** 310 618-6099
Web: www.kddi.com

HISTORICAL FINANCIALS
Company Type: Public

Income Statement — FYE: March 31

	REVENUE ($mil)	NET INCOME ($mil)	NET PROFIT MARGIN	EMPLOYEES
03/23	42,585	5,086	11.9%	86,331
03/22	44,778	5,528	12.3%	86,009
03/21	47,980	5,883	12.3%	82,560
03/20	48,247	5,893	12.2%	83,308
03/19	45,874	5,577	12.2%	78,337
Annual Growth	(1.8%)	(2.3%)	—	2.5%

2023 Year-End Financials
Debt ratio: 0.1%   No. of shares ($ mil.): 2,158
Return on equity: 13.4%   Dividends
Cash ($ mil.): 3,605   Yield: 3.1%
Current Ratio: 1.86   Payout: 20.8%
Long-term debt ($ mil.): 6,864   Market value ($ mil.): 33,283

	STOCK PRICE ($) FY Close	P/E High/Low	Earnings	Dividends	Book Value
03/23	15.42	0 0	2.33	0.48	17.82
03/22	16.33	0 0	2.46	0.54	18.46
03/21	15.49	0 0	2.56	0.57	18.86
03/20	14.60	0 0	2.54	0.51	17.53
03/19	10.72	0 0	2.34	0.43	16.04
Annual Growth	9.5%	—	(0.1%)	2.9%	2.7%

KE Holdings Inc

EXECUTIVES
Chief Executive Officer, Executive Director, Yongdong Peng
Chief Financial Officer, Tao Xu
Chief Operating Officer, Wangang Xu
Chairman, Director, Hui Zuo
Executive Director, Yigang Shan
Independent Director, Xiaohong Chen
Independent Director, Yu Chen
Director, Zhaohui Li
Auditors : PricewaterhouseCoopers Zhong Tian LLP

LOCATIONS
HQ: KE Holdings Inc
  Oriental Electronic Technology Building, No. 2 Chuangye Road, Haidian District, Beijing 100086
Phone: (86) 10 5810 4689
Web: www.ke.com

HISTORICAL FINANCIALS
Company Type: Public

Income Statement — FYE: December 31

	REVENUE ($mil)	NET INCOME ($mil)	NET PROFIT MARGIN	EMPLOYEES
12/22	8,794	(200)	—	98,540
12/21	12,719	(82)	—	110,082
12/20	10,776	424	3.9%	119,658
12/19	6,613	(313)	—	87,706
12/18	4,164	(68)	—	0
Annual Growth	20.5%	—	—	—

2022 Year-End Financials

Debt ratio: 0.1%
Return on equity: (-2.0%)
Cash ($ mil.): 2,814
Current Ratio: 2.11
Long-term debt ($ mil.): —
No. of shares ($ mil.): 3,757
Dividends
  Yield: —
  Payout: 0.0%
Market value ($ mil.): 52,461

	STOCK PRICE ($) FY Close	P/E High/Low	PER SHARE ($) Earnings	Dividends	Book Value
12/22	13.96	— —	(0.06)	0.00	2.66
12/21	20.12	— —	(0.02)	0.00	2.97
12/20	61.54	242 110	0.05	0.00	2.92
Annual Growth	(52.4%)		—	—	(2.4%)

Keiyo Bank, Ltd. (The) (Japan)

Keiyo Bank aims to be chief in Chiba. Founded in 1943, the regional bank operates mainly in the urban areas in and surrounding Chiba Prefecture, Japan. Among its commercial banking services are ATM, consumer loans, and foreign currency deposits. Keiyo operates via some 262 locations including a Tokyo branch and 114 in Chiba proper. Japan Trustee Services Bank claims a 5.37% stake in the bank alongside Nipponkoa Insurance (4.33%), and The Chiba Bank (4.19%).

EXECUTIVES

President, Representative Director, Toshiyuki Kumagai
Deputy President, Representative Director, Kiyoshi Hashimoto
Senior Managing Executive Officer, Director, Satoru Akiyama
Director, Tatsushi Ichikawa
Director, Kazuo Fujisaki
Director, Seiji Sato
Outside Director, Yasushi Saito
Outside Director, Katsusada Akiyama
Outside Director, Hiroshi Uchimura
Outside Director, Tomoko Tobe
Auditors : Ernst & Young ShinNihon LLC

LOCATIONS

HQ: Keiyo Bank, Ltd. (The) (Japan)
  5-45 Chibaminato, Chuo-ku, Chiba 260-0026
Phone: (81) 43 222 2121
Web: www.keiyobank.co.jp

COMPETITORS

AICHI BANK, LTD.,
HACHIJUNI BANK, LTD., THE
HOKKOKU BANK, LTD., THE
NISHI-NIPPON CITYBANK,LTD.
UNITED OVERSEAS BANK LIMITED

HISTORICAL FINANCIALS
Company Type: Public

Income Statement   FYE: March 31

	ASSETS ($mil)	NET INCOME ($mil)	INCOME AS % OF ASSETS	EMPLOYEES
03/21	50,151	66	0.1%	3,062
03/20	46,013	51	0.1%	3,071
03/19	44,204	95	0.2%	3,055
03/18	45,104	114	0.3%	3,108
03/17	41,128	104	0.3%	3,130
Annual Growth	5.1%	(10.5%)		(0.5%)

2021 Year-End Financials

Return on assets: 0.1%
Return on equity: 2.5%
Long-term debt ($ mil.): —
No. of shares ($ mil.): 130
Sales ($ mil.): 569
Dividends
  Yield: —
  Payout: 33.7%
Market value ($ mil.): —

Kering SA

Kering (pronounced as "caring") has transformed itself from a conglomerate to the world's largest luxury group. The Paris-based company's stable of global luxury brands includes Italian high end label Gucci as well as Alexander McQueen, Brioni, Balenciaga, Bottega Veneta, Pomellato, and Saint Laurent. About 40% of Kering's sales are generated from Asia Pacific (excluding Japan). François Pinault founded the firm in 1963 as Pinault Group, which eventually became Pinault-Printemps-Redoute (PPR) and later Kering.

Operations

Kering's top three brands by revenue include Gucci (approximately 55% of the company's revenue), Saint Lauren (nearly 15%), and Bottega Veneta (nearly 10%). Other houses account for the remainder.

In terms of product category, leather goods account for approximately 50% of Kering's revenue. Other major categories include shoes (about 20%), ready-to-wear (some 15%), and watches and jewelry (about 10%).

By distribution channel, sales from directly operated stores bring in about 80% of the company's sales, while wholesale sales, royalties and other revenue account for more than 20%.

Geographic Reach

Paris-based Kering rings up about 40% of its sales in Asia Pacific. Western Europe and North America are also important markets for the luxury goods maker, representing about 25% each of sales. Japan accounts for about 5% of sales, and the rest comes from the rest of the world.

Kering operates approximately 1,565 direct operated stores, of which about 330 are in Western Europe, around 250 are in North America, and nearly 235 are in Japan. Approximately 750 direct operated stores are located in emerging markets.

Sales and Marketing

Kering's retail channel operates a directly operated store network and its wholesale channel includes department stores, independent high-end multi-brand stores, and franchise stores.

Financial Performance

Note: Growth rates may differ after conversion to US Dollars.

Company's revenue for fiscal 2021 increased by 35% to EUR 17.6 billion compared from the prior year with EUR 13.1 billion.

Net income for fiscal 2021 decreased to EUR 168.4 million compared from the prior year with EUR 2.1 billion.

Cash held by the company at the end of fiscal 2021 increased to EUR 4.5 billion. Cash provided by operations was EUR 4.9 billion, while cash used for investing and financing activities were EUR 451.5 million and EUR 2.9 billion, respectively. Main uses of cash were for acquisitions and dividends paid.

Strategy

A major player in a fast-growing market around the world, Kering enjoys solid fundamentals and a balanced portfolio of complementary brands with strong potential. Its strategic priorities are straightforward. The company and its Houses seek to achieve same-store revenue growth while ensuring the targeted and selective expansion of their retail networks. Kering aims to grow its Houses in a sustainable manner, enhance the exclusivity of its distribution and secure its profitable growth trajectories. The company is also investing proactively to develop cross-business growth platforms in the areas of e-commerce, omni-channel distribution, logistics and technological infrastructure, digital expertise and innovative tools.

Company Background

Sixteen-year-old François Pinault left school in 1952 to join the family timber business. He took over the firm when his father died in 1963; that year the company was renamed Pinault Group. Pinault diversified the company into wood importing and retailing, eventually building a flourishing enterprise. In 1973 Pinault began to show his talent for the art of the deal. Sensing the demand for timber was peaking, he sold 80% of the business, buying it back two years later at an 85% discount.

Pinault began to diversify outside the timber industry in the 1990s. It acquired a series of companies, including Au Printemps (owner of Printemps stores and 54% of catalog company Redoute) in 1992. The firm then became the Pinault-Printemps Group. In 1993 the group reorganized into four divisions: retail, business-to-business, financial services, and international trade and eventually renamed itself Pinault-Printemps-Redoute (PPR).

In 2005 François-Henri Pinault, the son of the company's founder, joined the company as its new CEO. During his 10 years at the helm, Weinberg oversaw the transformation of the company from a business-to-business concern to a focused luxury retail group. To underscore the company's transformation begun in 2005, in 2013 PPR became Kering.

HISTORY

Sixteen-year-old François Pinault left school in 1952 to join the family timber business. He took over the firm when his father died in 1963; that year the company was renamed Pinault Group. Pinault diversified the company into wood importing and retailing, eventually building a flourishing enterprise. In 1973 Pinault began to show his talent for the art of the deal. Sensing the demand for timber was peaking, he sold 80% of the business, buying it back two years later at an 85% discount.

During the 1970s Pinault bought struggling timber businesses and turned them around. (He was helped, in part, by a policy of the French government that subsidized purchases of failing companies in order to preserve jobs.) Pinault purchased bankrupt wood panel manufacturer Isoroy in 1986 for a token fee. In 1987 he bought ailing paper company Chapelle Darblay, selling it three years later at a 40% profit. By 1988, when it filed to go public on the Paris exchange, Pinault Group was a vertically integrated timber manufacturing, trading, and distribution company.

Pinault began to diversify outside the timber industry in the 1990s. It acquired electrical equipment distributor CFAO (Compagnie Française de l'Afrique Occidentale) in 1990, the Conforama furniture chain in 1991, and Au Printemps (owner of Printemps stores and 54% of catalog company Redoute) in 1992. The firm then became the Pinault-Printemps Group. The purchase of Au Printemps left the company heavily in debt, and it sold some of its noncore assets during the early 1990s.

In 1993 the group reorganized into four divisions: retail, business-to-business, financial services, and international trade. That year Pinault-Printemps bought a majority stake in Groupelec and merged it with electrical equipment subsidiary CDME, forming Rexel. In 1994 the company completed its acquisition of Redoute. After renaming itself Pinault-Printemps-Redoute (PPR), it bought a majority stake in French book and music retailer Fnac (buying the rest in 1995). In 1995 Rexel head Serge Weinberg took over the company after CEO Pierre Blayau ran afoul of Pinault over strategy. PPR added West African pharmaceuticals distributor SCOA in 1996. While Rexel gobbled up 11 companies in Europe and the US that year, PPR launched a new chain of women's lingerie stores called Orcanta and started its own venture capital fund.

PPR acquired Becob, France's #3 building materials distributor, in 1997. Expanding globally, Redcats (Redoute's new name) launched the Vertbaudet (children's wear) and Cyrillus (sportswear) catalogs in the UK that year.

In 1998 PPR bought a majority stake in Guilbert, the European leader in office supplies and furniture, and a 44% stake in Brylane (renamed Redcats USA in 2004), the US's #4 mail-order company. PPR also opened a new store format in France called Made in Sport (sporting goods). In addition, it began offering phone cards through subsidiary Kertel.

PPR bought the remainder of Brylane in 1999 and also launched a new division to oversee the online efforts of its various businesses. Later that year, PPR sparked a string of legal battles between it and LVMH when it purchased 42% of luxury goods maker Gucci. (The move thwarted LVMH's efforts to take over Gucci by diluting LVMH's stake in the firm.) In early 2000 PPR bought France's largest computer retailer, Surcouf.

In March 2001 a Dutch court granted a request by LVMH and ordered an investigation into the legality of the alliance of PPR and Gucci. In a deal to end years of litigation, PPR purchased LVMH's stake in Gucci for $806.5 million in October 2001, increasing its ownership to 53.2%.

The company sold Yves Saint Laurent's haute couture division to French dressmaking company SLPB Prestige Services in March 2002. Guilbert's mail-order business was sold to US office supplies retailer Staples in October of that year for $815 million. (The rest of Guilbert was later sold to Office Depot in May 2003.) In June 2003, PPR's timber wholesale business, Pinault Bois & Matériaux, was sold to the UK's Wolseley plc. In December PPR sold 14.5% of Finaref and Finaref Nordic to Agricole. Also in 2003, PPR increased its stake in Gucci to 67.58%.

To fund its transformation, the company sold Guilbert and Pinault Bois & Matériaux (lumber and building supplies) to shore up its balance sheet and fund its offer for the rest of Gucci in 2004. In November, PPR finalized a deal to sell its controlling stake in electrical equipment distributor Rexel to Ray Acquisition SCA, a consortium made up of three investment firms.

In March 2005 François-Henri Pinault, the son of the company's founder, joined the company as its new CEO, succeeding Serge Weinberg. During his 10 years at the helm, Weinberg oversaw the transformation of the company from a business-to-business concern to a focused luxury retail group. At the annual general meeting in May shareholders approved the offical name change to PPR from Pinault-Printemps-Redoute.

In August 2006, as part of its strategy to focus on its luxury business, PPR sold its Paris-based department store chain Printemps to Italy's La Rinascente for about $1.3 billion. The divestiture included all of the chain's 17 stores. In September, PPR's Redcats Group acquired The Sportman's Guide, a catalog and online marketer, for about $265 million. In July 2008 Redcats Group's US division completed the sale of its Missy Group apparel line, which included the Chadwick's of Boston, metrostyle, and Closeout Catalog Outlets brands, to the US private equity fund Monomoy Capital Partners for about $24 million.

To secure a foothold in the international premium footwear market, PPR increased its nearly 30% stake in PUMA in July 2007 to more than 60%. The deal, valued at more than $7 billion, placed the German athletic shoemaker in PPR's brand portfolio alongside its luxury holdings.

In a bid to increase its presence in the luxury watch business, PPR in 2008 acquired a 23% stake in the Swiss watchmaking company Sowind Group, the maker of high-end Girard-Perregaux and JeanRichard watches.

In December 2009 PPR sold a majority stake in its indirect subsidiary CFAO to the public. The ?806 million ($1.2 billion) in proceeds from the offering of the African car distributor went to Discodis, a wholly-owned subsidiary of PPR. In addition to auto distribution, CFAO's other business units include: Eurapharma, a distributor of pharmaceuticals; CFAO Technologies; and CFAO Industries & Trading. The shares trade on Euronext Paris.

The company sold its Conforama chain of household furniture and appliance stores to South Africa's Steinhoff International Holdings (SIH) in early 2011. The deal, valued at ?1.2 billion (about $1.6 billion), allowed PPR to devote more attention to its core Gucci and PUMA units. In June PPR made US youth brand Volcom, Inc. a wholly-owned subsidiary via a tender offer for the California company's shares in a deal valued at $608 million.

To underscore the company's transformation begun in 2005, in June 2013 PPR became Kering. The name change reaffirms the Group's international scope while acknowledging its origins in the Brittany region of France. (In Breton ker means "home" and "place to live in.")

EXECUTIVES

Chairman, Chief Executive Officer, Francois-Henri Pinault
Managing Director, Non-Independent Director, Jean-Francois Palus
Chief Client and Digital Officer, Gregory Boutte
Chief Sustainability Officer, Marie-Claire Daveu
Chief Financial Officer, Jean-Marc Duplaix
Chief Communications and Image Officer, Valerie Duport
Chief People Officer, Beatrice Lazat
Lead Independent Director, Sophie L'Helias
Independent Director, Yseulys Costes
Independent Director, Jean Liu
Independent Director, Daniela Riccardi

Independent Director, Tidjane Thiam
Independent Director, Emma Watson
Non-Independent Director, Jean-Pierre Denis
Non-Independent Director, Heloise Temple-Boyer
Non-Independent Director, Baudouin Prot
Director, Concetta Battaglia
Director, Claire Lacaze
Auditors : Deloitte & Associés

LOCATIONS
HQ: Kering SA
40 Rue de Sevres, Paris 75007
Phone: (33) 1 45 64 61 00   Fax: (33) 1 45 64 60 00
Web: www.kering.com

2015 Sales
	% of total
Western Europe	31
Asia/Pacific	26
North America	23
Japan	10
Other countries	10
Total	**100**

PRODUCTS/OPERATIONS
2015 Sales
	% of total
Luxury	68
Sports & Lifestyle	32
Total	**100**

Selected Brands
Luxury
    Alexander McQueen
    Balenciaga
    Bottega Veneta
    Boucheron
    Brioni
    Christopher Kane
    Girard-Perregaux
    Gucci
    JeanRichard
    Sergio Rossi
    Stella McCartney
    Yves Saint Laurent
Sport & lifestyle
    Electric
    Puma
    Volcom

Selected Operations
Luxury Goods
    Gucci Group N.V. (99.39%, leather goods and apparel)
        PUMA (athletic footwear)
    Sowind Group (50.1%, watches)
Retail
    Fnac (electronics, books, music; Belgium, Brazil, France, Italy, Monaco, Portugal, Spain, Switzerland, and Taiwan)
        Volcom, Inc. (US, young men's and women's apparel)

COMPETITORS
Bertelsmann SE & Co. KGaA
COMPAGNIE FINANCIERE RICHEMONT SA
KINGFISHER PLC
Koninklijke Ahold Delhaize N.V.
MUSGRAVE GROUP PUBLIC LIMITED COMPANY
RALLYE
RECKITT BENCKISER GROUP PLC
TARGET CORPORATION
Victoria Retail Group B.V.
WINMARK CORPORATION

HISTORICAL FINANCIALS
Company Type: Public

Income Statement   FYE: December 31

	REVENUE ($mil)	NET INCOME ($mil)	NET PROFIT MARGIN	EMPLOYEES
12/22	21,735	3,859	17.8%	47,227
12/21	19,971	3,594	18.0%	42,811
12/20	16,077	2,639	16.4%	38,553
12/19	17,833	2,592	14.5%	38,068
12/18	15,649	4,254	27.2%	34,795
Annual Growth	8.6%	(2.4%)		7.9%

2022 Year-End Financials
Debt ratio: 23.5%   No. of shares ($ mil.): 122
Return on equity: 26.4%   Dividends
Cash ($ mil.): 4,631   Yield: —
Current Ratio: 1.37   Payout: 4.0%
Long-term debt ($ mil.): 4,642   Market value ($ mil.): 6,192

	STOCK PRICE ($) FY Close	P/E High/Low		PER SHARE ($) Earnings	Dividends	Book Value
12/22	50.66	3	2	31.30	1.28	122.32
12/21	80.51	4	2	28.85	1.47	121.76
12/20	72.45	4	2	21.11	0.89	116.13
12/19	65.36	4	2	20.66	5.84	92.31
12/18	46.76	2	1	33.77	5.38	90.14
Annual Growth	2.0%		—	(1.9%)	(30.1%)	7.9%

Kingfisher PLC

Kingfisher is an international home improvement company that operates more than 1,470 B&Q, Screwfix, Castorama, TradePoint, Koçtas, and Brico Dépôt stores in eight countries across Europe. The UK is the company's home market where the majority of its stores are located. Customers visit Kingfisher in-store and online to buy an array of home improvement products under the categories outdoor and garden, home and bedroom, building and hardware, and kitchen and bathroom. Kingfisher operates the Koçtas joint venture in Turkey. It generates about 50% of sales in the UK and Ireland.

Operations
Kingfisher operates under retail banners including B&Q, Castorama, Brico Dépôt, Screwfix, TradePoint and Koçtas. The company offers home improvement products and services to consumers and trade professionals.

In the UK, Kingfisher's biggest market, the company offers around 40,000 home improvement and garden products at B&Q. Screwfix, which has more than 11,000 items in stock, serves a professional customer base via mail-order and in store with trade tools, plumbing, electrical products, and products for fixing and improving bathrooms and kitchens. In France and Poland, Castorama-branded stores stock nearly 50,000 products; and Brico Dépôt addresses similar markets at a lower price.

Geographic Reach
Kingfisher operates more than 1,470 stores in total. It has more than 1,100 in the UK and Ireland, roughly 230 in Turkey, almost 215 in France, some 90 in Poland, approximately 35 in Romania, about 30 in Spain, and three in Portugal.

Overall, Kingfisher generates about 50% of revenue in the UK and Ireland, nearly 35% in France, and more than 15% in other international.

Sales and Marketing
Kingfisher reaches customers via several different touchpoints. Its physical locations are its primary channel but it also offers online delivery and, for professional customers, mail-order. In the UK, B&Q is aimed at DIYers while Screwfix serves wholesalers, tradesmen, and DIY experts.

Financial Performance
Note: Growth rates may differ after conversion to US Dollars.

The company's revenue for fiscal 2021 increased by 7% to £13.2 billion compared to £12.3 billion in the prior year. The increase was largely driven by a strong sales performance in the UK and France.

Cash held by the company at the end of fiscal 2021 decreased to £809 million. Cash provided by operations was £1.2 billion while investing and financing activities used £385 million and £1.0 billion, respectively. Main cash uses were purchase of property, plant and equipment and intangible assets; and principal element of lease rental payments.

Strategy
Two years ago, the company launched its new strategy, 'Powered by Kingfisher'. This strategy seeks to make the most of the company's considerable scale and the advantaged market positions occupied by its various banners. New compact store formats were tested in the UK, France and Poland, and the early learnings are proving extremely valuable. In e-commerce, Screwfix launched a one hour delivery service. More recently, Kingfisher launched its first online product marketplace, via B&Q's powerful digital platform. This initiative significantly increases the range of products the company can offer its customers, including for the first time, products from third party providers.

Company Background
Kingfisher traces its lineage back to the international expansion efforts of US retailer Woolworth, which set up shop in Liverpool in 1909. The company grew quickly and went public in 1931, with Woolworth retaining a majority stake. Activity kicked up a notch in 1980, following which it acquired do-it-yourself chain B&Q, was bought out by private equity, acquired electronics retailer Comet, renamed F.W. Woolworth stores as Woolworths, acquired Superdrug, and two further drugstore chains. At the end of the 1980s the company changed its name to Kingfisher. In the next few decades, further acquisitions followed, including several businesses (such as Castorama) in France, as

did spin-offs and divestitures, such as Woolworth's and Superdrug in 2001.

HISTORY

The beginning of Kingfisher is directly tied to the former US Woolworth chain (now Foot Locker). With the success of F.W. Woolworth general merchandise stores in the US, founder Frank Woolworth expanded overseas, first to Canada, then in 1909 to Liverpool, England. By 1914 Woolworth's UK subsidiaries had 31 stores.

Growing quickly, the company went public in 1931, with its US parent retaining a 53% stake. The company spent most of the postwar years rebuilding bombed stores and had 762 stores by 1950.

The company opened its first Woolco Department Store, modeled after the US Woolco stores of its parent, in 1967. However, other retailers had cut into sales, and by 1968 it lost its place as Britain's leading retailer to Marks and Spencer. In 1973 it opened Shoppers World, a catalog showroom. It made its first takeover in 1980, buying B&Q, a chain of 40 do-it-yourself stores.

An investment group acquired Woolworth in 1982 using the vehicle Paternoster Stores. (The US parent sold its stake in Woolworth.) The company, renamed Woolworth Holdings, closed unprofitable Woolworth stores and sold its Shoppers World stores in 1983 and its Ireland Woolworth stores in 1984. It also acquired Comet, a UK home electronics chain, and continued to expand B&Q.

Two years later all of its F.W. Woolworth stores were renamed Woolworths, and food and clothing lines were abandoned. Also in 1986 the company sold its Woolco stores and bought record and tape distributor Record Merchandisers (later renamed Entertainment UK). The next year Woolworth Holdings acquired Superdrug, a chain of 297 discount drugstores. Adding to its Superdrug chain, in 1988 the company acquired and integrated two UK pharmacy chains: 110-store Tip Top Drugstores and 145-store Share Drug.

To reflect its growing diversity of businesses, the company was renamed Kingfisher in 1989. Also that year it bought drug retailer Medicare, with 86 stores. Expanding further into electronics, in 1993 Kingfisher acquired Darty, with 130 stores. Adding music retail to music distribution, that year the firm founded Music and Video Club (MVC).

In 1998 Kingfisher increased its presence in France by taking control of electronics chain BUT. It also merged its B&Q chain with the do-it-yourself stores of France's Castorama in 1998 and gained a 55% stake in the new group (though as part of the deal Kingfisher received only 50% of the group's voting rights).

Following the lead of rival Dixons, in 1999 Kingfisher launched its own free Internet access service in France called Libertysurf. Soon thereafter, Libertysurf acquired 70% of Objectif Net and its website, Nomade.fr. Kingfisher's planned purchase of food retailer ASDA Group collapsed in June 1999 after being outbid by Wal-Mart Stores.

Kingfisher sold its 35% stake in Libertysurf to Italian ISP Tiscali in 2001, and it sold its Superdrug chain to Kruidvat, a Dutch health and beauty group. Kingfisher demerged Woolworths Group the same year in a public offering. With Woolies went electronic entertainment companies EUK, MVC, VCI, and Streets Online. Also in 2001 Kingfisher bought 25% plus one share of the unlisted ordinary voting shares of Germany's Hornbach Holding, a family-owned group that owns 80% of one of Germany's leading DIY chains, Hornbach-Baumarkt.

In 2002 Kingfisher acquired the remainder of Castorama and bought 17.4% of Hornbach's listed non-voting preference shares (which with the 2001 purchase represents a 21.2% stake in Hornbach). Kingfisher additionally bought 5.5% of the ordinary shares of Hornbach-Baumarkt.

CEO Geoffrey Mulcahy stepped down in 2002 and was replaced by Gerry Murphy, formerly CEO for Carlton (now ITV plc), in 2003. Kingfisher sold its 20 retail parks for $1.1 billion to a consortium that includes real estate firms Pillar Property and Capital & Regional Properties the same year. Also in 2003 Kingfisher sold ProMarkt, with about 190 stores in Germany, to its former owners, Michael and Matthias Wegert.

To focus on DIY, Kingfisher floated its electrical businesses as a new company, Kesa Electricals, in 2003. Kesa Electricals includes Darty, France's leading electrical retailer with more than 180 stores, and Comet, with some 260 stores in the UK. Kingfisher sold two home-improvement chains that year. RÃ©no-DÃ©pÃ´t, which operates about 20 home-improvement stores in Canada, was sold to RONA. NOMI, with about 40 stores in Poland, was acquired by Enterprise Investors.

And in 2003 Kingfisher sold Dubois Materiaux, a French building materials dealer, to Saint-Gobain Building Distribution.

In June 2005 the company acquired its biggest competitor in Asia, OBI Asia, which added about a dozen stores in China and its first outlet in South Korea. The next year Kingfisher entered its 11th market, Russia, with its first Castorama store there. In May, Sir Francis Mackay retired as chairman of the company and was succeeded by Peter Jackson.

Kingfisher named Ian Cheshire as its new chief executive in 2008, succeeding Gerry Murphy, who resigned in late 2007. Cheshire joined B&Q in 1998. Also in 2008 Kingfisher sold its Italian Castorama business to France's Groupe ADEO for $871 million. In addition, the company sold its Castorama business in Spain in search of higher returns elsewhere in Europe. The retailer also closed its unprofitable Trade Depot format in the UK.

Daniel Bernard took over the chairman's seat from Jackson in 2009.

EXECUTIVES

Chief Executive Officer, Executive Director, Thierry Garnier
Chief Financial Officer, Executive Director, Bernard Ladislas Bot
Secretary, Chloe Barry
Chairman, Non-Executive Director, Andrew Cosslett
Non-Executive Director, Senior Independent Director, Catherine Bradley
Non-Executive Director, Claudia I. Arney
Non-Executive Director, Jeff Carr
Non-Executive Director, Sophie A. Gasperment
Non-Executive Director, Rakhi Goss-Custard
Non-Executive Director, Bill Lennie
Auditors : Deloitte LLP

LOCATIONS

HQ: Kingfisher PLC
One Paddington Square, London W2 1GG
Phone: (44) 20 7372 8008 **Fax:** (44) 20 7644 1001
Web: www.kingfisher.com

2019 Sales

	% of total
UK & Ireland	43
France	37
Poland	12
Others	8
Total	100

2019 Stores

	No. of Stores
UK & Ireland	923
France	224
Poland	76
Spain	29
Romania	38
Spain	28
Russia	20
Germany	19
Portugal	3
Total	1,331

COMPETITORS

CARREFOUR
CEV Handelsimmobilien Holding GmbH
DEBENHAMS PLC
HOWDEN JOINERY GROUP PLC
J SAINSBURY PLC
KERING
Koninklijke Ahold Delhaize N.V.
MUSGRAVE GROUP PUBLIC LIMITED COMPANY
Tengelmann Warenhandelsgesellschaft KG
WM MORRISON SUPERMARKETS P L C

HISTORICAL FINANCIALS

Company Type: Public

Income Statement   FYE: January 31

	REVENUE ($mil)	NET INCOME ($mil)	NET PROFIT MARGIN	EMPLOYEES
01/23	16,088	580	3.6%	80,000
01/22	17,677	1,130	6.4%	82,000
01/21	16,924	811	4.8%	78,000
01/20	15,110	10	0.1%	78,000
01/19	15,345	286	1.9%	79,000
Annual Growth	1.2%	19.3%	—	0.3%

2023 Year-End Financials

Debt ratio: 1.2%
Return on equity: 7.0%
Cash ($ mil.): 352
Current Ratio: 1.30
Long-term debt ($ mil.): 125
No. of shares ($ mil.): 1,940
Dividends
Yield: 3.9%
Payout: 94.6%
Market value ($ mil.): 13,289

	STOCK PRICE ($) FY Close	P/E High/Low	PER SHARE ($) Earnings	Dividends	Book Value
01/23	6.85	35 21	0.29	0.27	4.23
01/22	8.91	25 17	0.53	0.30	4.40
01/21	7.55	31 12	0.38	0.11	4.27
01/20	5.34	1753 1232	0.01	0.24	3.61
01/19	5.97	95 52	0.13	0.25	4.14
Annual Growth	3.5%	— —	21.2%	1.5%	0.5%

Kirin Holdings Co Ltd

Kirin is a pure holding company structure, consisting of some 145 consolidated subsidiaries and about 30 equity accounted investees. Kirin is a top beer maker in Japan through its Kirin Brewery Co. In addition to its domestic Kirin-branded beers, the company owns brewers that serve overseas markets, such as Australia's Lion and Philippines-based San Miguel Brewery. The beer brewer also makes soft drinks (coffee, tea drinks, and mineral water), the alcoholic fruit drink chu-hi, and owns Japanese wine producer Mercian Corporation. Beyond beverages, Kirin also has operations in health and dairy foods, and pharmaceutical-manufacturing sectors. About 65% of its revenue comes from its domestic operations.

Operations

Kirin operates through four segments: Japan Beer and Spirits Businesses, Japan Nonalcoholic Beverages Business, Oceania Adult Beverages Business, and Pharmaceuticals Business.

Japan Beer and Spirits Businesses, for which Kirin Brewery Company, Limited oversees the operations, conducts production and sale of alcoholic beverages, such as beer, happo-shu, new genre, wine, whiskey, and spirits, in Japan. The segment accounts for about 35% of revenue.

Pharmaceuticals Business, for which Kyowa Kirin Co., Ltd. oversees the operations, conducts production and sale of pharmaceutical products. The segment generates some 20% of revenue.

Japan Non-alcoholic Beverages Business, for which Kirin Beverage Company, Limited oversees the operations, conducts production and sale of soft drinks in Japan. The segment brings in nearly 15% of revenue.

Oceania Adult Beverages Business, for which Lion Pty Limited oversees the operations, conducts production and sale of beer, whiskey, spirits and other products in the Oceania region. The segment accounts for about 10% of revenue.

Geographic Reach

Outside Japan, Kirin has established local operations in Australia, China, Germany, Myanmar, the Philippines, Singapore, South Korea, Taiwan, the UK, the US, and Vietnam. In the US, it owns soft-drink bottler Coca-Cola Bottling Beverages Northeast, Inc. in New Hampshire and bourbon maker Four Roses Distillery in Kentucky.

Its home country, Japan, accounts for around 65% of total revenue, while America brings in more than 15% of revenue, Oceania and other regions generate roughly 10% each of revenue.

Financial Performance

The company reported total revenue of 1.8 trillion yen in 2021, a 2% decrease from the previous year's total revenue.

In 2021, the company had a net income of 99.6 billion yen, a 20% decrease from the previous year's net income of 124.6 billion yen.

The company's cash at the end of 2021 was 149.5 billion yen. Operating activities generated 219.3 billion yen, while investing activities used 56.4 billion yen, mainly for acquisition of property, plant and equipment and intangible assets. Financing activities used another 180.5 billion yen, mainly for decrease in commercial paper.

Strategy

In the 2022-2024 Medium-Term Business Plan, KV2027's basic direction will remain unchanged and Kirin Holdings will continue to strengthen its existing businesses and create new value by promoting CSV as the core of its management. Specifically, Kirin Holdings will make growth investments and strategic investments in the following three domains: (1) Increase profit in the Food & Beverages Domain, (2) Strengthen the operating base of the Pharmaceuticals Domain's global base, and (3) Scaling up the Health Science Domain, aiming for sustainable growth. To achieve these goals, Kirin Holdings will continue to work on strengthening the Kirin Group's organizational capabilities towards innovation. In addition, Kirin Holdings will build a solid organizational foundation by thoroughly adhering to the Kirin Group's DNA of focusing on quality, building an SCM*1 system that balances efficiency and sustainability, and strengthening governance to support value creation. Through these efforts, Kirin Holdings will achieve its financial targets of a normalized EPS CAGR of at least 11% by 2024*2 and ROIC of at least 10% as of 2024, and ride a new growth track toward achieving KV2027.

Company Background

Kirin Brewery Co., Ltd. was established on February 23, 1907, taking over the business of The Japan Brewery Co., Ltd., which had started marketing Kirin Beer in 1888.

Kirin Ichiban Shibori, which first hit the market in 1990, went on to become one of the most popular beers in Japan. Kirin Brewery's soft-drink business division was spun off to become Kirin Beverage Co., Ltd. in 1991.

In 2007, celebrating its 100th anniversary, Kirin Brewery changed its trade name to Kirin Holdings Co., Ltd., established as a pure holding company for the Kirin Group.

HISTORY

American William Copeland went to Yokohama, Japan, in 1864 and five years later established the Spring Valley Brewery, the first in Japan, to provide beer for foreign nationals. Lacking funds to continue the brewery, Copeland closed it in 1884. The next year a group of foreign and Japanese businessmen reopened it as Japan Brewery. The business created the Kirin label in 1888 and was soon profitable.

The operation was run primarily by Americans and Europeans at first, but by 1907 Japanese workers had filled the ranks and adopted the Kirin Brewery Company name. Sales plummeted during WWII when the government limited brewing output. After the war, the US occupation forces inadvertently assisted Kirin when they split Dai Nippon Brewery (Kirin's main competitor) into two companies (Asahi and Sapporo Breweries) while leaving Kirin intact. The company became Japan's leading brewer during the 1950s.

During the 1970s Kirin introduced several soft drinks and in 1972 branched into hard liquor through a joint venture with Seagram (Kirin-Seagram).

The firm bought several Coca-Cola bottling operations in New England and Japan in the 1980s. Kirin also entered the pharmaceuticals business, in part through a joint venture with US-based Amgen. In 1988 the brewer signed an agreement with Molson to produce Kirin beer for the North American market. In 1989 Kirin bought Napa Valley's Raymond Vineyards.

In 1991 Kirin formed a partnership to market Tropicana drinks in Japan. It also entered an alliance with Sankyo (Japan's #2 drug company) in 1991 to market Kirin's medication for anemia, which it had developed with Amgen.

Chairman Hideyo Motoyama resigned in 1993 after four company executives were arrested for allegedly paying a group of racketeers who had threatened to disrupt Kirin's annual meeting. Joint venture Kirin-Amgen won the rights to make thrombopoietin (TPO), a blood platelet growth stimulator, in 1995.

Yasuhiro Satoh became president of Kirin in 1996. The brewer moved into China that year through an agreement with China Resources (Shenyang) Snowflake Brewery. To brew its beers in the US, the company formed Kirin Brewery of America, also in 1996.

In response to losing market share to Asahi, Kirin cut its workforce in 1998 and introduced Tanrei, a cheaper, low-malt beer that quickly captured half its market. Building on its presence in China, Kirin bought 46% of brewer Lion Nathan (based in Australia and New Zealand) for $742.5 million that year. It became a licensed brewer of Anheuser-Busch in 1999.

Like other Japanese brewers, Kirin struggled against dwindling demand for its most expensive brews in 2000. Koichiro Aramaki was named president of the company the following year and began to expand and diversify Kirin's operations to overcome slow growth domestically. In 2002 the company bought 15% of Philippine food and drink giant San Miguel for about $530 million. It also boosted ties with beverage giant Pernod Ricard by purchasing 32% of SIFA, a French food services firm, for an estimated $155 million. In 2002 Kirin also formed Flower Season Ltd., a joint venture with Dole Food Company, to sell flowers to Japanese retailers. Also in 2002 Kirin launched its new Pure Blue brand of "shochu" distilled liquor.

In 2006 Aramaki stepped down as president (he remained chairman) and turned the reins over to former managing director Kazuyasu Kato. The following year Kirin reorganized as a holding company.

The company added to its international dairy holdings with its 2007 acquisition of Australian milk and cheese producer National Foods. The following year National Foods acquired Australian dairy company Australian Co-operative Foods Limited (dba Dairy Farmers) for about $763 million. With some 2,000 members, Dairy Farmers is one of the biggest dairy product makers in Australia. These acquisitions made Kirin a top player in the Oceania dairy sector, which is part of the company's larger strategy to focus and grow in the Asian and Oceania markets.

In 2009 Kirin acquired a 100% interest in San Miguel Brewery of the Philippines. Following Kirin's successful tender offer to acquire the remainder of Lion Nathan's shares, later that year Lion Nathan and National Foods were consolidated under Kirin's Australian holding company, which was renamed Lion Nathan National Foods.

Early in 2010 company veteran Senji Miyake was named president and CEO of the Japanese brewer (among other top management changes). Miyake joined Kirin Brewery Company in 1970. In December Kirin made Mercian Corp. a wholly owned subsidiary following a scandal at Mercian's fish feedstuffs division.

EXECUTIVES

President, Chief Executive Officer, Representative Director, Yoshinori Isozaki
Executive Vice President, Representative Director, Keisuke Nishimura
Director, Toshiya Miyoshi
Director, Takeshi Minakata
Director, Junko Tsuboi

Outside Director, Masakatsu Mori
Outside Director, Hiroyuki Yanagi
Outside Director, Chieko Matsuda
Outside Director, Noriko Shiono
Outside Director, Rod Eddington
Outside Director, George Olcott
Outside Director, Shinya Katanozaka
Auditors: KPMG AZSA LLC

LOCATIONS

HQ: Kirin Holdings Co Ltd
NAKANO CENTRAL PARK SOUTH, 4-10-2 Nakano, Nakano-ku, Tokyo 164-0001
Phone: (81) 3 6837 7015
Web: www.kirinholdings.co.jp

2013 Sales

	% of total
Japan	65
Asia/Oceania	22
Others	13
Total	100

PRODUCTS/OPERATIONS

2013 sales

	% of total
Japan integrated beverages	45
Overseas integrated beverages	35
Pharmaceuticals and bio-chemicals	17
Others	3
Total	100

COMPETITORS

ANHEUSER-BUSCH COMPANIES, LLC
ASAHI GROUP HOLDINGS,LTD.
Anheuser-Busch InBev
COCA - COLA HELLENIC BOTTLING COMPANY S.A.
DANONE
Heineken N.V.
LION PTY LTD
MOLSON COORS BEVERAGE COMPANY
SAPPORO HOLDINGS LIMITED
UNITED BISCUITS TOPCO LIMITED

HISTORICAL FINANCIALS

Company Type: Public

Income Statement — FYE: December 31

	REVENUE ($mil)	NET INCOME ($mil)	NET PROFIT MARGIN	EMPLOYEES
12/22	15,097	842	5.6%	34,550
12/21	15,824	519	3.3%	33,592
12/20	17,944	697	3.9%	36,214
12/19	17,880	549	3.1%	35,717
12/18	17,555	1,493	8.5%	36,376
Annual Growth	(3.7%)	(13.3%)	—	(1.3%)

2022 Year-End Financials

Debt ratio: 0.2%
Return on equity: 11.8%
Cash ($ mil.): 668
Current Ratio: 1.40
Long-term debt ($ mil.): 3,101
No. of shares ($ mil.): 811
Dividends
 Yield: —
 Payout: 49.6%
Market value ($ mil.): 12,356

	STOCK PRICE ($) FY Close	P/E High/Low	PER SHARE ($) Earnings	Dividends	Book Value
12/22	15.22	0 0	1.03	0.51	9.16
12/21	16.16	0 0	0.62	0.59	9.31
12/20	23.80	0 0	0.83	0.61	9.76
12/19	21.82	0 0	0.63	0.54	9.61
12/18	20.78	0 0	1.67	0.45	9.49
Annual Growth	(7.5%)	— —	(11.5%)	2.9%	(0.9%)

Kobe Steel Ltd

One of Japan's leading steel companies, Kobe Steel (aka Kobelco) makes aluminum, copper, and titanium products, and it produces welding products, such as welding robots, and industrial machinery, including compressors and crushers. The company also provides wholesale power supply, operating six power plants in Kobe and Moka. Kobe Steel's real estate division rents, manages and sells properties. Kobe Steel's joint venture with PRO-TEC Coating Company -- produces hot-dipped galvanized steel sheets, and cold-rolled, and high-strength steel sheets. With more than 200 subsidiaries and about 50 affiliates, the company has global operations in more than 20 countries.

Operations

The company operates in seven segments: Steel & Aluminum (about 45% of revenue), Construction Machinery (over 15%), Electric Power (nearly 15%), Advanced Materials (about 10%), Machinery (more than 5%), Engineering (about 5%), Welding, and Other (accounts for the rest).

The Steel & Aluminum segment is achieving maximum synergies as the only producer of both steel and aluminum offering steel wire rods and bars, steel sheets, steel billets, aluminum rolled products, and aluminum castings and forgings, among others.

The Construction Machinery segment accelerates the construction of a global system to meet the needs of different regions and applications, by establishing a network of local subsidiaries and distributors in locations worldwide. Its main products and businesses include civil engineering and construction machinery, environmental recycling, crawler cranes, and wheel cranes.

The Electric Power segment provides a stable supply of electricity for the region. It is also currently pursuing plans to construct additional plants.

The Advanced Materials segment is one of the leading producers in Japan, contributing to the weight reduction of cars, planes, trains, ships, and more. It offers aluminum (extrusions, suspensions, castings, and forgings), titanium, steel castings and forgings, copper, and steel powder products, among others.

The Machinery segment offers a wide

range of products, including industrial machinery, compressors, and energy equipment. Kobe Steel creates distinctive products to meet global demand in key growth fields, such as the automotive, environmental, and energy industries, while also striving to build optimal production networks and strengthen its manufacturing capabilities.

The Engineering segment has engineering capabilities that combine and integrate original, industry-leading processes, technologies, and expertise. Kobe Steel contributes to society by providing value-added solutions that flexibly meet a wide variety of customer needs.

The Welding segment offers total welding solutions that combine welding materials, robotic welding systems, welding technology, and more.

Other segment includes an extensive range of businesses that are being continuously refined through repeated selection and concentration. These businesses include Real estate development, construction, sales, brokering, remodeling; leasing, building management; condominium management; special alloys and other new materials (target materials, etc.); material analysis and testing; high-pressure gas cylinder manufacturing; superconducting products; and general trading company.

Geographic Reach

Hyogo, Japan-based, Kobelco has offices in Tokyo, Osaka, Nagoya, Hokkaido, Tohoku, Hokuriku, Chigoku and Shikoku, Kyushu, Okinawa, and Hyogo (R&D laboratories). It also has a manufacturing plant located in Hyogo, Osaka, Hiroshima, and Kyoto. Additionally, it also has regional headquarters and offices in the US, China, Thailand, and Germany.

Sales and Marketing

The company serves a wide range of industries including natural resources and energy savings, energy and chemicals, electronics, automobiles, engineering, eco solutions, transport, and industry and life.

Financial Performance

Kobe Steel's increased to JPY2.5 trillion compared to the prior year with JPY2.1 billion. Despite a decline in sales volume, sales increased due to selling price improvements and an increase in the unit selling price of electricity associated with a sharp rise in the market price of thermal coal in the electric power business.

Net income for fiscal 2022 increased to JPY72.5 billion compared to the prior year with JPY60.0 billion. The increase was primarily due to higher revenues offsetting the increase in expenses.

Cash held by the company at the end of fiscal 2022 decreased to JPY145.4 billion. Cash provided by operations was JPY69.8 million while cash used for investing activities was JPY70.0 billion.

Company Background

In 1905, general partnership trading company Suzuki Shoten acquired a steel business in Wakinohama, Kobe, called Kobayashi Seikosho operated by Seiichiro Kobayashi and changed its name to Kobe Seikosho. Then, in 1911 Suzuki Shoten spun off the company to establish Kobe Steel Works, Ltd. with a capital of Â¥1.4 million of Wakinohamacho, Kobe. This was the beginning of the company that is today known as Kobelco.

EXECUTIVES

President, Representative Director, Mitsugu Yamaguchi
Executive Vice President, Representative Director, Yoshihiko Katsukawa
Executive Vice President, Representative Director, Hajime Nagara
Executive Vice President, Masamichi Takeuchi
Executive Vice President, Makoto Mizuguchi
Director, Koichi Sakamoto
Director, Shinji Miyaoka
Outside Director, Hiroyuki Baba
Outside Director, Yumiko Ito
Outside Director, Shinsuke Kitagawa
Director, Hiroshi Ishikawa
Director, Gunyu Matsumoto
Outside Director, Masaaki Kono
Outside Director, Kunio Miura
Outside Director, Nobuko Sekiguchi
Auditors : KPMG AZSA LLC

LOCATIONS

HQ: Kobe Steel Ltd
2-2-4 Wakinohama-Kaigandori, Chuo-ku, Kobe, Hyogo 651-8585
Phone: (81) 78 261 5194 **Fax:** (81) 78 261 4123
Web: www.kobelco.co.jp

PRODUCTS/OPERATIONS

2017 Sales

	% of total.
Materials Businesses	
Iron & Steel	37
Aluminum & Copper	18
Welding	4
Machinery Business	
Construction Machinery	19
Machinery	8
Engineering	6
Electric Power Business	
Electric Power	4
Other Businesses	4
Total	100

Selected Products

Aluminum and Copper
    Aluminum plate
    Copper sheet and strip
Construction Machinery
    Crawler cranes
    Environmental Recycling Machinery
    Hydraulic excavators
    Mini hydraulic excavators
    Wheel cranes
Electric Power
    Kobe Power Plant
Engineering
    Advanced Urban Transit System
    Iron Unit Field
Iron and Steel
    Steel bars
    Steel castings and forgings
    Steel plates
    Steel powder
    Steel sheets
    Titanium
    Wire rod and bars
Machinery
    Standard compressors
    Rotating machinery
    Tire and rubber machinery
    Plastic processing machinery
    Advance Technology Equipment
    Rolling Mill
    Ultra High Pressure Equipment
    Energy & Chemical Field
Welding
    Electrodes
    Flux-cored wires
    Metallic flux-cored wire
    Solid wires
    Welding fluxes

COMPETITORS

AK STEEL HOLDING CORPORATION
CARPENTER TECHNOLOGY CORPORATION
COMMERCIAL METALS COMPANY
HBIS Company Limited
JFE HOLDINGS, INC.
NIPPON STEEL CORPORATION
NIPPON STEEL NISSHIN CO., LTD.
NUCOR CORPORATION
UNITED STATES STEEL CORPORATION
thyssenkrupp AG

HISTORICAL FINANCIALS

Company Type: Public

Income Statement   FYE: March 31

	REVENUE ($mil)	NET INCOME ($mil)	NET PROFIT MARGIN	EMPLOYEES
03/23	18,564	544	2.9%	44,938
03/22	17,121	493	2.9%	43,888
03/21	15,403	209	1.4%	46,428
03/20	17,225	(626)	—	47,807
03/19	17,805	324	1.8%	45,404
Annual Growth	1.0%	13.8%		(0.3%)

2023 Year-End Financials

Debt ratio: 0.2%   No. of shares ($ mil.): 396
Return on equity: 8.3%   Dividends
Cash ($ mil.): 1,528   Yield: —
Current Ratio: 1.35   Payout: 0.0%
Long-term debt ($ mil.): 5,193   Market value ($ mil.): —

Koc Holdings AS

Led by its energy businesses, KoÃ§ Holding is Turkey's dominant industrial conglomerate. The company operates through its around 105,000 employees and a distribution network composed of over 800 bank branches and some 11,000 dealers and after-sales service points. Through these, the company serves more than 12.5 million customers. The company's Tofas unit, an alliance with Fiat, is Turkey's champion carmaker; KoÃ§'s joint venture with Ford Motor sells imported Ford models. Other businesses include consumer goods such as large household appliances (ArÃ§elik, teaming up with LG Electronics) and energy (distribution of liquefied petroleum gas). Subsidiaries engage in food production, retail, tourism, and IT. The KoÃ§ family, one of the wealthiest in Turkey, controls the company.

Operations

KoÃ§ Holding is organized under five core business segments: Energy, Automotive, Consumer durables, Finance, and Other.

The Energy segment that generates more than 40% of total revenue, offers petroleum products. The Koc Group continues to play a leading role to meet Turkey's demand for petroleum fuel products. TÃœPRAS continued to fulfill the country's need for petroleum products, while leading its sector with its innovative practices, which it has put forward with the vision of being a pioneering company that is respectful of environment and life values, and whose performance is admired.

Automotive, generates around 25% of total revenue, offers automotive retailing and car rentals, commercial vehicles, buses, passenger cars, and trucks.

Consumer durables, generates about 15% of total revenue, offers white goods and appliances. The Koc Group maintained its domestic leadership in the Turkish white goods market. It has maintained its number 2 position in the overall white goods market in the European region, including Turkey, with its global brand Beko, and its market leadership with its brands Arctic in Romania and Defy in South Africa. ArÃ§elik-LG, meanwhile, is the leader in the Turkish air conditioning market.

The company's finance segment generates about 15% of total revenue. It operates the Yapi Kredi, the KoÃ§ Group's flagship company in finance, is the 3rd largest private bank with TL 781 billion of total assets.

Other business lines that generates some 5% of total revenue, offers tourism, Food production, IT support, and retail.

Geographic Reach

Koc Holding A.S. is headquartered in Nakkastepe, Turkey. It operates in more than 150 countries with some 80 production facilities worldwide located in Australia, Egypt, China, Spain, France, and Russia.

Sales and Marketing

KoÃ§ serves more than 12.5 million customers for the year 2021 through some 11,000 dealers and aftersales service points.

Financial Performance

The company's revenue in 2021 increased to TL 346.7 billion compared to TL 183.8 billion in the prior year.

Net income in 2021 increased to TL 26.2 billion compared to TL 12.6 billion in the prior year.

Cash held by the company at the end of 2021 increased to TL 144.7 billion. Operating and financing activities provided TL 50.7 billion and TL 10.2 billion, respectively. Investing activities used TL 53.6 billion, mainly for purchases of property, plant and equipment and intangible assets.

Strategy

The company's innovations strategies are: Building a culture of innovation and creating the right working environment to enhance its innovation capacity; cultivating corporate entrepreneurship across the company and supporting employees' entrepreneurial efforts; extending innovative endeavors not only across product and service development activities, but in all business units and operations ; increasing partnership with external stakeholders, an important source of innovation, and managing these collaborations more effectively; and managing innovative operations via clear processes to ensure sustainability.

In order to implement its innovation strategy, KoÃ§ Holding has been conducting the KoÃ§ Innovation Program since 2014. Accordingly, innovation management infrastructures are built up at Koc companies in line with the self-developed KoÃ§ Innovation Management Model.

HISTORY

In 1917, 16-year-old Vehbi KoÃ§ and his father opened a small grocery store in Ankara, Turkey. With the fall of the Ottoman Empire after WWI, Turkey's capital was moved to Ankara, which was then only a village. The KoÃ§s recognized an opportunity and expanded into construction and building supplies, winning a contract to repair the roof of the Turkish parliament building. By age 26, KoÃ§ was a millionaire.

Ford Motor made KoÃ§ its Turkish agent in 1928. In 1931 Mobil Oil and KoÃ§ entered an exclusive agreement to search for oil in Turkey. The company incorporated in 1938 as KoÃ§ Ticaret Corporation, the first Turkish joint stock company with an employee stock-ownership program.

Despite Turkey's neutrality in WWII, the fighting disrupted KoÃ§'s business. The nation became isolationist after the war and restricted foreign concerns to selling through local agents; KoÃ§ benefited by importing foreign products.

General Electric and KoÃ§ entered a joint venture in 1946 to build Turkey's first lightbulb factory. In 1955 KoÃ§ set up ArÃ§elik, the first Turkish producer of refrigerators, washing machines, and water heaters; TÃ¼rk Demir DÃ¶kÃ¼m, the first Turkish producer of radiators and, later, auto castings; and Turkay, the country's first private producer of matches. In 1959 KoÃ§ constructed Turkey's first truck assembly plant (Otosan).

Other firsts followed in the 1960s as the company leveraged its size and government influence to attract more ventures. These included a tire factory (with Uniroyal), a cable factory (with Siemens), production of electric motors and compressors (with GE), and the production of Anadol, the first car to be made entirely in Turkey (by Otosan, under license from Ford). In 1974 KoÃ§ expanded into retailing with the purchase of Migros, Turkey's largest chain of supermarkets.

The Turkish military imposed martial law in 1980 and restricted foreign exchange payments, forcing KoÃ§ to limit its operations. In 1986, a year after foreign companies were allowed to export products directly to Turkey, KoÃ§ and American Express started KoÃ§-Amerikan Bank (which KoÃ§ bought out and renamed KoÃ§bank in 1992). In the late 1980s Vehbi's only son, Rahmi, took over the company's leadership. Vehbi KoÃ§ died in 1996.

Auto sales fell sharply in 1996 as buyers awaited the country's entry into the European Union's customs union. In an effort to offset market risks, KoÃ§ forged a number of alliances in 1997. It participated in a British-Canadian-Turkish consortium that was building a large power plant in central Turkey.

Reflecting a greater willingness to open the company to foreign investors, KoÃ§ announced plans to offer $250 million in shares in a public offering in 1998, but it soon canceled the offering because of market volatility. A year later the company completed an auto plant in Samarkand, Uzbekistan, to build Otoyol-Iveco buses and trucks.

KoÃ§ entered into a joint venture -- KoÃ§ Finansal Hizmetler -- with Unicredito Italiano in 2002 in an effort to further consolidate its financial holdings.

Significant company moves in 2008 included selling its Otomotiv Lastikleri Tevzi (Oltas) to Germany's Continental AG. Oltas had distributed Continental tires and related products since 2003. The company's interest in supermarkets dwindled to less than 50% with the sale of its stake in Migros. Its sway, however, in the IT data processing business of KoÃ§Net Haberlesme Teknolojileri ve Iletisim Hizmetleri A.S. increased to almost 100%. The company picked up military aero and marine tech simulator Kaletron, an arm of Kale Group, too.

In 2009 the global recession curtailed industrial output and demand and hurt the company's revenues. However, its diversified portfolio and cost saving measures enabled it to post a modest improvement in net income.

EXECUTIVES

Chief Executive Officer, Director, Levent Cakiroglu
Chief Financial Officer, Polat Sen
Energy Group President, Yagiz Eyuboglu
Consumer Durables Group President, Fatih Kemal Ebiclioglu
Automotive Group President, Haydar Yenigun
Banking Group President, Gokhan Erun
President, Tourism, Food and Retailing Group President, Ozgur Burak Akkol
Audit Group President, Kemal Uzun
Chief Legal and Compliance Officer, Kenan Yilmaz

Honorary Chairman, Rahmi M. Koc
Chair, Omer M. Koc
Vice-Chairman, Director, Ali Y. Koc
Independent Director, Emily K. Rafferty
Independent Director, Cem M. Kozlu
Independent Director, Peter Matyr
Independent Director, Michel Ray de Carvalho
Director, Semahat Sevim Arsel
Director, Caroline N. Koc
Director, Ipek Kirac
Director, Jacques A. Nasser
Auditors : PwC Bagimsiz Denetim ve Serbest Muhasebeci Mali Müsavirlik A.S.

LOCATIONS

HQ: Koc Holdings AS
 Nakkastepe, Azizbey Sokak No. 1, Istanbul, Kuzguncuk 34674
Phone: (90) 216 531 0000 **Fax:** (90) 216 531 0099
Web: www.koc.com.tr

2016 Sales

	% of total
Domestic	74
Foreign	26
Total	100

PRODUCTS/OPERATIONS

2016 Sales

	% of total
Energy	42
Automotive	26
Finance	15
Consumer durables	11
Other	6
Total	100

Core Businesses
Automotive
Construction and mining
Durable goods
Food/Beverage/Tobacco
Energy
Financial services
Information technology
International trade
Marinas
New business development
Tourism and services

COMPETITORS

ACCIONA, SA
Franz Haniel & Cie. GmbH
HACI OMER SABANCI HOLDING ANONIM SIRKETI
IBERDROLA, SOCIEDAD ANONIMA
ITOCHU CORPORATION
Itausa S/A
KUKA AG
MITSUBISHI CORPORATION
SHV Holdings N.V.
SOJITZ CORPORATION

HISTORICAL FINANCIALS

Company Type: Public

Income Statement FYE: December 31

	REVENUE ($mil)	NET INCOME ($mil)	NET PROFIT MARGIN	EMPLOYEES
12/22	48,176	3,728	7.7%	0
12/21	25,919	1,135	4.4%	0
12/20	24,720	1,247	5.0%	0
12/19	25,798	737	2.9%	92,990
12/18	27,074	1,046	3.9%	92,631
Annual Growth	15.5%	37.4%	—	—

2022 Year-End Financials

Debt ratio: 1.3% No. of shares ($ mil.): —
Return on equity: 65.5% Dividends
Cash ($ mil.): 15,094 Yield: —
Current Ratio: 0.86 Payout: 0.0%
Long-term debt ($ mil.): 8,151 Market value ($ mil.): —

	STOCK PRICE ($) FY Close	P/E High/Low	Earnings	Dividends	Book Value
12/22	22.39	1 0	1.47	0.19	0.00
12/21	10.53	3 1	0.45	0.27	0.00
12/20	13.50	4 2	0.49	0.12	0.00
12/19	17.05	10 7	0.29	0.26	0.02
12/18	13.20	8 5	0.41	0.32	0.02
Annual Growth	14.1%	—	37.4%	(12.5%)	

Komatsu Ltd

EXECUTIVES

Chairman, Director, Tetsuji Ohashi
President, Chief Executive Officer, Representative Director, Hiroyuki Ogawa
Senior Managing Executive Officer, Representative Director, Masayuki Moriyama
Senior Managing Executive Officer, Director, Takeshi Horikoshi
Director, Kiyoshi Mizuhara
Outside Director, Takeshi Kunibe
Outside Director, Arthur M. Mitchell
Outside Director, Naoko Saiki
Outside Director, Michitaka Sawada
Auditors : KPMG AZSA LLC

LOCATIONS

HQ: Komatsu Ltd
 2-3-6 Akasaka, Minato-ku, Tokyo 107-8414
Phone: (81) 3 5561 2604
Web: www.komatsu.jp

HISTORICAL FINANCIALS

Company Type: Public

Income Statement FYE: March 31

	REVENUE ($mil)	NET INCOME ($mil)	NET PROFIT MARGIN	EMPLOYEES
03/23	26,605	2,450	9.2%	70,608
03/22	23,038	1,849	8.0%	67,755
03/21	19,774	959	4.9%	65,620
03/20	22,522	1,417	6.3%	68,879
03/19	24,608	2,316	9.4%	68,674
Annual Growth	2.0%	1.4%	—	0.7%

2023 Year-End Financials

Debt ratio: 0.2% No. of shares ($ mil): 946
Return on equity: 13.6% Dividends
Cash ($ mil.): 2,177 Yield: 3.5%
Current Ratio: 2.07 Payout: 35.0%
Long-term debt ($ mil.): 4,251 Market value ($ mil.): 23,499

	STOCK PRICE ($) FY Close	P/E High/Low	Earnings	Dividends	Book Value
03/23	24.84	0 0	2.59	0.89	20.16
03/22	24.03	0 0	1.96	0.69	19.41
03/21	31.23	0 0	1.02	0.54	18.26
03/20	16.41	0 0	1.50	1.05	17.27
03/19	23.30	0 0	2.45	0.89	17.36
Annual Growth	1.6%	—	1.4%	(0.2%)	3.8%

Kone OYJ

EXECUTIVES

President, Chief Executive Officer, Henrik Ehrnrooth
Secretary, General Counsel, Johannes Frande
Chief Financial Officer, Ilka Hara
Chief Technology Officer, Maciej Kranz
Chairman, Director, Antti Herlin
Vice Chair, Director, Jussi Herlin
Director, Matti Alahuhta
Director, Susan Duinhoven
Director, Iiris Herlin
Director, Ravi Kant
Director, Krishna Mikkilineni
Director, Jennifer Xin-Zhe Li
Auditors : Ernst & Young Oy

LOCATIONS

HQ: Kone OYJ
 Keilasatama 3, P.O. Box 7, Espoo FIN-02150
Phone: (358) 9 204 751 **Fax:** (358) 9 204 75 4309
Web: www.kone.com

HISTORICAL FINANCIALS

Company Type: Public

Income Statement FYE: December 31

	REVENUE ($mil)	NET INCOME ($mil)	NET PROFIT MARGIN	EMPLOYEES
12/23	12,130	1,025	8.5%	63,536
12/22	11,648	827	7.1%	63,277
12/21	11,900	1,147	9.6%	62,720
12/20	12,197	1,152	9.5%	61,380
12/19	11,207	1,045	9.3%	59,825
Annual Growth	2.0%	(0.5%)	—	1.5%

2023 Year-End Financials

Debt ratio: 7.0% No. of shares ($ mil.): 517
Return on equity: 33.1% Dividends
Cash ($ mil.): 470 Yield: —
Current Ratio: 1.13 Payout: 48.3%
Long-term debt ($ mil.): 485 Market value ($ mil.): 12,911

	STOCK PRICE ($) FY Close	P/E High/Low		PER SHARE ($) Earnings	Dividends	Book Value
12/23	24.96	16	12	1.98	0.96	5.89
12/22	25.83	22	14	1.59	1.11	5.86
12/21	35.75	21	17	2.22	1.34	6.94
12/20	40.64	26	15	2.22	0.95	7.52
12/19	32.63	18	13	2.02	0.93	6.88
Annual Growth	(6.5%)	—	—	(0.5%)	0.8%	(3.8%)

Koninklijke Ahold Delhaize NV

Koninklijke Ahold Delhaize is a family of great local brands serving millions of customers in the US, Europe, and Indonesia with over 7,450 stores. Formed in 2016 from the merger of Royal Ahold and Delhaize Group, the company's operations include Giant Food, Stop & Shop, Food Lion, and other banners in the US. Other interests include meal kit delivery service Peapod in the US, Gall & Gall liquor stores in the Netherlands, and joint ventures in Portugal and Indonesia. Serving approximately 55 million customers online and in stores, Ahold Delhaize owns about 20 retail brands. Most of the company's sales were generated from the US, accounting to approximately 60% of total sales.

Operations

Ahold Delhaize's retail operations are presented in two reportable segments: the US and Europe. In addition, Other retail, consisting of Ahold Delhaize's unconsolidated joint ventures JMR ? Gestão de Empresas de Retalho, SGPS, S.A. (JMR), and P.T. Lion Super Indo (Super Indo), as well as Ahold Delhaize's Global Support Office.

The US segment includes Stop & Shop, Food Lion, The GIANT Company, Hannaford, Giant Food, FreshDirect, and Peapod. The Europe segment includes Albert Heijn (including the Netherlands and Belgium), Delhaize (Delhaize Le Lion including Belgium and Luxembourg), bol.com (including the Netherlands and Belgium), Albert (Czech Republic), Alfa Beta (Greece), Mega Image (Romania), Delhaize Serbia (Republic of Serbia), Etos (the Netherlands), and Gall & Gall (the Netherlands).

Overall, the company's owned store sales generate about 80% of sales, while franchise and affiliate store sales and online sales account for the rest.

Geographic Reach

Ahold Delhaize is headquartered in Zaandam, the Netherlands. Its brands are active in Belgium, the Czech Republic, Greece, Luxembourg, the Netherlands, Romania, Serbia, and the US and participate in joint ventures in Indonesia and Portugal. Ahold Delhaize local brands have more than 7,450 local grocery, small format, and specialty stores. The US brings in approximately 60% of the company's revenue, while the Netherlands generates for more than 20%. The rest of the world accounts for the rest.

Sales and Marketing

Every month, millions of Ahold Delhaize's customers use its brands' websites and apps to do their shopping ? and it continues to invest in e-commerce growth and profitability.

Financial Performance

Note: Growth rates may differ after conversion to US Dollars.

The company's revenue has been rising in the last five years. It has an overall increase of 20% between 2018 and 2022.

Net sales for the financial year ending on January 2, 2022, were EUR 75.6 billion, an increase of EUR 865 million, or 1%, compared to net sales of EUR 74.7 billion for the financial year ending on January 3, 2021. At constant exchange rates, gasoline sales increased by 40%, driven by a reduction in pandemic measures during the year leading to an increase in gasoline volumes. In addition, gasoline prices increased considerably worldwide in 2021.

In 2021, the company had a net income of EUR 2.2 billion, a 61% increase from the previous year's net income of EUR 1.4 billion. This was primarily due to the higher volume of net sales for the year.

The company's cash at the end of 2021 was EUR 3 billion. Operating activities generated EUR 5.5 billion, while investing activities used EUR 2.6 billion, primarily for purchase of non-current assets. Financing activities used another EUR 3.1 billion, primarily for repayment of lease liabilities.

Strategy

The company's focus on driving omnichannel growth is centered around four areas:

Grow e-commerce and profitability. In years to come, it will scale Albert Heijn's premium subscription model and compact e-commerce models to select markets in Europe, starting with Albert in the Czech Republic;

Drive seamless omnichannel engagement. The company has announced plans for winning in the greater New York City area through a cooperative effort by Stop & Shop and FreshDirect. Bringing together the best of both brands and linking their digital and physical presences together will enable them to provide a unique and seamless omnichannel offering to more customers, delivering fresh and healthy food wherever, however and whenever they wish to shop;

Optimize its brick-and-mortar footprint. The company is expanding its footprint strategically, for example, through the acquisition of 38 DEEN stores in the Netherlands. Albert Heijn was able to finalize the conversion of stores and expand its reach before the important December 2021 sales period; and

Drive price, value and assortment. As part of its customer value proposition, the company's brands are investing in price. Its European brands will introduce around 1,500 "price favorites" ? high quality products that are always priced competitively ? to improve both price reality and price perception.

Company Background

Koninklijke Ahold Delhaize was formed in 2016 when supermarket giants Royal Ahold and Delhaize Group merged. The merger included bringing together Royal Ahold's 3,200 stores and Delhaize Group's 3,500 stores, some of which competed in the same markets in the US and Europe. Delhaize's major pre-merger brands included the Food Lion supermarket chain, as well as the Delhaize chain of stores in Europe, and Super Indo in Indonesia, while Royal Ahold's key brands comprised Giant Food, Stop & Shop, and Albert Heijn.

HISTORY

Albert Heijn and his wife took over his father's grocery store in Ootzaan, Netherlands, in 1887. By the end of WWI, the company had 50 Albert Heijn grocery stores in Holland, and at WWII's end it had almost 250 stores. In 1948 the company went public.

It opened its first self-service store in 1952 and its first supermarket in 1955. Growing into the #1 grocer in the Netherlands, Albert Heijn opened liquor and cosmetic stores in 1973. (It changed its name to Ahold that year to better reflect its range of businesses.) Ahold expanded outside the Netherlands in 1976 when it founded supermarket chain Cadadia in Spain (sold 1985).

Ahold entered the US in 1977 by purchasing BI-LO and furthered its expansion in 1981 by adding Pennsylvania-based Giant Food Stores. In 1987, in honor of its 100th anniversary, Ahold was granted the title Koninklijke (Dutch for "royal"). In 1988 it bought a majority stake in Dutch food wholesaler Schuitema.

The company added New York-based TOPS Markets in 1991. That year Royal Ahold founded food retailer and distributor Euronova (now called Ahold Czech Republic), and in 1992 it acquired 49% of Portuguese food retailer Jerónimo Martins Retail. In 1993 Cees van der Hoeven was promoted to chief executive and Royal Ahold was listed on the NYSE.

Other acquisitions included New England grocery giant The Stop & Shop Companies in 1996. That year saw the beginning of several Asian joint ventures that gave Royal Ahold stores in Singapore, Malaysia, and Thailand. It also formed a joint venture in 1998 with Argentina's Velox Retail Holdings (owner of about 90% of supermarket operators DISCO and Santa Isabel), and Royal Ahold added

Maryland-based grocer Giant Food Inc. (unrelated to Royal Ahold's Giant Food Stores).

Royal Ahold's moves in 1999 included the acquisition of several Spanish supermarket chains (with a total of about 200 stores), the purchase of Dutch institutional food wholesaler Gastronoom, and the acquisition of 50% of Sweden's top food seller, ICA AB. In Central America it acquired half of La Fragua, an operator of supermarkets and discount stores. However, North American expansion plans hit a snag when Royal Ahold backed out of a deal to buy Pathmark Stores.

In 2000 Royal Ahold acquired Spanish food retailer Kampio+, #2 and #4 foodservice distributors U.S. Foodservice and PYA/Monarch, US convenience store chains Sugar Creek and Golden Gallon, and all of the voting stock of Brazilian retailer BompreÃ§o. In June the firm bought a 51% stake in online grocer Peapod. Royal Ahold took over food retailer Superdiplo, which runs more than 300 stores in Spain (including the Canary Islands), in late 2000.

In March 2001 Royal Ahold began buying the remaining outstanding shares of BompreÃ§o with the intention of delisting the company from the Brazilian, Luxembourg, and New York stock exchanges (which it did in late December). Chicago-based Peapod became a wholly owned Royal Ahold subsidiary in 2001. The retailer also expanded its bricks-and-mortar US presence in 2001 by purchasing Alliant Exchange, parent of Alliant Foodservice, which distributes food to more than 100,000 customers, and Bruno's Supermarkets, which operates more than 180 stores in the Southeast. In December Ahold also agreed to buy the 32-store G. Barbosa supermarket chain, which would add to its holdings in Brazil.

Royal Ahold reported its first net loss in nearly 30 years in the second quarter of 2002. In August 2002 Royal Ahold assumed full control of Disco Ahold International Holdings, its former joint venture company with Velox Retail Holdings. Soon after the company increased its ownership stake in Chilean grocery chain Santa Isabel from 70% to 97% in a tender offer. In October the company integrated its Polish, Czech, and Slovak operations under the umbrella of Ahold Central Europe (ACE). ACE will manage more than 400 Albert supermarkets and Hypernova hypermarkets in Central Europe. In late 2002 subsidiary U.S. Foodservice agreed to buy Allen Foods, a major independent foodservice distributor in the Central Plains region.

In February 2003 CEO Cees van der Hoeven and CFO Michiel Meurs resigned following an announcement that the grocery giant would restate its financial results by at least $500 million because of accounting irregularities at U.S. Foodservice. (van der Hoeven is facing charges by Dutch prosecutors in connection with the scandal at U.S. Foodservice.) Chairman Henny de Ruiter became acting CEO of the company and Dudley Eustace, a British national who serves as a director of several Dutch companies, was named interim CFO in March. In May 2003 IKEA veteran Anders Moberg became acting CEO; de Ruiter remained chairman. Soon after, Ahold said it would restate earnings downward by $880 million (much more than the original $500 million projection) because of the accounting scandal at U.S. Foodservice. Further accounting investigations uncovered about $29 million in irregularities at the company's TOPS Markets US subsidiary.

In May, Ahold completed the sale of its De Tuinen natural product stores to NBTY's British subsidiary Holland & Barrett Europe. In June it sold its Jamin chain of candy stores to Jamin management. The Santa Isabel chain in Chile was sold in July to Cencosud for about $95 million, far less than the $150 million originally discussed. Adding to its woes, in July the public prosecutor in Amsterdam launched a criminal investigation into possible falsification of accounts by the company. Soon after, Ahold completed the sale of 22 stores in Indonesia to PT Hero Supermarket as well as its Malaysian retail business. In September the board of directors of Royal Ahold approved the appointment of Moberg and RyÃ¶ppÃ¶nen as CEO and CFO, respectively. Later in the month the global grocer sold its operations in Paraguay (Supermercados Stock S.A.) to A.J. Vierci for about $4 million.

In October 2003 Royal Ahold published its long-awaited 2002 results revealing a $1.27 billion loss, which the retailer attributed to special charges related to overstated profits at U.S. Foodservice. That month the company completed the sale of its 138-store Golden Gallon convenience chain to The Pantry for about $187 million, and de Ruiter resigned and was succeeded by Karel Vuursteen, previously a board member. In November, Royal Ahold sold two hypermarkets in Poland to Carrefour Poland as part of its overall strategy to restructure its retail portfolio. In December the Peruvian operations of its Santa Isabel chain were sold to Grupo Interbank and other investors led by Nexus Group.

In March 2004, Royal Ahold sold its 118-store BompreÃ§o chain in Brazil to Wal-Mart Stores and its credit card business (Hipercard) there to Unibanco S.A. for a combined price of about $500 million. Also in March, the Dutch chain sold its stake in CRC Ahold, operating in Thailand, to its partner, the Central Food Retail Co., completing the company's withdrawal from Asia. At a shareholders meeting in March, Ahold placed the blame for the accounting scandal, which nearly bankrupted the company in 2003, squarely on the shoulders of Jim Miller, the former CEO of U.S. Foodservice. (Later, Miller and Ahold agreed in late 2007 to settle litigation related to the matter with Miller paying Ahold $8 million.) In August Karel Vuursteen resigned as chairman of the supervisory board for personal reasons as was succeeded by RenÃ© Dahan. In September, Ahold reached a settlement with the Dutch public prosecutor in which the company agreed to pay ?8 million. In return, the Dutch prosecutor agreed not to undertake proceedings against Royal Ahold. In October the company reached a settlement with the US Securities and Exchange Commission that imposed no fines on Royal Ahold due, in part, to its "extensive co-operation" with the investigation. The company also finalized a deal to increase its stake in its Scandinavian retail joint venture, ICA AB. It paid its ?811 million for a 20% stake in the partnership sold by Canica. In December Ahold completed the sale of its retail activities in Spain and the Canary Islands (nearly 600 stores) to the Permira Funds.

In January 2005 the grocery giant sold its BI-LO and Bruno's chains in the southeastern US to an affiliate of Lone Star Funds for some $660 million. In February the Dutch retailer completed the sale of a dozen Hypernova hypermarkets in Poland to rival Carrefour, followed by the sale of a single large hypermarket to a local Polish firm two months later. Also in April Royal Ahold completed its exit from Brazil with the sale of 32 G. Barbosa hypermarkets there to ACON Investments, a US-based investment firm. In May the company announced completion of the sale of its 50% stake in Spanish winery Bodegas Williams & Humbert (formerly known as Luis Paez) to its joint venture partner Jose Medina y Cia SA for an undisclosed sum. In June Ahold completed the sale of its chain of 198 Wilson Farms and Sugarcreek convenience stores, part of its TOPS Markets subsidiary in the US, to WFI Acquisition for an undisclosed sum. In September Ahold sold its Deli XL foodservice operation in Belgium and the Netherlands to a subsidiary of South Africa-based The Bidvest Group for about ?140 million.

CFO Hannu RyÃ¶ppÃ¶nen resigned at the end of August 2005 to join Stora Enso, an integrated paper, packaging and forest products company. In October Royal Ahold completed the acquisition of 56 stores in the Czech Republic from Julius Meinl a.s. In November the company settled a US class action lawsuit by paying $1.1 billion to shareholders who purchased stock between July 3, 1999, and February 23, 2003; just before the 2003 accounting scandal broke. Concurrently, the company reached an agreement to settle litigation with the Dutch Shareholders' Association.

The grocery chain also sold 13 large

Hypernova hypermarkets in Poland to Carrefour and a local operator in early 2005. The company also moved its corporate headquarters from Zaandam to Amsterdam later in the year.

In 2006 the company sold three shopping centers in Poland and the Czech Republic for about ?108 million. In April, Jose Alvarez was named president and CEO of the combined Stop & Shop/Giant-Landover organization, succeeding Marc Smith, who retired. In September Royal Ahold was reported to be in talks with its Belgian counterpart, Delhaize, regarding a possible merger. However, negotiations were later suspended. In November the Dutch grocer completed the acquisition of 27 Konmar stores in the Netherlands from Laurus B.V. for about $130 million.

More than three years after teetering on the brink of bankruptcy as a result of one of Europe's largest financial scandals, a Dutch court found former CEO Cees van der Hoeven and former CFO Michael Meurs guilty of fraud. Van der Hoeven and Meurs were accused of improperly booking sales from four subsidiaries in Scandinavia, Argentina and Brazil. Both men were fined and given suspended sentences. Former executive board member Jan Andreae, who headed Ahold's European operations, was sentenced to four months in jail, suspended for two years, and fined.

CEO Anders Moberg left the company in July 2007. Also in July, U.S. Foodservice was finally sold to a consortium of Clayton, Dubilier & Rice and Kohlberg Kravis Roberts & Co. for about $7.1 billion. In November John Rishton, Ahold's CFO who had been serving as interim chief executive since Moberg's departure, was named to the post permanently. In December Royal Ahold sold its underperforming TOPS Markets chain to Morgan Stanley Private Equity for about $310 million.

In June 2008 the company completed sold its 73% stake in Schuitema N.V. to private equity firm CVC Capital Partners in return for cash and the transfer of 50-plus Schuitema stores to Ahold.

In 2009 Royal Ahold's Albert/Hypernova business in the Czech Republic and Slovakia closed 23 underperforming stores and downsized a dozen hypermarkets. It also finished converting its Hypernova stores to the Albert brand in the Czech Republic.

In February 2010 Ahold acquired 25 Ukrop's Super Market stores, inventory, equipment, and leases, in a $140 million transaction. The Ukrop's chain became part of Ahold USA's Giant-Carlisle division.

In March 2013 the company sold its 60% stake in the Sweden's largest food retailer, ICA AB, to Sweden's Hakon Invest for SEK 21.2 billion ($3.3 billion) in cash, to better stick to its strategy of focusing on businesses it controls.

EXECUTIVES

Chief Executive Officer, President, Frans Muller
Chief Financial Officer, Natalie Knight
Ahold Delhaize USA Chief Executive Officer, Kevin Holt
Europe and Indonesia Chief Executive Officer, Wouter Kolk
Chief Legal Officer, Jan Ernst de Groot
Chief Human Resources Officer, Natalia Wallenberg
Chief Information Officer, Ben Wishart
Independent Chairman, Peter Agnefjall
Independent Vice-Chairman, Bill McEwan
Independent Director, D. Rene Hooft Graafland
Independent Director, Katie Doyle
Independent Director, Helen Weir
Independent Director, Mary Anne Citrino
Independent Director, Frank van Zanten
Independent Director, Bala Subramanian
Independent Director, Jan Zijderveld
Auditors: PricewaterhouseCoopers Accountants N.V.

LOCATIONS

HQ: Koninklijke Ahold Delhaize NV
 Provincialeweg 11, Zaandam 1506 MA
Phone: (31) 88 659 5100
Web: www.aholddelhaize.com

2018 sales

	%
US	60
Netherlands	23
Belgium	8
Central and Southeastern Europe	9
Total	100

PRODUCTS/OPERATIONS

2018 sales

	%
Owned store sales	86
Franchise and affiliate store sales	9
Online sales	5
Wholesale sales	-
Other	-
Total	100

Selected Operations

Retail
 Europe
  Albert (supermarkets, Czech Republic and Slovakia)
  Albert Heijn (supermarkets, convenience stores)
  Alfa-Beta (supermarkets)
  Delhaize (supermarkets)
  Etos (drugstores, online shopping)
  Gall & Gall (liquor stores)
  MAXI (supermarkets)
  Mega Image (supermarkets)
  Shop & Go (convenience stores)
 US
  Food Lion (supermarkets)
  Giant-Carlisle (supermarkets & superstores)
  Giant-Landover (supermarkets)
  Stop & Go (convenience stores)
  Stop & Shop (supermarkets)

COMPETITORS

7-ELEVEN, INC
CARREFOUR
KERING
KINGFISHER PLC
LAURA ASHLEY HOLDINGS PLC
MUSGRAVE GROUP PUBLIC LIMITED COMPANY
Signet Jewelers Limited
THE GREAT ATLANTIC & PACIFIC TEA COMPANY, INC.
Tengelmann Warenhandelsgesellschaft KG
Victoria Retail Group B.V.

HISTORICAL FINANCIALS

Company Type: Public

Income Statement   FYE: January 1

	REVENUE ($mil)	NET INCOME ($mil)	NET PROFIT MARGIN	EMPLOYEES
01/23	92,902	2,719	2.9%	414,000
01/22	85,569	2,542	3.0%	413,000
01/21*	90,686	1,695	1.9%	414,000
12/19	73,853	1,968	2.7%	380,000
12/18	71,599	2,044	2.9%	372,000
Annual Growth	6.7%	7.4%	—	2.7%

*Fiscal year change

2023 Year-End Financials

Debt ratio: 12.5%   No. of shares ($ mil.): 977
Return on equity: 17.5%   Dividends
Cash ($ mil.): 3,291   Yield: —
Current Ratio: 0.72   Payout: 30.9%
Long-term debt ($ mil.): 4,835   Market value ($ mil.): 28,050

	STOCK PRICE ($) FY Close	P/E High/Low		PER SHARE ($) Earnings	Dividends	Book Value
01/23	28.70	13	10	2.71	0.84	16.83
01/22	34.40	16	11	2.46	0.76	15.36
01/21*	28.23	24	17	1.58	0.95	14.41
12/19	25.30	17	14	1.77	0.91	14.43
12/18	25.15	17	13	1.73	0.60	14.95
Annual Growth	3.4%		—	11.9%	8.6%	3.0%

*Fiscal year change

Koninklijke Philips NV

EXECUTIVES

Secretary, Vice-Chairman, Independent Director, Paul Stoffels
Chief Executive Officer, Executive Vice President, Roy Jakobs
Executive Vice President, Chief Financial Officer, Abhijit Bhattacharya
Executive Vice President, Chief Legal Officer, Marnix van Ginneken
International Markets Executive Vice President, International Markets Chief, Edwin Paalvast
Executive Vice President, Chief Innovation and Strategy Officer, Shez Partovi
Executive Vice President, Chief Human Resources Officer, Daniela Seabrook
Executive Vice President, Andy Ho
Executive Vice President, Deeptha Khanna
Executive Vice President, Bert van Meurs
Executive Vice President, Vitor Rocha
Executive Vice President, Kees Wesdorp

Chairman, Independent Director, Feike Sijbesma
Independent Director, Sock Koong Chua
Independent Director, Liz Doherty
Independent Director, Marc Harrison
Independent Director, Peter Loscher
Independent Director, Indra K. Nooyi
Independent Director, David E. I. Pyott
Independent Director, Herna Verhagen
Independent Director, Sanjay Poonen
Auditors : Ernst & Young Accountants LLP

LOCATIONS

HQ: Koninklijke Philips NV
Breitner Center, Amstelplein 2, Amsterdam 1096 BC
Phone: (31) 20 59 77 232
Web: www.philips.com

HISTORICAL FINANCIALS
Company Type: Public

Income Statement — FYE: December 31

	REVENUE ($mil)	NET INCOME ($mil)	NET PROFIT MARGIN	EMPLOYEES
12/23	20,124	(516)	—	69,656
12/22	19,040	(1,717)	—	77,233
12/21	19,418	3,756	19.3%	78,189
12/20	23,975	1,456	6.1%	81,592
12/19	21,873	1,310	6.0%	80,495
Annual Growth	(2.1%)	—		(3.6%)

2023 Year-End Financials
Debt ratio: 29.0%
Return on equity: (-3.6%)
Cash ($ mil.): 2,070
Current Ratio: 1.20
Long-term debt ($ mil.): 7,792
No. of shares ($ mil.): 906
Dividends
Yield: —
Payout: 0.0%
Market value ($ mil.): 21,146

	STOCK PRICE ($) FY Close	P/E High/Low	PER SHARE ($) Earnings	Dividends	Book Value
12/23	23.33	— —	(0.56)	0.94	14.70
12/22	14.99	— —	(1.94)	0.80	16.05
12/21	36.85	16 9	4.13	0.88	18.78
12/20	54.17	43 27	1.58	1.04	16.09
12/19	48.80	39 25	1.44	0.82	15.87
Annual Growth	(16.8%)		—	3.5%	(1.9%)

Korea Electric Power Corp

EXECUTIVES

President, Chief Executive Officer, Standing Director, Seung-Il Cheong
Comptroller, Auditor General, Standing Director, Young-Sang Jun
Senior Executive Vice President, Chief Business Management Officer, Standing Director, Jung-Bok Lee
Senior Executive Vice President, Chief Safety & Business Operations Officer, Standing Director, Jun-Ho Lee
Senior Executive Vice President, Chief Financial & Strategic Planning Officer, Standing Director, Heon-Gyu Park
Senior Executive Vice President, Chief Power Grid Officer, Standing Director, Tae-Ok Kim
Senior Executive Vice President, Chief Global & Nuclear Business Officer, Standing Director, Heung-Joo Lee
Chairperson, Non-Standing Director, Jong-Bae Park
Non-Standing Director, Jae-Shin Kim
Non-Standing Director, Su-Ran Bang
Non-Standing Director, Hyo-Sung Park
Non-Standing Director, Kee-Man Lee
Non-Standing Director, Kye-Sung Lee
Non-Standing Director, Jong-Woon Kim
Auditors : Ernst & Young Han Young

LOCATIONS

HQ: Korea Electric Power Corp
55 Jeollyeok-ro, Naju-si, Jeollanam-do 58322
Phone: (82) 61 345 4299   **Fax:** 201 613-40093
Web: www.kepco.co.kr

HISTORICAL FINANCIALS
Company Type: Public

Income Statement — FYE: December 31

	REVENUE ($mil)	NET INCOME ($mil)	NET PROFIT MARGIN	EMPLOYEES
12/23	67,945	(3,714)	—	0
12/22	56,274	(19,517)	—	49,237
12/21	50,428	(4,473)	—	48,809
12/20	53,224	1,829	3.4%	48,519
12/19	50,725	(2,031)	—	22,973
Annual Growth	7.6%			

2023 Year-End Financials
Debt ratio: —
Return on equity: (-12.6%)
Cash ($ mil.): 3,344
Current Ratio: 0.48
Long-term debt ($ mil.): 8,623
No. of shares ($ mil.): 641
Dividends
Yield: —
Payout: 0.0%
Market value ($ mil.): 4,654

	STOCK PRICE ($) FY Close	P/E High/Low	PER SHARE ($) Earnings	Dividends	Book Value
12/23	7.25	— —	(5.79)	0.00	43.00
12/22	8.64	— —	(30.40)	0.00	50.38
12/21	9.14	— —	(6.97)	0.54	83.61
12/20	12.27	0 0	2.85	0.00	99.18
12/19	11.83	— —	(3.16)	0.00	91.06
Annual Growth	(11.5%)		—	—	(17.1%)

Kubota Corp. (Japan)

Kubota is maker of tractors and farm equipment, from rice trans planters to combine harvesters. It also leads in producing iron ductile pipe for water supply systems as well as PVC pipe and the engines for its agricultural and industrial movers. The company has also entered into building environmental control plants and pumps. Its tractors and other equipment, with global production totaling more than 5.1 million units, help to support food production throughout the world. Kubota's lineup includes approximately 3,000 types of industrial engines for both internal use and external sale to meet a vast range of needs. Kubota generates around 75% of its revenue from outside of Japan.

Operations

Kubota operates in the three segments: farm and industrial machinery, water and environment, and other.

Farm and industrial machinery segment accounts for about 85% of the company's total revenue. It includes production of agricultural machinery and agricultural-related products such as tractors and combine harvesters, pumps, construction machinery inclusive of skid steer loaders and wheel loaders, and engines.

The water and environment systems segment produces pipe systems, water treatment facilities and plants for incinerating, melting, crushing and recycling wastes. It generates some 15% of total revenue.

Geographic Reach

Based in Osaka, Japan, Kubota manufactures its products not only in Japan but also in overseas countries like the Africa, Asia, Europe, Latin and North America, and Oceania. North America brings in more than 35% of total revenue, while Japan generates more than 25%, followed by Asia (excluding Japan) at almost 20% and Europe and others generates more than 15% of combined revenue.

Financial Performance

The company reported a total revenue of Â¥2.2 trillion in 2021, a 19% increase from the previous year's total revenue of Â¥1.9 trillion.

In 2021, the company had a net income of Â¥190.7 billion, a 35% increase from the previous year's net income of Â¥141.4 billion.

The company's cash at the end of 2021 was Â¥258.6 billion. Operating activities generated Â¥92.5 billion, while investing activities used Â¥127.4 billion, mainly for payments for acquisition of property, plant, and equipment and intangible assets. Financing activities provided another Â¥60.6 billion.

Strategy

Steadily developing its existing businesses is a vital part of supporting the creation of the foundations for the next generation. Based on the strengths of each business and market, the company will continue to promote the expansion of product lineups, business expansion that meets the needs, and business expansion by updating, maintaining, and managing social infrastructure. As part of its Mid-Term Business Plan 2025, the company has chosen four businesses to be its drivers of growth?construction machinery in North America, agricultural and construction machinery in the ASEAN region, global machinery and aftermarket services, and water environment solutions. In the past several years, the construction machinery business in North America has grown in particular.

This year, The company added another, fifth, driver of growth?the expansion of its business in India and entry into the basic machinery market. By maximizing synergy with Escorts, in whom the company raised its investment ratio, the company aims to increase its market share in India, which with 1 million units by 2030 is the world's biggest tractor market, to 25%, double its current share. The company also plans to expand its exports of basic machinery both within India and elsewhere, particularly to Africa. To respond to market needs, the company will reform how its own business should function, at a speed that exceeds customer expectations.

Company Background

Kubota Corporation was founded in 1890 as a casting manufacturer. The company developed the cultivator in 1947 and a tractor in 1960. It stated manufacturing mini-excavators in 1974. In 2011, it became the first company in the world to acquire the US CARB certificate. It established its manufacturing company in France in 2014 and water treatment facilities in Myanmar in 2015.

HISTORY

The son of a poor farmer and coppersmith, Gonshiro Oode left home in 1885 at age 14 and moved to Osaka to find work. He began as an apprentice at the Kuro Casting Shop, where he learned about metal casting. He saved his money and in 1890 opened Oode Casting.

Oode's shop grew rapidly, thanks to the industrialization of the Japanese economy and the expansion of the iron and steel industries. One of Oode's customers, Toshiro Kubota, took a liking to the hardworking young man, and in 1897 Kubota adopted him. Oode changed his own name to Kubota and also changed the name of his company to Kubota Iron Works.

Kubota made a number of technological breakthroughs in the early 1900s, including a new method of producing cast-iron pipe (developed in 1900). The company became the first to make the pipe in Japan, and it continued to grow as the country modernized its infrastructure.

Kubota began making steam engines, machine tools, and agricultural engines in 1917, and it also began exporting products to countries in Southeast Asia. In 1930 Kubota restructured and incorporated. It continued to add product lines, including agricultural and industrial motors.

Although WWII brought massive destruction to Japan, the peacetime that followed created plenty of work for Kubota's farm equipment and pipe operations as the country rebuilt. By 1960 the company was Japan's largest maker of farm equipment, ductile iron pipe, and cement roofing materials. That year Kubota introduced the first small agricultural tractor in Japan.

EXECUTIVES

President, Representative Director, Yuichi Kitao
Executive Vice President, Representative Director, Masato Yoshikawa
Executive Vice President, Director, Dai Watanabe
Senior Managing Executive Officer, Director, Hiroto Kimura
Senior Managing Executive Officer, Director, Eiji Yoshioka
Senior Managing Executive Officer, Yuji Tomiyama
Senior Managing Executive Officer, Kazuhiro Kimura
Senior Managing Executive Officer, Nikhil Nanda
Senior Managing Executive Officer, Nobuyuki Ishii
Director, Shingo Hanada
Outside Director, Yuzuru Matsuda
Outside Director, Koichi Ina
Outside Director, Yutaro Shintaku
Outside Director, Kumi Arakane
Outside Director, Koichi Kawana
Auditors : Deloitte Touche Tohmatsu LLC

LOCATIONS

HQ: Kubota Corp. (Japan)
1-2-47 Shikitsu-higashi, Naniwa-Ku, Osaka 556-8601
Phone: (81) 6 6648 2111   Fax: (81) 6 6648 2617
Web: www.kubota.co.jp

2015 Sales

	% of total
Asia	
Japan	42
Other Asian countries	19
North America	24
Europe	12
Other regions	3
Total	100

PRODUCTS/OPERATIONS

2015 Sales

	% of total
Farm & industrial machinery	76
Water & environment systems	21
Other	3
Total	100

Selected Products

Farm & industrial machinery
    Construction machinery (mini-excavators, wheel loaders)
    Engines (industrial applications)
    Farm equipment (tractors, combine harvesters, rice transplanters, power tillers, reaper binders)
Other
    Construction
    Services & other businesses
Social infrastructure
    Air conditioning equipment
    Electronic-equipped machinery
    Industrial castings
    Steel pipes
    Vending machines
Water & environment systems
    Ductile iron pipes
    Environmental control plants (water & sewage treatment plants, submerged membrane systems, biogas production systems, pulverizing facilities, irrigation systems)
    Plastic pipes & fittings
    Pumps
    Valves

COMPETITORS

AGCO CORPORATION
BLOUNT INTERNATIONAL, INC.
Buhler Industries Inc
CNH INDUSTRIAL N.V.
LINDSAY CORPORATION
MARUBENI CORPORATION
Neles Oyj
OXBO INTERNATIONAL CORPORATION
THE TORO COMPANY
thyssenkrupp AG

HISTORICAL FINANCIALS

Company Type: Public

Income Statement   FYE: December 31

	REVENUE ($mil)	NET INCOME ($mil)	NET PROFIT MARGIN	EMPLOYEES
12/22	20,329	1,185	5.8%	62,565
12/21	19,084	1,525	8.0%	46,649
12/20	17,980	1,246	6.9%	44,304
12/19	17,684	1,372	7.8%	43,907
12/18	16,825	1,260	7.5%	43,206
Annual Growth	4.8%	(1.5%)	—	9.7%

2022 Year-End Financials

Debt ratio: 0.3%	No. of shares ($ mil.): 1,190
Return on equity: 8.7%	Dividends
Cash ($ mil.): 1,713	Yield: —
Current Ratio: 1.45	Payout: 0.0%
Long-term debt ($ mil.): 7,362	Market value ($ mil.): 81,190

	STOCK PRICE ($) FY Close	P/E High/Low	PER SHARE ($) Earnings	Dividends	Book Value
12/22	68.17	1 1	0.99	1.67	12.00
12/21	111.72	1 1	1.26	1.82	12.15
12/20	110.34	1 1	1.03	1.66	11.85
12/19	79.00	1 1	1.12	1.62	10.89
12/18	70.45	1 1	1.02	1.52	9.89
Annual Growth	(0.8%)	— —	(0.7%)	2.3%	5.0%

Kuehne & Nagel International AG

Pass it on -- KuehneÂ + Nagel International is one of the world's top freight forwarding and logistics groups. KuehneÂ + Nagel (pronounced "KOO-nuh and NAH-gel") provides sea freight and airfreight forwarding, arranges the transportation of goods by road and rail, and offers customs brokerage services. The company's contract logistics unit offers warehousing and distribution services, and it managesÂ more thanÂ 7Â million sq. meters of warehouse space. Overall, KuehneÂ + Nagel operates from aboutÂ 900 locations in more thanÂ 100 countries worldwide. Executive chairman Klaus-Michael Kuehne, grandson of the company's co-founder, owns a controlling stake in KuehneÂ + Nagel.

HISTORY

Kuehne + Nagel (also KÃ¼hne + Nagel) was founded in 1890 in Bremen, Germany, by shipping veterans August Kuehne and Friedrich Nagel. The forwarding and commissioning agency's initial contracts were for glassware and cotton. Kuehne + Nagel convinced Hamburg sugar refiners to use its services to transport sugar by rail to the ice-free port of Bremen when the refiners' major export route, the Weser River, was frozen. By 1902 Kuehne + Nagel had an office in Hamburg. Nagel died in 1907.

Rebuilding after WWI, Kuehne + Nagel acquired the Weber & Freund import company in the early 1920s and expanded into Austria, Czechoslovakia, Switzerland, and the Balkans. In 1932, when August Kuehne died, sons Alfred and Werner became sole owners of Kuehne + Nagel. (Werner left the company in 1951.)

Kuehne + Nagel's headquarters in Bremen was destroyed in WWII. As postwar German trade recovered, Kuehne + Nagel grew rapidly, opening a subsidiary in Canada in 1953 and setting up branches across Germany, including Frankfurt (1949), Bonn and Hanover (1950), Wuppertal (1961), and Nuremberg (1963).

After the European Economic Community was founded, Kuehne + Nagel established a network of forwarding agents and subsidiaries across Europe, including offices in Antwerp, Belgium, and Rotterdam, the Netherlands, in 1954 and offices in Basel and Zurich, Switzerland, in 1963. Kuehne + Nagel took control of Greek forwarder Proodos in 1963 and set up an Italian subsidiary a year later.

Alfred Kuehne died in 1981. Heavy losses resulting from the expansion of the shipping fleet of Kuehne + Nagel prompted it to sell half of the company to British conglomerate Lonrho (renamed Lonmin in 1999). Alfred's son Klaus-Michael Kuehne, and Lonrho's Roland "Tiny" Rowland were appointed as joint chief executives.

In 1985 Kuehne + Nagel began expanding its transportation, warehousing, and distribution network by acquiring stakes in leading freight companies, including Domenichelli (Italy), Hollis Transportation (UK), and Van Vliet (the Netherlands). The Kuehne family expanded Kuehne + Nagel's presence in Switzerland (seen as a pan-European center) during the 1970s and 1980s, and in 1992 Kuehne + Nagel moved its global headquarters to Schindellegi, near Zurich.

In the early 1990s, after German reunification and the fall of the Soviet Union, Kuehne + Nagel acquired former East German state-owned forwarder VEB Deutrans. It also signed deals with local freight-forwarding operators in Russia and across Eastern Europe.

In 1992 Klaus-Michael Kuehne bought out Lonrho's stake and later sold a 33% stake to German conglomerate VIAG (later part of E.ON), which sold it back to Kuehne + Nagel in 1999. In 1994 Kuehne + Nagel went public.

To expand its rail network, the company in 1997 acquired a 51% stake in Swiss rail forwarder Ferroviasped, a major player in freight services for national railroads in Denmark, France, Spain, and Switzerland.

To stay competitive in a rapidly consolidating industry, Kuehne + Nagel formed an alliance in 1999 with French freight forwarder GEFCO, a subsidiary of Peugeot S.A. A year later Kuehne + Nagel formed an alliance with Singapore-based SembCorp Logistics, which later acquired a 20% stake in Kuehne + Nagel. In return, Kuehne + Nagel bought 5% of SembCorp Logistics.

In 2000 Kuehne + Nagel also made plans to expand operations in the US. The company followed through the next year when it bought Connecticut-based USCO Logistics for $300 million. USCO Logistics was renamed KuehneÂ + Nagel Logistics in 2004.

Also in 2004, Kuehne + Nagel and SembCorp LogisticsÂ terminated their alliance in order to proceed independently.

EXECUTIVES

Chief Executive Officer, Detlef Trefzger
Chief Financial Officer, Markus Blanka-Graff
Chief Human Resources Officer, Lothar A. Harings
Chief Information Officer, Martin Kolbe
Road Logistics and Sales Executive Vice President, Stefan Paul
Sea Logistics Executive Vice President, Horst Joachim Schacht
Air Logistics Executive Vice President, Yngve Ruud
Contract Logistics Executive Vice President, Gianfranco Sgro
Honorary Chairman, Klaus-Michael Kuehne
Non-Executive Chairman, Joerg Wolle
Non-Executive Vice-Chairman, Karl Gernandt
Non-Executive Director, Dominik Buergy
Non-Executive Director, Renato Fassbind
Non-Executive Director, David Kamenetzky
Non-Executive Director, Tobias B. Saehelin
Non-Executive Director, Hauke Stars
Non-Executive Director, Martin C. Wittig
Auditors : Ernst & Young Ltd

LOCATIONS

HQ: Kuehne & Nagel International AG
Kuehne & Nagel House, P.O. Box 67, Schindellegi CH-8834
Phone: (41) 44 786 95 11   **Fax:** (41) 44 786 95 95
Web: www.kuehne-nagel.com

COMPETITORS

Chocoladefabriken Lindt & SprÃ¼ngli AG
PHAROL - SGPS, S.A.
SEQUANA
Schindler Holding AG
Zurich Insurance Group AG

HISTORICAL FINANCIALS

Company Type: Public

Income Statement — FYE: December 31

	REVENUE ($mil)	NET INCOME ($mil)	NET PROFIT MARGIN	EMPLOYEES
12/21	35,933	2,226	6.2%	78,087
12/20	23,142	894	3.9%	78,249
12/19	21,820	825	3.8%	83,161
12/18	21,117	782	3.7%	81,900
12/17	19,051	755	4.0%	75,876
Annual Growth	17.2%	31.0%	—	0.7%

2021 Year-End Financials

Debt ratio: 3.0%
Return on equity: 72.4%
Cash ($ mil.): 2,525
Current Ratio: 1.16
Long-term debt ($ mil.): 219
No. of shares ($ mil.): 120
Dividends
  Yield: 1.7%
  Payout: 3.2%
Market value ($ mil.): 7,607

	STOCK PRICE ($) FY Close	P/E High/Low	Earnings	Dividends	Book Value
12/21	63.24	5 3	18.49	1.11	29.18
12/20	45.49	7 4	7.46	0.52	22.85
12/19	33.95	5 4	6.89	0.72	20.00
12/18	25.46	6 4	6.53	0.71	19.68
12/17	35.50	6 4	6.30	0.69	0.00
Annual Growth	15.5%	—	—	30.9%	12.9%

Kyocera Corp

EXECUTIVES

Chairman, Representative Director, Goro Yamaguchi
President, Representative Director, Hideo Tanimoto
Director, Hiroshi Fure
Director, Norihiko Ina
Director, Koichi Kano
Director, Shoichi Aoki
Outside Director, Akiko Koyano
Outside Director, Eiji Kakiuchi
Outside Director, Shigenobu Maekawa
Auditors : PricewaterhouseCoopers Kyoto

LOCATIONS

HQ: Kyocera Corp
6 Takeda Tobadono-cho, Fushimi-ku, Kyoto 612-8501
Phone: (81) 75 604 3500   **Fax:** (81) 75 604 3501
Web: www.kyocera.co.jp

HISTORICAL FINANCIALS

Company Type: Public

Income Statement
FYE: March 31

	REVENUE ($mil)	NET INCOME ($mil)	NET PROFIT MARGIN	EMPLOYEES
03/23	15,206	960	6.3%	81,209
03/22	15,118	1,220	8.1%	83,001
03/21	13,790	814	5.9%	78,490
03/20	14,731	992	6.7%	75,505
03/19	14,661	931	6.4%	76,863
Annual Growth	0.9%	0.8%	—	1.4%

2023 Year-End Financials

Debt ratio: —
Return on equity: 4.3%
Cash ($ mil.): 2,804
Current Ratio: 2.94
Long-term debt ($ mil.): 808
No. of shares ($ mil.): 1,435
Dividends
Yield: 10.6%
Payout: 0.0%
Market value ($ mil.): 74,841

	STOCK PRICE ($) FY Close	P/E High/Low	PER SHARE ($) Earnings	Dividends	Book Value
03/23	52.13	1 1	0.67	1.39	15.81
03/22	55.95	1 0	0.85	1.51	16.44
03/21	64.08	1 1	0.56	1.32	16.14
03/20	58.63	1 1	0.68	1.48	15.46
03/19	58.91	1 1	0.64	1.09	14.14
Annual Growth	(3.0%)	— —	1.0%	6.4%	2.8%

Kyushu Electric Power Co Inc

Kyushu Electric Power generates, transmits, and distributes electricity on Japan's southernmost island. The company serves customers in the Kyushu region providing nuclear, thermal, and hydroelectric power generation. The company's other operations include telecommunications, information system development business, and data center business. It also sells wholesale electricity and has international power production and consulting operations, primarily in Asia. Kyushu Electric was established in 1951. The power transmission and distribution business of Kyushu Electric Power was spun off as Kyushu Electric Power Transmission and Distribution Co., Inc. in 2020 to enhance the neutrality of the power transmission and distribution network.

Operations

Kyushu Electric's segments are Domestic Electric power (some 85% of sales), Other Energy Service (about 10%), Information and Communication Technology (ICT) Service (some 5%) and Other

The Domestic Electric Power segment is engaged in the business of power generation and retail electricity in Japan and electricity transmission and distribution in Kyushu region.

The Other Energy Service segment is engaged in the business that provides a stable supply of electric power, such as construction and maintenance of electricity-related facilities, selling gas and LNG, a renewable energy business, and overseas business.

The ICT Service segment is engaged in the data communication business, optical broadband business, construction and maintenance of telecommunications facilities, information system development business, and data center business.

Other segment is engaged in the real estate business, nursing home business, and other business.

Overall, about 90% of sales were generated from electric operations.

Geographic Reach

Headquartered in Fukuoka, Japan, Kyushu Electric has around 55 offices across Japan.

Financial Performance

In terms of income as of March 31 for 2020, consolidated operating revenues decreased 0.2% from the previous fiscal year to Â¥2.01 trillion despite an increase in sales in the ICT service business. Factors include a decrease in retail electricity sales and in electricity sales to other suppliers as well as an increase in renewable energy-related subsidies.

As a result of the foregoing factors, net income attributable to owners of the parent declined by Â¥31.3 billion over the previous fiscal year, to Â¥400 million.

Cash held by the company at the end of fiscal 2020 decreased to Â¥205.5 billion compared to Â¥245.3 billion in the prior. Cash provided by operation and financing activities were Â¥226.9 billion and Â¥158.0 billion, respectively. Cash used for investing activities was Â¥424.6 billion, mainly for capital expenditures including nuclear fuel.

Strategy

In recent years, there have been growing expectations toward efforts to bring about a sustainable society on a global scale. These include efforts to achieve the United Nations' sustainable development goals (SDGs) for the international community, and ESG investment that evaluates companies' consideration of factors such as the environment. The company recognizes the importance of meeting these expectations.

That is why its group strategy and ESG initiatives are inseparable. To name an example, its management vision includes a business performance target of contributing to the reduction of Kyushu's CO2 emissions by 70%. This is consistent with Japan's plan to combat global warming (a 26% reduction from 2013 levels in 2030) under the Paris Agreement. We have set three strategies for achieving its vision: Strategy I tied to E (Environment), Strategy II tied to S (Society), and Strategy III tied to G (Governance). Its entire management vision is linked to ESG.

In Strategy I, the company will contribute to a sustainable low-carbon society by improving our ratio of non-fossil fuel power sources Environment through the use of renewable and nuclear energy, and by promoting electricity usage in many fields. Strategy II will contribute to the resolution of various issues affecting communities and wider society by creating markets through new businesses and services. Strategy III will strengthen the business foundations that support the growth of the Kyuden Group.

Mergers and Acquisitions

In 2019, Kyushu Electric Power Co., Inc. participates in the management of EGCO, which is one of the largest Independent Power Producers in Thailand by acquiring indirect interest in the Electricity Generating Public Company Limited. With this participation, its equity ownership in overseas electricity generation project is approximately 2,300MW, which approaches its target in its mid-term management policy to expand equity ownership of 5,000MW by 2030. Terms were not disclosed.

EXECUTIVES

Chairman, Representative Director, Michiaki Uriu
President, Representative Director, Kazuhiro Ikebe
Executive Vice President, Representative Director, Ichirou Fujii
Executive Vice President, Representative Director, Makoto Toyoma
Executive Vice President, Representative Director, Naoyuki Toyoshima
Director, Yasuji Akiyama
Director, Junichi Fujimoto
Director, Yoshifumi Kuriyama
Director, Yoshiharu Senda
Outside Director, Sakie Tachibana Fukushima
Outside Director, Junji Tsuda
Director, Yasuaki Endo
Outside Director, Kazuko Fujita
Outside Director, Yuji Oie
Outside Director, Tomoka Sugihara
Auditors : Deloitte Touche Tohmatsu LLC

LOCATIONS

HQ: Kyushu Electric Power Co Inc
2-1-82 Watanabe-dori, Chuo-ku, Fukuoka 810-8720
Phone: (81) 92 761 3031
Web: www.kyuden.co.jp

PRODUCTS/OPERATIONS

2016 Sales

	% of total
Electric power	92
IT and Telecommunication	4
Energy related Business	3
Others	1
Total	100

COMPETITORS

ALLETE, INC.
ALLIANT ENERGY CORPORATION
CHUBU ELECTRIC POWER CO.,INC.
CHUGOKU ELECTRIC POWER COMPANY,INCORPORATED,THE

KANSAI ELECTRIC POWER COMPANY, INCORPORATED, THE
MANILA ELECTRIC COMPANY
QUANTA SERVICES, INC.
TOHOKU ELECTRIC POWER COMPANY,INCORPORATED
TOKYO GAS CO., LTD.
Uniper SE

HISTORICAL FINANCIALS
Company Type: Public

Income Statement — FYE: March 31

	REVENUE ($mil)	NET INCOME ($mil)	NET PROFIT MARGIN	EMPLOYEES
03/22	14,332	56	0.4%	21,226
03/21	19,253	290	1.5%	21,273
03/20	18,544	(3)	0.0%	21,180
03/19	18,214	279	1.5%	21,103
03/18	18,461	816	4.4%	20,968
Annual Growth	(6.1%)	(48.7%)	—	0.3%

2022 Year-End Financials
Debt ratio: 0.6%
Return on equity: 1.0%
Cash ($ mil.): 2,151
Current Ratio: 0.68
Long-term debt ($ mil.): 25,792
No. of shares ($ mil.): 473
Dividends
  Yield: —
  Payout: 0.0%
Market value ($ mil.): 3,493

	STOCK PRICE ($) FY Close	P/E High/Low	PER SHARE ($) Earnings	Dividends	Book Value
03/22	7.37	1 1	0.08	0.31	11.20
03/21	8.85	0 0	0.51	0.29	12.46
03/20	8.46	— —	(0.06)	0.32	11.87
03/19	12.13	0 0	0.43	0.23	12.18
03/18	11.65	0 0	1.36	0.24	12.50
Annual Growth	(10.8%)	—	(50.3%)	6.7%	(2.7%)

L'Air Liquide S.A. (France)

EXECUTIVES
Chief Executive Officer, Director, Francois Jackow
Executive Vice President, Michael J. Graff
Executive Vice President, Fabienne Lecorvaisier
Senior Vice President, Francois Abrial
Senior Vice President, Jean-Marc de Royere
Senior Vice President, Francois Venet
Senior Vice President, Pascal Vinet
Vice President, Ronnie Chalmers
Vice President, Marcelo Fioranelli
Vice President, Matthieu Giard
Vice President, Armelle Levieux
Vice President, Emilie Mouren-Renouard
Vice President, Jerome Pelletan
Vice President, Diana Schillag
Chairman, Benoit Potier
Independent Lead Director, Xavier Huillard
Independent Director, Annette Winkler
Independent Director, Sian Herbert-Jones
Independent Director, Genevieve B. Berger
Independent Director, Anette Bronder
Independent Director, Kim Ann Mink
Independent Director, Aiman Ezzat
Director, Philippe Dubrulle
Director, Fatima Tighlaline
Director, Bertrand Dumazy
Auditors : KPMG S.A.

LOCATIONS
HQ: L'Air Liquide S.A. (France)
   75, quai d'Orsay, Paris, Cedex 07 75007
Phone: (33) 1 40 62 55 55
Web: www.airliquide.com

HISTORICAL FINANCIALS
Company Type: Public

Income Statement — FYE: December 31

	REVENUE ($mil)	NET INCOME ($mil)	NET PROFIT MARGIN	EMPLOYEES
12/22	32,231	2,946	9.1%	67,109
12/21	26,668	2,911	10.9%	66,436
12/20	25,406	2,988	11.8%	64,445
12/19	24,836	2,516	10.1%	67,200
12/18	24,277	2,420	10.0%	66,000
Annual Growth	7.3%	5.0%	—	0.4%

2022 Year-End Financials
Debt ratio: 26.3%
Return on equity: 12.2%
Cash ($ mil.): 2,041
Current Ratio: 0.92
Long-term debt ($ mil.): 10,860
No. of shares ($ mil.): 522
Dividends
  Yield: —
  Payout: 10.1%
Market value ($ mil.): 14,770

	STOCK PRICE ($) FY Close	P/E High/Low	PER SHARE ($) Earnings	Dividends	Book Value
12/22	28.28	7 5	5.63	0.57	48.55
12/21	34.87	7 6	5.58	0.61	46.58
12/20	32.89	7 5	5.73	0.53	43.82
12/19	28.05	7 5	4.83	0.49	40.85
12/18	24.67	6 5	4.67	0.51	39.33
Annual Growth	3.5%	—	4.8%	2.9%	5.4%

L'Oreal S.A. (France)

EXECUTIVES
Chairman, Director, Jean-Paul Agon
Chief Executive Officer, Director, Nicolas Hieronimus
Research, Innovation and Technology Deputy Chief Executive, Barbara Lavernos
Chief Financial Officer, Christophe Babule
Travel Retail President, Vincent Boinay
Luxe President, Cyril Chapuy
Active Cosmetics President, Dermatological Beauty President, Myriam Cohen-Welgryn
Europe Zone President, Vianney Derville
Chief Digital and Marketing Officer, Asmita Dubey
North America President, David Greenberg
Professional Products President, Omar Hajeri
Chief Corporate Affairs and Engagement Officer, Blanca Juti
Chief Human Relations Officer, Jean-Claude Le Grand
North Asia Zone President, Fabrice Megarbane
Chief Corporate Sustainability Officer, Alexandra Palt
Consumer Products President, Alexis Perakis Valat
Latin America Zone President, Ersi Pirishi
Chief Global Growth Officer, Frederic Roze
South Asia Pacific, Middle East and North Africa Zones President, Vismay Sharma
Chief Operating Officer, Antoine Vanlaeys
Vice-Chairwoman, Director, Francoise Bettencourt Meyers
Vice-Chairman, Director, Paul Bulcke
Independent Director, Sophie Bellon
Independent Director, Patrice Caine
Independent Director, Fabienne Dulac
Independent Director, Belen Garijo
Independent Director, Ilham Kadri
Independent Director, Virginie Morgon
Independent Director, Alexandre Ricard
Director, Jean-Victor Meyers
Director, Nicolas Meyers
Director, Beatrice Guillaume-Grabisch
Director, Thierry Hamel
Director, Benny de Vlieger
Auditors : Deloitte & Associes

LOCATIONS
HQ: L'Oreal S.A. (France)
   41, rue Martre, Clichy Cedex 92117
Phone: (33) 1 47 56 70 00
Web: www.loreal.com

HISTORICAL FINANCIALS
Company Type: Public

Income Statement — FYE: December 31

	REVENUE ($mil)	NET INCOME ($mil)	NET PROFIT MARGIN	EMPLOYEES
12/22	40,864	6,094	14.9%	87,369
12/21	36,545	5,203	14.2%	85,412
12/20	34,354	4,373	12.7%	85,392
12/19	33,541	4,210	12.6%	87,974
12/18	30,848	4,460	14.5%	85,000
Annual Growth	7.3%	8.1%	—	0.7%

2022 Year-End Financials
Debt ratio: 9.2%
Return on equity: 22.4%
Cash ($ mil.): 2,795
Current Ratio: 1.02
Long-term debt ($ mil.): 3,222
No. of shares ($ mil.): 535
Dividends
  Yield: —
  Payout: 8.8%
Market value ($ mil.): 38,129

	STOCK PRICE ($) FY Close	P/E High/Low	PER SHARE ($) Earnings	Dividends	Book Value
12/22	71.25	9 6	11.33	1.00	54.24
12/21	95.42	12 8	9.29	1.83	49.86
12/20	76.15	12 8	7.78	0.87	63.56
12/19	58.87	9 7	7.48	0.86	59.18
12/18	45.66	7 6	7.92	0.86	55.11
Annual Growth	11.8%	—	9.4%	4.0%	(0.4%)

Larsen & Toubro Ltd

EXECUTIVES

Independent Non-Executive Director, Thomas Mathew T.
Auditors: Deloitte Haskins & Sells LLP

LOCATIONS

HQ: Larsen & Toubro Ltd
L&T House, Ballard Estate, Mumbai 400 001
Phone: (91) 22 6752 5656   **Fax:** (91) 22 6752 5893
Web: www.larsentoubro.com

HISTORICAL FINANCIALS

Company Type: Public

Income Statement				FYE: March 31
	REVENUE ($mil)	NET INCOME ($mil)	NET PROFIT MARGIN	EMPLOYEES
03/22	20,663	1,144	5.5%	50,267
03/21	18,584	1,583	8.5%	40,527
03/20	19,256	1,264	6.6%	45,467
03/19	20,378	1,286	6.3%	44,761
03/18	18,423	1,132	6.1%	42,924
Annual Growth	2.9%	0.3%	—	4.0%

2022 Year-End Financials
Debt ratio: 0.5%
Return on equity: 10.9%
Cash ($ mil.): 2,502
Current Ratio: 1.30
Long-term debt ($ mil.): 8,134
No. of shares ($ mil.): 1,405
Dividends
  Yield: —
  Payout: 35.6%
Market value ($ mil.): —

Laurentian Bank of Canada

Laurentian Bank of Canada is a financial institution that operates mainly across Canada. The bank caters for the needs of retail clients via its branch network based in Quebec. The bank stands out for its expertise among small and medium-sized enterprises and real estate developers owing to specialized teams across Canada. Its subsidiary, B2B Bank one of the major Canadian leaders in providing banking products and services investment accounts through financial advisors and brokers. Laurentian Banks Securities offers integrated brokerage services to clientele of institutional and retail investors. The banks line of business are Retail Services, Business Services, B2B Bank, Laurentian Bank Securities and Capital Markets and more.

EXECUTIVES

Chief Executive Officer, President, Executive Director, Rania Llewellyn
Chief Risk Officer, Executive Vice President, William Mason
Commercial Banking Executive Vice President, Eric Provost
Operations Executive Vice President, Yves Denomme
Executive Vice President, Chief Information Technology Officer, Beel Yaqub
Executive Vice President, Chief Human Resources Officer, Sebastian Belair
Executive Vice President, Chief Financial Officer, Yvan Deschamps
Capital Markets Executive Vice President, Kelsey Gunderson
Executive Vice President, Karine Abgrall-Teslyk
Chairman, Corporate Director, Michael Mueller
Corporate Director, Suzanne Gouin
Corporate Director, Sonia Baxendale
Corporate Director, Michael T. Boychuk
Corporate Director, Andrea Bolger
Corporate Director, David Morris
Corporate Director, David Mowat
Corporate Director, Michelle R. Savoy
Corporate Director, Susan Wolburgh Jenah
Corporate Director, Nicholas Zelenczuk
Auditors: Ernst & Young LLP

LOCATIONS

HQ: Laurentian Bank of Canada
1360 RenÃ©-LÃ©vesque Blvd. West, Suite 600, Montreal, Quebec H3G 0E5
Phone: —
Web: www.lbcfg.ca

2013 Loans

	% of total
Québec	60
Ontario	29
Rest of Canada	11
Total	100

PRODUCTS/OPERATIONS

2016 Revenue

	% of total
Interest income:	
loans	71
securities	2
Other, including derivatives	4
Other income:	
Fees and commissions on loans and deposits	10
Income from brokerage operations	5
Income from sales of mutual funds	3
Income from investment accounts	2
Insurance income, net	1
Income from treasury and financial market operations	1
Other	1
Total	100

2016 Loans

	% of total
Residential mortgage	71
Personal	29
Total	100

Selected Subsidiaries
B2B Bank
Laurentian Bank Securities Inc.
Laurentian Trust of Canada Inc.
LBC Financial Services Inc.
LBC Investment Management Inc.
LBC Trust
V.R. Holding Insurance Holding Company Ltd.

COMPETITORS

BOKF MERGER CORPORATION NUMBER SIXTEEN
CITY HOLDING COMPANY
COMMERCE BANCSHARES, INC.
FINANCIAL INSTITUTIONS, INC.
FIRST BUSINESS FINANCIAL SERVICES, INC.
HSBC Bank Canada
M&T BANK CORPORATION
TD BANK, N.A.
UMB FINANCIAL CORPORATION
WSFS FINANCIAL CORPORATION

HISTORICAL FINANCIALS

Company Type: Public

Income Statement				FYE: October 31
	ASSETS ($mil)	NET INCOME ($mil)	INCOME AS % OF ASSETS	EMPLOYEES
10/22	37,114	165	0.4%	3,000
10/21	36,491	46	0.1%	2,871
10/20	33,202	85	0.3%	3,048
10/19	33,672	131	0.4%	3,256
10/18	34,952	171	0.5%	3,642
Annual Growth	1.5%	(0.8%)	—	(4.7%)

2022 Year-End Financials
Return on assets: 0.4%
Return on equity: 8.3%
Long-term debt ($ mil.): —
No. of shares ($ mil.): 43
Sales ($ mil.): 1,299
Dividends
  Yield: —
  Payout: 35.9%
Market value ($ mil.): 888

	STOCK PRICE ($) FY Close	P/E High/Low		PER SHARE ($) Earnings	Dividends	Book Value
10/22	20.50	7	4	3.62	1.30	46.97
10/21	33.92	36	21	0.83	1.30	49.05
10/20	19.82	15	8	1.78	1.61	45.40
10/19	34.32	9	7	2.86	1.99	45.73
10/18	31.86	9	6	3.88	1.93	45.18
Annual Growth	(10.4%)	—	—	(1.7%)	(9.4%)	1.0%

Legal & General Group PLC

Legal & General Group (L&G) is one of the UK's largest financial services companies. The company operates across four broad business areas of retirement, investment management, capital investment and insurance through its subsidiaries and associates in the UK, the US and other countries around the world. With approximately Â£1.4 trillion assets under management, L&G's pensions business offers annuity contracts, longevity insurance contracts, lifetime mortgages, retirement interest only mortgages, and life time care plan. The UK's top life insurer operates in the US as Banner Life Insurance Company and William Penn Life Insurance Company of New York.

Operations

L&G divides its operations into four business segments, namely Legal & General Retirement (LGR), Legal & General Investment Management (LGIM), Legal & General Insurance (LGI), and Legal & General Capital (LGC).

LGIM generates about 80% of L&G's revenue and offers a range of pooled index funds, fixed income funds, and defined benefit pension scheme de-risking.

LGR, accounting for approximately 15% of the company's revenue, serves institutional and retail clients. It provides annuities, defined benefit pension scheme buy-ins and buyouts, lifetime mortgages, and longevity insurance.

LGC and LGI bring in about 10% of revenue combined. LGC makes capital investments in housing, urban regeneration, clean energy, and SME finance (including venture capital). LGI offers life insurance in the UK and US.

All in, L&G has more than Â£1.4 trillion in assets under management, making it the largest investment manager in the UK.

Geographic Reach
Based in the UK, L&G operates throughout North America, Asia Pacific, Europe and some other countries worldwide.

Sales and Marketing
L&G serves more than 9 million individual customers.

Financial Performance
The company's revenue for fiscal 2021 decreased to Â£45.3 billion compared from the prior year with Â£50.3 billion.

Net income for fiscal 2021 increased to Â£2.0 billion compared from the prior year with Â£1.6 billion.

Cash held by the company at the end of fiscal 2021 decreased to Â£16.5 billion. Cash provided by investing activities was Â£133 million while cash used for operations and financing activities were Â£169 million and Â£1.5 billion, respectively.

Strategy
Six long-term, global growth drivers shape its world and its markets. L&G's respond to these drivers through its strategic priorities:

Ageing demographics: the company aim to build a truly global asset management business, entering new markets and expanding its existing operations.

Globalization of asset markets: L&G aim to build a truly global asset management business, entering new markets and expanding its existing operations.

Investing in the real economy: By investing capital over the long term, the company aim to become leaders in direct investments whilst benefitting society through socially responsible investments.

Welfare reforms: the company want to help people take responsibility for their own financial security through insurance, pensions and savings.

Technological innovation: Technology and innovative solutions improve customers' lives and increase efficiency. The company aim to be market leaders in the digital provision of insurance and other financial solutions.

Addressing climate change: L&G are able to support the fight against climate catastrophe through the positioning of its own investments, L&G's influence as one of the world's largest asset managers and managing its own operational footprint.

HISTORY

The Legal in Legal & General's name comes from its founding mission -- to provide life insurance to members of the legal profession. The company was started in 1836 by six lawyers as the Legal & General Life Assurance Society; its first customer, solicitor Thomas Smith, ill-manneredly died four years later after paying less than 200 pounds on a 1,000-pound policy.

Throughout that century and into the next, the company made loans to individuals and corporations; it also moved into real estate. After struggling under claims during WWI and the 1918 flu pandemic, it moved into fire and accident coverage in 1920. It opened membership to nonlawyers in 1929. The company took over the UK operations of the US firm Metropolitan Life (MetLife) in 1933.

In 1934 Legal & General bought Gresham Life Assurance and Gresham Fire and Accident, to gain a presence in Australia. During WWII the company was hit hard by German air attacks, both physically (it had to relocate away from London for a time) and at the bottom line.

The postwar years were a time of expansion as the company moved into South Africa and also broadened its operations at home. In 1949 it moved into marine insurance and in 1956 inaugurated life insurance in Australia.

The company began expanding its product offerings in the 1970s with managed pension funds and retail unit trusts. It established a direct sales force for life and pensions in 1977. The company also formed alliances with several European insurance companies and sold its Gresham life subsidiary. In 1979 it formed Legal & General Group Limited as a holding company for its now-separate insurance, international, and investment management operations.

In 1981 Legal & General bought US auto insurer GEICO's two-thirds interest in Government Employees Life Insurance Company, changing the subsidiary's name to Banner Life. Three years later it bought the Dutch operations of Unilife Assurance and created a subsidiary in the Netherlands. Despite all this activity, however, the company's performance during the 1980s was poor, and it brought in David Prosser (who became CEO in 1991) to goose its asset management operations.

In 1989 the company bought William Penn Life Insurance from Continental Corp. and opened its first real estate agency -- just in time for the real estate market crash. Legal & General and other mortgage guarantee insurers were also squeezed by the resulting increase in mortgage default rates as homebuyers were caught between high interest rates and high unemployment.

The company formed a joint venture with Woolwich Building Society to provide Woolwich customers with insurance products in 1995. The next year it followed the insurance industry trend by establishing a bank of its own.

With each succeeding merger of its rivals, Legal & General became the target of rumors about its own fate. The company has remained adamantly independent, with Prosser claiming that Legal & General could instead benefit by picking up business left behind by the new entities.

In 1998 the British insurance industry was stung by scandalous revelations regarding improper pension sales in the late 1980s and early 1990s. Legal & General set aside about $1 billion to compensate victims; it also sold its Australian operations. In 1999 banking company National Westminster and Legal & General talked takeover, but the deal fell through. (NatWest was eventually bought by Royal Bank of Scotland.)

In 2001 Legal & General announced a deal with UK-based Barclays to provide the bank's customers with life insurance and pension products. In 2002 Legal & General extended its marketing agreement with UK financial services company Alliance & Leicester.

The company then discontinued its health insurance offerings and reduced its venture capital investment operations. In 2005, the company sold its Gresham Insurance subsidiary to Barclays Bank.

EXECUTIVES

Chief Executive Officer, Executive Director, Nigel D. Wilson

Chief Financial Officer, Executive Director, Stuart Jeffrey Davies

Corporate Affairs Director, John Godfrey

Human Resources Director, Emma Hardaker-Jones

Chief Risk Officer, Chris Knight

Chief Internal Auditor, Stephen Licence

Secretary, General Counsel, Geoffrey J. Timms

Chairman, John Oliver Frank Kingman

Senior Independent Non-Executive Director, Philip Broadley

Independent Non-Executive Director, Henrietta Baldock

Independent Non-Executive Director, Nilufer von Bismarck

Independent Non-Executive Director, Carolyn Johnson

Independent Non-Executive Director, Lesley Knox

Independent Non-Executive Director, Tushar Morzaria

Independent Non-Executive Director, George R. Lewis

Independent Non-Executive Director, Ric Lewis

Independent Non-Executive Director, Tushar Morzaria

Independent Non-Executive Director, Laura Wade-Gery

Auditors : KPMG LLP

LOCATIONS

HQ: Legal & General Group PLC
One Coleman Street, London EC2R 5AA
Phone: (44) 20 3124 2000   Fax: (44) 20 3124 2500
Web: www.legalandgeneralgroup.com

PRODUCTS/OPERATIONS

2018 operating profit

	%
LGR (Retirement)	
LGR Retail	44
LGR Institutional	16
LGIM (Investment Management)	16
LGI (Insurance)	12
LGC (Capital)	12
Total	100

Selected Subsidiaries

Banner Life Insurance Company Inc - long-term business; US
First British American Reinsurance Company II - reinsurance; US
First British Bermudan Reinsurance Company II Limited - reinsurance; Bermuda
First British Vermont Reinsurance Company II - reinsurance; US
First British Vermont Reinsurance Company - reinsurance; US
Legal & General (France) SA - long-term business
Legal & General (Portfolio Management Services) Limited - institutional fund management
Legal & General (Unit Trust Managers) Limited - unit trust management
Legal & General Assurance (Pensions Management) Limited - long-term business
Legal & General Assurance Society Limited - long-term and general insurance
Legal & General Bank (France) SA - financial services
Legal & General Finance PLC1 - treasury operations
Legal & General Insurance Limited - general insurance
Legal & General International (Ireland) Limited - long-term business
Legal & General Investment Management America Inc - institutional fund management
Legal & General Investment Management Limited - institutional fund management
Legal & General Nederland Levensverzekering Maatschappij NV - long-term business; Netherlands
Legal & General Partnership Services Limited - provision of services
Legal & General Pensions Limited - reinsurance
Legal & General Property Limited - property management
Legal & General Resources Limited1 - provision of services
Legal & General Risques Divers (France) SA - insurance company
LGV Capital Limited - private equity
Nationwide Life Limited - long-term business
Suffolk Life Annuities Limited - long-term business
Suffolk Life Pensions Limited - long-term business
William Penn Life Insurance Company of New York Inc - long-term business; US

COMPETITORS

E. SUN FINANCIAL HOLDING COMPANY, LTD.
LINCOLN NATIONAL CORPORATION
LIONTRUST ASSET MANAGEMENT PLC
LLOYDS BANKING GROUP PLC
MITSUBISHI UFJ FINANCIAL GROUP, INC.
MIZUHO FINANCIAL GROUP, INC.
STANDARD LIFE ABERDEEN PLC
THE HARTFORD FINANCIAL SERVICES GROUP, INC.
TP ICAP LIMITED
VIRGIN MONEY HOLDINGS (UK) PLC

HISTORICAL FINANCIALS

Company Type: Public

Income Statement
FYE: December 31

	ASSETS ($mil)	NET INCOME ($mil)	INCOME AS % OF ASSETS	EMPLOYEES
12/23	665,404	582	0.1%	0
12/22	617,895	2,757	0.4%	11,498
12/21	785,210	2,762	0.4%	10,741
12/20	778,655	2,193	0.3%	10,046
12/19	740,316	2,421	0.3%	8,542
Annual Growth	(2.6%)	(30.0%)	—	—

2023 Year-End Financials

Return on assets: —   Dividends
Return on equity: 5.3%   Yield: —
Long-term debt ($ mil.): —   Payout: 1244.3%
No. of shares ($ mil.): 5,917   Market value ($ mil.): 96,809
Sales ($ mil.): 50,657

	STOCK PRICE ($) FY Close	P/E High/Low		PER SHARE ($) Earnings	Dividends	Book Value
12/23	16.36	231	179	0.09	1.15	1.04
12/22	15.11	50	32	0.44	0.99	2.48
12/21	20.62	60	48	0.44	1.19	2.50
12/20	18.42	81	35	0.35	1.05	2.30
12/19	20.29	68	46	0.41	0.99	2.08
Annual Growth	(5.2%)	—	—	(30.9%)	3.8%	(16.0%)

Lenovo Group Ltd

Lenovo Group serves millions of customers in about 180 markets. The company is a leading company in the PC market expanding to infrastructure, mobile, solutions, and services. Through a series of acquisitions, the Hong Kong-based company is focused on a bold vision to deliver smarter technology for all. Besides ThinkPad-branded commercial PCs, Lenovo turns out tablets, and software. Its sales are evenly sourced from the major world markets of China, Asia Pacific, America, and Europe-Middle East-Africa (EMEA).

Operations

Lenovo group's operations are segmented to Intelligent Devices Group (IDG), Infrastructure Solutions Group (ISG) and Solutions and Services Group (SSG).

The IDG, which accounts for about 75% of the company's revenue, consists of the PC, tablet, smartphone, and other smart device businesses of the company. The ISG (about 20%) is one of the world's fastest-growing infrastructure solution providers. Lastly, the SSG offers services, which includes digital workplace, hybrid cloud and sustainability services, while protecting its core business with product-related services.

Geographic Reach

Lenovo Group operates in over 180 markets across the Americas, Asia Pacific, and the EMEA. Americas account for about 35% of the company's revenue, followed by China and the EMEA region, which accounts for about 25% each.

Sales and Marketing

The company sold less than 20% of its goods and services to its five largest customers. The company spent $1.1 billion and $815.8 million, respectively, for advertising and promotional expenses.

Financial Performance

Lenovo group's performance for the past five years has fluctuated with a decrease from 2022 to 2023, as its second highest performing year over the period.

The company's revenue decreased by $9.7 billion to $61.9 billion for 2023, as compared to 2022's revenue of $71.6 billion.

Lenovo's net profit decreased to $1.6 billion for fiscal year end 2023, as compared to the prior year's net profit of $2.0 billion.

About $232.8 million was held by the end of the year. Operating activities generated $89 million to the coffers. Investing activities and financing activities used $48.8 billion and $5.0 billion, respectively.

Strategy

Lenovo continues to be a leader and enabler of Intelligent Transformation, helping clients navigate a more complex world through smarter technology for all. Strong innovation, which goes hand-inhand with the pursuit of profitability growth, will further elevate the company's competitiveness in next-generation product design and solutions.

Mergers and Acquisitions

In the last two years Lenovo has made acquisitions to beef up its hardware offerings and support expansion in select markets. In 2014 it paid more than $5 billion to acquire two new major product lines. First it bought IBM's low-end x86 server business for $2.3 billion.

Also in 2014, Lenovo spent some $2.9 billion for Motorola Mobility from Google. As part of the deal, Lenovo owns the brands Moto X, Moto G, and the DROID Ultra series, while Google retained the patent portfolio.

Company Background

Liu Chuanzhi, an engineer at the Chinese Academy of Sciences who wrote industry research reports, established Legend Group Holdings Co. in 1984 in Beijing. Backed by a modest investment from the academy, Liu, who went on to become something of an entrepreneurial hero in China, and 10 other engineers were given a green light to form a retail business. They first bought and sold items ranging from TVs to roller skates, but later focused on distributing computer products and eventually moved into manufacturing PCs for AST Research. Legend introduced its first proprietary product, a Chinese character system for PCs, in 1985.

In 1988 the company formed Legend Holdings Limited, which was originally a Hong Kong-based PC distributor. The following year the parent company began designing and manufacturing motherboards and added systems integration services to its offerings. In 1990 China reduced import

HISTORY

Liu Chuanzhi, an engineer at the Chinese Academy of Sciences who wrote industry research reports, established Legend Group Holdings Co. in 1984 in Beijing. Backed by a modest investment from the academy, Liu, who went on to become something of an entrepreneurial hero in China, and 10 other engineers were given a green light to form a retail business. They first bought and sold items ranging from TVs to roller skates, but later focused on distributing computer products and eventually moved into manufacturing PCs for AST Research. Legend introduced its first proprietary product, a Chinese character system for PCs, in 1985.

In 1988 the company formed Legend Holdings Limited, which was originally a Hong Kong-based PC distributor. The following year the parent company began designing and manufacturing motherboards and added systems integration services to its offerings. In 1990 China reduced import tariffs, a move that opened the trade door for companies such as IBM and Compaq. That year Legend Group Holdings began making its own brand of PCs.

Legend Holdings went public in 1994, and the following year began absorbing operations from its parent company, which retained approximately 60% ownership in the subsidiary. By 1996 it was tied with IBM for PC market share in China; it became the country's top brand the following year.

In 1998 parent company Legend Group Holdings transferred Beijing Legend Group to its Hong Kong-based subsidiary. The following year Microsoft, looking to extend its operating system dominance into China, teamed up with Legend Holdings to create set-top boxes. In 2000 the company partnered with Pacific Century CyberWorks to provide broadband Internet services. The following year Legend spun off its distribution business, Digital China, as a separate public company. In 2001 Yang Yuanqing was named CEO of the company.

In 2002 Legend Holdings changed its English company name to Legend Group Limited. The company launched a corporate brand, Lenovo, the following year, and in 2004 it officially adopted Lenovo as its English name. It also sold its non-telecom IT services business to AsiaInfo Holdings, renamed AsiaInfo-Linkage, in 2004.

Lenovo acquired IBM's worldwide PC operations for approximately $1.75 billion in 2005. IBM executive Stephen Ward was named CEO of Lenovo at the time of the merger, but he was replaced by William Amelio before year's end. Amelio headed Dell's Asia/Pacific operations before joining Lenovo. In 2006 Lenovo launched a unit called Lenovo Services.

In 2007 Lenovo stopped using the IBM PC brand, to which it still held the rights, and began offering only Lenovo-branded machines. The following year it sponsored and supported the Olympic Summer Games in Beijing, providing more than 30,000 pieces of equipment and 600 engineers.

Looking to focus on its core PC operations, Lenovo sold its mobile phone business, Lenovo Mobile Communications, to Hony Capital in 2008. Hony, the private equity arm of Legend Holdings, paid $100 million for the unit.

A year later Lenovo bought back the mobile communications business for about $200 million in cash and stock. The company cited the growth of the mobile Internet market and the increasing convergence between the PC and wireless handset sectors for the about-face in product strategy. Lenovo's move came as Dell introduced a mobile phone for the Chinese market.

Citing a flagging economy, Lenovo announced a restructuring plan in 2009 that included a workforce reduction of 11%, executive pay cuts, and the consolidation of its China and the Asia/Pacific units. The company also initiated a management shakeup, including its chairman taking over as CEO. The change may in part have reflected a strategy shift for Lenovo. With corporate spending flagging, particularly in the US, the company planned to focus on China and other emerging markets, with an emphasis on consumers.

EXECUTIVES

Chairman, Chief Executive Officer, Director, Yuanqing Yang
President, Chief Operating Officer, Rory P. Read
Global Services Senior Vice President, Peter Bartolotta
Emerging Markets Senior Vice President, Emerging Markets President, Shaopeng Chen
Office of Operations Senior Vice President, Robert Cones
Human Resources Senior Vice President, Kenneth DiPietro
Senior Vice President, Chief Technology Officer, Zhiqiang He
Product Groups Senior Vice President, Product Groups President, Jun Liu
Senior Vice President, Yan Lu
Senior Vice President, General Counsel, Michael O'Neill
Senior Vice President, Chief Procurement Officer, Song Qiao
Senior Vice President, Chief Marketing Officer, David Roman
Senior Vice President, David Schmoock
Global Supply Chain Senior Vice President, Gerry Smith
Mature Markets Senior Vice President, Milko van Duijl
Senior Vice President, Chief Information Officer, Xiaoyan Wang
Senior Vice President, Chief Financial Officer, Wai Ming Wong
Planning Vice President, Corporate Strategy Vice President, Jian Qiao
Secretary, Chung Fu Mok
Vice-Chairman, Xuezheng Ma
Director, Linan Zhu
Director, James G. Coulter
Director, William O. Grabe
Director, Yibing Wu
Director, Chia-Wei Woo
Director, Lee Sen Ting
Director, Suning Tian
Director, Nicholas Charles Allen
Auditors : PricewaterhouseCoopers

LOCATIONS

HQ: Lenovo Group Ltd
23rd Floor, Lincoln House, Taikoo Place, 979 King's Road, Quarry Bay,
Phone: (852) 2590 0228   **Fax:** (852) 2516 5384
Web: www.lenovo.com

2018 Sales

	$ mil.	% of total
Americas (AG)	16,413.5	31
Europe, Middle east & Africa (EMEA)	12,502.5	28
China	12,357.5	25
Asia Pacific (AP)	9,764.4	16
Total	51,037.9	100

PRODUCTS/OPERATIONS

2019 Sales

	% of total
Personal Computers & Smart Devices	75
Mobile Business	13
Data Center Group	12
Total	100

Product Categories
Laptops
Desktops & All-in-Ones
Smartphones
Tablet PCs
Network Storage
Workstations
Accessories & Upgrades

COMPETITORS

AGILYSYS, INC.
ARROW ELECTRONICS, INC.
Acer Incorporated
COMPUCOM SYSTEMS, INC.
DELL TECHNOLOGIES INC.
FLEX LTD.
SCANSOURCE, INC.
SPEED COMMERCE, INC.
TECH DATA CORPORATION
Telefon AB LM Ericsson

HISTORICAL FINANCIALS

Company Type: Public

Income Statement   FYE: March 31

	REVENUE ($mil)	NET INCOME ($mil)	NET PROFIT MARGIN	EMPLOYEES
03/23	61,946	1,607	2.6%	77,000
03/22	71,618	2,029	2.8%	75,000
03/21	60,742	1,178	1.9%	71,500
03/20	50,716	665	1.3%	63,000
03/19	51,037	596	1.2%	57,000
Annual Growth	5.0%	28.1%	—	7.8%

2023 Year-End Financials

Debt ratio: 10.2%   No. of shares ($ mil.): 12,128
Return on equity: 32.0%   Dividends
Cash ($ mil.): 4,250   Yield: 4.3%
Current Ratio: 0.88   Payout: 730.2%
Long-term debt ($ mil.): 3,683   Market value ($ mil.): 260,270

	STOCK PRICE ($) FY Close	P/E High/Low	PER SHARE ($) Earnings	Dividends	Book Value
03/23	21.46	171 101	0.13	0.93	0.46
03/22	21.37	183 104	0.16	0.78	0.37
03/21	28.58	300 107	0.09	0.68	0.23
03/20	10.71	341 171	0.05	0.68	0.20
03/19	17.99	370 182	0.05	0.64	0.22
Annual Growth	4.5%	—	26.6%	10.0%	20.4%

Lewis (John) Partnership Plc

Diversified retailer John Lewis Partnership (JLP) is Britain's greatest purveyor of the middle-class lifestyle. JLP operates two major upmarket retail businesses: John Lewis, the department store chain that provides homeware, clothing, and electronics; and Waitrose, one of the UK's largest supermarket chains. The company operates about 35 John Lewis shops plus one outlet across the UK and about 330 Waitrose branches. John Lewis operates an e-commerce site, while Waitrose partners carry out online grocery service. The largest employee-owned business in the UK and amongst the largest in the world is owned in Trust by more than 74,000 partners. In addition, the retailer's omnichannel business also includes specialist online shops including waitrosecellar.com for wine and waitroseflorist.com for plants and flowers.

Operations

JLP operates through its two cherished retail brands - Waitrose and John Lewis. Through its retail brands, the company is enabling customers to shop the way they want with expert advice, brilliantly edited choices, and truly memorable experiences.

Waitrose (accounts for about 65% of the company's revenue) primarily markets and distributes grocery products including food, drink, household and other items. Waitrose also operates Waitrose farm which is part of the Leckford Estate in Hampshire. Leckford Farm produces arable crops including high-quality bread-making wheat which is used to make a range of Leckford label flour, as well as apples, pears, apple juice, cider, free-range eggs, chestnut mushrooms, and free range chickens to Waitrose shops.

John Lewis (some 35%) primarily markets and distributes home products such as products for bedrooms, living rooms, bathrooms, dining rooms, kitchens, home offices, laundry and utility rooms, and hallway gardens. It also sells home appliances and other electronics and gadgets such as televisions, soundbars, speakers, headphones, computers, monitors, IPads, tablets, projectors, printers, mobile phones, cameras, and fitness equipment, among others. Additionally, it also offers men, women, and kids apparel and accessories such as footwear, cashmere, coats, jackets, jeans, jumpers, cardigans, loungewear, handbags, bags, belts, hats, luggage, and more. Through John Lewis Finance, the company also offer a range of financial products from home insurance to foreign currency and its credit card, the Partnership Card.

The company's goods are split into four product lines: grocery (about 65% of the company's revenue), technology (nearly 15%), fashion (more than 10%), and home (about 10%). Services include free warranties on selected goods, which accounts for the rest of the revenue.

Geographic Reach

London-based, JLP operates about 35 John Lewis shops plus one outlet across the UK as well as johnlewis.com, and about 330 Waitrose shops in England, Scotland, Wales and The Channel Islands, including about 60 convenience branches, and another more than 25 shops at Welcome Break locations.

Sales and Marketing

The company primarily sells its products through its shops, online, and through its app. It has about 2.7 million ANYDAY customers. Its Waitrose business serves nearly a million customers annually. It also offers MyWaitrose loyalty program, which has about nine million members.

Financial Performance

Company's revenue for the past five fiscal years experienced increases and decreases starting from GBP 10.3 billion in 2019 to GBP 10.2 billion, GBP 10.8 billion, GBP 10.8 billion, and GBP 10.5 billion, for fiscal 2020 to 2023, respectively.

John Lewis' revenue for fiscal 2023 decreased to GBP 10.5 billion compared from the prior year with GBP 10.8 billion. The decrease was primarily due to lower revenues on every goods revenues aside from fashion sales.

Net loss for fiscal 2023 increased to GBP 197.6 million compared from the prior year with GBP 67.8 million. The increase in losses was primarily due to lower revenues offsetting the decrease in expenses.

Cash held by the company at the end of fiscal 2023 decreased to GBP1.0 billion. Cash provided by operations was GBP180.0 million while cash used for investing and financing activities were GBP242.8 million and GBP314.5 million, respectively. Main uses of cash were for purchase of property, plant and equipment; and payment of capital element of leases.

Company Background

Founded in 1864 by John Lewis, JLP became a partnership in 1929 when Lewis' son, Spedan, created a trust to own the company. All of the company's 85,500 employees (called partners) are beneficiaries of the trust and as such receive unique perks, as well as a share of the profits. A system of committees and councils, made up of partners, vote to determine the company's direction -- and trustees. The Leckford Farm, which supplies Waitrose supermarkets, is also available for partners to use as a retreat.

EXECUTIVES

Executive Chairman, Sharon E. White
Operations Director, Executive Director, Andrew Murphy
People Director, Executive Director, Tracey Killen
Partnership Services Financial Director, Executive Director, Patrick Lewis
Customer Service Director, Executive Director, Berangere Michel
Strategy & Commercial Development Director, Executive Director, Nina Bhatia
Secretary, Peter Simpson
Deputy Chairman, Non-Executive Director, Keith Williams
Non-Executive Director, Laura Wade-Gery
Non-Executive Director, Andy Martin
Director, Becky Wollam
Director, Ollie Killinger
Director, Nicky Spurgeon
Independent Non-Executive Director, Zarin Patel
Independent Non-Executive Director, Sharon L. Rolston
Auditors : KPMG LLP

LOCATIONS

HQ: Lewis (John) Partnership Plc
171 Victoria Street, London SW1E 5NN
Phone: (44) 207 828 1000
Web: www.johnlewispartnership.co.uk

PRODUCTS/OPERATIONS

2013 Stores

	No.
Waitrose supermarkets	255
Waitrose convenience	35
John Lewis department stores	30
John Lewis at home	9
Total	329

2013 Sales

	% of total
Waitrose	64
John Lewis	36
Total	100

Selected Subsidiaries

Greenbee (travel, leisure, and financial services)
Herbert Parkinson Limited (weaving and making up)
JLP Holdings BV (investment holding company, Holland)
JLP Insurance Limited (insurance, Guernsey)
JPL Scottish Limited Partnership (investment holding undertaking)
JPL Scottish Partnership (investment holding undertaking)
JLP Victoria Limited (investment holding company)
John Lewis Properties plc (property holding company)
Waitrose Limited (food retailing)
Waitrose (Guernsey) Limited (food retailing, Guernsey)
Waitrose (Jersey) Limited (food retailing, Jersey)

COMPETITORS

BI-MART CORPORATION
BJ'S WHOLESALE CLUB HOLDINGS, INC.
BJ'S WHOLESALE CLUB, INC.
COSTCO WHOLESALE CORPORATION
POUNDLAND LIMITED
SAM'S WEST, INC.
TESCO PLC
WAITROSE LIMITED
WH SMITH PLC
WM MORRISON SUPERMARKETS P L C

HISTORICAL FINANCIALS

Company Type: Public

Income Statement — FYE: January 29

	REVENUE ($mil)	NET INCOME ($mil)	NET PROFIT MARGIN	EMPLOYEES
01/22	14,510	(90)	—	78,600
01/21	14,769	(619)	—	80,900
01/20	13,286	141	1.1%	80,800
01/19	13,507	101	0.7%	83,900
01/18	14,540	105	0.7%	85,500
Annual Growth	(0.1%)	—		(2.1%)

2022 Year-End Financials

Debt ratio: 14.0%
Return on equity: (-2.9%)
Cash ($ mil.): 1,895
Current Ratio: 1.11
Long-term debt ($ mil.): 859
No. of shares ($ mil.): —
Dividends
Yield: —
Payout: 0.0%
Market value ($ mil.): —

LG Chem Ltd (New)

Founded in 1947, LG Chem is a leading chemical company and one of Korea's leading chemical companies. The company produces a variety of products, including petrochemicals. The Petrochemicals unit makes basic chemicals like ethylene, propylene, and derivatives, as well as PVC, acrylic, and plasticizers. The company's Advanced Materials segment various kinds of IT materials. LG Chem has manufacturing facilities located in Yeosu, Daesan, Ochang, Cheongju, Ulsan, Naju, Iksan, Paju, Osong, Onsan, Gimcheon, and overseas sites. The company went public in 2001, while LG still owns more than a third of LG Chem. China is the company's largest market.

Operations

The company operates through four operating segments:

The Petrochemical business includes production of olefin petrochemicals, such as ethylene, propylene, butadiene from Naphtha, and aromatic petrochemicals such as benzene. It also includes production of synthetic resin and synthetic components from olefin, and aromatic petrochemicals.

LG Energy Solution, Ltd. which was established through the split-off of Energy solution business from the Parent Company on December 1, 2020, and its subsidiaries mainly manufacture and supply batteries ranging from IT & New application batteries for mobile phones and laptop computers, to automotive batteries for electric vehicles and ESS (Energy Storage System) batteries.

The Advanced material business manufactures and supplies various kinds of IT materials such as automotive material, OLED film, semiconductor materials, OLED materials, battery materials and others and RO membranes, which will be the next growth engine for future.

The Life Sciences business manufactures and supplies pharmaceutical products, such as human growth hormone 'Eutropin', diabetes drug 'Zemiglo', bovine somatotropin 'Boostin', hyaluronic acid filler 'YVOIRE' and others, as well as fine chemical products, such as herbicide 'PYANCHOR' for rice farming and others.

Geographic Reach

Headquartered in Seoul, South Korea; LG Chem has its manufacturing facilities in Yeosu, Daesan, Ochang, Cheongju, Ulsan, Naju, Iksan, Paju, Osong, Onsan, Gimcheon and overseas sites.

Financial Performance

LG Chem's revenue for fiscal 2022 increased to KRW57.1 trillion compared to the prior year with KRW44.9 trillion. The increase was primarily due to higher revenues on every segment especially on its LG energy solutions segments.

Cash held by the company at the end of fiscal 2022 increased to KRW8.5 trillion. Cash provided by operations and financing activities were KRW569.9 billion and KRW13.3 trillion, respectively. Cash used for investing activities was KRW9.2 trillion, mainly for decrease in other receivables.

EXECUTIVES

Vice-Chairman, Chief Executive Officer, Peter Bahnsuk Kim
President, Chief Financial Officer, Director, Suk-Jeh Cho
Director, Yu-Sig Kang
Director, Ho-Soo Oh
Director, Seung-Mo Oh
Director, Il-Jin Park
Director, Ki-Myung Nam
Auditors : Samil PricewaterhouseCoopers

LOCATIONS

HQ: LG Chem Ltd (New)
LG Twin Towers, 128 Yeouido-dong, Youngdeungpo-gu, Seoul 07336
Phone: (82) 2 3777 1114   **Fax:** (82) 2 3773 7813

Web: www.lgchem.com

2015 Sales

	% of total
China	33
Korea	32
America	6
Southeast Asia	20
Western Europe	8
Other	1
Total	100

PRODUCTS/OPERATIONS

2015 Sales

	% of total
Basic materials and chemicals	71
Information Technology & Electronic Materials	11
Energy Solution	16
Advance Material	2
total	100

HISTORICAL FINANCIALS

Company Type: Public

Income Statement — FYE: December 31

	REVENUE ($mil)	NET INCOME ($mil)	NET PROFIT MARGIN	EMPLOYEES
12/22	41,372	1,472	3.6%	0
12/21	35,902	3,088	8.6%	0
12/20	27,635	471	1.7%	0
12/19	24,791	271	1.1%	0
12/18	25,278	1,320	5.2%	18,431
Annual Growth	13.1%	2.7%		

2022 Year-End Financials

Debt ratio: —
Return on equity: 6.9%
Cash ($ mil.): 6,778
Current Ratio: 1.80
Long-term debt ($ mil.): 9,465
No. of shares ($ mil.): 70
Dividends
Yield: —
Payout: 0.0%
Market value ($ mil.): —

LG Display Co Ltd

LG Display manufactures TFT-LCD and OLED technology-based display panels in a broad range of sizes and specifications primarily for use in IT products (comprising notebook computers, desktop monitors and tablet computers), televisions and mobile devices, including smartphones, and it is one of the world's leading suppliers of large-sized OLED television panels. It also manufactures display panels for industrial and other applications, including entertainment systems, automotive displays, portable navigation devices and medical diagnostic equipment. LG Electronics is LG Display's biggest shareholder as well as one of its biggest customers. Most of LG Display's sales are made to China.

Operations

LG Display sells through three product categories. The company's biggest product, IT products, accounts for over 40% of revenue. The Television product category supplies more than some 30% of revenue and the Mobile and other provides around 25% of revenue.

The IT products comprise notebook computers (utilizing display panels ranging from 11.6 inches to 17.3 inches in size), desktop monitors (utilizing display panels ranging from 15.6 inches to 49 inches in size) and tablet computers (utilizing display panels ranging from 7.85 inches to 12.9 inches in size).

The Televisions utilize large-sized display panels ranging from 23 inches to 98 inches in size, including "8K" Ultra HD television panels, which have four times the number of pixels compared to conventional HD television panels.

The Mobile and other applications, which utilize a wide array of display panel sizes, including smartphones and other types of mobile phones and industrial and other applications, such as entertainment systems, automotive displays, portable navigation devices and medical diagnostic equipment.

Geographic Reach

Headquartered in Korea, LG Display gets around 65% of revenue from sales to customers in China. Customers in other Asian countries comprise of approximately 10% of revenue, and in Korea, accounts for less than 5% of revenue. The remaining revenues are from customers in the US (about 10%), Europe (about 5%), and Poland (around 5%).

Sales and Marketing

LG Display sells through direct sales to end-brand customers and their system integrators and overseas subsidiaries. The company also sells through its affiliated trading company, LX International (formerly LG International), and its subsidiaries.

Sales to LG Electronics account for around 20% of revenue while LG Display's 10 biggest customers supply a significant majority of its sales.

Advertising expenses for the year ended in 2021 and 2020 were ?193 billion and ?114 billion, respectively.

Financial Performance

The company's revenue increased by 23% from ?24.3 trillion in 2020 to ?29.9 trillion in 2021. The increase in revenue resulted from increases in revenue derived from sales of panels for televisions, IT products and mobile and other applications, which were in turn mainly due to an increase in the number of those panels sold and an increase in the average selling prices of panels for televisions and IT products.

In 2021, the company had a net income of ?1.3 trillion.

The company's cash at the end of 2020 was ?3.5 trillion. Operating activities generated ?5.8 trillion, while investing activities used ?4.3 trillion, mainly for acquisition of property, plant and equipment. Financing activities used another ?2.5 trillion, primarily for repayments of current portion of long-term borrowings and bonds.

Strategy

In connection with its strategy to further enhance the diversity and capacity of its display panel production, the company anticipates that it will continue to incur significant capital expenditures for the construction of new production facilities and the maintenance and enhancement of existing production facilities, particularly in connection with its continued investments in OLED technology. LG's significant recent and pending capital expenditures include:

In August 2021, the company announced plans to make investments in an aggregate amount of up to ?3.3 trillion in a new fabrication facility in Paju, Korea, which would be used for the production of small- to mid-sized OLED panels. The company hasbegun construction in August 2021, which is expected to continue until the first quarter of 2024. The exact completion date is subject to change based on market conditions and any changes to its investment timetable.

In response to and in anticipation of growing demand in the China market, the company established a joint venture with the government of Guangzhou to construct a new fabrication facility to manufacture next generation large-sized OLED panels, which was established under the name of LG Display High-Tech (China) Co., Ltd., in July 2018. The company currently holds a 70% ownership interest in the joint venture and the government of Guangzhou holds the remaining 30% ownership interest. We have invested approximately W6 trillion in capital expenditures for the joint venture and commenced mass production of large-sized OLED panels at such fabrication facility in July 2020.

Company Background

LG Display was formed in 1999 when LG Electronics and Philips merged their LCD businesses. Philips no longer owns any part of LG Display.

EXECUTIVES

President, Chief Financial Officer, Chief Executive Officer, Director, James Ho-Young Jeong
Senior Vice President, Chief Financial Officer, Director, Donghee Suh
Chief Production Officer, Executive Vice President, Mun Shin Sang
Chief Technology Officer, Executive Vice President, Byeong Kang In
Director, Chairman, Young-Soo Kwon
Outside Director, Ho Lee Byoung
Outside Director, Kun Tai Han
Outside Director, Sik Hwang Sung
Outside Director, Yang Lee Chang
Auditors : KPMG Samjong Accounting Corp.

LOCATIONS

HQ: LG Display Co Ltd
  LG Twin Towers, 128 Yeoui-daero, Yeongdeungpo-gu, Seoul 07336
Phone: (82) 2 3777 1010   **Fax:** (82) 2 3777 0793
Web: www.lgdisplay.com

2017 Sales

	% of total
Asia/Pacific	
China	65
Other countries	8
Korea	7
Europe	9
Americas	10
Poland	1
Total	100

PRODUCTS/OPERATIONS

2017 Sales

	% of total
Televisions	42
Desktop monitors	16
Tablet products	9
Notebook computers	8
Mobile and others	25
Total	100

Products Selected

TV Display
Commercial Display
Monitor Display
Notebook Display
Mobile Display
Auto Display
IPS
AIT
Transparent flexible display
3D
OLED Light

COMPETITORS

AU Optronics Corp.
BEL FUSE INC.
BOE Technology Group Co., Ltd.
Infineon Technologies AG
LG Electronics Inc.
RENESAS ELECTRONICS AMERICA INC.
SOITEC
Samsung Electronics Co., Ltd.
TDK CORPORATION
UNIVERSAL DISPLAY CORPORATION

HISTORICAL FINANCIALS

Company Type: Public

Income Statement
FYE: December 31

	REVENUE ($mil)	NET INCOME ($mil)	NET PROFIT MARGIN	EMPLOYEES
12/23	16,428	(2,105)	—	0
12/22	20,861	(2,450)	—	69,656
12/21	25,148	998	4.0%	70,707
12/20	22,263	(82)	—	63,360
12/19	20,331	(2,450)	—	60,429
Annual Growth	(5.2%)			

2023 Year-End Financials

Debt ratio: —   No. of shares ($ mil.): 357
Return on equity: (-31.9%)   Dividends
Cash ($ mil.): 2,436   Yield: —
Current Ratio: 0.68   Payout: 0.0%
Long-term debt ($ mil.): 8,810   Market value ($ mil.): 1,725

	STOCK PRICE ($) FY Close	P/E High/Low		PER SHARE ($) Earnings	Dividends	Book Value
12/23	4.82	—	—	(5.88)	0.00	15.57
12/22	4.96	—	—	(6.85)	0.26	22.03
12/21	10.10	0	0	2.63	0.00	30.86
12/20	8.44	—	—	(0.23)	0.00	29.28
12/19	6.94	—	—	(6.85)	0.00	27.45
Annual Growth	(8.7%)	—	—	—	—	(13.2%)

LG Electronics Inc

LG Electronics is a world-class company with innovative technologies in the fields of electronics and home appliances, making products found in the kitchen, in the media room, and on the go. A leader in consumer electronics, mobile communications, and home appliances, the company operates in more than 140 business sites worldwide that design and make flat panel TVs, audio and video products, mobile handsets, air conditioners, washing machines, refrigerators, and more. About 35% of LG Electronics is owned by South Korea's LG Corp. The majority of its sales were generated from outside its home country, Korea.

Operations

The company operates in six operating segments: Home Appliance & Air Solutions (H&A), Home Entertainment (HE), Innotek, Vehicle Component Solutions (VS), Business Solutions (BS), and Other.

Home Appliances & Air Solutions with some 35% of revenue, manufactures and sells refrigerators, washing machines, vacuum cleaners, and residential and commercial air conditioners. Home Entertainment segment, which accounts for around 25% of revenue, manufactures and sells TVs, audio, beauty appliances, and other products.

Innotek (some 20%) offers camera modules, substrate and material, motor/sensor, and others. Vehicle Component Solutions segment (about 10%) designs and manufactures automobile parts. Business Solutions segment (nearly 10%) manufactures and sells monitors, PCs, information display, solar panels, and others.

Overall, sales of goods account for over 95% of sales.

Geographic Reach

LG Electronics is based in Seoul, South Korea. Approximately 70% of sales were generated in Korea, followed by North America and Asia with about 10% each, and Europe with approximately 5%. Other major markets are China, Middle East & Africa, South America, and Russia and others.

Financial Performance

Company's revenue for fiscal 2021 increased to KRW 74.7 trillion compared from the prior year with KRW 58.1 trillion.

Cash held by the end of fiscal 2021 increased to KRW 6.1 trillion. Cash provided by operations was KRW 2.7 trillion, while cash used for investing and financing activities were KRW 2.5 trillion and KRW 282.3 billion, respectively. Main uses of cash were acquisitions and repayment of borrowings.

Mergers and Acquisitions

In early 2022, LG Electronics acquired TISAX (Trusted Information Security Assessment Exchange), a global information security certification, in all major areas of the electronic devices business to strengthen competitiveness in the automotive parts business. In addition to the security certification, LG Electronics also received TISAX for its vehicle component solutions business' workplace, including LG Science Park in Gangseo-gu, Seoul, and LG Digital Park in Pyeongtaek, Gyeonggi-do. Last year, its ZKW, a subsidiary located in Austria, also obtained this certification.

In late 2021, LG Electronics approved the acquisition of Cybellum, a leading vehicle cybersecurity risk assessment solution provider based in Tel Aviv. The deal allows LG to assume an approximate 64% stake in the tech company valued at $140 million, a strategic move that will enhance LG's cybersecurity capabilities and accelerate its efforts to become an Innovation Partner for Future Mobility.

In early 2021, LG Electronics and Alphonso announced a significant investment by LG in Alphonso to bring together the two TV industry leaders' technologies and innovations to LG's smart TV lineup. With this investment of nearly $80 million, LG will become Alphonso's largest investor with a controlling stake of more than 50%. LG has made understanding customer tastes and consumer trends one of its highest priorities as part of its digital transformation strategy to deliver better customized services. LG plans to utilize Alphonso software and services ? including Alphonso's data analytics, media planning and activation, and Video AI capabilities ? with its broad range of home entertainment products.

EXECUTIVES

Vice-Chairman, Chief Executive Officer, Bon-Joon Koo
Vice-Chairman, Yu-Sig Kang
Digital Display President, Simon Kang
Asia President, Young-Woo Nam
President, Chief Technology Officer, Woo-Hyun Paik
Digital Appliance President, Young-Ha Lee
Vice President, Chief Financial Officer, Director, Do-Hyun Jung
Vice President, Chief Human Resources Officer, Young-Kee Kim
Chief Procurement Officer, Thomas K. Linton
Supply Chain Chief, Didier Chenneveau
Mobile Communications President, Skott Ahn
Europe President, James Kim
North America President, Michael Ahn
South & Central America President, Kyung-Hoon Byun
Korea President, Seong-Won Park
China President, Nam K. Woo
Digital Media President, B.B. Hwang
Director, In-Ki Joo
Director, Gyu-Min Lee
Director, Sang-Hee Kim
Director, Jong-Nam Joo

Auditors: Samil PricewaterhouseCoopers

LOCATIONS

HQ: LG Electronics Inc
LG Twin Towers, 128 Yeouido-dong, Yeongdeungpo-gu, Seoul 07336
Phone: (82) 2 3777 1114   **Fax:** (82) 2 3777 3428
Web: www.lge.com

2017 Sales

	% of total
Korea	33
North America	275
Asia	11
Europe	10
South America	7
Middle East & Africa	5
China	4
Other	3
Total	100

PRODUCTS/OPERATIONS

2017 Sales

	% of total
Home Appliance & Air Solution	31
Home Entertainment	30
Mobile communications	19
Innotek	11
Vehicle components	6
Other	3
Total	100

Selected Major Products & Services

Home Entertainment (LCD TVs, plasma TVs, audio, video, & optical storage)
Mobile Communication (mobile handsets, mobile accessory)
Home Appliance & Air Solution (washing machines, refrigerators, cooking appliances, vacuum cleaners, built-in appliances, air conditioners, and air purifiers)
Business Solutions (monitors, commercial displays, car infotainment, security business)
Vehicle Component Solutions (in-vehicle infotainment, HVAC and Motor, Vehicle Engineering)

COMPETITORS

CALAMP CORP.
CLEARONE, INC.
COMMSCOPE HOLDING COMPANY, INC.
COMTECH TELECOMMUNICATIONS CORP.
KVH INDUSTRIES, INC.
MONOLITHIC POWER SYSTEMS, INC.
SKYWORKS SOLUTIONS, INC.
STARHUB LTD.
Samsung Electronics Co., Ltd.
Zte Corporation

HISTORICAL FINANCIALS

Company Type: Public

Income Statement   FYE: December 31

	REVENUE ($mil)	NET INCOME ($mil)	NET PROFIT MARGIN	EMPLOYEES
12/21	62,892	868	1.4%	0
12/20	58,127	1,808	3.1%	0
12/19	53,962	27	0.1%	0
12/18	55,020	1,112	2.0%	37,698
12/17	57,589	1,618	2.8%	37,653

Annual Growth 2.2% (14.4%)

2021 Year-End Financials

Debt ratio: —
Return on equity: 6.3%
Cash ($ mil.): 5,216
Current Ratio: 1.16
Long-term debt ($ mil.): 6,763
No. of shares ($ mil.): 162
Dividends
Yield: —
Payout: 14.8%
Market value ($ mil.): —

LG Energy Solution Ltd

EXECUTIVES

Chief Executive Officer, Executive Director, Young-Soo Kwon
Director, Chang Sil Lee
Non-Standing Director, Bong Seok Kwon
Outside Director, Seung Soo Han
Outside Director, Mee Nam Shinn
Outside Director, Mee Sook Yeo
Auditors : Ernst & Young Han Young

LOCATIONS

HQ: LG Energy Solution Ltd
Parc1 tower1, 108 Yeoui-daero, Yeongdeungpo-gu, Seoul
Phone: (82) 2 3777 0114
Web: www.lgensol.com

HISTORICAL FINANCIALS

Company Type: Public

Income Statement — FYE: December 31

	REVENUE ($mil)	NET INCOME ($mil)	NET PROFIT MARGIN	EMPLOYEES
12/22	20,420	612	3.0%	0
12/21	15,025	667	4.4%	0
12/20	1,342	(418)	—	0
Annual Growth	290.0%	—	—	—

2022 Year-End Financials

Debt ratio: —
Return on equity: 5.7%
Cash ($ mil.): 4,736
Current Ratio: 1.64
Long-term debt ($ mil.): 4,181
No. of shares ($ mil.): 234
Dividends
Yield: —
Payout: 0.0%
Market value ($ mil.): —

LIXIL Corp

LIXIL is a maker of pioneering water and housing products. Through approximately 200 subsidiaries and affiliates, it makes products that improve how people live, from shower toilets to baths, kitchen systems, windows, doors, building exteriors and interior furnishings. Combined with its housing and building-related services, it meets the demand for better homes in markets worldwide. Through its global house of brands including INAX, GROHE and American Standard, as well as product brands in Japan such as RICHELLE and SPAGE, LIXIL provides bathroom and kitchen products that create unique experiences for today's discerning consumers of the world. Other operations include a real estate brokerage franchise, and ground inspections and improvement. Japan market accounts for more than 65% of revenue.

Operations

The company's products and services are categorized in four business segments: Water Technology (around 60% of sales), Housing Technology (more than 30%), Building Technology (more than 5%) and Housing and Services (less than 5%).

Lixil Water Technology makes attractive and purposefully designed products for bathrooms and kitchens through powerful global brands such as INAX, GROHE, and American Standard, as well as product brands such as RICHELLE and SPAGE.

Lixil Housing Technology's brands include TOSTEM, INTERIO, EXSIOR, SUPER WALL, NODEA and ASAHI TOSTEM and produce a range of housing-related products, from window sashes to entrance doors, exterior building materials, interior furnishing materials, and fabrics helping to make better homes a reality.

Building Technology segment manufactures products and offers services to support the construction of buildings that are environmentally conscious and which provide better spaces to live, work, study, and play. Major products are curtain walls, building window sashes, and store facades.

Housing and Services segment is divided into three businesses ? housing solution, real estate and financial services. Housing solution is responsible for the development of homebuilding franchise chains and construction on order. The real estate includes land, building and real estate management services and support for development of real estate franchise. Financial services business includes housing loans.

Geographic Reach

The company's head office is located in Tokyo, Japan. LIXIL has almost 80 manufacturing and sales sites worldwide. About 40 are in Japan, over 25 in Asia Pacific, nine in the Americas and four in Europe. LIXIL also operates about 110 showrooms in some 15 markets with around 85 of these in Japan.

Japan is the company's largest market, representing more than 65% of total sales. International market accounts for the remaining less than 35%.

Sales and Marketing

The company sells directly to customers such as dealers, sales agencies, construction companies, architectural firms, developers, wholesalers, volume retailers, and general consumers.

Financial Performance

The company reported a revenue of Â¥1,428.6 billion in 2022, a 4% increase from the previous year's revenue of Â¥1,378.3 billion.

In 2022, the company had a net income of Â¥48.6 billion, a 47% increase from the previous year's net income of Â¥33 billion.

The company's cash at the end of 2022 was Â¥100.4 billion. Operating activities generated Â¥118.3 billion, while investing activities used Â¥24.8 billion. Financing activities used another Â¥108.1 billion.

Strategy

The company has given management and employees a mandate to achieve sustainable growth that continuously adds value for all of the company's stakeholder interests. To achieve this, the LIXIL Playbook outlines its management direction, outlining the company's strategy for transformation and long-term growth through innovation.

Additionally, the company is continuing to implement a simplified business structure. With a simplified hierarchy and fewer corporate titles, the company can reduce costs and eliminate unnecessary management supervision. This is a central part of its drive to create an empowered, people-focused corporate culture.

Company Background

LIXIL was founded in 2011 through the merger of five of Japan's most successful building materials and housing companies? TOSTEM, INAX, Shin Nikkei, Sunwave, and TOEX. From the early 20th Century, the founding fathers of their legacy companies ushered in an era of innovation and laid down the principles that would make LIXIL one of the most respected names in the Japanese building and housing industry.

EXECUTIVES

Representative Executive Officer, President, Chief Executive Officer, Director, Kinya Seto
Representative Executive Officer, Executive Vice President, Chief Financial Officer, Director, Sachio Matsumoto
Representative Executive Officer, Senior Managing Executive Officer, Chief People Officer, Director, Hwa Jin Song Montesano
Senior Managing Executive Officer, Chief Digital Officer, Yugo Kanazawa
Senior Managing Executive Officer, Bi Joy Mohan
Senior Managing Executive Officer, Satoshi Yoshida
Senior Managing Executive Officer, Hiroyuki Onishi
Senior Managing Executive Officer, Shoko Kimijima
Outside Director, Jun Aoki
Outside Director, Shigeki Ishizuka
Outside Director, Shiho Konno
Outside Director, Mayumi Tamura
Outside Director, Yuji Nishiura
Outside Director, Daisuke Hamaguchi
Outside Director, Masatoshi Matsuzaki
Outside Director, Mariko Watabiki
Auditors : Deloitte Touche Tohmatsu LLC

LOCATIONS

HQ: LIXIL Corp
Osaki Garden Tower, 1-1-1 Nishi-Shinagawa, Shinagawa-ku, Tokyo 141-0033
Phone: (81) 50 1790 5765
Web: www.lixil.com

2018 Sales

	% of total
Japan	76
EMEA	9
Americas	8
Asia/Pacific	7
Total	**100**

PRODUCTS/OPERATIONS

2018 Sales

	% of total
LIXIL Water Technology (LWT)	42
LIXIL Housing Technology (LHT)	32
Distribution & Retail Business (D&R)	10
LIXIL Kitchen Technology (LKT)	7
LIXIL Building Technology (LBT)	6
Housing & Services Business (H&S)	3
Total	**100**

Selected Subsidiaries
Kawashima Selkon Textiles (fabric manufacturer)
LIXIL Group Finance (financial services)
LIXIL Housing Research Institute (homebuilding franchise chain)
LIXIL Realty (real estate services)
LIXIL Viva (operates Viva Home and Super Viva Home retail chains)
LIXIL ENERGY Co., Ltd.
LIXIL Building Materials Manufacturing Corporation

Selected Brands
Global
    INAX
    GROHE
    American Standard
    TOSTEM
    LIXIL
Global Specialty
    Kawashima Selkon
    Cobra
    DXV
    Jaxson
    SATO
Japan
    RICHELLE
    SPAGE
    INTERIO
    EXSIOR
    SUPER WALL
    AHAHI TOTEM

COMPETITORS

DIPLOMA PLC
EPWIN GROUP PLC
HALMA PUBLIC LIMITED COMPANY
Hiscox Ltd
INTERLINE BRANDS, INC.
Itausa S/A
LightInTheBox Holding Co., Ltd.
MITIE GROUP PLC
REXEL
WESFARMERS LIMITED

HISTORICAL FINANCIALS

Company Type: Public

Income Statement
FYE: March 31

	REVENUE ($mil)	NET INCOME ($mil)	NET PROFIT MARGIN	EMPLOYEES
03/23	11,232	120	1.1%	58,337
03/22	11,744	399	3.4%	59,091
03/21	12,447	298	2.4%	59,169
03/20	15,609	115	0.7%	73,426
03/19	16,548	(471)	—	76,182
Annual Growth	(9.2%)	—	—	(6.5%)

2023 Year-End Financials
Debt ratio: 0.2%
Return on equity: 2.5%
Cash ($ mil.): 800
Current Ratio: 1.14
Long-term debt ($ mil.): 2,593
No. of shares ($ mil.): 287
Dividends
Yield: 4.0%
Payout: 490.2%
Market value ($ mil.): 9,539

	STOCK PRICE ($) FY Close	P/E High/Low		PER SHARE ($) Earnings	Dividends	Book Value
03/23	33.23	1	1	0.42	1.34	16.36
03/22	37.56	0	0	1.31	1.44	17.32
03/21	56.28	1	0	0.98	1.32	17.19
03/20	24.45	1	0	0.37	1.94	15.95
03/19	27.72	—	—	(1.63)	1.58	16.61
Annual Growth	4.6%		—	—	(4.2%)	(0.4%)

Lloyds Banking Group Plc

One of Britain's largest lenders, Lloyds Banking Group serves retail and commercial banking, insurance, and savings. The bank provides services under the Lloyds Bank, Black Horse, Halifax, Bank of Scotland, Lex Autolease, MBNA, Schroders Personal Wealth, and Scottish Widows brands. Lloyds' retail division provides current accounts, savings accounts, credit cards, loans, mortgages, insurance, and motor finance. Lloyds Banking boasts approximately Â£886.6 billion in assets. The financial services group focused on retail and commercial customers ? with approximately 26 million customers in the UK, and a presence in nearly every community. Lloyds was formed in 2008 during the aftermath of the financial crisis via the merger of Lloyds TSB and HBOS.

Operations
Lloyds Banking's three divisions are Retail (brings in about 65% of the company's revenue), Commercial Banking (nearly 25%), and Insurance and Wealth approximately 10%.

Across its nearly 15 brands ? Lloyds Bank, Halifax, Bank of Scotland, Scottish Widows, Schroders Personal Wealth, MBNA, Black Horse, Lex Autolease, LDC, AMC, Birmingham Midshires and iWeb ? the Retail segment offers current accounts, savings, mortgages, credit cards, motor finance, and unsecured loans to personal and business banking customers. It professes more than 18 million online customers. Of these, more than 14 million are also mobile customers. Lex Autolease is the UK's largest vehicle-leasing business with a fleet of more than 329,000 cars and commercial vehicles. Black Horse offers motor finance loans on cars, caravans, motor homes, and motorbikes through a network of 5,000 motor dealers.

The Commercial Banking division provides lending, transactional banking, working capital management, debt financing, and risk management services.

The Insurance and Wealth division offers insurance, investment and wealth management products and services.

Net interest income accounts for more than 30% of company's total revenue.

Geographic Reach
Lloyds Banking is headquartered in London.

Sales and Marketing
Lloyds Banking targets consumers and businesses (including small to mid-sized enterprises, or SMEs) mostly in the UK.

The company's advertising and promotion costs were approximately Â£161 million, Â£187 million, and Â£170 million in 2021, 2020, and 2019, respectively.

Financial Performance
Company's revenue for fiscal 2021 increased to Â£37.4 billion compared from the prior year with Â£29.2 billion.

Profit for fiscal 2021 increased to Â£5.9 billion compared from the prior year with Â£1.4 billion.

Cash held by the company at the end of fiscal 2021 increased to Â£76.4 billion. Cash provided operations was Â£6.6 billion while cash used for investing and financing activities were Â£2.5 billion and Â£3.2 billion, respectively. Main uses of cash were purchase of financial assets and interest paid on subordinated liabilities.

Strategy
Building on its strong foundations, Lloyds Banking Group's purpose of Helping Britain Prosper forms the basis of its new strategy to profitably deliver for all of its stakeholders. Core to its purpose and strategy is its focus on building an inclusive society and supporting the transition to a low carbon economy. This is where Lloyds Banking Group can make the biggest difference, whilst creating new avenues for company's future growth. It is only by doing right by its customers, colleagues and communities that the company can achieve higher, more sustainable returns for shareholders.

Mergers and Acquisitions
In early 2022, Lloyds Banking Group completed its acquisition of Embark Group (Embark), a fast growing investment and retirement platform business. Embark enhances the group's capabilities to address the attractive mass market and self-directed wealth segment, completing its wealth proposition. Embark will also enable the group to re-platform its pensions and retirement proposition, delivering a market-leading platform for intermediaries and significantly strengthening its offering in retirement, an important growth market. A consideration of c.Â£390 million will be paid for the entire share capital of Embark upon completion.

Company Background
In 1765 John Taylor and Sampson Lloyd II founded Taylors and Lloyds bank in Birmingham, England; five years later their sons opened a London agency. In 1852 the last

Taylor involved with the bank died. In 1865 the bank converted to joint stock form and became Lloyds Banking Company Ltd. Over the next half century, it grew by merging with some 50 banks, becoming one of England's largest banks by the turn of the century.

After WWII, growth was hampered by high inflation. Lloyds added branches and products in the 1960s. By 1971 it had branches in 43 countries. It moved into insurance (1972), home mortgages (1979), real estate agency services (1982), and merchant banking (1986). Lloyds bought TSB Group in 1995.

The global economic crisis was a difficult time for Lloyds. The UK government took a 40% stake in the company after bailing it out, along with seven other top banks, in 2008. Lloyds accepted some Â£17 billion ($25 billion) in taxpayer money. As part of a restructuring plan (and to repay the UK government), Lloyds Banking Group launched one of the largest-ever capital raisings in Europe.

Around the same time of the government bailout, Lloyds TSB agreed to take over struggling HBOS, the UK's top mortgage lender and the operator of Halifax and Bank of Scotland, in a controversial (poorly timed) Â£12 billion deal. The combined bank served about one of every three UK consumers and controlled more than a quarter of the UK residential mortgage market.

In 2017, nearly nine years after the government bailout began, the British government sold its final stake in the Lloyds, making it fully private again.

HISTORY

In 1765 John Taylor and Sampson Lloyd II founded Taylors and Lloyds bank in Birmingham, England; five years later their sons opened a London agency. In 1852 the last Taylor involved with the bank died. In 1865 the bank converted to joint stock form and became Lloyds Banking Company Ltd. Over the next half century, it grew by merging with some 50 banks, becoming one of England's largest banks by the turn of the century.

Despite the post-WWI roller-coaster economy, the bank acquired Capital and Counties Bank (1918, bringing foreign connections); Fox, Fowler & Company (1921); and Cox & Company (1923). During both wars, deposits grew while lending dropped. After WWII, growth was hampered by high inflation.

Lloyds added branches and products in the 1960s. By 1971 it had branches in 43 countries. It moved into insurance (1972), home mortgages (1979), real estate agency services (1982), and merchant banking (1986).

In 1987 Latin American bank defaults pummeled Lloyds. Refocusing on domestic operations, the bank sold overseas subsidiaries (including Lloyds Bank Canada in 1990) and acquired 58% of life insurer Abbey Life (1988) and Cheltenham & Gloucester Building Society (1994). HSBC outbid Lloyds for Midland Bank in 1992; Lloyds bought TSB Group in 1995.

TSB Group evolved from the trustee savings banks (TSBs) formed in the 1800s. By 1860 there were 600 such banks, mainly in northern England and Scotland. During WWI many TSBs consolidated or closed. By WWII about 100 remained, and the mergers continued.

In the 1960s TSBs began offering checking accounts and trust services. Loans, credit cards, and other services came in 1973. In 1986 the four remaining TSBs (TSB Channel Islands, TSB England and Wales, TSB Northern Ireland, and TSB Scotland) agreed to merge and go public in order to gain equal footing with stock banks. TSB Group was born.

Flush with cash from its offering, TSB group defied the late 1980s recession to buy Target Group (life insurance, sold 1993), Hill Samuel (merchant banking), and other units; the purchases sent TSB sprawling.

As debt rose in the 1990s, TSB Group refocused on banking and insurance. TSB and Lloyds merged in 1995, linking their geographically complementary branch networks to fend off competition.

After the merger, Lloyds TSB focused on loans and insurance and dabbled in consumer finance, including the sale and delivery of big-ticket items (cars, large appliances). Returning overseas, it bought the consumer finance unit of Brazil's Banco Multiplic.

In late 1997 and 1998, the bank overhauled its operations to eliminate redundancies and began rebranding under one green and blue banner. In 1999 Lloyds TSB bailed out Abbey Life, which had nearly been bankrupted by the cost of settling pension mis-selling claims.

The bank in 2000 bought Scottish Widows to boost its fund management services. It sold the Abbey Life name and its new business to Zurich Financial Services' Allied Dunbar; Abbey Life continued to service existing business for Lloyds. Also that year, Lloyds TSB bought consumer and auto finance unit Chartered Trust from Standard Chartered. After a yearlong battle to buy London-based mortgage lender Abbey National, the UK government, in 2001, blocked the merger attempt because of concerns for the consumer.

Earlier in 2001 Lloyds TSB closed Bahamas-based subsidiary British Bank of Latin America because of alleged money-laundering links revealed in a US Senate report.

Lloyds TSB's asset finance operations bought First National Vehicle Holdings and Abbey National Vehicle Finance from Abbey National plc in 2002. The division also acquired Chartered Trust and Dutton-Forshaw Group, a car dealership. Lloyds TSB sold National Bank of New Zealand to Australia and New Zealand Bank Group in 2003.

Commerzbank unit Comdirect Bank sold its UK subsidiary, Comdirect Ltd, to Lloyds TSB unit Executive Services Group in 2004.

The company sold its Abbey Life unit to Deutsche Bank for nearly $2 billion in 2007. (The life insurer had been closed to new business since 2000.) The group also sold Lloyds TSB Registrars and car dealership The Dutton-Forshaw Group, which were noncore units of its wholesale and international business.

The global economic crisis was a difficult time for Lloyds. The UK government took a 40% stake in the company after bailing it out, along with seven other top banks, in 2008. Lloyds accepted some Â£17 billion ($25 billion) in taxpayer money. The government hoped the infusion of cash would loosen up credit markets and restore confidence in the financial system. As part of a restructuring plan (and to repay the UK government), Lloyds Banking Group launched one of the largest-ever capital raisings in Europe, which included a Â£9 billion ($13 billion) debt exchange and a nearly Â£14 billion ($20 billion) rights issue.

Around the same time of the government bailout, Lloyds TSB agreed to take over struggling HBOS, the UK's top mortgage lender. The controversial Â£12 billion ($22 billion) deal was announced after HBOS shares fell dramatically amid rising concerns surrounding the vitality of financial services companies worldwide. The combined bank served about one of every three UK consumers and controlled more than a quarter of the UK residential mortgage market. The UK government further capitalized the deal to ensure its viability.

Within weeks, though, Lloyds Banking Group revealed that HBOS had incurred some Â£11 billion ($18 billion) in losses, and shareholder unrest grew concerning the billions of pounds in toxic assets gained with the acquisition. The merger meant drastic cost cuts and job losses, as the company announced more than 42,000 job cuts.

Needless to say, not everyone was happy with the HBOS merger. At Lloyds Banking Group's annual meeting in 2009, a large group of shareholders loudly criticized the company's board for the HBOS deal, demanding resignations and threatening lawsuits over the merger. In 2010 one group of disgruntled shareholders launched legal action in order to recoup up to Â£14 billion ($20 billion) that they claim they lost as a result of the merger.

Lloyds Banking Group defended the merger, though, saying it helped improve the company's strategic position by improving its market position (it controlled about half of the savings market), brand recognition, and expanding its customer base. Although the deal brought short-term costs, company leaders were convinced that it was better positioned for future growth.

EXECUTIVES

Chief Executive Officer, Executive Director, Charlie Nunn
Chief Financial Officer, Executive Director, William Chalmers
Chief People and Places Officer, Sharon Doherty
Chief Internal Auditor, Laura Needham
Commercial Banking Interim Chief Operating Officer, David Oilfield
Staff Chief, Sustainable Business Chief, Sustainable Business Director, Staff Director, Janet Pope
Chief Risk Officer, Stephen Shelley
Corporate Affairs Director, Andrew Walton
Chief Legal Officer, Secretary, Kate Cheetham
Non-Executive Chairman, Independent Non-Executive Director, Robin Budenberg
Deputy Chairman, Senior Independent Director, Alan Dickinson
Independent Non-Executive Director, Cathy Turner
Independent Non-Executive Director, Harmeen Mehta
Independent Non-Executive Director, Sarah Catherine Legg
Independent Non-Executive Director, Amanda MacKenzie
Independent Non-Executive Director, Catherine Woods
Independent Non-Executive Director, Scott Wheway
Auditors : Deloitte LLP

LOCATIONS

HQ: Lloyds Banking Group Plc
25 Gresham Street, London EC2V 7HN
Phone: (44) 20 7626 1500
Web: www.lloydsbankinggroup.com

PRODUCTS/OPERATIONS

Selected Brands
Bank of Scotland
Cheltenham & Gloucester
Clerical Medical
Halifax
Lloyds
Scottish Widows

2016 Sales

	% of total
Net trading income	41
Interest	30
Insurance Premium income	20
Net fees & commissions	4
Other	5
Total	100

2017 Sales

	% of total
Retail	59
Commercial Banking	27
Insurance & Wealth	11
Other	3
Total	100

HISTORICAL FINANCIALS
Company Type: Public

Income Statement   FYE: December 31

	ASSETS ($mil)	NET INCOME ($mil)	INCOME AS % OF ASSETS	EMPLOYEES
12/23	1,123,400	6,958	0.6%	62,569
12/22	1,056,750	6,571	0.6%	0
12/21	1,194,750	7,794	0.7%	57,955
12/20	1,189,030	1,798	0.2%	61,576
12/19	1,101,210	3,862	0.4%	63,069
Annual Growth	0.5%	15.9%	—	(0.2%)

2023 Year-End Financials
Return on assets: 0.6%
Return on equity: 11.5%
Long-term debt ($ mil.): —
No. of shares ($ mil.): 63,569
Sales ($ mil.): 63,907
Dividends
Yield: —
Payout: 130.1%
Market value ($ mil.): 151,930

	STOCK PRICE ($) FY Close	P/E High/Low		PER SHARE ($) Earnings	Dividends	Book Value
12/23	2.39	36	26	0.10	0.12	0.95
12/22	2.20	36	25	0.09	0.10	0.85
12/21	2.55	36	23	0.10	0.07	1.01
12/20	1.96	288	104	0.02	0.06	0.96
12/19	3.31	101	72	0.04	0.16	0.91
Annual Growth	(7.8%)	—	—	20.8%	(6.7%)	1.0%

Loblaw Companies Ltd

EXECUTIVES

Chairman, President, Director, Galen G. Weston
Chief Financial Officer, Richard Dufresne
Chief Operating Officer, Robert Sawyer
Chief Administrative Officer, Robert Wiebe
Executive Vice President, Chief Legal Officer, Secretary, Nicholas Henn
Executive Vice President, Chief Technology and Analytics Officer, David Markwell
Executive Vice President, Chief Human Resources Officer, Mark Wilson
Corporate Affairs and Communications Senior Vice President, Kevin Groh
Discount Division President, Jocyanne Bourdeau
President's Choice Financial President, Barry K. Columb
Joe Fresh President, Ian Freedman
Shoppers Drug Mart President, Jeff Leger
Market Division President, Greg Ramier
Corporate Director, Scott B. Bonham
Corporate Director, Warren Bryant
Corporate Director, Christie J. B. Clark
Corporate Director, William A. Downe
Corporate Director, Janice Fukakusa
Corporate Director, M. Marianne Harris
Corporate Director, Claudia Kotchka
Corporate Director, Beth M. Pritchard
Corporate Director, Sarah E. Raiss
Director, Paviter S. Binning
Director, Daniel Debow
Auditors : PricewaterhouseCoopers LLP

LOCATIONS

HQ: Loblaw Companies Ltd
1 President's Choice Circle, Brampton, Ontario L6Y 5S5
Phone: 905 459-2500   **Fax:** 905 861-2206
Web: www.loblaw.ca

HISTORICAL FINANCIALS
Company Type: Public

Income Statement   FYE: December 30

	REVENUE ($mil)	NET INCOME ($mil)	NET PROFIT MARGIN	EMPLOYEES
12/23	44,912	1,584	3.5%	220,000
12/22*	41,779	1,420	3.4%	221,000
01/22	41,746	1,472	3.5%	215,000
01/21*	41,378	869	2.1%	220,000
12/19	36,687	825	2.3%	194,000
Annual Growth	5.2%	17.7%	—	3.2%

*Fiscal year change

2023 Year-End Financials
Debt ratio: 19.7%
Return on equity: 18.5%
Cash ($ mil.): 1,122
Current Ratio: 1.25
Long-term debt ($ mil.): 5,025
No. of shares ($ mil.): 309
Dividends
Yield: —
Payout: 26.7%
Market value ($ mil.): 29,902

	STOCK PRICE ($) FY Close	P/E High/Low		PER SHARE ($) Earnings	Dividends	Book Value
12/23	96.69	15	13	4.92	1.32	27.97
12/22*	89.96	16	12	4.25	1.17	25.88
01/22	81.92	15	9	4.28	1.10	27.29
01/21*	49.47	19	15	2.40	1.00	24.88
12/19	51.00	20	16	2.21	0.95	23.83
Annual Growth	17.3%	—	—	22.1%	8.6%	4.1%

*Fiscal year change

London Stock Exchange Group Plc

LSEG (London Stock Exchange Group) is a leading global financial markets infrastructure and data provider that operates connected businesses to serve customers across the entire financial markets value chain. LSEG is a top provider of financial indexing through FTSE Russell. The group offers benchmarking and analytics services, post-trade clearing and risk management, real-time market information and reference data, and trading technology to clients in capital markets. The group is home to several capital formation and execution venues: London Stock Exchange, AIM, Turquoise, CurveGlobal, FXall, Matching, and Tradeweb. Serving more than 190 countries, LSEG generates some 30% of revenue in the UK.

Operations
LSEG operates in three business divisions: Data & Analytics, Capital Markets, and Post Trade.

The Data & Analytics division provides high value data, analytics, indices, workflow solutions and data management capabilities. The division is split into five areas to address the different needs of its customers: Trading & Banking Solutions; Enterprise Data Solutions; Investment Solutions; Wealth Solutions; and Customer & Third-Party Risk Solutions. The division accounts for about 70% of total revenue.

The Capital Markets division (about 20%) provides businesses with access to capital through issuance and offers secondary market trading for equities, fixed income and foreign exchange (FX).

The Post Trade division (nearly 15%) provides a range of clearing, risk management, capital optimization and regulatory reporting solutions. The division is split into four areas by type of business and income: OTC Derivatives; Securities and Reporting; Non Cash Collateral; and Net Treasury Income.

Geographic Reach

LSEG is headquartered in the UK, with significant operations in about 65 countries across EMEA, North America, Latin America and Asia Pacific.

About 35% of the company's total revenue comes from USA, while some 30% comes from the UK, EU countries generates nearly 15%, and Asia and other countries account for around 20% of combined revenue.

Sales and Marketing

LSEG serves more than 45,000 customers, including the world's largest banks, asset managers, asset owners, wealth advisers, and hedge funds. Additionally, the group supports critical central banking and regulatory institutions with its solutions. The group has a sizeable and growing footprint across corporate communities, serving 48 of the top 50 largest corporates globally.

Financial Performance

Note: Growth rates may differ after conversion to US Dollars.

LSEG's revenue for fiscal 2022 increased by 6% to £7.7 billion compared from the prior year with £6.5 billion. The increase was primarily due to higher revenues on every segments aside from other and recoveries.

Net income for fiscal 2022 increased to £979 million compared from the prior year with £592 million. The increase was primarily due to higher revenues offsetting the increase in expenses.

Cash held by the company at the end of fiscal 2022 increased to £3.2 billion. Cash provided by operations was £3.2 billion while cash used for investing and financing activities were £909 million and £1.5 billion, respectively. Main uses of cash were purchase of intangible assets and dividends paid to equity holders of the parent.

Strategy

LSEG's new long-term strategic partnership with Microsoft is a win-win-win: a win for its customers, a win for Microsoft and a win for LSEG.

It is a transformative partnership for LSEG and will significantly accelerate its strategy to be the leading global financial markets infrastructure and data provider.

LSEG's long-term strategy builds on our strengths as a Group. The company are investing in solutions and services that can adapt and scale in evolving global financial markets. LSEG's strategy is to be: globally essential; multi-asset class; and seamlessly connected.

Mergers and Acquisitions

In late 2022, LSEG agreed to acquire Acadia, a leading provider of automated uncleared margin processing and integrated risk and optimisation services for the global derivatives community. The acquisition furthers LSEG's strategy to enhance and grow its multi-asset Post Trade offering for the uncleared derivatives space.

In 2022, LSEG has signed an agreement to acquire MayStreet, a leading market data solutions provider. The acquisition significantly enhances LSEG's Enterprise Data Solutions business, expanding LSEG's capabilities across the latency spectrum through a global low latency network of over 300 cross asset, exchange and trading venue feeds. This broadens and complements LSEG's real-time feeds and historical market data value proposition, particularly for front office customers, who use these solutions to support research and strategy development and to power electronic trading applications.

In early 2022, LSEG has agreed to acquire Global Data Consortium Inc (GDC), a global provider of high-quality identity verification data to support clients with Know Your Customer (KYC) requirements. LSEG to expand its global range of digital identity solutions through acquisition of Global Data Consortium Inc.

Company Background

For years, LSE and its rivals have been jockeying for dominance in the international stock market, fueled by the rise of electronic communication networks (ECNs) that has shaken up stodgy trading floors around the globe. At the same time, the establishment of the euro and the unified European market have the investment community crying out for a single, multinational stock exchange. The failed merger of LSE and TMX Group (operator of the Toronto Stock Exchange) was one of a handful announced in a wave of consolidation amongst the world's exchanges. It wasn't alone in its failure, however, as planned hookups of NYSE Euronext and Deutsche Börse, and the Singapore Exchange and the Australian Securities Exchange also hit the skids.

HISTORY

Who says coffeehouses are for poetry readings? The LSE (like Lloyd's insurance market in 1688) began as a London coffeehouse -- Jonathan's -- to which a group of rowdy brokers repaired after being ejected from the Royal Exchange in 1760. In 1773 the coffeehouse changed its name from Jonathan's to the Stock Exchange, and the organization grew as it helped finance England's Industrial Revolution.

In 1872 the exchange adopted the newest technological breakthrough, the ticker, which, at a breathtaking six words per minute, was a great improvement over earlier systems (such as carrier pigeons and semaphore relays) for reporting market activity. Eight years later, the LSE began to offer settlement services.

Early in the 20th century, the LSE benefited from consolidation among regional exchanges while its erstwhile competitor, the Royal Exchange, faded and finally closed in 1939.

Financial reform in the 1980s spurred the tradition-loving LSE to modernize. In 1986 the financial "Big Bang" deregulated commissions and opened up exchange membership, enabling the LSE to build a larger capital base. Trading also began moving off the floor with the introduction of the Stock Exchange Automated Quotations (SEAQ) system, modeled on Nasdaq. The reforms were successful. Overnight, the LSE began siphoning business away from other floor-based European exchanges and the once-somnolent market accelerated, taking on an American edge.

By 1995 the US boom in start-up trading inspired the LSE to open the Alternative Investment Market to woo high-growth stocks. Two years later the Stock Exchange Trading Service replaced the 11-year-old SEAQ system, highlighting LSE's resolve to not be left behind by the speed and lower cost of electronic communication networks. The LSE also started to use the CREST electronic settlement system run by CRESTCo.

Technology wasn't the only threat to LSE's European dominance. The birth of Europe's single currency had banks hungry for an efficient, centralized European stock exchange. Differences in rules, currency and practices (not to mention issues of national pride) prevented any single exchange from filling the role. Talks with Frankfurt's Deutsche Börse began. By 1998 the two exchanges formed an alliance to synchronize British and German securities trading.

In 2000, after two years of talks, LSE announced a merger with the once-sleepy Deutsche Börse to form iX international exchange, which would have had as an operating partner Nasdaq Europe (destined to be shuttered by parent Nasdaq three years later). Later that year Swedish concern OM Gruppen (now OMX), which owns the Stockholm exchange, launched a hostile bid for the LSE. The bid, which eventually failed, prompted the LSE to nix its deal with Deutsche Börse in order to focus on protecting itself. Also that year shareholder discontent over the Deutsche Börse deal prompted CEO Gavin Casey to resign; the company in 2001 replaced him with investment banker Clara Furse, the first woman CEO in the nearly three decades since the position was created and the first in any such high position at the exchange, where women weren't even members until the 1970s.

The LSE demutualized in 2000 and listed its shares the following year.

The company entered into a series of merger discussions that year but most attempts fizzled out, including talks with Germany's Deutsche Börse and a hostile takeover bid for the LSE by what is now OMX, owner of the Stockholm stock exchange. (The LSE did join forces with OMX in 2003 to launch derivatives exchange EDX London.) Even before Euronext's 2007 marriage to the NYSE, the LSE had been dealt a blow in its quest for pan-European dominance when Euronext won the bidding war for futures exchange LIFFE in 2001.

In 2006 NASDAQ offered $4 billion to acquire LSE, but was turned down as being an inadequate offer. After being spurned, NASDAQ went on to acquire a stake of some 30% in the LSE and launched a hostile takeover attempt. That bid, too, failed in 2007. (NASDAQ later sold its interests in LSE to Borse Dubai.) LSE's pre-eminent European position was further compromised in 2007 when a merger joined Euronext with the venerable and powerful New York Stock Exchange. LSE had tried to merge with Euronext itself two years earlier.

After pursuing a major merger partner for several years, LSE made another modest deal in 2007 when it bought Borsa Italiana. That deal gave the firm additional clearing and settlement operations and was part of its international expansion strategy. With an eye toward capturing some of the growing and lucrative Chinese equities market, the LSE opened an office in Beijing in 2008.

In 2010 LSE acquired 60% of electronic stock and derivative trading platform Turquoise. That acquisition expanded LSE's services across Europe and helped it keep pace with Euronext and Deutsche Börse.

In mid-2011 LSE and called off plans to join forces to create the combined LTMX Group. Billed as merger of equals, the transaction would have brought LSE's expertise in emerging markets together with TMX's clout in energy, mining, and minerals. However, before the deal was sealed, Maple Group, a consortium of Canadian banks, asset managers, and pension funds, stepped in with an unsolicited counteroffer for TMX an an effort to keep it Canadian-owned. Maple Group offered some £2.2 billion ($3.6 billion) for the exchange, about 20% more than LSE's bid. The board of TMX initially supported the LSE proposal, but the companies called the deal off when it looked like they didn't have enough shareholder support. Maple Group (now TMX Group Limited) took over TMX in 2012.

The company bought the remaining 50% stake in FTSE International that it already didn't own for £450 million ($705 million) in 2011. The move bolstered the exchange's presence in indices and analytics.

EXECUTIVES

Chief Executive Officer, Executive Director,
David Schwimmer
Chief Financial Officer, Executive Director,
Anna Manz
Chief Operating Officer, David Shalders
Chief People Officer, Erica Bourne
Chief Risk Officer, Balbir Bakhshi
Chief Information Officer, Anthony McCarthy
Chief Marketing Officer, Chief Corporate Affairs Officer, Brigitte Trafford
General Counsel, Catherine Johnson
Secretary, Lisa Margaret Condron
Chairman, Independent Non-Executive Director,
Don Robert
Senior Independent Director, Non-Executive Director, Cressida Hogg
Independent Non-Executive Director, Dominic Blakemore
Independent Non-Executive Director, Kathleen Traynor DeRose
Independent Non-Executive Director, Tsega Gebreyes
Independent Non-Executive Director, Valerie Rahmani
Independent Non-Executive Director, Ashok Vaswani
Independent Non-Executive Director, William Vereker
Non-Executive Director, Martin J. Brand
Non-Executive Director, Erin Brown
Non-Executive Director, Douglas M. Steenland
Non-Executive Director, Scott D. Guthrie
Auditors : Ernst & Young LLP

LOCATIONS

HQ: London Stock Exchange Group Plc
  10 Paternoster Square, London EC4M 7LS
Phone: (44) 20 7797 1000
Web: www.lseg.com

PRODUCTS/OPERATIONS

2018 Sales by Segment

	% of total
Information Services	39
Post-Trade Services LCH	31
Capital Markets	19
Post-Trade Services CC&G Monte Titoli	7
Technology Services	3
Other	1
Total	100

Selected Group Companies
BIt Market Services S.p.A. (IT, logistics, and advisory services)
Borsa Italiana S.p.A
Cassa di Compensazione e Garanzia S.p.A. (counterparty services, Italy)
FTSE International Limited (indices and analytics)
London Stock Exchange plc
Millennium Information Technologies Ltd (MillenniumIT, Sri Lanka)
Monte Titoli S.p.A. (post-trade services, Italy)
Proquote Limited (financial market software and data)
RUSSELL INVESTMENTS (institutional asset management, US)
Società per il Mercato dei Titoli di Stato S.p.A. (fixed-income trading, Italy)
Turquoise Trading Limited (pan-European trading)

COMPETITORS

3I GROUP PLC
Bertelsmann SE & Co. KGaA
Deutsche Börse AG
MAPFRE, SA
NEX INTERNATIONAL LIMITED
NYSE HOLDINGS LLC
PRUDENTIAL PUBLIC LIMITED COMPANY
RSA INSURANCE GROUP PLC
STANDARD LIFE ABERDEEN PLC
VIRTU KNIGHT CAPITAL GROUP LLC

HISTORICAL FINANCIALS

Company Type: Public

Income Statement   FYE: December 31

	REVENUE ($mil)	NET INCOME ($mil)	NET PROFIT MARGIN	EMPLOYEES
12/22	9,321	1,567	16.8%	24,441
12/21	9,083	4,216	46.4%	24,158
12/20	3,335	574	17.2%	5,219
12/19	3,055	550	18.0%	4,698
12/18	2,725	612	22.5%	4,405
Annual Growth	36.0%	26.5%	—	53.5%

2022 Year-End Financials
Debt ratio: 1.2%   No. of shares ($ mil.): 554
Return on equity: 5.2%   Dividends
Cash ($ mil.): 129,912   Yield: —
Current Ratio: 1.00   Payout: 9.5%
Long-term debt ($ mil.): 8,253   Market value ($ mil.): 11,874

	STOCK PRICE ($) FY Close	P/E High/Low		PER SHARE ($) Earnings	Dividends	Book Value
12/22	21.43	11	8	2.80	0.27	56.47
12/21	23.59	6	4	7.79	0.24	57.26
12/20	31.26	27	17	1.62	0.20	14.43
12/19	26.01	22	11	1.56	0.17	13.00
12/18	13.10	11	9	1.74	0.16	12.26
Annual Growth	13.1%	—		12.7%	14.0%	46.5%

lululemon athletica inc

lululemon athletica is principally a designer, distributor, and retailer of healthy lifestyle inspired athletic apparel and accessories. Its products include pants, shorts, tops, underwear, bags, yoga mats, and water bottles. The company specializes in making women's and clothing, but also serves men. lululemon operates about 575 company-owned stores in more than 15 countries (although most are in North America) and sells online and via mobile apps. Its clothing is manufactured by third-parties located mostly in South and Southeast Asia. Fast-growing lululemon was founded in 1998 by Dennis "Chip" Wilson. The US generates some 70% of the company's revenue.

Operations

lululemon reports its operations through two primary segments: company-operated stores and direct-to-consumer.

The company-operated stores segment includes its chain of about 575 retail stores, all but a handful of which operate under the lululemon name. These stores, located in malls and other spots in more than 15 countries, generate some 45% of total company revenue.

lululemon's direct-to-consumer segment, which accounts for about 45% of revenue, includes sales made via its website and mobile apps, including mobile apps on in-store devices that allow demand to be fulfilled via its distribution centers or other retail locations.

The remainder of revenue, less than 10%, comes from outlets, warehouse sales, wholesale operations, temporary locations, and licensing and supply agreements.

The company works with a group of about 40 vendors that manufacture its products.

Geographic Reach

Vancouver, Canada-based lululemon rings up some 70% of its sales in the US and approximately 15% in Canada; the rest comes from outside North America. The US is by far the largest market for its stores, accounting for around 55% of locations.

lululemon operates distribution centers in the US, Canada, and Australia. It also has warehouses, managed by third parties, in PRC and the Netherlands.

Sales and Marketing

lululemon relies on a community-based approach ? local brand ambassadors, digital marketing, social media, in-store community boards and grassroots initiatives ? to increase brand awareness.

The company's target customer is women, which generated over 65% of sales, followed by men with about 25%.

Financial Performance

Net revenue increased $1.9 billion, or 42%, to $6.3 billion in 2021 from $4.4 billion in 2020. The increase in net revenue was primarily due to increased company-operated store net revenue, which was the result of more extensive temporary store closures and COVID-19 operating restrictions that were in place during 2020. Direct to consumer net revenue and other net revenue also increased.

In 2021, the company had a net income of $975.3 million, a 66% increase from the previous year's net income of $588.9 million. The increase in net income in 2021 was primarily due to an increase in gross profit of $1.1 billion, an increase in other income (expense), net of $1.2 million partially offset by an increase in selling, general and administrative expenses of $616.0 million, an increase in income tax expense of $128.1 million, an increase in acquisition-related expenses of $11.6 million, and an increase in amortization of intangible assets of $3.6 million.

The company's cash at the end of 2021 was $1.3 billion. Operating activities generated $1.4 billion, while investing activities used $427.9 million, mainly for purchase of property and equipment. Financing activities used another $845 million, primarily for repurchase of common stock.

Strategy

In 2021, the company's new store growth will come primarily from company-operated store openings in Asia and in the US. Its real estate strategy over the next several years will not only consist of opening new company-operated stores, but also in overall square footage growth through store expansions and relocations.

Company Background

lululemon was founded in Vancouver by Dennis "Chip" Wilson in 1998. It began as a design studio by day and yoga studio by night and became a standalone store in late 2000.

EXECUTIVES

Chair, Director, Martha A.M. Morfitt
Chief Executive Officer, Director, Calvin R. McDonald, $576,923 total compensation
International Executive Vice President, Andre Maestrini
Chief Financial Officer, Meghan Frank
Chief Products Officer, Michelle Choe, $615,604 total compensation
Chief Brand Officer, Nicole Neuburger
Region Officer, Celeste Burgoyne, $625,165 total compensation
Lead Director, Director, David M. Mussafer
Director, Glenn K. Murphy, $357,310 total compensation
Director, Michael Casey
Director, Isabel Ge Mahe
Director, Stephanie L. Ferris
Director, Kathryn Henry
Director, Alison Loehnis
Director, Jon McNeill
Director, Emily C. White
Auditors : PricewaterhouseCoopers LLP

LOCATIONS

HQ: lululemon athletica inc
1818 Cornwall Avenue, Vancouver, British Columbia V6J 1C7
Phone: 604 732-6124   **Fax:** 604 874-6124
Web: www.lululemon.com

2018 Stores

	No.
US	285
Canada	64
Australia	29
China	22
UK	12
New Zealand	7
Singapore	3
South Korea	4
Germany	5
Japan	5
France	1
Ireland	1
Sweden	1
Switzerland	1
Total	**440**

2018 Sales

	$ mil.	% of total
US	2,363.4	72
Canada	565.1	17
Outside North America	359.8	11
Total	**3,288.3**	**100**

PRODUCTS/OPERATIONS

2018 Sales

	$ mil.	% of total
Corporate-owned stores	2,126.4	65
Direct to consumer	858.8	26
Other	303.1	9
Total	**3,288.3**	**100**

COMPETITORS

CENTRIC BRANDS LLC
DICK'S SPORTING GOODS, INC.
FIVE BELOW, INC.
GERRY WEBER International AG
JORDACHE ENTERPRISES INC.
KORET, INC.
RTW RETAILWINDS, INC.
ST. JOHN KNITS INTERNATIONAL, INCORPORATED
SUGARTOWN WORLDWIDE LLC
USPA ACCESSORIES LLC

HISTORICAL FINANCIALS

Company Type: Public

Income Statement — FYE: January 28

	REVENUE ($mil)	NET INCOME ($mil)	NET PROFIT MARGIN	EMPLOYEES
01/24	9,619	1,550	16.1%	38,000
01/23	8,110	854	10.5%	34,000
01/22	6,256	975	15.6%	29,000
01/21*	4,401	588	13.4%	25,000
02/20	3,979	645	16.2%	19,000
Annual Growth	24.7%	24.5%	—	18.9%

*Fiscal year change

2024 Year-End Financials

Debt ratio: —
Return on equity: 42.1%
Cash ($ mil.): 2,243
Current Ratio: 2.49
Long-term debt ($ mil.): —
No. of shares ($ mil.): 126
Dividends
  Yield: —
  Payout: 0.0%
Market value ($ mil.): 60,338

	STOCK PRICE ($) FY Close	P/E High/Low		PER SHARE ($) Earnings	Dividends	Book Value
01/24	478.03	42	24	12.20	0.00	33.53
01/23	310.85	60	38	6.68	0.00	24.73
01/22	315.91	64	38	7.49	0.00	21.32
01/21*	328.68	88	31	4.50	0.00	19.63
02/20	239.39	50	29	4.93	0.00	14.98
Annual Growth	18.9%	—	—	25.4%	—	22.3%

*Fiscal year change

LVMH Moet Hennessy Louis Vuitton

A family-run group, LVMH Moët Hennessy Louis Vuitton strives to ensure the long-term development of each of its Houses in keeping with their identity, their heritage and their expertise. LVMH makes wines and spirits (Dom Pérignon, Moët & Chandon, Veuve Clicquot, and Hennessy), perfumes (Christian Dior, Guerlain, and Givenchy), cosmetics (Make Up For Ever, Fresh, and Benefit), fashion and leather goods (Marc Jacobs, Givenchy, Kenzo, and Louis Vuitton), and watches and jewelry (TAG Heuer, Bulgari). LVMH's selective retail division includes Sephora cosmetics stores, Le Bon Marché, a Paris department stores, and DFS Group (duty-free shops). LVMH is owned by holding company Christian Dior and Bernard Arnault, the richest man in France. The majority of its sales were generated in Asia.

Operations
The company's brands and trade names are organized into six business groups. Four business groups ? Fashion & Leather Goods (about 50%), Watches & Jewelry (nearly 15%), Perfumes & Cosmetics (approximately 10%), and Wines and Spirits roughly 10% of sales) ? comprise brands dealing with the same category of products that use similar production and distribution processes. The Selective Retailing business group (about 20%) comprises the company's own-label retailing activities. The Other and holding companies business group comprises brands and businesses that are not associated with any of the above-mentioned business groups.

Geographic Reach
Headquartered in Paris, France, the company has nearly 5,555 stores in Europe, Asia, the US, and other regions. More than 40% of sales were generated from Asia, of which over 5% were generated from Japan; followed by the US with roughly 25%; the European countries with about 20% (roughly 5% from France); and other regions with the remaining. With approximately 110 production sites in France, the company operates in some 80 countries worldwide.

Sales and Marketing
Revenue mainly comprises retail sales within the company's store network (including e-commerce websites) and wholesale sales through agents and distributors. Direct sales to customers are mostly made through retail stores in Fashion and Leather Goods and Selective Retailing, as well as certain Watches and Jewelry and Perfumes and Cosmetics brands. Wholesale sales mainly concern the Wines and Spirits businesses, as well as certain Perfumes and Cosmetics and Watches and Jewelry brands.

Financial Performance
The company's revenue in 2021 increased to EUR 6.6 billion compared to EUR 5.2 billion in the prior year.

Profit in 2021 increased to EUR 684 million compared to EUR80 million in the prior year.

Strategy
The company's strategic priorities are: pursue value enhancing strategy; develop production capacities to ensure sustainable growth; further improve efficiency of distribution in key markets; and accelerate efforts to protect the environment, in particular in supply chains and packaging.

Mergers and Acquisitions
In early 2021, LVMH Moët Hennessy Louis Vuitton SE has completed the acquisition of US-based, Tiffany & Co., the global luxury jeweler. The acquisition of this iconic US jeweler will deeply transform LVMH's Watches & Jewelry division and complement LVMH's 75 distinguished Maisons. Terms were not disclosed.

HISTORY

Woodworker Louis Vuitton started his Paris career packing dresses for French Empress Eugenie. He later designed new types of luggage, and in 1854 he opened a store to sell his designs. In 1896 Vuitton introduced the LV monogram fabric that the company still uses. By 1900 Louis Vuitton had stores in the US and England, and by WWI Louis' son, Georges, had the world's largest retail store for travel goods.

Henry Racamier, a former steel executive who had married into the Vuitton family, took charge in 1977, repositioning the company's goods from esoteric status symbols to designer must-haves. Sales soared from $20 million to nearly $2.5 billion within a decade. Concerned about being a takeover target, Racamier merged Louis Vuitton in 1987 with Moët Hennessy (which made wines, spirits, and fragrances) and adopted the name LVMH Moët Hennessy Louis Vuitton.

Moët Hennessy had been formed through the 1971 merger of Moët et Chandon (the world's #1 champagne maker) and the Hennessy Cognac company (founded by Irish mercenary Richard Hennessy in 1765). Moët Hennessy acquired rights to Christian Dior fragrances in 1971.

Racamier tried to reverse the merger when disagreements with chairman Alain Chevalier arose. Racamier invited outside investor Bernard Arnault to increase his interest in the company. Arnault gained control of 43% of LVMH and became chairman in 1989. Chevalier stepped down, but Racamier fought for control for another 18 months and then set up Orcofi, a partner of cosmetics rival L'Oréal.

LVMH increased its fashion holdings with the purchases of the Givenchy Couture Group (1988), Christian Lacroix (1993), and Kenzo (1993). The company also acquired 55% of French media firm Desfosses International (1993), Celine fashions (1996), the Château d'Yquem winery (1996), and duty-free retailer DFS Group (1996). Next LVMH bought perfume chains Sephora (1997) and Marie-Jeanne Godard (1998). In 1998 LVMH integrated the Paris department store Le Bon Marché, which was controlled by Arnault.

LVMH accumulated a 34% stake in Italian luxury goods maker Gucci in early 1999 and planned to buy all of it. Fellow French conglomerate Pinault-Printemps-Redoute (PPR) later thwarted LVMH by purchasing 42% of Gucci.

Through its LV Capital unit, in 1999 LVMH began acquiring stakes in a host of luxury companies, including a joint venture with fashion company Prada to buy 51% of design house Fendi (LVMH bought Prada's 25.5% stake for $265 million in November 2001). It has since upped its Fendi stake to about 70%. LVMH later added the Ebel, Chaumet, and TAG Heuer brands to its new watch division.

In early 2000 LVMH bought Miami Cruiseline Services, which operates duty-free shops on cruise ships, auction house L'Etude Tajan, and 67% of Italian fashion house Emilio Pucci. The company later purchased 35% of French video game retailer Micromania and 51% of department store Samaritaine. In late 2000 LVMH acquired Gabrielle Studio, which owns all Donna Karan licenses. In 2001 the company bought Donna Karan International.

LVMH bought in 2001 the Newton and MountAdam vineyards for about $45 million. It then began marketing De Beers diamond jewelry in a 50-50 joint venture with the diamond powerhouse. In March LVMH prompted the investigation of a Dutch court into the PPR-Gucci alliance. The company sold its stake in Gucci to PPR for $806.5 million in October.

In October 2002 LVMH ceased trading on the Brussels and Nasdaq exchanges to concentrate on its Euronext investors. In October 2003 the company sold Canard-Duchene to the Alain Thienot Group. LVMH shed several of the less productive of its 50 brands in 2003, including auction house Phillips, de Pury & Luxemborg and fashion brand Michael Kors.

LVMH opened its biggest store -- a four-story emporium on New York's Fifth Avenue -- in February 2004. A few months later, the company added whisky-maker Glenmorangie PLC to its subsidiary roster. LVMH also made its debut in the South African market in October 2004, opening its first sub-Saharan boutique in Johannesburg. Also during the year, Bliss spas was sold off.

In early 2004 LVMH won a landmark lawsuit against Morgan Stanley, alleging that the firm had used biased research in misstatements about the financial health of LVMH that caused damage to the company's image. The presiding Parisian court ordered Morgan Stanley to pay 100 million euros (about $38 million) in damages. Morgan Stanley appealed the ruling later that year.

In late 2005 LVMH opened its largest store to date on the Champs-ElysÃ©es in Paris and the De Beers brand was introduced in the US with stores in New York and Los Angeles. Also that year, LVMH was the winning bidder for whisky maker Glenmorangie PLC, for which it paid Â£300 million. On the sell side, LVMH divested fashion design house Christian Lacroix SNC.

In May 2007 LVMH acquired a 55% stake in Chinese distillery Wenjun for an undisclosed amount. (Jiannanchun, the distillery's previous owner, retained a 45% stake in Wenjun.) In December 2007 the luxury goods firm acquired the French newspaper Les Echos from publisher Pearson. LVMH controls Les Echos' rival, the financial daily La Tribune, but has agreed to sell it. Group Les Echos deal includes the newspaper, Web site, business magazine Enjeux , and other financial information services.

In late 2008 Sephora SA acquired a 45% stake in the Russian perfume and cosmetics chain Ile de BeautÃ©. (The agreement, which gave Sephora the option to become a majority shareholder, allowed LVMH to up its share to 65% in mid-2011.) The firm acquired the luxury yacht-maker Royal Van Lent.

In August 2009 LVMH acquired 50% stakes in two French wine makers: privately-held Cheval Blanc; and La Tour du Pin, owner of the Chateau Quinault l'Enclose estate.

In early 2010 LVMH acquired a 40% stake in Dondup, an Italian apparel and denim brand for more than $43 million (or 30 million euros). Its plans are to expand Dondup's business internationally. Later in 2010 the company purchased a 70% stake in the Brazilian fragrance and cosmetics retailer Sack's. The acquisition, estimated to be worth R$250 million, is a move on LVMH's part to expand its Sephora beauty chain in Brazil, one of the fastest-growing beauty markets in the world.

Adding to its vast portfolio of luxury brands, in February 2011 LVMH acquired Ole Henriksen, a leading luxury botanical skincare company founded and owned by its namesake. Later that same week, LVMH bought a 70% stake in Nude Brands skin care, as the company continues to acquire niche brands. The four-year-old line - described as "biocompatible luxury skin care" - was founded by Bryan Meehan and Ali Hewson, wife of U2 front man Bono. In March, LVMH fired Dior star designer John Galliano amid charges of anti-Semitism. In September LVMH completed its tender offer from Rome-based Bulgari, acquiring about 98% of the shares.

EXECUTIVES

Chairman, Chief Executive Officer, Bernard Arnault
Managing Director, Director, Antonio Belloni
Development and Acquisitions Senior Vice President, Director, Nicolas Bazire
Human Resources and Synergies Executive Vice President, Chantal Gaemperle
Chief Financial Officer, Jean-Jacques Guiony
Strategy Member, Jean-Baptiste Voisin
Secretary, Marc-Antoine Jamet
Lead Independent Director, Charles de Croisset
Independent Director, Sophie Chassat
Independent Director, Clara Gaymard
Independent Director, Marie-Josee Kravis
Independent Director, Marie-Laure Sauty de Chalon
Independent Director, Yves-Thibault de Silguy
Independent Director, Natacha Valla
Independent Director, Hubert Vedrine
Director, Antoine Arnault
Director, Delphine Arnault
Director, Dominique Aumont
Director, Marie-Veronique Belloeil-Melkin
Director, Diego Della Valle
Auditors : Mazars

LOCATIONS

HQ: LVMH Moet Hennessy Louis Vuitton
22 avenue Montaigne, Paris 75008
Phone: (33) 1 44 13 22 22   **Fax:** (33) 1 44 13 21 19
Web: www.lvmh.com

2018 Stores

	No.
Europe	
France	514
Other countries	1,153
Asia	
Japan	422
Other countries	1,289
US	783
Other regions	431
Total	4,592

2018 Sales

	% of total
Europe	
France	10
Other countries	19
Asia	
Japan	7
Other countries	29
US	24
Other regions	11
Total	100

PRODUCTS/OPERATIONS

2018 Sales

	% of total
Fashion & leather goods	39
Selective retailing	28
Wines & spirits	11
Perfumes & cosmetics	13
Watches & jewelry	9
Total	100

Selected Brands and Operations

Fashion and leather goods
    Berluti
    Celine
    Donna Karan
    Emilio Pucci
    Fendi
    Gabrielle Studio (Donna Karan label)
    Givenchy
    Kenzo
    Loewe
    Loro Piana
    Louis Vuitton
    Marc Jacobs
    Thomas Pink
Retailing
    DFS Group
    La Samaritaine
    Le Bon Marché
    Miami Cruiseline Services (duty-free shops)
    Sephora
Fragrances and cosmetics
    Aqua di Parma
    BeneFit
    Bliss
    Fresh
    Guerlain
    Kenzo Parfums
    Make Up For Ever
    Marc Jacobs Fragrances
    Nude skin care
    Ole Henriksen
    Parfums Christian Dior
    Parfums Givenchy
Spirits and wines
    10 Cane
    Belvedere
    Canard-Duchêne
    Chandon Estates
    Château d'Yquem
    Dom Pérignon
    Hennessy
    Krug
    Mercier
    Moët & Chandon
    MountAdam
    Newton
    Ruinart
    Veuve Clicquot
Watches and jewelry
    Bulgari
    Chaumet
    De Beers
    Ebel
    Fred
    Omas
    TAG Heuer
    Zenith
Media (Desfosses International Group)
    Investir
    La Tribune
    Les Echos
    Radio Classique
Other
    Royal van Lent (luxury yachts)

COMPETITORS

ARCADIA GROUP LIMITED
CHRISTIAN DIOR
COMPAGNIE FINANCIERE RICHEMONT SA
Douglas Holding AG
INTER PARFUMS, INC.
KERING
Kering Holland N.V.
LAURA ASHLEY HOLDINGS PLC
NEIMAN MARCUS GROUP INC
SOCIETE ANONYME DES GALERIES LAFAYETTE

HISTORICAL FINANCIALS

Company Type: Public

Income Statement — FYE: December 31

	REVENUE ($mil)	NET INCOME ($mil)	NET PROFIT MARGIN	EMPLOYEES
12/23	95,423	16,806	17.6%	0
12/22	84,611	15,042	17.8%	0
12/21	72,697	13,623	18.7%	157,953
12/20	54,748	5,770	10.5%	150,479
12/19	60,290	8,051	13.4%	163,309
Annual Growth	12.2%	20.2%	—	—

2023 Year-End Financials

Debt ratio: 16.9%
Return on equity: 26.1%
Cash ($ mil.): 8,610
Current Ratio: 1.32
Long-term debt ($ mil.): 12,435
No. of shares ($ mil.): 499
Dividends
 Yield: —
 Payout: 8.2%
Market value ($ mil.): 81,146

	STOCK PRICE ($) FY Close	P/E High/Low		PER SHARE ($) Earnings	Dividends	Book Value
12/23	162.45	7	5	33.59	2.76	135.30
12/22	144.87	6	4	29.94	2.53	117.47
12/21	165.50	7	5	27.04	1.64	105.99
12/20	124.73	13	7	11.44	1.07	91.12
12/19	93.27	7	4	15.98	1.38	81.56
Annual Growth	14.9%	—	—	20.4%	18.9%	13.5%

LY Corp

Yahoo Japan Corporation operates Yahoo Japan, a Japanese online information portal that offers auctions, entertainment, news, and online shopping in addition to its search engine and Internet directory. It also provides registered users with e-mail, personalized Web pages, and access to topical message boards. Revenue is generated from advertising, e-commerce, and consumer and business services. The acquisitive company is working to capitalize on the growth of smartphones in the Japanese market. Tokyo-based technology investor SOFTBANK and US-based Internet portal Yahoo! jointly set up Yahoo Japan in 1996; the two firms each own about 35% of the company.

EXECUTIVES

President, Chief Executive Officer, Representative Director, Takeshi Idezawa
Group Chief Products Officer, Representative Director, Jungho Shin
Senior Managing Executive Officer, Chief Group Synergy Officer, Director, Takao Ozawa
Senior Managing Executive Officer, Director, Jun Masuda
Senior Managing Executive Officer, Chief Strategy Officer, Director, Taku Oketani
Outside Director, Yoshio Usumi
Outside Director, Maiko Hasumi
Outside Director, Tadashi Kunihiro
Outside Director, Rehito Hatoyama
Auditors : Deloitte Touche Tohmatsu LLC

LOCATIONS

HQ: LY Corp
1-3 Kioicho, Chiyoda-ku, Tokyo 102-8282
Phone: (81) 3 6779 4900
Web: www.lycorp.co.jp

PRODUCTS/OPERATIONS

2016 sales

Marketing Solutions Business	42
Other Business	9
Total	100

2016 sales

Business	39
Personal	20
Total	100

2016 sales

Goods	28
Total	100

COMPETITORS

ADTEGRITY.COM, INC.
ADUX
APOLLO INTERACTIVE, INC.
E-MACHITOWN CO., LTD.
HIBU PLC
MATCH GROUP, LLC
OVERSEE.NET
Rambler Media Group
THRYV, INC.
YAHOO! UK SERVICES LIMITED

HISTORICAL FINANCIALS

Company Type: Public

Income Statement — FYE: March 31

	REVENUE ($mil)	NET INCOME ($mil)	NET PROFIT MARGIN	EMPLOYEES
03/23	12,556	1,342	10.7%	41,165
03/22	12,886	635	4.9%	36,057
03/21	10,890	633	5.8%	34,332
03/20	9,700	752	7.8%	21,134
03/19	8,620	710	8.2%	18,055
Annual Growth	9.9%	17.3%	—	22.9%

2023 Year-End Financials

Debt ratio: 0.1%
Return on equity: 6.3%
Cash ($ mil.): 12,402
Current Ratio: 0.83
Long-term debt ($ mil.): —
No. of shares ($ mil.): 7,530
Dividends
 Yield: 1.5%
 Payout: 23.3%
Market value ($ mil.): 42,547

	STOCK PRICE ($) FY Close	P/E High/Low		PER SHARE ($) Earnings	Dividends	Book Value
03/23	5.65	0	0	0.18	0.09	2.91
03/22	8.63	1	1	0.08	0.10	2.95
03/21	9.91	1	0	0.13	0.16	3.19
03/20	6.30	1	0	0.16	0.32	1.49
03/19	4.86	1	0	0.13	0.08	1.45
Annual Growth	3.9%	—	—	7.6%	2.6%	19.0%

LyondellBasell Industries NV

EXECUTIVES

Chairman, Director, Jacques Aigrain
Chief Executive Officer, Director, Peter E.V. Vanacker
Executive Vice President, Chief Financial Officer, Principal Accounting Officer, Michael C. McMurray, $800,000 total compensation
Investor Relations Senior Vice President, Investor Relations Chief Accounting Officer, Chukwuemeka A. Oyolu
Executive Vice President, Chief Legal Officer, Jeffrey A. Kaplan, $601,110 total compensation
Division Officer, Torkel Rhenman
Division Officer, Kenneth Lane
Director, Lincoln E. Benet
Director, Jagjeet S. Bindra
Director, Robin Buchanan
Director, Stephen F. Cooper
Director, Nance K. Dicciani
Director, Claire S. Farley
Director, Michael Hanley
Director, Albert Manifold
Auditors : PricewaterhouseCoopers LLP

LOCATIONS

HQ: LyondellBasell Industries NV
4th Floor, One Vine Street, London W1J0AH
Phone: (44) 207 220 2600
Web: www.lyondellbasell.com

HISTORICAL FINANCIALS

Company Type: Public

Income Statement — FYE: December 31

	REVENUE ($mil)	NET INCOME ($mil)	NET PROFIT MARGIN	EMPLOYEES
12/23	41,107	2,121	5.2%	20,000
12/22	50,451	3,889	7.7%	19,300
12/21	46,173	5,617	12.2%	19,100
12/20	27,753	1,427	5.1%	19,200
12/19	34,727	3,397	9.8%	19,100
Annual Growth	4.3%	(11.1%)	—	1.2%

2023 Year-End Financials

Debt ratio: 30.4%
Return on equity: 16.5%
Cash ($ mil.): 3,390
Current Ratio: 1.84
Long-term debt ($ mil.): 10,333
No. of shares ($ mil.): 324
Dividends
 Yield: —
 Payout: 76.4%
Market value ($ mil.): —

Macquarie Bank Ltd

EXECUTIVES

Managing Director, Chief Executive Officer, Executive Director, Stuart D. Green
Executive Director, Shemara R. Wikramanayake
Legal and Governance Group Head, Evie Bruce
Risk Management Group Chief Risk Officer, Risk Management Group Head, A. Cassidy
Financial Management Group Chief Financial Officer, Financial Management Group Head, A. H. Harvey

Commodities and Global Markets Chief Operating Officer, Commodities and Global Markets Head, N. Sorbara
Banking and Financial Services Deputy Managing Director, Banking and Financial Services Head, G. C. Ward
Secretary, Dennis Leong
Assistant Secretary, Simone Kovacic
Independent Non-Executive Chairman, Peter H. Warne
Independent Non-Executive Director, Jillian R. Broadbent
Independent Non-Executive Director, Philip M. Coffey
Independent Non-Executive Director, Michael J. Coleman
Independent Non-Executive Director, Michelle A. Hinchliffe
Independent Non-Executive Director, Rebecca J. McGrath
Independent Non-Executive Director, Mike Roche
Independent Non-Executive Director, Glenn R. Stevens
Independent Non-Executive Director, Nicola M. Wakefield Evans
Auditors : PricewaterhouseCoopers

LOCATIONS

HQ: Macquarie Bank Ltd
50 Martin Place, Sydney, New South Wales 2000
Phone: (61) 2 8232 3333
Web: www.macquarie.com.au

HISTORICAL FINANCIALS
Company Type: Public

Income Statement — FYE: March 31

	REVENUE ($mil)	NET INCOME ($mil)	NET PROFIT MARGIN	EMPLOYEES
03/23	12,373	2,611	21.1%	0
03/22	7,931	2,032	25.6%	0
03/21	6,547	1,275	19.5%	0
03/20	5,536	899	16.2%	0
03/19	6,376	1,444	22.7%	0
Annual Growth	18.0%	16.0%	—	—

2023 Year-End Financials
Debt ratio: —
Return on equity: 20.3%
Cash ($ mil.): 27,825
Current Ratio: —
Long-term debt ($ mil.): —
No. of shares ($ mil.): 696
Dividends
Yield: —
Payout: 0.0%
Market value ($ mil.): —

Macquarie Group Ltd

Boasting assets under management of around A$399.2 billion, the holding company for Macquarie Bank and other subsidiaries operates an investment banking practice that provides asset management and finance, banking, advisory, lending, wealth management, and risk and capital services across debt, equity, and commodities for institutional, corporate, government, and retail clients. Founded in 1969, Macquarie Group has offices in about 35 countries. Domestic activities account for about 25% of the company's revenue.

Operations
Macquarie is divided into four Operating Groups, which are supported by four Central Service Groups: Risk Management Group, Legal and Governance, Financial Management Group and Corporate Operations Group.

The Operating Groups are split between annuity-style businesses and markets-facing businesses.

Annuity-style businesses are divided into two division -- Macquarie Asset Management (MAM) is a leading specialist global asset manager, and Banking and Financial Services (BFS), which serves the Australian market through personal banking, wealth management and business banking.

Marketing facing businesses include Commodities and Global Markets, and Macquarie Capital. CGM provides clients with an integrated, end-to-end offering across global markets including equities, fixed income, foreign exchange, commodities and technology, media and telecoms. Macquarie Capital has global capability in advisory and capital raising services, investing alongside partners and clients across the capital structure, providing clients with specialist expertise, advice and flexible capital solutions across a range of sectors.

Geographic Reach
Adelaide, SA, Australia-based Macquarie Group generates some 25% of its total revenue domestically. The Americas accounts for more than 45% and the Europe, Middle East, and Africa (EMEA), with nearly 25%. More than 5% comes from the Asia Pacific region. Macquarie and its subsidiaries have offices in nearly 35 markets in the Americas, EMEA, Asia, Australia, and New Zealand regions.

Sales and Marketing
Macquarie's customers include governmental, institutional, corporate, retail, and counterparties around the world, providing a diversified range of products and services. It has established leading market positions as a global specialist in a wide range of sectors, including resources and commodities, renewables, conventional energy, financial institutions, infrastructure and real estate and have a deep knowledge of Asia-Pacific financial markets.

Financial Performance
Note: Growth rates may differ after conversion to US dollars. This analysis uses financials from the company's annual report.

The company had a net interest income of $2.9 billion, 30% increase from the previous year's net income of $2.2 billion.

In 2022, the company had a net income of $4.7 billion, a 56% increase from the previous year's net income of $3 billion.

The company's cash at the end of 2022 was $84.3 billion. Operating activities generated $50.5 billion. Investing and financing activities generated $12 million, and $84.3 million, respectively.

Strategy
Consistent with the principles of What We Stand For, Macquarie's business strategy is focused on the medium-term with the following key aspects: Risk management approach; Strong balance sheet; Business mix; Diversification; Proven expertise; Adjacencies; as well as pursuit of growth opportunities.

Mergers and Acquisitions
In 2022, Macquarie Asset Management, on behalf of its European Logistics Real Estate Fund, has acquired a Dutch logistics real estate portfolio from the developer VDG Real Estate in an off-market transaction as the manager continues to increase its presence in Europe's logistics real estate sector. Christian Goebel, Co-Head of Macquarie Asset Management's Core/Core-Plus Real Estate strategy said: "With its strategic position along the spine of the EU's supply chain networks and future-facing facilities, this portfolio will help meet the demands of tenants and consumers as the digital economy continues to evolve."

Also in 2022, Macquarie Asset Management, on behalf of an institutional client, has reached an agreement to acquire a portfolio of Class A office buildings in Chile from Credit Suisse Asset Management which held the properties on behalf of one of its international real estate strategies. This acquisition marks Macquarie Asset Management's largest real estate transaction in Latin America to date through a private mandate.

In mid-2021, Macquarie announced that Macquarie Asset Management (MAM) has entered into a binding agreement to acquire AMP Capital's Global Equity and Fixed Income (GEFI) business, including fixed income, Australian listed equities, listed real estate and listed infrastructure, for a consideration of up to $A185 million. Post completion, Macquarie expects to acquire assets and teams focused on GEFI's global clients, as well as new and expanded investment capabilities in Australia and several international markets.

In 2021, Macquarie Capital Principal Finance (Macquarie Capital) announced the majority acquisition of Wavenet Group Holdings Limited (Wavenet), a multi-award-winning provider of telecoms and technology solutions ? serving thousands of small and medium-sized businesses and enterprises across the United Kingdom (UK). The new partnership with Macquarie Capital will boost this growth potential, by providing both expertise and flexible growth capital. This will enable more investment in the people at Wavenet and provide a renewed focus on strategic acquisitions.

In early 2021, Macquarie Asset Management and MAPFRE have acquired An der Alster 42, a prime office building in Hamburg, from Allianz Real Estate. The approximately 6,000m2 property is in the vibrant St. Georg district, near Hamburg's city centre and close to key transport connections. The six-storey office building overlooks the Outer Alster Lake and is leased on a long-term basis to two high-grade anchor tenants. The terms of the transaction have not been disclosed.

Company Background

Macquarie's predecessor organization, Hill Samuel Australia, launched in 1969 as a subsidiary of UK merchant bank Hill Samuel & Co. with three staff members. Macquarie Bank listed on the Australian Securities Exchange in 1996 and was established as non-operating holding company Macquarie Group in 2007.

HISTORY

Macquarie has made a slew of acquisitions in its past. It acquired several North America-based financial services companies, including investment bank Fox-Pitt Kelton Cochran Caronia Waller. In 2010 Macquarie expanded upon its individual and institutional asset management business when it acquired US-based Delaware Investments. It also bought the Canadian investment dealing business of Blackmont Capital, and rebranded it as Macquarie Private Wealth.

Two more US acquisitions were designed to enhance Macquarie Capital's advisory business. In 2010 Macquarie bought US-based specialist Presidio Partners, which performs real estate advisory and capital raising advisory services. Macquarie also bought Los Angeles-based investment bank Regal Capital Advisors, a specialist in strategic and financial advice for the gaming, lodging, and leisure industries.

Overseas, Macquarie acquired the cash equities sales and research business of German private bank Sal. Oppenheim Jr. & Cie. in 2010. The acquisition broadened Macquarie's European business, bolstering its presence in several key markets. Macquarie is looking to buy trading and investment banking businesses in Europe.

The company has also used acquisitions to bolster its position in the energy and other non-traditional banking markets.

In 2009 it acquired Canadian boutique investment bank Tristone Capital, which served the oil and gas industry. Macquarie also acquired the downstream natural gas trading operations of Constellation Energy. The company then combined that business with its Macquarie Cook Energy business to form Macquarie Energy, a larger North American wholesale gas company.

In 2010 Macquarie Energy acquired the wholesale electric marketing and trading portfolio of Integrys Energy Services in a deal that more than doubled Macquarie Energy's customer base and strengthened its position in key North American power markets. Also that year subsidiary Macquarie Aerospace agreed to purchase a portfolio of 53 aircraft from AIG unit International Lease Finance Corporation.

EXECUTIVES

Chief Executive Officer, Managing Director, Executive Director, Shemara R. Wikramanayake
Chief Risk Officer, Andrew Cassidy
Financial Management Group Chief Financial Officer, Financial Management Group Head, A. H. Harvey
Corporate Operations Group Chief Operating Officer, Corporate Operations Group Head, N. Sorbara
Macquarie Bank Chief Executive Officer, S. D. Green
Banking and Financial Services Deputy Managing Director, Banking and Financial Services Head, Greg C. Ward
Macquarie Asset Management Head, B. I. Way
Macquarie Capital Principal Finance Head, F. Herold
Commodities and Global Markets Head, Nicholas O'Kane
Co-Head of Macquarie Capital, Michael J. Silverton
Secretary, Dennis Leong
Chairman, Independent Non-Executive Director, Peter H. Warne
Independent Non-Executive Director, Jillian Rosemary Broadbent
Independent Non-Executive Director, Philip M. Coffey
Independent Non-Executive Director, Michael J. Coleman
Independent Non-Executive Director, Michelle A. Hinchliffe
Independent Non-Executive Director, Rebecca J. McGrath
Independent Non-Executive Director, Mike Roche
Independent Non-Executive Director, Glenn R. Stevens
Independent Non-Executive Director, Nicola M. Wakefield Evans
Auditors : PricewaterhouseCoopers

LOCATIONS

HQ: Macquarie Group Ltd
50 Martin Place, Sydney, New South Wales 2000
Phone: (61) 2 8232 3333
Web: www.macquarie.com

2018 Sales

	% of total
Australia	38
Europe, Middle East, and Africa	29
Americas	25
Asia/Pacific	8
Total	100

PRODUCTS/OPERATIONS

2018 Sales

	% of total
Lending	39
Financial markets	25
Asset & wealth management	18
Capital Markets	18
Total	100

2018 Sales

	% of total
Interest and similar income	38
Fee and commission income	36
Net trading income	15
Other operating income and charges	9
Others	2
Total	100

Selected Services

Bank Accounts
Transaction accounts
Savings account
Cash management accounts
Term deposits
Saving calculator
Credit Cards
Flexible Rewards
Qantas Rewards
Hilton Honors
Balance Transfer
Home Loans
Basic home loan
Offset home loan
Home loan calculators
Vehicle Loans
Car Loans
Motorcycle loans
Recreational vehicle loans
Investments
Online trading
Managed funds
Specialists investments
International Money Transfers
Macquarie Wrap
Private Bank
Financial Advice

COMPETITORS

ALTAMIR
CUSHMAN & WAKEFIELD PLC
DAIWA SECURITIES GROUP INC.
GGL GROUP NUMBER TWO LIMITED
INVESTEC PLC
MESIROW FINANCIAL HOLDINGS, INC
NOMURA HOLDINGS, INC.
RAYMOND JAMES FINANCIAL, INC.
ROBERT W. BAIRD & CO. INCORPORATED
ROTHSCHILD & CO

HISTORICAL FINANCIALS

Company Type: Public

Income Statement
FYE: March 31

	ASSETS ($mil)	NET INCOME ($mil)	INCOME AS % OF ASSETS	EMPLOYEES
03/22	298,642	3,520	1.2%	18,133
03/21	187,002	2,295	1.2%	16,459
03/20	156,194	1,667	1.1%	15,849
03/19	144,076	2,114	1.5%	15,700
03/18	147,250	1,967	1.3%	14,469
Annual Growth	19.3%	15.7%		5.8%

2022 Year-End Financials

Return on assets: 1.4%
Return on equity: 18.5%
Long-term debt ($ mil.): —
No. of shares ($ mil.): 368
Sales ($ mil.): 14,437
Dividends
Yield: 2.9%
Payout: 47.0%
Market value ($ mil.): 55,380

	STOCK PRICE ($) FY Close	P/E High/Low		PER SHARE ($) Earnings	Dividends	Book Value
03/22	150.32	13	9	9.21	4.39	58.00
03/21	116.82	14	8	6.28	2.22	48.41
03/20	52.95	12	6	4.67	4.19	37.83
03/19	92.21	10	8	6.16	3.68	38.88
03/18	80.26	11	8	5.72	3.75	39.03
Annual Growth	17.0%	—	—	12.6%	4.0%	10.4%

Magna International Inc

Through its various subsidiaries and divisions, Magna International operates like a start-up and innovate like a technology company. Besides being one of the world's largest automotive suppliers, Magna also considers itself a technology company delivering mobility solutions. The company makes body, exteriors and chassis, powertrain, active driver assistance, electronics, mechatronics, seating systems, roofing, and lighting systems and mirrors. Operations in North America and Europe represent nearly 90% of total revenues.

Operations

The company operates segments based on four global, product-oriented operating segments: Body Exteriors & Structures (accounts for about 40% of the company's total sales), Power & Vision (around 30%), Complete Vehicles (more than 15%), and Seating Systems (about 15%).

The company's operating results are primarily dependent on the levels of North American, European, Chinese car and light truck production by the customers. While Magna International supply systems and components to every major original equipment manufacturer, it do not supply systems and components for every vehicle, nor is the value of the content consistent from one vehicle to the next.

Geographic Reach

Based on Ontario, Canada, Magna boasts about 345 manufacturing facilities and roughly 90 product development, engineering, and sales centers in about 30 countries. Its operations in North America generates around 45% of its total sales, nearly 45% were produced in Europe, Asia pacific accounts for some 10% and the rest of the world for the remaining.

Sales and Marketing

A significant majority of Magna International's sales are to six customers: General Motors, BMW, Daimler, and Stellantis, which generate around 15% of sales each. Other customers, including Ford and Volkswagen, account for the remaining sales.

Financial Performance

The company had net sales of $36.2 billion in 2021, an 11% increase from the previous year's net sales of $32.6 billion. This was primarily due to a higher sales volume across all of the company's segments.

Net income attributable to Magna International increased $757 million to $1.514 billion for 2021 compared to $757 million for 2020 as a result of an increase in income from operations before income taxes of $942 million, partially offset by an increase of $119 million in income attributable to non-controlling interests and an increase in income taxes of $66 million.

The company's cash at the end of 2021 was $2.9 billion. Operating activities generated $2.9 billion, while investing activities used $2.3 billion, mainly for fixed asset additions. Financing activities used another $1.1 billion, primarily for repurchase of common shares.

Strategy

The company continues to implement a business strategy which is rooted in its best assessment as to the rate and direction of change in the automotive industry, including with respect to trends related to vehicle electrification and advanced driver assistance systems, as well as future mobility business models.

Mergers and Acquisitions

In mid-2021 Magna International has entered into a definitive merger agreement to acquire Stockholm, Sweden-based, Veoneer, a leader in automotive safety technology. Pursuant to the agreement, Magna will acquire all of the issued and outstanding shares of Veoneer for $31.25 per share in cash, representing an equity value of $3.8 billion, and an enterprise value of $3.3 billion. The acquisition builds on Magna's strengths and positions the company's advanced driver assistance systems ("ADAS") business as a global leader with comprehensive capabilities. The acquisition also expands Magna's ADAS business with major customers and provides access to new customers and regions, including in Asia.

Company Background

Magna International has historically expanded its product lines through acquisitions of other auto parts manufacturers. In early 2011, Magna Seating acquired Germany-based Vogelsitze GmbH, which made seats for buses and passenger trains. In 2012, Magna obtained Verwaltungs GmbH, a maker of automotive vacuum, engine, and transmission pumps with two facilities in Germany and one in each of China and Bulgaria. Also in 2012, to strengthen its automotive pump operations, Magna purchased the remaining 50% interest it didn't already own of STT Technologies, which made transmission and engine related pumps for the North American market.

HISTORY

Magna International is rooted in a tool and die shop founded by Frank Stronach and friend Tony Czapka in Ontario, Canada, in 1957. Austrian-born Stronach immigrated to Canada in 1954. By the end of 1957, the business, called Multimatic, had 10 employees. Multimatic delved into car parts when it landed a contract in 1960 to make sun visor brackets for a General Motors division in Canada.

To go public, Multimatic underwent a reverse merger in 1969 with Magna Electronics, a publicly traded maker of components for aerospace, defense, and industrial markets. (Stronach retained control of the company.) Annual sales reached $10 million that year. The company expanded its automotive operations during the early 1970s by adding more stamped and electronic components. Magna was renamed Magna International in 1973.

With sales increasing steadily among its auto parts businesses, Magna sold its aerospace and defense business (now part of Heroux-Devtek) in 1981. The new Magna consisted of five distinct automotive divisions that made seat tracks, door latches, electronic components, and other auto parts. During the 1980s the company expanded by adding factories and product lines. It also capitalized on car makers' penchant for outsourcing labor and bypassing unions. By 1987, when sales reached $1 billion, the company was producing systems for every area of the automobile. Stronach didn't spend all his time on cars, however; he owned race horses and restaurants. He had opened restaurants, tried various publishing ventures (which failed), and even made an unsuccessful run for a Canadian parliament seat in 1988.

Aggressive expansion during the 1980s eventually caught up with the company, and in 1989 Magna began to restructure, selling assets to pay off its debt. The company also was bailed out, in part, by two of its principal customers -- General Motors and Chrysler. Having recovered somewhat, Magna began acquiring small auto parts companies in Europe in 1992.

Magna expanded its European presence with the purchase of Austria-based Steyr-Daimler-Puch in 1998, adding about $1 billion in annual sales. The deal steered Magna into the auto assembly business. Stronach also added Santa Anita Park to his holdings that year. In late 1999 the company's racetrack interests were spun off as Magna Entertainment, with Magna retaining a 78% stake. Stronach's horse, Red Bullet, won the 2000 Preakness. Later that year Magna sold its 50% stake in Webasto Sunroofs to privately-owned German auto parts maker Webasto.

Early in 2001 Stronach's daughter Belinda was named vice chairman and CEO. The company then prepared to spin off Magna Steyr and Intier (now Magna's interiors and seating divisions) as public companies; Intier was spun off later in 2001.

Magna acquired rival automotive mirror maker Donnelly in 2002 in a stock-and-debt deal worth $320 million. The company divested its stake in Magna Entertainment in 2003.

Belinda Stronach stepped down as president, CEO, and director in order to make a bid for the leadership of Canada's new Conservative Party. Her father assumed the role of interim president in early 2004. Ms. Stronach's bid for the leadership of the Conservative Party was not successful. Mr. Stronach ran the company until 2005 when Magna adopted a co-CEO management structure with Donald Walker and Siegfried Wolf at the helm.

Magna and Daimler announced in 2004 that Magna would buy Daimler's drivetrain manufacturing subsidiary New Venture Gear for about $435 million. After approval by the European Commission, New Venture Gear was acquired by a newly created joint venture called New Process Gear, with Magna holding an 80% interest; Daimler held 20% until 2007, when Magna bought out its stake.

Russian conglomerate Basic Element, led by Russian aluminum magnate Oleg Deripaska, spent about $1.5 billion to purchase 20% of Magna in 2007. The transaction gave Magna entry to the Russian market, but late in 2008 Deripaska's bank, BNP Paribas, made a margin call that forced the businessman to give up his shares. In 2008 Magna International acquired Technoplast, a Russia-based manufacturer of plastic automotive interior and exterior parts, which bolstered its capacity in Eastern Europe and Russia.

On the heels of the General Motors bankruptcy filing in 2009, the German government selected Magna International as a partner for Adam Opel, and agreed to provide about ?1.5 billion (around $2 billion) in bridge loans while GM and Magna finalized the contract. A trusteeship for Opel was arranged to keep European operations separate from the Chapter 11 proceedings of GM.

Magna teamed up with Russian banking firm Sberbank to purchase a 55% interest in Opel and its UK-based Vauxhall unit. While GM initially agreed to the sale in September 2009, it backed out in November. The GM board decided to restructure Opel and its European operations instead, because business conditions were improving and the Opel brand was important to its global strategy. In Europe the decision was met with demands by the German government that its ?1.5 billion in bridge loans be returned, as well as protests and planned work stoppages by the German labor union.

The GM bankruptcy was brought on by the economic crisis of 2008 and 2009. Magna responded by implementing cost cutting measures, which included reducing its headcount by approximately 11,500, representing a 14% cutback between 2007 and 2009. It also sold off some of its non-core assets.

Founder and chairman Frank Stronach stepped down in 2010, citing the trend toward more regulatory limitations on company management as one of the reasons. He gave up his controlling share in the company, and with it his voting control. The company purchased and cancelled all of its Class B shares held by the Stronach Group and issued Class A Common shares. This capital transaction ended the company's dual class stock structure. The former premier of Ontario, Mike Harris, took Stronach's place. Co-CEO Siegfried ("Sigi") Wolf also resigned, which made co-CEO Donald Walker the sole CEO of Magna International as of mid-2011.

In early 2011, Magna Seating acquired Germany-based Vogelsitze GmbH, which made seats for buses and passenger trains. In 2012, Magna obtained Verwaltungs GmbH, a maker of automotive vacuum, engine, and transmission pumps with two facilities in Germany and one in each of China and Bulgaria.

EXECUTIVES

Power and Vision Chief Executive Officer,
Magna International Chief Executive Officer,
Magna Electronics Chief Executive Officer,
Executive Director, Seetarama Kotagiri
Chief Financial Officer, Vincent J. Galifi
Operations Chief Operating Officer, Tommy J. Skudutis
Chief Legal Officer, Executive Vice President, Bruce R. Cluney
Chief Human Resources Officer, Executive Vice President, Aaron D. McCarthy
Chief Sales & Marketing Officer, Executive Vice President, Eric J. Wilds
Operational Efficiency Executive Vice President, Uwe Geissinger
Corporate R&D Executive Vice President, Sherif S. Marakby
Systems & Portfolio Strategy Executive Vice President, Anton Mayer
Technology & Investments Executive Vice President, Boris Shulkin
Magna Europe President, Magna Asia President, Guenther F. Apfalter
Chairman, Director, Willian L. Young
Director, Scott B. Bonham
Director, Peter G. Bowie
Director, Mary S. Chan
Director, V. Peter Harder
Director, Kurt J. Lauk
Director, Robert F. MacLellan
Director, Cynthia A. Niekamp
Director, William A. Ruh
Director, Indira V. Samarasekera
Director, Lisa S. Westlake
Auditors : Deloitte LLP

LOCATIONS

HQ: Magna International Inc
337 Magna Drive, Aurora, Ontario L4G 7K1
Phone: 905 726-2462   **Fax:** 905 726-7164
Web: www.magna.com

2017 Sales

	$ mil.	% of total
North America	20,905	53
Europe	15,177	39
Asia	2,791	7
Rest of World	584	1
Corporate & Other	(511)	-
Total	38,946	100

PRODUCTS/OPERATIONS

2017 Sales

	$ mil.	% of total
Body systems and chassis systems	9,744	25
Powertrain systems	6,773	17
Exterior systems	5,325	14
Seating systems	5,203	13
Tooling, engineering & other	3,397	9
Complete vehicle assembly	2,944	8
Vision & electronic systems	2,891	7
Closure systems	2,669	7
Total	38,946	100

2017 Sales

	$ mil.	% of total
General Motors	6,854	18
Ford Motor Company	6,085	16
Fiat / Chrysler Group	5,502	14
Daimler AG	4,719	12
BMW	3,231	11
Volkswagen	4,025	10
Other	7,557	19
Total	38,946	100

Selected Operations, Products, and ServicesBody systems
   Chassis systems
   Seating
   Powertrain
   Electronics
   Mechatronics
   D-Optic headlights
   Clearview mirrors
   Vehicle engineering and manufacturing
   Hybrid dual clutch transmission
   Liteflex modular process
   48 volt edrive
   Driver monitoring systems
   MAX4 Autonomous Drive Platform

COMPETITORS

ALLISON TRANSMISSION HOLDINGS, INC.
AUTOLIV, INC.
GKN LIMITED
HILITE INTERNATIONAL, INC.
LEAR CORPORATION
MANN+HUMMEL FILTRATION TECHNOLOGY INTERMEDIATE HOLDINGS INC.
MOTORCAR PARTS OF AMERICA, INC.
Robert Bosch Gesellschaft mit beschränkter Haftung
TOWER INTERNATIONAL, INC.
VALEO

HISTORICAL FINANCIALS
Company Type: Public

Income Statement　　　　　　　　　　　FYE: December 31

	REVENUE ($mil)	NET INCOME ($mil)	NET PROFIT MARGIN	EMPLOYEES
12/23	42,797	1,213	2.8%	179,000
12/22	37,840	592	1.6%	158,000
12/21	36,242	1,514	4.2%	158,000
12/20	32,647	757	2.3%	158,000
12/19	39,431	1,765	4.5%	0
Annual Growth	2.1%	(9.0%)	—	—

2023 Year-End Financials
Debt ratio: 17.1%　　　　　　No. of shares ($ mil.): 286
Return on equity: 10.6%　　 Dividends
Cash ($ mil.): 1,198　　　　　Yield: —
Current Ratio: 1.06　　　　　Payout: 43.4%
Long-term debt ($ mil.): 4,175　Market value ($ mil.): 16,930

	STOCK PRICE ($) FY Close	P/E High/Low	PER SHARE ($) Earnings	Dividends	Book Value
12/23	59.08	16　11	4.23	1.84	41.47
12/22	56.18	44　23	2.03	1.80	38.24
12/21	80.94	21　14	5.00	1.72	39.74
12/20	70.80	29　10	2.52	1.60	37.83
12/19	54.84	10　 8	5.59	1.46	35.72
Annual Growth	1.9%	—	(6.7%)	6.0%	3.8%

Magnit PJSC

EXECUTIVES
Chief Executive Officer, J. G. Dunning
Auditors: Ernst & Young LLC

LOCATIONS
HQ: Magnit PJSC
15/5, Solnechnaya Street, Krasnodar 350072
Phone: (7) 861 210 98 10
Web: www.magnit-info.ru

HISTORICAL FINANCIALS
Company Type: Public

Income Statement　　　　　　　　　　　FYE: December 31

	REVENUE ($mil)	NET INCOME ($mil)	NET PROFIT MARGIN	EMPLOYEES
12/21	24,718	640	2.6%	0
12/20	20,771	441	2.1%	316,001
12/19	21,991	153	0.7%	308,432
12/18	17,748	485	2.7%	295,882
12/17	19,593	609	3.1%	0
Annual Growth	6.0%	1.3%	—	—

2021 Year-End Financials
Debt ratio: 0.3%　　　　　　No. of shares ($ mil.): 97
Return on equity: 26.5%　　 Dividends
Cash ($ mil.): 977　　　　　 Yield: —
Current Ratio: 0.77　　　　　Payout: 60.2%
Long-term debt ($ mil.): 2,733　Market value ($ mil.): —

Mahindra & Mahindra Ltd

Auditors: B S R & Co. LLP

LOCATIONS
HQ: Mahindra & Mahindra Ltd
Gateway Building, Apollo Bunder, Mumbai 400 001
Phone: (91) 22 22021031　　**Fax:** (91) 22 22875485
Web: www.mahindra.com

HISTORICAL FINANCIALS
Company Type: Public

Income Statement　　　　　　　　　　　FYE: March 31

	REVENUE ($mil)	NET INCOME ($mil)	NET PROFIT MARGIN	EMPLOYEES
03/22	12,027	868	7.2%	48,961
03/21	10,293	247	2.4%	40,619
03/20	12,741	16	0.1%	39,792
03/19	15,291	768	5.0%	42,875
03/18	14,432	1,154	8.0%	41,673
Annual Growth	(4.5%)	(6.9%)	—	4.1%

2022 Year-End Financials
Debt ratio: 0.6%　　　　　　No. of shares ($ mil.): 1,112
Return on equity: 14.8%　　 Dividends
Cash ($ mil.): 1,467　　　　 Yield: —
Current Ratio: 1.34　　　　　Payout: 19.6%
Long-term debt ($ mil.): 6,419　Market value ($ mil.): —

Manulife Financial Corp

Manulife Financial Corporation is a leading international financial services group that helps people make their decisions easier and lives better. It operates as Manulife across its offices in Canada, Asia, and Europe, and primarily as John Hancock in the US. Manulife provides financial advice, insurance, as well as wealth and asset management solutions for individuals, groups, and institutions. At the end of 2022, it had more than 116,000 agents, and thousands of distribution partners, serving more than 34 million customers. It has almost C$1.3 trillion in assets under management and administration. About 75% of Manulife's total revenue comes from outside of Canada.

Operations
Manulife's reporting segments are Asia, US, Canada, Wealth and Asset Management (Global WAM) and Corporate and Other. Asia, Global WAM, and Canada accounts for about 60%, 25%, and 15% of total revenue, respectively.

Insurance and annuity products (Asia, Canada and US) include a variety of individual life insurance, individual and group long-term care insurance and guaranteed and partially guaranteed annuity products. Products are distributed through multiple distribution channels, including insurance agents, brokers, banks, financial planners and direct marketing. Manulife Bank of Canada offers a variety of deposit and credit products to Canadian customers.

Global WAM segment include mutual funds and exchange-traded funds, group retirement and savings products, and institutional asset management services across all major asset classes. These products and services are distributed through multiple distribution channels, including agents and brokers affiliated with the company, independent securities brokerage firms and financial advisors pension plan consultants and banks.

Corporate and Other Segment comprised of investment performance of assets backing capital, net of amounts allocated to operating segments; costs incurred by the corporate office related to shareholder activities (not allocated to the operating segments); financing costs; Property and Casualty Reinsurance Business; and run-off reinsurance operations including variable annuities and accident and health.

Geographic Reach
Headquartered in Ontario, Canada, Manulife operates in the Americas (Canada, and the US), Europe, and the Asia region (Japan, Hong Kong, Macau, Singapore, mainland China, Vietnam, Indonesia, the Philippines, Malaysia and Cambodia, and Myanmar).

Asia generates nearly 75% of total revenue, while Canada accounts for about 25%, and other countries for less than 5%.

Sales and Marketing
Manulife distributes its insurance products through agents, brokers, banks, and financial planners. It also markets products directly to customers.

The group has over 116,000 contracted agents and more than 100 bank partnerships in Asia.

Financial Performance
Note: Growth rates may differ after conversion to US Dollars.

The company reported a total revenue of C$17.1 billion, a 72% decrease from the previous year's total revenue of C$61.8 billion. This was primarily due to the higher volume of realized and unrealized losses on assets supporting insurance and investment contract liabilities and on the macro hedge program.

In 2022, the company had a net income of C$7 billion, a 2% increase from the previous year's net income of C$6.9 billion.

The company's cash at the end of 2022 was C$18.6 billion. Operating activities generated C$17.7 billion, while investing activities used C$18.6 billion, mainly for purchases and mortgage advances. Financing activities used another C$3 billion, primarily for shareholders' dividends and other equity distributions.

Company Background

Manulife acquired US financial services giant John Hancock in a $10 billion deal in 2004, bringing Manulife into the top ranks of US and global life insurers. Manulife subsequently rebranded its US financial products with the more-recognizable John Hancock name and logo. Manulife also consolidated John Hancock's Canadian subsidiary, Maritime Life Assurance Company into its flagship subsidiary, The Manufacturers Life Insurance Company.

EXECUTIVES

Chief Executive Officer, Director, Roy Gori
General Account Investments Chief Investment Officer, Scott S. Hartz
Chief Marketing Officer, Karen A. Leggett
Chief Operations Officer, Rahul M. Joshi
Chief Risk Officer, Rahim Hirji
Chief Information Officer, Shamus E. Welland
Chief Human Resources Officer, Pamela O. Kimmet
Chief Financial Officer, Philip J. Witherington
General Counsel, James D. Gallagher
Chairman, Director, John M. Cassaday
Director, Leagh E. Turner
Director, May Siew Boi Tan
Director, Guy L.T. Bainbridge
Director, Joseph P. Caron
Director, Susan F. Dabarno
Director, Julie E. Dickson
Director, C. James Prieur
Director, Tsun-Yan Hsieh
Director, John R.V. Palmer
Director, Andrea S. Rosen
Director, Donald R. Lindsay
Auditors : Ernst & Young LLP

LOCATIONS

HQ: Manulife Financial Corp
200 Bloor Street East, Toronto, Ontario M4W 1E5
Phone: 416 926-3000 **Fax:** 416 926-5657
Web: www.manulife.com

2017 Sales

	% of total
US	41
Asia	37
Canada	21
Other	1
Total	100

PRODUCTS/OPERATIONS

2017 Sales

	% of total
Premiums	
Life & health	44
Annuities & pensions	8
Net investment income	27
Other	21
Total	100

COMPETITORS

AIA GROUP LIMITED
Endurance Specialty Holdings Ltd
GIBRALTAR LIFE INSURANCE CO., LTD., THE
INSURANCE AUSTRALIA GROUP LIMITED
LIVERPOOL VICTORIA FRIENDLY SOCIETY LTD
MASSACHUSETTS MUTUAL LIFE INSURANCE COMPANY
QBE INSURANCE GROUP LIMITED
REINSURANCE GROUP OF AMERICA, INCORPORATED
ROYAL LONDON MUTUAL INSURANCE SOCIETY,LIMITED(THE)
Sun Life Financial Inc

HISTORICAL FINANCIALS
Company Type: Public

Income Statement — FYE: December 31

	ASSETS ($mil)	NET INCOME ($mil)	INCOME AS % OF ASSETS	EMPLOYEES
12/23	660,590	3,850	0.6%	38,000
12/22	627,717	5,393	0.9%	0
12/21	720,487	5,578	0.8%	0
12/20	691,420	4,611	0.7%	0
12/19	621,362	4,301	0.7%	35,000
Annual Growth	1.5%	(2.7%)	—	2.1%

2023 Year-End Financials
Return on assets: 0.5%
Return on equity: 10.0%
Long-term debt ($ mil.): —
No. of shares ($ mil.): 1,806
Sales ($ mil.): 10,650
Dividends
Yield: —
Payout: 55.9%
Market value ($ mil.): 39,913

	STOCK PRICE ($) FY Close	P/E High/Low		PER SHARE ($) Earnings	Dividends	Book Value
12/23	22.10	8	7	1.97	1.10	19.76
12/22	17.84	6	4	2.72	0.98	21.69
12/21	19.07	6	5	2.78	0.93	23.10
12/20	17.82	7	3	2.30	1.13	20.77
12/19	20.29	7	5	2.13	0.75	19.27
Annual Growth	2.2%	—	—	(1.9%)	10.0%	0.6%

Mapfre SA

EXECUTIVES

Honorary Chairman, Jose Manuel Martinez Martinez
Chief Executive Officer, Chairman, Executive Director, Antonio Huertas Mejias
First Vice Chairman, Executive Director, Ignacio Baeza Gomez
Third Vice Chairman, Executive Director, Jose Manuel Inchausti Perez
Executive Director, Francisco Jose Marco Orenes
Member, Alfredo Castelo Marin
Member, Jesus Martinez Castellanos
Executive Director, Fernando Mata Verdejo
Member, Eduardo Perez de Lema
Member, Fernando Perez-Serrabona Garcia
Member, Elena Sanz Isla
Member, Jaime Tamayo Ibanez
Secretary, Angel L. Davila Bermejo
Vice Secretary, Jaime Alvarez de las Asturias Bohorques Rumeu
Second Vice Chairman, Independent External Director, Catalina Minarro Brugarolas
Independent External Director, Jose Antonio Colomer Guiu
Independent External Director, Ana Isabel Fernandez Alvarez
Independent External Director, Maria Leticia de Freitas Costa
Independent External Director, Rosa Maria Garcia Garcia
Independent External Director, Antonio Gomez Ciria
Independent External Director, Pilar Perales Viscasillas
External Director, Luis Hernando de Larramendi Martinez
External Director, Antonio Miguel-Romero de Olano
External Director, Alfonso Rebuelta Badias
Auditors : KPMG Auditores, S.L.

LOCATIONS

HQ: Mapfre SA
Carretera de Pozuelo 52. Madrid, Majadahonda 28222
Phone: (34) 91 581 1100 **Fax:** (34) 91 581 1143
Web: www.mapfre.com

HISTORICAL FINANCIALS
Company Type: Public

Income Statement — FYE: December 31

	ASSETS ($mil)	NET INCOME ($mil)	INCOME AS % OF ASSETS	EMPLOYEES
12/23	60,859	750	1.2%	30,873
12/22	63,682	685	1.1%	31,293
12/21	72,274	866	1.2%	32,341
12/20	84,870	646	0.8%	33,730
12/19	81,411	684	0.8%	34,324
Annual Growth	(7.0%)	2.3%	—	(2.6%)

2023 Year-End Financials
Return on assets: 1.1%
Return on equity: 8.5%
Long-term debt ($ mil.): —
No. of shares ($ mil.): 3,064
Sales ($ mil.): 27,763
Dividends
Yield: —
Payout: 93.1%
Market value ($ mil.): 13,483

	STOCK PRICE ($) FY Close	P/E High/Low		PER SHARE ($) Earnings	Dividends	Book Value
12/23	4.40	24	18	0.24	0.23	3.06
12/22	3.76	21	16	0.22	0.22	2.54
12/21	4.02	18	13	0.28	0.22	3.14
12/20	4.00	26	18	0.21	0.24	3.44
12/19	5.50	32	25	0.22	0.23	3.26
Annual Growth	(5.4%)	—	—	2.2%	(0.7%)	(1.6%)

Marks & Spencer Group PLC

Marks and Spencer (M&S) is a leading British retailer that operates as a family of businesses, selling high-quality, great-value, own-brand products and services, alongside a carefully selected range of third-party brands. The company sells its products through a network of over 1,485 stores and about 100 websites globally, and together, across its stores, support centers, warehouses, and supply chain. Its approximately 65,000 colleagues serve over 30 million customers annually. M&S is the UK's #1 retailer of womenswear, lingerie, menswear, kidswear, and home. M&S sells exclusively own-brand upmarket groceries and owns a 50% investment in Ocado's UK retail business. M&S generates the majority of its revenue in the UK.

Operations

M&S operates a family of parallel businesses. It predominantly sells own-brand products, manufactured and marketed exclusively under the M&S brand.

M&S Food sells sustainably sourced products of exceptional quality and value through five main categories: protein, deli and dairy; produce; ambient and in-store bakery; meals, dessert and frozen; hospitality; and food-on-the-move.

The company also sells stylish quality, sustainably sourced own-brand clothing and homeware through its principal product departments: womenswear, menswear, lingerie, kidswear, and home.

Through M&S Bank (operated by HSBC), the company provides a range of financial services, including credit cards, current account and savings, insurance and mortgages. M&S Energy is a competitive fully renewable energy source provider (operated by Octopus).

Lastly, M&S operates an active Property Development team to maximize the value of its property assets through investment and development opportunities.

The UK Food, accounts for about 60% of the company's revenue, includes the results of the UK retail food business and UK Food franchise operations, with the following five main categories: protein deli and dairy; produce; ambient and in-store bakery; meals, dessert and frozen; and hospitality and "Food on the Move"; and direct sales to Ocado Retail Limited. The UK Clothing & Home, bringing in approximately 30%, comprises the retailing of womenswear, menswear, lingerie, kidswear and home products through UK retail stores and online. International business consists of Marks and Spencer owned businesses in Europe and Asia and the international franchise operations. The business accounts for about 10%.

Geographic Reach

Based in London, M&S has a channel network of more than 1,485 stores and more than 100 international markets. The company generates the majority of its revenue in the UK.?

Sales and Marketing

M&S serves about 30 million customers annually from across the UK. It has a channel network of stores and online services in the UK and more than 100 international markets. To promote the benefits of the M&S app and encourage more customers to download and start using it, the company ran a two week app-focused campaign, including its first ever Sparks TV advert.

Financial Performance

Note: Growth rates may differ after conversion to US Dollars.

Group sales before adjusting items was Â£10.9 billion. Sales increased 7% versus 2019/20, driven by Food sales up 10%, Clothing & Home sales up 4% and International sales down 1%. Statutory revenue in the period was Â£10.9 billion, an increase of 7% versus 2019/20.

In 2021 the company had a net income of was Â£306.6 million, a 255% increase from the previous year's net loss of Â£198 million.

The company's cash at the end of 2021 was Â£1.8 billion. Operating activities generated Â£1.4 billion, while investing activities used Â£245.7 million, mainly for purchase of property, plant and equipment. Financing activities used another Â£595.9 million, primarily for payment of interest as well as repayment of lease liabilities.

Strategy

The aim of Marks & Spencer's transformation is to restore the company to sustainable profitable growth. However, in the new landscape?where the way it works and how customers shop may never be the same again?M&S is learning from the crisis to ensure that it is changed for good.

M&S will accelerate aspects of the transformation to increase its relevance in a new-consumer environment. M&S moved to 'trusted value' in Clothing & Home and option count reduction and supplier concentration brought forward. The reduction in range and shift towards fast moving product at great value necessitated by the crisis, resulting in a permanent reduction of 20% in autumn/winter store option count. The role of sourcing offices will be increased so that sampling, ordering, and quality issues are dealt with offshore. M&S is also developing a faster "near-sourcing" supply chain, to enable a test and re-order of seasonal fashion lines, particularly for the online business.

M&S is also establishing a store estate for the new world with the replacement of ageing stores already under way and shift in relationships with property providers to go faster. In addition, M&S is turbocharging growth to become an online winner in Clothing & Home and Food. The sharp growth of online grocery during the crisis is evidence of this, as is the strengthening performance of its online Clothing & Home.

Mergers and Acquisitions

In early 2021, Marks & Spencer purchased the Jaeger fashion brand from administrators, in a deal that excludes the retailers 63 remaining stores, as part of a strategy to bolster its clothing division with new names. No figures were disclosed.

HISTORY

Fleeing anti-Semitic persecution in Russian Poland, 19-year-old Michael Marks immigrated to England in 1882. Eventually settling in Leeds, Marks eked out a meager existence as a traveling peddler until he opened a small stall at the town market in 1884. Because he spoke little English, Marks laid out all of his merchandise and hung a sign that read, "Don't Ask the Price, It's a Penny," unaware at the time that self-service would eventually become the retailing standard. His methods were so successful that he had penny bazaars in five cities by 1890.

Finding himself unable to run the growing operation alone, Marks established an equal partnership with Englishman Tom Spencer, a cashier for a local distributor, forming Marks and Spencer in 1894. By the turn of the century, the company had 36 branches. Following the deaths of Spencer (1905) and Marks (1907), management of the company did not return to family hands until 1916, when Marks' 28-year-old son Simon became chairman.

Marks and Spencer broke with time-honored British retailing tradition in 1924 by eliminating wholesalers and establishing direct links with manufacturers. In 1926 the firm went public, and two years later it launched its now famous St Michael brand. The company turned its attention to pruning unprofitable departments to concentrate on goods that had a rapid turnover. In 1931 the Marks & Spencer stores (M&S) introduced a food department that sold produce and canned goods.

The company sustained severe losses during WWII, when bombing damaged approximately half of its stores. Marks and Spencer rebuilt, and in 1964 Simon's brother-in-law Israel Sieff became chairman. The company expanded to North America a decade later by buying three Canadian chains: Peoples (general merchandise, sold 1992), D'Allaird's (women's clothing, sold 1996), and Walker's (clothing shops, converted to M&S). Sieff's son Marcus Sieff became chairman in 1972. It opened its first store in Paris in 1975.

Derek Rayner replaced Marcus Sieff as chairman in 1984, becoming the first chairman hired from outside the Marks family since 1916. Under Rayner, Marks and Spencer moved into financial services by launching a charge card in 1985. The company purchased US-based Kings Super Markets and Brooks Brothers (upscale clothing stores) in 1988. Rayner retired in 1991, and CEO Richard Greenbury became chairman. During the 1990s M&S opened new stores in Germany, Hong Kong, Hungary, Spain, and Turkey.

In 1997 it paid Littlewoods $323 million for 19 UK stores, which it converted to M&S. Greenbury, facing criticism that the company was too slow to expand and embrace new ideas, was succeeded in 1999 as CEO by handpicked heir Peter Salsbury. That year, continued poor sales led Marks and Spencer to cut 700 jobs, close its 38 M&S stores in

Canada, and part ways with its clothing supplier of 30 years, William Baird. In early 2000 Marks and Spencer dodged a takeover attempt by investor Philip Green. Chairman Luc Vandevelde took over as CEO in September when Salsbury resigned.

In spring 2001 Marks and Spencer announced a recovery plan to salvage its struggling M&S chain by selling off many of its global operations, including its profitable US businesses (Brooks Brothers and Kings Super Markets). Unhappy with the company's direction and its departure from older values, Marks and Spencer board members Sir David Sieff (the last remaining founder member), Sir Ralph Robins, and Sir Michael Perry left the board in July 2001. Marks and Spencer sold Brooks Brothers to Retail Brand Alliance for $225 million (a loss from the $750 million the company paid for it in 1988) in November 2001 and nearly managed to sell its Kings Super Markets business to New York supermarket operator D'Agostino in July 2002, but the deal fell through later in the year due to a lack of financing.

Also in July 2002 Vandevelde -- who is credited with masterminding the M&S turnaround -- announced he would give up his role as CEO and hand the reins to managing director Roger Holmes. Vandevelde became the company's part-time chairman in January 2003.

In May 2004 both Vandevelde and Holmes left M&S. Stuart Rose, formerly head of Arcadia, was named CEO; non-executive board member Paul Myners was named interim chairman of the company. Prior to the shift in management, billionaire entrepreneur Philip Green (who owns Arcadia and Bhs in the UK) confirmed that he would mount a takeover bid for the retail group. Ultimately, Green's final proposal (the third he made for the retailer in a five week period) was rejected by the M&S board in July 2004. In October M&S bought the Per Una brand from designer George Davies for about £126 million and moved its head office from the old Baker Street location to Waterside House by the Grand Union Canal in London. In November Rose ousted more than a handful of company executives, including Maurice Helfgott, Mark McKeon, Laurel Powers-Freeling, Jean Tomlin, Jack Paterson, and 20-year veteran Alison Reed, who stepped down as CFO in April 2005.

M&S relaunched its Home catalogue in early 2005. In February of that year the company announced the sale of its former Baker Street headquarters, Michael House, to real estate company London & Regional Properties for £115 million. M&S, which is in a profit squeeze, said it plans to used the proceeds for "general corporate purposes." In August M&S sold its Lifestore in Gateshead to Active Asset Investment Management for £43 million. In December M&S won a ruling by the European Court of Justice that resulted in the company receiving a £30 million tax windfall from the Treasury.

In April 2006 M&S completed the sale of its 26-store Kings Super Markets chain in the US for about $61.5 million. Lord Burns, a former chairman of Abbey National, took up the post of chairman in July 2006 after joining Marks and Spencer as deputy chairman in 2005. Burns succeeded interim chairman Paul Myners.

In 2007 M&S opened three stores in Taiwan. (Marks & Spencer Taiwan is 60%-owned by the British retailer and 40% by President Chain Store.) The following year M&S opened its first store on the mainland, in Shanghai.

In June 2008 Lord Burns stepped down as chairman of the company and was succeeded by CEO Stuart Rose who became executive chairman. David Michels was appointed deputy chairman, as well. Rose stepped down as CEO in May 2010 to make way for Marc Bolland, thus decoupling the roles of chairman and chief executive at the firm.

EXECUTIVES

Food Chief Executive Officer, Executive Director, Steve Rowe
Chief Financial Officer, Eoin Tonge
Chief Strategy and Transformation Executive Director, Chief Strategy and Transformation Director, Executive Director, Katie Bickerstaffe
General Counsel, Secretary, Nick Folland
Chairman, Archie Norman
Senior Independent Director, Andy Halford
Non-Executive Director, Alison Brittain
Non-Executive Director, Tamara Ingram
Non-Executive Director, Sapna Sood
Non-Executive Director, Andrew C. Fisher
Non-Executive Director, Justin M. King
Non-Executive Director, Pip McCrostie
Auditors: Deloitte LLP

LOCATIONS

HQ: Marks & Spencer Group PLC
Waterside House, 35 North Wharf Road, London W2 1NW
Phone: (44) 20 7935 4222
Web: www.marksandspencer.com

2018 Sales

	% of total
UK	91
International	9
Total	100

PRODUCTS/OPERATIONS

2018 Sales

	% of total
UK	
Food	57
Clothing and Home	34
International	9
Total	100

COMPETITORS

ALBERTSON'S LLC
DAIEI, INC., THE
GNC HOLDINGS, INC.
NATURE'S SUNSHINE PRODUCTS, INC.
SPAR (UK) LIMITED
TEAVANA CORPORATION
THE BODY SHOP INTERNATIONAL LIMITED
THE GREAT ATLANTIC & PACIFIC TEA COMPANY, INC.
THE NATURE'S BOUNTY CO
VITACOST.COM INC.

HISTORICAL FINANCIALS

Company Type: Public

Income Statement — FYE: April 1

	REVENUE ($mil)	NET INCOME ($mil)	NET PROFIT MARGIN	EMPLOYEES
04/23	14,762	449	3.0%	0
04/22	14,294	402	2.8%	67,086
04/21*	12,661	(273)	—	69,846
03/20	12,438	28	0.2%	75,505
03/19	13,594	43	0.3%	78,597
Annual Growth	2.1%	78.9%		

*Fiscal year change

2023 Year-End Financials

Debt ratio: 49.3%
Return on equity: 12.7%
Cash ($ mil.): 1,321
Current Ratio: 0.80
Long-term debt ($ mil.): 3,939
No. of shares ($ mil.): —
Dividends
Yield: —
Payout: 0.0%
Market value ($ mil.): —

	STOCK PRICE ($) FY Close	P/E High/Low	PER SHARE ($) Earnings	Dividends	Book Value
04/23	4.22	23 12	0.22	0.00	0.00
04/22	4.12	43 22	0.20	0.00	1.95
04/21*	4.19		(0.14)	0.00	1.61
03/20	2.43	540 166	0.01	0.42	2.32
03/19	7.26	394 302	0.03	0.45	2.16
Annual Growth	(12.7%)		68.4%		

*Fiscal year change

Marubeni Corp.

One of Japan's largest sogo shosha (general trading companies), Marubeni conducts a broad range of import/export activities across numerous sectors. These include lifestyle, ICT business & logistics, forest products, food, agri business, chemicals, power business, energy, metals & mineral resources, plant, aerospace & ship, finance & leasing business, construction, auto & industrial machinery. Its footprint spans around 130 branches, including a dozen in Japan, around 55 overseas branches, and about 30 operated by overseas subsidiaries. The Marubeni traces the origins of its business to the linen cloth business started by its founder Chubei Itoh in 1858.

Operations

Marubeni Corporation and its consolidated subsidiaries use their broad business networks, both within Japan and overseas, to conduct importing and exporting (including third country trading), as well as domestic business, encompassing a diverse range of business activities across wide-ranging fields including lifestyle, IT solutions, food, agri business, forest products, chemicals, metals & mineral resources, energy, power, infrastructure project, aerospace & ship, finance, leasing & real estate business, construction, industrial machinery & mobility, next generation business development and next generation corporate development.

Geographic Reach

Headquartered in Tokyo, Japan; Marubeni have around 130 branches and offices, consisting of Head Office, about a dozen Japan branches and offices, 55 overseas branches and offices, and about 30 overseas corporate subsidiaries containing around 35 branches and offices.

Financial Performance

The company's revenue for fiscal 2022 increased to JPY8.5 trillion compared from the prior year with JPY6.3 trillion.

Net income for fiscal 2022 increased to JPY424.3 billion compared from the prior year with JPY223.3 billion.

Cash provided by operations JPY311.9 billion while cash used for investing and financing activities were JPY79.7 billion and JPY419.6 billion, respectively.

Strategy

The overall growth of the Marubeni Group is linked to that of the businesses conducted by the large number of companies in the Group. To enable each Group company to pursue growth independently, Marubeni oversees the business management of every Group company as the shareholder and business owner, based on a common set of Group policies and strategies. This system of operational execution and management is designed to help maximize corporate value.

To ensure this system, the Marubeni Group Governance Policy was established on April 1, 2017, with the following company-wide aims: to share and disseminate Marubeni Group management policies; to build and strengthen Group governance by clarifying the roles and responsibilities of the Corporation (as shareholder/ business owner) and Group companies; and to maintain and plan the codification of necessary systems, policies, and rules.

HISTORY

Marubeni's origins are closely linked to those of another leading Japanese trading company. ITOCHU founder Chubei Itoh set up Marubeni Shoten K. K. in 1858 as an outlet in Osaka for his textile trading business (originally C. Itoh & Co.). The symbol for the store was a circle (maru) drawn around the Japanese word for red (beni). As C. Itoh's global operations expanded, the Marubeni store served as headquarters.

Marubeni was split off from C. Itoh in 1921 to trade textiles, although it soon expanded its operations to include industrial and consumer goods. To mobilize for WWII, the Japanese government reunited Marubeni and C. Itoh in 1941, merging them with another trading company, Kishimoto, into a new entity, Sanko Kabushiki Kaisha. In 1944 Sanko, Daido Boeki, and Kureha Spinning were ordered to consolidate into a larger entity to be called the Daiken Co., but the war ended before all operations were fully integrated.

Spun off from Daiken in 1949, Marubeni began trading internationally. It opened a New York office in 1951 and diversified into food, metals, and machinery. During the Korean War, Marubeni benefited from the UN's use of Japan as a supply base.

In 1955 Marubeni merged with Iida & Company and changed its name to Marubeni-Iida. It received a government concession to supply silicon steel and iron sheets critical to the growing Japanese auto and appliance industries. The company expanded into engineering -- building factories, aircraft, and a nuclear reactor for the Japan Atomic Energy Research Institute -- and into petrochemicals, fertilizers, and rubber products.

Marubeni-Iida was behind the Fuyo keiretsu formed in the early 1960s. Fuyo (another word for Mt. Fuji) is a powerful assemblage of some 150 companies, including Canon, Hitachi, and Nissan, that form joint ventures and develop think tanks.

The firm became Marubeni Corp. in 1972, and a year later it bought Nanyo Bussan, another trading company. In 1973 Marubeni's image was tarnished by allegations that it had hoarded rice for sale on the Japanese black market.

In the 1990s Marubeni won several major construction contracts. Among them, Marubeni formed a venture in 1998 with John Laing and Turkey's Alarko Alsim to rebuild three airports in Uzbekistan.

Marubeni had begun offering Internet access in 1995, and two years later it launched an Internet-based long-distance telephone service. In 1999 the trading house formed two ventures with US firm Global Crossing, one to start operating Pacific Crossing One (the Japan-US cable) and another to lay a cable network in Japan.

That year Marubeni tied up with fellow trading company ITOCHU to integrate their steel processing subsidiaries in China to try to keep their Chinese businesses afloat. In 2000 ITOCHU and Marubeni formed an online steel trading joint venture with US-based e-commerce company MetalSite. The two companies also integrated their entire steel divisions in 2001, forming the Marubeni-Itochu Steel joint venture, among the largest steel companies in Japan.

Taking responsibility for the sharp downturn in Marubeni's financial performance, chairman Iwao Toriumi announced in 2001 that he would step down. The company launched a major restructuring effort the next year that was designed to give more autonomy to the managers of individual business units.

In 2005 Marubeni launched a large, power and water project in Abu Dhabi.

In 2007 Marubeni entered into the finance leasing industry in the US, launching subsidiary, CoActiv Capital Partners.

In 2008 Marubeni acquired US-based The PIC Group, Inc., an independent global provider of services and programs focused on power generation and other industrial facilities and services. In 2009 it acquired 49% of Invenergy Thermal Financing LLC, which owns three natural-gas fired power plants (with 1,014 MW of generating capcity) in the US.

In 2009 the company completed the Laffan Refinery in Qatar, which began commercial operations that year. It also signed a $2 billion deal to build the Shuweihat S2 Independent Water and Power Producer project in the United Arab Emirates.

EXECUTIVES

Chairman, Director, Fumiya Kokubu
President, Chief Executive Officer, Representative Director, Masumi Kakinoki
Executive Vice President, Representative Director, Akira Terakawa
Senior Managing Executive Officer, Chief Administrative Officer, Mutsumi Ishizuki
Senior Managing Executive Officer, Jun Horie
Senior Managing Executive Officer, Chief Strategy Officer, Kenichiro Oikawa
Senior Managing Executive Officer, Chief Financial Officer, Representative Director, Takayuki Furuya
Outside Director, Kyohei Takahashi
Outside Director, Yuri Okina
Outside Director, Masato Kitera
Outside Director, Shigeki Ishizuka
Outside Director, Hisayoshi Ando
Outside Director, Mutsuko Hatano
Auditors : Ernst & Young ShinNihon LLC

LOCATIONS

HQ: Marubeni Corp.
1-4-2 Ohtemachi, Chiyoda-ku, Tokyo 100-8088
Phone: (81) 3 3282 2111   **Fax:** (81) 3 3282 4241
Web: www.marubeni.com

2016 Sales

	% of total
Japan	53
US	33
Singapore	4
Other countries	10
Total	100

PRODUCTS/OPERATIONS

2019 Sales

	% of total
Food	54
Chemical & Forest Products	22
Energy & Metals	11
Consumer Products	5
Transportation & Industrial Machinery	5
Power projects & Plant	3
Total	100

2019 Sales

	% of total
Goods	97
Commission on service & trading margins	3
Total	100

COMPETITORS

CORE-MARK HOLDING COMPANY, INC.
George Weston Limited
ITOCHU CORPORATION
J.W. FILSHILL LIMITED
METCASH LIMITED
PERFORMANCE FOOD GROUP COMPANY
SMART & FINAL STORES LLC
SOJITZ CORPORATION
SUMITOMO CORPORATION
TOPCO ASSOCIATES, LLC

HISTORICAL FINANCIALS

Company Type: Public

Income Statement — FYE: March 31

	REVENUE ($mil)	NET INCOME ($mil)	NET PROFIT MARGIN	EMPLOYEES
03/23	69,005	4,077	5.9%	53,097
03/22	69,950	3,488	5.0%	53,145
03/21	57,190	2,035	3.6%	53,059
03/20	62,898	(1,818)	—	53,395
03/19	66,832	2,084	3.1%	50,540
Annual Growth	0.8%	18.3%	—	1.2%

2023 Year-End Financials

Debt ratio: 0.2%
Return on equity: 21.2%
Cash ($ mil.): 4,571
Current Ratio: 1.34
Long-term debt ($ mil.): 12,073
No. of shares ($ mil.): 1,696
Dividends
Yield: 4.1%
Payout: 238.9%
Market value ($ mil.): 228,557

	STOCK PRICE ($) FY Close	P/E High/Low	PER SHARE ($) Earnings	Dividends	Book Value
03/23	134.75	0 0	2.37	5.53	12.74
03/22	116.43	1 0	1.99	4.26	10.70
03/21	84.07	1 0	1.15	2.65	9.46
03/20	49.17	— —	(1.07)	3.17	8.04
03/19	70.47	1 1	1.18	3.21	10.29
Annual Growth	17.6%	— —	19.1%	14.5%	5.5%

Mazda Motor Corp. (Japan)

Mazda sells about 1.3 million passenger cars and pickup trucks in about 130 countries annually. The company has manufacturing operations in Japan, China, Thailand, Mexico, Vietnam, Malaysia, and Russia. Its lineup consists of the Mazda 2, 3, 6, and the MX-5 (passenger vehicles), the CX-3, -4, -5, -8, -30, -9 (crossover SUVs), and the BT-50 (pickup truck). The company produces the majority of its vehicles at home in Japan, although North America is its largest market. Mazda was founded in 1920.

Operations

The company's major product line includes MAZDA CX-3, CX-30, CX-4, CX-5, CX-8, CX-9, MAZDA 2, MAZDA 3, MAZDA 6, MAZDA MX-5, and MAZDA BT-50.

Overall, SUV/Crossovers accounts for about 60% of revenue and commercial vehicles and others (including micro-mini vehicles) account for the remaining some 40%.

Geographic Reach

Based in Hiroshima, Japan, North America is Mazda's biggest market at some 40% of total revenue. Japan accounts for over 25%, Europe and other markets account for the remaining revenue.

Mazda has major production sites in Japan, Mexico, Thailand, Malaysia, Vietnam, Russia and China. The company conducts sales in more than 130 countries and regions around the world.

Sales and Marketing

Mazda has around 210 sales companies in Japan and some 135 internationally.

Financial Performance

The company reported net sales of ¥3.1 trillion, an 8% increase from the previous year's net sales of ¥2.9 trillion.

In 2022, the company had a net income of ¥112.4 billion, a ¥110.2 billion increase from the previous year's net income of ¥2.2 billion.

The company's cash at the end of 2022 was ¥740.4 billion. Operating activities generated ¥189.2 billion, while investing activates used ¥136.2 billion, primarily for purchase of property, plant and equipment. Financing activities used another ¥86.4 billion, mainly for repayments of long-term loans payable.

HISTORY

Ingiro Matsuda founded cork producer Toyo Cork Kogyo in Hiroshima in 1920. The company changed its name to Toyo Kogyo in 1927 and began making machine tools. Impressed by Ford trucks used in 1923 earthquake-relief efforts, Matsuda had the company make a three-wheel motorcycle/truck hybrid in 1931.

During the 1930s the company supplied products to the Sumitomo industrial conglomerate. The Sumitomo Bank became a major shareholder of Toyo Kogyo.

The second Sino-Japanese War forced Toyo Kogyo to make rifles and cut back on its truck production. Although the company built a prototype passenger car in 1940, the outbreak of WWII refocused it on weapons. The August 1945 bombing of Hiroshima killed more than 400 Toyo Kogyo workers, but the company persevered, producing 10 trucks that December. By 1949 it was turning out 800 per month.

The company launched the first Mazda, a two-seat minicar, in 1960. The next year Toyo Kogyo licensed AUDI's new rotary engine technology. After releasing a string of models, the company became Japan's #3 automaker in 1964. Toyo Kogyo introduced the first Mazda powered by a rotary engine, Cosmo/110S, in 1967, followed by the Familia in 1968.

The company grew rapidly and began exporting to the US in 1970. However, recession, high gas prices, and concern over the inefficiency of rotary engines halted growth in the mid-1970s. Sumitomo Bank bailed out Toyo Kogyo. The company shifted emphasis back to piston engines but managed to launch the rotary engine RX-7 in 1978.

Ford's need for small-car expertise and Sumitomo's desire for a large partner for its client led to Ford's purchase of 25% of Toyo Kogyo in 1979. The company's early 1980s GLC/323 and 626 models were sold as Fords in Asia, Latin America, and the Middle East.

Toyo Kogyo changed its name to Mazda Motor Corporation in 1984. ("Mazda" is loosely derived from Matsuda's name, but the carmaker has never discouraged an association with the Zoroastrian god of light, Ahura Mazda.) The company opened a US plant in 1985, but a strong yen, expensive increases in production capacity, and a growing number of models led to increased overhead, soaring debt, and shrinking margins. By 1988 Mazda had begun to focus on sporty niche cars, launching the hot-selling Miata in 1989.

The company faced more problems with the early 1990s recession. In 1992 Mazda introduced a new 626 model. That year Mazda also sold half its interest in its Flat Rock, Michigan, plant to Ford. As the yen, development costs, and prices for its cars in the US all rose, sales in the US fell. In 1993 Mazda reorganized subsidiary Mazda of America by cutting staff.

Ford sank $481 million into Mazda in 1996, increasing its stake to 33%. That year the Ford-appointed former EVP of Mazda, Henry Wallace, became Mazda's president, making history as the first non-Japanese to head a major Japanese corporation. In 1997 Wallace resigned to become CFO of Ford's European operations, and former Ford executive James Miller replaced him. That year Mazda consolidated four US operations into Mazda North American Operations.

Restructuring continued in 1998 as Mazda consolidated some European operations and closed a plant in Thailand. In 1999 Mazda sold its credit division to Ford and its Naldec auto parts unit to Ford's Visteon unit. It announced plans to sell its stake in South Korean carmaker Kia Motors. Later in the year another American, Ford's Mark Fields, took over as president.

In 2000 Mazda recalled 30,000 of that year's MPV minivans to fix a powertrain control module and asked owners of all 2000 MPVs to bring in their vehicles for front-bumper reinforcement. Mazda also announced plans to close about 40% of its North American dealership outlets over the next three years. The following year Mazda completed a program to assume direct control over distribution in some European markets including France, Italy, Spain, and the UK.

In 2007 Mazda opened a new vehicle assembly plant in Nanjing, China, and also began building its passenger vehicle plant in Thailand. To strengthen its sales in Japan, the company introduced the Mazda Advantage Loan in 2007 in cooperation with PRIMUS Financial Services. Mazda acquired a 40% stake in PRIMUS in March 2008 to strengthen its auto financing business.

Ford's 33% stake in the company was reduced to about 13% in 2008 after the cash-starved company sold off approximately 20% of its holdings. A consortium of Hiroshima Bank, Panasonic (both Mazda business partners), and Mazda itself paid a combined sum of about $540 million to bring control of the company back to Japan.

EXECUTIVES

Chairman, Representative Director, Kiyotaka Shobuda

President, Chief Executive Officer, Representative Director, Masahiro Moro

Senior Managing Executive Officer, Chief Financial Officer, Representative Director, Jeffrey H. Guyton

Senior Managing Executive Officer, Director, Mitsuru Ono

Senior Managing Executive Officer, Director, Yasuhiro Aoyama

Senior Managing Executive Officer, Chief Technology Officer, Director, Ichiro Hirose

Senior Managing Executive Officer, Director, Takeshi Mukai

Senior Managing Executive Officer, Chief Strategy Officer, Director, Takeji Kojima

Senior Managing Executive Officer, Chief Financial Officer, Tetsuya Fujimoto

Senior Managing Executive Officer, Makoto Yoshihara

Chief Information Officer, Akihiro Kidani

Outside Director, Kiyoshi Sato

Outside Director, Michiko Ogawa

Director, Nobuhiko Watabe

Outside Director, Akira Kitamura

Outside Director, Hiroko Shibasaki

Outside Director, Masato Sugimori

Outside Director, Hiroshi Inoue

Auditors : KPMG AZSA LLC

LOCATIONS

HQ: Mazda Motor Corp. (Japan)
  3-1 Shinchi, Fuchu-cho, Aki-gun, Hiroshima 730-8670
Phone: (81) 82 282 1111
Web: www.mazda.co.jp

2017 Sales

	% of total
Japan	18
North America	34
Europe	20
Other regions	28
Total	100

PRODUCTS/OPERATIONS

Selected Models
BT-50 (pickup)
CX-3 (crossover SUV)
CX-4 (crossover SUV)
CX-5 (crossover SUV)
CX-8 (crossover SUV)
CX-9 (crossover SUV)
Mazda 2 (Demio)
Mazda 3 (Axela, hatchback sedan)
Mazda 6 (sport sedan)
Mazda 8 (MPV)
MX-5 (roadster)

Selected Subsidiaries and Affiliates
Mazda Australia Pty. Ltd.
Mazda Motor Logistics Europe NV (Belgium)
Mazda Motor of America, Inc.

COMPETITORS

FCA US LLC
FORD MOTOR COMPANY
HINO MOTORS, LTD.
NISSAN MOTOR CO.,LTD.
PEUGEOT SA
RENAULT
SUBARU CORPORATION
SUZUKI MOTOR CORPORATION
TOYOTA MOTOR CORPORATION
VOLKSWAGEN AG

HISTORICAL FINANCIALS

Company Type: Public

Income Statement   FYE: March 31

	REVENUE ($mil)	NET INCOME ($mil)	NET PROFIT MARGIN	EMPLOYEES
03/23	28,732	1,072	3.7%	48,481
03/22	25,652	670	2.6%	48,750
03/21	26,029	(285)	—	49,786
03/20	31,600	111	0.4%	50,479
03/19	32,188	573	1.8%	49,998
Annual Growth	(2.8%)	17.0%	—	(0.8%)

2023 Year-End Financials

Debt ratio: 0.1%   No. of shares ($ mil.): 629
Return on equity: 10.4%   Dividends
Cash ($ mil.): 4,715   Yield: 3.2%
Current Ratio: 1.37   Payout: 8.9%
Long-term debt ($ mil.): 2,968   Market value ($ mil.): 2,892

	STOCK PRICE ($) FY Close	P/E High/Low		PER SHARE ($) Earnings	Dividends	Book Value
03/23	4.59	0	0	1.70	0.15	17.16
03/22	3.65	0	0	1.06	0.16	16.99
03/21	4.09	—	—	(0.45)	0.09	16.95
03/20	2.66	0	0	0.18	0.16	17.19
03/19	5.56	0	0	0.91	0.16	17.48
Annual Growth	(4.7%)	—	—	16.9%	(1.8%)	(0.5%)

McKesson Europe AG

McKesson Europe is a global leader in healthcare supply chain management solutions, retail pharmacy, community oncology and specialty care, and healthcare information solutions. In addition to over 70 distribution centers serving more than 57,000 pharmacies, McKesson Europe owns and manages wholesale network that delivers to approximately 27,000 pharmacies every day in seven European countries and operates approximately 400 pharmacies and manage more than 300 pharmacies in four European countries. The companywas founded by Fraz Ludwig Gehe in 1833 and has a presence in about 10 European countries. Majority of its sales were generated in France.

Operations

McKesson Europe operates through two divisions: Pharmaceutical Distribution and Retail Pharmacy.

The Pharmaceutical Distribution business, accounts for about 95% of sales, delivers pharmaceutical and other healthcare-related products to pharmacies across Europe. This business functions as a vital link connecting manufacturers to retail pharmacies by supplying medicines and other products sold in pharmacies. Pharmaceutical and other healthcare-related products are stored at regional wholesale branches using technology-enabled management systems.

Bringing in over 5% of sales, Retail Pharmacy business serves patients and consumers directly through its own pharmacies and franchise pharmacies. The Lloyds Pharmacy brand operates in Belgium, Ireland and Italy. In addition, it partners with independent pharmacies under its franchise program and are involved in an associated company in the Netherlands.

Geographic Reach

Headquartered in Stuttgart, Germany, McKesson Europe generates about 70% of sales in France, over 10% from Belgium and over 5% in Italy. The Lloyds Pharmacy brand operates in Belgium, Ireland, Italy, and the UK.

Sales and Marketing

McKesson Europe serves patients and consumers in European countries directly through its own pharmacies and franchise pharmacies. The company partners with pharmaceutical manufacturers, providers, pharmacies, governments and other healthcare organizations to help provide the right medicines, medical products and healthcare services to the right patients. In addition, it also partners with independent pharmacies under its franchise program.

Its promotion and advertising expenses were EUR 8.1 million and EUR 7.9 million in 2022 and 2021, respectively.

Financial Performance

The company had a revenue of EUR 9.3 billion, a 9% increase from the previous year's revenue of EUR 8.5 billion.

In 2022, the company had a net loss of EUR 54.3 million, a 105% decrease from the previous year's net income of EUR 2.8 million.

The company's cash at the end of 2022 was EUR 1.9 billion. Operating activities generated EUR 0.9 million, while investing activities generated EUR 692.1 million. Financing activities generated another EUR 48.5 million.

Strategy

To achieve its goals, McKesson follows its McKesson Europe playbook which has three dimensions: foundational, transformational and aspirational. The foundational dimension is about strengthening the company's core business by delivering superior customer value with a competitive cost structure and by winning as one, inclusive team with an enterprise-first mindset. In the transformational dimension the company focuses on working smarter and growing smarter, e.g. position the business to benefit from digitalization and make progress towards McKesson's carbon-neutral goal in 2030. In the aspirational dimension, the company's goal is to be the preferred partner in patient care and become the best place to work in healthcare.

EXECUTIVES

Executive Board Member, Martin Fisher
Chief Financial Officer, Executive Board Member, Marion Helmes
Chairman, Stephen Borchert
Chairman, Stephan Gemkow
Deputy Chairman, Ihno Goldenstein
Director, Klaus Borowicz
Director, Hubertus Erlen
Director, Florian Funck
Director, Joerg Lauenroth-Mago
Director, Pauline Lindwall
Director, Susan Naumann
Director, Ulrich Neumeister
Director, W.M. Henning Rehder
Director, Patrick Schwarz-Schütte
Director, Hanspeter Spek
Director, Gabriele Katharina Stall
Auditors : Deloitte GmbH

LOCATIONS

HQ: McKesson Europe AG
Stockholmer Platz 1, Stuttgart 70137
Phone: (49) 711 5001 00   **Fax:** (49) 711 5001 12 60
Web: www.mckesson.eu

2013 Sales

	% of total
France	30
UK	22
Germany	21
Brazil	9
Other	18
Total	100

PRODUCTS/OPERATIONS

2013 Sales

	% of total
Pharmacy solutions	84
Customer solutions	16
Total	100

Selected Subsidiaries
Pharmacy Solutions (wholesale distribution division)
  AAH Pharmaceuticals Ltd. (UK)
  AFM S.p.A. (Italy)
  Cahill May Roberts Group Ltd (Ireland)
  GEHE Pharma Handel GmbH (Germany)
  GEHE Pharma Praha, spol. S r.o. (Czech Republic)
  Herba Chemosan Apotheker AG (Austria)
  Kemofarmacija d.d. (Slovenia, Romania, and Croatia)
  Laboratoria Flandria NV (Belgian)
  Norsk Medisinaldepot AS (Norway)
  OCP Repartition (France)
  OCP Portugal, Produtos Farmacêuticos SA (Portugal)
  Panpharma Participacoes S.A. (54%, Brazil)
  Pharma Belgium SA
  Rudolf Spiegel GmbH (Germany)
  Tjellesen Max Jenne A/S (Denmark)
Patient and Consumer Solutions (retail pharmacies division)
  Admenta Italia S.p.A.
  Apotheke DocMorris (retail franchise)
  Brocacef (45%, Netherlands)
  DocMorris Kooperationen GmbH (mail order)
  Lékárny Lloyds s.r.o. (Czech Republic)
  Lloyds Pharmacy Limited (UK)
  Lloydspharma SA (Belgium)
  Unicare Pharmacy Limited (Ireland)
  Vitusapotek AS (Norway)

COMPETITORS

AMERISOURCEBERGEN CORPORATION
CARDINAL HEALTH, INC.
China National Pharmaceutical Group Co., Ltd.
HIKMA PHARMACEUTICALS PUBLIC LIMITED COMPANY
MCKESSON CORPORATION
Mediq B.V.
PHOENIX Pharmahandel GmbH & Co KG
SUZUKEN CO., LTD.
THE HARVARD DRUG GROUP L L C
WALGREENS BOOTS ALLIANCE, INC.

HISTORICAL FINANCIALS

Company Type: Public

Income Statement   FYE: March 31

	REVENUE ($mil)	NET INCOME ($mil)	NET PROFIT MARGIN	EMPLOYEES
03/21	19,646	(12)	—	0
03/20	18,752	(272)	—	31,912
03/19	23,782	(66)	—	32,946
03/18	25,998	(368)	—	34,338
03/17	22,055	(1,033)	—	35,716
Annual Growth	(2.9%)			

2021 Year-End Financials
Debt ratio: 11.3%   No. of shares ($ mil.): —
Return on equity: (-0.5%)   Dividends
Cash ($ mil.): 1,398   Yield: —
Current Ratio: 1.26   Payout: 0.0%
Long-term debt ($ mil.): 621   Market value ($ mil.): —

	STOCK PRICE ($) FY Close	P/E High/Low	PER SHARE ($) Earnings	Dividends	Book Value
03/21	6.25	— —	(0.06)	0.13	0.00
03/20	3.91	— —	(1.34)	0.12	9.30
03/19	5.71	— —	(0.33)	0.12	10.94
03/18	6.37	— —	(1.81)	0.13	11.51
03/17	5.52	— —	(5.09)	0.12	9.85
Annual Growth	3.2%	—	—	2.2%	

Mediobanca Banca Di Credito Finanziario SpA

Mediobanca a premier specialized financial group offering Wealth Management, Consumer Banking and Corporate & Investment Banking services. The group is the number one merchant bank in Italy and a leader in Southern Europe. It provides top-tier advisory services and specialized lending solutions. Mediobanca serve its customers by prioritizing their interests and the most appropriate solutions, which range from the simplest to the most sophisticated on financial markets. The group also hold specialized asset management boutiques to offer an increasingly distinctive range of proprietary products. Its subsidiary Compass is a pioneer in consumer credit in Italy. Mediobanca generates vast majority of its revenue from Italy.

Operations
Mediobanca operates four main divisions: Wealth Management (WM); Consumer Banking (CB); Corporate and Investment Banking (CIB); and Insurance - Principal Investing (PI).

CB division accounts for more than 35% of total revenue and provides retail customers with a full range of consumer credit products: personal loans, special-purpose loans, salary-backed loans, credit cards, in addition to the buy-now-pay-later solution called "Pagolight". The division also includes Compass RE, which reinsures risks linked to insurance policies sold to clients, Compass Rent, which operates in second-hand vehicle and car hire, and the newly-incorporated Compass Link, which distributes Compass products and services via external collaborators.

WM division (some 25% of revenue) brings together all portfolio management services offered to the various client segments, plus asset management. It includes CheBanca!, which targets the Premier client bracket; the MBPB and CMB Monaco private banking networks, and the Asset Management companies (Cairn Capital, Mediobanca SGR, Mediobanca Management Company, and RAM Active Investment), plus Spafid.

CIB division (around 25%) includes investment banking (lending, advisory, capital markets activities) and proprietary trading (activities performed by Mediobanca and Mediobanca International, Mediobanca Securities and Messier et Associés); and Specialty Finance, which in turn consists of Factoring and Credit Management (including NPL portfolio acquisitions and management) performed by MBFACTA and MBCredit Solutions.

PI division generates almost 15% of

revenue and includes the group's portfolio of equity investments and shares, in particular the 12.8% stake in Assicurazioni Generali. The latter company has been the main component of the division for years and stands out for the solidity and consistency of its results, high profitability and contribution in terms of diversification and stabilization to the Mediobanca group's revenues.

Broadly speaking, about 50% of Mediobanca's revenue comes from net interest income, while some 30% comes from net fee and commission income and around 5% from net trading income.

Geographic Reach

Based in Italy, Mediobanca has a consolidated presence in some key markets, with branches and offices in Paris, New York, Madrid, London and Istanbul.

Italy generates about 90% revenue and International operations account for the rest.

Financial Performance

Note: Growth rates may differ after conversion to US dollars. This analysis uses financials from the company's annual report.

Company's revenue for fiscal 2022 increased by £726.5 million compared from the prior year with £627.3 million.

Net income for fiscal 2022 increased to £134.2 million compared from the prior year with £100.2 million.

Strategy

The macroeconomic scenario, defined in conjunction with the Group's budget, factors in central bank measures to dampen the inflationary pressure and a stabilization of the Russia/Ukraine conflict, resulting in a rise in interest rates and a moderate widening of the BTP/Bund spread. Growth in Italian GDP is expected to slow in 2023.

In this scenario, Mediobanca expects to continue to reach the objectives set in the Strategic Plan for 2023, on stable customer loans and growing AUM in Private Banking, supported by ongoing investments in technology and product innovation. Revenues should be boosted by higher fees and commissions, given the growing volumes of assets under management, and by higher net interest income due to the repricing of assets and availability of retail funding.

HISTORY

In 1946 the three Italian "banks of national interest," Banca Commerciale Italiana (Comit), Credito Italiano (now Unicredito Italiano), and Banco di Roma (now part of Banca di Roma), founded Mediobanca to offer medium-term credit, a market they were barred from.

Enrico Cuccia was with Comit at the time Mediobanca was formed and moved over to head the new institution. In 1955 he created the shareholder structure that later caused a twin uproar in Italian banking and politics: Although the state owned well more than half of the bank's shares, a group of wealthy shareholders who together owned less than 10% of the bank wielded the power.

Over the next several decades, Cuccia and Mediobanca operated on the behalf of these powerful shareholders and their family businesses, devising deals on terms that other companies could not get. Mediobanca also created a web of cross-holdings in other banks, which made money for the bank by selling its funds and other services.

In the 1960s and 1970s, the bank was at the center of a number of deals, not all of which were stellar successes. The bank engineered a merger between Pirelli and Dunlop, which fizzled, and also pushed the merger of chemical companies Montecatini and Edison into Montedison, which took a beating in the marketplace.

In 1982 Cuccia ostensibly retired, taking the title of honorary chairman. However, his influence never waned, and the 1980s brought a war for the soul of Italian business. In 1985 Romano Prodi, head of IRI, the state-run organization (liquidated in 2000) that owned nearly 60% of the bank, planned to privatize the bank. Instead the noble wing came up with its own privatization plan: The private shareholders requested that the state bring its stake in Mediobanca to below 50% by selling some of its shares to the Mediobanca cabal. In 1988 the privatization went through, but as part of the pact it was stipulated that the new shareholders would share decision-making powers with the Ala Nobile.

If the 1980s were wild, the 1990s were out of control. Italy's banking industry, hampered by red tape and old alliances, was left behind the rest of Europe. Many of Italy's banks became stock companies when banking laws changed, and many merged to compete in the European Union. Many of those deals threatened Mediobanca's hegemony, so it tried to block them. The bank nixed Unicredito's 1998 bid for Comit (which instead merged with Banca Intesa), as well as Sanpaolo IMI's 1999 offer for Banca di Roma.

In 2000 the bank, still keeping a grip on the wheels of finance, orchestrated investment firm Compart's buyout of Montedison (the merged entity took the Montedison name). That year the company launched an online private banking joint venture with Banca Mediolanum.

Also in 2000 its 46-year relationship with Lazard ended when the international investment banker announced plans to sell back to Mediobanca its 4% stake in the company along with its nearly 5% stake in Assicurazioni Generali.

After Cuccia's death in 2000, successor Vincenzo Maranghi battled such controlling shareholders as the Agnelli and Pirelli families and Deutsche Bank over the bank's future. These shareholders wanted to bring Mediobanca into the modern world by possibly merging it with another top Italian bank, or even separating its investment management operations from its investment banking, which generates a large majority of Mediobanca's profits.

However, in a bid to stick to the old ways, Maranghi arranged for backing (in exchange for a small stake in Mediobanca) from Swiss Life. Maranghi was blamed in part for the bank's decline: He forced out some of the investment banking division's top talent in the late 1990s and eventually resigned in 2003

Despite efforts to become more open, some of the mystery surrounding Mediobanca remains. The shareholder dispute erupted after the death of Cuccia (whose body was subsequently robbed from its grave and later found).

Maranghi's replacement, Gabriele Galateri di Genola, had his work cut out for him repairing cracks in Mediobanca's image, but he saw profits rise considerably. Under his watch, the group has made its first foray into operations abroad, opening an office in Paris. By 2004 the company posted improved financial results for a second consecutive year, including a 20% increase in investment banking fees.

Galateri di Genola resigned from Mediobanca in 2007 after he lost the support of the supervisory board. He was succeeded by Alberto Nagel, the company's general manager.

EXECUTIVES

Chairman, Renato Pagliaro
Deputy Chairman, Executive Deputy Chairman, Maurizia Angelo Comneno
Chief Executive Officer, Executive Director, Alberto Nagel
General Manager, Executive Director, Francesco Saverio Vinci
Executive Director, Gabriele Villa
Secretary, Massimo Bertolini
Director, Virginie Banet
Director, Maurizio Carfagna
Director, Laura Cioli
Director, Maurizio Costa
Director, Angela Gamba
Director, Valerie Hortefeux
Director, Maximo Ibarra
Director, Alberto Lupoi
Director, Elisabetta Magistretti
Director, Vittorio Pignatti Morano
Auditors : PricewaterhouseCoopers S.p.A.

LOCATIONS

HQ: Mediobanca Banca Di Credito Finanziario SpA
Piazzetta Enrico Cuccia 1, Milan 20121
Phone: (39) 02 8829 1 **Fax:** (39) 02 882 9367
Web: www.mediobanca.com

PRODUCTS/OPERATIONS

2015 Sales

	% of total
Retail and consumer banking	50
Corporate and private banking	32
Principal investing	15
Corporate center	3
Total	100

COMPETITORS

BANCA MONTE DEI PASCHI DI SIENA SPA
Bayerische Landesbank
NATWEST GROUP PLC
Nordea Bank AB
SANTANDER HOLDINGS USA, INC.
SYNOVUS FINANCIAL CORP.
Skandinaviska Enskilda Banken AB
Svenska Handelsbanken AB
UNICREDIT SPA
UniCredit Bank AG

HISTORICAL FINANCIALS
Company Type: Public

Income Statement — FYE: June 30

	ASSETS ($mil)	NET INCOME ($mil)	INCOME AS % OF ASSETS	EMPLOYEES
06/21	98,244	960	1.0%	4,754
06/20	88,392	672	0.8%	4,746
06/19	74,989	439	0.6%	986
06/18	84,244	1,006	1.2%	4,717
06/17	80,338	855	1.1%	4,798
Annual Growth	5.2%	2.9%	—	(0.2%)

2021 Year-End Financials

Return on assets: 0.9%
Return on equity: 7.7%
Long-term debt ($ mil.): —
No. of shares ($ mil.): 862
Sales ($ mil.): 3,771
Dividends
Yield: —
Payout: 70.9%
Market value ($ mil.): 10,029

	STOCK PRICE ($) FY Close	P/E High/Low		PER SHARE ($) Earnings	Dividends	Book Value
06/21	11.63	13	8	1.11	0.79	15.31
06/20	7.13	17	6	0.77	0.34	12.67
06/19	10.23	25	18	0.50	0.35	6.79
06/18	9.23	12	9	1.17	0.28	12.92
06/17	9.27	12	6	0.99	0.20	12.11
Annual Growth	5.8%		—	2.8%	40.8%	6.0%

Medipal Holdings Corp

Medipal Holdings controls, administers and supports the operating activities of companies in which it holds shares in the wholesale distribution of prescription and OTC pharmaceuticals, medical supplies, cosmetics, and personal sundries. In addition to supplying Japanese pharmacies and retail stores, Medipal distributes to hospitals and provides information technology support to its customers through its numerous subsidiaries and affiliates including Mediceo, Everlth, Atol, and Paltac. Its MP Agro subsidiary distributes animal health products. The company was founded in 1898.

Operations

The company operates in three segments: Prescription Pharmaceutical Wholesale Business (around 65% of sales), Cosmetics, Daily Necessities and OTC Pharmaceutical Wholesale Business (over 30%), and Animal Health Products and Food Processing Raw Materials Wholesale Business (less than 5%).

Its Prescription Pharmaceutical Wholesale Business operates through MEDICEO, EVERLTH, ATO, SPLine, MM CORPORATION, ASTEC, MVC, PharFeild, MEDIE, M.I.C., and Medipal Insurance Service subsidiaries. Its Cosmetics, Daily Necessities and OTC Pharmaceutical Wholesale Business operates through PALTAC. The Animal Health Products and Food Processing Raw Materials Wholesale Business operates through MP AGRO, and MEDIPAL FOODS sunbsidiary.

Geographic Reach

The company operates from more than 300 bases in Japan, where it is headquartered.

Sales and Marketing

The Prescription Pharmaceutical Wholesale Business conducts wholesale business for hospitals, clinics, dispensing pharmacies and other customers. The Cosmetics, Daily Necessities and OTC Pharmaceutical Wholesale Business conducts wholesale business for drugstores, home centers, convenience stores, supermarkets and other customers. The Animal Health Products and Food Processing Raw Materials Wholesale Business conducts wholesale business for animal hospitals, livestock and fish producers, processed food manufacturers and other customers.

Financial Performance

Company's revenue for fiscal 2022 increased to Â¥3.3 trillion compared from the prior year with Â¥3.2 trillion.

Net income for fiscal 2022 increased to Â¥29.4 billion compared from the prior year with Â¥23.9 billion.

Cash held by the company at the end of fiscal 2022 increased to Â¥260.5 billion. Cash provided by operations was Â¥61.2 billion while cash used for investing and financing activities were Â¥24.3 billion and Â¥16.5 billion, respectively. Main uses of cash were purchase of property, plant and equipment; and dividends paid.

Strategy

Company's three strategic focuses are: establishing business partnerships; expansion of new businesses; and innovation in existing businesses.

Company Background

Medipal was formed when Mediceo Holdings took over household products distributor Paltac in 2005. Paltac brought with it a distribution network and logistical prowess which allowed the new firm to move further into the OTC and non-drugs business. Previously, Mediceo Holdings become Japan's largest drug wholesaler in 2004, when it was formed through the merger of three smaller drug wholesalers (Kuraya Pharmaceuticals, Sanseido, and Tokyo Iyakuhin).

EXECUTIVES

President, Representative Director, Shuichi Watanabe
Executive Vice President, Director, Yasuhiro Choufuku
Senior Managing Director, Director, Toshihide Yoda
Director, Yuji Sakon
Director, Koichi Mimura
Director, Shinjiro Watanabe
Director, Kuniaki Imagawa
Director, Seiichi Kasutani
Outside Director, Mitsuko Kagami
Outside Director, Toshio Asano
Outside Director, Kuniko Shoji
Outside Director, Hiroshi Iwamoto
Auditors : KPMG AZSA LLC

LOCATIONS

HQ: Medipal Holdings Corp
2-7-15 Yaesu, Chuo-ku, Tokyo 104-8461
Phone: (81) 3 3517 5800
Web: www.medipal.co.jp

PRODUCTS/OPERATIONS

2017 Net Sales

	% of total
Prescription Pharmaceutical Wholesale	68
Cosmetics, Daily Necessities, and OTC Pharmaceutical Wholesale	30
Animal Health Products Raw Materials Wholesale	2
Total	100

Selected Divisions and Brands
Atol Co., Ltd.
Everlth Co., Ltd.
Mediceo Corporation
M.I.C. (Medical Information College) Inc.
MM Corporation
MP Agro Co., Ltd.
Paltac Corporation
Trim Co., Ltd.

COMPETITORS

ALFRESA HOLDINGS CORPORATION
DECHRA PHARMACEUTICALS PLC
DKSH Holding AG
ENDO INTERNATIONAL PUBLIC LIMITED COMPANY
MCKESSON CORPORATION
NUTRACEUTICAL INTERNATIONAL CORPORATION
PERRIGO COMPANY PUBLIC LIMITED COMPANY
STERIS LIMITED
SUZUKEN CO., LTD.
TOHO HOLDINGS CO.,LTD.

HISTORICAL FINANCIALS
Company Type: Public

Income Statement — FYE: March 31

	REVENUE ($mil)	NET INCOME ($mil)	NET PROFIT MARGIN	EMPLOYEES
03/22	27,055	241	0.9%	20,485
03/21	29,001	216	0.7%	20,588
03/20	29,968	349	1.2%	21,393
03/19	28,732	310	1.1%	21,731
03/18	29,630	327	1.1%	22,068
Annual Growth	(2.2%)	(7.3%)		(1.8%)

Medtronic PLC

EXECUTIVES

Strategy Chairman, Business Development Chairman, Business Development Chief Executive Officer, Strategy Chief Executive Officer, Chairman, Director, Geoffrey S. Martha, $1,100,000 total compensation
Executive Vice President, Chief Financial Officer, Karen L. Parkhill, $825,577 total compensation
Executive Vice President, Division Officer, Sean Salmon
Executive Vice President, Region Officer, Subsidiary Officer, Robert J.W. Ten Hoedt, $806,107 total compensation
Executive Vice President, Division Officer, Robert John (Bob) White
Lead Independent Director, Director, Craig Arnold
Director, Scott C. Donnelly
Director, Lidia L. Fonseca
Director, Andrea J. Goldsmith
Director, Randall J. Hogan
Director, Gregory Lewis
Director, Kevin E. Lofton
Director, Elizabeth G. Nabel
Director, Denise M. O'Leary
Director, Kendall J. (Ken) Powell
Director, Luca Benatti
Auditors : PricewaterhouseCoopers LLP

LOCATIONS

HQ: Medtronic PLC
  20 On Hatch, Lower Hatch Street, Dublin 2
Phone: (353) 1 438 1700
Web: www.medtronic.com

HISTORICAL FINANCIALS
Company Type: Public

Income Statement — FYE: April 28

	REVENUE ($mil)	NET INCOME ($mil)	NET PROFIT MARGIN	EMPLOYEES
04/23	31,227	3,758	12.0%	95,000
04/22	31,686	5,039	15.9%	95,000
04/21	30,117	3,606	12.0%	90,000
04/20	28,913	4,789	16.6%	90,000
04/19	30,557	4,631	15.2%	90,000
Annual Growth	0.5%	(5.1%)	—	1.4%

2023 Year-End Financials
Debt ratio: 26.8%
Return on equity: 7.2%
Cash ($ mil.): 1,543
Current Ratio: 2.39
Long-term debt ($ mil.): 24,344
No. of shares ($ mil.): 1,330
Dividends
Yield: —
Payout: 96.4%
Market value ($ mil.): —

2022 Year-End Financials
Debt ratio: —
Return on equity: 5.5%
Cash ($ mil.): 1,998
Current Ratio: 1.20
Long-term debt ($ mil.): —
No. of shares ($ mil.): 209
Dividends
Yield: —
Payout: 33.4%
Market value ($ mil.): —

Meituan

Auditors : PricewaterhouseCoopers

LOCATIONS

HQ: Meituan
  Block B&C, Hengjiweiye Building, No. 4 Wang Jing East Road, Chaoyang District, Beijing 100102
Phone: (86) 10 5737 6600
Web: www.about.meituan.com

HISTORICAL FINANCIALS
Company Type: Public

Income Statement — FYE: December 31

	REVENUE ($mil)	NET INCOME ($mil)	NET PROFIT MARGIN	EMPLOYEES
12/22	31,883	(969)	—	91,932
12/21	28,215	(3,707)	—	100,033
12/20	17,552	719	4.1%	69,205
12/19	14,016	321	2.3%	54,580
12/18	9,483	(16,788)	—	58,390
Annual Growth	35.4%	—	—	12.0%

2022 Year-End Financials
Debt ratio: 3.1%
Return on equity: (-5.2%)
Cash ($ mil.): 2,922
Current Ratio: 1.87
Long-term debt ($ mil.): 5,096
No. of shares ($ mil.): 6,193
Dividends
Yield: —
Payout: 0.0%
Market value ($ mil.): 273,985

	STOCK PRICE ($) FY Close	P/E High/Low		PER SHARE ($) Earnings	Dividends	Book Value
12/22	44.24	—	—	(0.16)	0.00	3.01
12/21	57.81	—	—	(0.61)	0.00	3.22
12/20	74.87	107	25	0.12	0.00	2.54
12/19	25.88	71	61	0.05	0.00	2.28
Annual Growth	19.6%	—	—	—	—	7.2%

Melrose Industries Plc

EXECUTIVES

Executive Vice-Chairman, Chairman, Christopher Miller
Executive Vice-Chairman, Chief Executive Officer, David Roper
Chief Executive Officer, Chief Operating Officer, Executive Director, Simon Peckham
Financial Director, Executive Director, Geoffrey Martin
Secretary, Jonathon Crawford
Non-Executive Chairman, Non-Executive Director, Justin Dowley
Senior Independent Director, Independent Non-Executive Director, Liz Hewitt
Independent Non-Executive Director, David George Lis
Independent Non-Executive Director, Archie G. Kane
Independent Non-Executive Director, Charlotte Twyning

Auditors : Deloitte LLP

LOCATIONS

HQ: Melrose Industries Plc
  Stratton House, 5 Stratton Street, London W1J 8LA
Phone: (44) 20 7647 4500   **Fax:** (44) 20 7647 4501
Web: www.melroseplc.net

HISTORICAL FINANCIALS
Company Type: Public

Income Statement — FYE: December 31

	REVENUE ($mil)	NET INCOME ($mil)	NET PROFIT MARGIN	EMPLOYEES
12/22	9,073	(370)	—	43,787
12/21	9,276	1,122	12.1%	40,046
12/20	11,968	(731)	—	51,395
12/19	14,482	(79)	—	56,092
12/18	10,986	(606)	—	62,350
Annual Growth	(4.7%)	—	—	(8.5%)

2022 Year-End Financials
Debt ratio: 12.9%
Return on equity: (-4.2%)
Cash ($ mil.): 427
Current Ratio: 0.96
Long-term debt ($ mil.): 1,725
No. of shares ($ mil.): 1,351
Dividends
Yield: —
Payout: 0.0%
Market value ($ mil.): —

MercadoLibre Inc

MercadoLibre is the largest online commerce ecosystem in Latin America based on unique visitors and page views. Its platform is designed to provide users with a complete portfolio of services to facilitate commercial transactions both digitally and offline. The company offers its users an ecosystem of six integrated e-commerce and digital payments services: the Mercado Libre Marketplace, the Mercado Pago Fintech platform, the Mercado Envios logistics service, the Mercado Libre Ads solution, the Mercado Libre Classifieds service, and the Mercado Shops online storefronts solution. The company serves more than 650 million users in about 20 countries; the majority of its sales come from Brazil.

Operations

MercadoLibre's reporting segment is based on geography: Brazil (about 55%), Argentina (more than 20%), Mexico (nearly 15%), and accounts for the rest, other countries include operations in Chile, Colombia, Costa Rica, Dominican Republic, Ecuador, Panama, Peru, Bolivia, Honduras, Nicaragua, El Salvador, Guatemala, Paraguay, Uruguay and the US.

Mercado Libre Marketplace is a fully-automated, topically-arranged and user-friendly online commerce platform, which can be accessed through its website and mobile app.

Mercado Envios logistics solution enables sellers on its platform to utilize third-party carriers and other logistics service providers, while also providing them with fulfillment and warehousing services.

Through Mercado Libre Classifieds, the company's online classified listing service, its users can also list and purchase motor vehicles, real estate, and services in the countries where it operates. Its classifieds pages are also a major source of traffic to the company's platform, benefitting both the Commerce and Fintech businesses.

Complementing the service, it offers the company's digital storefront solution, Mercado Shops, which allows users to set-up, manage and promote their own digital stores. These stores are hosted by Mercado Libre and offer integration with the rest of its ecosystem, namely Marketplaces, payment services and logistics services. Users can create a store at no cost, and can access additional functionalities and value added services on commission.

Geographic Reach

Headquartered in Montevideo, Uruguay, MercadoLibre has nearly 2,130 facilities primarily located in Argentina, Brazil, and Mexico, among others. In addition, the company has data centers located in Virginia. The company generates the majority of its sales in Brazil.

Sales and Marketing

Through the company's advertising platform, MercadoLibre's brands and sellers are able to display ads on its webpages through product searches, banner ads, or suggested products. Its advertising platform enables merchants and brands to access the millions of consumers that are on the company's Marketplaces at any given time with the Intent to purchase, which increases the likelihood of conversion.

The company carries out the majority of its marketing efforts on the Internet. It enters into agreements with portals, search engines, social networks, ad networks and other sites in order to attract Internet users to the Mercado Libre Marketplace and convert them into registered users and active traders on its platform.

The company spent approximately $35.5 million and $24.1 million on advertising for the years 2021 and 2020, respectively.

Overall, commerce brings in about 65% of the company's revenue by stream, while Fintech accounts for the rest.

Financial Performance

The company's net revenues grew 78% to $7.1 billion for 2021, as compared to the same period in 2020. The increase in net revenues was primarily attributable to the 36% increase in its gross merchandise volume, an increase of $629.6 million in the company's first-party sales and an increase of $357.6 million in shipping services billed net of carrier costs for 2021, as compared to the same period in 2020.

In 2021, the company had a net income of $240.6 million, a 196% increase from the previous year's net income of $81.3 million.

The company's cash at the end of 2021 was $3.6 billion. Operating activities generated $965 million, while investing activities used $1.6 billion, primarily for purchase of investments. Financing activities provided another $1.9 billion.

Strategy

MercadoLibre's main focus is to serve people in Latin America by enabling wider access to retail, digital payments and e-commerce services, and by providing compelling technology-based solutions that democratize commerce and money, thus contributing to the development of a large and growing digital economy in a region with a population of over 650 million people and one of the fastest-growing e-commerce and internet penetration rates in the world.

It serves buyers by giving them access to a broad and affordable variety of products and services, a selection it believes to be larger than otherwise available to them via other online and offline sources serving its Latin American markets. Additionally, the company provides payment settlement services and shipping solutions to facilitate such transactions, and advertising solutions to promote them. It also serves users by making capital more accessible through different credit products and fostering entrepreneurship and social mobility, with the goal of creating significant value for its stakeholders.

More broadly, the company strive to makes inefficient markets more efficient through technology and in that process generate value for all stakeholders.

To achieve these objectives, MercadoLibre intends to pursue the following strategies: Expand into additional transactional service offerings; Continue to improve the shopping experience for users; Continue to grow business and maintain market leadership; Increase monetization of its transactions; and Take advantage of the natural synergies that exist among its services.

Mergers and Acquisitions

In late 2021, MercadoLibre acquired Redelcom, a Chilean company that has been operating since 2010 as a payment services provider and that in October 2019 began offering point-of-sale (POS) terminals with the latest technology to retailers. The acquisition of Redelcom further strengthen the company's operation in Chile in the payment methods sector, especially in the physical world for SMEs, and to continue fulfilling its purpose of democratizing commerce and finance in the country.

In mid-2021, MercadoLibre agreed to acquire a $25 million stake in Aleph and additionally, will collaborate with IMS Internet Media Services on monetizing advertising space on MercadoLibre's digital properties in countries where MercadoLibre does not have local sales operations. Further, MercadoLibre and Aleph will partner to explore and collaborate in new business development opportunities in digital advertising.

EXECUTIVES

Chairman, President, Chief Executive Officer, Director, Marcos Eduardo Galperin, $552,767 total compensation
Corporate Affairs Executive Vice President, Juan Martin de la Serna
Executive Vice President, Chief Financial Officer, Pedro Arnt, $216,709 total compensation
Commerce Executive Vice President, Ariel Szarfsztejn
Executive Vice President, Chief Operating Officer, Daniel Rabinovich, $216,709 total compensation
Senior Vice President, Chief Accounting Officer, Marcelo Melamud, $581,940 total compensation
Senior Vice President, General Counsel, Secretary, Jacobo Cohen Imach
Payments Division Officer, Osvaldo Gimenez, $227,165 total compensation
Lead Independent Director, Director, Emiliano Calemzuk
Director, Susan Segal
Director, Mario Eduardo Vazquez
Director, Alejandro Nicolas Aguzin
Director, Nicolas Galperin
Director, Henrique Dubugras
Director, Richard A. Sanders
Director, Andrea Mayumi Petroni Merhy
Auditors : Pistrelli, Henry Martin y Asociados S.R.L.

LOCATIONS

HQ: MercadoLibre Inc
WTC Free Zone, Dr. Luis Bonavita 1294, Of. 1733, Tower II, Montevideo 11300
Phone: (598) 2 927 2770
Web: www.mercadolibre.com

HISTORICAL FINANCIALS

Company Type: Public

Income Statement — FYE: December 31

	REVENUE ($mil)	NET INCOME ($mil)	NET PROFIT MARGIN	EMPLOYEES
12/23	14,473	987	6.8%	58,313
12/22	10,537	482	4.6%	40,548
12/21	7,069	83	1.2%	29,957
12/20	3,973	(0)	0.0%	15,546
12/19	2,296	(171)	—	9,703
Annual Growth	58.4%	—	—	56.6%

2023 Year-End Financials

Debt ratio: 25.5%
Return on equity: 40.3%
Cash ($ mil.): 2,556
Current Ratio: 1.27
Long-term debt ($ mil.): 2,203
No. of shares ($ mil.): 50
Dividends
 Yield: —
 Payout: 0.0%
Market value ($ mil.): 79,320

	STOCK PRICE ($) FY Close	P/E High/Low		PER SHARE ($) Earnings	Dividends	Book Value
12/23	1,571.54	84	42	19.46	0.00	60.85
12/22	846.24	139	64	9.53	0.00	36.35
12/21	1,348.40	1188	631	1.67	0.00	30.38
12/20	1,675.22	—		(0.08)	0.00	33.12
12/19	571.94	—		(3.71)	0.00	41.88
Annual Growth	28.7%			—		9.8%

Mercedes-Benz AG

Mercedes-Benz, formerly Daimler AG, is one of the leading global suppliers of premium and luxury cars and one of the world's largest manufacturer of commercial vehicles. It also offers financing, leasing, fleet management, investments, insurance brokerage as well as innovative mobility services. As of 2022, the operational business activities of the Group have been managed in the business divisions Mercedes-Benz Cars and Vans, among others. Daimler sells its vehicles worldwide, but Europe represents about 40% of its net sales.

Operations

The Mercede-Benz group is divided to three segments namely, Mercedes-Benz Cars, Mercedes-Benz Vans, and Mercede-Benz Mobility.

The Mercedes-Benz Cars segment account for more than 70% of the company's revenue. The segment invests systematically in the development of efficient powertrains and is already setting the course for an all-electric future.

The Mercedes-Benz Vans segment is a global supplier of a complete portfolio of vans. Models offered in the commercial segment comprise the Sprinter large van, the Vito mid-size van (marketed as the Metris in the US), and the Citan urban delivery van. The range of Mercedes-Benz vans in the private-customer segment consists of the V-Class full-size multi-purpose vehicle, Marco Polo camper vans and recreational vehicles and, since 2022, the T-Class. The segment accounts more than 10% of the company's revenue.

Lastly, the Mercedes-Benz Mobility segment supports the sale of the company's vehicle brands worldwide with custom mobility and financial services. The services range from leasing and financing packages for end customers and dealers to insurance solutions, flexible subscription and rental models and fleet management services for business customers, with latter primarily offered via the Athlon brand. The segment accounts for about 20% of the company's revenue.

Geographic Reach

The company is headquartered in Stuttgart, Germany. Mercedes-Benz sells vehicles and provides in over 30 production facilities in Europe, North America and South America, Asia, and Africa. Europe and Asia accounts for about 30% of the company's revenue.

Financial Performance

Mercedes-Benz' performance for the past five years has fluctuated but had an overall increase with 2022 as the company's second highest year during the period.

The company's revenue increased by EUR 16.1 million to EUR 150.0 billion for 2022, as compared to 2021's revenue of EUR 133.9 billion.

Mercedes-Benz net income for fiscal year end 2022 decreased to EUR 14.8 billion, as compared to the prior year's net income of EUR 23.4 billion.

The company held about EUR 17.7 billion at the end of the year. Operating activities provided EUR 16.9 billion to the coffers. Investing activities and financing activities used EUR 3.4 billion and EUR19.0 billion, respectively. Main cash uses were for acquisition of marketable debt securities and similar investments, as well as repayment of long-term financing liabilities.

Strategy

Mercedes-Benz focuses in building the world's most desirable cars. For the Mercedes-Benz Vans offers its customers the most desirable vans and services worldwide. The Mercedes-Benz Mobility strategy is to achieve to be the number one financial and mobility service provider for luxurious driving in the electric era by 2025.

HISTORY

Daimler-Benz was formed by the merger of two German motor companies -- Daimler and Benz -- in 1926. Daimler-Benz bought Auto Union (Audi) in 1958 (sold to Volkswagen in 1966). The company's Mercedes cars gained international fame and sales expanded worldwide in the 1970s.

Daimler-Benz diversified in the 1980s, buying aerospace, heavy truck (Freightliner), and consumer and industrial electrical companies. Although diversification continued, sales slowed. Losses at its aerospace unit forced Daimler-Benz into the red in 1995. Also that year the company and ABB Asea Brown Boveri (now ABB) formed joint venture Adtranz, the #1 train maker in the world, and JÃ¼rgen Schrempp became chairman of the management board (CEO).

In 1998 Daimler-Benz acquired Chrysler and introduced a subcompact car, the smart, in Europe. The newly formed DaimlerChrysler rolled both companies' financial services units into DaimlerChrysler Interservices (DEBIS) in 1999.

EXECUTIVES

Chairman, Ola Kallenius
Production & Supply Chain Management, Jorg Burzer
Integrity & Legal Affairs, Renata Jungo Brungger
Human Resources and Director of Labor Relations, Sabine Kohleisen
Procurement Chief Technology Officer, Development Chief Technology Officer, Markus Schafer
Marketing & Sales, Britta Seeger
Greater China Region Officer, Greater China Management Board Member, Hubertus Troska
Finance & Controlling, Harald Wilhelm
Chairman, Supervisory Board Member, Bernd Pischetsrieder
Deputy Chairman, Supervisory Board Member, Ergun Lumali
Deputy Chairman, Supervisory Board Member, Michael Brecht
Supervisory Board Member, Sari Baldauf
Supervisory Board Member, Michael Bettag
Supervisory Board Member, Ben Van Beurden
Supervisory Board Member, Nadine Boguslawski
Supervisory Board Member, Martin Brudermuller
Supervisory Board Member, Liz Centoni
Supervisory Board Member, Michael Haberle
Supervisory Board Member, Timotheus Hottges
Supervisory Board Member, Olaf G. Koch
Supervisory Board Member, Roman Romanowski
Supervisory Board Member, Helene Svahn
Supervisory Board Member, Monika Tielsch
Supervisory Board Member, Elke Toenjes-Werner
Supervisory Board Member, Frank Weber
Supervisory Board Member, Roman Zitzelsberger
Auditors : KPMG AG Wirtschaftsprufungsgesellschaft

LOCATIONS

HQ: Mercedes-Benz AG
Mercedesstrasse 120, Stuttgart 70372
Phone: (49) 711 17 97875
Web: www.group.mercedes-benz.com

2018 Sales

	% of total
Europe	36
North America (NAFTA)	25
Asia	23
Other markets	6
Other revenue	10
Total	100

PRODUCTS/OPERATIONS

2018 Sales

	% of Sales
Mercedes-Benz Cars	53
Daimler Trucks	22
Daimler Financial Services	14
Mercedes-Benz Vans	8
Daimler Buses	2
Total	100

Selected Divisions and Brands

Mercedes-Benz Cars
    Mercedes-AMG
    Mercedes-Maybach
    Mercedes me
    smart
    EQ
Daimler Trucks
    Freightliner
    FUSO
    Mercedez-Benz
    Western Star
    BharatBenz
Mercedes-Benz Vans
    Mercedez-Benz
    Freightliner
Daimler Buses
    Mercedes-Benz
    Setra
    BharatBenz
Daimler Financial Services
    Mercedes-Benz Bank
    Daimler Truck Financial
    moovel
    Car2Go
    mytaxi

COMPETITORS

AB Volvo
ALLISON TRANSMISSION HOLDINGS, INC.
Bayerische Motoren Werke AG
CUMMINS INC.
DANA INCORPORATED
FORD MOTOR COMPANY
Hyundai Mobis Co., Ltd
LEAR CORPORATION
VOLKSWAGEN AG
WABCO HOLDINGS INC.

HISTORICAL FINANCIALS

Company Type: Public

Income Statement — FYE: December 31

	REVENUE ($mil)	NET INCOME ($mil)	NET PROFIT MARGIN	EMPLOYEES
12/23	169,705	15,795	9.3%	166,056
12/22	160,225	15,487	9.7%	168,797
12/21	151,549	26,039	17.2%	172,425
12/20	189,382	4,451	2.4%	288,481
12/19	193,952	2,668	1.4%	298,655
Annual Growth	(3.3%)	56.0%	—	(13.6%)

2023 Year-End Financials

Debt ratio: 45.7%
Return on equity: 16.0%
Cash ($ mil.): 17,679
Current Ratio: 1.26
Long-term debt ($ mil.): 70,581
No. of shares ($ mil.): 1,040
Dividends
Yield: —
Payout: 6.7%
Market value ($ mil.): 17,946

	STOCK PRICE ($) FY Close	P/E High/Low	PER SHARE ($) Earnings	Dividends	Book Value
12/23	17.24	2 1	14.91	1.01	97.65
12/22	16.35	2 1	14.47	0.93	85.27
12/21	23.59	1 1	24.34	0.41	76.12
12/20	17.52	5 2	4.16	0.16	69.62
12/19	13.58	7 5	2.49	0.62	64.38
Annual Growth	6.1%	— —	56.4%	12.9%	11.0%

Merck KGaA (Germany)

Merck KGaA is a leading science and technology company, operates across life science, healthcare and electronics. The company manufactures and sells prescription drugs including treatments for multiple sclerosis, cancers, growth disorders, infertility, and cardiovascular and metabolic diseases. Merck's specialty chemicals include liquid crystals, semiconductor materials, and coatings. It holds the global rights to the Merck name and brand. The only exceptions are Canada and the US. In these countries, it operates as EMD Serono in the biopharmaceutical business, as MilliporeSigma in the life science business, and as EMD Electronics in the high-tech materials business. About 35% of Merck's sales come from the Asia-Pacific region.

Operations

Merck operates through three segments: Life Science, Healthcare and Electronics.

Merck's Life Sciences segment generates about 45% of sales, makes tools, equipment, and chemicals used in pharmaceutical, biotech, and academic laboratories. Its product portfolio numbers some 300,000 and includes ultrapure reagents, testing kits, lab water systems, antibodies and cells, gene-editing technologies, and bioprocessing systems. The segment operates as MilliporeSigma in the US and Canada.

The Healthcare segment accounts for about 35% of sales, discovers, develops, manufactures, and markets innovative pharmaceutical and biological prescription drugs to treat cancer, multiple sclerosis (MS), infertility, growth disorders, and certain cardiovascular and metabolic diseases. Healthcare operates in four therapeutic areas: Neurology and Immunology, Oncology, Fertility, and General Medicine & Endocrinology. Its R&D pipeline positions with a clear focus on becoming a global specialty innovator in oncology, immuno-oncology, neurology, and immunology. The segment operates as EMD Serono in the US and Canada.

The Electronics segment, bringing in some 20% of sales, deals in high-tech chemicals for use in consumer electronics, semiconductors, automotive displays, lighting, pigments, coatings, and cosmetics. The business sector consists of three business units: Semiconductor Solutions, Display Solutions, and Surface Solutions. Comparing Electronics with a smartphone, Display Solutions represents the user interface, Semiconductor Solutions the intelligence, and Surface Solutions the aesthetics. The segment operates as EMD Electronics in the US and Canada.

Geographic Reach

Merck is headquartered in Germany with operations spread across around 65 countries. The Asia-Pacific region is the company's largest region, accounting for about 35% of sales, closely followed by Europe (roughly 30% of sales) and North America (almost 30%). Latin America and Middle East and Africa regions account for the remaining revenue.

Financial Performance

Note: Growth rates may differ after conversion to US Dollars.

Merck's revenue for fiscal 2022 increased to EUR22.2 billion compared from the prior year with EUR19.7 billion. This positive development was attributable to organic net sales growth of EUR1.3 billion or 6% and was driven by all of the company's business sectors.

Net income for fiscal 2022 increased to EUR3.3 billion compared from the prior year with EUR3.1 billion.

Cash held by the company at the end of fiscal 2022 decreased to EUR1.85 billion. Cash provided by operations was EUR4.3 billion while cash used for investing and financing activities were EUR2.7 billion and EUR1.6 billion, respectively. Main uses of cash were investments in property, plant and equipment; and repayment of bonds.

Strategy

Merck always takes the fundamentals into consideration when discussing and deciding on its Enterprise strategy.

Merck follows a risk diversification strategy with three distinct business sectors, and the company avoids overexposure to any single customer, industry, or geography. The company ensures resilience against business disruption and deep crises.

With its science and technology focus, the company wants to be leaders in its fields of expertise and markets, always pushing the boundaries to find new solutions and drive innovation. The company aims to create value for its business and for society.

Merck continues to operate under its current ownership with the Merck family as the majority owner.

The company delivers sustainable value, and Merck wants to maintain an attractive financial profile (for example, a strong credit rating) while assessing and considering the ESG (environmental, social, governance) impact of its growth ambition.

Mergers and acquisitions (M&A) are an important driver of the company's long-term value creation strategy with a focus on innovation-driven technology.

Mergers and Acquisitions

In late 2022, MilliporeSigma acquired Massachusetts-based Erbi Biosystems, a developer of the 2 ml micro-bioreactor platform technology, known as the Breez. The deal strengthens MilliporeSigma's upstream portfolio in therapeutic proteins by enabling scalable cell-based perfusion bioreactor processes from 2ml to 2000L with rapid lab-scale process development. It also offers future development opportunities in novel modality applications, including cell therapies. Financial terms were not disclosed.

In 2022, Merck will advance its bioprocessing portfolio with the acquisition of the MAST (Modular Automated Sampling Technology) platform from Lonza. The MAST platform is an automated, aseptic bioreactor sampling system developed in Bend, Oregon, USA. The acquisition of the MAST platform is another milestone to accelerate innovation in Merck's Process Solutions business unit, one of the company's three growth engines (Big 3), through targeted smaller to medium-sized acquisitions with high impact. The financial details of the deal were not disclosed.

Also in 2022, Merck acquired Exelead, a biopharmaceutical CDMO, specializes in PEGylated products and complex injectable formulations, for approximately USD 780 million in cash. The business combination is expected to enable Merck's Life Science business sector to provide its customers with comprehensive end-to-end contract development and manufacturing organization

(CDMO) services across the mRNA value chain. Merck plans to further invest over EUR 500 million to scale up Exelead's technology over the next ten years.

Company Background

Merck KGaA was founded in 1668 as a pharmacy and is the oldest pharmaceuticals business in the world.

The German firm is ancestor to US drug giant Merck & Co., but the American firm broke away during WWI. Subsequently, the company's current North American operations can't use the Merck name; they instead operate under the name EMD. Legal tussles over use of the name flare up sporadically as globalization brings the two into shared markets.

Merck launched an initiative in 2007 to transition from a classic pharmaceuticals and chemicals company to a science and technology company. The most significant move was the 2015 acquisition of Sigma-Aldrich, a research equipment maker, for $17 billion. Other major acquisitions include AZ Electronic Materials, a supplier of high-tech materials for the electronics industry, for $2.5 billion in 2014.

The firm sold its Biosimilars (generic biotech drugs) unit in 2017 to Fresenius for ?156 million plus ?497 in potential milestone payments.

HISTORY

In 1668 apothecary Friedrich Jacob Merck bought the Engel-Apotheke (Angel Pharmacy) in Darmstadt, establishing the family's presence in the drug business. Some 150 years later, descendant Emanuel Merck inherited the company; an experienced chemist, Merck transformed it into a drugmaker by 1827, producing morphine, codeine, cocaine, and other bulk pharmaceuticals. By the time Merck died in 1854, the company had sales around the world.

Two years later the company headed to the US. By the turn of the century, Merck had a production facility in New Jersey run by Emanuel's grandson George. When the US joined WWI, George turned over Merck's control of the US subsidiary (Merck & Co.) to the Alien Property Custodian, which sold the stock after the war. Merck lost its other overseas subsidiaries after WWI.

WWII left Merck struggling for supplies and labor, and its factories were decimated by Allied air raids. After the war, the military government allowed the firm to make drugs, then pesticides, food preservatives, reagents, and laboratory chemicals. Merck struggled along until the Wirthschaftswunder (economic miracle) in 1948 that turned around the German economy.

The war had lingering effects that cost the firm during the later half of the 20th century. Although Merck rebuilt its presence around the world, product development (particularly its ventures into biotechnology in the 1980s) was hampered by an exodus of talent to other countries and by certain protectionist policies of the German government.

Despite a sluggish economy and Germany's health care system reforms, Merck began an acquisition spree in 1990 that continued for several years. The firm diversified its pharmaceuticals and chemicals operations but drove itself into debt. In 1995 Merck offered a quarter of its stock to the public to pay its debt and continue its spree.

Some of its purchases in the late 1990s helped it establish itself in the cancer treatment niche; these buys included Lexigen Pharmaceuticals (1998). The next year the Merck family had to inject money into the company again to pay off debt from the acquisitions.

In 2004 the company sold its laboratory supplies distribution subsidiary, VWR International, to Clayton, Dubilier & Rice for $1.65 billion. VWR has since been sold to Madison Dearborn Partners.

In 2006 Merck made a failed $18 billion bid for Schering, which was instead acquired by Bayer.

That failed purchase was made up for through the $13 billion acquisition of Swiss biotech firm Serono (later Merck Serono) in 2007. The purchase made Merck the largest biotech company in Europe, adding biological operations focused on reproductive health, neurology, metabolism, and other areas. Following the acquisition, Merck combined Serono with its Merck Ethicals Division to form a new prescription pharmaceuticals division named Merck Serono. The Ethicals Division contributed cancer, cardiovascular, and other therapies, including marketing rights for ImClone's cancer drug Erbitux outside of the US and Canada.

In support of its status among the biggest players in the biotech field, Merck offloaded its generics unit, which had accounted for nearly 30% of the company's overall sales, that same year in order to pay down its debt from the Serono acquisition. Merck sold the unit to Mylan for a robust price of about $6.7 billion. Along with paying down debt, Merck used the money to fund additional acquisitions, targeting the over-the-counter medicine and chemical industries.

Merck moved to gain a tighter foothold in the Chinese chemical market in 2009 when it purchased pigment manufacturer Suzhou Taizhu Technology Development for $40 million. That same year the company increased its bioscience holdings in India by acquiring Bangalore Genei Private, an India-based company that specialized in making and selling genomics and proteomics research products, from the Sanmar Group.

Despite making some broad strokes at expansion, the company was hit by a decline in demand for its chemicals (including pigments) in 2009 and was forced to initiate some cutbacks in the division's manufacturing operations early in the year, primarily due to economic conditions and an ensuing lower demand for liquid crystals.

Merck launched a transformation initiative in 2007 to transition from a classic pharmaceuticals and chemicals company to a science and technology company. The most significant move was the 2015 acquisition of Sigma-Aldrich, a pharmaceutical equipment maker, for $17 billion. The acquisition positioned Merck as a leader in the life science industry. Other major acquisitions include AZ Electronic Materials, a supplier of high-tech materials for the electronics industry, for $2.5 billion in 2014.

Merck backed up its completed transformation with a complete re-branding in 2015, which included a re-naming of the separate division names such as Merck Serono and Merck Millipore in all geographies (bar the US and Canada), and bringing them under one Merck umbrella. The move is partly intended to boost awareness of the difference between the rival companies.

EXECUTIVES

Chairman, Chief Executive Officer, Belen Garijo
Chief Financial Officer, Marcus Kuhnert
Chairman, Independent Director, Wolfgang Buechele
Vice-Chairman, Director, Sascha Held
Independent Director, Michael Kleinemeier
Independent Director, Renate Koehler
Independent Director, Peter Emanuel Merck
Independent Director, Helene von Roeder
Independent Director, Helga Rubsamen-Schaeff
Independent Director, Daniel Thelen
Independent Director, Simon Thelen
Director, Gabriele Eismann
Director, Edeltraud Glanzer
Director, Jurgen Glaser
Director, Anne Lange
Director, Dietmar Oeter
Director, Alexander Putz
Director, Christian Raabe
Auditors : KPMG AG Wirtschaftsprüfungsgesellschaft

LOCATIONS

HQ: Merck KGaA (Germany)
  Frankfurter Strasse 250, Darmstadt 64293
Phone: (49) 6151 72 0   **Fax:** (49) 6151 72 5577
Web: www.emdgroup.com

2015 Sales

	% of total
Asia-Pacific	33
Europe	32
North America	21
Latin America	10
Middle East & Africa	4
Total	100

PRODUCTS/OPERATIONS

Metro Inc

METRO is a leader in food and pharmaceutical industry in Québec and Ontario. As a retailer, franchisor, distributor, and manufacturer, the company operates or services a network of some 950 food stores under several banners including Metro, Metro Plus, Super C and Food Basics, as well as some 650 drugstores primarily under the Jean Coutu, Brunet, Metro Pharmacy and Food Basics Pharmacy banners, providing employment to more than 90,000 people. METRO was founded in 1947.

Operations
METRO's reportable segments are food segment and pharmaceutical segment.

For consumers seeking a higher level of service and a greater variety of products, we operate 328 supermarkets under the Metro and Metro Plus banners. The 237 discount stores operating under the Super C and Food Basics banners offer products at low prices to consumers who are both cost and quality conscious. The Adonis banner, which currently has about 15 stores, is specialized in fresh products as well as Mediterranean and Middle-Eastern products. The company also operates Première Moisson, a banner specialized in premium quality artisan bakery, pastry, and deli products. Première Moisson sells its products to the company's stores, to restaurants and other chains as well as directly to consumers in its almost 25 stores. The company also acts as a distributor for independent neighborhood grocery stores.

The company also acts as franchisor and distributor for about 420 PJC Jean Coutu, PJC Health and PJC Health & Beauty drugstores as well as more than 155 Brunet Plus, Brunet, Brunet Clinique, and Clini Plus drugstores, held by pharmacist owners. The company operates some 75 drugstores in Ontario under Metro Pharmacy and Food Basics Pharmacy banners and their sales are included in the company's sales. Sales also include the supply of non-franchised drugstores and various health centres. The company is also active in generic drug manufacturing through its subsidiary Pro Doc Ltée.

Geographic Reach
Based in Montreal, METRO operates of network of some 950 food stores and 650 drugstores.

Financial Performance
Net income for fiscal 2021 increased to $1.12 billion compared from the prior year with $1.08 billion.

Cash held by the company at the end of fiscal 2021 increased to $445.8 million. Cash provided by operations was $1.6 billion while cash used for investing and financing activities were $471.6 million and $1.1 billion respectively. Main uses of cash were additions to fixed assets and investment properties; and shares redeemed.

Strategy
Metro's strategies remain customer-focused while considering the upcoming post-pandemic environment. The pandemic caused an increase in food consumption at home, and the company expect that a portion of this increase will remain in the short and midterm. Many consumers changed their habits and adopted new ways of shopping. In this regard, the company are well positioned with its e-commerce offer, providing operational flexibility to serve our customers in the way that is most convenient for them.

Metro's priorities for Fiscal 2022 are: increase its market share in the food sector; increase its leadership position in the pharmacy sector; continue to modernize its supply chain and accelerate the company's digital transformation; continue to develop its loyalty programs; develop the best team; and achieve its corporate responsibility objectives.

EXECUTIVES

President, Chief Executive Officer, Director, Eric Richer La Fleche
Executive Vice President, Chief Financial Officer, Treasurer, Francois Thibault
Executive Vice President, Marc Giroux
Executive Vice President, Carmine Fortino
National Procurement and Corporate Brands Senior Vice President, Serge Boulanger
The Jean Coutu Group (PJC) Inc. President, Alain Champagne
Real Estate and Engineering Vice President, Martin Allaire
Public Affairs and Communications Vice President, Marie-Claude Bacon
eCommerce and Digital Strategy Vice President, Christina Bedard
Technology Infrastructure Vice President, Sam Bernier
Human Resources Vice President, Genevieve Bich
Supply Chain Vice President, Dan Gabbard
Corporate Controller Vice President, Karin Jonsson
Information Systems Vice President, Frederic Legault
Vice President, General Counsel, Corporate Secretary, Simon Rivet
Marketing Vice President, Alain Tadros
Logistics and Distribution National Vice-President, Yves Vezina
Chairman, Director, Pierre Boivin
Director, Maryse Bertrand
Director, Francois J. Coutu
Director, Michel Coutu
Director, Stephanie L. Coyles
Director, Claude Dussault
Director, Russell Goodman
Director, Marc Guay
Director, Christian W. E. Haub
Director, Christine Magee
Director, Line Rivard
Auditors: Ernst & Young LLP

2015 Sales

	% of total
Healthcare	54
Life Sciences	26
Performance Materials	20
Total	100

Selected Pharmaceutical Products
Merck Serono
    Concor (antihypertensive)
    Erbitux (colorectal and neck cancer)
    Euthyrox (hypothyroid treatment)
    Glucophage (diabetes)
    Gonal-f (fertility)
    Pergoveris (fertility)
    Rebif (relapsing multiple sclerosis)
    Saizen (growth hormone deficiency)
    Serostim (HIV-associated wasting)
Consumer health care
    BION and MULTIBION (probiotic multivitamin)
    Cebion (vitamins and minerals)
    Fembion, Metfolin (multivitamins for women)
    Flexagil, Kytta, and Seven Seas (natural joint pain remedies and supplements)
    Kidabion (children's vitamins)
    Nasivin (cold remedy)
    Seven seas (diet supplement)
    Sangobion (anemia remedy)

COMPETITORS

AKORN, INC.
ASTRAZENECA PLC
BIOVERATIV INC.
BRISTOL-MYERS SQUIBB COMPANY
Bausch Health Companies Inc
Bayer AG
LIGAND PHARMACEUTICALS INCORPORATED
Novartis AG
SANOFI
TAKEDA PHARMACEUTICAL COMPANY LIMITED

HISTORICAL FINANCIALS

Company Type: Public

Income Statement   FYE: December 31

	REVENUE ($mil)	NET INCOME ($mil)	NET PROFIT MARGIN	EMPLOYEES
12/22	23,744	3,552	15.0%	64,232
12/21	22,282	3,457	15.5%	60,348
12/20	21,519	2,438	11.3%	58,096
12/19	18,134	1,482	8.2%	57,071
12/18	16,990	3,863	22.7%	51,749
Annual Growth	8.7%	(2.1%)	—	5.6%

2022 Year-End Financials
Debt ratio: 19.8%
Return on equity: 14.0%
Cash ($ mil.): 1,980
Current Ratio: 1.28
Long-term debt ($ mil.): 8,750
No. of shares ($ mil.): 129
Dividends
  Yield: —
  Payout: 3.2%
Market value ($ mil.): 4,986

	STOCK PRICE ($) FY Close	P/E High/Low		PER SHARE ($) Earnings	Dividends	Book Value
12/22	38.58	6	4	8.17	0.27	214.27
12/21	52.10	7	4	7.96	0.42	186.86
12/20	34.37	8	4	5.61	0.19	160.92
12/19	23.70	8	6	3.41	0.19	155.20
12/18	20.76	3	2	8.89	0.20	152.41
Annual Growth	16.8%	—	—	(2.1%)	7.4%	8.9%

PRODUCTS/OPERATIONS

2018 Sales

	% of total
Performance Products	31
Chemicals	32
Industrial Gases	17
Health Care	15
Other	5
Total	100

COMPETITORS

ARKEMA
CELANESE CORPORATION
DCC PUBLIC LIMITED COMPANY
Evonik Industries AG
LyondellBasell Industries N.V.
NEWMARKET CORPORATION
SASOL LTD
Ultrapar Participacoes S/A
VALLOUREC
VENATOR MATERIALS PLC

HISTORICAL FINANCIALS

Company Type: Public

Income Statement — FYE: March 31

	REVENUE ($mil)	NET INCOME ($mil)	NET PROFIT MARGIN	EMPLOYEES
03/23	34,797	721	2.1%	74,632
03/22	32,695	1,456	4.5%	76,081
03/21	29,420	(68)	—	75,638
03/20	32,984	498	1.5%	76,362
03/19	35,428	1,530	4.3%	79,578
Annual Growth	(0.4%)	(17.1%)	—	(1.6%)

2023 Year-End Financials

Debt ratio: 0.3%
Return on equity: 6.3%
Cash ($ mil.): 2,231
Current Ratio: 1.29
Long-term debt ($ mil.): 12,331
No. of shares ($ mil.): 1,424
Dividends
  Yield: —
  Payout: 141.0%
Market value ($ mil.): 42,693

	STOCK PRICE ($) FY Close	P/E High/Low	PER SHARE ($) Earnings	Dividends	Book Value
03/23	29.97	0 0	0.49	0.69	8.25
03/22	33.49	0 0	0.95	0.25	8.42
03/21	38.11	— —	(0.05)	0.22	7.84
03/20	32.31	1 1	0.32	0.29	7.57
03/19	35.24	0 0	0.99	0.36	8.74
Annual Growth	(4.0%)	—	(16.4%)	17.4%	(1.5%)

Mitsubishi Corp

EXECUTIVES

Chairman, Director, Takehiko Kakiuchi
President, Representative Director, Katsuya Nakanishi
Executive Vice President, Representative Director, Norikazu Tanaka
Managing Executive Officer, Chief Compliance Officer, Representative Director, Yutaka Kashiwagi
Representative Director, Yuzo Nouchi
Outside Director, Tsuneyoshi Tatsuoka
Outside Director, Shunichi Miyanaga
Outside Director, Sakie Akiyama
Outside Director, Mari Sagiya

Auditors : Deloitte Touche Tohmatsu LLC

LOCATIONS

HQ: Mitsubishi Corp
2-3-1 Marunouchi, Chiyoda-ku, Tokyo 100-8086
Phone: (81) 3 3210 2121   **Fax:** 212 605-2597
Web: www.mitsubishicorp.com

COMPETITORS

AMIRA C FOODS INTERNATIONAL DMCC
Empire Company Limited
ITOCHU CORPORATION
MARUBENI CORPORATION
Migros-Genossenschafts-Bund
SOJITZ CORPORATION
SUMITOMO CORPORATION
SYSCO CORPORATION
UNITED NATURAL FOODS, INC.
US FOODS, INC.

HISTORICAL FINANCIALS

Company Type: Public

Income Statement — FYE: March 31

	REVENUE ($mil)	NET INCOME ($mil)	NET PROFIT MARGIN	EMPLOYEES
03/23	161,969	8,865	5.5%	105,267
03/22	141,937	7,707	5.4%	104,176
03/21	116,366	1,558	1.3%	106,902
03/20	136,156	4,931	3.6%	110,006
03/19	145,414	5,334	3.7%	104,168
Annual Growth	2.7%	13.5%	—	0.3%

2023 Year-End Financials

Debt ratio: 0.2%
Return on equity: 15.7%
Cash ($ mil.): 11,690
Current Ratio: 1.36
Long-term debt ($ mil.): 26,234
No. of shares ($ mil.): 4,307
Dividends
  Yield: —
  Payout: 22.3%
Market value ($ mil.): —

Mitsubishi Electric Corp

EXECUTIVES

Representative Executive Officer, President, Chief Executive Officer, Director, Kei Uruma
Executive Vice President, Representative Executive Officer, Tadashi Matsumoto
Representative Director, Senior Managing Executive Officer, Chief Technology Officer, Kunihiko Kaga
Senior Managing Executive Officer, Noriyuki Takazawa
Chief Risk Management Officer, Satoshi Kusakabe
Chief Marketing Officer, Yoji Saito
Chief Information Officer, Eiichiro Mitani
Chief Financial Officer, Director, Kuniaki Masuda
Chief Productivity Officer, Chief Quality Officer, Yoshikazu Nakai
Chief Strategy Officer, Director, Satoshi Takeda
Chief Digital Officer, Hiroshi Sakakibara
Chief Human Resources Officer, Yasunari Abe
Outside Director, Mitoji Yabunaka
Outside Director, Kazunori Watanabe
Outside Director, Hiroko Koide

Outside Director, Tatsuro Kosaka
Outside Director, Hiroyuki Yanagi
Outside Director, Masako Egawa
Outside Director, Haruka Matsuyama
Director, Tadashi Kawagoishi
Director, Jun Nagasawa
Auditors : KPMG AZSA LLC

LOCATIONS

HQ: Mitsubishi Electric Corp
2-7-3 Marunouchi, Chiyoda-ku, Tokyo 100-8310
Phone: (81) 3 3218 2111
Web: www.mitsubishielectric.co.jp

HISTORICAL FINANCIALS

Company Type: Public

Income Statement — FYE: March 31

	REVENUE ($mil)	NET INCOME ($mil)	NET PROFIT MARGIN	EMPLOYEES
03/23	37,569	1,606	4.3%	149,655
03/22	36,804	1,672	4.5%	145,696
03/21	37,854	1,744	4.6%	145,653
03/20	41,110	2,043	5.0%	146,518
03/19	40,814	2,046	5.0%	145,817
Annual Growth	(2.0%)	(5.9%)	—	0.7%

2023 Year-End Financials

Debt ratio: —
Return on equity: 6.8%
Cash ($ mil.): 4,849
Current Ratio: 1.88
Long-term debt ($ mil.): 495
No. of shares ($ mil.): 2,113
Dividends
  Yield: 2.5%
  Payout: 80.3%
Market value ($ mil.): 50,233

	STOCK PRICE ($) FY Close	P/E High/Low	PER SHARE ($) Earnings	Dividends	Book Value
03/23	23.77	0 0	0.76	0.61	11.51
03/22	22.90	0 0	0.78	0.72	11.58
03/21	30.62	0 0	0.81	0.67	11.59
03/20	24.65	0 0	0.95	0.74	10.43
03/19	25.73	0 0	0.95	0.72	10.09
Annual Growth	(2.0%)	—	(5.5%)	(4.3%)	3.3%

Mitsubishi Estate Co Ltd

A comprehensive real estate developer, Mitsubishi Estate Co., Ltd. boasts the leading position in the Japanese market, operating a spectrum of businesses in diverse fields related to real estate, including an office building business centered on the Marunouchi district in central Tokyo, a retail property business, a residential business, a hotel business and airport business. The group's area of operations is not confined to Japan; it includes the US and the UK and extends to such Asian countries as China, Chinese Taipei, Singapore, Indonesia and Vietnam. The group subsidiary Mitsubishi Jisho Residence Co., Ltd., the developer of the Parkhouse condominium brand, has become Japan's leading supplier of condominiums.

Operations

The group operates through five primary segments: Commercial Property Business; Residential Business; International Business; Investment Management Business and Architectural Design & Engineering Business and Real Estate Services Business.

The largest segment, commercial property business (about 55% of revenue) engages in development of office buildings, retail properties, logistics facilities, hotels, and airports. Meanwhile, the residential business (nearly 30%) develops, markets, leases, manages and brokerage of condominiums and houses, new town development, leisure facility management and design and construction of custom-built housing.

Smaller segments include the international business (some 10% of revenue; operating in the US, the UK, and, increasingly, in growing Asian markets), architectural design and engineering and real estate service business (less than 5% of revenue; construction, agency, consulting, leasing, civil engineering, development planning, and consulting), and investment management (real estate assets such as REITs and private placement funds).

Geographic Reach
Based in Tokyo, Japan, the group area of operations is not confined to Japan; it includes the US and the UK and extends to such Asian countries as Singapore, Indonesia, Vietnam, Thailand, Malaysia, Philippines, Myanmar, Australia, China, and Taiwan.

Sales and Marketing
The company Marunouchi district tenants includes different types of business including finance (about 25%), manufacturing (about 25%), professional firms (about 20%), trading (some 10%), and information.

Financial Performance
Company's revenue for fiscal 2022 increased by Â¥141.9 billion to Â¥1.3 trillion compared from the prior year with Â¥1.2 trillion.

Net income for fiscal 2022 increased to Â¥155.6 billion compared from the prior year with Â¥135.7 billion.

Cash held by the company at the end of fiscal 2022 increased to Â¥234.2 billion. Cash provided by operations and financing activities were Â¥280.1 billion and Â¥91.0 billion, respectively. Cash used for investing activities was Â¥313.8 billion, mainly for purchase of property, plant and equipment.

EXECUTIVES

Chairman, Director, Junichi Yoshida
Representative Executive Officer, President, Director, Atsushi Nakajima
Representative Executive Officer, Executive Vice President, Futoshi Chiba
Representative Executive Officer, Executive Vice President, Kenji Hosokane
Representative Executive Officer, Senior Managing Executive Officer, Yuji Fujioka
Representative Executive Officer, Senior Managing Executive Officer, Director, Bunroku Naganuma
Representative Executive Officer, Senior Managing Executive Officer, Yutaro Yotsuzuka
Director, Naoki Umeda
Director, Mikihito Hirai
Director, Noboru Nishigai
Director, Hiroshi Katayama
Outside Director, Tsuyoshi Okamoto
Outside Director, Tetsuo Narukawa
Outside Director, Masaaki Shirakawa
Outside Director, Shin Nagase
Outside Director, Wataru Sueyoshi
Outside Director, Ayako Sonoda
Outside Director, Malanie Brock
Auditors: Ernst & Young ShinNihon LLC

LOCATIONS

HQ: Mitsubishi Estate Co Ltd
1-1-1 Otemachi, Chiyoda-ku, Tokyo 100-8133
Phone: (81) 3 3287 5100
Web: www.mec.co.jp

PRODUCTS/OPERATIONS

2014 Sales

	% of total
Building Business	44
Residential Business	37
International Business	7
Commercial Property Development & Investment Business	4
Hotel Business	3
Architectural Design & Engineering	2
Real Estate Services	2
Investment Management Business	1
Other	
Total	100

COMPETITORS

CBRE GROUP, INC.
JONES LANG LASALLE INCORPORATED
LINCOLN PROPERTY COMPANY
MAPELEY ESTATES LIMITED
MITSUI FUDOSAN CO., LTD.
PM REALTY GROUP, L.P.
STOCKLAND (UK) LIMITED
THE RELATED COMPANIES INC
TOKYU LAND CORPORATION
TRANSWESTERN COMMERCIAL SERVICES, L.L.C.

HISTORICAL FINANCIALS

Company Type: Public

Income Statement — FYE: March 31

	REVENUE ($mil)	NET INCOME ($mil)	NET PROFIT MARGIN	EMPLOYEES
03/23	10,345	1,241	12.0%	17,630
03/22	11,094	1,275	11.5%	17,268
03/21	10,906	1,225	11.2%	17,262
03/20	11,996	1,367	11.4%	16,951
03/19	11,407	1,215	10.7%	16,119
Annual Growth	(2.4%)	0.5%	—	2.3%

2023 Year-End Financials

Debt ratio: 0.3%
Return on equity: 7.9%
Cash ($ mil.): 1,689
Current Ratio: 1.89
Long-term debt ($ mil.): 18,309
No. of shares ($ mil.): 1,296
Dividends
  Yield: 2.4%
  Payout: 30.7%
Market value ($ mil.): 15,373

STOCK PRICE ($) FY Close	P/E High/Low	PER SHARE ($) Earnings	Dividends	Book Value
03/23 11.86	0 0	0.94	0.29	12.50
03/22 14.79	0 0	0.96	0.31	12.45
03/21 17.57	0 0	0.92	0.28	12.50
03/20 14.58	0 0	1.00	0.30	11.94
03/19 18.08	0 0	0.88	0.24	11.52
Annual Growth (10.0%)	—	1.9%	3.9%	2.1%

Mitsubishi HC Capital Inc

EXECUTIVES

Chairman, Representative Director, Seiji Kawabe
President, Representative Director, Takahiro Yanai
Executive Vice President, Representative Director, Kanji Nishiura
Executive Vice President, Director, Kazumi Anei
Executive Vice President, Director, Taiju Hisai
Director, Haruhiko Sato
Outside Director, Hiroyasu Nakata
Outside Director, Yuri Sasaki
Outside Director, Go Watanabe
Outside Director, Takuya Kuga
Director, Akira Hamamoto
Outside Director, Koichiro Hiraiwa
Outside Director, Hiroko Kaneko
Outside Director, Masayuki Saito
Auditors: Deloitte Touche Tohmatsu LLC

LOCATIONS

HQ: Mitsubishi HC Capital Inc
1-5-1 Marunouchi, Chiyoda-Ku, Tokyo 100-6525
Phone: (81) 3 6865 3004   **Fax:** 646 852-6845
Web: www.mitsubishi-hc-capital.com

HISTORICAL FINANCIALS

Company Type: Public

Income Statement — FYE: March 31

	REVENUE ($mil)	NET INCOME ($mil)	NET PROFIT MARGIN	EMPLOYEES
03/22	14,514	817	5.6%	10,372
03/21	8,077	499	6.2%	3,656
03/20	8,510	651	7.7%	3,578
03/19	7,803	621	8.0%	3,500
03/18	8,192	599	7.3%	3,481
Annual Growth	15.4%	8.0%		31.4%

2022 Year-End Financials

Debt ratio: 0.6%
Return on equity: 9.3%
Cash ($ mil.): 4,447
Current Ratio: 1.91
Long-term debt ($ mil.): 40,558
No. of shares ($ mil.): 1,436
Dividends
  Yield: —
  Payout: 75.1%
Market value ($ mil.): 14,577

	STOCK PRICE ($) FY Close	P/E High/Low		PER SHARE ($) Earnings	Dividends	Book Value
03/22	10.15	0	0	0.57	0.43	7.51
03/21	11.22	0	0	0.56	0.46	8.19
03/20	8.28	0	0	0.73	0.49	8.06
03/19	9.88	0	0	0.70	0.36	7.66
03/18	12.08	0	0	0.67	0.27	7.50
Annual Growth	(4.3%)	—	—	(4.1%)	12.1%	0.0%

Mitsubishi Heavy Industries Ltd

Mitsubishi Heavy Industries (MHI) Group is one of the world's leading industrial groups, spanning energy, logistics & infrastructure, industrial machinery, aerospace and defense. MHI operates through four business segments: Energy Systems, Logistics, Thermal and Drive Systems, Plants and Infrastructure Systems and Aircraft and Defense. The company's core market is Japan, but it also does business in other parts of Asia, North America, Europe, Central and South America, Africa, and the Middle East.

Operations

MHI operates through four reportable segments: Energy Systems, Logistics, Thermal and Drive Systems, Plants and Infrastructure Systems and Aircraft and Defense.

Energy Systems includes thermal power generation systems (Gas turbine combined cycle ["GTCC"] and Steam power), Nuclear power generation system (Light-water reactors, Nuclear fuel cycle & Advanced solutions), wind power generators, engines for aircrafts, compressors, Air Quality Control System ["AQCS"] and marine machinery. The segment accounts for more than 40% of revenue.

Logistics, Thermal & Drive Systems includes material handling equipment, turbochargers, engines, air-conditioning & refrigeration systems, and automotive thermal systems. The segment accounts for around 25% of revenue.

Plants & Infrastructure Systems includes metals machinery, commercial ships, engineering, environmental systems and mechatronics systems. The segment accounts for more than 15% of revenue.

Aircraft, Defense & Space includes commercial aircraft, defense aircraft, missile systems, naval ships, special vehicles, maritime systems (torpedoes) and space systems. The segment accounts for about 15% of revenue.

Geographic Reach

The company is based in Tokyo, Japan, and has a presence in North America, South America, Europe, the Middle East, Africa, China, Asia, Japan, and Oceania. Japan accounts for nearly 50% of its total revenue, and North America represents some 15%.

Financial Performance

The company reported a total revenue of Â¥3.9 trillion in 2021, a 4% increase from the previous year's total revenue of Â¥3.7 trillion.

In 2021, the company had net income of Â¥113.5 billion, a 179% increase from the previous year's net income of Â¥40.6 billion.

The company's cash for the year ended 2022 was Â¥314.3 billion. Operating activities generated Â¥285.6 billion, while financing activities used Â¥255.8 billion, mainly for the net increase in short-term borrowings. Investing activities provided another Â¥16.3 billion.

Strategy

The company is also pursuing initiatives for new business development under the guidance of the Growth Strategy Office, which the company sets up in April 2020. These include combining existing lines of business to develop products and services, and cultivating business domains beyond the reach of its existing business units. With regard to the M&A and alliances, the company is undertaking in various product areas, which take the business environment into consideration, through activities such as monitoring and screening at the point of entry, the company is putting initiatives aimed at smooth PMI into practice.

EXECUTIVES

Chairman, Director, Shunichi Miyanaga
President, Chief Executive Officer, Representative Director, Seiji Izumisawa
Executive Vice President, Representative Director, Hitoshi Kaguchi
Chief Technology Officer, Co-Chief Strategy Officer, Eisaku Ito
Chief Financial Officer, Managing Executive Officer, Representative Director, Hisato Kozawa
Chief Strategy Officer, Masayuki Suematsu
Outside Director, Ken Kobayashi
Outside Director, Nobuyuki Hirano
Outside Director, Mitsuhiro Furusawa
Director, Setsuo Tokunaga
Director, Ryutaro Takayanagi
Outside Director, Hiroo Unoura
Outside Director, Noriko Morikawa
Outside Director, Masako Ii
Auditors : KPMG AZSA LLC

LOCATIONS

HQ: Mitsubishi Heavy Industries Ltd
3-2-3 Marunouchi, Chiyoda-ku, Tokyo 100-8332
Phone: (81) 3 6275 6200   **Fax:** 346 308-8787
Web: www.mhi.co.jp

2018 Sales

	% of total
Asia	
Japan	46
Other countries	17
USA	15
Europe	11
Central and South America	4
Middle East	3
Africa	2
Other regions	2
Total	100

PRODUCTS/OPERATIONS

2018 Sales

	% of total
Industry & Infrastructure	45
Power Systems	35
Aircraft, Defense & Space	17
Others	3
Total	100

Selected Products

Aerospace
  Aeroengines
  Civil aircraft
  Defense aircraft
  Guided weapon systems
  Laser radar surveillance system
  Launch vehicles
  Rocket engines
  Space stations
General Machinery & Special Vehicles
  Agricultural machinery
  Construction machinery
  Forklift trucks
  Medium- and small-sized engines
  Tractors
  Turbochargers
Machinery & Steel Structures
  Air brakes
  Automated people movers
  Chemical plants
  CO2 recovery plants
  Crane and material handling systems
  Flue gas desulphurization plants
  Injection molding machines
  Monorails
  Production robots
  Rail transit systems
  Sludge treatment systems
  Testing equipment
Power Systems
  Boilers
  Desalination plants
  Fans and blowers
  Diesel engines
  Gas turbines
  Hydraulic equipment (actuators, generators, motors, pumps, and water pressure systems)
  Instrumentation and control systems
  Lithium-ion secondary batteries
  Solid oxide fuel cells
  Steam turbines
  Thin-film photovoltaic module
  Wind turbines
Shipbuilding & Ocean Development
  Cargo ships
  Floating facilities
  Marine engines
  Marine machinery
  Passenger ships
  Pure car carriers
  Special-purpose ships
  Tankers
Others
  Air conditioning and refrigeration systems
  Automotive thermal systems
  Centrifugal chillers
  Machine tools

COMPETITORS

BROADWIND ENERGY, INC.
CAPSTONE TURBINE CORPORATION
GENERAL ELECTRIC COMPANY
ITT INC.
MITSUBISHI POWER AMERICAS, INC.
SIA ENGINEERING COMPANY LIMITED
SOLAR TURBINES INCORPORATED
SUZLON ENERGY LIMITED
THERMON GROUP HOLDINGS, INC.
Wärtsilä Oyj Abp

HISTORICAL FINANCIALS

Company Type: Public

Income Statement — FYE: March 31

	REVENUE ($mil)	NET INCOME ($mil)	NET PROFIT MARGIN	EMPLOYEES
03/23	31,555	979	3.1%	84,317
03/22	31,736	933	2.9%	86,331
03/21	33,415	367	1.1%	90,322
03/20	37,230	802	2.2%	93,075
03/19	36,826	915	2.5%	93,173
Annual Growth	(3.8%)	1.7%	—	(2.5%)

2023 Year-End Financials

Debt ratio: 0.1%
Return on equity: 7.8%
Cash ($ mil.): 2,610
Current Ratio: 1.16
Long-term debt ($ mil.): 6,292
No. of shares ($ mil.): 336
Dividends
 Yield: —
 Payout: 33.4%
Market value ($ mil.): —

Mitsubishi Materials Corp.

EXECUTIVES

Chairman, Director, Akira Takeuchi
Representative Executive Officer, President, Chief Executive Officer, Director, Naoki Ono
Managing Executive Officer, Chief Governance Officer, Tetsuya Tanaka
Managing Executive Officer, Chief Financial Officer, Director, Nobuhiro Takayanagi
Managing Executive Officer, Chief Human Resources Officer, Makiko Nogawa
Representative Executive Officer, Managing Executive Officer, Chief Technical Officer, Chief Digital Officer, Director, Makoto Shibata
Outside Director, Mariko Tokuno
Outside Director, Hiroshi Watanabe
Outside Director, Hikaru Sugi
Outside Director, Tatsuo Wakabayashi
Outside Director, Koji Igarashi
Outside Director, Kazuhiko Takeda
Outside Director, Rikako Beppu
Auditors : KPMG AZSA LLC

LOCATIONS

HQ: Mitsubishi Materials Corp.
 3-2-3 Marunouchi, Chiyoda-ku, Tokyo 100-8117
Phone: (81) 3 5252 5226   **Fax:** 714 352-6190
Web: www.mmc.co.jp

COMPETITORS

Aurubis AG
CHINO MINES COMPANY
China Baowu Steel Group Corporation Limited
HANWA CO.,LTD.
Jiangxi Copper Company Limited
KAISER ALUMINUM CORPORATION
LuvHolding Oy
MATERION CORPORATION
MATERION TECHNICAL MATERIALS INC.
MINERALS TECHNOLOGIES INC.

HISTORICAL FINANCIALS

Company Type: Public

Income Statement — FYE: March 31

	REVENUE ($mil)	NET INCOME ($mil)	NET PROFIT MARGIN	EMPLOYEES
03/23	12,208	152	1.3%	21,341
03/22	14,894	370	2.5%	27,516
03/21	13,412	220	1.6%	31,565
03/20	13,966	(671)	—	34,260
03/19	15,016	11	0.1%	34,079
Annual Growth	(5.0%)	90.0%	—	(11.0%)

2023 Year-End Financials

Debt ratio: 0.2%
Return on equity: 3.4%
Cash ($ mil.): 1,067
Current Ratio: 1.36
Long-term debt ($ mil.): 2,714
No. of shares ($ mil.): 130
Dividends
 Yield: —
 Payout: 0.0%
Market value ($ mil.): —

Mitsubishi Motors Corp. (Japan)

Mitsubishi Motors Corporation is a global automobile company that has about 30,000 employees and a global footprint with production facilities in Japan, Thailand, Indonesia, Mainland China, the Philippines, Vietnam, and Russia. Mitsubishi Motors has a competitive edge in SUVs, pickup trucks and plug-in hybrid electric vehicles, and appeals to ambitious drivers willing to challenge convention and embrace innovation. Mitsubishi Motors traces its roots back to 1870. About 80% of sales come from outside of Japan.

Operations

The company operates in two reportable segments: automobiles and financial services.

The automobiles segment accounts for the vast majority of revenue and develops, designs, manufactures and sells automobiles and component parts. The financial services segment involves in the sales finance and leasing services of the company, including property sales associated with the expiration and cancellation of lease transactions.

Geographic Reach

Mitsubishi's largest market is Asia (excluding Japan), representing roughly 25% of revenue. Other major markets include Japan (about 20%), North America (nearly 20%), Europe (almost 15%), Oceania (about 15%), and other countries (more than 10%).

Based in Japan, Mitsubishi has about 30 facilities in nearly 15 countries and regions.

Financial Performance

The company's revenue for fiscal 2022 increased to JPY 2.0 trillion compared from the prior year with JPY 1.5 trillion.

Profit for fiscal 2022 was JPY 74.1 billion compared from the prior year with a loss of JPY 309.4 billion.

Cash held by the company at the end of fiscal 2022 increased to JPY 511.5 billion. Cash provided by operations was JPY 118.1 billion while cash used for investing and financing activities were JPY 69.1 billion and JPY 10.2 billion, respectively.

Company Background

Mitsubishi Motors Corporation was created in 1970 when Mitsubishi Heavy Industries spun off its motor vehicle division. Mitsubishi Heavy Industries was created in 1934 by the merger of Mitsubishi Aircraft and Mitsubishi Shipbuilding (which had been making cars since 1917).

EXECUTIVES

Chairman, Director, Tomofumi Hiraku
Representative Executive Officer, President, Chief Executive Officer, Director, Takao Kato
Representative Executive Officer, Executive Vice President, Hiroshi Nagaoka
Representative Executive Officer, Executive Vice President, Chief Financial Officer, Koji Ikeya
Representative Executive Officer, Executive Vice President, Tatsuo Nakamura
Director, Hitoshi Inada
Outside Director, Shunichi Miyanaga
Outside Director, Main Kohda
Outside Director, Kenichiro Sasae
Outside Director, Hideyuki Sakamoto
Outside Director, Yoshihiko Nakamura
Outside Director, Joji Tagawa
Outside Director, Takahiko Ikushima
Outside Director, Takehiko Kakiuchi
Outside Director, Kanetsugu Mike
Outside Director, Junko Ogushi
Auditors : Ernst & Young ShinNihon LLC

LOCATIONS

HQ: Mitsubishi Motors Corp. (Japan)
 3-1-21 Shibaura, Minato-ku, Tokyo 108-8410
Phone: (81) 3 3456 1111
Web: www.mitsubishi-motors.com

2015 Sales

	% of total
Europe	24
Japan	20
Asia	19
North America	13
Oceania	10
Other regions	14
Total	100

PRODUCTS/OPERATIONS

2015	%
Automobiles	99
Financial services	1
Total	100

Selected Models
Challenger
Colt
Diamante
Eclipse
Eclipse Spyder
Endeavor
Galant
i MiEV
Lancer
Lancer Evolution
Mirage
Outlander
Raider

COMPETITORS
AB Volvo
FIAT CHRYSLER AUTOMOBILES N.V.
FORD MOTOR COMPANY
GENERAL MOTORS COMPANY
HONDA MOTOR CO., LTD.
MAZDA MOTOR CORPORATION
MITSUBISHI CORPORATION
NISSAN MOTOR CO.,LTD.
TOYOTA MOTOR CORPORATION
VOLKSWAGEN AG

HISTORICAL FINANCIALS
Company Type: Public

Income Statement — FYE: March 31

	REVENUE ($mil)	NET INCOME ($mil)	NET PROFIT MARGIN	EMPLOYEES
03/23	18,456	1,266	6.9%	36,551
03/22	16,762	608	3.6%	36,744
03/21	13,145	(2,820)	—	36,525
03/20	20,914	(237)	—	39,729
03/19	22,706	1,199	5.3%	39,996
Annual Growth	(5.0%)	1.4%	—	(2.2%)

2023 Year-End Financials
Debt ratio: 0.1%
Return on equity: 23.9%
Cash ($ mil.): 4,474
Current Ratio: 1.46
Long-term debt ($ mil.): 1,862
No. of shares ($ mil.): 1,489
Dividends
  Yield: —
  Payout: 4.4%
Market value ($ mil.): —

Mitsubishi Shokuhin Co., Ltd.

Mitsubishi Shokuhin is a leading wholesale food distributor in Japan. It supplies retailers throughout the country with a wide assortment of products, including processed foods, seasonings and sauces, chilled and frozen foods, confectionery, and canned goods. In addition, the company distributes both alcoholic and non-alcoholic beverages. Trading company Mitsubishi Corporation owns just more than 50% of Mitsubishi Shokuhin. Formerly named Ryoshoku, the company adopted the Mitsubishi Shokuhin moniker in 2011. It also began absorbing three of its food wholesaling operations -- San-Esu, Food Service Network, and Meidi-ya. The integration is expected to be completed in 2012.

EXECUTIVES
President, Chief Sustainability Officer, Representative Director, Yutaka Kyoya
Managing Executive Officer, Chief Compliance Officer, Director, Koichi Enomoto
Managing Executive Officer, Chief Financial Officer, Director, Kazuaki Yamana
Managing Executive Officer, Chief Health Officer, Director, Yasuo Yamamoto
Director, Koji Tamura
Director, Wataru Kato
Outside Director, Tamaki Kakizaki
Outside Director, Nobuyuki Teshima
Outside Director, Masahiro Yoshikawa
Auditors: Deloitte Touche Tohmatsu LLC

LOCATIONS
HQ: Mitsubishi Shokuhin Co., Ltd.
 1-1-1 Koishikawa, Bunkyo-ku, Tokyo 112-8778
Phone: (81) 3 4553 5111
Web: www.mitsubishi-shokuhin.com

PRODUCTS/OPERATIONS
2016 sales

	% of total
Frozen and chilled foods business	39
Processed food business	32
Alcoholic beverages business	18
Confectioneries business	11
Total	100

COMPETITORS
MONOGRAM FOOD SOLUTIONS, LLC
NEWPORT MEAT NORTHERN CALIFORNIA, INC.
OMAHA STEAKS INTERNATIONAL, INC.
PDNC, LLC
SUPERIOR FOODS, INC.

HISTORICAL FINANCIALS
Company Type: Public

Income Statement — FYE: March 31

	REVENUE ($mil)	NET INCOME ($mil)	NET PROFIT MARGIN	EMPLOYEES
03/21	23,279	100	0.4%	6,441
03/20	24,455	105	0.4%	6,429
03/19	23,661	108	0.5%	6,427
03/18	23,669	101	0.4%	6,474
03/17	21,568	110	0.5%	6,407
Annual Growth	1.9%	(2.5%)	—	0.1%

2021 Year-End Financials
Debt ratio: —
Return on equity: 5.8%
Cash ($ mil.): 3
Current Ratio: 1.16
Long-term debt ($ mil.): —
No. of shares ($ mil.): 57
Dividends
  Yield: —
  Payout: 0.0%
Market value ($ mil.): —

Mitsubishi UFJ Financial Group Inc

Established in 2002, Mitsubishi UFJ Financial Group (MUFG) is a bank holding company incorporated as a joint stock company under the Companies Act of Japan. It is the holding company for MUFG Bank, Ltd. (formerly, The Bank of Tokyo-Mitsubishi UFJ, Ltd.), Mitsubishi UFJ Trust and Banking Corporation, Mitsubishi UFJ Securities Holdings Co., Ltd., Mitsubishi UFJ Morgan Stanley Securities Co., Ltd., Mitsubishi UFJ NICOS Co., Ltd., and other companies. It is one of the world's largest and most diversified financial groups with total assets of Â¥367.65 trillion as of March 31, 2022. It generates about 55% of its revenue from Japan.

Operations
The MUFG Group integrated the operations of its consolidated subsidiaries into seven business segments.?Digital Service, Retail & Commercial Banking, Japanese Corporate & Investment Banking, Global Commercial Banking, Asset Management & Investor Services, Global Corporate & Investment Banking, and Global Markets.

Digital Service Business Group (generates nearly 20% of revenue) covers digital-based non-face-to-face businesses servicing "mass-segment" customers or retail customers and small and medium-sized enterprise customers, of Mitsubishi UFJ NICOS, other consumer financing company and MUFG Bank in Japan.

Retail & Commercial Banking Business Group (some 15%) covers the domestic retail and commercial banking businesses. This business group mainly offers retail customers (with a strategic focus on high net-worth individual) and small and medium-sized enterprise customers in Japan an extensive array of commercial banking, trust banking and securities products and services.

Japanese Corporate & Investment Banking Business Group (some 15%) covers the large Japanese corporate businesses. This business group offers large Japanese corporations advanced financial solutions designed to respond to their diversified and globalized needs and to contribute to their business and financial strategies through the global network of the MUFG group companies.

Global Commercial Banking Business Group (nearly 20%) covers the retail and commercial banking businesses of MUFG Union Bank and Krungsri and Bank Danamon. This business group offers a comprehensive array of financial products and services such as loans, deposits, fund transfers, investments and asset management services for local retail, small and medium-sized enterprise, and corporate customers across the Asia-Pacific region.

Asset Management & Investor Services Business Group (nearly 10%) covers the asset management and asset administration businesses of Mitsubishi UFJ Trust and Banking, MUFG Bank and First Sentier Investors. By integrating the trust banking expertise of Mitsubishi UFJ Trust and Banking and the global strengths of MUFG Bank, the business group offers a full range of asset management and administration services for corporations and pension funds, including pension fund management and administration, advice on pension structures, and payments to beneficiaries, and also offer investment trusts for retail customers.

Global Corporate & Investment Banking Business Group (over 10%) covers the global corporate, investment and transaction banking businesses of MUFG Bank and Mitsubishi UFJ Securities Holdings. Through a global network of offices and branches, this business group provides non-Japanese large corporate and financial institution customers with a comprehensive set of solutions that meet their increasingly diverse and sophisticated financing needs.

Global Markets Business Group (some 10%) covers the customer business and the treasury operations of MUFG Bank, Mitsubishi UFJ Trust and Banking and Mitsubishi UFJ Securities Holdings. The customer business includes sales and trading in fixed income instruments, currencies, equities and other investment products as well as origination and distribution of financial products. The treasury operations include asset and liability management as well as global investments for the MUFG Group.

Other consists mainly of the corporate centers of MUFG, MUFG Bank, Mitsubishi UFJ Trust and Banking and Mitsubishi UFJ Morgan Stanley Securities. The elimination of duplicated amounts of net revenues among business segments is also reflected in Other.

Geographic Reach

The company operates in the US, Japan, and more than 50 countries in Europe, Asia/Oceania. About 55% of its revenue came from Japan and early 15% came from the US.

Sales and Marketing

The company aims to thoroughly refine its channels, products, services, and marketing by using digital technology, and provides the most advanced and optimal financial services for our customers. By freeing customers and employees from complicated flows of actions by simplifying workflow and utilizing digital technology, it seeks to provide customers with convenience and high-value-added services.

Financial Performance

Note: Growth rates may differ after conversion to US dollars.

MUFG's revenues declined by about 34% to Â¥3,925.7 billion in fiscal year 2022 (ended March 31) from Â¥5,909.8 billion in the prior year after recording sales decline across all its geographic locations.

The company suffered a net loss of Â¥83.3 billion in 2022 after recording a net income of Â¥1,117.3 billion in 2021.

Cash and cash equivalents at end of fiscal year 2022 was Â¥111,111,544. Operations provided Â¥909,355. Investing and financing activities provided another Â¥236,835 and Â¥5,385,042, respectively.

Strategy

In order to attain its vision for the three-year period to leverage its financial and digital capabilities to be the leading business partner that pioneers the future, MUFJ identified three strategic pillars of "Corporate Transformation," "Strategy for Growth," and "Structural Reforms."

Under its "Corporate Transformation" strategy, it will seek to change how it operates and executes. While focusing on "Digital transformation" and "Contribution to addressing environmental and social issues," it will also aim to "Transform our corporate culture" in order to accelerate decision making.

In order to attain its vision for the three-year period to leverage its financial and digital capabilities to be the leading business partner that pioneers the future, MUFJ identified three strategic pillars of "Corporate Transformation," "Strategy for Growth," and "Structural Reforms."

Under its "Corporate Transformation" strategy, it will seek to change how it operates and executes. While focusing on "Digital transformation" and "Contribution to addressing environmental and social issues," it will also aim to "Transform our corporate culture" in order to accelerate decision making.

MUFJ has a global strategic alliance with Morgan Stanley, under which it operates two joint venture securities companies in Japan, engage in joint corporate finance operations in the US and pursue other cooperative opportunities. It holds approximately 21.5% of the voting rights in Morgan Stanley as of March 31, 2022 and continue to hold approximately $521.4 million of perpetual non-cumulative non-convertible preferred stock with a 10% dividend.

Company Background

MUFG was formed in the 2005 merger of Mitsubishi Tokyo Financial Group and UFJ Holdings.

HISTORY

Mitsubishi Bank emerged from the exchange office of the original Mitsubishi zaibatsu (industrial group) in 1885. It evolved into a full-service bank by 1895 and became independent in 1919, though its primary customers were Mitsubishi group companies. The bank survived WWII, but a US fiat dismantled the zaibatsu after the war. Mitsubishi Bank reopened as Chiyoda Bank in 1948. After reopening offices in London and New York, the bank readopted the Mitsubishi name.

In the 1950s Mitsubishi Bank became the lead lender for the reconstituted Mitsubishi group (keiretsu). In the 1960s it followed its Mitsubishi partners overseas, helping finance Japan's growing international trade. In 1972 it acquired the Bank of California and began doing more business outside the group.

Japan's overinflated real estate market of the 1980s devastated many of the country's banks, including Nippon Trust Bank, of which Mitsubishi owned 5%. Japan's Ministry of Finance (MoF) urged Mitsubishi to bail Nippon out; as a reward for raising its stake in Nippon to 69% and assuming a mountain of unrecoverable loans, the MoF allowed Mitsubishi to begin issuing debt before other Japanese banks. In 1995 Mitsubishi Bank and Bank of Tokyo agreed to merge.

Bank of Tokyo (BOT) was established in 1880 as the Yokohama Specie Bank; the Iwasaki family, founders of the Mitsubishi group, served on its board. With links to the Imperial family, the bank was heavily influenced by government policy. With Japan isolated after the Sino-Japanese War, its international operations suffered greatly even before WWII. Completely dismantled after WWII, the bank was re-established in 1946 as the Bank of Tokyo, a commercial city bank bereft of its foreign exchange business. During the 1950s the government restored it as a foreign exchange specialist, but regulations limited its domestic business.

BOT evolved into an investment bank in the 1970s; its reputation as the leading foreign exchange bank brought in international clients and successful derivatives trading and overseas banking. By the time BOT and Mitsubishi Bank agreed to merge, BOT had 363 foreign offices (only 37 in Japan) with more foreign than Japanese employees.

The two banks merged in 1996 to form The Bank of Tokyo-Mitsubishi (BTM); Mitsubishi was the surviving entity. Their California banks merged to create Union Bank of California (UnionBanCal). The next year BTM reorganized its operations but had problems assimilating its disparate corporate cultures.

In 1998 Japanese banking regulators doled out nearly $240 billion to the industry to prop up failing banks and to strengthen healthier ones. Also that year BTM was fined for bribing MoF officials with entertainment gifts and posted a huge loss after writing off $8.4 billion in bad debt. Losses continued in 1999, and the bank responded by reorganizing operationally, cutting jobs and offices, and selling stock in UnionBanCal.

In 2000 BTM announced plans to form a financial group with Mitsubishi Trust Bank and Nippon Trust Bank. The following year the three banks unified and formed Mitsubishi Tokyo Financial Group. Before rolling into Mitsubishi Trust Financial Group, BTM paid back the money showered upon it by the Japanese government in 1998.

In 2004 MTFG introduced a new organizational structure that focused on its three core markets -- retail, corporate, and trust asset businesses. The company planned to unify business within each division and to improve decision-making companywide. The group also introduced a new executive officer system with the idea of separating company oversight and business execution. A mechanism for credit risk control was also added.

It was all to change in 2005, however. During this time, Mitsubishi Tokyo Financial Group merged with UFJ Holdings, emerging (at that time) as the world's largest bank by assets. As a result of the merger, the group was renamed Mitsubishi UFJ Financial Group (MUFG).

As with most of its peers, MUFG was not immune to the global credit crisis that began in 2007. Its NICOS consumer lending subsidiary had a disappointing year due to the credit crunch. The unit sold its installment credit, car loan, and car leasing businesses to JACCS in 2008. In 2009 MUFG announced plans to close 50 branches and cut nearly 1,000 jobs as a part of a long-term restructuring plan. In addition, the bank shut down some 200 ATMs and relocated another 1,000 employees.

In 2008 the group bought the rest of UnionBanCal and Mitsubishi UFJ NICOS it didn't already own and acquired a stake in bulge-bracket firm Morgan Stanley. MUFG also bought a 10% stake in UK-based Aberdeen Asset Management that year. (It later upped its interest to around 17%.)

EXECUTIVES

Chairman, Kanetsugu Mike
Deputy Chairman, Iwao Nagashima
Chief Executive Officer, President, Director, Hironori Kamezawa
Senior Managing Executive Officer, Chief Audit Officer, Yoshitaka Shiba
Senior Managing Executive Officer, Chief Financial Officer, Tetsuya Yonehana
Japanese Corporate & Investment Banking Senior Managing Executive Officer, Japanese Corporate & Investment Banking Head, Naomi Hayashi
Retail & Commercial Banking Senior Managing Executive Officer, Retail & Commercial Banking Head, Atsushi Miyata
Asset Management & Investor Services Senior Managing Executive Officer, Asset Management & Investor Services Head, Masamichi Yasuda
Senior Managing Executive Officer, Chief Human Resources Officer, Teruyuki Sasaki
Managing Executive Officer, Director, Makoto Kobayashi
Managing Corporate Executive, Deputy Chairman, Director, Junichi Hanzawa
Managing Executive Officer, Chief Digital Transformation Officer, Masakazu Osawa
Managing Corporate Executive, Chief Legal Officer, Hiroshi Mori
Managing Corporate Executive, Chief Strategy Officer, Yutaka Miyashita
Managing Corporate Executive, Chief Compliance Officer, Keitaro Tsukiyama

Global Corporate & Investment Banking Managing Corporate Executive, Global Corporate & Investment Banking Head, Fumitaka Nakahama
Managing Corporate Executive, Chief Information Officer, Toshiki Ochi
Global Markets Business Managing Corporate Executive, Global Markets Business Head, Hiroyuki Seki
Managing Corporate Executive, Chief Operating Officer, Hideaki Takase
Global Commercial Banking Managing Corporate Executive, Global Commercial Banking Head, Kenichi Yamato
Managing Corporate Executive, Chief Risk Officer, Shuichi Yokoyama
Outside Director, Mariko Fujii
Outside Director, Keiko Honda
Outside Director, Kaoru Kato
Outside Director, Satoko Kuwabara
Outside Director, Toby S. Myerson
Outside Director, Hirofumi Nomoto
Outside Director, Yasushi Shingai
Outside Director, Koichi Tsuji
Outside Director, Tarisa Watanagase
Director, Ritsuo Ogura
Director, Kenichi Miyanaga
Auditors: Deloitte Touche Tohmatsu LLC

LOCATIONS

HQ: Mitsubishi UFJ Financial Group Inc
7-1 Marunouchi 2-chome, Chiyoda-ku, Tokyo 100-8330
Phone: (81) 3 3240 8111 **Fax:** (81) 3 3240 7073
Web: www.mufg.jp

2018 Sales

	% of total
Japan	41
US	26
Europe	10
Asia/Oceania	15
Other regions	8
Total	**100**

PRODUCTS/OPERATIONS

2018 Sales

	% of total
Interest	
Loans, including fees	44
Deposits in other banks	2
Investment securities	
Interest	4
Dividends	3
Trading account assets	8
Other	2
Noninterest	
Fees & commissions	28
Foreign exchange gains	-
Trading accounts profits	-
Investment securities gains	6
Equity in earnings of equity method investees	4
Gains in sales of loans	-
Other	1
Total	**100**

2018 Sales

	% of total
Retail & Commercial Banking Business Group	41
Japanese Corporate & Investment Banking Business Group	13
Global Corporate & Investment Banking Business Group	9
Global Commercial Banking Business Group	16
Asset Management & Investor Services Business Group	5
Global Markets Business Group	15
Total	**100**

COMPETITORS

BANK OF YOKOHAMA,LTD.,
Credit Suisse Group AG
DEUTSCHE BANK AG
E. SUN FINANCIAL HOLDING COMPANY, LTD.
Hana Financial Group Inc.
LLOYDS BANKING GROUP PLC
MIZUHO FINANCIAL GROUP, INC.
SUMITOMO MITSUI TRUST HOLDINGS, INC.
Shinhan Financial Group Co., Ltd.
Woori Finance Holdings Co., Ltd.

HISTORICAL FINANCIALS

Company Type: Public

Income Statement — FYE: March 31

	ASSETS ($mil)	NET INCOME ($mil)	INCOME AS % OF ASSETS	EMPLOYEES
03/22	3,022,520	(684)	0.0%	158,100
03/21	3,195,540	10,090	0.3%	163,500
03/20	3,056,220	2,818	0.1%	168,400
03/19	2,756,170	6,489	0.2%	144,700
03/18	2,830,580	11,566	0.4%	144,000
Annual Growth	1.7%	—	—	2.4%

2022 Year-End Financials

Return on assets: —   Dividends
Return on equity: (-0.5%)   Yield: 3.7%
Long-term debt ($ mil.): —   Payout: 0.0%
No. of shares ($ mil.): 12,613   Market value ($ mil.): 78,079
Sales ($ mil.): 35,426

	STOCK PRICE ($) FY Close	P/E High/Low	PER SHARE ($) Earnings	Dividends	Book Value
03/22	6.19	— —	(0.06)	0.23	10.17
03/21	5.38	0 0	0.78	0.24	11.01
03/20	3.66	0 0	0.22	0.22	10.77
03/19	4.95	0 0	0.49	0.19	10.62
03/18	6.64	0 0	0.87	0.17	10.71
Annual Growth	(1.7%)	— —	—	8.0%	(1.3%)

Mitsui & Co., Ltd.

EXECUTIVES

Chairman, Representative Director, Tatsuo Yasunaga
President, Chief Executive Officer, Representative Director, Kenichi Hori
Executive Vice President, Representative Director, Motoaki Uno
Executive Vice President, Chief Human Resources Officer, Chief Compliance Officer, Representative Director, Yoshiaki Takemasu
Executive Vice President, Sayu Ueno

Senior Managing Executive Officer, Representative Director, Kazumasa Nakai
Senior Managing Executive Officer, Chief Financial Officer, Representative Director, Tetsuya Shigeta
Senior Managing Executive Officer, Chief Strategy Officer, Representative Director, Makoto Sato
Senior Managing Executive Officer, Chief Digital Information Officer, Representative Director, Toru Matsui
Senior Managing Executive Officer, Yoshiki Hirabayashi
Senior Managing Executive Officer, Motoyasu Nozaki
Senior Managing Executive Officer, Representative Director, Tetsuya Daikoku
Chief Strategy Officer, Kiyoshi Mori
Outside Director, Samuel Walsh
Outside Director, Takeshi Uchiyamada
Outside Director, Masako Egawa
Outside Director, Fujiyo Ishiguro
Outside Director, Sarah L. Casanova
Outside Director, Jessica Tan Soon Neo
Auditors: Deloitte Touche Tohmatsu LLC

LOCATIONS

HQ: Mitsui & Co., Ltd.
1-2-1 Otemachi, Chiyoda-ku, Tokyo 100-8631
Phone: (81) 3 3285 1111   **Fax:** 212 878-4800
Web: www.mitsui.com/jp/ja

HISTORICAL FINANCIALS

Company Type: Public

Income Statement — FYE: March 31

	REVENUE ($mil)	NET INCOME ($mil)	NET PROFIT MARGIN	EMPLOYEES
03/23	107,417	8,489	7.9%	55,874
03/22	96,661	7,520	7.8%	53,205
03/21	72,343	3,029	4.2%	54,230
03/20	63,427	3,606	5.7%	56,384
03/19	62,825	3,740	6.0%	54,347
Annual Growth	14.3%	22.7%	—	0.7%

2023 Year-End Financials

Debt ratio: 0.2%
Return on equity: 18.8%
Cash ($ mil.): 10,437
Current Ratio: 1.51
Long-term debt ($ mil.): 25,275
No. of shares ($ mil.): 1,528
Dividends
 Yield: —
 Payout: 347.7%
Market value ($ mil.): 953,946

	STOCK PRICE ($) FY Close	P/E High/Low		PER SHARE ($) Earnings	Dividends	Book Value
03/23	624.27	1	1	5.42	18.84	31.29
03/22	546.00	1	1	4.62	14.86	28.71
03/21	421.49	2	1	1.80	14.46	24.68
03/20	274.34	2	1	2.08	14.72	20.60
03/19	311.09	2	1	2.15	14.52	22.15
Annual Growth	19.0%	—		26.0%	6.7%	9.0%

Mitsui Chemicals Inc (Japan)

EXECUTIVES

Chairman, Director, Tsutomu Tannowa
President, Chief Executive Officer, Representative Director, Osamu Hashimoto
Senior Managing Executive Officer, Chief Technology Officer, Representative Director, Tadashi Yoshino
Senior Managing Executive Officer, Chief Financial Officer, Director, Hajime Nakajima
Senior Managing Executive Officer, Chief Human Resources Officer, Director, Yoshinori Andou
Outside Director, Yukiko Yoshimaru
Outside Director, Akira Mabuchi
Outside Director, Takayoshi Mimura
Auditors: Ernst & Young ShinNihon LLC

LOCATIONS

HQ: Mitsui Chemicals Inc (Japan)
2-2-1 Yaesu, Chuo-ku, Tokyo 104-0028
Phone: (81) 3 6880 7505   **Fax:** 914 253-0790
Web: jp.mitsuichem.com

COMPETITORS

CVC SPECIALTY CHEMICALS, INC.
DENKA COMPANY LIMITED
Elekeiroz S/A
HELM U.S. CORPORATION
KEMIRA CHEMICALS, INC.
MITSUBISHI GAS CHEMICAL COMPANY,INC.
NIPPON SYNTHETIC CHEMICAL INDUSTRY CO., LTD., THE
NISSAN CHEMICAL CORPORATION
Shanghai Taiqian Management Consulting Co., Ltd.
UBE INDUSTRIES, LTD.

HISTORICAL FINANCIALS

Company Type: Public

Income Statement — FYE: March 31

	REVENUE ($mil)	NET INCOME ($mil)	NET PROFIT MARGIN	EMPLOYEES
03/23	14,112	622	4.4%	18,933
03/22	13,258	904	6.8%	18,780
03/21	10,943	522	4.8%	18,051
03/20	12,335	349	2.8%	17,979
03/19	13,390	687	5.1%	17,743
Annual Growth	1.3%	(2.4%)	—	1.6%

2023 Year-End Financials

Debt ratio: 0.3%
Return on equity: 11.0%
Cash ($ mil.): 1,398
Current Ratio: 1.57
Long-term debt ($ mil.): 2,776
No. of shares ($ mil.): 190
Dividends
 Yield: 3.5%
 Payout: 0.0%
Market value ($ mil.): 2,463

	STOCK PRICE ($) FY Close	P/E High/Low		PER SHARE ($) Earnings	Dividends	Book Value
03/23	12.96	0	0	3.24	0.46	31.08
03/22	12.78	0	0	4.65	0.47	30.32
03/21	16.25	0	0	2.69	0.47	28.02
03/20	9.09	0	0	1.80	0.46	25.44
03/19	12.04	0	0	3.48	0.43	25.55
Annual Growth	1.9%	—		(1.8%)	1.9%	5.0%

Mitsui Fudosan Co Ltd

Mitsui Fudosan, the real estate arm of Mitsui & Co., builds, sells, leases, and manages a variety of luxury real estate, including office buildings, residential subdivisions, and condominiums. Its portfolio comprises retail facilities which accounts for about 15% of the company's total assets and over 50% office buildings in Japan alone. Known for its high-rises (the firm's Kasumigaseki Building in Tokyo is considered to be Japan's first skyscraper), the company also owns hotels and engages in real estate brokerage services. Besides Japan, the company operates offices in China, Hong Kong, Singapore, the UK, and the US. Mitsui Fudosan was established in 1941 when Mitsui Company's real estate division separated from its parent.

Operations

The company operates through four segments: Leasing (over 30% of sales), Property Sales (around 30%), Management (some 20%), and Other (more than 15%).

The Leasing segment includes revenue gained from the leasing of real estate. The Property Sales segment includes revenue gained from real estate property sales to individuals and investors. The Management segment includes revenue from fees gained through the management and operation of real estate, brokering deals, and other sources. The Other segment includes revenue gained from new construction of wooden housing under consignment and the operation of facilities such as hotels.

Geographic Reach

Headquartered in Japan, the company has business locations across Japan, as well as the US, UK, Singapore, Malaysia, Thailand, Australia, Taiwan, China, and Hong Kong.

Financial Performance

In fiscal 2021, although the COVID-19 pandemic situation continued, compared with the previous fiscal year, there was a recovery in the retail facilities' leasing business, growth in property sales to investors and an increase in revenues and profits from the Repark car park leasing business and Rehouse (retail residential brokerage). For these and other reasons, the company recorded revenue from operations of Â¥2.1 trillion, a 5% increase from the previous year's revenue.

In 2021, the company had a net income of Â¥177 billion, a 37% increase from the previous year's net income of Â¥129.6 billion.

The company's cash at the end of 2021 was Â¥142.7 billion. Operating activities generated Â¥271.5 billion, while investing activities used Â¥210.1 billion. Financing activities used another Â¥139.6 billion.

Strategy
The company's main initiatives consists of:

Driving evolution in the creation of neighborhoods. This initiative provides business and daily lifestyles to people, who are the centerpiece of the creation of neighborhoods, and realizes the creation of neighborhoods that improve with age and develop smart cities that serve as platforms for ultra-smart societies;

Innovating business models by harnessing real estate tech. This initiative enhances the competitiveness of existing businesses and create new businesses through Real Estate Ã— ICT, and accumulates and utilizes data from real physical spaces, such as offices, retail facilities, and residences; as well as

Dramatically growing the overseas business. This initiative expands business by leveraging the Mitsui Fudosan Group's strengths as a comprehensive and integrated developer, and promotes further localization and expand neighborhood creation development projects overseas.

Company Background
Mitsui Company, Japan's first holding company, was founded in 1909, and in 1914 its real estate section was established to manage land and buildings owned by the Mitsui family.

EXECUTIVES

Chairman, Representative Director, Masanobu Komoda
President, Representative Director, Takashi Ueda
Executive Vice President, Representative Director, Takashi Yamamoto
Senior Managing Executive Officer, Director, Takayuki Miki
Senior Managing Executive Officer, Director, Yoshihiro Hirokawa
Director, Shingo Suzuki
Director, Makoto Tokuda
Director, Hisashi Osawa
Outside Director, Tsunehiro Nakayama
Outside Director, Shinichiro Ito
Outside Director, Eriko Kawai
Outside Director, Mami Indo
Auditors : KPMG AZSA LLC

LOCATIONS
HQ: Mitsui Fudosan Co Ltd
2-1-1 Nihonbashi-Muromachi, Chuo-ku, Tokyo 103-0022
Phone: (81) 3 3246 3055

Web: www.mitsuifudosan.co.jp

PRODUCTS/OPERATIONS
FY2016 Sales

	% of total
Leasing	31
Property Sales	29
Management	20
Mitsui Home	14
Other	6
Total	100

Selected Group Companies
Housing
    Daiichi Engei Co., Ltd.
    MITSUI Designtec Co., Ltd.
    Mitsui Fudosan Housing Lease Co., Ltd.
    Mitsui Fudosan Realty Co., Ltd.
    Mitsui Fudosan Reform Co., Ltd.
    Mitsui Fudosan Residential Co., Ltd.
    Mitsui Fudosan Residential Service Chugoku Co., Ltd.
    Mitsui Fudosan Residential Service Co., Ltd.
    Mitsui Fudosan Residential Service Hokkaido Co., Ltd.
    Mitsui Fudosan Residential Service Kansai Co., Ltd.
    Mitsui Fudosan Residential Service Kyusyu Co., Ltd.
    Mitsui Fudosan Residential Service Tohoku Co., Ltd.
    Mitsui Home Co., Ltd.
    Mitsui Home Estate Co., Ltd.
Office Buildings
    First Facilities West Co., Ltd.
    Mitsui Fudosan Building Management Co., Ltd.
    Mitsui Fudosan Facilities Co., Ltd.
    NBF Office Management Co., Ltd.
    Nippon Building Fund Management Ltd.
Retail Properties
    Frontier REIT SC Management Co., Ltd.
    Mitsui Fudosan Frontier REIT Management Inc.
    Mitsui Fudosan Retail Management Co.,Ltd.
Accommodation
    Celestine Hotel Co., Ltd.
    Mitsui Fudosan Accommodations Fund Management.
    Mitsui Fudosan Hotel Management Co., Ltd.
    Mitsui Fudosan Housing Lease Co., Ltd.
Real Estate Solutions
    Mitsui Fudosan Investment Advisors, Inc.
Resort
    Kyusin Kaihatsu Inc.
    LaLaport Agency Co., Ltd.

COMPETITORS
Befimmo
FirstService Corporation
HEIWA REAL ESTATE CO.,LTD.
HELICAL PLC
KENNEDY WILSON EUROPE REAL ESTATE LIMITED
LONDONMETRIC PROPERTY PLC
MCKAY SECURITIES P L C
MITSUBISHI ESTATE COMPANY, LIMITED
NEWRIVER REIT PLC
PROLOGIS, INC.

HISTORICAL FINANCIALS
Company Type: Public

Income Statement   FYE: March 31

	REVENUE ($mil)	NET INCOME ($mil)	NET PROFIT MARGIN	EMPLOYEES
03/23	17,037	1,479	8.7%	38,668
03/22	17,271	1,455	8.4%	38,237
03/21	18,131	1,170	6.5%	38,230
03/20	17,555	1,694	9.7%	34,555
03/19	16,806	1,522	9.1%	32,327
Annual Growth	0.3%	(0.7%)	—	4.6%

2023 Year-End Financials
Debt ratio: 0.3%   No. of shares ($ mil.): 933
Return on equity: 6.9%   Dividends
Cash ($ mil.): 1,008   Yield: 2.4%
Current Ratio: 1.83   Payout: 92.5%
Long-term debt ($ mil.): 24,369   Market value ($ mil.): 52,640

	STOCK PRICE ($) FY Close	P/E High/Low		PER SHARE ($) Earnings	Dividends	Book Value
03/23	56.39	0	0	1.56	1.40	23.34
03/22	64.40	0	0	1.52	1.18	24.20
03/21	71.57	1	0	1.21	1.18	24.00
03/20	46.68	0	0	1.73	1.28	22.86
03/19	75.63	0	0	1.55	1.14	21.55
Annual Growth	(7.1%)	—	—	0.2%	5.2%	2.0%

Mitsui OSK Lines Ltd

Known as MOL, the company is one of the world's largest marine transportation companies and operates a fleet of about 700 vessels with an overall capacity of 50.8 million deadweight tons (DWT). The company's fleet includesvery large crude oil carriers (VLCCs) of more than 200,000 DWT and smaller vessels called Aframax tankers, contributing to the stable delivery of crude oil all around the world. The fleet also has various types of vessels that meet specific cargo characteristics - product tankers that transport refined petroleum products such as gas oils, naphtha, and gasoline, chemical tankers that transport liquid chemical products, and methanol carriers. In addition, the company provides logistics services such as warehousing and freight forwarding, operates marine terminals, and holds stakes in finance and real estate businesses. Japan generated majority of its sales.

Operations
The company operates through segments including Product Transport Business Unit (about 40% of sales), Dry Bulk Business Unit (about 30%), Energy and Offshore Business Unit (nearly 25%), and Associated Businesses, Others (some 10%).

The Product Transport Business Unit is composed of Containerships (around 20% of sales), and Car Carriers, Ferries and Coastal RoRo ships (about 20%). The Dry Bulk business includes iron ore and coal carriers, small- and medium-sized bulkers, wood chip carriers, short sea ships and multipurpose cargo ships, and open-hatch carriers, while Associated Businesses' and others include real estate and maritime affairs.

Geographic Reach
The company is headquartered in Tokyo, Japan. Japan generated about 80% of sales, Asia with about 15%, North America with some 5%, and Europe with less than 5%.

Financial Performance
The company's revenue for fiscal 2022 decreased to Â¥1.3 trillion compared to Â¥10.4 trillion in the prior year.

Cash held by the company at the end of fiscal 2022 increased to Â¥97.1 billion. Cash provided by operations was Â¥307.6 billion while cash used for investing and financing activities were Â¥107.5 billion and Â¥191.8 billion, respectively.

EXECUTIVES

Chairman, Director, Junichiro Ikeda
President, Representative Director, Takeshi Hashimoto
Executive Vice President, Representative Director, Toshiaki Tanaka
Senior Managing Executive Officer, Kenta Matsuzaka
Senior Managing Executive Officer, Yutaka Hinooka
Director, Junko Moro
Director, Hisashi Umemura
Outside Director, Hideto Fujii
Outside Director, Etsuko Katsu
Outside Director, Masaru Onishi
Outside Director, Mitsunobu Koshiba
Auditors : KPMG AZSA LLC

LOCATIONS

HQ: Mitsui OSK Lines Ltd
 2-1-1 Toranomon, Minato-ku, Tokyo 105-8688
Phone: (81) 3 3587 7026
Web: www.mol.co.jp

PRODUCTS/OPERATIONS

2016 Sales

	% of total
Bulkships	49
Containerships	42
Associated busines	6
Ferry & Domestic transport	3
Others	—
Total	100

Selected Services

Associated Businesses
Car Carriers
Containerships
Cruise Ship
Dry Bulkers
Ferries and Coastal Liners
Logistics
Offshore Business
Tankers
Terminal

COMPETITORS

China Ocean Shipping Co., Ltd.
Excel Maritime Carriers Ltd
GENCO SHIPPING & TRADING LIMITED
HMM Company Limited.
KAWASAKI KISEN KAISHA, LTD.
Odfjell Se
PREMUDA SPA
Torm A/S
Wallenius Wilhelmsen Ocean AS
YANG MING MARINE TRANSPORT CORPORATION

HISTORICAL FINANCIALS

Company Type: Public

Income Statement   FYE: March 31

	REVENUE ($mil)	NET INCOME ($mil)	NET PROFIT MARGIN	EMPLOYEES
03/23	12,103	5,977	49.4%	11,233
03/22	10,435	5,827	55.8%	11,041
03/21	8,953	813	9.1%	11,034
03/20	10,643	300	2.8%	11,308
03/19	11,143	242	2.2%	11,231
Annual Growth	2.1%	122.8%	—	0.0%

2023 Year-End Financials

Debt ratio: 0.2%   No. of shares ($ mil.): 361
Return on equity: 49.7%   Dividends
Cash ($ mil.): 705   Yield: 17.5%
Current Ratio: 0.66   Payout: 13.5%
Long-term debt ($ mil.): 5,137   Market value ($ mil.): 4,504

	STOCK PRICE ($) FY Close	P/E High/Low		PER SHARE ($) Earnings	Dividends	Book Value
03/23	12.45	0	0	16.49	2.18	39.97
03/22	35.75	0	0	16.12	1.93	29.06
03/21	15.30	0	0	2.26	0.08	14.57
03/20	10.31	0	0	0.81	0.08	13.22
03/19	10.68	0	0	0.65	0.05	13.26
Annual Growth	3.9%	—	—	124.1%	163.2%	31.8%

Miyazaki Bank, Ltd. (The)

Based in the Miyazaki Prefecture in Japan, The Miyazaki Bank is a leading Japanese regional bank offering checking and saving accounts, foreign currency deposits, credit cards, and other traditional banking products. Armed with eight subsidiaries and owning more than 90 branches, Miyazaki Bank additionally offers fund management and investment advisement services. Key subsidiary Miyagin Lease Co. provides general leasing services to the bank's customers as well. Miyazaki was initially established in 1932 as the Hyuga Industrial Bank; it changed its name to Miyazaki Bank in 1962.

EXECUTIVES

Chairman, Representative Director, Nobuya Hirano
President, Representative Director, Koji Sugita
Senior Managing Director, Director, Katsunori Kawachi
Director, Kazuhiro Hoshihara
Director, Tomoki Yamada
Director, Tetsuji Haraguchi
Director, Koji Yamashita
Outside Director, Junko Yamauchi
Outside Director, Hisatomo Shimazu
Outside Director, Hiromii Inamochi
Outside Director, Yoshinori Kashiwada
Auditors : Deloitte Touche Tohmatsu LLC

LOCATIONS

HQ: Miyazaki Bank, Ltd. (The)
 4-3-5 Tachibanadori-Higashi, Miyazaki 880-0805
Phone: (81) 985 27 3131
Web: www.miyagin.co.jp

COMPETITORS

HACHIJUNI BANK, LTD., THE
HYAKUGO BANK,LTD., THE
MIE BANK, LTD., THE
NISHI-NIPPON CITYBANK,LTD.
TOWA BANK,LTD., THE

HISTORICAL FINANCIALS

Company Type: Public

Income Statement   FYE: March 31

	ASSETS ($mil)	NET INCOME ($mil)	INCOME AS % OF ASSETS	EMPLOYEES
03/21	32,999	72	0.2%	1,928
03/20	30,631	65	0.2%	1,942
03/19	28,007	87	0.3%	2,000
03/18	27,937	82	0.3%	2,027
03/17	26,640	82	0.3%	2,014
Annual Growth	5.5%	(3.4%)		(1.1%)

2021 Year-End Financials

Return on assets: 0.2%   Dividends
Return on equity: 5.2%   Yield: —
Long-term debt ($ mil.): —   Payout: 21.6%
No. of shares ($ mil.): 17   Market value ($ mil.): —
Sales ($ mil.): 493

MMC Norilsk Nickel PJSC

EXECUTIVES

Chairman, President, Vladimir O. Potanin
Senior Vice President, Andrey Evgenyevich Bougrov
Senior Vice President, Chief Financial Officer, Sergey Malyshev
First Vice President, Chief Operating Officer, Executive Director, Sergey Barbashev
Vice President, Chief of Staff, Elena Savitskaya
Risk Management Vice President, Internal Control Vice President, Nina Plastinina
First Vice President, General Counsel, Executive Director, Marianna Aleksandrovna Zakharova
Strategy Senior Vice President, Procurement Senior Vice President, Strategic Projects Senior Vice President, Logistics Senior Vice President, Sergey Dubovitsky
Social Policy Senior Vice President, Public Relations Senior Vice President, Human Resources Senior Vice President, Larisa Zelkova
Corporate Secretary, Pavel Platov
Chairman, Independent Director, Gareth Peter Penny
Deputy Chairman, Non-Executive Director, Sergey L. Batekhin
Non-Executive Director, Alexey Bashkirov
Independent Director, Sergey Bratukhin

Independent Director, Roger Llewelyn Munnings
Independent Director, Robert Edwards
Independent Director, Sergey Volk
Independent Director, Maxim Poletaev
Non-Executive Director, Vyacheslav Solomin
Independent Director, Evgeny Shvarts
Non-Executive Director, Nikolay Abramov
Auditors : JSC KPMG

LOCATIONS

HQ: MMC Norilsk Nickel PJSC
18 building 13, Stromynka Street, Moscow 107996
Phone: (7) 495 989 76 50   Fax: (7) 495 780 73 67
Web: www.nornik.ru

HISTORICAL FINANCIALS
Company Type: Public

Income Statement				FYE: December 31
	REVENUE ($mil)	NET INCOME ($mil)	NET PROFIT MARGIN	EMPLOYEES
12/21	17,852	6,512	36.5%	0
12/20	15,545	3,385	21.8%	0
12/19	13,563	5,782	42.6%	0
12/18	11,670	3,085	26.4%	75,901
12/17	9,146	2,129	23.3%	78,950
Annual Growth	18.2%	32.2%	—	—

2021 Year-End Financials
Debt ratio: 43.6%   No. of shares ($ mil.): 153
Return on equity: —   Dividends
Cash ($ mil.): 5,547   Yield: —
Current Ratio: 1.22   Payout: 0.0%
Long-term debt ($ mil.): 8,616   Market value ($ mil.): —

MOL Magyar Olaj es Gazipari Reszvenytar

MOL Magyar Olaj-Ã‰os GÃ¡zipari Rt. (Hungarian Oil and Gas Company, or MOL) is a leading integrated Central Eastern European oil and gas corporation. It is an integrated, international oil and gas, petrochemicals and consumer retail company, active in over 30 countries. MOL's refineries produce 110 million barrels of oil equivalent per day, and it operates more than 2,000 gas stations in nine countries. Other activities include exploration and production in over 10 countries. Majority of the company's sales were generated outside the Hungary. The company was founded in 1991.

Operations

The company operates through five major operating business units: Downstream (about 65% of sales), Consumer Services (roughly 25%), Upstream (nearly 10%), Gas Midstream, and Corporate and other segments (less than 5% combined).

MOL's Downstream division turns crude oil into a range of refined products, which are moved and marketed for domestic, industrial and transport use. The products include gasoline, diesel, heating oil, aviation fuel, lubricants, bitumen, sulfur and liquefied petroleum gas (LPG). In addition, it produces and sells petrochemicals worldwide and holds a leading position in the petrochemical sector in the Central Eastern Europe region.

Its Consumer Services has built a leading fuel retail operation in the CEE region, with a 10 million retail customer base and one million daily transactions. MOL Group owns numerous service companies covering oil field services, asset operations and maintenance management.

Its FGSZ unit is currently the only company in Hungary that holds a natural gas transmission system operator's license. Aside from domestic natural gas transmission activity, FGSZ also performs transit activities for Serbia, Bosnia-Herzegovina, as well as cross border deliveries towards Romania and Croatia and the Ukraine.

MOL's Upstream portfolio consists of oil and gas exploration and production assets in nearly 15 countries with production activity in roughly 10 countries.

Overall, crude oil and oil products generated about 70% of sales, petrochemical products with nearly 20%, natural gas and gas products with around 5%, and other products, retail shop products, and services generated the rest.

Geographic Reach

Headquartered in Hungary, MOL is an integrated, independent, international oil and gas company with operations in some 30 countries. MOL's exploration and production activities are conducted in nearly 15 countries. The company operates four refineries and two petrochemicals plants, under integrated supply chain management, in Hungary, Slovakia and Croatia. MOL also has a network of service stations in nine countries across Central and South Eastern Europe.

Hungary generated over 25% of sales, Croatia with around 10%, Czech Republic and Slovakia with about 10% each, Italy and Romania with over 5% each, and the rest were generated from Poland, Austria, Serbia, UK, Germany, Bosnia-Herzegovina, Switzerland, Slovenia, Azerbaijan, Rest of Central-Eastern Europe, Rest of Europe, and Rest of the World.

Sales and Marketing

The company has no single major customer the revenue from which would exceed 10% of the total net sales revenues in 2021.

Financial Performance

The company reported net sales of HUF 6 trillion, a 49% increase from the previous year's net sales of HUF 4 trillion.

In 2021, the company had a net income of HUF 526.1 billion, an HUF 544.5 billion addition to the previous year's net loss.

The company's cash at the end of 2021 was HUF 367.4 billion. Operating activities generated HUF 918.1 billion, while investing activities used HUF 481.6 billion, primarily for capital expenditures. Financing activities used another HUF 272.5 billion, primarily for repayments of borrowings.

Strategy

MOL Group published in 2016 its 2030 strategy "Enter Tomorrow". The announcement of the 2030 "Enter Tomorrow" strategy put MOL as a front-runner amongst regional oil and gas companies in terms of publishing a comprehensive roadmap in response to anticipated long-term structural challenges to the oil and gas industry. The launch of the 2030 strategy sought not only to mitigate the low-carbon economy transition risks, but to capitalize on the opportunities created by it. With the strategy, MOL Group sought to gradually diversify the company's revenue streams away from traditional hydrocarbons by seeking opportunities for developing new low emission products and services in new markets.

The initial strategic shift rested on two pillars: 1) transform the company's refining operations by gradually shifting refining activities away from the production of fuels towards the production of feedstock for the company's petrochemical division, whilst simultaneously expanding the chemical value chain towards semi-commodity and specialty chemicals ("from fuel to chemicals"). Initial steps towards the group's petrochemical product diversification included expansion towards new products like synthetic rubber, polyol and propylene glycol. 2) The second pillar was to transform a traditional fuel retailer into a convenience retailer and alternative low-carbon mobility player ("from fuel retail to consumer goods"). Initial steps included the launch of the Fresh Corner concept store across the group's service station network, as well as the launch of mobility services.

Mergers and Acquisitions

In early 2022, MOL Group acquired ReMat Zrt., a recycler with production plants located in TiszaÃºjvÃ¡ros and Rakamaz, Hungary, and a logistics hub in Bratislava, Slovakia. ReMat is a market leading plastics recycler in Hungary with an annual processing capacity of 25,000 tons and almost 200 employees. The transaction fits into MOL's portfolio and its goal to become a key player in the low carbon circular economy in Central and Eastern Europe. Terms were not disclosed.

In early 2021. MOL Group announces the acquisition of 100% of Normbenz Slovakia s.r.o. by Slovnaft that includes 16 service stations in Slovakia operated under the Lukoil brand. MOL has also concluded a deal with MarchÃ© International AG to buy the company that operates 9 restaurants in Hungary under the MarchÃ© brand. SLOVNAFT Group is an integrated refining and petrochemical company based in Bratislava, Slovakia. The group's key company is SLOVNAFT, a.s., operating one of the most complex refineries in Europe and processing up to 6 million tons of crude oil annually.

Terms were not disclosed.

HISTORY

The oil refining industry in Hungary dates to the 1880s, when refineries were opened in Fiume (1882) and Budapest (1883). By 1913 Hungary had 28 plants.

Following Hungary's defeat in WWI, the country's refining industry fell into decline, as new national boundaries placed most of its former oil refineries and oil-producing regions outside its borders. By 1921 Hungary had only six operational refineries.

British and American investors set up the European Gas and Electric Company (EUROGASCO) in the US in 1931 to acquire oil and gas concessions in Central Europe and to build power plants. By 1937 EUROGASCO (controlled by Standard Oil of New Jersey) was producing oil. A year later Standard Oil set up the Hungarian-American Oil Industry Shareholding Co. (MAORT) to develop the fields, and in 1940 MAORT's production was meeting all of Hungary's oil needs.

During WWII, MAORT requisitioned all oil assets. The oil industry boomed as Hungary served as a major supplier for the German war machine. But by 1944, with German armies in retreat from the Eastern Front, much of Hungary's oil machinery and plants were dismantled. The remaining plants suffered heavy bombing from Allied forces or had equipment confiscated by Russian and Romanian troops.

After the war the Hungarian Soviet Crude Oil Co. began rebuilding Hungary's oil industry and started drilling on the Great Hungarian Plain in 1946. MAORT also ramped up oil production in the Trans-Danubian fields. In 1949, following charges of sabotage against MAORT managers, MAORT was nationalized and broken up into five national companies, which re-merged in 1952 with Hungarian Soviet Oil Co. (successor to Hungarian Soviet Crude Oil Co.).

In 1957 all operations of the Hungarian crude oil industry were consolidated under Crude Oil Trust, which took over the gas industry by 1960. That year the company was renamed National Crude Oil and Gas Trust (OKGT), and the focus of exploration soon shifted from Trans-Danubian fields to the Great Plain. By 1970 the Great Plain accounted for 67% of oil production and 96% of natural gas production.

Hungary began allowing foreign gasoline distributors to compete in domestic markets during the 1980s. Moving toward privatization, the Hungarian government founded MOL in 1991 as the successor to OKGT, which comprised nine oil and gas enterprises. In 1993 the socialist government sold 8% of MOL to the public. By 1998 the government had sold all but 25% of MOL.

During the 1990s the company also expanded in Central Europe. With Austria's OMV in 1994 it began building a 120-km pipeline linking Austria and Hungary, which gave it access to natural gas from Western Europe for the first time. MOL also opened up service stations in neighboring countries, beginning with one in Romania in 1996. By 2000 the company was operating about 80 stations in Romania, 18 in Slovakia, three in Ukraine, and two in Slovenia, in addition to its 330 stations in Hungary. MOL also acquired about 20% of chemical processor TVK in 1999 and upped the stake to nearly 33% by 2000. That year MOL also acquired 36% of Slovnaft, Slovakia's only oil refiner and its major retailer.

In 2003 MOL concluded a long-term crude oil supply agreement with Russian oil giant YUKOS.

The company agreed in 2004 to sell its gas businesses to E.ON Ruhrgas for about $1 billion. (After much scrutiny by Hungarian and EU regulators, the deal was completed in 2006.)

In 2005 MOL acquired the Romanian subsidiary of Royal Dutch Shell, including the purchase of 59 Shell filling stations. Royal Dutch Shell also sold MOL its Romania-based lubricants, aviation, and commercial businesses.

In 2007 MOL acquired two refining and marketing companies -- IES in Italy and Tifon in Croatia. Also that year MOL announced plans to merge with Austria's OMV, though those plans were abandoned the next year due to regulatory concerns from the European Commission. In 2009 OMV sold its 21% stake in MOL to Russian oil company Surgutneftegas. Eyeing new areas of exploration, that year MOL also acquired a 10% stake in Pearl Petroleum, giving it access to gas-condensate fields in Iraq.

In 2011 the Hungarian government acquired Surgutneftegas' 21% stake in MOL for about EUR 1.9 billion (US$2.6 billion).

EXECUTIVES

Chairman, Chief Executive Officer, Zsolt Hernadi
Exploration & Production Executive Vice President, Zoltan Aldott
Finance Executive Vice President, Jozsef Farkas Simola
Executive Vice President, Ferenc Horvath
Chief Financial Officer, Director, Jozsef Molnar
Vice-Chairman, Sandor Csanyi
Director, Laszlo Akar
Director, Mulham Al-Jarf
Director, Miklos Dobak
Director, Gabor Horvath
Director, Miklos Kamaras
Director, Erno Kemenes
Director, Iain Paterson
Auditors : Ernst & Young Kft.

LOCATIONS

HQ: MOL Magyar Olaj es Gazipari Reszvenytar
Oktober huszonharmadika u. 18, Budapest H-1117
Phone: (36) 1 209 0000
Web: www.mol.hu

2014 Sales

	%
Hungary	28
Croatia	12
Italy	9
Austria	9
Slovakia	9
Czech Republic	7
Romania	6
Poland	4
Germany	3
Bosnia-Herzegovina	3
Serbia	2
Slovenia	2
Switzerland	2
United Kingdom	1
Rest of Europe	2
Rest of the World	3
Total	100

PRODUCTS/OPERATIONS

2014 Sales

	% of total
Downstream	82
Upstream	10
Midstream	4
Corporate and other	4
Total	100

COMPETITORS

COMPAÑIA ESPAÑOLA DE PETROLEOS SAU
COSMO OIL CO., LTD.
ENI SPA
GAZPROM NEFT, PAO
HELLENIC PETROLEUM S.A.
Imperial Oil Limited
LUKOIL, PAO
NK ROSNEFT, PAO
OMV Aktiengesellschaft
Petroleo Brasileiro S A Petrobras

HISTORICAL FINANCIALS

Company Type: Public

Income Statement — FYE: December 31

	REVENUE ($mil)	NET INCOME ($mil)	NET PROFIT MARGIN	EMPLOYEES
12/21	18,237	1,610	8.8%	24,291
12/20	13,510	(53)	—	24,948
12/19	17,885	758	4.2%	26,032
12/18	18,435	1,074	5.8%	25,970
12/17	15,970	1,186	7.4%	25,959
Annual Growth	3.4%	7.9%		(1.6%)

2021 Year-End Financials

Debt ratio: —
Return on equity: 21.1%
Cash ($ mil.): 1,124
Current Ratio: 1.19
Long-term debt ($ mil.): 2,651
No. of shares ($ mil.): 625
Dividends
 Yield: —
 Payout: 5.7%
Market value ($ mil.): 2,332

	STOCK PRICE ($) FY Close	P/E High/Low		PER SHARE ($) Earnings	Dividends	Book Value
12/21	3.73	0	0	2.22	0.13	13.49
12/20	3.92	—	—	(0.07)	0.00	11.92
12/19	5.05	0	0	1.07	0.22	11.50
12/18	5.35	0	0	1.54	0.22	9.58
12/17	5.40	0	0	1.69	0.15	9.13
Annual Growth	(8.8%)			7.1%	(4.2%)	10.3%

Molson Coors Beverage Co

EXECUTIVES

Chairman, Director, Andrew T. Molson
Subsidiary Officer, Vice-Chairman, Director, Peter H. Coors, $850,000 total compensation
President, Chief Executive Officer, Director, Gavin D.K. Hattersley, $1,100,000 total compensation
Chief Financial Officer, Tracey L. Joubert, $662,188 total compensation
Chief Marketing Officer, Michelle St. Jacques
Deputy Chief Legal Officer, Secretary, Eric Gunning
Region Officer, Simon J. Cox, $456,617 total compensation
Division Officer, Peter John Marino
Division Officer, Director, David S. Coors
Director, Geoffrey E. Molson
Director Emeritus, Eric H. Molson
Director, Julia M. Brown
Director, Mary Lynn Ferguson-McHugh
Director, Nessa O'Sullivan
Director, Douglas D. Tough
Director, Louis Vachon
Director, James A. Winnefeld
Director, Roger G. Eaton
Director, Charles M. Herington
Director, H. Sanford Riley
Auditors : PricewaterhouseCoopers LLP

LOCATIONS

HQ: Molson Coors Beverage Co
111 Boulevard Robert-Bourassa, 9th Floor, Montreal, Quebec H3C 2M1
Phone: 514 521-1786
Web: www.molsoncoors.com

HISTORICAL FINANCIALS

Company Type: Public

Income Statement				FYE: December 31
	REVENUE ($mil)	NET INCOME ($mil)	NET PROFIT MARGIN	EMPLOYEES
12/23	11,702	948	8.1%	16,500
12/22	10,701	(175)	—	16,600
12/21	10,279	1,005	9.8%	16,300
12/20	9,654	(949)	—	17,000
12/19	10,579	241	2.3%	17,700
Annual Growth	2.6%	40.8%	—	(1.7%)

2023 Year-End Financials
Debt ratio: 23.6%
Return on equity: 7.3%
Cash ($ mil.): 868
Current Ratio: 0.70
Long-term debt ($ mil.): 5,312
No. of shares ($ mil.): 213
Dividends
Yield: —
Payout: 37.5%
Market value ($ mil.): 13,056

	STOCK PRICE ($) FY Close	P/E High/Low		PER SHARE ($) Earnings	Dividends	Book Value
12/23	61.21	16	11	4.37	1.64	61.87
12/22	51.52	—	—	(0.81)	1.52	58.67
12/21	46.35	13	9	4.62	0.68	61.83
12/20	45.19	—	—	(4.38)	1.71	57.06
12/19	53.90	59	45	1.11	1.96	62.04
Annual Growth	3.2%	—	—	40.9%	(4.4%)	(0.1%)

MS&AD Insurance Group Holdings

MS&AD Insurance Group is the holding company for several large Japanese insurance companies including Mitsui Sumitomo Insurance (MSI), Aioi Nissay Dowa Insurance (ADI), Mitsui Direct General, MSI Aioi Life, and MSI Primary Life. Together, the insurance companies offer property/casualty (e.g. auto, personal, fire, marine) and life insurance, as well as asset management (mutual funds, financial consulting) and risk management services. MS&AD Insurance's about 155 subsidiaries, which serve individuals and businesses in Japan, also offer products and services to customers in about 50 countries in Europe, Asia, and the Americas.

Operations
MS&AD has five primary operating divisions: domestic non-life insurance, domestic life insurance, international business, financial services, and risk-related services.

MS&AD's domestic non-life insurance business is operated by the following three subsidiaries and others in Japan: Mitsui Sumitomo Insurance Company, Limited (MSI) Aioi Nissay Dowa Insurance Company, Limited (ADI) Mitsui Direct General Insurance Company, Limited (Mitsui Direct General).

Domestic Life Insurance Business MS&AD's domestic life insurance business is operated by the following two subsidiaries and others in Japan: Mitsui Sumitomo Aioi Life Insurance Company, Limited (MSI Aioi Life) Mitsui Sumitomo Primary Life Insurance Company, Limited (MSI Primary Life).

International Business MS&AD's international business is operated by international divisions of domestic non-life insurance subsidiaries in Japan, and overseas subsidiaries, and overseas branches of domestic non-life insurance subsidiaries in overseas countries.

Financial Services Business MS&AD's financial services business, including asset management, financial guarantees, 401k, ART (alternative risk transfer), personal finance, and venture capital finance, is operated by domestic non-life insurance subsidiaries, Sumitomo Mitsui DS Asset Management Company, Limited, MITSUI SUMITOMO INSURANCE Venture Capital Co., Ltd, Leadenhall Capital Partners LLP and others.

Risk-Related Services Business MS&AD's risk-related services business, including risk management and the nursing care business, is operated by MS&AD InterRisk Research Institute & Consulting, Inc., Mitsui Sumitomo Insurance Care Network Company, Limited, and others.

Geographic Reach
Japan-based MS&AD operates in about 50 countries in the Asia/Pacific region, in Europe, and in the Americas.

Sales and Marketing
It has a strong customer base and the largest agent network in Japan with more than 80,000 agencies, 44.65 million individuals, and 2.6 million corporations.

Company Background
Formed in 2008 as a holding company for the Mitsui Sumitomo operations, MS&AD Insurance became the parent of a larger group of insurance companies through a three-way merger between Mitsui Sumitomo, Aioi Insurance, and Nissay Dowa General Insurance in 2010.

EXECUTIVES

Chairman, Director, Yasuyoshi Karasawa
Vice-Chairman, Representative Director, Yasuzo Kanasugi
President, Representative Director, Noriyuki Hara
Executive Vice President, Representative Director, Tetsuji Higuchi
Director, Tomoyuki Shimazu
Director, Yusuke Shirai
Outside Director, Mariko Bando
Outside Director, Junichi Tobimatsu
Outside Director, Rochelle Kopp
Outside Director, Akemi Ishiwata
Outside Director, Jun Suzuki
Auditors : KPMG AZSA LLC

LOCATIONS

HQ: MS&AD Insurance Group Holdings
2-27-2 Shinkawa, Chuo-ku, Tokyo 104-0033
Phone: (81) 3 5117 0270
Web: www.ms-ad-hd.com

PRODUCTS/OPERATIONS

2018 Sales
	% of total
Underwriting income	89
Investment income	11
Total	100

Selected Products
Compulsory Automobile Liability
Fire and Allied Insurance
Life
Marine
Personal Accident
Voluntary Automobile

COMPETITORS

AON GLOBAL LIMITED
AVIVA PLC

China Pacific Insurance (Group) Co., Ltd.
DAI-ICHI LIFE HOLDINGS, INC.
MAPFRE, SA
METLIFE, INC.
REINSURANCE GROUP OF AMERICA, INCORPORATED
SOMPO HOLDINGS, INC.
Sampo Oyj
XL GROUP PUBLIC LIMITED COMPANY

HISTORICAL FINANCIALS
Company Type: Public

Income Statement — FYE: March 31

	REVENUE ($mil)	NET INCOME ($mil)	NET PROFIT MARGIN	EMPLOYEES
03/23	37,959	1,212	3.2%	45,761
03/22	41,296	2,160	5.2%	48,065
03/21	43,494	1,304	3.0%	50,116
03/20	42,602	1,317	3.1%	50,633
03/19	48,721	1,740	3.6%	50,609
Annual Growth	(6.0%)	(8.6%)	—	(2.5%)

2023 Year-End Financials

Debt ratio: —
Return on equity: 5.1%
Cash ($ mil.): 36,445
Current Ratio: —
Long-term debt ($ mil.): —
No. of shares ($ mil.): 535
Dividends
Yield: 4.6%
Payout: 33.0%
Market value ($ mil.): 8,319

	STOCK PRICE ($) FY Close	P/E High/Low	PER SHARE ($) Earnings	Dividends	Book Value
03/23	15.53	0 0	2.25	0.73	42.20
03/22	16.19	0 0	3.90	0.73	48.95
03/21	14.68	0 0	2.31	0.71	49.92
03/20	13.81	0 0	2.29	0.67	39.71
03/19	15.24	0 0	2.97	0.61	42.56
Annual Growth	0.5%	—	(6.7%)	4.4%	(0.2%)

MTN Group Ltd (South Africa)

MTN Group is Africa's largest mobile network operator that provides voice, data, fintech, digital, enterprise, wholesale, and API services to more than 270 million subscribers across about 20 markets. The company has grown by investing in sophisticated communication infrastructure, developing new technologies and by harnessing the talent of its diverse people to now offer services to communities across Africa and the Middle East. The company partners with financial services companies to offer mobile banking services and money transfer services for clients without bank accounts. The company was established in South Africa at the dawn of democracy in 1994 as a leader in transformation. Majority of its sales were generated in Nigeria.

Operations
The group principally generates revenue from providing mobile telecommunications services, such as network services (comprising data, voice and SMS; about 75%), digital and fintech services (around 11%), interconnect and roaming services (about 10%), as well as from the sale of mobile devices (some 5%).

The network services and digital and fintech provides mobile telecommunication services, including network services and digital and fintech services. Network services (comprising data, voice and SMS) are considered to represent a single performance obligation as all are provided over the MTN network and transmitted as data representing a digital signal on the network. Digital and fintech services include value-added services, rich media services, MoMo, insurance, airtime lending, e-commerce, etc.

Geographic Reach
Headquartered in Gauteng, South Africa, MTN has operations in most African countries including Benin, Botswana, Cameroon, Ghana, Guinea Bissau, Guinea Conakry, Cote d'Ivoire, Kenya, Liberia, Namibia, Nigeria, Rwanda, South Africa, eSwatini, Uganda, and Zambia. It also provides service in Afghanistan, South Sudan, and Sudan. Nigeria accounted for about 35% of the revenue in 2021.

Financial Performance
The company's revenue for 2021 amounted to R181.6 billion, a 1% increase from the previous year's revenue of R179.4 billion.

In 2021, the company had a net income of R17 billion, a 14% decrease from the previous year's net income of R19.6 billion.

The company's cash at the end of 2021 was R39 billion. Operating activities generated R67.3 billion, while investing activities used R31 billion, primarily for the acquisition of property, plant and equipment. Financing activities used another R26.2 billion, primarily for repayment of borrowings.

Strategy
The company continued to implement the Enterprise Resource Planning (ERP) cloud system and processes with the following milestones being achieved: the adoption of a standard chart of accounts across the company, thereby enhancing transparent and consistent analysis and reporting. Design and deployment of a management company (ManCo) business intelligence (BI) platform to enhance analytic capabilities for the GSM, financial technology (FinCo) and FibreCo businesses. Configuration of the governance, risk and compliance advanced financial controls modules for transaction exception reporting and financial reporting compliance with deployment expected in 2022.

EXECUTIVES

President, Chief Executive Officer, Executive Director, R. T. Mupita
Chief Financial Officer, Executive Director, T. B. L. Molefe
Secretary, P. T. Sishuba-Bonoyi
Independent Non-Executive Director, M. H. Jonas
Independent Non-Executive Director, K. D. K. Mokhele
Independent Non-Executive Director, N. P. Gosa
Independent Non-Executive Director, C. W. N. Molope
Independent Non-Executive Director, P. B. Hanratty
Independent Non-Executive Director, S. Kheradpir
Independent Non-Executive Director, S. N. Mabaso-Koyana
Independent Non-Executive Director, S. P. Miller
Independent Non-Executive Director, N. L. Sowazi
Independent Non-Executive Director, B. S. Tshabalala
Independent Non-Executive Director, S. L. A. M. Sanusi
Non-Executive Director, V. M. Ragues
Auditors: PricewaterhouseCoopers Inc.

LOCATIONS
HQ: MTN Group Ltd (South Africa)
Innovation Centre, 216 - 14th Avenue, Fairland, Roodepoort, Gauteng 2195
Phone: (27) 11 912 3000   **Fax:** (27) 11 912 4093
Web: www.mtn.com

2014 Sales

	% of total
Nigeria	34
South Africa	24
Large opco cluster	20
Small opco cluster	14
Joint venture-Iran	7
Hyperinflation	1
Total	100

PRODUCTS/OPERATIONS

2014 Sales

	% of total
Outgoing voice	61
Data	19
Incoming voice	10
Devices	5
SMS	3
Other	1
Hyperinflation	1
Total	100

COMPETITORS
1&1 Drillisch AG
EMIRATES TELECOMMUNICATIONS GROUP COMPANY (ETISALAT GROUP) PJSC
HELLENIC TELECOMMUNICATIONS ORGANIZATION S.A.
HUGHES NETWORK SYSTEMS, LLC
KT Corporation
Koninklijke KPN N.V.
SAUDI TELECOM COMPANY
VIRGIN MEDIA FINANCE PLC
VODACOM GROUP LTD
VODAFONE GROUP PUBLIC LIMITED COMPANY

HISTORICAL FINANCIALS

Company Type: Public

Income Statement — FYE: December 31

	REVENUE ($mil)	NET INCOME ($mil)	NET PROFIT MARGIN	EMPLOYEES
12/22	12,231	1,142	9.3%	0
12/21	11,392	862	7.6%	0
12/20	12,223	1,160	9.5%	0
12/19	10,784	638	5.9%	19,288
12/18	9,358	606	6.5%	18,835
Annual Growth	6.9%	17.2%	—	—

2022 Year-End Financials

Debt ratio: 1.2%
Return on equity: 16.9%
Cash ($ mil.): 4,904
Current Ratio: 0.96
Long-term debt ($ mil.): 3,886
No. of shares ($ mil.): 1,806
Dividends
Yield: —
Payout: 20.1%
Market value ($ mil.): 13,437

	STOCK PRICE ($) FY Close	P/E High/Low	PER SHARE ($) Earnings	Dividends	Book Value
12/22	7.44	1 1	0.62	0.12	3.81
12/21	10.66	1 0	0.47	0.00	3.86
12/20	4.10	1 0	0.64	0.22	3.90
12/19	5.91	2 1	0.35	0.25	3.32
12/18	6.10	2 1	0.33	0.36	3.28
Annual Growth	5.1%	— —	16.7%	(23.6%)	3.8%

Muenchener Rueckversicherungs-Gesellschaft AG (Germany)

Münchener Rückversicherungs-Gesellschaft Aktiengesellschaft (Munich Re) is one of the world's leading reinsurers and operates in life, health and property-casualty business. Reinsurance coverage (insurance for insurers) includes fire, life, motor, and liability policies on both a facultative (individual risk) and treaty (categorized risk) basis. The company also provides direct insurance including life, health, and property coverage through Germany-based ERGO and other subsidiaries, and it provides asset management services through MEAG MUNICH ERGO. Generating about 50% of the company's total gross premiums written in Europe, the company's ERGO operates in about 25 countries.

Operations

Munich Re divides its business into five segments: Property-Casualty Reinsurance and Life and Health Reinsurance, which both operate globally; and ERGO Life and Health Germany (life and health and property-casualty insurance in Germany and global travel insurance), ERGO Property-Casualty Germany, and ERGO International.

Property-Casualty Reinsurance produces nearly 50% of total sales. Life and Health Reinsurance generates about 20% of total sales. It focuses on traditional reinsurance solutions that concentrate on the transfer of mortality risk. It is also active in the market of living benefits products such as occupational disability, long-term care and critical illness.

Overall, Reinsurance activities account for about 70% of total sales, while ERGO generates the rest.

Geographic Reach

Headquartered in Munich, Germany, Europe is Munich Re's largest market accounting for about 50% of the company's gross premiums written followed by North America that generates around 30% of gross premiums written. The remaining gross premiums written are from Asia and Australasia, Africa, Middle East and Latin America.

Sales and Marketing

Munich Re's ERGO serves approximately 35 million mostly retail customers. As a reinsurer, the company also writes its business in direct collaboration with primary insurers and also via brokers.

Financial Performance

Note: Growth rates may differ after conversion to US Dollars.

The company's revenue for fiscal 2021 increased to EUR59.6 billion compared from the prior year with EUR54.9 billion.

Cash held by the company at the end of fiscal 2021 decreased to EUR5.5 billion. Cash provided by operations was EUR5.2 billion, while cash used for investing and financing activities were EUR3.8 billion and EUR1.7 billion, respectively.

Strategy

Munich Re operates an integrated business model that combines primary insurance and reinsurance. This model enables the company to pool its industry-wide areas of expertise, share underlying know-how and data, and leverage synergies through risk diversification.

The company's strategy follows the three guiding principles of Scale, Shape, and Succeed, which are key pillars of the Munich Re Group Ambition 2025.

Scale represents growth in the company's core business. There are opportunities for organic growth in reinsurance in particular owing to recent improvements in market conditions. In asset management, the company want to boost its performance and reduce the yield erosion caused by low interest rates.

Shape stands for Munich Re's mission to develop new business models throughout the value chain, in turn shaping markets. In this environment, innovative and digital solutions will give rise to additional business opportunities.

Succeed symbolizes the added value that Munich Re generates for all its stakeholders.

Company Background

Munich Re dates back to 1880, where it gained an upper hand on an already mature reinsurance industry by taking an international approach to reinsurance. The company's guiding principles remain true to this day, namely independence from primary insurers, a broad spread of risks, an efficient system of treaty management, working in partnership with clients, and innovative insurance concepts.

HISTORY

Investors Carl Thieme and Theodor Cramer-Klett founded Munich Re in 1880. Within a month Munich Re opened offices in Hamburg, Berlin, Vienna, and St. Petersburg, establishing treaties with German and Danish insurers. In 1888 Munich Re went public; two years later, it opened an office in London and helped finance the creation of Allianz, which would soon come to dominate the German insurance industry. In 1892 the firm opened a branch in the US (it incurred severe losses from the 1906 San Francisco earthquake).

WWI interrupted Munich Re's UK and US operations. The company recovered after 1918, only to be hobbled again by the Great Depression. In 1933 Munich Re executive Kurt Schmitt became minister of economic affairs for the Nazis. Objecting to the evolving policies of National Socialism, he left after a year, returning to Munich Re, where he became chief executive in 1938.

Hitler's ignition of WWII wasn't quite the boom Munich Re needed; its international business was again disrupted. After the war, the Allies further limited overseas operations. Because of his involvement with the Nazi government, Schmitt was replaced by Eberhard von Reininghaus in 1945. The division of Germany further hampered the company's recovery.

Jump-started by the Marshall Plan in 1950, the West German Wirtschaftswunder (economic miracle) kicked into high gear, as the devastated country rebuilt. Relaxation of occupation-era trading limits also helped as the company rebuilt its foreign business. By 1969, Munich Re's sales topped DM 2 billion. Amid the global oil crisis and a rash of terrorist acts in Germany, the firm reported its first-ever reinsurance loss in 1977.

German reunification in 1990 provided new markets for Munich Re, but advantages from new business in the East were wiped out by claims arising from that year's harsh winter.

In 1992 an investigation by the German Federal Cartel Office prompted a realignment in the insurance business -- Allianz ceded its controlling interests in three life insurers (Hamburg-Mannheimer Versicherungs, Karlsruher Lebensversicherung, and Berlinische Lebensversicherung) to Munich Re, bringing it into direct insurance. Munich

Re took over Deutsche Krankenversicherung (DKV) in 1996. Also that year Munich Re acquired American Re.

During the 1990s reinsurance sales dwindled as competition increased, forcing lower premiums, and alternatives to insurance and reinsurance became more common. Munich Re looked to direct insurance, particularly individual property/casualty and life insurance, to compensate. In 1997 it merged Hamburg-Mannheimer and DKV with another insurer, Victoria AG, to form ERGO Versicherungsgruppe. Within a year, ERGO's insurance income accounted for half of all revenues.

Munich Re and ERGO launched asset management firm MEAG Munich ERGO AssetManagement in 1999. That year Munich Re experienced its worst year ever after natural disasters hit its reinsurance business hard. To recoup its losses, the next year the firm expanded both its reinsurance and primary insurance operations into key markets in Europe, North and South America, and Asia. Also in 2000, Munich Re bought CNA Financial's life reinsurance operations. Together with Swiss Re, the company launched Inreon, an online reinsurance exchange, in 2001.

As one of the companies hit hardest financially by the World Trade Center tragedy, Munich Re paid out some $2 billion in claims. In 2003 Allianz and Munich Re terminated their cooperation agreement, as their shareholdings in each other fell to under 15%. (The two companies gradually sold off nearly all of their ownership interests in following years.)

In 2004 Munich Re entered its first Asian market by forming a joint venture in China.

EXECUTIVES

Chairman, Joachim Wenning
Member, Thomas Blunck
Chief Investment Officer, Nicholas Gartside
Member, Stefan Golling
Member, Torsten Jeworrek
Chief Financial Officer, Christoph Jurecka
Member, Achim Kassow
Member, Markus Rieb
Chairman, Nikolaus von Bomhard
Deputy Chairman, Anne Horstmann
Director, Ann-Kristin Achleitner
Director, Clement B. Booth
Director, Ruth Brown
Director, Stephan Eberl
Director, Frank Fassin
Director, Ursula Gather
Director, Gerd Hausler
Director, Angelika Judith Herzog
Director, Renata Jungo Brungger
Director, Stefan Kaindl
Director, Carinne Knoche-Brouillon
Director, Gabriele Mucke
Director, Ulrich Plottke
Director, Manfred Rassy
Director, Carsten Spohr
Director, Karl-Heinz Streibich
Director, Markus Wagner
Director, Maximilian Zimmerer
Auditors : Ernst & Young GmbH Wirtschaftpruefungsgesellschaft

LOCATIONS

HQ: Muenchener Rueckversicherungs-Gesellschaft AG (Germany)
  Koeniginstrasse 107, Munich 80802
Phone: (49) 89 3891 2299 **Fax:** (49) 89 3891 3599
Web: www.munichre.com

2017 Premiums

	% of total
Europe	53
North America	32
Asia & Australasia	9
Latin America	3
Africa, Near & Middle East	3
Total	100

PRODUCTS/OPERATIONS

2017 Sales

	% of total
Reinsurance	
Property/casualty	35
Life and health	29
ERGO	
Life and health Germany	19
Property/casualty Germany	7
International	10
Total	100

Selected Brands
ERGO (primary insurance)
  Deutscher Automobil Schutz (D.A.S., auto insurance)
  Deutsche Krankenversicherung (DKV)
  ERV
ERGO Direkt (commercial customer consulting)
DKV (domestic health insurance)
Munich Health (international health insurance, domestic and international health reinsurance)
Munich Re
Munich Re America
  American Modern Insurance (specialty property/casualty insurance, life insurance, reinsurance)
  Hartford Steam Boiler (HSB, specialty property/casualty insurance and reinsurance)

COMPETITORS

AFLAC INCORPORATED
Allianz SE
CITIZENS, INC.
China Life Insurance Company Limited
GENERAL RE CORPORATION
Hannover Rück SE
MUTUAL OF OMAHA INSURANCE COMPANY
PRUDENTIAL FINANCIAL, INC.
Swiss Re AG
UNUM GROUP

HISTORICAL FINANCIALS

Company Type: Public

Income Statement — FYE: December 31

	ASSETS ($mil)	NET INCOME ($mil)	INCOME AS % OF ASSETS	EMPLOYEES
12/22	318,886	3,665	1.1%	41,389
12/21	353,600	3,319	0.9%	39,281
12/20	365,666	1,486	0.4%	39,642
12/19	322,855	3,058	0.9%	39,662
12/18	309,395	2,645	0.9%	41,410
Annual Growth	0.8%	8.5%		0.0%

2022 Year-End Financials
Return on assets: 1.1%
Return on equity: 13.2%
Long-term debt ($ mil.): —
No. of shares ($ mil.): 140
Sales ($ mil.): 76,741
Dividends
  Yield: —
  Payout: 0.0%
Market value ($ mil.): 4,539

	STOCK PRICE ($) FY Close	P/E High/Low		PER SHARE ($) Earnings	Dividends	Book Value
12/22	32.40	1	1	26.31	0.81	160.57
12/21	29.70	1	1	23.69	0.82	249.08
12/20	29.71	4	2	10.59	0.73	261.87
12/19	29.44	2	1	21.30	0.71	241.76
12/18	21.85	1	1	17.78	0.71	207.11
Annual Growth	10.3%	—		10.3%	3.2%	(6.2%)

Murata Manufacturing Co Ltd

Murata Manufacturing is one of the world's largest makers of passive electronic components, primarily capacitors, claiming large market share in several markets. The components, many of which are made of the ceramic materials that have been a Murata specialty since its founding, are used in electronic devices, such as computers, mobile phones, automotive, security & safety and medical equipment. Capacitors are its biggest product line, accounting for more than a third of sales. With a presence in North America, the Japan-based company also makes a wide variety of other components, including filters, antennas, resistors, power supplies, and sensors. About 90% of Murata's sales are outside of Japan's borders.

Operations

The company has two operating segment: Components (nearly 70%) and Modules (more than 30%).

Components segment is composed of: Capacitors, including products such as Multilayer ceramic capacitors, Polymer aluminum electrolytic capacitors, Silicon capacitors, High temperature film capacitors for automotive, etc.; Piezoelectric components products include SAW filters, Ultrasonic sensors, Resonators, Piezoelectric sensors, Ceramic filters, etc.; and Other component products include Inductors (coils), EMI suppression filters, Connectors, MEMS sensors, Thermistors, Lithium-ion batteries, etc.

Modules are essential compound components that wirelessly connect various devices. These are mounted on home appliances used in our daily lives, such as smart phones, tablet PCs, digital cameras and air conditioners, in-vehicle devices such as car navigation systems and in various settings, including enabling users to download and upload photos and music from the Internet, and hands-free calling while driving.

Geographic Reach

Headquartered in Tokyo, Japan, Greater China is the company's largest market, representing more than half of total sales. Other major markets include Asia generating over 15%, United States above 10%. Japan and Europe account for nearly 10% each.

Financial Performance

The company's net sales for fiscal 2021 increased to Â¥1.6 trillion compared from the prior year with Â¥1.5 trillion.

Net income for fiscal 2021 increased to Â¥237.0 billion compared from the prior year with Â¥183.0 billion.

Cash held by the company at the end of fiscal 2021 increased to Â¥407.7 billion. Cash provided by operations was Â¥373.6 billion while cash used for investing and financing activities were Â¥150.3 billion and Â¥118.2 billion, respectively.

Strategy

In order for Murata to continue to create value as an innovator in the drastically changing electronics industry, it is necessary to capture the global trends of technology and changes in society and reflect them in business management. In order to create various innovations looking ahead to the future from a long-term perspective, Murata uses a three-layer portfolio in its business management and focuses on four key fields with business opportunities to create value. The company's 3-layer portfolio are: creation of new business model; application-specific components business; and standard-products business

HISTORY

Akira Murata founded Murata Manufacturing Co. in 1944 to produce traditional ceramic tableware. However, the company quickly moved into high-performance ceramics for electronics, and expanded with new plants in Japan. (Its expansion of production capacity within Japan has remained consistent; since the 1960s Murata has opened at least three new domestic factories per decade.)

In 1963, the year it went public, Murata also opened an office in New York. The company created MurataBourns, a joint venture with Bourns, in 1966 to make industrial potentiometers, devices that control the amount of current that flows through a circuit.

Murata kept expanding overseas in the 1970s, with new operations in Singapore (1972), the US (1973), Hong Kong (1973), Germany (1975), and Taiwan (1978).

In 1981 the company bought the Canadian subsidiary of Erie Technological Products (electromagnetic filters) following a year-long regulatory battle. That year Murata shuttered its MurataBourns joint venture.

Murata continued to expand in the 1980s, with marketing, trading, and production offices in South Korea (1980), the UK (1982 and 1989), Brazil (1985 and 1986), Thailand (1988), Germany (1988), and the Netherlands (1989).

In 1991 Yasutaka Murata, who had joined the company in 1973, succeeded his father, Akira, as president. Akira became chairman.

More Asian offices opened during the 1990s in Malaysia (1990 and 1993) and the Philippines (1998). Murata began a major push into China in the mid-1990s, setting up operations in Beijing and Wuxi (1994), Shanghai (1995), and Suzhou (2001). Osamu Murata replaced his father as chairman in 1995. (Osamu retired as chairman in 2001; the post remained vacant until 2007.)

The company's profits surged in fiscal 2000 as a booming electronics market led to high demand for capacitors and other components; the next year, though, Murata warned of a sharp downturn in profits amid a steep slump in the worldwide electronics industry. The company took a big hit in the following years as the global chip industry went through its worst down period on record.

In 2004 Murata Electronics North America closed its plant in State College, Pennsylvania. Some functions were relocated to the US subsidiary's plant in Smyrna, Georgia. Later that year Murata Europe Management closed its capacitor taping operation in Plymouth, UK, shifting production to Japan and Singapore.

In 2005 Murata established a collaborative relationship with Nagano Japan Radio for switching power supplies, agreeing to manufacture each other's products. The company also created a joint venture with Superwave Corporation, called MTC Solutions, to make multi-task communication modules for wireless authentication systems. In 2005 Wuxi Murata Electronics began construction on its third plant to make chip monolithic ceramic capacitors in China.

Akira Murata died in 2006 at the age of 84. He had served as the company's honorary chairman since 1995.

In 2006 the company acquired SyChip, a US developer of radio-frequency (RF) semiconductors for digital music players, Global Positioning System (GPS) products, and PDAs, for about $137 million.

Yasutaka Murata, the first son of Akira Murata, became chairman of the company his father founded in 2007. That year Murata also acquired the Power Electronics division of C&D Technologies for $85 million in cash. The division makes power supplies and converters.

EXECUTIVES

Chairman, Representative Director, Tsuneo Murata
President, Representative Director, Norio Nakajima
Senior Managing Executive Officer, Director, Hiroshi Iwatsubo
Director, Masanori Minamide
Outside Director, Yuko Yasuda
Outside Director, Takashi Nishijima
Director, Yoshiro Ozawa
Outside Director, Hyo Kambayashi
Outside Director, Takatoshi Yamamoto
Outside Director, Naoko Munakata
Auditors : Deloitte Touche Tohmatsu LLC

LOCATIONS

HQ: Murata Manufacturing Co Ltd
   1-10-1 Higashikotari, Nagaokakyo, Kyoto 617-8555
Phone: (81) 75 955 6525   **Fax:** (81) 75 955 7359
Web: www.murata.com

2018 Sales

	% of total
Greater China	50
Asia and Others	17
The Americas	15
Japan	9
Europe	9
Total	100

PRODUCTS/OPERATIONS

2018 Sales

	% of total
Components	70
Modules	30
Others	-
Total	100

Selected Products

Ceramic Capacitors
   Disc
   High-frequency power
   High-voltage
   Monolithic
   Trimmer
   Microwave Components
   Chip dielectric and multilayer antennas
   Chip multilayer hybrid couplers
   Dielectric resonators
   Field-effect transistors (FETs)
   High-frequency coaxial connectors
   High-frequency microchip and monolithic ceramic capacitors
   Isolators/circulators
   Oscillators
   Radio-frequency (RF) diode switches
Piezoelectric Components
   Buzzers
   Diaphragms
   Ringers
   Speakers
Power Devices
   DC/DC converters
   High-voltage and switching power supplies
Sensors
   Electric potential

Magnetic pattern recognition
Non-contact potentiometers
Piezoelectric vibrating gyroscopes
Pyroelectric infrared sensors and modules
Rotary
Shock
Ultrasonic
Thermistors and Resistors
High-voltage resistors
Resistor networks
Thermistors
Trimmer potentiometers
Other
Chip coils
Delay lines
Electromagnetic interference (EMI) suppression filters
Filters
Flyback transformers
High-voltage multipliers
Resonators
TV/LCD tuners

COMPETITORS

LEGRAND FRANCE
NATIONAL SEMICONDUCTOR CORPORATION
PLUG POWER INC.
POWERSECURE INTERNATIONAL, INC.
RADIALL
RENISHAW P L C
SIGMATRON INTERNATIONAL, INC.
SOLAREDGE TECHNOLOGIES, INC.
SOLON SE
STATIC CONTROL COMPONENTS, INC.

HISTORICAL FINANCIALS

Company Type: Public

Income Statement — FYE: March 31

	REVENUE ($mil)	NET INCOME ($mil)	NET PROFIT MARGIN	EMPLOYEES
03/23	12,665	1,904	15.0%	73,164
03/22	14,901	2,582	17.3%	77,581
03/21	14,722	2,140	14.5%	75,184
03/20	14,132	1,685	11.9%	74,109
03/19	14,222	1,868	13.1%	77,571
Annual Growth	(2.9%)	0.5%	—	(1.5%)

2023 Year-End Financials

Debt ratio: —
Return on equity: 10.8%
Cash ($ mil.): 2,391
Current Ratio: 4.64
Long-term debt ($ mil.): 11
No. of shares ($ mil.): 1,889
Dividends
Yield: 2.5%
Payout: 18.0%
Market value ($ mil.): 28,753

	STOCK PRICE ($) FY Close	P/E High/Low	PER SHARE ($) Earnings	Dividends	Book Value
03/23	15.22	0 0	1.00	0.26	9.55
03/22	16.51	0 0	1.35	0.27	9.69
03/21	20.16	0 0	1.12	0.25	9.04
03/20	12.56	0 0	0.88	0.43	8.13
03/19	37.65	0 0	0.97	0.14	7.55
Annual Growth	(20.3%)	—	0.8%	18.0%	6.1%

Musashino Bank, Ltd.

The Musashino Bank serves the Saitama region to the north of Tokyo in Japan. The bank and its 8 subsidiaries do business from about 90 offices throughout the area. Musashino Bank provides leasing and lending services in addition to its standard consumer and commercial banking services. The bank provides capital for new small and medium-sized businesses through its Musashino New Business Fund. Musashino Bank was founded in 1952.

EXECUTIVES

Chairman, Director, Kikuo Kato
President, Representative Director, Kazumasa Nagahori
Senior Managing Director, Representative Director, Toshiyuki Shirai
Director, Ken Otomo
Director, Tsutomu Kainuma
Outside Director, Ryuichi Mitsuoka
Outside Director, Yukimitsu Sanada
Outside Director, Ayako Kobayashi
Auditors : Ernst & Young ShinNihon LLC

LOCATIONS

HQ: Musashino Bank, Ltd.
1-10-8 Sakuragi-cho, Omiya-ku, Saitama 330-0854
Phone: (81) 48 641 6111
Web: www.musashinobank.co.jp

COMPETITORS

JUROKU BANK,LTD., THE
MICHINOKU BANK, LTD., THE
NISHI-NIPPON CITYBANK,LTD.
OITA BANK,LTD., THE
YAMANASHI CHUO BANK, LTD., THE

HISTORICAL FINANCIALS

Company Type: Public

Income Statement — FYE: March 31

	ASSETS ($mil)	NET INCOME ($mil)	INCOME AS % OF ASSETS	EMPLOYEES
03/22	45,103	73	0.2%	2,869
03/21	48,046	72	0.2%	2,869
03/20	43,058	74	0.2%	2,920
03/19	41,772	48	0.1%	3,003
03/18	42,949	102	0.2%	3,117
Annual Growth	1.2%	(7.9%)	—	(2.1%)

2022 Year-End Financials

Return on assets: 0.1%
Return on equity: 3.6%
Long-term debt ($ mil.): —
No. of shares ($ mil.): 33
Sales ($ mil.): 585
Dividends
Yield: —
Payout: 33.4%
Market value ($ mil.): —

Nanto Bank, Ltd.

The Nanto Bank primarily serves the Nara region of Japan. The bank operates from about 135 offices, branches, and other facilities located in the Hyogo, Kyoto, Mie, Nara, Osaka, Tokyo, and Wakayama areas of the country. Nanto Bank provides a selection of financial services including consumer banking, credit card services, securities, leasing, and lending. The bank traces its historical roots back to 1934. Major subsidiaries include Nanto Credit Guarantee Co., Nanto Lease co., Nanto Estate Co., Nanto Staff Service Co., and Nanto Investment Management Co.

Strategy

The Nanto Bank aims to increase its balance of loans, deposits, and assets by expanding its branch net work mainly through the establishment of new branches. In Osaka Prefecture, identified as an important strategic area, two new branches -- the Eiwa branch and the Wakaeiwata branch -- were built and opened in Higashiosaka City in September 2012. The company also opened in 2013 its Joto corporate business office and the Hokusetsu corporate business office with a plan to eventually developing these into branches.

EXECUTIVES

President, Representative Director, Takashi Hashimoto
Deputy President, Representative Director, Satoshi Ishida
Senior Managing Executive Officer, Director, Kazuya Yokotani
Director, Kazunobu Nishikawa
Director, Tsuyoshi Sugiura
Director, Ryuichiro Funaki
Outside Director, Matazaemon Kitamura
Outside Director, Hidetaka Matsuzaka
Outside Director, Shuhei Aoki
Outside Director, Kozue Nakayama
Auditors : KPMG AZSA LLC

LOCATIONS

HQ: Nanto Bank, Ltd.
16 Hashimoto-cho, Nara 630-8677
Phone: (81) 742 22 1131
Web: www.nantobank.co.jp

COMPETITORS

HYAKUGO BANK,LTD., THE
IYO BANK, LTD., THE
JUROKU BANK,LTD., THE
MIE BANK, LTD., THE
OITA BANK,LTD., THE

HISTORICAL FINANCIALS

Company Type: Public

Income Statement — FYE: March 31

	ASSETS ($mil)	NET INCOME ($mil)	INCOME AS % OF ASSETS	EMPLOYEES
03/22	57,560	97	0.2%	3,352
03/21	59,248	97	0.2%	3,482
03/20	52,242	29	0.1%	3,677
03/19	52,362	100	0.2%	3,771
03/18	54,700	123	0.2%	3,830
Annual Growth	1.3%	(5.8%)	—	(3.3%)

2022 Year-End Financials

Return on assets: 0.1%
Return on equity: 4.0%
Long-term debt ($ mil.): —
No. of shares ($ mil.): 32
Sales ($ mil.): 638
Dividends
Yield: —
Payout: 0.0%
Market value ($ mil.): —

National Australia Bank Ltd.

National Australia Bank (NAB) is Australia's largest business bank that serves approximately eight million customers. It provides banking, wealth management, and investment banking services in Australia, as well as in New Zealand through its Bank of New Zealand (BNZ) subsidiary. NAB also offers financial and debt capital markets, specialized capital, custody and alternative investments for institutional clients. NAB funds some of the most important infrastructure in its communities ? including schools, hospitals, and roads.

Operations

NAB operates in five divisions: Business and Private Banking; Personal Banking; Corporate and Institutional Banking; New Zealand Banking; and Corporate Functions and Other.

Business and Private Banking focuses on NAB's priority small and medium (SME) customer segments. This division includes the leading NAB Business franchise, specialised Agriculture, Health, Government, Education and Community services along with Private Banking and JBWere, as well as the micro and small business segments. This division accounts for almost 40% of revenue.

Personal Banking provides customers with products and services through proprietary networks in NAB as well as third party and mortgage brokers. Customers are served through the Personal Banking network to secure home loans or manage personal finances through deposit, credit or personal loan facilities. The network also provides servicing support to individuals and business customers. The division accounts for about 30% of revenue.

Corporate and Institutional Banking provides a range of products and services including client coverage, corporate finance, markets, asset servicing, transactional banking and enterprise payments. The division services its customers in Australia and globally, including branches in the US, UK and Asia, with specialised industry relationships and product teams. It includes Bank of New Zealand's Markets Trading operations. The division accounts for about 15% of revenue.

New Zealand Banking provides banking and financial services across customer segments in New Zealand. It consists of Partnership Banking, servicing consumer and SME segments; Corporate and Institutional Banking, servicing Corporate, Institutional, Agribusiness, and Property customers, and includes Markets Sales operations in New Zealand. New Zealand Banking also includes the Wealth and Insurance franchises operating under the 'Bank of New Zealand' brand, but excludes the Bank of New Zealand's Markets Trading operations. The division accounts for 15% of revenue.

Corporate Functions and Other business includes UBank and enabling units that support all businesses including Treasury, Technology and Enterprise Operations, Strategy and Innovation, Support Units and Eliminations.

Geographic Reach

The company operates in more than 900 locations in Australia, New Zealand, and around the world.

Sales and Marketing

NAB served more than 8 million customers. Business and Private Banking serves small to medium businesses and investors; and also high net worth customers through Private Bank and JBWere.

NAB spent A$160 million on advertising and marketing expenses in 2021, compared to A$162 million in 2020.

Financial Performance

The company's revenue fell by about A$384 million to A$16.8 billion from A$17.2 billion from the prior year. Net interest income decreased by $74 million or 0.5%. Excluding large notable items of $49 million in the September 2020 full year, net interest income decreased by $123 million or 0.9%. This includes an increase of $192 million due to movements in economic hedges, offset in other operating income.

Net profit attributable to owners of NAB (statutory net profit) increased by $3,805 million. Excluding the impact of discontinued operations, statutory net profit increased by $2,973 million or 85.0%.

The company's cash in 2021 decreased by about A$24.2 billion to A$37.9 billion from the prior year. Cash provided by operating activities was A$759 million, while cash used by financing activities and investing activities were A$3.7 billion and $22 million, respectively. Main uses of cash were for repayments of bonds and deposits with central banks and other regulatory authorities.

Strategy

The company's strategic focus aligns with major global trends, with a particular focus on sustainability, infrastructure (including renewables), and private capital.

Mergers and Acquisitions

In 2021, NAB, completed the acquisition of 86 400 Holdings Ltd, the holding company of Australian digital bank, 86 400 ("86 400") for a total consideration of $261 million. Its strategy to grow UBank will be accelerated by the acquisition of 86 400. This brings together UBank's established business and 86 400's technology platform that will meet the changing needs of our customers. Together, the companies will develop a leading digital bank that attracts and retains customers at scale and creates a new generation of simple, fast and mobile banking solutions.

In the same year, NAB also announced its proposed acquisition of Citigroup's Australian consumer business, subject to regulatory approval. This planned transaction brings scale, customers and deep expertise, and supports NAB's strategic growth ambition for Personal banking.

EXECUTIVES

Chief Executive Officer, Managing Director, Executive Director, Ross McEwan
Chief Risk Officer, Shaun Dooley
Chief Financial Officer, Gary Lennon
Chief Operating Officer, Les Matheson
Chief Digital, Data and Analytics, Angela Mentis
Legal and Commercial Services Group Executive, Sharon Lee Cook
People and Culture Group Executive, Susan Ferrier
Corporate and Institutional Banking Group Executive, David Gall
Strategy and Innovation Group Executive, Nathan Goonan
Business and Private Banking Group Executive, Andrew Irvine
Personal Banking Group Executive, Rachel Slade
Technology and Enterprise Operations Group Executive, Patrick Wright
Managing Director, Chief Executive Officer, Daniel Huggins
Secretary, Louise Thomson
Secretary, Penelope MacRae
Secretary, Tricia Conte
Secretary, Ricardo Vasquez
Chairman, Independent Non-Executive Director, Philip Chronican
Independent Non-Executive Director, David Armstrong
Independent Non-Executive Director, Kathryn Fagg
Independent Non-Executive Director, Peeyush Gupta
Independent Non-Executive Director, Anne Loveridge
Independent Non-Executive Director, Douglas Mckay
Independent Non-Executive Director, Simon McKeon
Independent Non-Executive Director, Ann Sherry
Auditors : Ernst & Young

LOCATIONS

HQ: National Australia Bank Ltd.
Level 28, 395 Bourke Street, Melbourne, Victoria 3000
Phone: (61) 3 8872 2461
Web: www.nab.com.au

PRODUCTS/OPERATIONS

2015 Cash Earnings

	% of total
Australian banking	69
NZ banking	10
UK banking	10
NAB Wealth	8
Corporate function and others	3
Total	100

Selected Subsidiaries

Calibre Asset Management
Great Western Bancorporation
nabCapital (formerly Institutional Markets & Services)
National Australia Group Europe Limited
    Clydesdale Bank PLC
    Yorkshire Bank Home Loans Limited
    Yorkshire Bank Investments Limited
        National Australia Group Europe Services Limited
National Australia Group (NZ) Limited
    Bank of New Zealand
    BNZ International Funding Limited
National Australia Trustees Limited
National Wealth Management Holdings Limited
MLC Limited
    National Wealth Management International Holdings Limited

COMPETITORS

AUSTRALIA AND NEW ZEALAND BANKING GROUP LIMITED
Bank Of China Limited
COMMERZBANK AG
COMMONWEALTH BANK OF AUSTRALIA
DEUTSCHE BANK AG
HSBC HOLDINGS PLC
SHINSEI BANK, LIMITED
STANDARD CHARTERED PLC
UniCredit Bank AG
WESTPAC BANKING CORPORATION

HISTORICAL FINANCIALS

Company Type: Public

Income Statement — FYE: September 30

	ASSETS ($mil)	NET INCOME ($mil)	INCOME AS % OF ASSETS	EMPLOYEES
09/23	686,581	4,806	0.7%	38,516
09/22	682,000	4,454	0.7%	34,022
09/21	666,210	4,578	0.7%	34,217
09/20	616,749	1,821	0.3%	34,841
09/19	572,359	3,241	0.6%	33,950
Annual Growth	4.7%	10.3%	—	3.2%

2023 Year-End Financials

Return on assets: 0.7%
Return on equity: 12.3%
Long-term debt ($ mil.): —
No. of shares ($ mil.): 3,120
Sales ($ mil.): 33,654
Dividends
  Yield: —
  Payout: 34.2%
Market value ($ mil.): 29,055

	STOCK PRICE ($) FY Close	P/E High/Low		PER SHARE ($) Earnings	Dividends	Book Value
09/23	9.31	5	3	1.48	0.51	12.70
09/22	9.43	5	4	1.33	0.47	12.12
09/21	9.94	5	3	1.33	0.32	13.79
09/20	6.45	13	6	0.57	0.37	13.28
09/19	10.07	6	4	1.11	0.63	13.06
Annual Growth	(1.9%)	—	—	7.5%	(5.1%)	(0.7%)

National Bank of Canada

The National Bank of Canada offers financial services to individuals, businesses, institutional clients, and governments across Canada through Personal and Commercial Banking, Wealth Management, Financial Markets, and US Specialty Finance and International segments. The Personal and Commercial segment meets the financial needs of close to 2.6 million individuals and over 140,000 businesses across Canada. The bank also provides services such as treasury activities, bank funding, liquidity management, and asset and liability management. Founded in 1856, The bank's assets have grown to more than $356 billion.

Operations

The National Bank of Canada operates through four business segments: Personal and Commercial, Wealth Management, Financial Markets, and US Specialty Finance and International (USSF&I).

Personal and Commercial segment includes banking, financing, and investing services offered to individuals, advisors, and businesses as well as insurance operations. The segment accounts for more than 40% of the bank's total revenue.

Wealth Management segment comprises investment solutions, trust services, banking services, lending services, and other wealth management solutions offered through internal and third-party distribution networks. The segment accounts for nearly 25% of the total revenue.

Financial Markets segment provides corporate banking and investment banking and financial solutions for large and mid-size corporations, public sector organizations, and institutional investors. The segment accounts for nearly 25% of total revenue.

The USSF&I segment encompasses the specialty finance expertise provided by the Credigy subsidiary; the activities of the ABA Bank subsidiary, which offers financial products and services to individuals and businesses in Cambodia; and the activities of targeted investments in certain emerging markets. It accounts for more than 10% of the total revenue.

Geographic Reach

The National Bank of Canada is headquartered in Montreal and has some 385 branches and about 925 banking machines across Canada.

Sales and Marketing

The bank serves small-and-medium sized enterprises (SMEs), corporations, institutional clients and public sectors.

Financial Performance

The National Bank of Canada's financial performance for five years has continued to grow and increase year over year, with 2021 as its highest performing year.

For 2021, the bank recorded a 13% increase or about C$1 billion to C$8.9 billion compared to C$7.9 billion. This increase was driven by revenue growth across all of the bank's business segments.

The bank's net income increased by about C$1.1 billion to C$3.2 billion compared to C$2.1 billion in the prior year, a 53% year-over-year increase that was due to a significant decrease in provisions for credit losses on non-impaired loans, as macroeconomic and credit conditions improved from fiscal 2020, and to a significant reduction in provisions for credit losses on impaired loans. Also contributing to the net income growth was the excellent performance turned in by all the Bank's business segments, notably achieved through revenue growth.

Cash held by the bank at the end of the year amounted to C$33.9 billion. The bank's operating activities provided C$6.1 billion, while investing activities provided another C$1.4 billion. Financing activities used C$1.7 billion, mainly for dividends paid.

Mergers and Acquisitions

In 2021, the National Bank of Canada completed its acquisition of Flinks Technology Inc., a financial data aggregation and distribution company, for C$73 million. The acquisition strategically positions the bank in a high-growth market to continue to enhance customer experiences and benefit from future technology-driven innovation. After its initial transaction, the bank made another C$30 million investment in voting right preferred shares, giving it an 85.9% equity interest in Flinks.

Company Background

The National Bank of Canada was founded in 1859.

EXECUTIVES

President, Chief Executive Officer, Director, Laurent Ferreira

Market Risk Executive Vice President, Risk Management Executive Vice President, William E. Bonnell

Financial Markets Executive Vice President, Financial Markets Head, Denis Girouard

Internal Audit Chief Financial Officer, Finance Chief Financial Officer, Internal Audit Executive Vice President, Finance Executive Vice President, Ghislain Parent

Commerical Banking and Insurance Executive Vice President, Stephane Achard

Wealth Management Executive Vice President, Martin Gagnon

Internal Audit Executive Vice President, Employee Experience Executive Vice President, IT Delivery Management, Personal and Commercial Banking, Marketing and Operation Executive Vice President, Application Solutions Executive Vice President, Operations Executive Vice President, Transversal Support and Governance Executive Vice President, Brigitte Hebert

Personal Banking and Client Experience Executive Vice President, Lucie Blanchet

Operations Executive Vice President, Nathalie Genereux

Information Technology Executive Vice President, Julie Levesque

Chairman, Director, Jean Houde

Director, Manon Brouillette

Director, Karen A. Kinsley

Director, Andree Savoie

Director, Maryse Bertrand

Director, Yvon Charest
Director, Rebecca McKillican
Director, Macky Tall
Director, Pierre Blouin
Director, Patricia Curadeau-Grou
Director, Robert Pare
Director, Pierre Thabet
Director, Pierre Boivin
Director, Lino A. Saputo
Auditors : Deloitte LLP

LOCATIONS

HQ: National Bank of Canada
600 De La Gauchetiàre Street West, 7th Floor, Montreal, Quebec H3B 4L2
Phone: 514 394-5000 **Fax:** 514 394-8434
Web: www.nbc.ca

2016 sales

	% of total
Financial Markets	39
Personal and Commercial	38
Wealth Management	5
Other	18
Total	100

2016 sales

	% of total
Canada	89
United States	8
Other	3
Total	100

PRODUCTS/OPERATIONS

2016 Sales

	% of total
Interest	
Loans	50
Securities & other	8
Available-for-sale securities	4
Deposits with financial institutions	1
Noninterest	
Underwriting and advisory fees	5
Securities brokerage commissions	3
Mutual fund revenues	5
Trust service revenues	6
Credit fees	5
Card revenues	2
Deposit and payment service charges	3
Trading revenues (losses)	2
Gains (losses) on available-for-sale securities, net	1
Insurance revenues, net	1
Foreign exchange revenues, other than trading	1
Other	3
Total	100

Selected Subsidiaries
Natbank (banking, US)
NATCAN (75%, portfolio management and investments)
National Bank Direct Brokerage (online brokerage)
National Bank Financial (investment banking)
National Bank General Insurance (home and auto coverage)
National Bank Insurance Firm (insurance brokerage)
National Bank Life Insurance Company
National Bank Securities (mutual funds)
National Bank Trust (trust services)

COMPETITORS

BANCO BBVA ARGENTINA S.A.
BANCO ESPAÑOL DE CREDITO SA (EXTINGUIDA)
CONSUMERS BANCORP, INC.
CREDIT INDUSTRIEL ET COMMERCIAL
CROGHAN BANCSHARES, INC.
CTBC Financial Holding Co., Ltd.
EASTERN VIRGINIA BANKSHARES, INC.
PRINCETON NATIONAL BANCORP, INC.
QNB CORP.
THE ROYAL BANK OF SCOTLAND PUBLIC LIMITED COMPANY

HISTORICAL FINANCIALS
Company Type: Public

Income Statement   FYE: October 31

	ASSETS ($mil)	NET INCOME ($mil)	INCOME AS % OF ASSETS	EMPLOYEES
10/23	306,295	2,311	0.8%	31,243
10/22	295,455	2,398	0.8%	29,509
10/21	288,031	2,472	0.9%	26,920
10/20	249,297	1,445	0.6%	26,517
10/19	213,679	1,624	0.8%	25,487
Annual Growth	9.4%	9.2%	—	5.2%

2023 Year-End Financials
Return on assets: 0.7%   Dividends
Return on equity: 14.0%   Yield: 4.6%
Long-term debt ($ mil.): —   Payout: 56.6%
No. of shares ($ mil.): 338   Market value ($ mil.): 21,051
Sales ($ mil.): 16,892

	STOCK PRICE ($) FY Close	P/E High/Low		PER SHARE ($) Earnings	Dividends	Book Value
10/23	62.23	8	6	6.78	2.95	50.61
10/22	68.16	8	6	7.03	2.76	47.28
10/21	82.72	10	6	7.25	2.30	45.17
10/20	47.63	10	5	4.28	2.13	36.65
10/19	51.65	8	6	4.81	2.00	33.57
Annual Growth	4.8%	—	—	9.0%	10.2%	10.8%

National Grid plc

National Grid PLC owns and operates England and Wales' electricity infrastructure and operates Scotland's (Scotland's infrastructure is owned separately), which together span over 7,00 kilometers of overhead lines. National Grid PLC's UK customers are mainly electricity generation and gas shipping companies. In the US, subsidiary National Grid USA manages electricity generation & transmission assets and gas distribution networks in the New England region of the US. National Grid PLC also conducts liquefied natural gas (LNG) business in the UK and US. Majority of the company's sales were generated in the US.

Operations
The company operates through six business units:

UK Electricity Transmission own and operate the high-voltage electricity transmission (ET) network in England and Wales. Strategic Infrastructure (SI) is a new business unit, which, effective 1 April 2023, will deliver UK ET projects through the Accelerated Strategic Transmission Investment (ASTI) framework to connect 50 GW of offshore generation by 2030. The segment accounts for around 10% of the total revenue.

UK Electricity Distribution own and operate the electricity distribution networks for the Midlands, the South West and South Wales. The combined network makes us the largest distribution network operator (DNO) group in the UK. The segment accounts for around 10% of revenue.

UK Electricity System Operator currently operate as the electricity system operator across GB. As announced in April 2022, the ESO is expected to transfer out of National Grid to become part of the newly created Future System Operator (FSO) in 2024. The segment accounts for more than 20% of revenue.

New England own and operate electricity transmission facilities and distribution networks across Massachusetts, New Hampshire and Vermont as well as gas distribution networks across Massachusetts. The segment accounts for around 20% of revenue.

New York own and operate electricity transmission facilities and distribution networks across upstate New York. The company own and operate gas distribution networks across upstate New York, in New York City and on Long Island. The segment accounts for more than 30% of revenue.

National Grid Ventures operates separately from our core regulated units, is focused on competitive markets across the UK and US. Its portfolio includes electricity interconnectors, liquefied natural gas (LNG) storage and regasification, large-scale renewable generation, conventional generation and competitive transmission. The segment accounts for around 5% of revenues.

Other activities primarily relate to National Grid Partners (NGP), the venture investment and innovation arm of National Grid, as well as UK property, insurance and corporate activities. The segment accounts for less than 5%.

Geographic Reach
Headquartered in London, England; the company have ingenious network of specialist equipment is made up of 7,000km of overhead line, 350 substations and 22,000 pylons, which comprise the physical infrastructure of the electricity system.

Company's largest geographic market was the United States with around 55% of the total revenue.

Sales and Marketing
National Grid PLC is regulated by Ofgem in the UK. Its client base includes residential customers, industrial companies, and commercial enterprises.

Financial Performance
National Grid's revenue for fiscal 2023 increased to GBP21.8 billion compared to the prior year with GBP18.5 billion. The increase was primarily due to higher revenues in every operating segment aside from UK Electricity Transmission; and New England.

Cash held by the company at the end of

fiscal 2023 decreased to GBP163 million. Cash provided by operations and investing activities were GBP6.9 billion and GBP240 million, respectively. Cash used for financing activities were GBP7.2 billion, mainly for repayment of loans.

Strategy

National Grid's vision is to be at the heart of a clean, fair and affordable energy future. To deliver its vision in a focused way, the company has a strategy which sets the bounds of its business, guided by four strategic priorities. The four strategic focuses are: enable the energy transition for all; deliver for customers efficiently; grow its organizational capability; and empower colleagues for great performance.

Mergers and Acquisitions

In early 2021, National Grid plc entered into an agreement to acquire 100% of the share capital of PPL WPD Investments Limited (WPD), the holding company of Western Power Distribution plc, which is the UK's largest electricity distribution network operator. The total consideration for the transaction is Â£7.8 billion. The transaction is expected to complete in July 2021.

HISTORY

The National Grid Company was formed in 1990 as part of the privatization of the electricity industry in England and Wales. Until then, the Central Electricity Generating Board (CEGB), a state monopoly responsible for power generation in England and Wales, owned the national power grid (transmission system) and sold power to 12 area boards, the regional authorities that distributed electricity to customers.

The Electricity Act of 1989 paved the way for competition; in 1990 the CEGB was split into The National Grid Company and three power-generating firms: National Power, PowerGen, and Nuclear Electric. The 12 area boards transferred their assets to 12 regional companies, which jointly owned National Grid. The company, keeping its monopoly status, was charged to develop and operate an efficient, coordinated, and economical transmission system and to facilitate competition among power producers.

The company moved outside the UK when it invested in Citelec in 1993. An international consortium, Citelec controlled Transener, the surviving transmission system after Argentina privatized its electric utilities.

Also in 1993 National Grid set up Energis as a telecommunications firm to provide service to businesses. Piggybacking its fiber-optic lines on National Grid's transmission network, Energis introduced national services in 1994, and by 1996 it had won several major customers, including the BBC and Microsoft.

In 1995 National Grid went public as The National Grid Group. It also secured concessions to build transmission lines in Pakistan, but in 1997 a new Pakistani government put the project on hold. That year it also upped its stake in Citelec from 15% to 41%, which increased its control over the development of Argentina's transmission system. With partner CINergy Global, it also acquired 80% of the Power Division of Zambia Consolidated Copper Mines in 1997, and it was chosen as a joint venture partner by India's Karnataka Electricity Board to build a transmission line in that state.

The company sold 26% of Energis in 1997; in 1998 it announced plans to sell the rest of Energis and launch a new company under the National Grid banner to set up telecom firms overseas. That year it laid plans to enter the US by agreeing to acquire New England Electric System (NEES). (The $3.2 billion purchase closed in 2000.)

In 1999 the company cut its stake in Energis to 46% and announced plans to shop for more US energy holdings. A deal was struck to purchase New York Utility Niagara Mohawk Holdings the following year. (The deal was completed in 2002.) Also in 2000 and 2001 the company continued to slim its stake in Energis (33%).

National Grid sold some noncore businesses in 2001, including UK metering company Datum Services and US energy marketer Allenergy, and pulled out of the transmission project in India. It also agreed to manage the Alliance Regional Transmission Organization (RTO) in the US. In 2002 National Grid sold Niagara Mohawk's 50% interest in Canadian Niagara Power to Canadian utility Fortis.

The firm changed its name to National Grid Transco in 2002 upon completion of its acquisition of Lattice Group in a $21.5 billion deal.

In 2005 National Grid Transco sold four of its regional gas distribution networks; the North England network was acquired by a consortium that includes United Utilities and Cheung Kong Infrastructure; the South of England and Scotland networks were sold to Scottish and Southern Energy, Borealis Infrastructure, and Ontario Teachers' Pension Plan; and the Wales & West distribution network was purchased by a consortium managed by Macquarie Bank Limited. The company dropped Transco from its name in 2005.

National Grid dramatically boosted its North American assets in 2007 by acquiring gas distributor KeySpan for more than $7 billion. To comply with federal regulations connected to the KeySpan deal, in 2008 National Grid sold its 2,480-MW Ravenswood Generating Station in New York City to TransCanada for $2.9 billion.

In the second half of the decade, to raise cash and narrow its operational focus, the company jettisoned a number of noncore operations. National Grid sold its stakes in the alternative telecommunications network industry. The company also sold its telecom interests in Chile, Argentina, and Poland, and wrote off its 33% stake in bankrupt UK telecommunications firm Energis, which uses fiber-optic cable strung along National Grid's power lines. National Grid also sold former Lattice Group subsidiary 186k (fiber-optic networking) to Hutchison Whampoa, and exited its telecom venture in Brazil. It also sold its electricity interconnector linking Australia to the island state of Tasmania.

In 2010 a National Grid and TenneT joint venture began laying the first section of a high-voltage cable that will link the power grids in the UK and the Netherlands, bolstering power supply in both countries. The project will help the companies meet environmental goals by facilitating power flows from low-carbon generation plants.

With an eye on meeting ambitious European Union goals for carbon emission reductions, in 2009 National Grid released a report that by 2020 half of the UK's heating needs could be provided by biogas (converted from sewage and injected into the national gas distribution system), compensating for a decline in North Sea gas supply. In 2010 the company had one renewable gas plant under development in the US and two in the UK.

The company reported a major jump in revenues and income in 2010, primarily driven by a rebounding economy (prompting increased demand for power and gas) and by improved rates in the US market. Revenues grew by 40% in 2011 and net income by 30%, thanks to strong demand and higher prices in the UK and increased rates in the US.

In 2011 National Grid announced plans to save $200 million in a restructuring of its US operations, including cutting 1,200 jobs. Late in 2011 the company sold the Seneca-Upshur Petroleum subsidiary for approximately $152 million. The deal is a further move to return to core business operations in gas and electricity distribution. That year it also agreed to sell its non-regulated metering business in the UK (Onstream), to Macquarie Bank for about $440 million.

EXECUTIVES

Chief Executive Officer, Executive Director, John Pettigrew
Chief Financial Officer, Andy Agg
General Counsel, Secretary, Justine Campbell
Chair, Paula Rosput Reynolds
Independent Non-Executive Director, Senior Independent Director, Therese Esperdy
Independent Non-Executive Director, Jonathan Dawson
Independent Non-Executive Director, Liz Hewitt
Independent Non-Executive Director, Amanda Mesler
Independent Non-Executive Director, Anne Robinson
Independent Non-Executive Director, Earl Shipp
Independent Non-Executive Director, Jonathan Silver

Independent Non-Executive Director, Martha Brown Wyrsch
Independent Non-Executive Director, Ian Livingston
Independent Non-Executive Director, Tony Wood
Auditors : Deloitte LLP

LOCATIONS

HQ: National Grid plc
1-3 Strand, London WC2N 5EH
Phone: (44) 20 7004 3000   **Fax:** (44) 20 7004 3004
Web: www.nationalgrid.com

PRODUCTS/OPERATIONS

2018 sales

	%
US Regulated	66
UK Electricity Transmission	22
UK Gas Transmission	6
National Grid Ventures	6
Total	100

COMPETITORS

IBERDROLA, SOCIEDAD ANONIMA
ITALGAS RETI SPA
KINDER MORGAN ENERGY PARTNERS, L.P.
Korea Gas Corporation
LIBERTY POWER CORP, L.L.C.
OSAKA GAS CO., LTD.
SMARTESTENERGY LIMITED
SSE PLC
TOKYO GAS CO., LTD.
UNITED UTILITIES GROUP PLC

HISTORICAL FINANCIALS

Company Type: Public

Income Statement FYE: March 31

	REVENUE ($mil)	NET INCOME ($mil)	NET PROFIT MARGIN	EMPLOYEES
03/22	24,211	3,087	12.8%	29,292
03/21	20,345	2,257	11.1%	23,683
03/20	17,962	1,561	8.7%	23,069
03/19	19,561	1,979	10.1%	22,576
03/18	21,429	4,988	23.3%	23,023
Annual Growth	3.1%	(11.3%)	—	6.2%

2022 Year-End Financials

Debt ratio: 62.3%
Return on equity: 10.7%
Cash ($ mil.): 267
Current Ratio: 0.73
Long-term debt ($ mil.): 43,166
No. of shares ($ mil.): 3,645
Dividends
Yield: 4.4%
Payout: 377.6%
Market value ($ mil.): 280,197

	STOCK PRICE ($) FY Close	P/E High/Low		PER SHARE ($) Earnings	Dividends	Book Value
03/22	76.87	117	87	0.85	3.41	8.58
03/21	59.24	146	119	0.64	3.11	7.70
03/20	58.27	180	131	0.45	3.06	6.89
03/19	55.84	131	108	0.58	3.08	6.87
03/18	56.43	75	51	1.43	3.12	7.27
Annual Growth	8.0%	—		(12.2%)	2.3%	4.2%

National Westminster Bank Plc

National West Bank Public Limited Company (known as NatWest) offers mortgages, savings, loans, investments, credit cards, and insurance. NatWest Group (parent company) operates through its businesses and offers retail banking, commercial & institutional, private banking, and Ulster Bank RoI. NatWest aim to help its corporate and institutional customers access the financing they need, when they need it. The company provides its products depending on its customers which includes personal, premier, business, and corporate & institutes.

Operations

The company's products is divided into four categories: Personal, Premier, Business, and Corporates & Institutional.

Personal offers mortgages, savings, loans, investments, credit cards, insurance, reward accounts and cards, and overdrafts.

Premier offers Premier select account, Premier reward account, Premier reward black account, savings solutions, investing online and advice, tailored mortgage advice, discover its loans, and enhanced insurance cover.

Business offers bank accounts services, savings, cards, loans and finance, commercial mortgages, asset finance, trade finance, and businesses services.

Corporates & institutions offers everyday banking, financing, coverage and sector, FX and international trade, support disclosures, and market insights.

Geographic Reach

The company is headquartered at London, England.

EXECUTIVES

Chief Executive Officer, Executive Director, Alison Rose-Slade
Chief Financial Officer, Executive Director, Katie Murray
Chief Governance Officer, Secretary, Jan Cargill
Chairman, Howard Davies
Senior Independent Non-Executive Director, Graham Beale
Independent Non-Executive Director, Francesca Barnes
Independent Non-Executive Director, Ian Cormack
Independent Non-Executive Director, Patrick Flynn
Independent Non-Executive Director, Morten N. Friis
Independent Non-Executive Director, Robert Gillespie
Independent Non-Executive Director, Yasmin Jetha
Independent Non-Executive Director, Mike Rogers
Independent Non-Executive Director, Mark Seligman
Independent Non-Executive Director, Lena Wilson
Auditors : Ernst & Young LLP

LOCATIONS

HQ: National Westminster Bank Plc
250 Bishopsgate, London EC2M 4AA
Phone: (44) 20 7085 5000
Web: www.natwest.com

PRODUCTS/OPERATIONS

2018 sales

	% of total
Interest income	61
Fees and commissions receivable	17
Other non-interest income	22
Total	100

2018 sales

	% of total
UK Personal & Business Banking	55
Commercial and Private Banking	33
Central Items & other	17
Total	100

Services
Personal Banking
Credit card
Insurance
Loans
Mortgages
Saving Account
Private Banking
Credit Cards
Current Accounts
Insurance
Loans
Mortgages
Business Banking
International business
Startup business

COMPETITORS

CANARA BANK
COMMERCE BANCSHARES, INC.
FIRSTMERIT CORPORATION
HSBC Bank Canada
Industrial and Commercial Bank of China Limited
Laurentian Bank of Canada
SANTANDER UK GROUP HOLDINGS PLC
TCF FINANCIAL CORPORATION
TD BANK, N.A.
WSFS FINANCIAL CORPORATION

HISTORICAL FINANCIALS

Company Type: Public

Income Statement FYE: December 31

	ASSETS ($mil)	NET INCOME ($mil)	INCOME AS % OF ASSETS	EMPLOYEES
12/21	574,262	3,764	0.7%	0
12/20	519,412	518	0.1%	0
12/19	420,590	942	0.2%	51,700
12/18	395,717	3,343	0.8%	55,400
12/17	460,373	2,789	0.6%	14,400
Annual Growth	5.7%	7.8%	—	—

2021 Year-End Financials

Return on assets: 0.6%
Return on equity: 14.8%
Long-term debt ($ mil.): —
No. of shares ($ mil.): —
Sales ($ mil.): 13,972
Dividends
Yield: —
Payout: 0.0%
Market value ($ mil.): —

NatWest Group PLC

NatWest, formerly known as the Royal Bank of Scotland (RBS), is the largest business and commercial bank in the UK, with a leading retail business.. With total assets of nearly £38 billion, it offers retail banking, which provides a comprehensive range of banking products and related financial services including current accounts, mortgages, personal unsecured lending and personal deposits. Outside of Great Britain, RBS operates as Ulster Bank in Ireland and Northern Ireland and has additional small operations in Europe, the US, and Asia.

Operations
NatWest operates business segments including Retail Banking (about 40% of sales), Commercial Banking (around 50%), Private banking (about 5%), and Central Items & other (more than 5%).

Retail Banking serves personal customers in the UK. Private banking caters to UK-connected high net worth individuals and their business interests while Commercial banking serves start-up, SME, commercial, and corporate customers in the UK.

Overall, net interest income accounts for around 80% of sales while non-interest income account for some 20% of the company's sales.

Geographic Reach
NatWest is based in Edinburgh.

Sales and Marketing
NatWest serves customers, including individuals, high-net-worth individuals, SMEs, commercial enterprises, corporates, and financial institutions.

Financial Performance
Total income in 2021 was £1.8 billion, compared with £1.9 billion in 2020, impacted by the continued run-off of mortgage portfolios in Retail Banking, with intermediary new lending being originated through the NatWest Bank business.

Profit for 2021 was £776 million, compared with £366 million in 2020, reflecting a net impairment release of £360 million, due to continued low levels of realised losses to date.

Cash held by the company at the end of fiscal 2021 increased to £60.2 billion. Operating activities provided £15.8 billion. Investing activities provided £249 million while financing activities used £19 million. Main cash uses were for dividends paid and movement in subordinated liabilities.

Company Background
The group was crippled by both the global financial crisis and its ambitious international expansion, primarily its disastrous 2007 investment in Dutch bank ABN AMRO. In late 2008 the UK took a 60% stake in RBS, but the bank still ended up reporting an annual loss of some £28 billion ($41 billion) -- the largest loss in British corporate history. The government stepped in at least twice more to help RBS manage its debt and interest payments, intervening with the contingency that RBS make significant efforts to get back on solid ground. The UK government is progressively selling off its stake in RBS. Standing at around 62% in 2019, the government expects to sell its entire stake in the company by 2024.

HISTORY
Royal Bank of Scotland was founded in 1727, but its roots go back to the Darien Company, a merchant expedition that was established to set up a Scottish trading colony in Panama. The Darien expedition ended disastrously in 1699. In 1707 England voted to compensate Scottish creditors for the colony's failure (in part because England had promised support, then reneged, contributing to the collapse), and a small industry sprang up around paying creditors and loaning them money. In 1727 the Equivalent Company, the combined entity of these organizations, was granted a banking charter and became Royal Bank of Scotland.

In 1826 the Parliament voted to take away Scottish banks' right to issue banknotes for less than five pounds, which would have required banks to use gold or silver. Few banks had such reserves, and the move sparked an outcry. Novelist Sir Walter Scott's The Letters of Malachi Malagrowther, which defended the Scottish one-pound note, helped shoot down the proposal.

RBS expanded throughout Scotland over the next 50 years. It opened a London branch in 1874; it didn't establish a branch outside London until it bought Williams Deacon's Bank, which had a branch network in North England. RBS continued to use the Williams Deacon's name, as it did with Glyn, Mills & Co., which it purchased in 1939.

In 1968 RBS took on its modern persona as a public company when it merged with National Commercial Bank. The company moved overseas during the 1970s, establishing offices in Hong Kong and major US cities.

RBS spent the next 20 years trying to achieve another merger of the same scale as National Commercial. In 1981 the bank was wooed by Standard Chartered Bank and Hongkong and Shanghai Bank (now part of HSBC Holdings), but British regulators denied both suitors.

The bank moved into telephone operations in 1985, when it set up Direct Line for selling car insurance. In 1988 RBS bought New England bank Citizens Financial (but it plans to divest that business). In 1989 the company entered into an alliance with Banco Santander (now Santander Central Hispano), Spain's largest banking group. The alliance created a cross-pollination of ideas and strategies that boosted both banks' operations. The first fruit of the alliance came in 1991 with the launch of Interbank On-line Systems (IBOS), which connected several European banks and allowed for instantaneous money transfers.

In the 1990s RBS was linked with a variety of partners. It even made a bid for the much larger bank Barclays, in a move regarded as cheeky, but was rebuffed. In 1997 it announced a joint venture with Richard Branson's Virgin Group called Virgin Direct to offer personal banking. The company also bought Angel Trains Contract, a rolling stock leasing company, and established a transatlantic banking transfer system (similar to IBOS) with US bank CoreStates (now owned by First Union).

In 2000 RBS acquired NatWest after a prolonged takeover battle with rival Bank of Scotland (now part of HBOS plc). The bank sold Gartmore Investment Management, its fund management unit, to Nationwide Mutual Insurance Company. Royal Bank also sold the assets of NatWest's Equity Partners unit and launched NatWest Private Banking to target wealthy investors.

In 2004 RBS made several acquisitions to boost its US presence: It paid about $360 million for the credit card business of Connecticut-based People's Bank and bought payments processor Lynk Systems (now RBS Lynk), while Citizens Financial bought Cleveland-based bank Charter One Financial. Also that year Ulster Bank bought Ireland-based retail financial services provider First Active.

In 2007 RBS led the consortium that acquired the Dutch bank for ?71 billion in a deal that was called the largest ever in the banking industry. The buyers carved ABN AMRO into pieces; RBS took the global wholesale and international retail operations in Asia, Eastern Europe, and the Middle East. The ambitious takeover preceded the global economic crisis, though, and RBS was among the hardest hit financial groups.

The troubled company made several moves to try and raise capital. Early in 2008 the company announced a £12 billion rights issue. RBS also tried but failed to find a buyer for its insurance arm. However, other assets were divested that year. The company sold rolling stock leasing firm Angel Trains to Babcock & Brown and others, and it sold its joint venture Tesco Personal Finance back to supermarket giant Tesco. The efforts proved inadequate, though. The government took a controlling stake in the group in 2008, the same year that RBS reported the largest corporate loss in British history.

Also as part of the government rescue, RBS went through a management shakeup. Fred Goodwin, the architect of the bank's international expansion, was removed as CEO. He was replaced by Stephen Hester, formerly the CEO of British Land Company. Johnny Cameron, chairman of the group's global banking and markets segment (which lost the group's most money in 2008) was also ousted, and chairman Tom McKillop retired early.

RBS also shuffled its corporate structure in 2009. It split its UK retail and commercial banking division into three segments (retail, commercial, and wealth) and made Ulster Bank its own segment. The group folded its operations support division into other arms and established a segment to manage the selling and runoff of noncore operations. RBS retained the Global Banking & Markets, Global Transaction Services, US Retail & Commercial, and RBS Insurance (including Churchill Insurance) segments, although several of their components were transferred to the noncore segment.

RBS has scaled back on the international growth that weakened the group during the economic fallout, with the ultimate goal of reducing non-UK operations to less than a quarter of its assets. In 2009, the group sold its 4% stake in Bank of China for some Â£1.6 billion ($2.4 billion); it also sold most of its operations in Southeast Asia to Australia and New Zealand Banking Group for about $550 million. RBS divested units in Argentina, Colombia, Chile, the United Arab Emirates, Kazakhstan, and Pakistan -- all assets gained as part of its ABN AMRO transaction.

With the government having to step in at least twice to bail out the bank by 2011, RBC was forced to cut costs and sell non-core operations to refocus on its core banking business. In 2010, it sold more than 300 branches and offices to Banco Santander for some Â£1.65 billion ($2.6 billion). RBS sold its factoring and invoice financing unit to GE Capital and its payment services unit Global Merchant Services to Advent International and Bain Capital. It also sold its interest in RBS Sempra Commodities. In 2012, the company sold the international private banking business of Coutts to Royal Bank of Canada. Other divisions have been simply wound down and closed. RBS was ordered by the Federal Reserve in 2011 to improve its US operations or risk losing permission to do business in America. In October 2012, RBS sold a 30% stake in Direct Line Group, part of its insurance group, in an IPO valued at Â£2.6 billion ($4.2 billion).

EXECUTIVES

Chief Executive Officer, Executive Director, Alison Rose-Slade
Finance Chief Financial Officer, Executive Director, Katie Murray
Deputy Chief Governance Officer, Deputy Secretary, Jan Cargill
Independent Chairman, Director, Howard Davies
Senior Independent Non-Executive Director, Mark Seligman
Independent Non-Executive Director, Frank E. Dangeard
Independent Non-Executive Director, Roisin Donnelly
Independent Non-Executive Director, Patrick Flynn
Independent Non-Executive Director, Morten N. Friis
Independent Non-Executive Director, Yasmin Jetha
Independent Non-Executive Director, Mike Rogers
Independent Non-Executive Director, Lena Wilson
Auditors: Ernst & Young LLP

LOCATIONS

HQ: NatWest Group PLC
Gogarburn, P.O. Box 1000, Edinburgh EH12 1HQ
Phone: (44) 131 556 8555 **Fax:** (44) 131 626 3081
Web: www.natwestgroup.com

2018 Sales

	% of total
Net interest income	65
Net fees and commissions	18
Income from trading activities	10
Other operating income	7
Total	100

2018 Sales

	% of total
UK	92
Other countries	8
Total	100

PRODUCTS/OPERATIONS

2018 Sales by Segment

	% of total
Personal & Business Banking	
UK Personal & Business Banking	43
Ulster Bank	4
Commercial and Private Banking	
Commercial Banking	22
Private Banking	4
RBS International	4
NatWest Markets	17
Central items & other	2
Total	100

Selected Subsidiaries
Citizens Financial Group, Inc. (banking, US)
Coutts & Co (private banking)
Direct Line Insurance Group plc
National Westminster Bank Plc
The Royal Bank of Scotland plc
Ulster Bank Limited (Northern Ireland)

COMPETITORS
BANK OF AMERICA CORPORATION
COMMONWEALTH BANK OF AUSTRALIA
MEDIOBANCA S.P.A.
Nordea Bank AB
STANDARD CHARTERED PLC
Svenska Handelsbanken AB
The Toronto-Dominion Bank
UNICREDIT SPA
UniCredit Bank AG
WESTPAC BANKING CORPORATION

HISTORICAL FINANCIALS
Company Type: Public

Income Statement FYE: December 31

	ASSETS ($mil)	NET INCOME ($mil)	INCOME AS % OF ASSETS	EMPLOYEES
12/23	882,803	5,908	0.7%	61,600
12/22	866,819	4,320	0.5%	0
12/21	1,053,880	4,378	0.4%	58,735
12/20	1,091,070	(543)	0.0%	59,900
12/19	954,818	4,621	0.5%	62,900
Annual Growth	(1.9%)	6.3%	—	(0.5%)

2023 Year-End Financials
Return on assets: 0.6%   Dividends
Return on equity: 12.5%   Yield: —
Long-term debt ($ mil.): —   Payout: 64.7%
No. of shares ($ mil.): 8,991   Market value ($ mil.): 50,623
Sales ($ mil.): 32,349

	STOCK PRICE ($) FY Close	P/E High/Low	PER SHARE ($) Earnings	Dividends	Book Value
12/23	5.63	17 10	0.61	0.39	5.27
12/22	6.46	20 15	0.40	0.36	4.49
Annual Growth	(12.8%)	— —	10.7%	1.9%	4.1%

NEC Corp

EXECUTIVES

Chairman, Director, Takashi Niino
Representative Executive Officer, President, Chief Executive Officer, Director, Takayuki Morita
Chief Financial Officer, Director, Osamu Fujikawa
Director, Hajime Matsukura
Director, Shinobu Obata
Outside Director, Kuniharu Nakamura
Outside Director, Christina Ahmadjian
Outside Director, Masashi Oka
Outside Director, Kyoko Okada
Outside Director, Harufumi Mochizuki
Outside Director, Joji Okada
Outside Director, Yoshihito Yamada
Auditors: KPMG AZSA LLC

LOCATIONS

HQ: NEC Corp
5-7-1 Shiba, Minato-ku, Tokyo 108-8001
Phone: (81) 3 3454 1111
Web: www.nec.co.jp

HISTORICAL FINANCIALS
Company Type: Public

Income Statement FYE: March 31

	REVENUE ($mil)	NET INCOME ($mil)	NET PROFIT MARGIN	EMPLOYEES
03/23	24,875	859	3.5%	118,527
03/22	24,779	1,161	4.7%	117,418
03/21	27,040	1,351	5.0%	114,714
03/20	28,514	920	3.2%	112,638
03/19	26,307	362	1.4%	110,595
Annual Growth	(1.4%)	24.1%	—	1.7%

2023 Year-End Financials
Debt ratio: 0.1%   No. of shares ($ mil.): 266
Return on equity: 7.2%   Dividends
Cash ($ mil.): 3,149   Yield: —
Current Ratio: 1.46   Payout: 25.9%
Long-term debt ($ mil.): 2,408   Market value ($ mil.): —

Nedbank Group Ltd

Nedbank Group is one of the largest financial services group in Africa. The company offers a range of wholesale and retail banking services through its principal business clusters: Nedbank Corporate and Investment Banking, Nedbank Retail and Business Banking, Nedbank Wealth, Nedbank Africa Regions and Centre. Other services include property finance, credit card processing, insurance, and foreign exchange and securities trading. Nedbank has some 500 retail and commercial banking branches located primarily in South Africa's urban and suburban areas.

Operations

The company operates in five segments: Nedbank Retail and Business Banking (about 60% of sales), Nedbank Corporate and Investment Banking (over 25%), Nedbank Wealth (nearly 10%), Nedbank Africa Regions (around 5%), and Centre.

Nedbank Retail and Business Banking includes transactional accounts, home loans, vehicle and asset finance [including the Motor Finance Corporation (MFC)], card (both card-issuing and merchant-acquiring services), personal loans and investments. The business banking portfolio offers the full spectrum of commercial banking products and related services to entities.

Nedbank Corporate and Investment Banking offers the full spectrum of transactional, corporate, investment banking and markets solutions, characterized by a highly integrated partnership approach. These solutions include lending products, advisory services, leverage financing, trading, broking, structuring, hedging and client coverage.

Nedbank Wealth provides insurance, asset management and wealth management solutions to clients ranging from entry-level to high-net-worth individuals. Insurance provides life and non-life insurance solutions for individuals and businesses, including simple risk, funeral, vehicle, personal accident, credit life and investment solutions.

Nedbank Africa Regions is responsible for the group's banking operations and expansion activities on the rest of the African continent and has client-facing subsidiaries (retail and wholesale banking) in Eswatini, Lesotho, Namibia, Mozambique and Zimbabwe. The cluster also holds the around 20% investment in ETI, manages the Ecobank?Nedbank alliance and facilitates investment in other countries in Africa.

Centre is an aggregation of business operations that provide various support services to Nedbank Group Limited, and includes the following clusters: Group Finance; Group Technology; Group Strategic Planning and Economics; Group Human Resources; Group Compliance; Group Risk; and Group Marketing, Communications and Corporate Affairs. Centre also includes Group Balance Sheet Management, which is responsible for capital management, funding and liquidity risk management, the management of banking book interest rate risk, margin management and strategic portfolio tilt.

Overall, some 55% of sales were generated from net interest income, and the rest were generated from non-interest revenue and income, of which some 30% is frp, net commission and fees income.

In terms of loans, mortgage loans generated some 45%.

Geographic Reach

The company is headquartered in Sandton, South Africa.

Sales and Marketing

The Nedbank Retail serves the financial needs of all individuals (excluding high-net-worth individuals serviced by Nedbank Wealth) and small businesses.

Financial Performance

The company's revenue for fiscal 2021 increased to R57.5 billion compared to R54.2 billion in the prior year.

Net income for fiscal 2021 increased to R51.8 billion compared to R41.0 billion in the prior year.

Cash held by the company at the end of fiscal 2021 increased to R44.6 billion. Operating activities provided R12.1 billion while investing and financing activities used R2.1 billion and R7.4 billion, respectively.

Strategy

GIA's (Group Internal Audit) focus has been on fully implementing its digital transformation journey to align with the bank's digital strategy. The current skills mix, which includes data scientists, developers and cybersecurity specialists, will ensure GIA uses technology platforms effectively to obtain efficient and increased coverage, including data analytics and continuous auditing techniques.

EXECUTIVES

Chief Executive Officer, Executive Director, Michael William Thomas Brown
Chief Operating Officer, Executive Director, Mfundo Nkuhlu
Chief Financial Officer, Executive Director, Mike H. Davis
Secretary, Jackie Katzin
Non-Executive Chairman, P. Mpho Makwana
Lead Independent Director, Hubert Rene Brody
Independent Non-Executive Director, Brian A. Dames
Independent Non-Executive Director, Neo Phakama Dongwana
Independent Non-Executive Director, Errol M. Kruger
Independent Non-Executive Director, Rob A. G. Leith
Independent Non-Executive Director, Linda Makalima
Independent Non-Executive Director, Tshilidzi Marwala
Independent Non-Executive Director, Mantsika A. Matooane
Independent Non-Executive Director, Stanley S. Subramoney

Auditors: Ernst & Young Inc.

LOCATIONS

HQ: Nedbank Group Ltd
Nedbank 135 Rivonia Campus, 135 Rivonia Road, Sandown, Sandton 2196
Phone: (27) 11 294 4444 **Fax:** (27) 11 294 6540
Web: www.nedbankgroup.co.za

COMPETITORS

ACOM CO., LTD.
AIFUL CORPORATION
AMMB HOLDINGS BERHAD
BARCLAYS BANK PLC
HITACHI CAPITAL CORPORATION
HONG LEONG FINANCE LIMITED
HSBC Private Bank (Suisse) SA
RELIANCE CAPITAL LIMITED
SOR OR KOR PUBLIC COMPANY LIMITED
WELLS FARGO CAPITAL FINANCE (UK) LIMITED

HISTORICAL FINANCIALS

Company Type: Public

Income Statement — FYE: December 31

	ASSETS ($mil)	NET INCOME ($mil)	INCOME AS % OF ASSETS	EMPLOYEES
12/21	76,582	704	0.9%	0
12/20	83,695	236	0.3%	0
12/19	81,411	854	1.0%	29,403
12/18	72,600	930	1.3%	30,877
12/17	79,872	943	1.2%	31,531

Annual Growth (1.0%) (7.0%)

2021 Year-End Financials
Return on assets: 0.9%
Return on equity: 11.9%
Long-term debt ($ mil.): —
No. of shares ($ mil.): 485
Sales ($ mil.): 6,015
Dividends
Yield: 1.9%
Payout: 13.3%
Market value ($ mil.): 5,293

	STOCK PRICE ($) FY Close	P/E High/Low		PER SHARE ($) Earnings	Dividends	Book Value
12/21	10.90	1	0	1.42	0.21	12.85
12/20	8.83	2	1	0.48	0.65	12.53
12/19	15.40	1	1	1.75	0.76	12.96
12/18	19.32	1	1	1.89	0.77	12.21
12/17	20.68	1	1	1.93	0.77	13.80

Annual Growth (14.8%)   (7.3%) (27.5%) (1.8%)

Neste Oyj

Neste Oyj, or Neste Corporation in English (formerly Neste Oil), is the world's leading producer of sustainable aviation fuel, renewable diesel, and renewable feedstock solutions for various polymers and chemicals industry uses. Neste Oyj primarily sells its products domestically but also exports to customers in North America and Europe. It operates over 1,000 gas stations in Finland, Estonia, Latvia, and Lithuania. It has a crude oil refining capacity of some 10.5 million tons per year and renewable diesel production capacity of around 3.3 million tons per year. The company generated majority of its sales from Finland.

Operations

Neste Oyj operates through four segments: Oil Products (about 45% of sales), Renewable Products (nearly 35%), Marketing and Services (over 20%), and Other.

Oil Products produces, markets and sells an extensive range of low-carbon solutions that are based on high-quality oil products and related services to a global customer base. The product range includes diesel fuel, gasoline, aviation and marine fuels, light and heavy fuel oils, base oils, gasoline components, special fuels, such as small-engine gasoline, solvents, liquid gases, and bitumens.

Renewable Products produces, markets and sells renewable diesel, renewable jet fuels and solutions, renewable solvents as well as raw material for bioplastics based on Neste's proprietary technology to domestic and international wholesale markets. The Marketing & Services segment markets and sells cleaner fuels and oil products and associated services directly to end-users, of which the most important are private motorists, industry, transport companies, farmers, and heating oil customers. Other consists of the engineering and technology solutions company Neste Engineering Solutions and common corporate costs. Almost all of the company's sales were generated from the sale of goods.

Geographic Reach

Neste Oyj production facilities in Finland (headquarters), Singapore, the Netherlands and Bahrain and its retail sales network in Finland, Estonia, Latvia and Lithuania.

The company generated over 30% of sales from Finland, around 20% from North and South America, and about 10% from Baltic Rim.

Sales and Marketing

Neste Oyj serves a range of markets, including retailers, wholesale customers such as transport service companies, municipalities and other fleet owners or operators, airports, airlines, aviation fuel suppliers and corporate business travellers, as well as polymers and chemicals producers.

Financial Performance

Neste's revenue in 2021 totaled EUR15.1 billion (EUR11.8 billion). The change in revenue resulted from higher market and sales prices, which had a positive impact of approx.

In 2021, the company had a net income of EUR2 billion, a 149% increase from the previous year's net income of EUR786 million.

The company's cash at the end of 2021 was EUR1.7 billion. Operating activities generated EUR2 billion, while investing activities used EUR1.5 billion, mainly for purchases of property, plant and equipment. Financing activities used another EUR377 million, mainly for dividends paid.

Strategy

The company's strategy focuses on growing in renewable and circular solutions, creating readiness for the future, and boosting competitiveness and transformation. With the growth of renewable and circular solutions, it aims to help customers reduce their greenhouse gas emissions by at least 20 million tons of CO_2 annually by 2030. The company continues to serve existing and new customers with renewable and circular solutions, and by 2030, the company will have three strong renewables businesses: Renewable Aviation, Renewable Polymers and Chemicals, and Renewable Road Transportation. Growth in renewables also means expanding its production and raw material platform, which has been substantially strengthened through organic growth and acquisitions, and it will continue to grow the company's sourcing network and capabilities globally.

Company Background

In 2008 Neste Oil announced plans to build a major renewable diesel plant in Rotterdam, capable of producing 800,000 metric tons a day. Construction on the facility began in 2009. Completed in 2011 the plant expanded the company's green diesel production capacity to 2 million tons per year.

To expand its base oil business, the company completed a 400,000 metric tons-per-year joint venture base oil plant in Bahrain in 2011.

At the end of 2010, Neste Oil merged its Oil Products and Renewable Fuels businesses to create Oil Products and Renewables to improve operational efficiency and create synergies between the two businesses. That year the company posted a jump in revenues and income as the global economy bounced make from a recession. The rebound triggered stronger demand for oil and gas and higher commodity prices.

The Finnish government owns 50.1% of the company, which was founded shortly after WWII to ensure a steady oil supply for the country. Neste Oil was spun off by Fortum in 2005. In 2015, it changed its name to Neste Oyj (Neste Corporation).

EXECUTIVES

President, Chief Executive Officer, Peter E.V. Vanacker
Chief Financial Officer, Jyrki Maki-Kala
Sustainability and Corporate Affairs Senior Vice President, Minna Aila
Human Resources Senior Vice President, Hannele Jakosuo-Jansson
Innovation Senior Vice President, Lars Peter Lindfors
Renewable Polymers and Chemicals Executive Vice President, Mercedes Alonso
Marketing & Services Executive Vice President, Panu Kopra
Oil Products Executive Vice President, Markku Korvenranta
Renewable Aviation Executive Vice President, Thorsten Lange
Renewables Platform Executive Vice President, Matti Lehmus
Renewable Road Transportation Executive Vice President, Carl Nyberg
General Counsel, Christian Stahlberg
Chairman, Independent Director, Matti Kahkonen
Independent Non-Executive Director, John Abbott
Independent Non-Executive Director, Nick Elmslie
Independent Non-Executive Director, Martina Floel
Independent Non-Executive Director, Jean-Baptiste Renard
Independent Non-Executive Director, Jari Rosendal
Independent Non-Executive Director, Johanna Soderstrom
Independent Non-Executive Director, Marco Wiren
Auditors : KPMG OY AB

LOCATIONS

HQ: Neste Oyj
Keilaranta 21, Espoo 02150
Phone: (358) 10 458 11   **Fax:** (358) 10 458 4442
Web: www.neste.com

2013 Sales

	% of total
Europe	
Nordic countries	
Finland	46
Other	17
Baltic Rim	12
Other countries	25
North & South America	18
Other regions	2
Total	100

PRODUCTS/OPERATIONS

2013 Sales

	% of total
Oil products	65
Oil retail	22
Renewable fuels	12
Others	1
Total	100

COMPETITORS

COSMO OIL CO., LTD.
HOLLYFRONTIER CORPORATION
IDEMITSU KOSAN CO.,LTD.
INDIAN OIL CORPORATION LIMITED
Preem AB
REPSOL SA.
RS ENERGY K.K.
STATE OIL LIMITED
SURGUTNEFTEGAZ, PAO
Suncor Energy Inc

HISTORICAL FINANCIALS

Company Type: Public

Income Statement — FYE: December 31

	REVENUE ($mil)	NET INCOME ($mil)	NET PROFIT MARGIN	EMPLOYEES
12/22	27,456	2,016	7.3%	5,428
12/21	17,145	2,004	11.7%	4,845
12/20	14,421	873	6.1%	4,825
12/19	17,784	2,007	11.3%	4,413
12/18	17,084	890	5.2%	5,413
Annual Growth	12.6%	22.7%	—	0.1%

2022 Year-End Financials

Debt ratio: 15.7%
Return on equity: 24.6%
Cash ($ mil.): 1,357
Current Ratio: 1.92
Long-term debt ($ mil.): 1,644
No. of shares ($ mil.): 768
Dividends
  Yield: —
  Payout: 49.8%
Market value ($ mil.): 17,697

	STOCK PRICE ($) FY Close	P/E High/Low	PER SHARE ($) Earnings	Dividends	Book Value
12/22	23.04	11 7	2.63	1.31	11.57
12/21	24.50	16 10	2.60	0.79	10.29
12/20	36.52	39 13	1.14	0.58	9.47
12/19	17.32	30 7	2.60	0.42	8.66
12/18	38.20	287 120	0.02	0.98	0.10
Annual Growth	(11.9%)	—	250.5%	7.6%	225.1%

Nestle SA

Nestlé is one of the leading food and drinks companies that produces more than 2,000 brands including the world's leading coffee brand Nescafé, Haagen-Dazs ice cream, Purina pet food, DiGiorno pizza, KitKat chocolates, Perrier bottled water, and Starbucks Coffee At Home. The company's global business portfolio includes a wide range of brands from food and beverages to health care nutrition and petcare. Its brands, produced at around 355 factories globally, include global, regional, and local favorites. The Americas is Nestlé's biggest market. The company traces its roots back in 1866.

Operations

Nestlé's more than 2,000 brands are divided into seven product segments: Powdered and Liquid Beverages, PetCare, Nutrition and Health Science, Prepared Dishes and Cooking Aids, Milk Products and Ice Cream, Confectionary, and Water.

The Powdered and Liquid Beverages segment, which includes Nescafe, Nespresso, and Nesquik, generates more than 25% of sales.

PetCare makes pet food (about 20% of sales) under nine Purina sub-brands, including Felix and Pro Plan.

Nutrition and Health Science (approximately 15% of sales) sells baby food, infant nutrition, and skin care products under brands including Gerber, illuma, and Cerelac.

Prepared Dishes and Cooking Aids (nearly 15%) includes DiGiorno pizza and Maggi.

Milk Products and Ice Cream covers brands including Haagen-Dazs, Coffee Mate, and Nido and accounts for more than 10% of sales.

The Confectionery segment generated almost 10% of sales. The segment includes KitKat.

The Water segment consists of San Pellegrino water and soft drinks, Vittel, Perrier, and Pure Life. It generates some 5% of sales.

Geographic Reach

Nestlé divides its geographical operations across the regions of Americas (accounting for some 45% of sales); Europe, Middle East, and North Africa (approximately 30%); and Asia, Oceanic, and Africa (some 25%). The Swiss-based food giant has operations in some 185 countries worldwide and operates around 125 factories in Americas; about 135 in Europe, Middle East and North Africa; and nearly 95 in Asia, Oceanic and Africa.

Financial Performance

Company's revenue for fiscal 2021 increased by 3% to CHF 87.1 billion compared from the prior year with CHF 84.3 billion.

Profit for fiscal 2021 increased to CHF 16.9 billion compared from the prior year with CHF 12.2 billion.

Strategy

Nestle continued its portfolio transformation in 2021, investing in high-growth categories that contribute to its Nutrition, Health and Wellness strategy.

The company continue the strategic transformation of its global water business, completing the divestment of its North American Water brands. The focus is on its iconic international and premium mineral water brands as well as healthy hydration products. The acquisition of Essentia premium water expands its functional hydration offerings.

Beyond portfolio transformation, Nestle is investing in research and development (R&D) to make its portfolio more nutritious, delicious and sustainable. The company have increased capital expenditure to support its fast-growing categories ? particularly coffee and pet care ? to meet future demand.

Mergers and Acquisitions

In early 2022, Nestlé Health Science agreed to purchase a majority stake in Orgain, a leader in plant-based nutrition, from founder Dr. Andrew Abraham and Butterfly Equity, who will continue to be minority share owners. Orgain complements Nestlé Health Science's existing portfolio of nutrition products that support healthier lives.

In mid-2021, Nestlé Health Science announced the successful completion of its acquisition of the core brands of The Bountiful Company, including Nature's Bounty, Solgar, Osteo Bi-Flex, Puritan's Pride, Ester-C, and Sundown. The Bountiful Company is the number one pure-play leader in the highly attractive and growing global nutrition and supplement category. These brands will be integrated into Nestlé Health Science, creating a global leader in vitamins, minerals and nutritional supplements. The transaction price amounted to approximately $5.75 billion.

HISTORY

Henri Nestlé purchased a factory in Vevey, Switzerland, in 1843 that made products ranging from nut oils to rum. In 1867 he developed a powder made from cow's milk and wheat flour as a substitute for mother's milk. A year earlier Americans Charles and George Page had founded the Anglo-Swiss Condensed Milk Company in Cham, Switzerland, using Gail Borden's milk-canning technology.

In 1875 Nestlé sold his eponymous company, then doing business in 16 countries. When Anglo-Swiss launched a milk-based infant food in 1878, Nestlé's new owners responded by introducing a condensed-milk product. In 1905, a year after Nestlé began selling chocolate, the companies ended their rivalry by merging under the Nestlé name.

Hampered by limited milk supplies during WWI, the company expanded into regions less affected by the war, such as the US. In 1929 it acquired Cailler, the first company to mass-produce chocolate bars, and Swiss General, inventor of milk chocolate.

An investment in a Brazilian condensed-milk factory during the 1920s paid an unexpected dividend when Brazilian coffee growers suggested the company develop a water-soluble "coffee cube." Released in 1938, Nescafé instant coffee quickly became popular.

Other new products included Nestlé's Crunch bar (1938), Quik drink mix (1948), and Taster's Choice instant coffee (1966). Nestlé expanded during the 1970s with acquisitions such as Beringer Brothers wines (sold in 1995), Stouffer's, and Libby's.

Moving beyond foods in 1974, Nestlé acquired a 49% stake in Gesparal, a holding company that controls the French cosmetics company L'Oréal. It acquired pharmaceutical firm Alcon Laboratories three years later.

Helmut Maucher was named chairman and CEO in 1981. He began beefing up Nestlé's global presence. Boycotters had long accused Nestlé of harming children in developing countries through the unethical promotion of infant formula, and Maucher acknowledged the ongoing boycott by meeting with the critics and setting up a commission to police adherence to World Health Organization guidelines.

Nestlé bought Carnation in 1985. Maucher doubled the company's chocolate business in 1988 with the purchase of UK chocolate maker Rowntree (Kit Kat). Also in the 1980s Nestlé acquired Buitoni pastas.

The company expanded in the 1990s with the purchases of Butterfinger and Baby Ruth candies, Source Perrier water, Alpo pet food, and Ortega Mexican foods. Company veteran Peter Brabeck-Letmathe succeeded Maucher as CEO in 1997. He cleaned out Nestlé's pantry by selling non-core businesses (Contadina tomato products, Libby's canned meat products) but restocked with San Pellegrino (mineral water) and Dalgety's Spillers (pet food) in 1998.

By 1999 the company started rolling out its Nestlé Pure Life bottled water. It also sold its Findus brand (fish, vegetables) and its non-instant US coffee brands. That year Nestlé merged its US novelty ice-cream unit with operations of Pillsbury's Häagen-Dazs to form Ice Cream Partners USA. In 2000 Nestlé purchased snack maker PowerBar. In 2001 it bought Ralston Purina for $10.3 billion, making it the world's largest pet food maker. To win FTC approval, the companies agreed to sell Meow Mix and Alley Cat dry cat food brands to Hartz Mountain. In a deal that gives Nestlé a 99-year license to use the Häagen-Dazs brand in the US, the company agreed to pay $641 million to General Mills (which has bought Pillsbury from Britain's Diageo) for the other half of Ice Cream Partners.

In 2002 Nestlé acquired German ice-cream maker Schoeller Holding Group, as well as US food company Chef America, maker of Hot Pockets and Lean Pockets. That same year Nestlé also spun off eyecare subsidiary Alcon Laboratories, but retained about 75% ownership of it. The company renamed its water unit from Perrier Vittel SA to Nestlé Waters and bought Russian bottled water company Saint Springs. The company sold its savory flavor business, Food Ingredients Specialties (FIS), to Swiss flavoring company Givaudan, and its UK and Ireland ambient foods business to HM Capital Partners (then named Hicks, Muse, Tate & Furst). It also formed a joint venture with New Zealand dairy co-op Fonterra to produce and distribute dairy products in the Americas.

Nestlé and Cadbury Schweppes (now Cadbury) made a joint $10.5 billion bid for The Hershey Company in 2002 but Hershey called the sale off later that year.

While Nestlé already owned 30% of US ice cream powerhouse Dreyer's, in 2002 it proposed a merger of its US ice cream businesses. After months of antitrust scrutiny, the final deal gave Nestlé 67% of Dreyer's.

Seeking to further strengthen its position in the worldwide ice cream market, Nestlé acquired the ice cream and related products of Mövenpick, a Swiss food company 2003. The acquisition brought Nestlé licensing agreements with companies in Egypt, Finland, Germany, Norway, Sweden, and Saudi Arabia.

Other transactions in 2003 included the Nestlé USA unit selling its Ortega brand Mexican food products to B&G Foods and the parent company selling Mont Blanc, France's leading dessert brand, to French investment firm Activa Capital. Also that year the company added to its bottled-water business by acquiring Hutchison Whampoa's Powwow, which operates in Denmark, France, Germany, Italy, the Netherlands, Portugal, and the UK. In addition, it acquired Clear Water, a bottled-water home-and-office delivery company located in Russia.

In line with its strategy to concentrate on value-added products, in 2004 Nestlé sold its cocoa-processing facilities in Germany and the UK to Cargill. Also in 2004 the company acquired Finnish dairy company Valid's Valiojäätelö ice cream business and increased its stake in Israeli bakery company Osem to 53%. In addition, Nestlé sold its German frozen food distributor Eastman that year and Nestlé España bought Nestlé Portugal for about $682 million. Nestlé was ordered by the Brazilian government to sell its Chocolates Garoto in 2004 on the grounds that ownership of Garoto presented unfair market competition.

Later that same year, CEO Peter Brabeck-Letmathe announced he was considering reducing the number of outside directorships that he held because of increased demands as the leader of Nestlé. At the time Brabeck-Letmathe sat on the boards of Alcon, Credit Suisse, Dreyer's Grand Ice Cream, L'Oréal, Roche Holding, and "Winterthur" Swiss Insurance Company. (He has since left the "Winterthur" board.) And that year, in a tangle with a French union over retirement benefits, Nestlé threatened to sell Perrier or produce its popular water from another source. However, the company reached a settlement with the union and the production of Perrier continued.

Long-time chairman Rainer Gut retired in 2005 and Brabeck-Letmathe replaced him.

In 2005 it became a 90% owner of Dreyer's Grand Ice Cream. The next year, Nestlé became the owner of more than 90% of Dreyer's as the result of an exercise of a Put Right whereby Nestlé was required to purchase certain shareholders' Class A Callable Puttable Common Stock (or Class A shares). As a result of this "short form merger," Dreyer's ceased trading on the Nasdaq stock exchange.

In keeping with its strategy to concentrate on value-added products, during 2006 Nestlé sold its cocoa processing facilities in Germany and the UK to Cargill. Adding to its dominance in the European ice cream sector, the company acquired Finnish dairy company Valid's Valiojäätelö's ice cream business and Greece's Delta Ice cream, which has operations in Bulgaria, Greece, Macedonia, Montenegro, Romania, and Serbia. Later that year, Nestlé bought the Australian breakfast cereal, snack, and soup operations of Uncle Tobys from Burns Philp for $670 million. The cereal portion was integrated into Cereal Partners Worldwide. In another streamlining move, the company agreed to sell its canned liquid milk businesses in Southeast Asia to Singapore-based Fraser and Neave.

Hedging its bets, considering its food products (candy bars, ice cream) are on the opposite end of the waistline wars, Nestlé acquired Jenny Craig for $600 million in 2006.

In 2007 the company purchased the medical-nutrition business of Novartis for ?1.88 billion ($2.5 billion). The business, which has operations in 40 countries worldwide, makes food for hospital patients. The purchase was seen as a move by Nestlé to concentrate on higher-margin products. Brands in the acquisition included Boost and Resource nutritional supplements, and Optifast dieting products. Nestle divested some operations in France and Spain in order to settle competitive concerns surrounding the deal voiced by the European Commission.

On the food front, Nestlé subsidiary Dreyer's purchased the Eskimo Pie and Chipwich brands from Canadian ice cream maker, CoolBrands, in 2007 for almost $19 million.

Nestlé spooned out $5.5 billion in cash to purchase Gerber Products from Novartis in 2007. The deal made Nestlé the world's largest baby food company.

Due to the increased workload as chairman, Peter Brabeck-Letmathe stepped down as CEO in 2008; he remained in an active role as board chairman. Paul Bulcke, former head of Zone Americas for Nestlé, replaced Brabeck-Letmathe as CEO.

The company it added to its "out of home food and beverage" operations (i.e., foodservice) in 2009 with the purchase of Tampa-based Vitality Foodservice. Vitality provides commercial and non-commercial beverage services worldwide.

In August 2010 Nestlé acquired Liverpool-based Vitaflo, a maker of clinical nutrition products for people with metabolic disorders. Also in August it completed the sale of Alcon to Novartis. The pharmaceutical maker acquired Nestlé's stake in Alcon in two steps, beginning with the sale of a 25% stake for $11 billion in July 2008. Novartis exercised its option to buy Nestlé's remaining percentage of Alcon for $28 billion in 2010.

In November 2011, Nestlé acquired the Oscar stocks and sauces business from Paulig Group, building Nestlé Professional's presence in the culinary flavors sector. In late 2011 Nestlé paid $2.1 billion for a 60% interest in China-based confectionery Hsu Fu Chi. The deal put Nestlé at the helm of China's second-largest confectionery, and the purchase ranked as one of the largest foreign takeovers of a Chinese company.

In 2012 Nestlé made a historic $11.8 billion acquisition of Pfizer's nutrition business. The milestone deal enhanced Nestlé's infant nutrition business in key segments and geographies.

In July 2014, Nestlé acquired L'Oreal's 50% stake in Galderma, a joint venture formed by the two companies in 1981. Going forward, Galderma will operate as the pharmaceutical arm of Nestlé Skin Health S.A., established in June 2014 as a fully-owned Nestlé subsidiary.

EXECUTIVES

Executive Vice President, Laurent Freixe
Chief Executive Officer, Director, Ulf Mark Schneider

Executive Vice President, Marco Settembri
Executive Vice President, Chief Financial Officer, Francois-Xavier Roger
Research Executive Vice President, Innovation Technology Executive Vice President, Development Executive Vice President, Research Chief Technology Officer, Innovation Technology Chief Technology Officer, Development Chief Technology Officer, Stefan Palzer
Business Services Executive Vice President, Human Resources Executive Vice President, Beatrice Guillaume-Grabisch
Executive Vice President, General Counsel, Leanne Geale
Strategic Business Units, Marketing and Sales Executive Vice President, Bernard Meunier
Executive Vice President, Steven Wood Presley
Executive Vice President, Remy Ejel
Executive Vice President, David Xiqiang Zhang
Operations Executive Vice President, Stephanie Pullings Hart
Executive Vice President, David Rennie
Executive Vice President, Anna Mohl
Strategy Deputy Executive Vice President, Business Development Deputy Executive Vice President, Sanjay Bahadur
Deputy Executive Vice President, Chief Communications Officer, Lisa Gibby
Secretary, David P. Frick
Chairman, Director, Paul Bulcke
Vice-Chairman, Lead Independent Director, Henri de Castries
Director, Renato Fassbind
Director, Pablo Isla
Director, Patrick Aebischer
Director, Kimberly A. Ross
Director, Dick Boer
Director, Hanne de Mora
Director, Lindiwe Majele Sibanda
Director, Luca Maestri
Director, Chris Leong
Independent Director, Rainer Blair
Independent Director, Marie-Gabrielle Ineichen-Fleisch
Auditors : Ernst & Young Ltd

LOCATIONS

HQ: Nestle SA
Avenue Nestle 55, Vevey, Vaud CH 1800
Phone: (41) 21 924 2111 **Fax:** (41) 21 924 4800
Web: www.nestle.com

2018 sales

	% of total
Americas	45
EMENA	29
Zone Asia, Oceania and Africa	26
Total	100

2018 Factories

	No.
Americas	159
EMENA	146
Asia, Oceania & Africa	108
Total	413

PRODUCTS/OPERATIONS

2018 Product Sales

	% of total
Powdered & liquid beverages	24
Nutrition & health care	18
Milk products & ice cream	14
Prepared dishes & cooking aids	14
Pet care	13
Confectionery	9
Water	8
Total	100

Selected Products and Brands

Bouillons, soups, seasonings, pasta, and sauces
    Buitoni
    Maggi
    Thomy
    Winiary
Chilled Nestlé
    Chiquitin
    La Laitière
    La Lechera
    LC1
    Molico
    Ski
    Sveltesse
    Svelty
    Yoco
Chocolate, confectionery and biscuits
    Kit Kat
Coffee
    Bonka
    Loumidis
    Nescafé
    Nespresso
    Ricoré, Ricoffy
    Taster's Choice
    Zoégas
Foodservice and professional products
    Chef
    Davigel
    Minor's
    Santa Rica
Frozen foods (prepared dishes, pizzas)
    Buitoni
    California Pizza Kitchen (licensed)
    Delissio (Canada only)
    Hot Pockets
    Jack's Pizza
    Lean Cuisine
    Maggi
    Stouffer's
    Tombstone
Healthcare and nutrition
    Clinutren
    Modulen
    Nutren
    Peptamen
Ice cream
    Antica Gelateria del Corso
    Chipwich
    Dreyer's
    Drumstick/Extrême
    Edy's
    Eskimo Pie
    Häagen-Dazs
    Maxibon/Tandem
    Mega
    Mövenpick
    Parar
    Sin Parar/Sem
Infant food and nutrition
    Beba
    Cérélac
    Gerber
    Good Start
    Guigoz
    Lactogen
    Nan
    Neslac
    Nestlé
    Nestogen
    Nestum
Other beverages
    Carnation
    Caro
    Libby's
    Milo
    Nescau
    Nesquik
    Nestea
Performance nutrition
    PowerBar
    Pria
Pet care
    Alpo
    Beneful
    Cat Chow
    Dog Chow
    Fancy Feast
    Felix
    Gourmet
    Pro Plan
    Purina Friskies
    Purina ONE
    Tidy Cats
Refrigerated products (cold meat products, dough, pasta, pizzas, sauces)
    Buitoni
    Herta
    Nestlé
    Toll House
Shelf-stable products
    Bear Brand
    Carnation
    Coffee-Mate
    Gloria
    Klim
    La Lechera
    Milkmaid
    Moça
    Molico
    Nestlé Omega
    Nido
    Ninho
    Svelty
Water
    Acqua Panna
    Al Manhal
    Arrowhead
    Contrex
    Deer Park
    Hépar
    Ice Mountain
    Levissima
    Nestlé Aquarel
    Nestlé Pure Life
    Nestlé Vera
    Ozarka
    Perrier
    Poland Spring
    Quézac
    S.Pellegrino
    San Bernardo
    Vittel
    Zephyrhills

Selected Subsidiaries, Joint Ventures, and Affiliates

Beverage Partners Worldwide (50%, with The Coca-Cola Company, US)
Cereal Partners Worldwide (50%, with General Mills, US)
Galderma and Laboratoires innéov (29%, with L'Oreal, cosmetic and nutritional supplement products)
Gerber Products Company (infant nutrition, US)
Jenny Craig, Inc. (weight-loss centers and foods, US)
Uncle Tobys (soups, breakfast cereal, snacks, Australia)

COMPETITORS

Anheuser-Busch InBev
Axel Johnson AB
BUNZL PUBLIC LIMITED COMPANY
Barry Callebaut AG

DANONE
GENERAL MILLS, INC.
GREENCORE GROUP PUBLIC LIMITED COMPANY
GROUPE LACTALIS
Huhtamäki Oyj
UNILEVER PLC

HISTORICAL FINANCIALS
Company Type: Public

Income Statement   FYE: December 31

	REVENUE ($mil)	NET INCOME ($mil)	NET PROFIT MARGIN	EMPLOYEES
12/23	111,591	13,399	12.0%	270,000
12/22	102,741	10,048	9.8%	275,000
12/21	95,823	18,519	19.3%	276,000
12/20	96,148	13,888	14.4%	273,000
12/19	96,064	13,043	13.6%	291,000
Annual Growth	3.8%	0.7%	—	(1.9%)

2023 Year-End Financials

Debt ratio: 52.2%   No. of shares ($ mil.): 2,621
Return on equity: 28.8%   Dividends
Cash ($ mil.): 5,756   Yield: —
Current Ratio: 0.83   Payout: 69.6%
Long-term debt ($ mil.): 54,778   Market value ($ mil.): 303,102

	STOCK PRICE ($) FY Close	P/E High/Low		PER SHARE ($) Earnings	Dividends	Book Value
12/23	115.63	33	27	5.06	3.52	16.30
12/22	115.34	41	33	3.71	3.00	17.06
12/21	140.37	23	17	6.64	3.00	21.10
12/20	117.80	30	23	4.87	2.77	18.42
12/19	108.26	27	19	4.45	2.42	18.69
Annual Growth	1.7%	—	—	3.3%	9.8%	(3.4%)

NetEase, Inc

EXECUTIVES

Architect Chief Executive Officer, Director, William Lei Ding
Chief Financial Officer, Charles Zhaoxuan Yang
Independent Director, Alice Yu-Fen Cheng
Independent Director, Denny Ting Bun Lee
Independent Director, Joseph Tze Kay Tong
Independent Director, Lun Feng
Independent Director, Michael Man Kit Leung
Auditors : PricewaterhouseCoopers Zhong Tian LLP

LOCATIONS

HQ: NetEase, Inc
NetEase Building, No.599 Wangshang Road, Binjiang District, Hangzhou, Zhejiang Province 310052
Phone: (86) 571 8985 3378   **Fax:** (86) 10 8261 7823
Web: www.163.com

HISTORICAL FINANCIALS
Company Type: Public

Income Statement   FYE: December 31

	REVENUE ($mil)	NET INCOME ($mil)	NET PROFIT MARGIN	EMPLOYEES
12/22	13,987	2,948	21.1%	31,119
12/21	13,799	2,655	19.2%	32,064
12/20	11,263	1,844	16.4%	28,239
12/19	8,513	3,052	35.8%	20,797
12/18	9,763	894	9.2%	24,648
Annual Growth	9.4%	34.7%	—	6.0%

2022 Year-End Financials

Debt ratio: 2.3%   No. of shares ($ mil.): 3,223
Return on equity: 20.3%   Dividends
Cash ($ mil.): 15,921   Yield: —
Current Ratio: 2.32   Payout: 165.4%
Long-term debt ($ mil.): 529   Market value ($ mil.): 234,132

	STOCK PRICE ($) FY Close	P/E High/Low		PER SHARE ($) Earnings	Dividends	Book Value
12/22	72.63	17	9	0.89	1.48	4.71
12/21	101.78	27	16	0.79	0.82	4.59
12/20	95.77	149	23	0.55	0.92	3.75
12/19	306.64	49	32	0.94	1.96	2.74
12/18	235.37	173	99	0.27	0.33	2.06
Annual Growth	(25.5%)	—	—	34.3%	45.3%	23.0%

New World Development Co. Ltd.

New World Development Company (NWD) develops and invests in properties in Hong Kong, mainland China, and Southeast Asia. Its property and infrastructure developments include operations of roads, commercial aircraft leasing, construction, insurance, hotels, and other strategic business. Its portfolio includes development and investment in about 30 million sq. ft. of Hong Kong residential and commercial property and nearly 2.8 million sq. ft. in Mainland China, as well as investments in more than 15 hotels and department stores in Beijing, Shanghai, and other Chinese cities. NWD subsidiaries provide a diversified set of services in construction, aviation, roads, insurance, and investments. More than 60% of its total revenue accounts in Hong Kong.

Operations

NWD operates through seven segments: Property Development, Property Investments, Roads, Aviation, Construction, Insurance, Hotel Operations, and Others. Its three listed subsidiaries are New World China Land, NWS Holdings, and New World Department Store China (which has a network of more than 20 New World department stores, nearly 10 Ba Li Chun Tian department stores, and shopping malls in Shanghai).

Property development accounts for nearly 35% of revenue, while another nearly 30% from construction, and the remaining accounts in insurance, property investments, roads, hotel operations, and others.

Geographic Reach

Headquartered in Hong Kong's Central District, NWD operates in Hong Kong, mainland China. Its department stores are located in more than 15 major cities in mainland China including Beijing, Shanghai, and Chengdu.

More than 60% of its total revenue accounts in Hong Kong, while the remaining accounts in mainland China.

Sales and Marketing

The company marketing took place in the form of live broadcasting in its Mainland China properties due to the epidemic situation. Employees concerned from, sales and marketing, retail and digital marketing functions, have attended training about responsible marketing and advertising practices as well.

Financial Performance

In FY2020, the Company recorded consolidated revenues of HK$59.0 billion, which decreased by 23%. It was mainly attributable to the decline in contribution from the Hong Kong property development segment.

In FY2020, the Company's EBITDA amounted to HK$15.7 billion, of which EBITDA from Hong Kong and property-related segments accounted for 25% and 94%, respectively. In FY2019, EBITDA from Hong Kong and property-related segments accounted for 62% and 93%, respectively.

Cash held by the Company at the end of fiscal 2020 increased to HK$63.3 billion. Cash provided by financing activities was HK$ 28.5 billion while cash used for operations and investing activities were HK$10.3 billion and HK$17.1 billion, respectively. Main use for cash was additions of investment properties, property, plant and equipment, intangible assets and intangible concession rights.

Strategy

The Company continued with its strategy to dispose of non-core assets. In September 2019, the Company entered into an agreement to dispose of the entire interest in Hunan Success New Century Investment Company Limited at the consideration of RMB 2.2 billion subjects to the terms and conditions contained therein. The asset of this Company is Changsha La Ville New World. The disposal enables the Company to realize cash resources and unlock asset value at fair market value.

HISTORY

In 2004, NWS Holdings Limited, the group's infrastructure and service and rental operations, set up a 50/50 joint venture with Chow Tai Fook Enterprises Limited. The venture, Merryhill Group Limited, operates a range of transport services, including bus services, ferry services, and sightseeing ferry services.

In the same year, the New World also

inaugurated the Avenue of Stars, a tourist attraction honoring stars of Hong Kong's film industry. It also acquired its mobile service business unit, New World Mobile Holdings Limited, which offers mobile services, under the "New World Mobility" brand.

The company spun off its New World Department Store China unit in 2007; it plans to sell its Chinese herb and natural plant extracts provider Beijing New World Biotechnology Company to Walcom Group.

EXECUTIVES

Chairman, Executive Director, Henry Kar-Shun Cheng
Vice-Chairman, Chief Executive Officer, Executive Vice-Chairman, Executive Director, Adrian Chi-Kong Cheng
Executive Director, Chi-Heng Cheng
Executive Director, Chi-Man Cheng
Executive Director, Nam-Hoi Sitt
Executive Director, Echo Shaomei Huang
Executive Director, Jenny Wai-Han Chiu
Executive Director, Siu-Cheung Ma
Secretary, Man-Hoi Wong
Non-Executive Vice-Chairman, Non-Executive Director, William Wai Hoi Doo
Independent Non-Executive Director, Howard Ping-Leung Yeung
Independent Non-Executive Director, Hamilton Hau-Hay Ho
Independent Non-Executive Director, John Luen-Wai Lee
Independent Non-Executive Director, Thomas Cheung-Biu Liang
Independent Non-Executive Director, Albert Yuk-Keung Ip
Independent Non-Executive Director, Johnson Ow Chan
Non-Executive Director, Peter Kar-Shing Cheng
Auditors : PricewaterhouseCoopers

LOCATIONS

HQ: New World Development Co. Ltd.
  30/F., New World Tower, 16-18 Queen's Road Central,
Phone: (852) 2523 1056   **Fax:** (852) 2810 4673
Web: www.nwd.com.hk

PRODUCTS/OPERATIONS

2014 Sales

	% of total
Hong Kong	47
Mainland China	51
Others	2
Total	100

2014 Sales

	% of total
Property development	52
Property investment	4
Service	24
Infrastructure	4
Hotel operations	7
Department stores	7
Others	2
Total	100

COMPETITORS

ARVAL PHH HOLDINGS LIMITED
BUREAU VERITAS
CARILLION PLC
HANG LUNG PROPERTIES LIMITED
JOHN LAING LIMITED
JOHN SWIRE & SONS LIMITED
Link Real Estate Investment Trust
THE SYMPHONY GROUP PLC
TRANSPERFECT TRANSLATIONS INTERNATIONAL INC.
VIAD CORP

HISTORICAL FINANCIALS
Company Type: Public

Income Statement   FYE: June 30

	REVENUE ($mil)	NET INCOME ($mil)	NET PROFIT MARGIN	EMPLOYEES
06/23	12,149	114	0.9%	28,000
06/22	8,694	159	1.8%	28,000
06/21	8,785	150	1.7%	30,000
06/20	7,613	141	1.9%	44,000
06/19	9,830	2,325	23.7%	45,000
Annual Growth	5.4%	(52.8%)	—	(11.2%)

2023 Year-End Financials

Debt ratio: 3.9%   No. of shares ($ mil.): 2,516
Return on equity: 0.3%   Dividends
Cash ($ mil.): 6,796   Yield: 9.0%
Current Ratio: 0.96   Payout: 213.6%
Long-term debt ($ mil.): 17,637 Market value ($ mil.): 2,970

	STOCK PRICE ($) FY Close	P/E High/Low	PER SHARE ($) Earnings	Dividends	Book Value
06/23	1.18	5 3	0.05	0.11	12.35
06/22	1.76	5 3	0.06	0.11	6.61
06/21	2.59	20 5	0.06	0.11	6.89
06/20	2.30	8 4	0.06	0.11	6.33
06/19	3.07	1 0	0.91	0.10	6.15
Annual Growth	(21.3%)	—	(51.7%)	0.9%	19.0%

NH Foods Ltd

NH Foods (formerly Nippon Meat Packers) is one of Japan's top beef-, pork-, and chicken-processing firms. Its meat business includes all stages of production, from raising the animals and making their feed to processing the meat and delivering it to customers. NH Foods sells processed hams, sausages, and deli meats. Its fresh meat business includes chicken and other poultry, beef, and pork. The company owns some 155 farms, nearly 95 plants, about 320 sales and logistics facilities, and some 3 R&D labs. It also offers cheese and yogurt products under brands ROLF and Luna. Outside Japan, the NH Foods Group maintains operations in about 85 locations in 19 countries and regions.

EXECUTIVES

Chairman, Director, Tetsuhiro Kito
President, Representative Director, Nobuhisa Ikawa
Director, Fumio Maeda
Director, Masahito Kataoka
Director, Kohei Akiyama
Outside Director, Yasuko Kono
Outside Director, Hideo Arase
Outside Director, Tokushi Yamasaki
Auditors : Deloitte Touche Tohmatsu LLC

LOCATIONS

HQ: NH Foods Ltd
  BREEZE TOWER, 2-4-9 Umeda, Kita-ku, Osaka 530-0001
Phone: (81) 6 7525 3042
Web: www.nipponham.co.jp

2016 Sales

	% of total
Japan	90
Other countries	10
Total	100

PRODUCTS/OPERATIONS

2016 Sales

	% of total
Fresh Meats Business Division	63
Processed Foods Business Division	26
Affiliated Business Division	11
Total	100

2016 Sales

	% of total
Fresh meats	58
Processed foods	18
Hams and sausages	11
Marine products	8
Dairy products	2
Others	3
Total	100

Selected Divisions and Businesses
Affiliated
Hoko Co., Ltd
Marine Foods Corporation
Nippon Dry Foods Co., Ltd.
Nippon Luna, Inc.
Fresh meat
Day-Lee Foods, Inc.
Higashi Nippon Food, Inc.
Interfarm Co., Ltd.
Japan Food Corporation
Kanto Nippon Food, Inc.
Naka Nippon Food, Inc.
Nippon Food Group
Nippon Meat Packers Australia Pty. Ltd.
Nippon Pure Food, Inc.
Nippon White Farm Co., Ltd.
Nishi Nippon Food, Inc.
Texas Farm, LLC
Processed foods
Hakodate Carl Raymon Co., Ltd.
Kamakura Ham Tomioka Co., Ltd.
Shandong Rilong Foodstuffs Co., Ltd.
Thai Nippon Foods Co., Ltd.

COMPETITORS

A. Moksel GmbH
AMERICAN FOODS GROUP, LLC
HORMEL FOODS CORPORATION
LINDEN FOODS LIMITED
Maple Leaf Foods Inc
Marfrig Global Foods S/A
SMITHFIELD FOODS, INC.
SMITHFIELD PACKAGED MEATS CORP.
TYSON FOODS, INC.
TYSON FRESH MEATS, INC.

HISTORICAL FINANCIALS

Company Type: Public

Income Statement — FYE: March 31

	REVENUE ($mil)	NET INCOME ($mil)	NET PROFIT MARGIN	EMPLOYEES
03/23	9,458	124	1.3%	27,050
03/22	9,654	395	4.1%	27,649
03/21	10,621	294	2.8%	29,390
03/20	11,329	177	1.6%	30,130
03/19	11,144	176	1.6%	30,840
Annual Growth	(4.0%)	(8.3%)	—	(3.2%)

2023 Year-End Financials

Debt ratio: 0.2%
Return on equity: 3.4%
Cash ($ mil.): 487
Current Ratio: 1.54
Long-term debt ($ mil.): 744
No. of shares ($ mil.): 102
Dividends
Yield: —
Payout: 67.7%
Market value ($ mil.): —

Nidec Corp

Nidec claims to be the #1 comprehensive motor manufacturer for everything that spins and moves, from the smallest motors to some of the largest. The company holds the largest global market share for the automotive motors such as electric power steering motors and brake motors. It is primarily engaged in the development, manufacturing, and sales of small precision motors, automotive motors, home appliance motors, commercial and industrial motors, motors for machinery, electronic and optical components, and other related products. China is the company's largest markets, with around 25% of sales. Nidec was founded in 1973 by Shigenobu Nagamori and three other engineers as Nippon Densan Corporation.

Operations

The company operates in eight segments: ACIM (around 35% of sales), SPMS (over 15%), AMEC (some 10%), Nidec Sankyo (about 10%), Nidec Techno Motor (some 5%), Nidec Mobility (approximately 5%), Nidec Shimpo (roughly 5%), and Other (about 15%).

The ACIM segment mainly conducts research and development of motors, gears and control units for residential, commercial, home appliance and industrial uses, with respect to vehicle driving motors, encoders, elevator components and systems for industrial automation.

In the SPMS segment, research and development activities are currently conducted basic and applied research on precision small motors in general, such as precision small DC motors and fan motors, research and development for new products, and research to provide technical support to other research bases.

The AMEC segment is engaged in R&D aimed at the mass production of new products and new models of various in vehicle motors, including those for driving electric vehicles (EVs), which will contribute to the realization of a decarbonized society, and at the improvement of product quality.

The Nidec Sankyo segment develops stepping motors, smartphone/game-related products, motor drive unit products and system device-related products as part of its line-up of "karakuri-tronics" products integrating its "karakuri," or internal device mechanism technologies, with the motor technologies and servo technologies developed through its business diversification.

The Nidec Techno Motor segment develops air conditioner and home appliance motors in Fukui Prefecture in Japan and industrial motors in Fukuoka Prefectures in Japan.

The Nidec Mobility segment has development and design functions in six countries based on its automotive body control business and power electronics business. In the Body Control Business, it mainly develops body control modules, door peripheral control units including power window switches, and smart systems for motorcycles. In the Power Electronics Business, it mainly develops electric power steering, DC/DC converters for electric vehicles, and in-vehicle chargers.

In the Nidec Shimpo segment, it is developing products for reduction engines using integrated mechanical and electrical technologies in Japan, China and Germany. In addition, for press engine series product the company is developing a wide range of products in Japan, the US, and Spain, from compact high-speed precision presses to ultra-large servo presses, as well as peripheral high-speed feed devices.

In the Others segment, research and development activities are currently conducted on automotive products, machinery, electronic components and other small precision motors and others.

Among its products, appliance, commercial and industrial products account for over 40% of sales, followed by small precision motors with more than 20%, automotive products with over 20%, machinery with about 10%, and electronic and optical components with nearly 5%.

Geographic Reach

Headquartered in Kyoto, Japan, Nidec's largest single market is China, which accounts for around 25% of sales. The sales from the US accounts for more than 20%, Japan with nearly 20%, Thailand with about 5%, Germany and Italy, with roughly 10% combined, and the rest were generated from other countries.

Financial Performance

Consolidated net sales from continuing operations increased 19% to Â¥1.9 trillion for this fiscal year compared to the previous fiscal year of Â¥1.6 trillion.

In 2021, the company had a net profit of Â¥136.8 billion, a 12% increase from the previous year's net income of Â¥122.6 billion.

The company's cash for the year ended 2022 was Â¥199.7 billion. Operating activities generated Â¥95 billion, while investing activities used Â¥112.6 billion, mainly for additions to property, plant and equipment. Financing activities used another Â¥64.4 billion, primarily for purchase of treasury stock.

Strategy

NIDEC announces that it will achieve carbon neutrality in FY2040 as a major pillar of its new medium-term strategic goal Vision2025 and materiality initiatives, with the aim of contributing to the realization of a carbon-free society. To achieve this target, the company will first aim to substantially reduce the CO2 that NIDEC emits directly through its business activities at present (Scope 1), and CO2 that is emitted in the production stage of heat or energy used in business activities (Scope 2), by making its businesses more energy efficient and proactively introducing renewable energies. After building a solid foundation for renewable energy oriented CO2 emissions reduction, NIDEC will promote a shift to energy-saving, low-carbon fuels and employ carbon offset investments and other measures, thereby achieving carbon neutrality in its business activities in FY2040.

Mergers and Acquisitions

In early 2021, Nidec Corporation has completed the acquisitions of the shares of Japan-based Mitsubishi Heavy Industries Machine Tool Co., Ltd., a company that designs, manufactures, and sells machine tools, cutting tools, and related products, from Mitsubishi Heavy Industries, Ltd.; all the Mitsubishi Heavy Industries Group-owned shares of three overseas subsidiaries located in China, India, and the US that specialized in machine tool business; and the machine tool business run by overseas subsidiaries. The acquisition of machine tool business achieves a mutual complement with its existing businesses. Synergies are expected particularly in the machinery business, element technology development, manufacturing, sales, and other areas of its group's businesses. Terms were not disclosed.

HISTORY

A top engineer at tape deck manufacturer TEAC and machine tool maker Yamashina Siki in the early 1970s, Shigenobu Nagamori had developed a reputation as a brilliant engineer, but also as a young gun who was resistant to conformity and too indulged in personal challenges. Nagamori wasted no time in fulfilling his childhood dream of owning his own business. He lured away three engineers to start Nippon Densan Corporation (Nidec) out of his own home in 1973 when he was 29.

Nagamori knew he would have trouble selling his motors in Japan without an established reputation. (Most small businesses in Japan are founded with the acceptance that they will never grow beyond the role of subcontractor to one of the country's giant corporations.) But inspired by ancient Japanese traditions of self-determination and individualism, Nagamori decided to bypass the modern power structure and pitch his products overseas in the US. He arrived unannounced at 3M with a suitcase full of tiny motors. Despite his nervous presentation, 3M was impressed with the quality of Nidec motors and placed a small order.

In 1976 Nagamori established Nidec America Corporation to foster growing business in the US. The initial contract with 3M had ballooned into regular orders for thousands of motors, which 3M used in its high-speed cassette duplicators.

Still unable to secure a business loan in Japan, Nidec's staff took voluntary pay cuts to stay in business. (3M later offered a letter of credit on Nidec's behalf, forcing Japanese banks to reconsider.) Nagamori struggled to retain employees, who sought stability that only established companies such as NEC or Hitachi could provide. But Nagamori constantly improved his motors, which opened doors into new markets (computer disk drives) and kept the business alive.

EXECUTIVES

Chairman, Chief Executive Officer, Representative Director, Shigenobu Nagamori
President, Chief Operating Officer, Representative Director, Hiroshi Kobe
Director, Kazuya Murakami
Director, Hiroyuki Ochiai
Outside Director, Shinichi Sato
Outside Director, Yayoi Komatsu
Outside Director, Takako Sakai
Outside Director, Aya Yamada
Outside Director, Junko Watanabe
Outside Director, Hiroe Toyoshima
Auditors : PricewaterhouseCoopers Kyoto

LOCATIONS

HQ: Nidec Corp
338 Kuzetonoshiro-cho, Minami-ku, Kyoto 601-8205
Phone: (81) 75 935 6200   **Fax:** (81) 75 935 6101
Web: www.nidec.com

2018 Sales

	% of total
China	23
Japan	20
US	17
Thailand	9
Germany	9
Singapore	3
Other countries	19
Total	100

PRODUCTS/OPERATIONS

2018 Sales

	% of total
Nidec Motor	23
Nidec Motor & Actuators	16
Nidec Corporation	11
Nidec Sankyo	8
Nidec (H.K.)	7
Nidec Electronics (Thailand)	6
Nidec Techno Motor	5
Nidec Singapore	2
Nidec Copal	2
All Others	20
Total	100

2018 Sales

	% of total
Appliance, commercial and industrial products	35
Small precision motors	29
Automotive products	19
Machinery	12
Electronic and optical components	5
Other	
Total	

Selected Products
Mid-size DC motors
Pivot assemblies
Power supplies
Small high-precision AC motors
Small high-precision DC motors
Small high-precision fans

COMPETITORS

ALLIED MOTION TECHNOLOGIES INC.
BWX TECHNOLOGIES, INC.
ELECTROCOMPONENTS PUBLIC LIMITED COMPANY
GENERAC HOLDINGS INC.
GKN LIMITED
LENNOX INTERNATIONAL INC.
Nordex SE
PANASONIC CORPORATION
REGAL BELOIT CORPORATION
ZAP

HISTORICAL FINANCIALS
Company Type: Public

Income Statement   FYE: March 31

	REVENUE ($mil)	NET INCOME ($mil)	NET PROFIT MARGIN	EMPLOYEES
03/23	16,839	337	2.0%	128,002
03/22	15,769	1,125	7.1%	142,348
03/21	14,613	1,101	7.5%	136,186
03/20	14,139	553	3.9%	145,169
03/19	13,710	1,000	7.3%	137,791
Annual Growth	5.3%	(23.8%)	—	(1.8%)

2023 Year-End Financials
Debt ratio: 0.2%
Return on equity: 3.3%
Cash ($ mil.): 1,397
Current Ratio: 1.54
Long-term debt ($ mil.): 3,267
No. of shares ($ mil.): 575
Dividends
 Yield: 1.0%
 Payout: 0.0%
Market value ($ mil.): 7,472

	STOCK PRICE ($) FY Close	P/E High/Low	PER SHARE ($) Earnings	Dividends	Book Value
03/23	12.99	0 0	0.59	0.13	17.68
03/22	19.80	0 0	1.93	0.13	18.31
03/21	30.62	0 0	1.88	0.21	16.90
03/20	26.34	0 0	0.94	0.25	14.93
03/19	31.88	0 0	1.70	0.11	15.30
Annual Growth	(20.1%)	— (23.3%)	4.1%	3.7%

Nine Dragons Paper (Holdings) Limited

EXECUTIVES

Chairlady, Executive Chairlady, Yan Cheung
Deputy Chairman, Chief Executive Officer, Executive Deputy Chairman, Ming Chung Liu
Deputy Chairman, Deputy Chief Executive, Executive Deputy Chairman, Executive Director, Cheng Fei Zhang
Deputy Chairman, Vice President, Executive Deputy Chairman, Ken Liu
Vice President, Executive Director, Chun Shun Lau
Vice President, Executive Director, Lianpeng Zhang
Chief Financial Officer, Executive Director, Yuanfu Zhang
Executive Vice President, Michael LaVerdiere
Finance Assistant Controller, Finance Deputy Chief Financial Officer, Lianru Zhang
Deputy Chief Financial Officer, Ricky Yiu Kuen Chu
Investor Relations Director, Ho Yi Wan
Secretary, Judy Wai Chu Cheng
Independent Non-Executive Director, Maria Wai Chun Tam
Independent Non-Executive Director, Leung Sing Ng
Independent Non-Executive Director, Yiu Kin Lam
Independent Non-Executive Director, Kefu Chen
Auditors : PricewaterhouseCoopers

LOCATIONS

HQ: Nine Dragons Paper (Holdings) Limited
Unit 1, 22/F., One Harbour Square, 181 Hoi Bun Road, Kwun Tong, Kowloon.
Phone: (852) 3929 3800   **Fax:** (852) 3929 3890
Web: www.ndpaper.com

HISTORICAL FINANCIALS
Company Type: Public

Income Statement   FYE: June 30

	REVENUE ($mil)	NET INCOME ($mil)	NET PROFIT MARGIN	EMPLOYEES
06/22	9,627	488	5.1%	20,098
06/21	9,536	1,099	11.5%	19,599
06/20	7,258	589	8.1%	18,740
06/19	7,954	561	7.1%	18,500
06/18	7,972	1,185	14.9%	18,000
Annual Growth	4.8%	(19.9%)		2.8%

2022 Year-End Financials
Debt ratio: 6.2%
Return on equity: 7.0%
Cash ($ mil.): 1,446
Current Ratio: 1.79
Long-term debt ($ mil.): 5,499
No. of shares ($ mil.): 4,692
Dividends
 Yield: —
 Payout: 1428.5%
Market value ($ mil.): —

Nintendo Co., Ltd.

Nintendo wants everyone -- from apprentice Marios to alpha Donkey KongsÂ -- to play, preferably on one of its Nintendo DS handheld devices or its Wii home video game console. The market-leading game company achieved its status in part byÂ courting users that span generationsÂ and skill levels. Among the Big Three of the videogame console makers, Nintendo's Wii (pronounced "we") is #1, battling with Microsoft'sÂ Xbox and Sony's PlayStation for the hearts and dollars ofÂ devoted gamers. Also leading in handheld consoles, its DS device began in 2004,Â the most recent incarnation its no-glasses 3-D version launched in 2011, the 3DS. Wii successor Wii U, featuring aÂ controller with a touch screen, is planned for 2012.

HISTORY

Nintendo Co. was founded in 1889 as the Marufuku Company to make and sell hanafuda, Japanese game cards. In 1907 the company began producing Western playing cards. It became the Nintendo Playing Card Company in 1951 and began making theme cards under a licensing agreement with Disney in 1959.

During the 1950s and 1960s, Hiroshi Yamauchi took the company public and diversified into new areas (including a "love hotel"). The company took its current name in 1963. Nintendo began making toys at the start of the 1970s and entered the budding field of video games toward the end of the decade by licensing Magnavox's Pong technology. Then it moved into arcade games. Nintendo established its US subsidiary, Nintendo of America, in 1980; its first hit was Donkey Kong ("silly monkey") and its next was Super Mario Bros. (named after Nintendo of America's warehouse landlord).

The company released Famicom, a technologically advanced home video game system, in Japan in 1983. With its high-quality sound and graphics, Famicom was a smash, selling 15.2 million consoles and more than 183 million game cartridges in Japan alone. Meanwhile, in 1983 and 1984, the US home game market crashed, sending pioneer Atari up in flames. Nintendo persevered, successfully launching Famicom in the US in 1986 as the Nintendo Entertainment System (NES).

To prevent a barrage of independently produced, low-quality software (which had contributed to Atari's demise), Nintendo established stringent licensing policies for its software developers. Licensees were required to have approval of every game design, buy the blank cartridges from the company, agree not to make the game for any of Nintendo's competitors, and pay Nintendo royalties for the honor of developing a game.

As the market became saturated, Nintendo sought new products, releasing Game Boy in 1989 and the Super Family Computer game system (Super NES in the US) in 1991. The company broke with tradition in 1994 by making design alliances with companies like Silicon Graphics. After creating a 32-bit product in 1995, Nintendo launched the much-touted N64 game system in 1996. It also teamed with Microsoft and Nomura Research Institute on a satellite-delivered Internet system for Japan. Price wars between the top contenders continued in the US and Japan.

In 1998 Nintendo released PokÃ©mon, which involves trading and training virtual monsters (it had been popular in Japan since 1996), in the US. The company also launched the video game The Legend of Zelda: Ocarina of Time , which sold 2.5 million units in about six weeks. Nintendo issued 50 new games for 1998, compared to Sony's 131.

Nintendo announced in 1999 that its next-generation game system, Dolphin (later renamed GameCube), would use IBM's PowerPC microprocessor and Matsushita's (now Panasonic) DVD players.

The company bought a 3% stake in convenience store operator LAWSON in early 2000 in hopes of using its online operations to sell video games. Nintendo also teamed with advertising agency Dentsu to form ND Cube, a joint company that develops game software for mobile phones and portable machines.

In September 2001 Nintendo launched its long-awaited GameCube console system (which retailed at $100 less than its console rivals, Sony's PlayStation 2 and Microsoft's XBox); the system debuted in North America in November. In addition, the company came out with Game Boy Advance, its newest handheld model with a bigger screen and faster chip.

In April 2003 the company cut its royalty rates (charged to outside game developers), in an effort to enhance its video game titles portfolio. Later in the year Nintendo bought a stake (about 3%) in game developer and toy maker Bandai, a move expected to solidify cooperation between the two companies in marketing game software.

As part of its concentration on games, the company spun off its video game quality assurance division in 2009.

EXECUTIVES

President, Representative Director, Shuntaro Furukawa
Fellow, Representative Director, Shigeru Miyamoto
Senior Managing Executive Officer, Director, Shinya Takahashi
Director, Satoru Shibata
Director, Ko Shiota
Outside Director, Chris Meledandri
Director, Takuya Yoshimura
Outside Director, Katsuhiro Umeyama
Outside Director, Masao Yamazaki
Outside Director, Asa Shinkawa
Auditors : PricewaterhouseCoopers Kyoto

LOCATIONS

HQ: Nintendo Co., Ltd.
11-1 Kamitoba Hokotate-cho, Minami-ku, Kyoto 601-8501
Phone: (81) 75 662 9600
Web: www.nintendo.co.jp

2012 Sales

	% of total
The Americas	
US	33
Other Americas	6
Europe	33
Japan	23
Other	5
Total	100

PRODUCTS/OPERATIONS

2012 Sales

	% of total
Handheld Hardware	36
Handheld Software	20
Home Console Software	18
Home Console Hardware	18
Other	8
Total	100

Selected Consoles
3DS
3DS XL
DS
DS Lite
DSi
DSi XL
Wii
Wii U

Selected Games
Donkey Kong Country Returns
Kid Icarus: Uprising
Kirby Tilt 'n' Tumble
The Legend of Zelda
Mario & Sonic at the London 2012 Olympic Games
Mario Kart
Mario Party
Metroid Prime
Pokémon
Punch-Out!!
Sin and Punishment: Star Successor
Spider-Man
Super Mario Galaxy
Super Smash Bros. Brawl
Wii Fit Plus
Wii Play
Wii Sports Resort
Xenoblade Chronicles
Yoshi

Selected Subsidiaries
Nintendo Australia Pty. Ltd.
Nintendo Benelux B.V. (The Netherlands)
Nintendo Espa?a, S.A. (Spain)
Nintendo France S.A.R.L.
Nintendo of America, Inc. (US)
Nintendo of Canada Ltd.
Nintendo of Europe GmbH (Germany)

COMPETITORS

ATARI SA
EVERI GAMES HOLDING INC.
GAMELOFT SE
GAMEPLAY (GB) LIMITED
JAKKS PACIFIC, INC.
Mad Catz Interactive, Inc
SEGA CORPORATION

SONY CORPORATION
UBISOFT ENTERTAINMENT
WIZARDS OF THE COAST LLC

HISTORICAL FINANCIALS
Company Type: Public

Income Statement   FYE: March 31

	REVENUE ($mil)	NET INCOME ($mil)	NET PROFIT MARGIN	EMPLOYEES
03/23	12,025	3,249	27.0%	7,317
03/22	13,937	3,927	28.2%	6,717
03/21	15,885	4,338	27.3%	6,574
03/20	12,054	2,382	19.8%	6,200
03/19	10,840	1,751	16.2%	5,944
Annual Growth	2.6%	16.7%	—	5.3%

2023 Year-End Financials

Debt ratio: —   No. of shares ($ mil.): 1,164
Return on equity: 19.9%   Dividends
Cash ($ mil.): 9,488   Yield: 8.6%
Current Ratio: 4.34   Payout: 0.0%
Long-term debt ($ mil.): —   Market value ($ mil.): 11,281

	STOCK PRICE ($) FY Close	P/E High/Low		PER SHARE ($) Earnings	Dividends	Book Value
03/23	9.69	0	0	2.79	0.84	14.62
03/22	62.91	0	0	3.33	2.28	14.50
03/21	70.80	0	0	3.64	1.92	14.21
03/20	48.28	0	0	2.00	1.05	11.91
03/19	35.87	0	0	1.46	0.15	10.69
Annual Growth	(27.9%)	—	—	17.6%	54.2%	8.1%

Nippon Express Holdings Inc

Nippon Express us one of the world's leading companies with about 740 locations, spanning roughly 50 countries/regions. Besides general freight transportation, Nippon Express offers moving services and transportation of items such as cash and construction equipment. Nippon Express also provides warehousing services and air, ocean, and rail freight forwarding. The company operates from facilities throughout Japan, which accounts for the vast majority of its sale. Founded in 1937, Nippon Express also sells petroleum products and leases containers.

Operations
The company operates four segment reportable segments: Logistics, Logistic Support, Security Transportation, and Heavy Haulage & Construction.

The Nippon Express' logistics segment has grown as transport modes have expanded from railways to automobiles, ships, and airplanes. It generates around 80% of total revenue.

Logistic Support segment generates about 15% of total revenue, includes the sale e of distribution equipment, wrapping and packaging materials, vehicles, petroleum, liquefied petroleum (LP) gas, etc., lease, vehicle maintenance, insurance agency, mediation, planning, designing and management of real estate, investigation and research, logistics finance, automobile driving instruction, employee dispatching.

Security Transportation include security guard, and motor cargo transportation. Heavy Haulage & Construction includes heavy haulage and construction. Each of which accounts to a combined some 5% of Nippon Express' revenue.

Geographic Reach
The company operates in Japan, the Americas and Europe, and stretching into the rapidly developing markets of East Asia, South Asia and Oceania. It maintains a global presence with about 740 locations in some 310 cities spanning about 50 countries.

Sales and Marketing
The company caters to industries such as automotive, electric & telecommunications, fashion & retail, food, aerospace & aviation, railway, and pharmaceuticals.

Financial Performance
The company's revenue for fiscal 2022 decreased to JPY 1.8 trillion compared from the prior year with JPY 2.1 trillion.

Net income for fiscal 2022 decreased to JPY 54.0 billion compared from the prior year with JPY 56.1 billion.

Cash held by the company at the end of fiscal 2022 decreased to JPY 131.8 billion. Cash provided by operations and financing activities were JPY 155.4 billion and JPY 196.8 billion, respectively.

Strategy
In January 2022, the company transitioned to a holding company structure and made a fresh start with NIPPON EXPRESS HOLDINGS, INC. as its holding company.

By transitioning to a holding structure, the company will accelerate its global M&A strategy, which is essential for medium- to long-term corporate value enhancement, while implementing sustainable management from a long-term perspective, to become a logistics company with a presence in the global market, as stated in our long-term vision.

EXECUTIVES
Chairman, Representative Director, Kenji Watanabe
President, Representative Director, Mitsuru Saito
Director, Mamoru Akaishi
Outside Director, Sadako Yasuoka
Outside Director, Yojiro Shiba
Outside Director, Yumiko Ito
Auditors : Deloitte Touche Tohmatsu LLC

LOCATIONS
HQ: Nippon Express Holdings Inc
2 Kanda-Izumicho, Chiyoda-ku, Tokyo 101-8647
Phone: (81) 3 5801 1000
Web: www.nipponexpress-holdings.com

PRODUCTS/OPERATIONS
2015 Sales

	% of total
Combined business	39
Goods sales	22
Air freight forwarding	11
Marine & harbor transportation	6
Others	22
Total	100

Selected Services
Air Freight
Fine Arts Transport
Heavy Haulage
Logistics Design & IT
Marine Transport
Moving Service

COMPETITORS
A&R LOGISTICS, INC.
ABF FREIGHT SYSTEM, INC.
EUROPA EUROPEAN EXPRESS LIMITED
EXEL INC.
MAINFREIGHT, INC.
NIPPON YUSEN KABUSHIKI KAISHA
ODYSSEY LOGISTICS & TECHNOLOGY CORPORATION
U.S. XPRESS ENTERPRISES, INC.
USA TRUCK, INC.
YELLOW CORPORATION

HISTORICAL FINANCIALS
Company Type: Public

Income Statement   FYE: December 31

	REVENUE ($mil)	NET INCOME ($mil)	NET PROFIT MARGIN	EMPLOYEES
12/22	19,872	822	4.1%	85,988
12/21*	15,318	469	3.1%	86,688
03/21	18,778	506	2.7%	87,041
03/20	19,164	160	0.8%	89,024
03/19	19,310	445	2.3%	88,835
Annual Growth	0.7%	16.6%	—	(0.8%)

*Fiscal year change

2022 Year-End Financials

Debt ratio: 0.1%   No. of shares ($ mil.): 89
Return on equity: 15.5%   Dividends
Cash ($ mil.): 2,099   Yield: —
Current Ratio: 1.30   Payout: 0.0%
Long-term debt ($ mil.): 1,293   Market value ($ mil.): —

Nippon Paint Holdings Co Ltd

Japan's oldest paint company is also its largest. Founded in 1881, Nippon Paint produces paints and coatings for makers of cars, industrial products, and ships. It also makes paints for residential and commercial buildings and for the do-it-yourself market. Nippon Paint's fine chemicals unit produces adhesives, as well as surface treatment chemicals. The company's manufacturing operations are located principally in Asia, but also in North America and Europe. In the US, Nippon Paint makes automotive coatings and powder coatings through Nippon Paint (USA). Growing its US footprint, in 2016 the company agreed to buy California-based Dunn-Edwards Corp.

EXECUTIVES

Representative Executive Officer, Co-President, Director, Yuichiro Wakatsuki
Representative Executive Officer, Co-President, Director, Siew Kim Wee
Chairman, Director, Hup Jin Goh
Outside Director, Hisashi Hara
Outside Director, Peter M. Kirby
Outside Director, Hwee Hua Lim
Outside Director, Masataka Mitsuhashi
Outside Director, Toshio Morohoshi
Outside Director, Masayoshi Nakamura
Auditors : KPMG AZSA LLC

LOCATIONS

HQ: Nippon Paint Holdings Co Ltd
2-1-2 Oyodo Kita, Kita-ku, Osaka 531-8511
Phone: (81) 6 6455 9153
Web: www.nipponpaint-holdings.com

PRODUCTS/OPERATIONS

Selected Products
Paints and coatings
Automotive coatings (OEM paints, repair paints, plastics paints)
Industrial paints (paints for industrial products such as consumer electronic products, building materials, and metals)
Trade paints (for buildings, homes, bridges, plants, and condominiums)
Other paints (for do-it-yourselfers, boats, and roads)
Fine chemicals
Adhesives
Electronic materials
Life science chemicals
Surface-treatment chemicals, primarily for metals

COMPETITORS

AGC AMERICA, INC.
AKZO NOBEL PAINTS LLC
ASIAN PAINTS LIMITED
Akzo Nobel N.V.
COLOR WHEEL PAINT MFG., CO., INC.
Evonik Operations GmbH
H&R GmbH & Co. KGaA
Holdingselskabet af 19. Marts 2010 A/S
JACQUET METALS
SYNTHOMER PLC

HISTORICAL FINANCIALS

Company Type: Public

Income Statement				FYE: December 31
	REVENUE ($mil)	NET INCOME ($mil)	NET PROFIT MARGIN	EMPLOYEES
12/22	9,934	602	6.1%	41,130
12/21	8,672	586	6.8%	37,090
12/20	7,578	433	5.7%	27,318
12/19	6,373	338	5.3%	25,970
12/18	5,707	412	7.2%	20,402
Annual Growth	14.9%	10.0%	—	19.2%

2022 Year-End Financials
Debt ratio: 0.2%
Return on equity: 7.5%
Cash ($ mil.): 1,841
Current Ratio: 1.64
Long-term debt ($ mil.): 4,751
No. of shares ($ mil.): 2,348
Dividends
 Yield: —
 Payout: 32.5%
Market value ($ mil.): —

Nippon Paper Industries Co Ltd

Nippon Paper Industries Co. is the largest paper producer in Japan. The holding company operates through about 180 subsidiaries, affiliates, and related companies, manufacturing paper, paperboard for packaging and transportation, specialty paper, household paper goods under the Kleenex and Scottie brands, paper-based beverage cartons, films, chemicals, and lumber and building materials. Its Other division offers non-paper products and services, including soft drink bottling and logistics. Nippon Paper Industries changed its name from Nippon Paper Group in April 2013.

Operations
The company has major overseas subsidiaries and affiliates in Asia, Oceania, North America, South America, Europe, and Africa. Its R&D organization has three laboratories that focus on paper and pulp technologies; forestry and biotechnologies; and new product development.

Its operations are divided across several product segments: pulp and paper (nearly 80% of total sales) and paper-related (roughly 10%). The remaining revenues is generates from its wood products and construction-related and other segments.

Geographic Reach
Nippon Paper has about 30 mills in Japan, as well as extensive overseas operations.

Financial Performance
After peaking at $13.2 billion in revenue for 2011, Nippon Paper saw its revenues decrease in both 2012 and 2013. It also suffered a net loss of more than $500 million in 2012 due to climate disasters across Asia; however, it posted positive net income of $113 million in 2013.

Over the last two years the company's cash flow has also decreased due to additional investments for the purchases of property, plant, and equipment, and increased financing activities related to the the repayment of interest-bearing debt.

Strategy
Nippon Paper' strategy is to enhance the profitability of its core paper business, while also becoming more of a biomass-focused company that makes use of trees and wood in other fields, such as building materials, chemicals, and energy. Overseas, it is implementing measures to increase profits in Australia, deepening ties with partners like Lee & Man Paper Manufacturing and SCG Paper Public Company, and developing its business in emerging markets such as China and Southeast Asia.

Mergers and Acquisitions
In late 2019, Nippon Paper agreed to acquire the paperboard, fiber-based packaging businesses of Australia-based Orora Limited for AUD 1.7 billion. The deal will expand Nippon Paper's operations in Australia and New Zealand and enhance its integrated corrugated paperboard manufacturing capabilities.

EXECUTIVES

Chairman, Director, Fumio Manoshiro
President, Chief Executive Officer, Representative Director, Toru Nozawa
Executive Vice President, Representative Director, Masanobu Iizuka
Senior Managing Executive Officer, Yasuhito Obayashi
Director, Atsumi Yasunaga
Director, Mitsuhiro Sugino
Director, Tomoyasu Itakura
Outside Director, Makoto Fujioka
Outside Director, Yoko Hatta
Outside Director, Yutaka Kunigo
Auditors : Ernst & Young ShinNihon LLC

LOCATIONS

HQ: Nippon Paper Industries Co Ltd
4-6 Kandasurugadai, Chiyoda-ku, Tokyo 101-0062
Phone: (81) 3 6665 1111   **Fax:** (81) 3 6665 0300
Web: www.nipponpapergroup.com

PRODUCTS/OPERATIONS

2012 Sales

	% of total
Pulp & paper	78
Paper-related	9
Wood products & construction-related	6
Other	7
Total	100

HISTORICAL FINANCIALS

Company Type: Public

Income Statement				FYE: March 31
	REVENUE ($mil)	NET INCOME ($mil)	NET PROFIT MARGIN	EMPLOYEES
03/23	8,654	(378)	—	15,959
03/22	8,591	16	0.2%	16,129
03/21	9,097	28	0.3%	16,156
03/20	9,616	130	1.4%	12,592
03/19	9,650	(318)	—	12,943
Annual Growth	(2.7%)	—	—	5.4%

2023 Year-End Financials
Debt ratio: 0.4%
Return on equity: (-12.2%)
Cash ($ mil.): 1,083
Current Ratio: 1.24
Long-term debt ($ mil.): 4,939
No. of shares ($ mil.): 115
Dividends
 Yield: —
 Payout: 0.0%
Market value ($ mil.): —

Nippon Steel Corp (New)

Nippon Steel Corporation (formerly Nippon Steel & Sumitomo Metal), the world's fourth-largest steelmaker, manufactures pig iron and ingots, steel bars, plates, sheets, pipes, and tubes, as well as specialty, processed, and fabricated steel products. Nippon Steel's annual crude steel output is more than 95.6 million tons. The company's operations include steelmaking and steel fabrication, engineering, chemicals, new materials, and system solutions. It also delivers high-quality high-performance bars and rods to a wide range of industries including the automotive, construction, and industrial machinery industries.

Operations

Nippon Steel & Sumitomo Metal operates in four segments: Steelmaking and Steel Fabrication (about 90% of total revenue); Engineering and Construction; Chemicals and Materials; and System Solutions. The last three segments generated about 5% each.

Steelmaking and Steel Fabrication makes and markets steel products including pig iron and ingots, steel bars, plates, sheets, pipes, and tubes, and specialty, processed, and fabricated steel items.

Engineering and Construction makes and markets industrial machinery and equipment and steel structures. It also offers construction work under contract, waste processing and recycling services, and supplies electricity, gas, and heat.

Chemicals and Materials manufactures and sells coal-based chemical products, petrochemicals, electronic materials, materials and components for semiconductors and electronic parts, carbon fiber and composite products, and products that utilize technologies for metal processing.

The System Solutions segment includes computer system engineering and consulting services; IT-enabled outsourcing and other services.

Geographic Reach

Nippon Steel & Sumitomo Metal has operations in the Americas, Europe and the Middle East, and the Asia-Pacific region.

Its main operations are in Japan, but it also has major subsidiaries in Australia, Brazil, China, Indonesia, Thailand, and the US.

Financial Performance

Company's revenue for fiscal 2021 increased to JPY6.8 trillion compared from the prior year with JPY4.8 trillion.

Profit for fiscal 2021 was JPY816.6 billion compared from the prior year with a loss of JPY8.7 billion.

Cash held by the company at the end of fiscal 2021 increased to JPY551.0 billion. Cash provided by operations was JPY615.6 billion while cash used for investing and financing activities were JPY378.9 billion and JPY61.3 billion, respectively.

Strategy

Nippon Steel is strongly promoting digital transformation (DX).With the aim of becoming a digitally advanced company in the steel industry, we will work to innovate production and business processes by making full use of data and digital technology, and promote measures that will help speed up decision-making and fundamentally strengthen our problem-solving capabilities.

Company Background

As Japan prepared for war, the government in 1934 merged Yawata Works, the country's largest steel producer, and other Japanese steelmakers into one giant company ? Japan Iron & Steel.

As Japan lost the war, Japan Iron & Steel was ordered to dissolve by the Allied forces. Two new companies? Yawata Iron & Steel and Fuji Iron & Steel?emerged from the dissolution.

With Western assistance, the Japanese steel industry recovered from the war years in the 60s. Yawata and Fuji merged again in 1970 and became Nippon Steel, the world's largest steelmaker.

The company diversified in the mid-1980s to wean itself from dependence on steel. It has remained a leading steel company since.

In 2012, Nippon acquired Sumitomo Metal Industries, mating Japan's #1 and #3 steelmakers.

In 2019 the company shortened its name from Nippon Steel & Sumitomo Metal Corporation to Nippon Steel Corporation.

HISTORY

As Japan prepared for war, the government in 1934 merged Yawata Works, its largest steel producer, and other Japanese steelmakers into one giant company -- Japan Iron & Steel. During postwar occupation, Japan Iron & Steel was ordered to dissolve. Yawata Iron & Steel and Fuji Iron & Steel emerged from the dissolution, and with Western assistance the Japanese steel industry recovered from the war years. In the late 1960s Fuji Steel bought Tokai Iron & Steel (1967), and Yawata Steel took over Yawata Steel Tube Company (1968).

Yawata and Fuji merged in 1970 and became Nippon Steel, the world's largest steelmaker. In the 1970s the Japanese steel industry was criticized in the US; American competitors complained that Japan was "dumping" low-cost exports. Meanwhile, Nippon Steel aggressively courted China.

The company diversified in the mid-1980s to wean itself from dependence on steel. It created a New Materials unit in 1984, retraining "redundant" steelworkers to make silicon wafers and forming an Electronics Division in 1986. Nippon Steel began joint ventures with IBM Japan (small computers and software), Hitachi (office workstations), and C. Itoh (information systems for small and midsized companies) in 1988 as increased steel demand for construction and cars in Japan's "bubble economy" took the company to new heights.

In an atmosphere of economic optimism, the company spent more than four times the expected expense to build an amusement park capable of competing with Tokyo Disneyland. The company plowed ahead, spending some $230 million on the park. Space World amusement park opened on the island of Kyushu in 1990. The company's bubble burst that year. (The theme park declared bankruptcy in May 2005, and was sold to Kamori Kanko later that year.)

In response, Nippon Steel cut costs and intensified its diversification efforts by targeting electronics, information and telecommunications, new materials, and chemicals markets. Seeking to remake its steel operations, the company began a drastic, phased restructuring in 1993 that included a step most Japanese companies try to avoid -- cutting personnel. A semiconductor division was organized that year as part of the company's diversification strategy.

Upgrading its steel operations, Nippon Steel and partner Mitsubishi in 1996 introduced the world's first mass-production method for making hot-rolled steel sheet directly from smelted stainless steel. Profits were hurt that year by a loss-making project in the information and communications segment and by a steep decline in computer memory-chip prices.

The company began operation of a Chinese steelmaking joint venture, Guangzhou Pacific Tinplate, in 1997. The next year its Singapore-based joint venture with Hitachi, Ltd., began mass-producing computer memory chips in hopes of stemming semiconductor losses. But falling prices convinced Nippon Steel to get out of the memory chip business and in 1999 it sold its semiconductor subsidiary to South Korea's United Microelectronics.

That year the US imposed antidumping duties on the company's steel products. The next year Nippon Steel agreed to form a strategic alliance with South Korea-based Pohang Iron and Steel (POSCO), at that time the world's #1 steel maker. The deal called for the exploration of joint ventures, shared research, and joint procurement, as well as increased equity stakes in each other (at 2%-3%). Also in 2000 Nippon Steel agreed to provide Sumitomo Metal Industries and Nisshin Steel Co. with stainless steel products.

Early in 2001 Nippon Steel formed a cooperative alliance -- focused on automotive sheet products -- with French steel giant Usinor (now a part of ArcelorMittal). At the end of the year, Nippon Steel decided to form an alliance with Kobe Steel to pare down costs and share in distribution and production facilities. In 2002 the company continued its series of comprehensive alliances by forming alliances with Japanese steelmaker Nippon Metal Industry to exchange its semi-finished stainless steel technologies and with POSCO to build environment-related businesses.

The company reported a loss of Â¥51.69 billion ($430 million) for fiscal 2003 due to securities valuation losses and group restructuring charges. In 2004 Nippon Steel formed a joint venture with Baoshan Iron & Steel and Arcelor to manufacture high-grade automotive steel sheets.

Nippon Steel moved into the South American market in 2006, forming alliances with steelmaker Usiminas and iron miner CVRD. And the next year it created a JV with Baosteel and ArcelorMittal that produces automotive steel sheets.

The company joined up with Sumitomo Metal Industries in 2009 when the two companies agreed to form a joint venture that will combine their arc-welded stainless steel pipe and tube operations. Sumitomo will own 60% of the JV. The operations that make up the new company, which will be called Sumikin & Nippon Steel Stainless Steel Pipe Co., achieved sales of more than $250 million in 2008.

EXECUTIVES

Chairman, Representative Director, Kosei Shindo
President, Representative Director, Eiji Hashimoto
Executive Vice President, Representative Director, Naoki Sato
Executive Vice President, Representative Director, Takahiro Mori
Executive Vice President, Representative Director, Takashi Hirose
Executive Vice President, Representative Director, Kazuhisa Fukuda
Executive Vice President, Representative Director, Tadashi Imai
Executive Vice President, Representative Director, Hirofumi Funakoshi
Outside Director, Tetsuro Tomita
Outside Director, Kuniko Urano
Director, Shozo Furumoto
Director, Masayoshi Murase
Outside Director, Seiichiro Azuma
Outside Director, Hiroshi Yoshikawa
Outside Director, Masato Kitera
Auditors : KPMG AZSA LLC

LOCATIONS

HQ: Nippon Steel Corp (New)
2-6-1 Marunouchi, Chiyoda-ku, Tokyo 100-8071
Phone: (81) 3 6867 4111   **Fax:** 713 654-1261
Web: www.nipponsteel.com

2016 Sales

	% of total
Japan	66
Rest of Asia	22
Other	12
Total	100

PRODUCTS/OPERATIONS

2018 Sales

	% of total
Steelmaking & Steel Fabrication	88
Engineering & Construction	5
Chemicals	3
Systems Solutions	3
New Materials	1
Total	100

Selected Products and Services

Steelmaking and Steel Fabrication
　Fabricated and processed steels
　Pig iron and ingots
　Pipes and tubes
　Plates and sheets
　Sections
　Specialty sheets
Engineering and Construction
　Building construction
　Civil engineering
　Marine construction
　Plant and machinery
　Technical cooperation
Chemicals
　Aluminum products
　Ammonium sulfate
　Cement
　Ceramic products
　Coal tar
　Coke
　Ferrite
　Metallic foils
　Slag products
System Solutions
　Communications services
　Computers and equipment
　Data processing
　Systems development and integration
Urban Development
　Condominiums
　Theme parks
New Materials
　Semiconductor bonding wire
　Silicon wafers
　Titanium products
　Transformers
Other operations
　Services
　Energy services
　Financial services
　Insurance services
　Transportation
　Loading and unloading
　Marine and land transportation
　Warehousing

Selected Subsidiaries and Affiliates

Subsidiaries
　Nippon Steel & Sumikin Coated Sheet Corporation
　Nippon Steel & Sumikin Metal Products Co., Ltd.
　Nippon Steel & Sumikin Stainless Steel Corporation
　Nippon Steel & Sumikin Welding Co., Ltd.
　Nippon Steel Australia Pty. Limited
　Nippon Steel Blast Furnace Slag Cement Co., Ltd.
　Nippon Steel Drum Co., Ltd. 1,654
　Nippon Steel Logistics Co., Ltd.
　Nippon Steel Shipping Co., Ltd.
　Nippon Steel Transportation Co., Ltd.
　Nippon Steel U.S.A., Inc.
　Nittetsu Cement Co., Ltd.
　Nittetsu Elex Co., Ltd.
　Nittetsu Finance Co., Ltd.
　Nittetsu Steel Pipe Co., Ltd. 4,832
　Nittetsu Tokai Steel Wire Co., Ltd.
　NS Preferred Capital Limited
　Osaka Steel Co., Ltd.
　Siam Nippon Steel Pipe Co., Ltd.
　The Siam United Steel (1995) Co., Ltd.
Affiliates
　Daiwa Can Company
　Geostr Corporation
　Godo Steel, Ltd.
　Japan Casting & Forging Corporation
　Krosaki Harima Corporation
　Mitsui Mining Co., Ltd.
　Nichia Steel Works, Ltd.
　Nippon Steel Trading Co., Ltd.
　Sanko Metal Industrial Co., Ltd.
　Sanyo Special Steel Co., Ltd.
　Sanyu Co., Ltd.
　Suzuki Metal Industry Co., Ltd.
　Taihei Kogyo Co., Ltd.
　Topy Industries, Ltd.

COMPETITORS

AK STEEL HOLDING CORPORATION
ALLEGHENY TECHNOLOGIES INCORPORATED
HBIS Company Limited
JFE HOLDINGS, INC.
KOBE STEEL, LTD.
NIPPON STEEL NISSHIN CO., LTD.
NUCOR CORPORATION
STEEL TECHNOLOGIES LLC
TATA STEEL EUROPE LIMITED
thyssenkrupp AG

HISTORICAL FINANCIALS

Company Type: Public

Income Statement   FYE: March 31

	REVENUE ($mil)	NET INCOME ($mil)	NET PROFIT MARGIN	EMPLOYEES
03/23	59,883	5,210	8.7%	121,990
03/22	55,977	5,239	9.4%	123,806
03/21	43,615	(292)	—	125,038
03/20	54,551	(3,975)	—	126,324
03/19	55,785	2,268	4.1%	125,960
Annual Growth	1.8%	23.1%	—	(0.8%)

2023 Year-End Financials

Debt ratio: 0.2%　　　No. of shares ($ mil.): 921
Return on equity: 18.1%　Dividends
Cash ($ mil.): 5,033　　Yield: 5.5%
Current Ratio: 1.94　　Payout: 8.8%
Long-term debt ($ mil.): 16,741　Market value ($ mil.): 7,256

	STOCK PRICE ($) FY Close	P/E High/Low		PER SHARE ($) Earnings	Dividends	Book Value
03/23	7.87	0	0	5.04	0.44	34.05
03/22	17.98	0	0	5.41	0.71	30.91
03/21	17.30	—	—	(0.32)	0.09	27.04
03/20	8.60	—	—	(4.32)	0.46	26.39
03/19	17.74	0	0	2.54	0.24	31.64
Annual Growth	(18.4%)	—	—	18.7%	16.2%	1.9%

Nippon Steel Trading Corp

Nippon Steel Engineering is the steel-trading operation of Nippon Steel & Sumitomo Metal, Japan's steelmaker. The company trades a range of products, such as steel sheets, flat products, bar & wire rod, and construction products, which are distributed and manufactured in Asia, Europe, and North and Central America. Nippon Steel Engineering also imports steelmaking raw materials, through investing in raw material mines that enable the company to procure such raw materials. About 20% of iron ore and coking coal used in the company's steelmaking operations is from these mines. Steel products account for 85% of company sales. More than 70% of the company's total revenue comes from Japan. Nippon Steel Engineering started as the engineering division of Nippon Steel in 1974.

Operations

Nippon Steel Engineering operates in four segments: Steel (85% of total revenue); Foodstuffs (over 5%); Textiles (about 5%); and Industrial Supply and Infrastructure (less than 5%).

The Steel segment is engaged in a full range of steelmaking activities, from buying raw materials to the delivery of steel products to customers.

Foodstuffs offers imported meats (including beef, pork, and chicken), fishery products, agricultural products, and Other foodstuffs and processed foods.

Centering on OEM production for apparel makers, Textiles is engaged in everything from materials development to product planning, production, and distribution.

Industrial Supply and Infrastructure invests in new businesses with growth potential, such as industrial machinery, infrastructure businesses, and materials.

The company also has its non-steel segments, namely, Engineering and Construction, Chemicals and Materials, and System solutions.

Geographic Reach

Tokyo, Japan-based Nippon Steel Engineering has more than 10 manufacturing bases, which enables the company to produce more than 50 million tons of domestic crude steel per year. The company has overseas operations in ASEAN countries, China, India, the Middle East, North/Central America, South America, and Europe.

Japan accounts for more than 70% of total revenue, followed by Asia with over 20%.

Financial Performance

Note: Growth rates may differ after conversion to US Dollars.

Nippon Engineering has generally grown its revenues in the last five years, however had a slight decrease in performance from 2020 to 2021, slightly being higher than its 2018 performance.

The company's net sales dropped by Â¥407 billion to Â¥2.1 trillion in fiscal 2021 compared to Â¥2.5 trillion in the prior year.

Net income declined by Â¥5 billion to Â¥15.9 billion in 2021 compared to Â¥20.7 billion in the prior year.

The company held Â¥55.9 billion at the end of 2021. Operating activities generated Â¥47.3 billion. Investing activities and financing activities used Â¥6.5 billion and Â¥10 billion, respectively. Main cash uses were for purchases of properties, plants, and equipment as well as repayment of long-term debts.

Strategy

Nippon Steel Engineering's strategy is made up of its medium- to long-term management plan. These plans include the goal of the company to rebuild the domestic steel business and strengthen the group's management through restructuring. The plan also includes the deepening and expansion of the company's overseas operation. The company intends to establish a global capacity of 100 million tons of crude steel production. In addition, the company is also taking on the challenge of zero-carbon steel, which is achieved through the provision of their technology and products to those that benefit from them. Lastly, the company also aims to promote its digital transformation strategies through attentively collecting and analyzing the vast amounts of data generated at manufacturing and business sites to reduce costs and improve quality.

Company Background

In 2013 Nippon Steel Trading merged with Sumikin Bussan to form Nippon Steel & Sumikin Bussan Corporation.

EXECUTIVES

President, Representative Director, Shinichi Nakamura
Executive Vice President, Director, Hidetake Ishihara
Advisor, Director, Yasumitsu Saeki
Director, Yasuyuki Tomioka
Director, Kazuhiro Koshikawa
Director, Hiroshi Tashiro
Outside Director, Keishiro Kinoshita
Outside Director, Ryuko Inoue
Outside Director, Ryu Matsumoto
Auditors : Deloitte Touche Tohmatsu LLC

LOCATIONS

HQ: Nippon Steel Trading Corp
2-7-1 Nihonbashi, Chuo-ku, Tokyo 103-6025
Phone: (81) 3 6772 5098   **Fax:** 847 413-4030
Web: www.nst.nipponsteel.com

2016 Sales

	% of total
Japan	74
Asia	22
others	4
Total	100

PRODUCTS/OPERATIONS

2016 Sales

	% of Total
Steel	78
Industrial Supply and Infrastructure	5
Textiles	9
Foodstuffs	8
Others	
Reconciliations	-
Total	100

COMPETITORS

A.M. CASTLE & CO.
China Baowu Steel Group Corporation Limited
HANWA CO.,LTD.
NIPPON STEEL CORPORATION
NIPPON STEEL NISSHIN CO., LTD.
OLYMPIC STEEL, INC.
RBRG TRADING (UK) LIMITED
RELIANCE STEEL & ALUMINUM CO.
Russel Metals Inc
SSAB ENTERPRISES, LLC

HISTORICAL FINANCIALS

Company Type: Public

Income Statement   FYE: March 31

	REVENUE ($mil)	NET INCOME ($mil)	NET PROFIT MARGIN	EMPLOYEES
03/22	15,339	291	1.9%	6,584
03/21	18,724	143	0.8%	9,028
03/20	22,848	190	0.8%	7,971
03/19	23,031	209	0.9%	7,914
03/18	19,421	204	1.1%	7,785
Annual Growth	(5.7%)	9.2%	—	(4.1%)

2022 Year-End Financials

Debt ratio: 0.3%   No. of shares ($ mil.): 32
Return on equity: 13.1%   Dividends
Cash ($ mil.): 251   Yield: —
Current Ratio: 1.47   Payout: 0.0%
Long-term debt ($ mil.): 1,200 Market value ($ mil.): —

Nippon Telegraph & Telephone Corp (Japan)

EXECUTIVES

Chairman, Representative Director, Jun Sawada
General Affairs Department President, General Affairs Department Chief Executive Officer, Representative Director, Akira Shimada
Executive Vice President, Chief Technology Officer, Chief Information Officer, Representative Director, Katsuhiko Kawazoe
Executive Vice President, Chief Financial Officer, Chief Compliance Officer, Chief Human Resources Officer, Representative Director, Takashi Hiroi
Director, Akiko Kudo
Outside Director, Ken Sakamura
Outside Director, Yukako Uchinaga
Outside Director, Ryoji Chubachi
Outside Director, Koichiro Watanabe
Outside Director, Noriko Endo
Auditors : KPMG AZSA LLC

LOCATIONS

HQ: Nippon Telegraph & Telephone Corp (Japan)
Otemachi First Square, East Tower, 1-5-1 Otemachi, Chiyoda-ku, Tokyo 100-8116
Phone: (81) 3 6838 5481
Web: group.ntt

HISTORICAL FINANCIALS
Company Type: Public

Income Statement   FYE: March 31

	REVENUE ($mil)	NET INCOME ($mil)	NET PROFIT MARGIN	EMPLOYEES
03/23	98,630	9,108	9.2%	381,653
03/22	99,940	9,709	9.7%	378,183
03/21	107,871	8,274	7.7%	371,816
03/20	109,621	7,879	7.2%	370,826
03/19	107,273	7,716	7.2%	366,156
Annual Growth	(2.1%)	4.2%	—	1.0%

2023 Year-End Financials
Debt ratio: 0.2%   No. of shares ($ mil.): 85,262
Return on equity: 14.4%   Dividends
Cash ($ mil.): 5,961   Yield: 3.0%
Current Ratio: 0.97   Payout: 0.0%
Long-term debt ($ mil.): 47,979   Market value ($ mil.): 2,554,456

	STOCK PRICE ($) FY Close	P/E High/Low		PER SHARE ($) Earnings	Dividends	Book Value
03/23	29.96	2	2	0.10	0.91	0.75
03/22	29.11	2	2	0.11	0.98	0.77
03/21	25.91	3	2	0.09	0.92	0.75
03/20	23.62	6	2	0.09	0.88	0.92
03/19	42.72	6	4	0.08	0.72	0.87
Annual Growth	(8.5%)	—	—	7.1%	5.8%	(3.6%)

Nippon Yusen Kabushiki Kaisha

EXECUTIVES

Chairman, Director, Hitoshi Nagasawa
President, Representative Director, Takaya Soga
Executive Vice President, Representative Director, Akira Kono
Senior Managing Executive Officer, Director, Yutaka Higurashi
Outside Director, Hiroko Kuniya
Outside Director, Eiichi Tanabe
Outside Director, Nobukatsu Kanehara
Director, Eiichi Takahashi
Director, Keiko Kosugi
Outside Director, Hiroshi Nakaso
Outside Director, Satoko Kuwabara
Outside Director, Tatsumi Yamada
Auditors : Deloitte Touche Tohmatsu LLC

LOCATIONS

HQ: Nippon Yusen Kabushiki Kaisha
2-3-2 Marunouchi, Chiyoda-ku, Tokyo 100-0005
Phone: (81) 3 3284 5151
Web: www.nyk.com

COMPETITORS

BRAEMAR SHIPPING SERVICES PLC
CMA CGM ASIA PACIFIC LIMITED
EURONAV MI II INC.
GULFMARK OFFSHORE, INC.
INTERNATIONAL SHIPHOLDING CORPORATION
KAWASAKI KISEN KAISHA, LTD.
Odfjell Se
SEACOR HOLDINGS INC.
USA TRUCK, INC.
YANG MING MARINE TRANSPORT CORPORATION

HISTORICAL FINANCIALS
Company Type: Public

Income Statement   FYE: March 31

	REVENUE ($mil)	NET INCOME ($mil)	NET PROFIT MARGIN	EMPLOYEES
03/23	19,642	7,602	38.7%	46,545
03/22	18,750	8,296	44.2%	46,365
03/21	14,526	1,257	8.7%	46,044
03/20	15,369	286	1.9%	44,508
03/19	16,518	(401)	—	45,401
Annual Growth	4.4%	—	—	0.6%

2023 Year-End Financials
Debt ratio: 0.1%   No. of shares ($ mil.): 508
Return on equity: 48.3%   Dividends
Cash ($ mil.): 1,537   Yield: 46.0%
Current Ratio: 1.44   Payout: 0.0%
Long-term debt ($ mil.): 3,826   Market value ($ mil.): 2,380

	STOCK PRICE ($) FY Close	P/E High/Low		PER SHARE ($) Earnings	Dividends	Book Value
03/23	4.68	0	0	14.97	2.15	36.59
03/22	17.68	0	0	16.37	0.68	27.70
03/21	7.05	0	0	2.48	0.08	11.10
03/20	2.25	0	0	0.57	0.06	8.38
03/19	2.96	—	—	(0.79)	0.02	8.65
Annual Growth	12.1%	—	—	—	207.1%	43.4%

Nissan Motor Co., Ltd.

Nissan Motor is one of Japan's leading automakers. The company manufactures and sells related business of automotive products. The company has two major brands under its automotive business: Nissan and Infiniti. Infiniti is the premium brand from the company which is renowned for its world-first technologies and award-winning designs. Nissan generates the majority of its sales from North America.

Operations
Businesses of the Nissan are segmented into Automobile (about 90% of total revenue) and Sales financing (more than 10%) based on the features of products and services. The Automobile business includes manufacturing and sales of vehicles and parts. The Sales financing business provides sales finance services and leasing to support the sales activities of the Automobile business.

In 2022, the company produced 3.40 million vehicle units.

Geographic Reach
Nissan, headquartered in Kanagawa, Japan, manufactures in 15 markets and has 30 production facilities. The company has R&D facilities in more than 15 markets.

North America accounts for about 50% of total revenue, while Japan for over 20%, while Europe, Asia and other countries account for about 10% each.

Sales and Marketing
Nissan has major overseas sales network in North America & Mexico, Europe, Asia, Oceania, Latin America & Caribbean, Middle East & Gulf States, and Africa.

Financial Performance
Net sales in fiscal year 2022 increased by JPY 562.0 billion or 7.1% to JPY 8,424.6 billion from the prior fiscal year. As a result, operating income totaled JPY 247.3 billion, which improved by JPY398.0 billion from the prior fiscal year. This was mainly due to an improvement in the quality of sales and exchange rate fluctuations despite a decrease in sales volume and increase in raw material prices.

Net income attributable to owners of parent of JPY 215.5 billion was recorded, improved by JPY 664.2 billion from the prior fiscal year.

Nissan held cash and cash equivalents of JPY 1.8 billion in 2021. Operating activities generated JPY 847.2 million. Investing and financing activities used JPY 146.8 million and JPY 1.1 billion, respectively. Main cash uses were repayments of long-term borrowings, redemption of bonds, purchase of fixed assets and purchased of leased vehicles.

Strategy
In 2021, Nissan announced its Nissan Ambition 2030, its long-term vision for empowering mobility and beyond for a cleaner, safer, and more inclusive world. Nissan Ambition 2030 guides how the company will deliver superior value by empowering journeys and society through exciting, electrified vehicles and technological innovations. This effort has three focuses: accelerating electrified mobility with diverse choices and experiences; increasing accessibility and innovation and mobility; global ecosystem for mobility and beyond.

Company Background
In 1911 US-trained Masujiro Hashimoto established Tokyo-based Kwaishinsha Motor Car Works to repair, import, and manufacture cars. Kwaishinsha made its first car, sporting its DAT ("fast rabbit" in Japanese) logo, in 1913. Renamed DAT Motors in 1925, the company consolidated with ailing Jitsuyo Motors in 1926. DAT introduced the son of DAT in 1931 -- the Datsun minicar.

Tobata Casting (cast iron and auto parts) bought Datsun's production facilities in 1933. Tobata's Yoshisuke Aikawa believed there was a niche for small cars, and the car operations were spun off as Nissan Motors that year.

During WWII the Japanese government limited Nissan's production to trucks and airplane engines; Nissan survived postwar occupation, in part, due to business with the US Army. The company went public in 1951 and signed a licensing agreement the next year with Austin Motor (UK), which put it back in the car business.

Nissan entered the US market in 1958 with the model 211, using the Datsun name; it established Nissan Motor Corporation in Los Angeles in 1960. In the 1970s Nissan expanded exports of fuel-efficient cars such as the Datsun B210.

The company's name change in the US from Datsun to Nissan during the 1980s confused customers and took six years to complete. It launched its high-end Infiniti line in the US in 1989.

HISTORY

In 1911 US-trained Masujiro Hashimoto established Tokyo-based Kwaishinsha Motor Car Works to repair, import, and manufacture cars. Kwaishinsha made its first car, sporting its DAT ("fast rabbit" in Japanese) logo, in 1913. Renamed DAT Motors in 1925 and suffering from a strong domestic preference for American cars, the company consolidated with ailing Jitsuyo Motors in 1926. DAT introduced the son of DAT in 1931 -- the Datsun minicar ("son" means "damage or loss" in Japanese, hence the spelling change).

Tobata Casting (cast iron and auto parts) bought Datsun's production facilities in 1933. Tobata's Yoshisuke Aikawa believed there was a niche for small cars, and the car operations were spun off as Nissan Motors that year.

During WWII the Japanese government limited Nissan's production to trucks and airplane engines; Nissan survived postwar occupation, in part, due to business with the US Army. The company went public in 1951 and signed a licensing agreement the next year with Austin Motor (UK), which put it back in the car business. A 40% import tax allowed Nissan to compete in Japan even though it had higher costs than those of foreign carmakers.

Nissan entered the US market in 1958 with the model 211, using the Datsun name; it established Nissan Motor Corporation in Los Angeles in 1960. Exports rose as factory automation led to higher quality and lower costs. In the 1970s Nissan expanded exports of fuel-efficient cars such as the Datsun B210. The company became the leading US car importer in 1975.

The company's name change in the US from Datsun to Nissan during the 1980s confused customers and took six years to complete. In 1986 Nissan became the first major Japanese carmaker to build its products in Europe. It launched its high-end Infiniti line in the US in 1989.

EXECUTIVES

Outside Director, Chairman of the Board, Yasushi Kimura
Vice-Chairman of the Board, Director, Jean-Dominique Senard
Chief Financial Officer, Stephen Ma
Executive Vice President, Director, Hideyuki Sakamoto
Executive Vice President, Asako Hoshino
Executive Vice President, Kunio Nakaguro
Senior Managing Executive Officer, Joji Tagawa
Senior Managing Executive Officer, Hideaki Watanabe
Representative Executive Officer, President, Chief Executive Officer, Director, Makoto Uchida
Senior Managing Executive Officer, Noboru Tateishi
Senior Managing Executive Officer, Toru Ihara
Senior Managing Executive Officer, Takao Asami
Senior Managing Executive Officer, Takashi Hata
Senior Managing Executive Officer, Rakesh Kochhar
Senior Managing Executive Officer, Hari Nada
Senior Managing Executive Officer, Alfonso Albaisa
Senior Managing Executive Officer, Atul Pasricha
Senior Managing Executive Officer, Leon Dorssers
Senior Managing Executive Officer, Ivan Espinosa
Senior Managing Executive Officer, Shohei Yamazaki
Senior Managing Executive Officer, Guillaume Cartier
Senior Managing Executive Officer, Toshihiro Hirai
Senior Managing Executive Officer, Hiroki Hasegawa
Senior Managing Executive Officer, Yasuhiko Obata
Senior Managing Executive Officer, Jeremie Papin
Senior Managing Executive Officer, Junichi Endo
Senior Managing Executive Officer, Hitoshi Mano
Outside Director, Bernard Delmas
Outside Director, Keiko Ihara
Outside Director, Motoo Nagai
Outside Director, Andrew House
Outside Director, Brenda Harvey
Director, Pierre Fleuriot
Auditors : Ernst & Young ShinNihon LLC

LOCATIONS

HQ: Nissan Motor Co., Ltd.
1-1-1 Takashima, Nishi-ku, Yokohama, Kanagawa 220-8686
Phone: (81) 45 523 5523
Web: www.nissan.co.jp

PRODUCTS/OPERATIONS

Selected Products
Forklifts
    Engine-powerd forklifts
    Electric-powered forklifts
    Warehouse products
    Order pickers
    Pallet stackers
    Pallet transporters
    Reach trucks
Infiniti
    Infiniti Q50
    Infiniti Q60
    Infiniti Q70
    Infiniti Q70L
    Infiniti QX30
    Infiniti QX50
    Infiniti QX60
    Infiniti QX70
    Infiniti QX80
Nissan
    370Z
    370Z Roadster
    Altima
    Armada
    Frontier
    GT-R
    Juke
    Leaf EV
    Maxima
    Murano
    NV200 Cargo
    NV200 Taxi
    NV Passenger
    Pathfinder
    Rogue
    Rogue Sport
    Sentra
    Titan
    Titan XD
    Versa
    Versa Note

COMPETITORS

AUDI AG
Bayerische Motoren Werke AG
FIAT CHRYSLER AUTOMOBILES N.V.
FORD MOTOR COMPANY
HONDA MOTOR CO., LTD.
MAZDA MOTOR CORPORATION
MITSUBISHI MOTORS CORPORATION
PEUGEOT SA
TOYOTA MOTOR CORPORATION
VOLKSWAGEN AG

HISTORICAL FINANCIALS

Company Type: Public

Income Statement   FYE: March 31

	REVENUE ($mil)	NET INCOME ($mil)	NET PROFIT MARGIN	EMPLOYEES
03/23	79,563	1,666	2.1%	147,119
03/22	69,260	1,771	2.6%	149,857
03/21	71,010	(4,052)	—	148,559
03/20	91,007	(6,183)	—	155,811
03/19	104,514	2,881	2.8%	160,183
Annual Growth	(6.6%)	(12.8%)		(2.1%)

2023 Year-End Financials

Debt ratio: 0.3%
Return on equity: 4.5%
Cash ($ mil.): 13,503
Current Ratio: 1.68
Long-term debt ($ mil.): 30,568
No. of shares ($ mil.): 4,195
Dividends
  Yield: 0.9%
  Payout: 17.5%
Market value ($ mil.): 31,761

	STOCK PRICE ($) FY Close	P/E High/Low	PER SHARE ($) Earnings	Dividends	Book Value
03/23	7.57	0 0	0.43	0.07	9.19
03/22	8.90	0 0	0.45	0.04	8.98
03/21	11.28	— —	(1.04)	0.00	8.50
03/20	6.70	— —	(1.58)	0.71	8.93
03/19	16.42	0 0	0.74	0.99	11.42
Annual Growth	(17.6%)		(12.8%)	(47.9%)	(5.3%)

NN Group NV (Netherlands)

NN Group is an international financial services company, active in about 10 countries, with a strong presence in a number of European countries and Japan. With all its employees, the group provides retirement services, pensions, insurance, banking and investments to approximately 18 million customers. NN Group includes Nationale-Nederlanden, NN, ABN AMRO Insurance, Movir, AZL, BeFrank, OHRA and Woonnu. In 2022, NN Group completed the sales of its asset manager NN Investment Partners (NN IP) to Goldman Sachs. NN Group was spun off from ING to become a publicly traded company in 2014.

Operations

NN operating segments are Netherlands Life, Netherlands Non-Life, Insurance Europe, Japan Life, Asset Management, Banking, and Other.

Netherlands Life offers term life insurance as well as the full spectrum of pensions solutions including insured defined benefit (DB) and defined contribution (DC) via the NN-label; Premium Pension Institution (PPI) via its specialised label, BeFrank; an APF (general pension fund) solution via De Nationale; and pension fund administration services via AZLNetherlands. The segment accounts for about 45% of total revenue.

Netherlands Non-life (some 15%) offers a broad range of non-life insurance, including, motor, fire, liability, transport, travel, and disability and accident insurance to retail, self-employed SME and corporate customers. The segment comprises Nationale-Nederlanden Non-life, the non-life results of ABN AMRO Insurance, Movir, OHRA and HCS, and the broker results related to health insurance products.

Insurance Europe (about 15%) primarily offers life insurance and pension products to retail, self-employed and SME customers. In Belgium, Spain and Poland, it also offers non-life insurance products, and health insurance in Greece, Hungary and Romania. The countries in which Insurance Europe is active are a mixture of mature and growth markets. Its main brands are NN and Nationale-Nederlanden (in Spain and Poland).

Japan life offers a range of corporate-owned life insurance (COLI) products to owners and employees of SMEs through more than 5,000 registered independent agents and about 70 financial institution partners (banks and securities houses) supported by sales support office located in about 30 cities throughout Japan. The segment accounts for more than 10% of total revenue.

Accounting for less than 10% of revenue, Asset Management manages the assets of the NN's insurance businesses, offers retail and institutional customers a wide variety of actively managed investment products, and provides advisory services in all major asset classes and investment styles. In 2022, NN Group completed the sales of its asset manager NN Investment Partners (NN IP) to Goldman Sachs.

In Banking segment (about 5%), its NN Bank is the banking business of NN Group. It assist customers manage and protect their assets and income through mortgage loans, (internet) savings, bank annuities, consumer lending and retail investment products. In addition, NN Bank provides mortgage administration and management services to ING Bank N.V. (former WestlandUtrecht Bank), NN Life and NN Non-life in the Netherlands, NN Belgium, and the NN Dutch Residential Mortgage Fund.

Other comprises the businesses of Japan Closed Block VA, NN Re, the results of NN Group's holding company, and other results.

Geographic Reach

NN is based in Netherlands and active in about 10 countries, with a strong presence in a number of European countries and Japan.

Sales and Marketing

NN markets its high quality products and services to retail, SME, large corporate and institutional customers.

Financial Performance

Note: Growth rates may differ after conversion to US Dollars.

The company's revenue for fiscal 2021 increased to EUR 2.0 billion compared from the prior year with EUR 1.9 billion.

Profit for fiscal 2021 increased to EUR 3.3 billion compared from the prior year with EUR 1.9 billion.

Cash held by the company at the end of fiscal 2021 decreased to EUR 7.2 billion. Cash used for operations, investing and financing activities were EUR 2.6 billion, EUR 1.8 billion and EUR 5.2 billion, respectively. Main uses of cash were purchase of available-for-sale investments and proceeds from other borrowed funds.

Company Background

NN Group traces its roots back to the 1845 founding of De Nederlanden, a specialist in fire insurance.

EXECUTIVES

Chairman, Chief Executive Officer, David Knibbe
Vice-Chairman, Chief Financial Officer, Delfin Rueda
Chief Risk Officer, Bernhard Kaufmann
Chief Organization and Corporate Relations, Dailah Nihot
General Counsel, Secretary, Janet Stuijt
Chairman, Independent Director, David A. Cole
Vice-Chairman, Independent Director, Helene M. Vletter-van Dort
Independent Director, Inga K. Beale
Independent Director, Heijo J. G. Hauser
Independent Director, Robert W. Jenkins
Independent Director, Rob J. W. Lelieveld
Independent Director, Cecilia Reyes
Independent Director, Hans J. W. Schoen
Independent Director, Clara Christina F. T. Streit
Auditors : KPMG Accountants N.V.

LOCATIONS

HQ: NN Group NV (Netherlands)
Schenkkade 65, The Hauge 2595 AS
Phone: (31) 70 513 03 03
Web: www.nn-group.com

PRODUCTS/OPERATIONS

2018 Sales by Segment

	% of total
Netherlands Life	59
Insurance Europe	16
Investment Management	9
Japan Life	10
Netherlands Non-life	6
Total	100

COMPETITORS

AEGON N.V.
Achmea B.V.
ING Groep N.V.
Industrial Alliance Insurance and Financial Services Inc
MASSACHUSETTS MUTUAL LIFE INSURANCE COMPANY
METLIFE, INC.
MMC VENTURES LIMITED
Randstad N.V.
The Bank of Nova Scotia
Wolters Kluwer N.V.

HISTORICAL FINANCIALS

Company Type: Public

Income Statement — FYE: December 31

	ASSETS ($mil)	NET INCOME ($mil)	INCOME AS % OF ASSETS	EMPLOYEES
12/22	231,883	1,668	0.7%	16,104
12/21	284,760	3,710	1.3%	15,417
12/20	323,683	2,336	0.7%	15,118
12/19	279,116	2,202	0.8%	15,194
12/18	256,805	1,279	0.5%	14,953
Annual Growth	(2.5%)	6.9%		1.9%

2022 Year-End Financials

Return on assets: 0.6% — Dividends
Return on equity: 5.9% — Yield: —
Long-term debt ($ mil.): — — Payout: 19.0%
No. of shares ($ mil.): 281 — Market value ($ mil.): 5,732
Sales ($ mil.): 18,689

	STOCK PRICE ($) FY Close	P/E High/Low		PER SHARE ($) Earnings	Dividends	Book Value
12/22	20.37	5	4	5.44	1.04	67.44
12/21	27.12	3	2	11.78	1.79	128.35
12/20	21.56	4	2	7.20	1.09	152.18
12/19	18.91	4	3	6.46	0.87	113.41
12/18	19.59	7	6	3.61	0.76	84.27
Annual Growth	1.0%	—	—	10.8%	8.3%	(5.4%)

Nokia Corp

Nokia is one of the world's leading makers of the telecommunications infrastructure of mobile phone networks. The company is a B2B technology innovation leader, pioneering the future where networks meet cloud to realize the full potential of digital in every industry. The company's operations are segmented to Network Infrastructure, Mobile networks, Cloud and Network Services, and Nokia Technologies. Nokia has operations and customers in approximately 130 countries and about 87,000 employees. Finland's largest company, Nokia redoubled its commitment to telecom infrastructure with its acquisition of the telecom-equipment maker Alcatel-Lucent. Nokia generates roughly 40% of its revenue in North America.

Operations

Nokia has four business groups with each business group aiming to become a technology and market leader in their respective sector. The segments include, namely: Network Infrastructure; Mobile Networks; Cloud and Network Services; and Nokia Technologies.

The Network Infrastructure segment provides fiber, fixed wireless access technologies, copper, IP routing, data center, subsea and terrestrial optical networks, along with related services to customers including communications service providers, webscales (including hyperscalers), digital industries and governments.

The Mobile Networks segment creates products and services covering all network generations. Its portfolio includes products for radio access networks (RAN) and microwave radio links for transport networks, solutions for network management, as well as network planning, optimization, network deployment and technical support services.

The Cloud and Network Services enables CSPs and enterprises to deploy and monetize 5G, cloud-native software and as-a-Service delivery models. Lastly, the Nokia Technologies segment is responsible for managing Nokia's patent portfolio and monetizing Nokia's intellectual property, including patents, technologies, and the Nokia brand.

Geographic Reach

Nokia, headquartered in Espoo, Finland, has operations in North America (accounting for about 40%), Europe (about 30%), and Middle East & Africa. Other regional operations include India, Latin America, and the Asia Pacific.

Sales and Marketing

Nokia's customers include communications service providers, utility, energy, and transportation companies, the public sector, and other tech companies.

Financial Performance

Nokia's performance for the past five years has fluctuated but had an overall increase with 2022 as its highest performing year over the period.

The company recorded an increase in revenue of EUR 2.7 billion to EUR 24.9 billion for 2022, as compared to 2021's revenue of EUR 22.2 billion.

Nokia's net profit for fiscal year end 2022 also increased to EUR 4.3 billion, as compared to the prior year's net income of EUR 1.6 billion.

The company held EUR 5.5 billion by the end of the year. Operating activities provided EUR 1.5 billion to the coffers. Investing activities and financing activities used EUR 1.9 billion and EUR 837 million, respectively. Main cash uses were for purchase of interest-bearing financial investments and dividends paid and other contributions to shareholders.

Strategy

Nokia believes that networks are the key enabler for the digitalization of industries and the realization of the broader potential of the metaverse. As a result, we see opportunity to grow our business, expand into adjacencies and transform our business model. The company confidently asserts the value it brings through networking expertise, technology leadership, pioneering innovation, and collaborative advantage.

Company Background

Nokia has grown from its origins in 1865 as a papermill in Finland to one of the world's pre-eminent technology companies, and whose fortunes have a tangible impact on the lives of the Finnish population. Nokia has found and nurtured success in several sectors over the years, including cable, paper products, rubber boots and tires, mobile devices, and telecommunications infrastructure equipment. By 1998, Nokia was the world leader in mobile phones, a position it enjoyed for more than a decade.

However, its phones fell out of popularity in the smartphone era as the iOS and Android mobile operating systems vastly outperformed Nokia's Symbian software. A tie-up with Microsoft that saw Nokia's devices adopt Windows Phone 7 as their OS ultimately failed to save Nokia's device division as few people preferred Microsoft's OS, either, and Nokia sold the entire business to Microsoft.

The sale triggered a wholesale shift to telecoms equipment, which Nokia took to the next level with the 2016 acquisition of Alcatel-Lucent.

HISTORY

Nokia got its start in 1865 when engineer Fredrik Idestam established a mill to manufacture pulp and paper on the Tammerkoski rapids of the Nokianvirta River in Finland. Although Nokia flourished within Finland, the company was not well known to the rest of the world until it attempted to become a regional conglomerate in the early 1960s. French computer firm Machines Bull selected Nokia as its Finnish agent in 1962, and Nokia began researching radio transmission technology. In 1967, with the encouragement of Finland's government, Nokia merged with Finnish Rubber Works (a maker of tires and rubber footwear, formed in 1898) and Finnish Cable Works (a cable and electronics manufacturer formed in 1912) to form Nokia Corporation.

The company entered the phone business -- after a series of deals that expanded its industrial holdings -- when it acquired a 51% interest in the state-owned Finnish telecom company in 1981 and named it Telenokia.

Nokia caught the first wave of mobile phones, riding the popularity of its handsets in the late 1990s and early 2000s. It, however, didn't move fast enough to compete against smartphones and it eventually sold the handset business to Microsoft.

EXECUTIVES

President, Chief Executive Officer, Pekka Lundmark
Chief Financial Officer, Marco Wiren
Chief Strategy Officer, Chief Technology Officer, Nishant Batra
Chief Human Resources Officer, Stephanie Werner-Dietz
Customer Operations, Americas President, Ricky Corker
Fixed Networks President, Federico Guillen
Nokia Technologies President, Jenni Lukander
Mobile Networks President, Tommi Uitto
Chairman, Sari Baldauf, $521,000 total compensation
Director, Vice-Chairman, Kari Stadigh
Director, Bruce A. Brown
Director, Thomas Dannenfeldt
Director, Jeanette A. Horan
Director, Edward R. Kozel
Director, Elizabeth Nelson
Director, Soren Skou
Director, Carla Smits-Nusteling
Auditors : Deloitte Oy

LOCATIONS

HQ: Nokia Corp
  Karakaari 7, Espoo FI-02610
Phone: (358) 10 44 88 000   **Fax:** (358) 10 44 81 002
Web: www.nokia.com

2017 Sales

	% of total
Europe	29
North America	28
Asia/Pacific	
Greater China	11
Other	18
Middle East & Africa	8
Latin America	6
Total	100

2017 Sales

	% of total
United States	26
China	9
Finland	8
India	6
France	6
United Kingdom	3
Japan	3
Germany	2
Italy	2
Saudi Arabia	2
Other	33
Total	**100**

PRODUCTS/OPERATIONS

2017 Sales

	% of total
Nokia Networks	
Ultra Broadband Networks	39
IP Networks and Applications	25
Global Services	25
Nokia Technologies	7
Group common and other	4
Total	**100**

Selected Products
Nokia Flexi Multiradio
    Telco Cloud
    NetAct
    IP routers
Switching systems
    Radio contollers
    Base stations
    transmission systems
    mapping systems and software

COMPETITORS

ALCATEL LUCENT
AVAYA INC.
BIDSTACK GROUP PLC
Huawei Investment & Holding Co., Ltd.
INGENICO GROUP
MILLICOM INTERNATIONAL CELLULAR S.A.
ORANGE
TOUCHSTAR PLC
Telefon AB LM Ericsson
Telia Company AB

HISTORICAL FINANCIALS
Company Type: Public

Income Statement
FYE: December 31

	REVENUE ($mil)	NET INCOME ($mil)	NET PROFIT MARGIN	EMPLOYEES
12/23	24,653	736	3.0%	0
12/22	26,606	4,539	17.1%	86,900
12/21	25,129	1,837	7.3%	87,927
12/20	26,818	(3,096)	—	92,039
12/19	26,177	7	0.0%	98,322
Annual Growth	(1.5%)	211.1%	—	—

2023 Year-End Financials
Debt ratio: 11.6%
Return on equity: 3.1%
Cash ($ mil.): 6,904
Current Ratio: 1.65
Long-term debt ($ mil.): 4,028
No. of shares ($ mil.): 5,525
Dividends
  Yield: —
  Payout: 91.2%
Market value ($ mil.): 18,898

	STOCK PRICE ($) FY Close	P/E High/Low		PER SHARE ($) Earnings	Dividends	Book Value
12/23	3.42	43	26	0.13	0.12	4.12
12/22	4.64	8	6	0.80	0.06	4.08
12/21	6.22	22	12	0.33	0.09	3.49
12/20	3.91	—	—	(0.55)	0.11	2.72
12/19	3.71	—	—	0.00	0.11	3.07
Annual Growth	(2.0%)	—	—	—	2.0%	7.6%

Nomura Holdings Inc

Nomura Holdings is one of the leading financial services groups in Japan and provides services to individuals, institutions, corporates and governments through the company's three divisions ? Retail, Wholesale and Investment Management. It also makes private equity and venture capital investments, and oversees some Â¥126.6 trillion of retail client assets. Subsidiary Nomura Asset Management is one of Japan's largest asset management companies in terms of assets under management in investment trusts. In addition, Nomura Securities is the leading securities and investment banking company in Japan that provides individual investors and corporate clients with a broad range of services, including investment advisory services and securities underwriting. Operates in more than 30 countries and regions, Japan accounts for the majority of the company's revenue.

Operations

Nomura operates through three business divisions: Wholesale, Retail and Investment Management.

The Wholesale Division, generates approximately 50% of the company's revenue, consists of two businesses, Global Markets which is engaged in the trading, sales and structuring of financial products, and Investment Banking which is engaged in financing and advisory businesses.

In the company's Retail Division, Nomura conducts business activities by delivering a wide range of financial products and high quality investment services mainly for individuals and corporations in Japan primarily through a network of nationwide branches of Nomura Securities. The segment brings in about 15% of the company's revenue.

Accounts for some 10% of the company's revenue, Investment Management Division is responsible for the asset management business in a broad sense, aims to increase added value by combining various types of expertise that have been accumulated within the group, from traditional assets such as stocks and bonds, to alternative assets such as non-listed equities.

The company's revenue streams are fairly diversified. About 25% of its total revenue came from commissions, with another more than 20% coming from interest and dividends. Net gain on trading brings in nearly 20%, while asset management and portfolio service fees provide about 15%. The remainder of its revenue came from fees from investment banking, gain on investments in equity securities, gain on private equity and debt investments and others.

Geographic Reach

Based in Tokyo, Japan, Nomura operates offices in countries and regions worldwide, including Japan, the US, the UK, Singapore and Hong Kong. Generates most of its revenue in Japan, the Americas bring in nearly 15%, Europe provides approximately 10% and Asia and Oceania represent the remainder.

Sales and Marketing

The company offers its variety of financial services to individuals, corporations, financial institutions, governments and governmental agencies.

Financial Performance

Note: Growth rates may differ after conversion to US dollars.

Nomura Holdings' revenue for 2021 totaled Â¥1.6 trillion, a 17% decrease from the previous year's revenue of Â¥2 trillion. This was mainly due to a lower sales in the company's interest and dividends.

In 2021, the company had a net income of Â¥160.4 billion, a 27% decrease from the previous year's net income of Â¥219.4 billion.

The company's cash at the end of 2021 was Â¥3.2 trillion. Operating activities provided $665.8 billion, while investing activities used Â¥139 billion. Financing activities used another $270 billion, primarily for increase in short-term borrowings.

Strategy

Nomura has established a management vision for the year 2025, the 100th anniversary of its founding. In order to realize this management vision within the next five years, Nomura will promote three core values: Business growth, Trust from society, and Employee satisfaction. By the fiscal year 2023, Nomura aims to expand existing businesses and improve productivity. At the same time, the company will invest in and cultivate new business areas, thereby expanding the company's strategic options. By the fiscal year 2025, Nomura aims to expand its core business domain which is not just in the public but also private space to make a leap to a "Next Stage of Growth."

HISTORY

Tokushichi Nomura started a currency exchange, Nomura Shoten, in Osaka in 1872 and began trading stock. His son, Tokushichi II, took over and in 1910 formed Nomura's first syndicate to underwrite part of a government bond issue. It established the Osaka Nomura Bank in 1918. The bond department became independent in 1925 and became Nomura Securities. The company opened a New York office in 1927, entering stock brokerage in 1938.

The firm rebuilt and expanded retail operations after WWII. It encouraged stock market investing by promoting "million ryo savings chests" -- small boxes in which people saved cash (ryo was an old form of currency). When savings reached 5,000 yen, savers could buy into investment trusts. Nomura distributed more than a million chests in 10 years.

Nomura followed clients overseas in the 1960s, helped underwrite a US issue of Sony stock, and opened a London office. It became Japan's leading securities firm after a 1965 stock market crash decimated rival Yamaichi Securities. The firm grew rapidly in the 1970s, ushering investment capital in and out of Japan and competing with banks by issuing corporate debt securities.

As the Japanese economy soared in the 1980s, the company opened Nomura Bank International in London (1986) and bought 20% of US mergers and acquisitions advisor Wasserstein Perella (1988, sold 2001).

Then the Japanese economic bubble burst. Nomura's stock toppled 70% from its 1987 peak and underwriting plummeted. In 1991 and 1992, amid revelations that Nomura and other brokerages had reimbursed favored clients' trading losses, the firm was accused of manipulating stock in companies owned by Japanese racketeers. Nomura's chairman and president -- both named Tabuchi -- resigned, admitting no wrongdoing.

The firm trimmed staff and offices and focused on its most efficient operations. From 1993 to 2000, it seesawed from red to black and back again.

Junichi Ujiie became president after the payoff scandal; he restructured operations to prepare for Japan's financial deregulation. Nomura invested in pub chain Inntrepreneur and William Hill, a UK betting chain. It also created an entertainment lending unit to lend against future royalties or syndication fees, and spun off a minority stake in its high-risk US real estate business, which ceased lending altogether the next year.

In 1998 Nomura was dealt a double blow when Asian economies collapsed and Russia defaulted on its debts. Incurring substantial losses, the firm refocused on its domestic market and reduced overseas operations. That year it teamed with Industrial Bank of Japan for derivatives sales in the UK and pension plan consulting in Japan.

In 1999 Nomura bailed out ailing property subsidiary Nomura Finance, which had been crippled by the sinking Japanese real estate market. It also invested heavily in UK real estate and bought 40% of the Czech beer market with South African Breweries.

The next year the firm agreed to buy the business services arm of Welsh utilities firm Hyder; it also bought 114,000 flats in Germany with local government authorities, its first European deal outside the UK. Also in 2000 Nomura sold its assets in pachinko parlors and "love" hotels, Japanese cultural traditions with less-than-sparkling reputations. British authorities that year fined Nomura traders in relation to charges of trying to rig Australia's stock market in 1996.

The company converted to a holding company structure in 2001 and, months later, made its debut on the NYSE. It made two big deals in the UK that year, buying hotel chain Le MÃ©ridien and becoming the nation's largest pub owner via the purchase of some 1,000 locations from Bass. The company also bought a stake in Thomas Weisel Partners to increase its participation in M&A action between US and Japanese firms. In 2002 the company decided to sell the network of more than 4,100 pubs to a consortium of private investors for some $3 billion.

In 2007 Nomura acquired global agency brokerage Instinet. The deal allowed the company to begin offering electronic trading services.

In 2008 Japanese regulators chose a consortium led by Nomura to take control of troubled Ashikaga Bank from the government; Nomura's private equity arm took a stake of about 45% in Ashikaga. The deal marked Nomura's first foray into retail banking.

The global financial crisis heavily impacted Nomura, which reported steep declines in 2008 and 2009. The company lost some Â¥208 billion ($2 billion) in 2009 alone on trading and equity investments. The US subprime mortgage bust further hurt the group, which lost money on mortgage-backed securities.

In response, Nomura cut operating costs and fine-tuned its offerings. The following year, the company boosted its global investment banking capabilities by acquiring parts of the fallen bulge-bracket firm Lehman Brothers, including operations in Asia, Europe, and the Middle East, as well as the India-based back office operations. (In its post-acquisition transition, the company laid off some 11% of its UK workforce, or about 1,000 employees in its London office.) In an effort to boost its domestic asset management business, Nomura bought NikkoCiti Trust and Banking from Citigroup in 2009. The company also exited the US residential mortgage-backed securities business entirely.

The Lehman Brothers acquisition helped boost Nomura's profile in European equities and fixed-income trading. Adding on to that purchase, Nomura bought London-based Tricorn Partners -- a move that further complements its UK corporate finance advisory business.

Nomura Asset Management also bought a 35% stake in LIC Mutual Fund Asset Management Company of India. The deal gave Nomura a larger foothold in the Indian market and strengthened its credentials as an international asset manager.

EXECUTIVES

President, Chief Executive Officer, Representative Executive Officer, Director, Kentaro Okuda
Representative Executive Officer, Deputy President, Chief of Staff, Chief Compliance Officer, Director, Tomoyuki Teraguchi
Executive Managing Director, Toshiyasu Iiyama
Executive Managing Director, Chief Financial Officer, Takumi Kitamura
Executive Managing Director, Chief Risk Officer, Sotaro Kato
Executive Managing Director, Chief Strategy Officer, Toru Otsuka
Chairman, Director, Koji Nagai
Outside Director, Kazuhiko Ishimura
Outside Director, Takahisa Takahara
Outside Director, Noriaki Shimazaki
Outside Director, Mari Sono
Outside Director, Laura Simone Unger
Outside Director, Victor Chu
Outside Director, J. Christopher Giancarlo
Outside Director, Patricia Mosser
Director, Shoji Ogawa
Auditors: Ernst & Young ShinNihon LLC

LOCATIONS

HQ: Nomura Holdings Inc
13-1, Nihonbashi 1-chome, Chuo-Ku, Tokyo 103-8645
Phone: (81) 3 5255 1000   **Fax:** (81) 3 6746 7850
Web: www.nomuraholdings.com

2014 Sales

	% of total
Japan	69
Americas	13
Europe	13
Asia and Oceania	5
Total	100

PRODUCTS/OPERATIONS

2014 Sales

	% of total
Net gain on trading	28
Commissions	23
Interest and dividends	23
Asset management & portfolio service fees	11
Fees from investment banking	5
Gain on investments in equity securities	1
Other	9
Total	100

2014 Sales

	% of total
Wholesale	50
Retail	30
Asset Management	6
Others	14
Total	100

COMPETITORS

3I GROUP PLC
ABERDEEN ASSET MANAGEMENT PLC
HSBC HOLDINGS PLC
NEX INTERNATIONAL LIMITED
ROBERT W. BAIRD & CO. INCORPORATED
ROTHSCHILD & CO
SCHRODERS PLC
Sampo Oyj

Street Capital Group Inc
UBS AG

HISTORICAL FINANCIALS
Company Type: Public

Income Statement				FYE: March 31
	ASSETS ($mil)	NET INCOME ($mil)	INCOME AS % OF ASSETS	EMPLOYEES
03/22	356,899	1,175	0.3%	26,585
03/21	383,984	1,382	0.4%	26,402
03/20	405,341	1,999	0.5%	26,629
03/19	369,947	(906)	—	27,864
03/18	382,263	2,065	0.5%	28,048
Annual Growth	(1.7%)	(13.1%)	—	(1.3%)

2022 Year-End Financials
Return on assets: 0.3%
Return on equity: 5.0%
Long-term debt ($ mil.): —
No. of shares ($ mil.): 3,017
Sales ($ mil.): 5,666
Dividends
Yield: 4.9%
Payout: 50.8%
Market value ($ mil.): 12,735

	STOCK PRICE ($) FY Close	P/E High/Low		PER SHARE ($) Earnings	Dividends	Book Value
03/22	4.22	0	0	0.37	0.21	7.94
03/21	5.36	0	0	0.44	0.24	7.95
03/20	4.27	0	0	0.61	0.16	8.04
03/19	3.59	—	—	(0.27)	0.13	7.18
03/18	5.85	0	0	0.58	0.19	7.63
Annual Growth	(7.8%)	—	—	(10.6%)	2.5%	1.0%

Nordea Bank ABp

Nordea Bank is one of the largest financial services groups in the Nordic and Baltic Sea regions. Sweden is its home, but Nordea also has a major presence in Denmark, Finland, Norway, and Russia. The bank splits its operations into three main divisions: retail banking, wholesale banking, and wealth management. The bank also provides life and pension products. Originally founded in the 1820s, Nordea Bank now boasts a network of about 700 branches and serves some 11 million customers, including about 1 million corporate clients -- a key customer segment for Nordea. About 55% of its lending activity is to corporations.

Operations
The bank operates through three main segments. Retail Banking generates roughly 55% of the bank's overall income, and offers a wide range of traditional deposit and loan products for both household customers and corporate clients, mostly in the Nordic markets and the Baltic countries.

Wholesale Banking brings in another 25% of total revenue, and provides banking and other financial services to large Nordic and global corporate, institutional and public companies. This division also serves financial sector clients with funds and equity products as well as consulting services within asset allocation and fund sales. Nordea Bank Russia offers a full range of bank services to corporate and private customers in Russia.

Capital Markets unallocated includes the result in Capital Markets which is not allocated to the main business areas.

Roughly 15% of revenue comes from the Wealth Management division, which provides investment, savings and risk management products. It also manages customers' assets and gives financial advice to affluent and high net worth individuals and institutional investors.

Additionally, Nordea offers financing and other services to clients in the Shipping, Offshore & Oil Services industries. The bank also has a Life & Pensions business and an Asset Management division that is responsible for all actively-managed investment products.

Geographic Reach
Nordea Bank has an international network of branches, subsidiaries and representative offices in almost 20 countries around the world, with most of its operations in Denmark, Finland, Norway, and Sweden. More than 30% of revenue comes from Denmark, while Sweden generates another nearly 25%. Finland and Norway markets contribute more than 15% each. Other large markets include the Baltic countries and Russia.

Sales and Marketing
The bank serves private customers (from general retail to the highly-affluent), corporations, financial institutions, and other global institutional customers.

Nordea's mobile banking activity has been growing. In 2014, transaction volume from its mobile bank channels grew by 90%, with the number of active mobile banking users growing by 1,000 per day.

Financial Performance
Note: Growth rates may differ after conversion to US dollars.

Nordea's annual revenues have remained mostly stable for the past few years, while profits have steadily been rising. Revenue in 2014 grew by 3% to ?10.22 billion ($12.42 billion), mostly thanks to higher commission income from investment and lending services from the bank's growing Wealth Management and Retail Banking divisions.

Higher revenue in 2014 pushed profit higher for a third straight year, with net income rising by 7% to ?3.33 billion ($4.05 billion). Also helping the bank's bottom line, net loan loss provisions declined by 26% as its loan portfolio gained credit strength.

Cash levels fell despite higher earnings in 2014, with operations using ?10.82 billion ($13.15 billion), primarily as deposit funding from credit institutions and the broader public declined over the year.

Strategy
Nordea Bank has continued to focus more on its four key markets in the Nordic and Baltic regions (including Denmark, Finland, Norway, and Sweden). In mid-2014, to better concentrate resources on these key markets, Nordea exited its banking, life, and financing businesses in Poland through the sale of its Nordea Bank Polska S.A. to PKO Bank Polski SA for ?694 million ($927 million).

As the industry moves from brick-and-mortar branch banking to digital banking, Nordea has also been expanding its electronic offerings via its mobile, tablet, Netbank, and Facebook platforms. Indeed, during 2014, the bank reported that the number of mobile transactions grew by 90%, reflecting the change in consumer tastes in the banking industry. In late 2014, the company announced that it would increase its IT investments by 30-35% over the coming years, building new core banking and payment platforms to keep up with the digital banking trend.

Company Background
Sampo owns more than 20% of Nordea. The Swedish government held a nearly 20% stake in the bank but reduced that to 13% in 2011 as part of its plan to raise capital. It plans to sell more, and possibly all, of its Nordea stake over time.

Growth in European markets has been a focus for Nordea. In 2009, the company purchased a 75% stake in Russian bank JSB Orgresbank, rebranding it as OJSC Nordea Bank. Nordea also bought the Polish life insurance operations of Finnish banking group Sampo, doubling Nordea's customer base in Poland. However, Nordea put the breaks on aggressive growth and completely halted branch expansion in Russia and the Baltic countries in light of the global financial crisis.

HISTORY
Nordea traces its roots to 1974, when two Swedish government-owned banks, Postbanken and Sveriges Kreditbank, merged to form the country's largest bank, Post-och Kreditbanken (PKbanken), in order to compete with S-E-Banken and Svenska Handelsbanken.

PKbanken didn't hold on to the top spot long. By the early 1980s a recession and languid profits sank the company to third. However, the firm did expand, teaming with Norway's Christiana Bank og Kreditkasse to open joint offices in Hong Kong, Houston, London, SÃ£o Paolo, and Singapore.

As regulatory restrictions in Sweden eased, the government spun off 15% of its interest in the company on the Stockholm Stock Exchange in 1984.

PKbanken pulled out of its deal in London with Christiana Bank in 1986, but it bought a stake in London-based English Trust Group to expand its merchant banking services. In 1988 PKbanken acquired government-owned Carnegie Fondkommission, Sweden's largest brokerage, and in 1989 purchased the state-controlled

Swedish Investment Bank, a provider of funding to small and midsized businesses.

A year later PKbanken acquired regional Swedish bank Nordbanken and assumed the smaller firm's name. Soon after, the government axed the combined firm's top officers and installed new management. The purging didn't help, as another recession and a real estate market crash hammered the company's bottom line. In 1992 the Swedish government intervened again, acquiring all of the outstanding shares of Nordbanken that it did not already own. The company rebounded quickly after selling bad loans to the state and cutting staff by a fifth.

In 1994 the Swedish government transferred its ownership of Gota Bank to Nordbanken. The company resumed trading on the Stockholm Stock Exchange the following year.

Across the border in Finland, rivals Union Bank of Finland and Kansallis-Osake-Pankki merged in 1995 to create Merita Bank, the country's largest.

In 1997 Nordbanken and Merita Bank combined to form MeritaNordbanken, but their parents, Nordbanken Holdings and Merita Ab, remained separate. In 2000 the company bought Danish bank Unidanmark. MeritaNordbanken's holding companies united and assumed the name Nordic Baltic Holding. Later the company changed its name to Nordea, an amalgamation of "Nordic" and "idea."

In 2001 Nordea bought Christiania Bank og Kreditkasse and, later that year, attached the Nordea Bank name to its banking subsidiaries in Denmark, Finland, Norway, and Sweden.

By 2003 the company, composed primarily of the four national banking groups -- Nordea Bank Denmark, Nordea Bank Finland, Nordea Bank Norway, and Nordea Bank Sweden -- decided to change its complex legal structure and create one European company under the Nordea Bank banner.

Nordea acquired Denmark's Fionia Bank in 2009, including the bank's staff and its 29 branches but excluding some 2,000 troubled corporate customers. The Denmark government had taken control of the failing bank earlier in the year.

EXECUTIVES

Executive Vice President, Head of Wholesale Banking, Casper von Koskull
Executive Vice President, Head of Retail Banking, Lennart Jacobsen
Executive Vice President, Head of Group Corporate Center, Chief Financial Officer, Torsten Hagen Jorgensen
Executive Vice President, Chief Risk Officer, Head of Group Risk Managment, Ari Kaperi
Executive Vice President, Chief Operating Officer of Wholesale Banking, Peter Nyegaard
Executive Vice President, Head of Wealth Management, Gunn Waersted
Chairman, Bjorn Wahlroos
Vice-Chairwoman, Marie Ehrling
Director, Peter F. Braunwalder
Director, Elisabeth Grieg
Director, Svein S. Jacobsen
Director, Tom Knutzen
Director, Lars G. Nordstrom
Director, Sarah Russell
Director, Kari Stadigh
Director, Employee Representative, Kari Ahola
Employee Representative, Toni H Madsen
Employee Representative, Lars Oddestad
Employee Representative, Hans Christian Rise
Auditors : PricewaterhouseCoopers Oy

LOCATIONS

HQ: Nordea Bank ABp
Hamnbanegatan (Satamaradankatu) 5, Helsinki FI-00020
Phone: (46) 8 614 78 00   **Fax:** (46) 8 614 87 70
Web: www.nordea.com

2014 Sales

	% of total
Denmark	31
Sweden	24
Finland	18
Norway	17
New European markets	4
Other	6
Total	100

PRODUCTS/OPERATIONS

2014 Sales

	% of total
Banking products	61
Capital markets products	19
Savings products and asset management	10
Life and pensions	5
Other	5
Total	100

2014 Sales

	% of total
Retail Banking	56
Wholesale Banking	24
Wealth Management	16
Group Corporate Centre	4
Total	100

2014 Sales

	% of total
Net Interest income	54
Net Fee abd commission income	28
Net results on items at fair value	14
Other Operating income	4
Total	100

COMPETITORS

Coöperatieve Rabobank U.A.
NATWEST GROUP PLC
Skandinaviska Enskilda Banken AB
Svenska Handelsbanken AB
The Toronto-Dominion Bank

HISTORICAL FINANCIALS

Company Type: Public

Income Statement — FYE: December 31

	ASSETS ($mil)	NET INCOME ($mil)	INCOME AS % OF ASSETS	EMPLOYEES
12/22	635,320	3,819	0.6%	27,453
12/21	645,562	4,306	0.7%	27,402
12/20	677,660	2,746	0.4%	28,123
12/19	622,964	1,705	0.3%	29,300
12/18	631,470	3,515	0.6%	28,990
Annual Growth	0.2%	2.1%		(1.4%)

2022 Year-End Financials

Return on assets: 0.6%
Return on equity: 11.0%
Long-term debt ($ mil.): —
No. of shares ($ mil.): 3,640
Sales ($ mil.): 15,165
Dividends
Yield: —
Payout: 72.4%
Market value ($ mil.): 39,358

	STOCK PRICE ($) FY Close	P/E High/Low	PER SHARE ($) Earnings	Dividends	Book Value
12/22	10.81	13 9	1.01	0.73	9.21
12/21	12.22	13 8	1.08	0.92	9.64
12/20	8.16	18 10	0.68	0.88	10.25
12/19	8.12	25 16	0.43	0.52	8.73
12/18	8.39	0 0	87.03	0.79	9.30
Annual Growth	6.5%		(67.1%)	(1.8%)	(0.2%)

Norsk Hydro ASA

Norsk Hydro is a leading aluminum and energy company committed to a sustainable future. The company has approximately 6.2 million tons of alumina production. Its global operations include casthouse products, building systems, extruded and rolled products, and automotive and transport products, distributed worldwide. The company's business is present in a broad range of market segments for aluminum, energy, metal recycling, renewables, and batteries. Ranks among the world's largest aluminum producers, Norsk Hydro operates in more than 140 locations in approximately 40 countries, and serves more than 30,000 customers around the world. The majority of the company's sales were generated from customers from Europe.

Operations

Norsk Hydro has six operating segments: Hydro Extrusions, Metal Markets, Hydro Bauxite & Alumina, Hydro Aluminium Metal, and Hydro Energy.

Extruded Extrusions (more than 45% of sales) delivers products within extrusion profiles, building systems and precision tubing, and is present in about 40 countries.

Metal Markets (about 35%) includes all sales activities relating to products from its primary metal plants and operational responsibility for stand-alone recyclers as well as physical and financial metal trading activities.

Bauxite and Alumina (nearly 10%) includes bauxite mining activities, production of alumina and related commercial activities primarily the sale of alumina.

Aluminium Metal (about 5%) includes primary aluminum production and casting activities. The main products are comprised of extrusion ingots, foundry alloys, sheet ingot, and standard ingot.

Energy (less than 5%) includes operating and commercial responsibility for Hydro's power stations in Norway, a trading and wholesale business in Brazil, and energy sourcing for Hydro's world-wide operations.

Geographic Reach

Based in Norway, Norsk Hydro has primary metal production facilities in Europe, Canada, Australia, Brazil, and Qatar, and remelting plants in a range of countries in Europe and the US. It has employees in approximately 40 countries.

The company's key sourcing countries include the US, Brazil, Norway, Switzerland, Australia, Canada, Singapore, Germany, and China.

More than 45% of the company's revenue is from customers outside Europe. European Union brings in approximately 40%, while Europe accounts for about 10%.

Sales and Marketing

The company's products from Extruded Solutions are delivered to such sectors as construction, automotive and heating, ventilation, and air conditioning.

Financial Performance

Norsk Hydro's performance for the past five years with a downward trend for the first half, then increasing year-over-year since 2020, ending with 2022 as its highest performing year over the period.

The company's revenue for fiscal 2022 increased by NOK58.3 billion to NOK207.9 billion, as compared to 2021's revenue of NOK149.7 billion.

Net income for fiscal 2022 increased to NOK24.2 billion compared from the prior year's net income of NOK12.2 billion.

Cash held by the company at the end of fiscal 2022 increased to NOK21.2 billion. Cash provided by operations was at NOK4.7 billion. Investing activities used NOK226 million while financing activities provided NOK2 billion. Main cash uses were for purchases of short-term investments and paid dividends.

Strategy

In 2022, Norsk Hydro have taken key steps in the execution of its 2025 strategy, strengthening its low-carbon aluminium position as well as maturing business opportunities within new energy solutions.

Mergers and Acquisitions

In early 2022, Norsk Hydro made a tender offer for the purchase of all the shares in Alumetal, one of the largest producers of casting aluminum alloys in Europe. The transaction implies an enterprise value of approximately PLN 1.332 billion (approximately EUR 290 million) based on the latest reported net debt for FY2021 and dividends payable of PLN 106 million (approximately EUR 23 million). The transaction will strengthen Hydro's recycling position in Europe and widen its product offering in the low-carbon and scrap-based foundry alloy market.

HISTORY

Norwegian entrepreneurs Sam Eyde and Kristian Birkeland began Norsk Hydro-Elektrisk Kvaelstofaktieselskap (Norwegian Hydro-Electric Nitrogen Corp.) in 1905. The company used electricity generated from waterfalls to extract nitrogen from the air to produce fertilizer.

After WWII the Norwegian government seized German holdings in Norsk Hydro and took a 48% stake in the company. It grew to be the largest chemical firm in Scandinavia. In 1965, when Norway granted licenses for offshore petroleum exploration, the company formed partnerships with foreign companies. These included Phillips Petroleum, which spurred the North Sea boom in 1969 when its drilling rig Ocean Viking struck oil in the giant Ekofisk field, and Elf Aquitaine, which oversaw the Frigg discovery in 1971. The Norwegian state increased its share of Norsk Hydro to 51% in 1972.

The company also branched out with hydroelectric-powered aluminum processing at its Karmoy Works (1967) and with a fish-farming subsidiary, Mowi (1969). During much of the 1970s, it focused on oil and gas development, which added to the treasury and helped finance growth, often through acquisitions.

Norsk Hydro pushed into the European fertilizer market by buying Dutch company NSM in 1979; during the 1980s it acquired interests in fertilizer operations in France, Sweden, and the UK. In petrochemicals it expanded by buying two British PVC makers. Norsk Hydro-controlled Hydro Aluminum merged with ASV, another Norwegian aluminum company, in 1986, and the company consolidated its aluminum holdings two years later.

Hydro served as operator in the Oseberg field, which began production in 1988 and grew rapidly to become a major source of oil and gas. In 1990 it bought 330 Danish gasoline stations from UNO-X; in 1992 it purchased Mobil Oil's Norwegian marketing and distribution system. Two years later Norsk Hydro merged its oil and marketing operations in Norway and Denmark with Texaco's.

A weak world economy and increased competition limited its revenues in 1992 and 1993. The company countered slumping sales by selling noncore subsidiaries, including pharmaceutical unit Hydro Pharma (1992) and chocolate maker Freia Marabou (1993).

Norsk Hydro expanded further during the early 1990s, acquiring fertilizer plants in Germany, the UK, and the US, as well as W. R. Grace's ammonia plants in Trinidad and Tobago. The firm acquired Fisons' NPK fertilizer business in 1994. The company agreed to an asset swap with Petro-Canada in 1996, becoming a partner in oil and gas fields off the east coast of Canada. That year Norsk Hydro bought UNO-X's Swedish gas station operations.

The Norwegian government's stake in Norsk Hydro was reduced from 51% to about 45% in 1999 when the company and state-owned Statoil made a deal to take over Saga Petroleum, Norway's leading independent oil producer, to keep it out of foreign hands.

In light of major losses in 1999 by Hydro Agri, the company made plans in 2000 to close several European nitrogen fertilizer operations. However, it agreed to modernize and expand its Hydro Aluminum Sunndal facility, to make it the largest aluminum plant in Europe. That year the company also sold Saga UK (North Sea assets) to Conoco, and its fish-farming unit to Dutch company Nutreco.

In 2001 the company acquired a stake in Soquimich, an industrial minerals company in Chile, and majority control of Slovakian aluminum producer Slovalco.

The new decade brought with it a new focus; the company began to make aluminum its primary business lines. Toward that end Norsk Hydro bought VAW Aluminum from E.On AG for $2.8 billion in a deal that enabled it to expand its product base in Europe and the US, especially to key customers in the automobile industry. It then sold its flexible packaging unit to Alcan for about $545 million in 2003. Furthering the same goal, the company announced in 2003 and then followed through on a spinoff of its agrochemical unit the following year. The resultant company was Yara International.

Norsk Hydro sold its chemicals business to Ineos for $900 million in 2008.

In 2009 Svein Richard Brandtzà¦g took over as chief executive. He had been in charge of Hydro's Aluminum Products unit previously. Eivind Reiten resigned after eight years in charge of the company.

In 2011 Norsk Hydro acquired the Brazilian bauxite mining and alumina refining units of Vale SA for $5.7 billion, making it a major bauxite and alumina miner.

The Vale purchase gave Norsk Hydro control of the world's third-largest bauxite mine and the world's biggest alumina refinery, which have the capacity to supply the company with sufficient raw materials to operate without external suppliers for several decades. Norsk Hydro paid Vale about $1.1 billion in cash and a 22% stake in Norsk Hydro for the assets. The Norwegian government backed the deal, and reduced its stake in Norsk Hydro by about 20%.

Although the Vale acquisition positioned Norsk Hydro for growth, the aluminum markets have seen demand declining in 2011 and 30% of the aluminum producers losing money. Total demand growth declined to 7% in 2011 from a 19% increase in 2010. A drop in European demand has affected the market, due primarily to uncertainty over eurozone debt. A weakening economy has Chinese producers starting to cut back on production, and Hydro has stated that it would not restart its idled Sunndal smelter in Norway.

To raise cash, in 2011 Norsk Hydro divested its 21% ownership stake in Norwegian power production company SKS Produksjon AS to Salten Kraftsamband AS for $187 million. The deal did not affect Hydro's other power grid holdings.

In 2012 it agreed to form an aluminum manufacturing joint venture with Orkla. The proposed joint venture, which will retain the Sapa name (currently the aluminum products division of Orkla), will be equally owned by Norsk Hydro and Orkla, and will combine their respective profiles, building systems, and tubing business to create the world's largest manufactured aluminum products provider.

EXECUTIVES

President, Chief Executive Officer, Hilde Merete Aasheim
Chief Financial Officer, Executive Vice President, Pal Kildemo
Compliance Executive Vice President, Legal Executive Vice President, Anne-Lene Midseim
Energy & Corporate Development Executive Vice President, Arvid Moss
People & Safety Executive Vice President, Hilde Vestheim Nordh
Public Affairs Executive Vice President, Communications Executive Vice President, Inger Sethov
Division Officer, John G. Thuestad
Division Officer, Eivind Kallevik
Division Officer, Egil Hogna
Division Officer, Einar Glomnes
Division Officer, Erik Fossum
Chairperson, Non-Executive Director, Dag Mejdell
Deputy Chairman, Director, Irene Rummelhoff
Director, Arve Baade
Director, Rune Bjerke
Director, Liselott Kilaas
Director, Peter Kukielski
Director, Sten Roar Martinsen
Director, Ellen Merete Olstad
Director, Thomas Schulz
Director, Marianne Wiinholt
Auditors : KPMG AS

LOCATIONS

HQ: Norsk Hydro ASA
  Drammensveien 260, Oslo N-0240
Phone: (47) 22 53 81 00   **Fax:** (47) 22 53 85 53
Web: www.hydro.com

2016 sales
	% of total
European Union	49
Non-European Union	7
Norway	4
Outside Europe	40
Total	100

PRODUCTS/OPERATIONS

2016 sales
	% of total
Bauxite & Alumina	15
Primary metal	7
Metal market	48
Rolled Products	27
Energy	3
Other and eliminations	—
Total	100

Selected Operations
Aluminum products
  Hydro aluminum automotive
  Hydro aluminum extrusion
  Hydro aluminum rolled products and wire rod
Aluminum metal
Energy
  Hydroelectric power stations

COMPETITORS

3A COMPOSITES USA INC.
Companhia Brasileira de AlumÂnio
Fortum Oyj
Hydro Aluminium AS
KAISER ALUMINUM CORPORATION
Nordural Grundartangi ehf.
OMV Aktiengesellschaft
ORMET CORPORATION
Rio Tinto Alcan Inc
SASOL LTD

HISTORICAL FINANCIALS
Company Type: Public

Income Statement FYE: December 31

	REVENUE ($mil)	NET INCOME ($mil)	NET PROFIT MARGIN	EMPLOYEES
12/23	19,125	353	1.8%	32,724
12/22	21,279	2,456	11.5%	32,014
12/21	17,108	1,377	8.1%	31,264
12/20	16,237	216	1.3%	34,240
12/19	17,069	(206)	—	36,310
Annual Growth	2.9%	—	—	(2.6%)

2023 Year-End Financials
Debt ratio: 1.7%   No. of shares ($ mil.): 2,012
Return on equity: 3.5%   Dividends
Cash ($ mil.): 2,425   Yield: —
Current Ratio: 1.82   Payout: 306.2%
Long-term debt ($ mil.): 2,855   Market value ($ mil.): 13,440

	STOCK PRICE ($) FY Close	P/E High/Low		PER SHARE ($) Earnings Dividends		Book Value
12/23	6.68	5	3	0.17	0.53	4.93
12/22	7.53	1	0	1.20	0.68	5.10
12/21	7.90	1	1	0.67	0.29	4.64
12/20	4.58	5	3	0.11	0.14	4.25
12/19	3.69	—	—	(0.10)	0.14	4.44
Annual Growth	16.0%	—	—	—	39.0%	2.6%

North Pacific Bank Ltd

EXECUTIVES

President, Representative Director, Mitsuharu Yasuda
Deputy President, Representative Director, Minoru Nagano
Senior Managing Director, Director, Hitoshi Masuda
Director, Satoshi Shindo
Director, Masanori Abe
Director, Akira Yamada
Outside Director, Kazuaki Shimamoto
Outside Director, Naoki Nishita
Outside Director, Masako Taniguchi
Outside Director, Makiko Sasaki
Auditors : KPMG AZSA LLC

LOCATIONS

HQ: North Pacific Bank Ltd
  3-7 Odori-Nishi, Chuo-ku, Sapporo, Hokkaido 060-8661
Phone: (81) 11 261 1311
Web: www.hokuyobank.co.jp

COMPETITORS

CANDOVER INVESTMENTS PLC
Clairvest Group Inc.
EQUITY GROUP INVESTMENTS, L.L.C.
IAP WORLDWIDE SERVICES, INC.
KIYO HOLDINGS,INC.

HISTORICAL FINANCIALS
Company Type: Public

Income Statement FYE: March 31

	ASSETS ($mil)	NET INCOME ($mil)	INCOME AS % OF ASSETS	EMPLOYEES
03/22	111,346	96	0.1%	4,298
03/21	107,096	85	0.1%	4,546
03/20	92,013	69	0.1%	4,722
03/19	88,129	127	0.1%	4,955
03/18	89,469	128	0.1%	5,112
Annual Growth	5.6%	(6.9%)	—	(4.2%)

2022 Year-End Financials
Return on assets: —   Dividends
Return on equity: 2.7%   Yield: —
Long-term debt ($ mil.): —   Payout: 33.0%
No. of shares ($ mil.): 389   Market value ($ mil.): —
Sales ($ mil.): 1,024

Novartis AG Basel

EXECUTIVES

Chief Executive Officer, Vasant Narasimhan
Chief Financial Officer, Harry Kirsch
Chief People & Organization Officer, Robert Kowalski
Chief Legal Officer, Karen L. Hale
Chief Strategy & Growth Officer, Aharon Gal

Chief Ethics Officer, Chief Risk Officer, Chief Compliance Officer, Klaus Moosmayer
President, Victor Bulto
Operations President, Steffen Lang
President, Chief Commercial Officer, Marie-France Tschudin
Global Drug Development President, Global Drug Development Chief Medical Officer, Shreeram Aradhye
Corporate Secretary, Charlotte Pamer-Wieser
Independent Non-Executive Chairman, Joerg Reinhardt
Independent Non-Executive Director, Daniel Hochstrasser
Independent Non-Executive Director, Ana de Pro Gonzalo
Independent Non-Executive Director, Nancy C. Andrews
Independent Non-Executive Director, Ton Buechner
Independent Non-Executive Director, Patrice Bula
Independent Non-Executive Director, Elizabeth Doherty
Independent Non-Executive Director, Ann M. Fudge
Independent Non-Executive Director, Bridgette P. Heller
Independent Non-Executive Director, Frans van Houten
Independent Non-Executive Director, Simon E. Moroney
Independent Non-Executive Director, Andreas von Planta
Independent Non-Executive Director, Charles L. Sawyers
Independent Non-Executive Director, William T. Winters
Auditors : KPMG AG

LOCATIONS

HQ: Novartis AG Basel
   Lichtstrasse 35, Basel 4056
Phone: (41) 61 324 1111   **Fax:** (41) 61 324 7826
Web: www.novartis.com

HISTORICAL FINANCIALS
Company Type: Public

Income Statement				FYE: December 31
	REVENUE ($mil)	NET INCOME ($mil)	NET PROFIT MARGIN	EMPLOYEES
12/23	46,660	14,850	31.8%	76,057
12/22	51,828	6,955	13.4%	101,703
12/21	52,877	24,021	45.4%	104,323
12/20	49,898	8,072	16.2%	105,794
12/19	48,677	11,732	24.1%	103,914
Annual Growth	(1.1%)	6.1%	—	(7.5%)

2023 Year-End Financials
Debt ratio: 18.4%
Return on equity: 28.0%
Cash ($ mil.): 13,393
Current Ratio: 1.16
Long-term debt ($ mil.): 18,436
No. of shares ($ mil.): 2,044
Dividends
Yield: —
Payout: 32.0%
Market value ($ mil.): 206,386

	STOCK PRICE ($) FY Close	P/E High/Low		PER SHARE ($) Earnings	Dividends	Book Value
12/23	100.97	15	11	7.10	2.27	22.83
12/22	90.72	29	23	3.17	2.16	28.00
12/21	87.47	9	7	10.63	2.08	30.27
12/20	94.43	28	20	3.52	2.01	25.08
12/19	94.69	19	15	5.06	1.84	24.49
Annual Growth	1.6%	—	—	8.8%	5.4%	(1.7%)

Novatek Joint Stock Co

NOVATEK is a Russia's independent gas producer and one of a top global natural gas company. Established in 1994, NOVATEK accounts for approximately 80% of Russia's natural gas production. It explores for and processes natural gas and liquid hydrocarbons, producing 75 billion cubic meters of natural gas each year. It sells natural gas directly throughout the country, as well as internationally through traders. NOVATEK focuses its production on the prolific Yamal-Nenets Autonomous region (YNAO) in Western Siberia. Customers include end customers, and wholesale gas suppliers.

Operations
NOVATEK is engaged in the exploration and development, production, and processing of natural gas, gas condensate, and crude oil.

The YNAO is the most significant gas producing region in Russia, accounting for approximately 80% of Russia's natural gas production and over 15% of global gas production. The company has 65 licenses on exploration and production with 16.3 billion barrels of oil equivalent (boe) of SEC proved reserves. Marketable production of natural gas increased by about 10% and production of liquids decreased by less than 5%. It also produced 75 billion cubic meters of natural gas this year.

The company derives its revenue through products sales: natural gas (accounts for about half of the total revenue); Naphtha (more than 15%); crude oil (around 15%); liquefied petroleum gas (beyond 5%); stable gas condensate (5%); and other refined products (10%).

Geographic Reach
NOVATEK is headquartered in Russia. It carry commercial production of natural gas, gas condensate and crude oil at 20 fields. It stabilize gas condensate to Purovsky Plant and process stable gas condensate at Ust-Luga Complex.

Sales and Marketing
NOVATEK sell its natural gas to customers in the Russian domestic market, mainly through trunk pipelines and regional distribution networks, and deliver LNG purchased primarily from its joint ventures, OAO Yamal LNG and OOO Cryogas-Vysotsk, to international markets.

The company has advertising expenses of RR 531 million in 2019.

Financial Performance
NOVATEK's revenue was RUB 862.8 billion, a 4% increase from RUB 831.8 billion in 2018. The increase was caused by oil and gas sales, as well as other revenues.

Net income increased from RUB 163.7 billion to RUB 865.5 billion.

Cash and cash equivalents at the end of the year were RUB 53.2 billion, 28% higher than the previous year (RUB 41.5 billion). Operating activities provided RUB 307.4 billion to the coffers. Investing activities and financing activities used RUB 169 billion and RUB 119.4 billion, respectively. Main cash uses were purchases of property, plant, and equipment, and payment of dividends to shareholders.

Strategy
During 2019, NOVATEK obtained rights to use nine license areas located near the group's other assets in YNAO. These allowed the company to expand its resource base.

Company Background
NOVATEK was established in 1994, when AOOT FIK Novafininvest was established (the name was changed to OAO NOVATEK later). The new Company focused on oil and gas assets development from the very beginning.

EXECUTIVES

Chairman, Executive Director, Leonid V. Mikhelson
Strategic Planning First Deputy Chairman, Lev V. Feodosiev
First Deputy Chairman, Alexander M. Fridman
Economics and Finance Deputy Chairman, Viktor N. Belyakov
Communications Development Deputy Chairman, Communications Development Director, Denis B. Solovy?v
Legal Deputy Chairman, Legal Director, Tatyana S. Kuznetsova
Deputy Chairman, Eduard S. Gudkov
Deputy Chairman, Vladimir A. Baskov
Deputy Chairman, Evgeny A. Kot
Deputy Chairman, Mark A. Gyetvay
Chairman, Alexander E. Natalenko
Independent Director, Robert Castaigne
Independent Director, Burckhard Bergmann
Independent Director, Victor P. Orlav
Director, Michael Borrell
Director, Arnaud Le Foll
Director, Gennady N. Timchenko
Director, Andrei I. Akimov
Auditors : AO PricewaterhouseCoopers Audit

LOCATIONS

HQ: Novatek Joint Stock Co
   Ulitsa Pobedy 22a, Tarko-Sale, Yamal-Nenets Autonomous District 629850

Phone: (7) 495 730 60 00   Fax: (7) 495 721 22 53
Web: www.novatek.ru

PRODUCTS/OPERATIONS

2013 Sales

	% of total
Natural gas	69
Stable gas condensate	11
Naphtha	9
Liquefied petroleum gas	6
Crude oil	3
Other gas and gas condensate refined products	2
Total	100

COMPETITORS

ADANI ENTERPRISES LIMITED
CENTRAL GARDEN & PET COMPANY
DELTA NATURAL GAS COMPANY, INC.
DWM Energy AG
FIRST PACIFIC COMPANY LIMITED
GRAHAM PACKAGING COMPANY, L.P.
INPEX CORPORATION
MITSUI & CO. EUROPE PLC
SOCIETE INTERNATIONALE DE PLANTATIONS D'HEVEAS
TRIFAST PLC

HISTORICAL FINANCIALS

Company Type: Public

Income Statement   FYE: December 31

	REVENUE ($mil)	NET INCOME ($mil)	NET PROFIT MARGIN	EMPLOYEES
12/21	15,404	5,765	37.4%	0
12/20	9,515	906	9.5%	0
12/19	13,863	13,906	100.3%	15,445
12/18	11,934	2,349	19.7%	13,694
12/17	10,087	2,705	26.8%	8,145
Annual Growth	11.2%	20.8%	—	—

2021 Year-End Financials

Debt ratio: 0.1%
Return on equity: 24.6%
Cash ($ mil.): 1,412
Current Ratio: 1.48
Long-term debt ($ mil.): 892
No. of shares ($ mil.): 2,995
Dividends
. Yield: —
Payout: 35.6%
Market value ($ mil.): —

Novo-Nordisk AS

Novo Nordisk is a leading global healthcare company, founded in 1923. It makes modern insulin analogues Levemir and NovoLog (which mimic natural insulin regulation more closely than human insulin), Victoza for type 2 diabetes, and Saxenda, which treats obesity. The company also has products in the areas of hemostasis management (blood clotting), human growth hormone, and estrogen replacement therapy. The company has affiliates in some 80 countries and markets products in about 170 countries. It generates more than 50% of its revenue from North America. The not-for-profit Novo Nordisk Foundation, through its Novo A/S subsidiary, controls the voting power in Novo Nordisk.

Operations

Novo Nordisk operates in two business segments: Diabetes and Obesity (which covers insulins, oral anti-diabetic drugcs, and obesity therapies) and Rare disease (which covers rare blood disorders, rare endocrine disorders and hormone replacement therapy).

The Diabetes and Obesity segment accounts for about 90% of total revenue, primarily from diabetes treatments. Top product offerings include Levemir and Tresiba (long-acting insulin), NovoMix/NovoLog Mix (premix insulin), NovoRapid/NovoLog (fast-acting insulin), Victoza (type 2 diabetes and weight management), and Saxenda (obesity).

Rare disease segment accounts for more than 10% and includes the NovoSeven, Hemophilia A, and Hemophilia B.

Geographic Reach

Headquartered in Denmark, Novo Nordisk has some 15 production facilities and ten research and development centers located in Algeria, Brazil, China, Denmark, France, India, Japan, Russia, the UK, and the US.

Its primary markets are North America (about 50% of revenue), China, Japan, and major countries in Europe.

Financial Performance

Note: Growth rates may differ after conversion to US Dollars.

The company reported a total revenue of DKK177 billion, a 26% increase from the previous year's total revenue of DKK140.8 billion.

In 2022, the company had a net income of DKK55.5 billion, a 16% increase from the previous year's net income of DKK47.8 billion.

The company's cash at the end of 2022 was DKK12.7 billion. Operating activities generated DKK78.9 billion, while investing activities used DKK24.9 billion, mainly for purchase of property, plant and equipment. Financing activities used another DKK51.8 billion, primarily for dividends paid.

Strategy

The company's business is built around its clear purpose: driving change to defeat diabetes and other serious chronic diseases. Its key contribution is to discover and develop innovative medicines and make them accessible to patients throughout the world. The company aims to strengthen its leadership and treatment options in diabetes and obesity, secure a leading position within Rare Disease, and establish a strong presence in other serious chronic diseases, such as cardiovascular disease (CVD), non-alcoholic steatohepatitis (NASH), chronic kidney disease (CKD) and Alzheimer's disease (AD), and provide curative therapies based on its cell therapy platform.

Mergers and Acquisitions

In 2023, Novo Nordisk entered into exclusive negotiations for a controlling stake in BIOCORP, which would be followed by a mandatory simplified tender offer on all remaining outstanding shares in BIOCORP at a price of EUR 35.00 per share in cash, representing a total equity value of approximately EUR 154 million. BIOCORP is a French company specialised in the design, development and manufacturing of delivery systems and innovative medical devices, including Mallya, a Bluetooth enabled smart add-on device for pen injectors. Following the acquisition, Novo Nordisk would aim to preserve the agility and entrepreneurial spirit of BIOCORP, while investing further in the organization with the goal of delivering cutting edge devices and delivery solutions to improve care for people across the globe living with serious chronic diseases.

In late 2022, Novo Nordisk acquired Forma Therapeutics Holdings, Inc. (Forma), a clinical-stage biopharmaceutical company focused on transforming the lives of patients with sickle cell disease (SCD) and rare blood disorders. The acquisition of Forma Therapeutics, including its lead development candidate, etavopivat, is aligned with Novo Nordisk's strategy to complement and accelerate its scientific presence and pipeline in haemoglobinopathies, a group of disorders in which there is abnormal production or structure of the haemoglobin protein in the red blood cells.

Company Background

Novo Nordisk was formed by the 1989 merger of Danish insulin producers Novo and Nordisk. The company traces its roots to the founding of two Danish insulin companies, Nordisk Insulinlaboratorium and Novo Terapeutisk Laboratorium, in 1923 and 1925, respectively.

HISTORY

Novo Nordisk was formed by the 1989 merger of Danish insulin producers Novo and Nordisk.

Soon after Canadian researchers first extracted insulin from the pancreases of cattle, Danish researcher August Krogh (winner of the 1920 Nobel Prize in physiology) and physician Marie Krogh, his wife, teamed up with H. C. Hagedorn, also a physician, to found Nordisk Insulinlaboratorium. One of their lab workers was an inventor named Harald Pedersen, and in 1923 Nordisk hired Pedersen's brother, Thorvald, to analyze chemicals. The relationship was unsuccessful, however, and the brothers left the company.

The Pedersens decided to produce insulin themselves and set up operations in their basement in 1924. Harald also designed a syringe that patients could use for their own insulin injections. Within a decade their firm, Novo Terapeutisk Laboratorium, was selling its product in 40 countries.

Meanwhile, Nordisk introduced a slow-acting insulin in 1936. NPH insulin, launched in the US in 1950, soon became the leading longer-acting insulin. Nordisk later became a major maker of human growth hormone.

During WWII Novo produced its first enzyme, trypsin, used to soften leather. It began producing penicillin in 1947 and during the 1950s developed Heparin, a trypsin-based drug used to treat blood clots. The company unveiled more industrial enzymes in the 1960s.

In 1981 Novo began selling its insulin in the US through a joint venture with E. R. Squibb (now part of Bristol-Myers Squibb). The next year Novo was the first to produce human insulin (actually a modified form of pig insulin), and in 1983 Nordisk introduced the Nordisk Infuser, a pump that constantly released small quantities of insulin. Two years later Novo debuted the NovoPen, a refillable injector that looked like a fountain pen.

Novo was the world's #2 insulin maker (and the world's largest maker of industrial enzymes) when it merged with #3, Nordisk, in 1989. By combining their research and market share, they were better able to compete globally with then-#1 Eli Lilly. After the merger, Novo Nordisk introduced the NovoLet, the world's first prefilled, disposable insulin syringe.

Novo Nordisk introduced drugs for depression (Seroxat, 1992), epilepsy (Gabitril, 1995), and hemophilia (NovoSeven, 1995). The company entered a joint marketing alliance with Johnson & Johnson subsidiary LifeScan, the world's #1 maker of blood glucose monitors, in 1995. It also began working with Rhône-Poulenc Rorer on estrogen replacement therapies.

Eli Lilly raised a new challenge in 1996 with the FDA approval of Humalog (the US's first new insulin product in 14 years), which is absorbed faster, giving users more flexibility in their injection schedule. (Novo Nordisk's own fast-acting insulin product, NovoLog, received FDA approval four years later.) A 1998 marketing pact with Schering-Plough signaled Novo Nordisk's desire to boost sales of its diabetes drugs in the US, where Eli Lilly had historically dominated.

In 2000 Novo Nordisk split its health care and enzymes businesses; the split left Novo Nordisk with all the health care operations, while a new company, Novozymes, was formed to carry out the enzyme business. It bought out the remaining shares in its Brazilian subsidiary, Biobrás, in 2001. In 2002 the company spun off its US-based biotechnology firm, ZymoGenetics. It retained a one-third of the company until selling its shares to Bristol-Myers Squibb in 2010.

Further boosting its portfolio of diabetes and obesity intellectual property, the company acquired two US biopharmaceutical research firms (Calibrium and MB2) for undisclosed amounts in 2015.

EXECUTIVES

Chief Executive Officer, President, Lars Fruergaard Jorgensen

Chief Financial Officer, Executive Vice President, Karsten Munk Knudsen

Executive Vice President, Ludovic Helfgott

Executive Vice President, Doug Langa

Development Executive Vice President, Global Development Executive Vice President, Development Head, Global Development Head, Martin Holst Lange

Research Executive Vice President, Research Head, Research Chief Scientific Officer, Marcus Schindler

People & Organisation Executive Vice President, People & Organisation Head, Monique Carter

International Operations Executive Vice President, International Operations Head, Maziar Mike Doustdar

Corporate Affairs Executive Vice President, Commercial Strategy Executive Vice President, Corporate Affairs Head, Commercial Strategy Head, Camilla Sylvest

Product Supply, Quality & IT Executive Vice President, Product Supply, Quality & IT Head, Henrik Wulff

Auditors : Deloitte Statsautoriseret Revisionspartnerselskab

LOCATIONS

HQ: Novo-Nordisk AS
Novo Alle 1, Bagsvaerd DK-2880
Phone: (45) 4444 8888 **Fax:** (45) 4449 0555
Web: www.novonordisk.com

PRODUCTS/OPERATIONS

2016 Sales

	% of total
Diabetes and obesity care	
NovoRapid/Novolog	18
Levemir	15
Victoza	18
NovoMix/NovologMix	10
Human insulin	10
Other diabetes and obesity care (including Saxenda)	5
New-generation insulin	4
Biopharmaceuticals	
Haemophilia	9
Norditropin	8
Other products	3
Total	100

2016 sales

	$ mil.
USA	51
Europe	19
Region China	9
Pacific	8
other countries	13
Total	100

Selected Products

Diabetes products
    Human insulins
    Actrapid
    Insulatard
    Mixtard 30
    Glucagon-like Peptide-1
    Victoza
    Modern insulins
    Levemir
    NovoMix
    NovoRapid
    Oral antidiabetic agents
    NovoNorm
    PrandiMet
Biopharmaceuticals
    NovoSeven (recombinant hemophilia therapy)
    Norditropin (human growth hormone)
    Hormone replacement therapy
    Activelle
    Estrofem
    Novofem
    Vagifem

COMPETITORS

ADARE PHARMACEUTICALS, INC.
AMGEN INC.
ASTRAZENECA PLC
BIOMARIN PHARMACEUTICAL INC.
BRISTOL-MYERS SQUIBB COMPANY
ELI LILLY AND COMPANY
IONIS PHARMACEUTICALS, INC.
LES LABORATOIRES SERVIER
Roche Holding AG
VERTEX PHARMACEUTICALS INCORPORATED

HISTORICAL FINANCIALS

Company Type: Public

Income Statement — FYE: December 31

	REVENUE ($mil)	NET INCOME ($mil)	NET PROFIT MARGIN	EMPLOYEES
12/23	34,517	12,436	36.0%	63,370
12/22	25,414	7,974	31.4%	55,185
12/21	21,428	7,268	33.9%	48,478
12/20	20,939	6,950	33.2%	45,323
12/19	18,337	5,853	31.9%	43,258
Annual Growth	17.1%	20.7%	—	10.0%

2023 Year-End Financials

Debt ratio: 1.3%
Return on equity: 88.0%
Cash ($ mil.): 2,138
Current Ratio: 0.82
Long-term debt ($ mil.): 3,050
No. of shares ($ mil.): 4,458
Dividends
  Yield: —
  Payout: 27.2%
Market value ($ mil.): 461,211

	STOCK PRICE ($) FY Close	P/E High/Low		PER SHARE ($) Earnings	Dividends	Book Value
12/23	103.45	11	5	2.77	0.76	3.55
12/22	135.34	11	7	1.76	0.57	2.63
12/21	112.00	11	6	1.58	1.05	2.33
12/20	69.85	8	6	1.49	0.93	2.26
12/19	57.88	7	6	1.23	0.87	1.84
Annual Growth	15.6%	—	—	22.5%	(3.5%)	17.9%

Novolipetsk Steel

NLMK (formerly Novolipetsk Steel) is no run of the mill steel producer. One of the top steelmakers in Russia, producing 6.2 million tons annually, NLMK handles the entire steel production process, from mining iron ore to distribution of its finished products. The company produces hot and cold rolled, slab, pig iron, galvanized, pre-painted, and electrical steel through its steel-making and rolling businesses. It sells primarily to the automotive and construction industries in Europe and the US. Founded in the 1930s as a state-run company, it is now controlled by chairman Vladimir Lisin, who holds more than 80% of NLMK. More than 40% of the NLMK's total sales comes from Russia.

Operations

The company has identified six reportable segments of its business: Russian flat products; Russian long products; NLMK USA; NLMK DanSteel and Plates Distribution Network; Investments in NBH; and Mining.

The Russian flat products segment, which generates about 55% of the company's total revenue, is comprises of production and sales of steel products and coke, primarily pig iron, steel slabs, hot rolled steel, cold rolled steel, galvanised cold rolled sheet and cold rolled sheet with polymeric coatings and also electro-technical steel.

NLMK USA, comprising production and sales of steel products. The segment accounts for 15% of the revenue.

Investments in NBH (nearly 15%), comprising production of hot rolled, cold rolled coils and galvanised and pre-pained steel, and also production of a wide range of plates as well as a number of steel service centers.

The Russian long products segment (about 15% of revenue), comprising a number of steel-production facilities combined in a single production system beginning from scrap iron collection and recycling to steel-making, production of long products, reinforcing rebar and metalware.

NLMK DanSteel and Plates Distribution Network accounts for almost 5% and comprised of production and sales of plates.

Mining segment contributes the remaining revenue, which comprises mining, processing and sales of iron ore, fluxing limestone and metallurgical dolomite, and supplies raw materials to the steel segment and third parties.

Geographic Reach

NLMK has production assets in Russia, the US and the EU (in Belgium, Denmark, Italy and France). The company's single global production chain ensures efficient cost control and guarantees NLMK customers stable deliveries and the highest quality products.

More than 40% of the company's total revenue comes from Russia, followed by North America and EU with about 20% each, another 10% comes from Middle East including Turkey, and the remaining revenues comes from CIS, Central and South America, and Asia and Oceania.

The company is headquartered in Moscow, Russia.

Sales and Marketing

NLMK's key customers in Russia are construction and infrastructure companies. Products in Europe and the US are mainly sold to customers in the automotive industry; manufacturers of pipes; wind energy equipment manufacturers; heavy engineering companies and manufacturers of offshore drilling constructions.

Financial Performance

NLMK saw fluctuating revenues and profit in the last five years. Despite fluctuations, revenue grew 32% between 2015 and 2019, while profit rose 38% in the same five-year period. NLMK has a highly competitive cash cost among global manufacturers and one of the highest profitability levels in the industry.

Revenue decreased by 12% to $10.6 billion in 2019 amid falling steel product prices and lower sales due to major repairs at the NLMK Lipetsk BF and BOF facilities. Sales decreased to 171.1 million tons, 3% less from the year prior, due to lower steel output caused by the major repairs.

Net profit decreased by 40% to $1.3 billion in 2019 from $2.2 billion in 2018, mainly due to the decline in revenue as well as a higher effective income tax rate for that year.

Cash and cash equivalents at the end of the year were $713 million, a $456 million decrease from the year prior. Operating activities generated $2.6 billion in 2019, while investing and financing activities used $1.4 billion and $1.7 billion, respectively. NLMK's main cash uses in 2019 were dividends paid to shareholders, purchase and construction of property, plant and equipment and intangible assets, and placement of bank deposits.

Strategy

NLMK's Strategy 2022 is predicated on enhancing NLMK Group's competitive advantages through boosting operational efficiency across the entire production chain, growing cost-efficient steel production, enhancing vertical integration into key raw materials, increasing sales of high value-added (HVA) products, pursuing environmental, safety, and human capital development programs.

The key elements of Strategy 2022 include leadership in operational efficiency; growth in low-cost steel production; world-class sales portfolio; and leadership in sustainability and safety. In order to be a leader in operational efficiency, NLMK focuses on operational efficiency and working towards the best production practices; global leadership in the cash cost of steel production.

In terms of growth in low-cost steel production, NLMK aims to see growth of steel output at NLMMK Lipetsk; maintaining 100% self-sufficiency in iron ore; growth in energy self-sufficiency at NLMK Lipetsk; and decrease in coal consumption, including deficit grades.

In pursuit of having a world-class sales portfolio, NLMK also aims to see growth in its steel product sales, and in its high-value added (HVA) product output and sales.

Furthermore, NLMK works to minimize its environmental footprint and ensuring safe operations in order to become a leader in sustainability and safety.

Company Background

Founded in the 1930s as a state-run company.

EXECUTIVES

Management Board Chief Executive Officer, Management Board Chairman, Grigory Fedorishin
Energy Vice President, Sergey Chebotarev
Risk Management Vice President, Evgeny Ovcharov
Logistics Vice President, Sergey Likharev
Sales Vice PResident, Ilya Guschin
Operational & Efficiency Vice President, Tatyana Averchenkova
Human Resources & Management Vice President, Mikhail Arkhipov
Finance Vice President, Shamil Kurmashov
International Operation Vice President, Barend de Vos
Chairman, Non-Executive Director, Vladimir Lisin
Independent Director, Marjan Oudeman
Independent Director, Benedict Sciortino
Non-Executive Director, Director, Oleg Vladimirovich Bagrin
Independent Director, Joachim Limberg
Independent Director, Thomas Veraszto
Independent Director, Stanislav Shekshnia
Independent Director, Nikolai Gagarin
Independent Director, Karen Sarkisov
Auditors : AO PricewaterhouseCoopers Audit

LOCATIONS

HQ: Novolipetsk Steel
2, Metallurgov sq., Lipetsk 398040
Phone: (7) 4742 44 30 95   **Fax:** (7) 4742 442 317
Web: www.a-rnr.ru/

PRODUCTS/OPERATIONS

2014 Sales

	% of Total
Steel	63
Foreign rolled products	20
Long Products	14
Mining	3
All Other	-
Total	100

2014 Sales

	% of Total
Russia	42
European Union	18
Middle East, including Turkey	6
North America	20
Asia and Oceania	3
Other Regions	11
Total	100

Operating Businesses
Altai-koks
Stoilensky GOK
Stagdok
Dolomite
Tuapse Commercial Seaport
DanSteel
VIZ-Stal
Maxi-Group

COMPETITORS

A. FINKL & SONS CO.
AK STEEL HOLDING CORPORATION
ArcelorMittal
DC ALABAMA, INC.
ELKEM HOLDING, INC.
NIPPON DENKO CO., LTD.
NUCOR CORPORATION
READING ALLOYS, INC.
SEVERSTAL, PAO
Wugang Group Co., Ltd.

HISTORICAL FINANCIALS
Company Type: Public

Income Statement   FYE: December 31

	REVENUE ($mil)	NET INCOME ($mil)	NET PROFIT MARGIN	EMPLOYEES
12/21	16,196	5,036	31.1%	0
12/20	9,245	1,236	13.4%	0
12/19	10,554	1,339	12.7%	0
12/18	12,046	2,238	18.6%	0
12/17	10,065	1,450	14.4%	0
Annual Growth	12.6%	36.5%	—	—

2021 Year-End Financials
Debt ratio: 28.5%   No. of shares ($ mil.): 5,993
Return on equity: 90.3%   Dividends
Cash ($ mil.): 541   Yield: —
Current Ratio: 1.62   Payout: 676.0%
Long-term debt ($ mil.): 1,962   Market value ($ mil.): —

NTT Data Group Corp

EXECUTIVES

President, Representative Director, Yo Honma
Executive Vice President, Representative Director, Shigeki Yamaguchi
Executive Vice President, Representative Director, Toshi Fujiwara
Executive Vice President, Representative Director, Kazuhiro Nishihata
Outside Director, Eiji Hirano
Outside Director, Mariko Fujii
Director, Mapelli Patrizio
Outside Director, Fumihiko Ike
Outside Director, Shigenao Ishiguro
Outside Director, Katsura Sakurada
Outside Director, Akihioko Okada
Outside Director, Tomoko Hoshi
Outside Director, Mitsuko Inamasu
Auditors : KPMG AZSA LLC

LOCATIONS

HQ: NTT Data Group Corp
3-3-3 Toyosu, Koto-ku, Tokyo 135-6033
Phone: (81) 3 5546 8119
Web: www.nttdata.com

HISTORICAL FINANCIALS
Company Type: Public

Income Statement   FYE: March 31

	REVENUE ($mil)	NET INCOME ($mil)	NET PROFIT MARGIN	EMPLOYEES
03/22	20,979	1,175	5.6%	155,531
03/21	20,940	694	3.3%	143,081
03/20	20,882	692	3.3%	136,464
03/19	19,537	845	4.3%	126,953
03/18	19,938	547	2.7%	121,020
Annual Growth	1.3%	21.0%	—	6.5%

2022 Year-End Financials
Debt ratio: 0.1%   No. of shares ($ mil.): 1,402
Return on equity: 12.2%   Dividends
Cash ($ mil.): 2,030   Yield: —
Current Ratio: 1.26   Payout: 0.0%
Long-term debt ($ mil.): 3,236   Market value ($ mil.): 28,807

	STOCK PRICE ($) FY Close	P/E High/Low		PER SHARE ($) Earnings Dividends		Book Value
03/22	20.54	0	0	0.84	0.15	7.45
03/21	16.00	0	0	0.49	0.16	6.91
03/20	8.37	0	0	0.49	0.16	6.17
03/19	10.64	0	0	0.60	0.14	5.96
03/18	10.20	1	0	0.39	0.15	5.60
Annual Growth	19.1%	—	—	21.0%	1.0%	7.4%

Nutrien Ltd

EXECUTIVES

Chairman, Director, Russell K. Griling
Interim President, Chief Executive Officer, Kenneth A. Seitz
Executive Vice President, Chief Legal Officer, Noralee Bradley
Executive Vice President, Chief Financial Officer, Pedro Farah
Executive Vice President, Chief Information Officer, Brent Poohkay
Executive Vice President, Raef M. Sully
Executive Vice President, Chief Strategy Officer, Chief Sustainability Officer, Mark Thompson
Executive Vice President, Chief Human Resources Officer, Chief Administrative Officer, Michael R. Webb
Director, Christopher M. Burley
Director, Maura J. Clark
Director, Miranda C. Hubbs
Director, Raj Kushwaha
Director, Alice D. Laberge
Director, Consuelo E. Madere
Director, Keith G. Martell
Director, Aaron W. Regent
Director, Nelson L. C. Silva
Auditors : KPMG LLP

LOCATIONS

HQ: Nutrien Ltd
Suite 1700, 211 19th Street East, Saskatoon, Saskatchewan S7K 5R6
Phone: 306 933-8523   **Fax:** 306 933-8877
Web: www.nutrien.com

HISTORICAL FINANCIALS
Company Type: Public

Income Statement   FYE: December 31

	REVENUE ($mil)	NET INCOME ($mil)	NET PROFIT MARGIN	EMPLOYEES
12/23	29,056	1,258	4.3%	25,900
12/22	37,884	7,660	20.2%	24,700
12/21	27,712	3,179	11.5%	23,500
12/20	20,908	459	2.2%	23,100
12/19	20,023	992	5.0%	22,300
Annual Growth	9.8%	6.1%	—	3.8%

2023 Year-End Financials
Debt ratio: 21.9%   No. of shares ($ mil.): 494
Return on equity: 4.9%   Dividends
Cash ($ mil.): 941   Yield: —
Current Ratio: 1.17   Payout: 83.7%
Long-term debt ($ mil.): 8,913   Market value ($ mil.): 27,858

	STOCK PRICE ($) FY Close	P/E High/Low		PER SHARE ($) Earnings Dividends		Book Value
12/23	56.33	33	21	2.53	2.12	50.87
12/22	73.03	8	5	14.18	1.92	50.90
12/21	75.20	14	9	5.52	1.84	42.43
12/20	48.16	63	31	0.81	1.80	39.29
12/19	47.91	33	27	1.70	1.76	39.91
Annual Growth	4.1%	—	—	10.5%	4.8%	6.2%

NXP Semiconductors NV

NXP Semiconductors is a global semiconductor company and a long-standing supplier in the industry. It provides leading solutions that leverage its combined portfolio of intellectual property, deep application knowledge, process technology and manufacturing expertise in the domains of cryptography-security, high-speed interface, radio frequency (RF), mixed-signal analog-digital (mixed A/D), power management, digital signal processing and embedded system design. In addition to its former parent Philips, NXP's customers include Apple, Bosch, Aptiv, Denso, Continental, Samsung, and Visteon. Customers in China account for about 40% of sales for the Netherlands-based company.

Operations
Its product groups are focused on four primary end-markets: Automotive (about 50%), Industrial IoT (over 20%), Communication Infrastructure & Other (around 15%), and Mobile (nearly 15%).Its product groups are focused on four primary end-markets: Automotive (about 50%), Industrial IoT (over 20%), Communication Infrastructure & Other (around 15%), and Mobile (nearly 15%).

Its broad portfolio of semiconductor products includes microcontrollers, application processors, communication processors, connectivity chipsets, analog and interface devices, RF power amplifiers, security controllers and sensors.

Geographic Reach
Headquartered in Eindhoven, the Netherlands, NXP has operations in three regions encompassing over 30 countries. China is its largest single market with about 40% of sales, followed by Singapore with over 10%, and US with roughly 10%.

Sales and Marketing
NXP markets its products and solutions worldwide to a variety of OEMs, Original

Design Manufacturers (ODMs), contract manufacturers and distributors. Its ten largest OEM end customers, some of whom are supplied by distributors, in alphabetical order, are Apple, Aptiv, Bosch, Continental, Denso, LG, Samsung, Vitesco, and Visteon. It also has a strong position with its distribution partners, including its three largest, Arrow, Avnet and WT Micro. Avnet is its largest customer which accounts for about 20% of sales. The company's sales from distributors account for over 55% of sales, while OEM/EMS account for over 40%.

Financial Performance

Revenue in 2021 was $11.1 billion compared to $8.6 billion in 2020, an increase of $2.5 billion or 29% year-on-year, as a result of resurgent growth across all of the company's four focus end markets, with substantial growth in its strategic focused Automotive and Industrial end markets.

Net income in 2021 increased to $1.9 billion compared to $80 million in the prior year.

Cash held by the company at the end of 2021 increased to $2.8 billion. Operating activities provided $3.1 billion while investing and financing activities used $914 million and $1.6 billion, respectively. Main cash uses were capital expenditures and purchase of treasury shares and restricted stock unit withholdings.

Strategy

A key element of its strategy is to offer highly integrated and secure solutions that are increasingly sought by its customers to simplify their development efforts and shorten their time to market. The company believes it has the broadest ARM processor portfolio in the industry, from microcontrollers to crossover processors and from application processors to communication processors.

EXECUTIVES

Chairman, Director, Peter L. Bonfield
Vice-Chairman, Director, Peter Smitham
President, Chief Executive Officer, Executive Director, Kurt Sievers
Executive Vice President, Chief Financial Officer, Bill Betz
Sales Executive Vice President, Marketing Executive Vice President, Steve Owen
Executive Vice President, General Counsel, Secretary, Jennifer B. Wuamett
Executive Vice President, Chief Human Resources Officer, Christopher Jensen
Director, Kenneth A. Goldman
Director, Annette K. Clayton
Director, Anthony R. Foxx
Director, Josef Kaeser
Director, Lena Olving
Director, Julie Southern
Director, Jasmin Staiblin
Director, Gregory L. Summe
Director, Karl-Henrik Sundstrom

Auditors: Ernst & Young Accountants LLP

LOCATIONS

HQ: NXP Semiconductors NV
60 High Tech Campus, Eindhoven 5656 AG
Phone: (31) 40 272 9999
Web: www.nxp.com

2018 Sales

	$ in mil.	% of total
China	3,430	36
Netherlands	349	4
United States	919	10
Singapore	1,220	13
Germany	531	6
Japan	735	8
South Korea	357	4
Malaysia	112	2
Other countries	1,754	17
Total	9,407	100

PRODUCTS/OPERATIONS

Selected Products
Audio
    Amplifiers
    Digital signal processors (DSPs)
    Radio receivers
    Synthesizers
Discrete devices
    Diodes
    Rectifiers
    Sensors
    Thyristors
    Transistors (automotive, communications, industrial, and lighting applications)
Display drivers
Identification and security devices
Logic devices
    Buffer/drivers
    Encoders and decoders
    Multiplexers and demultiplexers
    Phase-locked loops (PLLs)
    Timers
    Transceivers
Microcontrollers (MCUs)
    32-bit ARM MCUs
    Controller area network (CAN) devices
Peripheral interconnect
    Bus switches
    Universal serial bus (USB) hubs, interface devices, and transceivers
Standard analog devices
    Data interface devices
    Motor control devices
    Power supply management
    Regulators
Video
    Amplifiers
    Converters
    Demodulators
    Encoders and decoders

COMPETITORS

ARD Holdings S.A.
ASML Holding N.V.
CYPRESS SEMICONDUCTOR CORPORATION
Gemalto B.V.
LyondellBasell Industries N.V.
MMC VENTURES LIMITED
RENESAS ELECTRONICS CORPORATION
SKYWORKS SOLUTIONS, INC.
Signify N.V.
TomTom N.V.

HISTORICAL FINANCIALS

Company Type: Public

Income Statement — FYE: December 31

	REVENUE ($mil)	NET INCOME ($mil)	NET PROFIT MARGIN	EMPLOYEES
12/23	13,276	2,797	21.1%	34,200
12/22	13,205	2,787	21.1%	34,500
12/21	11,063	1,871	16.9%	31,000
12/20	8,612	52	0.6%	29,000
12/19	8,877	243	2.7%	29,400
Annual Growth	-10.6%	84.2%	—	3.9%

2023 Year-End Financials

Debt ratio: 45.9%
Return on equity: 34.7%
Cash ($ mil.): 3,862
Current Ratio: 1.91
Long-term debt ($ mil.): 10,175
No. of shares ($ mil.): 257
Dividends
  Yield: —
  Payout: 37.9%
Market value ($ mil.): —

Obayashi Corp

Obayashi Corporation provide all types of buildings such as offices, condominiums, commercial facilities, factories, hospitals and schools that meet diverse needs including reduced environmental load and energy conservation, comfort and convenience as well as seismic resistance and disaster readiness for securing business continuity. It builds infrastructure essential to people's lives, such as tunnels, bridges, dams, riverbanks, railroads, and expressways. Obayashi develop and own excellent leasing properties in prime locations, primarily in metropolitan areas. In the urban redevelopment business, it has experience in numerous projects as a project partner and specified agent. It promotes renewable energy, PPP and agriculture business. Founded in 1892 by Yoshigoro Obayashi.

Operations

Obayashi operates four core business segments. Its Domestic Building Construction business (which generated 55% of net sales in fiscal 2020, ended March), builds offices, condos, commercial facilities, factories, hospitals, and schools, and designs for customers concerned with environmental harm, energy conservation, seismic resistance, and disaster readiness. Its Domestic Civil Engineering business (16% of net sales) builds various types of infrastructure, such as tunnels, bridges, dams, riverbanks and more.

The company's Overseas Construction business (23% of net sales) builds infrastructure such as railroads, bridges and expressway. Its Real Estate business (3% of net sales) works on redevelopment projects across Japan as a project partner or specified agent, and sells properties for lease in favorable locations (mainly urban areas).

Geographic Reach

Obayashi Corporation is based in Japan. The company offices are internationally located in London, Auckland, Sydney, Guam,

Taipei, Jakarta, Hanoi, Phnom Penh, Kuala Lumpur, Bangkok, Yangon, Dhaka, and Japan.

Sales and Marketing

Obayashi Corporation markets its products and services through its websites by its projects such as public facility such as government, hospital, educational, and cultural. Office/ Industrial Facility; Logistic, Research and Development, Infrastructure; Telecommunications, Dam, Power Plant, Railway, Airport, Amusement/Hospitality; Retail/Shopping Center, Hotel, Historical Building Structure, Urban/Land Development, Residence and Outsider Japan.

Financial Performance

Note: Growth rates may differ after conversion to US dollars. This analysis uses financials from the company's annual report.

The company's revenue for fiscal 2020 increased to Â¥2.1 trillion from Â¥2.0 trillion.

In 2020, net income decreased to Â¥113.1 billion from the prior year's Â¥113.2 billion.

Cash held by the company at the end of fiscal 2020 increased to Â¥298.9 billion. Operating activities provided Â¥237.6 billion while investing and financing activities used Â¥47.3 billion and Â¥49.4 billion, respectively.

Strategy

In 2020, construction investment was steady in Obayashi's major markets. These included large-scale redevelopment of urban areas in Japan and building, maintenance, and repair of infrastructure.

The company's business strategy based on medium-term business plan includes:

Realize stable earnings by enhancing competitive advantages in growth markets and areas and providing integrated high-value-added services for buildings, centered on leveraging the company's total capabilities and global network.

Improve productivity by building next-generation production systems utilizing IoT, AI, and robotics, transforming business processes by basing then on BIM, and developing labor-saving construction methods, etc.

Eradicate serious accidents and quality and construction defects by implementing diverse education programs and rigorously managing safety and quality by ICT.

Secure production capacity by improving the working environment at construction sites, developing multiskilled workers, securing skilled workers, and providing educational support, etc.

Enhance earnings capacity and expand business domains by collaborating with local partners and sharing the company's technology in its overseas building construction business.

HISTORY

With the first wave of Japanese modernization in 1892, Yoshigoro Ohbayashi opened a small construction operation in Osaka. He won the bid for construction of the Abe Paper Mill. In 1898 he joined with partner Kamezo Shirasugi to lay the foundations for the Obayashi Corporation.

Obayashi's first big contract came in 1901, for the construction of buildings for Osaka's Fifth National Industry Fair. During the Russo-Japanese War, the young corporation built 100 barracks in three weeks, a feat that helped it win a contract to build Tokyo Station (completed 1914). Obayashi executives were invited to the US by the Fluor Company in the early 1920s to study advanced construction techniques. After a 1923 earthquake and firestorm leveled much of Tokyo, Obayashi applied the technology it learned from Fluor to build quake-resistant, fireproof buildings.

Like many Japanese companies, Obayashi is quiet about its history in the years leading up to WWII and the rebuilding that followed. However, the Korean War increased demand for company projects such as the Tokyo Station annex, the Japan Broadcasting Corporation building, and the first of 50 major dam projects.

In the 1960s Obayashi became the first Japanese construction firm to build an internal R&D facility. Its Technical Research Institute developed the OWS-Soletanche Diaphragm Wall Construction Method, which it used on the New Osaka building in 1961 and has adapted to many other buildings since. In 1965 the company began its first major civil engineering project overseas, doing its part in a 32-year-long excavation in Singapore that reclaimed about 3% of that country's land mass from the sea. Also that year Obayashi completed the first high-rise in Japan, Yokohama's 21-story Hotel Empire.

Expo '70 in Osaka showcased Obayashi's air-membrane dome and roof lift-up method. During the 1970s the company played key roles in Japan's massive highway-building projects. In 1979 it was the first Japanese construction company to be awarded a public works contract in the US.

Obayashi completed thousands of projects during the 1980s. It helped build the Tsukuba Expo '85 and restored the Katsura Rikyu Detached Palace, a national treasure.

In 1994 two former Obayashi executives were found guilty of giving a 10 million yen (about $100,000) bribe to the mayor of Sendai two years earlier. The company was one of several major construction companies involved in the scandal.

In the 1990s Obayashi "mole" machines chewed through the earth to create the Tokyo Bay Aqualine tunnel. In 1996 the company developed anti-earthquake construction methods for structures built on soft ground (almost a fifth of buildings in Tokyo).

Obayashi was hard hit in 1998 and 1999 as financial crises created turmoil in Japan's construction industry. The company responded by reducing its workforce by about 5%, taking advantage of economies of scale in materials purchasing, and working with subcontractors to cut costs. Beefing up its project orders is another key strategy. New projects secured by Obayashi in 2000 included the Taiwan North-South High Speed Rail Project and a new head office for Japanese advertising giant Dentsu.

In 2002 the group completed the NHK Osaka Broadcasting Station and the renovation of Kobe Wing Stadium, a site for part of the 2002 World Cup soccer finals. Obayashi and Kobe Steel won the contract to operate the stadium for 15 years.

Obayashi was caught in a building scandal in its home country in 2005, when it came to light that an outside architect had falsified documents regarding earthquake resistance for one of its projects, a hotel. Obayashi said that the falsifications were too skillfully done to catch at the construction stage.

EXECUTIVES

Chairman, Director, Takeo Obayashi
President, Chief Executive Officer, Representative Director, Kenji Hasuwa
Executive Vice President, Director, Toshihiko Murata
Executive Vice President, Representative Director, Atsushi Sasagawa
Executive Vice President, Representative Director, Akinobu Nohira
Executive Vice President, Director, Toshimi Sato
Senior Managing Executive Officer, Naoki Kajita
Senior Managing Executive Officer, Seiji Nagai
Outside Director, Naoki Izumiya
Outside Director, Yoko Kobayashi
Outside Director, Masako Orii
Outside Director, Hiroyuki Kato
Outside Director, Yukiko Kuroda
Auditors : Ernst & Young ShinNihon LLC

LOCATIONS

HQ: Obayashi Corp
2-15-2 Konan, Minato-ku, Tokyo 108-8502
Phone: (81) 3 5769 1017   **Fax:** 650 589-8384
Web: www.obayashi.co.jp

2014 Sales

	% of total
Japan	81
Overseas	
North America	10
Asia	8
Others	1
Total	100

Obayashi has operations in Cambodia, China, Indonesia, Japan, Malaysia, the Philippines, Singapore, Taiwan, Thailand, the UK, the US, and Vietnam.

PRODUCTS/OPERATIONS

2014 Sales	% of total
Domestic Building Construction Business	56
Domestic Civil Engineering Business	20
Overseas Construction Business	18
Real Estate Business	3
Other Business	3
Total	100

Selected Subsidiaries and Affiliates
Atelier G&B Co., Ltd.
E.W. Howell Co., Inc. (US)
James E. Roberts-Obayashi Corporation (50%, housing projects, US)
Mutsuzawa Green Co., Ltd. (golf club and restaurant operations)
Naigai Technos Corporation
Obayashi Real Estate Corporation
Obayashi Road Corporation
OC Finance Corporation
OC Real Estate Management, LLC (US)
SOMA Environment Service Corporation
Taiwan Obayashi Corporation
Thai Obayashi Corporation Limited (49%)

COMPETITORS
Bilfinger SE
COLAS SA
EIFFAGE
KELLER GROUP PLC
PETER KIEWIT SONS', INC.
SKANSKA USA CIVIL INC.
STERLING CONSTRUCTION COMPANY, INC.
STRABAG SE
TAISEI CORPORATION
TAKENAKA CORPORATION

HISTORICAL FINANCIALS
Company Type: Public

Income Statement — FYE: March 31

	REVENUE ($mil)	NET INCOME ($mil)	NET PROFIT MARGIN	EMPLOYEES
03/23	14,895	583	3.9%	19,257
03/22	15,808	321	2.0%	18,967
03/21	15,957	892	5.6%	19,058
03/20	19,097	1,041	5.5%	18,879
03/19	18,418	1,021	5.5%	18,832
Annual Growth	(5.2%)	(13.1%)	—	0.6%

2023 Year-End Financials
Debt ratio: 0.1%
Return on equity: 7.9%
Cash ($ mil.): 3,149
Current Ratio: 1.23
Long-term debt ($ mil.): 1,818
No. of shares ($ mil.): 718
Dividends
 Yield: —
 Payout: 0.0%
Market value ($ mil.): —

Ogaki Kyoritsu Bank, Ltd.

The Ogaki Kyoritsu Bank provides banking and other financial services in the Gifu prefecture in central Japan. The bank serves consumers and businesses from more than 140 domestic branch locations and from 3 international offices in Hong Kong, Shanghai, and New York. Services include banking, credit cards, credit guaranty, and leasing. Ogaki Kyoritsu Bank was established in 1896.

EXECUTIVES
President, Representative Director, Toshiyuki Sakai
Director, Satoshi Tsuchiya
Director, Takaharu Hayashi
Director, Masayuki Nogami
Director, Masaki Kakehi
Outside Director, Masaaki Kanda
Outside Director, Yasutake Tango
Outside Director, Yuko Moriguchi
Auditors : KPMG AZSA LLC

LOCATIONS
HQ: Ogaki Kyoritsu Bank, Ltd.
 3-98 Kuruwa-machi, Ogaki, Gifu 503-0887
Phone: (81) 584 74 2111
Web: www.okb.co.jp

COMPETITORS
CHIBA BANK,LTD., THE
EHIME BANK, LTD., THE
HACHIJUNI BANK, LTD., THE
NISHI-NIPPON CITYBANK,LTD.
YAMANASHI CHUO BANK, LTD., THE

HISTORICAL FINANCIALS
Company Type: Public

Income Statement — FYE: March 31

	ASSETS ($mil)	NET INCOME ($mil)	INCOME AS % OF ASSETS	EMPLOYEES
03/22	63,477	87	0.1%	4,133
03/21	67,291	72	0.1%	4,285
03/20	55,118	50	0.1%	4,401
03/19	52,678	61	0.1%	4,484
03/18	54,190	91	0.2%	4,499
Annual Growth	4.0%	(1.1%)	—	(2.1%)

2022 Year-End Financials
Return on assets: 0.1%
Return on equity: 3.3%
Long-term debt ($ mil.): —
No. of shares ($ mil.): 41
Sales ($ mil.): 948
Dividends
 Yield: —
 Payout: 27.5%
Market value ($ mil.): —

Oita Bank Ltd (Japan)

EXECUTIVES
President, Representative Director, Tomiichiro Goto
Senior Managing Director, Representative Director, Masayuki Takeshima
Senior Managing Director, Representative Director, Yasuhide Takahashi
Director, Nobuhiko Okamatsu
Director, Hiroaki Shimonomura
Outside Director, Akiko Yamamoto
Director, Masayuki Sagara
Director, Hiroyuki Hirakawa
Outside Director, Yoshimi Osaki
Outside Director, Mitsuo Kawano
Outside Director, Sachiko Oro
Auditors : Deloitte Touche Tohmatsu LLC

LOCATIONS
HQ: Oita Bank Ltd (Japan)
 3-4-1 Funaimachi, Oita 870-0021
Phone: (81) 97 534 1111
Web: www.oitabank.co.jp

HISTORICAL FINANCIALS
Company Type: Public

Income Statement — FYE: March 31

	ASSETS ($mil)	NET INCOME ($mil)	INCOME AS % OF ASSETS	EMPLOYEES
03/22	35,437	44	0.1%	2,492
03/21	34,442	32	0.1%	2,587
03/20	31,257	46	0.1%	2,656
03/19	30,049	52	0.2%	2,711
03/18	30,325	56	0.2%	2,786
Annual Growth	4.0%	(5.9%)	—	(2.7%)

2022 Year-End Financials
Return on assets: 0.1%
Return on equity: 2.6%
Long-term debt ($ mil.): —
No. of shares ($ mil.): 15
Sales ($ mil.): 460
Dividends
 Yield: —
 Payout: 23.5%
Market value ($ mil.): —

Oji Holdings Corp

One of Japan's top paper makers, along with Nippon Paper Industries Co., Oji Holdings produces pulp and paper and converted paper products through nearly 190 subsidiaries and affiliates worldwide. Its business segments include: Industrial Materials, Household and Consumer Products, Functional Materials, Forest Resources and Environment Marketing, Printing and Communications Media and other businesses which focus on real estate, engineering, trading business and logistic. Products include container board and corrugated containers, boxboard and folding cartons, among others. Japan is responsible for more 70% of the sales. Customers include overseas and domestic companies in the retail and energy sectors. The company was founded in 1873.

Operations
The company has four operating segments. These being: Household and Industrial Materials accounting for nearly 40%, Functional Faterials generates some 15%, Forest Resource and Environment Marketing brings in more than 15% and Printing and Communications Media gets less than 20%.

Industrial Materials segment focuses on containerboard and corrugated containers, boxboard and folding cartons. Household and Consumer Products segment centers on tissue, toilet tissue and wet wipes. Functional Materials segment provides specialty paper, thermal paper and film. Forest Resources and Environment Marketing segment concentrates on pulp, energy, plantation service and lumber processing. Printing and Communications Media segment makes newsprint, printing and publication and communications paper.

Geographic Reach

Headquartered in Tokyo, Japan is Oji Holdings' largest market accounting for 70%. Other sales are made in Asia which accounts for nearly 20%, Oceania, Europe, and the Americas, each contributes some 5%.

Sales and Marketing

It serves various industries such as energy, retail, film, packaging and newsprint, among others.

Financial Performance

Oji Holdings' net sales has been in the ¥1.4 billion to ¥1.6 billion range for the past five years, recording a 5% increase from 2015 to 2019. Meanwhile, the company's net income has achieved year-over-year growth after its decline in 2017. Net income increased by 358% from 2015 to 2019.

Net sales decreased from ¥1.6 billion in 2018 to ¥1.5 billion in 2019. Household and Industrial Materials remains to have the top net sales per business segment, comprising 38.8% of the company's 2019 revenue. This was followed by the Printing and Communications Media segment (16.5%), Other (16.4%), Forest Resources and Environment Marketing Business (16.1%), and Functional Materials (12.2%).

Cash and cash equivalents at the end of the year were ¥82.4 billion, similar to the previous year. Cash provided by operations was ¥124.5 billion. Investing activities used ¥64.8 billion primarily for payment for acquisition of property, plant, equipment, and intangible assets. Financing activities, on the other hand, used ¥58.1 billion primarily for repayment of long-term loans payable.

Strategy

Oji Holdings' new corrugated container plant in Funabashi City, Chiba Prefecture, has started commercial production in July 2020, to meet the growth in demand for corrugated containers in the Kanto region. The Industrial Materials Company will enhance its competitive strength in the corrugated container business in the Kanto region, by aggressively capturing new demand for corrugated containers, and expanding its supply volume. At the same time, as part of its initiatives to restructure manufacturing in response to structural changes in domestic demand, we will shut down the manufacturing facilities at the Oji Materia Nayoro Mill and transfer other facilities to Oji Paper Tomakomai Mill, and production facilities for newsprint at the Tomakomai Mill are now in the midst of modification for containerboard and kraft paper. To further reinforce earnings bases through the integration of material and converting, a range of investments will be made for the optimization of the domestic business structure.

The Industrial Materials Company conducts business at 45 sites in nine countries in Southeast Asia, India, and Oceania. It has been focusing mainly on expanding converting sites to respond to growing packaging demand, and now, it will install new containerboard production facilities in Malaysia, which is scheduled to start commercial operation in 2021. Through these efforts, the company will further progress the development of overseas businesses by integrating material and converting.

HISTORY

Eiichi Shibusawa established Oji Paper in 1873 as Shoshi-Gaisha. Production began two years later at the company's mill in Oji. The company, which was partially funded by the Mitsui Group, was the first in Japan to use Western papermaking technology. During the 1890s the Mitsui Group granted the company additional funding to install the latest papermaking technology in Shoshi-Gaisha's facilities, but the Group removed Shibusawa from the company's management team soon after. The company was renamed Oji Paper Manufacturing Company in 1893. Oji Paper enjoyed great success and expansion under the management of the Mitsui Group and during WWI, as Japan's exports tripled, the company's sales substantially increased.

In 1933 Oji Paper acquired Fuji Paper and Karafuto Industries and soon was producing about 80% of the country's paper needs. The company prospered through WWII despite significant shortages of raw materials. During the Allied occupation that followed the war, the company was forced to split into three companies: Jujo Paper, Honshu Paper, and Tomakomai Paper. Tomakomai was renamed Oji Paper shortly after the split. Experiencing a shortage of imported pulp after the war, the company propositioned US government officials to create a company that would import pulp from Alaska. In 1953 the Alaska Pulp Company was established and began supplying pulp to Oji Paper and its affiliates.

The company modernized its facilities during the 1960s, which led to cutbacks in its workforce; the cutbacks were followed by strikes and lockouts during that period. The 1970s brought acquisitions that included Kita Nippon Paper and Nippon Pulp Industries. The company also built mills in New Zealand (1971) and Brazil (1972). Throughout the 1970s and 1980s, Oji Paper enhanced its line of specialty and consumer paper products; it added its own line of disposable diapers in 1989. The company also increased its newsprint output that year when it purchased Toyo Pulp Company. Despite apparent decreases in demand for newsprint from the late 1980s, the company continued to grow into the 1990s due to its higher reliance on other paper products.

The company's acquisitions of Kanzaki Paper (1993) and Honshu Paper (1996) reinforced its influence in international paper markets. In 1999, amid a recession in Japan, the company began implementing major cutbacks on its operations that included reducing staff, eliminating or stopping some of its paper machines, and consolidating some of its divisions such as its self-adhesive products unit. The cutbacks proved successful, and Oji Paper bounced back to profitability in 2000. To keep operating costs low, the company is now expanding into Asia with new facilities planned or already open in China.

In 2002 Oji Paper continued to restructure and cut costs as Japan's slumping information technology and advertising business negatively affected its paper business, and depressed sales of home appliances led to poor sales in its paperboard segment.

In mid-2006 Oji made an (ultimately unsuccessful) unsolicited $1.2 billion bid for rival Hokuetsu Paper Mills. The deal made a stir because it is highly unusual for Japanese firms to make unsolicited takeover bids. Oji's takeover attempt eventually inspired competitors Nippon Paper and Rengo to combine forces around cardboard manufacturing, a segment that Oji had been leading.

In 2007 the company agreed to a partnership with Mitsubishi Paper Mills to combat increasing raw material costs and a shrinking domestic market. Mitsubishi plans to up its capacity at its mills to accommodate Oji orders while Oji has agreed to supply Mitsubishi paper with thermostatic recording paper from its Thailand subsidiary.

EXECUTIVES

Chairman, Representative Director, Masatoshi Kaku
President, Representative Director, Hiroyuki Isono
Executive Vice President, Representative Director, Fumio Shindo
Senior Managing Director, Director, Kazuhiko Kamada
Director, Shigeki Aoki
Director, Akio Hasebe
Director, Takayuki Moridaira
Director, Yuji Onuki
Outside Director, Michihiro Nara
Outside Director, Sachiko Ai
Outside Director, Seiko Nagai
Outside Director, Hiromichi Ogawa
Auditors : Deloitte Touche Tohmatsu LLC

LOCATIONS

HQ: Oji Holdings Corp
4-7-5 Ginza, Chuo-ku, Tokyo 104-0061
Phone: (81) 3 3563 1111 **Fax:** (81) 3 3563 1135
Web: www.ojiholdings.co.jp

PRODUCTS/OPERATIONS

2016 Sales

	% of total
Household and industrial materials	42
Printing and communication media	21
Forest resource and environment marketing	19
Functional materials	15
Others	3
Total	100

COMPETITORS

ARJOWIGGINS
Catalyst Paper Corporation
DS SMITH PLC
Flsmidth & Co. A/S
Franz Haniel & Cie. GmbH
Holmen AB
KUKA AG
Salzgitter Klöckner-Werke GmbH
UPM-Kymmene Oyj
Voith GmbH & Co. KGaA

HISTORICAL FINANCIALS

Company Type: Public

Income Statement
FYE: March 31

	REVENUE ($mil)	NET INCOME ($mil)	NET PROFIT MARGIN	EMPLOYEES
03/23	12,814	424	3.3%	37,845
03/22	12,086	719	6.0%	35,608
03/21	12,273	448	3.7%	36,034
03/20	13,888	535	3.9%	36,810
03/19	14,005	469	3.4%	36,309
Annual Growth	(2.2%)	(2.5%)	—	1.0%

2023 Year-End Financials

Debt ratio: 0.3%
Return on equity: 6.3%
Cash ($ mil.): 381
Current Ratio: 1.15
Long-term debt ($ mil.): 3,570
No. of shares ($ mil.): 992
Dividends
Yield: —
Payout: 266.7%
Market value ($ mil.): 39,262

	STOCK PRICE ($) FY Close	P/E High/Low		PER SHARE ($) Earnings	Dividends	Book Value
03/23	39.54	1	1	0.43	1.14	7.09
03/22	49.63	1	1	0.73	1.16	7.05
03/21	67.94	1	1	0.45	1.26	6.84
03/20	56.44	1	1	0.54	0.55	6.43
03/19	61.82	1	1	0.47	0.99	6.17
Annual Growth	(10.6%)	—	—	(2.5%)	3.6%	3.5%

OMV AG (Austria)

Oil and chemicals group OMV is Austria's largest industrial company. A leading oil and gas company in Central and Eastern Europe, it explores, develops, and produces oil and gas in its core regions and operates three refineries in Europe, Schwechat (Austria) and Burghausen (Germany). It is also one of the world's leading providers of advanced and circular polyolefin solutions. In 2022, OMV reported proved reserves of 1 billion barrels of oil equivalent; it produced about 500,000 barrels of oil equivalent per day. The majority of its sales were generated outside Austria and Germany. The company was founded in 1956.

Operations

OMV's segments includes Chemicals & Materials (about 20%), Refining & Marketing (roughly 40%), Exploration & Production (more than 40%), and Corporate & Other.

The Chemicals & Materials segment is one of the world's leading providers of advanced and circular polyolefin solutions. The segment is also a European market leading in base chemicals, fertilizers, and plastics recycling.

The Refining & Marketing segment operates three refineries in Europe, Schwechat (Austria), and Burghausen (Germany), which features integrated petrochemical production.

The Exploration & Production segment explores, develops, and produces oil and gas in the company's four core regions.

Geographic Reach

OMV, headquartered in Austria, has three refineries in Europe, Schwechat (Austria), and Burghausen (Germany). Austria and Germany are the company's largest market accounting for about 25% each. The company's other markets include Romania, the UAE, New Zealand, and Norway, among other countries.

Financial Performance

OMV's performance for the past five years has fluctuated but had an overall increase with 2022 as its highest performing year over the period.

The company recorded a EUR26.7 billion increase of its revenues to EUR62.3 billion, as compared to 2021's revenue of EUR35.6 billion.

OMV's net income for fiscal year end 2022 also increased to EUR5.2 billion, as compared to the prior year's net income of EUR2.8 billion.

The company held EUR8.1 billion by the end of the year. Operating activities generated EUR7.8 billion to the coffers. Investing activities and financing activities used EUR2 billion and EUR2.7 billion, respectively. Main cash uses were for intangible assets and property, plant, and equipment as well as repayments of long-term borrowings.

Strategy

The company's goal is to transform from an integrated oil, gas, and chemicals company into a leader in innovative sustainable fuels, chemicals, and materials, leveraging opportunities in the circular economy. The Group aims to become a net-zero emissions company by 2050 for all three scopes of greenhouse gas emissions. By taking this path, OMV expects to deliver an operating cash flow excluding net working capital effects of around EUR 6 billion by 2025 and at least EUR 7 billion by 2030.

Mergers and Acquisitions

In 2021, OMV and MOL Group, a leading international, integrated oil and gas company headquartered in Budapest, Hungary, announced the agreement for MOL Group to acquire OMV Slovenia. The agreement encompasses 120 filling stations as well as OMV's wholesale business in Slovenia. The agreed purchase price amounts to EUR 301 million (100% share). This transaction will reduce OMV's debt by approx. EUR 290 million before consideration of taxes from OMV's perspective (92.25% share), which will have a positive impact on OMV's gearing.

HISTORY

Oil exploration began in Austria in the 1920s, largely as joint ventures with foreign firms such as Shell and Socony-Vacuum. Full-scale production did not get underway until 1938, when the Anschluss (the absorption of Austria by Germany) paved the way for Germany to exploit Austria's natural resources to fuel its growing war machine. In the division of spoils following WWII, Russia gained control of Austria's oil reserves.

The Russian-administered oil assets were transferred to the new Austrian government in 1955, which authorized the company Österreichische Mineralölverwaltung (ÖMG) in 1956 to control state oil assets. ÖMG, state-controlled by the Austrian Mineral Oil Administration, set about building a major refinery in 1960 and acquiring marketing companies Martha and Ö-ROP in 1965.

In 1968 Ö-MG became the first Western company to sign a natural gas supply contract with Russia. In 1974 the company commissioned the Trans-Austria Gas Pipeline, which enabled the supply of natural gas to Italy. That year Ö-MG changed its name to Ö-MV Aktiengesellschaft (Ö-MV became OMV in 1995 for international markets).

During the 1970s OMV expanded its crude supply arrangements, tapping supplies from Iran, Iraq, Libya, and other Middle Eastern countries. It moved into oil and gas exploration in the mid-1980s, forming OMV Libya (acquiring 25% of Occidental's Libyan production) and OMV UK.

With Austria moving toward increasing privatization, in 1987 about 15% of OMV's shares were sold to the public. The government sold another 10% two years later. In 1989 OMV acquired PCD Polymere. With the aim of merging state-owned oil and chemical activities, OMV acquired Chemie Linz in 1990. The company also opened its first OMV-branded service station that year. In 1994 OMV reorganized itself as an integrated oil and gas group based in Central Europe, with international exploration and production activities, and with other operations in the chemical and petrochemical sectors.

In 1995 OMV acquired TOTAL-AUSTRIA, expanding its service stations by 59. The company introduced OMV lubricants to the Greek market in 1996. It also expanded its OMV service station network in Hungary to 66 stations after acquiring 31 Q8 (Kuwait) sites. In 1997 the Stroh Company's retail network in Austria was merged into OMV.

Expanding its retail network even farther, OMV acquired BP's retail network in the

Czech Republic, Slovakia, and Hungary in 1998. It also sold its stake in Chemie Linz and acquired a 25% stake in major European polyolefin producer Borealis, which in turn acquired PCD Polymere. In 1999 the company pushed its retail network into Bulgaria and Romania. That year OMV also acquired Australian company Cultus Petroleum.

OMV and Shell agreed to develop North Sea fields together in 2000. That year OMV also formed a joint venture with Italy's Edison International to explore in Vietnam and acquired more than 9% of Hungarian rival MOL. It upped that stake to 10% in 2001.

In 2002 OMV opened its first gas station in Serbia and Montenegro. It also increased its German gas station count from 79 to 151 with the purchase of 32 units from Royal Dutch Shell and 40 stations from Martin GmbH & Co.

In 2003 the company acquired Preussag Energie's exploration and production assets for $320 million. That year the company moved into Bosnia-Herzegovina, opening nine gas stations.

During 2004 the company bought up 51% of Romania's Petrom, making it the top oil and gas producer in Central Europe. As part of the deal, OMV chose to divest itself of its quarter-chunk of Rompetrol.

In 2006 Russian energy giant Gazprom signed long-term contracts for gas deliveries with OMV.

In a major consolidation move, in 2006 OMV agreed to buy Austrian power firm Verbund for $17 billion, but the move was rebuffed by government regulators. The next year the company announced plans to merge with Hungary's energy powerhouse MOL, but those plans were called off as well, due to European Commission regulatory concerns in 2008.

After plans to merge with Hungary's MOL went south, OMV the next year sold its 21% stake in it to Russian oil company Surgutneftegas for ?1.4 billion ($1.85 billion). Also in 2009, in keeping with its focus on retail markets in the Danube region, southeastern Europe, and the Black Sea region, OMV sold subsidiary OMV Italia; San Marco Petroli acquired the network of about 100 gas stations in the northern Italian region of Triveneto.

OMV has been disposing of some of its heating oil operations. In 2008 it unloaded Bayern GmbH, and it plans to sell its OMV Wärme VertriebsgmbH by the end of 2010. At that point, the sale of heating oil to private clients will be handled by partners, but OMV will continue to service corporate customers.

Eyeing new areas of exploration, that year OMV also acquired a 10% stake in Pearl Petroleum, giving it access to gas-condensate fields in Iraq.

In 2010 the company boosted its share of Turkey-based oil products company Petrol Ofisi (renamed OMV Petrol Ofisi) from 42% to 96%, by acquiring a 54% stake from Dogan Holding for about $1.4 billion. The deal gave OMV access to not only Turkey but the Caspian region and the Middle East.

The acquisition of full control (in 2010) of Petrol Ofisi, Turkey's leading filling station and retail business with the only nationwide filling station network in the country (approximately 2,300 stations), built a strategic bridge in the growth market of Turkey.

In a further push to grow in the Middle East, in 2011 the company acquired two Tunisia-based exploration and production units from Pioneer Natural Resources for $866 million. It also boosted its footprint in Pakistan, acquiring Petronas Carigali (Pakistan) Ltd. in 2011.

In 2012 the company sold its gas station subsidiary in Croatia. That year it boosted it E&P assets, entering Abu Dhabi, and acquiring natural gas assets in Norway.

EXECUTIVES

Chief Executive Officer, Chairman, Member, Alfred Stern
Deputy Chief Executive, Deputy Chairman, Member, Johann Pleininger
Chief Financial Officer, Reinhard Florey
Member, Elena Skvortsova
Member, Martijn van Koten
Chairman, Mark Garrett
Deputy Chairman, Christine Catasta
Director, Stefan Doboczky
Director, Karl Rose
Director, Elisabeth Stadler
Director, Christoph Swarovski
Director, Cathrine Trattner
Director, Gertrude Tumpel-Gugerell
Director, Alexander Auer
Director, Hubert Bunderla
Director, Nicole Schachenhofer
Director, Angela Schorna
Director, Gerhard Singer
Auditors : Ernst & Young Wirtschaftsprufungsgesellschaft m.b.H.

LOCATIONS

HQ: OMV AG (Austria)
  Trabrennstrasse 6-8, Vienna 1020
Phone: (43) 1 40440 0
Web: www.omv.com

2016 Sales

	% of total
Austria	25
Turkey	25
Romania	16
Germany	14
Rest of CEE	13
Rest of Europe	5
Rest of world	2
Total	100

PRODUCTS/OPERATIONS

2016 Sales

	% of total
D/S	95
U/S	5
Total	100

COMPETITORS

BG GROUP LIMITED
CONOCOPHILLIPS
ENI SPA
Equinor ASA
GAZPROM, PAO
HESS CORPORATION
LUKOIL, PAO
MOL Magyar Olaj- és Gázipari Nyilvánosan Működő Részvénytársaság
SEAENERGY PLC
SURGUTNEFTEGAZ, PAO

HISTORICAL FINANCIALS

Company Type: Public

Income Statement FYE: December 31

	REVENUE ($mil)	NET INCOME ($mil)	NET PROFIT MARGIN	EMPLOYEES
12/21	40,243	2,368	5.9%	22,434
12/20	20,311	1,543	7.6%	25,291
12/19	26,341	1,884	7.2%	19,845
12/18	26,259	1,646	6.3%	20,231
12/17	24,241	521	2.2%	20,721
Annual Growth	13.5%	46.0%	—	2.0%

2021 Year-End Financials

Debt ratio: 20.7%   No. of shares ($ mil.): 327
Return on equity: 14.3%   Dividends
Cash ($ mil.): 5,715   Yield: 21.9%
Current Ratio: 1.36   Payout: 20.8%
Long-term debt ($ mil.): 9,835   Market value ($ mil.): 18,558

	STOCK PRICE ($) FY Close	P/E High/Low		PER SHARE ($) Earnings	Dividends	Book Value
12/21	56.75	10	6	7.24	3.11	53.67
12/20	40.15	16	5	4.73	1.49	51.57
12/19	55.70	12	9	5.76	1.42	44.69
12/18	44.32	15	10	5.04	1.27	41.73
12/17	63.37	49	30	1.59	1.05	41.18
Annual Growth	(2.7%)	—	—	46.0%	31.2%	6.8%

Orange

Orange is an operator of mobile and internet services in Europe and Africa and a global leader in corporate telecommunication services. The company is able to serve its customers through its employees located in France, Spain, Poland, Africa, the Asia-Pacific, and the US. Currently, the company has more than 140,000 employee and over 250 million customers. It is a leading European wireless operator and broadband service provider, as well as sales of equipment including mobile terminals and broadband equipment among others. Orange's services for corporate clients are provided by its Orange Business Services unit, which offers a wide range of managed business networking and data services.

Operations

The operating segments are: France

(Enterprise excluded); Spain and each of the Other European countries (including the business segments Poland, Belgium and Luxembourg and each of the Central European countries); the Sonatel subgroup (in Senegal, Orange Mali, Orange Bissau, Orange in Guinea and Orange in Sierra Leone), Enterprise which brings together dedicated communication solutions and services for businesses in France and around the world; International Carriers & Shared Services (IC&SS); and Mobile Financial Services which includes the Orange Bank entity.

Geographic Reach

The company is able to serve its customers through its employees located in France, Spain, Poland, Africa, the Asia-Pacific, and the US.

Sales and Marketing

Advertising, promotion, sponsoring, communication and brand marketing costs are recorded as expenses during the period in which they are incurred. The company spent EUR783 million, EUR736 million, and EUR823 million, for years 2021, 2020, and 2019, respectively.

Financial Performance

Note: Growth rates may differ after conversion to US Dollars.

For the last five years, the company's performance has remained almost the same staying at an almost stagnant level but still ended the period with 2021 as its highest performing year.

In fiscal 2021 the company grew its sales to EUR42.5 which is EUR252 million higher than 2020's revenue of EUR42.3 billion.

However, consolidated net income decreased to EUR782 million in 2021 as compared to the prior year's net income of EUR5.1 billion.

Orange's cash position was at EUR8.6 million billion at the end of 2021. Operating activities provided EUR11.2 billion. Financing activities and investing activities used EUR5.9 billion and EUR4.8 billion, respectively Main cash uses include purchases of property, plant and equipment and intangible assets and medium and long-term debt redemptions and repayments.

Strategy

Orange's strategy is to accelerate its business in growth areas with a particular focus on mobile financial services (including Mobile Banking), B2B IT services and cyber security. Although building on the Group's strengths (digital expertise, distribution strength, capacity for innovation, brand image and a strong presence in the MEA Region), the development of these new businesses requires substantial resources, without any guarantee that the corresponding services will gain sufficient traction to generate a return on these investments.

The company has its new strategic plan named Engage 2025. With the Engage 2025 strategic plan, Orange is staking its claim as an engaged and committed leader. The company's strength lies in reconciling business performance and a sustainable approach with customers, employees, stakeholders, partners and society in general. With Engage 2025, Orange is capitalising on these strong choices and setting ambitious new targets for 2025 while making a responsible commitment to its employees, customers and society at large.

Company Background

Orange's history dates back to the foundation of the telegraph network in France. Much like BT Group in Britain which shares a similar timeline, Orange in its present form is a result of the privatization of France's department for telecommunications. The department became an independent public entity in 1991 and was renamed France Télécom, before being privatized six years later, becoming a société anonyme (limited company) on 31 December 1996.

Over the next decade or so, France Télécom grew organically and via acquisitions, which included the purchase of Orange, a British-founded mobile network sold by Vodafone as part of an anti-competition ruling. By the mid-00s, France Télécom had become one of the world's largest telecoms companies and had built up significant operations outside France. It decided a new, unifying brand identity was needed to replace the explicitly French "France Télecom", and with the use of mobile services on the sharp increase, it settled on using Orange. Over the next decade the company brought its varied operations across the globe under the Orange brand and officially renamed itself Orange SA in 2013.

HISTORY

Shortly before he abdicated, King Louis Philippe laid the groundwork for France's state-owned telegraphic service. Established in 1851, the operation became part of the French Post Office in the 1870s, about the time Alexander Graham Bell invented the telephone. The French government licensed three private companies to provide telegraph service, and during the 1880s they merged into the Société Générale de Téléphones (SGT). In 1883 the country's first exchange was initiated in Rheims. Four years later an international circuit was installed connecting Paris and Brussels. The government nationalized SGT in 1889.

By the turn of the century, France had more than 60,000 phone lines, and in 1924 a standardized telephone was introduced. Long-distance service improved with underground cabling, and phone exchanges in Paris and other leading cities became automated during the 1930s.

WWII proved a major setback to the French government's telephone operations, Direction Générale des Télécommunications (DGT), because a large part of its equipment was destroyed or damaged. For the next two decades France lagged behind other nations in telephony infrastructure development. An exception to this technological stagnation was Centre National d'Etudes des Télécommunications (CNET), the research laboratory formed in 1944 that eventually became France Telecom's research arm.

In 1962 DGT was a key player in the first intercontinental television broadcast, between the US and France, via a Telstar satellite. The company began to catch up with its peers when it developed a digital phone system in the mid-1970s. In 1974 CNET was instrumental in the launch of France's first experimental communications satellite. In another technological advance, DGT began replacing its paper directories with the innovative Minitel online terminals in 1980.

The French government created France Telecom in 1988. In 1993 France Telecom and Deutsche Telekom (DT) teamed up to form the Global One international telecommunications venture, and Sprint joined the next year. Global One was formally launched in 1996. Also that year France Telecom began providing Internet access, though Minitel still reigned as the country's top online service.

In 1997 the government sold about 20% of France Telecom to the public. With Europe's state telephone monopolies ending in 1998, France Telecom reorganized and brought prices in line with those of its competitors.

EXECUTIVES

Chief Executive Officer, Chairman, Stephane Richard
Finance Deputy Managing Director, Strategy Deputy Managing Director, Ramon Fernandez
Strategy Senior Executive Vice President, Cyber Security Senior Executive Vice President, Hugues Foulon
Senior Executive Vice President, Secretary, Nicolas Guerin
Branding Senior Executive Vice President, Communications Senior Executive Vice President, Beatrice Mandine
Independent Director, Alexandre Bompard
Independent Director, Anne-Gabrielle Heilbronner
Independent Director, Christel Heydemann
Independent Director, Helle Kristoffersen
Independent Director, Bernard Ramanantsoa
Independent Director, Frederic Sanchez
Independent Director, Jean-Michel Severino
Auditors : KPMG Audit

LOCATIONS

HQ: Orange
111 quai du President Roosevelt, Issy-les-Moulineaux 92130

Phone: (33) 1 44 44 21 05
Web: www.orange.com

2017 sales

	% of total
France	42
Enterprise	17
Spain	13
Africa & Middle-East	12
Poland	6
Central European countries	4
International Carriers & Shared Services	4
Belgium & Luxembourg	2
Total	100

PRODUCTS/OPERATIONS

Selected Operations
Audience and advertising (Internet advertising business)
Content (partnerships with content providers and development of related technology platforms)
Enterprise communication services (communication services to companies)
Health (services to the health care industry)
Home communication services (residential communication services, especially fixed-line broadband)
Personal communication services (communication services for individuals using mobile devices)

COMPETITORS

BT GROUP PLC
CHARTER COMMUNICATIONS, INC.
COMPUTACENTER PLC
Deutsche Telekom AG
GLOBALSTAR, INC.
IDT CORPORATION
LEVEL 3 PARENT, LLC
Proximus
SPRINT CORPORATION
XO HOLDINGS, INC

HISTORICAL FINANCIALS
Company Type: Public

Income Statement — FYE: December 31

	REVENUE ($mil)	NET INCOME ($mil)	NET PROFIT MARGIN	EMPLOYEES
12/21	48,132	263	0.5%	139,698
12/20	51,875	5,917	11.4%	142,150
12/19	47,432	3,375	7.1%	146,768
12/18	47,392	2,237	4.7%	150,711
12/17	49,271	2,284	4.6%	151,556
Annual Growth	(0.6%)	(41.7%)	—	(2.0%)

2021 Year-End Financials
Debt ratio: —
Return on equity: 0.6%
Cash ($ mil.): 9,757
Current Ratio: 0.95
Long-term debt ($ mil.): —
No. of shares ($ mil.): 2,658
Dividends
 Yield: 8.8%
 Payout: 0.0%
Market value ($ mil.): 28,050

	STOCK PRICE ($) FY Close	P/E High/Low	PER SHARE ($) Earnings	Dividends	Book Value
12/21	10.55	— —	0.00	0.93	13.77
12/20	11.86	10 6	2.10	0.71	15.88
12/19	14.59	16 14	1.15	0.78	13.44
12/18	16.19	28 24	0.71	0.81	13.24
12/17	17.40	30 26	0.74	0.78	13.74
Annual Growth	(11.8%)	— —	—	4.7%	0.0%

Orbia Advance Corp SAB De CV

Orbia (formerly Mexichem) is one of the largest pipe producers in Europe and Latin America and a leader in the production of PVC resin in Latin America. It makes such chemical building blocks as chlorine, caustic soda, resin and fluorite compounds, and fluorite. Orbia's chemical and petrochemical output find use in a range of consumer and industrial products, including soaps and detergents as well as for use in water treatment and the manufacture of PVC. The company also mines and processes fluorite, which is used in the production of steel, ceramics, glass and cement. While focusing on North and Latin America, Orbia also exports products to more than 110 countries through its nearly 120 production plants and two fluorspar mines. Mexico, the US and Northwest Europe account for the majority of sales.

Operations
Orbia's operations consist of five business groups: Polymer Solutions (around 35% of sales), Building & Infrastructure (some 30%), Precision Agriculture (over 10%), Data Communications (around 10%), and Fluorinated Solutions (about 10%).

Polymer Solutions is as universal and dynamic as the materials it produces. It focuses on the production of general and special PVC resins and other vinyl polymers with a wide range of applications, creating solutions that support its customers' everyday life, such as pipes, cables, floors, automobile parts, household appliances, clothing, packaging and medical devices.

The Building and Infrastructure is redefining today's pipe and fittings industry by creating innovative solutions with longer life and less installation work. It also develops sustainable technologies for water management systems, as well as systems for heating and cooling water in homes.

Precision Agriculture helps the world to grow more with less. Precision Agriculture's cutting-edge digital farming technologies, services and irrigation systems enable farmers to achieve significantly higher yields and better-quality food while using less water, fertilizer and other inputs. By helping farmers grow more with less, Precision Agriculture enables farmers around the world to feed the planet more efficiently and sustainably.

Data Communications operates under the belief that every organization, every community, and every inhabitant on the planet deserves the chance to benefit to the fullest from modern technology. The company annually produces more than 400 million meters of essential and innovative infrastructure, including conduit, FuturePath, cables-in-conduit and accessories, which create the physical pathways for fiber optics and other network technologies that connect cities, homes and people. It is the world leader in the manufacture and distribution of such products in a highly dynamic industry and in conduit and a leading company in HDPE based products for cable and fiber optics, as well as pressurized pipes from natural gas and other solutions.

Fluorinated Solutions provides products, technologies and other applications of fluorinated materials that support modern life in countless ways. With the world's largest fluorite mine, solid knowledge and vast production experience, this segment develops value-added chemicals, as well as propellants and advanced materials used in a wide range of applications, including automotive, infrastructure, health and medicine, HVAC and food cold chain.

Geographic Reach
Headquartered in Mexico, the company has a global presence in some 50 countries where it's about 120 production plants were located. It has concessions for the exploitation of two fluorite mines in Mexico, eight training academies, and about 20 research and development laboratories. It also has commercial activities in over 110 countries.

The US accounts for around 20% of sales, followed by Northwest Europe with over 15%, Southwest Europe, bringing in about 15%, and Mexico with around 10%. Colombia, AMEA, Brazil, Central and Eastern Europe, Israel, Central America, Peru, Southeast Europe and Ecuador represent for the remaining sales.

Sales and Marketing
The clients of the Salt-Chloro-Sose-Ethylene-VCM Process are located mainly in the secondary sector, the petrochemical, secondary chemical, agrochemical and pharmaceutical industries; PVC resin production, plastics processing, soap and detergents, cellulose and paper, matches, and polymers such as polyurethane products for hygiene and cleaning of hospitals and homes, water treatment, bottling and metal-mechanical industry.

For product sales, Orbia has long-term contracts with some customers, for which it has established sales schemes that promote loyalty through discounts for volume acquired during specific periods of time.

In addition, PVC products are used by customers in the manufacture of pipes and fittings, flexible and rigid profiles, upholstery, flexible and rigid films, bottles and containers, synthetic floors, blinds, laminated polystyrene, toy industry, footwear and articles for the medical industry, among others.

Financial Performance
The company had net sales of $8.8 billion in 2021, a 37% increase from the previous year's net sales of $6.4 billion. This was primarily due to a higher volume of Polymer Solutions sales for the year.

The company had a net income of $772 million, a 142% increase from the previous year's net income of $319 million.

Strategy

In the course of business, Orbia enters into strategic partnerships with third parties. Specifically, Orbia has a 50:50 strategic alliance joint venture with OxyChem for production of ethylene in a company called Ingleside Ethylene, LLC located in Ingleside, Texas, US.

Mergers and Acquisitions

In late 2021, Koura, part of the Orbia community of companies, announced that it has signed a definitive agreement to acquire Madison, Wisconsin-based Silatronix, a leading battery technology start-up. Koura is executing on a comprehensive energy materials strategy and this acquisition complements its capabilities in energy storage deployment ? presently, an area of accelerated need and demand for a renewable future.

In early 2021, Alphagary, a division of Orbia's Polymer Solutions business group, announced that it will acquire majority share ownership of Shakun Polymers Private Limited (Shakun), a privately held and family-owned market leader in the production of compounds for the wire and cable markets in the Indian subcontinent, the Middle East, Southeast Asia and Africa. Shakun's semi-conductive and cross-linkable compounds expand Alphagary's portfolio, offer a growth platform and meet customer requirements.

Also in early 2021, Netafim, an Orbia company, has signed a definitive agreement to acquire Dutch turn-key greenhouse project provider Gakon Horticultural Projects. The acquisition is synergistic, combining Netafim's global presence and expertise and Gakon's greenhouse technology. Gakon brings unique expertise in all aspects of greenhouse project execution, glasshouse manufacturing capabilities, and a proven track record in key verticals.

EXECUTIVES

Chairman, Juan Pablo del Valle Perochena
Honorary Chairman, Antonio Del Valle Ruiz
Chief Executive Officer, Director, Antonio Carrillo Rule
Chief Financial Officer, Rodrigo Guzman Perera
General Counsel, Alvaro Soto Gonzalez
Director, Antonio del Valle Perochena
Director, Francisco Javier Del Valle Perochena
Director, Adolfo Del Valle Ruiz
Director, Ignacio Del Valle Ruiz
Director, Jaime Ruiz Sacristan
Director, Ricardo Gutierrez Munoz
Director, Divo Milan Haddad
Director, Fernando Ruiz Sahagun
Director, Jorge Corvera Gibsone
Director, Guillermo Ortiz Martinez
Director, Eduardo Tricio Haro
Director, Juan Francisco Beckmann Vidal
Director, Valentin Diez Morodo
Director, Eugenio Clariond Reyes
Auditors : Galaz, Yamazaki, Ruiz Urquiza, S.C. (member of Deloitte & Touche Tohmatsu)

LOCATIONS

HQ: Orbia Advance Corp SAB De CV
Avenida Paseo de la Reforma 483, Piso 47, Mexico City, Cuauhtemoc 06500
Phone: (52) 55 5366 4000   **Fax:** (52) 55 5397 8836
Web: www.orbia.com

2015 Sales

	% of total
Mexico	22
NorthWest Europe	16
USA	16
Southwest Europe	10
Colombia	9
Brazil	7
Central and Eastern Europe	4
Central America	3
SouthEast Europe	3
Ecuador	2
Peru	2
Argentina	1
Japan	1
Venezuela	-
Other Europe	1
Others	3
Total	100

PRODUCTS/OPERATIONS

2015 Sales

	% of total
Fluent	53
Vinyl	36
Fluorine	10
Holding Entity	1
Total	100

COMPETITORS

AUREA
China Baowu Steel Group Corporation Limited
DOWA HOLDINGS CO.,LTD.
INEOS OXIDE LIMITED
MITSUI CHEMICALS AMERICA, INC.
Refratechnik Holding GmbH
RÅœTGERS GmbH
VENATOR MATERIALS PLC
VINYTHAI PUBLIC COMPANY LIMITED
VOTORANTIM PARTICIPACOES S.A.

HISTORICAL FINANCIALS

Company Type: Public

Income Statement   FYE: December 31

	REVENUE ($mil)	NET INCOME ($mil)	NET PROFIT MARGIN	EMPLOYEES
12/21	8,782	657	7.5%	0
12/20	6,419	194	3.0%	21,688
12/19	6,987	206	3.0%	22,123
12/18	7,198	354	4.9%	22,107
12/17	5,828	194	3.3%	17,671
Annual Growth	10.8%	35.6%	—	—

2021 Year-End Financials

Debt ratio: 33.2%   No. of shares ($ mil.): —
Return on equity: 25.1%   Dividends
Cash ($ mil.): 781   Yield: —
Current Ratio: 1.41   Payout: 0.0%
Long-term debt ($ mil.): 3,279 Market value ($ mil.): —

Origin Energy Ltd

Origin Energy has a rich heritage in energy exploration, production, power generation and retailing. It is a leading provider of energy to homes and businesses throughout Australia. It also invests in renewable energy technologies. The company is a major retailer of natural gas, electricity, and liquefied petroleum gas (LPG) in Australia with some 4.5 million customers (mostly in Victoria). The company has extensive operations across Australia, Papua New Guinea and the South Pacific covering electricity generation, upstream unconventional gas and LNG and LPG.

Operations

Origin Energy gets majority of its revenue from its Business and Wholesale segment, which account for 50% of the company's revenue, followed by the Retail segment at 35%. Other segments include LPG, solar and energy gas, and integrated gas.

The retail electricity segment provides standard service offerings with discounts on published tariff rates. For the company's business and wholesale segment, transfer of renewable energy certificates (RECs) is included to its offerings.

The company's solar and energy services related to the sales of solar, batteries and Community Energy Services. Sales from this segment includes the sale, installation, repairs and maintenance services of solar photovoltaic systems, and battery solutions, to residential and business customers.

Geographic Reach

Origin Energy offers its services throughout Australia, with its LPG segment focused on Pacific countries such as Apia, Pago Pago, Rarotonga, Lautaka, Labasa, and Suva, among others.

Financial Performance

Origin Energy's performance for the past five years has fluctuated but had an overall increase, ending with 2023 as the company's highest performing year over the period.

The company's revenue increased by $2 billion to $16.5 billion for fiscal year end 2023, as compared to 2022's revenue of $14.5 billion.

Origin Energy recorded a net income of $1.1 billion for 2023, as compared to the prior year's net loss of $1.4 billion.

The company held $463 million at the end of 2023. Operating activities used $633 million. Investing activities provided $1.2 billion, while financing activities used $721 million. Main cash uses were for acquisition of property, plant and equipment, and repayment of borrowings.

Strategy

Over the past year, execution of Origin's strategy has accelerated leading to increasing confidence as to its future prospects as the energy transition gathers momentum. The company is rapidly building its pipeline of renewable and storage projects. It approved the first phase of a large-scale Eraring battery, acquired the Warrane prospective wind development site in the New England renewable energy zone and progressed several renewable and brownfield battery development options across the portfolio.

Origin Energy released its first Climate Transition Action Plan (CTAP) outlining the company's strategy and ambition to lead the energy transition through cleaner energy and customer solutions. The CTAP includes new targets to accelerate emissions reduction across Origin and create value for shareholders, towards a long-term ambition to be net zero emissions by 2050.

EXECUTIVES

Chief Executive Officer, Managing Director, Executive Director, Frank G. Calabria
Chief Financial Officer, Lawrie Tremaine
Retail Executive General Manager, Jon Briskin
Energy Supply and Operations Executive General Manager, Greg Jarvis
General Counsel, Kate Jordan
Secretary, Helen Hardy
Independent Non-Executive Chairman, Independent Non-Executive Director, Scott W. Perkins
Independent Non-Executive Director, John H. Akehurst
Independent Non-Executive Director, Ilana R. Atlas
Independent Non-Executive Director, Maxine N. Brenner
Independent Non-Executive Director, Greg Lalicker
Independent Non-Executive Director, Mick McCormack
Independent Non-Executive Director, Bruce W. D. Morgan
Independent Non-Executive Director, Steven Sargent
Independent Non-Executive Director, Joan Withers
Auditors : Ernst & Young

LOCATIONS

HQ: Origin Energy Ltd
Level 32, Tower 1, 100 Barangaroo Avenue, Barangaroo, New South Wales 2000
Phone: (61) 2 8345 5000 **Fax:** (61) 2 9252 9244
Web: www.originenergy.com.au

2016 Sales

	% of total
Australia	98
New Zealand	1
Others	1
Total	100

PRODUCTS/OPERATIONS

2016 Sales

	% of total
Energy Markets	94
Integrated Gas	4
Contact Energy	2
Total	100

COMPETITORS

AVANGRID, INC.
CALPINE CORPORATION
CH ENERGY GROUP, INC.
COMMERCE ENERGY GROUP, INC.
DYNEGY NORTH AMERICA, INC.
INPEX CORPORATION
NOCO ENERGY CORP.
SOUTH JERSEY INDUSTRIES, INC.
TransAlta Corporation
Vattenfall Europe AG

HISTORICAL FINANCIALS

Company Type: Public

Income Statement — FYE: June 30

	REVENUE ($mil)	NET INCOME ($mil)	NET PROFIT MARGIN	EMPLOYEES
06/23	10,939	698	6.4%	11,260
06/22	10,052	(983)	—	5,174
06/21	9,112	(1,719)	—	5,000
06/20	9,053	56	0.6%	5,200
06/19	10,336	848	8.2%	5,360
Annual Growth	1.4%	(4.8%)	—	20.4%

2023 Year-End Financials

Debt ratio: 0.7%
Return on equity: 11.1%
Cash ($ mil.): 306
Current Ratio: 1.04
Long-term debt ($ mil.): —
No. of shares ($ mil.): 1,721
Dividends
Yield: 3.1%
Payout: 41.2%
Market value ($ mil.): 9,379

	STOCK PRICE ($) FY Close	P/E High/Low		PER SHARE ($) Earnings	Dividends	Book Value
06/23	5.45	9	6	0.40	0.17	3.42
06/22	3.82	—	—	(0.56)	0.10	4.01
06/21	3.65	—	—	(0.98)	0.11	4.19
06/20	4.35	126	58	0.03	0.16	4.94
06/19	5.05	10	6	0.48	0.06	5.24
Annual Growth	1.9%	—	—	(4.3%)	32.1%	(10.1%)

Orix Corp

ORIX Corporation is a financial services group which provides innovative products and services to its customers by constantly pursuing new businesses. The company has expanded from its original leasing business into an enterprise active in operations and investing in a diverse array of areas around the world, delivering a wide variety of products and services to corporate and individual customers, communities, and in infrastructure. Established in 1964, ORIX has spread its businesses globally by establishing locations in about 30 countries and regions across the world. Its home country, Japan, generates more than 75% of the company's revenue.

Operations

ORIX organizes its businesses into ten segments: Insurance about 20% of total revenue), Corporate Financial Services and Maintenance Leasing (nearly 20%), Real Estate (about 15% of revenue), PE Investment and Concession (about 15% of revenue), ORIX Europe (some 10%), Environment and Energy (about 5%), ORIX USA (about 5%), Asia and Australia (about 5%), Banking and Credit (about 5%), and Aircraft and Ships (less than 5%).

The Insurance segment is its largest segment and consists of life insurance; Corporate Financial Services and Maintenance Leasing segment is involved in finance and fee business; leasing and rental of automobiles, electronic measuring instruments and ICT-related equipment; and Yayoi; Real Estate segment consists of real estate development, rental and management, facility operation, and real estate asset management; PE Investment and Concession segment consists of private equity investment, and concession; ORIX Europe segment consists of asset management of global equity and fixed income; Environment and Energy segment consists of domestic and overseas renewable energy, electric power retailing, ESCO services, sales of solar panels and battery energy storage system, and recycling and waste management; ORIX USA segment consists of finance, investment and asset management in the Americas; Asia and Australia segment consists of finance and investment businesses in Asia and Australia; Banking and Credit segment consists of banking and consumer finance; and Aircraft and Ships segment consists of aircraft leasing and management, and ship-related finance and investment.

Overall, services income accounts for nearly 35% of revenue, while operating leases and life insurance premiums and related investment income generate around 20% each of revenue, goods and real estate income brings in more than 15% and finance revenues account for more than 10%.

Geographic Reach

ORIX, headquartered in Tokyo, Japan, operates more than 1,650 offices in Japan (where it earns more than 75% of its revenue) and about 475 overseas. The Americas is ORIX's second-largest market, comprising another 10% of total revenue.

Financial Performance

Company's revenue for fiscal 2022 increased by 10% to Â¥2.5 trillion compared from the prior year with Â¥2.3 trillion.

Net income for fiscal 2022 increased by Â¥312.1 billion compared from the prior year with Â¥192.4 billion.

Cash held by the company at the end of fiscal 2022 was Â¥1.1 trillion. Cash provided by operations was Â¥1.1 trillion while cash used for investing and financing activities were Â¥808.8 billion and Â¥306.6 billion, respectively.

Strategy

During the fiscal year ended March 31, 2022 the COVID-19 has not subsided worldwide yet. Due to the increase of uncertainty in the operating environment stemming from a shortage of semiconductors, rising crude oil prices, interest-rate hikes and a sharp depreciation of the yen, ORIX Group exercised extreme caution in managing its various business segments. In fiscal 2022, ORIX Group achieved a significant increase in profits primarily due to an increase in gains on sales of subsidiaries and affiliates resulting from the sale of the business of Yayoi. The business environments in the facility operation business in the Real Estate Segment, the concession business in the PE Investment and Concession Segment, and the aircraft leasing business in the Aircraft and Ships Segment did not recover from the previous fiscal year when it was affected by the impact of the COVID-19 pandemic.

Mergers and Acquisitions

In 2021, ORIX announced that it has completed its acquisition of Elawan Energy S.L. (Elawan), developer and operator of wind and solar power plants in about 15 countries around the world, with a focus on Europe and North and South America. European subsidiary ORIX Corporation Europe N.V. successfully gained regulatory approvals to acquire 80% of Elawan's issued shares, and becomes the majority shareholder in the business. These capabilities align well with ORIX's renewable energy business, and Elawan will form an integral part of its global renewable energy strategy, complementing an already leading market position in Japan with an enhanced presence in other core markets around the world.

In early 2021, ORIX announced that it has completed its acquisition of shares in Greenko Energy Holdings ("Greenko"), one of the two major Indian renewable energy operators. Simultaneous to acquiring issued shares in Greenko, ORIX integrated its entire wind power generation business in India into Greenko in exchange for new additional shares of Greenko. Accordingly, ORIX has acquired approximately 21.8% of Greenko for a total value of approximately U$961 million.

Also in early 2021, ORIX announced today that it has completed its acquisition 70% of shares in Gravis Capital Management Ltd ("Gravis"), an alternative asset management company, that manages funds investing primarily in the UK. infrastructure, renewable energy and real estate sectors, with a significant ESG focus. As a result of this acquisition, ORIX will be able to support further growth of Gravis including expansion of its existing fund portfolios and formation of new funds.

EXECUTIVES

Chief Executive Officer, President, Representative Executive Officer, Director, Makoto Inoue

Senior Managing Executive Officer, Director, Shuji Irie
Senior Managing Executive Officer, Assistant Chief Executive, Director, Shoji Taniguchi
Senior Managing Executive Officer, Director, Satoru Matsuzaki
Senior Managing Executive Officer, Director, Yoshiteru Suzuki
Senior Managing Executive Officer, Kiyoshi Fushitani
Managing Executive Officer, Yasuaki Mikami
Global Managing Executive Officer, Global General Counsel, Director, Stan H. Koyanagi
Outside Director, Heizo Takenaka
Outside Director, Michael Cusumano
Outside Director, Sakie Akiyama
Outside Director, Hiroshi Watanabe
Outside Director, Aiko Sekine
Outside Director, Chikatomo Hodo
Auditors : KPMG AZSA LLC

LOCATIONS

HQ: Orix Corp
World Trade Center Building, South Tower, 2-4-1 Hamamatsu-cho, Minato-ku, Tokyo 105-5135
Phone: (81) 3 3435 1274 **Fax:** (81) 3 3435 1276
Web: www.orix.co.jp

2018 Sales

	% of total
Japan	83
Americas	4
Others	13
Total	100

PRODUCTS/OPERATIONS

2018 Sales by Business Segment

	% of total
Corporate Financial Services	4
Maintenance Leasing	10
Real Estate	6
Investment and Operation	49
Retail	15
Overseas Business	16
Total	100

Selected Subsidiaries and Segments

ORIX Aircraft (aircraft leasing)
ORIX Asset Management & Loan Services Corporation (commercial mortgage servicing)
ORIX Auto (car rental and leasing)
ORIX Buffaloes Baseball Club (professional baseball team)
ORIX Life Insurance
ORIX Real Estate (real estate development and investment)
ORIX Real Estate Investment Advisors (asset management)
ORIX Rentec (rental operations)
ORIX Trust and Banking
ORIX USA
SUN Leasing Corporation (medical equipment leasing)

COMPETITORS

BGC PARTNERS, INC.
CATERPILLAR FINANCIAL SERVICES CORPORATION
F&C EQUITY PARTNERS PLC
FORD MOTOR CREDIT COMPANY LLC
HEWLETT-PACKARD FINANCIAL SERVICES COMPANY
INVESTEC PLC
MITSUBISHI UFJ LEASE & FINANCE COMPANY LIMITED
OPPENHEIMER HOLDINGS INC.
SILVERFLEET CAPITAL LIMITED
TOKYO CENTURY CORPORATION

HISTORICAL FINANCIALS

Company Type: Public

Income Statement — FYE: March 31

	ASSETS ($mil)	NET INCOME ($mil)	INCOME AS % OF ASSETS	EMPLOYEES
03/22	117,322	2,566	2.2%	32,235
03/21	122,494	1,737	1.4%	33,153
03/20	120,382	2,788	2.3%	31,233
03/19	109,938	2,923	2.7%	32,411
03/18	107,603	2,948	2.7%	31,890
Annual Growth	2.2%	(3.4%)	—	0.3%

2022 Year-End Financials

Return on assets: 2.2%
Return on equity: 9.9%
Long-term debt ($ mil.): —
No. of shares ($ mil.): 1,193
Sales ($ mil.): 20,551
Dividends
Yield: 3.6%
Payout: 158.6%
Market value ($ mil.): 119,161

	STOCK PRICE ($) FY Close	P/E High/Low	PER SHARE ($) Earnings	Dividends	Book Value
03/22	99.85	0 0	2.13	3.68	22.47
03/21	84.79	1 0	1.40	3.59	22.47
03/20	59.10	0 0	2.18	3.73	21.98
03/19	71.87	0 0	2.28	3.12	20.44
03/18	89.86	0 0	2.30	2.66	19.74
Annual Growth	2.7%		(1.9%)	8.5%	3.3%

Orsted A/S

The Danish energy giant company, Ãrsted, renamed from DONG (Danish Oil and Natural Gas) Energy in 2017 after selling off its upstream oil and gas production (or black energy) assets, becoming a renewable energy company. Ãrsted develops, constructs, and operates offshore and onshore wind farms, solar farms, energy storage facilities, and bioenergy plants, and provides energy products to its customers. Ãrsted is the only energy company in the world with a science-based net-zero emissions target as validated by the Science Based Targets initiative (SBTi). The Denmark generates about 75% of total revenue. The company begins in 1973 when the Danish State established a company called Dansk Olie & Naturgas A/S (Danish Oil and Natural Gas), also known as DONG.

Operations

Ãrsted's three business units are Offshore, Bioenergy & Other, and Onshore.

In offshore segment, Orsted develops, constructs, owns, and operates offshore wind farms in the UK, Germany, Denmark, the Netherlands, the US, Taiwan, Japan, and South Korea. The segment accounts for some 60% of revenue.

Bioenergy & Other segment (nearly 40%) provides around one quarter of Denmark's district heating and around one third of Denmark's thermal power through our CHP plants, making our CHP business a leading provider of heat, power, and ancillary services in Denmark.

Onshore segment (less than 5%) develops, operates, and owns onshore wind, solar PV, and storage projects across the southern and midwestern US (primarily in ERCOT, SPP, and the South-East) and in Europe (UK and Ireland).

Overall, roughly 35% of sales were generated from the sale of power, around 20% each from sale of gas and generation of power, about 10% from revenue from construction of offshore wind farms and transmission assets, and nearly 5% each from generation and sale of heat and steam and others. Around 10% from government grants.

Geographic Reach
Denmark-based Ãrsted has operations in Germany, the Netherlands, Taiwan, US and the UK. About 75% of sales were generated from Denmark, UK with about 20%, while Germany, US, Taiwan and Others generated over 5% combined.

Sales and Marketing
No single customer accounted for more than 10 % of its consolidated sales.

Financial Performance
Revenue for the year increased by 55% to DKK77.7 billion in 2021. The increase was primarily due to the significantly higher gas and power prices across all markets and the divestment of the offshore transmission asset at Hornsea 1 in 2021.

In 2021, the company had a net income of DKK10.2 billion, a 32% decrease from the previous year's net income of DKK15.1 billion. This was primarily due to the higher volume of cost of sales for the year.

The company's cash at the end of 2021 was DKK8.6 billion. Operating activities generated DKK12.1 billion, while investing activities used DKK12.6 billion, mainly for purchase of intangible assets, and property, plant, and equipment. Financing activities provided another DKK3.4 billion.

Mergers and Acquisitions

Company Background
Orsted was founded in 1972 as Dansk Naturgas A/S.

EXECUTIVES

President, Chief Executive Officer, Executive Director, Mads Nipper
Deputy Chief Executive, Chief Commercial Officer, Executive Director, Martin Neubert
Chief Financial Officer, Executive Director, Marianne Wiinholt
Independent Chaiman, Thomas Thune Andersen
Independent Deputy Chairman, Lene Skole
Independent Director, Julia King
Independent Director, Peter Korsholm
Independent Director, Lynda Armstrong
Independent Director, Dieter Wemmer
Independent Director, Jorgen Kildahl
Director, Henrik Poulsen
Employee Representative, Ole Henriksen
Employee Representative, Daniel Tas Sandermann
Employee Representative, Benny Gobel
Auditors : PricewaterhouseCoopers Statsautoriseret Revisionspartnerselskab

LOCATIONS
HQ: Orsted A/S
Kraftvaerksvej 53, Fredericia DK-7000
Phone: (45) 99 55 11 11
Web: www.orsted.com

2016 Sales
	% of total
UK	47
Denmark	25
Germany	18
Netherlands	9
Other	1
Total	100

PRODUCTS/OPERATIONS
2016 Sales
	% of total
Distribution & Customer Solutions	58
Wind Power	34
Bio energy & Thermal Power	8
Other activities/ eliminations	-
Total	100

COMPETITORS
CLP HOLDINGS LIMITED
ENGIE
ENTERPRISE PRODUCTS PARTNERS L.P.
ETP LEGACY LP
IBERDROLA, SOCIEDAD ANONIMA
KINDER MORGAN INC
TC Energy Corporation
THE WILLIAMS COMPANIES INC
Uniper SE
Vattenfall AB

HISTORICAL FINANCIALS
Company Type: Public

Income Statement — FYE: December 31

	REVENUE ($mil)	NET INCOME ($mil)	NET PROFIT MARGIN	EMPLOYEES
12/22	18,998	2,172	11.4%	8,027
12/21	11,821	1,668	14.1%	6,836
12/20	8,272	2,572	31.1%	6,179
12/19	10,579	1,079	10.2%	6,526
12/18	11,581	2,799	24.2%	6,080
Annual Growth	13.2%	(6.1%)	—	7.2%

2022 Year-End Financials
Debt ratio: 2.9%
Return on equity: 17.4%
Cash ($ mil.): 2,323
Current Ratio: 1.51
Long-term debt ($ mil.): 8,682
No. of shares ($ mil.): 420
Dividends
Yield: —
Payout: 7.7%
Market value ($ mil.): 12,687

	STOCK PRICE ($) FY Close	P/E High/Low		PER SHARE ($) Earnings	Dividends	Book Value
12/22	30.19	1	1	4.97	0.38	31.28
12/21	42.73	3	2	3.70	0.40	29.72
12/20	68.35	2	1	5.94	0.33	37.15
12/19	34.65	2	1	2.33	0.31	30.89
12/18	22.00	1	0	6.50	0.31	29.84
Annual Growth	8.2%	—	—	(6.5%)	5.2%	1.2%

Osaka Gas Co Ltd (Japan)

Osaka Gas keeps Osaka, Hyogo, Kyoto, Shiga, and Wakayama cooking. A large Japanese gas supplier, the utility serves more than 9 million customers in the Kansai region. The company imports a large amount of its gas and has production operations in Australia and Indonesia; it also owns liquefied natural gas (LNG) terminals and tankers. Osaka Gas has branched out into electricity: It generates and markets power to wholesale and large retail customers in Japan and abroad. It maintains a pipeline of approximately 62,400 km and a power generation capacity of 2 megawatts in Japan. Other operations include gas appliance sales, pipeline installation, real estate management, and leasing. Osaka Gas was established in 1897.

Operations
Osaka Gas operates through four reporting segments: Domestic Energy/Gas; Life & Business Solutions; Domestic Energy/Electricity; and International Energy.

Domestic Energy/Gas (more than 65% of revenues) manufactures, supplies, and sells city gas and gas appliances, conducts gas pipelines installations, and sells LNG, LPG, and industrial gas.

Life and Business Solutions includes real estate development and leasing, IT services, the marketing of fine materials, and carbon material products. This segment represents 15% of the company's total sales.

Domestic Energy/Electricity produces and sell electricity, and it accounts for about 15% of the revenue.

Comprised the remaining revenue, International Energy Business includes overseas energy supply, LNG vessel chartering business, and petroleum and natural gas business development and investment.

Geographic Reach
The company's main natural gas reserves in Algeria, Australia, Brunei, Canada, China, Egypt, Indonesia, Iran, Iraq, Kuwait, Malaysia, Nigeria, Norway, Oman, Papua New Guinea, Qatar, Russia, Saudi Arabia, Turkmenistan, the UAE, the US, and Venezuela.

Headquartered in Osaka, Japan has also office in Tokyo, and about 10 offices overseas located in the Australia, Indonesia, the Philippines, Singapore, Thailand, UK, and the US.

Sales and Marketing
Osaka Gas provides solutions that meets various needs of more than 9 million customers for household, factories, and offices.

The company also serves residential, commercial, and industrial customers.

Financial Performance
Osaka Gas has seen fluctuating revenue

for the last five years, recording a 4% increase from 2016 to 2020. The same trend as revenue was seen in the company's net income, but with a recorded 50% decrease from 2016 to 2020.

Revenue was Â¥1.4 trillion, Â¥3.2 billion less than in the previous year. Domestic Energy/Gas contributed the highest revenue per segment, comprising 70% of the company's 2020 revenue. This was followed by Domestic Energy/Electricity (15%) and Life and Business Solutions (12%).

Net income increased from Â¥33.6 billion in 2019 to Â¥41.8 billion in 2020.

Cash and cash equivalents at the end of the year were Â¥146.8 billion, Â¥31 billion more than in the previous year. Operating activities provided Â¥182.9 billion to the coffers. Investing activities used Â¥232.3 billion primarily for purchase of property, plant, and equipment, while financing activities provided Â¥79.3 billion mostly from proceeds from issuance of bonds.

Strategy

In 2020, Osaka Gas made significant progress in its International Energy Business, especially in the US, such as the commencement of commercial operations of the Freeport LNG Project and the Fairview natural gas-fired power plant as well as the acquisition of all shares in Sabine Oil and Gas Corporation, a shale gas development company.

The company aims to maximize value for its customers and to reach the goals under the current Medium-term Management Plan as it develops strategies for future growth while preventing the spread of the coronavirus.

Mergers and Acquisitions

In late 2020, Osaka Gas has acquired issued shares of Palette Cloud (Japan based), which provides Palette Kanri, the property management system provided by Palette Cloud, for rental housing management companies. Palette Kanri is a cloud-based tenant management system designed exclusively for the real estate industry. The two companies aim to make the most of their respective strengths and produce a good synergy between them to contribute to greater convenience in rental collective housing and help continuous advancement in consumer and business life.

In late 2019, the company wholly-owned subsidiary, Gas and Power Co Ltd, has acquired all the equity help by JGC Holdings Corporation of the issued shares of JGC Mirai Solar Co Ltd, a photovoltaic power generation business operator based in Oita City, Oita Prefecture. As a result of the equity acquisition, JGC Mirai will change its corporate name to Daigas Oita Mirai Solar Co Ltd as wholly-owned subsidiary of G&P.

In mid-2019, Osaka Gas entered into a definitive agreement with Texas based Sabine Oil & Gas Holding to acquire 100% of the outstanding shares of its subsidiary, Oil & Gas Corporation (Sabine). Sabine holds acreage in East Texas located in Harrison, Panola, Rusk, and Upshur counties, among others, totaling 175,000 net acres which is producing shale gas in the amount of 210 mmcfed with approximately 1,200 wells at present, showing a significant drilling inventory on the Haynesville and Cotton Valley formation. Through this acquisitions, Osaka Gas has also gained operatorship of the upstream business along with Sabine's excellent management and operations capabilities.

Company Background

Osaka Gas was established in 1897.

EXECUTIVES

Chairman, Director, Takehiro Honjo
President, Representative Director, Masataka Fujiwara
Executive Vice President, Representative Director, Tadashi Miyagawa
Executive Vice President, Representative Director, Takeshi Matsui
Executive Vice President, Representative Director, Takayuki Tasaka
Director, Fumitoshi Takeguchi
Outside Director, Kazutoshi Murao
Outside Director, Tatsuo Kijima
Outside Director, Yumiko Sato
Outside Director, Mikiyo Niizeki
Auditors : KPMG AZSA LLC

LOCATIONS

HQ: Osaka Gas Co Ltd (Japan)
 4-1-2 Hiranomachi, Chuo-ku, Osaka 541-0046
Phone: (81) 6 6205 4537   **Fax:** 713 354-9101
Web: www.osakagas.co.jp

PRODUCTS/OPERATIONS

2015 Sales

	% of total
Gas	72
LPG, Electricity and Other Energies	16
Life & Business Solutions	11
International Energies	1
Total	100

COMPETITORS

KINDER MORGAN ENERGY PARTNERS, L.P.
Korea Gas Corporation
NATIONAL GRID PLC
NATURGY ENERGY GROUP SA.
PHOENIX NATURAL GAS LIMITED
SMARTESTENERGY LIMITED
SOUTH JERSEY INDUSTRIES, INC.
TOHO GAS CO., LTD.
TOKYO GAS CO., LTD.
eni gas & power

HISTORICAL FINANCIALS

Company Type: Public

Income Statement   FYE: March 31

	REVENUE ($mil)	NET INCOME ($mil)	NET PROFIT MARGIN	EMPLOYEES
03/23	17,082	428	2.5%	21,792
03/22	13,046	1,054	8.1%	23,504
03/21	12,319	730	5.9%	23,520
03/20	12,608	384	3.1%	23,265
03/19	12,387	303	2.4%	23,044
Annual Growth	8.4%	9.0%		(1.4%)

2023 Year-End Financials
Debt ratio: 0.2%   No. of shares ($ mil.): 415
Return on equity: 4.3%   Dividends
Cash ($ mil.): 638   Yield: —
Current Ratio: 1.70   Payout: 0.0%
Long-term debt ($ mil.): 6,093   Market value ($ mil.): —

OSB Group plc

OneSavings Bank, which does business as Kent Reliance across the UK (primarily in Kent) and the Channel Islands, holds subsidiaries specializing in mortgaging banking loans, including residential, and commercial buy-to-rent mortgages. Its subsidiaries include: specialty mortgage lender Kent Reliance for Intermediaries, Jersey-based personalized-mortgage provider Jersey Home Loans, Guernsey Home Loans, and Reliance Property Loans, which administers mortgages assets acquired by OneSavings Bank. India-based subsidiary Easiprocess performs back-office processing services for other financial firms. OneSavings Bank was formed in 2011 after merging with Kent Reliance Building Society, which traced its roots back to 1847. OneSavings merged with Charter Court, a rival mortgage lender, in 2019.

Operations

OneSavings Bank operates three business segments: Buy-to-Let/SME, Residential Mortgages, and Personal Loans.

Beyond its lending activities, the company also offers regular savings accounts products, including NISAs. Its residential loan product lines include first charge, second charge, and shared ownership residential mortgage loans, as well as secured loans.

Company Background

In 2011 the operations of Kent Reliance Building Society (which traced its roots back more than 150 years) were transferred to the newly created OneSavings Bank.

EXECUTIVES

Chief Executive Officer, Executive Director, Andy John Golding
Chief Financial Officer, Executive Director, April Talintyre
Commercial Operations Group Director,
Commercial Operations Chief Risk Officer, Jens Bech

Mortgages Group Managing Director, Alan Cleary
Chief Information Officer, Richard Davis
Chief Risk Officer, Peter Charles Elcock
Secretary, General Counsel, Jason Elphick
Chief Information Officer, John Gaunt
Chief Risk Officer, Hasan Kazmi
Chief Operating Officer, Clive Kornitzer
Group Chief Internal Auditor, Lisa Odendaal
Savings Group Managing Director, Paul Whitlock
Chief Credit Officer, Richad Wilson
Chairman, David Avery Weymouth
Senior Independent Director, Noel Harwerth
Independent Non-Executive Director, Graham Allatt
Independent Non-Executive Director, Rajan Kapoor
Independent Non-Executive Director, Sarah Hedger
Independent Non-Executive Director, Mary McNamara
Auditors : Deloitte LLP

LOCATIONS

HQ: OSB Group plc
 OSB House, Quayside, Chatham Maritime, Chatham, Kent ME4 4QZ
Phone: (44) 1634 848944
Web: www.osb.co.uk

HISTORICAL FINANCIALS
Company Type: Public

Income Statement — FYE: December 31

	ASSETS ($mil)	NET INCOME ($mil)	INCOME AS % OF ASSETS	EMPLOYEES
12/21	33,061	465	1.4%	1,755
12/20	30,916	267	0.9%	1,816
12/19	28,282	209	0.7%	1,279
12/18	13,355	179	1.3%	989
12/17	11,601	171	1.5%	813
Annual Growth	29.9%	28.4%	—	21.2%

2021 Year-End Financials
Return on assets: 1.4%
Return on equity: 18.9%
Long-term debt ($ mil.): —
No. of shares ($ mil.): 447
Sales ($ mil.): 1,062
Dividends
 Yield: —
 Payout: 34.5%
Market value ($ mil.): —

Otsuka Holdings Co., Ltd.

EXECUTIVES

Chairman, Representative Director, Ichiro Otsuka
President, Chief Executive Officer, Representative Director, Tatsuo Higuchi
Executive Vice President, Director, Yoshiro Matsuo
Chief Strategy Officer, Director, Shuichi Takagi
Chief Financial Officer, Director, Yuko Makino
Director, Masayuki Kobayashi
Director, Noriko Tojo
Director, Makoto Inoue
Outside Director, Yukio Matsutani
Outside Director, Ko Sekiguchi
Outside Director, Yoshihisa Aoki
Outside Director, Mayo Mita
Outside Director, Tatsuaki Kitachi
Auditors : KPMG AZSA LLC

LOCATIONS

HQ: Otsuka Holdings Co., Ltd.
 Shinagawa Grand Central Tower 12F, 2-16-4 Konan, Minato-ku, Tokyo 108-8241
Phone: (81) 3 6717 1410 **Fax:** 415 986-5361
Web: www.otsuka.com

HISTORICAL FINANCIALS
Company Type: Public

Income Statement — FYE: December 31

	REVENUE ($mil)	NET INCOME ($mil)	NET PROFIT MARGIN	EMPLOYEES
12/22	13,189	1,017	7.7%	38,868
12/21	13,016	1,089	8.4%	38,210
12/20	13,804	1,437	10.4%	38,220
12/19	12,860	1,171	9.1%	37,837
12/18	11,748	750	6.4%	36,998
Annual Growth	2.9%	7.9%	—	1.2%

2022 Year-End Financials
Debt ratio: —
Return on equity: 6.3%
Cash ($ mil.): 3,546
Current Ratio: 2.21
Long-term debt ($ mil.): 711
No. of shares ($ mil.): 542
Dividends
 Yield: —
 Payout: 20.6%
Market value ($ mil.): 8,834

	STOCK PRICE ($) FY Close	P/E High/Low	PER SHARE ($) Earnings	Dividends	Book Value
12/22	16.28	0 0	1.87	0.39	31.12
12/21	18.25	0 0	2.01	0.45	32.21
12/20	21.43	0 0	2.64	0.47	33.14
12/19	22.28	0 0	2.13	0.46	30.00
12/18	20.22	0 0	1.38	0.46	28.61
Annual Growth	(5.3%)	— —	8.0%	(4.1%)	2.1%

Paltac Corp

EXECUTIVES

Chairman, Chief Executive Officer, Representative Director, Kunio Mikita
President, Chief Operating Officer, Representative Director, Seiichi Kasutani
Senior Managing Executive Officer, Director, Masahiro Noma
Senior Managing Executive Officer, Director, Akiyoshi Moriya
Senior Managing Executive Officer, Hirotake Ito
Director, Masaharu Shimada
Outside Director, Katsutoshi Yogo
Outside Director, Kaori Oishi
Outside Director, Katsumi Asada
Outside Director, Mineko Orisaku
Auditors : KPMZ AZSA LLC

LOCATIONS

HQ: Paltac Corp
 2-46 Honmachibashi, Chuo-ku, Osaka 540-0029
Phone: (81) 6 4793 1050 **Fax:** (81) 6 4793 1053
Web: www.paltac.co.jp

HISTORICAL FINANCIALS
Company Type: Public

Income Statement — FYE: March 31

	REVENUE ($mil)	NET INCOME ($mil)	NET PROFIT MARGIN	EMPLOYEES
03/21	9,331	174	1.9%	2,169
03/20	9,639	234	2.4%	2,196
03/19	9,167	178	1.9%	2,207
03/18	9,103	164	1.8%	2,217
03/17	8,247	130	1.6%	2,221
Annual Growth	3.1%	7.5%	—	(0.6%)

2021 Year-End Financials
Debt ratio: —
Return on equity: 8.5%
Cash ($ mil.): 339
Current Ratio: 1.55
Long-term debt ($ mil.): 1
No. of shares ($ mil.): 63
Dividends
 Yield: —
 Payout: 0.0%
Market value ($ mil.): —

Pan Pacific International Holdings Corp

EXECUTIVES

President, Chief Executive Officer, Representative Director, Naoki Yoshida
Senior Managing Executive Officer, Director, Kenji Sekiguchi
Senior Managing Executive Officer, Chief Merchandising Officer (Global), Director, Kazuhiro Matsumoto
Chief Strategy Officer, Director, Hideki Moriya
Chief Administrative Officer, Director, Yuji Ishii
Founding Chairman, Advisor, Director, Takao Yasuda
Director, Hitomi Ninomiya
Outside Director, Isao Kubo
Outside Director, Yasunori Yoshimura
Outside Director, Jumpei Nishitani
Outside Director, Masaharu Kamo
Auditors : UHY Tokyo & Co.

LOCATIONS

HQ: Pan Pacific International Holdings Corp
 2-19-10 Aobadai, Meguro-ku, Tokyo 153-0042
Phone: (81) 3 5725 7532 **Fax:** (81) 3 5725 7322
Web: www.ppi-hd.co.jp

HISTORICAL FINANCIALS

Company Type: Public

Income Statement — FYE: June 30

	REVENUE ($mil)	NET INCOME ($mil)	NET PROFIT MARGIN	EMPLOYEES
06/23	13,382	457	3.4%	60,516
06/22	13,436	454	3.4%	60,416
06/21	15,459	487	3.2%	55,689
06/20	15,611	466	3.0%	47,709
06/19	12,338	448	3.6%	48,351
Annual Growth	2.1%	0.5%	—	5.8%

2023 Year-End Financials

Debt ratio: 0.3%
Return on equity: 15.6%
Cash ($ mil.): 1,672
Current Ratio: 1.50
Long-term debt ($ mil.): 3,690
No. of shares ($ mil.): 596
Dividends
 Yield: 0.7%
 Payout: 16.6%
Market value ($ mil.): 10,685

	STOCK PRICE ($) FY Close	P/E High/Low	PER SHARE ($) Earnings	Dividends	Book Value
06/23	17.91	0 0	0.76	0.13	5.26
06/22	15.87	0 0	0.75	0.14	4.83
06/21	21.03	0 0	0.77	0.14	5.98
06/20	22.08	0 0	0.73	0.10	5.47
06/19	15.89	0 0	0.71	0.09	4.84
Annual Growth	3.0%	— —	2.0%	10.5%	2.1%

Panasonic Holdings Corp

Panasonic has been a prolific electronics manufacturer since 1918. Its offerings include automotive and industrial systems (including car infotainment products) and home appliances; the company also makes lighting products, energy systems, avionics systems, and process automation machines and equipment. The company operates worldwide, but generates nearly half its revenue from Japan.

Operations

Panasonic has five primary business segments: Lifestyle (about 50% of company's total revenue), Automotive (some 15%), Connect (more than 10%), Industry (about 15%), and Energy (around 10%).

Panasonic's lifestyle segment includes air conditioners, TVs, cameras, and devices.

The automotive segment includes car infotainment systems, head-up displays, automotive speakers, and automotive switches, among others.

The connect segment includes aircraft in-flight entertainment systems and communications services, electronic components-mounting machines, welding equipment, and projectors, among others.

The industry segment includes relays, switches, power supplies, touch panels, and motors, among others.

The energy segment includes cylindrical lithium-ion batteries for in-vehicle use, dry batteries, and storage battery modules/systems, among others.

Geographic Reach

Japan-based Panasonic sells its products and services in the Americas, Europe, and Asia. The company is highly reliant on its home continent, Japan, which accounts for nearly half of total revenue.

Financial Performance

Note: Growth rates may differ after conversion to US dollars.

The company's consolidated sales increased by 10% to ¥7.4 trillion from a year ago. Domestic sales increased from the previous year due to favorable sales of products for the industrial and information & communication sectors. Overseas sales increased from the previous year due to demand-driven growth in automotive batteries and the new consolidation of Blue Yonder.

Net profit for fiscal 2022 was ¥255.3 billion, compared to ¥165.1 billion in the previous fiscal year.

Cash held by the company at the end of fiscal 2022 decreased to ¥1.2 trillion. Operating and investing activities provided ¥252.6 billion. Investing activities used ¥96.1 billion, while financing activities provided another ¥58.9 billion.

Strategy

Panasonic has transitioned to an operating company system in which each business operates with a high degree of independence and has reorganized its reportable segments into the following five segments: Lifestyle, Automotive, Connect, Industry, and Energy.

Mergers and Acquisitions

In 2021, Panasonic completed the acquisition of Blue Yonder, the leading end-to-end, digital fulfillment platform provider. Panasonic has now purchased the remaining 80% of shares of Blue Yonder, adding to the 20% which Panasonic acquired in July 2020. The investment values Blue Yonder at USD8.5 billion. The acquisition accelerates Panasonic's and Blue Yonder's shared vision for an Autonomous Supply Chain.

Company Background

Grade school dropout Konosuke Matsushita took $50 in 1918 and went into business making electric plugs (with his brother-in-law, Toshio Iue, founder of SANYO). His mission, to help people by making high-quality, low-priced conveniences while providing his employees with good working conditions, earned him the sobriquet "god of business management." The company grew across the decades, expanding into new regions (it opened its first manufacturing facility outside Japan -- in Thailand -- in 1961) and new products (washing machines, TVs, and refrigerators were launched in the 1950s). In 2008 it took the name Panasonic Corporation and consolidated all its brands under the Panasonic name.

HISTORY

Grade school dropout Konosuke Matsushita took $50 in 1918 and went into business making electric plugs (with his brother-in-law, Toshio Iue, founder of SANYO). His mission, to help people by making high-quality, low-priced conveniences while providing his employees with good working conditions, earned him the sobriquet, "god of business management." Matsushita Electric Industrial grew by developing inexpensive lamps, batteries, radios, and motors in the 1920s and 1930s.

During WWII the Japanese government ordered the firm to build wood-laminate products for the military. Postwar occupation forces prevented Matsushita from working at his firm for four years. Thanks to unions' efforts, he rejoined his namesake company shortly before it entered a joint venture with Dutch manufacturer Philips in 1952. The following year it moved into consumer goods, making televisions, refrigerators, and washing machines and later expanding into high-performance audio products. Matsushita bought a majority stake in Victor Company of Japan (JVC, originally established by RCA Victor) in 1954. Its 1959 New York subsidiary opening began Matsushita's drive overseas.

Sold under the National, Panasonic, and Technics names, the firm's products were usually not cutting-edge but were attractively priced. Under Masaharu Matsushita, the founder's son-in-law who became president in 1961, the company became Japan's largest home appliance maker, introducing air conditioners, microwave ovens, stereo components, and VCRs in the 1960s and 1970s. JVC developed the VHS format for VCRs, which beat out Sony's Betamax format.

Matsushita built much of its sales growth on new industrial and commercial customers in the 1980s. The company expanded its semiconductor, office and factory automation, auto electronics, audio-visual, housing, and air-conditioning product offerings that decade. Konosuke died in 1989.

EXECUTIVES

Chairman, Director, Kazuhiro Tsuga
President, Chief Executive Officer, Chief Strategy Officer, Representative Director, Yuki Kusumi
Executive Vice President, Representative Director, Tetsuro Homma
Executive Vice President, Chief Risk Management Officer, Representative Director, Mototsugu Sato
Executive Vice President, Chief Financial Officer, Representative Director, Hirokazu Umeda
Chief Human Resources Officer, Executive Officer, Shigeki Mishima

Chief Technology Officer, Executive Officer, Tatsuo Ogawa
Chief Strategy Officer, Kazuyo Sumida
Chief Information Officer, Hajime Tamaoki
Executive Vice President, Director, Yoshiyuki Miyabe
Outside Director, Shinobu Matsui
Outside Director, Keita Nishiyama
Outside Director, Kunio Noji
Outside Director, Michitaka Sawada
Outside Director, Kazuhiko Toyama
Outside Director, Yoshinobu Tsutsui
Director, Ayako Shotoku
Auditors : KPMG AZSA LLC

LOCATIONS

HQ: Panasonic Holdings Corp
 1006 Oaza Kadoma, Kadoma, Osaka 571-8501
Phone: (81) 6 6908 1121
Web: www.panasonic.com/jp

2018 Sales

	% of total
Japan	47
Americas	17
China	12
Europe	10
Other Asia	14
Total	100

PRODUCTS/OPERATIONS

2018 Sales

	% of total
Automotive and industrial systems	32
Appliances	29
Eco solutions	18
Connected solutions	13
Other	8
Total	100

COMPETITORS

AURA SYSTEMS, INC.
EAST PENN MANUFACTURING CO.
ELECTROCOMPONENTS PUBLIC LIMITED COMPANY
HITACHI AUTOMOTIVE SYSTEMS AMERICAS, INC.
HITACHI, LTD.
JABIL INC.
KIMBALL ELECTRONICS GROUP, LLC
MAXWELL TECHNOLOGIES, INC.
PRESTOLITE WIRE LLC
ROBERT BOSCH LLC

HISTORICAL FINANCIALS

Company Type: Public

Income Statement — FYE: March 31

	REVENUE ($mil)	NET INCOME ($mil)	NET PROFIT MARGIN	EMPLOYEES
03/23	62,911	1,993	3.2%	233,391
03/22	60,744	2,099	3.5%	240,198
03/21	60,499	1,490	2.5%	243,540
03/20	69,005	2,079	3.0%	259,385
03/19	72,263	2,565	3.6%	271,869
Annual Growth	(3.4%)	(6.1%)	—	(3.7%)

2023 Year-End Financials

Debt ratio: 0.1%
Return on equity: 7.8%
Cash ($ mil.): 6,153
Current Ratio: 1.32
Long-term debt ($ mil.): 7,884
No. of shares ($ mil.): 2,334
Dividends
 Yield: 1.2%
 Payout: 26.2%
Market value ($ mil.): 20,774

	STOCK PRICE ($) FY Close	P/E High/Low	PER SHARE ($) Earnings	Dividends	Book Value
03/23	8.90	0 0	0.85	0.11	11.64
03/22	9.70	0 0	0.90	0.22	11.15
03/21	13.04	0 0	0.64	0.24	10.04
03/20	7.50	0 0	0.89	0.28	7.89
03/19	8.67	0 0	1.10	0.27	6.92
Annual Growth	0.7%	— —	(6.1%)	(20.6%)	13.9%

Parkland Corp

Established in 2010, Parkland is an independent supplier and marketer of fuel and petroleum products and a leading convenience store operator. Parkland services customers across Canada, the United States, the Caribbean region and the Americas through three channels: Retail, Commercial and Wholesale. Parkland optimizes its fuel supply across these three channels by operating and leveraging a growing portfolio of supply relationships and storage infrastructure. Parkland provides trusted and locally relevant fuel brands and convenience store offerings in the communities it serves. About 50% of the company's total revenue comes from Canada.

Operations

Parkland has four operating segments: Canada; International; USA; and Supply.

Canada generates around 40% of the total sales. It operates and services a network of retail gas stations in Canada operating under many key retail brands including Ultramar, Esso, Fas Gas Plus, Chevron, and Pioneer. In addition, Parkland operates a convenience store brand, On the Run / MarchÃ© Express, as well as other convenience store brands.

International includes operations in about 25 countries predominantly located in the Caribbean and northern coast of South America. International operates and services a network of retail service stations under brands including Esso, Shell and Sol. This segment accounts for about 25% of revenue.

The USA (over 20%) delivers fuel, lubricants and other related products and services to commercial and wholesale customers, and operates a network of retail fuel and convenience stores including On the Run, Arco, Cenex, Chevron, Conoco, Exxon, Mr. Gas, U-Gas, and other brands, and cardlocks under various brands throughout the US. USA operates a wide variety of terminals, storage facilities and trucks, and contracts pipeline, storage facilities and third-party carriers to support its network.

Supply is responsible for managing Parkland's fuel supply contracts, purchasing fuel from refiners, refining and marketing fuel, transporting and distributing fuel through ships, rail and highway carriers, and storing fuel in owned and leased facilities. This segment contributes about 15% of revenue.

Corporate includes centralized administrative services and expenses incurred to support operations. Due to the nature of these activities, these costs are not specifically allocated to Parkland's operating segments.

Overall, about 95% of sales were generated from Fueland Petroleum product revenue, while the rest were generated from convenience and other non-fuel revenue.

Geographic Reach

Parkland is headquartered in Calgary, Alberta with more than five regional offices located in Burnaby, Dartmouth, Minot, Montreal, and Victoria. Its international segment has sales and operations in about 25 countries in the Caribbean.

About 50% of company's total revenue comes from Canada, and over 30% contributes by the US, while other countries generated the remaining roughly 20%.

Sales and Marketing

Parkland delivers a range of refined fuel and petroleum products to motorists, businesses, consumers, resellers, aviation, and wholesale customers. Canada Retail and Canada Commercial segments contracts sell fuel and petroleum products to retail and commercial consumers. The company also sells branded and private label lubricants to commercial, industrial and wholesale customers.

Financial Performance

The company reported a revenue of $21.5 billion in 2021, a 54% increase from the previous year's revenue of $14 billion.

The company had a net income of $126 million, a 13% increase from the previous year's net income of $112 million.

The company's cash at the end of 2021 was $326 million. Operating activities generated $904 million, while investing activities used $1.5 billion, mainly for acquisitions. Financing activities provided another $655 million.

Mergers and Acquisitions

In early 2022, Parkland as entered into an agreement to acquire M&M Food Market, a premium, restaurant-quality frozen food retailer who brings high-quality, convenient food choices to Canadians. This acquisition provides a platform to grow its food offer, expand its proprietary brands, and advance its digital and loyalty strategy. The acquisition includes over 300 well-located standalone franchise and corporate owned stores, over 2,000 M&M Express locations, and a well-established rewards program with approximately two million active members. Terms were not disclosed.

In 2021, Parkland announced it has entered into an agreement to acquire Conrad & Bischoff Inc. and its related companies. C&B is a well-established retail, commercial, wholesale and lubricants business with annual fuel and petroleum product volume of approximately 700 million litres. Through this acquisition, Parkland will establish a fourth

U.S. ROC in Idaho Falls, Idaho. The transaction includes 58 retail locations, comprising 19 high-quality company owned sites featuring proprietary branded backcourts and 39 retail dealer sites. In addition, terminal operations with combined tank storage of 30 million litres and capacity for 88 rail cars adds significant supply optionality in the Rocky Mountains PADD IV.

In early 2021, Parkland completed the acquisition of Story, a well-established retail and commercial fuel business headquartered in Bozeman, Montana. This acquisition adds scale and density to Parkland's existing Northern Tier ROC and expands its presence in the high-growth Montana and Idaho markets.

Company Background
Parkland Fuel was formed in 2010.

EXECUTIVES

Chairman, James Pantelidis
Retail Market Chief Executive Officer, Retail Market President, Executive Director, Robert B. Espey
Integration Senior Vice President, Strategy Senior Vice President, Corporate Development Senior Vice President, Darren Smart
Strategic Marketing Senior Vice President, Strategic Marketing and Innovation Senior Vice President, Ian White
Chief Financial Officer, Marcel Teunissen
People and Culture Senior Vice President, Ferio Pugliese
Senior Vice President, General Counsel, Secretary, Christy Elliott
Director, John F. Bechtold
Director, Lisa Colnett
Director, Timothy Hogarth
Director, Richard Hookway
Director, Angela John
Director, Domenic Pilla
Director, Steven Richardson
Director, David A. Spencer
Director, Deborah S. Stein
Auditors : PricewaterhouseCoopers LLP

LOCATIONS

HQ: Parkland Corp
Suite 1800, 240 4 Ave. S.W., Calgary, Alberta T2P 4H4
Phone: 403 567-2500
Web: www.parkland.ca

2015 sales

	% of total
Canada	88
United States	12
Total	100

PRODUCTS/OPERATIONS

2015 sales

	% of total
Retail Fuels	34
Commercial Fuels	19
Parkland USA	12
Supply and Wholesale	35
Corporate	—
Total	100

COMPETITORS

Agrium Inc
CENTRICA PLC
Koninklijke DSM N.V.
LSB INDUSTRIES, INC.
MARATHON PETROLEUM CORPORATION
MURPHY USA INC.
TERRA NITROGEN COMPANY, L.P.
THE SCOTTS MIRACLE-GRO COMPANY
URALKALI, PAO
Yara International ASA

HISTORICAL FINANCIALS

Company Type: Public

Income Statement   FYE: December 31

	REVENUE ($mil)	NET INCOME ($mil)	NET PROFIT MARGIN	EMPLOYEES
12/22	26,221	229	0.9%	6,284
12/21	16,855	76	0.5%	5,946
12/20	11,004	64	0.6%	4,389
12/19	14,170	317	2.2%	4,635
12/18	10,605	151	1.4%	3,051
Annual Growth	25.4%	10.9%	—	19.8%

2022 Year-End Financials

Debt ratio: 32.7%
Return on equity: 12.3%
Cash ($ mil.): 482
Current Ratio: 1.39
Long-term debt ($ mil.): 4,544
No. of shares ($ mil.): 175
Dividends
Yield: —
Payout: 67.1%
Market value ($ mil.): 3,847

	STOCK PRICE ($) FY Close	P/E High/Low		PER SHARE ($) Earnings	Dividends	Book Value
12/22	21.93	15	9	1.42	0.95	12.80
12/21	27.50	55	40	0.50	0.98	10.03
12/20	31.94	70	28	0.42	0.90	10.04
12/19	36.67	14	10	1.96	0.91	10.15
12/18	25.76	22	13	1.12	0.86	9.89
Annual Growth	(3.9%)			6.0%	2.6%	6.7%

PDD Holdings Inc

EXECUTIVES

Chairman, Chief Executive Officer, Lei Chen
Operations Senior Vice President, Junyun Xiao
Product Development Senior Vice President, Zhenwei Zheng
Finance Vice President, Jing Ma
General Counsel, Jianchong Zhu
Independent Director, Anthony Kam Ping Leung
Independent Director, Qi Lu
Independent Director, Nanpeng Shen
Independent Director, George Yong-Boon Yeo
Director, Haifeng Lin
Auditors : Ernst & Young Hua Ming LLP

LOCATIONS

HQ: PDD Holdings Inc
First Floor, 25 St Stephen's Green, Dublin 2 19711
Phone: (353) 1 5397938
Web: www.pddholdings.com

HISTORICAL FINANCIALS

Company Type: Public

Income Statement   FYE: December 31

	REVENUE ($mil)	NET INCOME ($mil)	NET PROFIT MARGIN	EMPLOYEES
12/22	18,925	4,571	24.2%	12,992
12/21	14,798	1,223	8.3%	9,762
12/20	9,096	(1,097)	—	7,986
12/19	4,331	(1,001)	—	5,828
12/18	1,907	(1,485)	—	3,683
Annual Growth	77.5%			37.0%

2022 Year-End Financials

Debt ratio: 0.9%
Return on equity: 32.7%
Cash ($ mil.): 4,975
Current Ratio: 1.85
Long-term debt ($ mil.): 228
No. of shares ($ mil.): 5,278
Dividends
Yield: —
Payout: 0.0%
Market value ($ mil.): 430,449

	STOCK PRICE ($) FY Close	P/E High/Low		PER SHARE ($) Earnings	Dividends	Book Value
12/22	81.55	15	4	0.79	0.00	3.23
12/21	58.30	133	35	0.21	0.00	2.34
12/20	177.67	—	—	(0.23)	0.00	1.86
12/19	37.82	—	—	(0.22)	0.00	0.76
12/18	22.44	—	—	(0.50)	0.00	0.61
Annual Growth	38.1%					51.5%

Permanent TSB Group Holdings Plc

EXECUTIVES

Chief Executive Officer, Executive Director, Jeremy Masding
Chief Financial Officer, Executive Director, Eamonn Crowley
Chief Risk Officer, Executive Director, Michael Frawley
Chief Technology Officer, Tom Hayes
Human Resources Director, Ger Mitchell
Chief Legal Officer, Legal Counsel, Andrew Walsh
Operations Director, Shane O'Sullivan
Product Assurance Director, Breege Timoney
Banking Director, Patrick Farrell
Internal Audit Head, Paul Redmond
Secretary, Conor Ryan
Independent Non-Executive Chairman, Robert Elliott
Senior Independent Director, Julie O'Neill
Independent Non-Executive Director, Ken Slattery
Independent Non-Executive Director, Ronan O'Neill
Independent Non-Executive Director, Andrew Power

Independent Non-Executive Director, Donal Courtney
Independent Non-Executive Director, Ruth Wandhofer
Non-Executive Director, Marian Corcoran
Auditors : PricewaterhouseCoopers

LOCATIONS

HQ: Permanent TSB Group Holdings Plc
56 - 59, St. Stephen's Green, Dublin 2
Phone: —
Web: www.permanenttsbgroup.ie

COMPETITORS

ALLIED IRISH BANKS, PUBLIC LIMITED COMPANY
BANK OF ENGLAND
BANK OF JAPAN
Bank of Canada
FEDERAL RESERVE BANK OF NEW YORK

HISTORICAL FINANCIALS

Company Type: Public

Income Statement — FYE: December 31

	ASSETS ($mil)	NET INCOME ($mil)	INCOME AS % OF ASSETS	EMPLOYEES
12/23	30,741	75	0.2%	3,330
12/22	27,697	238	0.9%	0
12/21	25,166	(22)	—	2,236
12/20	25,755	(198)	—	2,435
12/19	22,767	33	0.1%	2,379
Annual Growth	7.8%	22.3%	—	8.8%

2023 Year-End Financials

Return on assets: 0.2%
Return on equity: 2.8%
Long-term debt ($ mil.): —
No. of shares ($ mil.): 545
Sales ($ mil.): 963
Dividends
Yield: —
Payout: 0.0%
Market value ($ mil.): 1,026

	STOCK PRICE ($) FY Close	P/E High/Low	PER SHARE ($) Earnings	Dividends	Book Value
12/23	1.88	68 40	0.05	0.00	4.91
12/22	1.85	4 3	0.48	0.00	4.69
12/21	1.80	— —	(0.10)	0.00	4.45
12/20	0.95	— —	(0.47)	0.00	5.27
12/19	1.30	42 27	0.05	0.00	4.93
Annual Growth	9.7%	— —	1.4%	—	(0.1%)

Pernod Ricard S.A. (France)

Created in 1975 through the merger of former rivals Ricard and Pernod, this titan of French spirits lays claim to the top global brands of vodka and Scotch whisky. Pernod Ricard's vast portfolio of wine and spirits comprises iconic labels ABSOLUT vodka and Chivas Regal and Ballantine's scotch; premium spirits, such as Beefeater gin and Malibu; prestige spirits and champagnes (e.g., Martell cognac and G.H. Mumm champagne); and best-selling Irish whiskey, Jameson. Absolut sold approximately 12 million cases worldwide, while Jameson sold some 10 million and Ballantine's approximately 9 million. The company generates most of its sales in Asia and other regions.

Operations

Pernod Ricard's House of Brands encompasses five brand categories: Strategic International Brands, Strategic Local Brands, Specialty Brands, Prestige Brands, and Strategic Wines.

Strategic International Brands represent the largest part of the company's business (accounts for about 65% of the company's revenue) and its international potential. They are the company's worldwide top priorities and the reference brands in each category. These brands include Absolut, Jameson, Ballantine's, Malibu, Havana Club, Chivas Regal, Ricard, and Beefeater, among others.

Strategic Local Brands (brings in about 20%) are strongly rooted in a limited number of specific markets. They benefit from very strong local consumer loyalty. This part of the company's portfolio often boosts its route-to-market. Its revenue is driven by Seagram's Indian whiskies, Kahlua, Olmeca, and Seagram's Gin.

Specialty Brands meet a growing demand for smaller-scale "craft" products. Authentic, these brands offer a unique and comprehensive value proposition that responds to new consumer trends and expectations. Provides roughly 10% of the company's revenue, Specialty Brands include Altos, Ceders, Del Maguey, Italicus, Jefferson's, Lillet, Monkey 47, Pernod, and Smooth Ambler, among others.

Prestige Brands (accounts for around 5%), the company's portfolio of highly desirable global luxury brands, target its most affluent consumers all over the world. It is the industry's most comprehensive portfolio, spanning all major luxury categories and moments of conviviality. Prestige portfolio comprises Absolut Elyx, Ballantine's, Chivas, The Glenlivet, Havana Club, KI NO BI, L'Orbe and more.

Strategic Wines contributes nearly 5% of the company's revenue. The category covers a wide range of origins and tastes. Shared over a meal with friends or on more formal occasions, wine is increasingly appreciated around the world by a growing variety of consumers. Brands include Brancott Estate, Campo Viejo, Church Road, George, Wyndham, Jacob's Creek, Kenwood, St Hugo, Stoneleigh, and Ysios.

Geographic Reach

Paris-based Pernod Ricard does business in more than 160 countries. In addition, the company has about 95 production sites in approximately 25 countries. The company generates more than 40% of revenue in Asia and other regions. Europe provides around 30% while the Americas bring in another roughly 30%.

Financial Performance

The company reported net sales of EUR 10.7 billion in 2022, a 21% increase from the previous year's net sales of EUR 8.8 billion.

In 2022, the company had a net income of EUR 2 billion, a 53% increase from the previous year's net income of EUR 1.3 billion.

The company's cash at the end of 2022 was EUR 2.5 billion. Operating activities generated EUR 2.3 billion, while investing activities used EUR 1.2 billion. Financing activities used another EUR 683 million.

Strategy

The company's growth model is referred to as The Conviviality Platform.

With The Conviviality Platform, Pernod Ricard is defining the company's strategic priorities for the future. A purposeful and powerful growth model, The Conviviality Platform unites its existing competitive advantages with new technologies to deliver on the company's mission to unlock the magic of human connection by bringing Good Times from a Good Place.

This long-term model translates into concrete action plans through the next phase of Transform & Accelerate, its three-year strategic plan. With the broadest brand portfolio in the industry, which covers all moments of consumption, creating moments of conviviality is the core value proposition of Pernod Ricard's steady growth. By analysing both consumer demand as well as every aspect of the company's business using responsibly sourced data and ethically developed AI, the company is able to generate and fulfil demand, with precision at scale, offering the right products at the right price to the right consumer, for every occasion and in every market.

The first dimension of the company's growth model is structured around three growth axes to get more value out of its existing portfolio: Activating more brands with the right level of investment; Maximizing the pricing power of brands; Growing the company's positions within the Prestige market.

Mergers and Acquisitions

In late 2021, Pernod Ricard announced the signing of an agreement for the acquisition of The Whisky Exchange, a leading spirits online and physical retailer and a reference for global whisky and fine spirits lovers. This acquisition is in line with Pernod Ricard's consumer centric strategy of meeting new consumer needs and expectations, in a context of solid e-commerce growth and strong demand for premiumization. Pernod Ricard will leverage synergies between The Whisky Exchange's expertise and its in-house platforms such as Drinks&Co and Bodeboca.

Company Background

The hard-won acquisition of The Absolut Company (formerly known as Vin&Sprit) in 2008 was a transformative purchase for Pernod Ricard in that it enlarged its premium brand portfolio and geographic presence. The whopping $8-billion deal, under which $546 million in debt was assumed, secured Pernod Ricard's share of the vodka market in the US, where annually some 5 million cases of ABSOLUT are sold.

HISTORY

Henri-Louis Pernod inherited Pernod Fils, an absinthe distillery, from his father-in-law in 1805 and immediately moved it to Pontarlier, France, to avoid stiff French import taxes. Demand for absinthe, a potent liqueur, spread quickly, and by the 1870s the liqueur was the toast of Paris. It was even featured in Impressionist paintings, and rumor has it that Vincent Van Gogh's psychosis might have been caused by it.

In the late 1800s serious competition for the absinthe market emerged from distiller Pernod Avignon, run by Jules Pernod (no relation to Henri-Louis). In 1906 Switzerland banned absinthe and France followed suit in 1915. In 1926 Henri-Louis joined with another anise distiller, Aristide Hemard, and formed Etablissements Hemard et Pernod Fils. Jules joined them in 1928. The resulting company was named Pernod.

Four years later the ban on pastis was lifted by the French government, and Paul Ricard, who made pastis illegally beforehand, began selling it openly. The licorice-flavored drink became popular in France. His company, Ricard, became a successful spirits maker and went public in 1962. Ricard acquired the Biscuit cognac brand in 1966.

Pernod and Ricard merged in 1975 to form Pernod Ricard. The company's operations included Campbell (scotch), SEGM (spirits exporter), and JFA Pampryl (fruit juice). In 1976 the group acquired CDC (Cinzano, Dubonnet). Two years later Patrick Ricard, son of Paul, became chairman and CEO.

Expanding through acquisitions in the 1980s, Pernod Ricard bought US-based Austin Nichols (Wild Turkey) from du Ligget Group in 1980 and acquired control of both Sias-MPA (fruit preparations) in 1982 and Compagnie Francaise des Produits Orangina (soft drinks) in 1984. The next year the firm added Ramazzotti (spirits, Italy) and IGM (distribution, Germany) to its mix, and in 1988 it bought Irish Distillers (whiskey), Yoo-Hoo Industries (US), and BWG (distribution, Ireland; sold in 2002). Australia's Orlando Wyndham Wines was added to the company's wine list in 1989 and merged with Pernod Ricard's Wyndham Estate winery the following year.

The group also acquired Spain's Larios gin, the Czech Republic's Becherovka liqueurs, and Italcanditi, a fruit preparations firm. Pernod Ricard added Mexican distillery Tequila Viuda de Romero (Real Hacienda tequila) to its liquor cabinet in January 2000.

Pernod Ricard later teamed up with liquor giant Diageo to bid on Seagram's spirits and wine business. Their collective bid of $8.2 billion (with Pernod Ricard paying $3.2 billion) was accepted in December 2000, with Pernod Ricard agreeing to acquire such brands as Chivas Regal, Glenlivet, and Glen Grant (which was sold to Campari in 2006).

In early 2001 the company agreed to pay $71 million for 80% of Polmos Poznan, maker of one of Poland's top vodka brands, Wyborowa in a deal including export rights. In October the company sold its soft-drink business in Continental Europe, North America, and Australia to Cadbury Schweppes for about $640 million to help finance the Seagram's deal. (Cadbury later spun off its soft drink business and became Dr Pepper Snapple Group.) After months of delay, the company finalized its deal to buy a part of Seagram's drinks business from Vivendi Universal after finally gaining FTC approval in December 2001. Pernod Ricard and brand co-owner Diageo licensed Seagram's nonalcoholic mixers to The Coca-Cola Company in 2002; it also sold sold Polish juice-making subsidiary Agros Fortuna that year.

By 2005 Pernod was back in a shopping mood. To help allay anti-competitive concerns, Pernod Ricard enlisted the help of Fortune Brands for its friendly bid for rival distiller Allied Domecq. As part of the deal, Fortune Brands ended up with Pernod Ricard's Larios gin, as well as several brands from Allied Domecq (including Canadian Club whisky, Clos du Bois wine, Courvoisier cognac, Maker's Mark bourbon, and Sauza tequila). Pernod Ricard paid about $14 billion for its former chief competitor Allied Domecq. Fortune Brands anted up about $5 billion for its part of the acquisition.

Pernod became the owner of Dunkin' Donuts and Baskin-Robbins ice cream operations as a result of the Allied Domecq buyout; in 2006 it sold both companies to a consortium of buyers that included Bain Capital, Carlyle Group, and Thomas H. Lee Partners.

As part of the juggling that took place in the Allied Domecq acquisition, Pernod Ricard also sold its Bushmills Irish whisky to competitor Diageo, and its Braemar, Glen Grant, and Old Smuggler brands to Campari. The Allied Domecq purchase also prompted a round of reorganization at Pernod Ricard, which in early 2006 outlined a new structure that divided the company into four main brand units (Chivas Brothers, Martell Mumm Perrier-Jouët, Ricard, and Pernod) and its distribution operations into four geographic regions (Americas, Asia, Europe, and Pacific).

In 2008 the company sold off 14 labels, including wine brands Farmingham, Canei, La Ina and Rio Viejo, and Spanish brandy brands Carlos I, Carlos III, and Filipe II. The next year it sold the Tia Maria coffee liqueur to Illva Saronno for ?125 million ($177 million) in cash.

In July 2011 Pernod Ricard addded "ultra-premium" tequila to its drinks portfolio through the formation of a joint venture with Tequila Avion.

EXECUTIVES

Chairman, Chief Executive Officer, Executive Director, Alexandre Ricard
Global Business Development Managing Director, Christian Porta
Corporate Communications Executive Vice President, Public Affairs Executive Vice President, Corporate Social Responsibility Executive Vice President, Conor McQuaid
Finance, IT & Operations Executive Vice President, Helene de Tissot
Human Resources, Sustainability & Responsibility Executive Vice President, Cedric Ramat
General Counsel, Compliance Officer, Anne-Marie Poliquin
Lead Independent Director, Director, Patricia Barbizet
Independent Director, Wolfgang Colberg
Independent Director, Virginie Fauvel
Independent Director, Ian Gallienne
Independent Director, Anne Lange
Independent Director, Philippe Petitcolin
Independent Director, Namita Shah
Independent Director, Kory Sorenson
Director, Patricia Ricard Giron
Director, Brice Thommen
Director, Cesar Giron
Director, Veronica Vargas
Director, Maria Jesus Carrasco Lopez
Auditors : KPMG S.A.

LOCATIONS

HQ: Pernod Ricard S.A. (France)
5, Cours Paul Ricard, Paris, Cedex 08 75380
Phone: (33) 1 70 93 16 00
Web: www.pernod-ricard.com

2018 Sales

	% of total
Asia & other regions	41
Europe	31
Americas	28
Total	100

PRODUCTS/OPERATIONS

2018 Sales

	% of total
Strategic International Brands	63
Strategic Local Brands	19
Strategic Wines	5
Other products	13
Total	100

Selected Brands

Local brands
    100 Pipers whisky (Thailand)
    Amaro Ramazzotti bitters (Germany)
    Ararat brandy (Russia)
    Becherovka bitters (Czech Republic)
    Blender's Pride whisky (Argentina)
    Clan Campbell premium whisky (France)
    Imperial whisky (South Korea)
    Montilla rum (Brazil)
    Olmeca tequila (Russia)
    Passport whisky (Brazil)

Pastis 51 spirit (France)
Royal Stag whisky (India)
Ruavieja liqueur (Spain)
Seagram's Gin (US)
Something Special whisky (Venezuela)
Suze bitters (France)
Wiser's whisky (Canada)
Wyborowa vodka (Poland)

Top 14
Global icons
ABSOLUT vodka
Chivas Regal Scotch whisky
Premium spirits
Ballentine's Scotch whisky
Beefeater gin
Havana Club rum
Jameson Irish whiskey
Kahlúa liqueur
Malibu liqueur
Ricard pastis
Prestige spirits and champagne
The Glenlivet Scotch whisky
G.H. Mumm champagne
Martell cognac
Perrier-Jouët champagne
Royal Salute Scotch whisky

Wine
Brancott Estate (formerly Montana)
Campo Viejo
Graffigna
Jacob's Creek

COMPETITORS

Anheuser-Busch InBev
BEAM SUNTORY INC.
COCA - COLA HELLENIC BOTTLING COMPANY S.A.
DANONE
DIAGEO PLC
DISTIL PLC
Heineken N.V.
REMY COINTREAU
UNITED BISCUITS TOPCO LIMITED
WILLIAM GRANT & SONS GROUP LIMITED

HISTORICAL FINANCIALS

Company Type: Public

Income Statement   FYE: June 30

	REVENUE ($mil)	NET INCOME ($mil)	NET PROFIT MARGIN	EMPLOYEES
06/23	13,173	2,455	18.6%	20,617
06/22	11,120	2,074	18.7%	19,480
06/21	10,495	1,552	14.8%	18,306
06/20	9,458	368	3.9%	18,776
06/19	10,447	1,655	15.8%	19,140
Annual Growth	6.0%	10.4%	—	1.9%

2023 Year-End Financials
Debt ratio: 32.8%   No. of shares ($ mil.): 253
Return on equity: 14.2%   Dividends
Cash ($ mil.): 1,746   Yield: 2.2%
Current Ratio: 1.73   Payout: 10.5%
Long-term debt ($ mil.): 10,692   Market value ($ mil.): 11,118

	STOCK PRICE ($) FY Close	P/E High/Low		PER SHARE ($) Earnings	Dividends	Book Value
06/23	43.90	5	4	9.56	0.98	67.36
06/22	36.72	6	5	7.99	0.72	64.48
Annual Growth	19.6%	—	—	4.6%	8.2%	1.1%

Persol Holdings Co Ltd

EXECUTIVES

Chairman, Director, Masamichi Mizuta
President, Chief Executive Officer, Representative Director, Takao Wada
Executive Vice President, Representative Director, Hirotoshi Takahashi
Outside Director, Ryosuke Tamakoshi
Outside Director, Naohiro Nishiguchi
Outside Director, Masaki Yamauchi
Outside Director, Kazuhiro Yoshizawa
Director, Daisuke Hayashi
Outside Director, Chisa Enomoto
Outside Director, Kazuhiko Tomoda
Auditors : Deloitte Touche Tohmatsu LLC

LOCATIONS

HQ: Persol Holdings Co Ltd
2-1-1 Yoyogi, Shibuya-ku, Tokyo 151-0053
Phone: (81) 3 3375 2220
Web: www.persol-group.co.jp

HISTORICAL FINANCIALS

Company Type: Public

Income Statement   FYE: March 31

	REVENUE ($mil)	NET INCOME ($mil)	NET PROFIT MARGIN	EMPLOYEES
03/22	8,721	259	3.0%	60,675
03/21	8,586	143	1.7%	54,760
03/20	8,941	70	0.8%	50,774
03/19	8,359	219	2.6%	45,434
03/18	6,801	73	1.1%	37,812
Annual Growth	6.4%	37.2%	—	12.5%

2022 Year-End Financials
Debt ratio: 0.1%   No. of shares ($ mil.): 2,320
Return on equity: 18.5%   Dividends
Cash ($ mil.): 884   Yield: —
Current Ratio: 1.71   Payout: 0.0%
Long-term debt ($ mil.): 328   Market value ($ mil.): —

PetroChina Co Ltd

A subsidiary of state-owned China National Petroleum Corporation (CNPC), PetroChina is the largest oil and gas producer and seller occupying a leading position in the oil and gas industry in China, one of the largest companies in China in terms of sales revenue, and also one of the largest companies in the world. Its principal business lines include the exploration, development, transmission, production, and marketing of crude oil and natural gas; the refining of crude oil and petroleum products, as well as the production and marketing of basic petrochemical products, derivative chemical products and other chemical products; the marketing and trading of refined oil products and non-oil products; and the sale of natural gas. The company has proved reserves of some 6.1 billion barrels of crude oil and 74.9 billion cu. ft. of natural gas. More than 60% of its revenue comes from its Mainland China.

Operations

The company's operating segments comprise: Exploration and Production, Refining and Chemicals, Marketing, and Natural Gas and Pipeline.

The Marketing segment (nearly 70% of revenue) is engaged in the marketing of refined products and non-oil products, and the trading business.

The Natural Gas and Pipeline segment (about 15% of revenue) is engaged in the transportation and sale of natural gas.

The Refining and Chemicals segment (more than 10% of revenue) is engaged in the refining of crude oil and petroleum products, production and marketing of primary petrochemical products, derivative petrochemical products and other chemical products.

The Exploration and Production segment (around 5% of revenue) is engaged in the exploration, development, transportation, production and marketing of crude oil and natural gas.

The Head Office and Other segment relates to cash management and financing activities, the corporate center, research and development, and other business services supporting the other operating business segments of the company.

Geographic Reach

Substantially all of its total estimated proved crude oil and natural gas reserves are located in China, principally in Northeastern, Northern, Southwestern, and Northwestern China. In addition, PetroChina operates around 35 enterprises located in nine provinces, four autonomous regions and three municipalities for its refining and chemicals segment.

Its natural gas supply covers all provinces, municipalities under direct administration of the central government, autonomous regions and Hong Kong of China, except Macau and Taiwan. The Bohai Rim, the Yangtze River Delta and the Southwestern region in China are its principal markets for natural gas. In addition, provinces such as Inner Mongolia, and Anhui consume more and more natural gas and have become another significant natural gas market for the company. PetroChina supplies natural gas to these regions primarily through pipelines except for Tibet where it supplies natural gas by LNG tanker trucks.

Its home country, China, accounts for more than 60% of total revenue.

Sales and Marketing

The company sell natural gas primarily to industrial companies, power plants, fertilizer, and chemical companies, commercial users and municipal utilities owned by local governments.

PetroChina markets its refined products through some 35 regional sales companies including two distribution branch companies and one convenience store chain company, PetroChina uSmile Company Limited, operated under the trade name uSmile, as well as through an extensive network of sales personnel and independent distributors and a broad wholesale and retail distribution network across China.

Financial Performance

The company's revenue for fiscal 2021 increased to RMB 2.6 trillion compared from the prior year with RMB 1.9 trillion.

Profit for fiscal 2021 increased to RMB 92.2 billion compared from the prior year with RMB 19.0 billion.

Cash held by the company at the end of fiscal 2021 increased to RMB 136.8 billion. Cash provided by operations was RMB 341.5 billion, while cash used for investing and financing activities were RMB 213.0 billion and RMB 108.0 billion, respectively. Main uses of cash were repayments of short-term borrowings and capital expenditures.

EXECUTIVES

Supervisor, Lifu Jiang
Staff Supervisor, Jiamin Li
Supervisor, Fengshan Zhang
Staff Supervisor, Xianhua Liu
Chief Financial Officer, Board Secretary, Board Secretary (Acting), Shouping Chai
Staff Supervisor, Suotang Fu
Supervisor, Yaozhong Lu
Supervisor, Liang Wang
Supervisory Committee Chairman, Bo Lv
President, Executive Director, Director, Yongzhang Huang
General Engineer, Jigang Yang
Non-executive Director, Director, Yuezhen Liu
Non-executive Director, Director, Liangwei Duan
Independent Non-executive Director, Independent Director, Aishi Liang
Independent Non-executive Director, Independent Director, Henry Simon
Non-executive Director, Director, Fangzheng Jiao
Chairman, Houliang Dai
Independent Non-executive Director, Independent Director, Jinyong Cai
Independent Non-executive Director, Independent Director, Xiaoming Jiang
Independent Non-executive Director, Independent Director, Liren Dedi
Auditors : KPMG Huazhen (Special General Partnership)

LOCATIONS

HQ: PetroChina Co Ltd
 No. 9 Dongzhimen North Street, Dongcheng District, Beijing 100007
 Phone: (86) 10 5998 6270   **Fax:** (86) 10 6209 9557
 Web: www.petrochina.com.cn

2013 Sales

	% of total
Mainland China	67
Other countries	33
Total	100

PRODUCTS/OPERATIONS

2013 Sales

	% of total
Marketing	51
Refining & chemicals	23
Exploration & production	20
Natural gas & pipeline	6
Total	100

COMPETITORS

ANDEAVOR LLC
BG GROUP LIMITED
CNOOC LIMITED
China National Petroleum Corporation
ECOPETROL S A
ESSAR ENERGY LIMITED
GAIL (INDIA) LIMITED
OMV Aktiengesellschaft
SURGUTNEFTEGAZ, PAO
Suncor Energy Inc

HISTORICAL FINANCIALS

Company Type: Public

Income Statement   FYE: December 31

	REVENUE ($mil)	NET INCOME ($mil)	NET PROFIT MARGIN	EMPLOYEES
12/22	469,537	21,652	4.6%	0
12/21	411,796	14,516	3.5%	0
12/20	295,682	2,905	1.0%	0
12/19	361,703	6,564	1.8%	0
12/18	342,176	7,645	2.2%	0
Annual Growth	8.2%	29.7%		

2022 Year-End Financials

Debt ratio: 1.1%   No. of shares ($ mil.): —
Return on equity: 11.3%   Dividends
Cash ($ mil.): 32,622   Yield: —
Current Ratio: 0.98   Payout: 0.0%
Long-term debt ($ mil.): 24,588   Market value ($ mil.): —

Petroleo Brasileiro SA

Petroleo Brasileiro S.A. Petrobras (Petrobras) operates and produces the majority of Brazil's oil and gas. Petrobras has proved oil and gas reserves, and produced average daily production of more than 2.2 million barrels of oil equivalent. In Brazil, it operates a dozen refineries and an extensive oil and gas pipeline network. Other units operate electricity (approximately 15 thermal power plants), petrochemicals, and natural gas assets. Petrobras is controlled by the Brazilian government and generates the majority of sales in Brazilian market.

Operations

Petrobras operates through three business segments: Refining, Transportation and Marketing, Exploration and Production, and Gas and Power.

The Refining, Transportation, and Marketing segment is Petrobras' most lucrative, at over 85% of sales. The company operates the company's activities of refining, logistics, transport, marketing and trading of crude oil and oil products in Brazil and abroad, exports of ethanol, petrochemical operations, such as extraction and processing of shale, as well as holding interests in petrochemical companies in Brazil.

Gas and Power, accounting for around 10% of sales, covers Petrobras' natural gas and electricity logistics and trading of natural gas and electricity, transportation and trading of LNG, generation of electricity by means of thermoelectric power plants, as well as holding interests in transportation and distribution companies of natural gas in Brazil and abroad. It also includes natural gas processing and fertilizer operations.

The Exploration and Production segment covers Petrobras' upstream activities, including the exploration, development, and production of crude oil, natural gas, and natural gas liquids (NGLs) in Brazil and elsewhere. The segment represents the rest of total revenue.

The company also generates sales from corporate and other businesses. It include Petrobras' distribution and biofuels activities.

Overall, approximately 60% of sales were generated from oil products.

Geographic Reach

Rio de Janeiro-based Petrobras does most of its business in Brazil but also explores for and produces oil in Argentina, Bolivia, Colombia, Uruguay, Netherlands, the UK, the US, and Singapore. In addition to its explorations activities, the company also has support activities such as trade and financial in Rotterdam, Houston, and Singapore.

Sales and Marketing

Petrobras distributes its oil products through a company-owned retail network, wholesale channels, and by supplying other fuel wholesalers and retailers.

Crude oil is primarily sold through long-term contracts and also in the spot market. The company's overseas portfolio includes approximately 30 clients, such as refiners that process or have processed Brazilian oils regularly. The Natural gas is marketed to around 20 clients, most of which are distributors.

Financial Performance

In 2021, sales revenues increased 56% compared to 2020, reaching $84 billion, due to the 70% increase in Brent price and the increase in demand in the domestic market, mainly due to the economic recovery after the height of the Covid-19 pandemic. An additional factor was the increase in sales of natural gas and electricity, as a result of the increase in thermoelectric generation in 2021 and industrial demand recovery.

Net income attributable to shareholders was $19.9 billion in 2021, a 1642% increase compared to $1.1 billion in 2020, mainly as a result of higher Brent prices and reversal of impairment in 2021 as compared to impairment expenses in 2020.

The company's cash at the end of 2021 was $10.5 billion. Operating activities generated $37.8 billion, while financing activities used $40.8 billion, mainly for repayments of debt. Investing activities provided another $2.2 billion.

Strategy

The company continues to strengthen its initiatives related to ESG matters, with a firm commitment to accelerate decarbonization in its operations and prioritize acting ethically and transparently, with a particular focus on safe operations and respect for people and the environment. The strategic model it has adopted remains anchored in the assumption that producing oil and gas can be compatible with accelerated general decarbonization efforts, by adopting the concept of double resilience. Double resilience is composed of two parts: (1) economic, which means resiliency towards low oil price scenarios, and (2) environmental, characterized by a focus on a low carbon footprint. Currently, the company has reached a prominent position in the production of low carbon emission oil, particularly with respect to its pre-salt fields, which makes the company a relevant player in the offshore oil and gas industry in relation to this requirement. It will keep pushing for further reductions, investing in new technology and CO2 injection.

The Strategic Plan maintains active portfolio management, with expected divestments ranging from $15 to $25 billion, which the company believes will contribute to further business efficiency improvements, value creation, higher return on capital and strong cash flow to maintain an adequate level of debt. This active portfolio management allow the company to explore better investments opportunities by focusing its activities on assets that have more potential to raise its portfolio's expected rate of return in a sustainable way.

HISTORY

"O petrÃ³leo Ã© nosso!"

"The oil is ours!" proclaimed the Brazilian nationalists' slogan in 1953, and President GetÃºlio Vargas approved a bill creating a state-run monopoly on petroleum discovery, development, refining, and transport. The same year that PETRÃ"LEO BRASILEIRO (PETROBRAS) was created, a team led by American geologist Walter Link reported that the prospects of finding petroleum in Brazil were slim. The report outraged Brazilian nationalists, who saw it as a ploy for foreign exploitation. PETROBRAS proved it could find oil, but Brazil continued to import crude oil and petroleum products. By 1973 the company produced about 10% of the nation's needs.

When oil prices soared during the Arab embargo, the government, instead of encouraging exploration for domestic oil, pushed PETROBRAS into a program to promote alcohol fuels. The company was forced to raise gasoline prices to make the more costly gasohol attractive to consumers. During the 1979 oil crunch the price of gasohol was fixed at 65% of gasoline. But during the oil glut of the mid-1980s, PETROBRAS' cost of making gasohol was twice what it cost to buy gasoline -- in other words, PETROBRAS lost money.

PETROBRAS soon began overseas exploration. In 1980 it found an oil field in Iraq, an important trading partner during the 1980s. The company also drilled in Angola and, through a 1987 agreement with Texaco, in the Gulf of Mexico.

In the mid-1980s PETROBRAS began production in the deepwater Campos basin off the coast of Rio de Janeiro state. Discoveries there in 1988, in the Marlim and Albacora fields, more than tripled its oil reserves. It plunged deep into the thick Amazon jungle in 1986 to explore for oil, and by 1990 Amazon wells were making a significant contribution to total production. That year, to ease dependence on imports, PETROBRAS launched a five-year, $16.9 billion plan to boost crude oil production. It also began selling its mining and trading assets.

Before the invasion of Kuwait, Brazil relied heavily on Iraq, trading weapons for oil. After the invasion spawned increases in crude prices, PETROBRAS raised pump prices but, yielding to the government's anti-inflation program, still did not raise them enough to cover costs. It lost $13 million a day.

The company sold 26% of Petrobras Distribuidora to the public in 1993 and privatized several of its petrochemical and fertilizer subsidiaries. A 1994 presidential order, bent on stabilizing Brazil's 40%-per-month inflation, cut the prices of oil products. In 1995 the government loosened its grip on the oil and gas industry and allowed foreign companies to enter the Brazilian market. In the wake of this reform, PETROBRAS teamed up with a Japanese consortium to build Brazil's largest oil refinery.

In 1997 PETROBRAS appealed a $4 billion judgment from a 1992 shareholder lawsuit; the suit alleged PETROBRAS had undervalued shares during the privatization of the loss-making Petroquisa affiliate. (The appeal was granted in 1999.)

As part of an effort to boost oil production, PETROBRAS also began to raise money abroad in 1999. The next year PETROBRAS and Spanish oil giant Repsol YPF agreed to swap oil and gas assets in Argentina and Brazil in a deal worth more than $1 billion.

In 2000 the company announced plans to change its corporate name to PETROBRAX, but fierce political and popular reaction forced the company to abort this plan in 2001. In an even greater public relations disaster that year, one of PETROBRAS' giant rigs sank off of Brazil and 10 workers were killed. In 2001 PETROBRAS announced that it was going to spend as much as $3 billion to buy an oil company in order to increase its production in the Gulf of Mexico.

In 2002 the company expressed an interest in buying Argentina's major oil company (YPF) from Spanish/Argentine energy giant Repsol YPF. That year PETROBRAS bought control (59%) of Argentine energy company Perez Companc in a deal valued at $1 billion. PETROBRAS also reported its first oil find in Argentina in 2002.

In 2006 the company acquired a 50% stake in a deepwater block in Equatorial Guinea from a private group of companies for an undisclosed sum.

The company also restructured the Brazilian petrochemical industry to make it more efficient. Its actions included the purchase of the petrochemical assets of the Ipiranga Group in 2007 and Suzano PetroquÃmica, a leader in Latin American polypropylene resin production, in 2008.

In 2007 PETROBRAS announced a major offshore oil discovery in the Tupi. In 2008 it reported it had discovered a major natural gas field near the Tupi find.

In 2011 it was operating more than 130 production platforms. PETROBRAS has made a number of major offshore oil discoveries in offshore Brazil since 2000, including the Tupi field (found in 2007) and which has the potential to boost Brazil's oil reserves by 40%. In 2010 PETROBRAS announced another major discovery, a 3.7 to 15 billion-barrels-of-oil-reserves find (offshore of Rio de Janeiro) that could double Brazil's known reserves.

Streamlining its Petrobras Argentina operations, in 2011 the company acquired that unit's Brazilian petrochemicals business (Innova SA), for $332 million.

In 2012 it teamed up with GE Oil & Gas in a $1.1 billion deal through which the GE unit will supply 380 subsea wellhead systems to a number of PETROBRAS' oil and gas fields in offshore Brazil.

Brazil's government owns more than 55% of PETROBRAS.

EXECUTIVES

Chief Executive Officer, Executive Director,
Roberto da Cunha Castello Branco
Chief Trading and Logistics Officer, Andre Barreto Chiarini
Chief Financial Officer, Chief Investor Relations Officer, Andrea Marques de Almeida
Chief Exploration and Production Officer, Carlos Alberto Pereira de Oliveira
Chief Governance and Compliance Executive Officer, Marcelo Barbosa de Castro Zenkner
Chief Digital Transformation and Innovation Executive Officer, Nicolas Simone

Chief Institutional Relations and Sustainability Executive Officer, Roberto Furian Ardenghy
Chief Refining and Natural Gas Officer, Rodrigo Costa Lima e Silva
Chief Production Development Officer, Rudimar Andreis Lorenzatto
Chairman, Eduardo Bacellar Leal Ferreira
Independent Director, Joao Cox Neto
Independent Director, Leornado Pietro Antonelli
Independent Director, Marcelo Mesquita de Siqueira Filho
Independent Director, Nivio Ziviani
Independent Director, Omar Carneiro da Cunha Sobrinho
Independent Director, Paulo Cesar de Souza e Silva
Independent Director, Rodrigo de Mesquita Pereira
Independent Director, Rosangela Buzanelli Torres
Independent Director, Ruy Flaks Schneider
Auditors : KPMG Auditores Independentes Ltda.

LOCATIONS

HQ: Petroleo Brasileiro SA
Avenida Republica do Chile, 65, Rio de Janeiro 20231-912
Phone: (55) 21 3224 4477
Web: www.petrobras.com.br

2018 Sales

	% of total
Brazil	76
Other countries	24
Total	100

PRODUCTS/OPERATIONS

2018 Sales

	% of total
Refining, transportation & marketing	44
Exploration & production	32
Distribution	17
Gas & Power	7
Biofuels	—
Total	100

Selected Subsidiaries

Downstream Participações S.A. (asset exchanges between Petrobras and Repsol-YPF)
Petrobras Argentina (59%; oil and gas, Argentina)
Petrobras Comercializadora de Energia Ltda
Petrobras Distribuidora SA (BR; distribution and marketing of petroleum products, fuel alcohol, and natural gas)
Petrobras Gás SA (Gaspetro, management of the Brazil-Bolivia pipeline and other natural gas assets)
Petrobras Internacional SA (Braspetro; overseas exploration and production, marketing, and services)
Petrobras International Finance Company - PIFCO (oil imports)
Petrobras Negócios Eletrônicos S.A.
Petrobras Química SA (Petroquisa, petrochemicals)
Petrobras Transporte SA (Transpetro, oil and gas transportation and storage)

COMPETITORS

COMPAÑIA ESPAÑOLA DE PETROLEOS SAU
COSMO OIL CO., LTD.
ENI SPA
Equinor ASA
HESS CORPORATION
HOLLYFRONTIER CORPORATION
MOL Magyar Olaj- és Gázipari Nyilvãnosan Működő Részvénytársaság
NK ROSNEFT, PAO
ROYAL DUTCH SHELL plc
Suncor Energy Inc

HISTORICAL FINANCIALS

Company Type: Public

Income Statement   FYE: December 31

	REVENUE ($mil)	NET INCOME ($mil)	NET PROFIT MARGIN	EMPLOYEES
12/23	105,513	25,679	24.3%	46,730
12/22	124,474	36,623	29.4%	45,149
12/21	83,966	19,875	23.7%	45,532
12/20	53,683	1,141	2.1%	49,050
12/19	76,589	10,151	13.3%	57,983
Annual Growth	8.3%	26.1%	—	(5.3%)

2023 Year-End Financials

Debt ratio: 3.4%
Return on equity: 55.3%
Cash ($ mil.): 12,697
Current Ratio: 0.96
Long-term debt ($ mil.): 24,422
No. of shares ($ mil.): 7,442
Dividends
  Yield: 0.1%
  Payout: 128.0%
Market value ($ mil.): 118,852

	STOCK PRICE ($) FY Close	P/E High/Low		PER SHARE ($) Earnings	Dividends	Book Value
12/23	15.97	2	1	1.97	2.52	10.53
12/22	10.65	6	3	2.81	6.34	9.34
12/21	10.98	8	5	1.52	1.98	9.33
12/20	11.23	181	48	0.09	0.17	7.97
12/19	15.94	23	16	0.78	0.21	5.62
Annual Growth	0.0%	—		26.1%	86.2%	17.0%

Petroleos Mexicanos (Pemex) (Mexico)

Petróleos Mexicanos (PEMEX) is the largest company in Mexico. It operates through the whole chain of value of the industry, from exploration and production - upstream- to industrial transformation, logistics and marketing ?downstream. The company carries out extensive exploration and extraction projects every year, generating approximately 2.5 million barrels of oil daily and more than 6 million of cubic feet of natural gas. It has six refineries, eight petrochemical complexes and nine gas processing complexes. Logistically, it has about 85 land and maritime terminals, as well as oil and gas pipelines, maritime vessels, and varying fleets of ground transportation in order to supply over 10,000 service stations throughout the country. Petróleos Mexicanos is a productive state-owned company, wholly owned by the Mexican Government.

Operations

PEMEX operates through four main segments:

The industrial transformation segment is comprised of four principal activities: refining, gas and aromatics, ethylene and derivatives and fertilizers. Pemex Industrial Transformation converts crude oil into gasoline, jet fuel, diesel, fuel oil, asphalts and lubricants. It processes wet natural gas to produce dry natural gas, ethane, liquefied petroleum gas (LPG) and other natural gas liquids, along with aromatic derivatives chain products such as toluene, benzene and xylene. Pemex Industrial Transformation produces, distributes and markets ethane and propylene derivatives. Its fertilizer business integrates the ammonia production chain. The segment accounts for more than 45% of total revenue.

Its exploration and production segment (about 30% of revenue) operates through the productive state-owned subsidiary Pemex Exploration and Production and explores for and produces crude oil and natural gas, primarily in the northeastern and southeastern regions of Mexico and offshore in the Gulf of Mexico.

The international trading segment (some 20%) provides international trading, distribution, risk management, insurance and transportation services. This segment operates through P.M.I. Comercio Internacional, P.M.I. Trading, P.M.I. Norteamérica, and Mex Gas International, S.L. (which, together with the PMI Subsidiaries, collectively refer to as the Trading Companies). Certain of the Trading Companies sell, buy and transport crude oil, refined products and petrochemicals in world markets, and provide related risk management, insurance, transportation and storage services.

The logistics segment operates through the productive state-owned subsidiary Pemex Logistics and provides land, maritime and pipeline transportation, storage and distribution services to some of its subsidiaries and other companies, including Tesoro México Supply & Marketing, S. de R.L. de C.V. (a subsidiary of Marathon Petroleum Corporation), which we refer to as Tesoro, local gas stations and distributors. In 2021, PEMEX injected about 1,272.9 thousand barrels per day of crude oil and petroleum products into its pipelines.

Geographic Reach

Based in Mexico, PEMEX operations are geographically dispersed throughout Mexico, and it has presences in almost every states. The Trading Companies have offices in Mexico City, Houston, and Singapore.

Financial Performance

Total sales increased by 57% or $541.9 billion in 2021, from $953.7 billion in 2020 to $1.5 trillion in 2021, primarily due to increases in domestic sales prices of gasoline, diesel, fuel oil, jet fuel, natural gas and natural gas liquids and an 86% increase in the weighted average price of Mexican crude oil for export sales.

In 2021, the company had a net loss of $294.5 billion, a 42% decrease from the previous year's net loss of $509.1 billion.

The company's cash at the end of 2021 was $76.5 billion. Operating activities generated $189.2 billion, while investing activities used $12.7 billion, mainly for acquisition of wells, pipelines, properties, plant and equipment. Financing activities provided another $99.4 billion.

Strategy

As part of its commercial strategy, the company operates wholesale and retail service stations, some of which are PEMEX-branded and others of which are unbranded. The unbranded stations buy products through marketing contracts and, when appropriate, have access to discounts and credit. In the case of its PEMEX-branded stations, both Pemex marketers and associate distributors can sell products with the Pemex brand. Retailers to the public may only buy products through marketing contracts, just as they may only sell Pemex brand products through a franchise agreement or a Pemex brand sublicensing agreement.

HISTORY

Histories of precolonial Mexico recount the nation's first oil business: Natives along the Tampico coast gathered asphalt from naturally occurring deposits and traded with the Aztecs.

As the 20th century began, Americans Edward Doheny and Charles Canfield struck oil near Tampico. Their success was eclipsed in 1910 by a nearby well drilled by British engineer Weetman Pearson, leader of the firm that became Pearson PLC.

President Porfirio Díaz had welcomed foreign ownership of Mexican resources, but revolution ousted Díaz, and the 1917 Constitution proclaimed that natural resources belonged to the nation. Without enforcing legislation, however, foreign oil companies continued business as usual until a 1925 act limited their concessions. During a bitter labor dispute in 1938, President Lázaro Cárdenas expropriated foreign oil holdings -- the first nationalization of oil holdings by a non-Communist state. Subsequent legislation created Petróleos Mexicanos (PEMEX).

Without foreign capital and expertise, the new state-owned company struggled, and Mexico had to import petroleum in the early 1970s. But for many Mexicans, PEMEX remained a symbol of national identity and economic independence. That faith was rewarded in 1972 when a major oil discovery made PEMEX one of the world's top oil producers again. Ample domestic oil supplies and high world prices during the Iranian upheaval in the late 1970s fueled a boom and a government borrowing spree in Mexico. Between 1982 and 1985 PEMEX contributed more than 50% of government revenues.

When oil prices collapsed in 1985, Mexico cut investment in exploration, and production dropped. To decrease its reliance on oil, Mexico began lowering trade barriers and encouraging manufacturing, even allowing some foreign ownership of petrochemical processing.

Elected in 1988, President Carlos Salinas de Gortari began to reform PEMEX. Labor's grip on the company was loosened in 1989 when a union leader was arrested and jailed after a gun battle. In 1992, after a PEMEX pipeline explosion killed more than 200 people in Guadalajara, four of its executives and several local officials were sent to prison, amid public cries for company reform.

President Ernesto Zedillo appointed Adrián Lajous Vargas head of PEMEX in 1994. Under the professorial Lajous, PEMEX began to adopt modern business practices (such as trimming its bloated payroll), look for more reserves, and improve its refining capability. Lajous tried to sell some petrochemical assets in 1995, but had to modify the scheme the next year after massive public protests by the country's nationalists. Still, PEMEX began selling off natural gas production, distribution, and storage networks to private companies.

Though oil prices were dropping, in 1998 Mexico finally upped PEMEX's investment budget and PEMEX dramatically increased exploration and production. In spite of 2000's looming national election (elections traditionally had caused bureaucrats to keep a low profile to protect their jobs), Lajous again fanned the flames of the opposition: In 1998 he signed a major deal to sell Mexican crude to Exxon's Texas refinery, and in 1999 a four-year-old PEMEX/Shell joint venture announced it would expand its US refinery.

In 1999 Lajous resigned and was replaced by Rogelio Montemayor, a former governor. The next year Vicente Fox was elected as Mexico's new president, the country's first non-Institutional Revolutionary Party (PRI) leader in seven decades. He announced plans to replace PEMEX's politician-staffed board with professionals -- Montemayor was among the casualties -- and modernize the company, but he ruled out privatizing PEMEX as politically unfeasible.

Fox appointed Raúl Muñoz, formerly with Dupont Mexico, in 2003 to lead PEMEX. Muñoz, however, was engulfed in a scandal involving the misuse of funds and forced to resign the following year. His replacement, Luis Ramírez, lasted until the next national election, when incoming President Felipe Calderón appointed Jesús Reyes.

Reyes was replaced by Juan José Suárez Coppel in 2009.

In 2011 the company reported a major gas find in the Gulf of Mexico with estimated reserves of 400 to 600 billion cubic feet. The discovery is the tenth deepwater gas discovery PEMEX has made since 2004. However, because of the persistence of low natural gas commodity prices, the development of these fields is on hold while the company focuses on crude oil production (supported by high crude oil prices) mainly in southeast Mexico.

EXECUTIVES

Chairperson, Norma Rocio Nahle Garcia
Chief Executive Officer, General Director, Octavio Romero Oropeza
Chief Financial Officer, Alberto Velazquez Garcia
Management and Services Corporate Director, Marcos Manuel Herreria Alamina
Planning, Coordination and Performance Corporate Director, Victor Manuel Navarro Cervantes
Legal Director, Luz Maria Zarza Delgado
Independent Director, Juan Jose Paullada Figueroa
Independent Director, Jose Eduardo Beltran Hernandez
Independent Director, Rafael Espino de la Pena
Independent Director, Humberto Domingo Mayans Canabal
Director, Arturo Herrera Gutierrez
Director, Maria Luisa Albores Gonzalez
Director, Manuel Bartlett Diaz
Auditors : KPMG Cardenas Dosal S.C.

LOCATIONS

HQ: Petroleos Mexicanos (Pemex) (Mexico)
Avenida Marina Nacional 329, Colonia Verónica Anzures, Mexico City 11300
Phone: (52) 55 9126 2940
Web: www.pemex.com

PRODUCTS/OPERATIONS

2016 Sales

	% of total
Domestic sales	62
Export sales:	
United States	21
Europe	6
Canada, Central and South America	1
Other	9
Services income	1
Total	

2016 Sales

	% of total
Trading Companies	35
Industrial Transformation	34
Exploration and Production	27
Logistics	3
Ethylene	1
Drilling and Service	-
Cogeneration and Services	-
Fertilizers	-
Corporate and other subsidiary companies	-
Total	100

Selected Subsidiaries

PEMEX Exploración y Producción (petroleum and natural gas exploration and production)
PEMEX Gas y Petroquímica Básica (natural gas, liquids from natural gas, and ethane processing)
PEMEX Petroquímica (petrochemical production)
PEMEX Refinación (refining and marketing)
P.M.I. Comercio Internacional (international trading)

COMPETITORS

ANADARKO PETROLEUM CORPORATION
CONOCOPHILLIPS
Equinor ASA
GAZPROM NEFT, PAO
GAZPROM, PAO
LUKOIL, PAO
OMV Aktiengesellschaft
SEAENERGY PLC
TATNEFT, PAO
YPF S.A.

HISTORICAL FINANCIALS
Company Type: Public

Income Statement				FYE: December 31
	REVENUE ($mil)	NET INCOME ($mil)	NET PROFIT MARGIN	EMPLOYEES
12/22	121,809	5,131	4.2%	116,063
12/21	73,147	(14,404)	—	120,798
12/20	47,997	(25,611)	—	120,936
12/19	74,101	(18,356)	—	122,646
12/18	85,491	(9,172)	—	124,818
Annual Growth	9.3%	—		(1.8%)

2022 Year-End Financials
Debt ratio: 4.8%
Return on equity: —
Cash ($ mil.): 3,292
Current Ratio: 0.57
Long-term debt ($ mil.): 83,075
No. of shares ($ mil.): —
Dividends
  Yield: —
  Payout: 0.0%
Market value ($ mil.): —

Phoenix Group Holdings PLC

EXECUTIVES

Chief Executive Officer, Executive Director, Andy Briggs
Human Resources Director, Stephen Jefford
Chief Operating Officer, Tony Kassimiotis
Financial Director, Executive Director, James Mcconville
Chief Risk Officer, Jonathan Pears
Deputy Group Finance Director, Rakesh Thakrar
Corporate Development Director, Corporate Development Chief Actuary, Simon True
General Counsel, Quentin Zentner
Corporate Secretary, Gerald Watson
Chairman, Nicholas Lyons
Senior Independent Non-Executive Director, Alastair Barbour
Non-Executive Director, Campbell Fleming
Independent Non-Executive Director, Karen Green
Independent Non-Executive Director, Wendy Mayall
Independent Non-Executive Director, John Pollock
Independent Non-Executive Director, Belinda Richards
Independent Non-Executive Director, Nicholas Shott
Independent Non-Executive Director, Kory Sorenson
Non-Executive Director, Mike Tumilty
Auditors : Ernst & Young LLP

LOCATIONS

HQ: Phoenix Group Holdings PLC
Juxon House, 100 St Paul's Churchyard, London EC4M 8BU
Phone: —
Web: www.thephoenixgroup.com

COMPETITORS

3I GROUP PLC
AON GLOBAL LIMITED
AVIVA PLC
AXA
Argo Group International Holdings, Ltd.
LEGAL & GENERAL GROUP PLC
NEW YORK LIFE INSURANCE COMPANY
PRUDENTIAL PUBLIC LIMITED COMPANY
STANDARD LIFE ABERDEEN PLC
THE HARTFORD FINANCIAL SERVICES GROUP, INC.

HISTORICAL FINANCIALS
Company Type: Public

Income Statement				FYE: December 31
	ASSETS ($mil)	NET INCOME ($mil)	INCOME AS % OF ASSETS	EMPLOYEES
12/22	343,294	(2,201)	—	8,333
12/21	449,854	(1,128)	—	8,045
12/20	456,256	1,089	0.2%	7,653
12/19	320,470	112	0.0%	4,417
12/18	293,629	483	0.2%	4,088
Annual Growth	4.0%	—		19.5%

2022 Year-End Financials
Return on assets: (-0.5%)
Return on equity: (-33.3%)
Long-term debt ($ mil.): —
No. of shares ($ mil.): 1,000
Sales ($ mil.): (-38,220)
Dividends
  Yield: —
  Payout: 0.0%
Market value ($ mil.): —

Ping An Insurance (Group) Co of China Ltd.

Ping An Insurance is one of China's largest insurance companies. It specializes in life and health coverage but offers a variety of other products, including auto insurance, corporate property and casualty insurance, engineering insurance, cargo insurance, liability insurance, guarantee insurance, credit insurance, home contents insurance, accident and health insurance, as well as international reinsurance business. The company also provides stock trading, equity investment funds and bonds, property leasing, and asset management services through Ping An Trust, Ping An Financial Leasing, and Ping An Asset Management. Its Ping An Bank subsidiary offers retail banking and other consumer services, such as credit card and mortgage lending. The group also includes Ping An Health Insurance.

Operations

Ping An Insurance operates through Life and Health Insurance, Property & Casualty Insurance, Banking, Other Asset Management, Technology, Trust, and Securities.

The largest segment, Life and Health Insurance, brings in more than 45% of the company's total revenue. It offers a comprehensive range of life insurance products to individual and corporate customers, including term, whole-life, endowment, annuity, investment-linked, universal life and health care and medical insurance, reflecting performance summary of life insurance, annuity insurance and health insurance subsidiaries.

Property & Casualty Insurance segment offers a wide variety of insurance products to individual and corporate customers, including auto insurance, non-auto insurance, accident and health insurance. The segment brings in some 25% of total revenue. The Banking segment provides loan and intermediary business with corporate and retail business customers. It also provides wealth management and credit card services to individuals. It accounts for about 20% of revenue.

The Other Asset Management segment provides finance leasing, investment management, and other asset management services. It brings in about 5% of revenue.

The Technology provides various financial and daily-life services through internet platforms such as financial transaction information service platform, health care service platform, reflecting performance summary of the technology business subsidiaries, associates and jointly controlled entities. Its operating units include Lufax Holding, OneConnect and Ping An Health. The segment brings in less than 5% of revenue.

The smallest segments are Trust, which operates through Ping An Trust; and Securities, which provides securities brokerage, futures brokerage, investment banking, asset management, and financial advisory services through Ping An Securities and its subsidiaries.

Geographic Reach

Ping An is based in Shenzhen, China and operates mainly in China. Ping An Bank has about 110 branches (including the Hong Kong branch) and about 1,190 business outlets.

Sales and Marketing

The company has nearly 227 million retail customers and more than 693 million internet users.

Financial Performance

Note: Growth rates may differ after conversion to US Dollars.

The company reported a total revenue of RMB 1.2 trillion, a 5% decrease from the previous year's total revenue. This was primarily due to the lower volume of Investment income for the year.

In 2022, the company had a net income of RMB 83.8 billion, an 18% decrease from the previous year's net income of RMB 101.6 million.

The company's cash at the end of 2022 was RMB 442.9 billion. Operating activities generated RMB 485.9 billion, while investing activities used RMB 224 billion, mainly for purchases of investments. Financing activities used another RMB 230.7 billion, primarily for repayment of borrowings.

Strategy

Ping An's integrated finance strategy is focused on the development of both retail customers (1) and corporate customers under a customer-centric philosophy. In retail business, Ping An leverages its ecosystems to build a brand of heartwarming financial services by providing one-stop integrated finance solutions. In corporate business, under a "1 + N" services model (one customer + N products), Ping An focuses on tiered customer development of large and medium-sized enterprises, small and microenterprises, and financial institutions.

Company Background

Ping An Insurance was founded in 1988 as China's first joint-stock insurance company. It ventured beyond insurance in 1995 by establishing Ping An Securities.

EXECUTIVES

Vice-Chairman, Executive Vice President, Standing Deputy General Manager, Deputy General Manager, Jianyi Sun
Deputy General Manager, Senior Vice President, Kexiang Chen
Supervisory Committee Chairman, Liji Gu
Chief Financial Officer, Deputy General Manager, Standing Deputy General Manager, Executive Director, Bo Yao
Supervisor, Wangjin Zhang
Outside Supervisor, Baokui Huang
General Manager, Deputy General Manager, Executive Director, Yonglin Xie
Board Secretary, Ruisheng Sheng
Staff Supervisor, Zhiliang Wang
Deputy General Manager, Executive Director, Fangfang Cai
Deputy General Manager, Baoxin Huang
Deputy General Manager, Standing Deputy General Manager, Executive Director, Xinying Chen
Chief Operating Officer, Xiaolu Zhang
Chairman, Mingzhe Ma
Non-executive Director, Jiren Xie
Non-executive Director, Xiaoping Yang
Independent Non-executive Director, Hui Ouyang
Non-executive Director, Yongjian Wang
Independent Non-executive Director, Yiyun Chu
Independent Non-executive Director, Hong Liu
Independent Non-executive Director, Chengye Wu
Non-executive Director, Wei Huang
Independent Non-executive Director, Li Jin
Independent Non-executive Director, Gangping Wu
Auditors : PricewaterhouseCoopers Zhong Tian LLP

LOCATIONS

HQ: Ping An Insurance (Group) Co of China Ltd.
47th, 48th, 109th, 110th, 111th and 112th Floors, Ping An Finance Center, No. 5033 Yitian Road, Futian District, Shenzhen, Guangdong Province 518033

Phone: (86) 400 8866 338 **Fax:** (86) 755 8243 1029
Web: www.pingan.cn

PRODUCTS/OPERATIONS

2018 Sales by Segment

	% of total
Life and Health Insurance	51
Property & Casualty Insurance	21
Banking	19
Other Asset Management	4
Fintech & Healthtech	3
Trust	1
Securities	1
Total	100

2018 Sales

	% of total
Net earned premiums	62
Interest revenue from banking operations	15
Interest revenue from non-banking operations	8
Fees & commission revenue from non-insurance operations	4
Investment income	3
Share of profits & losses of associates & jointly controlled entities	2
Reinsurance commission revenue	1
Other revenue & other gains	5
Total	

Selected Subsidiaries and Affiliates
China Ping An Insurance Overseas (Holdings) Limited
    China Ping An Insurance (Hong Kong) Company Limited (75%)
        Ping An of China Asset Management (Hong Kong) Company Limited
China Ping An Trust & Investment Co., Ltd.
    Ping An Securities Co., Ltd.
Ping An Annuity Insurance Company of China, Ltd.
Ping An Health Insurance Company of China, Ltd.
Ping An Life Insurance Company of China, Ltd.
Ping An Property & Casualty Insurance Company of China, Ltd.
Shenzhen Ping An Bank Co., Ltd.

COMPETITORS

China Pacific Insurance (Group) Co., Ltd.
HEALTHPLAN HOLDINGS, INC.
Industrial Alliance Insurance and Financial Services Inc
JELF LIMITED
JLT GROUP HOLDINGS LIMITED
KEOGHS LLP
NATIONAL FARMERS UNION MUTUAL INSURANCE SOCIETY LIMITED(THE)
SCOR SE
SECURIAN FINANCIAL GROUP, INC.
WARRANTECH CORPORATION

HISTORICAL FINANCIALS

Company Type: Public

Income Statement   FYE: December 31

	ASSETS ($mil)	NET INCOME ($mil)	INCOME AS % OF ASSETS	EMPLOYEES
12/22	1,614,400	12,143	0.8%	0
12/21	1,597,510	16,006	1.0%	0
12/20	1,456,810	21,879	1.5%	0
12/19	1,181,760	21,471	1.8%	0
12/18	1,038,480	15,614	1.5%	376,900
Annual Growth	11.7%	(6.1%)	—	—

2022 Year-End Financials
Return on assets: 0.7%
Return on equity: 10.0%
Long-term debt ($ mil.): —
No. of shares ($ mil.): —
Sales ($ mil.): 5,808
Dividends
Yield: —
Payout: 88.5%
Market value ($ mil.): —

	STOCK PRICE ($) FY Close	P/E High/Low	PER SHARE ($) Earnings	Dividends	Book Value
12/22	13.15	3 2	0.69	0.61	0.00
12/21	14.34	5 2	0.90	0.59	0.00
12/20	24.50	3 2	1.23	0.50	0.00
12/19	23.80	3 2	1.20	0.45	0.00
12/18	17.39	4 3	0.87	0.48	4.43
Annual Growth	(6.7%)	— —	(5.9%)	6.0%	

Piraeus Financial Holdings SA

Greece is the word and Piraeus has most certainly heard. Piraeus Bank provides retail banking, investment banking, leasing, and insurance services in the Mediterranean and in Central and Eastern Europe. Its network of branches across Greece numbers more than 1,000, plus it has about 400 more in Albania (Tirana Bank), Romania, Bulgaria, Serbia, the Ukraine, and the US (New York's Marathon Bank). Piraeus Bank also provides its services through its electronic Winbank business, which includes about 1,900 ATMs, Internet, and phone banking. The company maintains a diverse loan portfolio with energy and transportation loans making up 30% of its portfolio. Piraeus Bank was founded in 1916 and under state control until 1991.

EXECUTIVES

Chief Executive Officer, Managing Director, Executive Director, Christos Ioannis Megalou
Secretary, Maria Zapanti
Non-Executive Chairman, George P. Handjinicolaou
Vice-Chairman, Independent Non-Executive Director, Karel De Boeck
Independent Non-Executive Director, Venetia Kontogouris
Independent Non-Executive Director, Arne Berggren
Independent Non-Executive Director, Enrico Tommaso Cucchiani
Independent Non-Executive Chairman, David Hexter
Non-Executive Director, Solomon A. Berahas
Non-Executive Director, Alexander Blades
Non-Executive Director, Periklis Dontas
Auditors : Deloitte Certified Public Accountants S.A.

LOCATIONS

HQ: Piraeus Financial Holdings SA
4 Amerikis str., Athens 105 64
Phone: (30) 210 333 5000   **Fax:** (30) 210 333 5080
Web: www.piraeusbankgroup.com

Branch Locations	No.
Greece	1,037
Romanis	140
Bulgaria	83
Albania	53
Serbia	42
Egypt	41
Ukraine	37
Cyprus	14
London	1
Frankfurt	1
Total	1,449

PRODUCTS/OPERATIONS

Selected Subsidiaries
ATEbank
ETBA Industrial Areas S.A.
Marathon Bank of New York (USA)
OJSC Piraeus Bank ICB (Ukraine)
Picar S.A.
Piraeus Asset Management Mutual Funds S.A.
Piraeus Bank AD Beograd (Serbia)
Piraeus Bank Bulgaria AD
Piraeus Bank (Cyprus) Ltd
Piraeus Bank Egypt SAE
Piraeus Capital Management
Piraeus Card Services
Piraeus Direct Services S.A.
Piraeus Insurance and Reinsurance Brokerage S.A.
Piraeus Insurance Agency S.A.
Piraeus Factoring S.A.
Piraeus Leaases SA
Piraeus Leasing Bulgaria
Piraeus Bank Romania S.A.
Piraeus Leasing Romania
Piraeus Private Equity
Piraeus Real Estate S.A.
Piraeus Securities S.A.
Piraeus Wealth Management
Tirana Bank S.A. (Albania)
Tirana Leasing (Albania)

COMPETITORS
ALPHA BANK A.E.
BANK OF CYPRUS PUBLIC COMPANY LIMITED
EUROBANK ERGASIAS SERVICES AND HOLDINGS S.A.
Islandsbanki hf.
NORTHERN BANK LIMITED

HISTORICAL FINANCIALS
Company Type: Public

Income Statement — FYE: December 31

	ASSETS ($mil)	NET INCOME ($mil)	INCOME AS % OF ASSETS	EMPLOYEES
12/23	84,676	872	1.0%	8,087
12/22	80,809	1,014	1.3%	8,658
12/21	90,310	(3,411)	—	10,425
12/20	87,844	(800)	—	11,395
12/19	68,748	314	0.5%	12,613
Annual Growth	5.3%	29.1%	—	(10.5%)

2023 Year-End Financials
Return on assets: 1.0%
Return on equity: 11.3%
Long-term debt ($ mil.): —
No. of shares ($ mil.): 1,245
Sales ($ mil.): 3,847
Dividends
  Yield: —
  Payout: 0.0%
Market value ($ mil.): 4,348

STOCK PRICE ($) FY Close	P/E High/Low		PER SHARE ($) Earnings	Dividends	Book Value
12/23	3.49	6	2	0.70	0.00	6.49
12/22	1.34	2	1	0.81	0.01	5.60
12/21	1.40	—	—	(3.97)	0.04	5.24
12/20	3.16	—	—	(30.58)	0.00	327.22
12/19	6.50	1	0	6.11	0.00	325.02
Annual Growth	(14.4%)	—	—	(41.9%)	—	(62.4%)

PJSC Magnitogorsk Iron & Steel Works

EXECUTIVES
Sales Head, Alexey Kuzmin
Logistics Head, Pavel Kravchenko
Financial Resources Department Head, Maria Nikulina
Chief Executive Officer, Chairman, Director, Pavel V. Shilyaev
External Communications Deputy Chief Executive, Vladimir Ruga
Chief Information Technology Specialist, Vadim Feoktistov
Chief Legal Officer, Sergey Shepilov
Secretary, Pavel Chereshenkov
Production Deputy General Director, Oleg Shiryaev
Chairman, Victor F. Rashnikov
Independent Director, Valeriy Martsinovich
Independent Director, Tav Morgan
Independent Director, Nikolay Nikiforov
Security Director, Sergey Semenov
Corporate Matters and Social Programmes Director, Sergey V. Krivoshchekov
Economics Director, Andrey Eremin
Human Resources Director, Oleg Kiykov
Occupational Health, Industrial Safety and the Environment Director, Grigory Schurov
Director, Zumrud Kh. Rustamova
Director, Kirill Y. Liovin
Commercial Operations Director, Sergey Nenashev
Auditors : AO PricewaterhouseCoopers Audit

LOCATIONS
HQ: PJSC Magnitogorsk Iron & Steel Works
93 Kirova Street, Magnitogorsk, Chelyabinsk 455000
Phone: (7) 3519 24 40 09 Fax: (7) 3519 24 73 09
Web: www.mmk.ru

HISTORICAL FINANCIALS
Company Type: Public

Income Statement — FYE: December 31

	REVENUE ($mil)	NET INCOME ($mil)	NET PROFIT MARGIN	EMPLOYEES
12/21	11,869	3,118	26.3%	0
12/20	6,395	603	9.4%	56,609
12/19	7,566	850	11.2%	17,663
12/18	8,214	1,315	16.0%	0
12/17	7,546	1,184	15.7%	0
Annual Growth	12.0%	27.4%		

2021 Year-End Financials
Debt ratio: 9.9%
Return on equity: 57.2%
Cash ($ mil.): 843
Current Ratio: 1.86
Long-term debt ($ mil.): 528
No. of shares ($ mil.): 11,174
Dividends
  Yield: —
  Payout: 546.9%
Market value ($ mil.): —

POSCO Holdings Inc

POSCO is one of the largest steel producers in the world. The company has approximately 45.3 million tons of annual crude steel and stainless steel production capacity, including some 40.7 million tons of production capacity in Korea. The company exports a wide range of steel products including hot rolled sheets, plate, wire rod, cold rolled sheets, galvanized sheets, and stainless steel globally, earning worldwide recognition for its superb technology and excellent quality. Beyond steel, the company also engages in power generation, materials trading and resource development activities. POSCO's Pohang and Gwangyang plants in Korea are the largest steel facilities in the world by production. The company generates the majority of its sales Korea.

Operations
POSCO operates through four reportable operating segments ? a steel segment, a trading segment, a construction segment and a segment that contains operations of all other entities.

The steel segment (nearly 55% of revenue) includes production of steel products and sale of such products.

The trading segment (around 35% revenue) consists primarily of global trading activities and natural resources development activities of POSCO International. POSCO International exports and imports a wide range of steel products and commodities, including iron and steel, raw materials for steel production, non-ferrous metals, chemicals, automotive parts, machinery and plant equipment, electronics products, agricultural commodities, and textiles, that are both obtained from and supplied to POSCO, as well as between other suppliers and purchasers in Korea and overseas.

The construction segment (about 10% revenue) includes planning, designing and construction of industrial plants, civil engineering projects and commercial and

Strategy

Power's value creation strategy is focused upon three levers:

OpCo Organic. Capitalize on significant past investments to drive higher organic earnings growth; Enhance communications to provide greater visibility of earnings to the market;

OpCo M&A. Augment earnings and value through acquisitions and associated synergies; Exit businesses that do not meet return thresholds; and

Power Company Level. Create value through investment platforms; Create and realize value from standalone businesses; Return capital to shareholders; and Enhance communications to allow the market to measure value creation.

EXECUTIVES

Chairman, Director, Paul Desmarais
Deputy Chairman, Director, Andre Desmarais
Vice-Chairman, Michel Plessis-Belair
Vice-Chairman, Amaury de Seze
President, Chief Executive Officer, Director, Robert Jeffrey Orr
Executive Vice President, Chief Financial Officer, Gregory D. Tretiak
Executive Vice President, Claude Genereux
Senior Vice President, Olivier Desmarais
Senior Vice President, Paul Desmarais III
Senior Vice President, Paul C. Genest
Vice President, Controller, Denis Le Vasseur
Vice President, Henry Yuhong Liu
Vice President, Richard Pan
Vice President, Pierre Piche
Human Resources Vice President, Administration Vice President, Luc Reny
Assistant General Counsel, Edouard Vo-Quang
Vice President, General Counsel, Secretary, Stephane Lemay
Lead Director, Director, Anthony R. Graham
Director, Pierre Beaudoin
Director, Marcel R. Coutu
Director, Gary A. Doer
Director, J. David A. Jackson
Director, Sharon MacLeod
Director, Paula B. Madoff
Director, Isabelle Marcoux
Director, Christian Noyer
Director, T. Timothy Ryan
Director, Siim A. Vanaselja
Auditors : Deloitte LLP

LOCATIONS

HQ: Power Corp. of Canada
751 Victoria Square, Montreal, Quebec H2Y 2J3
Phone: —
Web: www.powercorporation.com

2017 sales by geographic location

	% of total
Canada	42
US	19
Europe	39
Total	100

PRODUCTS/OPERATIONS

2017 sales

	% of total
Premium income, net	66
Net investment income	16
Fees income	16
Other revenue	2
Total	100

2017 sales

	% of total
Lifeco	91
IGM	6
Corporate	-
Other	3
Total	100

Selected Investments

Communications
  Gesca Ltée (newspaper publisher)
  Square Victoria Communications Group Inc.
  Square Victoria Digital Properties Inc.
Financial Services
  Great-West Lifeco Inc. (68%)
  The Canada Life Assurance Company
  Great-West Life & Annuity Insurance Company
  The Great-West Life Assurance Company
  London Life Insurance Company
  Putnam Investments, LLC
  IGM Financial Inc. (57%)
  Investment Planning Counsel (91%)
  Investors Group
  Mackenzie Financial Corporation
  Power Financial Corporation (66%)
  Victoria Square Ventures Inc.
Other
  Pergesa Holding S.A. (Switzerland)
  Eagle Creek Renewable Energy
  Lumenpulse Group
  Portage Ventures
  Wealthsimple
  Personal Capital

COMPETITORS

CLAYTON, DUBILIER & RICE, INC.
Canaccord Genuity Group Inc
EVERCORE INC.
FORESIGHT GROUP LLP
INVESTEC PLC
MS&AD INSURANCE GROUP HOLDINGS, INC.
NUMIS CORPORATION PLC
OCTOPUS INVESTMENTS LIMITED
PERMIRA ADVISERS LLP
WESTERN & SOUTHERN FINANCIAL GROUP, INC.

HISTORICAL FINANCIALS

Company Type: Public

Income Statement

FYE: December 31

	ASSETS ($mil)	NET INCOME ($mil)	INCOME AS % OF ASSETS	EMPLOYEES
12/22	542,469	38	0.0%	0
12/21	519,481	40	—	33,700
12/20	494,094	40	0.0%	29,900
12/19	366,498	39	0.0%	30,600
12/18	332,140	38	0.0%	0
Annual Growth	13.0%	0.2%	—	—

2022 Year-End Financials

Return on assets: —
Return on equity: 0.2%
Long-term debt ($ mil.): —
No. of shares ($ mil.): 612
Sales ($ mil.): 35,980
Dividends
Yield: —
Payout: 70.7%
Market value ($ mil.): 14,406

	STOCK PRICE ($) FY Close	P/E High/Low		PER SHARE ($) Earnings	Dividends	Book Value
12/22	23.53	11	8	2.07	1.46	29.01
12/21	33.08	8	5	3.35	1.44	30.74
12/20	22.99	9	4	2.42	1.72	28.02
12/19	25.71	10	7	1.94	1.23	28.83
12/18	17.96	9	6	2.03	1.10	26.62
Annual Growth	7.0%	—	—	0.5%	7.3%	2.2%

Prudential Plc

Prudential is a leading provider of life and health insurance products and asset management in Asia and Africa. It is focused on delivering profitable regular premium health and protection insurance products and fee-based earnings. In asset management, Eastspring manages $258.5 billion across some 10 markets in Asia and provides focused investment solutions to third-party retail and institutional clients as well as to its internally sourced life funds. About 18.6 million of Prudential's customers are in Asia. Prudential plc was formed in 1848 to offer life insurance and loans to the professional people, and is not affiliated with US insurance giant Prudential Financial.

Geographic Reach

Headquartered in London, Prudential is focused on Asia and Africa. In Asia, Prudential has operations in roughly 15 markets, including Hong Kong, Singapore, Indonesia, Malaysia, China, Thailand, Vietnam, Taiwan, Philippines, Cambodia, Laos, Myanmar, and India.

Hong Kong is Prudential's largest market by revenue at some 40%, followed by Singapore at more than 25%.

Sales and Marketing

Prudential distributes products primarily through extensive distribution networks, across digital, agency and bancassurance channels. With a diverse customer base, Prudential's five largest customers account for less than 30% of its revenue.

Financial Performance

The company's revenue for fiscal 2021 decreased to $26.5 billion compared from the prior year with $36.2 billion.

Net income for fiscal 2021 decreased to $3.0 billion compared from the prior year with $3.2 billion.

Cash held by the company at the end of fiscal 2021 decreased to $7.2 billion. Cash provided by operations and financing activities were $278 million and $1.3 billion, respectively. Cash used for investing activities was $1.3 billion, mainly for acquisitions.

Strategy

The company are developing the capacity to serve up to 50 million customers by 2025 through investing in its multi-channel distribution capabilities, applying digital capabilities to increase the efficiency of its operations and introducing products and services that allow the company to develop more diverse customer bases in its markets. Prudential continue to invest in its people and systems to ensure the company have the resources to deliver on its long-term growth strategy and to evolve its operating model to keep pace with its opportunities as an exclusively Asian and African business. Prudential seek to achieve this by: delivering profitable growth in a socially responsible way; digitalizing its products, services and experiences; and humanizing its company and advice channels.

Company Background

Knock knock. Who's there? It's the Man from the Pru -- one of Prudential plc's famous army of door-to-door salesmen and financial advisors. Or at least that was the story for around 150 years before the Pru went all modern in 2001. With the acquisition of Jackson National it entered the US in 1986 and (re)entered life insurance in Asia at the turn of the millennium. In 2019 Prudential demerged its UK and Europe business, M&G Prudential, to focus on the US and Asia.

HISTORY

Actually, prudence almost killed Prudential before it ever got started. Founded in 1848 as Prudential Mutual Assurance Investment and Loan Association, the firm initially insured middle-class customers. The Dickensian conditions of the working poor made them too risky for insurers. Unfortunately the company found few takers of the right sort, and by 1852 Prudential was in peril.

Two events saved Prudential: The House of Commons pressed for insurance coverage for all classes, and Prudential's own agents pushed for change. The company expanded into industrial insurance, a modest coverage for the working poor. In 1864, to quell criticism of the insurance industry, Prudential brought in independent auditors to confirm its soundness. This soon became a marketing tool and business took off. The Pru, as it came to be known, became the leading industrial insurer by the 1880s. It covered half the country's population by 1905. The firm's salesmen were known for making personal visits to customers (the "Man from the Pru" became a ubiquitous icon in the 1940s and was revived in 1997).

During the two world wars, Prudential boosted its reputation by honoring the policies of war victims when it could have legally denied them. Between wars the company added fire and accident insurance in Europe.

The 1980s were volatile for insurance companies, especially in the wake of Britain's financial deregulation in 1986. Therefore, in 1982, under the direction of CEO Brian Corby, the Pru reorganized product lines and in 1985 entered the real estate business. In 1986 it entered the US market by buying US-based Jackson National Life Insurance.

Prudential, which had considered selling Mercantile and General Reinsurance in the early 1990s (purchased in 1969), sold the reinsurer back to Swiss Re in 1996. It also formed Prudential Bank and created an Asian emerging-market investment fund that year.

Insurance regulators reprimanded the company for mis-selling financial products in 1997. In 1998 Jackson National bought a California savings and loan, enabling it to sell investment products in the US. Also that year the Pru sold its Australian and New Zealand businesses, and Prudential Bank launched its pioneering Internet bank Egg Banking.

In 1999 Prudential bought investment manager M&G Group. The company then changed its name to Prudential plc and began talks with the Prudential Insurance Company of America to resolve confusion of their similar names as they expanded into new markets. Also in 1999 the Pru joined forces with the Bank of China to offer pension and asset management in Hong Kong.

The company announced plans in 2000 to sell a chunk of its institutional fund management business as well as its traditional balanced pension business to Deutsche Bank. That year the company spun off 20% of Egg (it sold the rest in 2007).

Entering the Japanese life insurance market, Prudential bought Orico Life in 2001. Prudential's hopes of capturing the lucrative annuities market by acquiring American General were dashed that year as American General instead embraced American International Group, leaving the Pru with a $600 million break-up fee. To consolidate operations, the firm sold its general insurance business in 2001 to Swiss insurer Winterthur (a subsidiary of Credit Suisse).

In early 2006 Prudential rejected a takeover offer from larger rival Aviva valued at nearly $30 billion.

After helping oversee the shift in focus that brought the company growth in Asia and stability during the 2008 economic downturn, CEO Mark Tucker stepped down at the end of September 2009. The company chose CFO Tidjane Thiam to replace him. Thiam, a native of Ivory Coast, became the first black CEO of a FTSE 100 company.

In early 2010 the company expanded its operations in Singapore by acquiring United Overseas Bank's life insurance unit for S$428 million ($307 million). Along with becoming owner of UOB Life Assurance Ltd., Prudential entered into an agreement through which UOB sells Prudential's life, accident, and health insurance policies for 12 years at the bank's more than 400 branches in Singapore, Indonesia, and Thailand, giving Prudential a greater presence in those markets. In 2011 Prudential targeted the business of Singapore's class of "rising rich" individuals as an important area for growth.

Prudential made a splashy bid on AIG's Hong Kong-based American International Assurance (AIA) business in 2010. The $35.5 billion deal ($25 billion in cash, $8.5 billion in securities, and $2 billion in stock) would have made Prudential the largest life insurer in Hong Kong and allowed AIG to pay off a chunk of its debt to the US government. However, Prudential's shareholders were not impressed and raised a ruckus over the deal. To appease them, Prudential attempted to reduce its offer to $30 billion -- which AIG coolly refused -- and then simply withdrew its entire offer.

EXECUTIVES

Chief Executive Officer, Executive Director, Anil Wadhwani
Chief Financial Officer, Executive Director, James Turner
Chief Risk Officer, Chief Compliance Officer, Avnish Kalra
Human Resources Director, Jolene Chen
Secretary, Tom Clarkson
Senior Independent Non-Executive Director, Philip J. Remnant
Independent Non-Executive Director, Chua Sock Koong
Independent Non-Executive Director, Ming Lu
Independent Non-Executive Director, Jeremy Anderson
Independent Non-Executive Director, David Law
Independent Non-Executive Director, Thomas R. Watjen
Independent Non-Executive Director, Amy Yip
Independent Non-Executive Director, Jeanette Wong
Independent Non-Executive Director, Arijit Basu
Independent Non-Executive Director, George Sartorel
Independent Non-Executive Director, Claudia Suessmuth Dyckerhoff
Auditors : KPMG LLP

LOCATIONS

HQ: Prudential Plc
13th Floor, One International Finance Centre, 1 Harbour View Street, Central,
Phone: (852) 2918 6300
Web: www.prudentialplc.com

2017 Sales

	% of total
US	39
UK and Europe	33
Asia	28
Other	-
Total	100

COMPETITORS

AMERICAN INTERNATIONAL GROUP, INC.

AVIVA PLC
AXA
Allianz SE
MAPFRE, SA
NIPPON LIFE INSURANCE COMPANY
PRUDENTIAL FINANCIAL, INC.
RSA INSURANCE GROUP PLC
STANDARD LIFE ABERDEEN PLC
Sampo Oyj

HISTORICAL FINANCIALS
Company Type: Public

Income Statement — FYE: December 31

	ASSETS ($mil)	NET INCOME ($mil)	INCOME AS % OF ASSETS	EMPLOYEES
12/22	165,942	998	0.6%	14,681
12/21	199,102	(2,042)	—	14,486
12/20	704,322	2,890	0.4%	17,256
12/19	599,818	1,034	0.2%	24,676
12/18	649,418	3,843	0.6%	28,206
Annual Growth	(28.9%)	(28.6%)	—	(15.1%)

2022 Year-End Financials
Return on assets: 0.5%
Return on equity: 5.8%
Long-term debt ($ mil.): —
No. of shares ($ mil.): 2,749
Sales ($ mil.): (-8,190)
Dividends
Yield: —
Payout: 96.4%
Market value ($ mil.): 75,561

	STOCK PRICE ($) FY Close	P/E High/Low	PER SHARE ($) Earnings	Dividends	Book Value
12/22	27.48	100 50	0.37	0.35	6.17
12/21	34.43	— —	(0.78)	0.32	6.22
12/20	36.93	1 0	111.36	5.83	10.92
12/19	38.09	2 1	40.01	6.47	9.89
12/18	35.37	43 29	1.49	1.28	8.49
Annual Growth	(6.1%)	— —	(29.7%)	(27.6%)	(7.7%)

PT Bank Mandiri Persero Tbk

Bank Mandiri has a mandate for banking in Indonesia. Boasting nearly $70 billion in assets, the bank is the country's largest lender and commercial bank by assets, and serves consumers and businesses through nearly 2,400 branches and some 17,340 ATMs throughout Indonesia. The group's other products and services include trade finance, Islamic banking, and investment banking through subsidiary Mandiri Sekuritas. AXA Mandiri Financial Services (a joint venture of Bank Mandiri and insurance titan AXA) offers financial advisory services, including wealth planning and insurance. The government owns 60% of Bank Mandiri.

Operations
Bank Mandiri generated roughly 69% of its total operating income from net interest income (mostly from a mix of wholesale and retail loans) in 2014. Another 16% of its total operating income came from other fees and commissions (mostly consisting of administration fees, transfer/retail transaction fees, and credit card fees), while about 5% came from net premium income from insurance sales. The rest came from foreign exchange gains, gains from bond appreciation and sales, and other sources of income.

About 53% of Bank Mandiri's loan portfolio was evenly split between corporate and commercial loans at the end of 2014, while another 11% of the portfolio was made up of small business loans. Another 12% of the portfolio was made up of consumer loans (two-thirds of which were mortgages and auto loans, with some credit card, payroll, and home equity loans as well), while 7% of the loan portfolio was tied to the group's fast-growing micro loan business.

Geographic Reach
Nearly 99% of Bank Mandiri's operating income came from business in Indonesia. The rest came from operations in Asia (Singapore, Hong Kong, Timor Leste, Shanghai, and Malaysia), Western Europe (England), and the Cayman Islands.

Financial Performance
Note: Growth rates may differ after conversion to US dollars. This analysis uses financials from the company's annual report.

Bank Mandiri's annual operating income has nearly doubled since 2010 to a record 56.9 trillion Rp ($4.6 billion) at the end of 2014 thanks to aggressive branch expansion and loan business growth. Indeed, its loan assets have more than doubled since 2010, growing from 246.2 trillion Rp ($27 billion) to 530 trillion Rp ($42.6 billion) at the end of 2014.

Strategy
Bank Mandiri has grown its business through an aggressive branch expansion over the past several years. The group has more than doubled the size of its domestic branch network since 2009, from 1,095 branches to more than 2,380 branches by late 2015.

The group also seek growth through the acquisition of other banks as well as insurance, multifinance companies, and other financial services firms.

Company Background
In 2009, Bank Mandiri purchased a 51% stake in automotive financing company Tunas Financindo, which helped the company tap further into the consumer credit market.

Bank Mandiri was formed in the 1998 government-mandated merger of Bank Bumi Daya, Bank Dagang Negara, Bank Ekspor Impor, and Bank Pembangunan Indonesia. The predecessor banks were among dozens taken over by the government in the wake of the 1997-1998 Asian financial crisis.

Auditors : Kantor Akuntan Publik Tanudiredja, Wibisana, Rintis & Rekan

LOCATIONS
HQ: PT Bank Mandiri Persero Tbk
Plaza Mandiri, Jl. Jenderal Gatot Subroto Kav. 36-38, Jakarta 12190

Phone: (62) 21 5265045 **Fax:** (62) 21 5274477
Web: www.bankmandiri.co.id

2014 Sales
	% of total
Indonesia	99
Asia	1
Other	-
Total	100

PRODUCTS/OPERATIONS
2014 sales
	% of total
Micro and retail	34
Treasury, financial institution and SAM	26
Commercial and business	10
Consumer	10
Corporate	6
Subsidiary-Sharia	6
Subsidiary- other than Sharia and insurance	5
Subsidiary-insurance	2
Institutional banking	1
Head Office	-
Total	100

Selected Subsidiaries & Affiliates
PT AXA Mandiri Financial Services (49%, insurance)
Bank Mandiri (Europe) Limited (UK, commercial banking)
PT Bank Syariah Mandiri (BSM) (99.99%, Islamic banking)
PT Bumi Daya Plaza (93%, property management)
PT Mandiri Sekuritas (96%, securities)
PT Usaha Gedung Bank Dagang Negara (99%, property management)

COMPETITORS
CANARA BANK
EASTERN BANK CORPORATION
FIRST FINANCIAL CORPORATION
HSBC USA, INC.
MALAYAN BANKING BERHAD
PT. BANK CENTRAL ASIA TBK
SHINSEI BANK, LIMITED
Shanghai Pudong Development Bank Co., Ltd.
TURKIYE GARANTI BANKASI ANONIM SIRKETI
YAPI VE KREDI BANKASI ANONIM SIRKETI

HISTORICAL FINANCIALS
Company Type: Public

Income Statement — FYE: December 31

	REVENUE ($mil)	NET INCOME ($mil)	NET PROFIT MARGIN	EMPLOYEES
12/23	11,336	3,562	31.4%	38,965
12/22	9,629	2,658	27.6%	38,176
12/21	9,025	1,967	21.8%	37,840
12/20	8,318	1,222	14.7%	38,247
12/19	8,642	1,982	22.9%	39,065
Annual Growth	7.0%	15.8%	—	(0.1%)

2023 Year-End Financials
Debt ratio: —
Return on equity: 22.4%
Cash ($ mil.): 15,886
Current Ratio: —
Long-term debt ($ mil.): —
No. of shares ($ mil.): 93,333
Dividends
Yield: —
Payout: 1341.2%
Market value ($ mil.): 1,468,133

	STOCK PRICE ($) FY Close	P/E High/Low	PER SHARE ($) Earnings	Dividends	Book Value
12/23	15.73	0 0	0.04	0.51	0.18
12/22	12.72	0 0	0.03	0.33	0.29
12/21	9.88	0 0	0.02	0.21	0.29
12/20	8.90	0 0	0.01	0.54	0.21
12/19	11.10	0 0	0.02	0.24	0.22
Annual Growth	9.1%	— —	15.8%	21.1%	(5.1%)

PT Telekomunikasi Indonesia (Persero) TBK

Telkom is the largest telecommunications company in Indonesia. The primary provider of telecommunication services in Indonesia, PT Telekomunikasi Indonesia -- more commonly known as Telkom -- operates around 9 million fixed lines. Its mobile service subsidiary, Telkomsel, is one of the largest Indonesian cellular operator with some 9 million subscribers. Telkom also offers leased lines and data transport services, as well as data and Internet services. The company is facing increased competition from other telecommunications service providers, due to regulatory reforms, yet it continues to grow, largely on the strength of cellular services and Internet services. The Indonesian government owns over 50%% of Telkom. Vast majority of its sales come from Indonesia.

Operations
Telkom operates through five business segments. The Mobile segment, which generated around 45% of sales, is the company's biggest. It comprises mobile broadband services, mobile digital services that include financial services, video on demand (VOD), music, gaming, IoT solutions, big data analytics, digital ads, and mobile legacy services such as mobile voice and SMS. The Enterprise segment, which accounts for more than 20% of revenue, mainly comprises ICT and digital platform that covers enterprise-grade connectivity services, including satellite, IT services, data center and cloud, business process outsourcing, and other adjacent services. The Wholesale and International Business (WIB) segment (over 15%) comprises wholesale telecommunications carrier services, international business, tower business, and infrastructure and network management services. The Consumer segment (about 15% of revenue) comprises fixed voice services, fixed broadband services, IPTV, and related consumer digital services.

In all, data, internet and information technology service revenues generated over 55% of sales, Indihome with about 20%, and telephone revenues with more than 10%.

Geographic Reach
Headquartered in Bandung, West Java in Indonesia, Telkom has an extensive reach in its neighborhood and beyond. It has operations in Singapore, Hong Kong, Timor Leste, Australia, Macau, Taiwan, the US, Malaysia, Myanmar, and Saudi Arabia. Approximately 95% of sales were generated from Indonesia, while the rest were generated from foreign countries.

Sales and Marketing
Telkom serves approximately 176 million cellular customers through its mobile segment. Enterprise segment caters corporate customers, small and medium business (SMBs), and government institutions, while WIB segment serves customers including other licensed operators, service providers, and digital players at domestic and overseas.

The company's marketing expenses were Rp 3.6 trillion, Rp 3.5 trillion, and Rp 3.4 trillion for the years 2021, 2020, and 2019, respectively.

Financial Performance
The company's revenue for fiscal 2021 increased to Rp 143.2 trillion compared from the prior year with Rp 136.4 trillion.

Net income for fiscal 2021 increased to Rp 34.1 trillion compared from the prior year with Rp 29.9 trillion.

Cash held by the company at the end of fiscal 2021 increased to Rp 18.2 trillion. Cash provided by operations was Rp59.0 trillion while cash used for investing and financing activities were Rp35.9 trillion and Rp 22.2 trillion, respectively.

Strategy
As the largest telecommunications company in Indonesia, Telkom intend to become the preferred digital telecommunications company in Indonesia that contributes to the prosperity and competitiveness of Indonesia while creating and delivering value to its stakeholders. The company intend to rapidly build sustainable digital infrastructure and smart platforms that will be competitively priced, affordable, and accessible to a wide range of customers. Telkom also nurture best-in-class digital talents who will contribute to the development of Indonesia's digital capabilities and increase the penetration of digital technologies and services, as well as improve our customers' experience through the development of a comprehensive digital ecosystem.

The company have been strengthening its digital capabilities and intend to further expand its leadership in connectivity-driven business and provide end-to-end digital experience its customers. The company have been enhancing our digital connectivity offering to businesses, invested in its digital platform, and diversified its digital service offering as Telekom pursue maximizing value to its customers and stakeholders through cash flow optimization, value creation and the enhancement of synergies. To that end, the company have been expanding the backbone network infrastructure and broadband network access throughout Indonesia and expanded and improved its offering of digital services.

Mergers and Acquisitions
In 2022, PT Telkom Indonesia Tbk (Telkom) strengthens its B2B IT Digital Services business through the acquisition of PT Sigma Cipta Caraka (TelkomSigma) with a capital investment of Rp 2.6 trillion. This equity participation is in the context of strengthening and transforming the company in accordance with the strategic transformation plan which is part of the group strategy that makes TelkomSigma a direct subsidiary of Telkom, which was previously a subsidiary of Telkom Metra. This is one of the strategic initiatives to accelerate TelkomSigma to become a B2B IT Digital Service Leader.

EXECUTIVES

President Director, Director, Ririek Adriansyah
Finance Director, Director, Heri Supriadi
Network, Information Technology and Solution Director, Director, Herlan Wijanarko
Consumer Service Director, Director, F. M. Venusiana R.
Digital Business Director, Director, Muhamad Fajrin Rasyid
Strategic Portfolio Director, Director, Budi Setyawan Wijaya
Wholesale and International Service Director, Director, Dian Rachmawan
Human Capital Management Director, Enterprise and Business Service Director, Director, Edi Witjara
Secretary, Andi Setiawan
Auditors : Purwantono, Sungkoro & Surja

LOCATIONS

HQ: PT Telekomunikasi Indonesia (Persero) TBK
Jl. Japati No. 1, Bandung 40133
Phone: (62) 22 4521404   Fax: (62) 22 7206757
Web: www.telkom.co.id

2016 Sales

	% of total
Indonesia	98
Foreign countries	2
Total	100

PRODUCTS/OPERATIONS

2016 Sales

	% of total
Data, internet and information technology service revenues	51
Telephone revenues	40
Interconnection revenues	3
Network revenues	1
Other revenues	5
Total	100

2016 Sales

	% of total
Personal	54
Corporate	36
Home	8
Others	2
Total	100

COMPETITORS

HUGHES NETWORK SYSTEMS, LLC
IBASIS, INC.
LEVEL 3 PARENT, LLC
ROSTELEKOM, PAO
SAUDI TELECOM COMPANY
SINGAPORE TELECOMMUNICATIONS LIMITED
Shaw Communications Inc
TDS TELECOMMUNICATIONS CORPORATION
TELSTRA CORPORATION LIMITED
UNITEK GLOBAL SERVICES, INC.

HISTORICAL FINANCIALS
Company Type: Public

Income Statement — FYE: December 31

	REVENUE ($mil)	NET INCOME ($mil)	NET PROFIT MARGIN	EMPLOYEES
12/21	10,053	1,746	17.4%	23,756
12/20	9,740	1,502	15.4%	25,348
12/19	9,777	1,375	14.1%	24,272
12/18	9,091	1,237	13.6%	24,071
12/17	9,462	1,632	17.2%	24,065
Annual Growth	1.5%	1.7%	—	(0.3%)

2021 Year-End Financials
Debt ratio: —
Return on equity: 22.2%
Cash ($ mil.): 2,689
Current Ratio: 0.89
Long-term debt ($ mil.): 2,549
No. of shares ($ mil.): 99,062
Dividends
 Yield: 5.7%
 Payout: 4989.1%
Market value ($ mil.): 2,871,814

	STOCK PRICE ($) FY Close	P/E High/Low		PER SHARE ($) Earnings	Dividends	Book Value
12/21	28.99	0	0	0.02	1.68	0.09
12/20	23.52	0	0	0.02	0.80	0.07
12/19	28.50	0	0	0.01	1.16	0.07
12/18	26.21	0	0	0.01	1.21	0.07
12/17	32.22	0	0	0.02	0.87	0.07
Annual Growth	(2.6%)	—	—	1.7%	18.0%	5.8%

PTT Exploration & Production Public Co Ltd

PTT Exploration and Production (PTTEP) was established for the sole purpose of searching for gold -- black gold, that is. The company engages in petroleum exploration and production, with more than 40 active projects in Algeria, Australia, Bahrain, Bangladesh, Cambodia, Egypt, Indonesia, Iran, Malaysia, Myanmar, New Zealand, Oman, Thailand, and Vietnam. The company has proved reserves of 846 million barrels of oil equivalent. Its end products include crude oil, natural gas, liquid propane gas, and condensate. PTTEP also operates natural gas pipelines. In 2014 it bought Hess' oil and gas assets in Thailand for $1 billion. PTTEP was founded in 1985; PTT Public Co. owns 66% of its shares.

EXECUTIVES

Chief Executive Officer, Director, Montri Rawanchaikul
Finance Senior Vice President, Orachon Ouiyamapun
Accounting Senior Vice President, Sermsak Satchawannakul
Human Resources, Corporate Affairs, and Assurance Group Executive Vice President, Chayong Borisuitsawat
Strategy and Business Development Group Executive Vice President, Natruedee Khositaphai
Operations Support Group Executive Vice President, Suksant Ongvises
Finance and Accounting Group Executive Vice President, Sumrid Sumneing
, Geosciences, Subsurface, and Exploration Group Executive Vice President, Piya Sukhumpanumet
Production Asset Group Executive Vice President, Nirandorn Rojanasomsith
Engineering and Development Group Acting Executive Vice President, Kanita Sartwattayu
Financial Accounting Vice President, Vanasanan Boonyalerdlak
Taxes Vice President, Yasa Vudhivorn
Capital Market and Financial Planning Vice President, Nuchanong Sangkeaw
Accounting Policy and Solutions Vice President, Pratamaporn Deesrinthum
Vice President, Anutra Bunnag
Managerial Accounting Vice President, Sakchai Sarawek
Insurance Vice President, Netrsuda Pokkasorn
Senior Vice President, Corporate Secretary, Maneeya Srisukhumboworncha
Chairman, Independent Director, Krairit Euchukanonchai
Vice-Chairman, Tanarat Ubol
Independent Director, Veerathai Santiprabhob
Independent Director, Nimit Suwannarat
Independent Director, Achapom Charuchinda
Independent Director, Pitipan Tepartimargorn
Independent Director, Dechapiwat Na songkhla
Independent Director, Bundhit Eua-arporn
Independent Director, Angkarat Priebjrivat
Independent Director, Penchun Jarikasem
Director, Wattanapong Kurovat
Director, Auttapol Rerkpiboon
Director, Patchara Anuntasilpa
Director, Atikom Terbsiri
Auditors : PricewaterhouseCoopers ABAS Ltd.

LOCATIONS

HQ: PTT Exploration & Production Public Co Ltd
555/1 Energy Complex Building A, 6th & 19th - 36th Floor, Vibhavadi-Rangsit Road, Chatuchak, Bangkok 10900
Phone: (66) 2 537 4000   Fax: (66) 2 537 4444
Web: www.pttep.com

2013 Sales
	% of total
Southeast Asia	
Thailand	72
Other countries	18
North America	4
Middle East, Africa & other regions	6
Total	100

COMPETITORS

COMPAÃ'IA ESPAÃ'OLA DE PETROLEOS SAU
CPC CORPORATION, TAIWAN
ENI SPA
HELLENIC PETROLEUM S.A.
IDEMITSU KOSAN CO.,LTD.
KUNLUN ENERGY COMPANY LIMITED
QATARGAS OPERATING COMPANY LIMITED
RAS GAS COMPANY LIMITED
STATE OIL LIMITED
TransAtlantic Petroleum Corp

HISTORICAL FINANCIALS
Company Type: Public

Income Statement — FYE: December 31

	REVENUE ($mil)	NET INCOME ($mil)	NET PROFIT MARGIN	EMPLOYEES
12/22	9,838	2,052	20.9%	0
12/21	7,074	1,171	16.6%	0
12/20	5,592	757	13.5%	0
12/19	6,674	1,638	24.5%	0
12/18	5,461	1,119	20.5%	0
Annual Growth	15.9%	16.4%	—	—

2022 Year-End Financials
Debt ratio: 0.3%
Return on equity: 16.0%
Cash ($ mil.): 3,540
Current Ratio: 1.72
Long-term debt ($ mil.): 2,810
No. of shares ($ mil.): 3,969
Dividends
 Yield: —
 Payout: 0.0%
Market value ($ mil.): 41,685

	STOCK PRICE ($) FY Close	P/E High/Low		PER SHARE ($) Earnings	Dividends	Book Value
12/22	10.50	1	0	0.52	0.37	3.41
12/21	7.25	1	1	0.29	0.25	3.15
12/20	7.11	2	1	0.19	0.31	2.98
12/19	8.35	1	1	0.39	0.33	3.02
12/18	7.19	1	1	0.27	0.24	3.04
Annual Growth	9.9%	—	—	17.9%	11.3%	2.9%

PTT Global Chemical Public Co Ltd

PTT Global Chemical (formerly PTT Chemical) is the leading producer of petrochemicals in Asia. It has an olefins and aromatics production capacity of 8.7 million tons per year and petroleum production capacity of 280,000 barrels per day. PTT Global Chemical also produces chemicals used to make adhesives, paint, rubber, and solvents and is Thailand's largest producer of olefins. It is also an investor in US-based NatureWorks. PTT Chemical was formed in 2005 when oil and gas company PTT acquired National Petrochemical Public Co. Ltd. and combined it with its Thai Olefins unit. In 2011 PTT Chemical merged with PTT Aromatics and Refining to form integrated petrochemical and refining company PTT Global Chemical.

EXECUTIVES

President, Chief Executive Officer, Secretary, Executive Director, Kongkrapan Intarajang
Green Chemicals Business Unit Chief Operating Officer, Value Added Products Chief Operating Officer, Green Chemicals Business Unit Acting Senior Vice President, Value Added Products Acting Senior Vice President, Varit Namwong

Base and Intermediate Chemicals Chief Operating Officer, Toasaporn Boonyapipat
Center of Excellence Chief Operating Officer, Wiboon Chuchepchunkamon
International Business Chief Operating Officer, Narongsak Jivakanun
Accounting Executive Vice President, Finance Executive Vice President, Pattaralada Sa-Ngasang
Corporate Strategy Executive Vice President, Warawan Tippawanich
Marketing, Commercial and Supply Chain Executive Vice President, Saroj Putthammawong
Organizational Effectiveness Executive Vice President, Pirun Krimwongrut
Polymers Business Unit Executive Vice President, Pornsak Mongkoltrirat
Olefins Executive Vice President, Pukpong Wungrattanasopon
Specialy Business Senior Vice President, Mergers & Acquisitions Senior Vice President, Specialy Business Acting Senior Vice President, Mergers & Acquisitions Acting Senior Vice President, Rattiya Chandavasu
Internal Audit Senior Vice President, Amorn Putiphrawan
Technical, Engineering and Maintenance Senior Vice President, Jeeranee Pimthanothai
Corporate Secretary and Legal Senior Vice President, Pilasphan Udomjarumanee
Refinery Senior Vice President, Ratchada Sawasdirak
Aromatics Senior Vice President, Anutin Chuaypen
EO-Based Performance Business Unit Senior Vice President, Vitaya Pinmuangngarm
Phenol Business Unit Senior Vice President, Paisarn Sarapee
Utilities Senior Vice President, Supasit Tongsupachok
Downstream Strategy and Business Development Senior Vice President, Chananchida Wiboonkanarak
CAPEX Excellence Senior Vice President, Khomson Piyawattanaviroj
Quality, Safety, Occupational Health and Environment Senior Vice President, Sakesiri Piyavej
Transformation Excellence Senior Vice President, Chatsuda Kanjanarat
Procurement Senior Vice President, Paranai Waitayasewee
Science and Innovation Senior Vice President, Long Term Innovation and Corporate Venture Capital Senior Vice President, Science and Innovation Acting Senior Vice President, Long Term Innovation and Corporate Venture Capital Acting Senior Vice President, Kamel Ramdani
Sustainability Executive Vice President, Chaya Chandavasu
US Second Home Senior Vice President, Panod Awaiwanond
Chairman, Independent Non-Executive Director, Piyasvasti Amranand
Independent Non-Executive Director, Watanan Petersik
Independent Non-Executive Director, Somkit Lertpaithoon
Independent Non-Executive Director, Nithi Chungcharoen
Independent Non-Executive Director, Pakorn Nilprapunt
Independent Non-Executive Director, Don Wasantapruek
Independent Non-Executive Director, Apisak Tantivorawong
Independent Non-Executive Director, Grisada Boonrach
Non-Executive Director, Sarawut Kaewtathip
Non-Executive Director, Noppadol Pinsupa
Non-Executive Director, Chansin Treenuchagron
Non-Executive Director, Disathat Panyarachun
Non-Executive Director, Peekthong Thongyai
Non-Executive Director, Pantip Sripimol
Auditors : Deloitte Touche Tohmatsu Jaiyos Audit Co., Ltd.

LOCATIONS

HQ: PTT Global Chemical Public Co Ltd
555/1 Energy Complex, Building A, 14th - 18th Floor, Vibhavadi Rangsit Road, Chatuchak, Bangkok 10900
Phone: (66) 2 265 8400   **Fax:** (66) 2 265 8500
Web: www.pttgcgroup.com

PRODUCTS/OPERATIONS

Selected Businesses
Aromatics
Eo-Based Performance
Green Chemicals
High Volume Specialties
Olefins
Polymers
Refinery & Shared Facilities

HISTORICAL FINANCIALS

Company Type: Public

Income Statement — FYE: December 31

	REVENUE ($mil)	NET INCOME ($mil)	NET PROFIT MARGIN	EMPLOYEES
12/21	14,140	1,356	9.6%	0
12/20	10,999	6	0.1%	0
12/19	13,858	392	2.8%	0
12/18	16,032	1,238	7.7%	6,427
12/17	13,503	1,279	9.5%	6,334
Annual Growth	1.2%	1.5%	—	—

2021 Year-End Financials
Debt ratio: 1.1%
Return on equity: 15.0%
Cash ($ mil.): 1,676
Current Ratio: 1.41
Long-term debt ($ mil.): 6,777
No. of shares ($ mil.): 4,508
Dividends
  Yield: —
  Payout: 0.0%
Market value ($ mil.): —

PTT Public Co Ltd

Established on 1978, PTT is a fully integrated national petroleum and petrochemical company that operates through investment in subsidiaries, joint ventures, and associates (PTT Group), which are engaged in exploration and production, liquefied natural gas, petrochemical and refining, oil and retail, power and utilities, coal and service businesses. Gas Business covers supplying natural gas to both domestic and international, industrial factories and petroleum service stations. PTT also has Petroleum Exploration and Production that focuses on exploration of natural gas, condensate and crude oil (in Thailand and elsewhere).

Operations

PTT's major segments involve: Upstream petroleum and Natural gas; Downstream petroleum; and the new business and infrastructure.

The upstream petroleum and natural gas segment involve the petroleum exploration and production business that operate and invests with leading petroleum exploration and production companies both domestically and overseas. The natural gas segment conducts natural gas business including procurement, natural pipeline transmission, distribution, and natural gas separation. Products from the natural gas separation plants are used as feedstock for the petrochemical industry as fuel in the household, transportation, and industry sectors. The segment also involves the company's coal business.

The downstream petroleum business involves the company's oil and retail, international trading, and petrochemical and refining.

Lastly, the new business and infrastructure group was established to develop new businesses in accordance with the company's "Powering Life with Future Energy and Beyond" vision, that focuses in sectors such as renewable energy, energy storage, EV value chain and hydrogen business.

Oil products account for about 60% of the company's sales, followed by gas products and petrochemical products at about 20% each.

Geographic Reach

PTT's operates globally but has bulk of it domestically in Thailand, with about 60% of the company's revenues. Its overseas projects are located in Southeast Asia, Australia, America, and Africa.

Sales and Marketing

PTT conducts petroleum exploration and production businesses in both domestic and international. The target markets are both domestic and overseas where the company has invested. In 2021, the total sales ratio of natural gas to liquid was 64% : 36%. PTTEP sells its outputs from domestic and regional projects primarily to the Thai market through PTT, the major buyer and processor of all products. PTT then turns the processed products to power sector, petrochemical sector, transportation sector, industry sector, and household sector.

The marketing of petroleum products varies with their characteristics and field location, which results in differentiation of the market and sales price structures.

Financial Performance

PTT's performance for the past five years has fluctuated with a downward trend in the first half, then increasing year-over-year from 2020 and ending with 2022 as its highest performing year over the period.

The company's revenue for 2022 increased by Baht 1.1 trillion to Baht 3.4 trillion, as compared to 2021's revenue of Baht 2.3 billion.

However, PTT's net income for fiscal year end 2022 decreased to Baht 91.2 billion, as compared to Baht 108.4 billion.

PTT held Baht 340.1 billion by the end of the year. Operating activities provided Baht 164,916 to the coffers. Investing activities and financing activities used Baht 58,760 and Baht 69,958, respectively. Main cash uses were for cash payment of property, plant and equipment and repayment of long-term borrowings.

Strategy

PTTEP, moreover, has invested in new business outside petroleum exploration and production field in pursuit of long-term growth. These investments focus on the development of its current technologies and R&D capabilities that support its current business. PTTEP has urgently expanded its artificial intelligence (AI) and robotics businesses, its renewable energy business, and new energy business. For example, it has invested in AI & Robotics Ventures Company Limited (ARV) to develop a platform of AI and robotic innovations. Not only that, ARV aims to become a tech leader in AI and robotics field, but it also intends to provide forums where young talents are able to apply their concepts and technologies for the commercial market in a systematic manner and make positive changes to the world.

Mergers and Acquisitions

In late 2021, PTTEP is looking to further expand investment in the Sharjah Emirate of the United Arab Emirates (UAE) by acquiring 25% participating interest in the Concession Area C onshore the Emirate of Sharjah, from Eni Sharjah B.V. The investment aligns with PTTEP's strategic focus on petroleum prolific area in the Middle East. Upon the completion of the acquisition, Eni Sharjah B.V. (Operator) will hold 50% participating interest while SNOC will hold 25% and PTTEP MENA 25% accordingly. Terms were not disclosed.

Company Background

Thailand, which created PTT to secure energy supplies during the oil crunch of the late 1970s, sold a third of the company in a 2001 IPO.

In 2008, as part of PTT's energy diversification drive, the company opened the world's largest NGV (natural gas vehicle) gas station in Thailand to respond to the growing number of NGV vehicles in the country.

EXECUTIVES

Secretary, President, Chief Executive Officer, Director, Auttapol Rerkpiboon
Chief Financial Officer, Pannalin Mahawongtikul
Upstream Petroleum and Gas Business Group Chief Operating Officer, Atikom Terbsiri
Downstream Petroleum Business Group Chief Operating Officer, Kris Imsang
Chief New Business and Infrastructure Officer, Noppadol Pinsupa
Innovation and New Ventures Senior Executive Vice President, Buranin Rattanasombat
Engineering and Infrastructure Senior Executive Vice President, Chansak Chuenchom
Gas Business Unit Senior Executive Vice President, Wuttikorn Stithit
Corporate Strategy Senior Executive Vice President, Terdkiat Prommool
Downstream Business Group Alignmen Senior Executive Vice President, Peekthong Thongyai
International Trading Business Unit Senior Executive Vice President, Disathat Panyarachun
Organization Management and Sustainability Senior Executive Vice President, Suchat Ramarch
Office Senior Executive Vice President, Office General Counsel, Peangpanor Boonklum
Chairman, Independent Director, Thosaporn Sirisumphand
Independent Director, Teerawat Boonyawat
Independent Director, Jatuporn Buruspat
Independent Director, Narongdech Srukhosit
Independent Director, Chayodom Sabhasri
Independent Director, Danucha Pichayanan
Independent Director, Krisada Chinavicharana
Independent Director, Krishna Boonyachai
Independent Director, Don Wasantapruek
Independent Director, Rungroj Sangkram
Independent Director, Payong Srivanich
Director, Chayotid Kridakon
Director, Premrutai Vinaiphat
Director, Phongsthorn Thavisin
Auditors : EY Office Limited

LOCATIONS

HQ: PTT Public Co Ltd
 555 Vibhavadi-Rangsit Road, Chatuchak, Bangkok 10900
Phone: (66) 2 537 2000   **Fax:** (66) 2 537 3498 9
Web: www.pttplc.com

PRODUCTS/OPERATIONS

2011 Sales

	% of total
International trading	53
Oil	21
Natural gas	16
Exploration & production	6
Petrochemical	3
Coal	1
Other	—
Total	100

Selected Subsidiaries and Affiliates:
PetroAsia (Huizhou) Co., Ltd. (25%)
PTT Exploration and Production Public Co., Ltd. (66%)
PTT Mart Co., Ltd. (49%)
PTT Natural Gas Distribution Co., Ltd. (58%)
Star Petroleum Refining Co., Ltd. (36%)
Thai Lube Blending Co., Ltd. (49%)
Thai Oil Plc. (50%)

COMPETITORS

China National Petroleum Corporation
ECOPETROL S A
EXTERRAN CORPORATION
GAIL (INDIA) LIMITED
IDEMITSU KOSAN CO.,LTD.
INDIAN OIL CORPORATION LIMITED
ISRAMCO, INC.
QEP RESOURCES, INC.
SURGUTNEFTEGAZ, PAO
THAI OIL PUBLIC COMPANY LIMITED

HISTORICAL FINANCIALS
Company Type: Public

Income Statement — FYE: December 31

	REVENUE ($mil)	NET INCOME ($mil)	NET PROFIT MARGIN	EMPLOYEES
12/22	97,464	2,639	2.7%	0
12/21	68,110	3,267	4.8%	0
12/20	53,967	1,261	2.3%	0
12/19	74,518	3,120	4.2%	0
12/18	72,215	3,699	5.1%	0
Annual Growth	7.8%	(8.1%)	—	—

2022 Year-End Financials
Debt ratio: 0.9%   No. of shares ($ mil.): 28,562
Return on equity: 8.8%   Dividends
Cash ($ mil.): 9,842   Yield: —
Current Ratio: 1.76   Payout: 0.0%
Long-term debt ($ mil.): 26,772   Market value ($ mil.): —

Publicis Groupe S.A.

Publicis is one of the world's largest advertising and media firms. The European holding company provides a range of marketing services through four operating segments: Publicis Communications, Publicis Sapient, Publicis Media, and Publicis Health. It works with well-known agency brands such as Leo Burnett, Digitas, BBH, Fallon, and Saatchi & Saatchi, among others. Marcel Bleustein-Blanchet founded Publicis in 1926 and named it after the French word for advertising combined with the French word for six, his favorite number. The group serves clients in over 100 countries but generates the majority of its sales in North America.

Operations

Publicis is organized into four segments: Publicis Communications, Publicis Media, Publicis Sapient, and Publicis Health.

Its Publicis Communications segment is the creative communications hub and includes Leo Burnett, Saatchi & Saatchi, Publicis Worldwide, BBH, Marcel, Fallon, MSLGROUP, and Prodigious networks. Publicis Sapient is the group's digital and technology arm. Publicis Media operates media planning and buying services through agencies such as Zenith, Digitas, Spark, Performics, and Starcom. It creates value for clients through global media agency brands and scaled capabilities across investment, strategy, insights and analytics, data and technology, commerce, performance marketing, and content. Publicis Health's mission is to be the indispensable force for health and wellness business transformation through the alchemy of creativity and technology.

Geographic Reach

Publicis is headquartered in Paris and has operations in more than 100 countries. North America accounts for the largest share of the company's revenue at around 60% of total, followed by Europe (nearly 25%), Asia Pacific (some 10%), and Latin America and Middle East/Africa (approximately 5% combined).

Sales and Marketing

Publicis serves about 3,575 main clients in financial, automotive, TMT, non-food consumer products, food and beverages, healthcare, and leisure/energy/luxury, and retail sectors.

Automotive is Publicis's largest sector, accounting for some 15% of total revenue.

Financial Performance

The company's revenue for fiscal 2021 increased 8% to EUR 10.5 billion compared with EUR 9.7 billion in the prior year.

Net income for fiscal 2021 increased to EUR 1 billion compared to EUR 576 million in the prior year.

Mergers and Acquisitions

In mid-2022, Publicis announced the acquisition of Profitero, a leading SaaS global ecommerce intelligence platform helping brands accelerate commerce sales and profitability. Profitero's solutions provide actionable insights and product visibility to more than 4,000 brands and 70 million products on more than 700 retailer websites, in over 50 countries every day. Its products will further scale and supercharge the group's existing commerce capabilities around the world.

In early 2022, Publicis announced the acquisition of Romania-based Tremend, one of the fastest-growing and largest independent software engineering companies in Central and Eastern Europe. Tremend currently reaches approximately 60 million of its clients' end users with its proven technology and will serve as the newest global delivery center for Publicis Sapient. "We're impressed with the Tremend team's vision, the breadth of its skillset and capabilities around agile engineering and its deep industry expertise. Bringing Tremend into Publicis Sapient is a powerful expansion of our global distributed delivery model and we expect to rapidly grow headcount to 2,500 people by 2025 as well as our geographic footprint in the region," said Nigel Vaz, CEO of Publicis Sapient.

In mid-2021, Publicis announced the acquisition of CitrusAd, a software as a service (SaaS) platform optimizing brands marketing performances directly within retailer websites. With more than 50% of its activities in the US, CitrusAd is present across more than 20 countries and six industries. The Australian-based company provides its world-class technology to more than 70 major retailers globally and over 4,000 brands are utilizing their self-served platform.

Company Background

In 1926 Marcel Bleustein, then 19 years old, started France's first advertising agency, which he called Publicis (a takeoff on "publicity" and "six"). The company has spent the subsequent decades expanding globally through partnerships and acquisitions.

A major purchase was Saatchi & Saatchi, which it acquired in 2000 for about $1.9 billion. Along with the deal, the company inherited Saatchi's 50% of media buying unit Zenith Media (jointly owned by Cordiant Communications). In 2001 it merged Optimedia and Zenith, with Publicis owning 75% of the new business.

HISTORY

In 1926 Marcel Bleustein, then 19 years old, started France's first advertising agency, which he called Publicis (a takeoff on "publicity" and "six"). He launched his own radio station, Radio Cite, after the French government banned all advertising on state-run stations, and by 1939 he had expanded into film distribution and movie theaters. With the outbreak of WWII, Bleustein fled to London to serve with the Free French Forces.

Having adopted the name Bleustein-Blanchet, he returned to France following the liberation and revived his advertising business. In 1958 he bought the former Hotel Astoria on the Champs-Elysées and opened the first Le Drugstore. The original structure burned in a 1972 fire, and legend has it that Bleustein-Blanchet tapped Maurice Lévy to lead the company after he found Lévy salvaging records amid the ruins.

To expand its business, Publicis formed an alliance -- Chicago-based Foote, Cone & Belding Communications (FCB) -- in 1988. The partnership soured five years later, however, when Publicis acquired France's Groupe FCA. (FCB claimed the acquisition was a breach of contract and countered by establishing a new holding company for itself, True North Communications.) Bleustein-Blanchet died in 1996, and his daughter, Elisabeth Badinter, was named chair of the supervisory board.

In 1997 Publicis and True North divided their joint network, Publicis Communications, with True North getting the European offices and Publicis getting Africa, Asia, and Argentina. Later that year Publicis attempted a $700 million hostile bid for the 81.5% of True North it didn't already own to stop True North's acquisition of Bozell, Jacobs, Kenyon & Eckhardt. The bid failed, and Publicis' stake in True North was reduced to 11%. (True North was later acquired by Interpublic Group in 2001.)

The company gained new ground in the US through its acquisitions of Hal Riney & Partners and Evans Group in 1998. That year Lévy helped soothe a bitter feud among the descendants of Marcel Bleustein: Elisabeth Badinter had battled with her sister Michele Bleustein-Blanchet over Bleustein-Blanchet's desire to sell her stake in Publicis' holding company. Lévy's solution allowed Bleustein-Blanchet to sell her shares and left Badinter with control of the company.

Continuing its US expansion, in 1999 Publicis bought a 49% stake in Burrell Communications Group (one of the largest African-American-owned ad agencies in the US).

In 2000 the company bought advertising outfit Fallon McElligott (now Fallon Worldwide), marketing firm Frankel & Co., and media buyer DeWitt Media (which was merged into Optimedia). Publicis capped off the year by acquiring Saatchi & Saatchi for about $1.9 billion. Along with the deal, it inherited Saatchi's 50% of media buying unit Zenith Media (jointly owned by Cordiant Communications). In 2001 it merged Optimedia and Zenith, with Publicis owning 75% of the new business.

2002 was a big year for Publicis and the ad industry in general; the decision to acquire Bcom3 catapulted the company into the really big leagues and created a distinct size difference between the top four advertising conglomerates and everyone else.

From 2002 to 2005, the company worked on integrating Bcom3 and Saatchi & Saatchi into its operational infrastructure, as well as making small but selective acquisitions in order to maximize debt reduction.

In 2007, Publicis substantially beefed up its digital offerings when it bought US-based Digitas for $1.3 billion. A few months later, Publicis acquired Business Interactif, an interactive marketing agency based in France. The acquisition bolstered its French Digitas operations.

About that same time, Publicis also snatched up Communication Central Group (CCG), one of the largest interactive marketing agencies in China. CCG was later rebranded as Digitas Greater China. In late 2008, Publicis acquired the search marketing business of DoubleClick's Performics operations. The deal gave Publicis 130 additional clients and 200 specialists in the Internet search marketing arena. Also in 2008, Leo Burnett's Asia/Pacific network got a boost when Publicis acquired W&K Communications, an agency specializing in advertising, promotion, television production, and media buying services, and owning a presence in Beijing and Guangzhou, China. W&K was later renamed Leo Burnett W&K Beijing Advertising Co.

EXECUTIVES

Chairman, Chief Executive Officer, Arthur Sadoun

Finance Executive Vice President, Jean-Michel Etienne

Chief Financial Officer, Michel-Alain Proch
Secretary, Anne-Gabrielle Heilbronner
Chief Operating Officer, Steven King
Chairman, Maurice Levy
Supervisory Board Vice-Chairman, Elisabeth Badinter
Supervisory Board Member, Simon Badinter
Supervisory Board Member, Jean Charest
Supervisory Board Member, Sophie Dulac
Supervisory Board Member, Thomas H. Glocer
Supervisory Board Member, Marie-Josee Kravis
Supervisory Board Member, Andre Kudelski
Supervisory Board Member, Enrico Letta
Supervisory Board Member, Suzan LeVine
Supervisory Board Member, Antonella Mei-Pochtler
Supervisory Board Member, Cherie Nursalim
Supervisory Board Member, Pierre Penicaud
Supervisory Board Member, Patricia Velay-Borrini
Auditors : Mazars

LOCATIONS

HQ: Publicis Groupe S.A.
133, avenue des Champs-Elysees, Paris 75008
Phone: (33) 1 44 43 70 00
Web: www.publicisgroupe.com

2016 Sales

	% of total
North America	54
Europe	28
Asia Pacific	11
Latin America	4
Middle East Africa	3
Total	100

COMPETITORS

BULL
Bertelsmann SE & Co. KGaA
CAPGEMINI
DENTSU INTERNATIONAL LIMITED
KCOM GROUP LIMITED
KERING
LAGARDERE SCA
THE INTERPUBLIC GROUP OF COMPANIES, INC.
VIVENDI SE
WPP PLC

HISTORICAL FINANCIALS

Company Type: Public

Income Statement — FYE: December 31

	REVENUE ($mil)	NET INCOME ($mil)	NET PROFIT MARGIN	EMPLOYEES
12/21	13,285	1,162	8.7%	88,531
12/20	13,240	706	5.3%	79,051
12/19	12,351	944	7.6%	83,235
12/18	11,395	1,052	9.2%	75,588
12/17	11,615	1,033	8.9%	77,767
Annual Growth	3.4%	3.0%	—	3.3%

2021 Year-End Financials

Debt ratio: 12.5%
Return on equity: 13.0%
Cash ($ mil.): 4,141
Current Ratio: 0.94
Long-term debt ($ mil.): 3,900
No. of shares ($ mil.): 249
Dividends
  Yield: 5.4%
  Payout: 11.9%
Market value ($ mil.): 4,218

	STOCK PRICE ($) FY Close	P/E High/Low		PER SHARE ($) Earnings	Dividends	Book Value
12/21	16.90	4	3	4.62	0.93	38.94
12/20	12.34	6	3	2.92	0.34	35.89
12/19	11.32	4	3	3.99	0.59	35.07
12/18	14.16	5	3	4.49	0.59	33.94
12/17	16.99	5	4	4.48	0.56	31.55
Annual Growth	(0.1%)	—	—	0.7%	13.5%	5.4%

Puma SE

PUMA designs and makes sporting footwear, apparel, and accessories sold under the PUMA and Cobra Golf labels, was formed when German brothers Rudi and Adi Dassler feuded and split their family firm into adidas and PUMA. While shoes are PUMA's heritage, apparel accounts for a growing portion of sales. It has been expanding its athletic apparel styles to include men's golf, sailing, motorsports, and denim items. PUMA also operates its own retail stores and controls product distribution in many countries. PUMA, which holds long-term sponsorship arrangement with leading sports teams such as Manchester City, AC Milan, and the Italian national soccer team, is one of the world's leading athletic shoe companies, along with NIKE and adidas.

HISTORY

German brothers Adolph and Rudolph Dassler (Adi and Rudi) began business together in Herzogenaurach as Gebrœder Dassler Schuhfabrik ("Dassler Brothers Shoe Factory") in 1924. The company distinguished itself by tailoring specific shoes to different sports. Its first big success came in 1936 when American Jesse Owens, donning Dassler shoes, ran into the record books at the Olympic Games.

The Dasslers prospered until the Nazis took over the factory to make soldiers' boots. Late in WWII, when American troops occupied the area, Adi befriended them and even made shoes for an American soldier who would compete in the 1946 Olympics. Meanwhile, Rudi was a soldier and eventually wound up in an American prison camp. After WWII the brothers again scrounged for material for their shoes and even paid employees with things like firewood and yarn.

Rudi and Adi parted ways in 1948 over war-related politics. One story says Rudi believed that Adi failed to use his Allied contacts to free him from the prison camp. The brothers agreed that neither would use the Dassler name on their products. Adi remained in the factory as adidas, and Rudi opened shop across the river as PUMA Schuhfabrik Rudolph Dassler.

In 1948 members of Germany's team won the first post-WWII international soccer match wearing PUMA's Atom shoes. The company became PUMA-Sportschuhfabriken Rudolf Dassler KG in 1959 when Rudi's wife and two sons, Armin and Gerd, joined the team.

In 1974 Rudi died and Armin took over the company. The new regime continued the innovations, introducing shoe technologies and new products during the jogging boom of the 1970s. The period lifted PUMA's fortunes, and by 1977 it was selling its shoes in nearly 150 countries, turning out 40,000 pairs of shoes from plants in seven countries and raking in $100 million a year.

The mid-1980s brought the company more publicity as first Martina Navratilova and then Boris Becker won Wimbledon wearing PUMA shoes. In 1986 the company went public on the Munich and Frankfurt exchanges, raising DM86.7 million ($41 million). Before PUMA went public, Armin stepped down as head of the company (citing ill health); he retained 70% of the voting shares.

PUMA faded to the back of the pack in the mid-1980s. Though it did well in Europe, it missed important trends in the fashion-conscious US, a key sports market. For fiscal 1986 PUMA lost $21.6 million and blamed the US market, where it competed with giants Reebok and NIKE.

Jochen Zeitz became CEO in 1993 and began a reorganization. After a series of ownership changes, the company landed in the hands of Swiss company Proventus in 1995. After PUMA turned a profit, paying its first dividend since going public, Proventus sold all but a 25% stake to the public in 1996. The same year the company purchased its North American licensee and committed to growth in the US. In 1997 US film production company Monarchy Enterprises purchased Proventus' 25% of PUMA.

PUMA raised its visibility in 1998 by signing tennis phenom Serena Williams and buying 25% of sportswear firm LogoAthletic. PUMA accomplished part of its US comeback in 1999 when, with LogoAthletic, it became an official supplier of the NFL and NBA. PUMA also bought back its UK licensing from sporting goods manufacturer Dunlop Slazenger and opened a store, its first, in California. In 2000 the company teamed up with Porsche and SPARCO to release a shoe for racecar drivers. PUMA's licensing deal with the NFL and NBA ended in 2001. Reebok later bought the assets of bankrupt LogoAthletic and landed the exclusive licenses to outfit the NBA and NFL players. The company sponsored four teams in the 2002 World Cup soccer series, a major marketing opportunity in the eyes of company officials.

In 2003 film production company Monarchy Enterprises, which held approximately 39% ownership of PUMA by then, sold off all of its stake. In 2005 Gunter and Daniela Herz (who made their fortune through the TCHIBO coffee group, now maxingvest) raised their stake in PUMA to a blocking minority of 25%.

In October 2006 the company opened a 5,300-sq.-ft. store in Manhattan to serve as the model for all the company's future stores worldwide. In late 2007 PUMA extended the contract of chairman and CEO Zeitz through 2012. It also appointed Melody Harris-Jensbach, a management board member since mid-2007, as deputy CEO effective January 2008. Also in early 2008 Puma appointed designer Hussein Chalayan as its creative director, while acquiring a majority stake in Chalayan's fashion brand. PUMA's licensing agreement with Schiesser Lifestyle expired at the end of 2008.

In January 2010 PUMA sold its stake in the Hussein Chalayan fashion brand to its partner Chalayan LLP. As a result, the Hussein Chalayan brand is now managed independently from PUMA. In April the company completed the acquisition of the Cobra golf brand from Acushnet, owned by Fortune Brands. The sale included the Cobra Golf brand, its inventory, intellectual property, and endorsement contracts.

PUMA became a European Corporation -- PUMA SE -- in 2011.

EXECUTIVES

Chief Executive Officer, Bjorn Gulden
Chief Sourcing Officer, Anne-Laure Descours
Chief Financial Officer, Hubert Hinterseher
Chief Commercial Officer, Arne Freundt
Independent Chairman, Jean-Francois Palus
Independent Director, Deputy Chairman, Thore Ohlsson
Independent Director, Fiona May
Independent Director, Heloise Temple-Boyer
Director, Martin Koppel
Director, Bernd Illig
Auditors : KPMG AG Wirtschaftsprüfungsgesellschaft

LOCATIONS

HQ: Puma SE
 PUMA Way 1, Herzogenaurach 91074
Phone: (49) 9132 81 0 **Fax:** (49) 9132 81 22 46
Web: www.puma.com

PRODUCTS/OPERATIONS

Selected Products
Apparel
 Dresses
 Jackets
 Pants
 Shirts
 Shorts
 Skirts
Shoes
 Auto racing
 Basketball
 Baseball
 Lifestlye
 Running
 Soccer
 Tennis
Eyewear

COMPETITORS

B & B REALISATIONS LIMITED
BOARDRIDERS, INC.
COLUMBIA SPORTSWEAR COMPANY
CONVERSE INC.
HUGO BOSS AG
PENTLAND GROUP LIMITED
SPEEDO USA INC.
UNDER ARMOUR, INC.
VF OUTDOOR, LLC
adidas AG

HISTORICAL FINANCIALS
Company Type: Public

Income Statement FYE: December 31

	REVENUE ($mil)	NET INCOME ($mil)	NET PROFIT MARGIN	EMPLOYEES
12/22	9,041	377	4.2%	18,071
12/21	7,702	350	4.5%	16,125
12/20	6,424	96	1.5%	14,374
12/19	6,177	294	4.8%	14,332
12/18	5,323	214	4.0%	12,894
Annual Growth	14.2%	15.2%		8.8%

2022 Year-End Financials
Debt ratio: 1.2%
Return on equity: 15.0%
Cash ($ mil.): 494
Current Ratio: 1.48
Long-term debt ($ mil.): —
No. of shares ($ mil.): 149
Dividends
 Yield: —
 Payout: 1.8%
Market value ($ mil.): 906

	STOCK PRICE ($) FY Close	P/E High/Low		PER SHARE ($) Earnings	Dividends	Book Value
12/22	6.05	5	2	2.52	0.05	17.63
12/21	12.29	6	4	2.34	0.01	16.75
12/20	11.74	22	10	0.65	0.20	14.13
12/19	8.00	38	4	1.98	0.24	14.07
12/18	52.96	45	28	1.44	0.10	13.05
Annual Growth	(41.9%)	—	—	15.1%	(17.4%)	7.8%

Qatar Islamic Bank

EXECUTIVES

Acting Chief Executive Officer, Ahmad Meshari
Chief Risk Officer, Syed Maqbul Quader
General Manager, Murtada Khidir
General Manager, Ahmed A. Al Kuwar
General Manager, Salah Al-Hail
Director, Mansour Al Muslah
Auditors : KPMG

LOCATIONS

HQ: Qatar Islamic Bank
 Grand Hamad Ave., P.O. Box 559, Doha
Phone: (974) 4409409 **Fax:** (974) 4412700
Web: www.qib.com.qa

HISTORICAL FINANCIALS
Company Type: Public

Income Statement FYE: December 31

	ASSETS ($mil)	NET INCOME ($mil)	INCOME AS % OF ASSETS	EMPLOYEES
12/23	51,966	1,182	2.3%	0
12/22	50,549	1,100	2.2%	0
12/20	47,900	842	1.8%	0
12/19	44,922	839	1.9%	0
12/18	42,096	756	1.8%	0
Annual Growth	4.3%	9.3%		

2023 Year-End Financials
Return on assets: 2.3%
Return on equity: 3.2%
Long-term debt ($ mil.): —
No. of shares ($ mil.): 2,362
Sales ($ mil.): 3,146
Dividends
 Yield: —
 Payout: 41.9%
Market value ($ mil.): —

QBE Insurance Group Ltd.

QBE Insurance Group is one of the world's largest insurance and reinsurance companies, with operations in all the major insurance markets. QBE's captive reinsurer, Equator Re, provides reinsurance protection to its divisions in conjunction with the QBE's external reinsurance programs. The QBE story began in October 1886, when young Scotsmen James Burns and Robert Philp ? already partners in a shipping business ? established The North Queensland Insurance Company Limited (QI).

Operations

QBE operates through three primary segments: North America, International and Australia Pacific.

North America writes general insurance, reinsurance and Crop business in the US.

International writes general insurance business in the UK, Europe and Canada. It also writes general insurance and reinsurance business through Lloyd's; worldwide reinsurance business through offices in the United Kingdom, US, Ireland, Bermuda and mainland Europe; and provides personal and commercial insurance covers in Hong Kong, Singapore, Malaysia and Vietnam.

Australia Pacific primarily underwrites general insurance risks throughout Australia, New Zealand and the Pacific region, providing all major lines of insurance for personal and commercial risks.

Geographic Reach

QBE is headquartered in Sydney, Australia, and has operations in more than 25 countries in Australia, Europe, North America, Asia and the Pacific.

Financial Performance

The company's revenue for fiscal 2021 increased by 10% to $13.4 billion compared from the prior year with $11.7 billion.

Net income for fiscal 2021 was $750

million compared from the prior year with a net loss of $1.5 billion.

Cash held by the company at the end of fiscal 2021 increased to $819 million. Cash provided by operations and financing activities were $2.8 billion and $101 million, respectively. Cash used investing activities was $2.8 billion, mainly for net payments for purchase of interest-bearing financial assets.

Strategy

Meaningful progress was achieved against each of its 2021 strategic priorities of performance, modernization, customer focus and culture. The company saw significant progress on a number of activities underpinning the performance agenda with the reinvigoration of cell reviews, delivery against key sustainability and climate commitments and targeted growth. QBE's modernization journey continues with ongoing efforts to upgrade critical foundational capabilities and to further embed its digital capabilities across the organization. Embedding automation across underwriting, distribution and claims to support the evolving needs of its customers and partners remains an ongoing focus. While there are still key programs of work to deliver, the company are now well progressed with its modernization journey.

Company Background

QBE was formed in 1973 with the merger of Australia's Queensland Insurance, Bankers' and Traders' Insurance, and Equitable Probate and General Insurance.

Queensland Insurance was founded in 1886 and by 1890 operated more than 36 agencies in London, Hong Kong, Singapore, New Zealand, and the Pacific Islands. In 1904, it opened its own offices in London and New York. Bankers' and Traders' started operations in 1921.

QBE is now one of the top 20 global insurance companies.

EXECUTIVES

Group Chief Executive Officer, Andrew Horton
Group Chief Financial Officer, Inder Singh
Group Chief Risk Officer, Fiona Larnach
Group Chief Underwriting Officer, Sam Harrison
Technology Group Executive, Operations Group Executive, Matt Mansour
People and Culture Group Executive, Amanda Hughes
Sustainability Group Executive, Corporate Affairs Group Executive, Vivienne Bower
International Chief Executive Officer, Jason Harris
Asia Pacific Chief Executive Officer, Sue Houghton
North America Chief Executive Officer, Todd Matthew Jones
Group General Counsel, Secretary, Carolyn Scobie
Deputy Secretary, Peter Smiles
Independent Chair, Michael Wilkins
Deputy Chairman, Independent Non-Executive Director, John M. Green
Independent Non-Executive Director, Tan Le
Independent Non-Executive Director, Eric Smith
Independent Non-Executive Director, Stephen Fitzgerald
Independent Non-Executive Director, Kathryn Mary Lisson
Independent Non-Executive Director, Jann Skinner
Independent Non-Executive Director, Brian Pomeroy
Independent Non-Executive Director, Rolf Albert Wilhelm Tolle
Auditors : PricewaterhouseCoopers

LOCATIONS

HQ: QBE Insurance Group Ltd.
Level 18, 388 George Street, Sydney, New South Wales 2000
Phone: (61) 2 9375 4444   **Fax:** (61) 2 9231 6104
Web: www.qbe.com

COMPETITORS

AIA GROUP LIMITED
AMERICAN INTERNATIONAL GROUP, INC.
CNA FINANCIAL CORPORATION
Endurance Specialty Holdings Ltd
INSURANCE AUSTRALIA GROUP LIMITED
LIVERPOOL VICTORIA FRIENDLY SOCIETY LTD
MAIN STREET AMERICA GROUP, INC.
MAPFRE, SA
Manulife Financial Corporation
Talanx AG

HISTORICAL FINANCIALS

Company Type: Public

Income Statement — FYE: December 31

	ASSETS ($mil)	NET INCOME ($mil)	INCOME AS % OF ASSETS	EMPLOYEES
12/22	49,502	770	1.6%	0
12/21	49,303	750	1.5%	11,651
12/20	46,624	(1,517)	—	11,000
12/19	40,035	550	1.4%	11,704
12/18	39,582	390	1.0%	0
Annual Growth	5.8%	18.5%	—	—

2022 Year-End Financials
Return on assets: 1.5%   Dividends
Return on equity: 8.6%   Yield: —
Long-term debt ($ mil.): —   Payout: 80.9%
No. of shares ($ mil.): 1,485   Market value ($ mil.): —
Sales ($ mil.): 14,063

Raiffeisen Bank International Ag Wien

EXECUTIVES

Chief Risk Officer, Johann Strobl
Chief Financial Officer, Martin Gruell
Chief Operating Officer, Aris Bogdaneris
Executive Member, Karl Sevelda
Executive Member, Peter Lennkh
Executive Member, Klemens Breuer
First Deputy Chairman, Erwin Hameseder
Second Deputy Chairman, Ludwig Scharinger
Assistant Chairman, Markus Mair
Director, Steward D. Gager
Director, Kurt Geiger
Director, Hannes Schmid
Director, Johannes Schuster
Director, Friedrich Sommer
Director, Christian Teufl
Director, Martin Prater
Director, Rudolf Kortenhof
Director, Peter Anzeletti-Reikl
Director, Sabine Chadt
Director, Helge Rechberger
Auditors : Deloitte Audit Wirtschaftsprufungs GmbH

LOCATIONS

HQ: Raiffeisen Bank International Ag Wien
Am Stadtpark 9, Vienna 1030
Phone: (43) 1 71 707 0   **Fax:** (43) 1 71 707 1715
Web: www.rbinternational.com

HISTORICAL FINANCIALS

Company Type: Public

Income Statement — FYE: December 31

	REVENUE ($mil)	NET INCOME ($mil)	NET PROFIT MARGIN	EMPLOYEES
12/22	13,760	3,873	28.2%	44,414
12/21	8,587	1,552	18.1%	46,185
12/20	8,816	986	11.2%	45,414
12/19	8,837	1,377	15.6%	46,873
12/18	5,561	1,454	26.1%	47,079
Annual Growth	25.4%	27.8%	—	(1.4%)

2022 Year-End Financials
Debt ratio: —   No. of shares ($ mil.): 328
Return on equity: 22.5%   Dividends
Cash ($ mil.): 57,335   Yield: 0.2%
Current Ratio: —   Payout: 0.0%
Long-term debt ($ mil.): —   Market value ($ mil.): 1,314

	STOCK PRICE ($) FY Close	P/E High/Low		PER SHARE ($) Earnings	Dividends	Book Value
12/22	4.00	1	0	11.49	0.85	57.36
12/21	7.55	2	1	4.40	0.21	49.83
12/20	5.00	3	2	2.72	0.59	50.30
12/19	6.24	2	1	3.97	0.16	44.26
12/18	6.18	3	2	4.21	0.11	40.82
Annual Growth	(10.3%)	—	—	28.5%	66.6%	8.9%

Rakuten Group Inc

EXECUTIVES

Chairman, President, Chief Executive Officer, Representative Director, Hiroshi Mikitani
Vice-Chairman, Representative Director, Masayuki Hosaka
Executive Vice President, Chief Operating Officer, Representative Director, Kentaro Hyakuno

Executive Vice President, Chief Financial Officer, Director, Kenji Hirose
Outside Director, Kazunori Takeda
Outside Director, Sarah J. M. Whitley
Outside Director, Charles B. Baxter
Outside Director, Takashi Mitachi
Outside Director, Jun Murai
Outside Director, Takaharu Ando
Outside Director, Tsedal Neeley
Outside Director, Shigeki Habuka
Auditors : Ernst & Young ShinNihon LLC

LOCATIONS

HQ: Rakuten Group Inc
Rakuten Crimson House, 1-14-1 Tamagawa, Setagaya-ku, Tokyo 158-0094
Phone: (81) 50 5581 6910
Web: corp.rakuten.co.jp

HISTORICAL FINANCIALS

Company Type: Public

Income Statement — FYE: December 31

	REVENUE ($mil)	NET INCOME ($mil)	NET PROFIT MARGIN	EMPLOYEES
12/22	14,630	(2,829)	—	32,079
12/21	14,610	(1,162)	—	28,261
12/20	14,121	(1,107)	—	23,841
12/19	11,641	(293)	—	20,053
12/18	10,016	1,293	12.9%	17,214
Annual Growth	9.9%	—	—	16.8%

2022 Year-End Financials

Debt ratio: —
Return on equity: (-39.0%)
Cash ($ mil.): 50,829
Current Ratio: 482.45
Long-term debt ($ mil.): —
No. of shares ($ mil.): 1,590
Dividends
Yield: —
Payout: 0.0%
Market value ($ mil.): 7,078

	STOCK PRICE ($) FY Close	P/E High/Low	PER SHARE ($) Earnings	Dividends	Book Value
12/22	4.45	— —	(1.78)	0.07	3.88
12/21	10.00	— —	(0.76)	0.04	6.01
12/20	9.67	— —	(0.81)	0.04	4.33
12/19	8.51	— —	(0.22)	0.04	5.00
12/18	6.65	0 0	0.95	0.04	5.21
Annual Growth	(9.6%)	—	—	12.9%	(7.1%)

Ramsay Health Care Ltd. (Australia)

Ramsay Health Care provides quality health care through a global network of clinical practice, teaching, and research. The company's global networks extend across 10 countries with over eight million admission/patients visits facilities in more than 530 locations. As the continent's largest private hospital group, the company operates more than 70 hospitals and day surgery facilities in Australia. In Europe, it operates in 350 locations in five countries. In France, it has more than 130 facilities. In Denmark, Norway and Sweden, Ramsay Santé operates about 210 facilities including primary care units, specialist clinics and hospitals. Ramsay Santé also operates a 93-bed hospital in Italy. In Asia, it operates three hospitals in Indonesia, three hospitals and a nursing college in Malaysia and one-day surgery in Hong Kong.

Operations

Ramsay Health Care has four operating segments: Asia Pacific, UK, France and Nordics.

In Asia, Ramsay Sime Darby Health Care Sdn Bhd operates four hospitals in Indonesia, four hospitals and a nursing college in Malaysia and a one-day surgery in Hong Kong. The business employs more than 4,000 people. Ramsay Sime Darby is a 50:50 joint venture arrangement with Malaysian multinational conglomerate Sime Darby Berhad. The Asia segment accounts for about 40% of total revenue.

In France (more than 35 of total revenue), Ramsay Santé has a market leading position with more than 130 acute care and mental health facilities. In Denmark, Norway and Sweden (around 15% of revenue), Ramsay Santé operates 210 facilities including primary care units, specialist clinics and hospitals. Ramsay Santé also operates a 93-bed hospital in Italy.

Ramsay UK (less than 10% of revenue) has a network of about 35 acute hospitals and day procedure centres providing a comprehensive range of clinical specialities to private and self-insured patients as well as to patients referred by the NHS. Ramsay UK also operates a diagnostic imaging service and provides neurological services through its three neuro-rehabilitation facilities.

Geographic Reach

Based in Sydney, Australia, Ramsay Health care generates about 50% of revenue in Europe, while around 40% coming from Asia Pacific and some 10% from the UK.

Financial Performance

The company's revenue for fiscal 2021 increased to $13.3 billion compared from the prior year with $12.4 billion.

Net income for fiscal 2021 increased to $449 million compared from the prior year with $284 billion. C

ash held by the company at the end of fiscal 2021 was $1 billion. Cash provided by operations was $1.5 billion while cash used for investing activities were $2.5 billion. Main uses of cash were for purchase of property, plant and equipment; and business combinations consideration held in escrow. Financing activities provided another $584 million.

Strategy

During the year, the Board and management team undertook a deep dive into Ramsay's strategic direction, looking at where the business wants to be by 2030 and what needs to be done to get there. Its overarching vision is to leverage Ramsay's global platform to be a leading patient-centric, integrated health care provider of the future. The 2030 strategy balances the needs of all the company's stakeholders, taking into account a rapidly changing environment.

Ramsay is significantly increasing its development pipeline in fiscal year 2022 (FY22) and investment is expected to continue to be at elevated levels over the next few years. Over the medium term, returns from this investment are expected to be in-line with previous achievements.

Mergers and Acquisitions

In 2021, Ramsey Health Care has agreed to acquire UK-based private hospital group Spire Healthcare for approximately $1.4bn (£999.6m). The terms of the deal states that Spire shareholders will receive $3.4 (£2.40) per share in cash, which represents a 24.4% premium to Spire's closing price.

EXECUTIVES

Chief Executive Officer, Managing Director, Executive Director, Craig R. McNally
Chief Financial Officer, Martyn Roberts
Ramsay Health Care Australia Chief Executive Officer, Daniel A. Sims
Group General Counsel, Secretary, Henrietta Rowe
Chairman, Non-Independent Non-Executive Director, Michael S. Siddle
Deputy Chairman, Non-Independent Non-Executive Director, Peter J. Evans
Independent Non-Executive Director, Lead Independent Director, David I. Thodey
Independent Non-Executive Director, James McMurdo
Independent Non-Executive Director, Alison Deans
Independent Non-Executive Director, Karen Penrose
Independent Non-Executive Director, Claudia R. Sussmuth Dyckerhoff
Auditors : Ernst & Young

LOCATIONS

HQ: Ramsay Health Care Ltd. (Australia)
Suite 18.03, Level 18, 126 Phillip Street, Sydney, New South Wales 2000
Phone: (61) 2 9220 1000 **Fax:** (61) 2 9220 1001
Web: www.ramsayhealth.com

2016 Sales

	% of total
Asia Pacific	51
France	39
UK	10
Total	100

COMPETITORS

AMSURG CORP.
BRITISH UNITED PROVIDENT ASSOCIATION LIMITED(THE)
HCA HEALTHCARE, INC.
HENRY SCHEIN, INC.
NUFFIELD HEALTH
SHANDS TEACHING HOSPITAL AND CLINICS, INC.
SONIC HEALTHCARE LIMITED

SWEDISH HEALTH SERVICES
TEXAS CHILDREN'S HOSPITAL
UNITED SURGICAL PARTNERS INTERNATIONAL, INC.

HISTORICAL FINANCIALS
Company Type: Public

Income Statement — FYE: June 30

	REVENUE ($mil)	NET INCOME ($mil)	NET PROFIT MARGIN	EMPLOYEES
06/23	10,173	197	1.9%	179,000
06/22	9,477	188	2.0%	88,000
06/21	10,007	337	3.4%	80,000
06/20	8,512	194	2.3%	80,000
06/19	8,124	382	4.7%	77,000
Annual Growth	5.8%	(15.2%)	—	23.5%

2023 Year-End Financials
Debt ratio: 18.7% No. of shares ($ mil.): 228
Return on equity: 7.3% Dividends
Cash ($ mil.): 434 Yield: —
Current Ratio: 1.02 Payout: 16.8%
Long-term debt ($ mil.): 3,879 Market value ($ mil.): 2,123

	STOCK PRICE ($) FY Close	P/E High/Low		PER SHARE ($) Earnings	Dividends	Book Value
06/23	9.31	10	7	0.83	0.14	12.05
06/22	12.19	12	9	0.80	0.24	11.88
06/21	11.61	7	6	1.45	0.08	13.29
06/20	12.72	10	7	0.89	0.22	11.29
06/19	12.56	5	4	1.84	0.23	8.57
Annual Growth	(7.2%)	—	—	(18.2%)	(11.6%)	8.0%

Reckitt Benckiser Group Plc

EXECUTIVES

Chief Executive Officer, Executive Director, Laxman Narasimhan
Chief Financial Officer, Jeff Carr
Chief Transformation Officer, Kris Licht
Chief Transformation Officer, Volker Kuhn
Chief Human Resources Officer, Ranjay Radhakrishnan
Chief Information & Digitisation Officer, Filippo Catalano
Chief Supply Officer, Sami Naffakh
Chief R&D Officer, Angela Naef
Corporate Affairs Head, Corporate Affairs Chief Sustainability Officer, Miguel Veiga-Pestana
General Counsel, Secretary, Catheryn O'Rourke
Chairman, Non-Executive Director, Christopher A. Sinclair
Senior Independent Director, Nicandro Durante
Non-Executive Director, Olivier Bohuon
Non-Executive Director, Andrew R.J. Bonfield
Non-Executive Director, Margherita Della Valle
Non-Executive Director, Mary Harris
Non-Executive Director, Mehmood Khan
Non-Executive Director, Pamela J. Kirby
Non-Executive Director, Sara Mathew
Non-Executive Director, Elane B. Stock

Auditors : KPMG LLP

LOCATIONS
HQ: Reckitt Benckiser Group Plc
103 – 105 Bath Road, Slough, Berkshire SL1 3UH
Phone: (44) 1753 217800
Web: www.reckitt.com

HISTORICAL FINANCIALS
Company Type: Public

Income Statement — FYE: December 31

	REVENUE ($mil)	NET INCOME ($mil)	NET PROFIT MARGIN	EMPLOYEES
12/22	17,398	2,804	16.1%	40,000
12/21	17,835	(43)	—	41,800
12/20	19,096	1,619	8.5%	43,900
12/19	16,963	(4,863)	—	42,400
12/18	16,083	2,759	17.2%	42,400
Annual Growth	2.0%	0.4%	—	(1.4%)

2022 Year-End Financials
Debt ratio: 35.9% No. of shares ($ mil.): 715
Return on equity: 27.6% Dividends
Cash ($ mil.): 1,392 Yield: —
Current Ratio: 0.63 Payout: 9.5%
Long-term debt ($ mil.): 8,248 Market value ($ mil.): 10,085

	STOCK PRICE ($) FY Close	P/E High/Low		PER SHARE ($) Earnings	Dividends	Book Value
12/22	14.09	5	4	3.91	0.37	15.88
12/21	17.50	—	—	(0.06)	0.45	13.96
12/20	18.12	13	8	2.27	0.41	17.45
12/19	16.56	—	—	(6.86)	0.41	17.42
12/18	15.13	6	5	3.89	0.42	26.60
Annual Growth	(1.8%)	—	—	0.1%	(2.9%)	(12.1%)

Recruit Holdings Co Ltd

EXECUTIVES

Chairman, Representative Director, Masumi Minegishi
President, Chief Executive Officer, Representative Director, Hisayuki Idekoba
Chief Operating Officer, Managing Executive Officer, Chief Strategy Officer, Chief Human Resources Officer, Chief Risk Officer, Director, Ayano Senaha
Director, Rony Kahan
Outside Director, Naoki Izumiya
Outside Director, Hiroki Totoki
Outside Director, Keiko Honda
Auditors : Ernst & Young ShinNihon LLC

LOCATIONS
HQ: Recruit Holdings Co Ltd
1-9-2 Marunouchi, Chiyoda-ku, Tokyo 100-6640
Phone: (81) 3 6835 1111
Web: www.recruit.co.jp

HISTORICAL FINANCIALS
Company Type: Public

Income Statement — FYE: March 31

	REVENUE ($mil)	NET INCOME ($mil)	NET PROFIT MARGIN	EMPLOYEES
03/22	23,608	2,440	10.3%	53,653
03/21	20,495	1,186	5.8%	48,520
03/20	22,104	1,657	7.5%	51,900
03/19	20,865	1,573	7.5%	48,305
03/18	20,467	1,428	7.0%	42,483
Annual Growth	3.6%	14.3%	—	6.0%

2022 Year-End Financials
Debt ratio: — No. of shares ($ mil.): 1,622
Return on equity: 24.1% Dividends
Cash ($ mil.): 5,504 Yield: 0.4%
Current Ratio: 1.70 Payout: 2.3%
Long-term debt ($ mil.): 282 Market value ($ mil.): 14,193

	STOCK PRICE ($) FY Close	P/E High/Low		PER SHARE ($) Earnings	Dividends	Book Value
03/22	8.75	0	0	1.49	0.04	6.91
03/21	9.84	0	0	0.72	0.05	6.03
03/20	5.16	0	0	1.00	0.05	5.52
03/19	5.70	0	0	0.94	0.05	5.22
Annual Growth	15.4%	—	—	12.1%	(5.0%)	7.3%

Reliance Industries Ltd

EXECUTIVES

Managing Director, Chairman, Executive Director, Mukesh Dhirubhai Ambani
Executive Director, Nikhil R. Meswani
Executive Director, Hital R. Meswani
Executive Director, P. M. S. Prasad
Executive Director, Pawan Kumar Kapil
Non-Independent Non-Executive Director, Nita M. Ambani
Lead Independent Director, Mansingh L. Bhakta
Independent Director, Arundhati Bhattacharya
Independent Director, Shumeet Banerji
Independent Director, Raminder Singh Gujral
Independent Director, Adil Zainulbhai
Independent Director, Yogendra P. Trivedi
Independent Director, Dipak C. Jain
Independent Director, Raghunath A. Mashelkar
Auditors : DTS & Associates LLP

LOCATIONS
HQ: Reliance Industries Ltd
3rd Floor, Maker Chambers IV, 222, Nariman Point, Mumbai 400 021
Phone: (91) 22 3555 5000   **Fax:** (91) 22 2204 2268
Web: www.ril.com

HISTORICAL FINANCIALS

Company Type: Public

Income Statement — FYE: March 31

	REVENUE ($mil)	NET INCOME ($mil)	NET PROFIT MARGIN	EMPLOYEES
03/22	97,241	8,014	8.2%	342,982
03/21	68,699	6,714	9.8%	236,334
03/20	82,823	5,210	6.3%	26,488
03/19	85,216	5,721	6.7%	28,967
03/18	64,280	5,544	8.6%	29,533
Annual Growth	10.9%	9.6%	—	84.6%

2022 Year-End Financials

Debt ratio: 0.2%
Return on equity: 8.2%
Cash ($ mil.): 4,776
Current Ratio: 1.12
Long-term debt ($ mil.): 24,779
No. of shares ($ mil.): 6,765
Dividends
Yield: —
Payout: 12.6%
Market value ($ mil.): —

RELX PLC

RELX PLC is a global provider of information-based analytics and decision tools for professional and business customers. The company serves customers in over 180 countries and has offices in about 40 countries. Additionally, the company's Scientific, Technical & Medical market segment takes the global top spot, while its exhibition segment takes the second highest spot in events business globally. Majority of the company's sales were generated in North America.

Operations

The company operates through four operating segments:

Risk provides customers with information-based analytics and decision tools that combine public and industry-specific content with advanced technology and algorithms to assist them in evaluating and predicting risk and enhancing operational efficiency. The segment accounts for around 35% of the total revenue.

Scientific, Technical & Medical provides information and analytics that help institutions and professionals progress science, advance healthcare and improve performance. STM accounts for around 35% of revenues.

Legal provides legal, regulatory and business information and analytics that help customers increase their productivity, improve decision-making and achieve better outcomes. The segment accounts for around 20% of revenues.

Exhibitions combines industry expertise with data and digital tools to help customers connect digitally and face-to-face, learn about markets, source products and complete transactions. Exhibitions segment accounts for around 10% of the total revenues.

Geographic Reach

Headquartered in London, England; RELX serves customers in more than 180 countries and has offices in about 40 countries. Company's largest market was North America with around 60% of total revenue followed by Europe with around 20% of revenue.

Financial Performance

RELX's revenue for the past five fiscal years experienced decreases and increases starting from 2018 with GBP7.5 billion, to GBP7.9 billion, GBP7.1 billion, GBP7.2 billion and GBP8.6 billion, for fiscal years 2019 to 2022, respectively.

Company's revenue for fiscal 2022 increased to GBP8.6 billion compared from the prior year with GBP7.2 billion. The increase was primarily due to higher revenues on every segment.

Cash held by the company at the end of fiscal 2022 increased to GBP334 million. Cash provided by operations was GBP2.4 billion while cash used for investing and financing activities were GBP1.2 billion and GBP474 million, respectively. Main uses of cash were acquisitions and repayment of term debt.

Strategy

RELX's number one strategic priority continues to be the organic development of increasingly sophisticated information-based analytics and decision tools that deliver enhanced value to professional and business customers across the industries that the company serve.

The company aim to build leading positions in long-term global growth markets and leverage its skills, assets and resources across RELX, both to build solutions for its customers and to pursue cost efficiencies.

RELX are systematically migrating all of its information solutions across RELX towards higher value-add decision tools, adding broader data sets, embedding more sophisticated analytics and leveraging more powerful technology, primarily through organic development.

Company Background

The company was originally incorporated in 1903. The company combined with RELX NV in 1993. In 2015, the company simplified its structure so that all of the business into one jointly controlled company, the RELX Group plc. RELX NV merged into RELX PLC forming a single parent company in 2018.

EXECUTIVES

Chief Executive Officer, Executive Director, Erik Engstrom
Chief Financial Officer, Executive Director, Nick L. Luff
Risk Chief Executive Officer, Mark Kelsey
Scientific, Technical and Medical Chief Executive Officer, Kumsal Bayazit
Legal Chief Executive Officer, Mike Walsh
Exhibitions Chief Executive Officer, Hugh M. Jones IV
Chief Human Resources Officer, Rose Thomson
Risk Chief Technology Officer, Vijay Raghavan
Chief Legal Officer, Secretary, Henry A. Udow
Chief Strategy Officer, Jelena Sevo
Independent Non-Executive Chairman, Paul Walker
Senior Independent Non-Executive Director, Wolfhart Hauser
Independent Non-Executive Director, June Felix
Independent Non-Executive Director, Charlotte Hogg
Independent Non-Executive Director, Marike E. Van Lier Lels
Independent Non-Executive Director, Suzanne H. Wood
Independent Non-Executive Director, Robert MacLeod
Independent Non-Executive Director, Andrew Sukawaty
Auditors: Ernst & Young LLP

LOCATIONS

HQ: RELX PLC
1-3 Strand, London WC2N 5JR
Phone: (44) 20 7166 5500 **Fax:** (44) 20 7166 5799
Web: www.relx.com

2018 sales

	% of total
North America	55
Europe	24
Rest of world	21
Total	100

PRODUCTS/OPERATIONS

2018 sales

	% of total
Scientific, Technical & Medical	34
Risk & Business Information	28
Legal	22
Exhibitions	16
Total	100

COMPETITORS

ATOS SYNTEL INC.
BAZAARVOICE, INC.
CORNERSTONE ONDEMAND, INC.
EUROVESTECH PLC
FIVE9, INC.
HEALTHSTREAM, INC.
INTRALINKS HOLDINGS, INC.
IQVIA HOLDINGS INC.
MEDIDATA SOLUTIONS, INC.
RELX GROUP PLC

HISTORICAL FINANCIALS

Company Type: Public

Income Statement — FYE: December 31

	REVENUE ($mil)	NET INCOME ($mil)	NET PROFIT MARGIN	EMPLOYEES
12/23	11,675	2,269	19.4%	36,500
12/22	10,296	1,967	19.1%	33,200
12/21	9,762	1,982	20.3%	33,500
12/20	9,703	1,670	17.2%	33,200
12/19	10,398	1,987	19.1%	33,200
Annual Growth	2.9%	3.4%	—	2.4%

2023 Year-End Financials

Debt ratio: 55.5%
Return on equity: 49.2%
Cash ($ mil.): 197
Current Ratio: 0.52
Long-term debt ($ mil.): 6,606
No. of shares ($ mil.): 1,881
Dividends
Yield: —
Payout: 59.2%
Market value ($ mil.): 74,622

	STOCK PRICE ($)	P/E	PER SHARE ($)		
	FY Close	High/Low	Earnings	Dividends	Book Value
12/23	39.66	43 31	1.19	0.71	2.34
12/22	27.72	35 29	1.02	0.61	2.38
12/21	32.61	43 30	1.02	0.67	2.26
12/20	24.66	45 31	0.86	0.58	1.49
12/19	25.27	35 28	1.02	0.54	1.48
Annual Growth	11.9%	— —	4.1%	7.0%	12.2%

RenaissanceRe Holdings Ltd.

RenaissanceRe is a global provider of reinsurance and insurance. Through its Renaissance Reinsurance subsidiary, the Bermuda-based firm indemnifies insurance companies around the globe against excess losses on natural catastrophes, paying insurance claims after they exceed a certain retained amount. Its Syndicate 1458 offers insurance through Lloyd's of London. Top Layer Re, a joint venture with State Farm, provides excess non-US property catastrophe reinsurance. Another RenaissanceRe venture, DaVinci Reinsurance, covers catastrophes and specialty risks such as terrorism. RenaissanceRe was established in 1993.

Operations

RenaissanceRe operates in two primary segments -- the Property segment and the Casualty and Specialty segment. The segments account for an evenly split of gross premiums written.

Property, which is comprised of catastrophe and other property (re)insurance written on behalf of its operating subsidiaries, joint ventures and managed funds; and Casualty and Specialty, which is comprised of casualty and specialty (re)insurance written on behalf of its operating subsidiaries, joint ventures and managed funds.

Overall, about 95% of its revenue comes from net premiums earned and the remaining revenue comes from net investment income.

Geographic Reach

RenaissanceRe is headquartered in Bermuda and leases office space in the US, Australia, Ireland, Singapore, Switzerland, and the UK.

The US and Caribbean bring in around 50% of RenaissanceRe's gross premiums written.

Sales and Marketing

RenaissanceRe primarily markets its products through reinsurance brokers. Three brokerage firms ? AON, Marsh, and Arthur J. Gallagher ? account for about 80% of the company's gross premiums written.

Financial Performance

Company's revenue for fiscal 2021 increased to $5.3 billion compared form the prior year with $5.2 billion.

Net loss for fiscal 2021 was $103.4 million compared from the prior year with a profit of $993.1 million.

Cash held by the company at the end of fiscal 2021 increased to $1.9 billion while cash used for investing and financing activities were $816.3 million and $302.5 million, respectively. Main uses of cash were for purchases of fixed maturity investments trading and RenaissanceRe common share repurchases.

Strategy

RenaissanceRe's mission is to match desirable, well-structured risks with efficient sources of capital to achieve its vision of being the best underwriter. The company believe that this will allow the company to produce superior returns for its shareholders over the long term, and to protect communities and enable prosperity. The company's strategy for achieving these objectives, which is supported by its core values, its principles and its culture, is to operate an integrated system of what it believes are its three competitive advantages: superior customer relationships, superior risk selection and superior capital management. The company believe all three competitive advantages are required to achieve its objectives, and RenaissanceRe aim to seamlessly coordinate the delivery of these competitive advantages for the benefit of its shareholders, ceding insurers, brokers, investors in its joint ventures and managed funds, and other stakeholders.

EXECUTIVES

President, Chief Executive Officer, Director, Kevin J. O'Donnell, $1,070,000 total compensation
Executive Vice President, Group Chief Underwriting Officer, Subsidiary Officer, David Marra
Executive Vice President, Chief Financial Officer, Robert (Bob) Qutub, $610,000 total compensation
Executive Vice President, Chief Portfolio Officer, Ross A. Curtis, $654,167 total compensation
Executive Vice President, Chief Risk Officer, Ian D. Branagan, $572,923 total compensation
Senior Vice President, Chief Investment Officer, Sean G. Brosnan
Senior Vice President, Group General Counsel, Corporate Secretary, Shannon Lowry Bender
Senior Vice President, Chief Accounting Officer, James C. Fraser
Non-Executive Chairman, Director, James L. Gibbons
Director, Shyam Gidumal
Director, Henry Klehm
Director, Valerie Rahmani
Director, Carol P. Sanders
Director, Cynthia M. Trudell
Director, David C. Bushnell
Director, Anthony M. Santomero
Director, Brian G.J. Gray
Director, Duncan P. Hennes

Auditors : PricewaterhouseCoopers Ltd.

LOCATIONS

HQ: RenaissanceRe Holdings Ltd.
Renaissance House, 12 Crow Lane, Pembroke HM 19
Phone: (1) 441 2954513 **Fax:** (1) 441 2959453
Web: www.renre.com

PRODUCTS/OPERATIONS

2017 Sales by Segment

	% of total
Casualty and Specialty	52
Property	48
Total	100

2017 Sales

	$ mil.	% of total
Net premiums earned	1,717.6	82
Net investment income	222.2	11
Net realized and unrealized gains on investments	135.8	6
Net foreign exchange gains	10.6	1
Equity in earnings of other ventures	8.0	-
Other	9.4	-
Total	2,095.6	100

COMPETITORS

AMERICAN EQUITY INVESTMENT LIFE HOLDING COMPANY
AMTRUST FINANCIAL SERVICES, INC.
CRAWFORD & COMPANY
DONEGAL GROUP INC.
HALLMARK FINANCIAL SERVICES, INC.
KANSAS CITY LIFE INSURANCE COMPANY
PRIMERICA, INC.
THE NASSAU COMPANIES OF NEW YORK
UNITED FIRE GROUP, INC.
W. R. BERKLEY CORPORATION

HISTORICAL FINANCIALS

Company Type: Public

Income Statement   FYE: December 31

	ASSETS ($mil)	NET INCOME ($mil)	INCOME AS % OF ASSETS	EMPLOYEES
12/23	49,007	2,561	5.2%	0
12/22	36,552	(1,061)	—	718
12/21	33,959	(40)	—	649
12/20	30,820	762	2.5%	604
12/19	26,330	748	2.8%	566
Annual Growth	16.8%	36.0%	—	—

2023 Year-End Financials

Return on assets: 5.9%   Dividends
Return on equity: 34.6%   Yield: —
Long-term debt ($ mil.): —   Payout: 2.9%
No. of shares ($ mil.): 52   Market value ($ mil.): —
Sales ($ mil.): 9,134

Renault S.A. (France)

EXECUTIVES

Chief Executive Officer, Luca de Meo
Deputy Chief Executive, Clotilde Delbos
Group Industry Executive Vice President, Jose Vicente de los Mozos
Group Quality Executive Vice President, Philippe Guerin-Boutaud
Group Advanced Product & Planning Executive Vice President, Ali Kassai

Renesas Electronics Corp

Renesas Electronics is a global leader in microcontrollers, analog, power, and SoC products and provides comprehensive solutions for a broad range of automotive, industrial, home electronics, office automation, and information communication technology applications that help shape a limitless future. Its products are used in automotive (in the auto factory as well as in the auto), industrial, and consumer electronics applications. With operations in more than 30 countries, the majority of Renesas' revenue comes from outside Japan. Established in 2002, Renesas is built on the foundation that combines the rich culture of technology and innovation of Hitachi, Mitsubishi and NEC.

Operations

Renesas Electronics operates in two main segments: Industrial/Infrastructure/IoT Business and Automotive Business ? accounts for an evenly split of revenue.

The Industrial/Infrastructure/IoT segment includes the product categories Industrial, Infrastructure, and "IoT" which support the smart society. It mainly supplies MCUs and SoCs in each of these categories.

The automotive segment includes the product categories Automotive control, comprising semiconductor devices for controlling automobile engines and bodies, and Automotive information, comprising of semiconductor devices used in sensing systems for detecting environments inside and outside the vehicle as well as automotive information devices such as IVI (in-vehicle infotainment) and instrument panels used to give various information to the driver of the vehicle.

Geographic Reach

More than 30% of Renesas Electronics' revenue comes from customers in Japan while nearly 25% from China and another some 20% from other Asian countries. The company's European and North American markets combined to provide about a quarter of revenue.

Headquartered in Tokyo, Japan, the company has sales operations in Asia, North America, South America, Middle East, and Europe. Its manufacturing and engineering facilities are in Japan and Asia.

Sales and Marketing

Renesas' major customers are Ryosan Company and WT Microelectronics, which accounts for about 15% each of revenue.

Financial Performance

The company reported a revenue of ¥994.4 billion in 2021, a 39% increase from the previous year's revenue of ¥715.7 billion.

In 2021, the company had a net income of ¥127.3 billion, a 179% improvement from the previous year's net income of ¥45.6 million.

The company's cash at the end of 2021 was ¥221.9 billion. Operating activities generated ¥307.4 billion, while investing activities used ¥663.1 billion, mainly for payments for acquisitions of subsidiaries. Financing activities provided another ¥340.9 billion, mainly for repayments of long-term borrowings.

Strategy

The company announced the "Mid-Term Growth Strategy" and "Financial Model" on February 17, 2020. The company set as a long-term target of achieving sales growth exceeding that of the market through concentrated investment of management resources in markets on which the company is focusing its attention. The company also set non-GAAP financial targets of achieving a 50% gross margin and a 20% or more operating margin by optimizing production efficiency, improving the product mix and realizing synergies from the integration of IDT.

The targets in the "Mid-Term Growth Strategy" and "Financial Model" are the company's long-term management objectives as of the date of filing and the company cannot guarantee that these will be achieved. Results may be affected by a number of risk factors and other changes in the external environment, including the matters described under "Risk Factors" in the Management's Discussion and Analysis of Operations.

Mergers and Acquisitions

In mid-2022, Renesas Electronics announced that it has entered into a definitive agreement to acquire Steradian Semiconductors Private Limited (Steradian), a fabless semiconductor company based in Bengaluru, India, that provides 4D imaging radar solutions, in an all-cash transaction. The acquisition of Steradian's radar technology will enable Renesas to extend its reach in the radar market and boost its automotive and industrial sensing solution offerings.

In 2022, Renesas Electronics announced the completion of the acquisition of US-based Reality Analytics, Inc. (Reality AI), a leading provider of embedded AI solutions. Combining Reality AI's best-in-class AI inference technologies with Renesas' extensive MCU and MPU product portfolios will enable seamless implementation of machine learning and signal processing. The acquisition will allow Renesas to expand its tool suite and software offerings for AI applications and increase its in-house capability to provide highly optimized endpoint solutions that combine both hardware and software.

In late 2021, Renesas Electronics announced the successful completion of acquisition of Israel-based Celeno Communications, the leading provider of smart, innovative Wi-Fi solutions, under

---

Group Engineering Executive Vice President, Gilles Le Borgne
Executive Vice President, Denis Le Vot
Executive Vice President, Chief Turnaround Officer, Nicolas Maure
Human Resources Executive Vice President, Francois Roger
Alliance Purchasing Organization Executive Vice President, Veronique Sarlat-Depotte
Group Design Executive Vice President, Laurens van den Acker
, Group IS IT/Digital Executive Vice President, Frederic Vincent
Chairman, Jean-Dominique Senard
Lead Independent Director, Pierre Fleuriot
Independent Director, Catherine Barba
Independent Director, Miriem Bensalah-Chaqroun
Independent Director, Marie-Annick Darmaillac
Independent Director, Pascal Sourisse
Independent Director, Patrick Thomas
Independent Director, Annette Winkler
Independent Director, Bernard Delpit
Director, Frederic Barrat
Director, Thomas Courbe
Director, Richard Gentil
Director, Benoit Ostertag
Director, Eric Personne
Director, Yu Serizawa
Director, Joji Tagawa
Director, Martine Vial
Auditors : KPMG Audit

LOCATIONS

HQ: Renault S.A. (France)
13-15, quai Le Gallo, Boulogne-Billancourt, Cedex 92513
Phone: (33) 1 76840404
Web: www.groupe.renault.com

HISTORICAL FINANCIALS

Company Type: Public

Income Statement — FYE: December 31

	REVENUE ($mil)	NET INCOME ($mil)	NET PROFIT MARGIN	EMPLOYEES
12/22	49,547	(360)	—	0
12/21	52,306	1,005	1.9%	0
12/20	53,355	(9,828)	—	170,158
12/19	62,355	(158)	—	179,565
12/18	65,755	3,781	5.8%	183,002
Annual Growth	(6.8%)	—	—	—

2022 Year-End Financials

Debt ratio: 56.6% No. of shares ($ mil.): 290
Return on equity: (-1.2%) Dividends
Cash ($ mil.): 23,255 Yield: —
Current Ratio: 1.12 Payout: 0.0%
Long-term debt ($ mil.): 9,662 Market value ($ mil.): 1,923

	STOCK PRICE ($) FY Close	P/E High/Low		PER SHARE ($) Earnings	Dividends	Book Value
12/22	6.62	—	—	(1.32)	0.00	105.91
12/21	6.86	3	2	3.67	0.00	106.21
12/20	8.73	—	—	(36.22)	0.00	104.41
12/19	9.42	—	—	(0.58)	0.80	133.28
12/18	12.30	2	1	13.89	0.83	140.05
Annual Growth	(14.3%)	—	—	—	—	(6.7%)

which Renesas will acquire Celeno in an all cash transaction valuing Celeno at approximately $315 million. In addition to expanding the solution offering, the acquisition also increases Renesas' engineering and design scale with Celeno's design center in Israel and by welcoming R&D staff based in Israel, Ukraine, India, China, Taiwan and more. This further strengthens Renesas' global engineering and software development talent base, allowing Renesas to bring more seamless and expanded services to customers around the globe.

In mid-2021, Renesas Electronics Corporation and Dialog Semiconductor Plc (Dialog), a leading provider of battery and power management, Wi-Fi, Bluetooth low energy and Industrial edge computing solutions, announced the successful completion of Renesas' acquisition of the entire issued and to be issued share capital of Dialog. Renesas will fund the cash consideration payable to Dialog shareholders of approximately EUR 4.8 billion. The closing of the acquisition of Dialog, following the landmark acquisitions of Intersil and IDT, reinforces Renesas as a premier embedded solution provider. Renesas will expand its market presence with an even broader range of product portfolio by combining Dialog's low-power mixed signal products, low-power Wi-Fi and Bluetooth connectivity expertise, flash memory, battery and power management as well as its long-standing experience and in-depth knowledge in providing configurable mixed-signal (CMIC) solutions and more.

EXECUTIVES

President, Chief Executive Officer, Representative Director, Hidetoshi Shibata
Outside Director, Jiro Iwasaki
Outside Director, Selena Loh LaCroix
Outside Director, Noboru Yamamoto
Outside Director, Takuya Hirano
Auditors : PricewaterhouseCoopers Aarata LLC

LOCATIONS

HQ: Renesas Electronics Corp
  3-2-24 Toyosu, Koto-ku, Tokyo 135-0061
  Phone: (81) 3 6773 3000   **Fax:** (81) 3 6773 3333
  Web: www.renesas.com/jp/ja

2017 Sales

	% of total
Automotive	52
Industrial	27
Broad-based business	13
Other	8
Total	100

PRODUCTS/OPERATIONS

Selected Products
Development software
Discrete devices
Electrically erasable programmable read-only memories
General-purpose linear devices
Low-latency DRAMs
Microcontrollers
Microprocessors
Power integrated circuits
Radio-frequency (RF) and microwave devices
Standard logic devices
Static random-access memories
Transistors

HISTORICAL FINANCIALS
Company Type: Public

Income Statement   FYE: December 31

	REVENUE ($mil)	NET INCOME ($mil)	NET PROFIT MARGIN	EMPLOYEES
12/22	11,389	1,947	17.1%	21,017
12/21	8,638	1,105	12.8%	20,962
12/20	6,943	442	6.4%	18,753
12/19	6,615	(54)	—	18,958
12/18	6,879	463	6.7%	20,231
Annual Growth	13.4%	43.2%	—	1.0%

2022 Year-End Financials
Debt ratio: 0.2%   No. of shares ($ mil.): 1,796
Return on equity: 19.0%   Dividends
Cash ($ mil.): 2,378   Yield: —
Current Ratio: 1.36   Payout: 0.0%
Long-term debt ($ mil.): 4,824   Market value ($ mil.): 7,889

	STOCK PRICE ($) FY Close	P/E High/Low		PER SHARE ($) Earnings	Dividends	Book Value
12/22	4.39	0	0	1.02	0.00	6.48
12/21	6.20	0	0	0.59	0.00	5.18
12/20	5.23	0	0	0.25	0.00	3.45
12/19	3.42	—	—	(0.03)	0.00	3.34
12/18	2.23	0	0	0.28	0.00	3.26
Annual Growth	18.5%	—	—	38.6%	—	18.7%

Repsol S.A.

Repsol is a global multi-energy provider that has an integrated business model that ranges from oil and gas exploration and production to the commercialization of energy solutions for the home and mobility. The company sells its products in more than 90 countries and serves approximately 24 million customers. It is a group of companies, with a vision of being a multi-energy efficient, sustainable and competitive company, performs activities in the hydrocarbon sector throughout its entire value chain (exploration, development and production of crude oil and natural gas, refining, production, transportation and sale of a wide range of oil and petrochemical products, oil derivatives and natural gas), as well as activities for the generation and sale of electricity. The company started in 1927. Majority of its sales were generated from Spain.

Operations
Repsol's reporting segments are: Industrial (some 60% of sales); Commercial and Renewables (about 35%) Exploration and Production (over 5%).

The Industrial segment includes refining activities, petrochemicals, trading and transportation of crude oil and oil products, and sale, transportation and regasification of natural gas and liquefied natural gas (LNG).

Commercial and Renewables segment integrates the businesses of low-carbon power generation and renewable sources, sale of gas and power, mobility and sale of oil products, and liquefied petroleum gas (LPG).

The Exploration and Production segment include activities for the exploration, development and production of crude oil and natural gas reserves.

Geographic Reach
Madrid-based, Repsol sells its products in over 90 countries and has seven industrial complexes in Spain, Portugal, and Peru. The Spain generated about 50% of sales, while the US, Peru and Portugal generated around 5% each.

Sales and Marketing
The company serves 24 million customers, with 1.4 electricity and gas customers. Repsol also operates more than 4,600 service stations in Spain, Portugal, Peru, and Mexico.

Financial Performance
The company's revenue in 2021 increased to EUR 52.1 billion compared to EUR 35.0 billion in the prior year.

Net income in 2021 was EUR 2.5 billion compared to a net loss of EUR 3.3 billion in the prior year.

Cash held by the company at the end of 2021 increased to EUR 5.9 billion. Operating activities provided EUR 5.5 billion while investing and financing activities used EUR2.6 billion and EUR1.5 billion, respectively.

Strategy
In December 2019, Repsol was the first energy firm to announce its commitment to become a net zero emissions company by 2050, thus starting a strategic change of course.

The Strategic Plan 2021-2025 (SP 21-25 or the Plan) seeks to bring about the company's transformation and sets the tone for accelerating the energy transition, following a cost-effective and realistic path and ensuring profitability, future success and maximum value for shareholders.

The Plan envisions two distinct periods: the first (2021-2022) is focused on ensuring financial robustness by prioritizing efficiency, investment reduction and capital optimization, while developing projects to lead the energy transition; the second (2023-2025), once the impact of the COVID-19 crisis is behind the company, will focus on accelerating transformation and growth.

Mergers and Acquisitions
In early 2022. Repsol has acquired Capital Energy's portfolio of 25,000 residential and SME electricity customers. With this transaction, Repsol reinforces its growth in this business and now has 1.35 million electricity and gas customers. The acquisition reinforces Repsol's growth as a major player in the electricity and gas market in Spain, where it already has more than 1.3 million customers. In addition, this transaction is

another step towards achieving the commitments set out in its strategy, which envisages having 2 million electricity, gas and electric mobility customers by 2025. Terms were not disclosed.

In mid-2021, Repsol has acquired 100% of Klikin, the startup founded by entrepreneur Gustavo GarcÃa Brusilovsky, which has driven Waylet to emerge as a payment and loyalty app with more than two million users. Repsol has acquired the remaining 30%, which had been held by the founding partners. This transaction is part of Repsol's digital customer growth strategy, as outlined in the 2021-2025 Strategic Plan, and will consolidate Waylet as the leading mobility payment app in Spain. Terms were not disclosed.

In early 2021, Repsol signed an agreement to acquire 40% of Hecate Energy, a US-based PV solar and battery storage project developer. The transaction is Repsol's first foray into the US renewables market and complements the company's capabilities and portfolio and adds a solid platform with strong growth potential.

HISTORY

The Repsol Group emerged during Spain's negotiations to join the European Union, named after REPESA's premium lubricant brand, Repsol.

It was created in 1987 by the National Hydrocarbons Institute during the reorganization of the Spanish energy sector. The company went fully private in 1997.

EXECUTIVES

Chairman, Non-Executive Director, Antonio Brufau Niubo
Chief Executive Officer, Executive Director, Josu Jon Imaz San Miguel
Chief Financial Officer, Antonio Lorenzo Sierra
Investor Relations Executive Managing Director, Customer & Low Carbon Generation Executive Managing Director, Finance Executive Managing Director, Maria Victoria Zingoni
Exploration Executive Managing Director, Production Executive Managing Director, Tomás García Blanco
Corporate Responsibility Executive Managing Director, Institutional Relatioins Executive Managing Director, Communications Executive Managing Director, Arturo Gonzalo Aizpiri
Legal Affairs Executive Managing Director, Miguel Klingenberg Calvo
Industrial Transformation & Circular Economy Executive Director, Juan Abascal
People & Organization Corporate Director, Carmen Munoz
Digitalization & Global Services Corporate Director, Valero Marin
Chairman Office Executive Managing Director, Communications Executive Managing Director, Begona Elices Garcia

Sustainability Executive Managing Director, Technology Development, Resources Executive Managing Director, Luis Cabra Duenas
General Counsel, Non-Executive Director, Luis Suarez de Lezo Mantilla
Deputy Chairman, Manuel Manrique Cecilia
Director, Jose Manuel Loureda Mantinan
Independent Director, Ignacio Martín San Vicente
Independent Director, Maite Ballester Fornés
Non-Executive Director, Henri Philippe Reichstul
Independent Director, Arantza Estefania Larranaga
Independent Director, Mariano Marzo Carpio
Independent Director, Rene Dahan
Independent Director, J. Robinson West
Independent Director, Carmina Ganyet i Cirera
Independent Director, Isabel Torremocha Ferrezuelo
Independent Director, Teresa Garcia-Mila Lloveras
Auditors : PricewaterhouseCoopers Auditores, S.L.

LOCATIONS

HQ: Repsol S.A.
Calle Mendez Alvaro 44, Madrid 28045
Phone: (34) 91 75 38 100
Web: www.repsol.com

2018 sales

	%
Spain	51
US	6
Peru	6
Portugal	5
Other	32
Total	100

PRODUCTS/OPERATIONS

2018 Sales

	% of total
Downstream	90
Upstream	10
Total	100

COMPETITORS

BP P.L.C.
DCC PUBLIC LIMITED COMPANY
ENI SPA
IBERDROLA, SOCIEDAD ANONIMA
LUKOIL, PAO
NATURGY ENERGY GROUP SA.
RWE AG
SASOL LTD
TOTAL SE
Uniper SE

HISTORICAL FINANCIALS

Company Type: Public

Income Statement — FYE: December 31

	REVENUE ($mil)	NET INCOME ($mil)	NET PROFIT MARGIN	EMPLOYEES
12/22	80,902	4,540	5.6%	23,770
12/21	57,163	2,828	4.9%	23,900
12/20	40,080	(4,036)	—	23,739
12/19	55,396	(8,568)	—	24,634
12/18	57,263	2,680	4.7%	24,506
Annual Growth	9.0%	14.1%	—	(0.8%)

2022 Year-End Financials

Debt ratio: 20.1%
Return on equity: 17.8%
Cash ($ mil.): 6,955
Current Ratio: 1.55
Long-term debt ($ mil.): 8,251
No. of shares ($ mil.): 1,327
Dividends
Yield: —
Payout: 16.4%
Market value ($ mil.): 21,142

	STOCK PRICE ($) FY Close	P/E High/Low		PER SHARE ($) Earnings	Dividends	Book Value
12/22	15.93	6	4	3.16	0.52	20.36
12/21	11.84	8	6	1.86	0.55	17.34
12/20	10.01	—	—	(2.61)	0.71	16.52
12/19	15.68	—	—	(2.78)	0.82	19.35
12/18	16.03	14	11	1.66	0.83	23.33
Annual Growth	(0.2%)		—	17.5%	(11.1%)	(3.4%)

Resona Holdings Inc
Osaka

Resona Holdings resonate in Japan's retail banking market. It's the holding company of Resona Bank and smaller regional banks Kinki Osaka Bank and Saitama Resona Bank, which operate nearly 1,450 branches across Japan mainly in the greater Tokyo area and the Kansai region. While it focuses on consumer and small business banking services, Resona Bank also provides corporate pension management and real estate services, corporate and personal trust services, personal loans, asset management, and estate planning services. Altogether, Resona Holdings boasts over Â¥45 trillion ($375 billion) in total assets and Â¥24 trillion ($20 billion) in trust assets.

Operations

Resona Holdings operates three core business segments: Consumer Banking, which provides consumer loans, asset management, and asset succession services; Corporate Banking, which provides corporate loans, trust asset management, real estate services, corporate pension management, and asset succession services; and Market Trading, which provides short-term lending, borrowing, bond purchase and sale, and derivatives trading in financial markets.

About 54% of its total revenue came from interest income in fiscal 2015 (ended March 31), while 23% came from non-trust fees and commissions and 3% came from trust fees. About 85% of its total loans and bills discounted were loans to small and medium-sized enterprises (SMEs). More than 60% of its deposits were from individuals.

Geographic Reach

Tokyo-based Resona Holdings has more than 1,440 branches across Japan, including more than 820 in the Kanto region, and 579 in the Kansai region. Its Kinki Osaka Bank subsidiary has 128 manned branches mainly in the Kinki region. About 40% of its branches are manned, while the majority are unmanned.

Financial Performance

Note: Growth rates may differ after conversion to US dollars.

Resona Holdings' revenues and profits have trended lower over the past several years mostly due to shrinking interest margins on loans amidst the low-interest environment.

The company had a breakout year in fiscal 2015 (ended March 31), however, as its revenue rose by 4% to Â¥861.4 billion ($7.2 billion) on higher fee and commission income from sales of its investment trust and insurance products. Its interest income continued to slide downward due to low interest margins.

Despite generating higher revenue in FY2015, the group's net income fell by 4% to Â¥211.4 billion ($1.77 billion) mostly due to higher income taxes and a Â¥23 billion charge related to the reversal of deferred tax assets in line with the reduction of the effective corporate tax rate. Resona's operating cash levels fell in half to Â¥1,103 billion ($9 billion) for the year mostly as it extended more of its cash toward loans and bills discounted.

Strategy

Resona Holdings in early 2015 launched its "New Mid-term Management Plan" for the next decade, which set its sights on becoming the "No. 1 Retail Bank" through more proactive measures toward continued growth. Continuing to focus on its retail banking business and lending to SMEs, the bank planned to "maximize customer value by maintaining its fundamental stance that 'Customers' joy and happiness are Resona's.'

The company also in 2015 outlined its three "ACL" initiatives, which included: "All Resona," which aimed to offer collaboration of companies and services to provide SME customers with management consulting and other services as they grew; "Cross-selling promotion," which aimed to cross sell life insurance to the group's mortgage customers which numbered 560,000 borrowers and grew by 40,000 new borrowers annually; and "Low-cost operations," which rely on productivity-boosting initiatives such as installed communication terminals that allow tellers to serve customers more securely and efficiently.

Resona Holdings has significant market strength in its key markets in the greater Tokyo metro area and the Kansai region (the most populated and economically active parts of Japan). During 2015, it held 40% of the deposit market in the Saitama and Osaka Prefectures, and nearly 20% of the loan market in the region as well.

EXECUTIVES

Representative Executive Officer, President, Chief Executive Officer, Director, Masahiro Minami

Executive Officer, Executive Vice President, Chief Strategy Officer, Chief Risk Officer, Director, Shigeki Ishida

Chief Information Officer, Chief Process Reengineering Officer, Executive Officer, Director, Mikio Noguchi

Executive Officer, Chief Administrative Officer, Koichi Akiyama

Chief Financial Officer, Narunobu Ota

Chief Compliance Officer, Yukinobu Murao

Chief Human Resources Officer, Hideo Sekiguchi

Chief Digital Information Officer, Shinichiro Isa

Director, Hisahiko Oikawa

Outside Director, Chiharu Baba

Outside Director, Kimie Iwata

Outside Director, Setsuko Egami

Outside Director, Fumihiko Ike

Outside Director, Sawako Nohara

Outside Director, Masaki Yamauchi

Outside Director, Katsuyuki Tanaka

Outside Director, Ryuji Yasuda

Auditors : Deloitte Touche Tohmatsu LLC

LOCATIONS

HQ: Resona Holdings Inc Osaka
1-5-65 Kiba, Koto-ku, Tokyo 135-8582
Phone: (81) 3 6704 3111
Web: www.resona-gr.co.jp

PRODUCTS/OPERATIONS

2014 Sales

	% of total
Interest income	57
Fees and commissions	23
Other operating income	4
Trust fees	3
Other	13
Total	100

Selected Subsidiaries

Daiwa Guarantee Co., Ltd. (credit guarantee)
Resona Bank, Ltd. (bank)
Resona Guarantee Co., Ltd. (credit guarantee)
Saitama Resona Bank, Ltd. (bank)
Kinki Osaka Shinyo Hosho Co., Ltd. (credit guarantee)
The Kinki Osaka Bank, Ltd. (bank)
P.T. Bank Resona Perdania (bank)
Resona Kessai Service Co., Ltd. (collections agency)
Resona Card Co., Ltd. (credit cards)
Resona Capital Co., Ltd. (private equity)
Resona Research Institute Co., Ltd. (consulting)
Resona Business Service Co., Ltd. (staffing)

COMPETITORS

ALDERMORE GROUP PLC
BANKIA SA
BYLINE BANCORP, INC.
ENTERPRISE FINANCIAL SERVICES CORP
LIONTRUST ASSET MANAGEMENT PLC
METROPOLITAN BANK HOLDING CORP.
MIZUHO FINANCIAL GROUP, INC.
SHINSEI BANK, LIMITED
Shinhan Financial Group Co., Ltd.
Woori Finance Holdings Co., Ltd.

HISTORICAL FINANCIALS

Company Type: Public

Income Statement — FYE: March 31

	ASSETS ($mil)	NET INCOME ($mil)	INCOME AS % OF ASSETS	EMPLOYEES
03/23	561,718	1,204	0.2%	28,116
03/22	642,527	904	0.1%	29,337
03/21	665,595	1,124	0.2%	30,626
03/20	557,461	1,404	0.3%	31,425
03/19	533,755	1,581	0.3%	32,924
Annual Growth	1.3%	(6.6%)	—	(3.9%)

2023 Year-End Financials

Return on assets: 0.2%
Return on equity: 6.4%
Long-term debt ($ mil.): —
No. of shares ($ mil.): 2,376
Sales ($ mil.): 6,530
Dividends
  Yield: —
  Payout: 31.1%
Market value ($ mil.): —

Resonac Holdings Corp

EXECUTIVES

Chairman, Representative Director, Kohei Morikawa

President, Chief Executive Officer, Representative Director, Hidehito Takahashi

Chief Risk Officer, Director, Keiichi Kamiguchi

Chief Financial Officer, Director, Hideki Somemiya

Chief Strategy Officer, Director, Tomomitsu Maoka

Chief Technology Officer, Hiroshi Sakai

Outside Director, Kiyoshi Nishioka

Outside Director, Kozo Isshiki

Outside Director, Noriko Morikawa

Outside Director, Tetsuo Tsuneishi

Auditors : KPMG AZSA LLC

LOCATIONS

HQ: Resonac Holdings Corp
1-13-9 Shiba Daimon, Minato-ku, Tokyo 105-8518
Phone: (81) 3 5470 3384   **Fax:** (81) 3 3431 6215
Web: www.resonac.com

HISTORICAL FINANCIALS

Company Type: Public

Income Statement — FYE: December 31

	REVENUE ($mil)	NET INCOME ($mil)	NET PROFIT MARGIN	EMPLOYEES
12/22	10,568	233	2.2%	25,803
12/21	12,332	(105)	—	26,054
12/20	9,447	(740)	—	33,684
12/19	8,349	673	8.1%	10,813
12/18	9,021	1,013	11.2%	10,476
Annual Growth	4.0%	(30.7%)		25.3%

2022 Year-End Financials

Debt ratio: 0.4%
Return on equity: 5.7%
Cash ($ mil.): 1,420
Current Ratio: 1.70
Long-term debt ($ mil.): 7,075
No. of shares ($ mil.): 181
Dividends
  Yield: —
  Payout: 0.0%
Market value ($ mil.): 2,892

	STOCK PRICE ($)	P/E	PER SHARE ($)		
	FY Close	High/Low	Earnings	Dividends	Book Value
12/22	15.95	0 0	1.29	0.51	23.03
12/21	21.84	— —	(0.67)	0.55	24.62
12/20	21.39	— —	(5.07)	0.78	26.95
12/19	27.36	0 0	4.61	1.39	31.47
12/18	30.35	0 0	6.89	0.64	27.75
Annual Growth	(14.9%)	—	(34.2%)	(5.7%)	(4.6%)

Rexel S.A.

France-based Rexel distributes electrical parts and supplies that include wiring devices, cabling systems, lighting products, electrical tools, and climate control and security equipment. The company serves customers in the commercial sector; industrial markets such as utilities and automotive; and the residential market, including new construction and upgrade projects. Subsidiaries include Conectis (voice and networking products) as well as North American units Rexel USA and Rexel Canada Electrical. The company has over 1,900 branches and logistics centers in about 25 countries around the world. Rexel generates around 55% of revenue in Europe operations.

Operations

The company is mainly involved in the business of the distribution of low and ultra-low voltage electrical products to professional customers. The product offering covers electrical installation equipment, conduits and cables, lighting, security and communication, climate control, tools, renewable energies and energy management, and white and brown goods.

Overall, about 85% of sales were generated from warehouse sales, while direct sales generated around 15%.

Geographic Reach

Headquartered in Paris, France, Rexel operates through a network of more than 1,900 branches in roughly 25 countries. The company's largest market was around 55% from Europe which consist France, UK, Germany, Sweden, Switzerland, Belgium, Austria, the Netherlands, Norway, Finland, Spain, Ireland, Italy, Slovenia, Portugal, Russia and Luxembourg; followed by North America (US and Canada) with some 35%; and Asia-Pacific (Australia, China, New Zealand, India and Middle East) with about 10%, respectively.

Sales and Marketing

The company operates through a network of more than 1,900 branches and about 65 logistics center.

Financial Performance

The company's revenue for fiscal 2021 increased by 17% to EUR14.7 billion compared from the prior year with EUR12.6 billion.

Net income for fiscal 2021 increased to EUR597.6 million compared from the prior year with EUR261.3 million.

Cash held by the company at the end of fiscal 2021 decreased to EUR573.5 million. Cash provided by operations was EUR717.7 million while cash used for investing and financing activities were EUR542.3 million and EUR299.7 million, respectively.

Strategy

In 2021, the company experienced a strong sales growth in a constrained environment marked by product scarcity and price increases, showing its ability to fully capture market recovery driven by electrification and energy transition and to ensure business continuity for its customers.

Rexel also resumed its external growth policy and finalized five acquisitions of which the two main following ones in North America: Mayer, a major distributor of electrical products and services in the Eastern part of the USA; and A Utility distribution business in Canada.

Mergers and Acquisitions

In 2021, Rexel announces the closing of the acquisition of 100% of Mayer a major distributor of electrical products and services operating in the Eastern part of the US. This move is an important step in expanding Rexel's footprint in the US, the world's leading market for electrical supplies. Terms were not diclosed.

In early 2021, Rexel has acquired a minority stake in Trace Software International, a software edition company specialized in electrical design and calculation for non-residential building activity and 100% of Freshmile Services, an independent electrical vehicle charging station operator offering both services and supervision software. The ambition underpinning these 2 acquisitions is twofold: completes the current range of software solutions with a new proposition dedicated to the non-residential market to facilitate the daily work of our customers; and offers a full range of services to end users, from installed base monitoring to remote maintenance. Terms were not disclosed.

Company Background

Rexel was founded in 1967 as Compagnie de Distribution de Matériel Electrique (CDME) and went public on the Paris bourse in 1983. It entered the US market in 1986. CDME was acquired by Pinault in 1990 and changed its name to Rexel in 1993. The company entered international markets in South America, Asia Pacific, and Eastern Europe in the late 1990s.

EXECUTIVES

Chief Executive Officer, Non-Independent Director, Guilaume Texier
Chief Financial Officer, Laurent Delabarre
Purchasing, Supply Chain and Supplier Relationship Director, Guillaume Dubrule
Strategy Director, Constance Grisoni
Chief Human Resources and Communications Officer, Sabine Haman
Digital, IT and Sustainability Officer, Nathalie Wright
Secretary, Isabelle Hoepfner-Leger
Chairman, Independent Non-Executive Director, Ian Meakins
Deputy Chairman, Senior Independent Director, Francois Henrot
Independent Director, Francois Auque
Independent Director, Brigitte Cantaloube
Independent Director, Barbara Dalibard
Independent Director, Elen Phillips
Independent Director, Maria Richter
Independent Director, Agnes Touraine
Non-Independent Director, Marcus Alexanderson
Director, Toni Killebrew
Auditors : PricewaterhouseCoopers Audit

LOCATIONS

HQ: Rexel S.A.
13 boulevard du Fort-de-Vaux, CS 60002, Paris, Cedex 17 75838
Phone: (33) 1 42 85 85 00   **Fax:** (33) 1 42 85 92 02
Web: www.rexel.com

2018 Sales

	% of total
Europe	55
North America	36
Asia/Pacific	9
Total	100

Rexel distributes electrical products in more than 30 countries around the world.

PRODUCTS/OPERATIONS

2018 Sales

	% of total
Commercial	45
Industrial	30
Residential	25
Total	100

Selected Solutions:

Smart Building
Lighting
Climate Control
Security
Datacom
Photovoltaics
Home Automation
Electric Vehicles
Industrial Solutions
Production Parts

COMPETITORS

AMDOCS LIMITED
ANIXTER INTERNATIONAL, INC.
ATOS SE
DCC PUBLIC LIMITED COMPANY
DIPLOMA PLC
FLEX LTD.
IQGEO GROUP PLC
KEYSIGHT TECHNOLOGIES, INC.
LIXIL CORPORATION
SANMINA CORPORATION

HISTORICAL FINANCIALS

Company Type: Public

Income Statement — FYE: December 31

	REVENUE ($mil)	NET INCOME ($mil)	NET PROFIT MARGIN	EMPLOYEES
12/22	19,974	985	4.9%	25,906
12/21	16,627	675	4.1%	24,630
12/20	15,454	(320)	—	24,818
12/19	15,429	229	1.5%	26,537
12/18	15,306	172	1.1%	27,015
Annual Growth	6.9%	54.6%	—	(1.0%)

2022 Year-End Financials

Debt ratio: 29.5%
Return on equity: 18.7%
Cash ($ mil.): 956
Current Ratio: 1.55
Long-term debt ($ mil.): 3,008
No. of shares ($ mil.): 302
Dividends
 Yield: —
 Payout: 0.0%
Market value ($ mil.): —

Ricoh Co Ltd

Ricoh is a leading provider of digital services, information management, and print and imaging solutions designed to support digital transformation and optimize business performance. Ricoh makes fax machines, scanners, personal computers, servers, network equipment, related parts and supplies, services, support and service and solutions related to documents. Other products from the company, which operates about 225 subsidiaries and affiliates in more than 200 countries, include digital cameras, servers, software for its products, semiconductors, printed circuit boards, thermal paper labels, and optical equipment. Ricoh generates around 40% of its revenue from domestic operations.

Operations

Ricoh operates through five segments: digital services, digital products, graphic communications, industrial solutions, and other.

Digital Services account for more than 65% of revenue and sell office imaging equipment and consumables. These include MFPs and printers, with leading global market shares. It also provide other services to digitally resolve management issues and enhance customer productivity.

Digital Products (more than 15%) develop and produce (including on an OEM basis) office MFPs, in which the company is the global market leader, as well as printers and other imaging equipment and edge devices that support digital communication.

Graphic Communications (less than 10%) comprises of commercial printing and industrial printing. Commercial printing provides digital printing-related products and services for high-mix, low-volume printing to its customers in the printing industry. Industrial Printing manufactures and sells industrial inkjet heads, inkjet ink, and industrial printers for diverse applications. These include building materials, furniture, wallpaper, signage displays, and apparel fabrics.

Ricoh Industrial include thermal media and industrial business and accounts for about 5% of revenue. Thermal Media manufactures and sells thermal paper for point-of-sale, barcode, delivery, and other labels for food products, and thermal transfer ribbons for clothing price tags, brand tags, and tickets. Industrial Products provides precision device components and other products that employ optical and image processing technologies.

Other (less than 5%) include smart vision business and other businesses. Smart Vision includes 360° RICOH THETA cameras with software and cloud services to streamline real estate, construction, and architectural site work. Its other businesses include digital camera-related businesses, its business with PLAiR, a new plant-derived material that is an alternative to plastic, healthcare business, and social infrastructure and environmental businesses.

Geographic Reach

Sales in Ricoh's home country, Japan, account for about 40% of the company's revenue, followed by Europe, the Middle East, and Africa and the Americas for around 25% each, and other (China, South East Asia and Oceania), about 10%.

Financial Performance

Note: Growth rates may differ after currency conversion.

Consolidated sales for the term increased 5% from a year earlier, to JPY 1.8 trillion. This was despite various external factors hampering business activities. Among them were lost sales opportunities and production stoppages stemming from a global resurgence in COVID-19 infections, as well as container ship shortages and limited supplies owing to a lack of components.

Profit for fiscal 2021 was JPY 30.3 billion compared from the prior year with JPY 32.7 billion.

Cash held by the company at the end of fiscal 2022 decreased to JPY 234.0 billion. Cash provided by operations was JPY 82.5 billion, while cash used for investing and financing activities were JPY 59.4 billion and JPY 131.7 billion, respectively. Main uses of cash were expenditures for property, plant and equipment; and proceeds from purchase of investments in subsidiaries without change in scope of consolidation.

Strategy

The company will accelerate workplace transformation by leveraging the following strengths: a global sales and service network that underpins trust with customers; an array of edge devices employing proprietary technologies in such fields as optics, image processing, and printing; expertise based on internal deployments and customer successes; collaborating with business partners that offer expertise in various industries; digital experts who are close to customers; and the RICOH Smart Integration platform.

HISTORY

Ricoh began in 1936 as the Riken Kankoshi Company, making photographic paper. With founder Kiyoshi Ichimura at the helm, the company soon became the leader in Japan's sensitized paper market. It changed its name to Riken Optical Company in 1938 and started making cameras. Two years later it produced its first camera under the Ricoh brand.

By 1954 Ricoh cameras were Japan's #1 seller and also popular abroad. The next year it entered the office machine market with its compact mimeograph machine. Ricoh followed that in 1960 with an offset duplicator.

Ricoh built its business in the 1960s with a range of office machines, including reproduction and data processing equipment and retrieval systems. The company began establishing operations overseas, including US subsidiary Ricoh Industries U.S.A. in 1962. The US unit started marketing cameras but found greener pastures in the copier industry, where Ricoh's products were sold under the Pitney Bowes and Savin brand names. It changed its name to Ricoh Company in 1963. Two years later Ricoh entered the emerging field of office computers and introduced an electrostatic copier. In 1968 Ichimura died, and Mikio Tatebayashi took over as president for the next eight years.

EXECUTIVES

Chairman, Representative Director, Yoshinori Yamashita
President, Chief Executive Officer, Chief Technology Officer, Representative Director, Akira Oyama
Senior Managing Executive Officer, Katsunori Nakata
Senior Managing Executive Officer, Chief Financial Officer, Director, Takashi Kawaguchi
Chief Human Resources Officer, Mayuko Seto
Chief Digital Innovation Officer, Yasuyuki Nomizu
Outside Director, Keisuke Yokoo
Outside Director, Sadafumi Tani
Outside Director, Kazuhiko Ishimura
Outside Director, Shigenao Ishiguro
Outside Director, Yoko Takeda
Auditors : Deloitte Touche Tohmatsu LLC

LOCATIONS

HQ: Ricoh Co Ltd
1-3-6 Nakamagome, Ota-ku, Tokyo 143-8555
Phone: (81) 3 3777 8111
Web: www.ricoh.co.jp

2019 Sales

	% of total
Japan	39
The Americas	28
Europe, Middle East, Africa	23
Other	10
Total	100

PRODUCTS/OPERATIONS
2019 Sales

	% of total
Office Printing	55
Office Services	22
Commercial Printing	9
Industrial Printing	1
Thermal Media	3
Other	10
Total	100

Selected Products
Imaging and Solutions
    Imaging Solutions
    Diazo copiers
    Digital duplicators
    Digital monochrome and color copiers
    Fax machines
    Imaging supplies and consumables
    Wide-format copiers
    Printing systems (laser, multifunction)
    Scanners
    Network System Solutions
    Document management software
    Networking and applications software
    Network systems
    Personal computers
    Servers
    Services and support
Industrial
    Electronic components
    Measuring equipment
    Optical equipment
    Semiconductor devices
    Thermal media
Other
    Digital cameras and other photographic equipment
    Financing and logistics services
    Optical disks

COMPETITORS
EASTMAN KODAK COMPANY
ENTRUST CORPORATION
ESCALADE, INCORPORATED
FUJIFILM HOLDINGS CORPORATION
Francotyp-Postalia GmbH
KONICA MINOLTA, INC.
PITNEY BOWES INC.
QUADIENT, INC.
TELLERMATE LIMITED
XEROX CORPORATION

HISTORICAL FINANCIALS
Company Type: Public

Income Statement   FYE: March 31

	REVENUE ($mil)	NET INCOME ($mil)	NET PROFIT MARGIN	EMPLOYEES
03/23	16,024	408	2.5%	81,017
03/22	14,457	249	1.7%	78,360
03/21	15,191	(295)	—	81,184
03/20	18,503	364	2.0%	90,141
03/19	18,179	447	2.5%	92,663
Annual Growth	(3.1%)	(2.3%)	—	(3.3%)

2023 Year-End Financials
Debt ratio: 0.1%
Return on equity: 5.9%
Cash ($ mil.): 1,666
Current Ratio: 1.42
Long-term debt ($ mil.): 1,540
No. of shares ($ mil.): 609
Dividends
  Yield: —
  Payout: 34.1%
Market value ($ mil.): 4,455

	STOCK PRICE ($) FY Close	P/E High/Low		PER SHARE ($) Earnings	Dividends	Book Value
03/23	7.31	0	0	0.66	0.23	11.48
03/22	8.86	0	0	0.37	0.17	11.63
03/21	10.35	—	—	(0.41)	0.18	11.57
03/20	6.84	0	0	0.50	0.24	11.70
03/19	10.30	0	0	0.62	0.16	11.62
Annual Growth	(8.2%)	—	—	1.8%	9.4%	(0.3%)

Rio Tinto Ltd

Rio Tinto Limited is the Australian half of dual-listed sister companies, with Rio Tinto plc taking up residence in London. Although each company trades separately, the two Rio Tintos operate as one business. The company explores for a variety of commodities: bauxite, copper, diamonds, gold, iron ore, minerals (borates and titanium dioxide), and potash. Iron ore makes up approximately 55% of the company's sales. Operating in approximately 35 countries worldwide, the company has a major carbon footprint, significant scope 1 and 2 emissions and material indirect scope 3 emissions. China accounts for over 55% of the company's revenue.

Operations
Rio Tinto's portfolio includes iron ore, aluminum, bauxite, alumina, copper, diamonds, titanium dioxide, lithium, salt and borates. Company operating segments are:

Iron ore which includes iron ore mining and salt and gypsum production in Western Australia. The segment accounts for around 55% of revenues.

Aluminum which includes bauxite mining; alumina refining; aluminum smelting. The segment accounts for around 25% of revenue.

Copper operates mining and refining of copper, gold, silver, molybdenum and other by-products; exploration activities together with the Simandou iron ore project, which was the responsibility of the Copper product group chief executive during 2022. Copper segment accounts for around 10% of revenue.

Minerals includes businesses with products such as borates, titanium dioxide feedstock together with the Iron Ore Company of Canada (iron ore mining and iron concentrate/pellet production). Also includes diamond mining, sorting and marketing. The segment accounts for more than 10% of revenue.

Geographic Reach
Headquartered in Melbourne, Australia, the company operates in around 35 countries.

Financial Performance
Rio Tinto's revenue for the past five fiscal years continuously increased then decreased starting from $40.5 billion in 2018 to $43.2 billion, $44.6 billion, $63.5 billion, and $55.6 billion, for 2019 to 2022, respectively.

Company's revenue for fiscal 2022 decreased by 13% to $55.6 billion compared from the prior year with $63.5 billion. The decrease was primarily due to lower revenues on its iron ore segment.

Net income for fiscal 2022 decreased to $12.4 billion compared from the prior year with $21.1 billion. The decrease was primarily due to lower revenues while having a low decrease in expenses.

Cash held by the company at the end of fiscal 2022 decreased to $6.8 billion. Cash provided by operations was $16.1 billion while cash used for investing and financing activities were $6.7 billion and $15.5 billion, respectively. Main uses of cash were for purchases of property, plant and equipment and intangible assets; and equity dividends paid to owners of Rio Tinto.

Strategy
Rio Tinto will deliver its strategy through four clear objectives, which guide how it operate. These objectives enable its ambition, set a clear pathway to deliver long-term value, and drive its actions ? day in, day out. Delivering these with discipline will unlock capacity and allow Rio Tinto to grow with support from those who invest in the company and host its operations. The strategic pillars are best operator, excel in development, impeccable ESG, and social license.

Company Background
Rio Tinto Limited began life as the Zinc Corporation in 1905 to recover zinc from the tailings of the silver and lead mines around Australia's mineral-rich Broken Hill area. The company expanded steadily, extending its operations into a wide range of mining and metallurgical activities, primarily in Australia. By 1914 it had changed its name to Consolidated Zinc Corporation. The company discovered the world's largest deposit of bauxite (1955) and formed Hamersley Holdings with Kaiser Steel (1962) to mine iron ore.

Rio Tinto plc (UK) began with mining operations in Spain in 1873. It sold most of its Spanish holdings in 1954 and branched out to Australia, Africa, and Canada. In 1962 Rio Tinto and Australia's Consolidated Zinc merged to form RTZ. The companies merged their Australian interests as a partially owned subsidiary, CRA (from Conzinc Riotinto of Australia).

In 1968 RTZ bought U.S. Borax, which was built on one of the earth's few massive boron deposits. (The use of boron in cleansers was widespread in the late 19th century.) A 1927 discovery in the Mojave Desert led to development of a large boron mine. Until its Turkish mine was nationalized, RTZ controlled the world's boron supply. It sold U.S. Borax's consumer products operations in 1988.

RTZ opened a large copper mine at Bougainville in Papua New Guinea in 1969. Subsidiary CRA discovered diamonds in

Western Australia's Argyle region three years later. CRA then opened Australia's largest thermal-coal development at Blair Athol in 1984.

RTZ bought Kennecott Corporation in 1989 and expanded its copper operations. Kennecott had been formed by Stephen Birch and named for Robert Kennicott (a typo altered the spelling of the company's name); it had begun mining at Bingham Canyon, Utah, in 1904. Kennicott had died in Alaska while trying to establish an intercontinental telegraph line. Backed by J.P. Morgan and the Guggenheims, Birch also built a railroad to haul the ore. Kennecott merged its railroad and mine operations in 1915. Kennecott consolidated its hold on Chile's Braden copper mine (1925) and on the Utah Copper Company (1936) and other US mines. When copper prices slumped, British Petroleum's Standard Oil of Ohio subsidiary bought Kennecott (1981). In 1989 RTZ purchased British Petroleum's US mineral operations, including Kennecott.

By the 1990s RTZ and CRA (by then 49%-owned by RTZ) were increasingly competing for mining rights to recently opened areas of Asia and Latin America. RTZ sold the last of its nonmining holdings (building products group) in 1993. In 1995 RTZ brought CRA into its operations. Through Kennecott, RTZ purchased US coal mine operators Nerco, Cordero Mining Company, and Colowyo Coal Company. Also in 1995 the company acquired 13% of Freeport-McMoRan Copper & Gold (sold in 2004).

The RTZ and CRA company names were changed to Rio Tinto plc and Rio Tinto Limited, respectively, in 1997. Rio Tinto bought a Wyoming coal mine from Kerr-McGee for about $400 million in 1998. The next year Rio Tinto bought 80% of Kestrel (coal, Australia), increased its ownership of Blair Athol from 57% to 71%, and increased its stake in Comalco (aluminum) to 72%.

In 2000 CEO Leon Davis retired; his position passed to energy group executive Leigh Clifford. In a move that sparked an outcry from union officials, Davis accepted a position as non-executive deputy chairman (he retired from the board in 2005). Later that year Rio Tinto acquired both North Limited and Ashton Mining. The company also bought Comalco's outstanding shares and the Peabody Group's Australian subsidiaries.

Rio Tinto sold its Norzink Zink Smelter to Outokumpu in 2001. It also increased its holdings in Queensland Alumina, Coal & Allied Industr

HISTORY

Rio Tinto Limited began life as the Zinc Corporation in 1905 to recover zinc from the tailings of the silver and lead mines around Australia's mineral-rich Broken Hill area. The company expanded steadily, extending its operations into a wide range of mining and metallurgical activities, primarily in Australia. By 1914 it had changed its name to Consolidated Zinc Corporation. The company discovered the world's largest deposit of bauxite (1955) and formed Hamersley Holdings with Kaiser Steel (1962) to mine iron ore.

Rio Tinto plc (UK) began with mining operations in Spain in 1873. It sold most of its Spanish holdings in 1954 and branched out to Australia, Africa, and Canada. In 1962 Rio Tinto and Australia's Consolidated Zinc merged to form RTZ. The companies merged their Australian interests as a partially owned subsidiary, CRA (from Conzinc Riotinto of Australia).

In 1968 RTZ bought U.S. Borax, which was built on one of the earth's few massive boron deposits. (The use of boron in cleansers was widespread in the late 19th century.) A 1927 discovery in the Mojave Desert led to development of a large boron mine. Until its Turkish mine was nationalized, RTZ controlled the world's boron supply. It sold U.S. Borax's consumer products operations in 1988.

RTZ opened a large copper mine at Bougainville in Papua New Guinea in 1969. Subsidiary CRA discovered diamonds in Western Australia's Argyle region three years later. CRA then opened Australia's largest thermal-coal development at Blair Athol in 1984.

RTZ bought Kennecott Corporation in 1989 and expanded its copper operations. Kennecott had been formed by Stephen Birch and named for Robert Kennicott (a typo altered the spelling of the company's name); it had begun mining at Bingham Canyon, Utah, in 1904. Kennicott had died in Alaska while trying to establish an intercontinental telegraph line. Backed by J.P. Morgan and the Guggenheims, Birch also built a railroad to haul the ore. Kennecott merged its railroad and mine operations in 1915. Kennecott consolidated its hold on Chile's Braden copper mine (1925) and on the Utah Copper Company (1936) and other US mines. When copper prices slumped, British Petroleum's Standard Oil of Ohio subsidiary bought Kennecott (1981). In 1989 RTZ purchased British Petroleum's US mineral operations, including Kennecott.

By the 1990s RTZ and CRA (by then 49%-owned by RTZ) were increasingly competing for mining rights to recently opened areas of Asia and Latin America. RTZ sold the last of its nonmining holdings (building products group) in 1993. In 1995 RTZ brought CRA into its operations. Through Kennecott, RTZ purchased US coal mine operators Nerco, Cordero Mining Company, and Colowyo Coal Company. Also in 1995 the company acquired 13% of Freeport-McMoRan Copper & Gold (sold in 2004).

The RTZ and CRA company names were changed to Rio Tinto plc and Rio Tinto Limited, respectively, in 1997. Rio Tinto bought a Wyoming coal mine from Kerr-McGee for about $400 million in 1998. The next year Rio Tinto bought 80% of Kestrel (coal, Australia), increased its ownership of Blair Athol from 57% to 71%, and increased its stake in Comalco (aluminum) to 72%.

In 2000 CEO Leon Davis retired; his position passed to energy group executive Leigh Clifford. In a move that sparked an outcry from union officials, Davis accepted a position as non-executive deputy chairman (he retired from the board in 2005). Later that year Rio Tinto acquired both North Limited and Ashton Mining. The company also bought Comalco's outstanding shares and the Peabody Group's Australian subsidiaries.

Rio Tinto sold its Norzink Zink Smelter to Outokumpu in 2001. It also increased its holdings in Queensland Alumina, Coal & Allied Industries, and Palabora Mining, and it began developing the Hail Creek Coal Project in Australia, which is based on one of the l

EXECUTIVES

Interim Chief Financial Officer, Peter Cunningham
Chief Executive Officer, Executive Director, Jakob Stausholm
Chief Operating Officer, Arnaud Soirat
Chief Commercial Officer, Alf Barrios
Chief People Officer, James Martin
Chief Legal Officer & External Affairs, Barbara Levi
Secretary, Tim Paine
Director, Chairman, Simon Thompson
Senior Independent Director, Sam Laidlaw
Senior Independent Director, Simon McKeon
Independent Non-Executive Director, Megan Clark
Independent Non-Executive Director, Hinda Gharbi
Independent Non-Executive Director, Simon Henry
Independent Non-Executive Director, Michael L'Estrange
Independent Non-Executive Director, Jennifer Nason
Independent Non-Executive Director, Ngaire Woods
Auditors : KPMG

LOCATIONS

HQ: Rio Tinto Ltd
   Level 7, 360 Collins Street, Melbourne, Victoria 3000
Phone: (61) 3 9283 3333
Web: www.riotinto.com

2015 Sales

	% of total
China	42
US	15
Other Asia	14
Japan	11
Europe (Excluding UK)	8
Canada	4
Australia	3
UK	1
Other	2
Total	100

PRODUCTS/OPERATIONS

2015 Sales

	% of total
Iron Ore	41
Aluminum	27
Copper	9
Coal	8
Industrial Minerals	6
Gold	3
Diamonds	2
Other	4
Total	100

Selected Holdings

Aluminum
    Bell Bay
    Boyne Island (59%, smelting)
    Queensland Alumina Ltd. (80%)
    Tiwai Point (79%, New Zealand)
    Weipa (Australia)
Iron Ore
    Hamersley Iron Pty. Ltd.
    Channar (60%)
    Marandoo mine (Pilbara, Australia)
    Nammuldi
    Iron Ore Co. of Canada (59%)
    Robe River Iron Associates (53%)
Energy & Minerals
    Coal
    Bengalla (30%, Australia)
    Blair Athol Coal (71%)
    Hail Creek Coal (82%)
    Hunter Valley Operations (76%)
    Kestrel (80%)
    Mt Thorley (61%)
    Warkworth (42%)
    Rio Tinto Diamonds & Minerals
    Rio Tinto Diamond (diamonds, Australia, Canada, Zimbabwe)
    Rio Tinto Minerals (borates, titanium dioxide, Argentina/Australia/US)
Copper Products
    Escondida (30%, Chile)
    Grasberg (40%, Indonesia)
    Kennecott Utah Copper (US)
    Northparkes (80%)
    Palabora (58%, South Africa)
Gold
    Barneys Canyon (US)
    Bingham Canyon (US)
    Escondida (30%, Chile)
    Rawhide (51%, US)

COMPETITORS

ASARCO LLC
BHP GROUP PLC
Capstone Mining Corp
FRANKLIN MINING, INC.
Fortune Minerals Limited
Kinross Gold Corporation
Magellan Minerals Ltd
NEWMONT CORPORATION
Philex Gold Inc
Turquoise Hill Resources Ltd

HISTORICAL FINANCIALS

Company Type: Public

Income Statement   FYE: December 31

	REVENUE ($mil)	NET INCOME ($mil)	NET PROFIT MARGIN	EMPLOYEES
12/21	59,617	21,094	35.4%	49,345
12/20	41,848	9,769	23.3%	47,474
12/19	43,165	8,010	18.6%	46,007
12/18	40,522	13,638	33.7%	47,458
12/17	40,030	8,762	21.9%	46,807
Annual Growth	10.5%	24.6%		1.3%

2021 Year-End Financials

Debt ratio: 10.7%
Return on equity: 42.8%
Cash ($ mil.): 12,807
Current Ratio: 1.93
Long-term debt ($ mil.): 11,032
No. of shares ($ mil.): 370
Dividends
  Yield: —
  Payout: 58.6%
Market value ($ mil.): —

Rio Tinto Plc

Founded in 1873, Rio Tinto works in 35 countries ? in mines, smelters and refineries, as well as in sales offices, data centers, research and development labs and with artificial intelligence. In Western Australia, it produces five iron ore products, including the Pilbara Blend?, the world's most traded brand of iron ore. Its Dampier Salt operations in Western Australia are the world's largest exporter of seaborne salt, produced from evaporating seawater. Its vertically integrated aluminium portfolio spans high-quality bauxite mines, alumina refineries and smelters which, in Canada, are powered entirely by clean, renewable energy. Rio Tinto generates over 55% of its revenue from China.

Operations

Rio Tinto consists of four business units based on their primary products: Iron Ore, Aluminum, Copper, and Minerals.

In the Pilbara region of Western Australia, Rio Tinto produces five iron ore products, including the Pilbara Blend, the world's most traded brand of iron ore. Its vertically integrated aluminium portfolio spans high-quality bauxite mines, alumina refineries and smelters which, in Canada, are powered entirely by clean, renewable energy.

In addition to copper, Rio Tinto's product group also includes the Simandou iron ore project in Guinea, the largest known undeveloped high-grade iron ore deposit in the world. Its Minerals product group provides materials essential to a wide variety of industries, ranging from agriculture to renewable energy and electric vehicles.

Sales of iron ore account for around 65% of the total, aluminum some 20%, industrial minerals and coppers account for about 5% each.

Geographic Reach

Based in London, Rio Tinto has mining and corporate functions spanning the world, but its areas of particular strength are Australia, where it mines all the company's major ores, and North America, with significant additional other businesses in Asia, Europe, Africa, and South America. China is Rio Tinto's largest geography by sales, accounting for more than 55% of the total. Followed by the US with nearly 15% of total sales. The remaining sales are generated from: Asia excluding China and Japan (nearly 10%); Japan (nearly 10%); Europe excluding the UK (about 5%); Canada, Australia, the UK and other countries (almost 10% combined).

Sales and Marketing

The Energy and Minerals portfolio includes titanium dioxide; rutile and zircon; borates; iron ore concentrate and pellets; and uranium.

The company's operations around the world are at various stages in the mining lifecycle, from exploration to program rehabilitation. Alongside copper, the company also produce gold, silver, molybdenum and other materials such as rhenium. Rio Tinto supply customers in China, Japan and the US.

Financial Performance

Rio Tinto' performance continues to grow and has an upward trend in its overall financial performance since 2017 and up to this year, 2021.

Rio Tinto's revenue rose by more than 40% to $63.5 billion in 2021 compared to $44.6 billion in 2020.

The company's net income increased by about 115% or $11.3 billion from $9.8 billion in 2020 to $21.1 billion in 2021. The increase reflected the higher prices, the impact of closure provision increases at Energy Resources of Australia (ERA) and other non-operating sites, $0.5 billion of exchange and derivative gains and $0.2 billion of impairments.

Cash at the end of the year totaled $22.6 billion, another $12.2 billion increase from the previous year. Cash from operations generated $25.3 billion. Investing and financing activities used $7.2 billion and $15.9 billion, respectively.

Strategy

In 2021, Rio Tinto announced a new integrated strategy bringing together a set of new commitments across three pillars of activity with four objectives guiding how it seeks to improve its business: Accelerate the decarbonization of its assets; Develop products and technologies that help its customers decarbonize; and Grow in materials enabling the energy transition.

Accelerate the decarbonization of its assets - To achieve its raised decarbonization ambition and targets, Rio Tinto will switch to renewables at scale, with a priority focus in the Pilbara. It will accelerate the electrification of its mobile equipment and processes, and empower its people to think differently about energy solutions.

Develop products and technologies that help its customers decarbonize ? Rio Tinto will increase its investment in research and development to speed up the development of products and technologies that will enable its customers to decarbonize. This includes the continued development of ELYSISTM for aluminium, finding future pathways for Pilbara ores as the industry transitions to green steel, and studying a hydrogen-based hot briquetted iron (HBI) plant in Canada.

Grow in materials enabling the energy transition ? Rio Tinto will seek to grow further in copper and battery materials, and to bring additional tonnes of high-grade iron ore to market from the Iron Ore Company of Canada (IOC) and the Simandou project in Guinea.

Delivering on its strategy depends on four objectives set out at the start of 2021: to be the best operator, to achieve impeccable environmental, social and governance (ESG) credentials, to excel in development, and to protect its social license. These essential components will help improve productivity and reduce capital intensity, and assist the company in becoming a partner of choice globally.

HISTORY

Following a tough 2009 in which the global recession depressed commodity prices, Rio Tinto rebounded strongly in 2010, posting a 35% increase in overall revenues due primarily to increased sales volumes and prices generated by the beginnings of an economic recovery. Leading the pack for Rio Tinto was its Iron Ore segment, which saw an increase of 91% over the previous year, followed by the Copper segment with a hike of 24%, and the Energy unit with 15%. Profitability soared in 2010, as net income jumped more than 184% due to lower operating costs and significant reductions in debt.

Despite its failed effort the previous year to hike its 9% stake in Rio Tinto to 19%, Aluminum Corporation of China (Chinalco) formed a joint venture with Rio Tinto in 2010 to operate an iron ore project in Guinea, West Africa. A Chinalco subsidiary will hold 47% of Rio Tinto's Simandou project, which is expected to begin producing up to 70 million tons of ore per year by 2015.

In 2011 Rio Tinto and Chinalco teamed up again on a new joint venture that will focus on mineral exploration in China. Chinalco is seeking to find and develop domestic sources of copper, coal, and potash to offset the cost of importing those raw materials. Chinalco will hold a 51% interest in the joint venture, Chinalco Rio Tinto Exploration, with Rio Tinto holding the remaining 49%.

One of the world's largest producers of copper, Rio Tinto operates the Oyu Tolgoi project in Mongolia, along with Canada's Ivanhoe Mines and the Mongolian government. Vancouver-based Ivanhoe controlled one of the world's largest untapped copper and gold deposits in Mongolia, and Rio Tinto expects the mine to be one of the world's top 10 copper producers, as well as one of the top gold producers, by 2018. In 2012, Rio Tinto upped its holding in Ivanhoe from 49% to 51% to become the majority owner.

Also in early 2012, Rio Tinto completed its offer for Canada-based uranium producer Hathor Exploration, valued at $578 million, after rival Cameco Corp. made a takeover bid for the company in 2011. Hathor supplies about a fifth of the world's uranium.

In 2011 the company also started slimming its aluminum operations. It placed 13 assets on the chopping block, allowing Rio Tinto Alcan to focus on its high-quality, tier one assets (mostly in Canada) and improve performance. The company also planned to transfer its stakes in six Australian and New Zealand operations to a new business unit, Pacific Aluminium.The new unit, managed and reported separately from Rio Tinto Alcan, would include the company's Gove bauxite mine and alumina refinery, Boyne Smelters and Gladstone Power Station, Tomago smelter, and Bell Bay smelter in Australia. In New Zealand it would include the New Zealand Aluminium Smelters.

For at least a while longer the company is holding on to seven noncore assets managed by Rio Tinto Alcan, including operations in France, Germany, the UK, and the US. The company is in no hurry to sell and may wait until the economy improves before divesting certain operations. Rio Tinto has tried a similar divestment strategy before. It embarked on a divestment plan in the mid-2000s, with the long-term goal of turning out $15 billion from its divestments. By 2010, the company had gained more than $10 billion from the divestment program.

Rio Tinto was formed in 1972.

EXECUTIVES

Chief Executive Officer, Executive Director, Jakob Stausholm
Australia Chief Executive Officer, Kellie Parker
Chief Financial Officer, Executive Director, Peter Cunningham
Chief Operating Officer, Arnaud Soirat
Chief Technical Officer, Mark Davies
Chief Legal Officer, Governance & Corporate Affairs, Isabelle Deschamps
Chief Commercial Officer, Alf Barrios
Chief People Officer, James Martin
Secretary, Steve Allen
Chairman, Dominic Barton
Senior Independent Director, Independent Non-Executive Director, Sam Laidlaw
Independent Non-Executive Director, Ben Wyatt
Independent Non-Executive Director, Megan Clark
Independent Non-Executive Director, Simon Henry
Independent Non-Executive Director, Simon McKeon
Independent Non-Executive Director, Jennifer Nason
Independent Non-Executive Director, Ngaire Woods
Independent Non-Executive Director, Kaisa H. Hietala
Auditors : KPMG LLP

LOCATIONS

HQ: Rio Tinto Plc
6 St. James's Square, London SW1Y 4AD
Phone: (44) 20 7781 2000   **Fax:** (44) 20 7781 1800
Web: www.riotinto.com

2017 Sales by Destination

	$m	% of total
China	17,706	44
US	5,716	14
Asia (excl. China and Japan)	5,108	13
Japan	4,701	12
Europe (excl. UK)	3,015	7
Canada	1,111	3
Australia	710	2
UK	449	1
Other Countries	1,514	4
Total	40,030	100

PRODUCTS/OPERATIONS

2017 sales

	$m	% of total
Iron ore	20,010	50
Aluminum	10,864	27
Copper	1,760	4
Coal	2,822	7
Industrial minerals	2,060	5
Gold	378	1
Diamonds	706	2
Other	1,430	4
Total	40,030	100

COMPETITORS

ANGLO PACIFIC GROUP PLC
BARRICK TZ LIMITED
BHP GROUP LIMITED
BHP GROUP PLC
MONTERRICO METALS LIMITED
Nexa Resources
POLYMETAL INTERNATIONAL PLC
VEDANTA RESOURCES LIMITED
Vale S/A
WEATHERLY INTERNATIONAL PUBLIC LIMITED COMPANY

HISTORICAL FINANCIALS

Company Type: Public

Income Statement   FYE: December 31

	REVENUE ($mil)	NET INCOME ($mil)	NET PROFIT MARGIN	EMPLOYEES
12/23	54,041	10,058	18.6%	57,000
12/22	55,554	656	1.2%	53,726
12/21	63,495	1,481	2.3%	49,345
12/20	44,611	631	1.4%	47,474
12/19	43,165	(1,038)	—	46,007
Annual Growth	5.8%	—	—	5.5%

2023 Year-End Financials

Debt ratio: 1.1%   No. of shares ($ mil.): 1,622
Return on equity: 19.2%   Dividends
Cash ($ mil.): 9,673   Yield: —
Current Ratio: 1.69   Payout: 36.4%
Long-term debt ($ mil.): —   Market value ($ mil.): 120,814

	STOCK PRICE ($) FY Close	P/E High/Low		PER SHARE ($) Earnings	Dividends	Book Value
12/23	74.46	13	9	6.17	2.25	33.64
12/22	71.20	11	7	7.62	7.46	40.15
12/21	66.94	7	5	12.95	9.63	41.21
12/20	75.22	13	6	6.00	3.86	37.74
12/19	59.36	13	9	4.88	6.35	32.43
Annual Growth	5.8%	—	—	6.0%	(22.9%)	0.9%

Roche Holding Ltd

One of the world's largest pharmaceutical companies, Roche has operations in over 100 countries. Roche's prescription drugs include cancer therapies MabThera/Rituxan and Avastin, Perjeta and Kadcyla for HER2-positive breast cancer, idiopathic pulmonary fibrosis drug Esbriet, Tarceva, which is used for treatment of patients with advanced non-small cell lung cancer and Tamiflu, which is used for infectious diseases. The company markets many of its bestsellers through California-based subsidiary Genentech and Japanese affiliate Chugai Pharmaceutical. Roche generates the majority of its revenue in North America.

Operations

Roche operates in two divisions: Pharmaceuticals and Diagnostics.

Its pharmaceuticals division accounts for about 70% of total revenue, focuses in oncology, neuroscience, infectious diseases, immunology, and ophthalmology.

Diagnostics segment, which accounts for nearly 30% of total revenue, is a leading maker of in vitro (test tube) clinical diagnostic tests through its professional diagnostics segment; it is also an established provider of diabetes tests and glucose monitors.

Geographic Reach

Roche, based in Basel, Switzerland, generates around 45% of its total revenue in North America, while more than 25% in Europe and almost 25% in Asia.

In the Asia/Pacific region, it operates in about 25 countries including Hong Kong, India, Indonesia, Japan, Philippines, Taiwan, Thailand, UAE, Vietnam, Pakistan, Singapore, China and Malaysia. The company also has a solid stance in the Japanese drug market through its 61.2% stake in Chugai Pharmaceutical.

Sales and Marketing

In total, three US national wholesale distributors represents approximately a third of total revenues. The three US national wholesale distributors are McKesson Corp., AmerisourceBergen Corp., and Cardinal Health, Inc.

Financial Performance

Note: Growth rates may vary after conversion to US Dollars.

The company had a revenue of CHF 62.8 million in 2021, an 8% increase from the previous year's revenue of CHF 58.3 billion. The increase was primarily due to higher sales volumes for the year.

In 2021, the company had a net income of CHF 13.9 billion a 3% decrease from the previous year's net income of CHF 14.3 billion.

The company's cash at the end of 2021 was CHF 6.9 billion. Operating activities generated CHF 21 billion, while investing activities used CHF 6.6 billion, mainly for purchase of property, plant and equipment. Financing activities used another CHF 13.1 billion, primarily for share repurchase.

Mergers and Acquisitions

Acquisitions are also key elements in Roche's R&D growth strategy, and have expanded its pharmaceutical segment in focused therapeutic areas.

In late 2021, Roche acquired a 100% controlling interest in Protocol First, Inc. ('Protocol First'), a privately owned US company based in Salt Lake City, Utah. The acquisition provides Roche an access to Protocol First's software solutions which enhance clinical research efficiency. Protocol First is reported in the Pharmaceuticals Division. The total consideration was US$55 million, which was paid in cash.

Also in late 2021, Roche acquired a 100% interest in TIB Molbiol Group ('TIB Molbiol'), a privately owned group based in Berlin, Germany. TIB Molbiol is a manufacturer of custom oligonucleotides that has been collaborating with Roche for more than 20 years. The acquisition of TIB Molbiol will enhance the Roche's broad portfolio of molecular diagnostics solutions with a wide range of assays for infectious diseases. TIB Molbiol is reported in the Diagnostics Division. The total consideration was EUR 492 million, which was paid in cash.

In 2021, Roche acquired a 100% controlling interest in GenMark Diagnostics, Inc. ('GenMark'), a publicly owned US company based in Carlsbad, California, that had been listed on Nasdaq. GenMark provides multiplex molecular diagnostic solutions that are designed to detect multiple pathogens from a single patient sample. The addition of GenMark's proprietary multiplex technology complements the Group's diagnostic offering, addressing a broad range of infectious disease testing needs, including respiratory and bloodstream infections. GenMark is reported in the Diagnostics Division. The total consideration was US$1.9 billion, which was paid in cash.

Company Background

Roche can trace a direct line back to the foundation in 1896 of F.Hoffmann-La Roche & Co by entrepreneur Fritz Hoffman-La Roche. Pharmacist Carl Schaerges, the first head of research, together with chemist Emil C. Barell, demonstrated the presence of iodine in thyroid extracts. This results in Roche's first patent and scientific publications. The company became the first to synthetic vitamin C on a mass scale in 1934, and in 1957 developed the benzodiazepines class of tranquilizers. Over the years, Roche has expanded in Switzerland and abroad by making numerous acquisitions, including Genentech in the US for a whopping $46.8 billion.

HISTORY

Fritz Hoffmann-La Roche, backed by family wealth, began making pharmaceuticals in a lab in Basel, Switzerland, in 1894. At the time, drug compounds were mixed at pharmacies and lacked uniformity. Hoffmann was not a chemist, but saw the potential for mass-produced, standardized, branded drugs.

By WWI, Hoffman had become successful, selling Thiocal (cough medicine), Digalen (digitalis extract), and other products on four continents. During the war, the Bolsheviks seized the firm's St. Petersburg, Russia, facility, and its Warsaw plant was almost destroyed. Devastated, Hoffmann sold company shares outside the family in 1919 and died in 1920.

As WWII loomed, Roche divided its holdings between F. Hoffman-La Roche and Sapac, which held many of Roche's foreign operations. US operations became more important during the war. Roche synthesized vitamins C, A, and E (eventually becoming the world's top vitamin maker) and built plants and research centers worldwide.

Roche continued to develop such successful products as tranquilizers Librium (1960) and Valium (1963) -- the world's best-selling prescription drug prior to anti-ulcer successors Tagamet (SmithKline Beecham, now part of GlaxoSmithKline) and Prilosec (AstraZeneca). Roche made its first fragrance and flavor buy, Givaudan, in 1963.

In the 1970s, after several governments accused it of price-gouging on Librium and Valium, Roche agreed to price restraints. The company was fined for vitamin price-fixing in 1976. It was also rapped that year for its slow response to an Italian factory dioxin leak that killed thousands of animals and forced hundreds of families to evacuate.

Roche became one of the first drugmakers to sell another's products when it agreed to sell Glaxo's Zantac ulcer treatment in the US in 1982. The move let Roche maintain its large US sales force at the time when Valium went off patent, decimating the company's drug sales.

Roche acquired a product pipeline when it bought a majority stake in genetic engineering firm Genentech in 1990. In 1994 it bought the struggling Syntex, solidifying its position in North America. The company gained Aleve and other products in 1996 when it bought out its joint venture with Procter & Gamble and also acquired Cincinnati-based flavors and fragrances firm Tastemaker.

In its biggest acquisition ever, Roche bought Corange in 1998 for $10.2 billion; its subsidiary Boehringer Mannheim was renamed Roche Molecular Biochemicals. In 1999 Roche announced it had located the gene that causes osteoarthritis. The company began to market anti-obesity pharmaceutical Xenical in the US that year, despite reports of some unpleasant side effects.

EXECUTIVES

Chief Executive Officer, Executive Director, Severin Schwan
Chief Financial and Information Officer, Alan Hippe
Chief People Officer, Cristina A. Wilbur
Chief Compliance Officer, Pascale Schmidt
General Counsel, Claudia Bockstiegel
Secretary, Annette Luther
Chairman, Independent Non-Executive Director, Christoph Franz
Vice-Chairman, Independent Non-Executive Director, Andre Hoffmann
Independent Non-Executive Director, Jorg Duschmale
Independent Non-Executive Director, Patrick Frost
Independent Non-Executive Director, Anita Hauser
Independent Non-Executive Director, Richard P. Lifton
Independent Non-Executive Director, Bernard J. Poussot
Independent Non-Executive Director, Claudia Suessmuth Dyckerhoff
Auditors : KPMG AG

LOCATIONS

HQ: Roche Holding Ltd
  Grenzacherstrasse 124, Basel CH-4070
Phone: (41) 61 688 11 11   **Fax:** (41) 61 688 13 96
Web: www.roche.com

2017 Sales

	% of total
America	50
Europe	26
Asia	21
Africa, Australia & Oceania	3
Total	100

PRODUCTS/OPERATIONS

2017 Sales

Pharmaceuticals	% of total
Oncology	48
Immunology	14
Neuroscience	3
Ophthalmology	3
Infectious disease	2
Other	7
Diagnostics	23
Total	100

Selected Products
Top Products (listed alphabetically)
  Actemra/RoActemra (rheumatoid arthritis)
  Activase/TNKase (cardiovascular)
  Alecensa
  Avastin (colorectal cancer, non-small cell lung cancer, breast cancer, kidney cancer)
  Bactrim (anti-infective)
  Bondronat (bone disease in breast cancer patients)
  Bonviva/Boniva (osteoporosis)
  CellCept (transplantation)
  Cotellic
  Dilatrend
  Dormicum (sedation)
  Erivedge (basal cell carcinoma)
  ESBRIET
  FoundationOne
  FoundationOne Heme
  Fuzeon (HIV)
  Gazyva/Gazyvaro
  Harmony Prenatal test
  Hemlibra
  Herceptin (HER2-positive breast cancer)
  Invirase (HIV)
  Kadcyla
    Kytril (nausea and vomiting induced by chemotherapy or radiation therapy)
    Lariam
    Lucentis (wet age-related macular degeneration, diabetic macular edema)
    MabThera SC/Rituxan Hycela
    MabThera/Rituxan (non-Hodgkin's lymphoma, rheumatoid arthritis, chronic lymphocytic leukemia)
    Madopar (Parkinson's disease, restless leg syndrome)
    MIRCERA (predialysis)
    NeoRecormon (anemia, oncology)
    Neupogen
    Ocrevus
    Pegasys (hepatitis B and C)
    Perjeta (breast cancer)
    Pulmozyme (cystic fibrosis)
    Rocaltrol (osteoporosis)
    Rocephin (bacterial infections)
    Roferon-A (hepatitis C, hairy cell leukemia, AIDS-related Kaposi's sarcoma)
    Tamiflu (treatment and prevention of influenza)
    Tarceva (advanced non-small cell lung cancer, advanced pancreatic cancer)
    Tecentriq
    Toradol (acute pain)
    Valcyte (cytomegalovirus infection)
    Valium (anxiety disorders)
    Vesanoid (leukemia)
    Viracept (HIV)
    Xeloda
    Xenical (weight loss, weight control)
    Xolair (asthma)
    Zelboraf (metastatic melanoma)

COMPETITORS

AMDIPHARM MERCURY HOLDCO UK LIMITED
ASTRAZENECA PLC
BUNZL PUBLIC LIMITED COMPANY
CHILTERN INTERNATIONAL LIMITED
Clariant AG
ELI LILLY AND COMPANY
Gambro AB
KYOWA KIRIN INTERNATIONAL PLC
PFIZER INC.
U C B

HISTORICAL FINANCIALS
Company Type: Public

Income Statement				FYE: December 31
	REVENUE ($mil)	NET INCOME ($mil)	NET PROFIT MARGIN	EMPLOYEES
12/23	70,188	13,744	19.6%	103,605
12/22	72,005	13,464	18.7%	103,613
12/21	72,138	15,260	21.2%	100,920
12/20	68,514	16,230	23.7%	101,465
12/19	65,947	13,961	21.2%	97,735
Annual Growth	1.6%	(0.4%)	—	1.5%

2023 Year-End Financials
Debt ratio: 38.6% No. of shares ($ mil.): 797
Return on equity: 40.1% Dividends
Cash ($ mil.): 6,426 Yield: —
Current Ratio: 1.35 Payout: 5.1%
Long-term debt ($ mil.): 29,656 Market value ($ mil.): 28,884

	STOCK PRICE ($) FY Close	P/E High/Low		PER SHARE ($) Earnings	Dividends	Book Value
12/23	36.23	3	2	17.11	0.89	43.96
12/22	39.15	3	3	16.66	0.79	37.50
12/21	51.69	3	2	17.75	0.77	31.10
12/20	43.84	3	2	18.76	0.72	47.84
12/19	40.66	3	2	16.16	0.68	39.27
Annual Growth	(2.8%)	—	—	1.4%	7.0%	2.9%

Rogers Communications Inc

Founded in 1960, Rogers Communications is Canada's #1 mobile phone outfit, with about 14 million subscribers across the country. Rogers' networks connect millions of Canadians through 5G, wireless, connected homes, and media. The company launched and expanded Canada's first and largest 5G network to over 170 cities and towns and started rolling out Canada's first 5G standalone core network. The late founder Ted Rogers started the company with a single radio station. The company is dedicated to providing industry-leading wireless, cable, sports, and media to millions of customers across Canada. head office is in Toronto, Ontario and it has numerous offices across Canada.

Operations
Almost 60% of Rogers Communications' revenue is generated by its wireless unit, which provides mobile broadband data services such as web access and streaming media in addition to standard voice and messaging services. The company's wireless brands are Rogers, Fido, and chatr.

Cable telecommunications operations (nearly 30%), including Internet, television, telephony (phone), and smart home monitoring services for Canadian consumers and businesses, and network connectivity through its fibre network and data centre assets to support a range of voice, data, networking, hosting, and cloud-based services for the business, public sector, and carrier wholesale markets.

Media segment (over 10%) includes diversified portfolio of media properties, including sports media and entertainment, television and radio broadcasting, specialty channels, multi-platform shopping, and digital media.

Geographic Reach
Based in Ontario, Toronto, Rogers Communications provides services throughout Canada. The company's LTE

reaches about 95% of the Canadian population while 5G network 70% of population.

Sales and Marketing

Rogers' sales teams and third-party retailers sell services to the enterprise, public sector, and carrier wholesale markets. An extensive network of third-party channel distributors deals with IT integrators, consultants, local service providers and other indirect sales relationships. This diverse approach gives greater breadth of coverage and allows for strong sales growth for next-generation services.

Rogers distributes its residential cable products using various channels, including: company-owned Rogers and Fido retail stores; customer self-serve using rogers.com and fido.ca; its contact centers, outbound telemarketing, and door-to-door agents; and major retail chains.

Financial Performance

Rogers Communications' revenue has fluctuated over the last five years. Net income has slightly declined from 2018 to 2021. Sales increased 5% to $14.7 billion in 2021, a $1.4 billion increase from 2020 primarily driven by a 23% increase in Media revenue and a total of 6% increase in Wireless and Cable revenue.

Rogers's net income fell 2% to $1.6 billion in 2021 from 2020 primarily as a result of the decrease in adjusted EBITDA.

The company had $715 million in cash and equivalents in 2021 compared to $2.5 billion in 2020. In 2021, operations generated $4.2 billion, while investing activities used $6.1 billion mostly for acquisitions and other strategic transactions, net of cash acquired. Financing activities provided $203 million in 2021.

Strategy

Rogers communications set annual objectives to measure progress on its six strategic priorities and to address short-term opportunities and risks. The company's long-term vision builds on its strengths, including a unique mix of technology and media assets. Its focus is clear: deliver best-in-class engagement, a best-in-class customer experience, and industry-leading shareholder value.

To achieve this vision, Rogers' strategic priorities are: Create best-in-class customer experiences by putting its customers first in everything the company does; Invest in its networks and technology to deliver leading performance, reliability, and coverage; Drive growth in each of its lines of business; Drive best-in-class financial outcomes for its shareholders; Develop its people, drive engagement, and build a high-performing and inclusive culture; and become a strong, socially and environmentally responsible leader in its communities.

One of its objectives is to enhance its marketing and sales capabilities to propel consistent and sustainable customer additions; grow its business in key regional markets across Canada; create products, services, and content that customers will love; and anchor its media strategy in sports and diversify into digital and sports-related growth areas.

Company Background

Edward Rogers, at age 21, transmitted Canada's first radio signal across the Atlantic in 1921. He invented the first alternating current (AC) radio tube in 1925, which revolutionized the home-receiver industry.

The son of a wealthy businessman, Rogers founded Rogers Majestic in Toronto in the mid-1920s to make his radio tubes. He also established several radio stations, including CFRB ("Canada's First Rogers Batteryless"), which later commanded the country's largest audience.

In 1931 Rogers won the first experimental license to broadcast TV, but his businesses were sold when he died in 1939. His son Ted Rogers Jr. was only five at the time, but even as a youngster he showed business acumen, buying up shares of Standard Broadcasting. In his twenties he bought CHFI, a Toronto radio station that pioneered FM broadcasting.

Rogers moved into cable TV and in 1967 was awarded licenses for Toronto, Brampton, and Leamington. Rogers Cable TV expanded when it bought Canadian Cablevision (1979) and Premier Cablevision (1980). With the takeover of UA-Columbia Cablevision in 1981, Rogers became Canada's largest cable operator.

HISTORY

Edward Rogers, at age 21, transmitted Canada's first radio signal across the Atlantic in 1921. He invented the first alternating current (AC) radio tube in 1925, which revolutionized the home-receiver industry.

Son of a wealthy businessman, Rogers founded Rogers Majestic in Toronto in the mid-1920s to make his radio tubes. He also established several radio stations, including CFRB ("Canada's First Rogers Batteryless"), which later commanded the country's largest audience.

In 1931 Rogers won the first experimental license to broadcast TV, but his businesses were sold when he died in 1939. His son Ted Rogers Jr. was only five at the time, but even as a youngster he showed business acumen, buying up shares of Standard Broadcasting. In his twenties he bought CHFI, a Toronto radio station that pioneered FM broadcasting.

Rogers moved into cable TV and in 1967 was awarded licenses for Toronto, Brampton, and Leamington. Rogers Cable TV expanded when it bought Canadian Cablevision (1979) and Premier Cablevision (1980). With the takeover of UA-Columbia Cablevision in 1981, Rogers became Canada's largest cable operator.

EXECUTIVES

Corporate Development Chair, Emerging Business Chair, Chair, Director, Edward S. Rogers
President, Chief Executive Officer, Director, Joseph M. Natale
Chief Customer Officer, Eric P. Agius
Chief Technology and Information Officer, Jorge Fernandes
Chief Legal and Regulatory Officer, Secretary, Graeme McPhail
Chief Communications Officer, Sevaun T. Palvetzian
Chief Human Resources Officer, James M. Reid
Chief Financial Officer, Anthony Staffieri
Deputy Chair, Director, Melinda M. Rogers-Hixon
Non-Executive Vice Chair, Director, Philip B. Lind
Lead Director, John A. MacDonald
Director, Bonnie R. Brooks
Director, Robert Depatie
Director, Robert J. Gemmell
Director, Alan D. Horn
Director, Ellis Jacob
Director, Isabelle Marcoux
Director, David R. Peterson
Director, Loretta A. Rogers
Director, Martha L. Rogers
Auditors : KPMG LLP

LOCATIONS

HQ: Rogers Communications Inc
333 Bloor Street East, Toronto, Ontario M4W 1G9
Phone: 416-935-7777
Web: www.rogers.com

PRODUCTS/OPERATIONS

2018 Sales

	% of total
Wireless	60
Cable operations	26
Media	14
Corporate items and intercompany eliminations	
Total	100

Selected Operations

Wireless Communications
    Cellular service
    Data service
    Digital PCS
Cable and Telephone
    Cable television
    Broadband Internet access
    Dial-up Internet access
    Local access
    Long-distance
    Teleconferencing
Media
    Content
    e-Commerce
    Radio
    TV broadcasting
    Televised shopping
    Publishing
    Sports entertainment

COMPETITORS

ARRIS GLOBAL LTD.
AT&T INC.
BCE Inc

COMCAST CORPORATION
MTS, PAO
Manitoba Telecom Services Inc
SK Telecom Co.,Ltd.
SKY LIMITED
Swisscom AG
TELECOM ITALIA O TIM SPA

HISTORICAL FINANCIALS
Company Type: Public

Income Statement   FYE: December 31

	REVENUE ($mil)	NET INCOME ($mil)	NET PROFIT MARGIN	EMPLOYEES
12/23	14,567	640	4.4%	0
12/22	11,383	1,242	10.9%	22,000
12/21	11,506	1,223	10.6%	23,000
12/20	10,929	1,250	11.4%	23,500
12/19	11,575	1,568	13.6%	25,300
Annual Growth	5.9%	(20.1%)	—	—

2023 Year-End Financials
Debt ratio: 46.4%   No. of shares ($ mil.): 530
Return on equity: 8.2%   Dividends
Cash ($ mil.): 603   Yield: —
Current Ratio: 0.89   Payout: 123.4%
Long-term debt ($ mil.): 29,993   Market value ($ mil.): 24,810

	STOCK PRICE ($) FY Close	P/E High/Low		PER SHARE ($) Earnings	Dividends	Book Value
12/23	46.81	31	23	1.22	1.51	14.86
12/22	46.84	17	11	2.45	1.48	14.78
12/21	47.63	17	14	2.41	1.60	16.38
12/20	46.59	17	12	2.46	1.51	14.89
12/19	49.67	14	12	3.05	1.50	14.32
Annual Growth	(1.5%)	—	—	(20.4%)	0.1%	0.9%

Rolls-Royce Holdings Plc

Rolls-Royce Holdings doesn't make cars so luxurious you'll cry (see Motor Cars), but it sure can make an aircraft engine whine. One of the world's largest aircraft engine makers, Rolls-Royce, through its Civil and Defense Aerospace businesses, makes commercial and military engines for a broad customer base, including airlines, corporate and utility aircraft and helicopter operators, and armed forces around the world. Beyond aviation, its Energy unit supplies gas turbine power generation to the oil and gas industry, while its Marine segment makes propulsion systems that power 70 navies worldwide. Rolls-Royce has operations in North America, Europe, and Asia, with an emerging presence in the Middle East.

Operations
The company operates two divisions: Aerospace, and Land & Sea.

The Aerospace division covers both civil and military aviation, for which it develops, manufactures, markets and sells engines and power systems. The division's engines are found in the aircraft such as the Airbus A380, and on the defense side of things, Rolls-Royce commands approximately one-quarter of the world's military engine manufacturing market share. Its portfolio covers all major sectors -- combat, helicopters, unmanned and tactical aircraft, training, and transport. The Land & Sea division has three interests of power systems, marine propulsion, and nuclear power generation and propulsion. Its PWR2 nuclear propulsion system is found in the Royal Navy's Trident submarine fleet.

Geographic Reach
Headquartered in London, Rolls-Royce has operations in over 50 countries and customers in over 150 worldwide. Europe is the company's biggest market at around 35% of sales, followed by North America at 30% and Asia at 20%.

Financial Performance
Note: Growth rates may differ after conversion to US Dollars.

After a few years of growth from 2011, sales have flattened, coming in at £13.7 billion in 2014 and 2015. Sales in Land & Sea were marginally lower than prior year due to weakness in Marine sales. Net income nudged up £14 million in 2015 to £83 million due to a decrease in taxation and commercial and administrative costs. Cash flow from operations fell 16% to £1.1 billion due to changes in provisions.

Strategy
Rolls-Royce is carrying out a streamlining process to enhance operational efficiency, which included the axing of 600 management jobs since mid-2015 and the consolidation of its Civil Aerospace repair and overhaul activities, allowing for the closure of sites in Brazil and the UK. It also sold its Michell Bearings business in November 2015 for £12.6 million and its L'Orange diesel parts maker to Woodward, a US company, for $859 million.

Rolls-Royce expects to see an uptick in its overseas business following the sharp fall in value of the Pound Sterling subsequent to the EU referendum in mid-2016.

Rolls-Royce is possibly weighing up an escalation of its nuclear activities after the UK government announced a £250 million competition to encourage development of small modular reactor (SMR) technologies, which have potential uses as part of a 7 gigawatt network of SMRs.

Mergers and Acquisitions
In mid-2016, Rolls-Royce announced the purchase of the remaining 53% of shares in Industria de Turbo Propulsores (ITP) for ?720 million in order to strengthen its large engine growth program. ITP brings with it long-term aftermarket revenue, including the high volume Trent 1000 and Trent XWB engines. The acquisition completed at the end of 2017.

In 2015, the company acquired R.O.V Technologies, which makes products that allow for the remote inspection and cleaning of boiling/pressurized water reactors, complementing Rolls-Royce's existing nuclear activities.

HISTORY
In 1906 automobile and aviation enthusiast Charles Rolls and engineer Henry Royce unveiled the Silver Ghost, an automobile that earned Rolls-Royce a reputation as maker of the best car in the world.

A year after Rolls' 1910 death in a biplane crash, Royce suffered a breakdown. From his home Royce continued to design Rolls-Royce engines such as the Eagle, its first aircraft engine, in 1914, and other engines used to power airplanes during WWI -- but management of the company fell to Claude Johnson, who remained chief executive until 1926.

Although the company returned primarily to making cars after WWI, its engines were used in several history-making flights and, in 1931, set world speed records for land, sea, and air. Rolls-Royce bought the Bentley Motor Company that year. In 1933 it introduced the Merlin engine, which powered the Spitfire, Hurricane, and Mustang fighters of WWII. Rolls-Royce began designing a jet engine in 1938, and over the years it pioneered the turboprop engine, turbofan, and vertical takeoff engine.

Realizing that it had to break into the lucrative US airliner market to stay alive, Rolls-Royce bought its main British competitor, Bristol-Siddley Engines, in 1966. With Bristol-Siddley came its contract to build the engine for the Anglo-French Concorde in 1976 and a US presence.

Lockheed ordered the company's RB211 engine for its TriStar in 1968, but Rolls-Royce underestimated the project's technical and financial challenges and entered bankruptcy in 1971. The British government stepped in and nationalized the aerospace division and sold the auto group. The RB211 entered service on the TriStar in 1972 and on the Boeing 747 in 1977.

Rolls-Royce was reprivatized in 1987. In a diversification effort two years later, the company bought mining, marine, and power plant specialist Northern Engineering Industries. In the early 1990s the aerospace market was hurt by military spending cutbacks and a recession; the company cut more than 18,000 jobs.

A joint venture with BMW launched the BR710 engine for Gulfstream and Canadair's long-range business jets in 1990. The company bought Allison Engine in 1995.

Rolls-Royce sold Parsons Power Generation Systems to Siemens in 1997. Also that year it won a contract to supply Trent 892 engines for Boeing 777 jets being built for American Airlines (a subsidiary of AMR Corporation) in a deal worth $1 billion.

In 1998 the British government approved a repayable investment of about $335 million in the company to develop a new model of Trent aircraft engines. Narrowing its focus, the company sold its power transmission and distribution business to Austria-based VA Technologie.

Rolls-Royce pumped up its gas and oil equipment business in 1999 by buying the rotating compression equipment unit of Cooper Cameron (now Cameron International); it became one of the world leaders in marine propulsion by acquiring Vickers. The company then bought the aero and industrial engine repair service of First Aviation Services and took full control of its aircraft-engine joint venture with BMW; in return BMW received a 10% stake in Rolls.

In 2000 subsidiary Rolls-Royce Energy Systems India Private was awarded its first order: producing a Bergen gas engine for Garden Silk Mills for powering a textile plant in India. That year Rolls-Royce won a contract to supply engines for Israel's El Al airline's Boeing 777s. Late in 2000 it was reported that the company would cut about 5,000 jobs over three years.

Early in 2001 Rolls-Royce sold most of its Vickers Turbine Components business. In October the company cut about 11% of its workforce in response to the worldwide crisis in the commercial jet business.

In 2002 the company announced that it had inked a 10-year, $2 billion deal to supply engines to Gulfstream Aerospace. That year Rolls-Royce sold its Vickers Defence Systems unit, which made tanks and armored vehicles, to Alvis Plc. In 2003 Sir Ralph Robins, who had been executive chairman for more than a decade, retired from his post.

Early in 2004 Rolls-Royce and GE Aircraft Engines were picked to supply engines for Boeing's upcoming 787 Dreamliner. Rolls-Royce was also selected to supply engines for Airbus' upcoming behemoth A380.

In late 2007 it scored one of its largest contracts, a $42 million project to provide steering gear and deck machinery for Chinese shipbuilder Sinopacific.

In 2008 it entered into a joint venture with Goodrich Corporation called Aero Engine Controls to produce engine controls for Rolls-Royce aircraft. It also partnered with France's AREVA to construct the first new nuclear reactors built in the UK in more than 20 years.

In 2009 the company focused on developing four advanced manufacturing research centers in the US, the UK, and Singapore. Rolls-Royce invested Â£300 million (more than $450 million) in its UK factories as part of its almost Â£2 billion (over $3 billion) capital replacement plan to be carried out over a period of 10 years. That year Rolls-Royce engines allowed the BAE Systems' Mantis UAV, and AgustaWestland's Lynx Wildcat helicopter to take flight.

Rolls-Royce's nuclear market was strengthened in 2009 by its agreement with electric service provider EDF Energy (formerly known as London Electricity Group) to enter into a joint venture, with EDF Energy giving support to the UK facility. The following year the company introduced its STOVL (short take-off and vertical landing) Rolls-Royce LiftSystem.

The bell of financial crisis knelled in 2008, causing the company to implement cost-cutting measures, which included headcount reductions of almost 10%. The company, in partnership with GE Aviation, continued development of the F136 engine for the F-35 Joint Strike Fighter and its Trent 1000 engine took its first flight in the Boeing 787 Dreamliner. Also in 2008 Rolls-Royce established its civil nuclear business to tap a growing global market.

EXECUTIVES

Chief Executive Officer, Executive Director, Tufan Erginbilgic
Chief Financial Officer, Executive Director, Panos Kakoullis
Chief Governance Officer, Pamela Coles
Chair, Non-Executive Director, Anita M. Frew
Senior Independent Non-Executive Director, George Culmer
Independent Non-Executive Director, Paul Adams
Independent Non-Executive Director, Birgit A. Behrendt
Independent Non-Executive Director, Jitesh Gadhia
Independent Non-Executive Director, Beverly K. Goulet
Independent Non-Executive Director, Nick L. Luff
Independent Non-Executive Director, Mike Manley
Independent Non-Executive Director, Wendy Mars
Independent Non-Executive Director, Kevin Smith
Independent Non-Executive Director, Angela Strank
Auditors: PricewaterhouseCoopers LLP

LOCATIONS

HQ: Rolls-Royce Holdings Plc
 Kings Place, 90 York Way, London N1 9FX
Phone: (44) 20 7222 9020
Web: www.rolls-royce.com

2015 Sales

	% of total
Europe	36
North America	30
Asia	21
Middle East	6
South America	3
Australasia	2
Africa	1
Other	1
Total	100

PRODUCTS/OPERATIONS

2015 Sales (by market)

	% of total
Civil Aerospace	52
Power Systems	18
Defence Aerospace	15
Marine	10
Nuclear	5
Total	100

Selected Products and Services

Aircraft engines
Automation and control equipment
Bearings and seals
Diesel and gas turbine engines
Electric propulsion systems
Engine support services
Helicopter engines
Fuel cells
Generators
Offshore drilling equipment
Overhaul and repair services
Ship designs
Technical publications
Training

Selected Subsidiaries

Civil aerospace
 Optimized Systems and Solutions Limited (OSyS) (advanced controls and predictive data management)
  Rolls-Royce Leasing Limited (engine leasing)
  Rolls-Royce Total Care Services Limited (aftermarket support services)
Corporate
 Rolls-Royce International Limited (international support and commercial information services)
 Rolls-Royce Power Engineering plc (power generation and marine systems)
Energy
 Rolls-Royce Fuel Cell Systems Limited (fuel cell system development)
 Rolls-Royce Power Development Limited (project development)
  Tidal Generation Limited (development of tidal generation systems)
Marine
 ODIM ASA (offshore drilling, naval, and power generation equipment)
 Rolls-Royce Marine Electrical Systems Limited (marine electrical systems)
 Rolls-Royce Power Development Limited (generation of electricity from independent power projects)
 Rolls-Royce Marine Power Operations Limited (nuclear submarine propulsion systems)
 Rolls-Royce Power Engineering plc (energy and marine systems)
p>#

COMPETITORS

BAE SYSTEMS PLC
Bombardier Inc
CIRRUS DESIGN CORPORATION
GKN LIMITED
GULFSTREAM AEROSPACE CORPORATION
KAMAN CORPORATION
Pratt & Whitney Canada Cie
SAFRAN AIRCRAFT ENGINES
TEXTRON INC.
THE BOEING COMPANY

HISTORICAL FINANCIALS

Company Type: Public

Income Statement — FYE: December 31

	REVENUE ($mil)	NET INCOME ($mil)	NET PROFIT MARGIN	EMPLOYEES
12/22	16,275	(1,527)	—	41,800
12/21	15,118	161	1.1%	44,000
12/20	16,136	(4,326)	—	48,200
12/19	21,904	(1,736)	—	51,700
12/18	20,082	(3,065)	—	54,500
Annual Growth	(5.1%)	—	—	(6.4%)

2022 Year-End Financials

Debt ratio: 24.3%
Return on equity: —
Cash ($ mil.): 3,138
Current Ratio: 1.15
Long-term debt ($ mil.): 6,737
No. of shares ($ mil.): 8,367
Dividends
Yield: —
Payout: 0.0%
Market value ($ mil.): 8,953

	STOCK PRICE ($) FY Close	P/E High/Low		PER SHARE ($) Earnings	Dividends	Book Value
12/22	1.07	—	—	(0.18)	0.00	(0.87)
12/21	1.62	136	83	0.02	0.00	(0.75)
12/20	1.58	—	—	(0.72)	2.00	(0.80)
12/19	9.01	—	—	(0.31)	0.29	(0.79)
12/18	10.46	—	—	(0.57)	0.22	(0.25)
Annual Growth	(43.4%)	—	—	—	—	—

Rosneft Oil Co OJSC (Moscow)

Rosneft is the leader of the Russian oil industry and the largest publicly traded oil company in the world. Its core activities include hydrocarbon prospecting and exploration, production of oil, gas and gas condensate, implementation of offshore field development projects, refining, sales of oil, gas and refined products in Russia and abroad. It has proved reserves of 5 million barrels of oil equivalent per day, and thirteen refineries. Rosneft operates shipping and pipeline companies, and a national network of around 2,995 gasoline stations. The company was established in 1889.

Operations

Rosneft ranks among the world's top publicly traded oil and gas companies. It is primarily engaged in exploration and production of hydrocarbons, production of petroleum products and petrochemicals, and marketing of refined products.

Almost all of its sales were generated from the oil, gas, petroleum products, and petrochemicals sales.

Geographic Reach

Rosneft is headquartered in Moscow, Russia.

Financial Performance

In 2021, revenue increased by 52% year-on-year to RUB 8.8 trillion on the back of rising global oil prices and a recovery of demand for crude oil and petroleum products in the global market to almost pre-crisis levels.

In 2021, the company had a net income of RUB 883 billion, a 569% increase from the previous year's net income of RUB 132 billion.

The company's cash at the end of 2021 was RUB 659 billion. Operating activities generated RUB 1.2 trillion, while investing activities used RUB 1.3 trillion, mainly for capital expenditures. Financing activities used another RUB 19 billion, primarily for repayment of long-term loans and borrowings.

Strategy

Originally developed in 2014, the Long-Term Development Program (the Program) is subject to annual updates. In 2021, the company revised the program, taking into account the company's performance, action plans to achieve certain strategic goals, and updated initiatives drafted pursuant to the Russian Government's directives. The updated Program was approved by the company's Board of Directors. The Program details the company's strategic focus areas, targets and goals for all business areas and corporate functions. It also includes a list of key initiatives to achieve the company's strategic goals. The main priorities, key performance indicators (KPIs) and action plans under the current Innovation Development Program, Import Substitution and Equipment Localization Program, and Energy Saving Program take into account the Program provisions and are integrated into the current version of the document. The performance indicators include an integrated KPI for innovations. Rosneft's Investment Program aims to help the company achieve its strategic objectives stipulated in the Strategy and the Program (Investment Program in 2021 section) for key business areas. The company completed the Program's key initiatives planned for core businesses and functional units in 2021.

HISTORY

Rosneft was formed in 1993.

In 2004 Rosneft acquired YUKOS' main oil unit -- Yugansk -- in a controversial $9.4 billion deal. The acquisition of Yugansk (also known as Yuganskneftegaz) has been more complicated than Rosneft may have wished, as questions were raised about how the deal was handled and how the transaction was funded. In 2004 the company agreed to merge with Russian energy giant Gazprom. The Yugansk acquisition threw the merger with Gazprom into disarray, with Rosneft claiming that terms of the deal should be renegotiated to account for the change in value of Rosneft's assets. In addition, Group Menatep (majority owner of YUKOS) called for Rosneft to repay a loan estimated at about $900 million that is secured by Yugansk assets. In response Rosneft filed an $11 billion suit against YUKOS for unpaid taxes related to Yugansk.

In 2005 Rosneft approved the deal with Gazprom, though the acquisition would exclude the Yugansk assets acquired from YUKOS. After months of conflicting reports, state-controlled Gazprom abandoned the deal.

In 2006 Rosneft and BP teamed up to develop energy projects in Russia's Arctic. Rosneft raised $10.4 billion in a 2006 IPO (during which BP acquired a $1 billion stake).

In a move toward becoming a global oil company, in 2011 Rosneft formed a strategic alliance with BP (involving a stock swap of 5% of BP's shares for 9.5% of Rosneft's) to help fund the exploration of three blocks on the Russian Arctic continental shelf. The blocks have a production capacity on a par with the UK North Sea. However, rival Russian partners at TNK-BP (BP's established Russian joint venture) objected to the proposed deal, saying that have the legal right to have first choice on BP expansion activities in Russia. An arbitration tribunal in the UK supported their position. BP subsequently agreed to pursue the Rosneft deal through TNK BP. This move was unsuccessful and in May 2011 the BP/Rosneft deal fell through.

It followed this by forming a joint venture with Exxon Mobil to explore oil and gas fields in the Arctic. (This plan was stymied by US sanctions imposed in 2014).

Growing its European refinery footprint, in 2011 it also acquired a 50% stake in German refinery Ruhr Oel from PDVSA for about $1.6 billion. BP owns the other 50%.

Beefing up its Russian assets, in 2012 also bought 51% of NGK ITERA LLC, one of the largest independent producers and traders of natural gas in Russia, for RUB 7 billion (US $227 million).

EXECUTIVES

Chief Executive Officer, Deputy Chairman, Igor Sechin

Deputy Chairman, Zeljko Runje

Internal Audit Vice President, Gennady Ivanovich Bukaev

Financial Director, Peter Ivanovich Lazarev

State Secretary, Vice President, Zavaleeva Elena Vladimirovna

Vice President, Yuri Igorevich Kurilin

Vice President, Andrey Aleksandrovich Polyakov

Security Service Vice President, Ural Alfretovich Latypov

Chairman, Independent Director, Gerhard Schroeder

Deputy Chairman, Matthias Warnig

Non-Executive Director, Andrey Belousov

Independent Director, Oleg Viyugin

Non-Executive Director, Robert Dudley

Non-Executive Director, Guillermo Quintero

Non-Executive Director, Alexander Novak

Independent Director, Hans-Joerg Rudloff

Auditors : Ernst & Young LLC

LOCATIONS
HQ: Rosneft Oil Co OJSC (Moscow)
26/1, Sofiyskaya Embankment, Moscow 117997
Phone: (7) 499 517 88 99 **Fax:** (7) 499 517 72 35
Web: www.rosneft.com

PRODUCTS/OPERATIONS

2016 Sales

	% of total
Oil, gas, Petroleum products & petrochemicals	98
Support services & other	2
Equity share in profits of associates & joint ventures	—
Total	**100**

2016 Sales

	% of total
Refining and distribution	66
Exploration and production	33
Other	1
Total	**100**

COMPETITORS
COSMO OIL CO., LTD.
ENI SPA
Equinor ASA
GAZPROM NEFT, PAO
LUKOIL, PAO
MARATHON PETROLEUM CORPORATION
MOL Magyar Olaj- Ã©s GÃ¡zipari NyilvÃ¡nosan
MÅ±kÃ¶dÃ¶ RÃ©szvÃ©nytÃ¡rsasÃ¡g
Petroleo Brasileiro S A Petrobras
RENEWABLE ENERGY GROUP, INC.
Suncor Energy Inc

HISTORICAL FINANCIALS
Company Type: Public

Income Statement   FYE: December 31

	REVENUE ($mil)	NET INCOME ($mil)	NET PROFIT MARGIN	EMPLOYEES
12/21	116,674	11,759	10.1%	0
12/20	76,960	1,965	2.6%	355,900
12/19	139,403	11,375	8.2%	334,600
12/18	118,200	7,877	6.7%	325,600
12/17	104,023	3,839	3.7%	318,000
Annual Growth	2.9%	32.3%		

2021 Year-End Financials
Debt ratio: 0.4%   No. of shares ($ mil.): 9,500
Return on equity: 17.2%   Dividends
Cash ($ mil.): 8,776   Yield: —
Current Ratio: 0.96   Payout: 0.0%
Long-term debt ($ mil.): 48,608 Market value ($ mil.): —

Royal Bank Canada (Montreal, Quebec)

Auditors: PricewaterhouseCoopers LLP

LOCATIONS
HQ: Royal Bank Canada (Montreal, Quebec)
Royal Bank of Canada, 200 Bay Street, Toronto, Ontario M5J 2J5
Phone: 888 212-5533
Web: www.rbc.com

HISTORICAL FINANCIALS
Company Type: Public

Income Statement   FYE: October 31

	REVENUE ($mil)	NET INCOME ($mil)	NET PROFIT MARGIN	EMPLOYEES
10/23	85,320	10,744	12.6%	91,398
10/22	49,058	11,557	23.6%	91,427
Annual Growth	73.9%	(7.0%)		0.0%

2023 Year-End Financials
Debt ratio: —   No. of shares ($ mil.): 1,400
Return on equity: 13.1%   Dividends
Cash ($ mil.): 110,766   Yield: 5.0%
Current Ratio: —   Payout: 7.1%
Long-term debt ($ mil.): —   Market value ($ mil.): 16,629

	STOCK PRICE ($) FY Close	P/E High/Low		PER SHARE ($) Earnings	Dividends	Book Value
10/23	11.87	1	1	7.59	0.69	60.75
10/22	14.23	2	1	8.09	0.71	57.18
Annual Growth	(16.6%)	—	—	(6.2%)	(3.7%)	6.2%

Royal Bank of Canada (Montreal, Quebec)

Royal Bank of Canada (RBC) is Canada's largest bank and one of the largest in the world by market capitalization. The bank provides a diversified set of personal and commercial banking, wealth management, insurance, investor and treasury services, and capital markets globally. It serves more than 17 million customers ? businesses and group clients, individual, and institutional clients -- through offices in Canada, the US, and about 30 other countries. RBC, which generates about 60% of revenue from Canada.

Operations
RBC operates six business segments: Personal & Commercial Banking, Wealth Management, Capital Markets, Insurance, Investor & Treasury Services, and Corporate support.

Personal & Commercial Banking generates about 40% of total revenue. It provides a broad suite of financial products and services.

Wealth Management provides a comprehensive suite of investment, trust, banking, credit, and other wealth solutions to high net worth and ultra-high net worth clients. It also offers asset management services to institutional and individual clients. The segment accounts about 30% of revenue.

Capital Markets segment brings in about 20% of revenue and provides the technological and operational foundation required to effectively deliver products and services to its clients.

More than 10% of revenue comes from Insurance -- life, health, home, auto, and other kinds of insurance. It includes insurance for individuals as well as reinsurance advice and solutions, and business insurance services to business and group clients.

The Investor & Treasury Services accounts for less than 5% of total revenue. It is a provider of asset services, a leader in Canadian cash management and transaction banking services, and a provider of treasury services to institutional clients worldwide.

The Corporate Support consists of Technology and Operations, which provides the technological and operational requirements needed to deliver services and products its customers.

Overall, net interest income accounts for about 40% of total revenue.

Geographic Reach
Ontario-based RBC has more than 17 million clients in Canada, the US, and about 30 other countries. The bank's Personal & Commercial Banking segment provides products and services in Canada, the Caribbean and the US.

Overall, RBC generates about 60% of its revenue from Canada, about 25% from the US, and some 15% from other international sources.

Sales and Marketing
RBC serves a wide range of customers including individuals, institutional groups, business clients, high-net-worth and ultra-high-net-worth individuals, and institutional clients.

Through its capital markets, RBC also serves the energy, mining and infrastructure, industrial, consumer, health care and technology markets, and financial services.

Financial Performance
Note: Growth rates may differ after conversion to US dollars.

Royal Bank of Canada's performance for five years starting from 2017 have seen steady growth year over year, ending with 2021 as its highest performing year.

Total revenue in 2021 increased by 5% or C$2.5 billion to C$49.7 billion compared to C$47.2 billion in the prior year, largely due to higher investment management and custodial fees, other revenue, mutual fund revenue, and underwriting and other advisory fees. Higher insurance premiums, investment and fee income (Insurance revenue) and credit fees also contributed to the increase.

RBC's net income in 2021 also increased by 40% or C$4.6 billion to C$16 billion compared to the prior year's C$11.4 billion. Its results reflected higher earnings in Personal & Commercial Banking, Capital Markets, Wealth Management, and Insurance, partially offset by lower earnings in Investor & Treasury Services.

Cash and due from banks at end of 2021 was C$113.8 billion. Operating activities generated C$61 billion. Investing activities and financing activities used C$57.3 billion and C$5.9 billion, respectively. Main cash uses were for purchases of investment securities, purchases of treasury shares and dividends payment.

Strategy

RBC's strategies revolve around transforming how it serves its clients. The bank aims to achieve this through reimagining their branch network to meet the evolving needs of their clients. In addition the bank aims to accelerate its growth by focusing on engaging key high-growth client segments and establishing key partnership, as well as the continuation of the investment in RBC ventures. Further, the bank aims to rapidly deliver digital solutions through personalized insights and enhancing the digital experience of small business and commercial clients. The bank's strategies also include investing on new tools and capabilities to become a more agile and efficient bank. RBC remains focused on its Caribbean and US operations.

Company Background

Royal Bank of Canada (RBC) was created as Merchants Bank in 1864 and incorporated in 1869. It changed its name to The Royal Bank of Canada in 1901 and to Royal Bank of Canada in 1990.

HISTORY

Royal Bank of Canada (RBC) has looked south of the border ever since its 1864 creation as Merchants Bank in Halifax, Nova Scotia, a port city bustling with trade spawned by the US Civil War. After incorporating in 1869 as Merchants Bank of Halifax, the bank added branches in eastern Canada. Merchants opened a branch in Bermuda in 1882. Gold strikes in Canada and Alaska in the late 1890s pushed it into western Canada.

Merchants opened offices in New York and Cuba in 1899 and changed its name to Royal Bank of Canada in 1901. RBC moved into new Montreal headquarters in 1907 and grew by purchasing such banks as Union Bank of Canada (1925). In 1928 it moved into the 42-story Royal Bank Building, then the tallest in the British Empire.

The bank faltered during the Depression but recovered during WWII. After the war RBC financed the expanding minerals and oil and gas industries. When Castro took power in Cuba, RBC tried to operate its branches under communist rule but sold out to Banco Nacional de Cuba in 1960.

RBC opened offices in the UK in 1979 and in West Germany, Puerto Rico, and the Bahamas in 1980. As Canada's banking rules relaxed, RBC bought Dominion Securities in 1987. The US Federal Reserve approved RBC's brokerage arm for participation in stock underwriting in 1991.

The bank faced a $650 million loss in 1992 after backing the Reichmann family's Olympia & York property development company, which failed under the weight of its UK projects. The next year an ever-diversifying RBC bought Royal Trustco, Canada's #2 trust company, and Voyageur Travel Insurance, its largest retail travel insurer. A management shakeup in late 1994 ended with bank president John Cleghorn taking control of the company.

In 1995 RBC listed on the New York Stock Exchange and the next year joined with Heller Financial (an affiliate of Japan's Fuji Bank) to finance trade between Canada and Mexico. It began offering PC home banking in 1996 and Internet banking in 1997. That year RBC became one of the world's largest securities-custody service providers with its acquisition of The Bank of Nova Scotia's institutional and pension custody operations.

The company and Bank of Montreal agreed to merge in 1998, but Canadian regulators, fearing the concentration of banking power seen in the US, rejected the merger. In response, the bank trimmed its workforce and orchestrated a sale-leaseback of its property portfolio (1999).

In the late 1990s RBC grew its online presence by purchasing the Internet banking operations of Security First Network Bank (now Security First Technologies, 1998), the online trading division of Bull & Bear Group (1999), and 20% of AOL Canada (1999). It also bought several trust and fiduciary services businesses from Ernst & Young.

It acquired US mortgage bank Prism Financial and the Canadian retail credit card business of BANK ONE in 2000. RBC also sold its commercial credit portfolio to U.S. Bancorp. The company agreed to pay a substantial fine after institutional asset management subsidiary RT Capital Management came under scrutiny from the Ontario Securities Commission for alleged involvement in illegal pension-fund stock manipulation. RBC ended up selling RT Capital to UBS AG the following year.

Also in 2001 RBC made another US purchase: North Carolina's Centura Banks (now RBC Centura Banks). It sold Houston-based home lender RBC Mortgage to New Century Financial in 2005. Also that year it acquired private bank Abacus Financial, which adding locations in the UK and Amsterdam.

RBC spent the decade prior to the global recession building up its US operations. The company moved into the US trust business in 2006 when it purchased American Guaranty & Trust, a unit of National Life Insurance Company. In 2007 it bought the electronic brokerage business of New York boutique Carlin Financial Group. Other acquisitions made during that period include debt securities investor Access Capital Strategies, energy advisory firm Richardson Barr, and DC-area investment bank Ferris, Baker Watts.

In 2008 RBC acquired community banks in Alabama, Georgia, and Florida, including Alabama National BanCorporation. That same year RBC agreed to buy back some $850 million in auction-rate securities and pay the New York State attorney general's office a nearly $10 million fine. Auction-rate securities were sold to investors as a low-risk investment, but as the economy worsened in 2007 and 2008, banks canceled the regular auctions, rendering the securities worthless. Customers and regulators claimed that banks continued to sell them the securities even though they knew the investments had become very high risk.

Also in 2008 RBC Bank expanded its finance operations when it bought the Canadian commercial leasing business of ABN AMRO. It renamed the unit RBC Equipment Finance Group.

To cement its place among the world's 10 largest wealth managers, RBC bought UK-based fixed income specialist BlueBay Asset Management for some $1.5 billion in 2010. Also that year it bought BNP Paribas Fortis' Hong Kong wealth management business.

In 2010 it also sold Liberty Life, its US life insurance subsidiary that had posted losses for two years, to Apollo affiliate Athene Holding. To boost brand recognition of another US unit, the company changed the name of Voyageur Asset Management to RBC Global Asset Management (US).

EXECUTIVES

Chief Executive Officer, President, Director, David I. McKay
Chief Financial Officer, Nadine Ahn
Chief Human Resources Officer, Kelly Pereira
Chief Legal Officer, Maria Douvas
Chief Risk Officer, Graeme Hepworth
Chief Administrative & Strategy Officer, Christoph Knoess
Senior Vice President, Associate General Counsel, Secretary, Karen E. McCarthy
Chairman, Kathleen P. Taylor
Corporate Director, Andrew A. Chisholm
Corporate Director, Toos N. Daruvala
Corporate Director, Roberta L. Jamieson
Corporate Director, Maryann Turcke
Corporate Director, Bridget A. van Kralingen
Director, Jacynthe Cote
Director, Frank Vettese
Director, David F. Denison
Director, Cynthia J. Devine
Director, Thierry Vandal
Director, Jeffery W. Yabuki
Director, Mirko Bibic
Auditors : PricewaterhouseCoopers LLP

LOCATIONS

HQ: Royal Bank of Canada (Montreal, Quebec)
200 Bay Street, Toronto, Ontario M5J 2J5
Phone: 416 974-6715
Web: www.rbc.com

2018 Sales

	% of total
Canada	60
US	23
Other international	17
Total	100

PRODUCTS/OPERATIONS

2018 Sales

	% of total
Net interest income	43
Non-interest income	57
Total	100

2018 Sales

	% of total
Personal & commercial banking	39
Wealth management	25
Capital markets	20
Insurance	10
Investor & treasury services	6
Total	100

COMPETITORS

AUSTRALIA AND NEW ZEALAND BANKING GROUP LIMITED
Banque de Montréal
COMMONWEALTH BANK OF AUSTRALIA
Canadian Imperial Bank Of Commerce
Credit Suisse Group AG
HUNTINGTON BANCSHARES INCORPORATED
ING Groep N.V.
KEYCORP
The Toronto-Dominion Bank
U.S. BANCORP

HISTORICAL FINANCIALS

Company Type: Public

Income Statement FYE: October 31

	ASSETS ($mil)	NET INCOME ($mil)	INCOME AS % OF ASSETS	EMPLOYEES
10/23	1,449,840	10,574	0.7%	91,398
10/22	1,403,010	11,557	0.8%	91,427
10/21	1,381,340	12,983	0.9%	85,301
10/20	1,221,240	8,593	0.7%	83,842
10/19	1,084,830	9,763	0.9%	82,801
Annual Growth	7.5%	2.0%	—	2.5%

2023 Year-End Financials

Return on assets: 0.7%
Return on equity: 12.9%
Long-term debt ($ mil.): —
No. of shares ($ mil.): 1,400
Sales ($ mil.): 85,320
Dividends
Yield: 4.9%
Payout: 68.1%
Market value ($ mil.): 111,873

	STOCK PRICE ($) FY Close	P/E High/Low		PER SHARE ($) Earnings	Dividends	Book Value
10/23	79.88	10	7	7.59	3.97	60.75
10/22	92.47	10	8	8.09	3.82	57.18
10/21	104.01	10	7	8.95	3.50	56.07
10/20	69.99	11	7	5.88	3.22	45.80
10/19	80.66	9	8	6.64	3.07	44.34
Annual Growth	(0.2%)	—		3.4%	6.6%	8.2%

Royal DSM NV

The clever folks at Netherlands-based Koninklijke DSM (DSM) produce nutritional products and performance materials. Its nutrition businesses, DSM Nutritional Products and DSM Food Specialties, manufacture vitamins, carotenoids, nutritional lipids for food, drink, and pharmaceuticals as well as enzymes, cultures, and sugar reduction. DSM Materials (DSM Engineering Materials, Resins & Functional Materials, and Additive Manufacturing) makes synthetic fibers, thermoplastics, and resins used in coatings. With upwards of 100 production facilities in more than 40 countries, DSM enjoys a global reach. Core customer sectors are animal nutrition companies, food and beverages makers, and the dietary supplements industry. The company generates majority of its revenue from Europe.

Operations

DSM divides its operations into three segments: Nutrition, Materials, and the Innovation Center.

The Nutrition segment is one of the world's leading suppliers of essential nutrients such as vitamins, carotenoids, nutritional lipids and other ingredients to the feed, food, pharmaceutical and personal care industries. Its Food Specialties unit is a major supplier of food enzymes, cultures, probiotics, bio-preservation, hydrocolloids, sugar reduction, and savory taste solutions. Nutrition products account for over 75% of DSM's annual sales.

The Materials segment cluster consists of DSM Engineering Materials, DSM Resins & Functional Materials, DSM Protective Materials and DSM Additive Manufacturing. DSM Engineering Materials is a global player in developing, manufacturing and marketing thermoplastics used in components for the electrical and electronics, automotive, building & construction, medical, food packaging and consumer goods industries. DSM Resins & Functional Materials is a leader in developing, manufacturing and marketing high-quality resins solutions for paints and coatings, UV-curable coatings for fiber-optic cables. DSM Protective Materials containing fiber for lightweight strength in ropes and synthetic chains and providing comfort and safety from footwear and to cut-resistant gloves to body armor. DSM Additive Manufacturing produce additives for 3D printing technologies. Materials products account for over 20% of sales.

The DSM's Innovation Center segment, which represents the remaining sales, has a general business development role, focusing on areas outside the current scope of the company's business groups. It has businesses with commercial potential, DSM Biochemical, DSM Bio-based Products & Services, DSM Advanced Solar, and DSM Venturing.

Geographic Reach

DSM's production footprint spans more than 100 commercial production facilities in upwards of 40 countries. Its revenue is geographically diversified, generating about 60% in Europe and nearly 15% in North America, more than 5% in Latin America and nearly 15% in China, around 5% in other Asian countries.

Sales and Marketing

Delivering local solutions across all regions, its end-market focus allows the company to better understand market needs, enable solution selling, and open up innovation headroom ? for example, more relevant solutions supporting early life nutrition and dietary supplements in Health, Nutrition & Care. With a significant and diverse premix footprint, together with superior formulations and delivery systems and increasing competences, in analytics and diagnostics, it is able to develop innovative and sustainable local solutions for its customers around the world.

Drawing on its emerging capabilities in digitization, it is swiftly developing an additional dimension to is future growth: precision & personalization. Developments in data science and bioscience are opening up exciting opportunities to address challenges in health and nutrition. Leveraging its reputation, science-based competences and global customer base, it seeks to create digital solutions that deliver unprecedented levels of precision.

Financial Performance

At EUR9.2 billion, net sales from continuing operations in 2021 were 14% higher than in 2020 (EUR 8.1 billion) after recording revenue increase in all its segments except in Innovation Center.

Net income for fiscal 2021 increased by over 230% to EUR 1.7 billion compared to EUR 508 million from the year.

Cash held by the company at the end of fiscal 2021 increased to EUR 1.6 billion. Cash provided by operations and investing activities were EUR 1.4 billion and EUR 208 million, respectively. Financing activities used EUR 984 million, mainly for repayment of loans and dividend paid.

Strategy

The company's long-term strategic focus remains on Health, Nutrition and Bioscience. Royal DSM' strategy aligns its unique competences and its purpose ('creating brighter lives for all') with its ambitions to address specific megatrends and targeted Sustainable Development Goals (SDGs).

In 2021, the company announced its decision to accelerate its journey toward becoming a company focused on Health, Nutrition & Bioscience, using its resources and capabilities to address the urgent societal and environmental challenges linked to the way the world produces and consumes food.

In the face of multiple systemic and interconnected food system challenges that impact the health and well-being of people, animals, and the planet, the Intergovernmental Panel on Climate Change (IPCC) Report of 2021 warns the world is rapidly approaching critical and irreversible tipping points. The company underpinned its transformation by creating three market-focused Business Groups in which it organizes its Health, Nutrition & Bioscience activities with effect from 1 January 2022: Animal Nutrition & Health, Health, Nutrition & Care, and Food & Beverage.

Company Background

DSM was established in 1902 by the Dutch government to mine coal reserves in the Southern Province of Limburg.

The company's evolution has continued unabated after it closed the last coal mine in the early 70s. In the past 20 years, it transformed once again, as it began to focus more on creating science-based solutions in health, nutrition and sustainable living.

HISTORY

Koninklijke DSM began in 1902 with the Dutch government's desire to establish a source for coal. Previously all coal used in Holland was either imported or held by foreign companies.

In 1920 DSM began selling coke-oven gas as an energy source. In 1929, as the use of coke-oven gas began to diminish, DSM expanded to produce chemicals such as fertilizer. Although chemical production increased, the fuel shortage following WWII translated into growth for DSM's coal and coke operations. The company built a research lab in 1945, and the chemicals business expanded to produce plastics.

The 1960s saw coal energy become unfeasible, so the decision to phase out coal mining came in 1965. With two-thirds of its sales and profits gone, DSM expanded its line of chemicals. It became an unquoted public company in 1967.

DSM replaced its use of coke-oven gas with natural gas and petroleum products to produce chemicals in 1970. After spinning off its fertilizer business to a subsidiary, the company turned its focus to industrial chemicals (plastics and resins). DSM restructured in the 1980s to include a wider variety of fine chemicals. It became publicly traded in 1989.

DSM restructured again and created an engineering plastics products division in Brussels (1990), followed by the creation of three other units (fine chemicals, hydrocarbons, and fertilizers) in 1992. A 1995 joint venture with Jiangsu Jiangyin to make thermoplastic compounds and a 1996 contract with Ford gave DSM access to the automotive market. In 1998 DSM aligned itself with Japan's JSR Engineering Plastics to sell its line of auto, electronic, and connector parts. For the purpose of making semi-synthetic penicillin, DSM entered into a joint venture with China-based Zhang Jia Kou in 1999.

Early in 2001 DSM sold its engineering plastics operations to Quadrant Holding for $200 million. The rumors of DSM's possible bid for Rhodia were verified by the existence of such a bid -- which was turned down -- causing controversy among some Rhodia investors. In 2002 DSM sold its petrochemicals business to SABIC for about $2 billion. Later that year the company announced that it would acquire a vitamins and fine chemicals division from Roche, the Swiss-based health care group.

During the early 2000s DSM pared down and restructured many of its operations to control costs.

DSM made a strategic decision in 2007 to turn to life sciences and performance materials because the business lines offer better profit margins and more stable revenues than the company formerly had when it disproportionately relied on petrochemicals. To support its strategic focus, DSM not only divested itself of a number of noncore assets, it also made selective acquisitions.

The shift began to pay off in 2010, with the company rebounding from the global economic downturn. The company's focus on high-margin, high-quality businesses helped shield it from the impact of cyclicality. By cutting costs, working capital, and workforce, and by divesting several businesses, the company was able to reduce its net debt. Although the company's total sales for 2010 improved only slightly, its net income grew more than 33% from the previous year.

In 2012 the company, still following its new strategy, acquired the oilseed processing enzymes operations of industrial biotech company Verenium for $37 million. The buy gives DSM certain licenses for enzymes used in the food and beverage markets, including the Purifine brand products and those under development in the oilseed processing market.

Several divestments in 2010 enabled DSM to concentrate on growing sales in its target business areas: personalized nutrition, specialty packaging, biomedical, and industrial biotechnology. That year the company sold its DSM Agro and DSM Melamine operations to Egypt's Orascom Construction Industries for $416 million. It sold its DSM Special Products unit, which manufactured benzoic acid, sodium benzoate, benzaldehyde, and benzyl alcohol, to Emerald Performance Materials.

DSM agreed to sell the last of its citric acid businesses, Citrique Belge, to Adcuram in 2010. It also sold its thermoplastic elastomers business Sarlink to US-based polymer company Teknor Apex, and sold the remaining part of its elastomers unit to LANXESS for $415 million. The sale of its DSM Elastomers unit in December 2010 eliminated its base chemicals and materials operations. It also completed DSM's transformation to a life sciences and materials company.

Although it was busy divesting businesses in 2010, DSM also made key acquisitions and investments that year. They helped it grow both geographically and in product lines, particularly in Asia and North America. It picked up Mitsubishi Chemical's Novamid polyamide business in a no-cash exchange for its Xantar polycarbonate unit. DSM's acquisition of US-based specialty ingredients company Microbia from Ironwood Pharmaceuticals lets it take advantage of Microbia's proprietary platform and research and development capabilities.

Also in 2010, DSM acquired US-based Martek Biosciences for more than $1 billion. Martek makes products from microbial sources that promote health and wellness through nutrition The deal adds a new platform at DSM for polyunsaturated fatty acids, which have applications in the infant formula nutrition market.

DSM agreed to form a joint venture with DuPont in 2010 to develop, manufacture, and commercialize advanced surgical biomedical materials. The 50-50 venture will be called Actamax Surgical Materials. It formed another 50-50 joint venture, this time with Sinochem Group, for a biopharmaceutical venture to produce anti-infectives. The joint venture, DSM Sinochem Pharmaceuticals, is based in Hong Kong and includes all current DSM anti-infectives operations.

Later that year, through a subsidiary, DSM acquired a 51% stake in Taiwan-based AGI Corporation in a share purchase deal worth about $65 million. DSM's US-based subsidiary, DSM Resins, will use AGI's curable resins to strengthen its UV technology platform.

In 2011 DSM acquired Vitatene S.A.U., a Spain-based producer of carotenoids, a naturally occurring fat-soluble pigment that is synthesized by plants, algae, and certain bacteria. The acquisition allows DSM to strengthen the natural carotenoids offerings of its nutrition business as part of its strategy to grow in markets where consumer demand is high.

In 2013 JLL Partners and DSM combining DSM Pharmaceutical Products and Patheon Inc. into a new privately held company, named DPx, in which DSM holds a 49% share. That year DSM sold DSM's share in DEXPlastomers V.o.F. to Borealis for ?55 million. it also sold the Euroresins business in Germany, Austria, Switzerland, Poland and the Baltic states.

EXECUTIVES

Chief Financial Officer, Co-Chief Executive Officer, Geraldine Matchett
Chief Operating Officer, Co-Chief Executive Officer, Dimitri de Vreeze
Chair, Supervisory Board Member, Thomas Leysen
Deputy Chair, Supervisory Board Member, John Ramsay
Supervisory Board Member, Eileen Kennedy
Supervisory Board Member, Carla Mahieu
Supervisory Board Member, Erica L. Mann
Supervisory Board Member, Frits Dirk van Paasschen

Supervisory Board Member, Coerien M. Wortmann-Kool

Auditors : KPMG Accountants N.V.

LOCATIONS
HQ: Royal DSM NV
 Het Overloon 1, Heerlen, Limburg 6411 TE
Phone: (31) 45 578 2864   **Fax:** (31) 45 578 2595
Web: www.dsm.com

2018 Sales
	% of total
Western Europe (Excluding Netherlands)	24
North America	22
China	12
Latin America	12
Eastern Europe	7
Netherlands	4
Japan	3
India	3
Rest of Asia	10
Rest of the world	3
Total	**100**

PRODUCTS/OPERATIONS
2018 Sales
	% of total
Nutrition	66
Materials	32
Innovation Center	2
Corporate activities	—
Total	**100**

Selected Businesses
Nutrition
   DSM Nutritional Products
     Animal Nutrition & Health
     Human Nutrition & Health
   DSM Food Specialties
Performance Materials
   DSM Dyneema
   DSM Engineering Plastics
   DSM Resins
Polymer Intermediates
   DSM Fibre Intermediates
Pharma
   DSM Anti-infectives
   DSM Pharmaceutical Products

COMPETITORS
Agrium Inc
CRODA INTERNATIONAL PUBLIC LIMITED COMPANY
Evonik Industries AG
LANXESS SOLUTIONS US INC.
LSB INDUSTRIES, INC.
Parkland Corporation
TERRA NITROGEN COMPANY, L.P.
THE SCOTTS MIRACLE-GRO COMPANY
URALKALI, PAO
Yara International ASA

HISTORICAL FINANCIALS
Company Type: Public

Income Statement   FYE: December 31

	REVENUE ($mil)	NET INCOME ($mil)	NET PROFIT MARGIN	EMPLOYEES
12/22	8,960	1,809	20.2%	20,682
12/21	10,417	1,890	18.1%	21,358
12/20	9,948	612	6.2%	23,127
12/19	10,116	851	8.4%	22,174
12/18	10,612	1,233	11.6%	20,977
Annual Growth	(4.1%)	10.1%	—	(0.4%)

2022 Year-End Financials
Debt ratio: 17.7%   No. of shares ($ mil.): 173
Return on equity: 16.8%   Dividends
Cash ($ mil.): 2,942   Yield: —
Current Ratio: 3.15   Payout: 9.5%
Long-term debt ($ mil.): 2,989   Market value ($ mil.): —

RWE AG

RWE has become an electricity generation from renewables as the result of an asset swap with E.ON. Through its subsidiaries, RWE AG is a player in the field of renewable energy. Through innovation and investment, the new RWE is creating the foundation for a carbon neutral future. It also owns major UK and Netherlands-based utilities, and Germany-based electricity and gas supplier RWE Power. It generates over 35% of its revenue in Germany.

Operations
In its 2021 financial report, the company divided its operations to the following segments: Offshore Wind (less than 5% of revenue) is overseen by the RWE Renewables, the company's group; Onshore wind/Solar (some 10% of revenue) where the company pools their onshore wind, solar power and battery storage activities; Hydro/Biomass/Gas (around 5% of revenue) which is responsible for the run-of-river, pumped storage, biomass and gas power stations; Supply & trading (about 80% of revenue) where the company trades their energy commodities and is managed by RWE Supply and Trading; and Coal/Nuclear (about 5% of revenue), which was previously lignite and is the generating electricity in Germany produced from lignite, hard coal, and nuclear fuel.

Geographic Reach
RWE operates in Germany, the Netherlands/Belgium, the UK, Asia, and in Central Eastern and South Eastern Europe. Germany and UK accounted for approximately 35% of the company's revenue each.

Financial Performance
The company's revenue in 2021 increased to EUR 24.5 billion compared to EUR 13.7 billion in the prior year.

Net income in 2021 decreased to EUR 832 million compared to EUR 1.1 billion in the prior year.

Cash held by the company at the end of 2021 increased to EUR 5.8 billion. Cash provided by operations and financing activities were EUR 7.3 billion and EUR 1.5 billion, respectively. Cash used for investing activities was EUR 7.7 billion, mainly for capital expenditures.

Strategy
In November 2021, RWE informed the public about its growth and earnings targets for this decade and received very positive feedback. By 2030, RWE intend to invest EUR50 billion in renewables, battery storage, gas-fired power stations and electrolysers. Including proceeds from selling stakes in projects, it foresees net investments of EUR 30 billion. This will double its generation capacity in these technologies to 50 GW by 2030. At the same time, the company are successively phasing out electricity generated from coal and setting the stage for RWE to be carbon neutral by no later than 2040. This will not only make RWE greener, but also more profitable. RWE's 2030 goal is to achieve an adjusted EBITDA in its core business segments of EUR 5 billion. This would represent an increase of around 80?% compared to 2021.

Company Background
RWE traces its roots back to 1898, when Rheinisch-Westfälisches Elektrizitätswerk -- or RWE for short -- was established. In 1902, Hugo Stinnes, an industrialist from Mülheim, acquired control of the company. He worked to build a large-scale, efficient electricity supply.

HISTORY
Founded at the end of the 19th century, RWE mirrored the industrialization of Germany in its growth. It was formed as Rheinisch-Westfalisches Elektrizitatswerk in 1898 by Erich Zweigert, the mayor of Essen, and Hugo Stinnes, an industrialist from Mulheim, to provide electricity to Essen and surrounding areas. The company began supplying power in 1900.

Stinnes persuaded other cities -- Gelsenkirchen and Mulheim -- to buy shares in RWE in 1905. In 1908 RWE and rival Vereinigte Elektrizitatswerk Westfalen (VEW) agreed to divide up the territories that each would supply.

Germany's coal shortages, caused by WWI, prompted RWE to expand its coal operations, and it bought Rheinische Aktiengesellschaft für Braunkohlenbergbau, a coal producer, in 1932. RWE also built a power line network, completed in 1930, to connect populous northern Germany with the south. By 1939, as WWII began, the company had plants throughout most of western Germany. However, the war destroyed much of its infrastructure, and RWE had to rebuild.

The company continued to rely on coal for most of its fuel needs in the 1950s, but in 1961 RWE and Bayern Atomkraft sponsored the construction of a demonstration nuclear reactor, the first of several such projects, at Gundremmingen. The Gundremmingen plant was shut down in 1977, and to replace it RWE built two 1,300-MW reactors that began operation in 1984.

RWE began to diversify, and in 1988 it acquired Texaco's German petroleum and petrochemical unit, which became RWE-DEA. By 1990 RWE's operations also included waste management and construction. RWE reorganized, creating RWE Aktiengesellschaft as a holding company for group operations.

RWE-DEA acquired the US's Vista

Chemical in 1991, and RWE's Rheinbraun mining unit bought a 50% stake in Consolidation Coal from DuPont. (The mining venture went public in 1999 as CONSOL Energy.) RWE led a consortium that acquired major stakes in three Hungarian power companies in 1995.

Hoping to play a role in Germany's telecommunications market, RWE teamed with VEBA in 1997 to form the o.tel.o joint venture, and RWE and VEBA gained control of large German mobile phone operator E-Plus. The nation's telecom market was deregulated in 1998, but Mannesmann and former monopoly Deutsche Telekom proved to be formidable competitors. In 1999 RWE and VEBA sold o.tel.o's fixed-line business (along with the o.tel.o brand name) and cable-TV unit Tele Columbus. The next year the companies sold their joint stake in E-Plus.

Faced with deregulating German electricity markets, RWE Energie had begun restructuring as soon as the market opened up in 1998. It agreed to buy fellow German power company VEW in a $20 billion deal that closed in 2000. RWE also joined with insurance giant Allianz and France's Vivendi in a successful bid for a 49.9% stake in state-owned water distributor Berliner Wasserbetriebe (Vivendi later spurned an RWE offer to buy its energy businesses).

After taking advantage of deregulating markets in Germany, RWE moved to pick up other European utilities: It acquired UK-based Thames Water (later renamed RWE Thames Water) in 2000 and bought a majority stake in Dutch gas supplier Intergas the next year. In 2002 the company issued an exchange offer to acquire UK electricity supplier Innogy (later renamed RWE npower) for a total of about $4.4 billion in cash and $3 billion in assumed debt. It also completed a $3.7 billion purchase of Czech Republic gas supplier Transgas.

In a move to further streamline operations, RWE sold its 50% stake in refinery and service station subsidiary Shell & DEA Oil to Deutsche Shell and Shell Petroleum. To do battle in an increasingly competitive utility industry, RWE is acquiring stakes in other European utilities. In 2003 RWE also acquired North American utility American Water Works, which was combined with the US operations of RWE Thames Water, for $4.6 billion in cash and $4 billion in assumed debt.

Recognizing that its international acquisitions of water utilities in the early 2000s had left it overextended, RWE has been to selling its water assets in order to save cash and streamline its operations around its core power businesses. Overextended, in 2006 the company sold its Thames Water unit to Kemble Water Limited, a consortium led by Macquarie Bank's European Infrastructure Funds. It spun off its American Water unit in 2008.

The company saw its revenues drop in 2009 as the global recession hammered gas prices. However, the same lower gas prices helped RWE to save costs, enabling it to post an improved net income that year.

After being outmaneuvered by EDF in its plan to grow its Pan-European power footprint by acquiring British Energy, RWE in 2009 acquired top Dutch power utility Essent for $10.7 billion. The deal boost its position as one of the top electricity and gas utilities in Europe.

Growing its energy sources, in 2009 it also formed a joint venture with E.ON to develop 6,000 MW of nuclear power capacity in the UK. In a move to reduce its dependency on the wholesale gas markets, in 2009 RWE acquired 70% of the Breagh North Sea gas field for about $350 million.

The company announced CEO JÃœrgen GroÃŸmann, who fought Germany's decision to phase out nuclear power, stepped down in July 2012. GroÃŸmann was replaced by Peter Terium, the CEO of Essent. COO Rolf Martin Schmitz was named Deputy CEO.

EXECUTIVES

Chief Executive Officer, Markus Krebber
Chief Financial Officer, Michael Muller
Labour Chief Human Resources Officer, Labour Director, Zvezdana Seeger
Chairman, Werner Brandt
Director, Deputy Chairman, Ralf Sikorski
Director, Michael Bochinsky
Director, Sandra Bossemeyer
Director, Hans Friedrich Bunting
Director, Matthias Durbaum
Director, Ute Gerbaulet
Director, Hans-Peter Keitel
Director, Monika Kircher
Director, Thomas Kufen
Director, Reiner van Limbeck
Director, Harald Louis
Director, Dagmar Paasch
Director, Erhard Schipporeit
Director, Dirk Schumacher
Director, Ullrich Sierau
Director, Hauke Stars
Director, Helle Valentin
Director, Andreas Wagner
Director, Marion Weckes
Auditors : PricewaterhouseCoopers GmbH

LOCATIONS

HQ: RWE AG
   RWE Platz 1, Essen 45141
Phone: (49) 201 5179 0   **Fax:** (49) 201 5179 5299
Web: www.rwe.com

2017 Sales

	% of total
European Union	
Germany	62
UK	17
Other	19
Rest of Europe	1
Other	1
Total	100

PRODUCTS/OPERATIONS

2017 Sales by Segment

	% of total
innogy	88
Supply & Trading	7
European Power	2
Lignite & Nuclear	3
Other	-
Total	100

COMPETITORS

E.ON SE
E.ON UK PLC
ENDESA SA
IBERDROLA, SOCIEDAD ANONIMA
INTERNATIONAL POWER LTD.
REPSOL SA.
SHV Holdings N.V.
TOKYO ELECTRIC POWER COMPANY HOLDINGS, INCORPORATED
UNITED UTILITIES GROUP PLC
Vattenfall AB

HISTORICAL FINANCIALS

Company Type: Public

Income Statement   FYE: December 31

	REVENUE ($mil)	NET INCOME ($mil)	NET PROFIT MARGIN	EMPLOYEES
12/22	40,976	2,901	7.1%	18,627
12/21	27,760	816	2.9%	19,242
12/20	16,799	1,221	7.3%	19,630
12/19	14,736	9,541	64.7%	38,082
12/18	15,331	383	2.5%	58,441
Annual Growth	27.9%	65.8%	—	(24.9%)

2022 Year-End Financials

Debt ratio: 16.2%   No. of shares ($ mil.): 676
Return on equity: 12.6%   Dividends
Cash ($ mil.): 7,463   Yield: —
Current Ratio: 1.21   Payout: 16.3%
Long-term debt ($ mil.): 10,455   Market value ($ mil.): 29,970

	STOCK PRICE ($) FY Close	P/E High/Low		PER SHARE ($) Earnings	Dividends	Book Value
12/22	44.32	12	9	4.20	0.68	43.55
12/21	40.83	41	30	1.21	1.37	25.53
12/20	42.44	28	16	1.91	0.64	31.18
12/19	30.66	2	2	15.52	0.56	30.95
12/18	21.89	48	32	0.62	1.30	19.25
Annual Growth	19.3%	—	—	61.4%	(14.8%)	22.7%

Ryanair Holdings Plc

Ryanair Holdings is Europe's largest airline group and is the parent company of Buzz, Lauda, Malta Air & Ryanair. The carrier flies to over 240 destinations in over 40 countries. Ryanair specializes in short-haul routes between secondary and regional airports. It operates from some 90 bases in Europe and North America. The carrier maintains a fleet of about 485 Boeing 737-800s and about 30 Airbus A320 aircraft. Ryanair generates majority of revenue outside its home country, Ireland. Ryanair has operated as an international airline since commencing operations in 1985.

Operations
Ryanair operates a fleet of about 485 Boeing 737-800 aircraft and about 30 Airbus A320 aircraft. Ryanair plans for the purchases to enable it to lower fares and grow traffic. The company is comprised of four key separate airlines: Ryanair DAC, which generates about 85%; Buzz, Lauda, and Malta Air.

Overall, scheduled revenue accounts for some 55% of total sales. The remaining is from ancillary.

Geographic Reach
Ryanair operates approximately 3,000 daily flights. Its flights connect to over 240 destinations in more than 40 countries. Ireland and the UK collectively account for over 15% of its overall sales. Its largest market is Italy that brings in some 25%.

Ryanair is headquartered in Ireland.

Sales and Marketing
Ryanair primarily advertises its services in national and regional media across Europe. In addition, Ryanair uses advertising, email marketing and social media. Other marketing activities include the distribution of advertising and promotional material and cooperative advertising campaigns with other travel-related entities, including local tourist boards. Ryanair also regularly contacts people who have registered in its database to inform them about promotions and special offers.

Financial Performance
The company reported a revenue of EUR 4.8 billion in 2022, a 4% increase from the previous year's revenue of EUR 1.6 billion.

In 2022, the company had a net loss of EUR 240.8 million, a 76% improvement from the previous year's net loss of EUR 1 billion. The decrease in loss was primarily attributable to an 253% increase in traffic as European Governments gradually eased travel restrictions/lockdowns related to the Covid-19 pandemic.

The company's cash at the end of 2022 was EUR 2.7 billion. Operating activities generated EUR 1.9 billion, while investing activities used EUR 1.4 billion, mainly for capital expenditure - purchase of property, plant and equipment. Financing activities used another EUR 536.5 million, primarily for repayments of borrowings.

Strategy
Ryanair's objective is to establish itself as Europe's biggest scheduled passenger airline group, through continued improvements and expanded offerings of its low-fares service. In the highly challenging current operating environment, Ryanair seeks to offer low fares that generate increased passenger traffic while maintaining a continuous focus on cost-containment and operating efficiencies. The key elements of Ryanair's long-term strategy are:

Low-Fares. Ryanair sells seats on a one-way basis, thus eliminating minimum stay requirements from all travel on Ryanair scheduled services;

Customer Service. Ryanair's strategy is to deliver the best customer service performance in its peer group. Ryanair delivers industry leading punctuality and fewer lost bags than its peer group in Europe;

Frequent point-to-point flights on short-haul routes. Ryanair provides frequent point-to-point service on short-haul routes. In fiscal year 2021, Ryanair flew an average route length of approximately 776 miles and an average flight duration of approximately 1.88 hours. Short-haul routes allow Ryanair to offer its low fares and frequent service, while eliminating the need to provide unnecessary "frills", like free in-flight meals and movies, otherwise expected by customers on longer flights; and

Low Operating Costs. Ryanair strives to reduce or control four of the primary expenses involved in running a major scheduled airline group: (i) aircraft equipment and finance costs; (ii) personnel costs; (iii) customer service costs; and (iv) airport access and handling costs.

Company Background
Tony Ryan and his sons Declan and Cathal founded Ryanair in 1985.

EXECUTIVES

Chief Executive Officer, Director, Michael O'Leary
Finance Chief Financial Officer, Neil Sorahan
Safety and Security Chief Risk Officer, Carol Sharkey
Chief Technology Officer, John Hurley
Legal Secretary, Regulatory Affairs Secretary, Regulatory Affairs Chief Legal Officer, Legal Chief Legal Officer, Juliusz Komorek
Director, Chairman, Stan McCarthy
Senior Independent Non-Executive Director, Louise Phelan
Independent Non-Executive Director, Michael A. Cawley
Independent Non-Executive Director, Howard Millar
Independent Non-Executive Director, Mike O'Brien
Independent Non-Executive Director, Richard A. Milliken
Independent Non-Executive Director, Roisin Brennan
Independent Non-Executive Director, Emer Daly
Independent Non-Executive Director, Julie O'Neill
Independent Non-Executive Director, Geoff Doherty
Auditors : PricewaterhouseCoopers

LOCATIONS

HQ: Ryanair Holdings Plc
c/o Ryanair DAC, Dublin Office, Airside Business Park, Swords, County Dublin K67 NY94
Phone: (353) 1 945 1212   **Fax:** (353) 1 945 1213
Web: www.ryanair.com

COMPETITORS

AIR FRANCE - KLM
ALSTOM
AMERICAN SCIENCE AND ENGINEERING, INC.
ARVAL PHH HOLDINGS LIMITED
BOEING UNITED KINGDOM LIMITED
EASYJET PLC
SAS AB
SOUTHWEST AIRLINES CO.
STA TRAVEL LIMITED
VIAD CORP

HISTORICAL FINANCIALS

Company Type: Public

Income Statement   FYE: March 31

	REVENUE ($mil)	NET INCOME ($mil)	NET PROFIT MARGIN	EMPLOYEES
03/23	11,708	1,427	12.2%	22,261
03/22	5,329	(267)	—	19,116
03/21	1,918	(1,190)	—	15,016
03/20	9,306	710	7.6%	17,268
03/19	8,644	993	11.5%	16,840
Annual Growth	7.9%	9.5%		7.2%

2023 Year-End Financials
Debt ratio: 25.9%   No. of shares ($ mil.): 1,138
Return on equity: 23.4%   Dividends
Cash ($ mil.): 3,911   Yield: —
Current Ratio: 0.80   Payout: 0.0%
Long-term debt ($ mil.): 3,100   Market value ($ mil.): 107,366

	STOCK PRICE ($) FY Close	P/E High/Low		PER SHARE ($) Earnings	Dividends	Book Value
03/23	94.29	86	55	1.25	0.00	5.39
03/22	87.12	—	—	(0.24)	0.00	5.43
03/21	115.00	—	—	(1.07)	0.00	4.83
03/20	53.09	163	81	0.63	0.00	4.94
03/19	74.94	150	84	0.86	0.00	5.17
Annual Growth	5.9%			9.8%	—	1.0%

Safran SA

EXECUTIVES

Strategy and EAD Chief Executive Officer, Director, Olivier Andries
Chief Financial Officer, Pascal Bantegnie
International and Public Affairs Senior Executive Vice President, Alexandre Ziegler
Executive Vice President, Chief Digital Officer, Chief Information Officer, Frederic Verger
Communications Executive Vice President, Kate Philipps
R&T and Innovation Executive Vice President, Eric Dalbies
Production, Purchasing and Performance Executive Vice President, Marjolaine Grange
Corporate Human and Social Responsibility Executive Vice President, Stephane Dubois
Corporate Secretary, Karine Stamens
Chairman, Ross McInness
Lead Independent Director, Monique Cohen
Independent Director, Helene Auriol Potier
Independent Director, Patricia S. Bellinger
Independent Director, Jean-Lou Chameau

Independent Director, Fabienne Lecorvaisier
Independent Director, Laurent Guillot
Independent Director, Patrick Pelata
Independent Director, Robert Peugeot
Director, Alexandre Lahousse
Director, Celine Fornaro
Director, Christele Debarenne-Fievet
Director, Anne Aubert
Director, Marc Aubry
Director, Herve Chaillou
Auditors : Mazars

LOCATIONS

HQ: Safran SA
2, boulevard du General Martial-Valin, Paris 75015
Phone: (33) 1 40 60 80 80   **Fax:** (33) 1 40 60 81 02
Web: www.safran-group.com

HISTORICAL FINANCIALS

Company Type: Public

Income Statement — FYE: December 31

	REVENUE ($mil)	NET INCOME ($mil)	NET PROFIT MARGIN	EMPLOYEES
12/22	23,093	(2,626)	—	83,276
12/21	17,791	48	0.3%	76,765
12/20	20,139	432	2.1%	78,900
12/19	29,697	2,747	9.3%	95,443
12/18	25,177	1,469	5.8%	92,639
Annual Growth	(2.1%)	—	—	(2.6%)

2022 Year-End Financials

Debt ratio: 14.1%   No. of shares ($ mil.): 424
Return on equity: (-21.1%)   Dividends
Cash ($ mil.): 7,142   Yield: —
Current Ratio: 0.90   Payout: 0.0%
Long-term debt ($ mil.): 5,230   Market value ($ mil.): 13,263

	STOCK PRICE ($) FY Close	P/E High/Low	Earnings	Dividends	Book Value
12/22	31.24	— —	(6.15)	0.13	26.19
12/21	30.59	359 278	0.11	0.13	34.06
12/20	35.46	55 20	0.98	0.53	35.50
12/19	38.70	7 5	6.32	0.51	32.71
12/18	29.89	12 8	3.37	0.47	31.52
Annual Growth	1.1%	— —	—	(26.9%)	(4.5%)

Saipem SpA

Saipem is an advanced technological and engineering platform for the design, construction and operation of complex, safe and sustainable infrastructures and plants. The Milan-based firm provides construction and drilling services to oil and gas companies worldwide. Saipem is a leader in providing engineering, procurement, project management, and construction services with a preference for large-scale offshore and onshore projects. Its fleet of onshore drilling rigs numbers approximately 85 units. About a-third of the company's total revenue comes from the Middle East. Saipem was established in 1957.

Operations

Saipem has four business units: Onshore Engineering & Construction (about 50% of sales), Offshore Engineering & Construction (around 40%), Offshore Drilling (around 5%), and Onshore Drilling (some 5%).

The Onshore Engineering & Construction is focused on the execution of large-scale projects with a high degree of complexity in terms of engineering, technology, and operations, with a strong bias towards challenging projects in difficult environments and remote areas.

The Offshore Engineering & Construction Division is a leading "Global Solution Provider" in the energy industry, with a focus on SURF, fixed facilities and pipelines, renewable energies and decarbonization projects, as well as other technological services for the energy industry. The division's core activities include the development of subsea and conventional fields, laying of export pipelines and trunk lines, as well as acting as EPCI and T/I contractor for windfarms.

The Offshore Drilling fleet consisted of twelve vessels, divided as follows: six ultra-deep-water units for operations at depths in excess of 3,300 feet (the drillships Saipem 10000, Saipem 12000 and Santorini, and the semi-submersible drilling rigs Scarabeo 5, Scarabeo 8, and Scarabeo 9), five high specification jack-ups for operations at depths of up to 375 feet (Perro Negro 7, Perro Negro 8, Pioneer, Sea Lion 7, and Perro Negro 9), one standard jack-up for activities at depths of up to 150 feet (Perro Negro 4). All the rigs mentioned are self-owned with the exception of the jack-ups Pioneer, Sea Lion 7, Perro Negro 9, and the drillship Santorini, which are third party units and operated by Saipem.

The Onshore Drilling rig fleet comprises of around 65 units available for operations, in addition to over 15 rigs in Venezuela, which are unusable and entirely written off. Throughout the year, the Onshore Drilling Division managed one unit owned by a third party. The areas where Saipem operated were Latin America (Peru, Bolivia, Colombia, Ecuador, and Argentina), the Middle East (Saudi Arabia, Kuwait, and United Arab Emirates), and Africa (Congo and Morocco).

Overall, revenue from sales and E&C services generated about 90% of sales, while the rest were generated from sales and drilling services.

Geographic Reach

Italy-based, Saipem is present in more than 70 countries. Its largest market in terms of revenue is the Middles East, accounting for around 30%. Followed by Sub-Saharan Africa which contributes some 25%, Far East, Americas, and the rest of Europe represents around 10% each, CIS with over 5%, and about 5% from Italy.

The company's Offshore Drilling fleet operates in offshore Norway, in Egypt (both in the Mediterranean and the Red Sea), Angola, Ghana, Ivory Coast), Mozambique, Kenya, Mexico, and Saudi Arabia. The areas where Saipem operates were Latin America (Peru, Bolivia, Colombia, Ecuador and Argentina), the Middle East (Saudi Arabia, UAE, and Kuwait), and Africa (Congo and Morocco).

Financial Performance

Note: Growth rates may differ after conversion to US Dollars.

The company's revenue in 2021 decreased by 6% to EUR 6.9 billion compared to EUR 7.3 billion in the prior year.

Net loss in 2021 was EUR 2.5 billion compared to EUR 1.1 billion in the prior year.

Cash held by the company at the end of 2021 decreased to EUR 1.6 billion. Cash provided by operations and financing activities were EUR 90 million and EUR 331 million, respectively. Cash used for investing activities was EUR 490 million, mainly for disposals.

Strategy

The company's goal is to continue to develop, industrialize and adopt digital solutions in business and staff areas.

In order to provide comprehensive information and ensure continuity of its disclosure to corporate stakeholders, in addition to results and targets related to the material issues of the 2021 analysis, the section also presents results and targets for the issues of water resources management, recycling and waste reduction, and spill prevention and recovery and support and development of local communities, which are key components of the environmental management of operations and their impact on territories. Furthermore, in view of the strategic importance of the issue, results and objectives are also reported on the subject of advanced technologies and innovation.

Mergers and Acquisitions

In mid-2022, Saipem has been awarded an offshore E&C contract from Enimed, a company of the ENI SpA group, for the transport and installation of a gas pipeline that will connect the four wells of the Argo and Cassiopea fields to the Sicilian coast, for a value of about 300 million euros. The Cassiopea project represents a strategic infrastructure in the national energy landscape, recently hit by the deteriorating geo-political scenario, confirming Saipem as one of the main contractors able to effectively support customers and provide tangible solutions in response to the current energy crisis.

In late 2021, aipem has been awarded a new SURF EPCI contract awarded by Petrobras for the installation of a submarine system based on rigid risers relating to the Búzios 7 project, for the development of the pre-salt field located about 200 km off the coast of the state of Rio de Janeiro, at a depth of about 2,000 meters The project assigned to Saipem includes the engineering, procurement, construction and installation (EPCI) of the Riser Steel Lazy Wave (SLWR) and the corresponding interconnection flowlines between the 15 subsea wells and the FPSO unit, in addition to the related service lines and control umbilicals. Furthermore, Saipem will be responsible for the supply and installation of the anchors of the FPSO unit and for its attachment to the field. Terms were not disclosed.

In mid-2021, Saipem and Naval Energies, a subsidiary of Naval Group, yesterday signed an agreement for the acquisition of Naval Energies' activities in the floating wind energy sector, which consist of know-how engineering of Naval Energies in relation to floating units, in intellectual property rights and about thirty resources with modeling and simulation skills. This transaction has a completely marginal impact on the financial position of the Saipem group. Terms were not disclosed.

Company Background
Saipem was established in 1957.

HISTORY

Saipem has been operating as part of energy giant Eni since 1953, when the Italian government formed Ente Nazionale Idrocarburi (National Hydrocarbon Agency, or Eni). Eni's mission was to reduce Italy's dependence on international energy companies and sources. The agency began to emphasize oil field services and engineering activities in the late 1950s, primarily through Saipem and its subsidiaries.

The company was incorporated in 1969 as an international contractor offering a full range of services (including subsea pipelaying, platform installation, and drilling services) to the oil and gas industry. Saipem was first listed on the Milan stock exchange in 1984 and on the Paris stock exchange a year later.

As part of the Italian government's strategy to privatize its state industries during the 1990s, Eni became a joint stock company in 1992, with the government retaining a majority stake. During 1998 and 1999 Eni cut its holding in Saipem to 43%. In 2000 Saipem appointed Pietro Franco Tali, a former Saipem CFO, as chairman and CEO.

Delays in the development of large oil and gas fields in deep waters off of Brazil, the Gulf of Mexico, and West Africa, caused a drop in Saipem's 2000 revenues, despite robust oil prices.

In 2001 the company secured two contracts in Saudi Arabia (including the conversion of an oil pipeline into a gas pipeline for Saudi Aramco) worth $180 million.That year it also started construction on a major Turkish gas pipeline.

Saipem bought a 51% stake in French oil field construction contractor Bouygues Offshore in 2002. Later that year, the company increased its stake to 96.8%. In 2003, Saipem acquired International Development Process and Engineering, which was previously set to be acquired by Bouygues Offshore.

EXECUTIVES

Chief Executive Officer, Director, Alessandro Puliti
Chairman, Silvia Merlo
Independent Non-Executive Director, Paul Schapira
Non-Executive Director, Alessandra Ferone
Independent Director, Roberto Diacetti
Independent Director, Patrizia Michela Giangualano
Independent Director, Paola Tagliavini
Director, Davide Munanta
Director, Marco Reggiani
Auditors : KPMG SpA

LOCATIONS

HQ: Saipem SpA
Via Luigi Russolo, 5, San Donato Milanese, MI 20138
Phone: (39) 02 5201   **Fax:** (39) 02 52054295
Web: www.saipem.com

2015 Sales

	% of total
West Africa & Rest of Africa	24
Middle East	19
CIS	18
Americas	15
Rest of Europe	9
Far East	9
Italy	4
North Africa	2
Total	100

PRODUCTS/OPERATIONS

2015 Sales

	% of total
Offshore construction	60
Onshore construction	24
Offshore drilling	9
Onshore drilling	7
Total	100

Selected Subsidiaries
Intermare Sarda S.p.A.
Saipem Energy International S.p.A.
Saipem FPSO S.p.A
Saipem s.a
Saipem International B.V.

COMPETITORS

AMEC FOSTER WHEELER LIMITED
BEAZER HOMES USA, INC.
CALTON, INC.
CENTURY HOMEBUILDERS, LLC
CHAMPION ENTERPRISES HOLDINGS, LLC
HOVNANIAN ENTERPRISES, INC.
MCDERMOTT INTERNATIONAL INC
TOLL BROTHERS, INC.
UCP, INC.
Weatherford International Ltd.

HISTORICAL FINANCIALS
Company Type: Public

Income Statement   FYE: December 31

	REVENUE ($mil)	NET INCOME ($mil)	NET PROFIT MARGIN	EMPLOYEES
12/22	10,670	(223)	—	32,377
12/21	7,787	(2,792)	—	38,806
12/20	9,091	(1,394)	—	35,023
12/19	10,237	13	0.1%	36,986
12/18	9,777	(540)	—	34,129
Annual Growth	2.2%	—	—	(1.3%)

2022 Year-End Financials

Debt ratio: 21.3%   No. of shares ($ mil.): 1,995
Return on equity: (-17.4%) Dividends
Cash ($ mil.): 2,191   Yield: 0.2%
Current Ratio: 1.10   Payout: 0.0%
Long-term debt ($ mil.): 1,846   Market value ($ mil.): 439

	STOCK PRICE ($) FY Close	P/E High/Low	PER SHARE ($) Earnings	Dividends	Book Value
12/22	0.22	—	(0.23)	0.49	1.11
12/21	4.20	—	(28.18)	0.00	3.73
12/20	5.44	—	(14.11)	0.25	36.11
12/19	9.75	112 73	0.11	0.00	45.44
12/18	7.48	—	(5.27)	0.00	45.54
Annual Growth	(58.6%)		—	—	(60.5%)

Samsung Electronics Co Ltd

EXECUTIVES

Chairman, Chief Executive Officer, Kun-Hee Lee
Vice-Chairman, Chief Executive Officer, Yoon-Woo Lee
Vice-Chairman, Soon-Taek Kim
President, Chief Executive Officer, Director, Gee-Sung Choi
Vice-Chairman, Ho-Moon Kang
President, Chief Financial Officer, Director, Ju-Hwa Yun
President, Chief Operating Officer, Jae-Yong Lee
President, Nam-Sung Woo
President, Jong-Gyun Shin
President, Ki-Nam Kim
President, Sang-Gyun Kim
President, Hyun-Jong Kim
President, Bu-Geun Yoon
President, Won-Ki Jang
President, Sung-Ha Jee
President, Oh-Hyun Kwon
President, Dong-Soo Chun
President, Sang-Hoon Lee
Director, Dong-Min Yoon
Director, Chae-Woong Lee
Director, In-Ho Lee
Director, Oh-Soo Park
Auditors : Deloitte Anjin LLC

LOCATIONS

HQ: Samsung Electronics Co Ltd
129, Samsung-ro, Yeongtong-gu, Suwon-si, Gyeonggi-do 16677
Phone: (82) 31 200 1114   **Fax:** (82) 31 200 7538
Web: www.sec.co.kr

HISTORICAL FINANCIALS
Company Type: Public

Income Statement — FYE: December 31

	REVENUE ($mil)	NET INCOME ($mil)	NET PROFIT MARGIN	EMPLOYEES
12/21	235,341	33,031	14.0%	0
12/20	217,588	23,973	11.0%	0
12/19	199,548	18,625	9.3%	0
12/18	218,651	39,367	18.0%	0
12/17	224,719	38,780	17.3%	99,784

Annual Growth   1.2%   (3.9%)   —   —

2021 Year-End Financials
Debt ratio: —
Return on equity: 13.9%
Cash ($ mil.): 32,852
Current Ratio: 2.48
Long-term debt ($ mil.): 429
No. of shares ($ mil.): 5,969
Dividends
Yield: —
Payout: 0.0%
Market value ($ mil.): —

San-In Godo Bank, Ltd. (The) (Japan)

The San-in Godo Bank provides banking services in the Tottori and Shimane prefectures in western Japan. The bank also serves the adjacent Sanyo and Hyogo regions. It does business from more than 100 branches and 13 subsidiary companies. San-in Godo Bank operates overseas from offices in Dalian and Shanghai, China and New York City. The bank was established in 1941.

EXECUTIVES

Chairman, Representative Director, Fumio Ishimaru
President, Representative Director, Toru Yamasaki
Senior Managing Executive Officer, Director, Shuichi Ida
Senior Managing Executive Officer, Hideaki Furuyama
Senior Managing Executive Officer, Soichi Akishita
Director, Hiroshi Yoshikawa
Outside Director, Yasuyuki Kuratsu
Outside Director, Yasuhiro Goto
Outside Director, Chie Motoi
Director, Koji Miyauchi
Director, Mamiko Nakamura
Outside Director, Shoichi Imaoka
Outside Director, Tamaki Adachi
Outside Director, Tomoaki Seko
Auditors : Ernst & Young ShinNihon LLC

LOCATIONS

HQ: San-In Godo Bank, Ltd. (The) (Japan)
  10 Uomachi, Matsue, Shimane 690-8686
Phone: (81) 852 55 1000
Web: www.gogin.co.jp

COMPETITORS
BANK OF KYOTO,LTD., THE
HACHIJUNI BANK, LTD., THE
MUSASHINO BANK, LTD., THE
NISHI-NIPPON CITYBANK,LTD.
OGAKI KYORITSU BANK, LTD., THE

HISTORICAL FINANCIALS
Company Type: Public

Income Statement — FYE: March 31

	ASSETS ($mil)	NET INCOME ($mil)	INCOME AS % OF ASSETS	EMPLOYEES
03/22	55,699	119	0.2%	2,947
03/21	57,532	87	0.2%	3,217
03/20	52,431	96	0.2%	3,337
03/19	50,563	119	0.2%	3,366
03/18	52,253	128	0.2%	3,263

Annual Growth   1.6%   (2.0%)   —   (2.5%)

2022 Year-End Financials
Return on assets: 0.2%
Return on equity: 3.9%
Long-term debt ($ mil.): —
No. of shares ($ mil.): 156
Sales ($ mil.): 782
Dividends
Yield: —
Payout: 34.4%
Market value ($ mil.): —

Sandoz Group AG

EXECUTIVES

Chair, Independent Non-Executive Director, Gilbert Ghostine
Vice-Chairwoman, Independent Non-Executive Director, Karen J. Huebscher
North America President, Keren Haruvi
International President, Francisco Ballester
Europe President, Rebecca Guntern
Chief Executive Officer, Richard Saynor
Chief Financial Officer, Colin Bond
Chief Human Resources Officer, Tripti Jha
Chief Scientific Officer, Claire D'Abreu Hayling
Chief Commercial Officer, Pierre Bourdage
Manufacturing and Supply Officer Chief, Glenn A. Gerecke
General Counsel, Ingrid Sollerer
Independent Non-Executive Director, Shamiram R. Feinglass
Independent Non-Executive Director, François-Xavier Roger
Independent Non-Executive Director, Yannis Skoufalos
Independent Non-Executive Director, Aarti S. Shah
Independent Non-Executive Director, Maria Varsellona
Independent Non-Executive Director, Urs Riedener
Independent Non-Executive Director, Remco Steenbergen
Auditors : PricewaterhouseCoopers AG

LOCATIONS

HQ: Sandoz Group AG
  Suurstoffi 14, Rotkreuz 6343
Phone: (41) 44 239 47 03   **Fax:** (41) 44 239 69 14
Web: www.sandoz.com

HISTORICAL FINANCIALS
Company Type: Public

Income Statement — FYE: December 31

	REVENUE ($mil)	NET INCOME ($mil)	NET PROFIT MARGIN	EMPLOYEES
12/22	9,306	848	9.1%	21,738
12/21	9,678	908	9.4%	0
12/20	9,658	462	4.8%	0

Annual Growth   (1.8%)   35.5%   —   —

2022 Year-End Financials
Debt ratio: 1.2%
Return on equity: 10.0%
Cash ($ mil.): 74
Current Ratio: 0.76
Long-term debt ($ mil.): 30
No. of shares ($ mil.): —
Dividends
Yield: —
Payout: 0.0%
Market value ($ mil.): —

Sandvik AB (Sweden)

Sandvik is a global, high-tech engineering group with approximately 40,000 employees and sales in about 150 countries. It has a strong focus on enhancing customer productivity, profitability and sustainability. Its core values of Customer Focus, Innovation, Fair Play and Passion to Win represent the essence of the Sandvik culture. Together with its purpose "We make the shift ? advancing the world through engineering" and its Code of Conduct, the company can form a solid platform for its strategy. It manages risks and seize opportunities in the surrounding world and it has defined six strategic objectives for growth and operational excellence.

Operations
Sandvik has three business areas ? mining and rock solutions (generates more than 50% of revenue), rock and processing solutions (nearly 10%), and manufacturing and machining solutions (more than 40%).

Mining and rock solutions supply equipment and tools, parts, service, digital solutions and sustainability-driving technologies for the mining and infrastructure industries. Rock and processing solutions supply equipment, service and technical solutions for processing rock and minerals in the mining and infrastructure industries. Manufacturing and machining solutions manufactures tools and tooling systems for advanced metal cutting, expanding into digital manufacturing and software solutions, as well as technologies such as additive manufacturing and in-line metrology.

Geographic Reach
Headquartered in Sweden, Sandvik generates most of its revenue from Europe (more than 25%) and North America (some 25%). It also operates in Asia (nearly 20%), Australia (over 10%), Africa and Middle East (over 10%), and South America (over 5%).

Sales and Marketing
Sandvik generates its revenue from various market segment including mining

(nearly 50% of revenue), engineering (more than 20%), infrastructure (more than 10%), automotive (more than 5%), among others.

It delivers drill rigs, rock-drilling tools and systems, load and haul machines, tunneling equipment, continuous mining and mechanical cutting equipment, crushing and screening, service and sustainability-driving technologies to increase digitalization, automation, safety and customer productivity.

Financial Performance

The company's revenue has fluctuated over the last five years with 2022 gaining the highest revenue. Net profit also fluctuated between 2018 and 2022.

Revenue increased to SEK 112.3 million in 2022 from SEK 85.7 million in the previous year.

Profit fell from SEK 14.5 million in 2021 to SEK 11.2 million in 2022.

Cash and cash equivalents at the end of year was SEK 10.5 million. Operating and financing activities provided $10.5 million and SEK 6.2 million, respectively. Investing activities used SEK 20.3 million mainly for acquisition of companies and shares, net of cash acquired.

Strategy

Sandvik's strategy aims to create benefits for all its stakeholders ? customers, employees and communities, ultimately leading to shareholder value. It rests on the company's core values, explicit target setting in six strategic areas and a decentralized way of working.

Its strategy relies on a number of common strengths across the group: being close to the customer with a decentralized way of working and leading brands, digitalization and automation, a strong performance culture and first-class leadership that focuses on ensuring high employee engagement.

HISTORY

Sandvik's origins go back to 1862, when a steelworks called Hogbo Stal & Jernwerks was founded by Goran Fredrik Goransson in Sandviken, Sweden. Its products in the 1860s included steam hammers and rock drills. Hogbo Stal & Jernwerks' primary financial backer, Johan Holm, had money problems that left him and the company financially ruined; the company went bankrupt in 1866. Hogbo Stal & Jernwerks was reorganized and renamed Sandvikens Jernwerks AB, and Anders Henrik Goransson, the founder's son, took over as the new manager.

By the 1890s the company's steel products included cold-rolled steel rod and strip, and seamless tubing. It also made manufactured products such as saws, boiler tubes for steamships and railway engines, and wire for umbrellas. Sandvikens Jernwerks was listed on the Stockholm stock exchange in 1901.

EXECUTIVES

President, Chief Executive Officer, Director, Björn Rosengren
Chairman, Director, Anders Nyren
Honorary Chairman, Percy N. Barnevik
Communications Executive Vice President, Communications Head, Jessica Alm
Executive Vice President, Chief Financial Officer, Mats Backman
Executive Vice President, General Counsel, Secretary, Bo Severin
Human Resources Executive Vice President, Human Resources Head, Anna Vikstrom Persson
Research & Development Senior Vice President, Research & Development Head, Olle Wijk
Region Officer, Subsidiary Officer, Zhiqiang Zhang
Division Officer, Petra Einarsson
Division Officer, Dinggui Gao
Division Officer, Jonas Gustavsson
Division Officer, Gary Hughes
Information Technology Division Officer, Sourcing Division Officer, Strategy Division Officer, Sourcing Head, Strategy Head, Information Technology Head, Tomas Nordahl
Director, Jurgen M. Geissinger
Director, Johan Karlstrom
Director, Fredrik Lundberg
Director, Hanne de Mora
Director, Simon R. Thompson
Director, Lars Ask
Director, Jan Kjellgren
Director, Tomas Karnstrom
Deputy Board Member, Thomas Andersson
Deputy Board Member, Alicia Espinosa
Auditors : PricewaterhouseCoopers AB

LOCATIONS

HQ: Sandvik AB (Sweden)
 Kungsbron 1, Sektion G, Plan 6, Stockholm 111 22
Phone: (46) 8 456 11 00   **Fax:** (46) 26 26 10 22
Web: www.sandvik.com

2018 Sales

	%
Europe	38
North America	21
Asia	20
Africa/Middle East	9
Australia	7
South America	5
Total	100

PRODUCTS/OPERATIONS

2018 Sales

	% of total
Sandvik Mining & Rock Technology	43
Sandvik Machining Solutions	40
Sandvik Materials Technology	15
Other Operations	2
Total	100

2018 Sales by Customer

	% of total
Mining industry	34
Engineering industry	23
Automotive industry	12
Energy industry	11
Construction industry	9
Aerospace industry	6
Other	5
Total	100

COMPETITORS

ABB Ltd
ASSA ABLOY AB
Aperam
BODYCOTE PLC
CARPENTER TECHNOLOGY CORPORATION
ENERPAC TOOL GROUP CORP.
GKN LIMITED
INNERWORKINGS, INC.
Neles Oyj
TEAM, INC.

HISTORICAL FINANCIALS

Company Type: Public

Income Statement FYE: December 31

	REVENUE ($mil)	NET INCOME ($mil)	NET PROFIT MARGIN	EMPLOYEES
12/22	10,828	1,080	10.0%	40,489
12/21	10,939	1,596	14.6%	44,136
12/20	10,575	1,069	10.1%	37,125
12/19	11,097	917	8.3%	40,246
12/18	11,179	1,420	12.7%	41,705
Annual Growth	(0.8%)	(6.6%)	—	(0.7%)

2022 Year-End Financials

Debt ratio: 2.6% No. of shares ($ mil.): 1,254
Return on equity: 14.1% Dividends
Cash ($ mil.): 1,011 Yield: —
Current Ratio: 1.73 Payout: 136.8%
Long-term debt ($ mil.): 3,694 Market value ($ mil.): 22,704

	STOCK PRICE ($) FY Close	P/E High/Low		PER SHARE ($) Earnings	Dividends	Book Value
12/22	18.10	3	2	0.86	1.18	6.24
12/21	27.95	2	2	1.27	0.77	6.79
12/20	24.59	4	2	0.85	0.80	6.35
12/19	19.44	3	2	0.73	0.44	5.30
12/18	14.41	2	1	1.13	0.40	5.21
Annual Growth	5.9%			(6.6%)	31.1%	4.6%

Sanofi

Sanofi is a leading global healthcare company, focused on patient needs and engaged in the research, development, manufacture and marketing of therapeutic solutions. Its pharmaceutical unit specializes in rare diseases, multiple sclerosis (MS), oncology, immunology, diabetes, and cardiovascular illness; the big sellers are Aubagio (MS), Lantus (diabetes), Lovenox (thrombosis), and Plavix (atherothrombosis). Sanofi's vaccines business, Sanofi Pasteur, manufactures vaccines for flu, meningitis, and pneumonia and its consumer healthcare business makes cough and cold, pain, and digestive remedies. With business operations in approximately 90 countries and its products are available in more than 170 countries; the US is Sanofi's biggest market.

Operations

Sanofi operates through three segments: pharmaceuticals, vaccines, and consumer healthcare.

The pharmaceuticals segment generates around 70% of Sanofi's total revenue and consists of: Specialty Care (rare diseases, multiple sclerosis, oncology, rare blood disorders and immunology), and General Medicines (diabetes, cardiovascular and established prescription products).

Sanofi Pasteur produces vaccines and generates more than 15% of revenue and include immunizations against pertussis, flu, and meningitis, among other diseases. Its main brands are Pentacel, Vaxigrip, and Menactra (more than 100 million doses have been distributed since launch).

Sanofi also has one of the world's largest consumer healthcare portfolios (more than 10% of total revenue), which includes treatments for colds and allergies, pain, and heartburn. Leading brands include Allegra, Doliprane, Dulcolax, and Pharmaton.

Geographic Reach

Geographically, Sanofi's revenue is well diversified. Although the US is Sanofi's largest market at about 40% of revenue, Europe generates approximately 25% and the rest of the world accounts for the remainder. Based in Paris, France, Sanofi has business operations in about 90 countries and its products are available in more than 170 countries.

Sales and Marketing

Although specific distribution patterns vary by country, Sanofi sells prescription drugs primarily to wholesale drug distributors, independent and chain retail drug outlets, hospitals, clinics, managed-care organizations and government institutions. Rare diseases products are also sold directly to physicians.

The company uses a range of channels from in-person to digital to disseminate information about and promote its products among healthcare professionals, ensuring that the channels not only cover its latest therapeutic advances but also its established prescription products, which satisfy patient needs in some therapy areas. It regularly exhibits at major medical congresses. In some countries, products are also marketed directly to patients by way of television, radio, newspapers and magazines, and digital channels (such as the internet). National education and prevention campaigns can be used to improve patients' knowledge of their conditions.

Although Sanofi markets most of its products through its own sales forces, it has entered into and continue to form partnerships to co-promote/co-market certain products in specific geographical areas.

Financial Performance

Note: Growth rates may differ after conversion to US Dollars.

The company's revenue for fiscal 2021 increased by 7% to EUR38.6 billion compared from the prior year with EUR36.0 billion.

Net income for fiscal 2021 decreased to EUR6.2 billion compared from the prior year with EUR12.3 billion.

Cash held by the company at the end of fiscal 2021 decreased to EUR10.1 billion. Cash provided by operations was EUR10.5 billion while cash used for investing and financing activities were EUR7.3 billion and EUR7.1 billion, respectively.

Strategy

Sanofi pursue a strategy of selective acquisitions, in-licensing and collaborations in order to reinforce its pipeline and portfolio. The company are also proceeding to selective divestments to focus on key business areas. The implementation of this strategy depends on its ability to identify transaction opportunities, mobilize the appropriate resources in order to enter into agreements in a timely manner, and execute these transactions on acceptable economic terms.

The Sanofi "Play to Win" strategy is organized around four key priorities: focus on growth; lead with innovation; accelerate efficiency; and reinvent how we work to drive innovation and growth.

Mergers and Acquisitions

In 2022, Sanofi completed the acquisition of Amunix Pharmaceuticals, Inc, adding a promising pipeline of T-cell engagers and cytokine therapies, for $1 billion. The acquisition also provides access to Amunix Pro-XTEN, XPAT, and XPAC technology to deliver next generation Conditionally Activated Biologics. The technology platform is highly complementary to Sanofi's existing R&D platforms and supports Sanofi's efforts to accelerate and expand its contributions to innovative medicines for oncology patients, with approximately 20 molecules currently in development.

In late 2021, Sanofi completed its acquisition of Translate Bio, a clinical-stage mRNA therapeutics company, for approximately $38.00 per share in cash, which represents a total equity value of approximately $3.2 billion (on a fully diluted basis). The acquisition further accelerates the company's efforts to develop transformative vaccines and therapies using mRNA technology. It adds a critical pillar to the company's mRNA Center of Excellence which aims to unlock the potential of next-generation mRNA vaccines and other strategic areas such as immunology, oncology, and rare diseases.

Also in late 2021, Sanofi completed the acquisition of New York-based Kadmon Holdings, a biopharmaceutical company that discovers, develops, and markets transformative therapies for disease areas of significant unmet medical needs, for approximately $1.9 billion. The acquisition supports Sanofi's strategy to continue to grow its General Medicines core assets and will immediately add Rezurock (belumosudil) to its transplant portfolio. Rezurock is a recently FDA-approved, first-in-class treatment for chronic graft-versus-host disease (cGVHD) for adult and pediatric patients 12 years and older who have failed at least two prior lines of systemic therapy.

In 2021, Sanofi completed its acquisition of Kiadis, a clinical-stage biopharmaceutical company developing next generation, "off-the-shelf", NK cell-therapies. The acquisition continues to build on Sanofi's emerging presence in immuno-oncology aligned with the company's strategy to pursue best-in-class treatments in defined areas.

HISTORY

The Sanofi group got its start in 1973 when French oil conglomerate Elf Aquitaine (later part of TOTAL) merged several health care, cosmetics, and animal nutrition companies into one subsidiary. In 1977 Sanofi set up a Japanese subsidiary, through which it developed joint ventures with Japan's Meiji Seika Kaisha and Taisha Pharmaceutical firms. In 1979 Elf spun off Sanofi, although it retained ownership of more than half of the company. Almost from its founding Sanofi grew through acquisitions and alliances. During the 1980s it used a massive war chest to buy stakes and set up joint ventures, such as one with American Home Products in 1982.

The company bought couturier et parfumier Nina Ricci in 1988; such well-known fragrances as L'Air du Temps put it among the industry's top perfume houses. But Sanofi overreached the next two years and was outbid by American Home Products for AH Robins (the drug firm bankrupted by lawsuits over deaths from its Dalkon Shield IUD) and by RhÃ´ne-Poulenc (now part of Aventis) for Rorer. A chastened Sanofi and Kodak subsidiary Sterling Drug in 1991 entered into an alliance that didn't involve an exchange of cash.

In 1993 Sanofi made a splash when it bought the perfume business of fashion designer Yves Saint-Laurent. The next year it bought out much of the pharmaceutical joint venture with Kodak. Sanofi began divesting such noncore businesses as veterinarian and biotech operations in 1995. After suffering a loss in its perfume and beauty division in 1996, it sold Nina Ricci. The rest of its beauty division was sold in 1999 in preparation for the SynthÃ©labo merger.

SynthÃ©labo was founded in 1970 when drug firms Laboratoires Dausse and Laboratoires Robert et Carriere merged. In 1973 it became a 53%-owned subsidiary of beauty products maker L'OrÃ©al. In 1980 drug firm Metabio-Jouillie became a part of

Synthélabo, making it the #3 drug company in France. In 1983 Synthélabo and US drugmaker Searle created Lorex to market the French firm's products in the UK. (Synthélabo bought Searle's interest 10 years later.)

Throughout the 1980s Synthélabo acquired, merged, and formed joint ventures, including some in Japan with Mitsubishi Chemical, Fujisawa Pharmaceutical (1985), and Tanabe Seiyaku (1987). The company continued its acquisitive ways in the 1990s, buying several French rivals.

Synthélabo openly admitted its quest for a large international presence in 1996, announcing it wanted 80% of its sales to come from such foreign markets as Asia and the US. That year the company entered an alliance with Genset to research cancer-causing genes; it also signed on with SmithKline Beecham (now GlaxoSmithKline) and Human Genome Sciences to fund genetic research. Synthélabo's Hungarian subsidiary began planning to make drugs for the first time, rather than just selling its parent's products as in the past. The next year Synthélabo bought Pharmacia & Upjohn's German generic drug subsidiary Sanorania Pharma.

As Synthélabo and Sanofi merged in 1999, the new company's concentration on pharmaceuticals dictated several changes, including the sale of the company's interests in joint venture Pasteur Sanofi Diagnostics, as well as its beauty division, home to such well-known perfume lines as Yves Saint Laurent. It also sold its veterinary and animal feed division to what later became BNP Paribas.

EXECUTIVES

Chief Executive Officer, Executive Director, Paul Hudson
Chief Financial Officer, Executive Vice President, Jean-Baptiste Chasseloup de Chatillon
US Subsidiary Executive Vice President, Deputy Head of Legal Operations Executive Vice President, Legal Affairs Executive Vice President, US Subsidiary General Counsel, Deputy Head of Legal Operations General Counsel, Legal Affairs General Counsel, Karen Linehan
Executive Vice President, Chief Digital Officer, Arnaud Robert
Executive Vice President, Chief People Officer, Natalie Bickford
Global Industrial Affairs Executive Vice President, Philippe Luscan
Global Head of Research & Development Executive Vice President, John Reed
Chairman, Independent Director, Serge Weinberg
Independent Director, Bernard Charles
Independent Director, Patrick Kron
Independent Director, Lise Kingo
Independent Director, Gilles Schnepp
Independent Director, Rachel Duan
Independent Director, Fabienne Lecorvaisier
Independent Director, Melanie Lee
Independent Director, Carole Piwnica
Independent Director, Diane Souza
Independent Director, Thomas C. Sudhof
Director, Laurent Attal
Director, Marion Palme
Director, Christian Senectaire
Auditors : ERNST & YOUNG et Autres

LOCATIONS

HQ: Sanofi
 46 avenue de la Grande Armée, Paris 75017
Phone: (33) 1 53 77 40 00 Fax: (33) 1 53 77 43 03
Web: www.sanofi.com

2018 Sales

	% of total
US	33
Emerging Markets	
Asia	12
Latin America	8
Eurasia	3
Africa & Middle East	6
Europe	28
Rest of World	10
Total	100

PRODUCTS/OPERATIONS

2018 Sales

	% of total
Pharmaceuticals	72
Vaccines	15
Consumer Healthcare	13
Total	100

Selected Products

Prescription pharmaceuticals
 Actonel (osteoporosis)
 Acomplia/Zimulti (obesity)
 Allegra/Telfast (allergies)
 Amaryl (diabetes)
 Ambien/Stillnox/Myslee (insomnia)
 Apidra (diabetes)
 Aprovel/Avapro (hypertension)
 Copaxone (multiple sclerosis)
 Depakine (epilepsy)
 Eloxatine (colorectal cancer)
 Jevtana (prostate cancer)
 Lantus (long-acting insulin for diabetes)
 Lovenox/Clexane (deep vein thrombosis, other cardiovascular conditions)
 Multaq (atrial fibrillation and atrial flutter)
 Nasacort (allergic rhinitis)
 Plavix (arterial blood clots)
 Taxotere (breast and ovarian cancer)
 Tritace (hypertension)
 Vaxigrip (influenza vaccine)
 Xatral (benign prostatic hypertrophy)
Vaccines
 Adacel (diphtheria, tetanus, and pertussis adult booster vaccine)
 Fluzone (influenza vaccine)
 Insuman (diabetes)
 Menactra (meningitis and pneumonia vaccine)
 Pentaxim/Pentacel (Polio, pertussis, and HIB pediatric combination vaccine)
Consumer health
 Doliprane (pain)
 Enterogermina (intestinal health)
 Essentiale (liver therapy)
 Gold Bond (athlete's foot)
 Icy Hot (pain)
 Selsun Blue (dandruff)
 Unisom (sleep aid)
Animal health
 Frontline (antiparasitic)
 Heartgard (parasiticide)
 Ivomec (parasiticide)
Acquired Genzyme products
 Aldurazyme (genetic disease)
 Campath (oncology)
 Cerezyme (genetic disease)
 Clolar (oncology)
 Elaprase (genetic disease)
 Fabrazyme (genetic disease)
 Hectorol (kidney disease)
 Leukine (oncology)
 Mozobil (oncology)
 Myozyme/Lumizyme (genetic disease)
 Renagel/Renvela (kidney disease)
 Thymoglobulin (organ rejection)
 Thyrogen (endocrinology)

HISTORICAL FINANCIALS

Company Type: Public

Income Statement FYE: December 31

	NET REVENUE ($mil)	NET INCOME ($mil)	NET PROFIT MARGIN	EMPLOYEES
12/23	51,441	5,981	11.6%	87,994
12/22	48,477	8,940	18.4%	91,573
12/21	44,340	7,043	15.9%	95,442
12/20	45,862	15,112	33.0%	99,412
12/19	42,250	3,150	7.5%	100,409
Annual Growth	5.0%	17.4%	—	(3.2%)

2023 Year-End Financials

Debt ratio: 14.4% No. of shares ($ mil.): 1,251
Return on equity: 7.2% Dividends
Cash ($ mil.): 9,647 Yield: 0.1%
Current Ratio: 1.27 Payout: 123.9%
Long-term debt ($ mil.): 15,890 Market value ($ mil.): 62,230

	STOCK PRICE ($) FY Close	P/E High/Low		PER SHARE ($) Earnings	Dividends	Book Value
12/23	49.73	13	11	4.76	5.90	65.53
12/22	48.43	8	6	7.11	6.24	63.35
12/21	50.10	10	9	5.60	1.93	61.52
12/20	48.59	6	4	11.99	1.70	61.42
12/19	50.20	23	18	2.50	1.72	52.77
Annual Growth	(0.2%)			17.4%	36.1%	5.6%

SAP SE

SAP SE's enterprise resource planning software integrates back-office functions such as analytics, accounting, distribution and human resources, and comes in on-premises and cloud-linked forms. The company is able to give out its services through its about 110,000 employees. SAP is going all-in on cloud computing and software-as-a-service with its flagship application suite S/4HANA. Besides enterprise software, SAP Concur provides expenses management and SAP Fieldglass provides external workforce management. The company's cloud portfolio serves more than 20,000 partners in over 140 countries. The Americas is the company's largest market of more than 50% of industry's revenue.

Operations

SAP SE's segment includes Applications, Technology and Services and Qualtrics.

The services segment was dissolved and integrated into the former Applications,

Technology & Support segment, which was therefore re-named to Applications, Technology & Services. Revenues primarily come from the sale of software licenses, support offerings, and cloud subscriptions.

The Qualtrics segment derives its revenues mainly from the sale of experience management cloud solutions that run front-office functions across experience data, and from the sale of related services.

Geographic Reach

SAP is headquartered in Walldorf, Germany. Most of the company's revenues are from the Americas at more than 50% of the company's revenues. EMEA and APJ markets account for about 35% and 15%, respectively. Most of the company's subsidiaries operate in Switzerland, the UK, Spain, France, Italy, the Netherlands, Brazil, Canada, Mexico, Japan, Australia, China, and India.

Sales and Marketing

SAP's sales and marketing expenses consists mainly of personnel costs, direct sales costs, and the cost of marketing the company's products and services. The company used EUR 8.9 billion and EUR 7.5 billion for 2022 and 2021, respectively.

Financial Performance

SAP's performance for the past three years saw a year-over-year growth with 2022 as its highest performing year over the period.

The company's revenue increased by EUR 3.0 billion to EUR 30.9 billion in 2022, as compared to 2021's revenue of EUR 27.8 billion. SAP's net profit decreased to EUR 2.3 billion for fiscal year end 2022, as compared to the prior year's net profit of EUR 5.3 billion.

The company held EUR 9 billion by the end of the year. Operating activities provided EUR 5.6 billion to the coffers. Investing activities provided EUR 667 million, while financing activities used EUR 6.3 billion. Main cash uses were for purchase of equity or debt instruments of other entities and dividends paid.

Company Background

The company was founded in 1972 by former IBM employees, namely, Dietmar Hopp, Hasso Plattner, Hans-Werner Hector, Klaus Tchira und Claus Wellenreuther. Since then, the company have continued to expand their portfolio through various acquisitions. The company continues to grow through the SAP HANA, which enables customers in-memory computing.

HISTORY

Former IBM software engineers Hasso Plattner, Hans-Werner Hector, Dietmar Hopp, Claus Wellenreuther, and Klaus Tschira started SAP in 1972 when the project they were working on for IBM was moved to another unit.

While rival software firms made many products to automate the various parts of a company's operations, these engineers decided to make a single system that would tie a corporation together. In 1973 they launched an instantaneous, accounting transaction-processing program called R/1. By 1979 they had adapted the program to create R/2, mainframe software that linked external databases and communication systems.

The company went public in 1988. That year Plattner began a project to create software for the computer network market. In 1992, as sales of its R/2 mainframe software lagged, SAP introduced its R/3 software, which would later become its flagship SAP ERP.

EXECUTIVES

Chief Executive Officer, Member, Christian Klein
Chief People & Operating Officer, Member, Sabine Bendiek
Chief Financial Officer, Member, Luka Mucic
Chief Technology Officer, Member, Jurgen Mulller
Member, Scott Russell
Member, Thomas Saueressig
Chief Marketing and Solutions Officer, Member, Julia White
Chairman, Hasso Plattner
Member, Vice Chairperson, Lars Lamade
Member, Manuela Asche-Holstein
Member, Aicha Evans
Member, Gesche Joost
Member, Margret Klein-Magar
Member, Monika Kovachka-Dimitrova
Member, Peter Lengler
Member, Jennifer Xinzhe Li
Member, Qi Lu
Member, Gerhard Oswald
Member, Christine Regitz
Member, Friederike Rotsch
Member, Heike Steck
Member, Helmut Stengele
Member, Rouven Westphal
Member, Gunnar Wiedenfels
Member, James Wright
Auditors : KPMG AG Wirtschaftsprüfungsgesellschaft

LOCATIONS

HQ: SAP SE
Dietmar-Hopp-Allee 16, Walldorf 69190
Phone: (49) 0 6227 7 47474   **Fax:** (49) 0 6227 7 57575
Web: www.sap.com

2018 Sales

	% of total
Europe, Middle East & Africa	
Germany	15
Other countries	30
Americas	39
Asia/Pacific	16
Total	100

PRODUCTS/OPERATIONS

2018 Sales

	% of total
Software & Support	
Support	44
Licenses	19
Cloud Subscription & Support	20
Services	17
Total	100

Selected Customers
Aigo
City of Cape Town, South Africa
Danone
Beaumont Health System
McLaren Group

Selected Software
SAP Business All-in-One
SAP Business ByDesign
SAP Business One
SAP Business Suite
SAP ERP
SAP HANA
SAP NetWeaver

Selected Services
Application hosting
Business consulting
Custom development
Financing
Implementation
Maintenance
Training

Selected Acquisitions Concur (2014) Travel and expense management software for companiesHybris (2014) Real-time customer engagement and commerce platformSeeWhy (2014) Cloud-based behavioral target marketing softwareTicket-Web (2013) Ticketing software and customer relationship management (CRM) software for sports and entertainment.KMS Software (2013) Web-based personnel management softwareCamilion (2013) Product development, product lifecycle, and underwriting software for the insurance marketSmartOps (2013) Inventory and service-level optimization softwareKXEN (2013) Predictive analytics.Ariba (2012), A cloud-based business commerce networkSuccessFactors (2012; cloud-based, workforce management)
Right Hemisphere (2012; enterprise visualization)
TechniData (2010; environmental, health, and safety)
Sybase (2010, business intelligence and database management)
Clear Standards (2009, environmental)
Highdeal (2009, billing)
Visiprise (2008, manufacturing process management)
Business Objects (2008, business intelligence)
OutlookSoft (2007, business performance management)
Pilot Software (2007, business performance management)

COMPETITORS

BLACKLINE, INC.
CA, INC.
CALLIDUS SOFTWARE INC.
INFOR, INC.
MICRO FOCUS INTERNATIONAL PLC
MICROSTRATEGY INCORPORATED
ORACLE CORPORATION
SAP AMERICA, INC.
Software AG
VERSANT CORPORATION

HISTORICAL FINANCIALS

Company Type: Public

Income Statement   FYE: December 31

	REVENUE ($mil)	NET INCOME ($mil)	NET PROFIT MARGIN	EMPLOYEES
12/23	34,565	6,799	19.7%	107,602
12/22	32,971	2,439	7.4%	111,961
12/21	31,513	5,949	18.9%	107,415
12/20	33,551	6,314	18.8%	102,430
12/19	30,935	3,728	12.1%	100,330
Annual Growth	2.8%	16.2%	—	1.8%

2023 Year-End Financials

Debt ratio: 15.7%
Return on equity: 14.7%
Cash ($ mil.): 8,998
Current Ratio: 1.40
Long-term debt ($ mil.): 8,795
No. of shares ($ mil.): 1,167
Dividends
Yield: —
Payout: 28.4%
Market value ($ mil.): 180,442

	STOCK PRICE ($) FY Close	P/E High/Low		PER SHARE ($) Earnings	Dividends	Book Value
12/23	154.59	31	21	5.76	1.64	40.95
12/22	103.19	68	45	2.07	1.95	36.77
12/21	140.11	33	26	5.05	1.63	37.28
12/20	130.39	40	25	5.34	1.25	30.92
12/19	133.99	51	34	3.12	1.20	28.10
Annual Growth	3.6%	—	—	16.6%	8.1%	9.9%

Saputo Inc

Saputo produces markets and distributes a wide variety of dairy products such as cheese, fluid milk, extended shelf-life milk, and dairy ingredients. The company is one of the top ten dairy processors in the world, a leading cheese manufacturer and fluid milk and cream processors in Canada, a leading dairy processor in Australia, and the top dairy processor in Argentina. In the US, Saputo ranks among the top three cheese producers and is one of the top producers of extended shelf-life and cultured dairy products. In the UK, Saputo is the largest manufacturer of branded cheese and dairy spreads. Saputo products are sold in several countries under market-leading brands, as well as private label brands. The US generates more than 45% of the company's revenue.

Operations

Saputo reports its business under four sectors: Canada, the US, International, and Europe.

The Canada Sector, which consists of the Dairy Division (Canada), produces, markets, and distributes a variety of cheeses, including among others mozzarella and cheddar; specialty cheeses, such as ricotta, provolone; fine cheeses, such as brie and camembert; and other cheeses, including brick, Colby, farmer, Munster, Monterey jack, fresh curd, and processed cheeses. It also distributes fluid milk, cream, yogurt, sour cream, cottage cheese, and ice cream mixes, as well as certain other dairy and non-dairy products including butter, flavored cream, dips, and flavoured coffee whitener.

The US Sector through the Dairy Division (US), the company produces, markets and distributes a vast assortment of cheeses, including a broad line of mozzarella, American-style, and specialty cheeses. It also produces a variety of dairy and non-dairy extended shelf-life products, including among others cream and creamers, ice cream mixes, whipping cream, half and half, and value-added milks, as well as cultured products, such as sour cream and cottage cheese. Additionally, the company also produces and sells domestically and internationally, dairy ingredients such as whey powder, whey protein concentrates, lactose, and dairy ingredient blends.

The International Sector is comprised of the Dairy Division (Australia), which provides a variety of cheeses, butter and butter blends, milk and cream, as well as dairy ingredients, and the Dairy Division (Argentina) which offers a vast array of cheeses, butter and cream, as well as dairy ingredients.

The International Sector is comprised of the Dairy Division (Australia), which provides a variety of cheeses, butter and butter blends, milk and cream, as well as dairy ingredients, and the Dairy Division (Argentina) which offers a vast array of cheeses, butter and cream, as well as dairy ingredients.

Geographic Reach

Quebec, Canada-based, Saputo has about 65 plants located in Canada, the US, Australia, Argentina, and the UK. Additionally, Saputo's products are sold in over 60 countries.

Quebec, Canada-based, Saputo has about 65 plants located in Canada, the US, Australia, Argentina, and the UK. Additionally, Saputo's products are sold in over 60 countries.

Sales and Marketing

The company sells its products in three different market segments: retail, foodservice, and industrial.

In the retail segment (almost 50% of its revenue), the company sells its product to supermarket chains, mass-merchandisers, convenience stores, independent retailers, warehouse clubs, and specialty cheese boutiques under Saputo-owned or customer brand names. Its products are also sold directly to consumers through its e-commerce channels. In the foodservice segment (nearly 35%) the company sells its product to broad-line distributors, restaurants, hotels, and institutions under Saputo-owned or customer brand names. The industrial segment (about 20%) sells its product to food manufacturers.

Financial Performance

Company's revenue for fiscal 2023 increased to CAD17.8 billion compared to the prior year with CAD15.0 billion. The increase was primarily due to higher revenues on every market segments.

Net income for fiscal 2023 increased to CAD622 million compared to the prior year with CAD274 million. The increase is primarily due to higher adjusted EBITDA.

Cash held by the company at the end of fiscal 2023 increased to CAD263 million. Cash provided by operations was CAD1.0 billion while cash used for investing and financing activities were CAD632 million and CAD369 million, respectively. Main uses of cash were additions to property, plant and equipment; and repayment of long-term debt.

Strategy

Company's strategic focuses are:

Network Optimization & Capital Investments: Streamline and optimize our asset footprint, capital and operational investments, enhance manufacturing network to improve output, margin, utilization rates, and service levels, leveraging asset flexibility and automation.

Strategic Initiatives: New products and innovation, growth in dairy alternative products, process improvements, enhance value of ingredients through sales growth and cost containment initiatives.

Strengthen Core Business: Base business growth, pricing execution, improved reliability and growth of volume, channel and mix management, and shift to higher-margin product mix.

EXECUTIVES

Chair, President, Chief Executive Officer, Director, Lino A. Saputo
Chief Financial Officer, Secretary, Maxime Therrien
Human Resources Chief Human Resources Officer, Gaetane Wagner
Chief Acquisition and Strategic Development Officer, Martin Gagnon
President, Leanne Cutts
President, Carl Colizza
President, Frank C. Guido
President, Lyne Castonguay
President, Tom Atherton
President, Marcelo Cohen
President, Richard Wallace
Corporate Director, Louis-Philippe Carriere
Corporate Director, Henry E. Demone
Corporate Director, Karen Kinsley
Corporate Director, Diane Nyisztor
Director, Olu Fajemirokun-Beck
Director, Anthony M. Fata
Director, Annalisa King
Director, Tony Meti
Director, Franziska Ruf
Director, Annette Verschuren
Auditors: Deloitte LLP

LOCATIONS

HQ: Saputo Inc
6869 Metropolitain Blvd. East, St. Leonard, Montreal, Quebec H1P 1X8
Phone: 514 328-6662   **Fax:** 514 328-3322
Web: www.saputo.com

2019 Sales

	%
US	48
Canada	30
Australia	17
Argentina	5
Total	100

PRODUCTS/OPERATIONS
2019 Sales

	%
Retail	47
Foodservice	35
Industrial	18
Total	100

COMPETITORS

BEL
BEL BRANDS USA, INC.
Brf S/A
DEAN FOODS COMPANY
FONTERRA CO-OPERATIVE GROUP LIMITED
FOREMOST FARMS USA, COOPERATIVE
KRAFT HEINZ FOODS COMPANY
MONDELEZ INTERNATIONAL, INC.
SAPUTO CHEESE USA INC.
WH Group Limited

HISTORICAL FINANCIALS
Company Type: Public

Income Statement   FYE: March 31

	REVENUE ($mil)	NET INCOME ($mil)	NET PROFIT MARGIN	EMPLOYEES
03/23	13,168	459	3.5%	19,200
03/22	12,007	218	1.8%	18,600
03/21	11,344	496	4.4%	17,300
03/20	10,492	409	3.9%	17,200
03/19	10,061	562	5.6%	16,800
Annual Growth	7.0%	(5.0%)	—	3.4%

2023 Year-End Financials

Debt ratio: 18.5% No. of shares ($ mil.): 421
Return on equity: 9.1% Dividends
Cash ($ mil.): 194 Yield: —
Current Ratio: 1.62 Payout: 48.6%
Long-term debt ($ mil.): 2,172 Market value ($ mil.): 10,903

	STOCK PRICE ($) FY Close	P/E High/Low	PER SHARE ($) Earnings	Dividends	Book Value
03/23	25.86	19 12	1.09	0.53	12.50
03/22	23.80	51 32	0.53	0.57	12.47
03/21	30.07	20 15	1.21	0.55	12.40
03/20	24.03	22 14	1.02	0.47	11.27
03/19	33.46	18 14	1.44	0.49	10.35
Annual Growth	(6.2%)	—	(6.6%)	2.1%	4.8%

Saras Raffinerie Sarde SpA

EXECUTIVES

Chairman, Director, Massimo Moratti
Chief Executive Officer, General Manager, Director, Dario Scaffardi
Chief Financial Officer, Franco Balsamo
Director, Angelo Moratti
Director, Angelomario Moratti
Director, Gabriele Moratti
Director, Giovanni Emanuele Moratti
Lead Independent Director, Independent Non-Executive Director, Gilberto Callera
Independent Non-Executive Director, Adriana Cerretelli
Independent Non-Executive Director, Laura Fidanza
Independent Non-Executive Director, Isabelle Harvie-Watt
Independent Non-Executive Director, Francesca Luchi
Independent Director, Monica De Virgiliis
Auditors : EY SpA

LOCATIONS

HQ: Saras Raffinerie Sarde SpA
SS. Sulcitana 195, Km 19, Sarroch - Cagliari 09018
Phone: (39) 070 90911   **Fax:** (39) 070 900209
Web: www.saras.it

HISTORICAL FINANCIALS
Company Type: Public

Income Statement   FYE: December 31

	REVENUE ($mil)	NET INCOME ($mil)	NET PROFIT MARGIN	EMPLOYEES
12/21	9,775	10	0.1%	1,572
12/20	6,556	(338)	—	1,687
12/19	10,686	29	0.3%	1,745
12/18	11,906	160	1.4%	1,946
12/17	9,214	288	3.1%	1,944
Annual Growth	1.5%	(56.3%)	—	(5.2%)

2021 Year-End Financials

Debt ratio: 30.0% No. of shares ($ mil.): 951
Return on equity: 1.1% Dividends
Cash ($ mil.): 415 Yield: —
Current Ratio: 0.85 Payout: 0.0%
Long-term debt ($ mil.): 58 Market value ($ mil.): 3,034

	STOCK PRICE ($) FY Close	P/E High/Low	PER SHARE ($) Earnings	Dividends	Book Value
12/21	3.19	— —	0.01	0.00	0.94
12/20	3.19	— —	(0.36)	0.00	1.02
12/19	8.28	351 257	0.03	0.29	1.27
12/18	10.86	79 68	0.17	0.46	1.35
12/17	12.85	52 35	0.31	0.39	1.37
Annual Growth	(29.4%)	—	(56.3%)	—	(8.9%)

Sasol Ltd.

Sasol is a global chemicals and energy company that makes all manner of petrochemicals, liquid and gaseous fuels (gasoline, diesel, jet fuel, fuel alcohol, and fuel oils), synthetic fuels, and lubricants. The company also operates coal mines in South Africa and uses the coal as feedstock for its synthetic fuels and chemicals plants. Through proprietary technologies and processes the main products Sasol produce are fuel components, chemical components and co-products. From these main products and further value-adding processes it deliver diesel, petrol (gasoline), naphtha, kerosene, liquid petroleum gas (LPG), olefins, alcohols, polymers, solvents, surfactants, co-monomers, ammonia, methanol, crude tar acids, sulphur, illuminating paraffin, bitumen and fuel oil. Most of the company's operations are based in South Africa, but it also operates in numerous other countries throughout the world.

Operations

Sasol comprises two distinct market-focused businesses, namely: Chemicals (about 60% of sales) and Energy (some 40%).

The Chemicals business are grouped into Advanced Materials, Base Chemicals, Essential Care Chemicals and Performance Solutions. It also operates Chemicals Africa (about 25% of sales), Chemicals Eurasia (some 20%), and Chemicals America (some 15%).

The Energy business operates integrated value chains with feedstock sourced from the Mining and Gas operating segments and processed at our operations in Secunda, Sasolburg and Natref. There are also associated assets outside South Africa which include the Pande-Temane Petroleum Production Agreement (PPA) in Mozambique and ORYX GTL (gas to liquids) in Qatar. Mining is responsible for securing coal feedstock for the Southern African value chain, mainly for gasification, but also to generate electricity and steam. The Gas segment reflects the upstream feedstock, transport of gas through the ROMPCO pipeline, and external natural and methane rich gas sales. The Fuels segment comprises the sales and marketing of liquid fuels produced in South Africa, which generated over 35%.

Geographic Reach

Headquartered in South Africa, the company has presence in more than 20 countries. South Africa generated about 50% of sales, Europe with around 20%, US with some 15%, while the remaining sales were generated from the rest of the world.

Financial Performance

The company reported a revenue of R229.4 billion in 2022, a 5% increase from the previous year's revenue of R218 billion.

In 2022, the company had a net income of R40.5 billion, a 715% improvement from the previous year's net loss of R6.6 billion.

The company's cash at the end of 2022 was R43 billion. Operating activities generated R40.3 billion, while investing activities used R15.1 billion, mainly for additions to property, plant and equipment. Financing activities used another R15 billion, primarily for repayment of long-term debt.

Strategy

The company's strategic priorities consist of:

Strive to achieve a people-centered culture of safety by leading safety with both care and compliance; Intensify its focus on operational discipline and preventing high severity injuries and eliminating fatalities;

Strengthen stakeholder trust through continued delivery on community, regulatory and shareholder promises; Embrace diversity and inclusion to augment its culture and Employee Value Proposition; as well as Aligning a visible and integrated Just Transition program and incorporating localization and economic empowerment.

Company Background

The company, through Sasol Synfuels International, launched its first GTL plant with Qatar Petroleum in Qatar in 2007 and is constructing another in Nigeria. Although Sasol submitted a project application report in late 2009 for a CTL plant in China, it is still waiting for approval from the Chinese government. The company began a feasibility study in 2011 for a GTL plant near Lake Charles, Louisiana, which would be larger than its plant in Qatar and would produce diesel and naphtha. Sasol and Talisman Energy also began a feasibility study in 2011 for a GTL plant in western Canada. That year Sasol agreed to develop a GTL project in Uzbekistan, along with partners Uzbekneflegaz and PETRONAS.

In 2010 Sasol's fertilizer unit agreed to sell five blending plants and end ammonia imports in a deal struck with South Africa's Competition Commission to help cut fertilizer prices in South Africa. The company said it would dispose of its bulk blending and liquid fertilizer blending plants in Bellville, Durban, Endicott, Kimberley, and Potchefstroom by August 2011. The unit will continue producing limestone ammonium nitrate, ammonium sulfate, and a range of ammonium nitrate- and ammonium sulfate-based liquid and granular NPK fertilizer blends.

The company expanded its access to natural gas assets in Canada, buying a 50% stake in Talisman Energy's Farrell Creek shale assets for more than C$1 billion in 2011. As part of the deal, the two companies began the feasibility study to look into the viability of building a plant in western Canada to convert natural gas to liquid fuels using Sasol's proprietary technology. Sasol later completed a second C$1 billion deal with Talisman Energy in which it acquired 50% of the Cypress A shale gas asset in the Montney basin in British Columbia.

Also in 2011, a fuel sector strike in South Africa threatened the output of Sasol's basic chemicals production, with unions demanding more pay and a 40-hour workweek. Although the company's rate of chemicals output was reduced at its Secunda plant that year, Sasol experienced a 27% jump in earnings in 2011 over the previous year. Cost savings and higher global commodity prices helped it achieve higher margins, especially in its chemicals business. Its Sasol Polymers unit's operating profit increased by 65% over the prior year.

Sasol was founded in 1979.

EXECUTIVES

Chief Executive Officer, President, Executive Director, Fleetwood Rawstorne Grobler
Financial Control Services Chief Financial Officer, Executive Director, Paul Victor
Technology and Sustainability Executive Vice President, H. C. Brand
Chemicals Executive Vice President, B. V. Griffith
Human Resources Executive Vice President, Operations Executive Vice President, Bernard Ekhard Klingenberg
Executive Director, Vuyo Dominic Kahla
Energy Business Executive Vice President, B. P. Mabelane
Corporate Affairs Executive Vice President, Human Resources Executive Vice President, C. K. Mokoena
Chairman, Independent Non-Executive Director, G. M. Beatrix Kennealy
Lead Independent Director, Independent Non-Executive Director, Stephen Westwell
Independent Non-Executive Director, Manual J. Cuambe
Independent Non-Executive Director, Muriel Betty Nicolle Dube
Independent Non-Executive Director, Martina Floel
Independent Non-Executive Director, Katherine C. Harper
Independent Non-Executive Director, Nomgando Nomalungelo Angelina Matyumza
Independent Non-Executive Director, Zamani Moses Mkhize
Independent Non-Executive Director, Mpho Elizabeth Kolekile Nkeli
Independent Non-Executive Director, Sipho Abednego Nkosi
Independent Non-Executive Director, Peter James Robertson
Independent Non-Executive Director, S. Subramoney
Auditors : PricewaterhouseCoopers Inc.

LOCATIONS

HQ: Sasol Ltd.
Sasol Place, 50 Katherine Street, Sandton 2196
Phone: (27) 10 344 5000 **Fax:** (27) 11 788 5092
Web: www.sasol.com

2013 Sales by Geographic

	% of total
South Africa	48
Rest of South Africa	4
Europe	22
North America	11
Middle East and India	6
Far East	4
Southeast Asia and Australasia	3
South America	2
Total	100

PRODUCTS/OPERATIONS

2013 Sales

	% of total
Chemical cluster	55
South Africa energy cluster	41
International energy cluster	4
Total	100

Selected Locations
Asia
Australasia
Europe
Far East
Ireland
Middle East
Northern Asia
Rest of Africa
Southeast Asia
Southern Africa
The Americas
United Kingdom

COMPETITORS

BayWa AG
CARR'S GROUP PLC
DCC PUBLIC LIMITED COMPANY
Evonik Industries AG
FLUIDRA, SA
IDEMITSU KOSAN CO.,LTD.
INDIAN OIL CORPORATION LIMITED
REPSOL SA.
SURGUTNEFTEGAZ, PAO
TOTAL SE

HISTORICAL FINANCIALS

Company Type: Public

Income Statement FYE: June 30

	REVENUE ($mil)	NET INCOME ($mil)	NET PROFIT MARGIN	EMPLOYEES
06/23	15,254	463	3.0%	29,073
06/22	16,843	2,379	14.1%	28,630
06/21	14,122	631	4.5%	28,949
06/20	10,966	(5,248)	—	31,001
06/19	14,357	303	2.1%	31,429
Annual Growth	1.5%	11.2%		(1.9%)

2023 Year-End Financials

Debt ratio: 1.5%
Return on equity: 4.5%
Cash ($ mil.): 2,839
Current Ratio: 1.51
Long-term debt ($ mil.): 4,965
No. of shares ($ mil.): 640
Dividends
  Yield: 8.0%
  Payout: 135.4%
Market value ($ mil.): 7,931

	STOCK PRICE ($) FY Close	P/E High/Low		PER SHARE ($) Earnings	Dividends	Book Value
06/23	12.38	1	1	0.69	0.99	16.18
06/22	23.06	0	0	3.75	0.90	18.13
06/21	15.33	1	0	1.02	0.00	16.16
06/20	7.71			(8.49)	0.00	14.06
06/19	24.85	6	4	0.49	0.74	24.58
Annual Growth	(16.0%)			8.8%	7.7%	(9.9%)

Sberbank Of Russia

Whether you do your saving in Siberia or your asset management in Moscow, the Savings Bank of the Russian Federation, or Sberbank, has a branch for you. SberBank's national network features about a dozen regional banks with 14,200 branches in 83 of Russia's regions. SberBank is the historical successor of Savings Offices, which were established by the decree of Emperor Nicholas I, and later the State Labor Savings Offices.

Geographic Reach

The company is headquartered at Moscow, Russia.

Sales and Marketing

Sberbank serves individuals, institutions, and medium to large-sized businesses and corporations.

EXECUTIVES

Executive Chairman, Chief Executive Officer, Herman Gref
Deputy Chairman, Chief Financial Officer, Alexander Morozov
First Deputy Chairman, Alexander Vedyakhin
First Deputy Chairman, Lev Khasis
Deputy Chairman, Oleg Ganeev
Deputy Chairman, Executive Director, Bella Zlatkis
Deputy Chairman, Svetlana Kirsanova
Deputy Chairman, Stanislav Kuznetsov
Deputy Chairman, Anatoly Popov
Non-Executive Chairman, Sergey Ignatiev
Non-Executive Deputy Chairman, Sergei Shvetsov
Deputy Chairman, Senior Independent Director, Gennady Melikyan
Non-Executive Director, Valery Goreglyad
Non-Executive Director, Nadezhda Ivanova
Non-Executive Director, Maksim Oreshkin
Non-Executive Director, Olga Skorobogatova
Independent Director, Esko Tapani Aho
Independent Director, Leonid Boguslavskiy
Independent Director, Nikolay Kudryavtsev
Independent Director, Aleksandr Kuleshov
Independent Director, Nadya Wells
Auditors : AO PricewaterhouseCoopers Audit

LOCATIONS

HQ: Sberbank Of Russia
 19 Vavilova St., Moscow 117312
Phone: (7) 495 500 55 50   **Fax:** (7) 495 957 5731
Web: www.sberbank.com

PRODUCTS/OPERATIONS

Selected Subsidiary
DenizBank A.S.
Sberbank Europe AG
Sberbank Kazakhstan
BPS-Sberbank (Belarus)
Sberbank (Switzerland) AG

Selected Group companies
ActiveBusinessCollection LLC
Sberbank-Automated Trading System CJSC
Delovaya Sreda JSC
Sberbank Private Pension Funds JSC
Sberbank Leasing JSC
Sberbank-Services LLC
Sberbank Life Insurance LLC
Sberbank-Technology (Sbertech) JSC
Sovremennyye Tekhnologii LLC
Nonbanking Credit Institution Yandex.Money LLC

COMPETITORS

AKBANK TURK ANONIM SIRKETI
BANK OF INDIA
BANK VTB, PAO
BPCE
Banco Bradesco S/A
Banco do Brasil S/A
CAIXABANK SA
CANARA BANK
Shinhan Financial Group Co., Ltd.

Swedbank AB

HISTORICAL FINANCIALS
Company Type: Public

Income Statement — FYE: December 31

	REVENUE ($mil)	NET INCOME ($mil)	NET PROFIT MARGIN	EMPLOYEES
12/21	49,628	16,656	33.6%	287,866
12/20	42,910	10,174	23.7%	285,600
12/19	50,229	13,575	27.0%	281,300
12/18	39,817	11,950	30.0%	293,752
12/17	49,885	12,979	26.0%	310,277
Annual Growth	(0.1%)	6.4%	—	(1.9%)

2021 Year-End Financials
Debt ratio: —
Return on equity: 23.4%
Cash ($ mil.): 32,085
Current Ratio: —
Long-term debt ($ mil.): —
No. of shares ($ mil.): 22,456
Dividends
 Yield: —
 Payout: 0.0%
Market value ($ mil.): —

SBI Shinsei Bank Ltd

Shinsei Bank provides retail and corporate banking and several other financial services from about 25 branches and two local offices throughout Japan. Shinsei is a hybrid comprehensive financial group that is engaged in both bank and nonbank functions. It became a part of the SBI Group in 2021, and are now in the midst of actively incorporating the financial ecosystems and financial functions of the SBI Group. It offers retail banking services such as deposits, and investments, as well as trusts, securities brokerage services (through a partner institution), life and nonlife insurance (through partner institutions), housing loans, provision of financial transactions and services for individuals. Founded as the Long-Term Credit Bank of Japan in 1952, the company was reborn as Shinsei (Japanese for "new birth") Bank in 2000.

Operations

Shinsei Bank group operates two main business segments. The Individual Business segment which generates about 70% of Shinsei Bank's total revenue and around 30% from Institutional Business. Its Individual Business segment provides retail banking businesses with deposits, investment trusts and housing loans; unsecured loans; and credit card, shopping credit and payment services for individual customers. The Institutional Group includes the corporate business, which provides solutions to its corporate and financial institution customers; structured finance, which provides services such as real estate finance and project finance; services for private equity investments and business succession finance; the leasing business; and the markets business which provides market solutions for foreign exchange and interest rate derivatives, among others.

Broadly, about 60% of the bank's revenue came from interest income in FY2021, while around 15% came from fee and commission income. About 5% of its revenue came from net trading income, while the remaining roughly 25% of its revenue came from net other business income.

Geographic Reach

Shinsei Bank had about 25 branch outlets across Japan, with about 45% of them around Tokyo, six in the Kinki region, five in the Kanto (excluding Tokyo), two in Tohoku, and one each in the Chugoku, Tokai, Shikoku, Kyushi, Hokkaido, and Hokuriku/Koshinetsu regions of Japan.

Financial Performance

In fiscal 2021, total revenue decreased by Â¥4.3 billion to JPY217.5 billion, from Â¥221.9 billion in fiscal 2020, mainly due to the company's decision to record a loss on the sale of bonds in order to reduce the amount of interest rate risk in response to the rise in interest rates and for the future restructuring of the securities portfolio, despite an increase in interest income associated with the full-year effect of UDC Finance consolidation.

Profit for fiscal 2021 decreased to Â¥20.3 million compared from the prior year with Â¥45.1 million.

Strategy

The company's core strategies are:

Pursue value co-creation inside and outside the company. Regarding "value co-creation," it has traditionally promoted collaboration with external partner companies. Going forward, the company will expand the definition of "value co-creation" and promote it as an "open alliance" in a broad sense, including "value co-creation with the SBI Group companies," "value co-creation within the Shinsei Bank Group," "value co-creation with companies outside the company" and broadly defined nonorganic value co-strengthening its earnings base, and through these initiatives Shinsei will build a foundation for sustainable growth.

Enhance the company's strengths and realize a full range of service offerings. To deepen its strengths, the company have been focusing on small-scale financing and business with institutional investors. In the future, the company will add overseas business customers to this mix and enhance its expertise and deepen its experience as one of domains in which the Shinsei Bank Group possesses strengths.Achieve sustainability through business activities. The demand from society for sustainability is high, as it is for the Shinsei Bank Group.

Company Background

During the late 2000s, Shinsei had been battered by its exposure to toxic assets including loans to failed Lehman Brothers and structured asset-backed securities. It had also taken a hit in the domestic real estate market, in which the company had been a significant lender. Record losses reported for 2008 sparked rumors that Shinsei would merge with Aozora Bank, another struggling midsized bank that was nationalized in 2001. The two banks reached a merger agreement in 2009 but called those plans off due to strategic differences.

HISTORY

The Japanese government nationalized Shinsei Bank's debt-ridden Long-Term Credit Bank in 1998. It sold the bank to an international group led by US-based Ripplewood Holdings in 2000, making it one of the few major Japanese banks to come under foreign control. Ripplewood spun off the bank in 2004, placing it on the Tokyo Stock Exchange.

In 2007, Shinsei acquired a minority stake in global advisory firm Duff & Phelps.

In 2008, it acquired GE's consumer finance business in Japan, consisting of credit card, personal lending, and mortgage operations. In 2010 Shinsei Bank sold Shinsei Asset Management, its Mumbai-based asset management operation, to Daiwa Bank. The company would use the proceeds to pay down its debt.

EXECUTIVES

Chairman, Director, Hirofumi Gomi
President, Chief Executive Officer, Representative Director, Katsuya Kawashima
Senior Managing Executive Officer, Director, Katsumi Hatao
Director, Eisuke Terasawa
Outside Director, Yasuhiro Hayasaki
Outside Director, Ayumi Michi
Outside Director, Masahiro Terada
Outside Director, Yurina Takiguchi
Outside Director, Katsunori Tanizaki
Auditors : Deloitte Touche Tohmatsu LLC

LOCATIONS

HQ: SBI Shinsei Bank Ltd
2-4-3 Nihonbashi-Muromachi, Chuo-ku, Tokyo 103-8303
Phone: (81) 3 6880 7000
Web: www.shinseibank.com

PRODUCTS/OPERATIONS

2014 Sales

	% of total
Net interest income	54
Noninterest income	
Net fee and commission	12
Net trading income	7
Others	27
Total	100

COMPETITORS

AKBANK TURK ANONIM SIRKETI
CANARA BANK
China Construction Bank Corporation
HDFC BANK LIMITED
HSBC USA, INC.
PRIVATEBANCORP, INC.
PT. BANK MANDIRI (PERSERO) TBK
Shanghai Pudong Development Bank Co., Ltd.
Shinhan Financial Group Co., Ltd.
TURKIYE IS BANKASI ANONIM SIRKETI

HISTORICAL FINANCIALS
Company Type: Public

Income Statement FYE: March 31

	ASSETS ($mil)	NET INCOME ($mil)	INCOME AS % OF ASSETS	EMPLOYEES
03/23	102,825	321	0.3%	7,418
03/22	84,772	167	0.2%	7,304
03/21	96,999	407	0.4%	7,066
03/20	94,210	419	0.4%	6,738
03/19	86,426	472	0.5%	6,340
Annual Growth	4.4%	(9.2%)	—	4.0%

2023 Year-End Financials

Return on assets: 0.3%
Return on equity: 4.5%
Long-term debt ($ mil.): —
No. of shares ($ mil.): 204
Sales ($ mil.): 3,181
Dividends
Yield: —
Payout: 0.0%
Market value ($ mil.): —

Schindler Holding AG

Schindler is one of the world's leading suppliers of escalators, elevators, and moving walkways for use in airports, train and subway stations, and other public and government buildings, as well as in offices, commercial properties, and cruise ships. The company helps organize cities by moving people and goods, and connecting vertical and horizontal transportation systems. Schindler has operations in more than 100 countries and generates some 45% of its sales from Europe, Middle East, and Africa. Schindler was founded in 1874 in Central Switzerland.

Operations

Schindler operates through two segments: Elevators and Escalators and Finance.

The Elevators & Escalators segment is managed as one global unit and comprises an integrated business that specializes in the production and installation of elevators and escalators, as well as the modernization, maintenance, and repair of existing installations. The segment accounts for 100% of the company's total revenue.

Finance comprises the expenses of Schindler Holding Ltd. and BuildingMinds.

Geographic Reach

Based in Switzerland, Schindler operates in more than 100 countries around the globe. The company serves customers from more than 1,000 branches office worldwide, run production sites in eight countries, and six research and development facilities around the world.

Financial Performance

In 2022, the company had a total revenue of CHF11.3 billion, a 1% increase from the previous year's total revenue of CHF11.2 billion.

Net income was CHF659.0 million, a 25% decrease from the previous year's net income of CHF881.0 million.

The company's cash at the end of 2022 was CHF2.2 billion. Operating activities generated CHF688 million, while investing activities CHF646.0 million, mainly for additions to current and non-current financial assets. Financing activities used another CHF683.0 million, primarily for dividends paid to the shareholders of Schindler Holding Ltd.

HISTORY

Robert Schindler and Eduard Villiger established Schindler & Villiger in 1874 to make lift equipment and machinery in Lucerne, Switzerland. Villiger left the firm in 1892, and the enterprise became known as Robert Schindler, Machinery Manufacturer. The company added an iron foundry in 1895.

Robert sold the business to his brother, Alfred, in 1901 and the company was renamed Alfred Schindler. The following year it delivered its first electric passenger elevator with automatic push-button controls.

Alfred Schindler took on a partner in 1906 by the name of Fritz Geilfuss. The company's name was changed to Schindler & Cie. Around this time the company's first subsidiary was established in Berlin. Other subsidiaries soon followed in France and another in Germany. Sales offices were opened in Argentina (1910), Belgium and Russia (1912), and Egypt, Poland, and Spain (1914).

Schindler & Cie. continued to grow, adding elevator motor manufacturing (1915) and cranes (1920) to its product line. By 1923 the company had opened a factory in Mulhouse, France. Geilfuss died in 1920, and Adolf Sigg became Alfred Schindler's partner in 1925.

During WWI the company's iron foundry produced munitions; it eventually became independent in 1925. By 1931 the company had expanded into Bulgaria, China, Colombia, Ecuador, Egypt, Greece, Lithuania, Morocco, South Africa, and Yugoslavia. The firm was incorporated as Aufzüge und Elektromotorenfabrik, Schindler & Cie. AG in 1932. Schindler delivered its first escalator in 1936.

Sales fell off during WWII, as demand for elevators diminished, but the company managed to expand modestly (Venezuela, UK, South Africa). By 1959 Schindler had become Europe's largest elevator company. Schindler acquired a stake in Dutch firm Westdijk in 1967 and bought Wertheim-Werk of Austria in 1969.

The company was restructured under the name Schindler Holding AG in 1970. By 1974 it had 56 subsidiaries throughout Europe, South America, and South Africa. Schindler entered the US in 1979 with the purchase of Reliance Electric Cleveland's Haughton Elevator division in Toledo, Ohio.

The advent of the 1980s marked the beginning of a 15-year period of continued growth for Schindler. It established the first industrial joint venture with China in 1980 (another followed in 1988). Schindler went on to open an Australian subsidiary (1981) and strike a licensing deal with Bharat Bijlee Ltd., India's largest elevator company (1986). In 1987 Schindler bought a controlling interest in Japan's Nippon Elevator Industry Co. The company's 1988 purchase of a majority share of Swiss computer wholesaler ALSO Holding AG was deemed risky at the time, but after some restructuring measures were taken, the unit thrived. That year Schindler took over the North American elevator and escalator operations of Westinghouse.

During the first half of the 1990s, Schindler began to emphasize its role as a service provider (maintenance and repair) and focused on growing in the Middle East and Eastern Europe. The second half of the 1990s saw Schindler introduce several elevating innovations. The machine room-less elevator debuted in 1997. That year the company made it possible to order elevators online.

By 1999, the company's 125th anniversary, 40% of sales came from outside Europe, and non-elevator operations climbed to 20% of sales. In 2000 Schindler inked a deal with Mitsubishi Electric to supply each other with elevator components.

In a move to tap new markets, in 2002 Schindler acquired a 51% stake in Russian elevator maker Liftremont. The company closed factories in Brazil, France, Germany, Japan, Malaysia, Poland, and Turkey that year. In 2003 Schindler acquired South Korea's Joong Ang Elevator Company and Austria's Doppelmayr AufzÃ¼ge.

The ALSO Group sold its Systems Business unit to Germany's Bechtle in 2004. A year later ALSO bought majority control of GNT Holding, a Finnish distributor of IT products and consumer electronics.

2005 saw more acquisitions. Schindler bought Eletec Vytahy Spol (Czech Republic) and Mercury Ascensore (Japan). That year Schindler China opened an escalator factory in Shanghai, capable of producing more than 6,000 escalators a year.

In 2006 Schindler bought a one-quarter interest in Hyundai Elevator, the second largest vendor of elevators and escalators in South Korea. It also took full ownership of Certus, its long-time partner in Croatia, and established a Schindler Adriatic organization to represent the group's interests in the Balkans. ALSO made GNT Holding a wholly owned subsidiary in 2008.

Schindler's momentum was affected by a decision made by European Union regulators in 2007. The company was among five elevator manufacturers fined, following a three-year investigation into alleged anticompetitive practices in Belgium, Germany, Luxembourg, and the Netherlands from 1995 to 2004.

During 2008 Schindler increased its ownership in its Korean subsidiary from 70% to 100% and bought a 49% stake in Al Doha Elevators & Escalators WLL in Qatar. The company has been an exclusive distributor of Schindler products in Qatar since 2005. It was renamed Al Doha Schindler Elevators & Escalators.

EXECUTIVES

Chairman, Executive Chairman, Silvio Napoli
Chief Executive Officer, Thomas Oetterli
Deputy Chief Executive, David Clymo
Chief Financial Officer, Urs Scheidegger
Chief Technology Officer, Karl-Heinz Bauer
Executive Director, Tobias B. Staehelin
Vice-Chairman, Pius Baschera
Executive Director, Erich Ammann
Independent Non-Executive Director, Luc Bonnard
Independent Non-Executive Director, Patrice Bula
Independent Non-Executive Director, Monika Butler
Independent Non-Executive Director, Rudolph W. Fischer
Independent Non-Executive Director, Carole Visher
Non-Executive Director, Alfred N. Schindler
Auditors : PricewaterhouseCoopers AG

LOCATIONS

HQ: Schindler Holding AG
Seestrasse 55, Hergiswil CH-6052
Phone: (41) 41 632 85 50   Fax: (41) 41 445 31 44
Web: www.schindler.com

2015 Sales

	% of total
Europe	39
Americas	28
Asia-Pacific & Africa	33
Total	100

PRODUCTS/OPERATIONS

Selected Products & Services
Commercial elevators
Escalators (commercial, public transportation) & moving walks
E-tools (planning, analysis, reporting)
Freight & special elevators
High-rise elevators
Modernization (elevators, escalators)
Residential elevators
Service & maintenance

Selected Subsidiaries
Adams Elevator Equipment Company (US)
Administração e Comércio Jaguar Ltda. (Brazil)
Ascensores Schindler (Chile) SA
Ascensores Schindler de Colombia SA
Ascensores Schindler SA (90%, Argentina)
China-Schindler Elevator Co. Ltd. (63%)
Deve Hydraulic Lifts Pty. Ltd. (Australia)
Elevadores Schindler SA de CV (Mexico)
Elevator Car System (France)
Hovanes BV (The Netherlands)
Iran Schindler Lift Manufacturing Company Ltd. (15%)
Jardine Schindler Elevator Corp. (Philippines)
Jardine Schindler Lifts (Taiwan)
Jardine Schindler (Thai) Ltd.
Kibaek Specialfabrik Aps (Denmark)
Schindler Aufzügefabrik GmbH (Germany)
Schindler Elevator Corporation (Canada)
Schindler Elevator Corporation (US)
Schindler Elevator KK (Japan)
Schindler India PVT Ltd.
Schindler Ltd. (Egypt)
Schindler Ltd. (UK)
SA Schindler NV (Belgium)
Schindler SpA (Italy)
Stahl Heiser A/S (Norway)
Ternitz Druckguss GmbH (80%, Austria)

COMPETITORS

Chocoladefabriken Lindt & SprÃ¼ngli AG
EDP - ENERGIAS DE PORTUGAL, S.A.
HeidelbergCement AG
INCHCAPE PLC
KONE Oyj
LafargeHolcim Ltd
Rieter Holding AG
SEQUANA
Swiss Life Holding AG
Zurich Insurance Group AG

HISTORICAL FINANCIALS
Company Type: Public

Income Statement   FYE: December 31

	REVENUE ($mil)	NET INCOME ($mil)	NET PROFIT MARGIN	EMPLOYEES
12/21	12,309	907	7.4%	69,015
12/20	12,080	819	6.8%	66,674
12/19	11,659	892	7.7%	66,306
12/18	11,059	958	8.7%	64,486
12/17	10,429	844	8.1%	61,019
Annual Growth	4.2%	1.8%	—	3.1%

2021 Year-End Financials
Debt ratio: 10.0%   No. of shares ($ mil.): 107
Return on equity: 20.2%   Dividends
Cash ($ mil.): 3,112   Yield: —
Current Ratio: 1.39   Payout: 52.0%
Long-term debt ($ mil.): 982   Market value ($ mil.): —

Schlumberger Ltd

EXECUTIVES

Chairman, Director, Mark G. Papa
Chief Executive Officer, Director, Olivier Le Peuch, $1,400,000 total compensation
Finance Executive Vice President, Operations Executive Vice President, Finance Chief Financial Officer, Operations Chief Financial Officer, Stephane Biguet
Chief Legal Officer, Secretary, Dianne B. Ralston
General Counsel, Secretary, Alexander Juden, $750,000 total compensation
Division Officer, Khaled Al Mogharbel, $834,167 total compensation
Division Officer, Abdellah Merad
Division Officer, Rajeev Sonthalia
Division Officer, Gavin Rennick
Director, Ulrich Spiesshofer
Director, Vanitha Narayanan
Director, Peter John Coleman
Director, Samuel Georg Friedrich Leupold
Director, Maria Moræus Hanssen
Director, Patrick de La Chevardiere
Director, Miguel Matias Galuccio
Director, Tatiana Mitrova
Director, Henri Seydoux
Director, Jeffrey Wayne Sheets
Auditors : PricewaterhouseCoopers LLP

LOCATIONS

HQ: Schlumberger Ltd
42 Rue Saint-Dominique, Paris 75007
Phone: 713 513-2000
Web: www.slb.com

HISTORICAL FINANCIALS
Company Type: Public

Income Statement — FYE: December 31

	REVENUE ($mil)	NET INCOME ($mil)	NET PROFIT MARGIN	EMPLOYEES
12/23	33,477	4,203	12.6%	111,000
12/22	28,679	3,441	12.0%	99,000
12/21	23,077	1,881	8.2%	92,000
12/20	23,868	(10,518)	—	86,000
12/19	33,250	(10,137)	—	105,000
Annual Growth	0.2%	—	—	1.4%

2023 Year-End Financials

Debt ratio: 24.9%
Return on equity: 22.1%
Cash ($ mil.): 3,989
Current Ratio: 1.32
Long-term debt ($ mil.): 10,842
No. of shares ($ mil.): 1,427
Dividends
  Yield: —
  Payout: 34.3%
Market value ($ mil.): 74,282

	STOCK PRICE ($) FY Close	P/E High/Low		PER SHARE ($) Earnings	Dividends	Book Value
12/23	52.04	21	15	2.91	1.00	14.14
12/22	53.46	23	13	2.39	0.65	12.45
12/21	29.95	27	16	1.32	0.50	10.69
12/20	21.83	—	—	(7.57)	0.88	8.67
12/19	40.20	—	—	(7.32)	2.00	17.16
Annual Growth	6.7%	—	—	—	(15.9%)	(4.7%)

Schroders PLC

One of Europe's largest publicly traded money managers with more than £731.6 billion in assets under management, Schroders provides investment management services for such clients as major international companies, government agencies, pension funds, charities, and wealthy investors. It operates through three business segments of Asset Management, Wealth Management and Group. Asset Management provides equity, fixed income, multi-asset, private asset, and alternative investment advisory. Wealth Management conducts investment management, wealth planning, and banking. Group encompasses Schroders' investment capital, treasury management, business development, strategy, and management expense. More than 30% of Schroders' revenue earns from its domestic operations. Founded in London as J.F.Schröder & Co in 1800.

Operations

Schroders has three business segments: Asset Management, Wealth Management and the Group segment. The Asset Management segment (about 85% of total revenue) principally comprises investment management including advisory services in respect of equity, fixed income, multi-asset solutions and private assets and alternatives products. The Wealth Management segment (some 15% of total revenue) principally comprises investment management, wealth planning and financial advice, platform services and banking services. The Group segment principally comprises investment capital and treasury management activities, corporate development and strategy activities and the management costs associated with governance and corporate management.

Broadly speaking, more than 90% of total revenue came from management fees and the remaining revenue came from performance fees, carried interest, interest income earned by Wealth Management and other fees.

Geographic Reach

Based in London, UK, Schroders has more than 35 locations across Europe, the Americas, Asia, Australia and the Middle East.

Its home country, UK, generates more than 30% of Schroders' revenue, while Continental Europe and Middle East generate about 35% of revenue, Asia Pacific at more than 20% and Americas account for the remaining some 15%.

Sales and Marketing

Schroders' clients include individuals who invest directly and those who invest through businesses or financial advisers. It also serve the investment needs of institutions like insurance companies, pension funds and charities.

Financial Performance

Note: Growth rates may differ after conversion to US dollars. This analysis uses financials from the company's annual report.

Revenue for fiscal 2021 increased to £3.0 billion compared from the prior year with £2.5 billion.

Net income for fiscal 2021 increased to £2.6 billion compared from the prior year with £2.2 billion.

Cash held by the company at the end of fiscal 2021 increased to £5.1 billion. Cash provided by operations and investing activities were £1.2 billion and £117.4 million, respectively. Cash used for financing activities was £429.7 million, mainly for dividends paid.

Strategy

Changes in the investment industry continue to gather pace. The company's strategy looks decades ahead; it is carefully designed to benefit its clients, as Schroders' further diversify its business model towards higher demand areas. Schroders strategic focuses are:

Grow Asset Management. Schroder focus on offering products and solutions that are distinctive and of pinpoint relevance to each client. Product innovation is key to future proofing its business. As is geographically expanding its reach so the company can serve more clients in more jurisdictions.

Build closer relationships with end clients. End investors can benefit from the breadth of its expanding investment capabilities. The company have the opportunity to leverage our global investment expertise to build a leading Wealth Management franchise.

Expand Private Assets & Alternatives. Build on the surging client demand for new alternative sources of return. Schroders' Private Assets business is built to provide investors with a range of portfolio building blocks and customized private asset strategies. The company's teams have over two decades of experience in delivering risk-adjusted returns in all private asset classes, covering private equity, real estate, private debt and infrastructure.

Mergers and Acquisitions

In 2022, Schroders announced that it has completed the acquisition of a 75% shareholding in Greencoat Capital, one of Europe's largest investment managers dedicated to the high-growth renewable infrastructure market, for an initial consideration of £358 million. Greencoat, will become part of Schroders Capital, Schroders' growing private markets division. The business will be known as Schroders Greencoat.

In early 2022, Schroders completed the acquisition of Cairn Real Estate, a real estate fund and asset management business based in the Netherlands with ?1.3 billion of assets under management. The acquisition is expanding Schroders Capital's client offering in a key European growth market. It is also enhancing Schroders' access to Dutch real estate expertise and on-the-ground investment talent to meet the growing investment demand from its institutional investors.

In 2021, Schroders announced its intention to acquire River and Mercantile Group's UK Solutions Division consisting of its fiduciary management and derivatives businesses. The transaction is valued at approximately £230 million. The acquisition reaffirms Schroders strategy to provide clients with the highest quality solutions for their complex investment needs. This business has an excellent track record and market leading proposition. It will further strengthen Schroders ability to meet the requirements of pension funds as they evolve.

Also in 2021, Schroders announced its intention to acquire a 50.1% ownership stake in commercial real estate lending specialists RF Eclipse Limited - a leading alternative lender to small and medium sized enterprises in the real estate market. The business specialises in investment, development and construction financing across residential, commercial, retail and industrial properties. Following completion of the transaction, RF Eclipse will be renamed 'Schroder RF' recognising the complementary capabilities that both parent organisations bring to clients through the joint venture.

In early 2021, Schroders announced the acquisition of the remaining minority interest in Benchmark Capital, an award-winning, technology-driven wealth management business. The acquisition further builds on Schroders strategic priority of continuing to expand our wealth management offering.

HISTORY

By the 19th century, the Schroder family had established a global network of merchant houses from its base in Hamburg. In 1804 Johann Schroder joined his brother's London merchant house. Fourteen years later he opened J. Henry Schroder & Co.

The merchant bank expanded from the UK into North and South America and Asia. It grew both geographically and operationally, moving from trading to financing trade, then to raising capital for investment. In 1868 the firm entered Asia, building an investment fund in Japan. During the 1870s the company made its money distributing Peruvian guano.

Schroders built strong relationships in Germany and the US as the economies of those countries boomed at the turn of the century. However, the firm's loyalty was called into question with the outbreak of WWI; although family members hurriedly became British citizens, they were still targeted by anti-German sentiment.

In 1923 the firm opened J. Henry Schroder Bank & Trust in New York at the invitation of the US Federal Reserve. The company, which was nearly bankrupted when the German economy collapsed in 1931, used its interest in the New York bank to rebuild.

WWII and the beginning of the Cold War inhibited growth, and Schroders did not fully recover from its near-bankruptcy until the 1950s. In 1959 Schroders registered first as a private company then, two days later, went public.

In 1962 the company merged with rival merchant bank Helbert Wagg. Over the next two decades it grew its corporate finance, investment management, and lending services. In 1968 and 1969 Schroders entered the unit trust market (later sold in 1986 to National Mutual Life, although the firm continued to manage some of the funds).

While other banks were building branch networks during the 1980s, Schroders instead built a network of subsidiaries, including Schroder Investment Management (1985) and a 50% investment in US securities firm Wertheim & Co. (1986, increased to 100% in 1994). In 1985 the firm sold to Industrial Bank of Japan its Schroder Bank & Trust, which had been crippled by bad loans to Latin America. After the UK's Big Bang deregulation in 1986, Schroders shifted its focus to corporate finance and securities.

The end of the Cold War brought Schroders new opportunities in Europe; the firm advised the Hungarian, Czech, and Russian governments on privatizations. In 1994 the company opened its first branch in China, and Schroders continued to grow in Asia during the mid-1990s. ABN AMRO targeted the firm in 1995 for takeover, but the Schroder family refused to sell its controlling interest. As Europe privatized its pension funds, the company in 1996 launched its investment trust personal equity plans.

The financial crises in Asia and Russia in 1998 led Schroders to scuttle its investment operations in Asia. With its US operations struggling as well, the firm in 1999 entered merger talks with Beacon Group, led by Goldman Sachs veteran Geoffrey Boisi; when no deal resulted, Schroders repurchased IBJ Schroder International Bank, which it had planned to use as a launch pad into Latin America.

But in 2000 Schroders decided that, rather than competing with the US behemoths, it would sell its investment banking operations to Citigroup (which folded the unit into what is now its Citigroup Global Markets subsidiary), leaving Schroders as an asset management firm. At year's end, the company launched private bank Schroder & Co.

In 2006 Schroders bought London-based hedge fund manager NewFinance Capital; the following year it bought the property asset management division of Germany's Aareal Bank.

Schroders acquired the third-party fund management business of Swiss Re in 2008, bringing another £1 billion ($1.5 billion) to the firm's total assets under management. It also bought E.Sun Securities Investment Trust, which owned a securities investment trust enterprise license in Taiwan, allowing Schroders to establish an offshore fund there.

In 2010, the company sold its third-party private equity administration business to J.P. Morgan Worldwide Securities Services. The division was initially formed to complement Schroders' private equity business, which is no longer a part of the company. (Previously, Schroders exited investment banking with the sale to Salomon Smith Barney.)

EXECUTIVES

Chief Executive Officer, Executive Director, Peter Harrison
Chief Financial Officer, Executive Director, Richard Keers
Secretary, Graham Staples
Non-Executive Chairman, Michael Dobson
Chair designate, Independent Non-Executive Director, Dame Elizabeth Corley
Senior Independent Director, Non-Executive Director, Ian G. King
Independent Non-Executive Director, Matthew Westerman
Independent Non-Executive Director, Damon Buffini
Independent Non-Executive Director, Rhian Davies
Independent Non-Executive Director, Rakhi Goss-Custard
Independent Non-Executive Director, Deborah Waterhouse
Non-Executive Director, Claire Fitzalan Howard
Non-Executive Director, Leonie Schroder
Auditors : Ernst & Young LLP

LOCATIONS

HQ: Schroders PLC
1 London Wall Place, London EC2Y 5AU
Phone: (44) 20 7658 6000   **Fax:** (44) 20 7658 6965
Web: www.schroders.com

PRODUCTS/OPERATIONS

2018 Revenue

	% of total
Management fees	93
Performance fees	1
Carried interest	2
Other fees	2
Interest income earned by Wealth Management	2
Total	100

2018 Revenue

	% of total
Asset Management	88
Wealth Management	12
Group	-
Total	100

COMPETITORS

ABERDEEN ASSET MANAGEMENT PLC
ALLIANCEBERNSTEIN HOLDING L.P.
CLYDESDALE BANK PLC
DBRS Limited
GE COMMERCIAL FINANCE LIMITED
INSIGHT INVESTMENT MANAGEMENT LIMITED
NORTHERN TRUST CORPORATION
PENTA CAPITAL PARTNERS LIMITED
PRIMARY CAPITAL LIMITED
YORKSHIRE BANK PUBLIC LIMITED COMPANY

HISTORICAL FINANCIALS

Company Type: Public

Income Statement   FYE: December 31

	ASSETS ($mil)	NET INCOME ($mil)	INCOME AS % OF ASSETS	EMPLOYEES
12/22	25,683	585	2.3%	6,196
12/21	32,804	840	2.6%	5,650
12/20	29,577	663	2.2%	5,556
12/19	28,083	654	2.3%	5,359
12/18	25,068	644	2.6%	4,872
Annual Growth	0.6%	(2.4%)	—	6.2%

2022 Year-End Financials

Return on assets: 2.1%
Return on equity: 11.2%
Long-term debt ($ mil.): —
No. of shares ($ mil.): 1,551
Sales ($ mil.): 3,618
Dividends
Yield: —
Payout: 71.9%
Market value ($ mil.): —

SCOR S.E. (France)

A global, independent, Tier 1 reinsurance company, SCOR provides treaty (groups of risks) and facultative (individual risks) reinsurance, covering the risks of insurance underwriters around the globe. The company reinsures property/casualty, life, accident, and health insurance lines. SCOR's business is divided into three business units, which provide a broad range of innovative reinsurance solutions: SCOR Global P&C (Property & Casualty), SCOR Global Life and SCOR Global Investments. The company is structured around three regional management platforms, or organizational hubs: the EMEA Hub, the Americas Hub and the Asia-Pacific Hub. SCOR, the world's fourth largest reinsurer, is established in around 30 countries and provides services to over 4,900 clients worldwide.

Operations

SCOR operating segments are SCOR Global Life and SCOR Global P&C.

The SCOR Global Life segment operates worldwide through the subsidiaries and branches of SCOR SE. Via this network SCOR Global Life is represented in three business regions, EMEA, the Americas and Asia-Pacific, reinsuring Life and Health insurance risks along the three product lines Protection, Longevity and Financial Solutions with a strong focus on biometric risks. In order to achieve this, SCOR Global Life manages and optimizes the in-force book, deepens the franchise and aims at having the best team, organization and tools.

SCOR Global P&C is represented in three business regions, EMEA, the Americas and Asia-Pacific and operates in three business areas: Specialties Insurance (large corporate accounts underwritten through facultative insurance contracts, direct insurance, SCOR Channel, for which SCOR is the sole capital provider and MGA business, a specialized type of insurance agent/broker vested with underwriting authority from an insurer), Reinsurance (including Property, Casualty, Motor, Credit and Surety, Decennial Insurance, Aviation, Marine, Engineering, and Agricultural risks) and P&C Partners (including Cyber and Alternative Solutions).

The company's life insurance unit, SCOR Global Life, accounts for about 55% of gross written premiums, while SCOR Global P&C (property and casualty) brings in about 45%. Outside of its reinsurance operations, the company has a third, smaller business named SCOR Global Investments, which provides asset and investment management services to the other operating SCOR facilities.

Geographic Reach

Based in Paris, France, SCOR has about 35 offices throughout the Americas, Europe, Middle East, Africa (EMEA), and Asia-Pacific. SCOR generated about 35% of its gross written premiums in Europe, Middle East and Africa (EMEA), with significant market positions in France, Germany, Spain and Italy, about 45% of its gross written premiums are in the Americas and some 20% in Asia.

Sales and Marketing

Reinsurance is written either through brokers or directly. The Non-Life business unit wrote some 70% of gross written premiums through brokers and about 30% through direct business, while the Life business unit wrote more than 5% through brokers and around 95% through direct business.

Financial Performance

Net earned premiums for the year totaled EUR 13.9 billion, a 4% decrease from the previous year's net earned premiums of EUR 14.5 billion.

In 2021, the company had a net income of EUR 456 million, a 95% increase from the previous year's net income of EUR 234 million.

The company's cash at the end of 2021 was EUR 2.1 billion. Operating activities generated EUR 2.4 billion, while investing activities used EUR 1.5 billion, mainly for acquisitions of other insurance business investments. Financing activities used another EUR 674 million, primarily for dividends paid.

Strategy

In September 2021, SCOR extended "Quantum Leap" by one year until the end of 2022 and will present in Spring 2022 the orientations for the new strategic plan to start on January 1, 2023. The success of its various plans, along with the company's acquisitions of Revios (in 2006), Converium (in 2007), Transamerica Re (in 2011) and Generali US (in 2013), have contributed to the diversification strategy by balancing the proportion of the consolidated premiums written between its Non-Life and Life segments and have enabled the Group to preserve both its solvency and its profitability.

HISTORY

SCOR was founded in 1970 by the French government to compete against reinsurers like Munich Re and Swiss Reinsurance; the government eventually ceded control to a group of French insurers including AXA, UAP Re, and Groupe des Assurances Nationales. By 1972 SCOR was expanding internationally.

Growth continued throughout the 1970s and '80s. In 1989 the firm acquired Deutsche Continental Rückversicherungs in Germany. A year later the firm listed on the Paris stock exchange.

In the early 1990s SCOR's owners began setting up their own reinsurance operations and selling off their holdings in the company. In 1995 AXA and Assurances Generales de France were the last to sell their stakes. Also that year SCOR consolidated ownership in its subsidiaries and streamlined its Asian operations.

The year 1996 was a big one in the US for SCOR. It acquired the reinsurance business of Allstate and also listed on the New York Stock Exchange. As worldwide property/casualty markets took a downturn in 1996 and 1997, SCOR began expanding its life, accident, and health reinsurance.

Numerous natural disasters in 1998 and 1999 hobbled SCOR's already slumping property/casualty unit; losses were offset by increased business in other lines. SCOR acquired full control of its Commercial Risk Partners subsidiary in 1999, bolstering its specialty reinsurance business. In 2000 SCOR reorganized its industrial risk business to further offset recent losses. That year the company bought Partner Re's US subsidiary PartnerRe Life and Switzerland-based Veritas property/casualty reinsurance portfolio.

In 2001 SCOR joined Inreon, an online reinsurance exchange set up by industry bigwigs Swiss Re and Munich Re. In 2002 it liquidated and sold off subsidiary Commercial Risk Partners to reduce costs. Expanding internationally, the company opened offices in Korea and India in 2004 and 2005.

In 2007 SCOR acquired Swiss reinsurer Converium Holding, beginning with a buy-up of about a third of the company's shares. The purchase agreement went through several drafts (one resulting in a lawsuit alleging that SCOR had deliberately undervalued Converium), but was eventually accepted by both boards of directors. The acquisition added customers in Austria, Germany, Switzerland, and the UK and boosted SCOR into a spot among the top five global life reinsurers.

Also in 2007 SCOR transformed itself into a Societas Europaea, a legal structure that allows it more financial freedom in its European operations. In addition, the company voluntarily delisted from the New York Stock Exchange.

EXECUTIVES

Interim Chief Executive Officer, Francois de Varenne

Chief Financial Officer, Ian Kelly

Chief Sustainability Officer, Claire Le Gall-Robinson

Chief Risk Officer, Fabian Uffer

Chairman, Director, Denis Kessler

Vice-Chairman, Independent Director, Augustin de Romanet

Independent Director, Fabrice Bregier

Independent Director, Adrien Couret

Independent Director, Martine Gerow

Independent Director, Patricia Lacoste

Independent Director, Vanessa Marquette

Independent Director, Bruno Pfister

Independent Director, Thomas Saunier

Independent Director, Natacha Valla

Independent Director, Wang Zhen

Independent Director, Jane Fields Wicker-Miurin

Director, Marc Buker

Director, Pietro Santoro

Director, Claude Tendil

Auditors : Mazars

LOCATIONS

HQ: SCOR S.E. (France)
5, avenue Kleber, Paris 75116

Phone: (33) 1 58 44 70 00 Fax: (33) 1 58 44 85 00
Web: www.scor.com

2013 Gross Written Premiums

	% of total
Europe	42
Americas	39
Asia-Pacific & other regions	19
Total	**100**

PRODUCTS/OPERATIONS

2013 Premiums

	% of total
Global P&C	53
Global Life	47
Total	**100**

COMPETITORS

AMERICAN INTERNATIONAL GROUP, INC.
HEALTHPLAN HOLDINGS, INC.
JLT GROUP HOLDINGS LIMITED
KEOGHS LLP
Münchener Rückversicherungs-Gesellschaft AG in München
NATIONAL FARMERS UNION MUTUAL INSURANCE SOCIETY LIMITED(THE)
Ping An Insurance (Group) Company Of China, Ltd.
TESCO PLC
Talanx AG
WARRANTECH CORPORATION

HISTORICAL FINANCIALS

Company Type: Public

Income Statement   FYE: December 31

	ASSETS ($mil)	NET INCOME ($mil)	INCOME AS % OF ASSETS	EMPLOYEES
12/22	59,095	(321)	—	3,522
12/21	58,311	516	0.9%	3,590
12/20	56,721	287	0.5%	3,123
12/19	52,633	473	0.9%	3,028
12/18	50,827	368	0.7%	2,887
Annual Growth	**3.8%**	—	—	**5.1%**

2022 Year-End Financials

Return on assets: (-0.5%)   Dividends
Return on equity: (-5.2%)   Yield: —
Long-term debt ($ mil.): —   Payout: 0.0%
No. of shares ($ mil.): 179   Market value ($ mil.): 409
Sales ($ mil.): 21,069

	STOCK PRICE ($) FY Close	P/E High/Low		PER SHARE ($) Earnings	Dividends	Book Value
12/22	2.29	—	—	(1.80)	0.20	30.41
12/21	3.06	1	1	2.77	0.21	39.91
12/20	3.20	4	2	1.53	2.21	40.51
12/19	4.28	2	2	2.53	0.20	38.24
12/18	4.41	3	2	1.95	0.20	36.11
Annual Growth	**(15.2%)**	—	—	—	**(0.1%)**	**(4.2%)**

Sea Ltd

EXECUTIVES

Chairman, Chief Executive Officer, Executive Chairman, Executive Director, Forrest Xiaodong Li
Finance Chief Financial Officer, Executive Director, Tony Tianyu Hou
Chief Operating Officer, Executive Director, Gang Ye

Chief Corporate Officer, Secretary, General Counsel, Yanjun Wang
Independent Director, David Heng Chen Seng
Independent Director, Khoon Hua Kuok
Director, Yuxin Ren
Auditors: Ernst & Young LLP

LOCATIONS

HQ: Sea Ltd
1 Fusionopolis Place, #17-10, Galaxis, 138522
Phone: (65) 6270 8100
Web: www.sea.com

HISTORICAL FINANCIALS

Company Type: Public

Income Statement   FYE: December 31

	REVENUE ($mil)	NET INCOME ($mil)	NET PROFIT MARGIN	EMPLOYEES
12/22	12,449	(1,651)	—	0
12/21	9,955	(2,046)	—	67,300
12/20	4,375	(1,618)	—	33,800
12/19	2,175	(1,462)	—	29,800
12/18	826	(961)	—	22,600
Annual Growth	**97.0%**	—	—	—

2022 Year-End Financials

Debt ratio: 20.3%   No. of shares ($ mil.): 564
Return on equity: (-25.1%)   Dividends
Cash ($ mil.): 6,029   Yield: —
Current Ratio: 1.83   Payout: 0.0%
Long-term debt ($ mil.): 3,338 Market value ($ mil.): 29,384

	STOCK PRICE ($) FY Close	P/E High/Low		PER SHARE ($) Earnings	Dividends	Book Value
12/22	52.03	—	—	(2.96)	0.00	10.12
12/21	223.71	—	—	(3.84)	0.00	13.27
12/20	199.05	—	—	(3.39)	0.00	6.61
12/19	40.22	—	—	(3.35)	0.00	2.51
12/18	11.32	—	—	(2.84)	0.00	(0.71)
Annual Growth	**46.4%**	—	—	—	—	—

SEB SA

SEB is the world leader in small domestic equipment. Known for its portfolio of small appliances covering around 30 brand names (Krups, All-Clad, Moulinex, Rowenta, Tefal, and Arno), SEB makes cookware (frying pans, saucepans, and more), home and personal care(toasters, coffee makers, vacuums), and kitchen electrics (extra hoods, water purifiers). ASEB was founded in 1857 by Antoine Lescure, whose descendants still control the firm. Most of SEB's revenue comes from Western Europe.

Operations

SEB's operating segment id presented by geographical segment which includes EMEA (about 50% of sales), Asia (some 30%), and Americas (about 15%). Its professional business accounts for nearly 10%.

SEB owns four consumer brands, Tefal, Rowenta, Moulinex, Krups, and about 20 regional brands. It also owns four premium brands, as well as five professional brands. The company's product lines include: kitchen electrics, home and personal care, cookware, and professional business.

Overall, small electrical appliances account for some 60% of sales, cookware with around 30%, and professional coffee machines and hotels (nearly 10%).

Geographic Reach

SEB sells globally, with about 35% of revenue coming from Western Europe, followed by Asia-Pacific region (including China) which generates some 30% of revenue. Other EMEA generates about 15%, North America approximately 10%, and South America generates about 5%. SEB is headquartered in Ecully, France.

Sales and Marketing

SEB sells its products through distributors, its own more than 1,250 stores (including the Home & Cook banner) which include Supor Lifestores in China.

The company's advertising expenses for the years 2021 and 2020 were EUR 203.3 million and EUR 143.7 million, respectively.

Financial Performance

SEB's financials for the past five years show some fluctuation, with profits dipping slightly in 2019 and 2020, following growth in the prior years. Despite the recent challenges brought by the pandemic, the company has demonstrated resilience in the face of the crisis and even managed record-breaking growth.

In 2021, SEB achieved record performance with its revenues exceeding EUR 8 billion, driven by growth in its Small Electrical Appliances segment, which generated about EUR 5 billion of sales.

Profit for 2021 increased by over 50% to EUR 454 million from EUR 301 million the year prior. This growth results from a significant improvement in this year's operations due to results from the company's French entities in 2021, despite minimal cost increases.

SEB recorded EUR 2.3 billion in cash and cash equivalents at the end of 2021, representing a EUR 497.1 million increase from the year prior. Operations generated EUR 573.4 million, while investing activities provided another EUR 357.8 million from financial assets. Financing activities used EUR 488.5 million, mainly for borrowings and dividends.

Strategy

SEB pursues a multi-specialist strategy with top-ranking positions in small electrical appliances and a strong global leadership in cookware. Its mission is making consumers' everyday lives easier and more enjoyable and contributing to better living all around the world.

The company also pursues a virtuous innovation strategy consistent with a pragmatic approach to creating the product offering. Launching new products is the result of listening closely to what consumers want, conducting and in-depth analysis of their needs, inventing breakthrough concepts or unprecedented functionality, using new technologies, and creating one-of-a-kind designs. SEB focuses on energy consumption during manufacturing and use; reparability, recyclability or second-hand use, use of recycled materials; and ergonomics and inclusive designs.

HISTORY

Antoine Lescure formed his namesake firm in 1857 in Burgundy, France, to make metalware, including buckets and watering cans. The company expanded its product lines to include kitchen utensils and zinc tubs. Lescure's descendants renamed the firm Société d'Emboutissage de Bourgogne (Burgundy Metalware Company) in 1925.

The company began making pressure cookers in 1953, and in 1967 it entered the electrical appliance market with the introduction of an electric fryer. The next year the company acquired Tefal, a manufacturer specializing in nonstick cookware founded by Marc Gregoire in 1956. (Tefal is known as the world's first maker of nonstick frying pans). In 1972 the company bought Calor, known for its irons, hair dryers, and electric heaters. The next year the company was reorganized as a group structure (Groupe SEB) under a lead holding company (SEB SA). SEB went public in 1975, with the Lescure family retaining a controlling stake. A year later the company moved its headquarters to Ecully Cedex, France.

SEB expanded its geographic presence in 1988 when it bought Rowenta, a manufacturer of irons, coffee makers, toasters, and vacuum cleaners with factories in Germany and France. The next year the company opened a facility in Mexico to serve North America. Jacques Gairard was named CEO in 1990.

In the 1990s SEB opened offices in Eastern and Central Europe, China, and India. It began a joint venture to make irons in China in 1996. The company bought a 44% stake in Arno, Brazil's leader in electrical household appliances, in 1997 (increasing its stake to 98% in 1998). SEB bought Volmo, a small electrical appliance maker in Colombia and Venezuela, in 1998.

With sluggish sales, especially in Russia and Brazil, SEB began cutting its workforce in 1998. It also withdrew from businesses, including air conditioning and water treatment products, in which it wasn't the market leader. The company began outsourcing production of espresso machines and heaters in 1999. In 2000 SEB introduced a new line of Rowenta-brand bathroom scales and steam generators.

In 2001 SEB strengthened its global positioning with the acquisition of Krups-Moulinex, a transaction that was appealed by SEB's competitors and finally cleared by the French government in 2004.

The French appliance maker purchased Waterford Wedgwood's All-Clad subsidiary for about $250 million in 2004.

EXECUTIVES

Chief Executive Officer, Stanislas de Gramont
Chief Financial Officer, Executive Vice President, Nathalie Lomon
Human Resources Senior Executive Vice President, Delphine Segura-Vaylet
Legal Executive Vice President, Philippe Sumeire
EMEA President, Cyril Buxtorf
Cookware President, Pierre-Armand Lemoine
Industry President, Alain Leroy
Small Electrical Appliances President, Olivier Naccache
Public Affairs & Communication Executive Vice President, Public Affairs & Communication
Chief of Staff, Cathy Pianon
WMF President, Oliver Kastalio
Research Executive Vice President, Vincent Rouiller
Products and Innovation Senior Executive Vice President, Philippe Schaillee
Asia President, Vincent Tai
SEB Professional Executive Vice President, Martin Zouhar
America Executive Vice President, Oguzhan Olmez
Founding Chairman, Frederic Lescure
Founding Chairman, Henri Lescure
Founding Chairman, Emmanuel Lescure
Chairman, Thierry de La Tour d'Artaise
Independent Director, Yseulys Costes
Independent Director, Jean-Pierre Duprieu
Independent Director, Bertrand Finet
Independent Director, Catherine C. Pourre
Independent Director, Anne Guerin
Director, Delphine Bertrand
Director, Nora Bey
Director, Brigitte Forestier
Director, Caroline Chevalley
Director, Laurent Henry
Director, Thierry Lescure
Director, William Gairard
Director, Jerome Lescure
Director, Aude De Vassart
Director, Damarys Braida
Auditors: Deloitte & Associés

LOCATIONS

HQ: SEB SA
Campus SEB, 112 chemin du Moulin Carron, Ecully 69130
Phone: (33) 4 72 18 18 18   **Fax:** (33) 4 72 18 16 55
Web: www.groupeseb.com

2015 sales

	% of total
Asia Pacific	30
Europe	
France	16
Other Western EU	20
Central Europe and others	13
Americas	
North America	13
South America	8
Total	**100**

PRODUCTS/OPERATIONS

Selected Categories and Products
Appliances
Cookware
Electric cooking
Food and beverage preparation
Personal care
Linen care
Floor care & home comfort

Selected Brands
Airbake
All-Clad
Arno
Calor
Clock
Krups
Lagostina
Mirro
Moulinex
Panex
Regal
Rochedo
Rowenta
Samurai
Seb
Tefal/T-Fal
WearEver

2015 Sales

	% of total
Small appliances	67
Cookware	33
Total	**100**

HISTORICAL FINANCIALS

Company Type: Public

Income Statement — FYE: December 31

	REVENUE ($mil)	NET INCOME ($mil)	NET PROFIT MARGIN	EMPLOYEES
12/22	8,501	337	4.0%	30,863
12/21	9,121	513	5.6%	32,695
12/20	8,517	368	4.3%	32,847
12/19	8,256	426	5.2%	34,263
12/18	7,801	479	6.2%	33,974
Annual Growth	2.2%	(8.4%)	—	(2.4%)

2022 Year-End Financials
Debt ratio: 34.4%
Return on equity: 10.2%
Cash ($ mil.): 1,321
Current Ratio: 1.31
Long-term debt ($ mil.): 1,742
No. of shares ($ mil.): 55
Dividends
Yield: —
Payout: 54.8%
Market value ($ mil.): —

Seiko Epson Corp
Suwa

A top printer manufacturer, Seiko Epson (Epson Corp) produces office and home inkjet printers, commercial and industrial inkjet printers, POS printers, laser printers, dot matrix impact printers, scanners, label printers and printheads. Its product portfolio also includes projectors, scanners, and PCs; electronic devices and components, including semiconductors and LCDs; and precision products, such as lenses and factory automation equipment such as robots. Epson has sales and marketing sites, service sites, as well as production and R&D sites around the globe to accurately identify, and swiftly and flexibly meet the needs of customers in different regions. The company generates about 20% of its revenue in Japan.

Operations

The reportable segments of Epson are composed of three segments: Printing Solutions, Visual Communications and Wearable & Industrial Products.

Epson generates about 70% of its revenue from its Printing Solutions Business segment, which includes printers and its professional printing products and services. The Visual Communications Business segment, some 15% of revenue, develops and makes 3LCD projectors mainly for business, education, the home, and event as well as smart glasses and provide services related. The Wearable & Industrial Products Business segment comprises the manufacturing solutions business, wearable products business, microdevices business and the PC business and accounts for around 15% of revenue.

Geographic Reach

Seiko Epson, headquartered in Japan, operates facilities ? manufacturing sites, sales offices, and research and development centers ? around the world. Regional offices are in the US, China, the Netherlands, and Singapore.

About 80% of the company's revenue comes from international customers.

Financial Performance

The company reported a revenue of ¥1.1 trillion in 2022. The 113% increase was primarily due to higher sales volume across all of the company's segments.

In fiscal 2022, the company had a net income of ¥92.3 billion, a 198% increase from the previous year's net income of ¥31 billion.

The company's cash for the year ended 2022 was ¥335.2 billion. Operating activities generated ¥110.8 billion, while investing activities used ¥44.1 billion, mainly for purchase of property, plant and equipment. Financing activities used another ¥51.8 billion.

Strategy

The company's production strategy is to leverage changes caused by the spread of COVID-19 to accelerate the existing strategy. With regard to parts procurement, the company will continue to respond to the ongoing difficulties in procuring electronic parts and other components by securing parts in advance, changing product designs, and producing at multiple locations. As for securing logistics, the company will strengthen relations with shipping lines through load capacity contracts and proceed with the search for alternative transport routes. In the production automation, although there are challenges with strengthening and developing human resources at production sites, the company will promote digitalization of production equipment and launch of automated lines by developing hardware and data utilization technologies.

HISTORY

In 1881, 21-year-old Kitaro Hattori, who had begun working in the jewelry trade at age 13, opened a Tokyo watch shop and called it K. Hattori & Co. In 1892 Hattori started a factory in Seikosha to manufacture wall clocks and, later, watches and alarm clocks. K. Hattori & Co. went public in 1917. In 1924 it began using the Seiko brand on its timepieces. Kitaro's son Ganzo formed Daini Seikosha Co., precursor of Seiko Instruments, in 1937.

The company formed Daiwa Kogyo Ltd., a maker of mechanical watches, in 1942. In 1959 Daiwa Kogyo merged with the Suwa plant of Daini Seikosha to form Suwa Seikosha. Shinshu Seiki (renamed Epson in 1982) was established in 1961.

EXECUTIVES

Chairman, Director, Minoru Usui
President, Representative Director, Yasunori Ogawa
Senior Managing Executive Officer, Representative Director, Tatsuaki Seki
Outside Director, Mari Matsunaga
Outside Director, Tadashi Shimamoto
Outside Director, Masaki Yamauchi
Director, Masayuki Kawana
Outside Director, Yoshio Shirai
Outside Director, Susumu Murakoshi
Outside Director, Michiko Ohtsuka
Auditors : Ernst & Young ShinNihon LLC

LOCATIONS

HQ: Seiko Epson Corp Suwa
  3-3-5 Owa, Suwa, Nagano 392-8502
Phone: (81) 266 52 3131   Fax: 562 981-5220
Web: www.epson.jp

2016 Sales

	% of total
Japan	24
The United States	21
China	13
Other	42
Total	100

PRODUCTS/OPERATIONS

2016 Sales

	% of total
Printing Solutions	67
Visual Communications	17
Wearable & Industrial Products	16
Total	100

2016 Sales

	% of total
Sale of goods	99
Royalty income	-
Other	1
Total	100

Selected Products

Information-related equipment
  Printers
  Personal computers
  Projectors
  Scanners
Electronic devices
  Crystal devices
  LCDs
  Semiconductors
Precision products
  Factory automation
  Optical devices
  Watches

COMPETITORS

ASTRONOVA, INC.
CANON INC.
HP INC.
INVENTEC CORPORATION
KYOCERA CORPORATION
LEXMARK INTERNATIONAL INC.
PRINTRONIX, LLC
RICOH COMPANY,LTD.
XEROX CORPORATION
ZEBRA TECHNOLOGIES CORPORATION

HISTORICAL FINANCIALS

Company Type: Public

Income Statement   FYE: March 31

	REVENUE ($mil)	NET INCOME ($mil)	NET PROFIT MARGIN	EMPLOYEES
03/23	9,988	563	5.6%	79,906
03/22	9,281	758	8.2%	77,642
03/21	8,994	279	3.1%	79,944
03/20	9,613	71	0.7%	75,608
03/19	9,839	484	4.9%	76,647
Annual Growth	0.4%	3.8%	—	1.0%

2023 Year-End Financials

Debt ratio: 0.1%   No. of shares ($ mil.): 331
Return on equity: 10.7%   Dividends
Cash ($ mil.): 2,007   Yield: 3.1%
Current Ratio: 2.40   Payout: 14.0%
Long-term debt ($ mil.): 1,461   Market value ($ mil.): 2,351

	STOCK PRICE ($) FY Close	P/E High/Low		PER SHARE ($) Earnings	Dividends	Book Value
03/23	7.09	0	0	1.66	0.23	16.47
03/22	7.48	0	0	2.19	0.28	15.81
03/21	8.33	0	0	0.81	0.29	14.37
03/20	5.30	0	0	0.20	0.29	13.40
03/19	7.63	0	0	1.38	0.29	13.84
Annual Growth	(1.8%)	—	—	4.7%	(5.9%)	4.4%

Sekisui Chemical Co Ltd

Sekisui Chemical and its subsidiaries make up the SEKISUI CHEMICAL Group. It operates in over 190 companies throughout around 20 countries aim to contribute to improving the lives of the people of the world and the earth's environment. It holds the leading positions in its three diverse business divisions as well as top global market share in interlayer film, foam products, conductive particles and more. Its main segments include housing, urban infrastructure and environmental products, high performance plastics, and medical business. Other products include plastic pipes and fittings (used in water and sewage systems), medical multifrequency body fat meters, pipe valves, foams for automotive and construction applications, and rain gutters.

Operations
The company operates in four segments: Housing Company (about 45% of sales), High Performance Plastics Company (HPP; around 30%), Urban Infrastructure & Environmental Products Company (UIEP Company; about 20%), and Medical Business (over 5%).

The Housing Company is engaged in new housing construction activities as a specialist in the Unit Construction Method, an advanced factory-built approach that enables short construction periods and delivers functions in accordance with design plans.

The HPP Company business activities include leveraging its proprietary fine particle, adhesion, precise molding, and other technologies that provide advanced high-performance materials on a global basis that help bring about the further evolution of its customers' products and services for application in the Electronics, Mobility, and Building and Infrastructure material fields as well as various other industries.

The UIEP Company manufactures and markets water sewerage and supply pipe systems, in which it has a leading share in Japan, while also engaging in construction materials supply businesses, which collectively form the company's core operating platform.

The Medical Business consists the Diagnostics Business, which sells diagnostic reagents and equipment, and the Pharmaceutical Sciences Business, which is broken down into the pharmaceutical and fine chemicals business, which manufactures active pharmaceutical ingredients (APIs), etc., under contract, the drug development solutions business, which supports the R&D efforts of pharmaceutical companies, and the enzymes business, which manufactures precursors for diagnostic reagents and manufactures enzymes for the manufacture of biopharmaceuticals, the Medical Business is expanding its business globally.

Geographic Reach
The company has corporate headquarters in Osaka and Tokyo, Japan. It has about 175 companies located in the Americas, Europe, Asia & Oceania, and Japan, where it holds some 95 companies.

Financial Performance
The company reported a net sale of Â¥1.2 trillion, a 10% increase from the previous year's net sale of Â¥1.1 trillion.

In 2021, the company had a net income of Â¥83.2 million, a 10% decrease from the previous year's net income of Â¥91.9 million.

The company's operating activities for 2021 was Â¥105 billion, while financing activities used Â¥54.7 billion. Investing activities provided another Â¥2.7 billion.

Strategy
Vision 2030, the company's Long-term Vision, presents the vision statement of "Innovation for the Earth," which incorporates the company's resolute will to continuously drive innovation as a means of supporting the basis of LIFE and continuing to create peace of mind for the future to realize a sustainable society. This Vision lays down the four domains of Residential (Housing), Advanced Lifeline (Social Infrastructure), Innovative Mobility (Electric/Mobility), and Life Science (Health and Medical), and aims to double business by 2030 through the expansion of existing business while taking on the challenge of new domains along the strategy axis of business growth, reform, and creation centered on ESG management.

EXECUTIVES

Chairman, Director, Teiji Koge
President, Representative Director, Keita Kato
Senior Managing Executive Officer, Representative Director, Futoshi Kamiwaki
Senior Managing Executive Officer, Director, Yoshiyuki Hirai
Senior Managing Executive Officer, Director, Toshiyuki Kamiyoshi
Senior Managing Executive Officer, Director, Ikusuke Shimizu
Director, Kazuya Murakami
Outside Director, Hiroshi Oeda
Outside Director, Haruko Nozaki
Outside Director, Miharu Koezuka
Outside Director, Machiko Miyai
Outside Director, Yoshihiko Hatanaka
Auditors: KPMG AZSA LLC

LOCATIONS

HQ: Sekisui Chemical Co Ltd
 2-4-4 Nishitemma, Kita-ku, Osaka 530-8565
Phone: (81) 6 6365 4105
Web: www.sekisui.co.jp

2016 Sales

	% of total
Japan	74
Asia	11
America	8
Europe	6
Other	1
Total	100

PRODUCTS/OPERATIONS

2016 Sales

	% of total
Housing	43
High performance plastics	34
Urban infrastructure and environmental products	20
Other	3
Total	100

Selected Products
LCD fine particles, photosensitive materials,
Semiconductor materials
Optical adhesive tape and film, Double-faced tape, ITO film
Interlayer films for laminated glass
Polyolefin foam
Medical products
Packaging tape
CROSS-WAVE
Pipe materials
Pipeline rehabilitation
Industrial piping materials
Building materials and housing equipment
Performance materials
Housing

COMPETITORS
AMERICAN BUILDINGS COMPANY
BEHLEN MFG. CO.
BUTLER MANUFACTURING COMPANY
CHIEF INDUSTRIES, INC.
CORNERSTONE BUILDING BRANDS, INC.
HANDY & HARMAN LTD.
INDUSTRIAL ACOUSTICS COMPANY, INC.
MATERIAL SCIENCES CORPORATION
NCI GROUP, INC.
SUMITOMO HEAVY INDUSTRIES, LTD.

HISTORICAL FINANCIALS
Company Type: Public

Income Statement — FYE: March 31

	REVENUE ($mil)	NET INCOME ($mil)	NET PROFIT MARGIN	EMPLOYEES
03/23	9,329	520	5.6%	26,838
03/22	9,519	304	3.2%	26,419
03/21	9,542	375	3.9%	26,577
03/20	10,403	542	5.2%	27,003
03/19	10,318	596	5.8%	26,486
Annual Growth	(2.5%)	(3.4%)		0.3%

2023 Year-End Financials
Debt ratio: 0.1%
Return on equity: 10.0%
Cash ($ mil.): 758
Current Ratio: 1.90
Long-term debt ($ mil.): 722
No. of shares ($ mil.): 430
Dividends
 Yield: —
 Payout: 0.0%
Market value ($ mil.): —

Sekisui House, Ltd. (Japan)

Sekisui House could have written the book on Zen and the art of house building.

One of Japan's leading homebuilders, Sekisui House designs, prefabricates, and builds steel, wooden, and concrete houses and condominiums. It has built 2.2 billion homes. It is also involved in selling land, detached houses, and condominiums. Its real estate operations include leasing and managing houses, low-rise apartments, and commercial and retail buildings. Other operations include contract remodeling and landscaping. The company is also focusing on green building and sustainability in its new line of homes, and adds such features as fuel cells to its houses. Sekisui Chemical owns 10% of the company, which dates back to 1929.

EXECUTIVES

President, Chief Executive Officer, Representative Director, Yoshihiro Nakai
Vice-Chairman, Representative Director, Yosuke Horiuchi
Executive Vice President, Representative Director, Satoshi Tanaka
Senior Managing Executive Officer, Director, Toru Ishii
Senior Managing Executive Officer, Director, Hiroshi Shinozaki
Outside Director, Yukiko Yoshimaru
Outside Director, Toshifumi Kitazawa
Outside Director, Keiko Takegawa
Outside Director, Shinichi Abe
Outside Director, Yoshimi Nakajima
Auditors: Ernst & Young ShinNihon LLC

LOCATIONS

HQ: Sekisui House, Ltd. (Japan)
1-1-88 Oyodonaka, Kita-ku, Osaka 531-0076
Phone: (81) 6 6440 3111   **Fax:** (81) 6 6440 3331
Web: www.sekisuihouse.co.jp

PRODUCTS/OPERATIONS

Selected Subsidiaries and Affiliates
Sekisui House Umeda Operation Co., Ltd.
Sekiwa Real Estate Chubu, Ltd.
Sekiwa Real Estate Chugoku, Ltd.
Sekiwa Real Estate Kansai, Ltd.
Sekiwa Real Estate Kyushu, Ltd.
Sekiwa Real Estate Sapporo, Ltd.
Sekiwa Real Estate Tohoku, Ltd.
SGM Operation Co., Ltd

COMPETITORS

CADUS CORPORATION
CHAMPION ENTERPRISES HOLDINGS, LLC
CHRIS FREEMAN DESIGN LIMITED
CROWELL DON INC
DAVID POWERS HOMES, INC.
ENVOLVE CLIENT SERVICES GROUP, LLC
HOVNANIAN ENTERPRISES, INC.
RED SEAL DEVELOPMENT CORP.
ST JAMES GROUP LIMITED
TOLL BROTHERS, INC.

HISTORICAL FINANCIALS
Company Type: Public

Income Statement — FYE: January 31

	REVENUE ($mil)	NET INCOME ($mil)	NET PROFIT MARGIN	EMPLOYEES
01/23	22,453	1,414	6.3%	29,052
01/22	22,422	1,332	5.9%	28,821
01/21	23,358	1,179	5.0%	28,362
01/20	22,172	1,296	5.8%	27,397
01/19	19,886	1,183	6.0%	24,775
Annual Growth	3.1%	4.6%	—	4.1%

2023 Year-End Financials
Debt ratio: 0.1%
Return on equity: 11.8%
Cash ($ mil.): 2,552
Current Ratio: 2.00
Long-term debt ($ mil.): 1,359
No. of shares ($ mil.): 662
Dividends
Yield: 3.8%
Payout: 36.3%
Market value ($ mil.): 12,385

	STOCK PRICE ($) FY Close	P/E High/Low		PER SHARE ($) Earnings	Dividends	Book Value
01/23	18.70	0	0	2.12	0.73	18.90
01/22	20.23	0	0	1.97	0.74	18.91
01/21	19.47	0	0	1.73	0.82	18.60
01/20	21.51	0	0	1.89	0.73	17.01
01/19	15.09	0	0	1.71	0.71	15.83
Annual Growth	5.5%	—	—	5.4%	0.6%	4.5%

Seven & i Holdings Co. Ltd.

Japan's biggest retail conglomerate, Seven & i Holdings is a holding company that engages in a wide variety of business operations, including convenience stores, superstores, department stores, supermarkets, specialty stores, food services, and financial services. The company operates a network of about 85,000 stores globally and approximately 22,800 in Japan. Its convenience store operation mainly sells processed foods, fast foods, daily delivered foods, and non-food merchandise to customers visiting the directly managed corporate stores. With about 165 consolidated subsidiaries operating mainly in the retail business, the company was established in 2005 through share transfers between Seven-Eleven Japan Co., Ltd., Ito-Yokado Co., Ltd., and Denny's Japan Co., Ltd. It generates the majority of its revenue in North America.

Operations

Under the holding company structure, the company has classified its consolidated subsidiaries into six segments which are: Overseas convenience store operations (about 75% of the company's revenue), Superstore operations (more than 10%), Domestic convenience store operations (more than 5%), Department and specialty store operations (about 5%), Financial Services, and Others (together with financial services accounts for the rest).

The Overseas convenience store operations operate a convenience store business comprising directly managed corporate stores and franchised stores mainly under 7-Eleven, Inc.

The Superstore operations operate a retail business that provides a comprehensive range of daily life necessities such as food and other daily necessities.

The Domestic convenience store operations operate a convenience store business comprising directly managed corporate stores and franchised stores mainly under SEVEN-ELEVEN JAPAN CO., LTD.

The Department and specialty store operations operate a retail business that collects and provides various and high-dollar merchandise and services as well as advanced and unique merchandise and services.

The Financial Services operate a banking business, electronic money business, credit card business, and leasing business.

The Others operate several businesses including the real estate business.

Geographic Reach

Tokyo, Japan-based, the company operates approximately 85,000 stores globally and approximately 22,800 stores in Japan.

North America accounts for about 75% of the company's revenue, followed by Japan with about 25%, and the rest comes from other countries.

Sales and Marketing

The company primarily serves its customers through its convenience stores, superstores, supermarkets, specialty stores, and food services. It has approximately 59.9 million store visits per day globally and approximately 22 million store visits per day in Japan. Its financial services provides traditional banking services to individuals and businesses. The company's FCTI subsidiary is proud to be the exclusive ATM provider for 7-eleven stores throughout the US.

Financial Performance

Company's revenue for fiscal 2023 increased to JPY11.8 trillion compared from the prior year with JPY8.7 trillion. The increase was primarily due to higher revenues from overseas convenience store operations, offsetting the decrease in department and specialty store operations.

Cash held by the company at the end of fiscal 2023 increased to JPY1.7 trillion. Cash provided by operations was JPY928.5 billion while cash used for investing and financing activities were JPY413.2 billion and JPY27.4 billion, respectively. Main uses of cash were for acquisition of property and equipment, and dividends paid.

Strategy

7IN will continue to advance growth strategies in countries where the group already has stores and in those where it will open its first stores. By the fiscal year ending February 28, 2026, 7IN plans to establish a store network of 50,000 stores in areas outside

Japan and North America. By the fiscal year ending February 28, 2031, it plans to open stores in 30 countries and regions worldwide, including Japan and North America. Guided by these plans, 7IN will strive to achieve high-quality and speedy growth.

Company Background

Seven & i Holdings was founded in late 2005 to provide infrastructure and business services to its group of operating companies. 7-Eleven, Inc., became a wholly owned subsidiary shortly thereafter.

EXECUTIVES

President, Chief Executive Officer, Representative Director, Ryuichi Isaka
Executive Vice President, Chief Administrative Officer, Representative Director, Katsuhiro Goto
Senior Managing Executive Officer, Chief Sustainability Officer, Representative Director, Junro Ito
Senior Managing Executive Officer, Director, Fumihiko Nagamatsu
Senior Managing Executive Officer, Director, Joseph Michael DePinto
Managing Executive Officer, Chief Financial Officer, Director, Yoshimichi Maruyama
Managing Executive Officer, Chief Communications Officer, Chief Human Resources Officer, Kimiyoshi Yamaguchi
Managing Executive Officer, Chief Information Officer, Masaki Saito
Executive Officer, Chief Merchandising Development Officer, Masato Otake
Executive Officer, Chief Strategy Officer, Tamaki Wakita
Outside Director, Toshiro Yonemura
Outside Director, Yoshiyuki Izawa
Outside Director, Meyumi Yamada
Outside Director, Jenifer Simms Rogers
Outside Director, Shinji Wada
Outside Director, Fuminao Hachiuma
Outside Director, Paul K. Yonamine
Outside Director, Stephen Hayes Dacus
Outside Director, Elizabeth Miin Meyerdirk
Auditors : KPMG AZSA LLC

LOCATIONS

HQ: Seven & i Holdings Co. Ltd.
8-8 Nibancho, Chiyoda-ku, Tokyo 102-8452
Phone: (81) 3 6238 3000
Web: www.7andi.com

2018 Sales

	% of total
Japan	65
North America	33
Other regions	2
Total	100

PRODUCTS/OPERATIONS

2018 Sales

	% of total
Overseas convenience stores	33
Superstores	31
Domestic convenience stores	15
Department stores	11
Specialty stores	7
Financial services	3
Other	-
Total	100

Selected Subsidiaries and Affiliates

Convenience stores
  7-Eleven, Inc.
  Seven-Eleven (Beijing) Co.
  Seven-Eleven China Co.
  Seven-Eleven Hawaii, Inc.
  Seven-Eleven Japan Co.
Superstores
  Chengdu Ito-Yokado Co.
  Hua Tang Yokado Commercial Co.
  Ito-Yokado Co.
  KK. Sanei
  Marudai Co.
  SHELL GARDEN CO.
  York Mart Co.
  York-Benimaru Co.
Department stores
  Sogo & Seibu Co.
Specialty stores
  Barneys Japan
  Francfranc Corporation
  The Loft Co.
  Oshman's Japan Co.
  Seven & i Food Systems Co.
  Tower Records Japan
Financial services
  Seven Bank
  Seven Card Service Co.
  Seven Financial Service Co.

COMPETITORS

AEON CO., LTD.
BESTWAY (HOLDINGS) LIMITED
CASEY'S GENERAL STORES, INC.
CECONOMY AG
CFAO
EG GROUP LIMITED
ICELAND FOODS GROUP LIMITED
Itausa S/A
SPARTANNASH COMPANY
WESFARMERS LIMITED

HISTORICAL FINANCIALS

Company Type: Public

Income Statement   FYE: February 28

	REVENUE ($mil)	NET INCOME ($mil)	NET PROFIT MARGIN	EMPLOYEES
02/23	86,357	2,054	2.4%	167,248
02/22	75,733	1,824	2.4%	170,757
02/21	54,237	1,686	3.1%	135,332
02/20	61,118	2,006	3.3%	138,808
02/19	61,296	1,832	3.0%	144,628
Annual Growth	8.9%	2.9%	—	3.7%

2023 Year-End Financials

Debt ratio: 0.2%
Return on equity: 8.7%
Cash ($ mil.): 12,216
Current Ratio: 0.94
Long-term debt ($ mil.): 17,041
No. of shares ($ mil.): 2,653
Dividends
  Yield: 1.7%
  Payout: 49.2%
Market value ($ mil.): 59,392

	STOCK PRICE ($) FY Close	P/E High/Low		PER SHARE ($) Earnings	Dividends	Book Value
02/23	22.38	0	0	0.78	0.38	9.57
02/22	24.39	0	0	0.69	0.44	9.72
02/21	19.14	0	0	0.64	0.46	9.46
02/20	16.85	0	0	0.76	0.44	9.02
02/19	21.98	0	0	0.69	0.42	8.59
Annual Growth	0.5%			3.0%	(2.0%)	2.8%

SG Holdings Co Ltd

EXECUTIVES

Chairman, President, Representative Director, Eiichi Kuriwada
Representative Director, Hidekazu Matsumoto
Director, Masahide Motomura
Director, Shunichi Nakajima
Director, Katsuhiro Kawanago
Outside Director, Mika Takaoka
Outside Director, Osami Sagisaka
Outside Director, Masato Akiyama
Auditors : Deloitte Touche Tohmatsu LLC

LOCATIONS

HQ: SG Holdings Co Ltd
68 Kamitobatsunoda-cho, Minami-ku, Kyoto, Kyoto 601-8104
Phone: (81) 75 693 8850
Web: www.sg-hldgs.co.jp

HISTORICAL FINANCIALS

Company Type: Public

Income Statement   FYE: March 31

	REVENUE ($mil)	NET INCOME ($mil)	NET PROFIT MARGIN	EMPLOYEES
03/23	10,771	949	8.8%	52,268
03/22	13,058	877	6.7%	96,536
03/21	11,849	671	5.7%	97,774
03/20	10,810	435	4.0%	95,291
03/19	10,096	392	3.9%	92,982
Annual Growth	1.6%	24.7%		(13.4%)

2023 Year-End Financials

Debt ratio: 0.1%
Return on equity: 24.0%
Cash ($ mil.): 1,338
Current Ratio: 1.78
Long-term debt ($ mil.): 312
No. of shares ($ mil.): 630
Dividends
  Yield: —
  Payout: 7.8%
Market value ($ mil.): 10,531

	STOCK PRICE ($) FY Close	P/E High/Low		PER SHARE ($) Earnings	Dividends	Book Value
03/23	16.71	0	0	1.50	0.12	6.60
Annual Growth						

Shanghai Electric Group Co Ltd

EXECUTIVES

Board of Director Secretary, Rong Fu
Chief Technology Officer, President, Executive Director, Director, Ou Huang
President (Acting), President, Chief Executive Officer, Executive Director, Chairman, Jianhua Zheng
Chief Financial Officer, Kang Hu
Supervisor, Quanzhi Han
Staff Supervisor, Shengzhou Yuan
Staff Supervisor, Yan Zhang
Director, Non-executive Director, Minfang Yao
Director, An Li
Independent Director, Juntong Xi
Director, Zhaokai Zhu
Independent Director, Jianxin Xu
Independent Director, Yunhong Liu
Vice Chairman, Pin Gan
Auditors : PricewaterhouseCoopers Zhong Tian LLP

LOCATIONS

HQ: Shanghai Electric Group Co Ltd
No. 212 Qinjiang Road, Shanghai 200233
Phone: (86) 21 33261888   **Fax:** (86) 21 34695780
Web: www.shanghai-electric.com

HISTORICAL FINANCIALS

Company Type: Public

Income Statement				FYE: December 31
	REVENUE ($mil)	NET INCOME ($mil)	NET PROFIT MARGIN	EMPLOYEES
12/22	17,050	(516)	—	0
12/21	20,695	(1,573)	—	0
12/20	20,990	574	2.7%	0
12/19	18,324	503	2.7%	0
12/18	14,706	438	3.0%	0
Annual Growth	3.8%	—	—	—

2022 Year-End Financials

Debt ratio: 2.0%
Return on equity: (-6.3%)
Cash ($ mil.): 3,818
Current Ratio: 1.23
Long-term debt ($ mil.): 3,246
No. of shares ($ mil.): —
Dividends
Yield: —
Payout: 0.0%
Market value ($ mil.): —

Sharp Corp (Japan)

Sharp is primarily engaged in the manufacture and sale of telecommunications equipment, electrical equipment, electronic application equipment in general, and electronic components. The company's flagship products are LCDs, and PCs. The company also produces solar cells, laser diodes, and optical sensors. Other Sharp offerings are printers and cell phones; consumer audio and video products, such as Blu-ray disc players and LCD TVs; and a variety of appliances, such as air purifiers and steam ovens. Founded by Tokuji Hayakawa, Sharp traces its roots back to 1912 as metalworking shop in Matsui-cho, Honjo, Tokyo.

Operations

Sharp operates in three reportable segments: 8K Ecosystem (over 20% of total sales), Smart Life (over 15%), and ICT (nearly 15%).It also operates two devices businesses such as Display Device (nearly 35%) and Electronic Device (some 15%).

8K Ecosystem's products is comprised of color televisions, Blu-ray disc recorders, audio equipment, digital MFPs (multifunction printers), information displays, commercial projectors, POS systems, and audio equipment, among others. The Smart Life segment includes home appliances, telephones, storage batteries, and water foundries, while ICT's products are mobile phones and personal computers.

In addition, the Display device products include display modules and automotive cameras, while Electronic device offers camera modules, sensor modules, proximity sensors, dust sensors, wafer foundries, CMOS and CCD sensors, laser diodes.

Geographic Reach

Based in Osaka, Japan, Sharp has ten branches and five R&D facilities in Japan. It also has overseas R&D in US, China, Malaysia, and India.

Financial Performance

Company revenue for fiscal 2022 increased to JPY 2.5 trillion compared from the prior year with JPY 2.4 trillion.

Profit for fiscal 2022 increased to JPY 89.8 billion compared from the prior year with JPY 66.4 billion.

Cash held by the company at the end of fiscal 2022 decreased to JPY 239.4 billion. Cash provided by operations was JPY 75.2 billion while cash used for investing and financing activities were JPY 31.4 billion and JPY 124.3 billion, respectively.

Company Background

Tokuji Hayakawa established Hayakawa Electric Industry in 1912 to make a type of belt buckle he had designed. Three years later he invented the first mechanical pencil, named the Ever-Sharp, which was a commercial success. After an earthquake leveled much of Tokyo in 1923, including Hayakawa's business, he moved to Osaka and sold the rights to his pencil to finance a new factory. He introduced Japan's first crystal radio sets in 1925 and four years later debuted a vacuum tube radio.

Following WWII, Hayakawa Electric developed an experimental TV, which it began mass-producing in 1953. The company was ready with color TVs when Japan initiated color broadcasts in 1960. Hayakawa Electric grew tremendously during the 1960s, introducing microwave ovens (1962), solar cells (1963), the first electronic all-transistor-diode calculator (1964), and the first gallium arsenide LED (1969). The firm opened a US office in 1962. In 1970 the company began to make its own semiconductor devices and changed its name to Sharp Corp., a nod to the name of its first product.

HISTORY

Tokuji Hayakawa got started in manufacturing in 1912 when he established Hayakawa Electric Industry to make a type of belt buckle he had designed. Three years later he invented the first mechanical pencil, named the Ever-Sharp, which was a commercial success. After an earthquake leveled much of Tokyo in 1923, including Hayakawa's business, he moved to Osaka and sold the rights to his pencil to finance a new factory. He introduced Japan's first crystal radio sets in 1925 and four years later debuted a vacuum tube radio.

Following WWII, Hayakawa Electric developed an experimental TV, which it began mass-producing in 1953. The company was ready with color TVs when Japan initiated color broadcasts in 1960. Hayakawa Electric grew tremendously during the 1960s, introducing microwave ovens (1962), solar cells (1963), the first electronic all-transistor-diode calculator (1964), and the first gallium arsenide LED (1969). The firm opened a US office in 1962.

In 1970 the company began to make its own semiconductor devices and changed its name to Sharp Corporation, a nod to the name of its first product. It began mass production of LCDs in 1973. Sharp later introduced the first electronic calculator with an LCD (1973), solar-powered calculators (1976), and a credit card-sized calculator (1979).

EXECUTIVES

President, Chief Executive Officer, Representative Director, Po-Hsuan Wu
Executive Vice President, Representative Director, Masahiro Okitsu
Outside Director, Limin Hu
Outside Director, Steve Shyh Chen
Outside Director, Hsu-Tung Lu
Outside Director, Yasuo Himeiwa
Outside Director, Yutaka Nakagawa
Auditors : PricewaterhouseCoopers Aarata LLC

LOCATIONS

HQ: Sharp Corp (Japan)
1 Takumi-cho, Sakai-ku, Sakai, Osaka 590-8522
Phone: (81) 72 282 1221   **Fax:** 201 529-8425
Web: www.sharp.co.jp

PRODUCTS/OPERATIONS

2015 Sales

	% of total
Products business	54
Device business	46
Total	100

Selected Products

Consumer/information products
    Audiovisual and communication equipment
    Audio amplifiers
    Blu-ray disc players
    Digital cameras
    High-definition televisions

Liquid crystal display DVD televisions
Liquid crystal display televisions
Liquid crystal display video projectors
Mobile phones
Video cameras
Information equipment
Calculators
Digital copiers
Fax machines
Mobile business tools
Personal computers
Printers
Home appliances
Air cleaning systems
Superheated steam ovens
Electronic components
Flash memory
Integrated circuits
Laser diodes and other optoelectronic devices
Radio-frequency components
Satellite broadcasting components
Solar cells and other photovoltaic devices

COMPETITORS

BOSE CORPORATION
EMERSON RADIO CORP.
KOSS CORPORATION
MARSHALL AMPLIFICATION PLC
NATIONAL SEMICONDUCTOR CORPORATION
NIDEC CORPORATION
PGI, INC.
PHOTRONICS, INC.
PIONEER CORPORATION
ZENITH ELECTRONICS CORPORATION

HISTORICAL FINANCIALS

Company Type: Public

Income Statement — FYE: March 31

	NET REVENUE ($mil)	NET INCOME ($mil)	NET PROFIT MARGIN	EMPLOYEES
03/23	19,132	(1,958)	—	46,200
03/22	20,516	608	3.0%	47,941
03/21	21,909	481	2.2%	50,478
03/20	20,923	193	0.9%	52,876
03/19	21,672	670	3.1%	54,156
Annual Growth	(3.1%)	—	—	(3.9%)

2023 Year-End Financials

Debt ratio: 0.3%
Return on equity: (-78.6%)
Cash ($ mil.): 1,967
Current Ratio: 1.23
Long-term debt ($ mil.): 4,074
No. of shares ($ mil.): 649
Dividends
 Yield: 4.2%
 Payout: 0.0%
Market value ($ mil.): 1,123

	STOCK PRICE ($) FY Close	P/E High/Low		PER SHARE ($) Earnings	Dividends	Book Value
03/23	1.73	—	—	(3.06)	0.07	2.41
03/22	2.27	0	0	1.00	0.07	6.12
03/21	4.29	0	0	0.79	0.04	5.18
03/20	2.59	0	0	0.30	0.05	4.77
03/19	2.74	0	0	0.83	0.02	5.95
Annual Growth	(10.8%)	—	—	—	34.3%	(20.2%)

Shell plc

Royal Dutch Shell (Shell) boasts worldwide proved reserves of 1.3 billion barrels of oil equivalent. Operating in over 70 countries, the British-Dutch company pumps out 3.6 million barrels of crude oil, liquefied natural gas (LNG), natural gas, synthetic crude oil, and bitumen. Among the company's many and varied operations, it boasts the world's deepest oil and gas project in the Gulf of Mexico, the world's largest offshore floating LNG production plant off the Australian coast, and the world's largest retail fuel network at about 46,000 stations. Royal Dutch Shell also runs over 20 refineries, transports natural gas, trades gas and electricity, and develops renewable energy.

Operations

Shell divides its operations into five segments: Integrated Gas, Upstream, Oil Products, Chemicals and Corporate.

Its Oil Products business is part of an integrated value chain that refines crude oil and other feedstocks into products that are moved and marketed around the world for domestic, industrial and transport use. The products it sells include gasoline, diesel, heating oil, aviation fuel, marine fuel, low-carbon fuels, lubricants, bitumen and sulphur. It also trade crude oil, oil products and petrochemicals. It provides access to electric vehicle charge points at home, at work and on-the-go, including at its forecourts and at a range of public locations. The Oil Products generate some 70% of total sales.

Integrated Gas comprises the company's liquefied natural gas (LNG) operations, including exploration, extraction, and transportation. Other activities include the marketing and trading of crude oil, natural gas, LNG, electricity, and carbon-emission rights, and the sale of LNG as a fuel for heavy-duty vehicles and vessels. Shell's investments in renewable and other low-carbon energy forms, its New Energies business, are housed in this segment. The Integrated Gas segment accounts for nearly 20% of total sales.

Chemicals business supplies customers with a range of base and intermediate chemicals used to make products that people use every day. It has a major manufacturing plants which are located close to refineries, and its own marketing network. Chemicals represent more than 5% of total sales.

Shell's Upstream segment explores for and extracts crude oil, natural gas, and natural gas liquids. It also markets oil and gas and delivers them to market. The Upstream segment generates some 5% of total sales.

The Corporate segment covers the non-operating activities supporting Shell. It comprises Shell's holdings and treasury organisation, self-insurance activities and headquarters and central functions.

Geographic Reach

Listed in London but run out of The Hague in the Netherlands, Royal Dutch Shell has enormous global reach, producing oil and natural gas in more than 70 countries, including Australia, Brazil, Brunei, Canada, China, Denmark, Germany, Malaysia, the Netherlands, Nigeria, Norway, Oman, Qatar, Russia, the UK, and the US.

Shell operates about 46,000 fuel stations across 70 countries. Royal Dutch Shell's lubricants business produces, markets, and sells products in over 160 market and has four base oil manufacturing plants, more than 30 lubricant blending plants, eight grease plants, and four gas-to-liquid base oil storage hubs.

It makes about 35% of revenue from its Asia/Oceania/Africa reporting region, roughly 30% each from Europe, and US. Other Americas (Brazil in particular) account for the remainder.

Financial Performance

The company's revenue for fiscal 2020 decreased to $180.5 billion compared with $344.9 billion in the previous year.

Loss for fiscal 2020 was $21.7 billion compared to the prior year with an income of $15.8 billion.

Cash held by the company at the end of fiscal 2020 increased to $31.8 billion. Cash provided by operations was $34.1 billion, while cash used for investing and financing activities were $13.3 billion and $7.2 billion, respectively. Main cash uses were capital expenditures, dividends paid and repurchases of shares.

Strategy

Powering Progress sets out Shell's strategy to accelerate the transition of its business to net-zero emissions, in step with society. It is designed to deliver value for its shareholders, for its customers and for wider society. Powering Progress serves four main goals: generating shareholder value, achieving net-zero emissions, powering lives and respecting nature.

The company is transforming its company across its three business pillars of Growth, Transition and Upstream. The company's growth pillar includes its service stations, traditional and low-carbon fuels, integrated power, hydrogen, charging for electric vehicles, nature-based solutions, and carbon capture and storage. It focuses on working with its customers to accelerate the transition to net-zero emissions.

Shell's Transition pillar comprises its Integrated Gas, and its Chemicals and Products businesses, and produces sustainable cash flow. The company's Upstream pillar delivers the cash and returns needed to fund its shareholder distributions and the transformation of its company, by providing vital supplies of oil and natural gas.

HISTORY

In 1870 Marcus Samuel inherited an interest in his father's London trading company, which imported seashells from the Far East. He expanded the business and, after securing a contract for Russian oil, began selling kerosene in the Far East.

Standard Oil underpriced competitors to defend its Asian markets. Samuel secretly prepared his response and in 1892 unveiled the first of a fleet of tankers. Rejecting Standard's acquisition overtures, Samuel created "Shell" Transport and Trading in 1897.

Meanwhile, a Dutchman, Aeilko Zijlker, struck oil in Sumatra and formed Royal Dutch Petroleum in 1890 to exploit the oil field. Young Henri Deterding joined the firm in 1896 and established a sales force in the Far East.

Deterding became Royal Dutch's head in 1900 amid the battle for the Asian market. In 1903 Deterding, Samuel, and the Rothschilds (a French banking family) created Asiatic Petroleum, a marketing alliance. With Shell's non-Asian business eroding, Deterding engineered a merger between Royal Dutch and Shell in 1907. Royal Dutch shareholders got 60% control; "Shell" Transport and Trading, 40%.

After the 1911 Standard Oil breakup, Deterding entered the US, building refineries and buying producers. Shell products were available in every state by 1929. Royal Dutch/Shell joined the 1928 "As Is" cartel that fixed prices for most of two decades.

The post-WWII Royal Dutch/Shell profited from worldwide growth in oil consumption. It acquired 100% of Shell Oil, its US arm, in 1985, but shareholders sued, maintaining Shell Oil's assets had been undervalued in the deal. They were awarded $110 million in 1990.

Management's slow response to two 1995 controversies -- environmentalists' outrage over the planned sinking of an oil platform and human rights activists' criticism of Royal Dutch/Shell's role in Nigeria -- spurred a major shakeup. It began moving away from its decentralized structure and adopted a new policy of corporate openness.

In 1996 Royal Dutch/Shell and Exxon (now Exxon Mobil) formed a worldwide petroleum additives venture. Shell Oil joined Texaco (now part of Chevron) in 1998 to form Equilon Enterprises, combining US refining and marketing operations in the West and Midwest. Similarly, Shell Oil, Texaco, and Saudi Arabia's Aramco combined downstream operations on the US's East and Gulf coasts as Motiva Enterprises.

In 1999 Royal Dutch/Shell and the UK's BG plc acquired a controlling stake in Comgas, a unit of Companhia EnergÃ‰tica de SÃƒo Paulo and the largest natural gas distributor in Brazil, for about $1 billion.

In 2000 the company sold its coal business to UK-based mining giant Anglo American for more than $850 million. To gain a foothold in the US power marketing scene, Royal Dutch/Shell formed a joint venture with construction giant Bechtel (called InterGen). The next year the company agreed to combine its German refining and marketing operations with those of RWE-DEA. Royal Dutch/Shell tried to expand its US natural gas reserves in 2001 by making a $2 billion hostile bid for Barrett Resources, but the effort was withdrawn after Barrett agreed to be acquired by Williams for $2.5 billion.

In 2002, in connection with Chevron's acquisition of Texaco, Royal Dutch/Shell acquired ChevronTexaco's (now Chevron) stakes in the underperforming US marketing joint ventures Equilon and Motiva. That year the company, through its US Shell Oil unit, acquired Pennzoil-Quaker State for $1.8 billion. Also that year Royal Dutch/Shell acquired Enterprise Oil for $5 billion, plus debt. In addition, it purchased RWE's 50% stake in German refining and marketing joint venture Shell & DEA Oil (for $1.35 billion).

In 2004 the group signed a $200 million exploration deal with Libya, signaling its return to that country after a more than decade-long absence. Also that year the company reported that it had overestimated its reserves by 24%. The bad news resulted in the ouster of the chairman and CFO.

The Anglo-Dutch entity restructured to stay competitive. Revelations of overestimated oil reserves in 2004 prompted a push for greater transparency in the company's organizational structure. This led to the 2005 merger of former publicly traded owners Royal Dutch Petroleum and The "Shell" Transport and Trading Company into Royal Dutch Shell.

Searching for new oil assets, in 2006 the company acquired a large swath of oil sands acreage in Alberta, Canada. Further boosting its oil sands business, in 2007 the company acquired the 22% of Shell Canada that it did not already own. The company also began investing some $12 billion (in addition to the $2.6 billion already spent) in offshore projects near Dubai. In 2008 Royal Dutch Shell expanded its exploration assets in Alaska by acquiring 275 lease blocks in the Chukchi Sea, for $2.1 billion.

In 2009 the company made significant oil discoveries in the deepwater eastern Gulf of Mexico at West Boreas, Vito and the Cardamom Deep, and in 2010 at the Appomattox prospect in the Mississippi Canyon block. The finds expanded Shell Oil's long-term development plans in the area.

Further expanding its unconventional natural gas resources, in 2010 the company spent $4.7 billion to acquire East Resources, which holds 1 million acres of Marcellus Shale, one of the fastest-growing shale plays in the US.

On the conventional side of the oil business, the Gulf of Mexico produces 370,000 barrels of oil per day, or about 15% of Royal Dutch Shell's worldwide production. In 2010 the company claimed an industry record, starting production at the deepest floating drilling and production platform in the world. The Perdido Development operates in 8,000 ft. of water in the Gulf of Mexico. In response to the BP oil rig disaster in the Gulf of Mexico, the company joined forces with Exxon Mobil, Chevron, and ConocoPhillips to form a $1 billion rapid-response joint venture that will be able to better manage and contain future deepwater spills.

With an eye toward raising cash and focusing on its majority holdings and joint ventures, rather than on minority held businesses, in 2010 Royal Dutch Shell sold 10% of its 34% in Australian oil and gas enterprise Woodside Petroleum for $3.3 billion. Royal Dutch Shell also announced that it would seek to sell the rest of its stake in Woodside Petroleum over time. (Earlier in the year the company formed a $3.5 billion joint venture with PetroChina, which acquired Arrow Energy, a company with major natural gas assets in Northern Australia).

As part of its strategy of selling noncore downstream assets to raise cash, in 2010 Royal Dutch Shell sold its Finnish and Swedish operations (including a refinery in Gothenburg and 565 gas stations) to Finland-based St1 for $640 million. In 2011 it sold its UK-based Stanlow refinery to India's Essar Group for $350 million.

In 2010 the company formed a $12 billion joint venture with Brazil's Cosan to ramp up ethanol production.

EXECUTIVES

Chief Executive Officer, Executive Director, Wael Sawan
Chief Financial Officer, Executive Director, Sinead Gorman
Chief Human Resources Officer, Corporate Director, Ronan Cassidy
Sustainability Director, Corporate Relations Director, Strategy Director, Ed Daniels
Projects & Technology Director, Harry Brekelmans
Legal Director, Donny Ching
Secretary, Caroline J.M. Omloo
Chair, Independent Non-Executive Director, Andrew Mackenzie
Deputy Chairman, Senior Independent Director, Euleen Goh
Independent Non-Executive Director, Charles Roxburgh
Independent Non-Executive Director, Leena Srivastava
Independent Non-Executive Director, Dick Boer
Independent Non-Executive Director, Neil Carson
Independent Non-Executive Director, Ann Godbehere
Independent Non-Executive Director, Catherine J. Hughes
Independent Non-Executive Director, Martina Hund-Mejean
Independent Non-Executive Director, Abraham ("Bram") Schot
Independent Non-Executive Director, Jane H. Lute
Independent Non-Executive Director, Cyrus Taraporevala
Auditors : Ernst & Young LLP

LOCATIONS

HQ: Shell plc
  Shell Centre, London SE1 7NA
Phone: —
Web: www.shell.com

2018 Sales

	% of total
Asia, Oceania, Africa	39
Europe	31
USA	23
Other Americas	7
Total	100

PRODUCTS/OPERATIONS

2018 Sales

	% of total
Downstream	86
Integrated Gas	11
Upstream	3
Total	100

COMPETITORS

ARD Holdings S.A.
CHEVRON CORPORATION
CONOCOPHILLIPS
Chicago Bridge & Iron Company N.V.
Equinor ASA
Frank's International N.V.
Koninklijke Vopak N.V.
Louis Dreyfus Holding B.V.
LyondellBasell Industries N.V.
Nostrum Oil & Gas PLC

HISTORICAL FINANCIALS

Company Type: Public

Income Statement — FYE: December 31

	REVENUE ($mil)	NET INCOME ($mil)	NET PROFIT MARGIN	EMPLOYEES
12/23	323,183	19,359	6.0%	103,000
12/22	386,201	42,309	11.0%	87,000
12/21	272,657	20,101	7.4%	82,000
12/20	183,195	(21,680)	—	86,000
12/19	352,106	15,842	4.5%	83,000
Annual Growth	(2.1%)	5.1%		5.5%

2023 Year-End Financials

Debt ratio: 20.1%
Return on equity: 10.2%
Cash ($ mil.): 38,774
Current Ratio: 1.40
Long-term debt ($ mil.): 71,610
No. of shares ($ mil.): 6,486
Dividends
Yield: —
Payout: 86.8%
Market value ($ mil.): 426,798

	STOCK PRICE ($) FY Close	P/E High/Low	PER SHARE ($) Earnings	Dividends	Book Value
12/23	65.80	24 19	2.85	2.47	28.77
12/22	56.95	11 8	5.71	1.98	27.29
Annual Growth	15.5%	—	(15.9%)	5.7%	1.3%

Shiga Bank, Ltd.

Shiga Bank, established in 1933, has grown to become the largest bank in the Shiga prefecture. The bank and its 14 subsidiaries provide customers with typical banking products and services, credit card, leasing, and venture capital financing services, and accepts negotiable certificates of deposits and installment-deposits fixed-term savings products. Shiga Bank's primary customers are individuals and small and medium-sized businesses. The bank, which operates nearly 140 offices and branches in Japan, Hong Kong, and Thailand (as well as 10 agents), is banking on the region's expanding economy to improve local economies in the Kyoto and Shiga prefectures. Shiga Bank if controlled by Japan Trustee Service Bank.

EXECUTIVES

President, Representative Director, Shojiro Takahashi
Senior Managing Director, Representative Director, Motohiro Nishi
Senior Managing Director, Representative Director, Shinya Kubota
Director, Takahiro Saito
Director, Katsuyoshi Horiuchi
Director, Katsuyuki Nishikawa
Outside Director, Hajime Yasui
Outside Director, Minako Takeuchi
Director, Rikiya Hattori
Auditors: Deloitte Touche Tohmatsu LLC

LOCATIONS

HQ: Shiga Bank, Ltd.
1-38 Hamamachi, Otsu, Shiga 520-8686
Phone: (81) 77 521 9530
Web: www.shigagin.com

COMPETITORS

BANK OF AYUDHYA PUBLIC COMPANY LIMITED
CHUGOKU BANK, LIMITED, THE
EHIME BANK, LTD., THE
HACHIJUNI BANK, LTD., THE
NISHI-NIPPON CITYBANK, LTD.

HISTORICAL FINANCIALS

Company Type: Public

Income Statement — FYE: March 31

	ASSETS ($mil)	NET INCOME ($mil)	INCOME AS % OF ASSETS	EMPLOYEES
03/21	70,388	103	0.1%	3,439
03/20	57,899	114	0.2%	3,480
03/19	55,219	132	0.2%	3,487
03/18	55,327	130	0.2%	3,570
03/17	49,545	133	0.3%	3,627
Annual Growth	9.2%	(6.1%)	—	(1.3%)

2021 Year-End Financials

Return on assets: 0.1%
Return on equity: 2.6%
Long-term debt ($ mil.): —
No. of shares ($ mil.): 49
Sales ($ mil.): 799
Dividends
Yield: —
Payout: 18.1%
Market value ($ mil.): —

Shikoku Bank, Ltd. (Japan)

Shikoku Bank is primarily a provider of banking services to customers in Japan's Shikoku prefecture. The bank's financial services include both commercial and retail banking and lending among others. Shikoku Bank serves local businesses, individuals consumers, and public agencies through about 110 branches. The bank also operates six domestic subsidiaries.

EXECUTIVES

President, Representative Director, Fumiaki Yamamoto
Senior Managing Director, Representative Director, Yoshitsugu Ota
Director, Tatsuji Kobayashi
Director, Masahiko Suka
Director, Masato Hashitani
Director, Isao Shiraishi
Director, Hiroyuki Hamada
Director, Mitsufumi Ito
Outside Director, Yoshinori Ozaki
Director, Shinichiro Kumazawa
Outside Director, Masahiro Hamada
Outside Director, Chieko Inada
Outside Director, Yasushi Kanamoto
Outside Director, Toshikazu Sakai
Auditors: Ernst & Young ShinNihon LLC

LOCATIONS

HQ: Shikoku Bank, Ltd. (Japan)
1-1-1 Minami-Harimayacho, Kochi 780-8605
Phone: (81) 88 823 2111
Web: www.shikokubank.co.jp

COMPETITORS

CHUKYO BANK, LIMITED.
DAISAN BANK, LTD., THE
FUKUI BANK, LTD., THE
YAMAGATA BANK, LTD., THE
YAMANASHI CHUO BANK, LTD., THE

HISTORICAL FINANCIALS

Company Type: Public

Income Statement — FYE: March 31

	ASSETS ($mil)	NET INCOME ($mil)	INCOME AS % OF ASSETS	EMPLOYEES
03/22	29,865	65	0.2%	1,842
03/21	30,083	59	0.2%	1,908
03/20	27,617	28	0.1%	1,952
03/19	27,801	56	0.2%	1,998
03/18	28,510	67	0.2%	2,028
Annual Growth	1.2%	(0.8%)	—	(2.4%)

2022 Year-End Financials

Return on assets: 0.2%
Return on equity: 5.0%
Long-term debt ($ mil.): —
No. of shares ($ mil.): 41
Sales ($ mil.): 358
Dividends
Yield: —
Payout: 20.9%
Market value ($ mil.): —

Shimizu Corp.

Shimizu provides architectural, engineering, construction, and development services for commercial, industrial, infrastructure, and residential projects around the world. One of Japan's largest general contractors, the company has worked on major projects including Tokyo's Metro subway, Singapore's Changi Airport, and the Malaysia-Singapore Bridge. Other areas of specialization range from offices and power stations to railroads and dams. Shimizu has increasingly focused on green building and urban renewal projects. Needless to say, earthquake-resistant technologies and earthquake restoration projects are key to Shimizu's business. The company also provides facilities management. Shimizu was founded in 1804.

Operations
The company is engaged in construction, real estate development and other related businesses.

The Construction business is operated by branches located in various regions. The segment accounts for 90% of revenue.

The Real estate business involves in the development rental and sales. It is operated by the Investment and Development division. The segment accounts for the remaining 10% of revenue.

Geographic Reach
The company boasts more than 70 offices mostly across Japan, though it also operates in other parts of Asia, the Middle East, Europe, Africa, and North America.

Sales and Marketing
Shimizu mostly serves the office, medical and welfare, educational and cultural, production and research, logistics, and residential markets.

Financial Performance
Note: Growth rates may differ after conversion to US dollars.

The company's revenue increased to Â¥1.70 billion in fiscal 2020 compared to Â¥1.66 billion in the prior year.

Cash held by the company at the end of fiscal 2020 increased to Â¥352.7 billion. Cash provided by operations and financing activities were Â¥170.6 billion and Â¥68.7 billion, respectively. Cash used for investing activities was Â¥115.7 billion.

Strategy
Shimizu has positioned the five years of Mid-Term Management Plan (2019? 2023) as a period of advance investment to establish a new profit base. The company is pushing forcefully ahead on implementing this plan to expand and evolve the construction business, establish a profit base in non-construction businesses, and strengthen the management base to support growth. Shimizu will accelerate global expansion and pursue ESG management to enhance Shimizu's corporate value and contribute to the achievement of SDGs as its basic policy.

The company currently focuses on expanding and evolving the construction business; establishing a profit base in non-construction businesses; accelerating global expansion; and strengthening the management platform to support growth.

EXECUTIVES

Chairman, Representative Director, Yoichi Miyamoto
President, Representative Director, Kazuyuki Inoue
Executive Vice President, Director, Hiroshi Fujimura
Executive Vice President, Representative Director, Kentaro Ikeda
Executive Vice President, Toru Yamaji
Executive Vice President, Yoshito Tsutsumi
Senior Managing Executive Officer, Tatsuya Shinmura
Senior Managing Executive Officer, Masanobu Onishi
Senior Managing Executive Officer, Director, Takeshi Sekiguchi
Senior Managing Executive Officer, Takao Haneda
Senior Managing Executive Officer, Kouichi Yamashita
Senior Managing Executive Officer, Representative Director, Yoshiki Higashi
Senior Managing Executive Officer, Akira Yamazaki
Director, Noriaki Shimizu
Outside Director, Tamotsu Iwamoto
Outside Director, Junichi Kawada
Outside Director, Mayumi Tamura
Outside Director, Yumiko Jozuka
Auditors : Ernst & Young ShinNihon LLC

LOCATIONS

HQ: Shimizu Corp.
2-16-1 Kyobashi, Chuo-ku, Tokyo 104-8370
Phone: (81) 3 3561 1111 **Fax:** 770 956-7575
Web: www.shimz.co.jp

2014 Sales

	% of total
Japan	89
Asia	10
Other	1
Total	100

PRODUCTS/OPERATIONS

2014 Sales

	% of total
Construction contracts	90
Real estate development and other	10
Total	100

Selected Projects
Overseas Projects
Factory, Toyota Industries Compressor Parts America, Co. (TICA)HMSI 3rd FactoryKarawang Factory PT. SHARP ELECTRONICS INDONESIANipro Pharma Vietnam PlantUmiray BridgeUrban Suites
Domestic Project
Naoetsu LNG terminalOsaki Wiz CityShintakamatsu Data Center, PowericoYomiuri Shimbun, Tokyo Head OfficeSelected Subsidiaries
Daiichi Setsubi Engineering Corporation
Katayama Stratech Corp.
Milx Corporation
Shimizu Comprehensive Development Corporation
Super Regional, Inc.
The Nippon Road Co., Ltd.
TTK Corporation

COMPETITORS

AECOM
BOWMER AND KIRKLAND LIMITED
CREST NICHOLSON PLC
DAIWA HOUSE INDUSTRY CO., LTD.
HYDER CONSULTING GROUP HOLDINGS LIMITED
INSTALLED BUILDING PRODUCTS, INC.
LAING O'ROURKE PLC.
LENDLEASE CORPORATION LIMITED
LINDUM GROUP LIMITED
RENEW HOLDINGS PLC.

HISTORICAL FINANCIALS
Company Type: Public

Income Statement — FYE: March 31

	REVENUE ($mil)	NET INCOME ($mil)	NET PROFIT MARGIN	EMPLOYEES
03/23	14,519	368	2.5%	22,509
03/22	12,191	392	3.2%	22,286
03/21	13,154	697	5.3%	18,894
03/20	15,645	911	5.8%	18,475
03/19	15,034	899	6.0%	18,499
Annual Growth	(0.9%)	(20.0%)	—	5.0%

2023 Year-End Financials
Debt ratio: 0.2%   No. of shares ($ mil.): 740
Return on equity: 5.8%   Dividends
Cash ($ mil.): 2,798   Yield: —
Current Ratio: 1.34   Payout: 0.0%
Long-term debt ($ mil.): 2,576   Market value ($ mil.): —

Shin-Etsu Chemical Co., Ltd.

The Shin-Etsu Group makes a wide array of products for use in a broad range of industrial fields by drawing on the production technologies accumulated in the process of continuously diversifying and improving its product offerings. The company makes polyvinyl chloride (PVC) and more than 5,000 types of silicone, while its electronics materials unit makes semiconductor silicon, epoxy molding compounds, and rare earth magnets. Shin-Etsu also produces synthetic quartz used for fiber-optic communications and in LCD panels. Shin-Etsu operates in the US as Shintech, an integrated PVC production plant under construction in Louisiana. Majority of its sales were generated outside Japan. It was established in 1926 as Shin-Etsu Nitrogen Fertilizer Co., Ltd.

Operations
The company's four segment includes Infrastructure Materials (about 40% of sales), Electronic Materials (more than 30%), Functional Materials (roughly 20%), and Processing and Specialized Services (some 10%).

The Infrastructure Materials segment provides products indispensable to many aspects of life, from pipes for water supply and sewerage systems and other types of infrastructure to housing, agriculture, and daily necessities. These products include PVC, caustic soda, and polyvinyl alcohol (POVAL).

The Electronic Materials segment offers photoresists, photomask blanks, and encapsulant materials used in the semiconductor manufacturing process, while remaining at the forefront of the industry as the world's largest manufacturer of silicon wafers. It also supplies rare earth magnets, which are indispensable for reducing the size, weight, and power consumption of motors used in hybrid and electric vehicles, industrial equipment, and home appliances, as well as high purity synthetic quartz used as a material for optical fiber and large-scale photomask substrate.

The Functional Materials segment has developed over 5,000 different products that leverage the outstanding properties of silicone. It is now Japan's largest silicone manufacturer as well as on of the world's leading manufacturers. It also boast the largest market share in Japan for cellulose derivatives, which has a wide range of applications in the pharma, food, and industrial fields.

The Processing and Specialized Services segment applies and deploys fundamental technologies in the areas of materials and compounding, design, molding process, and evaluation and analysis for various resins such as PVC and silicone.

Geographic Reach

The company is headquartered in Tokyo, Japan. The company has over 25 plants and around 15 companies in Japan, and about 95 locations in about 20 countries, overseas. The US generated about 30% of sales, followed by Japan and Asia/Oceania (excluding China) with over 20% each, and Europe, China and others generated about 10% each.

Financial Performance

Net sales in FY2021 increased 39% or Â¥577.5 billion, compared to the previous year, amounting to Â¥2.1 trillion.

In 2022, the company had a net income of Â¥500.1 billion, a 73% increase from the previous year's net income of Â¥402.1 billion.

The company's cash at the end of 2022 was Â¥1 trillion. Operating activities generated Â¥553.5 billion, while investing activities used Â¥253.7 billion, mainly for purchases of property, plant and equipment. Financing activities used another Â¥122.5 billion, primarily for payment of cash dividends.

EXECUTIVES

Chairman of Board, Representative Director, Fumio Akiya

President, Representative Director, Yasuhiko Saitoh

Senior Managing Executive Officer, Director, Susumu Ueno

Senior Managing Executive Officer, Director, Masahiko Todoroki

Outside Director, Toshihiko Fukui

Outside Director, Hiroshi Komiyama

Outside Director, Kuniharu Nakamura

Outside Director, Michael H. McGarry

Outside Director, Mariko Hasegawa

Auditors : Ernst & Young ShinNihon LLC

LOCATIONS

HQ: Shin-Etsu Chemical Co., Ltd.
 1-4-1 Marunouchi, Chiyoda-ku, Tokyo 100-0005
Phone: (81) 3 6812 2300   **Fax:** 713 965-0629
Web: www.shinetsu.co.jp

2015 Sales

	% of total
Japan	28
US	22
Asia/Oceania (excluding china)	19
Europe	12
China	10
Others	9
Total	100

PRODUCTS/OPERATIONS

2015 Sales

	% of total
PVC/Chlor-Alkali	36
Semiconductor Silicon	18
Electronics & Functional Materials	15
Silicones	14
Speciality Chemicals	9
Diversified	8
Total	100

Selected products

PVC Chlor-Alkali
Polyvinyl chloride
Caustic soda
Chloromethane
Specialty Chemicals
Cellulose derivatives
Silicon metal
Poval (Polyvinyl alcohol)
Synthetic pheromones
Silicones
Semiconductor Silicon
Electronics & Functional Materials
Rare earth magnets
Encapsulation materials
Photoresists
Photomask blanks
Synthetic quartz products
Epoxy molding compounds
Pellicles
Diversified Business
Processed plastics
Export of plant equipment
International trading
Engineering
Information processing
Wafer container

COMPETITORS

AGC INC.
ARKEMA INC.
CLARIANT CORPORATION
EASTMAN CHEMICAL COMPANY
MPM HOLDINGS INC.
OXY CHEMICAL CORPORATION
SHINTECH INCORPORATED
THE HALLSTAR COMPANY
TORAY PLASTICS (AMERICA), INC.
UBE INDUSTRIES, LTD.

HISTORICAL FINANCIALS

Company Type: Public

Income Statement   FYE: March 31

	REVENUE ($mil)	NET INCOME ($mil)	NET PROFIT MARGIN	EMPLOYEES
03/23	21,089	5,317	25.2%	25,717
03/22	17,054	4,111	24.1%	24,954
03/21	13,519	2,652	19.6%	26,524
03/20	14,219	2,892	20.3%	25,697
03/19	14,393	2,791	19.4%	24,380
Annual Growth	10.0%	17.5%	—	1.3%

2023 Year-End Financials

Debt ratio: —   No. of shares ($ mil.): 2,017
Return on equity: 19.6%   Dividends
Cash ($ mil.): 10,884   Yield: 5.2%
Current Ratio: 5.64   Payout: 13.5%
Long-term debt ($ mil.): 141   Market value ($ mil.): 81,549

	STOCK PRICE ($) FY Close	P/E High/Low		PER SHARE ($) Earnings	Dividends	Book Value
03/23	40.42	0	0	2.61	0.86	14.42
03/22	37.93	0	0	1.98	0.64	13.18
03/21	42.41	0	0	1.28	0.52	12.24
03/20	24.45	0	0	1.39	0.49	11.76
03/19	21.03	0	0	1.31	0.16	10.69
Annual Growth	17.7%			18.8%	52.3%	7.8%

Shizuoka Bank Ltd (Japan)

EXECUTIVES

Chairman, Chief Executive Officer, Representative Director, Katsunori Nakanishi

President, Chief Operating Officer, Representative Director, Hisashi Shibata

Deputy President, Chief Financial Officer, Representative Director, Minoru Yagi

Senior Managing Director, Mitsuhide Sugita

Senior Managing Executive Officer, Director, Yutaka Fukushima

Director, Koichi Kiyokawa

Outside Director, Kumi Fujisawa

Outside Director, Motoshige Ito

Outside Director, Kazuto Tsubouchi

Outside Director, Kazutoshi Inano

Auditors : Deloitte Touche Tohmatsu LLC

LOCATIONS

HQ: Shizuoka Bank Ltd (Japan)
 1-10 Gofuku-cho, Aoi-ku, Shizuoka 420-8761
Phone: (81) 54 261 3131
Web: www.shizuokabank.co.jp

HISTORICAL FINANCIALS
Company Type: Public

Income Statement   FYE: March 31

	ASSETS ($mil)	NET INCOME ($mil)	INCOME AS % OF ASSETS	EMPLOYEES
03/22	122,645	342	0.3%	6,240
03/21	127,125	394	0.3%	6,311
03/20	115,548	356	0.3%	6,328
03/19	107,047	423	0.4%	6,422
03/18	108,608	472	0.4%	6,469
Annual Growth	3.1%	(7.7%)	—	(0.9%)

2022 Year-End Financials
Return on assets: 0.2%
Return on equity: 3.8%
Long-term debt ($ mil.): —
No. of shares ($ mil.): 564
Sales ($ mil.): 2,036
Dividends
  Yield: —
  Payout: 36.8%
  Market value ($ mil.): —

Shoprite Holdings, Ltd.

EXECUTIVES

Deputy Managing Director, Financial Director, Director, C. G. Goosen
Executive Director, Director, B. Harisunker
Executive Director, Director, A. E. Karp
Executive Director, Director, E. L. Nel
Chief Executive Officer, Director, J. W. Basson
Executive Director, Director, B. R. Weyers
Secretary, P. G. du Preez
Chairman, C. H. Wiese
Director, T. R. P. Hlongwane
Director, J. A. Louw
Director, J. F. Malherbe
Director, J. G. Rademeyer
Auditors: PricewaterhouseCoopers Inc.

LOCATIONS

HQ: Shoprite Holdings, Ltd.
Cnr William Dabbs Street and Old Paarl Roads, Brackenfell, Cape Town 7560
Phone: (27) 21 980 4000   Fax: (27) 21 980 4050
Web: www.shopriteholdings.co.za

HISTORICAL FINANCIALS
Company Type: Public

Income Statement   FYE: July 4

	REVENUE ($mil)	NET INCOME ($mil)	NET PROFIT MARGIN	EMPLOYEES
07/21*	11,635	335	2.9%	142,602
06/20	9,079	194	2.1%	141,452
06/19*	10,606	300	2.8%	147,268
07/18	10,563	378	3.6%	147,478
07/17	10,799	415	3.8%	143,802
Annual Growth	1.9%	(5.2%)	—	(0.2%)

*Fiscal year change

2021 Year-End Financials
Debt ratio: 0.6%
Return on equity: 23.2%
Cash ($ mil.): 550
Current Ratio: 1.13
Long-term debt ($ mil.): 157
No. of shares ($ mil.): 548
Dividends
  Yield: —
  Payout: 33.6%
  Market value ($ mil.): 5,898

	STOCK PRICE ($) FY Close	P/E High/Low	PER SHARE ($) Earnings	Dividends	Book Value
07/21*	10.76	1 1	0.61	0.20	2.66
06/20	6.12	2 1	0.35	0.13	2.08
06/19*	11.12	2 1	0.54	0.21	3.32
07/18	16.01	2 2	0.68	0.27	3.59
07/17	15.33	2 1	0.75	0.26	3.76
Annual Growth	(8.5%)	— —	(5.4%)	(6.3%)	(8.2%)

*Fiscal year change

Siam Cement Public Co. Ltd.

Siam Cement is a leading business conglomerate in the ASEAN region. It makes use of technology, enabling the development of innovative products, services, and solutions to meet the diverse application needs of consumers and the rapidly changing market conditions. The company is also known as Thailand's first cement manufacturer. The company provides strong domestic distribution network through sales campaign and activities to approximately 9,000 dealers nationwide, its cement products are offered to leading customer base, covering both public and private sectors domestically and internationally. About 55% of the company's revenue comes from Thailand.

Operations
The company's segments include the SCGP (Packaging Business), SCGC (Chemicals Business), and Cement-Building Materials Business.

The SCGC (Chemicals Business) accounts for about 25% of the company's revenue. The SCGP (Packaging Business) and Cement-Building Materials Business, both account for about 20% each. Others account for around 40%.

Geographic Reach
More than 50% of Siam Cement Public Limited come from Thailand. ASEAN operations and Global export and other operations account for about 20% each. Exports to ASEAN countries account for about 10%.

The company has majority of its assets in Vietnam, Indonesia, the Philippines, and Cambodia. Laos, Malaysia, and Singapore are some of the other countries that the company has its assets.

Financial Performance
Siam Cement Public's performance for the past five years decreased in the first half of the period, then recovered in 2020, ending with 2022 as its highest performing year over the period.

The company's revenue increased by Baht 39.5 billion to Baht 569.6 billion for 2022, as compared to 2021's revenue of Baht 530.1 billion.

Siam Cement Public's net income decreased to Baht 21.4 billion for fiscal year end 2022, as compared to the prior year's net income of Baht 47.2 billion.

The company held Baht 57.5 billion by the end of the year. The operating activities provided Baht 29.7 billion to the coffers. Investing activities used Baht 32.9 billion while financing activities provided Baht 55.1 billion. Main cash uses were for acquisition of equity and debt instruments of other entities and acquisition of property, plant, and equipment.

Company Background
In addition to the acquisition of a 90% stake in PT Indoris Printingdo, a high-value added packaging manufacturer in Indonesia with an annual capacity of 8,000 tons, in 2014, the company acquired Silathai Sanguan, which operates a crushing plant in Thailand; 55% of Panel World Co., Ltd., which operates cement-bonded particleboard in Thailand; 51% of Norner Holding, a leading Norway-based innovation and technology firm, specializing in material and polymer industries; and D-In-Pack Company Limited, which converts sheet boards to boxes and caters in Thailand.

In 2014 Siam Cement formed a joint venture with Florim Ceramiche S.p.A of Italy (with SCG Cement-Building Materials holding a 33% stake) to establish a plant to manufacture high-end ceramic tiles with an annual output capacity of 5 million square meters.

In 2013 the company acquired Prime Group, a major ceramic tiles producer in Vietnam.

In a 2011 deal to enhance Siam Cement's presence in the Indonesian market, the company acquired majority stakes in two firms, Keramika Indonesia Asosiasi Tbk (94%) and Kokoh Inti Arebama Tbk (70%). Keramika is a ceramics manufacturer, while Kokoh is a nationwide distributor of building materials. The transaction fits Siam Cement's strategy of acquiring assets that mesh closely with its existing business units. Also in 2011, it acquired Vietnam-based Alcamax Packaging for about $25 million.

Siam Cement has made major progress in its expansion in Southeast Asia, including the 2009 opening of a $185 million packaging paper plant in Vietnam. In 2010 Siam Cement acquired New Asia Industries Company, Vietnam's leading producer and distributor of corrugated containers, for $30 million.

Siam Cement is putting its money where the petrochemicals and packaging paper companies are. The company in 2006 formed a partnership with Dow Chemical to build a plastics manufacturing facility that began operations in 2010.

Thailand's first cement manufacturer, Siam Cement was founded in 1913 on orders from King Rama VI.

EXECUTIVES

President, Chief Executive Officer, Director, Roongrote Rangsiyopash
Investments Vice President, Finance Vice President, Investments Chief Financial Officer, Finance Chief Financial Officer, Chaovalit Ekabut
Corporate Administration Vice President, Aree Chavalitcheewingul
Secretary, Worapol Jennapar
Corporate Secretary, Pornpen Namwong
Treasurer, Padungdej Indralak
Director, Kamthon Sindhvananda
Director, Snoh Unakul
Director, Sumet Tantivejkul
Director, Pricha Attavipach
Director, Panas Simasathien
Director, Yos Euarchukiati
Director, Arsa Sarasin
Director, Chumpol NaLamlieng
Director, Tarrin Nimmanahaeminda
Director, Pramon Sutivong
Auditors : KPMG Phoomchai Audit Ltd.

LOCATIONS

HQ: Siam Cement Public Co. Ltd.
1 Siam Cement Road, Bangsue, Bangkok 10800
Phone: (66) 2 586 3333   **Fax:** (66) 2 586 2974
Web: www.scg.com

2014 Sales

	% of total
Thailand	61
China	7
Indonesia	6
Vietnam	6
Other	20
Total	100

PRODUCTS/OPERATIONS

2014 Sales

	% of total
Chemicals	50
Cement building materials	37
Paper	13
Other	-
Total	100

Selected Products

Chemicals
    Olefins
        Polyolefins
Paper & packaging
    Corrugated boxes
    Gypsum linerboard
    Industrial paper
    Printing paper
    Writing paper
Cement
    Dry mortar
    Gray cement
    Ready-mixed concrete
    White cement
Building products
    Ceramic tiles
    Concrete paving blocks
    Gypsum boards
    Roof tiles
    Sanitary fittings and wares

COMPETITORS

Freudenberg & Co. KG
IMERYS
INA-Holding Schaeffler GmbH & Co. KG
MASTEC, INC.
Marquard & Bahls AG
NIPPON STEEL NISSHIN CO., LTD.
SGL Carbon SE
TAIHEIYO CEMENT CORPORATION
Wood Canada Limited
thyssenkrupp Materials Services GmbH

HISTORICAL FINANCIALS

Company Type: Public

Income Statement   FYE: December 31

	REVENUE ($mil)	NET INCOME ($mil)	NET PROFIT MARGIN	EMPLOYEES
12/21	15,984	1,422	8.9%	58,283
12/20	13,358	1,140	8.5%	0
12/19	14,703	1,074	7.3%	0
12/18	14,789	1,383	9.4%	0
12/17	13,841	1,689	12.2%	0
Annual Growth	3.7%	(4.2%)	—	—

2021 Year-End Financials

Debt ratio: 1.0%
Return on equity: 13.7%
Cash ($ mil.): 1,085
Current Ratio: 1.38
Long-term debt ($ mil.): 6,220
No. of shares ($ mil.): 1,200
Dividends
Yield: —
Payout: 0.0%
Market value ($ mil.): 13,800

	STOCK PRICE ($) FY Close	P/E High/Low		PER SHARE ($) Earnings	Dividends	Book Value
12/21	11.50	0	0	1.19	0.41	9.19
12/20	12.67	0	0	0.95	0.33	8.93
12/19	12.88	1	0	0.90	0.42	7.84
12/18	12.83	0	0	1.15	0.47	7.14
12/17	16.84	0	0	1.41	0.46	6.68
Annual Growth	(9.1%)	—	—	(4.2%)	(2.9%)	8.3%

Siam Commercial Bank Public Co Ltd (The)

One of Thailand's largest commercial banks by total assets, deposits, and loans, The Siam Commercial Bank (SCB) offers deposits and lending and a wide range of other products and services. It is the country's oldest bank, established by Royal Charter in 1906 in response to the proliferation of foreign financial institutions in Thailand. It offers a variety of financial services, such as corporate and personal lending, retail and wholesale banking, credit cards, life insurance, foreign currency trading, and investment banking, among others. SCB operates through a network of about 700 branches and more than 8,880 ATMs. SCB had THB 3.3 trillion in total assets, THB 2.5 trillion in deposits, and THB 2.3 trillion in loans.

Operations

SCB's retail services include home loans, personal credit, car hire purchase, credit cards, ATM cards, debit cards, currency exchange facilities and overseas remittances as well as investment and insurance products. For corporate and SME customers, the bank offers cash management-related services, lending products, international trade financing, treasury products, debt and capital market products, corporate advisory, investment banking and other services.

Its brokerage arm, SCB Securities provides securities trading services as well as equity investment products and services to both institutional and retail investors. The SCB Asset Management specializes in asset management business that covers mutual funds, provident funds and private funds. In addition to SCB Securities Co., Ltd. and SCB Asset Management Co., Ltd., the Bank also has a subsidiary, namely SCB 10X, that specializes in pushing the frontier of digital and data analytics capabilities and using cutting-edge technologies to improve the banking business.

The bank's revenue came from three key segments: Corporate, SME, and Retail & Wealth. In 2021, the Retail & Wealth Segment contributed more than half of the bank's revenue, followed by the Corporate and SME Segments.

Overall, net interest income accounts for nearly 65% of total revenue and net interest income accounts for the remaining more than 35%.

Geographic Reach

Its head office and branch network is located in Thailand and has branches in Singapore, Hong Kong, Laos, Vietnam, China and Cayman Islands and its subsidiaries in Thailand, Singapore, Cambodia and Myanmar.

Sales and Marketing

SCB provides its financial products and services to corporate and commercial customers, small businesses, and individuals.

Financial Performance

Net interest income fell 2% year-on-year to THB 95.2 billion largely due to net interest margin compression in a currently low interest rate environment and the bank's focus on high quality loans.

In 2021, the company had a net income of THB 35.6 million, a 31% increase from the previous year's net income of THB 27.2 million.

The company's cash at the end of 2021 was THB 50.4 billion. Investing activities generated THB 81.4 billion, while operating activities used THB 68.5 billion. Financing activities used another THB 14.2 billion, primarily for dividends paid.

Strategy

Under the SCBX restructuring plan, SCB will continue to be the group's core revenue engine. However, in this business environment where the banking industry faces slower growth, intense competition and accelerating adoption of digital channels among customers, SCB will re-direct its business focus "to Be a Better Bank" that generates reasonable and sustainable returns.

SCB will pivot from a universal banking model to specializing in chosen business areas with a digital technology and digital banking focus.

EXECUTIVES

President, Chief Executive Officer, Director, Arthid Nanthawithaya
Senior Executive Vice President, General Counsel, Director, Bodin Asavanich
Senior Executive Vice President, Sirichai Sombutsiri
Senior Executive Vice President, Yol Phokasub
Senior Executive Vice President, Sarunthorn Chutima
Chief Financial Officer, Deepak Sarup
Chief Audit and Compliance Officer, Kannika Ngamsopee
Chief Risk Officer, Yokporn Tantisawetrat
Secretary, Siribunchong Uthayophas
Chairman, Anand Panyarachun
Director, Vichit Suraphongchai
Director, Maris Samaram
Director, Vicharn Panich
Director, Chumpol Na Lamlieng
Director, Sumate Tanthuwanit
Director, Kulpatra Sirodom
Director, Ekamol Kiriwat
Director, Chirayu Isarangkul Na Ayuthaya
Director, Disnadda Diskul
Director, Jada Wattanasiritham
Director, Supa Piyajitti
Director, Robert Ralph Parks
Director, Thosaporn Sirisamphand
Auditors : KPMG Phoomchai Audit Ltd.

LOCATIONS

HQ: Siam Commercial Bank Public Co Ltd (The)
9 Ratchadapisek Road, Jatujak, Bangkok 10900
Phone: (66) 2 544 1000   **Fax:** (66) 2 937 7721
Web: www.scb.co.th

PRODUCTS/OPERATIONS

2013 Sales

	% of total
Interest income	56
Net earned insurance premiums	23
Fees & service income	14
Net trading income	4
Dividend income	2
Net gain on investments	1
Total	100

Selected Group Companies
SCB Asset Management
SCB Life Assurance
SCB Securities
The Siam Commercial Bank

COMPETITORS

AKBANK TURK ANONIM SIRKETI
BANK OF AYUDHYA PUBLIC COMPANY LIMITED
BANK OF BARODA
China Merchants Bank Co., Ltd.
Industrial and Commercial Bank of China Limited
KASIKORNBANK PUBLIC COMPANY LIMITED
KEB Hana Bank Co., Ltd.
UNITED OVERSEAS BANK LIMITED
WGZ BANK AG Westdeutsche Genossenschafts-Zentralbank
Woori Finance Holdings Co., Ltd.

HISTORICAL FINANCIALS
Company Type: Public

Income Statement — FYE: December 31

	ASSETS ($mil)	NET INCOME ($mil)	INCOME AS % OF ASSETS	EMPLOYEES
12/21	99,944	1,073	1.1%	0
12/20	109,506	909	0.8%	0
12/19	99,495	1,357	1.4%	0
12/18	98,527	1,238	1.3%	0
12/17	92,823	1,324	1.4%	0
Annual Growth	1.9%	(5.1%)	—	—

2021 Year-End Financials
Return on assets: 1.0%   Dividends
Return on equity: 8.3%   Yield: —
Long-term debt ($ mil.): —   Payout: 0.0%
No. of shares ($ mil.): 3,395   Market value ($ mil.): 51,784
Sales ($ mil.): 5,352

	STOCK PRICE ($) FY Close	P/E High	P/E Low	Earnings	Dividends	Book Value
12/21	15.25	2	1	0.32	0.35	3.92
12/20	11.32	2	1	0.27	0.51	4.05
12/19	16.23	2	1	0.40	0.56	3.96
12/18	16.16	2	1	0.36	0.55	3.46
12/17	18.27	2	1	0.39	0.53	3.29
Annual Growth	(4.4%)	—	—	(5.1%)	(9.8%)	4.5%

Sibanye Stillwater Ltd

EXECUTIVES

Chief Executive Officer, Executive Director, Neal J. Froneman
Chief Financial Officer, Executive Director, Charl Keyter
Chief Technical Officer, Robert van Niekerk
Business Development Executive Vice President, Richard Stewart
Legal and Compliance Executive Vice President, Lerato Legong
Organisational Effectiveness Executive Vice President, Organisational Growth Executive Vice President, Jacob Dawid Mostert
Human Capital Executive Vice President, Corporate Affairs Executive Vice President, Themba Nkosi
Operations Executive Vice President, Group Technical Executive Vice President, SA PGM operations Executive Vice President, US PGM operations Executive Vice President, Wayne David Richard Robinson
SA PGM operations Executive Vice President, Johannes Dawid van Aswegen
Business Development Executive Vice President, Laurent Charbonnier
SA gold operations Executive Vice President, Richard Allen Cox
Secretary, Lerato Matlosa
Non-Executive Chairman, Independent Non-Executive Director, Vincent Maphai
Lead Independent Non-Executive Director, Richard P. Menell
Independent Non-Executive Director, Timothy J. Cumming
Independent Non-Executive Director, Savannah Danson
Independent Non-Executive Director, Harry Kenyon-Slaney
Independent Non-Executive Director, Nkosemntu Gladman Nika
Independent Non-Executive Director, Keith A. Rayner
Independent Non-Executive Director, Susan C. van der Merwe
Independent Non-Executive Director, Jerry S. Vilakazi
Independent Non-Executive Director, Elaine J. Dorward-King
Independent Non-Executive Director, Sindiswa Victoria Zilwa
Auditors : Ernst & Young Inc.

LOCATIONS

HQ: Sibanye Stillwater Ltd
Constantia Office Park, Cnr 14th Avenue & Hendrik Potgieter Road, Weltevreden Park 1709
Phone: (27) 11 278 9600   **Fax:** (27) 11 278 9863
Web: www.sibanyestillwater.com

HISTORICAL FINANCIALS
Company Type: Public

Income Statement — FYE: December 31

	REVENUE ($mil)	NET INCOME ($mil)	NET PROFIT MARGIN	EMPLOYEES
12/21	10,799	2,073	19.2%	0
12/20	8,681	1,997	23.0%	84,775
12/19	5,192	4	0.1%	84,521
12/18	3,522	(173)	—	63,518
12/17	3,729	(360)	—	66,472
Annual Growth	30.5%	—	—	—

2021 Year-End Financials
Debt ratio: 0.8%   No. of shares ($ mil.): 2,808
Return on equity: 44.5%   Dividends
Cash ($ mil.): 1,899   Yield: 10.5%
Current Ratio: 3.16   Payout: 168.8%
Long-term debt ($ mil.): 1,266   Market value ($ mil.): 35,217

	STOCK PRICE ($) FY Close	P/E High	P/E Low	Earnings	Dividends	Book Value
12/21	12.54	2	1	0.71	1.32	1.79
12/20	15.89	2	0	0.73	0.10	1.60
12/19	9.93	499	133	0.00	0.00	0.79
12/18	2.83	—	—	(0.08)	0.00	0.73
12/17	5.05	—	—	(0.19)	0.05	0.90
Annual Growth	25.5%	—	—	—	128.1%	18.7%

Siemens AG (Germany)

Siemens is a global powerhouse focusing

HOOVER'S HANDBOOK OF WORLD BUSINESS 2024

on the areas of electrification, automation and digitalization. One of the largest electronics and industrial engineering companies in the world. The German conglomerate makes everything from healthcare and building technologies to factory automation and power distribution equipment. Siemens has facilities in most corners of the world and serves a global customer base of manufacturers and construction, energy, and healthcare businesses. Formed in 1847 as Siemens & Halske, the company's technological innovations include the first long-distance telegraph system in Europe, a high-efficiency dynamo for generating electricity, and the SIMATIC industrial machine automation technology.

Operations

Siemens operates its business through six reportable segments.

Publicly traded and separately managed company, Siemens Healthineers generates about 30% of total sales. The division develops, manufactures, and sells health imaging and diagnostic technology and clinical consulting services globally to healthcare providers.

The Digital Industries segment offers automation technology, industrial software and services, and a cloud-based industrial internet of things (IoT) operating system primarily for manufacturing. This segment generates over 25% of sales.

Smart Infrastructure (roughly 25% of sales) connects energy systems, buildings and industries. The company do this from the macro to the micro level, physical products, components and systems to connected, cloud-based digital offerings and services. From intelligent grid control and electrification to smart storage solutions, from building automation and control systems to switches, valves and sensors.

Mobility segment (over 15%) combines all Siemens businesses in the area of passenger and freight transportation, including rail vehicles, rail automation systems, rail electrification systems, road traffic technology, digital solutions and related services. It also provides its customers with consulting, planning, financing, construction, service and operation of turnkey mobility systems.

Other segments include Financial Services and Portfolio Companies which accounts for less than 10% of sales combined.

Geographic Reach

Headquartered in Munich, Germany, Siemens has offices, warehouses, and R&D facilities in nearly every country across the globe and has diverse geographic revenue streams.

Siemens generates around half its revenue from the geographic region comprising Europe, CIS, Africa, and the Middle East. The Americas accounts for over 25% of sales, most of which comes from Siemens' largest single country, the US. It derives nearly 25% of sales from the Asia/Pacific region.

Sales and Marketing

Siemens serves a range of customers including infrastructure developers, construction companies and contractors; owners, operators and tenants of both public and commercial buildings including hospitals, campuses, airports and data centers; companies in heavy industries such as oil and gas, mining and chemicals; companies in discrete manufacturing industries such as automotive and machine building; and utilities and power grid network operators (transmission and distribution).

In its Smart Infrastructure segment, it serves its customers through a broad variety of channels, including its global product and systems sales organization, distributors, panel builders, original equipment manufacturers (OEM), value added resellers and installers, as well as by direct sales through the branch offices of its regional solutions and services units worldwide.

Financial Performance

Note: Growth rates may differ after conversion to US Dollars.

Siemens' revenue has fluctuated for five years, with 2017 as its highest performing year, slightly recovering in 2021 compared with the other years over the period.

The company's revenue increased by 13% to ?62.3 billion in fiscal 2021 compared to ?55.3 billion in the prior year. Revenue went up significantly year-over-year, led by double-digit growth in Siemens Healthineers and Digital Industries. Smart Infrastructure recorded a clear increase, while Mobility posted slightly higher revenue year-over-year. The revenue increase in emerging markets was driven by substantially higher demand in China and, to a lesser degree, India.

The company's net income also increased to ?6.7 billion compared to ?4.2 billion in the prior year. This improvement was due mainly to the aforementioned significantly higher Adjusted EBITA Industrial Business and the lower loss outside Industrial Business. In addition, discontinued operations, largely related to the sale of Flender, contributed income of ?1.1 billion in fiscal 2021.

Cash held by the company at the end of 2021 amounted to ?9.5 billion from 2020's cash held at about ?14.0 billion. Cash provided by operations was ?10.0 billion. Cash used for investing activities was ?15.5 billion while financing activities provided ?785 million. Main cash uses were for acquisition of businesses, repayment of long-term debt, dividends paid and additions to intangible assets and property, plant and equipment.

Strategy

A part of the company's strategy includes divesting its activities in some business areas and strengthening other areas through portfolio measures, including mergers and acquisitions. In addition, the company is primarily focused on highly attractive growth markets that support the global economy such as industry, infrastructure, transportation and healthcare.

Mergers and Acquisitions

In 2021, Siemens Healthineers completed the acquisition of Varian Medical Systems, Inc. (Varian) for US$16.4 billion. Varian becomes new business segment within Siemens Healthineers; important step in the implementation of its Strategy 2025. With Varian, Siemens Healthineers will leverage AI-assisted analytics to advance the development and delivery of data-driven precision care and redefine cancer diagnosis, care delivery and post-treatment survivorship. Through early and accurate detection as well as more efficient diagnosis, increased treatment quality and access, Siemens Healthineers will support and accelerate Varian's mission to reduce uncertainty for cancer patients and increase the level of cancer survivorship.

Company Background

Electrical engineer Werner von Siemens and craftsman Johann Halske formed Siemens & Halske in 1847. In 1874 the firm finished the first transatlantic telegraph cable, which ran from Ireland to the US. The company also created Europe's first electric power transmission system (1876), the world's first electrified railway (1879), and one of the first elevators (1880).

HISTORY

In 1847 electrical engineer Werner von Siemens and craftsman Johann Halske formed Siemens & Halske. The firm's first major project linked Berlin and Frankfurt with the first long-distance telegraph system in Europe (1848). In 1870 it completed a 6,600-mile telegraph line from London to Calcutta, India, and in 1874 it made the first transatlantic cable, linking Ireland to the US.

The company's history of firsts includes Europe's first electric power transmission system (1876), the world's first electrified railway (1879), and one of the first elevators (1880). In 1896 it patented the world's first X-ray tube and completed the first European subway, in Budapest, Hungary.

By the next century it had formed light-bulb cartel OSRAM with German rivals AEG and Auer (1919) and created a venture with Furukawa Electric called Fuji Electric (1923). It developed radios and traffic lights in the 1920s and began producing electron microscopes in 1939.

Siemens & Halske played a critical role in Germany's war effort in WWII and suffered heavy losses. During the 1950s it recovered by developing data processing equipment, silicates for semiconductors, and the first implantable pacemaker. It moved into the nuclear industry in 1959 when its first reactor went into service at Munich-Garching. In 1966 the company reincorporated as Siemens AG.

EXECUTIVES

President, Chief Executive Officer, Joe Kaeser
Deputy Chief Executive, Roland Busch
Member, Klaus Helmrich
Member, Cedrik Neike
Member, Ralf P. Thomas
Member, Matthias Rebellius
Member, Judith Wiese
Chairman, Jim Hagemann Snabe
First Deputy Chairman, Brigit Steinborn
Second Deputy Chairman, Werner Wenning
Director, Werner Brandt
Director, Michael Diekmann
Director, Andrea Fehrmann
Director, Bettina Haller
Director, Harald Kern
Director, Juergen Kerner
Director, Nicola Leibinger-Kammueller
Director, Benoit Potier
Director, Hagen Reimer
Director, Norbert Reithofer
Director, Baroness Nemat Shafik
Director, Nathalie von Siemens
Director, Michael Sigmund
Director, Dorothea Simon
Director, Matthias Zachert
Director, Gunnar Zukunft
Auditors : Ernst & Young GmbH

LOCATIONS

HQ: Siemens AG (Germany)
Werner-von-Siemens-Str. 1, Munich 80333
Phone: (49) 89 636 33443 **Fax:** (49) 89 636 30085
Web: www.siemens.com

2018 Sales

	% of total
Europe, CIS, Africa, Middle East	51
Americas	27
Asia, Australia	22
Total	100

PRODUCTS/OPERATIONS

2018 Sales

	% of total
Siemens Healthineers	16
Digital Factory	15
Power and Gas	15
Energy Management	14
Siemens Games Renewable Energy	11
Mobility	10
Process Industries and Drives	9
Building Technologies	8
Financial Services (SFS)	1
Total	100

Products & Services
Industrial Automation
Building Technologies
Drive Technology
Energy
Healthcare
Mobility
Financing
Consumer Products
Services
Solutions by Market
Aerospace
Automotive Manufacturing
Battery Manufacturing
Chemistry Industry
Cement
Cranes
Data Centers
Distributors
Electronics Industry
Fiber Industry
Food & Beverage
Glass Industry
Conveyor Technology
Machinery and Plant Construction
Marine
Mining Industry
Municipalities and DSOs
Oil & Gas
Panel Building
Pharmaceutical Industry
Power Utilities

COMPETITORS

ABB Ltd
AMETEK, INC.
COGNEX CORPORATION
FORTIVE CORPORATION
KEYSIGHT TECHNOLOGIES, INC.
MKS INSTRUMENTS, INC.
OMRON CO.,LTD.
SCHNEIDER ELECTRIC SE
TOSHIBA CORPORATION
YOKOGAWA ELECTRIC CORPORATION

HISTORICAL FINANCIALS

Company Type: Public

Income Statement FYE: September 30

	REVENUE ($mil)	NET INCOME ($mil)	NET PROFIT MARGIN	EMPLOYEES
09/23	82,395	8,421	10.2%	320,000
09/22	70,164	3,629	5.2%	311,000
09/21	72,072	7,131	9.9%	303,000
09/20	66,901	4,718	7.1%	294,000
09/19	94,740	5,644	6.0%	385,000
Annual Growth	(3.4%)	10.5%	—	(4.5%)

2023 Year-End Financials

Debt ratio: 34.0%   No. of shares ($ mil.): 789
Return on equity: 16.4%   Dividends
Cash ($ mil.): 10,683   Yield: —
Current Ratio: 1.35   Payout: 15.8%
Long-term debt ($ mil.): 41,439   Market value ($ mil.): 56,440

	STOCK PRICE ($) FY Close	P/E High/Low	PER SHARE ($) Earnings	Dividends	Book Value
09/23	71.45	9 5	10.50	1.67	64.10
09/22	48.95	16 10	4.47	1.67	60.14
09/21	82.14	11 8	8.79	7.67	64.02
09/20	69.65	14 7	5.77	1.56	53.31
09/19	53.59	9 7	6.89	1.60	64.59
Annual Growth	7.5%	— —	11.1%	1.0%	(0.2%)

Siemens Energy AG

Auditors : Ernst & Young GmbH
Wirtschaftpruefungsgesellschaft

LOCATIONS

HQ: Siemens Energy AG
Otto-Hahn-Ring 6, Munich 81739
Phone: (49) 89 636 00
Web: www.siemens-energy.com

HISTORICAL FINANCIALS

Company Type: Public

Income Statement FYE: September 30

	REVENUE ($mil)	NET INCOME ($mil)	NET PROFIT MARGIN	EMPLOYEES
09/21	32,968	(524)	—	0
09/20	32,148	(1,880)	—	92
09/19	31,413	172	0.5%	89
Annual Growth	2.4%	—	—	—

2021 Year-End Financials

Debt ratio: 7.2%   No. of shares ($ mil.): —
Return on equity: (-3.0%)   Dividends
Cash ($ mil.): 6,172   Yield: —
Current Ratio: 1.04   Payout: 0.0%
Long-term debt ($ mil.): 2,519   Market value ($ mil.): —

	STOCK PRICE ($) FY Close	P/E High/Low	PER SHARE ($) Earnings	Dividends	Book Value
09/21	27.01	— —	(0.73)	0.00	0.00
Annual Growth	—	— —	—	—	—

Siemens Gamesa Renewable Energy SA

Created in 2017 by the merger of Siemens Wind Power and Gamesa, Siemens Gamesa (formerly Gamesa Corporacion Tecnologica S.A.) specializes in the development and construction of wind farms, as well as the engineering solutions, design, production and sale of wind turbines. It supplies wind power solutions to customers all over the globe, the company have installed over 99 GW of capacity in about 80 countries. Siemens Gamesa is the world's only company operating at a global scale across the entire wind spectrum ? onshore, offshore and services that is well positioned to unlock the full potential of wind. The company has operations worldwide but generates majority of its sales in the Europe, Middle East, and Africa (EMEA) region.

Operations

The company operates in two business segments: Wind Turbines (around 80% of sales) and Operation and Maintenance (about 20%).

The Wind Turbines segment offers wind turbines for various pitch and speed technologies, as well as provides development, construction and sale of wind farms. The Operation and Maintenance segment is responsible for the management, monitoring and maintenance of wind farms.

Geographic Reach

Headquartered in Vizcaya, Spain, about 50% of sales were generated in Europe, Middle East & Africa (EMEA), while the other half was split to Americas, as well as Asia and Australia. The company also has operations in some 60 countries, and installed over 99GW of capacity of its onshore business across nearly 80 countries.

Sales and Marketing
Siemens Gamesa customers are mainly companies that are active within the energy sector which includes utilities, independent power producers, project developers, and others (including financial investors, oil & gas players, and companies that need to consume green energy).

Financial Performance
The company's revenue for fiscal 2021 increased to EUR 10.2 billion compared from the prior year with EUR 9.5 billion.

Net loss for fiscal 2021 decreased to EUR 625.9 million compared from the prior year with EUR 918.2 million.

Cash held by the company at the end of fiscal 2021 increased to EUR 2.0 billion. Cash provided by operations and financing activities were EUR 801.2 million and EUR 140.8 million, respectively. Cash used for investing activities was EUR 636.0 million, mainly for additions to intangible assets and property, plant and equipment.

Strategy
Launched in 2020, the LEAP program set clear priorities: innovation; productivity & asset management; operational excellence; sustainability and people; and digitalization.

In this context, its key objectives for the period until 2023 focus on:

Returning Onshore to sustainable profitability with a turnaround plan focused on the following priorities: Focus on profitable volume and de-risking the business; Introduction of new leading technology; Reduction of supply chain complexity; Reinforcement of project execution capabilities; and Reorganization to improve performance.

Capturing offshore market growth through a profitable leadership position with the following priorities: technological differentiation; globalization with market expansion and early customer engagement; and focus on execution excellence.

Sustainably growing faster than the market in service, with the following priorities: continuously develop new business models in partnership with customers; focus on innovation, productivity and operational excellence; and capture the potential of the profitable multi-brand business.

EXECUTIVES

Chief Executive Officer, Executive Director, Andreas Nauen
Chairman, Miguel Angel Lopez Borrego
Independent Director, Gloria Hernandez Garcia
Independent Director, Rudolf Krammer
Independent Director, Harald von Heynitz
Independent Director, Klaus Rosenfeld
External Director, Mariel von Schumann
External Director, Tim Oliver Holt
External Director, Maria Ferraro
External Director, Tim Dawidowsky
Auditors: Ernst & Young, S.L.

LOCATIONS
HQ: Siemens Gamesa Renewable Energy SA
Parque Tecnologico de Bizkaia, Edificio 222, Vizcaya, Zamudio 48170
Phone: (34) 944 03 73 52
Web: www.siemensgamesa.com

2012 Sales
	% of total
Latin America	32
Europe & other	27
US	20
India	12
China	9
Total	100

COMPETITORS
ACCIONA, SA
BROADWIND ENERGY, INC.
BayWa AG
CARR'S GROUP PLC
FUTUREN
IBERDROLA, SOCIEDAD ANONIMA
REPSOL SA.
VALLOUREC
Vattenfall AB
Ãrsted A/S

HISTORICAL FINANCIALS
Company Type: Public

Income Statement — FYE: September 30

	REVENUE ($mil)	NET INCOME ($mil)	NET PROFIT MARGIN	EMPLOYEES
09/21	11,804	(725)	—	26,182
09/20	11,103	(1,075)	—	25,458
09/19	11,156	152	1.4%	23,882
09/18	10,566	81	0.8%	23,799
09/17	7,724	(17)	—	22,432
Annual Growth	11.2%	—		3.9%

2021 Year-End Financials
Debt ratio: 10.2%
Return on equity: (-13.3%)
Cash ($ mil.): 2,269
Current Ratio: 0.79
Long-term debt ($ mil.): 1,259
No. of shares ($ mil.): 680
Dividends
  Yield: —
  Payout: 0.0%
Market value ($ mil.): 3,434

	STOCK PRICE ($) FY Close	P/E High/Low	PER SHARE ($) Earnings	Dividends	Book Value
09/21	5.05	— —	(1.06)	0.00	7.59
09/20	5.45	— —	(1.58)	0.01	8.50
09/19	2.77	17 9	0.23	0.00	10.07
09/18	2.57	34 21	0.12	0.00	10.11
09/17	2.59	— —	(0.04)	0.68	11.21
Annual Growth	18.2%		—	—	(9.3%)

Sika AG

EXECUTIVES
Executive Member, Paul Schuler
Chairman, Paul Haelg
Director, Monika Ribar
Director, Daniel J. Sauter
Director, Christoph Tobler
Auditors: Ernst & Young Ltd

LOCATIONS
HQ: Sika AG
Zugerstrasse 50, Baar 6340
Phone: (41) 58 436 68 00 **Fax:** (41) 58 436 68 50
Web: www.sika.com

HISTORICAL FINANCIALS
Company Type: Public

Income Statement — FYE: December 31

	REVENUE ($mil)	NET INCOME ($mil)	NET PROFIT MARGIN	EMPLOYEES
12/21	10,135	1,147	11.3%	27,059
12/20	8,944	936	10.5%	24,848
12/19	8,388	777	9.3%	25,141
12/18	7,202	694	9.6%	20,060
12/17	6,402	659	10.3%	18,484
Annual Growth	12.2%	14.9%	—	10.0%

2021 Year-End Financials
Debt ratio: 34.3%
Return on equity: 27.2%
Cash ($ mil.): 1,287
Current Ratio: 1.99
Long-term debt ($ mil.): 3,429
No. of shares ($ mil.): 143
Dividends
  Yield: 0.3%
  Payout: 2.1%
Market value ($ mil.): 5,944

	STOCK PRICE ($) FY Close	P/E High/Low	PER SHARE ($) Earnings	Dividends	Book Value
12/21	41.56	6 4	7.23	0.16	33.66
12/20	27.23	5 3	5.93	0.13	26.32
12/19	19.07	4 3	4.98	0.12	22.80
12/18	12.40	9 3	4.66	0.11	11.81
12/17	30.95	0 0	259.76	0.09	773.48
Annual Growth	7.6%		(59.2%)	13.4%	(54.3%)

Singapore Telecommunications Ltd

EXECUTIVES
Chief Executive Officer, Non-Independent Executive Director, Kuan Moon Yuen
Chief Financial Officer, Arthur Lang
Chief Information Officer/ Chief Digital Officer, William Woo
Chief People and Sustainability Officer, Aileen Tan
Chief Corporate Officer, Cheng Cheng Lim
Chief Technology Officer, Mark Chin Kok Chong
Assistant Secretary, Li Ching Lim
Chairman, Non-Independent Non-Executive Director, Theng Kiat Lee
Lead Independent Director, Independent Non-Executive Director, Gautam Banerjee
Independent Non-Executive Director, John Arthur
Independent Non-Executive Director, Venky Ganesan
Independent Non-Executive Director, Bradley Horowitz

Independent Non-Executive Director, Gail Patricia Kelly
Independent Non-Executive Director, Swee Say Lim
Independent Non-Executive Director, Christina Ong
Independent Non-Executive Director, Rajeev Suri
Independent Non-Executive Director, Swee Lian Teo
Independent Non-Executive Director, Siew Kim Wee
Independent Non-Executive Director, Hsin Yue Yong
Auditors : KPMG LLP

LOCATIONS

HQ: Singapore Telecommunications Ltd
31 Exeter Road, Comcentre, 239732
Phone: (65) 6838 3388   Fax: (65) 6732 8428
Web: www.singtel.com

HISTORICAL FINANCIALS

Company Type: Public

Income Statement   FYE: March 31

	REVENUE ($mil)	NET INCOME ($mil)	NET PROFIT MARGIN	EMPLOYEES
03/23	10,995	1,672	15.2%	24,070
03/22	11,329	1,439	12.7%	22,543
03/21	11,635	411	3.5%	22,892
03/20	11,601	753	6.5%	23,080
03/19	12,819	2,283	17.8%	24,071
Annual Growth	(3.8%)	(7.5%)	—	0.0%

2023 Year-End Financials

Debt ratio: 17.6%
Return on equity: 8.2%
Cash ($ mil.): 1,254
Current Ratio: 1.03
Long-term debt ($ mil.): 7,451
No. of shares ($ mil.): 16,514
Dividends
Yield: 6.2%
Payout: 872.5%
Market value ($ mil.): 304,818

	STOCK PRICE ($) FY Close	P/E High/Low	Earnings	Dividends	Book Value
03/23	18.46	158 129	0.10	1.16	1.18
03/22	19.48	166 139	0.09	0.47	1.26
03/21	18.15	626 443	0.03	1.22	1.19
03/20	17.77	380 242	0.05	1.23	1.15
03/19	22.41	139 112	0.14	1.25	1.35
Annual Growth	(4.7%)	— —	(7.8%)	(1.8%)	(3.2%)

Sinopec Shanghai Petrochemical Co., Ltd.

China's own entry into the world of giant petrochemical companies, Sinopec Shanghai Petrochemical Company is one of that country's largest producers of ethylene, a crucial ingredient in the manufacture of synthetic fibers and plastics. It also makes petroleum-based fuels and oils and other intermediate petrochemicals, such as benzene. The company operates primarily within China; most of its revenues are from eastern China. Though it was founded as a maker of synthetic fibers, that segment is Shanghai Petrochemical's smallest now; petroleum products account for almost half of sales. China Petroleum & Chemical (Sinopec), which is controlled by the Chinese government, owns about 55% of Shanghai Petrochemical.

HISTORY

The Mao-inspired Cultural Revolution of the 1960s restored the aging leader's political grip, but it also caused immense economic disruptions in China, including a virtual shutdown of foreign trade. In the early 1970s party reformists led by Zhou Enlai and Deng Xiaoping advocated improved contact with the outside world and the restoration of foreign trade, giving the Chinese economy access to much-needed technology. In 1972, the year President Nixon's visit to China restored Sino-US ties, China began contracting for plant and equipment imports, especially in the petrochemical areas of chemical fertilizers for agriculture and artificial fibers for industrial use. That year Shanghai Petrochemical Company was founded as China's first large petrochemical enterprise, using imported equipment and technology.

Under Sinopec's control, Shanghai Petrochemical fit squarely into the government's Four Modernizations policy (agriculture, industry, technology, and defense). Other factors in the firm's growth were the booming economies of the coastal cities in the east and south, made possible by economic liberalization policies that encouraged foreign investment. The Guangdong province in the south led the way as Hong Kong enterprise migrated there in the 1980s in search of lower wages and overhead. The expansion of industrial output there and in other provinces resulted in greatly increased demand for petrochemicals.

Emboldened by growth and further reforms in the oil industry, Sinopec restructured Shanghai Petrochemical in 1993 and listed it on the Hong Kong and New York stock markets. (It was the first Chinese company listed on the New York Stock Exchange.) The company formed a joint venture with US-based agribusiness giant Continental Grain in 1995 to build a liquid petroleum gas plant and teamed up with British Petroleum (now BP) to build an acrylonitrile plant. The company entered a joint venture with Union Carbide (purchased by Dow Chemical) in 1996 to build a polymer emulsion plant in China. Shanghai Petrochemical increased its market share for acrylics with its 1997 purchase of the Zhejiang Acrylic Fibre Plant, then a producer of about 40% of China's total acrylic-fiber output. Annual production grew to 130,000 tons by 1999.

Three broad-reaching events have hammered the company's profits: the Asian economic crisis, the decrease of Sinopec's subsidy on crude oil, and a global oversupply of petrochemicals. In 1997 Shanghai Petrochemical's product-mix adjustments, combined with cost cutting, offset some of the increased crude costs and lower prices. The company announced in 1998 that the Chinese government planned to crack down on the smuggling of foreign petrochemicals and help the domestic market. The firm remains vulnerable to policy changes, however. Additionally, consolidation of the Chinese petrochemical industry could translate into lost jobs. The company continued to modernize its facilities and increase its capacity in 2000 when it moved to upgrade operations in order to become a world-class production base for petrochemicals and derivatives.

EXECUTIVES

Executive Director, Vice President, Deputy General Manager, Qiang Jin
Production Department Executive Director, Production Department Vice President, Production Department Deputy General Manager, Executive Director, Wenmin Jin
Supervisory Committee Chairman, Yanhui Ma
Staff Supervisor, Hongjun Chen
Staff Supervisor, Feng Zhang
Supervisor, Tingji Cai
Independent Supervisor, Yunrui Zheng
Board Secretary, Deputy General Manager, Executive Director, Fei Huang
Deputy General Manager, Executive Director, Xiangyu Huang
General Manager, Vice Chairman, Zemin Guan
Supervisor, Xiaofeng Zhang
Chief Financial Officer, Deputy General Manager, Executive Director, Jun Du
Board Secretary, Gang Liu
Chairman, Executive Director, Haijun Wu
Independent Non-executive Director, Yuanqin Li
Independent Non-executive Director, Haifeng Chen
Independent Director, Song Gao
Director, Kun Peng
Independent Non-executive Director, Song Tang
Independent Director, Jun Yang
Director, Zhenglin Xie
Auditors : PricewaterhouseCoopers Zhong Tian LLP

LOCATIONS

HQ: Sinopec Shanghai Petrochemical Co., Ltd.
48 Jinyi Road, Jinshan District, Shanghai 200540
Phone: (86) 21 57943143   Fax: (86) 21 57940050
Web: www.spc.com.cn

PRODUCTS/OPERATIONS

2016 Sales

	% of total
Petroleum products	45
Trading of petrochemical products	27
Resins and plastics	13
Intermediate petrochemicals	12
Synthetic fibers	2
Others	1
Total	100

Selected Products
Petroleum Products
- Diesel
- Gasoline
- Jet oil
- Residual oil

Resins and Plastics
- LDPE film and pellets
- Polyester chips
- PP pellets
- PVA

Intermediate Petrochemicals
- Benzene
- Butadiene
- Ethylene
- Ethylene glycol
- Ethylene oxide

Synthetic Fibers
- Acrylic staple
- Acrylic top
- Polyester filament-POY
- Polyester staple
- PP fiber
- PVA fiber

COMPETITORS
COMPAÃIA ESPAÃ'OLA DE PETROLEOS SAU
COSMO OIL CO., LTD.
IDEMITSU KOSAN CO.,LTD.
INDIAN OIL CORPORATION LIMITED
MOL Magyar Olaj- Ã©s GÃ¡zipari NyilvÃ¡nosan
MÃ¼kÃ¶dÃ¶ RÃ©szvÃ©nytÃ¡rsasÃ¡g

HISTORICAL FINANCIALS
Company Type: Public

Income Statement — FYE: December 31

	REVENUE ($mil)	NET INCOME ($mil)	NET PROFIT MARGIN	EMPLOYEES
12/22	11,961	(416)	—	0
12/21	14,062	315	2.2%	0
12/20	11,422	96	0.8%	0
12/19	14,421	318	2.2%	0
12/18	15,667	767	4.9%	0
Annual Growth	(6.5%)			

2022 Year-End Financials
- Debt ratio: 0.8%
- Return on equity: (-10.1%)
- Cash ($ mil.): 579
- Current Ratio: 1.13
- Long-term debt ($ mil.): 101
- No. of shares ($ mil.): —
- Dividends
- Yield: —
- Payout: 0.0%
- Market value ($ mil.): —

Sinopharm Group Co., Ltd.

EXECUTIVES
President, Executive Director, Yulin Wei
Vice President, Guangpu Li
Vice President, Linian Shen
Vice President, Jun Lu
Board of Director Vice President, Board of Director Secretary, Board of Director Joint Company Secretary, Aimin Wu
Vice President, Jinming Shi
Vice President, Yong Liu
Vice President, Zhiming Li
Vice President, Zhongxi Cai
Vice President, Wanjun Ma
Vice President, Shuangjun Xu
Chief Financial Officer, Xiuchang Jiang
Joint Company Secretary, Wai Fung Ngai
Chairman, Non-Executive Director, Lulin She
Non-Executive Director, Qunbin Wang
Non-Executive Director, Wenhao Chen
Non-Executive Director, Bin Zhou
Non-Executive Director, Qiyu Chen
Non-Executive Director, Jindong Deng
Non-Executive Director, Banghan Fan
Non-Executive Director, Hailiang Liu
Independent Non-Executive Director, Fanghua Wang
Independent Non-Executive Director, Wuping Tao
Independent Non-Executive Director, Rong Xie
Independent Non-Executive Director, Bajun Zhou
Auditors : Ernst & Young

LOCATIONS
HQ: Sinopharm Group Co., Ltd.
Sinopharm Group Building, No. 385, East Longhua Road, Huangpu District, Shanghai 200023
Phone: (86) 21 2305 2666
Web: www.sinopharmgroup.com.cn

HISTORICAL FINANCIALS
Company Type: Public

Income Statement — FYE: December 31

	REVENUE ($mil)	NET INCOME ($mil)	NET PROFIT MARGIN	EMPLOYEES
12/22	80,037	1,235	1.5%	114,766
12/21	82,072	1,222	1.5%	0
12/16	37,209	669	1.8%	55,241
12/15	34,963	579	1.7%	54,735
12/14	32,246	463	1.4%	50,099
Annual Growth	12.0%	13.1%	—	10.9%

2022 Year-End Financials
- Debt ratio: 2.6%
- Return on equity: 13.1%
- Cash ($ mil.): 8,004
- Current Ratio: 1.36
- Long-term debt ($ mil.): 1,703
- No. of shares ($ mil.): 3,120
- Dividends
- Yield: —
- Payout: 110.4%
- Market value ($ mil.): 39,289

	STOCK PRICE ($) FY Close	P/E High/Low	Earnings	Dividends	Book Value
12/22	12.59	5 3	0.40	0.44	3.16
12/21	10.81	7 4	0.39	0.44	3.12
12/16	20.50	15 11	0.24	0.23	1.66
Annual Growth	(7.8%)		6.3%	8.1%	8.4%

Sinovac Biotech Ltd

Sinovac Biotech singles out infectious illnesses such as hepatitis A and pandemic influenza for its vaccine development programs. The company has commercialized vaccines for ailments such as hepatitis A (under the Healive brand), seasonal influenza (Anflu), and pandemic influenza strains (Panflu) in select global markets (primarily China). Sinovac has other vaccines under development for disease targets including pneumonia and meningitis. Through its Tangshan Yian subsidiary, the company is also researching vaccines with applications in the animal health industry. Parent company Sinovac (Cayman) is taking Sinovac Biotech private in a US$401.8 million transaction.

EXECUTIVES
Chief Executive Officer, President, Secretary, Chairman, Executive Director, Weidong Yin, $4,000 total compensation
Chief Financial Officer, Vice President, Nan Wang
Chief Operating Officer, Vice President, Research and Development, Qiang Gao
Vice President, Quality and Production, Jing Li
Independent Director, Simon Anderson
Independent Director, Yuk Lam Lo
Independent Director, Kenneth Lee
Independent Director, Meng Mei
Independent Director, Shan Fu
Auditors : Grant Thornton

LOCATIONS
HQ: Sinovac Biotech Ltd
No. 39 Shangdi Xi Road, Haidian District, Beijing 100085
Phone: (86) 10 5693 1800   **Fax:** (86) 10 5693 1800
Web: www.sinovac.com

COMPETITORS
AGENUS INC.
BRICKELL BIOTECH, INC.
DYNAVAX TECHNOLOGIES CORPORATION
IMCLONE SYSTEMS LLC
SANOFI PASTEUR INC.

HISTORICAL FINANCIALS
Company Type: Public

Income Statement — FYE: December 31

	REVENUE ($mil)	NET INCOME ($mil)	NET PROFIT MARGIN	EMPLOYEES
12/21	19,374	8,467	43.7%	4,281
12/20	510	110	21.6%	1,959
12/19	246	44	18.3%	910
12/18	229	21	9.5%	870
12/17	174	25	14.8%	800
Annual Growth	224.7%	325.6%	—	52.1%

2021 Year-End Financials
- Debt ratio: 0.2%
- Return on equity: —
- Cash ($ mil.): 11,608
- Current Ratio: 6.18
- Long-term debt ($ mil.): 22
- No. of shares ($ mil.): 99
- Dividends
- Yield: —
- Payout: 0.0%
- Market value ($ mil.): —

Sistema PJSFC

Sistema Public Joint Stock Financial Corporation or Sistema PJSFC is Russia's largest public investment company and one of the country's systemically important companies serving millions customers in the sectors of telecommunications, electric power, retail (including e-commerce), banking, high tech, hospitality, healthcare, pharmaceuticals, timber, agricultural and real estate industries. Major holdings include wireless network operator Mobile TeleSystems (MTS) and Ozon Holdings PLC (Ozon), one of Russia's largest e-commerce platform. The company was founded in 1993 by Chairman Vladimir Evtushenkov, one of the wealthiest men in Russia, owns a majority stake in Sistema PJSFC.

Operations

The company's investment portfolio is made up mostly of Russian companies operating across Russia and in more than 25 other countries. This includes MTS, Ozon, Segezha Group, Etalon group, MEDSI, Steppe Agroholding, Binnopharm Group, and other.

MTS is a leading telecom operator in Russia and the CIS offering mobile and fixed-line communication services, data transfer and Internet access, cable and satellite TV broadcasting; a provider of digital services, including fintech and media as part of ecosystems and mobile applications; a provider of IT solutions in the area of unified communications, the Internet of Things, monitoring, data processing and cloud computing.

Ozon is a leading multi-category online marketplace in Russia's e-commerce market with a broad product mix and extensive logistical infrastructure enabling the company to make one of the best offers to its customers.

Segezha Group is one of Russia's largest vertically integrated holding companies with a full cycle of logging and advanced wood processing. Segezha Group comprises forest, wood processing and pulp and paper assets in Russia and Europe.

Etalon Group is one of the largest and oldest real estate development companies in Russia specializing in mid-market housing construction projects. A leading player in St. Petersburg and Moscow, it is now actively expanding into other regions of Russia.

Medsi is Russia's biggest national private healthcare platform offering a full range of medical services, from primary and ambulance care to high-tech diagnostics, complex surgeries and rehabilitation programs, as well as a broad range of services aimed at improving the quality of life.

Steppe AgroHolding is one of Russia's largest vertically integrated agricultural players with 578 thsd ha of land and a diversified asset portfolio.

Binnopharm Group is Russia's leading pharmaceutical company specializing in the development, manufacturing, promotion and sales of drugs and medical products in the markets of Russia and the CIS.

Geographic Reach

Headquartered in Moscow, Russia, its investment portfolio is made up mostly of Russian companies operating across Russia and in more than 25 other countries.

Financial Performance

The company's revenue for fiscal 2021 increased by 11% to RUB 802.4 billion compared to RUB 691.6 billion in the prior year. driven by revenue growth at key assets: at MTS, thanks to higher consumption of telecoms services and internet traffic, increased consumption of ecosystem services and higher sales of handsets and accessories; at Segezha Group, on the back of an increase in production volumes and positive dynamics in prices for key products; at Steppe AgroHolding, thanks to an increased gross harvest in the Field Crops segment and increased milk production in the Dairy segment, as well as the successful development of agrotrading and the development of new business lines. The consolidation of Binnopharm Group's results in Sistema's financial statements from 25 June 2021 also had an impact on the company's revenue.

Net income for fiscal 2021 increased to RUB 17.3 billion compared to RUB 10.2 billion.

Strategy

Sistema's strategic goal is to ensure long-term growth of shareholder value by boosting return on investments in the existing assets and reinvesting available cash in new investment projects to diversify its portfolio and increase return on investments.

The key priorities of the company include further improvement of customer loyalty by expanding the product range and offering quality customer service; attraction of vendors by enhancing existing and creating new vendor solutions; development in other regions, including further expansion of operations in Belarus and Kazakhstan; development of promising business streams and enhancement of efficiency.

Mergers and Acquisitions

In late 2022, Sistema PJSFC has entered into binding agreements to acquire a 47.7% stake in Melon Fashion Group JSC, a leading Russian fashion manufacturer and retailer, from the Swedish Eastnine and East Capital Holding AB, as well as a group of individual investors, for RUB 15.8 billion. The completion of the Transaction is anticipated by the end of 2022 subject to further regulatory approvals and satisfaction of certain conditions stipulated by the parties to the Transaction.

In late 2021, Sistema PJSFC announced that JSC New Investment Holding as acquired Nearmedic International Limited, the 100% shareholder of LLC Nearmedic Plus, LLC Nearmedic Pharma, and several other pharmaceutical, biotech, and healthcare businesses in Russia and Italy. Sistema and the Sberbank group of companies have in equal parts provided the Buyer with RUB 1.2bn in equity financing that will go towards the partial repayment of Nearmedic's outstanding debt to Sberbank. Terms were not disclosed.

In early 2021, Sistema PJSFC announced that LLC Megapolis Invest, a joint venture between Sistema and LLC Sberbank Investments as acquired an additional 29.64% stake in JSC Elektrozavod from a private investor for RUB 5.8bn provided to the Purchaser by SberInvest in the form of debt financing. Elektrozavod Group includes transformer equipment production facilities in Moscow and Ufa, maintenance divisions, research and design institutes, an engineering centre and land plots totalling 19 hectares near the Elektrozavodskaya metro station in Moscow.

EXECUTIVES

Chairman, Co-Founder, Vladimir Evtushenkov
Chairman, President, Chief Executive Officer, Andrey Dubovskov
Auditors: AO Deloitte & Touche CIS

LOCATIONS

HQ: Sistema PJSFC
Building 1, 13 Mokhovaya Street, Moscow 125009
Phone: (7) 495 730 66 00
Web: www.sistema.com

PRODUCTS/OPERATIONS

2010 Sales

	$ in mil.	% of total
Oil & energy	13,316.7	47
Telecommunications	11,476.2	41
Consumer assets	1,949.7	7
Technology & industry	1,317.3	5
Other	38.6	—
Total	28,098.5	100

Selected Subsidiaries
Bashkirenergo (energy production)
Bashneft (oil and gas)
Binnofarm (pharmaceuticals distribution)
Detsky Mir-Center (retail and wholesale trading)
Intourist (travel services)
M2M Telematics (telecommunications)
Medsi (health care services)
Moscow Bank for Reconstruction and Development (financial services)
MTS (telecommunications)
Sistema Mass Media (cable TV, film production, advertising)
Sistema Shyam TeleServices Limited (telecommunications)

HISTORICAL FINANCIALS

Company Type: Public

Income Statement — FYE: December 31

	REVENUE ($mil)	NET INCOME ($mil)	NET PROFIT MARGIN	EMPLOYEES
12/21	10,685	230	2.2%	0
12/20	9,245	136	1.5%	0
12/19	10,554	459	4.4%	0
12/18	11,154	(658)	—	0
12/17	12,186	(1,636)	—	0
Annual Growth	(3.2%)	—	—	—

2021 Year-End Financials

Debt ratio: 0.6%
Return on equity: 23.0%
Cash ($ mil.): 1,090
Current Ratio: 0.62
Long-term debt ($ mil.): 8,543
No. of shares ($ mil.): 9,393
Dividends
Yield: —
Payout: 685.7%
Market value ($ mil.): 55,044

	STOCK PRICE ($) FY Close	P/E High/Low		PER SHARE ($) Earnings	Dividends	Book Value
12/21	5.86	5	3	0.02	0.17	0.12
12/20	7.75	7	3	0.01	0.07	0.09
12/19	4.74	2	1	0.05	0.07	0.07
12/18	2.20	—	—	(0.07)	0.06	0.03
12/17	3.45	—	—	(0.17)	1.05	0.09
Annual Growth	14.2%	—	—	—	(36.9%)	8.4%

Skandinaviska Enskilda Banken

SEB is a leading Nordic financial services group with a strong belief that entrepreneurial minds and innovative companies are key in creating a better world. SEB takes a long-term perspective and supports its customers in good times and bad. In Sweden and the Baltic countries, SEB offers financial advice and a wide range of financial services. In Denmark, Finland, Norway, Germany and UK the bank's operations have a strong focus on corporate and investment banking based on a full-service offering to corporate and institutional clients. The international nature of SEB's business is reflected in its presence in some 20 countries worldwide. Founded in 1856, the company boasts more than SEK 2.7 trillion in assets under management.

Operations

The company operates five main divisions: Large Corporates & Financial Institutions; Corporate & Private Customers; Baltic; Life and Investment Management.

Large Corporates & Financial Institutions division offer capital markets transaction services (equity and debt); financing as well as advice relating to investment banking activities (mergers and acquisitions, etc.); products and services for cash management and trade finance; brokerage and trading services; post trade investor services such as custody, risk and valuation services and collateral management; macroeconomic analysis and securities research. The division accounts for nearly 45% of total operating income.

Corporate & Private Customers division has a broad offering for both private and corporate customers, ranging from everyday banking services to private individuals and smaller companies, to Private Banking services with global reach for high-net-worth individuals in the Nordic countries. In addition, complex banking and advisory services are provided to medium-sized companies. The division also issues cards in the Nordic countries under SEB's own brand as well as for Eurocard and several other partner brands. It generates some 35% of total operating income.

Baltic division provides universal banking including advisory services to private individuals and all corporate customer segments in Estonia, Latvia and Lithuania, with significant market shares across key segments and products in all three countries. Baltic division accounts for about 10% of total operating income.

Life division provides life insurance solutions, including unit-linked, portfolio bond and traditional insurance as well as health and sickness insurance. The division aims to serve customers throughout life with long-term advice and solutions in order to provide companies and individuals with the right insurance coverage. The division makes up more than 5% of total operating income.

Investment Management offers asset management services through a broad range of funds and tailored portfolio mandates to institutional investors, as well as retail and Private Banking customers. Assets are managed across equities, fixed income, alternative investments and multi-strategy management. The division generates around 5% of total operating income.

More broadly, SEB generates almost 50% of its total operating income from net interest income, while about 40% from net fee and commission income and less than 15% from net financial income.

Geographic Reach

SEB generates more than 60% of its operating income in Sweden. Its other top markets are in the Nordic countries of Denmark, Finland, Germany, and Norway, as well as in Baltic countries such as Estonia, Latvia, and Lithuania.

Based in Sweden, SEB expands its business for large corporate customers in the Netherlands, Austria and Switzerland. It also has international presences in Beijing, Hong Kong, Kyiv, Luxembourg, New Delhi, New York, São Paulo, Shanghai, Singapore, St. Petersburg and Warsaw.

Sales and Marketing

SEB serves about four million corporate and private customers and 400,000 small and medium-sized businesses. SEB serves some 2,000 large corporations across a broad spectrum of industries.

Financial Performance

The company had a total operating income of SEK 54.6 billion, a 10% increase from the previous year's total operating income of SEK 49.7 billion. SEB's operating profit improved significantly compared with the challenging pandemic year of 2020, in line with the global economic recovery, rising stock markets and an improved sentiment.

In 2021, the company had a net income of SEK 25.4 billion, a 61% increase from the previous year's net income of SEK 15.7 billion.

The company's cash at the end of 2021 was SEK 445.7 billion. Operating activities generated SEK 130.3 billion, while investing activities used SEK 846 million, mainly for investments in intangible and tangible assets. Financing activities used another SEK 22.2 billion, primarily for dividends paid.

Strategy

As the banking industry changes and competition increases, SEB's core strengths as a bank are growing in importance. Over the last 15 years, the company has therefore adapted its strategic direction ? refocusing, strengthening and transforming SEB's core. This has entailed efforts such as a restructuring of SEB Group functions, corporate expansion in the Nordics and Germany, transformation of the Baltic and Retail divisions, and increased efforts aimed at achieving true customer centricity. During the past three years the company has focused on accelerating the transformation based on its three strategic focus areas of advisory leadership, operational excellence and extended presence.

SEB will continue to invest for the future, to ensure that it remains relevant for customers and that we continue to create long-term value for shareholders.

HISTORY

Skandinaviska Enskilda Banken (SEB) was incorporated in 1972 as a result of the merger between Stockholm's Enskilda Bank (founded in 1856 by the Wallenberg family) and Skandinaviska Banken (founded in 1864, and a pioneer in commercial lending in Scandinavia). By 1974 SEB had begun expanding its operations, forming an investment management subsidiary. It then became one of the first Swedish banks to go international when it took a stake in the German Deutsch-Skandinavische Bank in 1976. By the end of the 1970s SEB had reached halfway around the world, establishing a subsidiary in Singapore to handle Southeast Asian operations.

By the early 1980s SEB was leading the nation in industrial as well as private accounts, largely due to deregulation and the introduction of new financial instruments, including Swedish treasury bills, a commercial paper market, and market-rate state bonds. The bank continued to expand, opening branches in the Cayman Islands, Hamburg, London, and New York; it also began cross-border banking in Scandinavia through a regional alliance with Bergen Bank of Norway, Privatbanken of Denmark, and Union Bank of Finland.

In another step toward deregulation, the Swedish government lifted the ban on foreign banking in 1985. Within a year a dozen international banks had established themselves in Sweden, but SEB continued to expand; its investment banking subsidiary,

Enskilda Securities, opened branches in Hong Kong, London, New York, Paris, and Singapore in the latter half of the 1980s.

In 1990 the bank acquired an option to buy about a third of Skandia, Sweden's largest private insurance company. But facing strong resistance from Skandia's management, SEB accepted defeat and sold most of its option to two Scandinavian insurance companies. Winds of change blew through Sweden in the early 1990s as the country suffered a severe economic recession. Deregulation in the mid-1980s, followed by excessive lending to the property market, led to inflated real estate prices and then a collapse of the market. Banks investing in property experienced huge losses; many banks (including SEB) had to turn to the government for help to strengthen their capital bases. The mid-1990s saw the bank still trying to recover, selling several of its subsidiaries, including a vehicle finance unit, to GE Capital.

1997 saw SEB acquire Trygg-Hansa (now SEB Trygg Liv), one of Sweden's major insurers. The bank remained acquisitive in 1998, expanding aggressively into the Baltic by buying major stakes in banks in Estonia (Eesti Ãœhispank), Latvia (Latvija Unibanken), and Lithuania (Vilniaus Bankas).

In 1999 the bank further emphasized its Internet business, making it a separate unit. Also that year, SEB sold Trygg-Hansa's non-life business to Denmark's Codan Insurance in exchange for Codan's banking subsidiary and other assets. In 2000 the bank acquired Germany's almost 200-branch BfG Bank from CrÃ©dit Lyonnais; it then used BfG to create a cross-selling and Internet alliance with German insurer Gerling. Also in 2000 SEB upped its stake in Eesti Ãœhispank, Vilniaus Bankas, and Latvijas Unibanka.

The following year SEB announced plans to acquire fellow Swedish bank FÃ¶reningsSparbanken to create SEB SwedBank. EU regulators investigated the proposal and demanded significant concession. As a result, the two banks dropped plans for the merger later in 2001.

SEB continued to boost its offerings and services -- largely through acquisitions -- during the early years of the 21st century. Purchases included Europay in Norway (2002), Danish life insurer Codan Pension (2004), Ukraine's Bank Agio (2005), and Russia's PetroEnergoBank (2006). In 2007 it acquired nearly all of Factorial Bank, adding 65 branches in Eastern Ukraine. The following year it bought London-based hedge fund Key Asset Management.

EXECUTIVES

Deputy President, Deputy Chief Executive, Mats Torstendahl
Executive Vice President, Joachim Alpen
Chief Risk Officer, Mats Holmstrom
Acting Chief Financial Officer, Peter Kessiakoff
Chief Information Officer, Nicolas Moch
Executive Vice President, William Paus
Chief Sustainability Officer, Hans Beyer
General Counsel, Secretary, Hans Ragnhall
President, Chief Executive Officer, Director, Johan Torgeby
Chairman, Independent Director, Marcus Wallenberg
Vice-Chairman, Independent Director, Sven Nyman
Vice-Chairman, Independent Director, Jesper Ovesen
Independent Director, Signhild Arnegard Hansen
Independent Director, Anne-Catherine Berner
Independent Director, Winnie Fok
Independent Director, Lars Ottersgard
Independent Director, Helena Saxon
Director, Anna-Karin Glimstrom
Director, Charlotta Lindholm
Deputy Director, Annika Dahlberg
Deputy Director, Magnus Olsson
Auditors : Ernst & Young AB

LOCATIONS

HQ: Skandinaviska Enskilda Banken
  Kungstradgardsgatan 8, Stockholm SE-106 40
Phone: (46) 771 62 10 00
Web: www.sebgroup.com

2014 Operating Income

	% of total
Scandinavia	
Sweden	60
Norway	8
Denmark	7
Finland	4
Baltics	
Lithuania	3
Estonia	3
Latvia	2
Germany	7
Other	6
Total	100

PRODUCTS/OPERATIONS

2014 Sales by Segment

	% of total
Merchant Banking	38
Retail Banking	27
Life	10
Wealth Management	10
Baltic	8
Other	7
Total	100

COMPETITORS

Bayerische Landesbank
COMMONWEALTH BANK OF AUSTRALIA
CoÃ¶peratieve Rabobank U.A.
Landesbank Baden-WÃ¼rttemberg
NATWEST GROUP PLC
Nordea Bank AB
Svenska Handelsbanken AB
The Toronto-Dominion Bank
U.S. BANCORP
UniCredit Bank AG

HISTORICAL FINANCIALS

Company Type: Public

Income Statement   FYE: December 31

	ASSETS ($mil)	NET INCOME ($mil)	INCOME AS % OF ASSETS	EMPLOYEES
12/22	340,564	2,601	0.8%	16,500
12/21	364,718	2,806	0.8%	15,500
12/20	372,130	1,927	0.5%	16,193
12/19	307,085	2,168	0.7%	15,819
12/18	286,832	2,584	0.9%	15,562
Annual Growth	4.4%	0.2%	—	1.5%

2022 Year-End Financials

Return on assets: 0.7%   Dividends
Return on equity: 13.5%   Yield: —
Long-term debt ($ mil.): —   Payout: 47.8%
No. of shares ($ mil.): 2,113 Market value ($ mil.): —
Sales ($ mil.): 8,840

Smurfit Kappa Group PLC

Smurfit Kappa creates paper-based packaging solutions. It protects products in transit and precious resources for future generations while caring for each other, the environment and the planet. It owns approximately 68k hectares of forest globally, which are FSC or PEFC certified, promoting economic growth, protection of biodiversity and ecosystems and fostering social equity. It manufactures a wide range of papers mainly used for packaging purposes. Total global paper and board capacity is approximately 8.4 million tonnes per annum. It designs, manufactures and supplies paper-based packaging to package, promote and protect our customers' products. We manufacture corrugated packaging and also produce solidboard, folding carton and bag-in-box.

Operations

The group has identified two operating segments: Europe (generates more than 75% of revenue) and the Americas (nearly 25%).

The Europe and the Americas segments are each highly integrated. They include a system of mills and plants that primarily produce a full line of containerboard that is converted into corrugated containers within each segment. In addition, the Europe segment also produces other types of paper, such as solidboard, sack kraft paper, machine glazed ('MG') and graphic paper, and other paper-based packaging, such as honeycomb, solidboard packaging and folding cartons; and bag-in-box packaging. The Americas segment, which includes a number of Latin American countries and the United States, also comprises forestry; other types of paper, such as boxboard and sack paper; and paper-based packaging, such as folding cartons, honeycomb and paper sacks. Inter-segment revenue is not material.

Geographic Reach

Geographically, the major economic environments in which the group conducts its business are Europe (principally the Eurozone, Sweden and the United Kingdom) and the Americas (principally Argentina, Brazil, Colombia, Mexico and the United States).

It is located in 23 countries in Europe and 13 in the Americas. In Europe, it is the leader by production volume in corrugated packaging and containerboard and in Latin America, it is the only large-scale pan-regional player.

Sales and Marketing
The company offers an unrivalled portfolio of sustainable packaging solutions in a selection of materials and combine innovative structural design with high-quality print to maximize brand impact and drive increased sales.

Financial Performance
Revenue for the year increased by 27% to EUR 12.8 billion. EBITDA for the full year was EUR 2.4 billion, a 38% increase over 2021, with an EBITDA margin of 18.4%, ROCE of 21.8% and a net debt to EBITDA of less than 1.3x.

Profit for the financial year was EUR 945 million compared to EUR 679 million from the previous year.

Cash at the end of the year was EUR 771 million. Operation provided EUR 1.5 million while investing and financing activities used EUR 967 million and EUR 496 million, respectively. Main cash used was additions to property, plant and equipment and biological assets.

Strategy
The company's objective is to develop long-term customer relationships by providing customers with innovative, sustainable packaging solutions that enhance the customers' prospects of success in their end markets. The company strategic priorities include market position, partner of choice, operational excellence, investment in people, and capital allocation.

HISTORY

English tailor John Jefferson Smurfit began his career in box making as an advisor to a box maker that had been established in Dublin in 1934. In 1938, at the age of 29, he left his tailoring business in Belfast to fully control the Dublin company. Smurfit named it Jefferson Smurfit & Sons Limited in 1942. By 1950 the plant had expanded fivefold in size, and production had increased eight times.

After going public in 1964, the company went on a buying spree that included carton and box maker Temple Press Limited (1968), which doubled the company's size. Its size doubled again with the 1970 purchase of the Hely Group, a diversified company with holdings in packaging, radio and television distribution, and educational and office supplies. The company moved into the UK with its purchase of W. J. Noble and Sons (cartons and printing). In 1972 Jefferson Smurfit Group Limited became the company's name.

Expanding to overseas markets, the company bought 40% of US-based Time Industries (paper and plastics) in 1974, increased its share to 51% in 1976, and bought the rest in 1977 -- the same year Jefferson Smurfit's founder died. Jefferson Smurfit became full owner of Alton Box Board Company (US) in 1981. Two years later, in its effort to diversify, it formed Smurfit Paribas Bank, a joint venture with the French Bank Paribas. Also in 1983 the company established Jefferson Smurfit Corporation (JSC) to oversee its US operations.

Jefferson Smurfit diversified further with the 1984 purchase of a 76% stake in Executive Travel and full acquisition of Swains Packaging (plastic packaging). The company then moved into the newsprint business (1986), acquiring 80% of Publishers Paper Company (renamed Smurfit Newsprint Corporation). In a joint venture with Morgan Stanley Leveraged Equity Fund, Jefferson Smurfit purchased 50% of Mobil Oil's Container Corporation of America in 1986 for $1.2 billion.

In 1988 Jefferson Smurfit bought Sonofit Containers Limited and renamed it Smurfit Fibreboard Converters. Purchases in 1989 included Rolex Paper (paper tubes, UK) and Cartonera Nacional (corrugated packaging, Puerto Rico). Already a leading recycler of wastepaper, Jefferson Smurfit bought California-based Golden State Newsprint and Pacific Recycling in 1990. In 1994 it added the paper and packaging operations of France's Compagnie de Saint-Gobain, doubling its European operations. The following year it bought Les Papeteries du Limousin of France (corrugated packaging). Jefferson Smurfit also entered the Asian market through a joint venture with a company in China to establish a linerboard mill through its JSC unit.

In 1996 Jefferson Smurfit sold Swains Packaging and Smurfit Packaging Products to British Polythene Industries. The next year it bought majority shares in two Argentinian companies (paperboard and corrugated cases) and fully acquired two German trading companies (corrugated boxes and boards). It sold its Mexican Plastics division to Owens Illinois Group. JSC merged with Stone Container Corporation in 1998 to create the US's largest producer of containerboard, RockTenn PC (originally known as Smurfit-Stone Container). Jefferson Smurfit owned about 30% of the public company, but the holding was later spun off to shareholders. In 1999 the company began disposing of noncore operations -- timberlands, newsprint holdings, and finance businesses (Smurfit Finance and Smurfit Paribas Bank). Jefferson Smurfit doubled its converting capacity in Argentina in 2000 by buying corrugated plant FÃbrica Argentina de CartÃ"n Corrugado (FACCA).

In 2002 the company placed a revised bid to buy Swedish paper company MunksjÃ– as low paper prices in Europe led to an industry-wide devaluation. That June the shoe was on the other foot, however: US-based investment company Madison Dearborn Partners made a $3.5 billion cash bid for Jefferson Smurfit -- a 38% premium over where the stock was trading at the time -- and bought the company in July 2002. (Jefferson Smurfit did ultimately acquire MunksjÃ–, too.)

In 2003 the company acquired the European assets of its former US affiliate Smurfit-Stone Container in return for 50% of its Canadian unit and $200 million. Later that year, Jefferson Smurfit acquired 98% of Spanish paper company Papelera Navarra and changed the acquired company's name to Smurfit Navarra. In 2004, it acquired the remaining stake in the company.

In 2005, the company changed its name to Smurfit Kappa Group after acquiring rival Kappa Packaging.

Sharing in the global economic slowdown, SKG struggled to maintain its paper prominence by trimming assets faster than adding them. The company disposed of its non-core, non-productive businesses including newsprint, timberlands, and finance holdings. SKG exited the tissue and specialties business, dropping Smurfit MunksjÃ– in 2005. In 2008 the Group unloaded its 40% stake in the corrugated and containerboard manufacturer Duropack, and its ownership in the UK educational publisher EDCO.

EXECUTIVES

Chief Executive Officer, Director, Anthony Smurfit
Chief Financial Officer, Director, Ken Bowles
Secretary, G. Carson-Callan
Independent Non-Executive Chairman, Irial Finan
Senior Independent Non-Executive Director, Ganzalo Restrepo
Independent Non-Executive Director, Kaisa H. Hietala
Independent Non-Executive Director, Anne Anderson
Independent Non-Executive Director, Carol Fairweather
Independent Non-Executive Director, James Lawrance
Independent Non-Executive Director, Lourdes Melgar
Independent Non-Executive Director, John Moloney
Independent Non-Executive Director, Jorgen Buhl Rasmussen
Non-Executive Director, Frits Beurskens
Auditors : KPMG

LOCATIONS

HQ: Smurfit Kappa Group PLC
Beech Hill, Clonskeagh, Dublin 4 D04 N2R2
Phone: (353) 1 202 7000

Web: www.smurfitkappa.com

2018 Sales
	% of total
Europe	77
The Americas	23
Total	100

2018 Sales
	% of total
Ireland	1
Germany	15
France	12
United Kingdom	9
Mexico	9
The Netherlands	8
Other	46
Total	100

Selected Locations
Europe
  Austria
  Belgium (FR)
  Belgium (NL)
  Czech Republic
  Denmark
  Finland
  France
  Germany
  Greece
  Ireland
  Italy
  Latvia
  Lithuania
  Netherlands
  Norway
  Poland
  Portugal
  Russia
  Slovakia
  Spain
  Sweden
  Switzerland
  UK
The Americas
  Argentina
  Chile
  Colombia
  Costa Rica
  Dominican Republic
  Ecuador
  Mexico
  Puerto Rico
  US
  Venezuela

PRODUCTS/OPERATIONS

2018 sales
	%
Packaging	83
Paper	17
Total	100

Selected Products
Base materials graphic & printing
  Graphic board
Packaging
  Bag-in-box
  Food & groceries packaging
  Fresh food packaging
  Industrial packaging
  Primary packaging
  Retail ready packaging
  Standard products
Packaging intermediates
  Corrugated boards
  Fanfold
  Pre-printed liners
  Sheetfeeding
  Single face
Paper & board
  Containerboard
  Packaging board
  Solid board
  Specialty board
Raw & base materials
  Forest products
  Fresh fibre
  Recovered paper

HISTORICAL FINANCIALS
Company Type: Public

Income Statement   FYE: December 31

	REVENUE ($mil)	NET INCOME ($mil)	NET PROFIT MARGIN	EMPLOYEES
12/22	13,686	1,008	7.4%	48,624
12/21	11,439	768	6.7%	47,753
12/20	10,468	668	6.4%	46,375
12/19	10,158	534	5.3%	46,563
12/18	10,244	(739)	—	46,025
Annual Growth	7.5%	—	—	1.4%

2022 Year-End Financials
Debt ratio: 29.1%   No. of shares ($ mil.): 257
Return on equity: 20.0%   Dividends
Cash ($ mil.): 829   Yield: —
Current Ratio: 1.49   Payout: 23.8%
Long-term debt ($ mil.): 3,445   Market value ($ mil.): 9,559

	STOCK PRICE ($) FY Close	P/E High/Low		PER SHARE ($) Earnings	Dividends	Book Value
12/22	37.14	15	8	3.86	0.92	20.85
12/21	57.19	22	17	2.96	1.19	19.28
12/20	46.67	21	11	2.77	0.89	18.06
12/19	37.98	20	13	2.25	0.82	14.03
12/18	26.57	—	—	(3.13)	0.76	13.38
Annual Growth	8.7%		—	—	5.0%	11.7%

Societe Generale

EXECUTIVES

Deputy Chief Executive Officer, Philippe Aymerich
Deputy Chief Executive Officer, Diony Lebot
Chief Financial Officer, Claire Dumas
Chief Risk Officer, Stephane Landon
Chief Innovation Officer, Claire Calmejane
Chief Security Officer, Antoine Creux
Chief Information Officer, Carlos Goncalves
Deputy Chief Financial Officer, Xavier Lofficial
Chief Economist, Michala Marcussen
Chief Sustainability Officer, Hacina P.Y.
Chief Technology Officer, Alain Voiment
Chief Executive Officer, Director, Frederic Oudea
Secretary, Gilles Briatta
Chairman, Independent Director, Lorenzo Bini Smaghi
Independent Director, William Connelly
Independent Director, Jerome Contamine
Independent Director, Diane Cote
Independent Director, Kyra Hazou
Independent Director, Annette Messemer
Independent Director, Gerard Mestrallet
Independent Director, Juan Maria Nin Genova
Independent Director, Henri Poupart-Lafarge
Independent Director, Lubomira Rochet
Independent Director, Alexandra Schaapveld
Director, France Houssaye
Auditors: ERNST & YOUNG et Autres

LOCATIONS
HQ: Societe Generale
  29, Boulevard Haussman, Paris 75009
Phone: (33) 1 42 14 20 00
Web: www.societegenerale.com

HISTORICAL FINANCIALS
Company Type: Public

Income Statement   FYE: December 31

	ASSETS ($mil)	NET INCOME ($mil)	INCOME AS % OF ASSETS	EMPLOYEES
12/22	1,587,990	2,155	0.1%	117,576
12/21	1,657,560	6,384	0.4%	131,293
12/20	1,794,240	(316)	0.0%	133,251
12/19	1,523,030	3,646	0.2%	138,240
12/18	1,499,550	4,425	0.3%	149,022
Annual Growth	1.4%	(16.5%)	—	(5.8%)

2022 Year-End Financials
Return on assets: 0.1%   Dividends
Return on equity: 3.0%   Yield: —
Long-term debt ($ mil.): —   Payout: 19.1%
No. of shares ($ mil.): 849   Market value ($ mil.): 4,215
Sales ($ mil.): 60,900

	STOCK PRICE ($) FY Close	P/E High/Low		PER SHARE ($) Earnings	Dividends	Book Value
12/22	4.96	5	2	1.85	0.35	83.51
12/21	6.94	1	1	6.76	0.13	86.30
12/20	4.16	—	—	(1.25)	0.68	88.71
12/19	6.99	2	2	3.42	0.49	84.40
12/18	6.29	3	1	4.86	0.51	88.59
Annual Growth	(5.8%)	—	—	(21.5%)	(8.9%)	(1.5%)

Sodexo

Founded in 1966 by Pierre Bellon, Sodexo is the global leader in Quality of Life services. The company is a partner of over 100 million consumers in over 50 countries. With more than 422,000 employees worldwide, the company is the number one France-based private employer worldwide. The company has a wide range of services to meet the needs of clients and consumers. These services include on-site services, benefits & rewards services, and personal & home services. Sodexo's services contribute to the performance of their clients, the satisfaction of the company's consumers, the fulfillment of their teams and the economic, social and environmental development of their local communities.

Operations
Sodexo's portfolio of activities encompasses Food Services, Facilities Management Services, and Employee Benefit Solutions, as well as Hospitality services with Sodexo Live!

Geographic Reach
The company operates in more than 50 countries.

Financial Performance

Fiscal 2022 consolidated revenues reached EUR 21.1 billion, up 21% year-on-year, driven by organic growth of 17%, a net contribution from acquisitions and disposals of 1% and a strong positive currency impact of 6%.

Cash held by the company at the end of fiscal 2022 decreased to EUR 3.2 billion. Cash provided by operations was EUR 1.0 billion while cash used for investing and financing activities were EUR 386 million and EUR 1.1 billion, respectively. Main uses of cash were for acquisitions of property and dividends paid.

Strategy

Sodexo's strategic priorities are: boost US growth; accelerate the food model transformation; manage its portfolio more actively; and enhance the effectiveness of its organization.

HISTORY

The Bellon family had been luxury ship hospitality specialists since the turn of the century, 60 years before Pierre Bellon founded Sodexho in 1966. By 1971 Bellon had his first contract outside France to provide foodservice to a Brussels hospital. Sodexho continued to expand its services into the late 1970s, entering remote site management in Africa and the Middle East in 1975 and starting its service vouchers segment in Belgium and Germany in 1978.

Sodexho jumped the pond in 1980, expanding its businesses into North and South America. The company went public on the Paris Bourse exchange in 1983. Two years later it bought Seiler, a Boston vending machine company-turned-restaurateur. Sodexho then bought San Francisco's Food Dimensions in 1987. After beefing up its American operations with four other US acquisitions, the company merged Food Dimensions and Seiler in 1989. Sodexho's US river cruise company, Spirit Cruises -- an echo of the Bellon family's original calling -- was also included in the merger. The merged US companies were renamed Sodexho USA in 1993.

The 1990s proved an era of growth and acquisitions for Sodexho. The company expanded into Japan, Africa, Russia, and five Eastern European countries in 1993. The company acquired a 20% stake in Corrections Corporation of America the following year and virtually doubled its size with the acquisition of the UK's Gardner Merchant in 1995. The largest catering company in that region, Gardner Merchant had holdings that spanned Australia, Asia, northern Europe, the UK, and the US -- generally markets where Sodexho did not have a strong presence. That year the company also acquired Partena, a Swedish security and care company, from Volvo's Fortos.

Gardner Merchant's US business was officially merged with Sodexho USA in 1996 to make it the #4 foodservice company in the US. Also that year Sodexho acquired Brazilian service voucher company Cardapio. After a year of legal wrangling, Sodexho also lost a fight for control of Accor's Eurest France to rival caterer Compass Group and sold off its minority interest. The next year Sodexho acquired 49% of Universal Ogden Services, renamed Universal Services, an American remote site manager. To signify its efforts to maintain the individuality of the companies it acquires, Sodexho changed its name to Sodexho Alliance in 1997.

Marriott International merged its foodservice branch with Sodexho's North American foodservice operations in 1998. With a 48% stake, Sodexho Alliance became the largest shareholder; former Marriott International stockholders took the rest, with the Marriott family controlling 9%. Before the merger, Sodexho USA was less than one-fourth the size of Marriott International's foodservice division. Sodexho acquired GR Servicios Hoteleros in 1999, thereby becoming the largest caterer in Spain. The following year it agreed to merge its remote site management operations with Universal Services and rename it Universal Sodexho (later Sodexo Remote Sites).

In 2001 its initial $900 million bid to buy the 52% of Sodexho Marriott Services it didn't already own was rebuffed by its subsidiary's shareholders. Sodexho Alliance made a better offer (about $1.1 billion) and finally reached an agreement to purchase the rest of Sodexho Marriott Services. The deal was completed later that year and Sodexho Marriott Services changed its name to Sodexho, Inc. Also that year the company agreed to pay some $470 million for French rival Sogeres and US-based food management firm Wood Dining.

In 2002 the company announced it had detected accounting and management errors in its UK operations, causing the value of its stock to fall by nearly one-third. In addition, the company replaced its UK management team because of poor performance there.

Admitting no wrongdoing, Sodexho settled an $80 million race-bias lawsuit just before it was to go to trial in 2005. The suit, brought by the African-American employees of its American subsidiary, Sodexho, Inc., charged that African-Americans were routinely passed over for promotions and were segregated within the company. In addition to paying the monetary award, Sodexho agreed to increase company diversity through promotion incentives, monitoring, and training.

In 2005 Bellon, 75, stepped down as company CEO but remained chairman. He was replaced by Sodexho veteran Michel Landel. The company changed its name to Sodexo in 2008, a rebranding effort that eliminated both the word "Alliance" and the "h" from its name.

EXECUTIVES

Chief Executive Officer, Director, Chairwoman, Sophie Bellon
Chief Financial Officer, Marc Rolland
Chief Growth and Commercial Officer, Marc Plumart
Group Chief Communications and Public Affairs Officer, Anne Bardot
Group Chief Digital and Innovation Officer, Belen Moscoso del Prado Lopez-Doriga
Group Chief Strategy Officer, Alexandra Serizay
Group Chief Sales and Marketing Officer, Bruno Vanhaelst
Group Chief Human Resources Officer, Annick de Vanssay
Independent Director, Jean-Baptiste Chasseloup de Chatillon
Independent Director, Francoise Brougher
Independent Director, Lead Independent Director, Luc Messier
Independent Director, Federico J. Gonzalez Tejera
Independent Director, Sophie Stabile
Independent Director, Veronique Laury
Independent Director, Cecile Tandeau De Marsac
Director, Francois-Xavier Bellon
Director, Nathalie Bellon Szabo
Employee Representative, Philippe Besson
Employee Representative, Cathy Martin
Auditors: PricewaterhouseCoopers Audit

LOCATIONS

HQ: Sodexo
255, Quai de la Bataille de Stalingrad, Issy-les-Moulineaux, Cedex 9 92866
Phone: (33) 1 30 85 75 00
Web: www.sodexo.com

2018 Sales

	% of total
North America	45
Europe	39
Africa, Asia, Australia, LatAm, Middle East	16
Total	100

PRODUCTS/OPERATIONS

2018 Sales

	% of total
On-site Services	
Business & Administrations	54
Health Care and Seniors	23
Educations	10
Benefits & Services	4
Total	100

2018 sales

	% of total
On-site Services revenues	
Foodservices	65
Facilities management services	31
Benefits and Rewards Services	4
Total	100

COMPETITORS

ARAMARK
CANNAE HOLDINGS, INC.
COMPASS GROUP PLC
COMPUTACENTER PLC
HARLAN CASTLE INC

HAYS PLC
MCDONALD'S CORPORATION
MITCHELLS & BUTLERS PLC
SERCO GROUP PLC
SODEXO, INC.

HISTORICAL FINANCIALS
Company Type: Public

Income Statement — FYE: August 31

	REVENUE ($mil)	NET INCOME ($mil)	NET PROFIT MARGIN	EMPLOYEES
08/23	24,601	862	3.5%	429,941
08/22	21,121	694	3.3%	421,991
08/21	20,633	164	0.8%	412,088
08/20	23,013	(375)	—	422,712
08/19	24,235	734	3.0%	470,237
Annual Growth	0.4%	4.1%	—	(2.2%)

2023 Year-End Financials
Debt ratio: 29.2%
Return on equity: 17.7%
Cash ($ mil.): 2,200
Current Ratio: 1.16
Long-term debt ($ mil.): 5,490
No. of shares ($ mil.): 146
Dividends
Yield: 2.3%
Payout: 8.9%
Market value ($ mil.): 3,154

	STOCK PRICE ($) FY Close	P/E High/Low		PER SHARE ($) Earnings	Dividends	Book Value
08/23	21.55	4	3	5.85	0.51	33.72
08/22	15.31	4	3	4.69	0.45	30.11
08/21	16.50	22	14	1.11	2.37	25.65
08/20	14.40	—	—	(2.57)	0.64	22.51
08/19	22.61	5	4	4.97	0.61	33.69
Annual Growth	(1.2%)	—	—	4.2%	(4.3%)	0.0%

SoftBank Corp (New)

EXECUTIVES

Chairman, Representative Director, Ken Miyauchi
President, Chief Executive Officer, Representative Director, Junichi Miyakawa
Executive Vice President, Chief Operating Officer, Representative Director, Jun Shimba
Senior Managing Executive Officer, Chief Financial Officer, Director, Kazuhiko Fujihara
Executive Vice President, Chief Operating Officer, Representative Director, Yasuyuki Imai
Director, Masayoshi Son
Director, Kentaro Kawabe
Outside Director, Atsushi Horiba
Outside Director, Takehiro Kamigama
Outside Director, Kazuaki Oki
Outside Director, Kyoko Uemura
Outside Director, Reiko Hishiyama
Outside Director, Naomi Koshi
Auditors : Deloitte Touche Tohmatsu LLC

LOCATIONS
HQ: SoftBank Corp (New)
1-7-1 Kaigan, Minato-ku, Tokyo 105-7529
Phone: (81) 3 6889 2000
Web: www.softbank.jp

HISTORICAL FINANCIALS
Company Type: Public

Income Statement — FYE: March 31

	REVENUE ($mil)	NET INCOME ($mil)	NET PROFIT MARGIN	EMPLOYEES
03/22	46,783	4,254	9.1%	70,677
03/21	47,013	4,437	9.4%	65,920
03/20	44,783	4,358	9.7%	50,950
03/19	33,828	3,889	11.5%	29,609
03/18	33,738	3,773	11.2%	25,889
Annual Growth	8.5%	3.0%	—	28.5%

2022 Year-End Financials
Debt ratio: 0.3%
Return on equity: 32.4%
Cash ($ mil.): 12,716
Current Ratio: 0.77
Long-term debt ($ mil.): 28,155
No. of shares ($ mil.): 4,707
Dividends
Yield: 6.6%
Payout: 79.8%
Market value ($ mil.): 54,652

	STOCK PRICE ($) FY Close	P/E High/Low		PER SHARE ($) Earnings	Dividends	Book Value
03/22	11.61	0	0	0.89	0.77	2.93
03/21	13.12	0	0	0.93	0.81	2.91
03/20	12.90	0	0	0.90	0.39	1.94
03/19	11.50	0	0	0.81	0.34	2.35
Annual Growth	0.3%	—	—	2.5%	22.8%	5.6%

Sojitz Corp

Sojitz Corporation is a general trading company that engages in a wide range of businesses globally, including manufacturing, selling, importing, and exporting a variety of products, in addition to providing services and investing in diversified businesses, both in Japan and overseas. The company invests in various sectors and financing activities, including transportation, aerospace, medical, energy, marine, chemicals, defense, agriculture, forestry and more. Japan generates approximately 50% of the company's revenue. Sojitz traces its roots back to three trading companies ? Japan Cotton Trading Co., Ltd., Iwai & Co., Ltd., and Suzuki & Co., Ltd. ? with the oldest of its predecessors being Iwai Bunsuke Shoten, a company established in 1862.

Operations

Prior to the company's business divisions restructuring, Sojitz business divisions include Chemicals Division (brings in approximately 25% of the company's revenue), Metals & Mineral Resources Division (over 20%), Retail & Lifestyle Business Division (over 15%), Automotive Division (more than 10%), Foods & Agriculture Business Division (about 10%), Machinery & Medical Infrastructure Division (more than 5%), Energy & Social Infrastructure Division (about 5%), and Aerospace & Transportation Project Division and Industrial Infrastructure & Urban Development Division (account for the rest). As part of this restructuring, the Infrastructure & Healthcare Division was established to inherit certain businesses belonging to the prior Machinery & Medical Infrastructure Division, Energy & Social Infrastructure Division, and Industrial Infrastructure & Urban Development Division. In addition, the Consumer Industry & Agriculture Business Division and the Retail & Consumer Service Division were established to inherit certain businesses conducted by the prior Foods & Agriculture Business Division, Retail & Lifestyle Business Division, and Industrial Infrastructure & Urban Development Division. Meanwhile, the Metals & Mineral Resources Division was renamed the Metals, Mineral Resources & Recycling Division.

Sojitz's structure now consists of seven business divisions: Automotive Division, Aerospace & Transportation Project Division, Infrastructure & Healthcare Division, Metals, Mineral Resources & Recycling Division, Chemicals Division, Consumer Industry & Agriculture Business Division, and Retail & Consumer Service Division.

With automotive assembly and wholesale and retail sales as its core businesses, the Automotive Division develops its operations in growing markets, such as Asia, Russia, NIS countries, and Latin America, as well as in mature markets, such as Japan and the US. In addition, this division is actively enhancing its auto-financing business while developing automotive-related services that meet the needs of the changing times.

The Aerospace & Transportation Project Division develops aerospace industry businesses as a sales agent for commercial aircraft and defense systems and through its leasing, part-out, and business jet businesses. The division is also engaged in airport management, railroad, and other transportation infrastructure businesses as well as in-flight catering, freight car leasing, and other peripheral businesses. Meanwhile, this division's marine vessels business handles multiple types of new and secondhand vessels.

The Infrastructure & Healthcare Division provides new solutions to create value. Specific areas of operation include energy, telecommunications, urban infrastructure, and healthcare, where businesses are developed in response to global social issues, including the rising demand for infrastructure and healthcare due to economic growth in emerging countries, climate change, digitization, and the diversification of values.

In addition to upstream investment and trading in metal resources and ferrous materials, the Metals, Mineral Resources & Recycling Division has made a full-scale entry into the circular economy field, which includes recycling businesses, and this division is working to create and promote new businesses that respond to social needs.

The Chemicals Division conducts a wide variety of trading and businesses, ranging from basic chemicals, such as methanol, to functional materials focusing on plastic resins as well as inorganic chemicals like industrial salts and rare earths. It is also developing businesses in the environmental and life science fields to contribute to building a lowcarbon, recycling-oriented society.

The Consumer Industry & Agriculture Business Division is building sustainable business models in the fields of agribusiness, foodstuffs, marine products, animal feed, and forest products in order to contribute to food safety and security as well as comfortable living spaces.

The Retail & Consumer Service Division is focused on a diverse range of businesses that respond to consumer needs both in Japan and overseas. These businesses include food distribution, shopping center management, brand, consumer goods distribution, textile, and real estate.

Overall, sales of goods bring in about 95% of the company's revenue, while sales of services and others account for the rest.

Geographic Reach

Based in Tokyo, Japan, Sojitz has operations in Japan (generates approximately 50% of the company's revenue), Asia and Oceania (nearly 35%), the Americas (about 10%), and Europe (more than 5%). In addition to its five domestic branches and offices, the company has more than 75 overseas branches and offices.

Sales and Marketing

The company have engaged in wide variety of business in Japan and overseas such as food distribution business, commercial facility business, brand business, consumer goods distribution business, general commodities and lifestyle, textile business, and real estate business.

Financial Performance

Note: Growth rates may differ after conversion to US Dollars.

Revenue was down 9% year on year, to Â¥1.6 trillion, due to lower revenue in the Automotive Division, as a result of decreases in sales units in overseas automobile operations; in the Chemicals Division, a result of declines in the transaction volumes of plastic resins and falling methanol prices; and in the Retail & Lifestyle Business Division, as a result of lower lumber transactions.

Profit for the year amounted to Â¥29.4 billion, down Â¥35.2 billion year on year. Profit for the year (attributable to owners of the parent) decreased Â¥33.8 billion year on year, to Â¥27 billion.

The company's cash at the end of 2022 was Â¥287.6 billion. Operating activities generated Â¥85 billion, while investing activities used Â¥35.7 billion, mainly for purchase of investments. Financing activities used another Â¥40.6 billion, primarily for repayment of long-term borrowings.

Strategy

Medium-Term Management Plan 2023 lays out a growth strategy of concentrating management resources in fields in which the company can pursue competitiveness and growth markets based on sustainability. Specifically, the company have defined four initiatives for this growth strategy?Develop essential infrastructure and services to alleviate social issues, Expand "3R" (reduce, reuse, recycle) businesses, Strengthen retail efforts in ASEAN and India, and Create value by revitalizing domestic industries and rural regions. Alongside these initiatives, the company will utilize digital and new technologies and practice co-creation and sharing methodologies with partners inside and outside the company to achieve its goals. Based on this growth strategy, the company restructured its previous nine business divisions to form seven divisions.

Mergers and Acquisitions

In early 2022, Sojitz concluded a share transfer agreement with NH Foods Ltd. to acquire full ownership and related assets of Nippon Ham's subsidiary, The Marine Foods Corporation (Marine Foods). Shinagawa-ku, Tokyo-based, Marine Foods imports marine product raw materials, and the company is engaged in the manufacturing, processing, and sale of processed marine food products. In addition to Japan, Marine Foods procures a variety of marine product raw materials from Vietnam, Russia, Chile, and other countries around the world. Sojitz and Marine Foods will join forces to strengthen and expand the marine products business globally to greater Asia, North America, and other overseas regions.

Also in early 2022, Sojitz acquired additional shares through exercise of new stock acquisition rights in Royal Holdings Co., Ltd. (Royal Holdings), issued through third-party allotment for 36,540 out of 41,124 of its new stock acquisition rights to acquire an additional 3,654,000 shares of common stock in Royal Holdings. The company exercised its new stock acquisition rights, increasing its current shareholding ratio from 13.3% (5,820,700 shares of common stock) to 19.9% (9,474,700 shares of common stock). Sojitz also plans to exercise its stock acquisition rights for its remaining 4,854 new stock acquisition rights (458,400 shares of common stock). Additionally, Sojitz and Royal Holdings established a local subsidiary (Royal Holdings: 51%, Sojitz: 49%) in Singapore in 2021, and both companies will continue to jointly pursue new business development and M&A projects.

In early 2021, Sojitz acquired a 100% ownership interest in Southwest Rail Industries Inc. (SRI) through Sojitz Corporation of America, a fully owned subsidiary of Sojitz. SRI is a US company that operates a railcar leasing business headquartered in Texas. Sojitz Group aims to further expand its railway service business in North America and contribute to the realization of a decarbonized and sustainable society.

Company Background

In April 2003, Nichimen Corporation and Nissho Iwai Corporation established a joint holding company, integrating their businesses the following year to become the Sojitz Group. Both companies trace their history back to three trading company titans (Japan Cotton Trading Co., Ltd., Iwai & Co., Ltd. and Suzuki & Co., Ltd.) who played an instrumental role in the development of modern Japan.

HISTORY

The Nissho and Iwai companies got their acts together as Nissho Iwai in 1968, but each company dates back to the middle of the 19th century. In 1863 Bunsuke Iwai opened a shop in Osaka to sell imported goods such as glass, oil products, silk, and wine. The Meiji government, which came to power in 1868, encouraged modernization and industrialization, a climate in which Iwai's business flourished. In 1877 Iwajiro Suzuki established a similar trading concern, Suzuki & Co., that eventually became Nissho.

After cotton spinning machines were introduced in Japan in the 1890s, both Iwai and Suzuki imported cotton. Iwai began to trade directly with British trader William Duff & Son (an innovation in Japan, where the middleman, or shokan, played the paramount role in international trade). Iwai became the primary agent for Yawata Steel Works in 1901 and was incorporated in 1912. Meanwhile, Suzuki, solely engaged in the import trade, emerged as one of the top sugar brokers in the world and established an office in London.

To protect itself from foreign competition, Iwai established a number of companies to produce goods in Japan, including Nippon Steel Plate (1914) and Tokuyama Soda (1918). Stagnation after WWI forced Suzuki to restructure. In 1928 the company sold many of its assets to trading giant Mitsui and reorganized the rest under a new name, Nissho Co.

Both Iwai and Nissho subsequently grew as they helped fuel Japan's military expansion in Asia in the 1930s. But Japan's defeat in WWII devastated the companies. When the occupation forces broke up Mitsui and other larger trading conglomerates, both companies took advantage of the situation to move into new business areas. In 1949 Nissho established Nissho Chemical Industry, Nissho Fuel, and Nijko Shoji (a trading concern). It also opened its US operations, Nissho American Corp., in 1952.

Poor management by the Iwai family led the company into financial trouble in the 1960s and prompted the Japanese government to instruct the profitable Nissho to merge with Iwai in 1968.

In 1979 Nissho Iwai was accused of funneling kickbacks from US aircraft makers to Japanese politicians. The scandal led to arrests, the resignation of the company's chairman, and the suicide of another executive. Nissho Iwai exited the aircraft marketing business in 1980.

Despite Japan's recession in the 1990s, Nissho Iwai managed to make some significant investments. In 1991 the company teamed up with the Russian government to develop a Siberian oil refinery. A year later Nissho acquired a stake in courier DHL International, and in 1995 it set up a unit to process steel plates in Vietnam.

However, in the late 1990s rough economic conditions caught up with the firm. It dissolved its NI Finance unit (domestic financing) in 1998 after its disastrous performance. The large trading firm, or sogo shosha, also began a major restructuring effort to get back on track.

In 1999 Nissho Iwai sold its headquarters, its 5% stake in DHL International, and its stake in a Japanese ISP, Nifty. CEO Masatake Kusamichi resigned. He was replaced by Shiro Yasutake, who took charge of the firm's restructuring. In 2000 the company's ITX Corp. acquired five IT-related affiliates of Nichimen Corp.

As part of the group's streamlining efforts, in 2001 Nissho Iwai spun off its nonferrous marketing unit (Alconix) and agreed to merge the group's LNG operations with Sumitomo's LNG business. The next year Hidetoshi Nishimura replaced Yasutake as CEO.

In 2003 Nissho Iwai merged with the smaller Nichimen Corp. to form Nissho Iwai-Nichimen Holdings. Hidetoshi Nishimura, president and CEO of Nissho Iwai, and Toru Hambayashi, president of Nichimen, became co-CEOs of the new holding company. Former board member Akio Dobashi took over the reins as president and sole CEO early in 2004; in April he moved over to the chairman's seat and Yutaka Kase assumed the president and CEO titles. In June the company changed its name from Nissho Iwai-Nichimen Holdings to Sojitz Holdings Corporation.

As part of its ongoing reorganization in 2005, the company renamed itself again when it merged the holding company into Sojitz Corporation.

The company formed a subsidiary in China in 2009 to enter key businesses such as the automotive, ball bearing, textiles, and plastics industries. That year it transferred its domestic foodstuffs business to a wholly owned subsidiary called Sojitz Foods Corporation.

Sojitz also began searching in 2010 for sources other than China for rare earth metals. It signed a contract in mid-year with Lynas Corporation in Australia to purchase about 8,500 tons a year, some 30% of Japan's annual demand. It also entered a joint venture with Toyota Tusho to import another 3,000 tons from Vietnam. Shipments from China, which mines and sells most of the world's rare earth metals, were delayed in 2010 in a move Japan said was a de facto blockade. Rare earth metals, such as palladium, are a key element in the production of electronic components and lithium-ion batteries.

EXECUTIVES

President, Chief Executive Officer, Representative Director, Masayoshi Fujimoto
Executive Vice President, Representative Director, Ryutaro Hirai
Senior Managing Executive Officer, Representative Director, Yoshiki Manabe
Senior Managing Executive Officer, Director, Masaaki Bito
Senior Managing Executive Officer, Koichi Yamaguchi
Outside Director, Norio Otsuka
Outside Director, Naoko Saiki
Outside Director, Ungyong Shu
Outside Director, Haruko Kokue
Outside Director, Tsuyoshi Kameoka
Auditors : KPMG AZSA LLC

LOCATIONS

HQ: Sojitz Corp
   2-1-1 Uchisaiwai-cho, Chiyoda-ku, Tokyo 100-8691
Phone: (81) 3 6871 5000   **Fax:** (81) 3 6871 2430
Web: www.sojitz.com

2018 Sales

	% of total
Japan	47
Asia and Oceania	35
The Americas	8
Europe	8
Others	2
Total	100

PRODUCTS/OPERATIONS

2018 Sales

	% of total
Chemicals	28
Metals & Coal	18
Foods & Agriculture Business	8
Retail & Lifestyle	16
Automotive	11
Industrial Infrastructure & Urban Development	3
Aerospace & IT Business	4
Infrastructure & Environment Business	7
Energy	3
Others	2
Total	100

COMPETITORS

ASHLAND GLOBAL HOLDINGS INC.
BRENNTAG UK AND IRELAND LIMITED
HELM AG
ITOCHU CORPORATION
MARUBENI CORPORATION
NEXEO SOLUTIONS HOLDINGS, LLC
Ontex Group
SUMITOMO CORPORATION
UNIVAR SOLUTIONS INC.
WARWICK INTERNATIONAL GROUP LIMITED

HISTORICAL FINANCIALS

Company Type: Public

Income Statement   FYE: March 31

	REVENUE ($mil)	NET INCOME ($mil)	NET PROFIT MARGIN	EMPLOYEES
03/23	18,619	835	4.5%	26,423
03/22	17,270	676	3.9%	25,613
03/21	14,472	243	1.7%	24,141
03/20	16,166	560	3.5%	22,330
03/19	16,761	635	3.8%	21,909
Annual Growth	2.7%	7.1%	—	4.8%

2023 Year-End Financials

Debt ratio: 0.2%   No. of shares ($ mil.): 231
Return on equity: 14.2%   Dividends
Cash ($ mil.): 1,856   Yield: —
Current Ratio: 1.62   Payout: 0.0%
Long-term debt ($ mil.): 5,375   Market value ($ mil.): —

Sompo Holdings Inc

Sompo Holdings (formerly Sompo Japan Nipponkoa Holdings) is an insurance and financial company that owns several companies that are primarily engaged in the insurance sector. Its subsidiaries include property/casualty units Sompo Japan Insurance, Saison Automobile & Fire, and Mysurance, and a handful of overseas insurance companies. Domestic property/casualty insurance brings in about 55% of the company's total revenue. Other operations include asset and risk management services, pension plans, and some supplemental health insurance products. The company also owns SOMPO Care, which provides nursing care services. Sompo generates approximately 70% of its sales from its home country, Japan.

Operations

Sompo operates through four segments: Domestic P&C Insurance (which accounts for about 55% of total sales), Overseas Insurance (nearly 25%), Domestic Life Insurance (almost 10%), and Nursing Care & Healthcare (around 5%).

Domestic P&C insurance business consists mainly of underwriting of property and casualty insurance, investment, and related activities in Japan; Overseas insurance business consists mainly of underwriting of property and casualty insurance and investment activities overseas; Domestic life insurance business consists mainly of underwriting of life insurance and investment activities in Japan; and Nursing care & seniors business consists mainly of providing nursing care service.

Geographic Reach

Headquartered in Japan, Sompo has overseas subsidiaries, branch offices, and representative offices in about 30 countries and regions worldwide, including North America, Europe, the Middle East, Africa, Asia, Latin America, and Oceania.

About 70% of Sompo's total revenue comes from Japan, while more than 15%

comes from the US, and the remaining some 10% comes from other countries.

Financial Performance

Ordinary income increased by ¥321.1 billion to ¥4.2 trillion compared to the previous fiscal year, the components of which were underwriting income of ¥3.7 trillion, investment income of ¥338.4 billion and other ordinary income of ¥172.1 billion.

Net income for fiscal 2022 increased to ¥317.6 billion compared to ¥194.9 billion.

Cash held by the company at the end of fiscal 2022 increased to ¥1.2 trillion. Cash provided by operations was ¥600 billion while cash used for investing and financing activities were ¥348.5 billion and ¥170.1 billion, respectively. Main cash uses were purchase of securities and dividends paid.

Company Background

Sompo Holdings was created to hold two insurance companies: Sompo Japan and Nipponkoa Insurance. While already strong players in Japan's property/casualty and life insurance markets, when merger mania hit the industry they didn't want to be left out and formed the joint holding company in 2010. The two companies merged into one entity, Sompo Japan Nipponkoa Insurance, in 2014.

Why merge in the first place? Sompo cited pressures on its industry from several sources, including the country's declining birthrate, its rapidly aging population, and the effects of climate change. While those are real challenges to the industry, the Sompo/Nipponkoa merger also took place at the same time as several other large mergers among Japanese insurance companies.

EXECUTIVES

Representative Executive Officer, Chairman, Chief Executive Officer, Director, Kengo Sakurada
Representative Executive Officer, President, Chief Strategy Officer, Director, Mikio Okumura
Senior Managing Executive Officer, Koichi Narasaki
Chief Financial Officer, Chief Strategy Officer, Senior Managing Executive Officer, Masahiro Hamada
Chief Human Resources Officer, Senior Managing Executive Officer, Shinichi Hara
Chief Risk Officer, Yoshihiro Uotani
Outside Director, Scott Trevor Davis
Outside Director, Naoki Yanagida
Outside Director, Isao Endo
Outside Director, Hideyo Uchiyama
Outside Director, Kazuhiro Higashi
Outside Director, Takashi Nawa
Outside Director, Misuzu Shibata
Outside Director, Meyumi Yamada
Outside Director, Kumi Ito
Outside Director, Masayuki Waga
Director, Toshihiro Teshima
Director, Satoshi Kasai

Auditors: Ernst & Young ShinNihon LLC

LOCATIONS

HQ: Sompo Holdings Inc
1-26-1 Nishi-Shinjuku, Shinjuku-ku, Tokyo 160-8338
Phone: (81) 3 3349 3000   **Fax:** 212 471-1748
Web: www.sompo-hd.com

2018 Sales by Segment

	% of total
Domestic P&C Insurance	59
Overseas Insurance	17
Domestic Life Insurance	9
Nursing Care & Healthcare	3
Other	1
Adjustments	11
Total	100

2018 Sales

	% of total
Japan	79
US	10
Other	11
Total	100

Selected Locations
Belgium
Bermuda
France
Germany
Italy
Mexico
Singapore
Spain
Switzerland
UK
US

COMPETITORS

AMERICAN NATIONAL INSURANCE COMPANY
CNA FINANCIAL CORPORATION
DAI-ICHI LIFE HOLDINGS, INC.
Hiscox Ltd
MAPFRE, SA
MASSACHUSETTS MUTUAL LIFE INSURANCE COMPANY
MS&AD INSURANCE GROUP HOLDINGS, INC.
Sampo Oyj
T&D HOLDINGS, INC.
Talanx AG

HISTORICAL FINANCIALS

Company Type: Public

Income Statement   FYE: March 31

	REVENUE ($mil)	NET INCOME ($mil)	NET PROFIT MARGIN	EMPLOYEES
03/23	33,723	684	2.0%	90,541
03/22	33,907	1,848	5.5%	83,000
03/21	34,247	1,286	3.8%	82,118
03/20	34,115	1,128	3.3%	79,441
03/19	32,567	1,324	4.1%	81,115
Annual Growth	0.9%	(15.2%)		2.8%

2023 Year-End Financials

Debt ratio: —
Return on equity: 4.6%
Cash ($ mil.): 9,519
Current Ratio: —
Long-term debt ($ mil.): —
No. of shares ($ mil.): 333
Dividends
Yield: —
Payout: 96.1%
Market value ($ mil.): 6,660

	STOCK PRICE ($) FY Close	P/E High/Low	PER SHARE ($) Earnings	Dividends	Book Value
03/23	19.95	0 0	2.03	1.95	41.70
03/22	21.99	0 0	5.29	0.87	48.54
03/21	18.85	0 0	3.59	0.74	51.22
03/20	15.19	0 0	3.08	1.38	40.30
03/19	17.73	0 0	3.54	1.17	42.57
Annual Growth	3.0%		(13.0%)	13.6%	(0.5%)

Sony Group Corp

Sony develops, designs, produces, manufactures, and sells different kinds of electronic equipment, instruments and devices for consumer, professional and industrial markets such as network services, game hardware and software, televisions, audio and video recorders and players, still and video cameras, mobile phones, and image sensors. It is engaged in the development, production, manufacture, and distribution of recorded music and the management and licensing of the words and music of songs as well as the production and distribution of animation titles, including game applications based on animation titles. The company is also engaged in the production, acquisition and distribution of motion pictures and television programming and the operation of television and digital networks. In addition, Sony has several financial services businesses (insurance and banking). Japan and the US are the company's largest markets, together accounting for more than half of sales. In mid-2022, Sony acquired Bungie for approximately $3.6 billion. In 2021, Sony changed its company name from "Sony Corporation" to "Sony Group Corporation".

Operations

Sony reports revenue through seven business segments.

Its largest, accounting for more than 25% of sales, is Game & Network Services (G&NS), includes network services businesses, the manufacture and sales of home gaming products and production and sales of software.

The Electronics Products & Services (EP&S), accounting for about 25%, includes the Televisions business, the Audio and Video business, the Still and Video Cameras business, the smartphone business and internet-related service business.

The Financial Services, accounting for approximately 15%, represents individual life insurance and non-life insurance businesses in the Japanese market and a bank business in Japan.

The Pictures segment, accounting for over 10%, includes the Motion Pictures, Television Productions, and Media Networks businesses.

The Music segment, accounting for nearly 10% of sales, includes the Recorded Music, Music Publishing, and Visual Media and

Platform businesses.

The Imaging & Sensing Solutions (I&SS), accounting for about 10%, includes the image sensors business.

The All Other segment, accounting for less than 5%, consists of various operating activities, including the disc manufacturing and recording media businesses.

Geographic Reach

Based in Tokyo, Japan, Sony has facilities throughout the world, although its primary manufacturing plants are located in Japan. Other plant locations include China, Malaysia, Thailand, Europe, and the US.

Japan is also the company's single largest market by sales (nearly 30%), with the US and Europe accounting for almost 30% and 20% of sales, respectively.

Sales and Marketing

Sony's products are marketed worldwide by sales subsidiaries and unaffiliated distributors, as well as direct online sales and offers via the Internet. The company's electronics products and services are marketed under the trademark "Sony," which has been registered in more than 200 countries and territories.

Along with its global corporate functions in Japan, Sony Mobile also has sales and marketing operations in many major regions of the world, as well as a major manufacturing site in Thailand and product development sites in Japan and Sweden.

Advertising costs included in selling, general and administrative expenses for the fiscal years ended 2021 and 2022 were approximately Â¥261.4 billion and Â¥347.7 billion, respectively.

Financial Performance

The company had a revenue of Â¥9.9 trillion, a 10% increase from the previous year's revenue of Â¥9 trillion. This was mainly due to significant increases in sales in the Pictures, EP&S and Music segments.

In 2021, the company had a net income of Â¥493 million, a 29% decrease from the previous year's net income of Â¥693 million.

The company's cash for the year ended 2022 was Â¥889.1 billion. Operating activities generated Â¥459.7 billion, while investing activities used Â¥17.6 billion, mainly for payments for property, plant and equipment and other intangible assets. Financing activities used another Â¥50.1 billion, primarily for payment of dividends.

Strategy

Sony actively engages in acquisitions, joint ventures, capital expenditures and other strategic investments to acquire new technologies, efficiently develop new businesses and enhance its business competitiveness. For example, in September 2020, in order to achieve further growth and strengthen governance within the financial services business with the goal of enhancing the corporate value of the entire Sony Group, Sony acquired all of the common shares and related stock acquisition rights of Sony Financial Group Inc. ("SFGI") not held by Sony and made SFGI a wholly-owned subsidiary of Sony, spending Â¥396.7 billion.

Mergers and Acquisitions

In early 2022, Sony, through Sony Music Entertainment, completed its transaction to acquire Brazilian independent music company Som Livre. The acquisition will further enhance Sony Music's support for independent artists, songwriters and labels in Brazil and across the Latin music industry, in one of the most dynamic, competitive and fastest growing music markets in the world.

Also in early 2022, Sony announced its acquisition of Bungie, the developer of Destiny 2 and the studio that originally created Halo, in a deal worth approximately $3.6 billion. "Bungie's technical expertise, coupled with their track record of building highly engaged communities, make them a natural fit for collaboration with PlayStation Studios," said Herman Hulst, head of PlayStation Studios. "I believe that Bungie joining the PlayStation family will increase the capabilities of PlayStation Studios, and of Bungie, and achieve our vision of expanding PlayStation to hundreds of millions of gamers. For game creators, that's always our goal: to bring our vision to as many people as possible."

In mid-2021, Sony Pictures Entertainment Inc., a wholly-owned subsidiary of Sony, completed its acquisition of AT&T's Crunchyroll anime business through Funimation Global Group, LLC. Funimation is a joint venture between SPE and Sony Music Entertainment (Japan) Inc.'s subsidiary, Aniplex Inc. The deal provides the opportunity for Crunchyroll and Funimation to broaden distribution for their content partners and expand fan-centric offerings for consumers. The purchase price for the transaction is approximately $1.175 billion, subject to customary working capital and other adjustments, and the proceeds were paid in cash at closing.

In 2021, Sony invested in Bilibili Inc. and Epic Games, Inc. (Epic), and acquired minority interests in both companies, with the goal of accelerating business expansion in the area of entertainment. In the same month, the company acquired 100% of the shares and related assets of certain subsidiaries of Kobalt Music Group Limited (Kobalt), relating to AWAL, Kobalt's music distribution business mainly for independent recording artists, and Kobalt Neighbouring Rights, Kobalt's music neighboring rights management business. The consideration for this acquisition was Â¥49.8 billion.

Company Background

Tokyo Telecommunications Engineering Corporation, the predecessor of Sony, was established in 1946 with about 20 employees. It listed on the over-the-counter market of the Toyko Stock Exchange (TSE) in 1955 and three years later changed its name to Sony Corporation. The company also listed on the TSE that year.

HISTORY

Akio Morita, Masaru Ibuka, and Tamon Maeda (Ibuka's father-in-law) started Tokyo Telecommunications Engineering in 1946 with funding from Morita's father's sake business. The company produced the first Japanese tape recorder in 1950. Three years later Morita paid Western Electric (US) $25,000 for transistor technology licenses, which sparked a consumer electronics revolution in Japan. His firm launched one of the first transistor radios in 1955, followed by the first Sony-trademarked product, a pocket-sized radio, in 1957. The next year the company changed its name to Sony (from "sonus," Latin for "sound," and "sonny," meaning "little man"). It beat the competition to newly emerging markets for transistor TVs (1959) and solid-state videotape recorders (1961).

Sony launched the first home video recorder (1964) and the first solid-state condenser microphone (1965). Its 1968 introduction of the Trinitron color TV tube began another decade of explosive growth. Sony bet wrong on its Betamax VCR (1976), which lost to rival Matsushita's (now Panasonic Corp.) VHS as the industry standard. However, 1979 brought another success, the Walkman personal stereo.

Pressured by adverse currency rates and competition worldwide, Sony used its technology to diversify beyond consumer electronics and began to move production to other countries. In the 1980s it introduced Japan's first 32-bit workstation and became a major producer of computer chips and floppy disk drives. The purchases of CBS Records in 1988 ($2 billion) and Columbia Pictures in 1989 (a $4.9 billion deal, which included TriStar Pictures) made Sony a major force in the rapidly growing entertainment industry.

The firm manufactured Apple's PowerBook, but its portable CD player, Data Discman, was successful only in Japan (1991). In the early 1990s Sony joined Nintendo to create a new kind of game console, combining Sony's CD-ROM drive with the graphic capabilities of a workstation. Although Nintendo pulled out in 1992, Sony released PlayStation in Japan (1994) and in the US (1995) to great success. Two years later, in a joint venture with Intel, it developed a line of PC desktop systems.

Rather than support an industry-wide standard, in 1997 Sony teamed up with Philips Electronics to make another recording media, called Super Audio CD, which could replace videotapes and CDs. (Sony and Philips created the CD and continue to receive royalties from it.)

In 1998 Sony shipped its first digital, high-definition TV to the US, folded TriStar into Columbia Pictures, merged its Loews Theatres unit with Cineplex Odeon, and launched its Wega flat-screen TV.

Philips, Sun Microsystems, and Sony formed a joint venture in early 1999 to develop networked entertainment products. Also in 1999 Nobuyuki Idei became CEO, and the company introduced a Walkman with the capability to download music from the Internet.

In 2000 Sony formed PlayStation.com Japan to sell game consoles and software online; it also introduced its 128-bit PlayStation 2, which plays DVD movies and connects to the Internet. The company later restructured, placing all of its US entertainment holdings under a newly-formed umbrella company called Sony Broadband Entertainment.

In early 2001 Sony started an online bank with Japan's Sakura Bank and JP Morgan Chase. Struggling to coordinate its content units (music, movies, games, etc.) with its manufacturing operations (TVs, VCRs, radios, etc.), Sony announced yet another corporate restructuring plan; that move placed all electronics units under one upper-management group.

Adverse market conditions in 2001, aggravated by the September 11 attacks, led Sony Pictures Entertainment to consolidate its two domestic television operations, folding Columbia TriStar Network Television into Columbia TriStar Domestic Television (CTDT).

In February 2002 an investment group led by Onex Corporation acquired its Loews Theatres unit (which filed for bankruptcy in February 2001). In the course of the fiscal year ending March 2002, Sony laid off about 13,700 employees, primarily in its electronics and music businesses.

In an attempt to capitalize on the strength of its own brand, Sony Pictures Entertainment renamed its Columbia TriStar Domestic Television (CTDT) and Columbia TriStar International Television (CTIT) divisions in September 2002, designating them as Sony Pictures Television (SPT) and Sony Pictures Television International (SPTI), respectively. In October 2002 Sony transformed its Aiwa unit into a wholly-owned subsidiary and absorbed the struggling firm in December 2002.

In 2003 Sony adopted a US-style corporate governance model (made possible by a revision in Japan's Commercial Code) and acquired CIS Corp., a Japanese information system consulting firm. In an effort to cut costs through manufacturing consolidation, Sony closed its audio equipment plant in Indonesia that year.

Sony unveiled the Vaio Pocket in 2004, a portable music player designed to compete with Apple's iPod; Vaio Pocket debuted in the US later that year. Sony also introduced a similar product, Network Walkman -- its first Walkman with a hard drive -- in 2004. In October 2004 the company launched a music download system in Japan dubbed MusicDrop. The system utilizes Microsoft's Windows Media Player.

To manage its financial units (Sony Life Insurance Company, Sony Assurance, and Sony Bank), it created Sony Financial Holdings in 2004. The company announced in 2005 that Idei would be succeeded by foreigner Howard Stringer, who had been in charge of Sony's entertainment unit. In 2005 Sony sold its minority stake in music club Columbia House to BMG Direct, a subsidiary of Germany's Bertelsmann. In December 2005 the company spun off Sony Communication Network, the subsidiary that operates So-Net Internet service (which has nearly 3 million subscribers), through an IPO.

In June 2006 Sony created a holding company for its Japanese-based retail operations (Sony Plaza, Sony Family Club, B&C Laboratories, CP Cosmetics, Maxim's de Paris, and Lifeneo) and sold 51% of the holding company to investment firm Nikko Principal Investments Japan.

In late 2008 Sony bought out NEC's 45% stake in joint venture Sony Optiarc.

The company in 2010 sold the measuring equipment business of Sony Manufacturing Systems to Mori Seiki, a Japan-based precision tool maker, in a deal valued at about ¥6 billion (nearly $70 million). It also sold off its 90% stake in Sony Baja California, its main TV factory in North America located in Tijuana, Mexico, to Taiwanese company Hon Hai Precision Industry. It generated $217 million for its share in HBO Latin America, which it sold to Time Warner.

In February 2012 Sony acquired Telefonaktiebolaget LM Ericsson's 50% stake in Sony Ericsson Mobile Communications AB, marking the completion of the previously announced transaction. As a result, Sony Ericsson became a wholly-owned subsidiary of Sony and was renamed "Sony Mobile Communications."

EXECUTIVES

President Chairman, President President, President Chief Executive Officer, Chairman, Director, Kenichiro Yoshida
New Business Platform Strategy Executive Deputy President, New Business Platform Strategy Chief Financial Officer, Director, Hiroki Totoki
Senior Executive Vice President, Shiro Kambe
Senior Executive Vice President, Kazushi Ambe
Senior Executive Vice President, Toshimoto Mitomo
Senior Executive Vice President, Chief Technology Officer, Hiroaki Kitano
Director, Shuzo Sumi
Director, Tim Schaaff
Director, Toshiko Oka
Director, Sakie Akiyama
Director, Wendy Becker
Director, Yoshihiko Hatanaka
Director, Keiko Kishigami
Director, Joseph A. Kraft Jr.
Auditors: PricewaterhouseCoopers Aarata LLC

LOCATIONS

HQ: Sony Group Corp
7-1, Konan 1-Chome, Minato-Ku, Tokyo 108-0075
Phone: (81) 3 6748 2111
Web: www.sony.com

2018 Sales

	% of total
Japan	31
Europe	22
US	21
Asia/Pacific (except Japan and China)	12
China	8
Other	6
Total	100

PRODUCTS/OPERATIONS

2018 Sales

	% of total
Game & Network services	22
Home entertainment & sound	14
Mobile communications	8
Financial services	14
Semiconductors	10
Pictures	11
Imaging products & solutions	7
Music	9
Other	5
Total	100

COMPETITORS

AG&E HOLDINGS INC.
GAMELOFT SE
JAKKS PACIFIC, INC.
LEAPFROG ENTERPRISES, INC.
NINTENDO CO., LTD.
PIONEER CORPORATION
SONY CORPORATION OF AMERICA
TECHNICOLOR
TOMY INTERNATIONAL, INC.
UBISOFT ENTERTAINMENT

HISTORICAL FINANCIALS

Company Type: Public

Income Statement — FYE: March 31

	REVENUE ($mil)	NET INCOME ($mil)	NET PROFIT MARGIN	EMPLOYEES
03/23	86,644	7,036	8.1%	113,000
03/22	81,566	7,252	8.9%	108,900
03/21	81,276	10,582	13.0%	109,700
03/20	76,092	5,363	7.0%	111,700
03/19	78,249	8,273	10.6%	114,400
Annual Growth	2.6%	(4.0%)		(0.3%)

2023 Year-End Financials

Debt ratio: 0.1%
Return on equity: 13.0%
Cash ($ mil.): 11,119
Current Ratio: 0.62
Long-term debt ($ mil.): 9,276
No. of shares ($ mil.): 1,234
Dividends
Yield: 0.5%
Payout: 10.0%
Market value ($ mil.): 111,907

	STOCK PRICE ($) FY Close	P/E High/Low		PER SHARE ($) Earnings	Dividends	Book Value
03/23	90.65	0	0	5.67	0.53	43.97
03/22	102.71	0	0	5.80	0.54	47.48
03/21	106.01	0	0	8.46	0.47	40.64
03/20	59.18	0	0	4.25	0.37	31.15
03/19	42.24	0	0	6.39	0.27	27.05
Annual Growth	21.0%	—	—	(3.0%)	18.0%	12.9%

South African Reserve Bank

EXECUTIVES

Deputy Governor, Xolile Guma
Deputy Governor, Daniel Mminele
Deputy Governor, Lesetja Kganyago
Secretary, S. L.
Deputy Governor, Renosi Denise Mokate
Deputy Governor, Gill Marcus
Director, Len Konar
Director, Elias Masilela
Director, Thandi Orleyn
Director, Ben Smit
Director, Hans van der Merwe
Director, Fatima Jakoet
Director, Francois Engelbrecht Groepe
Deputy Governor, Xolile Pallo Guma
Director, Raymond Whitmore Knighton Parsons
Director, Zodwa Penelope Manase
Director, Stephen Mitford Goodson
Director, Thandeka Nozipho Mgoduso
Auditors : SizweNtsalubaGobodo Grant Thornton Inc.

LOCATIONS

HQ: South African Reserve Bank
370 Helen Joseph Street, Pretoria 0002
Phone: (27) 12 313 3911
Web: www.resbank.co.za

HISTORICAL FINANCIALS
Company Type: Public

Income Statement FYE: March 31

	ASSETS ($mil)	NET INCOME ($mil)	INCOME AS % OF ASSETS	EMPLOYEES
03/21	63,472	242	0.4%	2,251
03/20	62,466	159	0.3%	2,189
03/18	62,701	182	0.3%	1,967
03/17	56,623	90	0.2%	2,186
03/16	55,884	99	0.2%	2,233
Annual Growth	2.6%	19.4%	—	0.2%

2021 Year-End Financials
Return on assets: 0.3%
Return on equity: 14.4%
Long-term debt ($ mil.): —
No. of shares ($ mil.): 2
Sales ($ mil.): 1,318
Dividends
  Yield: —
  Payout: 0.0%
Market value ($ mil.): —

Spotify Technology SA

Spotify Technology S.A. is the world's most popular audio streaming subscription service with a community of 406 million MAUs, including some 180 million Premium Subscribers, across about 185 countries and territories. It offers both Premium and Ad-Supported Services. Its Ad-Supported Service serves as a funnel, driving a significant portion of our total gross added Premium Subscribers. Its portfolio of industry-leading original podcast content is created and produced by its wholly-owned subsidiaries, Spotify Studios, Gimlet Studios, Parcast, and The Ringer, along with partnerships with some of the world's most well-known creators. Almost all of its sales were generated outside Luxembourg.

Operations

Spotify operates and manages its business in two reportable segments?Premium (about 90% of sales) and Ad-Supported (over 10%).

Its Premium Service provides Premium Subscribers with unlimited online and offline high-quality streaming access to its catalog of music and podcasts. In addition to accessing its catalog on computers, tablets, and mobile devices, users can connect through speakers, receivers, televisions, cars, game consoles, and smart devices. The Premium Service offers a music listening experience without commercial breaks. It also offers a variety of subscription pricing plans for its Premium Service, including its Standard plan, Family Plan, Duo Plan, and Student Plan, among others, to appeal to users with different lifestyles and across various demographics and age groups.

Its Ad-Supported Service has no subscription fees and generally provides Ad-Supported Users with limited on-demand online access to its catalog of music and unlimited online access to its catalog of podcasts on their computers, tablets, and compatible mobile devices. It serves as both a Premium Subscriber acquisition channel and a robust option for users who are unable or unwilling to pay a monthly subscription fee but still want to enjoy access to a wide variety of high-quality audio content.

Geographic Reach

Headquartered in Luxembourg, the company operates in about 185 countries and territories. The US is its largest single market with about 40%, followed by the UK with some 10%, while other countries generated over half.

Sales and Marketing

The company has some 406 million monthly active users (MAUs), including 180 million Premium Subscribers. Its Premium Subscribers include all registered accounts in its Family Plan and Duo Plan. Its Family Plan consists of one primary subscriber and up to five additional sub-accounts, allowing up to six Premium Subscribers per Family Plan Subscription. Its Duo Plan consists of one primary subscriber and up to one additional sub-account, allowing up to two Premium Subscribers per Duo Plan Subscription.

The company's sales and marketing expenses were EUR 1.1 million, EUR 1.0 million, and EUR 0.8 million in 2021, 2020, and 2019, respectively.

Financial Performance

The company reported a revenue of EUR 9.7 billion in 2021, a 23% increase from the previous year's revenue of EUR 7.9 billion. Premium revenue increased by EUR 1.3 billion or 19%. The increase was attributable primarily to a 16% increase in Premium Subscribers. Ad-Supported revenue increased by EUR 463 million or 62%. This increase was due primarily to growth in music impressions sold and growth in CPM (cost per 1,000 impressions), which increased revenue in its direct and programmatic channels by EUR 181 million and EUR 87 million, respectively.

In 2021, the company had a net loss of EUR 34 million, a 94% improvement from the previous year's net loss of EUR 581 million. The improvement is primarily due to a higher volume of sales for the year.

The company's cash at the end of 2021 was EUR 2.7 billion. Operating activities generated EUR 361 million, while investing activities used EUR 187 million, mainly for purchases of short term investments. Financing activities provided another EUR 1.3 billion.

Strategy

Spotify is continuing to build a two-sided marketplace for users and creators, which leverages its relationships, data analytics, and software. The company has been instrumental in reshaping the way in which its users enjoy, discover, and share audio content, and with its marketplace strategy, Spotify empowers creators by offering unique insights and developing new tools designed to give creators more power and control and by unlocking new monetization opportunities for creators. Spotify is uniquely positioned to offer creators and fans access to one another, and to provide creators with analytics and tools that help them to better understand their fans, to support themselves, and to be able to live off of their creative work.

Mergers and Acquisitions

In late 2021, Spotify Technology has entered into a definitive agreement to acquire Findaway, a global leader in digital audiobook distribution based in Ohio. Spotify and Findaway will accelerate Spotify's entry into the rapidly growing audiobooks industry, enabling faster innovation and bringing audiobooks to Spotify's hundreds of millions of existing listeners. Findaway's technology infrastructure will enable Spotify to quickly scale its audiobook catalog and innovate on the experience for consumers, simultaneously providing new avenues for publishers, authors and independent creators to reach new audiences around the globe. The acquisition positions Spotify to revolutionize the space in the same way as music and podcasts, powering content to reach a wide audience on its global platform. Terms of the transaction were not disclosed.

Company Background

The company were incorporated in late 2006 as a Luxembourg private limited liability company (société à responsabilité limitée) and were transformed, in early 2009, into a Luxembourg public limited liability company (société anonyme).

EXECUTIVES

Chief Executive Officer, Chairman, Director, Daniel Ek, $440,281 total compensation
Chief Financial Officer, Paul Vogel
Chief Human Resources Officer, Katarina Berg
Chief Freemium Business Officer, Alex Norstrom, $389,335 total compensation
Chief Research and Development Officer, Gustav Soderstrom, $390,347 total compensation
Chief Content & Advertising Business Officer, Dawn Ostroff
General Counsel, Eve Konstan
Lead Independent Director, Christopher P. Marshall
Independent Director, Thomas O. Staggs
Independent Director, Padmasree Warrior
Independent Director, Mona K. Sutphen
Director, Martin Lorentzon
Director, Barry McCarthy, $560,000 total compensation
Director, Shishir Mehrotra
Director, Heidi O'Neill
Director, Ted Sarandos
Director, Cristina Stenbeck
Auditors : Ernst & Young AB

LOCATIONS

HQ: Spotify Technology SA
5, Place de la Gare, Luxembourg L-1616
Phone: —
Web: www.spotify.com

2017 Sales

	% of total
United States	39
United Kingdom	11
Other Countries	50
Total	100

PRODUCTS/OPERATIONS

2017 Sales

	% of total
Premium	90
Ad-Supported	10
Total	100

HISTORICAL FINANCIALS

Company Type: Public

Income Statement — FYE: December 31

	REVENUE ($mil)	NET INCOME ($mil)	NET PROFIT MARGIN	EMPLOYEES
12/23	14,672	(589)	—	0
12/22	12,524	(459)	—	8,359
12/21	10,942	(38)	—	6,617
12/20	9,671	(713)	—	5,584
12/19	7,594	(208)	—	4,405
Annual Growth	17.9%	—	—	—

2023 Year-End Financials

Debt ratio: 16.0% No. of shares ($ mil.): 197
Return on equity: (-21.6%) Dividends
Cash ($ mil.): 3,449 Yield: —
Current Ratio: 1.29 Payout: 0.0%
Long-term debt ($ mil.): 1,332 Market value ($ mil.): —

SSE PLC

EXECUTIVES

Chief Executive Officer, Executive Director, Alistair Phillips-Davies
Financial Director, Executive Director, Gregor Alexander
Energy and Commercial Director, Executive Director, Martin Pibworth
Human Resources Director, John Stewart
Corporate Affairs and Strategy Director, Sam Peacock
General Counsel, Liz Tanner
Investor Relations Secretary, Investor Relations Director, Sally Fairbairn
Chair, Non-Executive Director, John A. Manzoni
Senior Independent Director, Independent Non-Executive Director, Tony Cocker
Independent Non-Executive Director, Sue Bruce
Independent Non-Executive Director, Peter J. Lynas
Independent Non-Executive Director, Helen Mahy
Independent Non-Executive Director, Melanie Smith
Independent Non-Executive Director, Angela Strank
Auditors : Ernst & Young LLP

LOCATIONS

HQ: SSE PLC
Inveralmond House, 200 Dunkeld Road, Perth PH1 3AQ
Phone: (44) 1738 456000
Web: www.sse.com

HISTORICAL FINANCIALS

Company Type: Public

Income Statement — FYE: March 31

	REVENUE ($mil)	NET INCOME ($mil)	NET PROFIT MARGIN	EMPLOYEES
03/23	15,454	(152)	—	12,489
03/22	11,296	3,978	35.2%	10,754
03/21	9,397	3,133	33.3%	12,513
03/20	8,401	(72)	—	11,682
03/19	9,604	1,845	19.2%	20,370
Annual Growth	12.6%	—	—	(11.5%)

2023 Year-End Financials

Debt ratio: 39.8% No. of shares ($ mil.): 1,090
Return on equity: (-1.2%) Dividends
Cash ($ mil.): 1,103 Yield: 4.3%
Current Ratio: 1.21 Payout: 0.0%
Long-term debt ($ mil.): 8,556 Market value ($ mil.): 24,271

STOCK PRICE ($) FY Close	P/E High/Low		PER SHARE ($) Earnings	Dividends	Book Value
03/23	22.26	— —	(0.14)	0.97	11.88
03/22	23.06	8 7	3.76	1.05	11.23
03/21	20.13	10 7	3.01	1.03	8.82
03/20	16.10	— —	(0.07)	1.11	5.85
03/19	15.54	14 10	1.81	1.22	7.38
Annual Growth	9.4%		—	(5.6%)	12.6%

Standard Bank Group Ltd

Standard Bank Group sets the standard for sub-Saharan banking. Standard Bank, South Africa's largest bank, offers a variety of retail and commercial banking, corporate and investment banking, investment management, and life insurance services. The group currently operates in 20 countries in sub-Saharan Africa. Beyond Africa, the bank has offices in Asia, Europe, and the Americas, including many emerging markets. It serves individuals and business and corporate customers. Standard Bank holds a controlling stake in South African insurance firm Liberty Holdings. South Africa generated majority of its sales.

Operations

The company offers three client segments: Consumer & High Net Worth (CHNW; around 35% of sales), Corporate & Investment Banking (CIB; some 30%), and Business & Commercial (BCC; some 20%).

The CHNW segment offers tailored and comprehensive banking, investment, insurance and beyond financial solutions. It serves clients across Sub-Saharan Africa ranging from high net-worth, affluent, and main market by enabling their daily lives throughout their life journeys.

The CIB segment serves large companies (multinational, regional and domestic), governments, parastatals and institutional clients across Africa and internationally. Its clients leverage its in-depth sector and regional expertise, its specialist capabilities and its access to global capital markets for advisory, transactional, trading and funding support.

The BCC segment provides broad based client solutions for a wide spectrum of small- and medium-sized businesses as well as large commercial enterprises. Its client coverage support extends across a wide range of industries, sectors and solutions that deliver the necessary advisory, networking and sustainability support required by its clients to enable their growth.

Overall, interest income generated about 60% of sales, net fee and commission revenue generated about 20%, while income from investment management and life insurance activities generated over 10%.

Geographic Reach

Contributing almost 70% of Standard Bank Group's revenue, South Africa is its largest market by far. SBG also operates in some 20 countries in sub-Saharan Africa.

Financial Performance

The company reported a net interest income of R$62.4 billion, a 2% increase from the previous year's net interest income of R$61.4 billion.

In 2021, the company had a net income of R$24.9 billion, a 101% increase from the previous year's net income of R$12.4 billion. This was primarily due to the lower volume of interest expense for the year.

The company's cash at the end of 2021 was R$91.2 billion. Operating activities generated R$12.9 billion, while investing activities used R$4.7 billion, mainly for capital expenditure on property and equipment. Financing activities used another R$9.4 billion, primarily for payment of dividends.

Strategy

The company has shifted the business to be future-ready and client centric. Its reporting has changed to align to this principle. The client segments are responsible for designing and executing the client value proposition strategy. Client segments own the client relationship and create multi-product customer experiences to address life events distributed through its client engagement platforms.

The company supports a just transition that seeks to achieve the imperative for environmental sustainability in a manner that creates work opportunities and social inclusion, addresses Africa's energy poverty and acknowledges Africa's contribution to global emissions. It plans to reduce its financed emissions intensity while responsibly managing its exposure to fossil fuels, specifically where there is an energy transition roadmap that supports cleaner fuels.

The company has also adopted a phased and progressive approach to understanding its climate risk exposures and setting appropriate targets to reduce exposure and maximize opportunities. The first phase included the identification of four client sectors that face material climate-related risk and opportunity, namely: agriculture, gas, oil and thermal coal. It has undertaken a rigorous process of research, internal consultation and expert engagement to develop a clear understanding of risks and opportunities in each sector, set appropriate strategies and to determine appropriate targets to manage portfolio risk and maximize opportunity. Further, the company will support the transition by mobilizing sustainable finance across all banking products, with a cumulative target of R250 billion to R300 billion by the end of 2026.

EXECUTIVES

Chief Executive Officer, Executive Director, Simpiwe K. Tshabalala
Chief Finance & Value Management Officer, Executive Director, Arno Daehnke
Chief Risk & Corporate Affairs Officer, David W. P. Hodnett
Chief Strategy Officer, Adam Ikdal
Chief Operating Officer, Margaret Nienaber
Chief People and Culture Officer, Sharon C. Taylor
Independent Non-Executive Chairman, Independent Non-Executive Director, Nonkululeko Merina Cheryl Nyembezi-Heita
Senior Deputy Chairman, Non-Executive Director, Xueqing Guan
Deputy Chairman, Independent Non-Executive Director, Jacko Maree
Independent Non-Executive Director, Lead Independent Director, Trix Kennealy
Independent Non-Executive Director, Lwazi Bam
Independent Non-Executive Director, Paul L. H. Cook
Independent Non-Executive Director, Geraldine J. Fraser-Moleketi
Independent Non-Executive Director, Ben Kruger
Independent Non-Executive Director, Nomgando Nomalungelo Angelina Matyumza
Independent Non-Executive Director, Martin Oduor-Otieno
Independent Non-Executive Director, Atedo Peterside
Independent Non-Executive Director, John H. Vice
Non-Executive Director, Li Li
Non-Executive Director, Kgomotso Ditsebe Moroka
Auditors : PricewaterhouseCoopers Inc.

LOCATIONS

HQ: Standard Bank Group Ltd
9th Floor, Standard Bank Centre, 5 Simmonds Street, Johannesburg 2001
Phone: (27) 11 636 9111 **Fax:** (27) 11 636 4207
Web: www.standardbank.com

2011 Total Income

	% of total
South Africa	84
Rest of Africa	10
Outside of Africa	5
Central and other	1
Total	100

Selected Markets

Africa
    Angola
    Botswana
    DRC
    Ghana
    Kenya
    Lesotho
    Malawi
    Mauritius
    Mozambique
    Namibia
    Nigeria
    South Africa
    Swaziland
    Tanzania
    Uganda
    Zambia
Americas
    Argentina
    Brazil
    US
Europe/Asia Pacific
    China
    Hong Kong
    Isle of Man
    Japan
    Jersey
    Russia
    Singapore
    Taiwan
    Turkey
    United Arab Emirates
    United Kingdom

PRODUCTS/OPERATIONS

2011 Revenue

	% of total
Liberty	45
Personal & business banking	34
Corporate & investment banking	21
Central & other	-
Total	100

COMPETITORS

Hana Financial Group Inc.
LIONTRUST ASSET MANAGEMENT PLC
MITSUBISHI UFJ FINANCIAL GROUP, INC.
MIZUHO FINANCIAL GROUP, INC.
Nordea Bank AB
STANDARD CHARTERED PLC
Shinhan Financial Group Co., Ltd.
TP ICAP LIMITED
The Bank of Nova Scotia
Woori Finance Holdings Co., Ltd.

HISTORICAL FINANCIALS

Company Type: Public

Income Statement — FYE: December 31

	ASSETS ($mil)	NET INCOME ($mil)	INCOME AS % OF ASSETS	EMPLOYEES
12/22	170,399	2,046	1.2%	49,325
12/21	170,960	1,559	0.9%	49,224
12/20	172,615	842	0.5%	50,115
12/19	162,032	1,811	1.1%	50,691
12/18	147,922	1,909	1.3%	53,178
Annual Growth	3.6%	1.8%	—	(1.9%)

2022 Year-End Financials

Return on assets: 1.2% Dividends
Return on equity: 15.2% Yield: —
Long-term debt ($ mil.): — Payout: 35.9%
No. of shares ($ mil.): 1,648 Market value ($ mil.): 16,154
Sales ($ mil.): 15,300

	STOCK PRICE ($) FY Close	P/E High/Low	Earnings	Dividends	Book Value
12/22	9.80	1 0	1.24	0.44	8.56
12/21	8.78	1 0	0.98	0.29	8.47
12/20	8.64	1 1	0.53	0.44	8.08
12/19	11.88	1 1	1.13	0.52	8.14
12/18	12.73	1 1	1.19	0.53	7.60
Annual Growth	(6.3%)	—	1.1%	(4.2%)	3.0%

Standard Chartered Plc

Standard Chartered is a leading international banking group that operates in its target markets of Asia, the Middle East, and Africa, home to many of the world's fastest-growing economies. It has also operations in Europe and the Americas. The company offers products and services such as macro commodities and credit trading, sales and structuring, cash management, trade finance, working capital, investments, insurance, wealth advice, portfolio management, deposits, mortgages, credit card, personal loans, trade finance, and working capital, among others. In all, Standard Chartered has more than 775 branches in about 60 countries and serves customers in roughly 120 markets, with its largest market, Asia, accounting for about 70% of total revenue. Standard Chartered traces its roots back to 1853 when it first opened its doors in Mumbai, Kolkata, and Shanghai.

Operations

Standard Charter organizes its business around three client segment groups: Corporate, Commercial and Institutional Banking; Consumer, Private and Business Banking; and Ventures.

Corporate, Commercial and Institutional Banking segment, generates more than 60% of the company's total revenue, provides transaction services, corporate finance, financial markets, and borrowing.

Consumer, Private and Business Banking segment, which provides digital banking services with a human touch to its clients, with services spanning across deposits, payments, financing products and Wealth Management, pulls in over 35% of revenue.

Ventures promotes innovation, invests in disruptive financial technology and explores alternative business models. Its pipeline of over 30 ventures includes two cloud-native digital banks.

Geographic Reach

The UK-based Standard Chartered does business from more than 775 branches in around 60 markets, mostly in Asia, Africa and the Middle East, and Europe and the Americas.

The company's biggest territories are Asia (approximately 70% of revenue), followed by Africa & Middle East (more than 15%), and Europe & Americas (about 15%).

Sales and Marketing

The Corporate and Institutional Banking segment serves more than 20,000 clients worldwide, and Consumer, Private and Business Banking serves more than 10 million individuals and small businesses.

Financial Performance

The company reported a net interest income of $7.6 billion in 2022, a 12% increase from the previous year's net interest income of $6.8 billion. This was primarily due to the higher volume of Interest income for the year.

In 2022, the company had a net profit of $2.9 billion, a 27% increase from the previous year's net profit of $2.3 billion. This was primarily due to the higher volume of net interest income for the year.

The company's cash at the end of 2021 was $88.7 billion. Operating activities generated $15.2 billion, while investing activities used $22.6 billion, mainly for purchase of investment securities. Financing activities used another $772 million, primarily for repayment of senior debts.

Strategy

The company will continue to increase focus on:

Four strategic priorities: Network business, Affluent client business, Mass Retail business, and Sustainability.

Three critical enablers: People and Culture, Ways of Working, and Innovation.

Over the past year, the company has executed against its strategy. While there are adjacent areas it will continue focusing on, such as managing down low-returning risk-weighted assets (RWA) in Corporate, Commercial and Institutional Banking (CCIB), and accelerating cost-savings across Consumer, Private and Business Banking (CPBB), the company still believes its strategy is the right one. It has made good progress in the year and are on track to deliver its objectives.

Going forward, the company's strategic priorities and enablers will continue to be supported by its three Stands: Accelerating Zero, Lifting Participation and Resetting Globalization.

Company Background

Asia, Africa, and the Middle East have been among Stanchart's targeted areas for growth. It owns First Africa Group, which provides mergers and acquisitions advisory services to companies wanting to invest in Africa. Stanchart bought Barclays Bank's custody business in 2010, adding operations in eight African nations. In late 2011, the company bought the performing segment of Barclays' credit card business in India at a discount. In 2012, to expand its wholesale banking business in Turkey, Stanchart purchased Credit Agricole Yatirim Bankasi Turk A.S. (CAYBT), a fully-owned subsidiary of Credit Agricole Corporate and Investment Bank. It exited the equity capital markets in 2015. The company's trans-border nature means it sometimes falls foul of sanction regimes; it faces $900 million in fines from the US Government for violating sanctions against Iran and other countries.

HISTORY

Standard Chartered began in 1853 as the Chartered Bank of India, Australia and China to finance trade between the UK and its Asian colonies. It began establishing offices in 1858. Over the next 40 years, The Chartered Bank expanded throughout Asia. In the 20th century, the bank opened branches in Germany and the US. In 1957 Chartered entered the Middle East by acquiring Eastern Bank. In 1969 it agreed to merge with Standard Bank.

In 1862 schoolmaster John Paterson established the Standard Bank of British South Africa Ltd. to fund trade with mining businesses. Within two years the bank had 15 branches. Like Chartered, Standard had moved into Germany and the US by 1905 and operated in central and southern Africa by 1912.

In 1962 the bank was renamed The Standard Bank Ltd. Three years later it expanded into Gambia, Ghana, Nigeria, and Sierra Leone, but the end of colonialism meant instability; business was threatened and ruling parties often nationalized Standard's banks. In 1969 the bank agreed to merge with Chartered Bank.

Asian and Middle Eastern business flourished in the early 1970s, while South African branches struggled under growing international pressure on the country's apartheid regime. In response, the company diversified into metals trading and consumer finance. It also expanded in the US market with the purchase of Union Bancorp of California.

Standard Chartered failed in a 1981 attempt to gain entry to the UK market through purchasing Royal Bank of Scotland. Four years later that bank went public.

In 1986 Lloyds Bank tried to take over Standard Chartered, but investors Robert Holmes a Court, Yue-Kong Pao, and Khoo Teck Puat acquired enough of the company to block the play. Meanwhile, overseas financial deregulation brought more competition, and Hong Kong, Singapore, and Malaysia sank into recession.

Hit by trade sanctions against South Africa, the bank in 1987 sold its operations there. As the world tumbled deeper into recession, Standard Chartered's loan losses climbed. But the bank began to recover the next year as it trimmed its US bank holdings.

Scandal hit the bank in the 1990s. In 1992 Standard Chartered paid $515 million in restitution after a broker in its Mumbai, India office embezzled some $1.2 billion from Indian banks. In 1994 executives with Mocatta were convicted of bribery, and the Hong Kong government banned Standard Chartered Securities (sold in 1996) from underwriting stock offerings for nine months after it falsified six IPOs.

In 1997 Standard Chartered refocused on retail banking with its 1998 purchase of what is now Banco Standard Chartered in Latin America and its bank/insurance tie-ups with CGU (now CGNU) and Prudential plc. The promotion of Rana Talwar to CEO brought a strategic focus on emerging markets, from which other banks were withdrawing.

Standard Chartered in 1999 bought Thailand's Nakornthon Bank and the non-Swiss trade financing operations of UBS AG and expanded into China through a pact with the Bank of China. In 2000 the company bought Australia and New Zealand Banking Group's Grindlays operations in South Asia and the Middle East. The following year Stanchart began cutting 20% of its workforce. It also folded Grindlay's operations into its own, while retaining the brand's name.

In 2004 Stanchart bought the majority of Australia and New Zealand Banking Group's project finance business, which is headquartered in London. The business, which cost Stanchart about $1.5 billion, operates in four regions: the UK, the US, the Middle East, and South Asia (especially India).

In 2005 the bank acquired Korea First Bank (now SC First Bank); the deal was the biggest foreign investment ever for South Korea's financial sector. The following year, Stanchart paid about $1.2 billion for Taiwan's Hsinchu Bank, making it the first foreign bank owner in that country. Also in 2006, the bank acquired 20% of China Bohai Bank.

In 2008 the UK government responded to the global financial crisis by investing £50 billion ($87.9 billion) in the nation's top banks, including Stanchart. It agreed to guarantee another £250 billion ($438 billion) in bonds and provide additional liquidity of at least £200 billion ($350 billion) to the banks. The bailout plan was initiated to provide capital directly to the banks in order to revitalize lending activities.

Also in 2008 the company made some acquisitions for further international expansion. It bought Asia Trust and Investment Corporation, which added some 10 branches in the lucrative Taipei market. Stanchart also bought some of the Brazil operations of Lehman Brothers after that company filed for bankruptcy protection.

EXECUTIVES

Chief Executive Officer, Executive Director, Bill Winters
Chief Financial Officer, Executive Director, Andy N. Halford
Chief Technology, Operations and Transformation Officer, Roel Louwhoff
Chief Risk Officer, Sadia Ricke
General Counsel, Sandie Okoro
Secretary, Adrian de Souza
Chairman, Non-Executive Director, Jose Vinals
Senior Independent Director, Maria Ramos
Independent Non-Executive Director, Shirish Apte
Independent Non-Executive Director, Robin Lawther
Independent Non-Executive Director, Linda Yueh
Independent Non-Executive Director, Jackie Hunt
Independent Non-Executive Director, Gay Huey Evans
Independent Non-Executive Director, Phil Rivett
Independent Non-Executive Director, Jasmine M. Whitbread
Independent Non-Executive Director, David Philbrick Conner
Independent Non-Executive Director, David Tang
Independent Non-Executive Director, Carlson Tong
Auditors : Ernst & Young LLP

LOCATIONS

HQ: Standard Chartered Plc
32nd Floor, 4-4A Des Voeux Road, Central,
Phone: (44) 20 7885 8888   **Fax:** (44) 20 7885 9999
Web: www.sc.com

2018 Sales

	% of total
Greater China & North Asia	42
ASEAN & South Asia	27
Africa & the Middle East	18
Europe & Americas	11
Central and other	2
Total	100

PRODUCTS/OPERATIONS

2018 Sales

	% of total
Net Interest Income	59
Net Fee and Commission Income	24
Net Trading Income	11
Other Operating Income	6
Total	100

2018 Sales

	$mil	%
Corporate & Institutional Banking	6,606	45
Retail Banking	5,041	34
Commercial Banking	1,390	9
Private Banking	518	4
Central & Other Items	1,234	8
Total	14,789	100

COMPETITORS

ABERDEEN ASSET MANAGEMENT PLC
AUSTRALIA AND NEW ZEALAND BANKING GROUP LIMITED
CAPITALSOURCE INC.
CLOSE BROTHERS GROUP PLC
GENERAL ELECTRIC CAPITAL CORPORATION
HSBC HOLDINGS PLC
Islandsbanki hf.
KBC Groupe
NATIONAL BANK OF GREECE S.A.
Nordea Bank AB

HISTORICAL FINANCIALS

Company Type: Public

Income Statement   FYE: December 31

	ASSETS ($mil)	NET INCOME ($mil)	INCOME AS % OF ASSETS	EMPLOYEES
12/22	819,922	2,948	0.4%	83,266
12/21	827,818	2,315	0.3%	81,957
12/20	789,050	724	0.1%	83,657
12/19	720,398	2,303	0.3%	84,398
12/18	688,762	1,054	0.2%	85,402
Annual Growth	4.5%	29.3%	—	(0.6%)

2022 Year-End Financials

Return on assets: 0.3%   Dividends
Return on equity: 5.7%   Yield: —
Long-term debt ($ mil.): —   Payout: 23.7%
No. of shares ($ mil.): 2,867   Market value ($ mil.): 42,811
Sales ($ mil.): 24,992

	STOCK PRICE ($) FY Close	P/E High/Low	PER SHARE ($) Earnings	Dividends	Book Value
12/22	14.93	19 14	0.84	0.20	17.32
12/21	12.31	24 18	0.60	0.20	17.10
12/20	12.79	185 83	0.10	0.09	16.00
12/19	19.15	34 27	0.56	0.22	15.78
Annual Growth	(8.0%)	— —	10.6%	(2.3%)	2.4%

State Bank of India

EXECUTIVES

Managing Director, Executive Director, P. K. Gupta
Chairman, Executive Chairman, Rajnish Kumar
Managing Director, Executive Director, Arijit Basu
Managing Director, Executive Director, Dinesh Kumar Khara
Managing Director, Executive Director, Challa Sreenivasulu Setty
Director, Sanjiv Malhotra
Director, Bhaskar Pramanik
Director, Basant Seth
Director, B Venugopal
Director, Pushpendra Rai
Director, Purnima Gupta
Director, Sanjeev Maheshwari
Director, Debasish Panda
Director, Chandan Sinha
Auditors : Khandelwal Jain & Co.

LOCATIONS

HQ: State Bank of India
Corporate Centre, Madam Cama Road, Mumbai 400 021
Phone: (91) 22 2283 0535   **Fax:** (91) 22 2285 5348
Web: www.sbi.co.in

HISTORICAL FINANCIALS

Company Type: Public

Income Statement   FYE: March 31

	ASSETS ($mil)	NET INCOME ($mil)	INCOME AS % OF ASSETS	EMPLOYEES
03/22	707,727	4,669	0.7%	244,250
03/21	662,268	3,062	0.5%	245,652
03/20	555,704	2,617	0.5%	249,448
03/19	561,960	332	0.1%	257,252
03/18	555,855	(700)	—	264,041
Annual Growth	6.2%	—		(1.9%)

2022 Year-End Financials

Return on assets: 0.6%   Dividends
Return on equity: 12.1%   Yield: —
Long-term debt ($ mil.): —   Payout: 84.8%
No. of shares ($ mil.): 8,924   Market value ($ mil.): —
Sales ($ mil.): 53,836

Steel Authority of India Ltd

SAIL helps keep India's ship of industry afloat. Steel Authority of India Limited (SAIL) is among India's biggest steelmakers. The company's main steel products include flat products (coils, plates, and sheets), structurals (angles, beam, and channel), rail products (Corrosion Resistant Micro Alloyed Rail, Crane Rails, and high conductivity rails), and Long Products (TMT Bars, Wire Rods). SAIL produces iron and steel at five integrated plants and three special steel plants, located principally in the eastern and central regions of India and situated close to domestic sources of raw materials. The Government of India owns 75% of the company. About 95% of the company's total revenue comes from domestic sale. The company was founded in 1954.

Operations

SAIL is engaged in the manufacturing of iron and steel products and generate revenues from sale of iron and steel products and the same is only the reportable segment of the company. It accounts for almost of the company's revenue (more than 95%), while the remaining is from other products.

SAIL globally by supplying rails, structurals, merchant products, wire rods, rebars, plate mill plates, hot rolled coils, hot rolled plates / sheets, cold rolled steels, galvanised steels, cold rolled non-oriented (crno) coils, stainless steel sheets/coils, chequered plates, slabs, billets, blooms and pig iron, besides cut-to-size hot rolled and cold rolled materials in all continents.

Geographic Reach

SAIL produces iron and steel at five integrated plants and three special steel plants, located principally in the eastern and central regions of India and situated close to domestic sources of raw materials.

The company is head quartered in New Delhi, India. About 95% of the company's total revenue comes from domestic sale.

SAIL products have berthed successfully at Japan, China, Korea, Taiwan, Vietnam, Philippines, Singapore, Malaysia, Thailand, Indonesia, Australia, Mexico, Europe (UK, Germany, France, Belgium, Italy, Spain, Netherlands, and Portugal), Sudan, Oman, UAE, and many more, as well as in neighbouring countries such as Myanmar, Bangladesh, Sri Lanka and Nepal.

Sales and Marketing

The company growth in large steel-consuming sectors, including construction, automobiles, general engineering, and capital goods, bodes well for SAIL's prospects.

SAIL has been organizing seminars, workshops, lecture sessions, amongst opinion makers, consumers, designers, besides working amongst engineering students and academicians. The company organized around 180 "Gaon Ki Ore" workshops in more than 20 States/Union territories. Small consumers continued to be a focus area and 0.67 MT of steel was sold through the retail marketing channels.

Financial Performance

The company achieved a sales turnover of ?61,025 crores during the Financial Year 2019-20, which is lower by 8% as compared to the corresponding period of last year (CPLY) mainly due to a decrease in Net Sales Realisation (NSR) of Saleable Steel of 5 Integrated Steel Plants by about 12%.

Cash held by the company at the end of 2019 increased by ?118.8 crores to ?153.4 crores compared to the prior year with ?34.6 crores. Cash provided by operations was ? 10,117.1 crores, while cash used for investing and financing activities were ?650.6 crores and ?4,236.1 crores, respectively. Main use for cash were trade receivables and purchase of properties.

Strategy

The company has adopted a multi-pronged approach that includes organic growth, brown-field projects, technology leadership through strategic alliances, ensuring raw material security by developing new mines, diversifying in allied areas, etc. In line with the above approach, SAIL has formed Joint Venture Companies in different areas viz. power generation, rail wagon manufacturing, slag cement production, securing coking coal supplies from new overseas sources, etc. New initiatives are currently being explored in areas such as pellet manufacturing in a joint venture, outsourcing of power distribution and township maintenance services in SAIL townships, etc.

In the recent challenging period, the Corporate Communication function has become the cynosure of all eyes in the business world. The companies around the world realized the significance and the utmost need to have a full-fledged and evolved team of communicators, who in the regular as well as in times of crisis, keep the good word and works of the organization in proper perspective and public focus. Corporate Communication is a round-the-clock exercise where the communicators of the corporate strategize to bring the best image of the company to the world in tandem with the evolving realties, goals and targets of the company.

Company Background

The company was founded in 1954.

Auditors : KASG & CO.

LOCATIONS

HQ: Steel Authority of India Ltd
Ispat Bhawan, Lodi Road, New Delhi 110003
Phone: (91) 11 2436 7481   **Fax:** (91) 11 2436 7015
Web: www.sail.co.in

2013 Sales

	% of total
India	98
Other countries	2
Total	100

PRODUCTS/OPERATIONS

2013 Sales

	% of total
Steel products	96
Other products	4
Total	100

Selected Operations
Integrated Steel Plants
    Bhilai Steel Plant
    Bokaro Steel Plant
    Durgapur Steel Plant
    Indian Iron & Steel Co.
    Rourkela Steel Plant
Specialty Steel Plants
  Alloy Steels Plant
    Chandrapur Ferro Alloy Plant
    Salem Steel Plant
    Visvesvaraya Iron and Steel Plant

Selected Products
Ferro alloys
Ferro manganese
Silico manganese
Steel and Iron
    Flat products
    Cold rolled sheets
    Galvanized coils
    Galvanized sheets
    Hot rolled coils
    Hot rolled plates
    Wide and heavy plates
Structurals
    Angles
    Bars
    Channels
    Joists
    Rounds
    Wire rods
Tar products
Coal tar
Other products
    Pig iron
    Slabs
    Wheels and axles

COMPETITORS

CALIFORNIA STEEL INDUSTRIES, INC.
EREGLI DEMIR VE CELIK FABRIKALARI TURK ANONIM SIRKETI
Grupo Simec, S.A.B. de C.V.
KEYSTONE CONSOLIDATED INDUSTRIES, INC.
KOBE STEEL, LTD.
Maanshan Iron & Steel Company Limited
STEEL DYNAMICS, INC.
UNITED STATES STEEL CORPORATION
USS-POSCO INDUSTRIES, A CALIFORNIA JOINT VENTURE
Wugang Group Co., Ltd.

HISTORICAL FINANCIALS

Company Type: Public

Income Statement   FYE: March 31

	REVENUE ($mil)	NET INCOME ($mil)	NET PROFIT MARGIN	EMPLOYEES
03/22	13,774	1,616	11.7%	62,181
03/21	9,563	566	5.9%	65,564
03/20	8,283	280	3.4%	69,379
03/19	9,750	339	3.5%	72,339
03/18	9,127	(43)	—	76,870
Annual Growth	10.8%			(5.2%)

2022 Year-End Financials
Debt ratio: 0.1%
Return on equity: 24.5%
Cash ($ mil.): 103
Current Ratio: 0.73
Long-term debt ($ mil.): 1,074
No. of shares ($ mil.): 4,130
Dividends
 Yield: —
 Payout: 64.3%
Market value ($ mil.): —

Stellantis NV

Fiat Chrysler Automobiles (FCA) designs, engineers, and makes passenger cars, light commercial vehicles, components and production systems worldwide. Its automotive brands include Abarth, Alfa Romeo, Chrysler, Dodge, Fiat, Fiat Professional, Jeep, Lancia, Ram, SRT, and Maserati, as well as Mopar, its parts and service brand. FCA's businesses also include Comau (production systems), Magneti Marelli (components) and Teksid (iron and castings). Fiat (founded in 1899) .

Operations
Fiat Chrysler is the seventh largest automaker in the world. Activities are carried out through five reportable segments: NAFTA (North America and the Caribbean); LATAM (Latin America); APAC (the Asia-Pacific region including India); and EMEA (Western Europe, the Middle East and Africa) - Maserati, the company's global luxury brand segment.

The NAFTA region, the largest segment by sales at around 70% of total, comprises the North American countries (including the Caribbean). The Components segment produces lighting components, suspension, electronic systems and cast-iron components for engines and gearboxes, to list just a few.

Geographic Reach
FCA has operations in about 105 countries and generates sales in some 110. The NAFTA region is the company's largest by sales numbers at around 70 % of total.In Europe, FCA makes around 20% of vehicle sales in Italy.

Financial Performance
The company's revenue increased by ?2.2 billion to ?108.2 billion in 2019 compared from the prior year with ?110.4 million.

Net income in 2019 increased by 82% to ?6.6 billion primarily due to higher profit from discontinued operations.

The company's cash held at the end of 2019 increased by ?2.6 billion to ?15.0 billion compared from 2018 with ?12.5 billion. Cash provided by operations was ?10.5 billion, while cash used for investing and financing activities were ?3.0 billion and ?5.8 billion, respectively.

Strategy
The business plan and the additional measures mentioned above build upon the strategic actions taken in the prior plan to generate volume growth and margin expansion through the following: continued emphasis on building strong brands by leveraging renewals of key products and portfolio expansion; new white-space products with particular focus on the Jeep, Maserati and Alfa Romeo brands; improve the positioning of Maserati as a luxury brand, bridging product gap with specialty models, improving cadence of new model introduction, including a fully-electrified line-up, with new leadership team in place, new COO and other key appointments; refocus marketing in China to recently launched products, offer more efficient powertrain combinations along with continued product quality improvements, as well as changes in the leadership team; continue to focus on industrial rationalization to deliver cost savings through manufacturing and purchasing efficiencies and implement actions to increase capacity utilization, including local production of certain Jeep products, in EMEA; implementation of various electrified powertrain applications throughout the portfolio, supplemented with third-party agreements for the purchase of regulatory credits, as part of the company's regulatory compliance strategy; continue to explore opportunities to develop partnerships to share technologies and platforms, enhance skill set related to autonomous driving technologies, preserve full optionality and ensure speed to market; and maintain a disciplined approach to the deployment of capital and re-establish consistent shareholder remuneration actions.

Mergers and Acquisitions
In 2019, a proposed merger with French carmaker Renault fell through after opposition from the French government (Renault's largest single shareholder with a 15% stake in the company) caused Fiat to back out of the deal. Demands by the French included a corporate headquarters in Paris and job cuts to be made in the U.S. and Italy before any jobs were lost in France.

Later in 2019, FCA and Peugeot S.A. announced a planned merger that would combine the two companies to form the fourth-largest automaker in the world. The deal aims to create an automotive powerhouse with the scale and resources necessary to compete in a mobility-focused future of connected, electrified, shared, and autonomous vehicles. The combination would leverage FCA's strength in the North American market with trucks and SUVs and Peugeot's passenger car position in Europe.

EXECUTIVES

Chairman, Executive Director, John Elkann
Chief Executive Officer, Executive Director, Carlos Tavares
Chief Planning Officer, Olivier Bourges
Chief Financial Officer, Richard Keith Palmer
Enlarged Europe Chief Executive Officer, Maxime Picat
North America Chief Executive Officer, Mark Stewart
South America Chief Operating Officer, Antonio Filosa
Middle East & Africa Chief Operating Officer, Samir Cherfan
China Chief Operating Officer, Gregoire Olivier
India and Asia Pacific Chief Operating Officer, Carl Smiley
Americas Head, Michael Manley
Corporate General Counsel, Giorgio Fossati
Vice Chairman, Non-Executive Director, Robert Peugeot
Senior Independent Director, Non-Executive Director, Henri de Castries
Non-Executive Director, Andrea Agnelli
Non-Executive Director, Fiona Clare Cicconi
Non-Executive Director, Jacques de Saint-Exupery
Non-Executive Director, Nicolas Dufourcq
Non-Executive Director, Ann Frances Godbehere
Non-Executive Director, Wan Ling Martello
Non-Executive Director, Kevin Scott
Auditors : EY S.p.A

LOCATIONS

HQ: Stellantis NV
Taurusavenue 1, LS Hoofddorp 2132
Phone: (31) 23 700 1511
Web: www.stellantis.com

2013 Sales

	% of total
NAFTA (North America inc. Caribbean)	61
EMEA (Western Europe, Middle East, Africa)	18
LATAM (Latin America)	6
APAC (Asia-Pacific including India)	4
Components	9
Maserati	2
Total	100

HISTORICAL FINANCIALS
Company Type: Public

Income Statement — FYE: December 31

	REVENUE ($mil)	NET INCOME ($mil)	NET PROFIT MARGIN	EMPLOYEES
12/23	209,940	20,597	9.8%	258,275
12/22	191,812	17,942	9.4%	272,367
12/21	169,122	16,072	9.5%	281,595
12/20	106,377	35	0.0%	189,512
12/19	121,469	7,434	6.1%	191,752
Annual Growth	14.7%	29.0%	—	7.7%

2023 Year-End Financials
Debt ratio: 16.1%
Return on equity: 24.1%
Cash ($ mil.): 48,368
Current Ratio: 1.24
Long-term debt ($ mil.): 22,153
No. of shares ($ mil.): 3,023
Dividends
 Yield: —
 Payout: 26.0%
Market value ($ mil.): —

STMicroelectronics NV

EXECUTIVES

President, Chief Executive Officer, Jean-Marc Chery

Finance, Infrastructure & Services Chief Financial Officer, Finance, Infrastructure & Services President, Lorenzo Grandi

Chief Compliance Officer, Secretary, Philippe Dereeper
Technology, Manufacturing & Quality President, Orio Bellezza
Communications President, Sales President, Strategy Development President, Marketing President, Marco Luciano Cassis
Legal Counsel President, Steven Rose
Supply Chain Executive Vice President, Alberto Della Chiesa
Head of Back-End Manufacturing & Technology Executive Vice President, Fabio Gualandris
Digital & Smart Power Technology and Digital Front-End Manufacturing Executive Vice President, Joel Hartmann
Front-End Manufacturing, Analog and Power Executive Vice President, Michael Hummel
Integrated Marketing & Communications Executive Vice President, Claudia Levo
Corporate Treasury, Insurance, M&A, IP BU, Real Estate, and Italy Public Affairs Executive Vice President, Giuseppe Notarnicola
Europe and France Public Affairs Executive Vice President, Thierry Tingaud
Product Quality & Reliability Executive Vice President, Nicolas Yackowlew
Supervisory Board Member, Chairman, Maurizio Tamagnini
Supervisory Board Member, Vice-Chairman, Nicolas Dufourcq
Supervisory Board Member, Yann Delabriere
Supervisory Board Member, Janet G. Davidson
Supervisory Board Member, Ana de Pro Gonzalo
Supervisory Board Member, Heleen Kersten
Supervisory Board Member, Lucia Morselli
Supervisory Board Member, Alessandro Rivera
Supervisory Board Member, Frederic Sanchez
Auditors: Ernst & Young AG

LOCATIONS

HQ: STMicroelectronics NV
WTC Schiphol Airport, Schiphol Boulevard 265, Schiphol 1118 BH
Phone: (41) 22 929 29 29   **Fax:** (41) 22 929 29 88
Web: www.st.com

HISTORICAL FINANCIALS
Company Type: Public

Income Statement   FYE: December 31

	REVENUE ($mil)	NET INCOME ($mil)	NET PROFIT MARGIN	EMPLOYEES
12/22	16,128	3,960	24.6%	51,370
12/21	12,761	2,000	15.7%	48,254
12/20	10,219	1,106	10.8%	46,016
12/19	9,556	1,032	10.8%	45,554
12/18	9,664	1,287	13.3%	45,953
Annual Growth	13.7%	32.4%	—	2.8%

2022 Year-End Financials
Debt ratio: 13.6%
Return on equity: 36.1%
Cash ($ mil.): 3,258
Current Ratio: 2.56
Long-term debt ($ mil.): 2,542
No. of shares ($ mil.): 903
Dividends
  Yield: —
  Payout: 4.8%
Market value ($ mil.): 32,151

	STOCK PRICE ($) FY Close	P/E High/Low		PER SHARE ($) Earnings	Dividends	Book Value
12/22	35.57	11	7	4.19	0.20	14.04
12/21	48.88	24	15	2.16	0.19	10.16
12/20	37.12	34	13	1.20	0.16	9.33
12/19	26.91	24	10	1.14	0.20	7.90
12/18	13.88	18	9	1.41	0.20	7.08
Annual Growth	26.5%	—		31.3%	0.0%	18.7%

Stora Enso Oyj

Stora Enso is a leading provider of renewable products in packaging, biomaterials, wooden construction and paper, and one of the largest private forest owners in the world. The company also makes commercial and consumer packaging products (carton and corrugated cardboard), biomaterials (pulp and byproducts such as tall oil and turpentine), and wood products for construction as well as wood pellets for heating. Close to 75% of its sales are generated in Europe but the company operates in more than 30 countries.

Operations

Stora Enso's reportable segments are Packaging Materials, Packaging Solutions, Biomaterials, Wood Products, Forest, and Paper and the segment Other.

The Packaging Materials division aims to lead the development of circular packaging, providing premium packaging materials based on virgin and recycled fiber. Addressing the needs of today's eco-conscious consumers, Stora Enso helps customers replace fossil-based materials with low-carbon, renewable and recyclable alternatives for their food and drink, pharmaceutical or transport packaging. A wide selection of barrier coatings enables design optimization for various demanding packaging end-uses. The segment accounts for more than 35% of total revenue.

Accounting for more than 15% of revenue, wood products division is one of the largest sawnwood producers in Europe and a leading provider of sustainable wood-based solutions for the construction industry globally. The growing Building Solutions business offers building concepts to support low-carbon construction and eco-friendly designs. Stora Enso develops digital tools to simplify the design and construction of building projects with wood. In addition, it offers applications for windows, doors and packaging industries, as well as pellets for sustainable heating solutions.

In paper division (around 15%), Stora Enso is one of the major paper producers in Europe, with an established customer base and a wide product portfolio for print and office use. Customers benefit from Stora Enso's selection of paper grades made from recycled and virgin fiber, its technical and operational expertise and sustainability know-how, and its sales and customer service center network.

The Biomaterials division meets the growing demand for bio-based solutions to replace fossil-based and hazardous materials. Stora Enso uses all fractions of biomass, like lignin, to develop new solutions. Its work to replace fossil-based materials includes novel applications such as carbon for energy storage, bio-based binders and bio-based carbon fiber. Its pulp offering encompasses a wide variety of grades to meet the demands of paper, board, tissue and hygiene product producers, as well as materials from process side streams, such as tall oil and turpentine from biomass. The segment accounts for about 15% of revenue.

The Forest division creates value through sustainable forest management, competitive wood supply and innovation. Forests are the foundation for Stora Enso's renewable offerings. The division manages Stora Enso's forest assets in Sweden and a 41% share of Tornator, whose forest assets are mainly located in Finland. It is also responsible for wood sourcing for Stora Enso's Nordic, Baltic and Russian operations and B2B customers. Stora Enso is one of the biggest private forest owners in the world. The segment accounts for less than 10% of revenue.

The Packaging Solutions division (more than 5%) develops and sells premium fiber-based packaging products and services. Stora Enso's high-end eco-friendly packaging products are used by leading brands across multiple market sectors, including the retail, e-commerce and industrial sectors. The portfolio includes converting corrugated board and cartonboard, and converting new materials such as formed fiber and wood foams, as well as design and sustainability services, and circular and automation solutions.

The Other segment includes Stora Enso's shareholding in the energy company Pohjolan Voima (PVO), and the company's shared services and administration.

Geographic Reach

The company has operations in more than 30 countries worldwide. Stora Enso generates about 75% of revenue from Europe market, while more than 15% from Asia Pacific and around 10% from Americas and other market.

In Brazil, Stora Enso has a 50/50% investment with Suzano in the Veracel Cellulose pulp site. The Montes del Plata pulp site in Uruguay is a 50/50% joint operation between Stora Enso and Arauco. Its consumer board site in Guangxi, China, serves the Asian markets with virgin fiber-based board, and its operations also include eucalyptus plantations. The company supplies its customers in Asia through its global operations, from production sites in Europe, South America and China.

Sales and Marketing

Stora Enso serves markets for food and beverages, e-commerce, hygiene, personal care, retail and consumer goods, pharma, energy, adhesives, wooden construction, biomaterials, and more.

Financial Performance
In 2021, the company had sales amounting to EUR10.2 billion.

Strategy
Stora Enso's strategy is to focus on leading positions and accelerated growth in packaging, building solutions and the biomaterials innovation program. The company's innovation initiatives will be concentrated in the areas of new sustainable packaging materials, sustainable barriers and the biochemical platform in lignin. Forest, traditional wood products and market pulp make up the foundation for value creation in Stora Enso.

Its three focus areas for growth are:

Packaging Materials and Packaging Solutions, driven by high demand for plastic free and eco-friendly circular packaging. The company holds leading market positions and see attractive investment options;

Building Solutions, within its Wood Products division, driven by a growing wooden buildings market. Stora Enso offers alternatives to fossil-based construction material and are a leading global supplier; and

Biomaterials innovation, where our agenda is focused on lignin, and targets strong growth in new applications and markets.

Mergers and Acquisitions
In mid-2014 Stora Enso acquired US-based Virdia, a leading developer of extraction and separation technologies for conversion of cellulosic biomass into highly refined sugars and lignin.

HISTORY

Stora Enso's corporate ancestors were mining Kopparberg Mountain in Sweden as long ago as 1288. The mountain housed a copper mine that Swedish nobles and German merchants managed as a cooperative. By the 17th century King Karl IX instituted German mining methods to increase production. Copper became Sweden's largest export, at one point accounting for 60% of the country's gross national product.

Copper production slowed after two cave-ins in 1655 and 1687, and exploitation of the region's timber and iron ore resources began. By the early 1800s the company was producing pig and bar iron. In 1862 all of the company's activities were combined to form Stora Kopparbergs Bergslag. The role of copper became less important as the company consolidated its iron works and ventured into forest products. The firm reorganized as a limited liability company in 1888.

By 1915 Stora Kopparbergs had firmly established pulp and paper mills, as well as iron and steel works concentrated along the Dalalven River Basin. The company's activities revolved around these facilities for the next 60 years.

EXECUTIVES

President, Chief Executive Officer, Annica Bresky
Deputy Chief Executive, Chief Financial Officer, Seppo Parvi
Chief Strategy and Innovation Officer, Tobias Baarnman
Packaging Solutions Division Executive Vice President, David Ekberg
Sourcing Executive Vice President, Logistics Executive Vice President, Biomaterials Division Executive Vice President, Johanna Hagelberg
Head of Brand and Communications Executive Vice President, Rene Hansen
Packaging Materials Division Executive Vice President, Hannu Kasurinen
People and Culture Executive Vice President, Katariina Kravi
Legal Executive Vice President, Forest Division Executive Vice President, Per Lyrvall
Sustainability Executive Vice President, Annette Stube
Wood Products Division Executive Vice President, Lars Volkel
Acting General Counsel, Christian Swartling
Chair, Independent Director, Antti Makinen
Vice-Chairman, Independent Director, Hakan Buskhe
Independent Director, Elisabeth Fleuriot
Independent Director, Hock Goh
Independent Director, Helena Hedblom
Independent Director, Kari Jordan
Independent Director, Christiane Kuehne
Independent Director, Richard Nilsson
Independent Director, Hans Sohlstrom
Chairman, Director, Jorma Eloranta
Vice-Chairman, Director, Hans Straberg
Director, Mikko Helander
Auditors: PricewaterhouseCoopers Oy

LOCATIONS

HQ: Stora Enso Oyj
Salmisaarenaukio 2, Helsinki 00180
Phone: (358) 2046 111 **Fax:** (358) 2046 21206
Web: www.storaenso.com

2018 Sales by Destination

	% of total
Europe	73
Asia Pacific	18
North America	4
South America	2
Other	3
Total	100

PRODUCTS/OPERATIONS

2018 Sales

	% of total
Paper	22
Consumer Board	19
Wood Products	12
Biomaterials	12
Packaging Solutions	10
Other	25
Eliminations	-
Total	100

Selected Products
Book paper
Business forms
Cartonboards
Coreboards and tubes
Corrugated boxes
Digital papers
Directory paper
Document papers
Envelope papers
Fluff pulp
Foodservice boards
Graphic board
Graphic paper
Kraft papers
Laminated papers
Liquid packaging boards
Magazine paper
Newsprint
Paper-grade pulp
Sawn boards
Scholastic paper

COMPETITORS

CROWN HOLDINGS, INC.
Cascades Inc
DOMTAR CORPORATION
GREIF, INC.
HOKUETSU CORPORATION
INTERNATIONAL PAPER COMPANY
JAMES CROPPER PUBLIC LIMITED COMPANY
Resolute Forest Products Inc
SONOCO PRODUCTS COMPANY
UPM-Kymmene Oyj

HISTORICAL FINANCIALS

Company Type: Public

Income Statement — FYE: December 31

	REVENUE ($mil)	NET INCOME ($mil)	NET PROFIT MARGIN	EMPLOYEES
12/22	12,474	1,655	13.3%	20,110
12/21	11,504	1,432	12.5%	22,094
12/20	10,497	768	7.3%	23,189
12/19	11,289	988	8.8%	24,390
12/18	12,008	1,160	9.7%	26,129
Annual Growth	1.0%	9.3%	—	(6.3%)

2022 Year-End Financials
Debt ratio: 18.4%   No. of shares ($ mil.): 788
Return on equity: 13.3%   Dividends
Cash ($ mil.): 2,047   Yield: —
Current Ratio: 1.43   Payout: 27.9%
Long-term debt ($ mil.): 2,580   Market value ($ mil.): 11,088

	STOCK PRICE ($) FY Close	P/E High/Low	PER SHARE ($) Earnings	Dividends	Book Value
12/22	14.06	11 7	2.09	0.59	16.97
12/21	18.30	12 10	1.81	0.70	15.33
12/20	18.86	24 11	0.97	0.35	13.71
12/19	14.52	13 9	1.26	0.57	10.58
12/18	11.61	16 9	1.47	0.91	9.75
Annual Growth	4.9%	—	9.3%	(10.4%)	14.9%

Subaru Corporation

Subaru Corporation (formerly Fuji Heavy Industries) is the parent of Subaru of America, the automotive company known for its all-wheel-drive (AWD) technology found in crossover vehicles (a sedan drive with SUV looks) such as the Forester and Outback, and in the Impreza, Legacy, and Tribeca models. In addition to Subaru of America, based in the US, the company operates through more than 85 subsidiaries in Japan, China, and Taiwan, and seven equity-method affiliated companies. With more than 440 automobile sales locations in Japan plus location in more than 90 countries and regions, Subaru generates around 20% of its revenue from its home country, Japan.

Operations

The company operates in three business units: Automotive Business Unit, Aerospace Company, and Other Businesses.

The Automotive Business Unit manufactures cars equipped with outstanding safety and driving performance in a variety of driving conditions. This is reflected in the vehicles the company makes which has the Symmetrical All-Wheel Drive (AWD) System which features a symmetrically-laid-out drivetrain and the horizontally-opposed engine. The segment accounts for less than 100% of the company's total revenue.

The Aerospace Company develops and produces a wide variety of aircraft in various programs. It develops, manufactures, maintains, repairs, and provides technical support for products such as the UH1J and UH-2 utility helicopters used by the Japan Ground Self-Defense Force (JGSDF) for disaster relief and other purposes, the T-5 and T-7 for supporting pilot training at the Japan Maritime Self-Defense Force and the Japan Air Self-Defense Force, more than 15 models of unmanned aerial vehicles, and flight simulators. In the commercial program, the company participates in many international joint development projects for Boeing. For the 777X, Boeing's large passenger airliner, it is responsible for the Center Wing and its integration with the main landing gear (MLG) wheel well, as well as MLG doors, Wing-to-Body Fairings (forward), and side-of-body sections. The segment accounts for about 5% of total revenue.

Geographic Reach

The head office of Subaru Corporation is located in Tokyo, Japan. The company's Automotive Business Unit operates from four plants: Gunma Main plant, Yajima plant, Ota North plant and Oizumi plant. The Aerospace Company has three manufacturing plants located across Japan: Handa plant, Handa West plant, and Utsunomiya plant.

The company generates the majority of its revenue from North America, which represents nearly 75% of the company's sales followed by Japan which represents around 20%.

Sales and Marketing

The Aerospace Company develops and produces a wide variety of aircraft and components for major customers, such as Japan Ministry of Defense (JMOD) and Boeing.

Financial Performance

Company revenue for fiscal 2022 decreased to JPY2.7 trillion compared from the prior year with JPY2.8 trillion.

Net income for fiscal 2022 decreased to JPY70.6 billion compared from the prior year with JPY77.3 billion.

Cash held by the company at the end of fiscal 2022 decreased to JPY883.1 billion. Cash provided by operations was JPY195.7 billion while cash used for investing and financing activities were JPY179.7 billion and JPY98.5 billion, respectively.

Strategy

In the mid-term management vision "STEP" announced in 2018, we declared our goal of working toward zero fatal traffic accidents* by 2030, attaching particular importance to protecting lives. Up to now, Subaru has evolved its passive safety performance by adopting the Subaru Global Platform and the preventive safety performance of the EyeSight advanced driver assist system, strengths of the Subaru brand. However, the company will make efforts to integrate intelligent technologies and pursue greater levels of Enjoyment and Peace of Mind.

The next-generation EyeSight X system is an advanced driver assist system for highways. Subaru are also promoting the enhancement of connected safety, facilitating emergency rescue in the event of a serious accident through integration with Subaru STARLINK's connected services.

HISTORY

Chikuhei Nakajima started the Aircraft Research Laboratory north of Tokyo in 1917, renaming it the Nakajima Aircraft Company in 1931. Amid the ashes of WWII, Nakajima formed Fuji Sangyo to make products with aircraft technology in 1945. His motor scooters used bomber tail wheels, and he later added buses with unibody frames. Nakajima died in 1949.

Fuji Sangyo joined four other firms in 1953, and Fuji Heavy Industries was born. The Subaru car division debuted in 1958, and FHI went public two years later. The firm expanded product lines throughout the 1960s, and in 1968 Nissan Motor invested in FHI. The relationship lasted more than 30 years.

Subaru expanded to the US in 1968 with the help of furniture retailer Harvey Lamm. Lamm, visiting Japan, saw Subaru's utilitarian front-wheel-drive station wagon and recognized its potential. He convinced FHI to make him its US importer, and he set up Subaru of America. Lamm ultimately became chairman and CEO of the US subsidiary.

In 1975 FHI exported the four-wheel-drive Subaru GF to the US; it was the country's first four-wheel-drive car for the mass market. High energy prices and the appeal of a four-wheel-drive car drove sales in the 1970s and early 1980s. By 1986 Subaru achieved 12 straight years of record sales and profits.

The next year, however, a rising yen boosted Japanese car prices, and sales dips fueled round after round of incentives. Profits tanked, and Subaru responded by expanding trim levels and power train choices. The misstep confused shoppers and sales nose-dived.

Also in 1987 FHI and Isuzu teamed up to build an assembly plant (Subaru-Isuzu Automotive) in Indiana while other makers introduced minivans and sport utility vehicles. Focusing on cars, Subaru missed the start of the SUV boom. Even the arrival of the Legacy in 1989 failed to jumpstart sales. Lamm left Subaru in 1990, and two years later Subaru's US arm posted a record loss of $250 million.

Veteran CFO George Muller took over as president and COO of Subaru of America in 1993. Saddled with inventory, plummeting sales, and a poor brand image, he promptly launched one of the greatest turnarounds in US automotive history.

Muller refined the niche Lamm carved out in the 1970s. He cut every product from the lineup that lacked all-wheel-drive. Enlisting the Legacy, a car-SUV hybrid (Outback) was created in 1995 by lifting the body a few inches and adding beefy-looking body attachments.

Muller took aggressive steps at the corporate level to cut costs and build a culture of risk-taking, initiative, and speed. By 1999 profits were back to record levels. In Japan, though, trouble at parent FHI overshadowed Subaru's rejuvenation.

In 1998 revelations surfaced that FHI bribed legislator Yojiro Nakajima (a former official in Japan's defense agency and grandson of Chikuhei) to secure government contracts for a sea rescue aircraft. FHI had also illegally funneled cash to Nakajima to help his 1996 election bid. Nakajima, along with FHI's chairman and several former executives, was arrested. He later committed suicide, and FHI was barred from bidding on defense contracts for one year.

GM bought 20% of FHI for $1.5 billion in 1999. The deal included the 4% held by FHI's largest investor, Nissan. GM won access to FHI's all-wheel-drive technology and provided FHI resources to develop more-efficient fuel systems. Midway through 2000 Muller resigned from Subaru.

FHI struck a deal with Airbus in 2001 develop the company's new Airbus A380 airliner. Subaru and GM also unveiled plans to jointly produce an all-wheel-drive sport wagon to be built at the Subaru-Isuzu plant in the US.

FHI announced in 2002 that it would cease production of bus bodies and railway cars by March 2003. Later that year FHI bought Isuzu Motors' 49% stake in the companies' carmaking joint venture, Subaru-Isuzu Automotive. FHI renamed the company Subaru of Indiana Automotive.

That same year FHI implemented sweeping changes in an effort to focus on its core business -- building cars. The Fuji Dynamic Revolution-1 plan (FDR-1) aimed to increase sales by 35% by 2007 and to remake Subaru as a luxury brand. Part of the original plan was for the company to leverage its relationship with GM to reduce procurement and purchasing costs. GM, however, decided largely to terminate its relationship with FHI and has sold its 20% stake in the Japanese manufacturer, about 9% of it going to Toyota Motor. It sold the remaining 11% through Fuji's open-market share-buyback program and through regular market sales.

In the first product tie-up since Toyota became FHI's largest shareholder, the two companies announced in early 2006 that Toyota Camrys would be built at FHI's Subaru of Indiana plant. That production began the following year.

In 2006 FHI made a few adjustments to its FDR-1 plan. The company restructured its sales networks, and layed off about 700 workers to meet its cost reduction goals. The notion of transforming into a luxury brand, however, was deemed to be infeasible from a cost standpoint. FDR-1's successes were mixed. FHI managed to increase sales, but profits were hurt by poor sales at home in Japan and meager sales of higher-end Subaru models in the US, which were likely slowed by high fuel prices.

In 2007 FHI established its Overseas Sales and Marketing Divisions I & II. The first overseas division is dedicated to centralizing control of manufacturing and sales activities in the US. The move aimed to bring refinement and sophistication to the Subaru brand in the US while capitalizing on its reputation of offering affordable, compelling AWD vehicles.

EXECUTIVES

Chairman, Director, Tomomi Nakamura
President, Chief Executive Officer, Representative Director, Atsushi Osaki
Executive Vice President, Representative Director, Fumiaki Hayata
Senior Managing Executive Officer, Chief Financial Officer, Chief Risk Management Officer, Director, Katsuyuki Mizuma
Senior Managing Executive Officer, Chief Technology Officer, Director, Tetsuo Fujinuki
Senior Managing Executive Officer, Tomoaki Emori
Chief Quality Officer, Executive Officer, Osamu Eriguchi
Chief Information Officer, Kazuhiro Abe
Outside Director, Yasuyuki Abe
Outside Director, Miwako Doi
Outside Director, Fuminao Hachiuma
Auditors : KPMG AZSA LLC

LOCATIONS

HQ: Subaru Corporation
1-20-8 Ebisu, Shibuya-ku, Tokyo 150-8554
Phone: (81) 3 6447 8825   **Fax:** (81) 3 6447 8184
Web: www.subaru.co.jp

2018 Sales

	% of total
North America	68
Japan	20
Asia	4
Europe	3
Others	5
Total	100

PRODUCTS/OPERATIONS

2018 Sales

	% of total
Automobiles	94
Aerospace	4
Other	2
Total	100

Selected Products and Divisions

Aerospace
  AH-64D combat helicopter
  Center-wing section (Boeing B-777)
  Design and training simulators
  Fixed-wing aircraft
  T-1 Trainer
  Unmanned aircraft
Automobiles
  Dex
  Dias Wagon
  Exiga
  Forester
  Impreza (wagon, sedan)
  Legacy (touring, B4, Outback)
  Outback (sport, wagon, sedan)
  Sambar (van, truck, wagon)
  Stella (R1, R2, Pleo)
  Tribeca
Eco Technologies
  Clean Robot floor-cleaning system
  Intermediate refuse collection systems
  Maintenance and sanitation vehicles
  Refuse management systems
  Special purpose vehicles
  Sweepers and scrubbers
  Wind-power systems

Selected Subsidiaries:

Fuji Heavy Industries U.S.A., Inc.
Fuji Machinery Co., Ltd. (Japan)
Subaru Canada, Inc.
Subaru of China Ltd.
Subaru Europe N.V./S.A. (Belgium)
Subaru of America, Inc. (US)
Subaru of Indiana Automotive, Inc.

COMPETITORS

AUDI AG
FCA US LLC
FORD MOTOR COMPANY
HONDA MOTOR CO., LTD.
MAZDA MOTOR CORPORATION
Magna International Inc
NISSAN MOTOR CO.,LTD.
PEUGEOT SA
TOYOTA MOTOR CORPORATION
VOLKSWAGEN AG

HISTORICAL FINANCIALS

Company Type: Public

Income Statement   FYE: March 31

	REVENUE ($mil)	NET INCOME ($mil)	NET PROFIT MARGIN	EMPLOYEES
03/23	28,339	1,504	5.3%	45,605
03/22	22,563	575	2.6%	45,272
03/21	25,560	690	2.7%	45,511
03/20	30,807	1,405	4.6%	44,747
03/19	28,538	1,334	4.7%	43,057
Annual Growth	(0.2%)	3.0%	—	1.4%

2023 Year-End Financials

Debt ratio: 0.1%   No. of shares ($ mil.): 767
Return on equity: 10.0%   Dividends
Cash ($ mil.): 7,354   Yield: 3.0%
Current Ratio: 2.40   Payout: 12.4%
Long-term debt ($ mil.): 1,929   Market value ($ mil.): 6,101

	STOCK PRICE ($) FY Close	P/E High/Low	PER SHARE ($) Earnings	Dividends	Book Value
03/23	7.95	0 0	1.96	0.24	20.56
03/22	7.92	0 0	0.75	0.25	20.26
03/21	10.00	0 0	0.90	0.26	20.93
03/20	9.40	0 0	1.83	0.67	20.57
03/19	11.35	0 0	1.74	0.65	18.90
Annual Growth	(8.5%)	—	3.0%	(21.9%)	2.1%

Sumitomo Chemical Co., Ltd.

EXECUTIVES

Chairman, Representative Director, Masakazu Tokura
President, Representative Director, Keiichi Iwata
Executive Vice President, Director, Hiroshi Ueda
Executive Vice President, Director, Hiroshi Niinuma
Senior Managing Executive Officer, Representative Director, Masaki Matsui
Senior Managing Executive Officer, Representative Director, Nobuaki Mito
Senior Managing Executive Officer, Representative Director, Motoyuki Sakai
Senior Managing Executive Officer, Representative Director, Seiji Takeuchi
Senior Managing Executive Officer, Noriaki Takeshita
Outside Director, Hiroshi Tomono
Outside Director, Motoshige Itoh
Outside Director, Atsuko Muraki
Outside Director, Akira Ichikawa
Auditors : KPMG AZSA LLC

LOCATIONS

HQ: Sumitomo Chemical Co., Ltd.
2-7-1 Nihonbashi, Chuo-ku, Tokyo 103-6020
Phone: (81) 3 5201 0235   **Fax:** (81) 3 5201 0430
Web: www.sumitomo-chem.co.jp

HISTORICAL FINANCIALS
Company Type: Public

Income Statement   FYE: March 31

	REVENUE ($mil)	NET INCOME ($mil)	NET PROFIT MARGIN	EMPLOYEES
03/23	21,738	52	0.2%	37,235
03/22	22,734	1,332	5.9%	38,517
03/21	20,654	415	2.0%	38,648
03/20	20,504	284	1.4%	37,453
03/19	20,936	1,065	5.1%	36,384
Annual Growth	0.9%	(52.9%)	—	0.6%

2023 Year-End Financials
Debt ratio: 0.3%
Return on equity: 0.5%
Cash ($ mil.): 2,296
Current Ratio: 1.38
Long-term debt ($ mil.): 7,992
No. of shares ($ mil.): 1,635
Dividends
  Yield: 5.8%
  Payout: 3129.7%
Market value ($ mil.): 27,769

	STOCK PRICE ($) FY Close	P/E High	P/E Low	Earnings	Dividends	Book Value
03/23	16.98	5	4	0.03	0.99	5.38
03/22	22.86	0	0	0.82	0.85	6.13
03/21	26.09	1	0	0.25	0.56	5.63
03/20	14.58	1	1	0.17	1.01	5.20
03/19	23.36	0	0	0.65	1.04	5.52
Annual Growth	(7.7%)	—	—	(52.9%)	(1.3%)	(0.6%)

Sumitomo Corp. (Japan)

EXECUTIVES

Chairman, Director, Kuniharu Nakamura
President, Chief Executive Officer, Representative Director, Masayuki Hyodo
Executive Vice President, Representative Director, Shingo Ueno
Executive Vice President, Chief Administrative Officer, Chief Compliance Officer, Representative Director, Takayuki Seishima
Senior Managing Executive Officer, Masaki Nakajima
Senior Managing Executive Officer, Chief Financial Officer, Representative Director, Reiji Morooka
Senior Managing Executive Officer, Yoshiyuki Sakamoto
Senior Managing Executive Officer, Mitsuhiro Takeda
Senior Managing Executive Officer, Chief Strategy Officer, Representative Director, Hirokazu Higashino
Senior Managing Executive Officer, Katsuya Inubushi
Chief Digital Officer, Chief Information Officer, Tatsushi Tatsumi
Outside Director, Kimie Iwata
Outside Director, Hisashi Yamazaki
Outside Director, Akiko Ide
Outside Director, Takashi Mitachi
Outside Director, Takahisa Takahara

Auditors : KPMG AZSA LLC

LOCATIONS

HQ: Sumitomo Corp. (Japan)
2-3-2 Otemachi, Chiyoda-ku, Tokyo 100-8601
Phone: (81) 3 6285 5000   **Fax:** 212 207-0456
Web: www.sumitomocorp.co.jp

HISTORICAL FINANCIALS
Company Type: Public

Income Statement   FYE: March 31

	REVENUE ($mil)	NET INCOME ($mil)	NET PROFIT MARGIN	EMPLOYEES
03/23	51,190	4,243	8.3%	108,457
03/22	45,175	3,812	8.4%	102,422
03/21	41,951	(1,382)	—	103,443
03/20	48,823	1,578	3.2%	100,246
03/19	48,212	2,894	6.0%	91,362
Annual Growth	1.5%	10.0%	—	4.4%

2023 Year-End Financials
Debt ratio: 0.2%
Return on equity: 16.2%
Cash ($ mil.): 4,931
Current Ratio: 1.64
Long-term debt ($ mil.): 18,521
No. of shares ($ mil.): 1,234
Dividends
  Yield: 5.1%
  Payout: 27.2%
Market value ($ mil.): 21,806

	STOCK PRICE ($) FY Close	P/E High	P/E Low	Earnings	Dividends	Book Value
03/23	17.67	0	0	3.39	0.90	22.99
03/22	17.31	0	0	3.05	0.71	21.03
03/21	14.46	—	—	(1.11)	0.66	18.27
03/20	11.27	0	0	1.26	0.77	18.76
03/19	13.84	0	0	2.32	0.64	20.04
Annual Growth	6.3%	—	—	10.0%	9.0%	3.5%

Sumitomo Electric Industries, Ltd. (Japan)

Sumitomo Electric Industries (SEI) is Japan's largest producer of wire and cable, and makes several other products, including wiring harnesses for cars, flexible printed circuits, and optical fiber for telecommunications. The company has around 415 subsidiaries and affiliates around the globe. It sells more than 50% of its products to companies in the automotive industry; SEI also serves customers in the electronics, telecommunications, and environmental and energy industries. The company generates more than 40% of its business in Japan.

Operations

SEI operates five business segments categorized according to the products offered: Automotive, Environment and Energy, Industrial Materials, Electronics, and Info-communications (information and communications).

The Automotive business offers wiring harnesses, anti-vibration rubbers, automotive hoses, and car electronic components. The business segment accounts for more than 50% of the company's sales.

Environment and Energy offers electric conductors, power transmission wires/cables/equipment, magnet wires, air cushions for railroad vehicles, power system equipment such as substation equipment/control systems, charged beam equipment and processing, electrical/power supply work and engineering, and porous metals. The segment accounts for around 25% of sales.

Industrial Materials (approximately 10% of sales) includes tensioning materials for pre-stressed concrete, precision spring steel wires, steel tire cord, cemented carbide tools, diamond and CBN tools, laser optics, sintered powder metal parts, and semiconductors heat-spreader materials.

Electronics (nearly 10%) include wiring materials, electric beam irradiation products, flexible printed circuits, fluorine resin products, fasteners, metal parts, and chemical products.

Info-communications (more than 5%) comprises optical fiber cables and transceiver modules and optical and wireless devices.

Geographic Reach

Headquartered in Japan, SEI operates in about 415 companies located in about 40 countries. The company's primary operating facilities in Japan are located in Osaka, Kanagawa, Hyogo and Ibaraki. The company's largest market is Japan with more than 40% of revenue, followed by China and other Asian market (excluding Japan) with around 30% of sales, and the US and others with more than 15%. Europe and others account for the rest.

Financial Performance

Net sales were Â¥3.4 trillion, a 15% increase from preceding fiscal year's Â¥2.9 trillion. The increase was primarily due to the expanding sales of products such as optical wiring equipment for data centers, optical fibers for submarine cables, and access network equipment.

In 2021, the company had a net income of Â¥96.3 billion, a 71% increase from the previous year's net income of Â¥56.3 billion.

The company's cash at the end of 2021 was Â¥255.5 billion. Operating activities generated Â¥76 billion, while investing activities used Â¥165.1 billion, mainly for purchase of property, plant and equipment. Financing activities provided another Â¥82.8 billion.

Company Background

Sumitomo Electric Industries, as a part of the Sumitomo group business, began nearly 400 years ago with the paired talents of spiritual founder Masatomo Sumitomo (who had received training as a Buddhist priest) and his disciple and brother-in-law, Riemon Soga. Sumitomo wrote treatises on the conduct of commercial activity, and Soga applied his technological skill in extracting silver from copper ore, improving upon traditional Western methods, and opened a copper business in Kyoto in 1590 that soon transformed the copper refining industry in Japan.

The company later diversified its business to include flexible printed circuits (1960s), fiber optic cables for telecommunications (1970s), and wiring harnesses for automobiles made with its newly-developed aluminum alloy wires (2010s).

HISTORY

Sumitomo Electric Industries, as a part of the Sumitomo group business, began nearly 400 years ago with the paired talents of spiritual founder Masatomo Sumitomo (who had received training as a Buddhist priest) and his disciple and brother-in-law, Riemon Soga. Sumitomo wrote treatises on the conduct of commercial activity, and Soga applied his technological skill in extracting silver from copper ore, improving upon traditional Western methods, and opened a copper business in Kyoto in 1590 that soon transformed the copper refining industry in Japan.

Soga's prosperous copper business became the founding company of the Sumitomo group. After Soga died in 1636, his son, Tomomochi, married Masatomo's daughter (entering into the Sumitomo family) and became the company's leader.

By the late 1600s the family was one of Japan's top copper producers. The house of Sumitomo entered several other businesses by the mid-1800s in order to insulate itself from waning copper production. The family established the Sumitomo Copper Rolling Works in 1897 to produce bare copper wire.

In 1909 production of cable for Japan's telecommunications industry began, and in 1920 the family took their company public, renaming it Sumitomo Electric Wire & Cable Works. The next year the company added high-carbon steel wire manufacturing. Its name changed to Sumitomo Electric Industries (SEI) in 1939.

The company began making rubber products for use in aircraft fuel tanks in 1943. The decade drew to a close with the addition of overhead transmission cable engineering operations.

SEI continued to move into new businesses in the 1960s. In 1960 SEI took a 25% stake in Sumitomo 3M, a three-way joint venture with NEC (25%) and 3M (50%) to produce industrial cable in Japan. To capitalize on the boom in Japan's automobile and industrial equipment industries, SEI introduced disc brakes to its lineup in 1963. Also, SEI formally entered into management participation in Japan's Dunlop Tire Company, which was then renamed Sumitomo Rubber Industries. (It had initially invested in the tire maker in 1960.)

SEI hit pay dirt with its automotive businesses, producing brakes for manufacturers of passenger cars, commercial vehicles, motorcycles, construction and industrial equipment, and railcars. In the late 1960s SEI added traffic control systems.

With the introduction of compound semiconductors (used in wireless transmitters and electronic control devices) and cable television systems, the 1970s brought SEI into the arena of value-added high-tech products. SEI began producing optical-fiber cable in 1974.

SEI expanded further into fiber optics when it introduced its first LAN in 1981 and set up its US-based Sumitomo Electric Lightwave unit in 1983.

In 1987 the company began producing antilock brakes (ABS) and invested $45 million in an evenly split ABS manufacturing US joint venture (Lucas Sumitomo) with a unit of Lucas Varity. Lucas Varity was later bought by TRW, and Sumitomo eventually acquired its remaining 50%. SEI closed out the 1980s by adding satellite navigation systems to its growing automobile product offerings.

The 1990s saw wider global expansion through more alliances and acquisitions. In 1990 SEI teamed up again with Lucas Varity to establish a joint venture in the UK to make automobile wiring harnesses. (SEI, together with one of its own affiliates, bought Lucas' half share in the company in 1999.) That year SEI, through its Sumitomo Electric Wiring Systems unit, formed AutoNeural Systems, a joint venture with Ford-affiliated Visteon for automobile wiring harnesses.

In 2000 SEI set up ExceLight Communications (spun off from Sumitomo Electric Lightwave) to make optical components and subsystems for telecommunications, cable TV, and broadband equipment industries. The company restructured its electric power cable operations in early 2001, forming a manufacturing joint venture with Hitachi Cable and shutting one of its plants in Japan. Early the following year SEI acquired the Japan-based Calsonic Kansei Corporation's wiring harness business. SEI closed its electric furnaces in Japan and spun off its Sumitomo Steel Wire Corp. in late 2002. In early 2003 the company joined efforts with Hitachi Cable and Tatsuta Electric Wire & Cable to form Sumiden Hitachi Cable Ltd., a company that specialized in the manufacture of low-voltage power cables.

In 2006 the company acquired the former Volkswagen Bordnetze (now called Sumitomo Electric Bordnetze), a Germany-based manufacturer of wire harnesses, from its previous joint owners, Volkswagen and VDO Automotive.

Continuing to strengthen its European operations, the company, along with subsidiary Sumitomo Electric Sintered Alloy, acquired Germany-based Cloyes Europe, a sintered parts maker, in 2007. SEI will use this acquisition to supply Japanese auto parts makers that have manufacturing facilities in Europe.

Also in 2007, as part of a group realignment, SEI increased its ownership in Nissin Electric to more than 50%, and it acquired affiliate Toyokuni Electric Cable. The acquisitions are part of the company's efforts to position itself as a global player.

EXECUTIVES

Chairman, Representative Director, Masayoshi Matsumoto
President, Representative Director, Osamu Inoue
Executive Vice President, Representative Director, Mitsuo Nishida
Executive Vice President, Representative Director, Hideo Hato
Senior Managing Director, Representative Director, Akira Nishimura
Director, Masaki Shirayama
Director, Yasuhiro Miyata
Director, Toshiyuki Sahashi
Director, Shigeru Nakajima
Outside Director, Hiroshi Sato
Outside Director, Michihiro Tsuchiya
Outside Director, Christina Ahmadjian
Outside Director, Katsuaki Watanabe
Outside Director, Atsushi Horiba
Auditors : KPMG AZSA LLC

LOCATIONS

HQ: Sumitomo Electric Industries, Ltd. (Japan)
Sumitomo Bldg., 4-5-33 Kitahama, Chuo-ku, Osaka 541-0041
Phone: (81) 6 6220 4141 **Fax:** 212 490-6620
Web: www.sei.co.jp

2018 sales

	% of total
Japan	48
Asia	30
Americas	14
Europe and Others	8
Total	100

PRODUCTS/OPERATIONS

2018 sales

	% of total
Automotive	54
Environment and Energy	22
Industrial materials & other	11
Electronics	7
Information & communications	6
Total	100

Products
Automotive
Information and Communication System
Electronics / Consumer Electronics
Semiconductor / Device
Energy
Environment
Infrastructure
Industrial Product / Material
Bankruptcy
Wiring harnesses
Vibration-proof rubber
Automotive hoses

Car electrical equipment
Electronic wire products
Compound semiconductors
Metallic material for electronic parts
Electric-beam irradiation products
Flexible printed circuits
Fluorine resin products
Electric conductors
Power transmission wires/ cables/equipment
Magnet wires
Air cushions for railroad vehicles
Power systems
Equipment such as substation equipment/control systems
Charged beam equipment and processing
Electrical/power supply work and engineering, porous metals

COMPETITORS

Continental AG
DANA INCORPORATED
DENSO CORPORATION
GKN LIMITED
HILITE INTERNATIONAL, INC.
METHODE ELECTRONICS, INC.
NEWCOR, INC.
PULSE ELECTRONICS CORPORATION
Robert Bosch Gesellschaft mit beschrÄnkter Haftung
TENNECO INC.

HISTORICAL FINANCIALS
Company Type: Public

Income Statement				FYE: March 31
	REVENUE ($mil)	NET INCOME ($mil)	NET PROFIT MARGIN	EMPLOYEES
03/23	30,075	845	2.8%	334,716
03/22	27,687	791	2.9%	329,350
03/21	26,358	508	1.9%	325,011
03/20	28,622	669	2.3%	320,975
03/19	28,696	1,066	3.7%	312,930
Annual Growth	1.2%	(5.6%)	—	1.7%

2023 Year-End Financials
Debt ratio: 0.2%
Return on equity: 6.1%
Cash ($ mil.): 2,128
Current Ratio: 1.55
Long-term debt ($ mil.): 2,180
No. of shares ($ mil.): 780
Dividends
Yield: 2.8%
Payout: 0.0%
Market value ($ mil.): 10,079

	STOCK PRICE ($) FY Close	P/E High/Low	PER SHARE ($) Earnings	Dividends	Book Value
03/23	12.92	0 0	1.08	0.37	18.29
03/22	11.97	0 0	1.02	0.36	18.65
03/21	15.40	0 0	0.65	0.30	18.86
03/20	10.26	0 0	0.86	0.44	17.93
03/19	13.37	0 0	1.37	0.44	17.95
Annual Growth	(0.9%)	—	(5.6%)	(4.6%)	0.5%

Sumitomo Forestry Co., Ltd. (Japan)

EXECUTIVES

Chairman, Representative Director, Director, Akira Ichikawa

President, Representative Director, Toshiro Mitsuyoshi

Executive Vice President, Representative Director, Tatsuru Sato

Senior Managing Executive Officer, Director, Tatsumi Kawata

Senior Managing Executive Officer, Director, Atsushi Kawamura

Director, Ikuro Takahashi

Outside Director, Izumi Yamashita

Outside Director, Mitsue Kurihara

Outside Director, Yuko Toyoda

Auditors: Ernst & Young ShinNihon LLC

LOCATIONS

HQ: Sumitomo Forestry Co., Ltd. (Japan)
 1-3-2 Otemachi, Chiyoda-ku, Tokyo 100-8270
Phone: (81) 3 3214 2201
Web: sfc.jp

COMPETITORS

Antarchile S.A.
CADUS CORPORATION
CARLO CORP
CHAMPION ENTERPRISES HOLDINGS, LLC
CROWELL DON INC
HUMPHREY RICH CONSTRUCTION GROUP, INC.
PARK CORPORATION
RED SEAL DEVELOPMENT CORP.
SEKISUI HOUSE, LTD.
SIERRA PACIFIC INDUSTRIES

HISTORICAL FINANCIALS
Company Type: Public

Income Statement				FYE: December 31
	REVENUE ($mil)	NET INCOME ($mil)	NET PROFIT MARGIN	EMPLOYEES
12/22	12,671	824	6.5%	26,636
12/21	12,040	757	6.3%	26,100
12/20*	8,148	294	3.6%	25,253
03/20	10,171	256	2.5%	24,055
03/19	11,819	263	2.2%	23,692
Annual Growth	1.8%	33.0%		3.0%

*Fiscal year change

2022 Year-End Financials
Debt ratio: 0.2%
Return on equity: 19.3%
Cash ($ mil.): 977
Current Ratio: 2.17
Long-term debt ($ mil.): 2,109
No. of shares ($ mil.): 200
Dividends
Yield: —
Payout: 23.5%
Market value ($ mil.): —

Sumitomo Metal Mining Co Ltd

Sumitomo Metal Mining (SMM) focuses on Smelting and Refining, Mineral Resources, and Materials. Metals-related refining and processing (copper, gold, nickel, and zinc) lead SMM's operations. The company has smelting, refining, and mining operations in Japan, the US, Australia, Peru, Philippines, Chile and elsewhere. SMM also produces electronic materials, including bonding wire, lead frames, electric paste, and copper-clad polymide film for semiconductors and printed circuit boards. It also makes construction and housing materials and offers soil and water remediation services. With a history dating back to 1590, SMM, which was incorporated in 1950, is part of the Japanese keiretsu Sumitomo Group.

EXECUTIVES

Chairman, Director, Yoshiaki Nakazato

President, Representative Director, Akira Nozaki

Senior Managing Executive Officer, Representative Director, Toru Higo

Senior Managing Executive Officer, Director, Nobuhiro Matsumoto

Director, Masaru Takebayashi

Outside Director, Taeko Ishii

Outside Director, Manabu Kinoshita

Outside Director, Kanji Nishiura

Auditors: KPMG AZSA LLC

LOCATIONS

HQ: Sumitomo Metal Mining Co Ltd
 5-11-3 Shimbashi, Minato-ku, Tokyo 105-8716
Phone: (81) 3 3436 7926 **Fax:** (81) 3 3434 2215
Web: www.smm.co.jp

2016 Sales

	% of total
Asia	
Japan	60
East Asia	21
Southeast Asia	8
North America	9
Other regions	2
Total	100

PRODUCTS/OPERATIONS

2016 Sales

	% of total
Smelting & refining	73
Materials	19
Mineral resources	8
Total	100

Selected Operations
Metals (refining and sales of base and precious metals, including copper, gold, silver, nickel, and zinc)
Advanced materials (manufacturing and sale of metal powders, circuit board materials, and battery materials)
Electronics materials (integrated circuit package substrates, compound semiconductor crystals, printed circuit boards, electronic components, battery, electrode, and magnetic materials, and copper-clad polyimide film)
Mineral Resources (exploration, development, production, and sales of non-ferrous metal resources)
Other operations (construction materials and environmental business)

COMPETITORS

AMERICAN ZINC RECYCLING LLC
CHEM PROCESSING, INC.
DOWA HOLDINGS CO.,LTD.
H. C. STARCK INC.
KORPORATSIYA VSMPO-AVISMA, PAO
Korea Zinc Company, Ltd.
MITSUI MINING AND SMELTING COMPANY, LIMITED
SIPI METALS CORP.
Tongling Nonferrous Metals Group Holdings Co., Ltd.
UNITED STATES ANTIMONY CORPORATION

HISTORICAL FINANCIALS

Company Type: Public

Income Statement

FYE: March 31

	REVENUE ($mil)	NET INCOME ($mil)	NET PROFIT MARGIN	EMPLOYEES
03/23	10,684	1,205	11.3%	7,977
03/22	10,351	2,310	22.3%	7,928
03/21	8,364	854	10.2%	7,794
03/20	8,038	558	6.9%	7,539
03/19	8,237	603	7.3%	7,439
Annual Growth	6.7%	18.9%	—	1.8%

2023 Year-End Financials

Debt ratio: 0.1%
Return on equity: 10.4%
Cash ($ mil.): 1,614
Current Ratio: 2.17
Long-term debt ($ mil.): 2,243
No. of shares ($ mil.): 274
Dividends
Yield: 5.3%
Payout: 11.8%
Market value ($ mil.): 2,610

	STOCK PRICE ($) FY Close	P/E High/Low		PER SHARE ($) Earnings	Dividends	Book Value
03/23	9.50	0	0	4.39	0.51	44.59
03/22	12.69	0	0	8.41	0.47	43.24
03/21	10.82	0	0	3.11	0.14	36.61
03/20	4.97	0	0	2.03	0.14	33.59
03/19	7.23	0	0	2.19	0.27	34.42
Annual Growth	7.1%	—	—	18.9%	17.7%	6.7%

Sumitomo Mitsui Financial Group Inc
Tokyo

Sumitomo Mitsui Financial Group (SMFG) is the holding company for Sumitomo Mitsui Banking, which boasts some 455 domestic branches in Japan. As one of Japan's largest banks, SMFG provides retail, corporate, and investment banking; asset management; securities trading; and lending. Other units of SMFG include SMBC Trust Bank, SMFL, SMBC Nikko Securities, Sumitomo Mitsui Card Company, SMBC Finance Service Co, SMBC Consumer Finance, The Japan Research Institute, Sumitomo Mitsui DS Asset Management Company, and other subsidiaries and affiliates. SMFG was established in 2002.

Operations

SMFG operates four main business segments: the Wholesale Business Unit, the Retail Business Unit, the Global Business Unit, which was renamed from the International Business Unit in April 2020, and the Global Markets Business Unit, with the remaining operations recorded in Head office account and others.

The Wholesale Business Unit provides comprehensive solutions primarily for corporate clients in Japan that respond to wide-ranging client needs in relation to financing, investment management, risk hedging, settlement, M&A and other advisory services, digital services and leasing services. This business unit mainly consists of the wholesale businesses of SMBC, SMBC Trust Bank, SMFL, SMBC Nikko Securities, Sumitomo Mitsui Card and SMBC Finance Service, which changed its corporate name from Cedyna Financial Corporation upon merger with former SMBC Finance Service Co., Ltd. in July 2020.

The Retail Business Unit provides financial services to consumers residing in Japan and mainly consists of the retail businesses of SMBC, SMBC Trust Bank, SMBC Nikko Securities, Sumitomo Mitsui Card, SMBC Finance Service and SMBC Consumer Finance. This business unit offers a wide range of products and services for consumers, including wealth management services, settlement services, consumer finance and housing loans, in order to address the financial needs of all individual customers.

The Global Business Unit, which was renamed from the International Business Unit in April 2020, supports the global businesses of a diverse range of clients, such as Japanese companies operating overseas, non-Japanese companies, financial institutions and government agencies and public corporations of various countries. This business unit mainly consists of the international businesses of SMBC, SMBC Trust Bank, SMFL, SMBC Nikko Securities and their foreign subsidiaries.

The Global Markets Business Unit offers solutions through foreign exchange products, derivatives, bonds, stocks and other marketable financial products and also undertakes asset liability management operations, which help comprehensively control balance sheet liquidity risks and interest rate risks. This business unit consists of the Treasury Unit of SMBC and the global markets businesses of SMBC Nikko Securities.

Broadly speaking, about 45% of SMFG's revenue comes from net interest income, while almost 35% comes from net fee and commission income, and about 10% comes from net trading income. The rest of the revenue comes from net income from financial assets and liabilities, net investment income and other income.

Geographic Reach

About 60% of SMFG's operating income comes from its domestic business in Japan, while the rest comes from customers in the Americas (almost 20%), Europe and Middle East region (about 10% of operating income), and the Asia and Oceania region (around 15%).

Based in Japan, SMFG has a domestic network consisting of about 455 SMBC branch offices, more than 25 SMBC Trust Bank branch offices, some 110 SMBC Nikko Securities branch offices and around 725 SMBC Consumer Finance staffed and unstaffed branch offices.

Financial Performance

Note: Growth rates may differ after conversion to US dollars. This analysis uses financials from the company's annual report.

The company reported a net interest income of Â¥1.4 trillion, a 4% increase from the previous year's net interest income. This was primarily due to a lower volume of interest expense for the year.

In 2021, the company had a net income of Â¥499.6 billion, a 27% decrease from the previous year's net income of Â¥687.5 billion.

The company's cash at the end of 2021 was Â¥74.3 trillion. Operating activities generated Â¥5.1 trillion, while investing activities used Â¥2.7 trillion, mainly for purchases of financial assets at fair value through profit or loss and investment securities. Financing activities used another Â¥597.9 billion, primarily for redemption of subordinated bonds.

Strategy

Under its business strategy of "Transformation" and "Growth," the company has identified "Seven Key Strategies" as shown below:

Pursue sustainable growth of wealth management business; Improve productivity and strengthen solutions in the domestic wholesale business; Enhance overseas corporate and investment banking business to improve asset/capital efficiency; Hold the number one position in payment business; Enhance asset-light business on a global basis; Expand franchise in Asia and strengthen digital banking; and Develop digital solutions for corporate clients.

EXECUTIVES

Chief Executive Officer, President, Director, Jun Ohta
Chief Risk Officer, Senior Managing Executive Officer, Director, Teiko Kudo
Managing Executive Officer, Masahiko Oshima
Chief Human Resources Officer, Chief Compliance Officer, Deputy President, Corporate Executive Officer, Toshikazu Yaku
Chief Digital Innovation Officer, Senior Managing Director, Senior Managing Director (frmr), Katsunori Tanizaki
Chief Financial Officer, Senior Managing Corporate Executive Officer, Director, Toru Nakashima
Chief Compliance Officer, Senior Managing Executive Officer, Tetsuro Imaeda
Senior Managing Corporate Executive Officer, Masamichi Koike
Senior Managing Executive Officer, Akihiro Fukutome
Senior Managing Executive Officer, Muneo Kanamaru
Senior Managing Executive Officer, Takashi Yamashita
Senior Managing Executive Officer, Jun Uchikawa
Senior Managing Executive Officer, Yoshihiro Hyakutome

Senior Managing Executive Officer, Takeshi Mikami
Chairman, Takeshi Kunibe
Director, Makoto Takashima
Director, Atsuhiko Inoue
Director, Eriko Sakurai
Director, Toshihiro Isshiki
Director, Arthur M. Mitchell
Director, Shozo Yamazaki
Director, Masaharu Kohno
Director, Yoshinobu Tsutsui
Director, Katsuyoshi Shinbo
Director, Yasuyuki Kawasaki
Director, Masayuki Matsumoto
Auditors : KPMG AZSA LLC

LOCATIONS

HQ: Sumitomo Mitsui Financial Group Inc Tokyo
1-2 Marunouchi, 1-chome, Chiyoda-ku, Tokyo 100-0005
Phone: (81) 3 3282 8111   **Fax:** (81) 3 4333 9954
Web: www.smfg.co.jp

PRODUCTS/OPERATIONS

2013 Sales

	% of total
Interest	
Loans & advances	43
Investment securities	2
Other	1
Noninterest	
Fees & commissions	27
investment income	9
Trading profits	4
Other	14
Total	100

COMPETITORS

Bank of Communications Co.,Ltd.
Industrial and Commercial Bank of China Limited
MITSUBISHI UFJ FINANCIAL GROUP, INC.
MIZUHO FINANCIAL GROUP, INC.
OPPENHEIMER HOLDINGS INC.
RESONA HOLDINGS, INC.
SANTANDER UK GROUP HOLDINGS PLC
SUMITOMO MITSUI TRUST HOLDINGS, INC.
Shinhan Financial Group Co., Ltd.
Woori Finance Holdings Co., Ltd.

HISTORICAL FINANCIALS

Company Type: Public

Income Statement   FYE: March 31

	ASSETS ($mil)	NET INCOME ($mil)	INCOME AS % OF ASSETS	EMPLOYEES
03/22	2,040,170	4,107	0.2%	111,600
03/21	2,122,610	6,208	0.3%	98,100
03/20	1,954,470	1,842	0.1%	86,400
03/19	1,765,370	4,893	0.3%	99,800
03/18	1,809,790	7,157	0.4%	88,100
Annual Growth	3.0%	(13.0%)		6.1%

2022 Year-End Financials

Return on assets: 0.2%
Return on equity: 4.0%
Long-term debt ($ mil.): —
No. of shares ($ mil.): 1,370
Sales ($ mil.): 29,925
Dividends
 Yield: 5.6%
 Payout: 10.9%
Market value ($ mil.): 8,595

	STOCK PRICE ($) FY Close	P/E High/Low	PER SHARE ($) Earnings	Dividends	Book Value
03/22	6.27	0 0	3.00	0.36	76.10
03/21	7.25	0 0	4.53	0.37	80.45
03/20	4.79	0 0	1.34	0.34	73.15
03/19	7.03	0 0	3.50	0.32	72.98
03/18	8.50	0 0	5.07	0.30	75.19
Annual Growth	(7.3%)	—	(12.3%)	4.8%	0.3%

Sumitomo Mitsui Trust Holdings Inc

Sumitomo Mitsui Trust Holdings (formerly Chuo Mitsui Trust Holdings) holds Sumitomo Mitsui Trust Bank (retail trust, banking, real estate, and stock transfer services) and Sumitomo Mitsui Asset and Banking Company (pension and securities trusts). It also owns investment trust and private equity managers Sumitomo Mitsui Asset Management. It offers consulting to individuals and large corporations alike, specializing in brokerage, securitization, and investment advice related to real estate deals. Sumitomo also has operations in New York, London, Singapore, Hong Kong, Shanghai, and Thailand.

Operations
The firm operates six main business divisions that revolve around Sumitomo Mitsui Trust Bank, namely, Retail Business, Corporate Business, Investor Services Business, Real Estate Business, Global Markets Business, and Asset Management Business. These segments were derived from 2021's segments: the Global Markets Business, Asset Management Business, Fiduciary Services Business, Real Estate Business, Retail Total Solution Services Business, Wholesale Financial Services, and Stock Transfer Agency Services Business. Its Retail Financial Services business offers asset management administration, and succession services.

Before the changes in the segments for 2022, wholesale financial services account for about 40% of the industry. Other segments such as the Global Markets Business, Asset Management Business, Fiduciary Services Business, Real Estate Business, Retail Total Solution Services Business account for 10%, each.

Geographic Reach
While Sumitomo Mitsui Trust Holdings is present in several countries with Japan accounting for about 90% of the revenues. Other regions include Americas (5%), Europe (less than 5%), Asia and Oceania (less than 5%).

Financial Performance
Note: Growth rates may differ after conversion to US dollars. This analysis uses figures provided in the company's annual report.

Sumitomo's revenues and profits have been rising in the past five years with 2021 as the highest performing year over that period. The firm's net business profit rose in 2021 to Â¥346 billion as compared to 2020's revenue of Â¥294.7 billion.

The company's net income for the fiscal year end 2021 also increased by Â¥27 billion to Â¥169 billion as compared to the prior year's net income of Â¥142 billion, respectively.

The held Â¥15.7 trillion cash at the end of the fiscal year. The company's operating activities used Â¥120.3 billion. Investing activities and financing activities used Â¥879 billion and Â¥125 billion, respectively. Main cash uses were for purchase of securities and paid dividends.

Company Background
Chuo Mitsui Trust Holdings and Sumitomo Trust and Banking merged in 2012 to form Sumitomo Mitsui Trust Bank, one of Japan's largest asset management groups.

HISTORY

Before world markets were rocked by the shock waves of the US real estate and financial markets crash, CMHD received about Y430 billion ($4.4 billion) in government support. The company had been making steady payments since 2006 and planned to pay the remaining Y200 before the August 2009 deadline for the conversion of the government's preferred shares into ordinary shares. But mid-year the bank, along with several of its Japanese mid-level peers, announced it would be unable to meet the goal due to poor earnings.

Once the crisis passes, the company's strategy includes a focus on real estate lending, long a mainstay of business, and improving its position in the investment trust and real estate investing markets.

EXECUTIVES

Chairman, Director, Tetsuo Ohkubo
Representative Executive Officer, President, Director, Toru Takakura
Representative Executive Officer, Executive Vice President, Director, Atsushi Kaibara
Senior Managing Executive Officer, Director, Yasuyuki Suzuki
Director, Kazuya Oyama
Director, Masaru Hashimoto
Director, Kouji Tanaka
Director, Toshiaki Nakano
Outside Director, Isao Matsushita
Outside Director, Hiroko Kawamoto
Outside Director, Mitsuhiro Aso
Outside Director, Nobuaki Katoh
Outside Director, Kaoru Kashima
Outside Director, Tomonori Ito
Outside Director, Hajime Watanabe

Auditors : KPMG AZSA LLC

LOCATIONS

HQ: Sumitomo Mitsui Trust Holdings Inc
1-4-1 Marunouchi, Chiyoda-ku, Tokyo 100-8233
Phone: (81) 3 6256 6000
Web: www.smth.jp

PRODUCTS/OPERATIONS

2014 Sales

	% of total
SMTB	93
Other	7
Total	100

Selected Services
Fiduciary Services Business
Global Markets Business
Real Estate Business
Retail Financial Services Business
Stock Transfer Agency Services Business
Wholesale Financial Services Business

HISTORICAL FINANCIALS

Company Type: Public

Income Statement   FYE: March 31

	ASSETS ($mil)	NET INCOME ($mil)	INCOME AS % OF ASSETS	EMPLOYEES
03/23	518,245	1,434	0.3%	24,736
03/22	531,361	1,390	0.3%	24,224
03/21	561,428	1,284	0.2%	24,332
03/20	520,502	1,501	0.3%	23,807
03/19	514,964	1,570	0.3%	23,639
Annual Growth	0.2%	(2.2%)	—	1.1%

2023 Year-End Financials
Return on assets: 0.2%
Return on equity: 6.9%
Long-term debt ($ mil.): —
No. of shares ($ mil.): 727
Sales ($ mil.): 13,695
Dividends
Yield: 4.1%
Payout: 7.4%
Market value ($ mil.): 2,489

	STOCK PRICE ($) FY Close	P/E High/Low		PER SHARE ($) Earnings	Dividends	Book Value
03/23	3.42	0	0	1.94	0.14	28.81
03/22	3.32	0	0	1.85	0.14	29.78
03/21	3.57	0	0	1.71	0.14	32.45
03/20	2.88	0	0	2.00	0.14	31.40
03/19	3.60	0	0	2.07	0.12	31.66
Annual Growth	(1.2%)	—	—	(1.6%)	4.8%	(2.3%)

Sun Hung Kai Properties Ltd

EXECUTIVES

Chairman, Managing Director, Executive Chairman, Executive Director, Raymond Ping-luen Kwok
Deputy Managing Director, Executive Director, Mike Chik-wing Wong
Deputy Managing Director, Executive Director, Victor Ting Lui
Executive Director, Adam Kai-fai Kwok
Executive Director, Christopher Kai-wang Kwok
Executive Director, Eric Chi-ho Tung
Executive Director, Allen Yuk-lun Fung
Executive Director, Albert Tak-yeung Lau
Executive Director, Maureen Sau-yim Fung
Executive Director, Robert Hong-ki Chan
Chief Accountant, Frederick Ching-kam Li
Secretary, General Counsel, Sandy Sheung-tat Yung
Independent Non-Executive Director, Dicky Peter Yip
Independent Non-Executive Director, Richard Yue-chim Wong
Independent Non-Executive Director, Eric Ka-cheung Li
Independent Non-Executive Director, William Kwok-lun Fung
Independent Non-Executive Director, Norman Nai-pang Leung
Independent Non-Executive Director, Margaret Ko May-yee Leung
Independent Non-Executive Director, Henry Hung-ling Fan
Independent Non-Executive Director, Xiang-dong Wu
Non-Executive Director, William Cheuk-yin Kwan
Non-Executive Director, Geoffrey Kai-chun Kwok
Auditors : Deloitte Touche Tohmatsu

LOCATIONS

HQ: Sun Hung Kai Properties Ltd
45th Floor, Sun Hung Kai Centre, 30 Harbour Road,
Phone: (852) 2827 8111   **Fax:** (852) 2827 2862
Web: www.shkp.com

HISTORICAL FINANCIALS

Company Type: Public

Income Statement   FYE: June 30

	REVENUE ($mil)	NET INCOME ($mil)	NET PROFIT MARGIN	EMPLOYEES
06/23	9,084	3,050	33.6%	40,000
06/22	9,909	3,257	32.9%	40,500
06/21	10,978	3,436	31.3%	39,500
06/20	10,664	3,034	28.5%	39,500
06/19	10,923	5,751	52.7%	37,500
Annual Growth	(4.5%)	(14.7%)	—	1.6%

2023 Year-End Financials
Debt ratio: 2.0%
Return on equity: 3.9%
Cash ($ mil.): 1,949
Current Ratio: 4.55
Long-term debt ($ mil.): 14,999
No. of shares ($ mil.): 2,898
Dividends
Yield: 4.6%
Payout: 56.2%
Market value ($ mil.): 36,631

	STOCK PRICE ($) FY Close	P/E High/Low		PER SHARE ($) Earnings	Dividends	Book Value
06/23	12.64	2	1	1.05	0.59	26.51
06/22	11.84	2	1	1.12	0.59	26.47
06/21	14.95	2	1	1.19	0.60	26.38
06/20	12.72	2	1	1.05	0.59	25.63
06/19	17.01	1	1	1.98	0.56	25.20
Annual Growth	(7.2%)	—	—	(14.7%)	1.3%	1.3%

Sun Life Assurance Company of Canada

EXECUTIVES

Chief Executive Officer, Director, Donald A. Stewart
Executive Vice President, General Counsel, Thomas A. Bogart
Executive Vice President, Chief Financial Officer, Richard P. McKenney
Executive Vice President, Chief Risk Officer, Michael P. Stramaglia
Senior Vice President, Chief Marketing Officer, Mary De Paoli
Senior Vice President, Controller, Colm J. Freyne
Senior Vice President, Treasurer, Stephen C. Kicinski
Senior Vice President, Chief Human Resources Officer, K. Louise McLaren
Taxes Senior Vice President, Michael John O'Connor
Financial Planning and Analysis Senior Vice President, Dikran Ohannessian
Senior Vice President, Chief Auditor, Michael I. Percy-Robb
Senior Vice President, Chief Actuary, Robert W. Wilson
Vice President, Chief Medical Officer, Judith M. Beamish
Corporate Development Vice President, Thomas J. Clulow
Public and Corporate Affairs Vice President, Michel R. Leduc
Records Management Vice President, Records Management Chief Privacy Officer, Christine I. Mackiw
Vice President, Chief Compliance Officer, Natalie A. Ochrym
Investor Relations Vice President, Paul O. Petrelli
Vice President, Corporate Secretary, Joan M. Wilson
Chairman, Ronald W. Osborne
Director, James C. Baillie
Director, George W. Carmany
Director, John H. Clappison
Director, David A. Ganong
Director, Germaine Gibara
Director, Krystyna T. Hoeg
Director, David W. Kerr
Director, Idalene F. Kesner
Director, Mitchell M. Merin
Director, Bertin F. Nadeau
Director, Hugh D. Segal
Director, James H. Sutcliffe
Auditors : Deloitte LLP

LOCATIONS

HQ: Sun Life Assurance Company of Canada
1 York Street, 13st Floor, Toronto, Ontario M5J 0B6
Phone: 416 979-9966   **Fax:** 416 979-3209
Web: www.sunlife.com

HISTORICAL FINANCIALS

Company Type: Public

Income Statement — FYE: December 31

	ASSETS ($mil)	NET INCOME ($mil)	INCOME AS % OF ASSETS	EMPLOYEES
12/21	266,390	263	0.1%	0
12/20	253,387	222	0.1%	0
12/19	225,336	176	0.1%	0
12/18	196,809	218	0.1%	0
12/17	212,123	195	0.1%	0
Annual Growth	5.9%	7.7%	—	—

2021 Year-End Financials

Return on assets: 0.1%
Return on equity: 1.6%
Long-term debt ($ mil.): —
No. of shares ($ mil.): 481
Sales ($ mil.): 17,866
Dividends
Yield: —
Payout: 0.0%
Market value ($ mil.): —

Sun Life Financial Inc

Sun Life Financial is a leading international financial services organization providing asset management, wealth, insurance, and health solutions to individual and institutional clients. Sun Life's products and services are distributed through direct and independent sales agents and advisors, as well as banks and consultants. With about 97,400 advisors, Sun Life has about $1.33 trillion assets under management.

Operations

Sun Life Financial operates through five business segment: Canada, United States (US), Asset Management, Asia, and Corporate.

Canada segment accounts for about 50% of total revenue, operates through three business units: Individual Insurance & Wealth, Group Retirement Services, and Sun Life Health. The Individual Insurance & Wealth unit provides insurance and investment products to individuals and families. Group Retirement Services provides pension plans and defined benefit solutions to employers, while Sun Life Health offers life, dental, extended health care, disability and critical illness, and other insurance products to employers.

The US segment (more than 25%) operates through Group Benefits, Dental, and In-force Management. The Group Benefits unit offers life, disability, absence management, medical stop-loss, dental, vision, and voluntary insurance products. Dental provides Medicaid and Medicare Advantage products and services, as well as commercial group dental and vision solutions for employers of all sizes. In-force Management provides more than 85,000 individual life insurance policies.

The Asset Management segment (about 25%) operates through MFS Investment Management and SLC Management. MFS Investment Management manages assets for institutional and retail investors; it has more than $548 billion in assets under management. SLC Management is an institutional investment manager delivering alternative fixed income, private credit, infrastructure and global real estate solutions to institutional investors.

Asia segment (about 5%) operates through two business units: Local Markets and International Hubs. Local Markets provides asset management, wealth, protection and health solutions through a multi-channel distribution approach. International Hubs offers leading insurance and wealth products through agency and broker distribution, including life insurance solutions to High Net Worth families and individuals.

The Corporate segment includes the UK business (a run-off block of life and pension policies) and Corporate Support.

Geographic Reach

Sun Life has operations in a number of markets worldwide, including Canada (its home market), the US, the UK, Ireland, Hong Kong, the Philippines, Japan, Indonesia, India, China, Australia, Singapore, Vietnam, Malaysia, and Bermuda.

Sales and Marketing

Sun Life distributes its products through its own career sales force and through independent brokers, sales representatives, independent advisors, and benefits consultants, among others.

Financial Performance

Note: Growth rates may differ after conversion to US Dollars.

Sun Life's revenue for fiscal 2022 decreased to CAD23.3 billion compared from the prior year with CAD35.7 billion. The decrease was primarily due to the company having investment loss.

Net income for fiscal 2022 decreased to CAD3.1 billion compared from the prior year with CAD3.9 billion. The decrease was primarily due to lower revenues.

Cash held by the company at the end of fiscal 2022 decreased to CAD11.2 billion. Cash provided by operations was CAD4.3 billion while cash used for investing and financing activities were CAD2.9 billion and CAD71 million, respectively.

Strategy

Sun Life's strategy places the client at the center of everything the company do. The company's enterprise strategy, reflects both its priorities and its diversified business mix. The company believe by effectively executing on its strategy, the company can fulfill its purpose, create a positive impact for its clients, and achieve its goal to be a leader in each of its four pillars.

Sun Life's four strategic pillars are: Asset Management: A global leader in both public and alternative asset classes through MFS and SLC Management; Canada: A leader in health, wealth, and insurance; and Asia: A regional leader focused on fast-growing markets.

Mergers and Acquisitions

In 2023, Sun Life completes its acquisition of a 51% stakes in Advisors Asset Management, Inc. (AAM), a leading independent U.S. retail distribution firm. AAM will be part of SLC Management, Sun Life's institutional fixed income and alternatives asset manager. AAM will become the US retail distribution arm of SLC Management. This allows SLC Management to meet the growing demand among U.S. HNW investors for alternative assets.

In 2022, Sun Life completes its acquisition of DentaQuest, the second-largest dental benefits provider in the US by membership, for US$2.6 billion (approximately C$3.3 billion). Sun Life has acquired DentaQuest from CareQuest Institute for Oral Health, a US-based nonprofit organization, and minority shareholder Centerbridge Partners, L.P., a private investment management firm. DentaQuest is now part of the Sun Life US business, which offers dental benefits through employers for their employee benefits plans and has an extensive national commercial dental network.

Company Background

Sun Life was founded in 1865. It demutualized in 2000, and the money it raised as a publicly traded company helped finance growth. During the first 10 years of its public status, it grew through a steady pace of acquisitions beginning with its buy of Clarica Life in 2002. Clarica's products were later rebranded with the Sun Life name. International acquisitions have included Assurant Employee Benefits (2016), Genworth's US employee benefits group (2007), and insurance and pension operations in Hong Kong from Commonwealth Bank of Australia (2005).

EXECUTIVES

Chief Executive Officer, President, Director, Kevin D. Strain

Chief Financial Officer, Executive Vice President, Manjit Singh

Corporate Strategy and Global Marketing Executive Vice President, Linda M. Dougherty

Executive Vice President, Chief Risk Officer, Colm J. Freyne

Chief Legal Officer & Public Affairs Executive Vice President, Melissa J. Kennedy

Executive Vice President, Chief Information Officer, Laura A. Money

Executive Vice President, Chief Human Resources Officer, Communications Officer, Helena J. Pagano

Chairman, Director, William D. Anderson

Independent Director, Helen M. Mallovy Hicks

Independent Director, Barbara G. Stymiest

Director, Deepak Chopra

Director, Stephanie L. Coyles

Director, Martin J. G. Glynn

Director, Ashok K. Gupta

Director, M. Marianne Harris

Director, David H. Y. Ho
Director, Marie-Lucie Morin
Director, Scott F. Powers
Auditors : Deloitte LLP

LOCATIONS

HQ: Sun Life Financial Inc
1 York Street, 31st Floor, Toronto, Ontario M5J 0B6
Phone: 416 979-9966   Fax: 416 979-3209
Web: www.sunlife.com

PRODUCTS/OPERATIONS

2018 Sales by Segment

	% of total
SLF Canada	56
SLF U.S.	19
SLF Asset Management	15
SLF Asia	9
Corporate	1
Total	100

COMPETITORS

AIA GROUP LIMITED
AMERICAN NATIONAL INSURANCE COMPANY
AMERITRUST GROUP, INC.
Achmea B.V.
CNA FINANCIAL CORPORATION
Industrial Alliance Insurance and Financial Services Inc
LIVERPOOL VICTORIA FRIENDLY SOCIETY LTD
Manulife Financial Corporation
ROYAL LONDON MUTUAL INSURANCE SOCIETY,LIMITED(THE)
SECURIAN FINANCIAL GROUP, INC.

HISTORICAL FINANCIALS

Company Type: Public

Income Statement — FYE: December 31

	ASSETS ($mil)	NET INCOME ($mil)	INCOME AS % OF ASSETS	EMPLOYEES
12/23	251,419	2,387	0.9%	30,941
12/22	244,676	2,314	0.9%	29,169
12/21	271,167	3,168	1.2%	24,589
12/20	253,691	1,961	0.8%	23,816
12/19	228,233	2,083	0.9%	40,600
Annual Growth	2.4%	3.5%	—	(6.6%)

2023 Year-End Financials

Return on assets: 0.9%
Return on equity: 11.8%
Long-term debt ($ mil.): —
No. of shares ($ mil.): 584
Sales ($ mil.): 24,801
Dividends
Yield: —
Payout: 57.0%
Market value ($ mil.): 30,317

	STOCK PRICE ($) FY Close	P/E High/Low	PER SHARE ($) Earnings	Dividends	Book Value
12/23	51.86	10 9	3.97	2.26	31.02
12/22	46.42	10 8	3.85	2.04	36.93
12/21	55.69	8 7	5.25	1.85	37.53
12/20	44.46	13 7	3.22	1.64	34.68
12/19	45.57	11 8	3.38	1.58	31.99
Annual Growth	3.3%	—	4.1%	9.4%	(0.8%)

Suncor Energy Inc

Suncor Energy is strategically focused on developing one of the world's largest petroleum resource basins ? Canada's Athabasca oil sands. Suncor's operations include oil sands development, production and upgrading; offshore oil and gas; petroleum refining in Canada and the US; and the company's PetroCanada retail and wholesale distribution networks (including Canada's Electric Highway, a coast-to-coast network of fast-charging electric vehicle stations). Suncor also operates a renewable energy business and conducts energy trading activities focused principally on the marketing and trading of crude oil, natural gas, byproducts, refined products, and power. Majority of the company's sales were generated from the North America. The company was founded in 1967.

Operations

Suncor Energy operates through three operating segments:

Suncor's Oil Sands segment, with assets located in the Athabasca oil sands of northeast Alberta, produces bitumen from mining and in situ operations. Bitumen is either upgraded into SCO for refinery feedstock and diesel fuel, or blended with diluent for refinery feedstock or direct sale to market through the company's midstream infrastructure and its marketing activities. The segment includes the marketing, supply, transportation and risk management of crude oil, natural gas, power and byproducts. The segment accounts for around 40% of the total revenue.

Suncor's E&P segment consists of offshore operations off the east coast of Canada and in the U.K. North Sea, and onshore assets in Libya and Syria. This segment also includes the marketing and risk management of crude oil and natural gas. The segment accounts for more than 5% of revenue.

Suncor's R&M segment consists of two primary operations: the Refining and Supply and Marketing operations, as well as the infrastructure supporting the marketing, supply and risk management of refined products, crude oil, natural gas, power and byproducts. This segment also includes the trading of crude oil, refined products, natural gas and power. The segment accounts for approximately 55% of the total revenue.

Geographic Reach

Suncor Energy is headquartered at Alberta, Canada. The company mainly earns its revenue on its North America operations with more than 95% of the total revenue.

Sales and Marketing

The company's marketing operations sell refined petroleum products to retail customers primarily through a combination of company-owned Petro-Canada locations, branded-dealers in Canada and company-owned locations in the US marketed under other international brands. This includes Canada's Electric Highway, a coast-to-coast network of fast-charging electric vehicle stations. The company's marketing operations also sells refined petroleum products through a nationwide commercial road transportation network in Canada, and to other commercial and industrial customers, including other retail sellers, in Canada and the US.

Financial Performance

The company's revenue for fiscal 2022 increased to CAD58.5 billion compared to the prior year with CAD39.1 billion. The increase was primarily due to higher revenues on every segment offsetting the increase in expenses.

Net income for fiscal 2022 increased to CAD9.1 billion compared to the prior year with CAD4.1 billion. The increase was primarily due to higher revenues offsetting the increase in expenses.

Cash held by the company at the end of fiscal 2022 decreased to CAD2.0 billion. Cash provided by operations was CAD15.7 billion while cash used for investing and financing activities were CAD4.8 billion and CAD11.2 billion, respectively. The main uses of cash were capital and exploration expenditures; and the repurchase of common shares.

Strategy

Key components of Suncor's strategy include: optimizing value through integration and secured market access; optimizing asset portfolio; driving value through high-return investments; maximizing value through operational excellence and reliability; technology and people-enabled; and continuing to be an industry leader in sustainable development and the global energy expansion.

Mergers and Acquisitions

In 2023, Suncor Energy announced that it has agreed to purchase TotalEnergies EP Canada Ltd., which holds a 31.23% working interest in the Fort Hills oil sands mining project (Fort Hills) for $1.468 billion. The acquisition adds 61,000 barrels per day of net bitumen production capacity and 675 million barrels of proved and probable reserves to Suncor's existing oil sands portfolio.

Company Background

To focus on its growth markets and to pay down debt, in 2013 the company agreed to sell its conventional natural gas business in Western Canada to a Centrica and Qatar Petroleum partnership for $1 billion.

To further develop its oil sands assets, in 2010 the company formed a strategic alliance with TOTAL. As part of the deal, France-based TOTAL paid Suncor Energy about $1.7 billion to acquire 19% of Suncor Energy's 60% interest in the Fort Hills mining project and a 49% stake in the Voyageur Upgrader project near Fort McMurray. Suncor Energy acquired about 37% of TOTAL's stake in the Joslyn project.

Boosting its profile as an integrated energy company, in 2009 the company acquired Petro-Canada in a $15 billion deal. The acquisition created an energy behemoth with extensive holdings in oil sands, solid conventional exploration and production assets, and a major refining and retailing network. Following the Petro-Canada deal the company divested about $1.5 billion of non-core assets in Western Canada, the US, Trinidad and Tobago, and the North Sea. In 2010 Suncor Energy sold its North Sea exploration assets (of Petro Canada Netherlands) to Dana Petroleum for $393 million. Later that year it sold a pair of natural gas properties in Alberta to a subsidiary of Abu Dhabi National Energy Company for $285 million. It also sold its Wildcat Hills assets, which produce some 80 million cu. ft. of natural gas per day, to Direct Energy for about $360 million.

EXECUTIVES

Chief Executive Officer, President, Non-Independent Director, Mark Little
Chief Financial Officer, Alister Cowan
Chief Climate Officer, Martha Hall Findlay
Chief Transformation Officer, Bruno Francoeur
Human Resources Chief People Officer, Paul Gardner
Upstream Executive Vice President, Micheal R. MacSween
Downstream Executive Vice President, Corporate Development Executive Vice President, Trading Executive Vice President, Kris Smith
E&P and In Situ Senior Vice President, Shelley Powell
General Counsel, Chief Sustainability Officer, Arlene Strom
Independent Director, Patricia M. Bedient
Independent Director, John D. Gass
Independent Director, Russell Girling
Independent Director, Jean Paul Gladu
Independent Director, Dennis M. Houston
Independent Director, Brian MacDonald
Independent Director, Maureen McCaw
Independent Director, Lorraine Mitchelmore
Independent Director, Eira M. Thomas
Independent Director, Michael M. Wilson
Auditors : KPMG LLP

LOCATIONS

HQ: Suncor Energy Inc
150 - 6th Avenue S.W., Calgary, Alberta T2P 3E3
Phone: 403 296-8000
Web: www.suncor.com

COMPETITORS

DELEK US ENERGY, INC.
DELEK US HOLDINGS, INC.
ENI SPA
HOLLYFRONTIER CORPORATION
Imperial Oil Limited
MURPHY OIL CORPORATION
NOBLE ENERGY, INC.
Petroleo Brasileiro S A Petrobras
TC Energy Corporation
WESTERN REFINING, INC.

HISTORICAL FINANCIALS

Company Type: Public

Income Statement — FYE: December 31

	REVENUE ($mil)	NET INCOME ($mil)	NET PROFIT MARGIN	EMPLOYEES
12/23	38,286	6,258	16.3%	14,906
12/22	43,231	6,711	15.5%	16,558
12/21	30,700	3,234	10.5%	16,922
12/20	19,675	(3,392)	—	12,591
12/19	29,941	2,226	7.4%	12,889
Annual Growth	6.3%	29.5%		3.7%

2023 Year-End Financials

Debt ratio: 9.9%
Return on equity: 20.0%
Cash ($ mil.): 1,304
Current Ratio: 1.44
Long-term debt ($ mil.): 8,364
No. of shares ($ mil.): 1,290
Dividends
Yield: —
Payout: 33.2%
Market value ($ mil.): 41,335

	STOCK PRICE ($) FY Close	P/E High/Low		PER SHARE ($) Earnings	Dividends	Book Value
12/23	32.04	6	4	4.78	1.59	25.31
12/22	31.73	6	4	4.83	1.39	21.76
12/21	25.03	10	6	2.17	0.84	19.95
12/20	16.78	—	—	(2.22)	0.82	18.41
12/19	32.80	19	15	1.43	1.26	21.08
Annual Growth	(0.6%)	—	—	35.2%	5.9%	4.7%

Suncorp Group Ltd.

Suncorp-Metway (aka Suncorp Group) wants to be a rising star in Australia's insurance and banking sectors. The group owns Suncorp Insurance, which operates one of the country's largest general insurance companies, as well as a small but growing life insurance and wealth management business. The general insurance business sells personal and commercial property/casualty insurance under its Suncorp, AAMI, GIO, Vero, and Shannons brands. In addition to its insurance business, Suncorp also runs Suncorp Bank, an operator of some 200 branches in eastern Australia. Among other products, the bank offers personal and commercial banking accounts, financial planning, and loans to consumers and small to midsized businesses.

EXECUTIVES

Chief Executive Officer, Managing Director, Executive Director, Steve Johnston
Chief Information Officer, Adam Bennett
Insurance Product and Portfolio Chief Executive Officer, Lisa Harrison
Suncorp New Zealand Chief Executive Officer, Jimmy Higgins
Chief Risk Officer, Bridget Messer
Chief Financial Officer, Jeremy Robson
Insurance Chief Operating Officer, Suncorp New Zealand Chief Operating Officer, Paul Smeaton
People and Culture Group Executive, People, Culture and Advocacy Group Executive, Fiona Thompson
Banking and Wealth Chief Executive Officer, Clive van Horen
General Counsel, Belinda Speirs
Secretary, Darren C. Solomon
Chairman, Independent Non-Executive Director, Christine F. McLoughlin
Independent Non-Executive Director, Sylvia Falzon
Independent Non-Executive Director, Elmer Funke Kupper
Independent Non-Executive Director, Ian Hammond
Independent Non-Executive Director, Simon Machell
Independent Non-Executive Director, Sally Herman
Independent Non-Executive Director, Douglas F. Mctaggart
Independent Non-Executive Director, Lindsay Tanner
Independent Non-Executive Director, Duncan G. West
Auditors : KPMG

LOCATIONS

HQ: Suncorp Group Ltd.
Level 23, Heritage Lanes, 80 Ann Street, Brisbane, Queensland 4000
Phone: (61) 7 3362 1222   **Fax:** (61) 7 3135 2940
Web: www.suncorpgroup.com.au

PRODUCTS/OPERATIONS

2013 Sales

	% of total
General Insurance	
Personal	35
Commercial	23
Banking	19
Life and Wealth Management	13
New Zealand General Insurance	10
Total	100

Selected Subsidiaries

Asteron Group Ltd. (life insurance)
GIO General Ltd (general insurance products)
Suncorp Life & Superannuation Limited life (insurance products)
Suncorp Metway Insurance Ltd (general insurance products)
Suncorp Metway Investment Management Limited (investment schemes and provides investment management services)
Vero Insurance Ltd. (New Zealand general insurance)

COMPETITORS

BAKER BOYER BANCORP
BNCCORP, INC.
CONSUMERS BANCORP, INC.
CREDITO EMILIANO SPA
EXTRACO CORPORATION
LYONS NATIONAL BANK
RBC Insurance Holdings Inc
Skipton Building Society
UNIGARD INSURANCE COMPANY
UNITED FINANCIAL BANKING COMPANIES, INC.

HISTORICAL FINANCIALS
Company Type: Public

Income Statement				FYE: June 30
	ASSETS ($mil)	NET INCOME ($mil)	INCOME AS % OF ASSETS	EMPLOYEES
06/23	76,112	759	1.0%	13,000
06/22	73,186	468	0.6%	13,000
06/21	72,701	775	1.1%	13,505
06/20	65,611	625	1.0%	13,500
06/19	67,425	122	0.2%	0
Annual Growth	3.1%	57.8%	—	—

2023 Year-End Financials
Return on assets: 1.0%
Return on equity: 8.8%
Long-term debt ($ mil.): —
No. of shares ($ mil.): 1,266
Sales ($ mil.): 12,149
Dividends
 Yield: 3.2%
 Payout: 67.7%
Market value ($ mil.): —

Suntory Beverage & Food Ltd.

EXECUTIVES
President, Representative Director, Makiko Ono
Executive Vice President, Director, Shekhar Mundlay
Senior Managing Executive Officer, Director, Hachiro Naiki
Director, Peter Harding
Director, Hiroshi Miyamori
Outside Director, Yukari Inoue
Director, Yuji Yamazaki
Outside Director, Mika Masuyama
Outside Director, Mariko Mimura
Auditors : Deloitte Touche Tohmatsu LLC

LOCATIONS
HQ: Suntory Beverage & Food Ltd.
 3-1-1 Shibaura, Minato-ku, Tokyo 108-8503
Phone: (81) 3 5579 1837
Web: www.suntory.co.jp/softdrink/

HISTORICAL FINANCIALS
Company Type: Public

Income Statement				FYE: December 31
	REVENUE ($mil)	NET INCOME ($mil)	NET PROFIT MARGIN	EMPLOYEES
12/22	11,006	624	5.7%	24,779
12/21	11,023	596	5.4%	25,224
12/20	11,430	506	4.4%	25,618
12/19	11,968	634	5.3%	26,056
12/18	11,769	727	6.2%	26,164
Annual Growth	(1.7%)	(3.7%)	—	(1.4%)

2022 Year-End Financials
Debt ratio: 0.1%
Return on equity: 9.0%
Cash ($ mil.): 1,522
Current Ratio: 1.20
Long-term debt ($ mil.): 491
No. of shares ($ mil.): 308
Dividends
 Yield: —
 Payout: 0.0%
Market value ($ mil.): 5,247

	STOCK PRICE ($) FY Close	P/E High/Low	PER SHARE ($) Earnings	Dividends	Book Value
12/22	16.98	0 0	2.02	0.30	23.71
12/21	18.06	0 0	1.93	0.35	24.20
12/20	17.77	0 0	1.64	0.36	24.55
12/19	20.71	0 0	2.05	0.36	22.55
12/18	22.58	0 0	2.36	0.35	21.04
Annual Growth	(6.9%)	— —	(3.7%)	(4.1%)	3.0%

Suruga Bank, Ltd.

Just like its namesake bay at the foot of Mount Fuji, Suruga Bank wants to be deep and wide. Formed in 1895, the bank serves the greater Tokyo area through more than 125 branches. It offers mortgage loans, personal loans, credit cards, and wealth management products, deposit products, home loans for foreign residents, asset management, and small and medium enterprise (SME) lending services. It caters to SME markets, targeting the self-employed, working women, senior citizens, and the newly wealthy. Through an alliance with Japan Post Bank, it expanded its consumer loans business. Under the deal, Japan Post (with its branch network of more than 230 locations) handles home loans in partnership with Suruga.

EXECUTIVES
President, Representative Director, Kosuke Saga
Executive Vice President, Representative Director, Kosuke Kato
Director, Tomoaki Tsutsumi
Director, Tomoki Toya
Director, Takeshi Miyajima
Outside Director, Yoriyuki Kusaki
Director, Kazumasa Itakura
Outside Director, Emi Noge
Outside Director, Yoichi Namekata
Outside Director, Yasumine Satake
Auditors : Ernst & Young ShinNihon LLC

LOCATIONS
HQ: Suruga Bank, Ltd.
 23 Toriyoko-cho, Numazu, Shizuoka 410-8689
Phone: (81) 55 962 0080
Web: www.surugabank.co.jp

COMPETITORS
AOZORA BANK,LTD.
ARAB BANK PLC
BANK OF BARODA
DAISHI HOKUETSU BANK, LTD.
HANG SENG BANK, LIMITED

HISTORICAL FINANCIALS
Company Type: Public

Income Statement				FYE: March 31
	ASSETS ($mil)	NET INCOME ($mil)	INCOME AS % OF ASSETS	EMPLOYEES
03/22	29,513	65	0.2%	2,178
03/21	32,065	193	0.6%	2,280
03/20	32,073	233	0.7%	2,514
03/19	30,957	(877)	—	2,645
03/18	42,016	65	0.2%	2,661
Annual Growth	(8.5%)	(0.1%)		(4.9%)

2022 Year-End Financials
Return on assets: 0.2%
Return on equity: 2.8%
Long-term debt ($ mil.): —
No. of shares ($ mil.): 188
Sales ($ mil.): 757
Dividends
 Yield: —
 Payout: 0.0%
Market value ($ mil.): 6,712

	STOCK PRICE ($) FY Close	P/E High/Low	PER SHARE ($) Earnings	Dividends	Book Value
03/22	35.64	1 1	0.29	0.41	11.53
03/21	40.25	— —	0.84	0.45	11.14
03/20	40.25	0 0	1.01	0.05	10.21
03/19	227.00	— —	(3.79)	0.94	9.40
03/18	227.00	8 8	0.28	2.12	13.93
Annual Growth	(37.1%)	— —	0.1%	(33.5%)	(4.6%)

Suzuken Co Ltd

SUZUKEN is one of the largest distributors of drugs in Japan. It serves a network of customers that includes hospitals and health practitioners throughout the country. In addition to prescription and diagnostic pharmaceuticals, SUZUKEN also delivers select medical equipment and supplies. SUZUKEN purchases ethical drugs, diagnostic agents, medical equipment, medical materials, and medical food products from approximately 1,000 companies both in Japan and abroad; including pharmaceutical and medical equipment manufacturers, and supplies medical institutions and insurance pharmacies. Japan accounts for more than 90% of total revenue.

Operations
The company operates in four segments: Pharmaceutical Distribution, Pharmaceutical Manufacturing, Pharmacy, and Healthcare-Related Services. The largest segment, Pharmaceutical Distribution, sells pharmaceuticals, diagnostic reagents, and medical equipment and supplies to medical institutions and accounts for about 95% of total revenue. Pharmaceutical Manufacturing makes products including pharmaceuticals and reagents.

Meanwhile, Pharmacy prepares drugs based on prescriptions from medical centers. Healthcare-Related Services delivers specialty drugs for rare diseases, provides nursing care, makes medical equipment, and sells medical literature.

Geographic Reach

SUZUKEN has distribution centers, specialist logistics offices, and sales offices in all 47 prefectures in Japan.

Japan accounts for more than 90% of total revenue.

Financial Performance

Company's revenue for fiscal 2022 increased by 5% to Â¥2.2 trillion compared from the prior year with Â¥2.1 trillion.

Net income for fiscal 2022 increased by 82% to Â¥14.4 billion compared from the prior year with Â¥7.9 billion.

Cash held by the company at the end of fiscal 2022 decreased to Â¥168.2 billion. Cash provided by operations and investing activities were Â¥9.5 billion and Â¥1.4 billion, respectively. Cash used for financing activities was Â¥11.6 billion, mainly for dividends paid.

Strategy

The environment surrounding the company has changed drastically and rapidly beyond its expectations, due to the promotion of deregulation, entry of different industries, advancement of digitalization, and other factors. Accordingly, Suzuken recognize that the company are now at a major turning point. In order to address such changes in the environment, the company has worked on building a new business model and proceeding with initiatives toward low-cost management.

Company Background

SUZUKEN traces its history back to 1932, when Kenzo Suzuki established a sole proprietorship pharmaceutical wholesaler in the city of Nagoya. In the 1950s, the company began manufacturing drugs.

In the 1970s, the company began operating internationally; it also started manufacturing medical devices. In the following decade, SUZUKEN entered the diagnostics reagents market.

EXECUTIVES

Supreme Advisor, Director, Yoshiki Bessho
Chairman, Representative Director, Hiromi Miyata
President, Representative Director, Shigeru Asano
Senior Managing Executive Officer, Director, Hisashi Tamura
Director, Chie Takahashi
Outside Director, Yasunori Usui
Outside Director, Shunichi Samura
Outside Director, Keisuke Ueda
Outside Director, Toshiaki Iwatani
Outside Director, Takeshi Ogasawara
Auditors: Deloitte Touche Tohmatsu LLC

LOCATIONS

HQ: Suzuken Co Ltd
  8 Higashi-Katahamachi, Higashi-ku, Nagoya, Aichi 461-8701
Phone: (81) 52 961 2331
Web: www.suzuken.co.jp

PRODUCTS/OPERATIONS

2015 Sales

	% of total
Pharmaceutical distribution	
Ethical pharmaceuticals	83
Diagnostic reagents	4
Medical equipment & supplies	3
Other	1
Pharmaceutical manufacturing	3
Insurance pharmacy	4
Healthcare-related services	2
Total	100

Selected Distribution Units

ASTIS Co.
Nakano Yakuhin Co.
Sanki Corporation
Shoyaku Co.
Suzuken Iwate Co
Suzuken Okinawa Yakuhin

HISTORICAL FINANCIALS

Company Type: Public

Income Statement — FYE: March 31

	REVENUE ($mil)	NET INCOME ($mil)	NET PROFIT MARGIN	EMPLOYEES
03/22	18,356	118	0.6%	17,210
03/21	19,223	71	0.4%	18,305
03/20	20,391	259	1.3%	18,998
03/19	19,254	272	1.4%	19,122
03/18	20,002	177	0.9%	19,459
Annual Growth	(2.1%)	(9.6%)	—	(3.0%)

2022 Year-End Financials

Debt ratio: —
Return on equity: 3.4%
Cash ($ mil.): 1,162
Current Ratio: 1.27
Long-term debt ($ mil.): —
No. of shares ($ mil.): 87
Dividends
 Yield: —
 Payout: 0.0%
Market value ($ mil.): —

Suzuki Motor Corp. (Japan)

Suzuki Motor Corporation is a leading Japanese carmaker and a global motorcycle manufacturer. Suzuki's passenger car models include the Alto, Grand Vitara, Swift, Splash, and SX4. Its motorcycle products include cruiser, motocross, off road, scooter, street, and touring models, as well as ATVs. Suzuki Motor's non-vehicle products include outboard motors for boats and motorized wheelchairs. It builds its lineup on its own and through numerous subsidiaries and joint ventures overseas. Japan accounts for nearly 45% of sales. Suzuki Motor traces its roots back to 1909 when Michio Suzuki founded Suzuki Loom Works in Hamamatsu, Shizuoka Prefecture, Japan.

Operations

Suzuki divides its operations into four reportable segments: Automobile, Motorcycle, Marine and Other.

The Automobile segment generates around 90% of the company's total revenue and sells mini vehicles, sub-compact vehicles and standard-sized vehicles. Motorcycle segment (more than 5%) include motorcycles and all-terrain vehicles. Marine segment includes outboard motors and other segment (less than 5% of revenue) include motorized wheelchairs, solar power generation and real estate.

Geographic Reach

The company has production facilities in about 20 countries and serves more than 200 countries. Based in Japan (around 30% of its total revenue), Suzuki's Asian consumers represent nearly 45% of its revenue, whereas European and other regions account for some 15% and more than 10% of revenue, respectively.

Financial Performance

Company's revenue for fiscal 2021 increased by 12% to Â¥3.6 trillion compared from the prior year with Â¥3.2 trillion.

Profit for fiscal 2021 increased to Â¥274.3 billion compared from the prior year with Â¥241.1 billion.

Cash held by the company at the end of fiscal 2021 decreased to Â¥858.0 billion. Cash provided by operations was Â¥221.3 billion while cash used for investing and financing activities were Â¥153.5 billion and Â¥154.6 billion, respectively.

HISTORY

In 1909 Michio Suzuki started Suzuki Loom Works in Hamamatsu, Japan. The company went public in 1920 and continued producing weaving equipment until the onset of WWII, when it began to make war-related products.

Suzuki began developing inexpensive motor vehicles in 1947, and in 1952 it introduced a 36cc engine to motorize bicycles. The company changed its name to Suzuki Motor and launched its first motorcycle in 1954. Suzuki's entry into the minicar market came in 1955 with the Suzulight, followed by the Suzumoped (1958), a delivery van (1959), and the Suzulight Carry FB small truck (1961).

Suzuki's triumph in the 1962 50cc-class Isle of Man TT motorcycle race started a string of racing successes that brought international prominence to the Suzuki name. The company established its first overseas plant in Thailand in 1967.

In the 1970s Suzuki met market demand for motorcycles with large engines. Meanwhile, a mid-1970s recession and falling demand for low-powered cars in Japan led the minicar industry there to produce two-thirds fewer minicars in 1974 than in 1970. Suzuki responded by pushing overseas, beginning auto exports, and expanding foreign distribution. In 1975 it started producing motorcycles in Taiwan, Thailand, and Indonesia.

Suzuki boosted capacity internationally throughout the 1980s through joint ventures. Motorcycle sales in Japan peaked in 1982, then tapered off, but enjoyed a modest rebound in the late 1980s. In 1988 the company agreed to handle distribution of Peugeot cars in Japan.

Suzuki and General Motors began their longstanding relationship in 1981 when GM bought a small stake in Suzuki. The company began producing Swift subcompacts in 1983 and sold them through GM as the Chevy Sprint and, later, the Geo Metro. In 1986 Suzuki and GM of Canada jointly formed CAMI Automotive to produce vehicles, including Sprints, Metros, and Geo Trackers (Suzuki Sidekicks), in Ontario; production began in 1989.

Although sales via GM increased through 1990, US efforts with the Suzuki nameplate faltered shortly after Suzuki formed its US subsidiary in Brea, California, in 1986. A 1988 Consumer Reports claim that the company's Samurai SUV was prone to rolling over devastated US sales. The next year Suzuki's top US executives quit, apparently questioning the company's commitment to the US market.

Suzuki established Magyar Suzuki, a joint venture with Hungarian automaker Autokonszern Rt., C. Itoh & Co., and International Finance Corporation in 1991 to begin producing the Swift sedan in Hungary. The company expanded a licensing agreement with a Chinese government partner in 1993, becoming the first Japanese company to take an equity stake in a Chinese carmaking venture. The next year Suzuki introduced the Alto van, Japan's cheapest car, at just over $5,000, and the Wagon R miniwagon, which quickly became one of Japan's top-selling vehicles.

In a case that was later overturned, a woman was awarded $90 million from Suzuki after being paralyzed in a Samurai rollover in 1990. The company sued Consumers Union, publisher of Consumer Reports, in 1996, charging it had intended to fix the results in the 1988 Samurai testing.

GM raised its 3% stake in Suzuki to 10% in 1998. The company teamed up with GM and Fuji Heavy Industries (Subaru) in 2000 to develop compact cars for the European market. It was also announced that GM would spend about $600 million to double its stake in Suzuki to 20%. In 2001 Suzuki announced that it had agreed to cooperate with Kawasaki in the development of new motorcycles, scooters, and ATVs.

The following year Suzuki agreed to take control of Maruti Udyog Ltd., the state-owned India-based car manufacturer, in an $80 million rights issue deal.

GM sold almost all of its 20% stake in Suzuki in early 2006 to raise cash for its own beleaguered operations. GM divested the remaining 3% stake in late 2008 for about $230 million as it endured a dire cash crisis.

EXECUTIVES

President, Chairman of Executive Committee, Representative Director, Toshihiro Suzuki
Executive Vice President, Representative Director, Naomi Ishii
Senior Managing Director, Director, Masahiko Nagao
Senior Managing Director, Director, Toshiaki Suzuki
Senior Managing Director, Director, Kinji Saito
Senior Managing Director, Katsuhiro Kato
Outside Director, Hideaki Domichi
Outside Director, Shun Egusa
Outside Director, Naoko Takahashi
Auditors : Seimei Audit Corp.

LOCATIONS

HQ: Suzuki Motor Corp. (Japan)
300 Takatsuka-cho, Minami-ku, Hamamatsu, Shizuoka 432-8611
Phone: (81) 53 440 2030
Web: www.suzuki.co.jp

2016 Sales

	% of total
Asia	44
Japan	41
Europe	10
Other regions	5
Total	100

PRODUCTS/OPERATIONS

2016 Salles

	% of total
Automobiles	91
Motorcycles	7
Marine and power products	2
Total	100

List of Items
Automobiles
    Alto/CELERIO
    APV
    Grand Vitara SUV
    Jimny
    Kizashi sport sedan
    Splash
    Swift
    SX4 Crossover, Sport, SportBack
Motorcycles/ATV
    Cruiser
    Dual purpose
    Motocross
    Offroad
    Scooter
    Sport Enduro Tourer
    Street
    Supersport
Outboard motors
    Carburetor series (4-stroke)
    Electronic fuel injection series (4-stroke)
    Kerosene Outboards (2-stroke)

COMPETITORS

FORD MOTOR COMPANY
HINO MOTORS, LTD.
HONDA MOTOR CO., LTD.
MAZDA MOTOR CORPORATION
MITSUBISHI MOTORS CORPORATION
NISSAN MOTOR CO.,LTD.
PEUGEOT SA
RENAULT
TOYOTA MOTOR CORPORATION
YAMAHA MOTOR CO., LTD.

HISTORICAL FINANCIALS

Company Type: Public

Income Statement   FYE: March 31

	REVENUE ($mil)	NET INCOME ($mil)	NET PROFIT MARGIN	EMPLOYEES
03/23	34,850	1,660	4.8%	114,903
03/22	29,336	1,318	4.5%	109,695
03/21	28,703	1,322	4.6%	103,891
03/20	32,136	1,236	3.8%	102,572
03/19	34,958	1,614	4.6%	101,523
Annual Growth	(0.1%)	0.7%	—	3.1%

2023 Year-End Financials

Debt ratio: 0.1%   No. of shares ($ mil.): 486
Return on equity: 11.1%   Dividends
Cash ($ mil.): 7,196   Yield: 1.9%
Current Ratio: 1.47   Payout: 84.3%
Long-term debt ($ mil.): 3,129   Market value ($ mil.): 70,380

	STOCK PRICE ($) FY Close	P/E High/Low		PER SHARE ($) Earnings	Dividends	Book Value
03/23	144.78	0	0	3.42	2.79	32.10
03/22	136.90	1	0	2.71	3.51	31.79
03/21	182.84	1	0	2.72	3.20	31.38
03/20	94.75	1	0	2.64	2.73	28.23
03/19	177.25	1	0	3.57	2.95	27.25
Annual Growth	(4.9%)	—	—	(1.1%)	(1.4%)	4.2%

Svenska Handelsbanken

Svenska Handelsbanken is one of the world's strongest banks, and strives to provide the best bank offering within financing, savings and advisory services. Subsidiaries operate in several related areas, including life insurance, mortgages, pensions, fund management, and internet banking. The bank boast branches in countries, including Sweden, the UK, Denmark, Finland, Norway, and the Netherlands. Subsidiaries include corporate financing unit Handelsbanken Finans, Handelsbanken Asset Management, and Handelsbanken Liv. Founded in 1871, the bank's assets now exceed $3.3 billion. Sweden generated majority of its sales.

Operations

The bank operates in five business segments, mostly based on geography. These include branch operation segments in Sweden (about 65% of sales), the UK (some 15%), Norway (around 10%) and the Netherlands (less than 5%), as well as a Capital Markets segment (around 5%).

The bank made about 70% of its total revenue from interest income mostly from corporate loans and mortgage loans, but also from consumer loans. The majority of the remaining revenues came from fee and commission income from its investment banking (around 25%), as well as gains/losses on financial transactions with some 5%.

Geographic Reach

Svenska Handelsbanken generates approximately 70% of its revenue in Sweden, while its operations in UK brings in about 15%, and Norway with some 10% of total revenue. The banks other top markets include Denmark, Finland, and the Netherlands.

Financial Performance

Net interest income grew by 1%, or SEK312 million, to SEK 29.4 billion (29.1 billion). Continued robust growth, resulting from the bank's strong market position, particularly as regards mortgage loans and property finance, led to growing business volumes having a positive impact of SEK666 million.

In 2021, the company had a net income of SEK23.5 million, a 25% from the previous year's net income of SEK18.8 million.

The company's cash at the end of 2021 was SEK440 billion. Operating activities generated SEK49.4 billion, while investing activities used SEK752 million, mainly for acquisitions of property and equipment. Financing activities used another SEK26.8 million, primarily for dividend paid.

Strategy

In 2021, Handelsbanken made further advances in its sustainability activities. Early in the year, the bank presented a clear strategy for its continuing work within sustainability, and launched concrete, measurable sustainability goals for the Bank's core operations: financing, investment and advisory services. One of these objectives relates to achieving net zero emissions of greenhouse gases as soon as possible, or by 2040 at the latest. In the second quarter, the bank launched several new green loan offerings, for both private and corporate customers, to provide further support for customers' transitions. In late June, Handelsbanken became the first bank in the Nordic region to enter into a green EU taxonomy-adapted loan. Handelsbanken Fonder became the first Swedish fund management company to change the index of seven of its global and regional index funds to indices supporting the aims of the Paris Agreement (Paris-Aligned Benchmarks).

HISTORY

Svenska Handelsbanken (roughly translated as The Swedish Commercial Bank) was founded as Stockholms Handelsbank in 1871 by former directors of Stockholms Enskilda Bank who lost an internal power struggle. Industrialization in the latter stages of the 19th century saw Stockholms Handelsbank expand nationwide, with the bank pursuing an aggressive lending policy. Larger companies required larger financing, resulting in smaller local banks running into trouble and forcing them to merge with bigger ones. Through a series of mergers of this kind, Stockholms Handelsbank exploded in size and branches increased from seven (all Stockholm-based) to 250 nationwide by 1919.

To reflect this growth, the company changed its name to Svenska Handelsbanken the same year.

Sweden remained neutral during WWI, allowing business to prosper, but the depression hit hard. The bank had to write off millions in bad loans and additions to its reserves. During the 1930s Handelsbanken regained stability largely thanks to its geographical diversity; operations in areas with high economic activity made up for struggling regions.

Sweden once again remained neutral during WWII, but political uncertainty kept deposits high and it became difficult to maintain profitable loan volumes. In the 1940s Svenska Handelsbanken divested many of its industrial holdings and began to rededicate itself to small- and medium-scale lending.

Through a string of purchases in the 1950s and 1960s, the bank became the largest bank in Scandinavia and began looking to expand internationally. Joint ventures and acquisitions saw the company move into other parts of Europe and the US in the 1970s. Nordic American Banking, a US subsidiary, was set up to handle import and export financing for North and South American clients doing business with Scandinavian countries. The 1980s saw the company establish a merchant-banking subsidiary in London and enter the Asian market, forming Svenska Handelsbanken Asia (based in Singapore).

The bank remained acquisitive during the first half of the 1990s, including a purchase of life insurance company RKA (later renamed Handelsbanken Liv) and parts of the Finnish Skopbank. In 1996 Handelsbanken acquired Swedish mortgage company Stadshypotek.

During the latter half of the 1990s, it ventured into e-business and increased its presence in the Nordic countries and the UK. In 1999 the company acquired the Norwegian Bergensbanken after having been beaten by MeritaNordbanken in the chase for Christiania Bank (which was Norway's second-largest at the time). The next year Handelsbanken acquired Spartacus, a Danish consumer finance company. In 2001 it made another Danish purchase, Midtbank, making it one of Denmark's largest bankers. That year it also acquired Swedish life insurance company SPP.

In 2004 Handelsbanken bought Swedish fund manager XACT Fonder from OMHEX (now OMX).

The company bought Lokallbanken in Denmark in 2008. The deal added about 15 branches to Handelsbanken's network.

EXECUTIVES

Chief Executive Officer, President, Executive Vice President, Head of Regional Bank Stockholm, Non-Independent Director, Carina Akerstrom

Deputy Chief Executive, Per Beckman
Chief Financial Officer, Carl Cederschiold
Chief Sustainability and Climate Officer, Catharina Belfrage Sahlstrand
Chief Human Resources Officer, Magnus Ericson
Chief Risk Officer, Maria Hedin
Chief Strategy Officer, Martin Noreus
Chief Credit Officer, Robert E. Radway
Chief Legal Officer, Secretary, Martin Wasteson
Chief Information Officer, Mattias Forsberg
Capital Markets Head, Dan Lindwall
Product and Offerings Head, Anna Possne
Communications Head, Louise Sander
Chairman, Independent Director, Par Boman
Vice-Chairman, Independent Director, Fredrik Lundberg
Independent Director, Jon Fredrik Baksaas
Independent Director, Stina Bergfors
Independent Director, Hans Biorck
Independent Director, Kerstin Hessius
Independent Director, Ulf Riese
Independent Director, Arja Taaveniku
Auditors : Ernst & Young AB

LOCATIONS

HQ: Svenska Handelsbanken
Kungstradgardsgatan 2, Stockholm SE-106 70
Phone: (46) 8 701 10 00
Web: www.handelsbanken.se

2014 Sales

	% of total
Sweden	63
Norway	10
UK	10
Denmark	6
Finland	6
Netherlands	4
Other countries	1
Total	100

PRODUCTS/OPERATIONS

2014 Sales by Segment

	% of total
Branch operations	
Sweden	52
Other countries	33
Capital markets	15
Total	100

COMPETITORS

COMMONWEALTH BANK OF AUSTRALIA
Coöperatieve Rabobank U.A.
NATIONAL BANK OF GREECE S.A.
NATWEST GROUP PLC
Nordea Bank AB
STANDARD CHARTERED PLC
Skandinaviska Enskilda Banken AB
U.S. BANCORP
UNICREDIT SPA
UniCredit Bank AG

HISTORICAL FINANCIALS
Company Type: Public

Income Statement — FYE: December 31

	ASSETS ($mil)	NET INCOME ($mil)	INCOME AS % OF ASSETS	EMPLOYEES
12/23	353,338	2,907	0.8%	0
12/22	332,939	2,069	0.6%	10,954
12/21	369,413	2,155	0.6%	11,039
12/20	383,740	1,907	0.5%	12,474
12/19	329,985	1,819	0.6%	12,548
Annual Growth	1.7%	12.4%	—	—

2023 Year-End Financials
Return on assets: 0.8%
Return on equity: 14.5%
Long-term debt ($ mil.): —
No. of shares ($ mil.): 1,980
Sales ($ mil.): 17,569
Dividends Yield: —
Payout: 26.9%
Market value ($ mil.): 10,688

	STOCK PRICE ($) FY Close	P/E High	P/E Low	Earnings	Dividends	Book Value
12/23	5.40	0	0	1.47	0.40	10.34
12/22	4.98	0	0	1.04	0.24	9.54
12/21	5.37	1	0	1.09	0.48	10.13
12/20	4.98	1	1	0.96	1.00	10.60
12/19	5.31	1	1	0.92	0.30	8.68
Annual Growth	0.4%	—	—	12.3%	7.6%	4.5%

Swatch Group AG (The)

EXECUTIVES

Chief Executive Officer, President, Director, Georges Nicolas Hayek
Management Board Member, Florence Ollivier-Lamarque
Management Board Member, Raynald Aeschlimann
Management Board Member, Pierre-Andre Buhler
Management Board Member, Marc Alexander Hayek
Chief Financial Officer, Management Board Member, Thierry Kenel
Management Board Member, Peter Steiger
Management Board Member, Francois Thiebaud
Extended Management Board Member, Mireille Koenig
Extended Management Board Member, Matthias Breschan
Extended Management Board Member, Sylvain Dolla
Extended Management Board Member, Daniel Everts
Extended Management Board Member, Fadi Ghalayini
Extended Management Board Member, Hans-Rudolf Gottier
Extended Management Board Member, Lionel A. Marca
Extended Management Board Member, Calogero Polizzi
Extended Management Board Member, Michel Willemin
Corporate Secretary, Jennifer Meyer-Kluge
Chairwoman, Director, Nayla Hayek
Vice-Chairman, Director, Ernst Tanner
Director, Daniela Aeschlimann
Director, Claude Nicollier
Director, Jean-Pierre Roth
Auditors: PricewaterhouseCoopers AG

LOCATIONS
HQ: Swatch Group AG (The)
Seevorstadt 6, Biel CH-2501
Phone: (41) 32 343 68 11   **Fax:** (41) 32 343 69 11
Web: www.swatchgroup.com

HISTORICAL FINANCIALS
Company Type: Public

Income Statement — FYE: December 31

	REVENUE ($mil)	NET INCOME ($mil)	NET PROFIT MARGIN	EMPLOYEES
12/22	8,976	874	9.7%	32,061
12/21	8,340	838	10.0%	31,444
12/20	6,077	(57)	—	32,424
12/19	8,649	755	8.7%	36,089
12/18	9,440	858	9.1%	37,123
Annual Growth	(1.3%)	0.5%	—	(3.6%)

2022 Year-End Financials
Debt ratio: 0.1%
Return on equity: 6.8%
Cash ($ mil.): 2,358
Current Ratio: 9.23
Long-term debt ($ mil.): 2
No. of shares ($ mil.): 143
Dividends Yield: —
Payout: 5.0%
Market value ($ mil.): 2,038

	STOCK PRICE ($) FY Close	P/E High	P/E Low	Earnings	Dividends	Book Value
12/22	14.19	5	4	3.37	0.17	90.45
12/21	15.39	6	4	3.23	0.11	88.12
12/20	13.57	—	—	(0.23)	0.16	86.36
12/19	13.85	6	5	2.93	0.23	82.73
12/18	14.58	8	4	3.28	0.22	79.64
Annual Growth	(0.7%)	—	—	0.7%	(5.8%)	3.2%

Swedbank AB

EXECUTIVES

Chief Executive Officer, President, Jens Henriksson
Deputy Chief Executive, President, Tomas Hedberg
Chief Credit Officer, Lars-Erik Danielsson
Chief Compliance Officer, Ingrid Harbo
Chief Financial Officer, Anders C. Karlsson
Digital Banking & IT Chief Information Officer, Digital Banking & IT Head, Lotta Loven
Chief Risk Officer, Rolf Marquardt
Legal Chief Legal Officer, Legal Head, Charlotte Rydin
Large Corporates & Institutions Head, Pal Bergstrom
Swedish Banking Head, Mikael Bjorknert
Anti-Financial Crime Unit Head, Anders Ekedahl
Baltic Banking Head, Jon Lidefelt
Communication and Sustainability Head, Erik Ljungberg
Infrastructure Head, Human Resources Head, Carina Strand
Products & Advice Head, Kerstin Winlof
Chairman, Independent Director, Goran Persson
Vice-Chairman, Independent Director, Bo Magnusson
Independent Director, Bo Bengtsson
Independent Director, Goran Bengtsson
Independent Director, Annika Creutzer
Independent Director, Hans Eckerstrom
Independent Director, Kerstin Hermansson
Independent Director, Bengt Erik Lindgren
Independent Director, Anna Mossberg
Independent Director, Per Olof Nyman
Independent Director, Biljana Pehrsson
Director, Roger Ljung
Director, Ake Skoglund
Auditors: PricewaterhouseCoopers AB

LOCATIONS
HQ: Swedbank AB
Landsvaegen 40, Sundbyberg 17263
Phone: (46) 8 585 900 00   **Fax:** (46) 8 796 80 92
Web: www.swedbank.com

HISTORICAL FINANCIALS
Company Type: Public

Income Statement — FYE: December 31

	ASSETS ($mil)	NET INCOME ($mil)	INCOME AS % OF ASSETS	EMPLOYEES
12/22	275,211	2,108	0.8%	17,886
12/21	303,611	2,303	0.8%	17,700
12/20	317,568	1,582	0.5%	17,373
12/19	258,881	2,117	0.8%	16,327
12/18	250,924	2,364	0.9%	15,879
Annual Growth	2.3%	(2.8%)	—	3.0%

2022 Year-End Financials
Return on assets: 0.7%
Return on equity: 12.9%
Long-term debt ($ mil.): —
No. of shares ($ mil.): 1,123
Sales ($ mil.): 7,087
Dividends Yield: —
Payout: 57.1%
Market value ($ mil.): 19,025

	STOCK PRICE ($) FY Close	P/E High	P/E Low	Earnings	Dividends	Book Value
12/22	16.94	1	1	1.87	1.07	15.11
12/21	20.12	1	1	2.05	1.70	15.91
12/20	17.64	2	1	1.41	0.35	16.96
12/19	14.88	1	1	1.89	1.53	13.32
12/18	22.39	1	1	2.11	1.55	13.75
Annual Growth	(6.7%)	—	—	(2.9%)	(8.9%)	2.4%

Swire (John) & Sons Ltd.

John Swire & Sons is a holding company for a diverse group of businesses collectively known as the Swire group. Operations span the globe, but are concentrated in the Asia/Pacific region (Mainland China and Hong Kong), where it operates as Swire Pacific. Swire Pacific has interests in Property, Beverages, Trading and Industrial, Marine Services, and Aviation. Separately, John Swire & Sons owns businesses engaged in refrigerated warehousing (United States Cold Storage). The company was founded in 1816.

Operations

John Swire & Son's biggest operation is Swire Pacific, which generates the majority of the company's profits and in which John Swire holds a 60% stake.

John Swire's beverages and food chain businesses is Coca-Cola Company's biggest bottling partners. John Swire has exclusive rights to manufacture, market, and distribute Coca-Cola products in eleven Chinese provinces, the Shanghai Municipality, and Hong Kong, Taiwan, and a broad swath of Western US.

The Property business encompasses property interests in Hong Kong, China, Papua New Guinea Southeast Asia, and the US. These include investment, and trading interests as well as hotels. The principal businesses are grouped under Swire Properties Ltd., a leading developer, owner and operator of mixed-use, principally commercial, properties in the HKSAR and the Chinese mainland. Swire is also one of the largest operators of cold storage facilities in the US.

John Swire's Trading and Industrial activities encompass a wide spectrum of business interests that range from apparel to automotive trading. It includes Taikoo Motor group, which distributes and retails international brands of passenger cars, commercial vehicles, motorcycles and scooters, principally in Taiwan region. Through its subsidiary Steamships Trading Company, Swire has an interest in the manufacture and distribution of personal care items in Papua New Guinea.

John Swire's Aviation business includes airline, aircraft engineering, flight catering, cargo terminal operations and ground services operations, mainly grouped under the Cathay Pacific, which provides flight catering and ramp and passenger handling services, and owns and operates a cargo terminal at Hong Kong International Airport, as well as the Hong Kong Aircraft Engineering Company (HAECO), a global leader in aviation maintenance and repair services.

John Swire's Investment business takes minority interests in market-leading businesses that offer significant potential for further growth, with investments portfolio currently focusing on healthcare and sustainability. Swire has a financial interest in Green Monday Holdings, a business that produces and distributes plant-based food products across Asia and beyond.

Lastly, the Marine business includes Singapore-based Swire Shipping, the wholly owned shipping arm of John Swire & Sons. The company owns and manages a global vessel network, offering its customers high frequency liner shipping services and specialist shipping services to energy and infrastructure sectors in the project logistics market.

Geographic Reach

John Swire & Sons is headquartered in the UK., and has regional headquarters in Beijing, Hong Kong, Papua New Guinea, Thailand, Taiwan, Vietnam, and the US.

Company Background

John Swire & Sons is a product of Britain's colonial ambitions in the 19th Century, where merchants and traders flocked to Hong Kong, a British colony from 1842-1997, to trade with China.

EXECUTIVES

Group Financial Controller, J. A. Palfreyman
Secretary, David C. Morris
Chairman, Barnaby N. Swire
Deputy Chairman, Merlin Bingham Swire
Director, S. C. Pelling
Director, M. Cubbon
Director, Lydia Selina Dunn
Director, Nicholas Adam Hodnett Fenwick
Director, James Edward Hughes-Hallett
Director, G. D. McCallum
Director, J. S. Swire
Director, S. C. Swire
Director, W. J. Wemyss
Auditors : KPMG LLP

LOCATIONS

HQ: Swire (John) & Sons Ltd.
Swire House, 59 Buckingham Gate, London SW1E 6AJ
Phone: —

2017 sales

	%
Rest of Asia	34
Hong Kong	24
North America	22
Shipowning and operating	10
Australia	4
UK and Other Areas	3
Papua New Guinea	2
Africa	1
Total	100

PRODUCTS/OPERATIONS

Selected Businesses
Cathay Pacific Airways
HAECO (Hong Kong Aircraft Engineering Company)
Steamships Trading
Swire Pacific

2017 sales

	%
Beverages and food chain	39
Property	18
Aviation	14
Trading	11
Marine	11
Industrial	7
Total	100

HISTORICAL FINANCIALS

Company Type: Public

Income Statement FYE: December 31

	REVENUE ($mil)	NET INCOME ($mil)	NET PROFIT MARGIN	EMPLOYEES
12/21	16,284	657	4.0%	79,477
12/20	14,652	(758)	—	86,595
12/19	15,054	684	4.5%	91,022
12/18	13,508	511	3.8%	92,256
12/17	14,120	568	4.0%	94,235
Annual Growth	3.6%	3.7%	—	(4.2%)

2021 Year-End Financials

Debt ratio: 24.5%
Return on equity: 3.7%
Cash ($ mil.): 3,226
Current Ratio: 1.04
Long-term debt ($ mil.): 6,121
No. of shares ($ mil.): 100
Dividends
  Yield: —
  Payout: 0.0%
Market value ($ mil.): —

Swire Pacific Ltd.

Swire Pacific is a Hong Kong-based international conglomerate with a diversified portfolio of market leading businesses. It operates through three primary divisions: beverages, property, and aviation. It is one of the largest commercial landlords and operators of retail space, principally through the ownership and management of its core centers at Pacific Place and Taikoo Place. Swire Pacific is also a major Coca-Cola bottler in China and owns around 45% of Cathay Pacific Airways, Hong Kong's leading airline. Swire Pacific is controlled by its founding family through UK-based John Swire & Sons. Majority of its sales were generated outside Hong Kong. In mid-2022, Swire Pacific has struck a deal to buy Coca-Cola bottling operations in Vietnam and Cambodia for approximately $1.02 billion.

Operations

The company is organized on a divisional basis: Beverages (around 60%), Property (more than 15%), Aviation (about 15%), and Trading & Industrial (around 10%).

The Beverages division includes the Swire Coca-Cola which has the exclusive right to manufacture, market and distribute products of The Coca-Cola Company (TCCC) in eleven provinces and the Shanghai Municipality in the Chinese mainland and in Hong Kong, Taiwan, and an extensive area of the western USA.

Swire Properties is a leading developer, owner, and operator of mixed-use, principally commercial, properties in Hong Kong and the Chinese mainland, with a record of creating long-term value by transforming urban areas. Its property investment portfolio in Hong Kong comprises office and retail premises, serviced apartments and other luxury and high quality residential accommodation in prime locations. It also owns and manages two hotels in Hong Kong, The Upper House at Pacific Place and EAST Hong Kong at Taikoo Shing through Swire Hotels.

The Aviation Division comprises an associate interest in the Cathay Pacific group and the wholly-owned Hong Kong Aircraft Engineering Company (HAECO) group.

The Trading & Industrial Division includes Swire Resources, Taikoo Motors, Swire Foods, and Swire Environmental Services.

Overall, the company generates approximately 70% of sales from the sale of goods, followed by gross rental income from investment properties with nearly 15% and aircraft and engine maintenance services with nearly 10%.

Geographic Reach

Headquartered in Queensway, Hong Kong, the company generates about 55% of its sales in Chinese Mainland and Asia (excluding Hong Kong which accounts for about 20%), while the US accounts for more than 25%.

Sales and Marketing

The company's five largest customers account for less than 30% of sales.

Financial Performance

Company's revenue for fiscal 2021 increased to HK$15.9 billion compared from the prior year with HK$13.3 billion.

Cash held by the company at the end of fiscal 2021 decreased to HK$22.5 billion. Cash provided by operations were HK$11.7 billion while cash used for investing and financing activities were HK$6.3 billion and HK$12.3 billion, respectively. Main uses of cash were for purchase of shares in joint venture companies; and repayment of loans and bonds.

Strategy

Swire's aims are to deliver sustainable growth in shareholder value, achieved through sound returns on equity over the long term, and to return value to shareholders through sustainable growth in ordinary dividends. Company's strategy is focused on Greater China and South East Asia, where it seeks to grow its core divisions of Property, Beverages and Aviation. New areas of growth, such as healthcare and sustainable foods are being targeted under a new division, Swire Investments.

HISTORY

John Swire began a Liverpool trading company in 1816. By the time he died in 1847, John Swire & Sons derived much of its revenues from the US cotton trade. One of Swire's sons, John Samuel Swire, refocused the company on Chinese tea and textiles during the US Civil War. Unhappy with his representatives in Asia, Swire went to Shanghai and in 1866 partnered with customer Richard Butterfield. Butterfield & Swire (B&S) took Taikoo ("great and ancient") as a Chinese name. Butterfield soon left, but his name lived on with the company until 1974.

By 1868 B&S had offices in New York and Yokohama, Japan; it added a Hong Kong office two years later. The firm created China Navigation Company in 1872 to transport goods on the Yangtze River; the shipping line served all the major Pacific Rim ports by the late 1880s. Hong Kong-based Taikoo Sugar Refinery began operations in 1884.

The third John Swire took over B&S in 1898 and built the Taikoo Dockyard in Hong Kong. The company's Chinese operations were eventually devastated by the Japanese attack on China in 1937, WWII, and the Communist takeover in 1949. However, the company rebuilt in Hong Kong, and in 1948 it bought control of Cathay Pacific, a Hong Kong airline with six DC-3s.

In the 1950s and 1960s, the Swire family expanded the airline and established airport and aircraft service companies. Swire Pacific, the holding company for most of the family's Hong Kong interests, went public in 1959. It won the Coca-Cola bottling franchise for Hong Kong in 1965. The fifth generation of Swires, John and Adrian, took command of parent company John Swire & Sons in 1968 (Adrian became chairman in 1987). The Taikoo Dockyard merged its business with Hongkong & Whampoa Dockyard in 1972.

The 1984 agreement to return Hong Kong to Chinese control in 1997 plunged the colony into uncertainty. Capital flight and free-falling real estate values gave Swire an opportunity to pick up properties at bargain prices.

Meanwhile, Cathay Pacific had become a major Pacific carrier. In 1987 Swire sold about 12% of the airline to CITIC, China's state-owned overseas investment company. (CITIC later increased its share.) Three years later Swire bought 35% of Hong Kong's Dragonair, also partly owned by CITIC, and gave it Cathay Pacific's Shanghai and Beijing routes.

In the 1990s Swire's financial results and property values fluctuated along with confidence about the consequences of China's takeover. In 1997 Swire expanded its Chinese operations, acquiring the rights to distribute Volvo cars in China and Hong Kong. As Asian financial markets collapsed, Swire sold its insurance-underwriting businesses to focus on core operations. Adrian Swire stepped down that year, relinquishing the John Swire & Sons chairmanship to a nonfamily member, Edward Scott.

To expand its dwindling undeveloped property base a Swire-led consortium bought a reclaimed waterfront site on Hong Kong Island in 1998. Reflecting a rebounding economy, in 1999 the company sold more than 274,000 sq. ft. of Hong Kong office space to Time Warner and Cable & Wireless HKT.

In 2000 Swire sold health care and medical products trading unit Swire Loxley to CITIC Pacific, and in 2001 sold its 49% stake in Carlsberg Brewery Hong Kong Ltd., in order to focus on its growing regional soft drinks operations. The company sold its 49% stake in Schneider Swire Ltd. to joint venture partner Schneider Electric Industries in 2002.

Swire sold Chinese carrier Dragonair in 2006 to Cathay Pacific, still retaining an interest in the airline through its stake in Cathay Pacific. Two years later, it spun off its stake in SITA's waste management business to SUEZ Environment for $243 million and Shekou Container Terminals for $129 million.

EXECUTIVES

Chairman, Executive Director, Guy Martin Coutts Bradley
Executive Director, David Peter Cogman
Executive Director, Patrick Healy
Financial Director, Executive Director, Martin James Murray
Executive Director, Zhuo Ping Zhang
General Counsel, Secretary, Bernadette Mak Lomas
Independent Non-Executive Director, Paul Kenneth Etchells
Independent Non-Executive Director, Timothy George Freshwater
Independent Non-Executive Director, Chien Lee
Independent Non-Executive Director, Rose Wai Mun Lee
Independent Non-Executive Director, Gordon Robert Halyburton Orr
Independent Non-Executive Director, Ying Xu
Non-Executive Director, Martin Cubbon
Non-Executive Director, Merlin Bingham Swire
Non-Executive Director, Samuel Compton Swire
Auditors: PricewaterhouseCoopers

LOCATIONS

HQ: Swire Pacific Ltd.
33rd Floor, One Pacific Place, 88 Queensway,
Phone: (852) 2840 8093   **Fax:** (852) 2526 9365
Web: www.swirepacific.com

2018 Revenue

	% of total
Hong Kong	25
Asia (excluding Hong Kong)	48
US	23
Ship owning and operating activities	4
Others	-
Total	100

PRODUCTS/OPERATIONS

2018 Revenue

	% of total
Sales of goods	62
Aircraft and engine maintenance services	16
Gross rental income from investment properties	14
Charter hire	3
Rendering of other services	2
Hotels	2
Property trading	1
Total	100

2018 Revenue

	% of total
Beverages	49
Aviation	18
Property	17
Trading & Industrial	13
Marine Services	3
Head Office	-
Total	100

Selected Subsidiaries and Investments

Aviation
- Airline Training Property Limited (property investment, 43%)
- Cathay Kansei Terminal Services Company Limited (Japan, ground handling, 14%)
- Cathay Pacific Airways Limited (airline operations, 43%)
- Goodrich Asia-Pacific Limited (carbon brakes and wheel hubs, 37%)
- HAECO ATE Component Service Limited (component repairs, 75%)
- Honeywell TAECO Aerospace (Xiamen) Company Limited (Mainland China, component repairs, 24%)
- Hong Kong Aircraft Engineering Company Limited (aircraft maintenance, 75%)
- Singapore Aero Engine Services Private Limited (commercial engine overhaul services, 7%)
- Swire Aviation Limited (67%)
- Taikoo Engine Services (Xiamen) Company Limited (Mainland China, commercial engine overhaul services, 65%)
- Vogue Laundry Service Limited (laundry and dry cleaning services, 43%)

Beverages
- Mount Limited (holding company, 88%)
- Nanjing BC Foods Co., Ltd. (Mainland China, manufacture and sale, 45%)
- SPHI Holdings Limited (holding company)
- Swire Beverages Holdings Limited (holding company)
- Swire Coca-Cola HK Limited (manufacturing, 88%)
- Top Noble Limited (holding company)
- Xian BC Coca-Cola Beverages Limited (Mainland China, manufacture and sale, 75%)

Marine Services
- Lamor Swire Environmental Solutions Pte. Ltd. (Singapore, oil spill response services, 80%)
- Swire Offshore Arabia Company Limited (Saudi Arabia, ship maintenance and operations, 49%)
- Swire Pacific Offshore (Caspian) Limited (chartering and operating vessels)
- Swire Pacific Offshore NZ Limited (New Zealand, supply services to oil and gas exploration and development)
- Swire Pacific Offshore Pty. Limited (Australia, ship owning and operating)
- Swire Pacific Ship Management Limited (ship personnel management)

Other
- Spaciom Limited (Isle of Man, insurance underwriting)
- Swire Finance Limited
- Swire Pacific Capital Limited (Cayman Islands, financial services)

Properties
- Boom View Holdings Limited (British Virgin Islands, investment)
- Brickell CitiCenter West LLC (US, property trading)
- Cathay Limited (investment)
- Cityplaza Holdings Limited (investment)
- Coventry Estates Limited (investment)
- Festival Walk Holdings Limited (investment)
- Goldent Tent Limited (hotel investment)
- Hareton Limited (property trading, 50%)
- Island Delight Limited (property trading)
- Keen Well Holdings Limited (trading, 80%)
- One Queen's Road East Limited (investment)
- Oriental Landscapes Limited
- Pacific Place Holdings Limited (investment)
- Redhill Properties Limited (investment)
- Swire Properties (Finance) Limited
- Swire Properties Limited (holding company)
- Swire Properties Projects Limited (property management)
- Swire Properties Real Estate Agency Limited
- Taikoo Place Holdings Limited (investment)
- Ying Fen (Shanghai) Real Estate Development Company Limited (50%, investment)

Trading and Industrial
- Akzo Nobel Swire Paints (Guangzhou) Limited (Mainland China, manufacturing, 36%)
- Bel Air Motors Limited (automobile distribution in Taiwan)
- Liberty Motors Limited (automobile distribution in Taiwan)
- Swire Industrial Limited (holding company)
- Swire Resources (Shanghai) Trading Company Limited (apparel, footwear, and accessories)
- Taikoo Sugar Limited (food products)

HISTORICAL FINANCIALS
Company Type: Public

Income Statement   FYE: December 31

	REVENUE ($mil)	NET INCOME ($mil)	NET PROFIT MARGIN	EMPLOYEES
12/22	11,697	538	4.6%	58,784
12/21	11,644	431	3.7%	32,560
12/20	10,322	(1,418)	—	86,768
12/19	10,999	1,156	10.5%	94,000
12/18	10,802	3,016	27.9%	93,000
Annual Growth	2.0%	(35.0%)	—	(10.8%)

2022 Year-End Financials

Debt ratio: 2.0%
Return on equity: 1.5%
Cash ($ mil.): 1,490
Current Ratio: 0.98
Long-term debt ($ mil.): 7,458
No. of shares ($ mil.): 3,806
Dividends
 Yield: —
 Payout: 87.2%
Market value ($ mil.): 33,121

	STOCK PRICE ($) FY Close	P/E High/Low	Earnings	Dividends	Book Value
12/22	8.70	3 2	0.36	0.31	8.71
12/21	5.70	4 2	0.29	0.23	8.81
12/20	5.55	— —	(0.94)	0.27	8.72
12/19	9.25	2 1	0.77	0.36	9.03
12/18	10.56	1 1	2.01	0.26	8.88
Annual Growth	(4.7%)	—	(34.9%)	5.1%	(0.5%)

Swiss Life Holding AG

EXECUTIVES

Chairman, Director, Rolf Dorig
Vice-Chairman, Director, Frank Schnewlin
Chief Financial Officer, Matthias Aellig
Chief Executive Officer, Patrick Frost
Director, Thomas Buess
Director, Adrienne Corboud Fumagalli
Director, Ueli Dietiker
Director, Damir Filipovic
Director, Frank W. Keuper
Director, Stefan Loacker
Director, Henry Peter
Director, Martin Schmid
Director, Franziska Tschudi
Director, Klaus Tshutscher
Auditors : PricewaterhouseCoopers AG

LOCATIONS

HQ: Swiss Life Holding AG
General-Guisan-Quai 40, P.O. Box 2831, Zurich CH-8022
Phone: (41) 43 284 33 11 **Fax:** (41) 43 284 63 11
Web: www.swisslife.com

HISTORICAL FINANCIALS
Company Type: Public

Income Statement   FYE: December 31

	REVENUE ($mil)	NET INCOME ($mil)	NET PROFIT MARGIN	EMPLOYEES
12/21	24,340	1,366	5.6%	10,219
12/20	24,670	1,187	4.8%	9,823
12/19	25,157	1,240	4.9%	9,330
12/18	20,394	1,093	5.4%	8,624
12/17	19,231	1,031	5.4%	7,979
Annual Growth	6.1%	7.3%		6.4%

2021 Year-End Financials

Debt ratio: —
Return on equity: 7.4%
Cash ($ mil.): 7,896
Current Ratio: —
Long-term debt ($ mil.): —
No. of shares ($ mil.): 30
Dividends
 Yield: 3.0%
 Payout: 1.5%
Market value ($ mil.): 941

	STOCK PRICE ($) FY Close	P/E High/Low	Earnings	Dividends	Book Value
12/21	30.45	1 1	43.74	0.94	581.36
12/20	22.67	1 0	37.22	0.24	613.14
12/19	25.34	1 1	37.74	0.53	530.51
12/18	18.70	1 1	32.01	0.63	449.48
12/17	16.94	1 0	30.36	0.51	465.67
Annual Growth	15.8%	—	9.6%	16.3%	5.7%

Swiss Re Ltd

EXECUTIVES

Chief Executive Officer, Christian Mumenthaler
Chief Risk Officer, David A. Cole
Chief Strategy Officer, John R. Dacey
Chief Investment Officer, Guido Furer
Division Officer, Agostino Galvagni
Region Officer, Jean-Jacques Henchoz
Region Officer, Moses Ojeisekhoba
Chief Financial Officer, George Quinn
Region Officer, J. Eric Smith
Chief Underwriting Officer, Matthias Weber
Chief Operating Officer, Thomas Wellauer
Chairman, Walter B. Kielholz
Vice-Chairman, Renato Fassbind
Vice-Chairman, Mathis Cabiallavetta
Director, Jakob Baer
Director, Raymund Breu
Director, Raymond Kuo Fung Ch'ien
Director, John R. Coomber
Director, Rajna Gibson Brandon
Director, C. Robert Henrikson
Director, Malcom D. Knight
Director, Hans Ulrich Maerki
Director, Carlos E. Represas
Director, Jean-Pierre Roth
Auditors : KPMG AG

LOCATIONS

HQ: Swiss Re Ltd
Mythenquai 50/60, Zurich 8022

Phone: (41) 43 285 2121 Fax: (41) 43 285 2999
Web: www.swissre.com

HISTORICAL FINANCIALS
Company Type: Public

Income Statement — FYE: December 31

	ASSETS ($mil)	NET INCOME ($mil)	INCOME AS % OF ASSETS	EMPLOYEES
12/21	181,567	1,437	0.8%	13,985
12/20	182,622	(878)	—	13,189
12/19	238,567	727	0.3%	15,401
12/18	207,570	462	0.2%	14,943
12/17	222,526	398	0.2%	14,485
Annual Growth	(5.0%)	37.8%	—	(0.9%)

2021 Year-End Financials
Return on assets: 0.7%
Return on equity: 5.6%
Long-term debt ($ mil.): —
No. of shares ($ mil.): 317
Sales ($ mil.): 46,739
Dividends
Yield: 4.0%
Payout: 21.0%
Market value ($ mil.): 7,868

	STOCK PRICE ($) FY Close	P/E High/Low		PER SHARE ($) Earnings	Dividends	Book Value
12/21	24.78	5	4	4.78	1.01	74.23
12/20	23.69	—	—	(3.04)	1.51	85.47
12/19	28.12	11	9	2.39	1.40	89.34
12/18	22.91	19	16	1.37	1.27	82.48
12/17	23.38	24	21	1.03	1.22	97.65
Annual Growth	1.5%			46.8%	(4.7%)	(6.6%)

SwissCom AG

EXECUTIVES
Chief Executive Officer, Urs Schaeppi
Chief Financial Officer, Mario Rossi
Chief Procurement Officer, Klementina Pejic
Non-Executive Chairman, Hansueli Loosli
Non-Executive Deputy Chairman, Frank Esser
Non-Executive Director, Michael Rechsteiner
Non-Executive Director, Anna Mossberg
Non-Executive Director, Sandra Lathion-Zweifel
Non-Executive Director, Renzo Simoni
Non-Executive Director, Barbara Frei
Non-Executive Director, Alain Carrupt
Non-Executive Director, Roland Abt
Auditors : PricewaterhouseCoopers AG

LOCATIONS
HQ: SwissCom AG
Alte Tiefenaustrasse 6, Worblaufen CH-3048
Phone: (41) 58 221 99 11 Fax: (41) 58 221 81 54
Web: www.swisscom.com

HISTORICAL FINANCIALS
Company Type: Public

Income Statement — FYE: December 31

	REVENUE ($mil)	NET INCOME ($mil)	NET PROFIT MARGIN	EMPLOYEES
12/23	13,235	2,045	15.5%	19,729
12/22	12,045	1,736	14.4%	19,157
12/21	12,250	2,006	16.4%	18,905
12/20	12,603	1,737	13.8%	19,062
12/19	11,847	1,729	14.6%	19,317
Annual Growth	2.8%	4.3%	—	0.5%

2023 Year-End Financials
Debt ratio: 27.4%
Return on equity: 15.0%
Cash ($ mil.): 176
Current Ratio: 0.86
Long-term debt ($ mil.): 5,913
No. of shares ($ mil.): 51
Dividends
Yield: —
Payout: 6.6%
Market value ($ mil.): 3,117

	STOCK PRICE ($) FY Close	P/E High/Low		PER SHARE ($) Earnings	Dividends	Book Value
12/23	60.18	2	2	39.48	2.62	268.12
12/22	54.92	2	2	33.53	2.37	233.70
12/21	56.42	2	1	38.75	2.38	228.63
12/20	53.75	2	2	33.54	1.46	208.01
12/19	52.86	2	1	33.39	2.20	177.17
Annual Growth	3.3%	—	—	4.3%	4.5%	10.9%

T&D Holdings Inc

No mystery in a name here: T&D Holdings serves as the holding company for Japanese insurance companies Taiyo Life and Daido Life. Combined, the companies constitute one of Japan's top life insurers. Taiyo Life gears its products to individuals while Daido Life's products are targeted toward small businesses. Another subsidiary, T&D Financial Life, sells whole life policies through financial institutions the likes of banks, securities firms, and insurance shop agents. Other businesses under the T&D umbrella include T&D Asset Management, T&D Customer Services (administrative services), and Pet & Family (pet insurance), and T&D Information Systems (computer processing).

Operations
T&D Holdings' Taiyo Life division, which accounts for 40% of the holding company's annual revenues, serves households with comprehensive life products, including death benefits and medical or nursing care coverage. Meanwhile, the Daido Life unit (another 40% of sales) focuses on the sale of term life insurance and illness policies through business accounts. The third-largest business unit, T&D Financial Life, sells whole life policies.

Geographic Reach
The company operates in Japan.

Sales and Marketing
The operating units of T&D Holdings use targeted sales techniques. With a focus on selling to housewives and middle-aged women, Taiyo Life employs a sales force made up of some 8,600 women (similar in age to their target market base) who visit homes to present tailor-made coverage options. Daido Life gears its marketing efforts towards small and midsized businesses by partnering with enterprise associations (such as the National Federation of Corporate Taxpayers Association); it has some 3,800 in-house sales representatives. The company's T&D Financial Life unit markets through a network of some 120 agencies, including financial institutions.

Financial Performance
In fiscal 2014 (ended March), revenue decreased 14% to Â¥2,085 billion as new policy sales in the Taiyo Life and Daido Life units declined. The decline in new policies primarily reflected the impact of an increase in insurance premiums in 2013. It was partially offset by an increase in revenue from T&D Financial Life.

Net income rose 24% to Â¥78.9 billion in fiscal 2014 as provisions for policy and other reserves declined and operating expenses decreased. Cash flow from operations fell 75% to Â¥159 billion.

Strategy
T&D Holdings is seeking to grow by branching out beyond its traditional market segments. Its Taiyo Life unit is working to expand policy sales by marketing policies geared at men and children. Daido Life is adding products for business owners, such as living protection coverage, while T&D Financial Life is introducing new products for bereaved families and retirees. The group is also seeking to expand its international operations.

T&D Holdings is also growing its operations into the provision of short-term, small-amount policies for pet shops. The company seeks to expand in new and existing business fields through alliances and acquisitions, as well.

In 2014 Daido Life launched a new whole life product, Life Gift, which meets the growing demand for inheritance planning as Japan's population ages.

Company Background
T&D Holdings was formed through the merger of Taiyo Life and Daido Life in 2004. The companies first began working together through an alliance formed in 1999.

EXECUTIVES
President, Representative Director, Hirohisa Uehara
Executive Vice President, Representative Director, Kanaya Morinaka
Senior Managing Executive Officer, Director, Masahiko Moriyama
Senior Managing Executive Officer, Mitsuhiro Nagata
Senior Managing Executive Officer, Yasuro Tamura

Outside Director, Naoki Ohgo
Outside Director, Kensaku Watanabe
Outside Director, Chieko Matsuda
Director, Naoki Saejima
Director, Mutsuro Kitahara
Director, Takashi Ikawa
Director, Takashi Tojo
Outside Director, Seiji Higaki
Outside Director, Shinnosuke Yamada
Outside Director, Atsuko Taishido
Auditors : Ernst & Young ShinNihon LLC

LOCATIONS
HQ: T&D Holdings Inc
2-7-1 Nihonbashi, Chuo-ku, Tokyo 103-6006
Phone: (81) 3 3272 6104 **Fax:** (81) 3 3272 6552
Web: www.td-holdings.co.jp

PRODUCTS/OPERATIONS
2014 Sales
	% of total
Daido Life	40
Taiyo Life	37
T&D Financial Life	20
Other	3
Total	100

Selected Subsidiaries and Affiliates
AIC Private Equity Fund General Partner Ltd
Alternative Investment Capital Ltd.
Daido Life Insurance Company
Daido Management Service Co., Ltd.
Nihon System Shuno Inc.
Pet & Family Small-amount Short-term Insurance Company
T&D Asset Management Cayman Inc.
T&D Asset Management Co., Ltd.
T&D Confirm Ltd.
T&D Customer Services Co., Ltd.
T&D Financial Life Insurance Company
T&D Information System Ltd.
T&D Lease Co., Ltd.
Taiyo Credit Guarantee Co., Ltd.
Taiyo Life Insurance Company
Toyo Insurance Agency Co., Ltd.
Zenkoku Business Center Co., Ltd.

COMPETITORS
CITIZENS, INC.
DAI-ICHI LIFE HOLDINGS, INC.
DAIDO LIFE INSURANCE COMPANY
FUKOKU MUTUAL LIFE INSURANCE COMPANY
MAPFRE, SA
MS&AD INSURANCE GROUP HOLDINGS, INC.
PERSONAL GROUP HOLDINGS PLC
SOMPO HOLDINGS, INC.
STANDARD LIFE ABERDEEN PLC
Sampo Oyj

HISTORICAL FINANCIALS
Company Type: Public

Income Statement FYE: March 31

	ASSETS ($mil)	NET INCOME ($mil)	INCOME AS % OF ASSETS	EMPLOYEES
03/22	146,447	116	0.1%	20,605
03/21	161,457	1,465	0.9%	20,610
03/20	152,189	618	0.4%	20,106
03/19	142,624	657	0.5%	20,576
03/18	143,731	730	0.5%	20,960
Annual Growth	0.5%	(36.8%)	—	(0.4%)

2022 Year-End Financials
Return on assets: —
Return on equity: 0.9%
Long-term debt ($ mil.): —
No. of shares ($ mil.): 562
Sales ($ mil.): 20,869
Dividends
Yield: 3.3%
Payout: 106.7%
Market value ($ mil.): 3,848

	STOCK PRICE ($) FY Close	P/E High/Low	PER SHARE ($) Earnings	Dividends	Book Value
03/22	6.84	0 0	0.20	0.23	20.20
03/21	6.26	0 0	2.45	0.21	23.62
03/20	3.95	0 0	1.00	0.20	17.11
03/19	5.24	0 0	1.05	0.18	17.01
03/18	8.00	0 0	1.15	0.17	17.39
Annual Growth	(3.8%)	—	(35.4%)	8.8%	3.8%

Taisei Corp

EXECUTIVES
Chairman, Director, Takashi Yamauchi
Vice-Chairman, Kazuhiko Dai
President, Representative Director, Yoshiro Aikawa
Executive Vice President, Representative Director, Shigeyoshi Tanaka
Executive Vice President, Representative Director, Shigeyuki Sakurai
Executive Vice President, Representative Director, Norihiko Yaguchi
Senior Managing Executive Officer, Yoshinobu Shigeji
Senior Managing Executive Officer, Jirou Taniyama
Senior Managing Executive Officer, Hiroshi Tsuchiya
Senior Managing Executive Officer, Director, Hiroshi Kimura
Senior Managing Executive Officer, Keiji Hirano
Senior Managing Executive Officer, Director, Atsushi Yamamoto
Senior Managing Executive Officer, Director, Yoshihiro Teramoto
Senior Managing Executive Officer, Takeshi Kagata
Senior Managing Executive Officer, Shun Kitano
Senior Managing Executive Officer, Shimpei Oguchi
Outside Director, Atsuko Nishimura
Outside Director, Takao Murakami
Outside Director, Norio Otsuka
Outside Director, Fumiya Kokubu
Auditors : KPMG AZSA LLC

LOCATIONS
HQ: Taisei Corp
1-25-1 Nishi-Shinjuku, Shinjuku-ku, Tokyo 163-0606
Phone: (81) 3 3348 1111
Web: www.taisei.co.jp

HISTORICAL FINANCIALS
Company Type: Public

Income Statement FYE: March 31

	REVENUE ($mil)	NET INCOME ($mil)	NET PROFIT MARGIN	EMPLOYEES
03/22	12,687	587	4.6%	18,511
03/21	13,367	835	6.3%	18,571
03/20	16,133	1,124	7.0%	18,378
03/19	14,907	1,016	6.8%	18,082
03/18	14,931	1,194	8.0%	17,672
Annual Growth	(4.0%)	(16.3%)		1.2%

2022 Year-End Financials
Debt ratio: 0.1%
Return on equity: 8.3%
Cash ($ mil.): 4,103
Current Ratio: 1.40
Long-term debt ($ mil.): 874
No. of shares ($ mil.): 200
Dividends
Yield: 4.0%
Payout: 0.0%
Market value ($ mil.): 1,450

	STOCK PRICE ($) FY Close	P/E High/Low	PER SHARE ($) Earnings	Dividends	Book Value
03/22	7.23	0 0	2.88	0.29	35.63
03/21	9.90	0 0	4.00	0.31	36.87
03/20	8.06	0 0	5.28	0.31	32.70
03/19	12.00	0 0	4.62	0.31	29.82
03/18	13.00	0 0	5.29	0.26	28.02
Annual Growth	(13.6%)		(14.1%)	2.9%	6.2%

Taiwan Semiconductor Manufacturing Co., Ltd.

Taiwan Semiconductor Manufacturing Co. (TSMC) is the largest dedicated contract semiconductor manufacturer in the world, with roughly 30% market share. The company handles manufacturing for semiconductor and integrated device companies that don't have their own manufacturing facilities. The company offers a comprehensive range of wafer fabrication processes to manufacture complementary metal oxide silicon ("CMOS") logic, mixed-signal, radio frequency, embedded memory, and bipolar complementary metal oxide silicon. Taiwan Semiconductor Manufacturing Co's fabless customers include AMD, Broadcom, NVIDIA, and QUALCOMM. Geographically, TSMC's US customers account for about 70% of revenue.

Operations
Wafer manufacturing makes up more than 85% of sales, with the company's Arizona fabs expected to manufacture over 600,000 wafers per year, when finished.

More than 40% of revenue comes from Smartphone, roughly 40% is from High performance computing, Internet of Things generates nearly 10% of revenue and Digital consumer electronics, Automotive and Others generates about 5% of revenue each.

Geographic Reach

TSMC, headquartered in Hsinchu City, Taiwan, has offices around the world. Customers in the US account for about 70% of the company's revenue, followed by China with approximately 10% of company's revenue, and Taiwan with about 10% of company's revenue.

Most of TSMC's production capacity is in Taiwan, but it also has facilities in the US, Shanghai and Nanjing, China, among others.

Sales and Marketing

TSMC's revenue is tied to its 10 largest customers, who accounts for about 80% of company's net revenue.

TSMC spent NT$2,800 and NT$2,700 for marketing expenses in 2022 and 2021, respectively.

Financial Performance

Note: Growth rates may differ after conversion to US Dollars.

For the past five years, TSMC's performance has experienced an upward trend with a year-over-year increase, ending with 2022 as its highest performing year.

Its net revenue in 2022 increased by NT$676 billion to NT$2.3 trillion, as compared to 2021's revenue of NT$1.6 trillion.

Net income in fiscal year end 2022 increased to NT$1.1 trillion, as compared to the prior year's net income of NT$589.4 billion.

TSMC's cash and equivalents by the end of the year amounted to NT$1.3 trillion. Cash from operations amounted to NT$1.6 trillion. Investing activities and financing activities used NT$1.2 trillion and NT$200.2 billion, respectively. Main cash uses were for refundable deposits and cash dividends.

Strategy

TSMC relies on its competitive advantages that will enable them to prosper from the foundry segment's many attractive growth opportunities. For the five major markets, namely smartphones, high performance computing, the Internet of Things, automotive, and digital consumer electronics, and in response to the fact that the focus of customer demand is shifting from process-technology-centric to product-application-centric, the company has constructed five corresponding technology platforms to provide customers with comprehensive and competitive logic process technologies, specialty technologies, IPs and packaging and testing technologies to shorten customers' time to design and time to market.

Company Background

In 1987, Morris Chang founded Taiwan Semiconductor Manufacturing Company (TSMC) as the world's first dedicated contract semiconductor manufacturer -- the first silicon foundry. TSMC became profitable and throughout the 1990s, it continued to be among industry leaders both in production capacity and in deployment of cutting-edge technology.

HISTORY

The big foundries -- including TSMC's Taiwanese archrival United Microelectronics Corporation (UMC) -- played a major role in the growth of the worldwide fabless semiconductor industry in the 21st century. Foundries aim to save clients the costs and time associated with building expensive wafer fabrication plants (fabs) of their own. Their services are especially vital for fabless companies whose entire business model is predicated on outsourcing all manufacturing.

Morris Chang learned early to adapt to rapid change. The future founder and chairman of Taiwan Semiconductor Manufacturing Company (TSMC) lived in six cities before age 18, as his family fled the ravages of the Sino-Japanese War and WWII in China. Chang immigrated to the US to attend MIT and Stanford, where he ultimately earned a Ph.D. in electrical engineering.

In 25 years at Texas Instruments (TI), Chang worked his way up from the ranks of technical management into the executive suite. In 1983 he resigned from TI to become CEO of General Instrument, but in 1985 the Taiwanese government recruited him to head its Industrial Technology Research Institute (ITRI). He remained chairman of ITRI from 1988 to 1994.

Working from his position at ITRI, Chang became chairman of contract electronics manufacturer United Microelectronics Corporation (UMC) in 1987. Also that year he founded TSMC as the world's first dedicated contract semiconductor manufacturer -- the first silicon foundry. Chang's pioneering role in the foundry industry has earned him many accolades, including the first-ever Robert N. Noyce Medal of the Institute of Electrical and Electronics Engineers and the first-ever Exemplary Leadership award (subsequently named in his honor) of the Fabless Semiconductor Association (now the Global Semiconductor Alliance). Known for his analytical mind, Chang was once ranked among the top 1,000 players of contract bridge in the world.

TSMC became profitable within 15 months of its founding. Throughout the 1990s it continued to be among industry leaders both in production capacity and in deployment of cutting-edge technology.

EXECUTIVES

Business Development Chief Executive Officer, Vice-Chairman, C.C. Wei

Finance Chief Financial Officer, Finance Vice President, Wendell Huang

Corporate Information Technology Chief Information Officer, Corporate Information Technology Vice President, Chris Horng-Dar Lin

Europe & Asia Sales Senior Vice President, Human Resources Senior Vice President, Lora Ho

Research & Development Senior Vice President, Wei-Jen Lo

Corporate Strategy Office Senior Vice President, TSMC North America Senior Vice President, Rick Cassidy

Operations/Product Development Senior Vice President, Operations Senior Vice President, Y.P. Chin

Research & Development Second Vice Chairman, Technology Development Second Vice Chairman, Y.J. Mii

Information Technology and Materials Management & Risk Management Senior Vice President, J.K. Lin

Research & Development Senior Vice President, Europe & Asia Sales Senior Vice President, Cliff Hou

Operations/ Facility Vice President, Operations/ Fabs Facility Vice President, Arthur Chuang

Research & Development/ Integrated Interconnect & Packaging Vice President, K.C. Hsu

Research & Development/ Digital IPs Solution & TSMC Fellow Vice President, Research & Development/ Design & Technology Platform & TSMC Fellow Vice President, L.C. Lu

Legal Vice President, Legal General Counsel, Legal Corporate Governance Officer, Sylvia Fang

Research & Development Vice President, Operations Vice President, Y. L. Wang

Research & Development/ Integrated Interconnect & Packaging Vice President, Doug Yu

Business Development Vice President, Research & Development Vice President, Business Development Vice President (frmr), Research & Development Vice President (frmr), Kevin Zhang

Product Development Vice President, Operations Vice President, T.S. Chang

Research & Development Vice President, Technology Development/ Pathfinding Vice President, Min Cao

Research & Development/ Advanced Tool and Module Development Vice President, Simon Jang

Fab Operations Vice President, Fab Operations II Vice President, Operations/ Fab Operations II Vice President, Y.H. Liaw

Research & Development/ Platform Development Vice President, Michael Wu

Quality and Reliability Vice President, Jun He

Research & Development/ More than Moore Technologies Vice President, C.S. Yoo

Research & Development/ Platform Development Vice President, Geoffrey Yeap

Chairman, Mark Liu

Independent Director, Peter Leahy Bonfield

Independent Director, Kok-Choo Chen

Independent Director, Michael R. Splinter

Independent Director, Yancey Hai

Independent Director, Moshe N. Gavrielov

Independent Director, L. Rafael Reif

Director, Ming-Hsin Kung

Director: F.C. Tseng
Auditors: Deloitte & Touche

LOCATIONS
HQ: Taiwan Semiconductor Manufacturing Co., Ltd.
No. 8, Li-Hsin Road 6, Hsinchu Science Park, Hsinchu 300-096
Phone: (886) 3 563 6688   **Fax:** (886) 3 563 7000
Web: www.tsmc.com

2017 Sales by Geography

	% of total
United States	64
Asia	20
Taiwan	9
Europe, the Middle East and Africa	7
Total	100

2017 Sales by Region

	% of total
North America	64
China	12
Asia/Pacific	11
Europe, Middle East, and Africa	7
Japan	6
Total	100

PRODUCTS/OPERATIONS

2017 Sales

	% of total
Wafer	89
Others	11
Total	100

2017 Sales

	% of total
Fabless semiconductor companies/systems companies	80
Integrated device manufacturers	20
Total	100

2017 Sales

	% of total
Communication	59
Industrial/Standard	23
Computer	10
Consumer	8
Total	100

COMPETITORS

AMKOR TECHNOLOGY, INC.
APPLIED MATERIALS, INC.
ASM International N.V.
AXCELIS TECHNOLOGIES, INC.
ELECTRO SCIENTIFIC INDUSTRIES, INC.
INTEGRATED SILICON SOLUTION, INC.
LAM RESEARCH CORPORATION
LATTICE SEMICONDUCTOR CORPORATION
NATIONAL SEMICONDUCTOR CORPORATION
PHOTRONICS, INC.

HISTORICAL FINANCIALS
Company Type: Public

Income Statement   FYE: December 31

	REVENUE ($mil)	NET INCOME ($mil)	NET PROFIT MARGIN	EMPLOYEES
12/23	70,608	27,387	38.8%	0
12/22	73,885	33,176	44.9%	73,090
12/21	57,331	21,544	37.6%	65,152
12/20	47,656	18,428	38.7%	56,831
12/19	35,739	11,822	33.1%	51,297
Annual Growth	18.6%	23.4%	—	—

2023 Year-End Financials
Debt ratio: 0.5%   No. of shares ($ mil.): 25,932
Return on equity: 26.1%   Dividends
Cash ($ mil.): 47,864   Yield: —
Current Ratio: 2.40   Payout: 139.8%
Long-term debt ($ mil.): 29,993   Market value ($ mil.): 2,696,935

	STOCK PRICE ($) FY Close	P/E High/Low		PER SHARE ($) Earnings	Dividends	Book Value
12/23	104.00	3	2	1.06	1.48	4.36
12/22	74.49	3	2	1.28	1.41	3.71
12/21	120.31	6	5	0.83	1.48	3.02
12/20	109.04	5	2	0.71	1.36	2.54
12/19	58.10	4	3	0.46	1.60	2.08
Annual Growth	15.7%	—	—	23.4%	(2.0%)	20.3%

Takeda Pharmaceutical Co Ltd

The work of Takeda Pharmaceutical Company started way back in 1781, when its predecessor began selling traditional Japanese and Chinese remedies. Takeda is a global, values-based, research and development (R&D) driven biopharmaceutical company, which operates in approximately 80 countries and regions across the world. Top-selling products include ulcerative colitis drug Entyvio, stimulant medication for ADHD Vyanse, and Advate, a treatment for hemophilia A. Its largest market is the US, which brings in about 50% of revenue.

Operations
Product sales contribute more than 90% of Takeda's total revenue. The company also makes money on out-licensing and service.

The company is focused on four therapeutic areas: oncology, rare genetics and hematology, neuroscience, and gastroenterology (GI). The company also makes targeted R&D investments in plasma-derived therapies (PDT) and vaccines.

Gastroenterology provides about 25% of the company's total revenue. Rare disease accounts for about 20% of total revenue. PDT immunology, oncology and neuroscience account for about 15% each.

Geographic Reach
Headquartered in Japan, Takeda also has major regional locations in Austria, Japan, Ireland, Italy, Germany, Singapore, Switzerland, and the US.

The company's network span in more than 80 countries and regions in the Asia Pacific, the Americas, Europe, and Africa. The US is Takeda's largest market, bringing in nearly 50% of revenue, followed by Europe and Canada with about 20% of revenue. Japan accounts for nearly 20%, Asia and Latin America generate about 5% each, and Russia/CIS and other provide the remaining.

Sales and Marketing
Takeda sells its products to retail customers, government agencies, wholesalers, health insurance companies and managed healthcare organizations.

Financial Performance
The company's revenue for fiscal 2022 increased by 12% to JPY 3.6 trillion compared from the prior year with JPY 3.2 trillion.

Profit for fiscal 2022 decreased to JPY 230.2 billion compared from the prior year with JPY 376.2 billion.

Cash held by the company at the end of fiscal 2022 decreased to JPY 849.7 billion. Cash provided by operations was JPY 1.1 billion while cash used for investing and financing activities were JPY 198.1 billion and JPY 1.1 trillion.

Strategy
The company may also acquire new businesses to expand its R&D capabilities (including expanding into new methodologies) and to acquire new products (whether in the development pipeline or at the marketing stage) or enter other strategic regions. Similarly, the company divests from businesses and product lines to maintain its focus on key growth drivers and to manage its portfolio.

Mergers and Acquisitions
In 2022, Takeda announced the exercise of its option to acquire Adaptate Biotherapeutics (Adaptate), a UK company focused on developing antibody-based therapeutics for the modulation of variable delta 1 (Vd1) gamma delta (?d) T cells. Through the acquisition, Takeda will obtain Adaptate's antibody-based ?d T cell engager platform, including pre-clinical candidate and discovery pipeline programs. Adaptate's ?d T cell engagers are designed to specifically modulate ?d T cell-mediated immune responses at tumor sites while sparing damage to healthy cells.

In late 2021, Takeda announced to acquire GammaDelta Therapeutics Limited (GammaDelta), a company focused on exploiting the unique properties of gamma delta (?d) T cells for immunotherapy. The acquisition expands Takeda's immuno-oncology and innate immune cell therapy portfolio with novel platforms leveraging ?dT cells for the potential treatment of solid tumors and hematological malignancies. In addition to early-stage cell therapy programs, Takeda will obtain GammaDelta's allogeneic variable delta 1 (Vd1) gamma-delta (?d) T cell therapy platforms, which includes both blood-derived and tissue-derived platforms.

In early 2021, Takeda announced to acquire Maverick Therapeutics, a private biopharmaceutical company pioneering conditionally active bispecific T-cell targeted immunotherapies for up to approximately $525 million in upfront and potential milestone payments subject to certain adjustments. Under the agreement, Takeda will obtain Maverick's T-cell engager COBRA platform and a broad development portfolio, including Maverick's lead development candidate TAK-186 (MVC-101) currently in a Phase 1/2 study for the treatment of EGFR-expressing solid tumors, and TAK-280 (MVC-280), which is anticipated to enter the clinic in the second half of Takeda's fiscal year 2021 for the treatment of patients with B7H3-expressing solid tumors.

Company Background

In 1787 Chobei Takeda I started a business selling tradition Japanese and Chinese herbal medicines in Osaka, Japan. In the 1860s, with his great-grandson at the helm, the business started importing western medicines. The company entered the manufacturing business in 1895 and, in 1914, it established a research division so that it could develop its own products.

The company was incorporated as Chobei Takeda & Co. in 1925, transitioning from an individually owned business to a corporate organization. Chobei Takeda was renamed Takeda Pharmaceutical in 1943. It went public in 1949. In the 1960s Takeda began operating in other Asian markets. It entered the US and European markets in the 1990s.

EXECUTIVES

President, Chief Executive Officer, Representative Director, Christophe Weber
Chief Financial Officer, Director, Constantine Saroukos
Chair of Board Meeting, Outside Director, Masami Iijima
Representative Director, Masato Iwasaki
Director, Andrew Plump
Outside Director, Oliver Bohuon
Outside Director, Jean-Luc D. Butel
Outside Director, Ian Clark
Outside Director, Steven Gillis
Outside Director, John M. Maraganore
Outside Director, Michel Orsinger
Outside Director, Koji Hatsukawa
Outside Director, Yoshiaki Fujimori
Outside Director, Emiko Higashi
Outside Director, Kimberly A. Reed
Auditors : KPMG AZSA LLC

LOCATIONS

HQ: Takeda Pharmaceutical Co Ltd
  1-1, Nihonbashi-Honcho 2-Chome, Chuo-ku, Tokyo 103-8668
Phone: (81) 3 3278 2111   **Fax:** (81) 3 3278 2000
Web: www.takeda.co.jp

2018 Sales

	% of total
US	34
Japan	33
Europe & Canada	18
Latin America	6
Russia/CIS	4
Asia (excluding Japan) & other	4
Other	2
Total	100

PRODUCTS/OPERATIONS

Selected Products

Prescription drugs
  Actos (type 2 diabetes)
  Adecut (high blood pressure)
  Amasulin (anti-infective)
  Blopress (high blood pressure)
  Bronica (asthma)
  Ceuleuk (angiosarcoma)
  Dexilant (acid reflux)
  Eurodin (central nervous system)
  Lupron Depot (prostate cancer, endometriosis)
  Osten (osteoporosis)
  Pansporin (anti-infective)
  Prevacid (peptic ulcers)
  Rozerem (insomnia)
  Takesulin (anti-infective)
  Uloric (gout)
  Velcade (multiple myeloma)
Consumer health care
  Alinamin (vitamins)
  Benza (cold remedy)
  Scorba (athlete's foot)

Selected Subsidiaries

Amato Pharmaceutical Products, Ltd. (30%)
Millennium Pharmaceuticals, Inc. (US)
Nihon Pharmaceutical Co., Ltd. (88%)
Laboratoires Takeda (France)
Takeda America Holdings, Inc. (US)
Takeda Europe Holdings B.V. (Netherlands)
Takeda Cambridge Limited (UK)
Takeda Healthcare Products Co., Ltd.
Takeda Italia Farmacetici S.p.A. (77%)
Takeda Pharma AG (Switzerland)
Takeda Pharma GmbH (Germany)
Takeda Pharma Ireland Limited
Takeda Pharmaceuticals Europe Limited (UK)
Takeda Pharmaceuticals North America, Inc. (US)
Takeda Research Investment, Inc. (US)
Takeda San Diego, Inc. (US)
Takeda San Francisco, Inc. (US)
Takeda Singapore Pte Limited
Takeda (Thailand), Ltd. (48%)
Tianjin Takeda Pharmaceuticals Co., Ltd. (75%, China)

COMPETITORS

ALLERGAN LIMITED
BIOVERATIV INC.
BRISTOL-MYERS SQUIBB COMPANY
Bausch Health Companies Inc
CUBIST PHARMACEUTICALS LLC
ENDO HEALTH SOLUTIONS INC.
LIGAND PHARMACEUTICALS INCORPORATED
MERCK KG auf Aktien
SANOFI
TEVA PHARMACEUTICAL INDUSTRIES LIMITED

HISTORICAL FINANCIALS

Company Type: Public

Income Statement — FYE: March 31

	REVENUE ($mil)	NET INCOME ($mil)	NET PROFIT MARGIN	EMPLOYEES
03/22	29,341	1,891	6.4%	47,347
03/21	28,880	3,395	11.8%	47,099
03/20	30,319	407	1.3%	47,495
03/19	18,937	985	5.2%	49,578
03/18	16,673	1,759	10.6%	27,230
Annual Growth	15.2%	1.8%	—	14.8%

2022 Year-End Financials

Debt ratio: 0.3% No. of shares ($ mil.): 1,559
Return on equity: 4.2% Dividends
Cash ($ mil.): 6,985   Yield: 5.6%
Current Ratio: 1.21   Payout: 61.6%
Long-term debt ($ mil.): 34,047 Market value ($ mil.): 22,334

	STOCK PRICE ($) FY Close	P/E High/Low		PER SHARE ($) Earnings	Dividends	Book Value
03/22	14.32	0	0	1.20	0.80	29.96
03/21	18.26	0	0	2.16	0.85	29.64
03/20	15.18	1	0	0.26	0.83	27.61
03/19	20.37	0	0	1.02	0.81	29.77
03/18	24.41	0	0	2.24	0.86	23.68
Annual Growth	(12.5%)	—	—	(14.4%)	(1.5%)	6.1%

Tata Motors Ltd

Tata Motors is a company that operates in the automotive segment. The company produces passenger cars, including popular models such as Jaguar, Land Rover, Safari, and Sumo, and commercial vehicles, such as buses, trucks, tractor-trailers, light commercial vehicles, and defense and construction equipment. Furthermore, Tata Motors has OEMs offering an extensive range of integrated, smart and e-mobility solutions. Tata Motors sells its vehicles through an extensive dealer network in India and exports vehicles to countries in Africa, Asia, Europe, the Middle East, and South America. In addition, the company distributes Fiat-brand cars in India through its joint venture with Fiat. Tata Motors rolled out its first commercial truck in 1945. Its vehicles can now be found on the roads in more than 125 countries. The company generates majority of sales from international markets.

Operations

Tata Motors divides its operations through its business segments, commercial vehicles, passenger vehicles, electric vehicles, Jaguar land rover, and Tata Motors finance.

The company's commercial vehicle segment enables the company to be India's largest CV manufacturers with the widest product and service portfolio catering across cargo and passenger mobility segments. The passenger vehicle segment offerings include various body styles, powertrain options of Petrol, Diesel, and CNG.

The electric vehicles segment enables the company as the largest player in India's electric vehicle space with an 84% VAHAN market share and about 3,800 operational charging stations to date. Tata Motors' Jaguar Land Rover segment offers premium vehicles and exceptional driving experiences, with a significant investment in electric vehicles.

Geographic Reach

Tata Motors Limited operates across 125 countries, with majority of its operations in India, accounting for about 40% of the company's revenue. The company has operations in North America, the UK, India, and China.

Sales and Marketing

In 2022, the company scaled up their market coverage to reach 165 cities and tied up with 250 dealerships in fiscal year 2022 to

2023 increased presence across the country that will greatly increase the accessibility of its products.

Financial Performance

Tata Motors' performance for the past five years has fluctuated from year-to-year, with an overall increase, ending with 2023 as its highest performing year over the period.

The company's revenue increased by Crore67,513 to Crore345,966 for 2023, as compared to 2022's revenue of Crore278,453.

The company held Crore31,887 at the end of the year. Operating activities provided Crore35,388 to the coffers. Investing activities and financing activities used Crore16,804 and Crore26,243, respectively. Main cash uses were for payment for assets and net of issue expenses.

Strategy

Tata Motors has a unique advantage of having strong SUV portfolio, all powertrains - Petrol, Diesel, CNG?options and Leadership in the EV Space. SUVs will continue to garner larger share of the market owing to evolved consumer preference towards SUV. Post the BSVI Phase 2, most manufacturers have exited the diesel market, however, large set of customers are still looking to purchase diesel vehicles owing to its performance. CNG market is set to increase due to government's push and benefit of lower operating cost. In addition, EVs will gain traction with increasing acceptance and launch of new models. Thus, Tata Motors has an advantage to uniquely cater to the customer requirement to drive demand. The advantage is being further strengthened with launch of 'New Forever' interventions with innovative technologies.

Company Background

Tata Motors is part of the Tata Group, which was founded in 1868 by Jamsetji Tata. Tata Motors began manufacturing locomotives and other engineering products in 1945 and rolled out its first commercial truck?the TMB 312?in 1954. Tata Motors' 1210 series of vehicles began production in 1964 and in 1975, the company began producing the Tata 1210 semi-forward model.

In 1983, the company started making heavy commercial vehicles and in 2005, it launched its first fully built buses and coaches called GLOBUS and STARBUS brands. The popular Tata Nano mini car and Jaguar Land Rover were both introduced in 2009. In 2014, the company started making defense vehicles, the first being the Armoured Personnel Carrier (APC). Its first electric vehicle, the Tata Tigor, was launched in 2017.

EXECUTIVES

Chief Executive Officer, Managing Director, Guenter Butschek
Chief Financial Officer, Pathamadai Balachandran Balaji
Non-Executive Chairman, N. Chandrasekaran
Independent Director, Om Prakash Bhatt
Independent Director, Hanne Birgitte Breinbjerg Sorensen
Independent Director, Vedika Bhandarkar
Independent Director, Kosaraju Veerayya Chowdary
Non-Independent Non-Executive Director, Mitsuhiko Yamashita
Non-Executive Director, Thierry Bollore
Auditors : KPMG Assurance and Consulting Services LLP

LOCATIONS

HQ: Tata Motors Ltd
Bombay House, 24, Homi Mody Street, Mumbai, Maharashtra 400 001
Phone: (91) 22 6665 8282   Fax: (91) 22 6665 7790
Web: www.tatamotors.com

2018 Sales

	% of total
India	20
UK	17
Rest of Europe	16
United States	15
China	15
Rest of the World	17
Total	100

PRODUCTS/OPERATIONS

2018 Sales

	% of total
Jaguar Land Rover Vehicles	76
Tata and Flat Vehicles	20
Tata Daewoo Commercial Vehicles	2
Financial Revenues	1
Others	1
Total	100

Selected Products and Services

Cars and Sport Utility Vehicles
    Hatchbacks
    Sedans
    Sport Utility Vehicles
Defence
    Logistic
    Troop Carriers
    Water Tankers
    Tippers
    Load Carriers
    Prison Vans
    Fire tenders
    Aid & Development Vehicles
    Ambulances
    Buses
    Recovery Trucks
    Refrigerated Trucks
    Utility Trucks/Troop Carriers
    Armored Trucks
    Combat Vehicles
    Combat Support Vehicles
Trucks and Buses
    Trucks and Buses
    Municipal Solutions

Selected Subsidiaries

Concorde Motors (India) Limited
Jaguar Land Rover PLC-UK
PT Tata Indonesia
Sheba Properties Ltd-India
TAL Manufacturing Solutions Ltd-India
Tata Daewoo Commercial Vehicle Co Ltd- South Korea
Tata Hispano Motors Carrocera SA- Spain
Tata Marcopolo Motors Ltd-India.
Tata Motors (SA) Proprietary Ltd -South Africa.
Tata Motors European Technical center PLC -UK
Tata Motors Finance Ltd -India
Tata Motors Insurance Broking and Advisory Services Ltd-India
Tata Motors(Thailand) Ltd
Tata Precision Industries Pts Ltd-Singapore
Tata Technologies Ltd-India
TML Distribution Company Ltd-India
TML Drivelines Ltd-India
TML Holdings Pte Ltd- Singapore

COMPETITORS

AB Volvo
Bayerische Motoren Werke AG
China Faw Group Co., Ltd.
DAIMLER TRUCKS NORTH AMERICA LLC
Dongfeng Motor Group Co., Ltd
GENERAL MOTORS COMPANY
MAHINDRA AND MAHINDRA LIMITED
NISSAN MOTOR CO.,LTD.
PACCAR INC
VOLKSWAGEN AG

HISTORICAL FINANCIALS

Company Type: Public

Income Statement   FYE: March 31

	REVENUE ($mil)	NET INCOME ($mil)	NET PROFIT MARGIN	EMPLOYEES
03/22	36,512	(1,501)	—	73,608
03/21	33,917	(1,950)	—	75,278
03/20	34,345	(1,508)	—	78,906
03/19	43,264	(4,236)	—	82,797
03/18	44,311	1,024	2.3%	81,090
Annual Growth	(4.7%)			(2.4%)

2022 Year-End Financials

Debt ratio: 0.6%   No. of shares ($ mil.): 3,829
Return on equity: (-25.2%)   Dividends
Cash ($ mil.): 5,306   Yield: —
Current Ratio: 0.98   Payout: 0.0%
Long-term debt ($ mil.): 12,904   Market value ($ mil.): 107,025

	STOCK PRICE ($) FY Close	P/E High/Low	PER SHARE ($) Earnings	Dividends	Book Value
03/22	27.95	—	(0.39)	0.00	1.37
03/21	20.79	—	(0.54)	0.00	1.80
03/20	4.72	—	(0.44)	0.00	2.17
03/19	12.56	—	(1.25)	0.00	2.35
03/18	25.70	2 1	0.30	0.00	4.11
Annual Growth	2.1%				(24.0%)

Tata Steel Ltd

Tata Steel is one of the most geographically diversified steel producers around the world. The company's steelmaking and finishing facilities have the capacity to produce approximately 35 million tons of crude steel a year. Tata Steel's products include hot and cold rolled coils and sheets, tubes, wire rods, rings and bearings. Its domestic facilities are located in Jamshedpur in eastern India, and Tata Steel's international operations include UK-based subsidiary Tata Steel Europe, and Tata Steel Thailand. The company also owns interests in coal and iron projects that supply the steelmaker with raw materials. Tata Steel was established in in 1907.

Operations

The Indian product portfolio is divided into four segments ? Automotive and Special

Products; Industrial Products, Projects and Exports; Branded Products and Retail; and Services and Solutions. The Company supplies hot-rolled, cold-rolled, galvanized, branded solution offerings and more.

Tata Steel is one of the largest steel producers in Europe with a crude steel production capacity of over 12.4 MnTPA. The company established its presence in the European continent after acquiring Corus in 2007. The European operations produce a wide range of high-quality quality strip steel products for demanding markets such as construction, automotive, packaging and engineering.

Tata Steel's operations in Southeast Asia, with 2.2 MnTPA capacity, began in 2004 with the acquisition of NatSteel, Singapore. The operations are run by NatSteel Holdings Pte Ltd., a wholly-owned subsidiary of Tata Steel. The Company's flagship facility in Singapore is one of the largest single downstream rebar fabrication operations in the world. This plant is the only local steel mill with an integrated upstream and downstream operation, where steel is manufactured through recycling scrap, and fabricated according to customers' needs.

Geographic Reach

Headquartered in India; the company has manufacturing facilities in Jamshedpur, Netherlands and the United Kingdom, with downstream operations in the Netherlands, the United Kingdom, Germany, France, Belgium, Sweden, and Turkey. The company has a pan-Thailand distribution network and regularly exports steel to Laos, Cambodia, Indonesia, Malaysia, India, and Bangladesh.

Sales and Marketing

Tata Steel serves a wide array of industries such as automotive & ancillaries, construction retail, construction & infrastructure, downstream, packaging, engineering goods, trade & commercial, and energy.

Financial Performance

Tata Steel's revenue for fiscal 2022 decreased to INR2.43 trillion compared to the prior year with INR2.44 trillion. The slight decrease was primarily due to higher eliminations & adjustments offsetting the increase in some of its segments.

Net income for fiscal 2022 decreased to INR210.2 billion compared to the prior year with INR440.9 billion. The decrease was primarily due to higher expenditures accompanied by slightly lower revenues.

Cash held by the company at the end of fiscal 2022 decreased to INR8.6 billion. Cash provided by operations was INR142.2 billion while cash used for investing and financing activities were INR110.6 billion and INR49.8 billion, respectively. Main uses of cash were the purchase of capital assets; and repayments of short-term borrowings.

Strategy

At Tata Steel, the company aspires to be future-ready structurally, financially and culturally, in its pursuit to be the most valuable and respected steel company in the world. Following are the strategic objectives that Tata Steel aims to achieve across geographies: leadership in India; consolidate position as global cost leader; attain leadership position in adjacent businesses; and leadership in sustainability.

Company Background

Tata Steel was founded in 1907 as Asia's first private sector integrated steel company.

EXECUTIVES

Chief Executive Officer, Managing Director, Executive Director, T. V. Narendran
Chief Financial Officer, Executive Director, Koushik Chatterjee
Chief Legal Officer, Secretary, Parvatheesam Kanchinadham
Chairman, Ratan N. Tata
Non-Executive Chairman, Natarajan Chandrasekaran
Independent Director, Aman Mehta
Independent Director, O. P. Bhatt
Independent Director, Peter Blauwhoff
Independent Director, Mallika Srinivasan
Independent Director, Deepak Kapoor
Non-Executive Director, V. K. Sharma
Non-Executive Director, Saurabh Mahesh Agrawal
Auditors : Price Waterhouse & Co Chartered Accountants LLP

LOCATIONS

HQ: Tata Steel Ltd
 Bombay House, 24, Homi Mody Street, Fort, Mumbai 400 001
 Phone: (91) 22 6665 8282   Fax: (91) 22 6665 7724
 Web: www.tatasteel.com

2016 Sales

	% of total
Outside India	68
Within India	32
Total	100

PRODUCTS/OPERATIONS

2016 Sales

	% of total
Steel	91
Others	9
Total	100

Selected Operations

Steel
Ferroalloys & Minerals (chrome mines & manufacturing ferro chrome & ferro manganese)
Bearings (ball bearings, clutch release bearings & double row self-aligning bearings)
Tubes
Wire

COMPETITORS

AK STEEL HOLDING CORPORATION
ArcelorMittal
BLUESCOPE STEEL LIMITED
Gerdau S/A
JFE HOLDINGS, INC.
KOBE STEEL, LTD.
NIPPON STEEL CORPORATION
NIPPON STEEL NISSHIN CO., LTD.
TATA STEEL EUROPE LIMITED

UNITED STATES STEEL CORPORATION

HISTORICAL FINANCIALS
Company Type: Public

Income Statement   FYE: March 31

	REVENUE ($mil)	NET INCOME ($mil)	NET PROFIT MARGIN	EMPLOYEES
03/22	32,206	5,300	16.5%	72,551
03/21	21,361	1,023	4.8%	73,962
03/20	18,510	206	1.1%	70,212
03/19	22,786	1,476	6.5%	75,294
03/18	20,444	2,064	10.1%	65,144
Annual Growth	12.0%	26.6%	—	2.7%

2022 Year-End Financials
Debt ratio: 0.3%   No. of shares ($ mil.): 1,221
Return on equity: 42.5%   Dividends
Cash ($ mil.): 2,098   Yield: —
Current Ratio: 1.02   Payout: 6.1%
Long-term debt ($ mil.): 5,909   Market value ($ mil.): —

TC Energy Corp

TC Energy Corporation (formerly TransCanada) is a vital part of everyday life ? delivering the energy millions of people rely on to power their lives in a sustainable way. It owns about 54,750 miles of natural gas pipeline; connects growing supply in the most prolific basins on the continent to key markets. TC Energy has some 535 billion cu. ft. of natural gas storage assets. On the power side of its business portfolio it owns, operates, or controls seven power plants in Canada and the US, with about 4,260 MW of power generation capacity. About 45% of TC Energy's revenue comes from outside of Canada.

Operations

TC Energy operates in five business segments: US Natural Gas Pipelines, Canadian Natural Gas Pipelines, Liquids Pipelines, Mexico Natural Gas Pipelines, and Power and Storage. These segments offer different products and services, including certain natural gas, crude oil and electricity marketing and storage services. The company also has a Corporate segment, consisting of corporate and administrative functions that provide governance, financing and other support to the company's business segments.

The US Natural Gas Pipelines segment accounts for about 40% of total revenue, primarily consists of the company's investments in around 50,210 km (about 31,200 miles) of regulated natural gas pipelines, some 535 Bcf of regulated natural gas storage facilities and other assets.

The Canadian Natural Gas Pipelines segment (about 35% of total revenue) primarily consists of the company's investments in some 40,580 km (around 25,215 miles) of regulated natural gas pipelines currently in operation.

Over 15% of total revenue, the Liquids Pipelines segment primarily consists of the company's investments in around 4,855 km (about 3,020 miles) of crude oil pipeline systems which connect Alberta and US crude oil supplies to US refining markets in Illinois, Oklahoma and Texas.

The Mexico Natural Gas Pipelines segment (some 5%) primarily consists of the company's investments in about 2,505 km (about 1,555 miles) of regulated natural gas pipelines.

The Power and Storage segment (around 5%) primarily consists of the company's investments in seven power generation facilities and 118 Bcf of non-regulated natural gas storage facilities. These assets are located in Alberta, Ontario, QuÃ©bec and New Brunswick.

Overall, about 85% of sales were generated from capacity arrangements and transportation, around 10% from natural gas storage and other, and power generation and other with some 5% combined.

Geographic Reach

Headquartered in Canada, TC Energy's operations in the US is the largest markets in terms of revenue which accounts for over 50%, followed by Canada that contributes about 45%, and the remaining 5% revenue comes from Mexico.

The company has four natural gas-fired cogeneration facilities in Alberta, and seven power generation facilities ? enough to power more than 4 million homes.

Sales and Marketing

TC Energy's liquids business provides customers with a variety of crude oil marketing services including transportation, storage, and crude oil management, primarily through the purchase and sale of physical crude oil. Its natural gas pipeline network transports natural gas from supply basins to local distribution companies, power generation plants, industrial facilities, interconnecting pipelines, LNG export terminals and other businesses.

Financial Performance

The company's revenue has been fluctuating in the last five years. Net income was consistently rising until it dropped in 2021 for an overall decrease of 38% between 2017 and 2021.

The company's revenue totaled C$13.4 billion, a 3% increase from the previous year's revenue of C$13 billion. This was primarily due to a higher volume of sales in the company's US natural gas pipelines.

Net income for 2021 totaled C$2 billion, a 58% decrease from the previous year's net income of C$4.6 billion. This was primarily due to a higher volume of plant operating costs.

The company's cash at the end of 2021 was C$673 million. Operating activities generated C$6.9 billion, while investing activities used C$7.7 billion, mainly for capital expenditures. Financing activities used another C$88 million, mainly for long-term debts.

Strategy

The company's business consists of natural gas and crude oil transportation, storage and delivery systems in addition to power generation assets that produce electricity. These long-life infrastructure assets cover strategic North American corridors and are supported by long-term commercial arrangements and/or rate regulation, generating predictable and sustainable cash flows and earnings, the cornerstones of its low-risk business model. Its long-term strategy is driven by several key beliefs:

Natural gas will continue to play a pivotal role in North America's energy future; crude oil will remain an important part of the fuel mix; the need for renewables along with reliable, on-demand energy sources to support grid stability will grow significantly; as well as the value of existing infrastructure assets will become more valuable given the challenges to develop new greenfield, linear-energy infrastructure, in particular, pipelines.

Mergers and Acquisitions

In early 2021, TC Energy completed the previously announced merger pursuant to an agreement dated December 14, 2020. The merger resulted in TC Energy acquiring all of the outstanding publicly-held common units of TCP and TCP becoming an indirect, wholly owned subsidiary of TC Energy. The exchange ratio reflects a value for all the publicly-held common units of TCP of approximately US$1.68 billion, or 38 million TC Energy common shares based on the closing price of TC Energy's common shares on the New York Stock Exchange.

HISTORY

TransCanada had become financially overextended by branching into a range of energy businesses. It sold its gas marketing business to US energy marketer Mirant (now GenOn Energy) and divested its operations in Latin America. In the past few years the company has been growing its power business. In 2003 it acquired 33% of nuclear plant operator Bruce Power for C$376 million. It also has been building a 550 MW natural gas-fired cogeneration plant in Quebec. However, the group sold a power generation subsidiary, TransCanada Power, to EPCOR Utilities in 2005. The subsidiary operated 11 power generation plants in Canada and the US. That sale enabled TransCanada to focus on its larger, directly owned power businesses in Canada and the US.

Also sold was the company's general partner interest in ONEOK Partners, a subsidiary of ONEOK.

The company expanded its transportation and generation operations by acquiring Gas Transmission Northwest from bankrupt National Energy & Gas Transmission (NEGT) for $1.7 billion in 2004. It also acquired the hydroelectric generation assets of USGen New England, a NEGT subsidiary, in 2005.

The company became the operator of Northern Border Pipeline in early 2007. Northern Border Pipeline owns a 1,249-mile interstate pipeline system that transports gas from the Montana-Saskatchewan border to the upper Midwest region of the US. In a major move that expanded its US operations, in 2007 it acquired ANR Pipeline, its storage assets in Michigan, and control of Great Lakes Gas Transmission from El Paso Corporation for just over $4 billion (including assumed debt).

In 2008 the company was selected as the lead bidder for the proposed $26 billion Alaska Pipeline Project, which will link North Slope gas fields to end users across Canada and in the lower 48 states. In 2009 the company signed up Exxon Mobil to work with it in developing the project.

Pursuing an expansion strategy on the power side of the ledger, in 2008 TransCanada acquired the 2,480 MW Ravenswood Generating Station in New York City from National Grid for $2.9 billion. In 2009 the company announced plans to build a $1.2 billion power plant in Southern Ontario, due to begin producing power by the end of 2013. This segment is also developing wind farms as a green energy option.

To raise cash to pay down debt, in 2011 the company sold 25% of Gas Transmission Northwest and Bison Pipeline to subsidiary TC Pipelines for $605 million.

Expanding its pipeline business, in 2012 the company signed a deal with Phoenix Energy Holdings Limited to develop the $3 billion Grand Rapids (oil) Pipeline project in Northern Alberta. It also agreed to acquire BP's 40% stake in the Crossfield Gas Storage facility and BP's interest in CrossAlta Gas Storage & Services Ltd., a marketing joint venture between the two companies. This deal was valued at $210 million.

In 2019, the company changed its name from TransCanada to TC Energy (TC Ã‰nergie in French and TC EnergÃa in Spanish) to better reflect its position as an energy infrastructure company in all of North America.

EXECUTIVES

President, Chief Executive Officer, Director, François L. Poirier

Canadian Natural Gas Pipeline Executive Advisor, Tracy A. Robinson

Corporate Services Executive Vice President, Dawn E. de Lima

Strategy and Corporate Development Executive Vice President, Bevin M. Wirzba

Capital Markets Executive Vice President, Finance and Treasurer Executive Vice President, Corporate Finance Executive Vice President, Corporate Finance Chief Financial Officer, Capital Markets Chief Financial Officer, Finance and Treasurer Chief Financial Officer, Joel E. Hunter

U.S. and Mexico Natural Gas Pipelines Executive Vice President, U.S. and Mexico Natural Gas Pipelines President, Stanley G. Chapman

Stakeholder Relations Senior vice President, Patrick C. Muttart

Technical Centre Senior Vice President, Jawad A. Masud

Power, Storage and Origination Senior Vice President, Power, Storage and Origination President, Corey Hessen

Finance and Evaluations Vice President, Jonathan E. Wrathall

Corporate Development Law Vice President, Corporate Development Vice President, Law and Corporate Secretary Vice President, Finance Law Vice President, Christine R. Johnston

Risk Management Vice President, Gloria L. Hartl

Taxation Vice President, Dennis P. Hebert

Vice President, Controller, G. Glenn Menuz

Vice President, Treasurer, Nancy A. Johnson

Stakeholder Relations Executive Vice President, Stakeholder Relations General Counsel, Patrick M. Keys

Chair, Corporate Director, Siim A. Vanaselja

Corporate Director, Michael R. Culbert

Corporate Director, William D. Johnson

Corporate Director, Susan C. Jones

Corporate Director, Una M. Power

Corporate Director, Mary Pat Salomone

Corporate Director, D. Michael G. Stewart

Director, Stephen Cretier

Director, Randy L. Limbacher

Director, John E. Lowe

Director, David MacNaughton

Director, Indira V. Samarasekera

Director, Thierry Vandal

Auditors : KPMG LLP

LOCATIONS

HQ: TC Energy Corp
450 - 1st Street S.W., Calgary, Alberta T2P 5H1
Phone: 403 920-2000 **Fax:** 403 920-2467
Web: www.tcenergy.com

2014 Sales

	% of total
Canada	52
US	46
Mexico	2
Total	100

PRODUCTS/OPERATIONS

2014 Sales

	% of total
Natural gas pipeline	48
Energy	37
Liquids pipelines	15
Total	100

Selected Pipelines
Alberta System
Canadian Mainline
Foothills System
Keystone (under construction)
Great Lakes Gas Transmission Company (69%)
Gas Transmission Northwest (83%)
Iroquois Gas Transmission System (45%)
Northern Border Pipeline (17%)
Portland Natural Gas Transmission System (62%)
Tamazunchale Pipeline
Trans Québec & Maritimes (50%)
Tuscarora Gas Transmission (33%)

Selected Power Plants
Bear Creek (Alberta)
Bécancour (Québec)
Cancarb (Alberta)
Carseland (Alberta)
Coolidge (Arizona)
Deerfield River System
Grandview (New Brunswick)
Halton Hills (Ontario)
Kirby Wind Power
MacKay River (Alberta)
Ocean State (Rhode Island)
Ravenswood (New York)
Redwater (Alberta)

COMPETITORS

DOMINION ENERGY, INC.
DUKE ENERGY CORPORATION
ENERGY TRANSFER LP
ENTERPRISE PRODUCTS PARTNERS L.P.
ETP LEGACY LP
KINDER MORGAN INC
SEMPRA ENERGY
TARGA PIPELINE PARTNERS LP
TENNESSEE GAS PIPELINE COMPANY, L.L.C.
THE WILLIAMS COMPANIES INC

HISTORICAL FINANCIALS

Company Type: Public

Income Statement — FYE: December 31

	REVENUE ($mil)	NET INCOME ($mil)	NET PROFIT MARGIN	EMPLOYEES
12/23	12,021	2,204	18.3%	7,415
12/22	11,074	553	5.0%	7,477
12/21	10,510	1,534	14.6%	7,017
12/20	10,209	3,625	35.5%	7,283
12/19	10,179	3,179	31.2%	7,305
Annual Growth	4.2%	(8.7%)	—	0.4%

2023 Year-End Financials
Debt ratio: 38.1%   No. of shares ($ mil.): 1,037
Return on equity: 9.1%   Dividends
Cash ($ mil.): 2,774   Yield: —
Current Ratio: 0.96   Payout: 135.2%
Long-term debt ($ mil.): 45,466   Market value ($ mil.): 40,555

	STOCK PRICE ($) FY Close	P/E High/Low		Earnings	PER SHARE ($) Dividends	Book Value
12/23	39.09	16	12	2.07	2.81	21.49
12/22	39.86	86	62	0.47	2.66	24.69
12/21	46.54	29	22	1.46	2.76	26.63
12/20	40.72	13	8	3.72	2.41	26.23
12/19	53.31	13	9	3.28	2.27	25.17
Annual Growth	(7.5%)	—	—	(10.8%)	5.5%	(3.9%)

TDK Corp

TDK is a world leader in electronic solutions for the smart society. TDK's comprehensive, innovation-driven portfolio features passive components such as ceramic, aluminum electrolytic and film capacitors, as well as magnetics, high-frequency, and piezo and protection devices. The product spectrum also includes sensors and sensor systems such as temperature and pressure, magnetic, and MEMS sensors. In addition, TDK provides power supplies and energy devices, magnetic heads and more. These products are marketed under the product brands TDK, EPCOS, InvenSense, Micronas, Tronics and TDK-Lambda. TDK focuses on demanding markets in automotive, industrial and consumer electronics, and information and communication technology. With operations around the world, TDK generates about 90% of its sales outside of its home country.

Operations

TDK's four major reporting segments are Energy Application Products, Passive Components, Magnetic Application Products, and Sensor Application Components.

Energy application products (about 50% of total revenue) include energy devices such as lithium polymer batteries for smartphones, tablet devices, notebook computers, wearable devices, game consoles, drones and residential energy storage systems, and power supplies (DC-DC converters, onboard chargers and POL converters).

About 25% of revenue comes from passive components, which include ceramic chip capacitors, aluminum electrolytic capacitors, film capacitors, and 3-terminal feed-through capacitors.

Magnetic application products, some 15% of revenue, hard disk drive (HDD) heads, HDD suspension assemblies, power supplies, and magnet products.

Sensor application products (more than 5%) makes sensors for automotive, ICT and industrial and energy.

Geographic Reach

TDK, based in Tokyo, has more than 250 factories, research and development, and sales offices in more than 30 countries.

Most of TDK's revenue -- some 75% -- comes from customers in Asia (excluding Japan), about 10% comes from Europe with the US and Japan supplying 15% of combined revenue.

Financial Performance

The company reported a revenue of ¥1.9 trillion for the year ended March 2022, a 29% increase from the previous year's revenue of ¥1.5 trillion.

It has a net income of ¥131.3 billion.

HISTORY

Kanzo Saito, who had previously raised rabbits for their fur, took out a patent in 1935 on ferrite, a type of ceramic made mainly from iron oxide that held promise for electronics applications. (Japan's Yogoru Kato is credited with inventing the material.) Saito founded Tokyo Denkikagaku Kogyo K.K. (TDK) to pioneer the mass production of ferrite and output rose quickly as developers found countless new uses for the substance. Saito handed over the presidency of the company in 1946 to Teiichi Yamazaki, who expanded TDK's portfolio into products such as magnetic recording tape (1952).

The company's global thrust began when it opened a Los Angeles office in 1959. Two years later it was listing shares on the Tokyo Stock Exchange. TDK branched into cassette tapes in 1966 and electromagnetic wave absorbers in 1968, the year the company opened its first overseas manufacturing center in Taiwan.

During the 1970s TDK launched operations in Australia, Europe, and South America. It began listing its shares on the New York Stock Exchange in 1982. That year the company also introduced a solar battery. In 1983 TDK officially changed its name to TDK Corporation.

In 1987 Hiroshi Sato was appointed president of the company. TDK bought integrated circuit maker Silicon Systems in 1989 (sold in 1996 to Texas Instruments) as Sato began to modernize the company's offerings and organization. With a conservative management style, he'd often wait to see how other companies fared in new markets before committing TDK, prompting the industry to label him the "gambler who follows someone else." During his tenure, Sato gave the company solid footholds in niches such as optical disks, high-density heads, and cellular phone components.

EXECUTIVES

President, Representative Director, Noboru Saito
Senior Managing Executive Officer,
Representative Director, Tetsuji Yamanishi
Chairman, Director, Shigenao Ishiguro
Director, Shigeki Sato
Outside Director, Kozue Nakayama
Outside Director, Mutsuo Iwai
Outside Director, Shoei Yamana
Auditors : KPMG AZSA LLC

LOCATIONS

HQ: TDK Corp
  2-5-1 Nihonbashi, Chuo-ku, Tokyo 103-6128
Phone: (81) 3 6778 1068   **Fax:** 516 294-8318
Web: www.tdk.com

PRODUCTS/OPERATIONS

2019 Sales
	% of total
Energy Application Products	39
Passive Application Products	31
Magnetic Application Products	20
Sensor Application Products	6
Other	4
Total	100

2019 Sales
	% of total
Asia and others	72
Europe	12
Americas	8
Japan	8
Total	100

Selected Products
Data Storage
  Magnetic heads (hard disk drives)
  Thermal-assist magnetic heads (scheduled to begin production in March 2013)

Electronic Components
  Anechoic chambers
  Capacitors
  Converters
  Cores and magnets
  Ferrite
  Metal
  Inductors
  Power supplies
  Sensors
  Transformers
  Varistors
Other
  Factory automation equipment
  Organic EL displays

COMPETITORS

ADVANCED ENERGY INDUSTRIES, INC.
AMKOR TECHNOLOGY, INC.
HUTCHINSON TECHNOLOGY INCORPORATED
Infineon Technologies AG
KYOCERA CORPORATION
METHODE ELECTRONICS, INC.
PULSE ELECTRONICS CORPORATION
RENESAS ELECTRONICS AMERICA INC.
SOITEC
VICOR CORPORATION

HISTORICAL FINANCIALS
Company Type: Public

Income Statement   FYE: March 31

	REVENUE ($mil)	NET INCOME ($mil)	NET PROFIT MARGIN	EMPLOYEES
03/23	16,374	857	5.2%	102,908
03/22	15,637	1,079	6.9%	116,808
03/21	13,357	716	5.4%	129,284
03/20	12,556	532	4.2%	107,138
03/19	12,477	742	5.9%	104,781
Annual Growth	7.0%	3.7%	—	(0.4%)

2023 Year-End Financials
Debt ratio: 0.2%
Return on equity: 8.2%
Cash ($ mil.): 3,800
Current Ratio: 1.60
Long-term debt ($ mil.): 3,368
No. of shares ($ mil.): 379
Dividends
  Yield: 2.0%
  Payout: 32.6%
Market value ($ mil.): 13,567

	STOCK PRICE ($) FY Close	P/E High/Low		PER SHARE ($) Earnings	Dividends	Book Value
03/23	35.77	0	0	2.26	0.72	28.87
03/22	36.18	0	0	2.84	1.15	28.20
03/21	140.10	1	0	1.89	1.70	23.92
03/20	76.50	1	0	1.40	1.57	20.52
03/19	78.50	1	0	1.95	0.45	20.91
Annual Growth	(17.8%)	—	—	3.7%	12.6%	8.4%

TE Connectivity Ltd

TE Connectivity is known as the global industrial technology offering a broad range of connectivity and sensor solutions applied in industries such as transportation, industrial applications, medical technology, energy, data communications and home. Its devices are used in aerospace, automotive, datacomm, consumer electronics, energy, lighting products, and medical applications, as well as public safety, military, and telecom products. The company has about 90,000 employees globally, catering to clients in EMEA, Asia-Pacific, and the Americas. The company is headquartered in Switzerland.

Operations
TE Connectivity sorts its businesses into three divisions, namely, Transportation Solutions, Industrial Solutions, and Communications Solutions.

Transportation delivers about 60% of the company's revenue. It makes terminals and connector systems and components, sensors, relays, application tooling, and wire and heat shrink tubing. The segment caters to the automotive, commercial transportations, and sensors end markets.

Industrial solutions accounts for about 30% of revenue with its products that connect and distribute power, data, and signals, serving the industrial equipment, aerospace, defense, oil & gas, energy, and medical end markets.

Communications makes components for the data and devices and appliances markets, which generate about 15% of revenue.

Geographic Reach
TE Connectivity is a worldwide operation of manufacturing, warehousing, and offices in more than 50 countries.

In terms of revenue source, the Americas account for about 30% of the company's revenue, with EMEA and Asia-Pacific with about 40% each.

Sales and Marketing
TE Connectivity connects directly with its customers most of the time with 60% of revenue coming from its own sales force. The company sells their products through direct selling efforts to manufacturers.

Financial Performance
TE Connectivity's performance for the past five years has fluctuated but ending with 2022 as its highest performing year over the period.

For 2022, the company's revenues increased by $1.9 billion to $16.3 billion compared to $14.9 billion.

The company experienced another increase in its net income to $2.4 billion in 2021 compared to the prior year's net income of $2.3 billion.

TE Connectivity held cash of $1.8 billion at the end of 2022. Cash flow from operations amounted to $2.5 billion. Investing activities and financing activities used $878 million and $1.7 billion, respectively. Main cash uses were for capital expenditures and repurchase of common shares.

Company Background
TE Connectivity undertook its solo role on the world's stage of passive electronics in 2007. Tyco International had rewritten its corporate script, and moved to split off Tyco Electronics and Covidien (formerly Tyco Healthcare Group) from its security and engineered products operation; three stand-alone public companies resulted. The company changed its name to TE Connectivity in 2011 to better reflect its

operations after the ADC acquisition.

EXECUTIVES

Chairman, Director, Thomas J. Lynch, $443,077 total compensation
Chief Executive Officer, Director, Terrence R. Curtin, $1,136,539 total compensation
Executive Vice President, General Counsel, John S. Jenkins, $551,455 total compensation
Executive Vice President, Chief Financial Officer, Director, Heath A. Mitts, $628,277 total compensation
Global Human Resources Senior Vice President, Global Human Resources Chief Human Resources Officer, Timothy J. Murphy
Senior Vice President, Corporate Controller, Robert J. Ott
Vice President, Corporate Secretary, Harold G. Barksdale
Division Officer, Shadrak W. Kroeger
Division Officer, Steven T. Merkt, $627,361 total compensation
Division Officer, Aaron K. Stucki
Director, Carol A. (John) Davidson
Director, Lynn A. Dugle
Director, Syaru Shirley Lin
Director, William A. Jeffrey
Director, Abhijit Y. Talwalkar
Director, Mark C. Trudeau
Director, Jean-Pierre Clamadieu
Director, Dawn C. Willoughby
Director, Laura H. Wright
Auditors : DELOITTE & TOUCHE LLP

LOCATIONS

HQ: TE Connectivity Ltd
 Muhlenstrasse 26, Schaffhausen CH-8200
Phone: (41) 52 633 6661
Web: www.te.com

2018 Sales

	$ mil.	% of total
EMEA	5,255	38
APAC	4,762	34
Americas	3,971	28
Total	13,988	100

PRODUCTS/OPERATIONS

2018 Sales

	$ mil.	% of total
Transportation Solutions	8,290	59
Industrial Solutions	3,856	28
Communications Solutions	1,842	23
Total	13,988	100

Selected Products

Antennas
Application tooling
Circuit protection devices
Connector systems
Fiber optics
Heat shrink tubing
Intelligent building controls
Network interface devices
Racks and panels
Relays
Touch screens
Undersea telecommunication systems
Wire and cable

COMPETITORS

Adecco Group AG
Alpiq Holding SA
GROUPE CRIT
Garmin Ltd.
ICAHN ENTERPRISES L.P.
LafargeHolcim Ltd
MAXLINEAR, INC.
SANMINA CORPORATION
TCP International Holdings Ltd.
VIAVI SOLUTIONS INC.

HISTORICAL FINANCIALS

Company Type: Public

Income Statement — FYE: September 29

	REVENUE ($mil)	NET INCOME ($mil)	NET PROFIT MARGIN	EMPLOYEES
09/23	16,034	1,910	11.9%	90,000
09/22	16,281	2,428	14.9%	92,000
09/21	14,923	2,261	15.2%	89,000
09/20	12,172	(241)	—	82,000
09/19	13,448	1,844	13.7%	78,000
Annual Growth	4.5%	0.9%	—	3.6%

2023 Year-End Financials

Debt ratio: 19.4%
Return on equity: 17.1%
Cash ($ mil.): 1,661
Current Ratio: 1.77
Long-term debt ($ mil.): 3,529
No. of shares ($ mil.): 311
Dividends
 Yield: —
 Payout: 38.1%
Market value ($ mil.): —

Techtronic Industries Co. Ltd.

Techtronic Industries (TTI) is a fast-growing world leader in power tools, accessories, hand tools, outdoor power equipment, and floorcare and cleaning for Do-It-Yourself (DIY), professional and industrial users in the home improvement, repair, maintenance, construction, and infrastructure industries. The company is committed to accelerating the transformation of these industries through superior environmentally friendly cordless technology. The TTI brands like Milwaukee, Ryobi, and Hoover are recognized worldwide for their deep heritage and cordless product platforms of superior quality, outstanding performance, safety, productivity, and compelling innovation. Founded in 1985, the company generates the majority of its revenue in North America.

Operations

The company's operating segments are Power Equipment and Floorcare & Cleaning.

Power Equipment segment generates approximately 90% of the company's revenue. The segment includes sales of power tools, power tool accessories, outdoor products, and outdoor product accessories for consumer, trade, professional and industrial users. The products are available under the Milwaukee, Empire, AEG, Ryobi, Homelite, and Hart brands plus original equipment manufacturer (OEM) customers.

Floorcare & Cleaning segment, accounts for some 10% of the company's revenue, includes sales of floorcare products and floorcare accessories under the Hoover, Dirt Devil, Vax, and Oreck brands plus OEM customers.

Geographic Reach

Based in Hong Kong, TTI's operation around the world include manufacturing, R & D facilities as well as sales, marketing and administrative offices in North America, EMEA, Australia and New Zealand, Asia, and South America. North America brings in more than 75% of the company's revenue, Europe provides approximately 15%, and other countries account for nearly 10%.

Sales and Marketing

The company offers its products to consumers, professional, and industrial users in the home improvement, infrastructure, and construction industries. Its largest customer and five largest customers account for about 50% and around 60% respectively of the company's total revenue.

Financial Performance

The company reported a total revenue of $13.2 billion in 2021, a 35% increase from the previous year's total revenue of $9.8 billion. Increased strategic investments in new product, manufacturing capacity, geographic expansion, logistics, and the company's in-field marketing initiatives propelled the company's performance.

In 2021, the company had a net income of $1.2 billion, a 37% increase from the previous year's net income of $861.3 million.

The company's cash at the end of 2021 was $1.9 billion. Financing activities generated $1.5 billion, while operating activities used $100.9 million. Investing activities used another $1 billion, primarily for purchase of property, plant and equipment.

Strategy

In 2021, the company' continued to make progress on partnerships and initiatives that matter. Beyond aligning to the United Nations Sustainable Development Goals (SDGs) and continuing its membership with the Global Reporting Initiative (GRI), it began reporting against the Sustainability Accounting Standards Board (SASB) Standards and the recommendations of the Task Force on Climate-related Financial Disclosures (TCFD), while also prioritizing the company's de-carbonization agenda. As a founding member of the Better Mining Initiative (BMI) and active member of the Responsible Business Alliance (RBA), the company has forged ahead to collaborate with industry partners to effect change on crucial challenges in its supply chain.

EXECUTIVES

Chairman, Executive Director, Horst Julius Pudwill

Strategic Planning Vice-Chairman, Strategic Planning Executive Director, Vice-Chairman, Executive Director, Stephan Horst Pudwill
Chief Executive Officer, Executive Director, Joseph Galli
Operations Director, Executive Director, Patrick Kin Wah Chan
Chief Financial Officer, Executive Director, Frank Chi Chung Chan
Secretary, Veronica Ka Po Ng
Independent Non-Executive Director, Peter David Sullivan
Independent Non-Executive Director, Johannes-Gerhard Hesse
Independent Non-Executive Director, Robert Hinman Getz
Independent Non-Executive Director, Virginia Davis Wilmerding
Independent Non-Executive Director, Caroline Christina Kracht
Non-Executive Director, Roy Chi Ping Chung
Non-Executive Director, Camille Jojo
Auditors : Deloitte Touche Tohmatsu

LOCATIONS
HQ: Techtronic Industries Co. Ltd.
29/F, Tower 2, Kowloon Commerce Centre, 51 Kwai Cheong Road, Kwai Chung, New Territories,
Phone: (852) 2402 6888   **Fax:** (852) 2413 5971
Web: www.ttigroup.com

COMPETITORS
APEX TOOL GROUP, LLC
ARROYO PROCESS EQUIPMENT INC
BUFFALO PUMPS, INC.
BURNS BOLEKY CONTROLS, INC.
C&H DISTRIBUTORS, LLC
CAMPBELL HAUSFELD, LLC
CROWN EQUIPMENT CORPORATION
ECHO, INCORPORATED
HITACHI AMERICA LTD
SPEAR & JACKSON UK LIMITED

HISTORICAL FINANCIALS
Company Type: Public

Income Statement   FYE: December 31

	REVENUE ($mil)	NET INCOME ($mil)	NET PROFIT MARGIN	EMPLOYEES
12/22	13,253	1,077	8.1%	44,705
12/21	13,203	1,099	8.3%	51,426
12/20	9,811	800	8.2%	48,028
12/19	7,666	614	8.0%	33,177
12/18	7,021	552	7.9%	23,279
Annual Growth	17.2%	18.2%	—	17.7%

2022 Year-End Financials
Debt ratio: 23.7%
Return on equity: 21.6%
Cash ($ mil.): 1,428
Current Ratio: 1.37
Long-term debt ($ mil.): 1,198
No. of shares ($ mil.): 1,834
Dividends
Yield: —
Payout: 204.8%
Market value ($ mil.): 101,899

	STOCK PRICE ($) FY Close	P/E High/Low		PER SHARE ($) Earnings	Dividends	Book Value
12/22	55.54	172	79	0.59	1.20	2.84
12/21	99.40	187	118	0.60	1.03	2.57
12/20	71.36	170	63	0.44	0.68	2.13
12/19	41.02	122	77	0.34	0.57	1.85
12/18	26.25	112	76	0.30	0.46	1.67
Annual Growth	20.6%	—	—	18.2%	27.4%	14.1%

Teck Resources Ltd

Teck Resources is a Canadian-based exploration, mining, and processing company focused on steel-making coal (used in steel production), zinc, and copper. It produces some 26.2 million tonnes of coal, 705 thousand tonnes of zinc concentrate, and 294 thousand tonnes of copper each year. The company holds or owns interests in nine operating mines and operates a metallurgical facility. It mines copper in Canada, Chile, and Peru and has development projects in North and South America. Teck's Red Dog mine in Alaska holds some of the world's largest zinc reserves. Teck started out in 1913 as a gold mining company. Majority of the company's sales were generated in China.

Operations
Teck Resources' operates through three operating segments which are:

Copper segment is a significant copper producer in the Americas, with four operating mines in Canada, Chile and Peru, and eight significant copper development projects in North and South America. The segment accounts for around 20% of revenue.

Zinc segment is one of the world's largest producers of mined zinc, with production from the Red Dog mine in Alaska and from the Antamina copper mine in Peru, which has significant zinc co-product production, and one significant zinc development project in Alaska. Teck Resources also own one of the world's largest fully integrated zinc and lead smelting and refining facilities in British Columbia, Canada. The segment accounts for around 20% of revenue.

Steelmaking Coal segment are the world's second-largest seaborne exporter of steelmaking coal, with four low-carbon intensity operations in British Columbia, Canada that have significant high-quality steelmaking coal reserves. The segment accounts for around 60% of total revenue.

Geographic Reach
Headquartered in Vancouver, British Columbia (B.C.), Canada, it owns or have interests in nine operating mines, a large metallurgical complex, and several significant copper and zinc development projects, all in the Americas. Company's largest geographic market was China with more than 25% of revenue, followed by Japan and South Korea with more than 15% and over 10%, respectively.

Financial Performance
Company's revenue for fiscal 2022 increased to CAD17.3 billion compared from the prior year with CAD12.3 billion. The increase was primarily due to higher revenues on its steelmaking coal offsetting the decrease in copper segment.

Net income for fiscal 2022 increased to CAD4.1 billion compared from the prior year with CAD3.2 billion. The increase was primarily due to higher revenues offsetting the increase expenses.

Cash held by the company at the end of fiscal 2022 increased to CAD1.9 billion. Cash provided by operations was CAD8.0 billion while cash used for investing and financing activities were CAD5.7 billion and CAD2.0 billion, respectively. Main uses of cash were for expenditures on property, plant and equipment.

Strategy
Teck Reources' corporate strategy is focused on exploring for, acquiring, developing and operating world-class, long-life assets in stable jurisdictions that operate through multiple price cycles. The company maximize productivity and efficiency at its existing operations, maintain a strong balance sheet, and are nimble in recognizing and acting on opportunities. The pursuit of sustainability guides its approach to business, and it recognizes that its success depends on its ability to ensure safe workplaces, collaborative community relationships and a healthy environment.

EXECUTIVES
Chairman, Director, Sheila A. Murray
Vice-Chairman, Director, Norman B. Keevil
President, Chief Executive Officer, Executive Director, Donald R. Lindsay
Chief Financial Officer, Executive Vice President, Jonathan H. Price
Projects Senior Vice President, Technical Services Senior Vice President, Exploration Senior Vice President, Alex N. Christopher
Executive Vice President, Chief Operating Officer, Harry M. Conger
Marketing Senior Vice President, Logistics Senior Vice President, Real Foley
Corporate Development Senior Vice President, Nicholas P.M. Hooper
Asia and Europe Senior Vice President, Ralph J. Lutes
Energy Senior Vice President, Kieron McFadyen
Technology Senior Vice President, Innovation Senior Vice President, Technology Chief Transformation Officer, Innovation Chief Transformation Officer, Andrew K. Milner
Strategic Analysis Senior Vice President, Investor Relations Senior Vice President, H. Fraser Phillips
Commercial & Legal Affairs Senior Vice President, Peter C. Rozee

Senior Vice President, Robin B. Sheremeta
Corporate Affairs Senior Vice President, Sustainability Senior Vice President, External Affairs Senior Vice President, Marcia M. Smith
Human Resources Senior Vice President, Human Resources Chief Human Resources Officer, Dean C. Winsor
Logistics Vice President, Ian K. Anderson
Transformation Vice President, Greg J. Brouwer
Corporate Affairs Vice President, Douglas B. Brown
Security Vice President, Risk Vice President, Anne J. Chalmers
Corporate Affairs and Sustainability, South America Vice President, Amparo Cornejo
Maintenance Vice President, Larry M. Davey
Corporate Development Vice President, Sepanta Dorri
Vice President, Treasurer, Justine B. Fisher
Sustainable Development, Coal Vice President, C. Jeffrey Hanman
Assurance and Advisory Vice President, Sarah A. Huhges
Communities, Government Affairs & HSEC Systems Vice President, Amber C. Johnston-Billings
Business Development Vice President, M. Colin Joudrie
Environment Vice President, Scott E. Maloney
Exploration Vice President, Geoscience Vice President, Stuart R. McCracken
Health and Safety Vice President, Brianne L. Metzger-Doran
Project Development Vice President, Karla L. Mills
Taxes Vice President, Douglas J. Powrie
Vice President, Corporate Controller, Crystal J. Prystai
Vice President, Chief Innovation Officer, Kalev Ruberg
Planning and Innovation, Coal Vice President, Donald J. Sander
Marketing Vice President, Andre D. Stark
Legal Vice President, Nikola Uzelac
Corporate Secretary, Amanda R. Robinson
Director, Mayank M. Ashar
Director, Quan Chong
Director, Edward C. Dowling
Director, Toru Higo
Director, Tracey L. McVicar
Director, Kenneth W. Pickering
Director, Una M. Power
Director, Timothy R. Snider
Director, Masaru Tani
Director, Sarah A. Strunk
Director, Paul G. Schiodtz
Auditors : PricewaterhouseCoopers LLP

LOCATIONS
HQ: Teck Resources Ltd
Suite 3300, 550 Burrard Street, Vancouver, British Columbia V6C 0B3
Phone: 604 699-4000   **Fax:** 604 699-4729
Web: www.teck.com

PRODUCTS/OPERATIONS
2018 Sales

	% of total
Steel making Coal	50
Zinc	25
Copper	22
Energy	3
Total	100

Selected Products
Copper
Energy
Industrial Products & Fertilizers
Other Metals
Steelmaking Coal
Technology And Innovation
Zinc

Selected Operations
Coal
  Elk Valley Coal Partnership (40%, Canada)
  Fording Canadian Coal Trust
Copper
  Antamina (23%, Peru)
  Highland Valley Copper (98%)
  Louvicourt (25%, Canada)
Zinc
  Mines
  Pend Oreille Project (US)
  Red Dog mine (US, with Northwest Alaska Native Association)
  Smelters
  Trail Power
  Waneta hydroelectric dam
  Trail Smelter and Refineries (Canada)
Energy
  Fort Hills Energy (20%)
  Frontier and Equinox Oil Sands project (50%)

COMPETITORS
ASARCO LLC
Corporacion Nacional del Cobre de Chile
FREEPORT-MCMORAN INC.
First Quantum Minerals Ltd
GLENCORE PLC
Inmet Mining Corporation
PEABODY ENERGY CORPORATION
THOMPSON CREEK METALS COMPANY USA
Wallbridge Mining Company Limited
Zijin Mining Group Company Limited

HISTORICAL FINANCIALS
Company Type: Public

Income Statement   FYE: December 31

	REVENUE ($mil)	NET INCOME ($mil)	NET PROFIT MARGIN	EMPLOYEES
12/23	11,325	1,817	16.0%	12,600
12/22	12,803	2,452	19.2%	12,100
12/21	10,584	2,251	21.3%	10,600
12/20	7,027	(678)	—	10,000
12/19	9,164	(464)	—	0
Annual Growth	5.4%	—	—	—

2023 Year-End Financials
Debt ratio: 13.5%
Return on equity: 9.1%
Cash ($ mil.): 561
Current Ratio: 1.10
Long-term debt ($ mil.): 7,179
No. of shares ($ mil.): 517
Dividends
  Yield: —
  Payout: 21.7%
Market value ($ mil.): 21,867

	STOCK PRICE ($) FY Close	P/E High/Low		PER SHARE ($) Earnings	Dividends	Book Value
12/23	42.27	11	8	3.46	0.75	39.36
12/22	37.82	7	4	4.58	0.74	36.66
12/21	28.82	5	3	4.17	0.16	33.81
12/20	18.15	—	—	(1.27)	0.15	29.63
12/19	17.37	—	—	(0.83)	0.15	29.89
Annual Growth	24.9%	—	—	—	49.5%	7.1%

Telecom Italia SpA

Telecom Italia SpA (TIM) is one of Italy's leading telephone operators and offers fixed retail and wholesale access lines and mobile lines for retail and wholesale customers. It also operates in Brazil where its operations continue to grow through the enriching and increasing in value of their commercial offering. The company has about 62,000 lines in Brazil. TIM generates more about 80% of its sales in Italy.

Operations
The Domestic Business unit, which accounts for about 75%, involves the consumer segment, business segment, wholesale national market segment, and wholesale international market. The segments involve fixed and mobile voice and internet services and products managed; voice, data, and internet services and product; and management and development of the portfolio of regulated and unregulated wholesale services for fixed-line and mobile telecommunications operators.

Geographic Reach
About 80% of the company's revenues are from Italy, with the remaining 25% from Brazil.

Financial Performance
Telecom Italia's performance for the past five years fluctuated with a downward trend since 2018, then recovering slightly in 2022.

The company's revenues increased by EUR 472 million to EUR 15.8 billion in 2022, as compared to 2021's revenue of EUR 15.3 billion.

Telecom Italia's net loss for fiscal year end 2022 was at EUR 2.9 billion, followed by the previous year's net loss of EUR 8.7 billion.

The company held about EUR 3.6 billion at the end of the year. Operating activities provided EUR 4.9 billion to the coffers. Investing activities and financing activities used EUR 5.3 billion and EUR 2.9 billion, respectively. Main cash uses were for purchases of intangible, tangible and rights of use assets on a cash basis and repayments of non-current financial liabilities, including current portion.

Strategy
One of Telecom Italia's strategy includes the optimization of the customer base, applying a data driven logic, with the target of revenue maximization. To this end, a

transformation project is in progress for the construction of a fully-automated CVM platform based on machine learning algorithms and artificial intelligence to optimize investments and increase the effectiveness of the commercial actions.

Company Background

Telecom Italia S.p.A. is a leader in fixed-line and wireless telecommunication services in Italy. As a holding company with majority ownership in numerous subsidiaries, it provides domestic and international fixed-line and wireless telecommunication operations as well as Internet, information technology and satellite communication services. Its international operations include fixed-line and wireless communications in Latin America and the Mediterranean region. It is the majority owner of Telecom Italia Mobile (TIM), Italy's leading provider of wireless communications. Telecom Italia is the former government telephone monopoly, which was privatized in 1997 and controlled by Olivetti in 1999 in a hostile takeover. Telecom Italia faces increasing competition in both domestic and international markets.

HISTORY

After gaining political power in Italy, Benito Mussolini began a program of nationalization, focusing first on three major banks and their equity portfolios. Included were three local phone companies that became the core of Società Finanziaria Telefonica (STET), created in 1933 to handle Italy's phone services under the state's industrial holding company, Istituto per La Ricostruzione Industriale (IRI).

Germany and Italy grew closer in the years leading up to WWII, and Italian equipment makers entered a venture with Siemens to make phone equipment. STET came through the war with most of its infrastructure intact and a monopoly on phone service in Italy. Siemens' properties, along with those of other equipment makers, were taken over by another company, TETI, which was nationalized and put under STET's control in 1958. This expanded STET's monopoly to include equipment manufacturing.

Italy's industries were increasingly nationalized under IRI. Companies within the IRI family forged alliances with each other and with independent companies, which frequently were absorbed into STET.

STET's scope expanded during the 1960s and 1970s to include satellite and data communications, but its monopoly was undermined by new technologies such as faxes, PCs, and teleconferencing. In the technology race among equipment makers, STET fell behind. And in a satellite communications era, STET's status as a necessary long-distance carrier was threatened. Despite these pressures, change did not come easily to STET. State monopolies maintained popular support, not only on nationalistic grounds but also because of labor's strong anticompetitive stance.

Anticipating privatization, however, IRI reorganized STET in 1994 and poured new capital into the company. STET's five telecom companies -- SIP (domestic phone operator), Italcable (intercontinental), Telespazio (satellite), SIRM (maritime), and Iritel (domestic long distance) -- were merged into one, Telecom Italia. Its mobile phone business was spun off as Telecom Italia Mobile (TIM) in 1995.

To end political feuding, the government abruptly replaced the heads of STET and Telecom Italia in 1997. Telecom Italia was merged with STET, which took the Telecom Italia name and was privatized that year. Berardino Libonati became chairman, and Franco Bernabe, formerly CEO of oil company ENI, took the helm as CEO. The company began taking stakes in foreign telecom companies, including mobilkom austria, Spanish broadcaster Retevision, and -- as European Union competition began in 1998 -- Telekom Austria.

Erstwhile rival Olivetti launched a hostile takeover bid for Telecom Italia in 1999. Though Telecom Italia tried to fend off the smaller firm with various maneuvers, including a proposed merger with Deutsche Telekom, Olivetti gained 55% of Telecom Italia. Olivetti CEO Roberto Colaninno took over as chairman and CEO.

That year Telecom Italia sold 50% of Stream, its pay TV unit, to an investor group led by News Corp. The company also announced plans to spin off and sell a stake in its ISP, Tin.it. In 2000, however, Telecom Italia instead combined Tin.it with SEAT Pagine Gialle, a yellow pages directory publisher and Internet portal operator (spun off from the parent company and sold in 2003). Also that year the company sold off 81% of its telecom equipment unit, Italtel, and its 49% stake in installations firm Sirti.

In 2001 Colaninno and several other Telecom Italia officials were named as suspects in an investigation of whether the company had violated accounting, conflict of interest, and share manipulation laws. Colaninno was replaced when tire maker Pirelli and Edizione Holding, the parent company of the Benetton Group, acquired a 23% stake in Olivetti.

Telecom Italia teamed up with News Corp. to develop the Stream pay TV joint venture, renamed Sky Italia. The venture gained a kick-start when the two companies teamed to buy Italian pay-TV business Telepiu from Vivendi Universal in a cash and debt assumption deal that was valued at $871 million. The deal included agreements to drop disputes between Telepiu and Stream. Telecom Italia then sold a 30% stake in the venture to News Corp. It retained a 20% share with News Corp. controlling 80%.

In 2003 the company abandoned plans to acquire phone directories group Pagine Utili from Fininvest in a deal that would have been worth more than $130 million because of protests by Italian regulators who claimed the deal would breach competition laws. It also spun off its international services division starting in 2003 into a separate company, Telecom Italia Sparkle, which concentrated on services to other fixed-line operators, ISPs, and international corporations, and sold its nearly 62% stake in SEAT Pagine Gialle to an investor group for $3.55 billion.

Once the subsidiary, Telecom Italia became the parent company after the 2003 merger with former parent Olivetti. The reorganization simplified a corporate structure that was, at best, confusing: Olivetti, through its Tecnost unit, had acquired a controlling 55% stake in Telecom Italia in 1999. Two years later, tire maker Pirelli and the Benetton family teamed up to take control of Olivetti. Olivetti's largest shareholder was Olimpia, a company owned by Pirelli and the Benetton Group, among others.

Because Telecom Italia accounted for more than 95% of the revenues of Olivetti, the reorganization also kept the focus on the core business. The merger was met with favor among market watchers and some shareholders, although a group of international investors opposed the restructuring.

Reorganization continued at the company and it began selling some international fixed-line assets and putting some wireless operations outside Italy on the market. Disposals included Digitel, the Venezuelan wireless carrier, to Oswaldo Cisneros' Telvenco in a deal valued at about $425 million. It also sold its 81% stake in Greek wireless carrier Hellas Telecommunications, to US-based private equity firms Texas Pacific Group and Apax Partners in a deal valued at $1.4 billion; stakes in Spanish joint venture Auna and satellite unit Telespazio (to Leonardo - Finmeccanica); and in 2005 it sold its holdings in IT services and consulting company Finsiel, to Italian outsourcing firm Gruppo COS.

After spurning an offer from AT&T to buy the company, Telecom Italia named Pasquale Pistorio chairman in 2007, replacing Guido Rossi, who had held the position for only seven months. Telefonica subsequently won control of the company. Later that year Pistorio was replaced by Gabriele Galateri as chairman; Galateri was nominated by another top shareholder, Mediobanca.

In 2010 the company began selling off interests not related to its businesses in Italy or Brazil. It sold its 70% stake in Elettra, which specialized in laying submarine cables, to France Telecom (later renamed Orange) for ?20 million ($27 million); its Netherlands fixed-line provider BBNed to Tele2 for ?50 million ($64 million); and its German broadband unit, HanseNet, to Telefónica for the tidy sum of ?900 million ($1.2 billion) in cash. The following year Telecom Italia sold its 27% stake in the state-run Cuban phone company ETECSA for $706 million to Rafin SA, a financial services firm in that country. Also in 2011 the company sold subsidiary Loquendo to US-based Nuance Communications. The sales were part of Telecom Italia's ongoing effort to sell non-core businesses in order to reduce debt.

EXECUTIVES

Chief Executive Officer, Pietro Labriola
Chief Financial Officer, Giovanni Ronca
Chief Network, Operations & Wholesale Officer, Stefano Siragusa
Chief Strategy & Business Development Officer, Claudio Giovanni Ezio Ongaro
Chief Enterprise Market Officer, Massimo Mancini
Chief Regulatory Affairs and Wholesale Market Officer, Giovanni Gionata Massimiliano Moglia
Secretary, Agostino Nuzzolo
Independent Chairman, Salvatore Rossi
Lead Independent Director, Paola Sapienza
Independent Director, Federico Ferro Luzzi
Independent Director, Cristiana Falcone
Independent Director, Luca De Meo
Independent Director, Ilaria Romagnoli
Independent Director, Paola Camagni
Independent Director, Maurizio Carli
Independent Director, Paolo Boccardelli
Independent Director, Marella Moretti
Independent Director, Paola Bonomo
Director, Giovanni Gorno Tempini
Director, Frank Cadoret
Director, Arnaud Roy de Puyfontaine
Auditors : EY S.p.A

LOCATIONS

HQ: Telecom Italia SpA
Via Gaetano Negri 1, Milan 20123
Phone: (39) 06 36 88 1
Web: www.telecomitalia.com

2018 Sales

	% of total
Italy	79
Other regions	21
Total	100

PRODUCTS/OPERATIONS

2018 Sales

	% of total
Services	92
Equipment sales	8
Total	100

2017 Sales

	% of total
Domestic	79
Brazil	21
Total	100

COMPETITORS

AT&T INC.
BCE Inc

JAZZ TELECOM SAU (EXTINGUIDA)
Koninklijke KPN N.V.
MTS, PAO
Nortel Networks Limited
Proximus
SK Telecom Co.,Ltd.
TELEFONICA, SA
WIND TELECOMUNICAZIONI SPA

HISTORICAL FINANCIALS

Company Type: Public

Income Statement   FYE: December 31

	REVENUE ($mil)	NET INCOME ($mil)	NET PROFIT MARGIN	EMPLOYEES
12/22	17,686	(3,124)	—	50,392
12/21	18,181	(9,792)	—	51,929
12/20	20,272	8,865	43.7%	52,347
12/19	21,831	1,028	4.7%	55,198
12/18	22,733	(1,615)	—	57,901
Annual Growth	(6.1%)	—	—	(3.4%)

2022 Year-End Financials

Debt ratio: 45.2%   No. of shares ($ mil.): 15,213
Return on equity: (-18.0%)   Dividends
Cash ($ mil.): 3,796   Yield: —
Current Ratio: 0.72   Payout: 0.0%
Long-term debt ($ mil.): 22,922   Market value ($ mil.): 34,687

	STOCK PRICE ($) FY Close	P/E High/Low	PER SHARE ($) Earnings	Dividends	Book Value
12/22	2.28	— —	(0.15)	0.00	1.06
12/21	5.00	— —	(0.45)	0.09	1.30
12/20	4.57	20 10	0.41	0.08	2.12
12/19	6.18	162 121	0.04	0.01	1.51
12/18	5.55	— —	(0.08)	0.00	1.49
Annual Growth	(19.9%)	— —	—	—	(8.2%)

Telefonica SA

EXECUTIVES

Chief Executive Officer, Chairman, Executive Director, Jose Maria Alvarez-Pallete Lopez
Chief Finance and Control Officer, Laura Abasolo Garcia de Baquedano
Chief Corporate Affairs Officer, Chief Strategy Officer, Eduardo Navarro de Carvalho
Chief Strategy and Development Officer, Mark Evans
Chief Operating Officer, Executive Director, Angel Vila Boix
Internal Audit General Manager, Juan Francisco Gallego Arrechea
Global of Regulation Director, Global of Regulation Secretary, Pablo de Carvajal Gonzalez
Vice-Chairman, Non-Executive Director, Isidro Faine Casas
Vice-Chairman, Non-Executive Director, Jose Maria Abril Perez
Vice-Chairman, Non-Executive Director, Jose Javier Echenique Landiribar
Non-Executive Director, Juan Ignacio Cirac Sasturain
Non-Executive Director, Peter Erskine
Non-Executive Director, Carmen Garcia de Andres
Non-Executive Director, Maria Luisa Garcia Blanco

Non-Executive Director, Peter Loescher
Non-Executive Director, Veronica Pascual Boe
Non-Executive Director, Francisco Javier de Paz Mancho
Non-Executive Director, Francisco Jose Riberas de Mera
Non-Executive Director, Maria Rotondo Urcola
Non-Executive Director, Claudia Ramirez Sender
Auditors : PricewaterhouseCoopers Auditores, S.L.

LOCATIONS

HQ: Telefonica SA
Distrito Telefonica, Ronda de la Comunicacion, s/n, Madrid 28050
Phone: (34) 91 482 87 00   **Fax:** (34) 91 482 3817
Web: www.telefonica.com

HISTORICAL FINANCIALS

Company Type: Public

Income Statement   FYE: December 31

	REVENUE ($mil)	NET INCOME ($mil)	NET PROFIT MARGIN	EMPLOYEES
12/23	45,026	(987)	—	104,142
12/22	42,714	2,147	5.0%	103,651
12/21	44,456	9,209	20.7%	104,150
12/20	52,866	1,941	3.7%	112,797
12/19	54,366	1,282	2.4%	113,819
Annual Growth	(4.6%)	—	—	(2.2%)

2023 Year-End Financials

Debt ratio: 39.3%   No. of shares ($ mil.): 5,639
Return on equity: (-3.8%)   Dividends
Cash ($ mil.): 7,920   Yield: —
Current Ratio: 0.89   Payout: 0.0%
Long-term debt ($ mil.): 36,949   Market value ($ mil.): 21,993

	STOCK PRICE ($) FY Close	P/E High/Low	PER SHARE ($) Earnings	Dividends	Book Value
12/23	3.90	— —	(0.22)	0.34	4.29
12/22	3.57	17 11	0.33	0.32	4.75
12/21	4.24	4 3	1.55	0.40	4.46
12/20	4.04	33 14	0.29	0.46	2.54
12/19	6.97	52 39	0.19	0.45	3.76
Annual Growth	(13.5%)	— —	—	(6.8%)	3.4%

Telenor ASA

Telenor is a leading telecommunications provider, offering mobile, broadband, and TV services. The Norway-based company's mobile business has more than 172 million subscribers in its home country, Sweden, and Denmark, and across the world in Pakistan, Bangladesh, Thailand, Malaysia, and Myanmar. Telenor's products and services contribute to increase productivity and provide access to all digital content. Telenor generates the majority of its revenue from customers in Norway. The company was established in 1855.

Operations

Telenor's operating and reportable segments are based on business activities and geographical location. The main products and services are mobile communication and fixed line communication.

Its mobile communication business mainly includes voice, data, internet, content services, customer equipment and messaging. In Norway, Sweden, Denmark and Finland, the fixed line businesses are reported together with mobile operations. Fixed services comprise telephony, internet and TV and leased lines, as well as data services and managed services.

Other units consist of Corporate Functions, Telenor Infra, Telenor Satellite and Other Businesses. Corporate Functions comprise activities such as global shared services, research and development, strategic Group projects, Group Treasury, the internal insurance company, and support functions. Telenor Infra operates all passive infrastructure in Norway previously operated by Telenor Norway, Norkring and Telenor Real Estate. Telenor Satellite offers broadcasting and data communication services via satellite. Other Businesses consist mainly of mobile communication business at sea conducted by Telenor Maritime; Global Services, which is focused on interconnecting global operators and delivering key communications services on a global scale; Telenor Real Estate; Connexion, which is specialising in Internet of Things with capabilities to support the most advanced machine-to-machine-communication and Internet of Things customers worldwide; and other businesses, including internet based services and financial services, none of which are material enough to be reported as separate segments.

Overall, mobile subscription and traffic brings in more than 60% of the company's revenues, followed by fixed Internet/TV with approximately 10%. Fixed telephony, fixed data services, and others account for the rest.

Geographic Reach

Headquartered in Fornebu, Norway, Telenor operates in about 10 countries across the Nordics and Asia. Norway accounts for about 25% of the company's revenues, followed by Thailand with approximately 20%, Bangladesh with nearly 15%, and Malaysia and Sweden with more than 10% each. The remaining were generated from Finland, Pakistan, and Denmark.

Sales and Marketing

Telenor serves approximately 172 million subscribers across oil and energy, IT, healthcare, media, construction, agriculture, forestry, fishing, municipality, and transportation industries.

The company's advertising expenses were approximately NOK 1,763 million and NOK 1,761 million in 2021 and 2020, respectively.

Financial Performance

Revenues in 2021 were NOK 110.2 billion, 5% below the reported revenues of NOK 115.8 billion the previous year, driven by FX as currency adjusted revenues increased by 1%. For the full year 2021, organic subscription and traffic revenues were stable.

Net income for fiscal 2021 decreased to NOK4.6 billion compared from the prior year with NOK21.1 million. The decrease is primarily a result of a full write down of the operation in Myanmar of in total NOK 7.5 billion and gain on disposals last year of NOK 4.4 billion.

Cash held by the company at the end of fiscal 2021 increased to NOK15.1 billion. Operating activities provided NOK42.3 billion while investing and financing activities used NOK17.2 billion and NOK27.9 billion, respectively. Main cash uses were purchases of property, plant and equipment, intangible assets and prepayments for right-of-use and repayments of borrowings.

Strategy

Telenor has delivered on its strategy for the previous years and has built a solid platform for further modernization and a strengthened growth agenda while adhering to the core belief in doing business responsibly.

Telenor's strategy has delivered on the three ambitions from Capital Markets Day in 2020 to create shareholder value: growth, modernization and responsible business. The Group Strategic Action Plan forms the foundation for succeeding with Telenor's longer-term priorities.

Mergers and Acquisitions

In 2019 Telenor increased its stake in DNA, a mobile carrier in Finland, to more than 50% with the intention of eventually owning it outright. The deal will give Telenor control of the third-largest mobile operator in Finland, a country with the world's highest mobile data use in the world. DNA is also Finland's second-largest broadband service provider and operates its biggest cable-TV service.

HISTORY

Telecommunications arrived in Norway in 1855 when the first telegraph line was opened and the Norwegian Telegraph Administration was created. By 1880 telephone systems were being installed, followed by the first automatic phone exchange (1918), Telex services (1946), and a transmitter network for television, which debuted in 1960. Mobile phone service was introduced in 1966 but it was not until 1969 that the agency's name was changed to Norwegian Telecommunications Administration.

Norway had progressed to its first computer-controlled phone exchange by the mid 1970s and in 1976 launched a national satellite system (NORSAT) that linked North Sea oil explorers with Norway's mainland. It opened the world's first fully automated coastal earth station in 1982 to carry maritime traffic as part of the INMARSAT system and a year later automated its last manually operated phone exchange. (Telenor held a stake in INMARSAT until it sold it in 2006.)

In the mid-1980s the national carrier became known as Norwegian Telecom (Televerket). In 1984 it introduced an upgraded mobile phone system and a numeric paging system (alphanumeric paging followed in 1991). The first digital phone exchanges arrived in 1986 and two years later Televerket was reorganized into three units: the national operator (Televerket), a sales subsidiary (TBK), and a state regulatory agency for equipment approval (STF).

The company in 1990 organized its mobile services under a single division (Telemobil), which a year later became a limited company. Two years later data transmission was opened to competition and the resale of surplus leased line capacity was allowed.

In 1993 Televerket reorganized under the name Norwegian Telecom Group and joined a consortium of Nordic and Hungarian companies to win a mobile operator license in Hungary. A year later it became a state-owned company and in 1995 was renamed Telenor. That year it teamed up with British Telecommunications (now BT Group) and Tele Danmark (now TDC) to create the Swedish telecom competitor Telenordia (Telenor and BT became 50-50 owners in 2000).

EXECUTIVES

President, Chief Executive Officer, Sigve Brekke
Executive Vice President, Chief Financial Officer, Tone Hegland Bachke
Executive Vice President, Chief People & Sustainability Officer, Cecile Blydt Heuch
Executive Vice President, Chief Technology Officer, Ruza Sabanovic
Strategy Executive Vice President, External Relations Executive Vice President, Rita Skjaervik
Executive Vice President, Jorgen C. Arentz Rostrup
Executive Vice President, Petter-Borre Furberg
Executive Vice President, Jukka Leinonen
Chair, Gunn Waersted
Deputy Chair, Jorgen Kildahl
Director, Elisabetta Ripa
Director, Astrid Simonsen Joos
Director, Pieter Cornelis Knook
Director, Jacob Aqraou
Director, Jon Erik Reinhardsen
Employee Representative, Roger Ronning
Employee Representative, Jan Otto Eriksen
Employee Representative, Irene Vold
Auditors : Ernst & Young AS

LOCATIONS

HQ: Telenor ASA
   Snaroyveien 30, Fornebu N-1360
Phone: (47) 810 77 000
Web: www.telenor.com

2018 Sales

	% of total
Norway	26
Sweden	13
Other Nordic	5
Thailand	17
Malaysia	12
Bangladesh	12
Other Asia	13
Other Countires	2
Total	100

PRODUCTS/OPERATIONS

2018 Sales

	% of total
Mobile Subscription and Traffic	63
Fixed Internet/TV	8
Canal Digital DTH	4
Fixed Telephony	1
Fixed Data Services	1
Other Revenue	23
Total	100

COMPETITORS

Deutsche Telekom AG
EIRCOM LIMITED
Magyar Telekom Plc.
NETIA S A
Proximus
TDC A/S
TELSTRA CORPORATION LIMITED
Tele2 AB
Telekom Austria Aktiengesellschaft
Telia Company AB

HISTORICAL FINANCIALS

Company Type: Public

Income Statement				FYE: December 31
	REVENUE ($mil)	NET INCOME ($mil)	NET PROFIT MARGIN	EMPLOYEES
12/22	10,061	4,566	45.4%	14,000
12/21	12,491	173	1.4%	16,000
12/20	14,414	2,035	14.1%	18,000
12/19	12,934	884	6.8%	20,000
12/18	12,714	1,697	13.3%	21,000
Annual Growth	(5.7%)	28.1%		(9.6%)

2022 Year-End Financials

Debt ratio: 4.1% No. of shares ($ mil.): 1,399
Return on equity: — Dividends
Cash ($ mil.): 1,009 Yield: —
Current Ratio: 0.60 Payout: 29.3%
Long-term debt ($ mil.): 8,591 Market value ($ mil.): 12,997

	STOCK PRICE ($) FY Close	P/E High/Low		PER SHARE ($) Earnings	Dividends	Book Value
12/22	9.29	0	0	3.26	0.96	4.37
12/21	15.68	17	14	0.12	1.08	2.13
12/20	17.00	2	1	1.45	0.91	3.21
12/19	17.91	4	3	0.61	0.94	3.04
12/18	19.37	2	2	1.15	1.52	3.91
Annual Growth	(16.8%)	—	—	29.7%	(10.9%)	2.8%

Teleperformance SA

EXECUTIVES

Chairman, Chief Executive Officer, Daniel Julien

Chief Financial Officer, Deputy Chief Executive Officer, Olivier Rigaudy
Chief Operating Officer, Agustin Grisanti
Chief Client Officer, Miranda Collard
Chief Legal Officer, Chief Compliance Officer, Non-Independent Director, Leigh Ryan
Lead Independent Director, Independent Director, Patrick Thomas
Independent Director, Wai Ping Leung
Independent Director, Angela Maria Sierra-Moreno
Independent Director, Alain Boulet
Independent Director, Emily Abrera
Independent Director, Philippe Ginestie
Independent Director, Christobel Selecky
Independent Director, Robert Paszczak
Independent Director, Stephen Winningham
Non-Independent Director, Bernard Canetti
Non-Independent Director, Philippe Dominati
Non-Independent Director, Jean Guez
Director, Veronique deJocas
Director, Evangelos Papadopoulos
Auditors : KPMG Audit IS

LOCATIONS

HQ: Teleperformance SA
21-25 rue Balzac, Paris 75008
Phone: (33) 1 53 83 59 00 **Fax:** 786 276-8452
Web: www.teleperformance.com

HISTORICAL FINANCIALS

Company Type: Public

Income Statement				FYE: December 31
	REVENUE ($mil)	NET INCOME ($mil)	NET PROFIT MARGIN	EMPLOYEES
12/23	9,242	666	7.2%	360,980
12/22	8,708	688	7.9%	412,742
12/21	8,064	630	7.8%	418,742
12/20	7,045	397	5.6%	383,233
12/19	6,014	449	7.5%	331,065
Annual Growth	11.3%	10.4%	—	2.2%

2023 Year-End Financials

Debt ratio: 43.3% No. of shares ($ mil.): 60
Return on equity: 15.2% Dividends
Cash ($ mil.): 976 Yield: —
Current Ratio: 1.33 Payout: 18.9%
Long-term debt ($ mil.): 4,233 Market value ($ mil.): 4,421

	STOCK PRICE ($) FY Close	P/E High/Low		PER SHARE ($) Earnings	Dividends	Book Value
12/23	72.82	15	5	11.28	2.14	77.21
12/22	119.16	19	9	11.53	1.71	67.00
12/21	222.69	24	16	10.59	2.81	60.84
12/20	171.48	33	18	6.77	1.35	50.35
12/19	123.45	18	11	7.65	1.06	49.11
Annual Growth	(12.4%)	—	—	10.2%	19.1%	12.0%

Telstra Group Ltd

Telstra is Australia's #1 telecommunications carrier, serving more than 18.3 million retail mobile phone customers, 3.7 million fixed-line bundle and standalone data subscribers, and about 1.4 million standalone voice subscribers. It is also a leading ISP with more than 7.3 million fixed line broadband subscribers. Telstra's largest market is consumer and residential customers. The company also provides wholesale network services to other communications companies. Telstra has installed fifth generation (5G) network services in 10 Australian cities, preparing for the broader roll out of the technology in the coming years. Telstra has the Asia/Pacific region's largest subsea cable network, measuring about 400,000 kilometers.

Operations

Telstra operates through four segments: Telstra Consumer and Small Business (TC&SB), Telstra Enterprise (TE), Telstra InfraCo, and Networks and IT (N&IT).

The TC&SB segment, 55% of revenue, provides telecommunications products and mobile services, fixed and mobile broadband, telephone and Pay TV/IPTV, and digital content.

The TE segment, about a third of sales, manages Telstra?s business with larger companies. It manages data and internet protocol (IP) networks, mobility services, and network applications and services products such as managed network, unified communications, cloud, and integrated services

The Telstra InfraCo segment, about 10% of revenue, provides telecommunication products and services delivered over Telstra's network to other carries, carriage services providers, and inter-service providers.

The N&IT segment builds and manages the shared platforms, infrastructure, cloud services, software and technologies for internal functions.

Geographic Reach

Australia accounts for 95% of Telstra's revenue. The company's international operations, headquartered in Hong Kong, provide services to customers across the Asia/Pacific region, Europe, the Americas, the Middle East, and Africa.

Sales and Marketing

Telstra has many ways to reach its customers and prospective customers. It operates 362 branded retail stores, 90 Telstra Business Centers, and it has 127 business and enterprise partners. Its products are available in more 15,000 partner retail locations. A company initiative is to improve and expedite customer service. About 52% of its customer service interactions are handled online and 2.3 million customers use Telstra's smartphone app.

Financial Performance

Australian dollars are used in this financial report.

Telstra's revenue has been stagnant in the past five years as it has coped with increased competition in the Australian communications market.

In 2019 (ended June), revenue dropped to $27.8 billion, down about $1 billion from 2018. The company blamed the decrease on the National Broadband Network (nbn), a national wholesaler of broadband service that Telstra and other carriers buy service from. The company reported growth in its mobile, wholesale, and fixed-line businesses.

Telstra's profit also decreased, dropping to $2.1 billion in 2019, about 40% lower than the previous year, despite cost reductions made in 2019.

The company's coffers held $604 million in cash and equivalents at the end of 2019 compared to $620 million at the close of 2018. In 2019, operations generated $6.7 billion, while investing activities used $3.6 billion, and financing activities used about $3 billion.

Strategy

The launch of a national broadband network, known as nbn, has meant headaches for Telstra. In 2019 (ended June), the network cost the company about $600 million in revenue. As the top telecom provider in Australia, Telstra had been the de facto broadband provider in the country. But that role will go to nbn when the transition is complete. Telstra created its InfraCo segment in response to nbn and it positions the unit as an alternative infrastructure provider.

In the meantime, Telstra aims to improve its overall business through a plan of simplification. It is simplifying its business structure, cutting about $456 million in costs in 2019. It has made its offerings to consumers and businesses less complex, reducing the number of plans available to 20 from some 1,800.

Telstra is rolling out 5G service to more Australian cities and has begun selling 5G handsets. The emergence of the faster network could leapfrog the technologies sold by nbn and feed Telstra's revenue in the coming years.

Mergers and Acquisitions

The company acquired Pacnet Ltd., which operates undersea cables through Asia and from North America to Asia across the Pacific Ocean. The $697 million transaction brings Telstra an expanded data center network, more submarine cables, and major customers across the region. The move boosts Telstra's engagement with corporate customers.

HISTORY

When Australia gained independence in 1901, telecommunications were assigned to the new state-owned Postmaster-General's Department (PMG). Engineer H. P. Brown, who had managed the UK's telegraph and telephone system, became head of PMG in 1923. He set up research labs that year, oversaw the first overseas call to London in 1930, and streamlined operations until his reign ended in 1939.

During WWII Australia quickly expanded its communications infrastructure to assist the Allied Front in the South Pacific. Following the war, the government formed the Overseas Telecommunications Commission (OTC) in 1946 to handle international operations independent of PMG.

Even as new technology connected the continent and boosted the productivity of PMG, its postal operations steadily recorded losses in the postwar era. In 1974 a Royal Commission recommended that postal and telecom services be split. Australian Telecommunications Commission (Telecom Australia) was launched in 1975 (OTC retained overseas services); it turned a profit in its first year.

Looking to connect residents in the outback, the firm signed Japan's Nippon Electric (now NEC) in 1981 to set up a digital radio transmission system; by the next decade it connected some 50,000 outback users. Also in 1981 Telecom Australia took a 25% stake in government-owned satellite operator AUSSAT and launched nationwide paging and mobile phone service in Melbourne and Sydney.

Renamed Australian Telecommunications in 1989, the carrier got its first whiff of competition as others were allowed to provide phone equipment. Two years later Optus Communications began competing with Telecom Australia; for the privilege, it was forced to buy the unsuccessful AUSSAT. Long-distance competition began in 1991, and mobile phone competition began in 1992. In response, Telecom Australia merged with OTC to become Australian and Overseas Telecommunications Corporation (AOTC).

AOTC became Telstra Corporation in 1993 and launched a digital wireless GSM-based network. It joined with Rupert Murdoch's News Corp. to form pay TV operator FOXTEL in 1995.

EXECUTIVES

International Chief Executive Officer, International Managing Director, Executive Director, Andrew R. Penn
Strategy and Finance Chief Financial Officer, Consumer and Small Business Chief Financial Officer, Strategy and Finance Group Executive, Consumer and Small Business Group Executive, Vicki Brady
Telstra Consumer and Small Business Group Executive, Michael Ackland
Product and Technology Group Executive, Kim Krogh Andersen
Transformation and People Group Executive, Human Resources Group Executive, Alexandra Badenoch
Enterprise Group Executive, David Burns
Networks and IT Group Executive, Nikos Katinakis
Telstra Enterprise Chief Executive Officer, Telstra InfraCo Chief Executive Officer, Telstra Enterprise Group Executive, Telstra InfraCo Group Executive, Brandon Riley

Global Business Services Group Executive, Dean Salter
Sustainability, External Affairs & Legal General Counsel, Sustainability, External Affairs & Legal Group Executive, Lyndall Stoyles
Secretary, Sue Laver
Chairman, Non-Executive Director, John Patrick Mullen
Non-Executive Director, Eelco Blok
Non-Executive Director, Roy H. Chestnutt
Non-Executive Director, Craig W. Dunn
Non-Executive Director, Bridget Loudon
Non-Executive Director, Elana Rubin
Non-Executive Director, Nora L. Scheinkestel
Non-Executive Director, Niek Jan van Damme
Auditors: Ernst & Young

LOCATIONS

HQ: Telstra Group Ltd
  Level 41, 242 Exhibition Street, Melbourne, Victoria 3000
Phone: (61) 3 8647 4838 **Fax:** (61) 3 9650 0989
Web: www.telstra.com

2019 Sales

	% of total
Australia	94
Other countries	6
Total	100

PRODUCTS/OPERATIONS

2019 Sales

	% of total
Fixed	21
Mobile	42
Data & IP	9
Network applications & services	14
Media	3
Global connectivity	7
Other	4
Total	100

2015 Sales

	% of total
TC&SB	56
TE	33
Telstra InfraCo	11
N&IT	-
Other	-
Total	100

Selected Services

Advertising and directory services
Audio, video, and Internet conferencing
Broadband ISP
Cable TV
Data transmission
E-mail
Enhanced fax products and services
Freecall (toll-free 1-800 phone service)
Information technology (IT) services
Internet access
Mobile phone service
Prepaid telephony
Satellite transmission

COMPETITORS

CHARTER COMMUNICATIONS, INC.
IDT CORPORATION
LEVEL 3 PARENT, LLC
SK Telecom Co.,Ltd.
SPRINT CORPORATION
Shaw Communications Inc
TELEPHONE AND DATA SYSTEMS, INC.

VODAFONE GROUP PUBLIC LIMITED COMPANY
WINDSTREAM HOLDINGS, INC.
XO HOLDINGS, INC

HISTORICAL FINANCIALS
Company Type: Public

Income Statement — FYE: June 30

	REVENUE ($mil)	NET INCOME ($mil)	NET PROFIT MARGIN	EMPLOYEES
06/23	15,027	1,276	8.5%	31,761
06/22	14,638	1,161	7.9%	28,889
06/21	16,181	1,393	8.6%	27,015
06/20	16,248	1,246	7.7%	28,959
06/19	17,697	1,509	8.5%	29,769
Annual Growth	(4.0%)	(4.1%)	—	1.6%

2023 Year-End Financials
Debt ratio: 18.6%
Return on equity: 12.5%
Cash ($ mil.): 616
Current Ratio: 0.67
Long-term debt ($ mil.): 6,628
No. of shares ($ mil.): 11,554
Dividends
  Yield: 1.8%
  Payout: 234.1%
Market value ($ mil.): 162,571

	STOCK PRICE ($) FY Close	P/E High/Low	PER SHARE ($) Earnings	Dividends	Book Value
06/23	14.07	87 75	0.11	0.26	0.88
Annual Growth	—	— —	—	—	—

TELUS Corp

TELUS is a dynamic, world-leading communications technology company with some 18 million customer connections spanning wireless, data, IP, voice, television, entertainment, video and security. Data services include: internet protocol; television; hosting, managed information technology and cloud-based services; software, data management and data-analytics-driven smart-food chain technologies; and home and business security. Its TELUS International (TI) subsidiary provides customer experience and digital enablement transformation and designs, builds and delivers next-generation digital solutions to enhance the customer experience for clients across high-growth industry verticals.

Operations
TELUS operates through two divisions: TTech segment (about 90%) and DLCX segment (about 10%).

The TTech segment includes mobile technologies, which includes internet protocol, television, hosting, managed information technology and cloud-based services, and home and business security. The segments also include healthcare software and technology solutions, agriculture and consumer goods services, voice and other telecommunications services.

The DLCX segment, a digitally-led customer experience, is comprised of digital customer experience and digital-enablement transformation solutions, including artificial intelligence (AI), and content management.

Geographic Reach
TELUS offers its services to about 18 million customers in 160 countries globally. TELUS International operates in 30 countries globally.

Sales and Marketing
TELUS has an extensive sales network through TELUS-owned and branded stores across Canada, including its 50% ownership of the kiosk channel WOW! Mobile, and an extensive distribution network of exclusive dealers and large third-party national retail partners (Best Buy, Walmart and London Drugs), as well as online self-serve applications, intuitive virtual-assistant chatbots, mass marketing campaigns and customer care telephone agents. Through Mobile Klinik, we offer on-site professional smartphone and tablet repair services and sales.

Financial Performance
TELUS' performance for the past five years saw an upward trend with a year-over-year increase, ending with 2022 as its highest performing year over the period.

The company's revenue increased by 8.6% or $1.5 billion to $18.3 billion in 2022, as compared to 2021's revenue of $16.8 billion.

TELUS' net income for fiscal year end 2022 increased to $1.7 billion, as compared to the prior year's net income of $1.6 billion.

The company held $974 million by the end of the year. Operating activities provided $4.8 billion to the coffers. Investing activities used $5.4 billion, while financing activities provided $848 million. Main cash uses were for cash payments for capital assets, excluding spectrum licenses and redemptions and repayment of long-term debt.

Strategy
In 2022, the TELUS corporation advanced its mobile strategy: enhancing their reliable award-winning network, offering a world-leading 5G experience; elevating their customers' experience with their best-in-class customer service; focusing on high-quality, profitable customer growth, with easier access to latest smartphones; strengthening the company's business and public service offerings with tailored solutions by leveraging 5G network, including differentiated Internet of Things (IoT); and expanding their 'Mobility for Good of Indigenous Women at Risk of or Surviving Violence program.

Mergers and Acquisitions
In 2022, TELUS Corporation announced the completion of the previously disclosed acquisition of LifeWorks Inc., a world leader in providing digital and in-person solutions that support the total wellbeing of individuals ? mental, physical, financial and social, solidifying TELUS Health as one of the largest companies providing digital-first health and wellness services and solutions that empower individuals to live their healthiest lives. TELUS Health is now positioned to support corporate clients across more than 160 countries and covering more than 50 million lives and growing worldwide. The purchase price of the transaction was C$2.3 billion.

EXECUTIVES
Chairman, Director, R. H. Auchinleck
President, Chief Executive Officer, Director, Darren Entwistle
Executive Vice President, Chief Financial Officer, Doug French
Broadband Networks Executive Vice President, Broadband Networks Chief Customer Officer, Tony Geheran
Senior Vice President, Treasurer, Stephen Lewis
People and Culture Executive Vice President, People and Culture Chief Human Resources Officer, Sandy McIntosh
Chief Legal and Governance Officer, Andrea Wood
Director, W. Sean Willy
Director, Hazel Claxton
Director, Raymond T. Chan
Director, Lisa de Wilde
Director, Thomas E. Flynn
Director, Mary Jo Haddad
Director, Kathy Kinloch
Director, Christine Magee
Director, John Manley
Director, David Mowat
Director, Marc Parent
Director, Denise Pickett
Auditors : Deloitte LLP

LOCATIONS
HQ: TELUS Corp
23rd Floor, 510 West Georgia Street, Vancouver, British Columbia V6B 0M3
Phone: 604 697-8044   **Fax:** 604 899-1289
Web: www.telus.com

PRODUCTS/OPERATIONS
2018 Sales

	$ in mil.	% of total
Wireless	8,135	57
Wireline	6,233	43
Total	14,368	100

Selected Services
Data
  Data communications
  Digital data transmission
  Information services and consulting
  Internet services
  Network management
Health care
  Claims and benefits management
  Electronic health records
  Remote patient monitoring
  Pharmacy management
Wireless
  Cellular
  Digital PCS
  Satellite
  Wireless Data
Wireline
  Local exchange access
  Long-distance
  Telephone equipment sales and rentals

HISTORICAL FINANCIALS
Company Type: Public

Income Statement   FYE: December 31

	REVENUE ($mil)	NET INCOME ($mil)	NET PROFIT MARGIN	EMPLOYEES
12/23	15,093	634	4.2%	106,400
12/22	13,525	1,194	8.8%	108,500
12/21	13,220	1,299	9.8%	90,800
12/20	12,048	947	7.9%	78,100
12/19	11,203	1,340	12.0%	65,600
Annual Growth	7.7%	(17.1%)	—	12.9%

2023 Year-End Financials
Debt ratio: 36.9%
Return on equity: 5.1%
Cash ($ mil.): 651
Current Ratio: 0.67
Long-term debt ($ mil.): 17,620
No. of shares ($ mil.): 1,468
Dividends
Yield: —
Payout: 250.7%
Market value ($ mil.): 26,116

	STOCK PRICE ($) FY Close	P/E High/Low	PER SHARE ($) Earnings	Dividends	Book Value
12/23	17.79	38 28	0.44	1.10	8.28
12/22	19.31	22 17	0.85	1.00	8.56
12/21	23.57	19 16	0.96	1.02	8.66
12/20	19.80	46 16	0.74	0.89	7.35
12/19	38.73	27 24	1.11	0.85	6.69
Annual Growth	(17.7%)	— —	(20.8%)	6.7%	5.5%

Tenaris SA

Tenaris manufactures and distributes seamless steel pipe products used by several industries. Most of its products are oil country tubular goods company meant for the energy industry. Siderca, the company's Argentine producer, makes casings, tubing, and line pipe used in the oil and gas industry. Subsidiary Tubos de Acero de MÃ©xico, S.A. (Tamsa) also manufactures casings, tubing, line pipe, and other mechanical and structural seamless pipe. The Italian Dalmine makes seamless steel pipe used by the automotive and machinery industries. The company's Global Services unit provides sales and marketing services to the group's companies. In January 2019, Tenaris acquired 47.79% of the shares of Saudi Steel Pipe, a welded steel pipes producer for SAR 529.8 million (approximately $141 million). The acquired company (360,000 tons/year capacity) will help Tenaris expand its industrial presence in Saudi Arabia, one of the largest markets for line pipe products.

EXECUTIVES

Chairman, Chief Executive Officer, Executive Director, Paolo Rocca
Chief Financial Officer, Alicia Mondolo
Chief Industrial Officer, Antonio Caprera
Supply Chain Chief Supply Chain Officer, Gabriel Casanova
Chief Digital and Information Officer, Alejandro Lammertyn
Chief Human Resources Officer, Paola Mazzoleni
Chief Technology Officer, Marcelo Ramos
Director, Vice-Chairman, German Cura
Director, Vice-Chairman, Guillermo Vogel
Director, Simon Ayat
Director, Roberto Bonatti
Director, Carlos Alberto Condorelli
Director, Roberto Monti
Director, Gianfelice Mario Rocca
Director, Jamie Jose Serra Puche
Director, Yves Speeckaert
Director, Monica Tiuba
Director, Amadeo Vazquez y Vazquez
Auditors : PricewaterhouseCoopers, Societe cooperative

LOCATIONS

HQ: Tenaris SA
26, Boulevard Royal, 4th Floor, Luxembourg L-2449
Phone: (352) 26 47 89 78   **Fax:** (352) 26 47 89 79
Web: www.tenaris.com

COMPETITORS

CALIFORNIA STEEL INDUSTRIES, INC.
China Baowu Steel Group Corporation Limited
EARLE M. JORGENSEN COMPANY
General Steel Holdings, Inc.
Grupo Simec, S.A.B. de C.V.
Industrias CH, S.A.B. de C.V.
JACQUET METALS
JFE HOLDINGS, INC.
TUBACEX TUBOS INOXIDABLES SA
TUBOS REUNIDOS, SA

HISTORICAL FINANCIALS
Company Type: Public

Income Statement   FYE: December 31

	REVENUE ($mil)	NET INCOME ($mil)	NET PROFIT MARGIN	EMPLOYEES
12/23	14,868	3,918	26.4%	29,134
12/22	11,762	2,553	21.7%	25,292
12/21	6,521	1,100	16.9%	22,776
12/20	5,146	(634)	—	19,028
12/19	7,294	742	10.2%	23,200
Annual Growth	19.5%	51.6%		5.9%

2023 Year-End Financials
Debt ratio: 2.8%
Return on equity: 25.4%
Cash ($ mil.): 1,637
Current Ratio: 3.62
Long-term debt ($ mil.): 48
No. of shares ($ mil.): 1,167
Dividends
Yield: —
Payout: 32.5%
Market value ($ mil.): 40,596

	STOCK PRICE ($) FY Close	P/E High/Low	PER SHARE ($) Earnings	Dividends	Book Value
12/23	34.76	11 7	3.32	1.08	14.42
12/22	35.16	16 10	2.16	0.90	11.78
12/21	20.86	27 16	0.93	0.54	10.13
12/20	15.95	— —	(0.54)	0.14	9.54
12/19	22.64	48 32	0.63	0.82	10.16
Annual Growth	11.3%	—	51.5%	7.1%	9.2%

Tencent Holdings Ltd.

EXECUTIVES

Chairman, Chief Executive Officer, Executive Director, Huateng Ma
President, Executive Director, Martin Chi Ping Lau
Chief Information Officer, Chenye Xu
Chief Operating Officer, Yuxin Ren
Senior Executive Vice President, Xialong Zhang
Chief Strategy Officer, Senior Executive Vice President, James Gordon Mitchell
Senior Executive Vice President, Tao Sang Tong
Senior Executive Vice President, Shan Lu
Chief Exploration Officer, Senior Executive Vice President, David A. M. Wallerstein
Senior Vice President, Xiaoyi Ma
Senior Vice President, Ching-Hua Lin
Chief Financial Officer, Senior Vice President, John Shek Hon Lo
Senior Vice President, Kaitian Guo
Senior Vice President, Dan Xi
Senior Management Adviser, Kwok On Yeung
Independent Non-Executive Director, Dong Sheng Li
Independent Non-Executive Director, Ian Charles Stone
Independent Non-Executive Director, Siu Shun Yang
Independent Non-Executive Director, Yang Ke
Independent Non-Executive Director, Xiulan Zhang
Non-Executive Director, Jacobus Petrus Bekker
Non-Executive Director, Charles St. Leger Searle
Auditors : PricewaterhouseCoopers

LOCATIONS

HQ: Tencent Holdings Ltd.
Tencent Binhai Towers, No. 33 Haitian 2nd Road, Nanshan District, Shenzhen, Guangdong Province 518054
Phone: (86) 755 86013388   **Fax:** (86) 755 86013399
Web: www.tencent.com

HISTORICAL FINANCIALS
Company Type: Public

Income Statement   FYE: December 31

	REVENUE ($mil)	NET INCOME ($mil)	NET PROFIT MARGIN	EMPLOYEES
12/22	80,385	27,286	33.9%	108,436
12/21	88,226	35,412	40.1%	112,771
12/20	73,707	24,440	33.2%	85,858
12/19	54,221	13,410	24.7%	62,885
12/18	45,461	11,444	25.2%	54,309
Annual Growth	15.3%	24.3%	—	18.9%

2022 Year-End Financials
Debt ratio: 3.1%
Return on equity: 24.6%
Cash ($ mil.): 22,720
Current Ratio: 1.30
Long-term debt ($ mil.): 45,275
No. of shares ($ mil.): 9,489
Dividends
Yield: —
Payout: 48.5%
Market value ($ mil.): 401,965

	STOCK PRICE ($) FY Close	P/E High/Low	PER SHARE ($) Earnings	Dividends	Book Value
12/22	42.36	3 1	2.80	1.36	11.02
12/21	58.30	4 2	3.65	0.18	13.31
12/20	71.89	5 3	2.53	0.14	11.32
12/19	48.01	5 4	1.39	0.12	6.56
12/18	39.47	7 4	1.20	0.10	4.97
Annual Growth	1.8%	—	23.7%	91.4%	22.0%

Ternium S A

Ternium operates Latin America's largest steel entities and has become one of the leading flat steel producers. Luxembourg-based Ternium controls steel companies throughout the Americas, such as Ternium Argentina (formerly Siderar) and Mexico's Ternium Mexico. The company operates in places such as Mexico, Brazil, Argentina, Colombia, south US, and Central America. Ternium's facilities have an annual production capacity of 11.0 million tons. While it sells primarily to clients in the Americas it is developing a sales presence in Africa, Asia, and Europe as well. Majority of the company's sales were generated in Mexico.

Operations
Ternium is organized into two reportable segments: Steel and Mining.

The Steel segment generates most of the Ternium's total revenue (over 95%) and it includes the sales of steel products and other products like electricity and pig iron.

The Mining segment includes the sales of iron ore products, which are primarily consumed internally. This segment accounts for less than 5% of the revenue.

Among the company's products, hot-rolled and coated products account for the largest sales with more than 30% each, slabs account for about 10%, cold rolled with around 15%, and the rest comes from rolled formed and tubular, semi-finished, and other.

Geographic Reach
Luxembourg-based, Ternium has steel production facilities, service centers, distribution centers (DCs), and mining operations in Mexico, steel production facilities and service centers in the Southern Region, and steel production facilities, service centers and DCs in other markets, specifically Brazil, Colombia, the US and Central America.

The company has also over 10 steel production and processing units in Mexico, consisting of three integrated steel-making plants (two of which produce long steel products and one of which produces flat steel products and includes two steel service centers); five downstream flat steel processing plants, combining hot-rolling, cold-rolling and/or coating facilities (two of which include steel service centers); and four steel service centers.

About 55% of the company's sales were generated in Mexico, more than 20% in southern region, and the rest account for the others.

Sales and Marketing
The company's steel customers are in the construction, automotive, metal-mechanic and home appliances sectors, the packaging sector (for food, paints, sprays and petrochemicals), the agricultural equipment and capital goods sector, the tube and pipe sector (related to liquids and gas transportation and distribution), and steel processors. It also exports iron ore through the Manzanillo port that is located on Mexico's Pacific coast, mainly to customers in the Chinese iron ore market.

Financial Performance
Ternium's performance for the past five years have seen fluctuations but dipped from 2019 to 2020, then recovering in 2021 as the period's highest performing year.

Revenue increased by $7.4 billion to $16.1 billion in 2021 compared $8.7 billion in the prior year.

Ternium's net income increased in 2021 increased to $3.8 billion compared to the prior year's $778 million.

Cash and cash equivalents at the end of the year were $1.3 billion. Cash provided by operating activities was $2.7 billion. Investing activities and financing activities used $1 billion and $854.4 million, respectively. Main cash uses were for increase in other investments and paid dividends to company shareholders.

Strategy
Ternium's main strategic objective is to enhance shareholder value by strengthening Ternium's position as a competitive producer of steel products, in a manner consistent with minority shareholders' rights, while further consolidating Ternium's position as a leading steel producer in Latin America and a strong competitor in the Americas. The main elements of this strategy are: focus on higher margin value-added products; pursue strategic growth opportunities; implement Ternium's best practices; maximize the benefits arising from Ternium's broad distribution network; and enhance Ternium's position as a competitive steel producer.

Company Background
The Company was established as a Luxembourg sociÃ©tÃ© anonyme holding under Luxembourg's 1929 holding company regime.

EXECUTIVES

Chief Executive Officer, Maximo Vedoya
Chief Financial Officer, Pablo Brizzio
Planning General Director, Global Business Development General Director, Oscar Montero Martinez
Engineering, Industrial Coordination and Environment and Occupational Health and Safety Matters Director, Pablo Hernan Bassi
Quality Director, Ruben Herrera
Chief Information Officer, Roberto Demidchuck
Human Resources Director, Rodrigo Pina
Chairman, Paolo Rocca
Director, Vice-Chairman, Daniel Agustin Novegil
Independent Director, Gioia Ghezzi
Independent Director, Vincent Robert Gilles Decalf
Director, Ubaldo Jose Aguirre
Director, Roberto Bonatti
Director, Carlos Alberto Condorelli
Director, Adrian Lajous Vargas
Director, Gianfelice Mario Rocca
Auditors : PricewaterhouseCoopers Societe cooperative

LOCATIONS

HQ: Ternium S A
26 Boulevard Royal - 4th floor, Luxembourg L -2449
Phone: (352) 2668 3152   **Fax:** (352) 2653 8349
Web: www.ternium.com

2015 sales

	% of total
Mexico	56
Southern region	33
Others	11
Total	100

PRODUCTS/OPERATIONS

2015 sales

	% of total
Steel	97
Mining	3
Total	100

COMPETITORS

ACCIONA, SA
ArcelorMittal
Arcelormittal Brasil S/A
DEVRO PLC
Evraz Group S.A.
Gerdau S/A
IBERDROLA, SOCIEDAD ANONIMA
MetalÃºrgica Gerdau S/A.
Outokumpu Oyj
thyssenkrupp AG

HISTORICAL FINANCIALS
Company Type: Public

Income Statement — FYE: December 31

	REVENUE ($mil)	NET INCOME ($mil)	NET PROFIT MARGIN	EMPLOYEES
12/21	16,090	3,825	23.8%	20,142
12/20	8,735	778	8.9%	20,173
12/19	10,192	564	5.5%	20,061
12/18	11,454	1,506	13.2%	20,660
12/17	9,700	886	9.1%	21,255
Annual Growth	13.5%	44.1%	—	(1.3%)

2021 Year-End Financials
Debt ratio: 8.7%   No. of shares ($ mil.): 1,963
Return on equity: 42.9%   Dividends
Cash ($ mil.): 1,276   Yield: 6.6%
Current Ratio: 2.68   Payout: 239.6%
Long-term debt ($ mil.): 656   Market value ($ mil.): 85,433

	STOCK PRICE ($) FY Close	P/E High/Low		PER SHARE ($) Earnings	Dividends	Book Value
12/21	43.52	29	14	1.95	2.90	5.37
12/20	29.08	78	25	0.40	0.21	3.71
12/19	22.00	110	56	0.29	1.20	3.37
12/18	27.10	55	33	0.77	1.10	3.26
12/17	31.59	73	50	0.45	1.00	2.55
Annual Growth	8.3%	—	—	44.3%	30.5%	20.4%

Tesco PLC

EXECUTIVES

Group Chief Executive Officer, Executive Director, Ken Murphy
Chief Financial Officer, Executive Director, Imran Nawaz
Chief Customer Officer, Alessandra Bellini
Chief Technology Officer, Guus Dekkers
Communications Director, Christine Heffernan
Chief Products Officer, Ashwin Prasad
Chief People Officer, Emma Taylor
General Counsel, Adrian Morris
Secretary, Robert Welch
Chairman, John Allan
Senior Independent Non-Executive Director, Byron E. Grote
Independent Non-Executive Director, Melissa Bethell
Independent Non-Executive Director, Bertrand J. F. Bodson
Independent Non-Executive Director, Thierry Garnier
Independent Non-Executive Director, Alison Platt
Independent Non-Executive Director, Caroline Silver
Independent Non-Executive Director, Karen Whitworth
Independent Non-Executive Director, Stewart Gilliland
Independent Non-Executive Director, Carolyn Fairbairn
Auditors : Deloitte LLP

LOCATIONS

HQ: Tesco PLC
Tesco House, Shire Park, Kestrel Way, Welwyn Garden City AL7 1GA
Phone: (44) 1992 632222   **Fax:** (44) 1992 630794
Web: www.tescoplc.com

HISTORICAL FINANCIALS

Company Type: Public

Income Statement   FYE: February 25

	REVENUE ($mil)	NET INCOME ($mil)	NET PROFIT MARGIN	EMPLOYEES
02/23	78,825	892	1.1%	336,926
02/22	82,123	1,982	2.4%	354,744
02/21	80,586	8,551	10.6%	367,321
02/20	83,354	1,249	1.5%	423,092
02/19	83,156	1,720	2.1%	464,505
Annual Growth	(1.3%)	(15.1%)	—	(7.7%)

2023 Year-End Financials

Debt ratio: 19.1%
Return on equity: 5.3%
Cash ($ mil.): 2,954
Current Ratio: 0.72
Long-term debt ($ mil.): 6,689
No. of shares ($ mil.): 7,262
Dividends
  Yield: —
  Payout: 353.6%
Market value ($ mil.): 64,057

	STOCK PRICE ($) FY Close	P/E High/Low	Earnings	Dividends	Book Value
02/23	8.82	103 70	0.12	0.42	2.02
02/22	11.54	64 45	0.26	0.36	2.76
02/21	9.38	16 13	0.89	0.84	2.22
02/20	8.77	79 65	0.16	0.15	2.21
02/19	8.71	60 42	0.22	0.10	2.50
Annual Growth	0.3%	—	(14.5%)	45.1%	(5.2%)

Teva Pharmaceutical Industries Ltd

Teva Pharmaceutical Industries is a global leader in generics, biopharmaceuticals and specialty medicines with a portfolio consisting of more than 3,6500 products in nearly every therapeutic area. Teva has more than 1,100 generic products in its pre-approved global pipeline, which includes products in all stages of the approval process: pre-submission, post-submission and after tentative approval. In specialty medicines, the company focuses on three main areas ? the central nervous system (CNS) and pain, respiratory and oncology. The company operates in three segments: North America, Europe, and International Markets. Around half of the company's total revenue comes from the North America.

Operations

Teva operates its business through three segments: North America (accounts nearly 50% of company's revenue), Europe (about 30% of revenue) and International Markets (nearly 15% of revenue).

The North America segment includes the US and Canada. Its specialty portfolio has an established presence in central nervous system (CNS) medicines, and pain, respiratory and oncology.

Europe segment includes the European Union and certain other European countries. Its specialty portfolio focuses on three main areas: CNS and pain (including migraine), respiratory and oncology. Its OTC portfolio in Europe includes global brands such as SUDOCREM as well as local and regional brands such as NasenDuo in Germany and Flegamina in Poland.

The International Markets segment includes all countries in which the company operate other than those in its North America and Europe segments. These markets comprise more than 35 countries, covering a substantial portion of the global pharmaceutical market. Its specialty portfolio in International Markets focuses on three main areas: CNS and pain, respiratory and oncology.

Generic medicines produced by Teva include chemical and therapeutic versions of tablets, capsules, injectables, inhalants, liquids, ointments, and creams. It also offers a broad range of basic chemical entities, as well as specialized product families, such as sterile products, hormones, high-potency drugs and cytotoxic substances, in both parenteral and solid dosage forms. Specialty medicines include COPAXONE, AJOVY, AUSTEDO, BENDEKA and TREANDA, ProAir (ProAir HFA, ProAir Digihaler, and ProAir RespiClick), QVAR (QVAR and QVAR RediHaler), CINQAIR/CINQAERO, AirDuo RespiClick/ArmonAir RespiClick/AirDuo Digihaler and BRALTUS. In addition to focusing on therapeutic areas of CNS and respiratory medicines, Teva provides specialty medicines in oncology and selected other areas.

Teva operates about 40 finished dosage and packaging pharmaceutical plants in more than 25 countries. These plants manufacture solid dosage forms, sterile injectables, liquids, semi-solids, inhalers, transdermal patches and other medical devices. It produces approximately 76 billion tablets and capsules and approximately 680 million sterile units.

Overall, the company's sales of goods account for more than 85% of the company's total revenue, distribution generates nearly 10%, licensing arrangements and other represent the remaining.

Geographic Reach

Based in Israel, Teva operates about 80 manufacturing and R&D facilities. It also has principal executive offices in Parsippany, New Jersey and Amsterdam, the Netherlands. Its primary manufacturing technologies, solid dosage forms, injectables and blow-fill-seal, are available in North America, Europe, Latin America, India and Israel.

Sales and Marketing

Teva's generic sales in the US are made directly to retail drug chains, mail order distributors and wholesaler.

In North America, the company participates in pharmaceutical conferences and advertises in professional journals and on pharmacy websites.

The company's advertising costs for the years 2021, 2020 and 2019 were approximately $246 million, $225 million and $213 million, respectively.

Financial Performance

The company's revenue for fiscal 2021 decreased to $15.9 billion compared from the prior year with $16.7 billion.

Net income for fiscal 2021 was $456 million compared from the prior year with a net loss of $4.1 billion.

Cash held by the company at the end of fiscal 2021 increased to $2.2 billion. Cash provided by operations and investing activities were $798 million and $1.5 billion, respectively. Cash used for financing activities was $2.2 billion, mainly for repayment of senior notes and loans and other long term liabilities.

Strategy

The company's R&D activities span the breadth of its business, including generic medicines (finished goods and API), biosimilars, specialty medicines and OTC medicines.

All of its R&D activities are concentrated under one global group with overall responsibility for generics, biosimilars and specialty, enabling better focus and efficiency.

HISTORY

Teva traces its origins to Salomon, Levin and Elstein Ltd., a drug distribution firm based in Jerusalem, which, at the time, was a Jewish section of British-controlled Palestine.

Ironically, in the 1930s the company benefited from the emigration of Jewish people, many of whom were scientists, seeking to escape the Nazi regime in Germany, which at the time was the global leader in drug development. The company went public in 1951.

In 1968 Eli Hurvitz was appointed to Teva's board of directors, and scripted much of the company's growth. In 1970 Teva merged with Assia Chemical Laboratories (Hurvitz's old employer) and another company to form Teva Pharmaceutical Industries.

Ten years later Teva sold a 20% stake of itself to Koor Industries in exchange for Koor subsidiary Ikapharm, Teva's closest competitor. (Koor later launched a takeover bid, but the Founders Group, Teva's controlling shareholders, foiled the attempt.)

In 1985 Teva moved into the US. It formed a joint venture with W. R. Grace called TAG Pharmaceuticals (Teva bought out W. R. Grace's portion in 1991). In 1985 TAG bought Lemmon Co., famous -- or infamous -- for its tranquilizer Quaalude, which had gained notoriety as the recreational drug of choice for many young people. Lemmon, which ceased production of Quaalude prior to Teva's purchase, became the acquirer's generic manufacturing division.

Teva bought Abic, Israel's #2 drugmaker, in a complex 1988 transaction that gave Canadian investor and Seagram's heir Charles Bronfman a stake in the company. British publisher Robert Maxwell also bought a substantial stake in Teva. (Following Maxwell's mysterious death in 1993, his estate sold his stake.)

In the 1990s Teva turned its attention to Europe, buying companies in France, Hungary, Italy, and the UK. In 1996 the company bought US firm Biocraft Laboratories, merging it with Lemmon and forming Teva Pharmaceuticals USA.

In 1998 the company reorganized after officials realized that it had to evolve from being a collection of disparate operating entities to a more centralized operation. It also divested several operations -- including its Russian joint venture, its yeast and alcohol fermentation business, and some of its German operations -- in order to concentrate on pharmaceuticals.

EXECUTIVES

Chairman, Director, Sol J. Barer
President, Chief Executive Officer, Director, Kare Schultz, $2,000,000 total compensation
Portfolio Executive Vice President, Marketing Executive Vice President, Sven Dethlefs
Global Operations Executive Vice President, Eric Drapé
Global Research and Development Executive Vice President, Hafrun Fridriksdottir, $720,000 total compensation
Human Resources Executive Vice President, Human Resources Chief Human Resources Officer, Mark Sabag, $605,749 total compensation
Executive Vice President, Chief Legal Officer, David M. Stark
Executive Vice President, Chief Financial Officer, Eli Kalif
Division Officer, Gianfranco Nazzi
Region Officer, Richard Daniell
Region Officer, Brendan P. O'Grady
Director, Abbas Hussain
Director, Jean-Michel Halfon
Director, Nechemia (Chemi) J. Peres
Director, Janet S. Vergis
Director, Rosemary A. Crane
Director, Amir Elstein
Director, Gerald M. Lieberman
Director, Roberto A. Mignone
Director, Perry Nisen
Director, Ronit Satchi-Fainaro
Auditors: Kesselman & Kesselman (member of PricewaterhouseCoopers International Limited)

LOCATIONS

HQ: Teva Pharmaceutical Industries Ltd
124 Dvora HaNevi'a Street, Tel Aviv 6944020
Phone: (972) 3 914 8213
Web: www.tevapharm.com

2018 Sales

	$ mil.	% of total
North America	9,27	49
Europe	5,187	28
International Markets	3,005	16
Other activities	1,366	7
Total	18,854	100

PRODUCTS/OPERATIONS

2018 Sales

	$ mil.	% of total
Sales of goods	15,881	84
Distribution	1,956	10
Licensing arrangements	165	1
Other	852	5
Total	18,854	100

Selected Products
Branded products
  Central nervous system
  Azilect (Parkinson's)
  Copaxone (multiple sclerosis)
  Provigil (narcolepsy)
  Specialty respiratory
  ProAir (bronchial spasms)
  Qvar (chronic asthma)
Biosimilars
  Eporatio (erythopoietin, treatment for chemotherapy-induced anemia)
  Granulocyte Colony Stimulating Factor (anti-infective for oncology patients)
  Tev-Tropin (human growth hormone)
Generic products
  Amoxicillin (Amoxil)
  Atorvastatin (Lipitor)
  Bromatapp (Dimetapp)
  Candesartan (Atacand)
  Cimetidine (Tagamet)
  Ciprofloxacin (Cipro)
  Clemastine fumarate (Tavist)
  Clotrimazole (Lotrimin)
  Diclofenac extended release (Voltaren XR)
  Diltiazem HCl (Cardizem)
  Donepezil (Aricept)
  Fluconazole Injection (Diflucan)
  Fluoxetine (Prozac)
  Galantamine (Reminyl)
  Ketoconazole cream (Nizoral Cream)
  Lamivudine (Epivir)
  Lovastatin (Mevacor)
  Metronidazole (Flagyl)
  Quetiapine (Seroquel)
  Sotalol hydrochloride (Betapace)
  Sulfamethoxazole and Trimethoprim (Bactrim)
  Tizanidine (Zanaflex)
  Tramadol hydrochloride (Ultram/Ultracet)

COMPETITORS

ALLERGAN LIMITED
FAES FARMA, SA
LABORATORIO REIG JOFRE SA.
MANNATECH, INCORPORATED
NUTRACEUTICAL INTERNATIONAL CORPORATION
PFIZER INC.
SANOFI
TAKEDA PHARMACEUTICAL COMPANY LIMITED
TEVA PHARMACEUTICALS USA, INC.
USANA HEALTH SCIENCES, INC.

HISTORICAL FINANCIALS

Company Type: Public

Income Statement — FYE: December 31

	REVENUE ($mil)	NET INCOME ($mil)	NET PROFIT MARGIN	EMPLOYEES
12/23	15,846	(559)	—	36,472
12/22	14,925	(2,353)	—	36,826
12/21	15,878	417	2.6%	37,537
12/20	16,659	(3,990)	—	40,216
12/19	16,887	(999)	—	40,039
Annual Growth	(1.6%)	—	—	(2.3%)

2023 Year-End Financials

Debt ratio: 45.6%
Return on equity: (-7.2%)
Cash ($ mil.): 3,226
Current Ratio: 1.02
Long-term debt ($ mil.): 18,161
No. of shares ($ mil.): 1,121
Dividends
  Yield: —
  Payout: 0.0%
Market value ($ mil.): 11,704

	STOCK PRICE ($) FY Close	P/E High/Low		PER SHARE ($) Earnings	Dividends	Book Value
12/23	10.44	—	—	(0.50)	0.00	6.70
12/22	9.12	—	—	(2.12)	0.00	7.11
12/21	8.01	34	21	0.38	0.00	9.32
12/20	9.65	—	—	(3.64)	0.00	9.15
12/19	9.80	—	—	(0.91)	0.00	12.79
Annual Growth	1.6%	—	—	—	—	(14.9%)

TFI International Inc

TFI International (formerly known as TransForce) is one of North America's largest trucking companies, comprising dozens of subsidiaries offering truckload, less-than-truckload, logistics, and package and courier services across Canada and the US. Its vast e-commerce network spans more than 80 North American cities. The company boasts some 11,440 tractors, 38,090 trailers, and 6,905 independent contractors.

Operations

TFI operates through four segments: Package and Courier (P&C); Less-Than-Truckload (LTL); Truckload (TL); and Logistics.

The LTL segment accounting for around 45% of total revenue, pickups, consolidates, transports, and delivers smaller loads.

The TL segment (almost 30%) carries full loads directly from the customer to the destination using a closed van or specialized equipment to meet customers' specific needs. Includes expedited transportation, flatbed, tank, container and dedicated services.

The Logistics segment (about 20%) comprise of asset-light logistics services, including brokerage, freight forwarding and transportation management, as well as small package parcel delivery.

The P&C segment (more than 5% of total revenue) pickups, transports, and delivers items across North America

Geographic Reach

TFI's head office is in Montréal, Québec and its executive office is in Etobicoke, Ontario. The company has about 545 facilities, of which around 250 facilities are in Canada, including some 165 and 85 in Eastern and Western Canada, respectively. It also has about 295 facilities in the US.

The US is FTI's largest single market, accounting for around 70% of its total revenue.

Sales and Marketing

The company has a diverse customer base across a broad cross-section of industries, including retail, manufactured goods, automotive, building materials, metals and mining, food and beverage, services, chemicals and explosives, forest products, energy, maritime containers, and other industries.

Financial Performance

In 2022, the company had a total revenue of $8.8 billion, a 22% decrease from the previous year's total revenue of $7.2 billion. This was primarily due to the higher volume of sales in US and Canada.

Net income in 2022 was $823.2 million, a 9% increase from the previous year's net income of $754.4 million.

The company's cash at the end of 2022 was $147.1 million. Operating activities generated $971.6 million, while financing activities used $1.0 billion, mainly for repurchase of own shares. Investing activities provided another $223.4 million.

Strategy

A key part of the company's growth strategy is to acquire well-managed companies that are leaders in their market. It generally retains existing management and provides them with the requisite tools and support to excel. Its strategy is focused, disciplined, highly developed and proven.

Businesses under consideration must meet strict standards and be accretive to the company's financial performance in the near term. They must have demonstrable value in expanding its portfolio of companies by increasing the company's geographic reach, by providing complementary services, or by improving market penetration. Its preference is to acquire asset-light operations.

Smart, strategic acquisitions have been the key to the company's growth, expanding its reach, increasing its route density, and enhancing the company's capability to serve a large variety of customers, thereby promoting new platforms for further growth and strong shareholder returns.

Mergers and Acquisitions

In 2023, TFI acquired British Columbia-based Vedder Transportation Group (Vedder) which specializes in the tank truck transport of food grade liquids and dry bulk commodities. With the acquisition of Vedder, TFI adds the premier provider of such services in Western Canada along with a network of strategically located facilities, making TFI the premier Canadian coast-to-coast provider of food grade tank truck transportation services.

Also in 2023, TFI acquired Wisconsin-based JHT Holdings, Inc. (JHT), a leading asset light logistics and transportation provider in North America for Class 6-8 truck manufacturers. The acquisition brings a proprietary approach and potential synergies.

In early 2023, TFI acquired Axsun Group (Axsun), a North American provider of intermodal and freight brokerage services. Based in Montreal, Axsun operates out of multiple locations across Canada and the US, providing an integrated mix of intermodal services as well as over-the-road highway, drayage, logistics and warehousing on a primarily asset light basis. Axsun's existing business will prove complementary to TFI's service offerings in both Canada and the US, with many of its customers increasingly looking toward intermodal as a solution for their freight movement requirements. Terms of the transaction were not disclosed.

EXECUTIVES

Chairman, President, Chief Executive Officer, Director, Alain Bedard
Mergers & Acquisitions Chief Financial Officer, David Saperstein
Executive Vice President, Kal Atwal
Executive Vice President, Steven Brookshaw
Business Development Executive Vice President, Louis Gagnon
Executive Vice President, Rick Hashie
Executive Vice President, Brian Kohut
Executive Vice President, Robert McGonigal
Executive Vice President, Greg Orr
Information Technology Vice President, Daniel Auger
Finance and Operational Reporting Vice President, Daniel Chevalier
Finance & Control Vice President, Patrick Croteau
Marketing & Communications Vice President, Johanne Dean
Human Resources Vice President, Sylvain Desaulniers
Legal Affairs Vice President, Legal Affairs Corporate Secretary, Josiane M. Langlois
Insurance & Compliance Vice President, Chantal Martel
Finance Vice President, Martin Quesnel
Taxes Vice President, Ken Tourangeau
Director, Leslie Abi-Karam
Lead Director, Andre Berard
Director, Lucien Bouchard
Director, William T. England
Director, Diane Giard
Director, Richard Guay
Director, Debra J. Kelly-Ennis
Director, Neil D. Manning
Director, Joey Saputo
Director, Rosemary Turner
Auditors : KPMG LLP

LOCATIONS

HQ: TFI International Inc
8801 Trans-Canada Highway, Suite 500, Montreal, Quebec H4S 1Z6
Phone: 514 331-4113   **Fax:** 514 337-4200
Web: www.tfiintl.com

2018 Sales

	% of total
Canada	56
US	43
Mexico	1
Total	100

PRODUCTS/OPERATIONS

2018 Sales

	% of total
Truckload	46
Less-than-truckload	20
Logistics	20
Package & courier	15
Total	100

Selected Services
Less-Than-Truckload
Logistics
Package And Courier
Truckload

COMPETITORS

AMTRUST FINANCIAL SERVICES, INC.
ARCBEST CORPORATION
COVENANT LOGISTICS GROUP, INC.
KNIGHT TRANSPORTATION, INC.
KNIGHT-SWIFT TRANSPORTATION HOLDINGS INC.
LeasePlan Corporation N.V.
MAPFRE, SA
SCHNEIDER NATIONAL, INC.
SEACO GLOBAL LIMITED
WERNER ENTERPRISES, INC.

HISTORICAL FINANCIALS

Company Type: Public

Income Statement — FYE: December 31

	REVENUE ($mil)	NET INCOME ($mil)	NET PROFIT MARGIN	EMPLOYEES
12/22	8,812	823	9.3%	25,836
12/21	7,220	664	9.2%	29,539
12/20	3,781	275	7.3%	16,753
12/19	3,977	238	6.0%	17,150
12/18	3,762	214	5.7%	17,127
Annual Growth	23.7%	40.0%	—	10.8%

2022 Year-End Financials

Debt ratio: 23.9%
Return on equity: 35.1%
Cash ($ mil.): 147
Current Ratio: 1.31
Long-term debt ($ mil.): 1,278
No. of shares ($ mil.): 86
Dividends
Yield: —
Payout: 12.8%
Market value ($ mil.): 8,675

	STOCK PRICE ($) FY Close	P/E High/Low		PER SHARE ($) Earnings	Dividends	Book Value
12/22	100.24	12	8	9.02	1.16	28.46
12/21	112.11	17	7	6.97	0.96	24.09
12/20	51.58	17	6	3.03	0.80	19.17
12/19	33.80	9	7	2.79	0.75	14.20
12/18	25.94	11	7	2.36	0.66	13.40
Annual Growth	40.2%	—		39.8%	15.1%	20.7%

Thales

Thales develops and manufactures weapons, munitions, and equipment for waging war across all defensible spheres: land, air, water, space, and digital. Thales' primary customers are national defense forces across the globe with a particular focus on Europe, which accounts for nearly 55% of sales. Besides defense and security products, Thales' aerospace segment outfits commercial planes with in-flight entertainment and connectivity equipment and provides flight simulator-based pilot training, while a transport division provides rail signaling, monitoring, and ticketing for rail networks. Thales has operations in about 70 countries. The French government owns about 35% of Thales.

Operations

Thales divides its operations in three segments: Aerospace (about 30% of the company's revenue), Defense & Security (more than 50%), and Digital ID & Security (more than 20%).

Through the Aerospace segment, the company supports aircraft manufacturers, armed forces, airlines, operators, pilots, crews and passengers in making improvements to flight efficiency, safety, and comfort. The Defense & Security segment provides equipment and systems to logistics supports and related services, providing the needs of markets.

Over 30,000 organizations rely on the company's Digital Identity & Security solutions to verify the identities of people and of objects, to authorize access to digital services and to protect data. The segment solutions include physical and digital identity creation and management, authentication (including biometrics), connectivity, and data encryption.

Geographic Reach

Thales operates in about 70 countries, with Europe accounting for about 60% of the company's revenue. The company also has operations in North America (about 15%) and Asia (more than 10%). Other markets include the Middle East, Australia, and New Zealand.

Sales and Marketing

Customers include some of the world's largest corporations, as well as government. Almost 60% of Thales' revenues comes from government customers and more than 40% of its revenue comes from non-government customers (private operators of critical infrastructure, aircraft manufactures, etc.).

Financial Performance

Although Thales' performance for the past five years has fluctuated, there was an overall increase with 2022 as the company's second-highest performing year over the period.

The company's performance increased by EUR1.4 billion to EUR17.6 billion for 2022, as compared to 2021's revenue of EUR16.2 billion.

Thales's net income slightly decreased to EUR1.1 billion, almost the same as the prior year's net income of EUR1.1 billion.

The company held EUR5.3 billion at the end of the year. Thales generated EUR3 billion to the coffers. Investing activities and financing activities used EUR1.1 billion and EUR1.7 billion, respectively. Main cash uses were for acquisitions of subsidiaries and affiliates and repayment of debt.

Strategy

In recent financial years, to support its strategic Ambition 10 plan, the company has decided to step up its self funded R&D expenditure. In 2020, under the global Covid 19 crisis adaptation plan the company reduced its self financed R&D expenditure, while keeping it stable as a percentage of sales. In 2021, this expenditure rose faster than sales. It reached 6.3% of sales, up 20 basis points compared to 2020.

Targeted investment in R&D, in intangible and property plant and equipment as part of acquisitions as well as the purchase of equity interests are all major factors advancing the company's development strategy.

Mergers and Acquisitions

In 2022, Thales agreed to acquire two of European leading cybersecurity companies, S21sec and Excellium, gathered under the holding company Maxive Cybersecurity. This acquisition will complement Thales' cybersecurity portfolio, strengthening its incident detection and response services (Security Operations Centre ? SOC) as well as consulting, audit and integration services. The acquisition, for an enterprise value of EUR 120 million, is an important step forward for Thales in the highly dynamic market for cybersecurity consulting and managed services, which anticipates significant growth between 2020 and 2025.

Also in 2022, Thales acquired RUAG Simulation & Training, including its 500 employees and with sales worth approximately EUR 90 million in 2021. The consolidation will complement Thales's footprint in the land market in particular, meanwhile sustaining its field-proven expertise in helicopters and military aircraft solutions. This acquisition will provide an opportunity to reinforce local footprint in priority geographies (France, Switzerland, Germany, and UK), while increasing presence in UAE and Australia.

HISTORY

Compagnie Française Thomson-Houston (CFTH) began as a subsidiary for US-based tramway-equipment maker Thomson-Houston Electric Corporation in 1893. French investors bought the subsidiary when Thomson-Houston and Edison General Electric merged to become General Electric (GE). The fledgling company kept its founder's name and maintained a licensing agreement with GE. Early interests included power stations and the electrification of tramways. Diversification in the 1920s included the acquisition of Société des Usines du Pied-Selle (kitchen and heating equipment, 1920) and the formation of a finance company, Financiere Éelectricité (1925).

Alsthom was created in 1928 when Thomson and Société Alsacienne de Constructions Mécaniques joined to make industrial electrical equipment. Radio and TV receivers were added in 1929 when Thomson acquired Éetablissements Ducretet.

The 1930s brought the acquisition of Éetablissement Kraemer (radio equipment, 1936). During WWII, however, operations not used by the German military sat idle.

Postwar political conflict between France and the US, plus Thomson's involvement in defense and nuclear technology, caused it to end association with GE in 1953. A 1959 agreement with Pathé-Marconi began radio and TV production.

A 1966 merger with Hotchkiss-Brandt resulted in a new name, Thomson-Brandt. In 1968 another merger and another name change, Thomson-CSF, occurred when Compagnie Générale de TSF joined Thomson. In 1981 the French nationalized Thomson-Brandt, and in 1982 created holding company Thomson S.A. to manage it. Opposition to the government's nationalization in 1987 forced Thomson's return to the private sector, and the company formed semiconductor unit SGS-Thomson Microelectronics. In 1989 the company acquired defense electronics businesses MBLE (Belgium) and Signaal (Denmark) from Philips.

Arms sales declined in 1991 and the company began to produce consumer goods such as satellite TV dishes. A 1992 agreement introduced IBM technology to Thomson defense and space products. UK-based GEC and Thomson began making sonar and antisubmarine systems after a 1995 agreement.

Thomson sold its interests in Crédit Lyonnais Securities to the French government in 1996. The company sold its semiconductor unit in 1997. Thomson strengthened its defense business by taking a majority interest in Siemens Forvarssystemer (military communications, Norway) in 1998 and striking a $500 million deal with Raytheon to make control systems for NATO in 1999. That year Thomson also purchased a 42% stake in Singapore-based optronics company Avimo Group.

Late in 1999 Shorts Missile Systems Ltd. (SMS) -- Thomson's joint venture with Canada-based Bombardier-- won a long-term $319 million contract to make short-range Starstreak anti-aircraft missiles for the UK. In 2000 Thomson-CSF acquired UK-based Racal Electronics, a defense electronics firm, for $2.17 billion and bought out Bombardier's share in the SMS venture. Also in 2000 the company announced plans to sell Crouzet-Automatismes (its electro-mechanical components division) to Schneider Electric. In December Thomson-CSF changed its name to Thales and agreed to form a joint air-defense venture (Thales-Raytheon Systems) with Raytheon.

In 2001 the company acquired majority control over optronics company Avimo. The same year Thales sold its 48.8% stake in Alcatel Space to joint venture partner Alcatel for about $700 million. (That deal and another sale of Thales' stock late in the year reduced Alcatel's stake to about 16%.) Thales also agreed to buy Orbital Science's GPS businesses, Magellan Corporation, and Navigation Solutions LLC (NavSol), a joint venture with Hertz, for about $70 million. In November the company sold Thales Instruments (the former instruments business of Racal) to an investment firm consortium for about $120 million.

Thales agreed to sell its computer services arm, Thales IS, to French IT company GFI Informatique in 2002. However, GFI abandoned the deal, which would have been worth more than $300 million, soon after it was announced.

In 2004 Thales gained ground when BAE lost prime contractor status in building the Royal Navy's new carriers; but the two companies would ultimately work together, with US-based KBR coordinating things. The following year Thales inked a ?236 million deal to supply 18 facilities with Tiger combat helicopter simulators.

In 2006 Thales and Germany's Diehl Stiftung & Co. merged their aerospace activities, specifically cockpit avionics systems and flight and engine control, to create a new joint venture company, Diehl Aerospace GmbH. The two companies teamed up again to form Junghans Microtec GmbH, a combination of the two companies' ammunition fuse and safety device operations.

In exchange for a near 21% stake in Thales, plus cash, Thales acquired the satellite-building and homeland security businesses of telecom-equipment maker Alcatel-Lucent in 2006. The deal included Alcatel-Lucent's transport systems division, which makes signaling systems for railways and subway systems. As part of the acquisition, the French government's stake in Thales decreased.

Thales acquired a 25% slice of shipyard concern Direction des Constructions Navales (DCN) in 2007, with an option to increase its stake to as much as 35%. In return Thales handed over its Naval France business to DCN and a stake in three of Thales's concerns. The tie-up pushes Thales's system capabilities to the front of the European naval market. Also that same year, ITT Gilfillan and Thales inked a deal that would enable ITT radar systems to have the exclusive right to market and produce the Smart SMK II radar system for the US market. Thales also has a manufacturing facility in Maryland where it works on the Joint Tactical Radio System.

The company sold its Thales Computers unit to Kontron Modular Computers in 2008 for ?11 million (over $14 million). It also divested its electronic payment business that same year; American Group Hypercom purchased it for over ?93 million (almost $125 million).

To expand its information and communications systems security business, the company pocketed nCipher in 2008, a supplier of encryption products for government, financial institutions, and enterprises that need to protect sensitive data. Also in 2008 Thales joined Emirates Advanced Investments subsidiary C4 Advanced Solutions (C4AS) to step up military communication systems and equipment in the Middle East and Northern Africa. Holding a 49% stake in the Abu Dhabi-based joint venture (Thales Advanced Solutions), Thales supplies tactical radio maintenance, in-service support for products and systems, and software for communications systems to UAE armed forces. The joint venture extended Thales's regional influence; the company already won a deal to integrate communications at Abu Dhabi International Airport's air traffic control center tower. India is a customer too, and operates combat aircraft built by Dassault and Thales.

Thales purchased Israel-based medical imaging company CMT Medical Technologies in 2009 for about ?20 million (more than $28 million). While its medical imaging business took a giant hit during the recession, its joint venture with Philips and Siemens (Thales holds 51%) to make digital X-ray detectors offset the impact. The acquisition of CMT satisfies all the needs of OEM requirements.

EXECUTIVES

Performance Senior Executive Vice President, Operations Senior Executive Vice President, Performance Chief Executive Officer, Operations Chief Executive Officer, Chairman, Patrice Caine

Human Resources Senior Executive Vice President, Clement de Villepin

Operations and Performance Senior Executive Vice President, Jean-Loic Galle

International Development Senior Executive Vice President, Pascale Sourisse

Information Systems Senior Executive Vice President, Finance Senior Executive Vice President, Pascal Bouchiat

Ground Transportation Systems Executive Vice President, Millar Crawford

Digital Identity and Security Executive Vice President, Philippe Vallee

Space Executive Vice President, Herve Derrey

Avionics Executive Vice President, Yannick Assouad

Defence Mission Systems Executive Vice President, Philippe Duhamel

Strategy, Research and Technology Executive Vice President, Philippe Keryer

Land and Air System Executive Vice President, Christophe Salomon

Secure Communications Executive Vice President, Information Systems Executive Vice President, Marc Darmon

Executive Vice President, Secretary, General Counsel, Isabelle Simon

Independent Director, Philippe Knoche

Independent Director, Armelle de Madre

Independent Director, Anne-Claire Taittinger

Independent Director, Ann Taylor

Director, Anne Rigail

Director, Charles Edelstenne

Director, Bernard Fontana

Director, Loiek Segalen

Director, Delphine Geny-stephann

Director, Marie-Francoise Walbaum

Director, Emmanuel Moulin

Director, Eric Trappier

Director, Philippe Lepinay

Auditors : Mazars

LOCATIONS

HQ: Thales
Tour Carpe Diem, Place des Corolles â€" Esplanade Nord, Courbevoie 92400
Phone: (33) 1 57 77 80 00
Web: www.thalesgroup.com

2018 Sales

	% of total
Europe	55
Asia	14
Middle East	10
North America	9
Australia & New Zealand	5
Rest of the World	6
Total	100

PRODUCTS/OPERATIONS

2018 Sales

	% of total
Defense & Security	51
Aerospace	36
Transport	13
Total	100

Selected Divisions
Air operations
Avionics
Defense & security C4I systems
Defense mission systems
Land defense
Space
Transportation systems

Selected Subsidiaries
TDA Armements
Thales Air Systems
Thales Alenia Space
Thales Avionics
Thales Communications
Thales Electron Devices (TED)
Thales Optronique
Thales Raytheon Systems
Thales Security Solutions & Services SAS
Thales Services
Thales Systèmes Aéroportés
Thales Underwater Systems

COMPETITORS
CAPGEMINI
COBHAM LIMITED
FLEX LTD.
GENERAL DYNAMICS CORPORATION
GRIFFON CORPORATION
JOHNSON CONTROLS INTERNATIONAL PUBLIC LIMITED COMPANY
L3HARRIS TECHNOLOGIES, INC.
SPIRENT COMMUNICATIONS PLC
TECHNICOLOR
TT ELECTRONICS PLC

HISTORICAL FINANCIALS

Company Type: Public

Income Statement — FYE: December 31

	REVENUE ($mil)	NET INCOME ($mil)	NET PROFIT MARGIN	EMPLOYEES
12/21	18,327	1,232	6.7%	81,098
12/20	20,850	593	2.8%	80,702
12/19	20,660	1,259	6.1%	82,605
12/18	18,156	1,124	6.2%	66,135
12/17	18,934	985	5.2%	64,860
Annual Growth	(0.8%)	5.8%	—	5.7%

2021 Year-End Financials
Debt ratio: 20.4%
Return on equity: 18.7%
Cash ($ mil.): 5,715
Current Ratio: 1.06
Long-term debt ($ mil.): 5,209
No. of shares ($ mil.): 212
Dividends
 Yield: 2.7%
 Payout: 7.6%
Market value ($ mil.): 3,677

	STOCK PRICE ($) FY Close	P/E High/Low	PER SHARE ($) Earnings	Dividends	Book Value
12/21	17.27	4 3	5.78	0.47	34.45
12/20	18.36	11 6	2.79	0.10	29.49
12/19	21.07	2314 361	0.06	0.48	28.76
12/18	118.00	28 26	5.27	0.52	30.72
Annual Growth	(47.3%)	— —	2.4%	(2.5%)	2.9%

ThyssenKrupp AG

Thyssenkrupp (pronounced TISS-in kroop) is an international group of companies consisting largely of independent industrial and technology businesses. The German company's operations span about 740 sites and numerous sectors and fields, including industrial components, automotive technology, marine systems, material services, multi tracks and steel manufacture. Thyssenkrupp is active in about 50 countries worldwide but gets around 35% of total sales outside German-speaking areas. The company was formed in 1999 via the merger of German industrial companies Thyssen and Krupp.

Operations
The company operates through six operating segments:

Materials Services is the largest independent materials distributor and service provider in the western world (Europe and North America). ThyssenKrupp's portfolio ranges from high-quality materials and raw materials to technical services and intelligent processes for automation, extended supply chains, warehousing and inventory management. The segment accounts for more than 35% of total revenue.

Industrial Components comprises two business units: Bearings and Forged Technologies. The segment accounts for around 5% of revenue.

Automotive Technology is a leading German supplier and engineering partner to the international automotive industry. Its product and service portfolio comprises high-tech components, systems and automation solutions for vehicle manufacturing, as well as mechatronic solutions with electronics and internally developed software. The segment accounts for around 10% of revenues.

Steel Europe is the largest steel producer in Germany and concentrates on the attractive market segment of high-quality flat carbon steel, where it is one of the most important suppliers in its core European market. Its product portfolio comprises hot-rolled coil, sheet steel, premium cut-to-length sheets, coated products, tinplate, medium coil and grain-oriented and non-oriented electrical steel in a wide range of grades. The segment accounts for around 30%.

Marine Systems is a leading global manufacturer of conventional submarines, naval vessels and marine electronics and offers services to navies covering the full product lifecycle. As a fully integrated system supplier (platform, electronics, integration and services), the company develop and manufacture holistic solutions from a single source for its customers, both in Germany and in the customer's country. The segment accounts for around 5% of revenues.

In the Multi Tracks segment, thyssenkrupp bundles businesses where we see differences in potential and are therefore considering different development paths. This may be full or partial disposal, for example, or the continuation of a business with one or more external partners. The segment accounts for around 10% of revenue.

Geographic Reach
ThyssenKrupp operates through approximately 740 sites in around 50 countries across four continents.

Company's largest market was the German-speaking countries with around by 35% of total revenue; followed by North America and Western Europe with around 20%, each.

Sales and Marketing
Thyssenkrupp sells its products to industries including the automotive sector (some 30% of annual sales), steel and processing (about 15%), trading (around 10%), engineering (about 10%), public sector (around 5%), packaging (nearly 5%), construction and energy and utility (less than 5%), and other customer groups generates more than 20%.

Financial Performance
ThyssenKrupp's revenue for the past five fiscal years experienced decreases and increases starting from EUR41.5 billion in 2018, to EUR42.0 billion, EUR35.4 billion, EUR34.0 billion, and EUR41.1 billion, for fiscal 2019 to 2022, respectively.

Company's revenue for fiscal 2022 increased by 21% to EUR41.1 billion compared from the prior year with EUR34.0 billion. The increase was primarily due to higher revenues in every segment aside from Marine systems, and Multi Tracks.

Net income for fiscal 2022 was EUR1.2 billion compared from the prior year with a net loss of EUR25 million. The improvement was primarily due to higher revenues offsetting the increase in expenses.

Cash held by the company at the end of fiscal 2022 decreased to EUR7.6 billion. Cash provided by operation was EUR618 million while cash used for investing and financing activities were EUR277 million and EUR1.8 billion, respectively. Main uses of cash were capital expenditures and repayments of bonds

Strategy
The aim is to transform Thyssenkrupp into a high-performing and sustainable company with a lean management model and a clearly structured portfolio focused on growth opportunities. The framework for this is its brand and its values.

To develop the businesses of Thyssenkrupp AG in the best possible way, the Company's transformation will continue to focus on opportunities for our technologies arising from the issues of the future. In the green transformation in particular the company already sees enormous potential for further growth in the medium and long term, for example in the areas of hydrogen, green chemicals, renewable energies, electromobility and sustainable supply chains.

HISTORY

Formed separately in the 1800s, both Thyssen and Krupp flourished in their early years under family control. Friedrich Krupp opened his steel factory in 1811. He died in 1826 and left the nearly bankrupt factory in the hands of his 14-year-old son Alfred, who turned the business around. At the first World's Fair in 1851, Alfred unveiled a steel cannon far superior to earlier bronze models.

Twenty years later August Thyssen founded a puddling and rolling mill near Mulheim. He bought small factories and mines, and by WWI he ran Germany's largest iron and steel company. During the world wars the resources of both companies were turned toward military efforts.

Post-WWII years were tough for both companies. Thyssen was split up by the Allies, and when it began production again in 1953, it consisted of one steel plant. In the Krupp camp, Alfred's great-grandson Alfried was convicted in 1948 of using slave labor during WWII. Released from prison in 1951, Alfried rebuilt Krupp. After near ruin following WWII, both companies emerged and enjoyed a resurgence, along with the German economy, in which they prospered and expanded during the 1950s.

By the 1980s Thyssen's businesses included ships, locomotives, offshore oil rigs, specialty steel, and metals trading and distribution. Krupp continued to grow, and in 1992 it took over engineering and steelmaking concern Hoesch AG. (Eberhard Hoesch had begun making railroad tracks in the 1820s. The company grew and expanded into infrastructure and building products.)

The new Fried. Krupp AG Hoesch-Krupp bought Italian specialty steelmaker Acciai Speciali Terni, chemical-plant builder Uhde, and South African shipper J.H. Bachmann. Its automotive division formed a joint venture in Brazil and added production sites in China, Mexico, Romania, and the US.

In 1997 Thyssen expanded in North America with its $675 million acquisition of Giddings & Lewis (machine tools, US) and the purchase of Copper & Brass Sales (metals processing and distributing).

Krupp attempted a hostile takeover of Thyssen in 1997. The takeover failed, but the companies soon agreed to merge their steel operations to form Thyssen Krupp Stahl. Bigger plans were in the works, and in 1998 the two companies agreed to merge. That year Thyssen sold its Plusnet fixed-line phone business to Esprit Telecom Group.

In 1999 Krupp's automotive division (Krupp Hoesch Automotive) bought Cummins' Atlas Crankshaft subsidiary. Thyssen also bought US-based Dover's elevator business for $1.1 billion. Krupp and Thyssen completed their merger in 1999. The company planned to spin off its steel operations, but held off due to its success in 2000. ThyssenKrupp did, however, sell its Krupp Kunststofftechnik unit (plastic molding machines) for about $183 million. To speed corporate decision-making, the company made plans to scrap its dual-management structure in 2001.

Early in 2001 ThyssenKrupp agreed to buy 51% of Fiat unit Magneti Marelli's suspension-systems and shock-absorbers business. It also had the option of buying the remainder after 2004. In 2002 the company formed alliances with NKK and Kawasaki Steel to share its steel sheet making technologies while expanding its business with Japanese automotive makers in Europe. ThyssenKrupp's joint venture with Chinese steelmaker ANSC Angang New Steel, known as TAGAL, began producing galvanized coil of which about 80% will be used in China's burgeoning automotive industry.

In 2004 ThyssenKrupp sold its residential real estate unit for around $2.8 billion to a consortium of real estate funds operated by Morgan Stanley and Corpus-Immobiliengruppe. It divested the automotive segment of the capital goods unit in 2006, selling it off in pieces.

ThyssenKrupp opened three major, new steel facilities in the Americas in 2010. A new integrated steel mill in Santa Cruz, Brazil, started production in mid-year. The $7 billion plant, the company's biggest project ever, is a partnership with South American giant Vale SA, which owns a 25% stake in the venture. The company also began production at two plants in Calvert, Alabama: a $3.6 billion carbon steel plant and a $1.4 billion stainless steel rolling plant. The company also constructed -- and consolidated its corporate staff in -- a new headquarters building in Essen, Germany in 2010.

EXECUTIVES

Chief Executive Officer, Martina Merz
Chief Financial Officer, Klaus Keysberg
Labor Chief Human Resources Officer, Labor Member, Labor Director, Oliver Burkhard
Independent Chairman, Siegfried Russwurm
Vice-Chairman, Jurgen Kerner
Independent Director, Birgit A. Behrendt
Independent Director, Stefan Erwin Buchner
Independent Director, Wolfgang Colberg
Independent Director, Ursula Gather
Independent Director, Angelika Gifford
Independent Director, Bernhard Gunter
Independent Director, Friederike Helfer
Independent Director, Ingo Luge
Independent Director, Verena Volpert
Director, Achim Haas
Director, Tanja Jacquemin
Director, Daniela Jansen
Director, Christian Julius
Director, Thorsten Koch
Director, Tekin Nasikkol
Director, Peter Remmler
Director, Dirk Sievers
Director, Isolde Wurz
Auditors : PricewaterhouseCoopers GmbH Wirtschaftsprufungsgesellschaft

LOCATIONS

HQ: ThyssenKrupp AG
ThyssenKrupp Allee 1, Essen 45143
Phone: (49) 201 844 0   **Fax:** (49) 201 844 53600
Web: www.thyssenkrupp.com

Sales 2018
USA	16
China	7
Other	48
Total	100

PRODUCTS/OPERATIONS

Sales 2018
	%
Components Technology	17
Elevator Technology	17
Industrial Solutions	11
Materials Services	33
Steel Europe	21
Corporate	1
Total	100

COMPETITORS

Franz Haniel & Cie. GmbH
GEA Group AG
GKN LIMITED
Gerdau S/A
JFE HOLDINGS, INC.
MARUBENI CORPORATION
Outokumpu Oyj
RENISHAW P L C
VALEO
VALLOUREC

HISTORICAL FINANCIALS
Company Type: Public

Income Statement — FYE: September 30

	REVENUE ($mil)	NET INCOME ($mil)	NET PROFIT MARGIN	EMPLOYEES
09/23	39,768	(2,195)	—	99,981
09/22	40,103	1,107	2.8%	96,494
09/21	39,372	(133)	—	101,275
09/20	33,836	11,222	33.2%	103,598
09/19	45,811	(331)	—	162,372
Annual Growth	(3.5%)	—	—	(11.4%)

2023 Year-End Financials
Debt ratio: 9.6%
Return on equity: (-15.9%)
Cash ($ mil.): 7,775
Current Ratio: 1.83
Long-term debt ($ mil.): 1,391
No. of shares ($ mil.): 622
Dividends
Yield: —
Payout: 0.0%
Market value ($ mil.): 4,757

	STOCK PRICE ($) FY Close	P/E High/Low		PER SHARE ($) Earnings	Dividends	Book Value
09/23	7.64	—	—	(3.53)	0.10	20.15
09/22	4.23	6	2	1.77	0.15	22.24
09/21	10.55	—	—	(0.21)	0.00	19.34
09/20	5.00	1	0	18.03	0.00	18.45
09/19	13.98	—	—	(0.53)	0.11	3.07
Annual Growth	(14.0%)			—	(1.6%)	60.1%

Tochigi Bank Ltd.

Founded in 1942, the Tochigi Bank offers banking services to the Tochigi Prefecture in Japan (located about 60 miles north of Tokyo). Through more than 90 branches and 4 consolidated subsidiaries, Tochigi Bank offers conventional financial services products such as savings, lending, portfolio advisement, leasing, housing loan guarantees, credit cards, and foreign and domestic exchange services. The Tochigi Prefecture has developed into a production nucleus for agricultural and forestry products; as a result, the bank targets customers residing in these key sectors for assistance.

EXECUTIVES

President, Representative Director, Director, Junnosuke Kuromoto
Deputy President, Representative Director, Director, Sakae Ueki
Senior Managing Director, Director, Yoshifumi Inomata
Director, Yoshiaki Hashimoto
Director, Hiroshi Kondo
Director, Naohisa Isayama
Director, Hiroyuki Nakada
Director, Yoshimori Tomikawa
Outside Director, Toshimasa Aso
Outside Director, Akiko Kameoka
Outside Director, Jun Sekine
Outside Director, Yasuhisa Otani
Auditors : Deloitte Touche Tohmatsu LLC

LOCATIONS

HQ: Tochigi Bank Ltd.
 2-1-18 Nishi, Utsunomiya, Tochigi 320-8680
Phone: (81) 28 633 1241
Web: www.tochigibank.co.jp

COMPETITORS

AKBANK TURK ANONIM SIRKETI
AWA BANK, LTD., THE
DAISHI HOKUETSU BANK, LTD.
HIGO BANK, LTD., THE
KAGOSHIMA BANK, LTD., THE

HISTORICAL FINANCIALS
Company Type: Public

Income Statement				FYE: March 31
	ASSETS ($mil)	NET INCOME ($mil)	INCOME AS % OF ASSETS	EMPLOYEES
03/21	29,452	18	0.1%	2,209
03/20	26,943	16	0.1%	2,270
03/19	26,117	12	0.0%	2,331
03/18	27,031	42	0.2%	2,359
03/17	25,443	68	0.3%	2,276
Annual Growth	3.7%	(27.6%)	—	(0.7%)

2021 Year-End Financials
Return on assets: —
Return on equity: 1.2%
Long-term debt ($ mil.): —
No. of shares ($ mil.): 104
Sales ($ mil.): 364
Dividends
 Yield: —
 Payout: 25.1%
Market value ($ mil.): —

Toho Bank, Ltd. (The)

The Toho Bank is a regional bank serving the Fukushima Prefecture in Japan. Armed with more than 115 branches and ATMs installed at more than 230 locations, the bank offers local customers, businesses, and public institutions the traditional array of banking services including savings, lending, real estate, venture firm support and financing, and foreign and domestic exchange products. Toho Bank was established in 1941 and owns subsidiaries and affiliated companies such as The Toho Real Estate Service Co., The Toho Card Co., and The Toho Staff Service Co.

EXECUTIVES

President, Representative Director, Minoru Sato
Senior Managing Director, Representative Director, Hideho Suto
Director, Kiichi Yokoyama
Director, Shigeki Nanaumi
Outside Director, Masako Konishi
Outside Director, Hideya Takashima
Director, Takayuki Ishii
Outside Director, Hayao Watanabe
Outside Director, Satoshi Nagano
Outside Director, Ichiro Kawano
Auditors : Ernst & Young ShinNihon LLC

LOCATIONS

HQ: Toho Bank, Ltd. (The)
 3-25 Ohmachi, Fukushima 960-8633
Phone: (81) 24 523 3131
Web: www.tohobank.co.jp

COMPETITORS

CHUKYO BANK, LIMITED.
HYAKUGO BANK,LTD., THE
IYO BANK, LTD., THE
NANTO BANK,LTD., THE
TOWA BANK,LTD., THE

HISTORICAL FINANCIALS
Company Type: Public

Income Statement				FYE: March 31
	ASSETS ($mil)	NET INCOME ($mil)	INCOME AS % OF ASSETS	EMPLOYEES
03/22	58,661	55	0.1%	2,533
03/21	61,344	(42)	—	2,617
03/20	55,465	25	0.0%	2,725
03/19	53,367	32	0.1%	2,821
03/18	56,759	69	0.1%	2,927
Annual Growth	0.8%	(5.3%)	—	(3.5%)

2022 Year-End Financials
Return on assets: —
Return on equity: 3.5%
Long-term debt ($ mil.): —
No. of shares ($ mil.): 252
Sales ($ mil.): 495
Dividends
 Yield: —
 Payout: 0.0%
Market value ($ mil.): —

Toho Holdings Co Ltd

Toho is striving to become more specialized than before in the respective business segments of pharmaceutical wholesaling, dispensing pharmacy, manufacturing and sales of pharmaceutical and others. Subsidiary Toho Pharmaceutical is one of the country's leading pharmaceutical wholesalers, supplying medicines and other products to tens of thousands of customers, including clinics, hospitals, medical institutions, and pharmacies. The company purchases pharmaceuticals, medical and hygienic materials, and medical devices from some 1,100 manufacturers in Japan and beyond. Another Toho unit, PharmaCluster, operates as a dispensing pharmacy.

Operations

Toho operates through four segments: Pharmaceutical Wholesaling (accounts for more than 90% of revenue), Dispensing Pharmacy (more than 5%), Pharmaceutical Manufacturing and Sales, and Other Peripheral Businesses (about 5%).

Through Toho Pharmaceutical, it has more than 10 subsidiaries and affiliates that purchase pharmaceuticals and health-related products for distribution to hospitals, clinics, and pharmacies. To a lesser extent, the company is also engaged in the manufacturing of drugs. Dispensing pharmacy arm PharmaCluster operates through brands including Pharma-Daiwa, Shimizu Pharmacy, J. Miraimedical, Pharma Mirai, Vega Pharma, Cure, AOBADO, Kosei and Seiko Medical Brain.

Pharmaceutical manufacturing and sales business has one consolidated subsidiary (KYOSOMIRAI PHARMA) and three affiliates (AYM HD, AYUMI Pharmaceutical Holdings, AYUMI Pharmaceutical Corporation), which manufacture and sell pharmaceuticals. KYOSOMIRAI PHARMA (a consolidated subsidiary) manufactures and sells generic drugs and produces injection drugs on consignment. Generic drugs are mainly supplied to Toho Pharmaceutical. Other peripheral businesses engage in selling software to medical institutions (information processing) and assistance in in-house logistics at medical institutions (supply processing and distribution) to contribute to people's health and comfortable life.

Sales and Marketing

Toho purchase pharmaceuticals and health-related products, mainly from pharmaceutical manufacturers, for distribution primarily to hospitals, clinics, and dispensing pharmacies.

Financial Performance

The company's consolidated operating results for fiscal year ended March 31, 2022 recorded Â¥1.3 trillion yen for net sales (an increase of 5% on a year-on-year basis).

In 2021, the company had a net income of Â¥13.4 billion, a 168% increase from the previous year's net income of Â¥5 billion.

The company's cash at the end of 2021 was Â¥90 billion. Operating activities generated Â¥16.3 billion, while investing activities used Â¥11 billion, mainly for purchase of shares of subsidiaries and associates. Financing activities used another Â¥4.5 billion, primarily for repayments of long-term borrowings, as well as dividends paid.

EXECUTIVES

Chief Executive Officer, Representative Director, Atsushi Udoh
Chief Financial Officer, Representative Director, Hiromi Edahiro
Senior Managing Director, Chief Operating Officer, Director, Akira Umada
Director, Takeo Matsutani
Director, Masami Tada
Director, Kentaro Murakawa
Outside Director, Yoshiaki Kamoya
Outside Director, Shunsuke Watanabe
Outside Director, Hidehito Kotani
Auditors : Ernst & Young ShinNihon LLC

LOCATIONS

HQ: Toho Holdings Co Ltd
 5-2-1 Daizawa, Setagaya-ku, Tokyo 155-8655
Phone: (81) 3 3419 7893
Web: www.tohohd.co.jp

PRODUCTS/OPERATIONS

2017 Sales by Segment

	% of total
Pharmaceutical Wholesaling	92
Dispensing Pharmacy	8
Information Equipment	-
SMO	-
Total	**100**

HISTORICAL FINANCIALS

Company Type: Public

Income Statement   FYE: March 31

	REVENUE ($mil)	NET INCOME ($mil)	NET PROFIT MARGIN	EMPLOYEES
03/22	10,409	109	1.1%	10,145
03/21	10,931	45	0.4%	10,184
03/20	11,642	149	1.3%	10,319
03/19	11,036	125	1.1%	10,365
03/18	11,426	135	1.2%	10,135
Annual Growth	(2.3%)	(5.1%)		0.0%

2022 Year-End Financials

Debt ratio: —
Return on equity: 5.5%
Cash ($ mil.): 774
Current Ratio: 1.27
Long-term debt ($ mil.): 268
No. of shares ($ mil.): 70
Dividends
Yield: —
Payout: 17.1%
Market value ($ mil.): —

Tohoku Electric Power Co., Inc. (Japan)

The people of Tohoku, the northern part of Japan's main island, rely on Tohoku Electric Power for their electricity needs. Founded in 1951, the company produces power primarily through its thermal, hydroelectric, and nuclear power plants, although it is also developing solar and geothermal power plants to cut carbon emissions. Overall it has a generating capacity of about 16,695 MW. Tohoku Electric Power, one of Japan's top electric utilities, delivers electricity to roughly customers in Tohoku and Niigata.

Operations

Tohoku Electric Power generates, transmits, and sells electricity. It generates power via a variety of sources such as hydroelectric, thermal (coal, gas), geothermal, solar, and nuclear. In total, it has capacity to produce some 16,695 MW of electrical through about 225 generating stations. Its transmission facilities include some 15,385 km of transmission lines.

Its electricity business accounts for over 85% of total revenue.

Geographic Reach

Sendai, Japan-headquartered Tohoku Electric Power serves prefectures in northern Japan, including Aomori, Iwate, Akita, Miyagi, Yamagata, Fukushima and Niigata. Its power generation facilities are generally located in the same service area.

Sales and Marketing

The company's customers have included fuel futures market, electricity futures market, Japan Electric Power Exchange, and negotiated markets.

Financial Performance

Company's revenue for fiscal 2021 increased to Â¥2.3 trillion compared from the prior year with Â¥2.2 trillion.

Net income for fiscal 2021 decreased to Â¥29.4 billion compared from the prior year with Â¥63.1 billion.

Cash held by the company at the end of fiscal 2021 decreased to Â¥209.6 billion. Cash provided by operations was Â¥217.6 billion while cash used for investing and financing activities were Â¥255.0 billion and Â¥5.8 billion, respectively. Main uses of cash were for purchase of property, plant, and equipment; and redemption commercial papers.

Strategy

Company's three strategic focuses are: enhancing competitive strengths through comprehensive reforms in the power supply business; taking on the challenge of swiftly achieving profitability for smart society building business; and evolving the management foundation supporting corporate value creation.

EXECUTIVES

Chairman, Representative Director, Jiro Masuko
President, Representative Director, Kojiro Higuchi
Executive Vice President, Representative Director, Kazuhiro Ishiyama
Executive Vice President, Representative Director, Hiromitsu Takano
Executive Vice President, Chief Financial Officer, Representative Director, Satoshi Isagoda
Director, Sadahiro Ohno
Director, Sadao Kanazawa
Outside Director, Tsutomu Kamijo
Outside Director, Osamu Kawanobe
Outside Director, Mikito Nagai
Outside Director, Keiko Uehara
Director, Katsuaki Fujikura
Outside Director, Ikuko Miyahara
Outside Director, Kazuo Kobayashi
Outside Director, Akiko Ide
Auditors : Ernst & Young ShinNihon LLC

LOCATIONS

HQ: Tohoku Electric Power Co., Inc. (Japan)
 1-7-1 Honcho, Aoba-ku, Sendai, Miyagi 980-8550
Phone: (81) 22 225 2111
Web: www.tohoku-epco.co.jp

2016 Sales

	% of total
Electric Power Business	77
Construction Business	13
Other	10
Total	**100**

COMPETITORS

CAPSTONE TURBINE CORPORATION
CHUBU ELECTRIC POWER CO.,INC.
CHUGOKU ELECTRIC POWER COMPANY,INCORPORATED,THE
KANSAI ELECTRIC POWER COMPANY, INCORPORATED, THE
KYUSHU ELECTRIC POWER COMPANY, INCORPORATED
PG&E CORPORATION

PINNACLE WEST CAPITAL CORPORATION
TALEN ENERGY CORPORATION
Uniper SE
Vattenfall AB

HISTORICAL FINANCIALS
Company Type: Public

Income Statement FYE: March 31

	REVENUE ($mil)	NET INCOME ($mil)	NET PROFIT MARGIN	EMPLOYEES
03/23	22,579	(957)	—	24,528
03/22	17,301	(890)	—	24,833
03/21	20,653	265	1.3%	24,717
03/20	20,694	581	2.8%	24,870
03/19	20,265	419	2.1%	25,032
Annual Growth	2.7%	—	—	(0.5%)

2023 Year-End Financials
Debt ratio: 0.5% No. of shares ($ mil.): 500
Return on equity: (-20.4%) Dividends
Cash ($ mil.): 3,804 Yield: —
Current Ratio: 1.08 Payout: 0.0%
Long-term debt ($ mil.): 23,089 Market value ($ mil.): —

Tokio Marine Holdings Inc

Tokio Marine Holdings is Japan's oldest property/casualty insurance company. The firm has one of the largest insurance sales networks in Japan and has expanded its insurance operations to about 45 additional countries in Asia, Oceania, Europe, Africa, the Middle East, and the Americas. Through Tokio Marine & Nichido Fire Insurance (TMNF), Nisshin Fire and Marine Insurance, Philadelphia Insurance Companies, Kiln, HCC Insurance, and other subsidiaries, Tokio Marine provides marine, property/casualty, personal accident, fire, auto, and life insurance as well as reinsurance. It also offers asset management, pension plans, and other services.

Operations
Tokio Marine operates in four segments: Domestic Non-Life Insurance, Domestic Life Insurance, International Insurance, and Financial and Other.

Domestic Non-Life Insurance business, generates about 50% of the firm's revenue, primarily comprises underwriting of non-life insurance in Japan and related investments. International Insurance business (provides nearly 40%) primarily comprises underwriting of insurance overseas and related investments. Domestic Life Insurance business primarily comprises underwriting of life insurance in Japan and related investments. The segment contributes more than 10% of the firm's revenue. In Financial and Other businesses (accounts for the rest), the main businesses are investment advisory, investment trust services, staffing business, facility management business, and nursing care services.

Overall, non-Life insurance brings in nearly 75% of the firm's revenue, while life insurance accounts for about 25%.

Geographic Reach
Headquartered in Tokyo, the firm has insurance operations in about 45 countries throughout Asia and Oceania, Europe, the Middle East, and Africa, and the Americas. The majority of Tokio Marine's revenue comes from Japan (about 60%). The US brings in more than 25% of the firm's revenue, while other countries account for approximately 15%.

Sales and Marketing
Tokio Marine markets its products through a network of agents.

Financial Performance
In 2021, the company had a net income of Â¥554.3 billion, a 128% increase from the previous year's net income of Â¥243.2 billion.

The company's cash at the end of 2021 was Â¥912.2 billion. Operating activities generated Â¥1.1 trillion, while investing activities used Â¥665.4 billion, primarily for purchases of securities. Financing activities used another Â¥504.6 billion, primarily for the change in cash collateral under securities lending transactions.

Company Background
Japan's first insurance company, Tokio Marine and Fire Insurance, was founded in 1879 to provide marine insurance in Japan. The firm expanded overseas rapidly, establishing offices in London, Paris, and New York. It later added fire, personal accident, theft, and auto coverage.

In 1944 Tokio merged with Mitsubishi Marine Insurance and Meiji Fire Insurance. After the war Tokio slowly recovered and resumed overseas operations. During the 1950s and 1960s, the company grew its personal lines, adding homeowners coverage. Domestic business slowed during the 1970s and 1980s, and Tokio boosted operations overseas.

Millea Holdings was created in 2002 as the holding company for the merger between Tokio Marine and Fire and Nichido Fire and Marine. The two companies combined to become main operating subsidiary Tokio Marine & Nichido Fire Insurance in 2004. In 2008 Millea Holdings changed its name to Tokio Marine Holdings to reflect positive brand recognition associated with the Tokio Marine name.

Later acquisitions included Real Seguros (Brazil, 2005), Nisshin Fire and Marine (Japan, 2006), Asia General (Singapore, 2007), Nihon Kousei (Japan, 2007), Kiln (UK, 2008), Philadelphia Consolidated (US, 2008), Delphi Financial (US, 2012), and HCC (US, 2015).

HISTORY

After the US forced Japan to open to trade in 1854, Western marine insurers began operating there. In 1878 Japan's government organized backers for a Japanese marine insurance firm. Tokio Marine and Fire Insurance was founded the next year.

Tokio grew quickly, insuring trading companies like Mitsubishi and Mitsui; it soon had offices in London, Paris, and New York. Increased competition in the 1890s forced it to curtail its foreign operations and begin using brokers in most other countries.

Victory in the Russo-Japanese War of 1904-05 buoyed the country, but the economy slowed as it demobilized. Businesses responded by forming cooperative groups known as zaibatsu. Tokio Marine and Fire was allied with the Mitsubishi group.

Before WWI, Tokio expanded by adding fire, personal accident, theft, and auto insurance, and it continued to buy foreign sales brokers. Japan's insurance industry consolidated in the 1920s, and the company bought up smaller competitors. The 1923 Tokyo earthquake hit the industry hard, but Tokio's new fire insurance operations had little exposure.

Most of Tokio's foreign operations were seized during WWII. In 1944 Tokio merged with Mitsubishi Marine Insurance and Meiji Fire Insurance. Business grew in WWII, but wartime destruction left Tokio with nothing to insure and no money to pay claims.

After the war Tokio slowly recovered and resumed overseas operations. Although the US had dismantled the zaibatsu during occupation, Tokio allied once again with Mitsubishi when Japan's government rebuilt most of the old groups as keiretsu.

During the 1950s and 1960s, the company grew its personal lines, adding homeowners coverage. Domestic business slowed during the 1970s and 1980s, and Tokio boosted operations overseas. It added commercial property/casualty insurer Houston General Insurance (a US company sold in 1997), Tokio Reinsurance, and interests in insurance and investment management firms.

In the 1980s the firm invested heavily in real estate through jusen (mortgage companies). Japan's overheated real estate market collapsed in the early 1990s, dumping masses of nonperforming assets on jusen and their investors (the country's major banks and insurers, including Tokio).

Deregulation began in 1996, and economic recession soon followed. In 1998 Tokio joined other members of the Mitsubishi group, including Bank of Tokyo-Mitsubishi and Meiji Life Insurance, to form investment banking, pension, and trust joint ventures. The firm also formed its own investment trust and allied with such foreign financial companies as BANK ONE and United Asset Management to develop new investment products. Brokerage firm Charles Schwab Tokio Marine Securities, a joint venture, was launched in 1999. That year Tokio consolidated its foreign reinsurance operations into Tokio Marine Global Re in Dublin, Ireland, and kicked off a business push that included reorganizing its agent force and planning for online sales.

Millea Holdings was created in 2002 as the holding company for the merger between Tokio Marine and Fire and Nichido Fire and Marine. The two were combined and renamed Tokio Marine & Nichido Fire Insurance, a subsidiary of Millea Holdings.

The company's 2005 acquisition of Real Seguros allowed the company to bring its life insurance products to Brazil (renamed Tokio Marine Seguradora). In 2006 Millea acquired Nisshin Fire and Marine Insurance Company as a separately operated subsidiary. In 2007 the firm purchased Asia General Holdings and its life insurance subsidiaries, which operated in Singapore and Malaysia. It also purchased Japanese fire insurance provider Nihon Kousei Kyousaikai.

In 2008 Millea Holdings changed its name to Tokio Marine Holdings to reflect the positive brand recognition associated with the Tokio Marine name.

The company made several key acquisitions to further expand its international operations, including purchases of Kiln (UK, 2008), Philadelphia Consolidated (US, 2008), Delphi Financial (US, 2012), and HCC (US, 2015).

In late 2017, Tokio Marine subsidiary HCC acquired the medical stop-loss insurance operations of US giant AIG. The acquired business included some Â¥40.8 billion in gross written premiums.

EXECUTIVES

Chairman, Director, Tsuyoshi Nagano
President, Group Chief Executive Officer, Representative Director, Satoru Komiya
Executive Vice President, Representative Director, Akira Harashima
Senior Managing Director, Representative Director, Kenji Okada
Senior Managing Director, Director, Yoichi Moriwaki
Senior Managing Director, Kichiichiro Yamashita
Director, Yoshinori Ishii
Director, Kiyoshi Wada
Director, Shinichi Hirose
Outside Director, Akio Mimura
Outside Director, Masako Egawa
Outside Director, Takashi Mitachi
Outside Director, Nobuhiro Endo
Outside Director, Shinya Katanozaka
Outside Director, Emi Osono
Auditors : PricewaterhouseCoopers Aarata LLC

LOCATIONS

HQ: Tokio Marine Holdings Inc
 2-6-4 Otemachi, Chiyoda-ku, Tokyo 100-0004
Phone: (81) 3 6704 7700
Web: www.tokiomarinehd.com

PRODUCTS/OPERATIONS

Selected Mergers and Acquisitions
2008
Kiln (U.K.)
Philadelphia Consolidated Holding (US)
2012
Delphi Financial Group ($2.7 billion; specialty life insurer)
2015
HCC ($7.5 billion; specialty property/casualty)

COMPETITORS

AMERICAN INTERNATIONAL GROUP, INC.
AVIVA PLC
Allianz SE
Axis Capital Holdings Limited
MS&AD INSURANCE GROUP HOLDINGS, INC.
RSA INSURANCE GROUP PLC
SOMPO HOLDINGS, INC.
THE TRAVELERS COMPANIES INC
XL GROUP PUBLIC LIMITED COMPANY
Zurich Insurance Group AG

HISTORICAL FINANCIALS

Company Type: Public

Income Statement   FYE: March 31

	ASSETS ($mil)	NET INCOME ($mil)	INCOME AS % OF ASSETS	EMPLOYEES
03/23	207,979	2,826	1.4%	43,217
03/22	223,993	3,456	1.5%	43,048
03/21	232,698	1,461	0.6%	43,257
03/20	232,648	2,393	1.0%	41,101
03/19	203,455	2,479	1.2%	40,848
Annual Growth	0.6%	3.3%		1.4%

2023 Year-End Financials
Return on assets: 1.3%
Return on equity: 9.8%
Long-term debt ($ mil.): —
No. of shares ($ mil.): 1,993
Sales ($ mil.): 47,856
Dividends
 Yield: 7.3%
 Payout: 103.3%
Market value ($ mil.): 38,409

	STOCK PRICE ($) FY Close	P/E High/Low		PER SHARE ($) Earnings	Dividends	Book Value
03/23	19.27	0	0	1.41	1.42	13.68
03/22	58.17	0	0	1.68	1.96	16.24
03/21	47.65	1	1	0.70	2.18	15.92
03/20	45.50	0	0	1.13	2.03	14.85
03/19	48.50	0	0	1.15	0.72	15.24
Annual Growth	(20.6%)	—	—	5.1%	18.6%	(2.7%)

Tokyo Century Corp

Need to replace that aging industrial or office equipment? Century Tokyo Leasing specializes in the leasing and installment sale of office and information equipment, industrial machine tools, and medical technology as well as aircraft and vehicles. It provides financing, insurance, securities investment, factoring, and other related financial services products, too. Century Tokyo Leasing was formed in the 2009 merger of Century Leasing System and Tokyo Leasing (which began its leasing career in 1964); based in Tokyo, it has operations in China, India, Indonesia, Malaysia, Philippines, Singapore, Taiwan, Thailand, the UK, and the US.

Financial Performance

In fiscal 2015 (March year end), the company's revenue increased by 7%, led by leasing and installment sales which though grew by 6%.

That year the company's net income increased by 3% due to higher revenues offset by an increase in expenses (including selling, general and administrative expenses, gain on bargain purchase, along with derivatives other than for trading or hedging and increased taxes).

Century Tokyo Leasing's operating cash flows declined by 504% in 2014 due to increased cash outflows in trade notes and accounts payable and in loans receivable, offset by the increase in net income.

EXECUTIVES

Chairman, Representative Director, Masataka Yukiya
President, Representative Director, Koichi Baba
Executive Vice President, Director, Akihiko Okada
Executive Vice President, Director, Hiroshi Sato
Executive Vice President, Yoichiro Nakai
Senior Managing Executive Officer, Director, Toshio Kitamura
Senior Managing Executive Officer, Director, Mahoko Hara
Outside Director, Masao Yoshida
Outside Director, Akio Nakamura
Outside Director, Toshio Asano
Outside Director, Miho Tanaka
Outside Director, Tsuyoshi Numagami
Director, Tatsuya Hirasaki
Director, Shunichi Asada
Auditors : Deloitte Touche Tohmatsu LLC

LOCATIONS

HQ: Tokyo Century Corp
 3 Kanda-Neribeicho, Chiyoda-ku, Tokyo 101-0022
Phone: (81) 570 084390 **Fax:** (81) 3 5296 0230
Web: www.tokyocentury.co.jp

COMPETITORS

CATERPILLAR FINANCIAL SERVICES CORPORATION
CSI LEASING, INC.
FORD MOTOR CREDIT COMPANY LLC
GENERAL ELECTRIC CAPITAL CORPORATION
GRAINGER PLC
HITACHI CAPITAL (UK) PLC
MITSUBISHI UFJ LEASE & FINANCE COMPANY LIMITED
MITSUI FUDOSAN CO., LTD.
MIZUHO LEASING COMPANY, LIMITED
ORIX CORPORATION

HISTORICAL FINANCIALS

Company Type: Public

Income Statement   FYE: March 31

	REVENUE ($mil)	NET INCOME ($mil)	NET PROFIT MARGIN	EMPLOYEES
03/22	10,506	413	3.9%	12,390
03/21	10,839	443	4.1%	12,452
03/20	10,747	518	4.8%	12,704
03/19	9,640	471	4.9%	11,572
03/18	9,532	483	5.1%	9,290
Annual Growth	2.5%	(3.8%)		7.5%

2022 Year-End Financials
Debt ratio: 0.6%
Return on equity: 8.0%
Cash ($ mil.): 1,979
Current Ratio: 1.63
Long-term debt ($ mil.): 23,099
No. of shares ($ mil.): 488
Dividends
Yield: —
Payout: 34.9%
Market value ($ mil.): —

Tokyo Electric Power Company Holdings Inc

Tokyo Electric Power Company (TEPCO) is known as Japan's largest electricity operator which supplies power to the Kanto region, including the Tokyo Metropolitan Area. The company has total assets of about JPY 12.9 billion and electricity sales of about 233.8 TWh. Overall, the company has over 95 affiliated companies as its consolidated subsidiaries. TEPCO is still committed to carrying out the complex, multilayer and large-scale decommissioning project followed by the major crisis in 2011, when its Fukushima Dai-ichi nuclear plant complex experienced a partial meltdown at three reactors and radioactive material was released in the wake of a major earthquake and tsunami.

Operations
TEPCO holds five independent business entities: Tokyo Electric Power Company Holdings, TEPCO Energy Partner, TEPCO Power Grid, TEPCO Fuel & Power, and TEPCO Renewable Power.

The Tokyo Electric Power Company Holdings balances carbon neutrality with the stable supply of power. TEPCO Energy Partner, Inc. engages in the retail sale of electricity and gas in the Tokyo Metropolitan area. TEPCO Power Grid is a general power transmission and distribution operator in charge of providing a stable supply of power to the Tokyo Metropolitan area. TEPCO Fuel & Power handles the company's fuel and thermal power generation businesses. Lastly, TEPCO Renewable Power, Inc. manages the generation of power from renewable energies such as hydro, wind, solar, and geothermal power.

Overall, electricity generated around 90% of the company's sales.

Geographic Reach
TEPCO is headquartered in Tokyo, Japan and has offices in Washington, DC, and London.

Financial Performance
The company's revenue for fiscal 2022 decreased to JPY 5.3 trillion compared from the prior year with JPY 5.9 trillion.

Net income for fiscal 2022 decreased to JPY 5.6 billion compared from the prior year with JPY 180.9 billion.

Cash held by the company at the end of fiscal 2022 increased to JPY 861.8 billion. Cash provided by operations and financing activities were JPY 406.5 billion and JPY560.6 billion, respectively. Cash used for investing activities was JPY 559.8 billion, mainly for repayments of short-term loans.

Strategy
The 4th Comprehensive Special Business Plan objective of creating Â¥450 billion in profits annually cannot be achieved with its current business. The company need to make those additional profits through new businesses.

In anticipation of a carbon neutral society, the TEPCO Group is selecting and concentrating businesses outside of the electric industry, as well as exploring/commercializing new businesses. Through these initiatives the company shall build a business portfolio with high capital efficiency as it aim to achieve its goals.

HISTORY
The Tokyo Electric Power Company (TEPCO) descended from Tokyo Electric Light, which was formed in 1883. In 1887 the company switched on Japan's first power plant, a 25-KW fossil fuel generator. Fossil fuels were the main source of electricity in Japan until 1912, when long-distance transmission techniques became more efficient, making hydroelectric power cheaper.

In 1938 Japan nationalized electric utilities, despite strong objections from Yasuzaemon Matsunaga, a leader in Japan's utility industry and former president of the Japan Electric Association. After WWII Matsunaga championed public ownership of Japan's power companies, which helped in 1951 to establish the current system of 10 regional companies, each with a service monopoly. Tokyo Electric Power was the largest. That year it was listed on the Tokyo Stock Exchange and was regulated by the Ministry of International Trade and Industry. (The ministry has regulated electric utilities since 1965.)

Fossil fuel plants made a comeback in Japan in the postwar era because they could be built more economically than hydroelectric plants. When the OPEC oil embargo of the 1970s demonstrated Japan's dependence on foreign oil, TEPCO increased its use of liquefied natural gas (LNG) and nuclear energy sources. (It brought its first nuke online in 1971.) In 1977 it formed the Energy Conservation Center to promote conservation and related legislation.

To further reduce its oil dependence TEPCO joined other US and Japanese firms in building a coal gasification plant in California's Mojave Desert in 1982. Two years later TEPCO announced it would begin building its first coal-burning generator since the oil crisis. It established Tokyo Telecommunication Network (TTNet), a partnership to provide telecommunications services, in 1986 and TEPCO Cable TV in 1989.

As part of its interest in alternative energy systems, TEPCO established a global environment department in 1990 to conduct R&D on energy and the environment. Its environmental program has included reforestation and fuel cell research.

Liberalization in 1995 allowed Japan's electric utilities to buy power from independent power producers; TEPCO quickly lined up 10 suppliers. The company proceeded with energy experimentation in 1996, trying a 6,000-KW sodium-sulfur battery at a Yokohama transformer station. The next year the company announced that it would become the first electric utility to sell liquefied natural gas as part of its energy mix, and finished building the world's largest nuclear plant.

To gain experience in deregulating markets, TEPCO invested in US power generating company Orion Power in 1999. (It agreed to sell its 5% stake to Reliant Energy in 2001.) At home the firm joined Microsoft and SOFTBANK to form SpeedNet, which provides Internet access over TTNet's network. In 2000 TEPCO got its first taste of deregulation when large customers (accounting for about a third of the market) began choosing their electricity suppliers. Also in 2000 TEPCO joined a group of nine Japanese electric companies to create POWEREDCOM. (In 2005 TEPCO sold its stake in POWEREDCOM to KDDI in order to focus on its core power business).

In 2001 TEPCO joined up with Sumitomo and ElectricitÃ© de France to build Vietnam's first independent power plant.

To raise cash, in 2006 Mirant (now GenOn Energy) sold its power plants in the Philippines to TEPCO and Marubeni for $3.4 billion.

Public confidence was shaken by a rash of accidents within Japan's nuclear industry. The company had struggled to restore its credibility after the Japanese government shut down TEPCO's 17 nuclear reactors due to safety concerns, prompted by the company's admittance of falsifying safety data to cover up faults at several of its nuclear facilities in 2002. In 2009 it reopened the Kashiwazaki-Kariwa Nuclear Power Station, which was closed in 2007 due to a major earthquake in the region.

Through affiliates TEPCO also offers cable TV and Internet services, international consulting and investing in non-Japan-based independent power producers. Other businesses include construction, real estate, and transportation companies.

The company is developing new green energy sources, such as wind and solar in order to meet carbon emission reduction targets. In 2009 the company agreed to build a major solar project in Kawasaki, Kanagawa, to serve about 5,900 households. In 2010 it teamed up with Toyota Tsusho to fund wind power company Eurus Energy Holdings, which acquired solar power company Jindosun Park in 2011. Jindosun oversees the generation of 2,974 KW of electricity, mostly in South Korea, and activated a 45,000 KW plant in the US in mid-2011.

Broadening its international power assets, in 2011 the company agreed to buy 12% of Thailand-based independent power producer Electricity Generating PCL for about $274 million. However, the daunting financial impact of the Fukushima disaster has cast a pall over the company's international expansion plans.

In 2012 it agreed to sell its 67.5% stake in Australian power station Loy Yang A to the plant's minority owner AGL Resources for $1.6 billion.

EXECUTIVES

Chairman, Outside Director, Yoshimitsu Kobayashi
Representative Executive Officer, President, Director, Tomoaki Kobayakawa
Representative Executive Officer, Executive Vice President, Chief Financial Officer, Director, Hiroyuki Yamaguchi
Representative Executive Officer, Executive Vice President, Director, Daisuke Sakai
Executive Vice President, Chief Human Resources Officer, Mitsushi Saiki
Executive Vice President, Chief Innovation Officer, Director, Chikara Kojima
Executive Vice President, Director, Toshihiko Fukuda
Executive Vice President, Akira Ono
Chief Information Officer, Chief Information Security Officer, Tomomichi Seki
Chief Marketing Officer, Momoko Nagasaki
Chief Risk Management Officer, Masayuki Kishino
Outside Director, Shigeo Oyagi
Outside Director, Shoichiro Onishi
Outside Director, Asa Shinkawa
Outside Director, Junko Okawa
Outside Director, Takashi Nagata
Director, Shigehiro Yoshino
Director, Seiji Moriya
Auditors : Ernst & Young ShinNihon LLC

LOCATIONS

HQ: Tokyo Electric Power Company Holdings Inc
1-1-3 Uchisaiwai-cho, Chiyoda-Ku, Tokyo 100-8560
Phone: (81) 3 6373 1111
Web: www.tepco.co.jp

PRODUCTS/OPERATIONS

Selected Subsidiaries
TEPCO CABLE TELEVISION Inc. (85%, cable television)
TEPCO SYSTEMS CORPORATION (information software and services)
Toden Kogyo Co., Ltd. (facilities construction and maintenance)
Toden Real Estate Co., Inc. (property management)
Tokyo Densetsu Service Co., Ltd. (facilities construction and maintenance)
Tokyo Electric Power Environmental Engineering Company, Incorporated (facilities construction and maintenance)
Tokyo Electric Power Services Company, Limited (facilities construction and maintenance)

COMPETITORS

ACCIONA, SA
CHUBU ELECTRIC POWER CO.,INC.
E.ON UK PLC
ENDESA SA
IBERDROLA, SOCIEDAD ANONIMA
INTERNATIONAL POWER LTD.
KANSAI ELECTRIC POWER COMPANY, INCORPORATED, THE
RENEWABLE ENERGY SYSTEMS HOLDINGS LIMITED
RWE AG
UNITED UTILITIES GROUP PLC

HISTORICAL FINANCIALS
Company Type: Public

Income Statement FYE: March 31

	REVENUE ($mil)	NET INCOME ($mil)	NET PROFIT MARGIN	EMPLOYEES
03/23	58,555	(928)	—	40,413
03/22	43,653	46	0.1%	40,461
03/21	52,985	1,633	3.1%	40,530
03/20	57,498	467	0.8%	40,734
03/19	57,235	2,098	3.7%	44,042
Annual Growth	0.6%	—	—	(2.1%)

2023 Year-End Financials
Debt ratio: 0.3% No. of shares ($ mil.): 1,603
Return on equity: (-3.9%) Dividends
Cash ($ mil.): 5,390 Yield: —
Current Ratio: 0.50 Payout: 0.0%
Long-term debt ($ mil.): 22,376 Market value ($ mil.): 5,613

	STOCK PRICE ($) FY Close	P/E High/Low	PER SHARE ($) Earnings	Dividends	Book Value
03/23	3.50	— —	(0.58)	0.00	14.49
03/22	3.69	1 1	0.01	0.00	16.39
03/21	3.40	0 0	0.33	0.00	17.60
03/20	3.33	0 0	0.09	0.00	16.66
03/19	6.34	0 0	0.42	0.00	16.27
Annual Growth	(13.8%)				(2.8%)

Tokyo Electron, Ltd.

EXECUTIVES

President, Chief Executive Officer, Representative Director, Toshiki Kawai
Executive Vice President, Representative Director, Sadao Sasaki
Director, Yoshikazu Nunokawa
Outside Director, Michio Sasaki
Outside Director, Makiko Eda
Outside Director, Sachiko Ichikawa
Auditors : KPMG AZSA LLC

LOCATIONS

HQ: Tokyo Electron, Ltd.
5-3-1 Akasaka, Minato-ku, Tokyo 107-6325
Phone: (81) 3 5561 7000 **Fax:** 512 424-1001
Web: www.tel.co.jp

HISTORICAL FINANCIALS
Company Type: Public

Income Statement FYE: March 31

	REVENUE ($mil)	NET INCOME ($mil)	NET PROFIT MARGIN	EMPLOYEES
03/23	16,586	3,540	21.3%	17,204
03/22	16,473	3,593	21.8%	15,634
03/21	12,635	2,194	17.4%	14,479
03/20	10,384	1,706	16.4%	13,837
03/19	11,542	2,241	19.4%	12,742
Annual Growth	9.5%	12.1%	—	7.8%

2023 Year-End Financials
Debt ratio: — No. of shares ($ mil.): 469
Return on equity: 32.0% Dividends
Cash ($ mil.): 3,552 Yield: 5.1%
Current Ratio: 2.76 Payout: 26.8%
Long-term debt ($ mil.): — Market value ($ mil.): 41,823

	STOCK PRICE ($) FY Close	P/E High/Low	PER SHARE ($) Earnings	Dividends	Book Value
03/23	89.01	0 0	7.54	3.04	25.56
03/22	128.48	0 0	7.66	2.38	23.61
03/21	109.25	0 0	4.68	1.66	19.75
03/20	46.55	0 0	3.57	1.35	16.33
03/19	36.37	0 0	4.54	1.15	16.28
Annual Growth	25.1%	—	13.5%	27.4%	11.9%

Tokyo Gas Co Ltd

EXECUTIVES

Chairman, Director, Takashi Uchida
Representative Executive Officer, President, Chief Executive Officer, Director, Shinichi Sasayama
Senior Managing Executive Officer, Toshihide Kasutani
Senior Managing Executive Officer, Chief Technology Officer, Chief Digital Officer, Kentaro Kimoto
Senior Managing Executive Officer, Chief Risk Management Officer, Chief Human Resources Officer, Shinsuke Ogawa
Senior Managing Executive Officer, Satoshi Tanazawa
Senior Managing Executive Officer, Chief Financial Officer, Hirofumi Sato
Managing Executive Officer, Chief Information Officer, Ayumi Shigitani
Chief Digital Officer, Nobuhiro Sugesawa
Chief Risk Officer, Chief Human Resources Officer, Eito Tsuji
Director, Takashi Higo
Outside Director, Kazunori Takami
Outside Director, Junko Edahiro
Outside Director, Mami Indo
Outside Director, Hiromichi Ono
Outside Director, Hiroyuki Sekiguchi
Outside Director, Tsutomu Tannowa
Auditors : KPMG AZSA LLC

LOCATIONS

HQ: Tokyo Gas Co Ltd
1-5-20 Kaigan, Minato-ku, Tokyo 105-8527
Phone: (81) 3 5400 7736   Fax: 713 465-1802
Web: www.tokyo-gas.co.jp

HISTORICAL FINANCIALS

Company Type: Public

Income Statement   FYE: March 31

	REVENUE ($mil)	NET INCOME ($mil)	NET PROFIT MARGIN	EMPLOYEES
03/23	24,699	2,109	8.5%	15,963
03/22	17,636	729	4.1%	16,697
03/21	15,941	447	2.8%	16,858
03/20	17,735	399	2.3%	16,591
03/19	17,719	763	4.3%	16,708
Annual Growth	8.7%	28.9%	—	(1.1%)

2023 Year-End Financials

Debt ratio: 0.3%   No. of shares ($ mil.): 433
Return on equity: 20.1%   Dividends
Cash ($ mil.): 3,405   Yield: 2.6%
Current Ratio: 2.01   Payout: 0.0%
Long-term debt ($ mil.): 8,681   Market value ($ mil.): 4,061

	STOCK PRICE ($) FY Close	P/E High/Low	PER SHARE ($) Earnings	Dividends	Book Value
03/23	9.37	0 0	4.86	0.25	26.98
03/22	9.35	0 0	1.66	0.27	22.94
03/21	11.20	0 0	1.01	0.28	23.63
03/20	11.55	0 0	0.90	0.29	23.98
03/19	13.54	0 0	1.69	0.25	23.26
Annual Growth	(8.8%)	— —	30.1%	0.0%	3.8%

Toppan Inc

Toppan Inc. (formerly Toppan Printing) is a leading and diversified global provider committed to delivering sustainable, integrated solutions in fields including printing, communications, security, packaging, dÃ©cor materials, electronics, and digital transformation. The company produces commercial products (posters, catalogs, calendars), securities and cards, publications (magazines, books, and packaging products. In addition to traditional print products, Toppan also specializes in electronics materials, such as photomasks for semi-conductors and color filters for LCD TVs. The company boasts over 205 group companies across the Asia/Pacific region, as well as in Europe and North America. Toppan Printing was founded in 1900 by engineers from the printing bureau of Japan's Ministry of Finance. Majority of its sales were generated in Japan.

Operations

The company operates in three segments: Information & Communication (about 60% of sales), Living & Industry (roughly 30%), and Electronics (about nearly 15%).

The Information & Communication offers securities-related documents, passbooks, cards, business forms, catalogues and other commercial printing, magazines, books and other publication printing, and business process outsourcing (BPO).

The Living & Industry includes flexible packaging, folding cartons and other packaging products, plastic molded products, ink, transparent barrier film, decorative paper/film, wallpaper and other decorative material.

The Electronics offers color filters for LCDs, TFT-LCDs, anti-reflection films, photomasks, and semiconductor packaging products.

Geographic Reach

Headquartered in Tokyo, Japan, The company has operations in Europe, Asia, North America, South America, and the Middle East and Africa. Over 70% of sales were generated from Japan, Asia with around 15%, and Other with more than 10%.

Financial Performance

The company's revenue for fiscal 2022 increased by 6% to Â¥1.5 trillion compared to Â¥1.47 trillion in the prior year, primarily due to increase in all segments.

Profit for fiscal 2022 increased by 50% to Â¥123.2 billion compared to Â¥82.0 billion in the prior year.

Cash held by the company at the end of fiscal 2022 decreased to Â¥414.3 billion. Operating and investing activities provided Â¥64.7 billion and Â¥32.8 billion, respectively. Financing activities used Â¥187.0 billion, mainly for redemption of bonds, dividends paid, and repayment of long-term borrowings.

Strategy

Toppan will strengthen its business continuity planning (BCP) in light of the COVID-19 pandemic and the situation in Ukraine, and will take steps to respond to changes in consumer behavior and values after the pandemic subsides. The company has positioned transforming the business portfolio, strengthening management foundations, and expanding ESG initiatives as priority measures for the medium to long term, and under the key concept of "Digital & Sustainable Transformation," the company will optimally allocate and effectively use management resources to expand business by pursuing the following initiatives.

HISTORY

Toppan Printing was established as Toppan Printing Limited Partnership in 1900 by engineers from Japan's Ministry of Finance who used the most advanced printing techniques of the day. It was renamed Toppan Printing Co. in 1908. In its early days the company focused primarily on securities (for the Ministry of Finance), books, and business forms.

Toppan flourished during and immediately after WWI as book and magazine publishing increased. In 1926 it opened the Koishikawa Paper Container Plant. Printing declined in the 1930s, however, as the Japanese dictatorship banned books and stifled writers and publishers. WWII brought a paper shortage and recession, which further depressed Japan's printing industry.

As the printing industry began to recover after the end of WWII, Toppan expanded into specialty packaging materials (1952) and industrial materials (1958). It also acquired children's book publisher Froebel-Kan in 1961 and became the first Japanese printer to open a Hong Kong plant in 1963. The company grew at a steady pace throughout the 1960s, eventually adding planning and designing to its stable of services. Toppan Moore Business Forms, a joint venture between Toppan and Canada's Moore Corporation, was established in 1965 (it would become Japan's largest business form printer by the 1980s).

Toppan formed a US subsidiary, Toppan Printing (America), in New York City in 1971 and became the first Japanese printer to establish a production plant in the US with the 1979 opening of a separation plant in Mountainside, New Jersey. During the late 1970s and early 1980s, the company made several important breakthroughs in containers and packing products; it developed long-term liquid storage containers (1976), easy-to-uncap heat seals for packaging (1978), and long-term food storage containers (1980). In 1983 Toppan Moore developed a smart card with two embedded integrated circuits. Two years later the company purchased decorating products manufacturer Kyodo Kako. By the end of the decade Toppan had moved into the production of videotext, batteries, compact discs, liquid crystal display filters, lottery tickets, postage stamps, and portable smart card systems. It also began emphasizing distribution and direct marketing services and created an industrial materials division.

By 1990 Toppan had 21 printing plants and more than 50 sales offices throughout Japan, as well as 21 international offices. That year the company formed a photomask joint venture company with Dallas-based Texas Instruments. Toppan executive Hiromichi Fujita was named president of the firm in 1991 (he later became chairman). The company established a multimedia unit in 1996 and acquired all of Toppan Moore -- renamed Toppan Forms -- the following year (it spun off Toppan Forms in a public offering in 1998).

In 1999 Toppan joined with Internet Initiative Japan, Intel, Sun Microsystems, and IBM Japan to create Bitway, which focuses on Internet marketing and distribution of digital content. The following year Toppan entered into a variety of partnerships and joint ventures with such firms as Chughwa Picture Tubes (photomasks), Gemplus (smart cards), and Baltimore Technologies Japan Co. (electronic authentication). Also in 2000 the company celebrated the 100th anniversary of its founding. In 2001 the company partnered with Taiwan's Powerchip Semiconductor

Corp. to make chips for other companies.

That year the company invested in another Internet opportunity, joining with NEC Corp. and SGI Japan Ltd. to support businesses using broadband Internet services.

EXECUTIVES

Chairman, Representative Director, Shingo Kaneko
President, Representative Director, Hideharu Maro
Executive Vice President, Representative Director, Kazunori Sakai
Senior Managing Executive Officer, Director, Masanori Saito
Director, Takashi Kurobe
Director, Hideki Soeda
Outside Director, Yoshinobu Noma
Outside Director, Ryoko Toyama
Outside Director, Mieko Nakabayashi
Auditors : KPMG AZSA LLC

LOCATIONS

HQ: Toppan Inc
  1-3-3 Suido, Bunkyo-ku, Tokyo 112-8531
Phone: (81) 3 3835 5665 **Fax:** 770 467-5905
Web: www.toppan.co.jp

2016 Sales

	% of total
Japan	85
Asia	11
Other	4
Total	100

PRODUCTS/OPERATIONS

Selected Offerings
Information & Networks
   Publications Printing
   Magazines
   Books
   Electronic publications
   Publication planning & editing
   Advertising
   Commercial Printing
   Posters
   Catalogs
   Brochures
   Flyers
   Direct mail
   Calendars
   Corporate communications materials
   Business Forms
   Cards
   Envelopes
   Continuous forms
Living Environment
   Packaging & industrial materials
   Interior decor materials
Electronics
   Displays
   Semiconductors

COMPETITORS

CENVEO, INC.
GINCOP, INC.
MACDERMID, INCORPORATED
MPS CHICAGO, INC.
OUTLOOK GROUP LLC
QUAD/GRAPHICS INC.
RENISHAW P L C

SANDY ALEXANDER, INC.
Torstar Corporation
WILLIAMSON PRINTING CORPORATION

HISTORICAL FINANCIALS
Company Type: Public

Income Statement FYE: March 31

	REVENUE ($mil)	NET INCOME ($mil)	NET PROFIT MARGIN	EMPLOYEES
03/23	12,304	457	3.7%	59,507
03/22	12,722	1,012	8.0%	60,109
03/21	13,248	740	5.6%	58,203
03/20	13,689	801	5.9%	58,102
03/19	13,226	370	2.8%	57,147
Annual Growth	(1.8%)	5.4%	—	1.0%

2023 Year-End Financials
Debt ratio: 0.1%
Return on equity: 4.5%
Cash ($ mil.): 3,241
Current Ratio: 2.37
Long-term debt ($ mil.): 1,383
No. of shares ($ mil.): 328
Dividends
  Yield: 1.6%
  Payout: 0.0%
Market value ($ mil.): 3,299

	STOCK PRICE ($) FY Close	P/E High/Low		PER SHARE ($) Earnings	Dividends	Book Value
03/23	10.05	0	0	1.39	0.17	30.31
03/22	8.96	0	0	3.00	0.18	33.43
03/21	8.82	0	0	2.14	0.27	34.76
03/20	8.26	0	0	2.40	0.18	31.26
03/19	7.41	0	0	1.09	0.18	32.53
Annual Growth	7.9%	—	—	6.3%	(1.4%)	(1.8%)

Toray Industries, Inc.

EXECUTIVES

Chairman, Representative Director, Akihiro Nikkaku
President, Representative Director, Mitsuo Ohya
Executive Vice President, Representative Director, Satoru Hagiwara
Executive Vice President, Director, Kazuyuki Adachi
Executive Vice President, Director, Kazuhiko Shuto
Senior Managing Executive Officer, Director, Tetsuya Tsunekawa
Director, Masahiko Okamoto
Director, Takashi Yoshiyama
Outside Director, Kunio Ito
Outside Director, Ryoji Noyori
Outside Director, Susumu Kaminaga
Outside Director, Kazuo Futagawa
Outside Director, Yuko Harayama
Auditors : Ernst & Young ShinNihon LLC

LOCATIONS

HQ: Toray Industries, Inc.
  2-1-1 Nihonbashi-Muromachi, Chuo-ku, Tokyo 103-8666
Phone: (81) 3 3245 5201 **Fax:** (81) 3 3245 5054
Web: www.toray.co.jp

HISTORICAL FINANCIALS
Company Type: Public

Income Statement FYE: March 31

	REVENUE ($mil)	NET INCOME ($mil)	NET PROFIT MARGIN	EMPLOYEES
03/23	18,690	546	2.9%	48,682
03/22	18,321	692	3.8%	48,842
03/21	17,011	413	2.4%	46,267
03/20	20,401	513	2.5%	48,031
03/19	21,570	716	3.3%	48,320
Annual Growth	(3.5%)	(6.5%)	—	0.2%

2023 Year-End Financials
Debt ratio: 0.2%
Return on equity: 4.9%
Cash ($ mil.): 1,681
Current Ratio: 1.73
Long-term debt ($ mil.): 4,010
No. of shares ($ mil.): 1,601
Dividends
  Yield: 2.1%
  Payout: 75.6%
Market value ($ mil.): 18,277

	STOCK PRICE ($) FY Close	P/E High/Low		PER SHARE ($) Earnings	Dividends	Book Value
03/23	11.41	0	0	0.34	0.25	7.20
03/22	10.40	0	0	0.43	0.22	7.22
03/21	12.96	0	0	0.26	0.24	6.98
03/20	8.52	0	0	0.32	0.29	6.30
03/19	12.72	0	0	0.45	0.29	6.39
Annual Growth	(2.7%)	—	—	(6.6%)	(3.6%)	3.0%

Toronto Dominion Bank

The Toronto-Dominion Bank, known as TD Bank, is one of the top 10 North American banks providing personal, small business, commercial banking solutions. It serves more than 25 million customers worldwide and ranks among the world's leading online financial service firms, with more than 15 million active online and mobile customers. In Canada, it operates more than 1,060 branches and over 3,300 automatic teller machines (ATMs). The company also has operations in the US under the TD Bank brand.

Operations

TD Bank operates three main business segments: Canadian Retail, US Retail, and Wholesale Banking.

Canadian Retail, which generates 60% of the bank's revenue, provides a full range of traditional banking products and other financial services to customers in the Canadian personal and commercial banking businesses, including wealth and insurance services.

The US Retail, which brings in 25% of revenue, operates under the brand TD Bank, and comprises the bank's US-based retail, commercial, and wealth management services. Retail provides a full suite of financial products and services through its network of 1,100-plus branches located along the east coast of the US.

Wholesale Banking, which contributes over 10% of bank revenue, provides a variety of capital market, investment banking, and corporate banking products and services. Operating under the TD Securities brand, this segment also provides services including underwriting and distribution of new debt and equity issues, offering advice on strategic acquisitions and divestitures, and meeting the investment brokerage needs of clients.

Geographic Reach

TD Bank mainly operates through its more than 1,060 branches spread across Canada. Its US subsidiary, TD Bank, operates some 1,150 branches from Maine to Florida.

Sales and Marketing

Most of the banking products sold by the company are offered to individual clients, business owners, and retail and institutional clients, among others.

Financial Performance

Reported revenue was C$42,693 million in 2021, a decrease of C$953 million, or 2%, compared with last year. Net interest income for the year was C$24,131 million, a decrease of C$366 million, or 1%, compared with last year. The decrease reflects lower margins in the Canadian and US Retail segments, and the impact of foreign exchange translation, partially offset by volume growth in the personal and commercial banking businesses, and higher trading net interest income.

Reported net income for the year was C$14.3 billion, an increase of $2.4 billion, or 20%, compared with last year. The increase primarily reflects lower PCL, higher revenues in the Canadian Retail business, and lower insurance claims and related expenses, partially offset by a net gain on sale of the Bank's investment in TD Ameritrade in the prior year, higher non-interest expenses, lower revenue in the US Retail business and a lower contribution from the bank's investment in Schwab as compared with the contribution from the Bank's investment in TD Ameritrade in the prior year.

The bank held cash and cash equivalents of C$6 billion in 2021. Operating activities generated C$50.1 billion. Financing and investing activities used C$5 billion and C$45.3 billion, respectively. Main cash uses were dividends paid and purchase of treasury shares.

Strategy

TD Bank continues to focus on its customers to provide enhanced offerings that meet evolving customer needs and expanding access to Canadians in rural, remote, and indigenous communities.

The bank has also accelerated its digital transformation, digitizing end-to-end daily banking and using new technologies to create legendary customer and employee experience across its platforms.

Mergers and Acquisitions

In 2021, TD Bank also acquired Headlands Tech Global Markets, LLC, a Chicago based quantitative fixed income trading company. The results of the acquired business have been consolidated from the acquisition date and included in the Wholesale segment.

Also in 2021, TD Bank acquired the Canadian Direct Equipment Finance business of Wells Fargo & Company. The results of the acquired business have been consolidated from the acquisition date and included in the Canadian Retail segment.

Company Background

The Bank of Toronto was established in 1855 by flour traders who wanted their own banking facilities. Its growth encouraged another group of businessmen to found the Dominion Bank in 1869. Dominion emphasized commercial banking and invested heavily in railways and construction.

As the new nation expanded westward, both banks established branch networks. They helped fund Canada's primary industries -- dairy, mining, oil, pulp, and textiles. After growing during and after WWII, The Bank of Toronto and Dominion Bank decided to increase their capital base, merging into a 450-branch bank in 1955.

HISTORY

The Bank of Toronto was established in 1855 by flour traders who wanted their own banking facilities. Its growth encouraged another group of businessmen to found the Dominion Bank in 1869. Dominion emphasized commercial banking and invested heavily in railways and construction.

As the new nation expanded westward, both banks established branch networks. They helped fund Canada's primary industries -- dairy, mining, oil, pulp, and textiles. True to its pioneering spirit, a Bank of Toronto official claimed to be the first to have set up a branch office with the help of aviation (in Manitoba in the 1920s).

The demand for agricultural products and commodities dropped after WWI, but production continued full throttle, creating a world grain glut that helped trigger the stock market crash of 1929. Both the Bank of Toronto and Dominion Bank contracted during the 1930s. After growing during and subsequent to WWII, The Bank of Toronto and Dominion Bank decided to increase their capital base, merging into a 450-branch bank in 1955.

In the 1970s TD Bank opened offices in Bangkok, Beirut, and Frankfurt, among other cities abroad. During the 1980s it was active in making loans to less-developed countries. After the deregulation of the Canadian securities industry in 1987, then-CEO Richard Thomson reduced international lending and began focusing on brokerage activities. The strategy paid off when several Latin American countries fell behind on their loans in the late 1980s.

As the North American economy slowed in the early 1990s, TD Bank's nonperforming loans increased and, with it, its loan loss reserves. The bank still made acquisitions, including Central Guaranty Trust (1993) and Lancaster Financial Holdings (1995, investment banking). It worked to build its financial services, expanding its range of service offerings and geographic coverage and buying New York-based Waterhouse Investor Services (1996); 97% of Australia-based Pont Securities (1997); and California-based Kennedy, Cabot & Co. (1997). In 1998 the bank sold its payroll services to Ceridian, and its Waterhouse Securities unit bought US discount brokerage Jack White & Co.

That year the government nixed TD Bank's merger with Canadian Imperial on the same day it voided the Royal Bank of Canada/Bank of Montreal deal. The banks believed the consolidation was necessary to stave off foreign banks' encroachment into Canada, but the government had domestic antitrust concerns: Though Canada has one-tenth the population of the US, its five top banks all ranked in the top 15 in North America.

In 1999 TD Bank bought Trimark Financial's retail trust banking business and spun off part of Waterhouse Investor Services, which would become part of TD Waterhouse Group. That year the bank ramped up its focus on Internet banking.

Not giving up on acquisition-fueled growth, in 2000 the company bought CT Financial Services (now TD Canada Trust) from British American Tobacco. As a condition for government approval, TD Bank had to sell its MasterCard credit portfolio (sold to Citibank Canada) and a dozen southern Ontario branches (to Bank of Montreal).

The company's plans to hitch a ride on the Wal-Mart gravy train derailed in 2001. Arrangements to open bank branches in some US-based Wal-Mart stores were squelched by regulators enforcing the banking and commerce barrier. TD Bank later closed all of its existing branches (more than 100 in all) inside Canadian Wal-Marts as part of a broader restructuring.

TD Bank suffered its first-ever annual loss during fiscal year 2002. Write-downs on loans to telecommunications, technology, and energy firms contributed mightily to the dismal results.

Frustrated by limited growth opportunities at home, in 2005 TD Bank ventured south of the border with its purchase of a stake in Banknorth. TD Bank paid about $4.8 billion in cash and stock for its original 51% stake (it bought the rest in 2007). Additionally, in 2006 the company assumed about a 40% ownership in TD AMERITRADE as part of the sale of TD Waterhouse.

In 2008 the company acquired New Jersey-based Commerce Bancorp. The $8.5 billion acquisition deal added some 450 branches along the eastern seaboard to TD Bank's US network and exemplified the company's plans to expand abroad. TD merged Commerce with its TD Banknorth unit to create TD Bank.

EXECUTIVES

Chair, Director, Brian M. Levitt
Chief Executive Officer, President, Director, Bharat B. Masrani
Chief Risk Officer, Ajai K. Bambawale
Treasury, Corporate Development, Strategic Sourcing and Real Estate Senior Executive Vice President, Barbara Hooper
Senior Executive Vice President, Chief Human Resources Officer, Kenn Lalonde
Enterprise Transformation, Enablement and Customer Experience Senior Executive Vice President, Christine Morris
Senior Executive Vice President, Chief Financial Officer, Kelvin V. Tran
General Counsel, Norie C. Campbell
Director, Cherie L. Brant
Director, Amy W. Brinkley
Director, Brian C. Ferguson
Director, Colleen A. Goggins
Director, Jean-Rene Halde
Director, David E. Kepler
Director, Alan N. MacGibbon
Director, Karen E. Maidment
Director, Irene Ruth Miller
Director, Claude Mongeau
Director, Joseph M. Natale
Director, S. Jane Rowe
Auditors : Ernst & Young LLP

LOCATIONS

HQ: Toronto Dominion Bank
66 Wellington Street West, Toronto, Ontario M5K 1A2
Phone: 416 944-6367   **Fax:** 416 982-6166
Web: www.td.com

PRODUCTS/OPERATIONS

FY2017 Revenue

	% of total
Interest	
Loans	53
Securities:	
Interest	9
Dividends	2
Deposits with banks	1
Non interest	
Investment and securities services	10
Insurance revenue	9
Service charges	6
Card services	6
Credit fees	3
Trading income	1
Total	**100**

FY2017 Revenue by Segment

	% of total
Canadian Retail	59
US Retail	28
Wholesale Banking	9
Corporate	4
Total	**100**

FY2017 Revenue by Country

	% of total
Canada	59
US	36
Other	5
Total	**100**

Selected Canadian Subsidiaries
CT Financial Assurance Company (99.9%)
Meloche Monnex Inc.
    Security National Insurance Company
    Primmum Insurance Company
    TD Direct Insurance Inc.
    TD General Insurance Company
    TD Home and Auto Insurance Company
TD Asset Finance Corp.
TD Asset Management Inc.
    TD Waterhouse Private Investment Counsel Inc.
TD Investment Services Inc.
TD Life Insurance Company
TD Mortgage Corporation
    The Canada Trust Company
    TD Pacific Mortgage Corporation
TD Mortgage Investment Corporation
TD Nordique Investments Limited
TD Parellel Private Equity Investors Ltd.
TD Securities Inc.
TD Timberlane Investments Limited
    TD McMurray Investments Limited
    TD Redpath Investments Limited
    TD Riverside Investments Limited
TD Vermillion Holdings ULC
    TD Financial International Ltd. (Bermuda)
    Canada Trustco International Limited (Barbados)
    TD Reinsurance (Barbados) Inc.
    Toronto Dominion International Inc. (Barbados)
TD Waterhouse Canada Inc.
    thinkorswim Canada
Truscan Property Corporation

Selected US Subsidiaries
TDAM USA Inc.
TD Prime Services
Toronto Dominion Holdings (U.S.A.), Inc.
    TD Holdings II Inc.
    TD Securities (USA) LLC
    Toronto Dominion (Texas) LLC
    Toronto Dominion Capital (U.S.A.) Inc.
    Toronto Dominion Investments, Inc.

Selected Other International Subsidiaries
Internaxx Bank S.A. (Luxembourg)
NatWest Personal Financial Management Limited (50%, UK)
    NatWest Stockbrokers Limited
TD Ireland
    TD Global Finance
TD Waterhouse Bank N.V. (The Netherlands)
TD Waterhouse Investor Services (UK) Limited
    TD Waterhouse Investor Services (Europe) Limited (UK)
Toronto Dominion (South East Asia) Limited (Singapore)

COMPETITORS

AUSTRALIA AND NEW ZEALAND BANKING GROUP LIMITED
Banque de Montréal
COMMONWEALTH BANK OF AUSTRALIA
Canadian Imperial Bank Of Commerce
ING Groep N.V.
KEYCORP
MUFG AMERICAS HOLDINGS CORPORATION
Royal Bank Of Canada
STANDARD CHARTERED PLC
U.S. BANCORP

HISTORICAL FINANCIALS
Company Type: Public

Income Statement   FYE: October 31

	ASSETS ($mil)	NET INCOME ($mil)	INCOME AS % OF ASSETS	EMPLOYEES
10/23	1,415,150	7,389	0.5%	103,257
10/22	1,403,240	12,564	0.9%	94,945
10/21	1,399,430	11,373	0.8%	89,464
10/20	1,289,890	8,741	0.7%	89,598
10/19	1,074,470	8,666	0.8%	89,031
Annual Growth	7.1%	(3.9%)		3.8%

2023 Year-End Financials
Return on assets: 0.5%
Return on equity: 9.1%
Long-term debt ($ mil.): —
No. of shares ($ mil.): 1,790
Sales ($ mil.): 73,819
Dividends
  Yield: 5.0%
  Payout: 65.6%
Market value ($ mil.): 99,993

	STOCK PRICE ($) FY Close	P/E High/Low	PER SHARE ($) Earnings	Dividends	Book Value
10/23	55.84	12 10	4.05	2.84	45.27
10/22	63.99	8 6	6.93	2.75	44.77
10/21	72.51	9 6	6.25	2.56	44.35
10/20	44.23	9 6	4.83	2.34	39.54
10/19	57.07	9 8	4.74	2.17	36.75
Annual Growth	(0.5%)		(3.9%)	7.0%	5.4%

Toshiba Corp

EXECUTIVES

Representative Executive Officer, President, Chief Executive Officer, Director, Taro Shimada
Representative Executive Officer, Senior Managing Executive Officer, Chief Financial Officer, Masayoshi Hirata
Representative Executive Officer, Senior Managing Executive Officer, Takayuki Konno
Representative Executive Officer, Senior Managing Executive Officer, Hiroyuki Sato
Director, Goro Yanase
Outside Director, Akihiro Watanabe
Outside Director, Paul J. Brough
Outside Director, Ayako Hirota Weissman
Outside Director, Jerome Thomas Black
Outside Director, George Raymond Zage III
Outside Director, Katsunori Hashimoto
Outside Director, Mikio Mochizuki
Outside Director, Ayumi Uzawa
Outside Director, Eijiro Imai
Outside Director, Nabeel Bhanji
Auditors : PricewaterhouseCoopers Aarata LLC

LOCATIONS

HQ: Toshiba Corp
1-1-1 Shibaura, Minato-ku, Tokyo 105-8001
Phone: (81) 3 3457 4511
Web: www.toshiba.co.jp

HISTORICAL FINANCIALS

Company Type: Public

Income Statement — FYE: March 31

	REVENUE ($mil)	NET INCOME ($mil)	NET PROFIT MARGIN	EMPLOYEES
03/23	26,482	950	3.6%	106,648
03/22	28,349	1,600	5.6%	116,224
03/21	28,442	1,029	3.6%	117,300
03/20	31,541	(1,056)	—	125,648
03/19	33,971	9,149	26.9%	128,697
Annual Growth	(6.0%)	(43.2%)	—	(4.6%)

2023 Year-End Financials

Debt ratio: 0.1%
Return on equity: 10.3%
Cash ($ mil.): 2,452
Current Ratio: 1.51
Long-term debt ($ mil.): 2,495
No. of shares ($ mil.): 432
Dividends
Yield: 6.3%
Payout: 49.8%
Market value ($ mil.): 7,272

	STOCK PRICE ($) FY Close	P/E High/Low	PER SHARE ($) Earnings	Dividends	Book Value
03/23	16.81	0 0	2.20	1.07	21.65
03/22	20.45	0 0	3.62	1.00	22.93
03/21	17.00	0 0	2.27	0.09	23.17
03/20	10.84	— —	(2.18)	0.18	19.09
03/19	15.86	0 0	14.83	0.09	24.30
Annual Growth	1.5%	— —	(38.0%)	85.0%	(2.8%)

TotalEnergies SE

Total SE, is a broad energy company that produces and markets fuels, natural gas, and electricity. The company operates in Australia, the US, Canada, France, and the UK. In 2020, the company finalized the acquisition of a 37.4% interest in Adani Gas. In terms of sales, Europe accumulated almost 50% of the total revenue. In early 2021, Total SE proposes to change its name to TotalEnergies as part of its plan to become a broad energy company amid the global clean energy transition.

Operations

TotalEnergies has four business segments: Exploration & Production; Integrated Gas, Renewables & Power; Refining & Chemicals; Marketing & Services.

The Refining & Chemicals segment, collecting 45% of annual sales, constitutes a major industrial hub comprising the activities of refining, petrochemicals and specialty chemicals. This segment also includes the activities of oil Supply, Trading and marine Shipping.

The Marketing and Services segments accounts for 25%. This segment includes the global activities of supply and marketing in the field of petroleum products.

The Integrated Gas, Renewables & Power segment is comprised of integrated gas (including LNG) and low carbon electricity businesses. It includes the upstream and midstream LNG activity that was previously reported in the Exploration & Production segment. The segment accounts for more than 10% of total revenue.

The Exploration & Production segment brings in about 20% of revenue.

Geographic Reach

France-based TotalEnergies has presence in Australia, the US, Canada, France, and the UK. Largest sales are evident in Europe for more than 40% of the total revenue, followed by France with around 20%.

Financial Performance

TotalEnergies' performance for the past five years has fluctuated with 2021 as its highest performing year over the period.

The company's revenue for 2021 increased by $64.9 billion to $184.6 billion as compared to 2020's revenue of $119.7 billion.

TotalEnergies recorded a net income of $16.3 billion in fiscal year end 2021 as compared to the prior year's net loss of $7.3 billion.

Cash held by the company at the end of 2021 increased to $21.3 billion. Cash provided by operations was $30.4 billion. Investing activities and financing activities used $13.6 billion and $25.5 billion, respectively. Main cash uses were for intangible assets and property, plant and equipment additions and decrease in current borrowings.

HISTORY

A French consortium formed the Compagnie Française des Pétroles (CFP) in 1924 to develop an oil industry for the country. Lacking reserves within its borders, France had a 24% stake in the Turkish Petroleum Company (TPC), acquired from Germany in 1920 as part of the spoils from WWI. When oil was discovered in Iraq in 1927, the TPC partners (CFP; Anglo-Persian Oil, later BP; Royal Dutch Shell; and a consortium of five US oil companies) became major players in the oil game.

After WWII, CFP diversified its sources for crude, opening a supply in 1947 from the Venezuelan company Pantepec and making several major discoveries in colonial Algeria in 1956. It also began supplying crude to Japan, South Korea, and Taiwan in the 1950s. To market its products in North Africa and France and other European areas, it introduced the brand name TOTAL in 1954. It began making petrochemicals in 1956. Decades later, in 1985, the company adopted its brand name as part of its new name, TOTAL Compagnie Française des Pétroles, shortened in 1991 to TOTAL.

EXECUTIVES

Chairman, Chief Executive Officer, Director, Patrick Pouyanne
Chief Financial Officer, Jean-Pierre Sbraire
Strategy-Innovation President, Strategy & Sustainability President, Helle Kristoffersen
Gas, Renewables & Power President, Stephane Michel
Marketing & Services President, Thierry Pflimlin
Refining & Chemicals President, Bernard Pinatel
People & Social Responsibility President, OneTech President, Namita Shah
Exploration & Production President, Nicolas Terraz
Lead Independent Director, Independent Director, Marie-Christine Coisne-Roquette
Independent Non-Executive Director, Patricia Barbizet
Independent Non-Executive Director, Jerome Contamine
Independent Non-Executive Director, Lise Croteau
Independent Non-Executive Director, Mark Cutifani
Independent Non-Executive Director, Maria van der Hoeven
Independent Non-Executive Director, Glenn Hubbard
Independent Non-Executive Director, Anne-Marie Idrac
Independent Non-Executive Director, Jean Lemierre
Independent Non-Executive Director, Jacques Aschenbroich
Director, Valerie Della Puppa Tibi
Director, Romain Garcia-Ivald
Director, Angel Pobo
Director, Emma de Jonge
Auditors : PricewaterhouseCoopers Audit

LOCATIONS

HQ: TotalEnergies SE
2, place Jean Millier, La Defense 6, Courbevoie 92400
Phone: (33) 1 47 44 45 46   **Fax:** (33) 1 47 44 49 44
Web: www.total.com

2018 Sales

	% of total
Europe	
France	23
Other countries	48
Africa	11
North America	11
Other regions	8
Total	100

PRODUCTS/OPERATIONS

2018 Sales

	% of total
Refining & Chemicals	49
Marketing & Services	27
Exploration & Production	17
Gas, Renewables & Power	7
Total	100

COMPETITORS

BP P.L.C.
BayWa AG
DCC PUBLIC LIMITED COMPANY
LyondellBasell Industries N.V.
PHILLIPS 66
REPSOL SA.
SASOL LTD
SURGUTNEFTEGAZ, PAO
Ultrapar Participacoes S/A
VALLOUREC

HISTORICAL FINANCIALS
Company Type: Public

Income Statement FYE: December 31

	REVENUE ($mil)	NET INCOME ($mil)	NET PROFIT MARGIN	EMPLOYEES
12/22	263,310	20,526	7.8%	101,279
12/21	184,634	16,032	8.7%	101,309
12/20	119,704	(7,242)	—	105,476
12/19	176,249	11,267	6.4%	107,776
12/18	184,106	11,446	6.2%	104,460
Annual Growth	9.4%	15.7%	—	(0.8%)

2022 Year-End Financials
Debt ratio: 17.3%
Return on equity: 18.3%
Cash ($ mil.): 33,026
Current Ratio: 1.15
Long-term debt ($ mil.): 36,987
No. of shares ($ mil.): 2,481
Dividends
Yield: 0.1%
Payout: 99.4%
Market value ($ mil.): 154,079

	STOCK PRICE ($) FY Close	P/E High/Low	PER SHARE ($) Earnings	Dividends	Book Value
12/22	62.08	8 6	7.85	7.80	45.01
12/21	49.46	9 7	5.92	3.06	42.87
12/20	41.91	— —	(2.90)	3.09	39.45
12/19	55.30	14 11	4.17	2.89	45.15
12/18	52.18	15 12	4.24	2.95	44.34
Annual Growth	4.4%	—	16.6%	27.5%	0.4%

Toyota Boshoku Corp

Toyota Boshoku primarily manufactures and sells automobile-related parts such as seats, interior components including door trims, exterior components such as bumpers, and unit components including air filters and stack manifolds. The company the top manufacturer of automotive interior components in Japan and ranks three in the world.. Founded in 1918 by Sakichi Toyoda, the company makes seats for Toyota Yaris model. Toyota Boshoku has over 90 companies around the globe. Majority of its sales were generated in Japan.

Operations
Toyota Boshoku operates in five geographical segments: Japan (around 45% of sales), North, Central and South America (around 20%), China as well as Asia and Oceania (about 15% each), and Europe and Africa (around 5%).

The company mainly engages in manufacture and sale of automotive components, and local companies incorporated within each region formulate a comprehensive strategy and operate business activities.

The company is responsible for Japan; TOYOTA BOSHOKU AMERICA, INC. is in charge of North, Central and South America, which includes the US and Canada as well as geographically close countries of Mexico, Brazil and Argentina; TOYOTA BOSHOKU ASIA CO., LTD. covers Asia and Oceania (mainly Thailand, India, Indonesia, Malaysia, the Philippines, Vietnam, and Australia, etc.) with a view to strengthening the community-based structure on both fronts of optimum production and supply network; and TOYOTA BOSHOKU (CHINA) CO., LTD. is responsible for China. TOYOTA BOSHOKU EUROPE N.V. is responsible for Europe and Africa (mainly France, Poland, Russia, Slovakia, Turkey, South Africa, etc.), and these regions are managed as one management unit.

In addition, it develops seats that elicit the maximum potential of each car, seats that make the vehicle easier to drive and that ensure the ultimate in comfort and pleasure. It also delivers automobile interior spaces in which people from every country and region of the world can create unforgettable moments with family, friends and other loved ones that will last a lifetime. It manufactures products that maximize engine performance while contributing to realizing a clean and comfortable vehicle interior space by developing next-generation filtration technology.

Geographic Reach
Toyota Boshoku has its head office in Kariya-shi, Aichi. The company operates above 90 companies in the Americas, Asia and Oceania, China, Europe and Africa, and in Japan.

Toyota Boshoku generates about 45% of total sales in Japan, while the US and China with about 15% each, and others generate the rest of sales.

Financial Performance
The company's revenue in 2022 decreased to JPY 1.3 trillion compared to JPY 1.4 billion in the prior year.

Profit in 2022 decreased to JPY 37.6 billion compared to JPY 46.0 billion in the prior year.

Cash held by the company at the end of 2022 increased to JPY195.2 billion. Cash provided by operations and financing activities were JPY 74.5 billion and JPY2.8 billion, respectively. Investing activities used JPY51.4 billion, mainly for purchase of property, plant and equipment.

Company Background
The company ramped up its interior operation in mid-2011 with the acquisition of Austria-based POLYTEC Holding's interior business. The deal will give Toyota Boshoku manufacturing and research facilities in Germany, Poland, and South Africa. Toyota Boshoku agreed in 2009 to merge its automotive fabric business with Kawashima Selkon Textiles and Toyota Tsusho Corporation. The new company, which is named TB Kawashima, will produce fabrics for seats and doors, headliners, as well as other interior fabrics for automobiles, trains, and aircraft. Toyota Boshoku holds a 35% stake in the joint venture. The company is also partnered with Japan-based automotive parts maker Aisin Seiki to produce car interior parts in Poland. The joint venture, which is 70% controlled by Toyota Boshoku, is called TBAI Poland. Production, scheduled to begin in 2011, will supply the company's seat plants in Russia and Turkey.

EXECUTIVES
Chairman, Representative Director, Shuhei Toyoda
Vice-Chairman, Director, Naoki Miyazaki
President, Representative Director, Masayoshi Shirayanagi
Director, Hiroshi Ioki
Director, Shunichi Iwamori
Outside Director, Akihiro Koyama
Outside Director, Junko Shiokawa
Outside Director, Takafumi Seto
Outside Director, Kenichiro Ito
Auditors : PricewaterhouseCoopers Aarata LLC

LOCATIONS
HQ: Toyota Boshoku Corp
1-1 Toyoda-cho, Kariya, Aichi 448-8651
Phone: (81) 566 23 6611   **Fax:** 859 525-1268
Web: www.toyota-boshoku.com

PRODUCTS/OPERATIONS
Selected Products
Air cleaners
Door trims
Electric sunshade system
Filters (oil, air, cabin, automatic transmission fluid, hydrocarbon absorption)
Floor carpets
Headliner lightings
Molded headliners
Package trays
Seats
Silencers
Textiles (seat fabrics, airbags, seatbelt webbing, uniforms, bumpers, fenders, partition net)

COMPETITORS
ADIENT PUBLIC LIMITED COMPANY
Continental AG
DENSO CORPORATION
FAURECIA EMISSIONS CONTROL SYSTEMS NA, LLC
HUSCO INTERNATIONAL, INC.
JTEKT CORPORATION
STRATTEC SECURITY CORPORATION
TENNECO INC.
TOYODA GOSEI CO., LTD.
WEBASTO ROOF SYSTEMS INC.

HISTORICAL FINANCIALS
Company Type: Public

Income Statement FYE: March 31

	REVENUE ($mil)	NET INCOME ($mil)	NET PROFIT MARGIN	EMPLOYEES
03/23	12,043	110	0.9%	53,430
03/22	11,686	322	2.8%	52,041
03/21	11,489	281	2.5%	50,899
03/20	12,644	228	1.8%	52,392
03/19	12,798	247	1.9%	51,991
Annual Growth	(1.5%)	(18.3%)	—	0.7%

2023 Year-End Financials
Debt ratio: 0.1%
Return on equity: 3.7%
Cash ($ mil.): 1,863
Current Ratio: 1.61
Long-term debt ($ mil.): 675
No. of shares ($ mil.): 186
Dividends
Yield: —
Payout: 89.1%
Market value ($ mil.): —

Toyota Industries Corporation (Japan)

Toyota Industries develops, produces, sells and provides services for a broad range of products, from industrial vehicles centered around a full lineup of lift trucks to materials handling systems. Lift trucks, which capture the top global market share, are delivered to customers around the world under the TOYOTA, RAYMOND and CESAB brands. It sells weaving machinery, spinning machinery, instruments for yarn testing and cotton classing, and other products. Toyota Industries has about 80 subsidiaries in and outside Japan. Its largest shareholders are Toyota Motor, which owns nearly 24.7% of the company. Toyota Industries generate some 30% of its revenue from its home country, Japan.

Operations
The company has three business activities: Material Handling Equipment (more than 65% of total sales), Automobile (nearly 30%) and Textile Machinery (less than 5%).

Materials Handling Equipment business activity provides materials handling products and service to customers around the world through Toyota Material Handling Group (TMHG), under the brands of TOYOTA, RAYMOND and CESAB. Toyota Industries develops, manufactures, and markets industrial vehicles, such as lift trucks, and other materials handling equipment and systems related to transportation, storage, and sorting of goods. In order to help customers, overcome logistics challenges, it offers optimized materials handling solutions based on its technological capabilities and materials handling know-how. Under the AICHI brand, the company provides aerial work platforms.

Automobile business activity develops and manufactures automobiles and automobile-related products, such as vehicles, engines, car air-conditioning compressors, car electronics components and devices, and stamping dies.

Textile Machinery business activity develops, manufactures, and markets textile machinery, the majority of which has been supplied to customers outside Japan. It has two main categories: spinning machinery and weaving machinery. Its textile machinery receives high praise from customers around the world for its high reliability and productivity as its products are developed through technological expertise accumulated over the years.

Geographic Reach
Headquartered in Kariya-shi, Toyota Industries operates through its subsidiaries in about 80 facilities located in Europe, Asia, North and Latin America and Oceania and has about 15 manufacturing plants in Japan.

Sales and Marketing
Toyota Industries' automobile and engine products are sold primarily to Toyota Motor, which accounts for nearly 15% of sales.

Financial Performance
Total consolidated net sales amounted to ¥2.7 trillion, an increase of 586.8 billion yen, or 28%, from the previous fiscal year.

The company had a net income of ¥246.1 billion, a 34% increase from the previous year's net income of ¥184 billion.

The company's cash for the year ended 2022 totaled ¥247.1 billion. Operating activities generated ¥321.1 billion, while investing activities used ¥229.8 billion, mainly for payments for bank deposits. Financing activities used another ¥92.1 billion, primarily for repayments of corporate bonds.

Strategy
Toyota Industries has made investments and promoted initiatives in growth fields while continuing manufacturing by swiftly responding to changes in the surrounding environment and risks. The company intends to focus on the following three actions in order to further strengthen the management platform and enhance corporate value.

Thoroughly adhere to the basics. Adhere to such basics as safety, health, quality and compliance, which constitute the foundation of any company, and continue to promote manufacturing while improving quality and productivity with safety as its top priority;

Strengthen management platform. The company will strengthen its efforts against various risks and build a flexible and robust organization so that the company can make an agile response in emergency situations. At the same time, the company will develop employees who learn, think and act quickly on their own while promoting the creation of organizations and workplaces where diverse human resources can demonstrate their capabilities to the fullest;

Lay the groundwork for further growth. Viewing changes in the markets and industries as opportunities for growth of the company, it will develop innovative technologies and products through the proactive use of digital technologies and open innovation and effort to provide services demanded by its customers. Through these initiatives, the company aims for sustainable growth of each business and strive to support industries and social foundations around the world and contribute to making the earth a better place to live, enriched lifestyles and a comfortable society as described in Toyota Industries' Vision 2030.

EXECUTIVES

Chairman, Representative Director, Tetsuro Toyoda
Vice-Chairman, Representative Director, Akira Onishi
President, Representative Director, Koichi Ito
Outside Director, Shuzo Sumi
Outside Director, Junichi Handa
Director, Kazunari Kumakura
Auditors : PricewaterhouseCoopers Aarata LLC

LOCATIONS

HQ: Toyota Industries Corporation (Japan)
2-1 Toyoda-cho, Kariya, Aichi 448-8671
Phone: (81) 566 22 2511 **Fax:** (81) 566 27 5650
Web: www.toyota-shokki.co.jp

PRODUCTS/OPERATIONS

Selected Products
Automobile
    Car air-conditioning compressors
    Diesel and gasoline engines
    Electronics components
    Foundry parts
    Passenger vehicles
Materials Handling Equipment
    Aerial work platforms
    Automated storage and retrieval systems
    Automatic guided vehicles
    Counterbalanced lift trucks
    Warehouse trucks
Logistics
    Collection and delivery of cash and management of sales proceeds
    Logistics planning
    Management, collection and delivery of corporate documents
    Operation of distribution centers
    Secure storage
    Transportation services
Textile Machinery
    Air-jet looms
    High-speed ring spinning frames
    High-speed roving frames
Other
    Semiconductor package substrates

COMPETITORS

BORGWARNER INC.
COOPER-STANDARD HOLDINGS INC.
CUMMINS INC.
Dongfeng Motor Group Co., Ltd
HONDA MOTOR CO., LTD.
MAHINDRA AND MAHINDRA LIMITED
MITSUBISHI MOTORS CORPORATION
NAVISTAR INTERNATIONAL CORPORATION
PACCAR INC
TATA MOTORS LIMITED

HISTORICAL FINANCIALS

Company Type: Public

Income Statement				FYE: March 31
	REVENUE ($mil)	NET INCOME ($mil)	NET PROFIT MARGIN	EMPLOYEES
03/23	25,377	1,448	5.7%	89,245
03/22	22,239	1,482	6.7%	84,707
03/21	19,131	1,234	6.5%	78,343
03/20	20,003	1,343	6.7%	79,266
03/19	20,000	1,379	6.9%	77,266
Annual Growth	6.1%	1.2%	—	3.7%

2023 Year-End Financials
Debt ratio: 0.2% No. of shares ($ mil.): 310
Return on equity: 4.9% Dividends
Cash ($ mil.): 4,676 Yield: 2.4%
Current Ratio: 1.76 Payout: 29.4%
Long-term debt ($ mil.): 8,855 Market value ($ mil.): 17,073

	STOCK PRICE ($) FY Close	P/E High/Low		PER SHARE ($) Earnings	Dividends	Book Value
03/23	54.99	0	0	4.66	1.35	92.80
03/22	69.27	0	0	4.77	1.44	104.02
03/21	90.65	0	0	3.98	1.36	94.13
03/20	47.34	0	0	4.33	1.47	72.36
03/19	50.50	0	0	4.44	1.40	72.12
Annual Growth	2.2%	—	—	1.2%	(0.8%)	6.5%

Toyota Motor Corp

Toyota Motor, also known as Toyota, primarily conducts business in the automotive industry. Toyota also conducts business in finance and other industries. Its business segments are automotive operations, financial services operations and all other operations. The company designs, manufactures, assembles, and sells passenger vehicles, minivans, and commercial vehicles such as trucks and related parts and accessories. While its financial service business provides retail installment credit and leasing through the purchase of installment and lease contracts originated by Toyota dealers. The company's international sales account for about 70% of the company's revenue.

Operations

The business segments of Toyota include automotive operations, financial services operations and all other operations. Automotive accounts for 90% of the company's total revenue. While its financial services operations, which include loans and leasing programs for customers and dealers, account for more than 5%.

Geographic Reach

Toyota and its affiliated companies produced automobiles and related components through more than 50 overseas manufacturing organizations in over 25 countries and regions besides Japan. The facilities are located principally in Japan, the US, Canada, the UK, France, Turkey, Czech Republic, Russia, Poland, Thailand, China, Taiwan, India, Indonesia, South Africa, Argentina, and Brazil.

In addition to its manufacturing facilities, Toyota's properties include sales offices and other sales facilities in major cities, repair service facilities and research and development facilities. Toyota's primary markets based on vehicle unit sales for fiscal 2022 were: Japan (about 25%), North America (some 30%), Europe (more than 10%), and Asia (roughly 20%).

In terms of sales, North America is the largest market, accounting for about 35%, followed by Japan at more than 30%, Asia accounts for about 15% and Europe brings in some 10%.

Sales and Marketing

Toyota's automotive sales distribution network is the largest in Japan. Toyota has about 255 dealers employing approximately 110 thousand personnel and operating approximately 4.6 thousand sales and service outlets. TOYOTA Mobility Tokyo Inc. is the only dealer owned by Toyota and the rest are independent.

Financial Performance

Toyota had net revenues for fiscal 2022 of JPY 31.4 trillion, an increase of JPY 4.2 billion, or 13%, compared to the prior fiscal year. The increase resulted mainly from the JPY 1.5 trillion impact of increased vehicle unit sales and changes in sales mix and the JPY1.4 trillion favorable impact of changes in exchange rates.

Net income attributable to the shareholders of Toyota Motor Corporation increased to JPY 2.9 trillion during fiscal 2022 compared to the prior fiscal year with JPY 2.3 trillion.

Cash held by the company at the end of fiscal 2022 increased to JPY 6.1 trillion compared to JPY 5.1 trillion in the prior year. Cash provided by operations was JPY 3.7 trillion and JPY 397.1 billion. Cash used for investing and financing activities were JPY 577.5 billion and JPY 2.5 trillion, respectively.

Strategy

The automotive industry is experiencing a once-in-a-century transformation. Toyota is now striving to transform the company into a mobility company. In an era, which it is hard to predict the future, Toyota has reflected on the path it has taken thus far and has formulated the "Toyota Philosophy" as a roadmap for the future.

Toyota's mission is "Producing Happiness for All" by expanding the possibilities of people, companies and communities through addressing the challenges of mobility as a mobility company. In order to do so, Toyota will continue to create new and unique value with various partners by relentlessly committing towards monozukuri (manufacturing), and by fostering imagination for people and society.

Toyota is accelerating its shift toward product-centered management under the "making ever-better cars" initiative, efforts to achieve carbon neutrality, and endeavors to develop essential technologies such as software and connected vehicles.

Company Background

Toyota was founded in 1937. During World War II, the company made military trucks and in the 1950s, it launched the four-wheel-drive Land Cruiser, full-sized Crown, and the small Corona. Toyota Motor Sales U.S.A. debuted the Toyota Corolla, which became the best-selling car of all time, in 1968. By 1970 Toyota was the world's fourth-largest automaker.

Toyota expanded rapidly in the US. During the 1970s the oil crisis caused demand for fuel-efficient cars, and Toyota was there to grab market share from US makers. In 1975 Toyota displaced Volkswagen as the US's #1 auto importer. Toyota began auto production in the US in 1984 through NUMMI, its joint venture with General Motors. The Lexus line was launched in the US in 1989.

Because of European restrictions on Japanese auto imports until 2000, Toyota's European expansion slowed. Toyota responded in 1992 by agreeing to distribute cars in Japan for Volkswagen and also by establishing an engine plant (later moved to full auto production) in the UK.

The SUV mania of the 1990s spurred Toyota's introduction of luxury minivans and light trucks. In 1997 Toyota introduced the Prius, a hybrid electric- and gas-powered car. That was the beginning of Toyota's push to provide an electrified version of all its models by 2025.

HISTORY

In 1926 Sakichi Toyoda founded Toyoda Automatic Loom Works. In 1930 he sold the rights to the loom he invented and gave the proceeds to his son Kiichiro Toyoda to begin an automotive business. Kiichiro opened an auto shop within the loom works in 1933. When protectionist legislation (1936) improved prospects for Japanese automakers, Kiichiro split off the car department, took it public (1937), and changed its name to Toyota.

During WWII the company made military trucks, but financial problems after the war caused Toyota to reorganize in 1950. Its postwar commitment to R&D paid off with the launch of the four-wheel-drive Land Cruiser (1951); full-sized Crown (1955); and the small Corona (1957).

Toyota Motor Sales U.S.A. debuted the Toyopet Crown in the US in 1957, but it proved underpowered for the US market. Toyota had better luck with the Corona in 1965 and with the Corolla (which became the best-selling car of all time) in 1968. By 1970 Toyota was the world's fourth largest carmaker.

Toyota expanded rapidly in the US. During the 1970s the oil crisis caused demand for fuel-efficient cars, and Toyota was there to grab market share from US makers. In 1975 Toyota displaced Volkswagen as the US's #1 auto importer. Toyota began auto production in the US in 1984 through NUMMI, its joint venture with General Motors. The Lexus line was launched in the US in 1989.

Because of European restrictions on Japanese auto imports until 2000, Toyota's European expansion slowed. Toyota responded in 1992 by agreeing to distribute cars in Japan for Volkswagen and also by establishing an engine plant (later moved to full auto production) in the UK.

The SUV mania of the 1990s spurred Toyota's introduction of luxury minivans and light trucks. Hiroshi Okuda, a 40-year veteran with Toyota and the first person from outside the Toyoda family to run the firm, succeeded

Tatsuro Toyoda as president in 1995. The next year Toyota consolidated its North American production units into Cincinnati-based Toyota Motor Manufacturing North America.

In 1997 Toyota introduced the Prius, a hybrid electric- and gas-powered car. The next year Toyota boosted its stake in affiliate Daihatsu Motor (mini-vehicles) to about 51% and started Toyota Mapmaster (51% owned), to make map databases for car navigation systems. Okuda became chairman in 1999, replacing Shoichiro Toyoda, and Fujio Cho became president (later chairman). Also that year Toyota agreed to form a joint venture with Isuzu Motors to manufacture buses.

In 2000 Toyota launched the WiLL Vi, a sedan aimed at young people. It announced that it was building an online replacement parts marketplace with i2 Technologies and formed a financial services company (Toyota Financial Service) and a brokerage firm (Toyota Financial Services Securities Corp.). Toyota also bought a 5% stake in Yamaha Motor (the world's #2 motorcycle maker) and raised its stake in truck maker Hino Motors from about 20% to around 34%.

International developments included Toyota's agreement with the Chinese government to produce passenger cars for sale in China built by Tianjin Toyota Motor Corp., a joint venture between Chinese carmaker Tianjin Automobile Xiali and Toyota. In 2001 Toyota opened a plant in France. Later that year Toyota also increased its stake in Hino Motors to 50%. With partners Toyoda Gosei and Horie Metal Co., Ltd., Toyota formed a joint venture in 2002 to manufacture resin fuel tank systems. In 2004 Toyota forged a joint venture agreement with Guangzhou Automobile Group to build engines in China. The following year Toyota established 14 Lexus dealerships in China. The company began joint car production in Europe with Peugeot S.A. in 2005. Also in 2005 Toyota bought just under 9% of Fuji Heavy Industries -- the Japanese maker of Subaru passenger vehicles. The two companies began production of Toyota Camrys at Fuji Heavy Industries' underutilized Subaru of Indiana plant in 2007.

After suffering through the Great Recession from 2008 to 2010, Toyota faced another unforeseen crisis. In March 2011 its business suffered unexpectedly from the Great East Japan Earthquake, which triggered a deadly tsunami and subsequent nuclear crisis that forced Tokyo Electric Power (Tepco) to shut down reactors at two nuclear power plants and five other conventional power plants. The events forced manufacturers to reduce their output or move production to other regions. Toyota, along with its rivals (Nissan, Honda, and Mazda), were forced to close their factories days after the devastation.

EXECUTIVES

Chairman, Representative Director, Takeshi Uchiyamada
Vice-Chairman, Representative Director, Shigeru Hayakawa
President, Representative Director, Akio Toyoda
Operating Officer, Representative Director, James Kuffner
Managing Executive Vice President, Managing Operating Officer, Representative Director, Kenta Kon
Managing Executive Vice President, Managing Operating Officer, Representative Director, Masahiko Maeda
Outside Director, Ikuro Sugawara
Outside Director, Philip Craven
Outside Director, Teiko Kudo
Auditors : PricewaterhouseCoopers Aarata LLC

LOCATIONS

HQ: Toyota Motor Corp
1 Toyota-cho, Toyota, Aichi 471-8571
Phone: (81) 565 28 2121   Fax: (81) 565 23 5800
Web: www.toyota.co.jp

2018 Sales

	% of total
Japan	43
North America	28
Asia	14
Europe	9
Other	6
Total	100

PRODUCTS/OPERATIONS

2018 Sales

	% of total
Automotive	88
Financial services	7
Other	5
Total	100

2018 Sales

	% of total
Sales of products	93
Financing operations	7
Total	100

Selected Products

Vehicles
    4Runner
    Allion (sold in Japan)
    Alphard (minivan sold in Japan)
    Aurus (hybrid)
    Avalon
    Camry (also hybrid)
    Corolla
    Corolla Rumion
    Crown
    FJ Cruiser
    Highlander (also hybrid)
    Land Cruiser
    Lexus
    GX
    LS600h (hybrid)
    LX (SUV)
    RX
    SC
    Mark X (sold in Japan)
    Matrix
    Premio (sold in Japan)
    Prius (hybrid)
    RAV4
    Scion
    Sequoia
    Sienna (minivan)
    Tacoma (truck)
    Tundra (truck)
    Vanguard
    Vellfire (minivan)
    Venza
    Wish (minivan sold in Japan)
    Yaris (marketed in Japan as the Vitz)
Other products
    Factory automation equipment
    Forklifts and other industrial vehicles
    Housing products

COMPETITORS

FORD MOTOR COMPANY
HONDA MOTOR CO., LTD.
MAZDA MOTOR CORPORATION
MITSUBISHI MOTORS CORPORATION
NISSAN MOTOR CO.,LTD.
SUZUKI MOTOR CORPORATION
TOYOTA MOTOR CORPORATION AUSTRALIA LIMITED
TOYOTA MOTOR NORTH AMERICA, INC.
TOYOTA MOTOR SALES, U.S.A., INC.
VOLKSWAGEN AG

HISTORICAL FINANCIALS

Company Type: Public

Income Statement   FYE: March 31

	REVENUE ($mil)	NET INCOME ($mil)	NET PROFIT MARGIN	EMPLOYEES
03/23	278,966	18,405	6.6%	375,235
03/22	257,977	23,431	9.1%	372,817
03/21	245,786	20,277	8.3%	366,283
03/20	275,725	19,126	6.9%	359,542
03/19	272,933	17,002	6.2%	370,870
Annual Growth	0.5%	2.0%	—	0.3%

2023 Year-End Financials

Debt ratio: 0.3%
Return on equity: 8.9%
Cash ($ mil.): 56,439
Current Ratio: 1.10
Long-term debt ($ mil.): 125,279
No. of shares ($ mil.): 13,565
Dividends
Yield: 1.2%
Payout: 479.8%
Market value ($ mil.): 1,922,050

	STOCK PRICE ($) FY Close	P/E High/Low	Earnings	Dividends	Book Value
03/23	141.69	1 1	1.35	1.76	15.69
03/22	180.25	1 1	1.69	4.55	15.66
03/21	156.06	1 1	1.44	4.24	15.12
03/20	119.95	1 1	1.34	4.02	13.70
03/19	118.02	1 1	1.17	3.95	12.65
Annual Growth	4.7%	— —	3.7%	(18.3%)	5.5%

Toyota Tsusho Corp

EXECUTIVES

Chairman, Director, Nobuhiko Murakami
President, Chief Executive Officer, Representative Director, Ichiro Kashitani
Chief Strategy Officer, Representative Director, Hiroshi Tominaga
Chief Financial Officer, Representative Director, Hideyuki Iwamoto
Outside Director, Kunihito Koumoto
Outside Director, Didier Leroy
Outside Director, Yukari Inoue
Outside Director, Chieko Matsuda
Auditors : PricewaterhouseCoopers Aarata LLC

LOCATIONS
HQ: Toyota Tsusho Corp
Century Toyota Bldg., 4-9-8 Meieki, Nakamura-ku, Nagoya, Aichi 450-8575
Phone: (81) 52 584 5482   **Fax:** (81) 52 584 5659
Web: www.toyota-tsusho.com

HISTORICAL FINANCIALS
Company Type: Public

Income Statement — FYE: March 31

	REVENUE ($mil)	NET INCOME ($mil)	NET PROFIT MARGIN	EMPLOYEES
03/23	73,946	2,133	2.9%	72,458
03/22	65,999	1,827	2.8%	69,630
03/21	56,981	1,215	2.1%	68,877
03/20	61,667	1,248	2.0%	71,033
03/19	61,066	1,197	2.0%	63,728
Annual Growth	4.9%	15.5%	—	3.3%

2023 Year-End Financials
Debt ratio: 0.2%
Return on equity: 15.5%
Cash ($ mil.): 5,793
Current Ratio: 1.52
Long-term debt ($ mil.): 9,573
No. of shares ($ mil.): 352
Dividends
 Yield: —
 Payout: 0.0%
Market value ($ mil.): —

Trane Technologies plc

EXECUTIVES
Chief Executive Officer, Chairman, Director, David S. Regnery, $730,000 total compensation
Executive Vice President, Chief Financial Officer, Christopher (Chris) J. Kuehn
Corporate Affairs Executive Vice President, Communications Executive Vice President, Human Resources Executive Vice President, Marketing Executive Vice President, Corporate Affairs Chief Human Resources Officer, Communications Chief Human Resources Officer, Human Resources Chief Human Resources Officer, Marketing Chief Human Resources Officer, Corporate Affairs Chief Communications Officer, Communications Chief Communications Officer, Human Resources Chief Communications Officer, Marketing Chief Communications Officer, Marcia J. Avedon, $643,750 total compensation
Innovation Executive Vice President, Innovation Chief Technology Officer, Innovation Chief Strategy Officer, Innovation Chief Sustainability Officer, Paul A. Camuti
Senior Vice President, General Counsel, Secretary, Evan M. Turtz
Vice President, Chief Accounting Officer, Principal Accounting Officer, Division Officer, Mark Majocha
Division Officer, Ray Pittard
Division Officer, Keith A. Sultana
Director, Kirk E. Arnold
Director, Ann C. Berzin
Director, April Miller Boise
Director, John G. Bruton
Director, Jared L. Cohon
Lead Independent Director, Director, Gary D. Forsee
Director, Linda P. Hudson
Director, Myles P. Lee
Director, John P. Surma
Director, Tony L. White
Director, Mark R. George
Director, Melissa Schaeffer
Auditors: PricewaterhouseCoopers LLP

LOCATIONS
HQ: Trane Technologies plc
170/175 Lakeview Dr., Airside Business Park, Swords, Co. Dublin
Phone: (353) 0 18707400
Web: www.tranetechnologies.com

HISTORICAL FINANCIALS
Company Type: Public

Income Statement — FYE: December 31

	REVENUE ($mil)	NET INCOME ($mil)	NET PROFIT MARGIN	EMPLOYEES
12/23	17,677	2,023	11.4%	40,000
12/22	15,991	1,756	11.0%	39,000
12/21	14,136	1,423	10.1%	37,000
12/20	12,454	854	6.9%	35,000
12/19	16,598	1,410	8.5%	50,000
Annual Growth	1.6%	9.4%	—	(5.4%)

2023 Year-End Financials
Debt ratio: 24.6%
Return on equity: 30.9%
Cash ($ mil.): 1,095
Current Ratio: 1.13
Long-term debt ($ mil.): 3,977
No. of shares ($ mil.): 227
Dividends
 Yield: —
 Payout: 34.2%
Market value ($ mil.): —

TSB Banking Group Plc

TSB is a retail bank with a trusted customer brand and heritage stretching back to the start of the savings bank movement 200 years ago. The company offer full retail banking to more than five million customers who are served through digital channels, over the phone and in branches. TSB is part of the Spanish banking group Sabadell. It offers a range of retail banking services and products to individuals and small business banking customers in the UK. TSB has a multi-channel model, including full digital (internet and mobile), telephone and national branch banking service.

Operations
The company offers personal and business banking products. Personal banking includes current accounts, savings, mortgages, loans, and insurance, while its Business banking products include savings, accounts, cards, loans and finance, and payment services.

In all, interest income generated about 90% of sales, while the rest were generated from other income.

Geographic Reach
The company is headquartered in Gresham Street, London.

Sales and Marketing
TSB offers a range of retail banking services and products to individuals and small business banking customers in the UK. TSB has a multi-channel model, including full digital (internet and mobile) and telephony capability and national branch coverage.

Financial Performance
The company had a net interest income of £868.9 million, an 11% increase from the previous year's net interest income of £786.4 million.

In 2021, the company had a net income of £157.5 million, a 177% improvement from the previous year's net loss of £204.6 million.

The company's cash at the end of 2021 was £4.9 billion. Operating activities used £2.1 billion. Financing activities generated £2.8 billion, while investing activities used £839.1 billion, mainly for purchase of debt securities.

Strategy
In January 2021, TSB published its pathway to reach operational net-zero carbon emissions by 2030, a key commitment in our responsible business strategy, the 'Do What Matters Plan'. As a member of the United Nation's Net Zero Banking Alliance, TSB has committed to aligning its lending portfolio with net-zero emissions by 2050. TSB will deliver a net-zero carbon pathway that meets international standards that is independently validated by the Science Based Targets initiative. This is supported by TSB's membership of the Partnership for Carbon Accounting Financials.

Company Background
TSB Banking Group's roots date back to the early 1800s, when several Trustee Savings Banks were established in the UK. However, the banks lost popularity by the second half of the century, largely as a result of the establishment of Post Office Savings Banks. After several years of consolidation, TSB Group plc was created and floated on the public exchange in 1986. The group merged with Lloyds Bank to become Lloyds TBC in 1995.

EXECUTIVES
Executive Chairman, Richard Meddings
Chief Executive Officer, Executive Director, Debbie Crosbie
Chief Financial Officer, Executive Director, Ralph Coates
Secretary, Keith Hawkins
Independent Non-Executive Director, Paulina Beato
Senior Independent Non-Executive Director, Dame Sandra Dawson
Independent Non-Executive Director, Graeme Hardie
Independent Non-Executive Director, Stephen Page

Independent Non-Executive Director, Andy Simmonds
Independent Non-Executive Director, Polly Williams
Non-Executive Director, Tomas Varela
Non-Executive Director, David Vegara
Auditors : KPMG LLP

LOCATIONS
HQ: TSB Banking Group Plc
20 Gresham Street, London EC2V 7JE
Phone: (44) 20 7003 9000
Web: www.tsb.co.uk

PRODUCTS/OPERATIONS
2016 Sales

	% of total
Interest and similar income	81
Fee and commission income	15
Other income	4
Total	100

HISTORICAL FINANCIALS
Company Type: Public

Income Statement — FYE: December 31

	ASSETS ($mil)	NET INCOME ($mil)	INCOME AS % OF ASSETS	EMPLOYEES
12/23	60,732	222	0.4%	0
12/22	59,528	123	0.2%	0
12/21	62,921	175	0.3%	6,137
12/20	57,872	(217)	—	7,068
12/19	52,189	34	0.1%	8,198
Annual Growth	3.9%	59.1%	—	—

2023 Year-End Financials
Return on assets: 0.3%
Return on equity: 8.6%
Long-term debt ($ mil.): —
No. of shares ($ mil.): 500
Sales ($ mil.): 2,676
Dividends
Yield: —
Payout: 0.0%
Market value ($ mil.): —

TUI AG

TUI is one of the world's leading tourism groups. The broad portfolio gathered under the company umbrella consists of strong tour operators, 1,600 travel agencies and leading online portals, five airlines with around 150 aircraft, over 400 hotels, some 15 cruise liners and many incoming agencies in all major holiday destinations around the globe. It covers the entire tourism value chain under one roof. This integrated offering enables it to provide its 27 million customers with an unmatched holiday experience in 180 regions. Germany accounts for more than 35% of total revenue.

Operations
TUI operates through Central Region; Western Region; North Region; Hotels and Resorts; TUI Musement; and Cruises.

The Central Region segment comprises the tour operators and airlines in Germany and tour operators in Austria, Poland and Switzerland. The segment accounts for about 50% of total revenue.

The Western Region segment comprises the tour operators and airlines in Belgium and the Netherlands and tour operators in France. The segment accounts for some 20% of total revenue.

The Northern Region segment comprises the tour operators and airlines in the UK, Ireland and the Nordic countries and the stake in the tour operation business of the Canadian company Sunwing as well as until its disposal end of March 2021 the associate TUI Russia. This segment also includes the tour operator TUI Lakes & Mountains, which plays a major role in securing the load factor for its UK aircraft fleet in winter. The segment accounts for more than 15% of total revenue.

The Hotels & Resorts segment comprises all company-owned hotels and hotel shareholdings of TUI Group. The company's hotel portfolio includes such well-known brands as Riu, TUI Blue and the premium club brand Robinson Clubs. The segments about 10% of total revenue.

The TUI Musement segment comprises the companies providing services in the destinations. The segment accounts some 5% of revenue.

The Cruises segment consists of the joint venture TUI Cruises, its subsidiary Hapag-Lloyd Cruises as well as the British cruise business Marella Cruises.

Geographic Reach
TUI's registered offices are located in Hanover and Berlin, Germany and serves more than 180 destinations around the world.

Germany is the company's largest market, accounting for more than 35% of total revenue, followed by UK (about 15%) and Spain. Other Europe accounts for some 40% of total revenue and North and South America accounts for nearly 5%.

Sales and Marketing
Available in all major holiday and city destinations to travelers around the world, including the 28 million annual TUI customers, there are currently more than 160,000 "things to do" - including excursions, activities, tickets and transfers. These are distributed through the Musement and TUI websites and apps, and B2B partners, including the world's leading OTAs, tour operators, cruise lines and travel companies.

Financial Performance
Note: Growth rates may differ after conversion to US Dollars.

In financial year 2021, TUI Group's revenue declined by 40% to EUR 4.7 billion due to the COVID-19 pandemic.

Loss for fiscal 2021 decreased to EUR 2.5 billion compared from the prior year with EUR 3.1 billion.

Cash held by the company at the end of fiscal 2021 increased to EUR 1.6 billion. Cash provided by investing activities was EUR 704.7 million while cash used for operations and financing activities were EUR 151.3 million and EUR 235.5 million, respectively.

Strategy
In particular, three megatrends will continue to drive the growth of tourism in the future. Firstly, TUI are seeing a shift in demographics with people living healthier, longer and with more money to spend which has a positive effect on travel and tourism. Secondly, middle classes continue to grow, particularly in South East Asia and Latin America. Thirdly, people are choosing experiences over the ownership of goods with increasing frequency. Therefore, tourism will continue to be an attractive growth market in the mid-term. Short-term, tourism markets have rebounded strongly from the COVID-19 crisis. The underlying desire of people to travel has been evident throughout the COVID-19 crisis, as it has seen immediate strong booking surges for its destinations on easing of governments' travel restrictions.

HISTORY
What became TUI was founded in Berlin in 1923 as Preussische Bergwerks-und Hutten-Aktiengesellschaft (Prussian Mine and Foundry Company) to operate former state-owned mining companies, saltworks, and smelters. Despite outmoded equipment and a war-shattered economy, the company prospered. So in 1929 the Prussian parliament combined Preussag with Hibernia and Preussischen Elektrizitats to form the state-run VEBA group, hoping to stimulate foreign investment.

Operating as part of VEBA didn't work out as well as Preussag had hoped, and WWII left the company a shell of its former self. In 1952, as restrictions on steel production were lifted and industry rebounded, Preussag relocated to Hanover. After taking steps to reestablish itself, Preussag made a public offering in 1959; VEBA kept about 22%.

A worldwide steel glut that lasted through the 1960s forced Preussag to diversify. Acquisitions included railroad tank car and transport agent VTG and shipbuilding and chemical companies. The company also formed oil exploration unit Preussag Energie in 1968. In 1969 VEBA sold its remaining stake in Preussag to Westdeusche Landesbank (WestLB).

When the 1970s oil crisis drove up steel costs, Preussag began international ventures to counter falling revenues at home. But the 1980s brought PR disasters. The European Commission fined Preussag and five other zinc producers for antitrust violations in 1984.

In 1989 Preussag reorganized into a holding company with four independent units: coal, oil, natural gas, and plant construction. But it was about to take a sharp business turn. Michael Frenzel, who had managed WestLB's industry holdings, became CEO in 1994 in the midst of another steel recession. Frenzel was determined to shift Preussag away from its rusting past and toward services and technology. In 1997 it acquired container shipping and travel firm Hapag-Lloyd, which had a 30% stake in Touristik Union International (TUI). By the end of 1998, the acquisitions of the rest of TUI, First Reisebuero Management, and a 25% stake in the UK's Thomas Cook (raised to 50.1% in 1999) had made Preussag Europe's top tourism group.

As part of its restructuring, Preussag traded its plant engineering units and half of its shipbuilding unit (HDW) to Babcock Borsig for a 33% stake in that company in 1999. Preussag then made plans to transfer another 25% of HDW to Sweden's Celsius in a deal (along with Babcock Borsig) to merge Celsius' Kockums submarine shipyards with HDW. That year Hapag-Lloyd and TUI were merged into Hapag Touristik Union (renamed TUI Group in 2000); VTG merged with Lehnkering, a 126-year-old freight forwarding group, becoming VTG-Lehnkering.

Preussag also acquired a stake in French package tour leader Nouvelles FrontiÃ¨res and sold a metals trading unit, W. & O. Bergmann, to Enron. By 2002 the company had sold off most of its non-tourism operations, changed its name to TUI, and restructured its business to concentrate on travel-related businesses.

In 2004 TUI sold a division of its VTG-Lehnkering logistics operation to investors for an undisclosed amount. Also that year TUI Travel Solutions GmbH sold 50% of its stake in TQ3 Travel Solutions to Navigant International. (It sold the rest of TQ3 to Navigant two years later.)

WestLB surrendered its majority shareholding of TUI in 2004, freeing up 90% of the company's shares for free float.

In 2005 the company purchased Canada-based CP Ships for almost $2 billion, making Hapag-Lloyd one of the world's largest container carriers.

Two years later, TUI expanded its travel business by buying First Choice Holidays and combining the UK-based company with its existing tourism operations to form TUI Travel, a publicly traded company in which TUI held a controlling stake. Around the same time, the company decided to shed its container shipping operations and focus solely on its tourism and travel services businesses. To this end, in March 2009, TUI sold Hapag-Lloyd to a German consortium but retained a 43% stake in the company. (TUI's stake in Hapag-Lloyd increased to about 50% as loans to the company were converted to equity.)

EXECUTIVES

Chief Investment Officer, Frank Rosenberger
Chief Human Resources Officer, Elke Eller
Chief Executive Officer, Friedrich Joussen
Markets & Airlines Chief Executive Officer, David Burling
Hotels & Resorts, Cruises, Destinations Experiences Chief Executive Officer, Sebastian Ebel
Chief Financial Officer, Birgit Conix
Chairman, Dieter Zetsche
Deputy Chairman, Peter Long
Deputy Chairman, Director, Frank Jakobi
Director, Stefan Weinhofer
Director, Ingrid-Helen Arnold
Director, Wolfgang Flintermann
Director, Maria Garana Corces
Director, Andreas Barczewski
Director, Peter Bremme
Director, Edgar Ernst
Director, Angelika Gifford
Director, Stefan Heinemann
Director, Valerie Gooding
Director, Dierk Hirschel
Director, Janis Kong
Director, Vladimir Lukin
Director, Coline McConville
Director, Alexey Mordashov
Director, Michael Ponipp
Director, Carola Schwirn
Director, Anette Strempel
Director, Joan Trian Riu
Director, Ortwin Strubelt
Auditors : Deloitte GmbH Wirtschaftspruefungsgesellschaft

LOCATIONS

HQ: TUI AG
 Karl-Wiechert-Allee 4, Hanover 30625
Phone: (49) 511 566 00   **Fax:** (49) 511 566 1901
Web: www.tuigroup.com

2018 sales

	%
UK	31
Germany	28
Spain	1
Other Europe	36
North and South America	4
Rest of the World	1
Total	100

PRODUCTS/OPERATIONS

2018 sales

	%
Markets & Airlines	
Northern Region	35
Central Region	34
Western Region	18
Holiday Experiences	
Hotels & Resorts	3
Cruise	5
Destination Experiences	1
All other segments	4
Total	100

COMPETITORS

CWT US, LLC
EXPEDIA GROUP, INC.
JET2 PLC
ROYAL CARIBBEAN CRUISES LTD.
SABRE CORPORATION
THOMAS COOK GROUP PLC
TRAVELPORT INC.
TRIPADVISOR, INC.
VACACIONES EDREAMS SL
VIAD CORP

HISTORICAL FINANCIALS

Company Type: Public
Income Statement   FYE: September 30

	REVENUE ($mil)	NET INCOME ($mil)	NET PROFIT MARGIN	EMPLOYEES
09/22	16,128	(270)	—	61,091
09/21	5,476	(2,855)	—	50,584
09/20	9,300	(3,686)	—	48,330
09/19	20,647	454	2.2%	71,473
09/18	22,613	848	3.8%	69,546
Annual Growth	(8.1%)			(3.2%)

2022 Year-End Financials

Debt ratio: 13.1%   No. of shares ($ mil.): 178
Return on equity: —   Dividends
Cash ($ mil.): 1,693   Yield: —
Current Ratio: 0.45   Payout: 0.0%
Long-term debt ($ mil.): 1,687   Market value ($ mil.): —

Turkiye Garanti Bankasi AS

TÃ¼rkiye Garanti Bankasi (Garanti Bank Turkey) is Turkey's second largest private bank. The bank is operating in all business lines of the banking sector, including corporate, commercial, SME, payment systems, retail, private, and investment banking. Garanti Bank has an extensive distribution network consisting of over 900 domestic branches, and about 10 branches across Cyprus, Malta, London, DÃ¼sseldorf, and Shanghai. Garanti Bank provides factoring, insurance, leasing, investment, private pension plans, portfolio management, and other services. As Turkey's second-largest private bank, Garanti serves more than 15 million customers. The bank was founded in 1946.

EXECUTIVES

Chairman, Suleyman Sozen
Chief Executive Officer, Director, Recep Bastug
SME Banking Executive Vice President, Cemal Onaran
Engineering and Data Executive Vice President, Ilker Kuruöz
Finance and Treasury Executive Vice President, Aydin Güler
Commercial Banking Executive Vice President, Selahattin Guldu
Customer Solutions and Digital Banking Executive Vice President, Isil Akdemir Evlioglu
Corporate, Investment Banking and Global Market Executive Vice President, Betul Ebru Edin
Talent and Culture Executive Vice President, Didem Dincer Baser
Retail Banking Executive Vice President, Mahmut Akten
Vice-Chairman, Independent Director, Jorge Sáenz-Azcúnaga Carranza
Independent Director, Mevhibe Canan Ozsoy
Independent Director, Sema Yurdum

Independent Director, Avi Aydin Düren
Director, Muammer Cuneyt Sezgin
Director, Jaime Saenz de Tejada Pulido
Director, Javier Bernal Dionis
Director, Rafael Salinas Martínez De Lecea
Director, Sait Ergun Ozen
Auditors : Güney Bagimsiz Denetim ve Serbest Muhasebeci Mali Müsavirlik Anonim Sirketi (A member firm of Ernst & Young Global Limited)

LOCATIONS

HQ: Turkiye Garanti Bankasi AS
Levent Nispetiye Mah., Aytar Cad., No. 2 Besiktas, Istanbul, Istanbul Province 34340
Phone: (90) 212 318 18 18 **Fax:** (90) 212 216 64 22
Web: www.garantibbva.com.tr

PRODUCTS/OPERATIONS

2014 Sales

	% of total
Interest income	80
Net fee and commission income	15
Other operting income	5
Total	100

2014 Sales

	% of total
Corporate Banking	33
Retail Banking	31
Investment Banking	13
Others	23
Total	100

COMPETITORS

AKBANK TURK ANONIM SIRKETI
AXIS BANK LIMITED
CANARA BANK
CITIZENS FINANCIAL GROUP, INC.
China Construction Bank Corporation
HSBC USA, INC.
Shanghai Pudong Development Bank Co., Ltd.
Shinhan Financial Group Co., Ltd.
TURKIYE IS BANKASI ANONIM SIRKETI
YAPI VE KREDI BANKASI ANONIM SIRKETI

HISTORICAL FINANCIALS

Company Type: Public

Income Statement — FYE: December 31

	ASSETS ($mil)	NET INCOME ($mil)	INCOME AS % OF ASSETS	EMPLOYEES
12/23	74,474	2,921	3.9%	18,966
12/22	69,635	3,125	4.5%	21,659
12/21	56,655	977	1.7%	18,354
12/20	72,760	848	1.2%	18,656
12/19	72,018	1,036	1.4%	18,784
Annual Growth	0.8%	29.6%	—	0.2%

2023 Year-End Financials

Return on assets: 4.9%
Return on equity: 43.4%
Long-term debt ($ mil.): —
No. of shares ($ mil.): 420,000
Sales ($ mil.): 12,392
Dividends
 Yield: —
 Payout: 802.2%
Market value ($ mil.): 865,200

	STOCK PRICE ($) FY Close	P/E High/Low		PER SHARE ($) Earnings	Dividends	Book Value
12/23	2.06	10	3	0.01	0.06	0.02
12/22	1.54	11	4	0.01	0.01	0.02
12/21	0.86	35	16	0.00	0.02	0.01
12/20	1.43	108	57	0.00	0.00	0.02
12/19	1.81	124	83	0.00	0.00	0.02
Annual Growth	3.3%	—	—	29.6%	—	(2.2%)

UBS Group AG

UBS Group AG is the world's leading wealth manager. It convenes the global ecosystem for investing, where people and ideas are connected and opportunities brought to life, and provides financial advice and solutions to wealthy, institutional and corporate clients worldwide, as well as to private clients in Switzerland. UBS offers investment solutions, products and impactful thought leadership, is the leading global wealth manager, provides large-scale and diversified asset management, focused investment banking capabilities, and personal and corporate banking services in Switzerland. The company was founded in 1747.

Operations

The company operates through four business divisions: Global Wealth Management (about 55% of sales), Investment Banking (over 25%), Personal and Corporate Banking (more than 10%), and Asset Management (over 5%).

The Global Wealth Management has over $3.3 trillion in invested assets. Its goal is to provide tailored financial services, advice and investable solutions to wealthy individuals and families around the world. The spectrum of its services ranges from investment management to estate planning and corporate finance advice, in addition to specific wealth management products and services.

The Investment Bank provides services to institutional, corporate and wealth management clients, helping them raise capital, invest and manage risks, while targeting attractive and sustainable risk-adjusted returns for shareholders.

The Personal & Corporate Banking provides comprehensive financial products and services to private, corporate and institutional clients. Personal & Corporate Banking is the core of its universal bank in Switzerland.

Asset Management is a large-scale and diversified global asset manager, with $1.2 trillion in invested assets. It offers investment capabilities and styles across all major traditional and alternative asset classes, as well as advisory support to institutions, wholesale intermediaries and Global Wealth Management clients around the world.

Overall, net fee and commission income generated about 60% of sales, net interest with around 25%, and other net income from financial instruments with some 15%.

Geographic Reach

Headquartered in Zurich, Switzerland, it also operates in London, New York, Hong Kong, and Singapore.

Sales and Marketing

The company caters to private, corporate and institutional clients.

Financial Performance

The company's revenue for fiscal 2021 increased to $35.5 billion compared to $32.4 billion in the prior year.

Profit for fiscal 2021 increased to $7.1 billion compared to $6.2 billion in the prior year.

Cash held by the company at the end of fiscal 2021 increased to $207.8 billion. Operating and financing activities provided $30.6 billion and $10.9 billion, respectively. Investing activities used $1.9 billion, mainly for purchase of financial assets measured at fair value through other comprehensive income.

Strategy

Five strategic imperatives will help UBS delivers on its strategy, bring its purpose to life, fulfill its client promise and achieve its vision. Behind these are a set of initiatives that will develop UBS along its strategic direction.

The company's focuses are: delivering the power of investing, play where UBS is positioned to win, make technology its differentiator, increase ease of doing business and enable its journey, and mobilize employees behind its future vision and act as one firm.

Mergers and Acquisitions

In early 2022, UBS and Wealthfront, an industry-leading, automated wealth management provider serving the next generation of investors, signed an agreement whereby UBS would acquire Wealthfront in an all-cash transaction valued at $1.4 billion. Through this acquisition, UBS will accelerate its growth ambitions in the US, broaden the firm's reach among affluent investors and expand its distribution and capabilities.

EXECUTIVES

Chief Executive Officer, Ralph A.J.G. Hamers
Chief Risk Officer, Christian Bluhm
Chief Financial Officer, Kirt Gardner
Human Resources Chief Operating Officer, Sabine Keller-Busse
Regulatory and Governance Chief Compliance Officer, Regulatory and Governance Chief Governance Officer, Markus Ronner
General Counsel, Markus U. Diethelm
Secretary, Markus Baumann
Non-Independent Non-Executive Chairman, Axel A. Weber

Vice-Chairman, Senior Independent Director, Non-Executive Director, Jeremy Anderson
Independent Non-Executive Director, William C. Dudley
Independent Non-Executive Director, Reto Francioni
Independent Non-Executive Director, Fred Hu
Independent Non-Executive Director, Mark Hughes
Independent Non-Executive Director, Julie G. Richardson
Independent Non-Executive Director, Beatrice Weder di Mauro
Independent Non-Executive Director, Dieter Wemmer
Independent Non-Executive Director, Jeanette Wong

Auditors : Ernst & Young Ltd.

LOCATIONS
HQ: UBS Group AG
Bahnhofstrasse 45, Zurich CH-8001
Phone: (41) 44 234 11 11
Web: www.ubs.com

HISTORICAL FINANCIALS
Company Type: Public

Income Statement				FYE: December 31
	REVENUE ($mil)	NET INCOME ($mil)	NET PROFIT MARGIN	EMPLOYEES
12/21	40,638	7,457	18.3%	71,385
12/20	39,106	6,557	16.8%	71,551
12/19	41,562	4,304	10.4%	68,601
12/18	43,077	4,516	10.5%	66,888
12/17	20,158	1,078	5.4%	61,253
Annual Growth	19.2%	62.1%	—	3.9%

2021 Year-End Financials
Debt ratio: —
Return on equity: 12.4%
Cash ($ mil.): 192,817
Current Ratio: —
Long-term debt ($ mil.): —
No. of shares ($ mil.): 3,399
Dividends
Yield: —
Payout: 24.2%
Market value ($ mil.): —

Ultrapar Participacoes SA

Brazil-based Ultrapar Participações is a holding company for a number of midstream and downstream liquefied petroleum gas (LPG) companies. Ultragaz distributes LPG to residential, commercial, and industrial customers; Ipiranga distributes gasoline, ethanol, disel, fuel oil, kerosene, natural gas for vehicles and lubricants from 7,090 service stations in Brazil and directly to large customers; Oxiteno manufactures ethylene oxide (plus derivatives) and specialty chemicals, including surfactants; and Ultracargo provides liquid storage via six terminals. Ultrapar also operates a chain of more than 415 drugstores under the Extrafarma banner. Ultra S.A holds a 20% stake in Ultrapar.

Operations
Ultrapar operates five main business segments: gas distribution, fuel distribution, chemicals, storage, and drugstores.

The fuel distribution segment (Ipiranga) operates the distribution and marketing of gasoline, ethanol, diesel, fuel oil, kerosene, natural gas for vehicles, and lubricants and related activities throughout all the Brazilian territory. Ipiranga sells fuel at 7,090 service stations and accounts for 85% of total sales.

The gas distribution segment (Ultragaz) distributes LPG to residential, commercial, and industrial consumers, especially in the South, Southeast, and Northeast regions of Brazil. Ultragaz has a roughly 25% share of the Brazilian market and generates about 10% of sales.

The chemicals segment (Oxiteno) produces ethylene oxide and its main derivatives and fatty alcohols, which are raw materials used in cosmetics, detergents, crop protection chemicals, packaging, textiles, and coatings. Oxiteno generates 5% of sales.

Extrafarma, the drugstore segment, retails pharmaceutical, hygiene, and beauty products through 415-plus drugstores in the states of Pará, Amapá, Maranhão, Tocantins, Pernambuco, Ceará, Bahia, Rio Grande do Norte, Paraíba, Sergipe and São Paulo. Extrafarma operates three distribution centers.

The storage segment (Ultracargo) operates liquid bulk terminals, especially in the Southeast and Northeast regions of Brazil. Accounting for one percent of sales.

The company also manufactures approximately 1,000 products used in various industrial sectors such as cosmetics, detergents, crop protection chemicals, packaging, textiles and coatings.

Geographic Reach
Ultrapar is headquartered in Sao Paulo and generates virtually all its revenue within Brazil. Subsidiary Ultragaz operates in all regions of Brazil through a distribution network comprising about 20 filling plants. Ipiranga's 7,090 service stations are spread across the country. Extrafarma operates in more than 10 states in Brazil and has three distribution centers in Benevides, Aquiraz and Guarulhos.

Subsidiary Oxiteno operates three plants in Mexico. Oxiteno's more than 10 international plants produce specialty chemicals. It also has commercial offices in Argentina, Belgium, China, and Colombia.

Sales and Marketing
Ultragaz distributes LPG to residential, commercial and industrial market segments. Ipiranga distributes gasoline, ethanol, diesel, NGV, fuel oil, kerosene and lubricants through a network of 7,090 service stations and directly to large customers. It delivers LPG to 11 million households and 55,000 business customers.

Financial Performance
Note: Growth rates may differ after conversion to US Dollars.

Ultrapar's fortunes are tied to commodity prices, fluctuations in the local currency (the reais), and the health of the Brazilian economy. Its revenues have steadily grown in the past years, despite a slight drop in 2019. Overall, revenue grew 18% between 2015 and 2019. Net income has also declined in 2019, following four years of profits averaging R$1.5 billion; net income fell 73% in the last five years.

Ultrapar's net revenue from sales and services decreased 2% from R$90.7 billion in 2018 to R$89.3 billion in 2019. This was due to decreases in revenues from Ipiranga and Oxiteno, offset by minimal increases in revenues from Utragaz, Ultracargo, and Extrafarma.

Net income in 2019 was R$402.9 million, a 64% decrease from R$1.1 billion in 2018, mainly due to the decline in operating income and share of profit of joint-ventures and associates between the periods and higher net financial expenses.

Ultrapar's cash on hand fell by R$1.8 billion during 2019, ending the year at $2.1 billion. The company's operations generated R$2.9 billion while its investing activities used R$1.8 billion and its financing used R$2.9 billion. Ultrapar's main cash uses in 2019 were capital increase in joint ventures, paid interests, lease payments, and redemption of non-controlling shares of Oxiteno Nordeste.

Strategy
Ultrapar has a multi-faceted strategy, each focusing on the company's key aspects for growth and development. The company intends to reinforce its high brand recognition associated with quality, safety and efficiency by continuing to supply high-quality products and services and to introduce new services and distribution channels.

The company also aims to maintain strong relationships with its resellers in the LPG and fuel distribution business. It plans to continue to invest in training its dealers, in order to maximize efficiency, to further strengthen its relationship and to promote the high standards for its distribution network. In parallel, it plans to continue to increase its operational efficiency and productivity at Ultragaz and Ipiranga.

Its sales strategy is to increase Ipiranga's market by improving the performance of the existing resale and expanding its network of service stations with high profitability and lower market share. Ipiranga's strategy also includes expanding its logistics infrastructure to support the growing demand for fuels in Brazil and initiatives aiming at differentiating its products and services.

It also aims to enhance its retail network. In 2019, Ipiranga launched Km de Vanatgens (KVM), a loyalty program through which customers and resellers may redeem rewards and benefits in areas of entertainment, tourism, magazines, airline tickets, car rental and others. With over 32 million participants in 2019, KMV has served as an important platform, strengthening relationships with Ipiranga's customers and resellers.

Company Background

In 2008 Ultrapar acquired Chevron's Texaco-branded fuel distribution business (2,000 gas stations) in Brazil for $720 million.

In 2010 it bought fuel distributor Distribuidora Nacional de Petroleo (DNP) for about $50 million. DNP has a network of 110 gas stations in the northern Brazilian states of Acre, Amazonas, Mato Grosso, Para, Rondonia, and Roraima.

EXECUTIVES

Chief Executive Officer, Frederico Pinheiro Fleury Curado

Chief Financial and Investor Relations Officer, Rodrigo de Almeida Pizzinatto

Chairman, Non-Executive Director, Pedro Wongtschowski

Vice-Chairman, Non-Executive Director, Lucio de Castro Andrade Filho

Non-Executive Director, Alexandre Teixeira de Assumpcao Saigh

Non-Executive Director, Ana Paula Vitali Janes Vescovi

Non-Executive Director, Flavia Buarque de Almeida

Non-Executive Director, Jorge Marques de Toledo Camargo

Non-Executive Director, Jose Gallo

Non-Executive Director, Jose Luiz Alqueres

Non-Executive Director, Jose Mauricio Pereira Coelho

Non-Executive Director, Marcos Marinho Lutz

Non-Executive Director, Otavio Lopes Castello Branco Neto

Auditors : KPMG Auditores Independentes Ltda.

LOCATIONS

HQ: Ultrapar Participacoes SA
Brigadeiro Luis Antonio Avenue, 1343, 9th Floor, Sao Paulo 01317-910
Phone: (55) 11 3177 7014
Web: www.ultra.com.br

PRODUCTS/OPERATIONS

2018 Sales

	% of total
Ipiranga	84
Ultragaz	8
Oxiteno	5
Extrafarma	2
Ultracargo	1
Total	100

Selected Subsidiaries
Ipiranga (fuels & lubricants)
Oxiteno (petrochemicals)
Ultracargo (transportation logistics)
Ultragaz (LPG distribution)

COMPETITORS
ARKEMA
BayWa AG
DCC PUBLIC LIMITED COMPANY
LyondellBasell Industries N.V.
PHILLIPS 66
RELIANCE INDUSTRIES LIMITED
REPSOL SA.
SASOL LTD
TOTAL SE
WILMAR INTERNATIONAL LIMITED

HISTORICAL FINANCIALS
Company Type: Public

Income Statement
FYE: December 31

	REVENUE ($mil)	NET INCOME ($mil)	NET PROFIT MARGIN	EMPLOYEES
12/21	19,691	152	0.8%	16,442
12/20	15,642	172	1.1%	15,946
12/19	22,215	92	0.4%	16,024
12/18	23,369	296	1.3%	17,034
12/17	24,151	475	2.0%	16,448
Annual Growth	(5.0%)	(24.7%)	—	0.0%

2021 Year-End Financials
Debt ratio: 7.5%
Return on equity: 8.6%
Cash ($ mil.): 409
Current Ratio: 1.98
Long-term debt ($ mil.): 2,424
No. of shares ($ mil.): 1,088
Dividends
 Yield: 4.0%
 Payout: 76.2%
Market value ($ mil.): 2,873

	STOCK PRICE ($) FY Close	P/E High/Low		PER SHARE ($) Earnings	Dividends	Book Value
12/21	2.64	6	3	0.14	0.11	1.66
12/20	4.53	6	2	0.16	0.09	1.68
12/19	6.26	42	11	0.09	0.13	2.17
12/18	13.54	20	9	0.27	0.20	2.24
12/17	22.73	17	13	0.44	0.26	2.61
Annual Growth	(41.6%)	—	—	(24.8%)	(19.8%)	(10.7%)

Umicore SA

Umicore provides clean-mobility solutions for all platform types and recycles these materials when they reach the end of their useful life. It also provides automotive catalysts for light-duty and heavy-duty vehicles of all fuel types, and the rechargeable battery materials and automotive catalysts that are required to power. Operating one of the world's most sophisticated precious metals recycling facilities and, across its activities, Umicore can recover about 30 precious and non-ferrous metals from industrial residues, used electronic scrap, batteries, automotive and industrial catalysts, fuel cells and more. The company owns around 40% of Element Six Abrasives, a joint venture with industrial diamond producer Element Six. Majority of its sales comes from Europe.

Operations

Umicore's operations are divided in three segments: Catalysis; Energy & Surface Technologies; and Recycling. Both the Catalysis segment and the Energy & Surface Technologies segment account for about 45% of the company's revenues.

The Catalysis segment comprises the Automotive Catalysts, Fuel Cells & Stationary Catalysts, and Precious Metals Chemistry Business Units. The segment focuses on the development and production of catalyst formulations and systems used to abate harmful emissions from combustion engines, for use in fuel cells, and chemical and life science applications.

The Energy & Surface Technologies segment consists of the company's innovative battery materials that power rechargeable lithium-ion batteries and enable the world's transition to electromobility.

Lastly, the Recycling segment, which accounts for more than 50% of the company's revenue, gives new life to used metals and recovers large number of precious and other metals from a wide range of waste streams and industrial residues.

Geographic Reach

Umicore has presence in Asia-Pacific, Europe, North and South America, and South Africa. The company is headquartered in Brussels, Belgium with about 45 different production sites, 15 research and development sites, and about 35% other sites such as sales and marketing offices.

Financial Performance

Umicore's performance for the past five years has increased year-over-year with 2022 as its highest performing year over the period.

The company's revenues increased by EUR 1.4 billion to EUR 25.4 billion for 2022, as compared to 2021's revenues of EUR 24.1 billion.

Umicore's net income for fiscal year end 2022 decreased to EUR 569.9 million, as compared to the prior year's net income of EUR 619 million.

The company held EUR 1.2 billion by the end of the year. Operating activities provided EUR 835.1 million to the coffers. Investing activities and financing activities used EUR 480.7 million and EUR 112.5 million, respectively. Main cash uses were for acquisition of property, plant, and equipment, as well as dividends paid to shareholders.

Strategy

Umicore's 2030 Rise Strategy, which was launched in June 2022, provided much-needed continuity in the company's strategic journey. The strategy comprises the company's focus on: reliable transformation partner; innovation and technology; sustainability champion; and excellence in execution.

HISTORY

Created in 1906 to exploit the rich mineral resources of the Belgian Congo (later called the Congo, then ZaÃ¯re, now simply Congo), the company, then known as Union MiniÃ¨re du Haut Katanga (UM), mined cobalt, copper, precious metals, tin, and zinc in Belgium's African colony. UM smelted the mined ores in Africa and then transported them to Belgium for refining.

UM first cast copper in the Belgian Congo at Elisabethville (now Lubumbashi) in

1911; tin production began in 1918, gold and silver recovery in 1921, and radium production in 1922. In 1924 the company began smelting cobalt at its Jadotville-Panda plant. It added production of zinc in 1937 and uranium in 1943. (It exited the uranium business in 1960.) That year the Congo gained independence from Belgium, and when widespread violence and unrest swept the country, the United Nations sent in troops to restore order. UN forces withdrew from the country in 1964.

In 1965 Joseph Mobutu rose to power and began a reign of terror. He nationalized UM's mines and smelting operations in 1968. Mobutu's action forced the company to develop new mining operations in the 1970s and 1980s. During that period the company became a subsidiary of conglomerate SociÃ©tÃ© GÃ©nÃ©rale de Belgique.

UM grew substantially in 1989, when it merged with Metallurgie Hoboken-Overplet (nonferrous and precious metals), Vielle-Montagne (zinc), and Mechim (engineering). Growth proved troublesome, however, and in 1995, saddled with high labor costs and too many noncore assets, the company began to sell off operations. By 1999 UM had sold Asturienne Penamet, Cananea, its CSO trading companies, Diamant Boart, Overpelt-Plascobel, Union Mines, and Zinkgruvan. The divestitures lowered sales, but returned the company to profitability.

With restructuring behind it, UM acquired a controlling interest in four businesses in 2000: Padaeng Industry (zinc, Thailand), Larvik Pigment (zinc for paint; Australia, Malaysia, Norway), and V&S Scientific and Tayside Optical Technology (both UK-based producers of finished optics products).

In 2001 UM acquired the 60% of optical materials maker Vertex (France) that it didn't own and sold its Sogemin metals trading unit to Belgian Natexis Banques Populaires (now called simply Natixis). That September UM changed its name to Umicore. The company continued its global growth in 2002, buying a zinc alloy processor in France and China's leading producer of zinc dust (used to make paint).

In 2003, the company acquired OM Group's precious metals group (PMG) for about $750 million, diversifying its business and expanding its operations in North and South America. Also that year Franco-Belgian utility Suez divested its 15% stake in the company (Suez had acquired a controlling stake when it bought SociÃ©tÃ© GÃ©nÃ©rale de Belgique).

In 2005 the company spun off its copper business as a separate company called Cumerio.

EXECUTIVES

Chief Executive Officer, Executive Director, Marc Grynberg
Chief Financial Officer, Filip Platteeuw
Chief Technology Officer, An Steegen
Human Resources Senior Vice President, Ignace de Ruijter
Communications Director, Christopher Smith
Government Affairs Senior Vice President, Egbert Lox
Corporate Research & Development Senior Vice President, Yves Van Rompaey
Information Systems Senior Vice President, Patrick Vermeulen
Group Treasurer Vice President, Alain Byl
Control Vice President, Accounting Vice President, Erik Brijs
Group Tax Vice President, Flavia Leone
Corporate Development Vice President, Digitalization Vice President, Thomas Jansseune
Executive Vice President, Chief Counsel, Secretary, Executive Director, Geraldine Nolens
Strategic Projects Senior Vice President, Guy Beke
Environment, Health & Safety Senior Vice President, Pierre Van De Bruaene
Purchasing & Transport Vice President, Sybolt Brouwer
Strategic Projects Vice President, Geert Bens
Chairman, Non-Executive Director, Thomas Leysen
Honorary Chairman, Karel Vinck
Independent Non-Executive Director, Liat Ben-Zur
Independent Non-Executive Director, Françoise Chombar
Independent Non-Executive Director, Koenraad Debackere
Independent Non-Executive Director, Mark Garrett
Independent Non-Executive Director, Ines Kolmsee
Non-Executive Director, Gerard Lamarche
Independent Non-Executive Director, Eric Meurice
Non-Executive Director, Laurent Raets
Non-Executive Director, Marc Van Sande
Auditors : EY Bedrijfsrevisoren BV

LOCATIONS

HQ: Umicore SA
 Rue du Marais 31 Broekstraat, Brussels B-1000
Phone: (32) 2 227 71 11 **Fax:** (32) 2 227 79 00
Web: www.umicore.com

2015 Sales

	% of total
Europe	65
Asia pacific	17
North America	13
South America	3
Africa	2
Total	100

PRODUCTS/OPERATIONS

2015 Sales

	% of total
Recycling	60
Catalysis	26
Energy & Surface Technologies	14
Total	100

Selected Business Units

Catalysis
Automotive Catalysts
Precious Metals Chemistry
Energy & Surface Technologies
Cobalt & Specialty Materials
Electro-Optic Materials
Electroplating
Rechargeable Battery Materials
Thin Film Products
Recycling
Battery Recycling
Jewellery & Industrial Metals
Platinum Engineered Materials
Precious Metals Management
Precious Metals Refining
Technical Materials
Other
Zinc Chemicals
Building Products - VMZINC

COMPETITORS

ABENGOA BIOENERGY US HOLDING LLC
BUCKMAN LABORATORIES, INC.
EASTMAN CHEMICAL COMPANY
Evonik Operations GmbH
HERAEUS HOLDING Gesellschaft mit beschrAonkter Haftung
IMERYS
LANXESS SOLUTIONS US INC.
MITSUBISHI CHEMICAL CORPORATION
SASOL CHEMICALS (USA) LLC
TAMINCO CORPORATION

HISTORICAL FINANCIALS

Company Type: Public

Income Statement FYE: December 31

	REVENUE ($mil)	NET INCOME ($mil)	NET PROFIT MARGIN	EMPLOYEES
12/21	27,426	700	2.6%	11,050
12/20	25,516	160	0.6%	10,859
12/19	19,767	323	1.6%	11,152
12/18	15,824	363	2.3%	13,600
12/17	14,408	254	1.8%	13,129
Annual Growth	17.5%	28.9%	—	(4.2%)

2021 Year-End Financials

Debt ratio: 26.2% No. of shares ($ mil.): 240
Return on equity: 21.8% Dividends
Cash ($ mil.): 1,351 Yield: 1.3%
Current Ratio: 1.71 Payout: 4.5%
Long-term debt ($ mil.): 1,880 Market value ($ mil.): 2,438

	STOCK PRICE ($) FY Close	P/E High/Low		PER SHARE ($) Earnings	Dividends	Book Value
12/21	10.13	7	4	2.90	0.14	14.64
12/20	11.90	27	16	0.66	0.05	13.04
12/19	12.15	10	6	1.34	0.13	12.09
12/18	9.86	11	7	1.50	0.13	12.40
12/17	11.94	50	12	1.16	0.13	9.85
Annual Growth	(4.0%)			25.6%	2.5%	10.4%

Unicredito SpA

UniCredit is one of the world's best bank for small and medium-sized enterprises. The financial services group operates in some 15 core European countries to over 15 million customers. Germany and Austria operates as UniCredit Bank and UniCredit Bank Austria. UniCredit's structure is based on four geographic-focused retail banking divisions, plus a corporate and investment bank and others. The bank has assets of approximately ? 920 billion and generates majority of sales in Italy. UniCredit is the result of the merger of several Italian banks in the late 1990s.

Operations
UniCredit operates through geographic areas: Italy; Germany; Central Europe (including Austria, Czech Republic and Slovakia, Hungary, Slovenia); Eastern Europe (including Bosnia and Herzegovina, Bulgaria, Croatia, Romania, Serbia, Russia).

Net interest income accounts for about 55% of sales, while fees and commissions generate about 35%.

Geographic Reach
From its Milan base, UniCredit through its about 90,000 employees cater to about 15 banks and four regions in Europe. Italy accounts for about 50% of UniCredit's sales, followed by Germany for nearly 25%.

Sales and Marketing
UniCredit boasts more than 15 million clients.

Financial Performance
Note: Growth rates may differ after conversion to US dollars.

UniCredit's performance for the past five years have fluctuated, with 2021 slightly recover from the prior year, which was the lowest performing year over the period.

In 2021, company's revenue were EUR 17.9 billion, a decreased of EUR 814 million compared to 2020's revenue of EUR 17.1 billion. In 2021, the company recorded a net profit of EUR 1.5 billion as compared to the prior year's net loss of EUR 2.8 billion.

Cash held by the company at the end of fiscal 2021 increased to EUR 9.6 billion. Operating activities, investing activities and financing activities used EUR 7.5 billion, EUR 699 billion and EUR 1.4 billion, respectively. Main cash uses were for purchases of property, plant and equipment and intangible assets.

HISTORY

UniCredito Italiano's ancestor Banca di Genova was formed in 1870, just after Italy unified. Within a year the bank was in a South American banking venture, Banco de Italia y Rio de la Plata. A banking crisis beginning in the late 1880s threatened the company, which was saved and reorganized with the aid of German banking interests. The changes gave the bank -- which was renamed Credito Italiano -- an advantage over home-grown rivals and pointed it in the direction of German-style universal banking, including making direct investments in Italy's late-blooming industrial sector.

In the early 20th century, Credito Italiano joined other banks in foreign ventures in Albania, Brazil, and China, and opened offices in London and New York.

After the 1929 crash, Credito Italiano acquired several failed banks. But Credito Italiano itself was none too healthy: Government attempts in the 1920s to peg the lira to the pound led to industrial stagnation, leaving the bank holding highly illiquid industrial investments, and by the early 1930s it was essentially an industrial holding company.

Credito Italiano's existence was threatened when the Depression hit in earnest. To save the bank and its peers, Mussolini established the Istituto per la Ricostruzione Industriale (IRI) in 1933 as a "temporary" Resolution Trust-style holding company (IRI was finally liquidated in 2000) to take over the industrial assets of Credito Italiano and several other banks. IRI was instantly a major shareholder in Credito Italiano. IRI-held banks were designated "banks of national interest" three years later and were allowed to provide only short-term commercial banking services, a limit that remained in effect for more than 50 years.

In 1946, to fill the need for long-term industrial credit to rebuild war-torn Italy, Credito Italiano joined with Banca Commerciale Italiana (now part of IntesaBci) and Banco di Roma to form Mediobanca.

Credito Italiano went public in 1969 (IRI sold its interest in the bank in 1993). As a bank of national interest, Credito Italiano was called upon to help bail out several of the country's industrial groups in 1979 (it did so reluctantly).

Changing laws allowed the company to expand its branch network in 1980, and in 1982 IRI allowed Credito Italiano to raise capital (although it was still obliged to prop up struggling state industries). But the 1987 US stock market crash caused Credito Italiano's earnings to plunge 33%. Two years later it bought a stake in Banca Nazionale dell'Agricoltura, then Italy's largest private bank.

In 1995 the company joined forces with Rolo Banca 1473 (named for the year its progenitor was founded) to form Credito Italiano Group. Two years later Alessandro Profumo became CEO. He would usher in more than a decade of rapid and agressive expansion.

Credito Italiano merged in 1998 with UniCredito, a collection of several northern Italian banks. One, Cassa di Risparmio di Verona Vicenza Belluno e Ancona (Cariverona), began in 1501 as a pawnshop operated by monks.

Foreshadowing the bank's shift to an Internet growth strategy (announced after talks with Spain's Banco Bilbao Vizcaya Argentaria fell through) UniCredito in 1999 announced plans for an electronic stock market, to include after-hours trading. It also continued to boost holdings in Eastern European banks. In 2000 the company entered into securities brokerage and mutual fund administration with its purchase of US-based Pioneer Investment Management.

In 2001 UniCredito bought 10% of the Pirelli/Benetton-owned holding company formed to control Italian telecommunications company Olivetti. The following year, the company partnered with KoÃ§ Holding to take a majority stake in Yapi Kredi.

The bank acquired HVB and Bank Austria in 2005 in an $18 billion cross-border deal, one of the largest such deals ever seen in Europe. The bank strengthened its hold at home in 2007 with the nearly $30 billion purchase of Italian bank Capitalia. Antitrust authorities ordered UniCredit to sell its stake in Assicurazioni Generali following the Capitalia transaction.

EXECUTIVES

Chief Executive Officer, Executive Director, Andrea Orcel

Secretary, Gianpaolo Alessandro

Independent Non-Executive Chairman, Pietro Carlo Padoan

Deputy Chairman, Independent Non-Executive Director, Lamberto Andreotti

Independent Non-Executive Director, Vincenzo Cariello

Independent Non-Executive Director, Elena Carletti

Independent Non-Executive Director, Jayne-Anne Gadhia

Independent Non-Executive Director, Jeffrey Alan Hedberg

Independent Non-Executive Director, Beatriz Angela Lara Bartolome

Independent Non-Executive Director, Luna Molinari

Independent Non-Executive Director, Maria Pierdicchi

Independent Non-Executive Director, Francesca Tondi

Independent Non-Executive Director, Alexander Wolfgring

Non-Executive Director, Renate Wagner

Auditors : KPMG S.p.A.

LOCATIONS

HQ: Unicredito SpA
Piazza Gae Aulenti 3 - Tower A, Milano 20154
Phone: (39) 2 88 621   **Fax:** (39) 2 8862 3463
Web: www.unicreditgroup.eu

2014 Sales

	% of total
Italy	48
Germany	20
Austria	9
Poland	7
Other countries	16
Total	100

PRODUCTS/OPERATIONS

2017 Sales

	% of total
Commercial banking Italy	36
Corporate & investment banking	20
Central & Eastern Europe	20
Commercial Banking Germany	13
Commercial Banking Austria	8
Asset gathering	3
Total	100

COMPETITORS

BANCA MONTE DEI PASCHI DI SIENA SPA
BANCO POPULAR ESPAÑOL SA (EXTINGUIDA)
BANCO SANTANDER SA
INTESA SANPAOLO SPA
MEDIOBANCA S.P.A.
NATWEST GROUP PLC
Nordea Bank AB
Skandinaviska Enskilda Banken AB
Svenska Handelsbanken AB
UniCredit Bank AG

HISTORICAL FINANCIALS

Company Type: Public

Income Statement   FYE: December 31

	ASSETS ($mil)	NET INCOME ($mil)	INCOME AS % OF ASSETS	EMPLOYEES
12/22	916,140	6,897	0.8%	82,995
12/21	1,037,550	1,743	0.2%	87,165
12/20	1,143,170	(3,418)	—	90,836
12/19	960,691	3,787	0.4%	94,514
12/18	952,194	4,457	0.5%	97,775
Annual Growth	(1.0%)	11.5%		(4.0%)

2022 Year-End Financials

Return on assets: 0.7%   Dividends
Return on equity: 10.3%   Yield: —
Long-term debt ($ mil.): —   Payout: 5.5%
No. of shares ($ mil.): 1,935 Market value ($ mil.): 13,244
Sales ($ mil.): 29,931

	STOCK PRICE ($) FY Close	P/E High/Low		PER SHARE ($) Earnings	Dividends	Book Value
12/22	7.05	3	1	3.26	0.18	34.96
12/21	7.64	11	6	0.76	0.05	31.55
12/20	4.53	—	—	(1.59)	0.00	32.64
12/19	7.25	5	3	1.63	0.10	30.88
12/18	5.62	6	3	1.95	0.12	28.67
Annual Growth	5.8%	—		13.7%	9.8%	5.1%

Unilever Plc

Unilever PLC, along with its Dutch counterpart, Unilever N.V., constitute a global food and refreshment, beauty and personal care, and home care products powerhouse. The group's vast portfolio of consumer products includes approximately 50 global brands ? including Hellmann's (mayonnaise), Knorr (soups), Lynx (fragrance), Magnum (ice cream), and Dove (soaps). Unilever's consumer goods are sold in more than 190 countries and its largest market is in the US. Based in the UK, Unilever works with around 53,000 supplier partners around the world.

Operations

Unilever's over 400 brands are divided into three groups.

The Beauty & Personal Care product category sells skin cleansing (soap, shower), skin care (face, hand and body moisturizers), hair care (shampoo, conditioner, styling) and deodorants ? brands include Axe, Dove, Lux, Rexona, and

Sunsilk ? as well as other household names such as TRESemmé, Signal, Lifebuoy, and Vaseline. It generates more than 40% of Unilever's total sales.

The Food & Refreshment primarily sells ice cream, savoury (soups, bouillons, seasoning), dressing (mayonnaise, ketchup) and tea. It comprises of brands, Knorr stocks, Hellmann's mayonnaise, Magnum, and more. The segment accounts for about 40% of sales.

The Home Care segment produces cleaning products of various kinds, led by the billion-euro Dirt is Good (Persil and Omo) and Surf brands, alongside Seventh Generation, Domestos, Sunlight, Cif, and more. It brings in some 20% of overall sales.

Geographic Reach

Based in London, UK, Unilever has operations in more than 190 countries.

Geographically, Unilever's revenue is highly diversified. The US is its single largest market that generates about 20% of sales, while the UK and India accounts for some 15% combined. Other countries generated the remaining over 65%.

Sales and Marketing

Unilever's household brands used by approximately 3.4 billion consumers every day. Its diverse line of customers ranges: from large traditional 'bricks and mortar' store partners (the largest group in terms of sales) to online-only retailers, small family-owned shops and value retailers.

Financial Performance

The company generated turnover of EUR 52.4 billion, a 3% increase from the previous year. Underlying sales growth was 5%, there was a net positive impact of 1% from acquisitions and disposals and a negative currency impact of 2% driven by weakening of currencies in the company's key markets such as US, Turkey, Brazil and India.

In 2021, the company had a net income of EUR 6.6 billion, a 9% increase from the previous year's net income of EUR 6.1 billion.

The company's cash at the end of 2021 was EUR 3.4 billion. Operating activities generated EUR 8 billion, while investing activities used EUR 3.2 billion, mainly for acquisition of businesses and investments in joint ventures and associates. Financing activities used another EUR 7.1 billion, primarily for dividends paid.

Strategy

In early 2021, Unilever set out in detail the Unilever Compass strategy to deliver its vision. The five clear, sharpened choices it has made in the company's Compass strategy ? portfolio, brands, markets, channels and culture ? along with the continued delivery of its 5 Growth Fundamentals, have been playing an important role in building momentum across the business.

Unilever's investments in high growth spaces continued in 2021. As well as its established businesses in hygiene and skin care where it continues to drive science-based innovation, the company is building sizeable new businesses in areas such as Prestige beauty, Functional nutrition and Plant-based foods, which are contributing to its growth. The company's Prestige beauty business, now including the digitally-led cruelty-free Paula's Choice brand which Unilever acquired in 2021, delivered strong double-digit growth in 2021 and reached ?1 billion turnover if it includes a full year of Paula's Choice.

Mergers and Acquisitions

In early 2021, Unilever has completed the acquisition of Paula's Choice, the digital-led skin care brand. Paula's Choice offers powerful content and digital tools to demystify the science behind skin care, including an extensive "Ingredient Dictionary" that breaks down the research behind nearly 4,000 ingredients, and Expert Advice, a curated online hub of skin care and ingredient knowledge. Terms of the deal were not disclosed.

Also in 2021, Unilever has signed an agreement to acquire Onnit, a holistic wellness and lifestyle company, based in Austin, Texas. Onnit's supplements are the foundation of the brands' offering and are made with scientifically proven and high-quality ingredients to provide improved cognitive function, mood and relaxation, gut health and immunity support. With its holistic health offering and digital-first model, Onnit perfectly complements the company's growing portfolio of innovative wellness and supplement brands that include OLLY, Equilibra, Liquid I.V., and SmartyPants Vitamins. Terms were not disclosed.

Company Background

Unilever traced its roots 1890's Although Unilever wasn't formed until 1930, the companies that joined forces to create the business we know today were already well established before the start of the 20th century. In 1929, With businesses expanding fast, companies set up negotiations intending to stop others producing the same types of products. But instead they agree to merge and so Unilever is created.

EXECUTIVES

Chief Executive Officer, Executive Director, Alan Jope

Chief Digital Officer, Chief Commercial Officer, Conny Braams
Ice Cream President, Matt Close
Chief Financial Officer, Executive Director, Graeme Pitkethly
Supply Chain Officer Chief Business Operations, Reginaldo Ecclissato
Nutrition President, Hanneke Faber
Beauty and Wellbeing President, Fernando Fernandez
Personal Care President, Fabian T. Garcia
South Asia President, Sanjiv Mehta
People Chief Transformation Officer, People Chief Officer, Nitin Paranjpe
Research & Development Chief Officer, Richard Slater
Home Care President, Peter ter Kulve
Chief Legal Officer, Secretary, Maria Varsellona
Chairman, Non-Executive Director, Nils Smedegaard Andersen
Vice-Chairman, Senior Independent Director, Andrea Jung
Independent Non-Executive Director, Judith Hartmann
Independent Non-Executive Director, Adrian Hennah
Independent Non-Executive Director, Susan Saltzbart Kilsby
Independent Non-Executive Director, Ruby Rong Lu
Independent Non-Executive Director, Strive Masiyiwa
Independent Non-Executive Director, Youngme E. Moon
Independent Non-Executive Director, Nelson Peltz
Independent Non-Executive Director, Hein Schumacher
Independent Non-Executive Director, Feike Sijbesma
Auditors : KPMG LLP

LOCATIONS

HQ: Unilever Plc
100 Victoria Embankment, London EC4Y 0DY
Phone: (44) 20 7822 5252 **Fax:** (44) 20 7822 5464
Web: www.unilever.com

2016 Sales

	% total
US	16
Netherlands / UK	7
Others	77
Total	100

PRODUCTS/OPERATIONS

2017 Sales

	% total
Personal Care	39
Foods	23
Refreshment	18
Home Care	20
Total	100

Selected Global Brands
Axe
Dirt is Good (OMO)
Dollar Shave Club
Dove
Family Goodness (Rama)
Hellmann's
Knorr
Lipton
Lux
Magnum
Rexona
Sunsilk
Surf

COMPETITORS

ASSA ABLOY AB
BUNZL PUBLIC LIMITED COMPANY
Barry Callebaut AG
Clariant AG
DIAMOND FOODS, LLC
INGENICO GROUP
INNERWORKINGS, INC.
Nestlé S.A.
THE KRAFT HEINZ COMPANY
Unilever N.V.

HISTORICAL FINANCIALS
Company Type: Public

Income Statement   FYE: December 31

	REVENUE ($mil)	NET INCOME ($mil)	NET PROFIT MARGIN	EMPLOYEES
12/23	66,017	7,185	10.9%	128,000
12/22	64,160	8,161	12.7%	0
12/21	59,359	6,846	11.5%	149,000
12/20	62,253	6,849	11.0%	150,000
12/19	58,361	6,315	10.8%	153,000
Annual Growth	3.1%	3.3%	—	(4.4%)

2023 Year-End Financials
Debt ratio: —   No. of shares ($ mil.): 2,500
Return on equity: 34.9%   Dividends
Cash ($ mil.): 4,606   Yield: —
Current Ratio: 0.76   Payout: 66.3%
Long-term debt ($ mil.): —   Market value ($ mil.): 121,220

	STOCK PRICE ($) FY Close	P/E High/Low		PER SHARE ($) Earnings	Dividends	Book Value
12/23	48.48	22	18	2.84	1.88	8.02
12/22	50.35	17	14	3.19	1.80	7.73
12/21	53.79	25	21	2.63	2.01	7.36
12/20	60.36	32	23	2.60	1.83	7.13
12/19	57.17	31	24	2.40	1.80	5.66
Annual Growth	(4.0%)	—	—	4.2%	1.2%	9.1%

United Overseas Bank Ltd. (Singapore)

One of Singapore's top financial institutions, United Overseas Bank (UOB) provides a range of commercial banking and personal financial services. Its offering includes consumer banking, private banking, commercial banking, transaction banking, investment banking and treasury services. Through its subsidiaries, UOB also provides asset management, private equity fund management and insurance services among others. Altogether, the bank has about 500 branches and offices and 1.25 million ATMs across some 20 countries in Asia Pacific, Europe and North America. Almost 55% of UOB's revenue comes from its domestic operations.

Operations

UOB is organized into three businesses ? Group Retail, Group Wholesale Banking and Group Global Markets.

The Group Wholesale Banking business provides customers with a broad range of products and services, including loans, trade services, cash management, capital markets solutions and advisory and treasury products. The business accounts for some 45% of total revenue.

The Group Retail business covers personal accounts, private banking, and small businesses. Customers have access to a diverse range of products and services, including deposits, insurance, card, wealth management, investment, loan and trade financing products which are available across the company's global branch network. It accounts for more than 40% of revenue.

The Group Global Markets business provides a comprehensive suite of treasury products and services across multi-asset classes which includes foreign exchange, interest rate, credit, commodities, equities and structured investment products to help customers manage market risks and volatility. GM also engages in market making activities and management of funding and liquidity. The business accounts for some 5% of revenue.

Overall, net interest income accounts for about 65% of revenue, while non ? interest income generates the remaining 35% of revenue.

Geographic Reach

Based in Singapore, UOB has a global reach spanning in about 20 countries across three continents.

Singapore is UOB's largest market, accounting for roughly 55% of revenue, followed by Malaysia (more than 10%), Thailand (about 10%) and Indonesia (some 5%).

Sales and Marketing

UOB serves personal and small enterprise customers. It also serves corporate and institutional client segments which include medium and large enterprises, local corporations, multi-national corporations, financial institutions, government-linked entities, financial sponsors and property funds.

Financial Performance

Company's revenue for fiscal 2021 increased to $9.8 billion compared from the prior year with $9.2 billion.

Net income for fiscal 2021 increased to $4.1 billion compared from the prior year with $2.9 billion.

Cash held by the company at the end of fiscal 2021 decreased to $31.0 billion. Cash provided by financing activities was $3.0 billion while cash used for operations and investing activities were $2.8 billion and $440 million, respectively. Main uses of cash were for loans to customers and purchase of properties and other fixed assets.

Strategy

Company's strategic focuses are: connect its customers seamlessly across ASEAN and its economic corridors with Greater China and the rest of the world through its sector specialization and ecosystem partnerships; attract and enable its colleagues to stay ahead through fostering care, development and well-being; help its customers achieve their personal and business financial goals through its omni-channel approach which melds the online and offline worlds seamlessly; and contribute to the progress of the economy, society and environment through responsible growth.

Mergers and Acquisitions

In 2021, UOB's subsidiaries have entered into agreements to acquire Citigroup's consumer banking businesses comprising its unsecured and secured lending portfolios, wealth management and retail deposit businesses (the Consumer Business) in Indonesia, Malaysia, Thailand and Vietnam (the Proposed Acquisition). As part of the Proposed Acquisition, UOB intends to bring onboard the employees in the Consumer Business. The Proposed Acquisition will further strengthen and deepen UOB's ASEAN franchise. The total cash consideration for the Proposed Acquisition, will be calculated based on an aggregate premium equivalent to S$915 million plus the net asset value of the Consumer Business as at completion.

Company Background

UOB was founded in 1935 as the United Chinese Bank and catered mainly to the Fujian community in Singapore. The bank changed its name to United Overseas Bank in 1965.

EXECUTIVES

Chief Executive Officer, Deputy Chairman, Executive Director, Ee Cheong Wee
Chief Risk Officer, Kok Seong Chan
Chief Financial Officer, Wai Fai Lee
President, Peter Moo Tan Tan
Chief Sustainability Officer, Eric Jin Huei Lim
President, Choon Hin Tan
Secretary, Joyce Ming Kuang Sia
Chairman, Independent Director, Kan Seng Wong
Non-Independent Non-Executive Director, Michael Jown Leam Lien
Non-Independent Non-Executive Director, Ee Lim Wee
Independent Director, Alvin Khirn Hai Yeo
Independent Director, Steven Swee Kim Phan
Independent Director, Tai Tee Chia
Independent Director, Tracey Kim Hong Woon
Independent Director, Lay Lim Teo
Auditors : Ernst & Young LLP

LOCATIONS

HQ: United Overseas Bank Ltd. (Singapore)
80 Raffles Place, UOB Plaza, 048624

Phone: (65) 6222 2121 **Fax:** (65) 6534 2334
Web: www.uobgroup.com

2012 Sales

	% of sales
Singapore	58
Malaysia	15
Thailand	8
Indonesia	7
China	6
Other	6
Total	100

Selected Subsidiaries

Far Eastern Bank Limited (Singapore)
PT Bank UOB Indonesia
United Overseas Bank (China)
United Overseas Bank (Malaysia)
United Overseas Bank (Philippines)
United Overseas Bank (Thailand)
United Overseas Insurance Limited Singapore
UOB Australia Limited
UOB Capital Investments Pte Ltd Singapore
UOB Capital Management Pte Ltd Singapore
UOB Holdings Private Limited Singapore
UOB Insurance (H.K.) Limited Hong Kong
UOB International Investment Private Limited

PRODUCTS/OPERATIONS

2012 Sales

	% of total
Interest income	61
Fees & commission	23
Other non-interest income	16
Total	100

2012 Sales

	% of total
Retail	36
Wholesale	36
Global markets & investment mgmt.	19
Other	9
Total	100

COMPETITORS

AUSTRALIA AND NEW ZEALAND BANKING GROUP LIMITED
BANK OF AYUDHYA PUBLIC COMPANY LIMITED
BANK OF BARODA
CIMB GROUP HOLDINGS BERHAD
China Merchants Bank Co., Ltd.
HANG SENG BANK, LIMITED
HSBC HOLDINGS PLC
HSBC USA, INC.
OVERSEA-CHINESE BANKING CORPORATION LIMITED
The Bank of Nova Scotia

HISTORICAL FINANCIALS

Company Type: Public

Income Statement — FYE: December 31

	ASSETS ($mil)	NET INCOME ($mil)	INCOME AS % OF ASSETS	EMPLOYEES
12/21	340,280	3,018	0.9%	0
12/20	326,703	2,205	0.7%	0
12/19	300,581	3,228	1.1%	26,872
12/18	285,005	2,943	1.0%	0
12/17	268,426	2,537	0.9%	0
Annual Growth	6.1%	4.4%	—	—

2021 Year-End Financials

Return on assets: 0.9%
Return on equity: 9.7%
Long-term debt ($ mil.): —
No. of shares ($ mil.): 1,671
Sales ($ mil.): 8,684
Dividends
Yield: 3.6%
Payout: 83.2%
Market value ($ mil.): 66,963

	STOCK PRICE ($) FY Close	P/E High/Low		PER SHARE ($) Earnings	Dividends	Book Value
12/21	40.05	17	14	1.76	1.47	18.89
12/20	34.17	24	16	1.27	1.65	18.50
12/19	39.32	16	14	1.89	1.81	17.66
12/18	36.12	19	15	1.71	1.71	16.59
12/17	39.64	20	15	1.48	1.05	16.59
Annual Growth	0.3%			4.4%	8.7%	3.3%

Vale SA

One of the largest metals and mining companies in the world, Vale is also the world's largest producers of iron ore and nickel, as well as iron ore pellets, copper, platinum group metals (PGMs), gold, silver and cobalt. With greenfield mineral exploration in five countries, Rio de Janeiro-based Vale maintains a network integrating its mines with railroads, ports, and ships. Additionally, it has hydroelectric plants in Brazil, Canada and Indonesia, and pursues investments in energy and steel businesses through affiliates and joint ventures. About 50% of its revenue comes from China.

Operations

The company operates through three operating segments:

Iron Solutions comprise of the production and extraction of iron ore, iron ore pellets, manganese, other ferrous products, and its logistic related services. The segment accounts for around 80% of the total revenue.

Energy Transition Materials includes the production and extraction of nickel and its by-products (gold, silver, cobalt, precious metals and others), and copper, as well as its by-products (gold and silver). The segment accounts for around 30% of the total revenue.

Other includes the revenues and cost of other products, services, research and development, investments in joint ventures and associates of other business and unallocated corporate expenses and costs related to the Brumadinho event.

Geographic Reach

Vale offer sales and technical support to its customers on a global basis through an established marketing network headquartered at its head office in Toronto (Canada). Vale have a well-established global marketing network for finished nickel with sales and technical support distributed around the world with presence in Singapore and Toronto (Canada) and have sales managers located in St. Prex (Switzerland), Paramus, New Jersey (United States) and at several locations throughout Asia.

Company's largest market was China with around 50% of the total revenue, followed by Japan and Brazil with around 10%, each.

Sales and Marketing

From its South Atlantic operations, the company sells most of our copper concentrates from Sossego and Salobo under medium- and long-term contracts to copper smelters in Europe and Asia. From its North Atlantic operations, Vale sells copper concentrates and copper matte produced in Sudbury domestically and to smelters in Europe and Asia under long-term contracts, as well as copper concentrates from Voisey's Bay under medium-term contracts. Also, from its North Atlantic operations, the company sells copper cathodes from Sudbury and Long Harbour under short-term contracts.

Financial Performance

In 2022, the company's net operating revenues from continuing operations decreased by $10.7 billion or 20% to $43.8 billion, from $54.5 billion in 2021. The decrease was mainly due to lower prices of Iron Solutions products due to the lower realized prices in the sale of iron ore, which reflects the drop in the market reference price (impact of $9.8 billion) and lower volume of iron ore sales (impact of $837 million).

Net income for fiscal 2022 decreased to $18.7 billion compared from the prior year with $22.4 billion. The decrease was primarily due to lower revenues while having higher operating expenses

Cash held by the company at the end of fiscal 2022 decreased to $4.7 billion. Cash provided by operations was $11.5 billion while cash used for investing and financing activities were $4.7 billion and $13.9 billion, respectively. Main uses of cash were capital expenditures and dividends and interest on capital paid to shareholders.

Strategy

Vale strategic guidelines are: promote sustainable mining; foster low carbon solution; and stay disciplined. Vale intend to continuously improve its processes for health, safety, environment and operational risk, prioritizing the use of technology to reduce risk, enhance controls and increase innovation to improve safety and dam management, and becoming a zero-fatality company.

The company has the ambition to lead low-carbon mining as the partner of choice with a rich product-based portfolio suited to future uses and a flexible approach to adapt to evolving technologies. Vale reaffirms its strong commitment to a sound balance sheet, a lean business portfolio and value creation for its stakeholders.

Company Background

HISTORY

During the 1890s, as land reforms opened the way for foreign investments in Brazil, the mineral-rich state of Minas Gerais caught the attention of mining companies from Europe and the US. British engineers founded the Itabira Iron Ore Company and took over the Doce River Valley's Vitã"ria-Minas Railroad. After Brazil's revolution (1930), Itabira was split up. One of the new companies, Itabira Mineraã‡Ãƒo, began shipping iron ore in 1940.

A 1942 agreement, prompted by the outbreak of WWII, established iron export regulations from Brazil to the US and the UK. Later that year the Companhia Vale do Rio Doce (CVRD) was formed, with the Brazilian government owning 80%. The new company received the assets of Itabira, including Brazil's "iron mountain," CauÃ‰ Peak. By the end of the 1940s, 80% of Brazil's iron ore exports were mined by CVRD. During the 1950s CVRD invested in land holdings and shipping operations. The company set up a shipping and logistics subsidiary in 1962.

CVRD teamed up with US Steel in 1970 to mine iron ore at CarajÃs in Amazonian Brazil; two years later the site was found to hold the world's largest iron ore reserves (18 billion tons). By 1975 CVRD had become the world's largest iron ore exporter. A year later the company finished doubling the tracks of the VitÃ"ria-Minas Railroad. It also set up a manganese mining company (Urucum Mineraã‡Ãƒo) and an alumina production facility (Alumina do Norte do Brasil, or Alunorte).

To support its CarajÃs mining operations, CVRD added the Estrada de Ferro de CarajÃs railway (finished 1985) and a hydroelectric project. In all, the giant CarajÃs project involved investments from the US, Japan, France, the European Economic Community, and the World Bank. (The CarajÃs area, like many mining sites in Brazil, has been the site of intense controversy because it attracts subsistence miners, including children, who work under dangerous circumstances.) By the late 1980s the company had become a major supplier of pelletized iron, used as feed for steel mill blast furnaces.

In 1992 CVRD expanded into the production of chemicals (Rio Capim QuÃmica, now ParÃ Pigmentos SA). The company acquired stakes in two steel mills -- SiderÃšrgica de TubarÃƒo and AÃ‡o Minas Gerais SA -- in 1993. In 1996 it invested in gold finds in ParÃ state. CVRD was privatized in 1997 and the next year set the sales record for a private Brazilian company.

The company listed ADR shares on the NYSE in 2000. Acquisitions that year included Brazilian iron ore companies SOCOIMEX and SAMITRI (73%). CVRD sold its 50% stake in pulp and paper group Bahia Sul, to Suzano for $320 million in 2001. It also sold its 51% share of pulp maker Cenibra and its share of steelmaker Companhia SiderÃšrgica Nacional (CSN).

In 2002 the Brazilian Treasury and the National Social and Economic Bank (BNDES) sold 33% of CVRD's shares, further privatizing the company. CVRD disposed of its last gold mine (Fazenda Brasileiro) in 2003. It also exited the dry bulk-shipping business that year.

Under pressure from increasing globalization, Vale had been forced to trim some of its operations (including its stake in CSN) to focus on mining and bulk transport. Those asset sales helped fund Vale's win over Australian mining giant BHP Billiton, the world's #2 iron ore producer, in a battle for Brazil's iron miner Caemi MineraÃ‡Ãƒo e Metalurgia, #4 worldwide. (From 2001 through 2006 the company picked up stakes in Caemi until it owned it fully.) The deal for Inco trumped offers from Canadian miner Teck and US copper producer Phelps Dodge.

Toward the end of 2007, the company -- then called Companhia Vale do Rio Doce -- decided that it wanted a new brand identity and so ditched its longtime nickname, CVRD, in favor of Vale. Two years later it changed its name legally, dropping the more formal Companhia Vale do Rio Doce.

EXECUTIVES

Integrated Bulk Operations Chief Executive Officer, Eduardo de Salles Bartolomeo

Investor Relations Chief Financial Officer, Investor Relations Executive Director, Luciano Siani Pires

Safety and Operational Excellence Executive Officer, Carlos Henrique Senna Medeiros

Institutional Relatioins Executive Officer, Communications Executive Officer, Luiz Eduardo Froes do Amaral Osorio

Business Support Executive Officer, Alexandre Gomes Pereira

Sustainability Executive Director, Maria Luiza de Oliveira Pinto e Paiva

General Counsel Executive Officer, Alexandre Silva D'Ambrosio

People Executive Director, Marina Barrenne de Artagao Quental

Chairman, Jose Mauricio Pereira Coelho

Vice-Chairman, Director, Fernando Jorge Buso Gomes

Independent Director, Isabella Saboya de Albuquerque

Independent Director, Marcelo Gasparino da Silva

Independent Director, Sandra Maria Guerra de Azevedo

Director, Eduardo de Oliveira Rodrigues Filho

Director, Jose Luciano Duarte Penido

Director, Lucio Azevedo

Director, Marcel Juviniano Barros

Director, Murilo Cesar Lemos dos Santos Passos

Director, Oscar Augusto de Camargo Filho

Director, Roger Allan Downey

Director, Toshiya Asahi

Auditors : PricewaterhouseCoopers Auditores Independentes Ltda.

LOCATIONS

HQ: Vale SA
Praia de Botafogo, 186 â€" offices 701 â€" 1901 â€" Botafogo, Rio de Janeiro 22250-145
Phone: (55) 21 3485 5000   **Fax:** (55) 21 3814 9935
Web: www.vale.com

2018 Sales

	$ mil.	% of total
China	15,242	42
Europe (excl. Germany)	4,454	12
Brazil	3,248	9
Japan	2,743	7
Germany	1,653	5
Asia, except Japan and China	3,666	10
Americas (excl. US and Brazil)	1,476	4
Middle East/Africa/Oceania	2,738	7
US	1,353	4
Total	36,575	100

PRODUCTS/OPERATIONS

2018 sales

	$ mil.	% of total
Ferrous minerals	27,933	76
Coal	1,643	5
Base metals	6,703	18
Others	296	1
Total	36,575	100

COMPETITORS

BHP GROUP LIMITED
BHP GROUP PLC
CLEVELAND-CLIFFS INC.
FORTESCUE METALS GROUP LTD
Galiano Gold Inc
LONMIN LIMITED
Nexa Resources
RIO TINTO PLC
VEDANTA LIMITED
Western Magnesium Corporation

HISTORICAL FINANCIALS
Company Type: Public

Income Statement — FYE: December 31

	REVENUE ($mil)	NET INCOME ($mil)	NET PROFIT MARGIN	EMPLOYEES
12/23	42,878	8,230	19.2%	66,807
12/22	42,834	18,139	42.3%	64,516
12/21	54,502	22,445	41.2%	72,266
12/20	40,018	4,881	12.2%	74,316
12/19	37,570	(1,683)	—	71,149
Annual Growth	3.4%	—	—	(1.6%)

2023 Year-End Financials

Debt ratio: 3.0%
Return on equity: 21.1%
Cash ($ mil.): 3,601
Current Ratio: 1.28
Long-term debt ($ mil.): 12,872
No. of shares ($ mil.): 4,299
Dividends
  Yield: —
  Payout: 61.4%
Market value ($ mil.): 68,196

	STOCK PRICE ($) FY Close	P/E High/Low	PER SHARE ($) Earnings	Dividends	Book Value
12/23	15.86	2 1	1.89	1.16	9.15
12/22	16.97	1 1	3.91	1.37	7.89
12/21	14.02	5 3	4.47	2.68	6.72
12/20	16.76	18 7	0.95	0.62	6.97
12/19	13.20	— —	(0.33)	0.22	7.81
Annual Growth	4.7%	—	—	51.2%	4.0%

Valeo SE

EXECUTIVES

Chief Financial Officer, Robert Charvier
Chief Ethics, Compliance and Data Protection Officer, Catherine Delhaye
Sales and Business Development Senior Vice President, Detlef Juerss
Communication and Investor Relations Senior Vice President, Francois Marion
Chief Human Resources Officer, Agnes Park
Corporate Strategy and Research & Development Chief Technology Officer, Research & Development and Product Marketing Chief Technology Officer, Strategy Chief Technology Officer, Corporate Strategy and External Relations Chief Technology Officer, Corporate Strategy and Research & Development Vice President, Research & Development and Product Marketing Vice President, Strategy Vice President, Corporate Strategy and External Relations Vice President, Geoffroy Bouquot
Powertrain Systems Business Group President, Xavier Dupont
Group Purchasing Vice President, Marc Guedon
Visibility Systems Business Group President, Maurizio Martinelli
Chief Executive Officer, Director, Christophe Perillat
Thermal Systems Business Group President, Francisco Moreno
Valeo Service President, Eric Schuler
Comfort & Driving Assistance Systems Business Group President, Marc Vrecko
General Counsel, General Secretary, Eric Antoine Fredette
Chairman, Lead Director, Independent Director, Gilles Michel
Independent Director, Bruno Bezard
Independent Director, Stephanie Frachet
Independent Director, Alexandre Dayon
Independent Director, Julie Avrane
Independent Director, Mari-Noelle Jego-Laveissiere
Independent Director, Director, Thierry Moulonguet
Independent Director, Patrick Sayer
Independent Director, Director, Ulrike Steinhorst
Independent Director, Veronique Weill
Director, Eric Poton
Director, Grzegorz Szelag
Auditors : Mazars

LOCATIONS

HQ: Valeo SE
100, rue de Courcelles, Paris, Cedex 17 75173
Phone: (33) 1 40 55 20 20   Fax: (33) 1 40 55 21 71
Web: www.valeo.com

HISTORICAL FINANCIALS
Company Type: Public

Income Statement — FYE: December 31

	REVENUE ($mil)	NET INCOME ($mil)	NET PROFIT MARGIN	EMPLOYEES
12/22	21,523	245	1.1%	109,900
12/21	19,263	198	1.0%	103,300
12/20	19,830	(1,336)	—	110,300
12/19	21,602	351	1.6%	114,700
12/18	21,773	625	2.9%	113,600
Annual Growth	(0.3%)	(20.8%)	—	(0.8%)

2022 Year-End Financials

Debt ratio: 32.6%
Return on equity: 6.1%
Cash ($ mil.): 3,555
Current Ratio: 0.89
Long-term debt ($ mil.): 4,760
No. of shares ($ mil.): 241
Dividends
  Yield: —
  Payout: 18.7%
Market value ($ mil.): 2,127

	STOCK PRICE ($) FY Close	P/E High/Low	PER SHARE ($) Earnings	Dividends	Book Value
12/22	8.82	16 8	1.00	0.19	16.93
12/21	15.21	26 16	0.81	0.29	17.30
12/20	19.60	— —	(5.58)	0.11	16.48
12/19	17.54	16 10	1.47	0.70	21.74
12/18	14.58	17 6	2.61	0.73	22.06
Annual Growth	(11.8%)	—	(21.3%)	(28.9%)	(6.4%)

Vedanta Ltd

EXECUTIVES

Corporate Social responsibility Head, Leena Verenkar
Health, Safety, Environment and Sustainability Head, Andrew Lewin
Asset Optimization Head, Philip Campbell
Non-Executive Chairman, Anil Agarwal
Auditors : S.R. Batliboi & Co. LLP

LOCATIONS

HQ: Vedanta Ltd
1st Floor, âC¨CâC™ wing, Unit 103, Corporate Avenue, Atul Projects, Chakala, Andheri (East), Mumbai , Maharashtra 400 093
Phone: (91) 022 6643 4500
Web: www.vedantalimited.com

HISTORICAL FINANCIALS
Company Type: Public

Income Statement — FYE: March 31

	REVENUE ($mil)	NET INCOME ($mil)	NET PROFIT MARGIN	EMPLOYEES
03/22	17,319	2,745	15.9%	16,738
03/21	11,871	1,542	13.0%	17,041
03/20	11,060	(810)	—	19,358
03/19	13,137	719	5.5%	20,068
03/18	14,044	210	1.5%	18,146
Annual Growth	5.4%	90.0%	—	(2.0%)

2022 Year-End Financials

Debt ratio: 0.4%
Return on equity: 34.0%
Cash ($ mil.): 1,144
Current Ratio: 1.05
Long-term debt ($ mil.): 4,779
No. of shares ($ mil.): 3,717
Dividends
  Yield: —
  Payout: 80.7%
Market value ($ mil.): —

Vestas Wind Systems A/S

Vestas designs, manufactures, installs, develops, and services wind energy and hybrid projects all over the world. With +169 GW of wind turbines installed in 88 countries, the company's sustainable energy solutions have already prevented 1.5 billion tonnes of CO2 being emitted into the atmosphere and contributed to a more sustainable energy system. It has more than 40 years of experience in wind energy and was the first company to reach the 100 GW landmarks for both the installation and service of wind turbines. The company generates about 20% of its revenue from the US.

Operations

In 2022, the company generated its revenue from two operating segments: Power Solutions (nearly 80% of revenue) and Service (more than 20%).

The Power Solutions segment contains sale of onshore and offshore wind power plants, wind turbines, development sites, among others. The Service segment contains sale of service contracts, spare parts and related activities.

Geographic Reach

The company recently has strong expansion in Europe and new markets such as the USA and South Korea and broader Asia Pacific. It has presence in more than 20 countries in Europe, Middle East, and Africa (EMEA), nearly 10 countries in the Americas, and more than 5 in the Asia Pacific region.

The company generates about 20% from the US, more than 5% from the UK, less than 4% from Denmark, and about 70% from other countries.

Sales and Marketing

Towards 2030, the USA and several core European markets with older installed fleets will likely see a significant share of new installations being realized through repowering. As installed fleets continue to age, the repowering market is expected to become a major driver of medium-and long-term demand.

Unlike offshore wind, where the company has installed turbines in more than 80 markets, offshore wind remains focused in key markets, meaning that the top 10 markets account for around 80% of volume. Offshore wind is also being expanded through the development of floating solutions, which are applicable for deep sea areas. The growing magnitude of offshore projects and the growing presence of oil majors and institutional investors necessitates strong partnerships to balance risk and address potential supply constraints.

Financial Performance

Note: Growth rates may differ after conversion to US Dollars.

The company's revenue has consistently increased over the last five years except for a slight decline in 2022. It recorded fluctuating profits between 2018 and 2022.

Revenue in 2022 amounted to EUR 14.5 billion, a decrease of 7% compared to EUR 15.6 billion in 2021. The decrease was mainly attributable to the Power Solutions segment challenged by transportation and project execution delays impacting deliveries across most geographical areas.

The company recorded a profit loss of about EUR 1.6 billion in 2022 compared to a profit gain of EUR 143 million in 2021.

Cash at the end of the year was EUR 2.4 billion. Operating and investing activities used EUR 195 million and EUR 758 million, respectively. Financing activities provided EUR 846 million.

Strategy

To continue growing its Development pipeline and business profitably, the company's strategy focuses on the origination of new pipeline; the improvement of project quality, scalability and efficiency; and levers to maximize value. Its focus on origination entails leveraging its capabilities and experience to grow its pipeline in existing and new markets, while also using Repowering and Power-to-X as key enablers.

It also seeks to improve its success rate further and ensure it has the right resources at the right time during project development. To maximize the value it generates, it continues to strengthen commercial and financial discipline. It is also enhancing its capabilities to de-risk projects, while building its network among potential investors.

Company Background

Vestas, which began manufacturing wind turbines in 1979, traces its roots back to the 19th century.

EXECUTIVES

Group President, Chief Executive Officer, Henrik Andersen
Executive Vice President, Chief Financial Officer, Hans Martin Smith
Power Solutions Executive Vice President, Anders Nielsen
Manufacturing & Global Procurement Executive Vice President, Tommy Rahbek Nielsen
Sales Executive Vice President, Javier Rodriguez Diez
Service Executive Vice President, Christian Venderby
People & Culture Executive Vice President, Kerstin Knapp
Digital Solutions & Development Executive Vice President, Thomas Alsbjerg
Chair, Bert Nordberg
Deputy Chairman, Anders Runevad
Director, Bruce Grant
Director, Eva Merete Sofelde Berneke
Director, Kentaro Hosomi
Director, Lena Olving
Director, Karl-Henrik Sundstrom
Director, Helle Thorning-Schmidt
Auditors : PricewaterhouseCoopers Statsautoriseret Revisionspartnerselskab

LOCATIONS

HQ: Vestas Wind Systems A/S
 Hedeager 42, Aarhus N. 8200
Phone: (45) 97 30 00 00 **Fax:** (45) 97 30 00 01
Web: www.vestas.com

2018 sales

	%
Americas	44
Europe, Middle East, and Africa	42
Asia/Pacific	14
Total	100

PRODUCTS/OPERATIONS

2018 sales

	%
Power Solutions	84
Service	16
Total	100

2018 sales

	%
Supply-and-install	43
Supply only	33
Service	16
Turnkey	8
Total	100

COMPETITORS

Aimia Inc
DYNATA, LLC
EnBW Energie Baden-Württemberg AG
FORRESTER RESEARCH, INC.
GARTNER, INC.
J.D. POWER
RENEWABLE ENERGY SYSTEMS HOLDINGS LIMITED
Reinet Investments S.C.A.
THE ADVISORY BOARD COMPANY
TOOLEY ENERGY LIMITED

HISTORICAL FINANCIALS

Company Type: Public

Income Statement — FYE: December 31

	REVENUE ($mil)	NET INCOME ($mil)	NET PROFIT MARGIN	EMPLOYEES
12/22	15,471	(1,678)	—	28,438
12/21	17,642	189	1.1%	29,427
12/20	18,187	938	5.2%	29,378
12/19	13,638	790	5.8%	25,541
12/18	11,605	783	6.7%	24,648
Annual Growth	7.5%	—	—	3.6%

2022 Year-End Financials

Debt ratio: 10.3% No. of shares ($ mil.): 1,006
Return on equity: (-40.3%) Dividends
Cash ($ mil.): 2,539 Yield: —
Current Ratio: 1.01 Payout: 0.0%
Long-term debt ($ mil.): 1,800 Market value ($ mil.): 9,660

	STOCK PRICE ($) FY Close	P/E High/Low		PER SHARE ($) Earnings	Dividends	Book Value
12/22	9.60	—	—	(1.67)	0.01	3.23
12/21	10.17	470	56	0.19	0.28	5.35
12/20	78.23	104	34	0.95	0.24	5.69
12/19	33.67	48	34	0.80	0.23	3.79
12/18	25.18	39	29	0.78	0.32	3.59
Annual Growth	(21.4%)	—	—	—	(57.0%)	(2.6%)

Vinci SA

VINCI is a global player in concessions, energy and construction businesses, operating in more than 120 countries. VINCI designs, finances, builds and manages, within the framework of public-private partnerships, transport infrastructures and public equipment which contribute to the development of mobility and territories. It operates in the motorway, des airport, bridge and tunnel, rail and stadium sectors. VINCI Energies' business and geographical footprint: Cobra IS has acknowledged expertise in delivering large energy EPC (Engineering, Procurement and Construction) projects and strong local positions in the Iberian Peninsula and Latin America. VINCI was founded in 1899 by two engineers from Polytechnique, an elite French engineering school, Alexandre Giros and Louis Loucheur, who founded Société Générale d'Entreprises (SGE), which became VINCI in 2000 following its merger with the GTM Group. About 45% of its revenue comes from France.

Operations

VINCI consists of six business lines in three businesses ? Concessions, Energy and Construction ? along with VINCI Immobilier, which is a business line that reports directly to the holding company.

VINCI Construction is organized into three pillars ? major projects (companies designing and carrying out projects that require general contractor capabilities because of their size, complexity or type); specialty networks (companies carrying out works requiring a high level of expertise in geotechnical and structural engineering, digital technology, nuclear energy or renewable thermal energy); and proximity networks (companies focused on a single core business area, such as buildings, civil engineering or infrastructure, and in a specific geographical area, working as closely as possible with their customers). The segment accounts for more than 45% of VINCI's revenue.

The Energy segment (about 35%) includes VINCI Energies, which provides services to the manufacturing sector, infrastructure, facilities management, and information and communication technology. It also includes Cobra IS, an EPC (engineering, procurement and construction) projects in the energy sector, manufacturing- and energy-related services, and the development of renewable energy concession projects.

The Consessions generate some 15% of VINCI's revenue and consist of three multi-billion euro businesses: VINCI Autoroutes (mortorway concessions in France), VINCI Airports (operates airports in France and in about 10 other countries under full ownership, concession contracts and/or delegated management), VINCI Highways (motorway and road infrastructure, mainly outside France), VINCI Railways (rail infrastructure) and VINCI Stadium (stadium management).

VINCI Immobilier provides property development (residential properties, commercial properties), operation of managed residences and property services.

Geographic Reach

Across its many subsidiaries, Vinci does business in almost all corners of the globe. Its home market of France generates some 45% of total revenue. Other important markets for the company include Germany and the UK. Beyond Western Europe, the company is active in Central and Eastern Europe, the Asia/Pacific region, Africa, the Americas, and the Middle East.

Headquartered in France, Vinci Construction operates in more than 100 countries. VINCI Energies ranks among the top players in France, Germany, Switzerland, Belgium, Netherlands, Portugal, Romania, Scandinavia (Sweden, Finland, and Norway), and the UK. VINCI Energies also operates in the rest of Europe, such as Austria, Italy, the Czech Republic or Poland. VINCI Energies is a long-time player in Africa, where it is a leader in Morocco and expanding its operations in West Africa. VINCI Energies also operates in the Middle East and has a solid foothold in New Zealand and Australia, as well as in South East Asia, with operations in Indonesia and Singapore. Vinci Airports is active in around 65airports in more than 10 countries, including Portugal, France, Cambodia, the Dominican Republic, Chile, Costa Rica, Serbia, the US, Japan, the UK, Sweden, and Brazil.

Financial Performance

Note: Growth rates may differ after conversion to US Dollars.

In 2022, the company had a total revenue of EUR62.3 billion, a 25% increase from the previous year's total revenue of EUR50 billion. This was primarily due to the higher volume of sales across all of the company's segments.

Consolidated net income attributable to owners of the parent was EUR4.3 billion or 7% of revenue, much higher than in 2021 (EUR2.6 billion and 5% of revenue).

The company's cash at the end of 2022 was EUR11.5 billion. Operating activities generated EUR9.4 billion, while investing activities used EUR5.3 billion, mainly for operating investments. Financing activities used another EUR2.8 billion, primarily for repayments of long-term borrowings.

Strategy

VINCI's business model is stable in its fundamentals and can be applied to ever expanding geographies and areas of expertise. This stability and versatility are what give it such immense resilience. The Group's strategy is to adapt and hone this robust model as it continues to develop across its three businesses ? Concessions, Energy and Construction. VINCI is also harnessing its innovation capacity while engaging in the environmental transition to achieve responsible, sustainable growth.

Mergers and Acquisitions

In 2023, VINCI Highways, a VINCI Concessions subsidiary, finalized the acquisition of a 55% stake in Entrevias from Patria, a Brazilian fund, and will hold the concession for two toll motorway sections in Brazil until 2047. With this first motorway concession in Brazil, VINCI Concessions is growing its operation in Latin America's largest economy.

Also in 2023, VINCI Energies acquired the Norwegian company Otera AS and its subsidiaries from Roadworks AS and Å… Energi AS. This transaction will enable VINCI Energies to strengthen and expand its offer and expertise in Norway through its Omexom brand, with ownership of one of the leading companies in the sector.

Company Background

HISTORY

VINCI's origins lie with French conglomerate Vivendi (now Vivendi Universal), which was founded in 1853 as Compagnie Générale des Eaux. Its mission was to irrigate French farmland and supply water to towns. The company won contracts to serve Lyons (1853), Nantes (1854), Paris (1860), and Venice (1880). Générale des Eaux moved into construction in 1972, building an office tower (and later hotels and houses) in Paris. The company also entered communications in the 1980s.

In 1988 Générale des Eaux acquired control of construction and civil engineering giant Société Générale d'Entreprises. SGE subsidiaries included Campenon Bernard SGE (part of Générale des Eaux since 1981), Sogea, Freyssinet, Cochery Bourdin Chaussé, Saunier Duval, Tunzini, Lefort Francheteau, and Wanner. SGE traces its construction roots to 1910. It became a subsidiary of Générale d'Electricité in 1966. Glassmaker Saint-Gobain acquired control of SGE in 1984. Under Générale des Eaux, SGE enhanced its European profile through acquisitions, including British builder Norwest Holst (1989), German road builder VBU (1991), and German pipe and duct maker MLTU (1992).

Générale des Eaux acquired publisher Havas in 1998 and took the name Vivendi -- representing vivacity and mobility. Its purchase of USFilter in 1999 made Vivendi the world's largest water company. Vivendi's SGE unit (renamed VINCI) agreed to acquire the construction arm of rival conglomerate Suez's GTM unit in 2000.

Groupe GTM traces its roots to Société Lyonnaise des Eaux et de L'Eclairage, a leading French water utility. Formed in 1880, Lyonnaise des Eaux built up its French and international operations to include water distribution, as well as gas and electricity production and distribution. A century later the company had diversified into such businesses as heating (Cofreth), waste management (Sita), and communications, acquiring a stake in Lyonnaise Communications (now Lyonnaise CÃ‚ble) in 1986.

In 1990 Lyonnaise des Eaux acquired construction firm Dumez, whose subsidiary GTM-Entrepose was France's largest car park manager. Four years later Dumez-GTM was formed to consolidate the construction and civil engineering businesses of Dumez and GTM-Entrepose. In 1997 Lyonnaise des Eaux and Compagnie de Suez merged to create a leading provider of private infrastructure services, Suez Lyonnaise des Eaux (which shortened its name to SUEZ in 2001). Compagnie Universal du Canal Maritime de Suez, the builder of the Suez Canal, was founded in 1858 and became FinanciÃ¨re de Suez in 1958. In 1967 FinanciÃ¨re de Suez acquired control of Lyonnaise des Eaux.

SGE changed its name to VINCI in 2000. That year, as part of their strategy to rationalize operations and focus on core businesses, Vivendi and SUEZ agreed to a friendly takeover of GTM by VINCI. SUEZ emerged as the combined company's largest shareholder, but by the following year both SUEZ and Vivendi Universal had exited most of VINCI's capital, leaving no core stockholder.

To better control its car park management operations, the company in 2001 created VINCI Park to operate as an umbrella of its VINCI Concessions unit. It expanded its concessions holdings even more in 2002 by hooking up with construction group Eiffage to grab a 17% stake in Europe's second-largest toll road operator, ASF, which was floated that year by the French government.

In 2003 the group won the contract to manage the restoration of the historic Hall of Mirrors. It also won the concession contract to operate, along with joint venture partner Keolis, the International Airport of Grenoble.

VINCI completed its acquisition of ASF in 2005. The deal was part of a government program to privatize motorway companies.

The company has had volatile internal struggles. There was unrest in the board room during 2006, as chairman Antoine Zacharias reportedly wanted to oust CEO Xavier Vuillard in favor of Nexity CEO Alain Dinin. Zacharias was the one who ended up resigning, and at the end of 2006, Dinin resigned from VINCI's board.

In 2007 VINCI's top French construction businesses, Sogea Construction and GTM Construction, merged to create VINCI Construction France, its domestic construction giant.

The company strengthened its position in the UK in 2008 when it bought British construction and facilities management firm Taylor Woodrow from Taylor Wimpey. The deal consolidated VINCI's position in UK facilities management and public-private partnership projects such as rail, airports, and energy infrastructure. In 2009, VINCI Construction acquired the troubled UK builder Haymills Group as that company teetered on the brink of collapse.

In 2008 Eurovia branched out from the road to the rails when it acquired rail infrastructure firm Vossloh Infrastructure Services (now ETF-Eurovia Travaux Ferroviaires) from Vossloh. The division specializes in rail track maintenance and installation.

EXECUTIVES

Chairman, Chief Executive Officer, Director, Xavier Huillard
Executive Vice President, Pierre Coppey
Executive Vice President, Chief Financial Officer, Christian Labeyrie
Corporate Communications Vice President, Pierre Duprat
Business Development Vice President, Christophe Pelissie du Rausas
Human Resources Vice President, Jocelyne Vassoille
General Counsel, Secretary, Patrick Richard
Independent Lead Director, Yannick Assouad
Independent Director, Benoit Bazin
Independent Director, Graziella Gavezotti
Independent Director, Caroline Gregoire Sainte Marie
Independent Director, Claude Laruelle
Independent Director, Marie-Christine Lombard
Independent Director, Rene Medori
Independent Director, Ana Paula Pessoa
Independent Director, Abdullah Hamad Al Attiyah
Non-Independent Director, Robert Castaigne
Non-Independent Director, Roberto Migliardi
Non-Independent Director, Dominique Muller Joly-Pottuz
Non-Independent Director, Alain Said
Non-Independent Director, Pascal Sourisse
Auditors : Deloitte & AssociÃ©s

LOCATIONS

HQ: Vinci SA
1973 boulevard de la DÃ©fense, Nanterre, Cedex 92000
Phone: (33) 1 57 98 61 00
Web: www.vinci.com

2018 Sales

	% of total
France	57
Germany	7
United Kingdom	5
Central and Eastern Europe	4
Benelux	3
Other European countries	7
North Americas	4
Central and South America	3
Africa	3
Russia, Asia Pacific and Middle East	3
Oceania	3
Total	100

PRODUCTS/OPERATIONS

2018 Sales

	% of total
Contracting	
VINCI Construction	32
VINCI Energies	28
Eurovia	20
Concessions	
VINCI Autoroutes	12
VINCI Airports	4
Other Concessions	1
VINCI Immobilier	3
Total	100

Selected Subsidiaries

VINCI Construction
    CFE (12.11%; Benelux)
    VINCI Construction France
    VINCI PLC (UK)
    VINCI Construction Filiales Internationales (Germany, Central Europe, overseas France, Africa)
        VINCI Construction Grands Projets
        Freyssinet (specialized civil engineering)
VINCI Concessions
VINCI Park
Eurovia
VINCI Energies
    Actemium (industry solutions)
    Axians (voice-data-image communication)
    CitÃ©os (urban lighting)
    Graniou (telecommunications infrastructure)
    Omexom (high-voltage power transmission)
    Opteor (maintenance)

COMPETITORS

ACCIONA, SA
AMEC FOSTER WHEELER LIMITED
ARCADIS N.V.
BOUYGUES
COLAS SA
EIFFAGE
ENGIE
FERROVIAL SA
STRABAG SE
WS ATKINS LIMITED

HISTORICAL FINANCIALS

Company Type: Public

Income Statement
FYE: December 31

	REVENUE ($mil)	NET INCOME ($mil)	NET PROFIT MARGIN	EMPLOYEES
12/22	66,791	4,548	6.8%	271,648
12/21	56,867	2,939	5.2%	218,569
12/20	53,966	1,524	2.8%	217,731
12/19	55,197	3,660	6.6%	222,397
12/18	50,894	3,416	6.7%	211,233
Annual Growth	7.0%	7.4%	—	6.5%

2022 Year-End Financials

Debt ratio: 28.6%
Return on equity: 17.4%
Cash ($ mil.): 13,433
Current Ratio: 0.86
Long-term debt ($ mil.): 25,237
No. of shares ($ mil.): 563
Dividends
    Yield: —
    Payout: 10.7%
Market value ($ mil.): 14,050

	STOCK PRICE ($) FY Close	P/E High/Low		PER SHARE ($) Earnings	Dividends	Book Value
12/22	24.93	4	3	7.98	0.86	49.16
12/21	26.31	6	5	5.10	0.80	45.63
12/20	24.92	15	8	2.70	0.57	45.56
12/19	27.63	5	3	6.53	0.75	41.37
12/18	20.51	5	4	6.09	0.75	39.60
Annual Growth	5.0%	—	—	7.0%	3.6%	5.6%

Vipshop Holdings Ltd

EXECUTIVES

Chief Executive Officer, Chairman, Eric Ya Shen
Chief Operating Officer, Vice-Chairman, Arthur Xiaobo Hong
Chief Financial Officer, David Cui
Co-Chief Technology Officer, Daniel Tsun-Ming Kao
Co-Chief Technology Officer, Pengjun Lu
Logistics Senior Vice President, Yizhi Tang
Non-Executive Director, Donghao Yang
Independent Director, Chun Liu
Independent Director, Frank Lin
Independent Director, Xing Liu
Independent Director, Kathleen Chien
Independent Director, Nanyan Zheng
Director, Martin Chi Ping Lau
Director, Jacky Yu Xu
Auditors: Deloitte Touche Tohmatsu

LOCATIONS

HQ: Vipshop Holdings Ltd
128 Dingxin Road, Haizhu District, Guangzhou 510220
Phone: (86) 20 2233 0025   **Fax:** (86) 20 2233 0111
Web: www.vip.com

HISTORICAL FINANCIALS
Company Type: Public

Income Statement — FYE: December 31

	REVENUE ($mil)	NET INCOME ($mil)	NET PROFIT MARGIN	EMPLOYEES
12/22	14,952	913	6.1%	6,815
12/21	18,438	737	4.0%	8,013
12/20	15,574	903	5.8%	7,567
12/19	13,364	577	4.3%	20,442
12/18	12,288	309	2.5%	57,638
Annual Growth	5.0%	31.1%	—	(41.4%)

2022 Year-End Financials

Debt ratio: 0.6%
Return on equity: 19.2%
Cash ($ mil.): 3,180
Current Ratio: 1.18
Long-term debt ($ mil.): —
No. of shares ($ mil.): 117
Dividends
Yield: —
Payout: 0.0%
Market value ($ mil.): 1,598

	STOCK PRICE ($) FY Close	P/E High/Low	PER SHARE ($) Earnings	Dividends	Book Value
12/22	13.64	0 0	7.12	0.00	40.51
12/21	8.40	1 0	5.31	0.00	37.85
12/20	28.11	1 0	6.54	0.00	32.10
12/19	14.17	0 0	4.25	0.00	23.39
12/18	5.46	1 0	2.27	0.00	18.88
Annual Growth	25.7%	—	33.1%	—	21.0%

Vivendi SE

Vivendi is one of the world's biggest media companies, offering music, movies and TV, games, and more. The company holds equity interests in leading entertainment groups including Universal Music Group, Lagardere, R. Enetertainment, MediaForEurope, MultiChoice Group, and Prisa and also in Telecom Italia. Canal+ Group is a pay-TV provider in France, Africa, Europe, and Asia. It also is a major producer and distributor of motion pictures. The Vivendi property Havas is a global advertising and public relations agency. The Gameloft unit develops and produces video games with an emphasis on mobile games such as Asphalt, Minion Rush, and Dragon Mania. France, Vivendi's home country, accounts for about 50% of revenue.

Operations

Vivendi's main businesses are aggregated within the following operating segments:

Canal+ Group is a publishing and distribution of premium and thematic pay-TV and free-to-air channels in France, Benelux, Poland, Central Europe, Africa and Asia, and production, sales and distribution of movies and TV series.

Havas Group is a communications group spanning all the communications disciplines (creativity, media expertise and healthcare/wellness).

Prisma Media is a market leader in French magazine publishing, online video and daily digital audience.

Gameloft is a leader in creation and publishing of downloadable video games for mobile phones, tablets, triple-play boxes and smart TVs.

Vivendi Village includes Vivendi Ticketing (in Europe, the US and the US through See Tickets) and live performances through Olympia Production, Festival Production, and the venues in Paris (l'Olympia and ThÃ©Ã¢tre de l'?uvre) and Africa (CanalOlympia).

New Initiatives includes Dailymotion (video content aggregation and distribution platform) and group Vivendi Africa (development of ultrahigh-speed Internet service in Africa).

Generosity and solidarity are the company's newest operating segment which includes CanalOlympia, previously part of Vivendi Village as well as the Vivendi Create Joy solidarity program, which supports initial and professional training projects in the Vivendi group's businesses.

The Corporate segment accounts for Vivendi's centralized services.

Geographic Reach

Paris-based, Vivendi has operations located in France (generates around 50% of total revenue), Americas (about 15%), Rest of Europe (around 25% of revenue), Asia and Oceania (around 5% of revenue), and Africa (around 10%).

Sales and Marketing

With about 9 million subscribers in mainland France, Canal+ Group boasts the largest portfolio of pay-TV customers.

Financial Performance

Vivendi's performance for the past five years has fluctuated with a decrease from 2019 to 2020, then increasing year-over-year since then, ending with 2022 as its highest performing year over the period.

In 2022, Vivendi's revenue increased by EUR878 million to EUR9.6 billion, as compared to 2021's revenue of EUR8.7 billion.

Net income in fiscal year end 2022 decreased to EUR343 million, as compared to the prior year's net income of EUR613 million.

Cash held by the company at the end of 2022 decreased to EUR 1.9 billion. Operating activities generated EUR748 million. Investing activities and financing activities used EUR695 million and EUR1.4 billion, respectively. Main cash uses were for investments and transactions on borrowings and other financial liabilities.

Strategy

Vivendi has three strategic pillars which includes Transformation, Internalizations, and Integration. The company is engaged in an extensive transformation and digitalization process; dedicated to having a meaning full impact around the world; and increasing development of joint projects between the company's segments.

Mergers and Acquisitions

In 2021, Vivendi completed its acquisition of Prisma Media, France's number one magazine publishing group, in print and digital, with some 20 leading brands. The Prisma Media acquisition is part of Vivendi's development strategy in media to gain a foothold in an industry that strongly complements its existing businesses.

HISTORY

Authorized by an imperial decree, Compagnie GÃ©nÃ©rale des Eaux was founded in 1853 by investors such as the Rothschild family and Napoleon III's half-brother to irrigate French farmland and supply water to towns. It won contracts to serve Lyons (1853), Nantes (1854), Paris (1860), and Venice (1880).

A supplier of water and other basic services for most of its history, the company that became Vivendi didn't move strongly into other areas until the 1980s when it made investments and acquisitions into telecommunications and then media and entertainment in the 1990s.

EXECUTIVES

Management Board Chairman, Management Board Chief Executive Officer, Arnaud Roy de Puyfontaine
Chief Compliance Officer, Management Board Member, General Counsel, Frederic Crepin
Chief Financial Officer, Management Board Member, Francois Laroze
Management Board Member, Claire Leost
Chief of HR Strategy and Corporate Culture, Management Board Member, Celine Merle-Beral
Management Board Member, Maxime Saada

Chairman, Director, Yannick Bollore
Vice-Chairman, Lead Independent Director, Philippe Benacin
Independent Director, Laurent Dassault
Independent Director, Maud Fentenoy
Independent Director, Cathia Lawson-Hall
Independent Director, Michele Reiser
Independent Director, Katie Stanton
Director, Cyrille Bollore
Director, Paulo Cardoso
Director, Dominique Delport
Director, Veronique Driot-Argentin
Director, Sandrine Le Bihan
Director, Athina Vasilogiannaki
Auditors : ERNST & YOUNG et Autres

LOCATIONS

HQ: Vivendi SE
42 avenue de Friedland, Paris, Cedex 08 75380
Phone: (33) 1 71 71 10 00   **Fax:** (33) 1 71 71 10 01
Web: www.vivendi.com

PRODUCTS/OPERATIONS

2018 Sales

	% of total
Universal Music Group	43
Canal+ Group	37
Havas	17
Gameloft	2
Vivendi Village	1
New Initiatives	-
Elimination	-

2018 Sales

Subscription Services	32
Advertising, Merchandising and Other	21
Total	100

COMPETITORS

Bertelsmann SE & Co. KGaA
Dalian Wanda Group Co., Ltd.
KERING
MATCH GROUP, INC.
MEREDITH CORPORATION
PUBLICIS GROUPE S.A.
SOFTBANK GROUP CORP.
TECHNICOLOR
TELEFONICA, SA
WARNER MEDIA, LLC

HISTORICAL FINANCIALS

Company Type: Public

Income Statement   FYE: December 31

	REVENUE ($mil)	NET INCOME ($mil)	NET PROFIT MARGIN	EMPLOYEES
12/22	10,503	(1,078)	—	35,000
12/21	10,936	27,947	255.6%	34,300
12/20	19,725	1,767	9.0%	42,526
12/19	17,854	1,777	10.0%	44,641
12/18	15,962	145	0.9%	41,600
Annual Growth	(9.9%)	—	—	(4.2%)

2022 Year-End Financials

Debt ratio: 12.6%
Return on equity: (-5.5%)
Cash ($ mil.): 2,037
Current Ratio: 1.11
Long-term debt ($ mil.): 3,151
No. of shares ($ mil.): 1,024
Dividends
Yield: —
Payout: 0.0%
Market value ($ mil.): 9,724

	STOCK PRICE ($) FY Close	P/E High/Low		PER SHARE ($) Earnings	Dividends	Book Value
12/22	9.49	—	—	(1.05)	0.27	18.10
12/21	13.48	2	1	25.89	28.13	20.55
12/20	32.10	26	17	1.55	0.65	17.70
12/19	28.95	23	18	1.44	0.56	14.73
12/18	24.15	284	233	0.11	0.55	15.64
Annual Growth	(20.8%)	—	—	—	(16.5%)	3.7%

Vodafone Group Plc

Vodafone is a European and African telecommunications company which transforms the way their customers live and work through their innovation, technology, connectivity, platforms, products, and services. The company operate mobile and fixed networks in more than 15 countries, with mobile partner networks in more than 45 countries. The company had an addition of more than 190,000 mobile contract customers and about 65,000 broadband customers, in Portugal alone. The company generates the majority of its business in Europe, where it is a leader in the wireless markets in the UK and Germany.

Operations

Vodafone's operations are attributed to a country based on the location of the Group company reporting the revenue, with majority of the company's revenues are from operations in Europe. About 95% of the company's revenue comes from contracts with customers.

Geographic Reach

The company, headquartered in Newbury, Berkshire, operate mobile and fixed networks in more than 15 countries, with mobile partner networks in more than 45 countries. Germany is Vodafone's biggest market, accounting for about 30% of the revenues, followed by Italy and the UK.

Financial Performance

Vodafone's performance for the past five years has fluctuated from 2020 to 2021, but had an overall increase with year-end 2023 as its highest performing year over the period.

The company's revenues increased by EUR 126 million to EUR 45.7 billion in 2023, as compared to 2022's revenue of EUR 45.6 billion.

Vodafone's net profit for 2023 increased to EUR 11.8 billion, as compared to the prior year's net profit of EUR 2.2 billion.

The company held EUR 11.6 billion by the end of the year. Operating activities provided EUR 18.1 billion to the coffers. Investing activities and financing activities used EUR 379 million and EUR 13.4 billion, respectively. Main cash uses were for purchases of property, plant, and equipment as well as repayment of borrowings.

Company Background

Vodafone was formed in 1983 as a joint venture between Racal Electronics (a UK electronics firm) and Millicom (a US telecom company), and was granted one of two mobile phone licenses in the UK (the other was held by Cellnet). Its service launched in 1985. In 1988 Racal offered 20% of Vodafone to the public; three years later the rest of the firm was spun off to become Vodafone Group. It made a landmark acquisition of Mannesmann in Germany, making it one of the country's largest carriers, and began its partner networks business model in 2011. Vodafone sold its 45% stake in Verizon Wireless for $130 billion in 2013, one of the biggest ever corporate deals.

HISTORY

Vodafone was formed in 1983 as a joint venture between Racal Electronics (a UK electronics firm) and Millicom (a US telecom company), and was granted one of two mobile phone licenses in the UK. It launched service in 1985 as a Racal subsidiary. Vodafone and Cellnet, the other licensee, were swamped with demand. In 1988 Racal offered 20% of Vodafone to the public; three years later the rest of the firm was spun off to become Vodafone Group.

Vodafone moved beyond the UK in the 1990s. By 1993 it had interests in mobile phone networks in Australia, Greece, Hong Kong, Malta, and Scandinavia.

EXECUTIVES

Chief Executive Officer, Executive Director, Nick Read
Financial Chief Financial Officer, Executive Director, Margherita Della Valle
Chief Human Resources Officer, Leanne Wood
External Affairs Director, Joakim Reiter
General Counsel, Secretary, Rosemary Martin
Independent Non-Executive Director, Chairman, Jean-Francois van Boxmeer
Senior Independent Non-Executive Director, Valerie Gooding
Independent Non-Executive Director, Sanjiv Ahuja
Independent Non-Executive Director, Crispin H. Davis
Independent Non-Executive Director, Michel Demare
Independent Non-Executive Director, Clara Hedwig Frances Furse
Independent Non-Executive Director, Renee Jo James
Independent Non-Executive Director, Maria Amparo Moraleda Matinez
Independent Non-Executive Director, David Nish
Auditors : Ernst & Young LLP

LOCATIONS

HQ: Vodafone Group Plc
Vodafone House, The Connection, Newbury, Berkshire RG14 2FN
Phone: (44) 1635 33251
Web: www.vodafone.com

2018 Sales

	% of total
Europe	
Germany	23
UK	15
Italy	13
Spain	11
Other Europe	11
Africa, Middle East and Asia Pacific (AMAP)	
Vodacom	12
Other AMAP	12
Common Functions	3
Total	**100**

PRODUCTS/OPERATIONS

2018 Sales

	% of total
Service revenue	88
Other revenue	12
Total	**100**

Countries of Operation (controlled interests)
Africa/the Middle East/Asia-Pacific
Australia
Democratic Republic of Congo
Egypt
Ghana
India
Lesotho
Mozambique
New Zealand
Qatar
South Africa
Tanzania
Europe
Albania
Czech Republic
Germany
Greece
Hungary
Ireland
Italy
Malta
Portugal
Romania
Spain
The Netherlands
Turkey
UK

COMPETITORS

3517667 Canada Inc
Altice Europe N.V.
BT GROUP PLC
CELLNEX TELECOM SA.
ILIAD
LIBERTY GLOBAL PLC
SK Telecom Co.,Ltd.
SOFTBANK GROUP CORP.
TELECOM ITALIA O TIM SPA
TELEFONICA, SA

HISTORICAL FINANCIALS

Company Type: Public

Income Statement — FYE: March 31

	REVENUE ($mil)	NET INCOME ($mil)	NET PROFIT MARGIN	EMPLOYEES
03/23	49,666	12,863	25.9%	98,103
03/22	50,596	2,317	4.6%	96,941
03/21	51,390	131	0.3%	96,506
03/20	49,269	(1,007)	—	95,219
03/19	49,038	(9,006)	—	98,996
Annual Growth	0.3%	—	—	(0.2%)

2023 Year-End Financials

Debt ratio: 33.6%
Return on equity: 20.0%
Cash ($ mil.): 12,719
Current Ratio: 0.89
Long-term debt ($ mil.): 44,934
No. of shares ($ mil.): 26,992
Dividends
Yield: 8.2%
Payout: 203.3%
Market value ($ mil.): 297,998

	STOCK PRICE ($) FY Close	P/E High/Low		Earnings	Dividends	Book Value
03/23	11.04	41	24	0.46	0.91	2.55
03/22	16.62	257	198	0.08	1.55	2.14
03/21	18.43	5045	3477	0.00	1.05	2.32
03/20	13.77	—	—	(0.03)	0.94	2.51
03/19	18.18	—	—	(0.33)	1.64	2.57
Annual Growth	(11.7%)	—	—	—	(13.7%)	(0.1%)

voestalpine AG

The voestalpine is the world's leading steel and technology company and one of the leading partners to the automotive and consumer goods industries in Europe and to the oil and gas industry around the world. The company produces steel in various forms for the automotive, railway, aerospace, and energy industries sold in approximately 50 countries worldwide. Its metal engineering division serves the railway industry with the manufacture of rails, wires, and tubes used in rail systems. voestalpine also engineers and manufactures automotive components. Voestalpine generates about 55% of the total revenue from the European Union market.

Operations

Voestalpine has four reportable segments: Steel Division (about 35% of total revenue); Metal Engineering Division (more than 20%); Metal Forming Division (over 20%); and High Performance Metals Division (approximately 20%).

The Steel Division produces advanced hot and cold rolled steel, as well as electrogalvanized, hot-dip galvanized and organically coated steel strip. Its other activities include electrical steel, heavy plate, a foundry, and downstream sectors ? the Steel & Service Center and Logistics Service.

The Metal Engineering Division is a global provider of complete welding solutions and is a European technology leader in premium wire products, providing high-tech seamless tubes for the oil and natural gas industries as well as for industrial applications.

The Metal Forming Division is the company's competence center for highly developed special sections, tube, and precision strip steel products as well as for pre-finished system components made of pressed, stamped, and roll-formed parts that are used in a wide range of industries, but especially in the premium automotive segment.

The High Performance Metals Division is the global market leader for tool steel and a leading provider of high-speed steel, valve steels and other products made from special steels, as well as powder materials, nickel-based alloys and titanium. It operates a global network of service centers with a focus on tool manufacturing, offering component processing, heat treatment, and coating services besides warehousing and preprocessing of special steels. The division also offers a broad range of services including logistics, distribution, and processing especially for the oil and natural gas industry.

The company's two financing entities, one raw materials purchasing companies as well as one personal services companies and the group-IT companies are included in the "Other" business segment. These companies are combined because their focus is on providing coordination services and support to the subsidiaries.

Geographic Reach

Headquartered in Linz, Austria, voestalpine operates in more than 50 countries on all five continents. About 55% of the total revenue comes from the European Union (without Austria), followed by USMCA which accounts for about 15%, another nearly 10% is from Asia; Austria represents about 10%, and South America brings in less than 5%. The rest of world accounts for the remainder.

Sales and Marketing

Voestalpine serves a diverse array of industries, including automotive, consumer goods, aerospace, oil and gas, railway systems, and tool steel sectors, among others.

About 30% of the company's revenue comes from automotive market, followed by energy and construction with about 15% each, railway systems and mechanical engineering with approximately 10% each, white goods/consumer goods with some 5%, and aerospace with less than 5%. Other markets generate the remainder.

Financial Performance

Voestalpine's performance for the past five years has fluctuated with a downward trend for the first half, then increasing year-over-year since then with 2022 as its highest performing year over the period.

The company's revenue for fiscal 2022 increased by EUR3.3 billion to EUR18.2 billion, as compared to 2021's revenue of EUR14.9 billion.

Profit for fiscal 2022 decreased to EUR1.2 billion, as compared to the prior year's net profit of EUR1.3 billion.

Cash held by the company at the end of fiscal 2022 increased to EUR1.1 billion. Cash provided by operations was EUR956.2 million. Investing activities and financing activities used EUR47.1 million and EUR685.9 million, respectively. Main cash uses were for additions to other intangible assets, property, plant, and equipment and repayment of non-current financial abilities.

Strategy

voestalpine's corporate strategy focuses

on leadership in innovation, technology, and quality. In the company's view, the continual development of new products and production processes is indispensable to its ability to distinguish itself from the competition and to defend its technology leadership. Research and Development (R&D) thus are a key to voestalpine's business model, because R&D-driven innovation ensures the company's success in the long term.

After declining in the crisis year 2020/21, both R&D expenditures in the business year 2021/22 and the R&D budget for the business year 2022/23 shot up to new highs. This continues previous years' overall trend and reflects the importance that the company attaches to research and development.

Company Background

Construction of an iron and steel factory begins in Linz, Austria, in 1938 as part of the German Nazi regime's war industry; its operations are launched incrementally starting in 1941.

EXECUTIVES

Chairman, Management Board Member, Herbert Eibensteiner
Chief Financial Officer, Management Board Member, Robert Ottel
Management Board Member, Peter Schwab
Management Board Member, Hubert Zajicek
Management Board Member, Franz Kainersdorfer
Management Board Member, Franz Rotter
Chairman, Wolfgang Eder
Deputy Chairman, Heinrich Schaller
Supervisory Board Member, Joachim Lemppenau
Supervisory Board Member, Franz Gasselsberger
Supervisory Board Member, Ingrid Jorg.
Supervisory Board Member, Florian Khol
Supervisory Board Member, Maria Kubitschek
Supervisory Board Member, Elisabeth Stadler
Supervisory Board Member, Josef Gritz
Supervisory Board Member, Sandra Fritz
Supervisory Board Member, Hans-Karl Schaller
Supervisory Board Member, Gerhard Scheidreiter
Auditors : Deloitte Audit Wirtschaftsprüfungs GmbH

LOCATIONS

HQ: voestalpine AG
Voestalpine Strasse 1, Linz 4020
Phone: (43) 70 50304 15 2090   **Fax:** (43) 70 50304 55 8981
Web: www.voestalpine.com

PRODUCTS/OPERATIONS

2016 Sales

	% of total
Steel	30
Metal Engineering Division	23
Special Steel Division	21
Metal Forming Division	18
Others	8
Total	100

COMPETITORS

CHARTER MANUFACTURING COMPANY, INC.
ERIKS N.V.
General Steel Holdings, Inc.
JACQUET METALS
PTC GROUP HOLDINGS CORP.
Rautaruukki Oyj
Salzgitter AG
TENARIS S.A.
TUBOS REUNIDOS, SA
voestalpine High Performance Metals GmbH

HISTORICAL FINANCIALS

Company Type: Public

Income Statement   FYE: March 31

	REVENUE ($mil)	NET INCOME ($mil)	NET PROFIT MARGIN	EMPLOYEES
03/23	19,804	1,158	5.8%	51,202
03/22	16,565	1,442	8.7%	50,225
03/21	13,216	49	0.4%	48,654
03/20	13,931	(243)	—	49,005
03/19	15,229	458	3.0%	50,102
Annual Growth	6.8%	26.1%	—	0.5%

2023 Year-End Financials

Debt ratio: 17.4%   No. of shares ($ mil.): 172
Return on equity: 14.7%   Dividends
Cash ($ mil.): 1,147   Yield: —
Current Ratio: 1.56   Payout: 2.6%
Long-term debt ($ mil.): 2,073   Market value ($ mil.): 1,141

	STOCK PRICE ($) FY Close	P/E High/Low		PER SHARE ($) Earnings	Dividends	Book Value
03/23	6.61	1	1	6.53	0.17	47.39
03/22	6.10	1	1	8.08	0.08	43.00
03/21	8.32	35	17	0.28	0.03	36.30
03/20	3.87	—	—	(1.36)	0.15	33.62
03/19	6.09	5	2	2.59	0.20	41.17
Annual Growth	2.1%	—	—	26.0%	(4.1%)	3.6%

Volkswagen AG

EXECUTIVES

Chair, Management Board Member, Oliver Blume
Management Board Member, Arno Antlitz
Management Board Member, Ralf Brandstatter
Management Board Member, Manred Doss
Management Board Member, Markus Duesmann
Management Board Member, Gunnar Kilian
Management Board Member, Thomas Schafer
Management Board Member, Thomas Schmall-Von Westerholt
Management Board Member, Hauke Stars
Management Board Member, Hiltrud Dorothea Werner
Chairman, Director, Hans Dieter Potsch
Deputy Chairman, Director, Jorg Hofmann
Director, Harald Buck
Director, Matias Carnero Sojo
Director, Daniela Cavallo
Director, Julia Willie Hamburg
Director, Marianne Heiß
Director, Arno Homburg
Director, Gunther Horvath
Director, Simone Mahler
Director, Peter Mosch
Director, Daniela Nowak
Director, Hans Michel Piech
Director, Ferdinand Oliver Porsche
Director, Wolfgang Porsche
Director, Jens Rothe
Director, Conny Schonhardt
Director, Stephan Weil
Auditors : Ernst & Young GmbH Wirtschaftpruefungsgesellschaft

LOCATIONS

HQ: Volkswagen AG
Letterbox 1848, Wolfsburg 38436
Phone: (49) 5361 9 0   **Fax:** (49) 5361 928282
Web: www.volkswagen.com

COMPETITORS

AUDI AG
Bayerische Motoren Werke AG
FORD MOTOR COMPANY
GENERAL MOTORS COMPANY
HONDA MOTOR CO., LTD.
MITSUBISHI MOTORS CORPORATION
NISSAN MOTOR CO.,LTD.
PEUGEOT SA
SUBARU CORPORATION
ZF Friedrichshafen AG

HISTORICAL FINANCIALS

Company Type: Public

Income Statement   FYE: December 31

	REVENUE ($mil)	NET INCOME ($mil)	NET PROFIT MARGIN	EMPLOYEES
12/22	298,232	15,878	5.3%	675,805
12/21	283,192	16,800	5.9%	672,800
12/20	273,543	10,228	3.7%	662,600
12/19	283,647	14,984	5.3%	671,200
12/18	270,093	13,544	5.0%	664,496
Annual Growth	2.5%	4.1%	—	0.4%

2022 Year-End Financials

Debt ratio: 37.8%   No. of shares ($ mil.): 295
Return on equity: 9.5%   Dividends
Cash ($ mil.): 31,156   Yield: —
Current Ratio: 1.23   Payout: 6.3%
Long-term debt ($ mil.): 124,378   Market value ($ mil.): 4,617

	STOCK PRICE ($) FY Close	P/E High/Low		PER SHARE ($) Earnings	Dividends	Book Value
12/22	15.65	1	1	31.65	2.01	598.56
12/21	29.20	1	1	33.49	0.74	554.06
12/20	20.85	1	1	20.37	0.37	528.40
12/19	19.29	1	1	29.87	0.35	463.35
12/18	15.60	1	1	26.99	5.50	454.51
Annual Growth	0.1%	—	—	4.1%	(22.3%)	7.1%

Volvo AB

AB Volvo is one of the world's largest manufacturers of heavy-duty trucks, construction equipment, buses and heavy-duty combustion engines as well as a leading supplier of marine and industrial engines. It has operations in the US, Brazil, India, France, and China, as well as sales of products in more than 190 markets. It makes trucks under the ten brands including Volvo, UD Trucks, Prevost, Renault Trucks, and Mack. The company also provides financing services though Volvo Financial Services and it generates more than 40% of sales from Europe. The company was founded in 1927.

Operations

AB Volvo's operations are segmented through product categories: Trucks (about 70% of the company's revenue) and Construction Equipment (more than 20%). Buses, Volvo Penta, Financial Services, and Group Functions & Other, account for less than 5% each.

Volvo Penta produces engines and power systems for marine and industrial applications, while financial services provide financial services to customers and dealers. Group functions & other include Nova Bus, Arquus, and common business support functions.

Geographic Reach

The Volvo Group is headquartered in Gothenburg, Sweden. The company has production in about 20 countries and sells its products in almost 190 markets.

The company garners about 40% of its revenues from Europe, followed by North America, which accounts for about 30%. Other markets include South America, Asia, Africa, and Oceania.

Sales and Marketing

The Volvo Group's global network of dealers and service centers staffed by competent and service-oriented personnel are key factors for customer satisfaction and success. The brand organizations within the Volvo Group support customers via efficient dealer workshops, and through service and maintenance agreements.

The company partners in alliances and joint ventures with SDLG, Eicher, and Dongfeng.

Financial Performance

AB Volvo's performance for the past five years fluctuated, but had an overall increase with 2022 as the company's highest performing year over the period.

The company's revenue increased by SEK101.3 billion to SEK473.5 billion, as compared to 2021's revenue of SEK372.2 billion.

AB Volvo's net income for 2022 slightly decreased to SEK32.7 billion, as compared to the prior year's net income of SEK32.8 billion.

The company held SEK83.9 billion at the end of the year. Operating activities provided SEK33.2 billion to the coffers. Investing activities and financing activities provided SEK13 billion and SEK11.8 billion, respectively. Main cash uses were for investments in tangible assets and repayments of borrowings.

Strategy

AB Volvo's focuses on creating value for its customers by improving their bottom-line profitability. The company aims to do this through: transforming the Volvo Group to become a leading end-to-end integrator; growing the service business and target selected industry verticals offering a portfolio of tailor-made solutions; securing a desirable and sustainable product and service portfolio with the right quality, leveraging new and well-known technologies, CAST, partnerships, and digital innovations; growing in Asia and the US; developing robust profitability throughout the decentralized regional value chains by leveraging global scale, digitalization, a purpose-fit footprint and continuous improvement using the Volvo Production System; selectively capturing, accelerating, and scaling-up new businesses and develop competencies and capabilities needed; and reinforcing value-based leadership and way of working where all colleagues are empowered to take action and are accountable for the results.

Company Background

Swedish ball bearing maker SKF formed Volvo (Latin for "I roll") as a subsidiary in 1915. Volvo began building cars in 1926, trucks in 1928, and bus chassis in 1932 in Gothenburg. Sweden's winters and icy roads made the company keenly attentive to engineering and safety. The Volvo Group sold its Volvo Cars division to Ford Motor Company in 1999; Volvo Cars was subsequently acquired by Chinese Zhejiang Geely Holding Group Co., Ltd in 2010.

EXECUTIVES

President, Chief Executive Officer, Director, Martin Lundstedt
Chief Purchasing Officer, Andrea Fuder
Finance Executive Vice President, Finance Chief Financial Officer, Jan Ytterberg
Executive Vice President, Chief Technology Officer, Lars Stenqvist
Executive Vice President, Jens Holtinger
Deputy Chief Executive, Jan Gurander
Executive Vice President, Roger Alm
Executive Vice President, Bruno Blin
Executive Vice President, Melker Jernberg
Human Resources Executive Vice President, Diana Niu
Executive Vice President, Joachim Rosenberg
Executive Vice President, Chief Digital Officer, Scott Rafkin
Executive Vice President, Martin Weissburg
Communications Executive Vice President, Kina Wileke
Legal Executive Vice President, Compliance Executive Vice President, Legal General Counsel, Compliance General Counsel, Compliance Secretary, Legal Secretary, Sofia Frandberg
Chairman, Carl-Henric Svanberg
Deputy, Camilla Johansson
Deputy, Mari Larsson
Director, Matti Alahuhta
Director, Martha Finn Brooks
Director, Eckhard Cordes
Director, Kurt Jofs
Director, Kathryn V. Marinello
Director, Eric Elzvik
Director, Martina Merz
Director, Hanne de Mora
Director, Helena Stjernholm
Director, Lars Ask
Director, Mats Henning
Director, Mikael Sallstrom
Auditors : Deloitte AB

LOCATIONS

HQ: Volvo AB
Volvo Bergegaards v., Göteborg SE-405 08
Phone: (46) 31 66 00 00   **Fax:** (46) 31 53 72 96
Web: www.volvogroup.com

2018 Sales

	% of total
Europe	41
North America	27
Asia	20
South America	5
Africa & Oceania	7
Total	100

PRODUCTS/OPERATIONS

2018 Sales

	% of total
Trucks	63
Construction Equipment	21
Buses	7
Volvo Penta	4
Group Functions & Other	2
Financial Services	3
Total	100

Selected Products & Brands

Volvo
Volvo Trucks
Volvo Buses
Volvo Construction Equipment
Volvo Penta
Volvo Penta Marine Leisure
Volvo Penta Marine Commercial
Volvo Penta Industrial
Terex Trucks
Renault Trucks
Prevost
Nova Bus Global
Mack Trucks
Arquus
Arrow Truck

COMPETITORS

ABB Ltd
ALLISON TRANSMISSION HOLDINGS, INC.
ALSTOM
ARVAL PHH HOLDINGS LIMITED
Atlas Copco AB
GKN LIMITED
NAVISTAR INTERNATIONAL CORPORATION
Neles Oyj
PACCAR INC
TKJP CORPORATION

HISTORICAL FINANCIALS
Company Type: Public

Income Statement — FYE: December 31

	REVENUE ($mil)	NET INCOME ($mil)	NET PROFIT MARGIN	EMPLOYEES
12/21	41,084	3,618	8.8%	95,850
12/20	41,423	2,364	5.7%	96,194
12/19	46,437	3,855	8.3%	103,985
12/18	43,662	2,781	6.4%	105,175
12/17	40,800	2,557	6.3%	99,488
Annual Growth	0.2%	9.1%	—	(0.9%)

2021 Year-End Financials
Debt ratio: 3.3%
Return on equity: 22.9%
Cash ($ mil.): 6,857
Current Ratio: 1.34
Long-term debt ($ mil.): 11,498
No. of shares ($ mil.): 2,033
Dividends
Yield: 12.3%
Payout: 153.7%
Market value ($ mil.): 46,952

	STOCK PRICE ($) FY Close	P/E High/Low		PER SHARE ($) Earnings	Dividends	Book Value
12/21	23.09	2	1	1.78	2.86	7.66
12/20	23.35	3	1	1.16	1.84	8.75
12/19	16.61	1	1	1.90	1.08	7.33
12/18	13.03	2	1	1.37	0.50	6.78
12/17	18.49	2	1	1.26	0.39	6.42
Annual Growth	5.7%	—	—	9.1%	64.1%	4.5%

Vontobel Holding AG

Vontobel Holding wants your business, if you're wealthy. The company owns Bank Vontobel, one of the largest players in the famously private world of Swiss banking. Bank Vontobel and the company's other subsidiaries provide investment funds and other investment banking and asset management services for private and institutional clients, primarily in Europe and North America. The family of former company chairman Hans-Dieter Vontobel (through various entities, including the Vontobel Foundation) control the company, which has more than $192 billion in assets under management.

EXECUTIVES

Chairman, Director, Herbert J. Scheidt
Vice-Chairman, Director, Frank Schnewlin
Chief Executive Officer, Zeno Staub
Chief Financial Officer, Thomas Heinzl
Chief Operating Officer, Felix Lenhard
Director, Bruno Basler
Director, Maja Baumann
Director, Elisabeth Bourqui
Director, David Cole
Director, Stefan Loacker
Director, Clara C. Streit
Director, Björn Wettergren
Auditors : Ernst & Young Ltd

LOCATIONS

HQ: Vontobel Holding AG
Gotthardstrasse 43, Zurich CH-8022

Phone: (41) 58 283 59 00 **Fax:** (41) 58 283 75 00
Web: www.vontobel.com

COMPETITORS

Grupo Financiero Banorte, S.A.B. de C.V.
MERCHANT HOUSE GROUP PLC
ROBERT W. BAIRD & CO. INCORPORATED
Sampo Oyj
THE ZS FUND L P

HISTORICAL FINANCIALS
Company Type: Public

Income Statement — FYE: December 31

	ASSETS ($mil)	NET INCOME ($mil)	INCOME AS % OF ASSETS	EMPLOYEES
12/23	34,840	256	0.7%	2,275
12/22	33,071	249	0.8%	2,295
12/21	35,491	409	1.2%	2,187
12/20	35,677	275	0.8%	2,094
12/19	27,144	259	1.0%	2,049
Annual Growth	6.4%	(0.3%)	—	2.7%

2023 Year-End Financials
Return on assets: 0.7%
Return on equity: 10.4%
Long-term debt ($ mil.): —
No. of shares ($ mil.): 55
Sales ($ mil.): 2,032
Dividends
Yield: —
Payout: 80.0%
Market value ($ mil.): —

Welcia Holdings Co Ltd

EXECUTIVES

Chairman, Representative Director, Takamitsu Ikeno
President, Chief Operating Officer, Executive Officer, Representative Director, Tadahisa Matsumoto
Executive Vice President, Chief Financial Officer, Executive Officer, Director, Norimasa Sato
Executive Vice President, Executive Officer, Director, Juichi Nakamura
Director, Motoya Okada
Outside Director, Yukari Narita
Outside Director, Tomoko Nakai
Outside Director, Kunio Ishizuka
Auditors : Deloitte Touche Tohmatsu LLC

LOCATIONS

HQ: Welcia Holdings Co Ltd
2-2-15 Sotokanda, Chiyoda-ku, Tokyo 101-0021
Phone: (81) 3 5207 5878
Web: www.welcia.co.jp

HISTORICAL FINANCIALS
Company Type: Public

Income Statement — FYE: February 28

	REVENUE ($mil)	NET INCOME ($mil)	NET PROFIT MARGIN	EMPLOYEES
02/21	8,931	263	2.9%	34,080
02/20	7,986	209	2.6%	30,552
02/19	7,032	157	2.2%	27,937
02/18	6,491	160	2.5%	24,252
02/17	5,551	128	2.3%	20,963
Annual Growth	12.6%	19.6%	—	12.9%

2021 Year-End Financials
Debt ratio: —
Return on equity: 16.3%
Cash ($ mil.): 488
Current Ratio: 1.06
Long-term debt ($ mil.): 86
No. of shares ($ mil.): 209
Dividends
Yield: —
Payout: 31.3%
Market value ($ mil.): —

Wesfarmers Ltd.

EXECUTIVES

Chief Financial Officer, Anthony Gianotti
Human Resources- Coles Chief Human Resources Officer, Business Development Chief Human Resources Officer, Human Resources- Coles Director, Business Development Director, Jenny Bryant
Wesfarmers Industrials division Financial Director, Finance Director of Coles Financial Director, Financial Services Financial Director, Wesfarmers Insurance Financial Director, Finance Director of Coles Managing Director, Financial Services Managing Director, Wesfarmers Insurance Managing Director, Wesfarmers Industrials division Managing Director, Finance Director of Coles Deputy Chief Executive, Financial Services Deputy Chief Executive, Wesfarmers Insurance Deputy Chief Executive, Wesfarmers Industrials division Deputy Chief Executive, Executive Director, Rob G. Scott
Bunnings Group Managing Director, Michael Schneider
Wesfarmers Industrials Managing Director, David Baxby
Officeworks Managing Director, Sarah Hunter
Executive General Manager, Company Secretariat & Group Risk, Aleksandra Spaseska
Kmart Group Managing Director, Ian Bailey
Corporate Affairs Executive General Manager, Naomi Flutter
Business Development Managing Director, Ed Bostock
General Counsel, Maya vanden Driesen
Chairman, Non-Executive Director, Michael Chaney
Non-Executive Director, Mike Roche
Non-Executive Director, Jennifer Westacott
Non-Executive Director, Bill English
Non-Executive Director, Wayne G. Osborn
Non-Executive Director, Sharon Warburton
Non-Executive Director, Vanessa M. Wallace
Non-Executive Director, Diane L. Smith-Gander

Auditors: Ernst & Young

LOCATIONS

HQ: Wesfarmers Ltd.
Level 14, Brookfield Place Tower 2, 123 St Georges Terrace, Perth, Western Australia 6000
Phone: (61) 8 9327 4211 Fax: (61) 8 9327 4216
Web: www.wesfarmers.com.au

HISTORICAL FINANCIALS

Company Type: Public

Income Statement — FYE: June 30

	REVENUE ($mil)	NET INCOME ($mil)	NET PROFIT MARGIN	EMPLOYEES
06/23	28,827	1,631	5.7%	120,000
06/22	25,343	1,618	6.4%	120,000
06/21	25,476	1,786	7.0%	114,000
06/20	21,138	1,162	5.5%	107,000
06/19	19,561	3,860	19.7%	105,000
Annual Growth	10.2%	(19.4%)	—	3.4%

2023 Year-End Financials

Debt ratio: 11.0%
Return on equity: 30.3%
Cash ($ mil.): 445
Current Ratio: 1.17
Long-term debt ($ mil.): 2,932
No. of shares ($ mil.): 1,134
Dividends
  Yield: 3.3%
  Payout: 36.6%
Market value ($ mil.): 18,583

	STOCK PRICE ($) FY Close	P/E High/Low	PER SHARE ($) Earnings	Dividends	Book Value
06/23	16.38	8 6	1.44	0.54	4.83
06/22	14.45	11 7	1.43	1.21	4.84
06/21	22.02	11 8	1.58	0.64	6.43
06/20	15.57	11 7	1.03	0.43	5.65
06/19	12.61	4 2	3.41	5.44	6.16
Annual Growth	6.7%	—	(19.4%)	(43.8%)	(5.9%)

West Japan Railway Co

West Japan Railway, known as JR-West, operates passenger train service across the western part of Japan's main island of Honshu, including connections between Osaka and Hakata. Its combined conventional and high-speed routes cover nearly 5,000 km (about 3,125 miles) covering over 15 prefectures. JR-West's network includes the high-speed intercity railway line Sanyo Shinkansen; Chugoku Area, the Kansai Urban Area, serving Hokuriku area; and other conventional railway lines. The company also provides ferry services and has retail, hotel, and real estate operations connected with its rail network.

EXECUTIVES

President, Representative Director, Kazuaki Hasegawa
Executive Vice President, Representative Director, Fumito Ogata
Executive Vice President, Representative Director, Keijiro Nakamura
Executive Vice President, Representative Director, Shoji Kurasaka
Outside Director, Hikaru Takagi
Outside Director, Yoshinobu Tsutsui
Outside Director, Haruko Nozaki
Outside Director, Kenji Iino
Outside Director, Yoshiyuki Miyabe
Director, Eiji Tsubone
Director, Hiroaki Maeda
Director, Masatoshi Miwa
Director, Hideo Okuda
Outside Director, Maki Ogura
Director, Makiko Tada
Outside Director, Emiko Hazama
Outside Director, Kenryo Goto
Auditors: Ernst & Young ShinNihon LLC

LOCATIONS

HQ: West Japan Railway Co
2-4-24 Shibata, Kita-ku, Osaka 530-8341
Phone: (81) 6 6375 2229
Web: www.westjr.co.jp

PRODUCTS/OPERATIONS

2016 sales

	% of total
Transportation	64
Sales of goods & food services	16
Real estate business	8
Other business	12
Total	100

COMPETITORS

ALASKA RAILROAD CORPORATION
CENTRAL JAPAN RAILWAY COMPANY
Canadian Pacific Railway Limited
Guangshen Railway Company Limited
KEIKYU CORPORATION
KEISEI ELECTRIC RAILWAY CO., LTD.
SEIBU RAILWAY CO., LTD.
TOBU RAILWAY CO., LTD.
Transport for London
UNION PACIFIC RAILROAD COMPANY

HISTORICAL FINANCIALS

Company Type: Public

Income Statement — FYE: March 31

	REVENUE ($mil)	NET INCOME ($mil)	NET PROFIT MARGIN	EMPLOYEES
03/23	10,478	664	6.3%	55,175
03/22	8,476	(930)	—	57,288
03/21	8,111	(2,106)	—	60,114
03/20	13,894	823	5.9%	60,940
03/19	13,809	927	6.7%	60,120
Annual Growth	(6.7%)	(8.0%)	—	(2.1%)

2023 Year-End Financials

Debt ratio: 0.3%
Return on equity: 8.8%
Cash ($ mil.): 2,178
Current Ratio: 1.09
Long-term debt ($ mil.): 10,642
No. of shares ($ mil.): 243
Dividends
  Yield: 1.7%
  Payout: 0.0%
Market value ($ mil.): 10,072

	STOCK PRICE ($) FY Close	P/E High/Low	PER SHARE ($) Earnings	Dividends	Book Value
03/23	41.31	0 0	2.73	0.74	31.86
03/22	41.89	— —	(4.24)	0.89	32.65
03/21	56.20	— —	(11.02)	1.30	40.26
03/20	66.75	0 0	4.30	1.69	53.83
03/19	75.51	0 0	4.82	1.51	50.65
Annual Growth	(14.0%)	—	(13.2%)	(16.3%)	(10.9%)

Weston (George) Ltd

George Weston Limited is a Canadian public company that owns two businesses in retail and real estate. The majority of the company's revenue comes from its majority-owned Loblaw Companies Limited (Loblaw), Canada's largest retailer that provides Canadians with grocery, pharmacy, pharmacy and healthcare services, health and beauty products, apparel, general merchandise, and financial services, through its grocery banners, Shoppers Drug Mart, Joe Fresh, and President's Choice Bank. In addition, its Choice Properties Real Estate Investment Trust (Choice Properties) business is a large and diversified owner, manager, and developer of a high-quality real estate portfolio comprising of more than 700 properties. The company was founded in 1882.

Operations

The company operates through its two reportable operating segments, Loblaw Companies Limited (Loblaw) and Choice Properties Real Estate Investment Trust (Choice Properties).

The Loblaw segment generates almost all of the company's revenue and it operates in two reportable operating segments, retail and financial services. Loblaw's retail segment consists primarily of food retail and drug retail. Lablow offers convenient grocery locations that span the value spectrum from discount to specialty, full-service pharmacies, banking services, affordable fashion and family apparel, digital retail presence, four of Canada's top consumer brands in President's Choice, Life Brand no name, and Farmer's Market, as well as Canada's leading loyalty program, PC Optimum.

Choice Properties segment (less than 5%) portfolio is comprised of retail properties, predominantly leased to necessity-based tenants, industrial, office, and residential assets concentrated in attractive markets and offers an impressive and substantial development pipeline.

Geographic Reach

Based in Toronto, George Weston operates across Canada.

Sales and Marketing

The company's Loblaw segment serves customers through its corporate and independently operated stores in communities across Canada. Tenants from its Choice

Properties segment include Staples, Lowe's, Wal-Mart, Sobeys, Canadian Tire, and TJX Companies among others.

Financial Performance

The company's revenue has been rising in the last five years. It has an overall increase of 17% between 2018 and 2022.

In 2022, the company had a total revenue of C$57 billion, a 6% increase from the previous year's total revenue of C$53.7 billion. The increase was primarily driven by an increase in retail sales of $3.2 billion, or 6%, and an improvement in financial services revenue of $156 million, or 13%.

Net income in 2022 was C$2.8 billion, a 97% increase from the previous year's net income of C$1.4 billion.

The company's cash at the end of 2022 was C$2.3 billion. Operating activities generated C$4.9 billion, while investing activities used C$2.5 billion, mainly for fixed asset and investment properties purchases. Financing activities used another C$3 billion, primarily for repayment of long-term debt.

Strategy

Loblaw is driven by its purpose to help Canadians Live Life Well which guides its strategic framework. This framework centers around a passion for customers and drives investments in three key strategic priorities: Everyday Digital Retail, Payments and Rewards, and Connected Healthcare. Enabling these investments comes from a sharp focus on leveraging data driven insights and process efficiency excellence to deliver strong financial performance. The framework is supported by colleagues with a shared set of CORE values and culture principles that encourages colleagues to be authentic, build trust and make connections.

Company Background

A baker's apprentice, George Weston began delivering bread in Toronto with a single horse in 1882. He added the Model Bakery in 1896 and began making cookies and biscuits in 1908.

Upon George's death in 1924, his son Garfield gained control of the company and took it public as George Weston Limited in 1928.

During the 1940s the company made a number of acquisitions, including papermaker E.B. Eddy (1943; sold 1998 to papermaker Domtar, giving it a 20% stake in Domtar), Southern Biscuit (1944), Western Grocers (1944, its first distribution company), and William Neilson (1948, chocolate and dairy products).

In 1953 it acquired a controlling interest in Loblaw Groceterias, Canada's largest grocery chain. George Weston continued its acquisitions during the 1950s and 1960s, adding grocer National Tea and diversifying into packaging (Somerville Industries, 1957) and fisheries (British Columbia Packers, 1962; Conners Bros., 1967).

HISTORY

A baker's apprentice, George Weston began delivering bread in Toronto with a single horse in 1882. He added the Model Bakery in 1896 and began making cookies and biscuits in 1908.

Upon George's death in 1924, his son Garfield gained control of the company and took it public as George Weston Limited in 1928. Having popularized the premium English biscuit in Canada, Garfield acquired bakeries in the UK to make cheap biscuits (uncommon at the time). He grouped the bakeries as a separate public company called Allied Bakeries in 1935 (it later became Associated British Foods and is still controlled by the Weston family).

Expansion-minded Garfield led the company into the US with the purchase of Associated Biscuit in 1939. By the late 1930s George Weston was making cakes, breads, and almost 500 kinds of candy and biscuits.

During the 1940s the company made a number of acquisitions, including papermaker E.B. Eddy (1943; sold 1998 to papermaker Domtar, giving it a 20% stake in Domtar), Southern Biscuit (1944), Western Grocers (1944, its first distribution company), and William Neilson (1948, chocolate and dairy products).

In 1953 it acquired a controlling interest in Loblaw Groceterias, Canada's largest grocery chain. George Weston continued its acquisitions during the 1950s and 1960s, adding grocer National Tea and diversifying into packaging (Somerville Industries, 1957) and fisheries (British Columbia Packers, 1962; Conners Bros., 1967).

By 1970, when Garfield's son Galen became president, the company's holdings were in disarray. Galen brought in new managers, consolidated the food distribution and sales operations under Loblaw Companies Limited, and cut back on National Tea (which shrank from over 900 stores in 1972 to 82 in 1993). When Garfield died in 1978, Galen became chairman.

Ever since Galen, a polo-playing chum of Prince Charles, was the target of a failed kidnapping attempt by the Irish Republican Army in 1983, the family has kept a low public profile.

George Weston became the #1 chocolate maker in Canada with its purchase of Cadbury Schweppes' Canadian assets in 1987. The 1980s concluded with a five-year price war in St. Louis among its National Tea stores, Kroger, and a local grocer. This ultimately proved fruitless, and Loblaw sold its US supermarkets in 1995, ending its US retail presence. As part of its divestiture of underachieving subsidiaries, the company sold its Neilson confectionery business back to Cadbury Schweppes in 1996 and sold its chocolate products company in 1998.

In early 1998 Loblaw set its sights on Quebec, buying Montreal-based Provigo.

Other George Weston acquisitions in the late 1990s included Oshawa Foods' 80-store Agora Foods franchise supermarket unit in eastern Canada and its Fieldfresh Farms dairy business, the frozen-bagel business of Quaker Oats, Pennsylvania-based Maier's Bakery, and Bunge International's Australian meat processor, Don Smallgoods. It also sold its British Columbia Packers fisheries unit.

Early in 2001 George Weston surprised analysts when it won Unilever's Bestfoods Baking Company (Entenmann's, Oroweat) with a bid of $1.8 billion. The company reduced its stake in Loblaw by 2% and sold its Connors canned seafood business to fund the purchase, which was completed in July 2001. To help pay down debt, in early 2002 the company sold its Orowheat business in the western US to Mexican bread giant Grupo Bimbo for $610 million.

In 2003 Weston's food distribution business introduced about 1,500 private label products. It sold its fisheries operations in Chile at a loss in 2004, for about $20 million. That September the company purchased Quebec-based Boulangerie Gadoua LtÃ©e, a family-owned baking business.

In 2005 the company sold its Heritage Salmon subsidiary, thus exiting the unprofitable fisheries business entirely. The company also restructured its US biscuit operations and opened a new fresh bakery plant in Orlando, Florida, in 2005 as part of its push to increase its business in the southeastern US. A new bakery in the midwestern US began production of bread and English muffins in late 2006.

In early 2007 Weston's Loblaw subsidiary announced it was writing down its operations in Quebec to the tune of $768 million tied to its struggling Provigo grocery stores.

In December 2008 the company sold the Neilson dairy division of Weston Foods Canada to Saputo for some C$465 million in cash (about $373 million). It will use the money to pay down debt. In January 2009 it completed the sale of its fresh bread and baked goods business in the US. Later in the year, Loblaw acquired T&T Supermarket, Canada's largest retailer of Asian food.

In September 2010 George Weston, through its Maplehurst Bakeries subsidiary, acquired Keystone Bakery Holdings for approximately $185 million. Keystone is comprised of three operating companies: Freed's Bakery of Manchester, New Hampshire, a leading supplier of frozen, thaw and sell iced cupcakes; Granny's Kitchens, of Frankfort, New York, a leading supplier of both frozen pre-fried and frozen, thaw and sell donuts; and Heartland Baking of DuQuoin, Illinois, a specialty supplier of frozen, thaw and sell cookies. In November Weston Foods acquired artisan and European-style bread manufacturer ACE Bakery for C$110 million (US$108 million). Based in Toronto, ACE was made a subsidiary of Weston Foods (Canada).

Its breads are distributed in Canada and the US.

Chairman and president Galen Weston stepped down as the company's president in late 2011, but remained chairman.

EXECUTIVES

Chairman, Chief Executive Officer, Galen G. Weston
President, Chief Financial Officer, Richard Dufresne
Executive Vice President, Chief Legal Officer, Gordon A. M. Currie
Executive Vice President, Chief Talent Officer, Rashid Wasti
Vice President, General Counsel, Secretary, Andrew Bunston
Vice President, Chief Risk Officer, Anemona Turcu
Strategy Chief Strategy Officer, Khush Dadyburjor
Controller Group Head, Lina Taglieri
Corporate Finance Group Treasurer, Corporate Finance Head, John Williams
Chairman Emeritus, Chairman, W. Galen Weston
Director, Deputy Chairman, Paviter S. Binning
Corporate Director, Nancy H. O. Lockhart
Corporate Director, Gordon M. Nixon
Corporate Director, Christi Strauss
Corporate Director, Barbara Stymiest
Director, Andrew Ferrier
Director, J. Robert S. Prichard
Auditors : KPMG LLP

LOCATIONS

HQ: Weston (George) Ltd
22 St. Clair Avenue East, Toronto, Ontario M4T 2S5
Phone: 416 922-2500 **Fax:** 416 922-4395
Web: www.weston.ca

2017 Sales

	% of total
Canada	97
US	3
Total	100

PRODUCTS/OPERATIONS

2017 Sales

	% of total
Loblaw	95
Weston Foods	5
Total	100

Selected Operations
Loblaw Companies Limited
Shoppers Drug Mart
Choice Properties REIT
President's Choice Financial
Weston Foods

COMPETITORS

ASSOCIATED BRITISH FOODS PLC
BATLEYS LIMITED
BURTON'S FOODS LIMITED
GENERAL MILLS, INC.
GREENCORE GROUP PUBLIC LIMITED COMPANY
METCASH LIMITED
RESER'S FINE FOODS, INC.
THE CHEFS' WAREHOUSE INC
TOPCO ASSOCIATES, LLC

Wessanen B.V.

HISTORICAL FINANCIALS
Company Type: Public

Income Statement — FYE: December 31

	REVENUE ($mil)	NET INCOME ($mil)	NET PROFIT MARGIN	EMPLOYEES
12/23	45,361	1,161	2.6%	220,000
12/22	42,181	1,342	3.2%	221,000
12/21	42,200	338	0.8%	215,000
12/20	42,964	756	1.8%	299
12/19	38,480	185	0.5%	194,000
Annual Growth	4.2%	58.1%	—	3.2%

2023 Year-End Financials
Debt ratio: 25.4%
Return on equity: 22.8%
Cash ($ mil.): 1,849
Current Ratio: 1.24
Long-term debt ($ mil.): 9,537
No. of shares ($ mil.): 134
Dividends
Yield: —
Payout: 26.0%
Market value ($ mil.): 16,154

	STOCK PRICE ($) FY Close	P/E High/Low		PER SHARE ($) Earnings	Dividends	Book Value
12/23	120.06	13	10	8.11	2.11	37.43
12/22	124.73	11	8	8.99	1.91	35.94
12/21	116.03	45	28	1.98	1.81	37.22
12/20	74.78	15	11	4.68	1.67	40.26
12/19	79.29	67	54	0.97	1.60	38.03
Annual Growth	10.9%		—	70.2%	7.1%	(0.4%)

Westpac Banking Corp

Westpac is Australia's first bank and oldest company, one of four major banking organizations in Australia and one of the largest banks in New Zealand. It provides a broad range of banking and financial services in these markets, including consumer, business and institutional banking and wealth management services. Through its unique portfolio of brands comprising Westpac, St.George, Bank of Melbourne, BankSA, BT and RAMS, Westpac support and serve over 13.9 million customers. It generates some 80% from its domestic operations. Established in 1817 as the Bank of New South Wales, the company changed its name to Westpac Banking Corporation in 1982.

Operations
Westpac comprises six major segments: Consumer; Business; Westpac Institutional Bank; New Zealand; Group Businesses; and Specialist Business.

Consumer segment serve consumers in Australia with a full range of banking products. The segment accounts for about 50% of total revenue.

Business segment serve the needs of small to medium businesses and commercial and agribusiness customers across Australia. This segment also includes its Private Wealth business, supporting the needs of high-net-worth individuals. The segment brings in some 20% of total revenue.

Westpac New Zealand delivers banking and wealth services to consumer, business and institutional customers across New Zealand. It generates nearly 15% of total revenue.

Westpac Institutional Bank (WIB) delivers a broad range of financial services to commercial, corporate, institutional, and government customers operating in, and with connections to, Australia and New Zealand. The segment generates more than 10% of total revenue.

Group Businesses comprising its head office and Australian support functions including treasury, customer services and technology, corporate services, and enterprise services. It accounts for about 5% of total revenue.

Specialist Businesses bringing together non-core businesses that ultimately plan to divest. These currently include superannuation, platforms and investments, along with its operations in Fiji and Papua New Guinea.

Overall, net interest income accounts for about 5% of total revenue, while net fee income generates for some 10%, net wealth management and insurance income brings in around 5% and trading income accounts the rest.

Geographic Reach
Its home country, Australia accounts for about 80% of Westpac's total revenue, while New Zealand accounts for another 20%. In addition to branches and subsidiaries located across Australia, New Zealand, and neighboring islands, Westpac's institutional division has offices in London, New York, and Singapore.

Financial Performance
Note: Growth rates may differ after conversion to US dollars.

The company's revenue for fiscal 2022 decreased to A$19.6 billion compared from the prior year with A$21.2 billion. The decrease was mainly due to the change on its other income from 2021 with A$952 million compared to 2022 with a loss of A$698 million.

Profit for fiscal 2022 increased to A$5.7 billion compared form the prior year with A$5.5 billion.

Cash held by the company at the end of fiscal 2022 increased to A$105.3 billion. Cash provided by operations, investing and financing activities were A$17.0 billion, A$2.8 billion and A$13.2 billion, respectively.

Strategy
Westpac's strategic priorities, Fix, Simplify and Perform, recognize its need to address its shortcomings, reshape the business to concentrate on its core businesses and markets, while lifting service and creating a stronger performance ethic. This will help the company to become a simpler, stronger bank.

Fix priorities address outstanding issues

such as risk management, risk culture, customer remediation, and IT complexity.

Simplify priorities streamline and focus the business which includes exit non-core businesses and consolidate international, reduce products, simplify fees, lines of Business operating model, and transform using digital and data to enhance the customer experience.

Perform priorities looks for sustainable long-term returns which includes customer service ? market leading, growth in key markets, reset cost base, enhance returns, optimize capital, strong balance sheet, and climate change ? focus on net-zero.

Mergers and Acquisitions
Company Background

Westpac Banking launched in 1817 as the Bank of New South Wales?the first bank established in the country. It changed its name to Westpac Banking Corporation in 1982 after it acquired the Commercial Bank of Australia. In 2011 it merged with St.George, which then launched the Bank of Melbourne.

HISTORY

Westpac proudly calls itself Australia's "First Bank." But when predecessor Bank of New South Wales was founded in 1817, some 90% of the eponymous colony's inhabitants were convicts or their relatives. (The penal colony was established just 30 years before the bank.) The British challenged the bank's charter, forcing it to become a joint-stock company.

New South Wales' parliament rechartered the company as a bank in 1850, amidst the country's first gold rushes. (Some bank branches consisted of tents in mining camps.) Heavy British investment and an influx of colonists kept the country growing. The bank's future partner, Commercial Bank of Australia, was founded in 1866 in Melbourne, in the neighboring colony of Victoria. More than half of the country's banks disappeared in a panic at the end of the century, when land speculation and a collapse in wool prices caused a depression.

Australia became a country with the onset of the 20th century, and its government formed Commonwealth Bank, a central bank. The Bank of New South Wales, now known as "The Wales," helped finance Australia's WWI efforts. Along with the rest of the world, the country and the bank rode up the Roaring '20s and down the Great Depression.

About 65% of the bank's male staff enlisted during WWII. Its New Guinea branches closed; others were hit by air raids. In 1947 the government moved to nationalize the prospering country's banks within the Commonwealth Bank, but the courts helped the banks fend off the attack on their independence.

The Bank of New South Wales moved into the newly opened savings banking market in 1956. The next year it bought into Australian Guarantee Corporation (it bought the rest in 1988).

The bank expanded abroad and diversified operations in the 1970s. Battered by a lagging, protectionist economy, Australia moved to deregulate banking in the 1980s. As foreign banks hustled in, Bank of New South Wales and Commercial Bank of Australia in 1982 made what was then the largest merger in Australia's history.

The new bank, known as Westpac (for its Western Pacific market area), began building its non-teller-based banking networks in the early 1980s. The company developed an extensive ATM network and established telephone and computerized banking. Later that decade it bought a stake in London gold dealer Johnson Matthey (1986) and all of William E. Pollock Government Securities (1987).

In 1992 Australia's wealthiest man, Kerry Packer, took a 10% share in troubled Westpac, gaining board seats for himself and friend "Chainsaw" Al Dunlap. Packer's power grab failed, and he sold the stake in 1993.

After buying itself into the equities market in the mid-1980s, Westpac sold its Ord Minnett brokerage division in 1993. The bank withdrew from Asia and expanded closer to home in the mid 1990s, buying Western Australia's Challenge Bank in 1995, Trust Bank of New Zealand in 1996, and Victoria's Bank of Melbourne in 1997.

In 1998 the bank agreed to merge its back-office operations with those of ANZ Banking Group, providing economies of scale while avoiding antitrust issues. The next year Westpac announced 3,000 job cuts, mainly through attrition, to ready itself for increased competition from changes in Australian law. Pacific operations caused waves in 2000: Westpac said it would pull out of Kiribati in response to government action, and a coup in Fiji prompted the bank to reduce employees' hours (a move that was criticized by the Fiji government). The next year, however, Westpac was strengthening ties to the Pacific market. It doubled its holdings in the Bank of Tonga (on the island of Tonga) and its share of Pacific Commercial Bank (on the island of Samoa).

In 2007 subsidiary Westpac Essential Services Trust formed a joint venture with another Australian firm to operate the Airport Link Company, a rail-to-airport passenger service in Sydney. The trust was established so investors could invest in public-private partnership (PPP) assets.

Westpac's acquisition of St.George Bank in 2008 catapulted Westpac from fourth to second among Australia's leading banks. The combination set Westpac and its St.George subsidiary behind only the National Australia Bank in terms of assets.

EXECUTIVES

Chief Executive Officer, Managing Director, Director, Peter King
Chief Financial Officer, Michael Rowland
Chief Transformation Officer, Yianna Papanikolaou
Chief Risk Officer, Ryan A. Zanin
Customer Services & Technology Group Executive, Scott Collary
Customer & Corporate Relations Group Executive, Corporate Services Group Executive, Carolyn McCann
Human Resources Group Executive, Christine Parker
General Counsel, Shannon Finch
Secretary, Tim Hartin
Chairman, Independent Non-Executive Director, John McFarlane
Independent Non-Executive Director, Nerida Caesar
Independent Non-Executive Director, Audette E. Exel
Independent Non-Executive Director, Michael J. Hawker
Independent Non-Executive Director, Christopher Lynch
Independent Non-Executive Director, Peter Ralph Marriott
Independent Non-Executive Director, Peter Stanley Nash
Independent Non-Executive Director, Nora L. Scheinkestel
Independent Non-Executive Director, Margaret Leone Seale
Auditors : PricewaterhouseCoopers

LOCATIONS

HQ: Westpac Banking Corp
275 Kent Street, Sydney, New South Wales 2000
Phone: (61) 2 9374 7113 **Fax:** (61) 2 8253 4128
Web: www.westpac.com.au

2018 Sales

	% of total
Australia	86
New Zealand	11
Other countries	3
Total	100

PRODUCTS/OPERATIONS

2018 Sales by Segment

	% of total
Consumer Bank	39
Business Bank	24
BT Financial Group Australia	10
Westpac Institutional Bank	13
Westpac New Zealand	10
Group Businesses	4
Total	100

2018 Sales

	% of total
Net interest income	74
Non-interest income	26
Total	100

Selected Products and Services
Bank accounts
Home loans
Credit cards
Personal loans
Travel money card

Share trading
Insurance
Savings accounts
Credit cards
Business loans
Merchant services

COMPETITORS

AUSTRALIA AND NEW ZEALAND BANKING GROUP LIMITED
Bank Of China Limited
COMMERZBANK AG
COMMONWEALTH BANK OF AUSTRALIA
DEUTSCHE BANK AG
NATIONAL AUSTRALIA BANK LIMITED
NATWEST GROUP PLC
Raiffeisen Zentralbank Ã–sterreich Aktiengesellschaft
STANDARD CHARTERED PLC
UniCredit Bank AG

HISTORICAL FINANCIALS

Company Type: Public

Income Statement — FYE: September 30

	ASSETS ($mil)	NET INCOME ($mil)	INCOME AS % OF ASSETS	EMPLOYEES
09/23	667,581	4,664	0.7%	36,146
09/22	655,546	3,680	0.6%	37,476
09/21	673,340	3,926	0.6%	40,143
09/20	649,047	1,629	0.3%	36,849
09/19	612,562	4,583	0.7%	33,288
Annual Growth	2.2%	0.4%	—	2.1%

2023 Year-End Financials

Return on assets: 0.7%
Return on equity: 10.0%
Long-term debt ($ mil.): —
No. of shares ($ mil.): 3,505
Sales ($ mil.): 30,749
Dividends
 Yield: —
 Payout: 103.9%
Market value ($ mil.): —

WH Group Ltd

EXECUTIVES

Chairman, Executive Chairman, Executive Director, Long Wan
Deputy Chairman, Executive Director, Hongwei Wan
Chief Executive Officer, Executive Director, Lijun Guo
Chief Legal Officer, Secretary, Ho Chau
Independent Non-Executive Director, Hui Zhou
Independent Non-Executive Director, Ming Huang
Independent Non-Executive Director, Don Jin Tin Lau
Non-Executive Director, Shuge Jiao
Auditors : Ernst & Young

LOCATIONS

HQ: WH Group Ltd
 Unit 7602B-7604A, Level 76, International Commerce Centre, 1 Austin Road West, Kowloon,
Phone: —
Web: www.wh-group.com

HISTORICAL FINANCIALS

Company Type: Public

Income Statement — FYE: December 31

	REVENUE ($mil)	NET INCOME ($mil)	NET PROFIT MARGIN	EMPLOYEES
12/22	28,136	1,370	4.9%	104,000
12/21	27,293	1,068	3.9%	107,000
12/20	25,589	828	3.2%	107,000
12/19	24,103	1,465	6.1%	101,000
12/18	22,605	943	4.2%	112,000
Annual Growth	5.6%	9.8%	—	(1.8%)

2022 Year-End Financials

Debt ratio: 17.0%
Return on equity: 14.9%
Cash ($ mil.): 1,394
Current Ratio: 1.61
Long-term debt ($ mil.): 2,504
No. of shares ($ mil.): 12,830
Dividends
 Yield: —
 Payout: 398.9%
Market value ($ mil.): 149,215

	STOCK PRICE ($) FY Close	P/E High/Low	Earnings	Dividends	Book Value
12/22	11.63	147 94	0.11	0.43	0.75
12/21	12.58	254 159	0.08	0.40	0.68
12/20	16.68	404 272	0.06	0.75	0.68
12/19	20.60	246 147	0.10	0.48	0.59
12/18	15.36	389 214	0.06	0.76	0.53
Annual Growth	(6.7%)	—	13.7%	(13.5%)	9.1%

Willis Towers Watson Public Ltd Co

EXECUTIVES

Chief Operating Officer, Alexis Faber
President, Chief Executive Officer, Director, Carl A. Hess
Chief Financial Officer, Andrew Krasner
Controller, Principal Accounting Officer, Joseph Kurpis
Division Officer, Julie Gebauer
Division Officer, Gene H. Wickes, $650,000 total compensation
Division Officer, Adam L. Garrard
Director, Stephen Chipman
Director, Paul D. Thomas
Director, Jackie Hunt
Director, Fumbi Chima
Director, Michael Hammond
Director, Michelle R. Swanback
Director, Inga K. Beale
Director, Fredric J. Tomczyk
Director, Paul C. Reilly
Auditors : Deloitte & Touche LLP

LOCATIONS

HQ: Willis Towers Watson Public Ltd Co
 c/o Willis Group Limited, 51 Lime Street, London EC3M 7DQ
Phone: (44) 20 3124 6000
Web: www.willistowerswatson.com

HISTORICAL FINANCIALS

Company Type: Public

Income Statement — FYE: December 31

	REVENUE ($mil)	NET INCOME ($mil)	NET PROFIT MARGIN	EMPLOYEES
12/23	9,483	1,055	11.1%	48,000
12/22	8,866	1,009	11.4%	46,600
12/21	8,998	4,222	46.9%	44,200
12/20	9,352	996	10.7%	46,100
12/19	9,039	1,044	11.5%	46,600
Annual Growth	1.2%	0.3%	—	0.7%

2023 Year-End Financials

Debt ratio: 18.0%
Return on equity: 10.8%
Cash ($ mil.): 1,424
Current Ratio: 1.06
Long-term debt ($ mil.): 4,574
No. of shares ($ mil.): 102
Dividends
 Yield: —
 Payout: 33.7%
Market value ($ mil.): —

Wipro Ltd

Wipro is a leading global information technology, consulting and business process services company. It provides digital strategy, customer centric design, consulting, infrastructure services, business process services, research and development, cloud, mobility and advanced analytics and product engineering for customers around the world. Operating in some 55 countries, the company generates about 60% of its revenue from the Americas (largely the US). Wipro offers services to companies in a wide range of industries including aerospace and defense, automotive, banking, communications, electronics, construction, healthcare, pharmaceuticals, retail, and oil, and gas. In 2021, Wipro acquired Capco for approximately $1.45 billion.

Operations

Wipro operates in three segments: IT Services, IT Products, and India State Run Enterprise (ISRE).

The company depends on its IT Services segment which accounts for almost all of its revenue. This segment provides a range of IT and IT-enabled services which include digital strategy, customer-centric design, consulting, infrastructure services, business process services, research and development, cloud, mobility and advanced analytics and product engineering to leading enterprises worldwide. The company was reorganized to four Strategic Market Units (SMUs) ? Americas 1, Americas 2, Europe, and Asia Pacific Middle East Africa (APMEA). Americas 1 and Americas 2 are primarily organized by industry sector, while Europe and APMEA are organized by countries. Americas 1 includes the entire business of LATAM and the following industry sectors in the US: healthcare and medical devices, consumer goods and life sciences, retail, transportation and services, communications, media and information services, technology products and platforms. Americas 2 includes the entire

Selected Services
Design and product development
Logistics
Outsourcing management
Prototyping
Repair
Safety and compliance testing
Supply chain management
Usability and reliability testing

COMPETITORS

3SERVE LTD
GETAC TECHNOLOGY CORPORATION
GLACIER COMPUTER, L.L.C.
Hewlett Packard Brasil Ltda
Hewlett-Packard GmbH
Hypertec Systems Inc
PREMIO, INC.
TOSHIBA AMERICA INFORMATION SYSTEMS, INC.
V.I.P. COMPUTER CENTRE LIMITED
WINTEC INDUSTRIES, INC.

HISTORICAL FINANCIALS

Company Type: Public

Income Statement — FYE: December 31

	REVENUE ($mil)	NET INCOME ($mil)	NET PROFIT MARGIN	EMPLOYEES
12/21	31,135	378	1.2%	0
12/20	30,069	308	1.0%	0
12/19	29,335	227	0.8%	0
12/18	29,084	160	0.6%	0
12/17	28,196	131	0.5%	0
Annual Growth	2.5%	30.3%	—	—

2021 Year-End Financials

Debt ratio: 1.3%
Return on equity: 14.0%
Cash ($ mil.): 2,533
Current Ratio: 1.15
Long-term debt ($ mil.): 1,180
No. of shares ($ mil.): 2,903
Dividends
Yield: —
Payout: 0.0%
Market value ($ mil.): —

Woodside Energy Group Ltd

Woodside Petroleum, now Woodside Energy, provides energy which Australia and the world needs to heat homes, keep lights on and enable industry. The company has a robust hydrocarbon business with a focus on LNG. Woodside has proved reserves of some 135.7 million barrels of oil equivalent. In Western Australia, it is building on and progressing development of the Scarborough gas resource through the world-class Pluto LNG facility. Offshore, it operates three floating production storage and offloading (FPSO) facilities. The Asian markets account for the majority of its sales.

Operations

In 2022, the company shifted the reporting of its segments to the nature and geographical location of the business and venture.

The Australia segment (about 75% of the company's revenues) includes exploration, evaluation, development, production and sales of liquified natural gas, pipeline gas, crude oil and condensate and natural gas liquids in Australia. The international segment (about 10%) involves the company's activities outside of Australia.

Woodside's marketing segment (about 15%) markets, ships, and trades oil and gas portfolio and optimization activities attributed to Marketing which have generated incremental value. Corporate/Other items segment is comprised of primarily corporate non-segmental items of revenue and expenses, as well as associated assets and liabilities not allocated to operating segments.

Geographic Reach

Headquartered in Perth, Western Australia, the Asian markets account for over 70% of sales, followed by European markets with about 20% and Americas with about 10%.

Sales and Marketing

The company has two major customers which account for around 10% of its external revenue each. The sales are generated by the Australia and Marketing operating segments.

Financial Performance

Although Woodside Energy recorded fluctuations in its performance for the past five years, with a sharp decrease from 2019 to 2020, then increasing year-over-year since then, ending with 2022 as its highest performing year over the period.

The company's revenues increased by $9.9 billion to $16.8 billion in 2022, as compared to 2021's revenue of $6.9 billion.

For fiscal year end 2022, the company's net income increased to $6.6 billion as compared to the prior year's net income of $2 billion.

The company's cash at the end of 2022 was $6.2 billion. Operating activities generated $8.8 billion to the coffers. Investing activities and financing activities used $2.3 billion and $3.3 billion, respectively. Main cash uses were for payments for capital and exploration expenditure and net of Dividend Reinvestment Plan.

Strategy

Woodside's strategy involves thriving through the energy transition by building al ow cost, lower carbon, profitable, resilient and diversified portfolio. The company focuses on safe, reliable, and efficient operations, and disciplined capital allocation, providing the foundation to progress key development projects and to navigate the energy transition.

HISTORY

The operator of the North West Shelf Project initially explored for oil and gas on the other side of Australia. In 1954 Rees Withers founded Woodside (Lake Entrance) Oil to explore in southeastern Victoria. Broker Geoff Donaldson, who helped finance the new company, became chairman in 1956. When Woodside failed to hit paydirt, the firm searched for better opportunities off the Australian coast.

In 1963 Woodside acquired permits to explore the relatively uncharted, storm-tossed waters off the remote northwestern coast of Australia. The expensive and risky venture prompted Woodside to get financial and technical support from major oil players, including Royal Dutch Shell, Burmah Oil, BP, and Chevron.

The company discovered three major gas fields in 1971. The North Rankin, Goodwyn, and Angel fields subsequently formed the nucleus of the North West Shelf Project, Australia's biggest energy resource development scheme. Woodside and Burmah combined their interests to form Woodside Burmah Oil, the project's manager. When Burmah Oil struggled financially in the 1970s, it sold its part of Woodside Burmah to Broken Hill Proprietary (BHP) in 1975. As the major shareholders, Royal Dutch Shell and BHP guided the firm during the late 1970s. The company became Woodside Petroleum Ltd. in 1977.

To bring the project's gas onshore, the firm and its partners built one of the world's largest offshore gas production platforms in the North Rankin field. In 1984 Woodside began piping natural gas to a processing plant near Dampier and delivering it under long-term contracts with western Australia's state-owned energy utility. That year Donaldson stepped down as chairman, and in 1985 Shell and BHP upped their stake in Woodside to 80%.

In 1985 Woodside moved into the second phase of the North West Shelf Project: liquefied natural gas (LNG) gas for export. This venture was divided among Woodside, BHP, BP, Royal Dutch Shell, Chevron, and a Mitsubishi-Mitsui joint venture. Over the next four years, the Woodside-led consortium built two LNG processing trains and four LNG storage tanks. It began exporting LNG in 1989 under 20-year contracts with eight Japanese power and gas utilities. Woodside regained some of its independence when BHP sold most of its shares in 1990; Royal Dutch Shell became Woodside's largest shareholder.

In the late 1980s the firm found crude oil on the North West Shelf, and in the Timor Sea in 1994. It began exporting liquefied petroleum gas in 1995.

To expand its resource base, Woodside began exploring in other areas in the late 1990s, including offshore Cambodia, Mauritania, and Papua New Guinea. In 1999 the company acquired a stake in a Gulf of Mexico exploration company. In 2000 Royal Dutch Shell announced a proposal to increase its stake in Woodside to 60%, but the Australian government blocked the deal the next year. Also in 2001 the company struck oil in Mauritania for the first time.

EXECUTIVES

Chief Executive Officer, Managing Director, Executive Director, Peter John Coleman
chief financial Officer, Executive Vice President, Sherry Duhe

Executive Vice President, Chief Operating Officer, Meg O'Neill
Development Executive Vice President, Robert Edwardes
Marketing, Trading and Shipping Executive Vice President, Reinhardt Matisons
Corporate and Legal Senior Vice President, Corporate and Legal General Counsel, Corporate and Legal Joint Secretary, Michael Abbott
Senior Vice President, Chief Technology Officer, Shaun Gregory
Secretary, Warren Baillie
Chairman, Director, Richard J. B. Goyder
Non-Executive Director, Chen Goh Swee
Director, Larry Archibald
Director, Melinda A. Cilento
Director, Frank C. Cooper
Director, Christopher M. Haynes
Director, Sarah Elizabeth Ryan
Director, Gene T. Tilbrook
Director, Ian J. Macfarlane
Director, Ann D. Pickard
Auditors: Ernst & Young

LOCATIONS

HQ: Woodside Energy Group Ltd
Mia Yellagonga, 11 Mount Street, Perth, Western Australia 6000
Phone: (61) 8 9348 4000   **Fax:** (61) 8 9214 2777
Web: www.woodside.com.au

2015 Sales

	% of total
Asia	84
Australia	11
Other	4
United States of America	1
Total	100

PRODUCTS/OPERATIONS

2015 Sales

	% of total
Pluto	47
North West Shelf	36
Australia Oil	10
Other	7
Total	100

COMPETITORS

BG GROUP LIMITED
CAIRN ENERGY PLC
CONOCOPHILLIPS
HILCORP ENERGY COMPANY
HUNT OIL USA, INC.
OMV Aktiengesellschaft
PREMIER OIL PLC
SAMSON INVESTMENT COMPANY
SEAENERGY PLC
SHELL OIL COMPANY

HISTORICAL FINANCIALS
Company Type: Public

Income Statement   FYE: December 31

	REVENUE ($mil)	NET INCOME ($mil)	NET PROFIT MARGIN	EMPLOYEES
12/23	13,994	1,660	11.9%	4,667
12/22	16,817	6,498	38.6%	4,376
12/21	6,962	1,983	28.5%	2,684
12/20	3,600	(4,028)	—	3,670
12/19	4,873	343	7.0%	3,834
Annual Growth	30.2%	48.3%		5.0%

2023 Year-End Financials

Debt ratio: 8.8%   No. of shares ($ mil.): 1,898
Return on equity: 4.6%   Dividends
Cash ($ mil.): 1,740   Yield: 0.1%
Current Ratio: 1.03   Payout: 510.9%
Long-term debt ($ mil.): 4,883   Market value ($ mil.): 40,045

	STOCK PRICE ($) FY Close	P/E High/Low		PER SHARE ($) Earnings	Dividends	Book Value
12/23	21.09	31	22	0.87	4.44	18.12
12/22	24.21	6	4	4.26	2.16	19.14
12/21	15.91	10	7	2.04	1.35	13.86
12/20	17.48	—	—	(4.24)	0.38	12.55
12/19	24.04	73	57	0.37	0.91	17.63
Annual Growth	(3.2%)	—	—	24.0%	48.6%	0.7%

Woolworths Group Ltd

Woolworths is Australia and New Zealand's largest retailer. The company is a food and everyday needs retailer united by the shared purpose of creating better experiences together for a better tomorrow. With more than 1,450 stores across its Woolworths Supermarkets, Countdown Supermarkets (New Zealand) and BIG W brands, B2B business serving wholesale and export markets, and a range of fast-growing eCommerce businesses. Woolworths employs more than 180,000 team members and serves more than 20 million customers a week. The company generates nearly 90% of revenue from its domestic operations.

Operations

Woolworths' four reportable segments are: Australian Food, Australian B2B, New Zealand Food and Big W.

Australian Food include procurement of food and related products for resale and provision of services to retail customers in Australia. The segment accounts for nearly 75% of total revenue.

New Zealand Food include procurement of food and drinks for resale and provision of services to retail customers in New Zealand. It generates more than 10% of total revenue.

Australian B2B include procurement and distribution of food and related products for resale to other businesses and provision of supply chain services to business customers in Australia. It accounts for more than 5% of total revenue.

BIG W (more than 5% of revenue) include procurement of discount general merchandise products for resale to retail customers in Australia.

Geographic Reach

With more than 1,450 stores, Woolworths generates nearly 90% of its revenue from its home country, Australia, and more than 10% of its revenue from New Zealand.

Sales and Marketing

Woolworths has served an average of more than 22.7 million customer per week.

Financial Performance

The company reported a revenue of $60.8 billion in 2021, a 9% increase from the previous year's revenue of $55.7 billion.

In 2021, the company had a net income of $1.5 billion.

The company's cash at the end of 2022 was $1 billion. Operating activities generated $3.4 billion while investing activities used $2.5 billion, mainly for payments for property, plant and equipment and intangible assets. Financing activities used another $1.3 billion, primarily for payments for share buy-back.

Strategy

A key strategic priority for Woolworths Supermarkets in F22 has been to tailor ranges and in-store experiences across three cohorts of store: Core, Value, and UP. This included the roll out of curated ranges, including a focus on a multicultural offer tailored to the local community. In Fiscal 2022 the company re-launched its latest concept stores in Miller (Value), Port Macquarie (Core) and Double Bay (UP). Curated range reviews now cover a quarter of sales, generating incremental sales, with strongest market share growth in the Value and UP cohorts. Woolworths Supermarkets also made good progress on its renewal program in Fiscal 2022, celebrating its 500th store renewal at Port Macquarie since the commencement of the renewal program.

Company Background

Woolworths was founded in 1924 by Percy Christmas as Woolworths Stupendous Bargain Basement, touting its wide range of goods offered at cheap prices. It took its name from a US chain, F.W. Woolworth, which did not hold the copyright to the Woolworth name in Australia at the time. It entered New Zealand shortly after, in 1929, and the next near-century was marked by steady organic and inorganic expansion and brand diversification. It began selling petrol in 1996 and liquor in 1998.

HISTORY

Harold Percival Christmas first tried a mail-order dress business before opening the popular Frock Salon retail store. Christmas and his partners opened a branch store in the Imperial Arcade in Sydney in 1924, renaming it "Woolworths Stupendous Bargain Basement" and luring customers with advertisements calling it "a handy place where good things are cheap ... you'll want to live at Woolworths." The company borrowed the name from Frank Woolworth's successful US chain, after determining that chain had no plans to open stores in Australia. Woolworths was listed on the Australian stock exchange in 1924.

Food sales came more than 30 years later. Woolworths opened its first freestanding, full-line supermarket in 1960, then diversified into specialty retail, buying the Rockmans women's clothing store chain the next year (sold in 2000). It expanded into discounting with the Big W chain in 1976 and further diversified when it bought 60% of the Dick Smith Electronics store chain in 1981 (buying the remainder in 1983).

The purchase of the Safeway grocery chain (the Australian operations of the US-based chain) put Woolworths on the top of the supermarket heap in 1985. But the company was hurting (it lost $13 million in 1985-86) because of a restructuring in the early 1980s that had weakened management by bulking up the front offices and dividing responsibilities. Woolworths got a shot in the arm from Paul Simons, who returned to the company in 1987 after running competitor Franklins. Simons cleaned house in the front offices, closed unprofitable stores, and began the successful "Fresh Food People" marketing strategy.

Industrial Equity Limited (IEL) bought the company in 1989; IEL then became part of the Adelaide Steamship group, which spun off Woolworths as a public company in 1993. Career Woolworths manager Reg Clairs took over as CEO the following year, following the untimely death (on a golf course) in 1993 of Harry Watts, who was being groomed for the job. As a result, the company has an unwritten rule of avoiding CEOs older than 60.

Clairs took the company in a variety of new directions. Woolworths began supplying fresh food to neighbor Asia in 1995. The company added Plus Petrol outlets adjacent to Woolworths Supermarkets in 1996. It also started a superstore concept for its Dick Smith Electronics chain (Power House) that year. In 1997 the company launched its Woolworths Metro store chain, which targets commuters and other on-the-run shoppers in urban areas, and it aggressively jumped into wholesaling to independent grocers.

Clairs (who was turning 60 in 1999) stepped down in late 1998 and Roger Corbett took over as CEO. Woolworths also began offering banking services to its customers and bought Dan Murphy's, a Victoria-based liquor chain, in 1998. It divested its Chisholm Manufacturing meat plants in 2000.

In 2001 Woolworths acquired two liquor store chains (Liberty Liquor, Booze Bros), more than 200 Tandy Electronics stores, and 72 Franklins supermarkets from Hong Kong-based Dairy Farm International Holdings (most of which were later converted to the Woolworths and Food for Less banners). It sold its Crazy Prices general merchandise stores and began restructuring its liquor operations into four distinctive formats.

Woolworths exited the New Zealand market in 2002 when it sold its supermarkets group there to Foodland Associated for $690 million.

Supermarket division chief Bill Wavish resigned in May 2003 and was replaced by former chief general manager of supermarket operations Tom Flood. Wavish was considered one of the top candidates to replace CEO Corbett. Also in 2003 the company discontinued its Australian Independent Wholesalers (AIW) operations. Flood, who, like Wavish, was considered a likely successor to Corbett, resigned abruptly in August 2004.

The company acquired Australia's biggest pub owner, Australian Leisure & Hospitality (ALH), in 2005. Woolworths operates ALH's retailing activities, leaving the pubs and gaming operations to its partner in the purchase, The Bruce Mathieson Group. (Previously, the duo had acquired a 16% stake in ALH.) In mid-2005 the company acquired the New Zealand supermarkets of Foodland Associated and 22 Action stores in Western Australia, Queensland, and New South Wales for about $1.8 billion.

In September 2006 the company announced it had purchased a 10% stake in New Zealand's The Warehouse retail chain. Corbett retired as CEO in October. He was succeeded by Michael Luscombe, the company's long-serving director of supermarkets.

Woolworths offered about $1.7 billion in 2008 to buy all of New Zealand's leading general merchandise retailer Warehouse Group. The purchase, however, which would have allowed Woolworths to expand from food into general merchandise in New Zealand, was blocked by that country's competition regulator in mid-2008. An attempt to take over Australia's JB Hi-Fi, an independent chain of home entertainment products, also failed.

In February 2011 Woolworths acquired The Cellarmasters Group from Archer Capital for A$340 million ($346 million). In October Grant O'Brien was named CEO of the company.

EXECUTIVES

Chief Executive Officer, Executive Director, Brad L. Banducci
Chief Legal Officer, Bill Reid
Chief Financial Officer, David P. Marr
Endeavour Drinks Managing Director, Steve Donohue
Woolworths Supermarkets Managing Director, Claire Peters
Group Portfolio Director, Colin Storrie
Secretary, Marcin Firek
Independent Non-Executive Chairman, Gordon McKellar Cairns
Independent Non-Executive Director, Jillian Rosemary Broadbent
Independent Non-Executive Director, Holly S. Kramer
Independent Non-Executive Director, Siobhan Louise McKenna
Independent Non-Executive Director, Scott Redvers Perkins
Independent Non-Executive Director, Kathryn A. Tesija
Independent Non-Executive Director, Jennifer Carr Smith
Independent Non-Executive Director, Michael James Ullmer
Auditors : Deloitte Touche Tohmatsu

LOCATIONS

HQ: Woolworths Group Ltd
1 Woolworths Way, Bella Vista, Sydney, New South Wales 2153
Phone: (61) 2 8885 0000
Web: www.woolworthsgroup.com.au

2016 Sales

	% of total
Australia	90
New Zealand	10
Total	

PRODUCTS/OPERATIONS

2018 Sales

	% of total
Australian Food	66
New Zealand Food	10
Endeavour Drinks	14
BIG W	6
Hotels	3
Unallocated	1
Total	100

Selected Brands

Australian Food
  Woolworths Supermarkets, Caltex Woolworths, Woolworths Rewards, Financial Services & Insurance
New Zealand Food
  Countdown
Endeavor Drinks
  Dan Murphy's, BWS, Cellarmasters, Langton's Portfolio
BIG W, ALH Group

COMPETITORS

7-ELEVEN, INC
ALBERTSONS COMPANIES, INC.
C&S WHOLESALE GROCERS, INC.
DELHAIZE AMERICA, LLC
J SAINSBURY PLC
KINGFISHER PLC
METCASH LIMITED
SUPERVALU INC.
THE GREAT ATLANTIC & PACIFIC TEA COMPANY, INC.
WM MORRISON SUPERMARKETS P L C

HISTORICAL FINANCIALS

Company Type: Public

Income Statement   FYE: June 25

	REVENUE ($mil)	NET INCOME ($mil)	NET PROFIT MARGIN	EMPLOYEES
06/23	42,970	1,081	2.5%	200,364
06/22	41,986	5,474	13.0%	198,000
06/21	42,285	1,574	3.7%	210,067
06/20	43,768	800	1.8%	215,000
06/19	42,026	1,886	4.5%	196,000
Annual Growth	0.6%	(13.0%)	—	0.6%

2023 Year-End Financials

Debt ratio: 7.5%
Return on equity: 26.1%
Cash ($ mil.): 758
Current Ratio: 0.54
Long-term debt ($ mil.): 2,198
No. of shares ($ mil.): 1,214
Dividends
Yield: —
Payout: 78.6%
Market value ($ mil.): —

WPP Plc (New)

Once upon a time WPP sold wiring and plastics products, but now it's the world's largest marketing and advertising agency. The company operates through more than 3,000 offices in upwards of 112 countries, and works with some 350 of the Fortune 500 Global Companies, among others. Its advertising agency networks, including Grey Worldwide, JWT, Ogilvy & Mather, and Young & Rubicam, offer creative campaign development and brand management services. WPP's holdings also include public relations firms, media buying and planning agencies, and many specialized marketing and communications units. In addition, its Kantar Group division is one of the world's leading market research organizations.

Operations

WPP operates four business segments: Advertising and Media Investment Management (45% of total revenue); Data Investment Management (20%); Public Relations & Public Affairs (8%); and Branding Identity, Healthcare and Specialist Communications (27%).

The Advertising segment produces advertising content across essentially all sectors, such as television, internet, radio, magazines and newspapers. The segment also includes GroupM, which is WPP's media investment management operation and is the largest global player in its field; GroupM boasts that it serves one in three adverts globally. In 2019 the WPP agreed to sell a 60% stake in marketing data consultancy Kantar to Bain Capital for proceeds of about $3.1 billion.

WPP's Data Investment Management segment is organized under the Kantar Group umbrella, which comprises 12 specialized operating brands that together aim to offer a complete view of consumers. Public Relations offers advice to clients looking to communicate to customers, governmental bodies, and other businesses. Lastly, the Branding & Identity segment offers branding and design services; marketing solutions for healthcare firms; and a range of specialist and customer services, including for sports, youth and entertainment marketing.

The company's nine 'billion-dollar brands' include Ogilvy, J. Walter Thompson, Mindshare, MEC, MediaCom, Y&R, MillwardBrown, TNS, and Wunderman.

Geographic Reach

WPP has a worldwide reach and operates out of upwards of 3,000 offices in 112 countries. North America (mostly the US) is the company's most valuable region by revenue at around 37% of total; the UK and Western Continental Europe pull in approximately 34%. The Asia-Pacific region, Latin America, the Middle East and North Africa and Eastern Europe make up the rest.

The company generated revenue of more than $1 billion in five markets: the US, the UK, Germany, Australia/New Zealand, and Greater China.

Financial Performance

Note: Growth rates may differ after conversion to US Dollars.

Total revenue in 2015 was up on prior year by 6% to £12.2 billion, after taking into account headwinds from foreign currency movements - the strength of the pound against the euro detracted from revenue by 1.4%. This was the fifth consecutive year of record sales. The strongest growth was in the Advertising and Media Investment Management segment, which grew by £400 million. The second-largest segment, Branding & Identity, brought in £3.3 billion. Factors behind the year's strong results include an industry-leading performance in winning new business and customer retention, as well as greater focus on emerging markets.

By region, North America generated sales of £4.5 billion - representing growth of around 15%. Western Continental Europe was the only region to see sales fall in 2015, down nearly 6% on prior year to £2.4 billion - this was due to a poor macroeconomic climate and unfavorable currency movements.

Net income was up to £1,245 for the year. Factors in this include exceptional gains of £296 million in 2015, which came from the sale of Kantar's internet measurement business and WPP's stakes in e-Rewards and Chime Communications. On the other hand, WPP incurred £106 million in restructuring costs, almost half of which was severance-related from the Data Investment Management business in Western Continental Europe.

The company's cash flow from operating activities fell from £1,703 million in 2014 to a still-considerable £1,360 million.

Strategy

WPP strategy comprises four key tenets: 'horizontality', which means closer links between the various WPP businesses via global client leaders and regional, sub-regional and country managers (there are 45 cross-group client teams today, up from 10 in 2010); a concerted effort to increase emerging market revenue to 40-45% of total sales (currently at 19%, up a point since 2010); a focus on expanding new media to 40-45% of revenue (currently at 38%, up 9 points since 2010); and hold firm in the more measureable marketing services, such as Data Investment Management, at 50% of revenue.

WPP aims to increase flexibility in cost structure, particularly in staffing costs, in order to mitigate against WWP's vulnerability and overreliance on large clients (the company's 10 largest customers account for 16% of revenue in 2015), which can scale back marketing budgets at short notice.

Acquisitions are a big part of WPP strategy, particularly as a means to access new markets. Of the 52 new acquisitions in 2015, 18 were in new markets and 37 in quantitative and digital. This was in line with the company's drive to expand the share of revenue in the Asia-Pacific region, Latin America, Eastern Europe and the Middle East and Africa to 40-45%, and in new media to 40-45% also.

Mergers and Acquisitions

WPP has long been exceptionally active on the acquisition front, and 2015 was no exception - indeed it was among the industry's most prolific acquirer for the year. The group made 40 acquisitions to a sum of £693.1 million, up 40% on 2014's £495 million (although down in number from 52). The most notable acquisition includes GroupM's purchase of a majority stake of Essence, the world's largest independent buyer of digital media, alongside a number of bolt-ons such as ABS Creative (?2.8 million revenue in 2015), Webling Interactive (A$4.4 million), and WANDA Digital ($3.4 million). Emerging market acquisitions include nudeJEH in Thailand and Ideal Group and Jüssi Intention Marketing in Brazil.

HISTORY

WPP Group began as Wire and Plastic Products, a maker of grocery baskets and other goods founded in 1958 by Gordon Sampson (who retired from the company in 2000). Investors led by former Saatchi & Saatchi advertising executive (and current WPP CEO) Martin Sorrell bought the company in 1985 and began acquiring marketing firms under the shortened name of WPP. In 1987 Sorrell used revenue from these businesses (and a sizable loan) to buy US advertising warhorse J. Walter Thompson (now JWT).

JWT was founded by William James Carlton as the Carlton & Smith agency in 1864. The New York City-based firm was bought by James Walter Thompson in 1877 and was later responsible for Prudential Insurance's Rock of Gibraltar symbol (1896). It began working for Ford (which is still a client) in 1943. JWT went public in 1969.

Following its acquisition of JWT, WPP formed European agency Conquest in 1988. The company (and its debt) grew the next year when it bought the Ogilvy Group (founded by David Ogilvy in 1948) for $860 million, making WPP the world's largest advertising company. But its acquisition frenzy also positioned the company for a fall in 1991, when depressed economies in the US and the UK slowed advertising spending. Saddled with debt, WPP nearly went into receivership before recovering the next year.

WPP began a period of controlled growth with no major acquisitions in 1993. It expanded internationally in 1994, opening new offices in South America, Europe, the Middle East, and Asia. Winning IBM's $500 million international advertising contract that year also aided WPP's financial recovery. However, this led to the loss of business from IBM's rivals, including AT&T, Compaq's European division (Compaq was purchased by Hewlett-Packard in 2002), and Microsoft.

By 1997 the company was again ready to flex its acquisition muscle. The firm bought 21 companies that year, including a stake in IBOPE (a market research firm in Latin America) and a share of Batey Holdings (the majority owner of Batey Ads, a prominent ad agency in the Asia/Pacific region). That year WPP also created its media planning unit Mindshare.

More acquisitions followed in 1998, including a 20% stake in Asatsu (the #3 advertising agency in Japan). The next year the company bought Texas-based market research firm IntelliQuest Information Group, which was merged with WPP's Millward Brown unit. Along with its acquisitions, WPP snagged some significant new accounts in 1998 and 1999, lining up business with Kimberly-Clark, Merrill Lynch, and the embattled International Olympic Committee.

In 2000 the company bought US-based rival Young & Rubicam for about $4.7 billion -- one of the largest advertising mergers ever. The move catapulted WPP to the top spot among the world's advertising firms. As if that wasn't enough, its Mindshare unit later snagged the $700 million media planning account of consumer products giant Unilever. WPP also took a 49% stake in UniWorld Group, the largest African-American-owned ad agency in the US.

Hamish Maxwell, chairman since 1996, retired in 2001 and was replaced by Philip Lader, the former US ambassador to the UK. That year, however, WPP's top ranking was stolen away by Interpublic Group following its acquisition of True North Communications. It later sparked a bidding war with Havas Advertising when it offered $630 million to buy UK media services firm Tempus Group. WPP grudgingly completed its acquisition of Tempus in 2002. The following year the company acquired Cordiant Communications.

WPP positioned itself for both short- and long-term growth in 2005 when it completed a $1.75 billion acquisition of US-based rival Grey Group, beating out bids from private equity players (including Kohlberg Kravis Roberts & Co.) and rival advertising firm Havas.

WPP in 2007 expanded its digital marketing and advertising services by acquiring 24/7 Real Media. The company snatched up Blast Radius, an interactive marketing agency, a few months later and aligned Blast Radius with Wunderman, a marketing communications unit of WPP's Young & Rubicam Brands division.

During the same year, WPP signed a lucrative $4.5 billion three-year deal for providing advertising and marketing services to Dell. In an unconventional move, WPP created a new agency, Enfatico, to cater to the computer giant during the three-year contract.

Throughout 2008 market research rival TNS rejected several unsolicited takeover bids from WPP (including a $2.1 billion offer in July). However, TNS eventually acquiesced to the proposal when more than 60% of its shareholders accepted WPP's offer in October. The deal greatly enhanced WPP's Kantar operations and created a global market research juggernaut. In late 2008 WPP also shortened its legal name from WPP Group plc to WPP plc.

The next year, WPP worked to streamline its operating structure when it integrated TNS Custom with its Research International subsidiary to create the world's largest custom research group. Throughout 2010, WPP focused on acquisitions and investments in the digital arena deriving from China, Brazil, Singapore, the UK, and the US.

EXECUTIVES

Chief Executive Officer, Executive Director, Mark Read
Chief Financial Officer, Executive Director, John Rogers
Chief Marketing and Growth Officer, Laurent Ezekiel
Chief Client Officer, Lindsay Pattison
Chief Technology Officer, Stepehn Pretorius
Chief Creative Officer, Rob Reilly
Chief People Officer, Jennifer Remling
Chief Operating Officer, Andrew Scott
Chief Counsel, Andrea Harris
Secretary, Balbir Kelly-Bisla
Chairman, Director, Roberto Quarta
Senior Independent Non-Executive Director, Nicole Seligman
Independent Non-Executive Director, Angela J. Ahrendts
Independent Non-Executive Director, Jacques Aigrain
Independent Non-Executive Director, Sandrine Dufour
Independent Non-Executive Director, Tarek Farahat
Independent Non-Executive Director, Tom Ilube
Independent Non-Executive Director, Cindy Rose
Independent Non-Executive Director, Sally Susman
Independent Non-Executive Director, Keith Weed
Independent Non-Executive Director, Jasmine M. Whitbread
Independent Non-Executive Director, Ya-Qin Zhang
Non-Executive Director, Simon Dingemans
Auditors : Deloitte LLP

LOCATIONS

HQ: WPP Plc (New)
Sea Containers, 18 Upper Ground, London SE1 9GL
Phone: (44) 20 7282 4600
Web: www.wpp.com

2015 Sales

	% of total
North America	37
Asia-Pacific, Latin America, Africa & Middle East and Central & Eastern Europe	29
Western Continental Europe	20
United Kingdom	14
Total	100

PRODUCTS/OPERATIONS

2015 Sales

	% total
Advertising and Media Investment Management	45
Branding Identity, Healthcare and Specialist Communications	27
Data Investment Management	20
Public Relations & Public Affairs	8
Total	100

Selected Operations
Advertising
    Asatsu-DK (21%, Japan)
    Bates Asia (China)
    Diamond Ogilvy
    Direct.com (US)
    Gallagher Group (US)
    Grey Worldwide (US)
    JWT (US)
    Kinetic Worldwide
    Malone Advertising (US)
    Ogilvy & Mather Worldwide (US)
    Red Cell (US)
    Soho Square (US)
    Studio.com (US)
    Tarantula
    The Weinstein Company (US)
    The Voluntarily United Group of Creative Agencies Y&R (US)
    Rainey Kelly Campbell Roalfe / Y&R (UK)
    SicolaMartin (US)
Media services
    GroupM
    MAXUS
    MediaCom Worldwide (US)
    Mediaedge:cia
    The Digital Edge
    Outrider
    Wunderman Media (US)
    Mindshare
    Performance
    Portland Outdoor
Research, information, and consulting
    The Kantar Group (US)
    Added Value Group
    Cheskin Added Value
    ASI/Kantar Research
    BPRI
    Cannondale Associates (US)

Center Partners (US)
Everystone
Fusion 5 (US)
The Futures Company
Glendinning Management Consultants
IMRB International (India)
KMR
AGBNielsen Media Research (50%)
BMRB International
Mediafax (Puerto Rico)
Lightspeed Research (US)
MVI
Mattson Jack Group (US)
Millward Brown (US)
Research International
RMS Instore
TNS
Ziment (US)
ohal

Public relations and public affairs
ABC Public Relations (Denmark)
BKSH (US)
Blanc & Otus
Buchanan Communications
Bulletin International
Burson-Marsteller (US)
Chime Communications (21%)
Clarion Communications
Cohn & Wolfe (US)
Federalist Group (US)
Finsbury
Hill & Knowlton (US)
Blanc & Otus (US)
Wexler & Walker Public Policy Associates (US)
Impact Employee Communications (Australia)
IPR Asia Holdings (China)
Ogilvy Public Relations Worldwide (US)
Penn, Schoen & Berland (US)
Quinn Gillespie (US)
Robinson Lerer & Montgomery (US)
Timmons & Company (US)
Wexler & Walker Public Policy Associates

Branding and corporate identity services
Addison Corporate Marketing
BDGMcColl
BDGworkfutures
The Brand Union
Coley Porter Bell
Dovetail
Fitch (US)
G2 Worldwide
Lambie-Nairn
Landor Associates (US)
The Partners
MJM Creative Services (US)
WalkerGroup (US)
Warwicks

Direct marketing, promotions, and relationship marketing
A. Eicoff & Company (US)
Bridge Worldwide
Dialog Marketing
Einson Freeman (US)
EWA
Good Technology
G2
G2 Branding & Design (US)
G2 Direct & Digital (US)
G2 Interactive (US)
G2 Promotional Marketing (US)
Headcount Worldwide Field Marketing
High Co. (34%, France)
Imaginet (US)
Mando Brand Assurance
Maxx Marketing (China)
OgilvyAction (formerly 141 Worldwide)
OgilvyOne Worldwide (US)
rmg:connect
RTC Relationship Marketing (US)
VML (US)
Wunderman
KBM Group (US)

Health care communications
Grey Healthcare Group (US)
Feinstein Kean Healthcare (US)
Geoff Howe Marketing Communications (US)
Ogilvy CommonHealth Worldwide (US)
Sudler & Hennessey (US)

Specialized communications
Alliance Agency (US)
Banner Corporation
The Bravo Group (US)
The Farm Group
The Food Group (US)
Forward
G WHIZ (US)
The Geppetto Group (US)
Global Sportnet (Germany)
JWT Specialized Communications (US)
Kang & Lee (US)
MosaicaMD (US)
Metro Group
Ogilvy Primary Contact
PACE (US)
PCI Fitch
Première Group
PRISM Group
Spafax
UniWorld Group (49%, US)
WING Latino (US)

COMPETITORS

CAPGEMINI
DENTSU GROUP INC.
DENTSU INTERNATIONAL LIMITED
HAVAS
MONSTER WORLDWIDE, INC.
OMNICOM GROUP INC.
PUBLICIS GROUPE S.A.
SIZMEK INC.
THE INTERPUBLIC GROUP OF COMPANIES, INC.
YUME, INC.

HISTORICAL FINANCIALS

Company Type: Public

Income Statement — FYE: December 31

	REVENUE ($mil)	NET INCOME ($mil)	NET PROFIT MARGIN	EMPLOYEES
12/23	18,919	140	0.7%	114,173
12/22	17,369	821	4.7%	115,473
12/21	17,251	859	5.0%	109,382
12/20	16,380	(4,049)	—	99,830
12/19	17,476	824	4.7%	106,786
Annual Growth	2.0%	(35.7%)	—	1.7%

2023 Year-End Financials

Debt ratio: 22.6%
Return on equity: 3.1%
Cash ($ mil.): 2,826
Current Ratio: 0.86
Long-term debt ($ mil.): 4,811
No. of shares ($ mil.): 1,074
Dividends
Yield: —
Payout: 1972.8%
Market value ($ mil.): 51,130

	STOCK PRICE ($) FY Close	P/E High/Low	PER SHARE ($) Earnings	Dividends	Book Value
12/23	47.57	652 422	0.13	2.54	4.00
12/22	49.16	118 70	0.74	2.01	4.14
12/21	75.55	143 96	0.71	1.83	4.22
12/20	54.08	— —	(3.31)	0.65	5.40
12/19	70.29	142 105	0.65	3.75	8.48
Annual Growth	(9.3%)	—	(33.4%)	(9.3%)	(17.1%)

WSP Global Inc

EXECUTIVES

President, Chief Executive Officer, Non-Independent Executive Director, Alexandre L'Heureux
Chief Financial Officer, Bruno Roy
Chief Operating Officer, Paul Dollin
Chief Legal Officer, Secretary, Philippe Fortier
Chief Corporate Services Officer, Robert Ouellete
Investor Relations Senior Vice President, Communications Senior Vice President, Isabelle Adjahi
Strategic Initiatives Senior Vice President, Operations Senior Vice President, Alain Michaud
Independent Non-Executive Chairman, Christopher Cole
Vice-Chairman, Pierre Shoiry
Non-Executive Director, Louis-Philippe Carriere
Non-Executive Director, Birgit Norgaard
Non-Executive Director, Linda Galipeau
Non-Executive Director, Suzanne Rancourt
Non-Executive Director, Paul Raymond
Auditors: PricewaterhouseCoopers LLP

LOCATIONS

HQ: WSP Global Inc
1600 Rene-Levesque Blvd West, Montreal, Quebec H3H 1P9
Phone: —
Web: www.wsp.com

HISTORICAL FINANCIALS

Company Type: Public

Income Statement — FYE: December 31

	REVENUE ($mil)	NET INCOME ($mil)	NET PROFIT MARGIN	EMPLOYEES
12/22	8,823	319	3.6%	66,000
12/21	8,070	371	4.6%	55,000
12/20	6,914	216	3.1%	47,000
12/19	6,847	220	3.2%	49,900
12/18	5,807	182	3.1%	48,000
Annual Growth	11.0%	15.1%	—	8.3%

2022 Year-End Financials

Debt ratio: 14.7%
Return on equity: 8.0%
Cash ($ mil.): 366
Current Ratio: 1.09
Long-term debt ($ mil.): 2,056
No. of shares ($ mil.): 124
Dividends
Yield: —
Payout: 41.8%
Market value ($ mil.): 14,394

	STOCK PRICE ($) FY Close	P/E High/Low	PER SHARE ($) Earnings	Dividends	Book Value
12/22	115.66	37 27	2.65	1.11	35.68
12/21	143.78	36 21	3.18	1.19	31.09
12/20	94.87	41 17	1.96	1.43	28.23
12/19	68.39	26 17	2.08	1.13	24.15
12/18	43.45	23 18	1.75	1.14	22.91
Annual Growth	27.7%	—	10.9%	(0.7%)	11.7%

Yamada Holdings Co Ltd

Yamada Denki is the #1 consumer electronics retailer in Japan and among the overall leading retailers in the country. The company's core products include appliances, audio and video equipment, personal computers, smart phones, and software. Yamada Denki's roughly 300 stores are located mainly in midsized and large cities throughout Japan; it also maintains a retail presence in China after entering the country in 2010. In addition to Yamada Denki stores, the company operates retailer KOUJIRO, which specializes in building and selling custom PCs under the Frontier brand. Its Daikuma discount department chain peddles food, bicycles, household goods, and electronics. Yamada Denki was established in 1973.

EXECUTIVES

Chairman, President, Chief Executive Officer, Representative Director, Noboru Yamada
Executive Vice President, Representative Director, Atsushi Murasawa
Senior Managing Executive Officer, Representative Director, Megumi Kogure
Director, Akira Fukui
Director, Takayuki Fukuda
Outside Director, Tsukasa Tokuhira
Outside Director, Miki Mitsunari
Outside Director, Kunimitsu Yoshinaga
Auditors : KPMG AZSA LLC

LOCATIONS

HQ: Yamada Holdings Co Ltd
1-1 Sakae-cho, Takasaki, Gunma 370-0841
Phone: (81) 570 078 181
Web: www.yamada-holdings.jp

PRODUCTS/OPERATIONS

2014

	%
Home electrical	59
Home Information	29
Other products	12
Total	100

COMPETITORS

ABT ELECTRONICS, INC.
AERUS LLC
EDION CORPORATION
GOME RETAIL HOLDINGS LIMITED
H2O ASSET MANAGEMENT CO., LTD.
HUSSMANN INTERNATIONAL, INC.
Macintosh Retail Group N.V.
P.C. RICHARD & SON, INC.
ROBERT DYAS HOLDINGS LIMITED
SHOP VAC CORPORATION

HISTORICAL FINANCIALS
Company Type: Public

Income Statement — FYE: March 31

	REVENUE ($mil)	NET INCOME ($mil)	NET PROFIT MARGIN	EMPLOYEES
03/22	13,313	415	3.1%	31,392
03/21	15,827	467	3.0%	33,558
03/20	14,846	226	1.5%	29,481
03/19	14,453	132	0.9%	28,373
03/18	14,821	280	1.9%	29,329
Annual Growth	(2.6%)	10.3%	—	1.7%

2022 Year-End Financials

Debt ratio: 0.1%
Return on equity: 7.7%
Cash ($ mil.): 470
Current Ratio: 1.59
Long-term debt ($ mil.): 913
No. of shares ($ mil.): 836
Dividends
  Yield: —
  Payout: 29.6%
Market value ($ mil.): —

Yamagata Bank Ltd. (The)

EXECUTIVES

President, Representative Director, Kichishige Hasegawa
Senior Managing Director, Representative Director, Shinichiro Miura
Senior Managing Executive Officer, Representative Director, Eiji Sato
Director, Hiroshi Koya
Director, Yutaka Touyama
Director, Izumi Hasegawa
Director, Tsutomu Komagome
Director, Tomokazu Kan
Director, Toshiyuki Komatsu
Director, Mitsuru Iokawa
Director, Hiroyuki Sasa
Outside Director, Yumiko Inoue
Outside Director, Keitaro Harada
Director, Takuro Taruishi
Outside Director, Yasumasa Gomi
Outside Director, Gisuke Ohara
Outside Director, Junichi Matsuda
Outside Director, Masanori Oshino
Auditors : Ernst & Young ShinNihon LLC

LOCATIONS

HQ: Yamagata Bank Ltd. (The)
3-1-2 Nanukamachi, Yamagata 990-8642
Phone: (81) 23 623 1221
Web: www.yamagatabank.co.jp

HISTORICAL FINANCIALS
Company Type: Public

Income Statement — FYE: March 31

	ASSETS ($mil)	NET INCOME ($mil)	INCOME AS % OF ASSETS	EMPLOYEES
03/22	29,089	27	0.1%	1,921
03/21	28,259	25	0.1%	1,970
03/20	24,441	23	0.1%	2,004
03/19	23,269	36	0.2%	2,072
03/18	24,656	46	0.2%	2,114
Annual Growth	4.2%	(12.2%)	—	(2.4%)

2022 Year-End Financials

Return on assets: 0.1%
Return on equity: 2.1%
Long-term debt ($ mil.): —
No. of shares ($ mil.): 32
Sales ($ mil.): 362
Dividends
  Yield: —
  Payout: 0.0%
Market value ($ mil.): —

Yamaha Motor Co Ltd

Yamaha Motor's core areas of expertise include powertrain technology originating from motorcycle development, and the chassis/hull technology that complements the performance of its vehicles and boats. Best known for its extensive line of motorcycles, Yamaha Motor also makes scooters, electric-hybrid bicycles, four-wheel ATVs, fishing boats and utility boats, electric wheelchairs, golf carts, and snowmobiles. Other products include engines, FRP swimming pools, electric wheelchairs, robots, Industrial use unmanned helicopters, and Industrial robots used to spray agricultural crops, among others. Founded in 1955, Yamaha Motor together with its more than 125 subsidiaries operates more than 45 sales bases, nearly 25 manufacturing plants, and about 20 development bases throughout the world. The majority of its revenue was generated in Asia.

Operations

The company operates in five segments: Land Mobility (about 65% of sales), Marine Products (almost 25%), Robotics (about 5%), Financial Services (about 5%), and Other products (account for the rest).

The Land Mobility segment primarily comprises the motorcycle, recreational vehicle (RV), and smart power vehicle (SPV) businesses, and offers a wide range of products tailored to the characteristics of each market, including products for practical daily transportation, as well as for leisure, commercial, and sports use.

The Marine Products segment offers a lineup that includes outboard motors, personal watercraft, and fiber-reinforced plastic (FRP) pools, and has established a world-leading presence in the marine market.

The Robotics segment develops products such as industrial robots for factory automation, surface mounting technology (SMT)-related equipment used for manufacturing printed circuit boards, semiconductor manufacturing equipment, and unmanned industrial-use helicopters and drones that utilize its core electronic control technology.

The Financial Services segment includes financing services and other related financial services to customers and dealerships.

Other Products segment manufactures and sells golf cars and land cars for golf courses and leisure facilities, generators and multipurpose engines based on small engine technology, and snow blowers for snowy regions.

Overall, the emerging market motorcycle business brings in about 65% of the company's revenue by main product category, followed by the developed market motorcycle business with more than 20%, recreational vehicles with roughly 10%, and smart power vehicles with about 5%.

Geographic Reach

Headquartered in Shizuoka-ken, Japan, the company operates in more than 180 countries and regions. The Overseas Market Development Operation (OMDO) business unit offers Yamaha products and after-sales services in approximately 140 countries and regions, mainly in Africa, Central America, and the Caribbean. It also has more than 125 subsidiaries in Europe, Asia (excl. Japan), the Americas, Oceania, and Japan.

About 40% of the company's revenue comes from Asia (excl. Japan), followed by North America with about 25%, Europe with about 15%, Japan with more than 5%, and the rest comes from other foreign markets.

Sales and Marketing

The company offers retail financing, wholesale financing, leases, insurance, and other financial services related to its products to customers and dealerships.

Financial Performance

Yamaha's revenue for the five fiscal years experienced decreases and increases starting from JPY1.67 trillion in 2018, to JPY1.66 trillion, JPY1.47 trillion, JPY1.81 trillion, and JPY2.25 trillion, for fiscal years 2019 to 2022, respectively.

Company's revenue for fiscal 2022 increased to JPY2.25 trillion compared from the prior year with JPY1.81 trillion. The increase was primarily due to strong demand for outboard motors in developed countries and the recovery of demand for motorcycles in emerging markets, despite the impact of supply shortages caused by global supply chain disruptions.

Net income for fiscal 2022 increased to JPY174.4 billion compared from the prior year with JPY155.6 billion. The increase was primarily due to higher revenues offsetting the increase in expenses.

Cash provided by operations and financing activities were JPY70.9 billion and JPY23.1 billion, respectively. Cash used for investing activities was JPY74.2 billion, mainly for purchase of fixed assets.

Strategy

Under its corporate mission to be a Kando Creating Company, Yamaha will work to realize its Long-Term Vision for 2030 of ART for Human Possibilities by carrying out its Medium-Term Management Plan from 2022 as phase two of the company's ongoing transformation. In recognition of the numerous challenges that must be addressed, including changes in the business environment, the rising awareness of sustainability, and the need for transformation, the company will continue with the growth strategies and reinforcement of management foundations that the company have pursued over the last three years, but while also strengthening its resolve for sustainability. In the rapidly changing business environment, the company will once again return to the essentials in fiscal 2023, especially growth strategies and reinforcement of its management foundations, to accelerate the pace of its transformation.

HISTORY

The origins of Yamaha Motor can be traced back to WWII. During the war Nippon Gakki Co. -- like most Japanese businesses -- retooled to make products for Japan's war effort. Nippon Gakki, which literally means "Japan musical instruments," switched from making pianos and organs to building propellers, fuel tanks, and wing parts for Japanese Zero fighter planes. This experience would later help Nippon Gakki (now called Yamaha Corporation) diversify into other industrial products during the years immediately after the war.

Nippon Gakki built its first motorcycle, the 125 cubic centimeter (cc) YA-1, in 1955. Later that year Yamaha Motor was created. Nippon Gakki retained partial ownership of the new company.

Yamaha Motor built its first sailboat using fiberglass-reinforced plastic in 1960. The company's line of marine products soon expanded to include powerboats, outboard motors, fishing vessels, and patrol boats for Japan's Maritime Safety Agency.

During the early 1960s Yamaha Motor (along with Honda and Suzuki) successfully penetrated the US market with a line of small, inexpensive motorcycles. Prior to the introduction of Japanese imports, the US motorcycle market had been dominated by heavy models built by the likes of Harley-Davidson and Triumph. Yamaha Motor's motorcycles also enjoyed success in Asian markets.

In 1966 Yamaha Motor provided the engine for Toyota's 2000GT sports car. By 1968 the company had introduced its first snowmobile (the SL350) and had opened its first overseas subsidiary, Yamaha Motor Europe NV (the Netherlands).

The company continued to expand geographically as it established Yamaha Motor do Brasil (1970) and Yamaha Motor Canada (1973). Product lines also grew in 1973 to include racing karts and generators. Yamaha Motor began marketing its first line of golf carts two years later. In 1977 the company created Yamaha Corporation, USA. The following year Yamaha Motor began marketing its first snow blower.

By 1981 the company had developed industrial assembly robots. Yamaha Motor introduced a four-wheel ATV in 1984. The following year the company entered into a development agreement with Ford for high-performance engines, and by 1986 the company offered personal watercraft. Yamaha Motor entered new markets in 1987 -- gas heat-pump (GHP) air conditioners (exited in 2000) and surface mounters for printed circuit boards.

Yamaha Motor started the Zhuzhou Nanfang Yamaha Motor Co. joint venture in China in 1993 for the production of motorcycles. The following year the company established two more joint ventures in China for the production of boats. Continuing to build upon its innovative traditions, Yamaha Motor developed the world's first auxiliary electric power unit for wheelchairs in 1996 and the PAS MII Super electro-hybrid bicycle in 1998.

In 1999 the company began producing motorcycles in Vietnam. Yamaha Corporation decreased its stake in Yamaha Motor to about 28% in 2000, and Toyota Motor took a 5% stake in the company to become Yamaha Motor's second-largest shareholder. In early 2001 Yamaha Motor announced that it would pursue legal action against the manufacturers of counterfeit motorcycles bearing the Yamaha name made in China.

The following year, in anticipation of its 50th anniversary in 2005, Yamaha announced its NEXT 50 mid-term management plan. The three-year plan increased net sales while strengthening Yamaha's position in China, India, and ASEAN (Southeast Asia) countries. In 2005 Yamaha launched a subsidiary in Russia, Yamaha Motor CIS, to sell Yamaha products at more than 80 dealers in that country. The same year it set up a subsidiary to sell motorcycles in India.

In 2006 the Japanese government filed a criminal complaint accusing Yamaha Motor of exporting unmanned helicopters to China in violation of regulations that forbid the unlicensed export of products that could have a military use.

EXECUTIVES

Chairman, Representative Director, Katsuaki Watanabe
President, Executive Officer, Representative Director, Yoshihiro Hidaka
Director, Heiji Maruyama
Director, Satohiko Matsuyama
Director, Motofumi Shitara
Outside Director, Takuya Nakata

Outside Director, Takehiro Kamigama
Outside Director, Yuko Tashiro
Outside Director, Tetsuji Ohashi
Outside Director, Jin Song Montesano
Auditors : Ernst & Young ShinNihon LLC

LOCATIONS

HQ: Yamaha Motor Co Ltd
  2500 Shingai, Iwata, Shizuoka 438-8501
Phone: (81) 538 32 1144
Web: www.yamaha-motor.co.jp

2015 Sales

	% of total
Asia	
Japan	10
Other countries	42
North America	22
Europe	13
Others	13
Total	100

PRODUCTS/OPERATIONS

2015 Sales

	% of total
Motorcycles	63
Marine products	19
Power products	10
Industrial machinery & robots	3
Other products	5
Total	100

Selected Products

Marine products
  Boats (power, sail & utility)
  Diesel engines
  Outboard motors
  Personal watercraft
  Swimming pools
Motorcycles
  Motocrossers
  Road racers
  Scooters
  Sports bikes
  Trail bikes
Power products
  All-terrain vehicles (ATVs)
  Generators
  Golf carts
  Multi-purpose engines
  Racing kart engines
  Side-by-side vehicles
  Snowmobiles
  Snow throwers
Other products
  Automotive components
  Automotive engines
  Electric wheelchairs
  Electro-hybrid bicycles (PAS)
  Industrial robots
  Surface mounters
  Unmanned helicopters

COMPETITORS

CYCLING SPORTS GROUP, INC.
DUCATI MOTOR HOLDING SPA
EDELBROCK, LLC
FOX FACTORY HOLDING CORP.
HARLEY-DAVIDSON, INC.
HERO MOTOCORP LIMITED
HONDA MOTOR CO., LTD.
PIAGGIO & C. SPA
SUZUKI MOTOR CORPORATION
YAMAHA MOTOR CORPORATION U.S.A.

HISTORICAL FINANCIALS

Company Type: Public

Income Statement — FYE: December 31

	REVENUE ($mil)	NET INCOME ($mil)	NET PROFIT MARGIN	EMPLOYEES
12/22	17,063	1,323	7.8%	64,162
12/21	15,745	1,351	8.6%	62,293
12/20	14,274	514	3.6%	63,367
12/19	15,333	697	4.5%	68,164
12/18	15,214	849	5.6%	67,071
Annual Growth	2.9%	11.7%	—	(1.1%)

2022 Year-End Financials

Debt ratio: 0.2%
Return on equity: 18.7%
Cash ($ mil.): 2,191
Current Ratio: 1.73
Long-term debt ($ mil.): 2,060
No. of shares ($ mil.): 1,014
Dividends
  Yield: —
  Payout: 24.4%
Market value ($ mil.): —

Yamanashi Chuo Bank, Ltd. (Japan)

The Yamanashi Chuo Bank serves customers primarily in the Yamanashi prefecture near Tokyo in Japan. The bank provides a range of standard banking services, including lending, savings, and financial planning, to the retail and commercial markets. Yamanashi Chuo Bank's other services include leasing and credit card services. The bank operates about 90 branch domestic branch locations and one office in Hong Kong.

EXECUTIVES

Chairman, Representative Director, Mitsuyoshi Seki
President, Representative Director, Yoshiaki Furuya
Senior Managing Director, Representative Director, Masahiko Yamadera
Director, Norihiko Tanaka
Director, Hideki Sato
Director, Tetsuya Naito
Outside Director, Michio Masukawa
Outside Director, Riyo Kano
Outside Director, Miki Ichikawa
Auditors : Deloitte Touche Tohmatsu LLC

LOCATIONS

HQ: Yamanashi Chuo Bank, Ltd. (Japan)
  1-20-8 Marunouchi, Kofu, Yamanashi 400-8601
Phone: (81) 55 233 2111
Web: www.yamanashibank.co.jp

COMPETITORS

CHUKYO BANK, LIMITED.
DAISAN BANK,LTD., THE
EHIME BANK, LTD., THE
NISHI-NIPPON CITYBANK,LTD.
OGAKI KYORITSU BANK, LTD., THE

HISTORICAL FINANCIALS

Company Type: Public

Income Statement — FYE: March 31

	ASSETS ($mil)	NET INCOME ($mil)	INCOME AS % OF ASSETS	EMPLOYEES
03/23	32,889	37	0.1%	2,289
03/22	36,746	34	0.1%	2,302
03/21	37,802	27	0.1%	2,316
03/20	32,348	34	0.1%	2,342
03/19	31,431	44	0.1%	2,394
Annual Growth	1.1%	(3.8%)	—	(1.1%)

2023 Year-End Financials

Return on assets: 0.1%
Return on equity: 2.5%
Long-term debt ($ mil.): —
No. of shares ($ mil.): 31
Sales ($ mil.): 455
Dividends
  Yield: —
  Payout: 27.8%
Market value ($ mil.): —

Yamato Holdings Co., Ltd.

The well-known black cat logo of express delivery giant Yamato Holdings crosses paths throughout Japan. The holding company's flagship unit, Yamato Transport, delivers billions of parcels and pieces of mail yearly from a network of thousands of delivery centers throughout Japan. Besides Yamato Transport and its signature next-day TA-Q-BIN (door-to-door parcel delivery) and Kuroneko Mail (document delivery) businesses, Yamato Holdings' operations include B2B logistics, information system development, financial transaction processing, fleet maintenance, and household moving services. Yamato Transport accounts for the bulk of the holding company's annual revenue. The company has more than 60 subsidiaries

EXECUTIVES

President, Representative Director, Yutaka Nagao
Executive Vice President, Representative Director, Toshizo Kurisu
Executive Vice President, Representative Director, Yasuharu Kosuge
Senior Managing Executive Officer, Tomoki Otani
Senior Managing Executive Officer, Shinji Makiura
Director, Kenichi Shibasaki
Outside Director, Mariko Tokuno
Outside Director, Yoichi Kobayashi
Outside Director, Shiro Sugata
Outside Director, Noriyuki Kuga
Outside Director, Charles Chuanli Yin
Auditors : Deloitte Touche Tohmatsu LLC

LOCATIONS

HQ: Yamato Holdings Co., Ltd.
  2-16-10 Ginza, Chuo-ku, Tokyo 104-8125
Phone: (81) 3 3541 4141
Web: www.yamato-hd.co.jp

2016 Sales
	% of total
Japan	98
North America	1
Other	1
Total	100

PRODUCTS/OPERATIONS
2016 Sales
	% of total
Delivery	78
BIZ-Logistics	8
Financial	5
Home Convenience	3
e-Business	3
Autoworks	2
Other	1
Total	100

2016 Sales
	% of total
TA-Q-BIN	66
Kuroneko DM-Bin	6
Other	28
Total	100

COMPETITORS
CASTLETON TECHNOLOGY LIMITED
CEVA LOGISTICS LIMITED
DIMENSION DATA HOLDINGS LTD
GEODIS
INTERSERVE PLC
OFFICETEAM 2 GROUP LIMITED
OZBURN-HESSEY HOLDING COMPANY LLC
PANTHER PREMIUM LOGISTICS, INC.
THE DUCHOSSOIS GROUP INC
UNIGROUP, INC.

HISTORICAL FINANCIALS
Company Type: Public

Income Statement — FYE: March 31

	REVENUE ($mil)	NET INCOME ($mil)	NET PROFIT MARGIN	EMPLOYEES
03/23	13,519	344	2.5%	210,197
03/22	14,745	460	3.1%	216,873
03/21	15,316	512	3.3%	223,191
03/20	15,017	205	1.4%	224,945
03/19	14,676	231	1.6%	225,125
Annual Growth	(2.0%)	10.4%	—	(1.7%)

2023 Year-End Financials
Debt ratio: —
Return on equity: 7.6%
Cash ($ mil.): 1,391
Current Ratio: 1.41
Long-term debt ($ mil.): —
No. of shares ($ mil.): 362
Dividends
Yield: —
Payout: 0.0%
Market value ($ mil.): 6,243

	STOCK PRICE ($) FY Close	P/E High/Low	PER SHARE ($) Earnings	Dividends	Book Value
03/23	17.21	0 0	0.95	0.34	12.63
03/22	18.73	0 0	1.24	0.47	13.23
03/21	26.62	0 0	1.37	0.37	13.40
03/20	14.95	0 0	0.52	0.27	13.28
03/19	25.01	0 0	0.59	0.25	12.96
Annual Growth	(8.9%)	— —	12.8%	8.7%	(0.6%)

YangMing Marine Transport Corp

A leading container shipping company, Yang Ming Marine Transport hauls big boxes full of freight from Taiwan to ports around the world. The company's fleet of about 90 vessels is made up primarily of containerships but also includes bulk carriers; it has an overall capacity of more than 4 million deadweight tons (DWT). Destinations served by the company include both the west and east coasts of the US, Europe, and the Asia/Pacific region. Yang Marine operates container terminals in the US as well as in Taiwan, and it offers logistics services related to ground transportation of containers. Taiwan-based customers account for nearly all of the company's sales.

EXECUTIVES
Chief Executive Officer, Chief Operation Officer, Chairman, Chih-Chien Hsieh
Senior Executive Vice President, Kun-Rong Pai
Chief Information Officer, Executive Vice President, Der-Shi Tsao
Chief Auditor, Executive Vice President, Shih-Fang Hsu
Chief Administrative Officer, Senior Vice President, Mei-Chi Shih
Chief Marine Technology Officer, Senior Vice President, Yeoung-Shuenn Ho
Chief Logistics Officer, Senior Vice President, Zheng-Xiong Zheng
Chief Strategy Officer, Senior Vice President, Shu-Chin Du
Chief Commercial Officer, Senior Vice President, Chao-Feng Chang
Chief Financial Officer, Senior Vice President, Hsiu-Chi Ho
Senior Vice President, Jia-Lin Wu
Senior Vice President, Jie-Li Zhu
Senior Vice President, Shi-Nan Huang
Senior Vice President, Yi-Da Wu
Senior Vice President, Chien-Chang Tzeng
Vice President, Dong-Hai Chen
Vice President, Li-Ping Xiong
Vice President, Xi-Chang Zhang
Vice President, Ping-Jen Tseng
Vice President, Zeng-Yu Qiu
Vice President, Yung-Kai Wang
Vice President, Leng-Hui Wang
Vice President, Yu-Wen Su
Vice President, Jia-Ting Dong
Vice President, Long-Xing Zhu
Vice President, Shun-Jin Yang
Vice President, Bao-Lin Li
Vice President, Chun-Jie Lu
Vice President, Wen-Zhong Ye
Vice President, Tai-Qi Tsai
Vice President, Zu-Wang Luan
Vice President, Guo-Liang Huang
Vice President, Men-Huo Tsai
Vice President, Li-Wen Liu
Director, Kun-Ching Liao
Director, Ping-Jen Tseng
Director, Cheng-mount Cheng
Director, Chien-Yi Chang
Director, Shao-Yuan Chang
Director, Wen-Ching Liu
Independent Director, Ming-Sheu Tsai
Independent Director, Tar-Shing Tang
Independent Director, Tze-Chun Wang
Auditors : Deloitte & Touche

LOCATIONS
HQ: YangMing Marine Transport Corp
271 Ming De 1st Road, Cidu District, Keelung 20646
Phone: (886) 2 2455 9988   **Fax:** (886) 2 2455 9985
Web: www.yangming.com

COMPETITORS
INTERNATIONAL SHIPHOLDING CORPORATION
KAWASAKI KISEN KAISHA, LTD.
NIPPON YUSEN KABUSHIKI KAISHA
Odfjell Se
TROPICAL SHIPPING & CONSTRUCTION COMPANY LIMITED

HISTORICAL FINANCIALS
Company Type: Public

Income Statement — FYE: December 31

	REVENUE ($mil)	NET INCOME ($mil)	NET PROFIT MARGIN	EMPLOYEES
12/21	12,051	5,968	49.5%	0
12/20	5,383	426	7.9%	0
12/19	4,982	(143)	—	0
12/18	4,637	(215)	—	0
12/17	4,420	10	0.2%	0
Annual Growth	28.5%	384.6%		

2021 Year-End Financials
Debt ratio: 0.2%
Return on equity: —
Cash ($ mil.): 2,074
Current Ratio: 3.09
Long-term debt ($ mil.): 573
No. of shares ($ mil.): 3,492
Dividends
Yield: —
Payout: 0.0%
Market value ($ mil.): —

Yankuang Energy Group Co Ltd

Yanzhou Coal Mining is helping fuel China's industrialization. The company is a controlled subsidiary of Yankuang Group. It is a leader in coal production in Eastern China, where most of its coal is generated, though Yanzhou also operates in Australia. The company produces about 106.4 million tons of raw coal and nearly 1.8 million tons of methanol; sold over 116.1 million tons of salable coal and around 1.8 million tons of methanol. Yanzhou Coal operates seven mines, producing both thermal coal for electric generation and coking coal for metallurgical production. It also owns major rail transport assets. About three-fourths of it sales came from China.

Operations
Yanzhou Coal is engaged primarily in the mining business. It is also engaged in the coal railway transportation business. The company does not currently have direct export rights in the PRC and all of its export sales is made through China National Coal Industry Import and Export Corporation, Minmetals Trading Co., Ltd. or Shanxi Coal Imp. & Exp. Group Corp. In addition to coal mining (accounts for about 95% of sales), its other principal activities include methanol, electricity and heat supply (some 5%), coal railway, and equipment manufacturing.

Geographic Reach
Most of Yanzhou Coal's sales are in China as well as Japan, South Korea, Singapore, Australia and other countries. The company is located in Jining City Shandong Province of East China, one of the most developed area of China and the frontal area for coal transferring from north to south. About 75% of the company's total sales were generated in China, Australia accounts for roughly 5%, and other countries account for the rest.

Sales and Marketing
The sales revenue attributable to the company's biggest customer is RMB 2.3 billion, representing about 5% over the annual sale revenue. In addition, the sales revenue attributable to the its top five customers is RMB 9.5 billion, accounting for nearly 15% of total annual sales revenue; the sales revenue attributable to connected parties among the top five customers is RMB1.7 billion, accounting for less than 5% of the total annual sales revenue.

Financial Performance
The Company's revenue in 2019 increased to RMB 67.8 billion compared to 2018, with RMB 67.4 billion. The increase was due to higher gross sales of coals.

Profit for the year 2019 was RMB 11.8 billion higher by RMB 504.1 million compared to the prior year.

Cash held by the Company at the end of 2019 decreased to RMB 22.8 billion. Cash provided by operations was RMB 16.4 billion, while cash used for investing and financing activities were RMB 11.4 billion and RMB 9.9 billion, respectively. Main uses for cash were payments for construction in progress and repayment of guaranteed notes.

Strategy
In 2019, the Company, by seizing policy opportunities of supply-side structural reform and replacement of the old growth drives with new ones in coal industry, has continuously improved the vitality and core competitiveness in various ways, such as optimizing the industrial structure, strengthening lean management, and accelerating changes in operating mechanisms. The coal industry focused on an integrated growth with high efficiency and significant achievements on intelligent coal mine construction. A group of Smart Fully-Mechanized Caving Workfaces, advanced at home and abroad, was built and put into normal operations. The percentage of high value-added products had been increased continuously through devoting great energy to implementing the win by clean coal strategy.

Company Background
The company had been increasing its reach abroad with the purchase of a mine in Australia in 2004. Yanzhou Coal Mining began expanding the production capacity and upgrading the technology at the mine the next year and commenced coal production in 2006.

However, the continuing industrialization of China has seen domestic sales take on greater importance to the company. By 2007, international sales had dipped below 10% of the company's total sales, where they had accounted for as nearly half at the beginning of this decade.

Still and all, the company joined other Chinese businesses with interest in the Australian minerals market when it bought coal miner Felix Resources for about A$3.3 billion ($2.7 billion US) in 2009. At the time the the deal was closed, it was the largest direct investment in Australia by a Chinese corporation.

Yanzhou Coal formed an $830 million joint mining venture in 2011 with its parent company, state-owned Yankuang Group.

EXECUTIVES

Supervisor, Shisheng Gu
Board Secretary, Qingbin Jin
Financial Controller, Chief Financial Officer, Director, Qingchun Zhao
Deputy General Manager, Director, Jing He
Supervisory Committee Vice Chairman, Hong Zhou
Deputy General Manager, Zhijie Gong
Deputy General Manager, Wei Li
General Engineer, Chunyao Wang
Deputy General Manager, Peng Wang
General Manager (Acting), Deputy General Manager, Yaomeng Xiao
Deputy General Manager, Chuanchang Zhang
Supervisor, Shipeng Li
Supervisor, Yanpo Qin
Staff Supervisor, Li Su
Staff Supervisor, Kai Zheng
Deputy General Manager, Zhaohua Tian
Chairman, Xiyong Li
Director, Xiangqian Wu
Independent Director, Zhaoguo Pan
Independent Director, Chang Cai
Director, Jian Liu
Independent Director, Hui Tian
Staff Director, Ruolin Wang
Independent Director, Limin Zhu

Auditors : SHINEWING (HK) CPA Limited

LOCATIONS
HQ: Yankuang Energy Group Co Ltd
298 Fushan South Road, Zoucheng, Shandong Province 273500
Phone: (86) 537 5382319 **Fax:** (86) 537 5383311
Web: www.yanzhoucoal.com.cn

PRODUCTS/OPERATIONS
2013 sales

	% of total
Coal mining revenue	97
Methanol, electricity and heat supply revenue	3
Railway transportation revenue	1
Unallocated and eliminations	(1)
Total	100

COMPETITORS
ALPHA NATURAL RESOURCES, INC.
ARCH RESOURCES, INC.
BHP GROUP PLC
China Coal Energy Company Limited
IRPC PUBLIC COMPANY LIMITED
Lotte Chemical Corporation
NIPPON COKE & ENGINEERING COMPANY, LIMITED
PEABODY ENERGY CORPORATION
RENTECH, INC.
WALTER COKE, INC.

HISTORICAL FINANCIALS
Company Type: Public

Income Statement — FYE: December 31

	REVENUE ($mil)	NET INCOME ($mil)	NET PROFIT MARGIN	EMPLOYEES
12/22	29,111	4,460	15.3%	0
12/21	23,940	2,561	10.7%	0
12/20	32,872	1,088	3.3%	0
12/19	28,835	1,245	4.3%	0
12/18	23,698	1,149	4.9%	0
Annual Growth	5.3%	40.3%	—	—

2022 Year-End Financials
Debt ratio: 3.7% No. of shares ($ mil.): —
Return on equity: 37.7% Dividends
Cash ($ mil.): 6,548 Yield: —
Current Ratio: 1.07 Payout: 287.8%
Long-term debt ($ mil.): 8,554 Market value ($ mil.): —

	STOCK PRICE ($) FY Close	P/E High/Low		PER SHARE ($) Earnings	Dividends	Book Value
12/22	30.42	7	3	0.91	2.61	0.00
12/21	19.72	7	2	0.53	0.00	0.00
12/20	7.90	7	5	0.22	0.00	0.00
12/19	9.00	6	4	0.25	0.00	0.00
12/18	7.94	11	5	0.23	0.00	0.00
Annual Growth	39.9%	—	—	40.3%	—	—

Yapi Ve Kredi Bankasi AS

Yapi ve Kredi Bankasi (Yapi Kredi for short) boasts over $80 billion in assets, making it Turkey's fourth-largest private bank. Yapi Kredi provides financial services -- including retail, corporate, and private banking services -- in Turkey through more than 1,000 branches and about 4,025 ATMs. It also operates in Bahrain and has subsidiary banks in Azerbaijan, Germany, the Netherlands, and Russia. Yapi Kredi, which launched Turkey's first credit card in 1988, now has 6 million cardholders. The bank also provides leasing, factoring, mutual funds, insurance, investment banking, and brokerage services. KoÃ§ Financial Services (KFS), jointly owned by UniCredit and KoÃ§ Holding, owns 82% of Yapi Kredi.

Operations

Yapi Kredi's operates three major business segments. Its Retail Banking segment serves individuals and small- to medium- enterprises (SMEs) with consumer loans (auto, mortgage, and general purpose) and commercial installment loans, respectively. About 59% of its loans were corporate and commercial loans in 2014, while retail loans and credit card receivables made up 27% and 14% of its total portfolio. The Retail Banking segment also provides card payment systems, investment accounts, insurance products, and payroll services.

Its Corporate & Commercial Banking segment has three subgroups: Corporate Banking for large-scale companies, Commercial Banking for medium-sized companies, and Multinational Companies Banking. Yapi Kredi's Private Banking and Wealth Management segment provides investment products to high net worth customers.

About 80% of Yapi Kredi's total revenue came from interest income (mostly from loans) in 2014, while another 14% came from fees and commissions income. The rest of its revenue came from trading gains (2%), and other miscellaneous income sources (4%).

Geographic Reach

Beyond its 1,000 branches in Turkey, Yapi Kredi has subsidiary-owned branches in Amsterdam, Moscow, Baku (in Azerbaijan), and an offshore branch in Bahrain.

Sales and Marketing

Yapi Kredi's retail banking arm serves individuals with up to T$500,000 (roughly $170,000) in financial assets and SMEs with annual turnovers of less than $10 million. Its commercial banking customers typically have annual turnover of more than $10 million, while its corporate banking customers are businesses with turnover of more than $100 million. The bank served more than 10 million customers in 2014.

Financial Performance

Note: Growth rates may differ after conversion to US dollars. This analysis uses financials from the company's annual report.

Yapi Kredi's revenue jumped 21% to T$15.9 billion ($6.8 billion) in 2014, mostly from higher interest income as its loan assets swelled by 26% (compared to sector growth of 18%), with growth in TL company, general purpose, and SME loans during the year. Its fee and commission income grew by 10%, despite new regulations, while deposits rose by 22%.

Even with revenue growth, the bank's net income fell 44% to T$2.06 billion ($887 million), mostly as its discontinued operations had generated some T$1.6 billion in 2013, but also because the bank incurred higher provisions for loan and other receivable impairments.

Yapi Kredi's operating cash levels jumped 72%, with operations using T$1.13 billion ($486 million) -- compared to T$3.97 billion ($1.86 billion) in 2013 -- mostly thanks to favorable working capital changes and higher cash earnings.

Strategy

Yapi Kredi has been moving toward digital banking channels that are quickly taking the industry by storm, allowing the bank to slow expensive branch-expansion plans and cut operating costs significantly while giving customers faster access to banking services.

To this end, the bank in 2015 planned to continue boosting its mobile and internet banking customer base (which reached 1.2 million and 4.2 million users at the end of 2014, respectively). It also would continue to expand its ATM network and self-service banking corners, implement video channel for digital banking customers, increase IVR self service usage for its call center, and divert more of its calls away from branches into a central location. Though its brick-and-mortar expansion plans have slowed compared to prior years, Yapi Kredi still added 54 physical branches to its network in 2014 to grow its business.

Yapi Kredi's aggressive expansion over the years has been effective at growing its customer base and overall business. Indeed, during 2014 the bank added 600,000 new customers to its business, growing its base about 2.7 times faster than in previous years and bringing its total customer count to 10.6 million.

The bank has been the market leader in credit card market share since 1988, and controlled nearly a 22% market share of the outstanding volume, nearly 20% of the issuing volume, and an 18% market share on the number of credit cards outstanding during 2014. Yapi Kredi was also the market leader in leasing and factoring, and was number two in mutual funds and brokerage categories.

Company Background

Yapi Kredi was previously controlled by Ã‡ukurova, one of Turkey's largest business congomerates. Ã‡ukurova fell to near-collapse in the aftermath of Turkey's economic crisis in 2001, and the group sold Yapi Kredi to KoÃ§bank owner KoÃ§ Financial Services (KFS) in 2005. The following year KFS merged Yapi Kredi and KoÃ§bank in what was the largest bank merger Turkey had seen. The combined group took the Yapi Kredi name.

KoÃ§ Financial Services (KFS), which is jointly owned by UniCredit and KoÃ§ Holding, owns 82% of Yapi Kredi, which was founded in 1944.

EXECUTIVES

Chief Executive Officer, Executive Director,
Gökhan Erün
Chief Operating Officer, Executive Director,
Marco Iannaccone
Chairman, Ali Y. Koc
Vice-Chairman, Niccolo Ubertalli
Director, Gianfranco Bisagni
Director, A. Umit Taftali
Director, Levent Cakiroglu
Director, Mirko D. G. Bianchi
Director, Carlo Vivaldi
Director, Ahmet F. Ashaboglu
Independent Director, Virma Sokmen
Independent Director, Ahmet Cimenoglu
Independent Director, Giovanna Villa
Independent Director, Wolfgang Schilk
Auditors : PwC Bagimsiz Denetim ve Serbest Muhasebeci Mali MÃ¼savirlik A.S.

LOCATIONS

HQ: Yapi Ve Kredi Bankasi AS
Yapi Kredi Plaza D Blok, Istanbul, Levent 34330
Phone: (90) 212 339 70 00   **Fax:** (90) 212 339 60 00
Web: www.yapikredi.com.tr

COMPETITORS

AKBANK TURK ANONIM SIRKETI
SHINSEI BANK, LIMITED
Shanghai Pudong Development Bank Co., Ltd.
TURKIYE GARANTI BANKASI ANONIM SIRKETI
TURKIYE IS BANKASI ANONIM SIRKETI

HISTORICAL FINANCIALS

Company Type: Public

Income Statement				FYE: December 31
	ASSETS ($mil)	NET INCOME ($mil)	INCOME AS % OF ASSETS	EMPLOYEES
12/23	63,029	2,300	3.6%	15,954
12/22	63,262	2,817	4.5%	16,339
12/21	58,376	784	1.3%	16,426
12/20	65,439	683	1.0%	16,938
12/19	69,101	604	0.9%	17,446
Annual Growth	(2.3%)	39.6%		(2.2%)

2023 Year-End Financials

Return on assets: 4.4%   Dividends
Return on equity: 44.5%   Yield: —
Long-term debt ($ mil.): —   Payout: 0.0%
No. of shares ($ mil.): 844,705   Market value ($ mil.): —
Sales ($ mil.): 11,054

Yorkshire Building Society

Yorkshire Building Society (YBS) provides mortgages, savings, personal loans, and brokerage services. One of the UK's largest mutually owned financial institutions, the group also offers insurance coverage including mortgage-payment policies and home and auto insurance. YBS's brands include the Chelsea Building Society, the Norwich & Peterborough Building Society, YBS Share Plans, and other subsidiaries including Accord Mortgages. It has around 3 million members and assets of more than £52.7 billion.

Operations
YBS is one of the largest building societies in the UK and as a mutual organization, is owned by and run for the benefit of members. It has no external shareholders. Its YBS Share Plans unit is one of the UK's largest specialist providers of tax-advantaged share plans.

Geographic Reach
Based in England, YBS has three main office locations in Bradford, Leeds, and Peterborough.

Company Background
The society merged with Chelsea Building Society in 2010 and with Norwich & Peterborough Building Society the following year; the two institutions continue to operate under their own brands.

The company was established in 1864 as the Huddersfield Equitable Permanent Benefit Building Society.

EXECUTIVES

Chief Executive Officer, Executive Director, Mike C. Regnier
Chief Financial Officer, Executive Director, Alasdair Lenman
Chief Operating Officer, Executive Director, Stephen C. White
Distribution Chief Customer Officer, Charles Canning
Chief Internal Audit Officer, Suzanne P. Clark
Chief People Officer, Orlagh Hunt
Chief Commercial Officer, David Morris
Chief Risk Officer, Richard Wells
Chief Strategy and Ventures Officer, Greg Willmott
Secretary, Simon Waite
Chairman, Non-Executive Director, John R. Heaps
Independent Non-Executive Director, Neeta A. K. Atkar
Independent Non-Executive Director, Guy L. T. Bainbridge
Independent Non-Executive Director, Alison E. Hutchinson
Independent Non-Executive Director, Gordon R. Ireland
Vice-Chairman, Senior Independent Non-Executive Director, Non-Executive Director, Mark A. Pain
Independent Non-Executive Director, Guy P. C. Parsons
Auditors: PricewaterhouseCoopers LLP

LOCATIONS
HQ: Yorkshire Building Society
Yorkshire House, Yorkshire Drive, Bradford BD5 8LJ
Phone: —
Web: www.ybs.co.uk

PRODUCTS/OPERATIONS
2015 Sales

	% of total
Interest receivable and similar income	96
Fees and commissions receivable	3
Other operating income	1
Total	100

COMPETITORS
COVENTRY BUILDING SOCIETY
KEYCORP
LIVERPOOL VICTORIA FRIENDLY SOCIETY LTD
NATWEST GROUP PLC
NEWCASTLE BUILDING SOCIETY
Nationwide Building Society
Nordea Bank AB
Svenska Handelsbanken AB
THE HANOVER INSURANCE GROUP INC
ZIONS BANCORPORATION

HISTORICAL FINANCIALS
Company Type: Public

Income Statement				FYE: December 31
	ASSETS ($mil)	NET INCOME ($mil)	INCOME AS % OF ASSETS	EMPLOYEES
12/21	71,054	346	0.5%	3,249
12/20	65,411	168	0.3%	3,344
12/19	58,471	170	0.3%	3,536
12/18	54,970	191	0.3%	3,906
12/17	56,792	168	0.3%	4,220
Annual Growth	5.8%	19.8%	—	(6.3%)

2021 Year-End Financials
Return on assets: 0.5%
Return on equity: 0.6%
Long-term debt ($ mil.): —
No. of shares ($ mil.): —
Sales ($ mil.): 1,413
Dividends
Yield: —
Payout: 0.0%
Market value ($ mil.): —

YPF SA

YPF is Argentina's leading energy company, operating a fully integrated oil and gas chain with leading market positions across the domestic upstream, downstream and gas and power segments. The company produces fuels, petrochemicals and lubricants at its La Plata, Luján de Cuyo and Plaza Huincul industrial complexes, offering a wide range of products, with a strong business presence in the retail, agriculture, industrial and LPG market sectors. It also built a logistics network of 2,400 trucks to supply its 1,600-plus service stations across the country. The company was founded in 1920s. Majority of its sales were generated in Argentina.

Operations
The company operates through three segments: Downstream (some 60% of sales), Upstream (about 30%), and Gas and Power (around 10%), Central Administration and Others generated the rest.

Its Upstream operations consist of the exploration, development and production of crude oil, natural gas and NGLs. The Downstream operations include the refining, marketing, transportation and distribution of oil and a wide range of petroleum products, petroleum derivatives, petrochemicals, LPG and biofuels. Additionally, through its Gas and Power business segment, we are active in the gas separation, natural gas distribution and power generation sectors both directly and through its investments in several affiliated companies.

Almost all of the company sales were generated from the sales of goods and services.

Geographic Reach
Headquartered in Buenos Aires, Argentina, over 85% of the company's petrochemical sales (including propylene) were made in the domestic market, while it exported the remainder to Mercosur countries, the rest of Latin America, Europe and the US.

In terms of sales, about 90% of sales were generated from Argentina.

Sales and Marketing
The company's trading division sells refined products and crude oil to international customers and purchases crude oil from domestic oil companies.

Financial Performance
For the past three years, YPF's performance has increased year-over-year with 2022 as its highest performing year over the period.

Revenues in 2022 increased by $5.1 billion to $18.7 billion, as compared to 2021's revenues of $13.7 billion.

For fiscal year end 2022, the company recorded a net income of $3.1 billion, as compared to the prior year's net income of $715 million.

The company's cash at the end of 2022 increased to $773 million. Operating activities generated $5.7 billion to the coffers. Investing activities and financing activities used $4 billion and $1.2 billion, respectively. Main cash uses were for acquisitions of property, plant, and equipment and intangible assets, as well as payments of loans.

Strategy
Its strategic pillars are:

Discipline in the allocation of capital, focused on the development of its unconventional hydrocarbon acreage with competitive advantages, generating value in a sustainable way;

Efficiency in costs and processes in all business segments, and particularly in the Vaca Muerta formation, with the aim of ensuring resilience even in low price scenarios;

Rationalization of the conventional asset portfolio, prioritizing profitability through the incorporation of technology and innovation to gain efficiency;

Adaptation of refineries to facilitate

greater shale processing and the expected evolution of the quality of fuels to be demanded by customers; and

Reduction of the company's specific CO2 emissions and the development of renewable energies through its participation in YPF Energía Eléctrica S.A. ("YPF EE"), as part of our commitment to sustainability.

HISTORY

An Argentine government team discovered oil while drilling for water in 1907. Determined to keep the oil under Argentine control, the government formed the world's first state-owned oil company, Direccion Nacional de los Yacimientos Petroliferos Fiscales (YPF), in 1922 to operate the newly discovered field. However, YPF lacked drilling equipment, capital, and staff; it found that the only way to increase domestic oil production was to allow in foreign oil companies. Although YPF's activities ebbed in the 1920s, it made major oil discoveries across Argentina in the 1930s.

A major turning point came with Juan Perón's rise to power in 1945. Perón extended state control over broad sections of the economy, including oil. He nationalized British and US oil holdings and gave YPF a virtual monopoly. In 1945 YPF accounted for 68% of the country's oil production; by 1955 it produced 84%. The company discovered a huge gas field two years later in western Argentina, making YPF -- and Argentina -- a major gas producer.

However, YPF's production failed to keep pace with the demands of the growing economy, and imports still dominated Argentina's oil market. Over the next 30 years, YPF experienced radical swings in government policy as ultranationalist military regimes alternated with liberal, reformist governments. YPF grew into a bloated and inefficient conglomerate. Between 1982 and 1989, despite a World Bank-financed program to modernize YPF's refineries, the firm lost more than $6 billion.

In 1989 Carlos Menem became Argentina's president, and YPF was privatized as part of his economic reform plan to cut loose 50 state-owned companies. To prepare YPF for its IPO, the president brought in a former head of Baker Hughes, José Estenssoro, to draft a plan for privatization. The plan was so impressive that Menem gave him the job as CEO of the company in 1990. Estenssoro cut 87% of YPF's staff and sold off $2 billion of noncore assets. By 1993 YPF was profitable and went public as YPF Sociedad Anónima, selling 45% of its shares to raise $3 billion.

A year later YPF began expanding beyond Argentina by shipping crude oil to Chile through a new 300-mile pipeline. It bought woebegone Texas oil company Maxus Energy in 1995 and turned it around at great expense. Estenssoro and three other YPF executives died in a plane crash that year; in 1997 YPF selected Roberto Monti, who had headed Maxus, to serve as its CEO.

In 1997 YPF and Astra C.A.P.S.A. -- in which Spanish oil firm Repsol had a controlling stake -- jointly purchased a 67% stake in Mexpetrol Argentina (an affiliate of Mexican state oil company PEMEX). Repsol was aggressively moving overseas. In 1998 Repsol lobbied hard to buy part of YPF; Spain's King Juan Carlos himself phoned up Menem to promote Repsol's interests.

A year later the Argentine government auctioned off a 15% stake in YPF to Repsol for $2 billion; Repsol then bought another 83% of the company for $13.2 billion. Repsol became Repsol YPF, while Monti was named VC and COO.

Monti retired the next year, after Repsol YPF increased its stake in YPF from 98% to 99%.

EXECUTIVES

Chief Executive Officer, Daniel Cristian Gonzalez Casartelli
Controller, Diego Martin Pandi
Chief Financial Officer, Luis Miguel Sas
Operations & Transformation Executive Vice President, Carlos Alberto Alfonsi
Corporate Affairs Executive Vice President, Marketing Executive Vice President, Communications Executive Vice President, Santiago Naranjo Alvarez
Strategy Vice President, Business Development Vice President, Business Development & Project Architecture Vice President, Sergio Fabian Giorgi
Upstream Legal Affairs Vice President, Legal Affairs Vice President, German Fernandez Lahore
Strategy Vice President, Business Development Vice President, Supply Chain Vice President, Fernando Pablo Giliberti
Chairman, Director, Guillermo Emilio Nielsen
Director, Norberto Alfredo Bruno
Director, Horacio Oscar Forchiassin
Director, Ignacio Perincioli
Director, Pedro Martin Kerchner Tomba
Director, Maria Cristina Tchintian
Director, Ramiro Gerardo Manzanal
Director, Hector Pedro Recalde
Director, Celso Alejandro Jaque
Director, Lorena Sanchez
Director, Arturo Carlos Giovenco
Auditors : Deloitte & Co. S.A.

LOCATIONS

HQ: YPF SA
  Macacha Guemes 515, Buenos Aires C1106BKK
Phone: (54) 11 5441 3500   Fax: (54) 11 5441 3726
Web: www.ypf.com

2016 Sales

	% of total
Argentina	92
Mercosur and associated countries	4
Europe	1
Rest of the world	3
Total	100

PRODUCTS/OPERATIONS

2016 Sales

	% of total
Downstream	52
Upstream	36
Gas and Power	9
Central Administration and Others	3
Total	100

COMPETITORS

CNOOC Petroleum North America ULC
GAZPROM NEFT, PAO
Gran Tierra Energy Inc
HARVEST NATURAL RESOURCES, INC.
HOVENSA, LLC
PHX MINERALS INC.
Petroleo Brasileiro S A Petrobras
Petróleos Mexicanos, E.P.E.
RANGE RESOURCES CORPORATION
SAUDI ARABIAN OIL COMPANY

HISTORICAL FINANCIALS
Company Type: Public

Income Statement — FYE: December 31

	REVENUE ($mil)	NET INCOME ($mil)	NET PROFIT MARGIN	EMPLOYEES
12/21	12,381	2	0.0%	21,321
12/20	7,952	(827)	—	0
12/19	11,333	(569)	—	22,932
12/18	11,565	1,024	8.9%	21,314
12/17	13,177	643	4.9%	0
Annual Growth	(1.5%)	(75.0%)		

2021 Year-End Financials

Debt ratio: 0.3%
Return on equity: —
Cash ($ mil.): 610
Current Ratio: 1.19
Long-term debt ($ mil.): 6,530
No. of shares ($ mil.): 393
Dividends
  Yield: —
  Payout: 0.0%
Market value ($ mil.): 1,502

	STOCK PRICE ($) FY Close	P/E High/Low	PER SHARE ($) Earnings	Dividends	Book Value
12/21	3.82	8 4	0.01	0.00	20.80
12/20	4.70	— —	(2.11)	0.00	20.46
12/19	11.58	— —	(1.45)	0.22	23.04
12/18	13.39	0 0	2.61	0.08	24.24
12/17	22.91	1 0	1.64	0.09	20.18
Annual Growth	(36.1%)		(75.1%)	—	0.8%

Yue Yuen Industrial (Holdings) Ltd.

Yue Yuen Industrial has two businesses, but only one focus: shoes. The company is one of the world's top manufacturers of branded footwear for international giants adidas, New Balance, Nike, Reebok, and Timberland, among others. It produces more than 322 million pairs of shoes annually, including athletic and casual shoes and sandals; it also makes components such as soles. In addition, Yue Yuen operates one of the largest networks of retail stores selling shoes and apparel across Greater China with nearly 5,885 directly-operated stores and approximately 3,950 sub-distributor stores. The US is the company's largest market, accounting for more 30% of revenue.

Operations
Yue Yuen generates about 45% of its revenue from its athletic shoe manufacturing operations, with around 10% from casual/outdoor shoes, and soles and components and sports sandals for about 5% combined. About 40% from retail while a small portion generated from apparel wholesale. Its core business include footwear manufacturing which is predominately athletic and casual/outdoor shoes and Pou Sheng for sportswear retail & sports services in the Greater China Region.

Geographic Reach
Hong Kong-based Yue Yuen generates more than 30% of its revenue from the US, Europe gives in nearly 30%, followed by Mainland China at approximately 15%, and the rest comes from other countries.

Sales and Marketing
The company partners with third party platforms such as T-Mall, JD, Vipshop, among others, as well as WeChat stores and shopping mall platforms.

Financial Performance
The company's revenue increased by 4% to $10.1 billion compared to the prior year, with $9.7 billion. The increase was primarily due to a 15% increase in the company's Pou Sheng operations.

Profit for the year decreased by 2% to $300.5 million in 2019.

Company Background
Founded in 1988, Yue Yuen is majority owned by Taiwanese athletic material maker Pou Chen.

EXECUTIVES

Chairman, Chi Neng Tsai
Managing Director, Director, David N. F. Tsai
General Manager, Director, Tai Yu Kuo
General Manager, Director, Chin Chu Lu
General Manager, Director, Sung Yen Kung
Executive Director, Director, Lu Min Chan
Executive Director, Director, Steve I Nan Li
Executive Director, Director, Patty Pei Chun Tsai
Executive Director, Director, Li Lien Kuo
Executive Director, Director, Shao Wu Lee
Executive Vice President, Chun Hui Yang
Executive Vice President, Wen Bin Hsiu
Executive Vice President, Nai Kun Tsai
Executive Vice President, Hsin Min Cheng
Executive Vice President, Pin Huang Lin
Vice President, Nai Chi Tsai
Vice President, Jerry Cheng Tien Lin
Vice President, Juei Chung Liu
Vice President, Ching Po Chiang
Vice President, Chin Yuan Huang
Vice President, Wen Hsien Shao
Vice President, Hsin Chien Chen
Senior Executive Manager, Teng Chen
Senior Executive Manager, Nai Yun Tsai
Senior Executive Manager, Tien Tzu Wu
Senior Executive Manager, Chen Chi Wu
Senior Executive Manager, Chang Li Lai
Senior Executive Manager, Chih Wen Chao
Senior Executive Manager, Te Shan Chin
Senior Executive Manager, Yung Hung Hsu
Senior Executive Manager, Tsai Yuan Hsiao
Senior Executive Manager, Cheng Chuan Lee
Senior Executive Manager, Tsung Ming Chou
Senior Executive Manager, Chia Li Chang
Senior Executive Manager, Chine Huei Chin
Senior Executive Manager, Shih Chung Chen
Senior Executive Manager, Shu Hua Cheng
Senior Executive Manager, Hung Pei Wu
Treasury Director, Finance Director, Dickens Chi Ming Chau
Senior Accounting Manager, Sai Kin Chow
Senior Manager, Christina Suet Fong Yau
Legal Corporate Secretary, Legal Head, William Lok Ming Ng
Investor Relations Head, Jerry Shum
Director, John J. D. Sy
Director, Len Yu Liu
Director, Yee Sik Leung
Director, Ming Fu Huang
Auditors : Deloitte Touche Tohmatsu

LOCATIONS

HQ: Yue Yuen Industrial (Holdings) Ltd.
22nd Floor, C-Bons International Center, 108 Wai Yip Street, Kwun Tong, Kowloon,
Phone: —
Web: www.yueyuen.com

2018 Sales

	$ mil.	% of total
People's Republic of China	4,186	43
US	2,177	22
Europe	1,774	18
Asia (ex. China)	1,014	11
Other	544	6
Total	9,695	100

PRODUCTS/OPERATIONS

2018 Sales

	$ mil.	% of total
Manufacturing		
Athletic shoes	4,268	44
Casual/Outdoor shoes	1,031	11
Soles and components and other	480	5
Sports sandals	92	1
Retail	3,794	39
Other	30	-
Total	9,695	100

2018 Sales

	$ mil.	% of total
Manufacturing business	5,881	61
Retailing Business	3,814	39
Total	9,695	100

HISTORICAL FINANCIALS
Company Type: Public

Income Statement — FYE: December 31

	REVENUE ($mil)	NET INCOME ($mil)	NET PROFIT MARGIN	EMPLOYEES
12/22	8,970	296	3.3%	310,000
12/21	8,533	115	1.3%	317,200
12/20	8,444	(90)	—	298,500
12/19	10,105	300	3.0%	347,100
12/18	9,695	307	3.2%	348,000
Annual Growth	(1.9%)	(0.9%)	—	(2.8%)

2022 Year-End Financials
Debt ratio: 18.1% No. of shares ($ mil.): 1,612
Return on equity: 7.1% Dividends
Cash ($ mil.): 1,018 Yield: —
Current Ratio: 2.07 Payout: 182.8%
Long-term debt ($ mil.): 928 Market value ($ mil.): 11,261

	STOCK PRICE ($) FY Close	P/E High/Low		PER SHARE ($) Earnings	Dividends	Book Value
12/22	6.99	48	27	0.18	0.34	2.60
12/21	8.37	181	110	0.07	0.20	2.54
12/20	10.69	—	—	(0.06)	0.40	2.42
12/19	14.46	94	69	0.19	0.88	2.54
12/18	15.68	128	67	0.19	0.88	2.55
Annual Growth	(18.3%)	—	—	(0.4%)	(21.3%)	0.4%

Zte Corp.

ZTE Corporation is one of the world's leading listed manufacturers of integrated communications equipment and providers of global integrated communications and information solutions dedicated to the provision of ICT products and solutions that satisfy the needs of customers, integrating design, development, production, sales and services with a special focus on carriers' networks, government and corporate business and consumer business. The company provides innovative technologies and integrated solutions, its portfolio spans all series of wireless, wireline, devices and professional telecommunications services. With business presence in more than 160 countries and regions, the majority of its revenue comes from China.

Operations
ZTE organized into business units based on its products and services and has three reportable operating segments: Carriers' network, Consumer Business, and Government and Corporate Business.

Carriers' network is focused on meeting carries' requirements in network evolution with the provision of wireless access, wireline access, bearer systems, core networks, server and storage and other innovative technologies and product solutions. The segment accounts for about 65% of the company's total revenue.

The Consumer Business is focused on bringing experience in smart devices to customers while also catering to the requirements of industry and corporate clients through the development, production and sale of products such as home information terminal, smart phones, mobile Internet terminals, innovative fusion terminals, as well as the provision of related software application and value-added services. The segment accounts for about 25% of the company's total revenue.

The Government and Corporate Business is focused on meeting requirements of government and corporate clients, providing informatisation solutions for the government and corporations through the application of products such as "communications networks, IOT, Big Data and cloud computing". The segment accounts for more than 10% of the company's total revenue.

Geographic Reach
ZTE's home country, China, accounts for about 80% of its total revenue, while Europe, America, and Oceania generate almost 15%, Asia (excluding China) brings in more than 10%, and Africa accounts for the remaining revenue.

Overall, The company provides products and services in more than 160 countries and regions.

Sales and Marketing
ZTE serves global telecom operators, government and enterprise customers, and consumers.

Financial Performance
Company revenue for fiscal 2022 increased to RMB123.0 million compared from the prior year with RMB114.5 million. The increase was primarily due to higher revenues in principal business accompanied by slight increase in other business.

Net income for fiscal 2022 increased to RMB7.8 million compared from the prior year with RMB7.0 million. The increase was primarily due to higher revenues and lower income tax offsetting the increase in operating expenses.

Cash held by the company at the end of fiscal 2022 increased to RMB47.1 million. Cash provided by operations and financing activities were RMB7.6 billion and RMB1.5 billion, respectively. Cash used for investing activities was RMB1.3 billion, mainly for acquisitions of investments.

EXECUTIVES

Product Research & Development Executive Vice President, Product Research & Development Supervisory Committee Chairman, Daxiong Xie
Staff Supervisor, Xiaoyue Xia
Staff Supervisor, Quancai Li
Chief Financial Officer, Board Secretary (Acting), Ying Li
President, Executive Director, Ziyang Xu
Supervisor, Xiaofeng Shang
Supervisor, Sufang Zhang
Board Secretary, Jianzhong Ding
Independent Non-executive Director, Manli Cai
Director, Non-executive Director, Rong Fang
Director, Executive Director, Junying Gu
Director, Non-executive Director, Buqing Li
Chairman, Zixue Li
Independent Non-executive Director, Jundong Wu
Director, Non-executive Director, Weimin Zhu
Independent Non-executive Director, Jiansheng Zhuang
Auditors : Ernst & Young Hua Ming LLP

LOCATIONS
HQ: Zte Corp.
ZTE Plaza, Keji Road South, Hi-Tech Industrial Park, Nanshan District, Shenzhen, Guangdong Province 518057
Phone: (86) 755 26770282   **Fax:** (86) 755 26770286
Web: www.zte.com.cn

PRODUCTS/OPERATIONS
2015 Sales

	% of total
Carriers' networks	57
Consumer business	32
Government and corporate business	11
Total	100

2015 Sales

Asia	% of total
PRC (People's Republic of China)	53
Other countries	15
Europe, the Americas and Oceania	25
Africa	7
Total	100

COMPETITORS
AVIAT NETWORKS, INC.
CALAMP CORP.
COMMSCOPE HOLDING COMPANY, INC.
COMTECH TELECOMMUNICATIONS CORP.
HARMONIC INC.
Huawei Investment & Holding Co., Ltd.
LG Electronics Inc.
MAXLINEAR, INC.
STEEL CONNECT, INC.
VIASAT, INC.

HISTORICAL FINANCIALS
Company Type: Public

Income Statement   FYE: December 31

	REVENUE ($mil)	NET INCOME ($mil)	NET PROFIT MARGIN	EMPLOYEES
12/22	17,822	1,171	6.6%	0
12/21	18,038	1,073	5.9%	0
12/20	15,511	651	4.2%	0
12/19	13,040	739	5.7%	0
12/18	12,432	(1,015)	—	0
Annual Growth	9.4%	—	—	—

2022 Year-End Financials
Debt ratio: 3.7%   No. of shares ($ mil.): —
Return on equity: 14.6%   Dividends
Cash ($ mil.): 8,167   Yield: —
Current Ratio: 1.76   Payout: 0.0%
Long-term debt ($ mil.): 5,091   Market value ($ mil.): —

Zurich Insurance Group AG

Active in nearly every country globally, Zurich Insurance Group is a major global provider of property and casualty and life insurance. Serving customers that include individuals, small businesses, and mid-sized and large companies, as well as multinational corporations, the company provides a wide range of products and services in more than 210 countries and territories. Its life insurance division offers life and health insurance, annuities, endowments, and other investment products. Zurich's Farmers Group business includes all reinsurance assumed from the Farmers Exchanges by the Group. It generates most of its sales from North America. The group was founded in 1872.

Operations
Zurich operates through five segments: Property & Casualty, Life regions, Farmers, Group Functions and Operations and Non-Core Businesses.

The Farmers provides, through Farmers Group, Inc. (FGI) and its subsidiaries, provides certain non-claims services and ancillary services to the Farmers Exchanges as attorney-in-fact. FGI receives fee income for providing services to the Farmers Exchanges, which are owned by their policyholders and managed by Farmers Group, Inc., a wholly owned subsidiary of the group. This segment also includes all reinsurance assumed from the Farmers Exchanges by the group. Farmers Exchanges are prominent writers of personal and small commercial lines of business in the US. In addition, this segment includes the activities of Farmers Life, a writer of individual life insurance business in the US.

Property & Casualty, offers insurance and reinsurance in Europe, Africa, North America, Latin America, and the Asia Pacific region. It offers motor, home, and commercial insurance and services to individuals and small to large businesses.

The Life segment also operates globally, offering comprehensive range of life and health insurance products for individuals and groups, including annuities, endowment and term insurance, unit-linked and investment-oriented products, as well as full private health, supplemental health and long-term care insurance.

Group Functions and Operations comprise the group's Holding and financing. Certain alternative investment positions not allocated to business operating segments are included within Holding and Financing. In addition, Group Functions and Operations includes operational technical governance activities relating to technology, underwriting, claims, actuarial and pricing.

Non-Core Businesses include insurance and reinsurance businesses that the group does not consider core to its operations and that are therefore mostly managed to achieve a beneficial run-off. Non-Core Businesses are mainly situated in the US, Bermuda and the Europe.

Geographic Reach

Headquartered in Zurich, Switzerland, Zurich has a strong position in North America and Europe as a provider of insurance to individuals, commercial operations and global corporate customers, with growing positions in Asia Pacific and Latin America. It generates about 35% of gross written premiums from North America. Europe, Middle East and Africa account for more than 45%, Latin America brings in about 10% and Asia Pacific represents around 10%. The company provides a wide range of property and casualty, and life insurance products and services in more than 210 countries and territories.

Sales and Marketing

All of Zurich's operating segments use a mixture of distribution channels to promote their products. The company has affiliated agents, and it also uses independent brokers, employee benefits consultants, financial advisors, bank representatives, travel providers, and car dealerships to promote its policies. Zurich markets its products to individual, small businesses, commercial, and corporate customers.

HISTORY

The roots of Zurich Financial Services stretch back to the 1872 founding of a reinsurer for Switzerland Transport Insurance. The company soon branched out into accident, travel, and workers' compensation insurance and in 1875 it changed its name to Transport and Accident Insurance plc Zurich to reflect the changes. It then expanded into Berlin (the jumping-off point for its expansion into Scandinavia and Russia) and Stuttgart, Germany. The company exited marine lines in 1880; it later left the reinsurance business and expanded into liability insurance; in 1894 it changed its name to Zurich General Accident and Liability Insurance.

In 1912 Zurich crossed the Atlantic, expanding operations into the US. It agreed in 1925 to provide insurance for Ford cars at favorable terms. Zurich's business was hard hit during the war years of the late 1930s and 1940s. In 1955 the company changed its name to Zurich Insurance.

Starting in the 1960s, Zurich began buying other insurers, including Alpina (1965, Switzerland), Agrippina (1969, Germany), and Maryland Casualty Group (1989, US). It also bought the property liability operations of American General.

The company shifted its strategy in the early 1990s, expanding into what it deemed underrepresented markets in the UK and the US. Being big wasn't enough; Zurich needed to find a focus. It also jettisoned such marginal or unprofitable business lines as commercial fire insurance in Germany.

In 1995 Zurich bought struggling Chicago-based asset manager Kemper and in 1997 bought lackluster mutual fund manager Scudder Stevens & Clark, forming Scudder Kemper. That year it also bought failed Hong Kong investment bank Peregrine Investment Holdings.

Zurich merged in 1998 with the financial services businesses of B.A.T Industries, formerly known as the British-American Tobacco Co., created in 1902 as a joint venture between UK-based Imperial Tobacco and American Tobacco. As public disapproval of smoking grew in the 1970s, British-American Tobacco began diversifying; it changed its name to B.A.T Industries in 1976 and moved into insurance. In 1984 it rescued UK insurer Eagle Star from a hostile offer by German insurance giant Allianz. The next year it bought Hambro Life Assurance, renaming it Allied Dunbar. Moving into the large US market in 1988, B.A.T bought Farmers Insurance Group.

While B.A.T battled the antismoking army of the 1990s, the insurance industry struggled with stagnant growth. In 1997 Europe's largest insurance firms were named as defendants in class action lawsuits that sought recovery for unpaid claims on Holocaust-era insurance policies. In 1998 Zurich became a founding member of the International Commission on Holocaust Era Insurance Claims (ICHEIC).

Also in 1998 Zurich and B.A.T's insurance units merged to create Zurich Financial Services. The firm reshuffled some of its holdings and sold Eagle Star Reinsurance. In 1999 Zurich spun off its real estate holdings into PSP Swiss Property and, at the turn of the century, it focused on expansion, buying the new business of insurer Abbey Life, which it merged into Allied Dunbar. In 2000, the holding companies formed to own Zurich (Zurich Allied and Allied Zurich) were merged into the firm.

EXECUTIVES

General Insurance Chief Executive Officer, Mario Greco
Chief Information and Digital Officer, Ericson Chan
Chief Financial Officer, George Quinn
Chief Risk Officer, Chief Information Officer, Peter Giger
Chairman, Michel M Lies
Vice-Chairman, Christoph Franz
Director, Joan Lordi Amble
Director, Catherine Bessant
Director, Jasmin Staiblin
Director, Monica Machler
Director, Michael Halbherr
Director, Barry Stowe
Director, Alison Carnwath
Director, Kishore Mahbubani
Director, Sabine Keller-Busse
Auditors : Ernst & Young Ltd

LOCATIONS

HQ: Zurich Insurance Group AG
Mythenquai 2, Zurich 8002
Phone: (41) 0 625 25 25   **Fax:** (41) 0 625 35 55
Web: www.zurich.com

PRODUCTS/OPERATIONS

Selected Subsidiaries
Farmers Group, Inc. (property/casualty, US)
    21st Century Insurance Company (property/casualty, US)
    Farmers New World Life Insurance Company (life insurance, US)
    Foremost Insurance Company (specialty insurance, US)
    Bristol West Holdings, Inc. (specialty insurance, US)
Zurich American Insurance Company (general insurance, US)
Zurich Insurance plc (general insurance, UK)
Zurich International Life Limited (life insurance, UK)

COMPETITORS

AMERICAN INTERNATIONAL GROUP, INC.
AMUNDI
AVIVA PLC
Bâloise Holding AG
Credit Suisse Group AG
LIBERTY MUTUAL HOLDING COMPANY INC.
LafargeHolcim Ltd
RESOLUTION LIFE AAPH LIMITED
Swiss Life Holding AG
Swiss Re AG

HISTORICAL FINANCIALS

Company Type: Public

Income Statement				FYE: December 31
	ASSETS ($mil)	NET INCOME ($mil)	INCOME AS % OF ASSETS	EMPLOYEES
12/22	377,782	4,603	1.2%	0
12/21	435,826	5,202	1.2%	0
12/20	439,299	3,834	0.9%	55,089
12/19	404,688	4,147	1.0%	55,369
12/18	395,342	3,716	0.9%	53,535
Annual Growth	(1.1%)	5.5%	—	—

2022 Year-End Financials

Return on assets: 1.1%   Dividends
Return on equity: 14.2%   Yield: —
Long-term debt ($ mil.): —   Payout: 7.5%
No. of shares ($ mil.): 147   Market value ($ mil.): 7,059
Sales ($ mil.): 41,750

	STOCK PRICE ($) FY Close	P/E High/Low		PER SHARE ($) Earnings	Dividends	Book Value
12/22	47.85	2	1	30.77	2.33	180.54
12/21	44.00	1	1	34.66	2.17	255.45
12/20	42.22	2	1	25.56	0.13	257.77
12/19	41.00	1	1	27.69	1.90	236.42
12/18	29.81	1	1	24.83	1.86	205.00
Annual Growth	12.6%	—	—	5.5%	5.8%	(3.1%)

Hoover's Handbook of World Business

Executive Index

Index Of Executives

A

Aamund, Marie-Louise 216
Aasheim, Hilde Merete 452
Abaitua, Asis Canales 300
Abascal, Juan 504
Abaza, Hussein 172
Abbott, John 429
Abbott, Michael 674
Abdool-Samad, Tasneem 8
Abdullah, A. 9
Abe, Atsushi 263
Abe, Jun 287
Abe, Kazuhiro 583
Abe, Masanori 452
Abe, Noriaki 292
Abe, Shinichi 545
Abe, Yasunari 403
Abe, Yasuyuki 583
Abecasis, Joao 137
Abecasis, Teresa 265
Abelman, Jerome B. 122
Abgrall-Teslyk, Karine 363
Abi-Karam, Leslie 624
Abou-Zeid, Amani 172
Aboumrad, Carlos Hajj 83
Aboumrad, Daniel Hajj 43
Abraham, Joseph 172
Abraham, A. 9
Abramov, Alexander 243
Abramov, Nikolay 413
Abrera, Emily 617
Abrial, Francois 362
Abt, Roland 601
Abuzaakouk, Anas 102
Achard, Stephane 422
Achleitner, Ann-Kristin 418
Achleitner, Paul 103
Achten, Dominik von 279
Ackarapolpanich, Nipaporn 128
Acker, Laurens van den 502
Ackermann, Christina M. 101
Ackland, Michael 618
Acosta, Jose Humberto 85
Acut, Sabino E. 107
Adachi, Kazuyuki 636
Adachi, Tamaki 527
Adamo, Emma 65
Adams, Ken 71
Adams, Paul 516
Adamson, Clive 168
Adjahi, Isabelle 678
Adriansyah, Ririek 490
Adt, Katrin 143
Advaithi, Revathi 252
Aebischer, Patrick 432
Aellig, Matthias 600
Aeschlimann, Daniela 597
Aeschlimann, Raynald 597
Agarwal, Anil 656
Agarwal, Vikram 197
Ageborg, Katarina 66

Agg, Andy 424
Agius, Eric P. 514
Agnefjall, Peter 357
Agnelli, Andrea 243
Agnelli, Andrea 579
Agogue, Christophe 233
Agon, Jean-Paul 362
Agrawal, Saurabh Mahesh 607
Aguilar, Alvaro Gomez-Trenor 170
Aguirre, Ubaldo Jose 621
Agustsson, Magnus 198
Agutter, Giles 316
Aguzin, Alejandro Nicolas 396
Ahmadjian, Christina 427
Ahmadjian, Christina 585
Ahmadjian, Christina L. 57
Ahmed, B. 9
Ahn, Michael 370
Ahn, Nadine 519
Ahn, Skott 370
Aho, Esko 258
Aho, Esko Tapani 535
Ahola, Kari 450
Ahrendts, Angela J. 677
Ahuja, Sanjiv 661
Ai, Sachiko 461
Aigrain, Jacques 380
Aigrain, Jacques 677
Aihara, Risa 327
Aikawa, Yoshiro 602
Aila, Minna 429
Aivazis, Ioannis 281
Aizpiri, Arturo Gonzalo 504
Ajarti, Mourad 172
Akaishi, Mamoru 438
Akar, Laszlo 414
Akasaka, Yuji 326
Akbari, Homaira 84
Akehurst, John H. 467
Akerstrom, Carina 596
Akimov, Andrei I. 453
Akishita, Soichi 527
Akiya, Fumio 552
Akiyama, Katsusada 346
Akiyama, Kohei 434
Akiyama, Koichi 505
Akiyama, Masato 546
Akiyama, Sakie 327
Akiyama, Sakie 403
Akiyama, Sakie 468
Akiyama, Sakie 572
Akiyama, Satoru 346
Akiyama, Yasuji 361
Akkol, Ozgur Burak 353
Aklundh, Susanne Pahlen 61
Akman, Matthew 226
Akrasanee, Narongchai 23
Akten, Mahmut 646
Al-Essa, Tarek Sultan 216
Al-Haffar, Maher 144
Al-Hail, Salah 496
Al-Jarf, Mulham 414

Al-Saleh, Adel 125
Alahuhta, Matti 7
Alahuhta, Matti 354
Alahuhta, Matti 664
Alamina, Marcos Manuel Herreria 481
Alanis, David Penaloza 273
Albaisa, Alfonso 444
Albertoni, Walter Luis Bernardes 80
Albertson, Tim 32
Albrecht, Michael 261
Albuquerque, Isabella Saboya de 655
Aldach, Rene 279
Aldana, Denise Martinez 52
Aldott, Zoltan 414
Alessandro, Gianpaolo 651
Alexander, Gregor 574
Alexanderson, Marcus 506
Alexopoulos, Gergios 281
Alfonsi, Carlos Alberto 686
Alisov, Vladimir Ivanovich 266
Allain, Bernard 116
Allaire, Martin 400
Allak, Hasan 183
Allan, Graham 65
Allan, John 622
Allan, M. Elyse 124
Allatt, Graham 471
Allaway, Patrick 92
Allen, Charles 78
Allen, Jennifer 244
Allen, Nicholas Charles 167
Allen, Nicholas Charles 366
Allen, Simon 44
Allen, Steve 511
Allton, Nicholas 92
Alm, Jessica 528
Alm, Roger 664
Almaguer, Everardo Elizondo 144
Almaguer, Everardo Elizondo 273
Almanzar, Ben 171
Almeida, Andrea Marques de 479
Almeida, David 48
Almeida, Edmar de 265
Almeida, Flavia Buarque de 120
Almeida, Flavia Buarque de 649
Alonso, Jose Ramon de Jesus Martinez 171
Alonso, Joseph Anthony M. 93
Alonso, Mercedes 429
Alpen, Joachim 563
Alqueres, Jose Luiz 649
Alsbjerg, Thomas 657
Alshehhi, A. Z. 9
Altafim, Eric Andre 322
Althoff, Sven 277
Altman, Kobi 302
Altmayer, Dorothee 285
Alvarez, Ana Isabel Fernandez 386
Alvarez, Jose Antonio Alvarez 82
Alvarez, Jose Antonio Alvarez 84
Alvarez, Pilar Lopez 308
Alvarez, Santiago Naranjo 686

Amado, Nuno Manuel da Silva 86
Amaimo, Stephanie A. 256
Amamiya, Toshitake 345
Amano, Hiromasa 342
Amano, Reiko 219
Amano, Yutaka 193
Amatayakul, Parnsiree 85
Ambani, Mukesh Dhirubhai 499
Ambani, Nita M. 499
Ambe, Kazushi 572
Amble, Joan Lordi 689
Amend, Michael R. 270
Aminoach, Reem 302
Ammann, Erich 537
Amore, John J. 242
Amorim, Marta 265
Amorim, Paula 265
Amranand, Piyasvasti 492
Amsden, Mark 317
Amunátegui, Domingo Cruzat 228
An, Cong Hui 267
An, Qing Heng 267
Anand, Krishnan 122
Anapa, Pinar 29
Anayama, Makoto 321
Ancira, Carlos Eduardo Aldrete 171
Ancira, Carlos Eduardo Aldrete 254
Andersen, Eric C. 49
Andersen, Hans S. 137
Andersen, Henrik 657
Andersen, Jens Bjorn 216
Andersen, Kim Krogh 618
Andersen, Nils Smedegaard 31
Andersen, Nils Smedegaard 653
Andersen, Thomas Thune 469
Andersen, Tove 236
Anderson, Anne 564
Anderson, Elizabeth McKee 274
Anderson, Eric T. 134
Anderson, Ian K. 613
Anderson, Jeremy 488
Anderson, Jeremy 648
Anderson, Magali 290
Anderson, Nick 75
Anderson, R. Jamie 134
Anderson, Simon 560
Anderson, William D. 590
Andersson, Thomas 528
Anderton, Niall 35
Ando, Hiromichi 163
Ando, Hisayoshi 389
Ando, Takaharu 498
Ando, Yoshiko 335
Andou, Yoshinori 410
Andrade, Lineu Carlos Ferraz de 322
Andrade, Miguel Stilwell De 223
Andre, Carlos Jose Da Costa 268
Andree, Timothy 204
Andreotti, Lamberto 651
Andres, Carmen Garcia de 615
Andrew, Ewan 211
Andrews, Giles 88

HOOVER'S HANDBOOK OF WORLD BUSINESS 2024

INDEX OF EXECUTIVES

Andrews, Nancy C. 453
Andries, Olivier 524
Andrieux, Nathalie 140
Andronikakis, Spyridon A. 38
Androsov, Kirill Gennadievich 340
Anei, Kazumi 404
Ang, Lawrence Siu Lung 267
Angulo, Luis Carlos Sarmiento 271
Anscheit, Heike 173
Antlitz, Arno 663
Antonelli, Leornado Pietro 480
Antonov, Igor 266
Anuntasilpa, Patchara 491
Anzeletti-Reikl, Peter 497
Ao, Hong 40
Aoki, Jun 371
Aoki, Masakazu 287
Aoki, Shigeki 461
Aoki, Shoichi 360
Aoki, Shuhei 420
Aoki, Yoshihisa 471
Aoyagi, Shunichi 150
Aoyama, Yasuhiro 391
Apfalter, Guenther F. 384
Appel, Frank 209
Appére, Guillaume 140
Appert, Raphael 185
Appio, Thomas J. 101
Apte, Shirish 174
Apte, Shirish 577
Aqraou, Jacob 616
Aradhye, Shreeram 453
Arai, Yuko 191
Arakane, Kumi 359
Arakawa, Ryuji 33
Araki, Makoto 343
Aramburuzabala, Maria Asuncion 48
Arase, Hideo 434
Araujo, Leandro de Miranda 80
Aravena, Marcos Lima 184
Araya, Akihiro 30
Araya, Luis 83
Araya, Ramon Jara 225
Archibald, Larry 674
Archibald, Tania J. 111
Archila, Jorge Arturo Calvache 221
Ardalan, Natalie Bani 277
Arden, Elaine 294
Ardenghy, Roberto Furian 480
Ardila, Jaime 11
Arellano, Ian 91
Arfert, MajBritt 236
Arias, Fernan Ignacio Bejarano 221
Arias, Rolando Sanchez 80
Arima, Koji 202
Aris, Antoinette P. 60
Arison, Micky M. 138
Ariyoshi, Yoshinori 194
Arkhipov, Mikhail 456
Armada, Jose Sainz 300
Armstrong, David 421
Armstrong, Lynda 469
Arnault, Antoine 379
Arnault, Bernard 379
Arnault, Delphine 379
Arney, Claudia I. 349
Arnold, Craig 220
Arnold, Craig 395
Arnold, Helen 280

Arnold, Ingrid-Helen 646
Arnold, Kirk E. 644
Arnt, Pedro 396
Aro, Mikael 137
Arora, Nikesh 176
Arpin, Pam 133
Arrechea, Juan Francisco Gallego 615
Arrowsmith, Carol 148
Arrowsmith, Carol 180
Arroyo, Delfin Rueda 18
Arroyo, Manolo 170
Arsel, Semahat Sevim 354
Arseneault, Tom 75
Arthur, John 558
Arts, Frank 21
Asada, Katsumi 471
Asada, Shunichi 632
Asahara, Kenichi 321
Asahi, Toshiya 655
Asai, Keiichi 185
Asai, Takahiko 275
Asam, Dominik 27
Asami, Hidenori 249
Asami, Takao 444
Asano, Kikuo 341
Asano, Shigeru 594
Asano, Toshio 394
Asano, Toshio 632
Asavanich, Bodin 555
Ascençao, Léonel Pereira 239
Asche-Holstein, Manuela 531
Aschenbroich, Jacques 113
Aschenbroich, Jacques 639
Ashaboglu, Ahmet F. 684
Ashar, Mayank (Mike) M. 226
Ashar, Mayank M. 613
Ashby, Crystal E. 75
Ashby, Ian R. 47
Asher, Anique 91
Ashida, Kosuke 30
Ashitani, Shigeru 163
Ashley, Euan 66
Ashley, Mike 94
Ashley, Mike 96
Ashton, Helen 332
Ask, Lars 528
Ask, Lars 664
Aso, Mitsuhiro 588
Aso, Toshimasa 629
Assouad, Yannick 626
Assouad, Yannick 659
Aswegen, Johannes Dawid van 555
Athanassopoulos, Andreas D. 240
Atherton, Tom 532
Athreya, Ranganath 301
Atieh, Michael G. 160
Atiya, Sami 7
Atkar, Neeta A. K. 685
Atlas, Ilana R. 71
Atlas, Ilana R. 467
Attal, Laurent 530
Attavipach, Pricha 554
Attiyah, Abdullah Hamad Al 659
Attolini, Gerardo Estrada 254
Atwal, Kal 624
Aubert, Anne 525
Aubry, Marc 525
Auchincloss, Murray 117
Auchinleck, R. H. 619
Audi, Patricia Souto 82

Audier, Agnes 186
Auer, Alexander 463
Auerbacher, Petra 17
Aufreiter, Nora A. 91
Auger, Daniel 624
Aumont, Dominique 379
Auque, Francois 506
Auschel, Roland 17
Avdan, Berna 29
Avedon, Marcia J. 644
Averchenkova, Tatyana 456
Avila, Sergio 83
Avrane, Julie 656
Awaiwanond, Panod 492
Awaji, Mutsumi 150
Ayada, Yujiro 296
Ayala, Jaime Augusto Zobel de 93
Ayat, Simon 620
Aymerich, Philippe 565
Ayub, Alfredo Elias 273
Ayub, Arturo Elias 43
Ayuthaya, Chirayu Isarangkul Na 555
Azcarraga, Laura Renee Diez Barroso de 84
Azevedo, Lucio 655
Azevedo, Sandra Maria Guerra de 655
Azuma, Seiichiro 441

B

Baade, Arve 452
Baarnman, Tobias 581
Baba, Chiharu 505
Baba, Hiroyuki 352
Baba, Koichi 632
Babatz, Guillermo E. 91
Babiak, Janice M. 90
Babule, Christophe 362
Bacci, Marcelo Feriozzi 120
Bache, Carl 137
Bachke, Tone Hegland 616
Backman, Mats 528
Bacon, Marie-Claude 400
Badenoch, Alexandra 618
Baderschneider, Jean 255
Badia, Jose Maria Nus 82
Badias, Alfonso Rebuelta 386
Badinter, Elisabeth 495
Badinter, Simon 495
Bae, Joseph Y. 243
Baer, Jakob 600
Baez, Yeimy 221
Bagchi, Anup 301
Bagel-Trah, Simone 103
Bagel-Trah, Simone 284
Bagnarol, Stephen 91
Bagrin, Oleg Vladimirovich 456
Bahadur, Sanjay 432
Bahk, Byong-Won 486
Bai, Fugui 199
Bai, Jieke 153
Bai, Zhongen 157
Baier, Horst 103
Baier, Wolfgang 213
Bailey, Ian 665
Baillie, James C. 589
Baillie, Warren 674

Bailly, Maud 140
Bainbridge, Guy L. T. 685
Bainbridge, Guy L.T. 386
Baird, John Russell 133
Baker, Graham 330
Bakhshi, Balbir 376
Bakhshi, Sandeep 301
Baksaas, Jon Fredrik 237
Baksaas, Jon Fredrik 596
Bakstad, Gro 213
Balaji, Pathamadai Balachandran 606
Balbinot, Sergio 37
Baldauf, Sari 258
Baldauf, Sari 397
Baldauf, Sari 446
Baldock, Alex 189
Baldock, Henrietta 320
Baldock, Henrietta 364
Bali, Nayantara 307
Balkenende, Jan Peter (J.P.) 314
Ball, F. Michael 32
Ball, Tracey C. 256
Ballester, Francisco 527
Ballesteros, Juan Carlos Correa 52
Balling, Stephanie 261
Balsamo, Franco 533
Bam, Lwazi 575
Bambawale, Ajai K. 638
Bancroft, Charles 274
Band, Jonathon 138
Bando, Mariko 415
Banducci, Brad L. 675
Banerjee, Gautam 558
Banerji, Shumeet 499
Banet, Virginie 393
Banez, Rene G. 93
Bang, Bente 198
Bang, Su-Ran 358
Banister, Gaurdie E. 226
Banno, Masato 121
Bantegnie, Pascal 524
Baoshnakova, Sirma 37
Baquedano, Laura Abasolo Garcia de 615
Barba, Catherine 502
Barba, Ricardo Naya 144
Barbara, Antonio Jose da 80
Barbashev, Sergey 412
Barbeau, Patrick 315
Barber, Samantha 300
Barbizet, Patricia 476
Barbizet, Patricia 639
Barbosa, Fabio Colletti 40
Barbosa, Fabio Colletti 323
Barbosa, Vanessa de Souza Lobato 82
Barbosa, Vinicius Guimaraes 119
Barbour, Alastair 482
Barcelon, George T. 107
Barckhahn, Oswald 108
Barclay, Dan 90
Barczewski, Andreas 646
Bard, Margot 239
Bardin, Romolo 63
Bardin, Romolo 239
Bardot, Anne 566
Barer, Sol J. 623
Baril, Thierry 27
Barilla, Guido 197
Barksdale, Harold G. 611
Barnaba, Mark 255

INDEX OF EXECUTIVES

Barnes, Francesca 425
Barnes, Greg 44
Barnevik, Percy N. 528
Barnham, Stephen 190
Baroni, Paul 91
Barr, Kevin 168
Barragan, Alejandro M. Elizondo 52
Barragan, Bernardo Gonzalez 52
Barragan, Rodrigo Alberto Gonzalez 52
Barrat, Frederic 502
Barrena, Juan Muldoon 272
Barresi, John S. 101
Barrett, Deborah J. 270
Barrett, Katherine 48
Barrington, Martin J. (Marty) 48
Barrios, Alf 509
Barrios, Alf 511
Barron, Hal V. 274
Barros, Marcel Juviniano 655
Barroso, Gina Diez 84
Barry, Chloe 349
Bartel, Ricardo 83
Barth, Stefan 102
Bartlett, Rhian 325
Bartolome, Beatriz Angela Lara 651
Bartolomeo, Eduardo de Salles 655
Bartolotta, Peter 366
Barton, Dominic 511
Barton, Robert John Orr 220
Baschera, Pius 537
Baser, Didem Dincer 646
Bashkirov, Alexey 412
Basile, Cinzia V. 240
Baskov, Vladimir A. 453
Basler, Bruno 665
Bason, John 180
Bason, John G. 64
Bassa, Zarina BM 320
Bassi, Pablo Hernan 621
Basson, J. W. 553
Basten, Peter 182
Bastioli, Catia 168
Basto, Edgar 110
Bastoni, Elizabeth Ann 334
Bastos, Marcelo 47
Bastug, Recep 646
Basu, Arijit 488
Basu, Arijit 577
Batato, Magdi 137
Bate, Oliver 37
Batekhin, Sergey L. 412
Baticle, Jean-Michel 149
Batista, Joao Pinheiro Nogueira 119
Batista, Joesley Mendonca 331
Batista, Wesley 331
Batista, Wesley Mendonca 331
Batra, Nishant 446
Batra, Sandeep 301
Battaglia, Concetta 348
Baublies, Nicoley 207
Bauer, Charles-Eric 285
Bauer, Karl-Heinz 537
Bauer, Katja 218
Baumann, Maja 665
Baumann, Markus 647
Baumann, Werner 103
Baumscheiper, Michael 284
Baumstark, Achim 282
Baur, Wolfgang 143
Baxby, David 665

Baxendale, Sonia 363
Baxter, Celia 215
Baxter, Charles B. 498
Bayazit, Kumsal 500
Bayly, Walter 185
Bazin, Benoit 175
Bazin, Benoit 659
Bazire, Nicolas 379
Beal, Anne 274
Beale, Graham 425
Beale, Inga K. 445
Beale, Inga K. 670
Beamish, Judith M. 589
Beato, Paulina 644
Beaudoin, Pierre 487
Beaudry, France 299
Beaulieu, Valerie 15
Beber, Shawn 130
Bech, Jens 470
Bechtold, John F. 474
Becker, Sonja De 345
Becker, W. Marston 74
Becker, Wendy 572
Beckman, Per 596
Bedard, Alain 624
Bedard, Christina 400
Bedient, Patricia M. 592
Bednarz, Brian 35
Beeck, Hans van 32
Beerli, Andreas 79
Behle, Christine 207
Behlert, Bernd 261
Behrendt, Birgit A. 516
Behrendt, Birgit A. 628
Beilinson, Marc A. 68
Beke, Guy 650
Bekker, Jacobus Petrus 620
Belair, Sebastian 363
Belardi, James R. 68
Belec, Anne 299
Belismelis, Luis Enrique Romero 185
Bell, Genevieve 174
Bellemere, Gilles 32
Bellew, Peter 220
Bellezza, Orio 580
Belli, Tugrul 29
Bellinger, Patricia S. 524
Bellini, Alessandra 622
Bellini, Marina Fagundes 322
Belloeil-Melkin, Marie-Veronique 379
Bellon-Szabo, Nathalie 566
Bellon, Francois-Xavier 566
Bellon, Sophie 362
Bellon, Sophie 566
Belloni, Antonio 379
Belousov, Andrey 517
Beltran, Francisco Camacho 254
Beltran, Francisco Josue Camacho 280
Belyakov, Viktor N. 453
Ben-Zur, Liat 650
Ben, Shenglin 152
Benacin, Philippe 661
Benatti, Luca 395
Benchikh, Soraya 211
Bender, Shannon Lowry 501
Bendiek, Sabine 531
Benedetto, Paolo Di 63
Benet, Lincoln E. 380
Bengtsson, Bo 597
Bengtsson, Goran 597

Benitez, Enrique Zambrano 38
Benjumea, Francisco Javier Garcia-Carranza 84
Benner, Christiane 105
Benner, Christiane 183
Bennett, Adam 592
Bennett, David 168
Bennett, Ella 220
Bennetts, Michael 44
Bennink, Jan 170
Benoit-Cattin, Luc 56
Bens, Geert 650
Bensalah-Chaqroun, Miriem 502
Bentele, Roland 282
Beppu, Rikako 406
Berahas, Solomon A. 483
Berard, Andre 624
Berg, Katarina 574
Berger, Genevieve B. 362
Berger, Pascale 185
Bergfors, Stina 596
Berggren, Arne 483
Bergmann, Burckhard 453
Bergstedt, Mikael 70
Bergstrom, Pal 597
Berhend, Jurgen 247
Berlinger, Stefanie 119
Bermejo, Angel L. Davila 386
Bernabe, Estela P. 107
Bernardi, Carlo De 168
Bernardini, Roberto di 197
Bernardino, Daniel 247
Bernardo, Romeo L. 93
Berneke, Eva Merete Sofelde 657
Berner, Anne-Catherine 563
Bernicke, Jutta 284
Bernier, Jean 35
Bernier, Sam 400
Bernstein, David 138
Berry, C. J. 23
Berry, Robert 94
Berry, Robert 96
Berthelin, Michel 18
Bertolini, Massimo 393
Bertone, Andrea 41
Bertrand, Delphine 542
Bertrand, Jean-Marc 57
Bertrand, Maryse 400
Bertrand, Maryse 422
Berzin, Ann C. 644
Besga, Francisco Borja Acha 227
Besga, Francisco Borja Acha 228
Besharat, Alex 91
Besnier, Stephanie 233
Besombes, Beatrice 116
Bessant, Catherine 689
Bessho, Yoshiki 594
Besson, Philippe 566
Best, Catherine M. 132
Bester, Andrew 169
Bethell, Melissa 211
Bethell, Melissa 243
Bethell, Melissa 622
Bettag, Michael 397
Betz, Bill 458
Beullier, Alain 233
Beurden, Ben Van 397
Beurden, Joep van 18
Beurskens, Frits 564
Beutel, Eric 236

Bevan, John Andrew 111
Bey, Nora 542
Beyer, Hans 563
Bezard, Bruno 656
Bezzecheri, Maurizio 228
Bhagat, Smita 278
Bhagat, Vipul 107
Bhakta, Mansingh L. 499
Bhandarkar, Vedika 606
Bhanji, Nabeel 638
Bharucha, Kaizad 277
Bhat, Ashima 277
Bhatia, Nina 367
Bhatia, Raveesh K. 278
Bhatia, Vanisha Mittal 55
Bhatt, O. P. 607
Bhatt, Om Prakash 606
Bhattacharya, Abhijit 357
Bhattacharya, Arundhati 499
Bi, Mingjian 155
Biamonti, Jean-luc 239
Bianchi, Mirko D. G. 684
Bibby, Andrew J. 135
Bibic, Mirko 106
Bibic, Mirko 519
Bich, Genevieve 400
Bicho, Fernando Cardoso Rodrigues 86
Bickerstaffe, Katie 388
Bickford, Natalie 530
Bie, Maaike de 220
Biedenkopf, Sebastian 261
Bienfait, Robin A. 270
Biermann, Albert 298
Bierwirth, Andreas 220
Bievre, Martine 73
Bigne, Anne-Sophie De La 177
Bigos-Jaworowska, Sabina 94
Biguet, Stephane 537
Bihan, Sandrine Le 661
Bijapurkar, Rama 301
Billes, Martha G. 134
Billes, Owen G. 134
Billingham, Stephen 78
Billot, Thierry 140
Binbasgil, Sabri Hakan 29
Bindra, Jagjeet S. 380
Biner, Lilian Fossum 137
Bingham-Hall, Penny 255
Binham-Hall, Penelope 111
Binning, Paviter S. 374
Binning, Paviter S. 668
Biorck, Hans 596
Bird, Graham R. 270
Birnbaum, Leonhard 218
Birrell, Gordon 117
Birrell, Stuart 220
Bisagni, Gianfranco 684
Bischofberger, Norbert W. 103
Bismarck, Nilufer von 364
Bito, Masaaki 569
Bittencourt, Flavia Maria 120
Bittner, Carsten 7
Bitzer, Marc R. 105
Bjelis, Ivo 171
Bjerke, Rune 452
Bjorknert, Mikael 597
Black, Jerome Thomas 638
Blackburn, Gaston 297
Blackett, Karen 211
Blackett, Kelly S. 135

INDEX OF EXECUTIVES

Blackwell, Jean S. 337
Blades, Alexander 483
Blair, Rainer 432
Blakemore, Dominic 180
Blakemore, Dominic 376
Blanc, Amanda 73
Blanc, Amanda 118
Blanc, Jean-Sebastien 233
Blance, Andrea 73
Blanchet, Lucie 422
Blanco, Juan Sebastian Moreno 82
Blanco, Maria Luisa Garcia 615
Blanco, Roman 83
Blanco, Tomás García 504
Blanka-Graff, Markus 360
Blauwhoff, Peter 607
Blazquez, Pedro Azagra 300
Bleier, Info 238
Bleil, Lynn Dorsey 32
Blessing, Martin 198
Blidner, Jeffrey Miles 123
Blidner, Jeffrey Miles 124
Blidner, Jeffrey Miles 124
Blin, Bruno 664
Block, Philippe 290
Blok, Eelco 618
Blood, John 48
Bloom, Mark 19
Bloom, Mark 21
Blouin, Pierre 423
Blouin, Pierre J. 256
Bluhm, Christian 647
Blume, Oliver 663
Blunck, Thomas 418
Bobadilla, Luis Isasi Fernandez de 84
Boccardelli, Paolo 615
Boccon-Gibod, Isabelle 57
Bochinsky, Michael 523
Bock, Kurt Wilhelm 100
Bock, Kurt Wilhelm 105
Bockstiegel, Claudia 513
Bodson, Bertrand J. F. 622
Boe, Veronica Pascual 615
Boeck, Karel De 483
Boer, Dick 432
Boer, Dick 549
Boetger, Bruno D'Avila Melo 80
Bogart, Thomas A. 589
Bogdaneris, Aris 497
Bogdanovic, Zoran 171
Boguslavskiy, Leonid 535
Boguslawski, Nadine 397
Bohle, Birgit 209
Bohman, Staffan 3
Bohman, Staffan 70
Bohuon, Oliver 605
Bohuon, Olivier 499
Boillat, Pascal 174
Boinay, Vincent 362
Boise, April Miller 644
Boissard, Sophie 37
Boivin, Pierre 400
Boivin, Pierre 423
Boix, Angel Vila 615
Boizard, Christophe 21
Bok, Oscar de 208
Boleslawski, Alexandra 185
Bolger, Andrea 363
Bolland, Marc J. 243
Bolliger, Barbara 282

Bollore, Cyrille 661
Bollore, Thierry 606
Bollore, Yannick 661
Bom, Luis Todo 265
Boman, Par 596
Bomhard, Nikolaus von 208
Bomhard, Nikolaus von 418
Bomhard, Stefan 180
Bomhard, Stefan 304
Bompard, Alexandre 464
Bonatti, Roberto 620
Bonatti, Roberto 621
Bonavia, Paul J. 256
Bonchristiano, Antonio Carlos Augusto Ribeiro 40
Bond, Colin 527
Bonfield, Andrew R.J. 499
Bonfield, Peter L. 458
Bonfield, Peter Leahy 603
Bonham, Scott B. 91
Bonham, Scott B. 374
Bonham, Scott B. 384
Bonnafe, Jean-Laurent 113
Bonnard, Luc 537
Bonnechose, Benedicte De 177
Bonnell, William E. 422
Bonomo, Paola 615
Bonorino, Alessandro Rosa 120
Boondech, Prasobsook 128
Boonklum, Peangpanor 493
Boonpoapichart, Kriengchai 128
Boonrach, Grisada 492
Boonyachai, Krishna 493
Boonyalerdlak, Vanasanan 491
Boonyapipat, Toasaporn 492
Boonyawat, Teerawat 493
Boonyoung, Pridi 128
Booth, Clement B. 418
Borchert, Stephen 392
Borda, Rodolfo Velez 271
Borden, Robert L. 68
Bordin, Jose Sergio 80
Borgard, Lawrence T. 256
Borgne, Gilles Le 502
Borisuitsawat, Chayong 491
Borollossy, Hanan El 172
Borowicz, Klaus 392
Borrego, Miguel Angel Lopez 558
Borrell, Michael 453
Bortenlanger, Christine 185
Bortoloto, Emerson Macedo 322
Boselli, Lucas 61
Boss, Greg 187
Bosse, Christine 37
Bossemeyer, Sandra 523
Bostock, Ed 665
Bostoen, Alain 345
Bot, Bernard Ladislas 1
Bot, Bernard Ladislas 349
Botero, Maria Lorena Gutierrez 271
Botten, Peter R. 21
Bottger, Miriam 185
Bouchard, Alain 35
Bouchard, Lucien 624
Boucher, Richard 186
Bouchiat, Pascal 626
Bougrov, Andrey Evgenyevich 412
Boulanger, Francois 149
Boulanger, Serge 400
Boulet, Alain 617

Boulet, Jean-Francois 299
Bouquot, Geoffrey 656
Bourdage, Pierre 527
Bourdeau, Jocyanne 374
Bourges, Olivier 579
Bourke, Evelyn 88
Bourne, Erica 376
Bourqui, Elisabeth 665
Boursanoff, Alexander 173
Boutebba, Frederic 197
Boutinet, Martine 185
Boutte, Gregory 347
Bouygues, Cyril 116
Bouygues, Edward 116
Bouygues, Martin 116
Bouygues, Olivier 116
Bowen, Terry J. 110
Bower, Vivienne 497
Bowie, Peter G. 384
Bowles, Jack Marie Henry David 122
Bowles, Ken 564
Boxmeer, Jean-Francois M. L. van 280
Boxmeer, Jean-Francois van 661
Boxus, Joelle 31
Boyajian, Mark 149
Boychuk, Michael T. 363
Boyer, Bernard 56
Boyko, Eric 35
Boyle, Charlotte J. 172
Braams, Conny 653
Braathen, Kjerstin R. 213
Braca, Joan A. 339
Bracher, Candido Botelho 323
Brachlianoff, Estelle 285
Bradley, Bryan C. 132
Bradley, Catherine 349
Bradley, Catherine Biner 220
Bradley, Guy Martin Coutts 599
Bradley, Noralee 457
Brady, Vicki 618
Braga, Rogerio Carvalho 81
Bragança, Miguel de Campos Pereira de 86
Braida, Damarys 542
Braly, Angela F. 124
Branagan, Ian D. 501
Branco, Roberto da Cunha Castello 479
Brand, H. C. 534
Brand, Martin J. 376
Brandjes, Michiel 182
Brandler, Andrew Clifford Winawer 167
Brandon, Rajna Gibson 600
Brandstatter, Ralf 663
Brandt, Werner 523
Brandt, Werner 557
Brandtzæg, Svein Richard 213
Brant, Cherie L. 638
Brassac, Philippe 185
Bratt, Mikael 71
Bratukhin, Sergey 412
Braun, Henrique 172
Braunig, Guenther 209
Braunwalder, Peter F. 450
Brazier, Allan J. 51
Brecht, Michael 397
Breedon, Tim J. 96
Breeze, Diana 127
Bregier, Fabrice 233
Bregier, Fabrice 540

Brekelmans, Harry 549
Brekke, Sigve 616
Bremme, Peter 646
Brendish, Clay 176
Brennan, Roisin 524
Brenner, Maxine N. 467
Brenoe, Lars-Erik 198
Breschan, Matthias 597
Bresky, Annica 581
Brett, John 55
Breu, Raymund 600
Breuer, Kirsten Joachim 143
Breuer, Klemens 497
Breuer, Mark 201
Breum, Karsten 198
Breuninger, Barbara 279
Brewer, Andrew 35
Brewer, Andrew 44
Brewer, Nicola Mary 300
Brewster, David 172
Briatta, Gilles 565
Brich, Kirsten Ebbe 198
Brickley, Peter 170
Briggs, Andy 482
Bright, Craig 96
Brijs, Erik 650
Brilliant, Richard 138
Brinck, Soren 137
Brindamour, Charles J. G. 130
Brindamour, Charles J. G. 315
Brink, Dolf van den 280
Brink, Martin A. Van den 60
Brinkley, Amy W. 638
Brisac, Juliette 113
Briskin, Jon 467
Bristow, Mark 98
Brito, Carlos Alves de 40
Brito, Carlos Alves de 48
Brittain, Alison 388
Britton, Chris 215
Brizzio, Pablo 621
Brlas, Laurie 71
Broadbent, Jillian R. 381
Broadbent, Jillian Rosemary 382
Broadbent, Jillian Rosemary 675
Broadley, Philip 66
Broadley, Philip 364
Brochu, Anik 297
Brochu, Sophie 90
Brock, Gunnar 7
Brock, Malanie 404
Brock, Melanie 344
Broderick, Craig 90
Brodeur, Pierre 299
Brody, Hubert Rene 428
Broek, Harold van den 280
Broich, Andre Van 103
Brokhof, Markus 21
Bronder, Anette 362
Brook, Bruce 187
Brooks, Bonnie R. 514
Brooks, Conrad D. 74
Brooks, John Kenneth 133
Brooks, Martha Finn 182
Brooks, Martha Finn 664
Brookshaw, Steven 624
Broomhead, Malcolm 110
Brosnan, Sean G. 501
Brough, Paul J. 638
Brougher, Francoise 566

INDEX OF EXECUTIVES

Brouillette, Manon 422
Brouwer, Greg J. 613
Brouwer, Sybolt 650
Brown, Bruce A. 446
Brown, Douglas B. 613
Brown, Erin 376
Brown, Julia M. 415
Brown, Michael William Thomas 428
Brown, Palmer 180
Brown, Priscilla Sims 174
Brown, Ruth 418
Brown, Sébastien 239
Browne, Helen 73
Bruaene, Pierre Van De 650
Bruce, Evie 380
Bruce, Sue 574
Bruck, Jorge Bande 184
Bruder, Shauneen 131
Brudermuller, Martin 100
Brudermuller, Martin 397
Brueckner, Ronny 21
Brugarolas, Catalina Minarro 14
Brugarolas, Catalina Minarro 386
Brun, Nicolas 182
Brungger, Renata Jungo 397
Brungger, Renata Jungo 418
Brunila, Anne 258
Bruno, Norberto Alfredo 686
Bruton, John G. 644
Bruun-Hanssen, Haakon 236
Bruxelles, Henri 197
Bruzelius, Peggy B. 316
Bryan, Tracy 91
Bryant, Jenny 665
Bryant, John 170
Bryant, John 180
Bryant, Warren 374
Buberl, Thomas 73
Buc, Hernan Buchi 80
Buc, Marcos Buchi 184
Buchanan, Ian 88
Buchanan, John 223
Buchanan, Robin 380
Buchner, Stefan E. 183
Buchner, Stefan Erwin 628
Buck, Harald 663
Buckingham, Geraldine 295
Budenberg, Robin 374
Buechele, Wolfgang 399
Buechner, Ton 453
Buergy, Dominik 360
Buess, Thomas 600
Buffett, Howard W. 168
Buffini, Damon 539
Buhler, Pierre-Andre 597
Buhlmann, Jerry 307
Buhr, Gunnar de 173
Bukaev, Gennady Ivanovich 517
Buker, Marc 540
Bula, Patrice 453
Bula, Patrice 537
Bulcke, Paul 362
Bulcke, Paul 432
Bulnes, Juan Luis Ossa 184
Bulto, Victor 453
Bunce, John L. 55
Bunderla, Hubert 463
Bunnag, Anutra 491
Bunnenberg, Lutz 284
Bunston, Andrew 668

Bunting, Hans Friedrich 523
Bunyasaranand, Boonsong 85
Bunye, Ignacio R. 93
Buranamanit, Tanin 128
Burbidge, Eileen 189
Burckhardt, Andreas 79
Burger, J. P. 250
Burghardt, Stefan 173
Burgoyne, Celeste 377
Burgum, Melissa A. 11
Burke, Sheila P. 160
Burkhard, Oliver 628
Burkhardt-Berg, Gabriele 37
Burley, Christopher M. 457
Burling, David 646
Burnett-Kant, Eileen 167
Burns, David 618
Burns, M. Michele 48
Burrows, Richard 137
Burt, Tye 55
Burton, John 269
Buruspat, Jatuporn 493
Burzer, Jorg 397
Busch, Roland 557
Bushfield, Corine R. K. 39
Bushman, Julie L. 18
Bushnell, David C. 501
Buskhe, Hakan 4
Buskhe, Hakan 581
Butel, Jean-Luc D. 605
Butler, Monika 537
Butschek, Guenter 606
Butz, Stefan P. 213
Buxtorf, Cyril 542
Buys, Stefan 54
Byl, Alain 650
Byoung, Ho Lee 369
Byrne, Darragh 201
Byrne, Rory 213
Byun, Kyung-Hoon 370

C

Cabanis, Cecile 197
Cabiallavetta, Mathis 600
Cadav, Juana Francisca de Chantal Llano 272
Cadbury, Nicholas 316
Cadoret, Frank 615
Caesar, Nerida 669
Cahilly, Jason Glen 138
Cai, Chang 683
Cai, Dunyi 178
Cai, Fangfang 483
Cai, Haoyi 87
Cai, Hongbin 155
Cai, Hongping 128
Cai, Hongyu 98
Cai, Jin-Yong 49
Cai, Jinyong 478
Cai, Manli 688
Cai, Tianyuan 178
Cai, Tingji 559
Cai, Zhongxi 560
Cain, Steven 172
Caine, Patrice 362
Caine, Patrice 626
Cairnie, Ruth 65

Cairns, Gordon McKellar 675
Cairns, James 131
Cakiroglu, Levent 353
Cakiroglu, Levent 684
Calabria, Frank G. 467
Calari, Cesare 230
Caldwell, Nanci E. 130
Calemzuk, Emiliano 396
Callahan, Daniel H. 91
Callera, Gilberto 533
Callewaert, Katelijn 345
Callinicos, Brent 76
Callol, Ana 170
Calmejane, Claire 565
Caltagirone, Francesco Gaetano 63
Calvert, Victoria A. 39
Calvo, Domingo Armengol 80
Calvo, Miguel Klingenberg 504
Calvosa, Lucia 235
Camagni, Paola 615
Camara, Rogerio Pedro 80
Camargo, Jorge Marques de Toledo 649
Cambefort, Pierre 185
Camino, Javier Cavada 265
Cammisecra, Antonio 227
Camp, Victoria Van 4
Campbell, Bill 187
Campbell, Jeffrey C. 49
Campbell, Justine 424
Campbell, Norie C. 638
Campbell, Pauline 181
Campbell, Philip 656
Campelli, Fabrizio 206
Campos, Didier Mena 83
Campos, Vicente Falconi 40
Camuti, Paul A. 644
Canabal, Humberto Domingo Mayans 481
Canas, Cristian Toro 81
Candland, Paul 204
Canetti, Bernard 617
Canham, Rachel 125
Canning, Charles 685
Cannon, M. Elizabeth 132
Cano, Andre Rodrigues 80
Canova, Walter Fabian 221
Canseco, Leslie Pierce Diez 185
Cantaloube, Brigitte 506
Cantera, Jose Antonio Garcia 84
Cantu, Armando Ramos 38
Cantu, Javier Beltran 273
Cao, Haiyun 336
Cao, Liqun 309
Cao, Min 603
Cao, Qingyang 153
Cao, Zhiqiang 255
Capatides, Michael G. 130
Capellas, Michael D. 252
Cappi, Luiz Carlos Trabuco 80
Caprera, Antonio 620
Carbajal, Francisco Javier Fernandez 144
Carbajal, Francisco Javier Fernandez 254
Carbajal, Jose Antonio Fernandez 171
Carbajal, Jose Antonio Fernandez 254
Carbajal, Jose Antonio Fernandez 280
Carbajal, Jose Antonio Fernandez 280
Cardenas, Alvaro 211
Cardona, Andres Felipe Mejia 85

Cardoso, Paulo 661
Cardoso, Pureza 285
Carell, Thomas 100
Carfagna, Maurizio 393
Cargill, Jan 425
Cargill, Jan 427
Cariello, Vincenzo 651
Cariola, Gianfranco 235
Carletti, Elena 651
Carli, Maurizio 615
Carlier, Didier 141
Carlin, Peter H. 18
Carlson, Jan 71
Carlson, Jan 237
Carmany, George W. 589
Carnegie-Brown, Bruce 84
Carnegie, Maile 71
Carneiro, Vera de Morais Pinto Pereira 223
Carnwath, Alison 689
Carnwath, Dame Alison J. 100
Caron, Joseph P. 386
Carpio, Mariano Marzo 504
Carr, Jeff 349
Carr, Jeff 499
Carr, Roger 75
Carranza, Jorge Sáenz-Azcúnaga 646
Carriere, Jacques 299
Carriere, Louis-Philippe 532
Carriere, Louis-Philippe 678
Carro, Lourdes Maiz 80
Carroll, Cynthia 287
Carroll, Cynthia Blum 269
Carrothers, Douglas A. 299
Carrupt, Alain 601
Carson-Callan, G. 564
Carson, Neil 549
Carson, Seana 101
Carter, Bruce 92
Carter, Monique 455
Carter, Pamela L. 226
Cartier, Guillaume 444
Carvalho-Heineken, Charlene Lucille de 280
Carvalho, A.A.C. de 280
Carvalho, Eduardo Navarro de 615
Carvalho, M. R. de 280
Carvalho, Marcelo Arantes de 119
Carvalho, Maria Blini de 322
Carvalho, Michel R. de 280
Carvalho, Michel Ray de 354
Carvalho, Renato da Silva 322
Casamento, Michael 41
Casanova, Gabriel 620
Casanova, Sarah L. 410
Casartelli, Daniel Cristian Gonzalez 686
Casas, Isidro Faine 615
Casati, Gianfranco 11
Case, Gregory C. 49
Caser, Carlos Alberto 331
Casey, Geraldine 23
Casey, Keith M. 146
Casey, Michael 377
Casey, Theresa 332
Casper, David B. 90
Cass, Rafael Ramos 171
Cassaday, John M. 386
Cassidy, A. 380
Cassidy, Andrew 382

HOOVER'S HANDBOOK OF WORLD BUSINESS 2024

INDEX OF EXECUTIVES

Cassidy, Rick 603
Cassidy, Ronan 549
Cassin, Brian J. 325
Cassis, Marco Luciano 580
Cassista, Carl 297
Castaigne, Robert 453
Castaigne, Robert 659
Castelein, Kris 240
Castellanos, Jesus Martinez 386
Castillo-Schulz, Jorg Oliveri del 173
Castillo, Jaime Gutierrez 184
Castonguay, Lyne 532
Castries, Henri de 432
Castries, Henri de 579
Castro, Henrique de 84
Castro, Jones M. 107
Castro, Lorena Alba 308
Castro, Maria Luisa Jorda 272
Catalano, Filippo 499
Catalano, Giuseppe 63
Catasta, Christine 238
Catasta, Christine 463
Catoir, Christophe 15
Catoire, Caroline 185
Caubet, Maria Eugenia Bieto 227
Cavallo, Daniela 663
Cawley, Michael A. 524
Cebulla, Jorg 207
Cecilia, Manuel Manrique 504
Cederschiold, Carl 596
Celebioglu, Levent 29
Celorio, Victor Alberto Tiburcio 171
Celorio, Victor Alberto Tiburcio 254
Centoni, Liz 397
Cerda, Axel Juan Christensen de la 225
Cernko, Willibald 238
Cerqueira, Marcelo de Oliveira 119
Cerretelli, Adriana 533
Cerstelotte, Hilde 240
Ceruti, Franco 319
Cervantes, Victor Manuel Navarro 481
Cesar, Diana Ferreira 276
Cesaris, Ada Lucia De 235
Cestare, Andre Balestrin 322
Ch'ien, Raymond Kuo Fung 600
Ch'ien, Raymond Kuo Fung 156
Chabot, Rene 299
Chadt, Sabine 497
Chai, Shouping 478
Chaillou, Herve 525
Chairasmisak, Korsak 128
Chakraborty, Atanu 278
Chalendar, Pierre-Andre de 113
Chalendar, Pierre-Andre de 175
Challon-Kemoun, Adeline 177
Chalmers, Anne J. 613
Chalmers, Ronnie 362
Chalmers, Sabine 48
Chalmers, William 374
Chalon, Marie-Laure Sauty de 379
Chambers, Stuart J. 47
Chameau, Jean-Lou 524
Chamma, Andrea da Motta 119
Champagne, Alain 400
Chan, Alan Yee-Pong 159
Chan, Albert Hiu-Sang 159
Chan, Ericson 689
Chan, Frank Chi Chung 612
Chan, John Cho Chak 276
Chan, Johnson Ow 434

Chan, Kok Seong 654
Chan, Lu Min 687
Chan, Man 114
Chan, Mary S. 384
Chan, Patrick Kin Wah 612
Chan, Raymond T. 619
Chan, Robert Hong-ki 589
Chan, Sai-Cheong 159
Chandarasomboon, Amorn 85
Chandavasu, Chaya 492
Chandavasu, Rattiya 492
Chandel, Lalit Kumar 301
Chandrasekaran, N. 606
Chandrasekaran, Natarajan 607
Chandrashekar, Lavanya 211
Chaney, Michael 665
Chang, Baosheng 87
Chang, Chao-Feng 682
Chang, Cheng-Yung 242
Chang, Chia Li 687
Chang, Chia-Sheng 141
Chang, Chien-Yi 682
Chang, In-Hwa 486
Chang, Jason C. S. 58
Chang, Jimmy Ban Ja 250
Chang, K.H. 159
Chang, RC 12
Chang, Richard H. P. 58
Chang, Rutherford 58
Chang, Seung-Wha 486
Chang, Shao-Yuan 682
Chang, Susan 245
Chang, T.S. 603
Chang, Yang Lee 369
Chang, Zheng 199
Chanial, Victoria 247
Chant, Diana L. 134
Chao, Chih Wen 687
Chapman, Stanley G. 609
Chapot, Yves 177
Chapoulaud-Floque, Valerie 211
Chapuy, Cyril 362
Charbonnier, Laurent 555
Charest, Jean 131
Charest, Jean 495
Charest, Yvon 299
Charest, Yvon 423
Charles, Bernard 530
Charoen-Rajapark, Chatchawin 85
Charreton, Didier 47
Charuchinda, Achapom 491
Charur, Emilio Marcos 52
Charvier, Robert 656
Chassat, Sophie 379
Chatillon, Jean-Baptiste Chasseloup de 530
Chatillon, Jean-Baptiste Chasseloup de 566
Chatterjee, Koushik 607
Chatterjee, Rashmy 37
Chaturvedi, Girish Chandra 301
Chatzidis, Odysseus D. 209
Chau, Dickens Chi Ming 687
Chau, Ho 670
Chaumartin, Anik 24
Chavalitcheewingul, Aree 554
Chavez, Francisco Medina 43
Chearavanont, Narong 128
Chearavanont, Soopakij 128
Chearavanont, Suphachai 128

Chebotarev, Sergey 456
Checa, Hector Blas Grisi 83
Cheesewright, David 172
Cheetham, Kate 374
Chellew, Mark P. 44
Chen, Delin 309
Chen, Dong-Hai 682
Chen, Fung Ming 250
Chen, Grace 141
Chen, Guochuan 178
Chen, Guoyong 156
Chen, Haifeng 559
Chen, Hanwen 87
Chen, Hanwen 157
Chen, Hongjun 559
Chen, Hsin Chien 687
Chen, Huajhao 178
Chen, Jason 12
Chen, Jeffrey 58
Chen, Jhaoyi 159
Chen, Jolene 488
Chen, Junkui 87
Chen, Kangping 336
Chen, Kefu 436
Chen, Kexiang 483
Chen, Kok-Choo 603
Chen, Lei 474
Chen, Lijie 40
Chen, Liming 100
Chen, Mao-Cin 216
Chen, Meggy 12
Chen, Peiyuan 178
Chen, Qiyu 560
Chen, Ray Jui-Tsung 178
Chen, Ron-Chu 216
Chen, Shaopeng 366
Chen, Shaozong 87
Chen, Shengsyong 178
Chen, Shih Chung 687
Chen, Shuping 295
Chen, Siguan 178
Chen, Siqing 309
Chen, Sophia 12
Chen, Steve Shyh 547
Chen, Suka 216
Chen, Teng 687
Chen, Tianming 178
Chen, Tien-Szu 58
Chen, Tom Hsu Tang 250
Chen, Tsu-Pei 142
Chen, Wenhao 560
Chen, Xiaohong 345
Chen, Xinying 483
Chen, Y.S. 159
Chen, Yaohuan 155
Chen, Yifang 309
Chen, Yu 345
Chen, Yunian 335
Cheng, Adrian Chi-Kong 159
Cheng, Adrian Chi-Kong 434
Cheng, Alice Yu-Fen 433
Cheng, Cheng-mount 682
Cheng, Chi-Heng 434
Cheng, Chi-Man 434
Cheng, Conroy Chi-Heng 159
Cheng, Eva 114
Cheng, Hamilton Ping-Hei 159
Cheng, Heng 295
Cheng, Henry Kar-Shun 159
Cheng, Henry Kar-Shun 434

Cheng, Hong 156
Cheng, Hsin Min 687
Cheng, Humphrey 245
Cheng, Jennifer 71
Cheng, Judy Wai Chu 436
Cheng, Moses Mo Chi 154
Cheng, Pam P. 66
Cheng, Peter Kar-Shing 434
Cheng, Shu Hua 687
Cheng, Sophia 141
Cheng, Victor C.J. 672
Cheng, Will Wei 212
Cheng, Wilson Kam-Biu 159
Cheng, Yong 158
Cheng, Yu-Tung 159
Cheng, Yuanguo 152
Chenneveau, Didier 370
Cheong, Seung-Il 358
Chereshenkov, Pavel 484
Cherfan, Samir 579
Cherner, Anatoly 266
Cheruvatath, Nandakumar 220
Chery, Jean-Marc 579
Cheshire, Ian 125
Chestnutt, Roy H. 618
Cheung, David Chung Yan 267
Cheung, Yan 436
Cheval, Jean L. 38
Chevalier, Daniel 624
Chevalley, Caroline 542
Chevardiere, Patrick de La 537
Chevardiere, Patrick De La 177
Chevre, Claude 277
Chia, Tai Tee 654
Chiang, Ching Po 687
Chiang, Lai Yuen 276
Chiarini, Andre Barreto 479
Chiasson, Keith A. 145
Chiba, Futoshi 404
Chiba, Yuji 89
Chien, Kathleen 660
Chien, Mark 291
Chien, Victor 12
Chien, Wei-Chin 216
Chierchia, Giulia 118
Chiesa, Alberto Della 580
Chih, Yu Yang 249
Chikumoto, Manabu 402
Child, Peter 20
Chima, Fumbi 670
Chin, Chine Huei 687
Chin, Samuel Wai Leung 249
Chin, Te Shan 687
Chin, Y.P. 603
Chinavicharana, Krisada 493
Ching, Donny 549
Chipman, Stephen 670
Chirachavala, Arun 85
Chisholm, Andrew A. 519
Chitale, Uday M. 301
Chiu, Adolph Yeung 267
Chiu, Jenny Wai-Han 434
Chiu, Vivien Wai Man 276
Chng, Kai Fong 200
Chng, Sok Hui 200
Cho, Bonghan 200
Cho, Rose Mui 276
Cho, Suk-Jeh 368
Chocat, Noemie 175
Choe, Michelle 377

INDEX OF EXECUTIVES

Choi, Eun Soo 298
Choi, Gee-Sung 526
Choi, Jeong-Woo 486
Choi, Koon Shum 114
Chombar, Françoise 650
Chon, Jung-Son 486
Chong, Mark Chin Kok 558
Chong, Quan 613
Chong, Quince Wai Yan 167
Chopra, Deepak 590
Chou, Scott 216
Chou, Tsung Ming 687
Choufuku, Yasuhiro 394
Chow, Chung-Kong 22
Chow, Hong 108
Chow, Jacqueline 172
Chow, Liz Tan Ling 276
Chow, Paul Man Yiu 154
Chow, Sai Kin 687
Chowdary, Kosaraju Veerayya 606
Chretien, Benedicte 185
Christie, James R. 134
Christino, Genuino M. 54
Christopher, Alex N. 612
Chromik, Marcus 173
Chronican, Philip 421
Chryssikos, Georgios K. 240
Chu, Kok Wei 164
Chu, Ricky Yiu Kuen 436
Chu, Victor 27
Chu, Victor 448
Chu, Yiyun 483
Chua, Sock Koong 358
Chuang, Arthur 603
Chuaypen, Anutin 492
Chubachi, Ryoji 327
Chubachi, Ryoji 442
Chuchepchunkamon, Wiboon 492
Chuenchom, Chansak 493
Chuengviroj, Vichien 128
Chun, Dong-Soo 526
Chung, Eui Sun 298
Chung, Kenneth Patrick 152
Chung, Moon-Ki 486
Chung, Roy Chi Ping 612
Chung, Tsung-Ming 245
Chungcharoen, Nithi 492
Chutima, Sarunthorn 555
Chuvaev, Aleksander 258
Ciano, Pablo 208
Cicacovas, Aleksandras 198
Cicconi, Fiona Clare 579
Cifrian, Roberto Campa 254
Cilento, Melinda A. 674
Cimenoglu, Ahmet 684
Cinerari, Sergio 214
Cioli, Laura 393
Ciou, Pinghe 178
Cirelli, Jean-Francois 175
Cirera, Carmina Ganyet i 504
Ciria, Antonio Gomez 386
Cirillo, Mary A. 160
Cisneros, Gustavo A. 98
Citrino, Mary Anne 357
Clamadieu, Jean-Pierre 27
Clamadieu, Jean-Pierre 73
Clamadieu, Jean-Pierre 233
Clamadieu, Jean-Pierre 611
Clappison, John H. 589
Clark, Christie J. B. 25

Clark, Christie J. B. 374
Clark, Ian 605
Clark, Jack 182
Clark, Kevin P. 50
Clark, Kevin P. 51
Clark, Maura J. 256
Clark, Maura J. 457
Clark, Megan 187
Clark, Megan 509
Clark, Megan 511
Clark, Scott 177
Clark, Sue 304
Clark, Suzanne P. 685
Clarke, Alison 304
Clarke, Emmanuel 315
Clarke, Peter 244
Clarkson, Tom 488
Classon, Rolf A. 259
Clausade, Josseline de 140
Claxton, Hazel 619
Clayton, Annette K. 458
Cleary, Alan 471
Cleland, Abigail Pip 172
Clement, Luis Miguel Briola 272
Clementi, Enrich 218
Clements, James Dominic Luther 133
Clements, Sarah 316
Clemmer, Richard L. 50
Clemmer, Richard L. 51
Clemons, Jack 213
Clerc, Vincent 1
Clever, Xiaoqun 110
Clever, Xiaoqun 136
Clever, Xiaoqun 311
Clinck, Erik 345
Close, Matt 653
Cloutier, Jean 244
Clulow, Thomas J. 589
Cluney, Bruce R. 384
Clymo, David 537
Coallier, Robert 299
Coates, Peter 269
Coates, Ralph 644
Coates, Webster 190
Cobian, Mauricio Doehner 144
Coburn, Fergal 23
Coby, Paul 168
Cocenzo, Daniel 40
Cock, Alvaro Velasquez 271
Cockburn, Angus G. 59
Cocker, Tony 574
Cockerill, Ian 110
Cockroft, Graham 21
Cockwell, Jack L. 124
Coe, Sebastian 255
Coelho, Jose Mauricio Pereira 649
Coelho, Jose Mauricio Pereira 655
Coffey, Philip M. 381
Coffey, Philip M. 382
Cogman, David Peter 599
Cohade, Pierre E. 337
Cohen-Welgryn, Myriam 362
Cohen, David 174
Cohen, Marcelo 532
Cohen, Monique 113
Cohen, Monique 285
Cohen, Monique 524
Cohon, Jared L. 644
Coisne-Roquette, Marie-Christine 239
Coisne-Roquette, Marie-Christine 639

Colaco, Russ 331
Colberg, Wolfgang 476
Colberg, Wolfgang 628
Cole, Christopher 678
Cole, David 665
Cole, David A. 445
Cole, David A. 600
Coleman, Christopher L. 98
Coleman, Michael J. 381
Coleman, Michael J. 382
Coleman, Peter John 537
Coleman, Peter John 673
Coles, Pamela 516
Colgan, N. 186
Colizza, Carl 532
Collard, Miranda 617
Collary, Scott 669
Collins, Michelle L. 130
Colnett, Lisa 474
Colombas, Juan 314
Colombo, Paolo Andrea 319
Colpaert, Dries 240
Colruyt, Frans 240
Colruyt, Jef 240
Colruyt, Wim 240
Columb, Barry K. 374
Comadran, Sol Daurella 84
Comin, Luciano 122
Comneno, Maurizia Angelo 393
Comyn, Matthew 174
Concewitz, Robert Kunze 304
Concha, Raimundo Espinoza 184
Condorelli, Carlos Alberto 620
Condorelli, Carlos Alberto 621
Condron, Lisa Margaret 376
Cones, Robert 366
Conger, Harry M. 612
Conix, Birgit 60
Conix, Birgit 646
Conklin, James D. 18
Conlon, Kathleen Marie 111
Conn, Iain C. 125
Connelly, William 565
Connelly, William L. 19
Conner, David Philbrick 577
Connolly, Patrick J. 134
Connors, Michael P. 160
Conophy, F. Anthony 181
Conrad, Diana 274
Conrad, Melinda 44
Consing, Cezar Peralta 93
Constable, David 7
Constantine, Clem 192
Constantini, Carlos Fernando Rossi 322
Contamine, Jerome 565
Contamine, Jerome 639
Conte, Tricia 421
Conti, Fulvio 49
Conway, Heather E. 270
Cook, Alasdair 236
Cook, Paul L. H. 575
Cook, Sharon Lee 421
Coombe, Robert Neil 164
Coomber, John R. 600
Cooper, Frank C. 674
Cooper, Kirstine 73
Cooper, Nancy E. 50
Cooper, Nancy E. 51
Cooper, Nick 339

Cooper, Stephen F. 380
Coors, David S. 415
Coors, Peter H. 415
Cope, George A. 90
Coppens, Rika 240
Coppey, Pierre 659
Corbally, Kevin 71
Corces, Maria Garana 646
Corcoles, Francisco Martinez 300
Corcoran, Marian 475
Cordeiro, Daniel Wakswaser 40
Cordes, Eckhard 664
Corker, Ricky 446
Corley, Dame Elizabeth 539
Corley, Elizabeth 75
Cormack, Ian 425
Cormier, Michelle 297
Cornejo, Amparo 613
Cornhill, David W. 39
Cornhill, David W. 305
Correa, Alvaro 185
Correa, Daniel Sales 119
Corry, Carlos de la Isla 273
Corson, Bradley W. 305
Cortan, Ljiljana 314
Corte-Real, Ana Rita Pontifice Ferreira de Almeida 223
Cortes, Lydie 175
Cosec, Prism 243
Coslet, Jonathan J. 189
Cosslett, Andrew 349
Costa, Francisco Manuel Seixas da 334
Costa, Maria Leticia de Freitas 386
Costa, Maurizio 393
Costantini, Isela 98
Costes, Yseulys 347
Costes, Yseulys 542
Cote, Diane 565
Cote, Jacynthe 519
Cote, Sonya 315
Cotnoir, Frederic 315
Coull-Cicchini, Debbie 315
Coulter, James G. 366
Counsell, Debra J. 111
Courbe, Thomas 502
Courcy, Natasha Scotland 68
Couret, Adrien 540
Court, David C. 123
Court, David C. 134
Courtney, Donal 475
Courville, Isabelle 133
Cousin, Ertharin 103
Couto, Rodrigo Luis Rosa 81
Coutu, Francois J. 400
Coutu, Marcel R. 270
Coutu, Marcel R. 487
Coutu, Michel 400
Covarrubias, Jonathan 83
Cowan, Alister 592
Cox, Caroline 110
Cox, Richard Allen 555
Cox, Simon J. 415
Cox, William 124
Coyles, Stephanie L. 400
Coyles, Stephanie L. 590
Craen, Florian 285
Craig, Andronico Luksic 80
Craig, Gregory G. 134
Cramm, Bettina 73
Crane, Rosemary A. 623

HOOVER'S HANDBOOK OF WORLD BUSINESS 2024

INDEX OF EXECUTIVES

Craven, Philip 643
Crawford, Jonathon 395
Crawford, Millar 626
Crawford, Randall L. 39
Creel, Keith Edward 133
Creixell, Lorenzo Sendra 272
Crepin, Frederic 660
Cretier, Stephen 609
Creutzer, Annika 597
Creux, Antoine 565
Crew, Debra 211
Crisostomo, Michele 230
Crocker, Matthew R. 305
Croisset, Charles de 379
Cronin, Patrick 90
Crosbie, Debbie 644
Crosby, Ralph D. 27
Cross, Anna 94
Cross, Anna 96
Cross, Christine 170
Cross, Patricia 73
Crosthwaite, Perry K.O. 320
Croteau, Lise 297
Croteau, Lise 639
Croteau, Patrick 624
Crouch, Ewen Graham Wolseley 111
Crowley, Eamonn 474
Cruickshank, Nancy 253
Cruz, Rosemarie B. 93
Csanyi, Sandor 414
Cuambe, Manual J. 534
Cubbon, M. 598
Cubbon, Martin 599
Cucchiani, Enrico Tommaso 483
Cudjoe, Bindu 135
Cueva, Adrian G. Sada 273
Cuevas, Diego Gaxiola 272
Cui, David 660
Cui, Shanshan 76
Cui, Yong 152
Culbert, Michael R. 609
Culham, Harry 130
Culmer, George 73
Culmer, George 516
Cumming, Timothy J. 555
Cummings, Arthur 32
Cummins, John J. 8
Cunha, Gustavo Werneck da 268
Cunha, Jose Mauro Mettrau Carneiro da 119
Cunha, Maria da 317
Cunha, Paulo Roberto Simoes da 80
Cunningham, Peter 509
Cunningham, Peter 511
Cunningham, Susan M. 226
Cunnington, Kathleen K. 35
Cuppen, Tanja 7
Cura, German 620
Curadeau-Grou, Patricia 423
Curado, Frederico Fleury 7
Curado, Frederico Pinheiro Fleury 649
Curl, Gregory Lynn 165
Curran, Judy 247
Currie, Alistair 96
Currie, Gordon A. M. 668
Curtin, Terrence R. 611
Curtis, Ross A. 501
Cusumano, Michael 468
Cuthbertson, Andrew 187
Cutifani, Mark 639

Cutrale, Jose Luis 171
Cutrignelli, Raffaele 228
Cutts, Leanne 532
Czichowski, Frank 173

D

D'Ambrosio, Alexandre Silva 655
D'Amours, Jacques 35
d'Artaise, Thierry de La Tour 542
d'iribarne, Benoit 175
Dabarno, Susan F. 386
Dacey, John R. 600
Dacus, Stephen Hayes 546
Dadyburjor, Khush 668
Daehnke, Arno 575
Dagach, Fernando Aguad 81
Dahan, Rene 504
Dahl, Jacob 198
Dahlberg, Annika 563
Dahlin, P. Andrew 145
Dai, Houliang 478
Dai, Kazuhiko 602
Dai, Trudy Shan 34
Daikoku, Tetsuya 410
Dalal, Jatin Pravinchandra 671
Dalbies, Eric 524
Dalena, Fredrick K. 39
Daley, Matthew 47
Daley, Pamela 118
Dalibard, Barbara 177
Dalibard, Barbara 506
Dall'Orto, Leonardo Campo 120
Daly, Emer 524
Daly, Fiona 92
Dames, Brian A. 428
Damme, Alexandre Van 48
Damme, Niek Jan van 618
Daneau, Guy 299
Dangeard, Frank E. 427
Daniel, Patrick D. 130
Daniell, Richard 623
Daniels, Ed 549
Daniels, Michael E. 337
Danielsson, Lars-Erik 597
Dannenfeldt, Thomas 143
Dannenfeldt, Thomas 446
Danson, Savannah 555
Daochai, Predee 85
Darko, Alex B. 8
Darmaillac, Marie-Annick 502
Darmon, Marc 626
Daruvala, Toos N. 519
Das, Maarten 280
Dascupta, Anindya 304
Dassault, Laurent 661
Dassen, Roger J. M. 60
Dasso, Raimundo Morales 185
Dattels, Timothy D. 189
Daudin, Herve 140
Daunis-Opfermann, Sibylle 175
Daurella, Alfonso Libano 170
Daurella, Sol 170
Daveu, Marie-Claire 185
Daveu, Marie-Claire 347
Davey, Bradley 55
Davey, Larry M. 613
Davey, Peter W. 304

David-Borha, Olusola 172
David, Anastassis G. 172
David, Charlotte 285
Davidson, Carol A. (John) 611
Davidson, Janet G. 580
Davies, Christa 49
Davies, Howard 425
Davies, Howard 427
Davies, Mark 511
Davies, Rhian 539
Davies, Stuart Jeffrey 364
Davila, Alejandro Santo Domingo 48
Davis, Charles A. 74
Davis, Chris 169
Davis, Crispin H. 661
Davis, Darrell L. 35
Davis, Frank 214
Davis, Gareth 215
Davis, Greg 172
Davis, Mike H. 428
Davis, Richard 471
Davis, Scott Trevor 29
Davis, Scott Trevor 121
Davis, Scott Trevor 570
Davis, Stuart 91
Davydov, Andrey 243
Dawidowsky, Tim 558
Dawson, Dame Sandra 644
Dawson, Jonathan 424
Dayon, Alexandre 656
Dean, Johanne 624
Deans, Alison 498
Debackere, Koenraad 345
Debackere, Koenraad 650
Debarenne-Fievet, Christele 525
Debon, Marie-Ange 56
Debow, Daniel 374
Debroux, Laurence 243
Decalf, Vincent Robert Gilles 621
Dechant, Johann 311
Decker, Eva Vilstrup 137
Decoene, Ulrike 73
Dedi, Liren 478
Dee-Bradbury, Rebecca P. 111
Deeble, Helen 138
Deesrinthum, Pratamaporn 491
Deflesselle, Raphaelle 116
Dehaze, Alain 15
Dehl, Jaspreet 123
deJocas, Veronique 617
Dekkers, Guus 622
Dekkers, Sophie 220
Dekura, Kazuhito 194
Delabarre, Laurent 506
Delabriere, Yann 580
Delage, Jacinthe 233
Delaney, Emma 117
Delaporte, Thierry 175
Delaporte, Thierry 671
Delaunay, Nolwenn 247
Delbos, Clotilde 73
Delbos, Clotilde 501
DelFrari, Rhona M. 145
Delgado, Luz Maria Zarza 481
Delhaye, Catherine 656
Deli, Efthymia P. 240
Delia, Ronald S. 41
Dellaquila, Frank J. 51
Delmas, Bernard 444
Delorme, Marie Y. 135

Delpit, Bernard 502
Delport, Dominique 661
Deltenre, Ingrid 208
Delvaux, Nico 61
Demaille, Frank 233
Demare, Michel 66
Demare, Michel 661
Demidchuck, Roberto 621
Demirag, Levent 29
Demirtas, Ozgur 29
Demone, Henry E. 532
Denby, Nigel Christopher William 43
Dench, Robert G. 169
Deng, Jindong 560
Denham, Gillian H. 133
Denham, Robert Edwin 254
Denis, Jean-Pierre 348
Denison, David F. 106
Denison, David F. 519
Denomme, Yves 363
DeNunzio, Tony 189
Denzel, Nora M. 237
Depatie, Robert 514
Depickere, Franky 345
DePinto, Joseph Michael 546
Derbyshire, Mark E. 134
Dereeper, Philippe 580
Derman, Emre 29
DeRose, Kathleen Traynor 376
Derrey, Herve 626
Derville, Vianney 362
Desaulniers, Sylvain 624
Descalzi, Claudio 235
Deschamps, Ignacio 91
Deschamps, Isabelle 511
Deschamps, Yvan 363
Descours, Anne-Laure 496
Desforges, Odile 247
Desikan, Anantha N. 302
Desjardins, Kristi L. 305
Desjardins, Luc 130
Deslarzes, Jean-Christophe 15
Desmarais, Andre 270
Desmarais, Andre 487
Desmarais, Olivier 487
Desmarais, Paul 270
Desmarais, Paul 487
Destrebohn, Karine 32
Desvaux, Georges 73
Dethlefs, Sven 623
Devine, Cynthia J. 224
Devine, Cynthia J. 519
Dexter, Robert P. 106
Dhawan, Neelam 301
Diacetti, Roberto 526
Diamantopoulou, Anna 172
Diaz, Javier Monteoliva 308
Diaz, Manuel Bartlett 481
Diaz, Maria Angeles Alcala 300
Dibblee, Jennifer 299
Dicciani, Nance K. 380
Dickinson, Alan 374
Dickinson, Dan 236
Dickson, James M. 224
Dickson, Julie E. 386
Diderot, Matignon 140
Diekmann, Michael 37
Diekmann, Michael 261
Diekmann, Michael 557
Diethelm, Markus U. 647

INDEX OF EXECUTIVES

Diether, Tatjana 100
Dietiker, Ueli 600
Dietrich, Sabine U. 173
Dietz, Harry C. 274
Diez, Javier Rodriguez 657
Diezhandino, Cristina 211
Dijanosic, Michael 122
Dilley, Margarita K. 256
Dillon, Rick T. 18
Dincer, Suzan Sabanci 29
Ding, Feng 48
Ding, James 76
Ding, Jianzhong 688
Ding, William Lei 433
Dingemans, Simon 677
Dinkins, James Leonard 171
Dionis, Javier Bernal 647
DiPietro, Kenneth 366
Dirks, Thorsten 206
DiSanzo, Deborah 66
Diskul, Disnadda 555
Dittmeier, Carolyn G. 38
Dixon, Roger J. 46
Dixson-Decleve, Sandrine 223
Djurovic, Zarko 4
Dmitriev, Andrey 266
Dobak, Miklos 414
Dobber, Ruud 66
Doboczky, Stefan 463
Dobson, Julie A. 256
Dobson, Michael 539
Docherty, Alan 174
Dodig, Victor G. 130
Doer, Gary A. 270
Doer, Gary A. 487
Does, Pieter Willem van der 18
Doherty, Elizabeth 453
Doherty, Geoff 524
Doherty, Liz 358
Doherty, Sharon 374
Dohm, Karin 143
Doi, Miwako 583
Doi, Nobuhiro 89
Doig, John 91
Dolla, Sylvain 597
Dollin, Paul 678
Domichi, Hideaki 595
Dominati, Philippe 617
Dominguez, Andres Tagle 184
Dominguez, Christian Tauber 81
Dominguez, Jaime Muguiro 144
dominguez, Jose Eladio Seco 14
Domit, Carlos Slim 43
Domit, Patrick Slim 43
Donaghey, Elizabeth 44
Donck, Frank 345
Dong, Jia-Ting 682
Dong, Junqing 128
Dong, Xin 154
Dong, Yang 309
Donges, Jutta A. 173
Dongwana, Neo Phakama 428
Donkers, Wijnand P. 119
Donnelly, Roisin 427
Donnelly, Scott C. 395
Donnet, Philippe 63
Donofrio, John 337
Donofrio, Nicholas M. 50
Donofrio, Nicholas M. 51
Donohue, Steve 675

Donsion, Marie-Jose 56
Dontas, Periklis 483
Doo, William Junior Guiherme 88
Doo, William Wai Hoi 434
Dooley, Helen 23
Dooley, Shaun 421
Doppelt, Yoav 302
Doppstadt, Eric W. 55
Dorfler, Stefan 238
Dorig, Rolf 600
Dorlack, Jerome J. 18
Dormer, Alistair 287
Dorn, Mark 284
Dorner, Dan 7
Dorrego, Ana 83
Dorri, Sepanta 613
Dors, Laurence 185
Dorssers, Leon 444
Dort, Helene M. Vletter-van 445
Dorward-King, Elaine J. 555
Dosky, Jorg von 208
Doss, Manred 663
Dottori-Attanasio, Laura 130
Dotzenrath, Anja 117
Dou, Jian 156
Dougherty, Linda M. 590
Doughty, Stuart J. 78
Douglas, Carl 61
Douglas, William W. 172
Doukeris, Michel Dimitrios 40
Dourado, Esmeralda da Silva Santos 223
Doustdar, Maziar Mike 455
Douvas, Maria 519
Dowley, Justin 395
Dowling, Anne Melissa 74
Dowling, Caroline 201
Dowling, Edward C. 613
Downe, William A. 374
Downey, Roger Allan 655
Downing, John Matthew 179
Downing, John Matthew 304
Downing, Michael S. 68
Doyle, Katie 357
Drapé, Eric 623
Draper, Daniel J. 74
Dresser, Scott 236
Dreuzy, Pascaline de 116
Driesen, Maya vanden 665
Drinkwater, Anne 78
Drinkwater, Anne 236
Driot-Argentin, Veronique 661
Driscoll, Sharon 224
Drozdov, Anton V. 340
Drutman, Nadine R. 8
Dryburgh, Kerry 118
Du, Jun 559
Du, K.L. 159
Du, Shu-Chin 682
Duan, Liangwei 478
Duan, Rachel 15
Duan, Rachel 73
Duan, Rachel 295
Duan, Rachel 530
Duan, Wenwei 199
Dube, Benoit 149
Dube, Muriel Betty Nicolle 534
Dubey, Asmita 362
Dubois, Stephane 524
Dubourdeau, Pierre-Louis 177

Dubourg, Saori 100
Dubovitsky, Sergey 412
Dubovskov, Andrey 561
Dubrule, Guillaume 506
Dubrulle, Philippe 362
Dubuc, Nancy 253
Dubugras, Henrique 396
Dudley, Robert 517
Dudley, William C. 648
Duenas, Luis Cabra 504
Duesmann, Markus 663
Duffy, David 168
Dufour, Sandrine 677
Dufourcq, Nicolas 579
Dufourcq, Nicolas 580
Dufresne, Richard 374
Dufresne, Richard 668
Dugle, Lynn A. 611
Duh, Wu-Lin 216
Duhamel, Philippe 626
Duhe, Sherry 673
Duijl, Milko van 366
Duinhoven, Susan 354
Duke, Nora M. 256
Dulac, Fabienne 362
Dulac, Sophie 495
Dumas, Axel 285
Dumas, Claire 565
Dumas, Matthieu 285
Dumas, Pierre-Alexis 285
Dumazy, Bertrand 362
Dumont, Philippe 185
Dumurgier, Beatrice 140
Dunbar, Webster Roy 337
Dunkel, Gunter 183
Dunkerley, Mark B. 27
Dunn, Craig W. 618
Dunn, Lydia Selina 598
Dunning, J. G. 385
Dunnwald, Achim 317
Dunoyer, Marc 66
Dupin, Patrick 175
Duplaix, Jean-Marc 347
Dupont, Xavier 656
Duport, Valerie 347
Duprat, Pierre 659
Duprieu, Jean-Pierre 177
Duprieu, Jean-Pierre 542
Dupui, Jean Pierre 82
Dupuis, Patrick 671
Duran, Maria Juliana Alban 221
Durand, Olivier 247
Durand, Patrice 233
Durand, Xavier 32
Durante, Nicandro 499
Durbaum, Matthias 523
Durcan, Mark D. M. 60
Düren, Avi Aydin 647
Durongkaveroj, Pichet 85
Durrfeld, Katja 183
Duschmale, Jorg 513
Dussault, Claude 315
Dussault, Claude 400
Dutra, Felipe 48
Duz, Cetin 29
Dvorkovich, Arkady V. 340
Dy, Lucy C. 107
Dybal, Alexander 266
Dyck, Mark Van 180
Dyckerhoff, Claudia R. Sussmuth 498

Dyckerhoff, Claudia Suessmuth 488
Dyckerhoff, Claudia Suessmuth 513
Dynysiuk, Joanna 94
Dyson, Ian 332
Dyukov, Alexander Valerievich 266

E

Earp, Dawn 304
Earp, Pedro 48
East, Warren D. A. 60
Easterbrook, Jill 59
Eastwood, M. Glen 135
Eaton, Roger G. 415
Ebbe, Michael 216
Ebel, Gregory L. 226
Ebel, Sebastian 646
Eberl, Stephan 418
Ebicloglu, Fatih Kemal 353
Ebner, Bernhard 105
Ecclissato, Reginaldo 653
Echavarria, Luis Fernando Restrepo 85
Echavez, Luis Hernandez 144
Echeverri, Juan Emilio Posada 221
Echeverria, Jose Antonio 170
Eckardt, Daniela 143
Eckersley, Debra 92
Eckerstrom, Hans 597
Eckert, Jean-Blaise 176
Eckhardt, Sabine 143
Eda, Makiko 262
Eda, Makiko 634
Edahiro, Hiromi 630
Edahiro, Junko 634
Eddington, Rod 351
Eddington, Roderick I. 167
Eddy, Jodi Euerle 18
Edelstenne, Charles 626
Eder, Wolfgang 311
Eder, Wolfgang 663
Edgeworth, Allan L. 39
Edin, Betul Ebru 646
Edozien, Ngozi 304
Edwardes, Robert 674
Edwards, Christine A. 90
Edwards, N. Murray 132
Edwards, Robert 413
Egami, Setsuko 505
Egan, Jo 21
Egawa, Masako 403
Egawa, Masako 410
Egawa, Masako 632
Egeriis, Carsten Rasch 198
Egerth-Stadlhuber, Henrietta 238
Egloff, Francisco Rogelio Garza 38
Egloff, Francisco Rogelio Garza 52
Eguchi, Kouji 402
Eguia, Jose Antonio Chedraui 273
Eguiguren, Manuel Francisco Gana 225
Egusa, Shun 595
Ehrling, Marie 450
Ehrnrooth, Henrik 354
Eibensteiner, Herbert 663
Eichenbaum, Martin S. 90
Eichiner, Friedrich 37
Eichiner, Friedrich 311
Einarsson, Petra 528

INDEX OF EXECUTIVES

Eismann, Gabriele 399
Eitrheim, Pal 236
Ejel, Remy 432
Ek, Daniel 574
Ekabut, Chaovalit 554
Ekberg, David 581
Ekedahl, Anders 597
Ekholm, Borje E. 236
Eki, Yuji 286
Ekudden, Erik 237
El-Erian, Mohamed A. 94
Elcock, Peter Charles 471
Eldert-Klep, Cindy van 314
Eldessouky, Sam A. 101
Elfving, Ulrika 3
Elhedery, Georges 294
Eli, Ovadia 302
Eliasson, Thomas 4
Elizalde, Raul A. Anaya 81
Elizondo, Carlos Jose Garcia Moreno 43
Elkann, Ginevra 243
Elkann, John 243
Elkann, John 579
Eller, Elke 646
Elliott, Christy 474
Elliott, Matt 88
Elliott, Robert 474
Elliott, Shayne C. 71
Elliott, Shayne Cary 43
Ellis, Jeffrey Jerom 133
Ellis, Simon 61
Ellman, Mark A. 19
Elmin, Henrik 70
Elmslie, Nick 429
Eloranta, Jorma 581
Elphick, Jason 471
Elsner, Thomas 103
Elstein, Amir 623
Elvira, Susana 1
Elzen, Ronald den 280
Elzvik, Eric 664
Elzvik, Eric A. 237
Emmet, James 293
Emori, Tomoaki 583
Emory, Michael R. 236
Empey, Rachel Claire 105
Empey, Rachel Claire 259
Empey, Rachel Claire 261
Endicott, David J. 32
Endo, Isao 570
Endo, Junichi 444
Endo, Nobuhiro 632
Endo, Noriko 442
Endo, Yasuaki 361
Endrud, Nik 247
Engel, Hans-Ulrich 100
Engel, Marc 1
Engelfried, Annette 311
Engels, Stephen 198
Engelstoft, Morten Henrick 1
Engin, Eyup 29
England, William T. 624
English, Bill 665
Engstrom, Erik 500
Ennis, Patrick J. 671
Enns, Peter 160
Enomoto, Chisa 477
Enomoto, Koichi 407
Entwistle, Darren 619

Epaillard, Hugues 113
Epron, Daniel 185
Eremin, Andrey 484
Erenburg, Alexander 243
Erginbilgic, Tufan 201
Erginbilgic, Tufan 516
Ericksen, Susan 236
Ericson, Magnus 596
Eriguchi, Osamu 583
Eriksen, Jan Otto 616
Erlen, Hubertus 392
Ernst, Edgar 646
Ersek, Hikmet 238
Erskine, Peter 615
Erun, Gokhan 353
Erün, Gökhan 684
Ervasti-Vaintola, Ilona 258
Escajadillo, Ricardo Ernesto Saldivar 254
Escandar, Pedro Samhan 81
Escobar, Diana Hoyos 221
Esperdy, Therese 304
Esperdy, Therese 424
Espey, Robert B. 474
Espinola, Javier de Pedro 272
Espinosa, Alicia 528
Espinosa, Ivan 444
Espiritu, Octavio Victor R. 93
Esposito, Jose 185
Esser, Frank 601
Esser, Isabelle 197
Esser, Juergen 197
Etchells, Paul Kenneth 599
Etienne, Jean-Michel 494
Eua-arporn, Bundhit 85
Eua-arporn, Bundhit 491
Euarchukiati, Yos 554
Euchukanonchai, Krairit 491
Euris, Foncière 140
Evans, Aicha 531
Evans, Gay Huey 577
Evans, J. Michael 34
Evans, J. Michael 98
Evans, Mark 615
Evans, Nicola M. Wakefield 381
Evans, Nicola M. Wakefield 382
Evans, Peter J. 498
Evans, Richard B. 182
Evers, Sherri L. 305
Everts, Daniel 597
Evlioglu, Isil Akdemir 646
Evtushenkov, Vladimir 561
Ewerth, Maria Romberg 61
Ewing, Margaret 316
Exel, Audette E. 669
Eyuboglu, Yagiz 353
Ezekiel, Laurent 677
Ezzat, Aiman 136
Ezzat, Aiman 362

F

Faber, Alexis 670
Faber, Hanneke 653
Faber, Johanna W 103
Fabri, Eurico Ramos 80
Facchin, Claudio 287
Fagg, Jenny 92

Fagg, Kathryn 421
Fahima, Ilana 302
Fairbairn, Carolyn 622
Fairbairn, Dame Carolyn 295
Fairbairn, Sally 574
Fairweather, Carol 564
Fajemirokun-Beck, Olu 532
Fajerman, Sergio Guillinet 322
Fakude, Nolitha 46
Fakude, Nolitha 47
Falcone, Cristiana 615
Faldini, Roberto 119
Falero, Barbara 185
Fallowfield, Tim 325
Falzon, Sylvia 592
Fan, Banghan 560
Fan, Henry Hung-ling 589
Fan, Liangdong 159
Fang, Rong 688
Fang, Sylvia 603
Fappani, Silvia Alessandra 230
Farah, Pedro 457
Farahat, Tarek 677
Farahat, Tarek Mohamed Noshy Nasr Mohamed 331
Faria, Joao V. 220
Farias, Humberto Junqueira de 331
Farley, Claire S. 380
Farr, Sue 122
Farrell, Dawn L. 132
Farrell, Patrick 474
Farrell, Rebecca 41
Faruqui, Farhan 71
Fassbind, Renato 360
Fassbind, Renato 432
Fassbind, Renato 600
Fassin, Frank 418
Fata, Anthony M. 532
Faujour, Veronique 185
Faury, Guillaume 27
Faury, Guillaume 185
Fausing, Kim 290
Fauvel, Virginie 476
Favre, Juliette 239
Fearn, Ulrica 137
Fearon, Mark 249
Fearon, Richard H. 186
Fedorishin, Grigory 456
Fehrenbach, Franz 100
Fehrmann, Andrea 557
Feinglass, Shamiram R. 527
Felix, June 500
Fellmann, Beat 282
Feng, Bing 87
Feng, Lun 433
Feng, Weidong 309
Feng, Zhuo Zhi 152
Fenn, Grant Anthony 214
Fennebresque, Kim 102
Fentenoy, Maud 661
Fenwick, Nicholas Adam Hodnett 598
Feodosiev, Lev V. 453
Feoktistov, Vadim 484
Feral-Schuhl, Christiane 140
Ferguson-McHugh, Mary Lynn 415
Ferguson, Brian C. 638
Ferguson, Michael J. 214
Ferm, Peter 3
Fernandes, Jorge 514
Fernandes, Oswaldo Tadeu 80

Fernandes, Ruben 47
Fernandez, Eliseo Santiago Perez 331
Fernandez, Felipe Fernandez 223
Fernandez, Fernando 653
Fernandez, Jaime Sanchez 52
Fernandez, Jose Walfredo 300
Fernandez, Juan Ignacio Echeverria 83
Fernandez, Marcela Villareal 52
Fernandez, Ramon 73
Fernandez, Ramon 464
Fernandez, Ricardo Alonso 83
Fernkorn, Thomas 143
Ferone, Alessandra 526
Ferraby, Stephen 213
Ferran, Javier 211
Ferran, Javier 316
Ferrand, Carole 136
Ferrari, Gianfranco 185
Ferrari, Paolo 120
Ferraro, Maria 136
Ferraro, Maria 558
Ferraz, Joao Carlos 331
Ferreira, Eduardo Bacellar Leal 480
Ferreira, Jose de Paiva 82
Ferreira, Laurent 422
Ferrer, Antonio Garcia 13
Ferrezuelo, Isabel Torremocha 504
Ferrier, Andrew 668
Ferrier, Susan 421
Ferris, Stephanie L. 377
Ferro, Claudio Braz 48
Fewkes, Graham James 137
Fidanza, Laura 533
Fields, Janice L. 35
Figari, Alberta 63
Figueroa, Juan Jose Paullada 481
Figueroa, Julio Santiago 80
Filaretos, Spyros N. 38
Filho, Augusto Marques da Cruz 120
Filho, Edison Terra 119
Filho, Eduardo de Oliveira Rodrigues 655
Filho, Gesner Jose de Oliveira 119
Filho, Lucio de Castro Andrade 649
Filho, Marcelo Mesquita de Siqueira 480
Filho, Milton Maluhy 81
Filho, Milton Maluhy 322
Filho, Oscar Augusto de Camargo 655
Filipovic, Damir 600
Filippelli, Maria 135
Filosa, Antonio 579
Fimiani, Grazia 235
Finan, Irial 564
Finan, Pat 111
Finch, Shannon 669
Findlay, Martha Hall 592
Findlay, Michael 317
Finet, Bertrand 542
Fink, Monika 173
Finn, Sean 131
Fioranelli, Marcelo 362
Firek, Marcin 675
Firpo, Pablo 40
Fischer, Rudolph W. 537
Fish, Simon A. 90
Fisher, Andrew C. 388
Fisher, Justine B. 613
Fisher, Martin 392
Fitch, Laurie 223

INDEX OF EXECUTIVES

Fitzgerald, Stephen 497
Fitzpatrick, Dawn 94
Fitzpatrick, Dawn 96
Fitzpatrick, Eileen 88
Fitzwater, Matthew 96
Flatt, J. Bruce 124
Flatz, Alois 238
Fleche, Eric Richer La 90
Fleche, Eric Richer La 400
Fleischer, Egbert 102
Fleming, Campbell 482
Fleurant, James 293
Fleuriot, Elisabeth 581
Fleuriot, Pierre 444
Fleuriot, Pierre 502
Flint, Richard 253
Flintermann, Wolfgang 646
Floel, Martina 429
Floel, Martina 534
Florence, Cristian 83
Flores, Hector Avila 273
Flores, Jose Antonio Gonzalez 144
Florey, Reinhard 463
Florez, Maria Edith Gonzalez 271
Florian, Gerard 71
Flutter, Naomi 665
Flynn, Patrick 73
Flynn, Patrick 425
Flynn, Patrick 427
Flynn, Thomas E. 90
Flynn, Thomas E. 619
Foad, Keiran 84
Foden, Ross Neil 43
Fok, Canning K. N. 146
Fok, Winnie 563
Foley, Real 612
Foll, Arnaud Le 453
Folland, Nick 388
Follen, Geert 70
Follens, Geert 4
Fong, Christopher L. 132
Fonseca, Cristina 265
Fonseca, Lidia L. 395
Font, Felipe Cortes 52
Fontana, Bernard 626
Fontbona, Jean Paul Luksic 80
Fontes, Teresa Cristina Athayde Marcondes 322
Foo, Jixun 76
Foran, Mike 133
Forberg, Lars 7
Forchiassin, Horacio Oscar 686
Ford, James 274
Forese, James A. 295
Forestier, Brigitte 542
Fornaro, Celine 525
Fornés, Maite Ballester 504
Forrest, Andrew 255
Forsberg, Mattias 596
Forsee, Gary D. 644
Forssell, Johan 70
Fortier, Philippe 678
Fortin, Anne 315
Fortin, Richard 35
Fortino, Carmine 400
Fossati, Giorgio 579
Fosse, Gaelle de la 15
Fossum, Erik 452
Foulon, Hugues 464
Fournier, Jean-Rene 282

Fournier, Olivier 285
Fournier, Thierry 175
Fowler, Cameron 90
Fowler, Christopher H. 135
Foxx, Anthony R. 458
Frachet, Stephanie 182
Frachet, Stephanie 656
Framil, Leo 11
Franceschini, Luca 235
Franchini, Roberto 319
Francioni, Reto 172
Francioni, Reto 648
Francis, Cheryl A. 49
Francis, Mary 94
Francis, Mary 96
Franco, Jorge Elman Osorio 221
Franco, Juan David Escobar 85
Francoeur, Bruno 592
Francois-Poncet, Andre 73
Frandberg, Sofia 664
Frande, Johannes 354
Frank, Meghan 377
Franklin, Fabiam 179
Franz, Christoph 162
Franz, Christoph 513
Franz, Christoph 689
Fraser-Moleketi, Geraldine J. 575
Fraser, James C. 501
Fratto, Tanya D. 59
Frawley, Michael 24
Frawley, Michael 474
Frazier, Steve 134
Frazis, George 92
Fredette, Eric Antoine 656
Fredrickson, David 66
Fredrickson, Glenn H. 402
Freedman, Ian 374
Frega, Lorraine 177
Frei, Barbara 601
Freidberg, Luis Rubio 171
Freitas, Jorge Seabra de 265
Freitas, Pedro van Langendonck Teixeira de 119
Freixe, Laurent 431
French, Doug 619
Freshwater, Timothy George 599
Freudenstein, Richard J. 172
Freundt, Arne 496
Frew, Anita M. 516
Frew, Nicole 91
Freyne, Colm J. 589
Freyne, Colm J. 590
Friberg, Therese 3
Frick, David P. 432
Fridman, Alexander M. 453
Fridriksdottir, Hafrun 623
Friedland, David 320
Friese, Lard 19
Friis, Morten N. 425
Friis, Morten N. 427
Frisk, Mikael 258
Fritz, Sandra 663
Frohlich, Klaus 218
Frolov, Alexander 243
Fromont, Emmanuel 12
Froneman, Neal J. 555
Frost, Patrick 513
Frost, Patrick 600
Frutos, Pilar Gonzalez de 227
Fu, Rong 547

Fu, Shan 560
Fu, Suotang 478
Fuangfu, Chansak 85
Fuchs, Jaroslaw 94
Fuder, Andrea 664
Fudge, Ann M. 453
Fujie, Taro 29
Fujihara, Kazuhiko 567
Fujii, Hideto 412
Fujii, Hiroshi 73
Fujii, Ichirou 361
Fujii, Mariko 409
Fujii, Mariko 457
Fujikawa, Osamu 427
Fujikura, Katsuaki 630
Fujimori, Shun 321
Fujimori, Yoshiaki 605
Fujimoto, Junichi 361
Fujimoto, Masayoshi 569
Fujimoto, Tetsuya 391
Fujimoto, Tomoko 296
Fujimura, Hiroshi 551
Fujinuki, Tetsuo 583
Fujioka, Hiroshi 223
Fujioka, Makoto 439
Fujioka, Yuji 404
Fujisaki, Kazuo 346
Fujisawa, Kumi 552
Fujita, Kazuko 361
Fujita, Motohiro 20
Fujiwara, Ichiro 90
Fujiwara, Ken 402
Fujiwara, Masataka 470
Fujiwara, Satoru 296
Fujiwara, Shuichi 89
Fujiwara, Toshi 457
Fukai, Akihiko 275
Fukakusa, Janice 374
Fukakusa, Janice R. 124
Fukasawa, Yuji 219
Fukuchi, Junichi 329
Fukuda, Kazuhisa 441
Fukuda, Kyoichi 249
Fukuda, Naori 223
Fukuda, Nobuo 402
Fukuda, Takaharu 342
Fukuda, Takayuki 679
Fukuda, Toshihiko 634
Fukuhara, Keishi 93
Fukui, Akira 679
Fukui, Toshihiko 552
Fukujin, Yusuke 33
Fukumoto, Yasuaki 303
Fukunaga, Takehisa 73
Fukuoka, Takashi 190
Fukushima, Sakie Tachibana 361
Fukushima, Yutaka 552
Fukutome, Akihiro 587
Fukuyama, Masanori 93
Fukuzawa, Ichiro 45
Fulconis, Catherine 285
Fuller, David G. 270
Fumagalli, Adrienne Corboud 600
Funaki, Ryuichiro 420
Funaki, Toru 163
Funakoshi, Hirofumi 441
Funamoto, Kaoru 288
Funck, Florian 143
Funck, Florian 392
Fung, Allen Yuk-lun 589

Fung, Anita Yuen Mei 114
Fung, Maureen Sau-yim 589
Fung, Victor Kwok-King 159
Fung, William Kwok-lun 589
Furberg, Petter-Borre 616
Fure, Hiroshi 360
Furer, Guido 600
Furlan, Luiz Fernando 120
Furrer, Ivo 282
Furse, Clara Hedwig Frances 661
Furukawa, Hironari 277
Furukawa, Shuntaro 437
Furumoto, Shozo 441
Furusawa, Mitsuhiro 405
Furuse, Makoto 163
Furuta, Hidenori 263
Furutachi, Naoto 93
Furuya, Hiromichi 163
Furuya, Takayuki 389
Furuya, Yoshiaki 681
Furuyama, Hideaki 527
Fushitani, Kiyoshi 468
Futagawa, Kazuo 636

G

Gabbard, Dan 400
Gadbois, L. G. Serge 299
Gadhia, Jayne-Anne 651
Gadhia, Jitesh 516
Gadola, Marco 213
Gadomski, Marcin 94
Gaemperle, Chantal 379
Gagarin, Nikolai 456
Gager, Steward D. 497
Gagnon, Louis 624
Gagnon, Martin 422
Gagnon, Martin 532
Gaillard, Jean-Pierre 185
Gaines, Elizabeth Anne 255
Gairard, William 542
Gal, Aharon 452
Galan, Jose Ignacio Sanchez 300
Galbo, Julie 213
Galbraith, Susan 66
Galifi, Vincent J. 384
Galipeau, Linda 678
Gall-Robinson, Claire Le 540
Gall, David 421
Gallagher, James D. 386
Galle, Jean-Loic 626
Gallego, Emilio Garcia 13
Gallego, Luis 316
Galli, Joseph 612
Gallienne, Ian 17
Gallienne, Ian 476
Gallo, Jose 649
Gallo, Livio 228
Galperin, Marcos Eduardo 396
Galperin, Nicolas 396
Galtney, William F. 242
Galuccio, Miguel Matias 537
Galvagni, Agostino 600
Galvez, Jose Damian Bogas 227
Galvin, Donal 23
Gamba, Angela 393
Gammell, Damian P. 170
Gan, Kathleen Chieh Huey 276

INDEX OF EXECUTIVES

Gan, Larry Nyap Liou 43
Gan, Pin 547
Ganeev, Oleg 535
Ganesan, Venky 558
Ganong, David A. 589
Gansberg, David E. 55
Gantsho, Mandla Sizwe Vulindlela 304
Ganzin, Michel 185
Gao, Dinggui 528
Gao, Jianmin 335
Gao, Jie 267
Gao, Qiang 560
Gao, Song 559
Gao, Tongqing 154
Gaona, Amancio Ortega 308
Garcia-Ansorena, Ramiro Mato 84
Garcia-Ivald, Romain 639
Garcia, Alberto Velazquez 481
Garcia, Antonio Botella 13
Garcia, Begona Elices 504
Garcia, Belen Romana 73
Garcia, Belen Romana 84
Garcia, Claudio 48
Garcia, Fabian T. 653
Garcia, Federico Jose Reyes 171
Garcia, Fernando Perez-Serrabona 386
Garcia, Gloria Hernandez 558
Garcia, Ian Marcel Craig 171
Garcia, Miguel Moreno 225
Garcia, Norma Rocio Nahle 481
Garcia, Pierre Francis Haas 38
Garcia, Rosa Maria Garcia 386
Garcia, Washington Fabricio Ponce 171
Garcin-Meunier, Delphine 32
Gardner, Anthony 123
Gardner, Anthony L. 300
Gardner, Kirt 647
Gardner, Paul 592
Garg, Parag 168
Garijo, Belen 362
Garijo, Belen 399
Garling, Philip Stuart 214
Garnier, Thierry 349
Garnier, Thierry 622
Garrard, Adam L. 670
Garrett, Mark 463
Garrett, Mark 650
Garrido, Santiago Martinez 300
Gartner, Mathias 290
Gartside, Nicholas 418
Garza, Alfonso Garza 254
Garza, Alfonso Garza 254
Garza, Alvaro Fernandez 38
Garza, Eugenio Garza y 254
Garza, Jose Carlos Pons de la 38
Garza, Rafael Arana de la 273
Gasmen, Dino R. 93
Gasperment, Sophie A. 349
Gass, John D. 592
Gasselsberger, Franz 663
Gasssel, Helmut 311
Gather, Ursula 418
Gather, Ursula 628
Gattei, Francesco 235
Gatti, Anna 319
Gaunt, John 471
Gauto, Fladimir Batista Lopes 268
Gaveau, Nathalie 170
Gavezotti, Graziella 659

Gavgani, Bernard 113
Gavrielov, Moshe N. 603
Gaw, Christina 167
Gayares, Marita Socorro D. 93
Gaymard, Clara 116
Gaymard, Clara 197
Gaymard, Clara 379
Geale, Leanne 290
Geale, Leanne 432
Gealogo, Noravir A. 93
Gearhart, Jeffrey J. 138
Gebauer, Julie 670
Gebreyes, Tsega 376
Geheran, Tony 619
Geiger, Kurt 497
Geissinger, Jurgen M. 528
Geissinger, Uwe 384
Gelard, Yves Le 233
Gelink, G. G. 250
Gelsthorpe, Ed 75
Gemkow, Stephan 392
Gemkow, Stephen 27
Gemmell, Constance D. 305
Gemmell, Robert J. 514
Genc, Onur 80
Genereux, Claude 270
Genereux, Claude 487
Genereux, Nathalie 422
Genest, Paul C. 487
Genola, Gabriele Galateri di 63
Genova, Juan Maria Nin 565
Genster, Grit 261
Gentil, Richard 502
Gentoso, Jamie M. 290
Geny-stephann, Delphine 626
Geoghegan, Basil 24
George, Mark R. 644
George, Timothy M. 214
Geraghty, Sharon C. 270
Gerbaulet, Ute 523
Gerecke, Glenn A. 527
Germain, Jean-Marc 182
Germain, Maurice 299
Gernandt, Karl 360
Gerow, Martine 540
Gerrard, Ron 339
Gervais, Michel 299
Getz, Robert Hinman 612
Geva-Harel, Lilach 302
Ghalayini, Fadi 597
Gharbi, Hinda 509
Gheorghe, Mariana 314
Ghezzi, Gioia 621
Ghostine, Gilbert 527
Ghotmeh, Lina 175
Giancarlo, J. Christopher 448
Giangualano, Patrizia Michela 526
Gianotti, Anthony 665
Giansante, Filippo 235
Giard, Diane 236
Giard, Diane 624
Giard, Matthieu 362
Gibara, Germaine 589
Gibbons, James L. 501
Gibbs, John 316
Gibbs, Michael 312
Gibby, Lisa 432
Gibson-Brandon, Rajna 113
Gibsone, Jorge Corvera 466
Gidumal, Shyam 501

Giffin, Gordon D. 132
Gifford, Angelika 628
Gifford, Angelika 646
Gifford, William F. 48
Giger, Peter 689
Gilbert, Daryl H. 39
Gilbert, Martin J. 269
Gildea, Richard R. 38
Giliberti, Fernando Pablo 686
Gill, Byron 263
Gillespie, Robert 425
Gillet, Francois 240
Gillies, Crawford 96
Gilliland, Stewart 622
Gillis, Steven 605
Gilson, Jean-Marc 402
Gilvary, Brian 96
Gimenez, Osvaldo 396
Gimeno, Javier 175
Ginestie, Philippe 617
Gingras, Bruno 297
Ginneken, Marnix van 357
Giorgi, Sergio Fabian 686
Giovenco, Arturo Carlos 686
Girling, Russell 592
Giron, Cesar 476
Giron, Patricia Ricard 476
Girouard, Denis 422
Giroux, Marc 400
Girsky, Stephen J. 123
Given, Mark 325
Giza, Helen 259
Gladu, Jean Paul 592
Glanzer, Edeltraud 399
Glanzmann, Thomas H. 32
Glaser, Jurgen 399
Glebikowska-Michalak, Justyna 94
Glimstrom, Anna-Karin 563
Glocer, Thomas H. 495
Glomnes, Adrian 452
Glosser, Ludwig 143
Gluher, Alexandre da Silva 80
Gluskie, Kevin Gerard 279
Glynn, Martin J. G. 590
Gmur, Philipp 282
Go, Alvin C. 107
Goaer, Jean-Clade Le 37
Gobel, Benny 469
Gobert, Wilfred A. 132
Godbehere, Ann 549
Godbehere, Ann Frances 579
Godfrey, Darren 315
Godfrey, John 364
Godin, Julie 149
Godin, Serge 149
Goel, R. K. 152
Goggins, Colleen A. 103
Goggins, Colleen A. 638
Goh, Euleen 549
Goh, Hock 4
Goh, Hock 581
Goh, Hup Jin 439
Goiricelaya, Sara de la Rica 300
Gokcay, Gokhan 29
Goldberg, Gary J. 110
Golden, John L. 68
Goldenstein, Ihno 392
Golding, Andy John 470
Golding, Benjamin Kristoffer 213
Goldman, Kenneth A. 458

Goldsmith, Andrea J. 395
Golling, Stefan 418
Gomes, Fernando Jorge Buso 655
Gomez, Ignacio Baeza 386
Gomez, Oscar 83
Gomez, Pablo Fernando Quesada 83
Gomez, Sylvia Escovar 85
Gomi, Hirofumi 536
Gomi, Yasumasa 679
Gon, Cesar Nivaldo 323
Goncalves, Carlos 565
Goncalves, Hermenio Pinto 268
Goncalves, Rui Paulo 265
Gonda, Barbara Garza Laguera 84
Gonda, Barbara Garza Laguera 254
Gonda, Eva Maria Garza Laguera 254
Gonda, Mariana Garza Laguera 254
Gong, Shaozu 178
Gong, Zhijie 683
Gonzalez, Alberto Bailleres 254
Gonzalez, Alejandro Diego Cecchi 83
Gonzalez, Alvaro Soto 466
Gonzalez, Bertha Paula Michel 254
Gonzalez, Carlos Hank 273
Gonzalez, Cipriano Lopez 85
Gonzalez, Isaias Velazquez 273
Gonzalez, Jesus Viejo 52
Gonzalez, Maria Luisa Albores 481
Gonzalez, Monica Jimenez 221
Gonzalez, Pablo de Carvajal 615
Gonzalo, Ana de Pro 453
Gonzalo, Ana de Pro 580
Gonzalo, José 239
Gooding, Valerie 646
Gooding, Valerie 661
Goodman, Jesse 274
Goodman, Laurie S. 55
Goodman, Nicholas 124
Goodman, Richard A. 18
Goodman, Russell 499
Goodson, Stephen Mitford 573
Goonan, Nathan 421
Goosen, C. G. 553
Gopalan, Geeta 168
Gordillo, Rodrigo Echenique 83
Gordillo, Rodrigo Echenique 308
Gordon, Joseph F. 101
Gordon, Maria 243
Goreglyad, Valery 535
Gori, Roy 386
Gorin, Ariane 15
Gorman, Sinead 549
Gosa, N. P. 416
Goss-Custard, Rakhi 349
Goss-Custard, Rakhi 539
Gosse, Karen J. 256
Gosset-Grainville, Antoine 73
Goto, Akihiro 275
Goto, Katsuhiro 546
Goto, Kenryo 666
Goto, Shigeki 345
Goto, Teiichi 262
Goto, Tomichiro 460
Goto, Yasuhiro 527
Gottier, Hans-Rudolf 597
Gottschalk, Helmut 173
Gou, Hsiao Ling 250
Gou, Terry 291
Gouin, Suzanne 297
Gouin, Suzanne 363

INDEX OF EXECUTIVES

Goulaieff, Pierre 136
Goulding, Richard 88
Gouldson, Conor 24
Goulet, Beverly K. 516
Gourmelon, Nicole 185
Gouvea, Alexandre 185
Govil, Sucheta 185
Gowland, Glen 91
Goyal, Vijay 55
Goyder, Richard J. B. 674
Graafland, D. Rene Hooft 357
Grabe, Wiliam O. 366
Grace, Adrian 168
Graf, John A. 242
Graff, Michael J. 362
Graham, Anthony R. 487
Graham, Carolyn J. 135
Graham, James 172
Graham, Teresa A. 162
Graham, Wheeler 152
Gramont, Stanislas de 542
Granat, Carolina 7
Granata, Claudio 235
Granata, Matias 81
Granata, Matias 322
Grand, Jean-Claude Le 362
Grandi, Lorenzo 579
Grandisson, Marc 55
Grange, Marjolaine 524
Grange, Pascal 116
Granger, Alberto Consuegra 221
Grant, Bradley B. 39
Grant, Bruce 657
Grant, Mirella E. 213
Grant, Shane 197
Grassi, Massimo 61
Grau, Alberto 127
Grau, Penny S. 111
Gray, Brian G.J. 501
Gray, Denise 131
Grecco, Tatiana 322
Greco, Mario 689
Green, Gary 180
Green, John M. 497
Green, Karen 482
Green, S. D. 382
Green, Stuart D. 380
Greenberg, David 362
Greenberg, Evan G. 160
Greenberg, Mark 192
Greene, Michele 88
Greenhalgh, Neil 332
Greenspun, Brian L. 98
Gref, Herman 535
Gregg, Steven 44
Gregoriadi, Alice K. 240
Gregory, Shaun 674
Grenier, Emmanuel 140
Greve, Brad 75
Greve, Constantin 209
Grevy, Brian 17
Gri, Francoise 185
Grieber, Martin 238
Grieco, Maria Patrizia 227
Grieg, Elisabeth 450
Griffin, Rita 317
Griffith, B. V. 534
Griffiths, Anthony F. 244
Griffiths, Jane 75
Griffiths, Jane 339

Grigg, Christopher M. 75
Griling, Russell K. 457
Grillo, Ulrich 218
Grioli, Francesco 183
Grisanti, Agustin 617
Grisoni, Constance 506
Gritz, Josef 663
Grivet, Jerome 185
Grobler, Fleetwood Rawstorne 534
Groepe, Francois Engelbrecht 573
Groh, Kevin 374
Groot, Jan Ernst de 357
Gros-Pietro, Gian Maria 319
Grossman, Cynthia H. 52
Grossman, D. Keith 32
Grosso, Douglas G. Del 18
Grote, Byron E. 31
Grote, Byron E. 622
Groth, Anke 218
Gruber, Karl 243
Gruber, Peter 311
Gruell, Martin 497
Gruending, Colin K. 226
Grund, Burkhart 176
Grundler, Martina 37
Grundmann, Swen H. 176
Grynberg, Marc 650
Gu, Biquan 295
Gu, Chunyuan 167
Gu, Huizhong 158
Gu, Jianguo 295
Gu, Junying 688
Gu, Liji 483
Gu, Sheng 87
Gu, Shisheng 683
Guajardo, Pablo Roberto Gonzalez 43
Gualandris, Fabio 580
Guan, Xiaoguang 40
Guan, Xingshe 87
Guan, Xueqing 575
Guan, Yongmin 335
Guan, Zemin 559
Guat, Janet Har Ang 93
Guay, Marc 400
Guay, Richard 624
Gucht, Karel de 55
Gudduschat, Cordula 175
Gudgeon, Deborah 243
Gudkov, Eduard S. 453
Guedon, Marc 656
Guerin-Boutaud, Philippe 501
Guerin, Anne 542
Guerin, Nicolas 464
Guerra, Karen 122
Guerra, Karen J. 41
Guerra, Ricardo Ribeiro Mandacaru 322
Guerrand, Blaise 285
Guerrand, Julie 285
Guerrand, Olympia 285
Guerrand, Wilfried 285
Guerrero, Angel Alija 43
Guevarra, Lazaro Jerome C. 107
Guez, Jean 617
Guggenheimer, Steven 295
Gui, Sheng Yue 267
Guido, Frank C. 532
Guilarte, Juan Sanchez-Calero 227
Guilherme, Carlos Alberto Rodrigues 80

Guillaume-Grabisch, Beatrice 362
Guillaume-Grabisch, Beatrice 432
Guillen, Federico 446
Guillot, Laurent 525
Guillou, Marion 113
Guillouard, Catherine 27
Guindani, Pietro A. 235
Guiony, Jean-Jacques 379
Guiu, Jose Antonio Colomer 386
Gujral, Raminder Singh 499
Gularte, Miguel 331
Gulden, Bjorn 496
Guldu, Selahattin 646
Güler, Aydin 646
Gulich, Frank Ch. 213
Gulliver, Stuart 330
Gultekin, Ege 29
Gulzau, Gabriele 208
Guma, Xolile 573
Guma, Xolile Pallo 573
Gunderson, Kelsey 363
Gundlach, Robert 103
Gunn, Robert J. 244
Gunning, Eric 415
Gunter, Bernhard 628
Guntern, Rebecca 527
Guo, Hong 199
Guo, Hongjin 155
Guo, Kaitian 620
Guo, Lijun 670
Guo, Shiqing 156
Guo, Wei 158
Gupta, Ashok K. 590
Gupta, Jan 15
Gupta, P. K. 577
Gupta, Peeyush 421
Gupta, Piyush 200
Gupta, Purnima 577
Gupta, Rajiv L. 50
Gupta, Rajiv L. 51
Gurander, Jan 664
Gurdal, Hakan 279
Guschin, Ilya 456
Gustafson, Rickard 4
Gustavsson, Jan 172
Gustavsson, Jonas 528
Gut, Alexander 15
Guthertz, Patricia Lizarraga 185
Guthrie, Scott D. 376
Gutierrez, Alberto 27
Gutierrez, Arturo Herrera 481
Gutierrez, Jaime Alberto Villegas 85
Gutierrez, Jose M. 18
Gutierrez, Luis Alfonso Nicolau 171
Gutierrez, Luis Carlos Sarmiento 271
Gutierrez, Pedro Fernando Manrique 221
Gutovic, Miljan 290
Guyton, Jeffrey H. 391
Guzman, David Martinez 144
Guzman, Jorge Andres Saieh 81
Gyamlani, Moti 237
Gyetvay, Mark A. 453

H

Ha, Eon Tae 298
Haag, Markus 238

Haagensen, Thomas 220
Haas, Achim 628
Haas, Herbert K. 277
Haas, Kimberly J. 305
Haas, Rene 181
Haase, Margarete 314
Habeler-Drabek, Alexandra 238
Haberhauer, Regina 238
Haberle, Michael 397
Habib, Magda 172
Habu, Yuki 20
Habuka, Shigeki 402
Habuka, Shigeki 498
Hacchoji, Sonoko 326
Hachimura, Tsuyoshi 323
Hachiuma, Fuminao 546
Hachiuma, Fuminao 583
Haddad, Divo Milan 466
Haddad, Frederick S. 102
Haddad, Mary Jo 619
Hadders, Jan Zegering 21
Haelg, Paul 558
Haga, Yuko 401
Hagan, Annmarie T. 160
Hagelberg, Johanna 581
Haggerty, Gretchen R. 337
Hagino, Yoshinori 326
Hagiwara, Osamu 223
Hagiwara, Satoru 636
Hagleitner, Nikola 208
Hai, Yancey 603
Hainer, Herbert 37
Hainer, Herbert 207
Hajeri, Omar 362
Halbherr, Michael 689
Halde, Jean-Rene 638
Hale, Karen L. 452
Halfon, Jean-Michel 623
Halford, Andy 388
Halford, Andy N. 577
Halgouet, Eric du 285
Haller, Bettina 557
Halliday, Matthew 44
Halton, Jane 71
Hama, Naoki 262
Hamada, Hiroyuki 550
Hamada, Masahiro 550
Hamada, Masahiro 570
Hamada, Michiyo 28
Hamaguchi, Daisuke 371
Hamamoto, Akira 404
Haman, Sabine 506
Hamano, Miyako 275
Hamberger, Edward R. 133
Hamburg, Julia Willie 663
Hamel, Thierry 362
Hamers, Ralph A.J.G. 647
Hameseder, Erwin 497
Hamill, David 123
Hammerli, Annelis Luscher 282
Hammond, Ian 592
Hammond, Michael 670
Han, Bing 153
Han, Kun Tai 369
Han, Quanzhi 547
Han, Seung Soo 371
Han, Wensheng 158
Hanada, Shingo 359
Handa, Junichi 641
Handajani, Vera 164

HOOVER'S HANDBOOK OF WORLD BUSINESS 2024

INDEX OF EXECUTIVES

Handicott, Teresa G. 214
Handjinicolaou, George P. 483
Hanebeck, Jochen 311
Haneda, Takao 551
Hankonen-Nybom, Raija-Leena 198
Hanley, Michael 380
Hanman, C. Jeffrey 613
Hannasch, Brian P. 35
Hanratty, P. B. 416
Hansen, Cynthia L. 226
Hansen, Hakon 213
Hansen, Louise Aggerstrom 198
Hansen, Rene 581
Hansen, Signhild Arnegard 563
Hansert, Reiner 108
Hanssen, Maria Moræus 537
Hansson, Martin 108
Hanzawa, Junichi 409
Happe, Carolina Dybeck 237
Hara, Hisashi 439
Hara, Ilka 354
Hara, Mahoko 632
Hara, Noriyuki 415
Hara, Shinichi 570
Hara, Takeshi 33
Harada, Ikuhide 163
Harada, Kazuyuki 327
Harada, Keitaro 679
Haraguchi, Tetsuji 412
Harashima, Akira 632
Harayama, Yuko 636
Harazaki, Masaharu 93
Harbilas, D. James 39
Harbo, Ingrid 597
Hardaker-Jones, Emma 364
Hardegg, Maximilian 238
Harder, V. Peter 384
Hardie, Graeme 644
Harding, Peter 593
Harding, Richard Michael 214
Hardwick, Elanor R. 38
Hardwick, Elanor R. 74
Hardy, Anne 175
Hardy, Helen 467
Harings, Lothar A. 360
Harisunker, B. 553
Harlan, Joe 287
Harlin, Gerald J. 73
Harlow, Jo 325
Harnacke, Ulrich M. 119
Haro, Eduardo Tricio 466
Harper, Katherine C. 534
Harquail, David 90
Harreguy, Maite Aranzabal 185
Harris, Andrea 677
Harris, Jason 497
Harris, John D. 252
Harris, M. Marianne 374
Harris, M. Marianne 590
Harris, Mary 499
Harris, Sue 169
Harrison, John 27
Harrison, John Barrie 22
Harrison, Lisa 592
Harrison, Marc 358
Harrison, Peter 539
Harrison, Philip J. 78
Harrison, Sam 497
Hart, Cees't 137
Hart, Jeffrey R. 145

Hart, Stephanie Pullings 432
Hartin, Tim 669
Hartl, Gloria L. 609
Hartman, Peter F. 182
Hartmann, Joel 580
Hartmann, Judith 653
Hartung, Michael 252
Hartz, Scott S. 386
Hartzband, Meryl D. 242
Haruvi, Keren 527
Harvey, A. H. 380
Harvey, A. H. 382
Harvey, Brenda 444
Harvey, J. Brett 98
Harvie-Watt, Isabelle 533
Harwerth, Noel 471
Hasebe, Akio 461
Hasebe, Yoshihiro 344
Hasegawa, Eiichi 263
Hasegawa, Eiichi 303
Hasegawa, Hiroki 444
Hasegawa, Izumi 679
Hasegawa, Kazuaki 666
Hasegawa, Kichishige 679
Hasegawa, Mariko 552
Hasegawa, Masahiko 287
Hasegawa, Nobuyoshi 90
Hashie, Rick 624
Hashimoto, Eiji 441
Hashimoto, Hirofumi 189
Hashimoto, Katsunori 638
Hashimoto, Kiyoshi 346
Hashimoto, Masaru 588
Hashimoto, Osamu 410
Hashimoto, Takashi 420
Hashimoto, Takayuki 161
Hashimoto, Takayuki 402
Hashimoto, Takeshi 412
Hashimoto, Yasuhiko 344
Hashimoto, Yoshiaki 629
Hashitani, Masato 550
Hasumi, Maiko 380
Hasuwa, Kenji 459
Hata, Hiroyuki 89
Hata, Takashi 444
Hatanaka, Yasushi 277
Hatanaka, Yoshihiko 544
Hatanaka, Yoshihiko 572
Hatano, Mutsuko 389
Hatao, Katsumi 536
Hathaway, Richard Guy 179
Hato, Hideo 585
Hatoyama, Rehito 380
Hatsukawa, Koji 605
Hatta, Yoko 29
Hatta, Yoko 439
Hattab, Franck 140
Hattersley, Gavin D.K. 415
Hattori, Nobumichi 245
Hattori, Rikiya 550
Hattori, Satoru 90
Hattrem, Lillian 213
Hau, Douglas Tong 245
Haub, Christian W. E. 400
Haugel, Didier 32
Haughey, Douglas J. 256
Hauser, Anita 513
Hauser, Heijo J. G. 445
Hauser, Wolfhart 65
Hauser, Wolfhart 500

Hausfeld, Heike 103
Hausler, Gerd 418
Hauzy, Raphaële 140
Haward-Laird, Sharon 90
Hawker, Michael J. 669
Hawkins, Keith 644
Hayakawa, Shigeru 643
Hayama, Takatoshi 287
Hayasaki, Yasuhiro 536
Hayashi, Daisuke 477
Hayashi, Kingo 161
Hayashi, Makoto 20
Hayashi, Masahiro 263
Hayashi, Naomi 409
Hayashi, Nobuhide 344
Hayashi, Shinnosuke 202
Hayashi, Takaharu 460
Hayata, Fumiaki 583
Hayek, Georges Nicolas 597
Hayek, Marc Alexander 597
Hayek, Nayla 597
Hayes, Tom 474
Hayling, Claire D'Abreu 527
Haynes, Christopher M. 674
Hazama, Emiko 666
Hazou, Kyra 565
He, Jing 683
He, Jun 603
He, Zhiqiang 366
Healy, Patrick 599
Heaps, John R. 685
Hebert, Brigitte 422
Hebert, Dennis P. 609
Heckmann, Fritz-Juergen 279
Hedberg, Jeffrey Alan 651
Hedberg, Tomas 597
Hedblom, Helena 581
Hedengran, Petra 3
Hedger, Sarah 471
Hedin, Maria 596
Heffernan, Christine 622
Heiß, Marianne 663
Heilbronner, Anne-Gabrielle 464
Heilbronner, Anne-Gabrielle 495
Heim, Philippe 32
Heimpell, Claudia 83
Heinemann, Stefan 646
Heinz, Michael 100
Heinzl, Thomas 665
Heitmuller, Frauke 277
Helander, Mikko 581
Helber, Waldemar 100
Held, Sascha 399
Held, Thomas 208
Helfer, Friederike 628
Helfgott, Ludovic 455
Hellemondt-Gerdingh, Marjolien van 84
Heller, Bridgette P. 453
Helmes, Marion 280
Helmes, Marion 392
Helmrich, Klaus 557
Helten-Kindlein, Birgit 284
Hemstrom, Helena 70
Henaff, Thierry Le 56
Henaff, Thierry Le 177
Henchoz, Jean-Jacques 277
Henchoz, Jean-Jacques 600
Henderson, Frederick A. 18
Henn, Nicholas 374

Hennah, Adrian 325
Hennah, Adrian 653
Henne, Ilse 56
Hennes, Duncan P. 501
Henning, Mats 664
Henriksen, Ole 469
Henrikson, C. Robert 600
Henriksson, Henrik 3
Henriksson, Jens 597
Henrot, Francois 506
Henry, Kathryn 377
Henry, Laurent 542
Henry, Mike 110
Henry, Simon 509
Henry, Simon 511
Hepworth, Graeme 519
Herald, James Skip 243
Herbert-Jones, Sian 136
Herbert-Jones, Sian 362
Herbert, Clifford Francis 43
Herington, Charles M. 415
Herlin, Antti 354
Herlin, Iiris 354
Herlin, Jussi 354
Herlofsen, Rebekka Glasser 236
Herman, Benedikt-Richard Freiherr von 284
Herman, Sally 592
Hermann, Astrid 108
Hermann, Roswitha 17
Hermansson, Kerstin 597
Hermelin, Paul 136
Hernadi, Zsolt 414
Hernandez, Arturo Guitierrez 52
Hernandez, Enrique F. Senior 171
Hernandez, Jose Eduardo Beltran 481
Herold, F. 382
Herrera, Andres E. Garza 38
Herrera, Jesus Vicente Gonzalez 144
Herrera, Ruben 621
Herrero, Fernando Maria Masaveu 223
Herreros, Mariano Hernandez 14
Herscher, Penelope A. 247
Herscovici, Lucas 48
Herweijer, Celine 295
Herz, Wolfgang 108
Herzog, Angelika Judith 418
Hess, Beat W. 290
Hess, Carl A. 670
Hesse, Johannes-Gerhard 612
Hessel, Katja 209
Hessen, Corey 609
Hessius, Kerstin 596
Hester, Stephen Alan Michael 148
Hester, Stephen Alan Michael 220
Hetherington, Kim 127
Heuch, Cecile Blydt 616
Heuveldop, Niklas 237
Hewitt, Liz 269
Hewitt, Liz 395
Hewitt, Liz 424
Hewson, Carolyn 187
Hexter, David 483
Heya, Toshio 286
Heydemann, Christel 464
Heyman, Francois 186
Heymann, Andres Ergas 81
Heynitz, Harald von 558
Heywood, Suzanne 168
Hibberd, Sally-Ann 169

INDEX OF EXECUTIVES

Hicks, Greg 134
Hicks, Helen M. Mallovy 590
Hidai, Shohei 275
Hidaka, Yoshihiro 680
Hieronimus, Nicolas 362
Hiesinger, Heinrich 105
Hiesinger, Heinrich 208
Hiesinger, Heinrich 261
Hietala, Kaisa H. 511
Hietala, Kaisa H. 564
Higaki, Seiji 602
Higashi, Emiko 605
Higashi, Kazuhiro 292
Higashi, Kazuhiro 570
Higashi, Masahiro 120
Higashi, Yoshiki 551
Higashihara, Toshiaki 287
Higashino, Hirokazu 584
Higgins, Jimmy 592
Higgins, Nigel 94
Higgins, Nigel 96
Higginson, Andrew T. 332
Highnam, Alec 111
Higo, Takashi 634
Higo, Toru 586
Higo, Toru 613
Higuchi, Kojiro 630
Higuchi, Masayuki 262
Higuchi, Tatsuo 471
Higuchi, Tetsuji 415
Higurashi, Yutaka 443
Hikita, Sakae 189
Hilbert, Jonny 4
Hill, Jonathan S. 253
Hill, Mark 187
Hill, Sylvia 7
Himeiwa, Yasuo 547
Hinchli, Andrew 174
Hinchliffe, Michelle A. 110
Hinchliffe, Michelle A. 381
Hinchliffe, Michelle A. 382
Hinojosa, Claudio Melandri 83
Hinooka, Yutaka 412
Hinrichs, Lars 209
Hinshaw, John M. 294
Hinsley, Ronald J. 256
Hinterseher, Hubert 496
Hippe, Alan 513
Hirabayashi, Yoshiki 410
Hirai, Mikihito 404
Hirai, Ryutaro 569
Hirai, Toshihiro 444
Hirai, Yoshinori 21
Hirai, Yoshiyuki 544
Hiraiwa, Koichiro 404
Hirakawa, Hiroyuki 460
Hirako, Yuji 45
Hiraku, Tomofumi 406
Hiramoto, Tatsuo 163
Hirano, Atsuhiko 303
Hirano, Eiji 457
Hirano, Keiji 602
Hirano, Kotaro 287
Hirano, Nobuya 412
Hirano, Nobuyuki 405
Hirano, Takuya 503
Hiraoka, Tomoyo 402
Hirasaki, Tatsuya 632
Hirasawa, Juichi 45
Hirashima, Shoji 190

Hirata, Masayoshi 638
Hirji, Rahim 386
Hiroi, Takashi 442
Hirokawa, Yoshihiro 411
Hironaka, Yasuaki 327
Hirono, Michiko 327
Hirose, Ichiro 391
Hirose, Kenji 498
Hirose, Shinichi 632
Hirose, Takashi 441
Hirose, Wataru 249
Hirowatari, Kiyohide 329
Hirschel, Dierk 646
Hirshfeld, Alicia Alejandra Lebrija 273
Hisabayashi, Yoshinari 303
Hisai, Taiju 404
Hishiyama, Reiko 567
Hjalm, Rune 61
Hjertonsson, Johan 61
Hlongwane, T. R. P. 553
Ho, Andy 357
Ho, Bosco Hin Ngai 156
Ho, David H. Y. 591
Ho, George Joseph 192
Ho, Hamilton Hau-Hay 434
Ho, Hsiu-Chi 682
Ho, Lora 603
Ho, Mei-Yueh 58
Ho, Tian Yee 200
Ho, Yeoung-Shuenn 682
Ho, Yuet Mee 164
Hochstrasser, Daniel 453
Hodgins, Robert B. 39
Hodnett, David W. P. 575
Hodo, Chikatomo 402
Hodo, Chikatomo 468
Hoedt, Robert J.W. Ten 395
Hoeg, Krystyna T. 305
Hoeg, Krystyna T. 589
Hoepfner-Leger, Isabelle 506
Hoeven, Maria van der 639
Hoffman, Brent 242
Hoffmann, Andre 513
Hoffmann, Philippe 182
Hoffmann, Reiner 103
Hofmann, Jorg 663
Hogan, Randall J. 395
Hogarth, Timothy 474
Hogberg, Sofia Schorling 61
Hogg, Charlotte 500
Hogg, Cressida 75
Hogg, Cressida 376
Hogg, Sarah 317
Hogna, Egil 452
Hohmeister, Harry 206
Hohol, Linda M. O. 135
Hoidahl, Hans-Olav 35
Holdenried, Hans-Ulrich 311
Holguin, Maria Angela 334
Hollows, Nicole M. 214
Holmstrom, Mats 563
Holscher, Luise 208
Holt, Kevin 357
Holt, Tim Oliver 558
Holtinger, Jens 664
Homburg, Arno 663
Homma, Tetsuro 472
Homma, Toshio 136
Honda, Keiko 21
Honda, Keiko 409

Honda, Keiko 499
Hong, Arthur Xiaobo 660
Honjo, Takehiro 470
Honma, Yo 457
Hooft-Cheong, Choy van der 7
Hookway, Richard 474
Hooley, Joseph L. 50
Hooley, Joseph L. 51
Hooper, Barbara 638
Hooper, Nicholas P.M. 612
Hopgood, Daniel Roy 220
Horai, Eduardo Eiji 40
Horan, Jeanette A. 446
Horen, Clive van 592
Horgan, Brendan 59
Horgan, Tanya 24
Hori, Kenichi 409
Hori, Ryuji 277
Hori, Yutaka 249
Horiba, Atsushi 567
Horiba, Atsushi 585
Horie, Jun 389
Horie, Nobuyuki 275
Horie, Toshiyasu 57
Horiguchi, Tadayoshi 303
Horikoshi, Takeshi 354
Horiuchi, Katsuyoshi 550
Horiuchi, Yosuke 545
Hormozi, Mitra 68
Horn, Alan D. 514
Horn, Johann 105
Horowitz, Bradley 558
Horstmann, Anne 418
Horstmeier, Ilka 105
Horta-Osorio, António 243
Hortefeux, Valerie 393
Horton, Andrew 497
Horvat, Sinischa 100
Horvath, Ferenc 414
Horvath, Gabor 414
Horvath, Gunther 663
Hosaka, Masayuki 497
Hoshi, Tomoko 457
Hoshihara, Kazuhiro 412
Hoshino, Asako 444
Hoshino, Tsuguhiko 28
Hosokane, Kenji 404
Hosomi, Kentaro 657
Hottges, Timotheus 209
Hottges, Timotheus 397
Hou, Andrew 12
Hou, Ching-Ing 245
Hou, Cliff 603
Hou, Jinglei 212
Hou, Tony Tianyu 541
Hou, Yung-Hsung 216
Houde, Jean 422
Houghton, Chris 237
Houghton, Sue 497
Houle, Ghislain 131
Houle, Leo W. 168
Hountalas, Jon 130
Hourquebie, Philip A 320
House, Andrew 204
House, Andrew 444
Houssaye, France 565
Houston, Dennis M. 592
Houten, Frans van 453
Hove, Kjetil 236
Hovell-Patrizi, Allegra van 19

Howard, Claire Fitzalan 539
Howeg, Stephan 15
Howell, Justin M. 131
Howes, Richard Allan 127
Howle, Carol 118
Hoyos, Jaime Carvajal 179
Hoyt, Bert 332
Hoyt, Bob 294
Hryniewicz-Bieniek, Agnieszka 86
Hsiao, Tsai Yuan 687
Hsieh, Chih-Chien 682
Hsieh, Haydn 672
Hsieh, Louis T. 333
Hsieh, Tsun-Yan 386
Hsiu, Wen Bin 687
Hsiung, Ming-ho 142
Hsu, Ching-Hsiang 12
Hsu, David 330
Hsu, Jonathan Chung Chang 250
Hsu, Judie 142
Hsu, K.C. 603
Hsu, Rita Lai Tai Fan 88
Hsu, Rock Sheng-Hsiun 178
Hsu, Shih-Chun 245
Hsu, Shih-Fang 682
Hsu, Tai-Lin 58
Hsu, Wen-Bin 178
Hsu, Yung Hung 687
Hsuan, John Min-Chih 672
Hu, Changmiao 152
Hu, Fred 648
Hu, Kang 547
Hu, Limin 547
Hu, Shihai 40
Hu, Zhanyun 87
Hu, Zuliu 309
Huang, Baokui 483
Huang, Baoxin 483
Huang, Chaoquan 295
Huang, Chin Yuan 687
Huang, Ching Lu 141
Huang, Echo Shaomei 434
Huang, Fei 559
Huang, George 12
Huang, Guo-Liang 682
Huang, Jian 295
Huang, Jiang 18
Huang, Jiangfeng 128
Huang, Joe 216
Huang, Joseph N.C. 216
Huang, Liangbo 309
Huang, Lixin 295
Huang, Long 151
Huang, Ming 333
Huang, Ming 670
Huang, Ming Fu 687
Huang, Ou 547
Huang, Qing 157
Huang, Shi-Nan 682
Huang, Tetsai 291
Huang, Tiao-Kuei 142
Huang, Tiffany 12
Huang, Wei 483
Huang, Wendell 603
Huang, Wensheng 155
Huang, Xiangyu 559
Huang, Xiumei 153
Huang, Yongzhang 478
Huang, Yung-Jen 216
Huang, Zhenping 235

INDEX OF EXECUTIVES

Huat, Seek Ngee 124
Hubbard, Glenn 639
Hubbs, Miranda C. 305
Hubbs, Miranda C. 457
Huber, Doreen 143
Huber, Frank 247
Huber, Linda S. 90
Hudon, Isabelle 297
Hudson, Ian 56
Hudson, Isabel 73
Hudson, Isabel 125
Hudson, Linda P. 644
Hudson, Paul 530
Huebscher, Karen J. 527
Huerta, Javier 304
Huet, Jean-Marc 280
Hufenbecher, Constanze 311
Huggins, Daniel 421
Hughes-Hallett, James Edward 598
Hughes, Amanda 497
Hughes, Catherine J. 549
Hughes, Gary 528
Hughes, Mark 648
Hugin, ?Robert J. 160
Huhges, Sarah A. 613
Hui, Julian 330
Hui, Zhang 223
Huijsmans, Joris 137
Huillard, Xavier 362
Huillard, Xavier 659
Hulme, Philip 181
Hulst, Herman 314
Hummel, Michael 580
Hund-Mejean, Martina 549
Hundeshagen, Ilka 277
Hunt, Colin 23
Hunt, Graeme 21
Hunt, Jackie 577
Hunt, Jackie 670
Hunt, Orlagh 685
Hunter, Joel E. 608
Hunter, Melinda 21
Hunter, Sarah 665
Hurley, Alfred F. 253
Hurley, Imelda 214
Hurley, John 524
Hurlston, Michael E. 252
Hurtado, Luz Karime Vargas 271
Husain, M. 9
Hussain, Abbas 623
Huston, Peter Ernest 255
Hutchens, David G. 256
Hutchings, W. Preston 55
Hutchinson, Alison E. 685
Hutchinson, Richard Mark 111
Hwang, B.B. 370
Hwang, Po-Tuan 672
Hyakuno, Kentaro 497
Hyakutome, Yoshihiro 587
Hynes, Rose B. 214
Hyodo, Masayuki 584

I

Iannaccone, Marco 684
Ibanez, Jaime Tamayo 386
Ibarra, Inigo Victor de Oriol 300
Ibarra, Maximo 393

Icahn, Brett M. 102
Ichikawa, Akira 583
Ichikawa, Akira 586
Ichikawa, Miki 681
Ichikawa, Sachiko 634
Ichikawa, Tatsushi 346
Ichikura, Noboru 327
Ichimura, Yuji 402
Ida, Shuichi 527
Ide, Akiko 584
Ide, Akiko 630
Ide, Hiroshi 303
Ideguchi, Hiroki 57
Idekoba, Hisayuki 499
Idemitsu, Masakazu 303
Idezawa, Takeshi 380
Idrac, Anne-Marie 175
Idrac, Anne-Marie 639
Igarashi, Hiroshi 204
Igarashi, Koji 406
Iglhaut, Michael 183
Ignatiev, Sergey 535
Ihamuotila, Timo 7
Ihara, Ichiro 161
Ihara, Katsumi 287
Ihara, Keiko 444
Ihara, Toru 444
Ihlein, Michael 44
Ii, Masako 405
Iida, Jin 402
III, George Raymond Zage 638
III, Paul Desmarais 487
Iijima, Masami 342
Iijima, Masami 605
Iino, Kenji 666
Iio, Norinao 315
Iiyama, Toshiyasu 448
Iizuka, Atsushi 327
Iizuka, Masanobu 439
Ikawa, Nobuhisa 434
Ikawa, Takashi 602
Ikdal, Adam 575
Ike, Fumihiko 457
Ike, Fumihiko 505
Ikebe, Kazuhiro 361
Ikeda, Junichiro 412
Ikeda, Kentaro 551
Ikeda, Koji 286
Ikeda, Naoki 341
Ikeda, Norito 326
Ikeda, Norito 327
Ikemoto, Tetsuya 321
Ikeno, Takamitsu 665
Ikeya, Koji 406
Ikeyama, Masataka 303
Ikushima, Takahiko 406
Illek, Christian P. 209
Illig, Bernd 496
Ilube, Tom 677
Ilyukhina, Elena A. 266
Imach, Jacobo Cohen 396
Imaeda, Tetsuro 587
Imagawa, Kuniaki 394
Imai, Eijiro 638
Imai, Tadashi 441
Imai, Yasuyuki 567
Imaoka, Shoichi 527
Imokawa, Hisato 329
Imsang, Kris 493
In, Byeong Kang 369

Ina, Koichi 359
Ina, Norihiko 360
Inada, Chieko 550
Inada, Hitoshi 406
Inada, Koji 343
Inagaki, Seiji 190
Inamasu, Mitsuko 457
Inamochi, Hiromii 412
Inano, Kazutoshi 552
Indo, Mami 29
Indo, Mami 411
Indo, Mami 634
Indralak, Padungdej 554
Ineichen-Fleisch, Marie-Gabrielle 432
Ingelfinger, Thomas 108
Inglis, Mike 125
Ingram, Tamara 388
Inomata, Yoshifumi 629
Inoue, Atsuhiko 588
Inoue, Hiroshi 391
Inoue, Kazuyuki 551
Inoue, Keitaro 231
Inoue, Makoto 468
Inoue, Makoto 471
Inoue, Noriyuki 191
Inoue, Osamu 585
Inoue, Ryuko 185
Inoue, Ryuko 442
Inoue, Satoru 189
Inoue, Shinichi 45
Inoue, Yukari 593
Inoue, Yukari 643
Inoue, Yumiko 679
Inoue, Yuriko 190
Intarajang, Kongkrapan 491
Inubushi, Katsuya 584
Ioannou, Stavros E. 240
Iokawa, Mitsuru 679
Ioki, Hiroshi 640
Iordanou, Constantine P. 55
Ioschpe, Dan 120
Ip, Albert Yuk-Keung 434
Iqbal, Javed 122
Ireland, Gordon R. 685
Irie, Shuji 468
Irisawa, Hiroyuki 275
Iritani, Atsushi 193
Irvine, Andrew 421
Isa, Shinichiro 505
Isaacs-Lowe, Arlene 180
Isagoda, Satoshi 630
Isaka, Ryuichi 546
Isayama, Naohisa 629
Isaza, Sergio Restrepo 221
Ise, Katsumi 219
Ishibashi, Shuichi 120
Ishida, Satoshi 420
Ishida, Shigeki 505
Ishiguro, Akihide 341
Ishiguro, Fujiyo 410
Ishiguro, Shigenao 457
Ishiguro, Shigenao 507
Ishiguro, Shigenao 610
Ishihara, Hidetake 442
Ishihara, Kunio 327
Ishii, Atsuko 344
Ishii, Keita 323
Ishii, Naomi 595
Ishii, Nobuyuki 359
Ishii, Sonosuke 287

Ishii, Taeko 586
Ishii, Takayuki 629
Ishii, Toru 545
Ishii, Yoshinori 632
Ishii, Yuji 471
Ishikawa, Hiroshi 342
Ishikawa, Hiroshi 352
Ishikawa, Kensei 89
Ishimaru, Fumio 527
Ishimoto, Hiroshi 73
Ishimura, Kazuhiko 448
Ishimura, Kazuhiko 507
Ishiwata, Akemi 415
Ishiyama, Kazuhiro 630
Ishizuka, Kunio 323
Ishizuka, Kunio 665
Ishizuka, Shigeki 371
Ishizuka, Shigeki 389
Ishizuki, Mutsumi 389
Isla, Elena Sanz 386
Isla, Pablo 432
Isobe, Takeshi 263
Isono, Hiroyuki 461
Isozaki, Yoshinori 351
Isshiki, Kozo 505
Isshiki, Toshihiro 588
Itagaki, Toshiaki 162
Itakura, Kazumasa 593
Itakura, Tomoyasu 439
Ito, Akiko 323
Ito, Arata 249
Ito, Eisaku 405
Ito, Hirotake 471
Ito, Hisanori 161
Ito, Junro 546
Ito, Kenichiro 202
Ito, Kenichiro 640
Ito, Koichi 641
Ito, Kumi 570
Ito, Kunio 636
Ito, Mitsufumi 550
Ito, Motoshige 552
Ito, Satoko 341
Ito, Shinichiro 411
Ito, Shintaro 28
Ito, Tomonori 223
Ito, Tomonori 588
Ito, Toshiyasu 296
Ito, Yoji 262
Ito, Yujiro 194
Ito, Yumiko 352
Ito, Yumiko 438
Itoh, Atsuko 219
Itoh, Junichi 296
Itoh, Motoshige 219
Itoh, Motoshige 583
Iturrate, Orlando Poblete 83
Iunes, Fernando Fontes 268
IV, Hugh M. Jones 500
Ivanov, Aleksey 243
Ivanov, Nikolay 243
Ivanova, Nadezhda 535
Iwahashi, Toshiro 89
Iwai, Mutsuo 329
Iwai, Mutsuo 610
Iwamori, Shunichi 640
Iwamoto, Hideyuki 643
Iwamoto, Hiroshi 394
Iwamoto, Tamotsu 551
Iwamoto, Toshio 219

INDEX OF EXECUTIVES

Iwasaki, Jiro 503
Iwasaki, Masato 605
Iwata, Keiichi 583
Iwata, Kimie 29
Iwata, Kimie 505
Iwata, Kimie 584
Iwatani, Toshiaki 594
Iwatsubo, Hiroshi 419
Iwaya, Ryozo 401
Iwayama, Shinji 335
Iwayama, Toru 89
Iyer, Govind 312
Izawa, Yoshiyuki 546
Izdebski, Marcin 94
Izosimov, Alexander 243
Izumisawa, Seiji 405
Izumiya, Naoki 459
Izumiya, Naoki 499

J

Jaarsveld, Johan van 110
Jacinto, Jesus A. 107
Jackow, Francois 362
Jackson, J. David A. 487
Jackson, Peter 253
Jackson, Sally 274
Jacob, Ellis 514
Jacob, Renato Lulia 322
Jacobs, Charles R 320
Jacobsen, Lennart 450
Jacobsen, Svein S. 450
Jacquemin, Tanja 628
Jacques, Michelle St. 415
Jacubasch, Mario 208
Jagdishan, Sashidhar 277
Jagdishan, Sashidhar 278
Jager, Martine 92
Jain, Dipak C. 499
Jakobi, Frank 646
Jakobs, Roy 357
Jakoet, Fatima 573
Jakosuo-Jansson, Hannele 429
Jakubowski, Anna 86
Jamal, Arshil 270
Jamel, Nelson Jose 40
James, Renee Jo 661
Jamet, Marc-Antoine 379
Jamieson, Roberta L. 519
Jang, Simon 603
Jang, Won-Ki 526
Janjariyakun, Vichai 128
Janow, Merit E. 50
Jansen, Daniela 628
Jansen, Philip 125
Jansseune, Thomas 650
Jany, Patrick 1
Jaque, Celso Alejandro 686
Jaramillo, Alejandro Figueroa 271
Jaramillo, Mauricio Galvis 221
Jardine, W. R. 250
Jarikasem, Penchun 491
Jarlegren, Magnus 71
Jarupanich, Prasert 128
Jarvis, Greg 467
Jarvis, Kenton 220
Jarwaarde, Ewout van 119
Jaskolka, Norman 134

Jawa, Kanwal Jeet 191
Jayanthi, Aruna 177
Jeannin, Herve 136
Jearavisitkul, Pittaya 128
Jeavons, Mick 317
Jedrys, Grzegorz 86
Jee, Sung-Ha 526
Jefferies, Suzanne 127
Jefford, Stephen 482
Jeffrey, William A. 611
Jego-Laveissiere, Mari-Noelle 233
Jego-Laveissiere, Mari-Noelle 656
Jejdling, Fredrik 236
Jelito, Ernest 279
Jemmett-Page, Shonaid 73
Jenah, Susan Wolburgh 363
Jeng, T.R. 159
Jenisch, Jan 290
Jenkins, Donald M. 39
Jenkins, John S. 611
Jenkins, Robert W. 445
Jennapar, Worapol 554
Jennes, Stefan 173
Jensen, Alex 307
Jensen, Christopher 458
Jeong, James Ho-Young 369
Jeong, Tak 486
Jerchel, Kerstin 173
Jernberg, Melker 664
Jetha, Yasmin 425
Jetha, Yasmin 427
Jeworrek, Torsten 418
Jha, Rakesh 301
Jha, Tripti 527
Jhang, Bosyong 178
Jhang, Fucyuan 178
Jhang, Jhaosian 178
Jhang, Mingjhih 178
Jhang, Ying 178
Jhang, Yongcing 178
Jhang, Yongnan 178
Jhang, Zuen 159
Jhangiani, Nik 170
Jheng, Jhihcyuan 178
Jhou, Tingjyun 178
Jhou, Zongkai 291
Ji, Zhihong 152
Jia, Jinzhong 157
Jia, Yuzeng 153
Jian, Qin 154
Jiang, Jane Fang 34
Jiang, Lifu 478
Jiang, Wenbo 335
Jiang, Xiaoming 478
Jiang, Xin 114
Jiang, Xiuchang 560
Jiang, Yanbo 128
Jiang, Zhenying 155
Jiao, Fangzheng 478
Jiao, Shuge 670
Jimenez, Alejandro Cantu 43
Jimenez, Luis Arizpe 52
Jimenez, Pedro Lopez 14
Jin, Keyu 176
Jin, Li 483
Jin, Qiang 559
Jin, Qingbin 683
Jin, Shaoliang 21
Jin, Wenmin 559
Jin, Yongsheng 235

Jinnouchi, Yoshihiro 92
Jiraadisawong, Thupthep 128
Jirapongphan, Siri 85
Jivakanun, Narongsak 492
Jobin, Luc 122
Jochens, Birgit 279
Jocson, Ramon L. 93
Joerg, Ingrid 182
Jofs, Kurt 237
Jofs, Kurt 664
Johannpeter, Andre Bier Gerdau 268
Johannpeter, Claudio Gerdau 268
Johannpeter, Guilherme Chagas Gerdau 268
Johannson, Ernie 90
Johansson-Hedberg, Birgitta 258
Johansson, Bjarne 61
Johansson, Camilla 664
Johansson, Hasse 71
Johansson, Leif 61
Johansson, Leif 71
John, Angela 474
John, Steve 295
Johnson, Alan 304
Johnson, Carolyn 364
Johnson, Catherine 376
Johnson, Enda 88
Johnson, Nancy A. 609
Johnson, Rick 35
Johnson, Thomas H. 170
Johnson, William D. 609
Johnson, William P. 259
Johnston-Billings, Amber C. 613
Johnston, Christine R. 609
Johnston, Cynthia 39
Johnston, David L. 244
Johnston, Neil O. 189
Johnston, Steve 592
Jojo, Camille 612
Jolly, Bruce A. 305
Joly-Pottuz, Dominique Muller 659
Jonas, M. H. 416
Jones, Darrell R. 135
Jones, John Michael 179
Jones, Susan C. 609
Jones, Todd Matthew 497
Jonge, Emma de 639
Jonsson, Karin 400
Joo, In-Ki 370
Joo, Jong-Nam 370
Joong, Chi-Wei 142
Joos, Astrid Simonsen 616
Joosen, Andrea Gisle 189
Joost, Gesche 531
Jope, Alan 11
Jope, Alan 652
Jordan, Alister 172
Jordan, Kari 581
Jordan, Kate 467
Jordan, Mark 127
Jordan, Phil 325
Jorg., Ingrid 663
Jorge, Joao Nuno Lima Bras 86
Jorgensen, Lars Fruergaard 137
Jorgensen, Lars Fruergaard 455
Jorgensen, Torsten Hagen 450
Josefowicz, Gregory 224
Joseph, Pamela A. 18
Joseu, Alicia Koplowitz Romero de 227
Joshi, Mohit 73

Joshi, Rahul M. 386
Jotikasthira, Charamporn 85
Joubert, Tracey L. 415
Joudrie, M. Colin 613
Joussen, Friedrich 646
Jozuka, Yumiko 551
Jr., Joseph A. Kraft 572
Ju, Jiandong 87
Juarez, Jesus Santiago Martin 84
Juden, Alexander 537
Juerss, Detlef 656
Jukes, David C. 201
Julien, Daniel 617
Julius, Christian 628
Jun, Young-Sang 358
Jung, Andrea 653
Jung, Do-Hyun 370
Jung, Helga 209
Junior, Aod Cunha de Moraes 268
Junior, Jose Geraldo Franco Ortiz 322
Junior, Samuel Monteiro dos Santos 80
Junyent, Miquel Roca 14
Jurecka, Christoph 418
Jurjevich, Karen L. 244
Jurkovic, Philip Ryan 182
Juti, Blanca 362

K

Kabagambe, Anne 98
Kabla, Sagi 302
Kaczoruk, Stainslaw Ryszard 94
Kado, Maki 303
Kadoorie, Michael David 167
Kadoorie, Philip Lawrence 167
Kadri, Ilham 362
Kaeser, Joe 557
Kaeser, Josef 458
Kaewrathtanapattama, Taweesak 128
Kaewtathip, Sarawut 492
Kaga, Atsuko 343
Kaga, Kunihiko 403
Kagami, Mitsuko 394
Kagata, Takeshi 602
Kagawa, Ryohei 296
Kaguchi, Hitoshi 405
Kahan, Rony 499
Kahkonen, Matti 429
Kahla, Vuyo Dominic 534
Kai, Fumio 249
Kaiami, Makoto 327
Kaibara, Atsushi 588
Kaihara, Noriya 292
Kaindl, Stefan 418
Kainersdorfer, Franz 663
Kainuma, Tsutomu 420
Kainuma, Yoshihisa 401
Kaiwa, Makoto 327
Kajita, Emiko 45
Kajita, Naoki 459
Kajita, Yusuke 287
Kakar, Rajeev K. L. 172
Kakar, Rajeev K. L. 241
Kakehi, Masaki 460
Kakigi, Koji 335
Kakinoki, Masumi 389
Kakiuchi, Eiji 360
Kakiuchi, Takehiko 403

INDEX OF EXECUTIVES

Kakiuchi, Takehiko 406
Kakizaki, Tamaki 30
Kakizaki, Tamaki 407
Kakoullis, Panos 516
Kaku, Masatoshi 461
Kakuchi, Yuji 288
Kalif, Eli 623
Kallenius, Ola 397
Kallevik, Eivind 452
Kalmin, Steven 269
Kalogeraki, Naya 171
Kalra, Avnish 488
Kama, Kazuaki 190
Kamada, Kazuhiko 461
Kamanga, Deland 90
Kamaras, Miklos 414
Kambayashi, Hyo 419
Kambe, Shiro 572
Kamenetzky, David 360
Kameoka, Akiko 629
Kameoka, Tsuyoshi 569
Kamezawa, Hironori 409
Kamieth, Markus 100
Kamigama, Takehiro 567
Kamigama, Takehiro 681
Kamiguchi, Keiichi 505
Kamijo, Tsutomu 630
Kaminaga, Susumu 636
Kamiwaki, Futoshi 544
Kamiyoshi, Toshiyuki 544
Kamo, Masaharu 471
Kamoya, Yoshiaki 630
Kan, Tomokazu 679
Kanai, Takayuki 275
Kanamaru, Muneo 587
Kanamoto, Hideaki 296
Kanamoto, Yasushi 550
Kanan, A. 9
Kanasugi, Yasuzo 415
Kanazawa, Sadao 630
Kanazawa, Yugo 371
Kanchinadham, Parvatheesam 607
Kanda, Masaaki 460
Kanda, Yasumitsu 150
Kandholm, Joakim 4
Kane, Archie G. 395
Kanehana, Yoshinori 344
Kanehara, Nobukatsu 443
Kanei, Masashi 303
Kaneko, Hiroko 404
Kaneko, Shin 146
Kaneko, Shingo 636
Kanema, Yuji 288
Kang, Ho-Moon 526
Kang, Simon 370
Kang, Yu-Sig 368
Kang, Yu-Sig 370
Kanjanarat, Chatsuda 492
Kanno, Hitoshi 223
Kano, Koichi 360
Kano, Riyo 681
Kant, Ravi 354
Kantor, Ian R. 320
Kanzawa, Eiji 275
Kao, Daniel Tsun-Ming 660
Kao, Jerry 12
Kaperi, Ari 450
Kapil, Arvind 277
Kapil, Pawan Kumar 499
Kapilashrami, Tanuj 325

Kaplan, Jeffrey A. 380
Kaplan, Nadav 302
Kapoor, Deepak 607
Kapoor, Kishore 236
Kapoor, Navneet 1
Kapoor, Rajan 471
Kapoor, Sunir Kumar 80
Karaboutis, Adriana 49
Karalis, Veronique 240
Karasawa, Yasuyoshi 415
Karavias, Fokion C. 240
Kariyada, Fumitsugu 286
Karkkainen, Pentti O. 39
Karlsson, Anders C. 597
Karlsson, Arne 1
Karlsson, Eva 61
Karlstrom, Johan 186
Karlstrom, Johan 528
Karmilowicz, Mike 242
Karnad, Renu 278
Karnstrom, Tomas 528
Karp, A. E. 553
Karttinen, Timo 258
Karuth-Zelle, Barbara 37
Kasai, Satoshi 570
Kasama, Haruo 146
Kasama, Takayuki 327
Kaschke, Michael 284
Kashima, Kaoru 588
Kashitani, Ichiro 643
Kashiwada, Yoshinori 412
Kashiwagi, Yutaka 403
Kassai, Ali 501
Kassimiotis, Tony 482
Kassow, Achim 418
Kastalio, Oliver 542
Kasurinen, Hannu 581
Kasutani, Seiichi 394
Kasutani, Seiichi 471
Kasutani, Toshihide 634
Kaszynski, Michal 94
Katanozaka, Shinya 45
Katanozaka, Shinya 351
Katanozaka, Shinya 632
Kataoka, Masahito 434
Katase, Hirofumi 401
Katayama, Hiroshi 404
Katayama, Masanori 321
Katholm, Karen-Marie 31
Katinakis, Nikos 618
Kato, Hiromichi 163
Kato, Hiroyuki 459
Kato, Kaoru 409
Kato, Katsuhiro 595
Kato, Kazumaro 90
Kato, Keita 544
Kato, Kikuo 420
Kato, Kosuke 593
Kato, Nobuhisa 344
Kato, Nobuya 329
Kato, Sadanori 163
Kato, Sotaro 448
Kato, Takao 406
Kato, Tetsuya 296
Kato, Wataru 407
Kato, Yasumichi 277
Kato, Yuichiro 340
Katoh, Nobuaki 588
Katsu, Eijiro 45
Katsu, Etsuko 412

Katsukawa, Yoshihiko 352
Katsuki, Atsushi 57
Katsuki, Hisashi 33
Katsumi, Takeshi 342
Katsuno, Satoru 161
Katzin, Jackie 428
Kau, Melanie 35
Kauffmann, Herbert 17
Kaufman, Aviad 302
Kaufmann, Bernhard 445
Kaur, Pam 148
Kaur, Pam 295
Kavanagh, Sarah B. 102
Kawabe, Kentaro 567
Kawabe, Seiji 404
Kawachi, Katsunori 412
Kawada, Junichi 551
Kawada, Tatsuo 191
Kawagoishi, Tadashi 403
Kawaguchi, Takashi 507
Kawai, Eriko 411
Kawai, Shuji 193
Kawai, Toshiki 634
Kawakami, Yasushi 93
Kawakita, Hisashi 296
Kawamoto, Hiroaki 327
Kawamoto, Hiroko 219
Kawamoto, Hiroko 588
Kawamura, Atsushi 586
Kawamura, Hiroshi 327
Kawamura, Kanji 321
Kawamura, Yoshihiko 287
Kawamura, Yusuke 136
Kawana, Koichi 359
Kawana, Masatoshi 323
Kawana, Masayuki 543
Kawanago, Katsuhiro 546
Kawano, Ichiro 629
Kawano, Kenji 314
Kawano, Mitsuo 460
Kawanobe, Osamu 630
Kawasaki, Hiroko 231
Kawasaki, Yasuyuki 588
Kawase, Masatsugu 57
Kawashima, Katsuya 536
Kawata, Tatsumi 586
Kawazoe, Katsuhiko 442
Kazama, Masaru 342
Kazmi, Hasan 471
Ke, Qiubi 48
Ke, Yang 620
Keanly, Rose A. 8
Keens, David 325
Keers, Richard 539
Keese, Burkhard 173
Keeve, Thinus 172
Keevil, Norman B. 612
Kefalogiannis, Michael 281
Keitel, Hans-Peter 523
Keler, Sahin Alp 29
Kellan, H. S. 250
Kellaway, Racheal 92
Kelleher, Annette M. 339
Keller-Busse, Sabine 647
Keller-Busse, Sabine 689
Keller, Adrian T. 213
Keller, Andre 282
Keller, Andreas W. 213
Kellerhals, Jurgen 143
Kelly-Bisla, Balbir 677

Kelly-Ennis, Debra J. 624
Kelly, Gail Patricia 559
Kelly, Ian 540
Kelly, Kevin J. 130
Kelly, Roslyn 124
Kelly, Shaun 186
Kelly, Terri L. 60
Kelsey, Mark 500
Kemenes, Erno 414
Kemna, Angelien 73
Kemori, Nobumasa 335
Kempston-Darkes, Maureen 124
Kenel, Thierry 597
Kennealy, G. M. Beatrix 534
Kennealy, Trix 575
Kennedy, Eileen 521
Kennedy, Melissa J. 590
Kennedy, Patrick 88
Kenyon-Slaney, Harry 555
Keogan, Caoimhe 18
Keogh, John W. 160
Kepler, David E. 71
Kepler, David E. 638
Kerber, Meroonisha 304
Kermisch, Marc 168
Kern, Harald 557
Kerner, Juergen 557
Kerner, Jurgen 628
Kerr, David W. 589
Kerrien, Jean-Paul 186
Kersten, Heleen 580
Keryer, Philippe 626
Kesner, Idalene F. 589
Kessel, Alina 215
Kessiakoff, Peter 563
Kessler, Denis 540
Keswick, Adam 192
Keswick, Adam 330
Keswick, Ben 192
Keswick, Ben 330
Keuper, Frank W. 600
Kevin, Medica John 178
Key, John P. 71
Key, Matthew 125
Keys, Patrick M. 609
Keysberg, Klaus 628
Keyter, Charl 555
Kganyago, Lesetja 573
Khaili, Jawaan Awaidha Suhail Al 9
Khan, M. 9
Khan, Mehmood 499
Khan, Zafar 122
Khanani, A. Qadir 9
Khanna, Deeptha 357
Khara, Dinesh Kumar 577
Khasis, Lev 535
Khatu, Satish 183
Khazraji, W. Al 9
Kheradpir, S. 416
Khidir, Murtada 496
Khol, Florian 663
Khoo, Shulamite N. K. 164
Khositaphai, Natruedee 491
Khosrowshahi, Bijan 172
Khouri, Khaled Abdulla Neamat 9
Khuny, Marion 238
Kiba, Hiroko 146
Kicinski, Stephen C. 589
Kidani, Akihiro 391
Kidwai, Naina Lal 290

INDEX OF EXECUTIVES

Kielholz, Walter B. 600
Kiers, Deborah 92
Kijima, Tatsuo 470
Kikkawa, Takeo 303
Kikuchi, Kiyomi 402
Kikuchi, Maoko 287
Kikuta, Tetsuya 190
Kikuyama, Hideki 326
Kilaas, Liselott 452
Kilani, O. 9
Kildahl, Jorgen 469
Kildahl, Jorgen 616
Kildemo, Pal 452
Kilian, Gunnar 663
Killebrew, Toni 506
Killeen, S. L. 214
Killen, Tracey 367
Killinger, Ollie 367
Kilsby, Susan 211
Kilsby, Susan Saltzbart 653
Kim, Hae In 122
Kim, Hag-Dong 486
Kim, Hyun-Jong 526
Kim, Jae-Shin 358
Kim, James 370
Kim, Jong-Woon 358
Kim, Joo-Hyun 486
Kim, Joong Ho 152
Kim, Ki-Nam 526
Kim, Peter Bahnsuk 368
Kim, Sang-Gyun 526
Kim, Sang-Hee 370
Kim, Sang-Hyun 298
Kim, Shin-Bae 486
Kim, Soon-Taek 526
Kim, Sung-Jin 486
Kim, Tae-Ok 358
Kim, Yongah 236
Kim, Young-Kee 370
Kimijima, Shoko 286
Kimijima, Shoko 371
Kimm, Nicola 279
Kimmet, Pamela O. 386
Kimoto, Kentaro 634
Kimura, Hiroshi 602
Kimura, Hiroto 359
Kimura, Kazuhiro 359
Kimura, Yasushi 444
Kina, Leticia Rudge Barbosa 40
King, Annalisa 532
King, Ian G. 539
King, Julia 469
King, Justin M. 388
King, Peter 669
King, Steven 495
Kingman, John Oliver Frank 364
Kingo, Lise 185
Kingo, Lise 530
Kingsmill, Denise Patricia 308
Kingston, Jane 307
Kinjo, Tokei 93
Kinloch, Kathy 619
Kinnart, Peter 70
Kinney, Jane E. 146
Kinney, Jane E. 315
Kinoshita, Keishiro 442
Kinoshita, Manabu 33
Kinoshita, Manabu 586
Kinoshita, Takashi 219
Kinsley, Karen 532

Kinsley, Karen A. 422
Kinugawa, Kazuhide 327
Kirac, Ipek 354
Kirby, Pamela J. 31
Kirby, Pamela J. 127
Kirby, Pamela J. 201
Kirby, Pamela J. 499
Kirby, Peter M. 439
Kircher, Monika 523
Kiriwat, Ekamol 555
Kiriyama, Hiroshi 184
Kirk, Ewan 75
Kirkby, Allison 125
Kirsanova, Svetlana 535
Kirsch, Frank 37
Kirsch, Harry 452
Kirsch, Wolfgang 261
Kirsten, Artur Stefan 334
Kise, Yoichi 219
Kishida, Seiichi 33
Kishigami, Keiko 572
Kishino, Masayuki 634
Kita, Norio 342
Kitachi, Tatsuaki 471
Kitagawa, Hirokuni 288
Kitagawa, Ryoichi 57
Kitagawa, Shinsuke 352
Kitahara, Mutsuro 602
Kitajima, Motoharu 189
Kitajima, Yoshinari 189
Kitajima, Yoshitoshi 189
Kitamura, Akira 391
Kitamura, Kunitaro 262
Kitamura, Matazaemon 420
Kitamura, Takumi 448
Kitamura, Toshiaki 314
Kitamura, Toshio 632
Kitano, Hiroaki 572
Kitano, Shun 602
Kitano, Tatsuo 163
Kitano, Yoshihisa 335
Kitao, Yuichi 359
Kitazawa, Toshifumi 545
Kitcher, Julie 27
Kitera, Masato 329
Kitera, Masato 389
Kitera, Masato 441
Kito, Shunichi 303
Kito, Tetsuhiro 434
Kittaka, Kimihisa 314
Kittayarak, Kittipong 128
Kiuchi, Takahide 150
Kiykov, Oleg 484
Kiyokawa, Koichi 552
Kiyomune, Kazuo 286
Kiyono, Yukiyo 163
Kjellgren, Jan 528
Klasen, Eva 70
Klatten, Susanne 105
Klauke, Sabine 27
Klehm, Henry 501
Klein-Magar, Margret 531
Klein, Christian 17
Klein, Christian 531
Klein, Dorothea 131
Klein, Martin P. 68
Kleinemeier, Michael 399
Kleinman, Scott M. 68
Kleisterlee, Gerard J. 60
Kley, Karl Ludwig 218

Kley, Karl-Ludwig 207
Klingenberg, Bernard Ekhard 534
Klinken, Onno van 19
Klujsza, Marcelo 119
Knapp, Kerstin 657
Knapp, Pamela 175
Knauf, Isabel Corinna 183
Knibbe, David 445
Knight, Chris 364
Knight, Lester B. 49
Knight, Malcom D. 600
Knight, Natalie 357
Knobel, Carsten 207
Knobel, Carsten 284
Knoche-Brouillon, Carinne 418
Knoche, Philippe 626
Knoess, Christoph 519
Knof, Manfred 173
Knoll, Phillip R. 39
Knook, Pieter Cornelis 616
Knox, Lesley 364
Knudsen, Karsten Munk 455
Knutzen, Tom 450
Ko, Chen-En 216
Kobayakawa, Tomoaki 634
Kobayashi, Ayako 420
Kobayashi, Eizo 326
Kobayashi, Fumihiko 323
Kobayashi, Izumi 45
Kobayashi, Jun 303
Kobayashi, Kazuo 630
Kobayashi, Ken 405
Kobayashi, Kenichi 30
Kobayashi, Kenji 193
Kobayashi, Koji 28
Kobayashi, Makoto 409
Kobayashi, Masahiko 288
Kobayashi, Masayuki 471
Kobayashi, Nagahisa 296
Kobayashi, Soichi 303
Kobayashi, Tatsuji 550
Kobayashi, Toshinori 335
Kobayashi, Yoichi 681
Kobayashi, Yoko 459
Kobayashi, Yoshimitsu 634
Kobayashi, Yukari 121
Kobe, Hiroshi 436
Kobori, Hideki 57
Koc, Ali Y. 354
Koc, Ali Y. 684
Koc, Caroline N. 354
Koc, Omer M. 354
Koc, Rahmi M. 354
Koch, Nicole 209
Koch, Olaf G. 397
Koch, Thorsten 628
Kochhar, Rakesh 444
Kociancic, Mark 242
Kocsis, Andrea 208
Koda, Takayuki 29
Kodera, Akira 163
Kodera, Kazuhiro 303
Koehler, Martin 207
Koehler, Renate 399
Koenig, Mireille 597
Koeppel, Holly Keller 122
Koeppel, Holly Keller 253
Koeppel, Holly Keller 253
Koezuka, Miharu 327
Koezuka, Miharu 544

Kogame, Kotaro 163
Koge, Teiji 544
Kogure, Megumi 679
Koh, Beng Seng 114
Kohda, Main 329
Kohda, Main 406
Kohleisen, Sabine 397
Kohler, Annette G. 213
Kohler, Jens 105
Kohlpaintner, Christian 119
Kohn, Andreas 108
Kohno, Masaharu 588
Kohut, Brian 624
Koid, Phaik Gunn 43
Koide, Hiroko 403
Koike, Hiroshi 219
Koike, Masamichi 587
Koji, Akiyoshi 57
Kojima, Chikara 634
Kojima, Keiji 297
Kojima, Takeji 391
Kojo, Yoshiko 263
Kokubu, Fumiya 292
Kokubu, Fumiya 389
Kokubu, Fumiya 602
Kokue, Haruko 569
Kolbe, Martin 360
Kolbl, Konrad 261
Kolk, Wouter 357
Koll, Kathy Mitsuko 245
Koller, Patrick 247
Kollmann, Dagmar P. 170
Kollmann, Dagmar P. 209
Kolmsee, Ines 650
Kolobkov, Pavel 266
Koltze, Jan 108
Komagome, Tsutomu 679
Komatsu, Toshiyuki 679
Komatsu, Yasuhiro 190
Komatsu, Yayoi 436
Komiya, Satoru 632
Komiyama, Hiroshi 552
Komoda, Masanobu 411
Komorek, Juliusz 524
Kon, Kenta 286
Kon, Kenta 643
Konar, Len 573
Kondo, Fusakazu 190
Kondo, Hiroshi 629
Kondo, Jun 275
Kondo, Kazu 90
Kondo, Takao 90
Kong, Janis 646
Konieczny, Peter 41
Konig, Thomas 218
König, Wolfgang 284
Konishi, Masako 629
Konishi, Noriyuki 296
Konno, Hiroshi 249
Konno, Shiho 371
Konno, Takayuki 638
Kono, Akira 443
Kono, Masaaki 352
Kono, Yasuko 434
Konstan, Eve 574
Kontogouris, Venetia 483
Kontselidze, Archil 340
Koo, Bon-Joon 370
Koo, Tong-Fat 159
Koong, Chua Sock 488

INDEX OF EXECUTIVES

Kopp, Rochelle 415
Koppel, Martin 496
Kopra, Panu 429
Kornitzer, Clive 471
Korsholm, Peter 469
Kortenhof, Rudolf 497
Kortum, Franz-Josef 71
Korvenranta, Markku 429
Kosaka, Tatsuro 403
Koshane, Boitumelo 304
Koshi, Naomi 567
Koshiba, Mitsunobu 412
Koshijima, Keisuke 342
Koshikawa, Kazuhiro 442
Koskull, Casper von 450
Koso, Hiroshi 93
Kosokabe, Takeshi 194
Kostem, Orhun 29
Kostin, Andrey L. 340
Kosuge, Yasuharu 681
Kosugi, Keiko 443
Kot, Evgeny A. 453
Kotagiri, Seetarama 384
Kotani, Hidehito 630
Kotchka, Claudia 374
Koten, Martijn van 463
Kott, Boguslaw 86
Kotz, Christian 183
Kotzbauer, Michael 173
Koumoto, Kunihito 643
Koury, Jaime A. El 272
Kovachka-Dimitrova, Monika 531
Kovacic, Simone 381
Kowalski, Robert 452
Koya, Hiroshi 679
Koyama, Akihiro 640
Koyanagi, Stan H. 468
Koyano, Akiko 360
Kozawa, Hisato 405
Kozel, Edward R. 446
Kozlowska-Chyla, Beata 94
Kozlu, Cem M. 354
Kozminski, Andrzej 86
Kracht, Caroline Christina 612
Kraemer, Peter 48
Kralingen, Bridget A. van 519
Kramer, Christina 130
Kramer, Holly S. 675
Kramer, Lars 7
Krammer, Rudolf 558
Krantz, David 124
Kranz, Maciej 354
Krasner, Andrew 670
Kravchenko, Kirill 266
Kravchenko, Pavel 484
Kravi, Katariina 581
Kravis, Marie-Josee 379
Kravis, Marie-Josee 495
Krebber, Markus 523
Kreis, Melanie 208
Kreusel, Petra Steffi 209
Krick, Gerd 259
Kridakon, Chayotid 493
Krieger, Alexandra 173
Kriegner, Martin 290
Krimwongrut, Pirun 492
Kristiansen, Thore E. 265
Kristoffersen, Helle 464
Kristoffersen, Helle 639

Krivoshchekov, Sergey V. 484
Kroeger, Shadrak W. 611
Krog, Sverre 213
Kroll, Remy 285
Kron, Patrick 290
Kron, Patrick 530
Kronen, Petra 185
Krueger, Doris 207
Kruger, Ben 575
Kruger, Errol M. 428
Kruger, Harald 209
Krump, Paul J. 160
Kubitschek, Maria 663
Kubo, Isao 471
Kubohara, Kazunari 303
Kubota, Shinya 550
Kuchiishi, Takatoshi 277
Kudelski, Andre 495
Kudo, Akiko 442
Kudo, Hitoshi 249
Kudo, Koshiro 57
Kudo, Teiko 587
Kudo, Teiko 643
Kudo, Yasumi 231
Kudo, Yoko 161
Kudryavtsev, Nikolay 535
Kuehn, Christopher (Chris) J. 644
Kuehne, Christiane 581
Kuehne, Klaus-Michael 360
Kufen, Thomas 523
Kuffner, James 643
Kuga, Eiichi 163
Kuga, Noriyuki 681
Kuga, Takuya 404
Kuhn, Thorsten 208
Kuhn, Volker 499
Kuhnert, Marcus 399
Kuhnke, Frank 206
Kukielski, Peter 452
Kuleshov, Aleksandr 535
Kulve, Peter ter 653
Kumagai, Toshiyuki 346
Kumakura, Kazunari 340
Kumakura, Kazunari 641
Kumar, Rajnish 577
Kumazawa, Shinichiro 550
Kume, Yuji 341
Kumihashi, Kazuhiro 296
Kung, Chih-Jung 141
Kung, Ming-Hsin 603
Kung, Sung Yen 687
Kunibe, Takeshi 354
Kunibe, Takeshi 588
Kunigo, Yutaka 439
Kunihiro, Tadashi 380
Kunimasa, Kimiko 33
Kuniya, Hiroko 443
Kunzle, Hans C. 282
kuo-cheng, Chang 242
Kuo, Andrew Ming-Jian 142
Kuo, Li Lien 687
Kuo, Tai Yu 687
Kuo, Tung-Long 216
Kuok, Khoon Hua 541
Kuper, Jaime Zabludovsky 38
Kupper, Elmer Funke 592
Kuraishi, Seiji 292
Kurasaka, Shoji 666
Kurata, Hideyuki 21
Kurata, Isshu 223

Kurata, Yasuharu 277
Kuratsu, Yasuyuki 527
Kuri, Luis Alejandro Soberon 43
Kuribrena, Jose Antonio Meade 295
Kurihara, Mitsue 161
Kurihara, Mitsue 586
Kurilin, Yuri Igorevich 517
Kurisu, Toshizo 681
Kurita, Takuya 185
Kuriwada, Eiichi 546
Kuriyama, Yoshifumi 361
Kurmashov, Shamil 456
Kurobe, Takashi 636
Kuroda, Yukiko 459
Kurokawa, Hiroyuki 296
Kuromoto, Junnosuke 629
Kurovat, Wattanapong 491
Kuroyanagi, Masafumi 189
Kurpis, Joseph 670
Kurumado, Joji 246
Kuruöz, Ilker 646
Kusakabe, Satoshi 403
Kusaki, Yoriyuki 593
Kuse, Kazushi 57
Kushida, Shigeki 202
Kushwaha, Raj 457
Kusumi, Yuki 472
Kuula, Tapio 258
Kuwabara, Satoko 409
Kuwabara, Satoko 443
Kuwahara, Yasuaki 345
Kuwano, Yukinori 194
Kuwar, Ahmed A. Al 496
Kux, Barbara 284
Kuzmin, Alexey 484
Kuznets, Sergey I. 266
Kuznetsov, Alexander 243
Kuznetsov, Stanislav 535
Kuznetsova, Tatyana S. 453
Kvalheim, Grant 68
Kvisle, Harold N. 146
Kwan, Savio Ming Sang 122
Kwan, William Cheuk-yin 589
Kwiecinski, Jerzy 94
Kwist, C. M. 280
Kwok, Adam Kai-fai 589
Kwok, Christopher Kai-wang 589
Kwok, Clement King Man 276
Kwok, Eva L. 146
Kwok, Geoffrey Kai-chun 589
Kwok, Raymond Ping-luen 589
Kwon, Bong Seok 371
Kwon, Oh-Hyun 526
Kwon, Young-Soo 369
Kwon, Young-Soo 371
Kwong, Gordon Che-Keung 160
Kyoya, Yutaka 246
Kyoya, Yutaka 407

L

L., S. 573
L'Helias, Sophie 347
L'Heureux, Alexandre 678
L'Estrange, Michael 509
Laaksonen, Juha 258
Labelle, Bernard 149

Laber, Ilias 290
Laberge, Alice D. 457
Labeyrie, Christian 659
Labriola, Pietro 615
Lacaze, Claire 348
Lacerda, Eduardo Braga Cavalcanti de 40
Lacerda, Francisco de 227
Lacey, John S. 123
Lachapelle, Lise 299
Lacharrière, Fimalac Marc de 141
Lachenmann, Susanne 311
Lachs, Andreas 238
Lacorte, Jaime Felix Caruana 80
Lacoste, Patricia 32
Lacoste, Patricia 540
LaCroix, Selena Loh 503
Laegreid, Stig 236
Lafleur, Jean-Hugues 297
Lafon, Serge 177
Lafont, Bruno 55
LaForge, Melissa M. 226
Lagasse, Louis 297
Lageweg, Paul 122
Lagubeau, Julien 140
Lagunes, Jose Octavio Reyes 171
Lahey, Katie 138
Lahore, German Fernandez 686
Lahousse, Alexandre 525
Lai, Chang Li 687
Laidlaw, Sam 509
Laidlaw, Sam 511
Laing, Ian R. 305
Laing, Ronald K. 132
Laisathit, Niraman 85
Lake, Charles Ditmars 327
Lakshminarayanan, Ramesh 277
Lal, Punita 137
Lal, Punita 200
Lalicker, Greg 467
Lalonde, Kenn 638
Lam, Donald Yin Shing 276
Lam, Jeffrey Kin-Fung 160
Lam, Jocelyn Yin Shan 267
Lam, Maurice 316
Lam, Yiu Kin 436
Lamade, Lars 531
Lamarche, Gerard 650
Lambert, Christiane 186
Lambert, Jennifer Margaret 111
Lambert, Jerome 176
Lambert, Pippa 73
Lamlieng, Chumpol Na 555
Lammers, Patrick 218
Lammertyn, Alejandro 620
Lamont, David M. 110
Lamothe, Marie-Josee 35
Lamouche, Didier R. 15
Lamoureux, Claude 299
Lanaway, John B. 168
Lancaster, Richard Kendall 167
Landel, Michel 197
Landen, Gordana 15
Landiribar, Javier Echenique 13
Landiribar, Jose Javier Echenique 615
Landon, Stephane 565
Landon, Valerie 247
Landsnes, Bente Avnung 198
Lane, Kenneth 380

INDEX OF EXECUTIVES

Lang, Arthur 558
Lang, Steffen 453
Langa, Doug 455
Lange, Anne 308
Lange, Anne 399
Lange, Anne 476
Lange, Martin Holst 455
Lange, Thorsten 429
Langelier, Simon 304
Langer, Per 258
Langlois, Josiane M. 624
Langston, John 307
Laourde, Jean-Christophe 177
Lara, Rodrigo Brand de 83
Larnach, Fiona 497
Laroze, Francois 660
Larranaga, Arantza Estefania 504
Larrea, Jose Antonio Rivero 38
Larsen, Christine E. 130
Larson, Joshua 258
Larson, Michael 254
Larsson, Benny 70
Larsson, Mari 664
Laruelle, Claude 659
Lathauwer, Astrid de 240
Lathion-Zweifel, Sandra 601
Latypov, Ural Alfretovich 517
Lau, Albert Tak-yeung 589
Lau, Chun Shun 436
Lau, Don Jin Tin 670
Lau, Lawrence Juen-Yee 23
Lau, Martin Chi Ping 212
Lau, Martin Chi Ping 333
Lau, Martin Chi Ping 620
Lau, Martin Chi Ping 660
Lau, Siu Ki 250
Lauenroth-Mago, Joerg 392
Lauk, Kurt J. 384
Laury, Veronique 122
Laury, Veronique 566
Laut, Steve W. 132
Laver, Sue 618
LaVerdiere, Michael 436
Lavernos, Barbara 362
Lavin, Pablo Granito 80
Law, Alson Chun-tak 88
Law, David 488
Law, Fanny Fan Chiu Fun 167
Law, Quinn Yee Kwan 114
Law, Quinn Yee Kwan 235
Lawal, Kikelomo 130
Lawrance, James 564
Lawrence, Jake 91
Lawrenz, Jurgen 37
Lawson-Hall, Cathia 661
Lawson, Brian D. 124
Lawther, Robin 577
Layfield, Diana 66
Lazarev, Peter Ivanovich 517
Lazari, Octavio de 80
Lazat, Beatrice 347
Lazzarato, David A. 253
Le, Tan 497
Leach, Brian 68
Leach, Jeremy 182
Leal, Guilherme Muller 80
Leao, Mario Roberto Opice 82
Leary, Robert G. 315
Lebel, Anne 136
LeBlanc, Glen 106

Leblanc, Jacques 297
Lebot, Diony 565
Leboucher, Nathalie 32
LeBoutillier, John 299
Lecea, Rafael Salinas Martínez De 647
Lechner, Christoph 282
Lecorvaisier, Fabienne 362
Lecorvaisier, Fabienne 525
Lecorvaisier, Fabienne 530
Leduc, Michel R. 589
Lee, Amanda 21
Lee, Byung Kook 298
Lee, Chae-Woong 526
Lee, Champion 245
Lee, Chang Sil 371
Lee, Chang-Ken 141
Lee, Cheng Chuan 687
Lee, Chi-Jen 216
Lee, Chien 599
Lee, Dannis Cheuk Yin 267
Lee, Deborah 180
Lee, Delman 88
Lee, Delman 192
Lee, Denny Ting Bun 433
Lee, Dong Kyu 298
Lee, Gilbert Man Lung 276
Lee, Gyu-Min 370
Lee, Heung-Joo 358
Lee, In-Ho 526
Lee, Irene Yun Lien 276
Lee, Irene Yun-Lien 34
Lee, Jae-Yong 526
Lee, Ji-Ren 12
Lee, Jin Ming 250
Lee, John Luen-Wai 434
Lee, Judy 200
Lee, Jun-Ho 358
Lee, Jung-Bok 358
Lee, K.T. 159
Lee, Katherine 106
Lee, Kee-Man 358
Lee, Kenneth 560
Lee, Kitty 305
Lee, Kok Kwan 164
Lee, Kun-Hee 526
Lee, Kye-Sung 358
Lee, Melanie 530
Lee, Myles P. 644
Lee, Rannie Wah Lun 276
Lee, Rose Wai Mun 599
Lee, Sang-Hoon 526
Lee, Shao Wu 687
Lee, Sue 224
Lee, Sunny Wai Kwong 114
Lee, Tai-Chi 216
Lee, Theng Kiat 558
Lee, Wai Fai 654
Lee, Won Hee 298
Lee, Yoon-Woo 526
Lee, Young-Ha 370
Lee, Yuan Siong 22
Leeder, Nicholas 220
Lefebvre, Dominique 185
Lefebvre, Olivier 247
Lefevre, Deborah Hall 35
Legault, Frederic 400
Leger, Jeff 374
Legg, Sarah Catherine 374
Leggett, Karen A. 386
Legong, Lerato 555

LeGresley, David M. B. 236
Lehmann, Frauke 261
Lehmann, Lars 137
Lehmus, Matti 429
Lehti, Matti 258
Leibinger-Kammueller, Nicola 557
Leigh, John Andrew Harry 167
Leinonen, Jukka 616
Leite, Miguel Espregueira Mendes Pereira 223
Leith, Rob A. G. 428
Lelieveld, Rob J. W. 445
Lels, Marike E. Van Lier 500
Lema, Eduardo Perez de 386
Lemann, Paulo Alberto 48
Lemarchand, Agnes 175
Lemay, Stephane 487
Lemierre, Jean 113
Lemierre, Jean 639
Lemoine, Pierre-Armand 542
Lemppenau, Joachim 663
Lempres, Elizabeth C. 270
Lengler, Peter 531
Lenhard, Felix 665
Lenman, Alasdair 685
Lennartz-Pipenbacher, Ulrike 208
Lennie, Bill 349
Lennkh, Peter 497
Lennon, Carolan 253
Lennon, Gary 421
Lentz, Dennis 279
Leoka, Thabi 46
Leone, Flavia 650
Leonetti, Olivier C. 220
Leonetti, Olivier C. 337
Leong, Chris 432
Leong, Dennis 381
Leong, Dennis 382
Leost, Claire 660
Lepage, Philippe 233
Lepinay, Philippe 626
Lerberghe, Rose-Marie Van 116
Lerner, Ida 213
Leroux, Monique F. 35
Leroux, Monique F. 106
Leroux, Monique F. 177
Leroux, Sylvain 134
Leroy, Alain 542
Leroy, Didier 643
Leroy, Dominique 175
Lertpaithoon, Somkit 492
Lescure, Emmanuel 542
Lescure, Frederic 542
Lescure, Henri 542
Lescure, Jerome 542
Lescure, Thierry 542
Leston, Paula Mouzo 308
Letelier, Mauricio Baeza 81
Leten, Ronnie 237
Letta, Enrico 495
Leue, Torsten 277
Leukert, Bernd 206
Leung, Andrew Wing Lok 276
Leung, Anthony Kam Ping 474
Leung, Antony Kam Chung 152
Leung, Elsie Oi sie 156
Leung, Margaret Ko May-yee 589
Leung, Michael Man Kit 433
Leung, Mui Yin 235
Leung, Norman Nai-pang 589

Leung, Wai Ping 617
Leung, Yee Sik 687
Leupold, Samuel 230
Leupold, Samuel Georg Friedrich 537
Leventis, Anastasios I. 172
Leventis, Christodoulos 172
Lévêque, Didier 141
Lever, Viveca Brinkenfeldt 3
Levesque, Julie 422
Levi, Barbara 509
Levieux, Armelle 362
LeVine, Suzan 495
Levitt, Brian M. 638
Levo, Claudia 580
Levy, Jean-Bernard 247
Levy, Maurice 495
Lewin, Andrew 656
Lewiner, Colette 116
Lewis, George R. 364
Lewis, Gregory 395
Lewis, Jonathan 236
Lewis, Kevin A. 35
Lewis, Patrick 367
Lewis, Ric 364
Lewis, Sian 174
Lewis, Stephen 619
Lewis, Stuart Wilson 206
Leysen, Thomas 521
Leysen, Thomas 650
Lheureux, Pascal 186
Li, Adrian David Man-kiu 88
Li, An 547
Li, Arthur Kwok Cheung 88
Li, Aubrey Kwok-sing 88
Li, Bao-Lin 682
Li, Buqing 688
Li, Daniel Dong Hui 267
Li, David Kwok-po 88
Li, Dazhuang 40
Li, Defang 155
Li, Dong Sheng 620
Li, Eric Ka-cheung 589
Li, Fei-Fei 103
Li, Forrest Xiaodong 541
Li, Frederick Ching-kam 589
Li, Godwin Chi Chung 276
Li, Guangpu 560
Li, H 159
Li, Haifeng 295
Li, Huidi 154
Li, Jennifer Xin-Zhe 7
Li, Jennifer Xin-Zhe 354
Li, Jennifer Xinzhe 531
Li, Jiamin 478
Li, Jianmin 295
Li, Jiashi 158
Li, Jing 560
Li, Kit-Sang 159
Li, Kunyi 159
Li, Li 575
Li, Longcheng 87
Li, Lu 152
Li, Meocre Kwon-wing 88
Li, Min 212
Li, Mingguang 153
Li, Qian 128
Li, Quancai 688
Li, Qunfeng 48
Li, Robin Yanhong 76
Li, Ronghua 154

INDEX OF EXECUTIVES

Li, Samson Kai-cheong 88
Li, Sen 150
Li, Shipeng 683
Li, Shu Fu 267
Li, Shuqing 295
Li, Stephen Charles Kwok-sze 88
Li, Steve I Nan 687
Li, Tongbin 158
Li, Wei 683
Li, Xiande 336
Li, Xianhua 336
Li, Xiao Yun 152
Li, Xiaobo 48
Li, Xiaohui 87
Li, Xin 156
Li, Xiyong 683
Li, Yao 87
Li, Yi 165
Li, Ying 688
Li, Yonglin 155
Li, Yongzhao 128
Li, Yuanqin 559
Li, Zhaohui 345
Li, Zhiming 157
Li, Zhiming 560
Li, Zixue 688
Liang, Aishi 153
Liang, Aishi 478
Liang, Daguang 48
Liang, Dingpeng 159
Liang, Qing 335
Liang, Thomas Cheung-Biu 434
Liang, Victor Zhixiang 76
Liao, David Yi Chien 276
Liao, Jinwun 178
Liao, Kun-Ching 682
Liao, Lin 309
Liao, Xingeng 335
Liao, Yijian 87
Liao, Zihping 178
Liaw, Y.H. 603
Libnic, Samuel 81
Liceaga, Juan Carlos Rebollo 300
Licence, Stephen 364
Licht, Kris 499
Lidefelt, Bjorn 61
Lidefelt, Jon 597
Lieb, Eckhard 207
Liebelt, Graeme R. 41
Liebelt, Graeme R. 71
Lieberman, Gerald M. 623
Lien, Michael Jown Leam 654
Liepe, Andreas 105
Lies, Michel M 689
Lifton, Richard P. 513
Likharev, Sergey 456
Liljedal, Sara Hagg 70
Lilleyman, Greg 255
Lillikas, Yiorgos 56
Lim, Anthony Weng Kin 200
Lim, Cheng Cheng 558
Lim, Eric Jin Huei 654
Lim, Hwee Hua 439
Lim, Li Ching 558
Lim, Olivier Tse Ghow 200
Lim, Swee Say 559
Lima, Dawn E. de 608
Liman, Ulrich 185
Limbacher, Randy L. 609
Limbeck, Reiner van 523

Limberg, Joachim 456
Limcaoco, Jose Teodoro K. 93
Lin, Bough 58
Lin, Ching-Hua 620
Lin, Chong 295
Lin, Chris Horng-Dar 603
Lin, Dairen 153
Lin, Frank 660
Lin, Frank F.C. 672
Lin, Guangnan 178
Lin, Haifeng 474
Lin, Henry 672
Lin, Hong 152
Lin, Hsien-Ming 672
Lin, Hua 87
Lin, J.K. 603
Lin, Jen-Jen Chang 216
Lin, Jerry Cheng Tien 687
Lin, Jingzhen 114
Lin, Mingsong 178
Lin, Pin Huang 687
Lin, Sarena S. 103
Lin, Sue-Jean 32
Lin, Syaru Shirley 611
Lin, William 117
Lin, Xiaochun 158
Lin, Zhihong 87
Lin, Zhiquan 153
Lind, Philip B. 514
Lindbaek, Jannik 236
Lindén, Johan 214
Lindfors, Lars Peter 429
Lindgren, Bengt Erik 597
Lindholm, Charlotta 563
Lindqvist, Jenny 237
Lindsay, Donald R. 386
Lindsay, Donald R. 612
Lindwall, Dan 596
Lindwall, Pauline 392
Linehan, Karen 530
Ling, Yiqun 155
Lins, Clarissa 55
Linton, Joy 187
Linton, Thomas K. 370
Linton, William 224
Liovin, Kirill Y. 484
Lipowsky, Ursula 277
Lira, Lucas Machado 40
Lis, David George 395
Lis, Gregorio Maranon y Bertran de 179
Lisboa, Carlos Eduardo Klutzenschell 40
Lisboa, Marcos de Barros 40
Lisin, Vladimir 456
Lisson, Kathryn Mary 497
Lister, Paul 65
Little, Mark 592
Litvack, Karina A. 235
Litzen, Ulla 3
Liu, Changyue 158
Liu, Chenggang 114
Liu, Chengyu 291
Liu, Chun 660
Liu, Erfei 335
Liu, Fang 152
Liu, Fangyun 335
Liu, Gang 559
Liu, Genle 199
Liu, Guixin 156

Liu, Hailiang 560
Liu, Haoyang 87
Liu, Henry Yuhong 487
Liu, Hong 483
Liu, Hongbin 155
Liu, Huan 152
Liu, Jean 347
Liu, Jean Qing 212
Liu, Jian 683
Liu, Jianfeng 235
Liu, Jih-Gang 159
Liu, Jin 114
Liu, Jizhen 295
Liu, Juei Chung 687
Liu, Jun 87
Liu, Jun 152
Liu, Jun 366
Liu, Ken 436
Liu, Lanbiao 309
Liu, Len Yu 687
Liu, Li-Wen 682
Liu, Maoxun 151
Liu, Mark 603
Liu, Min 71
Liu, Ming Chung 436
Liu, Ming Hui 152
Liu, Quancheng 199
Liu, Ranxing 295
Liu, Richard Qiangdong 333
Liu, Tiantian 48
Liu, Wei 295
Liu, Wen-Ching 682
Liu, Xiang 151
Liu, Xianhua 478
Liu, Xiaoyong 156
Liu, Xiaozhi 48
Liu, Xiaozhi 71
Liu, Xiaozhi 339
Liu, Xike 335
Liu, Xing 660
Liu, Yingqiu 336
Liu, Yong 560
Liu, Yuezhen 478
Liu, Yunhong 547
Liu, Zhengjun 165
Liu, Zhengrong 108
Livingston, Ian 189
Livingston, Ian 425
Livingstone, Catherine 174
Lizaur, Jose Ignacio Perez 272
Ljung, Roger 597
Ljungberg, Erik 597
Llale, Tabego T. 304
Lleras, Jose Antonio Vargas 228
Llewellyn, Rania 363
Llorens, Juan Pi 80
Llosa, Reynaldo 185
Lloveras, Teresa Garcia-Mila 504
Lloyd, Jonathan 192
Lloyd, Jonathan 330
Lo, John Shek Hon 620
Lo, Raymond 58
Lo, Vincent Hong Sui 276
Lo, Wei-Jen 603
Lo, Winston Yau-lai 88
Lo, Yuk Lam 560
Loacker, Stefan 600
Loacker, Stefan 665
Lochray, Stuart I. 256
Lockhart, Nancy H. O. 668

Lodge, Jane Ann 201
Loebsack, Grita 108
Loehnis, Alison 377
Loescher, Peter 615
Lofficial, Xavier 565
Loffler, Carmen 183
Lofton, Kevin E. 395
Loganadhan, Vinodh 244
Logghe, Lieve 113
Logiurato, Liana 319
Lohr, Gernot 68
Lok, Finn 137
Lollgen, Frank 103
Lomas, Bernadette Mak 599
Lombard, Marie-Christine 659
Lombardi, Michele 168
Lombarte, Jordi 71
Lomelin, Carlos Vicente Salazar 80
Lomon, Nathalie 542
long-shung, Wang 242
Long, Andy 332
Long, Nicholas Tom 41
Long, Peter 646
Looney, Bernard 117
Loosli, Hansueli 601
Lopes, Alexsandro Broedel 322
Lopez-Doriga, Belen Moscoso del Prado 136
Lopez-Doriga, Belen Moscoso del Prado 566
Lopez-Jorrin, Alvaro 316
Lopez, Alejandro Arango 221
Lopez, Belen Garijo 80
Lopez, Jose Maria Alvarez-Pallete 615
Lopez, Maria Jesus Carrasco 476
Lopez, Rafael de Juan 179
Lorentzon, Martin 574
Lorenzatto, Rudimar Andreis 480
Lorenzini, Pedro Paulo Giubbina 322
Lorenzo, Juan Ramon Jimenez 84
Lorimer, Darren 236
Loscher, Peter 358
Losquadro, Geraldine (Gerri) 242
Loubser, R. M. 250
Loudon, Bridget 618
Louis, Harald 523
Loutfy, N. 9
Louw, J. A. 553
Louwhoff, Roel 577
Loven, Lotta 597
Loveridge, Anne 421
Lovold, Maria Ervik 213
Low-Friedrich, Iris 261
Low, C. 250
Lowe, John E. 609
Lowth, Simon 125
Lox, Egbert 650
Lozano, Adrian Jorge Lozano 52
Lozano, Marcelo Zambrano 144
Lozano, Rafael Garza 144
Lozano, Rogelio Zambrano 144
Lu, Chin Chu 687
Lu, Chun-Jie 682
Lu, Fang Ming 250
Lu, Fei 295
Lu, Gary 178
Lu, Hsu-Tung 547
Lu, Jun 560
Lu, L.C. 603
Lu, Ming 488

INDEX OF EXECUTIVES

Lu, Pengjun 660
Lu, Qi 474
Lu, Qi 531
Lu, Ruby Rong 653
Lu, Shan 620
Lu, Sidney 291
Lu, Yan 366
Lu, Yaozhong 478
Lu, Yongzhen 309
Luan, Zu-Wang 682
Lubascher, Rodolfo Krause 225
Lubek, David 140
Lucey, Kevin 201
Luchangco, Eric Roberto M. 93
Luchi, Francesca 533
Lucht, Udo 304
Lucki, Michael 78
Ludwig, Helmuth 287
Luff, Nick L. 500
Luff, Nick L. 516
Luge, Ingo 628
Luha, Eugen-Gheorghe 218
Luhabe, Wendy N. 176
Lui, Victor Ting 589
Lukander, Jenni 446
Lukin, Vladimir 646
Lumali, Ergun 397
Lund, Erik 137
Lund, Helge 117
Lund, Jens H. 216
Lundberg, Fredrik 528
Lundberg, Fredrik 596
Lundgren, Johan 220
Lundmark, Pekka 446
Lundstedt, Martin 664
Lundstrom, Paul R. 252
Luo, Laijun 158
Luo, Meijian 157
Luo, Nan 114
Luo, Rong 76
Lupica, John J. 160
Lupoi, Alberto 393
Luscan, Philippe 530
Lusk, Stephen 170
Lute, Jane H. 549
Lutes, Ralph J. 612
Luther, Annette 513
Luts, Erik 345
Lutz, Marcos Marinho 649
Luz, Lorival Nogueira 119
Luzzi, Federico Ferro 615
Lv, Bo 478
Lv, Dapeng 155
Lv, Lianggong 155
Lv, Xiangyang 128
Lyle, Mike Vacy 174
Lynas, Peter J. 574
Lynch, Christopher 669
Lynch, Kevin G. 131
Lynch, Thomas J. 611
Lyon, Mathias 4
Lyons, Daniel E. 305
Lyons, Mark Donald 55
Lyons, Nicholas 482
Lyons, Peter J. 214
Lyrvall, Per 581
Lyu, Fangming 291

M

M.C., McCarthy 152
Ma, Huateng 620
Ma, Jin Long 152
Ma, Jing 474
Ma, Jisiang 178
Ma, Mingzhe 483
Ma, Siu-Cheung 434
Ma, Stephen 444
Ma, Wanjun 560
Ma, Xiaoyi 620
Ma, Xuezheng 366
Ma, Xulun 158
Ma, Yanhui 559
Ma, Yongsheng 155
Ma, Zhixiang 235
Maas-Brunner, Melanie 100
Mabaso-Koyana, S. N. 416
Mabelane, B. P. 534
Mabuchi, Akira 410
Macbeath, Sharon 285
MacDonald, Brian 592
MacDonald, Doug 131
MacDonald, John A. 514
Maceiras, Oscar Garcia 308
Macfarlane, Alastair S. 304
Macfarlane, Ian J. 674
Macfarlane, John T. 71
MacGibbon, Alan N. 638
MacGregor, Catherine 233
Machell, Simon 592
Machenil, Lars 113
Machler, Monica 689
Mackay, Iain 274
MacKay, Michelle M. 189
Mackenna, Francisco Perez 81
MacKenzie, Amanda 374
Mackenzie, Andrew 549
Mackenzie, Don 123
MacKenzie, Ken N. 110
Mackiw, Christine I. 589
Maclean, Elaine 24
MacLellan, Robert F. 384
MacLeod, Fiona 168
MacLeod, Robert 500
MacLeod, Robert J. 339
MacLeod, Sharon 487
MacNaughton, David 609
MacNicholas, Garry 270
MacPhail, Keith A. 146
MacRae, Penelope 421
MacSween, Micheal R. 592
Madden, Teresa S. 226
Maddux, Franklin W. 259
Madere, Consuelo E. 457
Madero, Roger Saldana 144
Madhavan, S. 301
Madhavpeddi, Kalidas V. 269
Madoff, Paula B. 270
Madoff, Paula B. 487
Madon, Cyrus 123
Madre, Armelle de 626
Madsen, Jorn 35
Madsen, Thomas Lindegaard 1
Madsen, Toni H 450
Maeda, Fumio 434
Maeda, Hiroaki 666
Maeda, Kaori 287
Maeda, Koichi 190

Maeda, Masahiko 643
Maeda, Yuko 57
Maekawa, Shigenobu 360
Maerki, Hans Ulrich 600
Maes, Benoit 116
Maestri, Luca 432
Maestrini, Andre 377
Magaloni, Ana Laura 38
Magee, Christine 400
Magee, Christine 619
Mageza, Peter 46
Magistretti, Elisabetta 393
Magnusson, Bo 597
Maguire, Andy 24
Mahawongtikul, Pannalin 493
Mahe, Isabel Ge 377
Maher, Mary Lou 130
Maheshwari, Sanjeev 577
Maheshwari, Sunita 278
Mahieu, Carla 521
Mahjour, Morteza 169
Mahler, Simone 663
Mahmoud, Tirad 9
Mahon, Paul A. 270
Mahoney, Sean O. 50
Mahoney, Sean O. 51
Mahy, Helen 574
Mai, Jackson 216
Maia, Antonio Bernardo Vieira 179
Maidment, Karen E. 638
Maioli, Giampiero 185
Mair, Markus 497
Majcher, Marian 94
Majocha, Mark 644
Makalima, Linda 428
Makhmudova, Nigyar 197
Maki-Kala, Jyrki 429
Makinen, Antti 581
Makino, Akiji 191
Makino, Yuko 471
Makinose, Takashi 150
Makiura, Shinji 681
Makwana, P. Mpho 428
Malcolmson, Robert 106
Maldonado, Luis Santiago Perdomo 221
Malenfant, Dominique 131
Malherbe, J. F. 553
Malherbe, Josua 176
Malhotra, Sanjiv 577
Malloch-Brown, Lord 320
Malone, Mona 90
Maloney, Scott E. 613
Malrieu, Francoise 233
Malyshev, Sergey 412
Man-bun, Brian David Li 88
Manabe, Masaaki 288
Manabe, Seiji 343
Manabe, Sunao 190
Manabe, Yoshiki 569
Manase, Zodwa Penelope 573
Mancho, Francisco Javier de Paz 615
Mancini, Massimo 615
Mandine, Beatrice 464
Mandraffino, Erika 235
Manes, Gianna M. 256
Manifold, Albert 186
Manifold, Albert 380
Manley, John 619

Manley, Kelly 168
Manley, Michael 579
Manley, Mike 516
Mann, Erica L. 521
Manning, Neil D. 624
Manning, Robert A. 135
Mannings, Moni 220
Mano, Hitoshi 444
Manoshiro, Fumio 439
Mansour, Matt 497
Mantilla, Luis Suarez de Lezo 504
Mantinan, Jose Manuel Loureda 504
Manz, Anna 376
Manzanal, Ramiro Gerardo 686
Manzaro, Sidney Rogerio 120
Manzoni, John 211
Manzoni, John A. 574
Mao, Er Wan 152
Mao, Juan 158
Maoka, Tomomitsu 505
Maphai, Vincent 555
Maraganore, John M. 605
Marakby, Sherif S. 384
Maramag, Angela Pilar B. 93
Marca, Lionel A. 597
Marchetti, Walkiria Schirrmeister 80
Marchi, Alberto 230
Marchi, Victorio Carlos de 40
Marcial, Maria Theresa D. 93
Marcoccia, Loretta 91
Marcogliese, Richard J. 146
Marcote, Flora Perez 308
Marcotte, Louis 315
Marcoux, Isabelle 487
Marcoux, Isabelle 514
Marcus, Gill 269
Marcus, Gill 573
Marcussen, Michala 565
Maree, Jacko 575
Margerie, Victoire de 56
Marie, Caroline Gregoire Sainte 659
Marie, Fernando Fort 185
Marin, Alfredo Castelo 386
Marin, Juan Guitard 84
Marin, Valero 504
Marina, Gabriel Moneo 308
Marinello, Kathryn V. 664
Marino, Peter John 415
Marino, Ricardo Villela 81
Marino, Ricardo Villela 323
Marion, Francois 656
Markelov, Vitaly A. 266
Marks, Howard S. 124
Markscheid, Stephen 336
Markwell, David 374
Maro, Hideharu 636
Marquardt, Jan-Willem 207
Marquardt, Rolf 597
Marques, Ana Paula Garrido de Pina 223
Marques, Miguel Athayde 265
Marquette, Vanessa 540
Marquez, Ramon Martin Chavez 84
Marr, David P. 675
Marra, David 501
Marriott, Peter Ralph 669
Marroco, Tadeu Luiz 122
Mars, Wendy 516
Marsac, Cecile Tandeau De 566
Marsh, Adrian 215

HOOVER'S HANDBOOK OF WORLD BUSINESS 2024   715

INDEX OF EXECUTIVES

Marsh, Mary 293
Marshall, Christopher P. 574
Marshall, Ernest W. 220
Martel, Chantal 624
Martel, Christine 108
Martell, Angel Santodomingo 82
Martell, Keith G. 457
Martello, Wan Ling 34
Martello, Wan Ling 579
Martha, Geoffrey S. 395
Martin, Andy 367
Martin, Bradley 244
Martin, Bradley Paul L. 240
Martin, Cathy 566
Martin, Dalmacio D. 107
Martin, Geoffrey 395
Martin, James 509
Martin, James 511
Martin, Marcel 171
Martin, Maria Fuencisla Gomez 83
Martin, Rosemary 661
Martinelli, Maurizio 656
Martinez, Alberto Torrado 84
Martinez, Armando Martinez 300
Martinez, Guillermo Garza 52
Martinez, Guillermo Ortiz 466
Martinez, Jose Manuel Martinez 386
Martinez, Luis Fernando Barbosa 179
Martinez, Luis Hernando de Larramendi 386
Martinez, Maria Amparo Moraleda 27
Martinez, Miguel Largacha 271
Martinez, Oscar Montero 621
Martinez, Rodrigo Fernandez 38
Martinoli, Carolina 316
Martinsen, Sten Roar 452
Marton, Szilvia Pinczesne 218
Martsinovich, Valeriy 484
Maruyama, Heiji 680
Maruyama, Yoshimichi 546
Marwala, Tshilidzi 428
Marx, Kerstin 209
Masai, Yoshiteru 29
Masding, Jeremy 474
Mashego, T. S. 250
Mashelkar, Raghunath A. 499
Masilela, Elias 573
Masiyiwa, Strive 653
Maskell, Duncan 187
Masola, Diego 91
Mason, Barbara F. 91
Mason, Jonny 189
Mason, William 363
Masrani, Bharat B. 638
Massaro, Joseph R. 51
Masson, Michel Le 185
Masters, Blythe S.J. 1
Masud, Jawad A. 609
Masuda, Hiroya 327
Masuda, Hiroya 327
Masuda, Hiroya 327
Masuda, Hitoshi 452
Masuda, Jun 380
Masuda, Kenichi 121
Masuda, Koichi 190
Masuda, Kuniaki 403
Masukawa, Michio 681
Masuko, Jiro 630
Masuyama, Mika 593
Matchett, Geraldine 7

Matchett, Geraldine 521
Matheson, Les 421
Mathew, Sara 138
Mathew, Sara 499
Mathew, Shaji 312
Mathews, Ben J.S. 118
Mathieu, Michel 185
Matinez, Maria Amparo Moraleda 661
Matisons, Reinhardt 674
Matlosa, Lerato 555
Matooane, Mantsika A. 428
Matos, Lia Machado de 40
Matos, Nuno 294
Matsubara, Keiji 277
Matsubara, Takehisa 90
Matsubayashi, Shigeyuki 303
Matsuda, Akira 121
Matsuda, Chieko 57
Matsuda, Chieko 303
Matsuda, Chieko 351
Matsuda, Chieko 602
Matsuda, Chieko 643
Matsuda, Hiromichi 345
Matsuda, Junichi 679
Matsuda, Yuka 204
Matsuda, Yuzuru 359
Matsui, Gan 204
Matsui, Hidehiko 287
Matsui, Masaki 583
Matsui, Shinobu 473
Matsui, Takeshi 470
Matsui, Toru 410
Matsui, Yasushi 202
Matsukura, Hajime 427
Matsumaru, Ryuichi 150
Matsumoto, Gunyu 352
Matsumoto, Hidekazu 546
Matsumoto, Kazuhiro 471
Matsumoto, Masayoshi 585
Matsumoto, Masayuki 588
Matsumoto, Milton 80
Matsumoto, Nobuhiro 586
Matsumoto, Ryu 442
Matsumoto, Sachio 371
Matsumoto, Tadahisa 665
Matsumoto, Tadashi 403
Matsumoto, Takumi 340
Matsumura, Atsuko 401
Matsumura, Mikio 343
Matsunaga, Mari 57
Matsunaga, Mari 543
Matsuo, Yoshiro 471
Matsuoka, Takashi 401
Matsushima, Jun 342
Matsushita, Isao 588
Matsushita, Masa 193
Matsushita, Masaki 275
Matsuta, Masahiko 249
Matsutani, Takeo 630
Matsutani, Yukio 471
Matsuyama, Haruka 403
Matsuyama, Satohiko 680
Matsuzaka, Hidetaka 420
Matsuzaka, Kenta 412
Matsuzaki, Koichi 342
Matsuzaki, Masatoshi 371
Matsuzaki, Satoru 468
Matsuzaki, Takashi 191
Matsuzawa, Takumi 29
Matt, Peter R. 182

Mattheus, Daniela 173
Matthey, Alexander 18
Matute, Jorge Matute 225
Matyr, Peter 354
Matyumza, Nomgando Nomalungelo Angelina 534
Matyumza, Nomgando Nomalungelo Angelina 575
Maugis, Guy 182
Maure, Nicolas 502
Mauro, Beatrice Weder di 648
Maw, Scott Harlan 32
Maxson, Hilary 47
May, Fiona 496
May, Karen J. 32
May, Stefan 218
Mayall, Wendy 482
Mayer, Anton 384
Mayrhuber, Wolfgang 207
Mazoyer, Jean-Paul 185
Mazzarella, Maria 319
Mazzilli, Ines 63
Mazzoleni, Paola 620
Mazzucato, Mariana 230
Mbazima, Norman Bloe 46
McArthur, Susan J. 270
McBain, Fiona C. 189
McCall, H. Carl 68
McCallister, Terry D. 39
McCallum, G. D. 598
McCann, Carl 213
McCann, Carolyn 669
McCarthy, Aaron D. 384
McCarthy, Anthony 376
McCarthy, Barry 574
Mccarthy, Cormac Michael 201
McCarthy, Karen E. 519
McCarthy, Karen M. 256
McCarthy, Stan 524
McCaw, Maureen 592
McClure, Kathleen R. 11
McConville, Coline 646
Mcconville, James 482
McConville, Jim 73
McCool, Jim 127
McCormack, Mick 467
McCoy, Sherilyn S. 66
McCracken, Nicola 201
McCracken, Stuart R. 613
McCrory, Paul 122
McCrostie, Pip 388
McCulley, Tom 47
McDonagh, Brendan 24
McDonald, Andrew R. 189
McDonald, Calvin R. 377
McDonald, Lynn 236
McDonald, Marie E. 187
McElroy, David H. 55
McEwan, Bill 357
McEwan, Ross 421
McFadyen, Kieron 612
McFarland, R. William 244
Mcfarlane, Andrew 23
McFarlane, John 669
McGann, Gary 253
McGarry, Michael H. 552
McGonigal, Robert 624
Mcgowan, Murray 304
McGrath, Rebecca J. 381
McGrath, Rebecca J. 382

McGuire, Francis P. 299
McGuire, Tom 91
McInnes, Ross 233
McIntosh, Sandy 619
McIntyre, Bridget F. 21
McIntyre, Pamela A. 132
McKay, David I. 519
Mckay, Douglas 421
McKay, Lamar 196
McKay, Tim S. 132
McKenna, Frank J. 124
McKenna, Frank J. 132
McKenna, Siobhan Louise 675
McKenney, Richard P. 589
McKenzie, Jonathan M. 145
McKenzie, Margaret A. 131
McKenzie, Patricia 21
McKenzie, Paul 187
McKeon, Simon 421
McKeon, Simon 509
McKeon, Simon 511
McKillican, Rebecca 423
McKinstry, Nancy 11
McLaren, K. Louise 589
McLaughlin, Sarah 88
McLean, Christine N. 244
McLean, Jodie W. 189
McLeod, Ian 192
McLintock, Michael 65
McInness, Ross 524
McLoughlin, Christine F. 592
McMillan, Lorna 168
McMurdo, James 498
McMurray, Michael C. 380
McNally, Craig R. 498
McNamara, Mary 471
McNamee, Brian A. 187
McNeilage, Hazel M. 242
McNeill, Jon 377
McPhail, Graeme 514
McPherson, Julie F. 41
McQuaid, Conor 476
McSharry, Heather Ann 186
McSharry, Heather Ann 316
McSweeney, Erin L. 252
Mctaggart, Douglas F. 592
McTier, Charles H. 171
McVicar, Tracey L. 613
Mead, Fiona 187
Meakins, Ian 180
Meakins, Ian 506
Meaney, James 180
Meddings, Richard 644
Medeiros, Carlos Henrique Senna 655
Medina, Sergio Mauricio Menendez 144
Medlicott, Stella 237
Medline, Michael 224
Medori, Rene 659
Medvedev, Alexander Ivanovich 266
Medvedev, Yuri M. 340
Medvedovsky, Maxim 331
Megalou, Christos Ioannis 483
Megarbane, Fabrice 362
Meghen, Michael 214
Mehan, Daniel Joseph 250
Mehrotra, Shishir 574
Mehta, Aman 607
Mehta, Harmeen 374
Mehta, Sanjiv 653

INDEX OF EXECUTIVES

Mehta, Tarak 7
Mei-Pochtler, Antonella 63
Mei-Pochtler, Antonella 495
Mei, Meng 560
Mei, Yan 247
Meiras, Inigo 179
Meister, Paul M. 50
Meister, Paul M. 51
Meixner, Larry 402
Mejdell, Dag 452
Mejia, Luis Alberto Moreno 254
Mejias, Antonio Huertas 386
Melamud, Marcelo 396
Meldrum, Guy 122
Meledandri, Chris 437
Melgar, Lourdes 564
Melikyan, Gennady 535
Meline, David W. 7
Mellander, Carl 237
Mello, Spyros 172
Mello, Wilson 331
Mellquist, Helene 70
Melo, Pedro Augusto de 82
Melo, Ricardo Goncalves 40
Melo, Ricardo Morais Pereira de 40
Menchelli, Irzio Pinasco 185
Mendelsohn, Nicola S. 211
Mendes, Paul M. 132
Mendez, Norma Isaura Castaneda 272
Mendiguren, Ignacio Echevarria 171
Mendizabal, Cristina Garmendia 179
Menegaux, Florent 177
Menell, Richard P. 555
Menges, Kathrin 17
Menne, Simone 208
Menne, Simone 284
Menne, Simone 337
Menshikov, Sergey N. 266
Mentis, Angela 421
Menuz, G. Glenn 609
Meo, Francesco De 261
Meo, Luca de 501
Meo, Luca De 615
Mera, Francisco Jose Riberas de 615
Merad, Abdellah 537
Mercier, Denis 247
Merck, Peter Emanuel 399
Merckle, Ludwig 279
Merckle, Tobias 279
Merhy, Andrea Mayumi Petroni 396
Merin, Mitchell M. 589
Merkt, Steven T. 611
Merle-Beral, Celine 660
Merlo, Silvia 526
Merrick, Brent 44
Merrin, Patrice 269
Mertens, Peter 247
Merwe, Hans van der 573
Merwe, Kathryn van der 71
Merwe, Susan C. van der 555
Merz, Martina 207
Merz, Martina 628
Merz, Martina 664
Meshari, Ahmad 496
Meshulam, Amir 302
Mesler, Amanda 424
Messemer, Annette 565
Messer, Bridget 592
Messier, Luc 566
Messina, Carlo 319

Mestrallet, Gerard 565
Meswani, Hital R. 499
Meswani, Nikhil R. 499
Metaxas, Alexandros 281
Meti, Tony 532
Metzger-Doran, Brianne L. 613
Meunier, Bernard 432
Meurice, Eric 650
Meurs, Bert van 357
Mey, Jozef De 21
Meyer-Kluge, Jennifer 597
Meyer, Armin 41
Meyer, Melody 118
Meyer, Tobias 208
Meyerdirk, Elizabeth Miin 546
Meyers, Francoise Bettencourt 362
Meyers, Jean-Victor 362
Meyers, Nicolas 362
Mezzanotte, Bill 187
Mgoduso, Thandeka Nozipho 573
Mi, Dabin 295
Miaja, Rafael Robles 43
Miau, Feng-Chiang 142
Mibe, Toshihiro 292
Michaud-Ahmed, Anik 46
Michaud-Ahmed, Anik 47
Michaud, Alain 678
Michaud, Bruno 299
Michel, Berangere 367
Michel, Gilles 656
Michel, Jean-Paul 247
Michel, Madeleine 152
Michel, Stephane 639
Michelini, Matthew R. 68
Michi, Ayumi 536
Midseim, Anne-Lene 452
Midteide, Thomas 213
Miels, Luke 274
Migliardi, Roberto 659
Mignon, Laurent 57
Mignone, Roberto A. 623
Migoya, Alfonso Gonzales 171
Migoya, Alfonso Gonzalez 254
Miguel, Jose Marcos Ramirez 273
Miguel, Josu Jon Imaz San 504
Miguel, Mario Newton Nazareth 322
Miguez, Enrique 138
Mii, Y.J. 603
Mikami, Takeshi 588
Mikami, Yasuaki 468
Mike, Kanetsugu 406
Mike, Kanetsugu 409
Mikhailova, Elena Vladimirovna 266
Mikhelson, Leonid V. 453
Miki, Takayuki 411
Mikita, Kunio 471
Mikitani, Hiroshi 497
Mikkilineni, Krishna 354
Mikoshiba, Toshiaki 292
Milikin, Maurice Anthony 48
Millar, Howard 524
Millegan, Michael H. 74
Miller, Alexey Borisovich 266
Miller, Anthony 189
Miller, Bruce 190
Miller, Christopher 395
Miller, Craig W. 46
Miller, David 320
Miller, Irene Ruth 638
Miller, Klaus 277

Miller, S. P. 416
Miller, Steven D. 102
Miller, Timothy Alexander 35
Milleri, Francesco 239
Milliken, Richard A. 524
Mills, Karla L. 613
Mills, Robin 180
Milner, Andrew K. 612
Mimura, Akio 632
Mimura, Koichi 394
Mimura, Mariko 593
Mimura, Takayoshi 410
Minaka, Masatsugu 191
Minakata, Takeshi 351
Minakawa, Tsuyoshi 30
Minami, Masahiro 505
Minami, Shinsuke 321
Minamide, Masanori 419
Minamide, Masao 90
Minas, Mauricio Machado de 80
Minc, Alain 179
Minegishi, Masumi 45
Minegishi, Masumi 499
Mingo, Felix de Vicente 83
Mink, Kim Ann 362
Mintz, Jack M. 305
Miranda, Gerardo Jofre 184
Mire, Michael 73
Miron, Paulo Sergio 322
Mirt, Ramon A. 108
Mirtillo, Nunzio 237
Mirza, Jawaid 172
Mirza, Jawaid A. 241
Mishima, Shigeki 472
Mishima, Shin 341
Mishor, Miri 302
Misra, Kabir 34
Mita, Mayo 471
Mitachi, Takashi 498
Mitachi, Takashi 584
Mitachi, Takashi 632
Mitani, Eiichiro 403
Mitarai, Fujio 135
Mitchell, Arthur M. 354
Mitchell, Arthur M. 588
Mitchell, E. Gay 135
Mitchell, Ger 474
Mitchell, James Gordon 620
Mitchelmore, Lorraine 90
Mitchelmore, Lorraine 592
Mitic, Ljiljana 181
Mito, Nobuaki 583
Mitomo, Toshimoto 572
Mitrova, Tatiana 537
Mitsuhashi, Masataka 439
Mitsunari, Miki 679
Mitsuoka, Ryuichi 420
Mitsuoka, Tsugio 303
Mitsuya, Yuko 202
Mitsuya, Yuko 231
Mitsuya, Yuko 263
Mitsuyoshi, Toshiro 586
Mittal, Aditya 54
Mittal, Lakshmi N. 54
Mitts, Heath A. 611
Miura, Atsunori 73
Miura, Hiroyoshi 30
Miura, Kunio 352
Miura, Satoshi 287
Miura, Shinichiro 679

Miwa, Masatoshi 666
Miya, Kenji 189
Miyabe, Yoshiyuki 473
Miyabe, Yoshiyuki 666
Miyagawa, Tadashi 470
Miyahara, Ikuko 630
Miyai, Machiko 544
Miyaji, Shinji 21
Miyajima, Takeshi 593
Miyajima, Tsukasa 189
Miyakawa, Junichi 567
Miyake, Toru 189
Miyama, Minako 189
Miyamori, Hiroshi 593
Miyamoto, Shigeru 437
Miyamoto, Yoichi 551
Miyanaga, Kenichi 409
Miyanaga, Masato 163
Miyanaga, Shunichi 403
Miyanaga, Shunichi 405
Miyanaga, Shunichi 406
Miyanoya, Atsushi 89
Miyaoka, Shinji 352
Miyashita, Norio 249
Miyashita, Yutaka 409
Miyata, Atsushi 409
Miyata, Hiromi 594
Miyata, Tomohide 231
Miyata, Yasuhiro 585
Miyauchi, Ken 567
Miyauchi, Koji 527
Miyazaki, Kenji 321
Miyazaki, Naoki 640
Miyazaki, Yuko 401
Miyoshi, Toshiya 351
Mizrahi, Rafael Moises Kalach 43
Mizuguchi, Makoto 352
Mizuhara, Kiyoshi 354
Mizui, Toshiyuki 185
Mizuma, Katsuyuki 583
Mizuma, Satoshi 401
Mizuno, Hideki 90
Mizuno, Yasuhide 292
Mizuta, Hitoshi 343
Mizuta, Masamichi 477
Mizutani, Hitoshi 161
Mjoli-Mncube, Nonhlanhla S. 8
Mkhize, Zamani Moses 534
Mkhwanazi, Themba M. 47
Mlnarsky, Sabine 173
Mminele, Daniel 573
Mobley, Daniel 211
Mocatta, William Elkin 167
Moch, Nicolas 563
Mochizuki, Harufumi 427
Mochizuki, Mikio 638
Modise, Punkie E. 8
Mody, Zia 167
Moen, Anne Sigrun 213
Moffat, Nikki 106
Mogefors, Svante 71
Mogford, John 110
Mogharbel, Khaled Al 537
Moglia, Giovanni Gionata Massimiliano 615
Mohabeer, Dominique 105
Mohan, Bi Joy 371
Mohl, Anna 432
Moholi, Nombulelo T. 46
Moir, A. 9

INDEX OF EXECUTIVES

Mok, Chung Fu 366
Mok, Tony 66
Mokate, Renosi Denise 573
Mokhele, K. D. K. 416
Mokoena, C. K. 534
Mokwa, Christopher 247
Molefe, T. B. L. 416
Molinari, Luna 651
Moller, Jorgen 216
Mollerstad, Hilde 236
Molnar, Gary F. 146
Molnar, Jozsef 414
Moloko, Sello 8
Moloney, John 201
Moloney, John 564
Molope, C. W. N. 416
Molson, Andrew T. 415
Molson, Eric H. 415
Molson, Geoffrey E. 415
Moltke, James von 206
Mommeja, Renaud 285
Momoi, Mariko Y 162
Momper, Gilles 32
Mondardini, Monica 185
Mondolo, Alicia 620
Monesmith, Heath B. 220
Money, Laura A. 590
Mong, David Tak-yeung 88
Mongeau, Claude 146
Mongeau, Claude 638
Mongkoltrirat, Pornsak 492
Montecinos, Jose Miranda 228
Montemayor, David Juan Villarreal 273
Montes, Alfredo Villegas 80
Montes, Antonio Pardo de Santayana 82
Montesano, Hwa Jin Song 371
Montesano, Jin Song 681
Montesinos, Constantino Spas 171
Monti, Roberto 620
Montinola, Aurelio R. 93
Montoya, Esther America Paz 271
Montull, Daniel Javier Servitje 171
Montull, Daniel Javier Servitje 272
Moon, Youngme E. 653
Mooney, Andrew 127
Mooney, Beth E. 11
Moor, Andrew 236
Moorhouse, Barbara 78
Moosmayer, Klaus 453
Mora, Hanne de 432
Mora, Hanne de 528
Mora, Hanne de 664
Moraes, Pedro Luiz Bodin de 323
Moraleda, Amparo 1
Morales, Alfonso Gomez 83
Morales, Gustavo Arriagada 81
Morales, Manuel L. Barragan 52
Morales, Ramiro Gerardo Villarreal 144
Morano, Vittorio Pignatti 393
Moranville, Guy de Selliers de 21
Moratti, Angelo 533
Moratti, Angelomario 533
Moratti, Gabriele 533
Moratti, Giovanni Emanuele 533
Moratti, Massimo 533
Mordashov, Alexey 646
Moreau-Leroy, Helene 56
Moreira, Rogerio Bautista da Nova 119
Moreno, Ana Cristina Peralta 80

Moreno, Carlos Mario Giraldo 140
Moreno, Francisco 656
Moreno, Juan Antonio Gonzalez 273
Moreno, Julian Acuna 81
Moreto, Edson Marcelo 80
Moretti, Marella 615
Morfitt, Martha A.M. 377
Morgan-Silvester, Sarah A. 135
Morgan, Bruce W. D. 467
Morgan, Tav 484
Morgon, Virginie 362
Mori, Atsuhito 146
Mori, Hiroshi 409
Mori, Kazuhiko 303
Mori, Kimitaka 219
Mori, Kiyoshi 410
Mori, Masakatsu 351
Mori, Masashi 296
Mori, Nozomu 343
Mori, Takahiro 441
Mori, Yoshihiro 193
Moriani, Diva 63
Moriarty, Clodagh 325
Moribe, Shigeru 401
Moridaira, Takayuki 461
Moriguchi, Yuko 460
Morikawa, Kohei 505
Morikawa, Noriko 405
Morikawa, Noriko 505
Morimoto, Hideka 315
Morin, Francois 55
Morin, Marie-Lucie 591
Morinaka, Kanaya 601
Morissette, Benoit 315
Morita, Hideo 303
Morita, Mamoru 287
Morita, Takayuki 427
Moriwaki, Yoichi 632
Moriya, Akiyoshi 471
Moriya, Hideki 471
Moriya, Seiji 634
Moriyama, Masahiko 601
Moriyama, Masayuki 354
Moro, Junko 412
Moro, Masahiro 391
Morodo, Valentin Diez 466
Morohashi, Masahiro 30
Morohoshi, Toshio 439
Moroka, Kgomotso Ditsebe 575
Moroney, Simon E. 453
Morooka, Reiji 584
Morozov, Alexander 535
Morris, Adrian 622
Morris, Christine 638
Morris, David 363
Morris, David 685
Morris, David C. 598
Morris, Jennifer 255
Morrish, Jon 279
Morselli, Lucia 580
Morzaria, Tushar 118
Morzaria, Tushar 364
Morzaria, Tushar 364
Mosca, Fabrizio 319
Mosch, Peter 663
Moses, Marc 96
Moss, Arvid 452
Moss, Jeff 176
Mossberg, Anna 597
Mossberg, Anna 601

Mosser, Patricia 448
Mostert, Jacob Dawid 555
Motoi, Chie 527
Motomura, Masahide 546
Motta, Milena Teresa 319
Motta, Roberto Moses Thompson 40
Mottershead, Chris 339
Mottram, Heidi 148
Moue, Hidemi 287
Moulin, Emmanuel 626
Moulonguet, Thierry 656
Moura, Carlos Alberto Bezerra de 119
Moura, Gabriel Amado de 81
Mouren-Renouard, Emilie 362
Mowat, David 363
Mowat, David 619
Moynot, Sebastien 56
Mozos, Jose Vicente de los 501
Mu, Nini 235
Mu, Xuan 295
Mucic, Luka 279
Mucic, Luka 531
Mucke, Gabriele 418
Muehlemann, Werner 315
Mueller, Klaus-Peter 261
Mueller, Michael 363
Mueller, Ralf 207
Muenz, David J. 344
Mufamadi, Sydney 304
Muhlen, Alexander von zur 206
Mujica, Fernando Borja 84
Mukai, Chiaki 263
Mukai, Chiaki 344
Mukai, Takeshi 391
Muldoon, Fiona 88
Mulhern, Carmel 174
Mulhern, George 237
Mullen, John Patrick 618
Muller, Beat 282
Muller, Frans 357
Muller, Klaus-Peter 173
Muller, Michael 523
Muller, Nicolaas Johannes 304
Muller, Udo 17
Mulligan, Margaret J. 135
Mulligan, Richard C. 102
Mullller, Jurgen 531
Mulye, Vishakha V. 301
Mumenthaler, Christian 600
Munaiz, Manuel Moreu 300
Munakata, Naoko 419
Munanta, Davide 526
Mundlay, Shekhar 593
Mundra, Hari L. 301
Munekata, Hisako 90
Munnings, Roger Llewelyn 413
Munoz, Carmen 504
Munoz, David Ibarra 43
Munoz, Elena Leon 300
Munoz, Feliciano Gonzalez 290
Munoz, Ricardo Gutierrez 466
Munyantwali, Swithin J. 8
Mupita, R. T. 416
Muracciole, Nathalie 57
Muracciole, Odile 141
Murai, Jun 498
Murakami, Ippei 50
Murakami, Kazuya 436
Murakami, Kazuya 544
Murakami, Nobuhiko 643

Murakami, Takao 602
Murakawa, Kentaro 630
Muraki, Atsuko 583
Murakoshi, Susumu 543
Murao, Kazutoshi 470
Murao, Yukinobu 505
Murasawa, Atsushi 679
Murase, Masayoshi 441
Murase, Yukio 341
Murata, Nanako 303
Murata, Toshihiko 459
Murata, Tsuneo 419
Murata, Yoshiyuki 194
Muratoglu, Gamze Sebnem 29
Muratore, Emiliano 83
Murayama, Seiichi 231
Muriel, Rodolfo Garcia 144
Murphy, Andrew 367
Murphy, Conor 201
Murphy, Donal 201
Murphy, Gerry 189
Murphy, Glenn K. 377
Murphy, James 122
Murphy, John 171
Murphy, Ken 622
Murphy, Kevin 249
Murphy, Michael R. 55
Murphy, Senan 186
Murphy, Stephen 135
Murphy, Timothy J. 611
Murray, Bradley 71
Murray, Donald A. 134
Murray, Eileen K. 295
Murray, Katie 425
Murray, Katie 427
Murray, Martin James 599
Murray, Patrick R. 226
Murray, Sheila A. 106
Murray, Sheila A. 612
Murray, Vanda 127
Murria, Vinodka 127
Musca, Xavier 136
Musca, Xavier 185
Muschal, Thorsetn 247
Muslah, Mansour Al 496
Mussafer, David M. 377
Muta, Hidemitsu 93
Muto, Koichi 286
Muttart, Patrick C. 609
Myerson, Toby S. 409
Mytilinaios, Stefanos N. 38

N

N., Sreedhar 175
Nabel, Elizabeth G. 395
Naccache, Olivier 542
Nachbar, Moacir 80
Nada, Hari 444
Nadeau, Bertin F. 589
Nadeau, Marie-Jose 233
Nadeau, Marie-Jose 297
Naef, Angela 499
Naffakh, Sami 499
Nagahori, Kazumasa 420
Nagai, Koji 448
Nagai, Mikito 630
Nagai, Motoo 444

INDEX OF EXECUTIVES

Nagai, Seiji 459
Nagai, Seiko 461
Nagamatsu, Fumihiko 546
Nagamori, Shigenobu 436
Nagano, Katsuya 287
Nagano, Minoru 452
Nagano, Satoshi 629
Nagano, Tsuyoshi 146
Nagano, Tsuyoshi 262
Nagano, Tsuyoshi 632
Naganuma, Bunroku 404
Nagao, Masahiko 595
Nagao, Yutaka 681
Nagaoka, Hiroshi 406
Nagaoka, Susumu 73
Nagara, Hajime 352
Nagarajan, Hina 118
Nagasaki, Momoko 634
Nagasawa, Hitoshi 443
Nagasawa, Jun 403
Nagase, Shin 404
Nagase, Toshiya 194
Nagashima, Hidemi 277
Nagashima, Iwao 409
Nagashima, Yukiko 329
Nagata, Mitsuhiro 601
Nagata, Ryoko 292
Nagata, Takashi 634
Nagel, Alberto 393
Nagle, Gary 269
Naidoo, Dhanasagree 8
Naidoo, Dhanasagree 46
Naidoo, P. D. 250
Naidu, Tulsi 671
Naiki, Hachiro 593
Nair, Leena 125
Nair, Radhakrishnan 301
Naito, Fumio 343
Naito, Tetsuya 681
Naka, Hiroyuki 323
Nakabayashi, Mieko 636
Nakada, Hiroyuki 629
Nakada, Koichi 288
Nakagawa, Yoichi 277
Nakagawa, Yutaka 547
Nakaguro, Kunio 444
Nakahama, Fumitaka 409
Nakahara, Toshiya 231
Nakahata, Hidenobu 287
Nakahira, Yuko 402
Nakai, Kamezou 277
Nakai, Kazumasa 410
Nakai, Tomoko 665
Nakai, Yoichiro 632
Nakai, Yoshihiro 545
Nakai, Yoshikazu 403
Nakajima, Atsushi 404
Nakajima, Hajime 410
Nakajima, Masahiro 286
Nakajima, Masaki 584
Nakajima, Norio 419
Nakajima, Shigeru 585
Nakajima, Shunichi 546
Nakajima, Yasuhiro 121
Nakajima, Yoshimi 545
Nakamori, Makiko 323
Nakamura, Akihiko 146
Nakamura, Akio 632
Nakamura, Atsushi 296
Nakamura, Juichi 665

Nakamura, Kazunori 287
Nakamura, Kazuya 288
Nakamura, Keijiro 666
Nakamura, Kuniharu 427
Nakamura, Kuniharu 552
Nakamura, Kuniharu 584
Nakamura, Makoto 275
Nakamura, Mamiko 527
Nakamura, Masayoshi 439
Nakamura, Shinichi 442
Nakamura, Shinzaburo 92
Nakamura, Tatsuo 406
Nakamura, Tomomi 583
Nakamura, Yoshihiko 406
Nakanishi, Katsunori 552
Nakanishi, Katsuya 403
Nakanishi, Kiyoshi 223
Nakanishi, Yoshiyuki 303
Nakano, Kei 329
Nakano, Toshiaki 588
Nakano, Yoshiaki 179
Nakashima, Toru 587
Nakaso, Hiroshi 443
Nakata, Hiroyasu 404
Nakata, Katsunori 507
Nakata, Naofumi 30
Nakata, Takuya 680
Nakatani, Hiroshi 344
Nakayama, Joji 29
Nakayama, Kozue 321
Nakayama, Kozue 420
Nakayama, Kozue 610
Nakayama, Tsunehiro 411
Nakazato, Yoshiaki 586
Nakazawa, Hiroshi 288
Nakazawa, Keiji 327
NaLamlieng, Chumpol 554
Nam, Ki-Myung 368
Nam, Young-Woo 370
Nambo, Masaru 263
Namekata, Yoichi 593
Namwong, Pornpen 554
Namwong, Varit 491
Nanaumi, Shigeki 629
Nanbu, Masami 296
Nanda, Nikhil 359
Nanninga, Stephan 127
Nanthawithaya, Arthid 555
Naouri, Jean-Charles 140
Napoli, Silvio 220
Napoli, Silvio 537
Nara, Michihiro 461
Nara, Tomoaki 327
Narasaki, Koichi 570
Narasimhan, Laxman 499
Narasimhan, Vasant 452
Narayanan, Vanitha 537
Narendran, T. V. 607
Narita, Yukari 665
Narro, Alejandro Jose Arizpe 52
Narukawa, Tetsuo 404
Narukawa, Yoshihiro 287
Narvinger, Per 237
Nascimento, Renato Barbosa do 322
Nash, Peter Stanley 669
Nasi, Alessandro 168
Nasi, Alessandro 243
Nasikkol, Tekin 628
Nason, Jennifer 509
Nason, Jennifer 511

Nasser, Jacques A. 354
Natale, Joseph M. 514
Natale, Joseph M. 638
Natalenko, Alexander E. 453
Natrusov, Artem 243
Nauen, Andreas 558
Naumann, Susan 392
Naus, Harold 314
Navarro, Isabel María Aguilera 144
Nawa, Takashi 570
Nawaz, Imran 622
Nayager, Dayalan 211
Nayak, Chitra 312
Nayar, Arun 41
Nazzi, Gianfranco 623
Neate, James 91
Nebbia, Luciano 319
Nedeljkovic, Milan 105
Needham, Laura 374
Neeley, Tsedal 498
Negoro, Masakazu 344
Negus, Warwick Martin 92
Neike, Cedrik 557
Neiles, Byron C. 226
Neilson, Derek 168
Nejade, Henri 119
Nekoshima, Akio 344
Nel, E. L. 553
Nelles, Philip 183
Nellis, Anthony J. 71
Nelson, Elizabeth 446
Nelson, Judith 192
Nemat, Claudia 27
Nemat, Claudia 209
Nemoto, Naoko 288
Nenadyshina, Viktoriya 266
Nenashev, Sergey 484
Neo, Jessica Tan Soon 410
Neoh, Anthony Francis 165
Nesle, Alban de Mailly 73
Nesmes, Anne-Francoise 180
Neto, Jean Jereissati 40
Neto, Joao Cox 119
Neto, Joao Cox 480
Neto, Jorge Novis 81
Neto, Jose Ramos Rocha 80
Neto, Jose Virgilio Vita 322
Neto, Julio Soares de Moura 119
Neto, Otavio Lopes Castello Branco 649
Netto, Alberto Monteiro de Queiroz 82
Netto, Pedro Gutemberg Quariguasi 179
Netto, Rubens Fogli 322
Neubert, Martin 469
Neuburger, Nicole 377
Neumann, Kristin 119
Neumeister, Ulrich 392
Neuss, Sabine 183
Neves, Eduardo 81
Neves, Joao Carvalho das 223
Nevistic, Vesna 176
Newham, Paul 92
Ng, Albert Kong Ping 34
Ng, Daryl Win Kong 88
Ng, Jimmy Keng Joo 200
Ng, Kenneth Sing Yip 276
Ng, Leung Sing 436
Ng, Veronica Ka Po 612
Ng, William Lok Ming 687

Ngai, Wai Fung 560
Ngamsopee, Kannika 555
Ngonyama, Babalwa 304
Nibuya, Susumu 303
Nickl, Wolfgang 103
Nickolds, Paula 325
Nicks, Damien 21
Nicol, Sylvie 284
Nicollier, Claude 597
Niekamp, Cynthia A. 384
Niekerk, Robert van 555
Nielsen, Anders 657
Nielsen, Guillermo Emilio 686
Nielsen, Jan Thorsgaard 198
Nielsen, Tommy Rahbek 657
Niemann, Douglas 68
Nienaber, Margaret 575
Nieto, Carlos Andres Santos 221
Nieuwdorp, Roel 21
Nightingale, Anthony J. L. 192
Nightingale, Anthony J. L. 330
Nigris, Ernesto Lopez de 52
Nihot, Dailah 445
Niimi, Tsutomu 341
Niino, Masahiro 249
Niino, Takashi 427
Niinuma, Hiroshi 583
Niisato, Shinji 89
Niizeki, Mikiyo 470
Nika, Nkosemntu Gladman 555
Nikiforov, Nikolay 484
Nikkaku, Akihiro 636
Nikulina, Maria 484
Nilekani, Nandan M. 312
Niljianskul, Chokechai 85
Nilprapunt, Pakorn 492
Nilsson, Jannicke 236
Nilsson, Richard 581
Nilsson, Thomas 70
Nimmanahaeminda, Tarrin 554
Nimocks, Suzanne P. 124
Ninomiya, Hitomi 471
Nipper, Mads 469
Nisen, Perry 623
Nish, David 661
Nish, David Thomas 295
Nishi, Hirokazu 73
Nishi, Motohiro 550
Nishibori, Satoru 249
Nishida, Mitsuo 585
Nishigai, Noboru 404
Nishiguchi, Naohiro 477
Nishiguchi, Toru 344
Nishihata, Kazuhiro 457
Nishii, Shigeru 288
Nishii, Takaaki 190
Nishii, Takaaki 344
Nishijima, Takashi 419
Nishikawa, Katsuyuki 550
Nishikawa, Kazunobu 420
Nishikawa, Kuniko 275
Nishikawa, Tomoo 315
Nishimura, Akira 585
Nishimura, Atsuko 315
Nishimura, Atsuko 602
Nishimura, Keisuke 351
Nishimura, Motohiko 344
Nishimura, Shingo 231
Nishimura, Taisuke 190
Nishino, Hiroshi 303

HOOVER'S HANDBOOK OF WORLD BUSINESS 2024   719

INDEX OF EXECUTIVES

Nishioka, Keiko 296
Nishioka, Kiyoshi 505
Nishioka, Seiichiro 231
Nishita, Naoki 452
Nishitani, Jumpei 471
Nishiura, Kanji 404
Nishiura, Kanji 586
Nishiura, Yuji 371
Nishiyama, Keita 473
Nishiyama, Mitsuaki 287
Nishizawa, Hitoshi 275
Nishizawa, Nobuhiro 343
Nitcher, Eric 118
Niu, Diana 664
Niu, Dongxiao 199
Niubo, Antonio Brufau 504
Niwa, Shunsuke 146
Nixon, Gordon M. 106
Nixon, Gordon M. 668
Nkeli, Mpho Elizabeth Kolekile 304
Nkeli, Mpho Elizabeth Kolekile 534
Nkosi, Sipho Abednego 534
Nkosi, Themba 555
Nkuhlu, Mfundo 428
Noda, Seiko 73
Noda, Yumiko 303
Nogami, Masayuki 460
Nogawa, Makiko 406
Noge, Emi 593
Noguchi, Mikio 505
Nogueira, Andre 331
Nohara, Sawako 190
Nohara, Sawako 505
Nohira, Akinobu 459
Noji, Kunio 473
Nolan, Helen 214
Nolens, Geraldine 650
Noma, Masahiro 471
Noma, Yoshinobu 636
Nomizu, Yasuyuki 507
Nomoto, Hirofumi 409
Nomura, Takao 342
Nomura, Takaya 223
None, Shigeru 401
Nonka, Helena 47
Nonnenmacher, Rolf 183
Nonnenmacher, Rolf 185
Nooyi, Indra K. 358
Nordahl, Tomas 528
Nordberg, Bert 657
Nordh, Hilde Vestheim 452
Nordmann, Dirk 183
Nordstrom, Lars G. 450
Noreus, Martin 596
Norgaard, Birgit 678
Norgaard, Birgit Woidemann 216
Noriega, Alfonso de Angoitia 273
Noriega, Jose Borda 52
Norman, Archie 388
Normoyle, Helen 24
Noronha, Marcelo de Araujo 80
Norris, Mike J. 181
Norrman, Steve 4
Norstrom, Alex 574
Nosko, Roland 17
Nosohara, Etsuko 163
Nota, Pieter 105
Notarnicola, Giuseppe 580
Notebaert, Richard C. 49
Noteboom, Ben J. 19

Nouchi, Yuzo 403
Nout, Wellink 309
Novak, Alexander 517
Novegil, Daniel Agustin 621
Novikov, Vitaliy 172
Novozhenov, Denis 243
Nowak, Alojzy 86
Nowak, Daniela 663
Nowlan, John 111
Nowotne, Doreen 119
Noyer, Christian 113
Noyer, Christian 487
Noyori, Ryoji 636
Nozaki, Akira 586
Nozaki, Haruko 544
Nozaki, Haruko 666
Nozaki, Motoyasu 410
Nozawa, Toru 439
Numagami, Tsuyoshi 632
Nunes, Adolfo Mesquita 265
Nunes, Regina Helena Jorge 300
Nunez, Maria Eugenia de la Fuente 83
Nunn, Charlie 374
Nunoi, Tomoko 249
Nunokawa, Yoshikazu 634
Nursalim, Cherie 495
Nutzenberger, Stefanie 143
Nuzzolo, Agostino 615
Nyasulu, Hixonia 47
Nyberg, Carl 429
Nyegaard, Peter 450
Nyembezi-Heita, Nonkululeko Merina Cheryl 47
Nyembezi-Heita, Nonkululeko Merina Cheryl 575
Nyisztor, Diane 532
Nyman, Per Olof 597
Nyman, Sven 563
Nyren, Anders 528

O

O'Brien, Ann 24
O'Brien, Mike 524
O'Byrne, Barry 294
O'Byrne, Kevin 148
O'Byrne, Kevin 325
O'Callaghan, Jeremiah Alphonsus 331
O'Connor, James E. 131
O'Connor, Michael John 589
O'Connor, Stephen 293
O'Donnell, Kevin J. 501
O'Donnell, Lord 124
O'Dwyer, Fergal 24
O'Grady, Brendan P. 623
O'Grady, Myles 88
O'Higgins, John 339
O'Keeffe, John 211
O'Leary, Denise M. 395
O'Leary, Michael 524
O'Malley, Paul 174
O'Neill, Heidi 574
O'Neill, Julie 474
O'Neill, Julie 524
O'Neill, Michael 366
O'Neill, Ronan 474
O'Reilly, David 122
O'Shea, Ana Patricia Botin-Sanz de Sautuola y 84

O'Shea, Chris 148
O'Shea, Javier Botin-Sanz de Sautuola y 84
O'Sullivan, Nessa 415
O'Sullivan, Shane 474
O'Dea, Regan P. 256
O'Kane, Nicholas 382
O'Mahony, David 238
O'Neill, Meg 674
O'Reilly, Christine 71
O'Reilly, Christine 110
O'Reilly, Lindsay 96
O'Rourke, Catheryn 499
O'Sullivan, Paul D. 71
Obara, Shinobu 89
Obata, Shinobu 427
Obata, Yasuhiko 444
Obayashi, Takeo 459
Obayashi, Yasuhito 439
Obermann, Rene 27
Ocampo, Marie Josephine M. 93
Ochi, Toshiki 409
Ochiai, Hiroyuki 436
Ochrym, Natalie A. 589
Oddestad, Lars 450
Odell, Stephen T. 243
Odendaal, Lisa 471
Oduor-Otieno, Martin 575
Oeda, Hiroshi 544
Oelrich, Stefan 103
Oeter, Dietmar 399
Oetterli, Thomas 537
Offer, Scott 252
Oga, Kimiko 223
Ogasawara, Takeshi 594
Ogata, Fumito 666
Ogata, Masaki 219
Ogawa, Hiromichi 461
Ogawa, Hiroyuki 354
Ogawa, Marie 288
Ogawa, Michiko 391
Ogawa, Shinsuke 634
Ogawa, Shoichi 249
Ogawa, Shoji 448
Ogawa, Tatsuo 473
Ogawa, Yasunori 543
Ogawa, Yoichiro 292
Ogden, Peter 181
Ogi, Akira 286
Ogilvie, Thomas 208
Ogiso, Satoshi 286
Oguchi, Shimpei 602
Ogura, Maki 666
Ogura, Ritsuo 409
Ogushi, Junko 406
Oguz, Bulent 29
Oh, Ho-Soo 368
Oh, Seung-Mo 368
Ohannessian, Dikran 589
Ohara, Gisuke 679
Ohara, Hiroyuki 163
Ohara, Masayoshi 50
Ohashi, Hideyuki 190
Ohashi, Shigeki 33
Ohashi, Tetsuji 57
Ohashi, Tetsuji 354
Ohashi, Tetsuji 681
Ohgo, Naoki 602
Ohkubo, Tetsuo 588
Ohlmeyer, Harm 17

Ohlsson-Leijon, Anna 3
Ohlsson-Leijon, Anna 70
Ohlsson, Thore 496
Ohno, Sadahiro 630
Ohr, Eugene M. 298
Ohta, Jun 587
Ohtsu, Keiji 292
Ohtsuka, Michiko 543
Ohtsuki, Masahiko 190
Ohya, Mitsuo 636
Oie, Yuji 361
Oikawa, Hisahiko 505
Oikawa, Kenichiro 389
Oilfield, David 374
Oishi, Kaori 471
Oizumi, Taku 288
Ojeisekhoba, Moses 600
Oka, Masashi 427
Oka, Tomoaki 90
Oka, Toshiko 231
Oka, Toshiko 287
Oka, Toshiko 572
Okada, Akihiko 632
Okada, Akihioko 457
Okada, Joji 427
Okada, Kenji 632
Okada, Kyoko 427
Okada, Motoya 20
Okada, Motoya 665
Okada, Yoshifumi 73
Okafuji, Masahiro 323
Okamatsu, Nobuhiko 460
Okamoto, Iwao 340
Okamoto, Masahiko 636
Okamoto, Shigeaki 329
Okamoto, Tsukasa 193
Okamoto, Tsuyoshi 57
Okamoto, Tsuyoshi 327
Okamoto, Tsuyoshi 404
Okawa, Junko 345
Okawa, Junko 634
Okazaki, Takeshi 245
Oketani, Taku 380
Oki, Kazuaki 567
Okihara, Takamune 343
Okina, Yuri 121
Okina, Yuri 389
Okitsu, Masahiro 547
Okkerse, Liesbet 345
Okomo-Okello, Francis 8
Okoro, Sandie 577
Okray, Thomas B. 220
Oku, Masayuki 88
Okuda, Hideo 666
Okuda, Kentaro 448
Okuda, Osamu 162
Okuhara, Kazushige 287
Okumiya, Kyoko 345
Okumura, Mikio 570
Okuno, Minako 89
Okuzawa, Hiroyuki 190
Oladokun, Olayide 137
Olaguibel, Rafael Alberto Suarez 171
Olano, Antonio Miguel-Romero de 386
Olayan, Hutham S. 124
Olcott, George 351
Oldorff, Frithjof R. 71
Oleas, Jurg 290
Olesen, Soren-Peter Fuchs 137

INDEX OF EXECUTIVES

Oliveira, Aurelio Ricardo Bustilho de 228
Oliveira, Carlos Alberto Pereira de 479
Oliveira, Raul Catarino Galamba de 80
Oliver, George R. 337
Olivier, Gaelle 197
Olivier, Gregoire 579
Oliveira, Ramon de 73
Olivieri, Fernando Angel Gonzalez 144
Ollagnier, Jean-Marc 11
Ollivier-Lamarque, Florence 597
Ollmann, Michael 277
Olmez, Oguzhan 542
Olsen, Jens Peter Due 213
Olson, Timothy J. 55
Olsovsky, Jo-ann dePass 131
Olsson, Magnus 563
Olstad, Ellen Merete 452
Olving, Lena 61
Olving, Lena 458
Olving, Lena 657
Omloo, Caroline J.M. 549
Omoteyama, Kyoko 30
Omura, Yukiko 293
Onaran, Cemal 646
Ong, Christina 559
Ong, Estrellita V. 107
Ongaro, Claudio Giovanni Ezio 615
Ongvises, Suksant 491
Onishi, Akira 641
Onishi, Hiroyuki 371
Onishi, Masanobu 551
Onishi, Masaru 412
Onishi, Shoichiro 634
Onishi, Tadashi 288
Onishi, Yasuo 73
Ono, Akira 634
Ono, Hiromichi 634
Ono, Makiko 593
Ono, Masayasu 150
Ono, Mitsuru 391
Ono, Naoki 406
Ono, Naotake 245
Ono, Taneki 327
Onoyama, Tadahiko 249
Onuki, Yuji 461
Oodaira, Takashi 321
Oomi, Hideto 50
Oommen, Dilip 55
Oosterman, Wade 106
Opedal, Anders 236
Opstad, Alexander 213
Or, Raymond Ching-Fai 160
Orcel, Andrea 651
Ordan, Stephanie 61
Ordonez, Fabio Castellanos 271
Orellana, Pedro 83
Orenes, Francisco Jose Marco 386
Oreshkin, Maksim 535
Orii, Masako 459
Orisaku, Mineko 471
Orlav, Victor P. 453
Orleyn, Thandi 573
Orlopp, Bettina 173
Ormaza, Xabier Sagredo 300
Ormerod, John 182
Oro, Sachiko 460
Oropeza, Octavio Romero 481
Orr, Gordon Robert Halyburton 599
Orr, Greg 624

Orr, Robert Jeffrey 270
Orr, Robert Jeffrey 487
Orrego, Eduardo Ebensperger 80
Orsinger, Michel 605
Ortberg, Robert K. 50
Ortberg, Robert K. 51
Ortiz, Juan Carlos Andrade 241
Osaki, Atsushi 583
Osaki, Yoshimi 460
Osawa, Hisashi 411
Osawa, Masakazu 409
Osborn, Wayne G. 665
Osborne, Ronald W. 589
Oshima, Masahiko 587
Oshima, Taku 146
Oshimi, Yoshikazu 342
Oshino, Masanori 679
Oshita, Hajime 335
Osono, Emi 632
Osorio, Jose Luiz 120
Osorio, Luiz Eduardo Froes do Amaral 655
Ossadnik, Victoria 218
Osswald, Oliver 290
Ostertag, Benoit 502
Ostroff, Dawn 574
Osugi, Kazuhito 275
Oswald, Gerhard 531
Ota, Katsuyuki 231
Ota, Narunobu 505
Ota, Yoshitsugu 550
Otagiri, Junko 89
Otake, Masato 546
Otani, Noriko 163
Otani, Tomoki 681
Otani, Yasuhisa 629
Otazua, John Anthony Santa Maria 171
Otomo, Hirotsugu 194
Otomo, Ken 420
Otsuka, Ichiro 471
Otsuka, Norio 569
Otsuka, Norio 602
Otsuka, Toru 448
Ott, Robert J. 611
Ottel, Robert 663
Ottersgard, Lars 563
Oudea, Frederic 136
Oudea, Frederic 565
Oudeman, Marjan 456
Ouellete, Robert 678
Ouiyamapun, Orachon 491
Ouvrier-Buffet, Gerard 186
Ouyang, Hui 483
Ovcharov, Evgeny 456
Ovelmen, Karyn F. 55
Overall, Laura 168
Overbeck, Karin 3
Overmars, Pieter Sipko 18
Owen, Steve 458
Owens, J. Michael 134
Owens, William Arthur 671
Oxley, Stephen 339
Oyabu, Chiho 89
Oyagi, Shigeo 634
Oyama, Akira 507
Oyama, Kazuya 588
Oyama, Kiichiro 296
Oyolu, Chukwuemeka A. 380

Ozaki, Yoshinori 550
Ozawa, Takao 380
Ozawa, Yoshiro 419
Ozben, Yunus Emre 29
Ozdemir, Yusuf 208
Ozen, Sait Ergun 647
Ozer-Armon, Tzipi 302
Ozsoy, Mevhibe Canan 646
Ozturk, Zeynep 29

P

P.Y., Hacina 565
Paalvast, Edwin 357
Paasch, Dagmar 523
Paasschen, Frits Dirk van 521
Paatero-Kaarnakari, Maria 258
Paavola, Teppo 15
Pabon, Luis Fernando Pabon 271
Pace, Robert 131
Paco, Oscar Romero De 261
Padbury, Mary 174
Padoan, Pietro Carlo 651
Pagano, Helena J. 590
Page, Gregory R. 220
Page, Stephen 644
Paglia, Louis J. 56
Pagliaro, Renato 393
Pagnutti, Louis P. 106
Pahk, Hee-Jae 486
Pai, Kun-Rong 682
Pai, Satish 7
Pai, Satish 118
Paik, Woo-Hyun 370
Pain, Mark A. 685
Paine, Tim 509
Paiva, Maria Luiza de Oliveira Pinto e 655
Paja, David 51
Palacios, Maria de Lourdes Melgar 84
Palazuelos, Alberto Sanchez 52
Palfreyman, J. A. 598
Palme, Marion 530
Palmer, John R.V. 386
Palmer, Richard Keith 579
Palombo, Grace M. 270
Palt, Alexandra 362
Palus, Jean-Francois 347
Palus, Jean-Francois 496
Palvetzian, Sevaun T. 514
Palzer, Stefan 432
Pamer-Wieser, Charlotte 453
Pan, Lincoln 189
Pan, Nicholas D. Le 130
Pan, Richard 487
Pan, Zhaoguo 683
Panayotopoulos, Dimitri 122
Panda, Debasish 577
Pandi, Diego Martin 686
Pando, Antonio Cosio 43
Pang, Y. K. 192
Pang, Y. K. 330
Pangalos, Menelas 66
Paniagua, Angel Jesus Acebes 300
Panich, Vicharn 555
Panizza, Pablo 48
Panossian, Hratch 130
Pant, Vandita 110

Pantalakis, Theodoros 281
Pantelias, Spyridon 281
Pantelidis, James 474
Pantelidis, Jim 299
Panyarachun, Anand 555
Panyarachun, Disathat 492
Panyarachun, Disathat 493
Pao, Yi Hsin 250
Paoli, Alberto de 227
Paoli, Mary De 589
Paolo, Primiano Di 37
Papa, Mark G. 537
Papadimitriou, Georgios 265
Papadopoulo, Nicolas 55
Papadopoulos, Evangelos 617
Papagaryfallou, Lazaros A. 38
Papagiannopoulos, Constantinos 281
Papakonstantinou, Georgios 281
Papalexopoulou, Alexandra 172
Papanikolaou, Yianna 669
Papathanasiou, Ioannis 281
Papazoglou, Loukas 281
Papier, Olaf 108
Papin, Jeremie 444
Papirnik, Vladimira 345
Paquette, Sylvie 315
Paranjpe, Nitin 280
Paranjpe, Nitin 653
Paravicini, Lukas 304
Pardo, Felipe Bayon 221
Pardo, Jaime Chico 272
Pardo, Marcela Leonor Jimenez 81
Pare, Robert 423
Parekh, Salil 312
Parekh, Sandeep 278
Parent, Ghislain 422
Parent, Marc 619
Parente, Pedro Pullen 120
Parezanovic, Sanda 171
Parigi, Bruno Maria 319
Parikh, Bobby 312
Paris, Roberto de Jesus 80
Park, Agnes 656
Park, Heon-Gyu 358
Park, Hyo-Sung 358
Park, Il-Jin 368
Park, Jong-Bae 358
Park, Oh-Soo 526
Park, Seong-Won 370
Park, Taemin 57
Parker, Christine 669
Parker, Kellie 511
Parkes, David 75
Parkhill, Karen L. 395
Parks, Robert Ralph 555
Parmentier, Thierry 56
Parr, Jeremy 192
Parra, Carolina 135
Parris, Colin J. 50
Parris, Colin J. 51
Parsons, Guy P. C. 685
Parsons, Raymond Whitmore Knighton 573
Participations, Societe Carpinienne de 140
Partovi, Shez 357
Parvi, Seppo 581
Paschke, Werner P. 182
Pasquesi, John M. 55
Pasquier, Bernard 81

INDEX OF EXECUTIVES

Pasricha, Atul 444
Passos, Murilo Cesar Lemos dos Santos 655
Pastore, Daniel Sposito 322
Paszczak, Robert 617
Patalano, Nicholas 57
Patel, Malay 278
Patel, Nadir 134
Patel, Zarin 367
Pateman, Steve 88
Paterson, Iain 414
Paterson, Nigel 189
Patrizio, Mapelli 457
Pats, Jean-Claude 177
Patterson, Lynn K. 91
Pattison, Lindsay 677
Paul, Stefan 360
Paula, Jefferson de 54
Paull, Matthew H. 133
Paulson, John A. 101
Paus, William 563
Pavez, Ivan Antonio Perez 225
Payan, Juan Manuel Rojas 221
Payer, Gabriela Maria 282
Paz, Avisar 302
Peacock, Lynne 317
Peacock, Sam 574
Pearce, Stephen W. 47
Pearce, Stephen W. 76
Pears, Jonathan 482
Pearson, John 208
Peat, Michael 243
Peckham, Simon 395
Pedini, Claire 175
Pehrsson, Biljana 597
Peirson, James 168
Peixoto, Neil Hamilton dos Guimaraes 120
Pejic, Klementina 601
Pelata, Patrick 525
Pelisson, Gilles C. 11
Pellegrini, Mirella 230
Pelletan, Jerome 362
Pellicioli, Lorenzo 63
Pelling, S. C. 598
Pelouch, Miroslav 218
Peltz, Nelson 653
Pena, Eduardo Guillermo Hernández 171
Pena, Rafael Espino de la 481
Penchienati-Bosetta, Veronique 197
Peng, Kun 559
Peng, Philip 672
Peng, Phillip 12
Peng, Yongdong 345
Penicaud, Pierre 495
Penido, Jose Luciano Duarte 655
Penn, Andrew R. 618
Penner, Michael D. 91
Penner, Timothy H. 315
Penny, Gareth Peter 412
Penrose, Karen 92
Penrose, Karen 498
Pentland, Louise 287
Pepin, Normand 299
Perakis-Valat, Alexis 362
Percy-Robb, Michael I. 589
Pereda, Maria Dolores Herrera 300
Pereira, Alexandre Gomes 655
Pereira, Daniella 172

Pereira, Kelly 519
Pereira, Rodrigo de Mesquita 480
Pereira, Simon 181
Perera, Rodrigo Guzman 466
Peres, Nechemia (Chemi) J. 623
Perez, Arnaldo 138
Perez, Arturo Manuel Fernandez 272
Perez, Jose Luis del Valle 13
Perez, Jose Manuel Inchausti 386
Perez, Jose Maria Abril 615
Perez, Juan Pedro Santa Maria 83
Perez, Karina Paola Awad 171
Perez, Marta Ortega 308
Perez, Vicente S. 107
Perica, Adrian 212
Perillat, Christophe 656
Périllat, Christophe 32
Perincioli, Ignacio 686
Perkins, Scott Redvers 675
Perkins, Scott W. 467
Perl, Lionel 21
Pernot, Laurance 175
Perochena, Antonio del Valle 466
Perochena, Francisco Javier Del Valle 466
Perochena, Juan Pablo del Valle 466
Perreault, Paul 187
Perrier, Yves 185
Perrotti, Roberto 63
Perry, Jocelyn H. 256
Pershing, John E. 134
Personne, Eric 502
Persson, Anna Vikstrom 528
Persson, Fredrik 3
Persson, Goran 597
Persson, Mats 61
Pessanha, Jose Miguel Bensliman Schorcht da Silva 86
Pessoa, Ana Paula 659
Peter, Henry 600
Peter, Nicolas 105
Peters, Claire 675
Petersen, Peter 137
Peterside, Atedo 575
Petersik, Watanan 492
Peterson, David R. 299
Peterson, David R. 514
Peticov, Glaucimar 80
Petitcolin, Philippe 476
Petrelli, Paul O. 589
Petrillo, Louis T. 55
Pettigrew, Jim 24
Pettigrew, Jim 168
Pettigrew, John 424
Peuch, Olivier Le 537
Peugeot, Robert 247
Peugeot, Robert 525
Peugeot, Robert 579
Peverett, Jane L. 130
Peverett, Jane L. 133
Pfau, Lorenz 183
Pfister, Bruno 540
Pflanz, Frederic 108
Pflimlin, Thierry 639
Phan, Steven Swee Kim 654
Pharaon, Fadi 237
Phelan, Louise 524
Philipps, Kate 524
Phillips-Davies, Alistair 574
Phillips, Davis S. 74

Phillips, Elen 506
Phillips, H. Fraser 612
Phillips, Robert L. 131
Phillips, Robert L. 135
Phillips, Robin 316
Phokasub, Yol 555
Phornprapha, Phornthep 85
Phutrakul, Tanate 314
Pianalto, Sandra 220
Pianon, Cathy 542
Piasecki, Nicole W. 76
Pibworth, Martin 574
Picard, Rachel 73
Picat, Maxime 579
Picaud, Geraldine 290
Picaud, Geraldine 311
Picca, Bruno 319
Piccinno, Emanuele 235
Pichayanan, Danucha 493
Pichler, Barbara 238
Pichottka, Andrea 284
Pickard, Ann D. 674
Pickel, Michael 277
Pickering, Kenneth W. 613
Pickett, Denise 619
Pictet, Guillaume 176
Piech, Hans Michel 663
Pieder, Erik 61
Pierdicchi, Maria 651
Pietracci, Bruno 172
Pilenko, Thierry 56
Pilla, Domenic 474
Pimthanothai, Jeeranee 492
Pina, Rodrigo 621
Pinatel, Bernard 639
Pinault, Francois-Henri 347
Pinczuk, Ana G. 50
Pinczuk, Ana G. 51
Pineres, Ernesto Gutierrez de 221
Pinheiro, Miguel Maya Dias 86
Pinmuangngarm, Vitaya 492
Pinsupa, Noppadol 492
Pinsupa, Noppadol 493
Pinter, Jozef 238
Pinto, Carlos 265
Pinto, Helena Sofia Silva Borges Salgado Fonseca Cerveira 223
Pinto, Marcio Percival Alves 331
Pioche, Emmanuel 247
Piquemal, Thomas 141
Piramal, Swati A. 239
Pires, Luciano Siani 655
Pirishi, Ersi 362
Pisani, Alberto Maria 319
Pischetsrieder, Bernd 397
Pistelli, Lapo 235
Pitchford, Lloyd 127
Pitkethly, Graeme 653
Pittard, Ray 644
Pitz, Laird Joseph 133
Piwnica, Carole 530
Piyajitti, Supa 555
Piyavej, Sakesiri 492
Piyawattanaviroj, Khomson 492
Pizzinatto, Rodrigo de Almeida 649
Planta, Andreas von 282
Planta, Andreas von 453
Plante, Gilles 43
Plastinina, Nina 412

Plata, Jorge Adrian Rincon 271
Plath, Claudia 143
Platov, Pavel 412
Platt, Alison 622
Platt, Gillian L. 186
Platt, James 49
Platteeuw, Filip 650
Plattner, Hasso 531
Plazas, Hernando Ramirez 221
Pleines, Thomas 79
Pleininger, Johann 463
Plenborg, Thomas 216
Plessis-Belair, Michel 297
Plessis-Belair, Michel 487
Plessis, Jan du 125
Ploey, Wouter De 113
Ploog, Jens 143
Ploss, Ines 279
Ploss, Reinhard 311
Plottke, Ulrich 418
Plourde, Real 35
Plumart, Marc 566
Plump, Andrew 605
Pobo, Angel 639
Poddar, Mahima 236
Poelvoorde, Geert Van 55
Pohls, Rene 218
Poirier, François L. 608
Pojamarnpornchai, Ronnakitt 128
Pokkasorn, Netsruda 491
Polack, Allan 198
Poletaev, Maxim 413
Poletto, Maurizio 238
Poliquin, Anne-Marie 476
Polizzi, Calogero 597
Pollak, Andrea 277
Pollath, Reinhard 108
Pollock, John 482
Pollock, Sam 124
Poloz, Stephen S. 226
Polyakov, Andrey Aleksandrovich 517
Pomeroy, Brian 497
Pomodoro, Livia 319
Pongritsakda, Wiwat 128
Ponipp, Michael 646
Pontoppidan, Caroline 1
Poohkay, Brent 457
Poomsurakul, Yuthasakk 128
Poonen, Sanjay 358
Pootrakool, Kobsak 85
Poots-Bijl, Jolanda 31
Pope, Darren 168
Pope, Janet 374
Popelier, Luc 345
Popov, Anatoly 535
Pordage, Simon M. 71
Porsche, Ferdinand Oliver 663
Porsche, Wolfgang 663
Porta, Christian 476
Porter, Brian J. 91
Porter, David 3
Portigliatti, Maude 177
Poschel, Ines 32
Posner, Brian S. 56
Possne, Anna 596
Post, Joachim 105
Potanin, Vladimir O. 412
Potier, Benoit 362
Potier, Benoit 557
Potier, Helene Auriol 524